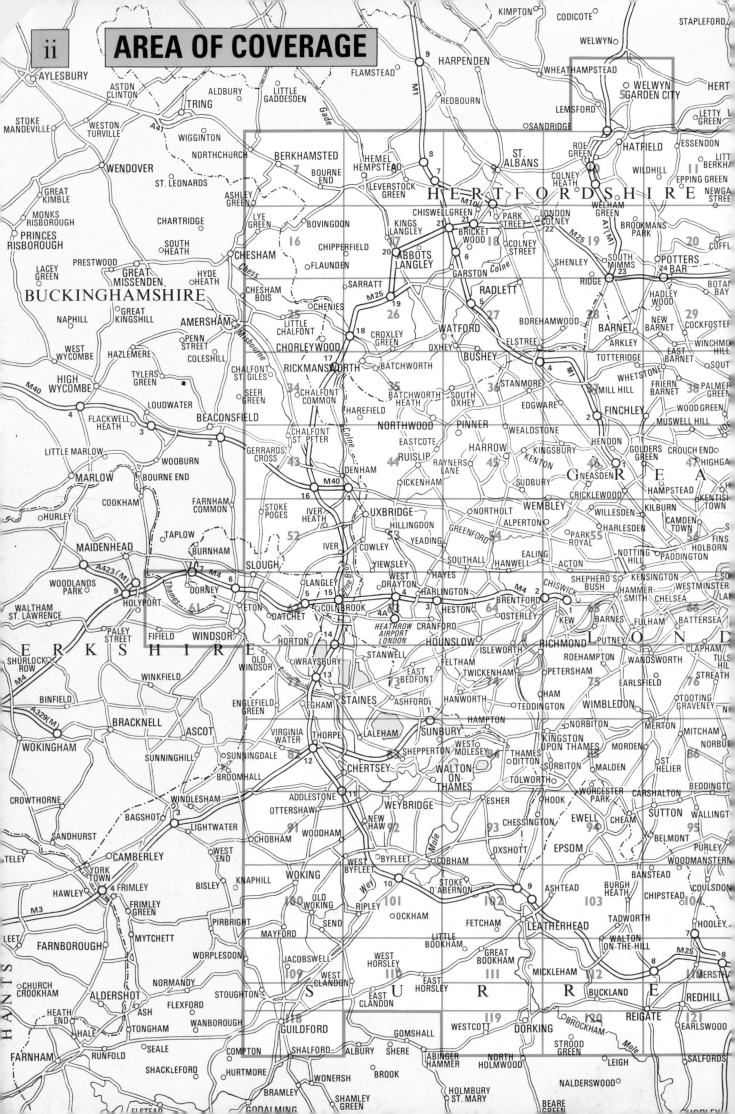

iii
Scale in miles
6 5 4 3 2 1 0
WADESMILL
SPELLBROOK
LITTLE HALLINGBURY
HIGH RODING
BROAD STREET
HATFIELD HEATH
WIDFORD
SAWBRIDGEWORTH
WARE
HUNSDON
HIGH WYCH
SHEERING
LEADEN RODING
GREAT WALTHAM
GREAT AMWELL
WHITE RODING
GOOD EASTER
STANSTEAD ABBOTS
CHURCHGATE STREET
ABBESS RODING
HERTFORD HEATH
HAILEY
HARLOW
MATCHING GREEN
CHALK END
ROYDON
POTTER STREET
HODDESDON
ROYDON HAMLET
BROXBOURNE
NAZEING
HASTINGWOOD
FYFIELD
WILLINGALE
GREAT OXNEY GREEN
CHELMSFORD
RADLEY GREEN
WRITTLE
DANBURY
WORMLEY
LOWER NAZEING
THORNWOOD COMMON
TYLER'S GREEN
HIGH ONGAR
GREAT BADDOW
GOFF'S OAK
BUMBLE'S GREEN
NORTH WEALD BASSETT
LOVES GREEN
CHESHUNT
EPPING
TOOT HILL
CHIPPING ONGAR
GALLEYWOOD
BICKNACRE
WALTHAM ABBEY
UPSHIRE
STONDON MASSEY
FRYERNING
MARGARETTING
WEST HANNINGFIELD
EAST HANNINGFIELD
M25
WALTHAM CROSS
THEYDON BOIS
HARE STREET
KELVEDON HATCH
DODDINGHURST
INGATESTONE
WOODHAM FERRERS
SEWARDSTONE
PASSINGFORD BRIDGE
E S S E X
HEYBRIDGE
STOCK
RETTENDON
ENFIELD
LOUGHTON
DEBDEN
NAVESTOCK
MOUNTNESSING
RAMSDEN HEATH
SOUTH WOODHAM FERRERS
PONDERS END
ABRIDGE
STAPLEFORD ABBOTTS
NAVESTOCK SIDE
HUTTON
CHINGFORD
Roding
CHIGWELL
LAMBOURNE END
BOURNEBRIDGE
PILGRIMS HATCH
SHENFIELD
BILLERICAY
RAMSDEN BELLHOUSE
HULLBRIDGE
BUCKHURST HILL
HARP HILL
HAROLD HILL
BROOK STREET
BRENTWOOD
WICKFORD
RAWRETH
EDMONTON
HIGHAMS PARK
HAINAULT
COLLIER ROW
WARLEY
INGRAVE
SOUTH GREEN
CRAYS HILL
TOTTENHAM
WOODFORD GREEN
GIDEA PARK
GREAT WARLEY
HERONGATE
RAYLEIGH
HIGHAM HILL
SNARESBROOK
BARKINGSIDE
LAINDON
BASILDON
THUNDERSLEY
WALTHAMSTOW
NEWBURY PARK
ROMFORD
HORNCHURCH
VANGE
PITSEA
HADLEIGH
LEYTONSTONE
WANSTEAD
ILFORD
CHADWELL HEATH
UPMINSTER
SOUTH BENFLEET
LEYTON
FOREST GATE
BECONTREE
ELM PARK
BULPHAN
HACKNEY
STRATFORD
BARKING
DAGENHAM
CORBETS TEY
NORTH OCKENDON
HORNDON ON THE HILL
FOBBING
CANVEY ISLAND
BETHNAL GREEN
WEST HAM
EAST HAM
CORRINGHAM
CANVEY
STEPNEY
Lea
BECKTON
RAINHAM
ORSETT
STANFORD LE HOPE
CORYTON
WHITECHAPEL
CANNING TOWN
SOUTH OCKENDON
POPLAR
NORTH WOOLWICH
THAMESMEAD
T H A M E S
BERMONDSEY
WOOLWICH
BELVEDERE
AVELEY
LITTLE THURROCK
CHADWELL ST. MARY
DEPTFORD
PLUMSTEAD
PURFLEET
GRAYS
WEST TILBURY
GREENWICH
ERITH
RIVER
CLIFFE
ST. MARY'S HOO
NEW CROSS
WELLING
TILBURY
COOLING
PECKHAM
BLACKHEATH
BEXLEYHEATH
GREENHITHE
HIGH HALSTOW
LEWISHAM
ELTHAM
DARTFORD
NORTHFLEET
SHARNAL STREET
CATFORD
NEW ELTHAM
BEXLEY
SWANSCOMBE
GRAVESEND
FOREST HILL
MOTTINGHAM
NORTH CRAY
WILMINGTON
CHATTENDEN
HOO
SYDENHAM
SOUTHEND
SIDCUP
FOOTS CRAY
DARENTH
SHORNE
HIGHAM
WAINSCOTT
BROMLEY
HEXTABLE
SOUTH DARENTH
LONGFIELD
STROOD
ROCHESTER
THORNTON HEATH
BECKENHAM
CHISLEHURST
ST. PAUL'S CRAY
SWANLEY
COBHAM
GILLINGHAM
BICKLEY
ST. MARY CRAY
SOLE STREET
CUXTON
CHATHAM
SOUTHBOROUGH
PETTS WOOD
CROCKENHILL
FARNINGHAM
HARTLEY
BORSTAL
ADDISCOMBE
HAYES
ORPINGTON
M20
MEOPHAM
RAINHAM
CROYDON
ADDINGTON
KESTON
CHELSFIELD
Darent
EYNSFORD
HALLING
Medway
HALE
M2
FARNBOROUGH
WEST KINGSDOWN
WALDERSLADE
SELSDON
NEW ADDINGTON
PRATT'S BOTTOM
SHOREHAM
CULVERSTONE GREEN
SNODLAND
BURHAM
DOWNE
STANSTED
SANDERSTEAD
HALSTEAD
K E N T
ECCLES
TROTTISCLIFFE
BIGGIN HILL
OTFORD
KEMSING
AYLESFORD
WARLINGHAM
KNOCKHOLT
WROTHAM
WROTHAM HEATH
DETLING
M26
WHYTELEAFE
TATSFIELD
IGHTHAM
BOROUGH GREEN
OFFHAM
WEST MALLING
WOLDINGHAM
SUNDRIDGE
RIVERHEAD
MAIDSTONE
CATERHAM
SEVENOAKS
EAST BARMING
BEARSTED
LIMPSFIELD
WESTERHAM
IVY HATCH
MEREWORTH
WATERINGBURY
LEEDS
GODSTONE
OXTED
IDE HILL
UNDER RIVER
SHIPBOURNE
NETTLESTEAD
LOOSE
LANGLEY HEATH
BLETCHINGLEY
TANDRIDGE
CROCKHAM HILL
SEVENOAKS WEALD
YALDING
BOUGHTON GREEN
HILDENBOROUGH
HADLOW
HALE STREET
LINTON
SOUTH GODSTONE
CROWHURST LANE END
FOUR ELMS
BENOVER
SUTTON VALENCE
MARLPIT HILL
CHIDDINGSTONE CAUSEWAY
HILDEN PARK
BARNES STREET
CHAINHURST
Beult
BLINDLEY HEATH
EDENBRIDGE
LEIGH
Medway
TONBRIDGE
COLLIER STREET
OUTWOOD
PADDOCK WOOD
MARDEN
LINGFIELD
PENSHURST
BIDBOROUGH

Published by

Nicholson
HarperCollins *Publishers*
77-85 Fulham Palace Road
London W6 8JB

 Nicholson

An Imprint of Bartholomew
A Division of HarperCollins*Publishers*

Maps (ii) (iii) (vi) (vii) 16-17 and map spreads numbered 5-123 at 1:20,000 are based upon the Ordnance Survey with the sanction of the Controller of H.M. Stationery Office. Crown Copyright Reserved.

All other mapping and information is generated from the Bartholomew Digital Databases.

The Ordnance Survey is not responsible for the
accuracy of the National Grid in this publication.

The London Underground map is reproduced by permission of London Regional Transport - LRT Registered User No. 93/1496.

Nicholson wishes to acknowledge the
co-operation of the Post Office in the preparation
of the postal information used in this atlas.

The greatest possible care and attention is taken in producing this atlas, but information can become out of date. Although the publishers can accept no responsibility for errors and omissions, they are always grateful for corrections and any other suggestions for improvement. Any information or queries relating to this atlas should be addressed to:

The Publishing Manager
Nicholson
HarperCollins Publishers
77-85 Fulham Palace Road
London W6 8JB

Printed in the U.K.

ISBN (cased edition) 0 7028 2137 3
93/1/15 E/J 6161 ENM
ISBN (paperback edition) 0 7028 2136 5
93/1/115 E/J 6159 ENM

GREATER LONDON STREET ATLAS

CONTENTS

LEAVE MOTORWAY HERE

Legend:
- ● Junction number
- 38 Mileage Clockwise
- 38 Mileage Anti-Clockwise

	1	2	3	4	5	6	7	8	9	10	11	12	13	14	15	16	17	18	19	20	21	22	23	24	25	26	27	28	29	30	31
1 DARTFORD		4	8	12	22	25	28	35	41	46	48	51	53	55	59	53	52	49	48	45	40	37	34	28	25	21	13	10	5	5	4
2 A2	4		3	7	11	21	24	27	34	40	45	47	50	52	54	59	54	50	49	46	41	38	35	29	26	22	14	11	6	5	5
3 M20	8	4		4	8	18	21	24	31	37	42	44	47	49	51	56	57	53	52	49	44	41	38	32	29	25	17	14	9	8	8
4 A21	12	7	4		4	14	17	20	27	33	38	40	43	45	47	52	58	57	56	53	48	45	42	36	33	29	21	18	13	12	12
5 M26	22	11	8	4		10	13	16	23	29	34	36	39	41	43	48	54	58	59	57	52	49	46	40	37	33	25	22	17	16	17
6 A22	25	21	18	14	10		3	6	13	19	24	26	29	31	33	38	44	54	58	59	56	53	49	43	37	33	29	26	22	26	26
7 M23	28	24	21	17	13	3		3	10	16	21	23	26	28	30	35	41	42	45	54	49	57	59	53	50	46	38	35	29	29	29
8 REIGATE	35	27	24	20	16	6	3		7	13	18	20	23	25	27	32	38	39	42	46	51	54	57	56	53	49	41	38	33	33	32
9 LEATHERHEAD	41	34	31	27	23	13	10	7		6	11	13	16	18	20	25	31	32	35	39	44	47	50	56	59	56	48	45	40	39	39
10 A3	46	40	37	33	29	19	16	13	6		5	7	10	12	14	19	25	26	29	33	38	41	44	50	53	57	54	51	46	45	45
11 CHERTSEY	48	45	42	38	34	24	21	18	11	5		2	5	7	9	14	20	21	24	28	33	36	39	45	48	52	59	56	51	51	50
12 M3	51	47	44	40	36	26	23	20	13	7	2		3	5	7	12	18	19	22	26	31	34	37	43	46	50	58	58	53	53	52
13 A30	53	50	47	43	39	29	26	23	16	10	5	3		2	4	9	15	16	19	23	28	31	34	40	43	47	55	58	56	55	55
14 HEATHROW 4	55	52	49	45	41	31	28	25	18	12	7	5	2		2	7	13	14	17	21	26	29	32	38	41	45	53	56	58	57	57
15 M4, HEATHROW 1-3	59	54	51	47	43	33	30	27	20	14	9	7	4	2		5	11	12	15	19	24	27	30	36	39	43	51	54	59	59	59
16 M40	53	59	56	52	48	38	35	32	25	19	14	12	9	7	5		6	7	10	14	19	22	25	31	34	38	46	49	54	54	55
17 RICKMANSWORTH	52	54	57	58	54	44	41	38	31	25	20	18	15	13	11	6		1	4	8	13	16	19	25	28	32	40	43	48	48	49
18 A404	49	50	53	57	58	54	42	39	32	26	21	19	16	14	12	7	1		3	7	12	15	18	24	27	31	39	42	47	47	48
19 WATFORD	48	49	52	56	59	58	45	42	35	29	24	22	19	17	15	10	4	3		4	9	12	15	21	24	28	36	39	44	44	45
20 A41	45	46	49	53	57	59	54	46	39	33	28	26	23	21	19	14	8	7	4		5	8	11	17	20	24	32	35	40	40	41
21 M1	40	41	44	48	52	56	49	51	44	38	33	31	28	26	24	19	13	12	9	5		3	6	12	15	19	27	30	35	36	36
22 ST. ALBANS	37	38	41	45	49	53	57	54	47	41	36	34	31	29	27	22	16	15	12	8	3		3	9	12	16	24	27	32	33	33
23 A1(M)	34	35	38	42	46	50	56	57	50	44	39	37	34	32	30	25	19	18	15	11	6	3		6	9	13	21	24	29	30	30
24 A111	28	29	32	36	40	47	53	56	56	50	45	43	40	38	36	31	25	24	21	17	12	9	6		3	7	15	18	23	24	24
25 A10	25	26	29	33	37	43	50	53	59	53	48	46	43	41	39	34	28	27	24	20	15	12	9	3		4	12	15	20	21	21
26 EPPING	21	22	25	29	33	37	46	49	56	57	52	50	47	45	43	38	32	31	28	24	19	16	13	7	4		8	11	16	17	17
27 M11	13	14	17	21	25	35	38	41	48	54	59	58	55	53	51	46	40	39	36	32	27	24	21	15	12	8		3	8	9	9
28 A12	10	11	14	18	22	32	35	38	45	51	56	58	58	56	54	49	43	42	39	35	30	27	24	18	15	11	3		5	6	6
29 A127	5	6	9	13	17	27	30	33	40	46	51	53	56	58	59	54	48	47	44	40	35	32	29	23	20	16	8	5		1	1
30 A13	5	5	8	12	16	26	29	33	39	45	50	53	55	57	59	55	48	47	44	40	36	33	30	24	21	17	9	6	1		1
31 A13	4	5	8	12	16	26	29	32	39	45	50	52	55	57	59	55	49	48	45	41	36	33	30	24	21	17	9	6	1	1	

ENTER MOTORWAY HERE

Note: This chart shows the shortest distance in miles between junctions. The colours indicate whether the distance is clockwise or anti-clockwise. The total distance around the M25 is approx. 117 miles.

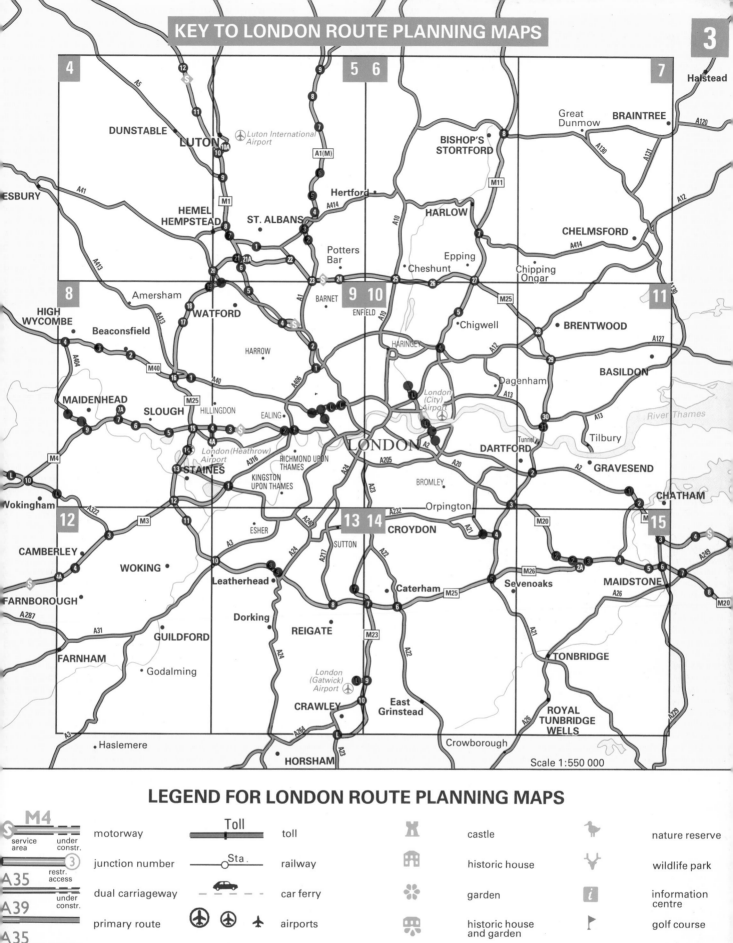

KEY TO LONDON ROUTE PLANNING MAPS

3

4 | **5** | **6** | **7**

Halstead

DUNSTABLE

LUTON

Luton International Airport

Great Dunmow

BRAINTREE

A120

BISHOP'S STORTFORD

A1(M)

Hertford

A414

HARLOW

CHELMSFORD

A414

HEMEL HEMPSTEAD

ST. ALBANS

Potters Bar

M11

A12

ESBURY

A41

A413

Epping

Chipping Ongar

Cheshunt

8

HIGH WYCOMBE

Amersham

WATFORD

BARNET

9 | **10**

ENFIELD

HARINGEY

Chigwell

A12

M25

11

BRENTWOOD

A127

BASILDON

Beaconsfield

HARROW

A404

A40

Dagenham

A13

MAIDENHEAD

SLOUGH

HILLINGDON

Ealing

London (City) Airport

A13

River Thames

Tilbury

M25

M40

LONDON

London (Heathrow) Airport

Richmond Upon Thames

A316

DARTFORD

Tunnel

GRAVESEND

A2

STAINES

Kingston Upon Thames

A205

A20

M4

A306

BROMLEY

CHATHAM

Wokingham

A3

A322

Orpington

A232

13 | **14**

CROYDON

M20

15

12

CAMBERLEY

M3

ESHER

SUTTON

A21

MAIDSTONE

WOKING

A24

A217

A22

Caterham

M25

Sevenoaks

A26

M20

FARNBOROUGH

Leatherhead

M26

A287

GUILDFORD

Dorking

REIGATE

M23

TONBRIDGE

A21

FARNHAM

Godalming

London (Gatwick) Airport

East Grinstead

ROYAL TUNBRIDGE WELLS

A26

Haslemere

CRAWLEY

A264

Crowborough

A29

HORSHAM

A23

Scale 1:550 000

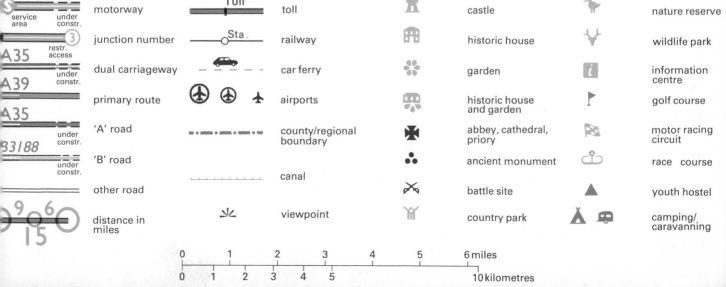

LEGEND FOR LONDON ROUTE PLANNING MAPS

M4 service area, under constr.	motorway	Toll — toll	castle		nature reserve
junction number		Sta. — railway	historic house		wildlife park
A35 restr. access, under constr.	dual carriageway	car ferry	garden		information centre
A39	primary route	airports	historic house and garden		golf course
A35 under constr.	'A' road	county/regional boundary	abbey, cathedral, priory		motor racing circuit
B3188 under constr.	'B' road	canal	ancient monument		race course
	other road		battle site		youth hostel
9 6 15	distance in miles	viewpoint	country park		camping/caravanning

0   1   2   3   4   5   6 miles

0 1 2 3 4 5   10 kilometres

4
Newton Longville
Little Brickhill
Great Brickhill
WOBURN ABBEY
Tingrith
A5120
Milton Bryan
Sharpenhoe
Harlington
A4146
Stoke Hammond
STOCKGROVE
Potsgrove
Toddington
Streatley
Toddington
Heath and Reach
Battlesden
Fancott
Upper Sundon
Soulbury
A5
Lower Sundon
North End
Hockliffe
Tebworth
Wingfield
B579
Chalton
B4032
LEIGHTON BUZZARD
A4012
A5120
Sundon Park
South End
Eggington
Linslade
LEIGHTON BUZZARD LIGHT RAILWAY
Houghton Regis
Limbury
Leagrave
Burcott
Stanbridge
Tilsworth
A505
Wing
ASCOTT (NT)
Billington
DUNSTABLE
A505
A5065
Ledburn
Eaton Green
Totternhoe
LUTON
A418
Slapton
Church End
Eaton Bray
A5
B4541
Mentmore
MENTMORE
B489
Caddington
Nup End
Wingrave
Horton
A4146
Kensworth
Edlesborough
Whipsnade
B4540
Slip End
B488
Ivinghoe Aston
Kensworth Common
B4540
Rowsham
Cheddington
ZOO
Whipsnade Park
Markyate
Pitstone Green
Ivinghoe
Hulcott
Long Marston
Dagnall
Studham
Cheverell's Green
Flamstead
A4146
Pitstone
Puttenham
Marsworth
Ringshall
Trowley Bottom
B489
B488
Wilstone
Little Gaddesden
B4506
Wilstone Res
Gaddesden Row
Buckland
New Mill
A41
Drayton Beauchamp
B486
Aldbury
ASHRIDGE
Great Gaddesden
Toll
Tring
Clinton
Water End
B4544
Halton
(NT)
Nettleden
Weston Turville
Wigginton
ZOOLOGICAL MUSEUM
PICCOTTS END
A4011
(RUINS)
Piccotts End
Hastoe
Potten End
HEMEL HEMPSTEAD
Nash Lee
Northchurch
Wendover
Hundreds
Three
Berkhamsted
A41
A414
Cross
Coombe Hill
(NT)
Cholesbury
St Leonards
Boxmoor
Leverstock Green
Buckland Common
Bourne End
Aylesbury
Ashley Green
Apsley
Whelpley Hill
Felden
Dunsmore
Bellingdon
Bedm
The Lee
A416
Lee Clump
Bovingdon
Kings Langley
Chartridge
(due to open summer 1993)
Little Hampden
A413
Ballinger Common
Lye Green
B4505
Newtown
B4505
Botley
Great Missenden
South Heath
Chipperfield
B485
CHESHAM
Flaunden
Prestwood
Hyde Heath
Waterside
Bucks Hill
Little Kingshill
A4128
Upper North Dean
Chesham Bois
Sarratt
Latimer
Great Kingshill
Little Missenden
Chiltern
Hundreds
Chenies
MANOR HO.
M25
Hughenden Valley
A404
Chandler's Cross
Holmer Green
Amersham
Cassiobury Park
Little Chalfont
Cryers Hill
B4442
Misbourne
Hazlemere
Penn Street
A404
Coleshill
Chorleywood
Chess
Croxley Green

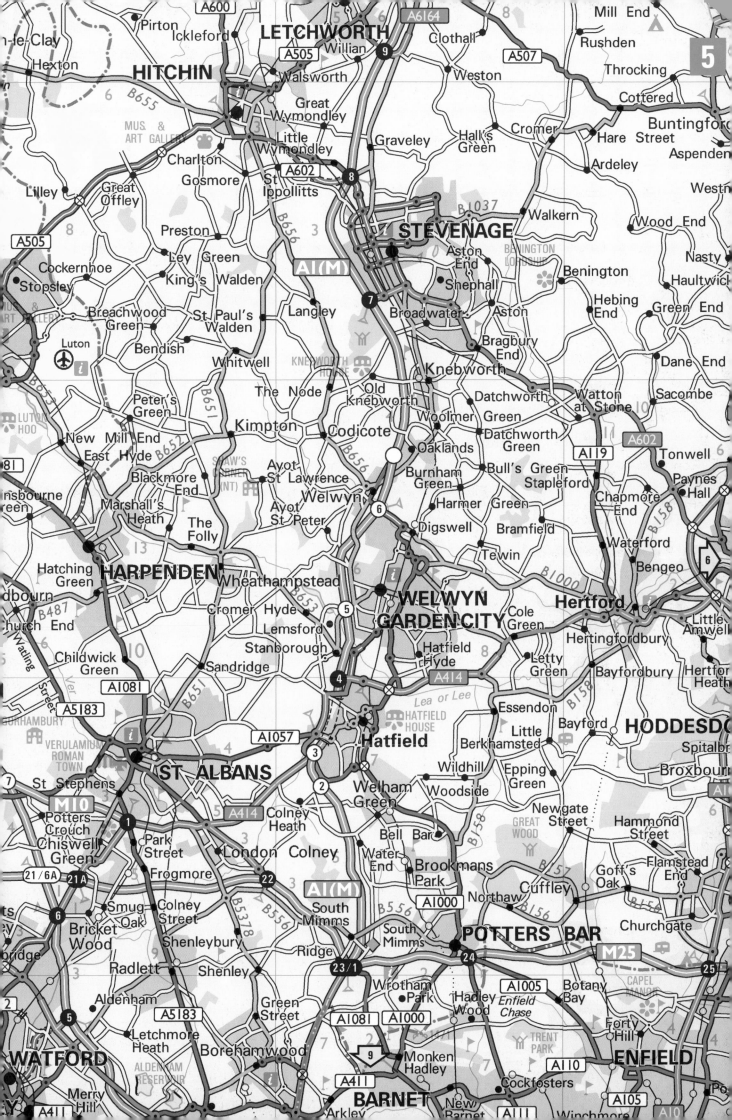
5
LETCHWORTH
HITCHIN
STEVENAGE
HARPENDEN
WELWYN GARDEN CITY
Hertford
HODDESDON
Hatfield
ST ALBANS
POTTERS BAR
WATFORD
BARNET
ENFIELD
Pirton
Ickleford
Hexton
Willian
Walsworth
Great Wymondley
Little Wymondley
Charlton
Gosmore
St Ippollitts
Graveley
Clothall
Weston
Mill End
Rushden
Throcking
Cottered
Buntingford
Hare Street
Aspenden
Cromer
Hall's Green
Ardeley
Walkern
Wood End
Nasty
Haultwick
Benington
Hebing End
Green End
Aston End
Shephall
Aston
Broadwater
Bragbury End
Knebworth
Old Knebworth
Datchworth
Watton at Stone
Sacombe
Dane End
Woolmer Green
Datchworth Green
Tonwell
Oaklands
Burnham Green
Bull's Green
Stapleford
Paynes Hall
Chapmore End
Harmer Green
Digswell
Bramfield
Waterford
Tewin
Bengeo
Cole Green
Hertingfordbury
Little Amwell
Hatfield Hyde
Letty Green
Bayfordbury
Hertford Heath
Essendon
Bayford
Little Berkhamsted
Spitalbrook
Broxbourne
Wildhill
Epping Green
Woodside
Welham Green
Newgate Street
Hammond Street
Bell Bar
Water End
Brookmans Park
Flamstead End
Goff's Oak
Cuffley
Northaw
Churchgate
South Mimms
Botany Bay
Wrotham Park
Hadley Wood
Enfield Chase
Forty Hill
Monken Hadley
Cockfosters
New Barnet
Winchmore
Arkley
Lilley
Great Offley
Preston
Ley Green
King's Walden
Cockernhoe
Stopsley
Breachwood Green
St Paul's Walden
Langley
Bendish
Whitwell
Luton
The Node
Codicote
Kimpton
Peter's Green
New Mill End
East Hyde
Ayot St Lawrence
Welwyn
Ayot St Peter
Blackmore End
Marshall's Heath
The Folly
Harpenden
Hatching Green
Wheathampstead
Cromer Hyde
Lemsford
Stanborough
Sandridge
Church End
Childwick Green
St Stephens
Potters Crouch
Chiswell Green
Park Street
London Colney
Colney Heath
Frogmore
Smug Oak
Colney Street
Bricket Wood
Shenleybury
Radlett
Shenley
Ridge
Aldenham
Green Street
Letchmore Heath
Borehamwood
Merry Hill
MUS & ART GALLERY
KNEBWORTH HOUSE
BENINGTON LORDSHIP
SHAW'S CORNER (NT)
HATFIELD HOUSE
VERULAMIUM ROMAN TOWN
GORHAMBURY
GREAT WOOD
CAPEL MANOR
TRENT PARK
ALDENHAM RESERVOIR
LUTON HOO
Watling Street
Ver
Lea or Lee
A600
A6164
A505
A507
A602
A1(M)
B1037
B656
B655
B653
B651
B652
B487
A1081
A5183
A1057
A414
B1000
A119
B158
M10
B5378
B556
A1000
B156
B157
M25
A1005
A110
A411
A105
A10
21/6A
21A
22
23/1
24
25

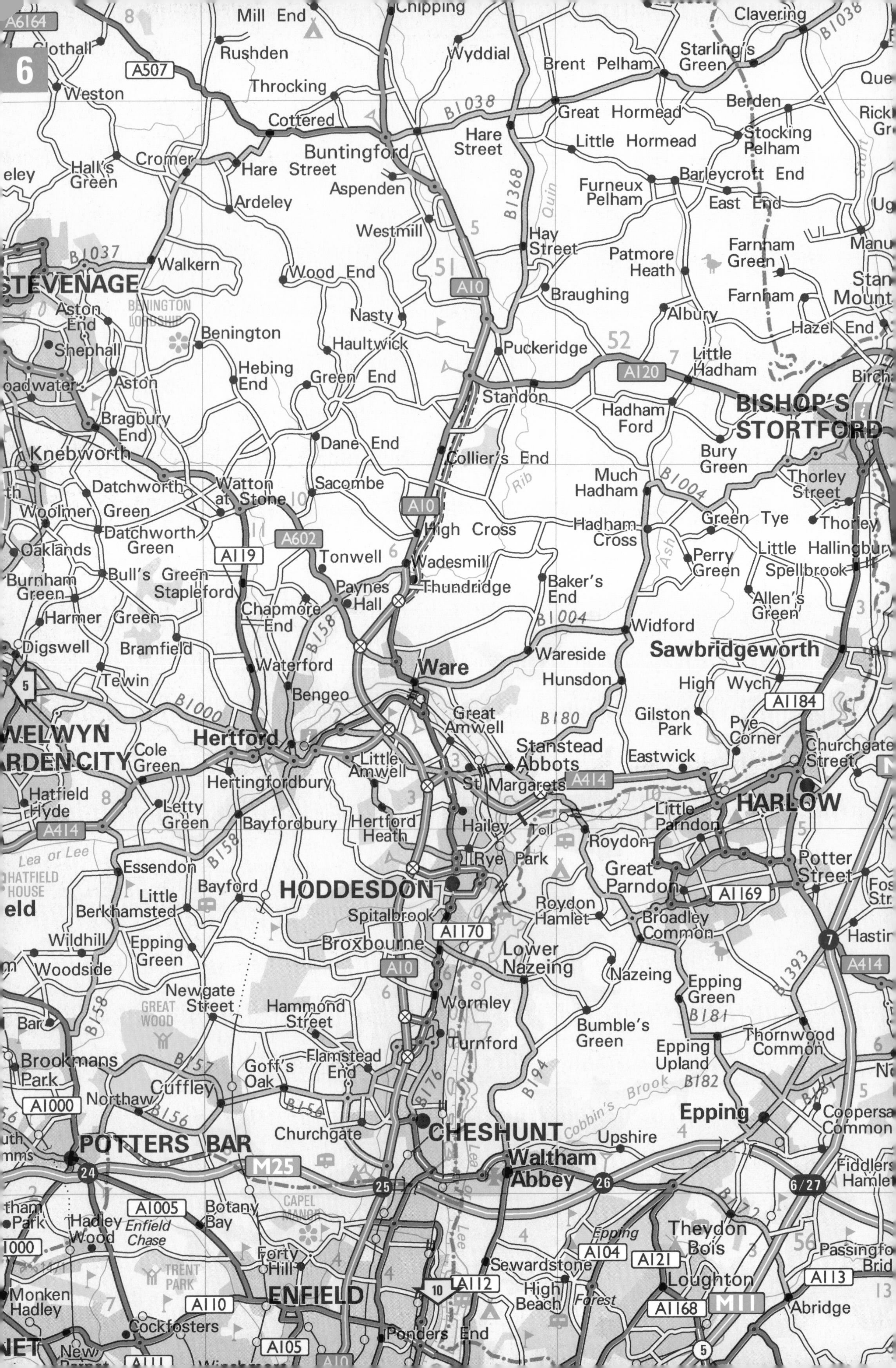

A6164
Clothall
A507
Weston
Mill End
Rushden
Throcking
Cottered
Buntingford
Hare Street
Aspenden
Chipping
Wyddial
Hare Street
B1038
Great Hormead
Little Hormead
Brent Pelham
Starling's Green
Clavering
Que
B1038
Berden
Stocking Pelham
Rick Gr
Manu
Hall's Green
Cromer
Hare Street
Ardeley
Westmill
B1368
Quin
Hay Street
Furneux Pelham
Barleycroft End
East End
Farnham Green
Stan Mount
B1037
Walkern
Wood End
51
A10
Braughing
Albury
52
Farnham
Hazel End
Birch
STEVENAGE
Aston End
Shephall
Benington
BENINGTON LORDSHIP
Nasty
Haultwick
Green End
Puckeridge
A120
Little Hadham
BISHOP'S STORTFORD
oadwater
Aston
Hebing End
Standon
Hadham Ford
Bury Green
Thorley Street
Bragbury End
Datchworth
Dane End
Sacombe
Collier's End
Rib
Much Hadham
B1004
Green Tye
Thorley
Knebworth
Woolmer Green
Watton at Stone
10
High Cross
Hadham Cross
Little Hallingbur
Spellbrook
Datchworth Green
A602
Ash
Perry Green
Allen's Green
Oaklands
A119
A602
Tonwell
Wadesmill
Thundridge
Baker's End
Widford
Sawbridgeworth
Burnham Green
Bull's Green
Stapleford
Chapmore End
Paynes Hall
B1004
Harmer Green
Digswell
Bramfield
B158
Waterford
Ware
Wareside
Hunsdon
High Wych
A1184
Bengeo
Great Amwell
B180
Gilston Park
Pye Corner
Churchgate Street
5
Tewin
B1000
WELWYN GARDEN CITY
Hertford
Cole Green
Hertingfordbury
Little Amwell
3
Stanstead Abbots
St Margarets
A414
Eastwick
HARLOW
Hatfield Hyde
A414
Letty Green
Bayfordbury
Hertford Heath
3
Hailey
Toll
Little Parndon
Rye Park
Roydon
Great Parndon
Rotter Street
Fos Str
eld
Lea or Lee
HATFIELD HOUSE
B158
Essendon
Bayford
HODDESDON
Spitalbrook
Roydon Hamlet
Broadley Common
A1169
Hastir
eld
Little Berkhamsted
Broxbourne
A1170
Lower Nazeing
Nazeing
Epping Green
B1393
A414
7
Wildhill
Woodside
Epping Green
Newgate Street
A10
Hammond Street
Wormley
Bumble's Green
B181
Epping Upland
Thornwood Common
Brookmans Park
A1000
GREAT WOOD
B157
Goff's Oak
Flamstead End
B176
Turnford
B194
Cobbin's Brook
B182
Epping
Northaw
B156
Churchgate
CHESHUNT
Upshire
Coopersa Common
POTTERS BAR
24
M25
25
Waltham Abbey
26
6/27
Fiddlers Hamle
tham Park
A1005
Botany Bay
Enfield Chase
CAPEL MANOR
TRENT PARK
Lee
Epping Forest
Theydon Bois
A104
A121
56
Passingfo Brid
1000
Monken Hadley
A110
Forty Hill
ENFIELD
10
A112
High Beach
Sewardstone
Loughton
A1168
M11
A113
13
NET
Cockfosters
A111
A105
Ponders End
A10
5

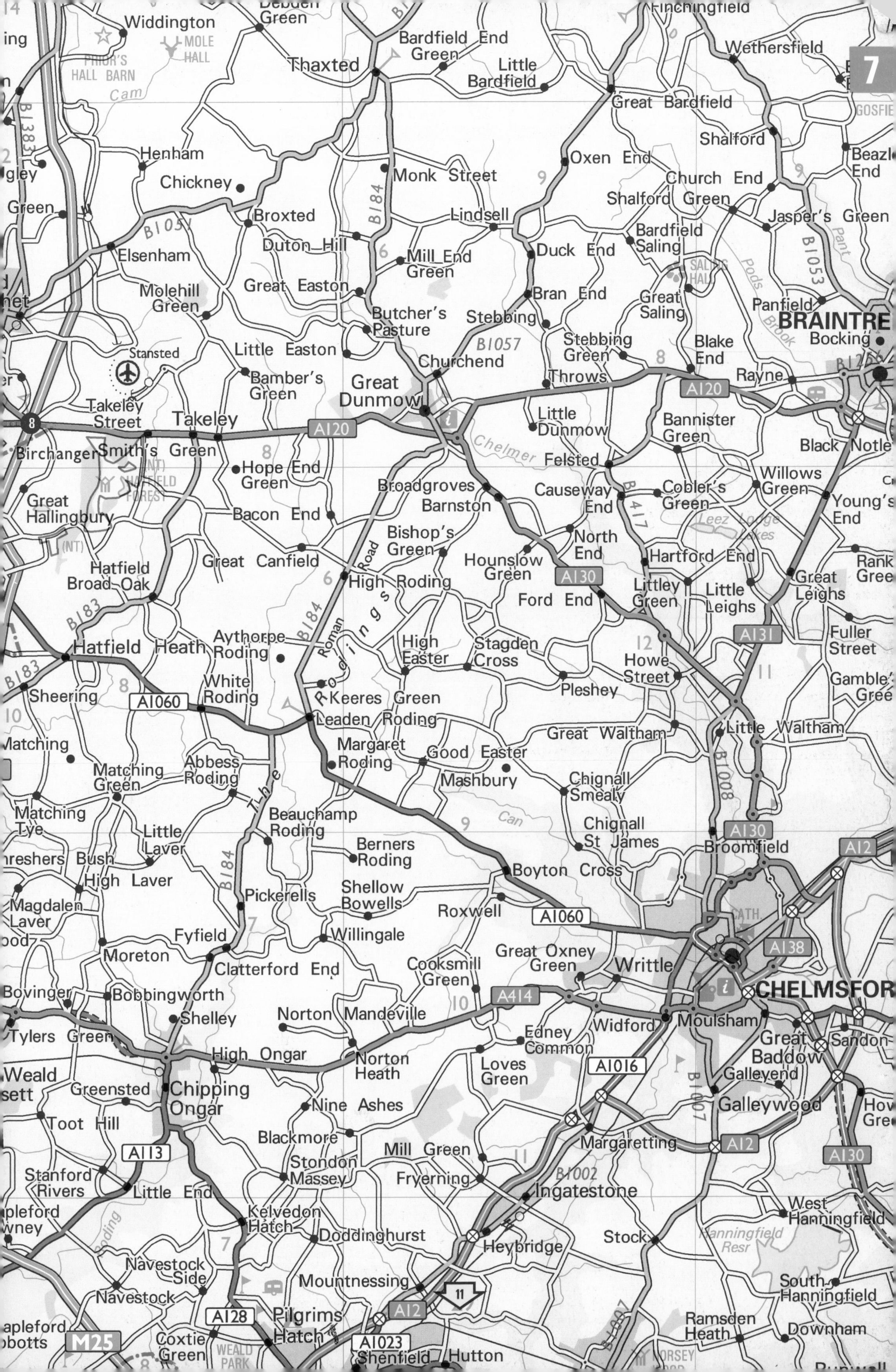

Widdington

MOLE HALL

PRIOR'S HALL BARN

Cam

Debden Green

Thaxted

Bardfield End Green

Little Bardfield

Finchingfield

Wethersfield

Great Bardfield

Shalford

Beazl End

GOSFIE

Henham

Chickney

Broxted

Duton Hill

Monk Street

Lindsell

Oxen End

Church End

Shalford Green

Jasper's Green

B184

Elsenham

Molehill Green

Great Easton

Mill End Green

Duck End

Bran End

Bardfield Saling

Great Saling

Panfield

BRAINTRE

Bocking

Stansted

Little Easton

Bamber's Green

Butcher's Pasture

Great Dunmow

Churchend

B1057

Stebbing

Stebbing Green

Blake End

Throws

Rayne

Black Notle

A120

Takeley Street

Takeley

Birchanger

Smith's Green

A120

Hope End Green

Bacon End

Broadgroves

Barnston

Chelmer

Little Dunmow

Felsted

Bannister Green

Cobler's Green

Willows Green

Young's End

Great Hallingbury

Great Canfield

Bishop's Green

High Roding

Hounslow Green

Causeway End

North End

Hartford End

Rank Gree

Hatfield Broad Oak

B183

B184

Roman Road

Aythorpe Roding

High Easter

Stagden Cross

Ford End

A130

Littley Green

Little Leighs

Great Leighs

Fuller Street

Gamble Gree

Hatfield Heath

White Roding

A1060

Keeres Green

Leaden Roding

Margaret Roding

Good Easter

Mashbury

Pleshey

Howe Street

Great Waltham

Little Waltham

A131

Sheering

Matching

Matching Green

Abbess Roding

B184

Beauchamp Roding

Berners Roding

Shellow Bowells

Roxwell

Boyton Cross

Chignall Smealy

Chignall St James

Broomfield

A130

Can

A1060

A12

Matching Tye

Little Laver

High Laver

Pickerells

Willingale

Great Oxney Green

Writtle

CHELMSFOR

Threshers Bush

Fyfield

Moreton

Clatterford End

Cooksmill Green

A414

Widford

Edney Common

Moulsham

A1016

Great Baddow

Galleyend

Magdalen Laver

Bovinger

Bobbingworth

Shelley

Norton Mandeville

Norton Heath

Loves Green

Galleywood

How Gree

Tylers Green

High Ongar

Nine Ashes

A12

Margaretting

A130

Weald Bassett

Greensted

Chipping Ongar

Blackmore

Mill Green

Fryerning

B1002

West Hanningfield

Toot Hill

A113

Stondon Massey

Ingatestone

Stock

Hanningfield Resr

Stanford Rivers

Little End

Kelvedon Hatch

Doddinghurst

Heybridge

South Hanningfield

pleford owney

Roding

Navestock Side

Navestock

A128

Mountnessing

Pilgrims Hatch

A12

11

Ramsden Heath

Downham

M25

Coxtie Green

WEALD PARK

A1023

Shenfield

Hutton

8
CHESHAM
Flaunden
Bucks Hill
Missenden
Heath
Prestwood
Little Kingshill
Hyde Heath
Waterside
Chesham Bois
A4128
North Dean
Great Kingshill
Little Missenden
Chiltern
Hundreds
Latimer
Sarratt
Chenies
M25
Chandler's Cross
Cassiobury Park
Hughenden Valley
Holmer Green
Amersham
A404
Little Chalfont
Cryers Hill
Hazlemere
Hughenden Manor
Penn Street
Coleshill
Misbourne
B4442
Chorleywood
Croxley Green
Winchmore Hill
Chalfont St Giles
Heronsgate
Tylers Green
A4145
RICKMANSW
HIGH WYCOMBE
Penn
Milton Cottage
A355
A413
Batchworth
Maple Cross
Batchworth Heath
Horn Hill
A40
Wycombe Marsh
Forty Green
Knotty Green
Seer Green
Jordans
Spindrift
Chalfont Common
West Hyde
Loudwater
Holtspur
Beaconsfield
Chalfont St Peter
Harefield
A404
Flackwell Heath
M40
A412
Mayhurst Wood
Ruislip Common
A4180
Well End
Wooburn Green
Gerrards Cross
Denham Green
Little Marlow
Wooburn
Hedsor
A355
Hedgerley
Bourne End
Dropmore
Farnham Common
Denham
Ickenham
Cookham Dean
Cookham
Cliveden
Burnham Beeches
Fulmer
16/1A
Cookham Rise
Uxbridge
Stoke Poges
A308
Furze Platt
A4094
Farnham Royal
Iver Heath
Pinkneys Green
Taplow
Hitcham
Burnham
A412
HILLIN
MAIDENHEAD
Cowley
A4
Iver
George Green
A408
A437
Salt Hill
SLOUGH
Bray Wick
Bray
Dorney
Yiewsley
Thorney
West Drayton
A404(M)
Richings Park
Upton
Woodlands Park
Eton Wick
Langley
A4
Holyport
Boveney
15/4B
Sipson
Harmondsworth
Clewer Village
Eton
M4
Colnbrook
Stud Green
A308
Fifield
Datchet
Touchen End
Oakley Green
Poyle
Longford
Paley Street
B3024
WINDSOR
Heathrow (London)
A330
Safari Park
Spital
Horton
Hawthorn Hill
Old Windsor
M25
Stanwell Moor
Stanwell
Maiden's Green
Windsor Forest
Windsor
A308
Wraysbury
Hythe End
A3095
Warfield
Winkfield
Cranbourne
Great
Cooper's Hill
A3044
A30
Feltham
A332
Park
Ashford
Newell Green
Winkfield Row
Woodside
Englefield Green
STAINES
EGHAM
A308
Burleigh
North Ascot
Cheapside
Virginia Water
A320
Ascot
Virginia Water
Thorpe
Laleham
Littleton
BRACKNELL
A329
Sunninghill
South Ascot
Sunningdale
M3
A332
A330
Longcross Sta.
Lyne
Shepperton
A244
12
Chobham Common
CHERTSEY
A322
A30
B386
M3
B3020
A317
Weybridge
Longcross

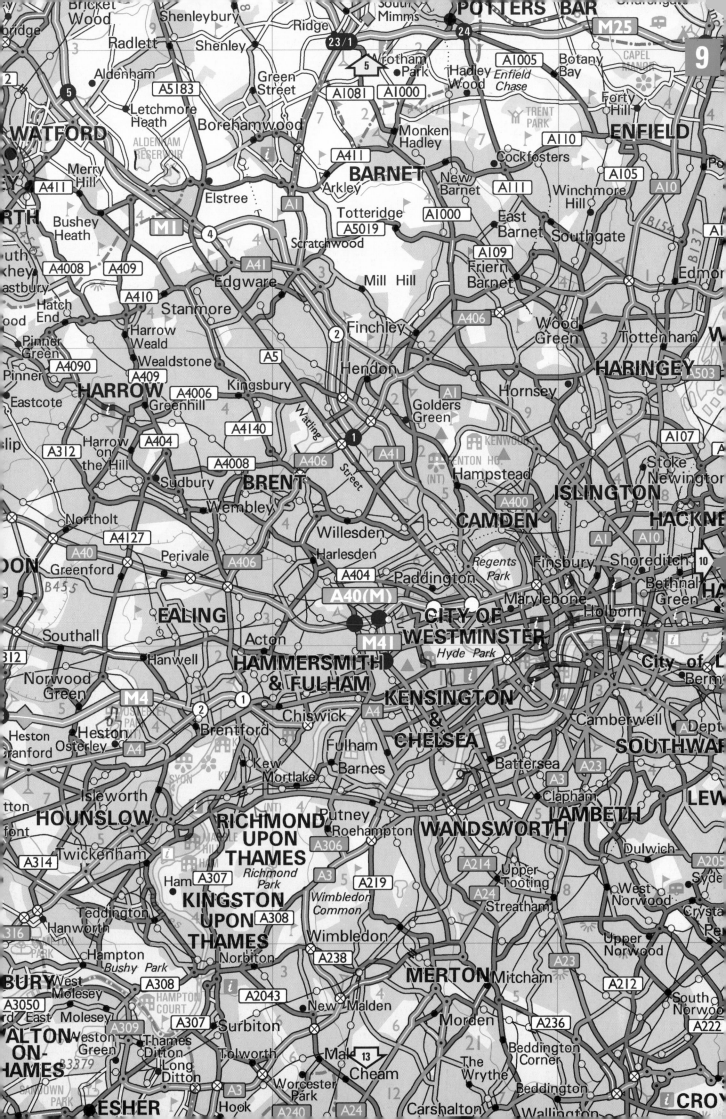

9
POTTERS BAR
M25
South Mimms
Shenleybury
Ridge
Radlett
Shenley
Aldenham
Green Street
Wrotham Park
Hadley Wood
Enfield Chase
Botany Bay
Forty Hill
CAPEL MANOR
TRENT PARK
ENFIELD
A1005
A1081
A1000
A5183
Letchmore Heath
Borehamwood
Monken Hadley
WATFORD
ALDENHAM RESERVOIR
A411
A110
Cockfosters
Merry Hill
BARNET
Arkley
New Barnet
A111
A105
A10
Winchmore Hill
Elstree
A1
Totteridge
A1000
Bushey Heath
M1
A5019
East Barnet
Southgate
Scratchwood
A109
A4008
A409
A41
Edgware
Mill Hill
Friern Barnet
Edmonton
A410
Stanmore
Hatch End
A406
Wood Green
Tottenham
Harrow Weald
Finchley
Pinner Green
A4090
Wealdstone
Hendon
HARINGEY
A503
Pinner
A409
HARROW
A4006
Kingsbury
Hornsey
Eastcote
Greenhill
Golders Green
Watling Street
A4140
KENWOOD
A107
Harrow on the Hill
A404
A312
A4008
A406
A41
KENWOOD HO.
Stoke Newington
Hampstead
(NT)
Sudbury
BRENT
ISLINGTON
A400
Wembley
HACKNEY
Northolt
CAMDEN
Willesden
A4127
A1
A10
A40
Perivale
Harlesden
Regents Park
Finsbury
Shoreditch
Greenford
A406
10
B455
A404
Paddington
Bethnal Green
A40(M)
Marylebone
CITY OF WESTMINSTER
Holborn
EALING
Southall
Acton
M41
A312
Hanwell
Hyde Park
HAMMERSMITH & FULHAM
City of London
Bermondsey
Norwood Green
M4
KENSINGTON & CHELSEA
Chiswick
A4
Camberwell
Deptford
Heston
Brentford
Osterley
Fulham
SOUTHWARK
Cranford
A4
Kew
Battersea
Barnes
A23
Mortlake
A3
SYON
Clapham
Isleworth
LAMBETH
LEWISHAM
HOUNSLOW
RICHMOND UPON THAMES
Putney
Roehampton
WANDSWORTH
A306
Twickenham
Dulwich
A314
A214
A205
Upper Tooting
Ham
A307
Richmond Park
A3
A219
Sydenham
KINGSTON UPON THAMES
A24
West Norwood
Wimbledon Common
Streatham
Crystal Palace
Teddington
A308
Hanworth
A316
Wimbledon
Upper Norwood
Hampton
Norbiton
A238
A23
Bushy Park
A308
MERTON
Mitcham
A212
West Molesey
HAMPTON COURT
A2043
A3050
New Malden
South Norwood
East Molesey
A309
A307
Surbiton
Morden
A236
A222
WALTON-ON-THAMES
Weston Green
Thames Ditton
Beddington Corner
Long Ditton
Tolworth
13
The Wrythe
B3379
Cheam
Worcester Park
Beddington
ESHER
A3
Hook
Carshalton
Wallington
A240
A24
SANDOWN PARK
CROYDON

Potters Bar
M25
24
25
26
6/27
Waltham Abbey
Fiddlers Hamlet
Hadley Wood
Enfield Chase
A1005
Botany Bay
Capel Manor
6
Theydon Bois
Passingford Bridge
Epping
A104
A121
Forty Hill
Sewardstone
Trent Park
A112
High Beach
Forest
Loughton
A113
Monken Hadley
A110
ENFIELD
A1168
M11
Abridge
Cockfosters
Ponders End
5
New Barnet
A105
A111
A10
Winchmore Hill
Chingford
Buckhurst Hill
Lambourne End
A1000
East Barnet
Southgate
B154
B137
A1055
CHIGWELL
Hainault
B160
A109
Friern Barnet
Edmonton
Woodford Green
B173
Chigwell Row
Grange Hill
Hill
A112
Hainault
A406
Wood Green
Woodford
Woodford Bridge
A1112
Tottenham
WALTHAM FOREST
4
Marks Gate
Barkingside
HARINGEY
A503
Walthamstow
A1400
REDBRIDGE
A1
Hornsey
Golders Green
Wanstead
A12
Seven Kings
A118
Kenwood
A107
A104
A123
A1083
Kenton Ho.
(NT)
Hampstead
Stoke Newington
Leyton
A616
Ilford
Becontree
A11
ISLINGTON
A400
A406
A124
A1240
CAMDEN
HACKNEY
Forest Gate
BARKING
DAGENHAM
A102(M)
West Ham
A1
A10
Barking
9
Regents Park
Finsbury
Shoreditch
TOWER HAMLETS
East Ham
Paddington
Bethnal Green
NEWHAM
Creekmouth
Marylebone
A102
Stepney
A13
Holborn
CITY OF WESTMINSTER
Beckton
Thamesmead
Hyde Park
Poplar
London City
A1011
A117
A2016
City of London
Isle of Dogs
Abbey Wood
Erith
Bermondsey
A102(M)
KENSINGTON & CHELSEA
GREENWICH
Woolwich
Plumstead
A206
Camberwell
Deptford
A205
Charlton
East Wickham
SOUTHWARK
Shooter's Hill
Battersea
A23
Kidbrooke
Welling
A3
A2
A207
Bexley
Clapham
LEWISHAM
Eltham
WANDSWORTH
LAMBETH
Hither Green
Eltham Palace
BEXLEY
Dulwich
Catford
A214
A205
Grove Park
A2212
A20
New Eltham
Upper Tooting
Sydenham
A24
West Norwood
Streatham
Mottingham
Sidcup
A223
Foots Cray
Crystal Palace
A21
Penge
Chislehurst
Upper Norwood
A23
Beckenham
A222
St Paul's Cray
MERTON
Mitcham
BROMLEY
A212
B251
Bickley
South Norwood
(NT)
Morden
A236
A21
A222
Eden Park
Bromley Common
A208
St Mary Cray
A214
Beddington Corner
West Wickham
Hayes
B265
14
Orpington
The Wrythe
A232
A232
Shirley
Beddington
Locksbottom
A224
Carshalton
CROYDON
Addington
A223

11
A113
Stanford Rivers
Little End
Stondon Massey
Mill Green
Fryerning
Margaretting
A12
A130
Ingatestone
B1002
Kelvedon Hatch
Doddinghurst
Heybridge
Stock
West Hanning
Hanningfield Resr
Navestock Side
Navestock
Mountnessing
South Hanningfield
A128
Pilgrims Hatch
A12
29
Ramsden Heath
Downham
M25
Coxtie Green
WEALD PARK
A1023
Shenfield
Hutton
NORSEY WOOD
Runwell
Bournebridge
Noak Hill
South Weald
BRENTWOOD
A129
Billericay
Ramsden Bellhouse
South Green
Wickford
Tye Common
A1023
Havering-atte-Bower
28
Brook Street
A128
Ingrave
A129
Crouch
Crays Hill
Harold Hill
B186
THORNDON PARK
Little Burstead
Great Burstead
A132
Roman Road
Great Warley
Little Warley
Herongate
Dunton Wayletts
A176
A127
Harold Wood
Gidea Park
40
North Be
Childerditch
A127
BASILDO
Romford
29
East Horndon
Laindon
B148
A132
Pitsea
B1006
Langdon Hills
Vange
Cranham
West Horndon
Westley Heights
A176
A13
A124
Hornchurch
Rush Green
HAVERING
Upminster
B186
Bulphan
B1007
Dry Street
16
A125
B1421
WESTLEY HEIGHTS
ONE TREE HILL
Elm Park
North Ockendon
A128
B1420
Dagenham
A13
South Hornchurch
Horndon on the Hill
Fobbing
Corringham
BELHUS WOOD
South Ockendon
B188
Orsett
A1014
Coryton
Rainham
Baker Street
Stanford-le-Hope
Thames
Wennington
B1335
North Stifford
A13
Mucking
Aveley
30
A128
Blythe Sand
Danger Zone
Thames
Thurrock
Linford
Chadwell St Mary
31
Little Thurrock
The Lower Hope
Purfleet
A1090
A126
West Tilbury
West Thurrock
GRAYS
A126
East Tilbury
Slade Green
A282
A1089
Tilbury
Cliffe
Dartford Tunnel & Bridge
Toll
FORT
A206
Crayford
1A
Greenhithe
Northfleet
Danger Zone
HALL PLACE
Stone
A226
GRAVESEND
Church Street
Cliffe Woods
Swanscombe
MILTON CHANTRY
Chalk
DARTFORD
1B
Lower Higham
Perry Street
A2
A226
B2000
Wilmington
2
A2
Bean
Betsham
Singlewell or Ifield
Shorne
Higham
Wainscott
Hawley
Lane End
B262
Southfleet
A2
A289
Hextable
Darenth
Green Street Green
Hook Green
Thong
Shorne Ridgeway
Frindsbury
Sutton at Hone
South Darenth
Istead Rise
1
Swanley
Farningham Rd Sta.
B260
Longfield
OWLETTS
Strood
New Barn
Cobham
COBHAM HALL
ROCHESTER
3/1
Horton Kirby
NEW COLLEGE
Hartley
Longfield Hill
Sole Street
2
CHATHAM
Farningham
Camer
Cuxton
Borstal
(RUINS)
Hook Green
CAMER
A229
M25
Fawkham Green
15
Luddesdown
Medway
M2
A20
Meopham
ROMAN VILLA (RUINS)
Eynsford
LULLINGSTONE
New Ash Green
Meopham Green
Halling
Wouldham

12
EGHAM
BRACKNELL
North Ascot
Ascot
Cheapside
Virginia Water
Sunninghill
South Ascot
Sunningdale
Longcross Sta.
Chobham Common
Thorpe
Laleham
Littleton
Lyne
Shepperton
CHERTSEY
Weybridge
Addlestone
Crowthorne
Surrey Hill
Bagshot
Windlesham
Longcross
Ottershaw
Row Town
New Haw
Burrowhill
Lightwater
Woodham
Bagshot Heath
Chobham
Camberley
CAMBERLEY
Blackwater
Donkey Town
West End
Byfleet
West Byfleet
Bisley
Knaphill
Horsell
Wisley
Chobham Ridges
Danger Zone
WOKING
Pyrford
FRIMLEY
St John's
Brookwood
Newark Priory
Martyr's Green
Farnborough Green
Deepcut
Old Woking
Ripley
Ockham
West Heath
Frimley Green
Mayford
Send Marsh
Cove
Mytchett
Pirbright
Worplesdon Sta.
Send
FARNBOROUGH
Sutton Green
Sutton Place
Henley Park
Worplesdon
Pitch Place
Hatchlands
West Clandon
West Horsley
Ash Vale
Normandy
Stoughton
Burpham
North Town
Wood Street
East Clandon
Ash
Wanborough Sta.
Merrow
Clandon Park (NT)
ALDERSHOT
Flexford
Heath End
Tongham
Wanborough
Onslow Village
Newland's Corner
Badshot Lea
Hog's Back
GUILDFORD
Albury
Seale
Puttenham
Loseley
Chilworth
Albury Park
Shere
Runfold
Compton
Albury Heath
FARNHAM
The Sands
Shalford
Blackheath
Lower Bourne
Shackleford
Hurtmore
Farncombe
Wonersh
Farley Green
Waverley Abbey
Charleshill
Bramley
Peaslake
Eashing
Shamley Green
Tilford
Peper Harow
Elstead
Godalming
Hurtwood Common
Stroud Common
Milford
Busbridge
Thorncombe Street
Millbridge
Milford Sta.
Grafham
Witley Common (NT)
Winkworth Arboretum (NT)
Rowly
Frensham Gt. Pond
Frensham
Wheelerstreet
Hydestile
Ewhurst
Rushmoor
Hascombe
Thursley
Witley
Bowlhead Green
Wormley
Hambledon
Cranleigh
Churt
Witley Sta.
Loxhill
Beacon Hill
Brook
Sandhills
Vachery Pond
Headley Down
Hindhead
Gibbet Hill
Dunsfold
Alfold Crossways
Grayshott
Grayswood
Chiddingfold
Haslemere
Alfold
M3
A3
A31
A320
A332
A330
A30
A322
A3095
A319
A3046
A324
A317
A318
A245
A247
A321
A323
A325
A3014
A3100
A25
A248
A287
A281
A286
A283
A244
B3020
B386
B383
B3015
B311
B382
B380
B3032
B3000
B3001
B2130
B2128
B2127
B2039
B374
B365
B376
B3002

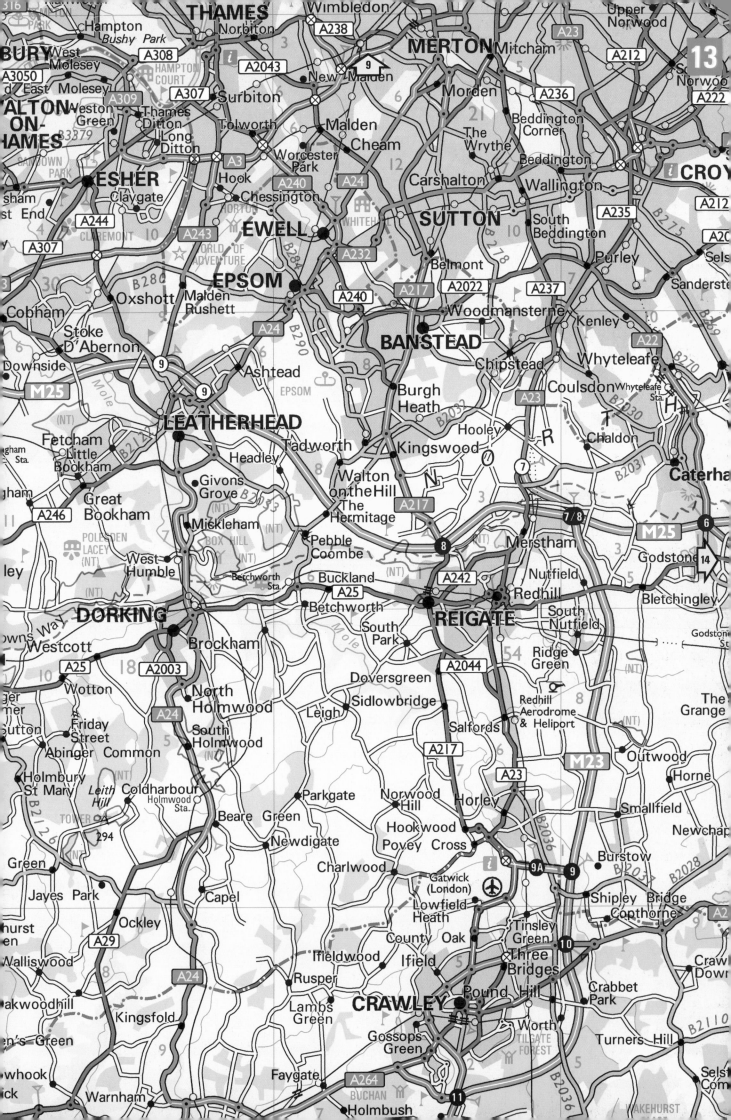

316
13
THAMES
Wimbledon
Upper Norwood
Hampton
Bushy Park
Norbiton
A238
MERTON
Mitcham
A23
A212
West Molesey
A308
HAMPTON COURT
A2043
New Malden
A3050
East Molesey
A307
Surbiton
Morden
A236
Norwood
A222
A309
Weston Green
Thames Ditton
Malden
Beddington Corner
ON-
B3379
Tolworth
The Wrythe
Long Ditton
Cheam
SANDOWN PARK
A3
Worcester Park
Beddington
ESHER
Hook
A240
A24
Carshalton
Wallington
CROY
Claygate
Chessington
A212
A244
CLAREMONT
HORTON
A243
EWELL
WHITEHALL
SUTTON
South Beddington
A235
B275
A307
WORLD OF ADVENTURE
B284
A232
B278
Belmont
Purley
B280
EPSOM
A217
A2022
A237
Oxshott
Malden Rushett
A240
Woodmansterne
Sanderstead
Cobham
Kenley
Stoke D'Abernon
A24
B290
BANSTEAD
A22
Downside
Ashtead
Chipstead
Whyteleafe
B270
M25
Mole
EPSOM
Burgh Heath
Coulsdon
Whyteleafe Sta.
(NT)
LEATHERHEAD
B2032
Hooley
B2030
Fetcham
Little Bookham
Tadworth
Headley
Kingswood
Chaldon
Walton on the Hill
B2031
Caterham
Givons Grove
Great Bookham
A246
B2033
Mickleham
The Hermitage
A217
Merstham
M25
POLESDEN LACEY
BOX HILL
Pebble Coombe
Godstone
West Humble
Betchworth Sta.
Buckland
A242
Nutfield
A25
Redhill
Bletchingley
DORKING
Betchworth
REIGATE
South Nutfield
Westcott
Brockham
South Park
Mole
Ridge Green
A25
A2003
A2044
Wotton
North Holmwood
Doversgreen
Sidlowbridge
Redhill Aerodrome & Heliport
The Grange
Friday Street
Leigh
Salfords
A24
South Holmwood
Abinger Common
A217
Outwood
M23
Holmbury St Mary
Leith Hill
Coldharbour
A23
Horne
Holmwood Sta.
Parkgate
Norwood Hill
Horley
Smallfield
TOWER
Beare Green
Hookwood
294
B2126
B2036
Newchap
Newdigate
Povey Cross
Burstow
Green
Charlwood
Gatwick (London)
B2028
Jayes Park
Capel
Lowfield Heath
Shipley Bridge
Copthorne
Ockley
Tinsley Green
County Oak
A29
Three Bridges
Ifieldwood
Ifield
Walliswood
Crabbet Park
A24
Rusper
Pound Hill
Lambs Green
CRAWLEY
Kingsfold
Worth
TILGATE FOREST
Gossops Green
Turners Hill
B2110
Faygate
A264
BUCHAN
Warnham
Holmbush
B2036
WAKEHURST

14
Upper Norwood
Chislehurst
Beckenham
BROMLEY
A222
St Paul's Cray
Mitcham
A23
A212
South Norwood
Bickley
Morden
A236
A222
10
Eden Park
A21
Bromley Common
A208
St Mary Cray
Beddington Corner
The Wrythe
A214
West Wickham
Hayes
Orpington
A232
Shirley
A232
Beddington
Carshalton
Wallington
CROYDON
Addington
Locksbottom
A224
A223
Keston
Farnborough
Chelsfield
SUTTON
A235
A212
South Beddington
New Addington
Green Street Green
Knockholt Sta.
A21
A2022
Purley
Selsdon
Leaves Green
Downe
Pratt's Bottom
Belmont
A2022
A237
Sanderstead
Farleigh
A233
Hazelwood
Halstead
A217
Woodmansterne
Kenley
Down House
Cudham
Knockholt Pound
ANSTEAD
A22
Biggin Hill
Chelsham
Chipstead
Whyteleafe
Warlingham
Knockholt
Burgh Heath
Coulsdon
Whyteleafe Sta.
Chevening
A23
Tatsfield
Hooley
Woldingham
Kingswood
Chaldon
267
Chipstead
Brasted
Caterham
Titsey
Quebec Ho.
A217
Westerham
Limpsfield
Brasted Ch
Oxted
A25
M25
Squerryes Court
Merstham
Godstone
Chartwell
Toy's Hill
13
Nutfield
A242
Redhill
Tandridge
Holland
Crockham Hill
Bletchingley
REIGATE
South Nutfield
Godstone Sta.
South Godstone
Ridge Green
Marlpit Hill
Four Elms
A2044
Crowhurst Lane End
Bough Beech
Redhill Aerodrome & Heliport
The Grange
Crowhurst
Salfords
Blindley Heath
Haxted
Edenbridge
A217
Mill & Museum
Outwood
M23
Hever
A23
Horne
Lingfield
Marsh Green
Horley
A22
Smallfield
Markbeech
Newchapel
Lingfield
Greathed Manor
Cowden Pound
Burstow
Felcourt
Dormansland
Cowden Sta
Claydene
Gatwick (London)
Dormans Park
Cowden
Lowfield Heath
Shipley Bridge
Copthorne
A264
Felbridge
Holtye Common
Tinsley Green
A264
Ifield
Three Bridges
East Grinstead
Hammerwood
Sackville College
Hammerwood Park
Crawley Down
Pound Hill
Crabbet Park
Brockhurst
Sunnyside
Hartwell
Forest Way
Ashurstwood
Worth
Tilgate Forest
Turners Hill
Saint Hill
Brambletye
A22
Hartfield
Standen
Forest Row
Weir Wood Res.
Selsfield Common
Kidbrooke Park
Upper Hartfield
Coleman's
Wakehurst
Spring Hill Wildfowl
B2036
B2110
B2028
B2026
B269

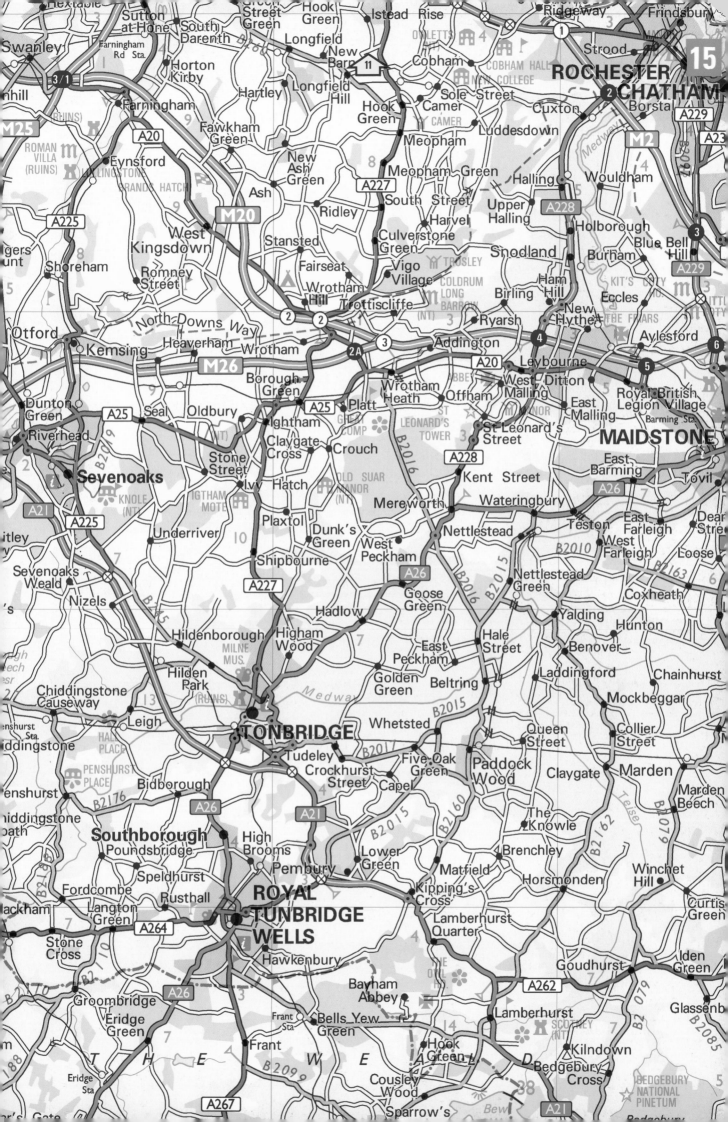

15
ROCHESTER
CHATHAM
MAIDSTONE
TONBRIDGE
ROYAL TUNBRIDGE WELLS
Sevenoaks
Southborough
Swanley
Sutton at Hone
South Darenth
Horton Kirby
Farningham
Eynsford
West Kingsdown
Shoreham
Otford
Kemsing
Heaverham
Wrotham
Borough Green
Ightham
Seal
Oldbury
Riverhead
Dunton Green
Longfield
New Barn
Hartley
Fawkham Green
New Ash Green
Ash
Ridley
Stansted
Fairseat
Wrotham Hill
Trottiscliffe
Vigo Village
Culverstone Green
Meopham
Meopham Green
South Street
Harvel
Cobham
Sole Street
Camer
Luddesdown
Cuxton
Strood
Frindsbury
Borstal
Halling
Upper Halling
Snodland
Wouldham
Holborough
Burham
Blue Bell Hill
Eccles
Aylesford
Birling
Ham Hill
New Hythe
Ryarsh
Addington
Leybourne
West Malling
Ditton
Offham
East Malling
Royal British Legion Village
Wrotham Heath
Platt
St Leonard's Street
Crouch
Claygate Cross
Stone Street
Ivy Hatch
Plaxtol
Dunk's Green
Shipbourne
West Peckham
Mereworth
Kent Street
Wateringbury
Nettlestead
Nettlestead Green
Teston
East Barming
Tovil
East Farleigh
West Farleigh
Loose
Coxheath
Yalding
Hunton
Benover
Laddingford
Chainhurst
Mockbeggar
Collier Street
Marden
Marden Beech
Hale Street
East Peckham
Beltring
Golden Green
Hadlow
Goose Green
Higham Wood
Hildenborough
Hilden Park
Underriver
Sevenoaks Weald
Nizels
Chiddingstone Causeway
Leigh
Penshurst
Bidborough
Tudeley
Crockhurst Street
Capel
Five Oak Green
Whetsted
Paddock Wood
Queen Street
Claygate
The Knowle
Brenchley
Matfield
Horsmonden
Winchet Hill
Curtis Green
High Brooms
Pembury
Lower Green
Kipping's Cross
Lamberhurst Quarter
Goudhurst
Iden Green
Glassenbury
Poundsbridge
Speldhurst
Rusthall
Fordcombe
Langton Green
Stone Cross
Groombridge
Eridge Green
Hawkenbury
Bayham Abbey
Bells Yew Green
Frant
Lamberhurst
Kilndown
Bedgebury Cross
Hook Green
Cousley Wood
Sparrow's
THE WEALD
M25
M20
M26
M2
A20
A225
A227
A25
A228
A26
A21
A229
A262
A264
A267
B2016
B2015
B2010
B2163
B2017
B2160
B2162
B2079
B2176
B2099
B2085
North Downs Way
Medway
Teise
BEDGEBURY NATIONAL PINETUM
KNOLE (NT)
IGTHAM MOTE
PENSHURST PLACE
HALL PLACE
MILNE MUS.
COBHAM HALL
NEW COLLEGE
TROSLEY
COLDRUM LONG BARROW (NT)
KIT'S COTY HO.
THE FRIARS
ST LEONARD'S TOWER
OLD SUAR MANOR (NT)
SCOTNEY (NT)

16
INNER LONDON ROUTE MAP
Edgware
Burnt Oak
Queensbury
Kingsbury
Kenton
The Hyde
HENDON
FINCHLEY
North Finchley
FRIERN BARNET
New Southgate
Church End
East Finchley
Muswell Hill
Hampstead Garden Suburb
Highgate
Golders Green
Archway
Holloway
HAMPSTEAD
HAMPSTEAD HEATH
Gospel Oak
Kentish Town
Camden Town
Neasden
Cricklewood
WEMBLEY
Stonebridge Park
WILLESDEN
Harlesden
Alperton
Kilburn
St. John's Wood
REGENT'S PARK
Maida Vale
Park Royal
Hanger Hill Park
EALING
ACTON
East Acton
Shepherds Bush
Mayfair
Hyde Park
Kensington Gardens
KENSINGTON
HAMMERSMITH
CHISWICK
BRENTFORD
Gunnersbury
CHELSEA
Pimlico
Olympia
Kew
FULHAM
Castelnau
BARNES
Putney
Mortlake
East Sheen
RICHMOND
Roehampton
BATTERSEA
Clapham
Nine Elms
WANDSWORTH
Earlsfield
Balham
Upper Tooting
Petersham
Ham
RICHMOND PARK
M1
A40(M)
M41
M4
Crown Copyright Reserved
Based upon the Ordnance Survey of the Controller of H.M.

17
M11
REFERENCE
Motorways
Circular & Ring Roads
Primary Routes
Class A Roads
Class B Roads
Railway Stations (B.R.)
Underground Stations
B.R. & Underground Stas.
Landmarks
Golf Courses
Principal Sports Grounds
21
113
225
ILFORD
QUEENSWAY
STRATFORD
Hospital
18 Holes
9 Holes
Rugby
Football
Cricket
0
1 Mile
Scale
EDMONTON
Woodford Wells
Woodford
Highams Park
Larkswood Park
Pymmes Park
Southgate Hospital
North Middlesex Hospital
Banbury Reservoir
Walthamstow Stadium
Tottenham F.C.
Noel Park
TOTTENHAM
Lido Lordship Rec. Grd.
WALTHAMSTOW
Whipps Cross
Snaresbrook
Royal Wanstead Sch.
Whipps Cross Hosp.
Gates Corner
The Eagle
The George
Reservoirs
St. Ann's General Hospital
Stamford Hill
Leytonstone
Leytonstone Ho. Hosp.
Green Man
Finsbury Park
Clissold Park
STOKE NEWINGTON
Arsenal F.C.
HIGHBURY
Hackney Downs
Leyton Marshes
Hackney Marshes
LEYTON
Orient F.C.
Wanstead Flats
Ilford
ILFORD
South Park
Forest Gate
Manor Park
HACKNEY
Eastern Hosp.
Hackney Wick Stadium
Stratford
Langthorne Hosp.
Barking Park
Plashet Park
Dalston
A102(M)
Stratford Marsh
Victoria Park
West Ham Park
WEST HAM
Upton Park
ISLINGTON
St. Leonard's Hospital
London Hospital (Mile end)
Bow
Bow Bridge
West Ham United F.C.
Plaistow
EAST HAM
Bethnal Green
Queen Mary College
Stepney
St. Clement's London Hosp.
BROMLEY
St. Andrew's Hosp.
Newham Hosp.
McMillan Stadium
London Mus.
River Lea
Canning Town
Beckton
St. Paul's
The Tower
Tower Bri.
POPLAR
Limehouse Basin
Rotherhithe Tunnel
Canary Wharf
Blackwall Tunnel
Royal Victoria Dock
Royal Albert Dock
King George V. Dock
East London River Crossing
Silvertown
Thames Barrier
RIVER
THAMES
Woolwich Free Ferry
Royal Dockyard
Thamesmead
D
O
N
Bermondsey
Southwark Park
Greenland Dock
Millwall
Millwall Dock
ISLE OF DOGS
Elephant & Castle
Deptford Park
Royal Naval College
Maryon Park
Maryon Wilson Park
Barracks
WOOLWICH
Kennington
DEPTFORD
Greenwich Dist. Hosp.
National Maritime Museum
CHARLTON
Charlton Park
R.A. Tactical School
Shrewsbury Park
Millwall F.C.
New Cross Gen. Hosp.
GREENWICH
Greenwich Park
Blackheath
Woolwich Common
Shooters Hill
St. Giles Hosp.
CAMBERWELL
Peckham
New Cross
Marquis of Granby
Brook Hosp.
Water Tower
King's Coll. Hosp.
Ruskin Park
Nunhead
Blackheath
Kidbrooke
Eltham Common
Woolwich Meml. Hosp.
Oxleas Wood
Jack Wood
Brockley
LEWISHAM
Hilly Fields
Clock Tower
Peckham Rye Park
Dulwich Hospital
Herne Hill
East Dulwich
Lee
New Tigers Head
Sutcliffe Park
Eltham
Eltham Warren
Lee Green
Hither Green
Hither Green Hospital
Lewisham Hospital
Ladywell Rec. Grd.
One Tree Hill
Brockwell Park
Cycle Track
Dulwich
Dulwich Park
Horniman Gardens
Horniman Museum
Forest Hill
Guy's Hospital R.F.C.
Catford Stadium
Catford
Yorkshire Grey
Clifton's Corner
Eltham Palace
Avery Hill Training Coll
Royal Blackheath
Royal Hotel
New Eltham
Mottingham
Eltham Coll.
Grove Park Hosp.
Dulwich College
Dulwich & Sydenham Hill
West Dulwich
CIRCULAR
BROMLEY
© Nicholson 1993

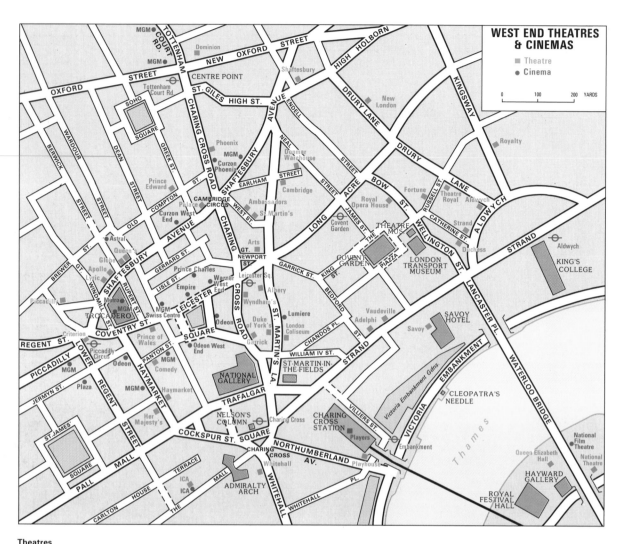

WEST END THEATRES & CINEMAS
- ■ Theatre
- ● Cinema

0   100   200   YARDS

Theatres

ADELPHI	The Strand	071 836 7611
ALBERY	St. Martin's Lane	071 867 1115
ALDWYCH	Aldwych	071 836 6404
ALMEIDA	Almeida St N1	071 359 4404
AMBASSADORS	West St	071 836 1171
APOLLO	Shaftesbury Av	071 437 5070
*APOLLO VICTORIA	Wilton Rd SW1	071 828 8665
ARTS	Gt. Newport St	071 836 2132
*BARBICAN	Barbican Centre	071 638 8891
CAMBRIDGE	Earlham St	071 379 5299
*COCKPIT	Gateforth St	071 262 7907
COMEDY	Panton St	071 867 1045
CRITERION	Piccadilly Circus	071 839 4488
DOMINION	Tottenham Court Rd	071 580 9562
DONMAR WAREHOUSE	Earlham St	071 867 1126
DUCHESS	Catherine St	071 494 5075
DUKE OF YORK'S	St. Martin's Lane	071 836 5122
FORTUNE	Russell St	071 836 2238
GARRICK	Charing Cross Rd	071 494 5085
GLOBE	Shaftesbury Av	071 494 5065
*GREENWICH	Crooms Hill SE10	081 858 7755
*HAYMARKET	Haymarket	071 930 8800
(Theatre Royal)		
HER MAJESTY'S	Haymarket	071 494 5400
ICA	The Mall	071 930 3647
*LONDON PALLADIUM	Argyll St	071 494 5020
LYRIC	Shaftesbury Av	071 494 5045
*MERMAID	Blackfriars EC4	071 410 0102
NATIONAL THEATRE	South Bank	071 928 2252
NEW LONDON	Drury Lane	071 405 0072
*OLD VIC	Waterloo Rd SW1	071 928 7616
*OPEN AIR THEATRE	Regent's Park	071 486 2431
PALACE	Shaftesbury Av	071 434 0909
PHOENIX	Charing Cross Rd	071 867 1044
PICCADILLY	Denman St	071 867 1118
PLAYHOUSE	Northumberland Av	071 839 4401
PRINCE EDWARD	Old Compton St	071 734 8951
PRINCE OF WALES	Coventry St	071 839 5987
QUEEN'S	Shaftesbury Av	071 494 5040
*ROYAL COURT	Sloane Sq SW1	071 730 1745
ROYALTY	Kingsway	071 494 5090
ST. MARTIN'S	West St	071 836 1443
SAVOY	Strand	071 836 8117
SHAFTESBURY	Shaftesbury Av	071 379 5399
STRAND	Aldwych	071 930 8800
THEATRE ROYAL	Drury Lane	071 494 5000
VAUDEVILLE	Strand	071 836 9987
*VICTORIA PALACE	Victoria St SW1	071 834 1317
WHITEHALL	Whitehall	071 867 1119
WYNDHAM'S	Charing Cross Rd	C71 867 1116

Concert Halls, Opera and Ballet

*BARBICAN HALL	Barbican Centre	071 638 8891
LONDON COLISEUM	St. Martins Lane	071 836 3161
QUEEN ELIZABETH HALL	South Bank	071 928 3002
ROYAL OPERA HOUSE	Covent Garden	071 240 1066
*SADLER'S WELLS	Rosebery Av EC1	071 278 8916

Cinemas

ASTRAL	Brewer St	071 734 6387
CHELSEA	King's Rd SW3	071 351 3742
*CURZON MAYFAIR	Curzon St W1	071 465 8865
CURZON PHOENIX	Charing Cross Rd	071 240 9661
CURZON WEST END	Shaftesbury Av	071 439 4805
EMPIRE	Leicester Sq	071 437 1234
ICA	The Mall	071 930 3647
LUMIERE	St. Martin's Lane	071 836 0691
METRO	Rupert St	071 437 0757
MGM BAKER STREET	Baker St	071 935 9772
MGM CHELSEA	King's Rd	071 352 5096
*MGM FULHAM ROAD	Fulham Rd	071 370 2636
MGM HAYMARKET	Haymarket	071 839 1527
MGM OXFORD STREET	Oxford St	071 636 0310
MGM PANTON STREET	Panton St	071 930 0631
MGM PICCADILLY	Piccadilly	071 437 3561
MGM SHAFTESBURY AV	Shaftesbury Av	071 836 6279
MGM SWISS CENTRE	Leicester Sq	071 439 4470
MGM TOTTENHAM COURT ROAD	Tottenham Court Rd	071 636 6148
MGM TROCADERO	Trocadero Centre	071 434 0032
*MINEMA	Knightsbridge	071 235 4225
ODEON HAYMARKET	Haymarket	0426 915353
*ODEON KENSINGTON	Kensington	0426 914666
ODEON MARBLE ARCH	Marble Arch	0426 914501
ODEON MEZZANINE	Leicester Sq	0426 915683
*ODEON WEST END	Leicester Sq	0426 915574
PLAZA	Lower Regent St	071 437 1234
PRINCE CHARLES	Leicester Sq	071 437 8181
*RENOIR	Brunswick Sq	071 837 8402
*SCREEN ON BAKER STREET	Baker St	071 935 2772
WARNER WEST END	Leicester Sq	071 439 0791

*NOT SHOWN ON THE MAP

EY TO MAP PAGES

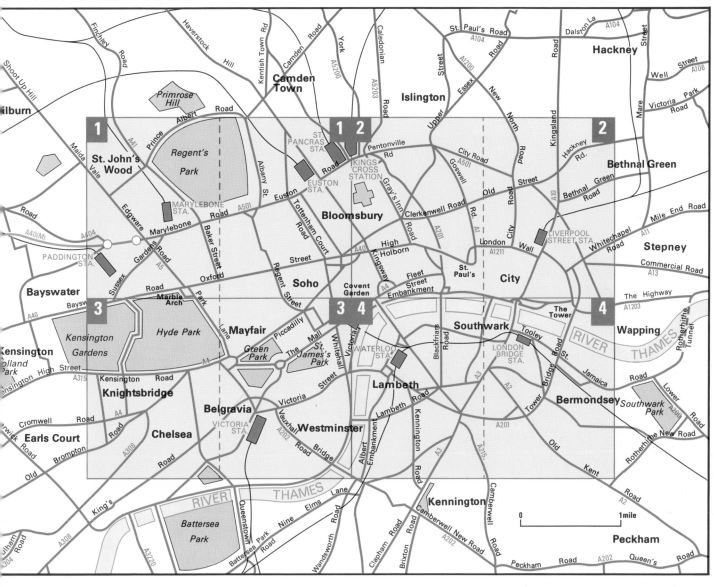

KEY TO MAP SYMBOLS

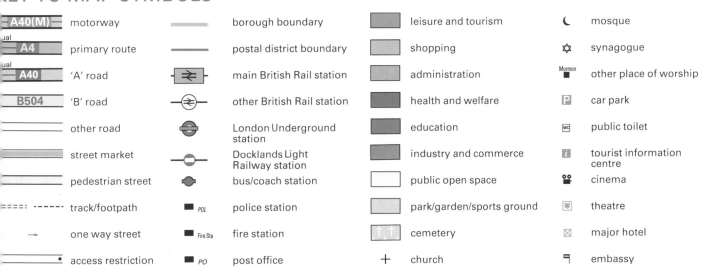

A40(M) motorway	borough boundary	leisure and tourism	☾ mosque
A4 primary route	postal district boundary	shopping	✡ synagogue
A40 'A' road	⇌ main British Rail station	administration	Mormon ■ other place of worship
B504 'B' road	⊖ other British Rail station	health and welfare	P car park
other road	⊖ London Underground station	education	WC public toilet
street market	⊖ Docklands Light Railway station	industry and commerce	i tourist information centre
pedestrian street	⊖ bus/coach station	public open space	🎥 cinema
track/footpath	■ POL police station	park/garden/sports ground	theatre
one way street	■ Fire Sta fire station	cemetery	⊠ major hotel
access restriction	■ PO post office	+ church	embassy

Scale 1:10,000 (6.3 inches to 1 mile)

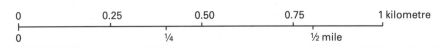

MAIN LONDON MAPS

KIMPTON
CODICOTE
STAPLEFORD
WADESMILL
WELWYN
FLAMSTEAD
WHEATHAMPSTEAD
WARE
ALDBURY
LITTLE GADDESDEN
TRING
REDBOURN
WELWYN GARDEN CITY
HERTFORD
GREAT AMWELL
STAN
Gade
LEMSFORD
LETTY GREEN
Lea
HERTFORD HEATH
HAILEY
A41
WIGGINTON
SANDRIDGE
NORTHCHURCH
BERKHAMSTED
HEMEL HEMPSTEAD
ST. ALBANS
ROE GREEN
HATFIELD
ESSENDON
HODDESDON
RO
ST. LEONARDS
BOURNE END
LEVERSTOCK GREEN
COLNEY HEATH
WILDHILL
LITTLE BERKHAMSTED
BROXBOURN
ASHLEY GREEN
HERTFORDSHIRE
EPPING GREEN
NEWGATE STREET
WORMLEY
LOWER NA
BUCKINGHAMSHIRE
CHISWELLGREEN
PARK STREET
LONDON COLNEY
WELHAM GREEN
CHARTRIDGE
LYE GREEN
BOVINGDON
KINGS LANGLEY
BRICKET WOOD
BROOKMANS PARK
GOFF'S OAK
SOUTH HEATH
CHESHAM
CHIPPERFIELD
ABBOTS LANGLEY
COLNEY STREET
CUFFLEY
CHESHUNT
GREAT MISSENDEN
HYDE HEATH
Chess
FLAUNDEN
GARSTON
Colne
SHENLEY
SOUTH MIMMS
POTTERS BAR
WALTHAM ABBEY
SARRATT
RIDGE
M25
WALTHAM CROSS
CHESHAM BOIS
RADLETT
HADLEY WOOD
BOTANY BAY
CHASE SIDE
SEWARDS
CHENIES
BOREHAMWOOD
BARNET
NEW BARNET
COCKFOSTERS
ENFIELD
HOLMER GREEN
LITTLE CHALFONT
AMERSHAM
Misbourne
CROXLEY GREEN
WATFORD
ARKLEY
WINCHMORE HILL
PONDERS END
LOU
HAZLEMERE
PENN STREET
CHORLEYWOOD
OXHEY
ELSTREE
EAST BARNET
COLESHILL
BUSHEY
TOTTERIDGE
SOUTHGATE
CHIN
CHALFONT ST. GILES
RICKMANSWORTH
BATCHWORTH
WHETSTONE
TYLERS GREEN
STANMORE
FRIERN BARNET
PALMERS GREEN
EDMONTON
HIGHAMS PARK
SEER GREEN
CHALFONT COMMON
BATCHWORTH HEATH
SOUTH OXHEY
MILL HILL
LOUDWATER
HAREFIELD
EDGWARE
FINCHLEY
WOOD GREEN
TOTTENHAM
BEACONSFIELD
NORTHWOOD
PINNER
WEALDSTONE
MUSWELL HILL
Hornsey
HIGHAM HILL
WOOBURN GREEN
CHALFONT ST. PETER
Colne
EASTCOTE
HARROW
HENDON
GOLDERS GREEN
CROUCH END
STAMFORD HILL
WALTHAMSTOW
GERRARDS CROSS
RUISLIP
RAYNERS LANE
KINGSBURY
KENTON
HIGHGATE
LEYTONSTONE
WOOBURN
BOURNE END
DENHAM
ICKENHAM
SUDBURY
NEASDEN
GREATER
LEYTON
M40
CRICKLEWOOD
HAMPSTEAD
HOLLOWAY
COOKHAM
FARNHAM COMMON
STOKE POGES
IVER HEATH
UXBRIDGE
NORTHOLT
WEMBLEY
WILLESDEN
KILBURN
KENTISH TOWN
DALSTON
HACKNEY
STRATFORD
WEST HAM
HILLINGDON
ALPERTON
CAMDEN TOWN
ISLINGTON
BETHNAL GREEN
TAPLOW
GREENFORD
HARLESDEN
SHOREDITCH
BURNHAM
IVER
COWLEY
YEADING
PARK ROYAL
FINSBURY
STEPNEY
Lea
MAIDENHEAD
SLOUGH
YIEWSLEY
SOUTHALL
HANWELL
EALING
ACTON
NOTTING HILL
PADDINGTON
HOLBORN
CITY
WHITE-CHAPEL
POPLAR
Colne Brook
WEST DRAYTON
HAYES
SHEPHERD'S BUSH
KENSINGTON
SOUTHWARK
BERMONDSEY
DORNEY
LANGLEY
HARLINGTON
M4
CHISWICK
WESTMINSTER
BRAY
Thames
ETON
COLNBROOK
HESTON
BRENTFORD
HAMMERSMITH
CHELSEA
LAMBETH
DEPTFORD
GREENWICH
DATCHET
HEATHROW AIRPORT LONDON
CRANFORD
OSTERLEY
KEW
BARNES
FULHAM
BATTERSEA
CAMBERWELL
NEW CROSS
FIFIELD
WINDSOR
HORTON
HOUNSLOW
RICHMOND
PUTNEY
LONDON
PECKHAM
BLA
BRIXTON
BERKSHIRE
OLD WINDSOR
WRAYSBURY
STANWELL
ISLEWORTH
ROEHAMPTON
WANDSWORTH
CLAPHAM
TULSE HILL
DULWICH
LEWISHAM
WINKFIELD
FELTHAM
TWICKENHAM
PETERSHAM
EAST BEDFONT
STREATHAM
CATFORD
MOTTIN
EARLSFIELD
FOREST HILL
SOUTH
ENGLEFIELD GREEN
EGHAM
STAINES
ASHFORD
HANWORTH
HAM
WIMBLEDON
TOOTING GRAVENEY
WEST NORWOOD
SYDENHAM
TEDDINGTON
HAMPTON
NORBITON
MERTON
BROMLEY
ASCOT
VIRGINIA WATER
THORPE
LALEHAM
SUNBURY
KINGSTON UPON THAMES
MITCHAM
THORNTON HEATH
BECKENHAM
SUNNINGHILL
SUNNINGDALE
SHEPPERTON
WEST MOLESEY
THAMES DITTON
MORDEN
NORBURY
SOUTHBO
M3
M25
SELHURST
BROOMHALL
CHERTSEY
WALTON ON-THAMES
SURBITON
MALDEN
ST. HELIER
ADDISCOMBE
HAYES
TOLWORTH
WORCESTER PARK
CARSHALTON
BEDDINGTON
CROYDON
WINDLESHAM
ADDLESTONE
WEYBRIDGE
ESHER
HOOK
ADDINGTON
OTTERSHAW
SUTTON
WALLINGTON
BAGSHOT
LIGHTWATER
NEW HAW
CHESSINGTON
EWELL
CHEAM
SELSDON
NEW ADDINGTON
WOODHAM
Mole
BELMONT
CHOBHAM
OXSHOTT
EPSOM
PURLEY
SANDERSTEAD
WEST END
WEST BYFLEET
BYFLEET
COBHAM
WOODMANSTERNE
BANSTEAD
WOKING
KNAPHILL
Wey
STOKE D'ABERNON
ASHTEAD
BURGH HEATH
COULSDON
WARLINGHAM
BISLEY
OLD WOKING
WHYTE LEAFE
CHIPSTEAD
FRIMLEY GREEN
RIPLEY
OCKHAM
TAT
PIRBRIGHT
SEND
TADWORTH
WOLDINGHAM
HOOLEY
FETCHAM
LEATHERHEAD
MYTCHETT
MAYFORD
WALTON-ON-THE-HILL
CATERHAM
LITTLE BOOKHAM
WORPLESDON
GREAT BOOKHAM
JACOBSWELL
WEST HORSLEY
MERSTHAM
LIMPSFIELD
MICKLEHAM
M25
GODSTONE
NORMANDY
WEST CLANDON
EAST HORSLEY
OXTED
STOUGHTON
SURREY
BUCKLAND
FLEXFORD
EAST CLANDON
REDHILL
BLETCHINGLEY
TANDRIDGE
ASH
WANBOROUGH
REIGATE
TONGHAM
GUILDFORD
WESTCOTT
DORKING
BROCKHAM
EARLSWOOD
GOMSHALL
SOUTH GODSTONE
CROWHURST LANE END
SEALE
Mole
COMPTON
SHALFORD
ALBURY
SHERE
STROOD GREEN
M23
ABINGER HAMMER
NORTH HOLMWOOD
LEIGH
SALFORDS
SHACKLEFORD
HURTMORE
BROOK
OUTWOOD
BLINDLEY HEATH
WONERSH
NALDERSWOOD
BRAMLEY
SHAMLEY GREEN
HOLMBURY ST. MARY
ELSTEAD
GODALMING
BEARE GREEN
LINGF

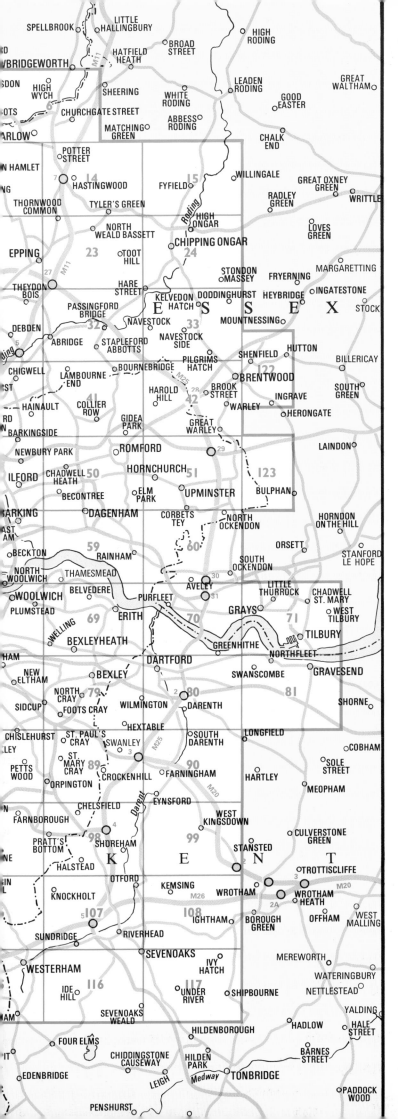

KEY TO SYMBOLS ON MAIN LONDON MAPS

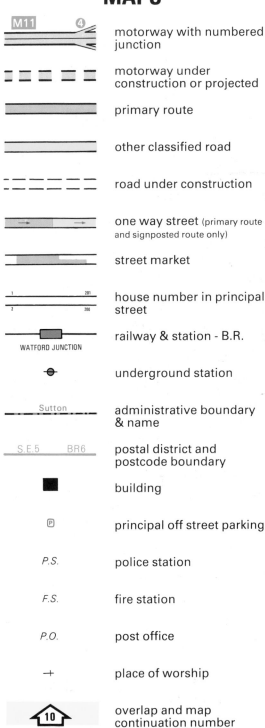

M11 ——— 4	motorway with numbered junction
– – – – –	motorway under construction or projected
════	primary route
————	other classified road
- - - - -	road under construction
→ →	one way street (primary route and signposted route only)
	street market
1 ——— 201 / 2 ——— 200	house number in principal street
WATFORD JUNCTION	railway & station - B.R.
⊖	underground station
Sutton	administrative boundary & name
S.E.5 BR6	postal district and postcode boundary
■	building
℗	principal off street parking
P.S.	police station
F.S.	fire station
P.O.	post office
+	place of worship
⌂ 10	overlap and map continuation number

SCALE

1: 20,000 (3.17 inches to 1 mile)

0   ¼   ½   ¾ mile

0   ½   1 Kilometre

1
REGENT'S PARK
LONDON ZOO
RUNNING TRACK
Tennis Cts
ST. JOHN'S WOOD
LORD'S CRICKET GROUND
MUSEUM
St. John's Wood Church
Winfield House
Hanover Lodge
London Central Mosque
HANOVER GATE
BOATING LAKE
OPEN AIR THEA
QUEEN MARY'S GARDENS
INNER CIRCLE
Bandstand
LONDON BUSINESS SCH
ROYAL COLL OF OBSTETRICIANS & GYNAECOLOGISTS
REGENT'S COLLEGE
Clarence Gate
YORK BRIDGE
LISSON GREEN EST
LISSON GROVE
CHURCH STREET ESTATE
Electricity Sta
MAIDA VALE HOSP
PADDINGTON GREEN
PADDINGTON COLLEGE
St. David's (Welsh)
St. Mary
Sylvia Young Theatre Sch
ST. EDWARDS CONV.
SHERLOCK HOLMES MUS
MADAME TUSSAUD'S
PLANETARIUM
BAKER STREET
MARYLEBONE
MARYLEBONE RD
WESTMINSTER TOWN HALL
OPHTHALMIC HOSP
SAMARITAN HOSP
EDGWARE ROAD
North Westminster Comm Sch
PADDINGTON
ST. MARY'S HOSP
MEDICAL SCHOOL
Paddington Basin
Great Western Royal
Norfolk Towers
FITZROY NUFFIELD HOSPITAL
Bryanston Court
Holiday Inn
Christian Science
WALLACE COLLECTION
HEINZ GALL
PORTMAN SQUARE
W1
WIGMORE ST
SELFRIDGES
OXFORD ST
MARBLE ARCH
Mount Royal
C&A
M&S
Speaker's Corner
CUMBERLAND GATE
BAYSWATER ROAD
NORTH CARRIAGE DRIVE
LANCASTER GATE
Victoria Gate
Marlborough Gate
The Fountains
Lancaster Gate
Grosvenor House
PARK LANE
SEYMOUR STREET
EDGWARE RD
SUSSEX GARDENS
PRAED ST
WELLINGTON ROAD
PRINCE ALBERT ROAD
PARK ROAD
ST. JOHN'S WOOD RD
GLOUCESTER PLACE
ORCHARD ST
PORTMAN ST
3
OXFORD STREET where marked is closed to through traffic (except buses & taxis) from 7a.m. - 7p.m. Monday - Saturday
A B C D E F G H
1 2 3 4 5 6 7 8 9 10

1
REGENT'S PARK
NW1
SOMERS TOWN
ST. PANCRAS
KING'S CROSS
EUSTON
EUSTON SQUARE
WARREN ST
GT. PORTLAND ST
REGENT'S PARK
UNIVERSITY COLLEGE LONDON
UNIVERSITY OF LONDON
BLOOMSBURY
THE BRITISH MUSEUM AND BRITISH LIBRARY
GOODGE ST
TOTTENHAM COURT ROAD
OXFORD CIRCUS
OXFORD ST
SOHO
COVENT GARDEN
LEICESTER SQ
STRAND
MAYFAIR
PICCADILLY CIR
EUSTON ROAD
MARYLEBONE ROAD
GOWER STREET
TOTTENHAM COURT RD
REGENT ST
PORTLAND PLACE
NEW BOND ST
SHAFTESBURY AVE
CHARING CROSS ROAD
HIGH HOLBORN
NEW OXFORD ST
BLOOMSBURY WAY
SOUTHAMPTON ROW
CAMDEN TOWN HALL
New British Library (Opening 1993)
J
K
L
M
N
P
Q
2
3
4
5
6
7
8
9
10

2
A
B
C
D
E
F
G
H
1
2
3
4
5
6
7
8
9
10
KING'S CROSS
KING'S CROSS ST. PANCRAS
THAMESLINK
PENTONVILLE
PENTONVILLE RD
ANGEL
CITY ROAD
FINSBURY
CALEDONIAN RD
WHARFDALE RD
KINGSWAY COLLEGE
MOUNT PLEASANT POST OFFICE
FARRINGDON RD
ROSEBERY AVE
GRAY'S INN ROAD
ST. PANCRAS
WC1
CORAM'S FIELDS
THE HOSP FOR SICK CHILDREN
CLERKENWELL
CLERKENWELL RD
ST. BARTHOLOMEW'S MEDICAL COLL
GRAY'S INN GDNS
CHANCERY LANE
FARRINGDON
BLOOMSBURY
SOUTHAMPTON ROW
THEOBALD'S RD
HIGH HOLBORN
HOLBORN
LINCOLN'S INN FIELDS
ROYAL COURTS OF JUSTICE
PUBLIC RECORD OFFICE
HOLBORN VIADUCT
ST. BARTHOLOMEW'S HOSPITAL
CENTRAL CRIMINAL COURT (Old Bailey)
NEWGATE ST
FLEET STREET
CITY THAMESLINK
EC4
BLACKFRIARS
KINGSWAY
ALDWYCH
STRAND
COVENT GARDEN
WC2
SOMERSET HOUSE
TEMPLE
VICTORIA EMBANKMENT
RIVER THAMES
KING'S REACH
HMS PRESIDENT
HQS WELLINGTON
4

2
HOXTON
SHOREDITCH
ST. LUKE'S
BROADGATE
BARBICAN
HAGGERSTON
EC1
EC2
EC3
SHOREDITCH PARK
MOORFIELDS EYE HOSPITAL
BUNHILL FIELDS
LIVERPOOL STREET
Site of Old Spitalfields Market
ALDGATE
ALDGATE EAST
MOORGATE
BANK
MONUMENT
MANSION HOUSE
CANNON ST
TOWER HILL
TOWER GATEWAY
FENCHURCH ST
THE TOWER
Bank of England
Stock Exch
Lloyds of London
Nat West Tower
St. Paul's Cathedral
OLD STREET
CITY ROAD
NEW NORTH ROAD
EAST RD
KINGSLAND ROAD
HACKNEY ROAD
COLUMBIA ROAD
BETHNAL GREEN RD
COMMERCIAL ST
BISHOPSGATE
LONDON WALL
WHITECHAPEL HIGH ST
COMMERCIAL RD
MINORIES
LEMAN STREET
ROYAL MINT ST
LOWER THAMES ST
CHISWELL STREET
CHEAPSIDE
QUEEN VICTORIA ST
CORNHILL
LEADENHALL ST
HOUNDSDITCH
MIDDLESEX ST
BRICK LANE
A10
A1208
A1209
A1202
A5201
A501
A1211
A1210
B101
B144
B100
B122
B118
B135
B134
B126
J
K
L
M
N
P
Q
1
2
3
4
5
6
7
8
9
10

3
OXFORD STREET where marked is closed to through traffic (except buses & taxis) from 7a.m. - 7p.m. Monday - Saturday
HYDE PARK
KENSINGTON GARDENS
THE SERPENTINE
THE LONG WATER
SW7
SW3
BROMPTON
IMPERIAL COLLEGE
NATURAL HISTORY MUSEUM
VICTORIA & ALBERT MUSEUM
SCIENCE MUSEUM
HARRODS
SOUTH KENSINGTON
SLOANE SQUARE
KNIGHTSBRIDGE
LANCASTER GATE
MARBLE ARCH
HYDE PARK CORNER

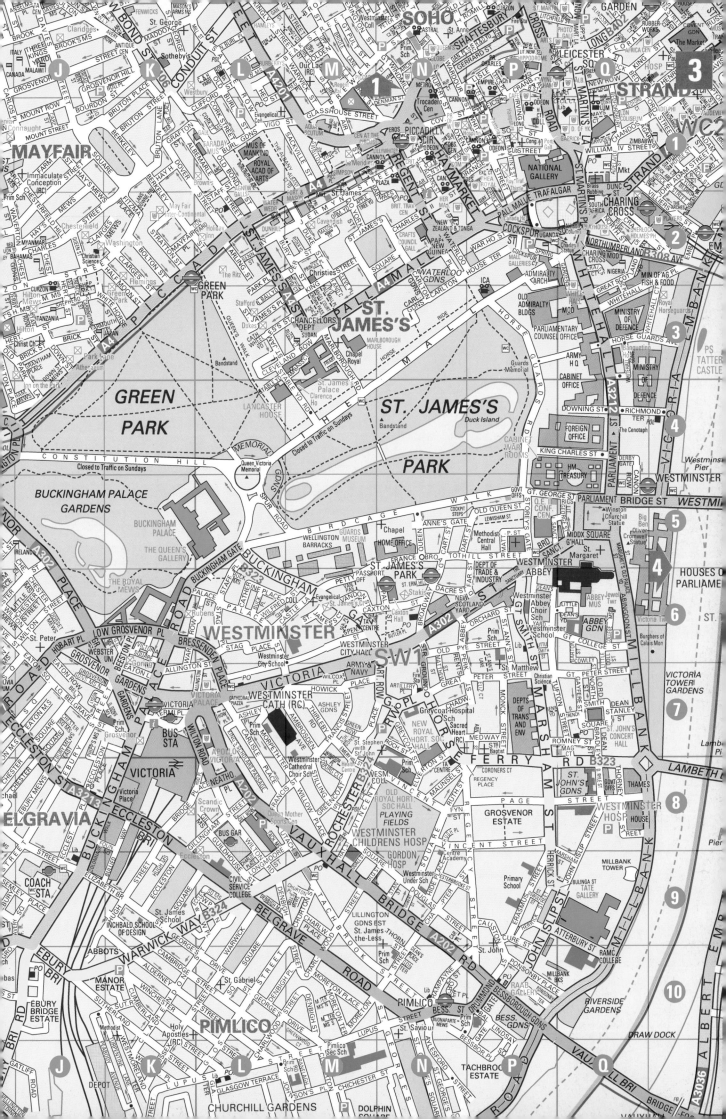
3
SOHO
MAYFAIR
STRAND
WC2
SHAFTESBURY
LEICESTER SQ
PICCADILLY CIR.
HAYMARKET
REGENT ST
PICCADILLY
NATIONAL GALLERY
TRAFALGAR
CHARING CROSS
PALL MALL
ST. JAMES'S
GREEN PARK
ST. JAMES'S PARK
Duck Island
CONSTITUTION HILL
Closed to Traffic on Sundays
Queen Victoria Memorial
BUCKINGHAM PALACE GARDENS
BUCKINGHAM PALACE
THE QUEEN'S GALLERY
THE ROYAL MEWS
BIRDCAGE WALK
WELLINGTON BARRACKS
GUARDS MUSEUM
HOME OFFICE
WHITEHALL
MINISTRY OF DEFENCE
DOWNING ST
FOREIGN OFFICE
HM TREASURY
CABINET WAR ROOMS
PARLIAMENT ST
WESTMINSTER
PARLIAMENT SQUARE
BRIDGE ST
HOUSES OF PARLIAMENT
Big Ben
WESTMINSTER ABBEY
Victoria Twr
VICTORIA TOWER GARDENS
MILLBANK
WESTMINSTER
SW1
VICTORIA
VICTORIA ST
WESTMINSTER CATH (RC)
BUS STA
COACH STA
ELGRAVIA
BUCKINGHAM PALACE ROAD
ECCLESTON BRI
VAUXHALL BRIDGE RD
HORSEFERRY RD
MARSHAM ST
GROSVENOR ESTATE
TATE GALLERY
MILLBANK TOWER
BELGRAVE ROAD
WARWICK WAY
PIMLICO
CHURCHILL GARDENS
LUPUS ST
RIVERSIDE GARDENS
DRAW DOCK
ALBERT EMB
VAUXHALL BRI
A4
A4201
A3212
A302
A202
B323
B324
A3213
A3036
J
K
L
M
N
P
Q
1
2
3
4
5
6
7
8
9
10

4
STRAND
WC2
CHARING CROSS
EMBANKMENT
WESTMINSTER
WESTMINSTER BRI
HOUSES OF PARLIAMENT
VICTORIA TOWER GARDENS
MILLBANK
LAMBETH BRI
LAMBETH
ALBERT EMBANKMENT
WATERLOO BRI
RIVER THAMES
KING'S REACH
ALDWYCH
TEMPLE
SOMERSET HOUSE
HMS PRESIDENT
HQS WELLINGTON Master Mariners
EC4
BLACKFRIARS
BLACKFRIARS BRI
BLACKFRIARS ROAD
NATIONAL THEATRE
QUEEN ELIZABETH HALL AND PURCELL ROOM
ROYAL FESTIVAL HALL
HAYWARD GALLERY
Festival Pier
HUNGERFORD BRI
Cleopatra's Needle
Charing Cross Pier
The London Television Centre
STAMFORD STREET
UPPER GROUND
Shell Centre
JUBILEE GDNS
Old County Hall
Westminster Pier
WATERLOO
WATERLOO EAST
WATERLOO ROAD
THE CUT
THE YOUNG VIC
THE OLD VIC
TANSWELL ESTATE
PEABODY SQUARE
ST. GEORGE'S CATHEDRAL
ST. GEORGE'S CIRCUS
BOROUGH ROAD
SOUTHWARK
UNION STREET
SOUTH BANK POLY
FLORENCE NIGHTINGALE MUSEUM
ST. THOMAS' HOSP
LAMBETH PALACE RD
LAMBETH PALACE GDNS
ARCHBISHOP'S PARK
LAMBETH ROAD
IMPERIAL WAR MUS
GERALDINE MARY HARMSWORTH PARK
ELEPHANT AND CASTLE
NEWINGTON BUTTS
KENNINGTON ROAD
KENNINGTON LANE
KENNINGTON PARK ROAD
KENNINGTON
SE11
Lambeth
Lilian Baylis Sec School
LAMBETH WALK
BLACK PRINCE ROAD
VAUXHALL GDNS EST
Power Station (Disused)
British Library (India Office & Records)
LONDON COLLEGE OF PRINTING
SURREY GARDENS
ALBERTA EST
A B C D E F G H
1 2 3 4 5 6 7 8 9 10

4
J
K
L
M
N
P
Q
1
2
3
4
5
6
7
8
9
10
MANSION HOUSE
CANNON ST
MONUMENT
FENCHURCH ST
EC3
TOWER HILL
TOWER GATEWAY
PRESCOT ST
ROYAL MINT
Southwark Bridge Steps
Swan Lane Pier
St. Magnus the Martyr
Site of Old Billingsgate Mkt
Custom House
LOWER THAMES ST
All Hallows by the Tower and Brass Rub. Cen
THE TOWER
Tower Pier
London Commodity Exchange
EAST SMITHFIELD
World Trade Centre
ST. KATHARINE'S DOCK
Ivory House
Tower Thistle
Alderman Stairs
ST. KATHARINE'S WAY
SCHOONER KATHLEEN & MAY
LONDON BRIDGE HOSPITAL
HMS BELFAST
City Pier
CLINK EXHIBITION
SOUTHWARK CATHEDRAL
Hay's Galleria
SOUTHWARK CROWN COURT
TOOLEY ST
TOWER BRIDGE MUSEUM & EXHIBITIONS
TOWER BRI
TOWER BRIDGE APPR
SOUTHWARK BRIDGE
SOUTHWARK BRI ROAD
LONDON BRI
KING WILLIAM ST
A300
A200
A100
B300
LONDON BRIDGE
Borough Mkt
ST THOMAS ST
GUY'S HOSP
BERMONDSEY STREET
SOUTH LONDON COLL
ST. OLAVE'S EST
DESIGN MUS
ST. SAV. DOCK
Mill Stairs
POMEROY PURDY GALLERY
JACOB ST
JAMAICA ROAD
DICKENS EST
CRUCIFIX LANE
DRUID ST
St. George the Martyr
THE BOROUGH
LOCKYER EST
TYERS EST
WHITES GRDS EST
ST. JOHN'S EST
TANNER STREET
LEATHERMARKET ST
KIPLING EST
Bermondsey Leather Mkt
SOUTHWARK COLLEGE Bermondsey Centre
PURBROOK EST
ST. SAVIOUR'S ESTATE
LONG LANE
A2198
TABARD GARDEN ESTATE
TABARD GARDENS
REC GRD
ELIM EST
CLUNY EST
St. Mary Magdalen
ABBEY STREET
B202
AYLWYN ESTATE
NECKINGER ESTATE
BERMONDSEY
GREAT DOVER ST
A2
SE1
Holy Trinity
HARPER ROAD
B240
LAWSON ESTATE
Geoffrey Chaucer Sec Sch
SOUTH BANK POLY Rachel McMillan Annexe
Brotherhood of the Cross & Star
MEAKIN EST
GRANGE ED CEN
GRANGE ROAD
A2206
SPA ROAD
TOWN HALL
BERMONDSEY SPA
VAUBAN ESTATE
HAROLD ESTATE
St. Saviour's & St. Olave's Sec Sch
Bricklayer's Arms
CREASY EST
GUINNESS BLDGS
NEW KENT ROAD
A201
Aylwin Sec School
SOUTHWARK PARK RD
NEWINGTON
INDUSTRIAL ESTATE
MANDELA WAY
OLD KENT ROAD
B203
DUNTON RD
LONGFIELD ESTATE
LYNTON EST
ROLLS ROAD
ALVEY EST
EAST STREET
WALWORTH
BROWNING EST
Walworth Lower School
SURREY SQUARE PARK
KINGLAKE EST
FARADAY GDNS
Walworth Sec Sch
THOMAS-A-BECKET PH
Southwark
LONGLAND COURT
MAWBEY ESTATE
St. Philip with St. Mark
MICHAEL FARADAY HOUSE
AYLESBURY EST
A215
English Martyrs (RC)
DAWES HOUSE
St. John the Evangelist

5
Codicote Rd.
Dowdell's Wood
Fish Wood
Warren Wood
Threegroves Wood
Cherrytree Spring
Coneydell Spring
Bladder Wood
Ayot Bury
Rectory Wood
Whitehill Farm
Ayot St. Peter
Ayot Place
AL6
Saul's Wood
Gregg's Wood
The Frythe
Home Farm
Long Spring
Little Hocketts Wood
Mitchell's Wood
Manor Farm
Homer's Wood
Cooks Wood
Sandybottom Wood
Crossway
Uplands
Malms Wood
Rectory Wood
Digswell Hill
Sherrards Training Centre
Digswell Place
New Wood
Conduit Field
Sherrardspark Wood
Reddings Plantation
Robinson's Wood
St. Albans
Hunter's Bridge
Sparrowhall Farm
Waterend Lane
Soray's Farm
Bowle's Wood
Ayot Green
Gray's Wood
Cowpers Spring
Crackendell Wood
Waterend House
Ford
Waterend
Park Mead Spring
Fancy Plantation
A1(M)
Brockswood Lane
B653
David's Dingle
Charlie's Croft
Keepers Cottage
Reservoir Plantation
Bluebell Hill Wood
Chalkdell Farm
Coleman Green La.
Brocket Hall
Brocket Park
Golf Course
AL8
Flint Bridge Plantation
Warren Farm
The Broadwater
Marford Road
Welwyn Garden City
Lamb's Grove
Four Gate Plantation
AL4
Upper Cromer Hyde Farm
Handside
Templehill Plantation
Lodgehill Plantation
Sprite Field Spring
Fletcher's Wick
Cromer Hyde Lane
Crooked Chimney P.H.
Roeback
Lemsford
Benstead's Wood
Wet Grove
Long Spring Grove
Long Grove Plantation
Brocket Corner
Lemsford House
Rec. Grd.
River Lea or Lee
Titnol's Wood
Cromerhyde Farm
College Annex
School
Swimming Pool
Stanborough Park
Dogsheart Spring
Brocket Road
County Police H.Q.
Chalkdell Wood
Symondshyde Farm
Hammonds
Boating Lake
"The Bull"
Stanborough
Sailing Lake
Stanborough Bury
Symondshyde Great Wood
Great North Road
Coopers Green Lane
Great Braitch Lane
Furze Field
AL10
Manor Road
A414
Astwick Manor Farm
School
Mt. Pleasant La.
Astwick Manor
Playing Fields
Birchwood Industrial Site
Cooper's Green
Hatfield Garden Village
BM
BN
BO
BP
BQ
10

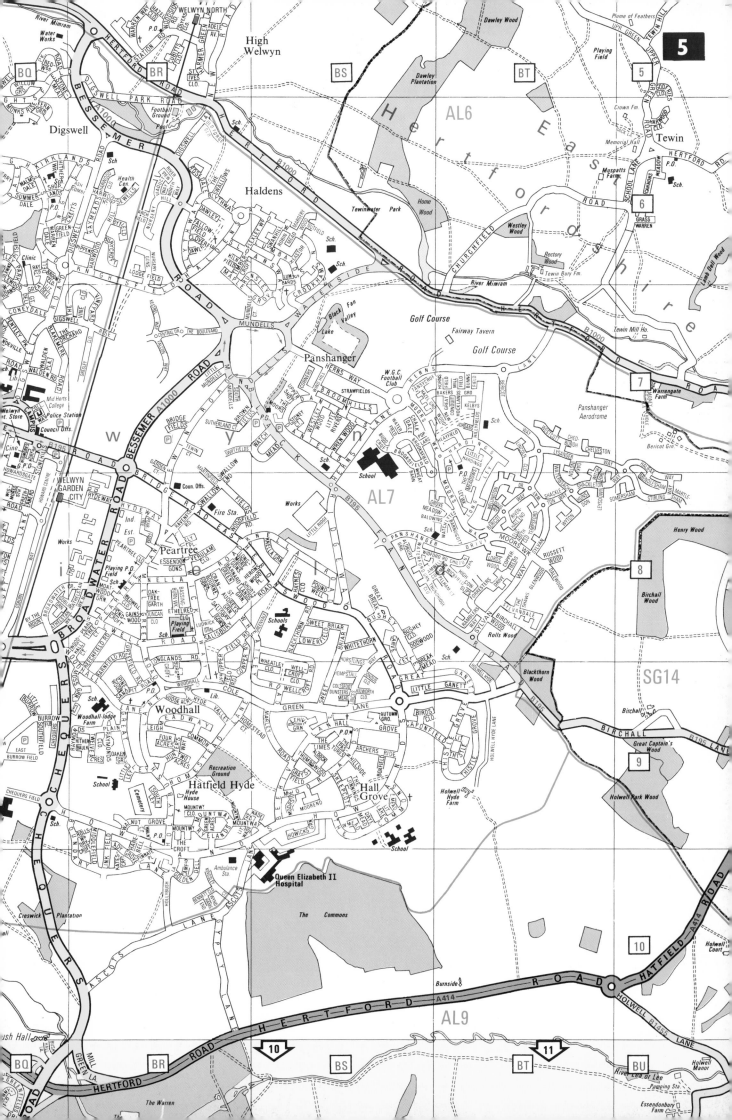
5
Welwyn North
High Welwyn
Digswell
Haldens
Tewin
Dawley Wood
Dawley Plantation
Home Wood
Westley Wood
Rectory Wood
Twinwater Park
Tewin Bury Fm.
River Mimram
Golf Course
Fairway Tavern
Panshanger
Panshanger Aerodrome
W.G.C. Football Club
Hertfordshire
Welwyn Garden City
Peartree
Woodhall
Hatfield Hyde
Hall Grove
Queen Elizabeth II Hospital
The Commons
Creswick Plantation
Recreation Ground
Cemetery
Henry Wood
Birchall Wood
Blackthorn Wood
Great Captain's Wood
Holwell Park Wood
Holwell Hyde Farm
Holwell Court
Holwell Manor
Essendonbury Farm
Burnside
The Warren
River Lea or Lee
AL6
AL7
AL9
SG14
BQ
BR
BS
BT
BU
HERTFORD ROAD
BESSEMER ROAD
BROADWATER ROAD
CHEQUERS
HATFIELD ROAD
10
11

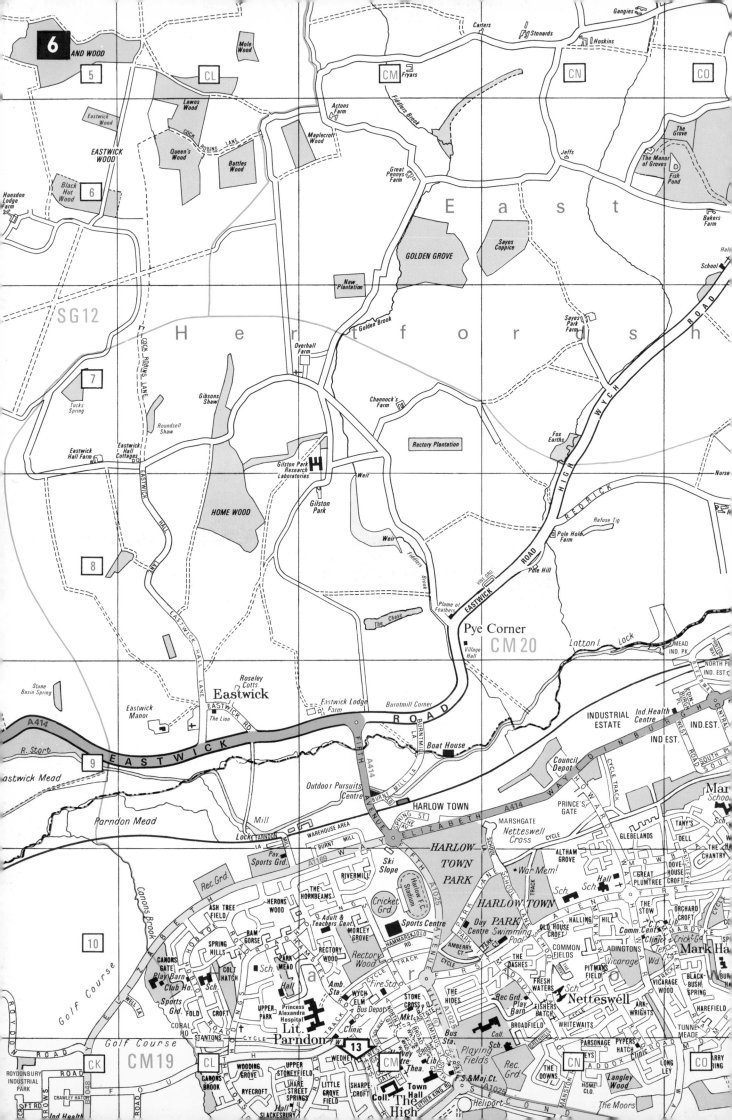

6
Eastwick Wood
Eastwick
Pye Corner
Harlow Town
Harlow Town Park
Lit. Parndon
Netteswell
Golden Grove
Home Wood
Gilston Park
Gilston Park Research Laboratories
Eastwick Road
Edinburgh Way
Fifth Avenue
High Wych Road
Elizabeth Way
Industrial Estate
Parndon Mead
Eastwick Mead
Golf Course
Princess Alexandra Hospital
SG12
CM20
CM19

SAWBRIDGEWORTH
Claylane Farm
School
Football Ground
CAMBRIDGE RD.
Pol. Sta.
Rec. Grd.
Sch.
April Place
Burtons Mill
SAWBRIDGEWORTH
Malthouse
Great Hyde Hall
Oak Spring
Cowicks
STATION ROAD
BELL STREET
Council Offs.
Cricket Grd.
Lib.
Fire Sta.
P.O.
School
Malthouse
HALLINGBURY ROAD
SHEERING LOWER ROAD
CM 21
Nursery
Police Ho.
WYCH ROAD
Riding Stables
Rowney Wood
LONDON ROAD
A1184
Scout Hut
Nursery Wood
Nursery
Oak Walk
Stort Navigation
Lock
Rec. Grd.
BACK LANE
Nursery
Newhouse
Quickbury
CM 22
Sheering
THE STREET
Rowney Farm
Nursery
PISHIOBURY DRIVE
Feakes Lock
Union Wood
Rowneybury
Nursery
Ashplant
HARLOW ROAD
Hall Common
Glyn's Spring
Durrington Hall
Sheering Hall
Aylmers
Earthworks
Pincey Brook
Harlow Lock
HARLOW MILL
SITE ROMAN TEMPLE
Works
HART RD.
THE CRESCENT
MARSH
Ealing Bridge
Weir
Campions
SHEERING ROAD
B183
EPPING FOREST
The Mores
M11
Mayfield Farm
THE HOO
GUILFORDS
Harlowbury
A414
PRIORY AVENUE
STATION ROAD
Drill Hall Sch.
THE OXLEYS
Clinic
Windmill Fields
Moor Hall
MOORHALL ROAD
MATCHING ROAD
Moat
Housham Hall
Moorhall Wood
CM17
Elmbridge
Mulberry Green
STAFFORDS
Hotel
Churchgate Street
Fire Sta.
Cricket Gd.
CHIPPINGFIELD
Cor. Off.
Lib.
Sch.
GILDEN WAY
Feltimores Farm
Feltimores
Housham hall Gate
Morehall Farm
Matching Mill
FIRST AVENUE
School
Playing Fields
Recreation Ground
Recreation Ground
Cycle Mus.
FELMONGERS
Sports Grd.
Markhall Wood
The Kennels
Hillingdon House
Harlow Tye
Franklins
Newpond Spring
Gravelpit Spring
Gravelpit Farm
Hubbards Hall
Allotment Gardens
Hobbs Cross
Brenthall Wood
Barnsley Wood
Barnsley Cottage
Roffey Hall
New Way
CO CP CQ CR CS
5 6 7 8 9 10

14

7
Norcott Court Farm
Norcott Court
NORTHCHURCH COMMON
Hill Farm
Frithsden Beeches
10
AP
AQ
AR
AS
Northchurch Farm
Dudswell House
Dudswell
11
Dudswell Farm
Hamberlins Farm
Grand Union Canal
Allotments
Ashridge
TRING RD
HIGH ST
Sports Ground
Rec. Grd.
R. Bulbourne
Caravan Park
Northchurch
BERKHAMSTED
HP4
Berkhamsted Place
Castle Hill Farm
Well Farm
Berkhamsted Hill
School
D
a
c
12
Sports Ground
CASTLE
The Rookery
Woodcock Hill
Cox Dell
Sch.
Sports Centre
Recreation Ground
Allotments
GOSSOMS END
HIGH STREET
LONDON ROAD
Oak Corner
ROSSWAY LANE
SHOOTERSWAY
13
Marlin Farm
Shootersway
PROPOSED A41 BERKHAMSTED BY-PASS
Playing Fields
Sports Ground
KINGSHILL WAY
Schools
Playing Fields
Rec. Grd.
School
Marlin Chapel Farm
Kingshill
Cemetery
Brickhill Green Pond
Ashlyns Farm
Ashlyns Hall Old Peoples Home
Model Farm
Furzefield Wood
Firs Wood
HOG LANE
Pancake Wood
House Spring
Long Green
The Rookery
Icedell Wood
Sandpit Green
14
Willow Wood
Hockeridge Wood
Hog Lane Farm
Johns Lane Farm
Heresfoot
Haresfoot Farm
Dropping's Wood
Bottom Farm
Coker's Spring
Nursery
Capon's Spring
15
Harriot's End Farm
Harriot's End Spring
The Larches
Heathen Grove
Mount's Hill
Old Oak Farm
Snowhill Farm
Police Ho.
Community Centre
Ashley Green
Village Hall
Ashley Green Farm
Flamstead Farm
Great Wood
Short Wood
16
AO
C
h
i
l
t
e
r
HP5
Sale's Farm
Spencer's Farm
Hemming Farm
A416
CHESHAM ROAD
WHITE HILL

7
AS
AT
AU
AV
10
11
12
13
14
15
8
16
NETTLEDEN RD.
NETTLEDEN ROAD
Hollybush Farm
Frithsden Vines
Great Frithsden Copse
Little Frithsden Copse
Heizdins Wood
HOLLYBUSH HILL
Noake Mill
River
Brown's Spring
Hollybush
Wood
Catstail Wood
Sports Ground
F COURSE
Grim's Ditch
VICARAGE ROAD
Pottenend Farm
Potten End
THE FRONT
P.O.
Sch
The Green
THE COMMON
HEMPSTEAD ROAD
Dell Wood
Boxted
Old Court Green
Haresfoot Senior Sch.
Amersfort
The Pheasantries
BERKHAMSTED RD.
FENNYCROFT
Playing Fields
Sch.
Gutteridge Wood
Little Heath Small Farm
Little Heath House
Boxted Ho.
FIELDS END LANE
PULLEYS LANE
Warners End Valley
Littleheath Great Farm
Fields End Farm
Warner's End
HAWTHORN LANE
CHAULDEN LANE
WARNERS END RD.
Bullbeggar's Wood
BULLBEGGARS LANE
LITTLE HEATH LANE
POUCHEN END LANE
Northridge Park
Shrub Hill
Chaulden
Lock
Grand Union Canal
R.Bulbourne
A41
LONDON ROAD
Pouchen End
Broadway Farm
Pix Farm
PIX FARM LANE
Sch. Hall
P.O.
School Playing Field
Rugby Grnd.
R. Bulbourne
Motel
SUGAR LANE
Bourne End
GRAND UNION
Moorend Fm
HEMEL HEMPSTEAD
Roughdown Co
Crittell's Wood
Bourne Grove
Hanging Wood
Westbrook Hay
Hay Wood
Club Ho.
Lit Hay Fm
Club House
Little Hay Golf Course
Coleshill Wood
SHEETHANGER COMMON
GOLF COURSE
HP3
Felden
Water Tower
Felden Lo.
Howes Retreat
Ramacre Wood
Lwr Dads Wood
BURY WOOD
BOX LANE
LONGCROFT LA
Longcroft Fm
Felden Grange
FEATHERBED

8
10
11
12
13
14
15
7
17
AW
AX
AY
AZ
Varney's Wood
Wood Farm
Lovett's End
DODDS LANE
LEIGHTON BUZZARD ROAD
Thrift Wood
Noake Mill
River Gade
Nurs.
Catstail Wood
Dell Wood
Grove Hill Fields
Cupid Green
Piccotts End
PICCOTTS END LANE
Boar's Head
Home Park
Marchmont Arms
Gadebridge
Howe Grove
Council Depot
REDBOURN ROAD
Yewtree Wood
HP2
School
Marchmont Grn.
Randall Park
St. Paul's Wing Hosp.
Keen's Fields
QUEENSWAY
GADEBRIDGE PARK
Warners End Valley
Warner's End
Old Town Hall
Council Offs.
Tech. Coll.
Civic Cent.
Lockers Park
HEMEL HEMPSTEAD
West Herts Hospital
Ind. Est.
Adeyfield
Highfield
Chaulden
Northridge Park
Shrub Hill
Convent
Cemetery
Boxmoor
ST. ALBANS ROAD
Jarman Fields
Ski Slopes
School Playing Field
Rugby Grnd.
GRAND UNION CANAL
Lock
Cricket Ground
STATION RD.
TWO WATERS RD.
A41 LONDON ROAD
HEMEL HEMPSTEAD
Duckhall
Gas Wks.
Two Waters
L.C.B.S. Garage
Roughdown Common
Threefields
Frogmore End
Apsley End
Home Wood
Felden
Water Tower
COMMON COURSE
Felden Lo.
Howe's Retreat
Boys Brigade Training Cen.
FEATHERBED LANE
LONGCROFT LA.
Felden Grange
Felden Orchard
Hen's Head Wood
Sports Ground
APSLEY
Apsley Mills
River Gade
Dolittle Meadows Business P.
Playing Field
HP3
Bennetts End
Sch.
Hall
P.O.

M1
M10
PUNCH BOWL LANE
HOGG END LANE
BREAKSPEAR WAY
A414
HEMEL HEMPSTEAD ROAD
A4147
LEVERSTOCK GREEN WAY
Oil Depot
Leverstock Green
Motorway Police Sta
St. Albans
AL3
AL2
WD5
Three Rivers
Pimlico
Potterscrouch
Westwick Hall
Gorhambury (ruin)
Great Furzefield Wood
Potterscrouch Plantations
Blackwater Wood
Brickkiln Wood
Windmillhill Wood
Kentish Wood
The Vistas
Oak Wood
Square Wood
Appspond Wood
Long Deans
Woodend Farm
Cherrytree Farm
Southend Farm
Baker's Farm
Bohemia Farm
Hill Farm
Beech Hyde Farm
Butler's Farm
Kettlewell's Farm
Megdell Farm
Woodwell's Farm
Westwick Farm
Westwick Row Farm
Hill End Farm
Maidenscrouch Fm
Bunker's Fm
Well Fm
Highwoodhall Fm
Rose Acre Fm.
Corner Fm.
Three Cherrytrees Farm
Lower Cherrytree Farm
Squash Club
Sports Ground
Cemetery
Motel
Site of Heliport
High Wood
The Swan
AZ
BA
BB
BC
10
11
12
13
14
15
9
17
7
8

9
Dane-end Farm
10
BD
BE
BF
BG
Bush Wood
Childwick Bury
Wood
Bohemia Farm
Hill Farm
New Jerome's Cottage
WATLING
A5183
BOWL
11
Baker's Farm
LANE
Shafford Farm
BATCH WOOD
Ladies Grove Wood
ST.
Bow Bri
Fish Ponds
Beech Hyde Farm
HOGG END
Butler's Farm
S
t
A
I
Batchwood Hall
Bowling Green
Ten. Cts
Putting Green
Batchwood Hall Golf Course
WATLING (Roman Road)
Mayne's Fm
12
Kettlewell's Farm
GORHAMBURY
STREET
REDBOURN
Pre' Hotel
Windmillhill Wood
AL 3
River Ver
A5183
RD.
City Hospital
Gorhambury
ROMAN WALL (Course of)
DRIVE
Gorhambury (ruin)
Oak Wood
13
THE FOSSE
8
SITE OF THEATRE
Kingsbury Mill
Mus.
FISHPOOL
Sch.
ST MICHAELS
St Michaels Manor Ho
Verulamium Museum
VERULAMIUM (Site of)
ROMAN WALL (Course of)
A4147
BLUEHOUSE HILL
VERULAMIUM (Open Space)
Hypocaust
PRAE WOOD
Square Wood
LAKE
St Albans Sch.
Abbey Mill
ROMAN WALL (Course of)
THE CAUSEWAY (Site of)
KING HARRY
Verulam Hills
Sports Arena
Swimming Pool
Hyper-mkt.
Sch.
ROAD
HEMPSTEAD
HEMEL
A4147
14
Hill End Farm
7
BEDMOND
LANE
WESTFIELD
ROWLATT DR
ST STEPHENS AV
P.O.
St Columba's Coll.
ST STEPHENS HILL
A5183
MIDWAY
WESTFIELDS
NETHERWAY
CHALK HILL ROAD
WATLING
Schs
TITHE BARN EST.
BIRCH WOOD
Maidenscrouch Fm
APPS POND LANE
Windridge Fm
M10
15
M1
Appspond Wood
WINDRIDGE
Holly Bush
Long Spring
Park Wood
Westfield's Farm
ROBERT
Potterscrouch
BEDMOND LA
East Farm
RAGGED HALL LANE
Cuckman's Fm
Ragged Hall
Potterscrouch Farm
Square Wood
Scrubs Wood
18
Cuckman's Wood
WD 5
BD
BE
BF
BG
WATFORD
STANLEY AV
St Julians Wood
Schs.
LABURNUM GROVE
AL2
NORTH ORBITAL RD.
A405
B4630
FURZEBUSH LANE
ST ALBAN'S LANE
CHISWELL

9
Station
BG
BH
BJ
BK
10
11
12
13
14
15
18
AL4
AL1
Townsend
Fleetville
ST. ALBANS
Tyttenhanger Green
HARPENDEN ROAD
A1081
SANDRIDGE ROAD
ST ALBANS ROAD
B651
MARSHALSWICK LANE
SANDPIT LANE
HATFIELD ROAD
A1057
LONDON ROAD
NORTH ORBITAL ROAD
A414
COLNEY HEATH LA.
HILL END LANE
NIGHTINGALE LA.
CELL BARNES LA.
CAMP ROAD
VICTORIA ST.
ST. PETERS ST.
CLARENCE PARK
CEMETERY
Industrial Site
Railway Cottages
Sports Ground
Ancient Briton
Heathlands Sch.
Amb. & Fire Sta.
Open Space
Play Fld
CHARMOUTH CT
Beaumont Sch.
Irene Stebbings House
Home Wood
Oaklands Agricultural Institute
Oak Farm
Nashe's Fm
Hill End Hospital
Cell Barnes Hosp.
Nurses Quarters
Recreatn Grd.
Hill End Fm
Playing Fields
Playing Field
Golf Course
Club Ho.
Verulam Golf Course
Newbarns Mill
Sopwell
Lit. Sopwell Farm
Sopwell Nunnery Site of
Old Mile Ho
Tennis Cts.
Sports Grd.
Birklands Polytechnic
Nurses Home
High Wick Hosp.
Coppice Wood
Chalkdell Wood
Hedges Fm
Rugby Grd.
Cricket Grd.
Allots
Civic Centre
Town Hall
ST. ALBANS Station

10
BL
BM
BN
BO
5
9
19
AL4
FURZE FIELD
Sutton's Farm
Fairfold's Farm
W.T. Station
Woodcock Hill
Manor Rd.
Astwick Manor Farm
Astwick Manor
Coopers Green Lane
Cooper's Green
Hook's Wood
Sleeve Hall Wood
Cut Field Wood
Ball's Covert
Oak Wood
Home Covert
Beech Farm
Oak Farm
Ash Green
HATFIELD AERODROME
British Aerospace
Nashe's Fm
Pirton Clo.
Lincoln Clo.
Sandringham
Langham Clo.
Holborn Clo.
Chancery
Craiglands
Portman Clo.
Twyford Rd.
Beverley Gdns.
Harvesters
Ripon Way
Villiers
Briar Rd.
Spring Wood Walk
Arden Way
Harness Way
Glade Side
Crescent
Newgate Clo.
Buxton Clo.
Sandpit Lane
Coopers Lane
St. Albans Rd. West
Comet Hotel
Selwyn Cres.
Selwyn Av.
Poplars
Bramble Rd.
Popefield Fm
Ellenbrook Lane
Ellenbrook
The Springs
Crossbrook
Railway Cotts
A1001 (A1)
Oaklands Agricultural Institute
Sports Grd.
East Drive
Oaklands La.
The Horseshoes
Boggymead Spring
Wilkin's Green
Wilkins Green Lane
Nast Hyde Farm
Springfield Rd.
Station Road
Smallford Nurseries
Sch.
Beaumont Sch.
Home Wood
Hatfield Road
A1057
Wynchlands Cr.
Newood Clo.
Cedarwood Drive
Longacres
P.O.
Gresford Clo.
St Yon Ct.
Sewell Clo.
Firwood Av.
Cranbrook Dr.
Fourways
Ind. Est.
Alban Park
Acrewood Way
Lyon Way
Ryders Av.
College
Sleapshyde Farm
Sleapshyde Lane
Smiths Cres.
Sleap Cross Gardens
Smallford Lane
A414
Hobbs Clo.
Swans Clo.
Boissy Clo.
Colney Heath Lane
Playing Fields
Smallford Farm
Hill End Hosp
Hixberry Lane
Council Nursery
Recn Grd
Cell Barnes Hosp.
Recreatn Grd.
Highfield Lane
Johnson's Spring
COLNEY HEATH
Roundhouse Farm
Sports Grd
St Marks Clo.
Church La.
Westlea
Park La.
High Street
Tel.Ex.
Roestock Lane
Pumping Sta.
Admirals Clo.
Bullen's Green Lane
Fellowes
Tollgate Rd.
Colney Heath Fm.
Fredericks Wood
Tollgate Fm
Hill End Fm
Tyttenhanger Green
Barley Mow Lane
Barley Mow
Parkgate Corner
Water Works
R. Colne
Highfield Farm
Knight's Wood
Nurses Home
High Wick Hosp
Blount Spring
North Orbital Road
Warren Fm.
Coursers Road
Tyttenhanger Farm
Coppice Wood
Whitehorse
Hertsmere
Garden Wood
Tyttenhanger Park
The New Plantation
Coursers Farm
The Osierbed
Alexander
Five Acres
Oldfield Rd.
A1081
A405

BO
BP
BQ
BR
5
11
12
13
14
15
19
2
HATFIELD
Hatfield House
HATFIELD PARK
Welwyn Hatfield
Old Hatfield
Bishops Palace
HOME PARK
The Warren
The Vineyard
The Broadwater
THE LONG RIDE
Sewage Works
HERTFORD ROAD
A414
MT. PLEASANT LA.
Bush Hall
CHEQUERS
A1000
ASCOTS LANE
MILL GREEN LA.
GYPSY LANE
Playing Fields
BIRCHWOOD INDUSTRIAL SITE
The Ryde
Bus Depot
A1001 (A1)
BARNET BY-PASS
TUNNEL
Sports Ground
Fire Sta.
Mid Herts Teachers Centre
ST. ALBANS RD. EAST
A1057
Town Centre
Mem. Hall
Lib
Swim Pool
QUEENSWAY
CAVENDISH WAY
School
Sch.
Hillend Farm
The Furze Field
Pollard Wood
Brickkiln Wood
Conduit Wood
Wellington Wood
The Roughs
Coombe Wood
Home Fm
Howe Dell
GREAT NORTH ROAD
Pump Sta.
Sports Centre
South Hatfield
AL9
GREEN STREET
Woodside Place Farm
Woodside
WILDHILL ROAD
MILLWARD'S PARK
Halfwayoak Pond
Sports Grd.
SOUTHWAY
A1001
The Downs
Parsonage Farm
Marshmoor
TRAVELLERS LA.
POOLEY'S LA.
Works
The Rookery
WELHAM GREEN
Lower Woodside
Lower Woodside Farm
GRUBBS LANE
WOODSIDE LA.
Caravan Park
The Fir
White Lodge Farm
Swan Lo.
Nursery
Fox's Nursery
Bell Bar
BELL LA.
The Legg
Bush Wood
A1(M)
WELHAM GREEN Wood
MOAT
Potterells Farm
Skimpans Farm
Peplin's Wood
North Mymms
DIXONS HILL RD.
Potterells
Flinter's Wood
Round Wood
Home Farm
Club Ho.
Golf

11
HERTFORD ROAD
A414
HATFIELD
Holwell Court
Burnside
BS
BT
BU
BV
5
HOLWELL LANE
Sewage Works
The Warren
The Broadwater
River Lea or Lee
Holwell Manor
Holwell Bridge
LOW ROAD
South Lodge
Pumping Sta.
Essendonbury Farm
THE LONG RIDE
Hillend Farm
Ox Wood
Larkinshill Grove
B158
ESSENDON HILL
BEDWELL AVENUE
HOME PARK
WEST END LANE
Field House Farm
HANBURY LA.
CHURCH ST.
GLEBE CLO.
Poundfield Wood
RECTORY CLO.
GLEBE COTTS.
EAST VIEW
SCHOOL LANE
School
ESSENDON CLO.
Sports Ground
P.O.
Essendon
Backhouse Wood
The Furze Field
Lower Westend Farm
Upper West End Farm
West End Farm
Pollard Wood
Brickkiln Wood
Flint Farm
West End
Bedwellpark Farm
HATFIELD PARK
Conduit Wood
Edward's Wood
HIGH ROAD
Sandpit Grove
Essendon Place
Wellington Wood
Deeve Wood
Long Wood
Essendon Place Farm
10
The Roughs
Pope's Farm
Harefield Wood
Bedwell Park
Berkhamsted Place
AL9
Bath Wood
CUMBERLOW HILL
Belvedere Farm
BERKHAMSTED LANE
GREEN STREET
Home Wood
Panther's Wood
Bedwell Lodge Farm
CUMBERLOW LANE
Duncan's Wood
Wildhill
Camfield Place
Cucumber Hall Farm
Woodside Place Farm
Woodside
Brewhouse Farm
WILDHILL ROAD
Camfield Farm
Hoppett's Wood
Wildhill
Whitbury Wood
WOODSIDE
Riding Sch.
HORNBEAM LANE
Nine Acre Wood
Warren Wood
Lower Woodside
GRUBBS LANE
Lower Woodside Farm
WOODSIDE LA.
Caravan Park
House
Woodhill Farm
Chestnut Farm
MOAT LANE
Westfield
WOODFIELD
Woodfield Farm
The Firs
Sch.
LANE
Coldharbour Farm
GREAT NORTH ROAD
15
Barbers Lodge Farm
White Lodge Farm
Swan Lo.
Nursery
BELL LANE
Kentish Lane Farm
A1000
Bell Bar
Water Tower
Brookmans Park Transmitting Sta.
The Legg
20
Coldharbour Plantation
Broombarns Wood
Home Farm
Round Wood
UPLANDS
PINE GROVE
KENTISH LANE
B158
Club Ho.
Sch.
George's Wood
EN6
Golf

11
SG14
BV
BW
BX
BY
10
11
12
13
14
15
The Pightle
Roxford
Moat
Weir
River Lea
Bayfordbury
Home Farm
Observatory
SAILOR'S GROVE
Clements Farm
Gravefield Grove
Hook's Grove
Spring Wood
Gravel Pits
Water Hall Farm
LOWER B158 HATFIELD ROAD
LONDON B158 ROAD
Broadgreen Cottages
BROAD GREEN
BROAD GRN WOOD
Sewage Works
Broadgreen Wood
Weepings Wood
Pumping Station
Gravel Pit
STOCKING LANE
ROBINS NEST HILL
Bayfordhall Farm
Bayford Hall
Pav
Owls Hatch Cottages
HARMOND'S WOOD
East
Longacre Wood
Little Stockings
Great Stockings
Culver Wood
STOCKING LA.
Farm
War Memorial
CHURCH LANE
WELL ROW
Warren House
Place Farm
BAYFORD GREEN
Culverwood House
Culverwood Farm
GREAT GROVES
Bayford
Sewage Farm
BACK LANE
Filter Beds
Manor House
Furze Field
Sch.
BAYFORD
BAYFORD WOOD
Caravan Park
Memorial Hall
BAYFORD ROAD
Fanshaws
Brickendon
Hertfordshire
Breach Lane
Little Berkhamsted House
Monument
GOLF COURSE
Fanshaws Farm
FANSHAWS
Farmer's Boy
Bayford House
Danes Farm
LANE
ORCHARD CLO.
CHURCH
Little Berkhamsted
BUCKS ALLEY
Gidner's Wood
Brickendon Green
PEMBRIDGE
Rec. Grd.
P.O.
GODDARDS CLO.
CHURCH ROAD
Bayford Wood
New Pond Fm.
Eves Lot
Keepers Cottage
Morley Grove
Brickendon Grange
Buck's Alley Wood
Buck's Farm
Bell's Wood
SG13
BLACKFAN WOOD
Claypits Wood
Bush Farm
ASHENDENE
Starch Grove
BROX
Radio Navigational Beacon
WHITE STUBBS LANE
Nursery
Old Claypits Farm
The Beehive
Ashendene Farm
Ashen Grove
DEVILS LANE
Woodcock Lodge
Epping Ho. School
P.O.
Epping Green
Epping Green Farm
Howewood
Calais Wood
Ponsbourne Lodge Fm.
Calves Grove
PONSBOURNE TUNNEL
Woodcock Lodge Farm
TYLERS CAUSEWAY
Tylers Causeway
NEWGATE STREET
WORMLEY WOOD
The Warren
The Roughs
Ponsfall Farm
Wellfield Grove
Westfield Grove
Ponsbourne Ho.
Ponsbourne Park
DERRY WOOD
NEW PARK ROAD
New Park House
Long Grove
Hazel Grove
Baisley Wood
P.O.
Sch.
Ponsbourne Manor Ho.
Calves Croft
Tanfield Stud
Hell Wood
Newgate Street
Hall
NEWGATE ST VILLAGE
TOLMERS MS.
20
St. Lawrence Farm
Recreation Grd.
Tolmers Pk. Hosp.
Pumping Sta.
EN7
Nurseries
DARNICLE HILL
Res.
HAMMOND STREET
Newgate Street Bridge
e
l
d

Bayfordbury
Observatory
SAILOR'S GROVE
Brickendon Bury
BALLS WOOD
Brides Farm
HIGH WOOD
Hobbyhorse Wood
Clements Farm
Blackfields Farm
Elbow Lane Farm
BOX WO
LIGHTS WOOD
Owls Hatch Cottages
Edwards Green
Monk's Wood
Dalmonds
DALMONDS WOOD
Goose Green
The Huntsman
HARMOND'S WOOD
SG13
East
Hertfordshire
Sewards Farm
Gas Valve Compound
Japps Fm
Highfield Farm
Jepps Wood
Monks Green
GREAT GROVES
Sewage Farm
Poultry Houses
HODDESDONPARK WOOD
HIGHFIELD WOOD
Fanshaws
Bourne Orchard
Brickendon
BRAMBLE'S WOOD
Bourne Wood
Farmer's Boy
Fanshaws Farm
Round Grove
Brickendon Green
DANEMEAD WOOD
COWHEATH WOOD
Morley Grove
GOLF COURSE
PONSBOURNE TUNNEL
Claypits Wood
Nursery Grove
BROAD RIDING WOOD
Refuse Tip
Starch Grove
Hedgerows Wood
BROXBOURNE WOOD
Hedgegrove Farm
Broxbourne Special Scho
Edgewood Farm
Home Farm
Lower White Stubbs
Cold Hall
Pembridge Lane Farm
Ettridge Farm
STOCKING WOOD
Upper White Stubbs
Broxbourne Zoological Gardens
Calais Wood
Birch Farm
Bencroft Wood
Wormley Hill House
WORMLEY WOOD
Nut Wood
Wormley West End
Westlea
Manor Farm
Manor House
Bury Farm
Woodman
Holborn Stud Farm
Fins Wood
Wormleybury
Biggs Grove
Westfield Grove
Beech Grove
New Plantation
DERRY WOOD
Beaumont Manor
Baisley's Wood
Bramble Grove
THUNDERFIELD GROVE
Factory Farm
Hazel Grove
Calves Croft
Bread & Cheese Br
MOAT
Kitchenme Wood
Tanfield Stud Fm.
Spring Wood
EN7
Nurseries
Res.
Gammon Farm
Paradise House
Doggett Hill
MANGROVE LANE
BRICKENDON LANE
BACK LANE
ERMINE STREET
ELBOW LANE
LORD LANE
RED HILLS
COCK LANE
PEMBRIDGE LANE
WHITE STUBBS LANE
DEVILS LANE
CHURCH LANE
SPRING WALK
PARK LANE
WEST END ROAD
HOLY CROSS HILL
BEAUMONT ROAD
BREAD AND CHEESE LA
GAMMONS LANE
PARADISE HILL
HAMMOND ST
FORD
BZ
CA
CB
CC
10
11
12
13
14
15
21

Lea Valley Experimental Horticultural Station
Boxwood Lodge
CC
CD
CE
CF
10
11
12
13
14
15
21
Dells Wood
Woollensbrook
B1197
A10
BY PASS
HODDESDON BY PASS
A1170
WARE ROAD
Cemetery
Rye Park
EN11
HODDESDON
Spitalbrook
Broxbourne
BROXBOURNE
EN10
EN9
CM19
Wentworth Cottages
Wormley
Queens Head P.H.
Turnford
Turnford Coll. of Further Educ.
Turnford Marsh
Hell Wood
Lanthorn's Wood
Highleigh Farm
High Leigh
Lowfield Cricket Ground
Icehouse Grove
Playing Fields
Wormley Play. Fields
Sports Ground
Recreation Ground
Boating Centre
Broxbourne Lido
Keyser's Estate
Nazeing Marsh
Sewage Wks
Marshgate
Payne's Farm
Clayton Hill
St Leonards
Netherkidder Farm
Langridge
Kings Weir
Towing Path
River Lea
River Lea Navigation
River Stort
River Lynch
New River
Boating Lake
Sand and Gravel Works
Gasholder Station
Watercress Beds
Electricity Transformer Station
Electricity Transformer
Cooling Towers
Power Station
Broxbourne Junction
Industrial Area
RYE HOUSE
Rye House Hotel
Rye House Stadium
Rye Meads Purificati
Toll Gate
Feilde's Weir Lock
Dobb's Weir Bridge
Dobb's Weir Lock
Nursery
Nurseries
Curringtons
Mulberries
Epping Forest
Herts C.C. Adult Training Centre
Allotment Gardens
Rec. Grd.
Foot-ball Grd.
DUKE ST.
DINANT LINK RD.
HIGH STREET
HIGH ROAD
STATION ROAD
CONDUIT LA. W.
CHARLTON WAY
ESSEX ROAD
PINDAR ROAD
DOBB'S WEIR ROAD
NAZEING NEW ROAD
NAZEING RD.
MEADGATE RD.
GREEN LANE
PAYNES LANE
NURSERY RD.
ST LEONARD'S ROAD
NORTH STREET
MIDDLE STREET
WESTERN RD.
SHOOTERS DRIVE
HYDE MEAD
TATSFIELD AV.
LAUNDRY LA.
CHURCH LANE
SLIPE LANE
WEST SIDE
COZENS LANE EAST
BAAS HILL
PARK LANE
COCK LANE
LORD STREET
WESTFIELD ROAD
AMWELL ST.
BURFORD ST.
WHITLEY ROAD
HAWTHORN RD.
LILAC ROAD
MIDDLEFIELD RD.
STANSTEAD ROAD
RYE ROAD
RATTY'S LANE
CHARLTON MEAD LANE

13
ROYDON
River Stort
Toll Gate
Lock
Roydon Lodge
ROYDON
Rye Meads Sewage Purification Works
East Herts
Temple Farm
Eastend Farm
Rye House
Rye House Hotel
RYE HOUSE
Rye House Stadium
Works
School
Tel. Ex.
Beaumont Hall
Lightfoot Farm
ROYDON PARK
River Stort Navigation
Broxbourne
Industrial Area
Nursery
Kingmead (School)
Feilde's Weir Lock
The Grove
CM19
Power Station
Cooling Towers
Downe Hall Farm
Didgemere Hall
New Barns Farm
Brickfield Wood
Electricity Transformer
EN11
NETHERHALL COMMON
Epping
Netherhall Farm
Nurseries
Totwellhill Bushes
Hallsgreen
Roydon Hamlet
Boating Lake
Paradise Farm
STONESHOT COMMON
Tylers Cross
EN10
'Black Swan'
Broadley Common
Lake
Curringtons
Maplecroft
Nazeing
Rookswood
Sun Inn
Harknett's Gate
Pol. Sta.
White's Wood
Old P.O.
Lower Nazeing
Mansion Ho.
Nazeing Park Sch.
EN9
Sch.
Mulberries
Middle Street
NAZEING COMMON
Payne's Farm
Perry Hill Fm.
Convalescent Home
Clayton Hill
Belchers
WALNUT TREE COTT
Tel. Ex.
Sch. Ho.
King Harold's Head
Netherkidders Farm
Bumble's Green
Nazeing Gate
St Leonards
St. Lawrence Farm
Allmains
Copy Wood
22
Nazeing Long Green

Mark Hall South
13
HARLOW
Lit. Parndon
Netteswell
The High
Hare Street
Katherines
Great Parndon
Passmores
Tye Green
Brays Grove
Latton Bush
Kingsmoor
Stewards
Sumners
Epping Green
Rye Hill
Hospital Wood
Parndon Wood
Risdens Wood
Marles Wood
Epping Forest
Long Green
CM16
CM18
CM20
CK
CL
CM
CN
6
22
14
11
12
13
14
15

14
Mark Hall South
Netteswell
HARLOW
Potter Street
Tye Green
Brays Grove
Latton Bush
Foster Street
HARLOW COMMON
HARLOW PARK
Hastingwood
Thornwood Common
Thornwood
CM20
CM18
CM17
CM16
CO
CP
CQ
CR
11
12
13
14
15
6
13
23
7
M11
A414
A1025
A1169
B1393
SECOND AVENUE
HARLOW BY-PASS
POTTER STREET
LONDON RD.
HIGH RD.
CANES LANE
RAYLEY LANE
FOSTER STREET
HASTINGWOOD RD
UPLAND ROAD
WEALD HALL LANE
RYE HILL RD
RYE HILL ROAD
HARLOW COMMON ROAD
COMMONSIDE ROAD
SOUTHERN WAY
TUMBLER ROAD
LATTON COMMON ROAD
Epping
Recreation Ground
Markhall Wood
Gravelpit Spring
Gravelpit Farm
Hubbards Hall
Brenthall Wood
Barnsley Wood
Barnsley Cottage
Kitchen Hall
Town Side
Clock Tr.
Playing Fields
Latton Common
Mark Bushes
LATTON PARK
Rundell's Grove
Randells
LATTON PRIORY (Remains of) CHURCH
MOAT
Priory Fm.
Rye Hill Common
Rivetts Fm.
Horseshoes Farm
Depot
Cross Keys
Esgors
High Elms
Rose Fm.
Hayleys Manor Farm
Currance Farm
Rugby Grd.
Council Depot
Weald Hall
Marles Farm
Canes Wood
CAMNES Site of Canes
Delved Bri.
Hastingwood House
Paris Hall
Church Farm
Wyntersbrook Farm
Shonks
Seale's Farm
Langley Wood
The Moors
Motel
School
Sch.
Special Sch.
Sports Ground
Spts. Grd.
Rec. Gd.

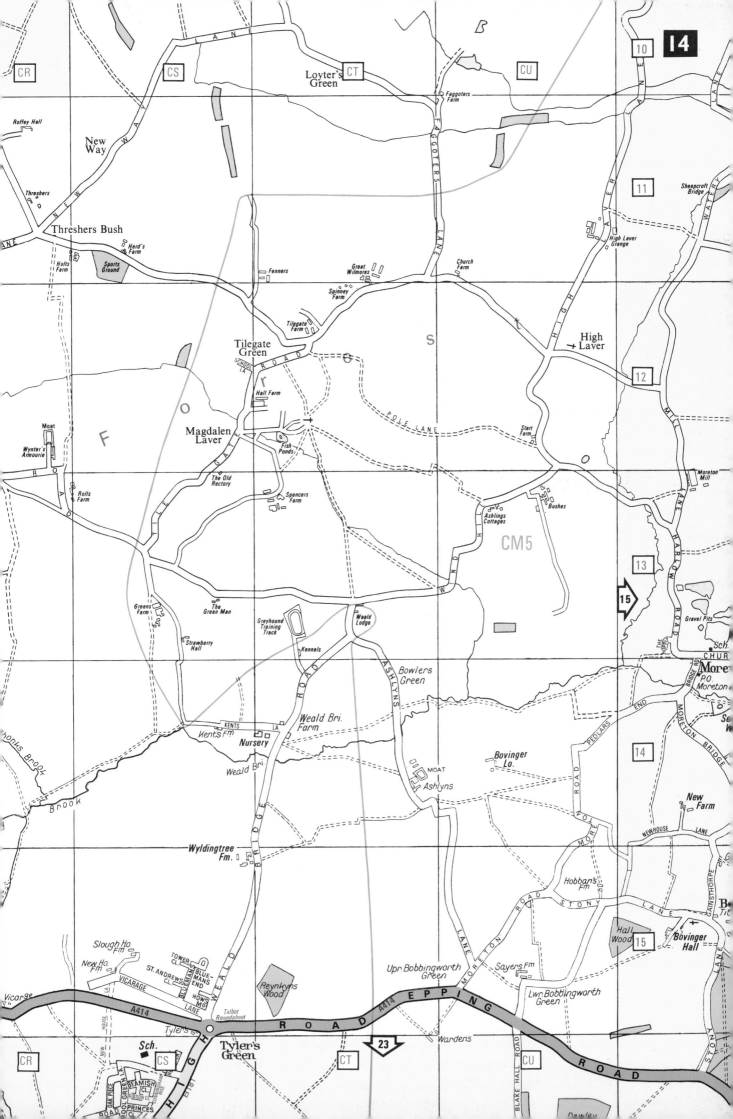
Loyter's Green
Faggoters Farm
Roffey Hall
New Way
NEW WAY
LANE
Threshers
Threshers Bush
Herd's Farm
Holts Farm
Sports Ground
Fenners
Great Wilmores
Spinney Farm
Church Farm
FAGGOTERS LANE
High Laver Grange
HIGH LAVER
High Laver
Sheepcroft Bridge
WATERY
Tilegate Farm
Tilegate Green
SCHOOL LA
ROAD
Hall Farm
Magdalen Laver
Fish Ponds
Moat
Wynter's Armourie
ROAD
POLE LANE
Start Farm
Moreton Mill
MILL LANE
The Old Rectory
Rolls Farm
Spencers Farm
Ashlings Cottages
Bushes
CM5
TILEGATE
WIND HILL
HARLOW ROAD
Greens Farm
The Green Man
Greyhound Training Track
Weald Lodge
Gravel Pits
Strawberry Hall
Kennels
Sch.
THE HOPPIT
CHUR
BRIDGE RD
Bowlers Green
ASHLYNS
P.O. Moreton
ROAD
KENTS LA
Kent's Fm
Nursery
Weald Bri. Farm
PEDLARS END
MORETON BRIDGE
Bovinger Lo.
Weald Bri.
Brook
MOAT
Ashlyns
ROAD
BRIDGE
New Farm
NEWHOUSE LANE
MORETON
Wyldingtree Fm.
Hobbans Fm
GAINSTHORPE
STONY LANE
ROAD
Hall Wood
Bovinger Hall
LANE
Slough Ho Fm
TOWER CL.
BLUE-MANS END
New Ho. Fm
ST. ANDREWS CL.
VICARAGE LANE
HOWS MD
WEALD
Reynkyns Wood
Upr. Bobbingworth Green
Sayers Fm
MORETON
Lwr. Bobbingworth Green
Vicarage
A414
EPPING ROAD
A414
Talbot Roundabout
Tyler's
Wardens
Sch.
Tyler's Green
HIGH
NEW HOUSE LA
BLAKE HALL ROAD
STONY LANE
ROAD
BEAMISH CL.
GIBSON CL.
CUNNINGHAM RISE
OAK PIECE
POOL GREEN LA
PRINCES CL.
ROAD
Dewley
FOREST
CR
CS
CT
CU
10
11
12
13
14
15
15
23

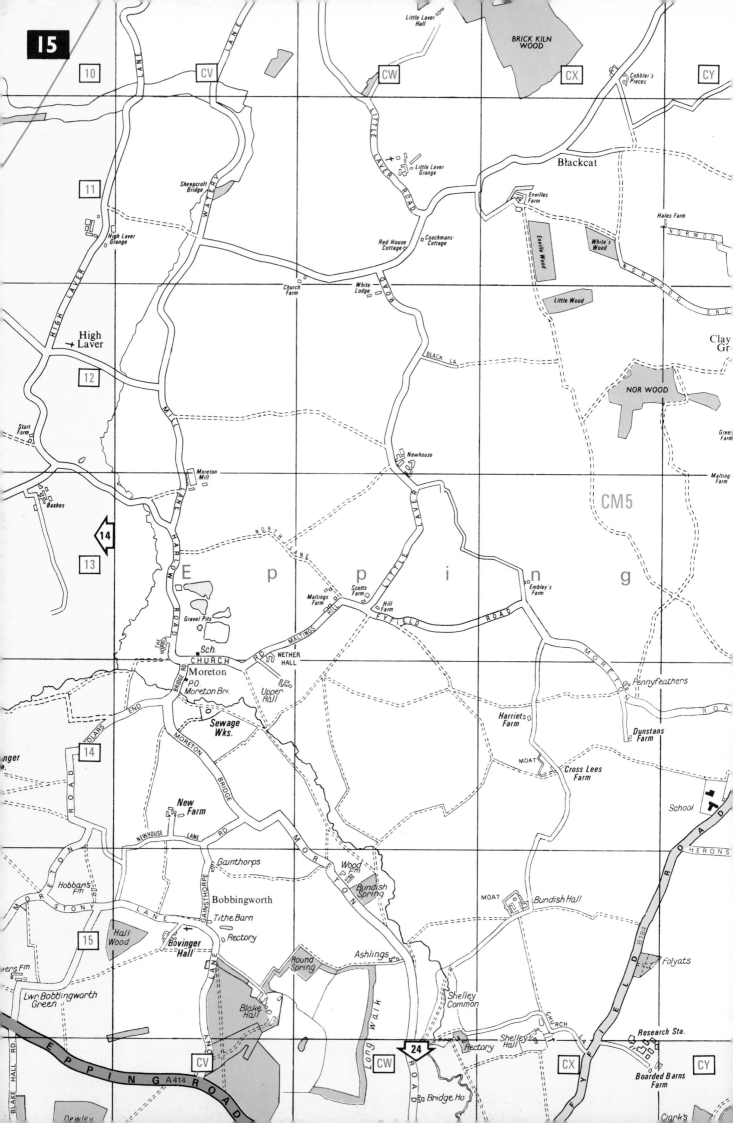

15
10
11
12
13
14
15
CV
CW
CX
CY
14
24
Little Laver Hall
BRICK KILN WOOD
Cobbler's Pieces
LANE
WATERY
Sheepcroft Bridge
LITTLE LAVER ROAD
Little Laver Grange
Blackcat
Envilles Farm
Enville Wood
Hales Farm
NORWOOD END
White's Wood
High Laver Grange
HIGH LAVER
High Laver
Red House Cottage
Coachmans Cottage
Church Farm
White Lodge
Little Wood
Clay Gr
BLACK LA.
NOR WOOD
Start Farm
MILL
Newhouse
Moreton Mill
Malting Farm
Bushes
HARLOW
LITTLE LAVER
CM5
NORTH LANE
E p p i n g
Embley's Farm
Maltings Farm
Scotts Farm
Hill Farm
FYFIELD ROAD
Gravel Pits
MALTINGS HILL
THE HOPPET
Sch.
CHURCH RD
NETHER HALL
Moreton
BRIDGE RD
P.O.
Moreton Bri.
Upper Hall
MORETON ROAD
Pennyfeathers
Harriets Farm
Dunstans Farm
END
Sewage Wks.
MORETON BRIDGE
MOAT
Cross Lees Farm
New Farm
School
NEWHOUSE LANE RD
HERONS
Gainthorps
Wood Fm
Bundish Spring
Hobbans Fm
MORETON
STONY LANE
Bobbingworth
GAINSTHORPE
Tithe Barn
Rectory
MOAT
Bundish Hall
Hall Wood
Bovinger Hall
Ashlings
Round Spring
B184
Folyats
Lwr. Bobbingworth Green
Blake Hall
Long Walk
Shelley Common
CHURCH LA.
Shelley Hall
Rectory
Research Sta.
FYFIELD ROAD
EPPING ROAD
A414
BLAKE HALL RD
Boarded Barns Farm
Bridge Ho
Dewley
Clark's

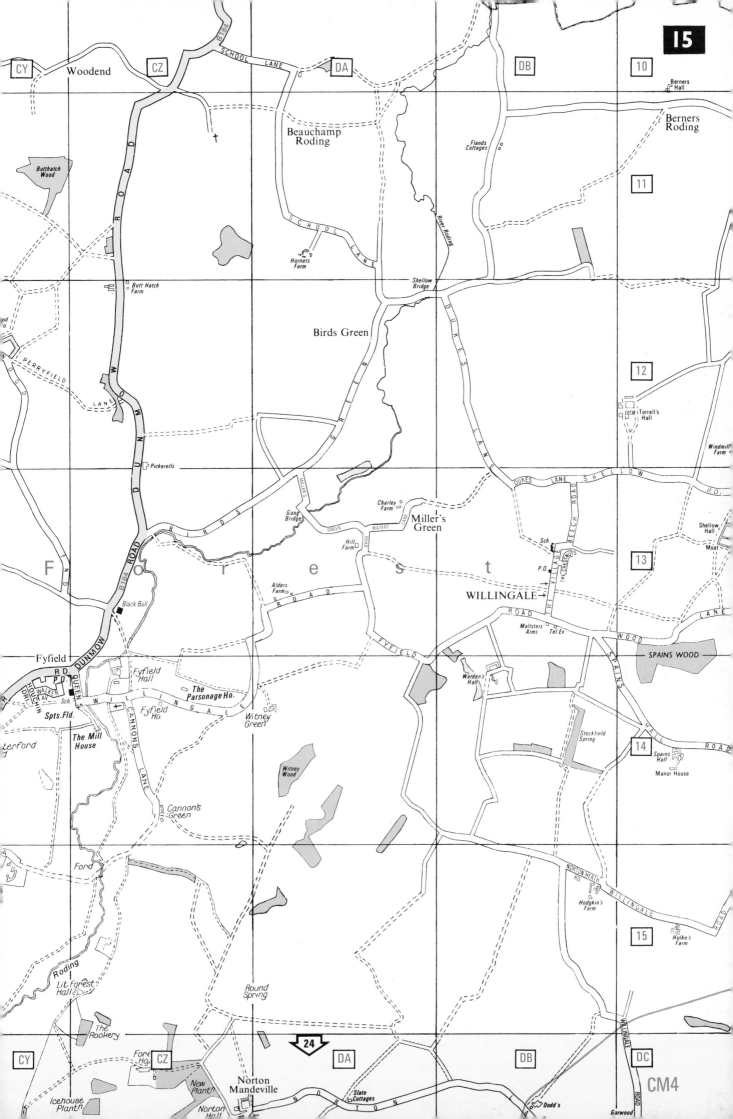
Woodend
Beauchamp Roding
Berners Hall
Berners Roding
Butthatch Wood
Flands Cottages
River Roding
Hornets Farm
Butt Hatch Farm
Shellow Bridge
Birds Green
Perryfield Lane
Dunmow Road
B184
School Lane
Dukes Lane
Torrell's Hall
Windmill Farm
Pickerells
Shellow Road
Charley Farm
Miller's Green
Gang Bridge
Millers Green
Watery Lane
Hill Farm
Shellow Hall
Moat
Forest
Alders Farm
Willingale
The Chestnuts
The Village
Beech Road
P.O.
Sch.
Black Bull
Maltsters Arms
Tel.Ex.
Wood Lane
Spains Wood
Fyfield
Fyfield Road
Fyfield Hall
Warden's Hall
The Parsonage Ho.
Willingale Road
Fyfield Ho.
Witney Green
Queens
Walker Av.
Houchin Dri.
Spts. Fld.
The Mill House
Cannons Lane
Stockfield Spring
Spains Hall Road
Spains Hall
Manor House
Witney Wood
Cannon's Green
Ford
Norton Heath Rd.
Willingale Road
Hodgkin's Farm
Hulke's Farm
Roding
Lit. Forest Hall
Round Spring
The Rookery
Forest Hall
New Plantn
Norton Mandeville
Slate Cottages
Norton Lane
Icehouse Plantn
Norton Hall
Dodd's
Garwood
Willingale Road
CM4
24
CY
CZ
DA
DB
DC
10
11
12
13
14
15

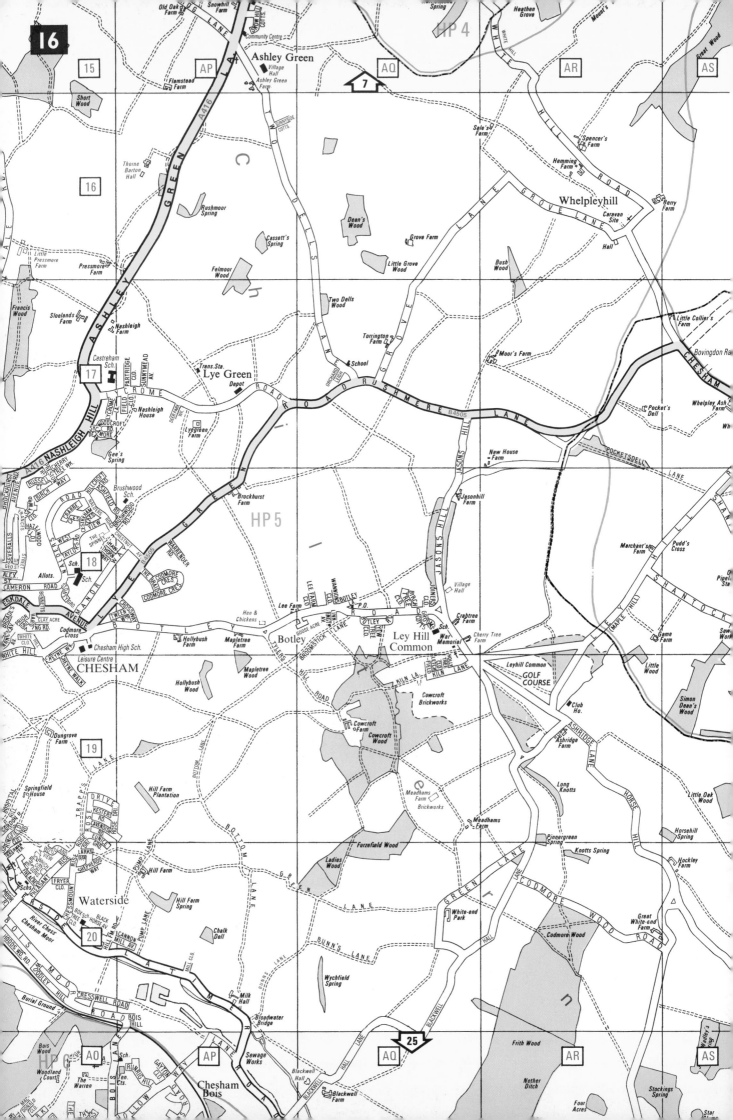
Old Oak Farm
Snowhill Farm
Community Centre
Ashley Green
Village Hall
Ashley Green Farm
Heathen Grove
HP 4
Mount's
Great Wood
15
AP
AQ
AR
AS
7
Flamstead Farm
Short Wood
SUNNYSIDE COTTS.
Sale's Farm
Spencer's Farm
Hemming Farm
WHITE HILL
Thorne Barton Hall
16
Rushmoor Spring
Dean's Wood
Whelpleyhill
Berry Farm
Caravan Site
Hall
GROVE LANE
Cassett's Spring
Grove Farm
Little Pressmore Farm
Pressmore Farm
Felmoor Wood
Little Grove Wood
Bush Wood
Francis Wood
Sloelands Farm
Two Dells Wood
TWO DELLS LANE
Nashleigh Farm
Torrington Farm
Little Collier's Farm
Moor's Farm
Bovingdon Ra
Cestreham Sch.
17
Trans.Sta.
Lye Green
Depot
School
ORCHARD LEIGH
CHESHAM
LYCROME ROAD
RUSHMERE LANE
B4505
Nashleigh House
Lyegreen Farm
Pocket's Dell
Whelpley Ash Farm
NASHLEIGH HILL
A416
ASHLEY GREEN LANE
Gee's Spring
New House Farm
POCKETSDELL LANE
Brushwood Sch.
Brockhurst Farm
Jasonhill Farm
JASONS HILL
HP 5
Marchant's Farm
Pudd's Cross
18
Sch.
Allots.
CAMERON ROAD
WARRENDER RD.
CODMORE CRES.
Village Hall
ESKDALE AVENUE
MANOR
Hen & Chickens
Lee Farm
P.O.
Crabtree Farm
SHANTOCK
Codmore Cross
Chesham High Sch.
Leisure Centre
CHESHAM
Hollybush Farm
Mapletree Farm
Botley
BOTLEY ROAD
Ley Hill Common
Sch.
War Memorial
Cherry Tree Farm
Game Farm
WHITE HILL
Mapletree Wood
Hollybush Wood
TYLERS HILL ROAD
KILN LANE
Leyhill Common
GOLF COURSE
Little Wood
Cowcroft Brickworks
Club Ho.
Simon Dean's Wood
Dungrove Farm
Cowcroft Farm
Cowcroft Wood
Ashridge Farm
ASHRIDGE LANE
19
Springfield House
Hill Farm Plantation
BOTTOM LANE
Long Knotts
Meadhams Farm
Brickworks
Little Oak Wood
Meadhams Farm
HORSE HILL
Horsehill Spring
Pinnergreen Spring
Knotts Spring
Hockley Farm
Furzefield Wood
Ladies Wood
Hill Farm
Waterside
Hill Farm Spring
GREEN LANE
White-end Park
CODMORE WOOD ROAD
Great White-end Farm
River Chess
Chesham Moor
20
Chalk Dell
BUNN'S LANE
Codmore Wood
Wychfield Spring
CRESSWELL ROAD
Burial Ground
BOIS MOOR ROAD
Milk Hall
Broadwater Bridge
BLACKWELL HALL LANE
25
Bois Wood
AO
Sch.
Sewage Works
Frith Wood
Woodland Court
The Warren
Ten. Cts.
Chesham Bois
Blackwell Hall
Blackwell Farm
Nether Ditch
Stockings Spring
Four Acres
HP 6

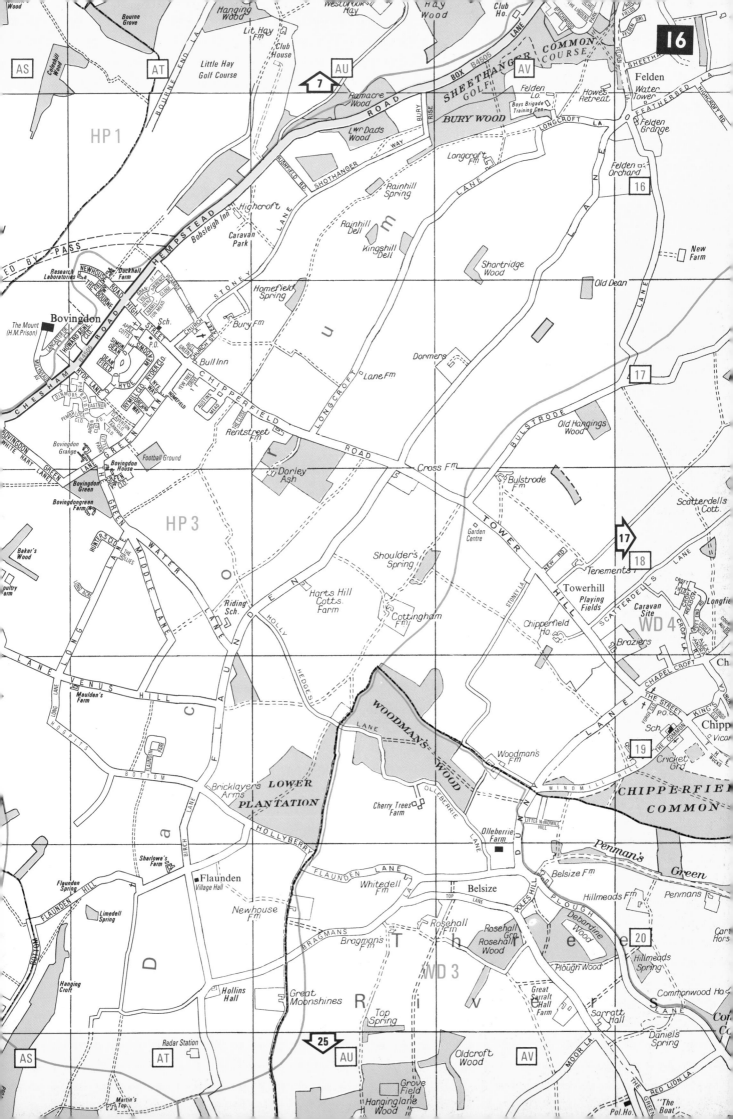
Bourne Grove
Hanging Wood
Westbrook Hay
Hay Wood
Club Ho.
Lit Hay Fm
Club House
Little Hay Golf Course
Coleshill Wood
BOURNE END LA
AS
AT
AU
AV
7
Ramacre Wood
SHEETHANGER COMMON GOLF COURSE
BOX LANE
B4505
Felden Lo.
Howe's Retreat
Boys Brigade Training Cen.
Felden
Water Tower
FEATHERBED LA
HIGHCROFT RD.
Felden Grange
BURY WOOD
BURY RISE
LONGCROFT LA
HP 1
Lwr Dads Wood
SHOTHANGER WAY
BUSHFIELD RD.
Longcroft Fm
Felden Orchard
16
Rainhill Spring
Highcroft
Bobsleigh Inn
HEMPSTEAD ROAD
Caravan Park
Rainhill Dell
Kingshill Dell
LONGCROFT LANE
New Farm
Shortridge Wood
Old Dean
BY-PASS
Research Laboratories
NEWHOUSE ROAD
Duckhall Farm
VICARAGE CLOSE
STONEY LANE
Homefield Spring
The Mount (H.M.Prison)
Bovingdon
Sch.
HIGH STREET
CHURCH ST.
Bury Fm
HOWARD AGNE CLO.
P.O.
Bull Inn
Dormers
CHESHAM ROAD
HYDE LANE
RYDER CLO.
NYE WAY
HOMEFIELD
Lane Fm
17
CHIPPERFIELD ROAD
DINMORE
PEMBRIDGE CLO.
EASTNOR
AUSTINS MEAD
BULSTRODE LANE
Old Hangings Wood
Rentstreet Fm
Bovingdon Grange
Football Ground
Darley Ash
Cross Fm
BOVINGDON GREEN
WHITE HART LANE
Bovingdon House
Bovingdon Green
Bulstrode Fm
Scatterdells Cott.
Bovingdongreen Farm
HP 3
Garden Centre
TOWER HILL
17
18
Baker's Wood
HUNTERS CLO.
THE HOLLIES
WATER LANE
MIDDLE LANE
Shoulder's Spring
NEW RD
Tenements
Harts Hill Cotts. Farm
Towerhill
Playing Fields
SCATTERDELLS LANE
Caravan Site
Longfield
Poultry Farm
LONG ACRE
LONG LANE
Riding Sch.
Cottingham Fm
STONEY LA.
Chipperfield Ho.
WD 4
CROFT LA.
HOLLY HEDGES
FLAUNDEN LANE
Braziers
LANE
VENUS HILL
CHAPEL CROFT
Maulden's Farm
THE STREET
P.O.
Sch.
THE COMMON
Chipp
Vicar
WOODMAN'S WOOD
KING'S
HOGPITS BOTTOM
FLAUNDEN PARK
Woodman's Fm
19
Cricket Grd
LOWER PLANTATION
Bricklayers Arms
WINDMILL HILL
CHIPPERFIELD COMMON
Cherry Trees Farm
OLLEBERRIE LANE
LITTLE WINDMILL HILL
HOLLYBERRY
BIRCH LANE
Olleberrie Farm
DUNNY LANE
Penman's Green
Sharlowe's Farm
Flaunden
Village Hall
FLAUNDEN LANE
Belsize Fm
Whitedell Fm
Belsize
Hillmeads Fm
Penmans
Flaunden Spring
FLAUNDEN HILL
TOP LANE
POLES HILL
PLOUGH LANE
Limedell Spring
Newhouse Fm
Debardine Wood
Rosehall Fm
Rosehall Grn
Rosehall Wood
BRAGMANS LANE
Bragman's Fm
Three Rivers
20
WD 3
Plough Wood
Hillmeads Spring
BOTTOM
Hanging Croft
Hollins Hall
Great Moonshines
Great Sarratt Hall Farm
Commonwood Ho
Top Spring
Sarratt Hall
Radar Station
25
Daniels Spring
Oldcroft Wood
MOOR LA
Grove Field
Hanginglane Wood
Martin's Top
RED LION LA.
THE GREEN
Pol.Ho.
"The Boat"

Threefields
Frogmore End
Apsley End
Apsley Mills
River Gade
LONDON RD.
HEMPSTEAD ROAD
A41
APSLEY
HP3
Felden
Water Tower
Felden Lo.
Howes Retreat
Boys Brigade Training Cen.
LONGCROFT LA.
FEATHERBED LANE
HIGHCROFT RD.
Felden Grange
Felden Orchard
Home Wood
KING EDWARD ST.
WEYMOUTH ST.
HIGHRIDGE RD.
Hen's Head Wood
Sports Ground
Sports Ground
Harling Farm
Shendish
Bowling Green
Great Wood
Phasels Wood
New Farm
Old Dean
Scout Camp
RUCKLERS LANE
Rucklers Green
Doolittle Meadows Business Park
Eagle
Barnes Lo
The Hangings
The Nucket
Barnes Fm
BARNES LANE
Badgerdell Wood
Old Hangings Wood
FLAUNDEN LANE
BULSTRODE LA.
Bulstrode Fm
D a c o r u m
SCATTERDELLS WOOD
The Grove
The Wings
Scatterdells Cott.
SCATTERDELLS LANE
Sch.
Kings Langley Common
Cricket Grd
Hill Farm
VICARAGE LANE
Priory
Sch.
Sch.
LANGLEY HILL
Westmeon
GREAT PARK
KING'S LANGLEY
HIGH ST.
Village Hall
Comm Cen.
Whippendell Farm
Whippendell Ho.
WHIPPENDELL ROAD
Whippendell Bottom
Ballspond Fm
Riding Sch.
CHIPPERFIELD ROAD
Longfield
Caravan Site
Braziers
Towerhill
Playing Fields
Chipperfield Ho.
TOWER HILL
Clements Fm
Chapel Croft
Chipperfield
Vicarage
Rookery Wood
Manor Ho
Kings Langley Lodge
CHIPPERFIELD COMMON
Cricket Grd
Woodman's Fm
WINDMILL HILL
LITTLE WINDMILL HILL
Penman's Green
Belsize Fm
POLES HILL
Hillmeads Fm
Penmans
Little Callipers
Callipers Hall
Jefferys Fm
BERRYBUSHES WOOD
Model Fm
Cart & Horses
QUICKMOOR LANE
BUCKS HILL
Hillmeads Spring
Plough Wood
Great Sarratt Hall Farm
Sarratt Hall
Commonwood Ho
Commonwood Common
Buckshill
Rose & Crown
Lukes Journey Dell
Sheepcot Spring
Beechen Bottom
M25
T h r e e
WD3
Daniels Spring
Little Westwood Fm
Great Westwood Farm
OUSE LANE
High Spring
MOOR LA.
RED LION LANE
THE GREEN
"The Boat"
Pol. Ho.
BOTTOM LANE
Deadmans
AW
AX
AY
AZ
16
17
18
19
20
8
16
26

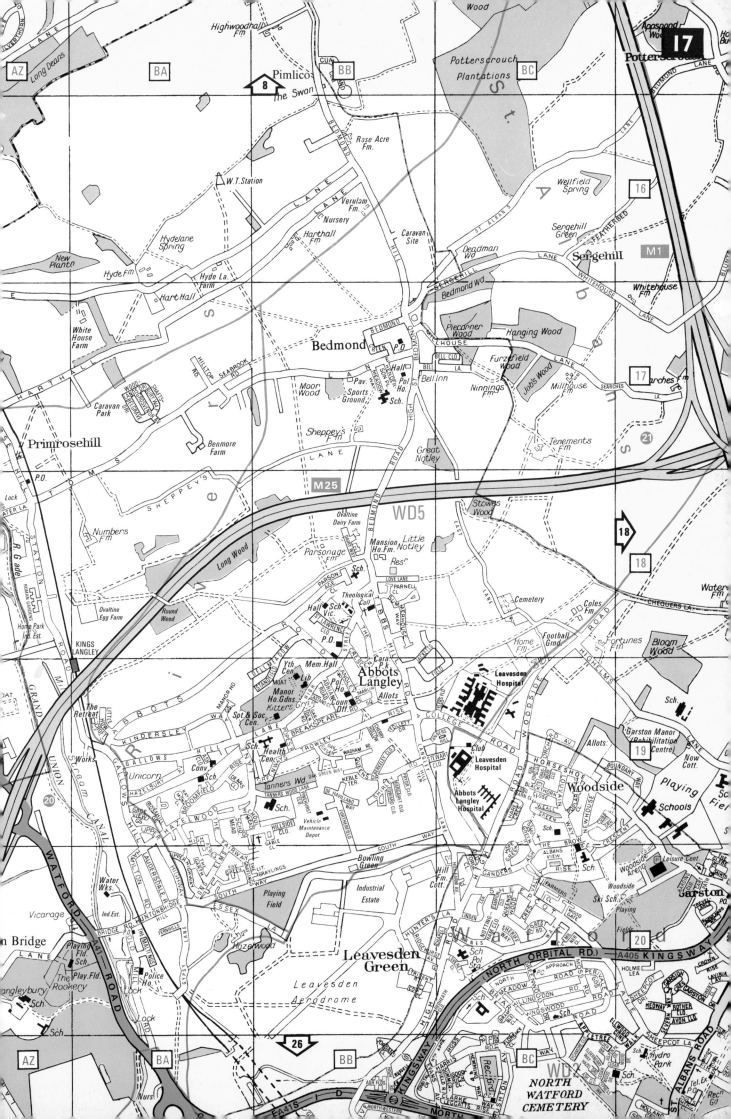
17
Pimlico
The Swan
8
Potterscrouch Plantations
Bedmond
Primrosehill
Sergehill
M1
M25
WD5
18
Abbots Langley
Leavesden Hospital
Abbots Langley Hospital
Woodside
Leavesden Green
Leavesden Aerodrome
Garston
26
North Watford Cemetery
WD2
AZ
BA
BB
BC
16
19
20

18
Potterscrouch
Appspond Wood
Holly Bush
Long Spring
Park Wood
Westfield's Farm
East Fm.
Square Wood
Potterscrouch Farm
Cuckman's Fm.
Cuckman's Wood
Ragged Hall
St. Julians Wood
Plaistowes Fm.
Bone Hill
Rose Soc. Gardens
Chiswellgreen
Daneswick
Sergehill Green
Sergehill
WD 5
Whitehouse Fm.
Plaistowe's Wood
Hanging Wood
Holt Wood
Holt Fm.
Noke Fm.
The Noke Hotel
Burston Manor Fm.
Birchwood Farm
Birch Wood
Nursery
Job's Wood
Millhouse Fm.
Searches Fm.
Tenements Fm.
Tenterden House
"Spielplatz"
The Spinney
Winch Hill Wood
M25
M1
M10
AL 2
Cricket Grd.
Waterdell Farm
Cemetery
Coles Fm.
Home Fm.
Football Grnd.
Fortunes Fm.
Bloom Wood
Black Boy
Woodside Retreat
Bricket Wood
Bricket Wood
Running Track
College
Nottlers Wood
Nottlers Ho.
Three Rivers
Garston Manor (Rehabilitation Centre)
Woodside
Playing Schools
Sch. Fields
Corner Cottage
Building Research Station
BRICKET WOOD
BRICKETWOOD COMMON
New Plantn.
R. Colne
Pumping
Ford
Mutchetts Wood
Little Munden Fm.
Four Acre Plantation
Woodside Arena
Leisure Cent.
Garston
Three Horse Shoes
Watford
GARSTON PARK
Coldharbour Plantn.
Crab Wood
Peartree Wood
Munden Spring
Munden Ho.
NORTH ORBITAL RD. KINGSWAY
NORTH ORBITAL ROAD
WATFORD ROAD
ST. ALBANS ROAD
A405
A412
B4630
WD 2
NORTH WATFORD CEMETERY
Open Air Theatre
BD
BE
BF
BG
9
16
17
18
19
20
27

Sopwell
Lit. Sopwell Farm
Verulam Golf Course
AL1
AL4
BG
BH
BJ
BK
9
Birklands Polytechnic
NORTH ORBITAL ROAD
A414
Chalkden Wood
Hedges Fm.
Napsbury La.
Nurs.
Rugby Grd.
Cricket Grd.
Sports Grd.
Allots
Coppice Wood
Nurses Home
Wick Hosp.
River Ver
Park Street
Allots
AERODROME
(Disused)
Park Industrial Estate
Recreation Grd.
Sch.
Napsbury Fm
Napsbury Hospital
Cricket Ground
Nurses Home
SHEEPHOUSE LANE EST
Playing Fields
Rec. Centre
Kings Head
Lib.
Pol.Sta.
Recreation Grd.
LONDON COLNEY
Riverside Industrial Estate
Waterside Hotel
16
17
Fir Tree Farm
Barley Mo Farm
Broad Colney Lakes
Broad Colney
Frogmore
Vicarage
Ford
Caravan Centre
R. Ver
R. Colne
M25
All Saints Convent
Chap.
Plant Maintenance Depot
19
18
Warehouse Area
Springfield Farm
Colney Park
Sewage Plant (Disused)
Sports Ground
OLD PARKBURY LA.
INDUSTRIAL EST.
Colney Street
Parkbury
Old Parkbury
Waterside
Shenleybury
Shenleybury Farm
Club Ho.
Harperbury Hospital
Colneystreet Bridge
Pumping Sta.
Netherwylde Cott.
Shenleybury Cottages
Shenleybury House
B556
HARPER LANE
Houndswood Farm
Houndswood
Hounds Wood
NINE ACRES
Model Fm
MARGARET COTTS.
Netherwylde Farm
Harper House
Wild Fm
Cow Banks
Monks Wood
Shenley Hospital
Social Club
Ford
Hill Fm
WATLING STREET
A5183
RADLETT ROAD
West Herts Main Drainage Authorities (Blackbirds Works)
High Bridge
Golf Course
WD7
Sand Plant
Cricket Grd
20
Club House
Pol.Sta.
Fire Sta.
Radlett Hall
Starveacres
The Folly
Tel. Ex.
27
B462
War Meml.
The Gorse
Auriol Farm
RADLETT
OAKRIDGE LANE
SHENLEY HILL
RADLETT ROAD
B5378
LONDON ROAD
NEWBERRIES

LONDON COLNEY
Bowmansgreen
SHENLEY
Shenleybury
Harperbury Hospital
Shenley Hospital
COLNEY HEATH
Broad Colney
Tyttenhanger Park
Coppice Wood
Garden Wood
The New Plantation
Coursers Farm
University College of London Athletics Ground
SALISBURY HALL
COMBE WOOD
Shenley Lodge
Redwell Wood Farm
Round Wood
Bigpursley Wood
Littleridge Wood
Littlepursley Wood
Crossoaks Farm
The Gorse
NEWBERRIES
Auriol Farm
Kitwells Cotts
Cricket Field
Football Ground
Pursley Farm
Ravenscroft Fm
Sewage Works
St Catherines Fm
Rabley Pk Fm
Pit (Closed)
Pinks Hotel
Keepers Cott.
R.S.P.C.A
Swallow Hole
Shenley Hall
Stud Farm
Rectory
Social Club
Nursery
Sand Plant
Cricket Grd
Wild Fm
Cow Banks
Shenleybury House (Hosp. Annexe)
Shenleybury Cottages
Shenleybury Farm
Dell Grove
Plant Maintenance Depot
Tennis Ct.
Pav.
Farm
Ridgeview Res Club
Waterslash Hotel
Riverside Industrial Estate
Bowmans Green Farm
Recreation Grd.
Playing Fields
Kings Head
Rec Centre
Pol. Sta.
Lib.
Sch.
Broad Colney Lakes
Chap.
Nurses Home
High Wick Hosp.
Blount Spring
Warren Fm.
Frederick's Wood
Tollgate Fm
Tyttenhanger Farm
NORTH ORBITAL ROAD
A414
LONDON COLNEY BY-PASS
A1081
COURSERS
BELL LANE
B556
B5378
BLACK LION HILL
LONDON RD
RECTORY
MIMMS LANE
PACKHORSE LANE
CROSSOAKS
GREEN ST.
M25
AL2
AL4
WD6
WD7
H e r t
10
16
17
18
19
20
22
28
BL
BM
BN
BO

19
WELHAM GREEN
Wood
MOAT
BO
BP
BQ
BR
10
Potterells Farm
Skimpans Farm
WELHAM GREEN
Fox's Nursery
White Lodge Farm
Swan Lo.
Nursery
Bell Bar
BULL'S LANE
STATION
The Legg
Peplin's Wood
North Mymms
DIXONS HILL CLO
DIXONS
SWANLAND
ROAD
Potterells
Flinter's Wood
Round Wood
Home Farm
Club Ho.
Sch.
Golf Course
16
Brookmans Park
MYMMS
PARK
Cricket Grd
Home Farm
Water End
Mimmshall Brook
BRADMORE LANE
Brick Kiln Wood
AL9
PEPLINS WAY
BRADMORE WAY
Bradmore Green
P.O.
Lib.
BROOKMAN'S
AVENUE
GEORGE'S
MOFFATS
Moffats
THE GROVE
CALDER AV
BROOKMAN'S PARK
STATION
BLUEBRIDGE
OAKLANDS
WESTLAND
THE GARDENS
Waterend Green
WARRENGATE
ROAD
ABDALE LA.
WISE'S LANE
Pumping Sta.
Abdale House
Gobions Garden
Gobions Pond
17
GOBIONS WOOD
Cangsley Grove
LOVE LANE
Royal Veterinary College
Northumberland Ho.
HAWKSHEAD
Cherry Dell
Sports Ground
Hawkshead Bridge
The Folly
LANE
HAWKSHEAD WOOD
Vinegar Spring
Lodge
Pilvage Wood
Bolons Park Coll.
20
CAMP
Old Castle Quarry
MYMMSHALL WOOD
18
Cranborne Industrial Estate
CRANBORNE
Furzefield Wood
Warrengate Farm
Potters Bar Golf Course
Lodge House
Woodhill Farm
A1(M)
Mimms Hall
King George V. Playing Field
Swimming Baths
MUTTON LANE
B556
P.O.
Youth Centre
Club Ho.
Little
BLACKHORSE LANE
Town Farm
ST. ALBANS ROAD
B556
CECIL ROAD
Mimmshall Brook
EN6
19
POTTERS BAR
LADBROOKE DRIVE
South Mimms
P.O.
Sch.
ST. GILES AV.
GREYHOUND LANE
Bridgefoot
Bridgefoot House
BRIDGEFOOT
Dugdale Hill
Grasmere
Sch.
Rydal Mount
Coun. Depot
Sch.
Allots
20
Cem.
Play Area
Motel
South Mimms Service Area
Mimms Wash
1
23
M25
SAWYERS LANE
Blanche Farm
BLANCHE LANE
28
A1081
Wash Farm
BAKER
Elm Farm
BENTLEY HEATH
Bentleyheath Farm
White Ho.
EN5
Bentley Heath
Village Hall
Duke of York
Dancershill

20
DERRY WOOD
Newgate Street
Tolmers Pk. Hosp.
Ponsbourne Manor Ho.
Hazel Grove
Long Grove
St. Lawrence Farm
Pumping Sta.
Newgate Street Bridge
HAMMOND STREET
Burleigh Farm
Nurseries
CHESHUNT COMMON
Lucas End
Goff's Oak
HOME WOOD
CUFFLEY
Cuffley Hill
Thorntons Farm
Nyn Manor Farm
Sports Grd.
Coles Hill
Colesdale Farm
Burnt Farm
Cattlins
Dysons Osiers
Nursery Plantation
Cattlegate Wood
Cattlegate
Cattlegate Farm
St. Raphaels (Barvin Park) School
Barvin Hill
South Hill
Glasgow Stud Farm
Sanders's Corner
Crews Hill Golf Course
Whitewebbs Wood
Sloemans Farm
M25
SG 13
EN 7
EN 2
11
16
17
18
19
20
21
29
BV
BW
BX
BY

DERRY WOOD
SG13
Baisley's Wood
Beaumont Manor
BEAUMONT ROAD
Bramble Grove
THUNDERFIELD GROVE
New Plantation
Factory Farm
Hazel Grove
Calves Croft
BZ
CA
CB
CC
12
Bread & Cheese Br.
MOAT
Spring Wood
Tanfield Stud Fm.
EN 10
GAMMON'S LANE
PARADISE HILL
PARADISE
Nurseries
Res.
HAMMOND
16
Gammon Farm
Appleby Street
Paradise House
Doggett Hill
Cromwell Wood
Appleby Street Farm
NEWGATE
STREET
Cheshunt Park Farm
Hammond Street
CHESHUNT PARK
ROAD
DIGDAG HILL
Lucasend Farm
Nursery
Golf Course
CROUCH LANE
Lucas End
ROSEDALE
LONGFIELD
Club Ho.
CHESHUNT RESERVOIR (North)
Poultry Farm
Rags Brook
17
Sch.
ST JAMES'S ROAD
ST ANDREW'S ROAD
Flamstead End
Play. Flds.
Goff's Hotel
Goff's Oak
Rosedale Sports Ground
CUFFLEY HILL
GOFF'S LANE
Village Hall
Lib.
Goffsoak House
Playing Field
B156
McGREDY
CHURCH
20
18
Colesgrove Manor
Swimming Pool
Poyndon Farm
EN 7
HALF MOAT MANOR HO (SITE OF)
Sports Field
Play. Field
Public Open Space
Borough Offices
SILVER STREET
Halstead Hill House
FLAMSTEAD END
Schs.
CEMETERY
COLLEGE RD
Churchgate
The Bungalow
Adath Yisroel Cemetery
Nurseries
BARROW LANE
Elm Lodge
Playing Field
Woodgreen Farm
Broadfield Farm
NEW RIVER
Theobalds Brook
Burnt Farm
Bury Green Farm
RELIEF ROAD
B198
19
OLD PARK RIDE
Cattlins
Dysons Osiers
Burygreen Plantation
HOME WOOD
Cuffley
Hanging Plantation
Gate
Home Plantation
Spring Farm
Theobalds Manor
Temple Bar
Temple House
Sports Ground
THEOBALD'S PARK
Theobalds Park College
Theobalds Pk Farm
GREAT CAMBRIDGE ROAD A10
Gunsite Stud
South Osiers
20
Riding Sch.
Bullscross Farm
Camp Site
M25
Western Cemetery (Jewish)
25
Sanders's Corner
Gate
Whitewebbs Farm
Sloemans Farm
30
WHITEWEBBS ROAD
EN 2
Pumping Sta.
Whitewebbs Wood
White Webbs
Municipal Golf Course
Roam Cott
Capel Ho.
BULLSMOOR LANE
Bull's Cross
THEOBALDS PARK

21
Wormley
Turnford
CHESHUNT
WALTHAM CROSS
WALTHAM ABBEY
Holyfield
Clayton Hill
St Leonards
Langridge
Turnford Marsh
Aqueduct Lock
Cheshunt Lock
Holyfield Marsh
Hooks Marsh
Thistly Marsh
Hall Marsh
WALTHAM MARSH
Fish Pond
Playing Field
Lower Island
Rammey Marsh
GALLEYHILL WOOD
Government Research Establishment
Sand & Gravel Works
Elec. Transformer Sta.
Sailing Club
Weir
Stubbings Nursery
Fishers Green
Holyfield Farm
Monkhams Hall
The Rookery
Homefield Wood
Kennel Wood
Hayes Hill Fm. (Lea Valley Show Farm)
Holyfieldhall Farm
Netherkidders Farm
Marsh Hill
Quintonhill Farm
RIVER LEA
RIVER LEA NAVIGATION
Small River Lea
HODDESDON BY-PASS
EN 8
EN 9
M25
12
22
30
16
17
18
19
20
CC
CD
CE
CF

Clayton Hill
Perry Hill Fm.
Convalescent Home
Middle St.
Walnut Tree Cott
Belchers
Belchers La.
Nazeing Common
Tel. Ex.
Sch. Ho.
King Harold's Head
Bumble Green
13
CG
CH
CJ
CK
Laundry La.
Netherkidders Farm
St Leonards
St Leonards Rd.
Cemetery Lane
St. Lawrence Farm
Allots.
Road
Allmains Cl.
Galleyhill Road
Allmains
Nazeing Gate
Copy Wood
Nazeing Long Green
Harolds Park Fm
16
Colemans Lane
B194
Felsteads
Lane
Lousehall La.
Waltham Road
Galleyhill Green
Holyfieldhall Farm
Marsh Hill
The Springs
Deerpark Wood
Parvills
Galley Hill
Kennels
Clavenhambury Farm
Hayes Hill Fm.
Lea Valley
(Show Farm)
17
Galleyhill Wood
Holyfield Road
Broadgate Springs
Brayshill Spring
Road
Clavenhambury
Galleyhill
Holyfield
North Lodge Farm
Holyfield
Longcroft Grove
Stocking Grove
Scatterbushes Wood
Puck Lane
Aimes Grn.
Aimesgn Farm
EN9
Cobbinsend Farm
Cobbinsend Road
Homefield Wood
21
Epping
Maple Springs
Monkhams Rifle Range
18
Caravan Park
Sewage Wks.
Kennel Wood
Lane
Lodge
Breach Barns Farm
Fernhall Farm
Fernhall Wood
Clapgate
Nursery
Dallance Farm
Obelisk Wood
Cobbins Brook
Brookmeadow Wood
Long Street
Fernhall Lane
Home Farm
Nicholls Farm
Cobbin Pond
Nurseries
Copthall Green
19
Galleyhill Road
Warlies Park
Burgess Farm
West Hill
Waltham Abbey
Sports Grd.
Nursery
Pick Hill
Pickhill Farm
Warlies School
Horseshoe Hill
P.O.
Parklands
Paternoster Hill
Harries Crt
Amesbury
Homefield
Conybury Ct.
Upshire Road
Sch.
Sch's
C.C.
Saxon Way
Tudor Way
Monkswood Ave
Halfhides
Broomstick Hall Rd.
Sports Centre
Ninefields
Loughton Ct.
Sergeants Grn.
Upshire
Old Sch. Ho.
Rugged La.
Copthall Green
Woodgreen Rd.
Sergeants Green La.
Oxleys Wood
P.O.
Farm Hill Road
A121
20
Indust. Est
Rec. Grd.
Honey Lane
Cullings Ct.
Mallion Ct.
Hillhouse
Abbots Dr.
Wood Green
Blind Green
Lane
Brambly Shaw
Morris Ct.
Gant Ct.
Harlton Ct.
Haywood Ct.
Woodgreen Farm
A112
Denny Av.
Roundhills
Downlands
Fairways
Playing Fld.
School
Woodgreen Potteries
Wood Green
Woodredon
F.S.
Indust. Est
Cem.
Cemy.
Sewardstone Rd.
Gilsand
Upshire Hall
31
Conybury Wood
Woodredon Farm
Stag Shaw
Lodge La.
Beechfield Wk.
Quintonhill Farm
Greylands
Lane
A121
26
Skillet Hill
Volunteer
Woodridge

Epping Green
P.O.
CK
CL
CM
CN
13
Site of SHINGLE HALL
MOAT
Marles Wood
Rose Fm.
Hayleys Manor Farm
Currance Farm
All Saints' Vicarage
PUMP LA.
Sch.
B181
UPLAND ROAD
Pinch Timber Farm
All Saints' Ch.
Takeleys on Site of MANOR HOUSE
Epping Upland
Hunter's Hall Farm
Chambers Manor Farm
16
Orange Wood
Ballhill Wood
Gills Farm
Cobbin's Br.
Sewage Wks.
Orange Peel
Orange Field Plant.n
Gills Plant.n
Cobbins Brook
Wintry Wood
17
Winthry Farm
B181
Bury Farm
BURY
LINDSEY
Playing Fld.
Shaftesbury Farm
Almshos
THORNWOOD
CM16
23
Spratt's Hedgerow Wood
Spratt's Hedgerow
F o r e s t
B182
BOLT CELLAR
Pond Field Plant.n
Jenkins's Plantation
The Green
18
Little Rookery Wood
Fitches Plantation
Playing Fld.
Theydon Grove
EPPING
Cemetery
Sec.y Sch.
Sports Grd.
Gov. Offs.
Wood House
New Farm
Home Farm
Griffin's Wood
Griffin's Wood
Copped Hall
Sports Grd
LOWER BURY LA.
HIGH ST.
Bower Hill
19
Bell Inn
WESTERN ROAD
Gas Works
COPTHALL PARK
Selvage
M25
Ladder Stile
B1393
EPPING RD.
Common
Bell
Res.
Forestgate Inn
Ivy Chimneys
Sch.
IVYCHIMNEYS ROAD
BRIDGE HILL
BROOK RD.
STEWARDS
Tunnel
THE WARREN
Theydon Towers
Great Gregories Farm
Lodges
Green Ride
AMBERSBURY BANKS
EPPING FOREST
20
LODGE ROAD
Club House
Little Gregories
Golf Course
B1393
THEYDON ROAD
LITTLE GREGORIES LANE
Riding Sch.
31
CK
CL
CM
CN
EPPING
Green Ride
PIERCING
Wansfell

Esgors
Thornwood
CO
CP
CQ
CR
14
Rose Fm.
High Elms
Hayleys Manor Farm
UPLAND ROAD
Rugby Grd.
Council Depot
Sewage Works
WEALD HALL LANE
Weald Hall
Currance Farm
Thornwood Common
MOAT
16
Disused Camp Site
CARPENTERS ARMS LA.
P.O.
Blacksmiths' Arms
Thornwood
MOAT
Site of MARSHALLS
NORTH WEALD AERODROME
Depot
Woodside
WOODSIDE
Park Place
ROAD
HIGH ROAD
Wintry Wood
EPPING FOREST
STUMP RD.
17
Wintry Park Farm
Playing Fld.
The Lake
Hosp.
B181
B1393
Roughtalley's Wood
Shaftesbury Farm
LINDSEY ST.
LANE
Epping Plain
PLAIN RD.
ONGAR RD.
THORNWOOD RD.
Almshos
St. Margaret's Hospital
PARKLANDS
Coopersale Common
COOPERSALE COMMON
Inst.
M11
Gernon Bushes
The Green
Res. Pav.
Playing Field
Childs Home
Vic.
18
22
Binching Coppice
Postern-lane Spring
Epping
CM16
Theydon Grove
Mount Wood
HIGH STREET
EPPING
Redyn's Wood
Forty Acres
Sch.
Pub. Ho.
Coopersale Ho.
Gov. Offs.
STONARDS HILL
Ongar Down
Stonards
Coopersale Street
Gaynes Park
Mount Quarter
Bower Hill
Almhos
Lo
EPPING
19
GAYNESPARK (Site of)
Gravelpit Wood
BANKS LANE
Gas Works
School
Steward's Green
Fiddlers Hamlet
MOUNT ROAD
Mount End
IVYCHIMNEYS RD.
BRIDGE HILL
BROOK RD.
STEWARD'S GREEN ROAD
Merry Fiddlers
Searles Farm
BLACKSMITHS HILL
BEACH WOOD
Little Thornhall
20
M11
North Ho.
Sewage Works
Long Plantation
6
Gardners
Coopersale Hall
BRICK KILN HILL
CROSS ROAD
32
27
M25
HOBBS CROSS RD.
Barber's Wood
PRIVATE ROAD
Icehouse Plantn
Coleman Farm

North Weald Bassett
Tylers Green
Ongar Radio Station
Ongar Park Hall
NORTH WEALD STA.
Cold Hall Farm
ONGAR PARK WOOD
Forest
Colliers Hatch
Moat Ho.
Woodhatch
Mole Trap
Nickerlands
Northlands Wood
Long Spring
Hanging Spring
Round Spring
Park Spring
Little Tawney Hall
Howfield
The Grove
Knightsland Wood
Berwick Farm
Berwick Lane
Icehouse Wood
Twentyacre Wood
Cesslands Farm
Freemans Farm
Does Fm
Toot Hill
Steers Farm
Wealds Farm
Blake's Farm
Stewarts Farm
Caravan Site
Greensted Green
Greensted Ho.
Hardings
Greensted Wood
Dewley Wood
Perrills
Millers Grove
Dolman's Spring
Pickle's Gardens
Widow's Farm
Burrows Farm
Newhouse
Coleman's Farm
Draper's Corner
Drill Ho.
Clark's Farm
Rockett's Cotts.
Stanford Rivers
Stanford Hall
Rectory
Murrells Farm
Traceys Farm
White Bear
LONDON ROAD A113
EPPING ROAD A414
HIGH RD.
Talbot Roundabout
Upr. Bobbingworth Green
Lwr. Bobbingworth Green
Sayers Fm.
Wardens
Bovinger Hall
Reynkyns Wood
Slough Ho. Fm
New Ho. Fm
Sch.
P.O.
Skips Corner
Sewage Wks.
CM5
CR
CS
CT
CU
14
16
17
18
19
20
24
32

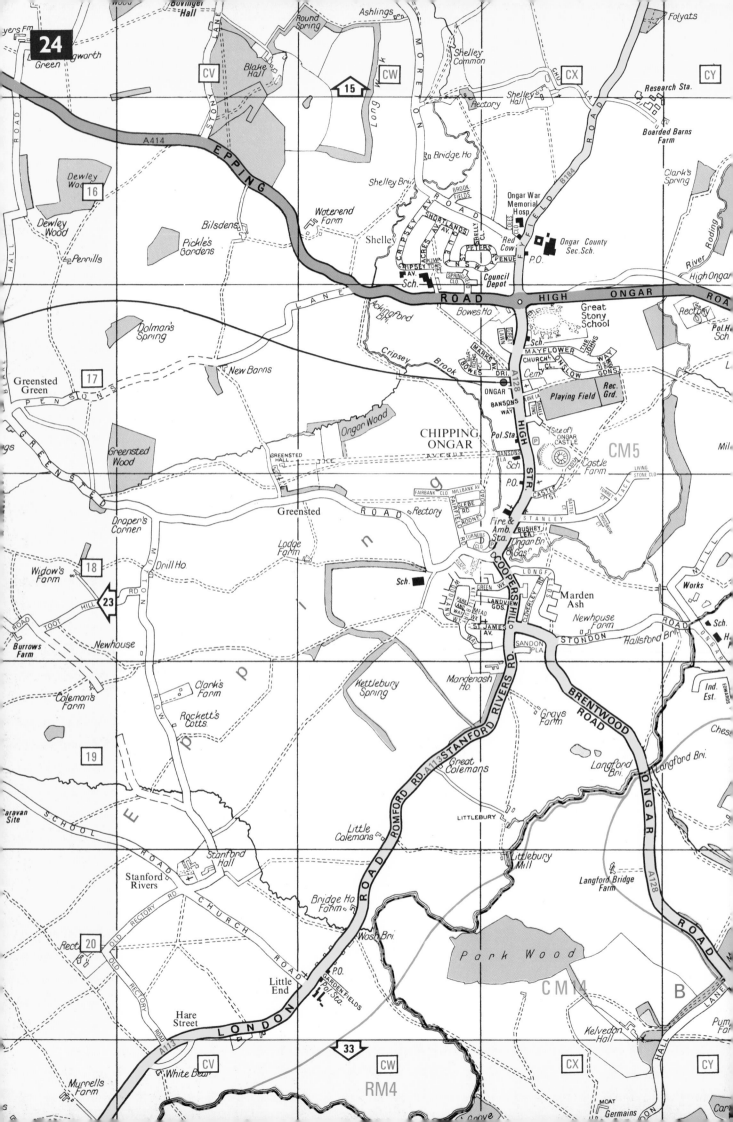

Bovinger Hall
Ashlings
Folyats
Round Spring
Blake Hall
Shelley Common
CV
CW
CX
CY
15
Long Walk
MORETON
STONY LANE
Rectory
Shelley Hall
Research Sta.
Boarded Barns Farm
A414
EPPING
ROAD
HIGH ONGAR
Dewley Wood
16
Bridge Ho
Shelley Bri.
Clark's Spring
Waterend Farm
Bilsdens
Pickle's Gardens
Shelley
Ongar War Memorial Hosp.
Ongar County Sec. Sch.
FYFIELD ROAD
B184
Red Cow
P.O.
Council Depot
Sch.
Perrills
River Roding
High Ongar
LANE
Bowes Ho
Great Stony School
Rectory
Akingford Bri.
Dolman's Spring
Cripsey Brook
MAYFLOWER WAY
CHURCH CL.
ONSLOW GDNS.
Cem.
New Barns
Greensted Green
17
PENSONS
A128
ONGAR
Playing Field
Rec. Grd.
BANSONS WAY
Ongar Wood
CHIPPING ONGAR
HIGH STR.
Pol. Sta.
(Site of) ONGAR CASTLE
CM5
GREENSTED HALL
AVENUE
Sch.
Castle Farm
Greensted Wood
GREENSTED
P.O.
CASTLE ST.
FAIRBANK CLO.
MILLBANK AV.
GLEBE RD
FAIRFIELD
RODNEY
Greensted
ROAD
Rectory
STANLEY
Draper's Corner
Fire & Amb. Sta.
BUSHEY LEA
Ongar Br.
Lodge Farm
Drill Ho.
COOPERSHILL
Widow's Farm
18
23
MUTTON ROW
Sch.
Epping
LONGFIELD
Marden Ash
Works
GREEN WK
LANDVIEW GDS.
TOOT HILL RD
ST. JAMES AV.
Newhouse Farm
STONDON ROAD
Hallsford Bri.
Newhouse
Burrows Farm
SANDON PLA.
Mardenash Ho.
Ind. Est.
Clark's Farm
Coleman's Farm
Kettlebury Spring
BRENTWOOD ROAD
Grays Farm
Rockett's Cotts.
STANFORD RIVERS RD.
A113
ROMFORD RD.
19
Great Colemans
Langford Bri.
Langford Bri.
Caravan Site
SCHOOL ROAD
LITTLEBURY
ONGAR ROAD
Little Colemans
Littlebury Mill
Stanford Hall
Stanford Rivers
Langford Bridge Farm
CHURCH ROAD
OLD RECTORY RD
Bridge Ho. Farm
Wash Bri.
Rect.
20
Park Wood
P.O.
Little End
Pol. Sta.
GARDEN FIELDS
CM14
B
Hare Street
LONDON ROAD
Kelvedon Hall
HALL LANE
33
White Bear
Murrells Farm
RM4
MOAT
Germains

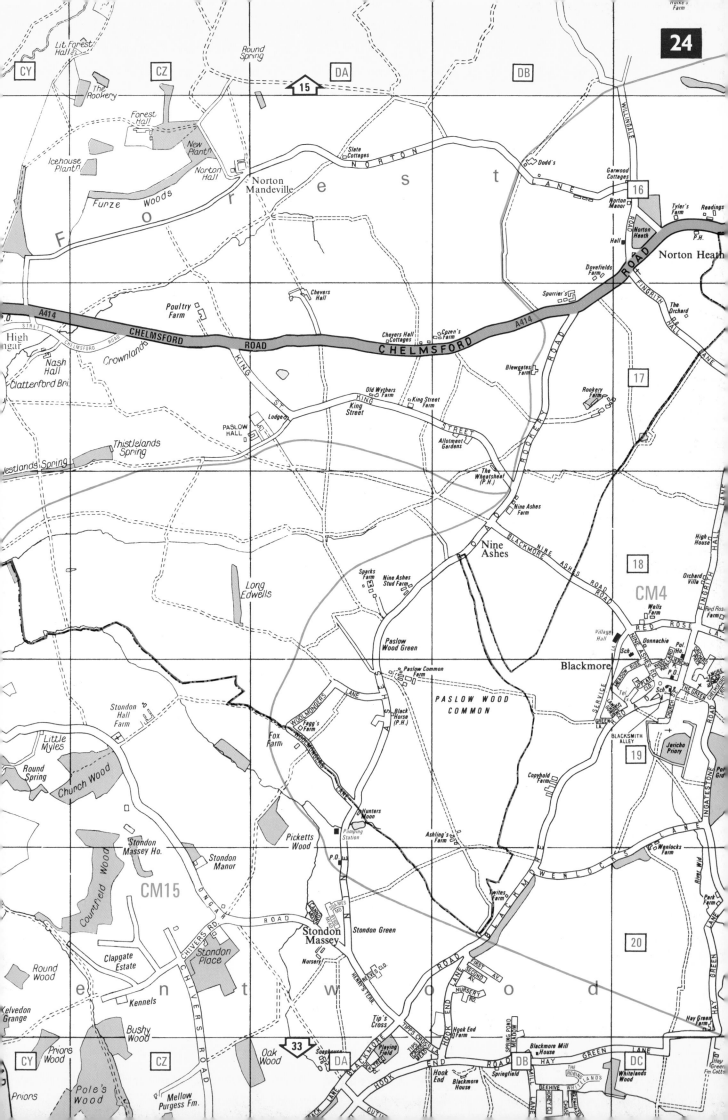
Lit. Forest Hall
The Rookery
Round Spring
Forest Hall
New Plantn
Icehouse Plantn
Norton Hall
Norton Mandeville
Furze Woods
Slate Cottages
NORTON LANE
Dodd's
Garwood Cottages
Norton Manor
WILLINGALE ROAD
Tyler's Farm
Readings
Norton Heath
Norton Heath
P.H.
Dovefields Farm
Spurrier's
FINGRITH HALL LANE
The Orchard
Chevers Hall
Poultry Farm
A414
CHELMSFORD ROAD
Chevers Hall Cottages
Cozen's Farm
High Ongar
Nash Hall
Crownland
Clatterford Bri.
Blewgates Farm
Rookery Farm
ROOKERY ROAD
Old Wythers Farm
King Street Farm
KING STREET
King Street
Lodge
PASLOW HALL
Allotment Gardens
Thistlelands Spring
Westlands Spring
The Wheatsheaf (P.H.)
Nine Ashes Farm
Nine Ashes
BLACKMORE NINE ASHES ROAD
High House
Orchard Villa
Long Edwells
Sparks Farm
Nine Ashes Stud Farm
CM4
Wells Farm
Red Rose Farm
RED ROSE LA.
Village Hall
Donnachie
Pol. Ho.
Sch.
Blackmore
P.O.
Paslow Wood Green
Paslow Common Farm
PASLOW WOOD COMMON
WOOLMONGERS LANE
Black Horse (P.H.)
Stondon Hall Farm
Fagg's Farm
Fox Farm
THE GREEN
SERVICE RD.
GREEN LA.
BLACKSMITH ALLEY
Jericho Priory
Little Myles
Round Spring
Church Wood
Copyhold Farm
INGATESTONE ROAD
Hunters Moon
Pumping Station
Picketts Wood
Ashling's Farm
Stondon Massey Ho.
Stondon Manor
Countfield Wood
Wenlocks Farm
WENLOCKS LANE
River Wid
CM15
P.O.
Twites Farm
Park Farm
ONGAR ROAD
Stondon Massey
Stondon Green
Stondon Place
CHIVERS RD.
Clapgate Estate
Nursery
REEVES CL.
HENRY'S TERR.
FIRST AV.
SECOND AV.
NURSERY RD.
BLACKMORE ROAD
Round Wood
Kennels
Kelvedon Grange
Tip's Cross
TIPPS CROSS LA.
HOOK END LANE
Hook End Farm
SPRING POND MEADOW
Hay Green Farm
HAY GREEN LANE
Bushy Wood
Priors Wood
Oak Wood
Soaphouse
Playing Field
Blackmore Mill House
HAY GREEN LANE
THE ROBINS
WHITELANDS
Whitelands Wood
Hay Green Fm Cotts.
Hook End
Blackmore House
Springfield
BEEHIVE
HONEY CL.
CHASE
MILL LANE
HOOK END ROAD
Pole's Wood
Priors
Mellow Purgess Fm.
CHIVERS ROAD
Brentwood
CY
CZ
DA
DB
DC
15
16
17
18
19
20
33

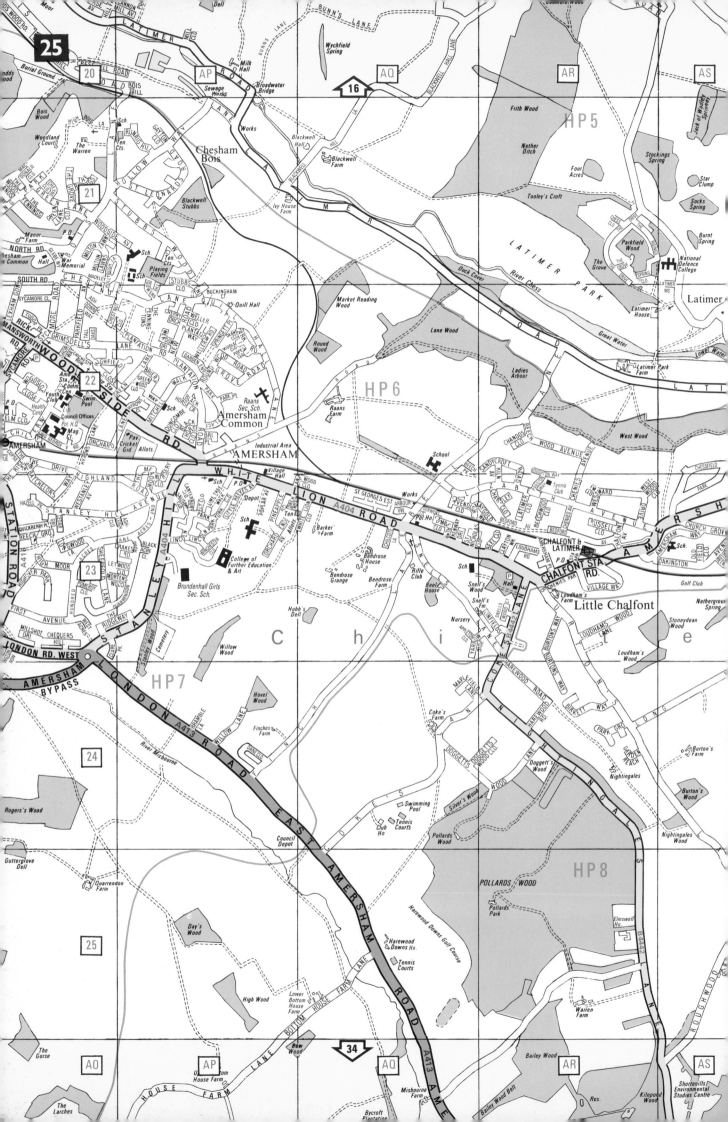

Chesham Bois
Amersham Common
AMERSHAM
Little Chalfont
Latimer
HP5
HP6
HP7
HP8
16
34
LATIMER ROAD
WHITE LION ROAD
A404
LONDON ROAD
EAST AMERSHAM ROAD
A413
AMERSHAM BYPASS
STATION ROAD
STANLEY HILL
WOODSIDE RD.
NIGHTINGALES LANE
B4442
LATIMER PARK
River Chess
Chiltern

HP3
WD3
AS
AT
AU
AV
16
34
26
Hollins Hall
Great Moonshine
Top Spring
Great Sarratt Hall Farm
Sarratt Hall
Plough Wood
Rosehall Wood
Bragmans Fm
Hanging Croft
Radar Station
Oldcroft Wood
Daniels Spring
Grove Field
Hanginglane Wood
Limeshill Wood
Martin's Top
Geary's Plantation
Baldwin's Wood
Flaunden Grove
Dacorum
Three Rivers
Valley Farm
Albert Cott.
Dawes Common
Providence Hall
"The Boat"
Pol.Ho
Village Hall
Greenend Farm
Sandfield Wood
Rectory
Sarratt Bottom
Nobles
Church End
Cock
Farm
Mill Farm
R. Chess
Holloway Lane
MOUNT WOOD
Chenies Pla.
Placehouse Copse
Coney Wood
Greathouse Farm
Cricket Grd.
Manor House
Chenies
Back Lane
Mountwood Fm
'Bedford Arms'
P.O.
Nicholas Spring
Turveylane Wood
Goldingtons
Sarrattmill Ho
New Road
Football Grnd.
Claypits Cotts.
Cricket Grnd.
Wyburn Wood
A404
Bullscroft Spring
Scrubs Wood
New Mo Farm
Blunts Wood
Mead Spring
Chilton's Wood
Little Greenstreet Fm
Great Greenstreet Fm
Old Hanging Wood
Halsey's Wood
Lodge Copse
Lodge Farm
St.Clement Danes Sch.
Marlins Clo.
Field Study Centre
Dell Fm
Dell Wood
Millfield plantation
M25
Coun. Offs. (Chorleywood Ho)
Cem.y
Chorleywood West
CHORLEYWOOD
Rickmansworth Rd
Chenies Road
Whitelands Wood
Carpenter's Wood
Hillas Wood
Whiteland Avenue
Green Lane
The Orchard
Cricket Grd.
Greenbury Clo
Scout Hut
Colley La
Club Ho.
Mem. Hall
The Sportsman Hotel
CHORLEYWOOD Golf Course COMMON
Newhouse Farm
Sch.
Blacketts Wood Dr.
Station Approach
Lib.
Black Horse
Home Wood
Kennel Lane
Crosslane Wood
Burton's Lane
Chalfont Lane
Philipshill Farm
Roughwood Park
Commongate Rd
Valley Road
Solomons Wood
Green-Hills Cl.
The Hall
Catlip's Farm
Hill Farm
The Swillet
Shepherds Lane
Long Lane
Philipshill Wood
Bullsland Farm
Heronsgate
Coombe Hill Rd
Beacon Way
Sch.
P.O.

26
Sarratt
Commonwood Common
Buckshill
Church End
Chorleywood
Chandler's Cross
Three Rivers
RICKMANSWORTH
CROXLEY
GREAT WOOD
HARROCKS WOOD
Welling Grove
Beechengrove Wood
Rickmansworth Masonic School (Girls)
RICKMANSWORTH PARK
M25
WD3
WD4
AW
AX
AY
AZ
17
19
18
21
22
23
24
25
35

Leavesden Green
Leavesden Aerodrome
17
AZ
BA
BB
BC
NORTH ORBITAL RD.
KINGSWAY
WATFORD ROAD
A41
Police Ho.
The Rookery
Play. Fld.
Langleybury
GADE SIDE
KINGSWAY
A405
NORTH WESTERN AV.
LEGGATT'S RISE
NORTH WATFORD CEMETERY
Rec. Grd.
Playing Field
Harebreaks Recreation Grd.
Heath Wood
LANGLEYBURY
The Grove
THE GROVE PARK
Grove Mill
Water Wks
Weir
GROVE MILL
R. Gade
HEMPSTEAD ROAD
A411
COURTLANDS
RIDGEWAY
NASCOT WOOD ROAD
GAMMON'S
Playing Field
Rec. Grd.
Rounton
WD2
ST. ALBANS ROAD
A412
WATFORD NORTH
BUSHEY MILL LANE
Gasometer
Ind. Est.
21
22
23
24
25
27
WATFORD JUNC.
COLONIAL INDUSTRIAL ESTATE
Open Space
School Sports Grd.
Sports Ground
West Herts Golf Course
WHIPPENDELL WOOD
Jacott's Hill
Iron Bridge Lock
GRAND UNION CANAL
CASSIOBURY DRIVE
WOODLAND DRIVE
CASSIOBURY PARK
Paddling Pool
Watercress Beds
R. Gade
Rousebarn Farm
ROUSEBARN LANE
WATFORD
WD1
Town Hall
College
Sports Ground
Council Offices
Cemetery
Coll. Annexe
PARK AVENUE
RICKMANSWORTH RD.
A412
Cassiobridge House
Lock
Marina
Cassio Bri.
CROXLEY GREEN
WHIPPENDELL
KING GEORGE'S AV.
SYDNEY RD.
Sports Ground
Recreation Ground
CROXLEY
WATFORD ROAD
Croxley Mills
Common Moor Lock
Long Valley Wood
HOLYWELL INDUSTRIAL EST.
WATFORD WEST
WATFORD STADIUM (Match days only)
Watford General Hosp. (Shrodells)
Watford Football Ground
VICARAGE ROAD
A4145
Allotments
Rec. Grd.
Holywell Farm
King George V. Playing Flds.
Community Centre
Tolpits Caravan Site
TOLPITS LANE
35
Gravel Pit
RIVER COLNE
Business Park
Moor Lane Crossing
COMMON MOOR
Wiggenhall Br.
Sports Gd.
Depot
OXHEY PARK
Caravan Park
WATFORD HIGH ST
Water Wks
Harlequin Centre
Rec. Grd.

27
NORTH WATFORD CEMETERY
KINGSWAY
NORTH ORBITAL RD.
GARSTON PARK
GARSTON
Coldharbour Plantn
Crab Wood
Peartree Wood
Munden Spring
Munden Ho.
St. Albans
Open Air Theatre
University of Hertfordshire
M1
18
A41 LEGGATT'S RISE
NORTH WESTERN AV.
A41 WESTERN WAY
ST. ALBANS ROAD
A412
Gasometer
Ind. Est.
WATFORD NORTH
River Colne
Binghams
Golf Course
WD2
Aldenham
Playing Field
Church Farm
Sports Centre
RADLETT LANE
HARTSPRING LANE
Busheymill Bri.
Pumping Sta.
BERRY GROVE LA.
Bushey Hall Farm
Knutsford Recn Ground
Industrial Estate
Caravan Site
The Three Compasses
Patchetts Green
Delrow House
Motel
Hall
Sch.
Sports Cen.
WATFORD JUNC.
COLONIAL INDUSTRIAL ESTATE
ORPHANGE RD.
PARK AVE
LINK RD.
Playgd.
Scotts Wood
Royal Caledonian Schools
Playing Field
Bushey Hall Golf Course
American Sch.
Police Sports Club
Jewish Cemetery
LITTLE BUSHEY LANE
Icedale Wood
Club Ho
Town Hall
Baths
Sports Ground
Coll. Annexe
Cemetery
Watford General Hosp. (Shrodells)
Watford Football Ground
Allotments
Harlequin Centre
WATFORD COLLEGE
WATFORD HIGH ST.
Eastern Gas Board
Water Wks
International University of Europe
Allots
Moat-field Recn Grd.
WD1
Wiggenhall Br.
Sports Gd.
Depot
OXHEY PARK
Caravan Park
Grange Park School
Royal Masonic Sch. (Junr.)
Council Offices
Comm. Cen.
Hall
P.O. Bushey Ho.
British Leg.
LONDON A411 ROAD
HIGH ST.
OXHEY
Rec. Gd.
Hayden Hill
36
BUSHEY
Swim Pool
St. Margaret's Sch.
Swimming Pool
SPARROWS
CHALK HILL
A4008
A4125
BD
BE
BF
BG
21
22
23
24
25
26
5

West Herts Main Drainage Authorities (Blackbirds Works)
Golf Course
Cricket Grd
Sand Plant
High Bridge
Club House
18
Starveacres
The Folly
RADLETT
Radlett Hall
Pol Sta.
Fire Sta.
Tel. Ex.
War Meml.
The Gorse
NEWBERRIES PARK
Auriol Farm
Wood Hall Farm
Wood Hall
Kemprow Fm
WD7
Tykes Water
Playing Field
Cobden Hill
Cobdenhill Dell
Battlers Green
Battlers Green Farm
Moses Dell
Brick Wks.
Kendal Wood
Little Organ Hall
Little Kendals Farm
Kendals Country Club
The Fruit Farm
Little Kendals Wood
Letchmore Heath
Bhaktivedanta Manor
Sanatorm
Aldenham School
Slades Fm
Nth Medburn Farm
28
Letchmore Lo.
Electricity Transformer Station
MOATS
Hilfield Fm
Elstree Aerodrome (Private)
ALDENHAM PARK
Haberdasher's Aske's Schools
Tykes Water Lake
WD6
Elstree Golf Course
Hilfield Castle
HILFIELD PARK RESERVOIR
Aldenham Country Park
Home Fm
Lister Cotts
Radnor Hall
Cem.
ALDENHAM RESERVOIR
Sports Grd
ELSTREE
The Fishery
Open Space
M1
36
Little Bushey
Harrow
Barnet
ELSTREE OPEN SPACE
Edgwarebury Country Club
WESTERN AVENUE
WATFORD BY-PASS
A5183
A411
A41
A409
B462
BG
BH
BJ
BK
21
22
23
24
25

28
Sand Plant
Cricket Grd
Nursery
RADLETT LANE
BL
BM
BN
BO
19
Bigpursley Wood
Ridge
CROSSOAKS LANE
SUMMERSWOOD LANE
PACKHORSE LA
NEWCOMBE RD
NEW RD
BIRCH WOOD
NEW COME PATH
LONDON RD
Football Ground
Cricket Field
GREEN ST B5378
Littlepursley Wood
Crossoaks Farm
Crossoaks Wood
The Gorse
WD7
Auriol Farm
NEWBERRIES PARK
WOODHALL LANE
Kitwells Cotts
Wood Hall Farm
21
Wood Hall
Kitwells Lo.
Villa Scalabrini
Birch Wood
High Canons
Holmshill House
Lyndhurst
Rest
Silver Hill
WOODHALL LANE
High Canons Farm
HIGH CANONS
Buckettsland Farm
BUCKETTSLAND LANE
WELL END RD
Green Street
COWLEY HILL
THEOBALD ST
22
Ford
Campions
Cowleyhill Farm
Well End Lodge
Well End
Holly Cot.
Health Centre
Schools
STAPLETON RD
REDWOOD RISE
STANBOROUGH AVENUE
PURSLEY RD
RESTON PATH
Recreation Gd.
Rec Gd.
P.O.
Nicholas Hawksmoor Sch.
Sports Centre
ROWLEY LANE
Rowley Farm
ALEXANDRA RD
POTTERS
Schools
AYCLIFFE RD
Sch.
CROWN RD
ALBAN CRES
Aberford Lake
GATESHEAD RD
BROOK RD
23
27
Tykes Water
Meadow pk.
Football Grd
Bowl. Grn.
HANCOCK CT
Industrial Park
B'wd
Sports Gd.
Syn.
Hall
Sch.
Civic Cen.
Borehamwood Swim. Coll. Pool
Health Cen.
Lib.
Sta.
A5135
YORK WAY
Elstree House
Sports Ground
North Medburn Farm
KINGSLEY AV
ASHDOWN DR.
CROXDALE RD
Television Studios
ELSTREE WAY
Fire & Amb. Sta.
BULLHEAD RD
MANOR WAY
INDUSTRIAL EST.
Elect. Brd. Dpt.
CHESTER RD
WARWICK RD
Elstree Moat House
Elstree Golf Course
Boulevard 25
Elstree Studios
Borehamwood
King Georges Field
Sch.
A5183
24
PARK AV
SHENLEY RD
FURZEHILL RD
KENILWORTH DRIVE
C.C.
Hillside Sec. and Monksmead Prim. Schs.
Rec. Grd.
Play. Fld.
Tykes Water Lake
LANE
ELSTREE
Gas Works
Sch.
Hall
P.O.
C.C.
Rec. Grd.
Athletic Grd
Fire Research Sta.
Scout Hut
Hall
RIPON WAY
ALLUM LANE A5135
Radnor Hall
Cem.
LODGE AVENUE
THE RISE
BARNET LANE
ASHLEY DRIVE
FARRIERS WAY
Met. Pol. Cadet Playing Fields
25
ELSTREE HILL NTH
THE BARTONS
ELSTREE
Syn.
A411
WOODCOCK HILL
LANE A411 BARNET
Elstree Tunnel
Deacons Heights
Deacons Hill
A411 LANE
Stirling Corner
Car Pk.
SCRATCHWOOD OPEN SPACE
BARNET WAY A1
BARNET LANE
Penniwells
37
DEACONS HILL OPEN SPACE
BM
Hyver Hall
BL
BN
BO
Boys Hill Wood
Edgwarebury Country Club
ELSTREE OPEN SPACE
M1
Thistle Wood
N.W.7

South Mimms Service Area
Mimms Wash
EN6
M25
BO
BP
BQ
BR
19
Blanche Farm
BLANCHE LANE
A1081
Wash Farm
SAWYERS LANE
Elm Farm
BENTLEY HEATH
Bentleyheath Farm
White Ho.
Bentley Heath
Village Hall
Duke of York
Dancershill Farm
Dancershill Ho.
Dancers Hill
Norfolk Lodge
HILL ROAD
21
DYRHAM LANE
Dyrham Park Farm
Mimmshall Brook
BOTTOM
TROTTERS
BY PASS
A1
Wrotham Park
WROTHAM PARK
A1000
Deadman's
Green Dragon
ST ALBANS ROAD
DYRHAM PARK
Dyrham Park (Country Club)
Knightsland Farm
Home Farm
Kitt's End
22
Valentine's Farm
GALLEY
EN4
Monkey Mead
Allots
Golf Course
Club Ho.
High Stone
Fold Farm
Moat
Glebe Farm
Saffron Green
HADLEY GREEN
29
23
The Grove
Monken Hadley
EN5
Byng Road Playing Fields
Hadley Ho.
Homestead Farm
GALLEY LANE
Sch.
Burial Grd
King George's Field
Playing Fld.
Queen Elizabeths Boys Sch.
Cricket Grd.
ARKLEY
WOOD ST.
A411
BARNET
24
HIGH BARNET
Barnet Gen Hosp
Elmbank
Oaklands
Arkley Golf Course
Arkley Hall
Arkley
ROWLEY GREEN ROAD
BARNET COMMON
St. Stephens Hosp.
Underhill
Barnet F.C.
Cricket Grd.
25
Playing Fields
GREAT NORTH ROAD
Whitings Hill
MAYS LANE
Dollis Brook
Totteridgevale Fm.
Grange Playing Fields
37
N.20
Pinefield Priory
B552
HENDON
GATE LANE
SOUTH HERTS
OAKLANDS ROAD

M25
EN7
South Hill
Holly Hill Farm
BV
BW
BX
BY
20
CATTLEGATE
CREWS HILL
CREWS HILL ROAD
Club Ho.
Glasgow Stud Farm
Sanders's Corner
Sloemans Farm
Nurseries
WHITEWEBBS
THEOBALDS PARK ROAD
Pumping Sta.
Crews Hill Golf Course
BEECH AV
CYPRESS A.
ROSEWOOD DR.
Whitewebbs Wood
21
King's Oak Farm
Wildwood
King's Oak Plain
Turkey Brook
THE RIDGEWAY
A1005
Foley Cottage
Parting Hill
Playing Fld.
Sch.
Botany Bay
Botany Bay Farm
EAST LODGE LANE
East Lodge
Little Beechhill Wood
Duncan's Wood
STRAYFIELD RD.
Clay Hill Lo.
FLASH LANE
CLAY HILL
Claysmore
Kingswood
Clay Hill
Rectory Farm
Rendlesham Viaduct
EN2
HILLY FIELDS PARK
22
CHASE
LAVENDER HILL CEMETERY
COOK'S HOLE RD.
PHIPPS HATCH LA.
Park Side Ho.
MOAT
HADLEY ROAD
Parkside Farm
Pumping Sta.
Enfield District Hosp.
GORDON HILL
Camlet Hill
Wolverton
Leeging Beech Gutter
Hog Hill
LAVENDER
FAIRVIEW RD.
30
23
Chase Side
TRENT PARK
Middlesex Polytechnic
Country Park
Monument
Shaws Wood
The Rookery
Sports Ground
Rec. Gd.
Merryhills Brook
SLADES HILL A110
WINDMILL HILL
ENFIELD ROAD A110
Triangular Wd.
Golf Course
24
Salmon's Brook
PICCADILLY LINE
Public Golf Course
OAKWOOD
Highlands Hospital
South Lodge Hospital
Grange Park
Sports Grd.
Park Corner
GRANGE PARK
Golf Course
Old Park
25
TOWN PARK
New River
Bush
OAKWOOD PARK
Yachting Pond
N14
N21
38
Playing Flds.
Church Army Home
Bowling Green
PICCADILLY
GREEN DRAGON LANE
RIDGE

Broxbourne
EN7
M25
21
BZ
CA
CB
CC
25
Sanders's Corner
Whitewebbs Farm
Sloemans Farm
Western Cemetery (Jewish)
Bullscross Farm
Pumping Sta.
Whitewebbs Wood
White Webbs
Municipal Golf Course
WHITE WEBBS PARK
Golf Filter Bed
New River (Old Course)
Roam Cott.
Bull's Cross
Capel Ho.
King's Oak Farm
Wildwood
Myddleton Ho. (Lee Valley Regional Park Authority)
Clay Hill Lo.
Claysmore
Club Ho.
Bramley Ho.
FORTY HALL ESTATE
Maiden's Bri.
Roselands
Crematorium
EN2
Clay Hill
22
HILLY FIELDS PARK
Forty Hall Museum
Forty Hill
LAVENDER HILL CEMETERY
Enfield District Hosp.
Refuse Disposal Plant
Adath Yisroel Cemetery
29
Sports Ground
23
Chase Side
Queen Elizabeth Stadium
ENFIELD PLAYING FIELDS
EN1
Playing Fields
Schools
ENFIELD
24
ENFIELD CHASE
ENFIELD TOWN
Palace Gardens Precinct
Enfield Football Stadium
Swimming Pool
TOWN PARK
Golf Course
New River
BUSH HILL PARK
Rec.n Ground
SOUTHBURY
Middlesex University
Grange Park
25
Golf Course
Old Park
Bush Hill
BUSH HILL PARK
Halliwick
N.21
N.9
JUBILEE PARK
WINCHMORE
39
GREAT CAMBRIDGE ROAD
A10
A110
A105
A1010
HERTFORD ROAD
SOUTHBURY ROAD
LONDON ROAD
WINDMILL HILL
CHURCH STREET

WALTHAM CROSS
WALTHAM ABBEY
Lower Island
Caravan Park
M25
EN8
EN9
EN3
IG10
E.4
A1010
A1055
A121
A112
A110
A1069
Cobbins Brook
Rammey Marsh Lock
Government Establishment
Research
Quintonhill Farm
Sewage Works (Sludge Disposal)
ENFIELD LOCK
Welches Fm
ALBANY PARK
School
Pumping Sta.
Aqueduct
Riding Stables
Sewardstone Hall
Nursery
The Grange
High Beech Nursery
Avey Nursery
AVEY LANE
Thompson's Wood
Golden Row
Netherhouse Farm
Royal Oak
Sewardstone
Bach Hill
Fernhill Wood
Police Cadet Training College
Watersmill Business Centre
Enfield Highway
Goldsdown Rec. Grd.
Brimsdown
KING GEORGE'S RESERVOIR
RIVER LEA NAVIGATION
Riding School
Village Hall
Pick's Farm
Carrolls Farm
Gilwell Park
Essex
Golf Course
Swim. Pool
Reservoir
Kennels
Fox & Hounds
Yardley Hill
Bury Farm
Filter Beds
Club Ho.
Sewardstone Bury
Hawk Wood
Jubilee Retreat
EPPING FOREST
Waltham Forest
CHINGFORD PLAIN
Pole Hill Obelisk (Referring Object Due North From Greenwich)
PUBLIC GOLF COURSE
Royal Forest Hotel
South Marsh
Ponders End Lock
PONDERS END
Riverside Industrial Estate
Filter Tanks
Enfield Sewage Wks.
LEA VALLEY ROAD
CHINGFORD
CC
CD
CE
CF
21
22
23
24
25
31
39

WALTHAM ABBEY
31
HONEY LANE
School
Honeylands
M25
EN9
22
Upshire Hall
Woodgreen Farm
Woodgreen Potteries
Wood Green
Potkiln Wood
Brambly Shaw
Conybury Wood
Woodredon
Woodredon Farm
Stat Shaw
SKILLET HILL
WOODRIDDEN
A121
26
Quintonhill Farm
Jews Cemetery
Honeylane Plain
Volunteer
Poplar Shaw
Round Hills
Beech Hill Park
Forest Side
CLAYPIT HILL
AVEY LANE
Avey Nursery
Aveylane Farm
Golf Course
Club Ho.
High Beech Nursery
The Grange
SEWARDSTONE
Riding Sch.
PYNESTGREEN
WELLINGTON
Duke of Wellington
Dick Turpin's Cave
Rushey Plain
Wake Valley Pond
Wake Valley
MONK
Mount Pleasant
High Beech
Epping Forest Conservation Centre
King's Oak Hotel
Nursery
Nursery
MOTT
Thompson's Wood
Netherhouse Farm
Golden Row
Manor Farm
Manor House
MANOR RD.
Almsh. Sch.
STREET
MOTT ST.
Wallsgrove House
Little Monk
Blackweir Hill
Broom Hill
Sewardstone
Aldergrove Wood
Barn Hill
30
BLIND LA.
LIPPITTS HILL
PEPPER ALLEY
LOUGHTON CAMP
Fernhill Wood
Field Study Cent.
Robin Hood
IG 10
Pipers Farm
Caravan Site
Owl (P.H.)
Police Cadet Training College
CHURCH RD.
Keeper's Cotts.
Whitehouse Plain
EARL'S PATH
Staple's Hill
Carrolls Farm
West Essex Golf Course
Gilwell Park
Round Thicket
North Long Hills
Almshouse Plain
Caravan Site
Ludgate House
Ludgate Plain
Swim. Pool
Reservoir
Nursery
FAIRMEAD
Fairmead Bottom
EPPING NEW ROAD
A104
E.4
Bury Farm
Filter Beds
Long Hills
Club Ho.
Sewardstonebury
Bury Wood
Cuckoo Pits
Grimstons Oak
The Warren
ALBION HILL
WARREN HILL
HIGH ROAD
Hawk Wood
Jubilee Retreat
Magpie Hill
Connaught Water
Warren Hill Ho.
Warren Hill
EPPING FOREST
Waltham Forest
CHINGFORD PLAIN
PUBLIC GOLF COURSE
Qn. Elizabeth's Hunting Lodge
RANGERS ROAD
A1069
40
MANOR ROAD
North Farm
Holmhurst
Warrenwood Ho.
The Warren Pond
CHINGFORD
Children's Playground
Oak Hall
CG
CH
CJ
CK
21
23
24
25

31
M25
CK
CL
CM
CN
22
21
23
24
25
32
40
THEYDON BOIS
DEBDEN ESTATE
Debden Green
Abridge
Wake Arms
Theydon Green
Debden Green
CM16
RM4
IG7
M11
Epping Forest
Ambersbury Banks
Oak Hill Enclosure
Wansfell Coll.
Birch Hall Farm
Oak Hill Fm.
Redoak Wood
Gaunt's Wood
Ripley Grange
Residential Further Education Centre
Thrifts Hill Farm
Blunt's Farm
Parsonage Farm
Springhouse
Theydon Hall
Piggott's Fm.
Long Shaw
Broadfield Shaw
Bank of England Printing Works
Sports Field
Woolston Hall
Turnours Hall
Great Downs Farm
Marchings
Sewage Wks.
Caravan Pk.
Rolls Park
Site of Barringtons
Grange Farm
Loughton Hall Sports Centre
Loughton Coll.
Recreation Ground
River Roding
Loughton Bri.
Oakwood Hill Ind. Est.
Open Space
Open Space Rectory Green
Golding's Hill Ponds
Arewater Green
Allotments
DEBDEN
Viaduct
Central Line
A121
A113
A1168
A112
B172
B1393

32
Sewage Works
North Ho.
Coopersale Hall
CO
CP
CQ
CR
23
Long Plantation
Barber's Wood
PRIVATE ROAD
Peaks Farm
BRICK KILN HILL
M11 6
M25 27
CM16
Hill Hall
Icehouse Plantn
21
THEYDON BOIS STA.
Blunt's Farm
Parsonage Farm
The Priory
Theydon Garnon
Hobbs Cross
Hobbs Cross Farm
HOBBS CROSS ROAD
LANE
MOUNT HALL (Site of)
COOPERSALE
ABRIDGE
B172
Thrifts Hill Farm
Springhouse
Hilly Spring
Bush Grove
Abridge Golf & Country Club
22
Cem.
Hydes
Brook Ho.
EPPING LANE
Skinners Farm
Theydon Hall
31
M11
Hill's Farm
Sewage Wks.
Jackson's Fm.
23
A113
Nursery
Stapleford Aer
ROAD
EPPING
Bloody Mead
Piggott's Fm.
Long Shaw
Pryors
Plessey Thorn Elect
Theydon Mead
White Hart
ONGAR
Ape's Grove
Patch Park
Foxburrow Wood
Abridge
P.O.
Blue Boar
MARKET PL.
THE POPLARS
THE MEAD
PANCROFT
FIELD CLO.
ALDERWOOD
KNIGHTS WALK
MIDDLE BOY
NEW FARM DR.
New Farm
Alder Wood
Jubilee Plantatn
Sewage Wks.
Caravan Pk.
Sch
24
LONDON ROAD
RM4
CHURCH LANE
LAMBOURNE HALL
Soapley's Wood
Great Wood
Great Downs Farm
Knoll's Wood
St Mary & All Saints Ch.
ABRIDGE RD
GRAVEL LANE
A113
Turnours Hall
Conduit Wood
CONDUIT WELL
BISHOP'S MOAT
Bishop's Hall
DEUX HALL (Site of)
Broom Grove
Marchings
25
Clark's Wood
Poultry Farm
IG7
St John's Farm
NEW LANE
Miss Rm
Gallman's End Fm.
Blackbush Farm
Isabella Cotts
KNOW HILL
Knollshill Fm.
The Shaws
Pettits Hall
41
CO
CP
ROAD
Church Ho.
FEATHERBED
CQ
ouse Fm.
BOURN BRIDGE
CR
Young's Fm.
MANOR
LORD'S
B174
E P P I N G F

CR

Hanging
Spring

Long
Spring

CS

CT

Berwick
Farm

CM5

Icehouse
Wood

CU

Rectory

OLD RECTORY RD

21

White Bear

Park
Spring

Round
Spring

Little Tawney
Hall

BELL'S
COTTS.

Howfield
The
Grove

Berwick
Ham

Twentyacre
Wood

Tracey's
Farm

Murrells
Farm

Tenacre
Wood

Stanyrocks
Plantation

Broom Wood

N A

The Old
Rectory

The Moors

Langford Bottom

Bob's Barn

Wayletts

A113

22

Stapleford
Tawney

Bob's Barn Wood

SHONKS

Lawns

STAPLEFORD TAWNEY HALL
(Site of)
Great Tawney
Hall

Shales More

Railmead
Plantation

Mitchells
Farm

Shonk's Mill
Bridge

MILL

Mill Spring

Flook
Wood

ROAD

Shales More
Cotts.

LONDON

A113

Suttans

Playing
Fields

Playing
Fields

Playing
Flds

Gravel
Pit

Howletts
Hall

Dabbs Fm

BOUNCE HILL

33

23

Yewtree
Farm

LANE

Passingford
Mill

P.O.

Passingford
Bridge

Randalls
Fm

P.O.

Loft
Hall

ROAD

Waters
Fm

Tel.
Ex.

Green Farm

M25

24

onds

B175

Bons
Fm

Albyns

CURTISMILL

GREEN

Lodge Fm.

Brook Fm.

CHURCH LA.

Deerbarn
Wood

CURTIS

LA.

Jenkins
Fm

Lee Farm

Stapleford
Abbotts

Rect

Bentleyfield
Wood

Martins
Hern

CURTIS MILL LA.

STAPLEFORD

Sch.

Brook

RING

Grove
Ho.

Stapleford
Hall
Farm

Bourne

Tyseahill
Fm

Spring Fm

25

Dycots

B175

High House
Farm

Olives
Fm

Works

Watton's
Green

Watton Fm.

Navestock

Common

CM14

ROAD

LANE

CR

CS

Pinchbacks
Bri.

TURNBRIDGE LA.

OAK HILL

41

Lyngs
Fm

CT

LYSEAH?

HILL

Asheton Fm

CHURCH RD

Skips Corner
Fa

CU

HORSEMAN SIDE

23

Rectory
Little End
P.O.
GARDENFIELDS
Pol. Sta.
Park Wood
CM5
Epping Forest
Hare Street
CV
CW
24
CX
CY
Kelvedon Hall
LONDON ROAD
A113
White Bear
Murrells Farm
Ireland Grove
MOAT
Germains Farm
KELVEDON HALL
21
Aspen Wood
Colliers Spring
Hollingford Spring
Highash Wood
Carts Wd
Stonyrocks Plantation
Lit. Aspen Wood
Cook's Wood
Merlin Wood
Broom Wood
NAVESTOCK
PARK
Red Wood
Slades Farm
Beaconhill Farm
Lady's Pond
SLADES (Site of)
CROWN RD
CHURCH
Beacon Hill
Little Beaconhill Fm
Lawns
Engine House Wood
Church Wood
BEACON HILL
LODGE RD
Howard Lo.
22
Lady's Hill
DRAKES HILL
DUDBROOK
Dudbrook
Navestock Hall Fm.
Fortification Wood
BOIS HALL
SHONKS MILL ROAD
Rose Hall Farm
Hazle Spring
Strawberry Spring
Shonk's Mill Bridge
Hook Wood
Shonk's Mill Spring
DUDBROOK
Redgate Wood
Twostile Wood
Upper Boishall Wood
Alder Shaw
PRINCES
Shaw
Strawberry Wood
Lower Boishall Wood
Paynes Shaw
Heronlands
MILL LA.
32
RM4
Gipsy Bottom
CM14
Green Man
23
BOUNCE HILL
Dabbs Fm
Yewtree Fm.
CHURCH RD.
Navestock
Brent
WATER LA.
P.O.
Nave Side
Randalls Fm
Marleys
SABINES
ROAD
Princes Gate
NAVESTOCK SIDE
P.O.
Sch.Ho.
Plough
Sabines Green
Lashe's Farm
PRINCES RD
SNAKES
LANE
Loft Hall
OLD ROAD
ROAD
HOUSE LANE
TAN
Sabines Farm
Tan Ho.
The Mores
Bower Fm.
24
OLD
ROAD
Weald
Common
DYTCHLEYS
Wheelers Cotts
WHEELERS
Navestock Heath Ho.
WARWICK PL
Coxtie Green
Fm.
MURTHERING
Horseman Side
LANE
Honeysuckle Cotts.
Alma Arms
SIDE
Oakhurst Farm
GREEN
Jenkins Fm
South
COXTIE
Dytchleys
Coxtie Ho.
Oakhurst Wood
Lee Farm
M25
Waterhale Farm
Waterhale
Gilstead Hall
Gilstead Wood
25
Lincoln
Waterhales
HORSEMAN
Weald Side
Dycots
Watton Fm.
Watton's Green
Navestock Common
"The Chequers"
Frieze Hall
CHEQUERS RD.
Locksmith Wood
LINCOLNS
Skips Corner Farm
42
Goldsmith Wd
CHURCH RD.
CV
CW
CX
CY
Havering Plain
Havering
Wabbings Plantation
ROAD
Frieze Hill
Fm
Old

33
CM4
CM15
CY
CZ
DA
DB
DC
21
22
23
24
25
24
42
122
Round Wood
Clapgate Estate
Stondon Place
Kennels
Bushy Wood
Priors Wood
Pole's Wood
Priors
Oak Wood
Mellow Purgess Fm.
Clapgate
Chivers
The Coppice
Hatch Farm
Sch.
Radio Stn.
Kelvedon Hatch
P.O.
Pol.Off.
"Eagle"
The Swan
Fox Hatch
Brizes
Brizes Wood
Doddinghurst Common
Cow Farm
Kennels
Caravan Park
Alders Wood
The Warren
Bentley
Bentley Golf & Country Club
Ashwells Farm
Pilgrims' Hatch Common
Cedar Ho.
Nursery
Tel.Ex.
Nurs.
Kennels
Crow Green
Pilgrims Hall
Elm Ho.
Moat Ho.
Lib.
"Black Horse"
Pilgrim's Hatch
Cricket Grd.
Larch Wood
Fox Wd
Broom Wood
Shepherd's Spinney
Langton's Wood
The Forest
Langtons
High Wood
Schs.
Rose & Crown
Bishops Hall Park
Sports Centre & Swimming Pool
Sawyers Hall Farm
Playing Field
Robin Hd
Sch.
Nursery
Soaphouse Farm
Tip's Cross
Playing Field
Hook End Farm
Hook End
Blackmore House
Springfield
Blackmore Mill House
Whitelands Wood
Hay Green Farm
Hay Farm
Barfield Farm
Brooklyn
Church Wood
Doddinghurst Place (Site of)
Place Farm
Furze Wd.
Red House Farm
Cowes Farm
Waterworks Spring
Steeple Way
Schools
Hall
Playing Field
Doddinghurst
The Hurst
Wyatt's Green
Wyatt's Farm
Works
Brick Bridge House
Wolves Farm
Brick Bridge
Adelaide Farm
Peartree Green
Peartree Farm
Emblands Bridge
The Emblems
Shop Farm Nurseries
Pettits Farm
Park Farm
Park Wood
America Farm
Wishfields Farm
Sumner's Farm
Howe's Farm
Palmer
Days Farm
Brickhouse Farm
Brickhouse Wood
Canterbury Tye Farm
Canterbury Tye Spring
Six Acre Spring
Shenfield Hall
Hall Wood
Pye Wood
Nursery
A128
A12
A1023
ONGAR ROAD
BRENTWOOD A12 BY-PASS
HOOK END ROAD
BLACKMORE ROAD
BACK LANE
SCHOOL ROAD
CHIVERS ROAD
CHURCH LANE
DAGWOOD LANE
STOCKS LANE
DAYS LANE
SOLID LANE
WARREN LANE
FROG STREET
KENNEL LANE
DODDINGHURST ROAD
HAY GREEN LANE
MILL LANE
OUTINGS LANE
WYATTS GREEN ROAD
BROOK LANE
MOUNTNESSING LANE
PETTITS LANE
ASHWELLS ROAD
HULLETTS LANE
WELL LANE
DAYS LANE
CROW GREEN ROAD
SANDPIT LANE
BELL-HOUSE LANE
PILGRIMS LANE
HATCH ROAD
DANES WAY
ORCHARD LANE
MAGNOLIA WAY
WEALD PARK

25
26
27
28
29
30
AO
AP
AQ
AR
AS
25
43
HP8
HP9
Chalfont St. Giles
Chalfont St. Peter
Seer Green
Jordans
A413 AMERSHAM ROAD
A413 AMERSHAM ROAD
LONDON ROAD
GRAVEL HILL
B4442
VACHE LANE
NIGHTINGALES LANE
DEADHEARN LANE
GORELANDS LANE
CHESHAM LANE
BOTTOM HOUSE FARM LANE
BOTTOM HOUSE LANE
BOTTRELLS LANE
RAWLINGS LANE
NEWBARN LANE
THREE HOUSEHOLDS
BACK LANE
NARCOT LANE
BOWSTRIDGE LANE
TWITCHELLS LANE
WELDERS LANE
LAYTER'S GREEN LANE
POTKILN LANE
LONG BOTTOM LANE
JORDANS LANE
DEAN WOOD RD.
MUMFORDS LANE
High Wood
Lower Bottom House Farm
Bow Wood
Upper Bottom House Farm
The Gorse
The Larches
Hales Wood
Welpley's Wood
Works
Hodgemoor Woods
Bycroft Plantation
Perryfield Plantation
Rushcroft Wood
Misbourne Farm
Misbourne House
Mill Farm
Bailey Wood
Bailey Wood Belt
Res.
The Vache
Kilnpond Wood
Shortenills Environmental Studies Centre
Shortenills Wood
Downs Ho.
Tennis Courts
Maternity Home
Lib.
Church Farm House
Allotments
River Misbourne
Miltons Cottage
School
Playing Field
Pavilion
Cemetery
Top Farm
Dibden Hill
Dibden Hill Farm
Bramkys Farm
Narcot Farm
Greyhound Training Track
Abattoir
Bowstridge
Turner's Wood Farm
Ashwell's Farm
Sports Ground
Foxdell Wood
Widmer Farm
Rawlings Farm
Ponds Farm
Depot
Big Copse
The Princess Marina Centre
Little Copse
Bowles's Farm
Butlers Cross
Allotments
Recreation Ground
Nursery
Manor Farm
Green Wood Cem.
Long Wood
Grove Farm
Farm Wood
Middle Wood
Chalfont Grove
Round Wood
Pond Warren Wood
Jordans Farm
Crutches Wood
Tennis Court
Tennis Courts
Youth Hostel
Dean Farm
Pumping Sta.
Dean Wood
Club
SEER GREEN
Wheatsheaf Wood
Stone Dean Farm
Welders House
Tennis Court
Welders Wood
Swimming Pool
Grove Wood
Spring Wood
Mountain Wood
Weedons Dell
The Ash Beds
Thirty Acre Knoll
Pitlands Wood
Birchland Wood
Great Legs Wood
Malms Wood
Outfield Farm
Windmill Farm
Woodlands Farm
Tennis Courts
Playing Field
Community Centre
Leisure Centre
Hosp.
Ambulance Station
Convent
Library
Goldhill Common
Layter's Green
Layter's Green Farm
Caravan Park
Stampwell Farm
Birchland Wood
High Wood
Beech Wood
Austenwood
Sports Ground
Hollytree Farm
Austenwood Common
Lower Pyebushes
Birch Wood
KINGSWAY

Solomons Wood
The Hall
Catlips Farm
Hill Farm
Sch.
P.O.
AS
AT
AU
AV
25
M25
Philipshill Wood
Bullsland Farm
Heronsgate
Ladywalk
17
WD3
26
Rec Grd.
Sch.
Allots.
Mill
St.Peters Hostel
Newland Park
College of Education
NEWLAND PARK
BOTTOM WOOD
Longlane Farm
UXBRIDGE RD.
A412
A405
27
Playing Field
Five Plantations
Rowan Farm
Model Farm
Pollardshill Wood
Woodoaks Farm
Froghall Farm
Brawlings Farm
Eight Acre Wood
INDUSTRIAL ESTATE
Maple Cross
Lock
Springwell Farm
COLNE
RIVER
Chalfont Common
Horn Hill
Kiln Wood
Tubb's Cottages
Recreation Ground
Beechen Wood
Maplelodge Farm
Rec Grnd.
28
35
Sewage Wks
Roberts's Farm
Williams Spring
Sch.
West Hyde Playing Fields
Lynsters
Roberts's Wood
M25
Round Rocket Plantation
Refuse Tip
Gravel Pit
Lynsters Lake
29
Bloom Wood
Cemetery
Rec. Grnd.
Pynesfield Lake
West Hyde
Works
Sports Gd.
Warren Farm Cottages
SL9
Mount Pleasant
GRAND UNION CANAL
Chalfont Heights Scout Camp
Troy Mill
30
Hogtrough Wood
Jacks Mill
Troy
Golf Course
Mopes Farm
Pond
Little Halings Wood
Little Halings
43
Chalfont Lodge
UB9
Club House
Gerrards Cross Golf Course
Research Laboratories
KNOCKHILL
WOOD
Beaconsfield
The Rivers
CHALFONT LANE
HORNHILL RD
DENHAM WAY
SHIRE LANE
ROBERTS LANE
WEST HYDE LANE
COPPERMILL
TILEHOUSE
UXBRIDGE ROAD
SLADE OAK

M25
Solomons Wood
Rickmansworth Masonic School (Girls)
RICKMANSWORTH
RICKMANSWORTH PARK
26
AW
AX
AY
AZ
WATFORD
HIGHFIELD
UPPER HILL RISE WAY
THE MOUNT
BEACON WAY
SHEPHERDS WAY
PHEASANTS WAY
QUEENS DRIVE
OAKFIELD
CHILTERN DRIVE
COOMBE HILL RD
P.O.
Sch.
Cemetery
Scotsbridge Mill
Scotsbr.
Crick. Gd
Playing Fld
SCOTS HILL
PARK RD.
Fortune Com.
CROXLEY HALL WOOD
Croxleyhall Farm
Coun. Offs.
Caravan Lane
A412
RICKMANSWORTH BY-PASS
RICKMANSWORTH
HIGH ST
CHURCH ST.
Lib.
Pol. Amb. & Fire Sta.
RECTORY RD.
NIGHTINGALE RD
Tennis Crts
MEADOW WAY
MONEY HILL RD
Hall
THE HIGHLANDS
BERRY CL.
BERRY LANE
MIDDLETON RD
Recn Grd.
Play Fld
Sch.
The Bury
Lock
Locks
Weir
Depot
Water Wks
RIVERSIDE DRIVE
ROAD
Mill End
Moneyhill
RIVER COLNE
Batchworth Lake
The Aquadrome
Bury Lake
Bury Farm
Footbridge
Allots.
MILL WAY
SPRINGWELL AV
UXBRIDGE RD
A412
A405
LONG LA
Longlane Farm
27
Drayton Ford
GRAND UNION CANAL
Stocker's Lock
Stocker's Farm
Stocker's Lake
HAREFIELD RD
The Grove
Batchworth
MOOR LANE
A4145
Club Ho.
Rickmansworth
LONDON RD
BATCHWORTH HILL
A404
West
MOOR
High
Course
Moor Park Farm
WD3
Froghall Farm
INDUSTRIAL ESTATE
Old Chalk Pit
Andrews Ley Fm.
Juniper Hill
Gareth Wood
High Wood
Shepherds Close Dell
Greenbroom Spring
Sandfield Spring
Cemetery
Lock
Springwell Chalk Pit
SPRINGWELL LANE
COLNE RIVER
Springwell Farm
34
28
Sixteen Acre Spring
Pipers Farm
Home Farm
BATCHWORTH
Cooks Wood
Bush Spring
Howard Spring
WOODCOCK HILL ROAD
Woodcock Hill
Rose & Crown
Whipping Spring
Sewage Wks.
Hyde Fields
Lynsters
Long Spring
Park Wood
Cripps Farm
Willingrove Wood
SHRUBS
BISHOP'S WOOD
Poor field
LOCKWELL WOOD
Weybeards Fm.
Harefieldgrove Farm
Vernon Arms
Lynsters Lake
White Heath Farm
Harefield Grove
Old Res.
Resr
WHITE HILL
ROAD
French Grove
29
Hill End
Watts Common
Battlerwells Fm
PARK WOOD
Harefield Hosp.
Recreation Grd.
Top Wood
Battlers Wells Wood
Pynesfield Lake
Lock
Pearson's Wood
UB9
Works
Sports Gd.
BELFRY AV.
SUMMERHOUSE LA.
ROMAN CLO.
MILNE WAY
MT. PLEASANT
Harefield Hosp.
RICKMANSWORTH ROAD
NEWDIGATE RD.
Sch.
Shepherds Hill House
Deadman's Grove
Mount Pleasant
PARK LANE
GRAND UNION CANAL
Furzefield
NORTHWOOD RD.
ASH GROVE
The Green
Lib.
Schs.
Colney Farm
30
Troy Mill
MERLE AVE
Harefield
Ashain Spring
Jacks Mill
BLACK JACKS
HIGH ST
Harefield Ho.
Crick. Gd
BREAKSPEAR ROAD
Spotted Dog
Kiln Pond
Claypits
Troy
Newstead House
DOVEDALE CLO.
BIRD LA.
Cricket Grd.
Knightscote Farm
Dell
Badminton Shooting Ground
Pond
COUNTESS CLO.
Langley Farm
44
White Horse
LOVETT RD.
CHURCH HILL
ROAD
Highbones
AW
AX
AY
AZ
RIVER
A412
Bourne Farm
ST. MARYS
Breakspear
BREAKSPEAR ROAD NORTH
T
h
R
i
v
H
i
l

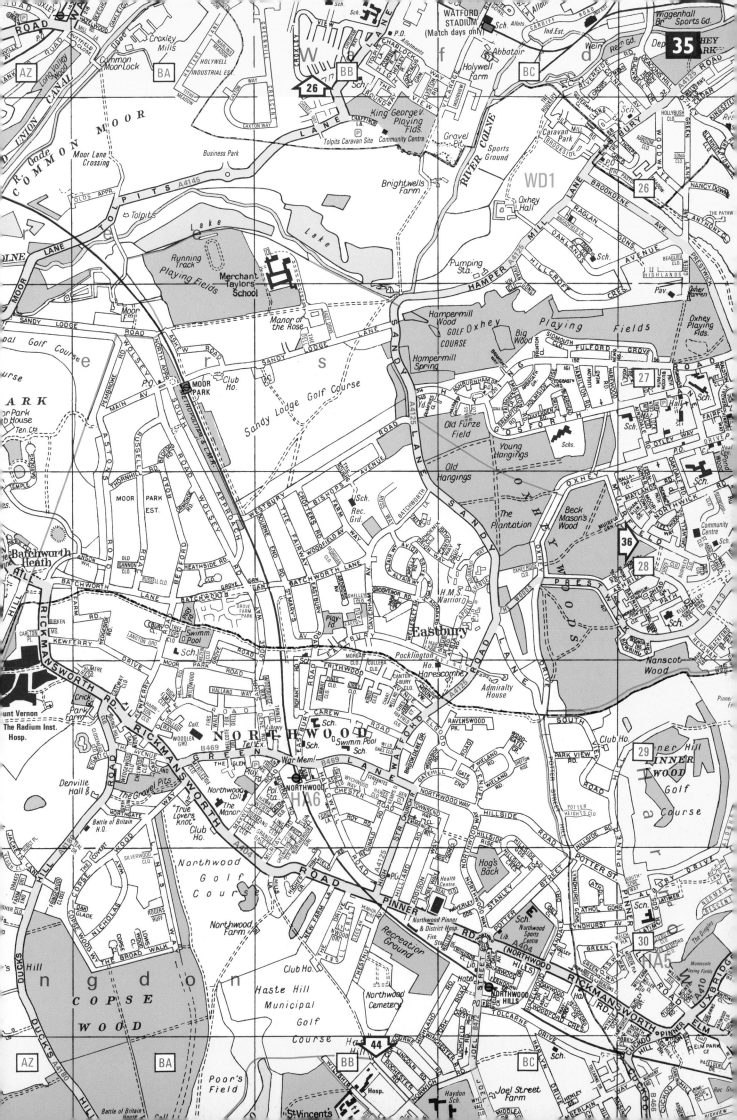
WATFORD STADIUM (Match days only)
Croxley Mills
Common Moor Lock
Long Valley Wood
UNION CANAL
HOLYWELL INDUSTRIAL EST.
Allotments
Holywell Farm
Abbatoir
Ind. Est.
Wiggenhall Sports Gd.
COMMON MOOR
R. Gade
Moor Lane Crossing
Business Park
King George V. Playing Flds.
Tolpits Caravan Site
Community Centre
Gravel Pit
Sports Ground
RIVER COLNE
Caravan Park
WD1
Brightwells Farm
Oxhey Hall
TOLPITS
Tolpits
Lake
Running Track
Playing Fields
Merchant Taylors' School
Pumping Sta.
HAMPER MILL LANE
Moor Fm.
Manor of the Rose
Hampermill Wood
GOLF COURSE
Oxhey Playing Fields
Big Wood
Oxhey Warren
Hampermill Spring
SANDY LODGE
Golf Course
MOOR PARK
Club Ho.
Sandy Lodge Golf Course
Old Furze Field
Young Hangings
Old Hangings
The Plantation
Beck Mason's Wood
OXHEY WOODS
MOOR PARK EST.
Community Centre
Batchworth Heath
H.M.S. Warrior
Eastbury
Pocklington Ho.
Harescombe
Admiralty House
Nanscot Wood
Swimm. Pool
Mount Vernon
The Radium Inst. Hosp.
Crick. Gd.
Park Farm
NORTHWOOD
Swimm. Pool
War Mem.
NORTHWOOD
HA6
Denville Hall
The Gravel Pits
Northwood Coll.
The Manor
"True Lovers Knot"
Club Ho.
Battle of Britain H.Q.
Northwood Golf Course
Hog's Back
Northwood Farm
Recreation Ground
Northwood Pinner & District Hosp.
Northwood Sports Centre
NORTHWOOD HILLS
Pinner Hill
PINNER WOOD
Golf Course
HA5
Montesole Playing Fields
The Dingles
COPSE WOOD
Ducks Hill
Club Ho.
Haste Hill Municipal Golf Course
Northwood Cemetery
Haydon Sch.
Joel Street Farm
Poor's Field
Hosp.
St. Vincent's
Battle of Britain House
RICKMANSWORTH RD.
PINNER RD.
TOLCARNE DRIVE
AZ
BA
BB
BC
26
27
28
29
30
36
44

36
OXHEY
BUSHEY
Watford Heath
Merry Hill
HARTSBOURNE
GOLF
COURSE
GRIMSDYKE
GOLF COURSE
HARROW WEALD COMMON
SOUTH OXHEY
Carpenders Park
Nanscot Wood
Pinner Hill
PINNER WOOD
Golf
Course
HATCH END
PINNER PARK
PINNER
WD1
WD2
HA5
HA2
BD
BE
BF
BG
27
45
35
26
27
28
29
30
Sherwoods Wood
Margeholes Wood
Oxhey Playing Flds.
Playing Fields
Beck Mason's Wood
Sir James Altham Sch.
Carpenders Park Cemetery
Harrow Arts Centre
Hatch End High Sch.
Bedford Ladies College Sports Ground
Old Millhillians R.U.F.C.
British Rail Sports Ground
Shaftesbury Playing Fields
Montesole Playing Fields
Saddler's Mead Recreation Ground
St. Margaret's Sch.
Levels Wood
Weald Wood
Stony Wood
Grim's Dyke Country Hotel
Oxhey Woods
Prestwick Road
Little Oxhey Lane
Oxhey Lane
Uxbridge Road
Rickmansworth Rd.
Elm Park Rd.
High Street
London Road
Chalk Hill
Headstone Lane

ALDENHAM RESERVOIR
WESTERN AVENUE A41
DAGGER LA.
ELSTREE ROAD A411
WATFORD BY-PASS A41
WATFORD RD.
BARNET LANE A411
ELSTREE HILL SOUTH
HIGH ST. ELSTREE
THE BARTONS
Sports Grd
The Fishery
Open Space
WD6
M1
27
BG
BH
BJ
BK
ELSTREE OPEN SPACE
Edgwarebury Country Club
26
27
28
29
30
37
45
4
Little Bushey
Bushey and Dist. Hosp.
B.U.P.A. Hosp.
BUSHEY HEATH
Allots.
Water Works
Reservoirs
Reservoir
Heathbourne Ho.
HEATHBOURNE ROAD A409
HILFIELD LA.
MAGPIE HALL RD.
Waterfall
STANMORE COMMON
The Grove
Drill Ho.
Obelisk
Lymes Fm.
Royal National Orthopaedic Hospital
Brockleyhill Fm.
Brockley Grange
Brockleyhill Ho.
SYLLONIACAE (Roman Site)
NUTT GROVE
ELSTREE ROAD A5
BROCKLEY HILL
EDGWARE WAY A41
Limes Ho.
Pear Wood
Cloisters Wood
WOOD LANE
WARREN LANE
Cricket Grd.
Reservoir
Harrow Rugby Ground
Springbok Ho. O.P. Home
Little Common
THE COMMON A4140
Kestrel Grove
Glenthorne
Bentley Priory
HARROW WEALD COMMON
BENTLEY PRIORY PARK
DEER PARK
Boat Ho.
Landing Stage
Priory Close O.P. Home
The Kiln
The Hare
Priory Ho.
Stanmore Hall
The Abercorn
STANMORE
EDGWARE
EDGWAREBURY GOLF COURSE
Cricket Grd
SPUR ROAD A410
STONEGROVE
HA8
Sports
GLANLEAM ROAD
LONDON ROAD A410
THE BROADWAY
Recreation Grd.
STANMORE
Rec. Ground
The Lake
North London Collegiate Sch.
CANONS PARK
Kg. George V Memorial Gardens
BROOKSHILL DR.
Hillside
The Glade
Bentley Wood High Sch.
Boating Lake
UXBRIDGE ROAD A410
Swimming Pool
Stanmore Park R.A.F. Station
HA7
Orme Lodge
Elm Park College
Cottage Hospital
Weald College
Council Offs.
Cemetery
HA3
Harrow Weald
Bus Depot
Recreation Ground
Club Ho.
STANMORE GOLF COURSE
Sports Ground
Gas Works
Stanmore Marsh
CANONS PARK
WHITCHURCH LANE B461
Green Man Playing Fields
N.L. Poly Sports Ground
Prince Edward Playing Fields
Mountview High Sch.
CENTENARY PARK
Park High Sch.
Playing Fld.
Stanmore Residential Nursery
WEALDSTONE
Byron Recreation Ground
Cemetery
Kodak Works
Industrial Park
HONEYPOT LANE A4140
KENTON LANE
HIGH ST. A409

ELSTREE
Hertsmere
WD6
BL
BM
BN
BO
28
DEACONS HILL OPEN SPACE
SCRATCHWOOD OPEN SPACE
Deacons Heights
Stirling Corner
Elstree Tunnel
ELSTREE OPEN SPACE
M1
26
Edgware Bury
Bury Fm.
Scatchwood Service Area
Motel
MILL HILL GOLF COURSE
Boys Hill Wood
Thistle Wood
Clump of Trees Wood
Hemmings Wood
Stoney Wood Lake
Stoney Wood
Hyver Hall
MOAT
Target Wood
The Shrubbery
Nut Wood
Mill Hill High Sch.
Brockley Grange
SYLLONIACAE (Roman Site)
27
Sports Ground
EDGWAREBURY PARK
EDGWAREBURY GOLF COURSE
Mill Hill High Sch.
Stoneyfield Park
John Groom's Crippleage
Convent of St. Mary at the Cross
HA7
36
STANMORE
Cricket Grd.
Sports Ground
Edgware Sch.
Rec. Ground
The Lake
Stone Grove Park
North London Collegiate Sch.
CANONS PARK
K. George V Memorial Gardens
The Basin
EDGWARE
HA8
Bus Depot
War Memorial
Cine.
Gas Works
29
Stanmore Marsh
CANONS PARK
Sports Ground
Chandos Recreation Ground
Blood Transfus. Centre
Edgware General Hosp.
WATLING
WATLING PARK
Playing Field
Burnt Oak
BURNT OAK
MILL HILL BROADWAY
Lyndhurst Park
Green Man
Playing Fields
N.L. Poly. Sports Ground
Prince Edward Playing Fields
Sports Ground
Clinic
30
CENTENARY PARK
Park High Sch.
Stanmore Residential Nursery
QUEENSBURY
BRIXTON ESTATE
Silkstream Park
Bald Faced Stag
Montrose Playing Fields
Silk Stream
Colindale Hospital
NORTHERN LINE
N.W.9
46
HERON TRADING ESTATE
CAPITOL INDUSTRIAL PARK
Brent
Brit. Musm. Newspaper Repository
Eton Grove
Royal Dental Hosp.
A41
A5
A410
A1
A411
A5100
A5109
A4140
B461

Barnet Playing Fields
EN5
BO
BP
BQ
BR
28
Dollis Brook
Grange Playing Fields
Whitings Hill
Mays Lane
Playing Field
May's Lane
Gate
Pinefield Priory
Barnet
Hendon Wood Lane
Hendon Wood Lane Open Space
South Herts Golf Course
26
Oaklands Road
Grange Avenue
Totteridge Ho.
Grave Yard
Totteridge Park
Totteridge Common
Redings
Wykeham Rise
Totteridge
Montebello
N.20
St. Edwards College
Oak Lodge
Totteridge Lodge
Ellern Mede Fm.
The Warren
Fairlawn
Totteridge Village
The Dorlands
Garden Hill
Harmsworth Way
Pine Grove
Trevanion
Hendon Park
Highwood Hill
Highwood Ho.
Holcombe Dale
Totteridge Ornamental Waters
Lynells
Strathearn
27
Coppice Walk
Laurel Way
Laurel Fm.
Boat Ho.
N.W.7
St. Mary's Abbey and School
Swimming Pool
Sports Grd.
Belmont
Folly Fm.
Burton Hole Playing Fields
Playing Field
Holcombe Hill
The Mill Field
Drapers Cottage Homes
West Grove
St. Joseph's R.C. College
Three Hammers
Cemetery
Sanatorium
Mill Hill School
Playing Fields
Burton Hole La.
Northiam
38
N.12
Sports Ground
Shakespeare Rd.
Milton Rd.
Tennyson R.
St. Vincent's Central Ho.
St. Vincent's Sch.
National Inst. for Medical Research
The Ridgeway
Oakfields
Burton Hole La.
Chanctonbury Riverside Walk
28
Collinson Ho.
The Priory
Drivers Hill
Parkfield
School
Wills Park
Daws Lane
Swimming Pool
Mill Hill
Mylesdown Milespit Hill
Watch Tower Ho.
Partingdale Lane
Frith Manor Ho.
Lullington Garth
Sch.
Cissbury Ring
Arrandene
Arrandene Recreation Ground
Paddington Cemetery
Inglis Barracks
Reading Way
Mill Hill Park
Observatory
Watford Way
Featherstone Hill
Woodcote Av.
Rushden Gdns.
Bittacy Hill Park
Bittacy Hill
Nether Court Club Ho.
Finchley Golf Course
West Finchley
29
Sports Grd. Copthall Girls Sch.
Page Street
Mill Hill East
North Thames Gas Board
Athletic Ground
Bunn's Lane
Sports Ground
Club Ho.
Devonshire Rd.
Hendon
Oakhampton Road
Holders Hill Circus
Dollis Brook
Christ's Coll. Playing Fields
Finchley
Hasmonean Sch.
Swim. Pool
Longfield Av.
Copthall Sports Centre
Stadium
Golf
Hendon Park Cemetery and Crematorium
Finchley Central
Sch.
St. James R.C. High Sch.
R.A.F. Museum
Sports Field
N.W.4
Course
Holder's Hill
Hendon Avenue
Church End
Christ's Coll.
Municipal Offices
30
Sunny Hill Park
Great North Way A1
Windsor Open Space
Meml. Coll.
Cypress Av.
East End Road
A504
A598
Regent's Park Road
Convent Sch.
46
Hendon Hall
Swim Pool
Waverley Gr.
Allandale Avenue
A41
A406

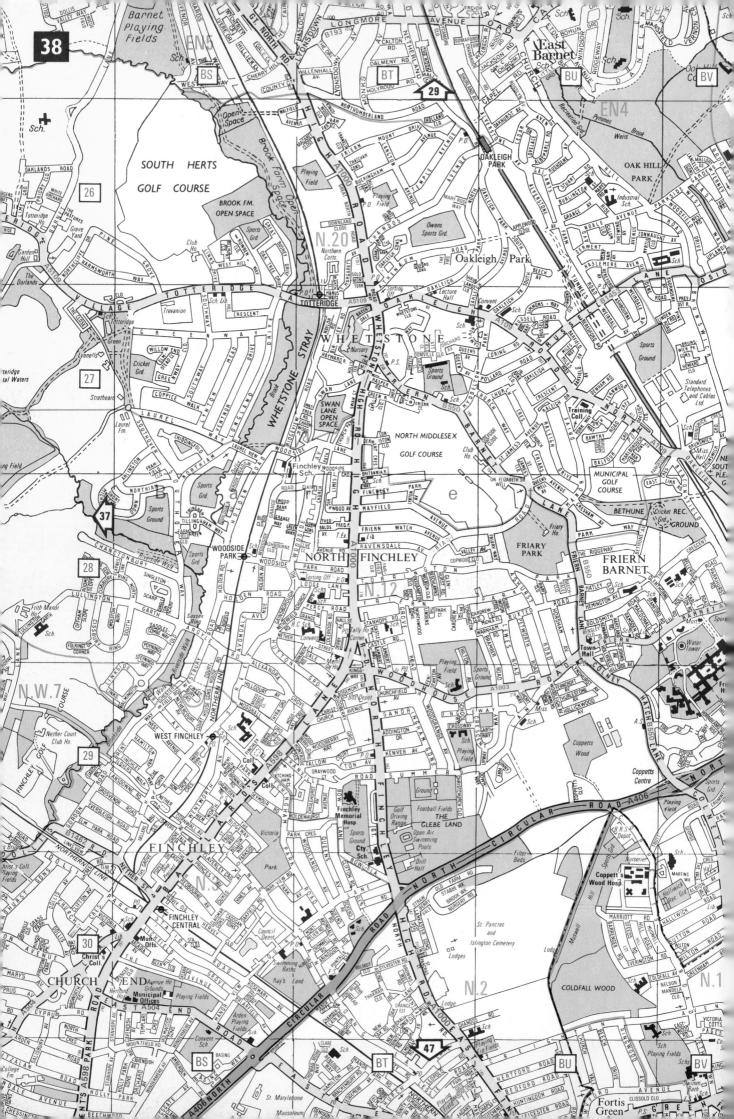
Barnet Playing Fields
EN5
BS
BT
BU
BV
29
East Barnet
EN4
Oak Hill Park
SOUTH HERTS GOLF COURSE
BROOK FM. OPEN SPACE
26
27
28
29
30
37
47
N.20
Oakleigh Park
OAKLEIGH PARK
Totteridge
TOTTERIDGE LA.
TOTTERIDGE
WHETSTONE
WHETSTONE STRAY
SWAN LANE OPEN SPACE
NORTH MIDDLESEX GOLF COURSE
MUNICIPAL GOLF COURSE
Friary Park
FRIARY PARK
FRIERN BARNET
NORTH FINCHLEY
N.12
WOODSIDE PARK
WEST FINCHLEY
FINCHLEY
N.3
FINCHLEY CENTRAL
CHURCH END
N.W.7
Finchley Memorial Hosp.
THE GLEBE LAND
St. Pancras and Islington Cemetery
COLDFALL WOOD
Coppetts Wood
Coppetts Centre
Coppett's Wood Hosp.
N.2
N.10
Fortis Green
Victoria Park
Kay's Land
St. Marylebone Mausoleum
NORTH CIRCULAR ROAD
A406
A1000
A109
A5109
A598
A504
A1003
B550
B1453
B1462
HIGH ROAD
GREAT NORTH ROAD
BALLARDS LANE
REGENTS PARK ROAD
EAST END ROAD
FRIERN BARNET LANE
COLNEY HATCH LANE
WOODHOUSE ROAD
OAKLEIGH ROAD NORTH
EAST FINCHLEY
Municipal Offices
Town Hall
Training Coll
Standard Telephones and Cables Ltd.

OAKWOOD PARK
GROVELANDS PARK
WINCHMORE HILL
SOUTHGATE
PALMER'S GREEN
BROOMFIELD PARK
ARNOS PARK
NEW SOUTHGATE
BOUNDS GREEN
BOWES PARK
WOOD GREEN
MUSWELL HILL GOLF COURSE
ALEXANDRA PARK
Noel Park
Bowes
MUSWELL HILL
TURNPIKE LANE

Bush Hill
EN1
BZ
CA
CB
CC
30
26
27
28
29
38
48
WINCHMORE HILL
NCHMORE HILL
RIDGE AVENUE
Jubilee Park
Bury Street
Salmon's Brook
Edmonton Cemetery
Firs Farm Playing Field
Clowes Sports Ground
Recreation Ground
LOWER EDMONTON
UPPER EDMONTON
Jewish Cemetery
Tottenham Park Cemetery
Tatem Recreation Ground
PYMME'S PARK
Lake
SILVER ST
STERLING WAY
CIRCULAR ROAD
A406
A10
A1010
GREAT CAMBRIDGE ROAD
North Middlesex Hosp.
CRAIG PARK
ANGEL RD
Eastern Gas Board
Gothic Wks.
Bowes
Greentrees Hosp.
Wesleyan Sports Grd.
New River Sports Centre
The Weymarks
WHITE HART LANE
Wingate Trading Est.
Tottenham Hotspur Foot. Grd.
Tottenham Cemetery
The Moselle
BRUCE CASTLE PARK
Bruce Castle (Museum)
Tower Gdn.
THE ROUNDWAY
LORDSHIP LANE
TOTTENHAM
BRUCE GROVE
Lordship Recreation Ground
Model Traffic Area
NORTHUMBERLAND PARK
TOTTENHAM MARSHES
River Lea Navigation
Stonebridge Lock
LOCKWOOD RESERVOIR
Down Lane Recreation Ground
Athletic Grd.
DOWNHILLS PARK
TURNPIKE LANE
Noel Park
N.9
N.13
N.17
N.18
N.21
N.22

CHINGFORD
Chingford Hatch
HIGHAMS PARK
Hale End
HIGHAM HILL
WILLIAM GIRLING RESERVOIR
BANBURY RESERVOIR
LARKSWOOD PARK
MANSFIELD PARK
RIDGEWAY PARK
Chingford Mount Cemetery
Walthamstow Stadium
Grammar School
Waltham Forest College
Town Hall
LEA VALLEY VIADUCT
NORTH CIRCULAR ROAD
WADHAM RD.
SOUTHEND ROAD
FOREST ROAD
CHINGFORD PLAIN
PUBLIC GOLF COURSE
E.4
E.17

40
EPPING FOREST
CHINGFORD PLAIN
PUBLIC GOLF COURSE
Connaught Water
Magpie Hill
Warren Hill
IG10
CHINGFORD
BUCKHURST HILL
Forest Hosp.
PALMERSTON ROAD
RODING LANE
IG9
E4
EPPING FOREST
Lord's Bushes
Knighton Wood
Woodford Wells
RODING VALLEY
CENTRAL LINE
WOODFORD GOLF COURSE
Chingford Hatch
HIGHAMS PARK
IG8
WOODFORD GREEN
Woodford High School
RAY PARK
WOODFORD
Hale End
SOUTHEND ROAD
NORTH CIRCULAR RD.
SOUTH WOODFORD
E17
E18
FOREST ROAD
WOODFORD TRADING EST.
IG4
M11
A406
A104
A110
A1009
A113
A121
CG
CH
CJ
CK
31
39
49
26
27
28
29
30

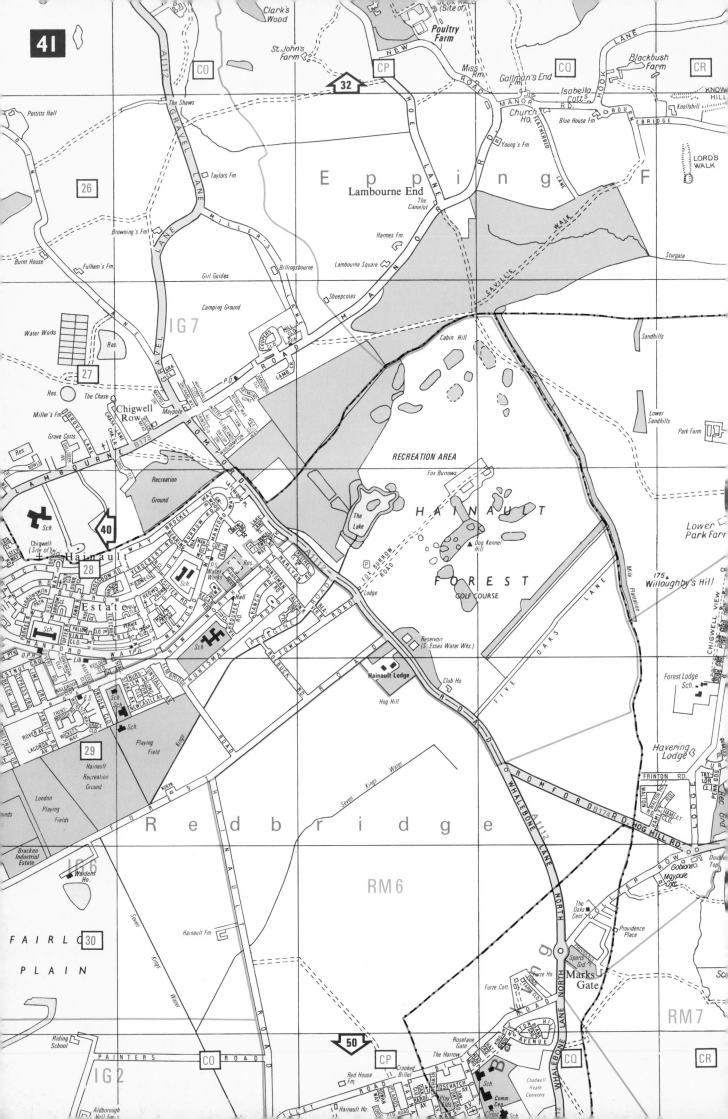
32
40
50
CO
CP
CQ
CR
26
27
28
29
30
IG7
IG6
IG2
RM6
RM7
Epping Fo
Redbridge
Clark's Wood
Poultry Farm
St. John's Farm
New Road
Miss Rm
Gallman's End Fm.
Blackbush Farm
Hook Lane
Isabella Cotts.
Knollshill
Manor Rd.
Church Ho.
Blue House Fm.
Bournebridge
Young's Fm.
Featherbed Lane
Lord's Walk
Pettitts Hall
The Shaws
Gravel Lane
Hoe Lane
Taylors Fm.
Lambourne End
The Camelot
Miller's Lane
Browning's Fm.
Harmes Fm.
Cavill's Walk
Sturgate
Burnt House
Fulham's Fm.
Girl Guides
Camping Ground
Billingsbourne
Lambourne Square
Manor Road
Sheepcotes
Water Works
Res.
Cabin Hill
Sandhills
Lower Sandhills
Park Farm
The Chase
Chigwell Row
Miller's Fm.
Grove Lane
Grove Cotts.
Maypole
P.O.
Romford Road
Lambourne Rd.
B173
Recreation Ground
Recreation Area
Fox Burrows
Hainault Forest
Golf Course
The Lake
Dog Kennel Hill
Fox Burrow Road
Lodge
Lower Park Farm
Willoughby's Hill
Mile Plantation
Chigwell View
Sch.
Chigwell (Site of)
Hainault Estate
Manford Way
New North Rd.
Huntsman Rd.
Peregrine Road
Fowler Road
Roebuck Rd.
Reservoir (S. Essex Water Wks.)
Hainault Lodge
Hog Hill
Club Ho
Five Oaks Lane
Forest Lodge Sch.
Havering Lodge
Frinton Rd.
Hog Hill Rd.
Romford Rd.
B174
Whalebone Lane
A1112
Forest Road
Hainault Road
Seven Kings Water
Playing Field
Hainault Recreation Ground
London Playing Fields
Bracken Industrial Estate
Wardens Ho.
Fairlop Plain
Hainault Fm.
Gobions
Maypole Cott.
Double Top
The Oaks Cent.
Providence Place
Sports Grd.
Marks Gate
Furze Ho.
Furze Cott.
Kingston Hill Avenue
Roselane Gate
The Harrow
Crooked Billet
Red House Fm.
Hainault Ho.
Riding School
Painters Road
Aldborough Hall Fm.
Chadwell Heath Cemetery
Comm. Cen.
Whalebone Lane North

Hall Farm
High House Farm
Olives Fm
Works
Spring Fm
Dycots
Watton Fm
Wattons Green
Navestock Common
CM14
Brentwood
Skips Corner Farm
Asheton Fm
Pyrgo Wood
Old Crown
STAPLEFORD ROAD
OAK HILL RD.
MURTHERING LANE
TYSEA HILL
CHURCH ROAD
Pinchback Bri.
R. Rom
Boyland's Oak Farm
Butcher's Fm
Towneley Cotts
Lyngs Fm
Bourne Br.
RM 4
Straights Plantation
Palace Plantation
Sandpits Plantation
Witch Hill Plantation
Home Farm
PYRGO PARK
Widdrington Fm
Tench Pond Plantation
Caravan Park
Playing Fld.
Bower Fm
BOWER FARM ROAD
HAVERING PARK
HAVERING ATTE-BOWER
The Green
Foxburrow Wood
Lodge
BROXHILL ROAD
Havering Park
WELLINGTONIA AVENUE
HAVERING PLA.
NORTH ROAD
Pine Wood
PINEWOOD ROAD
ORANGE TREE HILL
Bower Wood
Bower Ho.
BOWER PARK
Upper Bedfords
Broxhill Common
NOAK HILL ROAD
Larch Wood
BEDFORDS PARK
Chase Cross Schools
Special Sch.
Havering
Chase Cross
Lower Bedfords
LOWER BEDFORDS RD.
STRAIGHT ROAD
RM5
L.B. OF HAVERING GOLF COURSE
Club House
Rise Park
BOBS LANE
Lawns Park
Collier Row
Sports Grounds
EASTERN AVENUE EAST
A12
Romford Golf Course
GIDEA PARK
RM 2
Club Ho.
Sports Grd.
Gallows Corner
RAPHAEL PARK
Hare Street
MAIN ROAD
A118
Lake
King George
HAINAULT RD.
32
42
50
26
27
28
29
30
CR
CS
CT
CU

Waterhales
Dycots
Watton Fm.
Wattons Green
Weald Side
"The Chequers"
Frieze
Locksmith Wood
Goldsmith Wd
Frieze Hill
CV
CW
CX
CY
33
Havering
Wabbing's Plantation
Plain
Pyrgo Wood
26
Old Crown
Hou Hatch
St. Vincent's Hamlet
Wrightsbridge Fm.
Wrights Bri.
Wealdside
Weald
RM4
Sandpits Plantation
Spice Pit Wood
Spice Pits Farm
Open Space
Widdrington Fm.
Birdcage Cottage
M25
Noak Hill
Tench Pond Plantation
The Osiers
27
Priory
Caravan Park
Foxburrow Wood
Bear Inn
Manor Fm.
Lodge
DAGNAM PARK
Playing Fields
Fir Wood
Cock Wood
HAROLD HILL
HATTERS WOOD
Maylands Golf Course
Broxhill Common
28
41
Duck Wood
Maylands
Indoor Swimming Pool
CENTRAL PARK
Health Cen.
Comm. Centre
Sports Ground
Harold Park
R.C. Sch.
RM3
29
A12
London Borough of Havering Technical Offs.
HAROLD HILL INDUSTRIAL EST.
Tel. Ex.
Paine's Brook
Ingrebourne River
Brentwood Teachers Training College (Annexe)
Sports Grounds
EASTERN AVE. EAST
COLCHESTER ROAD
HAROLD WOOD
HAROLD WOOD
Harold Wood Hospital
30
Romford Golf Course
Sports Grd.
Gallows Corner
SOUTHEND ARTERIAL ROAD
Cockabourne Bri.
Ivy Lodge Farm
DEA ARK
RM2
Pages Farm
Miniature Golf Course
Harold Wood Park
Comm. Cen.
Club Ho.
MAIN ROAD
A118
A127
51
Hare Street
P.O.
Sch.

BRENTWOOD
South Weald
Brook Street
Warley
Great Warley
Little Warl
CM13
CM14
CM15
WEALD PARK
Country Park
Deer Park
High Wood Hospital
St. Faith's Hospital
Warley Hospital
Marillac Hospital
Brentwood District Hosp.
Nuffield Nursing Home
Moat Ho. Hotel
Halfway House Farm
Bishops Hall Park
Sports Centre & Swimming Pool
The Chelmer Inst. of Higher Education
Seven Arches
King George's Playing Field
Hart's Wood
Donkey Lane Plantation
Barrack Wood
Ellen's Wood
Holden's Wood
Golf Range & Ski Slopes
HOME PARK
GREAT PARK
GOLF COURSE
Boyles Court
Mascalls
Jackson's Wood
Tylers Shaw
Gibblings Shaw
Sewage Works
Stonyhylls Farm
Coombe Lo.
Great Readings
Beredens
Warley Place
Warley Lea Fm
Thatchers Arms
'Horse & Groom'
Fords
Coun. Depot
Kents Wood
Devil's Hd. Plantation
Little Warley Common
Scrub Hill
LONDON ROAD
HIGH STREET
SHENFIELD ROAD
BROOK ST.
WARLEY ROAD
GREAT WARLEY STREET
MAGPIE LA.
EAGLE WAY
WARLEY GAP
BRENTWOOD BY-PASS
A12
A128
A1023
B186
M25
33
51
122
CY
CZ
DA
DB
DC
26
27
28
29
30
1 CANTERBURY WAY
2 BIRCHWOOD CLO.
3 ASHBEAM CLO.
4 HAVENWOOD CLO.
5 COVERLEY CLO.
6 WILMOT GREEN
7 EVELYN WALK
8 BUNYONS CLO.
9 GIBRALTAR CLO.
10 GREENFIELDS CLO.
11 FLEMINGS
12 MEADSWAY

AO
AP
AQ
AR
AS
34
52
31
32
33
34
35
Chalfont St. Peter
Layter's Green
Caravan Park
Layter's Green Farm
Thirty Acre Knoll
Pitlands Wood
Birchland Wood
Great Legs Wood
Malms Wood
Stampwell Farm
High Wood
Beech Wood
Austenwood
Sports Ground
Lower Pyebushes
Birch Wood
Bell House Hotel
Siblet's Wood
Chantry Wood
Mumford's Farm
MUMFORDS LANE
OXFORD ROAD
A40
Wapsey's Wood
Further Warren Wood
Went Plantation
BULSTRODE PARK
Bulstrode
Moat Farm
HEDGERLEY LANE
Slade Wood
Slade Farm
WAPSEYS LANE
Hedgerley Green
Manor Farm
Sutton's Wood
Leith Grove
M40
Moll Hayes Wood
Hedgerley
Church Wood
Subway
KILN LANE
Kiln Wood
Hanging Wood
Yewtree Wood
MOUNT HILL LANE
Dukes Kiln
STEVENSON RD.
GREGORY RD.
ELKINS RD.
COTTAGE PARK
HEDGERLEY PARK
Mounthill Wood
Fulmer Valley Farm
Scout Hut
Black Grove
One Pin Fm.
PARISH LANE
LONGFIELD
SL2
COLLUM GREEN ROAD
Tara
Parkside Cemetery
Pickeridge Wood
South
Timber Wood
Stoke Wood
GYPSY LANE
STOKE WOOD LA.
Pickeridge Farm
The Pickeridge
Fulmer Chase
Fulmer
Fulmer Hall
Fulmer Place
Fulmer House
Templemead
WINDSOR ROAD
STOKE COMMON ROAD
Lerchmoor
STOKE COMMON
Duffield Farm
GERRARDS CROSS ROAD
B416
The Grange
Ingram's Copse
Brockhurst Wood
BICKMANS LANE
DUFFIELD LANE
Fulmer Gardens
Home Farm
Penn Wood
SL3
Frame Wood
Mill House Farm
Fulmer Court
Wexham Place
Farnham Common
Parson's Wood
CLEVEHURST CLO.
ELBERFIELD
FULMER COMMON ROAD
Fulmer Common
WINDMILL ROAD
GERRARDS CROSS
SL9
GERRARDS CROSS COMMON
BULSTRODE WAY
WEST COMMON
Braid House
The Bull
Camp
CAMP ROAD
Cricket Ground
DUKES WOOD
HOWARDS THICKET
FULMER DRIVE
HOWARDS WOOD DRIVE
THE UPLANDS
DUKES RIDE
Maltmans
MALTMANS LANE
Tennis Court
Playing Field
Hollytree Farm
Austenwood Common
Sch.
School
LATCHMOOR AV.
ORCHEHILL AVENUE
PACKHORSE ROAD
KINGSWAY
NORTH PARK
STATION APP.
P.O.

Hogtrough Wood
Golf Course
Mopes Farm
Troy Mill
Jacks Mill
WD3
Troy
AS
AT
AU
AV
34
Pond
RIVER
Little Halings Wood
Little Halings
Tile House
JUNIPER WOOD
Chalfont Lodge
Gerrards Cross Golf Course
Pavilion
R. Misbourne
Club House
Research Laboratories
CHALFONT PARK
Chalfont Park
M25
KNOCKHILL WOOD
Square Copse
Quarters Wood
Round Copse
Coldharbour Farm
GERRARDS CROSS
Great Halings Wood
Halings House (M.O.D. Hostel)
Wyatt's Covert
Caravan Site
Northmoon Hill Wood
A412
31
Lake
Hillingdon
MARISH LANE
HALINGS LANE
The Marish
TILEHOUSE LANE
Battlesford Wood
COLNE
Ranston Covert
Labs.
The Tudors
MARSHAM LA.
Diss Park
Oakend Wood
Denham Marsh Wood
SLADE OAK LA.
MIRRIE LANE
The Mirrie
Denham Aerodrome
Denham Country Club
32
Broadwater Park Industrial Estate
Thorn Ho.
THE WOODLANDS
WOODLANDS CLO.
Isle of Wight Farm
OVER THE MISBOURNE
Nurs.
Denham Golf Course
Newstead Wood
Sch.
Colsels Wood
Golf Club House
DENHAM GREEN LANE
ST FRANCIS RD.
ST MARY'S RD.
ASHCROFT DR.
TILEHOUSE WAY
NORTH ORBITAL ROAD
Yth. Cen.
HILLCREST WAYE
BEECH WAYE
AVENUE
WOODHILL
MORELANDS DRIVE
Mill Wood
DENHAM GOLF CLUB
DOGGETS FARM RD
UPPER RD.
MIDDLE ROAD
LOWER RD.
OLD RECTORY LANE
STATION APP.
DENHAM
UB9
44
Woodhill
Gallows Wood
Sewage Works
Comm. Cen.
A413
33
REUSDEN WAY
Little Gallows Wood
Moorhouse Farm
River Misbourne
The Rancho
A40
Fire Sta.
Police Sta.
P.O.
Tatling End
BROKEN GATE
BAKERS WOOD
Denham Place
VILLAGE RD.
St. Huberts
SKYLARK RD.
HOLLYBUSH
REDHILL
Huntwyk
VILLAGE
Vill. Hall
Denham
St. Hubert's Home Farm
ST HUBERTS LANE
Little Prestwick
Old Prestwick
BLACKSMITH'S LANE
MOUNT LA.
Redhill Farm
ASHMEAD
Court Farm
Hollybush Farm
Naboth
Alderbourne Manor
Gladwin's Wood
Refuse Tip.
CHEAPSIDE
Sch.
Rec Grd
34
Priory Covert
Denham Mount
FROGGY LANE
FIELD ROAD
Small Holdings
SOUTHLANDS RD.
PRIORY CLOSE
Oldhouse Farm
ULMER
Hawk's Wood
Holly Bush
M25
16
Furzeney
Hawk's Wood
HAWKSWOOD LANE
1
Rush Green
M40
New House Farm
Rush Green Fm.
GOSSAMS WOOD
WILLETS LANE
A4020
M40
1A
35
Brown's Wood
Alder Bourne
Oldhouse Wood
Small Holdings
Ivy House Farm
Kingcup Fm.
Alderbourne Farm
ALDERBOURNE LANE
SEVENHILLS ROAD
Blanchard's Farm
Parkspring Wood
Mount Fidget Wood
52
LONG COPPICE
SOUTHLANDS ROAD
A412
SL0
CHERRY TREE LANE
HAWKSWOOD GRO.
Cha.
Cangley Corner
COMMON
FULMER
Dromenagh
Southlands Manor
Nurs.
KNIGHTON WAY LA.

Troy Mill
Jacks Mill
Pond
River Colne
AW
AX
AY
AZ
35
Harefield Ho.
Crick. Gd
Spotted Dog
Cricket Gd
Ashain Spring
Kiln Pond
Claypits
Knightscote Farm
Dell
Badminton Shooting Ground
Langley Farm
Newstead House
Dove Dale Clo.
Bird La.
Countess Clo.
Lovett Rd.
White Horse
Highbones
Bourne Farm
Breakspear
North Breakspear Road
Harefield Pla. (Site of)
Park Lodge Farm
Warren Farm
Bayhurst Wood
Willow Farm
A412
31
Wyatts Covert
Caravan Site
Northmoon Hill Wood
Lake
North Orbital Rd.
Battleford Wood
Ranston Covert
Labs.
Rec. Grd.
Lock
Harefield Moor
Halfway House
Pumping Sta.
Moorhall Cottages
Moorhall Rd.
32
Newstead Wood
Sch.
Broadwater Park Industrial Estate
Yth. Cen.
Savay Farm
UB9
Tilehouse Lane
Tilehouse Way
43
Denham
P.O.
Pumping Sta.
Dewe's Dell
Highway Farm
Newyears Green
Newyears Lane
Hillingdon Sailing Base
Dewe's Farm
Newyears Green Covert
St. Leonard's Farm
Elmwood
Altcar Covert
33
Widows Cruise Covert
Camping Site
Misbourne
Denham Place
Flagmoor Covert
Harefield Place (Public)
Golf Course
Brackenbury Farm
Copthall Covert
Moat
Pumping Sta.
Village Rd.
Vill. Hall
Denham
Court Farm
Denham Court
Copthall Farm
Home Farm
Denham Avenue A412
Ashmead
Rec. Grd.
34
Weir
St. John's Covert
Priory Covert
Club Ho.
Harefield Place
Breakspear Road
Green Acres Av.
Small Holdings
Southlands Rd.
Denham Lock
Frays River
Canal
Harvil Road
B467
The Lea
Harefield Pl. Estate
Highfield Drive
Swakeleys
Oxford Road
A40 Western Avenue
M40
New House Farm
35
Weirs
Willowbank
Grand Union Canal
Uxbridge Circus
Vyners Sch.
Warren Road
UB10
Tennis Ccs.
Park Wd.
R. Pinn
Halford
A4020
Ivy House Farm
Community Centre
Factory
Ski Centre
Sports Ground
Running Track
Kingcup Fm
Willets Lane
Southlands Road
Nurs.
New Denham
Lock
Uxbridge Common
53
UB8
B483
Swimming Pool
Southlands Manor
High Br.
North

AZ
BA
BB
BC
35
31
32
33
34
35
45
53
HA6
HA5
HA4
COPSE WOOD
BESS WOOD
Young Wood
DUCKS HILL
Poor's Field
Battle of Britain House
Coll.
Ruislip Common
RUISLIP LIDO
Pav.
Haste Hill Municipal Course
Haste Hill
Club Ho.
Northwood Cemetery
St. Vincent's Orthopaedic Hospital
Hosp.
NORTHWOOD HILLS
RICKMANSWORTH RD.
TOLCARNE DRIVE
JOEL STREET
Joel Street Farm
Haydon Sch.
Playing Field
Haydon Hall
Cuckoo Hill
Tennis Cts.
PARK WOOD
Crematm
Open Space
Fire Sta.
Cannon Bridge
FINE BUSH LANE
BROADWOOD AVENUE
KINGS COLLEGE FIELDS
KINGS COLLEGE RD.
EASTCOTE
Eastcote Ho.
HIGH RD.
Swimming Pool
Bishop Ramsey C.E.Sch.
Recreation Ground
RUISLIP
Mill Farm
Manor Fm
Rec. Gnd.
EASTCOTE RD.
BURY ST.
HIGH ST.
RUISLIP MANOR
ELM AVENUE
PARK WAY
WEST END RD.
KINGS END
Ruislip Municipal Golf Course
Club Ho.
Cricket Gd.
Ickenham Green
WEST RUISLIP
PICCADILLY & MET.
Sports Ground
Playing Fields
Bessingby Fields
Cavendish Sports Gd.
Pine Gds. Open Space
New Pond Fields Farm
Yeading Brook
Recreation Ground
RUISLIP GARDENS
Open Space
HILL FARM ROAD
ICKENHAM
Ickenham Youth Centre
Douay Martyrs R.C. Sch.
Manor Farm
Longlane Farm
Ickenham Marsh
Canal Feeder
Master Brewer Motel
NORTHOLT AERODROME
Sports Gd.
British Airways
Sports Gnd
Polish War Mem!
A40
A4180
B466
B467
B472
A404

45
PINNER PARK
Pinner Park Farm
BD
BE
BF
BG
36
31
32
33
34
35
44
54
HA5
HA4
HA2
UB5
PINNER
Cuckoo Hill
EASTCOTE
Harrow Garden Village
NORTH HARROW
WEST HARROW
SOUTH HARROW
RAYNERS LANE
Haydon Hall
Eastcote Ho
South Ruislip
SOUTH RUISLIP
Northolt Park
NORTHOLT PARK
Wood End
ROXBOURNE PARK
ALEXANDRA PARK
WOODLANDS OPEN SPACE
Yeading Brook Open Space
Pinner Village Garden Recreation Ground
Pinner Memorial Garden
The Croft Open Space
Cavendish Sports Gd.
Bessingby Fields
Headstone Manor Recreation Ground
West Harrow Recreation Ground
Whitmore High Sch.
Roxbourne Hospital
Nower Hill High Sch.
Rooks Heath High Schs
Queensmead Sch.
S.Ruislip Leisure Centre
LORD HALSBURY MEMORIAL PLAYING FIELDS
Kodak Sports Ground
British Rail Sports Ground
Old Lyonians Sports Grd.
Harrow Borough F.C.
MET. & PICCADILLY LINE
MET. LINE
PINNER ROAD
ALEXANDRA AVENUE
RAYNERS LANE
MARSH ROAD
UXBRIDGE ROAD
RICKMANSWORTH RD.
ELM PARK RD.
BRIDGE ST.
HIGH ST.
GEORGE V AVENUE
IMPERIAL DRIVE
VICTORIA ROAD
NORTHOLT ROAD
WHITTON AV.
WOODLANDS
EASTCOTE LANE
A404
A4090
A312
A410
B463
B466

45
BG
BH
BJ
BK
36
31
32
33
34
35
46
54
HA7
HA3
HA1
HA9
HA0
UB6
WEALDSTONE
HARROW & WEALDSTONE
Byron Recreation Ground
Cemetery
Swimming Pool
Harrow Leisure Centre
Civic Centre
Kodak Works
Industrial Park
Mountview High Sch.
Park High Sch.
CENTENARY PARK
Playing Fld.
Stanmore Residential Nursery
KENTON
Kenton Sports Grd.
Kenton Recreation Ground
Central Depot L.B. of H.
Wealdstone Foot. Grd.
Harrow Recreation Ground
HARROW ON THE HILL
Greenhill Coll.
Gayton High Sch. For Boys
Sports Ground
NORTHWICK PARK
Harrow College of Higher Education
Northwick Park Hospital
Harrow School Bathing Place
NORTHWICK PARK
Masonic Centre
St.Gregory's R.C High Sch.
Wealdstone Brook
WOODCOCK PARK
Claremont High Sch.
Playing Field
Electricity Sub Station
MET. LINE
HARROW
Rifle Range
Football Grd.
HARROW SCHOOL PLAYING FIELDS
Harrow School Sports Ground
Harrow School Fm.
Football Grounds
Music Room
Parade Grd.
Chapel
Harrow School
Gymnasium
Highmead Church Fields
Cricket Ground
The Park
Newlands
Harrow Sch. Lake
The Lodge
Parkfield
The Chalet
Kennet Ho.
Julianhill
Julian Cott.
Nurses Ho.
Harrow Hosp.
St.Dominic's Sixth Form College
Chasewood Park
The Clementine Churchill Hosp.
Orley Farm Sch.
Crick.Ground
Swimming Pool
Harrow Cricket Club
TUNNEL
SUDBURY HILL
War Mem.
Sudbury Towers
Open Space
PRESTON PARK
PRESTON ROAD
SOUTH KENTON
Preston Hotel
Forty Farm Sports Ground
G.E.C. Electrical Research Laboratory
G.E.C. Works
Wembley Commercial Centre
BAKERLOO LINE & B.R.
School Playing Fields
OPEN SPACE
NORTH WEMBLEY
VALE FARM SPORTS GROUND
Rugby Ground
Swimming Pool
Sports Centre
Wembley Foot. Grd.
Mitre
Recreation Ground
BUTLERS GRN.
SUDBURY
SUDBURY & HARROW RD.
BARHAM PARK
KING EDWARD VII PARK
WEMBLEY
WEMBLEY CENTRAL
SUDBURY TOWN
Horsenden Wood
Ballot Box
Allotments
Allot.
Youth & Teachers Cen.
Hosp.
STATION RD.
HIGH STREET
KENTON RD.
KENTON LANE
NORTHWICK AV.
WATFORD RD.
SUDBURY HILL
GREENFORD ROAD
WHITTON AVENUE
HARROW RD.
EAST LANE
HIGH RD.
LONDON RD.
SUDBURY COURT DR.
BESSBOROUGH ROAD
PETERBOROUGH RD.
A409
A404
A4006
A4005
A4088
A4127
A4090
A4140
A312

46
BL
BM
BN
BO
37
31
32
33
34
35
45
55
HA 8
HA 3
HA 9
NW 9
NW 10
QUEENSBURY
Stanmore Residential Nursery
BRIXTON ESTATE
HERON TRADING ESTATE
CAPITOL INDUSTRIAL PARK
Royal Dental Hosp Sports Ground
Montrose Playing Fields
Colindale Hospital
Brit. Musm. Newspaper Repository
NORTHERN LINE
QUEENSBURY PARK
Kingsbury Hosp.
Eton Grove Open Space
Roe Green
ROE GREEN PARK
Kingsbury High Sch. Playing Fields
Kingsbury Manor
Grove Park Sch.
Swimming Pool
KENTON ROAD
A4006
A4140
A5
KINGSBURY
KINGSBURY ROAD
Kenton Sports Grd.
Kenton Grange O.P.H.
Wealdstone Brook
St. Gregory's R.C. High Sch.
WOODCOCK PARK
Claremont High Sch. Playing Field
Police Training Area
Sports Ground
L.T.E. Sports Ground
Allotments
KINGSBURY GREEN
KINGSBURY TRADING EST.
SILVER JUBILEE PARK
WEST HENDON PLAYING FIELDS
FRYENT REGIONAL OPEN SPACE
FRYENT WAY
Church Lane Recreation Ground
JUBILEE LINE
MET. LINE
BARN HILL OPEN SPACE
Barn Hill
PRESTON ROAD
PRESTON PARK
SOUTH KENTON
Preston Hotel
Wembley Park
KINGSBURY
Brent Town Hall
Field Centre
WELSH HARP OPEN SPACE
Sailing Club
BRENT RESERVOIR
Pump House
Cemetery
Blackbird Cross
Forty Farm Sports Ground
Wembley Commercial Centre
G.E.C. Sports Ground
G.E.C. Works
Electrical Research Laboratory
Century Hotel
FORTY LANE
A4088
WEMBLEY PARK
BAKERLOO LINE & B.R.
NORTH WEMBLEY
JUBILEE & MET. LINE
T.V. Studios
Wembley Arena
Squash Centre
Conf. Centre
Pullman Kellogg Bldg.
Sunday Market Area
Cannon Ind Est
Exh.Cen.
Crest Hotel
Wembley Stadium
Kennels
KING EDWARD VII PARK
WEMBLEY
WEMBLEY STADIUM
SHERRENS FARM OPEN SPACE
L.T. Railway Wks.
B.R.
Iron Br.
NEASDEN
Neasden Circle
NEASDEN LANE
A406
NORTH CIRCULAR ROAD
Copland High Sch.
Brent House
Copland School Playing Fields
WEMBLEY CENTRAL
Wembley Hosp.
Youth & Teachers Cent.
Bowling Grn.
BRENT RECREATION GROUND
Neasden Hospital
Gibbons Recreation Ground
Mitchell Brook

46
Holder's Hill
SUNNY HILL PARK
R.A.F. Museum
CHURCH END
WINDSOR OPEN SPACE
Middlesex University
Town Hall
HENDON
HENDON CENTRAL
HENDON NORTHERN PARK
Hendon District Hosp.
Sturgess Park
BRENT CROSS SHOPPING CENTRE
BRENT CROSS
West Hendon
York Park
Colindeep Open Space
BIG WOOD
Little Wood
Prince's Park
Carmelite Convent
Jew's Cemetery
Crematorium
Garden of Remembrance
GOLDERS GREEN
Whitefield Sch.
Refuse Disposal Works
Solid Waste Transfer Station
Industrial Estate
CLITTERHOUSE PLAYING FIELDS
Hendon Football Ground
BASING HILL PARK
CHILDS HILL PARK
CHILDS HILL
Staples Corner
Sports Ground
John Kelly High Sch.
DOLLIS HILL ESTATE
Athletic Ground
Dollis Hill
Open Air Swim. Pool
GLADSTONE PARK
CRICKLEWOOD
Cricklewood Trading Estate
Athletic Grounds
Hampstead Cemetery
Fortune Green
Westfield Coll.
New College
Covered Reservoir
DOLLIS HILL
Tech. Coll.
CHAPMANS PK. IND. EST
WILLESDEN GREEN
KILBURN
WEST HAMPSTEAD
HAMPSTEAD
NORTH CIRCULAR ROAD
WATFORD WAY
HENDON WAY
EDGWARE ROAD
FINCHLEY ROAD
GREAT NORTH WAY
MET.L.& JUBILEE
NORTHERN LINE
BO
BP
BQ
BR
37
31
32
33
34
35
47
55

47
CHURCH END
Municipal Offices
Playing Fields
BS
BT
BU
BV
38
COLDFALL WOOD
Fortis Green
St. Marylebone Cemetery
Mausoleum
EAST FINCHLEY
EAST FINCHLEY
Nat. Hosp. of Nervous Dis.
CHERRY TREE WOOD
HIGHGATE WOOD
St. Luke's Woodside Hosp.
31
FALLODEN WAY
LYTTELTON ROAD
AYLMER RD.
ARCHWAY RD.
GREAT NORTH RD.
MARKET PL.
Little Wood
BIG WOOD
Lyttelton Playing Fields
Hampstead Garden Suburb
32
GOLF COURSE
HIGHGATE GOLF COURSE
Moorfields Hospital Annexe
Jew's Cemetery
Crematorium
Garden of Remembrance
HAMPSTEAD HEATH
Bunkers Hill
Turner's Wood
33
46
GOLDERS GREEN
Hippodrome
NORTH END
North End
Manor Ho. Hosp.
The Spaniards Inn
Kenwood Fm. Cottage
Ken Wood Ho. Museum and Art Gallery
Middlesex Hosp. Recovery Unit
KEN WOOD
Ladies Open Air Bathing Pond
CHILDS HILL PARK
GOLDERS HILL PARK
Leg of Mutton Pond
West Heath
HAMPSTEAD HEATH
Hampstead Ponds
Vale of Health
Jack Straw's Castle P.H.
Whitestone Pond
CHILDS HILL
34
Elm Park
PARLIAMENT HILL
Parliament Hill
Open Air Bathing Pool
Syston Coll.
Royal Free Hospital
HAMPSTEAD
HAMPSTEAD
HAMPS. HIGH ST.
ROSSLYN HILL
Keats Ho. Mus. and Lib.
HAMPSTEAD HEATH
GOSPEL OAK
Royal Free Hosp.
Westfield Coll.
Athletic Grounds
Fortune Green
Hampstead Cemetery
35
New College
Covered Reservoir
University Coll. Sch.
WEST HAMPSTEAD
Hampstead Cricket Club
FINCHLEY ROAD
56
Old Town Hall
BELSIZE PARK
BELSIZE PARK
HAVERSTOCK HILL
WEST HAMPSTEAD
W. HAMPSTEAD
KILBURN

47
38
56
31
32
33
34
35
48
BV
BW
BX
BY
N.22
N.8
N.4
N.7
N.17
N.5
N.19
ALEXANDRA PALACE
ALEXANDRA PARK
Alexandra Palace
Miniature Golf Course
Miniature Rifle Range
Cricket Ground
Reservoir
Filter beds
Football Grd.
The Lake
Pavilion
Ski Slope
WOOD GREEN COMMON
WOOD GREEN
Noel Park
Haringey
MUSWELL HILL
The Grove
Grove Lo. Gdns.
HORNSEY
HORNSEY HIGH ST.
PRIORY ROAD
PRIORY PARK
Hornsey Central Hosp.
Playing Fields
Swimm. Bath
Cricket Grd.
Shepherds Cott. Play. Fld.
QUEEN'S WOOD
CROUCH END
Hornsey Town Hall
Clock Tower
HIGHGATE
TURNPIKE LANE
TURNPIKE LA.
The Wellington
DOWNHILLS PARK
Downhills Rec. Grd.
Recreation Grd.
Model Traffic Area
The Black Boy
Chestnuts Rec. Grd.
HARRINGAY STADIUM
HARRINGAY
Cricket Ground
American Gardens
River Gate
Hornsey Gate
FINSBURY PARK
Manor Gate
MANOR HOUSE
Boating Lake
Seven Sisters Road Bri.
WEST RESERVOIR
CROUCH HILL
Crouch Hill Res. (Cov.)
STROUD GREEN
The Favourite
Elthorne Park
Whittington Hosp.
Highgate Cemetery
ARCHWAY
UPPER HOLLOWAY
UPR. HOLLOWAY
Whittington Park
Bus Depot
DARTMOUTH PARK
Royal Northern Hosp.
Equipment Depot
Cinema
St. George's Theatre
Sobell Sports Centre
ARSENAL
Arsenal Football Grd.
FINSBURY PARK
Bus Stn.
Islington
Hackney
TUFNELL PARK
Holloway Prison
HOLLOWAY
HOLLOWAY ROAD
DRAYTON PARK
HIGHBURY
Highbury Fields
Swim. Pool
Poly of N. London
KENTISH TOWN
CALEDONIAN ROAD
Caledonian Park
Clock Tower
HIGHBURY & ISLINGTON
CANONBURY
CLISSOLD PARK
ARCHWAY ROAD
JUNCTION ROAD
FORTESS ROAD
HOLLOWAY ROAD
SEVEN SISTERS ROAD
GREEN LANES
WEST GREEN ROAD
STROUD GREEN ROAD
HORNSEY RISE
HORNSEY ROAD
CAMDEN ROAD
PARKHURST ROAD
CALEDONIAN ROAD
A503
A400
A105
A5203
A1
B155

TOTTENHAM
BRUCE GROVE
39
BZ
CA
CB
CC
Lordship Recreation Ground
Playing Field
Open Air Thea.
The Moselle
Model Traffic Area
Recreation Grd.
DOWNHILLS PARK
Downhills Rec. Grd.
TURNPIKE LANE
31
MONUMENT WAY
FERRY LANE
HALE RD.
TOTTENHAM HALE
Down Lane Recreation Ground
Athletic Grd.
Sports Grd.
LOW MAYNARD RESERVOIR
Valve Towers
Town Hall
Tech. Sch.
Bus Garage
SEVEN SISTERS
High Cross Centre
RESERVOIR No. 2
RESERVOIR No. 1
RES. No. 3
WARWICK RESERVOIR (EAST)
WARWICK (WEST) RESERVOIR
Coppermill Lane Pumping Sta.
Markfield Recreation Ground
SOUTH TOTTENHAM
Chestnuts Rec. Grd.
St. Ann's Gen. Hosp.
32
HARRINGAY STADIUM
HARRINGAY
STAMFORD HILL
Cricket Ground
American Gardens
River Gate
Hornsey Gate
N.4
FINSBURY PARK
47
33
Boating Lake
SEVEN SISTERS
A503
A105
A10
EAST RESERVOIR
WEST RESERVOIR
Lordship Road Bri.
Seven Sisters Road Bri.
New River
STAMFORD HILL
GUINNESS TRUST DWELLINGS
Sports Ground
Playing Field
Hackney Rowing Centre
SPRINGFIELD PARK
WALTHAMSTOW
Copper Mills Junction
Coppermill Bri.
Horse Shoe Point
Horse Shoe Bri.
High Hill Ferry
UPPER CLAPTON
N.16
Abney Park Cemetery
STOKE NEWINGTON
BURY PARK
Pumping Sta.
CLISSOLD PARK
Municipal Offices & Library
34
STOKE NEWINGTON
RECTORY ROAD
CLAPTON
NORTH MILL FIELDS
E.5
LOWER CLAPTON
HACKNEY DOWNS
N.5
35
HIGHBURY
Poly. of North London
Arsenal Football Grd.
Swim. Pool
CANONBURY
57
KINGSLAND
DALSTON
HACKNEY DOWNS
HACKNEY CENTRAL STA.
German Hosp.
Tech. Coll.
Town Hall
N.1
HIGHBURY & ISLINGTON
BALLS POND RD.
Bus Depot

48
39
31
32
49
33
34
35
57
CC
CD
CE
CF
HIGHAM
WALTHAMSTOW
Waltham
Forest
E.17
WALTHAMSTOW CENTRAL
WALTHAMSTOW QUEENS ROAD
ST. JAMES STREET
BLACKHORSE ROAD
WOOD STREET
SNARESBROOK
LEYTON
E.10
LEYTON MIDLAND RD.
LEYTONSTONE
E.11
LEYTON
E.15
E.9
HACKNEY
Recreation
Ground
MARSHES
CLAPTON PARK
LEYTON MARSHES
MABLEY GREEN
Recreation Ground
Hackney Stadium
Hackney Hosp.
HOMERTON
MARYLAND
Whipps Cross Hosp.
Langthorne Hosp.
Waltham Forest College
Town Hall
Assembly Hall
Walthamstow Cemetery
St. Patrick's R.C Cemetery
Jewish Cemetery
County Cricket Ground
Orient Industrial Park
Temple Mills Sidings
Eastway Sports Centre
Electric Power Station
Hollow Pond
Whipps Cross Bathing Pool
Children's Boating Pool
ST. JAMES'S PARK
Low Hall Sports Ground
Filter Beds
Lea Bridge Riding School
Seymour Rd. Recreation Ground
Coronation Gdns.
Ruckholt (Site)
INTERNATIONAL FREIGHT TERMINAL
A503
A104
A112
A1006
A1007
A114
A11
A102(M)
FOREST ROAD
HOE STREET
LEA BRIDGE ROAD
WOODFORD ROAD
WHIPPS CROSS ROAD
HIGH ROAD
CHURCH ROAD
RUCKHOLT ROAD
EASTWAY
HOMERTON ROAD
TEMPLE MILL LANE
LEYTONSTONE ROAD
THE GROVE
R. Lea
River Lea
Hackney Cut Navigation
CENTRAL LINE

NORTH CIRCULAR RD.
WOODFORD
SOUTH WOODFORD
E.18
FOREST
WOODFORD ROAD
A104
A406
A503
CHIGWELL
HERMON HILL
M11
Hatton Special Sch.
P.D.S.A. Sanatorium
School Playing Fields
Beal High Sch.
IG4
Redbridge Rec. Grd
WOODFORD TRADING EST.
River Roding
Wanstead Hospital
SNARESBROOK ROAD
SNARESBROOK
Crown Court
Whipps Cross Bathing Pool
Hollow Pond
EPPING FOREST
WHIPPS CROSS
A114
Whipps Cross Hosp.
WANSTEAD
Recreation Ground
Rugby Football Grd.
Nutter Field
Tennis Cts.
REDBRIDGE
EASTERN AVENUE
A12
Wanstead Sports Centre
Wanstead High Sch.
GOLF COURSE
Sports Ground
The Heronry
Lincoln Island
Rook Island
A406
Play. Fld.
The High Stone
CAMBRIDGE PARK
Drill Hall
Leytonstone House Hosp.
E.11
BUSH ROAD
BLAKE HALL
A1008
The Basin
Sports Grd.
Wanstead House (Site Of)
WANSTEAD GOLF COURSE
WANSTEAD PARK
The Temple
Grotto
Chalet
Heronry Pond
Perch Pond
Shoulder of Mutton Pond
Reservoir Wood
Filter Beds Southern Sewage Works
Wanstead Park Rec. Grd.
Friends Meeting House
Bush Wood
LEYTONSTONE
E.10
Aldersbrook
ALDERSBROOK ROAD
A116
WANSTEAD FLATS
City of London Cemetery
Catacombs
Crematorium
Electric Power Station
St. Patrick's R.C. Cemetery
Langthorne Hosp.
Jewish Cemetery
West Ham Cemetery
Manor Park Cemetery
MANOR PARK
WOODGRANGE PARK
FOREST GATE
WANSTEAD PARK
ROMFORD ROAD
E.7
Woodgrange Park Cemetery
Jews Cemetery
MARYLAND
E.15
Mun. Offs.
HIGH ST.
CG
CH
CJ
CK
31
32
33
34
35
40
48
58

PLAIN
BARKINGSIDE
Mossford Green
CLAYHALL PARK
Aldborough Hatch
Fairlop Playing Fields
Cemetery
Recreation Ground
Dr. Barnardo's H.Q.
Mag. Ct.
GANTS HILL
Newbury Park
NEWBURY PARK
King George Hosp.
Goodmayes Hospital
School Playing Fields
SEVEN KINGS PARK
SEVEN KINGS
VALENTINE'S PARK
Valentines Mansion
GOLF COURSE
Open Air Swim. Pool
Boating Pool
Tennis Cts.
Cricket Grd.
Tennis Bowls
Bell Tower
The Lake
Landing Stage
Lodge
ILFORD
Town Hall
Exchange Shop. Cent.
Ilford Cemetery
Baths
Health Centre
Plessey Works
Carriage Sheds
Drill Ground
SOUTH PARK
Knox Playing Field
LOXFORD PARK
LITTLE ILFORD PARK
BARKING PARK
Barking Abbey Comp. Sch.
Barking Abbey Comp. Sch. (Annexe)
GOODMAYES PARK
Recreation Ground
North East London Poly. Barking Precinct
MAYES BROOK PARK
Boating Lakes
Riding School
Aldborough Hall Fm.
Dick Turpin
Aldborough Hatch Fm.
Rush Hall Sch.
William Torbitt Sch.
White's Fm.
Sports Grd.
CENTRAL LINE
EASTERN AVENUE
HIGH ROAD
A12
A123
A406
A118
A1083
A124
B177
IG1
IG2
IG3
IG5
IG6
CK
CL
CM
CN
31
32
33
34
35
40
50
58

PLAN
50
IG6
IG2
RM6
RM8
RM9
IG11
CO
CP
CQ
CR
41
49
59
31
32
33
34
35
Marks Gate
Aldborough Hatch
Little Heath
Goodmayes Hospital
Seven Kings Park
Chadwell Heath Hospital
Redbridge Tech. Coll.
St. Chads Park
Chadwell Heath
Goodmayes
Seven Kings
Goodmayes Park
Becontree
Valence Park
Parsloes Park
Dagenham
Mayesbrook Park
North East London Poly. Barking Precinct
Barking Abbey Comp Sch (Annexe)
Chadwell Heath Cemetery
Westlands Playing Field
Eastern Avenue
A12
A118
A1083
A124
A1112
A1153
High Road
Whalebone Lane North
Whalebone Lane South
Green Lane
Longbridge Road
Becontree Avenue
Valence Avenue
Goodmayes Lane
Painters Road
Billet Road
Hainault Road
Barley Lane
Mayesbrook
Seven Kings Water
Kings Water
Lake
Boating Lakes
Recreation Ground
Sports Ground
Playing Fields
District Line
Dagenham Heathway

Romford Golf Course
GIDEA PARK
RAPHAEL PARK
41
Hare Street
ROMFORD
Lodge Farm Park
Victoria Hosp.
Town Hall
Dolphin Leisure Centre
L.B. of Hav. Offices
Romford Brewery
Oldchurch Hosp.
Oldchurch Park
Rush Green
Cottons Park
Gas Works
Cemetery
Recreation Gd.
Ford Sports Grd.
Miniature Golf Course
CENTRAL PARK
Barking College of Technology
Rush Green Hospital
Fels Farm
Dagenham Cemetery
Hooks Hall Farm
Eastbrookend Farm
Sports Grd.
Stockdale Farm
Sterling Industrial Estate
Football Ground
Pondfield Park
DAGENHAM EAST
59
Hylands Park
Park Lane Playground
Roneo Corner
Heath Pk
Haynes Park
Harrow Lodge
Boating Lake
HORNCHURCH
Abbs Cross
ELM PARK
RM1
RM2
RM5
RM7
RM11
RM12
RM13
31
32
33
34
35
51

51
42
50
60
Hare Street
Gidea Park
Ardleigh Green
Harold Wood Park
Heath Pk
Emerson Park
Hornchurch
Upminster
Elm Park
Hacton
Corbets Tey
Nelmes
Lillyputs
Hylands Park
Upminster Park
Upminster Golf Course
Ingrebourne River
Haynes Park Golf Course
St. Georges Hospital
Park Corner Farm
Hacton Ho.
Rainham Lo.
Havering Tech. Coll
Campion R.C. Sch.
Abbs Cross
St. Andrews Park
Harold Wood Hospital
Gallows Corner
Romford Golf Course
Southend Arterial Road
A127
A124
A118
B1421
RM2
RM3
RM11
RM12
RM13
CV
CW
CX
CY
31
32
33
34
35

51
Little War
GOLF COURSE
GREAT PARK
Tooks Farm
Clapgate
Bluehouse Farm
Coombe Grn.
Coombe Lo.
Well Wood
Great Readings
Fairstead
Warley Elms
Lodge
Beredens
Norman's
Norman's Cottages
Cricket Ground
Parker's Shaw
St.Peter's Rectory
Warley Rose Garden
Dickenson's
Latchet's Shaw
CM13
Codham Hall Cottages
Codham Hall
Hulmers
Crossways
Brickhouse
WARLEY ST. FLYOVER
Warley Hall Wood
Pot Kilns
SOUTHEND ROAD
A127
Great Warley Hall
The Bungalow
Little Warley Hall
Hobbs Hole
Jax Folly
Gladstone Cottages
Factory
M25
Cranham Playing Fields
Upminster Hall
L.T. Railway Depot
Westbury
Cranham Court
Puddle Dock
Nursery
Monks Farm
Clay Tye Wood
Berry Farm
RM14
Wantz Br.
Cranham
Clay Tye Farm
Fairplay Farm
Claynes
Clay Tye Hill
Spring Wood
Middle Wd
Bonus Wood
South Essex Crematm.
Mortuary Chapel
Cem.
Cranham Place
Whitepost Farm
North Ockendon
The Orchard
Remembrance Cotts.
P.O.
Allot. Gdns.
Manor Farm
St. Marys Ch.
Hall Farm
Moat
Sand Pit
Redcrofts
Gt. Sunnings
OCKENDON ROAD
B1421
B187
B186
ST. MARYS LANE
CLAY TYE ROAD
WARLEY STREET
GREAT WARLEY ST.
CY
CZ
DA
DB
42
60
123
29
31
32
33
34
35

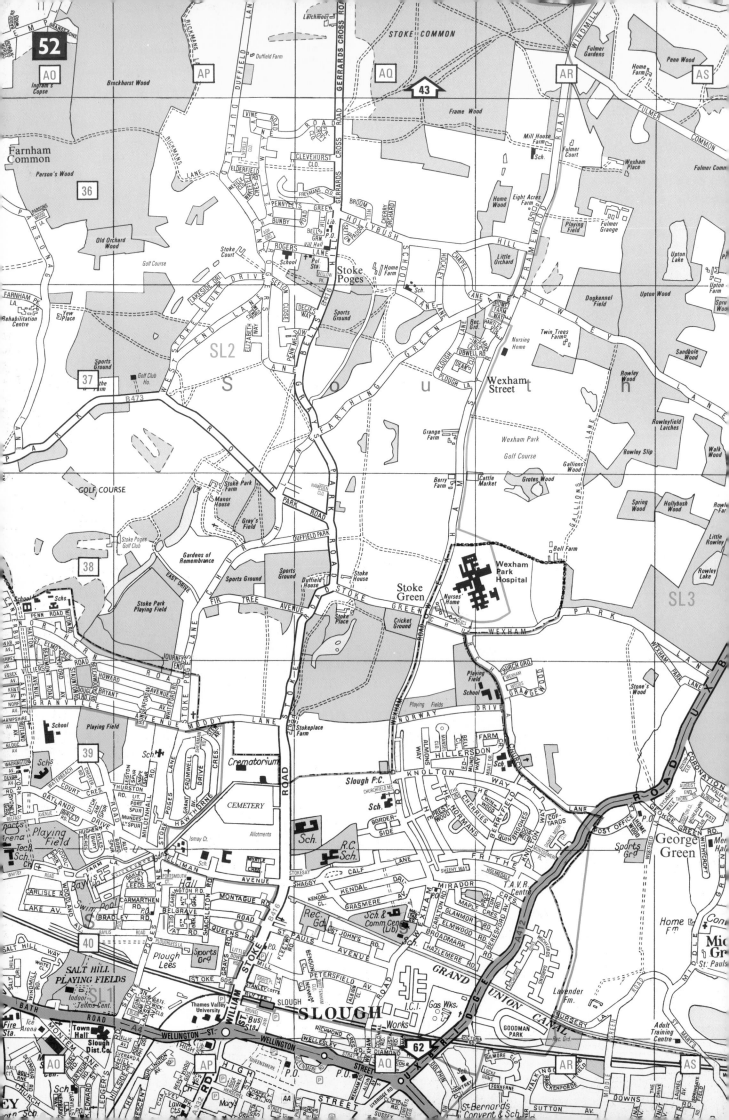

52
AO
AP
AQ
AR
AS
43
36
37
38
39
40
62
Stoke Common
Latchmoor
Duffield Farm
Brockhurst Wood
Ingram's Copse
Farnham Common
Parson's Wood
Old Orchard Wood
Golf Course
Farnham Pk La.
Rehabilitation Centre
Yew Place
Sports Ground
Golf Club Ho.
Stoke Court
Stoke Poges
School
Pol. Sta.
Lib.
P.O.
Vill Hall
Home Farm
Sports Ground
SL2
South
Frame Wood
Fulmer Gardens
Home Farm
Penn Wood
Fulmer Common
Mill House Farm
Fulmer Court
Wexham Place
Home Wood
Eight Acres Farm
Playing Field
Fulmer Grange
Little Orchard
Upton Lake
Upton Farm
Upton Wood
Dogkennel Field
Twin Trees Farm
Nursing Home
Sandbole Wood
Rowley Wood
Wexham Street
Rowleyfield Larches
Grange Farm
Wexham Park
Golf Course
Rowley Slip
Walk Wood
Gallions Wood
Berry Farm
Cattle Market
Grotes Wood
Spring Wood
Hollybush Wood
Little Rowley
Rowley Lake
Bell Farm
Wexham Park Hospital
Nurses' Home
Stoke Green
Cricket Ground
SL3
GOLF COURSE
Stoke Park Farm
Manor House
Gray's Field
Stoke Poges Golf Club
Gardens of Remembrance
Sports Ground
Duffield House
Stoke House
Stoke Place
Stoke Park Playing Field
Stoke Poges Lane
Stoneʼs Wood
Playing Field
School
Playing Fields
Stokeplace Farm
Crematorium
CEMETERY
Allotments
Slough F.C.
Sch.
R.C. Sch.
Ismay Ct.
Playing Field
Sports Arena
Tech Sch.
Swim Pool
Hall
Rec. Grd.
Sch. & Comm. Cent. (Lib)
T.A.V.R. Centre
George Green
Sports Grd
Home Fm
Plough Lees
Sports Grd
SALT HILL PLAYING FIELDS
SL1
Indoor Tennis Cent.
Ice Arena
Fire Sta.
Town Hall
Slough Dist.Co.
Thames Valley University
Bus Sta.
SLOUGH
I.C.I. Works
Gas Wks.
GRAND UNION CANAL
Lavender Fm.
GOODMAN PARK
Adult Training Centre
Rec. Grd.
St. Bernard's Convent & Sch.
St. Pauls
GERRARDS CROSS ROAD
DUFFIELD LANE
ROGERS LANE
HOLLYBUSH HILL
FRAMEWOOD ROAD
ROWLEY LANE
FULMER COMMON ROAD
PARK ROAD
STOKE ROAD
WEXHAM ROAD
NORWAY DRIVE
KNOLTON WAY
CHURCH LANE
WEXHAM PARK LANE
UXBRIDGE ROAD
WELLINGTON ST.
BATH ROAD
HIGH STREET
ELLIMAN AVENUE
MOODY LANE
GRANVILLE AVENUE
B416
B473
A4
A412
A332

AS
AT
AU
AV
43
62
53
36
37
38
39
40
UB9
SL0
M25
A412
A4007
B470
Alder Bourne
Small Holdings
Oldhouse Wood
Brown's Wood
Alderbourne Farm
Blanchard Farm
LONG COPPICE
SEVENHILLS ROAD
SEVEN HILLS ROAD
Dromenagh
Dromenagh Farm
The Clump
Round Coppice Farm
Southlands Manor
Watergete Fm.
Mansfield Farm
Electricity Sub Sta
Mount Fidget Wood
Parkspring Wood
HAWKSWOOD GRO
CHERRY TREE LANE
Langley Corner
COMMON ROAD
FULMER
Heathfield Plantation
Strawberry Wood
Pinewood Film Studios
PINEWOOD ROAD
PINEWOOD GREEN
PINEWOOD CLO.
ASHFORD RD
THORNBRIDGE RD
COPSE WOOD
HEATHERDEN GRN.
THE PARKWAY
LONGSTONE RD
Stag & Hounds
Rec. Grd
Coun. Depot
BANGORS ROAD NORTH
ANSLOW GDNS
ROSTREVOR GDNS
GLASTER WAY
HEATHWAY
LAURELS RD
KEEN ACRE
IVER HEATH
Ancoats Lodge
The Black Horse
Sch.
P.O.
Pol. Ho
Warren Ho. Fm.
Park Lo. Farm
Park Lodge
Diamond Wood
QUEEN'S DRIVE
PEACE ROAD
BLACK PARK
Blackpark Lake
BUCKS
CHURCH ROAD
DENHAM ROAD
SLOUGH ROAD
UXBRIDGE ROAD
Crooked Billet
WOOD LANE CLOSE
Sports Ground
Column Larches
SWALLOWDALE ESTATE
WHITE HOUSE WAY
GROSVENOR CLO.
LOWER MEAD
POTTERS CROSS
HARDINGS ROW
COOPERS ROW
BANGORS ROAD SOUTH
Bangors Park
Moorwards
Woodlands Park
Sea Rangers Hut
DELAFORD PARK
Palmer's Moor Fm
Palmers Moor Poultry Farm
Colne
Coppins
Coppins Farm
Lower Delaford
NORWOOD LA.
Nursery
Whip & Collar
SWALLOW STREET
Swallow Street
LOVE GREEN LA
Love Green
Hosp.
BARNFIELD
EVREHAM RD
Iver Lodge
Delaford Park
The Swan
HIGH STREET
IVER
Village Hall
The Bull
P.S.
Police Ho
STONECROFT AV.
DELAFORD CLOSE
VICTORIA CRES.
MARINA WAY
BARNES WAY
AVENUE DRIVE
BILLET LANE
Roughground Wood
BELLSWOOD LA.
Ashen Cross
Langley Park
Wood Lane Farm
Heath Lodge
Iver Grove
"The Gurkha"
Nursery
LANGLEY PARK ROAD
HOLLYBUSH LA.
Shreding Gr. Farm
Shreding Green
Rec. Grd.
Allots.
DUTTON WAY
GRANGE WAY
CHEQUERS ORCHARD
LANGLEY PARK
Love Hill Ho. Fm.
LOVE HILL LANE
IVERDALE CLO.
MANSION LANE
Nurs.
Mead's Cottages
HOLLOW HILL LA.
TRENCHES LA.
Camping Site
MOAT
The Orchards Residential Park
PICKFORD DRIVE
RIDGEWAY
Ridgeway Trading Estate
GRAND UNION CANAL
THORNEY LANE
Iver Court Farm
Water Treatment Works
Caravan Pk.
LANGLEY
ALDERBURY RD.
Langley College
Withy Bridge
BATHURST WALK
BATHURST CLO.
Thorney Farm
Tower
Huntsmoor Park Farm
Hunt
FORD LANE
Uxbridge Moor
Long Bridge
The Cut
KNIGHTON WAY LA.
Nurs.

53
44
52
63
36
37
38
39
40
AW
AX
AY
AZ
UB9
UB8
UB7
UB1
SL0
M25
A412
A4020
A4007
A408
B470
B467
B483
B465
Willowbank
Ivy House Farm
Community Centre
Kingcup Fm.
New Denham
Southlands Manor
Round Coppice Farm
Alder Bourne
Watergete Fm.
Mansfield Farm
Uxbridge Moor
Electricity Sub.Sta.
Long Br.
RIVER COLNE
High Br.
Industrial Estate
Recreation Grd.
Shopping Centre
Bus Sta.
UXBRIDGE
Civic Cent.
Uxbridge Common
Sports Ground
Ski Centre
Running Track
Swimming Pool
Tech. College
The Hermitage
Royal Air Force Uxbridge
American Community Sch.
Hillingdon Court Park
Hillingdon Golf Course
Club Ho.
War Meml.
Sport Grd
St.John's Hosp.
Brunel University
Uxbridge Cemetery
Cony Green
Sports Ground
Sea Rangers Hut
Woodlands Park
Moorwards
Delaford Park
Palmers Moor Fm.
Palmers Moor Poultry Farm
Coppins Farm
Lower Delaford
Iver Lodge
Delaford Park
The Swan
Village Hall
The Bull
IVER
Gas Wks.
Sports Gd.
Cowley Cott.
Uxbridge Foot. Grd.
Uxbridge Works
COWLEY
Clisby's Br.
Cowley Hall Recreation Grd.
Grand Union Canal
Huntsmoor Park
Huntsmoor Park Farm
Cowley Peachey
Clock House
Little Britain
Little Britain Bridge
Aqueduct
Pield Heath
Hillingdon Hosp
Colham Green
Convent
YIEWSLEY
Philpot's Fm.
Rec'n Gd.
Swim Bath
Town Hall
Rainbow Ind.Est.
Playing Flds.
Football Ground
Trout Lane
R. Colne
Ridgeway Trading Estate
Canal
Water Treatment Works
Coal Depot
West Drayton
Industrial Est.
Dock
Iver
Thorney Farm
West Drayton
R.A.F.

53
NORTHOLT
44
AERODROME
HA4
Ickenham Marsh
Manor Farm
Longlane Farm
Master Brewer Motel
Canal Feeder
A40 WESTERN AVENUE
Yeading Brook
Gutteridge Wood
Polish War Mem!
Underpass
36
Sports Field
Sports Gd.
Sports Grd
South Ruislip
A4180
WEST END ROAD
B455
Ten Acres
The Gorse
Lane Covert
SHARVEL LANE
MOAT
Down Barns
UB5
37
West London Shooting Grounds
Ealing
Hillingdon
GRANVILLE ROAD
RICHMOND
MERTON AV.
VICTORIA RD.
SEDGEWICK AV.
GROSVENOR
Play Fd.
Sch.
Clinic
School Playing Field
Home Covert
Hare Plantatn
Polehill Farm
CHARVILLE EST.
HAYSTALL CL.
FROGMORE FARM EST.
REGIONAL Grosvenor Playing Field
Hayes Shrub.
Hayes Park
Hillingdon Heath
Home Farm
School
OPEN SPACE
Grange Park
UB4
Canal Feeder
Youth Centre
Belmore Playing Fld.
54
38
Community Centre
KINGSHILL AVENUE
Hayes End
Mead House
Recreation Grd.
Recreation Ground
UXBRIDGE ROAD
A4020
Moorcroft
DRAYTON KINGSWAY
Rosedale Park
Wood End
Woodend Green
Hayes Park Farm
Stadium
Open Space
Cricket Ground
Town Hall
Town Hall Park
Dr. Tripletts Sch.
HAYES
The Grapes
Playing Field
39
Yeading
Goulds Green
Stockley Park Golf Course
Business Park
Rec. Ground
DAWLEY ROAD
A437
UB3
Minet Sch.
40
HAYES BYPASS
A312
Botwell Green
Swimming Pool
Sports Ground
63
R.C.Sch.
Starwell Br.
Abenglen Ind.Est.
Adler Ind.Est.
Dawley
Provident Ind.Est.
AZ
BA
BB
BC

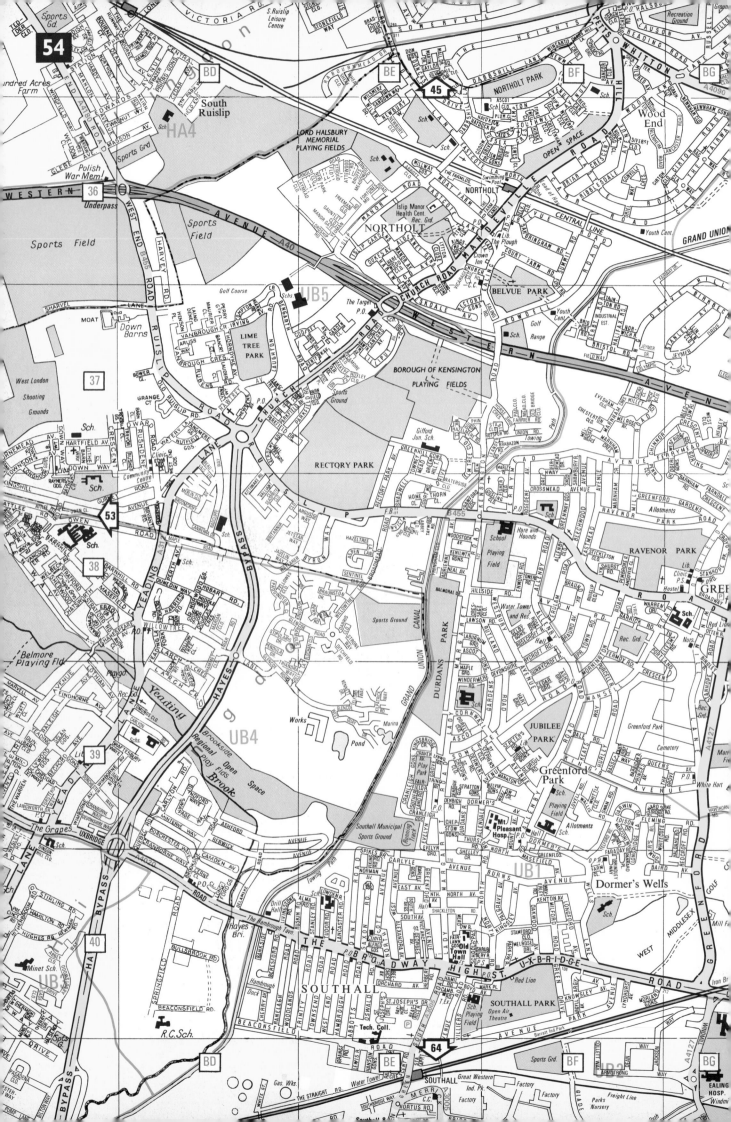

54
South Ruislip
HA4
Lord Halsbury Memorial Playing Fields
Northolt Park
Wood End
Open Space
Northolt
Western Avenue
Sports Field
Golf Course
UB5
Lime Tree Park
Borough of Kensington Playing Fields
Belvue Park
Rectory Park
West London Shooting Grounds
Down Barns
Ravenor Park
Durdans Park
Jubilee Park
Greenford Park
Belmore Playing Fld.
Yeading
UB4
Brookside Regional Play Fds
Open Space
Southall Municipal Sports Ground
Grand Union Canal
UB1
Dormer's Wells
Southall
Southall Park
The Broadway
High St.
Uxbridge Road
UB3
Hayes Bypass
Grand Union
Recreation Ground
Whitton Road
Sports Grd.
Southall
Greenford Road

SUDBURY
WEMBLEY
BARHAM PARK
Sudbury Towers
WHITTON AV.
WEST
A4090
45
HARROW RD.
A404
WEMBLEY CENTRAL
SUDBURY TOWN
Wembley Hosp.
Greenford Green
Horsenden Hill
Recreation Ground
HORSENDEN HILL
HORSENDEN HILL GOLF COURSE
Sudbury Heights
SUDBURY GOLF COURSE
PICCADILLY LINE
GRAND UNION CANAL
Alperton Cemetery
HA0
One Tree Hill Recreation Ground
ALPERTON
Alperton
GREENFORD
Rockware Glass Wks.
Perivale Wood
HORSENDEN LANE PUBLIC OPEN SPACE
Government Training Centre
UB6
PERIVALE INDUSTRIAL PARK
Ealing Central Sports Ground
WESTERN AVE
A40
SOUTH GREENFORD
PERIVALE
PERIVALE MUNICIPAL GOLF COURSE PARK
EALING GOLF COURSE
55
VIADUCT
HANGER LANE
GREYSTOKE PARK TERR.
Adult Training Centre
Gurnell Leisure Centre
PITSHANGER PARK
HANGER HILL PARK
Brentham
MONT PARK
W5
St. Augustines Priory
CASTLE BAR PARK
CLEVELAND PARK
Hospital for the Deaf
Elthorne Heights
W7
W13
BRENT VALLEY GOLF COURSE
Drayton Manor Sch.
DRAYTON GREEN
Drayton Green
WEST EALING
EALING BROADWAY
Town Hall
The Ealing Broadway Centre
EALING COMMON
Churchfields Recreation Ground
HANWELL
Kensington Cemetery
WEST UXBRIDGE RD.
BROADWAY
A4020
EALING
Pitshanger Manor Museum
WALPOLE PARK
B.B.C.T.V. Studios
Thames Valley University
City of Westminster Cemetery
64
Queen Victoria Hospital
HANWELL
A3002
BG
BH
BJ
BK
36
37
38
39
40

55
WEMBLEY
Wembley Stadium
WEMBLEY STADIUM
WEMBLEY CENTRAL
46
BL
BM
BN
BO
Copland School Playing Fields
Brent House
SHERRENS FARM OPEN SPACE
Tokyngton Recreation Ground
BAKERLOO LINE AND B.R.
STONEBRIDGE PARK
NORTH CIRCULAR ROAD
A406
A404
Gibbons Recreation Ground
Power Station
Stonebridge Rec. Grd.
HILLSIDE
CRAVEN PARK
HARLESDEN
One Tree Hill Recreation Ground
ALPERTON
Alperton
36
37
38
39
40
54
65
GRAND UNION CANAL
Sports Ground
OPEN SPACE
Council Depot
VIADUCT
HANGER LANE
A40
WESTERN AVENUE
Twyford Abbey
Park Royal
Guinness Brewery
Guinness Sports Ground
Central Middlesex Hosp.
TOWNSEND IND. EST.
WAXLOW ROAD
Freightliner Terminal
HANGER HILL PARK
St. Augustines Priory
Barclays Bank Athletic Ground
Ealing Cricket Ground
PARK ROYAL
NORTH EALING
WEST ACTON
NORTH ACTON
ACTON MAIN LINE
North Acton Playing Fields
Gipsy Corner
EALING BROADWAY
The Ealing Broadway Centre
Town Hall
EALING COMMON
N. Thames Gas Board Sports Ground
Springfield Gdns.
ACTON
HIGH STREET
ACTON CENTRAL
ACTON PARK
East Acton
Acton Hosp.
Thames Valley University
B.B.C.T.V. Studios
Victoria Ct. Cricket Ground
Public Playing Fields
W5
W3
HA0

55
46
56
65
36
37
38
39
40
BO
BP
BQ
BR
N.W.2
N.W.6
N.W.10
W.9
W.10
W.11
W.12
W.14
W.2
W.8
WILLESDEN
WILLESDEN GREEN
DOLLIS HILL
Tech. Coll.
CHAPMANS PK. IND. EST.
Willesden United Synagogue Cemetery
ROUNDWOOD PARK
Willesden General Hospital
Willesden Sports Centre
Swimming Pool
Brondesbury
BRONDESBURY
BRONDESBURY PARK
KILBURN
WEST HAMPSTEAD
W. HAMPSTEAD
KILBURN GRANGE PARK
KILBURN HIGH ROAD
KILBURN PARK
KENSAL RISE
KENSAL GREEN
Kensal Green Cemetery
QUEEN'S PARK
QUEENS PARK
Cemetery
WILLESDEN JUNCTION
GATEWAY TRADING EST.
St. Marys R.C. Cemetery
Cremat.
GRAND UNION CANAL
1 SWINBROOK RD.
2 TELFORD RD.
3 FARADAY RD.
4 ACKLAM RD.
5 MORGAN RD.
6 ORCHARD CLOSE
Paddington Recreation Ground
Running Track
MAIDA HILL
WESTBOURNE PARK
Paddington Com. Hosp.
WORMWOOD SCRUBS
LITTLE WORMWOOD SCRUBS
West London Stadium
Hammersmith Hosp.
Wormwood Scrubs Prison
OLD OAK EST.
St. Charles Hosp.
Princess Louise Hosp.
St. Charles' R.C. Coll.
NORTH KENSINGTON
LADBROKE GRO.
LATIMER ROAD
WESTWAY
A40(M)
A40
A404
A4020
M41
WHITE CITY
B.B.C. TV Centre
White City LRT Depot
WEST CROSS ROUTE
Hammersmith County Sch.
WORMHOLT PARK
SHEPHERDS BUSH
Sch. of Arts
Lime Gro. Studios B.B.C.
Shepherds Bush Centre
NOTTING HILL
NOTTING HILL GATE
HOLLAND PARK
Holland Park Sch.
King's Coll.
Town Hall
Ladbroke Square Gdns.
UXBRIDGE ROAD
HARROW ROAD
SCRUBS LANE
WOOD LANE

56
BS
BT
BU
BV
47
HAMPSTEAD
WEST HAMPSTEAD
W. HAMPSTEAD
FINCHLEY ROAD
BELSIZE PARK
SWISS COTTAGE
CHALK FARM
PRIMROSE HILL
KILBURN
BRONDESBURY
KILBURN GRANGE PARK
N.W.6
Brent
Cemetery
KILBURN HIGH ROAD
KILBURN PARK
SOUTH HAMPSTEAD
ST. JOHN'S WOOD
N.W.8
MAIDA VALE
MAIDA HILL
Lords Cricket Ground
Hosp. of St. John and St. Elizabeth
REGENTS PARK
London Zoo
Queen Mary's Gardens
Open Air Theatre
Winfield Ho.
Mosque
Boating Pool
Lake
Madame Tussauds
Planetarium
BAKER ST.
MARYLEBONE
Town Hall
Council Ho.
EDGWARE RD.
PADDINGTON
WARWICK AVENUE
Maida Vale Hosp.
Paddington Recreation Ground
Running Track
Cricket Ground
Paddington Sports Club
B.B.C. Studios
Tech. Inst.
55
36
37
38
39
40
WESTBOURNE PARK
Paddington Com. Hosp.
W E S T W A Y
A40(M)
ROYAL OAK
St. Mary's Hosp.
Paddington Basin
Fitzroy Nuff. Hosp.
MARBLE ARCH
OXFORD
BAYSWATER
QUEENSWAY
LANCASTER GATE
NOTTING HILL
NOTTING HILL GATE
Ladbroke Square Gdns.
HOLLAND PARK
Holland Park Sch.
HYDE PARK
OXFORD STREET where marked is closed to through traffic (except buses & taxis) between 7a.m.-7p.m. Monday-Saturday
Speakers corner
THE LONG WATER
THE SERPENTINE
Kensington Gardens
Round Pond
Kensington Palace
Peter Pan
Speke's Monument
Temple Lodge
Ranger's Lodge
Lido Pav.
Refreshment Room
66
ROTTEN ROW
KNIGHTSBRIDGE
Albert Memorial
KENSINGTON GORE
PARK LANE
A4202
A41
A5
A40
Kensington & Chelsea
HOLLAND PARK
Holland Ho

HIGHBURY
KENTISH TOWN
CAMDEN TOWN
BARNSBURY
ISLINGTON
SOMERS TOWN
MORNINGTON CRESCENT
CLERKENWELL
BLOOMSBURY
SOHO
SOUTHWARK
GREEN PARK
JAMES'S PARK
KINGS CROSS
ST. PANCRAS
EUSTON
WATERLOO
BLACKFRIARS
CHARING CROSS
EMBANKMENT
PENTONVILLE A501 ROAD
CALEDONIAN ROAD
CALEDONIAN ROAD & BARNSBURY
HIGHBURY & ISLINGTON
ANGEL
FARRINGDON
BARBICAN
CHANCERY LANE
HOLBORN
TOTTENHAM COURT ROAD
OXFORD CIRCUS
PICCADILLY CIRCUS
LEICESTER SQUARE
COVENT GARDEN
ALDWYCH
TEMPLE
MANSION HOUSE
CANNON ST.
BOROUGH
RUSSELL SQUARE
GOODGE ST.
WARREN ST.
GT. PORTLAND ST.
REGENTS PARK
EUSTON SQ.
CAMDEN ROAD
British Museum
University College
KING'S REACH
STRAND
FLEET ST.
LONDON WALL
CHEAPSIDE
EMBANKMENT
WATERLOO BRI.
BLACKFRIARS BRI.
WESTMINSTER BRI.
BV
BW
BX
BY
47
36
37
38
39
40
57
66

57
HIGHBURY
CANONBURY
DALSTON
HACKNEY
HOXTON
HAGGERSTON
SHOREDITCH
SPITALFIELDS
WHITECHAPEL
WAPPING
SOUTHWARK
BETHNAL GREEN
DALSTON KINGSLAND STA.
HACKNEY CENTRAL STA.
HACKNEY DOWNS
LONDON FIELDS
CAMBRIDGE HEATH
SHOREDITCH PARK
LIVERPOOL ST.
MOORGATE
BARBICAN
OLD STREET
ALDGATE
ALDGATE EAST
BANK
MANSION HOUSE
MONUMENT
CANNON ST.
BLACKFRIARS
FENCHURCH ST.
LONDON BRIDGE
TOWER GATEWAY
The Tower
CHEAPSIDE
LONDON WALL
CORNHILL
LEADENHALL ST.
COMMERCIAL A13 ROAD
WHITECHAPEL A11 RD.
KINGSLAND ROAD A10
A1200
A501
BZ
CA
CB
CC
48
56
67
36
37
38
39
40
E1

48
Hackney Stadium
HACKNEY WICK STA.
VICTORIA PARK
Cricket Ground
Football Ground
Running Track
Botanical Gds.
Boating Lake
E.9
WELL ST COMMON
HOMERTON
MABLEY GREEN
A102(M)
INTERNATIONAL FREIGHT TERMINAL
STRATFORD
E.15
S T R A T F O R D
Theatre Royal
Shop. Centre
MARYLAND
36
37
38
39
40
58
67
Stratford Marsh
River Lea
City Mill River
Waterworks River
BOW IND. EST.
OLD FORD
BLACKWALL
Grove Hall Pk.
Electric Power Sta.
Abbey Mills Sewage Pumping Sta.
Pumping Sta.
WEST HAM
Recreation Ground
E.3
BOW
BOW CHURCH
BROMLEY HIGH ST.
BROMLEY BY BOW
St. Andrew's Hosp.
Bow Lock & Flood Gates
The London Gas Museum
North Thames Gas Board
BROMLEY
Generating Sta.
Meath Gardens
The London Hosp. (Mile End)
The London Hosp. (St. Clement)
Queen Mary College
MILE END
Tower Hamlets Cemetery
STEPNEY GREEN
Hamlets
Stadium
S T E P N E Y
LIMEHOUSE
LIMEHOUSE (STEPNEY EAST)
Limehouse Basin
A13
EAST INDIA DOCK RD
P O P L A R
ALL SAINTS
CANNING TOWN
Poplar Bus. Park
WESTFERRY
POPLAR
WEST INDIA QUAY
E.14
WEST INDIA
Billingsgate Mkt.
CANARY WHARF
HERON QUAYS
Poplar Dock
Blackwall Basin
East India Dock
BLACKWALL TUNNEL
Blackwall Point
South Eastern Gas Board
S.E.10
West India & Millwall Dock Entrance
Nelson Dockyard Dry Dock
LIMEHOUSE REACH
St. Paul's Sports Grd.
Nature Park
Shop. Cent.
Council Offs
CC
CD
CE
CF

FOREST GATE
WOODGRANGE PARK
Woodgrange Park Cemetery
CG
CH
CJ
CK
49
MARYLAND
STRATFORD
36
University of East London
Passmore Edwards Mus.
WEST HAM PARK
The Cedars
Bowling Green
Clapton F.C. Grd
Spotted Dog
Jews Cemetery
PLASHET PARK
UPTON PARK
PRIORY PARK
DISTRICT LINE
PORTWAY
PLASHET ROAD
WEST HAM
37
PLAISTOW
Plaistow Hosp
Playing Field
Boleyn Castle
West Ham Football Grd
Abbey Mills Sewage
Pumping Sta.
WEST HAM
Northern Outfall Sewer
Athletic Ground
East London Crematorium Cemetery
Lister Gdns.
PLAISTOW Rec. Grd
Meml Recreation Ground
57
38
North Thames
The London Gas Museum
Recreation Ground
Newham General Hospital
Woodside Sch.
McMillan Stadium.
Brampton Park
Jewish Cem.
LONSDALE AV.
North Thames Gas Board
Generating Sta.
CANNING TOWN
39
Canning Town Recreation Grd.
NEWHAM WAY
A13
King George V Park
Albert Dock Hosp.
Sports Pavilion
Playing Fields
E.14
East India Dock
CUSTOM HOUSE
Seamen's Inst.
VICTORIA DOCK ROAD
ROYAL ALBERT DOCK SPINE RD.
E 16
Proposed D.
ROYAL VICTORIA DOCK
ROYAL
40
RIVER
Blackwall Point
BLACKWALL TUNNEL
London City Airport Pier
Pontoon Dock
Charles Street Trading Est.
CONNAUGHT CROSSING
Terminal Building
NORTH WOOLWICH ROAD
SILVERTOWN
South Eastern Gas Board
India & Millwall Dock Entrance
68
CG
CH
CJ
CK
S.E.10
South Eastern Gas
Hookness
Causeway

58
LITTLE ILFORD PARK
LOXFORD PARK
BARKING PARK
Barking Abbey Comp Sch.
Barking Abbey Comp Sch. (Annexe)
Boating Lakes
DISTRICT LINE
BARKING
UPNEY
Town Hall
Eastbury Comp Sch.
Maty. Hosp.
Barking Hosp.
Barking Road Rec.Grd.
Langdon Comp. Schs.
Recreation Ground
Sewage Works
GREAT FIELDS PARK
Gooseleys Playing Fields
BARKING BY PASS
ALFRED'S WAY
NEWHAM WAY
A13
A406
A124
A123
A117
Cemetery
Eastbury Level
Storage Channel
Creekmouth
Dagenham
Main Drainage Metropolis North Outfall Wks.
Main Drainage Metropolis (Northern Outfall)
Northern Outfall Sewer
London Industrial Park
BECKTON
New Beckton
NEW BECKTON PARK
North Thames Gas Board (Beckton Works)
Beckton Pier (No. 1)
Beckton Pier (No. 2)
Margaret or Tripcock Ness
Lighthouse
RIVER
GALLIONS REACH
PROPOSED EAST LONDON RIVER CROSSING
Gallions Park
SE 28
Thamesmere
Birchmere
ALBERT DOCK
KING GEORGE V. DOCK
LONDON CITY AIRPORT
NORTH WOOLWICH
Woolwich Pier
Greenwich
H.M. Prison
Barking or False Point
Tidal Barrier
Barking Creek Mouth
CK
CL
CM
CN
49
59
68
36
37
38
39
40

PARSLOES PARK
DAGENHAM
DAGENHAM HEATHWAY
BECONTREE
UPNEY
DISTRICT LINE
Mayesbrook Park
Boating Lakes
Barking Hosp.
Castle Green
Goresbrook Park
Ripple Road
A13
Container Depot
Ripple Level
Eastbury Level
Dagenham Marshes
DAGENHAM DOCK
Ford Motor Company
Creekmouth
Barking Power Station
Horse Shoe Corner
River Thames
Barking Reach
Halfway Reach
Cross Ness Lighthouse
Crossway Lake
Thamesmere
Southern Outfall Main Drainage Wks (G.L.C.)
Thames Water Authority
Crossway Park
Southmere Lake
Southmere Park
Birchmere Park
Erith Marshes
Thamesmead
Eastern Way
A2016
IG11
RM9
SE28
DA18
50
58
69

CR
CS
CT
CU
50
36
37
38
39
40
60
69
Sports Grd.
Stockdale Farm
E.R.
Football Ground
Pondfield Park
Pol. Sta.
DAGENHAM EAST
A1112
RM10
RM12
RM13
DA17
Bretons
Essex Water Company Pumping Sta.
Dagenham Beam Br.
Newtons Corner
Teresa Greene Occupational Centre
Dagenham Hospital
Swimming Pool
Clinic
THE LEYS
B178
A125
A13
B1335
RAINHAM ROAD
SOUTH DAGENHAM RD.
NEW ROAD
Brittons Playing Flds.
South Hornchurch
Community Cen. & Lib.
1 THAXTED WK.
2 NAZEING WK.
3 KELVEDON WK.
4 ABBERTON WK.
5 WRITTLE WK.
Gravel Pits
Ingrebourne R.
H a v e r i n g
Ford Motor Company
Car Works
Beam Bri.
Beam River
Level Crossing
Mudland Farm
Dovers Corner
Red Br.
Clock Tower
Rainham Rec. Gd
Sewage Works
HORNCHURCH MARSHES
RAINHAM
RAINHAM CREEK
Chemical Wks.
Rainham Rifle Ranges
Target No 1
Target No 2
Target No 3
Target No 4
Target No 5
Target No 6
RAINHAM MARSHES
Hornchurch Shoot
Jetty
Pier
Rainham Caves
Old Man's Head
Piers
Frog Island
Murex Works
Jenningtree Point
Belvedere Generating Station
RIVER
Chandlers Corner
Chafford Sports Centre
1 BAILLIE CLO.
2 REDBURY CLO.
3 CRAMMERVILLE WK.
4 MAGNUM CLO.
5 NORWAY WK.
South Hall
East Hall
WENNINGTON MAR
Sch.

St Georges Hospital
Hacton
Park Corner Farm
Corbets Tey
Parklands
Harwood Hall (Equestrian Cen.)
RM12
Gravel Pits
Rainham Lo.
Central Farm
G.L.C. Rubbish Tip
Gerpins
Damyns Hall
Abbey Wood
Berwick Pond
Berwickpond Farm
Berwick Ho.
Ingrebourne R.
White Post Corner
Warwick Woods
White Post Wood
Jewish Cemetery
Spring Farm Park
Spring Cottages
Chandlers Corner
RAINHAM
1 FAGUS AV.
2 ELDER WAY
3 BETULA WK.
4 ACER AV.
Launder's Barn
Bretts
Kenningtons
RM13
Chafford Sports Centre
South Hall
East Hall
Moor Hall
Wennington Hall
The Willows
Fire Sta.
Wennington
MARSHES
Hospital Shaw
Ponds Farm
WENNINGTON MARSHES
RM16
Target No5
Target No4
Sports Ground
Sports Gnd.
Tech. Coll.
Purfleet

North Ockendon
South Ockendon
South Ockendon Hospital
AVELEY ESTATE
Aveley
North Stifford
BELHUS PARK
RM14
RM15
RM16
M25
OCKENDON ROAD B1421
NORTH ROAD B186
WEST ROAD
STIFFORD ROAD B1335
WEST THURROCK A1306
Stubbers Outdoor Pursuits Centre
Brickkiln Wood
Whitehall Wood
Oak Wood
Hangmans Wood
Low Well Wood
Millard's Garden
Coombe Wood
Buckles Farm
Little Mollands Farm
Hill Farm
Ford Place
Groves Farm
Baldwins
Kemps
Freeman's Shaw
Cockhide
Nightingales Nest
Manor Farm
Middle Wd
Bonus Wood
Cranham Place
Whitepost Farm
The Orchard
The Wilderness
The Mount (Tumulus)
South Ockendon Hall
Little Palmer's Shaw
Great Palmer's Shaw
Middle Farm
Stifford Motel
Coppid Hall
Davy Down
Ardale Sch. (Approved Sch.)
Chalk Farm
CY
CZ
DA
DB
DC
36
37
38
39
40
51
70
30

Bray
Bray Wick
Dorney Reach
Dorney
Lake End
Fifield
Forest Green
Oakley Green
Water Oakley
Windsor
Bracknell
South Bucks
SL6
M4
A 308
B 3024
A 330
WINDSOR ROAD
FOREST GREEN
OAKLEY GREEN ROAD
DRIFT ROAD
FIFIELD ROAD
FIFIELD LANE
MONKEY ISLAND LANE
OLD MILL LANE
COURT LANE
LAKE END ROAD
ASCOT ROAD
UPPER BRAY ROAD
HOLYPORT ROAD
GAYS LANE
PRIMROSE LANE
TARBAY LANE
DEDWORTH
RIVER
Gravel Pit
Bray Marina
Queen's Eyot
Monkey Island
The Guild House
Bray International Film Centre
Oakley Court Hotel
Windsor Marina
Bullocks Hatch Bridge
WINDSOR FOREST
Holliday's Plain
Nobbscrook
FOLIEJON PARK
Jesus Hospital
Cannon Hill
Amerden House
Barge Farm
West Town Farm
Dorney Court
Stroud Farm
Coningsby Farm
Ledger Farm
Banham's Farm
Haws Hill Farm
Wakers Farm
New Lodge Farm
Foliejon Park Farm
Nobbscrook Farm
All Saints Church
Bray Wood
Mount Scipett Copse
The Rising Sun (P.H.)
Queen's Head (P.H.)
The Retreat Farm
Caravan Park
Football Ground
Cricket Ground
Forest Farm
Oakley Green Farm
Kimbers Farm
Tarbay Fm
Windsor Hill
Fish Pond

Cippenham
Village Green
Recreation Ground
BATH ROAD
A4
SALT HILL PLAYING FIELDS
Indoor Tennis Cent.
Town Hall
Slough Dist. Co.
Ice Arena
Fire Sta.
Montem Sports Cen.
Hindu Temple
CHALVEY
Recreatn Grd
SL1
M4
Moat
Superstore
Filter Beds
Sewage Works
THE WHEATBUTTS
Beaconsfield Dist. Council
Cricket Grd
Play. Fld.
WELLINGTON ST.
HIGH ST.
WINDSOR RD.
RAGSTONE ROAD
Eton Common Farm
Eton Little Common
Sewage Farm
Manor Farm
Bell Farm
Saddocks Fm
New Town
B3026
ETON WICK ROAD
NORTH FIELD
A332
Tennis Cts.
AGARS PLOUGH (Playing Fields)
Golf Course
Eton Great Common
Crown Fm.
Eton Wick
Memorial Gdns.
Depot
Swimming Pool
Colenorton Brook
Fifteen Arch Br.
SLOUGH ROAD
POCOCKS LANE
Playing Fields
SOUTH FIELD
Boveney Br.
Boveney Court Fm.
Boveney Lock
Weir
RACE COURSE
WINDSOR
Boveney Court
Boat Ho.
Grand Stand
Long Bridge
Mill Stream
A355
ETON
Eton College
Romney Lock
PUBLIC RECREATION GROUND
62
Playing Fd
Recreatn Grd
South Meadow
The Brocas
Bird Sanctuary
Elizabeth Bridge
Pedestrian Underpass
Clewer Park Allotments
Clewer
SL4
Leisure Pool
Windsor Town Bridge
Romney Weir
B470
KING EDWARD VII AV.
WINDSOR & ETON RIVERSIDE
MAIDENHEAD ROAD
Playing Field
WINDSOR & ETON CENTRAL
Madame Tussauds
Castle
East Lawn
Riding Sch.
Royal Mews
WINDSOR
Dedworth Manor
Recreation Ground
Play Field
Schs.
Dedworth
CLARENCE RD.
PEASCOD ST.
GOSLAR WAY
Sports Grd.
York House
44
Cricket Grd
Frogmore Cottage
Frogmore
MAUSOLEUMS
DEDWORTH ROAD
B3024
Clewer New Town
Clewer Manor (Sch.)
Playing Field
Combermere Barracks
King Edward VII Hosp.
ALMA RD.
OSBORNE ROAD
LONG WALK
Clewer Green
ST. LEONARDS ROAD
Windsor Cemetery
Football Grd.
Royal Free School
Playing Field
Allots
Kingsmead
Hog Common
Garrison Sports Ground
45
ALBERT ROAD
A308
Shaw Farm
Lake
St. Leonardshill
Queen Mary's Plantation
Ash Plantation
B3022
A332
KING'S RD.
SHEET ST. RD.
SAFARI PARK
Fish Pond
Diningroom Close
Spital Meadow
Cover
Paddockhill Copse
New Cover
Entrance to Park
Clayhall Farm
HOLLY DRIVE
AL
AM
AN
AO
41
42
43

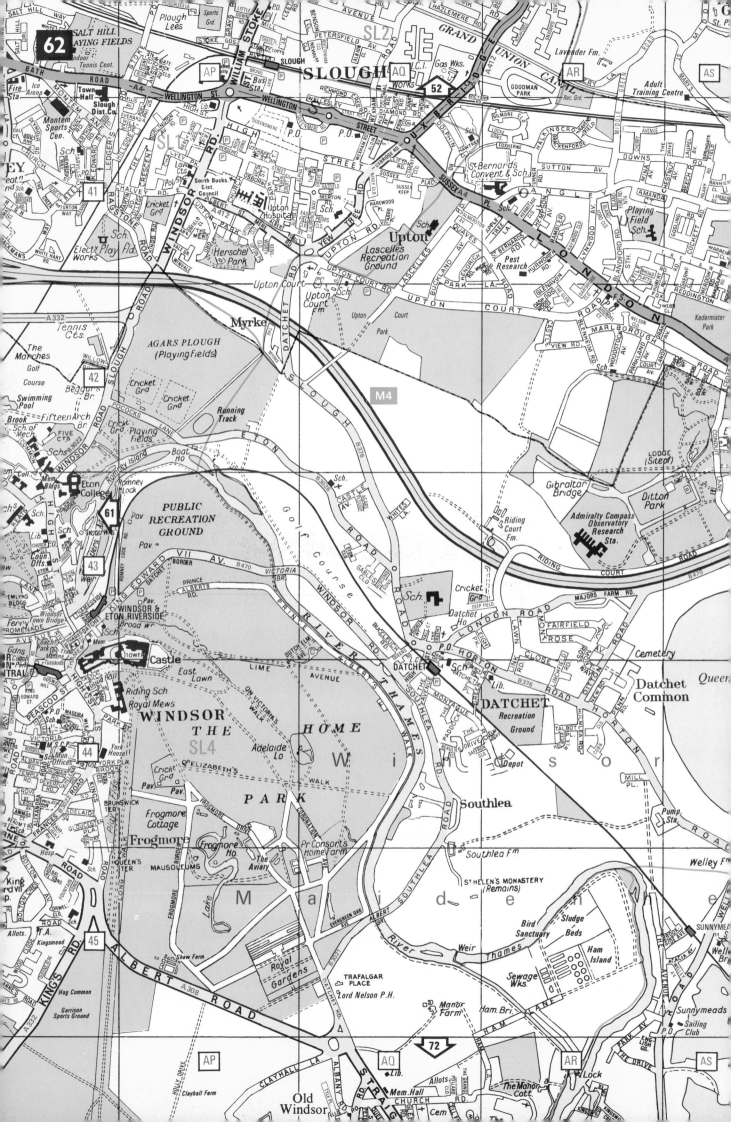

SLOUGH
SL1
SL2
SL4
M4
Salt Hill Playing Fields
Bath Road
Wellington St.
High St.
William St.
Stoke Gds.
Town Hall
Slough Dist. Co.
Montem Sports Cen.
Montem Lane
Ledgers Rd.
Chalvey
Ragstone Road
Windsor Rd.
Herschel Park
Upton Hospital
Upton
Upton Court
Upton Court Fm
Upton Park
Lascelles Recreation Ground
Upton Court Rd.
Sussex Pl.
London Road
Uxbridge Rd.
Grand Union Canal
Gas Wks.
Goodman Park
Lavender Fm.
Adult Training Centre
St. Bernards Convent & Sch.
Pest Research
Langley
Playing Field
Kedermister Park
Myrke
Datchet Rd.
Agars Plough (Playing Fields)
Running Track
Slough Road
Eton Road
Pococks Lane
Tennis Cts.
The Marches
Golf Course
Swimming Pool
Brook
Fifteen Arch Br.
Five Cts.
Eton College
Romney Island
Romney Lock
Boat Ho
Public Recreation Ground
King Edward VII Av.
Victoria Br.
Prince Alberts Rd.
Windsor & Eton Riverside
Windsor Town Bridge
Castle
East Lawn
Lime Avenue
Riding Sch.
Royal Mews
WINDSOR
THE HOME PARK
Windsor
Adelaide Lo
Queen Elizabeth's Walk
Frogmore Cottage
Frogmore
Frogmore Ho.
Mausoleums
Pr. Consort's Home Farm
The Aviary
Lake
Royal Gardens
Shaw Farm
Trafalgar Place
Lord Nelson P.H.
Albert Road
Kings Rd.
Hog Common
Garrison Sports Ground
Kingsmead
Old Windsor
Clayhall Farm
Clayhall La.
Straight Rd.
Church Rd.
Mem. Hall
Golf Course
Castle Av.
Whites La.
River Thames
Datchet
Datchet Ho
London Road
Horton Road
Datchet Recreation Ground
Datchet Common
Cemetery
Depot
Southlea
Southlea Road
Southlea Fm
St. Helen's Monastery (Remains)
Maidenhead
Bird Sanctuary
Sludge Beds
Ham Island
Sewage Wks.
Weir
Ham Bri.
Ham Lane
Manor Farm
The Manor Cott.
Lock
Sunnymeads
Sailing Club
Welley Fm
Pump. Sta.
Mill Pl.
Riding Court Fm.
Riding Court Road
Majors Farm Rd.
Gibraltar Bridge
Admiralty Compass Observatory Research Sta.
Ditton Park
Lodge (Site of)
Conduit Lane
Fairfield Av.
Montrose
AP
AQ
AR
AS
41
42
43
44
45
52
61
72

62
GRAND UNION CANAL
Langley College
Langley Hall
LANGLEY
Richings Park
Withy Bridge
Home Farm
Site of St LEONARD'S CHAPEL
Old Slade Farm
Sutton Court Farm
Oak Plantation
INDUSTRIAL ESTATE
Rec. Ground
M4
M25
Sewage Wks.
Thorney Ho.
Thorney Farm
Brand's Hill
Colnbrook
Recreation Grnd.
Hostel
Mildridge Farm
Sailing Centre
Reservoir
A4 COLNBROOK BY-PASS
(LONDON ROAD)
Cavenham Ho.
Tanhouse Fm
Colnbrook Bridge
Colne Brook
Poyle
Poyle Lodge
Poyle Mills
POYLE INDUSTRIAL AREA
BRITANNIA IND. EST.
Manor Fm
Poyle Farm
TRADING ESTATE
Golf Driving Range
Wraysbury River
Horton
Horton Lodge
Ashgood Farm
Berkin Manor
Gardners Country Home
Kennels
Horton Manor
Weir
Manor Farm
Stanwellmoor
Moor Stud Farm
Playing Grd
Gravel Wks.
Moor Bridge
Mad Bri.
Wraysbury Reservoir
AIRPORT A3113
William IV
Hotel
SL3
SL0
TW19
UB7
AS
AT
AU
AV
41
42
43
44
45
52
63
72

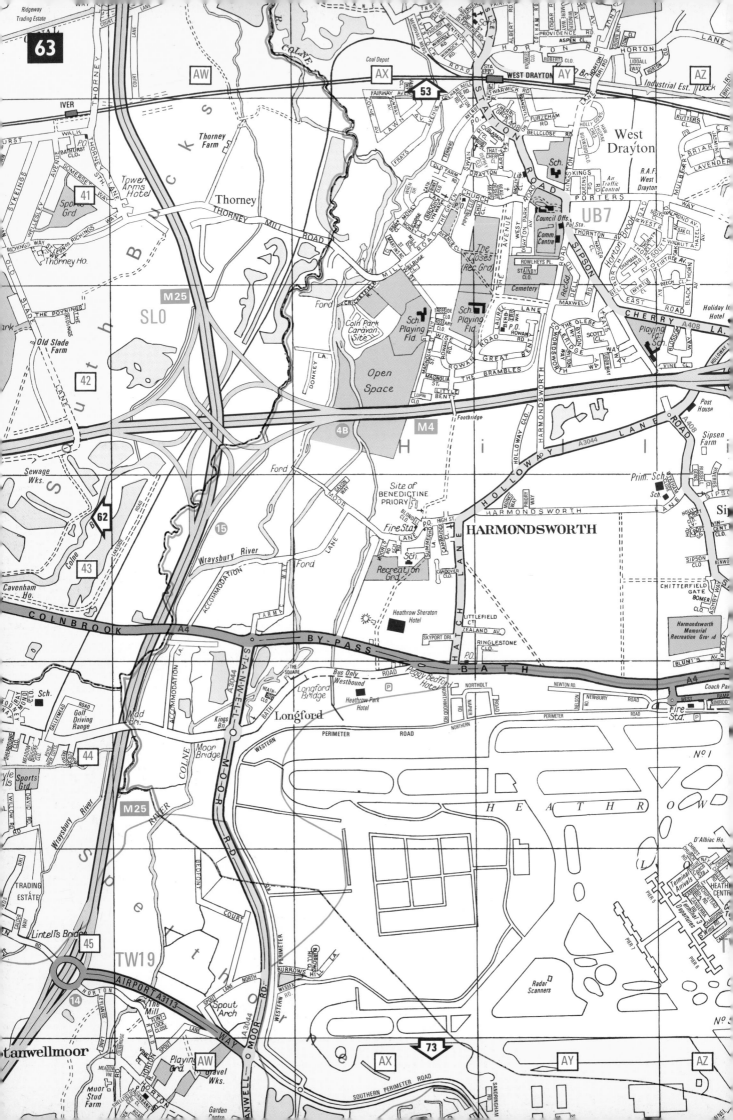

Ridgeway Trading Estate
AW
AX
AY
AZ
53
73
62
41
42
43
44
45
IVER
Coal Depot
WEST DRAYTON
Industrial Est.
West Drayton
R.A.F. West Drayton
Air Traffic Control
UB7
SL0
TW19
Thorney Farm
Thorney
Tower Arms Hotel
Thorney Ho.
THORNEY MILL ROAD
M25
M4
Old Slade Farm
Colne Park Caravan Site
Open Space
Sch. Playing Fld.
The Closes (Rec. Grd.)
Council Offs.
Comm. Centre
Pol. Sta.
Cemetery
Rec. Gd.
Horton Brook
Holiday Inn Hotel
CHERRY LA.
Post House
Sipsen Farm
Sewage Wks.
Cavenham Ho.
Colne
Ford
Site of BENEDICTINE PRIORY
Fire Sta.
HARMONDSWORTH
HOLLOWAY LANE
Recreation Grd.
Heathrow Sheraton Hotel
Harmondsworth Memorial Recreation Ground
Wraysbury River
ACCOMMODATION LANE
COLNBROOK BY-PASS
BATH ROAD
Longford
Longford Bridge
Heathrow Park Hotel
Peggy Bedford Hotel
Bus Only Westbound
PERIMETER ROAD
NORTHERN PERIMETER ROAD
WESTERN PERIMETER ROAD
SOUTHERN PERIMETER ROAD
Golf Driving Range
Mad Bri.
Kings Bri.
Moor Bridge
STANWELL MOOR RD.
Sports Grd.
TRADING ESTATE
Lintell's Bridge
HEATHROW
Radar Scanners
Terminal 1
Terminal 2
Terminal 3
D'Albiac Ho.
AIRPORT WAY A3113
Spout Arch
The Mill
Stanwellmoor
Playing Grd.
Gravel Wks.
Moor Stud Farm
Garden Centre
Spelthorne
South Bucks
Hillingdon

Business Park
GRAND UNION CANAL
Starwealt Br.
Dawley
Abenglen Ind.Est.
Adler Ind.Est.
Bournes Bri.
UB3
STATION HAYES & HARLINGTON
Botwell Green
Swimming Pool
Provident Ind.Est.
Minet Sch.
R.C.Sch.
SPRINGFIELD RD.
BEACONSFIELD RD.
HAYES BYPASS
UB2
Bulls Bridge
Sports Grd.
Playing Fld.
Pinkwell Park
Pinkwell Sch.
Sports Centre
Evening Inst.
Recreation Gd.
Cemetery
SHEPISTON LANE
MILLINGTON RD. INDUSTRIAL ESTATE
Cranford Park Sch.
Western International Market
Harlequin Centre
Site of MANOR HOUSE CRANFORD-LE-MOTE
Tennis Centre
M4
Subway
Little Harlington Field
Sports Ground
La. Meadows
Harlington
CRANFORD PARK
AVENUE PARK
R. Crane
THE PARKWAY
Heston Service Area
TW5
Redwood Est.
West End
Sipson House
Sipson Green
Excelsior Hotel
Skyway Hotel
Sheraton Skyline Hotel
Ariel Hotel
Heathrow Penta Hotel
Cranford Bri.
Berkeley Meads
Cranford
BATH ROAD
NORTHERN PERIMETER ROAD
RUNWAY
AIRPORT
Hangars
Queens Building
No2 RUNWAY
Speedbird Ho.
Comet Ho.
Allotments
Cranford Sch.
British Airways Training Sch.
PICCADILLY LINE
GT. SOUTH WEST RD.
A30
A312
A4
A437
THE CAUSEWAY
Trading Estate
Rifle Range
Beavers Sch.
TW4
Beavers Lane Camp
HATTON CROSS
Hatton Fm.
Hatton
TW14
NORTH FELTHAM TRADING EST.
Amb. Sta.
HEATHROW TERMINAL 4
Terminal 4
Babers Bri.
53
64
73
41
42
43
44
45
AZ
BA
BB
BC

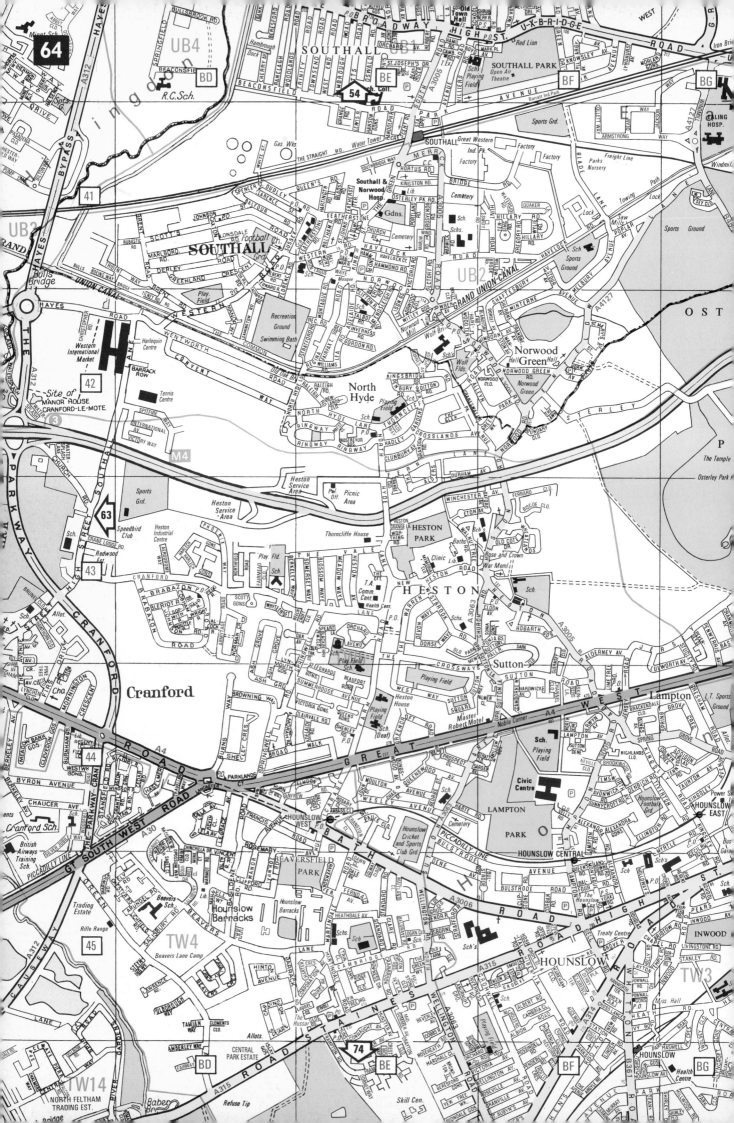

SOUTHALL
UB4
UB1
UB2
UB3
BD
BE
BF
BG
54
41
42
43
44
45
63
74
BROADWAY
HIGH ST.
UXBRIDGE ROAD
SOUTHALL PARK
Open Air Theatre
Red Lion
BEACONSFIELD RD.
R.C.Sch.
HAYES BYPASS
A312
THE STRAIGHT RD.
Gas Wks.
Water Tower
Great Western Ind. Pk.
Southall & Norwood Hosp.
Cemetery
EALING HOSP.
Freight Line
Parks Nursery
Sports Ground
GRAND UNION CANAL
UNION CANAL
Bulls Bridge
HAYES ROAD
Western International Market
Harlequin Centre
BARRACK ROW
Tennis Centre
Site of MANOR HOUSE CRANFORD-LE-MOTE
WESTERN
Recreation Ground
Swimming Bath
North Hyde
Norwood Green
Wolf Flds.
OSTERLEY LANE
The Temple
Osterley Park
M4
Heston Service Area
Picnic Area
Sports Grd.
Speedbird Club
Heston Industrial Centre
Redwood Est.
Thorncliffe House
HESTON PARK
Clinic
Rose and Crown War Meml.
HESTON
A3063
A3005
Sutton
Cranford
Lampton
L.T. Sports Ground
GREAT WEST ROAD
A4
Noble Corner
Master Robert Motel
Heston House
Civic Centre
LAMPTON PARK
Hounslow Cricket and Sports Club Grd.
HOUNSLOW WEST
HOUNSLOW CENTRAL
HOUNSLOW EAST
PICCADILLY LINE
BATH ROAD
A3006
BEAVERSFIELD PARK
Hounslow Barracks
GT SOUTH WEST ROAD
A30
Cranford Sch.
British Airways Training Sch.
Trading Estate
Rifle Range
TW4
Beavers Lane Camp
STAINES ROAD
A315
CENTRAL PARK ESTATE
Allots.
The Hussar
HOUNSLOW
Treaty Centre
INWOOD
TW3
TW14
NORTH FELTHAM TRADING EST.
Refuse Tip
Skill Cen.
Health Centre
B361
CAUSEWAY

64
EALING
HANWELL
Queen Victoria Hospital
GRAND UNION CANAL
Thames Valley University
WALPOLE PARK
Pitshanger Manor Museum
LAMMAS PARK
SOUTH EALING
NORTHFIELDS
ELTHORNE PARK
G.L.C. Playing Fields
LITTLE EALING
BOSTON MANOR
PICCADILLY LINE
M4
WYKE GREEN GOLF COURSE
BOSTON MANOR PARK
Boston Manor Ho.
GUNNERSBURY
BRENTFORD
GREAT WEST ROAD
Osterley
Spring Grove
Boro' Rd. College
SYON LANE
SYON PARK
Syon Ho.
Sites of The Battles of Brentford (A.D. 1016,1642)
RIVER THAMES
Royal Botanic Gdns
West Middlesex University Hosp.
ISLEWORTH
REDLEES PARK
OLD DEER PARK
Richmond upon Thames
Kew Observatory
Mid Surrey Golf Club
TW9
Maria Grey Training Coll.
RICHMOND
ST. MARGARET'S
National Coal Board
W. Middlesex Purification Works
TWICKENHAM ROAD
A316
A310
A4
54
65
74
41
42
43
44
45
BG
BH
BJ
BK

EALING COMMON
ACTON
ACTON PARK
ACTON CENTRAL
HIGH STREET
THE VALE
W5
W3
BL
BM
BN
BO
55
Heathfield Gdns.
Cricket Ground
Sports Ground
ACTON TOWN
South Acton
SOUTH ACTON
Bedford Park
SOUTH EALING
41
42
43
44
45
64
75
GUNNERSBURY PARK
MINIATURE GOLF COURSE
Gunnersbury Ho. (Mus)
Boating Lake
Horse Shoe Pond
Potomac Pond
Cricket and Football Ground
Kensington Cemetery
Acton Wks.
CHISWICK PARK
TURNHAM GREEN
CHISWICK COMMON
CHISWICK HIGH RD.
GUNNERSBURY
Gunnersbury
Mun. Offs.
CHISWICK
LITTLE EALING
Clayponds Hosp.
Carville Recreation
TW8
KEW BRIDGE
Living Steam Mus.
Piano Mus.
BRENTFORD
KEW BRIDGE RD.
GREAT WEST RD.
ELLESMERE ROAD
HOGARTH LA.
Hogarth Roundabout
St. Joseph's Hosp.
CHISWICK HOUSE GROUNDS
Chiswick Ho.
W.4
Grove Park
Chiswick Cemetery
Quintin Hogg Memorial Ground
Polytechnic Stadium
Duke Meadow Playing Fields
Civil Service Sports Grounds
Masonian Sports Grd.
DUKES MEADOWS
BARNES BRIDGE
Royal Botanic Gdns.
Herbarium
Kew Palace
Orangery
Aroid Ho. No.1
Seven Sisters
Rock Gdn.
Temple of Aeolus
Palm Ho.
Water Lily Ho.
Italian Gdn.
Temple of Bellona
King William's Temple
Temperate Ho.
North Gallery
Queens Cottage Grounds
Queens Cottage
King's Steps Gate
Pagoda
Lion Gate
Victoria Gate
Mount Pleasant
Site of Merlin's Cave
Isleworth Ferry Gate
Waterlily Pond
RIVER THAMES
Old England
Sites of The Battles of Brentford (A.D. 1016,1642)
KEW
KEW GARDENS
Redcliffe Training Coll.
Claims and Record Offices
Kew Pier
STRAND ON THE GREEN
Oliver's Ait
Pumping Ho.
Sewage Works
Mortlake Cremat.
Hammersmith Cemetery
North Sheen Cemetery (Fulham)
TW9
North Sheen
N. Sheen Rec. Grd.
Richmond
GOLF COURSE
Mid Surrey Golf Club
Richmond A.A. Ground
Richmond Sports Ground
Royal Hosp.
Richmond Swimming Baths
Recreation Ground
LOWER RICHMOND ROAD
MORTLAKE
Mortlake
Watneys Brewery
Mortlake Cemetery
Barnes Hosp.
SHEEN LANE
UPPER RICHMOND ROAD
NORTH SHEEN
EAST SHEEN
S.W.14
RICHMOND
Richmond Green
Black Horse
Pesthouse Common
East Sheen Cemetery
EAST SHEEN COMMON
Palewell Common

BO
BP
BQ
BR
55
SHEPHERDS BUSH
W.12
M41
White City LRT Depot
HOLLAND PARK
Holland Park Sch.
Kensington
KENSINGTON OLYMPIA
Olympia
RAVENSCOURT PARK
Royal Masonic Hosp.
Qn. Charlottes Maty. Hosp.
STAMFORD BROOK
HAMMERSMITH
Town Hall
GOLDHAWK ROAD
BROOK GREEN
KING STREET
GREAT WEST RD.
TALGARTH ROAD
WEST CROMWELL ROAD
WEST KENSINGTON
BARONS COURT
Hammersmith Cemetery
New Charing Cross Hosp.
Queen's Club
EARLS COURT
Earls Court Exhib. Hall
WEST BROMPTON
41
42
43
44
45
66
RIVER THAMES
Chiswick Eyot
St Pauls Sch.
CASTELNAU
Harrod's Depository
Riverside Studios
W. Middlesex Water Wks.
Reservoirs
S.W.13
Lillie Rd. Recreation Ground
Fulham Cemetery
FULHAM PALACE ROAD
WALHAM GREEN
FULHAM BROADWAY
S.W.6
EEL BROOK COMMON
PARSONS GREEN
FULHAM
KING'S ROAD
BARN ELMS PARK
Beverley Brook
BISHOPS PARK
Fulham Palace
Fulham Football Ground
HURLINGHAM PARK
Hurlingham Club Grds.
BARNES COMMON
BARNES
PUTNEY BRIDGE
Putney Cemetery
PUTNEY
Putney Hosp.
WANDSWORTH PARK
UPPER RICHMOND ROAD
S.W.15
75
EAST PUTNEY
ROEHAMPTON GOLF COURSE
A4
A205
A219
A306
A3220
S.W.18

BS
BT
BU
BV
56
Kensington Gardens
Round Pond
Kensington Palace
THE LONGWATER
THE SERPENTINE
PARK
ROTTEN ROW
HYDE PARK CORNER
KNIGHTSBRIDGE
HOLLAND PARK
KENSINGTON GORE
Roy. Albert Hall
Roy. Geog. Soc.
Imperial Coll.
Science Mus.
Nat. History Mus.
Geolog. Mus.
Victoria and Albert Mus.
The Oratory
BROMPTON
BELGRAVIA
HIGH ST. KENSINGTON
KENSINGTON
41
42
43
44
45
65
76
KENSINGTON OLYMPIA
WEST KENSINGTON
CROMWELL ROAD
GLOUCESTER ROAD
SOUTH KENSINGTON
EARLS COURT
Earls Court Exhib. Hall
WEST BROMPTON
Brompton Cemetery
Chelsea
SLOANE SQ.
Royal Marsden Hosp.
Brompton Hosp.
St. Stephens Hosp.
CHELSEA
Royal Hosp.
Burtons Court
Botanic Gdns.
CHELSEA EMBANKMENT
CHELSEA BRIDGE
RIVER
Peace Pagoda
BATTERSEA PARK
ALBERT BRIDGE
BATTERSEA BRIDGE
WALHAM GREEN
FULHAM BROADWAY
King's College
EEL BROOK COMMON
PARSONS GREEN
FULHAM
HURLINGHAM PARK
Hurlingham Club Grds.
SOUTH PARK
Chelsea Harbour
Chelsea College of Art & Design
Shell & Lensbury Terminal
Heliport
BATTERSEA
CLAPHAM JUNCTION
LAVENDER HILL
Town Hall
CLAPHAM COMMON NORTH SIDE
WANDSWORTH PARK
WANDSWORTH TOWN
WANDSWORTH BRIDGE
Enterprise Centre
St. John's Hosp.
St. Mary's Cemetery
SPENCER PARK
Bolingbroke Gro Hosp.
Mun. Bldgs. Town Hall
RICHMOND ROAD
BATTERSEA RISE

66
BV
BW
BX
BY
56
GREEN PARK
ST JAMES'S PARK
Buckingham Palace
WESTMINSTER
Houses of Parliament
Westminster Abbey
St. Thomas Hosp.
Lambeth Palace
ARCHBISHOP'S PARK
WATERLOO
South Bank
Old County Hall
Royal Festival Hall
CHARING CROSS
EMBANKMENT
BOROUGH
ELEPHANT & CASTLE
NEWINGTON
41
42
WALWORTH
LAMBETH
PIMLICO
Tate Gallery
VICTORIA
VAUXHALL
THAMES
KENNINGTON
KENNINGTON PARK
The Oval
OVAL
67
43
Battersea Power Station (disused)
New Covent Garden Mkt.
VAUXHALL PARK
SOUTH LAMBETH
STOCKWELL
44
MYATT'S FIELDS
LOUGHBOROUGH JUNCTION
King's Coll. Hosp.
CAMBERWELL
WANDSWORTH ROAD
CLAPHAM
CLAPHAM NORTH
CLAPHAM COMMON
South Western Hosp.
BRIXTON
Lambeth Town Hall
45
76
CLAPHAM PARK
QUEENS TOWN RD BATTERSEA

SOUTHWARK
LONDON BRI.
LONDON BRIDGE
Guy's Hosp.
57
BZ
CA
CB
CC
WAPPING
THE POOL
ROTHERHITHE TUNNEL
BERMONDSEY
JAMAICA ROAD
NEWINGTON
ELEPHANT & CASTLE
South Bank University
Coll. of Printing
Lambeth Hosp.
BOROUGH
41
42
43
44
45
66
77
WALWORTH
KENNINGTON
BURGESS PARK
SOUTHWARK PARK
South Eastern Gas Board
CAMBERWELL
PECKHAM
QUEENS ROAD PECKHAM
MYATT'S FIELDS
Maudsley Hosp.
DENMARK HILL
King's Coll. Hosp.
LOUGHBOROUGH JUNCTION
RUSKIN PARK
William Booth Meml. Traing Coll.
PECKHAM RYE
PECKHAM RYE COMMON
PECKHAM RYE PARK
NUNHEAD
EAST DULWICH
Dulwich Hosp.
S. London Art Gally.
Town Hall
St. Giles Hosp.
Camberwell Reception Cent.
SOUTH BERMONDSEY
Alleyn's Sch.
William Penn Sch.
Sports Ground

WEST INDIA
CANARY WHARF
Billingsgate Mkt.
DOCKS
Tower
Hamlets
E.14
57
Blackwall Basin
BLACKWALL TUNNEL
South Eastern Gas Board
West India & Millwall Dock Entrance
SOUTH QUAY
Council Offs.
L.D.D.C.
Millwall Inner Dock
London Arena
MILLWALL
Daily Telegraph
Millwall Outer Dock
ISLE OF DOGS
Cubitt Town
Mudchute Farm
MUDCHUTE
Millwall Recreation Ground
ISLAND GARDENS
Island Gdns.
A102(M)
41
42
LIMEHOUSE REACH
Nature Park
Daily Mail
S.E.16
REDRIFF ROAD
Greenland Dock
Sports Cent.
Greenland Pier
SURREY QUAYS
St. George's Stairs
DEPTFORD PARK
Running Track
Day Centre
Landing Stage
Supply Reserve Depot
Causeway
S.E.8
DEPTFORD
Electric Power Station
Royal Naval College
Cutty Sark
Greenwich Pier
GREENWICH FOOTWAY TUNNEL
National Maritime Museum
GREENWICH
68
43
Flamstead Ho. Mus.
GREENWICH PARK
Magnetic Observatory
Vanbrugh Cas.
The Wilderness (Deer Park)
MAZE HILL
CREEK RD.
GREEK BRI. ROAD
ROMNEY ROAD
TRAFALGAR RD.
EVELYN STREET
Millwall F.C. Grd.
NEW CROSS
NEW CROSS GATE
Town Hall
Goldsmith's Coll.
Fordham Pk.
Bus Depot
GREENWICH HIGH RD.
Town Hall
BLACKHEATH RD.
BLACKHEATH HILL
SHOOTERS HILL RD.
BLACKHEATH
44
S.E.3
Blackheath Gate
Folly Pond
ST. JOHN'S
S.E. London Tech. Coll.
LOAMPIT HILL
LOAMPIT VALE
LEWISHAM
Telegraph Hill
B2142
BROCKLEY
S.E.4
Cricket Grd.
HILLY FIELDS
Recreation Ground
Ladywell Cemetery
Brockley Cemetery
LEWISHAM
S.E.13
LEWISHAM HIGH ST.
LEE HIGH ROAD
A20
B220
St. Joseph's Academy
Playing Field
45
LEE
Manor House Gdns.
The Swan
77
LADYWELL
Ladywell
CROFTON PK.
CC
CD
CE
CF

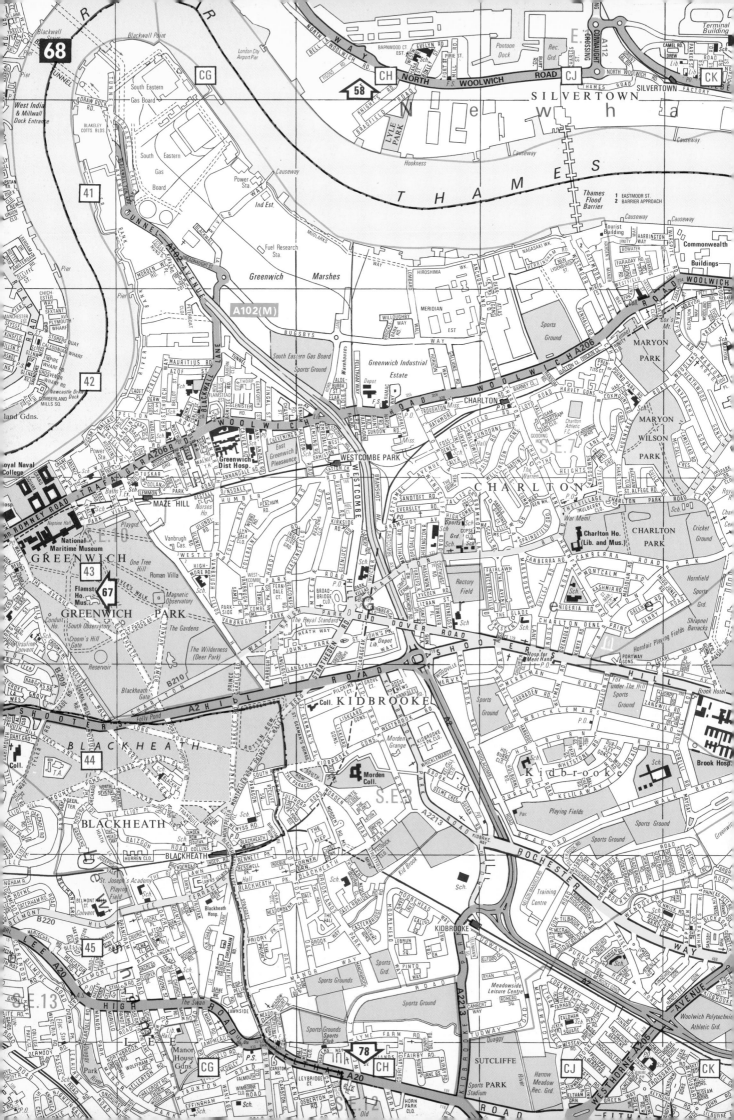
68
CG
CH
CJ
CK
58
41
42
43
44
45
67
78
Blackwall Point
South Eastern Gas Board
West India & Millwall Dock Entrance
London City Airport Pier
NORTH WOOLWICH ROAD
SILVERTOWN
CONNAUGHT CROSSING
A112
Terminal Building
Pontoon Dock
Rec. Grd.
LYLE PARK
Newham
Hookness
Causeway
THAMES
Thames Flood Barrier
1 EASTMOOR ST.
2 BARRIER APPROACH
Tourist Building
Commonwealth Buildings
Power Sta.
Ind Est.
Fuel Research Sta.
Greenwich Marshes
A102(M)
BLACKWALL TUNNEL AVENUE
BUGSBYS WAY
South Eastern Gas Board Sports Ground
Greenwich Industrial Estate
MERIDIAN EST
Sports Ground
WOOLWICH ROAD
A206
MARYON PARK
MARYON WILSON PARK
CHARLTON
S.E.7
Charlton Athletic F.C.
WESTCOMBE PARK
East Greenwich Pleasaunce
Greenwich Dist Hosp.
Royal Naval College
ROMNEY ROAD
TRAFALGAR ROAD
A206
MAZE HILL
National Maritime Museum
GREENWICH
S.E.10
Vanbrugh Cas.
One Tree Hill
Roman Villa
Magnetic Observatory
GREENWICH PARK
The Gardens
The Wilderness (Deer Park)
Flamsteed Ho. Mus.
South Observatory
Croom's Hill Gate
Reservoir
Blackheath Gate
Charlton Ho. (Lib. and Mus.)
CHARLTON PARK
Cricket Ground
War Meml.
Rectory Field
Hornfield Sports Grd.
Shrapnel Barracks
Hornfair Playing Fields
The Royal Standard
DOVER ROAD
SHOOTERS HILL
A2
Hosp. for Ment Hand.
Fox under The Hill Sports Ground
Brook Hotel
Brook Hosp.
KIDBROOKE
Coll.
Morden Grange
Morden Coll.
S.E.3
Kidbrooke
Playing Fields
Sports Ground
A2213
ROCHESTER WAY
Training Centre
KIDBROOKE
Sch.
BLACKHEATH
Folly Pond
SHOOTERS HILL ROAD
A2
BLACKHEATH
B210
B209
T.A.
St. Joseph's Academy Playing Field
Blackheath Hosp.
Convent
B220
LEE HIGH ROAD
A20
S.E.13
The Swan
LEE
Manor House Gdns.
Park
River
ELTHAM ROAD
A20
S.E.12
Sports Grounds
Sports Club
Sports Grd.
Meadowside Leisure Centre
Quaggy
SUTCLIFFE PARK
Sports Park Stadium
Harrow Meadow Rec. Grd.
River
KIDBROOKE PARK ROAD
A2213
WESTHORNE AVENUE
A205
Woolwich Polytechnic Athletic Grd.
Greenwich

68
CITY AIRPORT
GEORGE V. DOCK
CK
CL
CM
CN
58
NORTH WOOLWICH
Royal Victoria Gdns.
Woolwich Pier
Gallions Park
PROPOSED EAST LONDON RIVER CROSSING
EASTERN WAY
A2016
WESTERN WAY
S.E.28
H.M. Prison Bellmarsh
BROADWATERS ESTATE
WOOLWICH INDUSTRIAL ESTATE
Birchmere
Abbey
41
WOOLWICH HIGH ST.
WOOLWICH DOCKYARD
PLUMSTEAD ROAD
A206
WOOLWICH ARSENAL
WOOLWICH
S.E.18
Royal Artillery Barracks
PLUMSTEAD
PLUMSTEAD HIGH ST.
PLUMSTEAD COMMON
WINN'S COMMON
42
S.E.2
BOSTALL
Bostall Gdns.
Elizabeth Military Hosp.
Garrison Athletic Grd.
R.A.Tactical School
SHREWSBURY PARK
Shooters Hill
SHOOTER'S HILL GOLF COURSE
Woolwich Cemetery
Rockcliffe Gdns.
43
69
East Wickham
44
SHOOTER'S HILL
A207
ELTHAM COMMON
Castlewood Day Hosp
Meml. Hosp.
Severndroog Castle
Castle Wood
Jack Wood
Jackwood Ho.
OXLEAS WOOD
BELLEGROVE ROAD
WELLING
DA16
45
ROCHESTER WAY
WELLING WAY
FALCONWOOD
Falconwood Field
ELTHAM PARK
ROCHESTER WAY RELIEF ROAD
A2
Eltham Cemetery and Crematorium
ELTHAM WARREN GOLF COURSE
ELTHAM STN
78
EAST ROCHESTER WAY
DA15
A205

69
EASTERN WAY
A2016
CO
CP
CQ
CR
Southmere Lake
59
Southmere Park
Erith Marshes
DA 18
S.E.28
Birchmere
Thamesmead
Thamesmead Town Offices
Abbey Wood Estate
OPEN SPACE
H.M. Prison Bellmarsh
41
Greenwich
ABBEY WOOD
S.E.2
Recreation Ground
Lesnes Abbey (Remains)
Lesnes Park
LESNES ABBEY WOODS
Tumulus
Belvedere
42
A206
HIGH ST.
Bostall Gdns
BOSTALL HEATH
Bostall Ho.
Co-operative Woods
Caravan Site
BOSTALL HILL RD.
WOOLWICH RD.
BOSTALL WOODS
The Pines
COMMON
S.E.18
68
Clam Field Recreation Grd.
Goldie Leigh Hosp.
West Heath
Plumstead Cemetery
Woolwich Cemetery
43
East Wickham
White Horse
Stevens Park
Welling Sch. (Girls)
(Boys)
44
DA 16
WELLING
A207
45
Welling F.C.
DANSON PARK
The Mansion
The Lake
Boat Ho.
Swimming Pool
79
BEXLEYHEATH
BROADWAY
Sports Centre
Splashworld
Upton
DA 6
A2
A221

Jenningtree Point
Belvedere Power Station
RIVER
Pier
CR
CS
CT
CU
59
WENNINGTON MAR
RM 13
Havering
41
Sports Grd.
DA 17
New Hall
Great Coldharbour
Jetty
ERITH REACH
42
FRANKS PARK
Lessness Hth
ERITH
Railway Pier
Police Sta
Riverside
ERITH CEMETERY
Convent
70
43
Stadium
Recreation Grd.
DA 8
Erith Hosp.
Northumberland Heath
Sports Gd.
CRAYFORD MARSHES
Slade Green
North End
Howbury Grange (Tithe Barn)
SLADE GREEN
44
Bursted Wood
BARNEHURST
The Grange
Perry Street
Golf Course
Barnehurst
RIVER CRAY
Playing Flds.
Club Ho.
Adult Education Centre
45
DA 1
Martens Grove
Swimming Pool
Oakwood Play. Fld.
Crayside Ind. Est.
Crayford Sch.
Jolly Farmers
CRAYFORD MARSHES
79
Shenstone Park
Gas Wks.
INDUSTRIAL ESTATE
WATLING ST.
LONDON RD.
CRAYFORD
Stanham Farm
A206
A207
A220
A2000
A2016
THAMES ROAD
NORTHEND ROAD
SOUTH RD.

RM 13
WENNINGTON MARSHES
AVELEY MARSHES
Purfleet Rifle Ranges
Target No 5
Target No 4
Target No 3
Target No 2
Target No 1
LONDON ROAD
A13
ARTERIAL ROAD
Ponds Farm
PURFLEET
PRIVATE RD.
Sports Ground
Sports Gnd.
Tech. Coll.
Purfleet Ind. Park
Fanns Farm
Tele. Ex.
TANK HILL ROAD
A1090
Mar Dyke
Vehicle Test Cen.
PURFLEET
Beacon Hill
Oil Depot
Jetty
Pier
Circus Tavern
Watts
THAMES
Crayford Ness Beacon
Red House
DA 8
Sports Gd.
WALLHOUSE ROAD
Crayford Marshes
RIVER DARENT
Dartford Salt Marshes
West Kent Outfall Works
Sewage Bed
Works
Joyce Green Hospital
Lodge
Marsh Street
Littlebrook Power Station
Stone Marshes
Joyce Green Farm
Southfield Ho
Joyce Green Cem.
DA 1
Dartford Fresh Marshes
Slade Green
Council Depot
Howbury Grange (Tithe Barn)
Sports Grd.
The Grange
RIVER CRAY
Havering
Bexley
Dartford
CRAYFORD MARSHES
Stanham Farm
Rec. Grd.
Allots.
"Jolly Farmers"
A206
BURNHAM RD.
DARTFORD CREEK
VICTORIA
B.R.S. Depot
Works
TUNNEL ROAD
A282
Cotton Cottages
Toll
Mill
Sports Grd.
Play Grd.
Sch
R.C. Sch

60
69
80

70
60
71
80
CY
CZ
DA
DB
Aveley
North Stifford
Mar Dyke
Coppid Hall
Hangmans Wood
Low Well Wood
Brannett's Wood
Coombe Wood
Oak Wood
Davy Down
Sports Grd.
Rec. Gd.
Ardale Sch (Approved Sch.)
Arena Essex Motor Sports Complex
M25
Thurrock Service Area
Superstore
Lakeside Shopping Centre
Lakeside Retail Park
ARTERIAL ROAD
WEST THURROCK
Caravan Site
Causeway Bri.
Mar Dyke Farm
Tech. Coll.
A13 PURFLEET
Chafford Hundred
Outdoor Pursuits Centre
Chalk Quarries (Disused)
South Stifford
RM 16
RM 17
Askew Farm
Cement Works
Stonehouse Corner
DARTFORD TUNNEL APPROACH
West Thurrock
Tunnel Estate
Day Nursery
LONDON ROAD
Rec. Grd.
Wharf
Pier (Disused)
Piers
Pier
Power Sta.
RIV THA
Oil Storage Depot
St. Clement's or Fiddler's Reach
DARTFORD TUNNEL
QUEEN ELIZABETH II BRIDGE
Stoneness Lighthouse
Stone Ness
DA 11
Bell Wharf
Swanscombe Marsh
Sewage Works
Superstore
Pontoon
Dartford International Ferry Terminal
Jetty
Johnson's Wharf
Jetties
Pier
Greenhithe Foreshore
Paper Mills
Ingress Park
Ingress Abbey
Thames Nautical Training Coll.
Old Quarry
Cricket Gd.
Sports Gd.
DA 10
DA 9
Greenhithe
Eagle Cliff
Stone Crossing
Stone
Old Chalk Pit
Old Chalk
School Play Fld.

71
40
41
42
43
44
45
70
81
DC
DD
DE
DF
RM16
RM17
DA10
DA11
Mar Dyke
North Stifford
Coppid Hall
HIGH ROAD
Rec.Gd.
Sports Grd.
Hall
Davy Down
Ardale School (Approved Sch)
WEST THURROCK
A13
A1306
Chalk Pit Farm
Chafford Hundred
ELIZABETH RD.
HOGG LANE
A1012
Thurrock Hospital
Clinic
Rec.Grd.
FIELDWAY
School
Running Track
King George V Playing Fields
Civic Hall & Swimming Baths
Hangman's Wood
STANFORD
LODGE LANE
TENNYSON AVENUE
Allots.
School Play. Fld
Fire Sta.
Amb. Sta.
Outdoor Pursuits Centre
WARREN
Chalk Quarries (Disused)
South Stifford
Sports Grd
Askew Farm
MEESONS
PARKER ROAD
GRAYS
Thurrock
Little Thurrock
Industrial Estate
Grays New Cemetery
Playing Field
Rec. Grd.
Recreation Grd.
Tel.Ex.
Clinic
The Park Centre
Bus Depot
EASTERN WAY
ORSETT ROAD
PALMER'S AV.
A1013
A126
CLARENCE
EAST THURROCK RD.
BROADWAY
DOCK RD.
Sch. Playing Fields
Industrial Estate
Little Thurrock Marshes
DOCK APPROACH ROAD
A1089
THURROCK PARK WAY
Mission
Wharf
Pier
Pier (Disused)
Piers
Jetty
Jetties
The Beach
Boating Pool
Broadness Lighthouse
St Clement's or Fiddler's Reach
RIVER THAMES
Northfleet Hope
Gravesend Reach
Dock Extension
West Branch
Rolling Lift Bridge
Tilbury Ness
Beacon
Jetty
Lighthouse Jetty
Lighthouse
Swanscombe Marshes
Sewage Works
Botany Marshes
Bell Wharf
Cricket Gd.
Sports Gd.
Paper Mills
Old Quarry
Cement Wks.
GREEN MANOR WAY
Industrial Estate
Paper Mills
GALLEY HILL RD.
ROAD
A226
STONEBRIDGE
Sports Grd
Old Chalk Pit
SWANSCOMBE
G.P.O.

Whitecroft Fm.
Heath Place
Seaborough Hall
Grays & Orsett Golf Course
40
DF
DG
DH
DJ
DK
Walton's Hall
Brook Farm
Sutton's Farm
Orsett Heath
Ashen Shaw
Works
Linford
SS
41
Merrie Loo Farm
Terrels Heath
Highash Shaw
Muckingford
High Ho.
Beckland
Chadwell St. Mary
Mill Ho.
EAST TILBURY
42
Chadwell Place
Blue Anchor
Holford Farm
Shrove Hill Wood
CHADWELL BY-PASS
Hutts Hill
School
Manor Farm
SITE OF ST CHAD'S WELL
Hob Hill Farm
West Tilbury
Biggin
Broom Hill
Gunhill Farm
W. Tilbury Hall
Low Street
Tilbury Marshes
Hall Hill
St. James's Ch.
Sports Grd.
Gravelpit Farm
43
Hall Hill Common
Parsonage Shaw
Tilbury Marshes
Football Ground
Parsonage Common
RM18
Playing Field
Walton Common Level
West Tilbury Level
44
West Tilbury Marshes
TILBURY
Tilbury Power Sta.
45
Jetty
TILBURY RIVERSIDE
Tilbury Fort
Worlds End
Wharf
Tidal Basin
Pier
Port of London Authority
81
Gravesend Reach
DA12
GRAVESEND

72
62
82
AO
AP
AQ
AR
AS
45
46
47
48
49
50
Windsor
Maidenhead
Runnymede
SL4
TW20
River Thames
Weir
Royal Gardens
Trafalgar Place
Lord Nelson P.H.
Shaw Farm
Ham Island
Sewage Wks.
Manor Farm
Ham. Bri.
Albert Rd.
A308
B3021
Garrison Sports Grd.
Old Windsor
Clayhall La.
Clayhall Farm
Holly Drive
Straight Road
Lib.
Mem. Hall
Church Rd.
Moat
Tileplace Farm
Millers La.
Review Ground
Cem
The Avenue
Meadow Way
The Priory
The Manor Cott.
Lock
Friary Island
Manor Farm Estate
Ousley Road
Wharf Rd.
Riverside
The Embankment
Rec. Grd.
St. Peters C. of E. Sch.
Playing Field
Burfield
Crimp Hill
Kingsbury Dr.
Sch.
Walpole Rd.
Pelling Hill
Newmarket Plantation
Bear's Rails
Cemetery
King Edward VII Hospital
Woodside Farm
Rush Pond
Bear's Rails Pond
Prince of Wales Pond
The Long Walk
The Gallop
Old Windsor Wood
Withy Bed
Woodside
Beaumont
Runnymede Ho.
Sports Ground
Priest Hill
Magna Carta Island
Liddell Plantation
Old Covert
Duke of York Plantation
Wild Boar Enclosure
Sanat.
The Farm
Kennedy Memorial
St. John's R.C. School
Marchioness of Hertford Plantation
Prince Consort's Plantation
Princess Christian Plantation
Snow Hill
Spring Hill
Gore Plantation
Queen Victoria's Plantation
Cookes Hill
Windsor Great Park
Park Place
Beech Hill
The Dell
Ridgemead Road
Scaitcliffe School
Res.
Magna Carta Memorial
Coopers Hill
Cooper's Hill (National Trust)
Commonwealth Air Forces Memorial
All Saints Church
Royal Lodge
Bishops Gate Ho.
Bishopsgate Road
Roundoak
Englefield Green
Shoreditch Training College
Coopers Hill
Kingswood (Hall of Residence)
Ox Pond
Bishops Gate
Castlehill
Dell Park
Ham La.
Runnymede Park
Royal School
Cumberland Lodge
Cow Pond
Castlehill House
Crown Farm
Middle Hill
Prospect La.
Park Close
Pol. Sta.
Chapel Wood
Rhododendron Ride
Englefield Green
Wilderness
King's Lane
Towngreen Farm
St. Jude's Road
B388
Obelisk Ride
The Savill Gardens
Cemetery
Dane Hurst
Egham Hill
Royal Holloway College & Bedford New College
Smith's Lawn
Parkwood
Cork Clump
Cumberland Obelisk
Sandylands
Bagshot Rd.
Fuzzy Clump
Obelisk Pond
Harewarren Clump
Bellfields
Park Ho.
Bakeham Ho.
Prune Hill
Frank's Plantation
Egham Wick
Wick Lane
Scarletoak Plantation
The Bailiwick
Queenswood
Rusham Crossing
A30 London Road
Polo Grounds
Breakheart Hill
Weedon's Field
Windsor Great
Darkhole Clump
Heather Garden
Totem Pole
Ashleigh
Glenwood

72
62
73
82
AS
AT
AU
AV
46
47
48
49
50
Horton Manor Weir
Manor Farm
Stanwellmoor
Moor Stud Farm
Playing Grd.
Gravel Wks.
Garden Centre
Southern Farm
Sailing Club
WRAYSBURY RESERVOIR
Paper Mill
Nursery
P.O.
COPPERMILL
STATION RD.
WRAYSBURY
Wraysbury
Tithe Farm
Colne Brook
Lower Mill Farm
RIVER COLNE
Wyrardisbury River
Bone Head
KING GEORGE VI RESERVOIR
TW19
STAINES MOOR
Bonehead Ditch
Heron Lake
B376
ROAD
Hythe End
WRAYSBURY
Plant Hire Depot
Weir
Aquaduct
Thames Intake
Footbridge & Weir
Lock
Runnymede Hotel
Pleasure Ground
RIVERSIDE
A308
RUNNYMEDE
(National Trust)
Runnymede Br.
Queensmead Lake
Aqueduct
Moor Ho.
The Close
GLOUCESTER DR.
STAINES BY PASS
A30
Staines & Littleton Sports & Social Club
Staines Reservoirs Aqueduct
A3044
STANWELL NEW RD.
River Ash
Ashby Recreation Ground
Swimm Pool
Cem.
Trading Est.
Church Is.
THE MALTINGS
EGHAM BY-PASS
Water Works
CAUSEWAY
Staines Bri.
CLARENCE ST.
HIGH ST.
Elmsleigh Cen.
Bus Sta
Town Hall
LONDON RD.
Sports Ground
Strodes Coll.
Mus.
HIGH STREET
B3407
Manor Farm
Superstore
WENDOVER
Egham Hythe
Indoor Spts. Cen.
Swimm. Pool
Coun. Off.
Play. Fld.
Hythe First & Mid. Sch.
Social Cen. & Lib.
Magna Carta Sec. Sch.
STAINES
Leacroft Sch.
Staines Park
TW18
R.C. Sch.
Health Cent.
Mag. Ct.
EGHAM
Sports Centre
Thorpe Lea
Sports Field
B3376
THORPE LEA RD.
Bowling Club
M25
STROUDE ROAD
NEW WICKHAM LA.
Thorpe Lea First Sch.
Rec. Grd.
Mead Lake Ditch
A320
THORPE LEA ROAD
B388
Council Depot
COMMERCIAL
MEADWAY
Staines Town F.C.
Sweeps Bri.
Penton Hook Farm
MILTON PARK
Great Fosters
Thorpe Lea Nursery
Thorpe
CLOCKHOUSE LA.
TEMPLE GDNS.

73
Stanwellmoor
Stanwell Place
STANWELL
West Bedfont
KING GEORGE VI
RESERVOIR
STAINES
RESERVOIRS
Ashford
Hengrove
Ashford
Park
Cemetery
Shortwood Pond
Shortwood Common
STAINES
Ashford Manor
Golf
Course
QUEEN
RESERV
CARGO TERMINAL
Petroleum
Storage
Depot
Community Centre
Staines Cricket
& Hockey Club
Matthew
Arnold Sch.
Playing
Field
Penton Hook
Farm
TW 6
TW 19
TW 15
TW 18
TW 17
63
72
83
AW
AX
AY
AZ

AIRPORT
HEATHROW TERMINAL 4
Terminal 4
HATTON CROSS
Hatton
TW 14
TW 4
TW 12
TW 16
North Feltham
NORTH FELTHAM TRADING EST.
Fagg's Bridge
Crown & Sceptre
Duke of Northumberland's River
East Bedfont
Playing Field
Feltham Sports Arena
Glebelands Sports Grd.
Feltham Park Nursery
Blenheim Park
Golf Course
Clockhouse Roundabout
Royal Oak
Fairholme Prim.Sch.
Bedfont Ho.
Hounslow
FELTHAM
Grosvenor Park
Feltham Green
Bedfont Lake
Nursery
Borstal Institution
Lower Feltham
Cemetery
Sports Ground
HANWORTH PARK
Allotments
Rugby Ground
Felthamhill
Meadhurst Sports Club
Primary Filters Station
Reservoir
Filter Beds
Pumping Sta.
Reservoirs
Aqueduct
KEMPTON PARK (Race Days only)
Kempton Race Course
Grand Stand
Public Stand
Paddock
ASHFORD
Ashford Common
Reseach Centre
Sports Grd.
Water Works
SUNBURY
Superstore
GREAT SOUTH WEST RD.
STAINES RD.
STAINES ROAD WEST
STAINES ROAD EAST
ASHFORD ROAD
HOUNSLOW ROAD
HARLINGTON ROAD WEST
HARLINGTON ROAD EAST
HIGH STREET
BEDFONT ROAD
CHERTSEY ROAD
FELTHAMHILL ROAD
CASTLE WAY
A30
A315
A312
A244
A308
A316
B377
B3003
B3377
M3
63
83
46
47
48
49
50
74
AZ
BA
BB
BC

74
HOUNSLOW
BD
BE
BF
BG
64
TW 3
TW 4
TW 14
TW 13
TW 12
TW 16
CENTRAL PARK ESTATE
NORTH FELTHAM TRADING EST.
Fogg's Bridge
46
47
48
49
50
73
84
Refuse Tip
Golf
Course
HOUNSLOW HEATH
Mill Stream
Sports Ground
Skill Cen.
Heathland Comp. Sch.
The Warren Hotel
Hounslow Junction
Hounslow Cemetery
North Feltham
Feltham Park
Feltham Sports Arena
FELTHAM
Feltham Green
Whitton
WHITTON
Twickenham Cemetery
Heathfield Recreation Ground
CRANE PARK
S.W. Middlesex Cremat.
Feltham Baths
Mount Corner
HANWORTH PARK
HANWORTH TRADING EST
TWICKENHAM GOLF COURSE
FULWELL GOLF COURSE
New Hanworth
HANWORTH
Playing Field
Rectory Sch.
Hampton Sch.
Lady Eleanor Holles Sch.
Primary Filters Station
Reservoir
Pumping Sta.
Filter Beds
Aqueduct
Football Ground
Hatherop Road Playing Fields
Half Moon Covert
KEMPTON PARK
KEMPTON PARK (Race Days only)
Grand Stand
Public Stand
Race Course
Kempton Park Race Course
Spelthorne
CARLISLE PARK
HAMPTON
Hampton Cemetery
Community Centre & Sports Hall
Health Centre
STAINES ROAD
HANWORTH ROAD
UXBRIDGE ROAD
HOSPITAL BRIDGE ROAD
GREAT CHERTSEY ROAD
COUNTRY WAY
HAMPTON ROAD WEST
TWICKENHAM RD.
NELSON ROAD
HIGH STREET
A312
A314
A315
A316
A305
A311
A313
A244
B358

74
64
75
84
46
47
48
49
50
BG
BH
BJ
BK
TW 9
TW 7
TW 1
TW 2
TW 10
TW 11
KT 2
TWICKENHAM
ST. MARGARETS
RICHMOND
Richmond Hill
PETERSHAM
HAM
TEDDINGTON
STRAWBERRY HILL
HAMPTON WICK
KINGSTON
BUSHY PARK
MARBLE HILL PARK
ORLEANS PARK
RIVER THAMES
Eel Pie Island
Twickenham Rugby Union Football Ground
Royal Military School of Music (Kneller Hall)
Twickenham College
Strawberry Hill Golf Course
St. Mary's Training Coll.
Teddington Lock
Teddington Memorial Hosp.
National Physical Laboratory
Thames Television Studios
Hawker Aircraft Works
Normansfield Hosp.
Cassel Hosp.
Tiffin Girls Sch.
Star & Garter Home
Richmond College (Theological)
Old Deer Park Recreation Ground
Maria Grey Training Coll.
Petersham Meadows
Sudbrook Park Club Ho.
Thames Young Mariners Base
Ham Common

75
74
65
85
46
47
48
49
50
BL
BM
BN
BO
RICHMOND
NORTH SHEEN
EAST SHEEN
SW14
Richmond Green
Town Hall
Corporation Island
Richmond Hill
Richmond College (Theological)
Terrace Gdns.
Star & Garter Home
Richmond Gate
Petersham Meadows
PETERSHAM
German Sch.
HAM
Cassel Hosp.
Hawker Aircraft Works
HAM COMMON
Ham Gate
SUDBROOK PARK
GOLF COURSE
PETERSHAM PARK
East Sheen Cemetery
EAST SHEEN COMMON
Richmond Cemetery
Sheen Wood
Adams Pond
Roehampton Gate
PALEWELL COMMON
PALEWELL PARK
Bank of England Sports Grd.
RICHMOND PARK
Richmond upon Thames
TW10
Sidmouth Wood
Reservoir
Conduit Wood
Bog Lodge
Deer Pen
Saw Pit Plantation
Jubilee Plantation
White Lodge Plantations
White Lodge (Ballet Sch.)
Killcat Corner
Pen Ponds
Leg of Mutton Pond
Bailiff's Cott.
Whiteash Lodge
Pond Plantation
Lawn Plantation
Spankers Hill Wood
Treebox Wood
Pond Slade
Isabella Plantation
Broomfield Hill
Broomfield Hill Plantation
Robin Hood Gate
Deer Fold
High Wood
Thatchedhouse Lodge
Coronation Plantation
Ladderstile Gate
Kingston Hill
Kingston upon Thames
KT2
Kingston Gate
Kingston University
Coombe Hurst Kingston University
Kenry Ho.
COOMBE HILL GOLF COURSE
Coombe
COOMBE WOOD GOLF COURSE
Coombe Ridge Ho. Convent
Kingston Hosp.
Tiffin Girls Sch.
TW11
Teddington
Canbury Gardens
South Eastern Gas Board
KINGSTON
KT3

75
WANDSWORTH PARK
PUTNEY
S.W.15
EAST PUTNEY
UPPER RICHMOND ROAD
A205
A3209
A219
A306
A3
PUTNEY HEATH
PUTNEY HEATH
Roehampton
ROEHAMPTON LANE
ROEHAMPTON VALE A3
KINGSTON ROAD
TIBBET'S RIDE
Tibbet's Corner
WIMBLEDON PARK SIDE
PUTNEY HILL
Digby Stuart Coll.
Queen Mary's Hosp.
Manresa Ho. Jesuit Coll.
PUBLIC GOLF COURSE
Garnett College
Putney Vale
Putney Vale Cemetery
Crematorium
Royal Hosp. & Home
Whitelands Training Coll.
Wandsworth Sch.
SOUTHFIELDS
S.W.18
Recreation Ground
Wimbledon Park Lake
WIMBLEDON COMMON
Queens Mere
Windmill
Southland Coll.
Parkside Hosp.
S.W.19
All England Lawn Tennis & Croquet Club Grounds
WIMBLEDON PARK GOLF COURSE
WIMBLEDON PARK
Jubilee Clump
Stag Bog
GOLF COURSE
Hookhamslade Pond
Bluegate Gravel Pit (Disused)
Caesar's Camp
CANNIZARO PARK
ROYAL WIMBLEDON GOLF COURSE
Merton
HIGH STREET
WIMBLEDON
WIMBLEDON HILL
Town Hall
Centre Court Shopping Centre
SOUTH WIMBLEDON
Wimbledon R.C. Coll.
Atkinson Morley Hosp.
S.W.20
Cottenham Park
MERTON PARK
MERTON
KINGSTON BY-PASS
DISTRICT LINE
65
46
47
48
49
50
76
85
BO
BP
BQ
BR

76
66
46
47
48
49
50
75
86
BS
BT
BU
BV
WANDSWORTH PARK
WANDSWORTH TOWN
CLAPHAM JUNCTION
CLAPHAM COMMON NORTH SIDE
WANDSWORTH
WANDSWORTH COMMON
KING GEORGE'S PARK
EARLSFIELD
SOUTHFIELDS
WIMBLEDON PARK
SUMMERSTOWN
Wimbledon Stadium
Springfield Hosp.
Wandsworth Prison
Bolingbroke Gro. Hosp.
Qn. Elizabeth Ho.
BALHAM
TOOTING BEC
TOOTING GRAVENEY
TOOTING BROADWAY
TOOTING
St. Georges General Hosp.
Lambeth Cemetery
Wimbledon Cemetery
Streatham Cemetery
WIMBLEDON PARK GOLF COURSE
Wimbledon Park Lake
WIMBLEDON
SOUTH WIMBLEDON
Colliers Wood
MERTON PARK
MERTON
Gorringe Park
FIGGE'S MARSH
Wandsworth Sch.
Emanuel Sch.
Spencer Park
Garratt Park
Garratt Green
Nelson Gdns
Haydons Rd.

76
BV
BW
BX
BY
66
46
47
48
49
50
77
86
BRIXTON
CLAPHAM COMMON
CLAPHAM PARK
S.W.4
CLAPHAM SOUTH
BALHAM HILL
BROCKWELL PARK
Brockwell Hall
HERNE HILL
S.E.24
TULSE HILL
Roupell Park
STREATHAM HILL
STREATHAM
TOOTING BEC COMMON
STREATHAM COMMON
S.W.16
LOWER STREATHAM
STREATHAM VALE PARK
WEST NORWOOD
S.E.27
South Metropolitan Cem.& W.Norwood Crem.
Knights Hill Playing Field
NORWOOD PARK
NORBURY
NORBURY PARK
Norwood Grove Rec. Grd.
Biggin Wood
Croydon
Lambeth Town Hall
Brixton Prison
Sports Field
Dulwich Cricket and Tennis Grd.
Knights Hill Allotments
PEABODY HILL EST
St. Joseph's R.C. Coll
Convent of The Faithful Virgin
CHRISTCHURCH
POYNDER'S ROAD
STREATHAM HIGH ROAD
LONDON ROAD
A23
A205
A214
A215
A216

77
67
46
47
48
49
50
76
87
BZ
CA
CB
CC
HERNE HILL
EAST DULWICH
DULWICH
WEST DULWICH
UPPER SYDENHAM
UPPER NORWOOD
PENGE
PECKHAM RYE COMMON
PECKHAM RYE PARK
BROCKWELL PARK
DULWICH PARK
DULWICH AND SYDENHAM GOLF COURSE
SYDENHAM WELLS PARK
CRYSTAL PALACE PARK
NORWOOD PARK
Westow Park
Camberwell Cemetery
Horniman Gardens
South Metropolitan Cem.&
W. Norwood Crem.
Dulwich Coll.
Dulwich Old Coll.
Stadium
Sports Hall
National Recreation Centre
Crystal Palace
Sydenham Hill
Gipsy Hill
Tulse Hill
North Dulwich
West Dulwich
Anerley
Penge West
Town Hall
DULWICH COMMON
LORDSHIP LANE
LONDON RD.
WESTWOOD HILL
CRYSTAL PALACE PARADE
CRYSTAL PALACE PARK ROAD
THURLOW PARK ROAD
Biggin Wood
Norwood Res.
St. Joseph's R.C. Coll
St. Christopher's Hospice

CC
CD
CE
CF
77
67
46
47
48
49
50
78
87
BROCKLEY
HILLY FIELDS
Recreation Ground
LEWISHAM
LEE
S.E.4
S.E.13
S.E.6
S.E.23
Ladywell Cemetery
Brockley Cemetery
Ladywell
LADYWELL
Lewisham Hosp.
LEWISHAM PARK
Manor House Gdns.
HITHER GREEN
Hither Green
Hither Green Hosp.
CROFTON PK.
Camberwell
New
Crematorium
PUBLIC OPEN SPACE
HONOR OAK PARK
Blythe Hill Fields
Brockley Hill
CATFORD
Catford Stadium
Ladywell Recreation Ground
CATFORD BRIDGE
St. Dunstan's College
Town Hall
MOUNTSFIELD PARK
Rushey Green
BROWNHILL ROAD
SOUTH CIRCULAR ROAD
STANSTEAD ROAD
A205
A21
Cricket Ground
Lewisham
Forest Hill Cricket Grd.
Athletic Ground
Prendergast Sch. Playing Fields
FORSTER MEMORIAL PARK
Bellingham
South Eastern Gas Board
KIRTLEY
SOUTHEND LANE
A2218
Southend Park
MAYOW PARK
LOWER SYDENHAM
Home Pk Rec. Grd.
BECKENHAM HILL
Recreation Ground
MUNICIPAL GOLF COURSE
BECKENHAM PLACE PARK
NEW BECKENHAM
Midland Bank Sports Ground
CATOR PARK
KENT HOUSE
BECKENHAM JUNCTION
RAVENSBOURNE
BR3
BR1
BR2
Bromley Park
SHORTLANDS GOLF COURSE
The Sloane Hosp.
BECKENHAM
Bromley

78
180
S.E.3
HIGH ROAD
LEE
CG
CH
68
CJ
CK
SUTCLIFFE PARK
Sports Park Stadium
Harrow Meadow Rec. Grd.
Meadowside Leisure Centre
ELTHAM ROAD
WESTHORNE AVENUE
Manor House Gdns.
46
HITHER GREEN
Hither Green
Hither Green Hosp.
Chiltonian Ind. Est.
LEE
Sports Centre
Old Colfeians Sports Grd.
Middle Park Field
Queenscroft Rec. Grd.
Eltham Palace (Remains)
SIDCUP ROAD
ST. MILDRED'S RD.
CIRCULAR ROAD A205
S.E.12
Crown Hotel
47
NORTHBROOK PARK
Lewisham
SE6
Hither Green Cemetery
Crematorium
Mottingham Hall
Mottingham
Elthan Coll.
Grove Park Hosp.
Grove Park
GROVE PARK
48
77
Prendergast Sch. Playing Fields
FORSTER MEMORIAL PARK
Recreation Ground
Downham Estate
Downham Recreation Ground
DOWNHAM
Mottingham Sports Ground
Lower Marvels Wood
Marvels Wood
Grove Park Cemetery
Elmstead Wood
Chinbrook Meadow Recreation Grd.
49
50
Shaftesbury Park
Bromley Hill Cemetery
Plaistow
Plaistow Cemetery
King's Meadow Pleasure Ground
BR1
SUNDRIDGE PARK GOLF COURSE
SUNDRIDGE PARK
Elmstead
ELMSTEAD WOODS
Sundridge Park Management Centre
Bromley Court Hotel
Bromley Park
SHORTLANDS GOLF COURSE
BR3
SUNDRIDGE PARK
88
BROMLEY NORTH
St. Joseph's Sch. Convent of the Holy Trinity
LONDON ROAD
BROMLEY HILL

FALCONWOOD
ELTHAM PARK
ROCHESTER WAY RELIEF ROAD
Open Air Swimming Pool
ELTHAM WARREN GOLF COURSE
ELTHAM STN
ELTHAM
ELTHAM HIGH ST.
BEXLEY ROAD
The University of Greenwich
AVERY HILL PARK
Avery Hill Hostel
Cambridge University Miss. Sports Ground
Unilever Sports Ground
S.E.9
ROYAL BLACKHEATH GOLF COURSE
South End
St. Thomas More Cth. Sch.
Parish Wood
Blackfen
HOLLY OAK PARK
DA 15
DA 16
Willersley Park
Marlborough Park
Lamorbey
The Hollies
Fairy Hill Recreation Ground
NEW ELTHAM
New Eltham
OLD FARM PARK
King George's Field
Longlands
Recreation Ground
SIDCUP
DA 14
SIDCUP BY-PASS
Crossways Hotel
Kemnal Corner
Kemnal Manor
Ashen Grove
Edgebury Cty. Prim. Sch.
BELMONT LANE OPEN SPACE
Chislehurst Cemetery
Playing Fields
Beaverwood Girls Sch.
Sidcup Place (Council Offs.)
Queen Mary's Hosp.
Frognall Corner
SCADBURY PARK
Chislehurst West
College of Art & Design
Walden Rec. Grd.
Whytes Woodlands
BR 7
Homewood
Stock Wells
Waterfall
CHISLEHURST GOLF COURSE
CHISLEHURST COMMON
Farringtons Sch. (Girls)
Bushy Clump
Icehouse Wood
Park Wood
Holbrook Wood
Camden Place Club Ho.
CHISLEHURST
PRINCE IMPERIAL ROAD
RED HILL
WHITE HORSE HILL
SIDCUP ROAD
A20
A210
A211
A222
A208
B2214
B264
CK
CL
CM
CN
68
79
88
46
47
48
49
50

79
DANSON PARK
69
Blackfen
Blendon
Upton
BEXLEYHEATH
Bridgen
BEXLEY
HOLLY OAK PARK
PENHILL PARK
Lamorbey
SIDCUP GOLF COURSE
Chislehurst and Sidcup Sch.
ABBEY HILL PARK
ALBANY PARK
SIDCUP
78
WARING PARK
NORTH CRAY
CRAY MEADOWS
FOOTS CRAY
Queen Mary's Hosp.
SCADBURY PARK
Ruxley
RUXLEY GOLF CENTRE
89
DA 15
DA 14
DA 6
BR 7
46
47
48
49
50
CO
CP
CR
Bromley

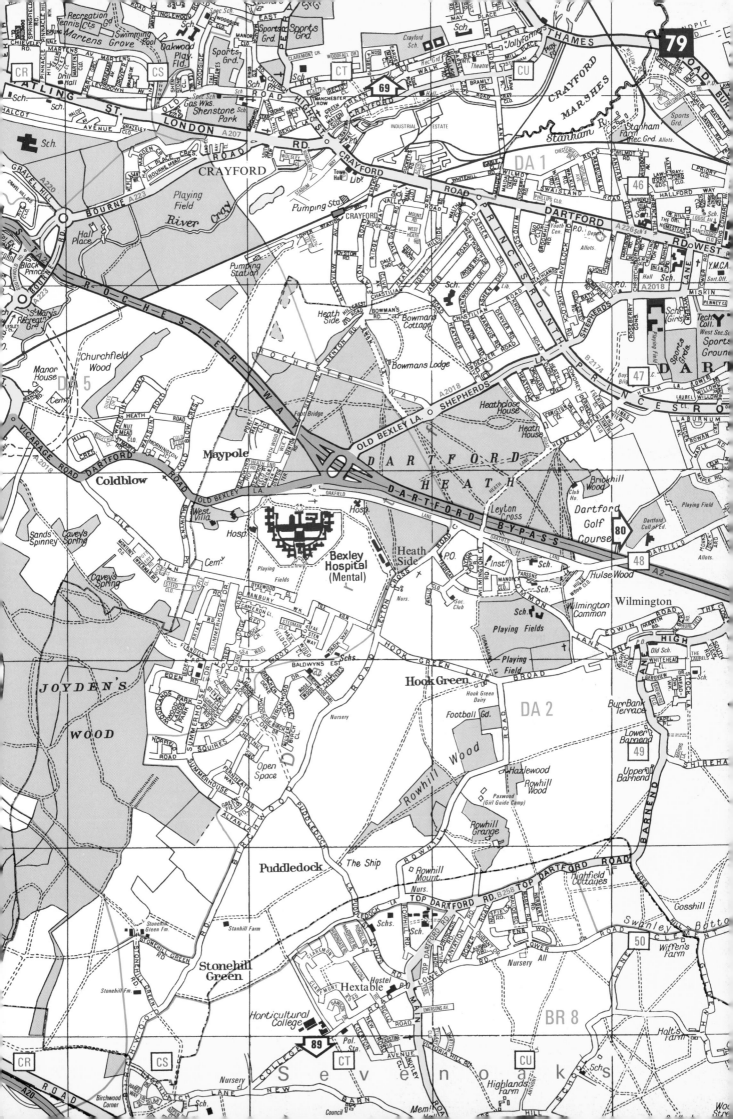

80
DARTFORD
FRESH MARSHES
CRAYFORD
MARSHES
DA 1
70
CV
CW
CX
CY
46
47
48
49
50
79
90
DARTFORD
Dartford Golf Course
Wilmington
Wilmington Common
New Town
Cobbs Croft
The Brent
Hesketh Park
Central Park
Brooklands Lake
Dartford Sportsdrome
Industrial Estate
Hawley Fishery
Sutton House
Hawley Manor
The Rookery
Hawley Mill
Darenth Water Works
DA 2
Hawley
Burnthouse
Shirehall Farm Cotts
Lower Barnend
Upper Barnend
BurrBank Terrace
Hazlewood
Rowhill Wood
Highfield Cottages
Gosshill
Sutton's Cottages
Swanley Bottom
Clement House
Clement Street
Wiffen's Farm
BR 8
Holt's Farm
Gildenhill
Wood Street
Sutton at Hone
Sutton Place
Broad Oak
Vicarage
Chequers
Darenth Court Farm
The Alders
Deer Park
St Johns (Nat.Trust)
Cotton Lane Cottages
Leisure Centre
Cemetery
Blackdale Farm Cotts.
Brickhill Wood
Oakfield Park
Playing Field
Sports Grounds
Swimming Pool
Min of Soc.Sec. & Dep.of Employ.
Brooklands House
Pumping Station (M.W.B.)
Stanham Farm
A206
A226
A2018
B2174
A225
A296
B2200
A282
B260
B258
A2
M25
BYPASS
PRINCES
HAWLEY
MAIN ROAD
DARTFORD TUNNEL ROAD
TOP DARTFORD ROAD
R. Darent

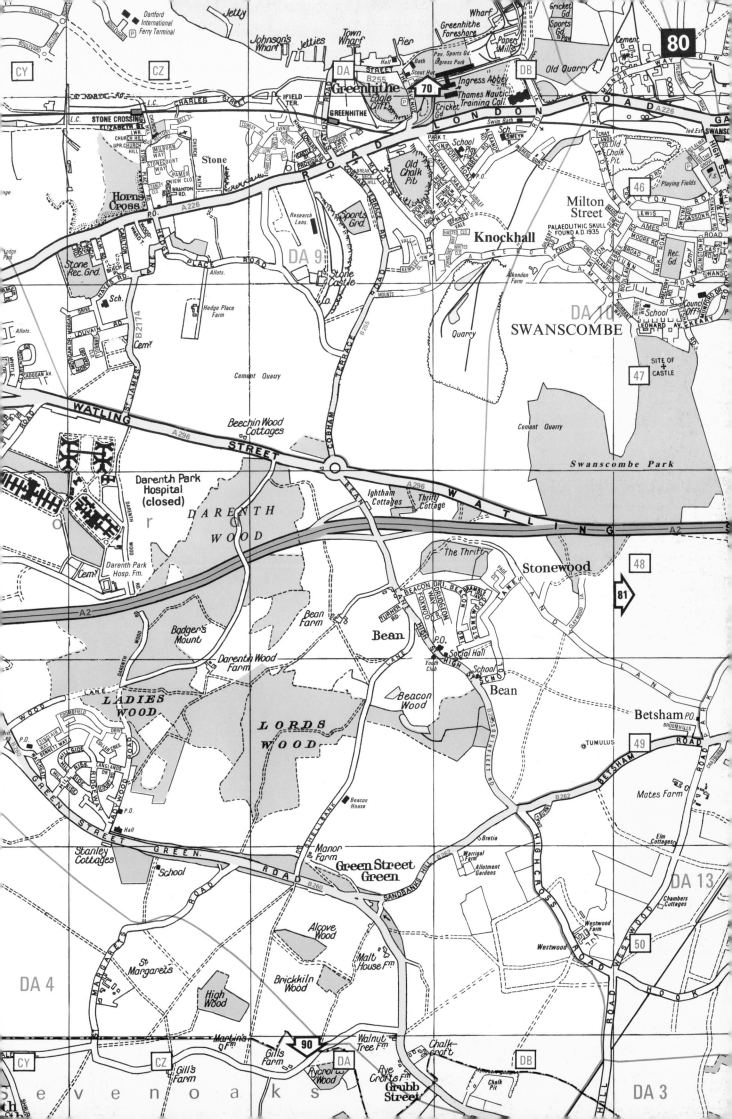
80
CY
CZ
DA
DB
Dartford International Ferry Terminal
Jetty
Johnson's Wharf
Jetties
Town Wharf
Pier
Wharf
Greenhithe Foreshore
Paper Mills
Gricket Gd.
Sports Gd.
Old Quarry
Cement Wks.
Pav. Sports Gd.
Ingress Park
Bath
Scout Hut
Hall
70
Ingress Abbey
Thames Nautic Training Coll.
Cricket Gd
Greenhithe
Eagle Cliff
B255
STREET
ST. MARY'S RD.
CHARLES STREET
IFIELD TER.
STATION ROAD
GREENHITHE
STONE CROSSING
ELIZABETH ST.
L.C.
LONDON ROAD
A226
Swim Bath
Sch.
SWEYN
Ind.Est.
SWANSCOMBE
HIGH ST.
Stone
MILBURN WAY
STONECOURT WAY
CHURCH PATH
BRANTON RD.
Horns Cross
P.O.
A226
Old Chalk Pit
School Play Fld
KNOCKHALL
Research Labs.
Sports Grd.
COBHAM TERRACE
MOUNTS ROAD
Knockhall
CRAYLANDS LANE
Old Chalk Pit
Milton Street
PALAEOLITHIC SKULL FOUND A.D.1935
46
Playing Fields
MILTON ROAD
SWANSCOMBE
DA 10
Rec. Gd.
Cem.y
School
Council Offs
LEONARD AV.
SITE OF CASTLE
47
ALKERDEN LA.
Alkerden Farm
Quarry
WOOD
HEDGE PLACE ROAD
Stone Rec. Grd.
HAYES RD.
Sch.
DA 9
Stone Castle
Allots.
Hedge Place Farm
LOUVAIN RD.
B2174
Cem.y
CADOGAN AV.
ST. JAMES RD.
Cement Quarry
Cement Quarry
WATLING STREET
A296
Beechin Wood Cottages
COBHAM TERRACE
Swanscombe Park
Darenth Park Hospital (closed)
DARENTH WOOD
BEAN LANE
Ightham Cottages
Thrift Cottage
A296
WATLING
A2
DARENTH WOOD RD.
Darenth Park Hosp. Fm.
Cem.y
The Thrift
Stonewood
48
81
A2
Badger's Mount
Bean Farm
BEACON DRI.
TURNER RD.
FOXWOOD
DRUDGEON WAY
STONEWOOD
Bean
HIGH ST.
P.O.
Social Hall
School
Youth Club
Bean
Darenth Wood Farm
LADIES WOOD
LORDS WOOD
Beacon Wood
CLAYWOOD LA.
Betsham P.O.
PARK
TUMULUS
49
BETSHAM ROAD
B262
Mates Farm
Elm Cottages
P.O.
Hall
LADYWOOD ROAD
B260
GREEN STREET GREEN ROAD
Stanley Cottages
School
SHELLBANK
Beacon House
Manor Farm
Green Street Green
SANDBANKS HILL
B262
Bretia
Warrigal Farm
Allotment Gardens
SOUTHFLEET RD
HIGHCROSS ROAD
Westwood Farm
Westwood
DA 13
Chambers Cottages
WESTWOOD
50
HOOK
B260
Alcove Wood
Malt House Fm.
Brickkiln Wood
High Wood
St. Margarets
MARGARETS
DA 4
Martin's Fm.
90
Gills Farm
Walnut Tree Fm.
Chalk-croft
Gill's Farm
Rycroft Wood
Rye Crofts Fm.
Grubb Street
Chalk Pit
HALL ROAD
DA 3
Sevenoaks

81
Rolling Lift Bridge
Cricket Gd.
Sports Gd.
Paper Mills
Botany Marshes
Wharf
Pier
Pier
Pier
Cement Wks.
Old Quarry
DC
DD
DE
DF
71
Industrial Estate
Tilbury Ness
Beacon
Jetty
Shell Mex & B.P.
Lighthouse Jetty
Lighthouse
Wharf
Wharf
Wharf
Jetty
Power Station
Paper Mills
GALLEY HILL RD.
A226
STONEBRIDGE RD
Sports Grd.
SWANSCOMBE
G.P.O.
Old Chalk Pit
Old Chalk Pit
Old Chalk Pit
Galley Hill
Playing Fields
46
Milton Street
DA10
PALAEOLITHIC SKULL FOUND A.D.1935
Rec. Gd.
HIGH STREET
NORTHFLEET
Sports Grd.
Ten Cts
SITE OF ROMAN BUILDING
LONDON
ANGLO-SAXON BURIAL GROUND
Alkenden Manor Farm
SWANSCOMBE
School
Play. Fld.
Rosherville
SITE OF CASTLE
47
Cement Quarry
Swanscombe Park
Sewage Works
DA11
Brook Vale
Day Centre
Council Depot
Springhead Enterprise Park
Recreation Grd.
Recreation Centre
Boys Schools
Playing Fields
Sports Centre Indoor Pool
Wombwell Park
Grammar School
Sch. for Girls
El. Sub. Sta.
Park Corner
Spring Head
Nurs.
A2
STREET
ROMAN ROAD (COURSE OF)
SITE OF ROMAN KILN
SITE OF ROMAN SETTLEMENT
ROMAN BURIAL GROUND
Stonewood
48
80
STATION RD
B259
B262
Betsham
DA 2
49
SITE OF SAXON BURIAL
Bathing Pool
Mates Farm
Manor Ho. Farm
DURNDALE
Disused
Vill. Hall
Northfleet Green
Northfleet Green Farm
Southfleet
Elm Cottages
Court Hill Cottages
Chapter Farm
Cricket Ground
Manor Farm
The Cottage
Madam Wood
DA13
Chambers Cottages
Allotment Gardens
The Limes
Hook Green
Hook Place Farm
Redstreet
Westwood Farm
Westwood
50
Banbury Villas
Axtane
Highview
Thomas's Cottages
Brakefield House
BROAD DITCH ROAD
FAIRVIEW
Court Wood
Courtwood Shaw
DA 3
Piggery
Elmlands Shaw

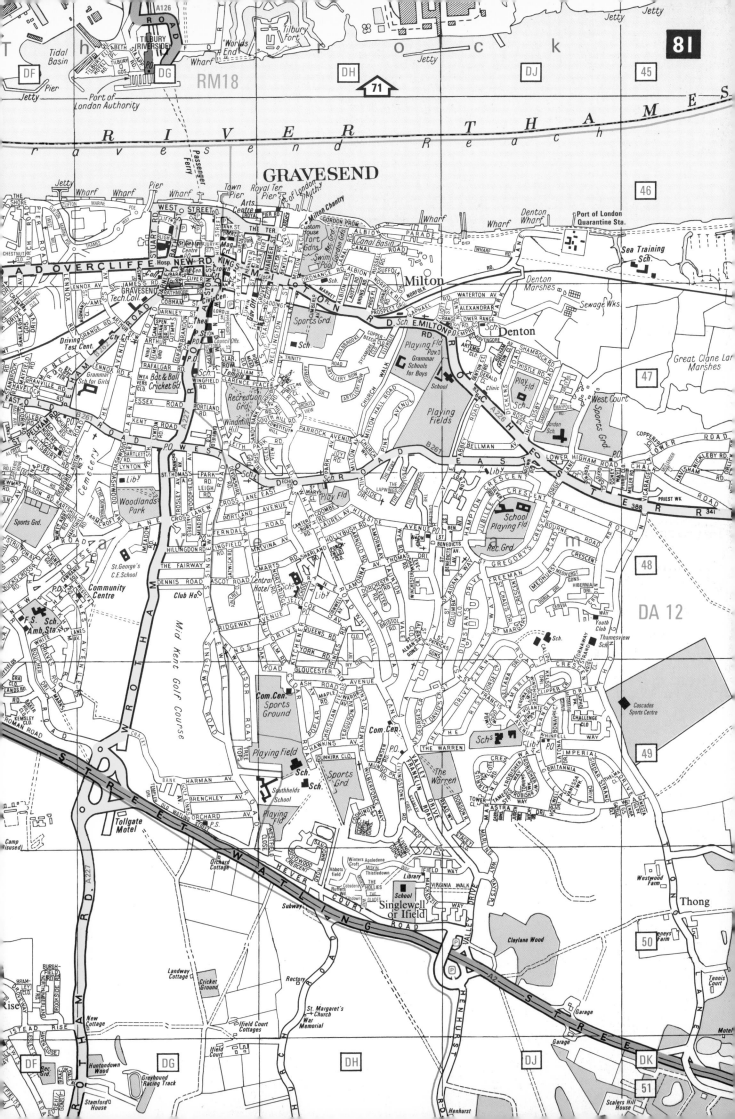
81
RIVER THAMES
Gravesend Reach
GRAVESEND
Tilbury Fort
Tidal Basin
Port of London Authority
Passenger Ferry
RM18
DF
DG
DH
DJ
DK
71
45
46
47
48
49
50
51
Milton
Denton
Denton Marshes
Sewage Wks.
Port of London Quarantine Sta.
Sea Training Sch.
Great Clane Lane Marshes
West Court Sports Grd.
Grammar Schools for Boys
Playing Fields
Woodlands Park
Cemetery
Mid Kent Golf Course
Community Centre
Central Hotel
Sports Ground
Playing Field
Southfields School
Tollgate Motel
The Warren
Cascades Sports Centre
Singlewell or Ifield
Claylane Wood
Cricket Ground
St. Margaret's Church
Thong
Westwood Farm
Huntondown Wood
Greyhound Racing Track
Stamford House
Henhurst
Scalers Hill House
DA 12
WATLING STREET
A2
A226
A227
B261
B262
OVERCLIFFE
WROTHAM RD.
SINGLEWELL
HENHURST RD.
THONG LANE

82
Cork Clump
Cumberland Obelisk
Fuzzy Clump
Obelisk Pond
Sandylands
Park Ho.
Royal Holloway College & Bedford New College
Bakeham Ho.
PRUNE HILL
WICK LANE
WICK ROAD
Egh Wick
72
AO
AP
AQ
AR
AS
Frank's Plantation
WINDSOR GREAT PARK
Scarletoak Plantation
The Bailiwick
Polo Grounds
Queenswood
TW20
Breakheart Hill
Weedon's Field
Heather Garden
Darkhole Clump
Totem Pole
Wick Pond
Ashleigh
Glenwood
51
Oxshed Clump
The Punch Bowl
The Valley Gardens
Broad Ride
Woodlee (Rehabilitation Centre)
Callow Hill
Virginia Water Plantations
The Dell
VIRGINIA WATER
Botany Bay Point
Glenridge Hotel
HOLLOW LANE
Merlewood
Frostfarm Plantation
Wheatsheaf Hotel
Kenwolde
Stroude Farm
BLACKNEST ROAD
A329
Worldsend Gate
52
SL5
CHRISTCHURCH ROAD
Virginia Water
Cascade Bridge
King's Copse
Waverley Copse
Belvedere Wood
CEDAR DRIVE
Virginia Wood
General's Copse
Belvedere Fort
B389
Cricket Ground
STATION APPROACH
LAKE ROAD
Duke's Copse
Broom Hill
Wentworth Pond
ABBOTS DRIVE
BROCKWAY
MONKS ROAD
NUNS WALK
KEEPERS WK.
VIRGINIA WATER
Lib.
GU25
Wentworth Golf Course
Wentworth Club
LONDON ROAD
A30
The Bourne
Waterloo Bridge
Wellington Bri.
WHARPESFORD AVENUE
SHERBOURNE DRI.
53
FIRWOOD RD.
NORTH DRIVE
PORTNALL DRIVE
Harpesford
HILLSIDE
CABRERA AVENUE
TRUMPSGREEN AVENUE
TRUMPSGREEN ROAD
Runnymede
The Dormy House
Wentworth
Ingliston House
Silverwood
Podenhale
HEATHERSIDE DRI.
Fish Ponds
CROWN ROAD
King George's Field
The Knowle
LYNE ROAD
WEST DRIVE
EAST DRIVE
BOURNESIDE
Knowle Hill
KNOWLE HILL
KNOWLE GROVE
Beech Wood
Trumps Farm
Knowle Grove
54
Wentworth Golf Course
SOUTH DRIVE
BEECHWOOD ROAD
Great Wood
MERESIDE PLA.
Longcross Bridge
Surrey
Burnt Hill
LONGCROSS
Bog Wood
Little Arm
M3
Chertsey Common
Hersham Farm
Ship Hill
BURMA ROAD
Barrowhills
Dicken's Wood
GU24
Long Arm
Memorial Cross
55
Grangewood
Longcross
LONDON ROAD
B386
Fairfields
Poultry Farm
ACCOMMODATION RD.
Oystershell Hill
Lily Pond Farm
LONGCROSS ROAD
Longcross House
Flutters Hill
CHERTSEY ROAD
CHOBHAM ROAD
CHOBHAM COMMON
The Heath
91

MILTON PARK
Great Fosters Hotel
Black Lane Farm
Luddington House
LUDDINGTON AV.
STROUDE ROAD
NEW WICKHAM LA.
Thorpe Lea Nursery
CLOCKHOUSE LA. E.
THORPE LEA ROAD
B388
Mead Lake Ditch
AYEBRIDGES AV.
WAVENDENE AV.
ASHLEIGH AV.
WARWICK AV.
Thorpe Industrial Estate
DELTAWAY
CRABTREE RD.
TEN ACRE LANE
Cemetery
Coldharbour
Eastly End
NORLANDS LANE
COLDHARBOUR LANE
Eastlyend House
The Grange
Thorpe House
Thorpe
VILLAGE ROAD
MILL LANE
Woodcock Farm
BOURNE MEADOW
MUCKHATCH LA.
WESTERN AV.
THE MIDWAY
ROSEMARY LA.
THE BENCE
First Sch.
YEW TREES
Longside Lake
Thorpe Green
Hurst Farm
HURST LANE
THORPE GREEN LANE
MILL HOUSE LANE
Fleet Lake
Manor Lake
THORPE PARK
Show Ground
Abbey Lake
St. Ann's Lake
Thorpe Water Park
Penton Hook Marina
Penton Hook Island
Penton Hook Farm
Penton Hook Lock
Weirs
MIXNAMS LANE
STAINES RD.
CHERTSEY LANE
A320
TEMPLE GDNS.
FERRY AV.
WEIR PL.
AYMER CLO.
LONG WAYS
BLACKETT CLO.
REDWOOD
WHEATSHEAF LA.
PENTON AV.
RIVERSIDE RD.
Staines Town F.C.
Sweeps Bri.
MEADWAY
CARLYLE RD.
TW18
Laleham Golf Course
Laleham
M25
M3
2
12
Anchor Copse
St Ann's Chapel (Remains)
St Ann's Hill Park
Monk's Grove
OLD COACH RD.
ST. ANNS HILL ROAD
RUXBURY ROAD
THORPE ROAD
B388
Sewage Works
Redlands
Lyne Farm
LYNE CROSSING ROAD
LYNE LANE
FARM CLO.
HARROW BOTTOM RD.
Lyne Place
The Rough
Merrywood Farm
Elm Farm Caravan Park
ALMNERS ROAD
HARDWICK LANE
WATERY LA.
Silver Birch Caravan Site
Lyne Copse
Recreation Ground
Lyne
Fangrove Caravan Park
FAN GROVE
Westbrook Farm
Fan Court Sch.
KT16
TRYS HILL
B386
Silverlands
France Farm
Botleys
HOLLOWAY HILL
White Lodge Centre
St. Peter's Hosp.
Botleys Park Hosp.
Fox Hills
Home Wood
Church Farm
Fish Pond
Great Cockcrow Railway
Cockcrow Hill
Hardwick Court Farm
Staines Lane
ST. ANN'S RD.
Pyrcroft Mid Sch.
Chilseygreen Fm.
Pyrcroft
Pyrcroft First Sch.
Nurs. Sch.
PYRCROFT RD.
CHILSEY GREEN RD.
COWLEY AVE.
BARKER RD.
Sports Ground
The Bourne
Abbey Mead
Abbey Bridge
Moat
Play. Fld.
COLONEL'S LANE
THE CEDARS
Old Town Hall
Mus.
LONDON ST.
CHERTSEY
Shopping Centre
Playing Fld.
R.C. Middle Sch.
FAIRWAY
CHERTSEY Play. Fld.
Sir William Perkin's School
Rec. Gd.
GUILDFORD ROAD
EASTWORTH RD.
HANWORTH TRADING EST.
Eastworth
Cemetery
Salesian Sch.
A317
Sandgates Convent
Pannell's Farm
Play. Fld.
Salesian Sch.
Police Traffic Cen.
Meadowcroft First Sch.
GREEN LANE
SANDLEWOOD
FERNDALE AV.
WAVERLEY
Huntingdon
BITTAMS LANE
ST. PETERS WAY
Cemetery
KT15
11
Simple Marsh Fm.
WESTON AV.
Convent
Abbeylands Sports Centre
SIMPLEMARSH RD.
OAKLANDS CT.
AS
AT
AU
AV
72
83
91
51
52
53
54
55

83
Staines Cricket & Hockey Club
Staines Town F.C.
Sweep Bri.
Penton Hook Farm
Pentonhook Lock
Weirs
Penton Hook Island
Penton Hook Marina
Thorpe Water Park
Fleet Lake
Abbey Lake
THAMES
TW18
Intake Channel
Pumping Station
Round Copse
QUEEN
RESERV
Spel
Manor Farm
Prim.Sch.
THE BROADWAY
Village Hall
War Mem.
Rec.n Grd.
Laleham
SHEPPERTON ROAD
Penton Park Est.
Club Ho.
Laleham Abbey
Recreation Ground
Laleham Golf Course
Laleham Burway
Laleham Park
Camping Site
Reservoirs
Nursery
Squires Bri.
Shepperton Studios
River Ash
LALEHAM
Littleton Sailing Club
Pool End
KT16
M3
Abbey Mead
Abbey Bridge
Play.Fld.
THE ABBEY (Site of)
THE CEDARS EST.
Home Farm
Abbey Chase
Black Ditch
Old Town Hall
Mus.
Sports Ground
The Bourne
Weir
Chertsey Lock
'Bridge Hotel'
CHERTSEY BRI. RD.
CHERTSEY RD.
Chertsey Bridge Recreation Grd.
Marina
Chertsey Meads
Dockett Eddy
Dockett Point
TOWPATH
Pharaoh's Island
Shepperton Weir
Shepperton Lock
Hamhaugh Island
CHERTSEY
R.C.Middle Sch.
William Perkin's School
Health Cen.
Caravan Pk.
Depot
Trading Est.
Gas Wks
Hanworth Trading Est.
Eastworth
Cemetery
Salesian Sch.
EASTWORTH ROAD
Sandgates Convent
Pannell's Farm
Play.Fld.
Fordwater Bri.
Clay Corner
Sec.Sch.
Youth Play.Fld. Cen.
Claybourne Sch.
Addlestonemoor
Fire Sta.
The Bourne
Woburn Place
WOBURN PARK
St.George's College
Cricket Ground
Hamm Court Farm
HAMM COURT EST.
Portmore Park
Hatch Farm
WOBURN HILL
M25
Meadowcroft First Sch.
ST. PETERS WAY
KT15
Simple Marsh Fm.
Victory Park
Sports Grd.
Meadowlands Caravan Park
WEYBRIDGE ROAD
Woburn Bri. Trading Est.
ADDLESTONE
Health Cen.
Abbeylands Sports Centre
Weybridge Lock
73
82
92
AW
AX
AY
AZ
51
52
53
54
55

83
73
84
92
51
52
53
54
55
AZ
BA
BB
BC
Ashford Common
Sunbury Common
Kempton Park (Race Days Only)
Kempton Park
Race Course
Sunbury
TW16
Charlton
M3
Upper Halliford
Lower Halliford
Shepperton
Walton on Thames
KT12
KT13
Weybridge
Ashley Park
Elmbridge
Apps Court
Thistlecroft
Water Works
Sports Grounds
Recreation Grd.
Refuse Transfer Sta.
Grange Farm Caravan Site
Vicarage Farm
Hawfield
Clock Ho.
Waterssplash Farm
Shepperton Marina
The Ashmere Club
Bishop Duppas Recreation Ground
Thames Meadow
Desborough Island
Reservoirs
Desborough Channel
Broad Water
Greenland's Farm
Dairy Farm
Elmbridge Leisure Centre
Thames Field Fm.
Sunbury Weir
Weir Hotel
Pumping House
River Thames
Sunbury Park
Town Hall
Cricket Ground
Marrowells
Walton Hosp.
Sandhills Meadow
War Close
Kennels
Walton Bridge Rd.
Staines Road East
Thames Street
Nursery Road
Hampton Court Road
Charlton Road
Upper Halliford Road
Gaston Bridge Road
Fordbridge Road
Green Lane
Russell Road
New Zealand Avenue
Oatlands Drive
Ashley Road
Hersham Road
Sunbury Lane
Terrace Road
Walton Lane
Station Avenue
Queens Road

84
KEMPTON PARK (RACE DAYS ONLY)
KEMPTON PARK
Kempton Race Course
Half Moon Covert
Reservoir
Grand Stand
Public Stand
TW16
Spelthorne
74
Football Grd
CARLISLE PARK
TW12
HAMPTON
Hampton Cemetery
Sports Grd.
St. Marys Cott. Hosp.
Works
UPPER SUNBURY ROAD
STAINES ROAD EAST
A308
THAMES STREET
Filter Beds
Reservoir
Engine Ho
Cricket Gd.
Sunbury Court
LOWER SUNBURY RD.
LOWER HAMPTON RD.
B375
RIVER THAMES
Platt's Ait
SUNBURY
Sunbury Park
Sunbury Lock
Sunbury Ct. Island
Swan's Rest
Rivermead I.
Police Cadet Train. Cen.
RESERVOIRS
Sunnyside Reservoir
HURST ROAD
A3050
Water Works
Apps Court Farm
Sunbury Weir
Weir Hotel
Pumping House
BESSBOROUGH RESERVOIR
KNIGHTS RESERVOIR
WALTON ROAD
B369
Elmbridge Leisure Centre
83
Thamesfield Fm.
QUEEN ELIZABETH II RESERVOIR
WALTON ON THAMES
WEST MOLESEY
Molesey Hosp.
Molesey Hurst Recreation Ground
Cemetery
Church Fm.
Neilson Recreation Ground
Dead River
ISLAND BARN RESERVOIR
Valve Tower
Elmb
Fieldcommon Fm.
Gravel Pit
Water Pollution Control Works
Sewage Wks.
River Mole
KT12
Sports Ground
Sandown Ind. Est.
Council Depot
HERSHAM TRADING EST.
Sewage Wks.
HERSHAM
Lower Green
SANDOWN PARK
Race Course
Trinity Sch.
Winning Post
Grandstand
The Warren
Waynflete's or Wolsey's Towers
Esher Place
South Waylands Fm.
Walton Hosp.
Elmgrove Recreation Ground
Swim. Pool
Playing Field
Coronation Play. Flds.
R.C.Mid.Sch.
WALTON ON THAMES
Thistlecroft
93
BD
BE
BF
BG
51
52
53
54
55

BUSHY PARK
Hampton Court Park
HAMPTON WICK
KINGSTON
EAST MOLESEY
HAMPTON COURT
THAMES DITTON
Giggs Hill
Weston Green
LONG DITTON
Southborough
SURBITON
Hinchley Wood
DITTON COMMON
LITTLEWORTH COMMON
HOOK
RIVER THAMES
HAMPTON COURT ROAD
PORTSMOUTH ROAD
KINGSTON BY-PASS
Hampton Court Palace
Kingston University
Surrey County Hall
Thames Ditton Hosp.
Esher Sixth Form College
Imber Ct. Trading Estate
KT1
KT6
KT7
KT8
KT9
KT10
TW11
74
85
93
51
52
53
54
55
BG
BH
BJ
BK

85
Coombe
Wood Course
Coombe Golf
75
Kingston Hosp.
KT2
Coombe Road
Coombe Lane
Kingston
Kingston University
Norbiton
Kingston Cemetery
Crematorium
Sewage Wks.
Kingston upon Thames
Surbiton Cemetery
Berrylands
Recreation Ground
Norbiton Common
Surbiton
KT5
KT6
Surbiton Hill Road
Ewell Road
Brighton Road
Portsmouth Road
Richmond Rd
London Road
Cambridge Rd
Kingston Road
Surrey County Hall
Coll. of Further Ed.
Guildhall
The Fairfield Recreation Ground
The Wilderness Parkfield
Claremont Hall
Masonic Hall
84
Southborough
Alexandra Rec. Ground
Tolworth
Tolworth Hosp.
Tolworth Tower Council Offices
Kingston By-Pass A3
Hogsmill Open Space
Malden Manor
Malden Homes
Maori Sports Ground
Tolworth Hall
Riverhill Sports Grd.
King George's Field
Running Track
Tolworth Court Bri.
Hogsmill River
Hook
KT9
94
Sports Centre
Playing Field
Hill Fm.
Worc
KT19
51
52
53
54
55
BL
BM
BN
BO

BO
BP
BQ
BR
75
86
94
51
52
53
54
55
Atkinson Morley Hosp.
Wimbledon R.C. Coll.
Cottenham Park
Cottenham Pk. Rec. Grd.
Holland Gdns.
Convent Sch.
Wimbledon Coll. Sports Grd.
W.O. Sports Ground
M. of W. Sports Grd.
MALDEN GOLF COURSE
RAYNES PARK
Raynes Park
Prince George's Playing Field
Merton Mans.
Messines Playing Fields
Joseph Hood Recreation Grd.
CANNON HILL COMMON
Cannon Hill
L.E.S.S.A. Sports Grd.
KINGSTON BY-PASS
KINGSTON ROAD
WIMBLEDON CHASE
Nelson Hosp.
JOHN INNES PARK
Playing Fields
MERTON PARK
MERTON
SOUTH MERTON
Mostyn Gdns.
BEVERLEY PARK
Beverley Brook
Schools Sports Grd.
Shannon Corner
Duke of Cambridge
KT3
West Barnes
King's College Sports Ground
G.L.C. Technical Schs. Sports Ground
Arch. Tenisons Sports Grd.
Sports Ground
MOTSPUR PARK
Motspur Park
London University Sports Ground
Sir Joseph Hood Memorial Playing Field
B.B.C. Sports Ground
North East Surrey Crematorium
Battersea New Cemetery
Lower Morden
G.L.C. Schools Playing Fields
Morden Playing Fields
SM4
Cycle Track
Swimming Baths
Morden Pk. Club Ho.
Tech. Coll.
MORDEN PARK
Peacock Fm. Nursery
East Pyl Brook
MORDEN SOUTH
ST. HELIER
Haig Homes
King George's Field
Carshalton, Merton and Morden
Morden Common
Cemetery
Sewage Disposal Wks.
Corporation Depot
MANOR PARK
Malden Green Fm.
WORCESTER PARK
KT4
Computer Centre
Cheam Hospital
St. Anthony's Hosp.
North Cheam
Cheam Common
Sutton Common Recreation Ground
Recreation Grd.
Sewage Works
Refuse Station
Highways Depot
Recreation Ground
SHADBOLT PARK
Cuddington Recreation Ground
L.R.T. Sports Ground
SM3
SM1
Health Cen.
Sports Centre
CHEAM
Sutton Utd. F.C.
Bus Depot
LONDON ROAD
ST. HELIER AVENUE
STONECOT HILL
CENTRAL ROAD
CHEAM COMMON ROAD
MALDEN ROAD
OLDFIELDS ROAD
ST. DUNSTAN'S HILL
A3
A24
A238
A298
A217
B282
B235
B279
B285
B286
B283
B281

86
SOUTH WIMBLEDON
Colliers Wood
Gorringe
MERTON PARK
MERTON
JOHN INNES PARK
Playing Fields
SOUTH MERTON
Mostyn Gdns.
MORDEN
MORDEN HALL PARK (National Trust)
Morden Hall
RAVENSBURY PARK (N.T.)
MITCHAM
MORDEN SOUTH
Morden Playing Fields
ST. HELIER
MORDEN
DEN PARK
POULTER PARK
Carshalton Playing Fields
Wandle Valley Hosp.
Sutton Common Recreation Ground
St. Helier Open Space
St. Helier Hosp.
ROSEHILL PARK
ROSEHILL
SUTTON COMMON
North Cheam
Cemetery
The Wrythe
ROYSTON PARK
HACKBRIDGE PARK
Recreation Ground
MERANTUN WAY
MORDEN ROAD
LONDON ROAD
BISHOPSFORD ROAD
ST. HELIER AVENUE
ROSE HILL
REIGATE AV.
ST. DUNSTAN'S HILL
CARSHALTON ROAD
WESTERN ROAD
SM4
SM3
SM5
SM1
BS
BT
BU
BV
51
52
53
54
55
76
85
95

86
STREATHAM
Lambeth
STREATHAM VALE PARK
BV
BW
BX
BY
76
NORBURY
NORBURY PARK
S.W.16
Biggin Wood
Sports Ground
Bank Sports Ground
Playing Field
South London Cremat.
Streatham Park Cemetery
Jew's Cemetery
Recreation Grd.
CR4
Recreation Ground
Norbury Hall
Barclays Bank Sports Ground
Thornton Heath Rec. Grd
Green Lane Rec. Grd
Football Ground
51
52
53
54
55
87
THORNTON HEATH
Sherwood Park
COMMON
CROYDON ROAD
BEDDINGTON LANE
Mill Ho.
Pond
Football Ground
Sports Ground
Cremat.
Croydon Cemetery
Mayday Hosp.
Queen's Hosp.
Queen's Road Cemetery
Ashworth Estate
Cement Works
Waddon Hosp.
Beddington Sewage Fm.
Beddington Fm.
Brit Air Power Sta.
Superstore
WADDON MARSH
CR0
WANDLE PARK
Stubbs Mead
Whitgift Centre
WEST CROYDON
Croydon Gen. Hosp.
Town Hall
BEDDINGTON PARK
Archery Grounds
Cricket Grd.
Carew Manor Sch.
Waddon
Waddon Park
Engineering Wks.
The Grange (Site of)
Boating Lake
SM6
BEDDINGTON
WADDON
95
Recreation Ground
DUPPAS HILL

87
UPPER NORWOOD
Westow Park
CRYSTAL PALACE
PENGE WEST
BZ
CA
77
CB
CC
PENGE
ANERLEY
Orchard Lodge
Beaulieu Heights
Sports Ground
S. Norwood Lake
Norbury Club
Grangewood Park
Playing Field
Green Lane Rec. Grd.
Football Ground
CR4
51
52
53
54
55
86
96
Thornton Heath Rec. Grd.
THORNTON HEATH
Cricket Ground
Mayday Hosp.
Queen's Hosp.
Queen's Road Cemetery
SELHURST
C.Palace Charlton Ath. Football Grd.
South Norwood Recreation Grd.
NORWOOD JUNCTION
SOUTH NORWOOD
Crystal Palace District Cemetery (Beckenham Crematorium)
S. Norwood Engine Ho.
Refuse Destructor
Croydon & Sports Arena
Rylands Fields
Golf Driving Range
WOODSIDE
ASHBURTON PARK
Playing Fields
S.E.25
S.E.20
WEST CROYDON
Croydon Gen. Hosp.
CROYDON
ADDISCOMBE
Recreation Grd.
EAST CROYDON
Whitgift Centre
Town Hall
WANDLE PARK
Park Hill Rec. Grd.
CR0
Playing Field
SHIRLEY PARK GOLF COURSE
Trinity Sch. of John Whitgift
DUPPAS HILL Recreation Ground
LLOYD PARK Playing Fld.
A215
A212
A213
A222
A232
A235
A236
A214

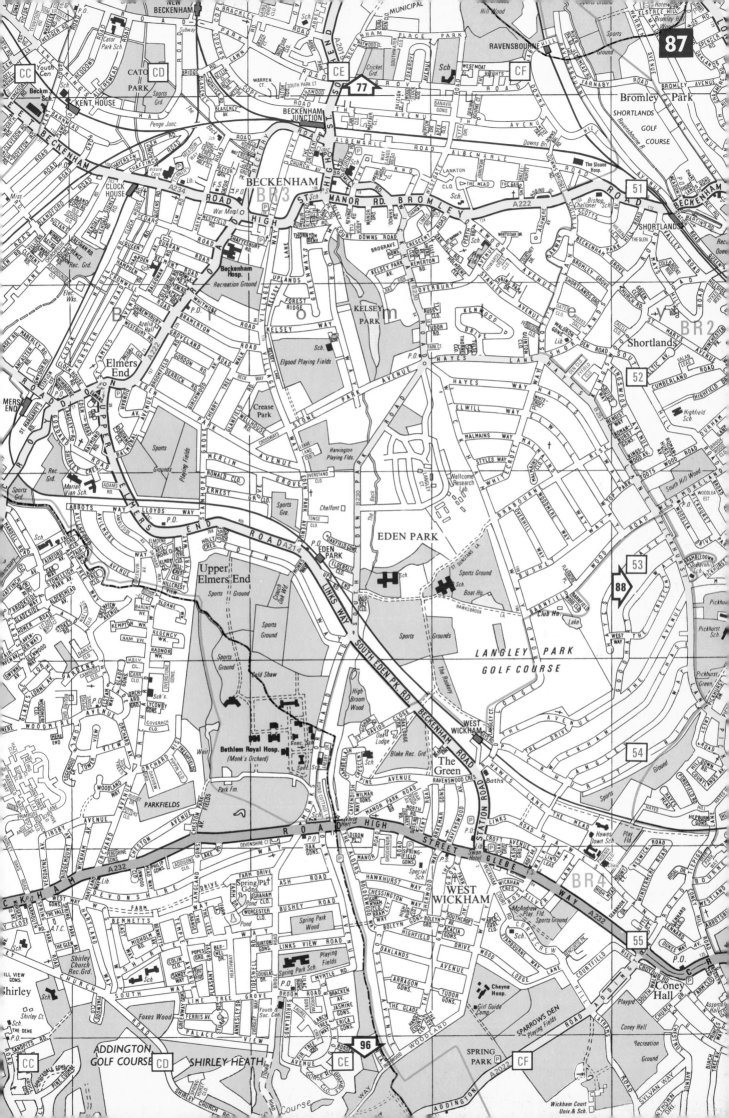
87
77
CC
CD
CE
CF
NEW BECKENHAM
RAVENSBOURNE
Bromley Park
SHORTLANDS GOLF COURSE
KENT HOUSE
CATOR PARK
BECKENHAM JUNCTION
BECKENHAM
BR3
CLOCK HOUSE
Beckenham Hosp.
Recreation Ground
KELSEY PARK
Elgood Playing Fields
Crease Park
Harvington Playing Flds.
Elmers End
Shortlands
BR2
51
52
53
54
55
88
EDEN PARK
LANGLEY PARK GOLF COURSE
Wellcome Research Lab.
Upper Elmers End
Bethlem Royal Hosp. (Monk's Orchard)
PARKFIELDS
WEST WICKHAM
The Green
BR4
Shirley
Coney Hall
Cheyne Hosp.
SPARROWS DEN Playing Fields
SPRING PARK
ADDINGTON GOLF COURSE
SHIRLEY HEATH
Wickham Court Univ. & Sch.
96
A222
A234
A214
A232
A2022
B230
B251

SUNDRIDGE PARK
Bromley Park
SHORTLANDS GOLF COURSE
The Sloane Hosp.
BECKENHAM LANE
SHORTLANDS
BROMLEY
BROMLEY NORTH
Town Hall
Bromley Coll.
Civic Centre
The Glades Shopping Centre
BROMLEY SOUTH
Widmore
Ravensbourne Sch. For Girls
Shortlands
Highfield Sch.
South Hill Wood
Bromley Gen. Hosp.
Bromley Football Grd. Cricket Grd.
NORMAN PARK
Sch. of Art
Bromley Tech. Coll.
Pickhurst Rec. Grd.
Pickhurst Sch.
HAYES
Hayes Street Fm.
Brook Wood
Mazzards Wood
Woodcock Grove
Lords Wood
Bolds Wood
Barnet Wood
Hayes Sch.
Hayes Sports Club
Five Elms
Colyer's Wood
Bromley Tech. High Sch.
West Wickham Common
HAYES COMMON
Coney Hall
Coney Hall Recreation Ground
SPARROWS DEN Playing Fields
Keston Mark
Wickham Common Sch.
Wickham Ct. Univ. & Sch.
BROMLEY
Sports Ground
Princes Plain Sch.
BR1
BR2
BR3
BR4
CG
CH
CJ
CK
78
87
97
51
52
53
54
55
A222
A21
A232
A233
B265
B228
CROYDON ROAD
HAYES LANE
MASONS HILL
BROMLEY COMMON
WIDMORE ROAD
BICKLEY ROAD

88
CHISLEHURST GOLF COURSE
CHISLEHURST COMMON
CHISLEHURST
78
CK
CL
CM
CN
SCADBURY PARK
Sunnymead
Farringtons Sch. (Girls)
Bushy Clump
Icehouse Wood
Park Wood
Holbrook Wood
The Larches
Moat Boat Ho.
BR7
Hawkwood
Coopers Sch.
Manor House
ST. PAULS CRAY COMMON
Gosshill Wood
Pond Wood
Walk Wood
Hawkwood Fm.
Tongs Fm.
HAWKSWOOD EST N.T.
PETTS WOOD (N.T.)
Hoblingwell Wood
51
52
53
54
55
BICKLEY
Kyd Brook
Moor Grove
Great Thrift
West Kent Hotel
Black Brook Wood
SOUTHBOROUGH
Thornet Wood
Sydney Shaw
Willetts Rec. Grd.
PETTS WOOD
BR5
Recreation Ground
Poverest Sch.
Southborough Sch. Playing Fields
Youth Centre
St. Luke's Cemetery
Parkfield Recreation Ground
Covert Wood
Poverest Recreation Ground
89
Sparrow Wood
Sparrow Common
Roundabout Wood
Crofton Sch.
Crofton Jun. Sch.
Broomhill Common
ORPINGTON
Civic Off.
College of Further Educ.
Crofton Heath
CROFTON HEATH
Clay Wood
Lennard Hosp.
Scrubs Fm.
Nobodys Wood
Pokeridden Wood
Civic Hall
ORPINGTON
STATION RD.
A232
CROFTON ROAD
ORPINGTON ROAD
CHISLEHURST ROAD
A208
A222
A223
A21
Broadstreet Green
Recreation Ground
Farnborough Hospital
BR6
Newstead Wood Girls Sch.
Public Swimming Pool
Darrick Wood
Darrick Wood Sch.
Playing Fields
97
Orpington Hosp.
Playing Field
St. Olave's Sch.
Pumping Sta.
FARNBOROUGH COMMON

SCADBURY PARK
Ruxley
RUXLEY GOLF CENTRE
CRAY VALLEY GOLF COURSE
St. Paul's Cray
PAULS CRAY HILL PARK
HOCKENDEN WOOD
ST. MARY CRAY
Kevington
ORPINGTON
GODDINGTON PARK
Orpington Hosp.
SEVENOAKS WAY
CRAY AVENUE
COURT ROAD
SPUR ROAD

Dartford
DA2
Stonehill Green
Stonehill Fm.
Hextable
Horticultural College
79
Pol. Sta.
Hostel
CR
CS
CT
CU
Nursery
COLLEGE
NEW BARN LANE
Council Depot
Mem. Hall
MAIN ROAD
B258
Highlands Farm
HIGHLANDS HILL
SWANLEY VILLAGE ROAD
Swanley Village
Sch.
Holt's Farm
Coldharbor Farm
WOOD ROAD
51
Birchwood Corner
LONDON RD.
B2173
Sch.
Swimming Pool
White Oaks Sports Cent.
Schs.
Nurs.
FIVE WAYS
Tweed Hill
M25
Franks Park
Birch Wood
Arts Centre
Sch.
SWANLEY LANE
SWANLEY
Sch.
Parkwood Hall Sch.
Windmill Hill Wood
Council Offices
Recreation Ground
Pol. Sta.
P.O.
HIGH STREET
STATION RD.
Schs.
Play. Fld.
Sch.
Play. Fld.
SWANLEY
BR8
Bus Depot
Olympic Leisure Centre
52
Night-ingale Place
Button Street
Tile Kilns Wood
M25
A20
BY-PASS
IND. EST.
M20
Rec. Grd.
Nursery
Petham Court
3
LONDON
53
A20
90
Sch.
The Green
Vill. Hall
BROADWAY
CRAY ROAD
B258
Cem.
Cherry Orchard
EYNSFORD ROAD
Gosenhill Farm
Crockenhill
Pol. Sta.
F'ball Grd.
Little Wested House
Willow Farm
Cacketshill Wood
Wested
Tunnel
54
Highcroft Hall
Heathfield Shaw
Horncross Shaw
Fountain Hoy
DA4
Baldwins Cotts.
Hulberry
Hulberry Farm
The Firs
55
LULLINGSTONE LANE
R. Darent
Hulberry Corner
Skeet Hill
LULLINGSTONE PARK
The Roughet
Lullingstone Villa
Newbarn
EYNSFORD
98
CR
CS
CT
CU
Doctor's Wood
Parkgate
Sevenoaks

Sutton at Hone
Deer Park
ST. JOHNS (Nat. Trust)
Swanley Village
Coldharbor
Wood Street
Gildenhill
Holt's Farm
Vicarage
Sch.
RAM'S WOOD
Tweed Hill
Franks Park
Hop Kiln Cottages
Homefield House
FARNINGHAM ROAD
S.R.
BR8
M25
Parkwood Hall Sch.
Olympic Leisure Centre
Button Street
FARNINGHAM WOOD
Franks Farm
Franks
The Folly
The Grange
Kirby Hall
CASTLE (Site of)
Eglantine Farm
Hill House
LONDON A20
M20
ROAD MAIN
Lion Hotel
FARNINGHAM
Hampton Court
GORSE HILL
Charton Farm
Polly Shaw
Eynsford Hill
Fountain Hoy
Beesfield Farm
Lincoln Kennels
Alchin's Wood
Firpound Shaw
Olivers Shaw
Eynsford Cas. (REMAINS OF)
War Mem!
Home Farm
Pumping Sta.
R. Darent
EYNSFORD
Lullingstone Roman Villa
Newbarn
Sandhole Shaw
Tunnel
CV
CW
CX
CY
80
89
99
51
52
53
54
55

90
80
99
51
52
53
54
55
CY
CZ
DA
DB
DC
DA2
DA13
DA4
DA3
TN15
St Margarets
Brickkiln Wood
Malt House Fm
High Wood
Martin's Fm
Gills Farm
Gill's Farm
Walnut Tree Fm
Rycrofts Wood
Rye Crofts Fm
Grubb Street
Chalk-croft
Chalk Pit
Gills Wood
White House
Mile End Green
Works
Allotment Gardens
Pinden
Sports Grd.
Rabbits Farm
RABBITS ROAD
GREEN STREET
GREEN ROAD
WHITEHILL ROAD
MAIN ROAD
NORTHDOWN RD.
Longfield
War Memorial
ESSEX
KENT
P.O.
STATION RD.
LONGFIELD
School
Dean Bottom Farm
Bramblefield Wood
Dean Bottom
Churchdown Wood
Hillside
Churchdown Farm
SITE OF MANOR HOUSE
Steepside
The Old Downs
CASTLE HILL
CANADA FARM RD.
Beeches Farm
Canada Farm
Hill Barn Farm
Rectory
Hartley Green
Sports Ground
Bowling Green
School
Gay Dawn Farm
Pennis Farm
Pennis House
FAIRBY LANE
Hartley
CHANTRY AV.
SCUDDERS HILL
VALLEY ROAD
Scudders Farm
Count Lodge
HORTON WOOD
THREE GATES ROAD
Grove Wood
Vill. Hall
School
North Lo.
Yewfield Shaw
Parkfield Wood
Pennis Wood
Northlands Shaw
Redlibbets Wood
Chapel Wood
Hopkins Spring Wood
Hatchfield Wood
Fawkham Manor
MANOR LANE
Speed Gate
White House Farm
SPEEDGATE HILL
Choaks Wood
Gabriel Spring Wood
GABRIEL STRING ROAD
SUN HILL
WEST YOKE ROAD
Westyoke Farm
Manns Farmhouse
Oliver's Farm
West Yoke
Ebenezer Chapel
Fawkham Green
P.O.
BRANDS HATCH ROAD
FAWKHAM GREEN RD.
Saxtens Wood
Brands Hatch Leisure Centre
Cage's Wood
ROGERS WOOD LANE
Brands Hatch
Woodlands
Crooked Billet
BILLET HILL
Landway Farm
Swan Meadows Farm
Grand Stand
Ind. Park
CHAPEL WOOD ROAD
New Ash Green
AYELANDS
MILLFIELD
TURNERS OAK SHAW
COLT STEAD
FOXBURY
NORTH ASH RD.
PUNCH CROFT
SEVEN ACRES
BUTLER'S PL.
St. Peter & St. Paul
Ash Place Farm

91
Longcross
Chobham Common
Chertsey Road
Oystershell Hill
Walk End
Chickabiddy Hill
Windsor Road
Staple Hill
Surrey Heath
Gracious Pond
Gracious Pond Road
Gracious Pond Farm
Butts Hill
Langshot Equitation & Livery Stables
Langshot Poultry Farm
Ram Bridge
Westways Farm
GU24
Burrowhill
Metco Works
Brimshot
Brimshot Farm
Paradise Farm
Little Heath
Little Heath Road
Windlesham Road
Henage Corner
Burrow Hill Farm
Manx Farm
Biddle Farm
Wood's Farm
Home Farm
The Cricketers
Chobham Place
Nursery
Pets Cemetery
Mincing Lane Nursery
Mincing Lane
Chobham Park Ho.
Chobham Park Farm
Chobham Park Lane
Partridge Farm
Tennis Courts
Blackberry Ho.
Marphil Boarding Kennels & Cattery
Stannershill Farm
Stanners Hill
Stonehill
Stonehill Road
Childown Farm
Fish Pond
Fern Hill
Stanyards Farm
Records Office Min. of Defence (Navy)
Larkenshaw Farm
Fishpool Bridge
Sowmoor Plantation
A319
Chobham House
Chobham
Bagshot Road
High Street
Mill Bourne
Emmett's Mill
Kelmstone Stud
Brooklands Farm
Sunfield Farm
Youngstroat Lane
Station Road
A3046
Recreation Ground
Cricket Ground
Village Hall
Flexlands School
Sandpit Hall Road
Piggery
Deewall House
Trotters Lane
Highfield
Focklesbrook Farm
Chobham Farm
Mimbridge
Coxhill Green
Coxhill Ho.
Heath-Hill Fm
Philpot Lane
The Bourne
Broadford
Broadford Lane
Refuse Tip
Sewage Works
Oakhurst Nursery
Milford Green
Castle Grove Road
Castle Grove Nurs.
Hagthorn Farm
Millbrook
Burnt Barn
Deeppool Fm
Carthouse Lane
Knap Hill Manor
Chobham Road
Bunyan's Lane
Romany Rd.
Wapshott Ho.
Shaws Fm
Young Stroat Farm
Mimbridge Cott
Chobham Road
Horsell Common
Horsell Recreation Centre
High Sch.
Mat. Hosp. Annex
Littlewick Road
Horsell Birch
Deep Pool
Cowslip La.
Holly Cotts
Parley Brook
Nurs.
Knaphill Nursery
Littlewick
82
100
56
57
58
59
60
AO
AP
AQ
AR
AS
M3
B386
B383

91
AS
AT
AU
AV
82
92
100
KT16
KT15
KT14
GU22
M25
A320
A319
A245
B385
B3121
B367
Botleys
France Farm
Holloway Road
St. Peter's Hosp.
Botleys Park Hosp.
Church Farm
Fish Pond
Sports Grd.
Sports Ground
Home Wood
Fox Hills
Kitchenride Corner
Golf Course
Stonehill Road
Foxhills Road
Huntingdon
Bittams Lane
St. Peters Way
Meadowcroft First Sch.
Simple Marsh Fm.
Weston Convent
Abbeylands Sports Centre
St. Pauls Mid. Sch.
Simplemarsh
School Lane
Church Rd.
Ether Hill
Recreation Ground
Ambulance Station
Ottershaw
Murray Road
Ottershaw Hosp.
Great Grove Farm
Spinney Hill
Hare Hill
Rowhill
Rec. Grd.
R.C. First Sch.
Coach House
Queenwood Farm
Chobham Road
Cross Lane Footpath
Ottershaw Prim. Sch.
Sch. Chaworth Sch.
Meath School
Spratts
Prim. Sch.
Bousley Rise
Nursery Farm
Nursery
The Common
Caravan Site
School
Nurseries
Tulk House
Playing Field
Ottershaw Sch.
Tennis Courts
Miniature Rifle Range
Long Copse
Guildford Road
Brox Copse
Brox Lane
Brox Wood
Rodwell Farm
Hall's Farm
The Bourne
Caravan Site
Little Blackmole Pond
Beech Hill Clump
Sandpit Plantation
Great Wood
Great Blackmole Pond
South Plantation
The Wey Farm
Woodlands Clo.
The Warren
Birch Wood
Ware Copse
Anningsley Park
Decoy Plantation
Grange Fm.
The Grange Prim. Sch.
Woodham Park Road
Queen Marys Dr.
Woodham
Old Farm
Dunford Bridge
Bonsey's Farm
The Larches
Hoyt Wood
Golf Course
Club Ho.
Durnford Farm
Martyr's Lane
Scotland Lock
Playing Field
Basingstoke Canal
West Byfleet
Club
Lock
Sheerwater Br.
Anthonys
New Zealand Golf Course
Danewell Hill
Danewell Gutter
Woodham Lane
Hall
Chertsey Road
Six Cross Roads
Sheerwater
Running Track
Rec. Grd.
Comm. Cen.
Youth Cen.
Sheerwater Business Centre
Club House
West Byfleet Golf Course
Allot.
Moslem Burial Grd.
Tumulus
Monument Br.
Council Depot
Genesis Business Park
Allotments
Coldharbour
Coldharbour Rd.
Oakcroft Road
Hare Hill
Lees Fm.
Ridgeway
Provident Place
Recrea Grd.

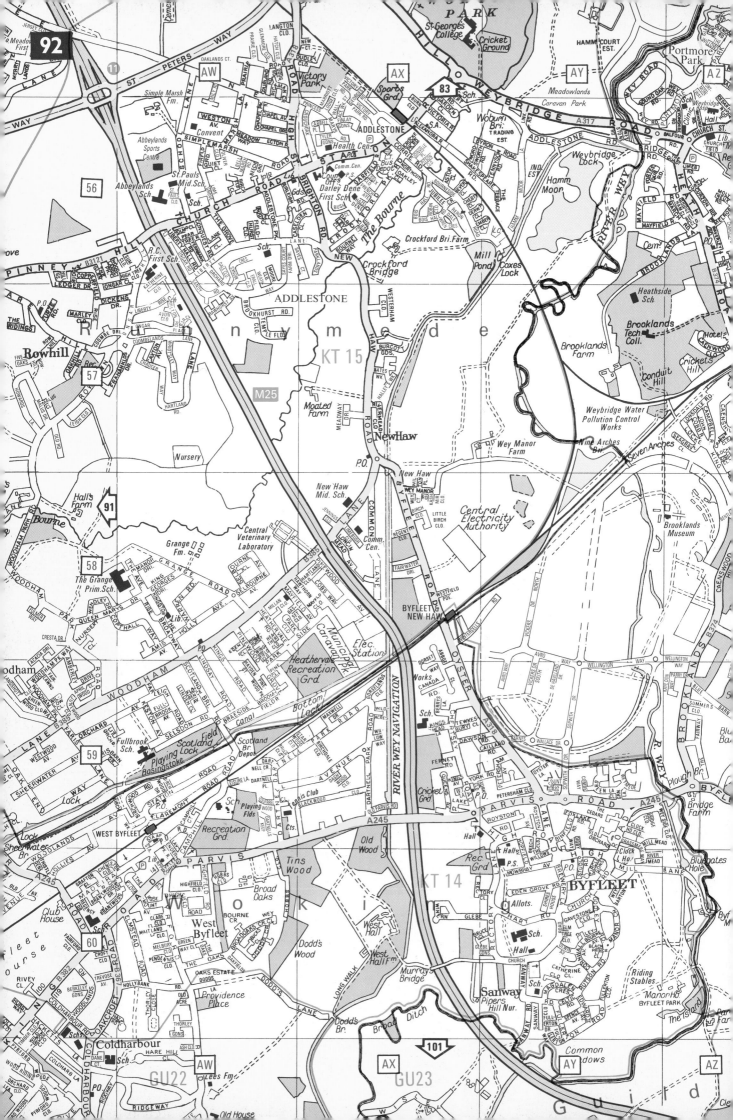
AW
AX
AY
AZ
56
57
58
59
60
83
91
101
PARK
St.George's College
Cricket Ground
HAMM COURT EST.
Portmore Park
Victory Park
Meadowlands Caravan Park
WEYBRIDGE ROAD
ST PETERS WAY
Simple Marsh Fm.
Abbeylands Sports Centre
Convent
ADDLESTONE
Health Cen.
Sports Grd.
Woburn Bri.
TRADING EST.
ADDLESTONE RD.
Weybridge Lock
Hamm Moor
IND. EST.
RIVER WEY
St.Pauls Mid.Sch.
Abbeylands Sch.
CHURCH ROAD
STATION
Darley Dene First Sch.
Bus Depot
The Bourne
Crockford Bri.Farm
Mill Pond
Coxes Lock
Crockford Bridge
R.C. First Sch.
PINNEY HILL
B3121
ADDLESTONE
Runnymede
KT 15
M25
Rowhill
Heathside Sch.
Brooklands Tech Coll.
Brooklands Farm
Crickets Hill
Conduit Hill
Moated Farm
New Haw
Nursery
Weybridge Water Pollution Control Works
Wey Manor Farm
Nine Arches Bri.
Seven Arches
Hall's Farm
Bourne
New Haw Mid. Sch.
Central Electricity Authority
Brooklands Museum
Central Veterinary Laboratory
Grange Fm.
The Grange Prim.Sch.
Comm. Cen.
BYFLEET & NEW HAW
Municipal Caravan Pk.
Elec. Station
Heathervale Recreation Grd.
WOODHAM
WOODHAM LANE
Bottom Lock
Scotland Lock
Playing Field
Fullbrook Sch.
Basingstoke Canal
Scotland Br. Depot
RIVER WEY NAVIGATION
OYSTER LANE
A318
WELLINGTON WAY
AVRO WAY
R. WEY
Plough Br.
Bridge Farm
Sheerwater Lock
Tennis Club
Cricket Grd
PARVIS ROAD
A245
WEST BYFLEET
Recreation Grd.
Old Wood
Tins Wood
Broad Oaks
KT 14
BYFLEET
Bluegates Hole
Club House
West Byfleet
Woking
Dodd's Wood
West Hall
West Hall Fm.
Murray's Bridge
Providence Place
Sanway
Pipers Hill Nur.
Riding Stables
Manor Ho.
BYFLEET PARK
The Island
Broad Ditch
Dodd's Br.
Coldharbour
Common Meadows
GU22
GU23
Lees Fm.
Old House
Guildford

WEYBRIDGE
Golf Course
Recreation Grd.
Ellesmere Hosp.
Burwood Park
Burwood Park (School)
Broad Water Lake
Walton on Thames
Thistlecroft
KT 12
KT 13
KT 11
Burvale Cemetery
Upper Common
Rabbitlane Ho.
Mud Town
Southwood Manor Farm
Park Cottage
Burhill Golf Course
Burhill Club Ho.
Whiteley Village
Home of Rest
St. George's Hill
Tennis Grd
Warren Pond
Rissington
Fox Oak
Strawberry Hill
Hill Farm
Turpins Cottage
Norwood Farm
River Mole
American Community School
Upper Pond
Club Ho.
Beards Hill
Burwood
Fairmile Hotel
Chippings Farm
Holmdene
Moorlands
Lingwood
Manor Pond
The Birches
Foxholme Covert
Fox Holme
Silver Mere
Silvermere
Silvermere Farm
Silvermere Golf Course
The Grange
Thirty Acre Wood
Seven Hills Motel
San Domenico
Belt Wood
Cobham Bri.
Pain's Hill
Painshill Park
The Broom
Wood Hill
Temple of Bacchus
Foxwarren Park
Wheel Island
OLD COMMON
COBHAM
Randalls Fm
Cott. Hosp
Rec Grd
Village Hall
Day Centre
Cricket Grd
Rose Lodge Wood
Cobham Court
BYFLEET ROAD
PORTSMOUTH ROAD
SEVEN HILLS ROAD
QUEENS ROAD
OATLANDS DRIVE
BURWOOD ROAD
ST GEORGES AVENUE
BETWEEN STREETS
STREET COBHAM
REDHILL ROAD
HERSHAM ROAD
STATION AVENUE
ONSLOW ROAD

83
93
101

HERSHAM
Thistlecroft
WALTON ON THAMES
Trinity Sch.
Sandown Park Golf Centre
Winning Post
Grandstand
The Warren
ESHER
Civic Centre
Waynflete's or Wolsey's Towers
Esher Place
South Waylands Fm.
KT12
Coronation Play. Flds.
R.C.Mid.Sch.
ESHER ROAD
HERSHAM BY-PASS
Rec. Grd.
Albany Br.
Recreation Ground
West End
Princess Alice Hospice
Glenhurst
Hawks Hill
Belvedere Hill
Milburn
Milburn Rough
Medical Cent.
Winterhouse Farm
MOAT
RIVER MOLE
WEST END COMMON
Southwood Manor Farm
Mud Town
Burhill Club Ho.
Claremont (School)
Claremont Landscape Gardens
CLAREMONT PARK
Island Pond
Stable Pond
Black Hill
Cowpond Wood
Albany Cotts
PORTSMOUTH ROAD
STONY HILL
The Ledges
WINTERDOWN WOOD
Winter Down
ESHER COMMON
Black Pond
Heywood
American Community School
Norwood Farm
Middle Pond
Spring Pond
Round Close
Fairmile
Fairmile Hotel
Fairmile Cottage
Chippings Farm
OLD COMMON
COBHAM
Randalls Fm.
Cott. Hosp.
Rec. Grd.
Village Hall
Day Centre
OXSHOTT HEATH
Oxshott Heath
Copse Wood
War Mem.
Heath Hill
OXSHOTT
Cocks Crossing
Little Heath
Knowle Hill
Beechmead
KT11
Weir
Rose Lodge Wood
Knott Park
A3
A244
A307
A245
A317
BD
BE
BF
BG
56
57
58
59
60
84
92
102

HINCHLEY WOOD
Fire Station
Government Offices
84
The Waffrons
Club Ho.
SURBITON GOLF COURSE
Telegraph Hill
Semaphore Ho.
Sports Ground
Couchmore Cotts.
Beazleys Fm.
KT10
Harelane Green
Loseberry
CLAYGATE
Wingham
Lower Wood
R.A.F. Chessington (Disused)
HOOK
Recreation Ground
Sports Ground
Playing Field
56
57
58
59
60
CHESSINGTON NORTH
Recreation Ground
Subway
Government Bldgs
Barwell Court
CHESSINGTON SOUTH
Fleetwood Sch.
KT9
Chessington
BARWELL TRADING ESTATE
Recreation Ground
Winey Hill Sports Ground
Sports Grd.
CLAYGATE COMMON
Ruxley Lodge
Horridon Farm
A3
Holroyd's Plantation
Birch Wood
Sixty Acre Wood
Chessington Zoo
Burnt Stub
Zoological Gardens
94
Park Farm
Peaked Riding
Stokesheath Farm
Jubilee Wood
Chessington Wood
Acrehill Farm
KT19
Malden Rushett
Milbournehold Plantation
Old Carpenters Plantation
The Heckets
Brickyard Plantation
Park Hospital
Glanmire Farm
Byhurst Farm
Stew Pond
KT18
Bunker's Hill
Rushet Farm
KT22
Oxshott
Adecroft Furze Field
Dane's Ct
Telegraph Hill
Reservoir
D'Abernon Chase
THE FOREST
KT21
102
Horns Hill
Oxshott Flat
Mole Valley
ASHTEAD COMMON
BG
BH
BJ
BK

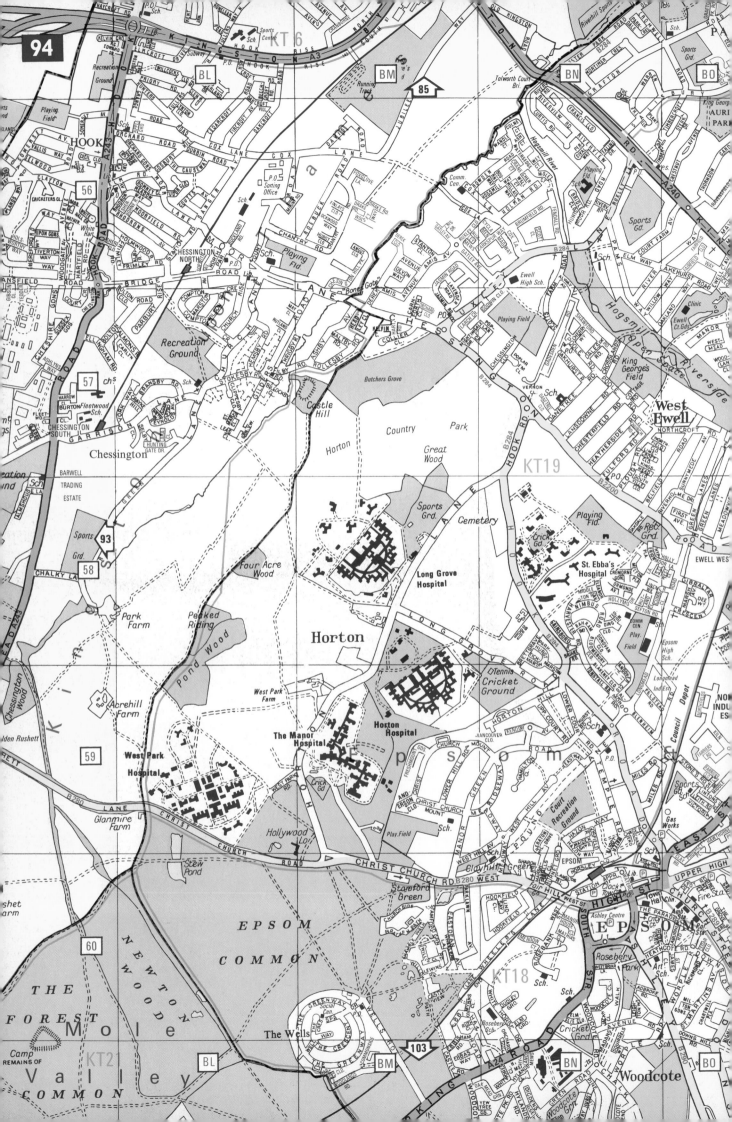

KT6
KT19
KT18
KT21
BL
BM
BN
BO
85
93
103
56
57
58
59
60
HOOK
Chessington
CHESSINGTON NORTH
CHESSINGTON SOUTH
BARWELL TRADING ESTATE
Recreation Ground
Playing Field
Castle Hill
Butchers Grove
Horton Country Park
Great Wood
Four Acre Wood
Peaked Riding
Pond Wood
Park Farm
Acrehill Farm
Chessington Wood
Horton
Long Grove Hospital
St. Ebba's Hospital
Horton Hospital
The Manor Hospital
West Park Hospital
West Park Farm
Glanmire Farm
Hollywood Lo.
Cemetery
Tennis Cricket Ground
Court Recreation Ground
Hogsmill Open Space
King George's Field
West Ewell
Ewell High Sch.
Epsom High Sch.
Stew Pond
Stamford Green
EPSOM COMMON
NEWTON WOOD
THE FOREST
Mole Valley
COMMON
The Wells
Woodcote
Rosebery Park
EPSOM
Ashley Centre
CHRIST CHURCH RD. B280
KINGSTON A3
HOOK ROAD A243
B284
B2200
A240
KINGSTON ROAD
A24 ROAD

STONELEIGH
NONSUCH PARK
Mansion House
Site of Nonsuch Palace
Diana's Dyke
Rems. of Banqueting Hall
Nonsuch High Sch for Girls
Playing Field
Harefield Br.
CHEAM
Cheam Recreation Ground
Cheam Park
Lower Cheam
Seear's Park
EWELL
EWELL EAST
Ewell Cnty. Tech. Coll.
Playing Fields
Priest Hill
Howell Hill
Cuddington Golf Course
Cuddington Hospital
BANSTEAD DOWNS
Golf Course
North Looe
Epsom College
Sports Ground
Recreation Ground
Lower Mill
Bourne Hall
Belmont Hosp.
WEST SUTTON
BANSTEAD
L.R.T. Sports Ground
Sutton & Epsom R.U.F.C.
Sports Ground
Drift Br.
85
95
103
56
57
58
59
60
BO
BP
BQ
BR
KT17
SM1
SM2
SM3
SM7
A24
A232
A240
A217
A2022
B283
B288
B2230
B291

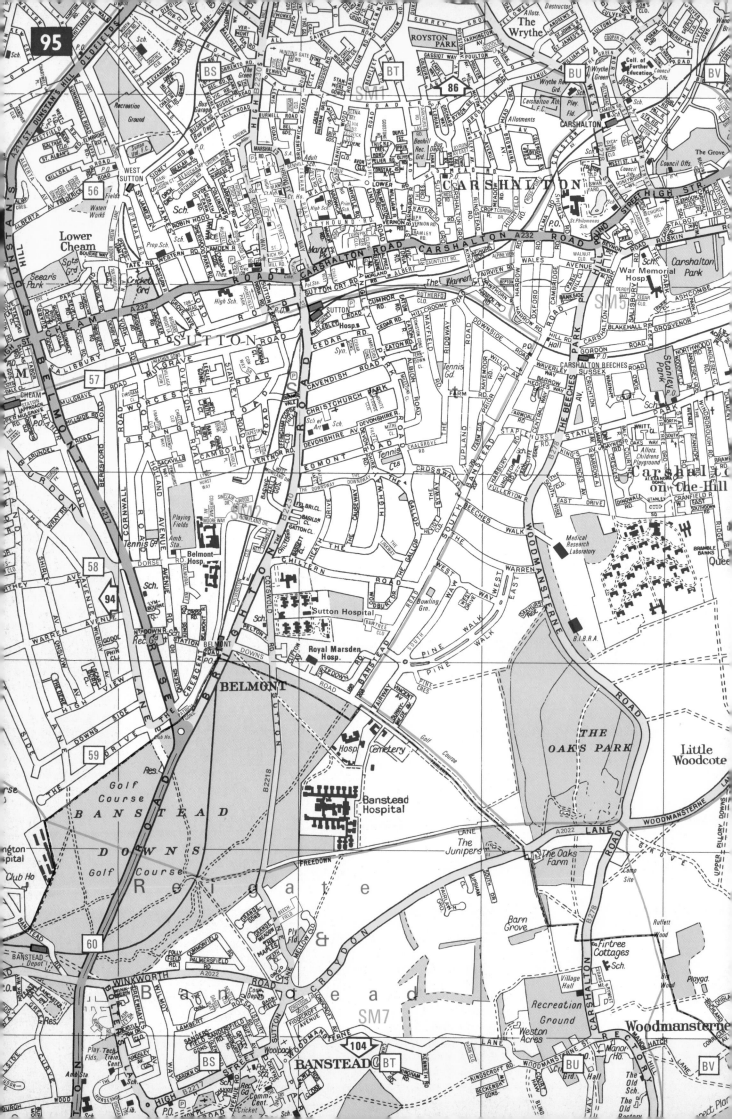
BS
BT
BU
BV
86
56
57
58
59
60
94
104
SM1
SM2
SM5
SM7
The Wrythe
Royston Park
Carshalton
Carshalton Beeches
Carshalton on-the-Hill
Carshalton Park
Stanley Park
War Memorial Hosp.
The Grove
Council Offs.
Coll. of Further Education
Carshalton Ath. F.C.
Allotments
St.Philomenas Sch.
West Sutton
Lower Cheam
Cheam
Sutton
Sutton Hospital
Royal Marsden Hosp.
Belmont
Belmont Hosp.
Medical Research Laboratory
B.I.B.R.A.
The Oaks Park
Little Woodcote
The Oaks Farm
The Junipers
Banstead Hospital
Banstead Downs
Golf Course
Reigate & Banstead
Barn Grove
Firtree Cottages
Ruffett Wood
Village Hall
Recreation Ground
Weston Acres
Woodmansterne
Banstead
Recreation Ground
Water Works
Seears Park
Playing Fields
Bowling Grn.
Cemetery
A217
A232
A2022
B2230
B2218
B2217
B278
Carshalton Road
Sutton Road
Cheam Road
Belmont Rise
Brighton Road
Banstead Road
Woodmansterne Road
Woodmansterne Lane
Croydon Lane
Carshalton Road
Rectory Lane
St. Dunstan's Hill
High Street
The Gallop
Chiltern Road
Downs Road
Sutton Lane
Winkworth Road
Freedown Lane
West Street
North Street
Pound Street
High Street
The Warren
Downside Road
Mulgrave Road
Egmont Road
Devonshire Avenue
Christchurch Park
Cavendish Road
Cedar Road
The Beeches Avenue
South Beeches
The Downsway
Pine Walk

BV
BW
BX
BY
86
56
57
58
59
60
96
104
WALLINGTON
BEDDINGTON
South Beddington
Bandon Hill
Waddon
Roundshaw Estate
Woodcote Green
Upper Woodcote
PURLEY
Little Roke
SM6
CR0
CR8
CR3
DUPPAS HILL
HALING PARK
PLAYING FIELDS
Woodcote Park Golf Course
Sports Ground
Russell Hill
Reedham
Smitham
Kenley

DUPPAS HILL
Recreation Ground
SHIRLEY PARK GOLF COURSE
Playing Field
LLOYD PARK
Playing Fld.
Coombe Fm.
Oaks Fm.
St. Margaret's Sch.
Spastics Cent.
ADDINGTON HILLS
Reservoir
Russell Sch.
Coombe Wood
BALLARDS PLANTATION
Warehousemen Clerks & Drapers Schools
Ballards Farm
Playing Fields
Sports Grd.
Sports Ground
Club House
Whitgift School
War Memorial
HALING PARK
Playing Field
SOUTH CROYDON
PLAYING FIELDS
Haling Manor High Sch.
Haling Grove Playing Flds
Croham Hurst
CROHAM HURST
Croham Hurst Golf Course
Thrift Wood
Littleheath Woods
Bramley Bank
Old Fox
Russell Hill Reservoir
South Croydon Recreation Ground
SANDERSTEAD
PURLEY OAKS
Purley Beeches
CR2
CR0
Purley Oaks Fm.
Sanderstead Plantatn
Selsdon
Selsdon Hill
Selsdon Park Hotel
Selsdon Court Hotel
Selsdon Park Golf Course
PURLEY
PURLEY DOWNS Golf Course
Club Ho.
RIDDLESDOWN
Sanderstead Recreation Grd
Sports Grd.
Mitchley Wood
Ragged Grove
Coombs Wood
Little Roke
Cricket Ground
Kenley Hotel
KENLEY
RIDDLESDOWN
Riddlesdown High Sch.
Barnfield Shaw
Ansley Berry Shaw
KINGSWOOD
Foxley Wood
Higher Dri. Recreatn Grd.
Recn Gd.
Pumping Sta.
Dipsley's Shaw
Hayes Ct.
School
Fire Sta.
BZ
CA
CB
CC
87
95
105
56
57
58
59
60
A212
A232
A235
A236
A22
A2022
A243
B275
B269
B2243
COOMBE ROAD
BRIGHTON ROAD
SOUTH END
CROHAM ROAD
UPPER SELSDON ROAD
ADDINGTON ROAD
LIMPSFIELD ROAD
MITCHLEY AVENUE
RIDDLESDOWN ROAD
GODSTONE ROAD
SANDERSTEAD HILL
ADDINGTON ROAD
CROHAM VALLEY ROAD
BALLARDS WAY
FARLEY ROAD
HALING PARK ROAD
WADDON WAY
PURLEY DOWNS ROAD
RECTORY PARK
FOXLEY ROAD

ADDINGTON GOLF COURSE
SHIRLEY HEATH
ADDINGTON PARK
Addington
Addington Palace Golf Course
RECREATION GROUND
Forestdale
New Addington
Addington Court Public Golf Course
FRITH WOOD
SELSDON WOOD
FRYLANDS WOOD
CRAB WOOD
Farleigh
Tandridge
Bromley
ROWDOWN WOOD
CR0
CR3
BR2
BR4
87
97
105

Coney Hall
West Wickham Common
Hayes Common
Keston Mark
Keston
Keston Common
White Shaw
Rouse Farm
Well Wood
Rouse Wood
Hazel Wood
Long Shaw
Cooper's Wood
Nash
Fox Hill
Old Chalk Pit
Wickham Court Farm
Wickham Court Univ.& Sch.
Coney Hall Recreation Ground
Sparrows Den Playing Fields
Miry Grove
Fox Hill Rd. Farm
Leafy Grove
Jackass Shaw
Waits' Cottages
Fuller's Wood
James's Wood
Baldwin Shaw
Bradmanshill Wood
War Bank
The Temple (Remains of)
Keston Ct.
Rushfield Shaw
Broomfieldbank Shaw
Rowdown Wood
New Addington
Blackness
May's Farm
Layham's Farm
Furze Bottom
Stagmanspit Cotts.
Sports Gd.
Crown Inn
Hoppershatch Shaw
Bradmoor
The Green
High Ho.
Leaves Green
Old House Fm
W. Wickham Reservoir
Playing Field
Higham's Hill
Club Ho.
Gushybank Shaw
Threecorner Grove
Playing Field
Fairchildes School
Jewels Wood
R.A.F. Married Quarters
Chapel Hill
Fairchildes
Bograms Wood
Beechfield Wood
Fairchildes Farm
Fickleshole Farm
Blackmans
TN16
Biggin Hill Aerodrome
Tandridge
Greathill Shaw
Crookedash Shaw
CR3
Five Acre Shaw
Midgley Shaws
Skid Hill
BR4
BR2
Bromley
Croydon
88
96
106
CG
CH
CJ
CK
56
57
58
59
60

FARNBOROUGH
GREEN STREET GREEN
Downe
Cudham
Single Street
Farthing Street
Locksbottom
Farnborough Hospital
Orpington Hosp.
CUCKOO WOOD
NEWYEARS WOOD
High Elms
Nature Centre
Golf Course
Downe Ho. Museum
Angas Convalescent Home for Seamen
St Peter & St Pauls Ch.
St Giles's Ch.
FARNBOROUGH WAY
FARNBOROUGH COMMON
SEVENOAKS WAY
BR6
TN14
88
98
106
CK
CL
CM
CN
56
57
58
59
60

89
97
107
CO
CP
CQ
CR
56
57
58
59
60
BR 6
Bromley
Goddington Ho.
GODDINGTON PARK
Playing Field
Pumping Sta
Orpington Hosp.
ORPINGTON A224
SEVENOAKS ROAD
SEVENOAKS ROAD
A21 SEVENOAKS
CHELSFIELD
Lilly's Wood
Lilly's Farm
Chelsfield Ho.
Cannock Sch.
Woodlands
Birch Wood
Chelsfield
Buck's Cross
Maypole
Court Lo Farm
St Martin of Tours ch
Court Lodge
High Beeches
World's End
Julian Brimstone
Tunnel
The Bo Peep
Hewitts
Coneyearth Wood
Goss Bushes
KNOCKHOLT
Chelsfield Hall
GREEN STREET GREEN
Chelsfield Hill Wood
Rounds Wood
Pratt's Bottom
Stonehouse Farm
Broke Farm
Pond
Watercrofts Wood
Little Molloms Wood
Charm Wood
Pratt's Bottom Wood
Pratt's Grove
Hook Wood
Rushmore Hill Wood
Birthday Wood
St Margaret's Ch.
Halstead Pla Sch.
Rectory
St MARGARETS CHURCH (Remains)
Colgates
Norsted Manor
Fairtrough
Lower Brooms Wood
Upper Brooms Wood
Lattice Coppice
Broom Wood
Homefield Spring
High Wood
Village Ho.
Pol. Off.
The Cock Inn
Halstead
Hazel Cottages
Lower Randle's Wood
Deerleap Wood
The Washneys
Perry Wood
Birchingbank Wd
Park Farm
New Stables Farm
NEWYEARS WOOD
Newlands Wood
Hayman's Wood
Piece Wood
Curry Farm
Birches Croft
Long Shaw
Single's Cross
Broomfield Wood
Chapel Croft
Jockey's Wood
Blueberry Farm
Nurs.
WARREN ROAD
CHURCH RD
CHELSFIELD HILL
LONDON ROAD
STONEHOUSE LANE
OLD STATION ROAD
SHOREHAM LA
CHURCH ROAD
OTFORD ROAD
RUSHMORE HILL
KNOCKHOLT RD
HARROW ROAD
POUND OR BOND LANE
SINGLES CROSS LANE
NORSTED LANE
CHARMWOOD LANE

CR
CS
CT
CU
89
Hulberry Corner
The Firs
Skeet Hill
The Roughet
Lullingstone Roman Villa
Newbarn
EYNSFORD
DA 4
LULLINGSTONE
PARK
Golf Course
Deer Park
Well House
Parkgate
Doctors Wood
FURMINGERS ROAD
Miss.
WELL HILL
Lullingstone
St Botolph's Ch.
Lullingstone Castle
Weir
56
UPPER BEECHEN WOOD
LOWER BEECHEN WOOD
HOME WOOD
WELL HILL ROAD
REDMANS LANE
Cockerhurst
M25
West Wood
CASTLE (Remains)
Castle Fm.
57
COCKERHURST ROAD
CASTLE FARM ROAD
Coombe Hollow
Coombe Firs
Preston Hill Plantation
Rifle Ranges
99
58
Targets
Preston Hill
R. DARENT
Preston Farm
4
BARNETT'S WOOD
CHELSFIELD LA.
Saunders
Timbenden Farm
Timberden Bottom
SHACKLANDS ROAD
Darenthdale
Osbourne Fm.
The Mill Ho.
MILL LA.
CROWN RD.
Badgers Mount
CHARLES RD.
HIGHLAND RD.
Sevenoaks
Gold Hill
Dunstall Priory
DUNSTALL WOODS
JENKIN'S NECK WOOD
Shacklands
ANDREW'S WOOD
MEENFIELD WOOD
Recreation Ground
Hall
HIGH ST.
The Mount
SHOREHAM
CHURCH ST.
STATION ROAD
SHOREHAM
Capt Hall
59
MILDMAY PL.
Sch.
Pol. Ho.
MESNE WAY
Robsack Wood
TN 14
Shoreham Pla.
White Hill
FACKENDEN LA.
Black Eagle P.H.
A224
LONDON ROAD
Tunnel
Shepherds Barn Cottages
WATER LA
Filston Hall
MOAT
Home Farm
PILOTS WOOD
The Aero
Sepham Heath
LANE
Polhill Arms
60
EYNSFORD ROAD
SHOREHAM ROAD
A225
Lower Barn
Sepham Farm
107
POLHILL
BECKMAN CLO.
FORT RD.
CROW DR.
ARMSTRONG CLO.
GREENHILL RD
HILLYDEAL RD
COOMBE RD.
R. DARENT

EYNSFORD
Lullingstone
Lullingstone Roman Villa
Lullingstone Castle
St Botolph's Ch.
Pumping Sta.
Pol Ho.
STATION RD
POLLYHAUGH
ST MARTINS DR
EYNSFORD RISE
Newbarn
Weir
Reservoir
A225
EYNSFORD ROAD
SHOREHAM ROAD
Chalkhurst
Chalkhurst Wood
UPPER AUSTIN LODGE ROAD
Lower Austin Lodge
Upper Austin Lodge
Eynsford Range (Gun Testing)
BOWER LANE
Park Ho Farm
Park House Cotts
Res.
UPPER PARK WOOD
HARTNIPS WOOD
The Strikes
DA4
Olivers Shaw
Sandhole Shaw
MAPLESCOMBE
Lower Park Wood
Maplescombe Farm
Adder Bank Shaw
Countfield Shaw
CHAPEL (Remains)
THE BIRCHES
Coombe Fins
Preston Hill Plantation
Rifle Ranges
Targets
Preston Hill
Preston Farm
R. DARENT
HOG WOOD
HIGH CASTLE WOOD
ASHEN GROVE
ASHEN GROVE ROAD
Trailer Park
Caravan Park
East Hill Farm
EAST HILL
Sevenoaks
Lower Wood
BROOM WOOD
Upper Wood
Gold Hill
Dunstall Priory
DUNSTALL WOODS
TN14
SHOREHAM
Copt Hall
White Hill
FACKENDEN LA
Austin Spring
Dunstall Farm
Pig & Whistle
Romney Street Farm
Romney Street
Countfield Wood
Lit. Countfield Wood
LEIZE WOOD
PECKEN WOOD
East Hill
Warren Shaw
Lib
P.O.
Magpie Bottom
Doctor's Wood
Kit's Wood
Highfield Wood
Highfield
Sevenacre Stubs
ROWDOW
Littlehurst Fm.
Porters Fm.
Eastdown
LANE
GODDBURY RD
Goodbury Farm
CROSS ROAD
CLARKE'S GREEN RD.
TINKERPOT
COTMANS
GREAT WOOD
Paine's Farm
Greenhill Wood
Hillydeal Wood
GREENHILL RD
HILLYDEAL RD.
DOWNS WAY
Beech Lees Wood
Carpenters Wood
Monks in the Hole
SHOREHILL LA
Shorehill Farm
Fabs Wood
Four Acre Wood
ROWDOW WOOD
Flatdeal Wood
CV
CW
CX
CY
90
98
108
56
57
58
59
60

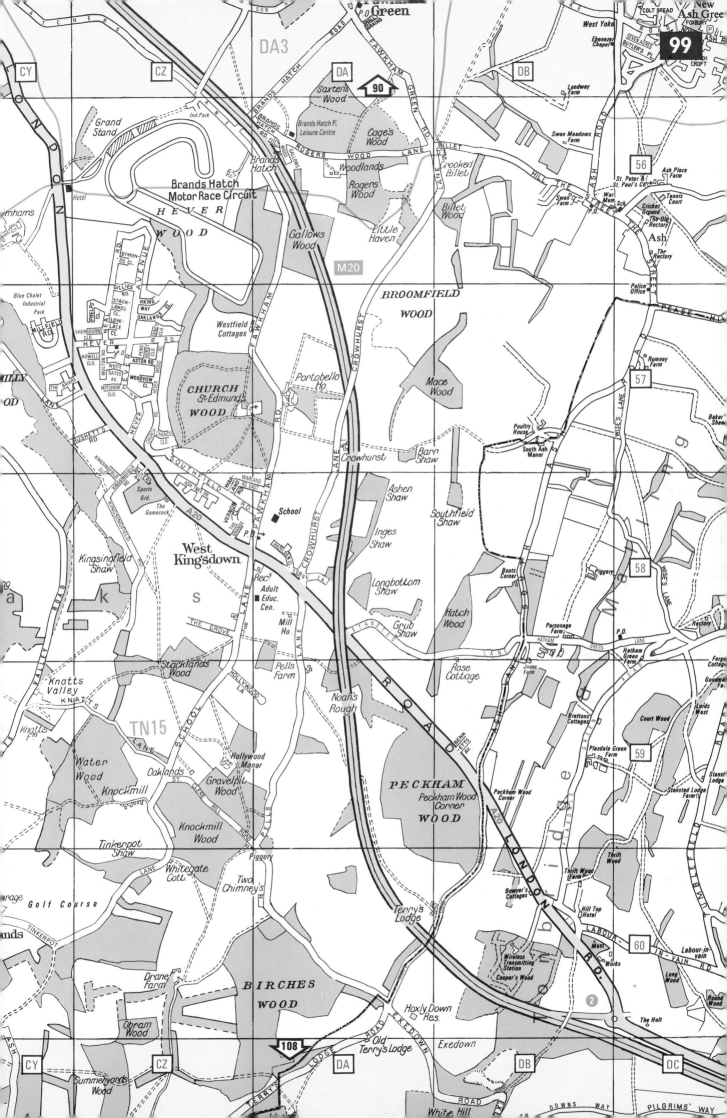

99
Brands Hatch Motor Race Circuit
West Kingsdown
Brands Hatch
Crowhurst
Church Wood
Broomfield Wood
Peckham Wood
Birches Wood
Knatts Valley
Ash
Knockmill
Terry's Lodge
Exedown
White Hill
M20
A20
DA3
TN15
90
108
56
57
58
59
60
CY
CZ
DA
DB
DC

100
GU24
GU21
GU22
GU3
GU4
AO
AP
AQ
AR
AS
91
109
61
62
63
64
65
CARTHOUSE LANE
Knap Hill Manor
CHOBHAM ROAD
A3046
HORSELL COMMON
Holly Cotts.
Nurs.
Parley Brook
LITTLEWICK ROAD
Littlewick Common
Knaphill Nursery
Lipscombe Farm
Nursery House
Whitfield Court
Waterers Park
Knaphill
Tracious Copse
Cricketers' Inn
Goldsworth Park IND. AREA
Allots.
Lake
Sch.
Social Centre
Horsell
Parish Hall
Horsell Recreation Centre
High Sch.
Mat. Hosp. Annex.
Cemy.
Horsell Moor
WOKING
Sports Grd
GOLDSWORTH
Step Bri.
Prim.Sch.
Mid.Sch.
LOCKFIELD DRIVE
ST JOHN'S ROAD
Locks
Sports Ground
The Winston Churchill Sch.
Brookwood Hospital
HERMITAGE ROAD
A324
Crematorium
Kiln Bridge
St. John's Lye
Cricket Ground
Basingstoke Canal
Hermitage Bridge
BROOKWOOD LYE RD.
Wych Street
WYCH HILL
STAR HILL
HOOK HEATH AV.
Ten. Club
Sports Gd
Allen House Park
Club Ho.
PONDMILE ROAD
GOLF CLUB RD
Hook Heath Golf Course
Hook Heath
New Copse
West Hill
Golf Course
Nursery
Gorse Hill
Hook Hill
Fishers Hill
Saracens
Brook Farm
Nurseries
BLACKHORSE ROAD
SAUNDERS LANE
Sanderslane Fm
Vill. Hall
Mayfield Centre
EGLEY ROAD
A320
Scout Hall
Sch.
Hoe Stream
Westfield Common
Pav. Cricket Grd.
Loampit Farm
Mayford
Loanbarn Farm
Crastock Farm
SMARTS HEATH RD.
B380
SMART'S HEATH
Worplesden Golf Course
Nurseries
Ellis Place
The House by the Green
Bridley Pond
Bridley Manor
Bridley Cross
Bridley Copse
BERRY LANE
BAGSHOT RD.
PREY HEATH
Kemishford Br.
WORPLESDON
Burdenshot Hill
BURDENSHOT HILL
Havering Farm
Stanford Brook
Blanketmill Farm
Stony Yarrows
Mayford Manor Hotel
Whitehouse Farm
Pyle Hill
Frog Lane Farm
GUILDFORD ROAD

100
KT14
GU23
AS
AT
AU
AV
91
101
109
61
62
63
64
65
Six Cross Roads
West Byfleet Golf Course
Coldharbour
Maybury
Woking
Kingfield
Westfield
Old Woking
Cartbridge
Send
Sendmarsh
Pyrford
Pyrford Common
Burntcommon
Sendbarns
Moslem Burial Grd.
Monument Br.
Tumulus
Council Depot
Genesis Business Park
Playing Field
Allotments
Shah Jehan Mosque
St. Peter's Home
St. Dunstan's Sch.
Maybury Inn
Fox Hill
The Hanger
The Rough
Pyrford Rough
Pyrford Court
Stone Farm
Church Farm
Wheeler's Fm.
Roundhill Farm
Monument Hill
Roundbridge Farm
Hoebridge Fm.
Hoe Bridge
Sewage Farm
Sewage Works
Carters Lane
Wokingpark Farm
Old Hall
Moat
R. Wey
Abbey Stream
Priory Church
Newark Priory
Newark Lane
Caravan Site
Seven Stars
Homewood Farm
Papercourt Lock
Papercourt Farm
Broadmead Cut
Broad Mead
R. Wey Navigation
Gravel Pit
Prews Farm
Papercourt Sailing Club
Boughton Hall Farm
Boughton Hall Hotel
Jovial Sailor
Garlick's Arch Copse
Send First Sch.
St. Bedes Mid. Sch.
Cricketshill Farm
Crickets Hill
Cricket Ground
Sedholme
Cemetery
Send Barns Farm
Triggs Lock
River Wey
Wareham's Farm
Runtleywood Farm
Chamberlands Br.
Runtley Wood
Fishers Fm.
Moorlane Fm.
Sports Grd.
Works
Mill Moor
Hipley Br.
Broadmead Br.
St. Peter's Church
Childs Home
St. John Comp. Sch.
Woking College
Sports Ground
Beechcroft Hosp.
Victoria Hosp.
Chertsey Rd. Br.
Rowley Bristow Orthopaedic Hospital
Youth Club
Crick. Gd.
Lees Fm.
Pyrford Place
Send Hill
Recn. Grd.
Depot
Lock
A245
A320
A247
B382
B367
B368
B380
B2215
Chertsey Road
Woodham Road
Old Woking Road
Pyrford Common Road
Upshott Lane
Coldharbour Road
Pyrford Road
Warren La.
Hockering Road
Heathside Park Rd.
Ashwood Rd.
Rose Lane
White Rose L.
Elm Bridge Lane
Rydens Way
High Street
Vicarage Rd.
Broadmead Rd.
Send Road
Send Barns La.
Sendmarsh Rd.
Tannery La.
Papercourt Lane
Polesden La.
Potters Lane
Portsmouth Rd.
Boughton Hall Avenue
Woodhill
Runtley Wood La.
Robin Hood Lane
Linden Way
Loop Rd.
Newark Lane
Ridgeway
Hare Hill Cl.
Teggs La.
Lovelace Dr.
East Hill
College Rd.
Maybury Hill
Princess Rd.
Balmoral Drive
Forest Rd.
Pinetree Hill
Lincoln Dr.
Hamilton Drive

101
Coldharbour
Pyrford
Pyrford Green
Wisley
Sanway
Ripley
Ripley Green
Ockham Park
Sendmarsh
Burntcommon
Woking
Guildford
GU22
GU23
KT14
M25
A3
River Wey
Wisley Common
Royal Horticultural Society's Gdns
Rowley Bristow Orthopaedic Hospital
Newark Priory
Walsham Meadow
Townslow Meadow
The Decoy
Papercourt Sailing Club
Oldlands Copse
Hungry Hill
92
110
100

101
92
102
110
AZ
BA
BB
BC
61
62
63
64
65
KT11
KT23
KT24
M25
A3
A245
B366
B2039
PAINSHILL PARK
Cobham Bri.
Pain's Hill
San Domenico
WOOD
The Broom
Temple of Bacchus
Wood Hill
The Lake
The Tower
Tower Hill
Red Hill
Wheel Island
Weir
Foxwarren Park
STREET COBHAM
BETWEEN STREETS
Cricket Grd
Rec. Grd
Village Hall
Day Centre
ANVIL LANE
DOWNSIDE BRIDGE ROAD
HIGH ST.
CHURCH ST.
RIVER HILL
MILL RD
STOKE RD
FREELANDS RD
HOGSHILL LANE
Lib.
Sch.
Rose Lodge Wood
Cobham Court
Downside Bridge
Cobham Tilt
P.O.
RIVER MOLE
CHATLEY WOOD
Chatley Fm.
Breach Hill Wood
Telegraph Hill
CHATLEY HEATH
OCKHAM COMMON
The Bogs
POINTERS ROAD
Pointers
Lodge Copse
Bramble Wood
Halfpenny Cross
PLOUGH LANE
Cobham Park
Park Wood
Mill Race
Cobham Stud Fm.
Curtain Pond Cottages
Cassins Farm
Chilbrook Farm
CHILBROOK FARM RD.
Pointers Green
Pointers Farm
Pondtail Farm
Brickfield Copse
Lit. Brickfield Copse
Downside Common
Downside
DOWNSIDE COMMON RD.
Downside Farm
BOOKHAM
HATCHFORD WOOD
HATCHFORD PARK
Hatchford Park School
St. Matthew's Church
Hatchford Farm
NORTON LA.
GOOSE GRN.
Cold Norton
Norton Wood
Parsonage
Hatchford Cotts
Hatchford End
Wilderness Farm
Hunt's Copse
HATCH LA.
OLD LANE
New Barn Farm
HORSLEY ROAD
Bull Riding Farm
Withy Bed
Martyr's Green
OCKHAM LANE
Pound Farm
Mays Green
OLD OAK COMMON
The New Preserve
Peaked Rough
Roundabout
Upton Farm
Tanner's Copse
HATCH LANE
Trulliber Copse
Chaffers Copse
HOOK WOOD
STUMPS GROVE
New Barn Wood
Newmarsh Farm
N. Surrey Gun Club
Nursery
Brick Kiln Copse
Clamp Rough
Bushy Thicket
Thicket Copse
Little Mornshill Wood
BANK'S LANE
National Trust
Blackmoor Farm
Gallows Grove
Bramble Cottage
Slade Farm
EFFINGHAM JUNC.
P.O.
BLUE RIDE
BARNSTHORNS WOOD
Club Ho.
Golf Course
Slater's Oak
Norwood Farm
LOWER FARM RD
EFFINGHAM COMMON
EFFINGHAM COMMON RD
The Drift
THE FOREST
FOREST RD
ORCHARD CLO.
Lower Farm
Mallards
Waterloo Farm
Broom House
Football Ground
NIGHTINGALE AV.
NORTHCOTE RD
Duncombe Farm
THE HIGHLANDS
PARKSIDE CLO.
WILD WOOD CLO.
FOREST CLO.
HOOKE RD
HEATH RIDE
NIGHTINGALE RD
THE RIDINGS
MOAT
Upper Lee
Manor Farm
HORSLEY
WHITEHILL LA.
BUNGALOW RD.
GREEN LANE
Even Wood

102
93
101
111
BD
BE
BF
BG
61
62
63
64
65
KT11
KT24
KT23
M25
A245
Rec Grd
Leigh Court
Little Heath
Knowle Hill
Knott Park
E l m b r i d g e
Rose Lodge Wood
Downside Bridge
Cobham Tilt
Cobham Cemetery
Cobham Park
Cobham Stud Fm
Curtain Pond Cottages
Cossins
Chilbrook Farm
Downside Common
Downside
Downside Farm
Park Wood
Mill Race
Little Roundabout
River Mole
Mill
COBHAM & STOKE D'ABERNON
Sports Fields
Lower Farm
Stoke D'Abernon
Upper Farm
Woodlands Farm
Woodlands Park (Hotel)
Old Parks
Parkside School
Old Parks Copse
R. Mole
Stoke D'Abernon Br
Muggeridge Wood
Wrens Hill Wood
Thornets Wood
Slyfield House
Little Wood
Yehudi Menuhin Music School
Bushy Copse
Sheepbell Farm
New Barn Farm
Down Wood
Spring Meadow Wood
Bookham Lodge
Chasemore Wood
Lady Chewtons Wood
Bull Riding Farm
Withy Bed
Peaked Rough
Chestnore Farm
Hundred Pound Bridge Wood
The Birches
Ashspring Copse
Monksgreen Farm
New Barn Wood
Hundred Pound Br
Newmarsh Farm
N. Surrey Gun Club
Nurs.
GREAT BOOKHAM COMMON
National Trust
BANK'S COMMON
LITTLE BOOKHAM COMMON
Banks Fm
Bushy Thicket
Thicket Copse
Little Mornshill Wood
Isle of Wight
GREAT MORNSHILL WOOD
Sewage Wks.
Slater's Oak
Norwood Farm
Bookham Grange Hotel
BOOKHAM
Bookham Tunnel
Herons Reach
Mallards Mere
Lower Farm
OAKEN WOOD
Little Bookham
THORNET WOOD
Upper Lee Wood Farm
MOAT
Youth Club
Old Barn Hall
Sch.
P.O.
Hall
Ind. Est.

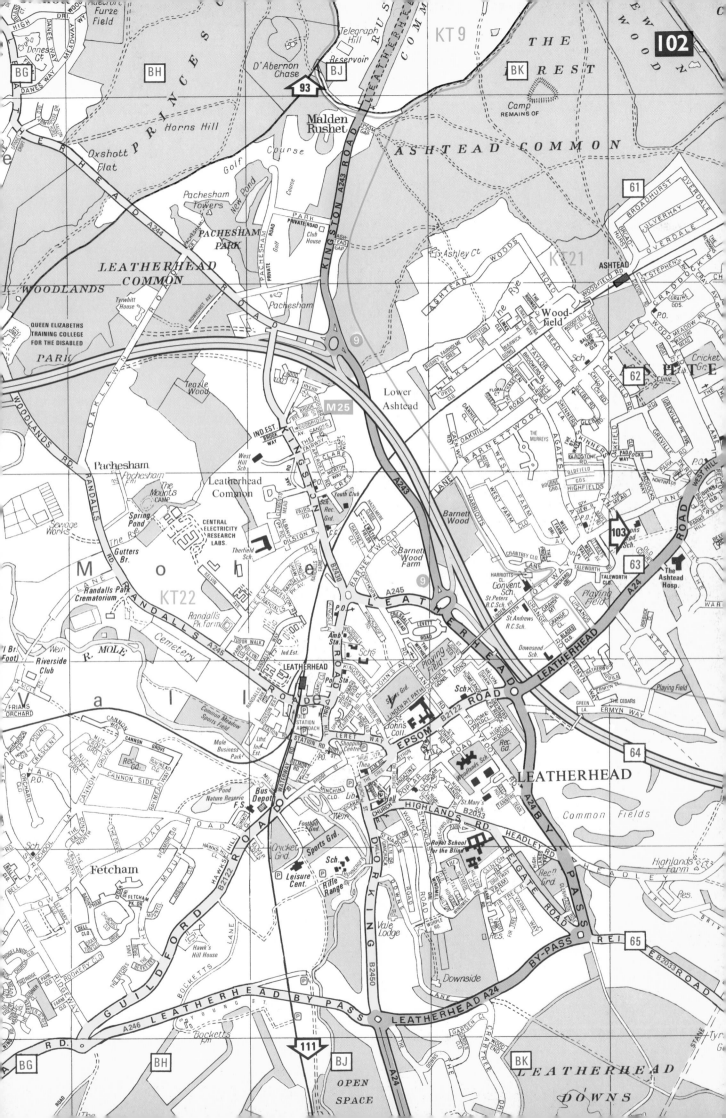

KT9
THE FOREST
Camp REMAINS OF
ASHTEAD COMMON
Telegraph Hill
Reservoir
D'Abernon Chase
93
Malden Rushet
PRINCES COVERTS
Horns Hill
Oxshott Flat
Golf Course
Pachesham Towers
New Pond
PACHESHAM PARK
Club House
KINGSTON A243 ROAD
LEATHERHEAD COMMON
WOODLANDS
Tyrwhitt House
QUEEN ELIZABETHS TRAINING COLLEGE FOR THE DISABLED
PARK
Pachesham
KT21
Ashley Ct.
ASHTEAD WOODS ROAD
The Rye
Wood-field
ASHTEAD
61
62
63
64
65
ASHTEAD
Lower Ashtead
M25
Teazle Wood
IND. EST.
West Hill Sch.
Pachesham
The Mounts CAMP
Spring Pond
Sewage Works
CENTRAL ELECTRICITY RESEARCH LABS.
Leatherhead Common
Therfield Sch.
Youth Club
Barnett Wood
Barnett Wood Farm
BARNETTWOOD LANE
The Murreys
Harriotts Cl.
Convent Sch.
St. Peters R.C.Sch.
St.Andrews R.C.Sch.
Downsend Sch.
Playing Field
103
The Ashtead Hosp.
Gutters Br.
Mole
KT22
Randalls Park Crematorium
Randalls Pk.Farm
Cemetery
R. MOLE
Riverside Club
RANDALLS A245 ROAD
LEATHERHEAD
Vale
Common Meadow Sports Field
Mole Business Park
St. John's Coll.
EPSOM B2122 ROAD
Woodlands Sch.
LEATHERHEAD
Common Fields
A24 BY PASS
Pond Nature Reserve
Bus Depot
F.S.
Football Gnd.
Cricket Grd.
Sports Grd.
Leisure Cent.
Rifle Range
Royal School for the Blind
HEADLEY RD.
REIGATE ROAD
Highlands Farm
Res.
Fetcham
GUILDFORD B2122 ROAD
Hawk's Hill House
BOCKETTS LANE
DORKING B2450 ROAD
Vale Lodge
Downside
A246 LEATHERHEAD BY PASS
LEATHERHEAD A24 BY-PASS
REIGATE B2033 ROAD
Bocketts Fm
111
OPEN SPACE
LEATHERHEAD DOWNS
BG
BH
BJ
BK

103
ASHTEAD
LEATHERHEAD
Woodcote
The Wells
Ashtead Park
Langley Vale
Woodfield
KT21
KT18
KT22
M25
A24
94
102
112
LEATHERHEAD DOWNS
NOWER WOOD
GREAT HURST WOOD
Epsom District Hosp.
City of London Freemens School
Headley Court Rehabilitation Centre
The Ashtead Hosp.
Golf Course
Common Fields
Addlestead Wood
Hook Wood
Tyrrells Wood Golf Course
DORKING ROAD
EPSOM ROAD
LEATHERHEAD ROAD
REIGATE ROAD
A24 BY-PASS
HEADLEY ROAD

BANSTEAD
Playing Field
Depot
A2022 ROAD
P.O.
NORK GDNS
Res
BO
BP
BQ
BR
94
COLLEGE ROAD
FIR TREE ROAD
Drift Br.
Drift Br. Ho.
Sports Ground
Tennis Ct.
Epsom College
KT17
Golf Club Ho.
LONGDOWN LANE SOUTH
EPSOM DOWNS
Res
B284
B291
B288
A240
Scout Hut
Hall
Play. Fld.
Schs.
ROUNDWOOD WAY
PARSONSFIELD ROAD
NORK RISE
NORK WAY
BEACON WAY
Comm. Cent.
Park Wood
NORK PARK
SM7
HILLSIDE
BURGH WOOD
Amb. Sta.
Sch.
Lib.
P.O.
61
HIGH ST
B2217
GARRATTS LANE
DICELAND RD.
FERNDALE RD.
LYME REGIS ROAD
STILLING CLO.
CHIPSTEAD ROAD
THORNFIELD ROAD
The Council House
Nork Park Sch.
THE BRINDLES
THE DRIVE
PICQUETS WAY
HEIGHTS CL.
Recreation Ground
CHURCH LANE
Nork Park
Nork
YEWTREE BOTTOM RD.
Buckle's Gap
Golf Course
GRAND STAND ROAD
OLD LONDON ROAD
Grand St.
TATTENHAM CORNER RD.
Race Course
Res
Tattenham Corner
TATTENHAM CORNER
Lib.
Clinic
Shawley Wd.
SHAWLEY WAY
Play. Fld.
Sch.
B2221
TATTENHAM WAY
GREAT TATTENHAMS
62
WOOD LA.
Wood Lo.
Canons Wood
Pages Acre
Ruffett Wood
Lambert's Shaw
Res.
BURGH HEATH
REIGATE ROAD
A217
BRIGHTON ROAD
BURGH HEATH
Playing Field
De Burgh Sch.
Merland Rise Recreation Ground
Sports Centre
Fir Wood
Sch.
Hall
P.O.
Canons Farm
Read's Rest Cottages
63
104
Temple Bar Sports Grd.
St. Monica's
OLD LONDON RD.
Race Course
Sth. Tadworth Farm
EPSOM LANE
B290
EPSOM DOWNS
CHETWODE ROAD
PRESTON LANE
COPTHILL LANE
FURZE HILL
WATERHOUSE LANE
Highhurst Woods
FOREST DRIVE
KINGSWOOD
64
Tadworth Ct. Childrens Hosp.
The Wilderness
Red House
KT20
BONSOR DRIVE
B2032
Sch.
Odeon Pond
TADWORTH
TADWORTH
Tunnel
Pond
Sch.
St. Cross Brit. Transport Pol. Train. Sch.
Tadworth Country Club Pond
Withybed Corner
Mere Pond
Mill Ho.
Nylenfield Walton Mill (Disused)
Hockey Grd.
CAMPS
Little Dowding
Castle House
112
War Memorial
Kingswood
Kingswood Warren (B.B.C. Research) Dept.
WARREN DRIVE
THE WARREN
65
Warren Farm
Club Ho.
Smugglers Pit Plantation
Bottom
Kingswood Golf
Sandhill Wood
WALTON STREET
P.O.
All.
Hall
WALTON ON THE HILL
BO
BP
BQ
BR
Club Ho.
Rec. Gd.
DORKING ROAD
BANSTEAD
CHIPSTEAD LANE
Hogden
Sports Grd.
Pav.
Millfield Wood
The Press at Kingswood
Reigate and Banstead

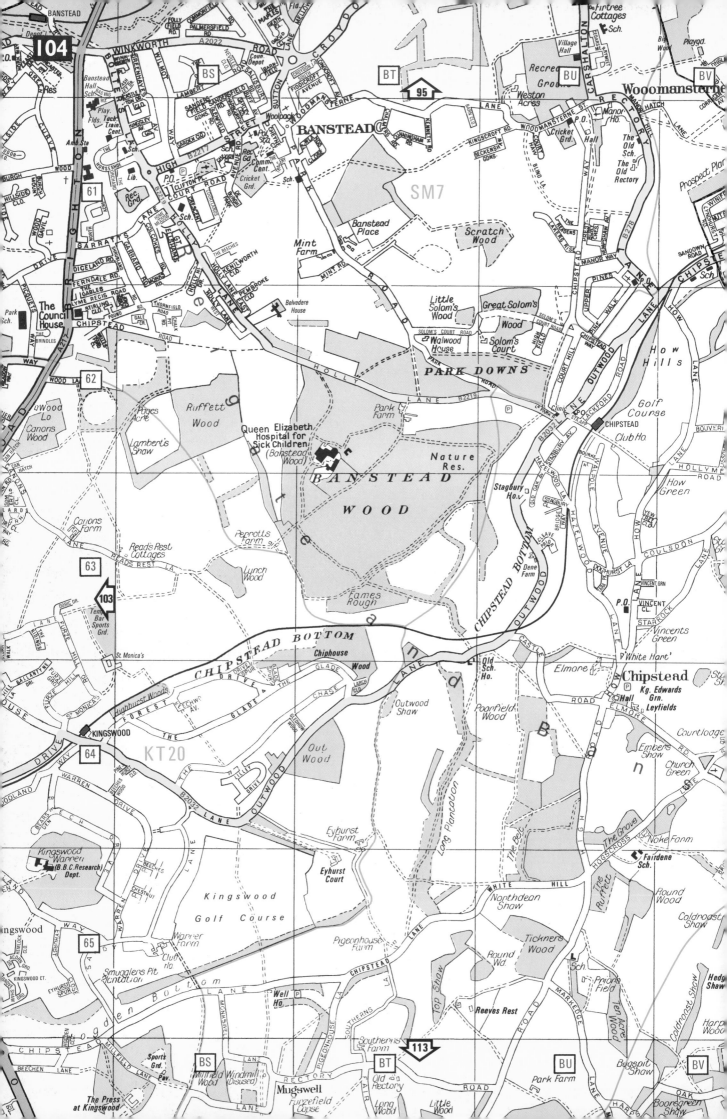
104
95
113
103
BANSTEAD
Woodmansterne
Chipstead
KINGSWOOD
CHIPSTEAD
SM7
KT20
BANSTEAD WOOD
PARK DOWNS
CHIPSTEAD BOTTOM
Queen Elizabeth Hospital for Sick Children (Banstead Wood)
Nature Res.
Kingswood Golf Course
Golf Course
The Council House
Mugswell
Kingswood Warren (B.B.C. Research) Dept.
Banstead Place
Mint Farm
Scratch Wood
Ruffett Wood
Lunch Wood
Fames Rough
Chiphouse Wood
Outwood Shaw
Out Wood
Poorfield Wood
Long Plantation
Tickners Wood
Northdean Shaw
Reeves Rest
Eyhurst Court
Eyhurst Farm
Pigeonhouse Farm
Warren Farm
Smugglers Pit Plantation
Southerns Farm
Park Farm
Windmill (Disused)
The Press at Kingswood
Fairdene Sch.
Noke Farm
Round Wood
Coldroast Shaw
How Hills
How Green
Vincents Green
Elmore
Kg. Edwards Grn.
Leyfields
Church Green
Courtlodge
Embers Shaw
Dene Farm
Stagbury Ho.
Canons Farm
Canons Wood
Reads Rest Cottages
Perrotts Farm
Pages Acre
Lamberts Shaw
Walwood House
Solom's Court
Great Solom's Wood
Little Solom's Wood
Belvedere House
Weston Acres
Village Hall
Firtree Cottages
Prospect Plan
Old Sch. Ho.
Temple Bar Sports Grd.
St. Monica's
Highhurst Woods
Sports Grd.
Millfield Wood
Furzefield Copse
Old Rectory
Well Ho.
Priors Field
Ten Acre Wood
The Ruffett
The Grove
Top Shaw
Round Wd.
Bugspit Shaw
Boorsgreen Shaw
Coldroast Shaw
Hedge Shaw
WINKWORTH ROAD
CHIPSTEAD ROAD
HOLLY LANE
OUTWOOD LANE
HIGH STREET
PARK ROAD
WHITE HILL
MARKEDGE LANE
RECTORY LANE
HOGSCROSS LANE
HOLLYMEAD ROAD
COULSDON LANE
STARROCK
CASTLE ROAD
ELMORE ROAD
HOW LANE
FOREST DRIVE
THE GLADE
CHIPSTEAD LANE
Hogden Bottom
BS BT BU BV
61 62 63 64 65

104
95
105
113
BV
BW
BX
BY
61
62
63
64
65
COULSDON
Old Coulsdon
Coulsdon Common
Chaldon
Waddington
Kenley
Smitham
Coulsdon South
Cane Hill Hospital
Netherne Hospital
St Lawrence's Hospital
Farthing Downs
Alderstead Heath
Woodcote Park Golf Course
Coulsdon Court (Club Ho.)
Public Golf Course
Happy Valley
Croydon
Tandridge
CR5
RH1
M23

Little Roke
RIDDLESDOWN
Kenley Hotel
Cricket Ground
Riddlesdown
CR2
96
Barnfield Shaw
Ansley Berry Shaw
Dipsley's Shaw
Hamsey Green
The Gorse
Rose & Crown
Chalk Pit
Warlingham Court Farm
Batts Farm
The Dobbin (Public Open Space)
Pumping Sta.
Swimming Bath
Bourne Park
KENLEY
Watendone Manor
Gas Works (Disused)
Kenley House
Whyteleafe
KENLEY COMMON
Whyteleafe Rec. Ground
UPPER WARLINGHAM
Sports Ground
Betts Mead Recreation Ground
Waddington
KENLEY AERODROME
Joysons Hill
WHYTELEAFE SOUTH
White Ho.
Kooringa
Blize Wood
Rydons Wood
Taunton Manor High Sch.
CATERHAM ON-THE-HILL
COULSDON COMMON
MANOR PARK
Burntwood Hill
Portley Ho. Sch.
Subways
CR3
Birchwood Ho.
Stony Hill
Caterham Valley
St Lawrence's Hospital
Westway Common
Clifton Arms
Home Wood
Fryern Farm
Fryern Broom Wood
QUEENS PARK
Cemetery
CATERHAM
Recreation Grd.
Tillingdown Fm
Youth Centre
Willey Heath or Chaldon Common
Round Wood
Playing Field
Willey Broom Wood
White Knobs
GODSTONE ROAD
CATERHAM BY-PASS
A22
B2030
B2031
B2208
B269
CHALDON
ROOK LANE
114
104
61
62
63
64
65
BZ
CA
CB
CC

Farleigh
Chelsham
WARLINGHAM
WOLDINGHAM
Woldingham Garden Village
Warlingham Park Hospital
GREATPARK WOOD
HOLT WOOD
LEDGERS PARK
WORMS HEATH
LUMBERDINE WOOD
GREENHILL SHAW
CR6
RH8
96
106
114
61
62
63
64
65
CC
CD
CE
CF

BIGGIN HILL
AERODROME
BIGGIN HILL
Pimlico
TATSFIELD
Titsey
Fairchildes Farm
Fickleshole Farm
Blackmans
Skid Hill
Greathill Shaw
Crookedash Shaw
Five Acre Shaw
Midgley Shaws
Honeyoak Wood
St Leonard's Church
Mollards Wood
Owls Wood
Jerry Reddins Shaw
Long Coppice
Norheads
Broom Lodge
Chelsham Court
Cony Crook
Cowyard Shaw
Round Wood
Cherry Tree Shaw
Home Wood
Parsons Shaw
Milberry Cottage
Beddlestead
LUMBERDINE WOOD
Ashen Shaw
Beech Fm
Kitchen Grove
Cheverells Fm
Longlands Shaw
Westmore Green
Village Hall
Furze Corner
PITCHERS WOOD
Church Farm
Clarks Lane Farm
The Old Rectory
High Trees
Botleyhill Fm
TITSEY PLANTATION
Pilgrims Farm
Titsey Place
Hell Shaw
Flint Ho.
Church Wood
Square Wood
TITSEY PARK
Manor Ho.
Tatsfield Green
Old Ship
Kennels
Costar Farm
Cem.
Recreatn Grd.
Fire Sta.
Youth Centre
Clacket
Res.
CR3
RH8
CG
CH
CJ
CK
61
62
63
64
65
97
105
115
B269
B2024
A233
MAIN ROAD
HIGH HILL ROAD
FAIRCHILDES
PARK RD.
BLACKMAN'S LANE
SKID HILL LANE
BOUNDARY RD.
CROWN LANE
ASH LANE
RAILPIT LANE
HESIERS ROAD
HESIERS HILL
CHELSHAM COURT ROAD
BEDDLESTEAD LANE
BEECH FARM RD.
NORHEADS LANE
OAKLANDS LANE
VICTORIA GDS.
SUNNINGVALE AV.
CHRISTY RD.
ARTHUR RD.
CAMELOT CLO.
KINGS RD.
HIGHFIELD ROAD
BEECH ROAD
ROSE-HILL RD.
STOCK HILL
CHURCH RD.
SUTHERLAND AV.
THE GROVE
RICKETTS HILL
LUSTED HALL LA.
KEMSLEY RD.
PAYNESFIELD AV.
GOATSFIELD RD.
CROSSWAYS
JOHNS RD.
MAESMAUR RD.
NINEHAMS RD.
SHIP HILL
CHURCH LANE
CLARKS LANE
APPROACH RD.
TATSFIELD LANE
WHITE LANE
TITSEY HILL
TITSEY ROAD
BOTLEY HILL
PILGRIMS LANE
BROOMLANDS LANE
PILGRIMS WAY
RECTORY RD.
CROWN ROAD
CUDHAM RD.
RAG HILL
Sch.
P.S.

106
97
107
115
BR6
TN14
TN16
CK
CL
CM
CN
61
62
63
64
65
Spencers Grove
Luxted
Single Street
Twenty Acres Shaw
DOWNE ROAD
CHALKEY HILL
St Peter & St Paul's Ch
Angas Convalescent Home for Seamen
Foxburrow Wood
Hook Wood
NEWYEARS WOOD
Newlands Wood
Birches Croft
Bird House Wood
Swim. Bath
Southfield Shaw
Strakes Shaw
Bottom Barn
CHURCH HILL
Cudham
Cudham Hall
Recn. Grd.
Cocket's Farm
CACKETS
P.O.
Vic.
BERRY'S HILL
LANE
Sch.
Old Jail
Letts Green
Cophall Wood
Shelleys
SHELLEYS
Brickyard Farm
RESTAVON CARAVAN SITE
Blackbush Shaw
Berry's Green
Broom Wood
NEW BARN LANE
Baston Wood
Horns Green
CHERRY LODGE GOLF COURSE
Pimlico Wood
Newbarn
THRIFT LA.
Knockholt Wood
MOUNT HILL
MAIN
The Mount
ROYAL OAK HILL
BURLINGS
STONEINGS
Park Cotts
BERRYS GREEN RD.
CUDHAM FRITH
SOUTH LANE
Fox & Hounds
Withins Wood
HARROW
Shellem Wood
LANE
Bombers Lodge
BOMBERS LA.
Scotts Lodge
THE NOWER
NORTH DOWNS
BRASTED
Brasted Farm
Shoothe Wood
South Street
GRAYS' WOOD
Southwood
VIEWLANDS AV.
The Nower
Painter's Wood
Great South Street Fm
BUCKHURST
WESTERHAM ROAD
A233
Joeland's Wood
SILVERSTED LA.
GRAYS
Gray's Stud Fm
HOGTROUGH
Hawley's Corner
Broomcocks Wood
PALACE AVENUE
CHESNUT AV.
CHESNUT
Res.
Old Quarry
Pilgrims Ho.
Hogtrough Hill
PILGRIMS
Court Farm
The Homestead
Round Shaw
The Mount
Watercress Beds
THE AVENUE
Pumping Station
Hill Park
Hill Sch
WAY
PILGRIMS
Betsomshill Fm
Holywell Shaw
Park Wood
Gaysham
GREEN LA.
Green Leas
Force Green
BEGGARS LANE
HARTLEY WOOD
WESTERHAM WOOD
HILL
CROYDON ROAD
B2024
Park Fm
Charmans Farm
Rec. Grd.
Gaysham Cottages
Cupids Coppice
Court Lodge
M25
ASH RD.
ELM RD.
HARTLEY
OAK RD.
BLOOMFIELD
MADAN
Pol Ho
CLARENCE RD
WOODBURY RD
CORONATION TER.
Westerham
Biggin Hill
Knockholt
Valley

107
NEWYEARS WOOD
Newlands Wood
Hayman's Wood
Piece Wood
98
Birches Croft
Long Shaw
Singles Cross
Jockey's Wood
Blueberry Farm
Knockholt Pound
Cophall Wood
Letts Green
Shelleys
Ivy Farm
The Grange
Chine Farm
Homefield
Knockholt House
Lees Wood
Park Corner
Chapel Croft
Broom Wood
Knockholt
Baston Wood
COOPER'S WOOD
Ashfield Wood
Minny Wood
Knockholt Wood
Knockholt Beeches
The Mount
PARK WOOD
Park Ho.
Sundridge Hill Fm
Roughfields Wood
Hagbush Wood
Scott's Lodge
106
St Botolph's Ch.
Chevening
Shootfield
Chevening House
Brasted Hill Farm
Shootfield Wood
Home Farm
CHEVENING
PARK
Home Wood
The Nower
Chevening Cross
Oveny Green Fm
Combe Bank Farm
Claypit Shaw
Hogtrough Hill
Court Lodge Farm
COMBE BANK WOOD
M25
Watercress Beds
Holywell Shaw
Park Wood
Little Combe Bank
Sand & Gravel Pit
St Martin's Church
The Old Rectory
Brasted
Sundridge
TN16
Park Fm
Charmans Farm
Brasted Place
The Rookeries
Warren Fm.
116
Sundridge Place Farm
The Red Ho
Birch field
CO
CP
CQ
CR
61
62
63
64
65
Sevenoaks

OTFORD
Dunton Green
Longford
RIVERHEAD
Chipstead
Bessel's Green
St. John's
SEVENOAKS
Sand & Gravel Pit
Rye Wood
Broughton House
Broughton Manor
Twitton Ho
New Barn Farm
Rakefield Wood
Cold Arbor Wood
Obelisk Wood
Brittains Farm
Salters Heath
TN14
TN13
M25
M26
A225
A224
A25
A21
R. DARENT
98
108
116

108
CV
CW
CX
CY
99
GREAT WOOD
Greenhill Wood
Hillydeal Wood
Paine's Farm
Beech Lees Wood
Carpenters Wood
Four Acre Wood
ROWDOW WOOD
Flatdeal Wood
Otford Court (Sch.)
Monks in the Hole
Shorehill Farm
Fabs Wood
New Park Wood
Shore Hill
Old Quarry
61
OTFORD
THE PALACE
ST THOMAS A BECKET'S WELL
PILGRIMS' WAY EAST
Chalk Pit
Recreation Ground
Stud Farm
TN14
Youth Hostel
Sch.
Hall
Library
Kemsing
Pol. Ho.
Long Lodge Oast House
Oxenhill Shaw
Eatwell Shaw
Dyne's Farm
Hill's Wood
62
M26
Bushy Wood
Sevenoaks
Child's Bridge
107
IND. EST.
Noah's Ark
Cockney's Wood
DARENT
Sealcroft Cotts.
Noah's Ark Bri.
HONEYPOT
63
The Moors
Penfield
Tanners Cross
Sevenoaks Gas Works
Greatness
Pol. Off.
School
BAT & BALL
Playing Field
Cem.y
Recreation Ground
Fire Sta.
SEAL
Money Shaw
Fullers Hill
SEAL ROAD A25
HIGH ST.
The Wildernesse Secondary School for boys
Millpond Wood
Playing Field
Hearth Wood
SEAL HILL A25
East Paddock Wood
64
Hosp.
Lib
Sevenoaks Hosp.
Town Council
Wildernesse
School For Blind
Wildernesse
The Grove
Club Ho.
Golf Course
St. John's
Sch.
Playing Field
CHANCE WOOD
Oak Bank Sch.
Seal
Chapel Wood
Richardsons Wood
Brickkiln Wood
Guy's Wood
Apps's Wood
Hall Place
65
Recn Grnd
Vine Lodge
Blackhall
TN13
Golf Course
Duchess Plantn
Buck's Head Inn
Vine Cricket Grd
Hosp.
Fire Sta.
Council Off.
Drill Hall
117
Furze Field
Godden Green
Marys Mead
Hudson's Wood
GODDEN WOOD
Rec. Grnd
Sch.
SEVENOAKS
Swimming Pool
Stake Farm

BIRCHES WOOD
Drane Farm
Obram Wood
Summeryards Wood
Hoxly Down Res.
Exedown
Old Terry's Lodge
OLD TERRY'S LODGE ROAD
Shoulder of Mutton
White Hill
NORTH DOWNS WAY
PILGRIMS' WAY
KEMSING ROAD
St Clere
Coney Shaw
East Lodge
West Yaldham Farm
Yaldham Manor
Heaverham
Lower St Clere
Chequers
West Lo.
Broughton Cotts.
Martin Spring Wood
New House Farm
New House Farm Cottages
Blacksole Field
FEN POND RD.
M20
M26
A20
The Scrub
Wireless Transmitting Station
Cooper's Wood
Labour-in-vain
Round Wood
Hook Wood
Rumleys Wood
Osier Bed Wood
Clay Pits
Patchgrove Wood
Ruffits Wood
Ashplat Wood
The Wilderness
Ightham Court
Boundary House
MOUND
Westlands Cottage
Cricketts Farm
Sand Pit
West Bank
Brick Works
TN15
CHAUCER INDUSTRIAL PARK
KEMSING
Pumping Station
Stonepitts Manor
WATERY LANE
Broomsleigh
Chart Farm
Fountain
Fern Villa
Styants Bottom
Tonbridge & Malling
The Toll
Oldbury Hill
Oldbury Farm Ho.
Oldbury
OLDBURY LANE
OLDBURY CAMP
OLDBURY WOOD
NATIONAL TRUST
Heron Shaw Wood
IGHTHAM BY-PASS
A25
A227
BOROUGH GREEN ROAD
SEVENOAKS RD.
Dark Hill Farm
Borough Green
Stone Crushing Works
Quarry
Stangate Bridge
Ightham
Trycewell Farm
Ash Tree Farm
The Rectory
Double Dance
Chalklin's Shaw
Belmont Lodge
Cricket Ground
Piggery
Ightham Warren
Warren Farm
Gibbons Lodge
Gibbons Place
Main field
Tebb's Copyhold
Tebb's Corner
Ightham Common
Bewley Farm
Bewley Bar
Golding Hop Farm
Sheet Hill Farm
Brookside Farm
Crowhurst Farm
King's Cottages
Goddens Cottages
Quarry Site
Larchwood Farm
Styants Wood
CHART CROWN POINT
SEVENOAKS ROAD
Crown Point
Frankfield Ho.
Fish Ponds Wood
RASPIT HILL
Raspit Hill
Beaconsmount
Rose Wood
The Knoll
Wood Chart
Flaneswood
Stone Street
Res.
Lord's Spring Fm.
CY
CZ
DA
DB
DC
99
117
61
62
63
64
65

AO
AP
AQ
AR
AS
100
118
66
67
68
69
70
GU1
GU2
GU3
GU4
Bridley Manor
Bridley Cross Roads
Bridley Copse
Stanford Brook
Blanketmill Farm
Brook Farm
Rickford Common
Norton Farm
Gooserye Farm
Hockley Lands
Woodcorner Farm
Kemishford Br.
Burdenshot Hill
PREY HEATH
WORPLESDON
Mayford Hotel
Whitehouse Farm
Pyle Hill
Havering Farm
Whitmoor Pond
Whitmoor Wood
Whitmoor House
Whitmoor Farm
Poor Jack's Wood
Frog Lane Farm
Cox's Farm
GUILDFORD ROAD
WOKING ROAD
BAGSHOT ROAD
WORPLESDON ROAD
ALDERSHOT ROAD
SALT BOX ROAD
THE CHURCH LANE
GOOSE LANE
BURDENSHOT ROAD
WHITMOOR LANE
CLAY LANE
Worplesdon
Worplesdon Place Hotel
Fish Pond
Cricket Ground
Perry Hill
Perry Hill Farm
Vine Farm
Maryland
St. Mary's Ch.
WHITMOOR COMMON
School
Sudpré Farm
Pitmore Farm
Nursery
Fairlands Farm
Worplesdon Chase
Field Res. Stn.
Pitch Place
Stables
Frosbury Fm.
Liddington Hall Fm.
Ryde's Hill
BROAD STREET COMMON
Hunt's Farm
Worplesdon First & Mid.Sch.
Hook Farm
Willow Grange
Britten's Pond
Stringers Common
Jacobswell
Queen Elizabeth Park (W.R.A.C.Barracks)
Play.Fld.
Youth Centre
Stoke Hill First Sch.
Abattoir
Cattle Market
Slyfield Ind.Est.
Enterprise Est.
Slyfield Green
Ladymead
Allots.
Sewage Wks.
Hort. Soc.
Stoke Lock
Bellfields
Corporation Depot
Pumping Sta.
Stoke Mill
Marina
Clinic
Mid.Sch.
Bishop Reindrop Sch.
Hall
Stoke New Cemetery
Stoke Cem.
River
Water Meadows
Waterside Centre
Stoughton Rec. Grd.
Stoughton
STOUGHTON ROAD
Convent & R.C.Sch.
St.Marys R.C. First Sch.
St.Josephs R.C. Mid. Sch.
Barnwood First Sch.
Youth Cen.
WESTBOROUGH
Westborough First Sch.
Training Centre
PARK BARN EST
Park Barn Sch.
Westwood Park Middle Sch.
LADYMEAD
PARKWAY
WOODBRIDGE RD.
BY PASS
A3
A320
A322
A323
A3100
INDUSTRIAL ESTATE
Sports Grd.
Cathedral Hill Ind.Est.
Guildford Business Park
University of Surrey
Spts Hall
Lib.
Cathedral
Rec. Grd.
Sports Gd.
Fire Sta.
Amb.Sta.
The Lido
Indoor Bowling Green
Guildford Coll. of Art & Tech.
STOKE
Tennis Cts.
Pool
Tech.Coll. Anx.
GUILDFORD
Riverside Business Centre
Royal Surrey Hosp.
Running Track
Play. Flds.
Philip Trenman Sports Ground
Biological Res. Centre
The Priestley Centre
Queen Eleanor Mid.Sch.
Sports Centre
Friary Centre
Village

109
AS
AT
AU
AV
100
110
118
66
67
68
69
70
Chamberlands Br.
Runtleywood Farm
Cricketshill Farm
Send Hill
St.Bedes Mid.Sch.
Send First Sch.
Boughton Hall Hotel
Garlick's Arch Copse
Burntcommon
Triggs Lock
Wareham's Farm
River Wey
River Wey Navigation
Sutton Green
Manor House
Crickets Hill
Cricket Ground
Sendholm
Cemetery
Sendcourt Farm
Fell Hill
Send Grove
Send Barns Farm
Sendbarns
GU23
Nursery
Tithebarns House
Hazelhurst Cottage
HIGHCOTTS WOOD
Ladygrove Farm
Sutton Park
Sutton Place
Whitehouse Farm
Nuthill Farm
Broadoak Bridge
Weir
Bower's Lock
Dedswell Manor Farm
FRITHYS WOOD
COTTS WOOD
Gosden Hill Fm.
Cuckoo Fm
Brit.Ley. Recreation Ground
CLANDON PARK
Burpham
Burpham First Sch.
Vill. Hall
Superstore
Park
Council Depot.
Surrey Police Traffic Centre
Merrow Common
GU4
George Abbot Comp.Sch.
Play. Fld.
Amb. Sta.
Temple Court
Clandon House
The Wilderness
St.Peters & Merrow Grange Comp. Sch.
Mid. Sch.
Merrow
Play.Fld.
Hall
Convent & R.C.Sch.
Sports Grd.
Temple Court Sch.
Cricket Ground
Tormead Sch.
Prep Sch.
Govern't Offs.
Golf Club Ho.
Golf Course
MERROW DOWNS
Urn Field
Newlands House
LONDON ROAD
EPSOM ROAD
A246
A25
A3
A247
A3100
B2215
THE STREET
SHERE RD.
CLANDON RD.
PORTSMOUTH RD.
BOXGROVE RD.
TRODDS LANE
MERROW LANE
INN LANE
NEW INN LANE
DOWNSIDE RD.
GREEN LANE
VICARAGE LANE
SEND BARNS LANE
WOODHILL
SEND HILL

Boughton Hall Farm
Boughton Hotel
Grove Heath Farm
Copse
Catherinehams
Ryde Farm
Pond
Hangover House
Hungry Hill
Garlic Arch Copse
AW
AX
AY
AZ
101
GU23
Burntcommon
OLDLANDS COPSE
Nursery
Sheppardsgrove Copse
Bramblenide Copse
Jury Farm
66
Tithebarns House
Tithebarns Farm
Sussex Farm
August Hill
Oak Ride Farm
HIGHCOTTS WOOD
Hazelhurst Cottage
Holride Farm
Furze Copse
109
Hungry Hill Nursery
Detention Centre
67
EAST CLANDON COMMON
Humphrey's Copse
Lower Hammonds Farm
Nursery
Dedswell Manor Farm
ROAM WELLS
Martin Furze
GASON WOOD
Birch Farm
Buttinham Copse
Cammocks Wood
CLANDON
Cuckoo Farm
68
Great Wix Wood
Withybed Plantation
Norcote Wood
Recreation Ground
Home Farm
CLANDON PARK
West Clandon
Summers Farm
Hatchlands N.T.
Fullers Farm
Old Manor Farm
Clandon Regis
East Clandon
Woolgars Farm
New Park
New Manor Ho.
69
Tanfield Place
A246
EPSOM ROAD
Temple Court
Blakes Lane Farm
GU4
Springfield House
118
Clandon House
The Wilderness
A246 ROAD
West Clandon
High Clandon Farm
70
Long Acres Farm
Sunray Farm
Barnet Wood
CLANDON DOWNS
Dean Bottom
Wellhouse Farm
Golf Course
Sun Valley Farm
Old Scotland Farm
AW
AX
AY
AZ
Harrowhill Copse
Newlands Corner Hotel
Netherlands
Tickners Copse
Staplelane Copse
Newlands House
New Scotland
SHERE ROAD
A25
THE STREET
A247

EFFINGHAM COMMON
RIDE
THE FOREST
The Drift
Golf
101
111
119
AZ
BA
BB
BC
66
67
68
69
70
Broom House
Football Ground
Waterloo Fa.
Raleigh First & Middle Sch.
NIGHTINGALE AV.
NIGHTINGALE CRESCENT
NORTHCOTE CRESCENT
NORTHCOTE CLO.
NORTHCOTE RD.
EDWIN RD.
HEATHER DENE
MEADOW WAY
HOWARD CLO.
WESTON LEA
THE HIGHLANDS
B2039
Manor Farm
Depot
Nurs.
FARLEY'S CLO.
WOODSIDE
GRETA BANK
LOLLESWORTH WOOD
HORSLEY
Roundtree Farm
LOLLESWORTH LA.
Cricket Ground
RICKSONS LA.
Parkrow Copse
Lolleswoth Wood
Grovelands
TINTELLS LA.
KENYONS
SILKMORE LA.
P.O.
FAIRVIEW
PINCOTT LA.
St Mary's First Sch.
OVERBROOK
Pol. Ho.
MOUNT
PLEASANT
CRANMORE LA.
West Horsley
Nursery
Cranmore Sch.
Poultry Farm
Play. Fld.
EPSOM
BUTLERS HILL
SHERE RD.
JEFFRIES RD.
Wix Hill Stables
Weston Wood
Sheep Leas
Daws Dene
Pebblehill Fm.
PEBBLE HILL
Kennels
Hillside Farm
Hookwood Farm
Woodcote Lodge
Hazel Copse
Woodcote Farm
Elbridge Wood
Upper Common
Upper Weston Wood
Little Jarvis
Rogers Brook
Mountain Wood
Green Dene Plantation
KT24
ORCHARD CLO.
HEATHWAY
FOREST LA.
WILD WOOD CLO.
PARKSIDE CLO.
PARKSIDE PL.
THE RIDINGS
FOREST CLO.
NIGHTINGALE RD.
HOOKE RD.
HEATH RD.
NORRELS RIDE
NORRELS DR.
COBHAM WAY
THE RIDE
THE CHASE
HIGH PARK AV.
GLENDENE AV.
KINGSTON AV.
P.O. Lib.
THE BIRCHES
OLD RECTORY LA.
Whites Hill
WOODLAND DRI.
OCKHAM ROAD SOUTH
OAK WOOD DR.
OAKWOOD CLO.
PENNYMEAD DRI.
RISE
Recn. Grd.
Frenchlands Copse
FRENCHLANDS HATCH
HIGHER DR.
MEADOW BANK
LYNX HILL
PARK CORNER DR.
Park Corner
LOWER PERYERS
MANOR GRO.
MANOR CL.
HIGHFIELDS
FARM LA.
Timber Pond
House Pond
West Horsley Place
Place Farm
HOLMWOOD CLO.
BISHOPSMEAD PARADE
Horsley Towers
Elec. Council Training Cen.
FEARN CLO.
ST. MARTIN'S CLO.
GUILDFORD LODGE DRI.
EAST HORSLEY
A246
ROAD
GUILDFORD
LONGHURST RD.
WELLINGTON COTTS.
THE WARREN
ROWBARNS WAY
Rowbarns Manor
GREEN DENE
Rowbarns Plantation
LARK RISE
Woods Plantation
CHALK LANE
London Cross
Oak Field Plant.
CROCKNORTH
Round Wood
Robin Hood Bridge
Coles Copse
Bird Common
Scotch Plantation
Green Hill
HONEYSUCKLE BOTTOM
Larch Plantation
Dick Focks Common
Briery Hill Wood
SHEEPWALK LANE
King's Hills
Mole Valley
GU5
Hook Farm
MOAT
Lower Farm
Upper Lee Wood Farm
GREATLEE WOOD
LITTLELEE WOOD
Grt. Ridings Plantation
LEEWOOD WAY
OLD LONDON RD.
VIEW
Ridings Wood
The Walleys
Park Wood
Gravel Hill Pond
Pennymead Lake
PINE WALK
Brook Hill
PARK WOOD
Orestan Farm
ORESTAN LA.
Parrotts Coppice
The Short Wood
DIRTHAM LANE
CALVERT RD.
CHESTER RD.
Whistlers Farm
Standard Hill
SALMONS RD.
Dancing Pit
PARK HORSLEY
Warren Farm
Brockholes Cross
Outdowns Plantation
LONDON LANE
Thistle Cuts
Oldlands Plantation
OUTDOWNS
Golf Cours
Crown of the Hill Plantation
Pump Pond Wood
Crocknorth Farm
RH5
Osborne Plantation
The Hermitage
SHEEPWALK
Burrows Wood
Dunley Hill Farm
Ranmore Country Club
EFFINGHAM UPPER COM
DROVE
OAKEN GROVE
Mallards Mere
LOWER FARM RD.
Francis

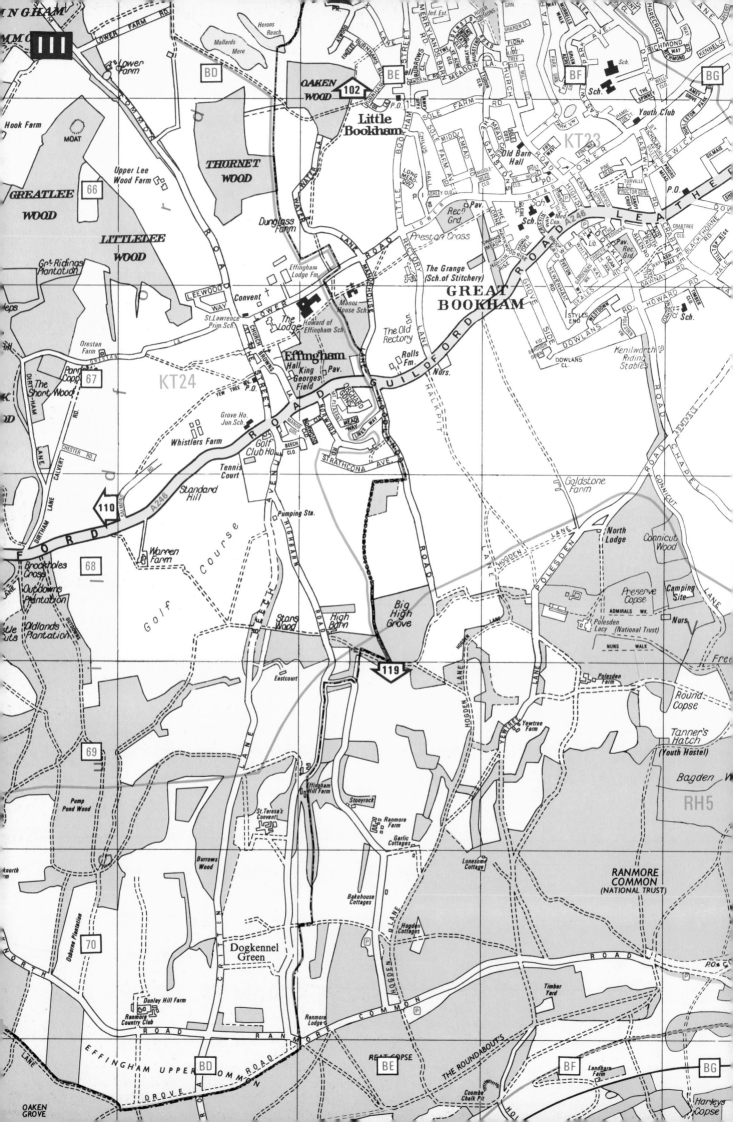

111
102
110
119
BD
BE
BF
BG
66
67
68
69
70
KT23
KT24
RH5
Little Bookham
GREAT BOOKHAM
Effingham
OAKEN WOOD
THORNET WOOD
GREATLEE WOOD
LITTLELEE WOOD
Hook Farm
MOAT
Lower Farm
Upper Lee Wood Farm
Mallards Mere
Herons Reach
Dunglass Farm
Effingham Lodge Fm.
Convent
St.Lawrence Prim.Sch.
The Lodge
Howard of Effingham Sch.
Manor House Sch.
Effingham Hall
King Georges Field
Orestan Farm
The Short Wood
Grove Ho. Jun.Sch.
Whistlers Farm
Golf Club Ho
Tennis Court
Standard Hill
Pumping Sta.
Warren Farm
Brockholes Cross
Outdowns Plantation
Oldlands Plantation
Golf Course
Stars Wood
High Barn
Big High Grove
Eastcourt
Old Barn Hall
Prestor Cross
The Grange (Sch.of Stitchery)
The Old Rectory
Rolls Fm.
Kenilworth Riding Stables
Goldstone Farm
North Lodge
Connicut Wood
Preserve Copse
Camping Site
Polesden Lacy (National Trust)
Polesden Farm
Round Copse
Tanner's Hatch (Youth Hostel)
Bagden
Yewtree Farm
Pump Pond Wood
Effingham Hill Farm
Stonyrock
St. Teresa's Convent
Ranmore Farm
Garlic Cottages
Lonesome Cottage
Burrows Wood
Bakehouse Cottages
Hogden Cottages
RANMORE COMMON (NATIONAL TRUST)
Dogkennel Green
Osborne Plantation
Dunley Hill Farm
Ranmore Country Club
Ranmore Lodge
Timber Yard
REAT COPSE
Landbarn Farm
Coombe Chalk Pit
Harleys Copse
OAKEN GROVE
EFFINGHAM UPPER COMMON
RANMORE COMMON ROAD
THE ROUNDABOUTS
GUILDFORD ROAD
A246
LOWER ROAD
THE STREET
BEECH AVENUE
HIGHBARN ROAD
WOODLANDS ROAD
HALKPIT LANE
POLESDEN LANE
HOGDEN LANE
YEWTREE LANE
CRITTEN LANE
NORTH ROAD
DRAVE ROAD
LOWER FARM RD.
COMMON ROAD
WATER LA.
MANOR HOUSE LANE
RECTORY LANE
LITTLE BOOKHAM STREET
SOLE FARM RD.
LOWER SHOTT
DOWLANS RD.
HOWARD RD.
CHURCH RD.
EASTWICK RD.
STRATHCONA AVE.
DIRTHAM LANE
CALVERT RD.
CHESTER RD.
CONNICUT LANE
CHAPEL LANE

LEATHERHEAD BY-PASS
A246
A24
BG
BH
BJ
BK
102
Hawk's Hill House
Downside
Bocketts Fm
KT22
OPEN SPACE
LEATHERHEAD DOWNS
GIVONS GROVE
Cherkley Court
66
STANE STREET
(Roman Road)
The Hazels
Bridge Croft
MICKLEHAM DRI.
CHERKLEY HILL
FETCHAM DOWNS
UPDOWN WOOD
Icehouse Combe
The Priory
Walnut Tree Clump
NORBURY
Nursery
BYTTOM HILL
112
THE SCRUBS
Denshire Hill
Norbury Park
PARK
R. MOLE
MICKLEHAM DOWNS
Sch.
Rec. Grd.
MICKLEHAM
Swanworth Fm
Cricket Gd.
DELL CLOSE
Rectory
67
WHITE HILL
National Trust
Warren Farm
Druids Grove
SWANWORTH LA
P.O.
St. Michaels Ch
Mickleham Hall
Mole
Valley
Lodge Farm
B2209
JUNIPERHILL WOOD
Juniperhill
HEADLEY
Cowslip Fm.
Cowslip Cottage
Fredley Manor
BEECHY WOOD
Chapel Wd.
Crabtree Cotts.
Juniper Hall
(Field Study Cent.)
St. Faiths
Nicols Field
CRABTREE
68
National Trust
The Thorns
Juniper Bottom
Foxbury Shaw
Chapel Wood
Pinehurst
The Tower
Lodge Hill
BY PASS
Chapel Hill
Foxbury
ZIG-ZAG ROAD
CHAPEL LA
Chapel Fm.
CAMILLA
119
West Humble
Burford Bri. Hotel
Swim. Pool
Bagden Fm
Camilla Lacey
Burford Bri.
Lodge Hill National Trust
Box Hill
KT20
WESTHUMBLE ST.
BOXHILL & WEST-HUMBLE
BURNEY
ADLERS
PILGRIMS WAY
PILGRIMS CLO.
Ashcombe Wood
Old Dean Cott.
RANMORE COMMON RD.
Dorking Wood
Gravel Pit Plant
Playing Field
Pav. Playing Field
Burford Lodge
69
Keepers Lodge
Fort Cottage
120
ZIG - ZAG ROAD
Stepping Stones
Memorial
Boxlands
Bradley Farm
BRADLEY LA.
LONDON ROAD
Boxhurst
Ashcombe Wood
Pixholme Court
Playing Fields
RIVER MOLE
Denbies Farm
NORTH DOWNS WAY
Offices
PIXHAM LA
Pixham Firs
70
Sewage Wks.
BOXHILL RD.
Denbies
Sch.
CHICHESTER ROAD
CALVER
DORKING
Sports Grd.
PIXHOLME GRO.
OLD REIGATE
Deepdene Bri.
Boxhill Bri.
KEPPEL RD.
RANMORE
PILGRIMS WAY
Depot
ASHCOMBE ROAD
A2003
CROFT AV.
LINCOLN RD.
DEEPDENE
DOWNSVIEW
CHESTER CLO.
LESLIE RD.
YEW TREE RD.
Playing Field
FAIRFIELD
DEEPDENE AV.
CEMETERY
A25
REIGATE
Riding Stables
COMBE RD.
CHALKPIT LA.
PIPPBROOK GDNS.
Mag. Ct.
Lib.
Recreat. Grd.
Mill Pond
DORKING TOWN
Gas Holders
STATION RD.
Football Gd.
RH4
RH5
BETCHWORTH
Golf Course
Clay Copse
Swim. Cent.

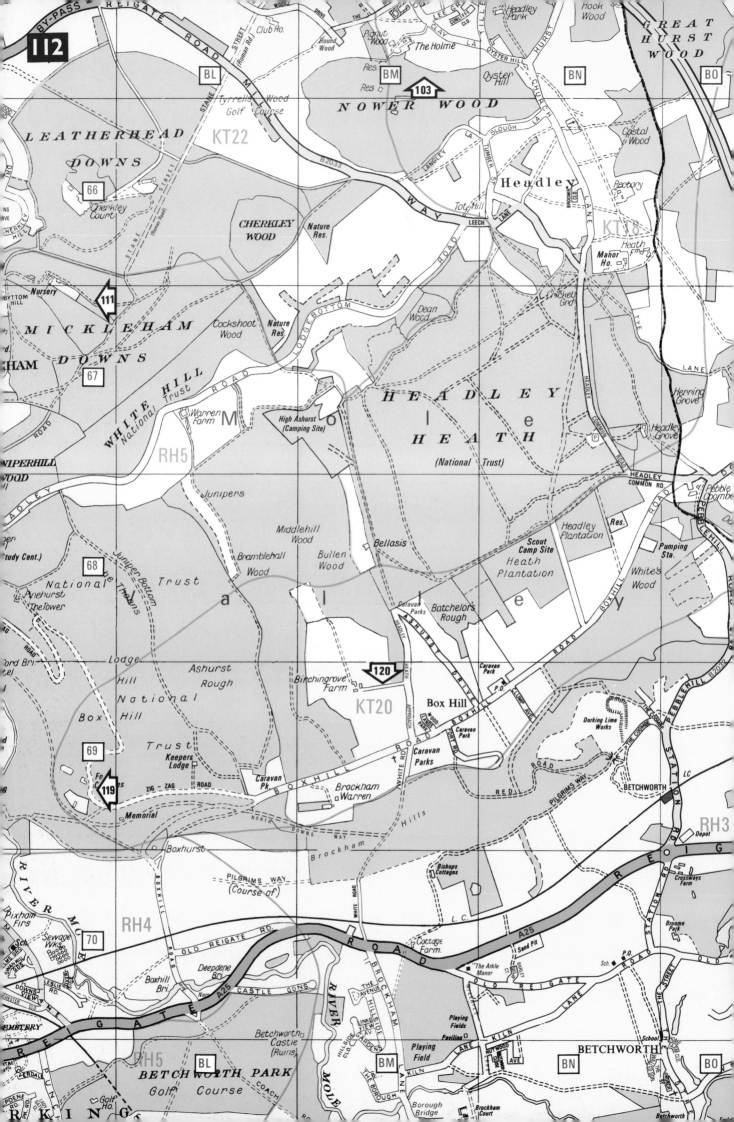

LEATHERHEAD DOWNS
Cherkley Court
CHERKLEY WOOD
Nature Res.
NOWER WOOD
Tyrrells Wood Golf Course
KT22
REIGATE ROAD
B2033
Headley
KT18
GREAT HURST WOOD
Oyster Hill
Hook Wood
Headley Park
The Holme
Castal Wood
Rectory
Manor Ho.
Heath Fm.
MICKLEHAM DOWNS
Cockshoot Wood
Nature Res.
LODGE BOTTOM
Dean Wood
HEADLEY HEATH
(National Trust)
WHITE HILL
National Trust
Warren Farm
High Ashurst (Camping Site)
RH5
Mole Valley
Junipers
Middlehill Wood
Bramblehall Wood
Bullen Wood
Bellasis
Headley Plantation
Scout Camp Site
Heath Plantation
Batchelor's Rough
White's Wood
Pumping Sta.
Herring Grove
Headley Grove
Pebble Coombe
Juniper Bottom
National Trust
Ashurst Rough
Birchingrove Farm
KT20
Box Hill
Lodge Hill National Trust
Box Hill National Trust
Keepers Lodge
ZIG-ZAG ROAD
Memorial
Brockham Warren
Dorking Lime Works
BETCHWORTH
PILGRIMS WAY
NORTH DOWNS WAY
Brockham Hills
Boxhurst
RH3
Bishops Cottages
Crossways Farm
Broome Park
PILGRIMS WAY (Course of)
RH4
A25
REIGATE ROAD
RIVER MOLE
Pixham Firs
Sewage Wks.
Deepdene Bri.
Boxhill Bri.
CASTLE GDNS.
Betchworth Castle (Ruins)
Cottage Farm
The Arkle Manor
Sand Pit
Playing Fields
Playing Field
BETCHWORTH PARK Golf Course
Borough Bridge
Brockham Court
BL
BM
BN
BO
66
67
68
69
70
103
111
119
120

WALTON ON-THE-HILL
BANSTEAD HEATH
WALTON HEATH
KT20
Reigate and Banstead
M25
MARGERY WOOD
Lower Kingswood
Mogador
LITTLE HEATH
Walton Oaks
Experimental Farm
Bushfield Wood
Round Wood
Watson's Wood
Buckland Hills
Mount Hall
Colley Hill
National Trust
Juniper Hill
Queens Park
REIGATE National Trust
Colleyland Shaw
Colley Pit
Buckland
A25
REIGATE HEATH
RH2
Buckland Lodge
Dungate's Farm
Club House
Skimmington
Wonham Manor
Wonham Mill
Garthlands
Priory Pond
Cricket Field
Playing Field
Kemp's Farm
Underhill Farm
Sturts Ho.
Hedgecroft
Lovelands
Sandhill Wood
Castle House
Little Dowding
Hockey Grd.
Smugglers Pit Plantation
The Press at Kingswood
Caravan Park
Red Lo.
Grub Wood
Millfield Wood
Rookery Cottages
Oxford Cottages
Council Yard
Kingswood Grange
Kingswood Manor
Manor Fm. Stables
Natural Gas Pressure Reducing Sta.
Dent's Fm.
Margery
Margery Ho.
Margery Fm.
Funzefield Copse
Kiln Field Pit
Water Tower
Pilgrims Holt
Broadleas
Colley Copse
Colley Wood
Clears Cotts
Sports Ground
Tennis Cts.
Black Horse
Cricket Grd.
Bowling Grn
Castle Grounds
Town Hall
103
113
120
121
66
67
68
69
70
BO
BP
BQ
BR

Smugglers Pit Plantation
Club Ho.
Well Ho.
Chipstead
Southerns Farm
Reeves Rest
Round Wd.
Wood
Priors Field
Ten Acre Wood
Coldcoast Shaw
BS
BT
BU
BV
104
CR3
Chipstead
Beechen Lane
Millfield Lane
Sports Grd.
Pav.
Millfield Wood
Windmill (Disused)
Rectory
Old Rectory
Road
Park Farm
Bugspit Shaw
Mugswell
Funzefield Copse
Long Wood
Little Wood
Upper Gatton Wood
Boorsgreen Shaw
Boorsgreen Farm
The Press at Kingswood
66
Caravan Park
Grub Wood
Green
Gutwick Wood
Colts Bushes
Dell Wood
Funzefield Shaw
Hill
Brier Lea
112
The Mount
Orchard Way
Upper Gatton Park
UPPER GATTON PARK
Gatwick Fm.
Ashtead
M25
P.O.
Lower Kingswood
Lovelands Farm
Oxford Cottages
Council Yard
Mint House
Park Shaw
Rookery Cottages
CH.
67
Ten. Cts.
Babylon Lane
Kingswood Grange
Kingswood Manor
The Crossways
Crossways Fm.
Gatton
Whitehall Fm.
The Orpington Nursery
Manor Fm. Stables
Majority Plantation
Glebe Shaw
Jubilee Plantation
Road
Stubbs
Caravan Pk.
Gatlands Shaw
Tower Wood
Gatton
THE PA
KT20
Mint Lane
Manor La.
Buckland
Reigate
Roy. Alexandra & Albert Sch.
Cedar Walk
Margery
Margery Lane
Blackhorse
Gatton Park
8
Margery Ho.
Pilgrims' Way
The Burpit
Hop Garden Pond
Res.
Halfmoon Clump
Margery Fm.
Funzefield Copse
Engine Pond
The Serpentine
The Lake
68
Reigate Hill
Great Buck Wood
Water Tower
Banstead
Pilgrims Holt
North Downs Way
Motel
Nut Wood Nat. Trust
Nutwood Lo.
Temple Wood
London Road
Queens Park
Fort
Reigate Hill National Trust
121
A242
RH2
Gatton Park Road
Sheep Walk
Coppice La.
Pilgrims Way
Underhill Rd.
Yew Tree La.
Quarry Hill Park
Gatton Cl.
Cent. for Blind
Playing Fld.
St. Bedes Sch.
Sch.
Broadle
69
Washington Clo.
Raglan
Harewood Clo.
Greystones Dri.
Millview Cl.
Carlton Grn.
Colley Copse
120
Colley Wood
Merrywood Park
Raglan
Timperley Gs.
Redhill Tennis Club
Brookland Way
Hurstleigh Dri.
Sports Gd.
Ply. Fld.
Training Cent.
Batts Hill
Manor Rd.
Tennis Cts.
Somers Rd.
Wray Park Rd.
Fire Brigade H.Q.
Hall
Wray Common
Schs.
R.C.Sch.
North St.
Gloucester Rd.
Sports Grd.
Reigate
Holmesdale Rd.
Croydon Road
Albert Road
Yorke Rd.
Rushworth
Doods Rd.
P.O.
Madeira
T.A. Centre
Rec. Cent.
Linkfield Corner
Oxford Rd.
Station Rd.
Queensway
Redhill
Princess Way
70
West St.
A25
London Rd.
Castle Grounds
Town Hall
Church St.
Southwalk
Mus.
Deerings Rd.
Wray Common Rd.
The Cedars
Hatchlands Rd.
Redstone Hill
High St.
Cromwell Rd.
Bowling Grn.
Cricket Gd.
Reigate Road
Millway
Div. Pol. H.Q.
Grove Rd.
Oakdene Rd.
Monks Wk.
Church Walk
Playing Fld.
Prep. Sch.
Cemetery
E. Surrey Coll. (Art Dept.)
Health Cent.
Whitepost Hill
Ridgeway Rd.
Playing Field
Sch.
Bell St.
Bus Depot
Blackborough Rd.
Brighton Rd. A23
Rugby Club
Allots.
Priory Pond
Cricket Field
Blanford Rd.
Oak Way
Redhill Common
Reigate
Reigate Park
Hooley
Dunottar

113
104
114
121
BV
BW
BX
BY
66
67
68
69
70
CR3
RH1
M23
M25
A23
A25
B2031
Alderstead Heath
Fryern Broom Wood
Fryern Farm
Rook Lane
Rook Hill
Vill. Hall
Sch.
Willey Broom Wood
Willey Broom La.
Six Brothers Field (N.T.)
Round Wood
Chaldon Common Road
Birchwood
Alderstead Farm
Alderstead La.
Reservoir
The Shrubbery
Merstham Tunnel
Beech Rd.
Shepherds Hill
Tollsworth
Pilgrims Way
Hilltop Farm
Hilltop Lane
Hilltop House
W.T.Sta.
Ridgebushes Wood
Scouts Camp Site
Willey Park Farm
Chalkpit (Disused)
Church Hill
Lime Works Rd.
Jolliffe Rd.
London Rd. Nth.
Ockley Hill
Grubs Wood
Quarry Hangers
Spring Bottom
Bedlams Bank
North Downs Way
Rockshaw Road
Albury Edge
New Pond
Spring Bottom Road
Quarry Cotts
Rockshaw Ho.
Furzefield Wood
Rocky Shaw
Quarry Wd.
Merstham Ho.
Vill. Hall
Merstham
Merstham Grange
High St.
School Hill
Radstock Way
Mansfield Drive
Delabole Rd.
Chesterton Dr.
Dundrey Cres.
Bolsover Gro.
Oakley Farm
Warwick Wold
Warwick Wold Road
Oakwood Rd.
Yew Tree Cottage
Black Bushes
Bletchingley Road
Portland Dr.
Worsted Green
Taunton Dri.
Sunstone Gr.
Greystone Sch.
Clinic
Lib.
Comm.Cent.
South Merstham
Rec. Gd.
Play.Fld.
Allots.
Speyns Fm.
London Rd. A23 South
The Crossways
Albury Rd.
Devon Rd.
Melton Rd.
Bourne Rd.
Orpin Rd.
Battlebridge Ho.
Battlebridge La.
Sewage Works
Redhill Brook
Merstham Road
Pendell Farm
Pendell House
Pendell Court
Pendell Road
Water Lane
Brewerstreet Farm
The Old Rectory
Brewer Street
Whitehill Lane
Caravan Site
Sand & Silicon Wks.
Ford Br.
Nutfield Marsh Rd.
Nutfield Rd.
Mercers Farm
Manor House
Lake Farm
Cricket Ground
Pav.
Chilmead Lane
Chilmead Farm
Peyton's Cotts.
Cockley Plantation
Sandy Lane
Glebe House
Great Common
Little Common
Stychens Lane
Dormers Farm
Allotments
Nursery
Whitehill Lane
Redhill Brook
Sand Pit
Mercers Farm
Nutfield Court
The Rectory
Bletchingley Road
Castle Street
Big Common Lane
Botery's Cross
Barfields
Playing Field
High Street
Castle Hill
Castle Place
Bletchingley
Works
Cem.
Pimlico Hill
Sports Ground
Nutfield
Church Hill
High Street
P.O.
Coopers Hill Road
Robert Denholme House
Coombes Coppice
Stanley's Wood
Castlehill Farm
Research Labs.
Patteson Court
Nutfield Road
North Park
Playing Field
Furze Hill
Holmesdale
Nutfield Priory (Sch.for Deaf)
South Park
Priory Farm
Mid Street
Steners Hill
Steners Hill Park Farm
Sandhills
Cormongers Lane
Little Cormongers Farm
Kentwins
Bowerhill Wood
Philanthropic Road
Hogtrough La.
Fullers Wood La.
Cemetery
Thornthrift
Redstone Hill
Elmethorpe
Trowers Way

CATERHAM
Queen's Park
Chaldon Common
Playing Field
Fryern Farm
Rook Hill
Vill. Hall
Sch.
Willey Broom Wood
Round Wood
CR3
White Knobs
Tillingdown Fm
Recreation Grd.
Youth Centre
Government Offs.
Harestone Valley
Caterham Sch
Sports Grd.
Shirley Goss (Sch.)
Mottrams Sch
Eight Acre Wood
Paddock Wood
Ockley Wood
The Mardens
Ridgebushes Wood
Scouts Camp Site
Hilltop House
W.T.Sta
Willey Park Farm
Grubs Wood
Harrow P.H.
Whitehill Tower
War Coppice Garden Village
OLDPARK WOOD
Ten Acre Shaw
Tupwood Scrubs
Fosterdown Fort
The Devils Hole
Dialbank Wood
Quarry Hangers
Spring Bottom
Rocky Shaw
Quarry Wd.
The Mound
Gravelly Hill
View Point
Kennel Shaw
Black Bushes
Conduit Shaw
Roughets Ho.
White Hill Ho.
Whitehills Roughets
Fosterdown Farm
Yew Tree Cottage
M25
Kitchen Copse
Tandridge
North Park Farm
Tylers Green
Big Pickle
Little Pickle
Hopgarden Shaw
Place Farm
Brewerstreet Farm
Pendell Farm
Pendell Court
Pendell House
Manor House
Lake Farm
The Old Rectory
RH1
The Roughets
Godstone
Village Hall
Bay Pond
Youth Centre
Godstone Green
Nursery
Stangrave Hall
Ivy Mill Farm
Waterhouse Farm
Chevington Farmhouse
Cockley Plantation
Great Common
Dormers Farm
Allotments
Little Common
Playing Field
Cemetery
Court Lodge Farm
Garston Park
Stratton
BLETCHINGLEY ROAD
GODSTONE ROAD
CASTLE STREET
HIGH STREET
M23
Castle Hill
Castle Place
Bletchingley
Sports Ground
Town Farm
School
Playing Fields
Coombes Coppice
Harlings Shaw
Castlehill Farm
Pound Farm
Tilburstowhill or Tilbusterhill Plantation
Sand Pit
Penduck Shaw
Steners Hill Park Farm
Sandhills
Coldharbour Farm
Crookedfield
Springfield Shaw
Moor's Wood
Long Shaw
Tilburstowhill Farm
Home Farm
BZ
CA
CB
CC
66
67
68
69
70
71
105
113
121
A25
A22
B2236

114
105
115
CC
CD
CE
CF
66
67
68
69
70
71
M25
A25
A22
RH8
RH9
OXTED
Upper Court
Little Church Wood
Whistlers Wood
Hell Shaw
TITSEY
Templehill Plantation
Hollingden
Club Ho.
Golf Course
Convent of the Sacred Heart
Great Church Wood
Oxted Tunnel
WOLDINGHAM ROAD
THE RIDGE
Flint Ho.
Beech Plantn
Chalk Pit
Stubbs Copse
The Rumps
Whitefield Plantatn
Horse Shaw
Chaldons Fm.
Tandridge Hill
Hanging Wood
GANGERS HILL
PILGRIMS WAY
HOGTROUGH LA.
Rye Wood
Robins Grove Wood
The Abbeys
Armitage Wood
Hamfield Shaw
Lodge Wood
Barrow Green Ct
Blunt Ho.
The Bogs
MASTER PARK
Flint Hall Farm
Palmers Wood
Flower Wood
ROOKS NEST PARK
Duckpit Wood
Sand Pit
The Priory
Kennels
Streete Court School
School Plantation
Nursery
Club House
Midland Bank College
GODSTONE ROAD
TANDRIDGE GOLF COURSE
Garden Centre
Church Town
The Glebe House
Little Court Farm
Oxted Place
Broadham Green
HURST GREEN
Tanhouse Farm
Stonehall Farm
Leigh Place
Leigh Place Pond
Tandridge Court
Tandridge Court Farm
Oldpark Wood
Tandridge
TANDRIDGE PARK
Southlands
Perrysfield Farm
Perrysfield
THE ENTERDENT
Village Hall
Tandridge Hall
Stocketts Manor
Stocketts Manor Farm
Cottsford
Kings Green
Stow Coppice
Wonham House Hotel
Newhouse Farm
GODSTONE BY-PASS
SOUTHLANDS LANE
GROVE ROAD
BROADHAM GREEN
POPES LANE
BROOK LANE
JACKASS LANE
Leisure Centre
EAST HILL
WEST HILL
Oxted & Limpsfield Hosp.

CR3
CG
CH
CJ
CK
106
114
RH8
66
67
68
69
70
71
M25
TITSEY PLANTATION
Hell Shaw
Flint Ho.
Beech Plantn.
Titsey Place
Pilgrims Farm
Clacket
Titsey
Church Wood
Clacket Wood
Square Wood
TITSEY PARK
Limpsfield Lodge Fm.
Park Farm
TITSEY WOOD
Ashen Coppice
Broomlands Fm.
Sand Pits
Moorhouse Sand Pits
Limpsfield Grange (Sch.)
Hookwood
Furzedown
The Rips
LIMPSFIELD
Tennis Club
Oxted & Limpsfield Hosp.
Play'g Fld
Nursing Home
Blunt Ho.
The Bogs
MASTER PARK
Lib.& Health Centre Council Off.
Leisure Centre
Fire Sta.
LIMPSFIELD COMMON
Lakestreet Green
Limpsfield Common
St. Michaels School
Allot.
LIMPSFIELD COMMON (National Trust)
GOLF COURSE
Briars Cross
WESTERHAM ROAD
EAST HILL
WEST HILL
KENT HATCH
OXTED
WEST HEATH
Hazelwood Sch.
Midland Bank College
Stonehall Farm
The Alders
Boulthurst Farm
Tenchleys Park
Tenchleys Wood
Loampit Wood
HURST GREEN
Tanhouse Farm
Broadham Green
Moor Ho. School
Pol.Ho.
Doghurst
Tenchleys Farm
ITCHINGWOOD COMMON
Playing Field
Perrysfield Farm
Perrysfield
Mill Pond
Cottsford Mill
FAIRVIEW EST.
Rec.Grd.
Stocketts Manor
T.D.C.Depot
Parishcroft Wood
Stockenden Farm
Stocketts Manor Farm
Kings Green
Honesland Wood
Collesters Wood
Mollstones Wood

Gaysham
Green Leas
Force Green
HARTLEY WOOD
WESTERHAM WOOD
CK
CL
CM
CN
106
M25
A233
B2024
Gaysham Cottages
Cupids Coppice
CROYDON ROAD
Charmans Farm
Park Fm
Rec. Grd.
A25
Wet Wood
Devil of Kent
Court Lodge
Church Hill School
Sch.
Pol Ho
Recreation Ground
Tennis Cts.
R. Darent
SEVENOAKS
66
Valence School
Green Croft
FARLEY COMMON
Lib.
Sta
P.O.
Fire Sta
Quebec Ho (WOLFE'S HO.)
HIGH STREET
LONDON RD.
Wolfe Statue
Churchill Statue
Drill Hall
Squerryes Lodge
Westwood Fm
Brick & Tile Works
Brewery
WESTERHAM
Dunsdale
Dunsdale Wood
VALENCE WOOD
Fish Pond
Resr
TN16
67
Grasshopper
Moorhouse Bank
Squerryes Court
Lodges Wood
GODDLEY STOCK ROAD
Hosey Hill
Gillhams
Moor Ho.
SQUERRYES PARK
Cricket Gd
Chart's Edge
Sch.
Manning's Wood
Moorhouse Bank Common
TOWER WOOD
HOSEY COMMON
HOSEY COMMON ROAD
B2026
French Street
Frenchstreet Farm
68
116
THE HIGH CHART
Horns Hill
Long Wood
Goodley Stock
Fort
Chart
Crockham House
MOORHOUSE
THE CHART
Round Wood
Woodlands N.T.
CROCKHAM HILL COMMON
B269 ROAD
TREVEREUX
Conv. Home
Scearn Bank
KENT HATCH
Chartwell N.T.
Chartwell Farm
The Grove N.T.
69
Castle G.
Crockham Hill Farm
Froghole Farm
Mariners
MAPLETON ROAD
FROGHOLE LANE
Little Mariners
Gudge Wood
PUDDEDOCK LANE
Trevereux
HILL
Derby Wood
SMITHS LANE
OAKDALE LANE
Sch
P.O. Lib
Crockham Hill
DEANERY RD.
Ties Wood
70
SWAYNESLAND ROAD
youth hostel
Pol Ho
MAIN ROAD
POOTINGS
TN8
DAIRY LANE
Hurst Farm
Old Dairy Farm
DENNETTSLAND RD.
Grange Farm N.T.
Crockham Grange
Obriss
Row Wood
Longcroft Wood
Haftcroft Wood
Redland Farm
71
Guildables
Coakham Farm

Brasted
Sundridge
The Old Rectory
Church
Park Fm
Charmans Farm
Rec. Grd.
HIGH ST.
MAIN ROAD
A25
Pol. Ho.
Parish Hall
CHAPMANS RD.
MANOR RD.
WOODSIDE RD.
P.O.
Sch.
Pond
Brasted Place
The Rookeries
107
CO
CP
CQ
CR
The Red Ho.
Sundridge Place Farm
GREYSTONE PARK
Birchfield Farm
Birchfield Wood
Woodside
CHURCH ROAD
Haverswood Farm
Colinette Farm
Valence School
66
OAKS
Dunsdale
VALENCE WOOD
Dunsdale Wood
Vines Gate Shaw
Park Shaw
Lodge Farm Barn
Hill Water Bottom Wood
GREAT WOOD
The Hollies
PIPERS LANE
CHART LANE
Sundridge Hospital
WILLOW WOOD
TN16
67
Brasted Chart
Chapman's Wood
Penn Wood
Gillhams
PIPERS GREEN ROAD
QUORNDEN WOOD
Penn Farm
Manning's Wood
ROUND WOOD
Quornden
Brook Place
115
Phillippines
Frenchstreet Farm
Hendenfoot
Great Norman Street Farm
Cordons Farm
68
S
e
v
e
n
Emmetts N.T.
THE CHART
Long Wood
Goath Comm
Scords Wood N.T.
Pol. Ho.
CAMBERWELL LANE
School
Round Wood
Woodlands N.T.
Ritherden
Ide Hill
WHEATSHEAF HILL
Chartwell N.T.
69
The Grove N.T.
Toy's Hill N.T.
TOYS HILL
Ide Hill N.T.
Chartwell Farm
Castle Grove
Toy's Hill
Quinten Wood
Hanging Bank
B2042
The Guzzle
PUDDLEDOCK LANE
Gudge Wood
Chains Farm
Derby Wood
Tanhouse Wood
Round Wood
Ties Wood
Toy's Hill Wood
70
Hayes Coppice
TN8
Henden Manor
Stockyard Bungalow
IDE HILL ROAD
Obriss Farm
Row Wood
Boons Wood
Oak Lodge Farm
The Roughet
"Red Lion"
71
Pond Wood

116
107
117
SEVENOAKS
Kippington
GREAT BRITAINS WOOD
MILL BANK WOOD
WHITLEY FOREST
RED GROVE
COLD ARBOR WOOD
Sevenoaks Weald
Sevenoaks School
Sevenoaks Common
TONBRIDGE ROAD
SEVENOAKS BY-PASS
HYDE'S FOREST
BOWZELL WOOD
TN13
TN14
TN15

117
108
116
SEVENOAKS
Knole (N.T.)
KNOLE PARK
Golf Course
Echo Mount
The Wilderness
Running Track
Playing Field
Sevenoaks School
Furze Field
GODDEN WOOD
Godden Green
Bucks Head Inn
Blackhall
Brickkiln Wood
Guy's Wood
Apps's Wood
Hall Place
Marys Mead
Hudson's Wood
Lords Spring Wood
Stake Farm
Bow Petts Cottage
Rambles Wood
Bakers Wood
South Field Shaw
Lower Fawke Farm
Little Fawke Farm
Fawke Common
Fawke Wood
Redlands Wood
Clacketts Wood
Carter's Hill
ROMAN CEMETERY (Site of)
One Tree Hill (N.T.)
TN13
TN14
TN15
CV
CW
CX
CY
66
67
68
69
70
71
HIGH STREET
TONBRIDGE ROAD
A225
A21
B245
B2019
A224
LONDON RD
TONBRIDGE
RIVER HILL
SEVENOAKS
LONDON ROAD
BY-PASS
BROAD WALK
DUCHESS'S WALK
CHESTNUT WALK
ST. JULIANS ROAD
FAWKE COMMON RD
CARTERS HILL
UNDERRIVER HOUSE
Greensand Way
Sevenoaks Common
Beechmont Bank
Hubbards Hill
Weald Place
Brimstonewell Wood
St.Julian's
Rumshott Manor
Kettleshill Farm
Kettleshill House
Black Charles Barn
Absalom's Farm
Forge View
Valley Farm
The Forge
Underriver
School
River Hill
Park Wood
Riverhill House
Georges Shaw
St.Julians Farm
Panthurst
Recreation Ground
Sevenoaks Weald
Hall
Hillanvale Farm
Morleys Farm
Lansdown Wood
Stony Wood
Elses Farm
Chestnut Wood
Bank Wood
Thomas's Wood
Kentlands
The Red House Farm
Wood End
Oakhurst Farm
Oakhurst Wood
Nizels Wood
Robsacks Wood
Pitts Farm
Nizels
Nizels Farm
Crofton
Cock Wood
Whitesteppes
Irons Wood
Sewage Wks.
Old Cock
F.B.
Stidolph's Farm
Chequers Shaw
Blue House Farm
Priory Wood
Mansers Farm
The Limes Farm
New House Farm
Long Barn
Brook Farm
Pol. Ho.
Dale Farm
WINDMILL ROAD
CHURCH ROAD
MORLEYS
SCABHARBOUR ROAD
EGGPIE
LONG BARN ROAD
HUBBARDS HILL
BEECHMONT ROAD
WEALD ROAD
SOLEFIELDS
LETTER BOX LANE
WHITE HART WOOD
THE RISE
GRASSY LANE
Council Off.
Fire Sta.
Drill Hall
Rec. Grnd.
Swimming Pool
Vine Cricket Grd
Cem
Hosp.
Sch.

Flaneswood
WOOD
Fish Ponds Wood
Ightham Common
RASPIT
HILL
108
Tebb's Copyhold
Gibbons Place
King's Cottages
Goddens Cottages
CY
CZ
DA
DB
DC
Sch
Res.
Tebb's Corner
Bewley Farm
Rose Wood
Raspit Hill
Foxbury Farm
Stone Street
Beaconsmount
Lords Spring Fm
Bitchets Farm
Broomfield Wood
Broomfield
STONE STREET RD
POND LA
CHURCH RD.
SANDY LANE
COACH RD
PINETREE LA.
ISMAYS RD
BACK LANE
BEWLEY LANE
Golding Hop Farm
Sheet Hill Farm
Brookside Farm
Bewley Bar
Colebank Shaw
TONBRIDGE RD.
A227
Ivy Hatch
P.O.
Ivy Hatch Court
66
Boot Wood
Scatts Dene
Bourne Hill Farm
Yopps Green Farm
Vopps Green
BOURNE LA.
BROADHEATH
Cricket Gd
HIGH CROSS ROAD
High Cross
East Bank Wd
The Dell
Lady's Wood
Bartons Farm
BACK LANE
The Grange
Bitchet Green
BROADHOATH WOOD
Scathes Wood
Wright's Farm
HIGH CROSS RD.
East Moat
West Bank Wood
Plaxtol
67
HIGH ST
Plaxtol County Primary School
Cricket Grnd.
Martin's Wood
IGHTHAM MOTE
MOTE
Fairlawne
Fairlawne Park
PECKHAM WALK AVENUE
SCHOOL LANE
Rooks Hill Ho.
Mote Farm
Plantation Farm
Cinderfield Wood
Wilmot Hill
Fatting Pen.
Home Coverts
Wilmot Cottage
Pav.
Spts Grnd.
South Seers Wood
Brakybank Wood
Budd's Dell
N. Leys Shaw
Fairlawne Home Farm
68
STUMBLE HILL TONBRIDGE
Inst.
Point Corner
Ducks Grove
Underriver House
Budds Green
Great Budds
Cold Blows
UPPER GREEN
LADY VANE CL.
P.O.
Shipbourne
REEDS LANE
Little Budds
MOTE ROAD
Kilnfield Wood
Long Slope Wood
School
BACK LANE
Nether St.
Kennels
Martins
Budd's Toll
SHIPBOURNE ROAD
Woodhall Farm
West Green Farm
Barr Wood
Hoad Common
Point Wood
69
SHIPBOURNE FOREST
Hollanden Wood
Marchurst
Peacock Wood
Kiln Wood
Tinley Lodge Farm
The Court House
Hoad Wood
Claygate Wood
SHIPBOURNE ROAD
Wilderness Wood
Twelve Acre Plantation
Dene Park Farm
Tinley Lodge Toll
TN11
Lees Wood
Sawpit Wood
Lodge Wood
Pitman Hall
Girls Home
Park Shaw
Fox Wood
Princess Christians Hospital
Cold Harbour Toll
70
Dene Park (Further Ed. Cent.)
N. Lodge
Coldharbour Farm
Spring Wood
Upper Lodge Wood
Roughetts Wood
The Ruffets
Upper Hollanden Farm
Coldharbour
Thomas Delarue School
HIGHAM LANE
ASHES LA.
COLDHARBOUR LANE
Stacey's Wood
Horns Lodge
STARVECROW CL.
Starvecrow Wood
71
Trench Farm
Medway Valley Walk
Tonbridge

109
AO
AP
AQ
AR
AS
69
70
71
72
73
74
GU3
GU2
Frosbury Fm.
Liddington Hall
Worplesdon First & Mid.Sch.
Hook Farm
Broad Street Common
Ryde's Hill
Stables
Queen Elizabeth Park (W.R.A.C.Barracks)
Worplesdon
Aldershot
A323
A322
A320 Road
Woking
Moorfield
Slyfield Ind.Est.
Abattoir
Cattle Market
Enterprise Est.
Slyfield Green
Woodlands Rd.
Youth Centre
Stoke Hill First Sch.
Bishop Reindrop Sch.
Stoke New Cemetery
Stoke Cem.
Sewage Wks.
Allots.
Ladymead
Bellfields
Corporation Depot
Pumping Sta.
Stoke Lock
Stoke Mill
Marina
River
Water Meadows
Waterside Centre
Stoughton Rec. Grd.
Stoughton
Stoughton Road
Barnwood First Sch.
St. Marys R.C. First Sch.
St. Josephs R.C. Mid. Sch.
Youth Cen.
Play Fld.
Westborough
Westborough First Sch.
Training Centre
Park Barn Sch.
Westwood Park Middle Sch.
Weston
A3
Ladymead Parkway
Woodbridge
Industrial Estate
The Lido
Indoor Bowling Green
Guildford Coll. of Art & Tech.
Stoke
Nightingale
Tech. Coll. Anx.
Guildford Business Park
Cathedral Hill Ind. Est.
Sports Grd.
University of Surrey
Lib.
Cathedral
Spts Hall
Riverside Business Centre
Running Track
Play. Flds.
Royal Surrey Hosp.
Philip Henman Sports Ground
Biological Res. Centre
Strawberry Grove
The Priestley Centre
Village Onslow
Hotel
Queen Eleanor Mid.Sch.
Guildford
Farnham Road Hosp.
Guildford Sch.
Onslow First Sch.
Recn Grd.
Inst. of Adult Educ.
A31
Dean Bottom
Manor Copse
Manor Fm.
Guildford By-Pass
Middleton Road
Manor Way
Farnham Road
Hog's Back
Godalming By-Pass
Henley Grove
School Camp
Site of Anglo Saxon Burial Ground
Guildown Av.
Guildown Road
Artington Ho.
Cemetery
Castle (Ruins)
Racks Close
Council Offs.
Weir Ho. (NT)
Rowing Club
River Wey
Portsmouth Road
High Street
London Road Guildford Station
Civic Hall
Inst. of Adult Educ.
Fort
A281 Shalford
Chantry View Road
Shalford Park
Ferry
Pilgrims Way
Sports Ground
St. Catherine's House
Braboeuf Manor (College of Law)
Sandy Lane
North Downs Way
Piccard's Rough
Police H.Q.
Munstead View
East Warren
West Warren
Bowling Green
Sports Ground
Artington Manor Farm
Shalford Junction
River Wey Navigation
Orange Grove
Orange Court
Orange Court Farm
Littleton
Rush Croft
Rushy Platts Farm
Loseley Park
Loseley House
The Grove
Ashen Copse
Puddock Copse
Rushcroft Farm
Caravan Site
Cemetery
Shalford
Shalford Station
The Street
Tilehouse Farm
Dagley Lane
Polsted Manor
Compton Wood
Brook House
Mellersh's
Brickfields Farm
Old Claypits Wood
A3100
A248
Kings
Ashcroft

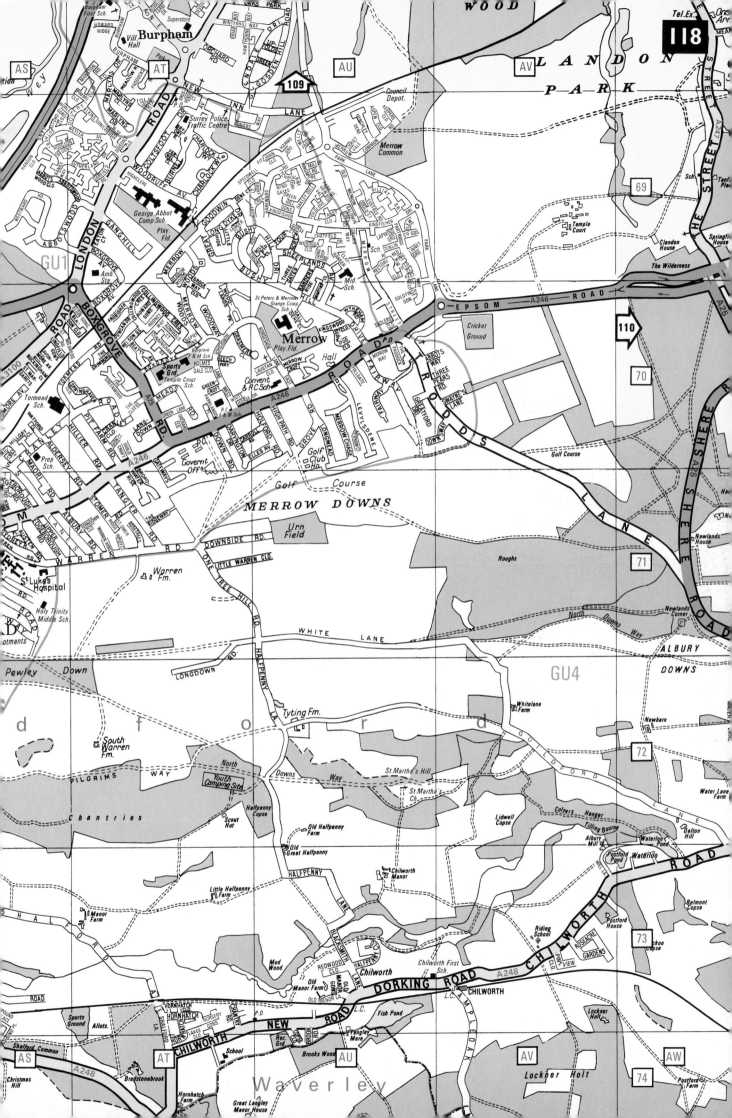
Burpham
Merrow
MERROW DOWNS
CLANDON PARK
EPSOM ROAD
LONDON ROAD
WARREN RD.
WHITE LANE
ONE TREE HILL RD.
HALFPENNY LANE
DORKING ROAD
CHILWORTH ROAD
NEW ROAD
SHERE ROAD
TRODDS LANE
GUILDFORD LANE
PILGRIMS WAY
North Downs Way
Chantries
ALBURY DOWNS
Pewley Down
Chilworth
CHILWORTH
St Luke's Hospital
George Abbot Comp.Sch.
Golf Course
Roughs
Urn Field
Warren Fm.
Tyting Fm.
St.Martha's Hill
Lockner Holt
Waverley
GU1
GU4
109
110

119
Brockholes Cross
KT24
Golf Course
Oldlands Plantation
BD
BE
BF
BG
Stars Wood
High Barn
Big High Grove
111
Preserve Copse
Camping Site
Admirals Wk.
Nurs.
Polesden Lacy (National Trust)
Nuns Walk
Eastcourt
Polesden Farm
Round Copse
Yewtree Farm
Tanner's Hatch (Youth Hostel)
Bayden
69
Pump Pond Wood
Effingham Hill Farm
Stonyrock
St. Teresa's Convent
Ranmore Farm
Garlic Cottages
Guildford
Burrows Wood
110
Lonesome Cottage
RANMORE COMMON (NATIONAL TRUST)
Osborne Plantation
Bakehouse Cottages
Hogden Cottages
70
Dogkennel Green
North
Crittenden Lane
Hogden Lane
Yewtree Lane
Road
Timber Yard
Dunley Hill Farm
Ranmore Country Club
Ranmore Lodge
Ranmore Common Road
RH5
Effingham Upper Common
Drove Road
Great Copse
The Roundabout's
Landbarn Farm
Coombe Chalk Pit
Oaken Grove
Harley Copse
71
Pickett's Hole
Holehill Lane
Holehill Copse
Dunley Wood
The Dene
Rokefield
North Downs Way
Coomb Farm
Pipp Brook
Old Simm's Copse
Springfield Rd
Ashley
St Johns Rd
Dunley Wood
Westcott
Rec. Grd.
Coombe Copse
Westcott Mill
Mill Pond
Rookery Farm
Balchins Lane
The Paddock
72
Deerleap Rd.
Sandrock Rd.
Guildford
A25
Parsonage
Pointers
Coast Hill La.
Rectory
Westcott Heath
Park Farm
Westcott Hill Farm
The Rookery
Rookery Drive
Hildens
Leasers Barn
Deerleap Wood
Vale
Logmore Lane
Evershed's Rough
St Johns Church Road
Coast Hill
Applegarth Fm.
White Downs Lane
West Lane
Wotton
Fish Pond
Fir Plantation
Westlane Barn
(P.H.) Wotton Hatch
The School House
Coast Hill Farm
Bury Hill House
73
The Crossways
Guildford Road
A25
Sheephouse Green
Pipp Brook
Crossways Farm
Home Field Cottage
Manor Farm
Wotton Drive
Sylvanus Wood
Britt's Wood
Weir
Weir
Abinger Mill
Wotton House Gardens
Tilling Bourne
Wolvens Lane
Brook Farm
Gravel Pit
Brickyard Cottages
Firtree Plantation
Brick Yard La.
Wotton Drive
Sheephouse Lane
Weirs
Tillingbourne House
Wotton House Fire Service College
Damphurst Wood
BC
BD
BE
BF
BG
Raikes Lane
Abinger Lane
Townhurst Wood
Damphurst Hollow
Logmore Farm
74
Whitings Wood
Weir
Ellix Wood
Chandlers Wood

Chapel Wood
Chapel Hill
Foxbury Shaw
Foxbury
Chapel Fm.
CHAPEL LA.
111
BG
BH
BJ
BK
CAMILLA DR.
Camilla Lacey
West Humble
WESTHUMBLE ST.
BOXHILL & WEST-HUMBLE
Burford Bri.
Burford Bri. Hotel
Swim. Pool
Burford Lodge
Pinehurst
The Tower
National
Lodge Hill
Box Hill
National Trust
KT20
69
Keepers Lodge
Fort Cottages
ZIG - ZAG
Memorial
Boxhurst
Old Dean Cott.
Dorking Wood
RANMORE COMMON RD.
Ashcombe Wood
BURNEY RD.
ADLERS
PILGRIMS WAY
PILGRIMS CLO.
Gravel Pit Plant
Playing Field
Pav. Playing Field
Stepping Stones
Boxlands
Bradley Farm
BRADLEY LA.
Denbies Farm
NORTH DOWNS WAY
Denbies
Pixholme Court
Playing Fields
RIVER MOLE
Pixham Firs
Offices
Sewage Wks.
Sports Grd.
70
OLD REIGATE
Boxhill Bri.
Deepdene Bri.
DORKING
DORKING DEEPDENE
ASHCOMBE ROAD
A2003
Depot
PILGRIMS WAY
Riding Stables
DORKING WEST
Playing Field
Meadowbank Recreat. Grd.
Mill Pond
Football Gd.
CEMETERY
REIGATE
A25
120
BETCHWORTH
Golf Course
Club Ho.
Clay Copse
Pipp Brook
Gas Holders
INDUSTRIAL EST.
Milton Court
MILTONCOURT LA.
Milton Ct. Fm.
Milton Heath
WESTCOTT ROAD
A25
Sondes Pla.
Sondesplace Farm
HIGH ST.
WEST ST.
SOUTH ST.
VINCENT LA.
DORKING
Cotmandene
Deepdene House
DEEPDENE AV.
LADYEGATE ROAD
PUNCHBOWL LANE
71
Park Fm.
CHART PARK
Milton Brook
Westcott
Cricket Gd.
Milton Br.
Sondes Place Sch.
Remedial Cent.
LONGFIELD RD.
HAMPSTEAD LANE
Dorking Gen. Hosp.
Harrowlands Hosp.
The Glory Wood
Golf Course
WET GROVE
Tilehurst Fm.
Field Place
72
Goldenlands Farm
Osierbed Copse
THE NOWER
Observatory
Bury Hill
RH4
RH5
Osier Plant.
THE LAKE
Home Fm.
HARROW RD. W.
HARROW RD. E.
KNOLL RD.
RIDGEWAY RD.
Tennis Club
Res. Goodwyns Pla.
Starhurst Sch.
Comm. Cent.
CHART DOWNS ESTATE
Royal Oak
Stone Bridge
Bent Brook
Fir Plantation
Mad Horse Copse
COLDHARBOUR LANE
Rough Rew
HORSHAM ROAD
A24
FLINT HILL
BENTSBROOK RD.
HOLMESDALE RD.
Milehouse Farm
NORTH HOLMWOOD
Harelands Wood
Holmwood Farm
BENTSBROOK PARK
INHOLMS LANE
THE ORCHARD
Cricket Ground Pavilion
Beldham's Farm
Inholm's Farm
73
BLACKBROOK
Black Brook
Chadhurst Farm
Chadhurst Moor
STANE STREET
Hoop Copse
Inholms Farm
Blackbrook
The Plough
Blackbrook House
Woodlands Park

Box Hill
Brockham
Betchworth
Strood Green
Betchworth Park Golf Course
Betchworth Castle (Ruins)
Brockham Hills
Brockham Warren
Highridge Wood
Roothill Wood
Tweed Copse
Field Plantation
Mole Valley
River Mole
Tanner's Brook
Chart Park Golf Course
Wet Grove
Blackbrook
Pixham Firs
Boxhurst
Pilgrims Way (Course of)
Reigate Road
Dorking Lime Works
Research Laboratories Brockham Park
Oldpark Wood
Hook Copse
RH5
KT20
RH3

KT20
Colley
National Trust
Juniper Hill
Queens Park
Pilgrims Holt
REIGATE National
Underhill Farm
Kemp's Farm
Colleyland Shaw
Colley Pit
Buckland
A25
ROAD
Park Pit
Buckland Lodge
Dungate's Farm
REIGATE HEATH
Golf Course
Club House
Cricket Grd.
Black Horse
Broadleas
Clears Cotts
Colley Copse
Colley Wood
Sports Ground
Tennis Cts.
COLLEY MANOR DRIVE
BUCKLAND ROAD
WEST ST.
HIGH ST.
REIGATE
Castle Grounds
Town Hall
Bowling Grn
Cricket Gd.
Playing Field
Rugby Club
Allots.
Priory Pond
Cricket Field
REIGATE PARK
Park Hill
Res.
Skimmington
Disused Res.
Garthlands
Wonham Manor
Wonham Mill
River Mole
Wilderness Wood
The Old School Ho.
Trumpet Hill
Heathfield
Trumpets Hill
Little Santon Farm
Littleton Manor Fm.
Ede's Cotts
Littleton
Ricebridge Farm
Snowerhill Farm
Providence Cottage
Gilbert's Farm
Santon House
Wallace Brook
RH2
Clayhall Fm
South Park
Sports Gd
Hall
Sch.
Reigate and Banstead
Greenlane Cotts
Flanchford Farm
Knight's Gorse
Little Flanchford Farm
Flanchford Bridge
Mill Pond
Little Abbots Farm
Gad Brook
Slipshatch Wood
Keepers Cott.
Hilly Furze Field
Hartswood Manor
Playing Field
Mark Mead Plantation
Denshott Farm
Skeets Farm
Leigh Place
Moat
Bury's Court School
Kiln Field Plantation
River Mole
Ninetythree Plantation
Broad Ten Plantation
Twelve Acre Plantation
Butlers Shaw
School
P.O.
Leigh
Bures Manor
Alder Copse
Bell Copse
Institute
112
121
69
70
71
72
73
74
BO
BP
BQ
BR

121
Pilgrims Holt
Queens Park
Motel
Fort
113
Nut Wood
Nat. Trust
Nutwood Lo.
Temple Wood
The Serpentine
The Lake
REIGATE HILL
National Trust
REIGATE HILL
A217
GATTON PARK ROAD
A242
Playing Fld.
St. Bedes Sch.
Redhill Tennis Club
Colley Wood
Broadlands
69
Sports Gd.
Tennis Cts.
MANOR RD.
SOMERS RD.
Training Cent.
Fire Brigade H.Q.
Cent. for Blind
GREYSTONES
Wray Common
Schs.
R.C.Sch.
T.A. Centre
Linkfield Corner
STATION RD.
REDHILL
A25
WEST ST.
HIGH ST.
CHURCH ST.
REIGATE
Reigate Coll.
Castle Grounds
Town Hall
70
Bowling Grn
Cricket Gd.
Playing Field
Rugby Club
Allots.
Priory Pond
Cricket Field
REIGATE PARK
71
Res.
Park Hill
RH2
120
REIGATE ROAD
BELL ST.
A217
Cemetery
E. Surrey Coll. (Art Dept.)
Health Cent.
REDHILL COMMON
Dunottar Girls Sch.
Mead Vale
Woodhatch
Woodhatch Sch.
Redhill General Hosp.
St. Johns
EARLSWOOD
Golf Course
EARLSWOOD COMMON
Boating Lake
New Pond
Newpond Farm Nursery
A2044
Earlswood Sewage Works
Royal Earlswood Hospital
South Park
72
Garden Cent.
Comm. Cent.
Hall
Sch.
Slipshatch Wood
Keepers Cott.
Hartswood Manor
Doversgreen
DOVERS GREEN ROAD
Rec. Ground
Felland Copse
Dover's Fm
Playing Field
73
Kiln Field Plantation
Geals Copse
Ninetythree Plantation
Broad Ten Plantation
Twelve Acre Plantation
Home Grove
Petridge Wood
Benting Wood
Petridgewood Common
Brookside Farm
River Mole
Sidlow Bridge
Sidlowbridge
Sidlow Farm
74
Alder Copse
Institute
Lonesome Lodge
Salfords
BRIGHTON RD.
A23
HORLEY ROAD
WOODHATCH ROAD
BONEHURST RD.
BS
BT
BU
BV

113
114
Rec. Gd.
Play.Fld.
Allots.
Sewage Works
Redhill Brook
Pendell Farm
Water Lane
Brewerstreet Farm
The Old Rectory
Caravan Site
Sand & Silicon Wks.
Ford Br.
Mercers Farm
M23
Pendell House
Pendell Court
Manor House
Lake Farm
Cricket Ground
Pav.
Chilmead Lane
Nutfield Marsh Road
Peyton's Cotts.
Cockley Plantation
Chilmead Farm
Glebe House
Great Common
Dormers Farm
Allotments
Sand Pit
Little Common
Nutfield Court
The Rectory
Playing Field
Works
Sports Ground
Nutfield
Bletchingley Road
Castle Street
High Street
Nutfield Road
A25
Pimlico Hill
Cem.
Sch.
P.O.
Castle Hill
Castle Place
Castle Clo.
Bletchingley
Robert Denholme House
Coombes Coppice
Stanley's Wood
Research Labs.
Patteson Court
North Park
Holmesdale
Castlehill Farm
Playing Field
Furze Hill
Nutfield Priory (Sch.for Deaf)
South Park
Steners Hill
Steners Hill Park Farm
Sandhills
Priory Farm
Little Cormongers Farm
Kentwins
Bowerhill Wood
Philanthropic Road
Hogtrough La.
Sandy Lane
RH1
Kentwyns Rise
Home Farm
Cemetery
Queen's Ho.
Thornthrift
Lyttel Hall
Village Hall
Bray's Farm
Sports Grd.
South Nutfield
Colgate's Farm
Royal Philanthropic Society Sch.
Brook
Holmesdale Rd.
Oakwood Clo.
Nutfield
Cricket Ground
Gladstone's Ho.
Kingscross Lane
Thepps Shaw
Garston's Ho.
Thepps Clo.
Ridgegreen House
Crab Hill
Crab Hill House
Henhaw Farm
Hale Farm
Crabhill Farm
Bransland Wood
Staplehurst Fm.
Temple Wood
The Rookery
Nursery
Hazelhurst Fm.
Kings Mill Lane
Redhill Aerodrome and Heliport
Salfords Stream
Fish Pond
Lawn Hill
Burstow Park Farm
Pumping Station
Perimeter Road
Moats Lane
Mason's Bridge Road
Mason's Bridge Bungalow
The Plantation
South Hale Farm
Spring Field Wood
Dean Farm
Ruffet
Mason's Bridge
Dairy House Farm
Furzefield Wood
Prince of Wales Road
Coopers Hill Road
BV
BW
BX
BY
BZ
69
70
71
72
73
74

Mountnessing
Fitzwalters Dairy Farm
Heard's Farm
Palmer's Farm
Home Wood
Chainbridge Farm
River Wid
Arnold's Farm
Howe's Farm
Brick Farm
Canterbury Tye Farm
Canterbury Tye Spring
Arnold's Wood
Arnold's Shaw
Brickley Shaw
BRENTWOOD BY PASS ROAD
A12
A1023
B1002
CM15
Six Acre Spring
Wynbarn's Farm
'The Rose'
Sports Centre
Sch.
Recn Grd
Shenfield Hall Fm.
Hall Wood
Pye Wood
Playing Fields
School
Hutton Junc. Hotel
RAYLEIGH ROAD
A129
Hutton
Shenfield
SHENFIELD
Lib.
County Fire Brigade H.Q.
HUTTON ROAD
CHELMSFORD ROAD
SHENFIELD ROAD
Brentwood
The Chelmer Inst. of Higher Education
Amb.Sta.
Sports Grd.
Cricket Grd.
Nuffield Nursing Home
Brentwood Dist. Hosp.
Blood Trans. Cen.
Brockley Wd
Polo Field
Hunter Mem!
BRENTWOOD
Sports Ground
INGRAVE ROAD
Three Arch Bridge
Scout Camp
Thrift Wood
Thrift Green
Shenfield Common
Mat. Home
South Hove
Hall Wood
Ingrave Hall
SITE OF ST NICHOLAS'S CHURCH
Sutton Shaw
Highfield Wood
Birches Wood
CM13
CM14
Seven Arch Bri.
'Seven Arches'
King George's Playing Field
Walks Plantn
Golf Course
Hart's Wood
Ingrave Green
BRENTWOOD ROAD
A128
Dairy Farm
Salmond's Farm
Ingrave
Clinic
Donkey Lane Plantation
Kents Wood
Thorndon Hall
Long Plantation
Barrack
Coun. Depot
Marillac Hospital
School
Petroleum Depot
Hall
DC
DD
DE
DF
23
24
25
26
27
28
29
33
42

123
Little Warley
Childerditch
Childerditch Pond
GREAT PARK
Brentwood
CM13
A127 ARTERIAL ROAD
East Horndon
West Horndon
WEST HORNDON
St Peter's Rectory
Warley Hall Wood
Little Warley Hall
Great Warley Hall
Childerditch Hall
Hill Farm
Roses Farm
The Rookery
Menagerie Plantation
Old Hall Pond
Old Hall (Remains of)
St.Nicholas's Church (Site of)
Mill Wood
Jury Hill
Thick Shaw
Barrett's Shaw
Straight Path Shaw
Hollow Bottom Shaw
Round Shaw
Octagon Plantation
Cockridden Farm
Halfway Ho.
Glencar
East Horndon Hall
Broad Fields
Nuttys Farm
School
WEST HORNDON PLAYING FIELD
CADOGAN AVENUE
Engineering Works
Works
Orchard Cottages
Monks Farm
Old England
Little Tillingham Hall
Tillingham Hall
Moat
Field House
Barnards
Berry Farm
Fairplay Farm
Bullens and Herds
Home Farm
Corner Farm
Fen Farm
Blankets
Drakes Farm
Mar Dyke
Stone Hall
Harrow Inn (P.H.)
Caylock's Farm
Slough House
Hatch Farm
Brandon Hall
School Inst.
Bulphan Fen
Moat
RM14
RM15
Havering
Thurrock
BRENTWOOD ROAD
TILBURY ROAD
A128
B186
DC
DD
DE
DF
30
31
32
33
34
35
36
51

Notes

The street name and postal district or locality of an entry is followed by a grid reference and number of the map on which the name will be found, e.g. Abbey Rd, SW19 will be found in square **BT50** on map **76** and Norfolk Crescent, Sidcup in square **CN47** on map **78** (you will see from the map the latter location is in postcode boundary DA15).

The index contains some names for which there is insufficient space on the map. The adjoining thoroughfare to such roads is shown in italics, e.g. Agar Place, NW1 is off *Agar Grove* the latter being found in square **BW36** on map **56**.

A strict alphabetical order is followed in which Avenue, Close, Gardens etc, although abbreviated, are read as part of the preceding name. For example, Andrews Rd comes before Andrew St, and Abbey Orchard St before Abbey Rd.

Certain streets named in the Index are to be found both in the Central London enlarged-scale section, maps 1 to 4, as well as in parts of maps 56, 57, 66 and 67. In order to distinguish between the two the name of the street which is duplicated is given first in **bold type** (indicating the Central London Section), followed immediately by the same name in ordinary type.

ADDENDUM see page 408

Abbreviations of District Names

Alp.	Alperton	Dor.	Dorking	Long.	Longfield	Sun.	Sunbury-on-Thames
Amer.	Amersham	E.Mol.	East Molesey	Loug.	Loughton	Surb.	Surbiton
Ashf.	Ashford	Eden.	Edenbridge	Lthd.	Leatherhead	Sutt.	Sutton
Ash.	Ashtead	Edg.	Edgware	Maid.	Maidenhead	S.at H.	Sutton at Hone
Bans.	Banstead	Egh.	Egham	Mitch.	Mitcham	Swan.	Swanley
Bark.	Barking	Enf.	Enfield	Mord.	Morden	Swans.	Swanscombe
Barn.	Barnet	Epp.	Epping	New A.G.	New Ash Green	Tad.	Tadworth
Beac.	Beaconsfield	Eyns.	Eynsford	N.Mal.	New Malden	Tedd.	Teddington
Beck.	Beckenham	Farn.	Farningham	Nthlt.	Northolt	T.Ditt.	Thames Ditton
Belv.	Belvedere	Fawk.	Fawkham	Nthwd.	Northwood	Th.Hth.	Thornton Heath
Berk.	Berkhamsted	Felt.	Feltham	Ong.	Ongar	Til.	Tilbury
Betch.	Betchworth	Ger.Cr.	Gerrards Cross	Orp.	Orpington	Ton.	Tonbridge
Bex.	Bexley	God.	Godstone	Oxt.	Oxted	Twick.	Twickenham
Bexh.	Bexleyheath	Grav.	Gravesend	Pnr.	Pinner	Upmin.	Upminster
B. Stort.	Bishops Stortford	Grnf.	Greenford	Pot.B.	Potters Bar	Uxb.	Uxbridge
Borwd.	Borehamwood	Green.	Greenhithe	Pur.	Purley	Vir.W.	Virginia Water
Brent.	Brentford	Guild.	Guildford	Rad.	Radlett	Wall.	Wallington
Brwd.	Brentwood	Hmptn.	Hampton	Rain.	Rainham	Wal.Abb.	Waltham Abbey
Brom.	Bromley	Harl.	Harlow	Red.	Redhill	Wal.Cr.	Waltham Cross
Brox.	Broxbourne	Har.	Harrow	Reig.	Reigate	Walt.	Walton-on-Thames
Buck.H.	Buckhurst Hill	Hart.	Hartley	Rich.	Richmond upon Thames	Warl.	Warlingham
Bush.	Bushey	Hat.	Hatfield	Rick.	Rickmansworth	Wat.	Watford
Cars.	Carshalton	Hav.	Havering-atte-Bower	Rom.	Romford	Well.	Welling
Cat.	Caterham	Hem.H.	Hemel Hempstead	Ruis.	Ruislip	Welw.	Welwyn
Ch.St.G.	Chalfont St.Giles	Hert.	Hertford	St.Alb.	St.Albans	Welw.G.C.	Welwyn Garden City
Cher.	Chertsey	Hodd.	Hoddesdon	Saw.	Sawbridgeworth	Wem.	Wembley
Chesh.	Chesham	Horn.	Hornchurch	Sev.	Sevenoaks	West Dr.	West Drayton
Chess.	Chessington	Hort.K.	Horton Kirby	Shep.	Shepperton	West.	Westerham
Chig.	Chigwell	Houns.	Hounslow	Sid.	Sidcup	W.Mol.	West Molesey
Chis.	Chislehurst	Ilf.	Ilford	Slou.	Slough	W.Wick.	West Wickham
Chsnt.	Cheshunt	Ing.	Ingatestone	Sthl.	Southall	Wey.	Weybridge
Cob.	Cobham	Islw.	Isleworth	S.Croy.	South Croydon	Whyt.	Whyteleafe
Couls.	Coulsdon	Ken.	Kenley	S.Dnth.	South Darenth	Wdf.Grn.	Woodford Green
Croy.	Croydon	Kes.	Keston	S.Ock.	South Ockendon	Wind.	Windsor
Cuff.	Cuffley	K. Lang.	Kings Langley	Stai.	Staines	Wok.	Woking
Dag.	Dagenham	Kings.T.	Kingston on Thames	S.le H.	Stanford le Hope	Wor.Pk.	Worcester Park
Dart.	Dartford	Leyt.	Leytonstone	Stan.	Stanmore		

General Abbreviations

All.	Alley	Ct.	Court	La.	Lane	Rd.	Road
App.	Approach	Ctre.	Centre	Lo.	Lodge	S.	South
Arc.	Arcade	Dev.	Development	Mans.	Mansions	Shop.	Shopping
Av.	Avenue	Dr.	Drive	Mkt.	Market	Sq.	Square
Bdy.	Broadway	E.	East	Ms.	Mews	Sta.	Station
Bldgs.	Buildings	Embk.	Embankment	Mt.	Mount	St.	Street
Boul.	Boulevard	Esp.	Esplanade	N.	North	Ter.	Terrace
Bri.	Bridge	Est.	Estate	Par.	Parade	Trd.	Trading
Circ.	Circus	Gdns.	Gardens	Pass.	Passage	Vills.	Villas
Cft.	Croft	Gra.	Grange	Pk.	Park	Vw.	View
Clo.	Close	Grn.	Green	Pl.	Place	W.	West
Cor.	Corner	Gro.	Grove	Prom.	Promenade	Wf.	Wharf
Cotts.	Cottages	Ho.	House	Quad.	Quadrant	Wk.	Walk
Cres.	Crescent	Ind.	Industrial	Ri.	Rise	Yd.	Yard

A

Abberton Wk., Rain. 59 CT37
Abbess Clo. E6 58 CK39
Oliver Gdns.
Abbess Clo. SW2 76 BY47
Abbeville Rd. N8 47 BW31
Abbeville Rd. SW4 76 BW46
Abbey Ave., St.Alb. 9 BF15
Abbey Ave., Wem. 55 BL37
Abbey Clo., Hayes 53 BC40
Abbey Clo., Nthlt. 54 BE38
Abbey Clo., Pnr. 45 BD31
Abbey Clo., Wok. 100 AV61
Abbey Ct., Hmptn. 84 BF51
Abbey Ct., St.Alb. 9 BG14
Albert St.
Abbey Ct., Wal.Abb. 21 CE20
Abbey Cres., Belv. 69 CR42
Abbey Dr. SW17 76 BU49
Church La.
Abbey Dr., Stai. 83 AX52
Abbey Gdns. NW8 56 BT37
Abbey Gdns. W6 65 BR43
Abbey Gdns., Cher. 83 AW53
Abbey Gdns. Ms. NW8 56 BT37
Abbey Gro. SE2 69 CO42
Abbey La. E15 57 CF37
Abbey La., Beck. 77 CE50
Abbey Ms. E17 48 CE32
Leamington Ave.
Abbey Mill End, St.Alb. 9 BG14
Abbey Mill La., St.Alb. 9 BG14
Abbey Orchard St. SW1 3 P6
Abbey Orchard St. SW1 66 BW41
Abbey Pk., Beck. 77 CE50
Abbey Rd. E15 57 CF37
Abbey Rd. NW6 56 BS37
Abbey Rd. NW8 56 BT37
Abbey Rd. NW10 55 BM37
Abbey Rd. SE2 69 CP42
Abbey Rd. SW19 76 BT50
Abbey Rd., Bark. 58 CL36
Abbey Rd., Belv. 69 CP42
Abbey Rd., Bexh. 69 CQ45
Abbey Rd., Cher. 83 AW54
Abbey Rd., Croy. 86 BY55
Abbey Rd., Enf. 30 CA25
Abbey Rd., Grav. 81 DJ47
Abbey Rd., Green. 80 DB46
Abbey Rd., Ilf. 49 CM32
Abbey Rd., Shep. 83 AZ55
Abbey Rd., S.Croy. 96 CC58
Abbey Rd., Vir.W. 82 AR53
Abbey Rd., Wal.Cr. 21 CD20
Abbey Rd., Wok. 100 AR62
Abbey Rd. Est. NW8 56 BS37
Abbey St. E13 58 CH38
Abbey St. SE1 4 N6
Abbey St. SE1 67 CA41
Abbey Ter. NW10 55 BL37
Abbey Ter. SE2 69 CP42
Abbey Vw. NW7 37 BO27
Abbey Vw., Wal.Abb. 21 CE20
Abbey Vw. Rd., St.Alb. 9 BG13
Abbey Wk., E.Mol. 84 BF52
Abbey Wd. La., Rain. 60 CV37
Abbey Wd. Rd. SE2 69 CO42
Abbeydale Rd., Wem. 55 BL37
Abbeyfield Rd. SE16 67 CC42
Abbeyfields Clo. NW10 55 BM37
Abbeyhill Rd., Sid. 79 CP47
Abbot Clo., Stai. 73 AX50
Bingham Dr.
Abbot Clo., Wey. 92 AX59
Abbot Rd., Guil. 118 AR71
Abbot St. E8 57 CA36
Kingsland High St.
Abbots Ave., St.Alb. 9 BH15
Abbots Ave. W., St.Alb. 9 BG15
Abbots Clo. N1 57 BZ36
Alwyne Rd.
Abbots Clo., Brwd. 122 DD26
Abbots Clo., Guil. 118 AP72
Abbots Clo., Orp. 88 CM54
Abbots Clo., Rain. 60 CV37
Abbots Clo., Ruis. 45 BD34
Abbots Clo., Uxb. 53 AX39
Abbots Cres., Enf. 29 BY23
Abbots Dr., Har. 45 BF34
Abbots Dr., Vir.W. 82 AQ53
Abbots Dr., Wal.Abb. 22 CH20
Abbots Fld., Grav. 81 DH50
Abbots Ford Clo., Wok. 100 AT62
Onslow Cres.
Abbots Gdns. N2 47 BT31
Abbots La. SE1 4 N3
Abbots La. SE1 57 CA40
Abbots La., Ken. 105 BZ61
Abbots Manor Est. SW1 3 J10
Abbots Manor Est. SW1 66 BV42
Abbots Pk. SW2 76 BY47
Abbots Pk., St.Alb. 9 BJ15
Abbots Pl. NW6 56 BS37
Abbots Ri., Kings L. 17 AY16
Abbots Rd. E6 58 CJ37
Abbots Rd., Abb.L. 17 BA19
Abbots Rd., Edg. 37 BN29
Abbots Ter. N8 47 BX32
Abbots Tilt, Walt. 84 BE55
Abbots Vw., Kings L. 17 AY17
Abbots Wk., Cat. 105 CB64
Abbots Way, Beck. 87 CD53
Abbots Way, Guil. 118 AU70
Abbotsbury Clo. E15 57 CF37
Abbotsbury Clo. W14 65 BR41
Abbotsbury Gdns., Pnr. 45 BD33
Abbotsbury Rd. W14 65 BR41
Abbotsbury Rd., Brom. 88 CG55
Abbotsbury Rd., Mord. 86 BS53
Abbotsfield, Grav. 81 DH50
Abbotsford Ave. N15 48 BZ31
Abbotsford Gdns., Wdf.Grn. 40 CH30
Abbotsford Rd., Ilf. 50 CO34
Abbotshall Ave. N14 38 BW27
Abbotshall Rd. SE6 77 CF47
Abbotsleigh Clo., Sutt. 95 BS57
Camborne Rd.
Abbotsleigh Rd. SW16 76 BW49
Abbotsmede Clo., Twick. 74 BH48
Abbotstone Rd. SW15 65 BQ45
Abbotsweld, Harl. 13 CN12
Abbotswell Rd. SE4 77 CD46
Abbotswood, Guil. 118 AS69
Abbotswood Clo., Belv. 69 CQ41
Coptefield Dr.
Abbotswood Clo., Guil. 118 AS69
Abbotswood Dr., Wey. 92 BA59
Abbotswood Gdns., Ilf. 49 CK31
Abbotswood Rd. SW16 76 BW48
Abbotswood Way, Hayes 53 BC40
Abbott Ave. SW20 85 BQ51
Abbott Clo., Hmptn. 74 BE50
Abbott Clo., Nthlt. 54 BE36
Abbott Rd. E14 57 CF39
Abbotts Clo., Rom. 50 CR31
Abbotts Clo., Swan. 89 CU52
Abbotts Cres. E4 39 CF28
Abbotts Dr., Wem. 45 BJ34
Abbotts Grn., S.Croy. 96 CC57
Abbotts Pk. Rd. E10 48 CF33
Abbotts Rd., Barn. 29 BS24
Abbotts Rd., Mitch. 86 BW52
Abbotts Rd., Sthl. 54 BE40
Abbotts Rd., Sutt. 94 BR56
Abbotts Wk., Bexh. 69 CP43
Abbotts Wk., Wind. 61 AM44
Abbotts Way, Slou. 61 AL40
Abbs Cross Gdns., Horn. 51 CV33
Abbs Cross La., Horn. 51 CV34
Abchurch La. EC4 2 L10
Abchurch La. EC4 57 BZ40
Abchurch Yd. EC4 2 K10
Abchurch Yd. EC4 57 BZ40
Abchurch La.
Abdale La., Hat. 19 BP17
Abdale Rd. W12 55 BP40
Abel Clo., Hem.H. 8 AZ13
Abenbury Way, Brwd. 122 DD27
Aberavon Rd. E3 57 CD38
Abercairn Rd. SW16 76 BW50
Aberconway Rd., Mord. 86 BS52
Abercorn Clo. NW7 37 BR29
Abercorn Clo. NW8 56 BT38
Abercorn Clo., S.Croy. 96 CC59
Kersey Dr.
Abercorn Cres., Har. 45 BF33
Abercorn Est., Wem. 54 BK37
Abercorn Gdns., Har. 45 BK33
Abercorn Gdns., Rom. 50 CO32
Abercorn Gro., Ruis. 44 BA31
Abercorn Pl. NW8 56 BT38
Abercorn Rd. NW7 37 BR29
Abercorn Rd., Stan. 36 BK29
Abercorn Way, Wok. 100 AQ62
Abercrombie St. SW11 66 BU44
Abercrombie Way, Harl. 13 CM12
Aberdale Gdns., Pot.B. 19 BR19
Aberdare Clo., W.Wick. 87 CF55
Aberdare Gdns. NW6 56 BS36
Aberdare Gdns. NW7 37 BQ29
Aberdare Rd., Enf. 30 CB24
Aberdeen La. N5 47 BY35
Aberdeen Par. N18 39 CB28
Angel Rd.
Aberdeen Pk. N5 47 BY35
Aberdeen Pl. NW8 1 A4
Aberdeen Pl. NW8 56 BT38
Aberdeen Rd. N5 48 BZ35
Aberdeen Rd. N18 39 CB28
Aberdeen Rd. NW10 46 BO35
Aberdeen Rd., Croy. 96 BZ56
Aberdeen Rd., Har. 36 BH30
Aberdeen Ter. SE3 67 CF44
Aberdour Rd., Ilf. 50 CO34
Aberdour St. SE1 4 M8
Aberdour St. SE1 67 CA41
Aberfeldy St. E14 57 CF39
Aberford Gdns. SE18 68 CK44
Aberford Rd., Borwd. 28 BM23
Aberfoyle Rd. SW16 76 BW50
Abergeldie Rd. SE12 78 CH46
Abernethy Rd. SE13 68 CG45
Abersham Rd. E8 48 CA35
Abery St. SE18 68 CN42
Abingdon Clo. NW1 56 BW36
Abingdon Clo. SE1 4 Q9
Abingdon Clo. SW19 76 BT50
Abingdon Clo., Uxb. 53 AY37
Abingdon Clo., Wok. 100 AQ62
Winnington Way
Abingdon Pl., Pot.B. 20 BS19
Abingdon Rd. N3 38 BT30
Abingdon Rd. SW16 86 BX51
Abingdon Rd. W8 66 BS41
Abingdon St. SW1 3 Q6
Abingdon St. SW1 66 BX41
Abingdon Vill. W8 66 BS41
Abingdon Way, Orp. 98 CO56
Abinger Ave., Sutt. 94 BQ58
Abinger Clo., Brom. 88 CK52
Abinger Clo., Dor. 119 BK73
Abinger Clo., Ilf. 50 CO35
Abinger Clo., Wall. 95 BX56
Abinger Gdns., Islw. 64 BH45
Abinger Gro. SE8 67 CD43
Abinger La., Dor. 119 BC73
Abinger Ms. W9 56 BS38
Warlock Rd.
Abinger Rd. W4 65 BO41
Abinger Way, Guil. 109 AT68
Ablett St. SE16 67 CC42
Aboyne Dr. SW20 85 BP51
Aboyne Rd. NW10 46 BN34
Aboyne Rd. SW17 76 BT48
Abridge Clo., Wal.Cr. 30 CC21
Abridge Gdns., Rom. 41 CR29
Abridge Rd., Chig. 31 CM25
Abridge Rd., Epp. 31 CN22
Abridge Way, Bark. 59 CO37
Abyssinia Clo. SW11 66 BU45
Cairns Rd.
Acacia Ave. N17 39 BZ29
Acacia Ave., Brent. 64 BJ43
Acacia Ave., Hayes 53 BB39
Acacia Ave., Horn. 50 CT34
Acacia Ave., Ruis. 44 BC33
Acacia Ave., Shep. 83 AZ53
Acacia Ave., Stai. 62 AS45
Acacia Ave., Wem. 46 BL35
Acacia Ave., West Dr. 53 AY40
Acacia Ave., Wok. 100 AR63
Acacia Clo. SE20 87 CB51
Selby Rd.
Acacia Clo., Orp. 88 CM53
Acacia Clo., Stan. 36 BH29
Acacia Clo., Wey. 91 AU59
Acacia Dr.
Acacia Dr., Bans. 94 BQ60
Acacia Dr., Sutt. 85 BR54
Acacia Dr., Upmin. 51 CX35
Acacia Dr., Wey. 91 AV58
Acacia Gdns., Upmin. 51 CZ33
Acacia Gdns., W.Wick. 87 CF55
Acacia Gro. SE21 77 BZ48
Acacia Gro., Berk. 7 AQ13
Acacia Gro., N.Mal. 85 BN52
Acacia Ms. (Harmondsworth), West Dr. 63 AX43
High St.
Acacia Pl. NW8 56 BT37
Acacia Rd. E11 49 CG34
Acacia Rd. E17 48 CD32
Acacia Rd. N22 38 BY30
Acacia Rd. NW8 56 BT37
Acacia Rd. SW16 86 BX51
Acacia Rd. W3 55 BN40
Acacia Rd., Beck. 87 CD52
Acacia Rd., Dart. 80 CV47
Acacia Rd., Enf. 30 BZ23
Acacia Rd., Green. 80 CZ46
Acacia Rd., Guil. 118 AR70
Acacia Rd., Hmptn. 74 BF50
Acacia Rd., Mitch. 86 BV51
Acacia Rd., Stai. 73 AW49
Acacia St., Hat. 10 BP14
Acacia Wk., Swan. 89 CS51
Walnut Way
Acacia Way, Sid. 78 CN47
Academy Gdns., Croy. 87 CA54
Academy Gdns., Nthlt. 54 BD37
Academy Rd. SE18 68 CK44
Acanthus Rd. SW11 66 BV45
Accommodation La., West Dr. 63 AW44
Accommodation Rd. NW11 46 BR33
Accommodation Rd., Cher. 91 AS56
Acer Ave., Rain. 60 CV38
Acer Rd., West. 106 CJ61
Acers, St.Alb. 18 BG17
Acfold Rd. SW6 66 BS44
Achilles Clo., Hem.H. 8 AY12
Achilles Pl., Wok. 100 AR61
Beggars La.
Achilles Rd. NW6 47 BS35
Achilles St. SE14 67 CD43
Achilles Way W1 3 H3
Achilles Way W1 56 BV40
Acklam Rd. W10 55 BR39
Portobello Rd.
Acklington Dr. NW9 37 BO30
Ackmar Rd. SW6 66 BS44
Ackroyd Dr. E3 57 CD39
Ackroyd Rd. SE23 77 CC47
Ackroydon Est. SW19 75 BQ47
Ackworth Clo. N9 39 CC26
Turin Rd.
Acland Cres. SE5 67 BZ45
Acland Rd. NW2 55 BP36
Linacre Rd.
Acme Rd., Wat. 26 BC22
Acol Cres., Ruis. 44 BC35
Acol Rd. NW6 56 BS36
Acomb Rd., Dag. 59 CO37
Aconbury Rd., Dag. 59 CO37
Stamford Rd.
Acorn Clo. E4 39 CE28
The Lawns
Acorn Clo., Chis. 78 CM49
Acorn Clo., Enf. 29 BY23
Acorn Clo., Stan. 36 BJ29
Acorn Ct., Ilf. 49 CN32
Acorn Gdns. SE19 87 CA51
Acorn Gdns. W3 55 BN39
Acorn Gro., Hayes 63 BB43
Acorn Gro., Ruis. 44 BB35
Acorn Gro., Tad. 103 BR65
Acorn La., Cuffley 20 BX18
Acorn Par. SE15 67 CB43
Acorn Pl., Wat. 26 BC22
Acorn Rd., Dart. 79 CT46
Acorn Rd., Hem.H. 8 AZ14
Acorn Wk. SE16 57 CD40
Acorn Way SE23 77 CC48
Acorn Way, Orp. 97 CL56
Starts Hill Rd.
Acorns, The, Chig. 40 CN28
Acorns Clo., Hmptn. 74 BF50
Acorns Way, Esher 93 BG56
Acre La. SW2 66 BX45
Acre La., Cars. 95 BV56
Acre Pas., Wind. 61 AO44
Peascod St.
Acre Path, Nthlt. 54 BE36
Arnold Rd.
Acre Rd. SW19 76 BT50
Acre Rd., Dag. 59 CR36
Acre Rd., Kings.T. 85 BL51
Acre Vw., Horn. 51 CW31
Russetts
Acre Way, Nthwd. 35 BB30
Acre Wd., Hem.H. 8 AY14
Acrefield Rd., Ger.Cr. 43 AR31
Acres Ave., Ong. 24 CW16
Acres End, Amer. 25 AP23
Acres Gdns., Tad. 103 BQ63
Acrewood Way, St.Alb. 10 BL13
Acris St. SW18 76 BT46
Acton Clo. N9 39 CB27
Acton Clo., Chsnt. 21 CD19
Russells Ride
Acton Est. E8 57 CA37
Acton La. NW10 55 BN38
Acton La. W3 65 BN41
Acton La. W4 65 BN42
Acton Pk. Ind. Est. W3 55 BN40
Acton St. WC1 2 B3
Acton St. WC1 56 BX38
Acuba Rd. SW18 76 BS47
Ada Gdns. E14 57 CF39
Ada Gdns. E15 58 CG37
Ada Pl. E2 57 CB37
Ada Rd. SE5 67 CA43
Ada Rd., Wem. 45 BK34
Ada St. E8 57 CB37
Adair Clo. SE25 87 CB52
Adair Rd. W10 55 BR38
Adam & Eve Ct. W1 1 M8
Adam & Eve Ct. W1 56 BW39
Eastcastle St.
Adam & Eve Ms. W8 66 BS41
Adam Clo., Slou. 61 AN40
Adam Pl. N16 48 CA34
High St.
Adam St. WC2 4 A1
Adam St. WC2 56 BX40
Adam Wk. SW6 65 BQ43
Adams Clo. N3 38 BS29
Falkland Ave.
Adams Clo. NW9 46 BM34
Adams Ct. EC2 2 L8
Adams Gdns. Est. SE16 67 CC41
Adams Pl. N7 47 BX35
Georges Rd.
Adams Rd. N17 39 CA30
Adams Rd., Beck. 87 CD52
Adams Row W1 3 H1
Adams Row W1 56 BV40
Adams Sq., Bexh. 69 CP45
Adams Way, Croy. 87 CA53
Adamsfield, Wal.Cr. 21 CA16
Adamson Rd. E16 58 CH39
Adamson Rd. NW3 56 BT36
Adamsrill Clo., Enf. 30 BZ25
Adamsrill Rd. SE26 77 CC49
Adare Wk. SW16 76 BX48
Adcock Wk., Orp. 97 CN56
Adderley Gdns. SE9 78 CL49
Adderley Gro. SW11 76 BV46
Culmstock Rd.
Adderley Rd., Har. 36 BH30
Adderley St. E14 57 CF39
Addington Clo., Wind. 61 AN45
Addington Dr. N12 38 BT29
Addington Gro. SE26 77 CD49
Addington Rd. E3 57 CE38
Addington Rd. E16 58 CG38
Addington Rd. N4 47 BY32
Addington Rd., Croy. 86 BY54
Addington Rd., S.Croy. 96 CB59
Addington Rd., W.Wick. 96 CG56
Addington Sq. SE5 67 BZ43
Addington St. SE1 4 C5
Addington St. SE1 66 BX41
Addington Village Rd., Croy. 96 CD57
Addis Clo., Enf. 30 CC23
Addiscombe Ave., Croy. 87 CB54
Addiscombe Clo., Har. 45 BK32
Addiscombe Ct. Rd., Croy. 87 CA54
Addiscombe Gro., Croy. 87 BZ55
Addiscombe Rd., Croy. 87 BZ55
Addiscombe Rd., Wat. 26 BC24
Addison Ave. N14 29 BV25
Addison Ave. W11 55 BR40
Addison Ave., Houns. 64 BG44
Addison Bri. Pl. W14 65 BR42
Addison Clo., Cat. 105 BZ64
Addison Clo., Iver 52 AV39
Dutton Way
Addison Clo., Nthwd. 35 BB30
Addison Clo., Orp. 88 CM53
Addison Cres. W14 65 BR41
Addison Dr. SE12 78 CH46
Addison Gdns. W14 65 BQ41
Addison Gdns., Grays 71 DE42
Palmers Dr.
Addison Gdns., Surb. 85 BL52
Addison Gro. W4 65 BO41
Addison Pl. SE25 87 CB52
Addison Rd.
Addison Pl. W11 55 BR40
Addison Pl., Sthl. 54 BF40
Longford Ave.
Addison Rd. E11 49 CH32
Addison Rd. E17 48 CE32
Addison Rd. SE25 87 CB52
Addison Rd. W14 65 BR41
Addison Rd., Brom. 88 CJ53
Addison Rd., Cat. 105 BZ64
Addison Rd., Enf. 30 CC23
Addison Rd., Guil. 118 AS71
Addison Rd., Ilf. 40 CM30
Addison Rd., Tedd. 74 BJ50
Addison Rd., Wok. 100 AS62
Chertsey Rd.
Addison Way NW11 46 BR31
Addison Way, Hayes 53 BC39
Addison Way, Nthwd. 35 BB30
Addisons Clo., Croy. 87 CD55
Addle Hill EC4 2
Addle Hill EC4 56 B
Addle St. EC2 2
Addlestone Moor, Wey. 83 A
Addlestone Pk., Wey. 92 AV
Liberty La.
Addlestone Rd., Wey. 92 A
Adecroft Way, E.Mol. 84 BC
Adela Ave., N.Mal. 85 B
Adela St. W10 55 B
Kensal Rd.
Adelaide Ave. SE4 67 C
Adelaide Clo., Enf. 30 C
Adelaide Clo., Slou. 61 A
Amerden Way
Adelaide Clo., Stan. 36 B
Adelaide Cotts. W7 54 B
Adelaide Gdns., Rom. 50 C
Adelaide Gro. W12 55 B
Adelaide Pl., Wey. 92 B
Adelaide Rd. E10 48 C
Adelaide Rd. NW3 56 B
Adelaide Rd. W13 54 B
Adelaide Rd., Ashf. 73 A
Adelaide Rd., Chis. 78 C
Adelaide Rd., Houns. 64 B
Adelaide Rd., Ilf. 49 C
Adelaide Rd., Rich. 65 BL
Adelaide Rd., Sthl. 64 B
Adelaide Rd., Surb. 85 BL
Adelaide Rd., Tedd. 74 B
Adelaide Rd., Til. 71 D
Adelaide Rd., Walt. 83 BC
Adelaide Sq., Wind. 61 AC
Adelaide St. WC2 3
Adelaide St. WC2 56 BX
William IV St.
Adelaide St., St.Alb. 9 BG
Adelaide Wk. SW9 66 BY
Sussex Wk.
Adele Ave., Welw.G.C. 5 B
Adelina Gro. E1 57 CC
Adelina Ms. SW12 76 BW
Kings Ave.
Adeline Pl. WC1 1
Adeline Pl. WC1 56 BW
Adelphi Cres., Hayes 53 BB
Adelphi Cres., Horn. 50 CU
Adelphi Gdns., Slou. 62 A
Adelphi Rd., Epsom 94 BN
Adelphi Ter. WC2 4
Adelphi Ter. WC2 56 BX
Adam St.
Adelphi Way, Hayes 53 BB
Aden Gro. N16 48 BZ
Aden Lo. N16 48 BZ
Aden Rd., Enf. 30 CD
Aden Rd., Ilf. 49 CM
Aden Ter. N16 48 BZ
Adeney Clo. W6 65 BQ
Adenmore Rd. SE6 77 CE
Adeyfield Gdns., Hem.H. 8 AY
Adeyfield Rd., Hem.H. 8 AX
Adhara Rd., Nthwd. 35 BB
Adie Rd. W6 65 BQ
Adine Rd. E13 58 CH
Adingtons, Harl. 6 CN
Adler St. E1 57 CB
Adlers La., Dor. 119 BJ
Adley St. E5 48 CD
Admaston Rd. SE18 68 CM
Admiral Seymour Rd. SE9 68 CK
Admiral St. SE8 67 CE
Admirals Clo. E18 49 CH
Admirals Clo., St.Alb. 10 BO
Admirals Ct., Guil. 118 AT
Admirals Wk. NW3 47 BT
Admirals Wk., Couls. 104 BX
Admirals Wk., Hodd. 12 CE
Admirals Wk., St.Alb. 9 BJ
Admirals Way E14 67 CE
Admiralty Rd., Tedd. 74 BH
Adnams Wk., Rain. 59 CT
Adolf St. SE6 77 CE
Adolphus Rd. N4 47 BY
Adolphus St. SE8 67 CD
Adomar Rd., Dag. 50 CQ
Adpar St. W2 1
Adpar St. W2 56 BT
Adrian Clo., Uxb. 35 AX
Adrian Ms. SW10 66 BS
Adrian Rd., Abb.L. 17 BB
Adrienne Ave., Sthl. 54 BE
Adstock Ms., Ger.Cr. 34 AR
Church La.
Adstock Way, Grays 71 DC
Advice Ave., Grays 71 DC
Adys Rd. SE15 67 CA
Aerodrome Rd. NW9 37 BO
Aerodrome Way, Houns. 64 BD
Aeroville NW9 37 BO
Affleck St. N1 2
Affleck St. N1 56 BX
Pentonville Rd.
Afghan Rd. SW11 66 BU
Afton Dr., S.Ock. 60 DA
Agamemnon Rd. NW6 46 BR
Agar Clo., Surb. 85 BL
Agar Gro. NW1 56 BW
Agar Gro. Est. NW1 56 BW
Agar Pl. NW1 56 BW
Agar St. WC2 3
Agar St. WC2 56 BX
Chandos Pl.
Agars Plough (Eton), Wind. 62 AQ
Agate Clo. E16 58 CJ
Agate Rd. W6 65 BQ
Agates La., Ash. 102 BK
Agatha Clo. E1 57 CC
Agaton Rd. SE9 78 CM
Agave Rd. NW2 46 BQ
Agdon St. EC1 2

lon St. EC1 56 BY38
ncourt Rd. NW3 47 BU35
ster Rd., Chig. 41 CO28
nes Ave., Ilf. 49 CL34
nes Clo. E6 58 CL39
nes Gdns., Dag. 50 CP35
nes Rd. W3 55 BO40
nes Scott Ct., Wey. 83 AZ55
alace Dr.
nes St. E14 57 CD39
new Rd. SE23 77 CC47
aria Rd., Guil. 118 AQ71
icola Pl., Enf. 30 CA25
an Clo., Dag. 50 CQ34
een Wk. E15 58 CG36
sa Ave., Twick. 74 BJ46
sa Rd., Twick. 74 BJ46
sa St. E14 57 CF39
ger Rd. NW3 56 BU36
sdale Clo., Orp. 88 CM54
sdale Cres., Pnr. 45 BF31
sdale Rd. W5 54 BK38
sdale Rd., Wat. 36 BD27
sdale Way, Wok. 100 AQ62
sley Ave., Rom. 50 CR32
sley Clo. N9 39 CA26
sley St. E2 57 CB38
slie Wk. SW12 76 BV47
alham Gro.
slie Wd. Cres. E4 39 CE28
slie Wd. Gdns. E4 39 CE28
slie Wd. Rd. E4 39 CE28
sty St. SE16 67 CC41
runel Rd.
sworth Clo. NW2 46 BP34
sworth Rd. E9 57 CC36
sworth Rd., Croy. 86 BY54
sworth Way NW8 56 BT37
tree Ave. E6 58 CK37
tree Clo., Grav. 81 DG48
tree Clo., Slou. 62 AV44
tree Clo., Uxb. 53 AZ39
tree Cres., Ilf. 40 CM30
tree Est. SW6 65 BR43
tree Gro., Upmin. 51 CW34
tree Rd., Grnf. 54 BJ37
tree St. SW6 65 BR43
St. W1 3 M1
St. W1 56 BW40
lasshouse St.
drie Clo. N1 56 BX36
drie Clo., Hayes 54 BE39
lencoe Rd.
e Dr., S.Ock. 60 DA38
edale, Hem.H. 8 AY12
edale Ave. W4 65 BO42
edale Ave. S. W4 65 BO42
etheravon Rd. S.
edale Rd. SW12 76 BU47
edale Rd. W5 64 BK41
ey Neave Ct., Grays 71 DD41
rchard Dr.
field Way, Horn. 59 CU36
lie Gdns. W8 56 BS40
lie Gdns., Ilf. 49 CL33
port Way, Stai. 63 AW45
thrie Rd., Ilf. 50 CO34
gill Ave. W14 65 BR42
sher Rd. SE28 59 CP40
libie Rd. SE12 68 CG45
ken Rd. SE6 77 CE48
ken Rd., Barn. 28 BQ25
x Ave. NW9 46 BO31
x Rd. NW6 47 BS35
ehurst La., Sev. 117 CV66
ehurst St. SW15 75 BP46
eman Clo., St.Alb. 9 BE15
enside Rd. NW3 47 BT35
erman Rd. SW9 66 BY44
erman Rd., Surb. 84 BK53
ers La., Rick. 25 AU25
abama St. SE18 68 CM43
across Rd. W5 64 BK41
amein Gdns., Dart. 80 CY47
amein Rd., Swans. 80 DB46
an Clo., Dart. 70 CV45
an Dr., Barn. 28 BR25
an Gdns., Rom. 50 CR33
an Rd. SW19 75 BR49
an Tusing Rd., Guil. 118 AO70
an Way, Slou. 52 AS39
andale Dr., Pnr. 35 BC30
anthus Clo. SE12 78 CG46
aska St. SE1 4 D3
aska St. SE1 56 BY40
Cornwall Rd.
a Clo., Hayes 54 BE38
Ramulis Dr.
a Gdns. NW11 46 BR32
a Pl. W11 55 BR39
Portobello Rd.
acore Cres. SE13 77 CE46
ain Cres., Ashf. 73 AY48
an Ave., St.Alb. 9 BG12
an Cres., Borwd. 28 BM23
an Cres., Farn. 90 CX54
an Pk., St.Alb. 10 BL13
ans Vw., Wat. 17 BC20
any, The W1 3 L1
any, The W1 56 BW40
Vigo St.
any, The, Wdf.Grn. 40 CG28
any Clo. N15 47 BY31
any Clo. SW14 65 BM45
any Clo., Bex. 79 CP47
any Clo., Bush. 27 BG25
any Clo., Esher 93 BF58
any Clo., Reig. 121 BS69
any Clo., Uxb. 44 AZ35
any Cotts., Esher 93 BE57
any Ct., Epp. 22 CN18
any Ctyd. W1 3 M1
any Cres., Edg. 37 BM29
any Cres., Esher 93 BH57

Albany Mans. SW11 66 BU43
Albany Ms. SE17 67 BZ43
Albany Rd. SE5
Albany Ms., Kings.T. 74 BK50
Albany Pk. Rd.
Albany Pk. Ave., Enf. 30 CC23
Albany Pk. Rd., Kings.T. 74 BK50
Albany Pk. Rd., Lthd. 102 BJ63
Albany Pas., Rich. 75 BL46
Albany Pl. N7 47 BY35
Albany Pl., Brent. 64 BK43
Albany Rd.
Albany Pl., Egh. 72 AT49
Albany Reach, Surb. 84 BH53
Albany Rd. E10 48 CE33
Albany Rd. E12 49 CJ35
Albany Rd. E17 48 CD32
Albany Rd. N4 47 BY32
Albany Rd. N18 39 CC28
Albany Rd. SE5 67 BZ43
Albany Rd. SW19 76 BS49
Albany Rd. W13 54 BJ39
Albany Rd., Belv. 69 CQ43
Albany Rd., Bex. 79 CP47
Albany Rd., Brent. 64 BK43
Albany Rd., Brwd. 33 DA25
Albany Rd., Chis. 78 CL49
Albany Rd., Enf. 30 CC22
Albany Rd., Horn. 50 CU33
Albany Rd., N.Mal. 85 BN52
Albany Rd., Rich. 75 BL46
Albert Rd.
Albany Rd., Rom. 50 CQ32
Albany Rd., Walt. 93 BD56
Albany Rd., Wind. 61 AO44
Albany Rd. (Old Windsor), Wind. 72 AQ46
Albany Row N2 47 BT31
The Causeway
Albany St. NW1 56 BV37
Albany Ter. NW1 56 BV38
Euston Rd.
Albany Vw., Buck.H. 40 CH26
Albatross Gdns., S.Croy. 96 CC59
Albatross St. SE18 68 CM43
Albatross Way SE16 67 CC41
Albemarle SW19 75 BQ48
Albemarle App., Ilf. 49 CL32
Albemarle Ave., Chsnt. 21 CC17
Albemarle Ave., Pot.B. 20 BS19
Albemarle Clo., Grays 71 DD41
Albemarle Gdns., Ilf. 49 CL32
Albemarle Gdns., N.Mal. 85 BN52
Albemarle Pk., Stan. 36 BK28
Albemarle Rd., Barn. 38 BU26
Albemarle Rd., Beck. 87 CE51
Albemarle St. W1 3 L1
Albemarle St. W1 56 BV40
Albemarle Way EC1 2 F5
Albemarle Way EC1 56 BY38
Clerkenwell Rd.
Albeny Gate, St.Alb. 9 BG14
Albermarle Ave., Twick. 74 BE47
Alberon Gdns. NW11 46 BR31
Albert Ave. E4 39 CE28
Albert Ave. SW8 66 BX43
Albert Ave., Cher. 83 AW52
Albert Ave., Ilf. 49 CM34
High Rd.
Albert Bri. SW3 66 BU43
Albert Bri. SW11 66 BU43
Albert Bri. Rd. SW11 66 BU43
Albert Carr Gdns. SW16 76 BX49
Albert Clo. E9 57 CB37
Northiam St.
Albert Clo. N22 38 BW30
Albert Clo., Grays 71 DE41
Albert Clo., Slou. 62 AP41
Albert St.
Albert Ct. SW7 3 A5
Albert Ct. SW7 66 BT41
Albert Ct. SW19 75 BR47
Albert Cres. E4 39 CE28
Albert Dr. SW19 75 BR48
Albert Dr., Wok. 91 AU60
Albert Embk. SE1 66 BX42
Albert Gdns. E1 57 CC39
Albert Gate SW1 66 BU41
Rotten Row
Albert Gro. SW20 85 BQ51
Albert Hall Mans. SW7 3 A5
Albert Hall Mans. SW7 66 BT41
Prince Consort Rd.
Albert Mans. SW11 66 BU44
Albert Pl. N3 38 BS30
Popes Dr.
Albert Pl. W8 66 BS41
Albert Pl. (Eton Wick), Wind. 61 AN42
Common Rd.
Albert Rd. E10 48 CF34
Albert Rd. E16 58 CK40
Albert Rd. E17 48 CE32
Albert Rd. E18 49 CH31
Albert Rd. N4 47 BX33
Albert Rd. N15 48 CA32
Albert Rd. N22 38 BW30
Albert Rd. NW4 46 BQ31
Albert Rd. NW6 55 BR37
Albert Rd. NW7 37 BO28
Albert Rd. SE9 78 CK48
Albert Rd. SE20 77 CC50
Albert Rd. SE25 87 CB52
Albert Rd. W5 54 BJ38
Albert Rd., Ashf. 73 AY49
Albert Rd., Ash. 103 BL62
Albert Rd., Barn. 29 BT24
Albert Rd., Belv. 69 CQ42
Albert Rd., Bex. 79 CR47
Albert Rd., Brom. 88 CJ53
Albert Rd., Buck.H. 40 CJ27
Albert Rd., Dag. 50 CQ33
Albert Rd., Dart. 80 CV48
Albert Rd., Egh. 72 AR50

Albert Rd., Epsom 94 BO60
Albert Rd., Hmptn. 74 BG49
Albert Rd., Har. 45 BG31
Albert Rd., Hayes 63 BB41
Albert Rd., Houns. 64 BF45
Albert Rd., Ilf. 49 CM34
Albert Rd., Kings.T. 85 BL51
Albert Rd., Mitch. 86 BU52
Albert Rd., N.Mal. 85 BO52
Albert Rd., Orp. 98 CO56
Albert Rd. (St. Mary Cray), Orp. 89 CO53
Albert Rd., Red. 113 BW68
Albert Rd., Rich. 75 BL46
Albert Rd., Rom. 50 CT32
Albert Rd., Sthl. 64 BD41
Albert Rd., Sutt. 95 BT56
Albert Rd., Swans. 81 DC46
Albert Rd., Tedd. 74 BH50
Albert Rd., Twick. 74 BH47
Albert Rd., Warl. 105 CD62
Albert Rd., West Dr. 53 AY40
Albert Rd., Wey. 83 AX55
Albert Rd., Wind. 61 AP45
Albert Rd. Est., Belv. 69 CQ42
Albert Rd. N., Wat. 26 BC24
Albert Rd. S., Wat. 26 BC24
Albert Sq. E15 49 CG35
Albert Sq. SW8 66 BX43
Albert St. N12 38 BT28
Lodge La.
Albert St. NW1 56 BV37
Albert St., Brwd. 42 DB28
Albert St., St.Alb. 9 BG14
Albert St., Slou. 62 AP41
Albert St., Wat. 27 BD24
Queens Rd.
Albert St., Wind. 61 AN44
Albert Studios SW11 66 BU43
Albert Bri. Rd.
Albert Ter. NW1 56 BV37
Albert Ter. NW10 55 BN37
Albert Ter., Buck.H. 40 CK27
Albert Wk. E16 68 CL41
Alberta Ave., Sutt. 94 BR56
Alberta Est. SE17 4 G10
Alberta Est. SE17 66 BY42
Alberta Rd., Enf. 30 CA25
Alberta Rd., Erith 69 CS44
Alberta St. SE17 4 F10
Alberta St. SE17 66 BY42
Albertine Clo., Epsom 103 BP61
Albion Ave. N10 38 BV30
Albion Ave. SW8 66 BW44
Albion Bldgs. EC1 57 BZ39
Bartholomew Clo.
Albion Clo. W2 1 D10
Albion Clo. W2 56 BU40
Albion St.
Albion Clo., Rom. 50 CS32
Albion Clo., Slou. 52 AQ40
Albion Cres., Ch.St.G. 34 AQ27
Albion Dr. E8 57 CA36
Albion Est. SE16 67 CC41
Albion Gdns. W6 65 BP42
Albion Gate W2 56 BU40
Albion Gro. N16 48 BZ35
Albion Hill SE13 67 CE44
Albion Hill, Hem.H. 8 AX14
Albion Hill, Loug. 31 CJ25
Albion Ms. N1 56 BY36
Albion Ms. NW6 55 BR36
Kilburn High Rd.
Albion Ms. W2 1 D10
Albion Ms. W2 56 BU40
Albion Par., Grav. 81 DH46
Albion Pk., Loug. 31 CJ25
Albion Pl. EC1 2 F6
Albion Pl. EC1 56 BY39
Albion Pl. EC2 2 L7
Albion Pl. SE25 87 CB52
High St.
Albion Rd. E17 48 CF31
Albion Rd. N16 48 BZ34
Albion Rd. N17 39 CA30
Reform Row
Albion Rd., Bexh. 69 CR45
Albion Rd., Ch.St.G. 34 AQ27
Albion Rd., Grav. 81 DH47
Albion Rd., Hayes 53 BB39
Albion Rd., Houns. 64 BF45
Albion Rd., Kings.T. 85 BN51
Albion Rd., Reig. 121 BT71
Albion Rd., St.Alb. 9 BH13
Albion Rd., Sutt. 95 BT57
Albion Rd., Twick. 74 BH47
Albion Sq. E8 57 CA36
Albion St. SE16 67 CC41
Albion St. W2 1 D9
Albion St. W2 56 BU39
Albion St., Croy. 86 BY54
Albion Ter. E8 57 CA36
Albion Ter., Grav. 81 DH46
Albion Vill. Rd. SE26 77 CC48
Albion Way EC1 2 H7
Albion Way SE13 67 CF45
Albion Way, Wem. 46 BM34
Albrighton Rd. SE22 67 CA45
Albuhera Clo., Enf. 29 BY23
Albury Ave., Bexh. 69 CQ44
Albury Ave., Islw. 64 BH43
Albury Ave., Sutt. 94 BQ58
Albury Clo., Cher. 82 AQ55
Albury Clo., Hmptn. 74 BF50
Albury Ct., Croy. 96 BZ56
Albury Dr., Pnr. 36 BD30
Albury Gro. Rd., Chsnt. 21 CC18
Albury Pl., Red. 113 BW68
Albury Rd.
Albury Ride, Chsnt. 21 CC19
Albury Rd., Chess. 94 BL56
Albury Rd., Guil. 118 AS71
Albury Rd., Red. 113 BW68
Albury Rd., Walt. 92 BB57

Albury St. SE8 67 CE43
Albury Wk., Chsnt. 21 CC18
Albyfield, Brom. 88 CK52
Albyn Rd. SE8 67 CE44
Albyns Clo., Rain. 59 CU36
South End Rd.
Alcester Cres. E5 48 CB34
Alcester Rd., Wall. 95 BV56
Alcock Clo., Wall. 95 BW57
Alcock Rd., Houns. 64 BD43
Alcocks Clo., Tad. 103 BT63
Alcocks La., Tad. 103 BR64
Alconbury Rd. E5 48 CB34
Alcorn Clo., Sutt. 86 BS55
Alcott Clo. W7 54 BH39
Westcott Cres.
Aldam Pl. N16 48 CA34
High St.
Aldborough Rd., Dag. 59 CS36
Aldborough Rd., Upmin. 51 CW34
Aldborough Rd. N., Ilf. 49 CN32
Aldborough Rd. S., Ilf. 49 CN33
Aldborough Spur, Slou. 52 AP39
Aldbourne Rd. W12 55 BO40
Aldbridge St. SE17 4 N10
Aldbridge St. SE17 67 CA42
Aldbury Ave., Wem. 55 BM36
Aldbury Clo., St.Alb. 9 BK11
Sandringham Cres.
Aldbury Clo., Wat. 27 BD21
Aldbury Gro., Welw.G.C. 5 BS8
Aldbury Ms. N9 39 BZ26
Aldbury Rd., Rick. 34 AV26
Aldebert Ter. SW8 66 BX43
Aldeburgh Clo. E5 48 CB34
Southwold Rd.
Aldeburgh Pl., Wdf.Grn. 40 CH28
Aldeburgh St. SE10 68 CH42
Alden Ave. E15 58 CG38
Alden Vw., Wind. 61 AL44
Aldenham Ave., Rad. 27 BJ21
Aldenham Dr., Uxb. 53 AZ38
Aldenham Gro., Rad. 18 BJ20
Aldenham Rd., Borwd. 27 BJ24
Aldenham Rd., Bush. 27 BE25
Aldenham Rd., Rad. 27 BJ21
Aldenham Rd., Wat. 27 BD25
Aldenham St. NW1 1 M1
Aldenham St. NW1 56 BW37
Aldenholme, Wey. 92 BB57
Aldensley Rd. W6 65 BP41
Alder Ave., Upmin. 51 CW35
Alder Clo. SE15 67 CA43
Alder Clo., St.Alb. 18 BG17
Alder Clo., Slou. 61 AM40
Alder Cft., Couls. 104 BX61
Alder Gro. NW2 46 BP34
Alder Ms. N19 47 BW34
Bredgar Rd.
Alder Rd. SW14 65 BN45
Alder Rd., Sid. 78 CN48
Alder Rd., Uxb. 53 AX36
Alder Wk., Wat. 26 BC21
Alder Way, Swan. 89 CS51
Alderbourne La., Iver 43 AT35
Alderbourne La., Slou. 43 AR35
Alderbrook Rd. SW12 76 BV46
Alderbury Rd. SW13 65 BP43
Alderbury Rd., Slou. 62 AS41
Alderbury Rd. W., Slou. 62 AS41
Aldercoombe La., Cat. 114 CA67
Aldercroft, Couls. 104 BX61
Aldergrove Gdns., Houns. 64 BE44
Bath Rd.
Aldergrove Wk., Horn. 60 CV36
Airfield Way
Alderholt Way SE15 67 CA43
Alderley Ct., Berk. 7 AR13
Alderman Ave., Bark. 59 CO38
Alderman Clo., Hat. 10 BQ15
Alderman Judge Mall, Kings.T. 85 BL51
Eden St.
Aldermanbury EC2 2 J8
Aldermanbury EC2 57 BZ39
Aldermanbury Sq. EC2 2 J7
Aldermanbury Sq. EC2 57 BZ39
Aldermanbury
Aldermans Hill N13 38 BX28
Aldermans Wk. EC2 2 M7
Aldermans Wk. EC2 57 CA39
Bishopsgate
Aldermary Rd., Brom. 88 CH51
Aldermaston St. W10 55 BQ39
Alderminster Rd. SE1 67 CB42
Aldermoor Rd. SE6 77 CD48
Alderney Ave., Houns. 64 BF43
Alderney Gdns., Nthlt. 54 BE36
Alderney Rd. E1 57 CC38
Alderney Rd., Erith 69 CU43
Alderney St. SW1 3 K10
Alderney St. SW1 66 BV42
Alders, The N21 29 BY25
Alders, The, Felt. 74 BE49
Alders, The, Houns. 64 BE42
Alders, The, W.Wick. 87 CE55
Alders Ave., Wdf.Grn. 40 CG29
Alders Clo. E11 49 CH34
Alders Clo. W5 64 BK41
Olive Rd.
Alders Clo., Edg. 37 BN28
Alders Gro., E.Mol. 84 BG53
Alders Rd., Edg. 37 BN28
Alders Rd., Reig. 121 BS69
Aldersbrook Ave., Enf. 30 CA23
Aldersbrook Dr., Kings.T. 75 BL50
Aldersbrook La. E12 49 CK34
Aldersbrook Rd. E11 49 CH34
Aldersbrook Rd. E12 49 CH34
Aldersey Gdns., Bark. 58 CM36
Aldersey Rd., Guil. 118 AS70
Aldersford Clo. SE4 77 CC46
Aldersgate St. EC1 2 H6
Aldersgate St. EC1 57 BZ39

Aldersgrove, Wal.Abb. 22 CG20
Roundhills
Aldersgrove Ave. SE9 78 CJ48
Aldershot Rd. NW6 55 BR37
Aldershot Rd., Guil. 118 AO69
Aldershot Ter. SE18 68 CL43
Prince Imperial Way
Alderside Clo., Egh. 72 AS49
Alderside Wk., Egh. 72 AS49
Aldersmead Ave., Croy. 87 CC53
Aldersmead Rd., Beck. 77 CD50
Alderson St. W10 55 BR38
Kensal Rd.
Alderstead La., Red. 113 BW66
Alderton Clo. NW10 46 BN34
Alderton Clo., Brwd. 33 DA25
Alderton Clo., Loug. 31 CL24
Alderton Cres. NW4 46 BP32
Alderton Hall La., Loug. 31 CL24
Alderton Hill, Loug. 31 CK25
Alderton Ri., Loug. 31 CL24
Alderton Rd. SE24 67 BZ45
Alderton Rd., Croy. 87 CA54
Alderton Way NW4 46 BP32
Alderton Cres.
Alderton Way, Loug. 31 CL25
Alderville Rd. SW6 65 BR44
Alderwick Dr., Houns. 64 BG45
Alderwood Clo., Cat. 114 CA66
Alderwood Dr., Rom. 32 CO24
Alderwood Rd. SE9 78 CM46
Aldford St. W1 3 G2
Aldford St. W1 56 BV40
Aldgate EC3 2 P9
Aldgate Ave. E1 2 P8
Aldgate Ave. E1 57 CA39
Aldgate High St. EC3 2 P9
Aldgate High St. EC3 57 CA39
Aldin Ave. N., Slou. 62 AQ41
Aldin Ave. S., Slou. 62 AQ41
Aldine Ct. W12 65 BQ41
Aldine Pl. W12 65 BQ41
Aldine St. W12 65 BQ41
Aldingham Gdns., Horn. 50 CU35
Aldington Clo., Dag. 50 CP33
Aldington Rd. SE18 68 CJ41
Aldis Ms. SW17 76 BU49
Aldis St.
Aldis St. SW17 76 BU49
Aldock, Welw.G.C. 5 BS9
Aldred Rd. NW6 47 BS35
Aldren Rd. SW17 76 BT48
Aldrich Cres., Croy. 96 CF58
Aldrich Ter. SW18 76 BT48
Lidiard Rd.
Aldriche Way E4 39 CF29
Aldridge Ave., Edg. 37 BM27
Aldridge Ave., Enf. 30 CE22
Aldridge Ave., Ruis. 45 BD34
Aldridge Ave., Stan. 37 BL30
Aldridge Ri., N.Mal. 85 BO54
Aldridge Rd. Vill. W11 55 BR39
Aldridge Wk. N14 38 BX26
Aldrington Rd. SW16 76 BW49
Aldsworth Clo. W9 56 BS39
Amberley Rd.
Aldwick, St.Alb. 9 BJ14
Aldwick Clo. SE9 78 CM48
Aldwick Ct., Hem.H. 8 AX13
Aldwick Ct., St.Alb. 9 BJ14
Rodney Ave.
Aldwick Rd., Croy. 86 BX55
Aldworth Gro. SE13 77 CF46
Aldworth Rd. E15 58 CG36
Aldwych WC2 2 B10
Aldwych WC2 56 BX40
Aldwych Ave., Ilf. 49 CM31
Aldwych Clo., Horn. 50 CU34
Aldykes, Hat. 10 BO12
Alers Rd., Bexh. 79 CP46
Alestan Beck Rd. E16 58 CJ39
Alexander Ave. NW10 55 BP36
Alexander Clo., Barn. 29 BT24
Victoria Rd.
Alexander Clo., Brom. 88 CH54
Alexander Clo., Sid. 78 CN46
Alexander Clo., Twick. 74 BH48
Alexander Godley Clo., Ash. 103 BL63
Alexander La., Brwd. 122 DD25
Alexander Lo., Wey. 92 AZ56
Monument Hill
Alexander Ms. W2 56 BS39
Alexander St.
Alexander Pl. SW7 3 C8
Alexander Pl. SW7 66 BU42
Alexander Rd. N19 47 BX34
Alexander Rd., Bexh. 69 CP44
Alexander Rd., Chis. 78 CL49
Alexander Rd., Couls. 104 BV61
Alexander Rd., Egh. 72 AT49
Alexander Rd., Green. 80 DB46
Alexander Rd., Reig. 121 BS72
Alexander Rd., St.Alb. 18 BK16
Alexander Sq. SW3 3 C8
Alexander Sq. SW3 66 BU42
Alexander St. W2 56 BS39
Alexander St., Chesh. 16 AO18
Alexanders Wk., Cat. 114 CA66
Alexandra Ave. N22 38 BW30
Alexandra Ave. SW11 66 BV44
Alexandra Ave. W4 65 BN43
Alexandra Ave., Har. 45 BE33
Alexandra Ave., Sthl. 54 BE40
Alexandra Ave., Sutt. 86 BS55
Alexandra Ave., Warl. 105 CD62
Alexandra Clo., Ashf. 73 BA50
Alexandra Clo., Grays 71 DG41
Alexandra Clo., Har. 45 BF34
Alexandra Clo., Stai. 73 AX50
Alexandra Clo., Swan. 89 CT51
Northview
Alexandra Clo., Walt. 83 BC55
Alexandra Cotts. SE14 67 CD44

Alexandra Ct. N14 29 BW25
Alexandra Ct., Ashf. 73 BB50
Alexandra Rd.
Alexandra Ct., Wem. 46 BL35
Alexandra Cres., Brom. 78 CG50
Alexandra Dr. SE19 77 CA49
Alexandra Dr., Surb. 85 BM54
Alexandra Gdns. N10 47 BV31
Alexandra Gdns. W4 65 BO43
Alexandra Gdns., Cars. 95 BU58
Alexandra Gdns., Houns. 64 BF44
Alexandra Gro. N4 47 BY33
Alexandra Gro. N12 38 BS29
Alexandra Ms. N2 47 BU31
Fortis Grn.
Alexandra Pk. Rd. N10 38 BV30
Alexandra Pk. Rd. N22 38 BW30
Alexandra Pl. NW8 56 BT37
Alexandra Pl. SE25 87 BZ53
Alexandra Pl., Croy. 87 CA54
Alexandra Rd. E6 58 CL38
Alexandra Rd. E10 48 CF34
Alexandra Rd. E17 48 CD32
Alexandra Rd. E18 49 CH31
Alexandra Rd. N8 47 BY31
Alexandra Rd. N9 39 CB26
King Edwards Rd.
Alexandra Rd. N10 38 BV30
Alexandra Rd. N15 48 BZ32
Alexandra Rd. NW4 46 BQ31
Alexandra Rd. NW8 56 BT37
Alexandra Rd. SE26 77 CC50
Alexandra Rd. SW14 65 BN45
Alexandra Rd. SW19 75 BR50
Alexandra Rd. W4 65 BN41
Alexandra Rd., Ashf. 73 BA50
Alexandra Rd., Borwd. 28 BN22
Alexandra Rd., Brent. 64 BK43
Alexandra Rd., Brwd. 42 DB27
Alexandra Rd., Croy. 87 CA54
Alexandra Rd., Egh. 72 AR50
Alexandra Rd., Enf. 30 CC24
Alexandra Rd., Epsom 94 BO60
Alexandra Rd., Erith 69 CT43
Alexandra Rd., Grav. 81 DJ47
Alexandra Rd., Hem.H. 8 AX13
Alexandra Rd., Houns. 64 BF44
Alexandra Rd., Kings L. 17 AZ18
Alexandra Rd. (Chipperfield), Kings L. 17 AW18
Alexandra Rd., Kings.T. 75 BM50
Alexandra Rd., Mitch. 76 BU50
Alexandra Rd., Rain. 59 CT37
Alexandra Rd., Rich. 65 BL44
Alexandra Rd., Rick. 26 AW21
Alexandra Rd., Rom. 50 CT32
Alexandra Rd. (Chadwell Heath), Rom. 50 CP32
Alexandra Rd., St.Alb. 9 BH13
Alexandra Rd., Slou. 61 AO41
Alexandra Rd., T.Ditt. 84 BH53
Alexandra Rd., Til. 71 DF44
Alexandra Rd., Twick. 74 BK46
Alexandra Rd., Uxb. 53 AX37
Alexandra Rd., Warl. 105 CD62
Alexandra Rd., Wat. 26 BC23
Alexandra Rd., West. 106 CH63
Alexandra Rd., Wey. 92 AX56
Alexandra Rd., Wind. 61 AO44
Alexandra Sq., Mord. 86 BS53
Alexandra St. E16 58 CH39
Alexandra St. SE14 67 CD43
Alexandra Ter., Guil. 118 AS71
Alexandra Wk. SE19 77 CA49
Alexandra Way, Wal.Cr. 21 CD20
Alexandria Rd. W13 54 BJ40
Alexis St. SE16 67 CB42
Alf Lowne Ct., Grays 71 DG41
Chilton Rd.
Alfan La., Dart. 79 CS49
Alford Clo., Guil. 109 AS69
Alford Grn., Croy. 96 CF57
Alford Pl. N1 2 J1
Alford Pl. N1 57 BZ37
Alford Rd. SW8 66 BW44
Union Gro.
Alford Rd., Erith 69 CS42
Alfoxton Ave. N15 47 BY31
Alfred Gdns., Sthl. 54 BE40
Alfred Ms. W1 1 N6
Alfred Ms. W1 56 BW39
Alfred Pl. WC1 1 N6
Alfred Pl. WC1 56 BW39
Alfred Pl., Grav. 81 DF47
Alfred Rd. E15 49 CG35
Alfred Rd. SE25 87 CB53
Alfred Rd. W2 56 BS39
Alfred Rd. W3 55 BN40
Alfred Rd., Belv. 69 CQ42
Alfred Rd., Brwd. 42 DB27
Alfred Rd., Buck.H. 40 CJ27
Alfred Rd., Dart. 80 CW49
Alfred Rd., Erith 69 CT43
Alfred Rd., Felt. 74 BD48
Alfred Rd., Grav. 81 DG48
Alfred Rd., Kings.T. 85 BL52
Alfred Rd., S.Ock. 60 CY40
Alfred Rd., Sutt. 95 BT56
Alfred St. E3 57 CD38
Alfred St. E16 58 CG40
Dock Rd.
Alfred St., Grays 71 DE43
Alfreda St. SW11 66 BV44
Alfreds Gdns., Bark. 58 CN37
Alfreds Way, Bark. 58 CM37
Alfreton Clo. SW19 75 BQ48
Alfriston Ave., Croy. 86 BX54
Alfriston Ave., Har. 5 BF32
Alfriston Clo., Surb. 85 BL53
Alfriston Rd. SW11 66 BU45
Algar Clo., Islw. 64 BJ45
Algar Rd.
Algar Clo., Stan. 36 BH28
Algar Rd., Islw. 64 BJ45
Algarve Rd. SW18 76 BS47
Algernon Rd. NW4 46 BP32
Algernon Rd. NW6 56 BS37
Algernon Rd. SE13 67 CE45
Algers Clo., Loug. 31 CJ25
Algers Mead, Loug. 31 CJ25
Algers Rd., Loug. 31 CJ25
Algiers Rd. SE13 67 CE45
Alibon Gdns., Dag. 50 CR35
Alibon Rd., Dag. 50 CR35
Alice Gilliat Ct. W14 65 BR43
Alice Ruston Pl., Wok. 100 AR63
Alice St. SE1 4 M7
Alice St. SE1 67 CA41
Alice Way, Houns. 64 BF45
Alicia Ave., Har. 45 BJ31
Alicia Clo., Har. 45 BK31
Alicia Gdns., Har. 45 BJ31
Alie St. E1 2 Q9
Alie St. E1 57 CA39
Alington Cres. NW9 46 BN33
Alington Gro., Wall. 95 BW58
Alison Clo. E6 58 CL39
Alison Clo., Croy. 87 CC54
Shirley Oaks Rd.
Alison Clo., Wok. 100 AS60
Grange Rd.
Aliwal Rd. SW11 66 BU45
Alkerden La., Green. 80 DB46
Alkerden Rd. W4 65 BO42
Alkham Rd. N16 48 CA33
All Hallows Rd. N17 39 CA30
The Roundway
All Saints Clo. N9 39 CB27
All Saints Clo., Brwd. 33 DA21
All Saints Clo., Chig. 41 CO27
All Saints Clo., Swans. 81 DC46
High St.
All Saints Cres., Wat. 18 BD20
All Saints Dr. SE3 68 CG44
Royal Par.
All Saints Dr., S.Croy. 96 CA59
All Saints La., Rick. 26 AZ25
All Saints Ms., Har. 36 BH29
All Saints Pas. SW18 76 BS46
Wandsworth High St.
All Saints Rd. SW19 76 BT50
All Saints Rd. W3 65 BN41
All Saints Rd. W11 55 BR39
All Saints Rd., Grav. 81 DF47
All Saints Rd., Sutt. 86 BS55
All Saints St. N1 56 BX37
All Souls Ave. NW10 55 BP37
All Souls Pl. W1 1 K7
All Souls Pl. W1 56 BV39
Langham Pl.
Allan Barclay Clo. N15 48 CA32
High Rd.
Allan Clo., Dart. 80 CY47
Allan Clo., N.Mal. 85 BN53
Allan Way W3 55 BN39
Allanbrooke, Grav. 81 DH47
Allandale, Hem.H. 8 AX12
Allandale, St.Alb. 9 BF15
Allandale Ave. N3 46 BR31
Allandale Cres., Pot.B. 19 BR19
Allandale Pl., Orp. 89 CP55
Allandale Rd., Enf. 30 CC21
Allandale Rd., Hem.H. 8 AX12
Allandale Rd., Horn. 50 CT33
Allard Clo., Chsnt. 21 CA17
Allard Clo., Orp. 89 CP54
Allard Cres., Bush. 36 BG27
Allard Way, Brox. 12 CD14
Allardyce St. SW4 66 BX45
Allbrook Clo., Tedd. 74 BH49
Allcot Clo., Felt. 73 BB47
Allcroft Rd. NW5 47 BV35
Alldicks Rd., Hem.H. 8 AY14
Allen Clo. SE26 77 CC49
Allen Clo., Sun. 83 BC51
Allen Edwards Dr. SW8 66 BX44
Allen Ho. Pk., Wok. 100 AR63
Allen Rd. E3 57 CD37
Allen Rd. N16 48 CA35
Allen Rd., Beck. 87 CC51
Allen Rd., Croy. 86 BX54
Allen Rd., Lthd. 111 BF66
Allen Rd., Rain. 60 CV38
Allen Rd., Sun. 83 BC51
Allen St. W8 66 BS41
Allenby Ave., S.Croy. 96 BZ58
Allenby Clo., Grnf. 54 BF38
Allenby Cres., Grays 71 DD42
Allenby Dr., Horn. 51 CW33
Allenby Rd. SE23 77 CD48
Allenby Rd., Sthl. 54 BF38
Allenby Rd., West. 106 CK62
Allendale Ave., Sthl. 54 BF39
Allendale Clo. SE5 67 BZ44
Love Wk.
Allendale Clo. SE26 77 CC49
Trewsbury Rd.
Allendale Clo., Dart. 80 CY47
Princes Rd.
Allendale Rd., Grnf. 54 BJ36
Allens Rd., Enf. 30 CC25
Allensbury Pl. NW1 56 BX36
Allenswood Rd. SE9 68 CK45
Allerford Ct., Har. 45 BF32
Allerford Rd. SE6 77 CE48
Allerton Clo., Borwd. 28 BL22
Allerton Rd. N16 48 BZ34
Allerton Rd., Borwd. 28 BL22
Allerton Wk. N7 47 BX34
Durham Rd.
Allestree Rd. SW6 65 BR43
Alleyn Cres. SE21 77 BZ48
Alleyn Pk. SE21 77 BZ47
Alleyn Pk., Sthl. 64 BE42
Alleyn Pk. Est. SE21 77 CA49
Alleyn Rd. SE21 77 BZ48
Alleyndale Rd., Dag. 50 CP34
Allfarthing La. SW18 76 BS46
Allgood Clo., Mord. 85 BQ53
Allgood St. E2 2 Q1
Allhallows La. EC4 4 K1
Allhallows La. EC4 57 BZ40
Allhallows Rd. E6 58 CK39
Allhusen Gdns., Slou. 43 AS35
Alliance Clo., Wem. 45 BK35
Alliance Rd. E13 58 CJ38
Alliance Rd. SE18 69 CO43
Alliance Rd. W3 55 BM38
Allingham Clo. W7 54 BH40
Allingham Ct. NW3 47 BU35
Haverstock Hill
Allingham Rd., Reig. 121 BS72
Allingham St. N1 57 BZ37
Allington Ave. N17 39 CA29
Allington Ave., Shep. 83 BB52
Grange Fm. Caravan Site
Allington Clo. SW19 75 BQ49
Allington Clo., Grav. 81 DJ47
Farley Rd.
Allington Ct., Enf. 30 CC25
Allington Ct., Slou. 52 AP40
Myrtle Cres.
Allington Rd. NW4 46 BP32
Allington Rd. W10 55 BR37
Allington Rd., Har. 45 BG32
Allington Rd., Orp. 88 CM55
Allington St. SW1 3 K7
Allington St. SW1 66 BV41
Allison Clo. SE10 67 CF44
Allison Clo., Wal.Abb. 22 CH19
Allison Gro. SE21 77 CA47
Allison Rd. N8 47 BY32
Allison Rd. W3 55 BN39
Allitsen Rd. NW8 1 C1
Allitsen Rd. NW8 56 BU37
Allmains Clo., Wal.Abb. 22 CH16
Allnutt Way SW4 76 BW46
Allnutts Rd., Epp. 23 CO20
Alloa Rd. SE8 67 CC42
Alloa Rd., Ilf. 50 CO34
Allonby Dr., Ruis. 44 AZ32
Allonby Gdns., Wem. 45 BK33
Allotment La., Sev. 108 CV64
Alloway Clo., Wok. 100 AQ62
Inglewood
Alloway Rd. E3 57 CD38
Allsop Pl. NW1 1 F5
Allsop Pl. NW1 56 BU38
Allum Clo., Borwd. 28 BL24
Allum Gro., Tad. 103 BP64
Allum La., Borwd. 27 BK25
Allum Way N20 38 BT27
Manus Way
Allwood Clo. SE26 77 CC49
Allyn Clo., Stai. 72 AV50
Penton Rd.
Alma Ave. E4 39 CF29
Alma Ave., Horn. 51 CW35
Alma Clo., Wok. 100 AP62
Alma Cres., Sutt. 94 BR56
Alma Cut, St.Alb. 9 BH14
Alma Gro. SE1 4 Q9
Alma Gro. SE1 67 CA42
Alma Ho. E5 48 CB34
Downs Est.
Alma Pl. SE19 77 CA50
Church Rd.
Alma Pl., Th.Hth. 86 BY53
Alma Rd. N10 38 BV29
Alma Rd. SW18 66 BT45
Alma Rd., Berk. 7 AP12
Alma Rd., Cars. 95 BU56
Alma Rd., Enf. 30 CC25
Alma Rd., Esher 85 BH54
Alma Rd., Har. 36 BG30
Alma Rd., Orp. 89 CP55
Alma Rd., Reig. 121 BS70
Alma Rd., St.Alb. 9 BH14
Alma Rd., Sid. 79 CO48
Alma Rd., Sthl. 54 BE40
Alma Rd., Swans. 81 DC46
Alma Rd., Wind. 61 AO44
Alma Rd. (Eton Wick), Wind. 61 AM42
Alma Sq. NW8 56 BT38
Alma St. E15 57 CF36
Alma St. NW5 56 BV36
Alma Ter. SW18 76 BT47
Almack Rd. E5 48 CC35
Almeida St. N1 56 BY36
Almer Rd. SW20 75 BP50
Almeric Rd. SW11 66 BU45
Almington St. N4 47 BX33
Almners Rd., Cher. 82 AT54
Almond Ave. W5 65 BL41
Almond Ave., Buck.H. 40 CH27
Almond Ave., Cars. 86 BU55
Almond Ave., Uxb. 44 AZ34
Almond Ave., West Dr. 63 AZ41
Almond Ave., Wok. 100 AR63
Almond Clo. SE15 67 CB44
Almond Clo., Brom. 88 CL54
Almond Clo., Egh. 72 AQ50
Almond Clo., Grays 71 DG41
Almond Clo., Guil. 118 AR69
Almond Clo., Hayes 53 BB40
Almond Clo., Ruis. 44 BB34
Almond Clo., Shep. 83 BA51
Almond Clo., Wind. 61 AN44
Green La.
Almond Dr., Swan. 89 CS51
Almond Gro., Brent. 64 BJ43
Almond Rd. N17 39 CB29
Trulock Rd.
Almond Rd. SE16 67 CB42
Almond Rd., Dart. 80 CY47
Almond Rd., Epsom 94 BN59
Almond Wk., Hat. 10 BP14
Southdown Rd.
Almond Way, Borwd. 28 BM24
Whitehouse Ave.
Almond Way, Brom. 88 CL54
Almond Way, Har. 36 BF30
Almond Way, Mitch. 86 BW53
Almons Way, Slou. 52 AQ39
Almorah Rd. N1 57 BZ36
Almorah Rd., Houns. 64 BD44
Alms Heath, Wok. 101 AZ64
Almshouse La., Chess. 93 BK58
Almshouse La., Enf. 30 CB22
Alnwick Gro., Mord. 86 BS52
Abbotsbury Rd.
Alnwick Rd. E16 58 CJ39
Alnwick Rd. SE12 78 CH46
Alperton La., Wem. 54 BK38
Alperton St. W10 55 BR38
Alpha Clo. NW1 1 D3
Alpha Clo. NW1 56 BU38
Alpha Gro. E14 67 CE41
Alpha Pl. NW6 56 BS37
Alpha Pl. SW3 66 BU43
Alpha Rd. E4 39 CE27
Alpha Rd. N18 39 CB29
Alpha Rd. SE14 67 CD44
Alpha Rd., Brwd. 122 DE25
Alpha Rd., Croy. 87 CA54
Alpha Rd., Enf. 30 CD24
Alpha Rd., Surb. 85 BL53
Alpha Rd., Tedd. 74 BG49
Alpha Rd., Uxb. 53 AZ38
Alpha Rd., Wok. 100 AT61
Alpha Rd. (Chobham), Wok. 91 AP58
Alpha St. SE15 67 CB44
Alpha St. N., Slou. 62 AP41
Alpha St. S., Slou. 62 AP41
Alphea Clo. SW19 76 BU50
Courtney Rd.
Alpine Ave., Surb. 85 BH55
Alpine Clo., Croy. 87 CA55
Alpine Copse, Brom. 88 CL51
Alpine Rd. SE16 67 CC42
Alpine Rd., Red. 121 BV69
Alpine Rd., Walt. 83 BC54
Alpine Vw., Sutt. 95 BU56
Alpine Wk., Bush. 36 BN27
Alpine Way E6 58 CL39
Alresford Rd., Guil. 118 AQ71
Alric Ave. NW10 55 BN36
Alric Ave., N.Mal. 85 BO52
Alroy Rd. N4 47 BY33
Alsace Rd. SE17 4 M10
Alsace Rd. SE17 67 CA42
Alscot Rd. SE1 4 Q8
Alscot Rd. SE1 67 CA42
Alscot Way SE1 4 P8
Alsike Rd. SE2 69 CP41
Alsike Rd., Erith 69 CP41
Alsom Ave., Wor.Pk. 94 BP56
Alston Clo., Surb. 84 BJ54
Alston Rd. N18 39 CB28
Alston Rd. SW17 76 BT49
Alston Rd., Barn. 28 BR24
Alston Rd., Hem.H. 8 AW14
Alt Gro. SW19 75 BR50
Altair Clo. N17 39 CA29
Altair Way, Nthwd. 35 BB28
Altash Way SE9 78 CK48
Altenburg Ave. W13 64 BJ41
Altenburg Gdns. SW11 66 BU45
Alterton Clo., Wok. 100 AQ62
Altham Gro., Harl. 6 CN10
Altham Rd., Pnr. 36 BE29
Althea St. SW6 66 BS44
Althorne Gdns. E18 49 CG31
Althorne Rd., Red. 121 BV71
Althorne Way, Dag. 50 CR34
Althorp Rd. SW17 76 BU47
Althorp Rd., St.Alb. 9 BH13
Althorpe Gro. SW11 66 BT44
Westbridge Rd.
Althorpe Ms. SW11 66 BT44
Westbridge Rd.
Althorpe Rd. SW17 76 BU47
Althorpe Rd., Har. 45 BG32
Altmore Ave. E6 58 CK36
Alton Ave., Stan. 36 BH29
Alton Clo., Bex. 79 CQ47
Alton Clo., Islw. 64 BH44
Alton Ct., Stai. 82 AV51
Aymer Dr.
Alton Gdns., Beck. 77 CE50
Alton Gdns., Twick. 74 BG47
Alton Rd. N17 48 BZ31
Alton Rd. SW15 75 BP47
Alton Rd., Croy. 86 BY55
Alton Rd., Rich. 65 BL45
Alton St. E14 57 CE39
Altyre Clo., Beck. 87 CD53
Altyre Rd., Croy. 87 BZ55
Altyre Way, Beck. 87 CD53
Aluric Clo., Grays 71 DG42
Alva Way, Wat. 36 BD27
Alvanley Gdns. NW6 47 BS35
Alverstoke Rd., Rom. 42 CW29
Alverston Gdns. SE25 87 CA52
Alverstone Ave. SW19 76 BS48
Alverstone Ave., Barn. 38 BU26
Alverstone Gdns. SE9 78 CM47
Alverstone Rd. E12 49 CL35
Alverstone Rd. NW2 55 BQ36
Alverstone Rd., N.Mal. 85 BO52
Alverstone Rd., Wem. 46 BL33
Alverton, St.Alb. 9 BG12
Alverton St. SE8 67 CD42
Etta St.
Alveston Ave., Har. 45 BJ31
Alvey Est. SE17 4 M9
Alvey Est. SE17 67 CA42
Alvey St. SE17 4 M10
Alvey St. SE17 67 CA42
Alvia Gdns., Sutt. 95 BT56
Alvington Cres. E8 48 CA35
Alway Ave., Epsom 94 BN56
Alwen Gro., S.Ock. 60 DA39
Alwold Cres. SE12 78 CH46
Alwyn Ave. W4 65 BN
Alwyn Clo., Borwd. 28 BL
Alwyn Clo., Croy. 96 CE
Alwyn Gdns. NW4 46 BF
Handowe Clo.
Alwyn Gdns. W3 55 BM
Noel Rd.
Alwyne Ave., Brwd. 122 DD
Alwyne La. N1 56 BY
Alwyne Pl. N1 57 BZ
Alwyne Rd. N1 57 BZ
Alwyne Rd. SW19 75 BR
Alwyne Rd. W7 54 BH
Alwyne Sq. N1 57 BZ
Alwyne Vill. N1 56 BY
Alwyns Clo., Cher. 83 AW
Alwyns La., Cher. 82 AV
Alyngton, Berk. 7 AP
Alyth Gdns. NW11 47 BS
Amalgamated Dr., Brent. 64 BJ
Amanda Clo., Ilf. 40 CM
Amanda Ct., Slou. 62 AR
Amazon St. E1 57 CB
Hessel St.
Ambassador Clo., Houns. 64 BE
Ambassador Gdns. E6 58 CK
Viscount Dr.
Ambassador Sq. E14 67 CE
Cahir St.
Ambassadors Ct. SW1 3
Amber Ave. E17 39 CD
Amber St. E15 57 CF
Salway Rd.
Ambercroft Way, Couls. 104 BY
Amberdeen Ave. N3 47 BS
Ambergate Ct. E5 48 CC
Clapton Pk. Est.
Ambergate St. SE17 4 G
Ambergate St. SE17 66 BY
Amberley Clo., Orp. 97 CN
Warnford Rd.
Amberley Clo., Pnr. 45 BE
Amberley Clo., Wok. 109 AV
Amberley Ct., Sid. 79 CP
Amberley Dr., Wey. 91 AV
Amberley Gdns., Enf. 39 CA
Amberley Gdns., Epsom 94 BO
Amberley Gro. SE26 77 CB
Amberley Gro., Croy. 87 CA
Amberley Rd. E10 48 CE
Amberley Rd. N13 38 BX
Amberley Rd. SE2 69 CP
Amberley Rd. W9 56 BS
Amberley Rd., Buck.H. 40 CJ
Amberley Rd., Enf. 39 CA
Amberley Way, Houns. 74 BD
Amberley Way, Mord. 85 BR
Amberley Way, Rom. 50 CR
Amberley Way, Uxb. 53 AY
Amberry Ct., Harl. 6 CM
Amberwood Ri., N.Mal. 85 BN
Amblecote, Cob. 93 BD
Fair Acres
Amblecote Clo. SE12 78 CH
Amblecote Rd. SE12 78 CH
Ambler Rd. N4 47 BY
Ambleside, Brom. 77 CF
Ambleside, Epp. 23 CO
Ambleside Ave. SW16 76 BW
Ambleside Ave., Beck. 87 CD
Ambleside Ave., Horn. 50 CU
Ambleside Ave., Walt. 84 BD
Ambleside Clo. E9 48 CC
Ambleside Cres., Enf. 30 CC
Ambleside Dr., Felt. 73 BB
Ambleside Gdns., Ilf. 49 CK
Ambleside Gdns., S.Croy. 96 CC
Ambleside Gdns., Sutt. 95 BT
Ambleside Gdns., Wem. 45 BK
Ambleside Rd. NW10 55 BO
Ambleside Rd., Bexh. 69 CR
Ambleside Wk., Uxb. 53 AX
High St.
Ambleside Way, Egh. 72 AT
Ambrey Way, Wall. 95 BW
Ambrooke Rd., Belv. 69 CR
Gertrude Rd.
Ambrosden Ave. SW1 3
Ambrosden Ave. SW1 66 BW
Ambrose Ave. NW11 46 BR
Ambrose Clo. E6 58 CK
Bondfield Rd.
Ambrose Clo., Orp. 88 CN
Ambrose Ms. SW11 66 BU
Abercrombie St.
Ambrose St. SE16 67 CB
Southwark Pk. Rd.
Ambrose Wk. E3 57 CE
Malmesbury Rd.
Amelia St. SE17 4 H
Amelia St. SE17 66 BY
Amen Cor. EC4 2
Amen Cor. SW17 76 BU
Amen Ct. EC4 2
Amen Ct. EC4 56 BY
Amerden Way, Slou. 61 AN
America Sq. EC3 2 P
America St. SE1 4
America St. SE1 57 BZ
Great Guildford St.
Amerland Rd. SW18 75 BR
Amersham Ave. N18 39 BZ
Amersham By-pass, Amer. 25 AO
Amersham Clo., Rom. 42 CW
Amersham Dr., Rom. 42 CW
Amersham Gro. SE14 67 CD
Amersham Pl., Amer. 25 AR
Amersham Rd. SE14 67 CD
Amersham Rd., Amer. 25 AR
Amersham Rd., Ch.St.G. 25 AQ
Amersham Rd. (Chalfont Common), Ch.St.G. 34 AR
Amersham Rd., Croy. 87 BZ

ersham Rd., Ger.Cr. 43 AS31
ersham Rd., Har. 45 BH32
ersham Rd., Rom. 42 CW29
ersham Vale SE14 67 CD43
ersham Wk., Rom. 42 CW29
ersham Way, Amer. 25 AS23
ery Gdns. NW10 55 BP37
ery Gdns., Rom. 51 CV31
ery Rd., Har. 45 BJ34
es Rd., Swans. 81 DC46
esbury, Wal.Abb. 22 CH19
esbury Ave. SW2 76 BX48
esbury Clo., Epp. 22 CN19
esbury Clo., Wor.Pk. 85 BQ54
esbury Dr. E4 30 CE25
esbury Rd., Brom. 88 CJ52
esbury Rd., Dag. 59 CP36
esbury Rd., Epp. 22 CN19
esbury Rd., Felt. 74 BD48
ethyst Rd. E15 48 CF35
ey Dr., Lthd. 102 BG65
herst Ave. W13 54 BJ39
herst Clo., Orp. 89 CO52
herst Dr., Orp. 88 CN52
herst Gdns. W13 54 BK39
mherst Rd.
herst Hill, Sev. 107 CT64
herst Rd. W13 54 BK39
herst Rd., Sev. 107 CU64
hurst Gdns., Islw. 64 BH44
hurst Pk. N16 48 BZ33
hurst Pas. E8 48 CB35
hurst Rd. E8 48 CA35
hurst Rd. N16 48 CA35
hurst Ter. E8 48 CB35
hurst Wk. SE28 59 CO40
itfield Cres.
idas Gdns., Dag. 50 CO35
iel St. E1 57 CC38
Colebert Ave.
ies St. SW11 66 BU45
nis Ave., Epsom 94 BM57
nis Ave., Wey. 92 AW58
nis Rd., Wok. 100 AP63
nity Gro. SW20 85 BQ51
nity Rd. E15 58 CG37
nmanford Grn. NW9 46 BO32
Ruthin Clo.
nner Rd. SW11 76 BV46
nor Rd. W6 65 BQ41
nott Rd. SE15 67 CB45
noy Pl. E14 57 CE40
Birchfield St.
npere Way, Croy. 86 BX54
npleforth Rd. SE2 69 CO41
npthill Sq. Est. NW1 1 M1
npthill Sq. Est. NW1 56 BW37
npton Pl. WC1 2 B3
npton Pl. WC1 56 BX38
Ampton St.
npton St. WC1 2 B3
npton St. WC1 56 BX38
nroth Clo. SE23 77 CB47
nroth Grn. NW9 46 BO32
Fryent Gro.
nstel Way, Wok. 100 AP62
nsterdam Rd. E14 67 CF41
nwell Clo., Enf. 30 BZ25
nwell Common, Welw.G.C. 5 BS8
nwell Ct. N4 48 BZ33
nwell Ct., Hodd. 12 CE11
nwell Ct., Wal.Abb. 22 CG20
nwell St. EC1 2 D2
nwell St. EC1 56 BY38
nwell St., Hodd. 12 CE11
ny Rd., Oxt. 115 CG68
nyand Cotts., Twick. 74 BJ46
Amyand Pk. Rd.
nyand La., Twick. 74 BJ46
Beaconsfield Rd.
nyand Pk. Gdns., Twick. 74 BJ46
Amyand Pk. Rd.
nyand Pk. Rd., Twick. 74 BJ47
nyruth Rd. SE4 77 CE46
natola Rd. N19 47 BW34
ncaster Cres., N.Mal. 85 BP53
ncaster Rd., Beck. 87 CC52
ncaster St. SE18 68 CN43
nchor & Hope La. SE7 68 CH41
nchor Boul., Dart. 70 CY45
nchor Clo., Chsnt. 21 CC17
nchor Cres., Wok. 100 AO62
nchor Dr., Rain. 59 CU38
Wentworth Way
nchor Hill, Wok. 100 AO62
nchor La., Hem.H. 8 AW14
nchor Ms. SW12 76 BV46
Hazelbourne Rd.
nchor St. SE16 67 CB42
nchor Yd. EC1 2 J4
nchor Yd. EC1 57 BZ38
Old St.
nchorage Clo. SW19 76 BS49
ncill Clo. W6 65 BR43
ncona Rd. NW10 55 BP37
ncona Rd. SE18 68 CM42
ndalus Rd. SW9 66 BX45
nder Clo., Wem. 45 BK35
ndermass, Wind. 61 AL44
nderson Clo. W3 55 BN39
Cotton Ave.
nderson Clo., Epsom 94 BM59
nderson Clo., Uxb. 35 AW30
Belfry Ave.
nderson Dr., Ashf. 73 BA49
nderson Pl., Houns. 64 BF45
nderson Rd. E9 57 CC36
Daley St.
nderson Rd., Ilf. 49 CJ31
nderson Rd., Rad. 19 BM20
nderson Rd., Wey. 83 BA55
nderson St. SW3 3 E10
nderson St. SW3 66 BU42

Anderson Way, Belv. 69 CR41
Anderton Clo. SE5 67 CA45
Andover Clo., Epsom 94 BN58
Andover Clo., Grnf. 54 BF38
Andover Clo., Uxb. 53 AW37
Andover Ct., Wok. 100 AR63
Andover Pl. NW6 56 BS37
Andover Rd. N7 47 BX34
Andover Rd., Orp. 88 CN54
Andover Rd., Twick. 74 BG47
Andre St. E8 48 CB35
Andrew Borde St. WC2 1 P8
Andrew Borde St. WC2 56 BW39
Charing Cross Rd.
Andrew Clo., Bex. 79 CS46
Bourne Rd.
Andrew Clo., Ilf. 40 CM29
Andrew Pl. SW8 66 BW44
Andrew St. E14 57 CF39
Andrewes Clo. E6 58 CK39
Linton Gdns.
Andrews Clo., Buck.H. 40 CJ27
Andrews Clo., Epsom 94 BO60
Andrews Clo., Har. 45 BG33
Bessborough Rd.
Andrews Clo., Orp. 89 CP51
Andrews Clo., Wor.Pk. 85 BQ55
Andrews Crosse WC2 2 D9
Andrews Crosse WC2 56 BY39
Bell Yd.
Andrews La., Chsnt. 21 CB17
Andrews Pl. SE9 78 CL46
Andrews Rd. E8 57 CB37
Andrews Rd., Wal.Cr. 21 CA17
Andrews Wk. SE17 66 BY43
John Ruskin St.
Andrewsfield, Welw.G.C. 5 BT8
Rivenhall End
Androse Gdns., Brom. 88 CJ51
Widmore Rd.
Andwell Clo. SE2 69 CO41
Anerley Gro. SE19 77 CA50
Anerley Hill SE19 77 CA50
Anerley Pk. SE20 77 CB50
Anerley Pk. Rd. SE20 77 CB50
Anerley Rd. SE19 77 CB50
Anerley Rd. SE20 77 CB50
Anerley Sta. Rd. SE20 87 CB51
Anerley St. SW11 66 BU44
Dagnall St.
Anerley Vale SE19 77 CA50
Anfield Clo. SW12 76 BW47
Angas Ct., Wey. 92 BA56
Angel All. E1 2 Q8
Angel Clo. N18 39 CA28
Angel Ct. EC2 2 L8
Angel Ct. EC2 57 BZ39
Throgmorton St.
Angel Ct. SW1 3 M3
Angel Ct. SW1 56 BW40
King St.
Angel Ct. SW17 76 BU49
Angel Hill, Sutt. 86 BS55
Angel Hill Dr., Sutt. 86 BS55
Angel La. E15 57 CF36
Angel La., Hayes 53 BA39
Angel Ms. N1 2 E1
Angel Ms. N1 56 BY37
Angel Pas. EC4 4 K1
Angel Pas. EC4 57 BZ40
Upper Thames St.
Angel Pl. N18 39 CA28
Angel Clo.
Angel Pl. SE1 4 K4
Angel Pl. SE1 67 BZ41
Borough High St.
Angel Rd. N18 39 CB28
Angel Rd., Har. 45 BH32
Angel Rd., T.Ditt. 84 BJ54
Angel St. EC1 2 H8
Angel St. EC1 57 BZ39
Angel Wk. W6 65 BQ42
Angel Way, Rom. 50 CT32
Angelfield, Houns. 64 BF45
Angelica Gdns., Croy. 87 CC54
Angell Pk. Gdns. SW9 66 BY45
Angell Rd. SW9 66 BY44
Angerstein La. SE3 68 CG43
Angle Clo., Uxb. 53 AZ37
Angle Grn., Dag. 50 CP33
Angle Pl., Berk. 7 AQ13
Angle Rd., Grays 70 DB43
Anglefield Rd., Berk. 7 AQ13
Anglers Clo., Rich. 74 BK49
Anglers La. NW5 56 BV36
Angles Rd. SW16 76 BX49
Anglesea Ave. SE18 68 CL42
Anglesea Cen., Grav. 81 DG46
New Rd.
Anglesea Pl., Grav. 81 DG46
Clive Rd.
Anglesea Rd. SE18 68 CL42
Anglesea Rd., Kings.T. 84 BK52
Anglesea Rd., Orp. 89 CO53
Anglesey Clo., Ashf. 73 AZ48
Anglesey Ct. Rd., Cars. 95 BV57
Anglesey Dr., Rain. 59 CU38
Anglesey Gdns., Cars. 95 BV57
Anglesey Rd., Enf. 30 CB24
Anglesey Rd., Wat. 36 BD28
Anglesmede Cres., Pnr. 45 BF31
Anglesmede Way, Pnr. 45 BF31
Anglia Wk. E6 58 CK37
Napier Rd.
Anglo Rd. E3 57 CD37
Angus Clo., Chess. 94 BM56
Angus Dr., Ruis. 45 BD35
Angus Gdns. NW9 37 BN30
Angus Rd. E13 58 CJ38
Angus St. SE14 67 CD43
Anhalt Rd. SW11 66 BU43
Ankerdine Cres. SE18 68 CL43
Anlaby Rd., Tedd. 74 BH49
Anley Rd. W14 65 BQ41

Anmersh Gro., Stan. 36 BK30
Ann La. SW10 66 BT43
Ann St. SE18 68 CM42
Anna Neagle Clo. E7 49 CH35
Dames Rd.
Annabel Clo. E14 57 CE39
Annalee Gdns., S.Ock. 60 DA39
Annalee Rd., S.Ock. 60 DA39
Annan Way, Rom. 41 CS30
Annandale Gro., Uxb. 44 BA34
Tweedale Gro.
Annandale Rd. SE10 68 CG42
Annandale Rd. W4 65 BO42
Annandale Rd., Croy. 87 CB55
Annandale Rd., Guil. 118 AQ71
Annandale Rd., Sid. 78 CN47
Anne Boleyns Wk., Kings.T. 75 BL49
Anne Boleyns Wk., Sutt. 94 BR57
Anne Case Ms., N.Mal. 85 BO52
Sycamore Gro.
Anne of Cleves Rd., Dart. 80 CB46
Anne St. E13 58 CH38
Anne Way, E.Mol. 84 BF52
Anne Way, Ilf. 40 CM29
Anners Clo., Egh. 82 AU52
Village Rd.
Annes Wk., Cat. 105 CA63
Annesley Ave. NW9 46 BN31
Annesley Clo. NW10 46 BO34
Annesley Dr., Croy. 87 CD55
Annesley Rd. SE3 68 CH44
Annesley Wk. N19 47 BW34
Macdonald Rd.
Annett Clo., Shep. 83 BB52
Upper Halliford Rd.
Annett Rd., Walt. 83 BC54
Annette Clo., Har. 36 BH30
Spencer Rd.
Annette Cres. N1 57 BZ36
Essex Rd.
Annette Rd. N7 47 BX35
Annetts Gro. N1 57 BZ36
Essex Rd.
Annie Besant Clo. E3 57 CD37
Annifer Way, S.Ock. 60 DA39
Anning St. EC2 2 N4
Anning St. EC2 57 CA38
New Inn Yd.
Annington Rd. N2 47 BU31
Annis Rd. E9 57 CD36
Anns Clo. SW1 3 F5
Anns Clo. SW1 66 BV41
Kinnerton St.
Anns Pl. E1 2 P7
Annsworthy Ave., Th.Hth. 87 BZ52
Annsworthy Cres. SE25 87 BZ51
Lenham Rd.
Ansdell Rd. SE15 67 CC44
Ansdell St. W8 66 BS41
St. Albans Gro.
Ansdell Ter. W8 66 BS41
Ansell Gro., Cars. 86 BU54
Ansell Rd. SW17 76 BU48
Ansell Rd., Dor. 119 BJ71
Anselm Clo., Croy. 87 CA55
Anselm Rd. SW6 66 BS43
Anselm Rd., Pnr. 36 BE29
Ansford Rd., Brom. 77 CF49
Ansleigh Pl. W11 55 BQ40
Ansley Clo., S.Croy. 96 CB60
Anslow Gdns., Iver 52 AU37
Anson Clo., Hem.H. 16 AS17
Lancaster Dr.
Anson Clo., Ken. 105 BZ63
Anson Clo., Rom. 41 CR30
Anson Clo., St.Alb. 9 BJ14
Anson Clo. (Sandridge), St.Alb. 9 BK10
Anson Rd. N7 47 BW35
Anson Rd. NW2 46 BQ35
Anson Ter., Nthlt. 54 BF36
Anson Wk., Nthwd. 35 BA28
Anstead Dr., Rain. 59 CU37
Anstey Rd. SE15 67 CB45
Anstey Wk. N8 47 BY31
Anstice Clo. W4 65 BO43
Anstridge Rd. SE9 78 CM46
Antelope Ave., Grays 71 DD41
Antelope Rd. SE18 68 CK41
Anthony Clo. NW7 37 BO28
Anthony Clo., Sev. 107 CT63
Anthony Clo., Wat. 36 BD26
Anthony La., Swan. 89 CU51
Anthony Rd. SE25 87 CB53
Anthony Rd., Borwd. 28 BL23
Anthony Rd., Grnf. 54 BH37
Anthony Rd., Well. 69 CO44
Anthony St. E1 57 CB39
Commercial Rd.
Anthorne Clo., Pot.B. 20 BS19
Anthus Ms., Nthwd. 35 BB29
Antill Rd. E3 57 CD38
Antill Rd. N15 48 CB31
Antill Ter. E1 57 CC39
Antlers Hill E4 30 CE25
Antoinette Ct., Abb.L. 17 BB18
Dairy Way
Anton Cres., Sutt. 86 BS55
Anton Rd., S.Ock. 60 DA38
Anton St. E8 48 CB35
Antoneys Clo., Pnr. 36 BD30
Antonine Gate, St.Alb. 9 BF14
Antrim Gro. NW3 56 BU36
Antrim Mans. NW3 56 BU36
Antrim Rd. NW3 56 BU36
Antrobus Clo., Sutt. 94 BR56
Antrobus Rd. W4 65 BN42
Anvil Clo., Hem.H. 16 AT17
Anvil Ct., Slou. 62 AT42
Blacksmith Row
Anvil La., Cob. 92 BC60
Anvil Rd., Sun. 83 BC52
Anworth Clo., Wdf.Grn. 40 CH29

Anyards Rd., Cob. 92 BC60
Apeldoorn Dr., Wall. 95 BX58
Aperdele Rd., Lthd. 102 BJ62
Aperfield Rd., Erith 69 CT43
Aperfield Rd., West. 106 CK62
Apers Ave., Wok. 100 AS64
Apex Clo., Beck. 87 CF51
Apex Clo., Wey. 83 BA55
Apiary Ct., Welw.G.C. 5 BR5
Harmer Grn. La.
Apley Rd., Reig. 121 BS72
Aplin Way, Islw. 64 BH44
Osterley Rd.
Apollo Ave., Brom. 88 CH51
Hawes Rd.
Apollo Ave., Nthwd. 35 BC28
Apollo Clo., Horn. 50 CU34
Apollo Pl. SW10 66 BT44
Riley St.
Apollo Way SE28 68 CM41
Broadwater Rd.
Apollo Way, Hem.H. 8 AY12
Apothecary St. EC4 2 F9
Apothecary St. EC4 56 BY39
New Bri. St.
Appach Rd. SW2 76 BY46
Appian Way Est., Erith 69 CR42
Apple Cotts., Hem.H. 16 AT17
Apple Garth, Brent. 64 BK42
Apple Gro., Chess. 94 BL56
Apple Gro., Enf. 30 CA24
Apple Mkt., Kings.T. 84 BK51
Apple Orchard, Hem.H. 8 AY12
Apple Tree Ave., Uxb. 53 AY39
Apple Tree Ave., West Dr. 53 AY39
Apple Tree Yd. SW1 3 M2
Apple Tree Yd. SW1 56 BW40
Duke of York St.
Appleby Clo. E4 39 CF29
Appleby Clo. N15 48 BZ32
Penrith Rd.
Appleby Clo., Twick. 74 BG48
Appleby Dr., Rom. 42 CV28
Appleby Gdns., Felt. 73 BB47
Ambleside Dr.
Appleby Grn., Rom. 42 CV28
Appleby Rd. E8 57 CB36
Appleby Rd. E16 58 CG39
Appleby St. E2 2 P1
Appleby St. E2 57 CA37
Appleby St., Chsnt. 21 BZ16
Applecroft, St.Alb. 18 BF17
Applecroft Rd., Welw.G.C. 5 BP8
Appledore, Slou. 52 AP36
Duffield La.
Appledore Ave., Bexh. 69 CS44
Appledore Ave., Ruis. 44 BC34
Appledore Clo. SW17 76 BU48
Appledore Clo., Brom. 88 CG53
Appledore Clo., Edg. 37 BM30
Appledore Clo., Rom. 42 CV30
Appledore Cres., Sid. 78 CN48
Appledown Ri., Couls. 104 BW61
Applefield, Amer. 25 AR23
Amersham Pl.
Appleford Clo., Hodd. 12 CD11
Appleford Rd. W10 55 BR38
Applegarth, Croy. 96 CE57
Applegarth, Esher 93 BJ56
Applegarth Ave., Guil. 118 AO70
Applegarth Dr., Ilf. 49 CN31
Applegarth Rd. SE28 59 CO40
Applegarth Rd. W14 65 BQ41
Applegate, Brwd. 33 CZ25
Appleshaw Clo., Grav. 81 DG49
Chalky Bank
Appleton Clo., Amer. 25 AQ23
Appleton Gdns., N.Mal. 85 BP53
Appleton Rd. SE9 68 CK45
Appleton Rd., Loug. 31 CL24
Appleton Sq., Mitch. 86 BU51
Silbury Ave.
Appleton Way, Horn. 51 CV34
Appletree Clo., Brwd. 33 DB22
Appletree Cres.
Appletree Ct., Guil. 109 AU69
Old Merrow St.
Appletree Cres., Brwd. 33 DB22
Appletree Gdns., Barn. 29 BU24
Appletree La., Slou. 62 AR41
Appletree Wk., Chesh. 16 AO20
Cresswell Rd.
Appletree Wk., Wat. 17 BC20
Applewood Clo. N20 38 BU26
Applewood Clo. NW2 46 BP34
Appold St. EC2 2 M6
Appold St. EC2 57 CA39
Appold St., Erith 69 CT43
Apprentice Way E5 48 CB35
Clarence Rd.
Approach, The NW4 46 BQ32
Approach, The W3 55 BN39
Approach, The, Enf. 30 CB23
Approach, The, Lthd. 102 BE65
Approach, The, Orp. 88 CN55
Approach, The, Pot.B. 19 BR19
Approach, The, Upmin. 51 CX34
Approach Clo. N16 48 CA35
Cowper Rd.
Approach Rd. E2 57 CC37
Approach Rd. SW20 85 BQ51
Approach Rd., Ashf. 73 BA49
Approach Rd., Barn. 29 BT24
Approach Rd. (Cockfosters), Barn. 29 BV24
Approach Rd., E.Mol. 84 BF53
Approach Rd., Pur. 95 BY59
Approach Rd., St.Alb. 9 BH14
Apps Ct., Walt. 84 BD53
Apps Pond La., St.Alb. 8 BC15
Aprey Gdns. NW4 46 BQ31
April Clo. W7 54 BH40
April Clo., Felt. 73 BC48

April Clo., Orp. 97 CN56
Briarswood Way
April Glen SE23 77 CC48
Mayow Rd.
April Wd. Clo., Wey. 91 AV59
Apsledene, Grav. 81 DH50
Apsley Clo., Har. 45 BG32
Apsley Rd. SE25 87 CB52
Apsley Rd., N.Mal. 85 BN52
Apsley Way NW2 46 BP34
Aquarius Way, Nthwd. 35 BC28
Aquila Clo., Ash. 102 BK64
Aquila Clo., Nthwd. 35 BC28
Aquila St. NW8 56 BT37
Aquinas St. SE1 4 E3
Aquinas St. SE1 56 BY40
Arabella Dr. SW15 65 BO45
Arabia Clo. E4 39 CF26
Arabin Rd. SE4 67 CD45
Araglen Ave., S.Ock. 60 DA39
Aragon Ave., Epsom 94 BP58
Aragon Ave., T.Ditt. 84 BH53
Aragon Clo., Brom. 88 CK54
Seymour Dr.
Aragon Clo., Croy. 96 CG58
Aragon Clo., Enf. 29 BX22
Aragon Clo., Hem.H. 8 BA11
Aragon Clo., Rom. 41 CR29
Aragon Clo., Sun. 73 BB50
Aragon Dr., Ilf. 40 CM29
Aragon Dr., Ruis. 45 BD33
Field End Rd.
Aragon Ms. E1 57 CB40
Thomas More St.
Aragon Rd., Kings.T. 75 BL49
Aragon Rd., Mord. 85 BQ53
Aran Dr., Stan. 36 BK28
Aran Heights, Ch.St.G. 34 AQ28
Arandora Cres., Rom. 50 CO33
Arbery Rd. E3 57 CD38
Arbor Clo., Beck. 87 CE51
Arbor Ct. N16 48 BZ34
Arbor Rd. E4 39 CF27
Arborfield Clo., Slou. 62 AP41
Arbour Clo., Brwd. 42 DB28
Arbour Clo., Lthd. 102 BH65
Arbour Fld., Wok. 100 AS61
Arbour Rd., Enf. 30 CC24
Arbour Sq. E1 57 CC39
Arbour Vw., Amer. 25 AQ23
Bell La.
Arbour Way, Horn. 50 CU35
Arbroath Grn., Wat. 35 BC27
Arbroath Rd. SE9 68 CK45
Arbrook Clo., Orp. 89 CO52
Arbrook La., Esher 93 BG57
Arbury Ter. SE26 77 CB48
Wells Pk. Rd.
Arbuthnot La., Bex. 79 CQ47
Arbuthnot Rd. SE14 67 CC44
Arbutus Clo., Red. 121 BT71
Arbutus Rd., Red. 121 BT72
Arbutus St. E8 57 CA36
Arcade, The E17 48 CE31
Hoe St.
Arcade, The EC2 2 M7
Arcade, The EC2 57 CA39
Liverpool St.
Arcade Pl., Rom. 50 CT32
Arcadia Ave. N3 38 BS30
Arcadia St. E14 57 CE39
Arcadian Ave., Bex. 79 CQ46
Arcadian Clo., Bex. 79 CQ46
Arcadian Gdns. N22 38 BX29
Arcadian Rd., Bex. 79 CQ46
Arcany Rd., S.Ock. 60 DA38
Arch Fld., Welw.G.C. 5 BR6
Arch Rd., Walt. 84 BD55
Arch St. SE1 4 H7
Arch St. SE1 67 BZ41
Arch Way, Rom. 41 CU29
Archangel St. SE16 67 CC41
Archates Ave., Grays 71 DD41
Archbishops Pl. SW2 76 BX47
Archdale Rd. SE22 77 CA46
Archel Rd. W14 65 BR43
Archer Clo., Kings L. 17 AZ18
Archer Clo., Kings.T. 75 BL50
Archer Ho. SW11 66 BT44
Archer Ms., Hmptn. 74 BG50
Archer Rd. SE25 87 CB52
Archer Rd., Orp. 89 CO53
Archer St. W1 1 N10
Archer St. W1 56 BW40
Rupert St.
Archer Ter., West Dr. 53 AY40
Yew Ave.
Archer Way, Swan. 89 CU51
Archers, Harl. 13 CL13
Archers Dr., Enf. 30 CC23
Archers Ride, Welw.G.C. 5 BS9
Archery Clo. W2 1 D9
Archery Clo. W2 56 BU39
Archery Clo., Har. 45 BH31
Archery Rd. SE9 78 CK46
Arches, The WC2 4 A2
Arches, The, Har. 45 BG34
Archibald Ms. W1 3 J1
Archibald Rd. N7 47 BW35
Archibald Rd., Rom. 42 CX30
Archway Clo. N19 47 BW34
Archway Clo. SW19 76 BS49
Archway Mall N19 47 BW34
Archway Pl., Dor. 119 BJ71
Archway Rd. N6 47 BV33
Archway Rd. N19 47 BV33
Archway St. SW13 65 BO45
Arcola St. E8 48 CA35
Arctic St. NW5 47 BV35
Arcus Rd., Brom. 78 CG49
Ardbeg Rd. SE24 77 BZ46
Arden Clo., Bush. 36 BH26
Arden Clo., Har. 45 BG34
Arden Clo., Hem.H. 16 AT17

Ard–Ash

Arden Clo., Reig. 121 BS72
Arden Ct. Gdns. N2 47 BT33
Arden Cres. E14 67 CE42
Arden Cres., Dag. 59 CP36
Arden Est. N1 2 M1
Arden Est. N1 57 CA38
Arden Gro., Orp. 97 CL56
Pinecrest Gdns.
Arden Mhor, Pnr. 44 BC31
Arden Rd. N3 46 BR31
Arden Rd. W13 54 BJ40
Ardens Way, St.Alb. 9 BK12
Ardent Clo. SE25 87 CA52
Ardentinny, St.Alb. 9 BH14
London Rd.
Ardfern Ave. SW16 86 BY52
Ardfillan Rd. SE6 77 CF47
Ardgowan Rd. SE6 78 CG47
Ardilaun Rd. N5 48 BZ35
Ardleigh Clo., Horn. 51 CV31
Ardleigh Ct., Brwd. 122 DC26
Hutton Rd.
Ardleigh Gdns., Brwd. 122 DF26
Ardleigh Gdns., Sutt. 86 BS54
Ardleigh Grn. Rd., Horn. 51 CV32
Ardleigh Ms., Ilf. 49 CL34
Bengal Rd.
Ardleigh Rd. E17 39 CD30
Ardleigh Rd. N1 57 CA36
Ardley Clo. NW10 46 BO34
Ardley Clo. SE6 77 CD48
Ardley Clo., Ruis. 44 BA33
Ardlui Rd. SE27 77 BZ48
Ardmay Gdns., Surb. 85 BL53
Ardmere Rd. SE13 77 CF46
Ardmore Ave., Guil. 118 AQ69
Ardmore La., Buck.H. 40 CH26
Ardmore Rd., S.Ock. 60 DA38
Ardmore Way, Guil. 118 AQ69
Ardoch Rd. SE6 77 CF48
Ardross Ave., Nthwd. 35 BB28
Ardrossan Gdns., Wor.Pk. 85 BP55
Ardshiel Clo. SW15 65 BQ45
Bemish Rd.
Ardshiel Dr., Red. 121 BU71
Fairlawn Dr.
Ardsley Wd., Wey. 92 BB56
Ardwell Ave., Ilf. 49 CM32
Ardwell Rd. SW2 76 BX48
Ardwick Rd. NW2 47 BS35
Argall Ave. E10 48 CC33
Argent St. SE1 4 G4
Argent St., Grays 71 DD43
Argon Ms. SW6 66 BS43
Argosy Gdns., Stai. 72 AV50
Argosy La., Stai. 73 AX47
Clare Rd.
Argus Clo., Rom. 41 CR30
Lynton Ave.
Argus Way, Nthlt. 54 BE38
Argyle Ave., Houns. 74 BF46
Argyle Clo. W13 54 BJ38
Argyle Est. SW19 75 BQ48
Argyle Gdns., Upmin. 51 CY35
Argyle Pas. N17 39 CB30
Argyle Rd.
Argyle Pl. W6 65 BP42
Argyle Rd. E1 57 CC38
Argyle Rd. E15 49 CG35
Argyle Rd. E16 58 CH39
Argyle Rd. N12 38 BS28
Argyle Rd. N17 39 CB30
Argyle Rd. N18 39 CB28
Argyle Rd. W13 54 BJ38
Argyle Rd., Barn. 28 BQ24
Argyle Rd., Har. 45 BF32
Argyle Rd., Houns. 74 BF46
Argyle Rd., Ilf. 49 CL34
Argyle Rd., Sev. 116 CU66
Argyle Rd., Tedd. 74 BH49
Argyle Sq. WC1 2 A2
Argyle Sq. WC1 56 BX38
Argyle St. WC1 1 Q2
Argyle St. WC1 56 BX38
Argyle Wk. WC1 1 Q3
Argyll Ave., Sthl. 54 BF40
Argyll Gdns., Edg. 37 BM30
Argyll Rd. W8 66 BS41
Argyll Rd., Grays 71 DD42
Argyll Rd., Hem.H. 8 AY11
Argyll St. W1 1 L9
Argyll St. W1 56 BW39
Arica Rd. SE4 67 CD45
Ariel Clo., Grav. 81 DJ49
Ariel Rd. NW6 56 BS36
Ariel Way W12 55 BQ40
Arisdale Ave., S.Ock. 60 DA39
Aristotle Rd. SW4 66 BW45
Ark Ave., Grays 71 DD41
Arkell Gro. SE19 76 BY50
Arkindale Rd. SE6 77 CF48
Arkley Ct., Maid. 61 AH42
Arkley Cres. E17 48 CD32
Arkley Dr., Barn. 28 BP24
Arkley La., Barn. 28 BP24
Arkley Rd. E17 48 CD32
Arkley Rd., Hem.H. 8 AZ11
Arkley Vw., Barn. 28 BP24
Arklow Rd. SE14 67 CD43
Arkwright Rd. NW3 47 BT35
Arkwright Rd., Slou. 62 AV44
Arkwright Rd., S.Croy. 96 CA58
Arkwright Rd., Til. 71 DG44
Arkwright St. E16 58 CG39
Arkwrights, Harl. 6 CN10
Arlesford Rd. SW9 66 BX45
Arlesley Clo. SW15 75 BR46
Arlingford Rd. SW2 76 BY46
Arlington N12 38 BS28
Arlington Ave. N1 57 BZ37
Arlington Clo., Sid. 78 CN47
Arlington Clo., Sutt. 86 BS55
Arlington Clo., Twick. 74 BK46
Arlington Ct., Hayes 63 BB42
Arlington Cres., Wal.Cr. 21 CD20
Arlington Dr., Cars. 86 BU55
Arlington Dr., Ruis. 44 BA32
Arlington Gdns. W4 65 BN42
Arlington Gdns., Ilf. 49 CL33
Arlington Gdns., Rom. 42 CW30
Arlington Lo. SW2 66 BX45
Arlington Ms., Twick. 74 BK46
Arlington Rd.
Arlington Pas., Tedd. 74 BH49
Arlington Rd. N14 38 BV27
Arlington Rd. NW1 56 BV37
Arlington Rd. W13 54 BJ39
Arlington Rd., Ashf. 73 AY49
Arlington Rd., Rich. 74 BK48
Arlington Rd., Surb. 84 BK53
Arlington Rd., Tedd. 74 BH49
Arlington Rd., Twick. 74 BK46
Arlington Rd., Wdf.Grn. 40 CH30
Arlington Sq. N1 57 BZ37
Arlington St. SW1 3 L2
Arlington St. SW1 56 BW40
Arlington Way EC1 2 E2
Arlington Way EC1 56 BY38
Arliss Way, Nthlt. 54 BD37
Arlow Rd. N21 38 BY26
Armada Ct. SE8 67 CE43
Watergate St.
Armada St. SE8 67 CE43
Armadale Clo. N17 48 CB31
Armadale Rd. SW6 66 BS43
Armadale Rd., Felt. 73 BC46
Armadale Rd., Wok. 100 AQ62
Armagh Rd. E3 57 CD37
Armand Clo., Wat. 26 BB22
Armfield Clo., E.Mol. 84 BE53
Armfield Cres., Mitch. 86 BU51
Armfield Rd., Enf. 30 BZ23
Arminger Rd. W12 55 BP40
Armitage Clo., Rick. 26 AX24
Armitage Rd. NW11 46 BR33
Armitage Rd. SE10 68 CG42
Armor Rd., Grays 70 CY42
Armour Clo. N7 56 BX36
Armoury Dr., Grav. 81 DH47
Armoury Way SW18 76 BS46
Armstead Wk., Dag. 59 CR36
Armstrong Ave., Wdf.Grn. 40 CG29
Armstrong Clo. E6 58 CK39
Armstrong Clo., Dag. 50 CP33
Palmer Rd.
Armstrong Clo., Pnr. 44 BC32
Armstrong Clo., Sev. 107 CS61
Armstrong Clo., Walt. 83 BC53
Armstrong Cres., Barn. 29 BT24
Armstrong Pl., Hem.H. 8 AX13
High St.
Armstrong Rd. SW7 3 A7
Armstrong Rd. W3 55 BO40
Armstrong Rd., Egh. 72 AR50
Armstrong Rd., Felt. 74 BE49
Armstrong Way, Sthl. 64 BF41
Armytage Rd., Houns. 64 BD43
Arnal Cres. SW18 75 BR47
Arndale Wk. SW18 76 BS46
Arndale Cen.
Arndale Way, Egh. 72 AT49
Arne Gro., Orp. 88 CN55
Arne St. WC2 2 A9
Arne Wk. SE3 68 CG45
Arnett Clo., Rick. 26 AW25
Arnett Way, Rick. 26 AW25
Arneway St. SW1 3 P7
Arneway St. SW1 66 BW41
Horseferry Rd.
Arneways Ave., Rom. 50 CP31
Arnewood Clo. SW15 75 BP47
Arnewood Clo., Cob. 93 BF60
Arneys La., Mitch. 86 BV53
Arngask Rd. SE6 77 CF47
Arnhem Ave., S.Ock. 60 CY40
Arnhem Dr., Croy. 96 CF59
Arnhem Way SE22 77 CA46
Dulwich Gro.
Arnison Rd., E.Mol. 84 BG52
Arnold Ave. E., Enf. 30 CD22
Arnold Ave. W., Enf. 30 CD22
Arnold Circ. E2 2 P3
Arnold Circ. E2 57 CA38
Arnold Clo., Har. 46 BL33
Arnold Cres., Islw. 74 BG46
Arnold Est. SE1 4 Q5
Arnold Est. SE1 67 CA41
Arnold Gdns. N13 38 BY28
Arnold Pl., Til. 71 DG44
Kipling Ave.
Arnold Rd. E3 57 CE38
Arnold Rd. N15 48 CA31
Arnold Rd. SW17 76 BU50
Arnold Rd., Dag. 59 CQ36
Arnold Rd., Grav. 81 DH48
Arnold Rd., Nthlt. 54 BE36
Arnold Rd., Stai. 73 AX50
Arnold Rd., Wok. 100 AT61
Arnolds Ave., Brwd. 122 DE25
Arnolds Clo., Brwd. 122 DE25
Arnolds Fm. La., Brwd. 122 CF24
Arnolds La., S.at H. 80 CX50
Arnos Gro. N14 38 BW28
Arnos Rd. N11 38 BW28
Arnott Clo. SE28 59 CP40
Applegarth Rd.
Arnott Clo. W4 65 BN42
Fishers La.
Arnould Ave. SE5 67 BZ45
Arnsberg Rd., Erith 69 CT43
Arnsberg Way, Bexh. 69 CR45
Arnside Gdns., Wem. 45 BK33
Arnside Rd., Bexh. 69 CR44
Arnside St. SE17 67 BZ43
Arnulf St. SE6 77 CE49
Arnulls Rd. SW16 76 BY50
Arodene Rd. SW2 76 BX46
Arragon Gdns. SW16 76 BX50
Arragon Gdns., W.Wick. 87 CE55
Arragon Rd. E6 58 CJ37
Arragon Rd., Twick. 74 BJ47
Arran Clo., Erith 69 CS43
Arran Clo., Hem.H. 8 BA14
Arran Clo., Wall. 95 BW56
Arran Dr. E12 49 CJ33
Arran Rd. SE6 77 CE48
Arran Wk. N1 57 BZ36
Clephane Rd.
Arran Way, Esher 84 BF55
Arran Yews W5 55 BL40
Arras Ave., Mord. 86 BT53
Arretine Clo., St.Alb. 9 BE14
Arrol Rd., Beck. 87 CC52
Arrow Rd. E3 57 CE38
Arrowscout Wk., Nthlt. 54 BD38
Wayfarer Rd.
Arrowsmith Clo., Chig. 40 CN28
Arrowsmith Path, Chig. 40 CN28
Arrowsmith Rd., Chig. 40 CN28
Arrowsmith Rd., Loug. 31 CK24
Arsenal Rd. SE9 68 CK44
Artemis Clo., Grav. 81 DJ47
Arterberry Rd. SW20 75 BQ50
Arterial Ave., Rain. 59 CU38
Arterial Rd., Grays 70 DA41
Artesian Clo. NW10 55 BN36
Artesian Clo., Horn. 50 CT33
Artesian Rd. W2 56 BS39
Arthingworth St. E15 58 CG37
Arthur Ct. W2 56 BS39
Queensway
Arthur Gro. SE18 68 CM42
Arthur Henderson Ho. SW6 65 BR44
Arthur Rd. E6 58 CK37
Arthur Rd. N7 47 BX34
Arthur Rd. N9 39 CA27
Arthur Rd. SW19 76 BS48
Arthur Rd., Kings.T. 75 BM50
Arthur Rd., N.Mal. 85 BP53
Arthur Rd., Rom. 50 CP33
Arthur Rd., St.Alb. 9 BJ13
Arthur Rd., Slou. 61 AO41
Arthur Rd., West. 106 CJ61
Arthur Rd., Wind. 61 AO44
Arthur St. EC4 2 L10
Arthur St. EC4 57 BZ40
Arthur St., Bush. 27 BD24
Arthur St., Erith 69 CT43
Arthur St., Grav. 81 DG47
Arthur St., Grays 71 DE43
Arthur St. W., Grav. 81 DG47
Arthur Toft Ho., Grays 71 DD43
New Rd.
Arthurdon Rd. SE4 77 CE46
Arthurs Bri. Rd., Wok. 100 AR62
Artichoke Hill E1 57 CB40
Pennington St.
Artichoke Pl. SE5 67 BZ44
Camberwell Ch. St.
Artillery Clo., Ilf. 49 CM32
Artillery La. E1 2 N7
Artillery La. E1 57 CA39
Artillery Pas. E1 2 N7
Artillery Pl. SE18 68 CK42
Artillery Pl. SW1 3 N7
Artillery Rd., Guil. 118 AR70
Artillery Row SW1 3 N7
Artillery Row SW1 66 BW41
Artillery Row, Grav. 81 DH47
Artillery Ter., Guil. 118 AR70
Artillery Yd. EC2 57 CA38
Worship St.
Artington Clo., Orp. 97 CM56
Artington Wk., Guil. 118 AR72
Artizan St. E1 2 N8
Artizan St. E1 57 CA39
Harrow Pl.
Arundel Ave., Epsom 94 BP58
Arundel Ave., Mord. 85 BR52
Arundel Ave., S.Croy. 96 CB58
Arundel Clo. E15 49 CG35
Arundel Clo. SW11 76 BU46
Arundel Clo., Bex. 79 CQ46
Arundel Clo., Chsnt. 21 CB17
Arundel Clo., Croy. 86 BY55
Arundel Clo., Hmptn. 74 BF49
Arundel Clo., Hem.H. 8 AZ13
Arundel Ct., Slou. 62 AR42
Arundel Dr., Borwd. 28 BN24
Arundel Dr., Har. 45 BE35
Arundel Dr., Orp. 98 CO56
Arundel Dr., Wdf.Grn. 40 CH29
Arundel Gdns. N21 38 BY26
Arundel Gdns. W11 55 BR40
Arundel Gdns., Edg. 37 BN29
Cressingham Rd.
Arundel Gdns., Ilf. 50 CO34
Arundel Great Ct. WC2 2 C10
Arundel Gro. N16 48 CA35
Arundel Pl. N1 56 BY36
Arundel Rd., Barn. 29 BU24
Arundel Rd., Croy. 87 BZ53
Arundel Rd., Dart. 70 CV45
Arundel Rd., Dor. 119 BJ71
Arundel Rd., Houns. 64 BD45
Arundel Rd., Kings.T. 85 BM51
Arundel Rd., Rom. 42 CW30
Arundel Rd., Sutt. 94 BR57
Arundel Rd., Uxb. 53 AW37
Arundel Sq. N7 56 BY36
Arundel St. WC2 2 C10
Arundel St. WC2 56 BX40
Arundel Ter. SW13 65 BP43
Arvon Rd. N5 47 BY35
Ascalon St. SW8 66 BW43
Ascension Rd., Rom. 41 CS29
Ascham Dr. E4 39 CE29
Ascham End E17 39 CD30
Ascham St. NW5 47 BW35
Aschurch Rd., Croy. 87 CA54
Ascot Clo., Borwd. 28 BM25
Ascot Clo., Ilf. 40 CN29
Ascot Clo., Nthlt. 54 BF36
Ascot Gdns., Enf. 30 CC22
Ascot Gdns., Horn. 51 CW35
Ascot Gdns., Sthl. 54 BE39
Ascot Rd. E6 58 CK38
Ascot Rd. N15 48 BZ32
Ascot Rd. N18 39 CB28
Ascot Rd. SW17 76 BV50
Ascot Rd., Felt. 73 AZ48
Ascot Rd., Grav. 81 DG48
Ascot Rd., Maid. 61 AG42
Ascot Rd., Orp. 88 CN52
Ascot Rd., Wat. 26 BB25
Ascots La., Hat. 5 BR10
Ascott Ave. W5 65 BL41
Ash Clo. SE20 87 CC51
Ash Clo., Abb.L. 17 BA19
Ash Clo., Brwd. 33 CZ25
Ash Clo., Cars. 86 BU55
Ash Clo., Edg. 37 BN28
Ash Clo., Hat. 20 BS16
Ash Clo., N.Mal. 85 BN51
Ash Clo., Orp. 88 CM53
Ash Clo., Red. 113 BW68
Ash Clo., Rom. 41 CR29
Ash Clo., Sid. 79 CO48
Ash Clo., Slou. 62 AT41
Ash Clo., Stan. 36 BJ29
Ash Clo., Swan. 89 CS51
Ash Clo., Uxb. 35 AX30
Ash Clo., Wat. 26 BC21
Ash Clo., Wok. 100 AS63
Ash Clo., Wok. 101 AW61
Ash Ct., Epsom 94 BN56
Ash Dr., Hat. 10 BP14
Ash Dr., Red. 121 BV71
Ash Grn., Loug. 31 CK23
Ash Grn., Uxb. 53 AW36
Ash Gro. E8 57 CB37
Ash Gro. N13 39 BZ27
Ash Gro. NW2 46 BQ35
Ash Gro. SE20 87 CC51
Ash Gro. W5 65 BL41
Ash Gro., Enf. 39 CA26
Ash Gro., Felt. 73 BB47
Ash Gro., Guil. 118 AQ70
Ash Gro., Hayes 53 BA40
Ash Gro., Hem.H. 8 AY15
Ash Gro., Houns. 64 BD44
Ash Gro., Saw. 6 CR6
Ash Gro., Sthl. 54 BF39
Ash Gro., Stai. 73 AX50
Ash Gro., Uxb. 35 AX30
Ash Gro., Wem. 45 BJ35
Ash Gro., West Dr. 53 AY40
Ash Gro., W.Wick. 87 CF55
Ash Hill Clo., Bush. 36 BF26
Ash Hill Dr., Pnr. 45 BD31
Ash La., Croy. 95 BY56
Ash La., Horn. 51 CW31
Ash La., Rom. 41 CU29
Ash La., Sev. 99 DB59
Ash La., Wind. 61 AL44
Ash Platt Rd., Sev. 108 CW63
Ash Ride, Enf. 29 BY21
Ash Rd. E15 49 CG35
Ash Rd., Croy. 87 CE55
Ash Rd., Dart. 80 CV47
Ash Rd. (Hawley), Dart. 80 CW49
Ash Rd., Grav. 81 DH49
Ash Rd., Hartley 90 DC52
Ash Rd., Orp. 97 CN57
Ash Rd., Sev. 99 DB56
Ash Rd., Shep. 83 AZ52
Ash Rd., Sutt. 85 BR54
Ash Rd., West. 115 CM66
Ash Rd., Wok. 100 AS63
Ash Row, Brom. 88 CL54
Ash Tree Clo., Croy. 87 CD53
Ash Tree Clo., Sev. 99 CZ58
Ash Tree Dr.
Ash Tree Clo., Surb. 85 BL54
Ash Tree Dell NW9 46 BN32
Ash Tree Dr., Sev. 99 CZ58
Ash Tree Fld., Harl. 6 CL10
Ash Tree Way, Croy. 87 CD53
Ash Vale, Rick. 34 AU28
Ash Vw. Gdns., Ashf. 73 AY49
Ash Wk. SW2 76 BX47
Ash Wk., Wem. 45 BK34
Ashbeam Clo., Brwd. 42 DA28
Ashbourne Ave. E18 49 CH31
Ashbourne Ave. N20 38 BU27
Ashbourne Ave. NW11 46 BR32
Ashbourne Ave., Bexh. 69 CQ43
Ashbourne Ave., Har. 45 BG34
Ashbourne Clo. N12 38 BS28
Ashbourne Clo. W5 55 BM39
Ashbourne Clo., Couls. 104 BW62
Ashbourne Ct. E5 48 CC35
Clapton Pk. Est.
Ashbourne Gro. NW7 37 BN28
Ashbourne Gro. SE22 67 CA45
Ashbourne Gro. W4 65 BO42
Ashbourne Ri., Orp. 97 CM56
Ashbourne Rd. W5 55 BL38
Ashbourne Rd., Brox. 12 CD14
Ashbourne Rd., Mitch. 76 BV50
Ashbourne Rd., Rom. 42 CV28
Ashbourne Sq., Nthwd. 35 BB29
Rofant Rd.
Ashbourne Ter. SW19 75 BR50
Ashbourne Way NW11 46 BR32
Ashbourne Ave.
Ashbridge Rd. E11 49 CG33
Ashbridge St. NW8 1 C5
Ashbridge St. NW8 56 BU38
Ashbrook Rd. N19 47 BW33
Ashbrook Rd., Dag. 50 CR34
Ashbrook Rd., Wind. 72 AQ47
Ashburn Gdns. SW7 66 BT42
Ashburn Ms. SW7 66 BT42
Ashburn Pl. SW7 66 BT42
Ashburnham Ave., Har. 45 BH
Ashburnham Clo. N2 47 BT
Ashburnham Clo., Wat. 35 BC
Ashburnham Dr.
Ashburnham Dr., Wat. 35 BC
Ashburnham Gdns., Har. 45 BH
Ashburnham Gdns., Upmin. 51 CY
Ashburnham Gro. SE10 67 CE
Ashburnham Pk., Esher 93 BG
Ashburnham Pl. SE10 67 CE
Ashburnham Retreat SE10 67 CE
Ashburnham Rd. NW10 55 BO
Ashburnham Rd. SW10 66 BT
Ashburnham Rd., Belv. 69 CS
Ashburnham Rd., Rich. 74 BJ
Ashburton Ave., Croy. 87 CB
Ashburton Ave., Ilf. 49 CN
Ashburton Clo., Croy. 87 CB
Ashburton Ct., Pnr. 36 BD
Ashburton Est. SW15 75 BO
Ashburton Gdns., Croy. 87 CB
Ashburton Gro. N7 47 BY
Ashburton Rd. E16 58 CH
Ashburton Rd., Croy. 87 CB
Ashburton Rd., Ruis. 44 BC
Ashburton Ter. E13 58 CH
Grasmere Rd.
Ashbury Clo., Hat. 10 BO
St. Albans Rd. W.
Ashbury Cres., Guil. 118 AU
Ashbury Dr., Uxb. 44 AZ
Ashbury Gdns., Rom. 50 CP
Ashbury Rd. SW11 66 BU
Ashby Ave., Chess. 94 BM
Ashby Clo., Horn. 51 CX
Ashby Gdns., St.Alb. 9 BG
Ashby Gro. N1 57 BZ
Ashby Ms. SE4 67 CD
Ashby Rd. N15 48 CB
Ashby Rd. SE4 67 CD
Ashby Rd., Berk. 7 AO
Ashby Rd., Wat. 26 BC
Ashby St. EC1 2
Ashby St. EC1 56 BY
Ashby Wk., Croy. 87 BZ
Beulah Gro.
Ashby Way, West Dr. 63 AZ
Ashchurch Gro. W12 65 BP
Ashchurch Pk. Vill. W12 65 BP
Ashchurch Ter. W12 65 BP
Ashcombe, Welw.G.C. 5 B
Ashcombe Ave., Surb. 84 BK
Ashcombe Gdns., Edg. 37 BM
Ashcombe Pk. NW2 46 BO
Ashcombe Rd. SW19 76 BS
Ashcombe Rd., Cars. 95 BV
Ashcombe Rd., Dor. 119 BJ
Ashcombe Rd., Red. 113 BW
Ashcombe Sq., N.Mal. 85 BN
Ashcombe St. SW6 66 BS
Ashcombe Ter., Tad. 103 BP
Ashcroft, Pnr. 36 BF
Ashcroft Ave., Sid. 79 CO
Ashcroft Clo., Guil. 118 AS
Ashcroft Cres., Sid. 79 CO
Ashcroft Dr., Uxb. 43 AV
Ashcroft Pk., Cob. 93 BE
Ashcroft Ri., Couls. 104 BX
Ashcroft Rd. E3 57 CD
Ashcroft Rd., Chess. 85 BL
Ashdale, Lthd. 111 BF
Ashdale Clo., Stai. 73 AY
Ashdale Clo., Twick. 74 BF
Ashdale Gro., Stan. 36 BH
Ashdale Rd. SE12 78 CH
Ashdale Way, Twick. 74 BF
Ashdale Clo.
Ashdales, St.Alb. 9 BG
Ashdene, Pnr. 45 BD
Ashdene Clo., Ashf. 73 BA
Cambridge Rd.
Ashdon Clo., Wdf.Grn. 40 CH
Ashdon Rd. NW10 55 BO
Ashdon Rd., Bush. 27 BD
Ashdown Clo., Beck. 87 CE
Ashdown Cres. NW5 47 BV
Ashdown Cres., Chsnt. 21 CD
Ashdown Dr., Borwd. 28 BL
Ashdown Gdns., S.Croy. 105 CB
Ashdown Rd., Enf. 30 CC
Ashdown Rd., Epsom 94 BO
Ashdown Rd., Kings.T. 85 BL
Ashdown Rd., Reig. 121 BS
Ashdown Rd., Uxb. 53 AZ
Ashdown Rd., Wat. 36 BD
Woodhall La.
Ashdown Wk. E14 67 CE
Charnwood Gdns.
Ashdown Wk., Rom. 41 CR
Ashdown Way SW17 76 BV
Ashdown Way, Amer. 25 AO
Ashen Dr., Dart. 79 CU
Ashen Gro. SW19 76 BS
Ashen Gro. Rd., Sev. 99 CX
Ashen Vale, S.Croy. 96 CC
Ashenden Rd. E5 48 CC
Ashenden Rd., Guil. 118 AP
Ashenden Wk., Slou. 43 AO
Ashendene Rd., Hert. 11 BX
Ashentree Ct. EC4 56 BY
Whitefriars St.
Asher Way E1 57 CB
Ashes La., Ton. 117 DC
Ashfield Ave., Bush. 36 BF
Ashfield Ave., Felt. 73 BC
Ashfield Clo., Rich. 75 BL
Ashfield La., Chis. 78 CL
Ashfield Par. N14 38 BW
Ashfield Rd. N4 48 BZ
Ashfield Rd. N14 38 BW
Ashfield Rd. W3 55 BO

hfield Rd., Chesh. 16 AO18
hfield St. E1 57 CB39
hfields, Loug. 31 CK23
hfields, Wat. 26 BB21
hford Ave. N8 47 BX31
hford Ave., Ashf. 73 AZ50
hford Ave., Brwd. 42 DA27
hford Ave., Hayes 54 BD39
hford Clo. E17 48 CD32
hford Clo., Ashf. 73 AY49
hford Cres., Ashf. 73 AY48
hford Cres., Enf. 30 CC23
hford Gdns., Cob. 102 BD61
hford Grn., Wat. 36 BD28
hford La., Wind. 61 AK41
hford Rd. E6 58 CL36
hford Rd. E18 40 CH30
hford Rd. NW2 46 BQ35
hford Rd., Ashf. 73 BA50
hford Rd., Felt. 73 BA49
hford Rd., Iver 52 AU37
hford Rd., Stai. 83 AX51
hford St. N1 2 M2
hford St. N1 57 CA38
hgrove Rd., Ashf. 73 BA49
hgrove Rd., Brom. 77 CF50
hgrove Rd., Ilf. 49 CN33
hgrove Rd., Sev. 116 CU67
hingdon Clo. E4 39 CF27
hington Ct. SE26 77 CB49
hington Rd. SW6 65 BR44
hlake Rd. SW16 76 BX49
hland Pl. W1 1 G6
hland Pl. W1 56 BV39
hlar Pl. SE18 68 CL42
hlea Rd., Ger.Cr. 34 AS30
hleigh Ave., Egh. 72 AU50
hleigh Clo., Amer. 25 AP23
hleigh Ct. N4 48 BZ32
Wiltshire Gdns.
hleigh Gdns., Sutt. 86 BS55
hleigh Gdns., Upmin. 51 CY35
hleigh Rd. SE20 87 CB52
hleigh Rd. SW14 65 BO45
hley Ave., Epsom 94 BN60
Ashley Rd.
hley Ave., Ilf. 40 CL30
hley Ave., Mord. 86 BS53
hley Clo. NW4 37 BQ30
hley Clo., Lthd. 111 BE66
hley Clo., Pnr. 35 BC30
hley Clo., Sev. 107 CU65
hley Clo., Walt. 83 BB54
hley Clo., Welw.G.C. 5 BQ7
hley Ct., Hat. 10 BP12
hley Cres. N22 38 BY30
hley Cres. SW11 66 BV45
hley Dr., Bans. 95 BS60
hley Dr., Borwd. 28 BN25
hley Dr., Islw. 64 BH43
hley Dr., Twick. 74 BF47
hley Dr., Walt. 83 BC55
hley Gdns. N13 39 BZ28
hley Gdns. SW1 3 M7
hley Gdns., Grays 71 DE40
hley Gdns., Orp. 97 CN56
hley Gdns., Rich. 74 BK48
hley Gdns., Wem. 46 BL34
hley Grn. La., Chesh. 16 AO17
hley Gro., Loug. 31 CK24
hley La. NW4 37 BQ30
hley La., Croy. 95 BY56
hley Pk. Ave., Walt. 84 BB55
hley Pk. Cres., Walt. 83 BB54
hley Pk. Rd., Walt. 83 BC55
hley Pl. SW1 3 L7
hley Pl. SW1 66 BW41
hley Ri., Walt. 92 BB56
hley Rd. E4 39 CE29
hley Rd. E7 58 CJ36
hley Rd. N17 48 CB31
hley Rd. N19 47 BX33
hley Rd. SW19 76 BS50
hley Rd., Dor. 119 BG72
hley Rd., Enf. 30 CC23
hley Rd., Epsom 94 BN60
hley Rd., Hmptn. 84 BF51
hley Rd., Rich. 65 BL45
Jocelyn Rd.
hley Rd., St.Alb. 9 BK13
hley Rd., Sev. 107 CU65
hley Rd., T.Ditt. 84 BH53
hley Rd., Th.Hth. 86 BX52
hley Rd., Uxb. 53 AW37
hley Rd., Walt. 92 BB56
hley Rd., Wok. 100 AP62
hley Wk. NW7 37 BQ29
hleys, Rick. 34 AV26
hlin Rd. E15 48 CF35
hling Rd., Croy. 87 CB54
hlone Rd. SW15 65 BQ45
hlyn Clo., Bush. 27 BE24
hlyn Gro., Horn. 51 CV31
hlyns Ct., Berk. 7 AQ13
hlyns La., Epp. 14 CT13
hlyns Pk., Cob. 93 BE60
hlyns Rd., Berk. 7 AQ13
hlyns Rd., Epp. 22 CN18
hlyns Way, Chess. 93 BK57
hmead N14 29 BW25
hmead Dr., Uxb. 44 AW34
hmead La., Uxb. 44 AW34
hmead Rd. SE8 67 CE44
hmead Rd., Felt. 73 BC47
hmere Ave., Beck. 87 CF51
hmere Clo., Sutt. 94 BQ56
hmere Gro. SW2 66 BX45
hmill St. NW1 1 C6
hmill St. NW1 56 BU39
hmole Pl. SW8 66 BX43
hmole St. SW8 66 BX43
hmore Gdns., Hem.H. 8 AZ14
hmore Gro., Well. 68 CM45
hmore La., Kes. 97 CJ59
Ashmore Rd. W9 55 BR38
Ashmount Rd. N15 48 CA32
Ashmount Rd. N19 47 BW33
Ashmour Gdns., Rom. 41 CS30
Ashneal Gdns., Har. 45 BG34
Ashness Gdns., Grnf. 54 BJ36
Ashness Rd. SW11 76 BU46
Ashridge Clo., Har. 45 BK32
Ashridge Clo., Hem.H. 16 AS17
Pembridge Rd.
Ashridge Cres. SE18 68 CM43
Ashridge Dr., St.Alb. 18 BE18
Ashridge Dr., Wat. 35 BC28
Ashridge Gdns. N13 38 BW28
Ashridge Gdns., Pnr. 45 BE31
Ashridge La., Chesh. 16 AR19
Ashridge Ri., Berk. 7 AP12
Ashridge Way, Mord. 85 BR52
Ashridge Way, Sun. 73 BC50
Ashtead Gap, Lthd. 102 BJ61
Ashtead Rd. E5 48 CB33
Ashtead Wds. Rd., Ash. 102 BK62
Ashton Clo., Sutt. 94 BR56
Gander Grn. La.
Ashton Clo., Wey. 92 BC57
Ashton Gdns., Houns. 64 BE45
Ashton Gdns., Rom. 50 CQ32
Ashton Rd. E15 48 CF35
Ashton Rd., Enf. 30 CD21
Ashton Rd., Rom. 42 CV29
Ashton Rd., Wok. 100 AP62
Ashton St. E14 57 CF40
Ashtree Ave., Mitch. 86 BT51
Ashtree Clo., Orp. 97 CL56
Broadwater Gdns.
Ashtree Rd., Wat. 26 BC21
Ashtree Way, Hem.H. 8 AW14
Ashurst Clo. SE20 77 CB51
Ashurst Clo., Dart. 69 CT45
Ashurst Clo., Ken. 105 BZ61
Ashurst Clo., Nthwd. 35 BB29
Ashurst Dr., Ilf. 49 CL32
Ashurst Dr., Shep. 83 AY52
Ashurst Dr., Tad. 112 BM68
Ashurst Rd. N12 38 BU28
Ashurst Rd., Barn. 29 BU25
Ashurst Wk., Croy. 87 CB55
Ashvale Dr., Upmin. 51 CZ34
Ashvale Gdns., Rom. 41 CS28
Ashvale Gdns., Upmin. 51 CZ34
Ashvale Rd. SW17 76 BU49
Ashville Rd. E11 48 CF34
Ashwater Rd. SE12 78 CH47
Ashwell Clo. E6 58 CK39
Northumberland Rd.
Ashwell St., St.Alb. 9 BG13
Ashwells Rd., Brwd. 33 CY24
Ashwells Way, Ch.St.G. 34 AR27
Ashwin St. E8 57 CA36
Ashwindham Ct., Wok. 100 AP62
Ashwood, Warl. 105 CC63
Ashwood Ave., Rain. 59 CU38
Ashwood Ave., Uxb. 53 AZ39
Ashwood Gdns., Croy. 96 CF57
Ashwood Gdns., Hayes 63 BB42
Ashwood Pk., Lthd. 102 BG65
Ashwood Rd. E4 39 CF27
Ashwood Rd., Egh. 72 AQ50
Ashwood Rd., Pot.B. 20 BS20
Ashwood Rd., Wok. 100 AS62
Ashworth Pl., Guil. 118 AP70
Ashworth Rd. W9 56 BS38
Aske St. N1 2 M2
Aske St. N1 57 CA38
Pitfield St.
Askern Clo., Bexh. 69 CP45
Askew Bldgs. W12 65 BP41
Askew Rd.
Askew Cres. W12 55 BO40
Askew Fm. Rd., Grays 71 DC42
Askew Rd. W12 55 BO40
Askew Rd., Nthwd. 35 BA27
Askham Ct. W12 55 BP40
Askham Rd. W12 55 BP40
Askill Dr. SW15 75 BR46
Askwith Rd., Rain. 59 CS38
Asland Rd. E15 57 CF37
Aslett St. SW18 76 BT47
Asmar Clo., Couls. 104 BX61
Asmara Rd. NW2 46 BR35
Asmuns Hill NW11 47 BS32
Asmuns Pl. NW11 46 BR32
Aspasia Clo., St.Alb. 9 BH14
Aspdin Rd., Grav. 81 DE48
Aspect Row, Hem.H. 8 AW12
Aspen Clo. N19 47 BW34
Hargrave Pk.
Aspen Clo. W5 65 BL41
Aspen Clo., Cob. 102 BE61
Aspen Clo., Guil. 118 AU69
Aspen Clo., Orp. 98 CO56
Aspen Clo., Stai. 72 AV49
Moormede Cres.
Aspen Clo., Swan. 89 CS51
Aspen Clo., West Dr. 53 AY40
Aspen Copse, Brom. 88 CK51
Aspen Dr., Wem. 45 BJ34
Aspen Gdns. W6 65 BP42
Bridge Ave.
Aspen Gdns., Mitch. 86 BV53
Aspen Grn., Erith 69 CQ41
Aspen Gro., Upmin. 51 CW35
Aspen La., Nthlt. 54 BE38
Aspen Pk. Dr., Wat. 26 BC21
Aspen Way E14 57 CE40
Aspen Way, Bans. 94 BQ60
Aspen Way, Enf. 30 CC21
Aspenlea Rd. W6 65 BQ43
Aspern Rd. NW3 47 BU35
Aspinall Rd. SE4 67 CC45
Aspinden Rd. SE16 67 CB42
Aspledene, Grav. 81 DH50
Aspley Rd. SW18 76 BS46
Asplins Rd. N17 39 CB30
Asquith Clo., Dag. 50 CP33
Crystal Way
Ass Ho. La., Har. 36 BF28
Assam St. E1 57 CB39
Assembly Pas. E1 57 CC39
Assembly Wk., Cars. 86 BU54
Assher Rd., Walt. 84 BE55
Astall Clo., Har. 36 BH30
Astbury Rd. SE15 67 CC44
Aste St. E14 67 CF41
Astell St. SW3 3 D10
Astell St. SW3 66 BU42
Aster Pl. SE1 67 BZ41
Asteys Row N1 57 BZ36
Asthall Gdns., Ilf. 49 CM31
Astle St. SW11 66 BV44
Astleham Rd., Shep. 83 AY52
Astley, Grays 71 DC43
Astley Ave. NW2 46 BQ35
Astley Rd., Hem.H. 8 AX13
Aston Ave., Har. 45 BK33
Aston Clo., Ash. 102 BK62
Aston Clo., Sid. 79 CO48
Aston Grn., Houns. 64 BD44
Aston Mead, Wind. 61 AM44
Aston Ms., Rom. 50 CO33
Reynolds Ave.
Aston Rd. SW20 85 BQ51
Approach Rd.
Aston Rd. W5 54 BK39
Aston Rd., Esher 93 BH57
Aston St. E14 57 CD39
Aston Vw., Hem.H. 8 AZ10
Aston Way, Epsom 103 BO61
Aston Way, Pot.B. 20 BT19
Astons Rd., Nthwd. 35 BA27
Astonville St. SW18 76 BS47
Astor Ave., Rom. 50 CS32
Astor Clo., Kings.T. 75 BM50
Astor Clo., Wey. 92 AX56
Astor Rd., Sev. 99 CZ57
Astoria Wk. SW9 66 BY45
Astra Clo., Horn. 59 CU36
Astra Dr., Grav. 81 DJ49
Astrop Ms. W6 65 BQ41
Astrop Ter. W6 65 BQ41
Astwick Ave., Hat. 10 BO11
Astwood Ms. SW7 66 BS42
Asylum Arch Rd., Red. 121 BU72
Asylum Rd. SE15 67 CB43
Atalanta Clo., Pur. 95 BY58
Atalanta St. SW6 65 BQ44
Atbara Ct., Tedd. 74 BJ50
Atbara Rd., Tedd. 74 BJ50
Atcham Rd., Houns. 64 BG45
Atcost Rd., Bark. 59 CO39
Atheldene Rd. SW18 76 BS47
Athelney St. SE6 77 CE48
Athelstan Clo., Rom. 42 CW30
Athelstan Rd., Har. 36 BG30
Athelstan Rd., Kings.T. 85 BL52
Villiers Rd.
Athelstan Rd., Rom. 42 CW30
Athelstan Rd., Welw.G.C. 5 BQ8
Broadwater Cres.
Athelstan Wk. N., Welw.G.C. 5 BR8
Athelstan Wk. S., Welw.G.C. 5 BQ8
Athelstane Gro. E3 57 CD37
Athelstane Ms. N4 47 BY33
Stroud Grn. Rd.
Athelstone Rd., Hem.H. 8 AY15
Athena Clo., Har. 45 BG34
Athena Pl., Nthwd. 35 BB30
The Dr.
Athenaeum Rd. N20 38 BT26
Athenlay Rd. SE15 77 CC46
Atherden Rd. E5 48 CC35
Atherfield Rd., Reig. 121 BT72
Atherfold Rd. SW9 66 BX45
Atherley Way, Houns. 74 BE47
Heath Side
Atherstone Ms. SW7 66 BT42
Atherton Clo., Guil. 118 AS73
Atherton Clo., Stai. 73 AX46
Atherton Ct. (Eton), Wind. 61 AO43
Atherton Dr. SW19 75 BQ49
Atherton End, Saw. 6 CQ5
Atherton Gdns., Grays 71 DH42
Atherton Heights, Wem. 54 BK36
Bridgewater Rd.
Atherton Ms. E7 58 CG36
Atherton Pl., Har. 45 BG31
Atherton Pl., Sthl. 54 BF40
Longford Ave.
Atherton Rd. E7 49 CG35
Atherton Rd. SW13 65 BP43
Atherton Rd., Ilf. 40 CK30
Atherton St. SW11 66 BU44
Athlon Rd., Wem. 54 BK37
Athlone Clo. E5 48 CB35
Goulton Rd.
Athlone Clo., Esher 93 BH57
Athlone Clo., Rad. 27 BJ21
Athlone Gdns. W10 55 BR39
Faraday Rd.
Athlone Rd. SW2 76 BX47
Athlone Sq., Wind. 61 AO44
Ward Royal
Athlone St. NW5 56 BV36
Athol Clo., Pnr. 35 BC30
Athol Gdns., Pnr. 35 BC30
Athol Rd., Erith 69 CS42
Athol Sq. E14 57 CF39
Athol Way, Uxb. 53 AZ38
Athole Gdns., Enf. 30 CA25
Atholl Rd., Ilf. 50 CO33
Atkins Clo., Wok. 100 AQ62
Greythorne Rd.
Atkins Rd. E10 48 CE32
Atkins Rd. SW12 76 BW47
Atkinson Clo., Orp. 97 CN56
Atkinson Rd. E16 58 CJ39
Atlanta Boul., Rom. 50 CT32
Atlantic Rd. SW9 66 BY45
Atlas Gdns. SE7 68 CJ42
Atlas Ms. N7 56 BX36
Atlas Rd. E13 58 CH37
Atlas Rd. NW10 55 BO38
Atlas Rd., Wem. 46 BN35
Atley Rd. E3 57 CE37
Atney Rd. SW15 65 BR45
Atria Rd., Nthwd. 35 BC28
Atterbury Rd. N4 47 BY32
Wightman Rd.
Atterbury St. SW1 3 Q9
Atterbury St. SW1 66 BX42
Attewood Ave. NW10 46 BO34
Attewood Rd., Nthlt. 54 BE36
Attfield Clo. N20 38 BT27
Attimore Clo., Welw.G.C. 5 BP8
Attimore Rd., Welw.G.C. 5 BP8
Attle Clo., Uxb. 53 AZ37
Attlee Clo., Hayes 53 BC38
Attlee Ct., Grays 71 DD41
Lucas Rd.
Attlee Dr., Dart. 80 CX46
Attlee Rd. SE28 59 CO40
Attlee Rd., Hayes 53 BC38
Attlee Ter. E17 48 CE31
Attneave St. WC1 2 D3
Attneave St. WC1 56 BY38
Attwood Clo., S.Croy. 96 CB60
Atwater Clo. SW2 76 BY47
Atwell Clo. E10 48 CE32
Belmont Pk. Rd.
Atwell Rd. SE15 67 CB44
Atwood, Lthd. 102 BE65
Atwood Ave., Rich. 65 BM44
Atwood Rd. W6 65 BP42
Atwoods All., Rich. 65 BM44
Kew Gdns. Rd.
Atworth St. E14 67 CF41
Auberon St. E16 58 CK40
Aubert Pk. N5 47 BY35
Aubert Rd. N5 47 BY35
Aubretia Clo., Rom. 42 CW30
Sunflower Way
Aubrey Ave., St.Alb. 18 BK16
Aubrey Pl. NW8 56 BT37
Aubrey Rd. E17 48 CE31
Aubrey Rd. N8 47 BX32
Aubrey Rd. W8 55 BR40
Aubrey Wk. W8 55 BR40
Aubreys Rd., Hem.H. 7 AV14
Aubyn Hill SE27 77 BZ49
Aubyn Sq. SW15 75 BP46
Auckland Ave., Rain. 59 CT38
Auckland Clo. SE19 87 CA51
Auckland Clo., Enf. 30 CB22
Auckland Clo., Til. 71 DG44
Auckland Gdns. SE19 87 CA51
Auckland Hill SE27 77 BZ49
Auckland Ri. SE19 87 CA51
Auckland Rd. E10 48 CE34
Auckland Rd. SE19 87 CA51
Auckland Rd. SW11 66 BU45
Auckland Rd., Cat. 105 CA64
Auckland Rd., Ilf. 49 CL33
Auckland Rd., Kings.T. 85 BL52
Auckland Rd., Pot.B. 19 BQ19
Auckland St. SE11 66 BX42
Kennington La.
Auden Pl. NW1 56 BV37
Auden Pl. (Cheam), Sutt. 94 BQ56
Audleigh Pl., Chig. 40 CL29
Audley Clo. SW11 66 BV45
Audley Clo., Borwd. 28 BM24
Audley Clo., Wey. 92 AW56
Audley Ct. E18 49 CG31
Audley Ct., Pnr. 36 BD30
Audley Ct., Twick. 74 BG48
Audley Dr., Warl. 105 CC61
Audley Firs, Walt. 93 BD56
Audley Gdns., Ilf. 49 CN34
Audley Gdns., Loug. 31 CM23
Audley Gdns., Wal.Abb. 21 CF20
Audley Pl., Sutt. 95 BS57
Audley Rd. NW4 46 BP32
Audley Rd. W5 55 BL39
Audley Rd., Enf. 29 BY23
Audley Rd., Rich. 75 BL46
Audley Sq. W1 3 H2
Audley Wk., Orp. 89 CP53
Edmund Rd.
Audrey Clo., Beck. 87 CE53
Audrey Gdns., Wem. 45 BJ34
Audrey Rd., Ilf. 49 CL34
Audrey St. E2 57 CB37
Audric Clo., Kings.T. 85 BM51
Audwick Clo., Chsht. 21 CD17
Ashdown Cres.
Augur Clo., Stai. 72 AV49
Richmond Rd.
Augurs La. E13 58 CH38
August End, Slou. 52 AS39
Augusta Rd., Twick. 74 BG48
Augusta St. E14 57 CE39
Augustine Clo., Slou. 62 AV45
Augustine Rd. W14 65 BQ41
Augustine Rd., Har. 36 BG30
Augustine Rd., Orp. 89 CP52
Augustus Clo., Brent. 64 BK43
Augustus Clo., St.Alb. 9 BF14
Augustus Ct. SW16 76 BW48
Augustus La., Orp. 89 CO55
Augustus Rd. SW19 75 BQ47
Augustus St. NW1 1 K1
Augustus St. NW1 56 BV37
Aukingford Gdns., Ong. 24 CW17
Epping Rd.
Aultone Way, Cars. 86 BU55
Aultone Way, Sutt. 86 BS55
Aurelia Gdns., Croy. 86 BX53
Aurelia Rd., Croy. 86 BX53
Auriel Ave., Dag. 59 CS36
Auriga Ms. N16 48 BZ35
Auriol Clo., Wor.Pk. 85 BO55
Auriol Dr., Grnf. 54 BG36
Auriol Dr., Uxb. 53 AZ36
Auriol Pk. Rd., Wor.Pk. 85 BO55
Auriol Rd. W14 65 BR42
Aust Rd., Grav. 81 DH47
Austell Gdns. NW7 37 BO27
Austen Clo. SE28 59 CO40
Austen Clo., Green. 80 DB46
Austen Clo., Loug. 31 CM24
Austen Clo., Til. 71 DH44
Coleridge Rd.
Austen Gdns., Dart. 70 CW45
Austen Pl., Guil. 118 AS71
Austen Rd., Guil. 118 AS71
Austen Rd., Har. 45 BF34
Austenway, Ger.Cr. 43 AR31
Austenwood Clo., Ger.Cr. 34 AR30
Austenwood La., Ger.Cr. 34 AR30
Austin Ave., Brom. 88 CK53
Austin Clo. SE23 77 CD47
Brockley Vw.
Austin Clo., Ken. 104 BY62
Austin Clo., Twick. 74 BK46
Austin Friars EC2 2 L8
Austin Friars EC2 57 BZ39
Austin Friars Pas. EC2 2 L8
Austin Friars Pas. EC2 57 BZ39
Austin Friars
Austin Friars Sq. EC2 2 L8
Austin Rd. SW11 66 BV44
Austin Rd., Grav. 81 DF47
Austin Rd., Hayes 63 BB41
Austin Rd., Orp. 89 CO53
Austin St. E2 2 P3
Austin St. E2 57 CA38
Austin Waye, Uxb. 53 AX37
Austins La., Uxb. 44 BA34
Austins Mead, Hem.H. 16 AT17
Austins Pl., Hem.H. 8 AX13
Austral Clo., Sid. 78 CN48
Longlands Rd.
Austral Dr., Horn. 51 CV33
Austral St. SE11 4 F8
Austral St. SE11 66 BY42
Australia Rd. W12 55 BP40
Australia Rd., Slou. 62 AQ41
Austyn Gdns., Surb. 85 BM54
Autumn Clo., Enf. 30 CB23
Autumn Clo., Slou. 61 AM40
Autumn Glades, Hem.H. 8 BA14
Autumn Gro., Welw.G.C. 5 BS9
Autumn St. E3 57 CE37
Auxiliaries Way, Uxb. 43 AV32
Avalon Clo. W13 54 BJ39
Avalon Clo., Enf. 29 BY23
Avalon Clo., Orp. 89 CP55
Avalon Clo., Wat. 18 BE19
Avalon Rd. SW6 66 BS44
Avalon Rd. W13 54 BJ38
Avalon Rd., Orp. 89 CO55
Avard Gdns., Orp. 97 CM56
Isabella Dr.
Avarn Rd. SW17 76 BU50
Ave Maria La. EC4 2 G9
Avebury, Slou. 61 AN40
Avebury Pk., Surb. 84 BK54
Avebury Rd. E11 48 CF33
Avebury Rd. SW19 85 BR51
Avebury Rd., Orp. 88 CM55
Aveley By-Pass, S.Ock. 60 CY40
Aveley Clo., S.Ock. 60 CY40
High St.
Aveley Rd., Rom. 50 CS31
Aveley Rd., Upmin. 60 CX36
Aveline St. SE11 66 BX42
Aveling Clo., Pur. 95 BX60
Aveling Pk. Rd. E17 39 CE30
Avelon Rd., Rain. 59 CU37
Avelon Rd., Rom. 41 CS29
Avenell Rd. N5 47 BY34
Avening Rd. SW18 76 BS47
Avening Ter. SW18 76 BS46
Avenons Rd. E13 58 CH38
Avenue, The E4 39 CF29
Avenue, The E11 49 CH32
Avenue, The N3 38 BS30
Avenue, The N8 47 BY31
Avenue, The N10 38 BW30
Avenue, The N11 38 BV28
Avenue, The N17 39 BZ30
Avenue, The NW6 55 BR36
Avenue, The SE7 68 CJ43
Avenue, The SE10 67 CF43
Avenue, The SW4 76 BV46
Avenue, The SW18 76 BU47
Avenue, The W4 65 BO41
Avenue, The W13 54 BJ40
Avenue, The, Amer. 25 AO22
Avenue, The, Barn. 28 BR24
Avenue, The, Beck. 87 CE51
Avenue, The, Bet. 120 BM70
Avenue, The, Bex. 79 CP47
Avenue, The, Brwd. 122 DC29
Avenue, The, Brom. 88 CJ52
Avenue, The, Bush. 27 BE24
Avenue, The, Cars. 95 BV57
Avenue, The, Couls. 104 BW61
Avenue, The, Croy. 87 CA55
Avenue, The, Egh. 72 AT49
Avenue, The, Epsom 94 BQ57
Avenue, The, Esher 93 BH57
Avenue, The, Grav. 81 DG47
Avenue, The, Green. 70 DA45
Avenue, The, Guil. 118 AO74
Avenue, The, Hmptn. 74 BE50
Avenue, The, Harl. 6 CM9
Avenue, The, Har. 36 BH30
Avenue, The, Hem.H. 7 AV13
Avenue, The, Hodd. 12 CD13
Avenue, The, Horn. 51 CV34
Avenue, The, Houns. 74 BF46

Ave–Bal

Avenue, The (Cranford), Houns. 63 BC44
Avenue, The, Kes. 88 CJ55
Avenue, The, Loug. 31 CJ25
Avenue, The, Nthwd. 35 BA29
Avenue, The, Orp. 88 CN55
Avenue, The (St. Pauls Cray), Orp. 79 CO50
Avenue, The, Pnr. 45 BE32
Avenue, The (Hatch End), Pnr. 36 BE29
Avenue, The, Pot.B. 19 BR18
Avenue, The, Rad. 18 BJ20
Avenue, The, Red. 121 BX72
Avenue, The, Rich. 65 BL44
Avenue, The, Rom. 50 CS31
Avenue, The, Stai. 83 AW51
Avenue, The (Sunnymeads), Stai. 62 AR45
Avenue, The, Sun. 83 BC51
Avenue, The, Surb. 85 BL53
Avenue, The, Sutt. 94 BR58
Avenue, The, Tad. 103 BP64
Avenue, The, Twick. 74 BJ46
Avenue, The (Cowley), Uxb. 53 AX38
Avenue, The (Ickenham), Uxb. 44 AZ35
Avenue, The, Wat. 26 BC23
Avenue, The, Wem. 46 BL33
Avenue, The, West Dr. 63 AY41
Avenue, The, W.Wick. 87 CF54
Avenue, The, West. 106 CL65
Avenue, The, Wey. 92 AW58
Avenue, The, Whyt. 105 CB63
Avenue, The, Wind. 72 AQ46
Avenue, The, Wok. 91 AP58
Avenue, The, Wor.Pk. 85 BO55
Avenue App., Kings L. 17 AZ18
Avenue Clo. N14 29 BW25
Avenue Clo. NW2 55 BQ36
Avenue Clo. NW8 56 BU37
Avenue Clo., Houns. 63 BC44
Avenue Clo., Rom. 42 CW29
Avenue Clo., Tad. 103 BP64
Avenue Clo., West Dr. 63 AX41
Avenue Ct. N14 29 BW25
Avenue Rd.
Avenue Cres. W3 65 BM41
Avenue Cres., Houns. 63 BC43
Avenue Elmers, Surb. 85 BL53
Avenue Gdns. SE25 87 CA51
Avenue Gdns. SW14 65 BO45
Avenue Gdns. W3 65 BM41
Avenue Gdns., Houns. 63 BC43
Avenue Gdns., Tedd. 74 BH50
Avenue Ms. N10 47 BV31
Queens Ave.
Avenue Ms. NW6 47 BS35
Finchley Rd.
Avenue Pk. Rd. SE27 76 BY48
Avenue Ri., Bush. 27 BF25
Avenue Rd. E7 49 CH35
Avenue Rd. N6 47 BW33
Avenue Rd. N12 38 BT28
Avenue Rd. N14 38 BV26
Avenue Rd. N15 48 BZ32
Avenue Rd. NW3 56 BT36
Avenue Rd. NW10 55 BO37
Avenue Rd. SE20 87 CC51
Avenue Rd. SE25 87 CA51
Avenue Rd. SW16 86 BW51
Avenue Rd. SW20 85 BP51
Avenue Rd. W3 65 BM41
Avenue Rd., Bans. 104 BS61
Avenue Rd., Beck. 87 CC51
Avenue Rd., Belv. 69 CR42
Avenue Rd., Bexh. 69 CQ45
Avenue Rd., Brent. 64 BK42
Avenue Rd., Brwd. 42 DB28
Avenue Rd., Cat. 105 BZ64
Avenue Rd., Cob. 102 BD61
Avenue Rd., Epp. 31 CM21
Avenue Rd., Epsom 94 BN60
Avenue Rd., Erith 69 CS43
Avenue Rd., Felt. 73 BB48
Avenue Rd., Hmptn. 84 BF51
Avenue Rd., Hodd. 12 CF13
Avenue Rd., Islw. 64 BH44
Avenue Rd., Kings.T. 85 BL52
Avenue Rd., Maid. 61 AG40
Avenue Rd., N.Mal. 85 BO52
Avenue Rd., Pnr. 45 BE31
Avenue Rd. (Chadwell Heath), Rom. 50 CP33
Avenue Rd. (Harold Wd.), Rom. 42 CW29
Avenue Rd., St.Alb. 9 BH13
Avenue Rd., Sev. 108 CV65
Avenue Rd., Sthl. 54 BE40
Avenue Rd., Stai. 72 AU49
Avenue Rd., Sutt. 95 BS58
Avenue Rd., Tedd. 74 BJ50
Avenue Rd., Wall. 95 BW57
Avenue Rd., West. 106 CK63
Avenue Rd., Wdf.Grn. 40 CJ29
Avenue S., The, Surb. 85 BL54
Avenue Ter., N.Mal. 85 BN52
Avenue Ter., Wat. 27 BE25
Avenue Vill., Red. 113 BW68
Albury Rd.
Averil Gro. SW16 76 BY50
Averill St. W6 65 BQ43
Avern Gdns., E.Mol. 84 BF52
Avern Rd., E.Mol. 84 BF53
Avery Fm. Row SW1 3 J9
Avery Gdns., Ilf. 49 CK32
Avery Hill Rd. SE9 78 CM46
Avery Row W1 1 K10
Avery Row W1 56 BV40
Avey La., Wal.Abb. 31 CG22
Avia Clo., Hem.H. 8 AX15
Aviary Clo. E16 58 CG39
Aviary Rd., Wok. 101 AW61
Aviemore Clo., Beck. 87 CD53
Aviemore Way, Beck. 87 CD53
Avignon Rd. SE4 67 CC45
Avington Clo., Guil. 118 AS70
Avington Gro. SE20 77 CC50
Avington Way SE15 67 CA43
Avior Dr., Nthwd. 35 BB28
Avis Sq. E1 57 CC39
Avoca Rd. SW17 76 BV49
Avocet Ms. SE28 68 CM41
Avon Clo., Grav. 81 DH48
Avon Clo., Hayes 54 BD38
Avon Clo., Sutt. 95 BT56
Avon Clo., Wat. 18 BD20
Avon Clo., Wey. 92 AW57
Avon Clo., Wor.Pk. 85 BP55
Avon Ct., Guil. 118 AT70
Avon Grn., S.Ock. 60 DA39
Avon Ms., Pnr. 36 BE29
Avon Path, S.Croy. 96 BZ57
Avon Pl. SE1 4 J5
Avon Pl. SE1 67 BZ41
Avon Rd. E17 48 CF31
Avon Rd. SE4 67 CE45
Avon Rd., Grnf. 54 BF38
Avon Rd., Sun. 73 BB50
Avon Rd., Upmin. 51 CY32
Avon Sq., Hem.H. 8 AY11
Avon St. SE1 67 BZ41
Avon Way E18 49 CH31
Avondale Ave. N12 38 BS28
Avondale Ave. NW2 46 BO34
Avondale Ave., Barn. 38 BU26
Avondale Ave., Esher 84 BJ55
Avondale Ave., Stai. 72 AV50
Avondale Ave., Wor.Pk. 85 BO54
Avondale Clo., Loug. 40 CK26
Avondale Clo., Walt. 93 BD56
Avondale Ct. E16 58 CG39
Avondale Rd.
Avondale Ct. E18 40 CH30
Avondale Ct., St.Alb. 9 BH13
Upper Lattimore Rd.
Avondale Cres., Enf. 30 CD24
Avondale Cres., Ilf. 49 CJ32
Avondale Dr., Hayes 53 BC40
Avondale Dr., Loug. 40 CK26
Avondale Gdns., Houns. 74 BE46
Avondale Ms., Brom. 78 CG50
Avondale Rd.
Avondale Pk. Gdns. W11 55 BQ40
Avondale Pk. Rd. W11 55 BR40
Avondale Ri. SE15 67 CA45
Avondale Rd. E16 58 CG39
Avondale Rd. E17 48 CE33
Avondale Rd. N3 38 BT30
Avondale Rd. N13 38 BY27
Avondale Rd. N15 47 BY32
Avondale Rd. SE9 78 CK48
Avondale Rd. SW14 65 BN45
Avondale Rd. SW19 76 BS49
Avondale Rd., Ashf. 73 AX48
Avondale Rd., Brom. 78 CG50
Avondale Rd., Har. 45 BH31
Avondale Rd., S.Croy. 96 BZ57
Avondale Rd., Well. 69 CP44
Avondale Sq. SE1 67 CB42
Avonley Rd. SE14 67 CC43
Avonmead, Wok. 100 AR62
Silversmiths Way
Avonmore Ave., Guil. 118 AS70
Avonmore Pl. W14 65 BR42
Avonmore Rd.
Avonmore Rd. W14 65 BR42
Avonmouth Rd., Dart. 80 CV46
Avonmouth St. SE1 4 H6
Avontar Rd., S.Ock. 60 DA38
Avonwick Rd., Houns. 64 BF44
Avril Way E4 39 CF28
Avro Way, Wall. 95 BX57
Avro Way, Wey. 92 AY58
Awlfield Ave. N17 39 BZ30
Awliscombe Rd., Well. 68 CN44
Axe St., Bark. 58 CM37
Axholme Ave., Edg. 37 BM30
Axminster Cres., Well. 69 CP44
Axminster Rd. N7 47 BX34
Axtaine Rd., Orp. 89 CP54
Axtane Clo., S.at H. 90 CY51
Millstone Clo.
Axwood, Epsom 103 BN61
Aybrook St. W1 1 G7
Aybrook St. W1 56 BV39
Aycliffe Clo., Brom. 88 CK52
Aycliffe Dr., Hem.H. 8 AY11
Aycliffe Rd. W12 55 BP40
Aycliffe Rd., Borwd. 28 BL23
Ayebridges Ave., Egh. 72 AU50
Ayelands La., New A.G. 90 DC55
Aylands Rd., Enf. 30 CC21
Ayles Rd., Hayes 53 BC38
Aylesbury Clo. E7 58 CG36
Atherton Rd.
Aylesbury Cres., Slou. 52 AO39
Aylesbury Rd. SE17 67 BZ42
Aylesbury Rd., Brom. 88 CH52
Aylesbury St. EC1 2 F5
Aylesbury St. EC1 56 BY38
Aylesbury St. NW10 46 BN34
Aylesford Ave., Beck. 87 CD53
Aylesford St. SW1 66 BW42
Aylesham La., Rom. 42 CV28
Aylesham Rd., Orp. 88 CN54
Aylestone Ave. NW6 55 BQ36
Aylesworth Spur, Wind. 72 AQ47
Ashbrook Rd.
Aylett Rd. SE25 87 CB52
Aylett Rd., Islw. 64 BH44
Aylett Rd., Upmin. 51 CY34
Ayley Cft., Enf. 30 CB25
Ayliffe Clo., Kings.T. 85 BM51
Cambridge Gdns.
Aylmer Clo., Stan. 36 BJ28
Aylmer Dr., Stan. 36 BJ28
Aylmer Rd. E11 49 CG33
Aylmer Rd. N2 47 BU32
Aylmer Rd. W12 65 BO41
Aylmer Rd., Dag. 50 CQ34
Ayloffe Rd., Dag. 59 CQ36
Ayloffs Clo., Horn. 51 CW32
Ayloffs Wk., Horn. 51 CV32
Aylsham Dr., Uxb. 44 BA34
Aylsham Rd., Hodd. 12 CF11
Aylton Est. SE16 67 CC41
Aylward Rd. SE23 77 CC48
Aylward Rd. SW20 85 BR51
Aylward St. E1 57 CC39
Aylwards Ri., Stan. 36 BJ28
Aylwin Est. SE1 67 CA41
Aylwyn Est. SE1 4 N6
Aymer Clo., Stai. 82 AV51
Aymer Dr., Stai. 82 AV51
Aynho St., Wat. 26 BC25
Aynhoe Rd. W14 65 BQ42
Aynscombe Angle, Orp. 89 CO54
Aynscombe La. SW14 65 BN45
Aynscombe Path SW14 65 BN44
Thames Bank
Ayot Grn., Welw. 5 BP6
Ayot Little Grn., Welw. 5 BO6
Ayot Path, Borwd. 28 BM22
Ayot St. Peter Rd., Welw. 5 BO5
Ayr Ct. W3 55 BM39
Monks Dr.
Ayr Grn., Rom. 41 CS29
Ayr Way, Rom. 41 CT30
Ayres Clo. E13 58 CH38
Ayres Cres. NW10 55 BN36
Ayres St. SE1 4 J4
Ayres St. SE1 67 BZ41
Ayron Rd., S.Ock. 60 DA38
Aysrome Rd. N16 48 CA34
Ayrton Rd. SW7 3 A6
Aysgarth Pk., Maid. 61 AG42
Aysgarth Rd. SE21 77 BZ46
Aytoun Rd. SW9 66 BX44
Azalea Clo. W7 54 BH40
Azalea Clo., Ilf. 49 CL35
Tulip Dr.
Azalea Ct., Wok. 100 AR63
Azalea Dr., Swan. 89 CS52
Azalea Wk., Pnr. 44 BC32
Azalea Way, Slou. 52 AS39
Azenby Rd. SE15 67 CA44
Azof St. SE10 68 CG42

B

Baalbec Rd. N5 47 BY35
Baas Hill, Brox. 12 CC14
Baas Hill Clo., Brox. 12 CD14
Baas La., Brox. 12 CD14
Babbacombe Clo., Chess. 93 BK56
Babbacombe Gdns., Ilf. 49 CK31
Babbacombe Rd., Brom. 88 CH51
Baber Dr., Felt. 74 BD46
Babington Ri., Wem. 55 BM36
Babington Rd. NW4 46 BP31
Babington Rd. SW16 76 BW49
Babington Rd., Dag. 50 CP35
Babington Rd., Horn. 50 CU33
Babmaes St. SW1 3 N2
Babmaes St. SW1 56 BW40
Jermyn St.
Babylon La., Tad. 113 BS67
Bacchus Wk. N1 2 M1
Bachelors Acre, Wind. 61 AO44
Bachelors La., Wok. 101 AY65
Baches St. N1 2 L3
Baches St. N1 57 BZ38
Back, The, Berk. 7 AT11
Back All., Dor. 119 BJ71
Back Ch. La. E1 57 CB39
Back Grn., Walt. 93 BD57
Back Hill EC1 2 D5
Back Hill EC1 56 BY38
Back La. N8 47 BX32
New Rd.
Back La. NW3 47 BT35
Flask Wk.
Back La., Bark. 58 CM37
Broadway
Back La., Bex. 79 CR47
Back La., Bish. 6 CR6
Back La., Brent. 64 BK43
Back La., Brwd. 33 DA21
Back La., Ch.St.G. 34 AQ27
Back La., Edg. 37 BN30
Back La., Grays 70 DA41
Back La., Guil. 110 AX69
Back La., Hert. 12 BZ12
Back La., Rich. 74 BK48
Back La., Rick. 25 AT22
Back La., Rom. 50 CP33
Station Rd.
Back La. (Ivy Hatch), Sev. 108 DB65
Back La. (Mackerels Plain), Sev. 116 CR67
Back La. (Plaxtol), Sev. 117 DC67
Back La., Ton. 117 DB69
Back La., Wal.Abb. 13 CJ14
Back La., Wat. 27 BH23
Back La., Welw. 5 BT6
Back Path, Red. 114 BZ70
Back Rd., Sid. 79 CO49
Back St. W3 55 BM40
Back Swan Yd. SE1 67 CA41
Bermondsey St.
Backhouse Pl. SE17 4 N9
Bacon Gro. SE1 4 P7
Bacon Gro. SE1 67 CA41
Bacon La. NW9 46 BM31
Bacon La., Edg. 37 BM30
Bacon Link, Rom. 41 CR29
Bacon St. E1 2 Q4
Bacon St. E1 57 CA38
Bacon St. E2 2 Q4
Bacon St. E2 57 CA38
Bacons Dr., Cuffley 20 BX18
Bacons La. N6 47 BV33
Bacons Mead, Uxb. 44 AW34
Bacton St. E2 57 CC38
Digby St.
Badburgham Ct., Wal.Abb. 22 CG20
Ninefields
Baddow Clo., Dag. 59 CR37
Baddow Clo., Wdf.Grn. 40 CJ29
Baddow Wk. N1 57 BZ37
Popham St.
Baden Clo., Stai. 73 AW50
Baden Clo., Wey. 92 BB57
Baden Pl. SE1 4 K4
Baden Pl. SE1 67 BZ41
Baden Powell Clo., Surb. 85 BL55
Agar Clo.
Baden Powell Rd., Sev. 107 CT64
Baden Rd. N8 47 BW31
Baden Rd., Guil. 118 AQ69
Baden Rd., Ilf. 49 CL35
Bader Clo., Ken. 105 BZ61
Bader Clo., Welw.G.C. 5 BT8
Douglas Way
Bader Gdns., Slou. 61 AN41
Bader Wk., Grav. 81 DF48
Hillary Ave.
Bader Way, Rain. 59 CU36
Badger Clo., Guil. 118 AQ69
Badger Clo., Houns. 64 BD45
Chinchilla Dr.
Badger Way, Hat. 10 BP13
Badgers Clo., Ashf. 73 AY49
Fordbridge Rd.
Badgers Clo., Enf. 29 BY24
Badgers Clo., Felt. 73 BC49
Sycamore Clo.
Badgers Clo., Har. 45 BG32
Badgers Clo., Hayes 53 BB40
Badgers Clo., Wok. 100 AQ62
St. Johns Rd.
Badgers Copse, Orp. 88 CN55
Badgers Copse, Wor.Pk. 85 BO55
Badgers Ct., Epsom 94 BO60
The Gro.
Badgers Cft. N20 37 BR26
Badgers Cft. SE9 78 CL48
Badgers Cft., Brox. 12 CD14
Badgers Cft., Hem.H. 8 BA14
Pancake La.
Badgers Hill, Vir.W. 82 AR53
Badgers Hole, Croy. 96 CC56
Badgers La., Warl. 105 CC63
Badgers Mt., Grays 71 DF41
Badgers Ri., Sev. 98 CR58
Badgers Rd., Sev. 98 CR58
Badgers Wk., N.Mal. 85 BO51
Badgers Wk., Pur. 95 BW59
Badgers Wk., Whyt. 105 CA63
Badgers Wd., Cat. 114 BZ66
Badgers Wd., Slou. 43 AO35
Badingham Dr., Lthd. 102 BH65
Badlis Rd. E17 48 CD31
Badlow Clo., Erith 69 CT43
Badminton Clo., Borwd. 28 BM23
Stratfield Rd.
Badminton Clo., Har. 45 BH31
Badminton Clo., Nthlt. 54 BF36
Badminton Pl., Brox. 12 CD13
Badminton Rd. SW12 76 BV46
Badsworth Rd. SE5 67 BZ44
Bagden Hill, Dor. 111 BG68
Bagley Clo., West Dr. 63 AY41
Bagleys La. SW6 66 BS44
Bagleys Spring, Rom. 50 CQ31
Bagot Clo., Ash. 103 BL61
Bagshot Clo. SE18 68 CL44
Bagshot Rd., Egh. 72 AR50
Bagshot Rd., Enf. 39 CA26
Bagshot Rd., Guil. 109 AO66
Bagshot Rd., Wok. 100 AO65
Bagshot St. SE17 67 CA42
Bahram Rd., Epsom 94 BN58
Baildon St. SE8 67 CD43
Watsons St.
Bailey Clo. E4 39 CF28
Bailey Clo., Grays 70 CY42
Gabion Ave.
Bailey Clo., Wind. 61 AN44
Bailey Pl. SE26 77 CC50
Bailey Rd., Dor. 119 BG72
Baillie Clo., Rain. 59 CU38
Baillie Rd., Guil. 118 AS71
Baillies Wk. W5 64 BK41
Bainbridge Rd., Dag. 50 CQ35
Bainbridge St. WC1 1 P8
Bainbridge St. WC1 56 BW39
Bainton Mead, Wok. 100 AQ62
Baird Ave., Sthl. 54 BF40
Baird Clo. NW9 46 BN32
Baird Clo., Bush. 27 BF25
Ashfield Ave.
Baird Clo., Slou. 61 AN41
Baird Gdns. SE21 77 CA49
Baird Rd., Enf. 30 CB24
Baird St. EC1 2 J4
Bairstow Clo., Borwd. 27 BK23
Baizdon Rd. SE3 68 CG44
Bakeham La., Egh. 72 AR50
Baker Boy La., Croy. 96 CD59
Baker Ct., Borwd. 28 BM23
Brook Rd.
Baker Hill Clo., Grav. 81 DF49
Baker La., Mitch. 86 BV51
Baker Rd. NW10 55 BN37
Baker Rd. SE18 68 CK43
Baker St. NW1 1 F5
Baker St. NW1 56 BU38
Baker St. W1 1
Baker St. W1 56 B
Baker St., Enf. 30 B
Baker St., Grays 71 D
Baker St., Pot.B. 28 B
Baker St., Wey. 92 A
Bakers All. SE1 57 C
Abbots La.
Bakers Ave. E17 48 C
Bakers Ave., Sev. 99 C
Bakers End SW20 85 B
Bakers Fld. N7 47 B
Bakers Gro., Welw.G.C. 5
Bakers Hill E5 48 C
Bakers Hill, Barn. 29 B
Bakers La. N6 47 B
North Hill
Bakers La. W5 54 B
The Gro.
Bakers La., Epp. 22 C
Bakers Mead, Gdse. 114 C
Bakers Meadow, Brwd. 33 D
Bakers Ms. W1 1
Bakers Ms. W1 56 B
Robert Adam St.
Bakers Pas. NW3 47 B
Oriel Pl.
Bakers Rents E2 2
Bakers Rd., Chsnt. 21 C
Bakers Rd., Uxb. 53 A
Bakers Row E15 58 CC
Bakers Row EC1 2
Bakers Row EC1 56 B
Bakers Wd., Uxb. 43 AU
Bakerscroft (Cheshunt), Wal.Cr. 21 C
High St.
Bakery Clo., Harl. 13 C
Harlow Rd.
Bakewell Ct. E5 48 CC
Clapton Pk. Est.
Bakewell Way, N.Mal. 85 BC
Bala Gdn. NW9 46 BC
Snowdon Dr.
Balaam St. E13 58 CH
Balaams La. N14 38 BW
Balaclava Rd. SE1 4
Balaclava Rd. SE1 67 CA
Balaclava Rd., Surb. 84 BK
Balben Rd. E9 57 CC
Balcaskie Rd. SE9 78 CK
Balchen Rd. SE3 68 C
Balchier Rd. SE22 77 CE
Balchins La., Dor. 119 BF
Balcombe St. NW1 1
Balcombe St. NW1 56 BU
Balcon Way, Borwd. 28 BN
Wilcox Clo.
Balcorne St. E9 57 CC
Balder Ri. SE12 78 CH
Balderton St. W1 1
Balderton St. W1 56 BV
Baldock St. E3 57 CE
Baldock Way, Borwd. 28 BL
Baldocks Rd., Epp. 31 CN
Baldry Gdns. SW16 76 BX
Baldwin Cres. SE5 67 BZ
Baldwin Cres., Guil. 118 AU
Baldwin St. EC1 2
Baldwin St. EC1 57 BZ
Baldwin Ter. N1 57 BZ
Baldwins, Welw.G.C. 5 B
Baldwins Gdns. EC1 2
Baldwins Gdns. EC1 56 BY
Baldwins Hill, Loug. 31 CK
Baldwins La., Rick. 26 AZ
Baldwins Pond, Loug. 31 CK
Baldwins Shore, Wind. 61 AO
Baldwyn Gdns. W3 55 BN
Baldwyns Est., Dart. 79 CT
Baldwyns Pk., Bex. 79 CS
Baldwyns Rd., Bex. 79 CS
Balfe St. N1 2
Balfe St. N1 56 BX
Balfern Gro. W4 65 BO
Balfern St. SW11 66 BU
Balfont Clo., S.Croy. 96 CB
Balfour App., Ilf. 49 CL
Balfour Rd.
Balfour Ave. W7 54 BH
Balfour Ave., Wok. 100 AS
Balfour Gro. N20 38 BU
Balfour Ho. W10 55 BQ
Balfour Ms. N9 39 CB
Bridge Rd.
Balfour Ms. W1 3
Balfour Pl. SW15 65 BP
Balfour Pl. W1 3
Balfour Rd. N5 48 BZ
Balfour Rd. N9 39 CB
Victoria Rd.
Balfour Rd. SE25 87 CB
Balfour Rd. SW19 76 BS
Balfour Rd. W3 55 BN
Balfour Rd. W13 64 BJ
Balfour Rd., Brom. 88 CJ
Balfour Rd., Cars. 95 BU
Balfour Rd., Grays 71 DE
Balfour Rd., Har. 45 BG
Balfour Rd., Houns. 64 BF
Balfour Rd., Ilf. 49 CL
Balfour Rd., Sthl. 64 BD
Balfour Rd., Wey. 92 AZ
Balfour St. SE17 4
Balfour St. SE17 67 BZ
Balgonie Rd. E4 39 CF
Balgores Cres., Rom. 50 CU
Balgores La., Rom. 50 CU
Balgores Sq., Rom. 50 CU
Balgowan Clo., N.Mal. 85 BO
Balgowan Rd., Beck. 87 CD
Balgowan St. SE18 68 CN
Balham Gro. SW12 76 BV
Balham High Rd. SW12 76 BV

ham High Rd. SW17 76 BV48
ham Hill SW12 76 BV47
ham New Rd. SW12 76 BV47
ham Pk. Rd. SW12 76 BU47
ham Rd. N9 39 CB27
ham Sta. Rd. SW12 76 BV47
kan Wk. E1 57 CB40
ennington St.
l La. N14 38 BW27
alaams La.
lamore Rd., Brom. 78 CH48
lance Rd. E9 57 CC36
lands N., The, Lthd. 102 BH64
lands S., The, Lthd. 102 BH65
lantine St. SW18 66 BT45
lantyne Dr., Tad. 103 BR64
lard Clo., Kings.T. 75 BN50
lard Grn., Wind. 61 AM43
lards Ave., S.Croy. 96 CB57
lards Clo., Dag. 59 CR37
lards Fm. Rd., 96 CB57
.Croy.
lards Grn., Tad. 103 BR63
lards La. N3 38 BS30
lards La. N12 38 BS30
lards La., Oxt. 115 CJ68
lards Ms., Edg. 37 BM29
igh St.
lards Ri., S.Croy. 96 CB57
lards Rd. NW2 46 BP34
lards Rd., Dag. 59 CR37
lards Way, Croy. 96 CB57
llards Way, S.Croy. 96 CB57
llast Quay SE10 67 CF42
llater Clo., Wat. 36 BD28
llater Rd. SW2 66 BX45
llater Rd., S.Croy. 96 CA56
llenger Ct., Wat. 26 BC24
alsey Rd.
llina St. SE23 77 CC47
llingdon Rd. SW11 76 BV46
llinger Ct., Berk. 7 AQ13
lliol Ave. E4 40 CG28
lliol Rd. N17 39 BZ30
lliol Rd. W10 55 BQ39
lliol Rd., Well. 69 CO44
lloch Rd. SE6 77 CF47
llogie Ave. NW10 46 BO35
llow Clo. SE5 67 BZ43
arris St.
lls Pond Rd. N1 57 BZ36
lmain Clo. W5 54 BK40
lmer Rd. E3 57 CD37
lmes Rd. N1 57 BZ37
lmoral Ave., Beck. 87 CD52
lmoral Clo. SW15 75 BQ46
Vestleigh Ave.
lmoral Cres., E.Mol. 84 BF52
lmoral Dr., Borwd. 28 BN24
lmoral Dr., Hayes 53 BB38
lmoral Dr., Sthl. 54 BE38
lmoral Dr., Wok. 100 AU61
lmoral Gdns. W13 64 BJ41
lmoral Gdns., Bex. 79 CQ47
lmoral Gdns., Ilf. 49 CN33
lmoral Gdns., Wind. 61 AO45
lmoral Gro. N7 56 BX36
Brewery Rd.
lmoral Ms. W12 65 BO41
Rylett Cres.
lmoral Rd. E7 49 CJ35
lmoral Rd. E10 48 CE34
lmoral Rd. NW2 55 BP36
lmoral Rd., Brwd. 33 DA25
lmoral Rd., Enf. 30 CC21
lmoral Rd., Har. 45 BF35
lmoral Rd., Horn. 51 CV34
lmoral Rd., Kings.T. 85 BL52
lmoral Rd., Rom. 50 CU32
lmoral Rd., S.at H. 80 CX50
lmoral Rd., Wat. 27 BD22
lmoral Rd., Wor.Pk. 85 BP55
lmoral Way, Sutt. 95 BS58
lmore Cres., Barn. 29 BV25
lmore St. N19 47 BV34
lmuir Gdns. SW15 65 BQ45
lnacraig Ave. NW10 46 BO35
lniel Gate SW1 3 P10
lniel Gate SW1 66 BW42
louhain Clo., Ash. 102 BK62
ltic Clo. SW19 76 BT50
ltic St. EC1 2 H5
ltic St. EC1 57 BZ38
ltimore Pl., Well. 68 CN44
lvernie Gro. SW18 75 BR47
mborough Gdns. W12 65 BQ41
mford Ave., Wem. 55 BL37
mford Ct. E15 48 CE35
mford Rd., Bark. 58 CM36
mford Rd., Brom. 77 CF49
mford Way, Rom. 41 CR28
mpfylde Clo., Wall. 86 BW55
mpton Rd. SE23 77 CC48
mpton Rd., Rom. 42 CW30
mpton Way, Wok. 100 AQ62
navie Gdns., Beck. 87 CF51
nbury Clo., Sutt. 95 BS57
nbury Ct. WC2 1 Q10
nbury Ct. WC2 56 BX40
Long Acre
nbury Rd. E9 57 CC36
nbury Rd. E17 39 CD29
nbury St. SW11 66 BU44
nbury St., Wat. 26 BC25
nbury Wk., Nthlt. 54 BF37
Leander Rd.
nchory Rd. SE3 68 CH43
nckside, Long. 90 DC52
ncroft Ave. N2 47 BU32
ncroft Ave., Buck.H. 40 CH27
ncroft Clo., Ashf. 73 AZ49
ncroft Ct., Nthlt. 54 BD37
ncroft Ct., Reig. 121 BS70
ncroft Gdns., Har. 36 BG30
Bancroft Gdns., Orp. 88 CN54
Bancroft Rd. E1 57 CC38
Bancroft Rd., Har. 36 BG30
Bancroft Rd., Reig. 121 BS70
Band La., Egh. 72 AS49
Banders Ri., Guil. 118 AU70
Bandon Ri., Wall. 95 BW56
Banes Down, Wal.Abb. 13 CG14
Bangalore St. SW15 65 BQ45
Bangor Clo., Nthlt. 45 BF35
Bangor Rd., Brent. 65 BL43
Bangors Clo., Iver 52 AV39
Bangors Rd. N., Iver 52 AU37
Bangors Rd. S., Iver 52 AV38
Banim St. W6 65 BP42
Banister Rd. W10 55 BQ38
Bank, The N6 47 BV33
Bank Ave., Mitch. 86 BT51
Bank Ct., Dart. 80 CW46
Bank Ct., Hem.H. 8 AX14
Bank End SE1 4 J2
Bank La. SW15 75 BO46
Bank La., Kings.T. 75 BL50
Bank La., Sev. 117 CX69
Bank Mill, Berk. 7 AS13
Bank Mill La., Berk. 7 AS13
Bank Pl., Brwd. 42 DB27
High St.
Bank St., Grav. 81 DG46
Bank St., Sev. 116 CU66
London Rd.
Bankfield Ct., Islw. 64 BH44
Bankfoot, Grays 71 DD42
Bankfoot Rd., Brom. 78 CG49
Bankhurst Rd. SE6 77 CD47
Banks La., Bexh. 69 CQ45
Banks La., Epp. 23 CQ19
Banks La., Lthd. 101 BC64
Banks Rd., Borwd. 28 BN23
Banks Spur, Slou. 61 AN41
Cooper Way
Banks Way, Guil. 118 AS69
Bankside SE1 4 H1
Bankside SE1 56 BY40
Bankside, Enf. 29 BY23
Bankside, Grav. 81 DE46
Bankside, S.Croy. 96 CA57
Bankside, Sthl. 54 BD40
Bankside, Wok. 100 AQ62
Bankside Ave., Nthlt. 53 BC37
Bankside Clo., Bex. 79 CS49
Bankside Clo., Cars. 95 BU57
Bankside Clo., West. 106 CJ62
Bankside Dr., T.Ditt. 84 BJ54
Bankside Way SE19 77 CA50
Central Hill Est.
Bankton Rd. SW2 66 BY45
Bankwell Rd. SE13 68 CG45
Bann Clo., S.Ock. 60 DA40
Banner Clo., Grays 70 CY42
Brimfield Rd.
Banner St. EC1 57 BZ38
Banning St. SE10 68 CG42
Bannister Clo. SW2 76 BY47
Bannister Clo., Grnf. 45 BG35
Bannister Clo., Slou. 62 AS41
Bannister Dr., Brwd. 122 DE25
Bannister Ho. E9 48 CC35
Bannisters Rd., Guil. 118 AP71
Bannockburn Rd. SE18 68 CN42
Bansons La., Ong. 24 CX17
Bansons Way, Ong. 24 CX17
Banstead Gdns. N9 39 CA27
Banstead Rd., Cars. 95 BT58
Banstead Rd., Cat. 105 BZ64
Banstead Rd., Epsom 94 BP59
Banstead Rd., Pur. 95 BY59
Banstead Rd. S., Sutt. 95 BT59
Banstead St. SE15 67 CC45
Banstead Way, Wall. 95 BX56
Banstock Rd., Edg. 37 BM29
Banton Clo., Enf. 30 CB23
Bantry St. SE5 67 BZ43
Banyard Rd. SE16 67 CB41
Southwark Pk. Rd.
Banyards, Horn. 51 CW32
Bapchild Pl., Orp. 89 CP52
Okemore Gdns.
Baptist Gdns. NW5 56 BV36
Queens Cres.
Barandon Wk. W11 55 BQ40
Lancaster Rd.
Barb Ms. W6 65 BQ41
Shepherds Bush Rd.
Barbara Brosnan Ct. NW8 1 A1
Barbara Clo., Shep. 83 AZ53
Barbauld Rd. N16 48 CA34
Barbel Clo., Wal.Cr. 21 CE20
Barber Clo. N21 38 BY26
Barberry Clo., Rom. 42 CV29
Barberry Rd., Hem.H. 8 AW13
Barbers All. E13 58 CH38
Barbers Rd. E15 57 CE37
Barbican, The EC2 2 H6
Barbican Rd., Grnf. 54 BF39
Barbican Site EC2 57 BZ39
Barbon Clo. WC1 2 A6
Barbot Clo. N9 39 CB27
Barchard St. SW18 76 BS46
Barchester Clo. W7 54 BH40
Barchester Clo., Uxb. 53 AX38
Barchester Rd., Har. 36 BG30
Barchester Rd., Slou. 62 AS41
Barchester St. E14 57 CE39
Barclay Clo. SW6 66 BS43
Barclay Clo., Lthd. 102 BF65
Barclay Ct., Hodd. 12 CE12
Barclay Oval, Wdf.Grn. 40 CH28
Barclay Rd. E11 49 CG33
Barclay Rd. E13 58 CJ38
Barclay Rd. E17 48 CF32
Barclay Rd. N18 39 BZ29
Barclay Rd. SW6 66 BS43
Barclay Rd., Croy. 87 BZ55
Barclay Way SE22 77 CB47
Wilkie Way
Barclay Way, Grays 70 CZ42
Barcombe Ave. SW2 76 BX48
Barcombe Clo., Orp. 88 CN51
Petersham Dr.
Bard Rd. W10 55 BQ40
Barden Clo., Uxb. 35 AX29
Barden St. SE18 68 CN43
Bardeswell Clo., Brwd. 42 DB27
Bardfield Ave., Rom. 50 CP31
Bardney Rd., Mord. 86 BS52
Bardolph Ave., Croy. 96 CD58
Bardolph Rd. N7 47 BX35
Bardolph Rd., Rich. 65 BL45
St. Georges Rd.
Bardon Wk., Wok. 100 AQ62
Bardsey Wk. N1 57 BZ36
Clephane Rd.
Bardsley Clo., Croy. 87 CB55
Bardsley La. SE10 67 CF43
Bardwell Ct., St.Alb. 9 BG14
Bardwell Rd.
Bardwell Rd., St.Alb. 9 BG14
Barfett St. W10 55 BR38
Barfield, S.at H. 90 CX51
Barfield Ave. N20 38 BU27
Barfield Rd. E11 49 CG33
Barfield Rd., Brom. 88 CL52
Barfields, Loug. 31 CL24
Barfields Cres., Red. 121 BY70
Barfields Gdns., Loug. 31 CL24
Barfields Path, Loug. 31 CL24
Barfolds, Hat. 10 BQ15
Barford Clo. NW4 37 BP30
Barford St. N1 56 BY37
Barforth Rd. SE15 67 CB45
Barfreston Way SE20 87 CB51
Bargate Clo. SE18 68 CN42
Bargate Clo., N.Mal. 85 BP54
Barge Ho. Rd. E16 68 CL41
Barge Ho. St. SE1 4 E2
Barge Ho. St. SE1 56 BY40
Barge Rd., E.Mol. 84 BG52
Barge Wk., Kings.T. 84 BK51
Bargery Rd. SE6 77 CE47
Bargrove Ave., Hem.H. 8 AW14
Bargrove Clo. SE20 77 CB50
Bargrove Cres. SE6 77 CD48
Elm La.
Barham Ave., Borwd. 28 BL24
Barham Clo., Brom. 88 CK54
Barham Clo., Chis. 78 CL49
Barham Clo., Rom. 41 CR30
Barham Clo., Wem. 54 BJ36
Barham Clo., Wey. 92 BA56
Barham Rd. SW20 75 BP50
Barham Rd., Chis. 78 CL49
Barham Rd., Dart. 80 CX47
Barham Rd., S.Croy. 96 BZ56
Baring Clo. SE12 78 CH48
Baring Rd. SE12 78 CH47
Baring Rd., Barn. 29 BT24
Baring Rd., Croy. 87 CB54
Baring St. N1 57 BZ37
Bark Burr Rd., Grays 71 DC41
Bark Hart Rd., Orp. 89 CO54
Bark Pl. W2 56 BS40
Barker Dr. NW1 56 BW36
Barker Rd., Cher. 82 AV54
Barker St. SW10 66 BT43
Barker Wk. SW16 76 BW48
Barker Way SE22 77 CB47
Wilkie Way
Barkham Rd. N17 39 BZ29
Barking By-pass, Bark. 58 CM38
Barking Rd. E6 58 CJ37
Barking Rd. E13 58 CG39
Barking Rd. E16 58 CG39
Barkis Way SE16 67 CB42
Egan Way
Barkston Gdns. SW5 66 BS42
Barkston Path, Borwd. 28 BM22
Barkway Ct. N4 48 BZ34
Kings Cres. Est.
Barkwood Clo., Rom. 50 CS32
Barkworth Rd. SE16 67 CB42
Barlborough St. SE14 67 CC43
Barlby Gdns. W10 55 BQ38
Barlby Rd. W10 55 BQ39
Barle Gdns., S.Ock. 60 DA39
Barley Clo., Bush. 27 BF25
Barley Cft., Harl. 13 CM13
Barley Cft., Hem.H. 8 BA13
Barley Fld., Brwd. 33 CZ22
Barley La., Ilf. 50 CO33
Barley La., Rom. 50 CO33
Barley Mow Clo., Wok. 100 AO62
Barley Mow Ct., Reig. 120 BN70
Barley Mow La., St.Alb. 10 BL14
Barley Mow La., Wok. 100 AO61
Barley Mow Pas. EC1 2 G7
Barley Mow Pas. W4 65 BN42
Heathfield Ter.
Barley Mow Rd., Egh. 72 AR49
Barley Mow Way, Shep. 83 AZ52
Petts La.
Barleycorn Way E14 57 CD40
Narrow St.
Barleycorn Way, Horn. 51 CW32
Barleycroft Grn., 5 BQ8
Welw.G.C.
Barleycroft Rd., 5 BQ8
Welw.G.C.
Barleyfields Clo., Rom. 50 CO32
Barlow Clo., Wall. 95 BX57
Redford Ave.
Barlow Pl. W1 3 K1
Barlow Pl. W1 56 BV40
Bruton La.
Barlow Rd. NW6 55 BR36
Barlow Rd. W3 55 BM40
Barlow Rd., Hmptn. 74 BF50
Barlow St. SE17 4 L9
Barlow St. SE17 67 BZ42
Barlow Way, Rain. 59 CS39
Barmeston Rd. SE6 77 CE48
Barmor Clo., Har. 36 BF30
Barmouth Ave., Grnf. 54 BH37
Barmouth Rd. SW18 76 BT46
Barmouth Rd., Croy. 87 CC55
Barn Clo., Ashf. 73 AZ49
Barn Clo., Bans. 104 BT61
Barn Clo., Hem.H. 8 AY15
Barn Clo., Nthlt. 54 BD37
Barn Clo., Rad. 27 BJ21
Barn Clo., Welw.G.C. 5 BQ8
Barn Ct., Saw. 6 CQ6
Station Rd.
Barn Cres., Pur. 96 BZ60
Barn Cres., Stan. 36 BK29
Barn Elms Pk. SW15 65 BQ44
Barn Fld., Epp. 23 CO17
Barn Hill, Harl. 13 CH13
Barn Hill, Wem. 46 BM33
Barn Lea, Rick. 35 AW26
Barn Mead, Brwd. 33 DB21
Barn Mead, Epp. 31 CN21
Barn Mead, Harl. 13 CN12
Barn Meadow Clo., Lthd. 102 BE65
Barn Meadow La.
Barn Meadow La., Lthd. 102 BE65
Barn Ri., Wem. 46 BM34
Barn Rd., Mitch. 86 BV52
Barn St. N16 48 CA34
Stoke Newington Ch. St.
Barn Way, Wem. 46 BM33
Barnabas Rd. E9 48 CC35
Barnaby Clo., Har. 45 BG34
Barnaby Way, Chig. 40 CL27
Barnacre Clo., Uxb. 53 AX39
Barnacres Cft., Hem.H. 8 AZ15
Barnacres Rd., Hem.H. 8 AY15
Barnard Acres, Wal.Abb. 13 CG15
Barnard Clo. SE18 68 CL41
Barnard Clo., Chis. 88 CM51
Barnard Clo., Hem.H. 8 AY14
Barnard Clo., Sun. 73 BC50
Barnard Clo., Wall. 95 BW57
Barnard Ct., Wok. 100 AP62
Ashwindham Ct.
Barnard Gdns., Hayes 53 BC38
Barnard Gdns., N.Mal. 85 BP52
Barnard Grn.,Welw.G.C. 5 BR8
Barnard Gro. E15 58 CG36
Vicarage La.
Barnard Hill N10 38 BV30
Barnard Rd. SW11 66 BU45
Barnard Rd., Enf. 30 CB23
Barnard Rd., Saw. 6 CQ5
Barnard Rd., Warl. 105 CE63
Barnardo Dr., Ilf. 49 CM31
Ashurst Dr.
Barnardo St. E1 57 CC39
Barnards Inn EC1 2 D8
Barnards Inn EC1 56 BY39
Fetter La.
Barnards Pl., S.Croy. 95 BY58
Pampisford Rd.
Barnby Rd., Wok. 100 AO62
Barnby St. E15 58 CG37
Barnby St. NW1 1 M2
Barnby St. NW1 56 BW37
Barncroft Clo., Loug. 31 CL25
Barncroft Clo., Uxb. 53 AZ39
Barncroft Rd., Berk. 7 AP13
Barncroft Rd., Loug. 31 CL25
Barncroft Way, St.Alb. 9 BJ14
Barndicott, Welw.G.C. 5 BT8
Barnehurst Ave., Bexh. 69 CS44
Barnehurst Ave., Erith 69 CS44
Barnehurst Clo., Erith 69 CS44
Barnehurst Rd., Bexh. 69 CR44
Barnend Dr., Dart. 80 CV49
Barnend La., Dart. 80 CV49
Barnes All., Hmptn. 84 BG51
Barnes Ave. SW13 65 BP43
Barnes Ave., Chesh. 16 AO18
Barnes Ave., Sthl. 64 BE42
Barnes Bri. SW13 65 BO44
Barnes Bri. W4 65 BO44
Barnes Clo. E12 49 CJ35
Barnes Ct. E16 58 CJ39
Ridgewell Rd.
Barnes Ct., Wdf.Grn. 40 CJ28
Durham Ave.
Barnes Cray Rd., Dart. 69 CU45
Barnes End, N.Mal. 85 BP53
Barnes High St. SW13 65 BO44
Barnes La., Kings L. 17 AW17
Barnes Pikle W5 54 BJ40
Mattock La.
Barnes Ri., Kings L. 17 AY17
Barnes Rd. N18 39 CC28
Barnes Rd., Ilf. 49 CM35
Barnes St. E14 57 CD39
Barnes Ter. SE8 67 CD42
Barnes Wallace Dr., Wey. 92 AY59
Barnes Way, Iver 52 AV40
Barnesdale Cres., Orp. 89 CO53
Barnet By-pass, Barn. 28 BO23
Barnet By-pass, Hat. 10 BO12
Barnet Dr., Brom. 88 CK55
Barnet Gate La., Barn. 28 BO25
Barnet Gro. E2 57 CB38
Barnet Hill, Barn. 28 BR24
Barnet La. N20 37 BR26
Barnet La., Borwd. 27 BK25
Barnet Rd. (Arkley), Barn. 28 BO25
Barnet Rd., Pot.B. 29 BS21
Barnet Rd., St.Alb. 19 BL17
Barnet Row, Guil. 109 AR68
Barnet Way NW7 37 BN28
Barnet Wd. Rd., Brom. 88 CJ55
Barnett Clo., Erith 69 CT44
Barnett Clo., Lthd. 102 BJ63
Barnett St. E1 57 CB39
Kinder St.
Barnetts Shaw, Oxt. 114 CF67
Barnettwood La., Ash. 102 BJ63
Barnettwood La., Lthd. 102 BJ63
Barney Clo. SE7 68 CJ42
Barnfield, Bans. 95 BS60
Barnfield, Hem.H. 8 AY15
Barnfield, Iver 52 AV39
Barnfield, N.Mal. 85 BN53
Barnfield, Slou. 61 AL40
Barnfield Ave., Croy. 87 CC55
Barnfield Ave., Kings.T. 74 BK49
Barnfield Ave., Mitch. 86 BV52
Barnfield Clo. N4 47 BX33
Crouch Hill
Barnfield Clo., Couls. 105 BZ63
Barnfield Clo., Hodd. 12 CE11
Barnfield Clo., Swan. 89 CS54
Barnfield Cres., Sev. 108 CW62
Barnfield Gdns., Kings.T. 75 BL49
Barnfield Gdns. Est. 68 CL43
SE18
Barnfield Pl. E14 67 CE42
Barnfield Rd. SE18 68 CL43
Barnfield Rd. W5 54 BK38
Barnfield Rd., Belv. 69 CQ43
Barnfield Rd., Edg. 37 BN30
Barnfield Rd., Orp. 89 CP52
Barnfield Rd., St.Alb. 9 BK12
Barnfield Rd., Sev. 107 CT65
Barnfield Rd., S.Croy. 96 CA58
Barnfield Rd., Welw.G.C. 5 BR9
Barnfield Rd., West. 106 CJ64
Barnfield Way, Oxt. 115 CH70
Barnfield Wd. Clo., Beck. 87 CF53
Barnfield Wd. Rd., Beck. 87 CF53
Barnham Rd., Grnf. 54 BG38
Barnham St. SE1 4 N4
Barnham St. SE1 67 CA41
Barnhill, Pnr. 45 BD32
Barnhill Ave., Brom. 88 CG53
Barnhill La., Hayes 53 BC38
Barnhill Rd., Hayes 53 BC38
Barnhill Rd., Wem. 46 BN34
Barnhurst Path, Wat. 36 BD28
Barningham Way NW9 46 BN32
Barnlea Clo., Felt. 74 BE48
Barnmead, Ong. 23 CT18
Barnmead, Wok. 91 AP58
Barnmead Gdns., Dag. 50 CQ35
Barnmead Rd., Beck. 87 CC51
Barnmead Rd., Dag. 50 CQ35
Barnsbury Clo., N.Mal. 85 BN52
Barnsbury Cres., Surb. 85 BN54
Barnsbury Gro. N7 56 BX36
Roman Way
Barnsbury La., Surb. 85 BM55
Barnsbury Ms. N1 56 BY36
Brooksby St.
Barnsbury Pk. N1 56 BY36
Barnsbury Rd. N1 56 BY37
Barnsbury Sq. N1 56 BY36
Barnsbury St. N1 56 BY36
Barnsbury Ter. N1 56 BY36
Barnscroft SW20 85 BP52
Barnsdale Ave. E14 67 CE42
Barnsdale Clo., Borwd. 28 BL23
Leeming Rd.
Barnsdale Rd. W9 55 BR38
Barnsfield Pl., Uxb. 53 AX36
Barnside Ct., Welw.G.C. 5 BQ8
Barnsley Rd., Rom. 42 CW29
Barnsley St. E1 57 CB38
Barnstaple Path, Rom. 42 CV28
Barnstaple Rd.
Barnstaple Rd., Rom. 42 CV28
Barnstaple Rd., Ruis. 45 BD34
Barnston Wk. N1 57 BZ37
Popham St.
Barnston Way, Brwd. 122 DE25
Barnsway, Kings L. 17 AY17
Barnway, Egh. 72 AR49
Barnwell Rd. SW2 76 BY46
Barnwood Clo. W9 56 BS38
Barnwood Clo., Guil. 118 AP69
Barnwood Clo., Ruis. 44 BA34
Barnwood Ct. E16 58 CH40
Barnwood Ct. Est. E16 58 CH40
Barnwood Rd., Guil. 118 AP70
Barnyard, The, Tad. 103 BP65
Baron Ct., Rom. 42 CW30
Oak Rd.
Baron Gdns., Ilf. 49 CM31
Baron Gro., Mitch. 86 BU52
Baron Rd., Dag. 50 CP33
Baron St. N1 2 D1
Baron St. N1 56 BY37
Baron Wk. E16 58 CG39
Baron Wk., Mitch. 86 BU52
Baroness Rd. E2 2 Q2
Baroness Rd. E2 57 CA38
Baronet Gro. N17 39 CB30
Baronet Rd. N17 39 CB30
Barons, The, Twick. 74 BJ46
Barons Ct. NW9 46 BN32
Barons Ct. Rd. W14 65 BR42
Barons Gate, Barn. 29 BU25
Barons Hurst, Epsom 103 BN61
Barons Keep W14 65 BR42
Gliddon Rd.
Barons Mead, Har. 45 BH31
Barons Pl. SE1 4 E5
Barons Pl. SE1 66 BY41
Barons Wk., Croy. 87 CD53
Barons Way, Egh. 72 AU50
Barons Way, Reig. 121 BS72
Baronsfield Rd., Twick. 74 BJ46
Baronsmead Rd. SW13 65 BP44
Baronsmede W5 65 BL41
Baronsmere Rd. N2 47 BU31
Barque Ms. SE8 67 CE43
Watergate St.
Barr Rd., Grav. 81 DJ48
Barr Rd., Pot.B. 20 BT20
Barra Clo., Hem.H. 8 AZ15

Barra Hall Rd., Hayes 53 BB40
Barrack La., Wind. 61 AO44
Barrack Path, Wok. 100 AP62
Barrack Rd., Guil. 118 AQ69
Barrack Rd., Houns. 64 BD45
Barrack Row, Grav. 81 DG46
Barrack Row, Sthl. 64 BD42
Barrards Way, Beac. 34 AO29
Barrat Way, Har. 45 BG31
Barratt Ave. N22 38 BX30
Barratt Ind. Pk., Sthl. 54 BF40
Barrenger Rd. N10 38 BU30
Barrens Brae, Wok. 100 AT62
Barrens Clo., Wok. 100 AT63
Barrens Pk., Wok. 100 AT63
Barrett Clo., Rom. 41 CU29
Barrett Rd. E17 48 CF31
Barrett Rd., Lthd. 111 BG66
Barrett St. W1 1 H9
Barrett St. W1 56 BV39
Barretts Grn. Rd. NW10 55 BN38
Barretts Gro. N16 48 CA35
Barretts Rd., Sev. 107 CS63
Barrhill Rd. SW2 76 BX48
Barricane Clo., Wok. 100 AQ63
Barrie Clo., Couls. 104 BV61
Barrie Est. W2 1 A10
Barrie Est. W2 56 BT40
Barriedale SE14 67 CD44
Barrier App. SE7 68 CJ41
Barringer Sq. SW17 76 BV49
Barrington Clo. NW5 47 BV35
Barrington Clo., Ilf. 40 CK30
Barrington Clo., Loug. 31 CM24
Barrington Ct. N10 38 BV30
Barrington Ct., Brwd. 122 DE25
Barrington Ct., Dor. 119 BJ72
Barrington Rd.
Barrington Grn., Loug. 31 CM24
Barrington Lo., Wey. 92 BA56
Princes Rd.
Barrington Pk. Gdns., Ch.St.G. 34 AR26
Barrington Rd. E12 58 CL36
Barrington Rd. N8 47 BW32
Barrington Rd. SW9 66 BY45
Barrington Rd., Bexh. 69 CP44
Barrington Rd., Dor. 119 BJ72
Barrington Rd., Loug. 31 CM24
Barrington Rd., Pur. 95 BW59
Barrington Rd., Sutt. 86 BS54
Barrington Vill. SE18 68 CL44
Barrisdale, Wok. 100 AU61
Barrons Clo., Ong. 24 CW17
Barrosa Dr., Hmptn. 84 BF51
Oldfield Rd.
Barrow Ave., Cars. 95 BU57
Barrow Clo. N21 38 BY27
Barrow Grn. Rd., Oxt. 114 CE68
Barrow Hedges Clo., Cars. 95 BU57
Barrow Hedges Way, Cars. 95 BU57
Barrow Hill Clo., Wor.Pk. 85 BO55
Barrow Hill Est. NW8 1 C1
Barrow Hill Est. NW8 56 BU37
Barrow Hill Rd. NW8 1 C1
Barrow Hill Rd. NW8 56 BU37
Barrow La., Chsnt. 21 CA19
Barrow Pt. Ave., Pnr. 36 BE30
Barrow Pt. La., Pnr. 36 BE30
Barrow Rd. SW16 76 BW50
Barrow Rd., Croy. 95 BY57
Barrow Wk., Brent. 64 BK43
Glenhurst Rd.
Barrow Way N7 47 BX34
Barrowdene Clo., Pnr. 36 BE30
Paines La.
Barrowell Grn. N21 38 BY27
Barrowfield Clo. N9 39 CB27
Barrowgate Rd. W4 65 BN42
Barrows Rd., Harl. 13 CK11
Barrowsfield, S.Croy. 96 CB59
Barrs La., Wok. 100 AO61
Barrs Rd. NW10 55 BN36
Barry Ave. N15 48 CA32
Craven Pk. Rd.
Barry Ave., Bexh. 69 CQ43
Barry Ave., Wind. 61 AO43
Barry Clo., Grays 71 DG41
Barry Clo., Orp. 88 CN55
Barry Clo., St.Alb. 18 BF16
Barry Pl., Wok. 100 AS62
Barry Rd. E6 58 CK39
Barry Rd. NW10 55 BN36
Barry Rd. SE22 77 CA46
Bars, The, Guil. 118 AR71
Barset Rd. SE15 67 CC45
Barson Clo. SE20 77 CC50
Barston Rd. SE27 77 BZ48
Barstow Cres. SW2 76 BX47
Bartel Clo., Hem.H. 8 BA14
Barter St. WC1 2 A7
Barter St. WC1 56 BX39
Barters Wk., Pnr. 45 BE31
High St.
Barth Rd. SE18 68 CN42
Bartholomew Clo. EC1 2 H7
Bartholomew Clo. EC1 57 BZ39
Bartholomew Clo. SW18 66 BT45
Bartholomew La. EC2 2 L9
Bartholomew La. EC2 57 BZ39
Threadneedle St.
Bartholomew Pl. EC1 2 H7
Bartholomew Rd. NW5 56 BW36
Bartholomew Sq. E1 57 CB38
Cudworth St.
Bartholomew Sq. EC1 2 J4
Bartholomew Sq. EC1 57 BZ38
Bartholomew St. SE1 4 L7
Bartholomew St. SE1 67 BZ41
Bartholomew Vill. NW5 56 BW36
Bartholomew Way, Swan. 89 CT52
Bartle Ave. E6 58 CK37
Bartle Rd. W11 55 BQ39

Bartlett Clo. E14 57 CE39
Bartlett Ct. EC4 2 E8
Bartlett Ct. EC4 56 BY39
New Fetter La.
Bartlett Rd., Grav. 81 DG47
Bartlett Rd., West. 115 CM66
Croydon Rd.
Bartlett St., S.Croy. 96 BZ56
Bartlow Gdns., Rom. 41 CS30
Barton, The, Cob. 93 BD59
Barton Ave., Rom. 50 CR33
Barton Clo. E6 58 CK39
Barton Clo. E9 48 CC35
Barton Clo. SE15 67 CB45
Barton Clo., Bexh. 79 CQ46
Barton Clo., Chig. 40 CM27
Barton Clo., Shep. 83 AZ53
Barton Clo., Wey. 92 AW57
Barton Grn., N.Mal. 85 BN51
Barton Meadows, Ilf. 49 CL31
Barton Rd. W14 65 BR42
Barton Rd., Horn. 50 CU34
Barton Rd., Sid. 79 CQ50
Barton Rd., Slou. 62 AS41
Barton Rd., S.at H. 90 CX51
Barton St. SW1 3 Q6
Barton St. SW1 66 BX41
Barton Way NW8 56 BT37
Barton Way, Borwd. 28 BM23
Barton Way, Rick. 26 AZ25
Bartons, The, Borwd. 27 BK25
Bartram Clo., Uxb. 53 AZ38
Bartram Rd. SE4 77 CD46
Bartrams La., Barn. 29 BT22
Barville Clo. SE4 67 CD45
St. Norbert Rd.
Barwell Trd. Est., Chess. 93 BK58
Barwick Rd. E7 49 CH35
Barwood Ave., W.Wick. 87 CE54
Basden Gro., Felt. 74 BF48
Basedale Rd., Dag. 59 CO36
Baseing Clo. E6 58 CL39
Basford Way, Wind. 61 AL45
Bashley Rd. NW10 55 BN38
Basil Ave. E6 58 CK38
Basil Gdns., Croy. 87 CC54
Basil St. SW3 3 E6
Basil St. SW3 66 BU41
Basildene Rd., Houns. 64 BD45
Basildon Ave., Ilf. 40 CL30
Basildon Clo., Sutt. 95 BT58
Basildon Rd. SE2 69 CO42
Basildon Rd., Bexh. 69 CQ44
Basildon Sq., Hem.H. 8 AY11
Basin Rd. E16 58 CG40
Basing Clo., T.Ditt. 84 BH54
Basing Ct. SE15 67 CA44
Basing Dr., Bex. 79 CQ46
Basing Est. N3 47 BS31
Basing Hill NW11 46 BR33
Basing Hill, Wem. 46 BL34
Basing Ho. Yd. E2 2 N2
Basing Ho. Yd. E2 57 CA38
Kingsland Rd.
Basing Pl. E2 2 N2
Basing Rd., Bans. 94 BR60
Basing Rd., Rick. 34 AV26
Basing St. W11 55 BR39
Basing Way N3 47 BS31
Basing Way, T.Ditt. 84 BH54
Basingdon Way SE5 67 BZ45
Basingfield Rd., T.Ditt. 84 BH54
Basinghall Ave. EC2 2 K7
Basinghall Ave. EC2 57 BZ39
Basinghall Gdns., Sutt. 95 BS58
Basinghall St. EC2 2 K8
Basinghall St. EC2 57 BZ39
Basire St. N1 57 BZ37
Baskerville Rd. SW18 76 BU47
Basket Gdns. SE9 78 CK46
Baslow Clo., Har. 36 BG30
Baslow Wk. E5 48 CC35
Clapton Pk. Est.
Basnett Rd. SW11 66 BV45
Bassano St. SE22 77 CA46
Bassant Rd. SE18 68 CN43
Bassein Pk. Rd. W12 65 BO41
Bassett Clo., Sutt. 95 BS58
Bassett Clo., Wey. 92 AW58
Bassett Gdns., Epp. 23 CR16
Bassett Gdns., Islw. 64 BG43
Bassett Rd. W10 55 BR39
Bassett Rd., Wok. 100 AU61
Bassett St. NW5 47 BV35
Bassett Way, Grnf. 54 BF39
Bassetts Clo., Orp. 97 CL56
Bassetts Way, Orp. 97 CL56
Bassil Rd., Hem.H. 8 AX14
Bassingbourne Clo., Brox. 12 CD13
Bassingburn Wk., Welw.G.C. 5 BR8
Bassingham Rd. SW18 76 BT47
Bassingham Rd., Wem. 54 BK36
Basswood Clo. SE15 67 CB45
Linden Gro.
Bastable Ave., Bark. 58 CN37
Bastion Rd. SE2 69 CO42
Baston Manor Rd., Brom. 88 CH55
Baston Rd., Brom. 88 CH54
Bastwick St. EC1 2 H4
Bastwick St. EC1 56 BY38
Basuto Rd. SW6 66 BS44
Batavia Clo., Sun. 83 BC51
Batavia Ms. SE14 67 CD43
Clifton Ri.
Batavia Rd. SE14 67 CD43
Batavia Rd., Sun. 83 BC51
Batchelor St. N1 56 BY37
Batchelors Way, Amer. 25 AO23
Batchwood Dr., St.Alb. 9 BF12
Batchwood Gdns., St.Alb. 9 BG12
Batchwood Grn., Orp. 89 CO52
Batchwood Vw., St.Alb. 9 BG12

Batchworth Heath Hill, Rick. 35 AZ28
Batchworth Hill, Rick. 35 AY27
Batchworth La., Nthwd. 35 AZ28
Bate St. E14 57 CD40
Three Colt St.
Bateman Clo., Bark. 58 CM36
Glenny Rd.
Bateman Rd. E4 39 CE29
Bateman Rd., Rick. 26 AZ25
Bateman St. W1 1 N9
Bateman St. W1 56 BW39
Dean St.
Batemans Bldgs. W1 1 N9
Batemans Row EC2 2 N4
Batemans Row EC2 57 CA38
Bates Cres., Croy. 95 BY56
Bates Hill, Sev. 108 DB64
Bates Rd., Rom. 42 CX29
Bates Wk., Wey. 92 AX57
Bateson St. SE18 68 CN42
Gunning St.
Bateson Way, Wok. 91 AU60
Batford Clo., Welw.G.C. 5 BS8
Waterford Grn.
Bath Clo. SE15 67 CB43
Bath Ct. EC1 2 D5
Bath Ho. Rd., Croy. 86 BX54
Bath Pas., Kings.T. 84 BK51
Bath Pl., Barn. 28 BR24
Bath Rd. E7 58 CJ36
Bath Rd. N9 39 CB27
Bath Rd. W4 65 BO42
Bath Rd., Dart. 79 CU47
Bath Rd., Hayes 63 BC43
Bath Rd., Houns. 64 BF45
Bath Rd., Mitch. 86 BT52
Bath Rd., Rom. 50 CQ32
Bath Rd., Slou. 61 AN40
Bath Rd. (Poyle), Slou. 62 AV44
Bath Rd., West Dr. 63 AX44
Bath St. EC1 2 J3
Bath St. EC1 57 BZ38
Bath St., Grav. 81 DG46
Bath Ter. SE1 4 H7
Bath Ter. SE1 67 BZ41
Bathgate Rd. SW19 75 BQ48
Baths Rd., Brom. 88 CJ52
Bathurst Ave. SW19 86 BS51
Brisbane Ave.
Bathurst Clo., Iver 62 AV41
Bathurst Gdns. NW10 55 BP37
Bathurst Ms. W2 1 B10
Bathurst Ms. W2 56 BT40
Bathurst Rd., Hem.H. 8 AX12
Bathurst Rd., Ilf. 49 CL33
Bathurst St. W2 1 B10
Bathurst St. W2 56 BT40
Bathurst Wk., Iver 62 AV41
Bathway SE18 68 CL42
Market St.
Batley Rd. N16 48 CD34
Stoke Newington High St.
Batley Rd., Enf. 30 BZ23
Batman Clo. W12 55 BP40
Batoum Gdns. W6 65 BQ41
Batson St. W12 65 BP41
Batsworth Rd., Mitch. 86 BT52
Batten Ave., Wok. 100 AP63
Batten Clo. E6 58 CK39
Savage Gdns.
Batten St. SW11 66 BU45
Batterdale, Hat. 10 BQ12
The Bdy.
Battersby Rd. SE6 77 CF48
Battersea Bri. SW3 66 BT43
Battersea Bri. Rd. SW11 66 BU43
Battersea Ch. Rd. SW11 66 BT44
Battersea High St. SW11 66 BT44
Battersea Pk. Est. SW11 66 BV44
Dagnall St.
Battersea Pk. Rd. SW8 66 BU44
Battersea Pk. Rd. SW11 66 BU44
Battersea Ri. SW11 76 BT46
Battery Rd. SE28 68 CN41
Battis, The, Rom. 50 CT32
Battishill St. N1 56 BY36
Waterloo Ter.
Battle Bri. La. SE1 4 M3
Battle Bri. La. SE1 57 CA40
Tooley St.
Battle Bri. Rd. NW1 1 Q1
Battle Bri. Rd. NW1 56 BX37
Battle Clo. SW19 76 BT50
North Rd.
Battle Ct., Ong. 24 CX18
Battle Rd., Belv. 69 CS42
Battle Rd., Erith 69 CS42
Battlebridge La., Red. 113 BV68
Battledean Rd. N5 47 BY35
Battlefield Rd., St.Alb. 9 BH12
Battlefields Rd., Sev. 108 DC61
Battlers Grn. Dr., Rad. 27 BH21
Batts Hill, Red. 121 BU70
Batts Hill, Reig. 121 BU70
Batty St. E1 57 CB39
Baudwin Rd. SE6 78 CG48
Baugh Rd., Sid. 79 CP49
Baulk, The SW18 76 BS47
Bavant Rd. SW16 86 BX51
Bavaria Rd. N19 47 BX34
Bavent Rd. SE5 67 BZ44
Bawdale Rd. SE22 77 CA46
Bawdsey Ave., Ilf. 49 CN31
Bawtree Clo., Sutt. 95 BT58
Bawtree Rd. SE14 67 CD43
Bawtree Rd., Uxb. 53 AX36
Bawtry Rd. N20 38 BU27
Baxendale N20 38 BT27
Baxendale St. E2 57 CB38
Baxter Ave., Red. 121 BU70
Baxter Clo., Uxb. 53 AZ38
Baxter Rd. E16 58 CJ39
Baxter Rd. N1 57 BZ36

Baxter Rd. N18 39 CB28
Baxter Rd. NW10 55 BO38
Baxter Rd., Ilf. 49 CL35
Bay Ct. W5 65 BL41
Bay Ct., Berk. 7 AQ13
Bay Manor La., Grays 70 CZ43
Bay Path, Gdse. 114 CC69
Bay Tree Clo., Brom. 88 CJ51
Bay Tree Wk., Wat. 26 BC22
Bayards, Warl. 105 CC62
Bayeaux, Tad. 103 BQ64
Bayes Clo. SE26 77 CC49
Bayfield Rd. SE9 68 CJ45
Bayford Clo., Hem.H. 8 BA11
Bayford Grn., Hert. 11 BY12
Bayford La., Hert. 11 BX11
Bayford Rd. NW10 55 BQ38
Bayford St. E8 57 CB36
Bayham Pl. NW1 56 BW37
Bayham Rd. W4 65 BN41
Bayham Rd. W13 54 BJ40
Bayham Rd., Mord. 86 BS52
Bayham Rd., Sev. 108 CV65
Bayham St. NW1 56 BW37
Bayhurst Dr., Nthwd. 35 BB29
Kings Clo.
Bayley St. WC1 1 N7
Bayley St. WC1 56 BW39
Bayley Wk. SE2 69 CQ43
Bayleys Hill, Sev. 116 CT69
Bayleys Mead, Brwd. 122 DE27
Baylis Rd. SE1 4 D5
Baylis Rd. SE1 66 BY41
Baylis Rd., Slou. 52 AO40
Bayliss Ave. SE28 59 CP40
Bayly Rd., Dart. 80 CX46
Baymans Wd., Brwd. 122 DC27
Bayne Clo. E6 58 CK39
Savage Gdns.
Bayne Hill, Beac. 34 AO29
Bayne Hill Clo., Beac. 34 AO29
Baynes Clo., Enf. 30 CB23
Baynes Ms. NW3 56 BT36
Belsize La.
Baynes St. NW1 56 BW36
Bayonne Rd. W6 65 BR43
Bayston Rd. N16 48 CA34
Bayswater Rd. W2 56 BS40
Baythorne St. E3 57 CD39
Baytree Clo., Sid. 78 CN47
Larch Gro.
Baytree Rd. SW2 66 BX45
Baywood Sq., Chig. 41 CO28
Bazalgette Clo., N.Mal. 85 BN53
Bazalgette Gdns.
Bazalgette Gdns., N.Mal. 85 BN53
Bazely St. E14 57 CF40
Bazes Shaw, Dart. 90 DC55
Church Rd.
Bazile Rd. N21 29 BY25
Beach Gro., Felt. 74 BF48
Beacham Clo. SE7 68 CJ42
Beachborough Rd., Brom. 77 CF49
Beachcroft Rd. E11 49 CG34
Beachcroft Way N19 47 BX33
Hornsey Ri.
Beachy Rd. E3 57 CE36
Beacon Clo., Bans. 103 BQ61
Beacon Clo., Ger.Cr. 34 AS30
Joiners La.
Beacon Clo., Uxb. 44 AX35
Beacon Dr., Dart. 80 DA48
Beacon Gro., Cars. 95 BV56
Beacon Hill N7 47 BX35
Beacon Hill, Brwd. 33 CY22
Beacon Hill, Grays 70 CX42
Beacon Hill, Wok. 100 AQ63
Beacon Hill Rd., Brwd. 33 CX22
Beacon Ri., Sev. 116 CT66
Beacon Rd. SE13 77 CF46
Beacon Rd., Erith 69 CU43
Beacon Rd., Houns. 73 AZ46
Beacon Way, Bans. 103 BQ61
Beacon Way, Rick. 35 AW26
Beaconfields, Sev. 116 CT66
Beacons, The, Loug. 31 CL22
Beacons Clo. E6 58 CK39
Oliver Gdns.
Beaconsfield Ave., Epp. 22 CN18
Beaconsfield Clo. N11 38 BV28
Beaconsfield Clo. SE3 68 CH43
Beaconsfield Clo. W4 65 BN42
Beaconsfield Clo., Hat. 10 BQ11
Beaconsfield Pl., Epsom 94 BO59
Beaconsfield Rd. E10 48 CF34
Beaconsfield Rd. E16 58 CG38
Beaconsfield Rd. E17 48 CD32
Beaconsfield Rd. N9 39 CB27
Beaconsfield Rd. N11 38 BV27
Beaconsfield Rd. N15 48 CA31
Beaconsfield Rd. NW10 55 BO36
Beaconsfield Rd. SE3 68 CG43
Beaconsfield Rd. SE9 78 CK48
Beaconsfield Rd. SE17 67 CA42
Beaconsfield Rd. W4 65 BN41
Beaconsfield Rd. W5 64 BK41
Beaconsfield Rd., Bex. 79 CT48
Beaconsfield Rd., Brom. 88 CJ52
Beaconsfield Rd., Croy. 87 BZ53
Beaconsfield Rd., Enf. 30 CC22
Beaconsfield Rd., Epp. 22 CN18
Beaconsfield Rd., Epsom 103 BN63
Beaconsfield Rd., Esher 93 BH57
Beaconsfield Rd., Hat. 10 BQ12
Beaconsfield Rd., Hayes 54 BD40
Beaconsfield Rd., N.Mal. 85 BN51
Beaconsfield Rd., St.Alb. 9 BH13
Beaconsfield Rd., Sthl. 54 BD40
Beaconsfield Rd., Surb. 85 BL54
Beaconsfield Rd., Twick. 74 BJ46
Beaconsfield Rd., Twick. 74 BJ46
Beaconsfield Rd., Wok. 100 AS63
Beaconsfield Ter., Rom. 50 CQ32

Beaconsfield Ter. Rd. W14 65 BR
Maclise Rd.
Beaconsfield Wk. SW6 65 BR
Parsons Grn. La.
Beaconsfield Way, Epp. 23 CC
Beacontree Ave. E17 39 CF
Beacontree Rd. E11 49 CG
Beadles La., Oxt. 114 CF
Beadlow Clo., Cars. 86 BT
Olveston Wk.
Beadman St. SE27 76 BY
Beadnell Rd. SE23 77 CC
Beadon Rd. W6 65 BO
Beadon Rd., Brom. 88 CH
Beads Hall La., Brwd. 33 DA
Beadsfield E13 58 CH
Valetta Gro.
Beaford Gro. SW20 85 BR
Beagle Clo., Felt. 73 BC
Beagle Clo., Rad. 27 BH
Beagles Clo., Orp. 89 CP
Beak St. W1 1 M
Beak St. W1 56 BW
Beal Clo., Well. 69 CO
Beal Rd., Ilf. 49 CL
Beale Clo. N13 38 BY
Beale Pl. E3 57 CD
Beale Rd. E3 57 CD
Beales La., Wey. 83 AZ
Beales Rd., Lthd. 111 BF
Beam Ave., Dag. 59 CR
Beam Way, Dag. 59 CS
Beaminster Gdns., Ilf. 49 CL
Beamish Clo., Epp. 23 CS
Beamish Dr., Bush. 36 BG
Beamish Rd. N9 39 CB
Beamish Rd., Orp. 89 CP
Bean La., Dart. 80 DA
Bean Rd., Bexh. 69 CP
Beanacre Clo. E9 57 CD
Mallard Clo
Beanshaw SE9 78 CL
Beansland Gro., Rom. 41 CQ
Bear All. EC4 2
Bear All. EC4 56 BY
Farringdon St.
Bear Clo., Rom. 50 CR
Fernden Way
Bear Gdns. SE1 4
Bear Gdns. SE1 57 BZ
Bear La. SE1 4
Bear La. SE1 56 BY
Bear Rd., Felt. 74 BD
Bear St. WC2 1 P
Bear St. WC2 56 BW
Long Acre
Beard Rd., Kings.T. 75 BL
Beardell St. SE19 77 CA
Beardow Gro. N14 29 BW
Beards Hill, Hmptn. 84 BH
Beards Hill Clo., Hmptn. 84 BF
Beards Rd., Ashf. 73 BB
Beardsfield E13 58 CH
Valetta Gro.
Beardsley Way W3 65 BN
Birkbeck Gro.
Bearfield Rd., Kings.T. 75 BL
Bearing Clo., Chig. 41 CO
Bearing Way, Chig. 41 CO
Bears Den, Tad. 103 BR
Bearstead Ri. SE4 77 CD
Bearwood Clo., Pot.B. 20 BT
Bearwood Clo., Wey. 92 AW
Ongar Pl.
Beasleys Ait La., Sun. 83 BB
Beatrice Ave. SW16 86 BX
Beatrice Ave., Wem. 46 BL
Beatrice Clo. E13 58 CH
Chargeable La.
Beatrice Clo., Pnr. 44 BC
Beatrice Ct., Wem. 46 BL
Beatrice Gdns., Grav. 81 DF
Beatrice Rd. E17 48 CE
Beatrice Rd. N4 47 BY
Beatrice Rd. N9 39 CC
Beatrice Rd. SE1 67 CB
Beatrice Rd., Oxt. 115 CG
Beatrice Rd., Rich. 75 BL
Albert Rd.
Beatrice Rd., Sthl. 54 BE
Beatson Wk. SE16 57 CC
Globe Pond Rd.
Beattie Clo., Lthd. 102 BE
Beattock Ri. N10 47 BV
Beatty Ave., Guil. 118 AT
Beatty Rd. N16 48 CA
Beatty Rd., Stan. 36 BK
Beatty St. NW1 56 BW
Beattyville Gdns., Ilf. 49 CL
Beauchamp Clo. W4 65 BN
Church Path
Beauchamp Gdns., Rick. 35 AW
Beauchamp Pl. SW3 3 D
Beauchamp Pl. SW3 66 BU
Beauchamp Rd. E7 58 CH
Beauchamp Rd. SE19 87 BZ
Beauchamp Rd. SW11 66 BU
Beauchamp Rd., E.Mol. 84 BF
Beauchamp Rd., Sutt. 95 BS
Beauchamp Rd., Twick. 74 BJ
Beauchamp St. EC1 56 BY
Leather La.
Beauchamp Ter. SW15 65 BP
Dryburgh Rd.
Beauclare Clo., Ash. 102 BK
Hatherwood
Beauclerc Rd. W6 65 BP
Beauclerk Clo., Felt. 73 BC
Florence Rd.
Beaudesert Ms., West Dr. 63 AY
Beaufort Ave., Har. 45 BJ
Beaufort Clo. E4 39 CE
Higham Sta. Ave.

aufort Clo. SW15 75 BP47
eaton Clo.
aufort Clo. W5 55 BL39
aufort Clo., Epp. 23 CR17
/ellington Rd.
aufort Clo., Reig. 120 BR70
aufort Clo., Rom. 50 CS31
aufort Clo., Wok. 100 AU61
aufort Ct., Rich. 74 BK49
aufort Dr. NW11 47 BS31
aufort Gdns. NW4 46 BQ32
aufort Gdns. SW3 3 D6
aufort Gdns. SW3 66 BU41
aufort Gdns. SW16 76 BX50
reen La.
aufort Gdns., Houns. 64 BE44
aufort Gdns., Ilf. 49 CL33
aufort Pk. NW11 47 BS31
aufort Pl., Maid. 61 AH41
aufort Rd. W5 55 BL39
aufort Rd., Kings.T. 85 BL52
aufort Rd., Reig. 120 BR70
aufort Rd., Rich. 74 BK49
aufort Rd., Ruis. 44 BA34
ysander Rd.
aufort Rd., Twick. 74 BK47
aufort Rd., Wok. 100 AU61
aufort St. SW3 66 BT43
aufort Way, Epsom 94 BP57
auforts, Egh. 72 AR49
aufoy Rd. N17 39 CA29
aufoy Rd. SW11 66 BV44
aufoy Wk. SE11 4 C9
aufoy Wk. SE11 66 BX42
aulieu Ave. SE26 77 CB49
aulieu Clo. NW9 46 BO31
aulieu Clo. SE5 67 BZ45
aulieu Clo., Mitch. 86 BV51
aulieu Clo., Slou. 62 AQ44
aulieu Clo., Twick. 74 BK46
aulieu Clo., Wat. 36 BD26
aulieu Dr., Pnr. 45 BD32
aulieu Gdns. N21 39 BZ26
aulieu Pl. W4 65 BN41
othschild Rd.
auly Way, Rom. 41 CT30
aumanor Gdns. SE9 78 CL49
eanshaw
aumaris Dr., Wdf.Grn. 40 CJ29
aumayes Clo., Hem.H. 8 AW14
aumont Ave. W14 65 BR42
aumont Ave., Har. 45 BF32
aumont Ave., Rich. 65 BL45
aumont Ave., St.Alb. 9 BJ12
aumont Ave., Wem. 45 BK35
aumont Clo., Kings.T. 75 BM50
aumont Clo., Rom. 42 CV30
aumont Cres. W14 65 BR42
aumont Cres., Rain. 59 CU36
aumont Dr., Ashf. 73 BA49
aumont Dr., Grav. 81 DF47
aumont Gdns. NW3 47 BS34
aumont Gdns., Brwd. 122 DE25
annister Dr.
aumont Gro. E1 57 CC38
aumont Ms. W1 1 H6
aumont Ms. W1 56 BV39
/arylebone High St.
aumont Pl. W1 1 M4
aumont Pl. W1 56 BW38
ottenham Ct. Rd.
aumont Pl., Barn. 28 BR22
aumont Ri. N19 47 BW33
aumont Rd. E10 48 CE33
aumont Rd. E13 58 CH38
aumont Rd. SE19 77 BZ50
aumont Rd. SW19 75 BR47
aumont Rd. W4 65 BN41
aumont Rd., Brox. 12 CA15
aumont Rd., Orp. 88 CM53
aumont Rd., Pur. 95 BY60
aumont Rd., Slou. 52 AO38
aumont Rd., Wind. 61 AO44
aumont Sq. E1 57 CC39
aumont St. W1 1 H6
aumont St. W1 56 BV39
aumont Vw., Chsnt. 21 BZ16
ear Tree Wk.
aumont Wk. NW3 56 BU36
delaide Rd.
auvais Ter., Nthlt. 54 BD37
auval Rd. SE22 77 CA46
aver Clo. SE20 77 CB50
aver Clo., Hmptn. 84 BF51
aver Gro., Nthlt. 54 BE38
etstar Way
aver Rd., Ilf. 41 CP28
averbank Rd. SE9 78 CM47
avercote Wk., Belv. 69 CQ43
)sborne Rd.
avers Clo., Guil. 118 AP70
avers Cres., Houns. 64 BD45
avers La., Houns. 64 BD45
averwood Rd., Chis. 78 CN49
avor La. W6 65 BP42
bbington Rd. SE18 68 CN42
bletts Clo., Orp. 97 CN56
c Clo., Ruis. 45 BD34
ccles Dr., Bark. 58 CN36
ccles St. E14 57 CD39
ck Clo. SE13 67 CE44
ck La., Beck. 87 CC52
ck River Pk., Beck. 87 CE51
ck Rd. E8 57 CB37
ck Way, Beck. 87 CD52
ckenham Gdns. N9 39 CA27
ckenham Gro., Brom. 87 CF51
ckenham Hill Rd. SE6 77 CE50
ckenham Hill Rd., 77 CE50
eck.
ckenham La., Brom. 88 CG51
ckenham Pl. Pk., Beck. 77 CE50
ckenham Rd., Beck. 87 CC51
ckenham Rd., W.Wick. 87 CE54

Beckenshaw Gdns., 104 BT61
Bans.
Beckers Est., The N16 48 CB34
Becket Ave. E6 58 CL38
Becket Clo. SE25 87 CB53
Becket Clo., Brwd. 42 DB29
Becket Fold, Har. 45 BH32
Becket Rd. N18 39 CC28
Becket St. SE1 4 K6
Becket St. SE1 67 BZ41
Beckets Sq., Berk. 7 AQ12
Bridle Way
Beckett Ave., Ken. 104 BY61
Beckett Clo. NW10 55 BN36
Beckett Clo. SW16 76 BW48
Beckett Clo., Belv. 69 CQ41
Tunstock Way
Beckett Wk., Beck. 77 CD50
Becketts Ave., St.Alb. 9 BG12
Becketts Clo., Felt. 73 BC46
Becketts Clo., Orp. 88 CN55
Becketts Pl., Hmptn. 84 BK51
Teddington Rd.
Beckford Pl. SE17 67 BZ42
Walworth Rd.
Beckford Rd., Croy. 87 CA53
Becklow Gdns. W12 65 BP41
Becklow Rd.
Becklow Rd. W12 65 BO41
Beckman Clo., Sev. 107 CS61
Becks Rd., Sid. 79 CO48
Beckton Rd. E16 58 CG39
Beckway Rd. SW16 86 BW51
Beckway St. SE17 4 M9
Beckway St. SE17 67 CA42
Beckwith Rd. SE24 77 BZ46
Beclands Rd. SW17 76 BV50
Becmead Ave. SW16 76 BW49
Becmead Ave., Har. 45 BJ32
Becondale Rd. SE19 77 CA49
Becontree Ave., Dag. 50 CO35
Bective Pl. SW15 65 BR45
Bective Rd. E7 49 CH35
Bective Rd. SW15 65 BR45
Becton Pl., Erith 69 CR44
Bedale Rd., Enf. 30 BZ22
Bedale Rd., Rom. 42 CX28
Bedale St. SE1 4 K3
Bedale St. SE1 57 BZ40
Bedale Wk., Dart. 80 CX47
Princes Ave.
Beddington Fm. Rd., 86 BX54
Croy.
Beddington Gdns., Wall. 95 BV57
Beddington Grn., Orp. 88 CN51
Beddington Gro., Wall. 95 BW56
Beddington La., Croy. 86 BW53
Beddington Path, Orp. 88 CN51
Beddington Rd., Ilf. 49 CN33
Beddington Rd., Orp. 88 CN51
Beddlestead La., Warl. 106 CG62
Bede Clo., Pnr. 36 BD30
Bede Rd., Rom. 50 CP32
Bedenham Way SE15 67 CA43
Hordle Prom. N.
Bedens Rd., Sid. 79 CQ50
Bedfont Clo., Felt. 73 BA46
Bedfont Ct., Stai. 63 AW45
Bedfont Lakes, Feltam 73 BA47
Bedfont La., Felt. 73 BA47
Bedfont La., Felt. 73 BB47
Bedfont Rd., Felt. 73 BA48
Bedfont Rd., Stai. 73 AY46
Bedford Ave. WC1 1 P7
Bedford Ave. WC1 56 BW39
Bedford Ave., Amer. 25 AR23
Bedford Ave., Barn. 28 BR25
Bedford Ave., Hayes 53 BC39
Bedford Clo. N10 38 BV29
Bedford Clo., Rick. 27 AT22
Bedford Ct. WC2 3 Q1
Bedford Ct. WC2 56 BX40
Bedford St.
Bedford Cres., Enf. 30 CD21
Bedford Gdns. W8 56 BS40
Bedford Gdns., Horn. 51 CV34
Bedford Hill SW12 76 BV47
Bedford Hill SW16 76 BV47
Bedford Pk., Croy. 87 BZ54
Bedford Pk. Mans. W4 65 BN42
Bedford Pk. Rd., St.Alb. 9 BH13
Bedford Pl. W1 56 BW39
Bedford Pl. WC1 1 Q6
Bedford Pl. WC1 56 BX39
Bedford Pl., Croy. 87 BZ54
Bedford Rd. E6 58 CL37
Bedford Rd. E17 48 CE31
Bedford Rd. E18 40 CH30
Bedford Rd. N2 47 BU31
Bedford Rd. N8 47 BW32
Bedford Rd. N9 39 CB26
Bedford Rd. N15 48 CA31
Bedford Rd. N22 38 BX30
Bedford Rd. NW7 37 BO27
Bedford Rd. SW4 66 BX45
Bedford Rd. W4 65 BN41
Bedford Rd. W13 54 BJ40
Bedford Rd., Brent. 65 BL42
Claypponds La.
Bedford Rd., Dart. 80 CX47
Bedford Rd., Grav. 81 DF48
Bedford Rd., Grays 71 DD42
Bedford Rd., Guil. 118 AR71
Bedford Rd., Har. 45 BG32
Bedford Rd., Ilf. 49 CL34
Bedford Rd., Nthwd. 35 BA27
Bedford Rd., Orp. 89 CO55
Bedford Rd., Ruis. 44 BB35
Bedford Rd., St.Alb. 9 BH14
Bedford Rd., Sid. 78 CN48
Bedford Rd., Twick. 74 BG48
Bedford Rd., Wor.Pk. 85 BQ55
Bedford Row WC1 2 C6
Bedford Row WC1 56 BX39

Bedford Sq. WC1 1 P7
Bedford Sq. WC1 56 BW39
Bedford St. WC2 1 Q10
Bedford St. WC2 56 BX40
Bedford St., Berk. 7 AS13
George St.
Bedford St., Wat. 26 BC23
Bedford Way WC1 1 P5
Bedford Way WC1 56 BW38
Bedfordbury WC2 3 Q1
Bedfordbury WC2 56 BX40
Chandos Pl.
Bedgebury Gdns. SW19 75 BR47
Bedgebury Rd. SE9 68 CJ45
Bedivere Rd., Brom. 78 CH48
Bedlow Way, Croy. 95 BX56
Nicholas Rd.
Bedmond Grn., Abb.L. 17 BB17
Bedmond Hill, Abb.L. 17 BB16
Bedmond La., St.Alb. 9 BE14
Bedmond La. 9 BD15
(Potterscrouch), St.Alb.
Bedmond Rd., Abb.L. 17 BB18
Bedmond Rd., Hem.H. 8 BA14
Bedonwell Rd. SE2 69 CQ43
Bedonwell Rd., Bexh. 69 CQ44
Bedser Dr., Grnf. 45 BG35
Bedster Gdns., E.Mol. 84 BG51
Bedwardine Rd. SE19 77 CA50
Bedwell Ave., Hat. 11 BV12
Bedwell Gdns. E., Hayes 63 BB42
Bedwell Gdns. W., Hayes 63 BB42
Bedwell Rd. N17 39 CA30
Bedwell Rd., Belv. 69 CQ42
Bedwin Way SE16 67 CB42
Bonamy Est. W.
Beeby Rd. E16 58 CH39
Beech Ave. N20 38 BU26
Beech Ave. W3 55 BO40
Beech Ave., Brent. 64 BJ43
Beech Ave., Brwd. 122 DC27
Beech Ave., Buck.H. 40 CH27
Beech Ave., Enf. 29 BY21
Beech Ave., Lthd. 111 BD68
Beech Ave., Rad. 18 BJ20
Beech Ave., Ruis. 44 BC33
Beech Ave., Sid. 79 CO47
Beech Ave., S.Croy. 96 BZ59
Beech Ave., Swan. 89 CT52
Beech Ave., Upmin. 51 CX35
Beech Ave., West. 106 CJ63
Beech Bottom, St.Alb. 9 BG12
Beech Pl.
Beech Clo. N9 30 CB25
Beech Clo. SE8 67 CD43
Clyde St.
Beech Clo. SW15 75 BP47
Beech Clo. SW19 75 BQ50
Beech Clo., Ashf. 73 BA49
Beech Clo., Cars. 86 BU55
Beech Clo., Cob. 93 BF59
Beech Clo., Dor. 119 BH71
Beech Clo., Hat. 10 BP13
Beech Clo., Horn. 50 CU34
Beech Clo., Lthd. 111 BD67
Beech Clo., Stai. 73 AX47
St. Marys Cres.
Beech Clo., Stai. 73 AX47
Diamedes Ave.
Beech Clo., Sun. 84 BD51
Beech Clo., Walt. 93 BD56
Beech Clo., West Dr. 63 AZ41
Beech Clo., Wey. 92 AY59
Beech Copse, Brom. 88 CK51
Beech Copse, S.Croy. 96 CB56
Beech Ct. SE9 78 CK46
Beech Ct., Cob. 93 BE59
Beech Ct., Tedd. 74 BK50
Broom Water
Beech Dell, Orp. 97 CK56
Beech Dr. N2 38 BU30
Beech Dr., Berk. 7 AR13
Beech Dr., Borwd. 28 BL23
Beech Dr., Reig. 121 BT70
Beech Dr., Saw. 6 CP7
Beech Dr., Tad. 103 BR64
Beech Dr., Wok. 100 AV65
Beech Fm. Rd., Warl. 105 CF63
Beech Fld., Bans. 95 BS60
Beech Gdns. W5 65 BL41
Beech Gdns., Dag. 59 CR36
Beech Gdns., Wok. 100 AR61
Beech Gro., Amer. 25 AO23
Beech Gro., Cat. 114 CA66
Beech Gro., Epsom 103 BP62
Beech Gro., Guil. 118 AP70
Beech Gro., Ilf. 40 CN29
Beech Gro., Mitch. 86 BW53
Beech Gro., N.Mal. 85 BN52
Beech Gro., S.Ock. 70 CY41
Beech Gro., Wey. 92 AW56
Beech Gro., Wok. 100 AR65
Beech Hall Cres. E4 39 CF29
Beech Hall Rd. E4 39 CF29
Beech Hill, Barn. 29 BT22
Beech Hill, Wok. 100 AR65
Beech Hill Ave., Barn. 29 BT23
Beech Hill Ct., Berk. 7 AR13
Beech Hill Gdns., 31 CH22
Wal.Abb.
Beech Holt, Lthd. 102 BK64
Beech Ho. Rd., Croy. 87 BZ55
Beech La., Beac. 34 AP29
Beech La., Buck.H. 40 CH27
Beech La., Guil. 118 AR72
Beech Lawn, Guil. 118 AS71
Beech Lawns N12 38 BT28
Beech Pk., Amer. 25 AQ22
Beech Pl., Epp. 22 CN19
Beech Pl., St.Alb. 9 BG12
Beech Rd. N11 38 BX29
Beech Rd. SW16 86 BX51
Beech Rd., Dart. 80 CV47
Beech Rd., Epsom 103 BO61

Beech Rd., Felt. 73 BB47
Beech Rd., Ong. 15 DB13
Beech Rd., Orp. 98 CO57
Beech Rd., Red. 113 BW66
Beech Rd., Reig. 121 BS69
Beech Rd., St.Alb. 9 BH12
Beech Rd., Sev. 116 CU66
Beech Rd., Slou. 62 AS41
Beech Rd., Wat. 26 BC22
Beech Rd., West. 106 CH62
Beech Rd., Wey. 92 BA56
St. Marys Rd.
Beech Row, Kings.T. 75 BL49
Beech St. EC2 2 H6
Beech St. EC2 57 BZ39
Beech St., Rom. 50 CS31
Beech Tree Clo., Stan. 36 BK28
Beech Tree Glade E4 40 CG26
Beech Tree La., Stai. 83 AW51
Beech Wk. NW7 37 BN29
Beech Wk., Dart. 69 CU45
Beech Wk., Epsom 94 BP59
Beech Wk., Hodd. 12 CD12
Beech Way NW10 55 BN36
Beech Way, Croy. 96 CC60
Beech Way, Epsom 103 BO61
Beech Way, Guil. 118 AT70
Beech Way, Twick. 74 BF48
Beech Waye, Ger.Cr. 43 AS33
Beech Wd. Ave., Amer. 25 AR22
Beechall, Cher. 91 AU57
Beechcroft, Ash. 103 BL63
Beechcroft, Chis. 78 CL50
Beechcroft Ave. NW11 46 BR33
Beechcroft Ave., Bexh. 69 CS44
Beechcroft Ave., Har. 45 BF33
Beechcroft Ave., Ken. 105 BZ61
Beechcroft Ave., N.Mal. 85 BN51
Beechcroft Ave., Rick. 26 BA25
Beechcroft Ave., Sthl. 54 BE40
Beechcroft Ave., S.le H. 71 DK42
Beechcroft Clo., Houns. 64 BE43
Beechcroft Clo., Orp. 97 CM56
Beechcroft Dr., Guil. 118 AO72
Beechcroft Gdns., Wem. 46 BL34
Beechcroft Manor, Wey. 83 BA55
Beechcroft Rd. E18 40 CH30
Beechcroft Rd. SW14 65 BN45
Beechcroft Rd. SW17 76 BU48
Beechcroft Rd., Bush. 27 BE25
Beechcroft Rd., Chess. 85 BL55
Beechcroft Rd., Orp. 97 CM56
Beechdale N21 38 BX27
Beechdale Rd. SW2 76 BX46
Beechdene, Tad. 103 BP64
Beechen Cliff Way, Islw. 64 BH44
Henley Clo.
Beechen Gro., Pnr. 45 BE31
Beechen Gro., Wat. 26 BC24
Beechen La., Tad. 112 BR66
Beechen Pl. SE23 77 CC48
Hindsley Pl.
Beechenlea La., Swan. 89 CU52
Beeches, The, Bans. 104 BS61
Beeches, The, Brwd. 42 DA27
Beeches, The, Lthd. 102 BH65
Beeches, The, Rick. 25 AV25
Beeches, The, St.Alb. 18 BG17
Sycamore Dr.
Beeches, The, Til. 71 DG44
Beeches Ave., The, Cars. 95 BU57
Beeches Clo. SE20 87 CC51
Genoa Rd.
Beeches Clo., Tad. 104 BS65
Beeches Rd. SW17 76 BU48
Beeches Rd., Sutt. 88 BR54
Ridge Rd.
Beeches Wk., Cars. 95 BT58
Beeches Wd., Tad. 103 BR64
Beechfield, Bans. 95 BS60
Beechfield, Kings L. 17 AY18
Beechfield, Saw. 6 CQ6
Beechfield Cotts., Brom. 88 CJ51
Beechfield Gdns., Rom. 50 CS33
Beechfield Rd. N4 48 BZ32
Beechfield Rd. SE6 77 CD47
Beechfield Rd., Brom. 88 CJ51
Beechfield Rd., Erith 69 CT43
Beechfield Rd., Hem.H. 8 AW14
Beechfield Rd., Welw.G.C. 5 BR9
Beechfield Wk., 30 CF21
Wal.Abb.
Beechhill Rd. SE9 78 CL46
Beechmont Ave., Vir.W. 82 AR53
Beechmont Clo., Brom. 78 CG49
Beechmont Rd., Sev. 116 CU68
Beechmore Gdns., Sutt. 85 BQ55
Beechmore Rd. SW11 66 BU44
Beechmount Ave. W7 54 BG39
Beecholme, Bans. 94 BQ60
Beecholme Ave., Mitch. 86 BV51
Beecholme Est. E5 48 CB34
Beechpark Way, Wat. 26 BB22
Beechtree Ave., Egh. 72 AQ50
Beechtree Pl., Sutt. 95 BS56
West St.
Beechvale Clo. N12 38 BU28
Beechway, Bex. 79 CP46
Beechwood Ave. N3 46 BR31
Beechwood Ave., Couls. 104 BV61
Beechwood Ave., Grnf. 54 BF38
Beechwood Ave., Har. 45 BF34
Beechwood Ave., Hayes 53 BA40
Beechwood Ave., Orp. 97 CN56
Beechwood Ave., Pot.B. 20 BS20
Beechwood Ave., Rich. 65 BM44
Beechwood Ave., Rick. 25 AT24
Beechwood Ave., Ruis. 44 BB34
Beechwood Ave., St.Alb. 9 BJ12
Beechwood Ave., Stai. 73 AW50
Beechwood Ave., Sun. 73 BC50
Beechwood Ave., Tad. 104 BS64
Beechwood Ave., Th.Hth. 86 BY52
Beechwood Ave., Uxb. 53 AZ39
Beechwood Ave., Wey. 92 BA56

Beechwood Clo. NW7 37 BO28
Beechwood Clo., Amer. 25 AR23
Beechwood Clo., Chsnt. 21 CA16
Beechwood Clo., Surb. 84 BK54
Beechwood Clo., Wey. 92 BB56
Beechwood Clo., Wok. 100 AP62
Beechwood Cres., Bexh. 69 CP45
Beechwood Dr., Cob. 93 BF59
Beechwood Dr., Kes. 97 CJ56
Beechwood Dr., Wdf.Grn. 40 CG28
Beechwood Gdns. NW10 55 BL38
St. Annes Gdns.
Beechwood Gdns., Cat. 105 CB64
Beechwood Gdns., Har. 45 BF34
Beechwood Gdns., Ilf. 49 CK32
Beechwood Gdns., Rain. 59 CU39
Beechwood Gdns., Slou. 62 AP41
Beechwood Gro. W3 55 BO40
East Acton La.
Beechwood Gro., Surb. 84 BK54
Beechwood Clo.
Beechwood La., Warl. 105 CC63
Beechwood Manor, Wey. 92 BB56
Beechwood Ms. N9 39 CB27
Winchester Rd.
Beechwood Pk. E18 49 CH31
Beechwood Pk., Hem.H. 7 AV15
Beechwood Pk., Lthd. 102 BK64
Beechwood Ri., Chis. 78 CL49
Beechwood Ri., Wat. 26 BC21
Beechwood Rd. E8 57 CA36
Beechwood Rd. N8 47 BW31
Beechwood Rd., Cat. 105 CB64
Beechwood Rd., Slou. 52 AO39
Beechwood Rd., S.Croy. 96 BZ58
Beechwood Rd., Vir.W. 82 AQ54
Beechwood Rd., Wok. 100 AP62
Beechwood Ter. E4 39 CF29
Larkshall Rd.
Beechwoods Ct. SE22 77 CA50
Crystal Palace Par.
Beechworth Clo. NW3 47 BS34
Beechy Lees Rd., Sev. 108 CW61
Beecot La., Walt. 84 BD55
Beecroft Rd. SE4 77 CD46
Beehive Chase, Brwd. 33 DB21
Beehive Clo., Borwd. 27 BK25
Beehive Clo., Uxb. 53 AY36
Honey Hill
Beehive Ct., Ilf. 49 CK32
Beehive Grn., Welw.G.C. 5 BS9
Beehive La., Ilf. 49 CK32
Beehive La., Welw.G.C. 5 BS9
Beehive Pas. EC3 2 M9
Beehive Rd., Chsnt. 20 BY17
Beehive Rd., Stai. 72 AV49
Beehive Way, Reig. 121 BS72
Beeken Dene, Orp. 97 CM56
Beel Clo., Amer. 25 AR23
Beeleigh Rd., Mord. 86 BS52
Beesfield La., Farn. 90 CX54
Beeston Clo. E8 48 CB35
Foxley Clo.
Beeston Clo., Wat. 36 BD28
Beeston Dr., Wal.Cr. 21 CC17
Beeston Pl. SW1 3 K7
Beeston Pl. SW1 66 BV41
Beeston Rd., Barn. 29 BT25
Berkeley Cres.
Beeston Way, Felt. 74 BD46
Beethoven Rd., Borwd. 36 BK26
Beethoven St. W10 55 BR38
Beeton Clo., Pnr. 36 BF29
Begbie Rd. SE3 68 CJ44
Beggars Bush La., Wat. 26 BA25
Beggars Hill, Epsom 94 BO57
Beggars Hollow, Enf. 30 BZ22
Beggars La., West. 106 CM65
Beggars La., Wok. 91 AO59
Beggars Roost La., Sutt. 95 BS57
Begonia Pl., Hmptn. 74 BF50
Gresham Rd.
Begonia Wk. W12 55 BO39
Du Cane Rd.
Beira St. SW12 76 BV47
Bekan Ct., Wat. 27 BD21
Bekesbourne St. E14 57 CD39
Ratcliffe La.
Belcher Rd., Hodd. 12 CE11
Amwell St.
Belchers La., Wal.Abb. 13 CJ15
Belcroft Clo., Brom. 78 CG50
Hope Pk.
Beldam Haw, Sev. 98 CR59
Beldham Gdns., E.Mol. 84 BF52
Belfairs Dr., Rom. 50 CP33
Belfairs Grn., Wat. 36 BD28
Heysham Dr.
Belfast Ave., Slou. 52 AO39
Belfast Rd. N16 48 CA34
Belfast Rd. SE25 87 CB52
Belfield Rd., Epsom 94 BN57
Belfont Wk. N7 47 BX35
Camden Rd.
Belford Gro. SE18 68 CL42
Belford Rd., Borwd. 28 BL22
Belfort Rd. SE15 67 CC44
Belfry Ave., Uxb. 35 AW29
Belfry La., Rick. 35 AX26
Belgrade Rd. N16 48 CA35
Belgrade Rd., Hmptn. 84 BF51
Belgrave Ave., Rom. 51 CV31
Belgrave Ave., Wat. 26 BB25
Belgrave Clo. N14 29 BW25
Belgrave Clo. W3 65 BM41
Avenue Rd.
Belgrave Clo., Orp. 89 CP52
Sandway Rd.
Belgrave Clo., St.Alb. 9 BK11
Portman Clo.
Belgrave Clo., Walt. 92 BC56
Belgrave Cres., Sun. 83 BC51
Belgrave Dr., Kings L. 17 BA17
Belgrave Gdns. N14 29 BW24

Belgrave Gdns. NW8 56 BS37
Belgrave Gdns., Stan. 36 BK28
Belgrave Grn. N., Slou. 52 AP40
Belgrave Grn. S., Slou. 52 AP40
Belgrave Manor, Wok. 100 AS63
Brooklyn Rd.
Belgrave Ms., Uxb. 53 AX38
Belgrave Ms. N. SW1 3 G5
Belgrave Ms. N. SW1 66 BV41
Belgrave Ms. S. SW1 3 H6
Belgrave Ms. S. SW1 66 BV41
Belgrave Ms. W. SW1 3 G6
Belgrave Pl. SW1 3 H6
Belgrave Pl. SW1 66 BV41
Belgrave Pl., Slou. 62 AQ41
Clifton Rd.
Belgrave Rd. E10 48 CF33
Belgrave Rd. E11 49 CH34
Belgrave Rd. E13 58 CJ38
Belgrave Rd. E17 48 CE32
Belgrave Rd. SE25 87 CA52
Belgrave Rd. SW1 3 L9
Belgrave Rd. SW1 66 BV42
Belgrave Rd. SW13 65 BO43
Belgrave Rd., Houns. 64 BE45
Belgrave Rd., Ilf. 49 CK33
Belgrave Rd., Mitch. 86 BT52
Belgrave Rd., Slou. 52 AP40
Belgrave Rd., Sun. 83 BC51
Belgrave Sq. SW1 3 G6
Belgrave Sq. SW1 66 BV41
Belgrave St. E1 57 CD39
Belgrave Ter., Wdf.Grn. 40 CH27
Belgrave Wk., Mitch. 86 BT52
Belgrave Yd. SW1 3 J7
Belgravia Gdns., Brom. 77 CF50
Belgravia Ms., Kings.T. 84 BK52
Belgrove St. WC1 2 A2
Belgrove St. WC1 56 BX38
Belham Rd., Kings L. 17 AY17
Belham Wk. SE5 67 BZ44
D'Eynsford Rd.
Belhaven Ct., Borwd. 28 BL23
Leeming Rd.
Belinda Rd. SW9 66 BY45
Belitha Vill. N1 56 BX36
Bell Ave., Rom. 41 CU30
Bell Ave., West Dr. 63 AY42
Bell Clo., Abb.L. 17 BC17
Bell Clo., Green. 80 CZ46
Bell Clo., Pnr. 36 BD30
Bell Clo., Ruis. 44 BB34
Bell Clo., Slou. 52 AQ39
Bell Cor., Upmin. 51 CY34
Bell Ct., Surb. 85 BM55
Bell Cres., Couls. 104 BV64
Bell Dr. SW18 75 BR47
Bell Fm. Ave., Dag. 50 CS34
Bell Gdns., Orp. 89 CP53
Bell Gate, Hem.H. 8 AY12
Bathurst Rd.
Bell Grn. SE26 77 CD49
Bell Grn., Hem.H. 16 AT17
Bell Grn. La. SE26 77 CD49
Bell Hill, Croy. 87 BZ55
Crown Hill
Bell Ho. Rd., Rom. 50 CS33
Bell Inn Yd. EC3 2 L9
Bell La. E1 2 P7
Bell La. E1 57 CA39
Bell La. E16 58 CH40
Bell La. NW4 46 BQ31
Bell La., Abb.L. 17 BB17
Bell La., Amer. 25 AQ23
Bell La., Berk. 7 AP12
Bell La., Brox. 12 CD14
Bell La., Enf. 30 CC22
Bell La., Hat. 11 BS15
Bell La., Hodd. 12 CE12
Bell La., Lthd. 102 BG65
Bell La., St.Alb. 19 BL18
Bell La., Twick. 74 BJ47
Bell La. (Eton Wick), Wind. 61 AM42
Bell La. Clo., Lthd. 102 BG65
Bell Mead, Saw. 6 CQ6
Bell Meadow SE19 77 CA49
Dulwich Wd. Ave.
Bell Meadow, Gdse. 114 CC69
Hickmans Clo.
Bell Par., Wind. 61 AM44
Bell Rd., E.Mol. 84 BG53
Bell Rd., Enf. 30 BZ23
Bell Rd., Houns. 64 BF45
Bell St. NW1 1 C6
Bell St. NW1 56 BU39
Bell St., Reig. 121 BS70
Bell St., Saw. 6 CQ6
Bell Vw., Wind. 61 AM45
Bell Vw. Clo., Wind. 61 AM44
Bell Wk., Saw. 6 CQ6
Bell Water Gate SE18 68 CL41
Bell Wf. La. EC4 57 BZ40
Upper Thames St.
Bell Yd. WC2 2 D9
Bell Yd. WC2 56 BY39
Bellamy Clo. SW5 65 BR42
Aisgill Ave.
Bellamy Clo., Uxb. 44 AZ34
Bellamy Clo., Wat. 26 BC23
Bellamy Dr., Stan. 36 BJ30
Bellamy Rd. E4 39 CE29
Bellamy Rd., Chsnt. 21 CD18
Bellamy Rd., Enf. 30 BZ23
Halifax Rd.
Bellamy St. SW12 76 BV47
Bellasis Ave. SW2 76 BX48
Bellclose Rd., West Dr. 63 AY41
Belle Vue, Grnf. 54 BG37
Belle Vue Clo., Stai. 83 AW51
Belle Vue Est. NW4 46 BQ31
Belle Vue Rd. E17 39 CF30
Belle Vue Rd., Bexh. 79 CQ46
Belle Vue Rd., Orp. 97 CL58
Standard Rd.
Bellefield Rd., Orp. 89 CO53
Bellefields Rd. SW9 66 BX45
Bellegrove Clo., Well. 68 CN44
Bellegrove Rd., Well. 68 CN44
Bellenden Rd. SE15 67 CA45
Bellestaines Pleasaunce E4 39 CE27
Belleville Rd. SW11 76 BU46
Bellevue La., Bush. 36 BG26
Bellevue Ms. N11 38 BV28
Bellevue Rd.
Bellevue Pk., Th.Hth. 87 BZ52
Bellevue Pl. E1 57 CC38
Bellevue Rd. N11 38 BV28
Bellevue Rd. NW4 46 BQ31
Bellevue Rd. SW13 65 BP44
Bellevue Rd. SW17 76 BU47
Bellevue Rd. W13 54 BJ38
Bellevue Rd., Horn. 51 CW33
Bellevue Rd., Kings.T. 85 BL52
Bellevue Rd., Rom. 41 CS29
Bellew St. SW17 76 BT48
Bellfield, Croy. 96 CD57
Bellfield Ave., Har. 36 BG29
Bellfield Rd., Guil. 118 AR69
Bellfields Rd., Guil. 118 AR69
Bellflower Clo. E6 58 CK39
Sorrell Gdns.
Bellflower Path, Rom. 42 CV29
Bellgate Ms. NW5 47 BV34
York Ri.
Bellhouse La., Brwd. 33 CZ25
Bellingham Grn. SE6 77 CE48
Bellingham Rd. SE6 77 CE48
Bellman Ave., Grav. 81 DJ47
Bellmarsh Rd., Wey. 92 AW56
Bellmount Wd. Ave., Wat. 26 BB23
Bellot St. SE10 68 CG42
Bellring Clo., Belv. 69 CR43
Bells All. SW6 66 BS44
Bells Gdns. Est. SE15 67 CB43
Bells Hill, Barn. 28 BQ25
Bells Hill, Slou. 52 AQ37
Bells Hill Grn., Slou. 52 AQ36
Bells La., Slou. 62 AT45
Bellswood La., Iver 52 AT39
Belltrees Gro. SW16 76 BX49
Bellvue Clo., Orp. 97 CL58
Bellweir Clo., Stai. 72 AT48
Wraysbury Rd.
Bellwood Rd. SE15 67 CC45
Belmarsh Rd. SE28 68 CN41
Belmont Ave. N9 39 CB26
Belmont Ave. N13 38 BX28
Belmont Ave. N17 48 BZ31
Belmont Ave., Barn. 29 BU25
Belmont Ave., Guil. 118 AP69
Belmont Ave., N.Mal. 85 BP52
Belmont Ave., Sthl. 64 BE41
Belmont Ave., Upmin. 51 CX34
Belmont Ave., Well. 68 CN44
Belmont Ave., Wem. 55 BL37
Belmont Circle, Har. 36 BJ30
Belmont Clo. E4 39 CF28
Falmouth Ave.
Belmont Clo. N20 38 BS26
Belmont Clo. SW4 66 BW45
Belmont Clo., Barn. 29 BU24
Belmont Clo., Uxb. 53 AX36
Belmont Clo., Wdf.Grn. 40 CH28
Belmont Ct. NW11 46 BR32
Belmont Ct., St.Alb. 9 BG14
Belmont Hill
Belmont Gro. SE13 67 CF45
Belmont Gro. W4 65 BN42
Belmont Hall Ct. SE13 67 CF45
Belmont Hill SE13 67 CF45
Belmont Hill, St.Alb. 9 BG14
Belmont La., Chis. 78 CL49
Belmont La., Stan. 36 BK29
Belmont Pk. SE13 67 CF45
Belmont Pk. Clo. SE13 67 CF45
Belmont Pk.
Belmont Pk. Rd. E10 48 CE32
Belmont Ri., Sutt. 94 BR57
Belmont Rd. N15 48 BZ31
Belmont Rd. N17 48 BZ31
Belmont Rd. SE25 87 CB53
Belmont Rd. SW4 66 BW45
Belmont Rd. W4 65 BN42
Belmont Rd., Beck. 87 CD51
Belmont Rd., Bush. 27 BE25
Belmont Rd., Chis. 78 CL49
Belmont Rd., Erith 69 CR43
Belmont Rd., Grays 71 DC43
Belmont Rd., Har. 45 BH31
Belmont Rd., Hem.H. 8 AY15
Belmont Rd., Horn. 51 CV34
Belmont Rd., Ilf. 49 CM34
Belmont Rd., Lthd. 102 BJ64
Belmont Rd., Reig. 121 BT71
Belmont Rd., Sev. 107 CU65
St. Botolphs Rd.
Belmont Rd., Sutt. 95 BS58
Belmont Rd., Twick. 74 BG48
Belmont Rd., Uxb. 53 AX36
Belmont Rd., Wall. 95 BV56
Belmont St. NW1 56 BV36
Belmont Ter. W4 65 BN42
Belmont Rd.
Belmor, Borwd. 28 BM25
Belmore Ave., Hayes 53 BC39
Belmore Ave., Wok. 100 AU61
Belmore La. N7 47 BW35
Belmore St. SW8 66 BW44
Beloe Clo. SW15 65 BP45
Belper Ct. E5 48 CC35
Clapton Pk. Est.
Belsham St. E9 57 CC36
Belsize Ave. N13 38 BX29
Belsize Ave. NW3 56 BT36
Belsize Ave. W13 64 BJ41
Belsize Clo., Hem.H. 8 AZ14
Belsize Clo., St.Alb. 9 BK11
Belsize Cres. NW3 47 BT35
Belsize Gdns., Sutt. 95 BS56
Belsize Gro. NW3 56 BU36
Belsize La. NW3 56 BT36
Belsize Ms. NW3 47 BT35
Belsize La.
Belsize Pk. NW3 56 BT36
Belsize Pk. Gdns. NW3 56 BU36
Belsize Pk. Ms. NW3 56 BT36
Belsize La.
Belsize Pl. NW3 47 BT35
Belsize Rd. NW6 56 BS37
Belsize Rd., Har. 36 BG29
Belsize Rd., Hem.H. 8 AZ14
Belsize Sq. NW3 56 BT36
Belsize Ter. NW3 56 BT36
Belson Rd. SE18 68 CK42
Belswains Grn., Hem.H. 8 AY15
Belswains La.
Belswains La., Hem.H. 8 AY15
Beltana Dr., Grav. 81 DJ49
Beltane Dr. SW19 75 BQ48
Belthorn Cres. SW12 76 BW47
Beltinge Rd., Rom. 51 CW31
Belton Rd. E7 58 CH36
Belton Rd. E11 49 CG35
Belton Rd. N17 48 CA31
Belton Rd. NW2 55 BP36
Belton Rd., Berk. 7 AQ12
Belton Rd., Sid. 79 CO49
Belton Way E3 57 CE39
Beltona Gdns., Chsnt. 21 CC17
Beltran Rd. SW6 66 BS44
Beltwood Rd., Belv. 69 CS42
Belvedere Ave. SW19 75 BR49
Belvedere Ave., Ilf. 40 CL30
Belvedere Bldgs. SE1 4 G5
Belvedere Bldgs. SE1 66 BY41
Belvedere Clo., Esher 93 BF56
Belvedere Clo., Grav. 81 DH47
Belvedere Clo., Guil. 118 AQ69
Belvedere Clo., Tedd. 74 BH49
Belvedere Clo., Wey. 92 AZ56
Belvedere Ct. N2 47 BT32
Belvedere Ct. SW15 65 BQ45
Upper Richmond Rd.
Belvedere Dr. SW19 75 BR49
Belvedere Gdns., E.Mol. 84 BE53
Belvedere Gdns., St.Alb. 18 BF17
Belvedere Gro. SW19 75 BR49
Belvedere Pl. SE1 4 G5
Belvedere Pl. SE1 66 BY41
Borough Rd.
Belvedere Rd. E10 48 CD33
Belvedere Rd. SE1 4 C4
Belvedere Rd. SE1 66 BX41
Belvedere Rd. SE2 59 CP40
Belvedere Rd. SE19 77 CA50
Belvedere Rd. W7 64 BH41
Trumpers Way
Belvedere Rd., Bexh. 69 CQ45
Belvedere Rd., Brwd. 42 CZ27
Belvedere Rd., West. 106 CK62
Belvedere Sq. SW19 75 BR49
Belvedere Strand NW9 37 BO30
Belvedere Way, Har. 46 BL32
Belvoir Clo. SE9 78 CK48
Nunnington Clo.
Belvoir Rd. SE22 77 CB47
Belvue Clo., Nthlt. 54 BF36
Belvue Rd., Nthlt. 54 BF36
Bembridge Clo. NW6 55 BQ36
Bembridge Ct., Slou. 62 AP41
Park St.
Bembridge Gdns., Ruis. 44 BA34
Bemerton St. N1 56 BX37
Bemish Rd. SW15 65 BQ45
Bempton Dr., Ruis. 44 BC34
Bemsted Rd. E17 48 CD31
Bemwell Ct., Sun. 83 BC51
Ben Hale Clo., Stan. 36 BJ28
Ben Jonson Rd. E1 57 CC39
Ben Smith Way SE16 67 CB41
Jamaica Rd.
Ben Tillet Clo., Bark. 59 CO36
Benares Rd. SE18 68 CN42
Benbow Clo., St.Alb. 9 BJ14
Benbow Rd. W6 65 BP41
Benbow St. SE8 67 CE43
Benbow Waye, Uxb. 53 AX39
Benbrick Rd., Guil. 118 AQ71
Benbury Clo., Brom. 77 CF49
Bence, The, Egh. 82 AT52
Bench, The, Rich. 74 BK48
Back La.
Bench Fld., S.Croy. 96 CA57
Bench Manor Cres., Ger.Cr. 34 AR30
Benchleys Rd., Hem.H. 7 AV14
Bencombe Rd., Pur. 95 BX60
Bencroft, Chsnt. 21 CB16
Bencroft Rd. SW16 76 BW50
Bencurtis Pk., W.Wick. 87 CF55
Bendall Ms. NW1 1 D6
Bendall Ms. NW1 56 BU39
Bell St.
Bendemeer Rd. SW15 65 BQ45
Bendish Rd. E6 58 CK36
Bendmore Ave. SE2 69 CO42
Bendon Valley SW18 76 BS47
Bendysh Rd., Bush. 27 BE24
Benedict Clo., Belv. 69 CQ41
Tunstock Way
Benedict Clo., Orp. 88 CN55
Benedict Dr., Felt. 73 BA47
Benedict Rd. SW9 66 BX45
Stockwell Pk.
Benedict Rd., Mitch. 86 BT52
Benedict Way N2 47 BT31
Benedictine Gate, Wal.Cr. 21 CD17
Benenden Grn., Brom. 88 CH53
Benenstock Rd., Stai. 73 AW46
Benets Rd., Horn. 51 CX33
Benett Gdns. SW16 86 BX51
Benfleet Clo., Cob. 93 BE59
Benfleet Clo., Sutt. 86 BT55
Benford Rd., Hodd. 12 CD13
Bengal Rd., Ilf. 49 CL35
Bengarth Dr., Har. 36 BG30
Bengarth Rd., Nthlt. 54 BD37
Bengeworth Rd. SE5 67 BZ45
Bengeworth Rd., Har. 45 BJ34
Benham Clo. SW11 66 BT45
Hope St.
Benham Clo., Couls. 104 BY62
Benham Gdns., Houns. 64 BE45
Benham Rd. W7 54 BH39
Benhams Pl. NW3 47 BT35
Holly Wk.
Benhill Ave., Sutt. 95 BS56
Benhill Rd. SE5 67 BZ43
Benhill Rd., Sutt. 86 BT55
Benhill Wd. Rd., Sutt. 86 BT55
Benhilton Gdns., Sutt. 86 BS55
Benhurst Ave., Horn. 50 CU35
Benhurst Clo., S.Croy. 96 CC58
Benhurst Ct. SW16 76 BY49
Benhurst Gdns., S.Croy. 96 CC58
Benhurst La. SW16 76 BY49
Benin St. SE13 77 CF47
Benison Ct., Slou. 62 AP41
Hencroft St.
Benjafield Clo. N18 39 CB28
Brettenham Rd.
Benjamin Clo., Horn. 50 CU32
Benjamin St. EC1 2 F6
Benjamin St. EC1 56 BY39
Benledi St. E14 57 CF39
Benn St. E9 57 CD36
Bennerley Rd. SW11 76 BU46
Bennet St. SW1 56 BW40
Arlington St.
Bennets Copse, Chis. 78 CK50
Wood Dr.
Bennets Hill EC4 2 G10
Bennetsfield Rd., West Dr. 53 AZ40
Bennett Clo., Kings.T. 84 BK51
Bennett Clo., Nthwd. 35 BB29
Bennett Clo., Well. 69 CO44
Bennett Clo., Welw.G.C. 5 BR10
Bennett Gro. SE13 67 CE44
Bennett Pk. SE3 68 CG45
Bennett Rd. E13 58 CJ38
Bennett Rd. N16 48 CA35
Bennett Rd., Rom. 50 CQ32
Bennett St. SW1 3 L2
Bennett St. W4 65 BO43
Bennett Way, Dart. 80 CY49
Bennett Way, Guil. 110 AW68
Bennetts, Chesh. 16 AO18
Bennetts Ave., Croy. 87 CD55
Bennetts Ave., Grnf. 54 BG37
Bennetts Ave., Sev. 99 DB59
Bennetts Castle La., Dag. 50 CP35
Bennetts Clo. N17 39 CB29
Bennetts Clo., Cob. 92 BC60
Bennetts Clo., St.Alb. 10 BN15
Bennetts Clo., Slou. 61 AN41
Bennetts End Clo., Hem.H. 8 AY14
Bennetts End Rd., Hem.H. 8 AZ14
Bennetts Gate, Hem.H. 8 AZ15
Bennetts End Rd.
Bennetts Way, Croy. 87 CD55
Bennetts Yd. SW1 3 P7
Bennetts Yd. SW1 66 BX41
Marsham St.
Benning Clo., Wind. 61 AL45
Benningholme Rd., Edg. 37 BO29
Bennington Rd. N17 39 CA30
Bennington Rd., Wdf.Grn. 40 CG29
Forest Dr.
Bennions Clo., Horn. 60 CV36
Franklin Rd.
Benns Wk., Rich. 65 BL45
Rosedale Rd.
Benrek Clo., Ilf. 40 CM30
Bensbury Clo. SW15 75 BQ47
Bensham Clo., Th.Hth. 87 BZ52
Bensham Gro., Th.Hth. 87 BZ51
Bensham La., Croy. 86 BY54
Bensham La., Th.Hth. 86 BY53
Bensham Manor Rd., Th.Hth. 87 BZ52
Benskin Rd., Wat. 26 BC25
Benskins La., Hav. 42 CV26
Bensley Clo. N11 38 BU28
Benson Ave. E6 58 CJ37
Benson Clo., Houns. 64 BF45
Benson Clo., Slou. 52 AQ40
Benson Clo., Uxb. 53 AY39
Benson Quay E1 57 CC40
Garnet St.
Benson Rd. SE23 77 CC47
Benson Rd., Croy. 86 BY55
Benson Rd., Grays 71 DD43
Benston Clo., Houns. 64 BF45
Staines Rd.
Bentfield Gdns. SE9 78 CJ48
Benthal Rd. N16 48 CB34
Benthall Gdns., Ken. 105 BZ62
Uplands Rd.
Bentham Ave., Wok. 100 AU61
Bentham Rd. E9 57 CC36
Bentham Rd. SE28 59 CO40
Bentham Wk. NW10 46 BN35
Lovett Way
Bentinck Clo., Ger.Cr. 43 AR32
Bentinck Ms. W1 1 H8
Bentinck Ms. W1 56 BV39
Marylebone La.
Bentinck Rd., West Dr. 53 AX40
Bentinck St. W1 1 H8
Bentinck St. W1 56 BV39
Bentley Dr., Ilf. 49 CM32
Bentley Dr., Wey. 92 AZ58
Bentley Heath La., Barn. 28 BR21
Bentley Rd. N1 57 CA
Tottenham Rd.
Bentley Rd., Slou. 61 AN
Bentley St., Grav. 81 DH
Bentley Way, Stan. 36 B.
Bentley Way, Wdf.Grn. 40 CH
Bentleys Meadow, Sev. 108 CV
Benton Rd., Ilf. 49 CM
Benton Rd., Wat. 36 BD
Bentons La. SE27 77 BZ
Bentons Ri. SE27 77 BZ
Bentry Clo., Dag. 50 CC
Bentry Rd., Dag. 50 CC
Bentsbrook Clo., Dor. 119 BJ
Spook Hill
Bentsbrook Pk., Dor. 119 BJ
Bentsbrook Rd., Dor. 119 BJ
Bentsley Clo., St.Alb. 9 BK
Bentworth Rd. W12 55 BP
Benwell Rd. N7 47 BY
Benwick Clo. SE16 67 CE
Aspinden Rd.
Benworth St. E3 57 CD
Benyon Path, S.Ock. 60 DE
Benyon Rd. N1 57 BZ
Berber Rd. SW11 76 BU
Ashness Rd.
Berberis Clo., Guil. 118 AR
Cypress Rd.
Berberis Wk., West Dr. 63 AY
Berceau Wk., Wat. 26 BB
Bercta Rd. SE9 78 CM
Bere St. E1 57 CC
Cranford St.
Berecroft, Harl. 13 CM
Beredens La., Upmin. 51 CZ
Berenger Wk. SW10 66 BT
Worlds End
Berens Rd. NW10 55 BQ
Berens Rd., Orp. 89 CP
Berens Way, Chis. 88 CN
Beresford Ave. N20 38 BU
Beresford Ave. W7 54 BG
Beresford Ave., Slou. 52 AR
Beresford Ave., Surb. 85 BM
Beresford Ave., Twick. 74 BK
Beresford Ave., Wem. 55 BL
Beresford Dr., Brom. 88 CK
St. Michaels Clo.
Beresford Dr., Wdf.Grn. 40 CJ
Beresford Gdns., Enf. 30 CA
Beresford Gdns., Houns. 74 BE
Beresford Gdns., Rom. 50 CQ
Beresford Rd. E4 40 CG
Beresford Rd. E17 39 CE
Beresford Rd. N2 47 BU
Beresford Rd. N5 48 BZ
Beresford Rd. N8 47 BY
Beresford Rd., Dor. 119 BJ
Beresford Rd., Grav. 81 DF
Beresford Rd., Har. 45 BG
Beresford Rd., Kings.T. 85 BL
Beresford Rd., N.Mal. 85 BN
Beresford Rd., Rick. 34 AV
Beresford Rd., St.Alb. 9 BJ
Beresford Rd., Sthl. 54 BD
Beresford Rd., Sutt. 94 BR
Beresford Sq. SE18 68 CL
Beresford St. SE18 68 CL
Beresford Ter. N5 48 BZ
Berestede Rd. W6 65 BO
Berger Clo., Orp. 88 CN
Berger Rd. E9 57 CC
Bergholt Ave., Ilf. 49 CK
Bergholt Cres. N16 48 CA
Bericot Way, Welw.G.C. 5 B
Bering Wk. E16 58 CJ
Leyes Rd.
Berkeley Ave., Bexh. 69 CP
Berkeley Ave., Grnf. 54 BG
Berkeley Ave., Houns. 63 BC
Berkeley Ave., Ilf. 40 CL
Berkeley Ave., Rom. 41 CS
Berkeley Clo., Abb.L. 17 BB
Berkeley Clo., Borwd. 28 BM
Berkeley Clo., Brent. 64 BJ
Berkeley Clo., Epsom 103 BN
Berkeley Clo., Horn. 51 CX
Berkeley Clo., Kings.T. 75 BL
Bank La.
Berkeley Clo., Orp. 88 CN
Buckingham Clo.
Berkeley Clo., Pot.B. 19 BR
Berkeley Clo., Ruis. 44 BC
Berkeley Clo., Stai. 72 AU
Moor La.
Berkeley Ct. EC1 56 BY
Briset St.
Berkeley Ct. N14 29 BW
Berkeley Ct., Guil. 118 AS
Berkeley Ct., Wey. 83 BB
Berkeley Cres., Barn. 29 BT
Berkeley Cres., Dart. 80 CW
Berkeley Dr., Horn. 51 CX
Berkeley Gdns. N21 39 BZ
Berkeley Gdns. W8 56 BS
Brunswick Gdns.
Berkeley Gdns., Esher 93 BJ
Berkeley Gdns., Walt. 83 BB
Berkeley Gdns., Wey. 91 AV
Berkeley Ms. W1 1
Berkeley Ms. W1 56 BU
Berkeley Pl. SW19 75 BQ
Berkeley Rd. E12 49 CK
Berkeley Rd. N8 47 BW
Berkeley Rd. N15 48 BZ
Berkeley Rd. NW9 46 BM
Berkeley Rd. SW13 65 BP
Berkeley Rd., Grav. 81 DG
Berkeley Rd., Uxb. 53 BA
Berkeley Sq. W1 3 K
Berkeley Sq. W1 56 BV
Berkeley Sq., Hem.H. 8 BA
Berkeley St. W1 3 K

keley St. W1 56 BV40
keley Wk. N7 47 BX34
urham Rd.
rkeley Waye, Houns. 64 BD43
keleys, The, Lthd. 102 BH65
khampstead Rd., 69 CR42
elv.
rkhamsted Ave., Wem. 55 BL36
rkhamsted Hill, Berk. 7 AS12
rkhamsted La., Hat. 11 BU13
rkhamsted Pl., Berk. 7 AQ12
rkhamsted Rd., Hem.H. 7 AU12
rkley Ave., Wal.Cr. 21 CC20
rkley Clo., St.Alb. 9 BK11
ortman Clo.
rkley Ct., Rick. 26 BA25
Aayfare
rkley Dr., E.Mol. 84 BE52
rkley Gro. NW1 56 BU36
erkley Rd.
rkley Rd. NW1 56 BU36
rks Hill, Rick. 25 AU25
rkshire Clo., Cat. 105 BZ64
rkshire Gdns. N13 38 BY29
rkshire Gdns. N18 39 CB28
rkshire Rd. E9 57 CD36
rkshire Sq., Mitch. 86 BX52
rkshire Way, Horn. 51 CX32
rkshire Way, Mitch. 86 BX52
rmans Clo., Brwd. 122 DD27
Hanging Hill La.
rmans Way NW10 46 BO35
rmondsey Sq. SE1 4 N6
rmondsey Sq. SE1 67 CA41
Tower Bri. Rd.
rmondsey St. SE1 4 M3
rmondsey St. SE1 57 CA40
rmondsey Wall E. 67 CB41
SE16
rmondsey Wall W. 67 CB41
SE16
Mill St.
rmuda Rd., Til. 71 DG44
rnal Clo. SE28 59 CP40
Haldane Rd.
rnard Ave. W13 64 BJ41
rnard Cassidy St. E16 58 CG39
Morgan St.
rnard Gdns. SW19 75 BR49
rnard Rd. N15 48 CA32
rnard Rd., Rom. 50 CS33
rnard Rd., Wall. 95 BV56
rnard St. WC1 1 Q5
rnard St. WC1 56 BX38
rnard St., St.Alb. 9 BG13
rnays Clo., Stan. 36 BK29
rnays Gro. SW9 66 BX45
rne Rd., Th.Hth. 87 BZ52
rnel Dr., Croy. 87 CD55
rner Est. E1 57 CB39
rners Dr. W13 54 BJ40
rners Dr., St.Alb. 9 BH15
rners Ms. W1 1 M7
rners Ms. W1 56 BW39
rners Pl. W1 1 M8
rners Pl. W1 56 BW39
rners Rd. N1 56 BY37
rners Rd. N22 38 BY30
rners St. W1 1 M7
rners St. W1 56 BW39
rners Way, Brox. 12 CD15
rney Rd., Croy. 87 BZ54
rnice Clo., Rain. 60 CV38
Arterial Ave.
rnville Way, Har. 46 BL32
Kenton Rd.
rnwell Rd. E4 40 CG27
rridge Est., Edg. 37 BL29
rridge Grn., Edg. 37 BM29
rridge Rd. SE19 77 BZ49
rries, The, St.Alb. 9 BJ11
rriman Rd. N7 47 BX34
rrin Way WC1 56 BX37
rriton Rd., Har. 45 BE33
rry Ave., Wat. 26 BC21
rry Clo. N21 38 BY26
rry Clo. NW10 55 BO36
rry Clo., Horn. 60 CV36
Airfield Way
rry Clo., Rick. 35 AW26
rry Gro. La., Bush. 27 BE22
rry Gro. La., Bush. 27 BF23
rry Hill, Stan. 36 BK28
rry La. SE21 77 BZ49
rry La., Guil. 100 AO65
rry La., Rick. 25 AU25
rry La., Rick. 26 AW25
rry La., Wok. 100 AO65
rry Meade, Ash. 103 BL62
rry Pl. EC1 2 G3
rry St. EC1 2 G4
rry St. EC1 56 BY38
Dallington St.
rry Wk., Ash. 103 BL63
rry Way W5 65 BL41
rry Way, Rick. 35 AW26
rrybank Clo. E4 39 CF27
Greenbank Clo.
rrydale Rd., Hayes 54 BE38
rryfield, Slou. 52 AR39
rryfield Clo. E17 48 CE31
rryfield Clo., Brom. 88 CK51
rryfield Rd. SE17 4 G10
rryfield Rd. SE17 66 BY42
rryhill SE9 68 CL45
rryhill Gdns. SE9 68 CL45
rrylands SW20 85 BQ52
rrylands, Orp. 89 CP55
rrylands, Surb. 85 BL53
rrylands Rd., Surb. 85 BL53
rryman Clo., Dag. 50 CP34
rrymans La. SE26 77 CC49
rrymead, Hem.H. 8 AY12
rrymead Gdns. W3 65 BN41

Berrymede Rd. W4 65 BN41
Berrys Cft. Ct., Stai. 73 AX50
Berrys Cft. Rd.
Berrys Cft. Rd., Stai. 73 AX50
Berrys Grn. Rd., West. 106 CL61
Berrys Hill, West. 106 CL61
Berrys La., Wey. 92 AX59
Bersham La., Grays 71 DC42
Bert Rd., Th.Hth. 87 BZ53
Bert Way, Enf. 30 CA24
Bertal Rd. SW17 76 BT49
Berther Rd., Horn. 51 CW33
Berthon St. SE8 67 CE43
Bertie Rd. NW10 55 BP36
Bertie Rd. SE26 77 CC50
Bertram Cotts. SW19 76 BS50
Bertram Rd. NW4 46 BP32
Bertram Rd., Enf. 30 CA24
Bertram Rd., Kings.T. 75 BM50
Bertram St. N19 47 BV34
Bertram Way, Enf. 30 CA24
Bertrand St. SE13 67 CE45
Bertrand Way SE28 59 CP40
Berwick Ave., Hayes 54 BD39
Berwick Clo., Stan. 36 BH29
Gordon Ave.
Berwick Clo., Wal.Cr. 21 CE20
Queens Dr.
Berwick Cres., Sid. 78 CN47
Berwick La., Ong. 23 CT20
Berwick Pond Clo., Rain. 60 CV37
Berwick Pond Rd., Rain. 60 CW37
Berwick Rd. E16 58 CJ39
Berwick Rd. N22 38 BY30
Berwick Rd., Borwd. 28 BL22
Berwick Rd., Rain. 60 CV37
Berwick Rd., Well. 69 CO44
Berwick St. W1 1 M8
Berwick St. W1 56 BW39
Berwick Way, Orp. 89 CO54
Vinson Clo.
Berwick Way, Sev. 107 CU63
Cramptons Rd.
Berwyn Ave., Houns. 64 BF44
Berwyn Rd. SE24 76 BY47
Berwyn Rd., Rich. 65 BM45
Beryl Ave. E6 58 CK39
Beryl Rd. W6 65 BQ42
Berystede, Kings.T. 75 BM50
Besant Ct. N1 48 BZ35
Mildmay Gro.
Besant Rd. NW2 46 BR35
Besant Way NW10 46 BN35
Besley St. SW16 76 BW50
Bessborough Gdns. SW1 3 P10
Bessborough Pl. SW1 3 N10
Bessborough Pl. SW1 66 BW42
Bessborough Rd. SW15 75 BP47
Bessborough Rd., Har. 45 BG33
Bessborough St. SW1 3 N10
Bessborough St. SW1 66 BW42
Bessels Grn. Rd., Sev. 107 CS65
Bessels Meadows, Sev. 107 CS65
Bessels Way
Bessels Way, Sev. 107 CS65
Bessemer Rd. SE5 67 BZ44
Bessemer Rd., Welw.G.C. 5 BR7
Bessingby Rd., Ruis. 44 BC34
Bessingham Wk. SE4 67 CD45
Frendsbury Rd.
Besson St. SE14 67 CC44
Bessy St. E2 57 CC38
Roman Rd.
Bestwood St. SE8 67 CC42
Beswick Ms. NW6 56 BS36
Lymington Rd.
Beta Rd., Wok. 91 AP58
Betam Rd., Hayes 63 BA41
Betchworth Clo., Sutt. 95 BT56
Turnpike La.
Betchworth Rd., Ilf. 49 CN34
Betchworth Way, Croy. 96 CF58
Betenson Ave., Sev. 107 CT64
Beth Rd., Wok. 100 AT61
Princess Rd.
Betham Rd., Grnf. 54 BG38
Bethany Waye, Felt. 73 BB47
Bethecar Rd., Har. 45 BH32
Bethel Rd., Sev. 108 CV65
Bethel Rd., Well. 69 CP45
Bethell Ave. E16 58 CG38
Bethell Ave., Ilf. 49 CL33
Bethersden Clo., Beck. 77 CD50
Bethnal Grn. Est. E2 57 CC38
Bethnal Grn. Rd. E1 2 P4
Bethnal Grn. Rd. E1 57 CA38
Bethnal Grn. Rd. E2 57 CA38
Bethune Ave. N11 38 BU28
Bethune Rd. N16 48 BZ33
Bethune Rd. NW10 55 BN38
Bethwin Rd. SE5 66 BY43
Betjeman Clo., Pnr. 45 BF31
Pinner Rd.
Betjeman Way, Hem.H. 8 AW12
Betley Ct., Walt. 83 BC55
Betony Clo., Croy. 87 CC54
Primrose La.
Betony Rd., Rom. 42 CV29
Betoyne Ave. E4 40 CG28
Betsham Rd., Erith 69 CT43
Betsham Rd., Grav. 80 DB49
Betsham Rd., Swans. 81 DC47
Betstyle Rd. N11 38 BV28
Betterton Dr., Sid. 79 CO48
Betterton Rd., Rain. 59 CT38
Betterton St. WC2 1 Q9
Betterton St. WC2 56 BX39
Bettles Clo., Uxb. 53 AX37
Bettons Pk. E15 58 CG37
New Plaistow Rd.
Bettridge Rd. SW6 65 BR44
Betts Clo., Beck. 87 CD51
Kendall Rd.

Betts La., Wal.Abb. 13 CJ14
Betts Rd. E16 58 CH40
Betts St. E1 57 CB40
Betts Way SE20 87 CB51
Anerley Rd.
Betts Way, Surb. 84 BJ54
Betula Clo., Ken. 105 BZ61
Betula Wk., Rain. 60 CB38
Between Sts., Cob. 92 BC60
Beulah Ave., Th.Hth. 87 BZ52
Beulah Rd.
Beulah Clo., Edg. 37 BM27
Beulah Cres., Th.Hth. 87 BZ51
Beulah Gro., Croy. 87 BZ53
Beulah Hill SE19 76 BY50
Beulah Path E17 48 CE32
Addison Rd.
Beulah Rd. E11 49 CG34
Cathall Rd.
Beulah Rd. E17 48 CE32
Beulah Rd. SW19 75 BR50
Beulah Rd., Epp. 23 CO18
Beulah Rd., Horn. 51 CV34
Beulah Rd., Sutt. 95 BS56
Beulah Rd., Th.Hth. 87 BZ52
Beulah Wk., Cat. 105 CD63
Beult Rd., Dart. 69 CU45
Bev Callender Clo. SW8 66 BV45
Heath Rd.
Bevan Ave., Bark. 59 CO36
Bevan Clo., Hem.H. 8 AX14
Bevan Ct., Croy. 95 BY56
Bevan Est., Barn. 29 BT24
Bevan Pl., Swan. 89 CT52
Bevan Rd. SE2 69 CO42
Bevan Rd., Barn. 29 BU24
Bevan St. N1 57 BZ37
Bevan Way, Horn. 51 CW35
Bevans Clo., Green. 80 DB46
Johnsons Way
Bevenden St. N1 2 L2
Bevenden St. N1 57 BZ38
Beveridge Rd. NW10 55 BO36
Curzon Cres.
Beverley NW8 1 C3
Beverley Ave. SW20 85 BO51
Beverley Ave., Houns. 64 BE45
Beverley Ave., Sid. 78 CN47
Beverley Clo. N21 39 BZ26
Beverley Clo. SW11 66 BT45
Maysoule Rd.
Beverley Clo. SW13 65 BP44
Beverley Clo., Brox. 12 CD14
Beverley Clo., Chess. 93 BK56
Beverley Clo., Enf. 30 CA24
Beverley Clo., Epsom 94 BQ59
Beverley Clo., Horn. 51 CW33
Beverley Clo., Wey. 83 BB55
Beverley Clo. (Addlestone), Wey. 92 AX56
Beverley Ct. N14 38 BW26
Beverley Ct. SE4 67 CD45
Beverley Ct., Slou. 62 AQ41
Dolphin Rd.
Beverley Cres., Wdf.Grn. 40 CH30
Beverley Dr., Edg. 46 BM31
Beverley Gdns. NW11 46 BR33
Beverley Gdns. SW13 65 BO45
Beverley Gdns., Chsnt. 21 CB19
Beverley Gdns., Grnf. 54 BH38
Western Ave.
Beverley Gdns., Horn. 51 CW33
Beverley Gdns., St.Alb. 9 BK11
Beverley Gdns., Stan. 36 BJ30
Beverley Gdns., Welw.G.C. 5 BT8
Wellington Dr.
Beverley Gdns., Wem. 46 BL33
Beverley Gdns., Wor.Pk. 85 BP54
Beverley Heights, Red. 121 BT71
Cronks Hill
Beverley Heights, Reig. 121 BS69
Beverley La., Kings.T. 75 BO50
Beverley Ms. E4 39 CF29
Beverley Rd.
Beverley Path SW13 65 BO44
Beverley Rd. E4 39 CF29
Beverley Rd. E6 58 CJ38
Beverley Rd. SE20 87 CB51
Beverley Rd. SW13 65 BO45
Beverley Rd. W4 65 BO42
Beverley Rd., Bexh. 69 CS44
Beverley Rd., Brom. 88 CK55
Beverley Rd., Dag. 50 CQ35
Beverley Rd., Kings.T. 84 BK51
Beverley Rd., Mitch. 86 BW52
Beverley Rd., N.Mal. 85 BP52
Beverley Rd., Ruis. 44 BC34
Beverley Rd., Sthl. 64 BE42
Beverley Rd., Sun. 83 BB51
Beverley Rd., Whyt. 105 CA61
Beverley Rd., Wor.Pk. 85 BO55
Beverley Way SW20 85 BO51
Beverley Way, N.Mal. 85 BO51
Beversbrook Rd. N19 47 BW34
Beverstone Rd. SW2 76 BX46
Beverstone Rd., Th.Hth. 86 BY52
Bevil Ct., Hodd. 12 CE10
Molesworth
Bevill Allen Clo. SW17 76 BU49
Bevin Clo. SE16 57 CD40
Stave Yd. Rd.
Bevin Ct. WC1 56 BX38
Bevin Rd., Hayes 53 BC38
Bevin Way WC1 2 D2
Bevington Rd. W10 55 BR39
Bevington Rd., Beck. 87 CE51
Bevington St. SE16 67 CB41
Bevis Clo., Dart. 80 CY47
Bevis Marks EC3 2 N8
Bevis Marks EC3 57 CA39
Bewcastle Gdns., Enf. 29 BX24
Bewdley St. N1 56 BY36
Bewick St. SW8 66 BV44
Bewley Clo., Chsnt. 21 CC19

Bewley La., Sev. 117 DB66
Bewley St. E1 57 CC40
Bewlys Rd. SE27 76 BY49
Bexhill Clo., Felt. 74 BE48
Bexhill Rd. N11 38 BW28
Bexhill Rd. SE4 77 CD46
Bexhill Rd. SW14 65 BN45
Bexhill Wk. E15 58 CG37
Manor Rd.
Bexley Clo., Dart. 79 CT46
Bexley Gdns. N9 39 BZ27
Bexley La., Dart. 79 CT46
Bexley La., Sid. 79 CP49
Bexley Rd. SE9 78 CL46
Bexley Rd., Erith 69 CS43
Bexley St., Wind. 61 AN44
Beyers Gdns., Hodd. 12 CE10
Beyers Prospect, Hodd. 12 CE10
Beynon Rd., Cars. 95 BU56
Bianca Ho. N1 57 CA37
Purcell St.
Bianca Rd. SE15 67 CA43
Bibsworth Rd. N3 37 BR30
Bibury Clo. SE15 69 CA43
St. Georges Way
Bicester Rd., Rich. 65 BM45
Bickenhall St. W1 1 F6
Bickenhall St. W1 56 BU39
Bickersteth Rd. SW17 76 BU50
Bickerton Rd. N19 47 BW34
Bickley Cres., Brom. 88 CK52
Bickley Pk. Rd., Brom. 88 CK52
Bickley Rd. E10 48 CE33
Bickley Rd., Brom. 88 CJ51
Bickley St. SW17 76 BU49
Bicknell Rd. SE5 67 BZ45
Bickney Way, Lthd. 102 BG65
Bicknoller Clo., Sutt. 95 BS58
Cotswold Rd.
Bicknoller Rd., Enf. 30 CA23
Bicknor Rd., Orp. 88 CN54
Bidborough Clo., Brom. 88 CG53
Bidborough St. WC1 1 Q3
Bidborough St. WC1 56 BW38
Biddenden Way SE9 78 CL49
Biddenden Way, Grav. 81 DF50
Biddenham Turn, Wat. 27 BD21
Bidder St. E16 58 CG38
Biddestone Rd. N7 47 BX35
Biddulph Rd. W9 56 BS38
Biddulph Rd., S.Croy. 96 BZ58
Bideford Ave., Grnf. 54 BJ38
Bideford Clo., Edg. 37 BM30
Bideford Clo., Felt. 74 BE48
Bideford Clo., Rom. 42 CV30
Bideford Gdns., Enf. 39 CA26
Bideford Rd., Brom. 78 CG48
Bideford Rd., Enf. 30 CD22
Bideford Rd., Ruis. 44 BC34
Bideford Rd., Well. 69 CO43
Bidhams Cres., Tad. 103 CO64
Bidwell Gdns. N11 38 BW29
Bidwell St. SE15 67 CB44
Big Common La., Red. 121 BY70
Big Hill E5 48 CB33
Bigbury Clo. N17 39 CA29
Biggerstaff Rd. E15 57 CF37
Biggerstaff St. N4 47 BY34
Biggin Ave., Mitch. 86 BU51
Biggin Hill SE19 86 BY51
Biggin La., Grays 71 DG43
Biggin Way SE19 76 BY50
Bigginwood Rd. SW16 76 BY50
Biggs Row SW15 65 BQ45
Felsham Rd.
Bigland St. E1 57 CB39
Bignell Rd. SE18 68 CL42
Bignold Rd. E7 49 CH35
Bigwood Ct. NW11 47 BS32
Bigwood Rd.
Bigwood Rd. NW11 47 BS32
Biko Clo., Uxb. 53 AX39
Sefton Way
Bill Hamling Clo. SE9 78 CK48
Billet Clo., Rom. 50 CP31
Billet Rd.
Billet Hill, Sev. 99 DB56
Billet La., Berk. 7 AQ12
Billet La., Horn. 51 CV33
Billet La., Iver 52 AT38
Billet La., Slou. 52 AT38
Billet Rd. E17 39 CC30
Billet Rd., Rom. 50 CO31
Billet Rd., Stai. 73 AW48
Billing Pl. SW10 66 BS43
Billing Rd. SW10 66 BS43
Billing St. SW10 66 BS43
Billingford Clo. SE4 67 CC45
Billington Rd. SE14 67 CC43
Billiter Sq. EC3 2 N9
Billiter Sq. EC3 57 CA39
Fenchurch Ave.
Billiter St. EC3 2 N9
Billiter St. EC3 57 CA39
Billockby Clo., Chess. 94 BL57
Billson St. E14 67 CF42
Billy Lows La., Pot.B. 20 BS19
Bilsby Gro. SE9 78 CJ49
Bilton Clo., Slou. 62 AV44
Colndale Rd.
Bilton Rd., Erith 69 CU43
Bilton Rd., Grnf. 54 BJ37
Bilton Way, Enf. 30 CD23
Bilton Way, Hayes 63 BC41
Bina Gdns. SW5 66 BT42
Bincote Rd., Enf. 29 BX24
Binden Rd. W12 65 BO41
Bindon Grn., Mord. 86 BS52
Bayham Rd.
Binfield Rd. SW4 66 BX44
Binfield Rd., S.Croy. 96 CA56
Binfield Rd., Wey. 92 AY59
Bingfield St. N1 56 BX37
Bingham Clo., S.Ock. 60 DA39

Bingham Dr., Stai. 73 AX50
Bingham Dr., Wok. 100 AP62
Bingham Pl. W1 1 G6
Bingham Pl. W1 56 BV38
Bingham Rd., Croy. 87 CB54
Bingham St. N1 57 BZ36
Binghams, The, Maid. 61 AG41
Bingley Rd. E16 58 CJ39
Bingley Rd., Grnf. 54 BG38
Bingley Rd., Hodd. 12 CF12
Bingley Rd., Sun. 73 BC50
Binney St. W1 1 H9
Binney St. W1 56 BV39
Binns Rd. W4 65 BO42
Binsey Wk. SE2 69 CP41
Binyon Cres., Stan. 36 BH28
Birbetts Rd. SE9 78 CK48
Birch Ave. N13 39 BZ27
Birch Ave., Cat. 105 BZ65
Birch Ave., West Dr. 53 AY39
Birch Clo. E16 58 CG39
Birch Clo. N19 47 BW34
Hargrave Pk.
Birch Clo. SE15 67 CB44
Bournemouth Rd.
Birch Clo., Amer. 25 AP22
Plantation Way
Birch Clo., Brent. 64 BJ43
Birch Clo., Buck.H. 40 CJ27
Birch Clo., Rom. 50 CR31
Birch Clo., Sev. 107 CU65
Birch Clo., Tedd. 74 BJ49
Birch Clo., Wey. 92 AX58
Birch Clo., Wok. 100 AR63
Birch Clo. (Sendmarsh), Wok. 109 AV66
Birch Copse, St.Alb. 18 BE18
Birch Cres., Horn. 51 CW31
Birch Cres., Uxb. 53 AY37
Birch Dr., Hat. 10 BP13
Birch Dr., Rick. 34 AU28
Birch Gdns., Dag. 50 CS34
Birch Grn. NW9 37 BO29
Clayton Fld.
Birch Grn., Hem.H. 7 AV12
Birch Grn., Stai. 72 AV48
Birch Gro. SE12 78 CG47
Birch Gro. W3 55 BM40
Birch Gro., Cob. 93 BD60
Birch Gro., Pot.B. 20 BS19
Birch Gro., Shep. 83 BB51
Birch Gro., Tad. 103 BR65
Birch Gro., Well. 69 CO45
Birch Gro., Wind. 61 AL44
Birch Gro., Wok. 100 AU61
Birch Hill, Croy. 96 CC56
Birch La., Hem.H. 16 AT20
Birch La., Pur. 95 BX59
Birch Leys, Hem.H. 8 AZ11
Hunters Oak
Birch Mead, Orp. 88 CL55
Birch Pk., Har. 36 BG29
Birch Pl., Green. 80 CZ46
Birch Rd., Berk. 7 AO11
Birch Rd., Felt. 74 BE49
Birch Rd., Rom. 50 CR31
Birch Row, Brom. 88 CL54
Birch Tree Ave., W.Wick. 97 CG56
Birch Tree Clo., Chesh. 16 AQ18
Birch Tree Wk., Wat. 26 BB22
Birch Tree Way, Croy. 87 CB55
Birch Vale, Cob. 93 BF59
Birch Vw., Epp. 23 CO18
Ongar Rd.
Birch Wk., Borwd. 28 BM23
Birch Wk., Erith 69 CS43
Birch Wk., Mitch. 86 BV51
Birch Wk., Wey. 92 AW59
Birch Way, Chesh. 16 AQ18
Birch Way, St.Alb. 18 BK17
Birch Way, Warl. 105 CD62
Birch Wd., Rad. 19 BM20
Birchall La., Welw.G.C. 5 BT9
Birchall Wd., Welw.G.C. 5 BT8
Birchanger Rd. SE25 87 CB53
Birchcroft Clo., Cat. 105 BZ65
Birchdale, Ger.Cr. 43 AR33
Birchdale Clo., Wey. 92 AX59
Birchdale Gdns., Rom. 50 CP33
Birchdale Rd. E7 49 CJ35
Birchdene Dr. SE28 59 CO40
Birchen Clo. NW9 46 BN34
Birchend Clo., S.Croy. 96 BZ57
Sussex Rd.
Birches, The N21 29 BX25
Birches, The SE7 68 CH43
Birches, The, Brwd. 122 DC27
Birches, The, Bush. 27 BG25
Birches, The, Epp. 23 CR16
Higham Vw.
Birches, The, Hem.H. 7 AV15
Birches, The, Lthd. 110 BB66
Birches, The, Orp. 97 CL56
Birches, The, Swan. 89 CT51
Birches, The, Wok. 100 AS62
Commercial Way
Birches Clo., Epsom 103 BO61
Birches Clo., Mitch. 86 BU52
Birches Clo., Pnr. 45 BD32
Birchfield Clo., Couls. 104 BX61
Birchfield Clo., Wey. 92 AW56
Birchfield Gro., Epsom 94 BO58
Birchfield Rd., Chsnt. 21 CB18
Birchfield St. E14 57 CE40
Birchgate Ms., Tad. 103 BQ64
Bidhams Cres.
Birchin Cross Rd., Sev. 108 CW61
Birchin La. EC3 2 L9
Birchin La. EC3 57 BZ39
Birchington Clo., Bexh. 69 CR44
Birchington Clo., Orp. 89 CP54
Hart Dyke Rd.
Birchington Rd. N8 47 BW32
Birchington Rd. NW6 56 BS37

Birchington Rd., Surb. 85 BL54
Birchington Rd., Wind. 61 AN44
Birchlands Ave. SW12 76 BU47
Birchmead, Wat. 26 BB22
Birchmead Ave., Pnr. 45 BD31
Birchmead Clo., St.Alb. 9 BG12
Birchmere Row SE3 68 CG44
Birchmore Wk. N5 48 BZ34
Birchville Ct., Bush. 36 BH26
Birchway, Hat. 10 BP11
Birchway, Hayes 53 BC40
Birchway, Red. 121 BV71
Birchwood, Wal.Abb. 22 CG20
Roundhills
Birchwood Ave. N10 47 BV31
Birchwood Ave., Beck. 87 CD52
Birchwood Ave., Hat. 10 BP11
Birchwood Ave., Sid. 79 CO48
Birchwood Ave., Wall. 86 BV55
Birchwood Clo., Brwd. 42 DA28
Birchwood Clo., Hat. 10 BP11
Birchwood Clo., Mord. 86 BS53
Birchwood Cotts., Hert. 11 BV15
Birchwood Ct. N13 38 BY28
Birchwood Ct., Edg. 37 BN30
Birchwood Dr. NW3 47 BS34
Birchwood Dr., Dart. 79 CT49
Birchwood Dr., Wey. 92 AW59
Birchwood Gro., Hmptn. 74 BF50
Birchwood La., Cat. 113 BY66
Birchwood La., Esher 93 BG58
Birchwood Pk. Ave., Swan. 89 CT52
Birchwood Rd. SW17 76 BV49
Birchwood Rd., Dart. 79 CS50
Birchwood Rd., Orp. 88 CM52
Birchwood Rd., Swan. 89 CS51
Birchwood Rd., Wey. 92 AW59
Birchwood Way, St.Alb. 18 BF17
Bird La., Brwd. 51 DB31
Bird La., Upmin. 51 CY32
Bird La., Uxb. 35 AX30
Bird St. W1 1 H9
Bird St. W1 56 BV39
Bird Wk., Twick. 74 BE47
Bird-in-bush Rd. SE15 67 CB43
Bird-in-hand La., Brom. 88 CJ51
Bird-in-hand Pas. SE23 77 CC48
Dartmouth Rd.
Birdbrook Clo., Brwd. 122 DE25
Poplar Dr.
Birdbrook Clo., Dag. 59 CS36
Birdbrook Rd. SE3 68 CJ45
Birdcage Wk. SW1 3 M5
Birdcage Wk. SW1 66 BW41
Birdcroft Rd., Welw.G.C. 5 BQ8
Birdham Clo., Brom. 88 CK53
Birdhouse La., Orp. 97 CL60
Birdhurst Ave., S.Croy. 96 BZ56
Birdhurst Gdns., S.Croy. 96 BZ56
Birdhurst Ri., S.Croy. 96 CA56
Birdhurst Rd. SW18 66 BT45
Birdhurst Rd. SW19 76 BU50
Birdhurst Rd., S.Croy. 96 CA56
Birdlip Clo. SE15 67 CA43
St. Georges Way
Birds, Wok. 100 AO63
Gorsewood Rd.
Birds Clo., Welw.G.C. 5 BS9
Birds Fm. Ave., Rom. 41 CR29
Birds Grn., Ong. 15 CZ13
Birds Hill Dr., Lthd. 93 BG60
Birds Hill Ri., Lthd. 93 BG60
Birds Hill Rd., Lthd. 93 BG59
Birdswood Dr., Wok. 100 AP63
Birdwood Clo., S.Croy. 96 CC59
Birdwood Clo., Tedd. 74 BH49
Birkbeck Ave. W3 55 BN40
Birkbeck Ave., Grnf. 54 BG37
Birkbeck Gdns., Wdf.Grn. 40 CH27
Birkbeck Gro. W3 65 BN41
Birkbeck Hill SE21 76 BY47
Birkbeck Pl. SE21 77 BZ47
Birkbeck Rd. E8 48 CA35
Birkbeck Rd. N8 47 BX31
Birkbeck Rd. N12 38 BT28
Birkbeck Rd. N17 39 CA30
Birkbeck Rd. NW7 37 BO28
Birkbeck Rd. SW19 76 BS49
Birkbeck Rd. W3 55 BN40
Birkbeck Rd. W5 64 BK42
Birkbeck Rd., Beck. 87 CC51
Birkbeck Rd., Brwd. 122 DE25
Birkbeck Rd., Enf. 30 BZ23
Birkbeck Rd., Ilf. 49 CM32
Birkbeck Rd., Rom. 50 CS33
Birkbeck Rd., Sid. 79 CO48
Birkbeck St. E2 57 CB38
Birkbeck Way, Grnf. 54 BG37
Birkdale Ave., Pnr. 45 BF31
Birkdale Ave., Rom. 42 CW29
Birkdale Clo., Orp. 88 CM54
Birkdale Gdns., Wat. 36 BD27
Birkdale Pl., Orp. 88 CM54
Birkdale Rd. SE2 69 CO42
Birkdale Rd. W5 55 BL38
Birken Ms., Nthwd. 35 AZ28
Birkenhead Ave., Kings.T. 85 BL51
Birkenhead St. WC1 2 A2
Birkenhead St. WC1 56 BX38
St. Chads St.
Birkett Way, Ch.St.G. 25 AR24
Birkhall Rd. SE6 77 CF47
Birkheads Rd., Reig. 121 BS70
Birklands La., St.Alb. 9 BJ15
Birklands Pk., St.Alb. 9 BJ15
London Rd.
Birkwood Clo. SW12 76 BW47
Birley Rd. N20 38 BT27
Birley Rd., Slou. 52 AO40
Birley St. SW11 66 BV44
Birling Rd., Erith 69 CS43
Birnam Clo., Wok. 101 AW65
Birnam Rd. N4 47 BX34
Birse Cres. NW10 46 BO35
Neasden La.
Birstall Grn., Wat. 36 BD27
Birstall Rd. N15 48 CA32
Birtley Path, Borwd. 28 BL23
Darrington Rd.
Biscay Rd. W6 65 BQ42
Biscoe Clo., Houns. 64 BF43
Biscoe Way SE13 67 CF45
Bisenden Rd., Croy. 87 CA55
Bisham Clo., Cars. 86 BU54
Bisham Gdns. N6 47 BV33
Bishop Craven Clo., Enf. 29 BY23
Chasewood Ave.
Bishop Duppas Pk., Shep. 83 BA54
Bishop Fox Way, T.Ditt. 84 BE52
Bishop Hall Rd., Brwd. 33 DA25
Bishop Ken Rd., Har. 36 BH30
Bishop Kings Rd. W14 65 BR42
Bishop Rd. N14 38 BV26
Bishop Rd. SW11 66 BU43
Bishop St. N1 57 BZ37
Bishops Ave. E13 58 CH37
Bishops Ave. SW6 65 BQ44
Bishops Ave., Borwd. 28 BL25
Bishops Ave., Brom. 88 CJ52
Bishops Ave., Nthwd. 35 BB28
Bishops Ave., Rom. 50 CP32
Bishops Ave., The N2 47 BT33
Bishops Bri. W2 56 BT39
Bishops Bri. Rd. W2 56 BS39
Bishops Clo. E17 48 CE31
Bishops Clo. N19 47 BW34
Wyndham Cres.
Bishops Clo. SE9 78 CM48
Bishops Clo., Barn. 28 BQ25
Bishops Clo., Couls. 104 BY62
Bishops Clo., Enf. 30 CB23
Bishops Clo., Hat. 10 BO12
College La.
Bishops Clo., Rich. 74 BK48
Bishops Clo., St.Alb. 9 BJ11
Bishops Clo., Sutt. 86 BS55
Bishops Clo., Uxb. 53 AZ37
Bishops Ct. EC4 2 F8
Bishops Ct. EC4 56 BY39
Old Bailey
Bishops Ct. WC2 2 D8
Bishops Ct. WC2 56 BY39
Chancery La.
Bishops Dr., Felt. 73 BA46
Bishops Fm. Clo., Wind. 61 AK44
Bishops Garth, St.Alb. 9 BJ11
Bishops Clo.
Bishops Gro. N2 47 BU32
Bishops Gro., Hmptn. 74 BF49
Bishops Hall, Kings.T. 84 BK51
Thames St.
Bishops Hill, Walt. 83 BC54
Bishops Mead, Hem.H. 8 AW14
Bishops Pk. Rd. SW6 65 BQ44
Bishops Pk. Rd. SW16 86 BX51
Bishops Ri., Hat. 10 BO12
Bishops Rd. N6 47 BV32
Bishops Rd. SW6 65 BR44
Bishops Rd. W7 64 BH41
Bishops Rd., Croy. 86 BY54
Bishops Rd., Hayes 53 BA39
Bishops Rd., Slou. 62 AQ41
Bishops Ter. SE11 4 E8
Bishops Ter. SE11 66 BY42
Bishops Wk., Chis. 88 CM51
Bishops Wk., Croy. 96 CC56
Bishops Wk., Pnr. 45 BE31
High St.
Bishops Way E2 57 CC37
Bishops Way NW10 55 BO36
Bishops Way, Egh. 72 AU50
Bishops Wd., Wok. 100 AP62
Bishopsfield, Harl. 13 CN12
Bishopsford, Cars. 86 BU53
Bishopsford Rd., Mord. 86 BT54
Bishopsgate EC2 2 N7
Bishopsgate EC2 57 CA39
Bishopsgate Chyd. EC2 2 M8
Bishopsgate Chyd. EC2 57 CA39
Bishopsgate Rd., Egh. 72 AQ48
Bishopsmead Par., Lthd. 110 BB67
Bishopsthorpe Rd. SE26 77 CC49
Bishopswood Rd. N6 47 BU33
Bisley Clo., Wal.Cr. 21 CC20
Bisley Clo., Wor.Pk. 85 BQ54
Bispham Rd. NW10 55 BL38
Bisson Rd. E15 57 CF37
Bisterne Ave. E17 48 CF31
Bitchet Rd., Sev. 117 CX67
Bittacy Clo. NW7 37 BQ29
Bittacy Hill NW7 37 BQ29
Bittacy Pk. Ave. NW7 37 BQ29
Bittacy Ri. NW7 37 BQ29
Bittacy Rd. NW7 37 BQ29
Bittams La., Cher. 91 AU56
Bittern Dr., Wok. 100 AP61
Bittern St. SE1 4 H5
Bittern St. SE1 67 BZ41
Bittoms, The, Kings.T. 84 BK52
Bixley Clo., Sthl. 64 BE42
Black Acre Clo., Amer. 25 AP23
Black Boy La. N15 48 BZ32
Black Boy Wd., St.Alb. 18 BF18
Black Cut, St.Alb. 9 BH14
Black Ditch Rd., Wal.Abb. 30 CF21
Black Fan Clo., Enf. 30 BZ23
Black Fan Rd., Welw.G.C. 5 BS7
Black Friars Ct. EC4 2 F10
Black Friars La. EC4 2 F10
Black Horse Ave., Chesh. 16 AO20
Black Horse Clo., Wind. 61 AL44
Black Horse Ct. SE1 4 L6
Black Horse La., Epp. 23 CS16
Black Horse Yd. E1 57 CA39
Middlesex St.
Black Jacks La., Uxb. 35 AW30
Black Lake Clo., Egh. 82 AT51
Black La., Ong. 15 CW12
Black Lion Hill, Rad. 19 BL19
Black Lion La. W6 65 BP42
Black Lion Yd. E1 57 CB39
Old Montague St.
Black Pk. Rd., Slou. 52 AS37
Black Path E10 48 CC33
Black Prince Clo., Wey. 92 AY60
Black Prince Rd. SE1 4 A9
Black Prince Rd. SE1 66 BX42
Black Prince Rd. SE11 4 C9
Black Prince Rd. SE11 66 BX42
Black Raven All. EC4 57 BZ40
Wharfside
Black Swan Yd. SE1 4 M4
Black Thorne Rd., West. 106 CK61
Black Tree Ms. SW9 66 BY45
Gresham Rd.
Blackacre Rd., Epp. 31 CN22
Blackall St. EC2 2 M4
Blackall St. EC2 57 CA38
Blackberry Clo., Shep. 83 BB52
Cherry Way
Blackberry Fm. Clo., Houns. 64 BE43
Blackbird Hill NW9 46 BN34
Blackbird Yd. E2 2 Q2
Blackbird Yd. E2 57 CA38
Ravenscroft St.
Blackbirds La., Wat. 18 BG20
Blackborne Rd., Dag. 59 CR36
Blackborough Clo., Reig. 121 BT70
Blackborough Rd., Reig. 121 BT71
Blackbridge Rd., Wok. 100 AR63
Blackbrook La., Brom. 88 CK53
Blackbrook Rd., Dor. 119 BK73
Blackburn, The, Lthd. 102 BE65
Little Bookham St.
Blackburn Rd. NW6 56 BS36
Blackburnes Ms. W1 1 G10
Blackburnes Ms. W1 56 BV40
Blackbury Clo., Pot.B. 20 BT19
Quakers La.
Blackbush Ave., Rom. 50 CP32
Blackbush Clo., Sutt. 95 BS57
Copse Hill
Blackbush Spring, Harl. 6 CO10
Blackdale, Chsnt. 21 CB17
Blackdown Ave., Wok. 100 AV61
Blackdown Clo., Wok. 100 AU61
Blackdown Ter. SE18 68 CK43
Blackett Clo., Stai. 82 AV51
Blackett St. SW15 65 BQ45
Blacketts Wd. Dr., Rick. 25 AT24
Blackfen Rd., Sid. 78 CN46
Blackford Clo., S.Croy. 95 BY58
Blackford Pl., Pur. 95 BY58
Pampisford Rd.
Blackford Rd., Wat. 36 BD28
Blackfords Path SW15 75 BP47
Roehampton High St.
Blackfriars Bri. EC4 56 BY40
Blackfriars Bri. SE1 56 BY40
Blackfriars La. EC4 56 BY40
Blackfriars Pas. EC4 2 F10
Blackfriars Pas. EC4 56 BY40
Blackfriars Rd. SE1 4 F2
Blackfriars Rd. SE1 66 BY41
Blackhall La., Sev. 108 CW65
Blackheath Ave. SE10 68 CG43
Blackheath Gro. SE3 68 CG44
Blackheath Hill SE10 67 CE44
Blackheath Pk. SE3 68 CG45
Blackheath Ri. SE13 67 CF44
Blackheath Rd. SE10 67 CE44
Blackheath Vale SE3 68 CG44
Blackheath Vill. SE3 68 CG44
Blackhills, Esher 93 BE58
Blackhorse Clo., Amer. 25 AP22
Blackhorse Clo., Grays 71 DE42
Richmond Rd.
Blackhorse Cres., Amer. 25 AP22
Blackhorse La. E17 48 CC31
Blackhorse La., Croy. 87 CB54
Blackhorse La., Pot.B. 19 BO18
Blackhorse La., Reig. 113 BS68
Blackhorse Ms. E17 48 CC31
Blackhorse Rd. E17 48 CC31
Blackhorse Rd. SE8 67 CD43
Blackhorse Rd., Sid. 79 CO49
Blackhorse Rd., Wok. 100 AO63
Blackland Ter. SW3 3 E9
Blacklands Dr., Hayes 53 BA38
Blacklands Mead, Red. 121 BX70
Blacklands Rd. SE6 77 CF49
Blacklands Ter. SW3 66 BU42
Blackley Clo., Wat. 26 BB22
Blackmans Clo., Dart. 80 CV47
Blackmans La., Warl. 97 CG60
Blackmoor La., Wat. 26 BA25
Blackmore Ave., Sthl. 54 BG40
Blackmore Clo., Grays 71 DE43
Richmond Rd.
Blackmore Ct., Wal.Abb. 22 CH20
Winters Way
Blackmore Cres., Wok. 100 AU61
Blackmore Mead, Ing. 24 DC19
Blackmore Rd., Brwd. 33 CZ22
Blackmore Rd., Buck.H. 40 CK26
Blackmore Rd., Ing. 24 DB18
Blackmore Way, Uxb. 53 AX36
Blackmores Gro., Tedd. 74 BJ50
Blackness La., Kes. 97 CJ57
Blackness La., Wok. 100 AS63
Blacknest Rd., Ascot 82 AO52
Blackpool Gdns., Hayes 53 BB38
Blackpool Rd. SE15 67 CB44
Blacks Rd. W6 65 BQ42
Blackshaw Pl. N1 57 CD36
Hertford Rd.
Blackshaw Rd. SW17 76 BT49
Blackshots La., Grays 71 DE40
Blacksmith All., Ing. 24 DC19
Blacksmith Clo., Ash. 103 BL63
Rectory La.
Blacksmith La., Guil. 118 AU73
Blacksmith Row, Slou. 62 AT42
Blacksmiths Clo., Rom. 50 CP32
Blacksmiths Hill, Epp. 23 CQ20
Blacksmiths Hill, S.Croy. 96 CB60
Blacksmiths La., Cher. 83 AW54
London St.
Blacksmiths La., Orp. 89 CP53
Blacksmiths La., Rain. 59 CT37
Blacksmiths La., St.Alb. 9 BF13
Blacksmiths La., Stai. 83 AX52
Blacksmiths La., Uxb. 43 AU34
Blackstock Ms. N4 47 BY34
Blackstock Rd.
Blackstock Rd. N4 47 BY34
Blackstock Rd. N5 47 BY34
Blackstone Clo., Red. 121 BU70
Blackstone Hill, Red. 121 BU70
Blackstone Rd. NW2 46 BQ35
Blackthorn Ave., West Dr. 63 AZ42
Blackthorn Clo., Reig. 121 BT71
Blackthorn Clo., St.Alb. 9 BK11
Blackthorn Clo., Sev. 99 CZ58
Ash Tree Dr.
Blackthorn Clo., Wat. 17 BC19
Blackthorn Ct., Houns. 64 BE43
Blackthorn Dell, Slou. 62 AR41
Hempson Ave.
Blackthorn Gro., Bexh. 69 CQ45
Blackthorn Pl., Guil. 118 AR69
Blackthorn Rd., Grays 71 DD40
Blackthorn Rd., Reig. 121 BT71
Blackthorn Rd., Welw.G.C. 5 BS8
Blackthorn St. E3 57 CE38
Blackthorn Way, Brent. 42 DB28
Blackthorne Ave., Croy. 87 CC54
Blackthorne Clo., Hat. 10 BO14
Blackthorne Dr. E4 39 CF28
Blackthorne Rd., Lthd. 111 BG66
Blackthorne Rd., Slou. 62 AV45
Blackwall La. SE10 68 CG41
Blackwall Tunnel App. SE10 68 CG41
Blackwall Tunnel Northern App. E14 57 CE37
Blackwall Way E14 57 CF40
Blackwater Clo., Rain. 59 CS39
Blackwater La., Hem.H. 8 BB15
Blackwater Rd., Sutt. 95 BS56
High St.
Blackwater St. SE22 77 CA46
Blackwell Ave., Guil. 118 AO70
Blackwell Clo. E5 48 CC35
Clapton Pk. Est.
Blackwell Clo., Har. 36 BG29
Blackwell Dr., Wat. 27 BD25
Blackwell Gdns., Edg. 37 BM27
Blackwell Hall La., Chesh. 25 AQ21
Blackwell Rd., Kings L. 17 AZ18
Blackwell St. SW9 66 BY43
Brixton Rd.
Blackwood Clo., Wey. 92 AX59
Blackwood St. SE17 4 K10
Blackwood St. SE17 67 BZ42
Blade Ms. SW15 65 BR45
Deodar Rd.
Bladen Clo., Wey. 92 BA57
Blades Clo., Lthd. 102 BK63
Bladindon Dr., Bex. 79 CP47
Bladon Clo., Guil. 118 AT70
Bladon Gdns., Har. 45 BF32
Blagdens Clo. N14 38 BW27
Blagdens La. N14 38 BW27
Blagdon Rd. SE13 77 CE46
Blagdon Rd., N.Mal. 85 BO52
Blagdon Wk., Tedd. 74 BK50
Blagrove Rd. W10 55 BR39
Blair Ave. NW9 46 BO33
Blair Ave., Esher 84 BG55
Blair Clo. N1 57 BZ36
Blair Clo., Hem.H. 8 AZ10
Braemar Turn
Blair Clo., Sid. 78 CN46
Boundary Rd.
Blair Ct., Beck. 87 CE51
The Knoll
Blair Dr., Sev. 107 CU65
Blair Rd., Slou. 52 AP40
Blair St. E14 57 CF39
Blairderry Rd. SW2 76 BX48
Blairhead Dr., Wat. 35 BC27
Blake Ave., Bark. 58 CN37
Blake Clo., Cars. 86 BU54
Blake Clo., Rain. 59 CT37
Blake Clo., St.Alb. 9 BJ15
Blake Clo., Well. 68 CN44
Blake Gdns. SW6 66 BS44
Blake Gdns., Dart. 70 CW45
Blake Hall Cres. E11 49 CH33
Blake Hall Rd. E11 49 CH33
Blake Hall Rd., Ong. 23 CU17
Blake Rd. E16 58 CG38
Blake Rd. N11 38 BW29
Blake Rd., Croy. 87 CA55
Blake Rd., Mitch. 86 BU52
Blake Way, Til. 71 DH44
Coleridge Rd.
Blakeden Dr., Esher 93 BH57
Blakehall Rd., Cars. 95 BU57
Blakemere Rd., Welw.G.C. 5 BQ7
Blakemore Rd. SW16 76 BX48
Blakemore Rd., Th.Hth. 86 BX53
Blakemore Way, Belv. 69 CQ41
Halifield Dr.
Blakeney Ave., Beck. 87 CD51
Blakeney Clo. E8 48 CB35
Foxley Clo.
Blakeney Clo. N20 38 BT26
Blakeney Clo., Epsom 94 BN59
Blakeney Rd., Beck. 77 CD50
Blakenham Rd. SW17 76 BL
Blaker Ct. SE7 68 C
Fairlawn
Blaker Rd. E15 57 CF
Blaker Rd. SE15 67 CA
Blakes Ave., N.Mal. 85 BC
Blakes Grn., W.Wick. 87 CF
Blakes La., Guil. 110 AY
Blakes La., N.Mal. 85 BC
Blakes Ter., N.Mal. 85 BF
Blakes Way, Til. 71 DH
Coleridge Rd.
Blakesley Ave. W5 54 BK
Blakesware Gdns. N9 39 BZ
Blakewood Clo., Felt. 74 BD
Blanch Clo. SE15 67 CC
Clifton Way
Blanchard Clo. SE9 78 CK
Shootery Clo.
Blanchard Way E8 57 CE
Lansdowne Dr.
Blanchards Hill, Guil. 109 AS
Blanche La., Pot.B. 19 BO
Blanche St. E16 58 CG
Blanchedowne SE5 67 BZ
Blanchland Rd., Mord. 86 BS
Blanchmans Rd., Warl. 105 CD
Bland St. SE9 68 C
Blandfield Rd. SW12 76 BV
Blandford Ave., Beck. 87 CD
Blandford Ave., Twick. 74 BF
Blandford Clo. N2 47 BT
Blandford Clo., Croy. 86 BX
Wandle Rd.
Blandford Clo., Rom. 50 CR
Blandford Clo., Slou. 62 AR
Blandford Rd. N.
Blandford Clo., Wok. 100 AT
Blandford Ct., Slou. 62 AR
Blandford Rd. S.
Blandford Cres. E4 39 CF
Blandford Rd. W4 65 BO
Blandford Rd. W5 64 BK
Blandford Rd., Beck. 87 CC
Blandford Rd., St.Alb. 9 BJ
Blandford Rd., Sthl. 64 BF
Blandford Rd., Tedd. 74 BG
Blandford Rd. N., Slou. 62 AR
Blandford Rd. S., Slou. 62 AR
Blandford Sq. NW1 1
Blandford Sq. NW1 56 BU
Blandford St. W1 1
Blandford St. W1 56 BU
Blandford Waye, Hayes 54 BD
Blaney Cres. E6 58 CL
Blanford Rd., Reig. 121 BT
Blanmerle Rd. SE9 78 CL
Blann Clo. SE9 78 CJ
Middle Pk. Ave.
Blantyre St. SW10 66 BT
Blantyre Wk. SW10 66 BT
Worlds End
Blashford St. SE13 77 CF
Blasker Wk. E14 67 CE
Rainbow Ave.
Blawith Rd., Har. 45 BH
Blaydon Clo. N17 39 CB
Blaydon Clo., Ruis. 44 BB
Blays Clo., Egh. 72 AR
Blays La.
Blays La., Egh. 72 AQ
Bleak Hill La. SE18 68 CN
Blean Gro. SE20 77 CC
Bleasdale Ave., Grnf. 54 BH
Blechynden St. W10 55 BQ
Bramley Rd.
Bleddyn Clo., Sid. 79 CP
Bledlow Clo. SE28 59 CP
Bledlow Ri., Grnf. 54 BG
Bleeding Heart Yd. EC1 2
Blegborough Rd. SW16 76 BW
Blencarn Clo., Wok. 100 AP
Blendon Dr., Bex. 79 CP
Blendon Path, Brom. 78 CG
Hope Pk.
Blendon Rd., Bex. 79 CP
Blendon Row SE17 67 BZ
Blendon Ter. SE18 68 CM
Blendworth Way SE15 67 CA
Hordle Prom. N.
Blenheim Ave., Ilf. 49 CL
Blenheim Clo. N21 39 BZ
Blenheim Clo. SW20 85 BQ
Blenheim Clo., Dart. 80 CV
Blenheim Clo., Grnf. 54 BG
Blenheim Clo., Rom. 50 CS
Blenheim Clo., Saw. 6 C
Blenheim Clo., Slou. 52 AS
Pickford Dr.
Blenheim Clo., Upmin. 51 CZ
Blenheim Clo., Wall. 95 BW
Blenheim Clo., Wat. 36 BD
Blenheim Clo., Wey. 91 AV
Madeira Rd.
Blenheim Ct. N19 47 BX
Blenheim Ct., Sid. 78 CM
Blenheim Cres. W11 55 BR
Blenheim Cres., Ruis. 44 BA
Blenheim Cres., S.Croy. 96 BZ
Blenheim Dr., Well. 68 CN
Blenheim Gdns. NW2 46 BQ
Blenheim Gdns. SW2 76 BX
Blenheim Gdns., Kings.T. 75 BM
Blenheim Gdns., S.Croy. 96 CB
Blenheim Gdns., S.Ock. 60 CX
Blenheim Gdns., Wall. 95 BW
Blenheim Gdns., Wem. 46 BL
Blenheim Gdns., Wok. 100 AQ
Blenheim Gro. SE15 67 CA
Blenheim Pk. Rd., S.Croy. 96 BZ
Blenheim Pas. NW8 56 BT
Blenheim Ri. N15 48 CA
Blenheim Rd. E6 58 CJ
Blenheim Rd. E15 49 CG

enheim Rd. E17 48 CC31
enheim Rd. NW8 56 BT37
enheim Rd. SE20 77 CC50
enheim Rd. SW20 85 BQ52
enheim Rd. W4 65 BO41
enheim Rd., Barn. 28 BQ24
enheim Rd., Brwd. 33 DA25
enheim Rd., Brom. 88 CK52
enheim Rd., Dart. 80 CV46
enheim Rd., Epsom 94 BN59
enheim Rd., Har. 45 BF32
enheim Rd., Nthlt. 54 BF36
enheim Rd., Orp. 89 CP55
enheim Rd., St.Alb. 9 BH13
enheim Rd., Sid. 79 CP47
enheim Rd., Slou. 62 AR42
enheim Rd., Sutt. 86 BS55
enheim St. W1 1 J9
enheim St. W1 56 BV39
enheim Ter. NW8 56 BT37
enheim Way, Epp. 23 CR17
enkarne Rd. SW11 76 BU46
enkin Clo., St.Alb. 9 BG11
eriot Rd., Houns. 64 BD43
essbury Rd., Edg. 37 BM30
essington Clo. SE13 67 CF45
essington Rd. SE13 67 CF45
etchingley Clo., Red. 113 BW68
etchingley Clo., Th.Hth. 86 BY52
Nutfield Rd.
etchingley Rd., Gdse. 114 CB69
etchingley Rd., Red. 121 BY70
etchingley Rd. 113 BW68
South Merstham), Red.
etchley Ct. N1 2 K1
etchley Ct. N1 57 BZ37
etchley St. N1 2 J1
etchley St. N1 57 BZ37
etchmore Clo., Hayes 63 BA42
etsoe Wk. N1 57 BZ37
Forston St.
ewett St. SE17 67 BZ42
Sandford Row
gh St., Grav. 81 DG46
Stuart Rd.
ghs Rd., Sev. 116 CU66
London Rd.
nco La., Slou. 52 AS39
ncoe Clo. SW19 75 BQ48
Thursley Gdns.
nd La., Bans. 104 BU61
nd La., Bet. 120 BN72
nd La., Loug. 31 CG23
nd La., Maid. 61 AG43
nd La., St.Alb. 19 BL17
nd La., Wal.Abb. 22 CJ20
ndmans La., Chsnt. 21 CC18
ss Cres. SE13 67 CE44
ssett St. SE10 67 CF44
sworth Clo., Hayes 54 BE38
Braunston Dr.
thbury Rd., Dag. 59 CO36
thdale Rd. SE2 69 CO42
thfield St. W8 66 BS41
Stratford Rd.
ockhouse Rd., Grays 71 DE43
ockley Rd., Wem. 45 BJ34
oemfontein Ave. W12 55 BP40
oemfontein Rd. W12 55 BP40
omfield Rd. W9 56 BS39
omfield St. EC2 2 L7
omfield St. EC2 57 BZ39
omfield Vill. W2 56 BS39
omville Rd., Dag. 50 CQ34
ondel St. SW11 66 BV44
ondell Clo., West Dr. 63 AX43
ondin Ave. W5 64 BK42
ondin St. E3 57 CE37
oom Gro. SE27 76 BY48
oom Pk. Rd. SW6 65 BR43
oomburg St. SW1 3 M9
oomburg St. SW1 66 BW42
Vincent Sq.
oomfield Cres., Ilf. 49 CL32
oomfield Pl. W1 1 K10
oomfield Rd. N6 47 BV32
oomfield Rd. SE18 68 CL43
oomfield Rd., Brom. 88 CJ53
oomfield Rd., Kings.T. 85 BL52
oomfield Ter. SW1 3 H10
oomfield Ter. SW1 66 BV42
oomfield Ter., West. 115 CN66
oomhall Rd. SE19 77 BZ49
oomsbury Clo. W5 55 BL40
oomsbury Clo., Epsom 94 BN58
oomsbury Ct. WC1 2 A7
oomsbury Ct., Pnr. 45 BE31
oomsbury Pl. SW18 76 BT46
Fullerton Rd.
oomsbury Pl. WC1 2 A6
oomsbury Pl. WC1 56 BX39
Southampton Row
oomsbury Sq. WC1 2 A7
oomsbury Sq. WC1 56 BX39
oomsbury St. WC1 1 P7
oomsbury St. WC1 56 BW39
oomsbury Way WC1 1 Q8
oomsbury Way WC1 56 BX39
ore Clo. SW8 66 BW44
Thessaly Rd.
ore Ct. W1 1 N10
ossom Clo. W5 65 BL41
ossom Clo., Croy. 96 CA56
ossom Clo., Dag. 59 CQ37
Burdetts Rd.
ossom La., Enf. 30 BZ23
ossom St. E1 2 N5
ossom St. E1 57 CA38
ossom Way, Uxb. 53 AY36
ossom Way, West Dr. 63 AZ42
ossom Waye, Houns. 64 BE43
ount St. E14 57 CD39
oxam Gdns. SE9 78 CK46
oxhall Rd. E10 48 CD33
Bloxham Cres., Hmptn. 74 BE50
Bloxworth Clo., Wall. 86 BW55
Blucher Rd. SE5 67 BZ43
Comber Gro.
Blue Anchor All., Rich. 65 BL45
Kew Rd.
Blue Anchor La. SE16 67 CB42
Blue Anchor La., Til. 71 DH42
Blue Anchor Yd. E1 57 CA40
Blue Ball La., Egh. 72 AS49
Blue Ball Yd. SW1 3 L3
Blue Ball Yd. SW1 56 BW40
St. James St.
Blue Barn La., Wey. 92 AZ59
Blue Cedars, Bans. 94 BR60
Bluebell Clo. SE26 77 CA49
Bluebell Clo., Hem.H. 7 AV14
Sundew Rd.
Bluebell Clo., Orp. 88 CL55
Bluebell Clo., Wall. 86 BV54
Bluebell Ct., Wok. 100 AR63
Bluebell Way, Ilf. 58 CL36
Blueberry Clo., St.Alb. 9 BG11
New Grns. Ave.
Blueberry Gdns., Couls. 104 BX61
Blueberry La., Sev. 107 CP61
Bluebridge Ave., Hat. 19 BR17
Bluebridge Rd., Hat. 19 BR17
Bluefield Clo., Hmptn. 74 BF49
Bluegates, Epsom 94 BP57
Bluehouse Hill, St.Alb. 9 BF14
Bluehouse La., Oxt. 115 CG67
Bluehouse Rd. E4 40 CG27
Bluemans, Epp. 14 CS15
Bluemans End, Epp. 14 CS15
Bluett Rd., St.Alb. 18 BK17
Blundell Clo., St.Alb. 9 BG11
Blundell La., Cob. 102 BE61
Blundell Rd., Edg. 37 BN30
Blundell St. N7 56 BX36
Blunden Clo., Dag. 50 CP33
Blunesfield, Pot.B. 20 BT19
Blunt Rd., S.Croy. 96 BZ56
Blunts Ave., West Dr. 63 AZ44
Blunts La., St.Alb. 18 BD16
Blunts Rd. SE9 78 CL46
Blurton Rd. E5 48 CC35
Blyth Clo. E14 67 CF42
Saunders Ness Rd.
Blyth Clo., Borwd. 28 BL23
Blyth Clo., Twick. 74 BH47
Grimwood Rd.
Blyth Rd. E17 48 CD33
Blyth Rd. SE28 59 CP40
Blyth Rd., Brom. 88 CG51
Blyth Rd., Hayes 63 BB41
Blyth Wk., Upmin. 51 CZ32
Blythe Clo. SE6 77 CD47
Blythe Clo., Iver 52 AV39
Grange Way
Blythe Clo., Twick. 74 BH47
Grimwood Rd.
Blythe Hill SE6 77 CD47
Blythe Hill, Orp. 88 CN51
Blythe Hill La. SE6 77 CD47
Blythe Rd. W14 65 BR41
Blythe Rd., Hodd. 12 CF13
Blythe St. E2 57 CB38
Blythe Vale SE6 77 CD47
Blythswood Rd., Ilf. 50 CO33
Blythway, Welw.G.C. 5 BR6
Blythwood Rd. N4 47 BX33
Blythwood Rd., Pnr. 36 BD30
Boades Ms. NW3 47 BT35
New End
Boadicea St. N1 56 BX37
Boakes Clo. NW9 46 BN31
Boakes Meadow, Sev. 98 CT59
Boar Clo., Chig. 41 CO28
Board Sch. Rd., Wok. 100 AS61
Boardman Ave. E4 30 CE25
Boars Rd., Harl. 14 CR11
Boathouse Wk. SE15 67 CA43
Bob Anker Clo. E13 58 CH38
Chesterton Rd.
Bob Marley Way SE24 66 BY45
Marcus Garvey Way
Bobbin Clo. SW4 66 BW45
Bobs La., Rom. 41 CT30
Bocketts La., Lthd. 102 BH65
Bockhampton Rd., Kings.T. 75 BL50
Bocking St. E8 57 CB37
Boddicott Clo. SW19 75 BR48
Bodell Clo., Grays 71 DD41
Bodiam Clo., Enf. 30 BZ23
Bodiam Rd. SW16 76 BW50
Bodle Ave., Swans. 81 DC47
Bodley Clo., N.Mal. 85 BO53
Bodley Rd., N.Mal. 85 BN53
Bodley St. SE17 67 BZ42
Wansey St.
Bodmin Clo., Har. 45 BE34
Bodmin Rd., Mord. 86 BS53
Bodmin St. SW18 76 BS47
Bodnant Gdns. SW20 85 BP52
Bodney Rd. E8 48 CB35
Bodwell Clo., Hem.H. 8 AW13
Bodwell Clo., Welw.G.C. 5 BR8
Boeing Way, Sthl. 63 BC41
Bogey La., Orp. 97 CK57
Bognor Gdns., Wat. 36 BD28
Bognor Rd., Well. 69 CP44
Bohemia Clo., Hem.H. 8 AY13
Bohemia Pl. E8 57 CB36
Mare St.
Bohun Gro., Barn. 29 BU25
Boileau Rd. SW13 65 BP43
Boileau Rd. W5 55 BL39
Bois Hall Rd., Wey. 92 AX56
Bois Hill, Chesh. 16 AP20
Bois La., Amer. 25 AO21
Bois Moor Rd., Chesh. 16 AO20
Bolden St. SE8 67 CE44
Bolderwood Way, W.Wick. 87 CE55
Boldmere Rd., Pnr. 45 BD33
Boleyn Ave., Enf. 30 CB23
Boleyn Ave., Epsom 94 BP58
Boleyn Clo. E17 48 CE31
Boleyn Clo., Hem.H. 8 BA11
Boleyn Clo., Stai. 72 AV49
Boleyn Dr., E.Mol. 84 BE52
Boleyn Dr., Ruis. 45 BD34
Boleyn Dr., St.Alb. 9 BG14
Boleyn Dr., Sev. 108 CW62
Boleyn Gdns., Brwd. 122 DD27
Boleyn Gdns., Dag. 59 CS36
Boleyn Gdns., W.Wick. 87 CE55
Boleyn Gro., W.Wick. 87 CE55
Boleyn Rd. E6 58 CJ37
Boleyn Rd. E7 58 CH36
Boleyn Rd. N16 48 CA35
Boleyn Wk., Lthd. 102 BH63
Boleyn Way, Barn. 29 BT24
Boleyn Way, Ilf. 40 CM29
Bolina Rd. SE16 67 CC42
Bolingbroke Gro. SW11 76 BU46
Bolingbroke Rd. W14 65 BQ41
Bolingbroke Wk. SW11 66 BU44
Bolingbroke Way, Hayes 53 BA40
Bollo Bri. Rd. W3 65 BM41
Bollo La. W3 65 BM41
Bollo La. W4 65 BM41
Bolney St. SW8 66 BX43
Bolney Way, Felt. 74 BE48
Bolsover Gro., Red. 113 BX68
Bolsover St. W1 1 K5
Bolsover St. W1 56 BV38
Bolstead Rd., Mitch. 86 BV51
Bolster Gro. N22 38 BW29
Bolt Cellar La., Epp. 22 CN18
Bolt Ct. EC4 2 E9
Bolt Ct. EC4 56 BY39
Gough Sq.
Bolters La., Bans. 94 BR60
Boltmore Clo. NW4 46 BQ31
Bolton Ave., Wind. 61 AO45
Bolton Clo. SE20 87 CB51
Selby Rd.
Bolton Clo., Chess. 94 BL57
Bolton Cres. SE5 66 BY43
Bolton Cres., Wind. 61 AO45
Bolton Gdns. NW10 55 BQ37
Bolton Gdns. SW5 66 BS42
Bolton Gdns., Brom. 78 CG50
Bolton Gdns., Tedd. 74 BJ50
Bolton Gdns. Ms. SW10 66 BT42
Bolton Rd. E15 58 CG36
Bolton Rd. N18 39 CA28
Bolton Rd. NW8 56 BS37
Bolton Rd. NW10 55 BO37
Bolton Rd. W4 65 BN43
Bolton Rd., Chess. 93 BK57
Bolton Rd., Har. 45 BG31
Bolton Rd., Wind. 61 AO45
Bolton St. W1 3 K2
Bolton St. W1 56 BV40
Bolton Wk. N7 47 BX34
Durham Rd.
Boltons, The SW10 66 BT42
Boltons, The, Wem. 45 BH35
Boltons Clo., Wok. 101 AW61
Boltons La., Hayes 63 AZ44
Boltons La., Wok. 101 AW61
Bombay St. SE16 67 CB42
Bombers La., West. 106 CM63
Bomer Clo., West Dr. 63 AZ43
Bomore Rd. W11 55 BQ40
Bon Marche Ter. SE27 77 CA49
Gipsy Rd.
Bonamy Est. E. SE16 67 CB42
Bonamy Est. W. SE16 67 CB42
Bonar Pl., Chis. 78 CK50
Bonar Rd. SE15 67 CB43
Bonavere Ct., Grav. 81 DJ49
Bonchester Clo., Chis. 88 CL51
Bonchurch Clo., Sutt. 95 BS57
Ventnor Rd.
Bonchurch Rd. W10 55 BR39
Bonchurch Rd. W13 54 BJ40
Bond Clo., Sev. 107 CP61
Bond Clo., West Dr. 53 AY39
Bond Ct. EC3 57 BZ39
Walbrook
Bond Ct. EC4 2 K9
Bond Gdns., Wall. 95 BW56
Bond Rd., Mitch. 86 BU51
Bond Rd., Surb. 85 BL55
Bond Rd., Warl. 105 CC62
Bond St. E15 49 CG35
Bond St. W1 56 BV39
Bond St. W4 65 BO42
Chiswick Common Rd.
Bond St. W5 54 BK40
Bond St., Egh. 72 AQ50
Bond St., Grays 71 DE43
Bondfield Rd. E6 58 CK39
Bondfield Wk., Dart. 70 CW45
Bonding Yd. Wk. SE16 67 CD41
Finland St.
Bondway SW8 66 BX43
Bonehurst Rd., Red. 121 BV74
Boneta Rd. SE18 68 CK41
Bonfield Ave., Hayes 53 BC38
Bonfield Rd. SE13 67 CF45
Bonham Gdns., Dag. 50 CP34
Bonham Rd. SW2 76 BX46
Bonham Rd., Dag. 50 CP34
Bonheur Rd. W4 65 BN41
Bonhill St. EC2 2 L5
Bonhill St. EC2 57 BZ38
Boniface Gdns., Har. 36 BF29
Boniface Rd., Uxb. 44 AZ34
Boniface Wk., Har. 36 BF29
Bonks Hill, Saw. 6 CP6
Bonner Hill Rd., Kings.T. 85 BL51
Bonner Rd. E2 57 CC37
Bonner St. E2 57 CC37
Bonner Wk., Grays 71 DC41
Bonners Clo., Wok. 100 AS64
Bonnersfield Clo., Har. 45 BH32
Bonnersfield La., Har. 45 BH32
Bonneville Gdns. SW4 76 BW46
Bonney Gro., Chsnt. 21 CB18
Bonney Way, Swan. 89 CT51
Bonnington Rd., Horn. 51 CV35
Bonnington Sq. SW8 66 BX43
Bonningtons, Brwd. 122 DD27
Bonny St. NW1 56 BW36
Bonnys Rd., Reig. 120 BQ71
Bonser Rd., Twick. 74 BH48
Bonsey Clo., Wok. 100 AS64
Bonsey La., Wok. 100 AS64
Bonseys La., Wok. 91 AS58
Bonseys Yd., Uxb. 53 AX36
George Sq.
Bonsor Dr., Tad. 103 BR64
Bonsor St. SE5 67 CA43
Bonville Gdns. NW4 46 BP31
Handowe Clo.
Bonville Rd., Brom. 78 CG49
Book Ms. WC2 1 P9
Booker Rd. N18 39 CB28
Bookham Ct., Lthd. 102 BE65
Church Rd.
Bookham Rd., Cob. 102 BD63
Boone St. SE13 68 CG45
Boones Rd. SE13 68 CG45
Boord St. SE10 68 CG41
Boot All., St.Alb. 9 BG13
Chequer St.
Boot St. N1 2 M3
Boot St. N1 57 CA38
Booth Clo. SE28 59 CO40
Booth Dr., Stai. 73 AX50
Booth Rd. NW9 37 BN30
Booth Rd., Croy. 86 BY55
Bourne St.
Boothby Rd. N19 47 BW34
Booths Clo., Hat. 10 BQ15
Booths Pl. W1 1 M7
Booths Pl. W1 56 BW39
Wells St.
Bordars Rd. W7 54 BH39
Bordars Wk. W7 54 BH39
Borden Ave., Enf. 30 BZ25
Border Cres. SE26 77 CB49
Border Gdns., Croy. 96 CE56
Border Rd. SE26 77 CB49
Bordergate, Mitch. 86 BU51
Bordergate Est., Mitch. 86 BU51
Borders La., Loug. 31 CL24
Borderside, Slou. 52 AQ39
Bordesley Rd., Mord. 86 BS53
Bordon Wk. SW15 75 BP47
Boreas Wk. N1 2 G1
Boreas Wk. N1 56 BY37
Nelson Pl.
Boreham Ave. E16 58 CH39
Boreham Clo. E11 48 CF33
Hainault Rd.
Boreham Holt, Borwd. 28 BL24
Boreham Rd. N22 39 BZ30
Borers Pas. E1 2 N8
Borers Pas. E1 57 CA39
Borgard Rd. SE18 68 CK42
Borkwood Pk., Orp. 97 CN56
Borkwood Way, Orp. 97 CM56
Borland Clo., Green. 80 DA46
Borland Rd. SE15 77 CC46
Borland Rd., Tedd. 74 BJ50
Bornedene, Pot.B. 19 BR19
Borneo St. SW15 65 BQ45
Borough, The, Bet. 120 BM71
Borough Grn. Rd., Sev. 108 DB64
Borough High St. SE1 4 J5
Borough High St. SE1 67 BZ41
Borough Hill, Croy. 86 BY55
Borough Rd. SE1 4 G6
Borough Rd. SE1 66 BY41
Borough Rd., Islw. 64 BH44
Borough Rd., Kings.T. 85 BM51
Borough Rd., Mitch. 86 BU51
Borough Rd., West. 106 CJ64
Borough Sq. SE1 4 H5
Borough Sq. SE1 67 BZ41
Great Suffolk St.
Borough Way, Pot.B. 19 BR19
Borrodaile Rd. SW18 76 BS46
Borrowdale, Hem.H. 8 AY12
Lonsdale
Borrowdale Ave., Har. 36 BJ30
Borrowdale Clo., Egh. 72 AT50
Derwent Rd.
Borrowdale Clo., Ilf. 49 CK31
Borrowdale Clo., S.Croy. 96 CA60
Borrowdale Dr., S.Croy. 96 CA59
Borthwick Ms. E15 49 CG35
Borthwick Rd.
Borthwick Rd. E15 49 CG35
Borthwick Rd. NW9 46 BO32
Borthwick St. SE8 67 CE42
Borwick Ave. E17 48 CD31
Bosanquet Clo., Uxb. 53 AX38
Bosanquet Rd., Hodd. 12 CF11
Bosbury Rd. SE6 77 CF48
Boscastle Rd. NW5 47 BV34
Boscobel Pl. SW1 3 H8
Boscobel Pl. SW1 66 BV42
Boscobel St. NW8 1 B5
Boscobel St. NW8 56 BT38
Boscombe Ave. E10 48 CF33
Boscombe Ave., Grays 71 DE42
Boscombe Ave., Horn. 51 CV33
Boscombe Clo. E5 48 CD35
Boscombe Clo., Egh. 82 AU51
Boscombe Gdns. SW16 76 BX50
Boscombe Rd. SW17 76 BV50
Boscombe Rd. SW19 86 BS51
Boscombe Rd. W12 55 BP40
Boscombe Rd., Wor.Pk. 85 BQ54
Bosgrove E4 39 CF26
Boss St. SE1 4 P4
Boss St. SE1 67 CA41
Bostal Row, Bexh. 69 CQ45
Bostall Hill SE2 69 CO42
Bostall Hill Rd. SE2 69 CP43
Bostall La. SE2 69 CO42
Bostall Manor Way SE2 69 CO42
Bostall Pk. Ave., Bexh. 69 CQ43
Bostall Rd., Orp. 79 CO50
Boston Gdns. W4 65 BO43
Boston Gdns., Brent. 64 BJ42
Boston Gro., Ruis. 44 BA32
Boston Manor Rd., Brent. 64 BJ42
Boston Pk. Rd., Brent. 64 BK42
Boston Pl. NW1 1 E5
Boston Pl. NW1 56 BU38
Boston Rd. E6 58 CK38
Boston Rd. E17 48 CE32
Boston Rd. W7 54 BH40
Boston Rd., Croy. 86 BX53
Boston Rd., Edg. 37 BN29
Boston Vale W7 64 BJ42
Bostonthorpe Rd. W7 64 BH41
Bosville Dr., Sev. 107 CU65
Bosville Rd., Sev. 107 CU65
Boswell Clo., Orp. 89 CP54
Killewarren Way
Boswell Ct. WC1 2 A6
Boswell Ct. WC1 56 BX39
Boswell Path, Hayes 63 BB42
Boswell Rd., Th.Hth. 87 BZ52
Boswell St. WC1 2 A6
Boswell St. WC1 56 BX39
Boswick La., Berk. 7 AO11
Bosworth Clo. E17 39 CD30
Bosworth Cres., Rom. 42 CV29
Bosworth Rd. N11 38 BW29
Bosworth Rd. W10 55 BR38
Bosworth Rd., Barn. 29 BS24
Bosworth Rd., Dag. 50 CR35
Botany Bay La., Chis. 88 CM51
Boteley Clo. E4 39 CF27
Boterys Cross, Red. 121 BY70
Botha Rd. E13 58 CH39
Botham Clo., Edg. 37 BM29
Pavilion Way
Bothwell Clo. E16 58 CG39
Bothwell Rd., Croy. 96 CF58
Bothwell St. W6 65 BQ43
Delorme St.
Botley La., Chesh. 16 AP18
Botley Rd., Hem.H. 8 AZ11
Botolph All. EC3 4 M1
Botolph La. EC3 4 M1
Botolph La. EC3 57 BZ40
Botsford Rd. SW20 85 BR51
Botsom La., Sev. 99 CY57
Bott Rd., Dart. 80 CW49
Bottom Ho. Fm. La., Ch.St.G. 34 AO27
Bottom La., Chesh. 16 AP19
Bottom La., Rick. 26 AW21
Bottrells La., Ch.St.G. 34 AO27
Botts Ms. W2 56 BS39
Chepstow Rd.
Botwell Common Rd., Hayes 53 BA40
Botwell Cres., Hayes 53 BB39
Botwell La., Hayes 53 BB40
Boucher Clo., Tedd. 74 BH49
Boucher Dr., Grav. 81 DF48
Bouchier Wk., Rain. 59 CU36
Deere Ave.
Boughton Ave., Brom. 88 CG54
Boughton Rd. SE28 68 CN41
Boughton Way, Amer. 25 AR22
Boulcott St. E1 57 CC39
Boulevard, The, Pnr. 45 BE31
Boulevard, The, Wat. 26 BA25
Boulevard, The, Welw.G.C. 5 BR7
Boulmer Rd., Uxb. 53 AX38
Boulogne Rd., Croy. 87 BZ53
Boulter Gdns., Horn. 59 CU36
Boulters Clo., Slou. 61 AN41
Amerden Way
Boulthurst Way, Oxt. 115 CH69
Boulton Rd., Dag. 50 CQ34
Boultwood Rd. E6 58 CK39
Bounce, The, Hem.H. 8 AX12
Bounce Hill, Rom. 32 CU23
Bounces La. N9 39 CB27
Bounces Rd. N9 39 CB26
Boundaries Rd. SW12 76 BU48
Boundaries Rd., Felt. 74 BD47
Boundary Clo. SE20 87 CB51
Haysleigh Gdns.
Boundary Clo., Ilf. 49 CM35
Loxford La.
Boundary Clo., Kings.T. 85 BM52
Boundary Clo., Sthl. 64 BF42
Boundary Ct., Welw.G.C. 5 BR10
Hollybush La.
Boundary Dr., Brwd. 122 DF26
Boundary La. E13 58 CJ38
Boundary La. SE17 67 BZ43
Camberwell Rd.
Boundary La., Welw.G.C. 5 BR9
Boundary Pas. E2 2 P4
Boundary Rd. E13 58 CJ37
Boundary Rd. E17 48 CD33
Boundary Rd. N9 30 CC25
Boundary Rd. N22 47 BY31
Boundary Rd. NW8 56 BS37
Boundary Rd. SW19 76 BT50
Boundary Rd., Ashf. 73 AX49
Boundary Rd., Bark. 58 CM37
Boundary Rd., Ger.Cr. 34 AR29
Boundary Rd., Pnr. 45 BD33
Boundary Rd., Rom. 50 CU32
Boundary Rd., St.Alb. 9 BH12
Boundary Rd., Sid. 78 CN46
Boundary Rd., Upmin. 51 CX34
Boundary Rd., Wall. 95 BV57

Boundary Rd., Wok. 100 AT61
Boundary Rd. S., Wall. 95 BV58
Boundary Row SE1 4 F4
Boundary Row SE1 66 BY41
Boundary St. E2 2 P3
Boundary St. E2 57 CA38
Boundary St., Erith 69 CT43
Boundary Way, Croy. 96 CE56
Boundary Way, Hem.H. 8 BA12
Boundary Way, Wat. 18 BD19
Boundary Yd., Wok. 100 AT61
Boundary Rd.
Boundfield Rd. SE6 78 CG48
Bounds Grn. Rd. N11 38 BW29
Bounds Grn. Rd. N22 38 BX29
Bourchier Clo., Sev. 116 CU66
Bourchier St. W1 1 N10
Bourchier St. W1 56 BW40
Wardour St.
Bourdon Pl. W1 1 K10
Bourdon Pl. W1 56 BV40
Bourdon St.
Bourdon Rd. SE20 87 CC51
Bourdon St. W1 3 J1
Bourdon St. W1 56 BV40
Bourke Clo. NW10 55 BO36
Mayo Rd.
Bourke Clo. SW4 76 BX46
Bourke Hill, Couls. 104 BU62
Bourlet Clo. W1 1 L7
Bourlet Clo. W1 56 BW39
Riding Ho. St.
Bourn Ave. N15 48 BZ31
Bourn Ave., Barn. 29 BT25
Bournbrook Rd. SE3 68 CJ45
Bourne, The N14 38 BW26
Bourne, The, Hem.H. 16 AT17
Bourne Ave. N14 38 BX27
Bourne Ave., Cher. 83 AW52
Eastern Ave.
Bourne Ave., Hayes 63 BA41
Bourne Ave., Ruis. 45 BD35
Bourne Ave., Uxb. 53 AZ38
Bourne Ave., Wind. 61 AO45
Bourne Clo., Brox. 12 CD13
Bourne Ct., Ruis. 44 BC35
Bourne Cres., Wey. 92 AW60
Bourne Dr., Mitch. 86 BT51
Bourne End, Horn. 51 CX33
Bourne End La., Berk. 7 AT15
Bourne End Rd., Nthwd. 35 BB28
Bourne Est. EC1 2 D6
Bourne Est. EC1 56 BY39
Bourne Gdns. E4 39 CE28
Bourne Gro., Ash. 102 BK63
Bourne Hill N13 38 BX27
Bourne Hill Clo. N13 38 BX27
Bourne Hill
Bourne La., Cat. 106 BZ64
Bourne La., Sev. 117 DC66
Bourne Mead, Bex. 79 CS46
Bourne Meadow, Cher. 82 AT52
Bourne Pk. Clo., Ken. 105 CA61
Bourne Pl. W4 65 BN42
Dukes Ave.
Bourne Rd. E7 49 CG34
Bourne Rd. N8 47 BX32
Bourne Rd., Berk. 7 AP12
Bourne Rd., Bex. 79 CR47
Bourne Rd., Brom. 88 CJ52
Bourne Rd., Bush. 27 BF25
Bourne Rd., Grav. 81 DJ48
Bourne Rd., Red. 113 BW68
Bourne Rd., Slou. 61 AO41
Bourne Rd., Vir.W. 82 AR53
Bourne St. SW1 3 G9
Bourne St. SW1 66 BV42
Bourne St., Croy. 86 BY55
Bourne Ter. W2 56 BS39
Bourne Vale, Brom. 88 CG54
Bourne Vw., Grnf. 54 BH36
Bourne Vw., Ken. 105 BZ61
Bourne Way, Brom. 88 CG55
Bourne Way, Epsom 94 BN56
Bourne Way, Sutt. 94 BR56
Bourne Way, Swan. 89 CS52
Bourne Way, Wey. 92 AX56
Bourne Way, Wok. 100 AR54
Bournebridge Clo., Brwd. 122 DF26
Bournebridge La., Rom. 41 CQ26
Bournefield Rd., Whyt. 105 CA62
Bournehall Ave., Bush. 27 BF25
Bournehall La., Bush. 27 BF25
Bournehall Rd., Bush. 27 BF25
Bournemead Ave., Nthlt. 53 BC37
Bournemead Clo., Nthlt. 53 BC37
Bournemead Way, Nthlt. 53 BC37
Bournemouth Rd. SE15 67 CB44
Bournemouth Rd. SW19 86 BS51
Bourneside, Vir.W. 82 AQ54
Bourneside Cres. N14 38 BW26
High St.
Bourneside Gdns. SE6 77 CF49
Bourneside Rd., Wey. 92 AX56
Bournevale Rd. SW16 76 BX49
Bournewood Rd. SE18 69 CO43
Bournewood Rd., Orp. 89 CO54
Bournville Rd. SE6 77 CE47
Bournwell Clo., Barn. 29 BU23
Bourton Clo., Hayes 53 BC40
Avondale Dr.
Bousfield Rd. SE14 67 CC44
Bousley Ri., Cher. 91 AU57
Boutflower Rd. SW11 66 BU45
Bouverie Gdns., Har. 45 BK32
Bouverie Ms. N16 48 CA34
Bouverie Rd.
Bouverie Pl. W2 1 B8
Bouverie Pl. W2 56 BT39
Bouverie Rd. N16 48 CA33
Bouverie Rd., Couls. 104 BV62
Bouverie Rd., Har. 45 BG32
Bouverie St. EC4 2 E9
Bouverie St. EC4 56 BY39
Bouverie Way, Slou. 62 AS42
Bouvier Rd., Enf. 30 CC22
Bovay Pl. N7 47 BX35
Bovay St. N7 47 BX35
Boveney Clo., Slou. 61 AN41
Amerden Way
Boveney New Rd. (Eton Wick), Wind. 61 AM42
Boveney Rd. SE23 77 CC47
Boveney Rd., Wind. 61 AL42
Bovey Way, S.Ock. 60 DA39
Bovill Rd. SE23 77 CC47
Bovingdon Ave., Wem. 55 BM36
Bovingdon Clo. N19 47 BW34
Bovingdon Cres., Wat. 18 BD20
Bovingdon Grn. La., Hem.H. 16 AS17
Bovingdon La. NW9 37 BO29
Bovingdon Rd. SW6 66 BS44
Bovingdon Sq., Mitch. 86 BX52
Bow Arrow La., Dart. 80 CX46
Bow Bri. Est. E3 57 CE38
Bow Chyd. EC4 2 J9
Bow Common La. E3 57 CD38
Bow Hay, Brwd. 122 DD27
Bow La. EC4 2 J9
Bow La. EC4 57 BZ39
Bow La. N12 38 BT29
Bow La., Mord. 85 BR53
Lower Morden La.
Bow Rd. E3 57 CD38
Bow Sprit, The, Cob. 102 BD61
Bow St. E15 49 CG35
Bow St. WC2 2 A9
Bow St. WC2 56 BX39
Bowater Clo. NW9 46 BN32
Bowater Clo. SW2 76 BX46
Loats Rd.
Bowater Pl. SE3 68 CH43
Bowater Rd. SE18 68 CJ41
Bowden Dr., Horn. 51 CW33
Bowden St. SE11 4 E10
Bowden St. SE11 66 BY42
Bowditch SE8 67 CD42
Bowdon Rd. E17 48 CE33
Bowen Dr. SE21 77 CA48
Bowen Rd., Har. 45 BG33
Bowen St. E14 57 CE39
Bowens Wd., Croy. 96 CD58
Bower Ave. SE10 68 CG44
Bower Clo., Nthlt. 54 BD37
Bower Clo., Rom. 41 CS29
Bower Ct., Epp. 23 CO19
Bower Ct., Wok. 100 AT61
Princess Rd.
Bower Fm. Rd., Hav. 41 CS27
Bower Hill, Epp. 23 CO19
Bower Hill Clo., Red. 121 BX72
Bower La., Eyns. 99 CX57
Bower Rd., Swan. 79 CU50
Bower St. E1 57 CC39
Stepney Causeway
Bower Ter., Epp. 23 CO19
Bower Vale, Epp. 23 CO19
Bowerdean St. SW6 66 BS44
Bowerhill La., Red. 121 BW71
Bowerman Ave. SE14 67 CD43
Bowerman Rd., Grays 71 DG42
Bowers Ave., Grav. 81 DF49
Mulberry Rd.
Bowers Clo., Guil. 109 AT68
Cotts Wd. Dr.
Bowers Fm. Dr., Guil. 109 AT68
Bowers La., Guil. 109 AS68
Bowers Rd., Sev. 98 CT59
Bowers Wk. E6 58 CK39
Northumberland Rd.
Bowes Clo., Sid. 79 CO46
Bowes Dr., Ong. 24 CW17
Bowes Rd. N11 38 BV28
Bowes Rd. N13 38 BV28
Bowes Rd. W3 55 BO40
Bowes Rd., Dag. 50 CP35
Bowes Rd., Stai. 72 AV50
Bowes Rd., Walt. 83 BC55
Bowes-Lyon Clo., Wind. 61 AO44
Ward Royal
Bowfell Rd. W6 65 BQ43
Bowford Ave., Bexh. 69 CQ44
Bowgate, St.Alb. 9 BH13
Bowhay, Brwd. 122 DD27
Bowhill Clo. SW9 66 BY43
Bowie Clo. SW4 76 BW47
Plummer Rd.
Bowland Rd. SW4 66 BW45
Bowland Rd., Wdf.Grn. 40 CJ28
Bowland Yd. SW1 3 F5
Bowlers Orchard, Ch.St.G. 34 AQ27
Bowles Grn., Enf. 30 CB21
Bowles Rd. SE1 67 CB43
Bowley La. SE19 77 CA49
Bowling Ct., Wat. 26 BB24
Mildred Ave.
Bowling Grn. Clo. SW15 75 BP47
Bowling Grn. Ct. EC2 2 N5
Bowling Grn. Ct. N1 57 CA38
Bowling Grn. La. EC1 2 E4
Bowling Grn. La. EC1 56 BY38
Bowling Grn. Pl. SE1 4 K4
Bowling Grn. Rd., Wok. 91 AP58
Bowling Grn. Row SE18 68 CK42
Samuel St.
Bowling Grn. St. SE11 66 BY43
Bowling Grn. Wk. N1 2 M2
Bowling Grn. Wk. N1 57 CA38
Bowls, The, Chig. 40 CN27
Bowls Clo., Stan. 36 BJ28
Bowman Ave. E16 58 CG40
Bowman Ms. SW18 75 BR47
Standen Rd.
Bowmans Clo. W13 54 BJ40
Bowmans Clo., Pot.B. 20 BT19
Bowmans Ct., Hem.H. 8 AX12
Fletcher Way
Bowmans Grn., Wat. 27 BE21
Bowmans Lea SE23 77 CC47
Dunoon Rd.
Bowmans Meadow, Wall. 86 BV55
Bowmans Ms. E1 57 CB39
Hooper St.
Bowmans Ms. N7 47 BX34
Seven Sisters Rd.
Bowmans Pl. N7 47 BX34
Hercules St.
Bowmans Rd., Dart. 79 CT47
Bowmead SE9 78 CK48
Bowmont Clo., Brwd. 122 DD25
Bowmore Wk. NW1 56 BW36
Agar Gro.
Bown Clo., Til. 71 DG45
Bowness Clo. E8 57 CA36
Rhodes St. Est.
Bowness Cres. SW15 75 BO49
Bowness Dr., Houns. 64 BE45
Bowness Rd. SE6 77 CE47
Bowness Rd., Bexh. 69 CR44
Bowness Way, Horn. 50 CU35
Bowood Rd. SW11 66 BV45
Bowood Rd., Enf. 30 CC23
Bowring Grn., Wat. 36 BD28
Bowrons Ave., Wem. 54 BK36
Bowry Dr., Stai. 72 AS46
Bowstridge La., Ch.St.G. 34 AR27
Bowyer Clo. E6 58 CK39
Hallywell Cres.
Bowyer Cres., Uxb. 43 AV32
Bowyer Pl. SE5 67 BZ43
Bowyer St. SE5 67 BZ43
Bowyers, Hem.H. 8 AX12
Bowyers Clo., Ash. 103 BL62
Bowzell Rd., Sev. 116 CT70
Box La., Bark. 59 CO37
Box La., Hem.H. 7 AV15
Box La., Hodd. 12 CD12
Box Ridge Ave., Pur. 95 BX59
Box Tree Clo., Chesh. 16 AO20
Box Tree Wk., Orp. 89 CP54
Boxall Rd. SE21 77 CA46
Boxfield, Welw.G.C. 5 BS9
Boxford Clo., S.Croy. 96 CC59
Boxgrove Ave., Guil. 118 AT69
Boxgrove La., Guil. 118 AT70
Boxgrove Rd. SE2 69 CO41
Boxgrove Rd., Guil. 118 AT70
Boxhill Rd., Dor. 120 BL70
Boxhill Rd., Tad. 120 BL69
Boxhill Way, Bet. 120 BM72
Boxley Rd., Mord. 86 BT52
Boxley St. E16 58 CH40
Boxmoor Rd., Har. 45 BJ31
Boxmoor Rd., Rom. 41 CS28
Boxoll Rd., Dag. 50 CQ35
Boxted Clo., Buck.H. 40 CK26
Boxted Rd., Hem.H. 7 AV12
Boxtree La., Har. 36 BG30
Boxtree Rd., Har. 36 BG29
Boxwell Rd., Berk. 7 AQ13
Boxwood Clo., West Dr. 63 AY41
Boxwood Way, Warl. 105 CC62
Boyard Rd. SE18 68 CL42
Boyce Clo., Borwd. 28 BL23
Boyce St. SE1 4 D3
Boyce St. SE1 56 BX40
Mepham St.
Boyce Way E13 58 CH38
Boycroft Ave. NW9 46 BN32
Boyd Ave., Sthl. 54 BE40
Boyd Clo., Kings.T. 75 BM50
Crescent Rd.
Boyd Rd. SW19 76 BT50
Boyd St. E1 57 CB39
Boydell Ct. NW8 56 BT37
Boyfield St. SE1 4 G5
Boyfield St. SE1 66 BY41
Boyland Rd., Brom. 78 CG49
Boyle Fm. Rd., T.Ditt. 84 BJ53
Boyle St. W1 1 L10
Boyle St. W1 56 BW40
Savile Row
Boyne Ave. NW4 46 BQ31
Boyne Ave., Stan. 36 BJ29
Boyne Rd. SE13 67 CF45
Boyne Rd., Dag. 50 CR34
Boyne Ter. Ms. W11 55 BR40
Boyseland Ct., Edg. 37 BM27
Boyson Rd. SE17 67 BZ43
Boythorn Way SE16 67 CB42
Bonamy Est. E.
Boyton Clo. E1 57 CC38
Stayners Rd.
Boyton Clo. N8 47 BX31
Boyton Rd. N8 47 BX31
Brabant Ct. EC3 2 M10
Brabant Ct. EC3 57 BZ40
Philpot La.
Brabant Rd. N22 38 BX30
Brabazon Ave., Wall. 95 BX57
Brabazon Rd., Houns. 64 BD43
Brabazon Rd., Nthlt. 54 BF37
Brabazon St. E14 57 CE39
Brabourn Gro. SE15 67 CC44
Brabourne Clo. SE19 77 CA49
Victoria Cres.
Brabourne Cres., Bexh. 69 CQ43
Brabourne Ri., Beck. 87 CF53
Bracewell Ave., Grnf. 45 BH35
Bracewell Rd. W10 55 BQ39
Bracewood Gdns., Croy. 87 CA55
Bracey St. N4 47 BX33
Bracken, The E4 30 CF26
Hortus Rd.
Bracken Ave. SW12 76 BV46
Bracken Ave., Croy. 87 CE55
Bracken Bri. Dr., Ruis. 45 BD34
Bracken Clo. E6 58 CK39
Bracken Clo., Slou. 43 AO35
Bracken Clo., Twick. 74 BF47
Bracken Clo., Wok. 100 AS62
Bracken Dene, Dart. 79 CT49
Bracken Dr., Chig. 40 CL29
Bracken End, Islw. 74 BG46
Harvesters Clo.
Bracken Gdns. SW13 65 BP44
Bracken Hill, Cob. 93 BF59
Bracken Hill, Ruis. 45 BE35
Bracken Hill Clo., Brom. 88 CG51
Bracken Hill La., Brom. 88 CG51
Bracken Ms., Rom. 50 CR32
Bracken Path, Epsom 94 BM60
Bracken Way, Guil. 118 AP69
Bracken Way, Wok. 91 AP58
Brackenbury Gdns. W6 65 BP41
Brackenbury Rd. N2 47 BT31
Brackenbury Rd. W6 65 BP41
Brackendale N21 38 BX26
Brackendale, Pot.B. 19 BR20
Brackendale Clo., Houns. 64 BF44
Brackendale Ct., Beck. 77 CE50
Brackendale Gdns., Upmin. 51 CY35
Brackendene, St.Alb. 18 BE18
Brackendene Clo., Wok. 100 AT61
Brackenforde, Slou. 62 AR41
Brackens, The, Enf. 39 CA26
Brackens, The, Hem.H. 8 AX13
Heather Way
Brackens, The, Orp. 98 CO56
Brackens Dr., Brwd. 42 DB28
Brackenwood, Sun. 83 BC51
Brackenwood Rd., Wok. 100 AO63
Brackley, Wey. 92 BA56
Brackley Clo., Wall. 95 BX57
Mollison Dr.
Brackley Rd. W4 65 BO42
Brackley Rd., Beck. 77 CD50
Brackley Sq., Wdf.Grn. 40 CJ29
Brackley St. EC1 2 J6
Brackley St. EC1 57 BZ39
Viscount St.
Brackley Ter. W4 65 BO42
Bracklyn Ct. N1 57 BZ37
Bracknell Clo. N22 38 BY30
Bracknell Gdns. NW3 47 BS35
Bracknell Gate NW3 47 BS35
Bracknell Pl., Hem.H. 8 AY11
Bracknell Way NW3 47 BS35
Bracondale, Esher 93 BG57
Bracondale Ave., Grav. 81 DF51
Bracondale Rd. SE2 69 CO42
Brad St. SE1 4 E3
Brad St. SE1 56 BY40
Bradbery, Rick. 34 AU28
Bradbourne Pk. Rd., Sev. 107 CU65
Bradbourne Rd., Bex. 79 CR47
Bradbourne Rd., Grays 71 DD43
Bradbourne Rd., Sev. 107 CU64
Bradbourne St. SW6 66 BS44
Bradbourne Vale Rd., Sev. 107 CT64
Bradbury Clo., Sthl. 64 BE42
Blandford Rd.
Bradbury Gdns., Slou. 43 AR35
Bradbury St. N16 48 CA35
Braddon Rd., Rich. 65 BL45
Braddyll St. SE10 68 CG42
Braden St. W9 56 BS38
Bradenham Ave., Well. 69 CO45
Bradenham Rd., Har. 45 BJ31
Bradenham Rd., Hayes 53 BB38
Bradenhurst Clo., Cat. 114 CA66
Bradfield Clo., Guil. 118 AT69
Sutherland Dr.
Bradfield Clo., Wok. 100 AS62
Bradfield Dr., Bark. 50 CO35
Bradfield Rd. E16 68 CH41
Bradfield Rd., Ruis. 45 BE35
Bradford Clo. SE26 77 CB49
Coombe Rd.
Bradford Clo., Brom. 88 CK54
Bradford Dr., Epsom 94 BO57
Bradford Rd. W3 65 BO41
Warple Way
Bradford Rd., Ilf. 49 CM33
Bradford Rd., Rick. 34 AU26
Bradgate, Cuffley 20 BW17
Bradgate Clo., Cuffley 20 BW17
Bradgate Rd. SE6 77 CE46
Brading Cres. E11 49 CH34
Brading Rd. SW2 76 BX47
Brading Rd., Croy. 86 BX53
Bradiston Rd. W9 55 BR38
Bradleigh Ave., Grays 71 DD42
Bradley Clo. N7 56 BX36
Blundell St.
Bradley Gdns. W13 54 BJ39
Bradley La., Dor. 119 BJ69
Bradley Ms. SW17 76 BU47
Bellevue Rd.
Bradley Rd. N22 38 BX30
Bradley Rd. SE19 77 BZ50
Bradley Rd., Enf. 30 CD22
Bradley Rd., Slou. 52 AO40
Bradleys Clo. N1 56 BY37
White Lion St.
Bradman Row, Edg. 37 BM29
Pavilion Way
Bradmead SW8 66 BV43
Bradmore Grn., Hat. 19 BR16
Bradmore La. W6 65 BQ42
Beadon Rd.
Bradmore La., Hat. 19 BQ16
Bradmore Pk. Rd. W6 65 BP42
Bradmore Way, Couls. 104 BX62
Bradmore Way, Hat. 19 BR16
Bradshaw Clo., Wind. 61 AM44
Bradshaw Rd., Wat. 27 BD23
Bradshawe Rd., Grays 71 DD40
Bradshawe Waye, Uxb. 53 AY39
Bradshaws, Hat. 10 BO14
Bradshaws Clo. SE25 87 CB
Bradstock Rd. E9 57 CC
Bradstock Rd., Epsom 94 BF
Bradstock Rd. Est. E9 57 CC
Bradwell Ave., Dag. 50 CR
Stour Rd.
Bradwell Clo. E18 49 CG
Bradwell Clo., Horn. 59 CU
Bradwell Grn., Brwd. 122 DE
Bradwell Ms. N18 39 CE
Lyndhurst Rd.
Bradwell Rd., Buck.H. 40 CK
Bradwell St. E1 57 CC
Brady Ave., Loug. 31 CM
Brady St. E1 57 CB
Brae Ct., Kings.T. 85 BM
Wolverton Ave.
Braefoot Ct. SW15 75 BO
Putney Hill
Braemar Ave. N22 38 BX
Braemar Ave. NW10 46 BN
Braemar Ave. SW19 76 BS
Braemar Ave., Bexh. 69 CS
Braemar Ave., S.Croy. 96 BZ
Braemar Ave., Th.Hth. 86 BY
Braemar Ave., Wem. 54 BK
Braemar Gdns. NW9 37 BN
Braemar Gdns., Horn. 51 CX
Braemar Gdns., Sid. 78 CM
Braemar Gdns., Slou. 61 AN
Braemar Gdns., W.Wick. 87 CF
Braemar Rd. E13 58 CG
Braemar Rd. N15 48 CA
Braemar Rd., Brent. 64 BK
Braemar Rd., Wor.Pk. 85 BP
Braemar Turn, Hem.H. 8 AZ
Braes Mead, Red. 121 BX
Braes St. N1 56 BY
Braeside, Beck. 77 CE
Braeside, Wey. 92 AW
Braeside Ave. SW19 85 BR
Braeside Ave., Sev. 107 CT
Braeside Clo., Pnr. 36 BF
Braeside Clo., Sev. 107 CT
Braeside Cres., Bexh. 69 CS
Braeside Rd. SW16 76 BW
Braesyde Clo., Belv. 69 CQ
Brafferton Rd., Croy. 96 BZ
Braganza St. SE17 66 BY
Bragmans La., Rick. 16 AU
Braham St. E1 2
Braham St. E1 57 CA
Braid, The, Chesh. 16 AP
Braid Ave. W3 55 BN
Braid Clo., Felt. 74 BE
Braidwood Rd. SE6 77 CF
Braidwood St. SE1 4
Braidwood St. SE1 57 CA
Brailsford Clo., Mitch. 86 BU
Longfield Dr.
Brailsford Rd. SW2 76 BY
Brain Clo., Hat. 10 BP
Brainton Ave., Felt. 73 BC
Braintree Ave., Ilf. 49 CK
Braintree Rd., Dag. 50 CR
Braintree Rd., Ruis. 44 BC
Braintree St. E2 57 CC
Braithwaite Ave., Rom. 50 CR
Braithwaite Gdns., Stan. 36 BK
Brakefield Rd., Grav. 81 DD
Brakey Hill, Red. 114 CA
Brakynbery, Berk. 7 AP
Brallings La., Ger.Cr. 34 AT
Bramah Grn. SW9 66 BY
Eyethorn Rd.
Bramalea Clo. N6 47 BV
Bramall Clo. E15 49 CG
Idmiston Rd.
Bramber Ct. W5 65 BL
Sterling Pl.
Bramber Ct., Slou. 61 AN
Avebury
Bramber Rd. N12 38 BU
Bramber Rd. W14 65 BR
Bramble Ave., Dart. 80 DB
Bramble Banks, Cars. 95 BV
Bramble Clo., Cat. 105 CA
Burntwood La.
Bramble Clo., Croy. 96 CE
Bramble Clo., Guil. 118 AP
Bramble Clo., Red. 121 BV
Bramble Clo., Shep. 83 BA
Bramble Clo., Stan. 36 BK
Bramble Clo., Uxb. 53 AY
Bramble Clo., Wat. 17 BC
Bramble Cft., Erith 69 CS
Bramble Down, Stai. 83 AW
Hereford Clo.
Bramble Fm. Clo., Uxb. 53 AZ
Bramble Gdns. W12 55 BO
Wallflower St.
Bramble La., Amer. 25 AP
Bramble La., Hodd. 12 CD
Bramble La., Sev. 116 CU
Bramble La., Upmin. 60 CY
Bramble Mead, Ch.St.G. 34 AQ
Bramble Ri., Cob. 102 BD
Bramble Ri., Harl. 6 CM
Hodings Rd.
Bramble Rd., Hat. 10 BN
Bramble Wk., Epsom 94 BM
Bramble Wk., Red. 121 BV
Hartspiece Rd.
Bramble Way, Wok. 100 AV
Linden Way
Bramblebury Rd. SE18 68 CM
Brambledene Clo., Wok. 100 AR
Silversmiths Way
Brambledown Clo., W.Wick. 88 CG
Brambledown Rd., Cars. 95 BV
Brambledown Rd., S.Croy. 96 BZ
Bramblefield Clo., Long. 90 DC

ambles, The, Chig.	40	CM29	Brandreth Rd. E6	58	CK39	Breakspeare Clo., Wat.	26	BC22	Brereton Ct., Hem.H.	8	AY14
ambles, The, St.Alb.	9	BG14	Brandreth Rd. SW17	76	BV48	Breakspeare Rd., Abb.L.	17	BB19	*Runham Rd.*		
Prospect Rd.			Brandries, The, Wall.	86	BW55	Breakspears Dr., Orp.	89	CO51	Brereton Rd. N17	39	CA29
ambles, The, West Dr.	63	AX42	Brands Hatch Rd., Fawk.	99	DA56	Breakspears Rd. SE4	67	CD45	**Bressenden Pl. SW1**	**3**	**K6**
ambles Clo., Islw.	64	BJ43	Brands Rd., Slou.	62	AT43	Bream Gdns. E6	58	CL38	Bressenden Pl. SW1	66	BV41
ambletye Pk.Rd., Red.	121	BU71	Brandsland, Reig.	121	BS72	Bream St. E3	57	CE36	Bressey Gro. E18	40	CG30
amblewood Clo., Cars.	86	BU54	Brandville Gdns., Ilf.	49	CL31	Breamore Clo. SW15	75	BP47	Bretlands Rd., Cher.	82	AV55
ambling Ri., Hem.H.	8	AY11	Brandville Rd., West Dr.	63	AY41	Breamore Ct., Ilf.	50	CO34	Brett Clo. N16	48	CA34
amblings, The E4	39	CF28	Brandy Way, Sutt.	95	BS57	Breamore Rd., Ilf.	49	CN34	Brett Clo., Nthlt.	54	BD38
amcote Ave., Mitch.	86	BU52	Branfill Rd., Upmin.	51	CX34	**Breams Bldgs. EC4**	**2**	**D8**	*Broomcroft Ave.*		
amcote Gro. SE16	67	CC42	Brangbourne Rd., Brom.	77	CF49	Breams Bldgs. EC4	56	BY39	Brett Cres. NW10	55	BN36
amcote Rd. SW15	65	BP45	Brangton Rd. SE11	66	BX42	Breamwater Gdns.,	74	BJ48	Brett Gdns., Dag.	59	CQ36
amdean Cres. SE12	78	CH47	*Loughborough St.*			Rich.			Brett Pl., Wat.	26	BC22
amdean Gdns. SE12	78	CH47	Brangwyn Cres. SW19	86	BT51	Brearley Clo., Edg.	37	BM29	Brett Rd. E8	48	CB35
amerton Rd., Beck.	87	CD52	Branksea St. SW6	65	BR43	*Pavilion Way*			Brett Rd., Barn.	28	BQ25
amerton St. SW3	66	BU43	Branksome Ave. N18	39	CA29	Brearley Clo., Uxb.	53	AY36	**Brettell St. SE17**	67	BZ42
amfield N4	48	BZ34	Branksome Clo., Hem.H.	8	AZ13	Breasley Clo. SW15	65	BP45	Brettenham Ave. E17	39	CE30
amfield Pl., Hem.H.	8	AZ10	Branksome Clo., Walt.	84	BD54	Brechin Pl. SW7	66	BT42	Brettenham Rd. E17	39	CD30
Ilstree Rd.			Branksome Rd. SW2	66	BX45	Brecken Clo., St.Alb.	9	BJ11	Brettenham Rd. N18	39	CB28
amfield Rd. SW11	76	BU46	Branksome Rd. SW19	86	BS51	Brecknock Rd. N7	47	BW35	Brettgrave, Epsom	94	BN58
amford Ct. N14	38	BW27	Branksome Way, Har.	46	BL32	Brecknock Rd. N19	47	BW35	Brevet Clo., Grays	70	CY42
amford Rd. SW18	66	BT45	Branksome Way, N.Mal.	85	BN51	Brecknock Rd. Est. N7	47	BW35	*Brimfield Rd.*		
amham Gdns. SW5	66	BS42	Bransby Rd., Chess.	94	BL57	Brecon Clo., Mitch.	86	BX52	Brewer Pl. SE18	68	CL42
amham Gdns., Chess.	93	BK56	Branscombe Gdns. N21	38	BY26	Brecon Clo., Wor.Pk.	94	BO32	*Charles Grindling Wk.*		
amhope La. SE7	68	CH43	Branscombe St. SE13	67	CE45	*Goldsmith Ave.*			**Brewer St. W1**	**1**	**M10**
amlands Clo. SW11	66	BU45	Bransdale Clo. NW6	56	BS37	Brecon Rd. W6	65	BR43	Brewer St. W1	56	BW40
amleas, Wat.	26	BB25	*West End La.*			Brecon Rd., Enf.	30	CC24	Brewer St., Red.	114	BZ69
amley Ave., Couls.	104	BW61	Bransell Clo., Swan.	89	CS53	Brede Clo. E6	58	CL38	Brewers Fld., Dart.	80	CV49
amley Ave., Shep.	83	BB52	Bransgrove Rd., Edg.	37	BL30	Bredgar Rd. N19	47	BW34	**Brewers Grn. SW1**	**3**	**M6**
Grange Fm. Caravan Site			Branston Cres., Orp.	88	CM54	Bredhurst Clo. SE20	77	CC50	Brewers La., Rich.	74	BK46
amley Clo. E17	39	CD30	Branstone Rd., Rich.	65	BL44	Bredon Rd. SE5	67	BZ45	Brewery Clo., Wem.	45	BJ35
amley Clo. N14	29	BV25	Brants Wk. W7	54	BH38	Bredon Rd., Croy.	87	CA54	Brewery La., Twick.	74	BH47
amley Clo., Cher.	83	AW54	Brantwood Ave., Erith	69	CS43	Bredune, Ken.	105	BZ61	Brewery La., Wey.	92	AY60
amley Clo., Grav.	81	DF50	Brantwood Ave., Islw.	64	BJ45	*Church La.*			Brewery Rd. N7	56	BX36
amley Clo., Hayes	53	BC40	Brantwood Clo. E17	48	CE31	Breech La., Tad.	112	BM66	Brewery Rd. SE18	68	CM42
Orchard Rd.			Brantwood Dr., Wey.	91	AV60	Breer St. SW6	66	BS45	Brewery Rd., Brom.	88	CK54
amley Clo., Orp.	88	CL54	Brantwood Gdns., Enf.	29	BX24	Breezers Hill E1	57	CB40	Brewery Rd., Hodd.	12	CE12
amley Clo., S.Croy.	95	BY56	Brantwood Gdns., Ilf.	49	CK31	*Pennington St.*			Brewery Rd., Wok.	100	AR62
amley Clo., Stai.	73	AX50	Brantwood Gdns., Wey.	91	AV60	Brember Rd., Har.	45	BG34	Brewhouse La. E1	57	CB40
Kingston Rd.			Brantwood Rd. N17	39	CA29	Bremer Rd., Stai.	73	AW48	*Wapping La.*		
amley Clo., Twick.	74	BG46	Brantwood Rd. SE24	77	BZ46	Bremner Clo., Swan.	89	CU52	Brewhouse Rd. SE18	68	CK42
amley Ct., Well.	69	CO44	Brantwood Rd., Bexh.	69	CR44	Bremner Rd. SW7	66	BT41	*Red Barracks Rd.*		
amley Cres., Ilf.	49	CL32	Brantwood Rd., S.Croy.	96	BZ58	*Queens Gate*			Brewhouse St. SW15	65	BR45
amley Gdns., Wat.	36	BD28	Brantwood Way, Orp.	89	CP52	Brenchley Ave., Grav.	81	DG49	Brewhouse Wk. SE16	57	CD40
amley Hill, S.Croy.	95	BY56	Brasher Clo., Grnf.	45	BG35	Brenchley Clo., Brom.	88	CG53	**Brewhouse Yd. EC1**	**2**	**F4**
amley Par. N14	29	BW24	*Bedser Dr.*			Brenchley Clo., Chis.	88	CL51	Brewhouse Yd. EC1	56	BY38
amley Pl., Dart.	69	CU45	Brassey Rd. NW6	55	BR36	Brenchley Gdns. SE23	77	CC46	*Compton St.*		
amley Rd. N14	29	BV25	Brassey Rd., Oxt.	115	CG68	Brenchley Rd., Orp.	88	CN51	**Bride Ct. EC4**	**2**	**F9**
amley Rd. W5	64	BK41	Brassey Sq. SW11	66	BV45	Brenda Rd. SW17	76	BU48	**Bride La. EC4**	**2**	**F9**
amley Rd. W10	55	BQ40	*Ashbury Rd.*			Brendans Clo., Horn.	51	CW33	Bride La. EC4	56	BY39
amley Rd., Sutt.	95	BT56	Brassie Ave. W3	55	BO39	Brende Gdns., E.Mol.	84	BF52	Bride St. N7	56	BX36
amley Rd. (Cheam),	94	BQ58	Brasted Clo. SE26	77	CC49	Brendon Ave. NW10	46	BO35	Bridewell Pl. E1	57	CB40
Sutt.			Brasted Clo., Bexh.	79	CP46	Brendon Clo., Erith	69	CT44	**Bridewell Pl. EC4**	**2**	**F9**
amley Shaw, Wal.Abb.	22	CG20	Brasted Clo., Orp.	89	CO55	Brendon Clo., Esher	93	BG57	Bridewell Pl. EC4	56	BY39
amley St. W10	55	BQ39	Brasted Hill, Sev.	116	CU68	Brendon Clo., Hayes	63	BA43	*Tudor St.*		
amley Way, Ash.	103	BL62	Brasted Hill Rd., West.	107	CO64	Brendon Dr., Esher	93	BG57	**Bridford Ms. W1**	**1**	**K6**
amley Way, Houns.	74	BE46	Brasted La., Sev.	107	CO63	Brendon Gdns., Har.	45	BF35	Bridford Ms. W1	56	BV39
amley Way, W.Wick.	87	CE55	Brasted Rd., Erith	69	CT43	Brendon Gdns., Ilf.	49	CN32	*Devonshire St.*		
ammas Clo., Slou.	61	AO41	Brathway Rd. SW18	76	BS47	Brendon Rd. SE9	78	CM48	Bridge, The W5	54	BK40
ampton Clo. E5	48	CB34	Bratley St. E1	57	CB38	Brendon Rd., Dag.	50	CQ33	Bridge, The, Har.	45	BH31
Comberton Rd.			*Weaver St.*			**Brendon St. W1**	**1**	**D8**	Bridge App. NW1	56	BV36
ampton Clo., Chsnt.	21	CB17	Brattle Wd., Sev.	116	CU68	Brendon St. W1	56	BU39	Bridge Ave. W6	65	BQ42
ampton Gdns. N15	48	BZ32	Braund Ave., Grnf.	54	BF38	Brendon Way, Enf.	39	CA26	Bridge Ave. W7	54	BG39
Brampton Rd.			Braundton Ave., Sid.	78	CN47	Brenley Clo., Mitch.	86	BV52	Bridge Ave., Upmin.	51	CX34
ampton Gdns., Walt.	93	BD56	Braunston Dr., Hayes	54	BE38	Brenley Gdns. SE9	68	CJ45	Bridge Clo., Brwd.	122	DC28
ampton Gro. NW4	46	BP31	Bravington Clo., Shep.	83	AY53	Brennan Rd., Til.	71	DG44	Bridge Clo., Enf.	30	CB23
ampton Gro., Har.	45	BJ31	Bravington Pl. W9	55	BR38	Brent, The, Dart.	80	CX47	Bridge Clo., Rom.	50	CT32
ampton Gro., Wem.	46	BL33	*Bravington Rd.*			Brent Clo., Bex.	79	CQ47	*Forge La.*		
ampton La. NW4	46	BQ31	Bravington Rd. W9	55	BR38	Brent Clo., Dart.	80	CX46	Bridge Clo., Sun.	83	BC52
Brampton Gro.			Braxfield Rd. SE4	67	CD45	Brent Ct. NW11	46	BQ33	Bridge Clo., Walt.	83	BB54
ampton Pk. Rd. N22	47	BY31	Braxted Pk. SW16	76	BX50	*Highfield Ave.*			Bridge Clo., Wey.	92	AY59
High Rd.			Bray Clo., Borwd.	28	BN23	Brent Cres. NW10	55	BL37	Bridge Clo., Wok.	100	AR62
ampton Rd. E6	58	CJ38	*Denham Way*			Brent Cross Shop. Cen.	46	BQ33	Bridge Cotts., Surb.	84	BJ54
ampton Rd. N15	48	BZ32	Bray Clo., Maid.	61	AH41	NW4			*Portsmouth Rd.*		
ampton Rd. NW9	46	BM31	Bray Clo., Maid.	61	AH42	Brent Grn. NW4	46	BQ32	Bridge Ct. E10	48	CD33
ampton Rd. SE2	69	CP43	Bray Cres. SE16	67	CC41	Brent La., Dart.	80	CW47	Bridge Dr. N13	38	BX28
ampton Rd., Bexh.	69	CP43	*Marlow Way*			Brent Lea, Brent.	64	BK43	Bridge End E17	39	CF30
ampton Rd., Croy.	87	CA53	Bray Dr. E16	58	CG40	Brent Pk. Rd. NW4	46	BP33	Bridge Gdns., Ashf.	73	BA50
ampton Rd., St.Alb.	9	BJ13	Bray Gdns., Wok.	100	AV61	Brent Pl., Barn.	28	BR25	Bridge Gdns., E.Mol.	84	BG52
ampton Rd., Uxb.	53	AZ37	Bray Pas. E16	58	CG40	Brent Rd. E16	58	CH39	Bridge Gate N21	39	BZ26
ampton Rd., Wat.	35	BC27	*Bray Dr.*			Brent Rd. SE18	68	CL43	Bridge Hill, Epp.	22	CN20
amsham Gdns., Wat.	36	BD28	**Bray Pl. SW3**	**3**	**E9**	Brent Rd., Brent.	64	BK43	Bridge Hill Clo., Guil.	109	AQ70
amshaw Ri., N.Mal.	85	BO53	Bray Pl. SW3	66	BU42	Brent Rd., S.Croy.	96	CB58	*Aldershot Rd.*		
amshaw Rd. E9	57	CC36	Bray Rd. NW7	37	BQ29	Brent Rd., Sthl.	64	BD41	Bridge Ho. Quay E14	57	CF40
amshill Clo., Chig.	40	CN28	Bray Rd., Cob.	102	BD61	Brent Side, Brent.	64	BK43	*Prestons Rd.*		
Tine Rd.			Bray Rd., Guil.	118	AQ71	Brent St. NW4	46	BQ31	Bridge La. NW11	46	BR31
amshill Gdns. NW5	47	BV34	Bray Rd., Maid.	61	AG40	Brent Ter. NW2	46	BQ33	Bridge La. SW11	66	BU44
amshill Rd. NW10	55	BO37	Brayards Rd. SE15	67	CB44	Brent Vw. Rd. NW9	46	BP32	Bridge La., Vir.W.	82	AS53
amshot Ave. SE7	68	CH43	Braybank, Maid.	61	AH41	Brent Way N3	38	BS29	Bridge Path, Wat.	26	BC23
amshot Way, Wat.	35	BC27	Braybourne Clo., Uxb.	53	AX36	Brent Way, Brent.	64	BK43	**Bridge Pl. SW1**	**3**	**K8**
amston Rd. NW10	55	BP37	Braybourne Dr., Islw.	64	BH43	Brent Way, Dart.	80	CX46	Bridge Pl. SW1	66	BV42
amwell Clo., Sun.	84	BD51	Braybrook St. W12	55	BO39	Brent Way, Wem.	55	BM36	Bridge Pl., Amer.	23	AP22
ancaster Rd. E12	49	CK35	Braybrooke Gdns. SE19	77	CA50	Brentcot Clo. W13	54	BJ38	Bridge Pl., Croy.	87	BZ54
ancaster Rd. SW16	76	BX48	*Fox Hill*			Brentfield NW10	55	BM36	Bridge Pl., Wat.	27	BD25
ancaster Rd., Ilf.	49	CM32	Brayburne Ave. SW4	66	BW44	Brentfield Clo. NW10	55	BN36	Bridge Rd. E6	58	CK36
ancepeth Gdns.,	40	CH27	Braycourt Ave., Walt.	83	BC54	Brentfield Gdns. NW2	46	BQ33	Bridge Rd. E15	57	CF36
Buck.H.			Braydon Rd. N16	48	CA33	Brentfield Rd. NW10	55	BN36	Bridge Rd. E17	48	CD33
anch Clo., Hat.	10	BQ11	Brayfield Rd., Maid.	61	AH41	Brentfield Rd., Dart.	80	CX47	Bridge Rd. N9	39	CB27
anch Hill NW3	47	BT34	Brayfield Ter. N1	56	BY36	Brentford Clo., Hayes	54	BD38	Bridge Rd. N22	38	BX30
anch Pl. N1	57	BZ37	*Lofting Rd.*			*Paddington Clo.*			Bridge Rd. NW10	55	BO36
anch Rd. E14	57	CD40	Brays Mead, Harl.	13	CN12	Brentham Way W5	54	BK38	Bridge Rd., Beck.	77	CD50
anch Rd., Ilf.	41	CO28	Brays Springs, Wal.Abb.	22	CG20	Brenthouse Rd. E9	57	CC36	Bridge Rd., Bexh.	69	CQ45
anch Rd., St.Alb.	9	BF13	*Roundhills*			Brenthurst Rd. NW10	55	BO36	Bridge Rd., Cher.	83	AW54
anch Rd. (Park St.),	18	BG17	Brayton Gdns., Enf.	29	BW24	Brentlands Dr., Dart.	80	CX47	Bridge Rd., Chess.	93	BL56
St.Alb.			Braywood Ave., Egh.	72	AS50	Brentmead Clo. W7	54	BH40	Bridge Rd., Croy.	87	BZ54
ancker Clo., Wall.	95	BX57	Braywood Rd. SE9	68	CM45	Brentmead Gdns. NW10	55	BL37	Bridge Rd., E.Mol.	84	BG53
ancker Rd., Har.	45	BK31	Brazil Clo., Croy.	86	BX54	Brentmead Pl. NW11	46	BQ32	Bridge Rd., Epsom	94	BO59
and St. SE10	67	CF43	Breach La., Dag.	59	CR38	Brenton St. E14	57	CD39	Bridge Rd., Erith	69	CT44
andlehow Rd. SW15	65	BR45	Breach La., Hert.	11	BW12	Brentside W13	54	BJ38	Bridge Rd., Grays	71	DD42
Brandon Est. SE17	**4**	**J9**	Breach Rd., Grays	70	CZ43	Brentside Clo. W13	54	BH39	Bridge Rd., Hodd.	70	DD43
andon Clo., Chsnt.	21	CA16	Bread & Cheese La.,	21	BZ16	Brentvale Ave., Sthl.	54	BG40	Bridge Rd., Houns.	64	BG45
andon Est. SE17	66	BY43	Chsnt.			Brentvale Ave., Wem.	55	BL37	Bridge Rd., Kings L.	17	BA20
andon Rd. E17	48	CF31	**Bread St. EC4**	**2**	**J10**	Brentwick Gdns., Brent.	65	BL42	Bridge Rd., Ong.	15	CV14
andon Rd. N7	56	BX36	Bread St. EC4	57	BZ39	Brentwood By-pass,	33	DA25	Bridge Rd., Orp.	89	CO53
andon Rd., Dart.	80	CX47	Break Mead, Welw.G.C.	5	BS8	Brwd.			Bridge Rd., Rain.	59	CU38
andon Rd., Sthl.	64	BE42	Breakfield, Couls.	104	BX61	Brentwood By-pass,	42	DA26	Bridge Rd., Sthl.	64	BE41
andon St. SE17	95	BS56	Breakneck Hill, Green.	80	DA46	Brwd.			Bridge Rd., Sutt.	95	BS57
andon St. SE17	**4**	**J9**	Breaks Rd., Hat.	10	BP12	Brentwood Clo. SE9	78	CM47	Bridge Rd., Twick.	74	BJ46
andon St. SE17	67	BZ42	Breakspear Ave., St.Alb.	9	BH14	Brentwood Pl., Brwd.	42	DB26	Bridge Rd., Uxb.	53	AX37
andon St., Grav.	81	DG47	Breakspear Rd., Ruis.	44	AZ32	Brentwood Rd., Brwd.	122	DD28	Bridge Rd., Wall.	95	BW56
andram Rd. SE13	68	CG45	Breakspear Rd. N., Uxb.	35	AX30	Brentwood Rd. (East	123	DF30	Bridge Rd., Welw.G.C.	5	BQ7
			Breakspear Rd. S., Uxb.	43	AY31	Horndon), Brwd.					
			Breakspear Way, Hem.H.	8	BA13	Brentwood Rd., Grays	71	DG42			
						Brentwood Rd., Ong.	24	CX19			
						Brentwood Rd., Rom.	50	CT32			

Bridge Rd., Wem. 46 BM34
Bridge Rd., Wey. 92 AY56
Bridge Rd. E., Welw.G.C. 5 BR8
Bridge Rd. Ms. SW19 76 BS50
Bridge Rd.
Bridge Row, Croy. 87 BZ54
Cross Rd.
Bridge St. SW1 3 Q5
Bridge St. SW1 66 BX41
Bridge St. W4 65 BN42
Bridge St., Berk. 7 AR13
Bridge St., Guil. 118 AR71
Bridge St., Hem.H. 8 AX14
Bridge St., Lthd. 102 BJ64
Bridge St., Pnr. 45 BE31
Bridge St., Rich. 74 BK46
Bridge St., Slou. 62 AU43
Bridge St., Stai. 72 AV49
Bridge St., Walt. 83 BB54
Bridge Ter. E15 57 CF36
Bridge Vw. W6 65 BQ42
Bridge Way N11 38 BW27
Bridge Way NW11 46 BR32
Bridge Way, Cob. 92 BB60
Bridge Way, Couls. 104 BU63
Bridge Way, Twick. 74 BG47
Bridge Way, Uxb. 44 AZ35
Bridge Way, Wem. 55 BL36
Bridge Wf., Cher. 83 AX54
Bridge Wf. Rd., Islw. 64 BJ45
Church St.
Bridge Yd. SE1 4 L2
Bridge Yd. SE1 57 BZ40
Bridgefield Clo., Bans. 103 BQ61
Bridgefield Rd., Sutt. 95 BS57
Bridgefields, Welw.G.C. 5 BR7
Bridgefoot SE1 66 BX42
Bridgefoot La., Pot.B. 19 BQ20
Bridgeford St. SW18 76 BT48
Bridgeham Clo., Wey. 92 AZ56
Bridgehill Clo., Guil. 118 AQ69
Aldershot Rd.
Bridgeland Rd. E16 58 CH40
Bridgeman Dr., Wind. 61 AN44
Bridgeman Rd. N1 56 BX36
Bridgeman Rd. W4 65 BN41
Bridgeman Rd., Tedd. 74 BJ50
Bridgeman St. NW8 1 C1
Bridgeman St. NW8 56 BU37
Bridgen Rd., Bex. 79 CQ47
Bridgend Rd. SW18 66 BT45
Bridgend Rd., Enf. 30 CC21
Bridgenhall Rd., Enf. 30 CA23
Bridgeport Pl. E1 57 CB40
Asher Way
Bridger Clo., Wat. 18 BE20
Bridges Ct. SW11 66 BT44
Bridges Dr., Dart. 80 CX46
Bridges La., Croy. 95 BX56
Bridges Pl. SW6 65 BR44
Bridges Rd. SW19 76 BS50
Bridges Rd., Stan. 36 BH28
Bridgetown Clo. SE19 77 CA49
St. Kitts Rd. Ter.
Bridgewater Clo., Chis. 88 CN52
Bridgewater Gdns., Edg. 37 BL30
Bridgewater Rd., Berk. 7 AQ11
Bridgewater Rd., Ruis. 44 BC35
Bridgewater Rd., Wem. 54 BK36
Bridgewater Rd., Wey. 92 BA57
Bridgewater Sq. EC2 2 H6
Bridgewater St. EC2 2 H6
Bridgewater St. EC2 57 BZ39
Viscount St.
Bridgewater Ter., Wind. 61 AO44
Goswell Rd.
Bridgewater Way, Bush. 36 BF26
Bridgeway, Bark. 58 CN36
Bridgeway St. NW1 1 M1
Bridgeway St. NW1 56 BW37
Bridgewood Clo. SE20 77 CB50
Castledine Rd.
Bridgewood Rd. SW16 76 BW50
Bridgewood Rd., Wor.Pk. 85 BP55
Bridgwater Clo., Rom. 42 CV28
Bridgwater Rd. E15 57 CF37
Bridgwater Rd., Rom. 42 CV28
Bridgwater Wk., Rom. 42 CV28
Bridle Clo., Enf. 30 CD22
Bridle Clo., Epsom 94 BN56
Bridle Clo., Kings.T. 84 BK52
Bridle Clo., St.Alb. 9 BH12
Bridle Clo., Sun. 83 BC52
Forge La.
Bridle End, Epsom 94 BO60
Bridle La. W1 1 M10
Bridle La. W1 56 BW40
Bridle Path, Croy. 86 BX55
Bridle Path, The, Epsom 94 BQ58
Bridle Path, The,Wdf.Grn. 40 CG29
Bridle Rd., Croy. 87 CE55
Bridle Rd., Epsom 94 BO60
Bridle Rd., Esher 93 BJ57
Bridle Rd., Pnr. 44 BC32
Bridle Rd., The, Pur. 95 BX58
Bridle Way, Berk. 7 AQ12
Bridle Way, Croy. 96 CE56
Bridle Way, Hodd. 12 CE10
Bridle Way, Orp. 97 CL56
Broadwater Gdns.
Bridle Way, The, Croy. 96 CD58
Bridle Way, The, Wall. 95 BW56
Bridle Way S., Hodd. 12 CE10
Bridlebarn La., Wok. 100 AR62
Bridlepath Way, Felt. 73 BB47
Bridleway Clo., Epsom 94 BQ58
Bridlington Clo., West. 106 CH63
Bridlington Rd. N9 39 CB26
Bridlington Rd., Wat. 36 BD27
Bridlington Spur, Slou. 61 AN41
Scarborough Way
Bridport Ave., Rom. 50 CR32
Bridport Pl. N1 57 BZ37
Bridport Rd. N18 39 CA28
Bridport Rd., Grnf. 54 BF37
Bridport Rd., Th.Hth. 86 BY52
Bridstow Pl. W2 56 BS39
Brief St. SE5 66 BY44
Brier Lea, Tad. 112 BR66
Brierley, Croy. 96 CE57
Brierley Ave. N9 39 CC26
Brierley Clo. SE25 87 CB52
Brierley Clo., Horn. 50 CU32
Brierley Rd. E11 48 CF35
Brierley Rd. SW12 76 BW48
Brierly Clo., Guil. 118 AQ69
Shepherds Hill
Brierly Gdns. E2 57 CC37
Cyprus St.
Briery Ct., Hem.H. 8 AZ13
Briery Fld., Rick. 26 AW24
Briery Rd., Hem.H. 8 AZ12
Briery Way, Amer. 25 AP22
Brigade St. SE3 68 CG44
Royal Par.
Brigadier Ave., Enf. 30 BZ23
Brigadier Hill, Enf. 30 BZ22
Bright Clo., Belv. 69 CP42
Bright Hill, Guil. 118 AS71
Bright St. E14 57 CE39
Brightfield Rd. SE12 78 CG46
Brightlands, Grav. 81 DF49
Henley Deane
Brightlands Rd., Reig. 121 BT69
Brightling Rd. SE4 77 CD46
Brightlingsea Pl. E14 57 CD40
Brightman Rd. SW18 76 BT47
Brighton Ave. E17 48 CD32
Brighton Clo., Uxb. 53 AZ36
Brighton Clo., Wey. 92 AW56
Burleigh Rd.
Brighton Dr., Nthlt. 54 BF36
Brighton Gro. SE14 67 CD44
Brighton Rd. E6 58 CL38
Brighton Rd. N2 38 BT30
Brighton Rd. N16 48 CA35
Brighton Rd., Bans. 94 BR60
Brighton Rd., Couls. 104 BW62
Brighton Rd., Croy. 96 BZ56
Brighton Rd., Pur. 95 BX60
Brighton Rd., Red. 121 BU71
Brighton Rd. (Hooley), Red. 104 BV65
Brighton Rd., Surb. 84 BK53
Brighton Rd., Sutt. 95 BT57
Brighton Rd., Tad. 103 BR62
Brighton Rd., Wat. 26 BC22
Brighton Rd., Wey. 92 AX56
Brighton Ter. SW9 66 BX45
Brights Ave., Rain. 59 CU38
Brightside, The, Enf. 30 CC23
Brightside Ave., Stai. 73 AX50
Brightside Rd. SE13 77 CF46
Brightwell Cres. SW17 76 BU49
Brightwell Rd., Wat. 26 BC25
Brigstock Rd., Belv. 69 CR42
Brigstock Rd., Couls. 104 BV61
Brigstock Rd., Th.Hth. 86 BY53
Brill Pl. NW1 1 P1
Brill Pl. NW1 56 BW37
Brim Hill N2 47 BT31
Brimfield Rd., Grays 70 CY42
Brimpsfield Clo. SE2 69 CO41
Brimsdown Ave., Enf. 30 CD23
Brimshot La., Wok. 91 AP58
Brimstone Clo., Orp. 98 CP57
Brindle Gate, Sid. 78 CN47
Brindles, Horn. 51 CW31
Brindles, The, Bans. 103 BR62
Brindles Clo., Brwd. 122 DE27
Brindles Clo., Til. 71 DK42
Beechcroft Ave.
Brindley St. SE14 67 CD44
Brindley Way, Sthl. 54 BF40
Brindwood Rd. E4 39 CD27
Brinkburn Clo. SE2 69 CO42
Brinkburn Clo., Edg. 37 BM30
Brinkburn Gdns., Edg. 46 BM31
Brinkley Rd., Wor.Pk. 85 BP55
Brinklow Cres. SE18 68 CL43
Brinkworth Rd., Ilf. 49 CK31
Brinkworth Way E9 57 CD36
Brinley Clo., Chsnt. 21 CC19
Brinsdale Rd. NW4 46 BQ31
Brinsley Rd., Har. 36 BG30
Brinsley St. E1 57 CB39
Watney St.
Brinsmead (Park St.), St.Alb. 18 BG17
Brinsmead Rd., Rom. 42 CX30
Brinsworth Clo., Twick. 74 BG47
Brinton Wk. SE1 4 F3
Brion Pl. E14 57 CF39
Briony Way, Sun. 73 BC50
Brisbane Ave. SW19 76 BS50
Brisbane Ho., Til. 71 DF44
Leicester Rd.
Brisbane Rd. E10 48 CE34
Brisbane Rd. W13 54 BJ40
Brisbane Rd., Ilf. 49 CL33
Brisbane St. SE5 67 BZ43
Briscoe Clo. E11 49 CG34
Briscoe Clo., Hodd. 12 CD11
Briscoe Rd. SW19 76 BT50
Briscoe Rd., Hodd. 12 CD11
Briscoe Rd., Rain. 60 CV37
Briset Rd. SE9 68 CJ45
Briset St. EC1 2 F6
Briset St. EC1 56 BY38
Briset Way N7 47 BX34
Bristol Clo., Stai. 73 AY46
Whitley Clo.
Bristol Gdns. W9 56 BS38
Bristol Ms. W9 56 BS38
Bristol Pk. Rd. E17 48 CD31
Hervey Pk. Rd.
Bristol Rd. E7 58 CJ36
Bristol Rd., Grav. 81 DH48
Bristol Rd., Grnf. 54 BF37
Bristol Rd., Mord. 86 BS53
Bristol Way, Slou. 52 AP40
Stoke Gdns.
Bristow Rd. SE19 77 CA49
Bristow Rd., Bexh. 69 CQ44
Bristow Rd., Croy. 95 BX56
Bristow Rd., Houns. 64 BF45
Britannia Clo. SW4 66 BW45
Clapham Cres.
Britannia Clo., Nthlt. 54 BD38
Britannia Dr., Grav. 81 DJ49
Britannia La., Twick. 74 BG47
Britannia Rd. N12 38 BT27
Britannia Rd. SW6 66 BS43
Britannia Rd., Brwd. 42 DB28
Britannia Rd., Ilf. 49 CL34
Britannia Rd., Surb. 85 BL54
Britannia Rd., Wal.Cr. 21 CD20
Britannia Row N1 56 BY37
Britannia St. WC1 2 B2
Britannia St. WC1 56 BX38
Britannia Wk. N1 2 K2
Britannia Wk. N1 57 BZ38
Britannia Way NW10 55 BM38
Britannia Way SW6 66 BS43
Britannia Way, Stai. 73 AX47
British Gro. W4 65 BO42
British Gro. Pas. W6 65 BO42
British Gro. S. W4 65 BO42
British Gro. Pas.
British Legion Rd. E4 40 CG27
British St. E3 57 CD38
Briton Clo., S.Croy. 96 CA59
Briton Cres., S.Croy. 96 CA59
Briton Hill Rd., S.Croy. 96 CA58
Brittain Rd., Dag. 50 CQ34
Brittain Rd., Walt. 93 BD56
Brittains La., Sev. 107 CT65
Britten Clo. NW11 47 BS33
Britten Clo., Borwd. 27 BK25
Beehive Clo.
Britten Dr., Sthl. 54 BE39
Thurston Rd.
Britten St. SW3 66 BU42
Brittenden Clo., Orp. 97 CN57
Brittens Clo., Guil. 109 AQ68
Brittens Ct. E1 57 CB40
Britton Ave., St.Alb. 9 BG13
Britton St. EC1 2 F5
Britton St. EC1 56 BY38
Brixham Cres., Ruis. 44 BC33
Brixham Gdns., Ilf. 49 CN35
Brixham Rd., Well. 69 CP44
Brixham St. E16 58 CK40
Brixton Est., Edg. 37 BM30
Brixton Hill SW2 76 BX47
Brixton Hill Pl. SW2 76 BX47
Brixton Oval SW2 66 BY45
Rushcroft Rd.
Brixton Rd. SW9 66 BY45
Brixton Rd., Wat. 26 BC23
Brixton Sta. Rd. SW9 66 BY45
Brixton Water La. SW2 76 BX46
Broad Acre, St.Alb. 18 BE18
Broad Acre, Stai. 73 AW49
Cherry Orchard
Broad Acres, Hat. 10 BO11
Broad Clo., Walt. 84 BE55
Broad Ct. WC2 2 A9
Broad Ct. WC2 56 BX39
Broad Ditch Rd., Grav. 81 DE50
Broad Grn., Hert. 11 BX11
Broad Grn. Ave., Croy. 86 BY54
Broad Grn. Wd., Hert. 11 BX11
Broad High Way, Cob. 102 BD61
Broad La. N8 47 BX32
Enfield Rd.
Broad La. N15 48 CA31
Broad La., Dart. 79 CU49
Broad La., Hmptn. 74 BE50
Broad Lawn SE9 78 CL48
Broad Meadow, Brwd. 33 CZ22
Broad Oak, Wdf.Grn. 40 CH28
Broad Oak Clo., Orp. 89 CO51
Mickleham Rd.
Broad Oaks, Surb. 85 BM54
Broadway
Broad Platts, Slou. 62 AR41
Broad Rd., Swans. 81 DC46
Broad Sanctuary SW1 3 P5
Broad Sanctuary SW1 66 BX41
Broad St., Dag. 59 CR36
Broad St., Guil. 118 AO69
Broad St., Hem.H. 8 AX13
Broad St., Tedd. 74 BH49
Broad St. Ave. EC2 2 M7
Broad St. Ave. EC2 57 CA39
Old Broad St.
Broad St. Pl. EC2 2 L7
Broad Strood, Loug. 31 CL22
Broad Vw. NW9 46 BM32
Broad Wk. N21 38 BX27
Broad Wk. NW1 56 BV37
Broad Wk. SE3 68 CJ44
Broad Wk. W1 3 G2
Broad Wk., Cat. 105 CA64
Broad Wk., Couls. 104 BV65
Broad Wk., Epsom 103 BO62
Broad Wk. (Burgh Heath), Epsom 103 BQ63
Broad Wk., Harl. 6 CM10
Broad Wk., Har. 45 BF31
Broad Wk., Houns. 64 BD44
Broad Wk., Orp. 89 CP55
Broad Wk., Sev. 117 CW67
Broad Wk., The W8 56 BS40
Broad Wk., The, Nthwd. 35 BA30
Broad Wk. La. NW11 46 BR33
Broad Wk. N., Brwd. 122 DD27
Broad Wk. S., The, Brwd. 122 DD28
Broad Yd. EC1 2 F5
Broad Yd. EC1 56 BY38
Broadacre Clo., Uxb. 44 AZ34
Broadacres, Guil. 118 AP69
Broadbent Clo. N6 47 BV33
Broadbent St. W1 1 J10
Broadbent St. W1 56 BV40
Grosvenor St.
Broadbridge Clo. SE3 68 CH43
Broadcoombe, S.Croy. 96 CC57
Broadcroft Ave., Stan. 36 BK30
Broadcroft Rd., Orp. 88 CM54
Broadfield, Harl. 6 CN10
Broadfield Clo. NW2 46 BQ34
Broadfield Clo., Croy. 86 BX55
Broadfield Clo., Rom. 50 CT32
Broadfield Clo., Tad. 103 BQ63
Broadfield Ct., Bush. 36 BH27
Broadfield La. NW1 56 BX36
Broadfield La., Wat. 35 BC26
Broadfield Pl., Welw.G.C. 5 BP8
Broadfield Rd. SE6 78 CG47
Broadfield Rd., Hem.H. 8 AY13
Broadfield Sq., Enf. 30 CB24
Broadfield Way, Buck.H. 40 CJ28
Broadfields, Chsnt. 20 BY18
Broadfields, E.Mol. 84 BG53
Broadfields, Har. 36 BF30
Broadfields, Saw. 6 CO6
Broadfields Ave. N21 38 BY26
Broadfields Ave., Edg. 37 BM28
Broadfields Way NW10 46 BO35
Broadford La., Wok. 91 AP59
Broadford Rd., Guil. 118 AR74
Broadgate, Wal.Abb. 22 CG20
Broadgate Circle EC2 2 M6
Broadgate Rd. E16 58 CJ39
Satanita Clo.
Broadgates Ave., Barn. 29 BS23
Broadgates Rd. SW18 76 BT47
Ellerton Rd.
Broadham Grn. Rd., Oxt. 114 CF69
Broadhead Strand NW9 37 BO30
Broadheath, Sev. 117 CZ66
Broadheath Dr., Chis. 78 CK49
Broadhinton Rd. SW4 66 BV45
Broadhurst, Ash. 103 BL61
Broadhurst Ave., Edg. 37 BM28
Broadhurst Ave., Ilf. 49 CN35
Broadhurst Clo. NW6 56 BS36
Broadhurst Gdns.
Broadhurst Clo., Rich. 75 BL46
Lower Gro. Rd.
Broadhurst Gdns. NW6 56 BS36
Broadhurst Gdns., Chig. 40 CM28
Broadhurst Gdns., Reig. 121 BS72
Broadhurst Gdns., Ruis. 45 BD34
Broadhurst Wk., Rain. 59 CU36
Broadlake Pl., St.Alb. 19 BL17
Broadlands, Grays 71 DC42
Broadlands, The, Felt. 74 BE48
Broadlands Ave. SW16 76 BX48
Broadlands Ave., Chesh. 16 AO18
Broadlands Ave., Enf. 30 CB24
Broadlands Ave., Shep. 83 BA53
Broadlands Clo. N6 47 BV33
Broadlands Clo. SW16 76 BX48
Broadlands Clo., Enf. 30 CB24
Broadlands Clo., Wal.Cr. 21 CC20
Raglan Ave.
Broadlands Dr., Warl. 105 CC63
Broadlands Rd. N6 47 BU33
Broadlands Rd., Brom. 78 CH49
Broadlands Way, N.Mal. 85 BO53
Broadlawns Clo., Har. 36 BH30
Broadley Rd., Harl. 13 CK13
Broadley St. NW8 1 B6
Broadley St. NW8 56 BT39
Broadley Ter. NW1 1 D5
Broadley Ter. NW1 56 BU38
Broadmark Rd., Slou. 52 AQ40
Broadmayne SE17 4 K10
Broadmead SE6 77 CE48
Broadmead, Ash. 103 BL62
Broadmead Ave., Wor.Pk. 85 BP54
Broadmead Clo., Hmptn. 74 BF50
Broadmead Clo., Pnr. 36 BE29
Broadmead Rd., Nthlt. 54 BE38
Broadmead Rd., Wdf.Grn. 40 CH29
Broadmeads, Wok. 100 AT64
Broadoak Ave., Enf. 30 CC21
Broadoak Rd., Erith 69 CS43
Broadoaks, Epp. 22 CN19
Broadoaks Cres., Wey. 92 AW60
Broadoaks Way, Brom. 88 CG53
Broadstone Pl. W1 1 G7
Broadstone Pl. W1 56 BV39
Broadstone Rd., Horn. 50 CU34
Broadview Ave., Grays 71 DE41
Broadview Rd. SW16 76 BW50
Broadwalk E18 49 CG31
Broadwall SE1 4 E2
Broadwall SE1 56 BY40
Broadwater SE28 68 CM41
Broadwater, Berk. 7 AR12
Broadwater, Pot.B. 20 BS18
Broadwater Clo., Stai. 72 AS47
Broadwater Clo., Walt. 92 BC56
Broadwater Clo., Wok. 91 AU59
Woodham La.
Broadwater Cres., Welw.G.C. 5 BQ8
Broadwater Gdns., Orp. 97 CL56
Broadwater Gdns., Uxb. 44 AW31
Broadwater La., Uxb. 44 AW31
Broadwater Pk., Maid. 61 AJ42
Barn Dr.
Broadwater Ri., Guil. 118 AT71
Broadwater Rd. N17 39 CA30
Broadwater Rd. SE28 68 CM41
Broadwater Rd. SW17 76 BU49
Broadwater Rd., Welw.G.C. 5 BR8
Broadwater Rd. N., Walt. 92 BC56
Broadwater Rd. S., Walt. 92 BC56
Broadwaters Est. SE28 68 CN
Broadway E13 58 CH
Broadway E15 57 CF
Broadway N20 38 BT
Broadway SW1 3
Broadway SW1 66 BW
Broadway SW16 76 BW
Broadway W6 65 BQ
Hammersmith Rd.
Broadway W7 54 BH
Broadway W13 54 BJ
Broadway, Bark. 58 CM
Broadway, Bexh. 69 CQ
Broadway, Edg. 37 BM
Broadway, Epsom 94 BP
Broadway, Grays 71 DE
Broadway, Grnf. 54 BG
Broadway, Hat. 10 BQ
Broadway, Rain. 59 CU
Broadway, Rom. 41 CU
Broadway, St.Alb. 9 BG
Broadway, Stai. 73 AW
Broadway, Surb. 85 BM
Broadway, Swan. 89 CS
Broadway, Til. 71 DF
Dock Rd.
Broadway, Wok. 100 AO
Broadway, The E4 39 CF
Broadway, The E13 58 CH
Broadway, The N8 47 BX
Broadway, The N9 39 CB
Broadway, The NW7 37 BO
Broadway, The SW19 75 BR
Broadway, The W3 65 BM
Gunnersbury La.
Broadway, The W5 54 BK
Broadway, The, Croy. 95 BX
Broadway, The, Dag. 50 CR
Broadway, The, Har. 36 BH
Broadway, The, Hat. 10 BQ
Broadway, The, Horn. 50 CU
Broadway, The, Loug. 31 CM
Broadway, The, Pnr. 36 BE
Broadway, The, Sthl. 54 BE
Broadway, The, Stai. 83 AX
Broadway, The, Stan. 36 BK
Broadway, The, Surb. 84 BH
Broadway, The, Sutt. 94 BR
Broadway, The, Wat. 27 BD
Broadway, The, Wey. 92 AW
Broadway, The, Wok. 100 AS
Broadway, The, Wdf.Grn. 40 CH
Broadway Ave., Croy. 87 BZ
Broadway Ave., Harl. 6 CC
Broadway Ave., Twick. 74 BJ
Broadway Clo., S.Croy. 96 CB
Broadway Clo., Wdf.Grn. 40 CH
Broadway Ct. SW19 76 BS
Broadway Gdns., Mitch. 86 BU
Broadway Mkt. E8 57 CB
Broadway Ms. N13 38 BX
Elmdale Rd.
Broadway Ms. N21 38 BY
Compton Rd.
Broadwick St. W1 1 M1
Broadwick St. W1 56 BW3
Broadwood Ave., Ruis. 44 BB3
Brocas Clo. NW3 56 BU
Fellows Rd.
Brocas St. (Eton), Wind. 61 AO4
Brock Grn., S.Ock. 60 DA
Brock Pl. E3 57 CE
Brock Rd. E13 58 CH
Brock St. SE15 67 CC4
Evelina Rd.
Brockdish Ave., Bark. 49 CN
Brockenhurst, E.Mol. 84 BE
Brockenhurst Ave., Wor.Pk. 85 BO
Brockenhurst Clo., Wok. 91 AS
Brockenhurst Gdns. NW7 37 BO2
Brockenhurst Gdns., Ilf. 49 CM3
Brockenhurst Rd., Croy. 87 CB
Brockenhurst Way SW16 86 BW
Brocket Clo., Chig. 40 CN2
Brocket Rd., Grays 71 DG4
Cherry Wk.
Brocket Rd., Hodd. 12 CE1
Brocket Rd., Welw.G.C. 5 BO
Brocket Way, Chig. 40 CN2
Brockett Clo., Welw.G.C. 5 BF
Brockham Clo. SW19 75 BR4
Brockham Cres., Croy. 96 CF5
Brockham Dr. SW2 76 BX4
Brockham Dr., Ilf. 49 CM3
Brockham La., Bet. 120 BM7
Brockham St. SE1 4 J
Brockham St. SE1 67 BZ4
Brockhamhurst Rd., Bet. 120 BM7
Brockhurst Clo., Stan. 36 BH2
Brockhurst Rd., Chesh. 16 AO1
Brockill Cres. SE4 67 CD4
Brocklebank Rd. SE7 68 CH4
Brocklebank Rd. SW18 76 BT4
Brocklehurst St. SE14 67 CC4
Brockles Mead, Harl. 13 CM1
Brocklesbury Clo., Wat. 27 BD2
Brocklesby Rd. SE25 87 CB5
Brockley Ave., Stan. 37 BL2
Brockley Ave. N., Stan. 37 BL2
Brockley Clo., Stan. 37 BL2
Brockley Combe, Wey. 92 BA5
Brockley Cres., Rom. 41 CS2
Brockley Cross SE4 67 CD4
Brockley Footpath SE14 67 CC4
Brockley Gdns. SE4 67 CD4
Brockley Gro. SE4 77 CD4
Brockley Gro., Brwd. 122 DD2
Brockley Hall Rd. SE4 77 CD4
Brockley Hill, Stan. 36 BK2
Brockley Ms. SE4 77 CD4
Brockley Pk. SE23 77 CD4
Brockley Ri. SE23 77 CD4
Brockley Rd. SE4 67 CD4

ockley Ter. SE17 67 CA42
Ivey St.
ockley Vw. SE23 77 CD47
ockley Way SE4 77 CC46
ockleyside, Stan. 37 BL28
ockman Ri., Brom. 77 CF49
ocks Dr., Sutt. 85 BR55
ockshot Clo., Brent. 64 BK43
ocksparkwood, Brwd. 122 DD27
ockswood La., 5 BP7
Welw.G.C.
ockton Clo., Rom. 50 CT31
ockway, Vir.W. 82 AR53
ockway Clo. E11 49 CG34
ockway Clo., Guil. 118 AT70
ockwell Clo., Orp. 88 CN53
ockwell Ct. SW2 76 BY46
ockwell Pk. Gdns. 76 BY47
E24
ockworth Clo. SE15 67 CA43
St. Georges Way
oderick Gro., Lthd. 111 BF66
oderick Rd. SE2 69 CO42
odewater Rd., Borwd. 28 BM23
odia Rd. N16 48 CA34
odie Rd. E4 39 CF26
odie Rd., Enf. 30 BZ22
odie Rd., Guil. 118 AS71
odie St. SE1 4 Q10
odie St. SE1 67 CA42
odlove La. E1 57 CC40
odrick Rd. SW17 76 BU48
ograve Gdns., Beck. 87 CE51
ograve Rd. N17 48 CB31
oke Ct., Guil. 118 AU69
oke Fm. Dr., Orp. 98 CP58
oken Furlong (Eton), 61 AN42
Wind.
oken Gate La., Uxb. 43 AU33
oken Wf. EC4 57 BZ40
okes Cres., Reig. 121 BS69
okes Rd., Reig. 121 BS69
okesley St. E3 57 CD38
omar Rd. SE5 67 CA45
omborough Grn., Wat. 36 BD28
ome Rd. SE9 68 CK45
omefield, Stan. 36 BK30
omefield Ct., Wal.Abb. 22 CH20
Winters Way
omehead St. E1 57 CC39
omells Rd. SW4 66 BW45
omet Clo., Wat. 26 BB22
omfelde Rd. SW4 66 BW45
omfelde Way SW4 66 BX44
omfield St. N1 56 BY37
omford Clo., Oxt. 115 CH70
omhall Rd., Dag. 59 CO36
omhedge SE9 78 CK48
omholm Rd. SE2 69 CO41
omleigh Clo., Chsnt. 21 CD17
Ashdown Cres.
omley, Grays 71 DC43
omley Ave., Brom. 78 CG50
omley Common, Brom. 88 CJ52
omley Cres., Brom. 88 CG51
omley Cres., Ruis. 44 BB35
omley Gdns., Brom. 88 CG51
omley Gro., Brom. 87 CF51
omley Hall Rd. E14 57 CF39
Lochnagar St.
omley High St. E3 57 CE38
omley Hill, Brom. 78 CG49
omley La., Chis. 78 CM50
omley Pl. W1 1 L6
omley Rd. E10 48 CE32
omley Rd. E17 48 CE31
omley Rd. N17 39 CA30
omley Rd. N18 39 BZ28
omley Rd. SE6 77 CE47
omley Rd., Beck. 87 CE51
omley Rd., Brom. 77 CE47
omley Rd., Chis. 88 CL51
omley St. E1 57 CC39
ompton Arc. SW3 3 E5
ompton Clo. SE20 87 CB51
Selby Rd.
ompton Clo., Houns. 74 BE46
ompton Dr., Erith 69 CU43
ompton Gro. N2 47 BU31
ompton Pk. Cres. SW6 66 BS43
ompton Pl. SW3 3 D6
ompton Pl. SW3 66 BU41
ompton Rd. SW1 3 E5
ompton Rd. SW1 66 BU42
ompton Rd. SW3 3 C8
ompton Rd. SW3 66 BU42
ompton Rd. SW7 3 C7
ompton Rd. SW7 66 BU42
ompton Sq. SW3 3 C6
ompton Sq. SW3 66 BU41
omwich Ave. N6 47 BV34
omyard Ave. W3 55 BO40
ondesbury Ct. NW2 55 BO36
ondesbury Pk. NW2 55 BP36
ondesbury Pk. NW6 55 BP36
ondesbury Rd. NW6 55 BR37
ondesbury Vill. NW6 55 BR37
onhill Ter. N17 39 CB30
Lansdowne Rd.
onsart Rd. SW6 65 BR43
onsdon Way, Uxb. 43 AV34
onson Rd. SW20 85 BQ51
onte Clo. E7 49 CH35
Bective Rd.
onte Clo., Ilf. 49 CL31
onte Clo., Til. 71 DH44
Coleridge Rd.
onte Cres., Hem.H. 8 AZ10
onte Gro., Dart. 70 CW45
onte Vw., Grav. 81 DH47
onti Clo. SE17 67 BZ42
onze St. SE8 67 CE43
ook Ave., Dag. 59 CR36
ook Ave., Edg. 37 BM29
Brook Ave., Wem. 46 BL34
Brook Clo. NW7 37 BR29
Brook Clo. SW20 85 BP52
Brook Clo., Chis. 88 CL51
Brook Clo., Dor. 119 BK70
Brook Clo., Rom. 41 CT30
Brook Clo., Ruis. 44 BB33
Brook Clo., Stai. 73 AY47
Brook Ct., Edg. 37 BM28
Brook Ct., Rad. 18 BJ20
Watling St.
Brook Cres. E4 39 CE28
Brook Cres. N9 39 CB28
Brook Dr. SE11 4 E7
Brook Dr. SE11 66 BY41
Brook Dr., Har. 45 BG31
Brook Dr., Rad. 18 BH20
Brook Dr., Ruis. 44 BB33
Brook Dr., Sun. 73 BB50
Brook End, Saw. 6 CP6
Brook Fm. Rd., Cob. 102 BD61
Brook Fld., Sev. 108 CW62
Brook Flds., Ong. 24 CW16
Brook Gdns. E4 39 CE28
Brook Gdns. SW13 65 BO45
Brook Gdns., Kings.T. 85 BN51
Brook Gate W1 3 F1
Brook Grn. W6 65 BQ41
Brook Hill, Oxt. 114 CF68
Brook Ho. Gdns. E4 40 CG28
Brook La. SE3 68 CH44
Brook La., Bex. 79 CP46
Brook La., Brwd. 33 DB22
Brook La., Brom. 78 CH50
Brook La., Saw. 6 CP6
Brook La., Wok. 100 AV64
Brook La. (Chobham), 91 AO59
Wok.
Brook La. Fld., Harl. 14 CO12
Brook La. N., Brent. 64 BK42
Brook Mead, Epsom 94 BO57
Brook Meadow N12 38 BS28
Brook Ms. N. W2 56 BT40
Brook Par., Chig. 40 CL27
Brook Pas. SW6 66 BS43
Moore Pk. Rd.
Brook Path, Loug. 31 CK24
Brook Pl., Barn. 29 BS25
Brook Ri., Chig. 40 CL27
Brook Rd. N8 47 BX31
Brook Rd. N22 47 BX31
Brook Rd. NW2 46 BO34
Brook Rd., Borwd. 28 BM23
Brook Rd., Brwd. 42 CZ27
Brook Rd., Buck.H. 40 CH27
Brook Rd., Epp. 23 CO20
Brook Rd., Grav. 81 DF47
Brook Rd., Guil. 118 AU73
Brook Rd., Ilf. 49 CN32
Brook Rd., Loug. 31 CK24
Brook Rd., Red. 121 BU71
Brook Rd. (Merstham), 113 BW68
Red.
Brook Rd., Rom. 41 CT30
Brook Rd., Saw. 6 CQ6
Brook Rd., Surb. 85 BL55
Brook Rd., Swan. 89 CS52
Brook Rd., Th.Hth. 87 BZ52
Brook Rd., Twick. 74 BJ46
Brook Rd., Wal.Cr. 21 CD20
Britannia Rd.
Brook Rd. S., Brent. 64 BK43
Brook St. N17 39 CA30
High Rd.
Brook St. W1 1 J10
Brook St. W1 56 BV40
Brook St. W2 1 B10
Brook St. W2 56 BT40
Brook St., Belv. 69 CR42
Brook St., Brwd. 42 CY28
Brook St., Kings.T. 85 BL51
Brook St., Wind. 61 AO44
Brook Wk. N2 38 BT30
Brook Wk., Edg. 37 BN29
Brook Way SE3 68 CH45
Brook Way, Chig. 40 CL27
Brook Way, Lthd. 102 BJ62
Brook Way, Rain. 59 CU39
Brookbank Ave. W7 54 BG39
Brookbank Rd. SE13 67 CE45
Brookdale N11 38 BW28
Brookdale Ave., Upmin. 51 CX34
Brookdale Clo., Upmin. 51 CX34
Brookdale Rd. E17 48 CD31
Brookdale Rd. SE6 77 CE46
Brookdale Rd., Bex. 79 CQ47
Brookdene Ave., Wat. 35 BC26
Brookdene Dr., Nthwd. 35 BB29
Brookdene Rd. SE18 68 CN42
Brooke Ave., Har. 45 BG34
Brooke Clo., Bush. 36 BG26
Brooke Rd. E5 48 CA34
Brooke Rd. E17 48 CF31
Brooke Rd. N16 48 CA34
Brooke Rd., Grays 71 DD42
Brooke St. EC1 2 D7
Brooke St. EC1 56 BY39
Brooke Way, Bush. 36 BG26
Richfield Rd.
Brookehowse Rd. SE6 77 CE48
Brookend Rd., Sid. 78 CN47
Brooker Rd., Wal.Abb. 21 CF20
Brookers Clo., Ash. 102 BK62
Brookes Ct. EC1 2 D6
Brookes Ct. EC1 56 BY39
Baldwins Gdns.
Brookfield N6 47 BV34
Brookfield, Wok. 100 AQ61
Brookfield Ave. E17 48 CF31
Brookfield Ave. NW7 37 BP29
Brookfield Ave. W5 54 BK38
Brookfield Ave., Sutt. 95 BT56
Brookfield Clo. NW7 37 BP29
Brookfield Clo., Brwd. 122 DE25
Brookfield Clo., Red. 121 BV73
Brookfield Ct., Grnf. 54 BG38
Brookfield Ct., Har. 45 BK32
Brookfield Cres. NW7 37 BP29
Brookfield Cres., Har. 45 BK32
Brookfield Est. NW5 47 BV34
Brookfield Gdns., Chsnt. 21 CC17
Brookfield Gdns., Esher 93 BH57
Brookfield La., Chsnt. 21 CB17
Brookfield Pk. NW5 47 BV34
Brookfield Path, Wdf.Grn. 40 CG29
Oak Hill
Brookfield Rd. E9 57 CD36
Brookfield Rd. N9 39 CB27
Brookfield Rd. W4 65 BN41
Brookfields, Enf. 30 CC24
Brookfields, Saw. 6 CP6
Brookfields Ave., Mitch. 86 BU53
Brookhill Clo. SE18 68 CL42
Brookhill Clo., Barn. 29 BU25
Brookhill Rd. SE18 68 CL42
Brookhill Rd., Barn. 29 BT25
Brookhouse Gdns. E4 40 CG28
Abbotts Cres.
Brookhurst Rd., Wey. 92 AW57
Brooking Rd. E7 49 CH35
Brookland Clo. NW11 47 BS31
Brookland Ri.
Brookland Garth NW11 47 BS31
Brookland Hill NW11 47 BS31
Brookland Ri. NW11 47 BS31
Brooklands App., Rom. 50 CS31
Brooklands Ave. SW19 76 BS48
Brooklands Ave., Sid. 78 CM48
Brooklands Clo., Cob. 102 BE61
Brooklands Clo., Rom. 50 CS31
Brooklands Clo., Sun. 83 BB51
Brooklands Ct., Enf. 30 BZ25
Bush Hill
Brooklands Ct., St.Alb. 9 BH13
Hatfield Rd.
Brooklands Dr., Grnf. 54 BK37
Brooklands Gdns., Horn. 51 CV32
Brooklands Gdns., Pot.B. 19 BR19
Brooklands La., Rom. 50 CS31
Brooklands La., Wey. 92 AZ56
Brooklands Pk. SE3 68 CH45
Brooklands Rd., Rom. 50 CS31
Brooklands Rd., T.Ditt. 84 BH54
Brooklands Rd., Wey. 92 AZ59
Brooklands St. SW8 66 BW44
Brooklands Way, Red. 121 BU69
Brooklea Clo. NW9 37 BO30
Brookleys, Wok. 91 AP58
Brooklyn Ave. SE25 87 CB52
Brooklyn Ave., Loug. 31 CK24
Brooklyn Clo., Cars. 86 BU55
Brooklyn Clo., Wok. 100 AS63
Brooklyn Ct., Loug. 31 CK24
High Rd.
Brooklyn Gro. SE25 87 CB52
Brooklyn Rd. SE25 87 CB52
Brooklyn Rd., Brom. 88 CJ53
Brooklyn Rd., Wok. 100 AS62
Brooklyn Way, West Dr. 63 AX41
Brookmans Ave., Grays 71 DE40
Brookmans Ave., Hat. 19 BR16
Brookmans Clo., Upmin. 51 CZ33
Brookmead Ave., Brom. 88 CK53
Brookmead Clo., Orp. 89 CO54
Brookmead Rd., Croy. 86 BW53
Brookmead Way, Orp. 89 CO53
Brookmeads Est., 86 BU53
Mitch.
Brookmill Rd. SE8 67 CE44
Brooks Ave. E6 58 CK38
Brooks Clo. SE9 78 CL48
Brooks Clo., Wey. 92 AZ58
Brooks Ct. E15 48 CE35
Brooks La. W4 65 BM43
Brooks Ms. W1 1 J10
Brooks Ms. W1 56 BV40
Brooks Rd. E13 58 CH37
Brooks Rd. W4 65 BM42
Brooks Way, Bush. 36 BG26
Richfield Rd.
Brooks Way, Orp. 89 CP51
Brooksbank St. E9 57 CC36
Brooksby Ms. N1 56 BY36
Brooksby St.
Brooksby St. N1 56 BY36
Brooksbys Wk. E9 48 CC35
Brookscroft, Croy. 96 CD58
Bowens Wd.
Brookscroft Rd. E17 39 CE30
Brooksfield, Welw.G.C. 5 BS7
Brookshill, Har. 36 BG28
Brookshill Ave., Har. 36 BG28
Brookshill Dr., Har. 36 BG28
Brookside N21 29 BX25
Brookside, Barn. 29 BU25
Brookside, Cars. 95 BV56
Brookside, Cher. 82 AV54
Brookside, Guilford 109 AR68
Brookside, Harl. 13 CK12
Brookside, Hat. 10 BN12
Brookside, Hodd. 12 CE12
Brookside, Horn. 51 CW32
Brookside, Ilf. 40 CM29
Brookside, Orp. 88 CN54
Brookside, Pot.B. 19 BP19
Brookside, Slou. 62 AU43
Brookside, Uxb. 53 AY36
Brookside, Wal.Abb. 22 CG19
Paternoster Hill
Brookside, Wat. 35 BC26
Brookside Ave., Ashf. 73 AX49
Brookside Ave., Stai. 62 AS45
Brookside Clo., Barn. 28 BR25
Brookside Clo., Felt. 73 BC48
Brookside Clo., Har. 45 BE35
Brookside Clo. (Kenton), 45 BK32
Har.
Brookside Cres., Cuffley 20 BX17
Brookside Cres., Wor.Pk. 85 BP54
Green La.
Brookside Gdns., Enf. 30 CB22
Brookside Rd. N9 39 CB28
Brookside Rd. N19 47 BW34
Brookside Rd. NW11 46 BR32
Brookside Rd., Grav. 81 DF50
Brookside Rd., Hayes 54 BD40
Brookside S., Barn. 38 BV26
Brookside Wk. NW11 46 BR31
Brookside Way, Croy. 87 CC53
Brooksville Ave. NW6 55 BR37
Brookvale, Erith 69 CR44
Brookview Rd. SW16 76 BV49
Brookville Rd. SW6 65 BR43
Brookwood Ave. SW13 65 BO44
Brookwood Clo., Brom. 88 CG52
Brookwood Lye Rd., 100 AO63
Wok.
Brookwood Rd. SW18 75 BR47
Brookwood Rd., Houns. 64 BF44
Broom Ave., Orp. 89 CO51
Broom Clo., Brom. 88 CK53
Broom Clo., Chsnt. 21 CB17
Spicersfield
Broom Clo., Esher 93 BF56
Broom Clo., Hat. 10 BO14
Broom Clo., Tedd. 74 BK50
Broom Ct., Rich. 65 BM44
Lichfield Rd.
Broom Gdns., Croy. 87 CE55
Broom Gro., Wat. 26 BC22
Broom Hall, Lthd. 93 BG60
Broom Hall Dr., Lthd. 93 BG60
Broom Hill, Hem.H. 7 AV14
Broom Hill, Slou. 52 AQ36
Broom Hill Ct., Wdf.Grn. 40 CH29
Broom La., Wok. 91 AP57
Broom Leys, St.Alb. 9 BK12
Broom Lock, Tedd. 74 BK50
Broom Water
Broom Mead, Bexh. 79 CR46
Broom Pk., Tedd. 74 BK50
Broom Rd., Croy. 87 CE55
Broom Rd., Tedd. 74 BJ49
Broom Water, Tedd. 74 BK50
Broom Water W., Tedd. 74 BK49
Broom Way, Wey. 92 BB56
Broomcroft Clo., Wok. 100 AU61
Broomcroft Dr.
Broomcroft Dr., Wok. 100 AU61
Broome Clo., Epsom 112 BN66
Broome Pl., S.Ock. 60 CY40
Park La.
Broome Rd., Hmptn. 74 BE50
Broome Way SE5 67 BZ43
Broomfield E17 48 CD33
Broomfield, Guil. 118 AP70
Broomfield, Harl. 6 CO9
Broomfield, St.Alb. 18 BG17
Broomfield, Sun. 83 BC51
Broomfield Ave. N13 38 BX28
Broomfield Ave., Brox. 21 CD16
Broomfield Ave., Loug. 31 CK25
Broomfield Ave., Sev. 107 CT64
Broomfield Clo., Guil. 118 AP69
Broomfield Clo., Rom. 41 CS29
Broomfield Ct., Wey. 92 AZ57
Broomfield La. N13 38 BX28
Broomfield Pk., Dor. 119 BG72
Broomfield Pl. W13 54 BJ40
Mattock La.
Broomfield Ride, Lthd. 93 BG80
Broomfield Ri., Abb.L. 17 BA19
Broomfield Rd. N13 38 BX28
Broomfield Rd. W13 54 BJ40
Broomfield Rd., Beck. 87 CD52
Broomfield Rd., Bexh. 79 CR46
Broomfield Rd., Rich. 65 BL44
Broomfield Rd., Rom. 50 CP33
Broomfield Rd., Surb. 85 BL54
Broomfield Rd., Swans. 81 DC46
Broomfield Rd., Tedd. 74 BK50
Melbourne Rd.
Broomfield Rd., Wey. 92 AW59
Broomfield St. E14 57 CE39
Broomfields, Esher 93 BG56
Broomgrove Gdns., Edg. 37 BM30
Broomgrove Rd. SW9 66 BX44
Broomhall End, Wok. 100 AS61
Broomhall La.
Broomhall La., Wok. 100 AS61
Broomhall Rd., S.Croy. 96 BZ58
Broomhall Rd., Wok. 100 AS61
Broomhill Ri., Bexh. 79 CR46
Broomhill Rd. SW18 76 BS46
Broomhill Rd., Dart. 79 CU46
Broomhill Rd., Ilf. 50 CO34
Broomhill Rd., Orp. 89 CO54
Broomhill Rd., Wdf.Grn. 40 CH29
Broomhills, Grav. 81 DC49
Broomhills, Welw.G.C. 5 BS7
Broomhouse La. SW6 66 BS44
Broomhouse Rd. SW6 66 BS44
Broomhurst Ct., Dor. 119 BJ72
Ridgeway Rd.
Broomlands La., Oxt. 106 CJ65
Broomloan La., Sutt. 86 BS55
Brooms Clo., Welw.G.C. 5 BQ6
Broomsleigh St. NW6 47 BS35
Broomstick Hall Rd., 22 CG20
Wal.Abb.
Broomstick La., Chesh. 16 AQ18
Broomwood Gdns., Brwd. 33 DA25
Broomwood Rd. SW11 76 BU46
Broomwood Rd., Orp. 89 CO51
Broseley Gdns., Rom. 42 CW28
Broseley Gro. SE26 77 CD49
Broseley Rd., Rom. 42 CW28
Broster Gdns. SE25 87 CA52
Brott St. E1 57 CC38
Mantus Rd.
Brougham Rd. E8 57 CB37
Brougham Rd. W3 55 BN39
Broughinge Rd., Borwd. 28 BM23
Broughton Ave. N3 46 BR31
Broughton Ave., Rich. 74 BK48
Broughton Ct. W13 54 BJ40
Broughton Rd.
Broughton Dr. SW9 66 BY45
Somerleyton Rd.
Broughton Gdns. N6 47 BW32
Broughton Hall Ave., 109 AV66
Wok.
Broughton Rd. SW6 66 BS44
Broughton Rd. W13 54 BJ40
Broughton Rd., Orp. 88 CM55
Broughton Rd., Sev. 107 CU61
Broughton Rd., Th.Hth. 86 BY53
Broughton St. SW8 66 BV44
Brouncker Rd. W3 65 BN41
Brow, The, Ch.St.G. 34 AR27
Brow, The, Red. 121 BV73
Spencer Way
Brow, The, Wat. 17 BC19
Brow Clo., Orp. 89 CP54
Brow Cres., Orp. 89 CP54
Browells La., Felt. 73 BC48
Brown Clo., Wall. 95 BX57
Brown Flds., Welw.G.C. 5 BR7
Brown Hart Gdns. W1 1 H10
Brown Hart Gdns. W1 56 BV40
Brown Rd., Grav. 81 DJ47
Brown St. W1 1 E8
Brown St. W1 56 BU39
Browne Clo., Rom. 41 CR28
Brownfield St. E14 57 CF39
Browngraves Rd., Hayes 63 BA43
Brownhill Rd. SE6 77 CE47
Browning Ave. W7 54 BH39
Browning Ave., Sutt. 95 BU56
Browning Ave., Wor.Pk. 85 BP54
Browning Clo., Hmptn. 74 BE49
Browning Clo., Well. 68 CN44
Browning Est. SE17 4 J10
Browning Est. SE17 67 BZ42
Browning Ms. W1 1 H7
Browning Ms. W1 56 BV39
New Cavendish St.
Browning Rd. E11 49 CG33
Browning Rd. E12 58 CK36
Browning Rd., Dart. 70 CW45
Browning Rd., Enf. 30 BZ22
Browning Rd., Lthd. 111 BG66
Browning St. SE17 4 J10
Browning St. SE17 67 BZ42
Browning Wk., Til. 71 DH44
Coleridge Rd.
Browning Way, Houns. 64 BD44
Brownlea Gdns., Ilf. 50 CO34
Brownlow Ms. WC1 2 C5
Brownlow Ms. WC1 56 BX38
Brownlow Rd. E7 49 CH35
Woodford Rd.
Brownlow Rd. E8 57 CA37
Brownlow Rd. N3 38 BS29
Brownlow Rd. N11 38 BX29
Brownlow Rd. NW10 55 BO36
Brownlow Rd. W13 54 BJ40
Broadway
Brownlow Rd., Berk. 7 AR12
Brownlow Rd., Borwd. 28 BM24
Brownlow Rd., Croy. 96 CA56
Brownlow Rd., Red. 121 BU70
Brownlow St. WC1 2 C7
Brownlow St. WC1 56 BX39
Brownrigg Rd., Ashf. 73 AZ49
Browns Bldgs. EC3 2 N9
Browns La. NW5 47 BV35
Browns La., Lthd. 111 BD67
Browns Rd. E17 48 CE31
Browns Rd., Surb. 85 BL54
Browns Spring, Berk. 7 AU11
Brownspring Dr. SE9 78 CL49
Brownswell Rd. N2 38 BT30
Brownswood Rd. N4 47 BY34
Brox La., Cher. 91 AU57
Brox Rd., Cher. 91 AU57
Broxash Rd. SW11 76 BV46
Broxbourne Ave. E18 49 CH31
Broxbourne Rd. E7 49 CH34
Broxbourne Rd., Orp. 88 CN54
Broxburn Dr., S.Ock. 60 DA39
Broxhill Rd., Hav. 41 CT27
Broxholm Rd. SE27 76 BY48
Broxted Ms., Brwd. 122 DE25
Broxted Rd. SE6 77 CD48
Broxwood Way NW8 56 BU37
Bruce Ave., Horn. 51 CV34
Bruce Ave., Shep. 83 BA53
Bruce Castle Rd. N17 39 CA30
Bruce Clo., Slou. 61 AN41
Bruce Clo., Well. 69 CO44
Bruce Clo., Wey. 92 AY60
Bruce Dr., S.Croy. 96 CC58
Bruce Gdns. N20 38 BU27
Bruce Gro. N17 39 CA30
Bruce Gro., Orp. 89 CO54
Bruce Gro., Wat. 27 BD22
Bruce Hall Ms. SW17 76 BV49
Brudenell Rd.
Bruce Rd. E3 57 CE38
Bruce Rd. NW10 55 BN36
Bruce Rd. SE25 87 BZ52
Bruce Rd., Barn. 28 BR24
Bruce Rd., Har. 36 BH30
Bruce Rd., Mitch. 76 BV50
Bruce Wk., Wind. 61 AL44
Tinkers La.
Bruce Way, Wal.Cr. 21 CC20
Bruces Wf. Rd., Grays 71 DD43
Brudenell, Wind. 61 AM45
Brudenell Rd. SW17 76 BU48
Bruffs Meadow, Nthlt. 54 BE36
Brumana Clo., Wey. 92 AZ57
Elgin Rd.
Brumfield Rd., Epsom 94 BN56
Brummell Clo., Bexh. 69 CS45

Brundall Clo., Hem.H. 8 AX14
Brune St. E1 2 P7
Brune St. E1 57 CA39
Brunel Clo. SE19 77 CA50
St. Aubyns Rd.
Brunel Clo., Houns. 63 BC43
Brunel Clo., Nthlt. 54 BE38
Brunel Clo., Til. 71 DG45
Brunel Est. W2 56 BS39
Brunel Pl., Houns. 54 BF39
Brunel Rd. SE16 67 CC41
Brunel Rd. W3 55 BO39
Brunel Rd., Wdf.Grn. 40 CK28
Brunel St. E16 58 CG39
Brunel Wk. N15 48 CA31
Brunel Wk., Twick. 74 BF47
Mallard Clo.
Brunel Way, Slou. 52 AP40
Brunner Clo. NW11 47 BS32
Brunner Ct., Cher. 91 AU56
Tringham Clo.
Brunner Rd. E17 48 CD32
Brunner Rd. W5 54 BK38
Bruno Pl., Wem. 46 BN34
Brunswick Ave. N11 38 BV27
Brunswick Ave., Upmin. 51 CZ33
Brunswick Cen. WC1 1 Q4
Brunswick Cen. WC1 56 BX38
Brunswick Clo., Bexh. 69 CP45
Brunswick Rd.
Brunswick Clo., Pnr. 45 BE32
Brunswick Clo., T.Ditt. 84 BH54
Brunswick Clo., Twick. 74 BG48
Brunswick Ct. EC1 56 BY38
Brunswick Ct. SE1 4 N4
Brunswick Ct. SE1 67 CA41
Brunswick Ct., Walt. 84 BD55
Brunswick Cres. N11 38 BV27
Brunswick Gdns. W5 55 BL38
Brunswick Gdns. W8 56 BS40
Brunswick Gdns., Ilf. 40 CM29
Brunswick Gro. N11 38 BV27
Brunswick Gro., Cob. 93 BD60
Brunswick Ms. SW16 76 BW50
Potters La.
Brunswick Ms. W1 1 F8
Brunswick Pk. SE5 67 BZ44
Brunswick Pk. Gdns. N11 38 BV27
Brunswick Pk. Rd. N11 38 BV27
Brunswick Pl. N1 2 L3
Brunswick Pl. N1 57 BZ38
Brunswick Pl. SE19 77 CB50
Brunswick Pl., Grav. 81 DH47
Brunswick Quay SE16 67 CC41
Brunswick Quay Gate SE16 67 CC41
Brunswick Quay
Brunswick Rd. E10 48 CF33
Brunswick Rd. E14 57 CF39
Brunswick Rd. N15 48 CA32
Brunswick Rd. W5 54 BK38
Brunswick Rd., Bexh. 69 CP45
Brunswick Rd., Kings.T. 85 BM51
Brunswick Rd., Sutt. 95 BS56
Brunswick Sq. N17 39 CA29
Brunswick Sq. WC1 2 A4
Brunswick Sq. WC1 56 BX38
Brunswick St. E17 48 CF32
Brunswick Ter., Wind. 61 AO44
Brunswick Vill. SE5 67 CA43
Brunswick Way N11 38 BV28
Brunton Pl. E14 57 CD39
Brushfield St. E1 2 N6
Brushfield St. E1 57 CA39
Brushrise, Wat. 26 BC21
Brushwood Dr., Rick. 25 AU24
Brushwood Rd., Chesh. 16 AP18
Brussels Rd. SW11 66 BT45
Bruton Clo., Chis. 78 CK50
Bullerswood Dr.
Bruton La. W1 3 K1
Bruton La. W1 56 BV40
Bruton Pl. W1 3 K1
Bruton Pl. W1 56 BV40
Bruton Rd., Mord. 86 BT52
Bruton St. W1 3 K1
Bruton St. W1 56 BV40
Bruton Way W13 54 BJ39
Bryan Ave. NW10 55 BP36
Bryan Clo., Sun. 73 BC50
Bryan Rd. SE16 67 CD41
Bryanston Ave., Twick. 74 BF47
Bryanston Clo., Sthl. 64 BE42
Blandford Rd.
Bryanston Ms. E. W1 1 E7
Bryanston Ms. W. W1 1 E7
Bryanston Ms. W. W1 56 BU39
Bryanston Pl. W1 1 E7
Bryanston Pl. W1 56 BU39
Bryanston Rd., Til. 71 DH44
Bryanston Sq. W1 1 E7
Bryanston Sq. W1 56 BU39
Bryanston St. W1 1 E9
Bryanston St. W1 56 BU39
Bryanstone Ave., Guil. 118 AQ69
Bryanstone Clo., Guil. 118 AP69
Bryanstone Gro., Guil. 109 AP68
Bryanstone Rd. N8 47 BW32
Bryanstone Rd., Wal.Cr. 21 CD20
Bryant Ave., Rom. 42 CV30
Bryant Ave., Slou. 52 AO39
Bryant Clo., Barn. 28 BR25
Bryant Rd., Nthlt. 54 BD38
Bryant St. E15 57 CF36
Bryantwood Rd. N7 47 BY35
Bryce Rd., Dag. 50 CP35
Brycedale Cres. N14 38 BW28
Bryden Clo. SE26 77 CD49
Brydges Pl. WC2 3 Q1
Brydges Rd. E15 48 CF35
Brydon Wk. N1 56 BX37
Outram Pl.
Bryer Pl., Wind. 61 AL45
Bryett Rd. N7 47 BX34

Brymay Clo. E3 57 CE37
Brympton Clo., Dor. 119 BJ72
Bryn-y-Mawr Rd., Enf. 30 CA24
Brynford Clo., Wok. 100 AS61
Brynmaer Rd. SW11 66 BU44
Bryony Clo., Uxb. 53 AY39
Bryony Rd. W12 55 BP40
Bryony Rd., Guil. 118 AT69
Bubblestone Rd., Sev. 107 CU61
Buccleuch Rd., Slou. 62 AQ43
Buccleuch Ter. E5 48 CB33
Clapton Common
Buchan Rd. SE15 67 CC45
Buchanan Clo., S.Ock. 60 CY40
Buchanan Ct., Borwd. 28 BN23
Buchanan Gdns. NW10 55 BP37
Bucharest Rd. SW18 76 BT47
Buck Clo., Horn. 51 CV32
Buck Hill Wk. W2 3 B1
Buck La. NW9 46 BN32
Buck Rd., Grav. 81 DE47
Buck Wk. E17 48 CF31
Buckbean Path, Rom. 42 CV29
Buckden Clo. SE12 78 CG46
Upwood Rd.
Buckettsland La., Borwd. 28 BN22
Buckfast Ct. W13 54 BJ40
Romsey Rd.
Buckfast Rd., Mord. 86 BS52
Buckfast St. E2 57 CB38
Buckham Thorns Rd., West. 115 CM66
Buckhold Rd. SW18 76 BS46
Buckhurst Ave., Cars. 86 BU54
Buckhurst Ave., Sev. 117 CV66
Buckhurst Clo., Red. 121 BU69
Buckhurst La., Sev. 117 CV66
Buckhurst Rd., West. 106 CL64
Buckhurst St. E1 57 CB38
Buckhurst Way, Buck.H. 40 CJ28
Buckingham Arc. WC2 4 A1
Buckingham Ave. N20 38 BT26
Buckingham Ave., E.Mol. 84 BF52
Buckingham Ave., Felt. 73 BC46
Buckingham Ave., Grnf. 54 BJ37
Buckingham Ave., Th.Hth. 86 BY51
Buckingham Ave., Well. 68 CN45
Buckingham Clo. W5 54 BK39
Buckingham Clo., Enf. 30 CA23
Buckingham Clo., Guil. 118 AS70
Buckingham Clo., Hmptn. 74 BE49
Buckingham Clo., Horn. 51 CV32
Woodlands Ave.
Buckingham Clo., Orp. 88 CN54
Buckingham Ct. NW4 37 BP30
Buckingham Ct., Amer. 25 AP22
Buckingham Dr., Chis. 78 CL49
Buckingham Gdns., E.Mol. 84 BF51
Buckingham Gdns., Edg. 37 BL29
Buckingham Gdns., Slou. 62 AP41
Buckingham Gdns., Th.Hth. 86 BY51
Buckingham Gate SW1 3 L5
Buckingham Gate SW1 66 BW41
Buckingham Gro., Uxb. 53 AY37
Buckingham Hill Rd., S.le H. 71 DK41
Buckingham La. SE23 77 CD47
Brockley Pk.
Buckingham Ms. NW10 55 BO37
Buckingham Ms. SW1 3 L6
Buckingham Palace Rd. SW1 3 J9
Buckingham Palace Rd. SW1 66 BV42
Buckingham Pl. SW1 3 L6
Buckingham Pl. SW1 66 BW41
Palace St.
Buckingham Rd. E10 48 CE34
Buckingham Rd. E11 49 CJ32
Buckingham Rd. E15 49 CG35
Buckingham Rd. E18 40 CG30
Buckingham Rd. N1 57 CA36
Buckingham Rd. N22 38 BX30
Buckingham Rd. NW10 55 BO37
Buckingham Rd., Borwd. 28 BN24
Buckingham Rd., Edg. 37 BL29
Buckingham Rd., Hmptn. 74 BE49
Buckingham Rd., Har. 45 BG32
Buckingham Rd., Ilf. 49 CM34
Buckingham Rd., Kings.T. 85 BL52
Buckingham Rd., Mitch. 86 BX53
Buckingham Rd., Rich. 74 BK48
Buckingham Rd., Wat. 27 BD22
Buckingham St. WC2 4 A1
Buckingham St. WC2 56 BX40
Watergate Wk.
Buckingham Ter., Sthl. 64 BF41
Havelock Rd.
Buckingham Way, Wall. 95 BW58
Buckland Ave., Slou. 62 AQ42
Buckland Cres. NW3 56 BT36
Buckland Cres., Wind. 61 AM44
Buckland La., Bet. 112 BP68
Buckland La., Tad. 112 BO68
Buckland Ri., Pnr. 36 BD30
Buckland Rd. E10 48 CF34
Buckland Rd., Chess. 94 BL56
Buckland Rd., Orp. 97 CN56
Buckland Rd., Reig. 120 BQ70
Buckland Rd., Sutt. 94 BQ58
Buckland Rd., Tad. 112 BR67
Buckland St. N1 2 L1
Buckland St. N1 57 BZ37
Buckland Wk., Mord. 86 BT53
Buckland Way, Wor.Pk. 85 BQ54
Bucklands Rd., Tedd. 74 BK50
Buckle St. E1 2 Q8
Buckle St. E1 57 CA39
Bucklebury Clo., Maid. 61 AH43
Buckleigh Ave. SW20 85 BR52
Buckleigh Rd. SW16 76 BW50

Buckleigh Way SE19 77 CA50
Stambourne Way
Buckler Gdns. SE9 78 CK49
Bucklers All. SW6 65 BR43
Haldane Rd.
Bucklers Clo., Brox. 12 CD14
Bucklers Ct., Brwd. 42 DB28
Brackens Dr.
Bucklers Way, Cars. 86 BU55
Bucklersbury EC4 2 K9
Bucklersbury EC4 57 BZ39
Walbrook
Buckles La., S.Ock. 60 DB39
Buckles Way, Bans. 103 BR61
Buckley Clo., Dart. 69 CT44
Buckley Rd. NW6 55 BR36
Buckley St. SE1 4 D3
Buckley St. SE1 56 BY40
Mepham St.
Buckmaster Rd. SW11 66 BU45
Bucknall St. WC2 1 P8
Bucknall St. WC2 56 BW39
Bucknalls Clo., Wat. 18 BE19
Bucknalls Dr., St.Alb. 18 BE19
Bucknalls La., Wat. 18 BD19
Bucknell Clo. SW2 66 BX45
Buckner Rd. SW2 66 BX45
Buckner St. W10 55 BR38
Bucknills Clo., Epsom 94 BN60
Ebbisham Rd.
Buckrell Rd. E4 39 CF27
Bucks All., Hert. 11 BW12
Bucks Ave., Wat. 36 BE26
Bucks Clo., Wey. 92 AW60
Bucks Cross Rd., Grav. 81 DF48
Bucks Cross Rd., Orp. 98 CQ56
Bucks Hill, Kings L. 17 AX20
Bucks Hill Rd., Kings L. 17 AW19
Buckstone Clo. SE23 77 CC46
Buckstone Rd. N18 39 CB28
Buckters Rents SE16 57 CD40
Buckthorne Rd. SE4 77 CD46
Buckton Rd., Borwd. 28 BL22
Budd Clo. N12 38 BS28
Budd Cft., Welw.G.C. 5 BS7
Buddings Circ., Wem. 46 BN34
Budebury Rd., Stai. 73 AW49
Budge Row EC4 2 K10
Budge Row EC4 57 BZ40
Cannon St.
Budgen Dr., Red. 121 BV69
Budgins Hill, Orp. 98 CO59
Budleigh Cres., Well. 69 CP43
Budoch Dr., Ilf. 50 CO34
Buer Rd. SW6 65 BR44
Buff Ave., Bans. 95 BS60
Bug Hill, Warl. 105 CC63
Bugsbys Way SE7 68 CH42
Bulbourne Clo., Berk. 7 AP12
Bulbourne Clo., Hem.H. 8 AW14
Bulganak Rd., Th.Hth. 87 BZ52
Bulinga St. SW1 3 Q9
Bulkeley Ave., Wind. 61 AN44
Bulkeley Clo., Egh. 72 AR49
Bull All., Well. 69 CO45
Bull Clo., Grays 71 DC41
Bull Hill, Lthd. 102 BJ64
Bull Inn Ct. WC2 4 A1
Bull Inn Ct. WC2 56 BX40
Strand
Bull La. N18 39 CA28
Bull La., Chis. 78 CM50
Bull La., Dag. 50 CR34
Bull La., Ger.Cr. 43 AR31
Bull Rd. E15 58 CG37
Bull Stag Grn., Hat. 10 BQ11
Bull Wf. La. EC4 2 J10
Bullace Clo., Hem.H. 8 AW13
Bullace La., Dart. 80 CW46
Bullace Row SE5 67 BZ44
Camberwell Rd.
Bullards Pl. E2 57 CC38
Bullbanks Rd., Belv. 69 CS42
Bullbeggars La., Berk. 7 AS13
Bullbeggars La., Wok. 100 AQ61
Bullbeggars Rd., Gdse. 114 CC69
Bullen St. SW11 66 BU44
Bullens Grn. La., St.Alb. 10 BO15
Buller Clo. SE15 67 CB43
Buller Rd. N17 39 CB30
Buller Rd. N22 38 BY30
Buller Rd. NW10 55 BQ38
Buller Rd., Bark. 58 CN36
Buller Rd., Th.Hth. 87 BZ51
Bullers Clo., Sid. 79 CQ49
Bullers Wd. Dr., Chis. 78 CK50
Bullescroft Rd., Edg. 37 BM27
Bullfields, Saw. 6 CQ5
Bullfinch Clo., Sev. 107 CS64
Bullfinch Dene, Sev. 107 CS64
Bullfinch La., Sev. 107 CS64
Bullfinch Rd., Croy. 96 CC59
Bullhead Rd., Borwd. 28 BN23
Bullied Way SW1 3 K9
Bullivant St. E14 57 CF39
Bullrush Clo., Hat. 10 BP13
Bullrush Gro., Uxb. 53 AX38
Iver La.
Bulls All. SW14 65 BN44
Bulls Bri. Rd., Sthl. 63 BC41
Bulls Cross, Enf. 30 CB22
Bulls Cross Ride, Wal.Cr. 30 CB21
Bulls Gdns. SW3 3 D8
Bulls Gdns. SW3 66 BU42
Walton St.
Bulls Head Pas. EC3 2 M9
Bulls Head Pas. EC3 57 CA39
Gracechurch St.
Bulls La., Hat. 10 BQ15
Bullsbrook Rd., Hayes 54 BD40
Bullsland Gdns., Rick. 25 AT25
Bullsland La., Rick. 25 AT25
Bullsmoor Clo., Wal.Cr. 30 CC21
Bullsmoor Gdns., Wal.Cr. 30 CB21

Bullsmoor La., Enf. 30 CB21
Bullsmoor Ride, Wal.Cr. 30 CC21
Bullsmoor Way, Wal.Cr. 30 CB21
Bullwell Cres., Chsnt. 21 CD18
Bulmer Gdns., Har. 45 BK33
Bulmer Ms. W11 56 BS40
Kensington Pk. Rd.
Bulmer Pl. W11 56 BS40
Bulmer Wk., Rain. 60 CV37
Bulow Ct. SW6 66 BS44
Bulstrode Ave., Houns. 64 BE44
Bulstrode Gdns., Houns. 64 BF45
Bulstrode La., Kings L. 16 AV17
Bulstrode Pl. W1 1 H7
Bulstrode Pl. W1 56 BV39
Bulstrode Rd., Houns. 64 BF45
Bulstrode St. W1 1 H8
Bulstrode St. W1 56 BV40
Bulstrode Way, Ger.Cr. 43 AR32
Bulwer Ct. Rd. E11 48 CF33
Bulwer Gdns., Barn. 29 BT24
Bulwer Rd.
Bulwer Rd. E11 48 CF33
Bulwer Rd. N18 39 CA28
Bulwer Rd., Barn. 29 BS24
Bulwer St. W12 55 BQ40
Bunby Rd., Slou. 52 AP36
Bunce Common Rd., Reig. 120 BN74
Buncefield La., Hem.H. 8 AZ12
Bunces Clo. (Eton Wick), Wind. 61 AN42
Bunces La., Wdf.Grn. 40 CG29
Bundys Way, Stai. 72 AV50
Bungalow Rd. SE25 87 CA52
Bungalow Rd., Wok. 101 AZ65
Bungalows, The SW16 76 BV50
Bungalows, The, Bush. 27 BE24
Bunhill Row EC1 2 K4
Bunhill Row EC1 57 BZ38
Bunhouse Pl. SW1 3 G10
Bunhouse Pl. SW1 66 BV42
Bourne St.
Bunkers Hill NW11 47 BT33
Bunkers Hill, Belv. 69 CR42
Bunkers Hill, Sid. 79 CQ48
Bunkers La., Hem.H. 17 AZ16
Bunns Fld., Welw.G.C. 5 BT7
Bunns La. NW7 37 BO29
Bunns La., Chesh. 16 AQ20
Bunsen St. E3 57 CD37
Kenilworth Rd.
Bunten Meade, Slou. 61 AN40
Bunting Clo., Mitch. 86 BU53
Buntingbridge Rd., Ilf. 49 CM32
Bunton St. SE18 68 CL41
Bunyan Rd. E17 48 CD31
Bunyans Clo., Brwd. 42 DA28
Bunyans La., Wok. 91 AO60
Bunyard Dr., Wok. 91 AU60
Buonaparte Ms. SW1 3 N10
Burbage Clo. SE1 4 K7
Burbage Clo. SE1 67 BZ41
Burbage Clo., Chsnt. 21 CD19
Burbage Rd. SE21 77 BZ46
Burbage Rd. SE24 77 BZ46
Burberry Clo., N.Mal. 85 BO51
Burbridge Rd., Shep. 83 AZ52
Burbridge Way N17 39 CA30
Ladysmith Rd.
Burch Rd., Grav. 81 DF46
Burcham St. E14 57 CE39
Burcharbro Rd. SE2 69 CP43
Burchell Ct., Bush. 36 BG26
Burchell Rd. E10 48 CE33
Burchell Rd. SE15 67 CB44
Burchett Way, Rom. 50 CQ32
Burchetts Way, Shep. 83 AZ53
Burchwall Clo., Rom. 41 CS29
Burcote, Wey. 92 BA57
Burcote Rd. SW18 76 BT47
Burcott Gdns., Wey. 92 AX57
Burcott Rd., Pur. 95 BY60
Burden Clo., Brent. 64 BK42
Burden Way E11 49 CH34
Burden Way, Guil. 109 AQ68
Burdenshot Hill, Guil. 100 AQ65
Burdenshott Ave., Rich. 65 BM45
Burder Clo. N1 57 CA36
Burder Rd.
Burder Rd. N1 57 CA36
Burdett Ave. SW20 85 BP51
Burdett Clo., Sid. 79 CQ49
Burdett Est. E14 57 CE39
Burdett Ms. NW3 56 BT36
Belsize Cres.
Burdett Rd. E3 57 CD38
Burdett Rd. E14 57 CD38
Burdett Rd., Croy. 87 BZ53
Burdett Rd., Rich. 65 BL44
Burdett St. SE1 4 D6
Burdett St. SE1 66 BY41
Pearman St.
Burdetts Rd., Dag. 59 CQ37
Burdock Clo., Croy. 87 CC54
Burdock Rd. N17 48 CB31
Burdon La., Sutt. 94 BR57
Burdon Pk., Sutt. 94 BR58
Burfield Clo. SW17 76 BT49
Burfield Clo., Hat. 10 BP11
Burfield Dr., Whyt. 105 CC63
Burfield Rd., Rick. 25 AU25
Burfield Rd., Wind. 72 AQ46
Burford Clo., Dag. 50 CP34
Burford Clo., Ilf. 49 CM31
Burford Clo., Uxb. 44 AY35
Burford Gdns. N13 38 BX27
Burford La., Epsom 94 BQ59
Burford Pl., Hodd. 12 CE12
Burford St.
Burford Rd. E6 58 CK38
Burford Rd. E15 57 CF37
Burford Rd. SE6 77 CD48
Burford Rd., Brent. 65 BL42

Burford Rd., Brom. 88 CK
Burford Rd., Sutt. 86 BS
Burford Rd., Wor.Pk. 85 BO
Burford St., Hodd. 12 CE
Burford Way, Croy. 96 CF
Burgate Clo., Dart. 69 CT
Burge St. SE1 4
Burges Clo., Horn. 51 CW
Burges Ct. E6 58 CL
Burges Rd. E6 58 CK
Burgess Ave. NW9 46 BN
Burgess Clo., Felt. 74 BE
Creswell Clo.
Burgess Hill NW2 47 BS
Burgess Rd. E15 49 CG
Burgess Rd., Sutt. 95 BS
Burgess St. E14 57 CE
Burgess Way, Stai. 73 AW
Burgett Rd., Slou. 61 AN
Burgh Heath Rd., Epsom 94 BO
Burgh Mt., Bans. 103 BR
Burgh St. N1 56 BY
Burgh Wd., Bans. 103 BR
Burghfield, Epsom 103 BO
Burghfield Rd., Grav. 81 DF
Burghill Rd. SE26 77 CC
Burghley Ave., Borwd. 28 BN
Burghley Ave., N.Mal. 85 BN
Burghley Rd. E11 49 CG
Burghley Rd. N8 47 BY
Burghley Rd. NW5 47 BV
Burghley Rd. SW19 75 BQ
Burgon St. EC4 2 G
Burgon St. EC4 56 BY
Carter La.
Burgos Gro. SE10 67 CE
Burgoyne Hatch, Harl. 6 CO
Burgoyne Rd. N4 47 BY
Burgoyne Rd. SE25 87 CA
Burgoyne Rd. SW9 66 BX
Burgoyne Rd., Sun. 73 BB
Burgundy Cft., Welw.G.C. 5 BR
Burham Clo. SE20 77 CC
Blenheim Rd.
Burhill Gro., Pnr. 36 BE
Barrow Pt. La.
Burhill Rd., Walt. 92 BC
Burke Clo. SW15 65 BO
Burke St. E16 58 CG
Burland Rd. SW11 76 BU
Burland Rd., Brwd. 42 DB
Burland Rd., Rom. 41 CS
Burlea Clo., Walt. 92 BC
Burleigh Ave., Sid. 78 CN
Burleigh Ave., Wall. 86 BV
Burleigh Clo., Wey. 92 AW
Burleigh Gdns. N14 38 BW
Burleigh Gdns., Ashf. 73 BA
Burleigh Ho. W10 55 BQ
Burleigh Mead, Hat. 10 BQ
Burleigh Pk., Cob. 93 BE
Burleigh Pl. SW15 75 BQ
Cambalt Rd.
Burleigh Pl., Mitch. 86 BU
Burleigh Rd., Chsnt. 21 CD
Burleigh Rd., Enf. 30 CA
Burleigh Rd., Hem.H. 8 BA
Burleigh Rd., St.Alb. 9 BJ
Burleigh Rd., Sutt. 85 BR
Burleigh Rd., Uxb. 53 AZ
Burleigh Rd., Wey. 92 AW
Burleigh St. WC2 2 A1
Burleigh St. WC2 56 BX
Tavistock St.
Burleigh Way, Cuffley 20 BX
Burleigh Way, Enf. 30 BZ
Burley Clo. E4 39 CE
Burley Clo. SW16 86 BW
Burley Orchard, Cher. 83 AW
Burley Rd. E16 58 CJ
Burlingham Clo., Guil. 118 AU
Gilliat Dr.
Burlings La., Sev. 106 CN
Burlington Arc. W1 3 L
Burlington Arc. W1 56 BW
Burlington Gdns.
Burlington Ave., Rich. 65 BM
Burlington Ave., Rom. 50 CS
Burlington Ave., Slou. 62 AP
Burlington Clo. E6 58 CK
Northumberland Rd.
Burlington Clo. W9 56 BS
Elgin Ave.
Burlington Clo., Brom. 88 CL
Crofton Rd.
Burlington Clo., Felt. 73 BA
Burlington Clo., Orp. 88 CL
Burlington Gdns. W1 3 L
Burlington Gdns. W1 56 BW
Burlington Gdns. W3 55 BN
Burlington Gdns. W4 65 BN
Burlington Gdns., Rom. 50 CQ
Burlington La. W4 65 BN
Burlington Ms. W3 55 BO
Burlington Gdns.
Burlington Pl., Wdf.Grn. 40 CH
Burlington Ri., Barn. 38 BU
Burlington Rd. N10 47 BV
Tetherdown
Burlington Rd. N17 39 CB
Burlington Rd. SW6 65 BR
Burlington Rd. W4 65 BN
Burlington Rd., Enf. 30 BZ
Burlington Rd., Islw. 64 BG
Burlington Rd., N.Mal. 85 BO
Burlington Rd., Slou. 62 AP
Burlington Rd., Th.Hth. 87 BZ
Burma Ct. N5 48 BZ
Green Las.
Burma Ms. N16 48 BZ
Burma Rd. N16 48 BZ
Burma Rd., Wok. 82 AP
Burman St. SE1 66 BY
Burmester Rd. SW17 76 BT

…n Clo., Wat. 27 BG24
…n Clo., Wey. 92 AX56
…n Side N9 39 CC27
…n Side, Ash. 103 BL62
…aby Cres. W4 65 BN43
…aby Gdns. W4 65 BM43
…aby Rd., Grav. 81 DF47
…aby St. SW10 66 BT43
…brae Clo. N12 38 BS29
…bury Rd. SW12 76 BW47
…croft Ave., Enf. 30 CC23
…e Jones Ho. W14 65 BR42
…ne St. NW1 1 C6
…nell Ave., Rich. 74 BK49
…nell Ave., Well. 69 CO44
…nell Gdns., Stan. 36 BK30
…nell Rd., Sutt. 95 BS56
…nell Wk. SE1 4 Q10
…nell Wk., Brwd. 42 DB29
…nels Ave. E6 58 CL38
…ness Clo. N7 56 BX36
…oman Way
…ness Clo., Uxb. 53 AX37
…hitehall Rd.
…net Ave., Guil. 118 AT69
…net Gro., Epsom 94 BN60
…nett Clo. E9 48 CC35
…nett Pk., Harl. 13 CL13
…nett Rd., Erith 70 CV43
…netts Rd., Wind. 61 AM44
…ney Ave., Surb. 85 BL53
…ney Clo., Lthd. 111 BG66
…ney Dr., Loug. 31 CL23
…ney Rd., Dor. 119 BJ69
…ney St. SE10 67 CF43
…nfoot Ave. SW6 65 BR44
…nham Ave., Uxb. 44 BA35
…nham Clo. SE1 4 Q9
…nham Clo., Enf. 30 CA22
…nham Clo., Wind. 61 AL44
…nham Clo., Wok. 100 AO62
…nham Ct. NW4 46 BQ31
…nham Cres. E11 49 CJ31
…nham Cres., Dart. 70 CV45
…nham Dr., Reig. 121 BS70
…nham Dr., Wor.Pk. 85 BQ55
…nham Gdns., Croy. 87 CA54
…nham Gdns., Hayes 63 BA41
…nham Gdns., Houns. 63 BC44
…nham Rd. E4 39 CD28
…nham Rd., Dag. 59 CO36
…nham Rd., Dart. 70 CV45
…nham Rd., Mord. 86 BS53
…nham Rd., Rom. 50 CS31
…nham Rd., St.Alb. 9 BJ13
…nham Rd., Sid. 79 CQ48
…nham Rd., Wok. 100 AO62
…nham St. E2 57 CC38
…nham St., Kings.T. 85 BM51
…nham Way W13 64 BJ41
…nhams Rd., Lthd. 102 BE65
…nhill Rd., Beck. 87 CE51
…nley Clo., Wat. 36 BD28
…nley Rd. NW10 46 BO35
…nley Rd. SW9 66 BX44
…nley Rd., Grays 70 DA43
…ns Ave., Felt. 73 BC46
…ns Ave., Sid. 79 CO46
…ns Ave., Sthl. 54 BF40
…ns Clo. SW19 76 BT50
…orth Rd.
…ns Clo., Cob. 102 BG61
…ns Clo., Erith 69 CT44
…ns Clo., Hayes 53 BB39
…ns Clo., Well. 68 CN44
…ns Dr., Bans. 94 BR60
…ns Dr., Hem.H. 8 AZ10
…ns Pl., Til. 71 DG44
…ns Rd. NW10 55 BO37
…ns Rd. SW11 66 BU44
…ns Rd. W13 64 BJ41
…ns Rd., Wem. 54 BK37
…ns Way, Brwd. 122 DE25
…ns Way, Houns. 64 BD44
…nsall St. SW3 3 D10
…nsall St. SW3 66 BU42
…nside, Hodd. 12 CD12
…nside, St.Alb. 9 BJ14
…nside, Saw. 6 CP6
…nside Clo. SE16 57 CC40
…nside Clo., Barn. 29 BS24
…leadway
…nside Clo., Hat. 10 BP11
…nside Clo., Twick. 74 BJ46
…nside Cres., Wem. 54 BK37
…nside Rd., Dag. 50 CP34
…nside Ter., Harl. 6 CQ9
…nt Ash Hill SE12 78 CG46
…nt Ash La., Brom. 78 CH50
…nt Ash Rd. SE12 78 CH46
…nt Common Clo., 109 AV66
…Vok.
…nt Fm. Ride, Enf. 20 BY20
…nt Mill, Harl. 6 CM9
…nt Mill Clo., Harl. 6 CM9
…urnt Mill La.
…nt Mill La., Harl. 6 CM9
…nt Oak Bdy., Edg. 37 BM30
…nt Oak Flds., Edg. 37 BM30
…ast Rd.
…nt Oak La., Sid. 78 CN46
…ntcommon La., Wok. 109 AV66
…nthouse La., Dart. 80 CW49
…nthwaite Rd. SW6 65 BR43
…ntmill La., Harl. 6 CM9
…ntwood, Brwd. 42 DB27
…errard Cres.
…ntwood Ave., Horn. 51 CV32
…ntwood Clo. SW18 76 BU47
…ntwood Clo., Brwd. 123 DE32
…ntwood Clo., Cat. 105 CB64
…ntwood Gro., Sev. 116 CU67
…ntwood La. SW17 76 BT48
…ntwood La., Cat. 105 CA64

Burntwood Rd., Sev. 116 CU67
Burnway, Horn. 51 CW33
Burpham La., Guil. 109 AT68
Burr Clo. E1 57 CB40
Burr Clo., Bexh. 69 CQ45
Burr Clo., St.Alb. 19 BL17
Burr Hill La., Wok. 91 AP58
Burr Rd. SW18 76 BS47
Burrage Gro. SE18 68 CM42
Burrage Pl. SE18 68 CL42
Burrage Rd. SE18 68 CM42
Burrard Rd. E16 58 CH39
Burrard Rd. NW6 47 BS35
Burrell, The, Dor. 119 BG72
Burrell Clo., Croy. 87 CD53
Burrell Clo., Edg. 37 BM27
Burrell Row, Beck. 87 CE51
High St
Burrell St. SE1 4 F2
Burrell St. SE1 56 BY40
Burrells Wf. Sq. E14 67 CE42
Burrfield Dr., Orp. 89 CP53
Burritt Rd., Kings.T. 85 BM51
Burroughs, The NW4 46 BP31
Burroughs Gdns. NW4 46 BP31
Burrow Clo., Chig. 40 CN28
Burrow Fld., Welw.G.C. 5 BQ9
Burrow Grn., Chig. 40 CN28
Burrow Hill Grn., Wok. 91 AO58
Windlesham Rd.
Burrow Rd., Chig. 40 CN28
Burrow Wk. SE21 77 BZ47
Rosendale Rd.
Burroway Rd., Slou. 62 AT41
Burrows Clo., Guil. 118 AP70
Burrows Clo., Lthd. 102 BE65
Burrows Hill Clo., Houns. 63 AX45
Burrows Hill La., Houns. 63 AW45
Burrows Ms. SE1 4 F4
Burrows Ms. SE1 66 BY41
Burrows Rd. NW10 55 BQ38
Bursdon Clo., Sid. 78 CN48
Burses Way, Brwd. 122 DE25
Bursland Rd., Enf. 30 CC24
Burslem Ave., Ilf. 41 CO29
Burslem St. E1 57 CB39
Burstead Clo., Cob. 93 BD59
Burstock Rd. SW15 65 BR45
Burston Dr., St.Alb. 18 BG17
Burston Rd. SW15 65 BQ45
Burstow Rd. SW20 85 BR51
Burt Rd. E16 58 CJ40
Burtenshaw Rd., T.Ditt. 84 BJ53
Burtley Clo. N4 48 BZ33
Burton Ave., Wat. 26 BC24
Burton Clo. NW7 37 BQ28
Burton Clo., Chess. 93 BK57
Burton Ct. SW3 66 BU42
Burton Dr., Loug. 31 CM24
Burton Gdns., Houns. 64 BE44
Burton Gro. SE17 67 BZ42
Burton La. SW9 66 BY44
Evandale Rd.
Burton La., Chsnt. 21 CA18
Burton Ms. SW1 3 H9
Burton Pl. WC1 1 P3
Burton Pl. WC1 56 BW38
Burton St.
Burton Rd. E18 49 CH31
Burton Rd. NW6 55 BR36
Burton Rd. SW9 66 BY44
Burton Rd., Kings.T. 75 BL50
Burton Rd., Loug. 31 CM24
Burton St. WC1 1 P3
Burton St. WC1 56 BW38
Burton Way, Wind. 61 AM45
Burtonhole La. NW7 37 BQ28
Burtons La., Ch.St.G. 25 AR23
Burtons Rd., Hmptn. 74 BF49
Burtons Way, Ch.St.G. 25 AR23
Burtwell La. SE27 77 BZ49
Burwash Ho. SE1 4 L5
Burwash Rd. SE18 68 CM42
Burway Cres., Cher. 83 AW52
Western Ave.
Burwell Ave., Grnf. 54 BH36
Burwell Clo. E1 57 CB39
Burwell Rd. E10 48 CD33
Burwell Wk. E3 57 CE38
Rounton Rd.
Burwood Ave., Brom. 88 CH55
Burwood Ave., Ken. 95 BY60
Burwood Ave., Pnr. 44 BC32
Burwood Clo., Guil. 118 AU70
Burwood Clo., Reig. 121 BT70
Burwood Clo., Surb. 85 BM54
Burwood Clo., Walt. 93 BD57
Burwood Gdns., Rain. 59 CT38
Burwood Pk. Rd., Walt. 92 BC56
Burwood Pl. W2 1 D8
Burwood Pl. W2 56 BU39
Burwood Rd., Walt. 92 BB57
Bury Ave., Hayes 53 BB37
Bury Ave., Ruis. 44 BA32
Bury Clo., Wok. 100 AR61
Bury Ct. EC3 2 N8
Bury Ct. EC3 57 CA39
Bury Grn., Hem.H. 8 AX13
Bury Grn. Rd., Chsnt. 21 CB19
Bury Gro., Mord. 86 BS53
Bury Hall Vill. N9 39 CA26
Bury Hill, Hem.H. 8 AW13
Bury Hill Clo., Hem.H. 8 AX13
Bury Holme, Brox. 12 CD15
Bury La., Epp. 22 CM17
Bury La., Rick. 35 AX26
Bury La., Wok. 100 AR61
Bury Meadows, Rick. 35 AX26
Bury Pl. WC1 1 Q7
Bury Pl. WC1 56 BX39
Bury Ri., Hem.H. 16 AU16
Bury Rd. E4 31 CG25
Bury Rd. N22 47 BY31

Bury Rd., Dag. 50 CR35
Bury Rd., Epp. 22 CN19
Bury Rd., Harl. 6 CP9
Bury Rd., Hat. 10 BQ12
Beaconsfield Rd.
Bury Rd., Hem.H. 8 AX13
Bury St. EC3 2 N9
Bury St. EC3 57 CA39
Bury St. N9 39 CA26
Bury St. SW1 3 M2
Bury St. SW1 56 BW40
Bury St., Guil. 118 AR71
Bury St., Ruis. 44 BA32
Bury St. W. N9 39 BZ26
Bury Wk. SW3 3 C9
Bury Wk. SW3 66 BU42
Burycroft, Welw.G.C. 5 BR6
Burydell La., St.Alb. 18 BG17
Buryfields, Guil. 118 AT71
Busby Ms. NW5 56 BW36
Torriano Ave.
Busby Pl. NW5 56 BW36
Busby St. E2 2 Q4
Busch Cor., Islw. 64 BJ44
Bush Clo., Ilf. 49 CM32
Bush Clo., Wey. 92 AX56
Bush Cotts. SW18 76 BS46
Putney Bri. Rd.
Bush Ct. N14 38 BW26
Bush Elms Rd., Horn. 50 CU33
Bush Fair, Harl. 13 CN12
Bush Gro. NW9 46 BN33
Bush Gro., Stan. 36 BK29
Bush Hall La., Hat. 10 BQ11
Bush Hill N21 39 BZ26
Bush Hill Rd. N21 30 BZ25
Bush Hill Rd., Har. 46 BL32
Bush Ind. Est. NW10 55 BN38
Bush La. EC4 2 K10
Bush La. EC4 57 BZ40
Cannon St.
Bush La., Wok. 100 AU65
Bush Rd. E8 57 CB37
Bush Rd. E11 49 CG33
Bush Rd. SE8 67 CC42
Bush Rd., Buck.H. 40 CJ28
Bush Rd., Rich. 65 BL43
Bush Rd., Shep. 83 AY53
Bushbaby Clo. SE1 4 M7
Bushbarns, Chsnt. 21 CB18
Bushberry Rd. E9 57 CD36
Bushbury La., Bet. 120 BM72
Bushby Ave., Brox. 12 CD14
Bushell Clo. SW2 76 BX48
Bushell Grn., Bush. 36 BG27
Bushell St. E1 57 CB40
Hermitage Wall
Bushell Way, Chis. 78 CL49
Bushetts Gro., Red. 113 BV68
Bushey Ave. E18 49 CG31
Bushey Ave., Orp. 88 CM54
Bushey Clo., Uxb. 44 AZ34
Bushey Clo., Welw.G.C. 5 BS8
Bushey Clo., Whyt. 105 CA61
Bushey Ct. SW20 85 BP51
Bushey Ct., Kings.T. 74 BK50
Bushey Cft., Harl. 13 CN12
Bushey Cft., Oxt. 114 CF68
High St.
Bushey Grn., Welw.G.C. 5 BS8
Bushey Ley
Bushey Gro. Rd., Bush. 27 BD24
Bushey Hall Dr., Bush. 27 BE24
Bushey Hall Rd., Bush. 27 BD24
Bushey Hill Rd. SE5 67 CA44
Bushey La., Sutt. 95 BS56
Bushey Lea, Ong. 24 CX18
Bushey Lees, Sid. 78 CN46
Fen Gro.
Bushey Ley, Welw.G.C. 5 BS8
Bushey Mill Cres., Wat. 27 BD22
Bushey Mill La., Bush. 27 BE23
Bushey Mill La., Wat. 27 BD22
Bushey Rd. E13 58 CJ37
Bushey Rd. N15 48 CA32
Bushey Rd. SW20 85 BP52
Bushey Rd., Croy. 87 CE55
Bushey Rd., Hayes 63 BB42
Bushey Rd., Sutt. 95 BS56
Bushey Rd., Uxb. 44 AZ34
Bushey Shaw, Ash. 102 BK62
Bushey Way, Beck. 87 CF53
Bushfield Clo., Edg. 37 BM27
Bushfield Cres., Edg. 37 BM27
Bushfield Dr., Red. 121 BV73
Bushfield Rd., Hem.H. 16 AU16
Bushfields, Loug. 31 CL25
Bushgrove Rd., Dag. 50 CP35
Bushmoor Cres. SE18 68 CL43
Bushnell Rd. SW17 76 BV48
Bushway, Dag. 50 CP35
Bushwood E11 49 CG33
Bushwood Clo., Hat. 10 BP15
Bushwood Dr. SE1 4 Q9
Bushwood Rd., Rich. 65 BM43
Bushy Down SW12 76 BV48
Bedford Hill
Bushy Hill Dr., Guil. 118 AT69
Bushy Pk. Cotts., Tedd. 74 BH50
Bushy Pk. Gdns., Tedd. 74 BG49
Bushy Pk. Rd., Tedd. 74 BJ50
Bushy Rd., Lthd. 102 BF65
Bushy Rd., Tedd. 74 BH50
Busk St. E2 57 CB37
Yorkton St.
Busty La., Sev. 108 DB64
Butcher Row E14 57 CC40
Butchers Rd. E16 58 CH39
Bute Ave., Rich. 75 BL48
Bute Ct., Wall. 95 BV56
Bute Rd.
Bute Gdns. W6 65 BQ42
Bute Gdns., Wall. 95 BW56
Bute Gdns. W., Wall. 95 BW56

Bute Rd., Croy. 86 BY54
Bute Rd., Ilf. 49 CL31
Bute Rd., Wall. 95 BW56
Bute St. SW7 3 A8
Bute St. SW7 66 BT42
Bute Wk. N1 57 BZ36
Clephane Rd.
Buthfield St. W8 66 BS41
Butler Ave., Har. 45 BG33
Butler Ho., Grays 71 DD43
Hawkes Clo.
Butler Pl. SW1 3 N6
Butler Pl. SW1 66 BW41
Palmer St.
Butler Rd. NW10 55 BO36
Curzon Cres.
Butler Rd., Dag. 50 CO35
Butler Rd., Har. 45 BG33
Butler St. E2 57 CC38
Digby St.
Butler St., Uxb. 53 AZ38
Butlers Clo., Wind. 61 AL44
Butlers Dene Rd., Cat. 105 CD63
Butlers Dr. E4 30 CF22
Butlers Hill, Lthd. 110 AZ68
Butlers Pl., New A.G. 90 DC55
Butt Fld. Vw., St.Alb. 9 BG15
Butter Cross La., Epp. 23 CO18
Butter Hill, Cars. 86 BV55
Butter Hill, Wall. 86 BV55
Buttercup Clo., Rom. 42 CV30
Copperfields Way
Buttercup Sq., Stai. 73 AX47
Diamedes Ave.
Butterfield La., St.Alb. 9 BH15
Butterfield Sq. E6 58 CK39
Guildford Rd.
Butterfields E17 48 CF32
Butterfly La. SE9 78 CL46
Butterfly La., Borwd. 27 BJ24
Butterfly Wk., Warl. 105 CC63
Butteridges Clo., Dag. 59 CQ37
Buttermere Clo. SW20 85 BQ53
Buttermere Clo., Felt. 73 BB47
Westmacott Dr.
Buttermere Clo., N.Mal. 85 BQ53
Grand Dr.
Buttermere Clo., St.Alb. 9 BJ14
Buttermere Dr. SW15 75 BR46
Buttermere Gdns., Pur. 96 BZ60
Buttermere Rd., Orp. 89 CP52
Buttermere Wk. E8 56 BY36
Rhodes Dev.
Buttermere Way, Egh. 72 AT50
Keswick Way
Buttersweet Ri., Saw. 6 CQ6
Butterwick W6 65 BQ42
Butterwick, Wat. 27 BE21
Buttesland St. N1 2 L2
Buttesland St. N1 57 BZ38
Buttfield Clo., Dag. 59 CR36
Buttlehide, Rick. 34 AU28
Buttmarsh Clo. SE18 68 CL42
Button St., Swan. 90 CV53
Buttondene Cres., Brox. 12 CE14
Butts, The, Brent. 64 BK43
Butts, The, Brox. 12 CD15
Butts, The, Sev. 107 CU62
Butts, The, Sun. 84 BD52
Butts Cotts., Felt. 74 BE48
Butts Cres., Felt. 74 BF48
Butts End, Hem.H. 8 AW12
Butts Fm. Est., Felt. 74 BE48
Butts Grn. Rd., Horn. 51 CV32
Butts Mead, Nthwd. 35 BA29
Butts Piece, Nthlt. 53 BC37
Longhook Gdns.
Butts Rd., Brom. 78 CG49
Butts Rd., Wok. 100 AS62
Chobham Rd.
Buttsbury Rd., Ilf. 49 CM35
Buxted Clo. E8 57 CA36
Buxted Rd. N12 38 BU28
Buxton Ave., Cat. 105 CA64
Buxton Clo., St.Alb. 9 BK12
Buxton Clo., Wdf.Grn. 40 CJ29
Buxton Ct. N1 2 J2
Buxton Cres., Sutt. 94 BR56
Buxton Dr. E11 49 CG31
Buxton Dr., N.Mal. 85 BN51
Buxton Gdns. W3 55 BM40
Buxton La., Cat. 105 BZ63
Buxton Path, Wat. 36 BD27
Buxton Rd. E4 39 CF26
Buxton Rd. E6 58 CK38
Buxton Rd. E15 49 CG35
Buxton Rd. E17 48 CD31
Buxton Rd. N19 47 BW33
Buxton Rd. NW2 55 BP36
Buxton Rd. SW14 65 BO45
Buxton Rd., Ashf. 73 AX49
Buxton Rd., Epp. 31 CN21
Buxton Rd., Erith 69 CS43
Buxton Rd., Grays 71 DF41
Buxton Rd., Ilf. 49 CN32
Buxton Rd., Th.Hth. 86 BY53
Buxton Rd., Wal.Abb. 22 CH20
Buxton St. E1 2 Q5
Buxton St. E1 57 CA38
By the Mt., Welw.G.C. 5 BQ8
By the Wd., Wat. 36 BE27
By-ways, The, Ash. 102 BK62
By-Wood End, Ger.Cr. 34 AS28
Roberts Wd. Dr.
Byam St. SW6 66 BT44
Byards Cft. SW16 86 BW51
Byatt Wk., Hmptn. 74 BE50
Victors Dr.
Bychurch End, Tedd. 74 BH49
Church Rd.
Bycliffe Ter., Grav. 81 DF47
Bycroft Rd., Sthl. 54 BF38
Bycroft St. SE20 77 CC50
Parish La.

Bycullah Ave., Enf. 29 BY24
Bycullah Rd., Enf. 29 BY23
Bye, The W3 55 BO39
Bye Way, The, Har. 36 BH30
Bye Ways, Twick. 74 BF48
Byefield Ct., Brwd. 123 DE32
Byegrove Rd. SW19 76 BT50
Byers Clo., Pot.B. 20 BT20
Byeway, The SW14 65 BN45
Byeway, The, Epsom 94 BO56
Byeway, The, Rick. 35 AY27
Byeways, The, Surb. 85 BM53
Byfeld Gdns. SW13 65 BP44
Byfield, Welw.G.C. 5 BR6
Byfield Ct., Brwd. 123 DE32
Byfield Ct., N.Mal. 85 BP52
Byfield Rd., Islw. 64 BJ45
Byfleet Cor., Wey. 92 AW60
Byfleet Rd., Cob. 92 AZ59
Byfleet Rd., Wey. 92 AX58
Byford Clo. E15 58 CG36
Bygrove, Croy. 96 CE57
Bygrove St. E14 57 CE39
Byland Clo. N21 38 BX26
Byland Clo. SE2 69 CO41
Finchale Rd.
Byland Dr., Maid. 61 AG42
Bylands, Wok. 100 AT63
Bylands Clo. SE16 57 CC40
Rotherhithe St.
Byne Rd. SE26 77 CC50
Byne Rd., Cars. 86 BU55
Bynes Rd., S.Croy. 96 BZ57
Byng Dr., Pot.B. 20 BS19
Byng Pl. WC1 1 N5
Byng Pl. WC1 56 BW38
Byng Rd., Barn. 28 BQ23
Byng St. E14 67 CE41
Bynghams, Harl. 13 CK12
Bynon Ave., Bexh. 69 CQ45
Byrd Mead, Brwd. 24 DA20
Byre Clo. N14 29 BV25
Byrefield Rd., Guil. 118 AP69
Byrne Rd. SW12 76 BV47
Byron, Slou. 62 AT42
Common Rd.
Byron Ave. E12 58 CK36
Byron Ave. E18 49 CG31
Byron Ave. NW9 46 BM31
Byron Ave., Borwd. 28 BM25
Byron Ave., Couls. 104 BX61
Byron Ave., Houns. 63 BC44
Byron Ave., Sutt. 95 BT56
Byron Ave., Wat. 27 BD23
Byron Ave. E., N.Mal. 85 BP52
Byron Ave. E., Sutt. 95 BT56
Byron Clo. E8 57 CA37
Brownlow Rd.
Byron Clo. SE28 59 CP40
Byron Clo., Hmptn. 74 BE49
Byron Clo., Walt. 84 BE54
Byron Clo., Wok. 100 AP62
Byron Ct., Enf. 29 BY23
Byron Ct., Rich. 74 BK49
Byron Dr. N2 47 BT32
Byron Gdns., Sutt. 95 BT56
Byron Gdns., Til. 71 DH44
Byron Hill Rd., Har. 45 BG33
Byron Pl., Hem.H. 8 AZ10
Byron Pl., Lthd. 102 BJ64
Byron Rd. E10 48 CE33
Byron Rd. E17 48 CE31
Byron Rd. NW2 46 BP34
Byron Rd. NW7 37 BP28
Byron Rd. W5 55 BL40
Byron Rd., Brwd. 122 DE26
Byron Rd., Dart. 70 CX45
Byron Rd., Har. 45 BH32
Byron Rd. (Wealdstone), Har. 36 BH30
Byron Rd., S.Croy. 96 CB58
Byron Rd., Wem. 45 BK34
Byron Rd., Wey. 92 AY56
Byron St. E14 57 CF39
Byron Ter. N9 39 CB26
Byron Ter., Har. 45 BH32
St. Anns Rd.
Byron Way, Hayes 53 BB38
Byron Way, Nthlt. 54 BE38
Byron Way, Rom. 42 CV30
Byron Way, West Dr. 63 AY42
Bysouth Clo., Ilf. 40 CL30
Bythorn St. SW9 66 BX45
Byton Rd. SW17 76 BU60
Byward Ave., Felt. 74 BD46
Byward St. EC3 4 N1
Byward St. EC3 57 CA40
Bywater St. SW3 3 E10
Bywater St. SW3 66 BU42
Byway, The, Pot.B. 20 BS20
Byway, The, Sutt. 95 BT58
Byways, Berk. 7 AS12
Byways, The, T.Ditt. 85 BM53
Bywell Pl. W1 1 L7
Bywood Ave., Croy. 87 CC53
Bywood Clo., Ken. 104 BY61
Byworth Wk. N19 47 BX33
Nyton Clo.

C

Cabbell Pl., Wey. 92 AX56
Cabbell St. NW1 1 C7
Cabbell St. NW1 56 BU39
Cabell Rd., Guil. 118 AO70
Cabinet Way E4 39 CD29
Cable Pl. SE10 67 CF43
Diamond Ter.
Cable St. E1 57 CB40

Cabot Way E6 58 CJ37
Parr Rd.
Cabrera Ave., Vir.W. 82 AR53
Cabrera Clo., Vir.W. 82 AR53
Cabul Rd. SW11 66 BU44
Cackets La., Sev. 106 CM61
Cactus Wk. W12 55 BO39
Du Cane Rd.
Cadbury Clo., Islw. 64 BJ44
Cadbury Clo., Sun. 73 BB50
Cadbury Rd., Sun. 73 BB50
Cadbury Way SE16 4 Q7
Caddington Clo., Barn. 29 BU25
Caddington Rd. NW2 46 BR34
Caddis Clo., Stan. 36 BH29
Caddy Clo., Egh. 72 AT49
Cade La., Sev. 117 CV67
Cade Rd. SE10 67 CF44
Cadell Clo. E2 2 Q1
Cader Rd. SW18 76 BT46
Cadet Dr. SE1 4 Q10
Cadet Pl. SE10 68 CG42
Cadiz Rd., Dag. 59 CS36
Cadiz St. SE17 67 BZ42
Cadley Ter. SE23 77 CC48
Cadmer Clo., N.Mal. 85 BO52
Cadmore La., Chsnt. 21 CC17
Cadogan Ave., Brwd. 123 DE32
Cadogan Ave., Dart. 80 CY47
Cadogan Clo. E9 57 CD36
Cadogan Ter.
Cadogan Clo., Brom. 87 CF51
Albermarle Rd.
Cadogan Clo., Har. 45 BF35
Cadogan Clo., Maid. 61 AG43
Cadogan Clo., Tedd. 74 BH49
Cadogan Ct. SW3 66 BU42
Draycott Ave.
Cadogan Ct., Sutt. 95 BS57
Cadogan Gdns. E18 49 CH31
Cadogan Gdns. N3 38 BS30
Cadogan Gdns. N21 29 BY25
Cadogan Gdns. SW3 3 F8
Cadogan Gdns. SW3 66 BU42
Cadogan Gate SW1 3 F8
Cadogan Gate SW1 66 BU42
Cadogan La. SW1 3 G7
Cadogan La. SW1 66 BV41
Cadogan Pl. SW1 3 F6
Cadogan Pl. SW1 66 BU41
Cadogan Rd., Surb. 84 BK53
Cadogan Sq. SW1 3 F7
Cadogan Sq. SW1 66 BU41
Cadogan St. SW3 3 E9
Cadogan St. SW3 66 BU42
Cadogan Ter. E9 57 CD36
Cadoxton Ave. N15 48 CA32
Cadwallon Rd. SE9 78 CL48
Caedmon Rd. N7 47 BX35
Caen Wd. Rd., Ash. 102 BK62
Caenshill Rd., Wey. 92 AZ57
Caenswood Hill, Wey. 92 AZ58
Caenwood Clo., Wey. 92 AZ57
Caerleon Clo., Sid. 79 CP49
Caerleon Ter. SE2 69 CO42
Caernarvon Clo., Hem.H. 8 AX13
Caernarvon Clo., Horn. 51 CX34
Caernarvon Clo., Mitch. 86 BX52
Caernarvon Dr., Ilf. 40 CL30
Caesars Wk., Mitch. 86 BU53
Caesars Way, Shep. 83 BA53
Nell Gwynne Ave.
Cage Pond Rd., Rad. 19 BL20
Cahill St. EC1 2 J5
Cahir St. E14 67 CE42
Caillard Rd., Wey. 92 AY59
Cains La., Felt. 73 BA46
Caird St. W10 55 BR38
Cairn Ave. W5 54 BK40
Cairn Way, Stan. 36 BH29
Cairndale Clo., Brom. 78 CG50
Cairnfield Ave. NW2 46 BO34
Cairngorm Clo., Tedd. 74 BJ49
Vicarage Rd.
Cairngorm Pl., Slou. 52 AO38
Northern Rd.
Cairns Ave., Wdf.Grn. 40 CK29
Cairns Clo., Dart. 80 CV46
Cairns Rd. SW11 76 BU46
Cairo New Rd., Croy. 86 BY55
Cairo Rd. E17 48 CE31
Caishowe Rd., Borwd. 28 BM23
Caistor Ms. SW12 76 BV47
Caistor Rd.
Caistor Pk. Rd. E15 58 CG37
Caistor Rd. SW12 76 BV47
Caithness Gdns., Sid. 78 CN46
Caithness Rd. W14 65 BQ41
Caithness Rd., Mitch. 76 BV50
Calabria Rd. N5 56 BY36
Calais St. SE5 66 BY44
Calbourne Ave., Horn. 50 CU35
Calbourne Rd. SW12 76 BU47
Calcott Clo., Brwd. 42 DA26
Calcott Wk. SE9 78 CJ49
Calcutta Rd., Til. 71 DF44
Caldbeck, Wal.Abb. 21 CF20
Caldbeck Ave., Wor.Pk. 85 BP55
Caldecot Rd. SE5 67 BZ44
Caldecot Way, Brox. 12 CD14
Caldecote Gdns., Bush. 36 BH26
Caldecote La., Bush. 36 BH26
Caldecott Way E5 48 CC34
Calder Ave., Grnf. 54 BH37
Calder Ave., Hat. 20 BS16
Calder Clo., Enf. 30 CA24
Calder Ct., Slou. 62 AS42
Ditton Pk. Rd.
Calder Gdns., Edg. 46 BM31
Calder Way, Slou. 62 AV45
Calderon Pl. W10 55 BQ39
St. Quintin Gdns.
Calderon Rd. E11 48 CF35
Caldervale Rd. SW4 76 BW46
Calderwood St. SE18 68 CL42
Caldew St. SE5 67 BZ43
Caldicot Grn. NW9 46 BO32
Snowdon Dr.
Caldwell Rd., Wat. 36 BD28
Caldwell St. SW9 66 BX43
Caldwell Yd. EC4 57 BZ40
Caldy Rd., Belv. 69 CR41
Caldy Wk. N1 57 BZ36
Cale St. SW3 3 C10
Cale St. SW3 66 BU42
Caleb St. SE1 4 H4
Caleb St. SE1 67 BZ41
Mint St.
Caledon Rd. E6 58 CK37
Caledon Rd., St.Alb. 18 BK16
Caledon Rd., Wall. 95 BV56
Caledonia Rd., Stai. 73 AY47
Caledonia St. N1 2 A1
Caledonia St. N1 56 BX37
Caledonian Rd. N1 2 A1
Caledonian Rd. N1 56 BX37
Caledonian Rd. N7 56 BX37
Caledonian Wf. E14 67 CF42
Caletock Way SE10 68 CG42
Glenister Rd.
Calfstock La., S.Dnth. 90 CW52
Caliban Twr. N1 57 CA37
Purcell St.
Calico Row SW11 66 BT45
York Pl.
Calidore Clo. SW2 76 BX46
Endymion Rd.
California La., Bush. 36 BG26
California Rd., N.Mal. 85 BN52
Caliph Clo., Grav. 81 DJ49
Callaby Ter. N1 56 BY36
St. Pauls Rd.
Callaghan Clo. SE13 68 CG45
Glenton Rd.
Callan Gro., S.Ock. 60 DA40
Callander Rd. SE6 77 CE48
Callard Ave. N13 38 BY28
Callcott Rd. NW6 55 BR36
Callcott St. W8 56 BS40
Callendar Rd. SW7 3 A6
Calley Down Cres., Croy. 96 CF59
Callis Fm. Clo., Stai. 73 AY46
Callis Rd. E17 48 CD32
Calliston Ct., Hem.H. 8 AY12
Callow Fold, Pur. 95 BY60
Higher Dr.
Callow Hill, Egh. 82 AR51
Callow Hill, Vir.W. 82 AR52
Callow St. SW3 66 BT43
Callowland Clo., Wat. 26 BC22
Calluna Ct., Wok. 100 AS62
Heathside Rd.
Calmington Rd. SE5 67 CA43
Calmont Rd., Brom. 77 CF50
Calmore Clo., Horn. 51 CV35
Calne Ave., Ilf. 40 CL30
Calonne Rd. SW19 75 BQ49
Calshot Rd., Houns. 63 AZ44
Calshot St. N1 56 BX37
Calshot Way, Enf. 29 BY24
Calshot Way, Houns. 63 AZ44
Calshot Rd.
Calthorpe Gdns., Edg. 37 BL28
Calthorpe Gdns., Sutt. 86 BY55
Calthorpe St. WC1 2 C4
Calthorpe St. WC1 56 BX38
Calton Ave. SE21 77 CA46
Calton Rd., Barn. 29 BT25
Calverley Clo., Beck. 77 CE50
Calverley Cres., Dag. 50 CR34
Calverley Gdns., Har. 45 BK33
Calverley Gro. N19 47 BW33
Calverley Rd., Epsom 94 BP57
Calvert Ave. E2 2 N3
Calvert Ave. E2 57 CA38
Calvert Clo., Belv. 69 CR42
Calvert Clo., Sid. 79 CQ50
Calvert Cres., Dor. 119 BJ70
Calvert Rd. SE10 68 CG42
Calvert Rd., Barn. 28 BQ23
Calvert Rd., Dor. 119 BJ70
Calvert Rd., Lthd. 110 BC68
Calvert St. NW1 56 BV37
Chalcot Rd.
Calverton Rd. E6 58 CL37
Calverts Bldgs. SE1 4 K3
Calvin Clo., Orp. 89 CP52
Calvin St. E1 2 P5
Calvin St. E1 57 CA38
Calydon Rd. SE7 68 CH42
Calypso Way SE8 67 CD41
Cam Grn., S.Ock. 60 DA39
Cam Rd. E15 57 CF37
Cam Ter., Chis. 78 CL50
Mill Pl.
Camac Rd., Twick. 74 BG47
Camarthen Grn. NW9 46 BO32
Snowdon Dr.
Cambalt Rd. SW15 75 BQ46
Camberley Ave. SW20 85 BP51
Camberley Ave., Enf. 30 CA24
Camberley Clo., Sutt. 85 BQ55
Camberley Rd., Houns. 63 AZ45
Cambert Way SE3 68 CH45
Camberwell Ch. St. SE5 67 BZ44
Camberwell Glebe SE5 67 BZ44
Camberwell Grn. SE5 67 BZ44
Camberwell Gro. SE5 67 BZ44
Camberwell La., Sev. 116 CQ69
Camberwell New Rd. SE5 66 BY43
Camberwell Pas. SE5 67 BZ44
Camberwell Rd.
Camberwell Rd. SE5 67 BZ43
Camberwell Sta. Rd. SE5 67 BZ44
Cambeys Rd., Dag. 50 CR35
Camborne Ave. W13 64 BJ41
Camborne Ave., Rom. 42 CV29
Camborne Clo., Houns. 63 AZ45
Camborne Dr., Hem.H. 8 AY11
Camborne Ms. W11 55 BR39
St. Marks Rd.
Camborne Rd. SW18 76 BS47
Camborne Rd., Croy. 87 CB54
Camborne Rd., Houns. 63 AZ45
Camborne Rd., Mord. 85 BQ53
Camborne Rd., Sid. 79 CP48
Camborne Rd., Sutt. 95 BS57
Camborne Rd., Well. 68 CN44
Camborne Rd. N., Houns. 63 AZ45
Camborne Rd.
Camborne Rd. S., Houns. 63 AZ45
Camborne Rd.
Camborne Wk., Rich. 74 BK46
Petersham Rd.
Camborne Way, Houns. 63 AZ45
Camborne Rd.
Camborne Way, Houns. 64 BF44
Camborne Way, Rom. 42 CW29
Cambourne Ave. N9 39 CC26
Cambray Rd. SW12 76 BW47
Cambray Rd., Orp. 88 CN54
Cambria Clo., Houns. 64 BF45
Cambria Clo., Sid. 78 CM47
Cambria Ct., Felt. 73 BC47
Cambria Ct., Slou. 62 AR41
Turner Rd.
Cambria Cres., Grav. 81 DJ49
Cambria Gdns., Stai. 73 AY47
Cambria Rd. SE5 67 BZ45
Cambria St. SW6 66 BS43
Cambrian Ave., Ilf. 49 CN32
Cambrian Clo. SE27 76 BY48
Cambrian Grn. NW9 46 BO32
Snowdon Dr.
Cambrian Gro., Grav. 81 DG47
Cambrian Rd. E10 48 CE33
Cambrian Rd., Rich. 75 BL46
Cambrian Way, Hem.H. 8 AY12
Cambridge Ave. NW6 56 BS37
Cambridge Ave., Grnf. 45 BH35
Cambridge Ave., N.Mal. 85 BO52
Cambridge Ave., Rom. 42 CV30
Cambridge Ave., Well. 68 CN45
Cambridge Barracks Rd. SE18 68 CK42
Cambridge Clo. SW20 85 BP51
Cambridge Clo., Chsnt. 21 CC18
Cambridge Clo., Houns. 64 BE45
Cambridge Clo., West Dr. 63 AX43
Cambridge Clo., Wok. 100 AP62
Cambridge Cotts., Rich. 65 BM43
Cambridge Cres. E2 57 CB37
Cambridge Cres., Tedd. 74 BJ49
Cambridge Cres., Wat. 27 BD24
Cambridge Dr. SE12 78 CH46
Cambridge Dr., Pot.B. 19 BQ19
Cambridge Dr., Ruis. 45 BD34
Cambridge Gdns. N10 38 BV30
Sydney Rd.
Cambridge Gdns. N13 38 BY28
Cambridge Gdns. N17 39 BZ29
Great Cambridge Rd.
Cambridge Gdns. N21 39 BZ26
Cambridge Gdns. NW6 56 BS37
Cambridge Gdns. W10 55 BQ39
Cambridge Gdns., Enf. 30 CB23
Cambridge Gdns., Grays 71 DG42
Cambridge Gdns., Kings.T. 85 BM51
Cambridge Gate NW1 1 K4
Cambridge Gate NW1 56 BV38
Cambridge Gate SE17 67 BZ43
Walworth Rd.
Cambridge Gate Ms. NW1 1 K4
Cambridge Gate Ms. NW1 56 BV38
Albany St.
Cambridge Grn. N9 39 CA26
Cambridge Grn. SE9 78 CL47
Cambridge Gro. SE20 87 CB51
Cambridge Gro. W6 65 BP42
Cambridge Gro. Rd., Kings.T. 85 BM52
Cambridge Heath Rd. E1 57 CB39
Cambridge Ho., Wind. 61 AO44
Ward Royal
Cambridge Mansion SW11 66 BU44
Cambridge Par., Enf. 30 CB23
Cambridge Pk. E11 49 CH33
Cambridge Pk., Twick. 74 BK46
Cambridge Pk. Est., Twick. 74 BK46
Cambridge Pk. Rd. E11 49 CG33
Cambridge Pl. NW6 56 BS38
Cambridge Rd.
Cambridge Pl. W8 66 BS41
Cambridge Rd. E4 39 CF26
Cambridge Rd. E11 49 CG32
Cambridge Rd. NW6 56 BS38
Cambridge Rd. SE20 87 CB52
Cambridge Rd. SW11 66 BU44
Cambridge Rd. SW13 65 BO44
Cambridge Rd. SW20 85 BP51
Cambridge Rd. W7 64 BH41
Cambridge Rd., Ashf. 73 BA50
Cambridge Rd., Bark. 58 CM36
Cambridge Rd., Brom. 78 CH50
Cambridge Rd., Cars. 95 BU57
Cambridge Rd., E.Mol. 84 BE52
Cambridge Rd., Hmptn. 74 BE50
Cambridge Rd., Har. 45 BF32
Cambridge Rd., Houns. 64 BE45
Cambridge Rd., Ilf. 49 CN33
Cambridge Rd., Kings.T. 85 BL51
Cambridge Rd., Mitch. 86 BV52
Cambridge Rd., N.Mal. 85 BN52
Cambridge Rd., Rich. 65 BM43
Cambridge Rd., St.Alb. 9 BJ14
Cambridge Rd., Saw. 6 CQ5
Cambridge Rd., Sid. 78 CN49
Cambridge Rd., Sthl. 54 BE40
Cambridge Rd., Tedd. 74 BJ49
Cambridge Rd., Twick. 74 BK46
Cambridge Rd., Uxb. 53 AX36
Cambridge Rd., Walt. 83 BC53
Cambridge Rd., Wat. 27 BD24
Cambridge Rd. N. W4 65 BM42
Cambridge Rd. S. W4 65 BM42
Cambridge Row SE18 68 CL42
Cambridge Sq. W2 1 C8
Cambridge Sq. W2 56 BU39
Cambridge St. SW1 3 K10
Cambridge St. SW1 66 BV42
Cambridge Ter. N9 39 CA26
Bury St. W.
Cambridge Ter. N13 38 BY28
Cambridge Ter. NW1 1 J3
Cambridge Ter. NW1 56 BV38
Outer Circle
Cambridge Ter., Berk. 7 AR13
Cambridge Ter. Ms. NW1 1 K3
Cambridge Ter. Ms. NW1 56 BV38
Albany St.
Cambus Clo., Hayes 54 BE39
Kilpatrick Way
Cambus Rd. E16 58 CH39
Camdale Rd. SE18 68 CN43
Camden Ave., Felt. 74 BD48
Camden Ave., Hayes 54 BD40
Camden Clo., Chis. 88 CM51
Camden Clo., Grays 71 DG42
Camden Gdns., Sutt. 95 BS56
Camden Gdns., Th.Hth. 86 BY52
Camden Gro., Chis. 78 CL50
Camden High St. NW1 56 BV36
Camden Hill Rd. SE19 77 CA50
Camden La. N7 47 BW35
Rowstock Gdns.
Camden Lock NW1 56 BV36
Camden Ms. NW1 56 BW36
Murray St.
Camden Pk. Rd. NW1 56 BW36
Camden Pk. Rd., Chis. 78 CK50
Camden Pas. N1 56 BY37
Camden Rd. E11 49 CH32
Camden Rd. E17 48 CD32
Camden Rd. N7 56 BW36
Camden Rd. NW1 56 BW36
Camden Rd., Bex. 79 CQ47
Camden Rd., Cars. 95 BU56
Camden Rd., Grays 71 DC41
Camden Rd., Sev. 107 CU64
Camden Rd., Sutt. 95 BS56
Camden Row SE3 68 CG44
Camden Sq. NW1 56 BW36
Camden Sq. SE15 67 CA44
Chepstow Way
Camden St. NW1 56 BW36
Camden Ter. NW1 56 BW36
North Vill.
Camden Wk. N1 56 BY37
Camden Way, Chis. 78 CK50
Camden Way, Th.Hth. 86 BY52
Camdenhurst St. E14 57 CD39
Camel Rd. E16 58 CJ40
Camelford Wk. W11 55 BQ40
Lancaster Rd.
Camellia Clo., Rom. 42 CW30
Columbine Way
Camellia Pl., Twick. 74 BF47
Camellia St. SW8 66 BX43
Camelot Clo. SE28 68 CM41
Camelot Clo. SW19 75 BR49
Camelot Clo., West. 106 CJ61
Camelot St. SE15 67 CB43
Camera Pl. SW10 66 BT43
Cameron Clo. N18 39 CB28
Cameron Clo. N20 38 BT27
Cameron Clo., Bex. 79 CS48
Cameron Clo., Brwd. 42 DB28
Cameron Dr., Wal.Cr. 21 CC20
Cameron Pl. E1 57 CB39
Cameron Rd. SE6 77 CD48
Cameron Rd., Brom. 88 CH53
Cameron Rd., Chesh. 16 AO18
Cameron Rd., Croy. 86 BY53
Cameron Rd., Ilf. 49 CN33
Cameron Sq., Mitch. 86 BU51
Silbury Ave.
Camerton Clo. E8 57 CA36
Laurel St.
Camfield, Welw.G.C. 5 BR10
Camilla Clo., Lthd. 111 BF66
Pine Dean
Camilla Clo., Sun. 73 BB50
Camilla Dr., Dor. 111 BJ68
Camilla Rd. SE16 67 CB42
Camille Clo. SE25 87 CB52
Camlan Rd., Brom. 78 CG49
Camlet St. E2 2 P4
Camlet St. E2 57 CA38
Camlet Way, Barn. 29 BS23
Camlet Way, St.Alb. 9 BF13
Camley St. NW1 56 BW37
Camm Ave., Wind. 61 AM45
Camm Gdns., Kings.T. 85 BL51
Church Rd.
Camm Gdns., T.Ditt. 84 BH54
Camomile Ave., Mitch. 86 BU51
Camomile St. EC3 2 M8
Camomile St. EC3 57 CA39
Camp End Rd., Wey. 92 BA59
Camp Rd. SW19 75 BP49
Camp Rd., Cat. 105 CD64
Camp Rd., Ger.Cr. 43 AR32
Camp Rd., St.Alb. 9 BH13
Camp Vw. SW19 75 BP49
Camp Vw. Rd., St.Alb. 9 BJ14
Campana Rd. SW6 66 BS44
Campbell Ave., Ilf. 49 CL31
Campbell Ave., Wok. 100 AS64
Campbell Clo. SW16 76 BW49
Campbell Clo., Hav. 41 CT29
Havering Rd.
Campbell Clo., Rom. 41 C
Campbell Clo., Ruis. 44 B
Campbell Clo., Twick. 74 B
Campbell Ct. NW9 46 B
Campbell Cft., Edg. 37 B
Campbell Est. SE18 68 C
Campbell Rd. E3 57 C
Campbell Rd. E6 58 C
Campbell Rd. E15 49 C
Trevelyan Rd.
Campbell Rd. E17 48 C
Campbell Rd. N17 39 C
Campbell Rd. W7 54 B
Campbell Rd., Cat. 105 B
Campbell Rd., Croy. 86 B
Campbell Rd., E.Mol. 84 B
Campbell Rd., Grav. 81 D
Campbell Rd., Twick. 74 B
Campbell Rd., Wey. 92 A
Campdale Rd. N7 47 B
Campden Cres., Dag. 50 C
Campden Cres., Wem. 45 B
Campden Gro. W8 66 B
Campden Hill W8 66 B
Campden Hill Gdns. W8 56 B
Campden Hill Pl. W11 55 B
Campden Hill Rd. W8 56 B
Campden Hill Sq. W8 55 B
Campden Ho. Clo. W8 66 B
Hornton St.
Campden Rd., S.Croy. 96 C
Campden Rd., Uxb. 44 A
Campden St. W8 56 B
Campen Clo. SW19 75 B
Queensmere Rd.
Camperdown St. E1 2
Camperdown St. E1 57 C
Leman St.
Campfield Rd. SE9 78 C
Campfield Rd., St.Alb. 9 B
Camphill Ct., Wey. 92 AV
Camphill Rd., Wey. 92 AV
Campion Clo. E6 58 C
Campion Clo., Croy. 96 C
Campion Clo., Grav. 81 D
Henley Deane
Campion Clo., Har. 46 B
Campion Clo. (Denham), Uxb. 44 AV
Campion Clo. (Hillingdon), Uxb. 53 A
Campion Clo., Wat. 17 B
Campion Ct., Grays 71 D
Churchill Rd.
Campion Ho., Islw. 64 B
Campion Pl. SE28 59 C
Campion Rd. SW15 65 B
Campion Rd., Hem.H. 7 A
Campion Rd., Islw. 64 B
Campion Ter. NW2 46 B
Campions, Epp. 23 C
Campions, Loug. 31 C
Campions, The, Borwd. 28 B
Campions Clo., Borwd. 28 B
Cample La., S.Ock. 60 D
Camplin Rd., Har. 46 B
Camplin St. SE14 67 C
Campsbourne, The N8 47 B
Rectory Gdns.
Campsbourne Rd. N8 47 B
Campsey Gdns., Dag. 59 C
Campsey Rd., Dag. 59 C
Campsfield Rd. N8 47 B
Campshill Pl. SE13 77 C
Campshill Rd.
Campshill Rd. SE13 77 C
Campus, The, Welw.G.C. 5 B
Campus Rd. E17 48 C
Camrose Ave., Edg. 37 B
Camrose Ave., Erith 69 C
Camrose Ave., Felt. 73 B
Camrose Clo., Croy. 87 C
Camrose Clo., Mord. 86 B
Camrose St. SE2 69 C
Canada Ave. N18 39 B
Canada Ave., Red. 121 B
Canada Cres. W3 55 B
Canada Dr., Red. 121 B
Canada Fm. Rd., S.Dnth. 90 D
Canada Gdns. SE13 77 C
Canada La., Brox. 21 C
Canada Rd. W3 55 B
Canada Rd., Cob. 93 B
Canada Rd., Slou. 62 A
Canada Rd., Wey. 92 A
Canada St. SE16 67 C
Canada Way W12 55 B
Canadas, The, Brox. 21 C
Rochford Clo.
Canadian Ave. SE6 77 C
Canal App. SE8 67 C
Canal Clo. E1 57 C
Canal Gro. SE15 67 C
Canal Head SE15 67 C
Peckham High St.
Canal Rd. E3 57 C
Canal Rd., Grav. 81 D
Canal St. SE5 67 B
Canal Wk. N1 57 B
Canal Wk. SE26 77 C
Venner Rd.
Canal Way NW1 56 B
Baynes St.
Canal Wf., Slou. 62 A
Canary Wf. E14 57 C
Canberra Clo. NW4 46 B
Aerodrome Rd.
Canberra Clo., Dag. 59 C
Canberra Clo., Horn. 51 C
Canberra Clo., St.Alb. 9 B
Canberra Cres., Dag. 59 C
Canberra Rd. E6 58 C
Barking Rd.
Canberra Rd. SE7 68 C

nberra Rd., Bexh. 69 CP43
nberra Rd., Houns. 63 AZ45
nberra Sq., Til. 71 DG44
nbury Ave., Kings.T. 85 BL51
nbury Ms. SE26 77 CB48
Wells Pk. Rd.
nbury Pk. Rd., Kings.T. 85 BL51
nbury Pas., Kings.T. 84 BK51
nbury Path, Orp. 89 CO52
nbury Pl., Kings.T. 85 BL51
Canbury Pas.
ncell Rd. SW9 66 BY44
ndahar Rd. SW11 66 BU44
nder Way, S.Ock. 60 DA40
ndlefield Clo., Hem.H. 8 AZ15
ndlefield Rd., Hem.H. 8 AZ15
ndlefield Wk., Hem.H. 8 AZ15
ndler St. N15 48 BZ32
ndover Clo., West Dr. 63 AX43
ndover Rd., Horn. 50 CU33
ndover St. W1 1 L7
ndover St. W1 56 BW39
oley St.
ndy Cft., Lthd. 111 BF66
ndy St. E3 57 CD37
neland Ct., Wal.Abb. 22 CG20
nes La., Harl. 14 CQ14
ney Ms. NW2 46 BQ34
Claremont Rd.
nfield Dr., Ruis. 44 BC35
nfield Gdns. NW6 56 BS36
nfield Pl. NW6 56 BT36
nfield Rd., Rain. 59 CT37
nfield Rd., Wdf.Grn. 40 CK29
nford Ave., Nthlt. 54 BE37
nford Clo., Enf. 29 BY23
nford Dr., Wey. 83 AW55
nford Gdns., N.Mal. 85 BN53
nford Rd. SW11 66 BV45
ngels Clo., Hem.H. 7 AV14
nham Rd. SE25 87 CA52
nham Rd. W3 65 BO41
nmore Gdns. SW16 76 BW50
nn Hall Rd. E11 49 CG35
nn Hatch, Tad. 103 BR62
nning Cres. N22 38 BX30
nning Cross SE5 67 BZ44
Grove La.
nning Pas. W8 66 BT41
Victoria Rd.
nning Pl. W8 66 BT41
nning Pl. Ms. W8 66 BT41
Canning Pl.
nning Rd. E15 58 CG37
nning Rd. E17 48 CD31
nning Rd. N5 47 BY34
nning Rd., Croy. 87 CA55
nning Rd., Har. 45 BH31
nnington Rd., Dag. 59 CP36
nnizaro Rd. SW19 75 BQ50
nnon Clo. SW20 85 BQ52
nnon Clo., Hmptn. 74 BF50
nnon Cres., Wok. 91 AP59
nnon Dr. E14 57 CE40
nnon Gro., Lthd. 102 BH64
nnon Hill N14 38 BX27
nnon Hill NW6 47 BS35
nnon Hill La. SW20 85 BQ53
nnon Hill Ms. N14 38 BX27
Cannon Hill
nnon La. NW3 47 BT34
nnon La., Pnr. 45 BE32
nnon Mill Ave., Chesh. 16 AP20
nnon Pl. NW3 47 BT34
nnon Pl. SE7 68 CK42
Maryon Rd.
nnon Rd. N14 38 BX27
nnon Rd., Bexh. 69 CQ44
nnon Rd., Wat. 27 BD25
nnon Row SW1 66 BX41
Bridge St.
nnon Side, Lthd. 102 BH64
nnon St. EC4 2 H9
nnon St. EC4 57 BZ39
nnon St., St.Alb. 9 BG13
nnon St. Rd. E1 57 CB39
nnon Way, E.Mol. 84 BF52
nnon Way, Lthd. 102 BH64
nnonbury Ave., Pnr. 45 BD32
nnons Cor., Edg. 37 BL28
nnons La., Ong. 15 CZ14
nnons Mead, Brwd. 24 DA20
nnons Meadow, Welw. 5 BU6
non Ave., Rom. 50 CP32
non Beck Rd. SE16 67 CC41
non Ct., Edg. 37 BL29
Stonegrove
non Hill, Maid. 61 AG41
non Hill Clo., Maid. 61 AH42
non Hill Way, Maid. 61 AG42
non Mohan Clo. N14 29 BV25
non Pk. Est., Stan. 36 BK28
non Rd., Brom. 88 CJ52
non Row SW1 3 Q5
non St. N1 57 BZ37
Prebend St.
nonbie Rd. SE23 77 CC47
nonbury Ave. N1 56 BY36
Canonbury Rd.
nonbury Gro. N1 57 BZ36
nonbury La. N1 56 BY36
nonbury Pk. N. N1 57 BZ36
nonbury Pk. S. N1 57 BZ36
nonbury Pl. N1 56 BY36
nonbury Rd. N1 56 BY36
nonbury Rd., Enf. 30 CA23
nonbury Sq. N1 56 BY36
nonbury St. N1 57 BZ36
nonbury Vill. N1 56 BY36
nons Brook, Harl. 13 CL11
nons Clo. N2 47 BT33
nons Clo., Edg. 37 BL29
nons Clo., Rad. 27 BJ21
Canons Clo., Reig. 120 BR70
Albert Rd. N.
Canons Dr., Edg. 37 BL29
Canons Gate, Harl. 6 CL10
Canons Hatch, Tad. 103 BR62
Canons Hill, Couls. 104 BY62
Canons La., Tad. 103 BR62
Canons Pk. Par., Edg. 37 BL29
Canons Wk., Croy. 87 CC55
Canonsleigh Rd., Dag. 59 CO36
Canopus Way, Nthwd. 35 BC28
Canopus Way, Stai. 73 AY47
Canrobert St. E2 57 CB37
Cantelowes Rd. NW1 56 BW36
Canterbury Ave., Ilf. 49 CK33
Canterbury Ave., Sid. 79 CO48
Canterbury Ave., Slou. 52 AO38
Canterbury Ave., Upmin. 51 CZ34
Canterbury Clo. E6 58 CK39
Canterbury Clo., Amer. 25 AP23
Canterbury Clo., Beck. 87 CE51
Canterbury Clo., Beck. 87 CE51
The Ave.
Canterbury Clo., Chig. 40 CN27
Canterbury Clo., Dart. 80 CX47
Canterbury Clo., Grnf. 54 BF39
Canterbury Clo., Nthwd. 35 BB29
Canterbury Cres. SW9 66 BY45
Canterbury Gro. SE27 76 BY49
Canterbury Par., S.Ock. 60 DB38
Canterbury Pl. SE17 4 G9
Canterbury Rd. E10 48 CF33
Canterbury Rd. NW6 56 BS37
Canterbury Rd., Borwd. 28 BM23
Canterbury Rd., Croy. 86 BX54
Canterbury Rd., Felt. 74 BE48
Canterbury Rd., Grav. 81 DH48
Canterbury Rd., Guil. 118 AP69
Canterbury Rd., Har. 45 BF32
Canterbury Rd., Mord. 86 BS54
Canterbury Rd., Wat. 26 BC23
Canterbury Ter. NW6 56 BS37
Canterbury Way, Brwd. 42 DA28
Canterbury Way, Grays 70 CZ42
Canterbury Way, Rick. 26 BA24
Cantley Gdns. SE19 87 CA51
Cantley Gdns., Ilf. 49 CM32
Cantley Rd. W7 64 BJ41
Canton St. E14 57 CE39
Cantrell Rd. E3 57 CD38
Cantwell Rd. SE18 68 CL43
Canute Gdns. SE16 67 CC42
Canvey St. SE1 4 G2
Canvey St. SE1 57 BZ40
Zoar St.
Cape Clo., Bark. 58 CL36
Cape Rd. N17 48 CB31
Cape Rd., St.Alb. 9 BJ13
Cape Yd. E1 57 CB40
Asher Way
Capel Ave., Wall. 95 BX56
Capel Clo. N20 38 BT27
Capel Clo., Brom. 88 CK54
Capel Ct. EC2 2 L9
Capel Ct. EC2 57 BZ39
Threadneedle St.
Capel Ct. SE20 87 CC51
Melvin Rd.
Capel Gdns., Ilf. 49 CN35
Capel Gdns., Pnr. 45 BE31
Capel Pl., Dart. 80 CV49
Capel Rd. E7 49 CH35
Capel Rd. E12 49 CJ35
Capel Rd., Barn. 29 BU25
Capel Rd., Enf. 30 CB21
Capel Rd., Wat. 27 BD25
Capel Vere Wk., Wat. 26 BB23
Capell Ave., Rick. 25 AU25
Capell Rd., Rick. 25 AU25
Capell Way, Rick. 25 AU25
Capella Rd., Nthwd. 35 BB28
Capeners Clo. SW1 3 G5
Capeners Clo. SW1 66 BV41
Kinnerton St.
Capern Rd. SW18 76 BT47
Cargill Rd.
Capital Ho. SE6 77 CE46
Capital Interchange Way, Brent. 65 BM42
Capital Pl., Croy. 95 BX56
Capitol Way NW9 46 BN31
Capland St. NW8 1 B4
Capland St. NW8 56 BT38
Caple Rd. NW10 55 BO37
Capon Clo., Brwd. 42 DA26
Caponfield, Welw.G.C. 5 BS9
Capper St. WC1 1 M5
Caprea Clo., Hayes 54 BD39
Triandra Way
Capri Rd., Croy. 87 CA54
Capstan Clo., Rom. 50 CO32
Capstan Ct., Dart. 70 CY45
Capstan Ride, Enf. 29 BY23
Capstan Rd. SE8 67 CD42
Capstan Sq. E14 67 CF41
Capstan Way SE16 57 CD40
Capstone Rd., Brom. 78 CG49
Captain Cook Clo., Ch.St.G. 34 AQ28
Captains Wk., Berk. 7 AR13
Capthorne Ave., Har. 45 BE33
Capthorne Ct., Har. 45 BE33
Capuchin Clo., Stan. 36 BJ29
Temple Mead Clo.
Capworth St. E10 48 CE33
Caractacus Grn., Wat. 26 BB25
Caradoc Clo. W2 56 BS39
Ledbury Rd.
Caradoc St. SE10 68 CG42
Caradon Clo. E11 49 CG34
Brockway Clo.
Caradon Clo., Wok. 100 AQ62
Caradon Way N15 48 BZ31
Caravan La., Rick. 35 AY26
Caravel Clo., Grays 71 DC41
Caravel Ms. SE8 67 CE43
Watergate St.
Caravelle Gdns., Nthlt. 54 BD38
Javelin Way
Caraway Pl., Guil. 109 AQ68
Carberry Rd. SE19 77 CA50
Carbery Ave. W3 65 BL41
Carbis Clo. E4 39 CF26
Carbis Rd. E14 57 CD39
Carbone Hill, Cuffley 20 BW17
Carburton St. W1 1 K6
Carburton St. W1 56 BV38
Carbury Clo., Horn. 60 CV36
Cardale St. E14 67 CF41
Plevna St.
Carden Rd. SE15 67 CB45
Cardiff Rd. W7 64 BJ41
Cardiff Rd., Enf. 30 CB24
Cardiff Rd., Wat. 26 BC25
Cardiff St. SE18 68 CN43
Cardigan Clo., Wok. 100 AP62
Cardigan Gdns., Ilf. 50 CO34
Cardigan Rd. E3 57 CD37
Cardigan Rd. SW13 65 BP44
Cardigan Rd. SW19 76 BT50
Cardigan Rd., Rich. 75 BL46
Cardigan St. SE11 4 D10
Cardigan St. SE11 66 BY42
Cardigan Wk. N1 57 BZ36
Ashby Gro.
Cardinal Ave., Borwd. 28 BM24
Cardinal Ave., Kings.T. 75 BL49
Cardinal Ave., Mord. 85 BR53
Cardinal Bourne St. SE1 4 L7
Cardinal Bourne St. SE1 67 BZ41
Cardinal Clo., Chsnt. 21 CA16
Adamsfield
Cardinal Clo., Chis. 78 CM50
Cardinal Clo., Mord. 85 BR53
Cardinal Clo., Wor.Pk. 94 BP56
Cardinal Ct., Borwd. 28 BM24
Cardinal Ave.
Cardinal Cres., N.Mal. 85 BN51
Cardinal Dr., Ilf. 40 CM29
Cardinal Dr., Walt. 84 BD54
Cardinal Gro., St.Alb. 9 BF14
Cardinal Pl. SW15 65 BQ45
Cardinal Rd., Felt. 73 BC47
Cardinal Rd., Ruis. 45 BD33
Cardinal Way, Har. 45 BH31
Wolseley Rd.
Cardinal Way, Rain. 60 CV37
Cardinals Wk., Hmptn. 74 BG50
Cardinals Wk., Sun. 73 BB50
Seymour Way
Cardinals Way N19 47 BW33
Cardingham, Wok. 100 AQ62
Cardington Sq., Houns. 64 BD45
Cardington St. NW1 1 M2
Cardington St. NW1 56 BW38
Cardozo Rd. N7 47 BX35
Cardrew Ave. N12 38 BT28
Cardrew Clo. N12 38 BT28
Cardross St. W6 65 BP41
Cardwell Rd. N7 47 BX35
Cardwell Rd. SE18 68 CL42
Cardwell Ter. N7 47 BX35
Cardwell Rd.
Cardy Rd., Hem.H. 8 AW13
Carew Clo. N7 47 BX34
Carew Clo., Couls. 105 BZ63
Carew Rd. N17 39 CB30
Carew Rd. W13 64 BK41
Carew Rd., Ash. 73 BA50
Carew Rd., Mitch. 86 BV51
Carew Rd., Nthwd. 35 BB29
Carew Rd., Th.Hth. 86 BY52
Carew Rd., Wall. 95 BW57
Carew St. SE5 67 BZ44
Carey Clo., Wind. 61 AN45
Carey Gdns. SW8 66 BW44
Stewarts Rd.
Carey La. EC2 2 H8
Carey La. EC2 57 BZ39
Gutter La.
Carey Pl. SW1 3 N9
Carey Pl., Wat. 27 BD24
Clifford St.
Carey Rd., Dag. 50 CQ35
Carey St. WC2 2 C9
Carey St. WC2 56 BX39
Careys Cft., Berk. 7 AQ12
Carfax Pl. SW4 66 BW45
Holwood Pl.
Carfax Rd., Hayes 63 BB42
Carfax Rd., Horn. 50 CT35
Carfree Clo. N1 56 BY36
Bewdley St.
Cargill Rd. SW18 76 BS47
Cargreen Pl. SE25 87 CA52
Cargreen Rd.
Cargreen Rd. SE25 87 CA52
Carholme Rd. SE23 77 CD47
Carisbrook Ave., Wat. 27 BD23
Carisbrook Clo., Stan. 36 BK30
Carisbrooke Ave., Bex. 79 CP47
Carisbrooke Clo., Enf. 30 CA23
Carisbrooke Clo., Horn. 51 CX34
Carisbrooke Ct., Slou. 52 AP40
Carisbrooke Gdns. SE15 67 CA43
Commercial Way
Carisbrooke Rd. E17 48 CD31
Carisbrooke Rd., Brwd. 33 DA25
Carisbrooke Rd., Brom. 88 CJ52
Carisbrooke Rd., Mitch. 86 BW52
Carisbrooke Rd., St.Alb. 18 BF16
Carkers La. NW5 47 BV35
Carleton Ave., Wall. 95 BW57
Carleton Clo., Esher 84 BG54
Carleton Pl., Hort.K. 80 CY52
Carleton Rd. N7 47 BW35
Carleton Rd., Chsnt. 21 CC17
Carlile Clo. E3 57 CD37
Carlingford Gdns., Mitch. 76 BU50
Carlingford Rd. N15 47 BY31
Carlingford Rd. NW3 47 BT35
Carlingford Rd., Mord. 85 BQ53
Carlisle Ave. EC3 2 P9
Carlisle Ave. EC3 57 CA39
Carlisle Ave. W3 55 BO39
Carlisle Ave., St.Alb. 9 BG12
Carlisle Clo., Kings.T. 85 BM51
Carlisle Gdns., Har. 45 BK33
Carlisle Gdns., Ilf. 49 CK32
Carlisle La. SE1 4 C7
Carlisle La. SE1 66 BX41
Carlisle Ms. NW8 1 B6
Carlisle Ms., Kings.T. 85 BM51
Carlisle Clo.
Carlisle Pl. N11 38 BV28
Carlisle Pl. SW1 3 L7
Carlisle Pl. SW1 66 BW41
Carlisle Rd. E10 48 CE33
Carlisle Rd. N4 47 BY33
Scarborough Rd.
Carlisle Rd. NW6 55 BR37
Carlisle Rd. NW9 46 BN31
Carlisle Rd., Dart. 80 CX46
Carlisle Rd., Hmptn. 74 BF50
Carlisle Rd., Rom. 50 CU32
Carlisle Rd., Slou. 52 AO40
Carlisle Rd., Sutt. 94 BR57
Carlisle St. W1 1 N9
Carlisle St. W1 56 BW39
Soho Sq.
Carlisle Wk. E8 57 CA36
Kirkland Wk.
Carlisle Way SW17 76 BV49
Carlos Pl. W1 1 H10
Carlos Pl. W1 56 BV40
Carlow St. NW1 56 BW37
Carlton Ave. N14 29 BW25
Carlton Ave., Felt. 74 BD46
Carlton Ave., Green. 80 CZ46
Carlton Ave., Har. 45 BJ32
Carlton Ave., Hayes 63 BB42
Carlton Ave., S.Croy. 96 BZ57
Carlton Ave. E., Wem. 45 BK34
Carlton Ave. W., Wem. 45 BJ34
Carlton Clo. NW3 47 BS34
Carlton Clo., Borwd. 28 BN24
Carlton Clo., Chess. 94 BL57
Carlton Clo., Edg. 37 BM28
Carlton Clo., Grays 71 DF41
Carlton Clo., Upmin. 51 CX34
Carlton Clo., Wok. 91 AT60
Carlton Ct. W9 56 BS37
Carlton Cres., Sutt. 94 BR56
Carlton Dr. SW15 75 BQ46
Carlton Dr., Ilf. 49 CM31
Carlton Gdns. SW1 3 N3
Carlton Gdns. SW1 56 BW40
Carlton Gdns. W5 54 BK39
Carlton Grn., Red. 121 BU69
Carlton Gro. SE15 67 CB44
Carlton Hill NW8 56 BS37
Carlton Ho. Ter. SW1 3 N3
Carlton Ho. Ter. SW1 56 BW40
Carlton Par., Orp. 89 CO54
Carlton Pk., Sev. 108 CV64
Carlton Pk. Ave. SW20 85 BQ51
Carlton Pl., Nthwd. 35 AZ28
Carlton Rd. E11 49 CG33
Carlton Rd. E12 49 CJ35
Carlton Rd. E17 39 CD30
Carlton Rd. N4 47 BY33
Carlton Rd. N11 38 BV28
Carlton Rd. SW14 65 BN45
Carlton Rd. W4 65 BN41
Carlton Rd. W5 54 BK40
Carlton Rd., Dart. 80 CX47
Carlton Rd., Erith 69 CR43
Carlton Rd., Grays 71 DF41
Carlton Rd., N.Mal. 85 BO51
Carlton Rd., Red. 121 BT69
Carlton Rd., Rom. 50 CT32
Carlton Rd., Sid. 78 CN49
Carlton Rd., Slou. 52 AQ40
Carlton Rd., S.Croy. 96 BZ57
Carlton Rd., Sun. 73 BB50
Carlton Rd., Walt. 83 BC54
Carlton Rd., Well. 69 CO45
Carlton Rd., Wok. 91 AT60
Carlton Sq. E1 57 CC38
Carlton St. SW1 3 N1
Carlton St. SW1 56 BW40
Regent St.
Carlton Ter. E7 58 CJ36
Carlton Ter. E11 49 CH32
Carlton Ter. N18 39 BZ27
Carlton Ter. SE26 77 CC48
Carlton Twr. Pl. SW1 3 F6
Carlton Vale NW6 56 BS38
Carlwell St. SW17 76 BU49
Carlyle Ave., Brom. 88 CJ52
Carlyle Ave., Sthl. 54 BE40
Carlyle Clo. N2 47 BT32
Carlyle Clo. NW10 55 BN37
Carlyle Clo., E.Mol. 84 BG51
Carlyle Gdns., Sthl. 54 BE40
Carlyle Pl. SW15 65 BQ45
Lacy Rd.
Carlyle Rd. E12 49 CK35
Carlyle Rd. SE28 59 CO40
Carlyle Rd. W5 64 BK42
Carlyle Rd., Croy. 87 CB55
Carlyle Rd., Stai. 73 AW50
Carlyle Sq. SW3 66 BT42
Carlyon Ave., Har. 45 BE35
Carlyon Clo., Wem. 55 BL37
Carlyon Clo., Wok. 100 AS62
Carlyon Rd., Hayes 54 BD39
Carlyon Rd., Wem. 55 BL37
Carmalt Gdns. SW15 65 BQ45
Carmalt Gdns., Walt. 93 BD56
Carmarthen Rd., Slou. 52 AP40
Carmelite Clo., Har. 36 BG30
Carmelite Rd., Har. 36 BG30
Carmelite St. EC4 2 E10
Carmelite St. EC4 56 BY40
Carmelite Wk., Har. 36 BG30
Carmelite Way, Har. 36 BG30
Carment St. E14 57 CE39
Carmichael Clo. SW11 66 BT45
Darien Rd.
Carmichael Clo., Ruis. 44 BC35
Carmichael Ms. SW18 76 BT46
Heathfield Rd.
Carmichael Rd. SE25 87 CA53
Carminia Rd. SW17 76 BV48
Carnaby Rd., Brox. 12 CD13
Carnaby St. W1 1 L9
Carnaby St. W1 56 BW39
Carnac St. SE27 77 BZ48
Carnach Grn., S.Ock. 60 DA40
Carnanton Rd. E17 39 CF30
Carnarvon Ave., Enf. 30 CA24
Carnarvon Dr., Hayes 63 BA42
Carnarvon Rd. E10 48 CF32
Carnarvon Rd. E15 58 CG36
Carnarvon Rd. E18 40 CG30
Carnarvon Rd., Barn. 28 BR24
Carnation St. SE2 69 CO42
Carnbrook Rd. SE3 68 CJ45
Carnecke Gdns. SE9 78 CK46
Carnegie Clo., Surb. 85 BL55
Fullers Ave.
Carnegie Pl. SW19 75 BQ48
Carnegie Rd., St.Alb. 9 BG11
Carnegie St. N1 56 BX37
Carnforth Clo., Epsom 94 BM57
Carnforth Gdns., Horn. 50 CU35
Carnforth Rd. SW16 76 BW50
Carnoustie Dr. N1 56 BX36
Carnwath Rd. SW6 66 BS45
Caro La., Hem.H. 8 AZ14
Carol St. NW1 56 BW37
Carolina Rd., Th.Hth. 86 BY51
Caroline Clo. N10 38 BV30
Caroline Clo. SW16 76 BX48
Caroline Clo., Croy. 96 CA56
Brownlow Rd.
Caroline Clo., Islw. 64 BH43
Osterley Rd.
Caroline Clo., West Dr. 63 AX41
Old Fm. Rd.
Caroline Ct., Ashf. 73 AZ50
Caroline Ct., Stan. 36 BJ29
The Chase
Caroline Gdns. E2 2 N2
Caroline Gdns. N1 57 CA38
Kingsland Rd.
Caroline Gdns. SE15 67 CB43
Caroline Pl. SW11 66 BV44
Caroline Pl. W2 56 BS40
Caroline Pl., Hayes 63 BB43
Nobel Dr.
Caroline Pl., Wat. 27 BE25
Caroline Pl. Ms. W2 56 BS40
Orme La.
Caroline Rd. SW19 75 BR50
Caroline St. E1 57 CC39
Caroline Ter. SW1 3 G9
Caroline Ter. SW1 66 BV42
Carolyn Clo., Wok. 100 AP63
Carolyn Dr., Orp. 89 CO55
Caroon Dr., Rick. 26 AW21
Carpenders Ave., Wat. 36 BE27
Carpenter Clo., Epsom 94 BO58
West St.
Carpenter Gdns. N21 38 BY27
Carpenter Path, Brwd. 122 DE25
Carpenter St. W1 3 J1
Carpenters Arms La., Epp. 23 CO16
Carpenters Clo., Epsom 94 BO58
West St.
Carpenters Ct., Twick. 74 BH48
Hampton Rd.
Carpenters Pl. SW4 66 BW45
Carpenters Rd. E15 57 CE36
Carpenters Rd., Enf. 30 CC21
Carpenters Way, Pot.B. 20 BT20
Carpenters Wd. Dr., Rick. 25 AT24
Carr Rd. E17 39 CD30
Carr Rd., Nthlt. 54 BF36
Carr St. E14 57 CD39
Carrara Wk. SW9 66 BY45
Somerleyton Dev.
Carriage Rd., The SW7 66 BT41
Carriageway, The, Sev. 107 CP65
Carrick Clo., Islw. 64 BJ45
Byfield Rd.
Carrick Dr., Ilf. 40 CM30
Carrick Dr., Sev. 107 CU65
Carrick Gdns. N17 39 BZ30
Flexmere Rd.
Carrick Gate, Esher 84 BG55
Carrick Ms. SE8 67 CE43
Watergate St.
Carrill Way, Belv. 69 CP42
Coptefield Dr.
Carrington Ave., Borwd. 28 BM25
Carrington Ave., Houns. 74 BF46
Carrington Clo., Barn. 28 BP25
Chartridge Clo.
Carrington Clo., Borwd. 28 BN25
Carrington Clo., Croy. 87 CD54
Carrington Gdns. E7 49 CH35
Woodford Rd.
Carrington Ho. SE8 67 CE44
Carrington Rd., Dart. 80 CW46
Carrington Rd., Rich. 65 BM45
Carrington Rd., Slou. 52 AP40
Carrington Sq., Har. 36 BG29
Carrington St. W1 3 J3
Carrington St. W1 56 BV40
Carrol Clo. NW5 47 BV35
Carroll Ave., Guil. 118 AT70
Carroll Clo. E15 49 CG35
Ash Rd.

Name	Pg	Ref
Carroll Hill, Loug.	31	CK24
Carron Clo. E14	57	CE39
Carronade Pl. SE28	68	CM41
Carroun Rd. SW8	66	BX43
Carrow Rd., Dag.	59	CO36
Carrow Rd., Walt.	84	BD55
Carroway La., Grnf.	54	BG37
Cowgate Rd.		
Carrs La. N21	30	BZ25
Carshalton Gro., Sutt.	95	BT56
Carshalton Pk. Rd., Cars.	95	BU57
Carshalton Pl., Cars.	95	BV56
Carshalton Rd., Bans.	95	BU60
Carshalton Rd., Mitch.	86	BV52
Carshalton Rd., Sutt.	95	BT56
Carshalton Rd. W., Sutt.	95	BS56
Carsington Gdns., Dart.	80	CV48
Carslake Rd. SW15	75	BQ46
Carson Rd. E16	58	CH38
Carson Rd. SE21	77	BZ47
Carson Rd., Barn.	29	BU24
Carstairs Rd. E5	77	CF48
Carston Clo. SE12	78	CG46
Carswell Clo., Brwd.	122	DE25
Carswell Clo., Ilf.	49	CJ31
Carswell Rd. SE6	77	CF47
Cart Path, Wat.	18	BD20
Cartel Clo., Grays	70	CY42
Gabion Ave.		
Carter Clo., Rom.	41	CR29
Carter Clo., Wall.	95	BW57
Carter Clo., Wind.	61	AN44
Carter Ct. EC4	56	BY39
Carter La.		
Carter Dr., Rom.	41	CR29
Carter La. EC4	2	G9
Carter La. EC4	56	BY39
Carter Pl. SE17	67	BZ42
Carter Rd. E13	58	CH37
Carter Rd. SW19	76	BT50
Carter St. SE17	67	BZ43
Carteret St. SW1	3	N5
Carteret St. SW1	66	BW41
Carteret Way SE8	67	CD42
Carterhatch La., Enf.	30	CA22
Carterhatch Rd., Enf.	30	CC23
Carters Clo., Loug.	31	CL25
Carters Clo., Wor.Pk.	85	BQ55
Carters Hill, Sev.	117	CX67
Carters Hill Clo. SE9	78	CJ47
Carters La. SE23	77	CD48
Carters La., Epp.	13	CL15
Carters La., Wok.	100	AU63
Carters Mead, Harl.	14	CP12
Carters Rd., Epsom	103	BO61
Carters Row, Grav.	81	DF48
Carters Row, Red.	121	BU71
Carters Yd. SW18	76	BS46
Wandsworth High St.		
Cartersfield Rd., Wal.Abb.	30	CF21
Carthew Rd. W6	65	BP41
Carthew Vill. W6	65	BP41
Carthouse La., Wok.	91	AP60
Carthusian St. EC1	2	H6
Carting La. WC2	4	A1
Carting La. WC2	56	BX40
Cartmel Clo. N17	39	CB29
Cartmel Clo., Red.	121	BU70
Cartmel Rd., Bexh.	69	CR44
Cartmell Gdns., Mord.	84	BT53
Carton St. W1	1	F8
Carton St. W1	56	BU39
Cartwright Gdns. WC1	1	Q3
Cartwright Gdns. WC1	56	BX38
Cartwright Rd., Dag.	59	CQ36
Cartwright St. E1	4	Q1
Cartwright St. E1	57	CA40
Carve Ley, Welw.G.C.	5	BS8
Carver Rd. SE24	77	BZ46
Carville Cres., Brent.	65	BL42
Cary Rd. E11	49	CG35
Carysfort Rd. N8	47	BW32
Carysfort Rd. N16	48	BZ34
Cascade Ave. N10	47	BW31
Cascade Clo., Buck.H.	40	CJ27
Cascade Rd.		
Cascade Clo., Orp.	88	CP52
Chalk Pit Ave.		
Cascade Rd., Buck.H.	40	CJ27
Cascades, Croy.	96	CG58
Caselden Clo., Wey.	92	AW56
Casella Rd. SE14	67	CC43
Casewick Rd. SE27	76	BY49
Casimir Rd. E5	48	CC34
Casino Ave. SE24	77	BZ46
Caslon Pl. E1	57	CB38
Cudworth St.		
Caspian St. SE5	67	BZ43
Caspian Wk. E16	58	CJ39
King George Ave.		
Cassandra Gate, Wal.Cr.	21	CD17
Casselden Rd. NW10	55	BN36
Cassidy Rd. SW6	66	BS43
Cassilda Rd. SE2	69	CO42
Cassilis Rd., Twick.	74	BJ46
Cassio Rd., Wat.	26	BC24
Cassiobridge Rd., Wat.	26	BB25
Cassiobury Ave., Felt.	73	BB46
Cassiobury Dr., Wat.	26	BB22
Cassiobury Pk. Ave., Wat.	26	BB24
Cassiobury Rd. E17	48	CC32
Cassis Ct., Loug.	31	CM24
Burton Dr.		
Cassland Rd. E9	57	CC36
Cassland Rd., Th.Hth.	87	BZ52
Casslee Rd. SE6	77	CD47
Cassocks Sq., Shep.	83	BA54
Russell Rd.		
Casson St. E1	57	CB39
Casstine Clo., Swan.	89	CT51
Castalia Sq. E14	67	CF41
Plevna St.		
Castalia St. E14	67	CF41
Castano Ct., Wat.	17	BB19
Castell Rd., Loug.	31	CM23
Castellain Rd. W9	56	BS38
Castellan Ave., Rom.	50	CU31
Castellane Clo., Stan.	36	BH29
Daventer Dr.		
Castello Ave. SW15	75	BQ46
Castelnau SW13	65	BP44
Castelnau Est. SW13	65	BP43
Castelnau Pl. SW13	65	BP43
Castelnau Row SW13	65	BP43
Lonsdale Rd.		
Casterbridge Rd. SE3	68	CH45
Castile Rd. SE18	68	CL42
Castillon Rd. SE6	78	CG48
Castlands Rd. SE6	77	CD48
Castle Ave. E4	39	CF29
Castle Ave., Epsom	94	BP58
Castle Ave., Rain.	59	CT36
Castle Ave., Slou.	61	AQ43
Castle Ave., West Dr.	53	AY40
Castle Baynard St. EC4	2	G10
Castle Clo. E9	48	CD35
Swinnerton St.		
Castle Clo. SW19	75	BQ48
Castle Clo., Brom.	88	CG52
Castle Clo., Bush.	27	BF25
Castle Clo., Hodd.	12	CF10
Castle Clo., Red.	114	BZ70
Castle Clo., Reig.	121	BS72
Castle Clo., Sun.	73	BB50
Millfarm Ave.		
Castle Ct. EC3	2	L9
Castle Ct. EC3	57	BZ39
Birchin La.		
Castle Dr., Ilf.	49	CK32
Castle Dr., Reig.	121	BS72
Castle Dr., Sev.	108	CW62
Castle Fm. Rd., Sev.	98	CT58
Castle Gdns., Dor.	120	BL70
Castle Gate Way, Berk.	7	AR12
Castle Grn. Rd., Wok.	91	AP59
Castle Grn., Wey.	83	BB55
Castle Hill, Berk.	7	AR12
Castle Hill, Guil.	118	AR71
Castle Hill, Hartley	90	DB53
Castle Hill, Wind.	61	AO44
Castle Hill Ave., Berk.	7	AR12
Castle Hill Ave., Croy.	96	CE58
Castle Hill Clo., Berk.	7	AR12
Castle Hill Rd., Egh.	72	AQ48
Castle La. SW1	3	L6
Castle La. SW1	66	BW41
Castle Mead, Hem.H.	8	AW14
Castle Ms. N12	38	BT28
Castle Ms. NW1	56	BV36
Castle Rd.		
Castle Pl. W4	65	BO42
Windmill Rd.		
Castle Rd. N12	38	BT28
Castle Rd. NW1	56	BV36
Castle Rd., Couls.	104	BU63
Castle Rd., Dag.	59	CO37
Castle Rd., Enf.	30	CD23
Castle Rd., Epsom	103	BM61
Castle Rd., Grays	71	DC43
Castle Rd., Hodd.	12	CE10
Castle Rd., Islw.	64	BH44
Castle Rd., Islw.	64	BH44
Castle Rd., Nthlt.	54	BF36
Castle Rd., St.Alb.	9	BJ13
Castle Rd., Sev.	98	CU57
Castle Rd., Sthl.	64	BE41
Warwick Rd.		
Castle Rd., Swans.	81	DC46
Castle Rd., Wey.	83	BB55
Castle Rd., Wok.	91	AS60
Castle Sq., Guil.	118	AR71
Castle Sq., Red.	114	BZ70
Castle St. E6	58	CJ37
Castle St., Berk.	7	AR13
Castle St., Green.	80	DA46
Castle St., Guil.	118	AR71
Castle St., Kings.T.	85	BL51
Castle St., Ong.	24	CX18
Castle St., Red.	121	BY70
Castle St., Slou.	62	AP41
Albert St.		
Castle St., Swans.	81	DC46
Castle Vw., Epsom	94	BM60
Castle Vw. Rd., Slou.	62	AR42
Castle Vw. Rd., Wey.	92	AZ56
Castle Wk., Reig.	121	BS70
High St.		
Castle Wk., Sun.	83	BD52
Elizabeth Gdns.		
Castle Way SW19	75	BQ48
Castle Way, Epsom	94	BP58
Castle Way, Felt.	74	BD49
Castle Yd. SE1	4	G2
Castle Yd., Rich.	74	BK46
Hill St.		
Castlebar Hill W5	54	BJ39
Castlebar Ms. W5	54	BJ39
Castlebar Pk. W5	54	BK39
Castlebar Rd. W5	54	BK39
Castlecombe Dr. SW19	75	BQ47
Castlecombe Rd. SE9	78	CK49
Castledine Rd. SE20	77	CB50
Castlefields, Grav.	81	DF51
Castlefields Rd., Reig.	121	BS70
Castleford Ave. SE9	78	CL47
Castlegate, Rich.	65	BL45
Castlehaven Rd. NW1	56	BV36
Castleleigh Ct., Enf.	30	BZ25
Castlemaine Ave., Epsom	94	BP58
Castlemaine Ave., S.Croy.	96	CA56
Castlereagh St. W1	1	D8
Castlereagh St. W1	56	BU39
Castleton Ave., Bexh.	69	CS44
Castleton Ave., Wem.	46	BL35
Castleton Clo., Bans.	104	BS61
Castleton Dr., Bans.	95	BS60
Castleton Rd. E17	39	CF30
Castleton Rd. SE9	78	CJ49
Castleton Rd., Ilf.	50	CO33
Castleton Rd., Mitch.	86	BW52
Castleton Rd., Ruis.	45	BD33
Castletown Rd. W14	65	BR42
Castleview Gdns., Ilf.	49	CK32
Castlewood Dr. SE9	68	CK44
Castlewood Rd. N15	48	CB32
Castlewood Rd. N16	48	CB32
Castlewood Rd., Barn.	29	BT24
Castor La. E14	57	CE40
Cat Hill, Barn.	29	BU25
Caterham Ave., Ilf.	40	CK30
Caterham By-pass, Cat.	105	CB65
Caterham Ct., Wal.Abb.	22	CG20
Caterham Dr., Couls.	104	BY62
Caterham Rd. SE13	67	CF45
Catesby St. SE17	4	L9
Catesby St. SE17	67	BZ42
Catford Bdy. SE6	77	CE47
Catford Hill SE6	77	CD48
Catford Rd. SE6	77	CE47
Cathall Rd. E11	48	CF34
Catham Clo., St.Alb.	9	BJ14
Cathay St. SE16	67	CB41
Cathay Wk., Nthlt.	54	BF37
Leander Rd.		
Cathcart Dr., Orp.	88	CN54
Cathcart Hill N19	47	BW34
Cathcart Rd. SW10	66	BS43
Cathcart St. NW5	47	BV35
Cathedral Pl. EC4	2	H9
Cathedral Pl. EC4	56	BY39
Newgate St.		
Cathedral St. SE1	4	K2
Cathedral St. SE1	57	BZ40
Cathedral Vw., Guil.	118	AP70
Catherall Rd. N5	48	BZ34
Catherine Clo., Brwd.	33	DA25
Catherine Clo., Hem.H.	8	AZ11
Catherine Clo., West Dr.	63	AX41
Catherine Clo., Wey.	92	AY60
Catherine Ct. N14	29	BW25
Catherine Dr., Sun.	73	BB50
Catherine Gdns., Houns.	64	BG45
Catherine Griffiths Ct. EC1	2	E4
Catherine Ho. SE10	67	CE44
Catherine Pl. SW1	3	L6
Catherine Pl. SW1	66	BW41
Catherine Rd., Enf.	30	CD21
Catherine Rd., Rom.	50	CU32
Catherine Rd., Surb.	84	BK53
Catherine St. WC2	2	B10
Catherine St. WC2	56	BX40
Catherine St., St.Alb.	9	BG13
Catherine Wheel All. E1	2	N7
Catherine Wheel Rd., Brent.	64	BK43
Catherine Wheel Yd. SW1	3	L3
Cathles Rd. SW12	76	BV46
Cathnor Rd. W12	65	BP41
Catisfield Rd., Enf.	30	CD22
Catkin Clo., Hem.H.	8	AW13
Catlin Cres., Shep.	83	BA53
Catlin St. SE16	67	CB42
Catlin St., Hem.H.	8	AW15
Catling Clo. SE23	77	CC48
Dacres Rd.		
Catlins La., Pnr.	44	BC31
Cato Rd. SW4	66	BW45
Cato St. W1	1	D7
Cato St. W1	56	BU39
Caton St. SE15	67	CA44
Cator Clo., Croy.	96	CF59
Cator Cres., Croy.	96	CF59
Cator La., Beck.	87	CD51
Cator Rd. SE26	77	CC50
Cator Rd., Cars.	95	BU56
Cator St. SE15	67	CA43
Catsey La., Bush.	36	BG26
Catsey Wds., Bush.	36	BG26
Catterick Way, Borwd.	28	BL23
Cattistock Rd. SE9	78	CK49
Cattle Mkt., Sev.	107	CU65
Cattlegate Hill, Pot.B.	20	BW19
Cattlegate Rd., Enf.	20	BX20
Cattlegate Rd., Pot.B.	20	BW19
Catton St. WC1	2	B7
Catton St. WC1	56	BX39
Cattsdell, Hem.H.	8	AY12
Caulfield Rd. E6	58	CK37
Caulfield Rd. SE15	67	CB44
Causeway, The N2	47	BT31
Causeway, The SW18	76	BS46
Causeway, The SW19	75	BQ49
Causeway, The, Cars.	86	BV55
Causeway, The, Chess.	94	BL56
Causeway, The, Egh.	72	AU49
Causeway, The, Esher	93	BH57
Causeway, The, Felt.	63	BC45
Causeway, The, Pot.B.	20	BT19
Causeway, The, St.Alb.	8	BF14
Causeway, The, Stai.	72	AU49
Causeway, The, Sutt.	95	BT58
Causeway, The, Tedd.	74	BH50
Causeway Clo., Pot.B.	20	BT19
Causeway, The, Wok.	100	AP62
Bingham Dr.		
Causey Pl., Wok.	100	AS62
Causey Way		
Causeyware Rd. N9	39	CB26
Causton Rd. N6	47	BV33
Causton St. SW1	3	P9
Causton St. SW1	66	BW42
Cautley Ave. SW4	76	BW46
Cavalier Clo., Rom.	50	CP31
Cavalry Cres., Houns.	64	BD45
Cavalry Cres., Wind.	61	AN45
Cavalry Gdns. SW15	75	BR46
Upper Richmond Rd.		
Cavan Dr., St.Alb.	9	BG11
Cavaye Pl. SW10	66	BT42
Fulham Rd.		
Cave Rd. E13	58	CH37
Cave Rd., Rich.	74	BK49
Cave St. N1	56	BX37
Cavell Cres., Dart.	70	CX45
Cavell Dr., Enf.	29	BY23
Cavell Rd. N17	39	BZ29
Cavell Rd., Chsnt.	21	CA17
Cavell St. E1	57	CB39
Cavendish Ave. NW8	1	A1
Cavendish Ave. NW8	56	BT38
Cavendish Ave. W13	54	BJ39
Cavendish Ave., Erith	69	CR43
Cavendish Ave., Har.	45	BG35
Cavendish Ave., Horn.	59	CU36
Cavendish Ave., N.Mal.	85	BP53
Cavendish Ave., Ruis.	44	BC35
Cavendish Ave., Sev.	107	CU64
Cavendish Ave., Sid.	79	CO47
Cavendish Ave., Well.	68	CN45
Cavendish Ave., Wdf.Grn.	40	CH30
Cavendish Clo. N18	39	CB28
Cavendish Clo. NW6	55	BR36
Cavendish Clo. NW8	1	B2
Cavendish Clo. NW8	56	BT38
Cavendish Clo. SW15	75	BR46
Cavendish Clo., Amer.	25	AQ23
Cavendish Clo., Hayes	53	BB39
Cavendish Clo., Sun.	73	BB50
Cavendish Ct. EC3	2	N8
Cavendish Ct. EC3	57	CA39
Houndsditch		
Cavendish Ct., Rick.	26	BA25
Mayfare		
Cavendish Ct., Sun.	73	BB50
Cavendish Rd.		
Cavendish Cres., Borwd.	28	BM24
Cavendish Cres., Horn.	59	CU36
Cavendish Dr. E11	48	CF33
Cavendish Dr., Edg.	37	BL29
Cavendish Dr., Esher	93	BH56
Cavendish Gdns., Bark.	49	CN35
Cavendish Gdns., Ilf.	49	CL33
Cavendish Gdns., Red.	121	BV70
Cavendish Gdns., Rom.	50	CQ32
Cavendish Ms. N. W1	1	K6
Cavendish Ms. N. W1	56	BV39
Hallam St.		
Cavendish Ms. S. W1	1	K7
Cavendish Ms. S. W1	56	BV39
Hallam St.		
Cavendish Pl. W1	1	K8
Cavendish Pl. W1	56	BV39
Cavendish Rd. E4	39	CF29
Cavendish Rd. N4	47	BY32
Cavendish Rd. N18	39	CB28
Cavendish Rd. NW6	55	BR36
Cavendish Rd. SW12	76	BV46
Cavendish Rd. SW19	76	BT50
Cavendish Rd. W4	65	BN44
Cavendish Rd., Barn.	28	BQ24
Cavendish Rd., Chesh.	16	AO19
Cavendish Rd., Croy.	86	BY54
Cavendish Rd., N.Mal.	85	BQ53
Cavendish Rd., Red.	121	BV70
Cavendish Rd., St.Alb.	9	BH13
Cavendish Rd., Sun.	73	BB50
Cavendish Rd., Sutt.	95	BT57
Cavendish Rd., Wey.	92	AZ58
Cavendish Rd., Wok.	100	AR63
Cavendish Sq. W1	1	K8
Cavendish Sq. W1	56	BV39
Cavendish Sq., Long.	90	DC52
Bramblefield Clo.		
Cavendish St. N1	2	K1
Cavendish St. N1	57	BZ37
Cavendish Way, Hat.	10	BO12
Cavendish Way, W.Wick.	87	CE54
Cavenham Clo., Wok.	100	AS63
Brooklyn Rd.		
Cavenham Gdns., Horn.	51	CV32
Cavenham Gdns., Ilf.	49	CM34
Caverleigh Way, Wor.Pk.	85	BP54
Caversham Ave. N13	38	BY27
Caversham Ave., Sutt.	85	BR55
Caversham Rd. N15	48	BZ31
Caversham Rd. NW5	56	BW36
Caversham Rd., Kings.T.	85	BL51
Caverswall St. W12	55	BQ39
Caveside Clo., Chis.	88	CL51
Cavills Wk., Rom.	41	CQ27
Cawcott Dr., Wind.	61	AM44
Cawdor Ave., S.Ock.	60	DA40
Cawdor Cres. W7	64	BJ41
Cawnpore St. SE19	77	CA49
Cawsey Way, Wok.	100	AS62
Caxton Ave., Wey.	92	AW57
Caxton Dr., Uxb.	53	AX37
Caxton Gdns., Guil.	118	AQ70
Weston Rd.		
Caxton Gro. E3	57	CE38
Caxton La., Oxt.	115	CK69
The Butts		
Caxton Rd. N22	38	BX30
Caxton Rd. SW19	76	BT49
Caxton Rd. W12	55	BQ40
Caxton Rd., Sthl.	64	BD41
Caxton St. SW1	3	M6
Caxton St. W1	66	BW41
Caxton St. N. E16	58	CG39
Caxton St. S. E16	58	CG40
Caxton Way, Wat.	26	B…
Caygill Clo., Brom.	88	C…
Cayley Clo., Wall.	95	B…
Cayton Pl. EC1	2	
Cayton Pl. EC1	57	B…
Cayton St.		
Cayton Rd., Grnf.	54	B…
Cayton St. EC1	2	
Cayton St. EC1	57	B…
Cazenove Rd. E17	39	C…
Cazenove Rd. N16	48	C…
CC30 Waterhall Clo. E17		
Cearn Way, Couls.	104	B…
Cecil Ave., Bark.	58	C…
Cecil Ave., Enf.	30	C…
Cecil Ave., Grays	71	C…
Cecil Ave., Horn.	51	C…
Cecil Ave., Wem.	46	B…
Cecil Clo., Ashf.	73	B…
Cecil Clo., Chess.	93	B…
Cecil Ct. WC2	3	
Cecil Ct. WC2	56	B…
St. Martins La.		
Cecil Ct., Barn.	28	B…
Cecil Ct., Croy.	87	C…
Cecil Cres., Hat.	10	B…
Cecil Pk., Pnr.	45	B…
Cecil Pl., Mitch.	86	B…
Cecil Rd. E11	49	C…
Cecil Rd. E13	58	C…
Cecil Rd. E17	39	C…
Cecil Rd. N10	38	B…
Cecil Rd. N14	38	B…
Cecil Rd. NW9	46	B…
Cecil Rd. NW10	55	B…
Cecil Rd. SW19	76	B…
Cecil Rd. W3	55	B…
Cecil Rd., Ashf.	73	B…
Cecil Rd., Chsnt.	21	C…
Cecil Rd., Croy.	86	B…
Cecil Rd., Enf.	30	C…
Cecil Rd., Grav.	81	D…
Cecil Rd., Har.	45	B…
Cecil Rd., Hodd.	12	C…
Cecil Rd., Houns.	64	B…
Cecil Rd., Ilf.	49	C…
Cecil Rd., Iver	52	A…
Cecil Rd., Pot.B.	19	B…
Cecil Rd., Reig.	121	B…
London Rd.		
Cecil Rd., Rom.	50	C…
Cecil Rd., St.Alb.	9	B…
Cecil Rd., Sutt.	94	B…
Cecil St., Wat.	26	B…
Cecil Way, Brom.	88	C…
Cecile Pk. N8	47	B…
Cecilia Clo. N2	47	B…
Cecilia Rd. E8	48	C…
Cedar Ave., Barn.	38	B…
Cedar Ave., Cob.	102	B…
Cedar Ave., Enf.	30	C…
Cedar Ave., Hayes	53	B…
Cedar Ave., Rom.	50	C…
Cedar Ave., Ruis.	45	B…
Cedar Ave., Sid.	78	C…
Cedar Ave., Twick.	74	B…
Cedar Ave., Upmin.	51	C…
Cedar Ave., Wal.Cr.	21	C…
Cedar Ave., West Dr.	53	A…
Cedar Clo. SE21	77	B…
Cedar Clo. SW15	75	B…
Cedar Clo., Borwd.	28	B…
Cedar Clo., Brwd.	122	D…
Cedar Clo., Brom.	88	C…
Cedar Clo., Buck.H.	40	C…
Cedar Clo., Cars.	95	B…
Cedar Clo., Dor.	119	B…
Cedar Clo., E.Mol.	84	B…
Cedar Clo., Epsom	94	B…
Cedar Clo., Esher	93	B…
Cedar Clo., Pot.B.	20	B…
Cedar Clo., Reig.	121	B…
Cedar Clo., Rom.	50	C…
Cedar Clo., Saw.	6	C…
Cedar Clo., Stai.	83	A…
Cedar Clo., Swan.	89	C…
Cedar Clo., Warl.	105	C…
Cedar Copse, Brom.	88	C…
Cedar Ct. N10	38	B…
Cedar Ct. SE9	78	C…
Cedar Ct. SW19	75	B…
Cedar Ct., Egh.	72	A…
Cedar Ct., Epp.	23	C…
Cedar Ct., St.Alb.	9	B…
Cedarwood Dr.		
Cedars, Brom.	88	C…
Cedar Dr. N2	47	B…
The Causeway		
Cedar Dr., Lthd.	102	B…
Cedar Dr., Pnr.	36	B…
Cedar Dr., S.at H.	90	C…
Cedar Dr., Uxb.	53	A…
Cedar Gdns., Sutt.	95	B…
Cedar Gdns., Upmin.	51	C…
Cedar Grn., Hodd.	12	C…
Cedar Gro. W5	65	B…
Cedar Gro., Amer.	25	A…
Cedar Gro., Bex.	79	C…
Cedar Gro., Sthl.	54	B…
Cedar Gro., Wey.	92	B…
Cedar Heights, Rich.	75	B…
Cedar Hill, Epsom	103	B…
Cedar Lawn Ave., Barn.	28	B…
Cedar Mt. SE9	78	C…
Cedar Pk. Gdns., Rom.	50	C…
Cedar Pk. Rd., Enf.	30	B…
Cedar Ri. N14	38	B…
Cedar Rd. N17	39	C…
Cedar Rd. NW2	46	B…
Cedar Rd., Berk.	7	A…
Cedar Rd., Brwd.	122	D…
Cedar Rd., Brom.	88	C…
Cedar Rd., Cob.	92	B…

Ced–Cha

ar Rd., Croy. 87 BZ55
ar Rd., Dart. 80 CV47
ar Rd., E.Mol. 84 BG52
ar Rd., Enf. 29 BY22
ar Rd., Erith 69 CU44
ar Rd., Felt. 73 BA47
ar Rd., Grav. 81 DH49
ar Rd., Grays 71 DG41
ar Rd., Hat. 10 BP13
ar Rd., Horn. 51 CV34
ar Rd., Houns. 64 BD44
ar Rd., Rom. 50 CS31
ar Rd., Sutt. 95 BT57
ar Rd., Tedd. 74 BJ49
ar Rd., Wat. 27 BD25
ar Rd., Wey. 92 AZ56
ar Rd., Wok. 100 AQ63
ar Ter., Rich. 65 BL45
ar Tree Gro. SE27 76 BY49
ar Wk., Hem.H. 8 AX14
ar Wk., Ken. 105 BZ61
ar Wk., Reig. 113 BU68
ar Wk., Tad. 103 BR63
ar Way NW1 56 BW36
ar Way, Berk. 7 AR13
ar Way, Guil. 118 AR69
ar Way, Slou. 62 AS42
ar Way, Sun. 73 BB50
ar Wd. Dr., Wat. 26 BC21
arcroft Rd., Chess. 94 BL56
arhurst Dr. SE9 78 CJ46
arne Rd. SW6 66 BS43
lham Rd.
ars, Bans. 95 BU60
ars, The, Buck.H. 40 CH26
ars, The, Guil. 118 AT69
ars, The, Har. 36 BG29
ars, The, Reig. 121 BT70
ars, The, Tedd. 74 BH50
ars, The, Wey. 92 AY59
ars Ave. E17 48 CE32
ars Ave., Mitch. 86 BV52
ars Ave., Rick. 35 AX26
ars Clo. NW4 46 BQ31
ars Clo., Ger.Cr. 34 AS28
ars Ct. N9 39 CA27
ars Est., Mitch. 86 BV52
ars Ms. SW4 66 BV45
ars Pl. SE7 68 CJ42
harlton Ch. La.
ars Rd. E15 58 CG36
ars Rd. N9 39 CB27
ars Rd. N21 38 BY27
ars Rd. SW4 66 BV45
ars Rd. SW13 65 BO44
ars Rd. W4 65 BN43
ars Rd., Beck. 87 CD51
ars Rd., Croy. 86 BX55
ars Rd., Kings.T. 84 BK51
ars Rd., Mord. 86 BS52
ars Wk., Wal.Abb. 21 CF20
arville Gdns. SW16 76 BX50
arwood Dr., St.Alb. 9 BK13
ra Ct. N16 48 CB33
ric Ave., Rom. 50 CT31
ric Rd. SE9 78 CM48
don Clo., Enf. 30 CD24
ndine Clo. E14 57 CE39
ndine Clo., S.Ock. 60 DB38
ndine Dr. SE28 59 CO40
ndine Rd., Walt. 93 BE56
ndine Way E15 58 CG38
emorial Ave.
edon Clo., Grays 71 DC41
estial Gdns. SE13 67 CF45
a Cres., Ash. 73 AX50
a Ho. N1 57 CA37
urcell St.
a Rd. N19 47 BW35
Barnes Clo., St.Alb. 9 BJ14
Barnes La., St.Alb. 9 BJ14
Fm. Ave., Wind. 72 AQ46
ic Ave., Brom. 88 CG52
ic Rd., Wey. 92 AY60
ic St. E14 57 CF39
nent Block Cotts., 71 DE42
rays
netery Hill, Hem.H. 8 AX14
netery La. SE7 68 CK43
netery La., Shep. 83 AZ54
netery La., Wal.Abb. 22 CG16
netery Rd. E7 49 CG35
netery Rd. N17 39 CA29
netery Rd. SE2 69 CO43
nmaes Ct. Rd., 8 AX13
em.H.
nmaes Mead, Hem.H. 8 AX13
acle Clo. NW3 47 BS34
taur St. SE1 4 C6
taur St. SE1 66 BX41
taury Ct., Grays 71 DE43
hurchill Rd.
tenary Rd., Enf. 30 CD24
tral Ave. E11 48 CF34
tral Ave. N2 38 BT30
tral Ave. N9 39 CA27
tral Ave. SW11 66 BU43
tral Ave. W3 55 BN40
tral Ave., E.Mol. 84 BE52
tral Ave., Enf. 30 CB23
tral Ave., Grav. 81 DG48
tral Ave., Grays 70 CZ42
tral Ave., Harl. 13 CM11
tral Ave., Hayes 53 BB40
tral Ave., Houns. 64 BG45
tral Ave., Pnr. 45 BE32
tral Ave., S.Ock. 70 CY41
tral Ave., Til. 71 DG44
tral Ave., Wal.Cr. 21 CD20
tral Ave., Well. 68 CN45
tral Circ. NW4 46 BP32
tral Dr., Horn. 51 CW34
tral Dr., St.Alb. 9 BK13
tral Dr., Welw.G.C. 5 BR7
Central Gdns., Mord. 86 BS53
Central Hill SE19 77 BZ49
Central Hill Est. SE19 77 CA50
Central Mkts. EC1 2 G7
Central Mkts. EC1 56 BY39
Central Par., Croy. 96 CF58
Central Pk. Ave., Dag. 50 CR34
Central Pk. Rd. E6 58 CJ37
Central Pl. SE25 87 CB52
Central Rd., Dart. 80 CW46
Central Rd., Harl. 6 CO9
Central Rd., Mord. 86 BW53
Central Rd., Wem. 45 BJ35
Central Rd., Wor.Pk. 85 BP54
Central Sq. NW11 47 BS32
Central Sq., E.Mol. 84 BE52
Central Sq., Wem. 55 BL36
Station Gro.
Central St. EC1 2 H2
Central St. EC1 57 BZ38
Central Way SE28 59 CO40
Central Way, Cars. 95 BU57
Central Way, Felt. 73 BC46
Central Way, Oxt. 114 CF67
Centre, The, Felt. 73 BC47
Centre Ave., Epp. 22 CN19
Centre Clo., Epp. 22 CN19
Centre Common Rd., 78 CL50
Chis.
Centre Dr., Epp. 22 CN19
Centre Rd. E7 49 CH34
Centre Rd. E11 49 CH34
Centre Rd. SE18 68 CL42
Centre Rd., Dag. 59 CR37
Centre Rd., New A.G. 90 DC55
Ash Rd.
Centre St. E2 57 CB37
Centre Way E17 39 CF29
Centre Way N9 39 CC27
Centre Way, Wal.Abb. 30 CF21
Centreway, Ilf. 49 CM34
Centurion Clo. N7 56 BX36
Centurion Way, Erith 69 CQ41
Centurion Way, Grays 70 CW42
Century Rd. E17 48 CD31
Century Rd., Egh. 72 AU49
Century Rd., Hodd. 12 CE11
Cephas Ave. E1 57 CC38
Cephas St. E1 57 CC38
Ceres Rd. SE18 68 CN42
Cerise Rd. SE15 67 CB44
Cerne Clo., Hayes 54 BD40
Cerne Rd., Grav. 81 DJ49
Cerne Rd., Mord. 86 BT53
Cerney Ms. W2 1 A10
Cerney Ms. W2 56 BT40
Gloucester Ter.
Cerotus Pl., Cher. 83 AV54
Barker Rd.
Cervantes Ct., Nthwd. 35 BB29
Cervia Way, Grav. 81 DJ48
Cestreham Cres., Chesh. 16 AO18
Ceylon Rd. W14 65 BQ41
Chace Ave., Pot.B. 20 BT19
Chadacre Ave., Ilf. 49 CK31
Chadacre Rd., Epsom 94 BP57
Chadbourn St. E14 57 CE39
Chadd Dr., Brom. 88 CK52
Chadd Grn. E13 58 CH37
Chadfields, Til. 71 DG43
Chadhurst Clo., Dor. 119 BK73
Wildcroft Dr.
Chadville Gdns., Rom. 50 CP32
Chadway, Dag. 50 CP33
Chadwell Ave., Chsnt. 21 CC17
Chadwell Ave., Rom. 50 CO33
Chadwell By-pass, 71 DF42
Grays
Chadwell Heath La., Rom. 50 CO31
Chadwell Hill, Grays 71 DG42
Chadwell Rd., Grays 71 DE42
Chadwell St. EC1 2 E2
Chadwell St. EC1 56 BY38
Chadwick Ave. E4 39 CF27
Chadwick Clo., Grav. 81 DF48
Chadwick Clo., Tedd. 74 BJ50
Chadwick Rd. E11 49 CG33
Chadwick Rd. NW10 55 BO36
Chadwick Rd. SE15 67 CA44
Chadwick Rd., Ilf. 49 CL34
Chadwick St. SW1 3 N7
Chadwick St. SW1 66 BW41
Chadwick Way SE28 59 CP40
Chadwin Rd. E13 58 CH39
Chadworth Way, Esher 93 BG56
Chaffers Mead, Ash. 103 BL61
Chaffinch Ave., Croy. 87 CC53
Chaffinch Clo., Croy. 87 CC53
Chaffinch La., Wat. 35 BB26
Chaffinch Rd., Beck. 87 CD51
Chaffinches Grn., Hem.H. 8 AZ15
Market Oak La.
Chafford Gdns., Brwd. 123 DE32
Chafford Wk., Rain. 60 CV37
Chafford Way, Grays 71 DD40
Chafford Way, Rom. 50 CP31
Chagford St. NW1 1 E5
Chagford St. NW1 56 BU38
Chailey Ave., Enf. 30 CA23
Chailey Clo., Houns. 64 BD44
Springwell Rd.
Chailey Pl., Walt. 93 BE56
Chailey St. E5 48 CC34
Chairmans Ave., Uxb. 43 AV32
Chalbury Wk. N1 56 BX37
Eckford St.
Chalcombe Rd. SE2 69 CO41
Chalcot Clo., Sutt. 95 BS57
Chalcot Cres. NW1 56 BU37
Chalcot Gdns. NW3 56 BU36
Chalcot Gdns., Surb. 84 BK54
Chalcot Rd. NW1 56 BV36
Chalcot Sq. NW1 56 BV36
Chalcots Est. NW3 56 BT36
Chalcroft Rd. SE13 78 CG46
Chaldon Common Rd., 105 BZ65
Cat.
Chaldon Rd. SW6 65 BR43
Chaldon Rd., Cat. 105 BZ65
Chaldon Way, Couls. 104 BX62
Chale Rd. SW2 76 BX46
Chale Wk., Sutt. 95 BS58
Hulverston Clo.
Chalet Clo., Berk. 7 AP13
Chalet Clo., Bex. 79 CS49
Chalfont Ave., Amer. 25 AR23
Chalfont Ave., Wem. 55 BM36
Chalfont Clo., Hem.H. 8 AZ11
Chalfont Grn. N9 39 CA27
Chalfont La., Ger.Cr. 34 AU29
Chalfont La., Rick. 25 AT25
Chalfont Pl., St.Alb. 9 BH13
Upper Lattimore Rd.
Chalfont Rd. N7 56 BY36
Sheringham Rd.
Chalfont Rd. N9 39 CA27
Chalfont Rd. SE25 87 CA52
Chalfont Rd., Beac. 34 AO28
Chalfont Rd., Ger.Cr. 34 AT27
Chalfont Rd., Hayes 63 BC41
Chalfont Sta. Rd., Amer. 25 AR23
Chalfont Wk., Pnr. 36 BD30
Willows Clo.
Chalfont Way W13 64 BJ41
Chalford Clo., E.Mol. 84 BF52
Chalford Rd. SE21 77 BZ49
Chalford Wk., Wdf.Grn. 40 CJ30
Chalforde Gdns., Rom. 50 CU31
Chalgrove Ave., Mord. 86 BS53
Chalgrove Cres., Ilf. 40 CK30
Chalgrove Gdns. N3 46 BR31
Chalgrove Rd. E9 57 CC36
Morning La.
Chalgrove Rd. N17 39 CB30
Chalgrove Rd., Sutt. 95 BT57
Chalice Clo., Wall. 95 BW57
Chalice Way SW2 76 BX47
Chalk Dale, Welw.G.C. 5 BS7
Chalk Fm. Rd. NW1 56 BV36
Chalk Hill, St.Alb. 9 BF15
Chalk Hill, Wat. 27 BD25
Chalk Hill Rd. W6 65 BQ42
Shortlands Ms.
Chalk La., Ash. 103 BL63
Chalk La., Barn. 29 BU24
Chalk La., Epsom 103 BN61
Chalk La., Harl. 6 CR9
Chalk La., Lthd. 110 BB68
Chalk Paddock, Epsom 103 BN61
Chalk La.
Chalk Pit Ave., Orp. 89 CP52
Chalk Pit Rd., Bans. 104 BS62
Chalk Pit Rd., Epsom 103 BN63
Chalk Pit Way, Sutt. 95 BT56
Chalk Rd. E13 58 CH39
Chalk Rd., Grav. 81 DK47
Chalkdell Flds., St.Alb. 9 BJ11
Chalkenden Clo. SE20 77 CB50
Castledine Rd.
Chalkey Hill, Sev. 97 CM60
Chalkhill Rd., Wem. 46 BM34
Chalklands, The, Wem. 46 BN34
Chalkpit La., Dor. 119 BJ71
Chalkpit La. (Bookman), 111 BE67
Lthd.
Chalkpit La., Oxt. 114 CF66
Chalkpit Ter., Dor. 119 BJ70
Chalkpit Wd., Oxt. 114 CF67
Chalks Ave., Saw. 6 CP5
Chalkstone Clo., Well. 69 CO44
Chalkwell Pk. Ave., Enf. 30 CA24
Chalky Bank, Grav. 81 DG49
Chalky La., Chess. 93 BK58
Challacombe Clo., 122 DD26
Brwd.
Challenge Clo., Grav. 81 DJ49
Challenge Rd., Ashf. 73 BA48
Challice Way SW2 76 BX47
Challin St. SE20 87 CC51
Challis Rd., Brent. 64 BK42
Challock Clo., West. 106 CJ61
Challoner Clo. N2 38 BT30
Challoner Cres. W14 65 BR42
Challoner St.
Challoner St. W14 65 BR42
Challoners Clo., E.Mol. 84 BG52
Chalmers Ct., Rick. 35 AY26
Chalmers La., Reig. 113 BT67
Chalmers Rd., Ashf. 73 AZ49
Chalmers Rd., Bans. 104 BT61
Chalmers Rd. E., Ashf. 73 BA49
Chalmers Ter. N16 48 CA34
Victorian Rd.
Chalmers Wk. SE17 66 BY43
Hillingdon St.
Chalmers Way, Felt. 73 BC46
Chalsey Rd. SE4 67 CD45
Chalton Dr. N2 47 BT32
Chalton St. NW1 56 BW37
Chalvey Gdns., Slou. 62 AP41
Chalvey Rd. E.
Chalvey Gro., Slou. 61 AN41
Chalvey Pk., Slou. 62 AP41
Chalvey Rd. E., Slou. 62 AP41
Chalvey Rd. W., Slou. 61 AO41
Chamber St. E1 2 Q10
Chamber St. E1 57 CA40
Chamberlain Clo. SE28 68 CM41
Garrick Dr.
Chamberlain Cotts. SE5 67 BZ44
Camberwell Gro.
Chamberlain Cres., 87 CE54
W.Wick.
Chamberlain La., Pnr. 44 BC31
Chamberlain Pl. E17 48 CD31
Higham St.
Chamberlain Rd. N2 38 BT30
Chamberlain Rd. N9 39 CB27
Chamberlain Rd. W13 64 BJ41
Midhurst Rd.
Chamberlain Sq. N1 56 BY36
Lofting Rd.
Chamberlain St. NW1 56 BU36
Regents Pk. Rd.
Chamberlain Wk., Felt. 74 BD49
Swift Rd.
Chamberlain Way, Pnr. 44 BC31
Chamberlain Way, Surb. 85 BL54
Chamberlayne Rd. NW10 55 BQ37
Chambers Gdns. N2 38 BT30
Chambers La. NW10 55 BP36
Chambers Rd. N7 47 BX35
Chambers St. SE16 67 CB41
Chambersbury La., 8 AZ15
Hem.H.
Chambersbury La., 17 AZ16
Hem.H.
Chambord St. E2 2 Q3
Chambord St. E2 57 CA38
Champion Cres. SE26 77 CD49
Champion Gro. SE5 67 CA45
Champion Hill SE5 67 BZ45
Champion Pk. SE5 67 BZ44
Champion Rd. SE26 77 CD49
Champion Rd., Upmin. 51 CX34
Champions Grn., Hodd. 12 CE10
Bridle Way S.
Champions Way, Hodd. 12 CE10
Lyttons Way
Champness Clo. SE27 77 BZ49
Rommany Rd.
Champneys Clo., Sutt. 94 BR57
Chance Clo., Grays 71 DC41
Chance St. E1 2 P4
Chance St. E1 57 CA38
Chance St. E2 57 CA38
Chancel Clo., Sev. 99 CZ57
Chancel St. SE1 4 F3
Chancel St. SE1 56 BY40
Dolben St.
Chancellor Ct., Guil. 118 AO71
Chancellor Gdns., S.Croy. 95 BY58
Chancellor Gro. SE21 77 BZ48
Chancellor Way, Sev. 107 CU64
Chancellors Rd. W6 65 BQ42
Chancellors St. W6 65 BQ42
Chancelot Rd. SE2 69 CO42
Chancery Clo., St.Alb. 9 BK11
Chancery La. WC2 2 D8
Chancery La. WC2 56 BX39
Chancery La., Beck. 87 CE51
Chanctonbury Chase, 121 BV70
Red.
Chanctonbury Clo. SE9 78 CL48
Chanctonbury Gdns., 95 BS57
Sutt.
Chanctonbury Way N12 37 BR28
Chandler Ave. E16 58 CH39
Chandler Clo., Hmptn. 84 BF51
Chandler Rd., Loug. 31 CL23
Chandler St. E1 57 CB40
Chandlers Clo., Felt. 73 BB47
Chandlers Cor., Rain. 60 CV38
Chandlers La., Rick. 26 AY21
Chandlers Ms. E14 67 CE41
Chandlers Rd., St.Alb. 9 BK11
Chandlers Wk., Brwd. 33 CZ22
Windmill Way
Chandlers Way, Rom. 50 CT32
Chandos Ave. E17 39 CE30
Chandos Ave. N14 38 BW27
Chandos Ave. N20 38 BT26
Chandos Ave. W5 64 BK42
Chandos Clo., Amer. 25 AR22
Chandos Clo., Buck.H. 40 CH27
Chandos Ct. N14 38 BW27
The Grn.
Chandos Cres., Edg. 37 BL29
Chandos Pl. WC2 3 Q1
Chandos Pl. WC2 56 BX40
Chandos Rd. E15 48 CF35
Chandos Rd. N2 38 BT30
Chandos Rd. N17 39 CA30
Chandos Rd. NW2 46 BQ35
Chandos Rd. NW10 55 BO38
Chandos Rd., Borwd. 28 BL23
Chandos Rd., Har. 45 BG32
Chandos Rd., Pnr. 45 BD33
Chandos Rd., Stai. 72 AU49
Chandos St. W1 1 K7
Chandos St. W1 56 BV39
Chandos Way NW11 47 BS33
Chandrye Clo. SE9 78 CK46
Change All. EC3 2 L9
Change All. EC3 57 BZ39
Birchin La.
Chanlock Path, S.Ock. 60 DA40
Carnach Grn.
Channel Clo., Houns. 64 BF44
Channelsea Rd. E15 57 CF37
Channing Clo., Horn. 51 CW33
Chant Sq. E15 57 CF36
Chant St. E15 57 CF36
Chanton Dr., Sutt. 94 BQ58
Chantrey Clo., Ash. 102 BK63
Chantrey Rd. SW9 66 BX45
Chantreywood, Brwd. 122 DD27
Brocksparkwood
Chantry, The, Harl. 6 CO9
Chantry, The, Uxb. 53 AY38
Chantry Ave., Hartley 90 DC53
Chantry Clo., Enf. 30 BZ22
Chantry Clo., Har. 46 BL32
Chantry Clo., Kings L. 17 AZ18
Chantry Clo., Sid. 79 CQ49
Ellenborough La.
Chantry Clo., West Dr. 53 AX40
Chantry Clo., Wind. 61 AN44
Chantry Ct., Hat. 10 BP13
Chantry Hurst, Epsom 103 BN61
Chantry La., Brom. 88 CJ53
Chantry La., Hat. 10 BO13
Chantry La., St.Alb. 18 BK16
Chantry Pl., Har. 36 BF30
Chantry Rd., Cher. 83 AW54
Chantry Rd., Chess. 94 BL56
Chantry Rd., Guil. 118 AT73
Chantry Rd., Har. 36 BF30
Chantry St. N1 56 BY37
Chantry Vw. Rd., Guil. 118 AR72
Chantry Way, Rain. 59 CS37
Chapel All, Brent. 65 BL43
High St.
Chapel Ave., Wey. 92 AW56
Chapel Clo. N2 47 BU31
Chapel Ct.
Chapel Clo., Dart. 79 CT46
Chapel Clo., Grays 70 DA43
Credo Way
Chapel Clo., Wat. 17 BC20
Chapel Ct. N2 47 BU31
Chapel Ct. SE1 4 K4
Chapel Ct. SE1 67 BZ41
Tennis St.
Chapel Cft., Kings L. 17 AW19
Chapel Cfts., Berk. 7 AP12
Kite Fld.
Chapel End, Ger.Cr. 34 AR30
Chapel End, Hodd. 12 CE12
Chapel Fm. Rd. SE9 78 CK48
Chapel Flds., Harl. 14 CP12
Chapel Gro., Epsom 103 BQ63
Chapel Gro., Wey. 92 AW56
Chapel High, Brwd. 42 DB27
Chapel Hill, Dart. 79 CT46
Chapel Hill, Pnr. 44 BC32
Chapel Hill Crossways, 111 BD67
Lthd.
Browns La.
Chapel Ho. Clo., Guil. 118 AP70
Park Barn Dr.
Chapel Ho. St. E14 67 CE42
Chapel La., Chig. 40 CN27
Chapel La., Dor. 119 BG72
Chapel La., Houns. 64 BF45
Chapel La., Lthd. 111 BG67
Chapel La. (Bookham), 111 BG68
Lthd.
Chapel La., Loug. 31 CK24
Chapel La., Ong. 24 CV20
Chapel La., Pnr. 45 BD31
Chapel La., Rom. 50 CP33
Station Rd.
Chapel La., Slou. 52 AQ36
Chapel La., Uxb. 53 AZ39
Chapel Mkt. N1 56 BY37
Chapel Pk. Rd., Wey. 92 AW56
Chapel Pl. EC2 2 M3
Chapel Pl. N1 56 BY37
Chapel Mkt.
Chapel Pl. N17 39 CA29
Chapel Pl. W1 1 J9
Chapel Pl. W1 56 BV39
Chapel Rd. SE27 76 BY49
Chapel Rd. W13 54 BJ40
Chapel Rd., Bexh. 69 CR45
Chapel Rd., Epp. 22 CN18
Chapel Rd., Houns. 64 BF45
Chapel Rd., Ilf. 49 CL34
Chapel Rd., Mitch. 86 BT52
Chapel Rd., Oxt. 115 CJ68
Chapel Rd., Red. 121 BU70
Chapel Rd., Sev. 108 DB64
Chapel Rd., Tad. 103 BQ65
Chapel Rd., Twick. 74 BK47
Chapel Rd., Warl. 105 CC62
Chapel Row, Uxb. 35 AX30
Chapel Side W2 56 BS40
Chapel Stones N17 39 CA30
Kings Rd.
Chapel St. E15 57 CF36
Chapel St. NW1 1 C7
Chapel St. NW1 56 BU39
Chapel St. SW1 3 H5
Chapel St. SW1 66 BV41
Chapel St., Berk. 7 AR13
Chapel St., Enf. 30 BZ24
Chapel St., Guil. 118 AR71
Chapel St., Hem.H. 8 AX13
Chapel St., Slou. 62 AP41
Chapel St., Uxb. 53 AX37
Cross St.
Chapel St., Wok. 100 AS62
High St.
Chapel Vw., S.Croy. 96 CC57
Chapel Wk. NW4 46 BP31
Chapel Way N7 47 BX34
Sussex Way
Chapel Way, Epsom 103 BQ63
Chapel Wd., Dart. 90 DC55
Chapel Wd. Rd., Fawk. 90 DC55
Chapel Yd. N18 39 CB29
Fore St.
Chapelmount Rd., 40 CK29
Wdf.Grn.
Chaplaincy Gdns., Horn. 51 CW33
Allenby Dr.
Chaplin Clo. SE1 4 E4
Chaplin Cres., Sun. 73 BB50
Chaplin Rd. E15 58 CG37
Chaplin Rd. N17 48 CA31
Forster Rd.
Chaplin Rd. NW2 55 BP36
Chaplin Rd., Dag. 59 CQ36
Chaplin Rd., Wem. 54 BK36
Chapman Clo., 63 AY41
West Dr.
Chapman Cres., Har. 46 BL32
Chapman Rd. E9 57 CD36
Chapman Rd., Belv. 69 CR42
Chapman Rd., Croy. 86 BY54
Chapman St. E1 57 CB39
Chapmans La. SE2 69 CP42
Chapmans La., Belv. 69 CP42
Abbey Rd.
Chapmans La., Orp. 89 CP51

Chapmans Pk. Ind. Est. NW10 55 BO36
Chapmans Rd., Sev. 107 CQ65
Chapone Pl. W1 1 N9
Chapples Clo., Loug. 31 CM25
Chapter Clo. W4 65 BN41
Beaumont Rd.
Chapter Clo., Uxb. 53 AY36
Chapter Ho. Ct. EC4 2 G9
Chapter Rd. NW2 46 BP35
Chapter Rd. SE17 66 BY42
Chapter St. SW1 3 N9
Chapter St. SW1 66 BW42
Chapter Way, Hmptn. 74 BF49
Bishops Gro.
Chara Pl. W4 65 BN43
Charcroft Gdns., Enf. 30 CC24
Chard Rd., Houns. 63 AZ44
Calshot Rd.
Chardin Rd. W4 65 BO42
Elliott Rd.
Chardins Clo., Hem.H. 7 AV13
Chardmore Rd. N16 48 CB33
Chardwell Clo. E6 58 CK39
Charecroft Way W12 65 BQ41
Charford Rd. E16 58 CH39
Chargate Clo., Walt. 92 BB57
Chargeable La. E13 58 CG38
Chargeable St. E16 58 CG38
Chargrove Clo. SE16 67 CC41
Marlow Way
Charing Clo., Orp. 97 CN56
Charing Cross WC2 3 Q2
Charing Cross Rd. WC2 1 P9
Charing Cross Rd. WC2 56 BW39
Chariotts Pl., Wind. 61 AO44
Peascod St.
Charlbert St. NW8 56 BU37
Charlbury Ave., Stan. 36 BK28
Charlbury Clo., Rom. 42 CV29
Charlbury Cres., Rom. 42 CV29
Charlbury Gdns., Ilf. 49 CN34
Charlbury Gro. W5 54 BK39
Charlbury Rd., Uxb. 44 AY34
Charldane Rd. SE9 78 CL48
Charlecote Gro. SE26 77 CB48
Charlecote Rd., Dag. 50 CQ34
Charlemont Rd. E6 58 CK38
Charles Barry Clo. SW4 66 BW45
Charles Burton Ct. E5 48 CD35
Meeson St.
Charles Clo., Sid. 79 CO49
Charles Cres., Har. 45 BG33
Charles Gdns., Slou. 52 AQ39
Borderside
Charles Grindling Wk. SE18 68 CL42
Charles Ho. W14 65 BR42
Charles Ho., Wind. 61 AO44
Ward Royal
Charles La. NW8 56 BU37
Charles Mills Ct. SW16 76 BX50
Charles Pl. NW1 1 M3
Charles Rd. E7 58 CJ36
Charles Rd. SW19 86 BS51
Shelton Rd.
Charles Rd. W13 54 BJ39
Charles Rd., Dag. 59 CS36
Charles Rd., Rom. 50 CP33
Charles Rd., Sev. 98 CR58
Charles Rd., Stai. 73 AX50
Charles II St. SW1 3 N2
Charles II St. SW1 56 BW40
Charles Sevright Dr. NW7 37 BQ28
Charles Sq. N1 2 L3
Charles Sq. N1 57 BZ38
Charles St. E16 58 CJ40
Charles St. SW13 65 BO45
Charles St. W1 3 J2
Charles St. W1 56 BV40
Charles St. W5 54 BK40
Lancaster Rd.
Charles St., Berk. 7 AQ13
Charles St., Cher. 82 AV54
Charles St., Croy. 87 BZ55
Charles St., Enf. 30 CA25
Charles St., Epp. 23 CO19
Charles St., Grays 71 DD43
Charles St., Green. 80 CZ46
Charles St., Hem.H. 8 AX14
Charles St., Houns. 64 BE44
Charles St., Uxb. 53 AZ38
Charles St., Wind. 61 AO44
Charlesfield SE9 78 CJ48
Charleston Clo., Felt. 73 BC48
Charleston St. SE17 4 J9
Charleston St. SE17 67 BZ42
Charleville Circ. SE26 77 CB49
Charleville Rd. W14 65 BR42
Charlieville Rd., Erith 69 CS43
Mill Rd.
Charlmont Rd. SW17 76 BU50
Charlock Way, Guil. 118 AT69
Charlock Way, Wat. 26 BB25
Charlotte Despard Ave. SW11 66 BV44
Charlotte Gdns., Rom. 41 CR29
Charlotte Ms. W1 1 M6
Charlotte Ms. W1 56 BW39
Tottenham St.
Charlotte Ms. W14 65 BR42
Munden St.
Charlotte Pl. NW9 46 BN32
Uphill Dr.
Charlotte Pl. SW1 3 L9
Charlotte Pl. W1 1 M7
Charlotte Pl. W1 56 BW39
Goodge St.
Charlotte Pl., Grays 70 DA43
Credo Way
Charlotte Rd. EC2 2 M3
Charlotte Rd. EC2 57 CA38
Charlotte Rd. SW13 65 BO44
Charlotte Rd., Dag. 59 CR36
Charlotte Rd., Wall. 95 BW57
Charlotte Row SW4 66 BW45
North St.
Charlotte Sq., Rich. 75 BL46
Greville Rd.
Charlotte St. W1 1 M6
Charlotte St. W1 56 BW39
Charlotte Ter. N1 56 BX37
Charlton, Wind. 61 AL44
Charlton Ave., Walt. 92 BC56
Charlton Ch. La. SE7 68 CJ42
Charlton Clo., Hodd. 12 CE12
Charlton Clo., Slou. 61 AN41
Charlton Clo., Uxb. 44 AZ34
Charlton Cres., Bark. 58 CN37
Charlton Dene SE7 68 CJ43
Charlton Dr., West. 106 CJ62
Charlton Gdns., Couls. 104 BW62
Charlton Kings, Wey. 83 BB55
Charlton Kings Rd. NW5 47 BW35
Charlton La. SE7 68 CJ42
Charlton La., Shep. 83 BA52
Charlton Mead La., Hodd. 12 CF12
Charlton Pk. La. SE7 68 CJ43
Charlton Pk. Rd. SE7 68 CJ43
Charlton Pl. N1 56 BY37
Charlton Pl., Wind. 61 AL44
Charlton
Charlton Rd. N9 39 CC26
Charlton Rd. NW10 55 BO37
Charlton Rd. SE3 68 CH43
Charlton Rd. SE7 68 CH43
Charlton Rd., Har. 45 BK31
Charlton Rd., Shep. 83 BA52
Charlton Rd., Wem. 46 BL33
Charlton Row, Wind. 61 AL44
Charlton
Charlton Sq., Wind. 61 AL44
Charlton
Charlton St., Grays 70 DB43
Charlton Wk., Wind. 61 AL44
Charlton
Charlton Way SE3 68 CG43
Charlton Way SE10 68 CG44
Charlton Way, Hodd. 12 CE12
Charlton Way, Wind. 61 AL44
Charlwood, Croy. 96 CD58
Charlwood Clo., Har. 36 BH29
Charlwood Dr., Cob. 102 BG61
Charlwood Pl. SW1 3 M9
Charlwood Pl. SW1 66 BW42
Charlwood Rd. SW15 65 BQ45
Charlwood St. SW1 3 M10
Charlwood St. SW1 66 BW42
Charlwood Ter. SW15 65 BQ45
Cardinal Pl.
Charman Rd., Red. 121 BU70
Charmans La., Reig. 120 BO74
Charmian Ave., Stan. 36 BK30
Charminster Ave. SW19 86 BS51
Charminster Ct., Surb. 84 BK54
Charminster Rd. SE9 78 CJ49
Charminster Rd., Wor.Pk. 85 BQ54
Charmouth Ct., St.Alb. 9 BJ12
Charmouth Rd., St.Alb. 9 BJ12
Charmouth Rd., Well. 69 CP44
Charmwood La., Orp. 98 CO58
Charne, The, Sev. 107 CU62
Charnock Ct. Cres., Swan. 89 CT52
Charnock Rd. E5 48 CB34
Charnwood Ave. SW19 86 BS51
Charnwood Clo., N.Mal. 85 BO52
Charnwood Dr. E18 49 CH31
Charnwood Gdns. E14 67 CE42
Charnwood Pl. N20 38 BT27
Charnwood Rd. SE25 87 BZ53
Charnwood Rd., Enf. 30 CB21
Charnwood Rd., Uxb. 53 AZ37
Charnwood St. E5 48 CB34
Charrington Rd., Croy. 86 BY55
Drayton Rd.
Charrington St. NW1 56 BW37
Charsley Clo., Amer. 25 AR23
Charsley Rd. SE6 77 CE48
Chart Clo., Brom. 88 CG51
Chart Clo., Croy. 87 CC53
Chart Clo., Dor. 119 BK72
Chart Downs Est., Dor. 119 BK72
Chart Gdns., Dor. 119 BK73
Chart La., Dor. 119 BK71
Chart La., Reig. 121 BS70
Chart La., West. 116 CO68
Chart La. S., Dor. 119 BK72
Chart St. N1 2 L2
Chart St. N1 57 BZ38
Chart Vw., Sev. 108 CX62
Chart Way, Reig. 121 BS70
Chartar Rd. E., Egh. 72 AU50
Chartar Rd. S., Egh. 72 AU50
Chartar Rd. W., Egh. 72 AU50
Charter Ave., Ilf. 49 CM33
Charter Clo., Slou. 62 AP41
Hencroft St.
Charter Cres., Houns. 64 BE45
Charter Dr., Bex. 79 CQ47
Charter Pl., Uxb. 53 AX37
Cross St.
Charter Rd., Kings.T. 85 BM52
Charter Rd., The, Wdf.Grn. 40 CG29
Charter Sq., Kings.T. 85 BM51
Charter Way N3 46 BR31
Regents Pk. Rd.
Charter Way N14 29 BW25
Charterhouse Ave., Wem. 45 BK3
Charterhouse Bldgs. EC1 2 G5
Charterhouse Bldgs. EC1 56 BY38
Goswell Rd.
Charterhouse Dr., Sev. 107 CU65
Charterhouse Rd., Orp. 89 CO55
Charterhouse Sq. EC1 2 G6
Charterhouse Sq. EC1 56 BY39
Charterhouse St. EC1 2 F6
Charterhouse St. EC1 56 BY39
Charteris Rd. N4 47 BY33
Charteris Rd. NW6 55 BR37
Charteris Rd., Wdf.Grn. 40 CH29
Charters Clo. SE19 77 CA49
Charters Cross, Harl. 13 CM12
Chartfield Ave. SW15 75 BP46
Chartfield Rd., Reig. 121 BT71
Chartfield Sq. SW15 75 BQ46
Chartham Gro. SE27 76 BY48
Royal Circ.
Chartham Rd. SE25 87 CB52
Chartley Ave. NW2 46 BO34
Chartley Ave., Stan. 36 BH29
Charton Clo., Belv. 69 CQ43
Chartridge Clo., Barn. 28 BP25
Chartridge Way, Hem.H. 8 BA13
Chartway, Sev. 108 CV65
Chartwell Clo. SE9 78 CM48
Chartwell Clo., Croy. 87 BZ54
Tavistock Rd.
Chartwell Clo., Wal.Abb. 22 CG20
Mason Way
Chartwell Dr., Orp. 97 CM56
Farnborough Hill
Chartwell Pl., Epsom 94 BO60
Chartwell Pl., Sutt. 85 BR55
Chartwell Rd., Nthwd. 35 BB29
Chartwell Way SE20 77 CB51
Jasmine Gro.
Charville Est., Hayes 53 BA37
Charville La., Hayes 53 BA38
Charville La. W., Uxb. 53 AZ38
Charwood SW16 76 BY49
Leigham Ct. Rd.
Chasden Rd., Hem.H. 7 AV12
Chase, The E12 49 CJ35
Chase, The SW4 66 BV45
Chase, The SW16 76 BX50
Chase, The SW20 85 BR51
Chase, The, Ash. 102 BK62
Chase, The, Bexh. 69 CR45
Chase, The, Brwd. 42 DB27
Chase, The (Ingrave), Brwd. 122 DE28
Chase, The (Warley), Brwd. 42 DA28
Cromwell Rd.
Chase, The, Brom. 88 CH52
Chase, The, Chsnt. 20 BY17
Chase, The, Chig. 40 CM28
Chase, The, Couls. 95 BW60
Chase, The, Edg. 37 BM30
Chase, The, Grays 70 DB43
Chase, The, Guil. 118 AQ71
Chase, The, Hem.H. 8 AY14
Chase, The (East Horsley), Lthd. 102 BG61
Chase, The (Oxshott), Lthd. 110 BB66
Chase, The, Pnr. 45 BE31
Chase, The (Eastcote), Pnr. 45 BD32
Chase, The, Rad. 27 BH21
Chase, The, Reig. 121 BT71
Chase, The, Rom. 50 CT31
Chase, The (Chadwell Heath), Rom. 50 CQ32
Chase, The (Rush Grn.), Rom. 50 CT34
Chase, The, Sev. 108 CW61
Chase, The, Stan. 36 BJ29
Chase, The, Sun. 83 BC51
Staines Rd.
Chase, The, Tad. 104 BS64
Chase, The, Upmin. 51 CZ34
Chase, The, Uxb. 44 AZ35
Chase, The, Wall. 95 BX56
Chase, The, Wat. 26 BB24
Chase Ct. Gdns., Enf. 30 BZ24
Chase Cross Rd., Rom. 41 CS29
Chase End, Epsom 94 BN59
Chase Gdns. E4 39 CE28
Chase Gdns., Twick. 74 BG46
Chase Grn., Enf. 30 BZ24
Chase Grn. Ave., Enf. 29 BY23
Chase Hill, Enf. 30 BZ24
Chase Ho. Gdns., Horn. 51 CW32
Great Nelmes Chase
Chase La., Chig. 40 CN27
Chase La., Ilf. 49 CM32
Chase Ridings, Enf. 29 BY23
Chase Rd. E18 40 CG30
Chase Rd. N14 29 BW25
Chase Rd. NW10 55 BN38
Chase Rd. W3 55 BN39
Chase Rd., Brwd. 42 DB27
Chase Rd., Epsom 94 BN59
Chase Side N14 29 BV25
Chase Side, Enf. 30 BZ24
Chase Side Ave. SW20 85 BR51
Chase Side Ave., Enf. 30 BZ23
Chase Side Clo., Rom. 41 CT29
Chase Side Cres., Enf. 30 BZ23
Chase Side Pl., Enf. 30 BZ23
Cricketers Arms Rd.
Chase Trd. Est., The NW10 55 BN38
Chase Way N14 38 BV27
Chasefield Clo., Guil. 118 AT69
Sutherland Dr.
Chasefield Rd. SW17 76 BU49
Chaseley St. E14 57 CD39
Chasemore Gdns., Croy. 95 BY56
Chaseside Gdns., Cher. 83 AW54
Chaseville Par. N21 29 BX25
Chaseville Pk. Rd.
Chaseville Pk. Rd. N21 29 BX25
Chaseways, Saw. 6 CP7
Chasewood Ave., Enf. 29 BY23
Chastilian Rd., Dart. 79 CT47
Chatfield Ct., Cat. 105 BZ64
Chatfield Dr., Guil. 118 AU69
Chatfield Pl. W5 55 BL39
Park Vw. Rd.
Chatfield Rd. SW11 66 BT45
Chatfield Rd., Croy. 86 BY54
Chatham Ave., Brom. 88 CG54
Chatham Clo. NW11 47 BS32
Chatham Clo., Sutt. 85 BR54
Chatham Hill Rd., Sev. 108 CV64
Chatham Pl. E9 57 CC36
Chatham Rd. E17 48 CD31
Chatham Rd. E18 40 CG30
Grove Hill
Chatham Rd. SW11 76 BU46
Chatham Rd., Kings.T. 85 BM51
Chatham Rd., Orp. 97 CM56
Chatham St. SE17 4 K8
Chatham St. SE17 67 BZ42
Chatsfield, Epsom 94 BP58
Cheam Rd.
Chatsworth Ave. NW4 37 BQ30
Chatsworth Ave. SW20 85 BR51
Chatsworth Ave., Brom. 78 CH49
Chatsworth Ave., Sid. 79 CO47
Chatsworth Ave., Wem. 46 BL35
Chatsworth Clo. NW4 37 BQ30
Chatsworth Clo., Borwd. 28 BM24
Chatsworth Clo., W.Wick. 88 CG55
Deer Pk. Way
Chatsworth Ct. W8 66 BS42
Chatsworth Cres., Houns. 64 BG45
Chatsworth Dr., Enf. 39 CB26
Chatsworth Est. E5 48 CC35
Chatsworth Gdns. W3 55 BM40
Chatsworth Gdns., Har. 45 BF33
Chatsworth Gdns., N.Mal. 85 BO53
Chatsworth Par., Orp. 88 CM53
Chatsworth Pl., Mitch. 86 BU52
Chatsworth Pl., Tedd. 74 BJ49
Chatsworth Ri. W5 55 BL38
Chatsworth Rd. E5 48 CC34
Chatsworth Rd. E15 49 CG35
Chatsworth Rd. NW2 55 BQ36
Chatsworth Rd. W4 65 BN43
Chatsworth Rd. W5 55 BL39
Chatsworth Rd., Croy. 87 BZ55
Chatsworth Rd., Dart. 70 CV45
Chatsworth Rd., Hayes 53 BC38
Chatsworth Rd., Sutt. 94 BQ56
Chatsworth Way SE27 76 BY48
Chatteris Ave., Rom. 42 CV29
Chattern Hill, Ashf. 73 AZ49
Chattern Rd., Ashf. 73 BA49
Chatterton Rd. N4 47 BY34
Chatterton Rd., Brom. 88 CJ52
Chatto Rd. SW11 76 BU46
Chaucer Ave., Hayes 53 BC39
Chaucer Ave., Houns. 63 BC44
Chaucer Ave., Rich. 65 BM44
Chaucer Ave., Wey. 92 AZ57
Chaucer Clo. N11 38 BW28
Chaucer Clo., Bans. 94 BR60
Chaucer Clo., Berk. 7 AP12
Chaucer Clo., Til. 71 DH44
Coleridge Rd.
Chaucer Dr. SE1 4 Q9
Chaucer Gdns., Sutt. 86 BS55
Chaucer Grn., Croy. 87 CC54
Chaucer Rd. E7 58 CH36
Chaucer Rd. E11 49 CH32
Chaucer Rd. E17 39 CF30
Chaucer Rd. SE24 76 BY46
Chaucer Rd. W3 55 BN40
Chaucer Rd., Ashf. 73 AY49
Chaucer Rd., Grav. 81 DE48
Chaucer Rd., Rom. 41 CU29
Chaucer Rd., Sid. 79 CP47
Chaucer Rd., Sutt. 95 BS56
Chaucer Rd., Well. 68 CN44
Chaucer Wk., Dart. 70 CW45
Chaucer Wk., Hem.H. 8 AZ10
Coleridge Cres.
Chaucer Way SW19 76 BT50
Chaucer Way, Dart. 70 CX45
Chaucer Way, Wey. 92 AW57
Chaulden Ho. Gdns., Hem.H. 7 AV14
Chaulden La., Hem.H. 7 AU14
Chaulden Ter., Hem.H. 7 AV14
Chauncey Ave., Pot.B. 20 BT20
Chauncey Clo. N9 39 CB27
Chauntler Rd. E16 58 CH40
Victoria Dock Rd.
Chave Cft. Ter., Tad. 103 BQ63
Chave Rd., Dart. 80 CW48
Chaworth Rd., Cher. 91 AU57
Cheam Clo., Tad. 103 BP64
Cheam Common Rd., Wor.Pk. 85 BP55
Cheam Pk. Way, Sutt. 94 BQ57
Cheam Rd., Epsom 94 BP58
Cheam Rd., Sutt. 94 BR57
Cheam St. SE15 67 CB45
Nunhead Gro.
Cheapside EC2 2 H9
Cheapside EC2 57 BZ39
Cheapside N13 39 BZ28
North Circular Rd.
Cheapside, Wok. 100 AR61
Cheapside La., Uxb. 43 AV34
Chedburgh, Welw.G.C. 5 BT7
Cheddar Rd., Houns. 63 AZ45
Cromer Rd.
Cheddar Waye, Hayes 53 BC39
Cheddington Rd. N18 39 CA27
Chedworth Clo. E16 58 CG39
Hallsville Rd.
Cheelson Rd., S.Ock. 60 DB37
Cheeseman Clo., Hmptn. 74 BE50
Victors Dr.
Cheffins Rd., Hodd. 12 CD10
Chelford Rd., Brom. 77 CF49
Chelmer Cres., Bark. 59 CO37
Chelmer Dr., Brwd. 122 D
Chelmer Rd. E9 48 C
Chelmer Rd., Grays 71 D
Chelmer Rd., Upmin. 51 C
Chelmsford Ave., Rom. 41 C
Chelmsford Clo. E6 58 C
Guildford Rd.
Chelmsford Clo. W6 65 B
Chelmsford Dr., Upmin. 51 CV
Chelmsford Gdns., Ilf. 49 C
Chelmsford Rd. E11 48 C
Chelmsford Rd. E17 48 C
Chelmsford Rd. E18 40 C
Chelmsford Rd. N14 38 BV
Chelmsford Rd., Brwd. 122 D
Chelmsford Rd., Ing. 24 D
Chelmsford Rd., Ong. 24 C
Chelmsford Sq. NW10 55 B
Chelsea Bri. SW1 66 B
Chelsea Bri. SW8 66 B
Chelsea Bri. Rd. SW1 3
Chelsea Bri. Rd. SW1 66 B
Chelsea Cloisters SW3 3
Chelsea Cloisters SW3 66 B
Makins St.
Chelsea Clo. NW10 55 B
Winchelsea Rd.
Chelsea Clo., Edg. 37 BN
Chelsea Clo., Hmptn. 74 B
Chelsea Ct. SW3 66 B
Chelsea Embk. SW3 66 B
Chelsea Gdns., Sutt. 94 B
Chelsea Harbour Dr. SW10 66 B
Chelsea Manor Est. SW3 66 B
Alpha Pl.
Chelsea Manor Gdns. SW3 66 B
Chelsea Manor St. SW3 66 BU
Chelsea Pk. Gdns. SW3 66 B
Chelsea Sq. SW3 3
Chelsea Sq. SW3 66 B
Chelsea Wf. SW10 66 B
Chelsfield Ave. N9 39 C
Chelsfield Gdns. SE26 77 C
Chelsfield Grn. N9 39 C
Chelsfield Ave.
Chelsfield Hill, Orp. 98 C
Chelsfield La., Orp. 89 C
Chelsfield La. (Chelsfield), Orp. 98 C
Chelsfield Rd., Orp. 89 C
Chelsham Clo., Warl. 105 C
Chelsham Ct. Rd., Warl. 105 C
Chelsham Rd. SW4 66 BV
Chelsham Rd., S.Croy. 96 B
Chelsham Rd., Warl. 105 C
Chelsing Ri., Hem.H. 8 B
Chelston Rd., Ruis. 44 BC
Chelsworth Clo., Rom. 42 CV
Chelsworth Dr. SE18 68 CM
Chelsworth Dr., Rom. 42 CV
Cheltenham Ave., Twick. 74 B
Cheltenham Clo., Nthlt. 54 BE
Cheltenham Gdns. E6 58 CK
Cheltenham Gdns., Loug. 31 CK
Cheltenham Pl. W3 55 BM
Cheltenham Pl., Har. 46 BL
Cheltenham Rd. E10 48 CF
Cheltenham Rd. SE15 67 CC
Cheltenham Rd., Orp. 89 CC
Cheltenham Ter. SW3 3
Cheltenham Ter. SW3 66 BU
Cheltenham Vill., Stai. 72 AV
Chelverton Rd. SW15 65 BQ
Chelveston, Welw.G.C. 5 B
Chelwood Ave., Hat. 10 BF
Chelwood Clo. E4 30 CE
Chelwood Clo., Epsom 94 BO
Chelwood Clo., Nthwd. 35 BA
Chelwood Gdns., Rich. 65 BM
Chelwood Gdns. Pas., Rich. 65 BM
Pensford Ave.
Chelwood Wk. SE4 67 CD
Chenappa Clo. E13 58 CH
Chenduit Way, Stan. 36 BH
Chene Dr., St.Alb. 9 BG
Cheney Rd. NW1 1
Cheney Rd. NW1 56 BX
Cheney Row E17 39 CD
Cheney St., Pnr. 45 BD
Cheneys Rd. E11 49 CG
Chenies, The, Dart. 79 CT
Chenies, The, Orp. 88 CN
Chenies Ave., Amer. 25 AP
Chenies Ct., Hem.H. 8 AZ
Chenies Ms. WC1 1
Chenies Ms. WC1 56 BW
Chenies Par., Amer. 25 AR
Chenies Pl. NW1 56 BW
Chenies Rd., Rick. 25 AU
Chenies St. WC1 1
Chenies St. WC1 56 BW
Chenies Way, Wat. 35 BB
Cheniston Clo., Wey. 91 AV
Cheniston Gdns. W8 66 BS
Chennells, Hat. 10 BO
Chepstow Ave., Horn. 51 CW
Chepstow Clo. SW15 75 BR
Chepstow Cres. W11 56 BS
Chepstow Cres., Ilf. 49 CN
Chepstow Gdns., Sthl. 54 BE
Chepstow Pl. W2 56 BS
Chepstow Ri., Croy. 87 CA
Chepstow Rd. W2 56 BS
Chepstow Rd. W7 64 BJ
Chepstow Rd., Croy. 87 CA
Chepstow Vill. W11 55 BR
Chepstow Way SE15 67 CA
Chequer St. EC1 2
Chequer St. EC1 57 BZ
Chequer St., St.Alb. 9 BG

equer Tree Clo., Wok. 100 AP61
reen Acre
equers, Welw.G.C. 5 BQ9
avensbury Rd.
equers Way, Orp. 88 CN52
erbury Ct. N1 57 BZ37
equers Gdns. N13 38 BY28
equers Hill, Amer. 25 AO23
equers La., Tad. 112 BP66
equers La., Wat. 18 BD18
equers Orchard, Iver 52 AV39
equers Pl., Dor. 119 BJ71
equers Rd., Brwd. 33 CW25
equers Rd., Loug. 31 CL25
equers Rd., Rom. 42 CW27
equers Sq., Uxb. 53 AX36
igh St.
equers Wk., Wal.Abb. 22 CG20
Mason Way
equers Way N13 38 BY28
erbury Clo. SE28 59 CP39
erbury Ct. N1 57 BZ37
erbury St. N1 2 L1
reen La.
erchefelle Ms., Stan. 36 BJ28
Green La.
erimoya Gdns., E.Mol. 84 BF52
eriton Rd. W7 54 BH40
eriton Ave., Brom. 88 CG53
eriton Ave., Ilf. 40 CK30
eriton Clo. W5 54 BK39
eriton Ct., St.Alb. 9 BK11
eriton Ct., Walt. 84 BD54
erkley Hill, Lthd. 111 BK66
erries, The, Slou. 52 AQ39
erry Acre, Ger.Cr. 34 AR28
erry Ave., Brwd. 122 DC27
erry Ave., Slou. 62 AR41
erry Ave., Sthl. 54 BD40
erry Ave., Swan. 89 CS52
erry Bounce, Hem.H. 8 AX12
erry Clo. E17 48 CE32
den Rd.
erry Clo. W5 64 BK41
erry Clo., Bans. 94 BQ60
erry Clo., Cars. 86 BU55
erry Clo., Mord. 85 BR52
erry Clo., Ruis. 44 BB34
erry Cres., Brent. 64 BJ43
erry Cft., Welw.G.C. 5 BQ6
erry Gdn. St. SE16 67 CB41
erry Gdns., Dag. 50 CQ35
erry Garth, Brent. 64 BK42
erry Grn. Clo., Red. 121 BV71
Hartspiece Rd.
erry Gro., Hayes 53 BC40
erry Gro., Uxb. 53 AZ39
erry Hill, Barn. 29 BS25
erry Hill, Rick. 26 AW24
erry Hill, St.Alb. 18 BF16
erry Hill Gdns., Croy. 95 BX56
erry Hollow, Abb.L. 17 BB19
erry La., West Dr. 63 AY42
erry Laurel Wk. SW2 76 BX46
eechdale Rd.
erry Orchard, Amer. 25 AP22
erry Orchard, Ash. 103 BM62
erry Orchard, Hem.H. 8 AX12
erry Orchard, Slou. 52 AQ36
erry Orchard, Stai. 73 AW49
erry Orchard, West Dr. 63 AY41
erry Orchard Clo., 89 CP53
Orp.
erry Orchard Gdns., 87 CA54
Croy.
Oval Rd.
erry Orchard Gdns., 84 BE52
E.Mol.
erry Orchard La., Brom. 88 CK55
erry Orchard Rd., Brom. 88 CK55
erry Orchard Rd., 87 BZ55
Croy.
E.Mol.
erry Ri., Ch.St.G. 34 AR27
erry Rd., Enf. 30 CC22
erry St., Rom. 50 CS32
erry St., Wok. 100 AS62
erry Tree Ave., Guil. 118 AP70
erry Tree Ave., St.Alb. 18 BK16
erry Tree Ave., Stai. 73 AW50
erry Tree Ave., West 53 AY39
Dr.
erry Tree Clo., Grays 71 DE43
Silverlocke Rd.
erry Tree Clo., Rain. 59 CT37
erry Tree Clo., Wem. 45 BH35
erry Tree Clo., Couls. 104 BX62
Coulsdon Rd.
erry Tree Dr. SW16 76 BX48
erry Tree Gdns., Croy. 87 BZ54
Oval Rd.
erry Tree Grn., S.Croy. 96 CB60
erry Tree La., Ger.Cr. 34 AR30
erry Tree La., Hem.H. 8 BA11
erry Tree La., Iver 52 AW37
erry Tree La., Pot.B. 20 BS20
erry Tree La., Rain. 59 CT38
erry Tree La., Rick. 34 AU26
erry Tree La., Slou. 52 AS36
erry Tree Ri., Buck.H. 40 CJ28
erry Tree Rd. E15 49 CG35
Wingfield Rd.
erry Tree Rd. N2 47 BU31
erry Tree Rd., Hodd. 12 CE11
erry Tree Rd., Wat. 26 BC21
erry Tree Wk., Beck. 87 CD52

Cherry Tree Wk., Chesh. 16 AO17
Cherry Tree Wk., W.Wick. 97 CG56
Cherry Tree Wk., West. 106 CJ61
Cherry Tree Way, Stan. 36 BJ28
Cherry Wk., Brom. 88 CH54
Cherry Wk., Grays 71 DG41
Cherry Wk., Rain. 59 CT37
Cherry Wk., Rick. 26 AX23
Cherry Way, Epsom 94 BN57
Cherry Way, Hat. 10 BP14
Cherry Way, Shep. 83 BB52
Cherry Way, Slou. 62 AU45
Mill La.
Cherrycot Hill, Orp. 97 CM56
Cherrycot Ri., Orp. 97 CM56
Cherrycroft Gdns., Pnr. 36 BE29
Westfield La.
Cherrydale, Wat. 26 BB24
Cherrydown, Grays 71 DE40
Cherrydown Ave. E4 39 CD27
Cherrydown Clo. E4 39 CD27
Cherrydown Rd., Sid. 79 CP48
Cherrydown Wk., Rom. 41 CR30
Cherrytree La., Iver 53 AW37
Cherrywood Ave., Egh. 72 AQ50
Cherrywood Clo., Beac. 34 AO28
Cherrywood Clo., Kings.T. 75 BM50
Alexandra Rd.
Cherrywood Ct., Tedd. 74 BJ49
Elmfield Ave.
Cherrywood Dr. SW15 75 BQ46
Cherrywood Dr., Grav. 81 DF49
Cherrywood La., Mord. 85 BR52
Cherston Gdns., Loug. 31 CL24
Cherston Rd., Loug. 31 CL24
Chertsey Bri. Rd., Cher. 83 AX54
Chertsey Clo., Ken. 104 BY61
Chertsey Cres., Croy. 96 CF58
Chertsey Dr., Sutt. 85 BR55
Chertsey La., Cher. 82 AV52
Chertsey La., Stai. 72 AV49
Chertsey Rd. E11 48 CF34
Chertsey Rd. W4 65 BM42
Chertsey Rd., Ash. 73 BA50
Chertsey Rd., Cher. 91 AO56
Chertsey Rd. (Longcross), 82 AP55
Cher.
Chertsey Rd., Felt. 73 BB49
Chertsey Rd., Ilf. 49 CM35
Chertsey Rd., Shep. 83 AY54
Chertsey Rd., Sun. 73 BA50
Chertsey Rd., Twick. 74 BJ46
Chertsey Rd. (Whitton), 74 BF48
Twick.
Chertsey Rd. 83 AW55
(Addlestonemoor), Wey.
Chertsey Rd. (Byfleet), 92 AX59
Wey.
Chertsey Rd., Wok. 100 AS61
Chertsey Rd., Wok. 100 AS62
Chertsey Rd. (Chobham), 91 AP58
Wok.
Chertsey St. SW17 76 BV49
Chertsey St., Guil. 118 AR71
Chervil Clo., Felt. 73 BC48
Charleston Clo.
Chervil Ms. SE28 59 CO40
Cherwell Clo., Rick. 26 AZ25
Cherwell Clo., Slou. 62 AT43
Tweed Rd.
Cherwell Ct., Epsom 94 BN56
Cherwell Gro., S.Ock. 60 DA40
Cherwell Way, Ruis. 44 BA32
Cheryls Clo. SW6 66 BS44
Cheselden Rd., Guil. 118 AS71
Cheseman St. SE26 77 CB48
Chesfield Rd., Kings.T. 75 BL50
Chesham Ave., Orp. 88 CL53
Chesham Clo. SW1 3 G7
Chesham Clo., Rom. 50 CS31
Chesham Clo., Sutt. 94 BR58
Chesham Ct., Berk. 7 AQ13
Ashlyns Rd.
Chesham Cres. SE20 77 CC51
Chesham La., Ch.St.G. 34 AS27
Chesham La., Ger.Cr. 34 AS28
Chesham Ms. SW1 3 G6
Chesham Ms. SW1 66 BV41
Chesham Ms., Guil. 118 AS71
Chesham Pl.
Chesham Pl. SW1 3 G7
Chesham Pl. SW1 66 BV41
Chesham Rd. SE20 87 CC51
Chesham Rd. SW19 76 BT49
Chesham Rd., Berk. 7 AQ14
Chesham Rd., Guil. 118 AS71
Chesham Rd., Hem.H. 16 AS17
Chesham Rd., Kings.T. 85 BM51
Chesham St. NW10 46 BN34
Chesham St. SW1 3 G7
Chesham St. SW1 66 BV41
Chesham Ter. W13 64 BJ41
Chesham Way, Wat. 26 BB25
Cheshire Clo. SE4 67 CD44
Malpas Rd.
Cheshire Clo., Cher. 91 AU57
Cheshire Clo., Horn. 51 CX32
Cheshire Clo., Mitch. 86 BX52
Cheshire Rd. EC4 65 BY39
Fleet St.
Cheshire Ct., Slou. 62 AQ41
Clements Clo.
Cheshire Gdns., Chess. 93 BK57
Cheshire Rd. N22 38 BX29
Cheshire St. E2 2 Q4
Cheshire St. E2 57 CA38
Chesholm Rd. N16 48 CA34
Chesholm Rd., Ashf. 73 BA50
Cheshunt Gate Ho., 21 CB18
Wal.Cr.
Cheshunt Pk., Chsnt. 21 CB17
Cheshunt Rd. E7 58 CH36

Cheshunt Rd., Belv. 69 CR42
Cheshunt Wash, Chsnt. 21 CD17
Chesil Way, Hayes 53 BB38
Chesilton Rd. SW6 65 BR44
Chesley Gdns. E6 58 CJ37
Chesney Cres., Croy. 96 CF57
Chesney St. SW11 66 BU44
Chesnut Gro. N17 48 CA31
Chesnut Rd.
Chesnut Rd. N17 48 CA31
Chess Clo., Chesh. 25 AR21
Chess Clo., Rick. 26 AX24
Chess Ct. E1 57 CA39
Old Castle St.
Chess Hill, Rick. 26 AX24
Chess La., Rick. 26 AX24
Chess Vale Ri., Rick. 26 AY25
Chess Way, Rick. 26 AW24
Chessfield Pk., Amer. 25 AS32
Chessholme Ct., Sun. 73 BB50
Scotts Ave.
Chessington Ave. N3 46 BR31
Chessington Ave., Bexh. 69 CQ43
Chessington Clo., 94 BN57
Epsom
Chessington Ct., Pnr. 45 BE31
Chessington Hall 93 BK57
Gdns., Chess.
Harrow Clo.
Chessington Hill Pk., 94 BM56
Chess.
Chessington Par., Chess. 93 BK56
Chessington Rd., Epsom 94 BM57
Chessington Way, 87 CE55
W.Wick.
Chessmount Ri., Chesh. 16 AO20
Chesson Rd. W14 65 BR43
Chesswood Way, Pnr. 36 BD30
Chester Ave., Rich. 75 BL46
Chester Ave., Twick. 74 BE47
Chester Ave., Upmin. 51 CZ34
Chester Clo. SW1 3 J5
Chester Clo. SW1 66 BV41
Chester Clo. SW13 65 BP45
Chester Clo., Ashf. 73 BA49
Chester Clo., Dor. 119 BK70
Chester Clo., Guil. 118 AP69
Chester Clo., Loug. 31 CM23
Chester Clo., Sutt. 86 BS55
Chester Clo., Uxb. 53 AZ39
Chester Clo. N. NW1 1 K2
Chester Clo. S. NW1 1 K3
Chester Cotts. SW1 3 G9
Chester Cotts. SW1 66 BV42
Bourne St.
Chester Ct. NW1 1 K2
Chester Ct. NW5 47 BV35
Chester Ct. W3 55 BM39
Monks Dr.
Chester Cres. E8 48 CA35
Chester Dr., Har. 45 BE32
Chester Gdns. W13 54 BJ39
Chester Gdns., Enf. 30 CB25
Chester Gdns., Mord. 86 BT53
Chester Gate NW1 1 J3
Chester Gate NW1 56 BV38
Outer Circle
Chester Grn., Loug. 31 CM23
Chester Gro. E2 57 CB38
Kelsey St.
Chester Gro. SE18 68 CM42
Chester Ms. SW1 3 J6
Chester Ms. SW1 66 BV41
Chester Path, Loug. 31 CM23
Chester Pl. NW1 1 J2
Chester Pl. NW1 56 BV38
Cumberland Ter.
Chester Rd. E7 58 CJ36
Chester Rd. E11 49 CH32
Chester Rd. E16 58 CG38
Chester Rd. E17 48 CC32
Chester Rd. N9 39 CB26
Chester Rd. N17 48 BZ31
Chester Rd. N19 47 BV34
Chester Rd. NW1 1 H3
Chester Rd. NW1 56 BV38
Chester Rd. SW19 75 BQ50
Chester Rd., Borwd. 28 BN24
Chester Rd., Chig. 40 CL27
Chester Rd., Houns. 64 BD45
Chester Rd. (Heathrow), 63 AZ45
Houns.
Chester Rd., Ilf. 49 CN33
Chester Rd., Lthd. 110 BC67
Chester Rd., Loug. 31 CL23
Chester Rd., Nthwd. 35 BB29
Chester Rd., Sid. 78 CN46
Chester Rd., Slou. 52 AO39
Chester Rd., Wat. 26 BC25
Chester Row SW1 3 G9
Chester Row SW1 66 BV42
Chester Sq. SW1 3 H8
Chester Sq. SW1 66 BV42
Chester Sq. Ms. SW1 3 J7
Chester St. E2 57 CB38
Chester St. SW1 3 H6
Chester St. SW1 66 BV41
Chester Ter. NW1 1 J2
Chester Ter. NW1 56 BV38
Chester Way SE11 4 E9
Chester Way SE11 66 BY42
Chesterfield Clo., Orp. 89 CQ52
Chesterfield Dr., Esher 84 BJ55
Chesterfield Dr., Sev. 107 CS64
Chesterfield Gdns. N4 41 BY32
Chesterfield Gdns. W1 3 J2
Chesterfield Gdns. W1 56 BV40
Chesterfield Gro. SE22 77 CA46
Chesterfield Hill W1 3 J2
Chesterfield Hill W1 56 BV40
Chesterfield Rd. E10 48 CF32
Chesterfield Rd. N3 38 BS29
Chesterfield Rd. W4 65 BN43
Chesterfield Rd., Ashf. 73 AX49

Chesterfield Rd., Barn. 28 BQ25
Chesterfield Rd., Enf. 30 CD22
Chesterfield Rd., Epsom 94 BN57
Chesterfield St. W1 3 J2
Chesterfield St. W1 56 BV40
Chesterfield Wk. SE10 67 CF44
Chesterfield Way, Hayes 63 BC41
Chesterford Gdns. NW3 47 BS35
Chesterford Rd. E12 49 CK35
Chesters, The, N.Mal. 85 BO51
Chesterton Clo. SW18 76 BS46
Ericsson Clo.
Chesterton Clo., Grnf. 54 BF37
Chesterton Dr., Red. 113 BX67
Chesterton Dr., Stai. 73 AY47
Chesterton Rd. E13 58 CH38
Chesterton Rd. W10 55 BQ39
Chesterton Ter. E13 58 CH38
Chesterton Ter., Kings.T. 85 BM51
Chesterton Way, Til. 71 DG44
Chesthunte Rd. N17 39 BZ30
Chestnut Ave. E7 49 CH35
Chestnut Ave. N8 47 BX32
Chestnut Ave. SW14 65 BO45
Thornton Rd.
Chestnut Ave., Brent. 64 BK42
Chestnut Ave., Buck.H. 40 CJ27
Chestnut Ave., Chesh. 16 AP18
Chestnut Ave., Edg. 37 BL29
Chestnut Ave., Epsom 94 BO56
Chestnut Ave., Esher 84 BG54
Chestnut Ave., Grays 71 DD41
Chestnut Ave., Guil. 118 AR72
Chestnut Ave., Hmptn. 74 BF50
Chestnut Ave., Horn. 50 CT34
Chestnut Ave., Nthwd. 35 BB30
Chestnut Ave., Rick. 26 AW25
Chestnut Ave., Slou. 62 AS41
Chestnut Ave., Tedd. 84 BH52
Chestnut Ave., Vir.W. 82 AP52
Chestnut Ave., Walt. 92 BB58
Chestnut Ave., Wem. 45 BJ35
Chestnut Ave., West Dr. 53 AY40
Chestnut Ave., W.Wick. 88 CG55
Chestnut Ave., West. 106 CK64
Chestnut Ave., Wey. 92 BA57
Chestnut Ave. N. E17 48 CF31
Chestnut Ave. S. E17 48 CF32
Chestnut Clo. N14 29 BW25
Chestnut Clo. N16 48 BZ34
Lordship Gro.
Chestnut Clo. SE6 57 CF49
Chestnut Clo. SE16 76 BY49
Leigham Ct. Rd.
Chestnut Clo., Amer. 25 AO22
Chestnut Clo., Ashf. 73 AZ49
Chestnut Clo., Berk. 7 AT12
Chestnut Clo., Buck.H. 40 CJ27
Chestnut Clo., Cars. 86 BU54
Chestnut Clo., Egh. 72 AQ50
Chestnut Clo., Ger.Cr. 34 AS30
Chestnut Clo., Grav. 81 DF46
Chestnut Clo., Hayes 53 BB40
Chestnut Clo., Horn. 51 CV35
Chestnut Clo., Orp. 98 CO56
Chestnut Clo., Red. 121 BV71
Haig Cres.
Chestnut Clo., Sun. 73 BB50
Cavendish Rd.
Chestnut Clo., Tad. 104 BS65
Chestnut Clo., West Dr. 63 AZ43
Chestnut Clo., Wey. 92 AX56
Chestnut Clo., Wok. 100 AV65
Chestnut Copse, Oxt. 115 CH69
Chestnut Ct., Amer. 25 AO22
Chestnut La.
Chestnut Dr. E11 49 CH32
Chestnut Dr., Berk. 7 AR13
Chestnut Dr., Bexh. 69 CP45
Chestnut Dr., Egh. 72 AR50
Chestnut Dr., Har. 36 BH29
Chestnut Dr., Pnr. 45 BD32
Chestnut Dr., St.Alb. 9 BJ12
Chestnut Dr., Wind. 61 AM45
Chestnut Gdns., Sutt. 95 BS56
Elm Gro.
Chestnut Glen, Horn. 50 CU34
Chestnut Grn., Stai. 73 AW49
Chestnut Gro. SW12 76 BV47
Chestnut Gro. W5 64 BK41
Chestnut Gro., Barn. 29 BU25
Chestnut Gro., Brwd. 42 DB27
Chestnut Gro., Dart. 79 CS49
Chestnut Gro., Ilf. 40 CN29
Chestnut Gro., Islw. 64 BJ45
Chestnut Gro., Mitch. 86 BW53
Chestnut Gro., N.Mal. 85 BN52
Chestnut Gro., S.Croy. 96 CB57
Chestnut Gro., Stai. 73 AX50
Chestnut Gro., Wem. 45 BJ35
Chestnut Gro., Wok. 100 AS63
Chestnut La. N20 37 BQ26
Chestnut La., Amer. 25 AO21
Chestnut La., Sev. 107 CU65
Chestnut La., Wey. 92 AZ56
Chestnut Manor Clo., 73 AW49
Stai.
Chestnut Mead, Red. 121 BU70
Oxford Rd.
Chestnut Ri. SE18 68 CM43
Chestnut Ri., Bush. 36 BF26
Chestnut Rd. SE27 76 BY48
Chestnut Rd. SW20 85 BQ51
Chestnut Rd., Ashf. 73 AZ49
Chestnut Rd., Dart. 80 CV47
Chestnut Rd., Enf. 30 CD21
Chestnut Rd., Guil. 118 AR70
Chestnut Rd., Kings.T. 75 BL50
Chestnut Rd., Twick. 74 BH48
Chestnut Rd. Pas., Twick. 74 BH48
Chestnut Wk., Ger.Cr. 34 AS29

Chestnut Wk., Sev. 117 CW67
Chestnut Wk., Shep. 83 BB53
Chestnut Wk., Walt. 92 BB58
Chestnut Wk., Wat. 26 BC22
Chestnut Wk., Wdf.Grn. 40 CH28
Chestnut Way, Felt. 73 BC48
Chestnuts, Brwd. 122 DD26
Chestnuts, The, Hem.H. 7 AV15
Beechwood Pk.
Chestnuts, The, Ong. 15 DB13
Chestnuts, The, Walt. 83 BC55
Cheston Ave., Croy. 87 CG54
Chestwood Gro., Uxb. 53 AY37
Cheswick Clo., Dart. 69 CT45
Woodfall Dr.
Chesworth Clo., Erith 69 CT44
Chettle Clo. SE1 4 K6
Chettle Clo. SE1 67 BZ41
Spurgeon St.
Chetwode Dr., Epsom 103 BQ62
Chetwode Pl., Epsom 103 BQ63
Chetwode Rd. SW17 76 BU48
Chetwode Rd., Epsom 103 BQ63
Chetwood Wk. E6 58 CK39
Remington Rd.
Chetwynd Ave., Barn. 38 BU26
Chetwynd Dr., Uxb. 53 AY37
Chetwynd Rd. NW5 47 BV35
Cheval Pl. SW7 3 D6
Cheval Pl. SW7 66 BU41
Cheval St. E14 67 CE41
Cheveley Clo., Rom. 42 CW30
Chevely Clo., Epp. 23 CP18
Cheveney Wk., Brom. 88 CH52
Marina Clo.
Chevening La., Sev. 107 CQ61
Chevening Rd. NW6 55 BQ37
Chevening Rd. SE10 68 CG42
Chevening Rd. SE19 77 BZ50
Chevening Rd., Sev. 107 CQ65
Chevenings, The, Sid. 79 CO48
Cheverton Rd. N19 47 BX33
Chevet St. E9 48 CD35
Chevington Way, Horn. 51 CV35
Cheviot Clo., Bans. 104 BS61
Cheviot Clo., Bexh. 69 CT44
Cheviot Clo., Bush. 27 BG25
Cheviot Clo., Enf. 30 BZ23
Cheviot Clo., Sutt. 95 BY58
Cheviot Gdns. NW2 46 BQ34
Cheviot Gate NW2 46 BR34
Cheviot Rd. SE27 76 BY49
Cheviot Rd., Horn. 50 CU33
Cheviot Rd., Slou. 62 AT42
Cheviot Way, Grnf. 54 BJ37
Cheviot Way, Ilf. 49 CN32
Cheviots, Hat. 10 BP14
Cheviots, Hem.H. 8 AY12
Chevremont, Guil. 118 AS71
Chewton Rd. E17 48 CD31
Cheyham Gdns., Sutt. 103 BQ58
Cheyham Way, Sutt. 94 BR58
Cheyne Ave. E18 48 CG31
Cheyne Ave., Twick. 74 BE47
Cheyne Clo. NW4 46 BQ32
Cheyne Clo., Amer. 25 AO21
Cheyne Clo., Brom. 88 CK55
Cheyne Clo., Ger.Cr. 43 AS33
Cheyne Clo. SW3 66 BU43
Flood St.
Cheyne Ct., Bans. 104 BS61
Cheyne Gdns. SW3 66 BU43
Cheyne Hill, Surb. 85 BL52
Cheyne Ms. SW3 66 BU43
Cheyne Path W7 54 BH39
Copley Clo.
Cheyne Pl. SW3 66 BU43
Cheyne Rd., Ashf. 73 BA50
Napier Rd.
Cheyne Row SW3 66 BU43
Cheyne Wk. N21 29 BY25
Cheyne Wk. NW4 46 BQ32
Cheyne Wk. SW3 66 BT43
Cheyne Wk. SW10 66 BT43
Cheyne Wk., Chesh. 16 AO18
Cheyne Wk., Croy. 87 CB56
Cheyneys Ave., Edg. 36 BK29
Chichele Gdns., Croy. 96 CA56
Chichele Rd. NW2 46 BQ35
Chichele Rd., Oxt. 115 CG67
Chicheley Gdns., Har. 36 BG29
Chicheley Rd., Har. 36 BG29
Chicheley St. SE1 4 C4
Chicheley St. SE1 66 BX41
Chichester Ave., Ruis. 44 BA34
Chichester Clo. E6 58 CK39
Chichester Clo. SE3 68 CJ44
Chichester Clo., Dor. 119 BJ70
Chichester Clo., S.Ock. 60 CY40
Chichester Ct., Stan. 94 BO58
Old Schools La.
Chichester Ct., Slou. 62 AQ41
Sussex Pl.
Chichester Ct., Stan. 46 BL31
Chichester Dr., Pur. 95 BX59
Chichester Dr., Sev. 116 CT66
Chichester Gdns., Ilf. 49 CK33
Chichester Ms. SE27 76 BY49
Chichester Rents WC2 2 D8
Chichester Rents WC2 56 BY39
Chancery La.
Chichester Ri., Grav. 81 DH49
Livingstone Rd.
Chichester Rd. E11 49 CG34
Chichester Rd. N9 39 CB26
Chichester Rd. NW6 55 BS37
Chichester Rd. W2 56 BS39
Chichester Rd., Croy. 87 CA55
Chichester Rd., Dor. 119 BJ70
Chichester Rd., Green. 80 CZ46
Chichester Row, Amer. 25 AO22
Chichester St. SW1 66 BW42
Chichester Way E14 67 CF42
Chichester Way, Felt. 74 BD46

Chichester Way, Wat. 18 BE20
Chickabiddy Hill, Wok. 91 AO56
Chicksand Est. E1 57 CB39
Chicksand St. E1 2 Q7
Chicksand St. E1 57 CA39
Chiddingfold N12 38 BS27
Chiddingstone Ave., Bexh. 69 CQ43
Chiddingstone St. SW6 66 BS44
Chieftan Dr., Grays 70 CX42
Chieveley Rd., Bexh. 69 CR45
Chiffinch Gdns., Grav. 81 DF48
  Riversdale
Chignell Pl. W13 54 BJ40
Chigwell High Rd., Chig. 40 CL28
Chigwell Hill E1 57 CB40
  Pennington St.
Chigwell Hurst Ct., Pnr. 36 BD20
Chigwell La., Loug. 31 CM24
Chigwell Pk. Dr., Chig. 40 CL28
Chigwell Ri., Chig. 40 CL27
Chigwell Rd. E18 49 CH31
Chigwell Rd., Wdf.Grn. 40 CJ29
Chigwell Vw., Rom. 41 CR28
Chilberton Rd., Red. 121 BW69
Chilcot Clo. E14 57 CE39
  Grundy St.
Chilcote La., Amer. 25 AQ23
Chilcott Rd., Wat. 26 BB21
Childebert Rd. SW17 76 BV48
Childerditch La., Brwd. 42 DC29
Childerditch La., Brwd. 123 DD30
Childerditch St., Brwd. 123 DD30
Childeric Rd. SE14 67 CD43
Childerley St. SW6 65 BR44
  Fulham Palace Rd.
Childers, The, Wdf.Grn. 40 CK28
Childers St. SE8 67 CD43
Childs Clo., Horn. 51 CV32
  Hill Cres.
Childs Cres., Swans. 80 DB46
Childs Hall Rd., Lthd. 111 BE66
Childs La. SE19 77 CA50
  Childs Pl.
Childs Pl. SW5 66 BS42
Childs St. SW5 66 BS42
Childs Wk. SW5 66 BS42
  Childs Pl.
Childs Way NW11 46 BR32
Childsbridge La., Sev. 108 CW62
Childsbridge Way, Sev. 108 CW63
Childwick Clo., Hem.H. 8 AZ15
Childwick Ct., Hem.H. 8 AZ15
Chilham Clo., Grnf. 54 BJ37
  Horsenden La. S.
Chilham Rd. SE9 78 CK49
Chilham Way, Brom. 88 CG54
Chillbrook Fm. Rd., Cob. 101 BC62
Chillerton Rd. SW17 76 BV49
Chillingworth Gdns., Twick. 74 BH48
  Tower Rd.
Chillingworth Rd. N7 47 BY35
Chilmans Dr., Lthd. 111 BF66
  Pine Dene
Chilmark Gdns., N.Mal. 85 BP53
Chilmark Gdns., Red. 113 BX68
Chilmark Rd. SW16 86 BW51
Chilmead La., Red. 121 BW69
Chilsey Grn. Rd., Cher. 82 AV53
Chiltern Ave., Amer. 25 AO22
Chiltern Ave., Bush. 27 BG25
Chiltern Ave., Twick. 74 BF47
Chiltern Clo., Berk. 7 AP12
Chiltern Clo., Bexh. 69 CT44
Chiltern Clo., Borwd. 28 BL23
Chiltern Clo., Bush. 27 BF25
Chiltern Clo., Chsnt. 20 BY17
Chiltern Clo., Croy. 87 CB55
Chiltern Clo., Uxb. 44 AZ34
Chiltern Clo., Wok. 100 AR64
Chiltern Dene, Enf. 29 BX24
Chiltern Dr., Rick. 34 AV26
Chiltern Dr., Surb. 85 BM53
Chiltern Gdns. NW2 46 BQ34
Chiltern Gdns., Brom. 88 CG52
Chiltern Gdns., Horn. 51 CV34
Chiltern Hill, Ger.Cr. 34 AS30
Chiltern Pk. Ave., Berk. 7 AQ12
Chiltern Rd. E3 57 CE38
Chiltern Rd., Grav. 81 DF48
Chiltern Rd., Ilf. 49 CN31
Chiltern Rd., Pnr. 45 BD32
Chiltern Rd., St.Alb. 9 BK11
Chiltern Rd., Sutt. 95 BS58
Chiltern St. W1 1 G6
Chiltern St. W1 56 BV39
Chiltern Vw. Rd., Uxb. 53 AX37
Chiltern Way, Wdf.Grn. 40 CH27
Chilterns, Berk. 7 AP12
Chilterns, Hat. 10 BP14
Chilterns, Hem.H. 8 AY12
  Malvern Way
Chilterns, The, Sutt. 95 BU58
Chilterns Clo., Bans. 104 BS61
  High St.
Chilthorne Rd. SE6 77 CD47
  Ravensbourne Pk. Cres.
Chilton Ave. W5 64 BK42
Chilton Ct., Walt. 92 BC56
Chilton Grn., Welw.G.C. 5 BT8
Chilton Gro. SE8 67 CC42
Chilton Rd., Edg. 37 BM29
Chilton Rd., Grays 71 DG41
Chilton Rd., Rich. 65 BM45
Chilton St. E2 2 Q4
Chilton St. E2 57 CA38
Chiltons, The E18 40 CH30
  Grove Hill
Chiltons Clo., Bans. 104 BS61
  High St.
Chilver St. SE10 68 CG42
Chilwell Gdns., Wat. 36 BD28
Chilworth Ct. SW19 75 BQ47
  Windlesham Gro.

Chilworth Gdns., Sutt. 86 BT55
Chilworth Ms. W2 1 A9
Chilworth Ms. W2 56 BT39
Chilworth New Rd., Guil. 118 AT74
Chilworth Rd., Guil. 118 AV73
Chilworth St. W2 56 BT39
Chimes Ms. N13 38 BY28
China La., Upmin. 123 DE35
Chinbrook Cres. SE12 78 CH48
  Chinbrook Rd.
Chinbrook Rd. SE12 78 CH48
Chinchilla Dr., Houns. 64 BD44
Chindits La., Brwd. 42 DB28
Chine, The N10 47 BW31
Chine, The N21 29 BY25
Chine, The, Wem. 45 BJ35
Ching Ct. WC2 1 Q9
Chingdale Rd. E4 40 CG27
Chingford Ave. E4 39 CE27
Chingford La., Wdf.Grn. 40 CG28
Chingford Mt. Rd. E4 39 CE28
Chingford Rd. E4 39 CE29
Chingley Clo., Brom. 78 CG50
Chinnery Clo., Enf. 30 CA22
Chinnor Cres., Grnf. 54 BF37
Chinthurst La., Guil. 118 AS74
Chipka St. E14 67 CF41
Chipley St. SE14 67 CD43
  Nynehead St.
Chipmunk Gro., Nthlt. 54 BE38
  Argus Way
Chippen Clo., Pnr. 44 BB31
Chippendale All., Uxb. 53 AX37
Chippendale Rd., Orp. 89 CO51
Chippendale St. E5 48 CC34
Chippendale Waye, Uxb. 53 AX36
Chippenham Ave., Wem. 46 BM35
Chippenham Clo., Rom. 42 CV28
Chippenham Gdns. NW6 56 BS38
  Malvern Rd.
Chippenham Ms. W9 56 BS38
Chippenham Rd. W9 56 BS38
Chippenham Rd., Rom. 42 CV28
Chippenham Wk., Rom. 42 CV29
Chipperfield Clo., Upmin. 51 CZ33
Chipperfield Rd., Hem.H. 8 AX15
Chipperfield Rd. (Bovingdon), Hem.H. 16 AT17
Chipperfield Rd., Kings L. 17 AX18
Chipperfield Rd., Orp. 89 CO51
Chipping Clo., Barn. 28 BR24
  Strafford Rd.
Chippingfield, Harl. 6 CP9
Chipstead Ave., Th.Hth. 86 BY52
Chipstead Clo. SE19 77 CA50
Chipstead Clo., Couls. 104 BV61
Chipstead Clo., Ger.Cr. 34 AR30
Chipstead Clo., Red. 121 BU71
Chipstead Ct., Wok. 100 AP61
  Creston Ave.
Chipstead Gdns. NW2 46 BP34
Chipstead La., Couls. 104 BT65
Chipstead La., Sev. 107 CS64
Chipstead La., Tad. 112 BR66
Chipstead Pk., Sev. 107 CS64
Chipstead Pk. Clo., Sev. 107 CS64
Chipstead Pl. Gdns., Sev. 107 CS64
  Chipstead La.
Chipstead Rd., Bans. 103 BR62
Chipstead Rd., Erith 69 CT43
Chipstead Rd., Houns. 63 AZ45
Chipstead St. SW6 66 BS44
Chipstead Valley Rd., Couls. 104 BV61
Chipstead Way, Bans. 104 BU62
Chirk Clo., Hayes 54 BE38
Chirton Wk., Wok. 100 AQ62
  Shilburn Way
Chisenhale Rd. E3 57 CD37
Chisholm Rd., Croy. 87 CA55
Chisholm Rd., Rich. 75 BL46
Chisledon Wk. E9 57 CD36
  Trowbridge Est.
Chislehurst Ave. N12 38 BT29
Chislehurst Rd., Brom. 88 CJ51
Chislehurst Rd., Orp. 88 CN52
Chislehurst Rd., Rich. 75 BL46
Chislehurst Rd., Sid. 79 CO49
Chislet Clo., Beck. 77 CE50
  Abbey La.
Chisley Rd. N15 48 CA32
Chiswell Sq. SE3 68 CH44
  Brook La.
Chiswell St. EC1 2 K6
Chiswell St. EC1 57 BZ39
Chiswellgreen La., St.Alb. 18 BE16
Chiswick Bri. SW14 65 BN44
Chiswick Bri. W4 65 BN44
Chiswick Clo., Croy. 86 BX55
Chiswick Ct., Pnr. 45 BE31
Chiswick Common Rd. W4 65 BN42
Chiswick Ct., Pnr. 45 BE31
Chiswick High Rd. W4 65 BM42
Chiswick La. W4 65 BO42
Chiswick La. S. W4 65 BP42
Chiswick Mall W4 65 BO43
Chiswick Quay W4 65 BN44
Chiswick Rd. N9 39 CB27
Chiswick Rd. W4 65 BN42
Chiswick Sq. W4 65 BO43
  Hogarth Roundabout
Chiswick Staithe W4 65 BN44
Chiswick Vill. W4 65 BM43
Chiswick Wf. W4 65 BO43
  Pumping Sta. Rd.
Chitty St. W1 1 M6
Chitty St. W1 56 BW39
Chittys La., Dag. 50 CP34
Chittys Wk., Guil. 109 AP68
Chivalry Rd. SW11 76 BU46
Chive Clo., Croy. 87 CC54
Chivers Rd. E4 39 CE28

Chivers Rd., Brwd. 24 CZ20
Choats Manor Way, Bark. 59 CP38
Choats Rd., Dag. 59 CQ38
Chobham Gdns. SW19 75 BQ48
Chobham La., Wok. 82 AP55
Chobham Pk. La., Wok. 91 AQ58
Chobham Pl., Wok. 91 AO57
Chobham Rd. E15 48 CF35
Chobham Rd., Cher. 91 AT57
Chobham Rd., Wok. 100 AS61
Chobham Rd. (Horsell), Wok. 91 AR60
Chobham Rd. (Knaphill), Wok. 100 AO61
Choir Grn., Wok. 100 AP62
Cholmeley Cres. N6 47 BV33
Cholmeley Pk. N6 47 BV33
Cholmley Gdns. NW6 47 BS35
  Fortune Grn. Rd.
Cholmley Rd., T.Ditt. 84 BJ53
Cholmondeley Ave. N 55 BP37
  NW10
Cholmondeley Wk., Rich. 74 BK46
Choppins Ct. E1 57 CB40
  Wapping La.
Chopwell Clo. E15 58 CG36
  West Ham La.
Chorleywood Bottom, Rick. 25 AU25
Chorleywood Clo., Rick. 35 AX26
  Nightingale Rd.
Chorleywood Cres., Orp. 88 CN51
Chorleywood Rd., Rick. 26 AW24
Choumert Gro. SE15 67 CB44
Choumert Rd. SE15 67 CA45
Choumert Sq. SE15 67 CB44
Chrichton St. SW8 66 BW44
  Westbury St.
Chrislaine Clo., Stai. 73 AX46
  High Street, Stanwell
Chrisp St. E14 57 CE39
Christ Ch. Mt., Epsom 94 BM59
Christ Ch. Rd. SW14 74 BM46
Christ Ch. Rd., Epsom 94 BL59
Christchurch Ave. N12 38 BT29
Christchurch Ave. NW6 55 BQ37
Christchurch Ave., Erith 69 CT43
Christchurch Ave., Har. 45 BH31
Christchurch Ave., Rain. 59 CT38
Christchurch Ave., Tedd. 74 BJ49
Christchurch Ave., Wem. 55 BL36
Christchurch Clo. N12 38 BT29
Christchurch Clo. SW19 86 BT51
Christchurch Clo., St.Alb. 9 BG13
  Worley Rd.
Christchurch Cres., Rad. 27 BJ21
Christchurch Gdns., Har. 45 BJ31
Christchurch Grn., Wem. 55 BL36
Christchurch Hill NW3 47 BT34
Christchurch La., Barn. 28 BR23
Christchurch Pk., Sutt. 95 BT57
Christchurch Pas. NW3 47 BT34
  Christchurch Hill
Christchurch Path, Hayes 63 BA41
Christchurch Rd. N8 47 BX32
Christchurch Rd. SW2 76 BX47
Christchurch Rd. SW19 86 BT51
Christchurch Rd., Beck. 87 CE51
  Fairfield Rd.
Christchurch Rd., Dart. 80 CV47
Christchurch Rd., Grav. 81 DH47
Christchurch Rd., Hem.H. 8 AX13
Christchurch Rd., Houns. 63 AZ45
Christchurch Rd., Ilf. 49 CL33
Christchurch Rd., Pur. 95 BY58
Christchurch Rd., Sid. 78 CN49
Christchurch Rd., Surb. 85 BL54
Christchurch Rd., Til. 71 DG44
Christchurch Rd., Vir.W. 82 AQ52
Christchurch Sq. E2 57 CC37
Christchurch St. SW3 66 BU43
Christchurch Way SE10 68 CG42
Christchurch Way, Wok. 100 AS62
  Church St. E.
Christian Flds. SW16 76 BY50
Christian Flds. Ave., Grav. 81 DH49
Christian Sq., Wind. 61 AO44
  Ward Royal
Christian St. E1 57 CB39
Christie Ct. N19 47 BX34
  Pine Gro.
Christie Gdns., Rom. 50 CO32
Christie La., Lthd. 111 BF66
Christie Rd. E9 57 CD36
Christina Sq. N4 47 BY33
  Adolphus Rd.
Christina St. EC2 2 M4
Christina St. EC2 57 CA38
Christopher Ave. W7 64 BJ41
Christopher Clo. SE16 67 CC41
Christopher Clo., Horn. 51 CV35
  Chevington Way
Christopher Clo., Sid. 78 CN46
  Blackfen Rd.
Christopher Clo., Tad. 103 BQ65
Christopher Ct., Hem.H. 8 AX15
  Seaton Rd.
Christopher Gdns., Dag. 50 CP35
  Wren Rd.
Christopher Ms. W11 55 BR40
  Penzance St.
Christopher Pl. NW1 1 P3
Christopher Pl., St.Alb. 9 BG13
  Market Pl.
Christopher St. EC2 2 L5
Christopher St. EC2 57 BZ38
Christy Rd., West. 106 CJ61
Chryssell Rd. SW9 66 BY43
Chubworth St. SE14 67 CD43
Chucks La., Tad. 103 BP65
Chudleigh Cres., Ilf. 49 CN35

Chudleigh Gdns., Sutt. 86 BT55
Chudleigh Rd. NW6 55 BQ36
Chudleigh Rd. SE4 77 CD46
Chudleigh Rd., Rom. 42 CW28
Chudleigh Rd., Twick. 74 BH46
Chudleigh St. E1 57 CC39
Chudleigh Way, Ruis. 44 BC33
Chulsa Rd. SE26 77 CB49
Chumleigh St. SE5 67 CA43
Chumleigh Wk., Surb. 85 BL52
Church All. EC2 57 BZ39
  Basinghall St.
Church All., Brent. 64 BK43
Church All., Croy. 86 BY54
Church All., Wat. 27 BG22
Church App. SE21 77 BZ48
Church App., Sev. 106 CM61
Church App., Stai. 73 AX46
Church Ave. E4 39 CF29
Church Ave. SW14 65 BN45
Church Ave., Beck. 87 CE51
Church Ave., Nthlt. 54 BE36
Church Ave., Pnr. 45 BE32
Church Ave., Ruis. 44 BA33
Church Ave., Sid. 79 CO49
Church Ave., Sthl. 64 BE41
Church Clo. N20 38 BU27
Church Clo. W8 66 BS41
Church Clo., Brwd. 33 CY22
Church Clo., Cuffley 20 BX18
Church Clo., Edg. 37 BN28
Church Clo., Hayes 53 BA39
Church Clo., Hert. 11 BW13
Church Clo., Lthd. 102 BG65
Church Clo., Loug. 31 CK23
Church Clo., Nthwd. 35 BC29
  Emmanuel Rd.
Church Clo., Stai. 83 AX52
  The Bdy.
Church Clo., Tad. 112 BR67
Church Clo., Uxb. 53 AW37
Church Clo., West Dr. 63 AW41
Church Clo., Wey. 92 AW56
Church Clo., Wok. 100 AR61
Church Ct., Rich. 74 BK46
Church Cres. E9 57 CC36
Church Cres. N3 37 BR30
Church Cres. N10 47 BV31
Church Cres. N20 38 BU27
Church Cres., St.Alb. 9 BG13
Church Cres., Saw. 6 CQ6
Church Cres., S.Ock. 60 DB38
Church Dr. NW9 46 BN33
Church Dr., Har. 45 BE32
Church Dr., Maid. 61 AH41
Church Dr., W.Wick. 88 CG55
Church Elm La., Dag. 59 CR36
Church End E17 48 CE31
Church End NW4 46 BP31
Church End, Harl. 13 CL12
Church Entry EC4 56 BY39
  Carter La.
Church Fm. Clo., Swan. 89 CS53
Church Fm. La., Sutt. 94 BR57
Church Fld., Sev. 107 CT64
Church Fld. Path, Chsnt. 21 CC18
Church Flds., E.Mol. 84 BF52
Church Flds., Loug. 31 CK24
Church Gdns. W5 64 BK41
Church Gdns., Wem. 45 BJ35
Church Gate SW6 65 BR45
  Myatts Flds. Dev.
Church Grn. SW9 66 BY44
Church Grn., Walt. 93 BD57
Church Gro. SE13 67 CE45
Church Gro., Amer. 25 AS23
Church Gro., Hayes 53 BB39
Church Gro., Kings.T. 84 BK51
Church Gro., Slou. 52 AR39
Church Hill E17 48 CE31
Church Hill N21 38 BX26
Church Hill SE18 68 CK41
Church Hill SW19 75 BR49
Church Hill, Barn. 29 BU25
Church Hill, Cat. 105 CA65
Church Hill, Dart. 80 CV48
Church Hill (Crayford), Dart. 69 CT45
Church Hill, Epp. 23 CO18
Church Hill, Green. 80 CZ46
Church Hill, Har. 45 BH33
Church Hill, Loug. 31 CK24
Church Hill, Orp. 89 CO54
Church Hill, Pur. 95 BY58
Church Hill (Merstham), Red. 113 BV66
Church Hill (Nutfield), Red. 121 BX70
Church Hill, Sev. 106 CM61
Church Hill, Uxb. 44 AX31
Church Hill, Welw.G.C. 5 BO8
Church Hill, West. 106 CJ64
Church Hill (Horsell), Wok. 100 AR61
Church Hill (Pyrford), Wok. 100 AV62
Church Hill, Warl. 105 CC62
Church Hill Rd. E17 48 CE31
Church Hill Rd., Barn. 38 BU26
Church Hill Rd., Surb. 85 BL53
Church Hill Rd., Sutt. 95 BQ55
Church Hill Wd., Orp. 88 CN53
Church Hollow, Grays 70 CX42
  Church La.
Church Holt, The, Slou. 43 AO33
Church Hyde SE18 68 CN43
  Old Mill Rd.
Church La. E11 49 CG33
Church La. E17 48 CE31
Church La. N2 47 BT31
Church La. N8 47 BX31
Church La. N9 39 CA27
Church La. N17 39 CA30

Church La. NW9 46 BN33
Church La. SW17 76 BU48
Church La. SW19 85 BR51
Church La. W5 64 BJ42
Church La. (Burgh Heath), Bans. 103 BQ62
Church La., Berk. 7 AP12
Church La. (Doddinghurst), Brwd. 33 DA21
Church La. (Great Warley), Brwd. 51 DE34
Church La., Brom. 88 CH53
Church La., Brox. 12 CC15
Church La., Cat. 104 BV64
Church La., Chsnt. 21 CC18
Church La., Chess. 94 BL56
Church La., Chis. 88 CM53
Church La., Couls. 104 BV64
Church La., Dag. 59 CR36
Church La., Enf. 30 CA24
Church La., Epp. 23 CO19
Church La. (Headley), Epsom 103 BM61
Church La., Ger.Cr. 34 AS30
Church La., Gdse. 114 CC71
Church La., Grays 70 CX42
Church La. (Worplesdon), Guil. 109 AO68
Church La., Har. 36 BH31
Church La., Hat. 10 BO14
Church La., Hem.H. 16 AT17
Church La., Hert. 11 BW13
Church La., Kings L. 17 AZ17
Church La., Loug. 31 CK24
Church La., Maid. 61 AH41
Church La., Ong. 15 CL10
Church La., Oxt. 114 CF69
Church La., Pnr. 45 BE31
Church La., Pot.B. 20 BV18
Church La. (Wennington), Rain. 60 CV38
Church La., Red. 114 BU69
Church La., Rick. 25 AV25
Church La., Rick. 26 AW24
Church La., Rom. 32 CT28
Church La., Rom. 50 CT32
Church La. (Stapleford Abbotts), Rom. 32 CS24
Church La., St.Alb. 10 BM10
Church La., Sev. 108 CX64
  Heaverham Rd.
Church La. (Stoke Poges), Slou. 52 AP36
Church La. (Wexham), Slou. 52 AO35
Church La., Tedd. 74 BH49
Church La., T.Ditt. 84 BJ53
Church La., Twick. 74 BJ48
Church La., Upmin. 60 DA34
Church La., Uxb. 53 AW37
Church La., Wall. 86 BW55
Church La., Warl. 105 CC61
Church La. (Chelsham), Warl. 105 CF61
Church La., West. 106 CJ64
Church La. (Send), Wok. 109 AR69
Church La. Ave., Couls. 104 BV64
Church La. Clo., Stai. 73 AX46
Church La. Dr., Couls. 104 BV64
Church Leys, Harl. 13 CM12
Church Manorway SE2 68 CN42
Church Manorway, Erith 69 CS43
Church Meadow, Surb. 84 BK55
Church Mt. N2 47 BT31
Church Par., Ashf. 73 AY49
  Church Rd.
Church Pas. EC2 57 BZ39
  Gresham St.
Church Pas., Rich. 74 BK46
  Red Lion St.
Church Pas., Surb. 85 BL52
Church Path E11 49 CH32
Church Path E17 48 CE31
  St. Mary Rd.
Church Path N5 47 BY36
Church Path N5 48 BZ36
Church Path N8 47 BX32
  Tottenham La.
Church Path N12 38 BT28
Church Path N17 39 CA29
Church Path N20 38 BT27
Church Path NW10 55 BO36
Church Path SW14 65 BN45
  North Worple Way
Church Path SW19 85 BR52
Church Path W4 65 BN41
Church Path W7 54 BH40
Church Path, Cob. 92 BC59
Church Path, Couls. 104 BY62
Church Path, Croy. 87 BZ55
Church Path, Green. 80 CZ46
Church Path, Maid. 61 AH41
Church Path, Mitch. 86 BU52
Church Path, Red. 113 BV66
Church Path, Wok. 100 AS62
  High St.
Church Pl. SW1 3 M11
Church Pl., Mitch. 86 BU52
Church Pl., Shep. 83 AZ53
  Church Rd.
Church Ri. SE23 77 CC47
Church Ri., Chess. 94 BL57
Church Rd. E10 48 CE33
Church Rd. E12 49 CK34
Church Rd. E17 39 CD31
Church Rd. N6 47 BV32
Church Rd. N17 39 CA30
Church Rd. NW4 46 BP31
Church Rd. NW10 55 BO36
Church Rd. SE19 87 CA50
Church Rd. SW13 65 BO44
Church Rd. (Merton) SW19 86 BT52

294

- ...rch Rd. (Wimbledon) ...V19 — 75 BR49
- ...rch Rd. W3 — 55 BN40
- ...rch Rd. W7 — 54 BG40
- ...rch Rd., Ashf. — 73 AY48
- ...rch Rd., Ash. — 102 BK62
- ...rch Rd., Bark. — 58 CM36
- ...rch Rd., Berk. — 7 AT12
- ...rch Rd., Bexh. — 69 CQ45
- ...rch Rd., Brwd. — 33 CY22
- ...rch Rd., Brom. — 88 CH51
- ...rch Rd. (Shortlands), rom. — 88 CG52
- ...rch Rd., Buck.H. — 40 CH26
- ...rch Rd., Cat. — 105 CA65
- ...rch Rd. (Woldingham), Cat. — 105 CD65
- ...rch Rd., Croy. — 86 BY55
- ...rch Rd., E.Mol. — 84 BG52
- ...rch Rd., Egh. — 72 AT49
- ...rch Rd., Enf. — 30 CC25
- ...rch Rd., Epsom — 94 BO59
- ...rch Rd. (West Ewell), psom — 94 BN57
- ...rch Rd., Erith — 69 CS42
- ...rch Rd., Esher — 93 BH51
- ...rch Rd., Felt. — 74 BD49
- ...rch Rd., Grav. — 81 DF47
- ...rch Rd. (Cobham), rav. — 81 DH51
- ...rch Rd. (West ilbury), Grays — 71 DJ43
- ...rch Rd., Guil. — 14 CP12
- ...rch Rd., Harl. — 90 DC52
- ...rch Rd., Hartley — 90 DC52
- ...rch Rd., Hav. — 42 CV26
- ...rch Rd., Hayes — 53 BB40
- ...rch Rd., Hem.H. — 8 BA14
- ...rch Rd., Hert. — 11 BW13
- ...rch Rd., Houns. — 63 BG42
- ...rch Rd. (Heston), ouns. — 64 BF43
- ...rch Rd., Ilf. — 49 CN32
- ...rch Rd., Islw. — 64 BG44
- ...rch Rd., Iver — 52 AU38
- ...rch Rd., Ken. — 105 BZ61
- ...rch Rd., Kes. — 97 CJ57
- ...rch Rd., Kings.T. — 85 BL51
- ...rch Rd., Lthd. — 102 BJ64
- ...rch Rd. (Bookham), thd. — 102 BE65
- ...rch Rd., Loug. — 31 CG24
- ...rch Rd., Maid. — 61 AQ40
- ...rch Rd., Mitch. — 86 BT51
- ...rch Rd., New A.G. — 90 DC55
- ...rch Rd., Nthlt. — 54 BD37
- ...rch Rd., Nthwd. — 35 BB29
- ...rch Rd. (Moreton), ing. — 15 CV14
- ...rch Rd. (Stanford ivers), Ong. — 24 CV20
- ...rch Rd., Orp. — 98 CP57
- ...rch Rd. (Farnborough), Orp. — 97 CM56
- ...rch Rd., Pot.B. — 20 BS18
- ...rch Rd., Pur. — 95 BX58
- ...rch Rd., Red. — 121 BU71
- ...rch Rd., Reig. — 121 BS71
- ...rch Rd., Rich. — 65 BL45
- ...rch Rd. (Ham), Rich. — 74 BK49
- ...rch Rd. (Harold Wd.), om. — 42 CX30
- ...rch Rd. (Navestock), Rom. — 33 CV23
- ...rch Rd. (Halstead), ev. — 98 CQ59
- ...rch Rd. (Seal), Sev. — 108 CW64
- ...rch Rd. (Sevenoaks Veald), Sev. — 116 CU69
- ...rch Rd. (Stone St.), ev. — 117 CZ66
- ...rch Rd. (Sundridge), Sev. — 116 CQ66
- ...rch Rd. (West ingsdown), Sev. — 99 CZ57
- ...rch Rd., Shep. — 83 AZ54
- ...rch Rd., Sid. — 79 CO49
- ...rch Rd. (Foots Cray), id. — 79 CP49
- ...rch Rd. (Sthl.) *Grosvenor Rd.* — 64 BE41
- ...rch Rd., Stan. — 36 BJ28
- ...rch Rd., Surb. — 84 BK54
- ...rch Rd., Sutt. — 94 BR57
- ...rch Rd., S.at H. — 80 CW50
- ...rch Rd., Swan. — 90 CV51
- ...rch Rd. Crockenhill, Swan. — 89 CS54
- ...rch Rd., Swans. — 81 DC46
- ...rch Rd., Tedd. — 74 BH49
- ...rch Rd., Til. — 71 DF44
- ...rch Rd. (Cowley), Uxb. — 53 AX38
- ...rch Rd. (Harefield), Uxb. — 44 AX31
- ...rch Rd., Wall. — 86 BW55
- ...rch Rd., Warl. — 105 CC62
- ...rch Rd., Wat. — 26 BC23
- ...rch Rd., Well. — 69 CO44
- ...rch Rd., Welw.G.C. — 5 BQ8
- ...rch Rd., West Dr. — 63 AX41
- ...rch Rd. (Biggin Hill), Vest. — 106 CJ62
- ...rch Rd. (Brasted), Vest. — 107 CO65
- ...rch Rd., Wey. — 92 AZ56
- ...rch Rd. (Addlestone), Ney. — 92 AW56
- ...rch Rd. (Byfleet), Ney. — 92 AY60
- ...rch Rd., Whyt. — 105 CA62
- ...rch Rd., Wind. — 72 AQ48
- ...rch Rd. (Horsell), Vok. — 100 AR61

- Church Rd. (St. Johns), Wok. — 100 AQ63
- Church Rd., Wor.Pk. — 85 BO54
- Church Row NW3 — 47 BT35
- Church Row SW6 *Moore Pk. Rd.* — 66 BS43
- Church Row, Chis. — 88 CM51
- Church Side, Epsom — 94 BM60
- Church Sq., Shep. — 83 AZ54
- Church St. E15 — 58 CG37
- Church St. E16 — 58 CL40
- Church St. N9 — 39 BZ26
- **Church St. NW8** — 1 B6
- Church St. NW8 — 56 BT39
- **Church St. W2** — 1 B6
- Church St. W2 — 56 BT39
- Church St. W4 — 65 BO43
- Church St., Bet. — 120 BO71
- Church St., Cob. — 101 BC61
- Church St., Croy. — 87 BZ55
- Church St., Dag. — 59 CR36
- Church St., Dor. — 119 BJ71
- Church St., Enf. — 30 BZ24
- Church St., Epsom — 94 BO60
- Church St. (Ewell), Epsom — 94 BP58
- Church St., Esher — 93 BF56
- Church St., Grav. — 81 DG46
- Church St. (Southfleet), Grav. — 81 DD49
- Church St., Grays — 71 DE43
- Church St., Hmptn. — 84 BG51
- Church St., Hat. — 10 BQ12
- Church St. (Essendon), Hat. — 11 BU12
- Church St., Hem.H. — 8 AX12
- Church St. (Bovingdon), Hem.H. — 16 AT17
- Church St., Ing. — 24 DC19
- Church St., Islw. — 64 BJ45
- Church St., Kings.T. *Clarence St.* — 84 BK51
- Church St., Lthd. — 102 BJ64
- Church St. (Effingham), Lthd. — 111 BD67
- Church St., Reig. — 121 BS70
- Church St., Rick. — 35 AY26
- Church St., St.Alb. — 9 BG13
- Church St., Saw. — 6 CQ6
- Church St. (Seal), Sev. — 108 CX64
- Church St. (Shoreham), Sev. — 98 CT59
- Church St., Slou. — 62 AP41
- Church St. (Chalvey), Slou. — 61 AO41
- Church St., Stai. — 72 AV49
- Church St., Sun. *High St.* — 83 BC52
- Church St., Sutt. — 95 BS56
- Church St., Twick. — 74 BJ47
- Church St., Wal.Abb. — 21 CF20
- Church St., Walt. — 83 BC54
- Church St., Wat. — 26 BC24
- Church St., Wey. — 92 AZ56
- Church St., Wok. — 100 AU64
- Church St. E., Wok. — 100 AS62
- **Church St. Est. NW8** — 1 B5
- Church St. Est. NW8 — 56 BT38
- Church St. N. E15 — 58 CG37
- Church St. Pas. E15 — 58 CG37
- Church St. W., Wok. — 100 AS62
- Church Stretton Rd., Houns. — 74 BG46
- Church Ter. N1 *Mortimer Rd.* — 57 CA36
- Church Ter. NW4 — 46 BP31
- Church Ter. SE13 — 68 CG45
- Church Ter. SW8 *Union Gro.* — 66 BW44
- Church Ter., Rich. *Wakefield Rd.* — 74 BK46
- Church Ter., Wind. — 61 AM44
- Church Vale N2 — 47 BU31
- Church Vale SE23 — 77 CC48
- Church Vw., Brox. — 12 CD13
- Church Vw., S.Ock. — 70 CY41
- Church Vw., Upmin. — 51 CX34
- Church Wk. N6 *Swains La.* — 47 BV34
- Church Wk. N16 — 48 BZ35
- Church Wk. NW2 — 46 BR34
- Church Wk. NW4 — 46 BQ31
- Church Wk. NW9 — 46 BN34
- Church Wk. SW13 — 65 BP44
- Church Wk. SW16 — 86 BW51
- Church Wk. SW20 — 85 BQ52
- Church Wk., Brent. — 64 BK43
- Church Wk., Brox. — 12 CD13
- Church Wk., Cher. — 83 AW53
- Church Wk., Dart. — 80 CV48
- Church Wk., Grav. — 81 DH47
- Church Wk., Hayes — 53 BB39
- Church Wk., Lthd. *The Cres.* — 102 BJ64
- Church Wk., Red. — 114 BZ70
- Church Wk., Reig. — 121 BS70
- Church Wk., Rich. — 74 BK46
- Church Wk., Saw. — 6 CQ6
- Church Wk., T.Ditt. — 84 BJ53
- Church Wk., Walt. — 83 BC54
- Church Wk., Wey. — 83 AZ55
- Church Way N20 — 38 BU27
- Church Way, Barn. — 29 BU24
- Church Way, Edg. — 37 BM29
- Church Way, Oxt. — 115 CG69
- Church Way, S.Croy. — 96 CA58
- **Church Yd. Row SE11** — 4 G8
- Church Yd. Row SE11 — 66 BY42
- Churchbury Clo., Enf. — 30 CA23
- Churchbury La., Enf. — 30 BZ24
- Churchbury Rd. SE9 — 78 CJ47
- Churchbury Rd., Enf. — 30 CA23
- Churchcroft Clo. SW12 *Endlesham Rd.* — 76 BV47
- Churchdown, Brom. — 78 CG49

- Churchfield, Harl. — 6 CO10
- Churchfield, Reig. — 120 BR70
- Churchfield Ave. N12 — 38 BS29
- Churchfield Clo., Har. — 45 BG31
- Churchfield Clo., Hayes *West Ave.* — 53 BB40
- Churchfield Ms., Slou. — 52 AQ39
- Churchfield Rd. W3 — 55 BN40
- Churchfield Rd. W7 — 64 BH41
- Churchfield Rd. W13 — 54 BJ40
- Churchfield Rd., Ger.Cr. — 34 AR30
- Churchfield Rd., Walt. — 83 BC55
- Churchfield Rd., Well. — 69 CO45
- Churchfield Rd., Welw. — 5 BT6
- Churchfield Rd., Wey. — 92 AZ56
- Churchfields E18 — 40 CH30
- Churchfields, Brox. — 12 CE13
- Churchfields, Dart. — 80 CV48
- Churchfields, E.Mol. — 84 BF52
- Churchfields, Guil. — 109 AT68
- Churchfields Ave., Felt. — 74 BE48
- Churchfields Ave., Wey. — 92 AZ56
- Churchfields La., Brox. — 12 CE13
- Churchfields Path, Wal.Cr. — 21 CC18
- Churchfields Rd., Beck. — 87 CC51
- Churchgate, Chsnt. — 21 CB18
- Churchgate Rd., Chsnt. — 21 CB18
- Churchgate St., Harl. — 6 CQ9
- Churchill Ave., Har. — 45 BJ32
- Churchill Ave., Uxb. — 53 AZ38
- Churchill Clo., Lthd. — 102 BH65
- Churchill Clo., Ong. — 24 CX17
- Churchill Clo., Uxb. — 53 AZ38
- Churchill Cres., Hat. — 10 BQ15
- Churchill Dr., Wey. — 92 BA56
- Churchill Gdns. W3 — 55 BM39
- Churchill Gdns. Rd. SW1 — 66 BV42
- Churchill Pl., Har. *Sandridge Clo.* — 45 BH31
- Churchill Rd. E16 — 58 CJ39
- Churchill Rd. NW2 — 55 BP36
- Churchill Rd. NW5 — 47 BV35
- Churchill Rd., Edg. — 37 BL29
- Churchill Rd., Grays — 71 DE43
- Churchill Rd., Guil. — 118 AS71
- Churchill Rd., Hort.K. — 90 CY52
- Churchill Rd., St.Alb. — 9 BJ13
- Churchill Rd., Slou. — 62 AS42
- Churchill Rd., S.Croy. — 96 BZ58
- Churchill Ter. E4 — 39 CE27
- Churchill Wk. E9 — 48 CC35
- Churchill Way, Sun. — 73 BC49
- Churchley Rd. SE26 — 77 CB49
- Churchmead Clo., Barn. — 29 BQ25
- Churchmead Rd. NW10 — 55 BP36
- Churchmore Rd. SW16 — 86 BW51
- Churchside Clo., West. — 106 CJ62
- Churchvale Ct. W4 *Harvard Rd.* — 65 BM42
- Churchview Rd., Twick. — 74 BG47
- **Churchway NW1** — 1 P2
- Churchway NW1 — 56 BW38
- Churchwell Path E9 — 48 CC35
- Churchyard Pas. SE5 *Camberwell Gro.* — 67 BZ44
- Churston Ave. E13 — 58 CH37
- Churston Clo. SW2 — 76 BY47
- Churston Dr., Mord. — 85 BQ53
- Churston Gdns. N11 — 38 BW29
- **Churton Pl. SW1** — 3 M9
- Churton Pl. SW1 — 66 BW42
- **Churton St. SW1** — 3 M9
- Churton St. SW1 — 66 BW42
- Chusan Pl. E14 — 57 CD39
- Chuters Clo., Wey. *High St.* — 92 AY60
- Chuters Gro., Epsom — 94 BO59
- Chyngton Clo., Sid. *Priestlands Pk. Rd.* — 78 CN48
- Cibber Rd. SE23 — 77 CC48
- Cicada Rd. SW18 — 76 BT46
- Cicely Rd. SE15 — 67 CB44
- Cillocks Clo., Hodd. — 12 CE11
- Cimba Wd., Grav. — 81 DJ49
- Cinder Path, Wok. *College La.* — 100 AR63
- Cinderford Way, Brom. — 78 CG49
- Cinnamon Gdns., Guil. *Oregano Way* — 109 AQ68
- Cinnamon Row SW11 *Clove Hitch Quay* — 66 BT45
- Cinnamon St. E1 — 57 CB40
- Cintra Pk. SE19 — 77 CA50
- Cippenham La., Slou. — 61 AN40
- Circle, The NW2 — 46 BO34
- Circle, The NW7 — 37 BN29
- Circle, The, Til. — 71 DG44
- Circle Gdns. SW19 — 86 BS51
- Circle Gdns., Wey. — 92 AY60
- Circle Rd., Walt. — 92 BB58
- Circuits, The, Pnr. — 45 BD31
- Circular Rd. N17 — 48 CA31
- Circular Way SE18 — 68 CK43
- Circus, The EC3 *Minories* — 57 CA40
- Circus, The, Til. — 71 DG44
- **Circus Ms. W1** — 1 E6
- **Circus Pl. EC2** — 2 L7
- Circus Pl. EC2 — 57 BZ39
- **Circus Rd. NW8** — 1 A2
- Circus Rd. NW8 — 56 BT38
- Circus Rd. SE18 — 67 CF43
- Cirencester St. W2 — 56 BS39
- Cissbury Ring N. N12 — 37 BR28
- Cissbury Ring S. N12 — 37 BR28
- Cissbury Rd. N15 — 48 BZ32
- **Citadel Pl. SE11** — 4 B10
- Citizen Rd. N7 — 47 BY35
- Citron Ter. SE15 *Nunhead Gro.* — 67 CB45

- **City Gdn. Row N1** — 2 G1
- City Gdn. Row N1 — 56 BY37
- **City Rd. EC1** — 2 F1
- City Rd. EC1 — 56 BY37
- Civic Sq., Til. — 71 DG44
- Civic Way, Ilf. — 49 CM31
- Civic Way, Wok. — 100 AS62
- **Clabon Ms. SW1** — 3 E7
- Clabon Ms. SW1 — 66 BU41
- Clack St. SE16 — 67 CC41
- Clacton Rd. E6 — 58 CJ38
- Clacton Rd. E17 — 48 CD32
- Claigmar Gdns. N3 — 38 BS30
- Claire Ct. N12 *Woodside Ave.* — 38 BT28
- Claire Ct., Pnr. — 36 BE29
- Claire Pl. E14 — 67 CE41
- Clairvale, Horn. — 51 CW33
- Clairvale Rd., Houns. — 64 BE44
- Clairview Rd. SW16 — 76 BV49
- Clairville Ct., Reig. *Wray Common* — 121 BT70
- Clairville Gdns. W7 — 54 BH40
- Clammas Waye, Uxb. — 53 AX39
- Clamp Hill, Stan. — 36 BG28
- Clancarty Rd. SW6 — 66 BS44
- Clandon Ave., Egh. — 72 AU50
- Clandon Clo. W3 *Avenue Rd.* — 65 BM41
- Clandon Clo., Epsom — 94 BO57
- Clandon Gdns. N3 — 47 BS31
- Clandon Rd., Guil. — 118 AS71
- Clandon Rd., Ilf. — 49 CN34
- Clandon Rd., Wok. — 109 AV66
- Clandon St. SE8 — 67 CE44
- Clandon Way, Wok. — 109 AV66
- Clanfield Way SE15 *Hordle Prom. W.* — 67 CA43
- Clanricarde Gdns. W2 — 56 BS40
- Clapgate La., Wal.Cr. — 21 CF18
- Clapgate Rd., Bush. — 27 BF25
- Clapham Common N. Side SW4 — 66 BU45
- Clapham Common S. Side SW4 — 76 BV46
- Clapham Common W. Side SW4 — 66 BU45
- Clapham Cres. SW4 — 66 BW45
- Clapham High St. SW4 — 66 BW45
- Clapham Manor St. SW4 — 66 BW45
- Clapham Pk. Est. SW2 — 76 BX47
- Clapham Pk. Est. SW4 — 76 BW46
- Clapham Pk. Rd. SW4 — 66 BW45
- Clapham Rd. SW9 — 66 BX45
- Clappers La., Wok. — 91 AO59
- Claps Gate La., Bark. — 58 CL38
- Clapton Common E5 — 48 CA33
- Clapton Pk. Est. E5 — 48 CC35
- Clapton Pas. E5 *Lower Clapton Rd.* — 48 CC35
- Clapton Sq. E5 — 48 CC35
- Clapton Ter. N16 — 48 CB33
- Clapton Way E5 — 48 CB35
- Clara Pl. SE18 *John Wilson St.* — 68 CL42
- Clara Pl. SE18 *Monk St.* — 68 CL42
- Clare Clo., Borwd. — 28 BL25
- Clare Clo., Wey. — 92 AW60
- Clare Cor. SE9 — 78 CL47
- Clare Cotts., Red. — 121 BY70
- Clare Ct., Cat. — 105 CE65
- Clare Cres., Lthd. — 102 BJ62
- Clare Gdns. E7 — 49 CH35
- Clare Gdns. W11 *Westbourne Pk. Rd.* — 55 BR39
- Clare Gdns., Bark. — 58 CN36
- Clare Gdns., Egh. — 72 AT49
- Clare Gdns., Stan. — 36 BK28
- Clare Hall Pl. SE16 *Litlington St.* — 67 CC42
- Clare La. N1 — 57 BZ36
- Clare Lawn Ave. SW14 — 75 BN46
- **Clare Mkt. WC2** — 2 B9
- Clare Mkt. WC2 *Portugal St.* — 56 BX39
- Clare Ms. SW6 *Waterford Rd.* — 66 BS43
- Clare Pk., Amer. — 25 AO23
- Clare Pl. SW15 *Minstead Gdns.* — 75 BO47
- Clare Rd. E11 — 48 CF32
- Clare Rd. NW10 — 55 BP36
- Clare Rd. SE14 — 67 CD44
- Clare Rd., Grnf. — 54 BG36
- Clare Rd., Houns. — 64 BE45
- Clare Rd., Stai. — 73 AX47
- Clare St. E2 — 57 CB37
- Clare Way, Bexh. — 69 CQ44
- Clare Way, Sev. — 117 CB67
- Claredale St. E2 — 57 CB37
- Clarehill Clo., Esher — 93 BF56
- Clarehill Rd., Esher — 93 BF47
- Claremont, Chsnt. — 21 CA18
- Claremont, St.Alb. — 18 BF19
- Claremont Ave., Esher — 93 BE57
- Claremont Ave., Har. — 46 BL32
- Claremont Ave., N.Mal. — 85 BP53
- Claremont Ave., Sun. — 83 BC51
- Claremont Ave., Walt. — 93 BD56
- Claremont Ave., Wok. — 100 AS63
- Claremont Clo. E16 — 58 CL40
- **Claremont Clo. N1** — 2 D1
- Claremont Clo. SW2 *Garden La.* — 76 BX47
- Claremont Clo., Grays *Premier Ave.* — 71 DE41
- Claremont Clo., Orp. — 97 CL56
- Claremont Clo., S.Croy. — 96 CB60
- Claremont Clo., Walt. — 93 BD56

- Claremont Ct., Dor. *Rose Hill* — 119 BJ72
- Claremont Cres., Dart. — 69 CT45
- Claremont Cres., Rick. — 26 BA25
- Claremont Dr., Esher — 93 BF58
- Claremont Dr., Wok. — 100 AS63
- Claremont End, Esher — 93 BF57
- Claremont Est. SW2 — 76 BX47
- Claremont Gdns., Dart. — 80 CY47
- Claremont Gdns., Ilf. — 49 CN34
- Claremont Gdns., Surb. — 85 BL52
- Claremont Gdns., Upmin. — 51 CY33
- Claremont Gro. W4 *Edensor Gdns.* — 65 BO43
- Claremont Gro., Wdf.Grn. — 40 CJ29
- Claremont La., Esher — 93 BF56
- Claremont Pk. N3 — 37 BR30
- Claremont Pk. Rd., Esher — 93 BF57
- Claremont Rd. E7 — 49 CH35
- Claremont Rd. E11 — 48 CF34
- Claremont Rd. E17 — 39 CD30
- Claremont Rd. N6 — 47 BV33
- Claremont Rd. NW2 — 46 BQ33
- Claremont Rd. W9 — 55 BR37
- Claremont Rd. W13 — 54 BJ39
- Claremont Rd., Barn. — 29 BT22
- Claremont Rd., Brom. — 88 CK52
- Claremont Rd., Croy. — 87 CB54
- Claremont Rd., Esher — 93 BH57
- Claremont Rd., Har. — 36 BH30
- Claremont Rd., Horn. — 50 CU32
- Claremont Rd., Red. — 121 BV69
- Claremont Rd., Stai. — 72 AU49
- Claremont Rd., Surb. — 85 BL53
- Claremont Rd., Swan. — 79 CT50
- Claremont Rd., Tedd. — 74 BH49
- Claremont Rd., Twick. — 74 BJ46
- Claremont Rd., Wey. — 92 AW59
- Claremont Rd., Wind. — 61 AQ44
- **Claremont Sq. N1** — 2 D1
- Claremont Sq. N1 — 56 BY37
- Claremont St. E16 — 58 CL40
- Claremont St. N18 — 39 CB29
- Claremont St. SE10 — 67 CE43
- Claremont Way NW2 — 46 BQ33
- Claremount Gdns., Epsom — 103 BQ62
- Claremount Gdns., Epsom — 103 BQ62
- Clarence Ave. SW4 — 76 BW47
- Clarence Ave., Brom. — 88 CK52
- Clarence Ave., Ilf. — 49 CL32
- Clarence Ave., N.Mal. — 85 BN51
- Clarence Ave., Upmin. — 51 CX34
- Clarence Clo., Bush. — 36 BH26
- Clarence Clo., Walt. — 92 BC56
- Clarence Cres. SW4 — 76 BW46
- Clarence Cres., Sid. — 79 CO48
- Clarence Cres., Wind. — 61 AO44
- Clarence Dr., Egh. — 72 AR49
- **Clarence Gdns. NW1** — 1 K3
- Clarence Gdns. NW1 — 56 BV38
- Clarence La. SW15 — 75 BO46
- Clarence Ms. E5 *Clarence Pl.* — 48 CB35
- **Clarence Pas. NW1** — 1 Q1
- Clarence Pl. E5 — 48 CB35
- Clarence Pl., Grav. — 81 DG47
- Clarence Rd. E5 — 48 CB35
- Clarence Rd. E12 — 49 CJ35
- Clarence Rd. E16 — 58 CG38
- Clarence Rd. E17 — 39 CC30
- Clarence Rd. N15 — 48 BZ32
- Clarence Rd. N22 — 38 BX29
- Clarence Rd. NW6 — 55 BR36
- Clarence Rd. SE9 — 78 CK48
- Clarence Rd. SW19 — 76 BS50
- Clarence Rd. W4 — 65 BM42
- Clarence Rd., Berk. — 7 AR13
- Clarence Rd., Bexh. — 69 CQ45
- Clarence Rd., Brwd. — 33 DA25
- Clarence Rd., Brom. — 88 CJ52
- Clarence Rd., Croy. — 87 BZ54
- Clarence Rd., Enf. — 30 CB25
- Clarence Rd., Grav. — 81 DH46
- Clarence Rd., Grays — 71 DD42
- Clarence Rd., Red. — 121 BT72
- Clarence Rd., Rich. — 65 BL44
- Clarence Rd., St.Alb. — 8 BH13
- Clarence Rd., Sid. — 79 CO48
- Clarence Rd., Sutt. — 95 BS56
- Clarence Rd., Tedd. — 74 BH50
- Clarence Rd., Wall. — 95 BV56
- Clarence Rd., Walt. — 92 BC56
- Clarence Rd., West. — 106 CK62
- Clarence Rd., Wind. — 61 AN44
- Clarence Row, Grav. — 81 DG47
- Clarence Row, Egh. — 72 AS50
- Clarence St., Kings.T. — 84 BK51
- Clarence St., Rich. — 65 BL45
- Clarence St., Sthl. — 64 BD41
- Clarence St., Stai. — 72 AV49
- **Clarence Ter. NW1** — 1 F4
- Clarence Ter. NW1 *Cornwall Ter.* — 56 BU38
- Clarence Ter., Houns. — 64 BF45
- Clarence Wk. SW4 — 66 BX44
- Clarence Wk., Red. — 121 BT72
- Clarence Way NW1 — 56 BV36
- Clarence Way Est. NW1 — 56 BV36
- Clarendon Ave. SE5 *Councillor St.* — 67 BZ42
- **Clarendon Clo. N1** — 1 C10
- Clarendon Clo. W2 *Clarendon Pl.* — 56 BU40
- Clarendon Clo., Orp. — 89 CO52
- Clarendon Ct. NW11 *Finchley Rd.* — 46 BR31
- Clarendon Ct., Slou. *Wexham Rd.* — 52 AQ40
- Clarendon Cres., Twick. — 74 BG48
- Clarendon Cross W11 *Portland Rd.* — 55 BR40
- Clarendon Dr. SW15 — 65 BQ45
- Clarendon Gdns. NW4 — 46 BP31

Cla–Clo

Clarendon Gdns. W9 56 BT38
Clarendon Gdns., Dart. 80 CY47
Clarendon Gdns., Ilf. 49 CK33
Clarendon Gdns., Wem. 45 BK35
Clarendon Grn., Orp. 89 CO52
Clarendon Gro. NW1 1 N2
Clarendon Gro. NW1 56 BW38
Phoenix Rd.
Clarendon Gro., Mitch. 86 BU52
Clarendon Gro., Orp. 89 CO52
Clarendon Ms. W2 1 C10
Clarendon Ms. W2 56 BU40
Clarendon Pl.
Clarendon Par., Wal.Cr. 21 CC18
Clarendon Path, Orp. 89 CO52
Clarendon Pl. W2 1 C10
Clarendon Pl. W2 56 BU40
Clarendon Ri. SE13 67 CF45
Clarendon Rd. E11 48 CF33
Clarendon Rd. E17 48 CE32
Clarendon Rd. E18 49 CH31
Clarendon Rd. N8 47 BX31
Clarendon Rd. N15 47 BY31
Clarendon Rd. N18 39 CB29
Clarendon Rd. N22 38 BX30
Clarendon Rd. SW19 76 BU50
Clarendon Rd. W5 55 BL38
Clarendon Rd. W11 55 BR40
Clarendon Rd., Ashf. 73 AY49
Clarendon Rd., Borwd. 28 BM24
Clarendon Rd., Chsnt. 21 CC18
Clarendon Rd., Croy. 86 BY55
Clarendon Rd., Har. 45 BH32
Clarendon Rd., Hayes 63 BB41
Clarendon Rd., Red. 121 BU70
Clarendon Rd., Sev. 116 CU66
Clarendon Rd., Wall. 95 BW57
Clarendon Rd., Wat. 26 BC24
Clarendon St. SW1 3 K10
Clarendon St. SW1 66 BV42
Clarendon Ter. W9 56 BT38
Maida Vale
Clarendon Wk. W11 55 BQ40
Lancaster Rd.
Clarendon Way N21 30 BZ25
Clarendon Way, Chis. 88 CN52
Clarendon Way, Orp. 88 CN52
Clarens St. SE6 77 CD48
Claret Gdns. SE25 87 CA52
Clareville Gro. SW7 66 BT42
Clareville Rd., Cat. 105 CB65
Clareville Rd., Orp. 88 CM55
Clareville St. SW7 66 BT42
Gloucester Rd.
Clarewood Wk. SW9 66 BY45
Somerleyton Rd.
Clarges Ms. W1 3 J2
Clarges Ms. W1 56 BV40
Clarges St. W1 3 K2
Clarges St. W1 56 BV40
Claribel Rd. SW9 66 BY44
Clarice Way, Wall. 95 BX58
Claridge Rd., Dag. 50 CP33
Clarina Rd. SE20 77 CC50
Clarissa Rd., Rom. 50 CP33
Clarissa St. E8 57 CA37
Clark Clo., Erith 69 CU44
Forest Rd.
Clark St. E1 57 CB39
Clark Way, Houns. 64 BE43
Springwell Rd.
Clarkbourne Dr., Grays 71 DE43
Clarke Path N16 48 CB33
Braydon Rd.
Clarke Way, Wat. 26 BC21
Clarkes Ave., Wor.Pk. 85 BQ54
Clarkes Dr., Uxb. 53 AY39
Clarkes Grn. Rd., Sev. 99 CX60
Clarkes Ms. W1 1 H6
Clarkes Rd., Hat. 10 BP12
Clarkhill, Harl. 13 CN12
Clarks Fld., Rick. 35 AW26
Church La.
Clarks La., Epp. 22 CN19
Hemnall St.
Clarks La., Sev. 98 CQ59
Clarks La., West. 106 CG65
Clarks Mead (Bushey), Wat. 36 BG26
Clarks Pl. EC2 2 M8
Clarks Rd., Ilf. 49 CM34
Clarkson Rd. E16 58 CG39
Clarkson St. E2 57 CB38
Clarksons, The, Bark. 58 CM37
Claston Clo., Dart. 69 CT45
Clatre Ct. N12 38 BT28
Claude Rd. E10 48 CF34
Claude Rd. E13 58 CH37
Claude Rd. SE15 67 CB44
Godman Rd.
Claude St. E14 67 CE42
Claudia Jones Way SW4 76 BX46
Loats Rd.
Claudia Pl. SW19 75 BR47
Augustus Rd.
Claudian Pl., St.Alb. 9 BF14
Claudian Way, Grays 71 DG41
Claughton Rd. E13 58 CJ37
Claughton Way, Brwd. 122 DE25
Clausen Way, Grnf. 54 BJ37
Clauson Ave., Nthlt. 45 BF35
Clave St. E1 57 CC40
Cinnamon St.
Claverdale Rd. SW2 76 BX47
Claverhambury Rd., Wal.Abb. 22 CG18
Clavering Ave. SW13 65 BP43
Clavering Clo., Twick. 74 BJ49
Clavering Gdns., Brwd. 123 DE32
Clavering Rd. E12 49 CJ33
Clavering Way, Brwd. 122 DE25
Claverley Gro. N3 38 BS30
Claverley Vill. N3 38 BS30
Claverley Gro.
Claverton Clo., Hem.H. 16 AT17
Claverton St. SW1 66 BW42
Claxton Gro. W6 65 BQ42
Clay Acre, Chesh. 16 AO18
Clay Ave., Mitch. 86 BV51
Clay Cft., Welw.G.C. 5 BS7
Hazel Gro.
Clay Hill, Bush. 27 BF25
Clay Hill, Enf. 29 BY22
Clay Hill Clo., Reig. 120 BP74
Clay La., Bush. 36 BH26
Clay La., Edg. 37 BM27
Clay La., Epsom 103 BM65
Clay La., Guil. 109 AR67
Clay La., Red. 121 BW71
Clay La., Stai. 73 AY47
Clay Ride, Loug. 31 CK25
Clay Rd., Epsom 94 BO60
Clay St. W1 1 F7
Clay St. W1 56 BU39
Dorset St.
Clay Tye Rd., Upmin. 51 DB35
Claybank Gro. SE13 67 CE45
Algernon Rd.
Claybourne Ms. SE19 77 CA50
Church Rd.
Claybridge Rd. SE12 78 CJ49
Claybrook Clo. N2 47 BT31
Long La.
Claybrook Rd. W6 65 BQ43
Clayburn Gdns., S.Ock. 60 DA40
Claybury, Bush. 36 BF26
Claybury Bdy., Ilf. 49 CK31
Claybury Rd., Wdf.Grn. 40 CK29
Claycroft, Welw.G.C. 5 BS7
Hazel Gro.
Claydon Dr., Croy. 95 BX56
Claydon End, Ger.Cr. 43 AS31
Claydon La., Ger.Cr. 43 AS31
Claydon Rd., Wok. 100 AQ61
Clayfarm Rd. SE9 78 CM48
Claygate Ave., Ilf. 49 CK31
Claygate Clo., Horn. 50 CT35
Carfax Rd.
Claygate Cres., Croy. 96 CF57
Claygate La., T.Ditt. 84 BJ54
Claygate Lo. Clo., Esher 93 BH57
Claygate Rd. W13 64 BJ41
Claygate Rd., Dor. 119 BJ72
Clayhall Ave., Ilf. 40 CK30
Clayhall La., Reig. 120 BQ72
Clayhall La., Wind. 72 AP46
Clayhanger, Guil. 118 AU69
Clayhill Cres. SE9 78 CJ49
Clayhill Rd., Reig. 120 BP74
Claylands Pl. SW8 66 BY43
Claylands Rd. SW8 66 BX43
Claymore Clo., Mord. 86 BS54
Claymore Rd., Hem.H. 8 AY11
Claypit Hill, Loug. 31 CJ22
Claypole Rd. E15 57 CF37
Clayponds Ave., Brent. 65 BL42
Clayponds Gdns. W5 64 BK42
Clayponds La., Brent. 65 BL42
Clays La. E15 48 CE35
Clays La., Loug. 31 CL23
Clays La. Clo. E15 48 CE35
Clayside, Chig. 40 CM28
Clayton Ave., Upmin. 51 CX35
Clayton Ave., Wem. 55 BL36
Clayton Clo. E6 58 CK39
Clayton Cres., Brent. 64 BK42
Clayton Cft. Rd., Dart. 79 CU48
Clayton Dr., Guil. 118 AP69
Clayton Fld. NW9 37 BO29
Clayton Rd. SE15 67 CB44
Clayton Rd., Chess. 93 BK56
Clayton Rd., Epsom 94 BO60
Clayton Rd., Hayes 63 BB41
Clayton Rd., Islw. 64 BH45
Clayton Rd., Rom. 50 CS33
Clayton St. SE11 66 BY43
Clayton Wk., Amer. 25 AR23
Clayton Waye, Uxb. 53 AX38
Claywood Clo., Orp. 88 CN54
Claywood La., Dart. 80 DB48
Clayworth Clo., Sid. 79 CO46
Cleall Ave., Wal.Abb. 21 CF20
Quaker La.
Cleanthus Rd. SE18 68 CL44
Clearbrook Way E1 57 CC39
West Arbour St.
Cleardene, Dor. 119 BJ71
Cleardown, Wok. 100 AT63
Clears, The, Reig. 120 BR69
Clearwell Dr. W9 56 BS38
Cleave Ave., Hayes 63 BB42
Cleave Ave., Orp. 97 CN57
Cleave Prior, Couls. 104 BU63
Cleaveland Rd., Surb. 84 BK53
Cleaver Sq. SE11 4 E10
Cleaver Sq. SE11 66 BY42
Cleaver St. SE11 4 E10
Cleaver St. SE11 66 BY42
Cleaverholme Clo. SE25 87 CB53
Cleeve, The, Guil. 118 AT70
Cleeve Ct., Wind. 61 AM45
Firs Ave.
Cleeve Hill SE23 77 CB47
Cleeve Pk. Gdns., Sid. 79 CO48
Faraday Ave.
Cleeve Rd., Lthd. 102 BJ63
Cleeves Clo., Hem.H. 8 AZ11
Cleeves Cres., Croy. 96 CF59
Clegg St. E1 57 CB40
Prusom St.
Clegg St. E13 58 CH37
Cleland Path, Loug. 31 CL23
Cleland Way, Ger.Cr. 34 AR30
Clem Attlee Ct. SW6 65 BR43
Clematis Clo., Rom. 42 CV29
Clematis St. W12 55 BP40
Clemence St. E14 57 CD39
Clement Ave. SW4 66 BW45
Clement Clo. NW6 55 BQ36
Clement Clo. W4 65 BN41
Winston Wk.
Clement Clo., Pur. 104 BY61
Clement Gdns., Hayes 63 BB42
Clement Rd. SW19 75 BR49
Clement Rd., Beck. 87 CC51
Clement Rd., Chsnt. 21 CD17
Clement St., Swan. 80 CV50
Clement Way, Upmin. 51 CW34
Clementhorpe Rd., Dag. 59 CP36
Clementina Rd. E10 48 CD33
Clementine Clo. W13 64 BJ41
Balfour Rd.
Clements Ave. E16 58 CH40
Clements Clo., Houns. 64 BD45
Clements Clo., Slou. 62 AQ41
Clements Inn WC2 2 C9
Clements Inn WC2 56 BX39
Strand
Clements Inn Pas. WC2 2 C9
Clements La. EC4 2 L10
Clements La. EC4 57 BZ40
Clements La., Ilf. 49 CL34
Clements Mead, Lthd. 102 BJ63
Clements Pl., Brent. 64 BK42
Challis Rd.
Clements Rd. E6 58 CK36
Clements Rd. SE16 67 CB41
Clements Rd., Ilf. 49 CL34
Clements Rd., Rick. 25 AU25
Clements Rd., Walt. 83 BC55
Clenches Fm. La., Sev. 116 CU66
Clenches Fm. Rd., Sev. 116 CU66
Clendon Way SE18 68 CM42
Clenham St. SE1 4 J4
Clenham St. SE1 67 BZ41
Southwark Bri. Rd.
Clenheadon Ri., Lthd. 102 BK65
Clensham Ct., Sutt. 86 BS55
Clensham La., Sutt. 86 BS55
Clenston Ms. W1 1 E8
Clenston Ms. W1 56 BU39
Seymour Pl.
Clephane Rd. N1 57 BZ36
Clere Pl. EC2 57 BZ38
Clere St.
Clere St. EC2 2 L4
Clere St. EC2 57 BZ38
Cleremont Rd. E9 57 CC37
Clerics Wk., Shep. 83 BA54
Russell Rd.
Clerkenwell Clo. EC1 2 E4
Clerkenwell Clo. EC1 56 BY38
Clerkenwell Grn. EC1 2 E5
Clerkenwell Grn. EC1 56 BY38
Clerkenwell Rd. EC1 2 D5
Clerkenwell Rd. EC1 56 BY38
Clerks Cft., Red. 114 BZ70
Clerks Piece, Loug. 31 CK24
Cleve Rd. NW6 56 BS36
Cleve Rd., Sid. 79 CP48
Clevedon, Wey. 92 BA56
Clevedon Clo. N16 48 CA34
Smalley Rd.
Clevedon Gdns., Hayes 63 BA41
Clevedon Gdns., Houns. 63 BC44
Clevedon Rd. SE20 87 CC51
Clevedon Rd., Kings.T. 85 BM51
Clevedon Rd., Twick. 74 BK46
Clevehurst Clo., Slou. 52 AQ36
Cleveland, Hem.H. 8 AZ12
Cleveland Ave. SW20 85 BR51
Cleveland Ave. W4 65 BO42
Cleveland Ave., Hmptn. 74 BE50
Cleveland Clo., Walt. 83 BC55
Cleveland Ct. W13 54 BJ39
Kent Ave.
Cleveland Cres., Borwd. 28 BN25
Cleveland Dr., Stai. 83 AW51
Cleveland Est. E1 57 CC38
Cleveland Gdns. N4 48 BZ32
Cleveland Gdns. NW2 46 BQ34
Cleveland Gdns. SW13 65 BO44
Cleveland Gdns. W2 56 BT39
Cleveland Gdns. W13 54 BJ39
Argyle Rd.
Cleveland Gdns., Wor.Pk. 85 BO55
Cleveland Gro. E1 57 CC38
Cleveland Way
Cleveland Ms. W1 1 L6
Cleveland Ms. W1 56 BW39
Maple St.
Cleveland Pk., Stai. 73 AY46
Cleveland Pk. Ave. E17 48 CE31
Cleveland Pk. Cres. E17 48 CE31
Cleveland Pl. SW1 3 M2
Cleveland Pl. SW1 56 BW40
King St.
Cleveland Ri., Mord. 85 BQ54
Cleveland Rd. E18 49 CH31
Cleveland Rd. N1 57 BZ36
Cleveland Rd. N9 39 CB26
Cleveland Rd. SW13 65 BO44
Cleveland Rd. W4 65 BN41
Cleveland Rd. W13 54 BJ39
Cleveland Rd., Ilf. 49 CL34
Cleveland Rd., Islw. 64 BJ45
Cleveland Rd., N.Mal. 85 BO52
Cleveland Rd., Uxb. 53 AX38
Cleveland Rd., Well. 68 CN44
Cleveland Rd., Wor.Pk. 85 BO55
Cleveland Row SW1 3 L3
Cleveland Row SW1 56 BW40
Cleveland Sq. W2 56 BT39
Cleveland St. W1 1 K5
Cleveland St. W1 56 BW38
Cleveland Ter. W2 56 BT39
Cleveland Way E1 57 CC38
Cleveland Way, Hem.H. 8 AZ12
Cleveley Clo. SE7 68 CJ42
Cleveley Cres. W5 55 BL37
Cleveleys Rd. E5 48 CB34
Cleverley Est. W12 55 BP40
Cleves Ave., Epsom 94 BP58
Cleves Clo., Cob. 92 BC60
Cleves Clo., Hem.H. 8 AZ11
Cleves Rd. E6 58 CJ37
Cleves Rd., Rich. 74 BK48
Cleves Rd., Sev. 108 CW62
Cleves Wk., Ilf. 40 CM29
Cleves Way, Hmptn. 74 BE50
Cleves Way, Ruis. 45 BD33
Cleves Way, Sun. 73 BB50
Cleves Wd., Wey. 92 BB56
Clewer Ave., Wind. 61 AN44
Clewer Ct. Rd., Wind. 61 AN43
Clewer Cres., Har. 36 BG30
Clewer Flds., Wind. 61 AN44
Clewer Hill Rd., Wind. 61 AM44
Clewer New Town, Wind. 61 AN44
Clewer Pk., Wind. 61 AN43
Clichy Est. E1 57 CC39
Clifden Rd. E5 48 CC35
Clifden Rd., Brent. 64 BK43
Clifden Rd., Twick. 74 BH47
Cliff End, Pur. 95 BY60
Cliff Gro., Grav. 81 DG47
Cliff Pl., S.Ock. 60 DB38
Cliff Rd. NW1 56 BW36
Cliff Ter. SE8 67 CE44
Cliff Vill. NW1 56 BW36
Cliff Wk. E16 58 CG39
Cliffe Rd., S.Croy. 96 BZ56
Cliffe Wk., Sutt. 95 BT56
Turnpike La.
Clifford Ave. SW14 65 BM45
Clifford Ave., Chis. 78 CK50
Clifford Ave., Ilf. 40 CL30
Clifford Ave., Wall. 95 BW56
Clifford Clo., Nthlt. 54 BE37
Clifford Ct. NW2 46 BO35
Clifford Dr. SW9 66 BY45
Clifford Gdns. NW10 55 BQ37
Clifford Gro., Ashf. 73 AZ49
Clifford Manor Rd., Guil. 118 AS72
Clifford Rd. E16 58 CG38
Clifford Rd. E17 39 CF30
Clifford Rd. N9 30 CC25
Clifford Rd. SE25 87 CB52
Clifford Rd., Barn. 29 BS24
Clifford Rd., Grays 71 DC41
Clifford Rd., Houns. 64 BD45
Clifford Rd., Rich. 74 BK48
Clifford Rd., Wem. 54 BK36
Clifford St. W1 3 L1
Clifford St. W1 56 BW40
Clifford St., Wat. 27 BD24
Clifford Way NW10 46 BO35
Cliffords Inn EC4 56 BY39
Fleet St.
Cliffview Rd. SE13 67 CE45
Clifton Ave. E17 48 CC31
Clifton Ave. N3 37 BR30
Clifton Ave. W12 65 BO41
Clifton Ave., Felt. 74 BD48
Clifton Ave., Stan. 36 BJ30
Clifton Ave., Sutt. 95 BS58
Clifton Ave., Wem. 55 BL36
Clifton Clo., Brwd. 123 DE32
Clifton Clo., Cat. 105 BZ65
Clifton Clo., Chsnt. 21 CD18
Clifton Clo., Orp. 97 CL56
Clifton Clo., Wey. 83 AW55
Clifton Ct. NW8 1 A4
Clifton Ct. NW8 56 BT38
Clifton Cres. SE15 67 CB43
Clifton Est. SE15 67 CB44
Clifton Gdns. N15 48 CA32
Clifton Gdns. NW11 46 BR32
Clifton Gdns. W4 65 BN42
Chiswick High Rd.
Clifton Gdns. W9 56 BT38
Clifton Gdns., Enf. 29 BX24
Clifton Gdns., Uxb. 53 AZ37
Clifton Gro. E8 57 CB36
Clifton Hill NW8 56 BS37
Clifton Marine Par., Grav. 81 DF46
Clifton Pk. Ave. SW20 85 BQ51
Approach Rd.
Clifton Pl. SE16 67 CC41
Canon Beck Rd.
Clifton Pl. W2 1 B9
Clifton Pl. W2 56 BT40
Clifton Pl., Bans. 104 BS61
Clifton Ri. SE14 67 CD43
Clifton Ri., Wind. 61 AL44
Clifton Rd. E7 58 CJ36
Clifton Rd. E16 58 CG39
Clifton Rd. N3 38 BT30
Clifton Rd. N8 47 BW32
Clifton Rd. N22 38 BW30
Clifton Rd. NW10 55 BP37
Clifton Rd. SE25 87 BZ52
Clifton Rd. SW19 75 BQ50
Clifton Rd. W9 56 BT38
Clifton Rd., Couls. 104 BV61
Clifton Rd., Grav. 81 DG48
Clifton Rd., Grnf. 54 BG38
Clifton Rd., Har. 46 BL32
Clifton Rd., Horn. 50 CU32
Clifton Rd., Houns. 63 AZ45
Conway Rd.
Clifton Rd., Ilf. 49 CM32
Clifton Rd., Islw. 64 BG44
Clifton Rd., Kings.T. 75 BL50
Clifton Rd., Loug. 31 CK24
Clifton Rd., Sid. 78 CN49
Clifton Rd., Slou. 62 AQ41
Clifton Rd., Sthl. 64 BE42
Clifton Rd., Tedd. 74 BH49
Clifton Rd., Wall. 95 BV56
Clifton Rd., Wat. 26 BC25
Clifton Rd., Well. 69 CO45
Clifton St. E8 57 CB36
Graham Rd.
Clifton St. EC2 2 M6
Clifton St. EC2 57 C
Clifton St., St.Alb. 9 B
Clifton Ter. N4 47 B
Clifton Vill. W9 56 B
Clifton Way SE15 67 C
Clifton Way, Borwd. 28 B
Clifton Way, Brwd. 122 D
Clifton Way, Wem. 55 B
Clifton Way, Wok. 100 A
Cliftons La., Reig. 120 B
Cliftonville, Dor. 119 B
Climb, The, Rick. 26 AV
Clinch Ct. E16 58 C
Cline Rd. N11 38 BV
Cline Rd., Guil. 118 A
Clink St. SE1 4
Clink St. SE1 57 B
Clinton Ave., E.Mol. 84 B
Clinton Ave., Well. 68 C
Clinton Clo., Wok. 100 A
Clinton Cres., Ilf. 40 C
Clinton Rd. E3 57 C
Clinton Rd. E7 49 C
Clinton Rd. N15 48 B
Clinton Rd., Lthd. 102 B
Clipper Boul., Dart. 70 C
Clipper Clo. SE16 67 C
Kinburn St.
Clipper Cres., Grav. 81 D
Clipper Way SE13 67 C
Limes Gro.
Clippesby Clo., Chess. 94 B
Clipstone Ms. W1 1
Clipstone Ms. W1 56 BV
Clipstone Rd., Houns. 64 B
Clipstone St. W1 1
Clipstone St. W1 56 BV
Clissold Clo. N2 47 BU
Clissold Ct. N4 48 B
Clissold Cres. N16 48 B
Clissold Rd. N16 48 B
Clitheroe Ave., Har. 45 B
Clitheroe Gdns., Wat. 36 BD
Clitheroe Rd. SW9 66 BX
Clitheroe Rd., Rom. 41 CS
Clitherow Ave. W7 64 B
Clitherow Rd., Brent. 64 B
Clitterhouse Cres. NW2 46 BO
Clitterhouse Rd. NW2 46 BO
Clive Ave. N18 39 CB
Clive Ave., Dart. 79 CT
Clive Clo., Pot.B. 19 BF
Clive Ct., Slou. 61 AO
Clive Ct., Surb. 85 BM
Clive Pas. SE21 77 BZ
Clive Rd.
Clive Pas. SE21 77 BZ
Chalford Rd.
Clive Rd. SE21 77 BZ
Clive Rd. SW19 76 BU
Clive Rd., Belv. 69 CO
Clive Rd., Brwd. 42 DE
Clive Rd., Enf. 30 CE
Clive Rd., Esher 93 BF
Clive Rd., Felt. 73 BC
Clive Rd., Grav. 81 DG
Clive Rd., Rom. 50 CU
Clive Rd., Twick. 74 BJ
Clive Way, Couls. 104 BX
Clive Way, Enf. 30 CE
Clive Way, Stai. 82 AV
Clive Way, Wat. 27 BD
Cliveden Clo. N12 38 BT
Cliveden Clo., Brwd. 122 DC
Cliveden Pl. SW1 3
Cliveden Pl., Shep. 83 AZ
Cliveden Rd. SW19 85 BR
Clivedon Rd. E4 40 CG
Clivesdale Dr., Hayes 53 BC
Avondale Dr.
Cloak La. EC4 2 K
Cloak La. EC4 57 BZ
Clock Ho. Clo., Wey. 92 AY
Clock Ho. La., Sev. 107 CU
Clock Ho. Mead, Lthd. 93 BF
Clock Ho. Rd., Beck. 87 CC
Clock Ter., Grav. 81 DH
Clock Twr. Pl. N7 56 BX
Clock Twr. Rd., Islw. 64 BH
Clockhouse Ave., Bark. 58 CM
Clockhouse Clo. SW19 75 BQ
Clockhouse La., Ashf. 73 AZ
Clockhouse La., Felt. 73 AZ
Clockhouse La., Grays 71 DC
Clockhouse La., Rom. 41 CR
Clockhouse La. E., Egh. 72 AT
Clockhouse La. W., Egh. 72 AT
Clocktower Ms. N1 57 BZ
Arlington Ave.
Clodhouse Hill, Wok. 100 AO
Cloister Clo., Rain. 59 CU
Cloister Gdns. SE25 87 CB
Cloister Gdns., Edg. 37 BN
Cloister Garth, Berk. 7 AR
Priory Gdns.
Cloister Garth, St.Alb. 9 BH
Cloister Rd. NW2 46 BR
Cloister Rd. W3 55 BN
Cloister Wk., Hem.H. 8 AX
Townsend
Cloisters, The, Rick. 35 AY
Cloisters, The, Welw.G.C. 5 BC
Parkway
Cloisters Ave., Brom. 88 CK
Clonard Way, Pnr. 36 BF
Clonbrock Rd. N16 48 CA
Cloncurry St. SW6 65 BQ
Clonmel Clo., Har. 45 BG
Clonmel Rd., Tedd. 74 BG
Clonmell Rd. N17 48 BZ
Clonmell Rd. SW6 65 BR
Clonmore St. SW18 75 BR
Cloonmore Ave., Orp. 97 CN
Clorane Gdns. NW3 47 BS

Clo–Col

Street	Page	Grid
ose, The E4	39	CF29
ose, The N14	38	BW27
ose, The N20	37	BR27
ose, The SE3	68	CG45
Heath La.		
ose, The, Barn.	29	BU25
ose, The, Beck.	87	CD52
ose, The, Bet.	120	BM72
ose, The, Bex.	79	CR47
ose, The, Brwd.	42	DB27
ose, The, Bush.	27	BF25
ose, The, Cars.	95	BU58
ose, The, Dart.	80	CV48
ose, The, Grays	71	DD41
ose, The, Har.	36	BG30
ose, The, Hat.	19	BR16
ose, The, Hem.H.	16	AT17
ose, The, Islw.	64	BG44
ose, The, Iver	52	AU38
ose, The, Mitch.	86	BU52
ose, The, N.Mal.	85	BN51
ose, The (Eastcote), Pnr.	45	BD33
ose, The (Rayners La.), Pnr.	45	BE33
ose, The, Pot.B.	20	BS19
ose, The, Pur.	95	BY58
ose, The, Pur.	95	BX58
Russell Hill		
ose, The, Rad.	18	BH20
ose, The, Reig.	121	BS71
ose, The, Rich.	65	BM45
ose, The, Rick.	35	AW26
ose, The, Rom.	50	CQ32
ose, The, Sev.	107	CT65
ose, The (Ightham), Sev.	108	DB63
ose, The, Sid.	79	CO49
ose, The, Sutt.	85	BR54
ose, The, Uxb.	53	AY36
ose, The (Hillingdon), Uxb.	53	AZ37
ose, The, Vir.W.	82	AR53
ose, The (Barnhill Rd.), Wem.	46	BN34
ose, The (Lyon Pk. Ave.), Wem.	55	BL36
ose, The, Wey.	92	AW60
osemead Clo., Nthwd.	35	BA29
oth Ct. EC1	**2**	**G7**
oth Fair EC1	**2**	**G7**
oth Fair EC1	56	BY39
oth St. EC1	**2**	**H6**
othier St. E1	57	CA39
Cutler St.		
oudberry Rd., Rom.	42	CV29
oudesdale Rd. SW17	76	BV48
oudesley Pl. N1	56	BY37
oudesley Rd. N1	56	BY37
oudesley Rd., Bexh.	69	CQ44
oudesley Rd., Erith	69	CT44
oudesley Sq. N1	56	BY37
oudesley St. N1	56	BY37
ouston Clo., Wall.	95	BX56
ova Rd. E7	58	CG36
ove Hitch Quay SW18	66	BT45
ove St. E13	58	CH38
ovelly Ave. NW9	46	BO31
ovelly Ave., Uxb.	44	BA35
ovelly Ave., Warl.	105	CB63
ovelly Clo., Pnr.	45	BD31
ovelly Clo., Uxb.	44	BA35
ovelly Ct., Horn.	51	CX34
ovelly Gdns. SE19	87	CA51
ovelly Gdns., Enf.	39	CA26
ovelly Gdns., Rom.	41	CR30
ovelly Rd. N8	47	BW31
ovelly Rd. W4	65	BN41
ovelly Rd. W5	64	BK41
ovelly Rd., Bexh.	69	CO43
ovelly Rd., Houns.	64	BF44
ovelly Way E1	57	CC39
Jamaica St.		
ovelly Way, Har.	45	BE34
ovelly Way, Orp.	88	CN53
Cotswold Ri.		
over Clo. E11	48	CF34
over Ct., Grays	71	DE43
Churchill Rd.		
over Ct., Wok.	100	AR62
over Fld., Harl.	14	CO12
over Hill, Couls.	104	BV64
over Leas, Epp.	22	CN18
over Ms. SW3	66	BU43
over Rd., Guil.	118	AP69
over Way, Hem.H.	8	AW13
over Way, Wall.	86	BV54
overdale Gdns., Sid.	78	CN46
overfield, Welw.G.C.	5	BR6
overland, Hat.	10	BO14
overley Rd., Ong.	24	CX18
overs, The, Grav.	81	DF49
Henley Deane		
owders Rd. SE6	77	CD48
owser Clo., Sutt.	95	BT56
oyster Wd., Edg.	36	BK29
ub Gdns. Rd., Brom.	88	CH54
ub Row E1	**2**	**P4**
ub Row E1	57	CA38
ub Row E2	**2**	**P4**
ub Row E2	57	CA38
ump, The, Rick.	26	AW25
ump Ave., Tad.	120	BN69
umps, The, Felt.	73	BA49
unas Gdns., Rom.	51	CV31
unbury Ave., Sthl.	64	BE42
unbury St. N1	**2**	**L1**
unbury St. N1	57	BZ37
uny Est. SE1	**4**	**M6**
uny Ms. SW5	66	BS42
uny Pl. SE1	**4**	**M6**
uny Pl. SE1	67	CA41
utton St. E14	57	CE39
ydach Rd., Enf.	30	CA24
Clyde Ave., S.Croy.	105	CB61
Clyde Circ. N15	48	CA31
Clyde Clo., Red.	121	BV70
Clyde Clo., Upmin.	51	CZ32
Clyde Ct., Red.	121	BV70
Clyde Clo.		
Clyde Cres., Upmin.	51	CZ32
Clyde Pl. E10	48	CE33
Clyde Rd. N15	48	CA31
Clyde Rd. N22	38	BW30
Clyde Rd., Croy.	87	CA55
Clyde Rd., Hodd.	12	CF13
Clyde Rd., Stai.	73	AX47
Clyde Rd., Sutt.	95	BS56
Clyde Rd., Wall.	95	BW56
Clyde Sq., Hem.H.	8	AY11
Clyde St. SE8	67	CD43
Clyde Ter. SE23	77	CC48
Clyde Vale SE23	77	CC48
Clyde Way, Rom.	41	CT30
Clydesdale, Enf.	30	CC24
Clydesdale Ave., Stan.	45	BK31
Clydesdale Clo., Borwd.	28	BN25
Clydesdale Gdns., Rich.	65	BM45
Clydesdale Path, Borwd.	28	BN25
Clydesdale Clo.		
Clydesdale Rd. W11	55	BR39
Clydesdale Rd., Horn.	50	CT33
Clydesdale Wk., Chsnt.	21	CD16
Tarpan Way		
Clydon Clo., Erith	69	CT43
Clyfford Rd., Ruis.	44	BB35
Clyfton Clo., Brox.	12	CD15
Clymping Dene, Felt.	73	BC47
Clyston Rd., Wat.	26	BB25
Clyston St. SW8	66	BW44
Coach & Horses Yd. W1	**1**	**L10**
Coach & Horses Yd. W1	56	BW40
Old Burlington St.		
Coach Ho. La. N5	47	BY35
Highbury Hill		
Coach Ho. La. SW19	75	BQ48
Coach Ho. Ms. SE23	77	CC47
Hengrave Rd.		
Coach Ho. Yd. NW3	47	BT35
Hampstead High St.		
Coach Rd., Bet.	120	BL71
Coach Rd., Cher.	91	AU57
Coach Rd., Dor.	120	BL71
Coach Rd., Sev.	108	DA65
Coachhouse Ms. SE20	77	CB50
Coachlands Ave., Guil.	118	AP70
Coal Rd., Til.	71	DJ42
Coal Wf. Rd. W12	65	BQ41
Shepherds Bush Pl.		
Coaldale Wk. SE21	77	BZ47
Rosendale Rd.		
Coalecroft Rd. SW15	65	BQ45
Coaley Row, Dag.	59	CQ37
Coast Hill, Dor.	119	BE73
Coast Hill La., Dor.	119	BF72
Coat Wicks, Beac.	34	AO29
Coate St. E2	57	CB37
Coates Dell, Wat.	18	BE20
Coates Hill Rd., Brom.	88	CL51
Coates Rd., Borwd.	36	BK26
Coates St., Harl.	13	CM11
Coates Wk., Brent.	65	BL42
Burford Rd.		
Coates Way, Wat.	18	BD20
Cob Clo., Borwd.	28	BN25
Hunter Path		
Cob Mead, Hat.	10	BP11
Cobb Clo., Slou.	62	AR44
Cobb Grn., Wat.	17	BC19
Cobb Rd., Berk.	7	AP13
Cobb St. E1	**2**	**P7**
Cobb St. E1	57	CA39
Leyden St.		
Cobbets Clo., Wok.	100	AQ62
Cobbets Hill, Wey.	92	AZ57
Cobbett, Guil.	118	AP70
Cobbett Rd. SE9	68	CK45
Cobbett Rd., Twick.	74	BF47
Cobbetts Ave., Ilf.	49	CJ32
Cobbins, The, Wal.Abb.	22	CG19
Cobbinsend Rd., Wal.Abb.	22	CJ18
Cobblers Wk., Tedd.	74	BG50
Cobbles, The, Brwd.	122	DC27
Cobbles, The, Upmin.	51	CZ33
Cobblestone Pl., Croy.	87	BZ54
Oakfield Rd.		
Cobbold Est. NW10	55	BO36
Cobbold Rd. E11	49	CG34
Cobbold Rd. NW10	55	BO36
Cobbold Rd. W12	65	BO41
Cobbs Rd., Houns.	64	BE45
Cobden Clo., Uxb.	53	AX37
Wellington Rd.		
Cobden Hill, Rad.	27	BJ21
Cobden Rd. E11	49	CG34
Cobden Rd. SE25	87	CB53
Cobden Rd., Orp.	97	CM58
Cobden Rd., Sev.	108	CV65
Cobham, Grays	71	DD41
Cobham Ave., N.Mal.	85	BP53
Cobham Clo. SW11	76	BU46
Cobham Clo., Brom.	88	CK54
Cobham Clo., Wall.	95	BX57
Redford Ave.		
Cobham Gate, Cob.	92	BC60
Cobham Pk. Rd., Cob.	101	BC62
Cobham Pl., Bexh.	79	CP46
Cobham Rd. E17	39	CF30
Cobham Rd. N22	47	BY31
Cobham Rd., Bark.	58	CM37
St. Margarets		
Cobham Rd., Cob.	102	BF62
Cobham Rd., Houns.	64	BD43
Cobham Rd., Ilf.	49	CN34
Cobham Rd., Kings.T.	85	BM51
Cobham Rd., Lthd.	102	BF62
Cobham Rd., Lthd.	102	BG64
Cobham St., Grav.	81	DG47
Cobham Ter. Rd., Green.	80	DA47
Cobham Way, Lthd.	110	BB66
Cobill Clo., Horn.	51	CV31
Cobland Rd. SE12	78	CJ49
Coborn Rd. E3	57	CD37
Coborn St. E3	57	CD38
Cobourg Rd. SE5	67	CA43
Cobourg St. NW1	**1**	**M3**
Cobourg St. NW1	56	BW38
Cobs Clo., Sev.	108	DB64
Cobs Way, Wey.	92	AW58
Cobsdene, Grav.	81	DH50
Coburg Clo. SW1	**3**	**M8**
Coburg Cres. SW2	76	BX47
Coburg Rd. N22	47	BX31
Cochrane Clo. NW8	56	BT37
Cochrane Ms. NW8	**1**	**B1**
Cochrane Ms. NW8	56	BT37
Cochrane Rd. SW19	75	BR50
Cochrane St. NW8	**1**	**B1**
Cochrane St. NW8	56	BT37
Cock Gro., Berk.	7	AO13
Cock Hill E1	**2**	**N7**
Cock Hill E1	57	CA39
New St.		
Cock La. EC1	**2**	**F7**
Cock La. EC1	56	BY39
Cock La., Hodd.	12	CB13
Cock La., Lthd.	102	BG64
Cock Robins La., Harl.	6	CL7
Cock Robins La., Ware	6	CL6
Cockayne Way SE8	67	CD42
Cocker Rd., Enf.	30	CB21
Cockerhurst Rd., Sev.	98	CS57
Cockett Rd., Slou.	62	AS41
Cockfosters Rd., Barn.	29	BU22
Cockmannings La., Orp.	89	CP54
Cockmannings Rd., Orp.	89	CP54
Cockpit Steps SW1	**3**	**P5**
Cockpit Yd. WC1	**2**	**C6**
Cockpit Yd. WC1	56	BX39
Northington St.		
Cocks Cres., N.Mal.	85	BO52
Cocksett Ave., Orp.	97	CN57
Cockshot Hill, Reig.	121	BS71
Cockshot Rd., Reig.	121	BS71
Cockspur Ct. SW1	**3**	**P2**
Cockspur Ct. SW1	56	BW40
Spring Gdns.		
Cockspur St. SW1	**3**	**P2**
Cockspur St. SW1	56	BW40
Cocksure La., Sid.	79	CR48
Code St. E1	**2**	**Q5**
Code St. E1	57	CA38
Codham Hall La., Brwd.	51	DB31
Codicote Dr., Wat.	18	BD20
Codicote Rd., Welw.	5	BN5
Codicote Row, Hem.H.	8	AZ10
Codicote Ter. N4	48	BZ34
Codling Clo. E1	57	CB40
Vaughan Way		
Codling Way, Wem.	45	BK35
Codmore Cres., Chesh.	16	AP18
Codmore Wd. Rd., Chesh.	16	AR20
Codrington Ct., Grav.	81	DH49
Codrington Ct., Wok.	100	AP62
Ashwindham Ct.		
Codrington Gdns., Grav.	81	DH49
Codrington Hill SE23	77	CD47
Codrington Ms. W11	55	BR39
Blenheim Cres.		
Codrington Ms. W11	55	BR40
Blenheim Cres.		
Cody Clo., Har.	45	BK31
Cody Clo., Wall.	95	BW57
Alcock Clo.		
Cody Clo., Wey.	92	AY59
Viscount Gdns.		
Cody Rd. E16	57	CF38
Coe Ave. SE25	87	CB53
Coe Spur, Slou.	61	AN41
Cooper Way		
Cofers Circ., Wem.	46	BM34
Coftards, Slou.	52	AR39
Cogan Ave. E17	39	CD30
Coin St. SE1	**4**	**D2**
Coin St. SE1	56	BY40
Coity Rd. NW5	56	BV36
Coke St. E1	57	CB39
Cokers La. SE21	77	BZ47
Perifield		
Cokes La., Ch.St.G.	25	AQ24
Colas Ms. NW6	56	BS37
Birchington Rd.		
Colbeck Ms. SW7	66	BS42
Colbeck Rd., Har.	45	BG33
Colberg Pl. N16	48	CA33
Colborne Way, Wor.Pk.	85	BQ55
Colbrook Ave., Hayes	63	BA41
Colbrook Clo., Hayes	63	BA41
Colburn Ave., Cat.	105	CA65
Colburn Ave., Pnr.	36	BE29
Colburn Cres., Guil.	118	AT69
Sutherland Dr.		
Colburn Way, Sutt.	86	BT55
Colby Rd. SE19	77	CA49
Colby Rd., Walt.	83	BC54
Colchester Ave. E12	49	CK34
Colchester Dr., Pnr.	45	BD32
Colchester Rd. E10	48	CF33
Colchester Rd. E17	48	CE32
Colchester Rd., Edg.	37	BN30
Colchester Rd., Nthwd.	35	BC30
Colchester Rd., Rom.	42	CV30
Colchester St. E1	**2**	**Q8**
Colcokes Rd., Bans.	104	BS61
Cold Arbor Rd., Sev.	107	CS65
Cold Blow Cres., Bex.	79	CS47
Cold Blows, Mitch.	86	BU52
Cold Harbour E14	57	CF40
Coldbath Sq. EC1	**2**	**D4**
Coldbath Sq. EC1	56	BY38
Topham St.		
Coldbath St. SE13	67	CE44
Coldblow La. SE14	67	CC43
Coldershaw Rd. W13	54	BJ40
Coldfall Ave. N10	38	BU30
Coldham Clo., Enf.	30	CD22
Standard Rd.		
Coldham Gro., Enf.	30	CD22
Standard Rd.		
Coldharbour Clo., Egh.	82	AV52
Coldharbour La.		
Coldharbour La. SE5	67	BZ45
Coldharbour La. SW9	66	BY45
Coldharbour La., Bush.	27	BF25
Coldharbour La., Dor.	119	BH74
Coldharbour La., Egh.	82	AU52
Coldharbour La., Hayes	53	BC40
Coldharbour La., Pur.	95	BY58
Coldharbour La., Red.	114	CA70
Coldharbour La., Ton.	117	CZ71
Coldharbour La., Wok.	100	AV61
Coldharbour Rd., Croy.	95	BY56
Coldharbour Rd., Grav.	81	DF48
Coldharbour Rd., Harl.	13	CK11
Coldharbour Rd., Wey.	91	AV60
Coldharbour Rd., Wok.	100	AV61
Coldharbour Way, Croy.	95	BY56
Coldshott, Oxt.	115	CH70
Coldstream Gdns. SW18	75	BR46
Cole Clo. SE28	59	CO40
Cole Gdns., Houns.	63	BC44
Sandringham Gdns.		
Cole Grn. La., Welw.G.C.	5	BR9
Cole Pk. Gdns., Twick.	74	BJ46
Cole Pk. Rd., Twick.	74	BJ46
Cole Rd., Twick.	74	BJ46
Cole Rd., Wat.	26	BC23
Cole St. SE1	**4**	**J5**
Cole St. SE1	67	BZ41
Colebeck Ms. N1	56	BY36
Colebert Ave. E1	57	CC38
Colebrook, Cher.	91	AU57
Colebrook Clo. SW15	75	BQ47
Colebrook Dr. E11	49	CH33
Colebrook Gdns., Loug.	31	CM23
Colebrook La., Loug.	31	CL23
Colebrook Path, Loug.	31	CL23
Colebrook Rd. E17	48	CD31
Colebrook Rd. SW16	86	BX51
Colebrook Way N11	38	BV28
Colebrooke Ave. W13	54	BJ39
Colebrooke Ri., Brom.	88	CG51
Colebrooke Rd., Reig.	121	BU69
Colebrooke Row N1	**2**	**F1**
Colebrooke Row N1	56	BY37
Coleby Path SE5	67	BZ43
Harris St.		
Coledale Dr., Stan.	36	BK30
Coleford Rd. SW18	76	BT46
Colegrave Rd. E15	48	CF35
Colegrove Rd. SE15	67	CA43
Coleherne Ct. SW5	66	BS42
Coleherne Ms. SW10	66	BS42
Coleherne Rd. SW10	66	BS42
Colehill Gdns. SW6	65	BR44
Fulham Palace Rd.		
Colehill La. SW6	65	BR44
Coleman Clo. SE25	87	CA51
Warminster Rd.		
Coleman Ct. SW18	76	BS47
Coleman Flds. N1	57	BZ37
Coleman Grn. La., St.Alb.	5	BM7
Coleman Rd. SE5	67	CA43
Coleman Rd., Belv.	69	CR42
Coleman Rd., Dag.	59	CQ36
Coleman St. EC2	**2**	**K8**
Coleman St. EC2	57	BZ39
Colemans Heath SE9	78	CL48
Colemans La., Wal.Abb.	21	CF16
Colenorton Cres. (Eton Wick), Wind.	61	AM42
Colenso Rd. E5	48	CC35
Colenso Rd., Ilf.	49	CN33
Colepits Wd. Rd. SE9	78	CM46
Coleraine Rd. N8	47	BY31
Coleraine Rd. SE3	68	CG43
Coleridge Ave. E12	58	CK36
Coleridge Ave., Sutt.	95	BU56
Coleridge Clo. SW8	66	BV44
Coleridge Clo., Brwd.	122	DE26
Byron Rd.		
Coleridge Cres., Hem.H.	8	AZ10
Coleridge Cres., Slou.	62	AV44
Coleridge Gdns. NW6	56	BT36
Coleridge La. N8	47	BX32
Coleridge Rd.		
Coleridge Rd. E17	48	CD31
Coleridge Rd. N4	47	BY34
Coleridge Rd. N8	47	BW32
Coleridge Rd. N12	38	BT28
Coleridge Rd., Ashf.	73	AY49
Coleridge Rd., Croy.	87	CC54
Coleridge Rd., Dart.	70	CX45
Coleridge Rd., Rom.	41	CU29
Coleridge Rd., Til.	71	DH44
Coleridge Wk. NW11	47	BS31
Coleridge Wk., Brwd.	122	DE26
Byron Rd.		
Coleridge Way, Hayes	53	BC39
Coleridge Way, Orp.	89	CO53
Coleridge Way, West Dr.	63	AY42
Coles Clo., Ong.	24	CX16
Coles Cres., Har.	45	BF34
Coles Grn., Bush.	36	BG26
Coles Grn., Loug.	31	CL23
Coles Grn. Ct. NW2	46	BP34
Coles Grn. Rd. NW2	46	BP33
Coles Hill, Hem.H.	8	AW12
Coles La., West.	107	CP65
Colesburg Rd., Beck.	87	CD52
Colescroft Hill, Pur.	104	BY61
Colesdale, Cuffley	20	BX18
Coleshill Rd., Tedd.	74	BH50
Colesmead Rd., Red.	121	BU69
Colestown St. SW11	66	BU44
Colet Gdns. W14	65	BQ42
Colet Rd., Brwd.	122	DE25
Colets Orchard, Sev.	107	CU61
Coley Ave., Wok.	100	AT62
Coley St. WC1	**2**	**C5**
Coley St. WC1	56	BX38
Colfe Rd. SE23	77	CD47
Colgrove, Welw.G.C.	5	BQ8
Colham Grn. Rd., Uxb.	53	AZ39
Colham Rd., Uxb.	53	AY38
Colham Rd., West Dr.	53	AY40
Colin Clo. NW9	46	BO31
Colin Clo., Croy.	87	CD55
Colin Clo., Dart.	80	CX46
Brent Clo.		
Colin Clo., W.Wick.	88	CG55
Colin Cres. NW9	46	BO31
Colin Dr. NW9	46	BO32
Colin Gdns. NW9	46	BO32
Colin Pk. Rd. NW9	46	BO31
Colin Rd. NW10	55	BP36
Colin Rd., Cat.	105	CB65
Colin Way, Slou.	61	AN41
Colina Rd. N15	47	BY32
Colindale Ave. NW9	46	BN31
Colindale Ave., St.Alb.	9	BH14
Colindeep Gdns. NW4	46	BP31
Colindeep La. NW9	46	BN31
Colinette Rd. SW15	65	BQ45
Colinton Rd., Ilf.	50	CO34
Coliston Rd. SW18	76	BS47
Collage Clo., Twick.	74	BG47
Collamore Ave. SW18	76	BU47
Collapit Clo., Har.	45	BF32
Collard Ave., Loug.	31	CM23
Collard Grn., Loug.	31	CM23
College App. SE10	67	CF43
College Ave., Egh.	72	AT50
College Ave., Epsom	94	BO60
College Ave., Grays	71	DD42
College Ave., Har.	36	BH30
College Ave., Slou.	62	AP41
College Clo. E9	48	CC35
College Clo. N18	39	CA28
College Clo., Grays	71	DD42
College Ave.		
College Clo., Har.	36	BH29
College Ct., Chsnt.	21	CC18
College Cres. NW3	56	BT36
College Cres., Wind.	61	AN44
College Cross N1	56	BY36
College Dr., Ruis.	44	BC33
College Gdns. E4	39	CE26
College Gdns. N18	39	CA28
College Gdns. SE21	77	CA47
College Gdns. SW17	76	BU48
College Gdns., Enf.	30	BZ23
College Gdns., Ilf.	49	CK32
College Gdns., N.Mal.	85	BO53
College Gate, Harl.	13	CM11
College Grn. SE19	77	CA50
College Hill EC4	**2**	**J10**
College Hill EC4	57	BZ40
College Hill Rd., Har.	36	BH29
College La. NW5	47	BV35
College La., Hat.	10	BO13
College La., Wok.	100	AR63
College Ms. SW1	**3**	**Q6**
College Ms. SW18	76	BS46
St. Anns Hill		
College Pk. Clo. SE13	67	CF45
College Pk. Rd. N17	39	CA29
College Rd.		
College Pl. E17	49	CG31
College Pl. NW1	56	BW37
College Pl., St.Alb.	9	BG13
College Rd. E17	48	CF32
College Rd. N17	39	CA29
College Rd. N21	38	BY27
College Rd. NW10	55	BQ37
College Rd. SE19	77	CA47
College Rd. SE21	77	CA47
College Rd. SW19	76	BT50
College Rd. W13	54	BJ39
College Rd., Abb.L.	17	BB19
College Rd., Brom.	88	CH51
College Rd., Chsnt.	21	CC18
College Rd., Croy.	87	BZ55
College Rd., Enf.	30	BZ23
College Rd., Epsom	94	BO60
College Rd., Grav.	81	DD46
College Rd., Grays	71	DE42
College Rd., Guil.	118	AR71
College Rd. (Harrow on the Hill), Har.	45	BH32
College Rd. (Harrow Weald), Har.	36	BH30
College Rd., Hodd.	12	CD11
College Rd., Islw.	64	BH44
College Rd., St.Alb.	9	BJ14
College Rd., Slou.	61	AM40
College Rd., Swan.	89	CT51
College Rd., Wem.	45	BK33
College Rd., Wok.	100	AT61
College Slip, Brom.	88	CH51
College St. EC4	**2**	**K10**
College St. EC4	57	BZ40
College St., St.Alb.	9	BG13
College Ter. E3	57	CD38
College Ter. N3	37	BR30
Hendon La.		
College Vw. SE9	78	CJ47
College Wk., Kings.T.	85	BL52
Grange Rd.		
College Way, Nthwd.	35	BA29
College Way, Welw.G.C.	5	BQ7
Collent St. E9	57	CC36
Coller Cres., Dart.	80	CZ49
Colless Rd. N15	48	CA32
Collet Clo., Chsnt.	21	CC17
Collet Gdns., Chsnt.	21	CC17
Collet Clo.		
Collet Rd., Sev.	108	CW62
Collett Rd. SE16	67	CB41

Collett Rd., Hem.H.	8	AX13	Colonial Rd., Slou.	62	AQ41	Comforts Fm. Ave., Oxt.	115	CG70	**Comus Pl. SE17**	**4**	**M9**	Coningsby Rd., S.Croy.	96	BZ
Colley Hill La., Slou.	43	AP34	Colonial Way, Wat.	27	BD23	Comfrey Ct., Grays	71	DE43	Comus Pl. SE17	67	CA42	Conington Rd. SE13	67	CE
Colley La., Reig.	120	BR70	**Colonnade WC1**	**2**	**A5**	Commerce Rd. N22	38	BX30	Comyn Rd. SW11	66	BU45	Conisbee Ct. N14	29	BW
Colley La., Rick.	25	AU24	Colonnade WC1	56	BX38	Commerce Rd., Brent.	64	BK43	Comyne Rd., Wat.	26	BB21	Conisborough Cres. SE6	77	CF
Colley Manor Dr., Reig.	120	BQ70	*Herbrand St.*			Commerce Way, Croy.	86	BX55	Comyns Clo. E16	58	CG39	Coniscliffe Rd. N13	39	BZ
Colley Way, Reig.	120	BR69	Colson Gdns., Loug.	31	CL24	Commercial Rd. E1	57	CB39	Comyns Rd., Dag.	59	CR36	Conista Ct., Wok.	100	AP
Collier Clo., Epsom	94	BM57	Colson Path, Loug.	31	CL24	Commercial Rd. E14	57	CD39	Conant Ms. E1	57	CB39	Coniston Ave., Bark.	58	CN
Collier Cres., Dart.	80	CZ49	Colson Rd., Croy.	87	CA55	Commercial Rd. N18	39	CA29	*Back Ch. La.*			Coniston Ave., Grnf.	54	BJ
Collier Dr., Edg.	37	BM30	Colson Rd., Loug.	31	CL24	Commercial Rd., Guil.	118	AR71	Conaways Clo., Epsom	94	BP58	Coniston Ave., Upmin.	51	CY
Collier Row La., Rom.	41	CR29	Colson Way SW16	76	BW49	Commercial Rd., Stai.	73	AW50	Concanon Rd. SW2	66	BX45	Coniston Ave., Well.	68	CN
Collier Row Rd., Rom.	41	CQ30	Colsterworth Rd. N15	48	CA31	**Commercial St. E1**	**2**	**P5**	**Concert Hall App. SE1**	**4**	**C3**	Coniston Clo. N20	38	BT
Collier St. N1	**2**	**B1**	Colston Ave., Cars.	95	BU56	Commercial St. E1	57	CA38	Concert Hall App. SE1	56	BX38	Coniston Clo. SW13	65	CN
Collier St. N1	56	BX37	Colston Cres., Chsnt.	20	BY17	Commercial Way NW10	55	BM37	Concord Clo., Nthlt.	54	BD38	*Lonsdale Rd.*		
Collier Way, Guil.	118	AU69	Colston Rd. E7	58	CJ36	Commercial Way SE15	67	CA43	Concord Rd. W3	55	BM38	Coniston Clo. SW20	85	BQ
Colliers Clo., Wok.	100	AQ62	Colston Rd. SW14	65	BN45	Commercial Way, Wok.	100	AS62	Concord Rd., Enf.	30	CB25	Coniston Clo. W4	65	BN
Colliers Shaw, Kes.	97	CJ56	Colt Hatch, Harl.	6	CL10	Commerell Pl. SE10	68	CG42	Concorde Clo., Houns.	64	BF44	Coniston Clo., Bark.	58	CN
Colliers St., Cat.	114	CB66	Coltishall Rd., Horn.	60	CV36	*Blackwall La.*			*Lampton Rd.*			*Coniston Ave.*		
Colliers Water La., Th.Hth.	86	BY53	Coltness Cres. SE2	69	CO42	Commerell St. SE10	68	CG42	Concorde Clo., Uxb.	53	AY37	Coniston Clo., Bexh.	69	CS
Collindale Ave., Erith	69	CR43	Colton Gdns. N17	48	BZ31	**Commodity Quay E1**	**4**	**Q1**	Concorde Dr. E6	58	CK39	Coniston Clo., Dart.	79	CU
Collindale Ave., Sid.	79	CO47	Coltsfoot, Welw.G.C.	5	BS9	Commodore St. E1	57	CD38	*Viscount Dr.*			Coniston Clo., Erith	69	CT
Collingbourne Rd. W12	55	BP40	Coltsfoot, The, Hem.H.	7	AV14	Common, The W5	55	BL40	Concorde Dr., Hem.H.	8	AX13	Coniston Clo., Hem.H.	8	BA
Collingham Pl. SW5	66	BS42	*The Foxgloves*			Common, The, Berk.	7	AS12	Concorde Way, Slou.	61	AQ40	Coniston Clo., N.Mal.	85	BQ
Collingham Rd. SW5	66	BS42	Coltsfoot Ct., Grays	71	DE43	Common, The, Hat.	10	BP12	Concourse, The N9	39	CB27	*Grand Dr.*		
Collings Clo. N22	38	BX29	Coltsfoot Dr., Guil.	118	AT69	Common, The, Kings L.	17	AW19	Concourse, The NW9	37	BO30	Coniston Ct., Wall.	95	BV
Whittington Rd.			Coltsfoot Path, Rom.	42	CV29	Common, The, Rich.	74	BK48	*Long Mead*			Coniston Gdns. N9	39	CC
Collington Clo., Grav.	81	DF47	Columbia Ave., Edg.	37	BM30	Common, The, Sthl.	64	BD42	Condell Rd. SW8	66	BW44	Coniston Gdns. NW9	46	BN
Beresford Rd.			Columbia Ave., Ruis.	44	BC33	Common, The, Stan.	36	BH27	Conder St. E14	57	CD39	Coniston Gdns., Ilf.	49	CK
Collingtree Ave., Surb.	85	BN54	Columbia Ave., Wor.Pk.	85	BO54	Common Clo., Wok.	91	AR60	Conderton Rd. SE5	67	BZ45	Coniston Gdns., Pnr.	44	BC
Collingtree Rd. SE26	77	CC49	Columbia Ct., N.Mal.	85	BO54	Common Grn., Berk.	7	AT12	*Bredon Rd.*			Coniston Gdns., Sutt.	95	BS
Collingwood Ave. N10	47	BV31	**Columbia Rd. E2**	**2**	**P2**	Common La., Dart.	79	CU48	Condor Path, Nthlt.	54	BF37	Coniston Gdns., Wem.	45	BK
Collingwood Clo. SE20	77	CB51	Columbia Rd. E2	57	CA38	Common La., Kings L.	17	AY17	*Leander Rd.*			Coniston Rd. N10	38	BV
Jasmine Gro.			Columbia Rd. E13	58	CG38	Common La., Red.	114	BZ69	Condor Rd., Stai.	83	AX52	Coniston Rd. N17	39	CB
Collingwood Clo., Twick.	74	BF46	Columbia Sq. SW14	65	BN45	Common La., Wat.	27	BH23	Condor Wk., Rain.	59	CU36	Coniston Rd., Bexh.	69	CS
Collingwood Cres., Guil.	118	AT70	*Upper Richmond Rd.*			Common La., Wey.	92	AX58	*Heron Flight Ave.*			Coniston Rd., Brom.	77	CF
Collingwood Est. E1	57	CB38	Columbia Wf. Rd., Grays	71	DD43	Common La. (Eton),	61	AO42	Condover Cres. SE18	68	CL43	Coniston Rd., Couls.	104	BW
Collingwood Pl. SE18	68	CL41	Columbine Ave. E6	58	CK39	Wind.			Condray Pl. SW11	66	BT44	Coniston Rd., Croy.	87	CD
Rodney St.			Columbine Ave., S.Croy.	95	BY57	Common Meadow La.,	18	BG20	*Battersea Ch. Rd.*			Coniston Rd., Kings L.	17	AY
Collingwood Pl., Walt.	83	BC55	Columbine Way SE13	67	CF44	Wat.			**Conduit Ct. WC2**	**1**	**Q10**	Coniston Rd., Twick.	74	BF
Trafalgar Dr.			Columbine Way, Rom.	42	CW30	Common Rd. SW13	65	BP45	Conduit La. N18	39	BZ28	Coniston Rd., Wok.	100	AT
Collingwood Rd. E17	48	CE32	Columbus Sq., Erith	69	CU43	Common Rd., Brwd.	122	DE28	*Hermitage La.*			Coniston Wk. E9	48	CC
Collingwood Rd. N15	48	CA31	*Frobisher Rd.*			Common Rd., Dor.	119	BG70	Conduit La., Enf.	31	CC26	*Churchill Wk.*		
Collingwood Rd., Mitch.	86	BU51	Colvestone Cres. E8	48	CA35	Common Rd., Esher	93	BJ57	Conduit La., Slou.	62	AS42	Coniston Way, Chess.	85	BL
Collingwood Rd., Sutt.	85	BR55	Colville Est. N1	57	BZ37	Common Rd., Lthd.	102	BE64	Conduit La., S.Croy.	96	CA56	Coniston Way, Egh.	72	AT
Collingwood Rd., Uxb.	53	AZ38	Colville Gdns. W11	55	BR39	Common Rd., Red.	121	BU71	Conduit La. E., Hodd.	12	CE12	Coniston Way, Horn.	50	CU
Collingwood St. E1	57	CB38	Colville Ho. W11	55	BR39	Common Rd., Rick.	25	AU24	Conduit La. W., Hodd.	12	CE12	Conistone Way N7	56	BX
Collins Ave., Stan.	37	BL30	Colville Ms. W11	55	BR39	Common Rd., Sev.	108	DA65	**Conduit Ms. W2**	**1**	**A9**	*Sutterton St.*		
Collins Dr., Ruis.	45	BD34	Colville Pl. W1	56	BW39	Common Rd., Slou.	62	AT42	Conduit Ms. W2	56	BT39	Conistone Way, Red.	121	BU
Collins Meadow, Harl.	13	CL11	*Colville Pl. W1*	**1**	**M7**	Common Rd., Stan.	36	BH27	**Conduit Pas. W2**	**1**	**A9**	Conlan St. W10	55	BR
Collins Rd. N5	48	BZ35	Colville Rd. E11	48	CF34	Common Rd., Wal.Abb.	13	CJ14	**Conduit Pl. W2**	**1**	**A9**	Conley Rd. NW10	55	BN
Collins Sq. SE3	68	CG44	Colville Rd. E17	39	CD30	Common Rd., Wind.	61	AL42	Conduit Pl. W2	56	BT39	Conley St. SE10	68	CG
Tranquil Vale			Colville Rd. N9	39	CB26	Common Rd. (Eton Wick),	61	AN42	*London St.*			Connaught Ave. E4	39	CF
Collins St. SE3	68	CG44	Colville Rd. W3	65	BM41	Wind.			Conduit Rd. SE18	68	CL42	Connaught Ave. SW14	65	BN
Collinson St. SE1	**4**	**H5**	Colville Rd. W11	55	BR39	Common Way, Esher	93	BG58	**Conduit St. W1**	**1**	**K10**	Connaught Ave., Ashf.	73	AX
Collinson St. SE1	67	BZ41	Colville Sq. W11	55	BR39	Commondale SW15	65	BQ45	Conduit St. W1	56	BV40	Connaught Ave., Barn.	38	BX
Collinson Wk. SE1	**4**	**H5**	Colville Sq. Ms. W11	55	BR39	Commonfield La. SW17	76	BU49	Conduit Way NW10	55	BN36	Connaught Ave., Enf.	30	CA
Collinson Wk. SE1	67	BZ41	*Portobello Rd.*			Commonfield Rd., Bans.	95	BS60	Conegar Ct., Slou.	52	AP40	Connaught Ave., Grays	71	DD
Scovell Rd.			Colville Ter. W11	55	BR39	Commonfields, Harl.	6	CN10	Conewood St. N5	47	BY34	Connaught Ave., Houns.	64	BE
Collinwood Ave., Enf.	30	CC24	Colvin Clo. SE26	77	CC49	Commongate Rd., Rick.	25	AU25	Coney Acre SE21	77	BZ47	Connaught Ave., Loug.	31	CJ
Collinwood Gdns., Ilf.	49	CK32	*Lawrie Pk. Rd.*			Commons, The, Welw.G.C.	5	BS9	Coney Berry, Reig.	121	BT72	Connaught Clo. E10	48	CD
Collis All., Twick.	74	BH47	Colvin Gdns. E4	39	CF27	Commons La., Hem.H.	8	AY13	Coney Burrows E4	40	CG27	**Connaught Clo. W2**	**1**	**C**
Albion Rd.			Colvin Gdns. E11	49	CH31	Commonside, Epsom	103	BM61	Coney Clo., Hat.	10	BP13	Connaught Clo. W2	56	BU
Colls Rd. SE15	67	CC44	Colvin Gdns., Ilf.	40	CM30	Commonside, Harl.	13	CN13	Coney Gdns., Saw.	6	CP5	*Connaught St.*		
Collum Grn. Rd., Slou.	43	AP34	Colvin Gdns., Wal.Cr.	30	CC21	Commonside, Kes.	97	CJ56	Coney Gro., Uxb.	53	AZ38	Connaught Clo., Enf.	30	CA
Collyer Ave., Croy.	95	BX56	Colvin Rd. E6	58	CK36	Commonside, Lthd.	102	BF65	Coney Hill Rd., W.Wick.	88	CG55	Connaught Clo., Hem.H.	8	AZ
Collyer Clo. N1	56	BX37	Colvin Rd., Th.Hth.	86	BY53	Commonside E., Mitch.	86	BV52	Coneybury, Red.	114	CA70	Connaught Clo., Sutt.	86	BT
Eckford St.			Colvin St. W6	65	BQ42	Commonside Rd., Harl.	13	CN13	Coneybury Clo., Warl.	105	CB63	Connaught Clo., Uxb.	53	BA
Collyer Pl. SE15	67	CA44	*Glenthorne Rd.*			Commonside W., Mitch.	86	BU52	Coneydale, Welw.G.C.	7	BQ7	Connaught Crossing E16	58	CJ
Peckham High St.			Colwell Rd. SE22	77	CA46	Commonwealth Ave.	55	BP40	Coneygrove Path, Nthlt.	54	BE36	Connaught Dr. NW11	47	BS
Collyer Rd., Croy.	95	BX56	Colwick Clo. N6	47	BW33	W12			*Arnold Rd.*			Connaught Gdns. N10	47	BV
Collyer Rd., St.Alb.	18	BK17	Colwith Rd. W6	65	BQ43	Commonwealth Ave.,	53	BA39	Conference Clo. E4	39	CF27	Connaught Gdns. N13	38	BY
Colman Clo., Epsom	103	BP62	Colwood Gdns. SW19	76	BT50	Hayes			*Greenbank Clo.*			Connaught Gdns., Berk.	7	AP
Colman Rd. E16	58	CJ39	**Colworth Gro. SE17**	**4**	**J9**	Commonwealth Rd. N17	39	CB29	Conference Rd. SE2	69	CP42	*St. Katherines Way*		
Colman Way, Red.	121	BU69	Colworth Gro. SE17	67	BZ42	Commonwealth Rd., Cat.	105	CB65	Congleton Gro. SE18	68	CM42	Connaught Gdns., Mord.	86	BT
Colmar Clo. E1	57	CC38	*Browning St.*			Commonwealth Way SE2	69	CO42	Congo Rd. SE18	68	CM42	Connaught Hill, Loug.	31	CJ
Alderney Rd.			Colworth Rd. E11	49	CG32	Community Clo., Uxb.	44	AZ34	Congress Rd. SE2	69	CP42	Connaught La., Ilf.	49	CM
Colmer Pl., Har.	36	BG29	Colworth Rd., Croy.	87	CB54	*Long La.*			Congreve Rd. SE9	68	CK45	**Connaught Ms. W2**	**1**	**E**
Colmer Rd. SW16	86	BX51	Colwyn Ave., Grnf.	54	BH37	Community Rd. E15	48	CF35	**Congreve St. SE17**	**4**	**M9**	Connaught Ms. W2	56	BU
Colmore Rd., Enf.	30	CC24	Colwyn Cres., Houns.	64	BG44	Community Rd., Grnf.	54	BG37	Congreve St. SE17	67	CA42	*Connaught Pl.*		
Colnbrook By-pass,	62	AU43	Colwyn Grn. NW9	46	BO32	Como Rd. SE23	77	CD48	Congreve Wk. E16	58	CJ39	**Connaught Pl. W2**	**1**	**E**
Slou.			*Snowdon Dr.*			Como St., Rom.	50	CS31	*Fulmer Rd.*			Connaught Pl. W2	56	BU
Colnbrook By-pass,	63	AW43	Colwyn Rd. NW2	46	BP34	Compass Hill, Rich.	75	BL46	Conical Cor., Enf.	30	BZ23	Connaught Rd. E4	40	CG
West Dr.			Colyer Clo. SE9	78	CL48	Compayne Gdns. NW6	46	BS36	Coniers Way, Guil.	118	AT69	*Springfield Rd.*		
Colnbrook St. SE1	**4**	**F7**	Colyer Clo. N1	56	BX37	Comport Grn., Croy.	97	CG59	Conifer Ave., Rom.	41	CR28	Connaught Rd. E11	48	CF
Colnbrook St. SE1	66	BY41	Colyer Rd., Grav.	81	DE48	Compton Ave. E6	58	CJ37	Conifer Clo., Orp.	97	CM56	Connaught Rd. E16	58	CJ
Colndale Rd., Slou.	62	AV44	Colyers Clo., Erith	69	CS44	Compton Ave. N1	56	BY36	*Beechcroft Rd.*			Connaught Rd. E17	48	CE
Colne Ave., Rick.	35	AW27	Colyers La., Erith	69	CS44	Compton Ave. N6	47	BU33	Conifer Clo., Reig.	121	BS69	Connaught Rd. N4	47	BY
Colne Ave., Wat.	26	BC25	Colyers Wk., Erith	69	CT44	Compton Ave., Brwd.	122	DE26	*Reigate Hill*			Connaught Rd. NW10	55	BO
Colne Ave., West Dr.	63	AX41	Colyton Clo., Well.	69	CP44	Compton Ave., Rom.	50	CU31	Conifer Clo., Wal.Cr.	21	CA18	Connaught Rd. SE18	68	CL
Colne Dr., Rom.	42	CW29	Colyton Clo., Wem.	54	BK36	**Compton Clo. NW1**	**1**	**K3**	Conifer Dr., Brwd.	42	DB28	Connaught Rd. W13	54	BJ
Colne Dr., Walt.	84	BD55	*Winnington Way*			Compton Clo. NW1	56	BW38	Conifer Gdns. SW16	76	BX48	Connaught Rd., Barn.	28	BQ
Colne Gdns., St.Alb.	19	BL17	Colyton Rd. SE22	77	CB46	*Robert St.*			Conifer Gdns., Enf.	30	CA25	Connaught Rd., Har.	36	BH
Colne Mead, Rick.	35	AW27	Colyton Way N18	39	CB28	Compton Clo. W13	54	BH39	Conifer Gdns., Sutt.	86	BS55	Connaught Rd., Horn.	51	CV
Uxbridge Rd.			Combe Ave. SE3	68	CG43	Compton Clo., Edg.	37	BM29	*Ashleigh Gdns.*			Connaught Rd., Ilf.	49	CM
Colne Orchard, Iver	52	AV39	Combe Bank Dr., Sev.	107	CQ64	*Pavilion Way*			Conifer La., Egh.	72	AU49	Connaught Rd., N.Mal.	85	BO
Colne Rd. E5	48	CD35	Combe La., Walt.	92	BB58	Compton Clo., Esher	93	BG56	Conifer Way, Hayes	53	BC40	Connaught Rd., Rich.	75	BL
Colne Rd. N21	39	BZ26	Combe Lea, Brom.	88	CK52	Compton Ct. SE19	77	CA49	*Longmead Rd.*			*Albert Rd.*		
Colne Rd., Twick.	74	BH47	Combe Ms. SE3	68	CG43	Compton Cres. N17	39	BZ29	Conifer Way, Swan.	89	CS51	Connaught Rd., St.Alb.	9	BG
Colne St. E13	58	CH38	Combe Rd., Wat.	26	BB25	Compton Cres. W4	65	BN43	Conifer Way, Wem.	45	BK34	Connaught Rd., Slou.	62	AQ
Colne St., Epsom	94	BN56	Combe St., Hem.H.	8	AX13	Compton Cres., Chess.	94	BL57	Conifers, Tedd.	74	BK50	Connaught Rd., Sutt.	86	BT
Colne Valley, Upmin.	51	CZ32	Combe Way, Wey.	93	AY59	Compton Cres., Nthlt.	54	BD37	Conifers, Wey.	92	BB56	Connaught Rd., Tedd.	74	BG
Colne Vw. Ter., St.Alb.	10	BL15	Combedale Rd. SE10	68	CH42	Compton Gdns., St.Alb.	18	BF16	Conifers, The, Hem.H.	7	AV15	**Connaught Sq. W2**	**1**	**E**
Colne Way, Hem.H.	8	AY11	Combermartin Rd. SW18	75	BR47	*Faringford Clo.*			Conifers, The, Wat.	27	BD21	Connaught Sq. W2	56	BU
Colne Way, Stai.	72	AT48	Comber Clo. NW2	46	BP34	**Compton Pas. EC1**	**2**	**G4**	Conifers Clo., Tedd.	74	BJ50	**Connaught St. W2**	**1**	**D**
Colne Way, Wat.	27	BE22	Comber Gro. SE5	67	BZ43	Compton Pas. EC1	56	BY38	Coniger Rd. SW6	66	BS44	Connaught St. W2	56	BU
Colnebridge, Stai.	73	AW46	Combermere Rd. SW9	66	BX45	*Compton St.*			Coningham Ms. W12	55	BP40	Connaught Way N13	38	BY
Colnebridge Clo., Stai.	72	AV49	Combermere Rd., Mord.	86	BS53	**Compton Pl. WC1**	**1**	**Q4**	*Percy Rd.*			Connell Cres. W5	55	BL
Clarence St.			Comberton Rd. E5	48	CB34	Compton Pl., Erith	69	CT43	Coningham Rd. W12	55	BP40	Connemara Clo., Borwd.	28	BN
Colnedale Rd., Uxb.	44	AX35	Combeside SE18	68	CN43	Compton Pl., Wat.	36	BE28	Coningsby Bank, St.Alb.	9	BG15	*Percheron Rd.*		
Colney Hatch La. N10	38	BV29	Combwell Cres. SE2	69	CO41	Compton Ri., Pnr.	45	BE32	Coningsby Clo., Hat.	10	BQ15	Connicut La., Lthd.	111	BF
Colney Hatch La. N11	38	BU29	Comely Bank Rd. E17	48	CE32	Compton Rd. N1	56	BY36	Coningsby Cotts. W5	64	BK41	Connington Cres. E4	39	CF
Colney Heath La., St.Alb.	10	BL14	Comeragh Clo., Wok.	100	AQ63	Compton Rd. N21	38	BY26	*Coningsby Rd.*			Connop Rd., Enf.	30	CC
Colney Rd., Dart.	80	CW46	Comeragh Ms. W14	65	BR42	Compton Rd. NW10	55	BQ38	Coningsby Dr., Pot.B.	20	BT20	Connor Rd., Dag.	50	CQ
Cologne Rd. SW11	66	BT45	*Comeragh Rd.*			Compton Rd. SW19	75	BR50	Coningsby Dr., Wat.	26	BB23	Connor St. E9	57	CC
Colomb St. SE10	68	CG42	Comeragh Rd. W14	65	BR42	Compton Rd., Croy.	87	CB54	Coningsby Gdns. E4	39	CE29	*Lauriston Rd.*		
Colombo Rd., Ilf.	49	CM33	Comerford Rd. SE4	67	CD45	Compton Rd., Hayes	53	BB40	Coningsby La., Maid.	61	AH44	Connors All. W6	65	BR
Colombo St. SE1	**4**	**F3**	Comet Clo., Grays	70	CX42	Compton Sq. N1	56	BY36	Coningsby Rd. N4	47	BY33	*Bayonne Rd.*		
Colombo St. SE1	56	BY40	Comet Clo., Wat.	17	BB20	*Canonbury Rd.*			Coningsby Rd. W5	64	BK41	Conolly Rd. W7	54	BH
Colonade Wk. SW1	**3**	**J9**	Comet Pl. SE8	67	CE43	**Compton St. EC1**	**2**	**F4**				Conquest Rd., Wey.	92	AW
Colonels La., Cher.	83	AW53	*Comet St.*			Compton St. EC1	56	BY38				Conrad Clo., Grays	71	DD
Colonels Wk., Enf.	29	BY24	Comet Rd., Hat.	10	BO12	Compton Ter. N1	56	BY36				*Conrad Gdns.*		
Colonial Ave., Twick.	74	BG46	Comet St. SE8	67	CE43	Comreddy Clo., Enf.	29	BY22				Conrad Dr., Wor.Pk.	85	BQ
Colonial Rd., Felt.	73	BB47										Conrad Gdns., Grays	71	DD
												Cons St. SE1	**4**	**E**

ns St. SE1 66 BY41
'indmill Wk.
nsfield Ave., N.Mal. 85 BP52
nsort Clo., Brwd. 42 DB28
ueen St.
nsort Ms., Islw. 74 BG46
nsort Rd. SE15 67 CB44
nstable Clo. NW11 47 BS32
nstable Clo., Hayes 53 BA37
nstable Cres. N15 48 CB32
nstable Gdns., Edg. 37 BM30
nstable Gdns., Islw. 74 BG46
nstable Rd., Grav. 81 DF48
nstable Wk. SE21 77 CA48
nstance Cres., Brom. 88 CG54
nstance Rd., Croy. 86 BY54
nstance Rd., Enf. 30 CA25
nstance Rd., Sutt. 95 BT56
nstance Rd., Twick. 74 BF47
nstance St. E16 58 CK40
nstantine Rd. NW3 47 BU35
nstitution Hill SW1 3 J4
nstitution Hill SW1 66 BV41
nstitution Hill, Grav. 81 DH47
nstitution Hill, Wok. 100 AS63
nstitution Ri. SE18 68 CL44
nsul Gdns., Swan. 79 CU50
rincess Rd.
ntent St. SE17 4 J9
ntent St. SE17 67 BZ42
ntessa Clo., Orp. 97 CM56
ntrol Twr. Rd., Houns. 63 AZ45
'hester Rd.
nvair Wk., Nthlt. 54 BD38
ittiwake Rd.
nvent Est. SE19 77 BZ50
nvent Gdns. W5 64 BK42
nvent Gdns. W11 55 BR39
nvent Hill SE19 77 BZ50
nvent La., Cob. 92 BB59
nvent Rd., Ashf. 73 AZ49
nvent Rd., Wind. 61 AM44
nvent Way, Sthl. 64 BD42
nway Clo., Rain. 59 CU36
nway Clo., Stan. 36 BJ29
nway Cres., Grnf. 54 BH37
nway Cres., Rom. 50 CP33
nway Dr., Ashf. 73 BA50
nway Dr., Hayes 63 BA41
nway Dr., Sutt. 95 BS57
nway Gdns., Enf. 30 CA22
nway Gdns., Grays 71 DD43
nway Gdns., Mitch. 86 BW52
nway Gdns., Wem. 45 BK33
nway Gro. W3 55 BN39
nway Ms. W1 1 L5
nway Rd. N14 38 BX27
nway Rd. N15 47 BY32
nway Rd. NW2 46 BQ34
nway Rd. SE18 68 CM42
nway Rd. SW20 85 BQ51
nway Rd., Felt. 74 BD49
nway Rd., Houns. 74 BE47
nway Rd. (Heathrow), 63 AZ45
Houns.
nway St. E13 58 CH38
'hilip St.
nway St. W1 1 L5
nway St. W1 56 BW38
nway Wk., Hmptn. 74 BE50
'earnley Cres.
nybeare NW3 56 BU36
Quickswood
nybury Clo., Wal.Abb. 22 CH19
nyer St. E3 57 CD37
nyerd Rd., Sev. 108 DC63
nyers Clo., Walt. 93 BD56
nyers Clo., Wdf.Grn. 40 CG29
nyers Rd. SW16 76 BW49
nyers Way, Loug. 31 CL24
oden Clo., Brom. 78 CH50
Plaistow La.
ok Sq., Erith 69 CT43
okes Clo. E11 49 CG34
okes La., Sutt. 94 BR57
Church Rd.
okham Cres. SE16 67 CC41
Marlow Way
okham Dene Clo., Chis. 88 CM51
okham Hill, Orp. 89 CR55
okham Rd., Sid. 79 CR50
okhill Rd. SE2 69 CO41
oks Clo., Rom. 41 CS30
oks Hole Rd., Enf. 29 BY22
oks Mead, Bush. 27 BF25
oks Rd. E15 57 CE37
oks Rd. SE17 66 BY43
oks Spinney, Harl. 6 CO10
oks Vennel, Hem.H. 8 AW12
ol Oak La. NW9 46 BO33
olfin Rd. E16 58 CH39
olgardie Ave. E4 39 CF28
olgardie Ave., Chig. 40 CL27
olgardie Rd., Ashf. 73 BA49
olhurst Rd. N8 47 BW32
omassie Rd. W9 55 BR38
Bravington Rd.
oombe, The, Bet. 120 BN69
oombe Ave., Croy. 96 CA56
oombe Ave., Sev. 107 CU63
oombe Bank, Kings.T. 85 BO51
oombe Clo., Edg. 37 BL30
oombe Clo., Houns. 64 BF45
oombe Cor. N21 38 BY26
oombe Cres., Hmptn. 74 BE50
oombe Dr., Ruis. 44 BC34
oombe Dr., Wey. 91 AV57
oombe End, Kings.T. 75 BN50
oombe Gdns. SW20 85 BP51
oombe Gdns., Berk. 7 AP12
oombe Gdns., N.Mal. 85 BO52
oombe Heights, Kings.T. 75 BO50
oombe Hill Glade, 75 BO50
Kings.T.

Coombe Hill Rd., Kings.T. 75 BO50
Coombe Hill Rd., Rick. 35 AW26
Coombe Ho. Chase, 85 BN51
N.Mal.
Coombe La., Croy. 96 CB56
Coombe La., Guil. 109 AO67
Coombe La. W., Kings.T. 85 BM51
Coombe Lea, Brom. 88 CK52
Coombe Moor, Kings.T. 75 BO50
Coombe Neville, Kings.T. 75 BN50
Coombe Pk., Kings.T. 75 BN49
Coombe Ridings, Kings.T. 75 BN49
Coombe Ri., Brwd. 122 DC26
Coombe Ri., Kings.T. 85 BN51
Coombe Rd. NW10 46 BN34
Coombe Rd. SE26 77 CB49
Coombe Rd. W4 65 BO42
Coombe Rd. W13 64 BJ41
Northcroft Rd.
Coombe Rd., Bush. 36 BG26
Coombe Rd., Croy. 96 BZ56
Coombe Rd., Grav. 81 DH48
Coombe Rd., Hmptn. 74 BE50
Coombe Rd., Kings.T. 85 BM51
Coombe Rd., N.Mal. 85 BO51
Coombe Rd., Rom. 51 CW31
Coombe Rd., Sev. 108 CV61
Coombe Vale, Ger.Cr. 43 AS33
Coombe Wk., Sutt. 86 BS55
Coombe Way, Wey. 92 AY59
Green La.
Coombe Wd. Hill, Pur. 96 BZ59
Coombe Wd. Rd., Kings.T. 75 BN49
Coombefield Clo., N.Mal. 85 BO53
Coombehurst Clo., Barn. 29 BU23
Coombelands La., Wey. 92 AW57
Coomber Way, Croy. 86 BW54
Coombermere Clo., 61 AN44
Wind.
Coombes Rd., Dag. 59 CQ37
Coombes Rd., St.Alb. 18 BK16
Coombewood Dr., Rom. 50 CR32
Coombfield Dr., Dart. 80 CZ49
Coombs St. N1 2 G1
Coombs St. N1 56 BY37
Remington St.
Coomer Rd. SW6 65 BR43
Cooms Wk., Edg. 37 BM30
East Rd.
Cooper Ave. E17 39 CD30
Cooper Clo. SE1 4 E5
Cooper Ct. E15 48 CE35
Holt Ct.
Cooper Cres., Cars. 86 BU55
Cooper Rd. NW10 46 BP35
Cooper Rd., Croy. 95 BY56
Cooper Rd., Guil. 118 AS71
Cooper St. E16 58 CG39
Cooper Way, Slou. 61 AN41
Coopers Clo. E1 57 CC38
Coopers Clo., Chig. 41 CO27
Coopers Clo., S.Dnth. 90 CY51
Paddock Clo.
Coopers Clo., Stai. 72 AV49
Coopers Grn. La., St.Alb. 10 BL12
Coopers Grn. La., 5 BN10
Welw.G.C.
Coopers Hill, Ong. 24 CX18
Coopers Hill La., Egh. 72 AR49
Coopers Hill Rd., Red. 121 BX70
Coopers Hill Rd., Red. 121 BY73
Coopers La. E10 48 CE33
Coopers La. NW1 1 P1
Coopers La. NW1 56 BW37
Coopers La. SE12 78 CH48
Coopers La., Pot.B. 20 BT19
Coopers La., Til. 71 DH43
Coopers La. Rd., Pot.B. 20 BU19
Coopers Rd. SE1 67 CA42
Coopers Rd., Grav. 81 DF47
Coopers Rd., Pot.B. 20 BT18
Coopers Row EC3 2 P10
Coopers Row EC3 57 CA40
Coopers Row, Iver 52 AU38
Coopers Wk., Chsnt. 21 CC17
Coopersale Clo., Wdf.Grn. 40 CJ29
Coopersale Common, 23 CP17
Epp.
Coopersale La., Epp. 32 CO22
Coopersale Rd. E9 48 CC35
Coopersale Rd., Epp. 23 CO18
Coopersale St., Epp. 23 CP19
Coote Gdns., Dag. 50 CQ34
Coote Rd., Bexh. 69 CQ44
Coote Rd., Dag. 50 CQ34
Cope Pl. W8 66 BS41
Cope St. SE16 67 CC42
Copeland Dr. E14 67 CE42
Barnsdale Ave.
Copeland Rd. E17 48 CE32
Copeland Rd. SE15 67 CB44
Copeman Clo. SE26 77 CC49
Copeman Rd., Brwd. 122 DE26
Copenhagen Gdns. W4 65 BN41
Copenhagen Pl. E14 57 CD39
Copenhagen St. N1 56 BX37
Copenhagen Way, Walt. 83 BC55
Copers Cope Rd., Beck. 77 CD50
Copeswood Rd., Wat. 26 BC23
Copford Clo., Wdf.Grn. 40 CK29
Green Wk.
Copford Wk. N1 57 BZ37
Popham St.
Copinger Wk., Edg. 37 BM30
North Rd.
Copland Ave., Wem. 45 BK35
Copland Clo., Wem. 45 BK35
Copland Rd., Wem. 55 BL36
Copleigh Dr., Tad. 103 BR63
Copleston Pas. SE5 67 CA45
Ivanhoe Rd.
Copleston Rd. SE15 67 CA45
Copley Clo. SE17 66 BY43
Hillingdon St.

Copley Clo. W7 54 BH39
Copley Clo., Red. 121 BU69
Copley Clo., Wok. 100 AP63
Copley Dene, Brom. 88 CJ51
Copley Pk. SW16 76 BX50
Copley Rd., Stan. 36 BK28
Copley St. E1 57 CC39
Stepney Grn.
Copley Way, Tad. 103 BQ63
Copmans Wick, Rick. 25 AU25
Copnor Way SE15 67 CA43
Hordle Prom. W.
Coppelia Rd. SE3 68 CG45
Coppen Rd., Dag. 50 CQ33
Copper Beech Clo., Hem.H. 7 AV15
Copper Beech Clo., Ilf. 40 CL30
Copper Beech Clo., Orp. 89 CP53
Rookery Gdns.
Copper Beech Gro., 61 AL44
Wind.
Copper Beech Rd., S.Ock. 60 DB38
Copper Beeches, Guil. 118 AS71
Copper Clo. SE19 77 CA50
Copper Mead Clo. NW2 46 BQ34
Copper Mill Dr., Islw. 64 BH44
St. Johns Rd.
Copper Mill La. SW17 76 BT49
Copper Mill Rd., Stai. 72 AT46
Copper Ridge, Ger.Cr. 34 AS28
Copperas St. SE8 67 CE43
Copperbeech Clo. NW3 47 BT35
Akenside Rd.
Copperbeech Clo., Grav. 81 DH47
Copperdale Rd., Hayes 63 BC41
Silverdale Gdns.
Copperfield, Chig. 40 CM28
Copperfield App., Chig. 40 CM29
Copperfield Ave., Uxb. 53 AZ39
Copperfield Clo., Grav. 81 DK47
Copperfield Clo., S.Croy. 96 BZ59
Copperfield Ct., Lthd. 102 BJ64
Kingston Rd.
Copperfield Gdns., Brwd. 42 DA26
Copperfield Ms. N18 39 CA28
Copperfield Orchard, 108 CW62
Sev.
Copperfields
Copperfield Ri., Wey. 91 AV56
Copperfield Rd. E3 57 CD38
Copperfield Rd. SE28 59 CP39
Copperfield St. SE1 4 G4
Copperfield St. SE1 66 BY41
Copperfield Way, Chis. 78 CM50
Dickens Dr.
Copperfield Way, Pnr. 45 BE31
Copperfields, Lthd. 102 BG64
Copperfields, Sev. 108 CW62
Copperfields, Welw.G.C. 5 BT8
Copperfields Wk., Sev. 108 CW62
Copperfields Way, Rom. 42 CV30
Coppergate Clo., Brom. 88 CH51
Coppermill La. E17 48 CC32
Coppermill La., Rick. 34 AV29
Coppermill La., Uxb. 35 AW29
Coppetts Clo. N12 38 BU29
Coppetts Rd. N10 38 BU29
Coppice, The, Ashf. 73 AZ50
School Rd.
Coppice, The, Beac. 34 AO29
School La.
Coppice, The, Brwd. 33 CZ21
Coppice, The, Enf. 29 BY24
Coppice, The, Hem.H. 8 AZ13
Coppice, The, Wat. 27 BD25
Coppice, The, West Dr. 53 AY39
Coppice Clo. SW20 85 BQ52
Coppice Clo., Guil. 118 AO70
Coppice Clo., Hat. 10 BO14
Coppice Clo., Ruis. 44 BA32
Coppice Clo., Stan. 36 BH29
Woodlands Dr.
Coppice Dr. SW15 75 BP46
Coppice Dr., Stai. 72 AR47
Coppice Est., Brom. 88 CL53
Coppice La., Reig. 120 BR69
Coppice Path, Chig. 41 CO27
Coppice Row, Epp. 31 CM21
Coppice Wk. N20 38 BS27
Coppice Way E18 49 CG31
Coppies Gro. N11 38 BV28
Copping Clo., Croy. 96 CA56
Coppings, The, Hodd. 12 CE10
Coppins, The, Croy. 96 CE57
Coppins, The, Har. 36 BH29
Coppins Clo., Berk. 7 AP13
Coppins La., Iver 52 AV39
Coppock Clo. SW11 66 BU44
Copse, The E4 40 CG26
Copse, The, Amer. 25 AO22
Copse, The, Cat. 114 CB66
Copse, The, Hem.H. 7 AV12
Copse, The, Lthd. 102 BF65
Copse Ave., W.Wick. 87 CE55
Copse Bank, Sev. 108 CW63
Copse Clo. SE7 68 CH43
Copse Clo., Guil. 118 AU73
Copse Clo., Nthwd. 35 BA30
Copse Clo., West Dr. 63 AX41
Copse Edge Ave., Epsom 94 BO60
Copse Glade, Surb. 84 BK54
Copse Hill SW20 85 BP51
Copse Hill, Pur. 95 BX60
Copse Hill, Sutt. 95 BS57
Copse La., Beac. 34 AP29
Copse Rd., Cob. 92 BC60
Copse Rd., Red. 121 BT71
Copse Rd., Wok. 100 AP62
Copse Side, Hartley 90 DC52
Copse Vw., S.Croy. 96 CC58
Copse Wd., Iver 52 AU37
Copse Wd. Way, Nthwd. 35 BA30
Copsem Dr., Esher 93 BG57
Copsem La., Esher 93 BG57
Copsem La., Lthd. 93 BG59

Copsem Way, Esher 93 BG57
Copsleigh Ave., Red. 121 BV74
Copsleigh Clo., Red. 121 BV73
Copsleigh Way, Red. 121 BV73
Copt Hall Rd., Sev. 108 DA65
Coptefield Dr., Belv. 69 CP41
Coptfold Rd., Brwd. 42 DB27
Copthall Ave. EC2 2 L8
Copthall Ave. EC2 57 BZ39
Copthall Bldgs EC2 57 BZ39
Telegraph St.
Copthall Bldgs. EC2 2 L8
Copthall Clo. EC2 2 K8
Copthall Clo. EC2 57 BZ39
Copthall Clo., Ger.Cr. 34 AS29
Copthall Cor., Ger.Cr. 34 AS29
Copthall Ct. EC2 2 L8
Copthall Ct. EC2 57 BZ39
Throgmorton St.
Copthall Dr. NW7 37 BP29
Copthall Gdns. NW7 37 BP29
Copthall Gdns., Twick. 74 BH47
Copthall La., Ger.Cr. 34 AS29
Copthall Rd. E., Uxb. 44 AZ34
Copthall Rd. W., Uxb. 44 AZ34
Copthall Way, Wey. 91 AV58
Copthill La., Tad. 103 BR63
Copthorn Clo., Shep. 83 BA53
Copthorne Ave. SW12 76 BW47
Copthorne Ave., Brom. 88 CK55
Copthorne Ave., Ilf. 40 CL29
Copthorne Clo., Ashf. 73 AY49
Ford Rd.
Copthorne Clo., Ilf. 40 CL29
Copthorne Clo., Rick. 26 AY25
Copthorne Gdns., Horn. 51 CX32
Copthorne Ms., Hayes 63 BB42
Copthorne Ri., S.Croy. 96 BZ60
Copthorne Rd., Lthd. 102 BJ63
Copthorne Rd., Rick. 26 AY25
Coptic St. WC1 1 Q7
Coptic St. WC1 56 BX39
Copwood Clo. N12 38 BT28
Coral Clo., Rom. 50 CP31
Coral Ho., Harl. 6 CL10
Coral Row SW18 66 BT45
Gartons Way
Coral St. SE1 4 E5
Coral St. SE1 66 BY41
Coralline Wk. SE2 69 CP41
Coram Clo., Berk. 7 AR13
Coram Grn., Brwd. 122 DE25
Coram St. WC1 1 Q5
Coram St. WC1 56 BX38
Coran Clo. N9 39 CC26
Corban Rd., Houns. 64 BF45
Corbar Clo., Barn. 29 BT23
Corbet Clo., Wall. 86 BV55
Corbet Ct. EC3 2 L9
Corbet Pl. E1 2 P6
Corbet Pl. E1 57 CA39
Calvin St.
Corbet Rd., Epsom 94 BO58
Corbets Ave., Upmin. 51 CX35
Corbets Tey Rd., Upmin. 51 CX35
Corbett Clo., Croy. 96 CF59
Corbett Gro. N22 38 BX29
Corbett Rd. E11 49 CJ32
Corbett Rd. E17 48 CF31
Corbett St. SW8 66 BX43
Corbetts Pas. SE16 67 CC42
Rotherhithe New Rd.
Corbicum E11 49 CG33
Corbiere Ct. SW19 75 BQ50
Thornton Rd.
Corbins La., Har. 45 BF34
Corbridge Cres. E2 57 CB37
Corby Clo., St.Alb. 18 BF16
Corby Cres., Enf. 29 BX24
Corby Dr., Egh. 72 AR50
Corby Rd. NW10 55 BN37
Corby Way E3 57 CE38
Knapp Rd.
Corbylands Rd., Sid. 78 CN47
Corbyn St. N4 47 BX33
Corcorans, Brwd. 33 DA25
Elizabeth Rd.
Cord Way E14 .67 CE41
Mellish St.
Cordelia Gdns., Stai. 73 AY47
Cordelia Rd., Stai. 73 AY47
Cordelia St. E14 57 CE39
Cordell Clo., Chsnt. 21 CD17
Corder Clo., St.Alb. 9 BF15
Corderoy Pl., Cher. 82 AV53
Cording St. E14 57 CE39
Cordingley Rd., Ruis. 44 BA34
Cordons Clo., Ger.Cr. 34 AR30
Cordova Rd. E3 57 CD38
Cordrey Gdns., Couls. 104 BX61
Cordwainers Wk. E13 58 CH37
Turpin Est.
Cordwell Rd. SE13 77 CF46
Corelli Rd. SE3 68 CK44
Corfe Ave., Har. 45 BF35
Corfe Clo., Ash. 102 BK62
Corfe Gdns., Slou. 61 AN40
Avebury
Corfield St. E2 57 CB38
Corfton Rd. W5 55 BL39
Coriander Cres., Guil. 109 AQ68
Oregano Way
Corinium Clo., Wem. 46 BL35
Corinium Gate, St.Alb. 9 BF14
Corinne Rd. N19 47 BW35
Corinth Par., Hayes 53 BB39
Corinthian Manorway, 69 CS42
Erith
Corinthian Rd., Erith 69 CS42
Corinthian Way, Stai. 73 AX47
Clare Rd.
Cork Sq. E1 57 CB40
Cork St. W1 3 L1
Cork St. W1 56 BW40

Cork St. Ms. W1 3 L1
Cork Tree Way E4 39 CD28
Corker Wk. N7 47 BX34
Corkers Path, Ilf. 49 CM34
Corkran Rd., Surb. 84 BK54
Corkscrew Hill, W.Wick. 87 CF55
Corlett St. NW1 1 C6
Corlett St. NW1 56 BU39
Bell St.
Cormongers La., Red. 121 BW70
Cormont Rd. SE5 66 BY44
Cormorant Clo. E17 39 CD29
Banbury Rd.
Cormorant Wk., Rain. 59 CU36
Heron Flight Ave.
Corn Cft., Hat. 10 BP11
Corn Mead, Welw.G.C. 5 BQ6
Corn Mill Dr., Orp. 88 CN54
Cornbury Rd., Edg. 36 BK29
Cornelia St. N7 56 BX36
Cornell Clo., Sid. 79 CQ50
Cornell Way, Rom. 41 CR28
Corner Grn. SE3 68 CH45
Corner Hall, Hem.H. 8 AX14
Corner Ho. St. WC2 3 Q2
Corner Mead NW9 37 BO30
Corner Vw., Hat. 10 BQ15
Dixons Hill Vw.
Cornerfield, Hat. 10 BP11
Cornerhall Ave., Hem.H. 8 AX14
Corners, Welw.G.C. 5 BS7
Cornerside, Ashf. 73 BA50
Corney Rd. W4 65 BO43
Cornfield Clo., Uxb. 53 AX37
Cornfield Rd., Bush. 27 BF24
Cornfield Rd., Reig. 121 BT71
Cornfields, Hem.H. 8 AW14
Cornflower La., Croy. 87 CC54
Cornflower Ter. SE22 77 CB46
Cornflower Way, Rom. 42 CW30
Cornford Clo., Brom. 88 CH53
Cornford Gro. SW12 76 BV48
Cornhill EC3 2 L9
Cornhill EC3 57 BZ39
Cornhill Clo., Wey. 83 AW55
Cornish Gro. SE20 87 CV51
Cornmill, Wal.Abb. 21 CE20
Cornmill La. SE13 67 CF45
Cornshaw Rd., Dag. 50 CP33
Cornsland, Brwd. 42 DB27
Cornthwaite Rd. E5 48 CC34
Cornwall Ave. E2 57 CC38
Cornwall Ave. N3 38 BS29
Cornwall Ave. N22 38 BX30
Cornwall Ave., Esher 93 BJ57
Cornwall Ave., Sthl. 54 BE39
Cornwall Ave., Well. 68 CN45
Cornwall Ave., Wey. 92 AY60
Cornwall Clo., Bark. 58 CN36
Cornwall Clo., Horn. 51 CX31
Cornwall Clo., Wal.Cr. 21 CD20
Cornwall Clo. (Eton Wick), 61 AM42
Wind.
Cornwall Cres. W11 55 BR40
Cornwall Dr., Orp. 79 CP50
Cornwall Gdns. NW10 55 BP36
Cornwall Gdns. SW7 66 BS41
Cornwall Gdns. Ms. SW7 66 BS41
Cornwall Gate, Grays 70 CX42
Water La.
Cornwall Gro. W4 65 BO42
Cornwall Lo., Kings.T. 75 BM50
Cornwall Rd. N4 47 BY33
Cornwall Rd. N15 48 BZ32
Cornwall Rd. N18 39 CB28
Cornwall Rd. SE1 4 D2
Cornwall Rd. SE1 56 BY40
Cornwall Rd., Brwd. 33 DA25
Cornwall Rd., Croy. 86 BY55
Cornwall Rd., Har. 45 BG32
Cornwall Rd., Pnr. 36 BE29
Cornwall Rd., Ruis. 44 BB34
Cornwall Rd., St.Alb. 9 BH14
Cornwall Rd., Sutt. 95 BS58
Cornwall Rd., Twick. 74 BJ47
Cornwall Rd., Uxb. 53 AX36
Cornwall St. E1 57 CB39
Watney St.
Cornwall Ter. NW1 1 F5
Cornwall Ter. NW1 56 BU38
Cornwall Ter. Ms. NW1 1 F5
Cornwall Way, Stai. 72 AV50
Cornwallis Ave. N9 39 CB27
Cornwallis Ave. SE9 78 CM48
Cornwallis Clo., Erith 69 CU43
Frobisher Rd.
Cornwallis Gro. N9 39 CB27
Cornwallis Rd. E17 48 CC31
Cornwallis Rd. N9 39 CB27
Cornwallis Rd. N19 47 BX34
Cornwallis Rd., Dag. 50 CP35
Cornwallis Wk. SE9 68 CK45
Cornwell Ave., Grav. 81 DH48
Cornwell Rd., Wind. 72 AQ46
Cornwood Clo. N2 47 BT32
Cornwood Dr. E1 57 CC39
Cornworthy Rd., Dag. 50 CP35
Corona Rd. SE12 78 CH47
Coronation Ave., Slou. 52 AS39
Coronation Ave., Wind. 62 AQ44
Coronation Clo., Bex. 79 CP46
Coronation Clo., Ilf. 49 CM31
Coronation Cres., Grays 71 DG41
Loewen Rd.
Coronation Dr., Horn. 50 CU35
Coronation Hill, Epp. 22 CN18
Coronation Rd. E13 58 CJ38
Coronation Rd. NW10 55 BL38
Coronation Rd., Hayes 63 BB42
Coronation Ter., West. 106 CK62
Coronation Wk., Twick. 74 BF47
Coronet St. N1 2 M3
Coronet St. N1 57 CA38
Corporation Ave., Houns. 64 BE45

nberry Clo., Nthlt. 54 BD37
nborne Ave., Sthl. 64 BF42
nborne Clo., Pot.B. 19 BR19
nborne Cres., Pot.B. 19 BR19
nborne Gdns., Upmin. 51 CX34
nborne Rd., Bark. 58 CM37
nborne Rd., Chsnt. 21 CC19
heobalds La.
nborne Rd., Hat. 10 BP12
nborne Rd., Hodd. 12 CE11
nborne Rd., Pot.B. 19 BR19
nborne Waye, Hayes 53 BC39
nbourn All. WC2 1 P10
nbourn Pas. SE16 67 CB41
Vilson Gro.
nbourn St. WC2 1 P10
nbourn St. WC2 56 BW40
ong Acre
nbourne Ave. E11 49 CH31
nbourne Ave., Surb. 85 BM55
nbourne Ave., Wind. 61 AM44
nbourne Clo. SW16 86 BX52
nbourne Clo., Slou. 61 AO40
anbourne Ct. E18 49 CH31
anbourne Dr., Pnr. 45 BD32
anbourne Gdns. NW11 46 BR32
anbourne Gdns., Ilf. 49 CM31
anbourne Gdns., 5 BR8
Velw.G.C.
anbourne Rd. E12 49 CK35
anbourne Rd. E15 48 CF35
anbourne Rd. N10 38 BV30
anbourne Rd., Nthwd. 44 BB31
anbourne Rd., Slou. 61 AO40
anbrook Clo., Brom. 88 CH53
anbrook Dr., Esher 84 BG55
anbrook Dr., Rom. 50 CU31
anbrook Dr., St.Alb. 10 BL13
anbrook Dr., Twick. 74 BF47
anbrook Est. E2 57 CC37
anbrook Ms. E17 48 CD32
anbrook Pk. N22 38 BX30
anbrook Ri., Ilf. 49 CK32
anbrook Rd. SE8 67 CE44
anbrook Rd. SW19 75 BR50
anbrook Rd. W4 65 BO42
anbrook Rd., Barn. 29 BT25
anbrook Rd., Bexh. 69 CQ44
anbrook Rd., Houns. 64 BE45
anbrook Rd., Ilf. 49 CL32
anbrook Rd., Th.Hth. 87 BZ51
anbrook St. E2 57 CC37
Roman Rd.
anbrook Ter. E2 57 CC37
Roman Rd.
anbury Rd. SW6 66 BS44
ane Ave. W3 55 BO40
Cumberland Pk.
ane Ave., Islw. 74 BJ46
ane Clo., Dag. 59 CR36
ane Ct. EC4 2 E9
ane Ct., Epsom 94 BN56
ane Gdns., Hayes 63 BB42
ane Gro. N7 56 BY36
Furlong Rd.
ane Lo. Rd., Houns. 63 BC43
ane Mead SE16 67 CC42
ane Pk. Rd., Twick. 74 BF48
ane Rd., Twick. 74 BH47
ane St. SE10 67 CF42
ane Way, Twick. 74 BG47
anebrook, Twick. 74 BG48
aneford Clo., Twick. 74 BH47
aneford Way, Twick. 74 BH47
anell Grn., S.Ock. 60 DA40
anes Dr., Surb. 85 BL52
anes Pk., Surb. 85 BL52
anes Pk. Ave., Surb. 85 BL52
anes Pk. Cres., Surb. 85 BL52
anes Water, Hayes 63 BB43
anes Way, Borwd. 28 BN25
aneswater Pk., Sthl. 64 BE42
anewood Clo., Wok. 100 AS63
Guildford Rd.
anfield Clo. SE27 77 BZ48
Dunelm Gro.
anfield Ct., Wok. 100 AQ62
Martindale Rd.
anfield Cres., Cuffley 20 BX18
anfield Dr. NW9 37 BO29
anfield Dr., Wat. 18 BE19
anfield Rd. SE4 67 CD45
anfield Rd. E., Cars. 95 BV58
anfield Rd. W., Cars. 95 BV58
anfield Row SE1 4 E6
anford Ave. N13 38 BX28
anford Ave., Stai. 73 AY47
anford Clo. SW20 75 BP50
anford Clo., Stai. 73 AY47
anford Cotts. E1 57 CC40
Cranford St.
anford Dr., Dart. 80 CW47
anford Dr., Hayes 63 BB42
anford La., Felt. 63 BB45
anford La., Hayes 63 BA43
anford La., Houns. 64 BD43
anford La. Est., Houns. 63 BC43
anford Pk. Rd., Hayes 63 BB42
anford Parkway, The, 63 BC42
Sthl.
anford Ri., Esher 93 BG56
anford Rd., Hayes 63 BB42
anford St. E1 57 CC40
anford Way N8 47 BX32
anham Gdns., Upmin. 51 CZ33
anham Rd., Horn. 50 CU32
anhurst Rd. NW2 46 BQ35
anleigh Clo. SE20 87 CB51
anleigh Clo., Bex. 79 CR46
anleigh Clo., Chsnt. 21 CB17
Valence Dr.
anleigh Clo., Orp. 88 CN55
anleigh Clo., S.Croy. 96 CB59
anleigh Dr., Swan. 89 CT53

Cranleigh Dr., Wal.Cr. 21 CB17
Cranleigh Gdns. N21 29 BY25
Cranleigh Gdns. SE25 87 CA52
Cranleigh Gdns., Bark. 58 CM36
Cranleigh Gdns., Har. 46 BL32
Cranleigh Gdns., Kings.T. 75 BL50
Cranleigh Gdns., Loug. 31 CK25
Cranleigh Gdns., S.Croy. 96 CB59
Cranleigh Gdns., Sthl. 54 BE39
Cranleigh Gdns., Sutt. 86 BS55
Cranleigh Ms. SW11 66 BU44
Cabul Rd.
Cranleigh Rd. N15 48 BZ32
Cranleigh Rd. SW19 85 BR52
Cranleigh Rd., Esher 84 BG54
Cranleigh Rd., Felt. 73 BB49
Cranleigh St. NW1 1 M1
Cranleigh St. NW1 56 BW37
Cranley Clo., Guil. 118 AT70
Cranley Dr., Ilf. 49 CM33
Cranley Dr., Ruis. 44 BB34
Cranley Gdns. N10 47 BV31
Cranley Gdns. N13 38 BX27
Cranley Gdns. SW7 66 BT42
Cranley Gdns., Wall. 95 BW57
Cranley Gro., Walt. 92 BB57
Cranley Ms. SW7 66 BT42
Cranley Ms., Ilf. 49 CM32
Cranley Rd.
Cranley Pl. SW7 3 A9
Cranley Pl. SW7 66 BT42
Cranley Rd. E13 58 CH39
Cranley Rd., Guil. 118 AS70
Cranley Rd., Ilf. 49 CM33
Cranley Rd., Walt. 92 BB56
Cranmer Ave. W13 64 BJ41
Cranmer Clo., Mord. 85 BQ53
Cranmer Clo., Pot.B. 20 BS18
Cranmer Clo., Ruis. 45 BD33
Cranmer Clo., Stan. 36 BK29
Cranmer Clo., Warl. 105 CD62
Cranmer Gdns.
Cranmer Clo., Wey. 92 AZ57
Cranmer Ct. SW3 3 D9
Cranmer Ct. SW3 66 BU42
Cranmer Ct. SW4 66 BW45
Cranmer Ct., Hmptn. 74 BF49
Cranmer Fm. Clo., Mitch. 86 BU52
Cranmer Gdns., Dag. 50 CS35
Cranmer Gdns., Warl. 105 CD62
Cranmer Rd. E7 49 CH35
Cranmer Rd. SW9 66 BY43
Cranmer Rd., Croy. 86 BY55
Cranmer Rd., Edg. 37 BM27
Cranmer Rd., Hmptn. 74 BF49
Cranmer Rd., Hayes 53 BA39
Cranmer Rd., Kings.T. 75 BL49
Cranmer Rd., Mitch. 86 BU52
Cranmer Rd., Sev. 107 CT65
Cranmer Ter. SW17 76 BT49
Cranmore Ave., Chis. 78 CK49
Cranmore Ave., Islw. 64 BG43
Cranmore Ct., St.Alb. 9 BH13
Avenue Rd.
Cranmore La., Lthd. 110 AZ68
Cranmore Pk. Est., Chis. 78 CK50
Cranmore Rd., Brom. 78 CG48
Cranmore Way N10 47 BW31
Cranston Clo., Guil. 109 AP68
Cranston Clo., Houns. 64 BE44
Cranston Clo., Reig. 121 BS71
Lymden Gdns.
Cranston Clo., Uxb. 44 BA34
Cranston Est. N1 2 L1
Cranston Est. N1 57 BZ37
Cranston Gdns. E4 39 CE28
Cranston Pk. Ave., Upmin. 51 CY35
Cranston Rd. SE23 77 CD47
Cranstoun Clo., Guil. 109 AP68
Keens Pk. Rd.
Cranswick Rd. SE16 67 CB42
Crantock Rd. SE6 77 CE48
Cranwell Clo. E3 57 CE38
Cranwell Gro., Shep. 83 AY52
Cranwell Rd., Houns. 63 AZ44
Cranwich Ave. N21 39 BZ26
Cranwich Rd. N16 48 BZ33
Cranwood St. EC1 2 L3
Cranwood St. EC1 57 BZ38
Cranworth Cres. E4 39 CF26
Cranworth Gdns. SW9 66 BY44
Craster Rd. SW2 76 BX47
Crathie Rd. SE12 78 CH46
Crathorn St. SE13 67 CF45
Cravan Ave., Felt. 73 BC48
Craven Ave. W5 54 BK40
Craven Ave., Sthl. 54 BE39
Craven Clo., Hayes 53 BC39
Craven Gdns. SW19 76 BS49
Craven Gdns., Bark. 58 CN37
Craven Gdns., Ilf. 40 CM30
Craven Gdns. (Collier 41 CR28
Row), Rom.
Craven Gdns. (Harold 42 CY29
Wd.), Rom.
Craven Hill W2 56 BT40
Craven Hill Gdns. W2 56 BT40
Craven Hill Ms. W2 56 BT40
Craven Ms. SW11 76 BV46
Taybridge Rd.
Craven Pk. NW10 55 BN37
Craven Pk. Ms. NW10 55 BN37
Craven Pk. Rd. N15 48 CA32
Craven Pk. Rd. NW10 55 BO37
Craven Pas. WC2 3 Q2
Craven Pas. WC2 56 BX40
Craven St.
Craven Rd. NW10 55 BN37
Craven Rd. W2 56 BT40
Craven Rd. W5 54 BK40
Craven Rd., Croy. 87 CB54
Craven Rd., Kings.T. 85 BL51
Craven Rd., Orp. 89 CP55
Craven St. WC2 3 Q2

Craven St. WC2 56 BX40
Craven Ter. W2 56 BT40
Craven Wk. N16 48 CB33
Crawford Ave., Grays 71 DD40
Crawford Ave., Wem. 45 BK35
Crawford Clo., Islw. 64 BH44
Crawford Compton Clo., 60 CV36
Horn.
Sarre Ave.
Crawford Est. SE5 67 BZ44
Crawford Gdns. N13 38 BY27
Crawford Gdns., Nthlt. 54 BE38
Crawford Ms. W1 1 E7
Crawford Pas. EC1 2 D5
Crawford Pas. EC1 56 BY38
Ray St.
Crawford Pl. W1 1 D8
Crawford Pl. W1 56 BU39
Crawford Rd. SE5 67 BZ44
Crawford Rd., Hat. 10 BP11
Crawford St. W1 1 D7
Crawford St. W1 56 BU39
Crawfords, Swan. 79 CT50
Dawson Dr.
Crawley Dr., Hem.H. 8 AY11
Crawley Hatch, Harl. 13 CK11
Crawley Rd. E10 48 CE33
Crawley Rd. N22 39 BZ30
Crawley Rd., Enf. 39 CA26
Crawshaw Dr., Cher. 91 AU57
Crawshay Clo., Sev. 107 CU65
Crawshay Rd. SW9 66 BY44
Crawthew Gro. SE22 67 CA45
Cray Ave., Ash. 103 BL61
Cray Ave., Orp. 89 CO54
Cray Clo., Dart. 69 CU45
Cray Rd., Belv. 69 CR43
Cray Rd., Sid. 79 CP50
Cray Rd., Swan. 89 CR53
Cray Valley Rd., Orp. 89 CO53
Craybrooke Rd., Sid. 79 CO49
Crayburne, Grav. 81 DC49
Craybury End SE9 78 CM48
Craydene Rd., Erith 69 CT44
Crayford Clo. E6 58 CJ39
Neatscourt Rd.
Crayford High St., Dart. 69 CT45
Crayford Rd. N7 47 BW35
Crayford Rd., Dart. 79 CT46
Crayford Rd., Erith 69 CT43
Crayford Way, Dart. 79 CT46
Crayke Hill, Chess. 94 BL57
Craylands, Orp. 89 CP52
Craylands La., Swans. 80 DB46
Craylands Sq., Swans. 80 DB46
Craymill Sq., Dart. 69 CT45
Norris Way
Crayonne Clo., Sun. 83 BB51
Crealock Gro., Wdf.Grn. 40 CG28
Crealock St. SW18 76 BS46
Creasey Clo., Horn. 50 CU34
Creasy Est. SE1 4 M7
Creasy St. SE1 67 CA41
Webb St.
Crebor St. SE22 77 CB46
Creden Hall Dr., Brom. 88 CK54
Lower Gravel Rd.
Credenhill St. SW16 76 BW50
Credenhill Way SE15 67 CB43
Ledbury St.
Crediton Hill NW6 47 BS35
Crediton Rd. E16 58 CH39
Crediton Rd. NW10 55 BQ37
Crediton Way, Esher 93 BJ56
Credo Way, Grays 70 DA43
Credon Rd. E13 58 CJ37
Credon Rd. SE16 67 CB42
Cree Way, Rom. 41 CT29
Creechurch La. EC3 2 N9
Creechurch La. EC3 57 CA39
Creechurch Pl. EC3 2 N9
Creed La. EC4 2 G9
Creed La. EC4 56 BY39
Creek, The, Sun. 83 BC53
Creek Rd. SE8 67 CE43
Creek Rd. SE10 67 CE43
Creek Rd., Bark. 58 CN38
Creek Rd., E.Mol. 84 BH52
Creekside SE8 67 CE43
Creekside, Rain. 59 CT38
Creeland Gro. SE6 77 CD47
Catford Hill
Crefeld Clo. W6 65 BR43
Creffield Rd. W3 55 BL40
Creffield Rd. W5 55 BL40
Creighton Ave. E6 58 CJ37
Creighton Ave. N2 47 BU31
Creighton Ave. N10 38 BU30
Creighton Ave., St.Alb. 9 BG15
Creighton Rd. N17 39 CA29
Creighton Rd. NW6 55 BQ37
Creighton Rd. W5 64 BK41
Cremarne Rd., Grav. 81 DF47
Cremer St. E2 2 P1
Cremer St. E2 57 CA37
Cremorne Est. SW10 66 BT43
Cremorne Gdns. SW10 66 BT43
Cremorne Gdns., Epsom 94 BN58
Cremorne Rd. SW10 66 BT43
Crescent, The E17 48 CD32
Crescent, The EC3 2 P10
Crescent, The N11 38 BV28
Crescent, The NW2 46 BP34
Crescent, The SW13 65 BO44
Crescent, The SW19 76 BS48
Crescent, The W3 55 BN39
Crescent, The (Abbots 17 BB18
Langley), Abb.L.
Crescent, The, Ashf. 73 AY49
Crescent, The, Barn. 29 BS23
Crescent, The, Beck. 87 CE51
Crescent, The, Bex. 79 CP47
Crescent, The, Cat. 105 CE65
Crescent, The, Cher. 83 AW52

Crescent, The, Croy. 87 BZ53
Crescent, The, E.Mol. 84 BE52
Crescent, The, Egh. 72 AS50
Crescent, The, Epp. 22 CN19
Crescent, The, Epsom 103 BM61
Crescent, The 81 DD46
(Northfleet), Grav.
Crescent, The (Perry St.), 81 DF48
Grav.
Crescent, The, Green. 80 DB46
Crescent, The, Guil. 118 AQ70
Crescent, The, Harl. 6 CP8
Crescent, The, Har. 45 BG33
Crescent, The, Hayes 63 BA43
Crescent, The, Ilf. 49 CL32
Crescent, The, Lthd. 102 BJ64
Crescent, The, Long. 90 DC52
Bramblefield Clo.
Crescent, The, Loug. 31 CJ25
Crescent, The, N.Mal. 85 BN52
Crescent, The, Reig. 121 BS70
Crescent, The, Rick. 26 AZ25
Crescent, The, St.Alb. 18 BF18
Crescent, The, Sev. 108 CV64
Crescent, The, Shep. 83 BB53
Crescent, The, Sid. 78 CN49
Crescent, The, Slou. 62 AP41
Crescent, The, Surb. 85 BL53
Crescent, The, Sutt. 95 BT56
Crescent, The (Belmont), 95 BS59
Sutt.
Crescent, The, Upmin. 51 CZ33
Crescent, The, Wat. 27 BD24
Crescent, The 27 BF22
(Aldenham), Wat.
Crescent, The, Wem. 45 BJ34
Crescent, The, W.Wick. 88 CG53
Crescent, The, Wey. 83 AZ55
Crescent Ave., Grays 71 DE42
Crescent Ave., Horn. 50 CT34
Crescent Ct., Surb. 84 BK53
Crescent Dr., Brwd. 122 DC26
Crescent Dr., Enf. 30 CC22
Crescent Dr., Orp. 88 CL53
Crescent E., Barn. 29 BT22
Crescent Gdns. SW19 76 BS48
Crescent Gdns., Ruis. 44 BC33
Crescent Gdns., Swan. 89 CS51
Crescent Gro. SW4 66 BW45
Crescent Gro., Mitch. 86 BU53
Crescent La. SW4 66 BW45
Crescent Pl. SW3 3 C8
Crescent Pl. SW3 66 BU42
Crescent Ri. N22 38 BW29
Crescent Ri., Barn. 29 BU25
Crescent Rd. E4 40 CG26
Crescent Rd. E6 58 CJ37
Crescent Rd. E10 48 CE34
Crescent Rd. E13 58 CH37
Crescent Rd. E18 40 CJ30
Crescent Rd. N3 37 BR30
Crescent Rd. N8 47 BW32
Crescent Rd. N9 39 CB26
Crescent Rd. N11 38 BU28
Glenthorne Rd.
Crescent Rd. N15 47 BY31
Carlingford Rd.
Crescent Rd. N22 38 BW30
Crescent Rd. SE18 68 CL42
Crescent Rd. SW20 75 BQ50
Crescent Rd., Barn. 29 BT24
Crescent Rd., Beck. 87 CE51
Crescent Rd., Brwd. 42 DA28
Crescent Rd., Brom. 78 CH50
Crescent Rd., Cat. 105 CB65
Crescent Rd., Dag. 50 CR34
Crescent Rd., Enf. 29 BY24
Crescent Rd., Erith 69 CT43
Crescent Rd., Hem.H. 8 AX13
Crescent Rd., Kings.T. 75 BM50
Crescent Rd., Red. 114 BZ70
Crescent Rd., Reig. 121 BS71
Crescent Rd., Sev. 107 CT63
Crescent Rd., Shep. 83 BA53
Crescent Rd., Sid. 78 CN48
Crescent Rd., S.Ock. 70 CY41
Central Ave.
Crescent Rd., Sthl. 64 BE41
Crescent Row EC1 2 H5
Crescent Row EC1 57 BZ38
Baltic St.
Crescent Stables SW15 65 BQ45
Upper Richmond Rd.
Crescent St. N1 56 BX36
Huntingdon St.
Crescent Vw., Loug. 31 CJ25
Crescent Wk., S.Ock. 70 CY41
Crescent Way N12 38 BU29
Crescent Way SE4 67 CE45
Crescent Way SW16 76 BX50
Crescent Way, Orp. 97 CN56
Crescent Way, S.Ock. 60 CY40
Crescent W., Barn. 29 BT22
Crescent Wd. Rd. SE26 77 CB48
Cresford Rd. SW6 66 BS44
Crespigny Rd. NW4 46 BP32
Cress End, Rick. 35 AW27
Springwell Ave.
Cress Rd., Slou. 61 AN41
Cressage Clo., Sthl. 54 BE38
Cressall Mead, Lthd. 102 BJ63
Cresset Rd. E9 57 CC36
Cresset St. SW4 66 BW45
Cressfield Clo. NW5 47 BV35
Cressida Rd. N19 47 BW33
Cressingham Gdns. Est. 76 BY47
SW2
Cressingham Gro., Sutt. 95 BT56
Cressingham Rd. SE13 67 CF45
Cressingham Rd., Edg. 37 BN29
Cressington Clo. N16 48 CA35
Wordsworth Rd.
Cresswell Gdns. SW5 66 BT42
Cresswell Gdns., Houns. 64 BE45

Cresswell Pk. SE3 68 CG45
Cresswell Pl. SW10 66 BT42
Cresswell Rd. SE25 87 CB52
Cresswell Rd., Chesh. 16 AO20
Cresswell Rd., Felt. 74 BE48
Cresswell Rd., Twick. 74 BK46
Cresswell Way N21 38 BY26
Cresswells Mead, Maid. 61 AG42
Cressy Ct. E1 57 CC39
Cressy Ct. W6 65 BP41
Cressy Pl. E1 57 CC39
Cressy Rd. NW3 47 BU35
Crest, The N13 38 BY28
Crest, The NW4 46 BQ32
Crest, The, Chsnt. 20 BY17
Crest, The, Saw. 6 CP6
Crest, The, Surb. 85 BM53
Crest Ave., Grays 71 DD43
Crest Clo., Sev. 98 CR59
Crest Dr., Enf. 30 CC22
Crest Pk., Hem.H. 8 BA13
Crest Rd. NW2 46 BO34
Crest Rd., Brom. 88 CG54
Crest Rd., S.Croy. 96 CB57
Crest Vw., Pnr. 45 BD31
Cresta Clo., Wey. 91 AV58
Cresta Ct. W5 55 BL38
Crestbrook Ave. N13 38 BY27
Crestbrook Pl. N13 38 BY27
Crestfield St. WC1 2 A2
Crestfield St. WC1 56 BX38
St. Chads St.
Cresthill Ave., Grays 71 DE42
Creston Ave., Wok. 100 AP61
Creston Way, Wor.Pk. 85 BQ55
Crestview Dr., Orp. 88 CL53
Crestway SW15 75 BP46
Crestwood Way, Houns. 74 BE46
Creswick Ct. W3 55 BM40
Creswick Ct., Welw.G.C. 5 BQ8
Goblins Grn.
Creswick Rd. W3 55 BM40
Creswick Wk. E3 57 CE37
Malmesbury Rd.
Creswick Wk. NW11 46 BR31
Crete Hall Rd., Grav. 81 DE46
Creton St. SE18 68 CL41
Crevington Way, Horn. 51 CV35
Crew Curve, Berk. 7 AP11
Crewdson Rd. SW9 66 BY43
Crewe Pl. NW10 55 BO38
Crewes Ave., Warl. 105 CC61
Crewes Clo., Warl. 105 CC62
Crewes Fm. La., Warl. 105 CC62
Crewes La., Warl. 105 CC61
Crews Hill, Enf. 20 BX20
Crews St. E14 67 CE42
Crewys Rd. NW2 46 BR34
Crewys Rd. SE15 67 CB44
Crichton Ave., Wall. 95 BW56
Crichton Gdns., Rom. 50 CR33
Crichton Rd., Cars. 95 BU57
Cricket Fld. Rd., Uxb. 53 AX37
Cricket Grn., Mitch. 86 BU52
Cricket Grd. Rd., Chis. 88 CL51
Cricket Hill, Red. 121 BX71
Cricket La., Beck. 77 CD50
Cricket Way, Wey. 83 BB55
Cricketers Arms Rd., Enf. 30 BZ23
Cricketers Clo. N14 38 BW26
Cricketers Clo., Chess. 93 BK56
Cricketers Clo., St.Alb. 9 BH13
Stonecross
Cricketers Ct. SE11 4 F9
Cricketfield Rd. E5 48 CB35
Cricketfield Rd., West Dr. 63 AX42
Cricklade Ave. SW2 76 BX48
Cricklade Ave., Rom. 42 CV29
Cricklewood Bdy. NW2 46 BQ35
Cricklewood La. NW2 46 BQ35
Cridland St. E15 58 CG37
Church St.
Crieff Ct., Tedd. 74 BK50
Crieff Rd. SW18 76 BT46
Criffel Ave. SW2 76 BW48
Crimp Hill, Wind. 72 AP47
Crimp Hill Rd., Wind. 72 AP47
Crimscott St. SE1 4 N7
Crimscott St. SE1 67 CA41
Crimsworth Rd. SW8 66 BW44
Crinan St. N1 56 BX37
Cringle St. SW8 66 BW43
Cripplegate St. EC2 2 H6
Cripsey Ave., Ong. 24 CW16
Crisp Rd. W6 65 BQ42
Crispen Rd., Felt. 74 BE49
Crispian Clo. NW10 46 BO35
Neasden La.
Crispin Clo., Ash. 103 BL62
Crispin Clo., Croy. 86 BX55
Crispin Cres., Croy. 86 BW55
Crispin Rd., Edg. 37 BN29
Crispin St. E1 2 P7
Crispin St. E1 57 CA39
Brushfield St.
Crispin Way, Slou. 43 AO35
Criss Cres., Ger.Cr. 34 AR30
Criss Gro., Ger.Cr. 34 AR30
Cristowe Rd. SW6 65 BR44
Criterion Ms. N19 47 BW34
St. Johns Vill.
Critten La., Dor. 119 BD70
Crockenhall Way, Grav. 81 DF50
Crockenhill La., Dart. 90 CV54
Crockenhill Rd., Orp. 89 CP53
Crockenhill Rd., Swan. 89 CQ53
Crockerton Rd. SW17 76 BU48
Crockery La., Guil. 110 AY68
Crockford Clo., Wey. 92 AX56
Crockford Pk. Rd.
Crockford Pk. Rd., Wey. 92 AX56
Crockham Way SE9 78 CL49
Crocknorth Rd., Dor. 110 BC70
Crocknorth Rd., Lthd. 110 BB69

Cro–Cuf

Crocus Clo., Croy. 87 CC54
Primrose La.
Crocus Fld., Barn. 28 BR25
Croffets, Tad. 103 BQ64
Croft, The NW10 55 BO37
Croft, The W5 55 BL39
Croft, The, Barn. 28 BQ24
Croft, The, Brox. 12 CD15
Croft, The, Houns. 64 BE43
Croft, The, Loug. 31 CL23
Croft, The, Pnr. 45 BE33
Croft, The, Ruis. 45 BD35
Croft, The, St.Alb. 18 BF16
Croft, The, Swan. 89 CS51
Croft, The, Welw.G.C. 5 BR9
Croft, The, Wem. 45 BK35
Croft Ave., Dor. 119 BJ70
Croft Ave., W.Wick. 87 CF54
Croft Clo. NW7 37 BO27
Croft Clo., Belv. 69 CQ42
Croft Clo., Chis. 78 CK49
Croft Clo., Hayes 63 BA43
Croft Clo., Kings L. 17 AW18
Croft Clo., Uxb. 53 AZ36
Croft End Rd., Kings L. 17 AW18
Croft Fld., Hat. 10 BP12
Croft Fld., Kings L. 17 AW18
Croft Gdns. W7 64 BJ41
Croft Gdns., Ruis. 44 BB33
Croft La., Kings L. 17 AW18
Croft Lo. Clo., Wdf.Grn. 40 CH29
Croft Meadow, Kings L. 17 AW18
Croft Rd. SW16 86 BY51
Croft Rd. SW19 76 BT50
Croft Rd., Brom. 78 CH50
Croft Rd., Cat. 105 CD64
Croft Rd., Enf. 30 CD23
Croft Rd., Ger.Cr. 34 AS30
Croft Rd., Sutt. 95 BT56
Croft Rd., West. 115 CL66
Croft St. SE8 67 CD42
Croft Wk., Brox. 12 CD15
Croft Way NW3 47 BS35
Croft Way, Sev. 116 CT66
Croft Way, Sid. 78 CN48
Croftdown Rd. NW5 47 BV34
Crofters, Wind. 72 AQ46
Crofters Clo., Islw. 74 BG46
Crofters End, Saw. 6 CQ5
Crofters Mead, Croy. 96 CD58
Crofters Rd., Nthwd. 35 BB28
Crofters Way NW1 56 BW37
Croftleigh Ave., Pur. 104 BY61
Crofton Ave. W4 65 BN43
Crofton Ave., Bex. 79 CP47
Crofton Ave., Orp. 88 CM55
Crofton Ave., Walt. 84 BD55
Crofton Clo., Cher. 91 AU57
Crofton Ct., Orp. 88 CM54
Crofton La., Orp. 88 CM55
Crofton Pk. Rd. SE4 77 CD46
Crofton Pound Hill, Orp. 88 CM55
Crofton Rd. E13 58 CH38
Crofton Rd. SE5 67 CA44
Crofton Rd., Grays 71 DF41
Crofton Rd., Orp. 88 CL55
Crofton Ter. E5 48 CD35
Durrington Rd.
Crofton Ter., Rich. 65 BL45
Crofton Way, Enf. 29 BY23
Croftongate Way SE4 77 CD46
Crofts, The, Hem.H. 8 AZ14
Crofts, The, Shep. 83 BB52
Crofts Path, Hem.H. 8 AZ14
Crofts Rd., Har. 45 BJ32
Croftway NW3 47 BS35
Croftway, Rich. 74 BJ48
Crogsland Rd. NW1 56 BV36
Croham Clo., S.Croy. 96 CA57
Croham Manor Rd., S.Croy. 96 CA57
Croham Mt., S.Croy. 96 CA57
Croham Pk. Ave., S.Croy. 96 CA56
Croham Rd., S.Croy. 96 BZ56
Croham Valley Rd., S.Croy. 96 CA57
Croindene Rd. SW16 86 BX51
Cromar Ct., Wok. 100 AR61
Cromartie Rd. N19 47 BW33
Crombie Clo., Ilf. 49 CK32
Crombie Rd., Sid. 78 CM47
Cromer Clo., Uxb. 53 BA39
Cromer Est. WC1 56 BX38
Cromer Hyde La., Welw.G.C. 5 BN8
Cromer Pl., Orp. 88 CN54
Andover Rd.
Cromer Rd. E10 48 CF33
Cromer Rd. N17 39 CB30
Sherringham Ave.
Cromer Rd. SE25 87 CB52
Cromer Rd. SW17 76 BV50
Cromer Rd., Barn. 29 BT24
Cromer Rd., Horn. 51 CV33
Cromer Rd., Houns. 63 AZ45
Cromer Rd., Rom. 50 CS32
Cromer Rd. (Chadwell Heath), Rom. 50 CQ32
Cromer Rd., Wat. 27 BD22
Cromer Rd., Wdf.Grn. 40 CH28
Cromer Rd. W., Houns. 63 AZ45
Camberley Rd.
Cromer St. WC1 2 A3
Cromer St. WC1 56 BX38
Cromer Ter. E8 48 CB35
Foxley Clo.
Cromer Vill. Rd. SW18 75 BR46
Cromford Clo., Orp. 88 CN55
Cromford Path E5 48 CC35
Clapton Pk. Est.
Cromford Rd. SW18 76 BS46
Cromford Way, N.Mal. 85 BN51
Cromlix Clo., Chis. 88 CL51
Crompton St. W2 1 A5
Crompton St. W2 56 BT38
Cromwall Ct., Enf. 30 CC25
Cromwell Ave. N6 47 BV33
Cromwell Ave. W6 65 BP42
Cromwell Ave., Brom. 88 CH52
Cromwell Ave., Chsnt. 21 CB18
Cromwell Ave., N.Mal. 85 BO53
Cromwell Clo. E1 57 CB40
Vaughan Way
Cromwell Clo. N2 47 BT31
Cromwell Clo. W3 55 BN40
Cromwell Clo., Brom. 88 CH52
Cromwell Clo., Ch.St.G. 34 AR27
Cromwell Clo., St.Alb. 9 BK11
Langham Clo.
Cromwell Clo., Walt. 83 BC54
Cromwell Cres. SW5 66 BS42
Cromwell Dr., Slou. 52 AP39
Cromwell Gdns. SW7 3 B7
Cromwell Gro. W6 65 BQ41
Cromwell Ms. SW7 3 B8
Cromwell Ms. SW7 66 BT42
Cromwell Pl. N6 47 BV33
Cromwell Ave.
Cromwell Pl. SW7 3 B8
Cromwell Pl. SW7 66 BT42
Cromwell Pl. SW14 65 BN45
Cromwell Pl. W3 55 BN40
Grove Pl.
Cromwell Rd. E7 58 CJ36
Cromwell Rd. E17 48 CF32
Cromwell Rd. N3 38 BT30
Cromwell Rd. N10 38 BV29
Cromwell Rd. SW5 66 BS42
Cromwell Rd. SW7 3 A8
Cromwell Rd. SW7 66 BS42
Cromwell Rd. SW9 66 BY44
Cromwell Rd. SW19 76 BS49
Cromwell Rd., Beck. 87 CD51
Cromwell Rd., Borwd. 28 BL23
Cromwell Rd., Brwd. 42 DA28
Cromwell Rd., Cat. 105 BZ64
Cromwell Rd., Chsnt. 21 CB17
Cromwell Rd., Croy. 87 BZ54
Cromwell Rd., Felt. 73 BC47
Cromwell Rd., Grays 71 DD42
Cromwell Rd., Hayes 53 BA39
Cromwell Rd., Kings.T. 85 BL51
Cromwell Rd., Red. 121 BU70
Cromwell Rd., Tedd. 74 BJ50
Cromwell Rd., Walt. 83 BC54
Cromwell Rd., Wem. 55 BL37
Cromwell Rd., Wor.Pk. 85 BN55
Cromwell St., Houns. 64 BF45
Cromwells Mere, Rom. 41 CS29
Crondace Rd. SW6 66 BS44
Crondall St. N1 2 M1
Crondall St. N1 57 BZ37
Cronks Hill, Red. 121 BT71
Cronkshill Clo., Red. 121 BT71
Cronkshill Rd., Red. 121 BT71
Crook Log, Bexh. 69 CP45
Crooke Rd. SE8 67 CC42
Crooked Billet SW19 75 BQ50
Crooked Billet Yd. N1 57 CA38
Kingsland Rd.
Crooked Mile, Wal.Abb. 21 CF18
Crooked Usage N3 46 BR31
Crooked Way, Wal.Abb. 13 CG14
Crookham Rd. SW6 65 BR44
Fulham Rd.
Crookhams, Welw.G.C. 5 BS7
Crookston Rd. SE9 68 CL45
Croombs Rd. E16 58 CJ39
Crooms Hill SE10 67 CF43
Crooms Hill Gro. SE10 67 CF43
Crop Common, Hat. 10 BP11
Cropley Ct. N1 57 BZ37
Cropley St. N1 57 BZ37
Croppath Rd., Dag. 50 CR35
Cropthorne Ct. W9 56 BT38
Maida Vale
Crosby Clo., Felt. 74 BE49
Crosby Ct. SE1 4 K4
Crosby Rd. E7 58 CH36
Crosby Rd., Dag. 59 CR37
Crosby Row SE1 4 K4
Crosby Row SE1 67 BZ41
Crosby Sq. EC3 2 M9
Crosby Sq. EC3 57 CA39
Crosby Wk. E8 57 CA36
Laurel St.
Crosier Way, Ruis. 44 BB34
Crosland Pl. SW11 66 BV45
Taybridge Rd.
Cross Acres, Wok. 100 AV61
Cross Deep, Twick. 74 BH48
Cross Deep Gdns, Twick. 74 BH48
Cross Keys Clo. W1 1 H7
Cross Keys Clo. W1 56 BV39
Marylebone La.
Cross Keys Clo., Sev. 116 CU67
Cross Keys Sq. EC1 57 BZ39
Little Britain
Cross Lances Rd., Houns. 64 BF45
Cross La. EC3 4 M1
Cross La. N8 47 BX31
Cross La., Bex. 79 CQ47
Cross La., Chesh. 91 AU57
Cross La. E., Grav. 81 DG48
Cross La. Footpath, Cher. 91 AT57
Cross Las., Ger.Cr. 34 AS28
Cross Las., Guil. 118 AS70
Cross Las. Clo., Ger.Cr. 34 AS28
Cross Las. W., Grav. 81 DG48
Cross Manorway SE28 59 CP40
Cross Oak Rd., Berk. 7 AQ13
Cross Oaks, Wind. 61 AN44
Cross Rd. E4 39 CF26
Cross Rd. N11 38 BV28
Cross Rd. N22 38 BY29
Cross Rd. SE5 67 CA44
Cross Rd. SW19 76 BS50
Cross Rd., Brom. 88 CK55
Cross Rd., Croy. 87 BZ54
Cross Rd., Dart. 80 CV46
Cross Rd. (Hawley), Dart. 80 CW49
Cross Rd., Enf. 30 CA24
Cross Rd., Felt. 74 BE49
Cross Rd., Grav. 81 DF46
Burch Rd.
Cross Rd., Har. 45 BG31
Cross Rd. (South Harrow), Har. 45 BF34
Cross Rd. (Wealdstone), Har. 36 BJ30
Cross Rd., Kings.T. 75 BL50
Cross Rd., Orp. 89 CO53
Cross Rd., Pur. 95 BY60
Cross Rd., Rom. 50 CR31
Cross Rd. (Chadwell Heath), Rom. 50 CP33
Cross Rd., Sid. 79 CO49
Cross Rd., Sutt. 95 BT56
Cross Rd. (Belmont), Sutt. 95 BS58
Cross Rd., Tad. 103 BQ64
Cross Rd., Wal.Cr. 21 CD20
Cross Rd., Wat. 27 BE25
Cross Rd., Wdf.Grn. 40 CK29
Cross Rds., Loug. 31 CH23
Cross St. N1 56 BY37
Cross St. N18 39 CB28
Raynham Rd.
Cross St. SW13 65 BO44
Cross St., Erith 69 CT43
Cross St., Hmptn. 74 BG49
Cross St., Harl. 13 CM11
Cross St., St.Alb. 9 BG13
Spencer St.
Cross St., Uxb. 53 AX37
Cross St., Wat. 27 BD24
Cross Way, The SE9 78 CJ48
Cross Way, The, Har. 36 BH30
Cross Ways, Berk. 7 AP13
Cross Ways, Hem.H. 8 AZ13
Crossbow Ct., Ong. 24 CX18
Crossbow Rd., Chig. 40 CN28
Crossbrook, Hat. 10 BO13
Crossbrook Rd. SE3 68 CK44
Crossbrook St., Chsnt. 21 CC19
Crossfell Rd., Hem.H. 8 AZ14
Crossfield Clo., Berk. 7 AP13
Crossfield Pl., Wey. 92 AZ57
Crossfield Rd. N17 48 BZ31
Crossfield Rd. NW3 56 BT36
Crossfield Rd., Hodd. 12 CE11
Crossfield Rd., Red. 121 BV70
Crossfield St. SE8 67 CE43
Crossfields, Loug. 31 CL25
Crossfields, St.Alb. 9 BF15
Crossford St. SW9 66 BX44
Lingham St.
Crossgate, Edg. 37 BM27
Crossgate, Grnf. 54 BJ36
Crossing Rd., Epp. 23 CO19
Crossland Rd., Th.Hth. 86 BY53
Crosslands Ave. W5 55 BL40
Crosslands Ave., Sthl. 64 BE42
Crosslands Rd., Epsom 94 BN57
Crosslet Sq. SE17 67 BZ42
Townsend St.
Crosslet St. SE17 4 L8
Crossley Clo., West. 106 CJ61
Crossley St. N7 56 BY36
Crossleys, Ch.St.G. 34 AR27
Crossleys Hill, Ch.St.G. 34 AR27
Crossmead SE9 78 CK47
Crossmead, Wat. 26 BC25
Crossmead Ave., Grnf. 54 BF38
Crossness Footpath, Belv. 69 CQ41
Crossness La. SE28 59 CQ40
Crossness Rd., Bark. 58 CN38
Crossoaks La. (South Mimms), Borwd. 19 BN20
Crosspath, The, Rad. 27 BJ21
Crossroads, The, Lthd. 111 BD67
Manor Gdns.
Crossthwaite Ave. SE5 67 BZ45
Crosswall EC3 2 P10
Crosswall EC3 57 CA40
Crossway N12 38 BT29
Crossway N16 48 CA35
Crossway NW9 46 BO31
Crossway SE28 59 CP39
Crossway SW20 85 BQ52
Crossway, Chesh. 16 AP18
Crossway, Dag. 50 CP34
Crossway, Enf. 39 CA26
Crossway, Hayes 53 BC40
Crossway, Orp. 88 CM52
Crossway, Pnr. 35 BC30
Crossway, Ruis. 45 BD35
Crossway, Walt. 83 BC55
Crossway, Welw.G.C. 5 BQ6
Crossway, Wdf.Grn. 40 CJ28
Crossway, The N22 38 BY29
Crossway, The SE9 78 CJ48
Crossway, The W13 54 BJ38
Crossway, The, Uxb. 53 AY37
Crossways N21 30 BZ25
Crossways, Brwd. 122 DD25
Crossways, Egh. 72 AU50
Crossways, Guil. 118 AP71
Crossways, Rom. 50 CU31
Crossways, S.Croy. 96 CD57
Crossways, Sun. 73 BB50
Staines Rd. W.
Crossways, Sutt. 95 BT57
Crossways, West. 106 CJ63
Crossways, The, Couls. 104 BX63
Crossways, The, Houns. 64 BE43
Crossways, The, Red. 113 BW68
Crossways, The, Wem. 46 BM34
Crossways Boul., Dart. 70 CY45
Crossways La., Reig. 113 BT67
Crossways Rd., Beck. 87 CE52
Crossways Rd., Mitch. 86 BV52
Crosswell Clo., Shep. 83 BA51
Charlton Rd.
Croston St. E8 57 CB37
Crothall Clo. N13 38 BX27
Crouch Ave., Bark. 59 CO37
Crouch Clo., Beck. 77 CE50
Abbey La.
Crouch Cft. SE9 78 CL48
Crouch End Hill N8 47 BW33
Crouch Hall Rd. N8 47 BW32
Crouch Hill N4 47 BX32
Crouch Hill N8 47 BX32
Crouch La., Chsnt. 21 BZ17
Crouch Rd. NW10 55 BN36
Crouch Rd., Grays 71 DG42
Crouch Valley, Upmin. 51 CZ33
Crouchfield, Hem.H. 8 AW14
Crouchman Clo. SE26 77 CB48
Crouchoak La., Wey. 92 AW56
Crow Clo., Warl. 105 CD62
Crow Dr., Sev. 107 CS61
Crow Grn. La., Brwd. 33 DA25
Crow Grn. Rd., Brwd. 33 CZ25
Crow La., Rom. 50 CQ33
Crowborough Dr., Warl. 105 CD62
Crowborough Path, Wat. 36 BD27
Crowborough Rd. SW17 76 BV50
Crowden Way SE28 59 CP40
Crowder St. E1 57 CB40
Crowhurst Clo. SW9 66 BY44
Crowhurst La., Sev. 99 DA58
Crowhurst Rd., Sev. 108 DB65
Crowhurst Way, Orp. 89 CP53
Crowland Ave., Hayes 63 BB42
Crowland Gdns. N14 38 BX26
Crowland Rd. N15 48 CA32
Crowland Rd., Th.Hth. 87 BZ52
Crowland Ter. N1 57 BZ36
Crowland Wk., Mord. 86 BS53
Crowlands Ave., Rom. 50 CR32
Crowley Cres., Croy. 95 BY56
Crowlin Wk. N1 57 BZ36
Clephane Rd.
Crowmarsh Gdns. SE23 77 CC47
Tyson Rd.
Crown Ash Hill, West. 97 CH60
Crown Ash La., West. 106 CH61
Crown Clo. E3 57 CE37
Wick La.
Crown Clo. NW6 56 BS36
Lymington Rd.
Crown Clo. NW7 37 BO27
Crown Clo., Bish. 6 CS7
Crown Clo., Hayes 63 BB41
Crown Clo., Orp. 98 CO56
Crown Clo., Walt. 84 BD54
Crown Ct. EC2 2 J9
Crown Ct. EC2 57 BZ39
Cheapside
Crown Ct. N10 38 BV29
Crown Ct. SE12 78 CH46
Crown Ct. WC2 2 A9
Crown Ct. WC2 56 BX39
Russell St.
Crown Ct., Brom. 88 CK53
Crown Ct., Til. 71 DG44
Newton Rd.
Crown Dale SE19 76 BY50
Crown Fld., Brox. 12 CE14
Crown Gate, Harl. 13 CM11
Crown Hill, Croy. 87 BZ55
Crown Hill, Wal.Abb. 22 CK20
Crown Hill Rd. NW10 55 BO37
Crown La. N14 38 BW26
Crown La. SW16 76 BY49
Crown La., Brom. 88 CJ53
Crown La., Chis. 88 CM51
Crown La., Mord. 86 BS52
Crown La., Vir.W. 82 AR53
Crown La. Gdns. SW16 76 BY49
Crown La.
Crown La. Spur, Brom. 88 CJ53
Crown Office Row EC4 2 D10
Crown Office Row EC4 58 BY40
Crown Par., Hayes 53 BB39
Crown Pas. SW1 3 M3
Crown Pas. SW1 56 BW40
King St.
Crown Pas., Wat. 27 BD24
Crown Pl. NW5 56 BV36
Crown Pt., Sev. 108 CZ64
Crown Pt. Par. SE19 76 BY50
Crown Ri., Wat. 18 BD20
Crown Rd. N10 38 BV29
Crown Rd., Borwd. 28 BM23
Crown Rd., Brwd. 33 CY23
Crown Rd., Enf. 30 CB24
Crown Rd., Grays 71 DD43
Crown Rd., Ilf. 49 CM31
Crown Rd., Mord. 86 BS52
Crown Rd., N.Mal. 85 BN51
Crown Rd., Orp. 98 CO56
Crown Rd., Sev. 98 CT58
Crown Rd., Sutt. 95 BS56
Crown Rd., Twick. 74 BJ46
Crown Rd., Vir.W. 82 AR53
Crown Rd., West. 106 CK63
Crown St. SE5 67 BZ43
Crown St. W3 55 BM40
Crown St., Brwd. 42 DB27
Crown St., Dag. 59 CS36
Crown St., Egh. 72 AT49
Crown St., Har. 45 BG33
Crown Ter., Rich. 65 BL45
Crown Wk., Uxb. 53 AX36
High St.
Crown Wk., Wem. 46 BL34
Crown Way, West Dr. 53 AY40
Crown Wds. La. SE9 68 CL44
Crown Wds. Way SE9 78 CM46
Crown Yd., Houns. 64 BG45
Crowndale Rd. NW1 56 BW37
Crownfield Ave., Ilf. 49 CN32
Crownfield Rd. E15 48 CF35
Crownfields, Sev. 116 C
Crownhill Rd., Wdf.Grn. 40 C
Crownmead Way, Rom. 50 C
Crownstone Rd. SW2 76 B
Crowntree Clo., Islw. 64 B
Stags Way
Crows Rd. E15 57 C
Crows Rd., Bark. 58 C
Crows Rd., Epp. 22 C
Crowshott Ave., Stan. 36 B
Crowstone Rd., Grays 71 D
Crowther Ave., Brent. 65 B
Crowther Rd. SE25 87 C
Crowthorne Clo. SW18 75 B
Crowthorne Rd. W10 55 B
Croxdale Rd., Borwd. 28 B
Croxden Clo., Edg. 46 B
Croxden Wk., Mord. 86 B
Croxford Gdns. N22 38 B
Croxford Way, Rom. 50 C
Croxley Clo., Orp. 89 C
Croxley Grn., Orp. 89 C
Croxley Rd. W9 55 B
Croxley Vw., Wat. 26 B
Croxted Clo. SE21 77 B
Croxted Rd. SE21 77 B
Croxted Rd. SE24 77 B
Croyde Ave., Grnf. 54 B
Croyde Ave., Hayes 63 B
Croyde Clo., Sid. 78 C
Croydon Gro., Croy. 86 B
Croydon La., Bans. 95 B
Croydon La. S., Bans. 95 B
Croydon Rd. E13 58 C
Croydon Rd. SE20 87 C
Croydon Rd., Beck. 87 C
Croydon Rd., Brom. 88 C
Croydon Rd., Cat. 105 C
Croydon Rd., Houns. 63 A
Croydon Rd., Mitch. 86 B
Croydon Rd., Reig. 121 B
Croydon Rd., Wall. 95 B
Croydon Rd., Warl. 105 C
Croydon Rd., W.Wick. 88 C
Croydon Rd., West. 106 C
Croyland Rd. N9 39 C
Croylands Dr., Surb. 85 B
Croysdale Ave., Sun. 83 B
Crozier Dr., S.Croy. 96 C
Crozier Rd., Uxb. 44 B
Crozier Ter. E9 48 C
Crucible Clo., Rom. 50 C
Crucifix La. SE1 4
Crucifix La. SE1 67 C
Cruden Rd., Grav. 81 D
Cruden St. N1 56 B
Cruick Ave., S.Ock. 60 D
Cruikshank Rd. E15 49 C
Cruikshank St. WC1 2
Cruikshank St. WC1 56 B
Crummock Gdns. NW9 46 B
Crumpsall St. SE2 69 C
Crundale Ave. NW9 46 B
Crunden Rd., S.Croy. 96 B
Crusader Clo., Grays 70 C
Centurian Way
Crusader Gdns., Croy. 87 C
Crushes Clo., Brwd. 122 D
Chelmer Dr.
Crusoe Rd., Erith 69 C
Crusoe Rd., Mitch. 76 B
Crutched Friars EC3 2 N
Crutched Friars EC3 57 C
Crutches La., Beac. 34 A
Crutchfield La., Walt. 83 B
Crutchley Rd. SE6 78 C
Crystal Ave., Horn. 51 C
Crystal Ct. SE19 77 C
Crystal Palace Par. SE19 77 C
Crystal Palace Pk. Rd. SE26 77 C
Crystal Palace Rd. SE22 67 C
Crystal Palace Sta. Rd. SE19 77 C
Crystal Ter. SE19 77 B
Crystal Vw. Ct., Brom. 77 C
Crystal Way, Dag. 50 C
Crystal Way, Har. 45 B
Cuba Dr., Enf. 30 C
Cuba St. E14 67 C
Cubitt St. WC1 2
Cubitt St. WC1 56 B
Cubitt St., Croy. 95 B
Cubitt Ter. SW4 66 B
Cubitts Clo., Welw.G.C. 5 B
Cubitts Yd. WC2 2 A
Cuckmans Dr., St.Alb. 18 B
Cuckoo Ave. W7 54 B
Cuckoo Dene W7 54 B
Cuckoo Hall La. N9 39 C
Cuckoo Hill, Pnr. 45 B
Cuckoo Hill Dr., Pnr. 45 B
Cuckoo Hill Rd., Pnr. 45 B
Cuckoo La. W7 54 B
Cuckoo La., Grays 71 D
Cuckoo Pound, Shep. 83 B
Cucumber La., Hat. 11 B
Cudas Clo., Epsom 94 B
Cuddington Ave., Wor.Pk. 85 B
Cuddington Clo., Tad. 103 B
Cuddington Way, Sutt. 94 B
Cudham Dr., Croy. 96 C
Cudham La. N., Sev. 97 C
Cudham La. S., Sev. 106 C
Cudham Pk. Rd., Sev. 97 C
Cudham Rd., Orp. 97 C
Cudham Rd., West. 106 C
Cudham St. SE6 77 C
Cudworth St. E1 57 C
Cuff Cres. SE9 78 C
Cuff Pt. E2 2
Cuff Pt. E2 57 C
Angela St.
Cuffley Ave., Wat. 18 B

ley Ct., Hem.H. 8 BA11
ley Hill, Chsnt. 20 BY18
ord Gdns. SW3 3 F9
ord Gdns. SW3 66 BU42
ord Gro. N1 57 CA36
ord Ms. N1 57 CA36
uthgate Rd.
ord Rd. N1 57 CA36
ord Rd., Grays 71 DE41
aith Gdns., Enf. 29 BX24
en Sq., S.Ock. 60 DB40
en Way NW10 55 BN38
era Clo., Nthwd. 35 BB29
esden Rd., Ken. 104 BY61
ng Rd. SE16 67 CC41
wer Rd.
ngs Ct., Wal.Abb. 22 CG20
ngton Clo., Har. 45 BJ31
ngworth Rd. NW10 46 BP35
oden Rd., Enf. 29 BY23
oden St. E14 57 CF39
um St. EC3 2 M10
um St. EC3 57 CA40
nington Rd. W13 54 BK40
nington Rd., S.Croy. 96 BZ57
nore Cross SW12 76 BV47
nore Rd. SE15 67 CB43
nstock Rd. SW11 76 BV46
eper Clo., Ilf. 40 CL29
oss Clo. N15 48 BZ31
oss St. W1 3 G1
oss St. W1 56 BV40
ac Rd., Surb. 85 BL55
er Dr., Oxt. 115 CG68
er Gro., Stan. 36 BK30
er Rd., St.Alb. 9 BH12
erden Rd. SW12 76 BW48
erden Rd., Wat. 35 BC27
erhay, Ash. 103 BL61
erhouse Gdns. SW16 76 BX48
erlands Clo., Stan. 36 BJ28
erley Rd. SE6 77 CE47
ers Ave., Cars. 86 BU55
ers Cft., Beac. 34 AO29
rmers Way
ers Retreat, Cars. 86 BU54
ers Way, Cars. 86 BU55
ers Yd., Brwd. 42 DB27
gh St.
erstone Clo., Brom. 88 CG53
ert La., Uxb. 53 AW37
ert Pl. SW11 66 BV44
ert Rd. N15 48 CA32
ert Rd. SW11 66 BU44
ey Clo., Hartley 90 DC53
worth St. NW8 1 C1
worth St. NW8 56 BU37
n Cum Hill, Hat. 11 BU13
nberland Ave. NW10 55 BM38
nberland Ave., Grav. 81 DH47
nberland Ave., Guil. 109 AQ68
nberland Ave., Horn. 51 CW34
nberland Ave., Well. 68 CN45
nberland Clo. E8 57 CA36
rest Rd.
nberland Clo. SW20 75 BQ50
nberland Clo., Amer. 25 AQ23
nberland Clo., Epsom 94 BN59
nberland Clo., Hem.H. 8 BB15
nberland Clo., Horn. 51 CW34
umberland Dr.
nberland Clo., Twick. 74 BJ46
nberland Ct., St.Alb. 9 BH13
arlisle Ave.
nberland Cres. W14 65 BR42
nberland Dr., Bexh. 69 CQ43
nberland Dr., Chess. 85 BL55
nberland Dr., Dart. 80 CW47
nberland Dr., Esher 84 BJ55
nberland Gdns. NW4 37 BQ30
nberland Gdns. WC1 2 C2
nberland Gdns. WC1 56 BX38
nberland Gate W1 1 E10
nberland Gate W1 56 BU40
nberland Mkt. NW1 1 K2
nberland Mkt. NW1 56 BV38
nberland Mkt. Est. W1 1 K2
nberland Mkt. Est. W1 56 BV38
nberland Mills Sq. 4 67 CF42
nberland Pk. W3 55 BN40
nberland Pl. NW1 1 J2
nberland Pl. NW1 56 BV38
uter Circle
nberland Pl., Sun. 83 BC52
nberland Rd. E12 49 CJ35
nberland Rd. E13 58 CH39
nberland Rd. E17 39 CD30
nberland Rd. N9 39 CC26
nberland Rd. N22 38 BX30
nberland Rd. SE25 87 CB53
nberland Rd. SW13 65 BO44
nberland Rd. W3 55 BN40
nberland Rd. W7 64 BH41
nberland Rd., Ashf. 73 AX48
nberland Rd., Brom. 88 CG52
nberland Rd., Har. 45 BF32
nberland Rd., Rich. 65 BM43
nberland Rd., Stan. 46 BL31
nberland St. SW1 3 K10
nberland St. SW1 66 BV42
nberland St., Stai. 72 AU49
nberland Ter. NW1 1 J1
nberland Ter. NW1 56 BV37
nberland Ter. Ms. W1 1 J1
nberlands, Ken. 105 BZ61
nberlow Ave. SE25 87 CA52
nberlow Pl., Hem.H. 8 BA14
nbernauld Gdns., in. 73 BB49
nberton Rd. N17 39 BZ30

Cumbrae Gdns., Surb. 84 BK54
Cumbrian Ave., Bexh. 69 CT44
Cumbrian Gdns. NW2 46 BQ34
Cumbrian Way, Uxb. 53 AX37
High St.
Cumley Rd., Epp. 23 CT18
Cumming Est. N1 57 BZ37
Cumming St. N1 2 C1
Cumming St. N1 56 BX37
Cummings Hall La., Rom. 42 CV27
Cumnor Gdns., Epsom 94 BP57
Cumnor Ri., Ken. 105 BZ62
Hayes La.
Cumnor Rd., Sutt. 95 BT57
Cunard Pl. EC3 2 N9
Cunard Pl. EC3 57 CA39
Bury St.
Cunard Rd. NW10 55 BN38
Cunard St. SE5 67 CA43
Cunard Wk. SE16 67 CD42
Cundy Rd. E16 58 CJ39
Cundy St. SW1 3 H9
Cundy St. SW1 66 BV42
Cundy St. Est. SW1 3 H9
Cundy St. Est. SW1 66 BV42
Cunliffe Clo., Epsom 103 BM65
Cunliffe Rd., Wor.Pk. 94 BO56
Cunliffe St. SW16 76 BW50
Cunningham Ave., Enf. 30 CD21
Cunningham Ave., Guil. 118 AT70
Cunningham Ave., St.Alb. 9 BH14
Cunningham Clo., Rom. 50 CP32
Chadwell Heath La.
Cunningham Clo., W.Wick. 87 CE55
Cunningham Hill Rd., St.Alb. 9 BH14
Cunningham Pk., Har. 45 BG32
Cunningham Pl. NW8 1 A4
Cunningham Pl. NW8 56 BT38
Cunningham Ri., Epp. 23 CS16
Cunningham Rd. N15 48 CB31
Cunningham Rd., Bans. 104 BT61
Cunningham Rd., Chsnt. 21 CD17
Cunnington St. W4 65 BN41
Cupar Rd. SW11 66 BV44
Cupid Grn. La., Hem.H. 8 AZ11
Cupola Clo., Brom. 78 CH49
Powster Rd.
Cureton St. SW1 3 P9
Cureton St. SW1 66 BW42
Curfew Bell Rd., Cher. 82 AV54
Guildford St.
Curfew Yd., Wind. 61 AO43
Datchet Rd.
Curlew Clo. SE28 59 CP40
Curlew Clo., Berk. 7 AR13
Curlew Clo., Croy. 96 CC59
Curlew Clo., S.Croy. 96 CC58
Curlew Gdns., Guil. 118 AU69
Curlew St. SE1 4 P4
Curlew St. SE1 67 CA41
Curlews, The, Grav. 81 DH48
Curling Clo., Couls. 104 BX63
Curling La., Grays 71 DC42
Curling Vale, Guil. 118 AQ71
Curnicks La. SE27 77 BZ49
Curnock Est. NW1 56 BW37
Curran Ave., Sid. 78 CN46
Curran Ave., Wall. 86 BV55
Curran Clo., Uxb. 53 AX38
Currey Rd., Grnf. 54 BG36
Curricle St. W3 55 BO40
Currie Hill Clo. SW19 75 BR49
Curry Ri. NW7 37 BQ29
Cursitor St. EC4 2 D8
Cursitor St. EC4 56 BY39
Curtain Rd. EC2 2 N3
Curtain Rd. EC2 57 CA38
Curthwaite Gdns., Enf. 29 BW24
Curtis Clo., Rick. 35 AW26
Curtis Dr. W3 55 BN39
Cotton Ave.
Curtis Fld. Rd. SW16 76 BX49
Curtis Gdns., Dor. 119 BJ71
Curtis Rd.
Curtis Mill La., Rom. 32 CT24
Curtis Rd., Dor. 119 BJ71
Curtis Rd., Epsom 94 BN56
Curtis Rd., Hem.H. 8 BA14
Curtis Rd., Horn. 51 CW33
Curtis Rd., Houns. 74 BE47
Curtis St. SE1 4 P8
Curtis St. SE1 67 CA42
Curtis Way SE1 4 P8
Curtis Way SE1 67 CA42
Curtis Way SE28 59 CO40
Curtis Way, Berk. 7 AR13
Curtismill Clo., Orp. 89 CO52
Curtismill Way, Orp. 89 CO52
Curvan Clo., Epsom 94 BO58
Curve, The W12 55 BP40
Curwen Ave. E7 49 CH35
Woodford Rd.
Curwen Rd. W12 65 BP41
Curzon Ave., Enf. 30 CC25
Curzon Ave., Stan. 36 BJ30
Curzon Clo., Orp. 97 CM56
Curzon Clo., Wey. 92 AZ56
Curzon Cres. NW10 55 BO36
Curzon Cres., Bark. 58 CN37
Curzon Dr., Grays 71 DD43
Curzon Gate W1 3 H3
Curzon Ho. W5 54 BJ38
Castlebar Pk.
Curzon Pl. W1 3 H3
Curzon Pl. W1 56 BV40
Curzon St.
Curzon Pl., Pnr. 45 BD32
Curzon Rd. N10 38 BV30
Curzon Rd. W5 54 BJ38
Curzon Rd., Th.Hth. 86 BX53

Curzon Rd., Wey. 92 AX56
Curzon St. W1 3 H3
Curzon St. W1 56 BV40
Cusack Clo., Twick. 74 BH49
Cussons Clo., Chsnt. 21 CB18
Custom Ho. Wf. EC3 57 CA40
Cut, The SE1 4 E4
Cut, The SE1 66 BY41
Cut Throat La., Hodd. 12 CD11
Cutcombe Rd. SE5 67 BZ44
Cutforth Rd., Saw. 6 CQ5
Cuthbert Gdns. SE25 87 CA52
Ross Rd.
Cuthbert Rd. E17 48 CF31
Cuthbert Rd. N18 39 CB28
Cuthbert Rd., Croy. 86 BY55
Cuthbert St. W2 1 A6
Cuthbert St. W2 56 BT39
Cuthill Wk. SE5 67 BZ44
Grove La.
Cutler St. E1 2 N8
Cutler St. E1 57 CA39
Cutlers Gdns. E1 2 N8
Cutlers Ter. N1 57 CA36
Balls Pond Rd.
Cutmere St., Grav. 81 DG47
Cutmore Dr., St.Alb. 10 BM14
Cutthroat All., Rich. 74 BK48
Cutting, The, Red. 121 BU71
Cuttsfield Ter., Hem.H. 7 AV14
Cuxton Clo., Bexh. 79 CQ46
Cyclamen Clo., Hmptn. 74 BF50
Gresham Rd.
Cyclamen Rd., Swan. 89 CS52
Cyclamen Way, Epsom 94 BN56
Cycle Track, Harl. 14 CO11
Cyclops Ms. E14 67 CE41
Westferry Rd.
Cygnet Ave., Felt. 74 BD47
Cygnet Clo. NW10 55 BN36
Kingfisher Way
Cygnet Clo., Borwd. 28 BN23
Cygnet Clo., Nthwd. 35 BA29
Cygnet Gdns., Grav. 81 DF48
Cygnet St. E1 2 Q4
Cygnet St. E1 57 CA38
Sclater St.
Cygnet Vw., Grays 70 CZ42
Cygnets, The, Felt. 74 BE49
Cymbran Ct., Hem.H. 8 AY11
Cynthia St. N1 2 C1
Cynthia St. N1 56 BX37
Cyntra Pl. E8 57 CB36
Mare St.
Cypress Ave., Enf. 29 BY21
Cypress Ave., Twick. 74 BG47
Cypress Clo., Wal.Abb. 21 CF20
Cypress Gro., Ilf. 40 CN29
Cypress Path, Rom. 42 CV29
Cypress Pl. W1 1 M5
Cypress Pl. W1 56 BW38
Maple St.
Cypress Rd. SE25 87 CA51
Cypress Rd., Guil. 118 AR69
Cypress Rd., Har. 36 BG30
Cypress Rd., Sun. 83 BB51
Harris Way
Cypress Wk., Egh. 72 AQ50
Cypress Wk., Wat. 26 BC21
Cypress Way, Bans. 94 BQ60
Cyprus Ave. N3 37 BR30
Cyprus Gdns. N3 37 BR30
Cyprus Pl. E2 57 CC37
Cyprus St.
Cyprus Pl. E6 58 CL40
Cyprus Rd. N3 37 BR30
Cyprus Rd. N9 39 CA27
Cyprus St. E2 57 CC37
Cyprus St. EC1 56 BY38
Cyrena Rd. SE22 77 CA46
Cyril Mans. SW11 66 BU44
Cyril Rd., Bexh. 69 CQ44
Cyril Rd., Orp. 89 CO54
Cyrus St. EC1 2 G4
Cyrus Way, St.Alb. 9 BG15
Czar St. SE8 67 CD43

D

Da Palma Ct. SW6 66 BS43
Racton Rd.
Dabbs Hill La., Nthlt. 45 BE35
D'Abernon Clo., Esher 93 BF56
D'Abernon Dr., Cob. 102 BD61
Dabin Cres. SE10 67 CF44
Dacca St. SE8 67 CD43
Dace Rd. E3 57 CE36
Dacorum Way, Hem.H. 8 AX13
Dacre Ave., Ilf. 40 CL30
Dacre Ave., S.Ock. 60 CY40
Dacre Clo., Chig. 40 CM28
Dacre Clo., Grnf. 54 BF37
Dacre Cres., S.Ock. 60 CY40
Dacre Gdns. SE13 68 CG45
Dacre Gdns., Borwd. 28 BN25
Dacre Gdns., Chig. 40 CM28
Dacre Pk. SE13 68 CG45
Dacre Pl. SE13 68 CG45
Dacre Rd. E11 49 CG33
Dacre Rd. E13 58 CH37
Dacre Rd., Croy. 86 BX54
Dacre St. SW1 3 N6
Dacre St. SW1 66 BW41
Dacres Rd. SE23 77 CC48
Dade Way, Sthl. 64 BE42
Daerwood Clo., Brom. 88 CK54
Daffodil Ave., Brwd. 33 DA25
Daffodil Clo., Croy. 87 CC54
Primrose La.

Daffodil Gdns., Ilf. 49 CL35
Lavender Pl.
Daffodil Pl., Hmptn. 74 BF50
Gresham Rd.
Daffodil St. W12 55 BO40
Dafforne Rd. SW17 76 BU48
Dagden Rd., Guil. 118 AS73
Dagenham Ave., Dag. 59 CQ37
Dagenham Rd. E10 48 CD33
Dagenham Rd., Dag. 50 CR35
Dagenham Rd., Rain. 59 CS36
Dagenham Rd., Rom. 50 CS33
Dagger La., Borwd. 27 BJ25
Daggs Dell Rd., Hem.H. 7 AV12
Dagley La., Guil. 118 AR73
Dagmar Ave., Wem. 46 BL35
Dagmar Gdns. NW10 55 BQ37
Dagmar Pas. N1 56 BY37
Cross St.
Dagmar Rd. N4 47 BY33
Dagmar Rd. N15 48 BZ32
Cornwall Rd.
Dagmar Rd. N22 38 BW30
Dagmar Rd. SE5 67 CA44
Dagmar Rd. SE25 87 CA52
Dagmar Rd., Dag. 59 CS36
Dagmar Rd., Kings.T. 85 BL51
Dagmar Rd., Sthl. 64 BE41
Dagmar Rd., Wind. 61 AO44
Dagmar Ter. N1 56 BY37
Dagnall Cres., Uxb. 53 AX39
Dagnall Pk. SE25 87 BZ53
Dagnall Rd. SE25 87 CA53
Dagnall St. SW11 66 BU44
Dagnam Pk. Clo., Rom. 42 CX28
Dagnam Pk. Dr., Rom. 42 CW28
Dagnam Pk. Gdns., Rom. 42 CX29
Dagnam Pk. Sq., Rom. 42 CX29
Dagnan Rd. SW12 76 BV47
Dagonet Gdns., Brom. 78 CH48
Dagonet Rd., Brom. 78 CH48
Dagwood La., Brwd. 33 DA22
Dahlia Dr., Swan. 89 CT51
Dahlia Gdns., Ilf. 58 CL36
Bluebell Way
Dahlia Gdns., Mitch. 86 BW52
Dahlia Rd. SE2 69 CO42
Dahomey Rd. SW16 76 BW50
Daiglen Dr., S.Ock. 60 DA40
Daimler Way, Wall. 95 BX57
Daines Clo. E12 49 CK34
Daines Clo., S.Ock. 60 DA38
Dainford Clo., Brom. 77 CF49
Dainton Clo., Brom. 88 CH51
Daintry Clo., Har. 45 BJ31
Daintry Way E9 57 CD36
Dairsie Rd. SE9 68 CL45
Dairy Clo., S.at H. 80 CX50
Dairy Clo., Th.Hth. 87 BZ51
Dairy La., Eden. 115 CL70
Dairy Ms. SW9 66 BX45
Andalus Rd.
Dairy Wk. SW19 75 BR49
Dairy Way, Abb.L. 17 BB18
Dairymans Wk., Guil. 109 AT68
Daisy Clo., Croy. 87 CC54
Primrose La.
Daisy Dormer Ct. SW9 66 BX45
Trinity Gdns.
Daisy La. SW6 66 BS45
Daisy Rd. E18 40 CH30
Dakota Gdns., Nthlt. 54 BE38
Argus Way
Dalberg Rd. SW2 66 BY45
Dalberg Way SE2 69 CP41
Lanridge Rd.
Dalby Rd. SW18 66 BT45
Dalby St. NW5 56 BV36
Dalcross Rd., Houns. 64 BE44
Dale, The, Kes. 97 CJ56
Dale, The, Wal.Abb. 22 CG20
Dale Ave., Edg. 37 BL30
Dale Ave., Houns. 64 BE45
Dale Clo. SE3 68 CH45
Dale Clo., Barn. 29 BS25
Dale Clo., Dart. 79 CT46
Dale Clo., Pnr. 35 BC30
Dale Clo., S.Ock. 60 DA39
Dale Clo., Wey. 92 AW56
Dale Ct., Saw. 6 CP6
The Crest
Dale Ct., Slou. 61 AO41
Dale Dr., Hayes 53 BB38
Dale End, Dart. 79 CT46
Dale Gdns., Wdf.Grn. 40 CH28
Dale Grn. Rd. N11 38 BV27
Dale Gro. N12 38 BT28
Dale Pk. Ave., Cars. 86 BU55
Dale Pk. Rd. SE19 87 BZ51
Dale Rd. NW5 47 BV35
Grafton Rd.
Dale Rd. SE17 66 BY43
Hillingdon St.
Dale Rd. SE18 68 CL43
Dale Rd., Dart. 79 CT46
Dale Rd., Grav. 81 DD49
Dale Rd., Grnf. 54 BF39
Dale Rd., Pur. 95 BY59
Dale Rd., Sun. 73 BB50
Dale Rd., Sutt. 94 BR56
Dale Rd., Swan. 89 CS51
Dale Rd., Walt. 83 BB54
Dale Row W11 55 BR39
St. Marks Rd.
Dale Side, Ger.Cr. 43 AS33
Dale St. W4 65 BO42
Dale Vw., Epsom 103 BM65
Dale Vw., Wok. 100 AQ62
Dale Vw. Ave. E4 39 CF27
Dale Vw. Cres. E4 39 CF27
Dale Vw. Gdns. E4 39 CF27
Dale Wk., Dart. 80 CY47
Dale Wd. Rd., Orp. 88 CN54

Dalebury Rd. SW17 76 BU48
Dalegarth Gdns., Pur. 96 BZ60
Daleham Ave., Egh. 72 AS50
Daleham Dr., Uxb. 53 AZ39
Daleham Gdns. NW3 56 BT36
Daleham Ms. NW3 56 BT36
Dalehead NW1 1 L1
Dales Path, Borwd. 28 BN25
Farriers Way
Dales Rd., Borwd. 28 BN25
Daleside, Orp. 98 CO56
Daleside Clo., Orp. 98 CO57
Daleside Dr., Pot.B. 19 BR20
Daleside Gdns., Chig. 40 CM27
Daleside Rd. SW16 76 BV49
Daleside Rd., Epsom 94 BN57
Daleview, Erith 69 CT44
Daleview Rd. N15 48 CA32
Dalewood, Welw.G.C. 5 BT8
Dalewood Clo., Horn. 51 CW33
Dalewood Gdns., Wor.Pk. 85 BP55
Daley St. E9 57 CC36
Daley Thompson Way SW8 66 BV45
Dalgarno Gdns. W10 55 BQ39
Dalgarno Way W10 55 BQ38
Dalgleish St. E14 57 CD39
Daling Way E3 57 CD37
Dalkeith Gro., Stan. 36 BK28
Dalkeith Rd. SE21 77 BZ47
Dalkeith Rd., Ilf. 49 CM34
Dallas Rd. NW4 46 BP33
Dallas Rd. SE26 77 CB49
Dallas Rd. W5 55 BL39
Dallas Rd., Sutt. 94 BR57
Dallas Ter., Hayes 63 BB41
Dallin Rd. SE18 68 CL43
Dallin Rd., Bexh. 69 CP45
Dalling Rd. W6 65 BP42
Dallinger Rd. SE12 78 CG46
Dallington Clo., Walt. 93 BD57
Dallington St. EC1 2 G4
Dallington St. EC1 56 BY38
Dalmain Rd. SE23 77 CC47
Dalmally Rd., Croy. 87 CA54
Dalmeny Ave. N7 47 BW35
Dalmeny Ave. SW16 86 BY51
Dalmeny Clo., Wem. 54 BK36
Dalmeny Cres., Houns. 64 BG45
Dalmeny Rd. N7 47 BW34
Dalmeny Rd., Barn. 29 BT25
Dalmeny Rd., Cars. 95 BV57
Dalmeny Rd., Erith 69 CR44
Dalmeny Rd., Wor.Pk. 85 BP55
Dalmeyer Rd. NW10 55 BO36
Dalmore Ave., Esher 93 BH57
Dalmore Rd. SE21 77 BZ48
Dalroy Clo., S.Ock. 60 DA39
Dalrymple Rd. SE4 67 CD45
Dalston Gdns., Stan. 37 BL30
Dalston La. E8 57 CA36
Dalton Ave., Mitch. 86 BU51
Dalton Clo., Hayes 53 BA38
Dalton Clo., Orp. 88 CN55
Dalton Rd., Har. 36 BG30
Dalton St. SE27 76 BY48
Dalton St., St.Alb. 9 BG13
Daltons, The, Stai. 73 AW50
Daltons Rd., Orp. 89 CR55
Daltons Rd., Swan. 89 CS54
Dalwood St. SE5 67 CA44
Daly Ct. E15 48 CE35
Holt Ct.
Dalyell Rd. SW9 66 BX45
Damascene Wk. SE21 77 BZ47
Lovelace Rd.
Damask Grn., Hem.H. 7 AV14
Dame St. N1 57 BZ37
Damer Ter. SW10 66 BT43
Ashburnham Rd.
Dames Rd. E7 49 CH34
Damien St. E1 57 CB39
Damigos Rd., Grav. 81 DJ47
Damon Clo., Sid. 79 CO48
Damphurst Hollow, Dor. 119 BF74
Damsonwood Clo., Sthl. 64 BF41
Havelock Rd.
Dan Leno Wk. SW6 66 BS43
Britannia Rd.
Danbrook Rd. SW16 86 BX51
Danbury Clo., Brwd. 33 CZ25
Danbury Clo., Rom. 50 CP31
Danbury Ms., Wall. 95 BV56
Danbury Rd., Loug. 40 CK26
Danbury Rd., Rain. 59 CT37
Danbury St. N1 56 BY37
Danbury Way, Wdf.Grn. 40 CJ29
Danby St. SE15 67 CA45
Dancer Rd. SW6 65 BR44
Fulham Rd.
Dancer Rd., Rich. 65 BM45
Dancers Hill Rd., Barn. 28 BQ21
Dancers La., Barn. 28 BQ21
Dandbridge Clo. SE10 68 CG42
Chilvers St.
Dando Cres. SE3 68 CH45
Dandridge Clo., Slou. 62 AR42
Dane Clo., Amer. 25 AP24
Dane Clo., Bex. 79 CR47
Dane Clo., Orp. 97 CM56
Dane Ct. N2 47 BT33
Dane Ct., Wok. 91 AV60
Dane Pl. E3 57 CD37
Roman Rd.
Dane Rd. N18 39 CC28
Dane Rd. SW19 86 BT51
Dane Rd. W13 54 BK40
Dane Rd., Ashf. 73 BA50
Dane Rd., Ilf. 49 CM35
Dane Rd., Sev. 107 CT62
Dane Rd., Sthl. 54 BE40
Dane Rd., Warl. 105 CC62
Dane St. WC1 2 B7

Dane St. WC1 56 BX39
Red Lion Sq.
Danebury, Croy. 96 CF57
Danebury Ave. SW15 75 BO46
Daneby Rd. SE6 77 CE48
Danecourt Gdns., Croy. 87 CA55
Danecroft Rd. SE24 77 BZ46
Danehill Wk., Sid. 79 CO48
Hatherley Rd.
Danehurst Gdns., Ilf. 49 CK32
Danehurst St. SW6 65 BR44
Daneland, Barn. 29 BU25
Danemead, Hodd. 12 CE10
Danemead Gro., Nthlt. 45 BF35
Danemere St. SW15 65 BQ45
Danes, The, St.Alb. 18 BG17
Park St. La.
Danes Clo., Grav. 81 DE48
Danes Clo., Lthd. 93 BG60
Danes Gate, Har. 45 BH31
Danes Hill, Wok. 100 AT62
Danes Rd., Rom. 50 CS33
Danes Way, Brwd. 33 DA25
Danes Way, Lthd. 93 BG60
Danesbury Rd., Felt. 73 BC47
Danescombe SE12 78 CH47
Winn Rd.
Danescourt Cres., Sutt. 86 BT55
Danescroft NW4 46 BQ32
Brent St.
Danescroft Ave. NW4 46 BQ32
Danescroft Gdns. NW4 46 BQ32
Danesdale Rd. E9 57 CD36
Daneshill, Red. 121 BU70
Daneshill Clo., Red. 121 BU70
Daneswood Ave. SE6 77 CF48
Daneswood Clo., Wey. 92 BA56
Danethorpe Rd., Wem. 54 BK36
Danetree Clo., Epsom 94 BN57
Danetree Rd., Epsom 94 BN57
Danette Gdns., Dag. 50 CR34
Daneville Rd. SE5 67 BZ44
Dangan Rd. E11 49 CH32
Daniel Bolt Clo. E14 57 CE39
Daniel Clo. N18 39 CC28
Daniel Clo. SW17 76 BU50
Daniel Clo., Grays 71 DG41
Daniel Clo., Grays 71 DC41
Daniel Gdns. SE15 67 CA43
Daniel Pl. NW4 46 BP32
Daniel Rd. W5 55 BL40
Daniel Way, Bans. 95 BS60
Daniells, Welw.G.C. 5 BS7
Daniels La., Warl. 105 CD61
Daniels Rd. SE15 67 CC45
Danses Clo., Guil. 118 AU69
Eustace Rd.
Dansey Pl. W1 1 N10
Dansington Rd., Well. 69 CO45
Danson Cres., Well. 69 CO45
Danson La., Well. 69 CO45
Danson Mead, Well. 69 CP45
Danson Rd., Bex. 79 CP46
Dante Pl. SE11 4 G9
Dante Rd. SE11 4 F8
Dante Rd. SE11 66 BY42
Danube St. SW3 3 D10
Danube St. SW3 66 BU42
Danvers Rd. N8 47 BW31
Danvers St. SW3 66 BT43
Danyon Clo., Rain. 60 CV38
Danziger Way, Borwd. 28 BN23
Dapdune Ct., Guil. 118 AR70
Woodbridge Rd.
Dapdune Rd., Guil. 118 AR70
Daphne Gdns. E4 39 CF27
Gunners Gro.
Daphne St. SW18 76 BT46
Daplyn St. E1 57 CB39
D'Arblay St. W1 1 M9
D'Arblay St. W1 56 BW39
Darby Clo., Cat. 105 BZ64
Darby Cres., Sun. 84 BD51
Darby Dr., Wal.Abb. 21 CF20
Sun St.
Darby Gdns., Sun. 84 BD51
Darcy Ave., Wall. 95 BW56
Darcy Clo. N20 38 BT27
D'Arcy Clo., Brwd. 122 DD26
Darcy Clo., Chsnt. 21 CD19
Darcy Clo., Couls. 104 BY63
D'Arcy Dr., Har. 45 BK31
D'Arcy Gdns., Dag. 59 CQ37
D'Arcy Gdns., Har. 45 BK31
D'Arcy Pl., Ash. 103 BL62
Darcy Rd. SW16 86 BW51
D'Arcy Rd., Ash. 103 BL62
D'Arcy Rd., Sutt. 94 BQ56
Dare Gdns., Dag. 50 CQ34
Darell Rd., Rich. 65 BM45
Darent Clo., Sev. 107 CR64
Darent Mead, S.at H. 90 CX51
Darenth Hill, Dart. 80 CY49
Darenth La., Sev. 107 CT64
Darenth La., S.Ock. 60 DA39
Darenth Rd. N16 48 CA33
Darenth Rd., Dart. 80 CW47
Darenth Rd., Well. 69 CO44
Darenth Wd. Rd., Dart. 80 CZ48
Darfield Rd. SE4 77 CD46
Darfield Rd., Guil. 118 AT69
Darfield Way W10 55 BQ40
Darfur St. SW15 65 BQ45
Dargate Clo. SE19 77 CA50
Chipstead Clo.
Darien Rd. SW11 66 BT45
Dark La., Brwd. 42 CZ28
Dark La., Chsnt. 21 CB18
Darkes La., Pot.B. 20 BS19
Darlan Rd. SW6 65 BR43
Darlaston Rd. SW19 75 BQ50
Darley Clo., Croy. 87 CD53
Darley Clo., Wey. 92 AX56
Darley Dr., N.Mal. 85 BN51
Darley Gdns., Mord. 86 BT53
Darley Rd. N9 39 CA26
Darley Rd. SW11 76 BU46
Darling Rd. SE4 67 CE45
Darling Row E1 57 CB38
Darlington Clo., Amer. 25 AO22
King George V Rd.
Darlington Gdns., Rom. 42 CV28
Darlington Path, Rom. 42 CV28
Darlington Rd. SE27 76 BY49
Darlton Clo., Dart. 69 CT44
Darlton Clo., Dart. 69 CT45
Darmaine Clo., S.Croy. 96 BZ57
Churchill Rd.
Darnets Fld., Sev. 107 CT61
Darnhills, Rad. 27 BH21
Darnicle Hill, Chsnt. 20 BY16
Darnley Pk., Wey. 83 AZ55
Portmore Pk. Rd.
Darnley Rd. E9 57 CB36
Darnley Rd., Grav. 81 DG47
Darnley Rd., Grays 71 DD43
Darnley Rd., Wdf.Grn. 40 CH30
Darnley St., Grav. 81 DG47
Darnley Ter. W11 55 BQ40
Darrell Clo., Slou. 62 AS42
Darrell Rd. SE22 77 CB46
Darren Clo. N4 47 BX33
Darrick Wd. Rd., Orp. 88 CM55
Darrington Rd., Borwd. 28 BL23
Darris Clo., Hayes 54 BE38
Darrs La., Berk. 7 AO12
Darsley Dr. SW8 66 BW44
Dart, The, Hem.H. 8 AZ11
Dart Clo., Slou. 62 AT43
Severn Cres.
Dart Clo., Upmin. 51 CY32
Dart Grn., S.Ock. 60 DA39
Dart St. W10 55 BR38
Dartfields, Rom. 42 CV29
Dartford Ave. N9 30 CC25
Dartford By-pass, Dart. 79 CU48
Dartford Rd., Bex. 79 CS47
Dartford Rd., Dart. 79 CU46
Dartford Rd. (The Brent), Dart. 80 CX47
Dartford Rd., Farn. 90 CW53
Dartford Rd., Sev. 108 CV64
Dartford St. SE17 67 BZ43
Dartford Tunnel App., Grays 70 CZ43
Dartmoor Wk. E14 67 CE42
Charnwood Gdns.
Dartmouth Ave., Wok. 91 AU60
Dartmouth Clo. W11 56 BS39
Ledbury Rd.
Dartmouth Grn., Wok. 91 AU60
Dartmouth Gro. SE10 67 CF44
Dartmouth Hill SE10 67 CF44
Dartmouth Pk. Ave. NW5 47 BV34
Dartmouth Pk. Hill N19 47 BV33
Dartmouth Pk. Hill NW5 47 BV33
Dartmouth Pk. Rd. NW5 47 BV35
Dartmouth Path, Wok. 91 AU60
Dartmouth Ave.
Dartmouth Pl. SE23 77 CC48
Dartmouth Pl. W4 65 BO43
Dartmouth Rd. E16 58 CH39
Dartmouth Rd. NW2 55 BQ36
Dartmouth Rd. NW4 46 BP32
Dartmouth Rd. SE23 77 CC48
Dartmouth Rd. SE26 77 CB48
Dartmouth Rd., Brom. 88 CH54
Dartmouth Rd., Ruis. 44 BC34
Dartmouth Row SE10 67 CF44
Dartmouth St. SW1 3 P5
Dartmouth St. SW1 66 BW41
Dartnell Ave., Wey. 92 AW59
Dartnell Cres., Wey. 92 AW59
Dartnell Pk. Rd., Wey. 92 AW59
Dartnell Pl., Wey. 92 AW59
Dartnell Rd., Croy. 87 CA54
Dartnells Keep, Wok. 92 AW59
Dartrey Wk. SW10 66 BT43
Worlds End
Dartview Clo., Grays 71 DE42
Chadwell Rd.
Darvell Clo., Wok. 100 AQ61
Darville Rd. N16 48 CA34
Darvills La., Slou. 61 AO41
Darwell Clo. E6 58 CL37
Darwin Clo. N11 38 BV28
Darwin Clo., Hem.H. 8 AZ10
Darwin Clo., Orp. 97 CM56
Darwin Clo., St.Alb. 9 BH11
Darwin Dr., Sthl. 54 BF39
Darwin Gdns., Wat. 36 BD28
Barnhurst Path
Darwin Pl. SE17 67 BZ42
Darwin St.
Darwin Rd. N22 38 BY30
Darwin Rd. W5 64 BK42
Darwin Rd., Slou. 62 AS41
Darwin Rd., Til. 71 DF44
Darwin Rd., Well. 68 CN45
Darwin St. SE17 4 L8
Darwin St. SE17 67 BZ42
Daryngton Dr., Grnf. 54 BG37
Daryngton Dr., Guil. 118 AT70
Dashes, The, Harl. 6 CN10
Dashwood Clo., Bexh. 79 CR46
Dashwood Clo., Slou. 62 AR42
Dashwood Clo., Wey. 92 AX59
Dashwood La., Grav. 81 DG48
Dashwood Rd. N8 47 BX32
Dashwood Rd., Grav. 81 DG47
Dassett Rd. SE27 76 BY49
Datchelor Pl. SE5 67 BZ44
Datchet Clo., Hem.H. 8 AZ11
Datchet Pl., Slou. 62 AQ44
Datchet Rd. SE6 77 CD48
Datchet Rd., Slou. 62 AP42
Datchet Rd. (Horton), Slou. 62 AS45
Datchet Rd., Wind. 61 AO43
Datchet Rd. (Old Windsor), Wind. 62 AQ45
Datchworth Ct. N4 48 BZ34
Kings Cres. Est.
Datchworth Turn, Hem.H. 8 BA13
Date St. SE17 67 BZ42
Daubeney Rd. E5 48 CD35
Daubeney Rd. N17 39 BZ29
Dault Rd. SW18 76 BT46
Davema Clo., Chis. 88 CL51
Brenchley Clo.
Davenant Rd. N19 47 BW34
Davenant Rd., Croy. 95 BY56
Davenant St. E1 57 CB39
Davenham Ave., Nthwd. 35 BB28
Davenport Clo., Tedd. 74 BJ50
Udney Pk. Rd.
Davenport Rd. SE6 77 CE46
Davenport Rd., Sid. 79 CP48
Daventer Dr., Stan. 36 BH29
Daventry Ave. E17 48 CE32
Daventry Clo., Slou. 62 AV44
Rodney Way
Daventry Gdns., Rom. 42 CV28
Daventry Grn., Rom. 42 CV28
Daventry Rd., Rom. 42 CV28
Daventry St. NW1 1 C6
Daventry St. NW1 56 BU39
Daver Ct. W5 54 BK39
Mount Ave.
Davern Clo. SE10 68 CG42
Davey Clo. N7 56 BX36
Davey Rd. E9 57 CE36
Davey St. SE15 67 CA43
David Ave., Grnf. 54 BH37
David Clo., Hayes 63 BB43
Nobel Dr.
David Dr., Rom. 42 CX29
David Ms. W1 1 G6
David Rd., Dag. 50 CQ34
David Rd., Slou. 62 AV44
David St. E15 57 CF36
Davidge St. SE1 4 G5
Davidge St. SE1 66 BY41
King James St.
Davids Rd. SE23 77 CC47
Davids Way, Ilf. 40 CN29
Davidson Gdns. SW8 66 BX43
Davidson La., Har. 45 BH33
Grove Hill
Davidson Rd., Croy. 87 CA54
Davidson Way, Rom. 50 CT33
Davies Clo., Croy. 87 CB53
Davies Clo., Rain. 60 CV38
Davies La. E11 49 CG34
Davies Ms. W1 1 J10
Davies Ms. W1 56 BV40
Davies St.
Davies St. W1 1 J10
Davies St. W1 56 BV39
Davies Way, Egh. 72 AU49
Davington Gdns., Dag. 50 CO35
Davington Rd., Dag. 59 CO36
Davinia Clo., Wdf.Grn. 40 CK29
Deacon Way
Davis Ave., Grav. 81 DF47
Davis Rd. W3 55 BO40
Davis Rd., Chess. 94 BM56
Davis Rd., Grays 71 DC41
Davis Rd., S.Ock. 60 CY40
Davis St. E13 58 CH37
Davison Dr., Chsnt. 21 CC17
Davisville Rd. W12 65 BP41
Davos Clo., Wok. 100 AS63
Davys Pl., Grav. 81 DJ50
Dawell Dr., West. 106 CJ62
Dawes Ave., Horn. 51 CV34
Dawes Ave., Islw. 64 BJ45
Dawes Ct., Esher 93 BF56
Dawes Ho. SE17 4 K9
Dawes La., Rick. 25 AV22
Dawes Moor Clo., Slou. 52 AR39
Dawes Rd. SW6 65 BR43
Dawes Rd., Uxb. 53 AY37
Dawes St. SE17 4 L10
Dawes St. SE17 67 BZ42
Dawley, Welw.G.C. 5 BR6
Dawley Ave., Uxb. 53 BA39
Dawley Ct., Hem.H. 8 AZ11
Dawley Grn., S.Ock. 60 DA39
Dawley Par., Hayes 53 BA40
Dawley Ride, Slou. 62 AV44
Dawley Rd., Hayes 53 BA40
Dawlish Ave. N13 38 BX28
Dawlish Ave. SW18 76 BS48
Dawlish Ave., Grnf. 54 BJ37
Dawlish Dr., Ilf. 49 CN35
Dawlish Dr., Pnr. 45 BE32
Dawlish Dr., Ruis. 44 BC34
Dawlish Rd. E10 48 CF33
Dawlish Rd. N17 48 CB31
Dawlish Rd. NW2 55 BQ36
Dawlish Wk., Rom. 42 CV30
Neave Cres.
Dawn Clo., Houns. 64 BE45
Dawn Redwood Clo., Slou. 62 AT45
Dawnay Gdns. SW18 76 BT48
Dawnay Rd. SW18 76 BT48
Dawnay Rd., Lthd. 111 BF66
Dawpool Rd. NW2 46 BO34
Daws Hill E4 30 CF23
Daws La. NW7 37 BO28
Dawson Ave., Bark. 58 CN36
Dawson Ave., Orp. 89 CO51
Dawson Clo. SE18 68 CM42
Dawson Clo., Hayes 53 BA39
Dawson Clo., Wind. 61 AN44
Dawson Dr., Dart. 79 CU46
Dawson Dr., Rain. 59 CU36
Dawson Gdns., Bark. 58 CN36
Dawson Ave.
Dawson Ho. SE5 67 CA44
Glebe Est.
Dawson Pl. W2 56 BS40
Dawson Rd. NW2 46 BQ35
Dawson Rd., Kings.T. 85 BL52
Dawson Rd., Wey. 92 AX59
Dawson St. E2 2 Q1
Dawson St. E2 57 CA37
Dawson Ter. N9 39 CC26
St. Alphege Rd.
Dax Ct., Sun. 84 BD52
Day Spring, Guil. 109 AQ68
Daybrook Rd. SW19 86 BS52
Daye Mead, Welw.G.C. 5 BS9
Daylesford Ave. SW15 65 BP45
Daylop Dr., Chig. 41 CO27
Daymer Gdns., Pnr. 44 BC31
Daymerslea Ridge, Lthd. 102 BK64
Days Acre, S.Croy. 96 CA58
Days Clo., Hat. 10 BO12
Days La., Brwd. 33 DA24
Days La., Sid. 78 CN47
Days Mead, Hat. 10 BO12
Daysbrook Rd. SW2 76 BX48
Dayton Dr., Erith 70 CV43
Dayton Gro. SE15 67 CC44
De Beauvoir Cres. N1 57 CA37
De Beauvoir Est. N1 57 CA37
De Beauvoir Rd. N1 57 CA37
De Beauvoir Sq. N1 57 CA36
De Bohun Ave. N14 29 BV25
De Burgh Pk., Bans. 104 BS61
De Crespigny Pk. SE5 67 BZ44
De Frene Rd. SE26 77 CC49
De Haviland Rd., Houns. 64 BD43
De Haviland Way, Stai. 73 AX46
De Havilland Clo., Hat. 10 BO12
De Havilland Dr., Wey. 92 AY59
De Havilland Rd., Edg. 37 BM30
De Havilland Rd., Wall. 95 BX57
De Havilland Way, Abb.L. 17 BB19
De Lapre Clo., Orp. 89 CP54
De Lara Way, Wok. 100 AR62
De Laune St. SE17 66 BY42
De Luci Rd., Erith 69 CS42
De Montfort Rd. SW16 76 BX48
De Morgan Rd. SW6 66 BS45
De Quincey Rd. N17 39 BZ30
De Salis Rd., Uxb. 53 BA38
De Tany Ct., St.Alb. 9 BH14
De Vere Gdns. W8 66 BT41
De Vere Gdns., Ilf. 49 CK34
De Vere Wk., Wat. 26 BB23
De Walden St. W1 1 H7
De Walden St. W1 56 BV39
Marylebone St.
Deacon Clo., Cob. 101 BC63
Deacon Clo., Pur. 95 BX58
Deacon Clo., St.Alb. 9 BG15
Creighton Ave.
Deacon Rd. NW2 46 BP35
Deacon Rd., Kings.T. 85 BL51
Deacon Way SE17 4 H8
Deacon Way SE17 67 BZ42
Deacon Way, Wdf.Grn. 40 CK29
Deacons Clo., Borwd. 28 BM24
Deacons Clo., Pnr. 35 BC30
Deacons Heights, Borwd. 28 BM25
Deacons Hill, Wat. 27 BD25
Deacons Hill Rd., Borwd. 28 BL24
Deacons Leas, Orp. 97 CM56
Deacons Wk., Hmptn. 74 BF49
Deaconsfield Rd., Hem.H. 8 AY15
Deadhearn La., Ch.St.G. 34 AS26
Deadmans Ash La., Rick. 26 AW21
Deakin Clo., Wat. 35 BB26
Chenies Way
Deal Porters Way SE16 67 CC41
Deal Rd. SW17 76 BV50
Deal St. E1 57 CB39
Deal Tree Clo., Brwd. 33 DA21
Deal Wk. SW9 66 BY43
Mandela St.
Deals Gateway SE10 67 CE44
Deptford Bri.
Dealtry Rd. SW15 65 BQ45
Dean Bradley St. SW1 3 Q7
Dean Bradley St. SW1 66 BX41
Dean Clo. E9 48 CC35
Dean Clo. SE16 57 CC40
Surrey Water Rd.
Dean Clo., Uxb. 53 AY36
Dean Clo., Wind. 61 AL45
Dean Clo., Wok. 100 AV61
Dean Ct., Wem. 45 BJ34
Dean Dr., Stan. 37 BL30
Dean Farrar St. SW1 3 P6
Dean Farrar St. SW1 66 BW41
Tothill St.
Dean Fld., Hem.H. 16 AT17
Dean Gdns. E17 48 CF31
Dean La., Red. 104 BW65
Dean Rd. NW2 55 BQ36
Dean Rd., Croy. 96 BZ56
Dean Rd., Hmptn. 74 BF49
Dean Rd., Houns. 74 BF46
Dean Ryle St. SW1 3 Q8
Dean Ryle St. SW1 66 BX42
Dean Stanley St. SW1 3 Q7
Dean Stanley St. SW1 66 BX41
Dean St. E7 49 CH35
Dean St. W1 1 N8
Dean St. W1 56 BW39
Dean Trench St. SW1 3 Q7
Dean Trench St. SW1 66 BX41
Tufton St.
Dean Wk., Edg. 37 BN29
Dean Wk., Lthd. 111 BF66
Dean Way, Cat. 114 BZ66
Dean Way, Ch.St.G. 34 AQ27
Dean Way, Sthl. 64 BF41
Dean Wd. Rd., Beac. 34 AO30
Deanacre Clo., Ger.Cr. 34
Deancroft Rd., Ger.Cr. 34
Deancross St. E1 57
Deane Ave., Ruis. 45
Deane Cft. Rd., Pnr. 44
Deane Way, Ruis. 44
Deanery Clo. N2 47
Deanery Ms. W1 3
Deanery Ms. W1 56
Deanery St.
Deanery Rd. E15 58
Deanery Rd., Eden. 115
Deanery St. W1 3
Deanery St. W1 56
Deanhill Ct. SW14 65
Deanhill Rd. SW14 65
Deans Bldgs. SE17 4
Deans Bldgs. SE17 67
Deans Clo. W4 65
Whitehall Gdns.
Deans Clo., Abb.L. 17
Deans Clo., Amer. 25
Deans Clo., Croy. 87
Deans Clo., Edg. 37
Deans Clo., Slou. 52
Deans Clo., Tad. 103
Deans Ct. EC4 2
Deans Ct. EC4 56
St. Pauls Chyd.
Deans Dr., Edg. 37
Deans Fld., Cat. 114
Deans Gdns., St.Alb. 9
Deans Gate Clo. SE23 77
Deans La., Edg. 37
Deans La., Tad. 112
Deans Ms. W1 1
Deans Ms. W1 56
Cavendish Sq.
Deans Pl. SW1 3
Deans Pl. SW1 66
Deans Rd. W7 54
Deans Rd., Brwd. 42
Cromwell Rd.
Deans Rd., Red. 113
Deans Rd., Sutt. 86
Deans Wk., Couls. 104
Deans Way, Edg. 37
Deans Yd. SW1 3
Deans Yd. SW1 66
Deansbrook Clo., Edg. 37
Deansbrook Rd., Edg. 37
Deanscroft Ave. NW9 46
Deansway N2 47
Deansway N9 39
Deansway, Hem.H. 8
De'Arn Gdns., Mitch. 86
Dearne Clo., Stan. 36
Deason St. E15 57
Debden Clo., Wdf.Grn. 40
Debden La., Loug. 31
Debden Rd., Loug. 31
Debden Wk., Horn. 59
Debenham Rd., Chsnt. 21
Debnams Rd. SE16 67
Rotherhithe New Rd.
Deborah Clo., Islw. 64
Osterley Rd.
Deborah Cres., Ruis. 44
Debrabant Clo., Belv. 69
DeBurgh Rd. SW19 76
Decies Way, Slou. 52
Decima St. SE1 4
Decima St. SE1 67
Deck Clo. SE16 67
Thame Rd.
Decoy Ave. NW11 46
Dedswell Dr., Guil. 110
Dedworth Dr., Wind. 61
Dedworth Rd., Wind. 61
Dee, The, Hem.H. 8
Dee Clo., Upmin. 51
Dee Rd., Rich. 65
Dee St. E14 57
Dee Way, Epsom 94
Dee Way, Rom. 41
Deeley Rd. SW8 66
Deena Clo. W3 55
Deep Fld., Slou. 62
Deep Pool La., Wok. 91
Deepdale SW19 75
Deepdale Ave., Brom. 88
Deepdene W5 55
The Ridings
Deepdene, Pot.B. 19
Deepdene Ave., Croy. 87
Deepdene Ave., Dor. 119
Deepdene Ave. Rd., Dor. 119
Deepdene Clo. E11 49
Deepdene Ct. N21 29
Deepdene Dr., Dor. 119
Deepdene Gdns. SW2 76
Deepdene Gdns., Dor. 119
Deepdene Pk. Rd., Dor. 119
Deepdene Path, Loug. 31
Deepdene Rd. SE5 67
Deepdene Rd., Loug. 31
Deepdene Rd., Well. 69
Deepdene Vale, Dor. 119
Deepdene Wd., Dor. 119
Deepfield Way, Couls. 104
Deepwell Clo., Islw. 64
Deepwood La., Grnf. 54
Deer Barn Rd., Guil. 118
Deer Leap Gro. E4 30
Deer Pk., Harl. 13
Deer Pk. Clo., Chesh. 16
Deer Pk. Clo., Kings.T. 75
Crescent Rd.
Deer Pk. Gdns., Mitch. 86
Deer Pk. Rd. SW19 86
Deer Pk. Way, W.Wick. 88
Deerbrook Rd. SE24 76
Deerdale Rd. SE24 67

ere Ave., Rain. 59 CU36
erfield Cotts. NW9 46 BO32
erhurst Clo., Felt. 73 BC49
erhurst Rd. NW2 55 BQ36
erhurst Rd. SW16 76 BX49
erings Dr., Pnr. 44 BC32
erings Rd., Reig. 121 BS70
erleap Rd., Dor. 119 BF72
erswood Ave., Hat. 10 BP13
eside Rd. SW17 76 BT48
eves Hall La., Pot.B. 19 BO20
fiance Wk. SE18 68 CK41
ntelope Rd.
fiant Way, Wall. 95 BX57
foe Ave., Rich. 65 BM43
foe Clo. SW17 76 BU50
foe Clo., Erith 69 CT44
elkirk Dr.
foe Par., Grays 71 DG41
foe Rd. N16 48 CA34
foe Way, Rom. 41 CR29
gema Rd., Chis. 78 CL49
har Cres. NW9 46 BP33
imos Dr., Hem.H. 8 AZ12
kker Rd. SE21 77 CA46
labole Rd., Red. 113 BX68
acourt Rd. SE3 68 CH43
Old Dover Rd.
afield Rd. SE7 68 CH42
afield Rd., Grays 71 DE42
aford Clo., Iver 52 AV39
aford Rd. SE16 67 CB42
aford St. SW6 65 BR43
agarde Rd., West. 115 CM66
lahay Ri., Berk. 7 AQ12
lamare Rd., Chsnt. 21 CD18
lamere Cres., Croy. 87 CC53
lamere Gdns. NW7 37 BN29
lamere Rd. SW20 85 BQ51
lamere Rd. W5 55 BL40
lamere Rd., Borwd. 28 BM23
lamere Rd., Hayes 54 BD40
lamere Rd., Reig. 121 BS72
lamere Ter. W2 56 BS39
lancey St. NW1 56 BV37
laporte, Epsom 94 BO59
lawthorne Pl.
largy Clo., Grays 71 DG41
onghouse Rd.
laware Rd. W9 56 BS38
lawyk Cres. SE24 77 BZ46
lcombe Ave., Wor.Pk. 85 BQ54
lderfield, Ash. 102 BK64
latherwood
lft Way SE22 77 CA46
ulwich Gro.
lhi Rd., Enf. 39 CA26
lhi St. N1 56 BX37
lia St. SW18 76 BS47
lius Clo., Borwd. 27 BK25
ll, The SE2 69 CO42
ll, The SE19 87 CA51
ll, The, Bex. 79 CT47
ll, The, Brent. 64 BK43
Boston Manor Rd.
ll, The, Brwd. 42 DA29
ll, The, Felt. 73 BC47
ll, The, Ger.Cr. 34 AS29
ll, The, Nthwd. 35 BB27
ll, The, Pnr. 36 BD30
ll, The, Rad. 27 BJ21
ll, The, Reig. 121 BS70
ll, The, St.Alb. 9 BJ12
ll, The, Tad. 103 BQ64
airacres
ll, The, Wall. 95 BW56
ll, The, Wem. 45 BJ35
ll, The, Wok. 100 AR62
ll, The, Wdf.Grn. 40 CH27
ll Clo. E15 57 CF37
ll Clo., Dor. 111 BK67
ll Clo., Lthd. 102 BH65
ll Clo., Wall. 95 BW56
ll Clo., Wdf.Grn. 40 CH27
ll Fm. Rd., Ruis. 44 BA32
ll La., Epsom 94 BP56
ll Lees, Beac. 34 AO29
ll Meadow, Hem.H. 8 AY15
ll Ri., St.Alb. 18 BF17
ll Rd., Berk. 7 AO11
ll Rd., Enf. 30 CC22
ll Rd., Epsom 94 BP57
ll Rd., Grays 71 DD42
ll Rd., Wat. 26 BC22
ll Rd., West Dr. 63 AY42
ll Side, Wat. 26 BC22
ll Wk., N.Mal. 85 BO51
ll Way W13 54 BK39
lla Path E5 48 CB34
Downs Est.
llbow Rd., Felt. 73 BC46
llcott Clo., Welw.G.C. 5 BP7
llcut Rd., Hem.H. 8 AZ12
llfield, St.Alb. 9 BH14
llfield Ave., Berk. 7 AQ12
llfield Clo., Beck. 77 CS50
oxgrove Rd.
llfield Clo., Berk. 7 AQ12
llfield Clo., Rad. 27 BH21
llfield Clo., Wat. 26 BC23
llfield Cres., Uxb. 53 AX38
llfield Rd., Hat. 10 BP12
llmeadow, Abb.L. 17 BB19
llors Clo., Barn. 28 BQ25
llow Clo., Ilf. 49 CM33
llow St. E1 57 CB40
lls, The, Hem.H. 8 AZ14
lls Clo. E4 30 CE25
lls Ms. SW1 3 M9
llside, Uxb. 44 AX32
llsome Gdns., St.Alb. 10 BO15
llsome La., Hat. 10 BP15
llsome Par., Hat. 10 BQ15
ellsome La.
Dellwood Clo., Rick. 35 AW26
Dellwood Gdns., Ilf. 49 CL31
Delmar Ave., Hem.H. 8 BA14
Delmare Clo. SW9 66 BX45
Brighton Ter.
Delme Cres. SE3 68 CH44
Delmey Clo., Croy. 87 CA55
Deloraine St. SE8 67 CE44
Delorme St. W6 65 BQ43
Delphian Ct. SW16 76 BY49
Leigham Ct. Rd.
Delta Clo., Wok. 91 AP58
Delta Clo., Wor.Pk. 85 BO55
Delta Ct. NW2 46 BP34
Delta Gain, Wat. 36 BD27
Delta Gro., Nthlt. 54 BD38
Kittiwake Rd.
Delta Rd., Brwd. 122 DE25
Delta Rd., Wok. 100 AT61
Delta Rd. (Chobham), Wok. 91 AP58
Delta Rd., Wor.Pk. 85 BO55
Delta St. E2 57 CB38
Wellington Row
Deltaway, Egh. 82 AU51
Delvers Mead, Dag. 50 CS35
Felhurst Cres.
Delverton Rd. SE17 66 BY42
Delves, Tad. 103 BQ64
Delvino Rd. SW6 65 BS44
Demesne Rd., Wall. 95 BW57
Demeta Clo., Wem. 46 BN34
Dempster Clo., Surb. 84 BK54
Dempster Rd. SW18 66 BT45
Den Clo., Beck. 87 CF52
Den Rd., Brom. 87 CF52
Denberry Dr., Sid. 79 CO48
Denbigh Clo. NW10 56 BO36
Denbigh Clo. W11 55 BR40
Denbigh Clo., Chis. 78 CK50
Denbigh Clo., Horn. 51 CW31
Denbigh Clo., Ruis. 44 BB34
Denbigh Clo., Sid. 79 CQ48
Riverside Rd.
Denbigh Clo., Sthl. 54 BE39
Denbigh Clo., Sutt. 94 BT56
Denbigh Dr., Hayes 63 BA41
Denbigh Gdns., Rich. 75 BL46
Denbigh Ms. SW1 3 L9
Denbigh Pl. SW1 3 L10
Denbigh Pl. SW1 66 BW42
Denbigh Rd. E6 58 CJ38
Denbigh Rd. W11 55 BR40
Denbigh Rd. W13 54 BJ40
Denbigh Rd., Houns. 64 BF44
Denbigh Rd., Sthl. 54 BE39
Denbigh St. SW1 3 L9
Denbigh St. SW1 66 BW42
Denbigh Ter. W11 55 BR40
Denbridge Rd., Brom. 88 CK51
Denby Rd., Cob. 93 BD59
Dendridge Clo., Enf. 30 CB22
Dendy St. SW12 76 BV47
Dene, The W13 54 BJ39
Templewood
Dene, The, Croy. 87 CC55
Dene, The, Dor. 119 BC73
Dene, The, E.Mol. 84 BE53
Dene, The, Sev. 116 CU66
Dene, The, Sutt. 94 BR59
Dene, The, Wem. 46 BL35
Dene Ave., Houns. 64 BE45
Dene Ave., Sid. 79 CO47
Dene Clo. SE4 67 CD45
Dene Clo., Brom. 88 CG54
Dene Clo., Dart. 79 CT49
Dene Clo., Wor.Pk. 85 BO55
Dene Ct., Guil. 118 AT69
Dene Dr., Orp. 89 CO55
Dene Gdns., Stan. 36 BK28
Dene Gdns., T.Ditt. 84 BJ55
Dene Holm Rd., Grav. 81 DE48
Dene Path, S.Ock. 60 DA39
Dene Pl., Wok. 100 AQ62
Caradon Clo.
Dene Rd. N11 38 BU26
Dene Rd., Ash. 103 BL63
Dene Rd., Buck.H. 40 CJ26
Dene Rd., Dart. 80 CW47
Dene Rd., Guil. 118 AS71
Dene Rd., Nthwd. 35 BA29
Dene St., Dor. 119 BJ71
Dene St. Gdns., Dor. 119 BJ71
Dene Wk., Long. 90 DC52
Denecroft Cres., Uxb. 53 AZ37
Denecroft Gdns., Grays 71 DE41
Denefield Dr., Ken. 105 BZ61
Denehurst Gdns. NW4 46 BQ32
Denehurst Gdns. W3 55 BM40
Denehurst Gdns., Rich. 65 BM45
Denehurst Gdns., Twick. 74 BG47
Denehurst Gdns., Wdf.Grn. 40 CH28
Denes, The, Hem.H. 8 AY15
Denewood, Barn. 29 BT25
Denewood Clo., Wat. 26 BB22
Denewood Rd. N6 47 BU32
Denfield, Dor. 119 BJ72
Dengie Wk. N1 57 BZ37
Basire St.
Denham Ave., Uxb. 43 AV34
Denham Clo., Hem.H. 8 AZ11
Sarratt Ave.
Denham Clo., Uxb. 44 AW34
Denham Clo., Well. 69 CP45
Park Vw. Rd.
Denham Ct. SE26 77 CB48
Halifax St.
Denham Cres., Mitch. 86 BU52
Denham Dr., Esher 93 BJ57
Denham Dr., Ilf. 49 CM32
Denham Grn. Clo., Uxb. 44 AW33
Denham Grn. La., Uxb. 43 AV32
Denham La., Ger.Cr. 34 AS29
Denham Rd. N20 38 BU27
Denham Rd. SE10 68 CH42
Denham Rd., Egh. 72 AT49
Denham Rd., Epsom 94 BO59
Denham Rd., Felt. 74 BD46
Denham Rd., Iver 52 AU37
Denham Rd., Uxb. 52 AU37
Denham Wk., Ger.Cr. 34 AS29
Denham Way, Bark. 58 CN37
Denham Way, Borwd. 28 BN23
Denham Way, Rick. 34 AV29
Denham Way, Uxb. 44 AW34
Denholm Gdns., Guil. 118 AT69
Denholme Rd. W9 55 BR38
Denholme Wk., Rain. 59 CT36
Denis Way SW4 66 BW45
Denison Clo. N2 47 BT31
Denison Rd. SW19 76 BT50
Denison Rd. W5 54 BK38
Denison Rd., Felt. 73 BB49
Deniston Ave., Bex. 79 CQ47
Denleigh Gdns. N21 38 BY26
Denleigh Gdns., T.Ditt. 84 BH53
Denman Dr. NW11 47 BS32
Denman Dr., Ashf. 73 AZ50
Denman Dr. N. NW11 47 BS32
Denman Dr. S. NW11 47 BS32
Denman Rd. SE15 67 CA44
Denman St. W1 3 N1
Denman St. W1 56 BW40
Denmark Ave. SW19 75 BR50
Denmark Ct., Mord. 86 BS53
Denmark Gdns., Cars. 86 BU55
Denmark Gro. N1 56 BY37
Denmark Hill SE5 67 BZ44
Denmark Hill Dr. NW9 46 BP31
Denmark Pl. WC2 1 P8
Denmark Rd. N8 47 BY31
Denmark Rd. NW6 55 BR37
Denmark Rd. SE5 67 BZ44
Denmark Rd. SE25 87 CB53
Denmark Rd. SW19 75 BQ50
Denmark Rd. W13 54 BJ40
Denmark Rd., Brom. 88 CH51
Denmark Rd., Cars. 86 BU55
Denmark Rd., Guil. 118 AS71
Denmark Rd., Kings.T. 85 BL52
Denmark Rd., Twick. 74 BG48
Denmark St. E13 58 CH39
Denmark St. N17 39 CB30
Denmark St. WC2 1 P9
Denmark St. WC2 56 BW39
Denmark St., Wat. 26 BC23
Denmark Wk. SE27 77 BZ49
Denmead Clo., Ger.Cr. 43 AS33
Denmead Rd., Croy. 86 BY54
Denmead Way SE15 67 CA43
Hordle Prom. S.
Dennan Rd., Surb. 85 BL54
Denner Rd. E4 39 CE27
Dennets, Wok. 100 AP62
Staveley Way
Dennett Rd., Croy. 86 BY54
Dennetts Gro. SE14 67 CC44
Dennetts Rd. SE14 67 CC44
Dennettsland Rd., Eden. 115 CM70
Denning Ave., Croy. 95 BY56
Denning Clo. NW8 56 BT38
Denning Clo., Hmptn. 74 BE49
Denning Rd. NW3 47 BT35
Dennington Clo. E5 48 CB34
Southwold Rd.
Dennington Pk. Rd. NW6 56 BS36
Denningtons, The, Wor.Pk. 85 BO55
Dennis Ave., Wem. 46 BL35
Dennis Clo., Ashf. 73 BA50
Chertsey Rd.
Dennis Clo., Red. 121 BU69
Dennis Gdns., Stan. 36 BK28
Dennis La., Stan. 36 BJ27
Dennis La. Est., Stan. 36 BJ28
Dennis Pk. Cres. SW20 85 BR51
Dennis Reeve Clo., Mitch. 86 BU51
Dennis Rd., E.Mol. 84 BG52
Dennis Rd., Grav. 81 DG48
Dennis Rd., Grnf. 54 BJ37
Dennis Rd., S.Ock. 60 DA37
Dennises La., Upmin. 60 CZ37
Denny Ave., Wal.Abb. 21 CF20
Denny Clo. E6 58 CK39
Linton Gdns.
Denny Cres. SE11 4 E10
Denny Cres. SE11 66 BY42
Denny St.
Denny Gdns., Dag. 59 CO36
Denny Gate, Wal.Cr. 21 CD17
Denny Rd. N9 39 CB26
Denny Rd., Slou. 62 AS42
Churchill Rd.
Denny St. SE11 4 E10
Denny St. SE11 66 BY42
Dens Pl., Wok. 100 AQ62
Densham Rd. E15 58 CG37
Densley Clo., Welw.G.C. 5 BQ7
Densole Clo., Beck. 87 CD51
Kings Hall Rd.
Densworth Gro. N9 39 CC27
Dent Clo., S.Ock. 60 DA39
Dunning Clo.
Denton Clo., Barn. 28 BQ25
Denton Clo., Red. 121 BV73
Denton Ct. Rd., Grav. 81 DJ47
Denton Gro., Walt. 84 BE55
Denton Rd. N8 47 BX32
Denton Rd. N18 39 CA28
Denton Rd. NW10 55 BN36
Denton Rd., Bex. 79 CT48
Denton Rd., Twick. 74 BK46
Denton Rd., Well. 69 CP43
Denton St. SW18 76 BS46
Denton St., Grav. 81 DJ47
Denton Ter., Bex. 79 CT48
Denton Way E5 48 CC34
Denton Way, Wok. 100 AP62
Dents Gro., Tad. 112 BR67
Dents Rd. SW11 76 BU46
Denvale Wk., Wok. 100 AQ62
Muirfield Rd.
Denver Clo., Orp. 88 CN53
Denver Rd. N16 48 CA33
Denver Rd., Dart. 79 CU47
Denyer St. SW3 3 D9
Denyer St. SW3 66 BU42
Denzil Rd. NW10 46 BO35
Denzil Rd., Guil. 118 AQ71
Denziloe Ave., Uxb. 53 AZ38
Deodar Rd. SW15 65 BR45
Deodora Clo. N20 38 BU27
Oakleigh Rd. N.
Depot Rd., Epsom 94 BO60
Depot Rd., Houns. 64 BG45
Depot St. SE5 67 BZ43
Deptford Bri. SE8 67 CE44
Deptford Bdy. SE8 67 CE44
Deptford Ch. St. SE8 67 CE43
Deptford Grn. SE8 67 CE43
Deptford High St. SE8 67 CE43
Deptford Strand SE8 67 CD42
Deptford Wf. SE8 67 CD42
Derby Arms Rd., Epsom 103 BO62
Derby Ave. N12 38 BT28
Derby Ave., Har. 36 BG30
Derby Ave., Rom. 50 CS32
Derby Ave., Upmin. 51 CW35
Derby Clo., Epsom 103 BP63
Derby Ct. E5 48 CC35
Clapton Pk. Est.
Derby Gate SW1 3 Q4
Derby Gate SW1 66 BX41
Derby Hill SE23 77 CC48
Derby Hill Cres. SE23 77 CC48
Derby Hill Est. SE23 77 CC48
Derby Rd. E7 58 CJ36
Derby Rd. E9 57 CC37
Derby Rd. E18 40 CG30
Derby Rd. N18 39 CB28
Derby Rd. SW14 65 BM45
Derby Rd. SW19 76 BS50
Derby Rd., Croy. 86 BY54
Derby Rd., Enf. 30 CB25
Derby Rd., Grays 71 DD43
Derby Rd., Grnf. 54 BF37
Derby Rd., Guil. 118 AP70
Derby Rd., Hodd. 12 CF13
Derby Rd., Surb. 85 BM54
Derby Rd., Sutt. 94 BR57
Derby Rd., Uxb. 53 AX37
Derby Rd., Wat. 27 BD24
Derby Stables Rd., Epsom 103 BO62
Derby St. W1 3 H3
Derby St. W1 56 BV40
Curzon St.
Derbyshire St. E2 57 CB38
Dereham Pl. EC2 2 N3
Dereham Pl. EC2 57 CA38
Dereham Rd., Bark. 49 CN35
Derek Ave., Epsom 94 BM57
Derek Ave., Wall. 95 BV56
Derek Ave., Wem. 55 BM36
Derek Clo., Epsom 94 BM56
Derham Gdns., Upmin. 51 CY34
Deri Ave., Rain. 59 CU38
Dericote Rd. E8 57 CB37
Croston St.
Deridene Clo., Stai. 73 AY46
Derifall Clo. E6 58 CK39
Hallywell Cres.
Dering Pl., Croy. 96 BZ56
Dering Rd., Croy. 96 BZ56
Dering St. W1 1 J9
Dering St. W1 56 BV39
Derinton Rd. SW17 76 BU49
Derley Rd., Sthl. 64 BD41
Dermody Gdns. SE13 77 CF46
Dermody Rd. SE13 77 CF46
Deronda Rd. SE24 76 BY47
Deroy Clo., Cars. 95 BU57
Derrick Ave., S.Croy. 96 BZ58
Derrick Gdns. SE7 68 CJ41
Derrick Rd., Beck. 87 CD52
Derry Ave., S.Ock. 60 DA39
Derry Down, Wok. 100 AR64
Derry Downs, Orp. 89 CP53
Derry Rd., Croy. 86 BX55
Derry St. W8 66 BS41
Dersingham Ave. E12 49 CK35
Dersingham Rd. NW2 46 BR34
Derwent Ave. N18 39 BZ28
Derwent Ave. NW7 37 BN29
Derwent Ave. NW9 46 BO32
Derwent Ave. SW15 75 BO49
Derwent Ave., Barn. 38 BU26
Derwent Ave., Pnr. 36 BE29
Derwent Ave., Uxb. 44 AZ34
Derwent Clo., Amer. 25 AQ23
Bell La.
Derwent Clo., Dart. 79 CU47
Derwent Clo., Esher 93 BH57
Derwent Clo., Felt. 73 BB47
Derwent Clo., Wey. 92 AX56
Derwent Cres. N20 38 BT27
Derwent Cres., Bexh. 69 CR44
Derwent Cres., Stan. 36 BK30
Derwent Dr., Hayes 53 BB39
Derwent Dr., Orp. 88 CM54
Derwent Dr., Pur. 96 BZ60
Derwent Gdns., Ilf. 49 CK31
Derwent Gdns., Wem. 45 BK33
Derwent Gro. SE22 67 CA45
Derwent Par., S.Ock. 60 DA39
Derwent Ri. NW9 46 BO32
Derwent Rd. N13 38 BX28
Derwent Rd. SE20 87 CB51
Derwent Rd. SW20 85 BQ53
Derwent Rd. W5 64 BK41
Derwent Rd., Egh. 72 AT50
Derwent Rd., N.Mal. 85 BQ53
Grand Dr.
Derwent Rd., S.Croy. 96 BZ60
Derwent Rd., Sthl. 54 BE39
Derwent Rd., Twick. 74 BF46
Derwent St. SE10 68 CG42
Derwent Wk., Wall. 95 BV57
Woodbourne Gdns.
Derwent Way, Horn. 50 CU35
Derwentwater Rd. W3 55 BN40
Derwentwater Rd., Hem.H. 8 BA14
Desborough Clo., Shep. 83 AZ54
Ferry La.
Desborough St. W2 56 BS39
Cirencester St.
Desenfans Rd. SE21 77 CA46
Desford Ct., Ashf. 73 AY48
Desford Rd. E16 58 CG38
Desford Way, Ashf. 73 AY48
Desmond Rd., Wat. 26 BB21
Desmond St. SE14 67 CD43
Despard Ave. SW11 66 BV44
Despard Rd. N19 47 BW33
Detillens La., Oxt. 115 CH68
Detling Clo., Horn. 51 CV35
Detling Rd., Brom. 78 CH49
Detling Rd., Erith 69 CS43
Detling Rd., Grav. 81 DE47
Detmold Rd. E5 48 CB34
Deva Clo., St.Alb. 9 BF14
Devalls Clo. E6 58 CL39
Devana End, Cars. 86 BU55
Devas Rd. SW20 85 BQ51
Devas St. E3 57 CE38
Devenay Rd. E15 58 CG36
Devenish Rd. SE2 69 CO41
Deventer Cres. SE22 77 CA46
Dulwich Gro.
Devereaux Rd., Grays 71 DC41
Davis Rd.
Deverell St. SE1 4 K7
Deverell St. SE1 67 BZ41
Devereux Ct. WC2 2 D9
Devereux Ct. WC2 56 BY40
Strand
Devereux Dr., Wat. 26 BB22
Devereux Rd. SW11 76 BU46
Devereux Rd., Wind. 61 AO44
Deveron Gdns., S.Ock. 60 DA39
Deveron Way, Rom. 41 CT30
Devils La., Egh. 72 AU50
Devitt Clo., Ash. 103 BM61
Devlan Clo. SE18 68 CL43
Llanover St.
Devoil Clo., Guil. 109 AT68
Devoke Way, Walt. 84 BD55
Devon Ave., Slou. 52 AO39
Devon Ave., Twick. 74 BG47
Devon Bank, Guil. 118 AR72
Portsmouth Rd.
Devon Clo. N17 48 CA31
Devon Clo., Buck.H. 40 CH27
Devon Clo., Grnf. 54 BK37
Devon Clo., Ken. 105 CA61
Devon Ct. W3 55 BM39
Links Rd.
Devon Ct., Dart. 90 CX51
Darent Mead
Devon Ct., Hmptn. 74 BF50
Devon Ct., St.Alb. 9 BH14
Old London Rd.
Devon Cres., Grnf. 54 BK37
Devon Cres., Red. 121 BT70
Devon Gdns. N4 47 BY32
Devon Ri. N2 47 BT31
Devon Rd., Bark. 58 CN37
Devon Rd., Red. 113 BW68
Devon Rd., Sutt. 94 BR58
Devon Rd., S.at H. 90 CX51
Devon Rd., Walt. 93 BD56
Devon Rd., Wat. 27 BD23
Devon St. SE15 67 CB43
Devon Way, Chess. 93 BK56
Devon Way, Epsom 94 BM56
Devon Waye, Houns. 64 BE43
Devon Waye, Uxb. 53 AY37
Devoncroft Gdns., Twick. 74 BJ47
Oak La.
Devonia Gdns. N18 39 BZ29
Devonia Rd. N1 56 BY37
Devonport Gdns., Ilf. 49 CK32
Devonport Ms. W12 65 BP41
Devonport Rd. W12 55 BP40
Devonport St. E1 57 CC39
Devons Est. E3 57 CE38
Devons Rd. E3 57 CE38
Devonshire Ave., Dart. 79 CU46
Devonshire Ave., Sutt. 95 BT57
Devonshire Ave., Wok. 91 AU60
Devonshire Clo. E15 49 CG35
Devonshire Clo. N13 38 BY27
Devonshire Clo. W1 1 J6
Devonshire Clo. W1 56 BV39
Devonshire Ct., Croy. 87 CD54
Devonshire Ct., Rich. 65 BL44
Holmesdale Rd.
Devonshire Cres. NW7 37 BQ29
Devonshire Dr. SE10 67 CE43
Devonshire Dr., Surb. 84 BK54
Devonshire Gdns. N17 39 BZ29
Devonshire Gdns. N21 39 BZ26
Devonshire Gdns. W4 65 BN43
Devonshire Gdns., S.le H. 71 DK41
Somerset Rd.
Devonshire Gro. SE15 67 CB43
Devonshire Hill La. N17 38 BY29
Devonshire Ms. W4 65 BO42
Glebe St.
Devonshire Ms. N. W1 1 J6
Devonshire Ms. N. W1 56 BV38
Park Cres. Ms. W.
Devonshire Ms. S. W1 1 J6
Devonshire Ms. S. W1 56 BV39
Devonshire Ms. W. W1 1 J5

Devonshire Ms. W. W1 56 BV38
Devonshire Pl. NW2 47 BS34
Devonshire Pl. W1 1 H5
Devonshire Pl. W1 56 BV38
Devonshire Pl. W4 65 BO42
Devonshire Pl. Ms. W1 1 H5
Devonshire Pl. Ms. W1 56 BV38
Devonshire Rd. E15 49 CG35
Devonshire Rd. E16 58 CH39
Devonshire Rd. E17 48 CE32
Devonshire Rd. N9 39 CC26
Devonshire Rd. N13 38 BX28
Devonshire Rd. N17 39 BZ29
Devonshire Rd. NW7 37 BQ29
Devonshire Rd. SE9 78 CK48
Devonshire Rd. SE23 77 CC47
Devonshire Rd. SW19 76 BU50
Devonshire Rd. W4 65 BO42
Devonshire Rd. W5 64 BK41
Devonshire Rd., Bexh. 69 CQ45
Devonshire Rd., Cars. 95 BV56
Devonshire Rd., Croy. 87 BZ54
Devonshire Rd., Felt. 74 BE48
Devonshire Rd., Grav. 81 DG48
Devonshire Rd., Grays 71 DC42
Devonshire Rd., Har. 45 BG32
Devonshire Rd., Horn. 51 CV34
Devonshire Rd., Ilf. 49 CM33
Devonshire Rd., Orp. 89 CO54
Devonshire Rd. (Eastcote), Pnr. 45 BD32
Devonshire Rd. (Hatch End), Pnr. 36 BE30
Devonshire Rd., Sthl. 54 BF39
Devonshire Rd., Sutt. 95 BT57
Devonshire Rd., Wey. 92 AZ56
Devonshire Row EC2 2 N7
Devonshire Row EC2 57 CA39
Devonshire Row Ms. W1 1 K5
Devonshire Sq. EC2 2 N7
Devonshire Sq. EC2 57 CA39
Devonshire Sq., Brom. 88 CH52
Masons Hill
Devonshire St. W1 1 H6
Devonshire St. W1 56 BV39
Devonshire St. W4 65 BO42
Devonshire Ter. W2 56 BT39
Devonshire Way, Croy. 87 CD55
Devonshire Way, Hayes 53 BC39
Dewar St. SE15 67 CB45
Dewberry Gdns. E6 58 CK39
Yarrow Cres.
Dewberry St. E14 57 CF39
Dewey Rd. N1 56 BY37
Dewey Rd., Dag. 59 CS36
Dewey St. SW17 76 BU49
Dewgrass Gro., Wal.Cr. 30 CC21
Holmesdale
Dewhurst Rd. W14 65 BQ41
Dewhurst Rd., Chsnt. 21 CB18
Dewlands, Gdse. 114 CC69
Dewlands Ave., Dart. 80 CX47
Dewport St. W6 65 BR43
Field Rd.
Dewsbury Clo., Pnr. 45 BE32
Dewsbury Clo., Rom. 42 CW29
Dewsbury Ct. W4 65 BN42
Chiswick Rd.
Dewsbury Gdns., Rom. 42 CW29
Dewsbury Gdns., Wor.Pk. 85 BP55
Dewsbury Rd. NW10 46 BP35
Dewsbury Rd., Rom. 42 CW29
Dewsbury Ter. NW1 56 BV36
Camden High St.
Dexter Clo., Grays 71 DD41
Dexter Rd., Barn. 28 BQ25
Deyncourt Gdns., Upmin. 51 CY34
Deyncourt Rd. N17 39 BZ30
Deynecourt Gdns. E11 49 CJ31
D'Eynsford Rd. SE5 67 BZ44
Diadem Ct. W1 1 N9
Dial Wk., The W8 66 BS41
Diamedes Ave., Stai. 73 AX47
Diamedes Cres., Stai. 73 AX47
Diameter Rd., Orp. 88 CL54
Diamond Clo., Dag. 50 CP33
Diamond Clo., Grays 71 DC41
Camden Rd.
Diamond Rd., Ruis. 45 BE35
Diamond Rd., Slou. 62 AQ41
Diamond Rd., Wat. 26 BC22
Diamond St. SE15 67 CA43
Diamond Ter. SE10 67 CF43
Diana Clo. E18 40 CH30
Diana Clo., Grays 71 DC41
Camden Rd.
Diana Clo., Slou. 52 AS39
Blinco La.
Diana Gdns., Surb. 85 BL55
Diana Pl. NW1 1 K4
Diana Pl. NW1 56 BV38
Diana Rd. E17 48 CD31
Dianthus Clo. SE2 69 CO42
Carnation St.
Dianthus Ct., Wok. 100 AR62
Diban Ave., Horn. 50 CU35
Dibden Hill, Ch.St.G. 34 AQ28
Dibden La., Sev. 116 CT66
Dibden St. N1 57 BZ37
Dibdin Clo., Sutt. 86 BS55
Dibdin Rd. SE1 66 BY41
Gerridge St.
Dibdin Rd., Sutt. 86 BS55
Dibna Clo., Slou. 52 AS39
Blinco La.
Diceland Rd., Bans. 103 BR61
Dicey Ave. NW2 46 BQ35
Dick Turpin Way, Felt. 63 BB45
Dickens Ave. N3 38 BT30
Dickens Ave., Dart. 70 CX45
Dickens Ave., Til. 71 DG44
Dickens Ave., Uxb. 53 AZ39
Dickens Clo., Hartley 90 DC53
Dickens Clo., Hayes 63 BB42
Croyde Ave.
Dickens Clo., Rich. 75 BL48
Dickens Clo., St.Alb. 9 BG13
Dickens Clo., Wal.Cr. 21 CB17
Dickens Ct., Hem.H. 8 AZ10
Sutton Pl.
Dickens Dr., Chis. 78 CM50
Dickens Dr., Wey. 92 AW56
Dickens Est. SE1 67 CB41
Dickens La. N18 39 CA28
Dickens Ri., Chig. 40 CL27
Dickens Rd. E6 58 CJ37
Dickens Rd., Grav. 81 DJ47
Dickens Sq. SE1 4 J6
Dickens Sq. SE1 67 BZ41
Dickens St. SW8 66 BV44
Dickenson Rd. N8 47 BX33
Dickenson Rd., Felt. 74 BD49
Dickenson St. NW5 56 BV36
Dalby St.
Dickensons La. SE25 87 CB53
Dickensons Pl. SE25 87 CB53
Dickerage La., N.Mal. 85 BN52
Dickerage Rd., N.Mal. 85 BN51
Dickins Clo., Chsnt. 21 CB17
Spicersfield
Dickinson Ave., Rick. 26 AZ25
Dickinson Sq., Rick. 26 AZ25
Dickson, Chsnt. 21 CA17
Dickson Rd. SE9 68 CK45
Dicksons Fold, Pnr. 45 BD31
Didsbury Clo. E6 58 CK37
Barking Rd.
Digby Cres. N4 48 BZ34
Digby Est. E2 57 CC38
Digby Gdns., Dag. 59 CR37
Digby Pl., Croy. 87 CA55
Digby Rd. E9 48 CC35
Digby Rd., Bark. 58 CN36
Digby St. E2 57 CC38
Digby Wk., Horn. 51 CV35
Digby Way, Wey. 92 AY59
Digdag Hill, Chsnt. 21 CA17
Digdens Ri., Epsom 103 BN61
Dighton Rd. SW18 76 BT46
Digswell Clo., Borwd. 28 BM22
Digswell Ct., Welw.G.C. 5 BQ7
Digswell Ri.
Digswell Hill, Welw.G.C. 5 BP6
Digswell Ho. Ms., Welw.G.C. 5 BQ6
Monks Ri.
Digswell La., Welw.G.C. 5 BR6
Digswell Lo., Welw.G.C. 5 BR7
Digswell Pk. Rd., Welw.G.C. 5 BQ5
Digswell Ri., Welw.G.C. 5 BQ7
Digswell Rd., Welw.G.C. 5 BQ7
Digswell St. N7 56 BY36
Holloway Rd.
Digswellbury, Welw.G.C. 5 BR6
Dilhorne Clo. SE12 78 CH48
Dilke St. SW3 66 BU43
Dillon Pl. N7 47 BX34
Dillwyn Clo. SE26 77 CD49
Dilston Clo., Nthlt. 54 BD38
Yeading La.
Dilston Gro. SE16 67 CC42
Abbeyfield Rd.
Dilston Rd., Lthd. 102 BJ63
Dilton Gdns. SW15 75 BP47
Dimes Pl. W6 65 BP42
King St.
Dimmock Dr., Grnf. 45 BG35
Dimmocks La., Rick. 26 AW21
Dimond Clo. E7 49 CH35
Stracey Rd.
Dimsdale Dr. NW9 46 BN33
Dimsdale Dr., Enf. 30 CB25
Dimsdale Wk. E13 58 CG37
Dinant Link Rd., Hodd. 12 CE11
Dingle, The, Uxb. 53 AZ38
Dingle Clo., Barn. 28 BO25
Dingle Gdns. E14 57 CE40
Dingle Rd., Ashf. 73 AZ49
Dingley La. SW16 76 BW48
Dingley Pl. EC1 2 J3
Dingley Pl. EC1 57 BZ38
Dingley Rd.
Dingley Rd. EC1 2 H3
Dingley Rd. EC1 57 BZ38
Dingon Hill Clo., Hayes 53 BC40
Dingwall Ave., Croy. 87 BZ55
Dingwall Gdns. NW11 47 BS32
Dingwall Pl., Croy. 87 BZ55
Dingwall Rd. SW18 76 BT47
Dingwall Rd., Cars. 95 BU58
Dingwall Rd., Croy. 87 BZ54
Dinmont Est. E2 57 CB37
Dinmont St. E2 57 CB37
Dinmore, Hem.H. 16 AS17
Dinsdale Clo., Wok. 100 AT62
Dinsdale Gdns. SE25 87 CA52
Dinsdale Gdns., Barn. 29 BS25
Dinsdale Rd. SE3 68 CG43
Dinsmore Rd. SW12 76 BV47
Dinton Rd. SW19 76 BT50
Dinton Rd., Kings.T. 75 BL50
Dione Rd., Hem.H. 8 AY12
Diploma Ave. N2 47 BU31
Dippers Clo., Sev. 108 CW62
Dirdene Clo., Epsom 94 BO59
Dirdene Gdns., Epsom 94 BO59
Dirdene Gro., Epsom 94 BO59
Dirleton Rd. E15 58 CG37
Dirtham La., Lthd. 110 BC67
Disbrowe Rd. W6 65 BR43
Discovery Wk. E1 57 CB40
Dishforth La. NW9 37 BO30
Disney Pl. SE1 4 J4
Disney Pl. SE1 67 BZ41
Disney St.
Disney St. SE1 4 J4
Disney St. SE1 67 BZ41
Dison Clo., Enf. 30 CC23
Disraeli Clo. SE28 59 CP40
Disraeli Clo. W4 65 BN41
Winston Wk.
Disraeli Ct., Slou. 62 AT43
Sutton Pl.
Disraeli Gdns. SW15 65 BR45
Fawe Pk. Rd.
Disraeli Rd. E7 58 CH36
Disraeli Rd. NW10 55 BN37
Disraeli Rd. SW15 65 BQ45
Disraeli Rd. W5 54 BK40
Diss St. E2 2 P2
Diss St. E2 57 CA38
Distaff La. EC4 2 H10
Distaff La. EC4 57 BZ39
Cannon St.
Distillery La. W6 65 BQ42
Distillery Rd. W6 65 BQ42
Distillery Wk., Brent. 65 BL43
Pottery Rd.
Distin St. SE11 4 D9
District Rd., Wem. 45 BJ35
Ditch All. SE10 67 CE44
Ditchburn St. E14 57 CF40
Ditches La., Couls. 104 BX63
Ditchfield Rd., Hayes 54 BE38
Ditchfield Rd., Hodd. 12 CE10
Dittisham Rd. SE9 78 CK49
Ditton Clo., T.Ditt. 84 BJ54
Ditton Gra. Clo., Surb. 84 BK54
Ditton Gra. Dr., Surb. 84 BK54
Ditton Hill Rd., Surb. 84 BK54
Ditton Lawn, T.Ditt. 84 BJ54
Ditton Pk. Rd., Slou. 62 AS43
Ditton Pl. SE20 87 CB51
Ditton Reach, T.Ditt. 84 BS53
Ditton Rd., Bexh. 79 CP46
Ditton Rd., Slou. 62 AR44
Ditton Rd., Slou. 62 AS43
Ditton Rd., Sthl. 64 BE42
Ditton Rd., Surb. 84 BK55
Divis Way SW15 75 BP46
Dover Pk. Dr.
Dixon Clo. E6 58 CK39
Brandreth Rd.
Dixon Pl., W.Wick. 87 CE54
Dixon Rd. SE14 67 CD44
Dixon Rd. SE25 87 CA52
Dixons All. SE16 67 CB41
West La.
Dixons Hill Clo., Hat. 19 BP16
Dixons Hill Rd., Hat. 19 BP16
Dobbin Clo., Har. 36 BJ30
Dobbs Weir Rd., Hodd. 12 CF12
Dobell Rd. SE9 78 CK46
Dobree Ave. NW10 55 BP36
Dobson Clo. NW6 56 BT36
Belsize Rd.
Dobson Rd., Grav. 81 DJ49
Dock App. Rd., Grays 71 DF43
Dock Rd. E16 58 CG40
Dock Rd., Brent. 64 BK43
Dock Rd., Grays 71 DE43
Dock Rd., Til. 71 DF44
Dock St. E1 57 CB40
Dockers Tanner Rd. E14 67 CE42
Dockett Eddy La., Shep. 83 AY54
Dockhead SE1 4 Q5
Dockhead SE1 67 CA41
Jamaica Rd.
Dockhill Ave. SE16 67 CC41
Dockland St. E16 58 CL40
Dockley Rd. SE16 67 CB41
Dockwell Clo., Felt. 63 BC45
Doctor Johnson Ave. SW17 76 BV48
Doctor Williams Wk., Guil. 109 AQ68
Doctors Clo. SE26 77 CC49
Lawrie Peak Rd.
Doctors Commons Rd., Berk. 7 AQ13
Doctors La., Cat. 104 BY65
Docwras Bldgs. N1 57 BZ36
Dod St. E14 57 CD39
Dodbrooke Rd. SE27 76 BY48
Doddinghurst Rd., Brwd. 42 DB26
Doddinghurst Rd. (Doddinghurst), Brwd. 33 DB22
Doddington Gro. SE17 66 BY43
Doddington Pl. SE17 66 BY43
Kennington Pk. Pl.
Dodds Cres., Wey. 92 AW60
Dodds La., Ch.St.G. 34 AQ27
Dodds La., Hem.H. 8 AX11
Dodds La., Wey. 92 AW60
Dodds Pk., Bet. 120 BM71
Dodsley Pl. N9 39 CB27
Dodson St. SE1 4 E5
Dodson St. SE1 66 BY41
Dodwood, Welw.G.C. 5 BS8
Doel Clo. SW19 76 BT50
Dog Kennel Hill SE22 67 CA45
Dog Kennel La., Hat. 10 BP12
Dog Kennel La., Rick. 25 AV25
Dog La. NW10 46 BO35
Dog Wd. Clo., Grav. 81 DF49
Doggets Clo., Barn. 29 BU25
Doggett Rd. SE6 77 CE47
Doggetts Cor., Horn. 51 CW34
Doggetts Fm. Rd., Uxb. 43 AU33
Doggetts Way, St.Alb. 9 BG15
Doggetts Wd. Clo., Ch.St.G. 25 AQ24
Doggetts Wd. La., Ch.St.G. 25 AQ24
Doghurst Ave., Hayes 63 AZ43
Doghurst Dr., West Dr. 63 AZ43
Doghurst La., Couls. 104 BU63
Dognell Grn., Welw.G.C. 5 BP7
Doherty Rd. E13 58 CH38
Dolben St. SE1 4 G3
Dolben St. SE1 56 BY40
Dolby Rd. SW6 65 BR44
Ewald Rd.
Dole St. NW7 37 BQ29
Dolland St. SE11 66 BX42
Dollis Ave. N3 37 BR30
Dollis Brook Wk., Barn. 28 BR25
Alan Dr.
Dollis Cres., Ruis. 45 BD33
Dollis Hill Ave. NW2 46 BP34
Dollis Hill Est. NW2 46 BP34
Dollis Hill La. NW2 46 BO35
Dollis Ms. N3 38 BS30
Dollis Pk.
Dollis Pk. N3 37 BR30
Dollis Rd. N3 37 BR29
Dollis Rd. NW7 37 BR30
Dollis Valley Way, Barn. 28 BR25
Dolman Rd. W4 65 BN42
Dolman St. SW4 66 BX45
Dolphin App., Rom. 50 CT31
Dolphin Clo. SE16 67 CC41
Kinburn St.
Dolphin Clo. SE28 59 CP39
Watersmeet Way
Dolphin Clo., Surb. 84 BK53
Dolphin Ct., Slou. 62 AQ41
Dolphin Rd.
Dolphin Ct., Stai. 73 AW48
Dolphin La. E14 57 CE40
Dolphin Rd., Nthlt. 54 BE37
Dolphin Rd., Slou. 62 AQ41
Dolphin Rd., Sun. 83 BB51
Dolphin Rd. N., Sun. 83 BB51
Dolphin Rd. S., Sun. 83 BB51
Dolphin Rd. W., Sun. 83 BB51
Dolphin Sq. SW1 66 BW42
Dolphin St., Kings.T. 85 BL51
Wood St.
Dombey St. WC1 2 B6
Dombey St. WC1 56 BX39
Dome Hill, Cat. 114 CA67
Dome Hill Pk. SE26 77 CA49
Dome Hill Peak, Cat. 114 CA66
Dome Way, Red. 121 BU70
Domett Clo. SE5 67 BZ45
Domingo St. EC1 2 H4
Domingo St. EC1 57 BZ38
Baltic St.
Dominion Dr., Rom. 41 CR29
Dominion Rd., Croy. 87 CA54
Dominion Rd., Sthl. 64 BE41
Featherstone Rd.
Dominion St. EC2 2 L6
Dominion St. EC2 57 BZ39
Dominion Way, Rain. 59 CU38
Domitian Pl., Enf. 30 CA25
Domonic Dr. SE9 78 CL49
Domville Clo. N20 38 BT27
Domville Gro. SE5 67 CA42
Don Phelan Clo. SE5 67 BZ44
Don Way, Rom. 41 CT29
Donald Dr., Rom. 50 CP32
Donald Rd. E13 58 CH37
Donald Rd., Croy. 86 BX54
Donaldson Rd. NW6 55 BR37
Donaldson Rd. SE18 68 CL44
Doncaster Dr., Nthlt. 45 BE35
Doncaster Gdns. N4 47 BY32
Stanhope Gdns.
Doncaster Gdns., Nthlt. 45 BE35
Doncaster Rd. N9 39 CB26
Doncaster Way, Upmin. 51 CW34
Donegal St. N1 2 C1
Donegal St. N1 56 BX37
Doneraile St. SW6 65 BQ44
Dongola Rd. E13 58 CH38
Dongola Rd. N17 48 CA31
Dongola Rd. W. E13 58 CH38
Donington Ave., Ilf. 49 CM32
Donkey All. SE22 77 CB47
Donkey La., Enf. 30 CB23
Donkey La., Farn. 90 CX55
Donkey La., West Dr. 63 AX42
Donne Gdns., Wok. 100 AV61
Donne Pl. SW3 3 D8
Donne Pl. SW3 66 BU42
Donne Pl., Mitch. 86 BV52
Donne Rd., Dag. 50 CP34
Donnefield Ave., Edg. 37 BL29
Donnington Rd. NW10 55 BP36
Donnington Rd., Har. 45 BK32
Donnington Rd., Sev. 107 CS63
Donnington Rd., Wor.Pk. 85 BP55
Donnybrook Rd. SW16 76 BW50
Donovan Ave. N10 38 BV30
Donovan Clo., Epsom 94 BN58
Doods Pk. Rd., Reig. 121 BT70
Doods Rd., Reig. 121 BT70
Doods Way, Reig. 121 BT70
Doon St. SE1 4 D2
Doon St. SE1 56 BY40
Doone Clo., Tedd. 74 BJ50
Dora Rd. SW19 76 BS49
Dora St. E14 57 CD39
Dorado Gdns., Orp. 89 CP55
Doral Way, Cars. 95 BU56
Carshalton Pk. Rd.
Doran Dr., Reig. 121 BT70
Doran Gdns., Reig. 121 BT70
Doran Gro. SE18 68 CM43
Doran Mans. N2 47 BU32
Doran Wk. E15 57 CF36
Dorcas Ct., St.Alb. 9 BH14
Old London Rd.
Dorchester Ave. N13 39 BZ28
Dorchester Ave., Bex. 79 CP47
Dorchester Ave., Har. 45 BF32
Dorchester Ave., Hodd. 12 CE11
Dorchester Clo., Dart. 80 CW47
Dorchester Clo., Nthlt. 45 BF35
Dorchester Clo., Orp. 79 CO50
Grovelands Rd.
Dorchester Ct. N14 38 BV26
Dorchester Ct. SE24 77 BZ46
Dorchester Ct., Rick. 26 B…
Mayfare
Dorchester Ct., Wok. 100 A…
Dorchester Dr. SE24 77 B…
Dorchester Dr., Felt. 73 B…
Dorchester Gdns. E4 39 C…
Dorchester Gdns. NW11 47 B…
Dorchester Gro. W4 65 BO…
Dorchester Rd., Grav. 81 D…
Dorchester Rd., Mord. 86 B…
Dorchester Rd., Nthlt. 45 B…
Dorchester Rd., Wey. 83 A…
Dorchester Rd., Wor.Pk. 85 BO…
Dorchester Way, Har. 46 B…
Dorchester Waye, Hayes 53 B…
Dorcis Ave., Bexh. 69 C…
Dordrecht Rd. W3 55 BO…
Dore Ave. E12 49 C…
Dore Gdns., Mord. 86 B…
Doreen Ave. NW9 46 B…
Dorell Clo., Sthl. 54 B…
Doria Dr., Grav. 81 D…
Doria Rd. SW6 65 B…
Dorian Rd., Horn. 50 C…
Doric Dr., Tad. 103 B…
Doric Way NW1 1
Doric Way NW1 56 BV…
Dorien Rd. SW20 85 BC…
Dorin Ct., Wok. 100 A…
Dorinium Clo., Wem. 46 B…
Lea Gdns.
Doris Ave., Erith 69 C…
Doris Rd. E7 58 C…
Doris Rd., Ashf. 73 BA…
Doris St. SE11 66 BY…
Tracey St.
Dorking Clo. SE8 67 CD…
Dorking Clo., Wor.Pk. 85 BC…
Dorking Gdns., Rom. 42 C…
Dorking Rd.
Dorking Glen, Rom. 42 CW…
Dorking Ri., Rom. 42 C…
Dorking Rd., Ash. 103 BM…
Dorking Rd., Epsom 103 BM…
Dorking Rd., Guil. 118 AU…
Dorking Rd., Lthd. 102 BJ…
Dorking Rd. (Bookham), Lthd. 111 B…
Dorking Rd., Rom. 42 CV…
Dorking Rd., Tad. 112 BC…
Dorking Wk., Rom. 42 CV…
Dorkins Way, Upmin. 51 CZ…
Dorlcote Rd. SW18 76 BT…
Dorling Dr., Epsom 94 BC…
Dorly Clo., Shep. 83 BE…
Dorman Pl. N9 39 CE…
Balham Rd.
Dorman Wk. NW10 55 BN…
Garden Way
Dorman Way NW8 56 BT…
Dormans Clo., Nthwd. 35 BA…
Dormay St. SW18 76 BS…
Dormer Clo. E15 58 CG…
Dormer Clo., Barn. 28 BO…
Dormers Ave., Sthl. 54 BE…
Dormers Ri., Sthl. 54 BF…
Dormers Wells La., Sthl. 54 BF…
Dormie Clo., St.Alb. 9 BG…
Dormy Wd., Ruis. 44 BB…
Dornberg Clo. SE3 68 CH…
Dornberg Rd. SE3 68 CH…
Banchory Rd.
Dorncliffe Rd. SW6 65 BF…
Dornels, Slou. 52 AR…
Dorney Gro., Wey. 83 AZ…
Dorney Reach Rd., Maid. 61 AJ…
Dorney Ri., Orp. 88 CN…
Dorney Way, Houns. 74 BE…
Dornfell St. NW6 46 BR…
Dornford Gdns., Couls. 105 BZ…
Dornton Rd. SW12 76 BV…
Dornton Rd., S.Croy. 96 BZ…
Dorothy Ave., Wem. 55 BL…
Dorothy Evans Clo., Bexh. 69 CR…
Dorothy Gdns., Dag. 50 CO…
Dorothy Rd. SW11 66 BU…
Dorriens Cft., Berk. 7 AP…
Dorrington Ct. SE25 87 CA…
Dorrington Gdns., Horn. 51 CV…
Dorrington St. EC1 2 …
Dorrington St. EC1 56 BY…
Dorrit Cres., Guil. 118 AP…
Dorrit Ms. N18 39 CA…
Dorrit Way, Chis. 78 CM…
Dickens Dr.
Dorrofield Clo., Rick. 26 BA…
Dors Clo. NW9 46 BN…
Dorset Ave., Hayes 53 BB…
Dorset Ave., Rom. 50 CS…
Dorset Ave., Sthl. 64 BF…
Dorset Ave., Well. 68 CN…
Dorset Bldgs. EC4 2 …
Dorset Bldgs. EC4 56 BY…
Dorset Ri.
Dorset Clo. NW1 1 …
Dorset Clo. NW1 56 BU…
Dorset Clo., Berk. 7 AP…
Dorset Clo., Hayes 53 BB…
Dorset Cres., Grav. 81 DJ…
Dorset Dr., Edg. 37 BL…
Dorset Dr., Wok. 100 AT…
Dorset Est. E2 2 C…
Dorset Est. E2 57 CA…
Dorset Gdns., Mitch. 86 BX…
Dorset Gdns., S.le H. 71 DK…
Somerset Rd.
Dorset Ms. SW1 3 …
Dorset Ms. SW1 66 BV…
Wilton St.
Dorset Pl. E15 57 CF…
Dorset Pl. SW1 3 N…
Dorset Pl. SW1 66 BW…
Rampayne St.

rset Ri. EC4 2 F9
rset Ri. EC4 56 BY39
rset Rd. E7 58 CJ36
rset Rd. N15 48 BZ31
rset Rd. N22 38 BX30
rset Rd. SE9 78 CK48
rset Rd. SW8 66 BX43
rset Rd. SW19 86 BS51
rset Rd. W5 64 BK41
rset Rd., Ashf. 73 AX48
rset Rd., Beck. 87 CC52
rset Rd., Har. 45 BG32
rset Rd., Mitch. 86 BU51
rset Rd., Sutt. 95 BS58
rset Rd., Wind. 61 AO44
rset Sq. NW1 1 E5
rset Sq. NW1 56 BU38
rset Sq., Epsom 94 BN58
Iollymoor La.
rset St. W1 1 F7
rset St. W1 56 BU39
rset Way, Twick. 74 BG47
rset Way, Wey. 92 AX59
rset Waye, Houns. 64 BE43
rset Waye, Uxb. 53 AY37
rville Cres. W6 65 BP41
rville Rd. SE12 78 CG46
thill Rd. SE18 68 CM43
uai Gro., Hmptn. 84 BG51
ubleday Rd., Loug. 31 CM24
ughty Ms. WC1 2 B5
ughty Ms. WC1 56 BX38
Roger St.
ughty St. WC1 2 B4
ughty St. WC1 56 BX38
uglas Ave. E17 39 CE30
uglas Ave., N.Mal. 85 BP52
uglas Ave., Rom. 42 CW30
uglas Ave., Wat. 27 BD22
uglas Ave., Wem. 55 BL36
uglas Clo., Guil. 109 AR67
uglas Clo., Stan. 36 BJ28
uglas Clo., Wall. 95 BX57
Mollison Dr.
uglas Cres., Hayes 54 BD38
uglas Dr., Croy. 87 CE55
uglas Est. N1 57 BZ36
uglas Gdns., Berk. 7 AP12
uglas La., Stai. 72 AS46
uglas Ms., Bans. 103 BR61
North Acre
uglas Pl. E14 67 CF42
uglas Rd. E4 40 CG26
uglas Rd. E16 58 CH39
uglas Rd. N1 57 BZ36
uglas Rd. N22 38 BY30
uglas Rd. NW6 55 BR37
uglas Rd., Esher 84 BF55
uglas Rd., Horn. 50 CT32
uglas Rd., Houns. 64 BF45
uglas Rd., Ilf. 50 CO33
uglas Rd., Kings.T. 85 BM52
uglas Rd., Reig. 121 BS70
Rushworth Rd.
uglas Rd., Slou. 52 AO39
uglas Rd., Stai. 73 AX46
uglas Rd., Surb. 85 BL55
uglas Rd., Well. 69 CO44
uglas Rd., Wey. 83 AW55
uglas Robinson Ct. W16 76 BX50
uglas Sq., Mord. 86 BS53
uglas St. SW1 3 N9
uglas St. SW1 66 BW42
uglas Way SE8 67 CD43
uglas Way, Welw.G.C. 5 BT8
ulton Ms. NW6 56 BS36
ymington Rd.
unesforth Gdns. SW18 76 BS47
unsell Ct., Brwd. 33 DA25
uro Pl. W8 66 BS41
uro St. E3 57 CE37
uthwaite Sq. E1 57 CB40
Torrington Pl.
ve App. E6 58 CK39
ve Clo., S.Croy. 96 CC59
ve Ct. EC2 2 K9
ve Ct., Hat. 10 BP13
ve Ho. Gdns. E4 39 CE27
ve La., Pot.B. 20 BS20
ve Ms. SW5 66 BT42
ve Pk., Pnr. 36 BF29
ve Pk., Rick. 25 AT25
ve Rd. N1 57 BZ36
ve Row E2 57 CB37
ve Wk. SW1 3 G10
ve Wk., Rain. 59 CU36
vecote Ave. N22 47 BY31
vecote Clo., Wey. 83 AZ55
vecott Gdns. SW14 65 BN45
North Worple Way
vedale Ave., Har. 45 BK32
vedale Ave., Ilf. 40 CL30
vedale Clo., Guil. 118 AT69
vedale Clo., Uxb. 35 AX30
vedale Clo., Well. 69 CO44
vedale Ri., Mitch. 76 BU50
vedale Rd. SE22 77 CB46
vedale Rd., Dart. 80 CY47
vedon Clo. N14 38 BX27
vehouse Cft., Harl. 6 CO10
vehouse Grn., Wey. 92 BA56
vehouse Mead, Bark. 58 CM37
vehouse St. SW3 3 C10
vehouse St. SW3 66 BT42
veney Clo., Orp. 89 CP52
ver Clo., Rom. 41 CS30
ver Ho. Rd. SW15 65 BP45
ver Pk. Dr. SW15 75 BP46
ver Rd. E12 49 CJ34
ver Rd. N9 39 CC27
ver Rd. SE19 77 BZ50
ver Rd., Grav. 81 DE47
ver Rd., Rom. 50 CQ32
Dover Rd. E., Grav. 81 DF47
Dover St. W1 3 K1
Dover St. W1 56 BV40
Dover Way, Rick. 26 BA24
Dover Yd. W1 3 K2
Dover Yd. W1 56 BU39
Berkeley St.
Dovercourt Ave., Th.Hth. 86 BY53
Dovercourt Gdns., Stan. 37 BL28
Dovercourt La., Sutt. 86 BT55
Dovercourt Rd. SE22 77 CA46
Doverfield, Wal.Cr. 21 BZ18
Doverfield Rd. SW2 76 BX46
Doverfield Rd., Guil. 118 AT69
Doveridge Gdns. N13 38 BY28
Dovers Cor., Rain. 59 CT38
Dovers Grn., Rad. 19 BN19
Dovers Grn. Rd., Reig. 121 BS73
Doversmead, Wok. 100 AP61
Doves Clo., Brom. 88 CK55
Doveton Rd., S.Croy. 96 BZ56
Doveton St. E1 57 CC38
Dowanhill Rd. SE6 77 CF47
Dowdells La., Welw. 5 BN5
Dowdeswell Clo. SW15 65 BO45
Dowding Pl., Stan. 36 BJ29
Dowding Rd., Uxb. 53 AY36
Dowding Rd., West. 106 CJ61
Dowding Wk., Grav. 81 DF48
Durndale La.
Dower Ave., Wall. 95 BV58
Dower Pk., Wind. 61 AM45
Dowgate Hill EC4 2 K10
Dowgate Hill EC4 57 BZ40
Dowland St. W10 55 BR38
Dowlans Clo., Lthd. 111 BF67
Dowlans Rd., Lthd. 111 BF67
Dowlas St. SE5 67 CA43
Dowlerville Rd., Orp. 97 CN57
Dowling Ct., Hem.H. 8 AY14
Woodman Rd.
Dowlings Par., Wem. 54 BK37
Bridgewater Rd.
Dowman Clo. SW19 86 BS51
Nelson Grn. Rd.
Down Ct., Hat. 10 BP14
Down Edge, St.Alb. 9 BF13
Down End SE18 68 CL43
Moordown
Down Hall Rd., Kings.T. 84 BK51
Down La., Guil. 118 AO72
Down Pl. W6 65 BP42
Bridge Ave.
Down Pl., Wind. 61 AK43
Down Rd., Guil. 118 AT70
Down Rd., Tedd. 74 BJ50
Down St. W1 3 J3
Down St. W1 56 BV40
Down St., E.Mol. 84 BF53
Down St. Ms. W1 3 J3
Down Way, Nthlt. 53 BC37
Down Way Clo., Nthlt. 53 BC37
Downage NW4 37 BQ30
Downage, The, Grav. 81 DG48
Downalong, Bush. 36 BG26
Downbank Ave., Bexh. 69 CS44
Downbarns Rd., Ruis. 45 BD35
Downbury Ms. SW18 76 BS46
Merton Rd.
Downderry Rd., Brom. 77 CF48
Downe Ave., Sev. 97 CM59
Downe Clo., Well. 69 CP43
Downe Rd., Kes. 97 CK58
Downe Rd., Mitch. 86 BU51
Downe Rd., Sev. 97 CM60
Downer Dr., Rick. 26 AW21
Downers Cotts. SW4 66 BW45
Downes Clo., Twick. 74 BJ46
St. Margarets Rd.
Downes Ct. N21 38 BY26
Downes Rd., St.Alb. 9 BJ11
Downes Ter., Rich. 75 BL46
Richmond Hill
Downfield, Wor.Pk. 85 BO54
Downfield Clo. W9 56 BS38
Downfield Rd., Chsnt. 21 CD19
Downfields, Welw.G.C. 5 BP9
Downham Clo., Rom. 41 CR29
Downham Rd. N1 57 BZ36
Downham Way, Brom. 78 CG49
Downhills Ave. N17 48 BZ31
Downhills Pk. Rd. N17 48 BZ31
Downhills Way N17 48 BZ31
Downhurst Ave. NW7 37 BN28
Downing Ave., Guil. 118 AP71
Downing Clo., Har. 45 BG31
Downing Dr., Grnf. 54 BG37
Downing Rd., Dag. 59 CQ37
Downing St. SW1 3 Q4
Downing St. SW1 66 BX41
Downings Wd., Rick. 34 AU28
Downland Clo. N20 38 BT26
Downland Clo., Couls. 95 BV60
Downland Clo., Epsom 103 BP62
Downland Gdns., Epsom 103 BP62
Downland Way, Epsom 103 BP62
Downlands, Wal.Abb. 22 CG20
Downlands Rd., Pur. 95 BX60
Downleys Clo. SE9 78 CK48
Downman Rd. SE9 68 CK45
Downs, The SW20 75 BQ50
Downs, The, Harl. 13 CN11
Downs, The, Hat. 10 BP13
Downs, The, Lthd. 111 BJ66
Downs Ave., Chis. 78 CK49
Downs Ave., Dart. 80 CX47
Downs Ave., Epsom 94 BO60
Downs Ave., Pnr. 45 BE32
Downs Bri. Rd., Beck. 87 CF51
Downs Ct. SW20 75 BQ50
Downs Ct. Rd., Pur. 95 BY59
Downs Hill, Beck. 77 CF50
Downs Hill, Grav. 81 DE50
Downs Hill Rd., Epsom 94 BO60
Downs Ho. Rd., Tad. 103 BO62
Downs La., Lthd. 102 BJ65
Downs Pk. Rd. E5 48 CA35
Downs Rd. E5 48 CB35
Downs Rd., Beck. 87 CE51
Downs Rd., Couls. 104 BW62
Downs Rd., Dor. 111 BK68
Downs Rd., Enf. 30 CA24
Downs Rd., Epsom 94 BO60
Downs Rd., Grav. 81 DE49
Downs Rd., Pur. 95 BY59
Downs Rd., Slou. 62 AR41
Downs Rd., Sutt. 95 BS58
Downs Rd., Th.Hth. 87 BZ51
Downs Side, Sutt. 94 BR59
Downs Valley, Long. 90 DC52
Downs Vw., Islw. 64 BH44
Downs Vw., Tad. 103 BP64
Downs Vw. Rd., Lthd. 111 BG67
Downs Way, Epsom 103 BO61
Downs Way, Lthd. 111 BG66
Downs Way, Orp. 97 CN56
Downs Way, Oxt. 115 CG67
Downs Way, Tad. 103 BP64
Downs Way Clo., Tad. 103 BP64
Downs Wd., Epsom 103 BP62
Downsell Rd. E15 48 CF35
Downsfield, Hat. 10 BP14
Sandfield
Downsfield Rd. E17 48 CD32
Downshall Ave., Ilf. 49 CN32
Downshire Hill NW3 47 BT35
Downside, Cher. 82 AV54
Downside, Epsom 94 BO60
Downside, Hem.H. 8 AY13
Downside, Sun. 83 BC51
Downside, Twick. 74 BH48
Downside Bri. Rd., Cob. 92 BC60
Downside Clo. SW19 76 BT50
Downside Common Rd., Cob. 101 BC62
Downside Cres. NW3 47 BU35
Downside Cres. W13 54 BJ38
Downside Orchard, Wok. 100 AT62
Downside Rd., Cob. 101 BC61
Downside Rd., Guil. 118 AT71
Downside Rd., Sutt. 95 BT57
Downside Wk., Nthlt. 54 BD38
Invicta Gro.
Downsland Dr., Brwd. 42 DB27
Downsview, Dor. 119 BK70
Downsview Ave., Wok. 100 AS64
Downsview Clo., Orp. 98 CP58
Downsview Clo., Swan. 89 CT52
Downsview Gdns. SE19 76 BY50
Downsview Rd. SE19 77 BZ50
Downsview Rd., Sev. 116 CT66
Downsway, Guil. 118 AV70
Downsway, S.Croy. 96 CA59
Downsway, Whyt. 105 CA61
Downsway, The, Sutt. 95 BS58
Downswood, Reig. 121 BT69
Downton Ave. SW2 76 BX48
Downtown Rd. SE16 67 CD41
Downview Clo., Cob. 101 BC63
Downway N12 38 BU29
Dowrey St. N1 56 BY37
Richmond Ave.
Dowry Wk., Wat. 26 BB22
Dowsett Rd. N17 39 CA30
Dowson Clo. SE5 67 BZ45
Doyce St. SE1 4 H4
Doyce St. SE1 67 BZ41
Southwark Bri. Rd.
Doyle Clo., Erith 69 CT44
Doyle Gdns. NW10 55 BP37
Doyle Rd. SE25 87 CB52
Doyle Way, Til. 71 DH44
Coleridge Rd.
D'Oyley St. SW1 3 G8
D'Oyley St. SW1 66 BV42
Doynton St. N19 47 BV34
Draco St. SE17 67 BZ43
Dragmire La., Mitch. 86 BT52
Dragon La., Wey. 92 AZ58
Dragoon Rd. SE8 67 CD42
Dragor Rd. NW10 55 BN38
Drake Ave., Cat. 105 BZ64
Drake Ave., Slou. 62 AR42
Drake Ave., Stai. 72 AV49
Drake Clo. SE16 67 CC41
Middleton Dr.
Drake Clo., Brwd. 42 DB28
Drake Ct., Har. 45 BE34
Drake Cres. SE28 59 CP39
Drake Rd. SE4 67 CE45
Drake Rd., Chess. 94 BM56
Drake Rd., Croy. 86 BX54
Drake Rd., Grays 71 DC41
Drake Rd., Har. 45 BE34
Drake Rd., Mitch. 86 BV53
Drake St. WC1 2 B7
Drake St. WC1 56 BX39
Theobalds Rd.
Drake St., Enf. 30 BZ23
Drakefell Rd. SE4 67 CD45
Drakefell Rd. SE14 67 CC44
Drakefield Rd. SW17 76 BV48
Drakely Ct. N5 47 BY35
Highbury Hill
Drakes Clo., Chsnt. 21 CC17
Drakes Clo., Esher 93 BF56
Drakes Dr., Nthwd. 35 AZ30
Drakes Dr., St.Alb. 9 BJ15
Drakes Grn., Esher 93 BF56
Drakes Rd., Amer. 25 AP23
Drakes Wk. E6 58 CK37
Drakes Way, Wok. 100 AR64
Drakewood Rd. SW16 76 BW50
Draper Clo., Belv. 69 CQ42
Drapers Rd. E15 48 CF35
Drapers Rd. N17 48 CA31
Drapers Rd., Enf. 29 BY23
Drappers Way SE16 67 CB42
St. James's Rd.
Draw Dock Rd. SE10 57 CF40
Drawell Clo. SE18 68 CN42
Drax Ave. SW20 75 BP50
Draxmont App. SW19 75 BR50
Dray Gdns. SW2 76 BX46
Draycot Rd. E11 49 CH32
Draycot Rd., Surb. 85 BM55
Draycott Ave. SW3 3 D8
Draycott Ave. SW3 66 BU42
Draycott Ave., Har. 45 BJ32
Draycott Clo., Har. 45 BJ32
Draycott Pl. SW3 3 E9
Draycott Pl. SW3 66 BU42
Draycott Ter. SW3 3 F9
Draycott Ter. SW3 66 BU42
Drayford Clo. W9 55 BR38
Drayson Ms. W8 66 BS41
Drayton Ave. W13 54 BJ40
Drayton Ave., Loug. 40 CK26
Drayton Ave., Orp. 88 CL54
Drayton Ave., Pot.B. 19 BR19
Drayton Bri. Rd. W7 54 BH40
Drayton Bri. Rd. W13 54 BJ39
Drayton Clo., Houns. 74 BE46
Drayton Clo., Lthd. 102 BH65
Drayton Gdns. N21 38 BY26
Drayton Gdns. SW10 66 BT42
Drayton Gdns. W13 54 BJ40
Drayton Gdns., West Dr. 63 AY41
Drayton Grn. W13 54 BJ40
Drayton Grn. Rd. W13 54 BJ40
Drayton Gro. W13 54 BJ40
Drayton Pk. N5 47 BY34
Drayton Rd. E11 48 CF33
Drayton Rd. N17 39 CA30
Drayton Rd. NW10 55 BO37
Drayton Rd. W13 54 BJ39
Drayton Rd., Borwd. 28 BM24
Drayton Rd., Croy. 86 BY55
Drayton Waye, Har. 45 BJ32
Dreadnought St. SE10 68 CG41
Drenon Sq., Hayes 53 BB40
Dresden Clo. NW6 56 BS36
Lymington Rd.
Dresden Rd. N19 47 BW33
Dresden Way, Wey. 92 AZ56
Dressington Ave. SE4 77 CE46
Chudleigh Rd.
Drew Ave. NW7 37 BQ29
Drew Gdns., Grnf. 54 BH36
Drew Rd. E16 58 CK40
Drewstead Rd. SW16 76 BW48
Drey, The, Ger.Cr. 34 AS28
Driffield Rd. E3 57 CD37
Drift, The, Kes. 88 CJ55
Drift La., Cob. 102 BE62
Drift Rd., Wind. 61 AG45
Drifts Way, Slou. 62 AU44
Driftway, Hem.H. 8 AY13
Driftway, The, Bans. 103 BQ61
Driftway, The, Lthd. 102 BK65
Driftway, The, Mitch. 86 BV51
Driftwood Ave., St.Alb. 18 BF16
Driftwood Dr., Ken. 105 BZ62
Drill Hall Rd., Cher. 83 AW54
Drinkwater Est., Felt. 73 BC46
Drinkwater Rd., Har. 45 BF34
Drive, The E4 39 CF26
Drive, The E17 48 CE31
Drive, The E18 49 CH31
Drive, The N2 47 BU32
Drive, The N3 38 BS29
Drive, The N7 47 BX36
Drive, The N11 38 BW29
Drive, The NW10 55 BO36
Longstone Ave.
Drive, The NW11 46 BR33
Drive, The SW16 86 BX52
Drive, The SW20 75 BQ50
Drive, The W3 55 BN39
Drive, The, Amer. 25 AO22
Drive, The, Ashf. 73 BA50
Drive, The, Bans. 103 BR62
Drive, The, Bark. 40 CN30
Drive, The, Bark. 58 CN36
Drive, The, Barn. 28 BR24
Drive, The (New Barnet), Barn. 29 BT25
Drive, The, Beck. 87 CE51
Drive, The, Bex. 79 CP47
Drive, The, Brwd. 42 DB29
Drive, The, Buck.H. 40 CJ26
Drive, The, Chsnt. 20 BY17
Drive, The, Chis. 88 CN52
Drive, The, Cob. 93 BE60
Drive, The, Couls. 95 BX60
Drive, The, Edg. 37 BM28
Drive, The, Enf. 30 BZ23
Drive, The, Epsom 94 BO57
Drive, The (Headley), Epsom 103 BM65
Drive, The, Erith 69 CR43
Drive, The, Esher 84 BG54
Drive, The, Felt. 73 BC47
Drive, The, Ger.Cr. 34 AS29
Drive, The, Grav. 81 DH49
Drive, The, Grays 70 CX43
Drive, The, Guil. 118 AP70
Beech Gro.
Drive, The, Guil. 118 AQ72
Drive, The (Onslow Village), Guil. 118 AP71
Drive, The, Harl. 6 CN10
Drive, The, Har. 45 BF32
Drive, The, Hat. 20 BS16
Drive, The, Hodd. 12 CE11
Drive, The, Houns. 64 BG44
Drive, The, Ilf. 49 CK32
Drive, The, Kings.T. 85 BN51
Drive, The, Lthd. 103 BL65
Drive, The (Fetcham), Lthd. 102 BH64
Drive, The, Loug. 31 CK24
Drive, The, Mord. 86 BT53
Drive, The, Nthwd. 35 BB30
Drive, The, Orp. 88 CN55
Drive, The, Pot.B. 19 BR20
Drive, The, Rad. 18 BJ20
Drive, The, Rick. 26 AW25
Drive, The, Rom. 41 CS29
Drive, The (Harold Wd.), Rom. 42 CW30
Drive, The, Saw. 6 CQ6
Drive, The, Sev. 107 CU65
Drive, The, Sid. 79 CO48
Drive, The, Slou. 62 AS41
Drive, The (Datchet), Slou. 62 AQ44
Drive, The, Stai. 72 AR46
Drive, The, Surb. 85 BL54
Drive, The, Sutt. 94 BR59
Drive, The, Th.Hth. 87 BZ52
Drive, The, Uxb. 44 AY35
Drive, The, Vir.W. 82 AS53
Drive, The, Wall. 95 BW58
Drive, The, Wat. 26 BB22
Drive, The, Wem. 46 BN34
Drive, The, W.Wick. 87 CF54
Drive, The, Wok. 100 AQ63
Drive Mead, Couls. 95 BX60
Drive Rd., Couls. 104 BW63
Drive Rd., Rick. 35 AX26
Drive Spur, Tad. 104 BS64
Driveway, The, Cuffley 20 BX17
Driveway, The, Hem.H. 8 AW14
Anchor La.
Droitwich Clo. SE26 77 CB48
Dromey Gdns., Har. 36 BH29
Dromore Rd. SW15 75 BR46
Dronfield Gdns., Dag. 50 CP35
Drood Yd. E1 57 CB40
Pennington St.
Droop St. W10 55 BQ38
Drop La., St.Alb. 18 BF18
Drove Rd., Dor. 119 BC71
Drove Way, Loug. 31 CL23
Drover La. SE15 67 CB43
Drovers Rd., S.Croy. 96 BZ56
Drovers Way, Beac. 34 AO29
Drovers Way, Hat. 10 BP11
Drovers Way, St.Alb. 9 BG13
Droveway, The, Grav. 81 DF50
Druce Rd. SE21 77 CA46
Drudgeon Way, Dart. 80 DB48
Druid St. SE1 4 N4
Druid St. SE1 67 CA41
Druids Clo., Ash. 103 BL63
Druids Way, Brom. 87 CF52
Drum St. E1 2 Q8
Drum St. E1 112 CA39
Drumaline Ridge, Wor.Pk. 85 BO55
Drummond Ave., Rom. 50 CS31
Drummond Clo., Erith 69 CT44
Drummond Cres. NW1 1 N2
Drummond Cres. NW1 56 BW38
Drummond Dr., Stan. 36 BH29
Drummond Gate SW1 3 P10
Drummond Gate SW1 66 BW42
Drummond Pl., Twick. 74 BJ46
Drummond Rd. E11 49 CH32
Drummond Rd. SE16 67 CB41
Drummond Rd., Croy. 87 BZ55
Drummond Rd., Guil. 118 AR70
Drummond Rd., Rom. 50 CS31
Drummond St. NW1 1 L4
Drummond St. NW1 56 BW38
Drummonds, The, Buck.H. 40 CH27
Drummonds, The, Epp. 23 CO18
Hartland Rd.
Drury Cres., Croy. 86 BY55
Drury La. WC2 2 A8
Drury La. WC2 56 BX39
Drury Rd., Har. 45 BG33
Drury Way NW10 46 BN35
Dryad St. SW15 65 BQ45
Dryburgh Gdns. NW9 46 BM31
Dryburgh Rd. SW15 65 BP45
Drycroft, Welw.G.C. 5 BR9
Dryden Ave. W7 54 BH39
Dryden Clo., Ilf. 40 CN29
Dryden Ct. SE11 4 E9
Dryden Ct., Guil. 118 AS71
Lower Edgeborough Rd.
Dryden Ho. SE5 67 CA44
Glebe Est.
Dryden Pl., Til. 71 DG44
Fielding Ave.
Dryden Rd. SW19 76 BT50
Dryden Rd., Enf. 30 CA25
Dryden Rd., Har. 36 BH30
Dryden Rd., Well. 68 CN44
Dryden St. WC2 2 A9
Dryden Way, Orp. 89 CO54
Dryfield Clo. NW10 55 BN36
Dryfield Rd., Edg. 37 BN29
Dryfield Wk. SE8 67 CE43
New King St.
Dryhill La., Sev. 107 CR65
Dryhill Rd., Belv. 69 CQ43
Dryland Ave., Orp. 97 CN56
Drylands Rd. N8 47 BX32
Drynham Pk., Wey. 83 BB55
Drysdale Ave. E4 39 CE26
Drysdale Clo., Nthwd. 35 BB29
Drysdale Pl. N1 2 N2
Drysdale Pl. N1 57 CA38
Drysdale St.
Drysdale St. N1 2 N2
Drysdale St. N1 57 CA38
Du Cane Clo. W12 55 BQ39
Du Cane Rd.
Du Cane Ct. SW17 76 BV47
Du Cane Rd. W12 55 BP39
Du Cros Dr., Stan. 36 BK29

Du Cros Rd. W3 55 BO40
Duarte Pl., Grays 71 DC41
Dubrae Clo., St.Alb. 9 BF14
Ducal St. E2 2 Q3
Ducal St. E2 57 CA38
Brick La.
Duchess Ms. W1 1 K7
Duchess Ms. W1 56 BV39
Duchess St.
Duchess of Bedfords Wk. W8 66 BS41
Duchess St. W1 1 K7
Duchess St. W1 56 BV39
Duchy Rd., Barn. 29 BT22
Duchy St. SE1 4 E2
Duchy St. SE1 56 BY40
Ducie St. SW4 66 BX45
Duck La. W1 1 N9
Duck La. W1 56 BW39
Broadwick St.
Duck La., Epp. 23 CP16
Duck Lees La., Enf. 30 CD24
Duckett Rd. N4 47 BY32
Duckett St. E1 57 CC38
Ducketts Rd., Dart. 79 CT46
Ducking Stool Ct., Rom. 50 CT31
Market Link
Duckling La., Saw. 6 CQ6
Fair Grn.
Ducks Hill, Nthwd. 35 AZ30
Ducks Hill Rd., Nthwd. 44 AZ31
Ducks Wk., Twick. 74 BK46
Ducksfoot La. EC4 57 BZ40
Upper Thames St.
Dudbrook Rd., Rom. 33 CW22
Dudden Hill La. NW10 46 BO35
Duddington Clo. SE9 78 CJ49
Dudley Ave., Har. 45 BK31
Dudley Ave., Wal.Cr. 21 CC19
Dudley Clo., Grays 71 DC41
Dudley Clo., Hem.H. 16 AT16
Dudley Clo., Wey. 83 AW55
Dudley Ct. NW11 46 BR31
Dudley Ct., Slou. 62 AQ41
Upton Rd.
Dudley Dr., Mord. 85 BR54
Dudley Dr., Ruis. 44 BC35
Dudley Gdns. W13 64 BJ41
Dudley Gdns., Har. 45 BG33
Dudley Gdns., Rom. 42 CV29
Dudley Gro., Epsom 94 BN60
Dudley Rd. E17 48 CE31
Dudley Rd. N3 38 BS30
Dudley Rd. NW6 55 BR37
Dudley Rd. SW19 76 BS50
Dudley Rd., Ashf. 73 AY49
Dudley Rd., Felt. 73 BA47
Dudley Rd., Grav. 81 CF47
Dudley Rd., Har. 45 BG34
Dudley Rd., Ilf. 49 CL35
Dudley Rd., Kings.T. 85 BL52
Dudley Rd., Rich. 65 BL44
Dudley Rd., Rom. 42 CV29
Dudley Rd., Sthl. 64 BD41
Dudley Rd., Walt. 83 BC53
Dudley St. W2 1 A7
Dudlington Rd. E5 48 CC34
Dudmaston Ms. SW3 3 B10
Dudmaston Ms. SW3 66 BT42
Dudsbury Rd., Dart. 79 CU46
Dudsbury Rd., Sid. 79 CO49
Dudset La., Houns. 63 BC44
Dudswell La., Berk. 7 AO10
Duff St. E14 57 CE39
Dufferin Ave. EC1 2 K5
Dufferin St. EC1 2 J5
Dufferin St. EC1 57 BZ38
Duffield Clo., Har. 45 BH32
Duffield La., Slou. 43 AP35
Duffield Pk., Slou. 52 AQ38
Duffield Rd., Tad. 103 BP65
Duffins Orchard, Cher. 91 AU57
Dufours Pl. W1 1 M9
Dufours Pl. W1 56 BW39
Broadwick St.
Dugdale Hill La., Pot.B. 19 BR20
Dugdales, Rick. 26 AZ24
Duke Gdns., Ilf. 49 CM31
Duke Rd.
Duke Humphrey Rd. SE3 68 CG44
Duke of Cambridge Clo., Twick. 74 BG46
Duke of Edinburgh Rd., Sutt. 86 BT55
Duke of Wellington Pl. SW1 3 H4
Duke of Wellington Pl. SW1 66 BV41
Duke of York St. SW1 3 M2
Duke of York St. SW1 56 BW40
Duke Rd. W4 65 BN42
Duke Rd., Ilf. 49 CM31
Duke Shore Pl. E14 57 CD40
Narrow St.
Duke St. SW1 3 M2
Duke St. SW1 56 BW40
Duke St. W1 1 H8
Duke St. W1 56 BV39
Duke St., Hodd. 12 CE11
Duke St., Rich. 74 BK46
Duke St., Sutt. 95 BT56
Duke St., Wat. 27 BD24
Duke St., Wind. 61 AO44
Duke St., Wok. 100 AS62
Duke St. Hill SE1 4 L2
Duke St. Hill SE1 57 BZ40
Duke St. Ms. NW8 56 BU38
Lisson Gro.
Dukes Ave. N3 38 BS30
Dukes Ave. N10 47 BW31
Dukes Ave. W4 65 BN42
Dukes Ave., Edg. 37 BL29
Dukes Ave., Epp. 31 CN21
Dukes Ave., Grays 71 DD41
Dukes Ave., Har. 45 BE32
Dukes Ave. (Wealdstone), Har. 45 BH31
Dukes Ave., Houns. 64 BE45
Dukes Ave., N.Mal. 85 BO52
Dukes Ave., Nthlt. 54 BE36
Dukes Ave., Rich. 74 BK49
Dukes Clo., Ashf. 73 BA49
Dukes Clo., Epp. 23 CR17
Dukes Clo., Ger.Cr. 43 AR33
Dukes Clo., Hmptn. 74 BE49
Dukes Clo., Kings.T. 74 BK49
Dukes Ct. E6 58 CL37
Dukes Hill, Warl. 105 CD63
Dukes Kiln Rd., Ger.Cr. 43 AR34
Dukes La. W8 66 BS41
Dukes La., Ger.Cr. 43 AR33
Dukes La., Ong. 15 DB12
Dukes Lo., Nthwd. 35 BB28
Eastbury Ave.
Dukes Meadows W4 65 BN44
Dukes Ms. N10 47 BV31
Dukes Ave.
Dukes Ms. W1 1 H8
Dukes Ms. W1 56 BV39
Duke St.
Dukes Orchard, Bex. 79 CS47
Dukes Pas. E17 48 CF31
Marlowe Rd.
Dukes Pl. EC3 2 N9
Dukes Pl. EC3 57 CA39
Dukes Pl., Brwd. 42 DB26
Wellesley Rd.
Dukes Ride, Dor. 119 BK73
Dukes Ride, Ger.Cr. 43 AS33
Dukes Ride, Uxb. 44 AY35
The Dr.
Dukes Rd. E6 58 CL37
Dukes Rd. W3 55 BM38
Dukes Rd. WC1 1 P3
Dukes Rd. WC1 56 BW38
Dukes Rd., Walt. 93 BD56
Dukes Way, Berk. 7 AQ12
Dukes Way, W.Wick. 88 CG55
Dukes Wd. Ave., Ger.Cr. 43 AS33
Dukes Wd. Dr., Ger.Cr. 43 AR33
Dukes Yd. W1 1 H10
Dukesthorpe Rd. SE26 77 CC49
Dulas St. N4 47 BX33
Everleigh St.
Dulford St. W11 55 BR40
Dulka Rd. SW11 76 BU46
Dulton Clo., Hem.H. 8 AX14
Dulverton Rd. SE9 78 CM48
Dulverton Rd., Rom. 42 CV29
Dulverton Rd., Ruis. 44 BC33
Dulverton Rd., S.Croy. 96 CC58
Dulwich Common SE21 77 CA47
Dulwich Oaks, The SE21 77 CA48
Dulwich Rd. SE24 76 BY46
Dulwich Village SE21 77 CA46
Dulwich Way, Rick. 26 AZ25
Dulwich Wd. Ave. SE19 77 CA49
Dulwich Wd. Pk. SE19 77 CA49
Dumbarton Ave., Wal.Cr. 21 CC20
Raglan Ave.
Dumbarton Rd. SW2 76 BX46
Dumbleton Clo., Kings.T. 85 BM51
Gloucester Rd.
Dumbreck Rd. SE9 68 CK45
Dumfries Clo., Wat. 35 BB27
Dumont Rd. N16 48 CA34
Dumpton Pl. NW1 56 BV36
Dunally Pk., Shep. 83 BA54
Dunbar Ave. SW16 86 BY51
Dunbar Ave., Beck. 87 CD52
Dunbar Ave., Dag. 50 CR34
Dunbar Clo., Hayes 53 BC39
Dunbar Ct., Walt. 84 BD55
Dunbar Gdns., Dag. 50 CR35
Dunbar Rd. E7 58 CH36
Dunbar Rd. N22 38 BY30
Dunbar Rd., N.Mal. 85 BN52
Dunbar St. SE27 77 BZ48
Dunblane Rd. SE9 68 CK45
Dunboe Pl., Shep. 83 BA54
Russell Rd.
Dunboyne Rd. NW3 47 BU35
Dunbridge St. E2 57 CB38
Duncan Clo., Barn. 29 BT24
Duncan Clo., Welw.G.C. 5 BR8
Duncan Ct., St.Alb. 9 BH14
Duncan Dr., Guil. 118 AT70
Duncan Gro. W3 55 BO39
Duncan Rd. E8 57 CB37
Duncan Rd., Rich. 65 BL45
Duncan Rd., Tad. 103 BR63
Duncan St. N1 56 BY37
Duncan Ter. N1 2 F1
Duncan Ter. N1 56 BY37
Duncan Way, Bush. 27 BE23
Duncannon Cres., Wind. 61 AL45
Duncannon St. WC2 3 Q1
Duncannon St. WC2 56 BX40
Strand
Dunch St. E1 57 CB39
Watney St.
Duncombe Clo., Amer. 25 AP22
Duncombe Hill SE23 77 CD47
Duncombe Rd. N19 47 BW33
Duncombe Rd., Berk. 7 AP12
Duncrievie Rd. SE13 77 CF46
Duncroft SE18 68 CN43
Duncroft, Wind. 61 AM45
Duncroft Clo., Reig. 120 BR70
Dundalk Rd. SE4 67 CD45
Dundas Gdns., E.Mol. 84 BF52
Dundas Rd. SE15 67 CC44
Dundee Rd. E13 58 CH37
Dundee Rd. SE25 87 CB53
Dundee St. E1 57 CB40
Green Bank
Dundela Gdns., Wor.Pk. 94 BP56
Dundonald Clo. E6 58 CK39
Northumberland Rd.
Dundonald Rd. NW10 55 BQ37
Dundonald Rd. SW19 85 BR51
Dundrey Cres., Red. 113 BX68
Dunedin Dr., Cat. 114 CA66
Dunedin Rd. E10 48 CE34
Dunedin Rd., Ilf. 49 CM33
Dunedin Rd., Rain. 59 CT38
Dunedin Way, Hayes 54 BD38
Dunelm Gro. SE27 77 BZ48
Dunelm St. E1 57 CC39
Dunfee Way, Wey. 92 AY59
Viscount Gdns.
Dunfield Gdns. SE6 77 CE49
Dunfield Rd. SE6 77 CE49
Dunford Rd. N7 47 BX35
Dungarvan Ave. SW15 65 BP45
Dungates La., Bet. 120 BP70
Dunheved Clo., Th.Hth. 86 BT53
Dunheved Rd. N., Th.Hth. 86 BY53
Dunheved Rd. S., Th.Hth. 86 BY53
Dunheved Rd. W., Th.Hth. 86 BY53
Dunholme Grn. N9 39 CA27
Dunholme La. N9 39 CA27
Dunholme Rd.
Dunholme Rd. N9 39 CA27
Dunkeld Rd. SE25 87 BZ52
Dunkeld Rd., Dag. 50 CO34
Dunkellin Gro., S.Ock. 60 DA39
Dunkellin Way, S.Ock. 60 DA39
Dunkery Rd. SE9 78 CH49
Dunkin Rd., Dart. 70 CX45
Dunkirk Clo., Grav. 81 DH49
Waring St.
Dunlace Rd. E5 48 CC35
Dunleary Clo., Houns. 74 BE47
Dunley Dr., Croy. 96 CE57
Dunlin, Hem.H. 8 AY11
Dunlin Clo., Red. 121 BU73
Dunlin Clo., Reig. 121 BU73
Dunlin Ri., Guil. 118 AU69
Dunloe Ave. N17 48 BZ31
Dunloe St. E2 2 Q1
Dunloe St. E2 57 CA37
Dunlop Pl. SE16 4 Q7
Dunlop Pl. SE16 67 CA41
Dunlop Rd., Til. 71 DF44
Dunmail Dr., Pur. 96 CA60
Dunmore, Guil. 118 AO70
Dunmore Pt. E2 2 P3
Dunmore Rd. NW6 55 BR37
Dunmore Rd. SW20 85 BQ51
Dunmow Clo., Felt. 74 BE49
Dunmow Clo., Loug. 31 CK25
Dunmow Clo., Rom. 50 CP32
Dunmow Dr., Rain. 59 CT37
Dunmow Gdns., Brwd. 123 DE32
Dunmow Rd. E15 48 CF35
Dunmow Rd., Ong. 15 CZ14
Dunmow Wk. N1 57 BZ37
Popham St.
Dunn Mead NW9 37 BO29
Dunn St. E8 48 CA35
Dunnents, Wok. 100 AP62
Staveley Way
Dunning Clo., S.Ock. 60 DA39
Dunningford Clo., Horn. 50 CT35
Dunnings La., Brwd. 123 DC33
Dunnings La., Upmin. 123 DD34
Dunnock Clo., Borwd. 28 BM24
Goldfinch Way
Dunnock Rd. E6 58 CK39
Dunns Pas. WC1 2 A8
Dunny La., Kings L. 16 AV19
Dunnymans Rd., Bans. 94 BR61
Basing Rd.
Dunollie Pl. NW5 47 BW35
Dunollie Rd.
Dunollie Rd. NW5 47 BW35
Dunoon Gdns. SE23 77 CC47
Devonshire Rd.
Dunoon Rd. SE23 77 CC47
Dunottar Clo., Red. 121 BT71
Dunraven Dr., Enf. 29 BY23
Dunraven Rd. W12 55 BP40
Dunraven St. W1 1 F10
Dunraven St. W1 56 BU40
Green St.
Dunsany Rd. W14 65 BQ41
Dunsbury Clo., Sutt. 95 BS58
Nettlecombe Clo.
Dunsdon Ave., Guil. 118 AQ71
Dunsfold Ri., Couls. 95 BW60
Dunsfold Way, Croy. 96 CE58
Dunsford Cres. SW18 76 BS47
Merton Rd.
Dunsford Way SW15 75 BP46
Dover Pk. Dr.
Dunsmore Clo., Bush. 27 BG25
Dunsmore Clo., Hayes 54 BD38
Kingsash Dr.
Dunsmore Rd., Walt. 83 BC53
Dunsmore Way, Bush. 27 BG25
Dunsmure Rd. N16 48 CA33
Dunspring La., Ilf. 40 CL30
Dunstable Clo., Rom. 42 CV29
Dunstable Ms. W1 1 H6
Dunstable Ms. W1 56 BV39
Dunstable Rd., E.Mol. 84 BE52
Dunstable Rd., Rich. 65 BL45
Dunstable Rd., Rom. 42 CV29
Dunstall Rd. SW20 75 BP50
Dunstall Way, E.Mol. 84 BF52
Dunstalls, Harl. 13 CL13
Dunstan Clo. N2 47 BT31
Thomas More Way
Dunstan Rd. NW11 46 BR33
Dunstan Rd., Couls. 104 BW62
Dunstans Gro. SE22 77 CB46
Dunstans Rd. SE22 77 CB47
Dunster Ave., Mord. 85 BQ54
Dunster Clo., Barn. 28 BQ24
Dunster Clo., Rom. 41 CS30
Dunster Clo., Uxb. 35 AW30
Dunster Ct. EC3 2 M10
Dunster Cres., Horn. 51 CX34
Dunster Dr. NW9 46 BN33
Dunster Gdns. NW6 55 BR36
Dunster Rd., Hem.H. 8 AZ10
Dunster Way, Har. 45 BE34
Dunsters Mead, Welw.G.C. 5 BS9
Dunsterville Way SE1 4 L5
Dunsterville Way SE1 67 BZ41
Dunston Rd. E8 57 CA37
Dunston Rd. SW11 66 BV44
Dunston St. E8 57 CA37
Dunton Clo., Surb. 84 BK54
Malcolm Dr.
Dunton Rd. E10 48 CE33
Dunton Rd. SE1 4 P9
Dunton Rd. SE1 67 CA42
Dunton Rd., Rom. 50 CT31
Duntshill Rd. SW18 76 BS47
Dunvegan Clo., E.Mol. 84 BF52
Dunvegan Rd. SE9 68 CK45
Dunwich Rd., Bexh. 69 CQ44
Dunworth Ms. W11 55 BR40
Portobello Rd.
Duplex Ride SW1 3 F5
Dupont Rd. SW20 85 BQ51
Dupont St. E14 57 CD39
Duppas Ave., Croy. 95 BY56
Violet La.
Duppas Clo., Shep. 83 BA53
Duppas Hill La., Croy. 95 BY56
Duppas Hill Rd., Croy. 95 BY56
Duppas Hill Ter., Croy. 86 BY55
Duppas La., Croy. 86 BY55
Duppas Rd., Croy. 86 BY55
Dupree Rd. SE7 68 CH42
Dura Den Clo., Beck. 77 CE50
Durand Clo., Cars. 86 BU54
Durand Gdns. SW9 66 BX44
Durand Way NW10 55 BN36
Durant Dr., Swan. 79 CU50
Durant St. E2 57 CB37
Durants Pk. Ave., Enf. 30 CC24
Durants Rd., Enf. 30 CC24
Durban Gdns., Dag. 59 CS36
Durban Ho. E7 58 CJ36
Durban Rd. E15 58 CG38
Durban Rd. E17 39 CD30
Durban Rd. N17 39 CA29
Durban Rd. SE27 77 BZ49
Durban Rd., Beck. 87 CD51
Durban Rd., Felt. 73 BC48
Durban Rd., Ilf. 49 CN33
Durban Rd. E., Wat. 26 BC24
Durban Rd. W., Wat. 26 BC24
Durbin Rd., Chess. 94 BL56
Durdans Rd., Sthl. 54 BE39
Durell Gdns., Dag. 50 CP35
Durell Rd., Dag. 50 CP35
Durfold Dr., Reig. 121 BT70
Durford Cres. SW15 75 BP47
Durham Ave., Brom. 88 CG52
Durham Ave., Houns. 64 BE42
Durham Ave., Rom. 51 CV31
Durham Ave., Wdf.Grn. 40 CJ28
Durham Clo. SW20 85 BP51
Durham Clo., Guil. 118 AP69
Durham Hill, Brom. 78 CG49
Durham Ho. St. WC2 4 A1
Durham Ho. St. WC2 56 BX40
Strand
Durham Pl. SW3 66 BU42
Durham Ri. SE18 68 CM42
Durham Rd. E12 49 CJ35
Durham Rd. E16 58 CG38
Durham Rd. N2 47 BU31
Durham Rd. N7 47 BX34
Durham Rd. N9 39 CB27
Durham Rd. SW20 85 BP51
Durham Rd. W5 64 BK41
Durham Rd., Borwd. 28 BN24
Durham Rd., Brom. 88 CG52
Durham Rd., Dag. 50 CS35
Durham Rd., Felt. 74 BD47
Durham Rd., Har. 45 BF32
Durham Rd., Sid. 79 CO49
Durham Row E1 57 CC39
Stepney High St.
Durham St. SE11 66 BX42
Durham Ter. W2 56 BS39
Durleston Pk. Dr., Lthd. 111 BG66
Durley Ave., Pnr. 45 BE33
Durley Gdns., Orp. 89 CO55
Durley Rd. N16 48 CA33
Durlston Rd. E5 48 CB34
Durlston Rd., Kings.T. 75 BL50
Durndale La., Grav. 81 DF49
Durnell Way, Loug. 31 CL24
Durnford St. N15 48 CA32
Durnford St. SE10 67 CF43
Greenwich Ch. St.
Durning Rd. SE19 77 BZ49
Durnsford Ave. SW19 76 BS48
Durnsford Rd. N11 38 BW30
Durnsford Rd. SW19 76 BS48
Durrant Way, Orp. 97 CM56
Durrant Way, Swans. 81 DC47
Durrants Clo., Rain. 60 CV37
Durrants Dr., Rick. 26 BA24
Durrants Hill Rd., Hem.H. 8 AX15
Durrants La., Berk. 7 AP13
Durrants La., Rick. 26 AY24
Durrants Rd., Berk. 7 AP12
Durrell Rd. SW6 65 BR44
Durrell Way, Shep. 83 BA53
Durrington Ave. SW20 75 BQ50
Durrington Pk. Rd. SW20 85 BQ51
Durrington Rd. E5 48 CD35
Durrington Rd. Dev. E5 48 CD35
Dursley Clo. SE3 68 CJ44
Dursley Gdns. SE3 68 CJ44
Dursley Rd. SE3 68 CJ44
Durward St. E1 57 C
Durweston Ms. W1 1
Durweston Ms. W1 56 B
Crawford St.
Durweston St. W1 1
Durweston St. W1 56 B
York St.
Dury Falls Clo., Horn. 51 C
Dury Rd., Barn. 28 B
Dutch Barn Clo., Stai. 73 A
Douglas Rd.
Dutch Gdns., Kings.T. 75 BN
Windmill Ri.
Dutch Yd. SW18 76 B
Wandsworth High St.
Dutton St. SE10 67 C
Dutton Way, Iver 52 A
Duxford Clo., Horn. 60 C
Duxons Turn, Hem.H. 8 A
Dyall Ho., Grays 71 D
Hawkes Clo.
Dye Ho. La. E3 57 C
Dyers Bldgs. EC1 2
Dyers Bldgs. EC1 56 B
Holborn
Dyers Hall Rd. E11 48 C
Dyers La. SW15 65 B
Dyers Way, Rom. 41 C
Dyke Dr., Orp. 89 C
Dykes Path, Wok. 100 A
Bentham Ave.
Dykes Way, Brom. 88 C
Dykewood Clo., Bex. 79 C
Dylan Clo., Brwd. 36 B
Sullivan Way
Dylan Rd., Belv. 69 C
Dylways SE5 67 B
Dymchurch Clo., Ilf. 40 C
Dymchurch Clo., Orp. 97 C
Dymes Path SW19 75 B
Queensmere Rd.
Dymock St. SW6 66 B
Dymoke Grn., St.Alb. 9 B
Dymoke Rd., Horn. 50 C
Dymokes Way, Hodd. 12 C
Dyne Rd. NW6 55 B
Dyneley Rd. SE12 78 C
Dynes Rd., Sev. 108 CW
Dynevor Pl., Guil. 109 AC
Dynevor Rd. N16 48 C
Dynevor Rd., Rich. 75 B
Dynham Rd. NW6 56 B
Dyott St. WC1 1
Dyott St. WC1 56 BW
Dyrham La., Barn. 28 B
Dysart Ave., Kings.T. 74 BK
Dysart St. EC2 2
Dysart St. EC2 57 B
Dyson Clo., Wind. 61 AN
Dyson Rd. E11 49 CG
Dyson Rd. E15 58 CG
Dysons Clo., Wal.Cr. 21 CC
Dysons Rd. N18 39 CE
Dytchleys La., Brwd. 33 CW

E

Eade Rd. N4 47 BZ
Eagans Clo. N2 47 B
Eagle Ave., Rom. 50 CC
Eagle Clo., Enf. 30 CC
Eagle Clo., Rain. 59 CU
Eagle Clo., Wal.Abb. 22 CH
Eagle Ct. EC1 2
Eagle Ct. EC1 56 BY
Albion Pl.
Eagle Hill SE19 77 BZ
Eagle La. E11 49 CH
Eagle La., Brwd. 33 CZ
Eagle Pl. SW1 3
Eagle Pl. SW1 56 BW
Jermyn St.
Eagle Rd., Guil. 118 AR
Eagle Rd., Wem. 54 BK
Eagle St. WC1 2
Eagle St. WC1 56 BX
High Holborn
Eagle Ter., Wdf.Grn. 40 CH
Eagle Way, Brwd. 42 DA
Eagle Way, Hat. 10 BF
Eagle Wf. Rd. N1 57 BZ
Eagles Dr., West. 106 CJ
Ricketts Hill
Eaglesfield Rd. SE18 68 CL
Eaglet Pl. E1 57 CC
Mile End Rd.
Ealdham Sq. SE9 68 CJ
Ealing Clo., Borwd. 28 BN
Ealing Downs Ct., Grnf. 54 BJ
Ealing Grn. W5 54 BK
Ealing Pk. Gdns. W5 64 BK
Ealing Pk. Ms. W5 64 BK
Ealing Rd.
Ealing Rd., Brent. 64 BK
Ealing Rd., Nthlt. 54 BF
Ealing Rd., Wem. 55 BL
Ealing Vill. W5 55 BL
Eamont Clo., Ruis. 44 AZ
Allonby Dr.
Eamont St. NW8 56 BU
Eardemont Clo., Dart. 69 CT
Eardley Cres. SW5 66 BS
Eardley Rd. SW16 76 BW
Eardley Rd., Belv. 69 CR
Eardley Rd., Sev. 107 CU
Earl Cotts. SE1 67 CA
Earl Ri. SE18 68 CM
Earl Rd. SE1 4 P
Earl Rd. SE1 67 CA

Rd. SW14 65 BN45
Rd., Grav. 81 DF48
St. EC2 2 L6
St. EC2 57 BZ39
St., Wat. 27 BD24
dom Rd. SW15 65 BQ45
e Gdns., Kings.T. 75 BL50
ham Gro. E7 49 CG35
ham Gro. N22 38 BX29
ham St. WC2 1 P9
ham St. WC2 56 BW39
s Ct. Gdns. SW5 66 BS42
s Ct. Rd. SW5 66 BS41
s Ct. Rd. W8 66 BS41
s Ct. Sq. SW5 66 BS42
s Cres., Har. 45 BH31
s La., Pot.B. 19 BO19
s Path, Loug. 31 CJ23
s Ter. W8 65 BR41
s Wk. W8 66 BS41
s Wk., Dag. 50 CO35
sbrook Rd., Red. 121 BU71
sferry Clo. N1 56 BX36
sferry Way N1 56 BX36
sfield, Maid. 61 AH42
sfield Rd. SW18 76 BT47
shall Rd. SE9 68 CK45
smead, Har. 45 BE35
smead Rd. N15 48 CA32
smead Rd. NW10 55 BQ38
sthorpe Ms. SW12 76 BV46
ightingale La.
sthorpe Rd. SE26 77 CC49
stoke St. EC1 2 F2
stoke St. EC1 56 BY38
pencer St.
stone Gro. E9 57 CB37
ictoria Pk. Rd.
swood, Cob. 93 BD59
swood Ave., Th.Hth. 86 BY53
swood Clo. SE10 68 CG42
arlswood St.
swood Gdns., Ilf. 49 CL31
swood Rd., Red. 121 BU71
swood St. SE10 68 CG42
y Ms. NW1 56 BV37
lington Rd.
nshaw St. WC2 1 P8
nshaw St. WC2 56 BW39
sby St. W14 65 BR42
by Cres., Mord. 86 BS53
ebourne Rd., Dag. 50 CP35
edale Dr., Horn. 50 CU35
ington Pl., Guil. 118 AS71
Maori Rd.
ington Way, S.Ock. 60 DA39
leys Ms. W1 1 H8
leys Ms. W1 56 BV39
Wigmore St.
t Acton La. W3 55 BO40
t Arbour St. E1 57 CC39
t Ave. E12 58 CK36
t Ave. E17 48 CE31
t Ave., Hayes 53 BB40
t Ave., Sthl. 54 BE40
t Ave., Wall. 95 BX56
t Ave., Walt. 92 BB58
t Bank N16 48 CA33
t Barnet Rd., Barn. 29 BT24
t Brook Clo., Wok. 100 AT61
t Burrow Fld., Welw.G.C. 5 BQ9
t Churchfield Rd. W3 55 BN40
t Clo. W5 55 BM38
t Clo., Barn. 29 BV24
t Clo., Grnf. 54 BG37
t Clo., Rain. 59 CU38
t Common, Ger.Cr. 43 AS32
t Ct., Wem. 45 BK34
t Cres. N11 38 BU28
t Cres., Enf. 30 CA25
t Cres., Wind. 61 AM44
t Cres. Rd., Grav. 81 DH46
t Cross Route E3 57 CD36
t Dr., Cars. 95 BU58
t Dr., Nthwd. 35 BB27
t Dr., Orp. 89 CO53
t Dr., St.Alb. 10 BL13
t Dr., Saw. 6 CQ6
t Dr., Slou. 52 AP38
t Dr., Vir.W. 82 AQ53
t Dr., Wat. 26 BC21
t Dulwich Est. SE22 67 CA45
t Dulwich Gro. SE22 77 CA46
t Dulwich Rd. SE22 67 CA45
t End Rd. N2 38 BS30
t End Rd. N3 38 BS30
t End Way, Pnr. 45 BE31
t Entrance, Dag. 59 CR37
t Ferry Rd. E14 67 CE42
t Ferry Rd. E14 67 CF41
t Flint, Hem.H. 7 AV13
t Gdn., Wok. 100 AU62
t Gdns. SW17 76 BU50
t Gate, Harl. 6 CM10
t Glade, Pnr. 45 BE31
t Grn., Hem.H. 17 AY16
t Hall Rd., Orp. 89 CQ54
t Ham Manor Way E6 58 CL39
t Harding St. EC4 2 E8
t Harding St. EC4 56 BY39
t Heath Rd. NW3 47 BT34
t Hill SW18 76 BS46
t Hill, Dart. 80 CW47
t Hill, Oxt. 115 CG68
t Hill, Sev. 99 CX59
t Hill, S.Croy. 96 CA58
t Hill, S.Dnth. 90 CY51
t Hill, Wem. 46 BM34
t Hill, West. 106 CH62
t Hill, Wok. 100 AU61
t Hill Dr., Dart. 80 CW47
t Hill Rd., Oxt. 115 CG68
t Holme, Erith 69 CS44
East Holme, Hayes 53 BC40
East India Dock Rd. E14 57 CE39
East India Dock Wall Rd. E14 57 CF40
East Kent Ave., Grav. 81 DE46
East La. SE16 67 CB41
East La., Abb.L. 17 BC18
East La., Kings.T. 84 BK52
High St.
East La., Lthd. 110 BA66
East La., Wem. 45 BJ34
East Lo. La., Enf. 29 BW21
East Mead, Welw.G.C. 5 BS9
East Mead, Wok. 100 AQ62
East Meads, Guil. 118 AQ71
East Milton Rd., Grav. 81 DH47
East Mt. St. E1 57 CB39
East Pk., Harl. 6 CO9
East Pk., Saw. 6 CQ6
East Pk. Clo., Rom. 50 CQ32
East Pas. EC1 2 H6
East Pl. SE27 77 BZ49
Pilgrim Hill
East Poultry Ave. EC1 2 F7
East Ramp, Houns. 63 AZ44
East Ridgeway, Cuffley 20 BX17
East Rd. E15 58 CH37
East Rd. N1 2 L2
East Rd. N1 57 BZ38
East Rd. SW19 76 BT50
East Rd., Barn. 38 BV26
East Rd., Belv. 69 CQ41
East Rd., Edg. 37 BM30
East Rd., Enf. 30 CC22
East Rd., Felt. 73 BA47
East Rd., Grays 70 CX43
East Rd., Harl. 6 CO9
East Rd., Kings.T. 85 BL51
East Rd., Reig. 112 BR70
East Rd. (Chadwell Heath), Rom. 50 CQ31
East Rd. (Rush Grn.), Rom. 50 CS33
East Rd., Well. 69 CO44
East Rd., West Dr. 63 AY42
East Rd., Wey. 92 BA57
East Rochester Way, Bex. 79 CQ46
East Rochester Way, Sid. 68 CM45
East Row E11 49 CH32
East Row W10 55 BR38
East Shalford La., Guil. 118 AS73
East Sheen Ave. SW14 75 BN46
East Smithfield E1 4 Q1
East Smithfield E1 57 CA40
East Sq. SE18 68 CL42
East St. EC2 57 BZ39
Blomfield St.
East St. SE17 4 J10
East St. SE17 67 BZ42
East St., Bark. 58 CM36
East St., Bexh. 69 CR45
East St., Brent. 64 BK43
East St., Brom. 88 CH51
East St., Epsom 94 BO59
East St., Grays 71 DE43
East St. (South Stifford), Grays 71 DC43
East St., Hem.H. 8 AX13
East St., Lthd. 111 BF66
East Surrey Gro. SE15 67 CA43
Commercial Way
East Tenter St. E1 2 Q9
East Tenter St. E1 57 CA39
East Ter., Grav. 81 DH46
East Thurrock Rd., Grays 71 DD43
East Tilbury Rd., S.le H. 71 DJ40
East Twrs., Pnr. 45 BD32
East Vw. E4 39 CF28
East Vw., Barn. 28 BR23
East Vw., Hat. 11 BU12
East Wk., Barn. 38 BV26
East Wk., Hayes 53 BC40
East Wk., Reig. 121 BS70
East Way E11 49 CH32
East Way, Brom. 88 CH54
East Way, Croy. 87 CD55
East Way, Guil. 118 AP70
East Way, Hayes 53 BC40
East Way, Wal.Abb. 30 CF21
East Woodside, Bex. 79 CQ47
Eastbank Rd., Hmptn. 74 BG49
Eastbourne Ave. W3 55 BN39
Eastbourne Gdns. SW14 65 BN45
Eastbourne Ms. W2 56 BT39
Eastbourne Rd. E6 58 CL38
Eastbourne Rd. E15 58 CG37
Eastbourne Rd. N15 48 CA32
Eastbourne Rd. SW17 76 BV50
Eastbourne Rd. W4 65 BN43
Eastbourne Rd., Brent. 64 BK42
Eastbourne Rd., Felt. 74 BD48
Eastbourne Rd., Gdse. 114 CC69
Eastbourne Ter. W2 56 BT39
Eastbournia Ave. N9 39 CB27
Eastbridge, Slou. 52 AQ40
Victoria Rd.
Eastbrook Ave. N9 39 CC26
Eastbrook Ave., Dag. 50 CS35
Eastbrook Dr., Rom. 50 CT34
Eastbrook Rd. SE3 68 CH43
Eastbrook Rd., Wal.Abb. 22 CG20
Eastbury Ave., Bark. 58 CN37
Eastbury Ave., Enf. 30 CA23
Eastbury Ave., Nthwd. 35 BB28
Eastbury Ct., St.Alb. 9 BH13
Lemsford Rd.
Eastbury Gro. W4 65 BO43
Dorchester Gro.
Eastbury Pl., Nthwd. 35 BB28
Eastbury Ave.
Eastbury Rd. E6 58 CL38
Eastbury Rd. W4 65 BO42
Eastbury Rd., Kings.T. 75 BL50
Eastbury Rd., Nthwd. 35 BB28
Eastbury Rd., Orp. 88 CM53
Eastbury Rd., Rom. 50 CS32
Eastbury Rd., Wat. 35 BC26
Eastbury Sq., Bark. 58 CN37
Eastbury Ter. E1 57 CC38
Eastcastle St. W1 1 L8
Eastcastle St. W1 56 BW39
Eastcheap EC3 2 L10
Eastcheap EC3 57 CA40
Eastchurch Rd., Houns. 63 BB44
Eastcombe Ave. SE7 68 CH43
Eastcote, Orp. 88 CN54
Eastcote Ave., E.Mol. 84 BE53
Eastcote Ave., Grnf. 45 BJ35
Eastcote Ave., Har. 45 BF34
Eastcote Gdns., Well. 68 CM44
Eastcote High Rd., Pnr. 44 BC32
Eastcote La., Har. 45 BE35
Eastcote La., Nthlt. 45 BE35
Eastcote La. N., Nthlt. 54 BE36
Eastcote Rd., Har. 45 BG34
Eastcote Rd., Pnr. 45 BD32
Eastcote Rd., Ruis. 44 BB33
Eastcote Rd., Well. 68 CM44
Eastcote St. SW9 66 BX44
Eastcote Vw., Pnr. 45 BD31
Eastcroft Rd., Epsom 94 BO57
Eastdean Ave., Epsom 94 BM60
Eastdene Dr., Rom. 42 CV28
Eastdown Pk. SE13 67 CF45
Eastern Ave., Cher. 83 AW52
Eastern Ave., Grays 70 CZ42
Eastern Ave., Ilf. 49 CH32
Eastern Ave., Pnr. 45 BD33
Eastern Ave., Rom. 50 CQ31
Eastern Ave., S.Ock. 70 CY41
Eastern Ave., Wal.Cr. 21 CD20
Eastern Ave. E., Rom. 41 CT30
Eastern Ave. W., Rom. 50 CQ31
Eastern Gateway Access Rd. E6 58 CL39
Eastern Ind. Est., Belv. 69 CR41
Eastern Perimeter Rd., Houns. 63 BB44
Eastern Rd. E13 58 CH37
Eastern Rd. E17 48 CF32
Eastern Rd. N2 47 BU31
Eastern Rd. N22 38 BX30
Eastern Rd. SE4 67 CE45
Eastern Rd., Grays 71 DE42
Eastern Rd., Rom. 50 CT32
Eastern Vw., West. 106 CJ61
Eastern Way SE28 69 CO41
Eastern Way, Erith 59 CQ40
Eastern Way, Grays 71 DD42
Easternville Gdns., Ilf. 49 CM32
Eastfield Ave., Wat. 27 BD23
Eastfield Clo., Slou. 62 AQ41
Eastfield Ct., St.Alb. 9 BK12
Southfield Way
Eastfield Gdns., Dag. 50 CR35
Eastfield Par., Pot.B. 20 BT19
Forbes Ave.
Eastfield Rd. E17 48 CE31
Eastfield Rd. N8 47 BX31
Eastfield Rd., Brwd. 42 DB27
Eastfield Rd., Dag. 50 CQ35
Eastfield Rd., Enf. 30 CC22
Eastfield Rd., Wal.Cr. 21 CD19
Eastfields, Pnr. 45 BD22
Eastfields Rd. W3 55 BN39
Eastfields Rd., Mitch. 86 BV51
Eastgate, Bans. 94 BR60
Eastgate Clo. SE28 59 CP39
Eastgate Gdns., Guil. 118 AS71
Eastglade, Nthwd. 35 BB28
Easthall La., Rain. 60 CV39
Eastham Cres., Brwd. 122 DD28
Eastholm NW11 47 BS31
Eastington Pl., Guil. 118 AS71
Maori Rd.
Eastlake Rd. SE5 67 BZ44
Eastlands Clo., Oxt. 114 CF67
Eastlands Cres. SE21 77 CA46
Eastlands Way, Oxt. 114 CF67
Eastlea Ave., Wat. 27 BE22
Eastleigh Ave., Har. 45 BF34
Eastleigh Clo. NW2 46 BO34
Eastleigh Clo., Sutt. 95 BS57
Eastleigh Rd., Bexh. 69 CS45
Eastleigh Rd., Felt. 63 BB45
Eastleigh Wk. SW15 75 BP47
Eastman Rd. W3 55 BN40
The Vale
Eastman Way, Hem.H. 8 AZ12
Eastmead, Ruis. 45 BD34
Eastmead Ave., Grnf. 54 BF38
Eastmead Clo., Brom. 88 CK51
Eastmearn Rd. SE21 77 BZ48
Eastminster E1 57 CA40
Royal Mint St.
Eastmont Rd., Esher 84 BH55
Eastmoor Pl. SE7 68 CJ41
Eastmoor St.
Eastmoor St. SE7 68 CJ41
Eastney Rd., Croy. 86 BY54
Eastney St. SE10 67 CF42
Eastnor, Hem.H. 16 AT17
Eastnor Rd. SE9 78 CM47
Eastnor Rd., Reig. 121 BS71
Easton Gdns., Borwd. 28 BO24
Easton St. WC1 2 D3
Easton St. WC1 56 BY38
Eastor, Welw.G.C. 5 BS6
Eastry Ave., Brom. 88 CG53
Eastry Rd., Erith 69 CR43
Eastside Rd. NW11 46 BR31
Eastview Ave. SE18 68 CN43
Eastville Ave. NW11 46 BR32
Eastway E9 57 CD36
Eastway, Epsom 94 BN59
Eastway, Mord. 85 BQ53
Eastway, Ruis. 44 BC33
Eastway, Wall. 95 BW56
Eastwell Clo., Beck. 87 CD51
Kings Hall Rd.
Eastwick Cres., Rick. 34 AV27
Eastwick Dr., Lthd. 102 BF65
Eastwick Hall La., Harl. 6 CL8
Eastwick Pk. Ave., Lthd. 102 BF65
Eastwick Rd., Harl. 6 CM9
Eastwick Rd., Lthd. 111 BF66
Eastwick Rd., Walt. 92 BC57
Eastwick Rd., Ware 6 CK9
Eastwick Row, Hem.H. 8 AZ14
Eastwood Clo. E18 40 CH30
Eastwood Ct., Hem.H. 8 AZ13
Eastwood Dr., Rain. 59 CU39
Eastwood Est. SW15 75 BP46
Eastwood Rd. E18 40 CH30
Eastwood Rd. N10 38 BV30
Eastwood Rd., Ilf. 50 CO33
Eastwood St. SW16 76 BW50
Eastworth Rd., Cher. 83 AW54
Eatington Rd. E10 48 CF32
Eaton Clo. SW1 3 G9
Eaton Clo. SW1 66 BV42
Eaton Clo., Stan. 36 BJ28
Eaton Ct., Guil. 118 AT69
Eaton Dr. SW9 66 BY45
Eaton Dr., Kings.T. 75 BM50
Eaton Dr., Rom. 41 CR29
Eaton Gdns., Dag. 59 CQ36
Eaton Gate SW1 3 G8
Eaton Gate SW1 66 BV42
Eaton Gate, Nthwd. 35 BA29
Eaton La. SW1 3 K7
Eaton La. SW1 66 BV41
Eaton Ms. N. SW1 3 G7
Eaton Ms. N. SW1 66 BV41
Eaton Ms. S. SW1 3 J7
Eaton Ms. S. SW1 66 BV42
Eaton Ms. W. SW1 3 H8
Eaton Ms. W. SW1 66 BV42
Eaton Pk., Cob. 93 BE60
Eaton Pk. Rd. N13 38 BY27
Eaton Pk. Rd., Cob. 93 BE60
Eaton Pl. SW1 3 G7
Eaton Pl. SW1 66 BV41
Eaton Ri. E11 49 CJ32
Eaton Ri. W5 54 BK39
Eaton Rd. NW4 46 BQ32
Eaton Rd., Enf. 30 CA24
Eaton Rd., Hem.H. 8 AZ12
Eaton Rd., Houns. 64 BG45
Eaton Rd., St.Alb. 9 BJ13
Eaton Rd., Sid. 79 CP48
Eaton Rd., Sutt. 95 BT57
Eaton Row SW1 3 J7
Eaton Row SW1 66 BV41
Eaton Sq. SW1 3 H8
Eaton Sq. SW1 66 BV42
Eaton Ter. SW1 3 G8
Eaton Ter. SW1 66 BV42
Eaton Ter. Ms. SW1 3 G8
Eaton Wk. SE15 67 CA44
Sumner Est.
Eaton Way, Dart. 70 CV45
Arundel Rd.
Eatons Mead E4 39 CE27
Eatonville Rd. SW17 76 BU48
Eatonville Vill. SW17 76 BU48
Eatonville Rd.
Ebbas Way, Epsom 103 BM61
Ebberns Rd., Hem.H. 8 AY15
Ebbisham Clo., Dor. 119 BJ71
Ebbisham Dr. SW8 66 BX43
Ebbisham La., Tad. 103 BP64
Ebbisham Rd., Epsom 94 BM60
Ebbisham Rd., Wor.Pk. 85 BQ55
Ebbsfleet Rd. NW2 46 BR35
Ebbsfleet Wk., Grav. 81 DD46
Ebdon Way SE3 68 CH45
Ebenezer St. N1 2 K2
Ebenezer St. N1 57 BZ38
Ebenezer Wk. SW16 86 BW51
Ebley Clo. SE15 67 CA43
St. Georges Way
Ebner St. SW18 76 BS46
Ebor St. E1 2 P4
Ebor St. E1 57 CA38
Ebrington Rd., Har. 45 BK32
Ebsworth St. SE23 77 CC47
Eburne Rd. N7 47 BX34
Ebury App., Rick. 35 AX26
Ebury Rd.
Ebury Bri. SW1 3 J10
Ebury Bri. SW1 66 BV42
Ebury Bri. Est. SW1 3 J10
Ebury Bri. Est. SW1 66 BV42
Ebury Bri. Rd. SW1 66 BV42
Ebury Clo., Kes. 88 CK55
Ebury Clo., Nthwd. 35 BA28
Ebury Ms. SE27 76 BY48
Ebury Ms. SW1 3 J8
Ebury Ms. SW1 66 BV42
Ebury Ms. E. SW1 3 J7
Ebury Rd., Rick. 35 AX26
Ebury Rd., Wat. 27 BD24
Ebury Sq. SW1 3 H9
Ebury Sq. SW1 66 BV42
Ebury St. SW1 3 H9
Ebury St. SW1 66 BV42
Eccles Hill, Dor. 119 BK73
Eccles Rd. SW11 66 BU45
Ecclesbourne Clo. N13 38 BY28
Ecclesbourne Gdns. N13 38 BY28
Ecclesbourne Rd. N1 57 BZ36
Ecclesbourne Rd., Th.Hth. 87 BZ53
Eccleston Bri. SW1 3 K8
Eccleston Bri. SW1 66 BV42
Eccleston Clo., Barn. 29 BU24
Carson Rd.
Eccleston Clo., Orp. 88 CM54
Eccleston Cres., Rom. 50 CO33
Eccleston Ms. SW1 3 H7
Eccleston Ms. SW1 66 BV41
Eccleston Pl. SW1 3 J8
Eccleston Pl. SW1 66 BV42
Eccleston Rd. W13 54 BJ40
Eccleston Sq. SW1 3 K9
Eccleston Sq. SW1 66 BV42
Eccleston Sq. Ms. SW1 3 K9
Eccleston Sq. Ms. SW1 66 BW42
Warwick Pl. N.
Eccleston St. SW1 3 H7
Eccleston St. SW1 66 BV41
Ecclestone Ct., Wem. 46 BL35
Ecclestone Ms., Wem. 46 BL35
Ecclestone Pl., Wem. 46 BL35
Echelforde Dr., Ashf. 73 AZ49
Echo Heights E4 39 CE26
Mount Echo Dr.
Echo Pit Rd., Guil. 118 AS72
Echo Sq., Grav. 81 DH48
Eckersley St. E1 57 CA38
Eckford St. N1 56 BY37
Eckstein Rd. SW11 66 BU45
Eclipse Rd. E13 58 CH39
Ecob Clo., Guil. 109 AP68
Ecton Rd., Wey. 92 AW56
Ector Rd. SE6 78 CG48
Edbrooke Rd. W9 56 BS38
Eddington St. N4 47 BY33
Everleigh St.
Eddiscombe Rd. SW6 65 BR44
Eddy Clo., Rom. 50 CR32
Eddy St., Berk. 7 AQ12
Eddystone Rd. SE4 77 CD46
Eddystone Wk., Stai. 73 AY47
Clare Rd.
Ede Clo., Houns. 64 BE45
Eden Clo. W8 66 BS41
Adam & Eve Ms.
Eden Clo., Bex. 79 CS49
Eden Clo., Slou. 62 AT42
Eden Clo., Wem. 54 BK37
Eden Clo., Wey. 92 AW58
Eden Ct. W5 55 BL39
Station Rd.
Eden Grn., S.Ock. 60 DA39
Eden Gro. E17 48 CE32
Eden Gro. N7 47 BX35
Eden Gro. Rd., Wey. 92 AY60
Eden Ms. SW17 76 BT48
Huntspill St.
Eden Pk. Ave., Beck. 87 CD52
Eden Rd. E17 48 CE32
Eden Rd. SE27 76 BY49
Eden Rd., Beck. 87 CD52
Eden Rd., Bex. 79 CS49
Eden Rd., Croy. 96 BZ56
Eden St., Kings.T. 85 BL51
Eden Way, Beck. 87 CD53
Eden Way, Warl. 105 CD62
Edenbridge Clo., Orp. 89 CP52
Edenbridge Rd. E9 57 CC36
Edenbridge Rd., Enf. 30 CA25
Edencourt Rd. SW16 76 BV50
Edendale Rd., Bexh. 69 CS44
Edenfield Gdns., Wor.Pk. 85 BO55
Edenhall Clo., Hem.H. 8 BA14
Edenhall Clo., Rom. 42 CV28
Edenhall Rd.
Edenhall Glen, Rom. 42 CV28
Edenhall Rd.
Edenhall Rd., Rom. 42 CV28
Edenham Way W10 55 BR39
Elkstone Rd.
Edenhurst Ave. SW6 65 BR45
Edenside Rd., Lthd. 102 BE65
Edensor Gdns. W4 65 BO43
Edensor Rd. W4 65 BO43
Edenvale Rd., Mitch. 76 BV50
Edenvale St. SW6 66 BS44
Ederline Ave. SW16 86 BX52
Edgar Clo., Swan. 89 CT52
Edgar Rd. E3 57 CE38
Edgar Rd., Houns. 74 BE47
Edgar Rd., Rom. 50 CP33
Edgar Rd., Sev. 108 CW62
Edgar Rd., S.Croy. 96 BZ58
Edgar Rd., West Dr. 53 AY40
Edgar Rd., West. 106 CJ64
Edgarley Ter. SW6 65 BR44
Edgars Ct., Welw.G.C. 5 BQ8
Broadwater Cres.
Edgbaston Rd., Wat. 35 BC27
Edge Clo., Wey. 92 AZ57
Edge Fld. Clo., Red. 121 BV73
Edge Hill SE18 68 CL43
Edge Hill SW19 75 BQ50
Edge Hill Ave. N3 47 BS31
Edge Hill Ct. SW19 75 BQ50
Edge St. W8 56 BS40
Edgeborough Way, Brom. 88 CJ51
Edgebury, Chis. 78 CL49
Edgebury Est., Chis. 78 CM49
Edgebury Wk., Chis. 78 CM49
Edgecombe Clo., Kings.T. 75 BN50
Edgecombe Rd. E11 49 CG33
Harvey Rd.
Edgecoombe, S.Croy. 96 CC57
Edgecot Gro. N15 48 CA32
Edgefield Ave., Bark. 58 CN36
Edgefield Clo., Dart. 80 CX47
Edgehill Ct., Walt. 84 BD54
Rodney Rd.
Edgehill Gdns., Dag. 50 CR35
Edgehill Gdns., Grav. 81 DF51

Edg–Elm

Edgehill Rd. W13 54 BJ39
Edgehill Rd., Chis. 78 CM48
Edgehill Rd., Mitch. 86 BV51
Edgehill Rd., Pur. 95 BY58
Edgel St. SW18 66 BS45
Ferrier St.
Edgeley, Lthd. 102 BE65
Edgeley La. SW4 66 BW45
Edgeley Rd. SW4 66 BW45
Edgell Clo., Vir.W. 82 AS52
Edgell Rd., Stai. 72 AV49
Edgepoint Clo. SE27 76 BY49
Knights Hill
Edgewood Dr., Orp. 97 CN58
Edgewood Grn., Croy. 87 CC54
Edgeworth Ave. NW4 46 BP32
Edgeworth Clo. NW4 46 BP32
Edgeworth Clo., Whyt. 105 CB62
Edgeworth Cres. NW4 46 BP32
Edgeworth Rd. SE9 68 CJ45
Edgeworth Rd., Barn. 29 BU24
Edgington Rd. SW16 76 BW50
Edgware Ct., Edg. 37 BM29
Edgware Rd. NW2 46 BP33
Edgware Rd. NW9 37 BN30
Edgware Rd. W2 1 A5
Edgware Rd. W2 56 BT38
Edgware Way, Edg. 36 BK26
Edgwarebury Gdns., Edg. 37 BM28
Edgwarebury La., Borwd. 37 BL26
Edgwarebury La., Edg. 37 BM28
Edinburgh Ave., Rick. 26 AW25
Edinburgh Clo., Uxb. 44 AZ35
Edinburgh Ct. SW20 85 BQ53
Edinburgh Cres., Wal.Cr. 21 CD20
Edinburgh Dr., Stai. 73 AX50
Edinburgh Dr. (Denham), Uxb. 43 AV32
Edinburgh Dr. (Ickenham), Uxb. 44 AZ35
Edinburgh Gdns., Wind. 61 AO44
Edinburgh Gate SW1 3 E5
Edinburgh Gate SW1 66 BU41
Edinburgh Ms., Til. 71 DG44
London Rd.
Edinburgh Pl., Harl. 6 CO9
Edinburgh Rd. E13 58 CH37
Edinburgh Rd. E17 48 CD32
Edinburgh Rd. N18 39 CB28
Edinburgh Rd. W7 64 BH41
Edinburgh Rd., Sutt. 86 BT55
Edinburgh Way, Harl. 6 CN9
Edington Rd. SE2 69 CO41
Edington Rd., Enf. 30 CC23
Edis St. NW1 56 BV37
Edison Ave., Horn. 50 CT33
Edison Clo., Horn. 50 CT33
Edison Dr., Sthl. 54 BF39
Edison Gro. SE18 68 CN43
Edison Rd. N8 47 BW32
Edison Rd., Brom. 88 CH51
Church Rd.
Edison Rd., Well. 68 CN44
Edith Dr. N11 38 BW29
Edith Gdns., Surb. 85 BM54
Edith Gro. SW10 66 BT43
Edith Rd. E6 58 CJ36
Edith Rd. E15 48 CF35
Edith Rd. SE25 87 BZ53
Edith Rd. SW19 76 BS50
Edith Rd. W14 65 BR42
Edith Rd., Orp. 98 CO56
Edith Rd., Rom. 50 CP33
Edith Row SW6 66 BS44
Edith St. E2 57 CA37
Edith Ter. SW10 66 BT43
Edith Yd. SW10 66 BT43
Worlds End
Edithna St. SW9 66 BX45
Ediths Rd., Sev. 108 CX62
Edlyn Clo., Berk. 7 AP12
Edmansons Clo. N17 39 CA30
Bruce Gro.
Edmondscote W13 54 BJ39
Cleveland Rd.
Edmund Beaufort Dr., St.Alb. 9 BH12
Harpenden Rd.
Edmund Rd., Mitch. 86 BU52
Edmund Rd., Orp. 89 CP53
Edmund Rd., Rain. 59 CT38
Edmund Rd., Well. 69 CO45
Edmund St. SE5 67 BZ43
Edmund Way, Slou. 52 AQ39
Edmunds Ave., Orp. 89 CP52
Edmunds Clo., Hayes 54 BD39
Edmunds Wk. N2 47 BU31
Edna Rd. SW20 85 BQ51
Edna St. SW11 66 BU44
Edric Rd. SE14 67 CC43
Edrick Rd., Edg. 37 BN29
Edrick Wk., Edg. 37 BN29
Edridge Clo., Bush. 27 BG25
Edridge Clo., Horn. 51 CV35
Edridge Rd., Croy. 87 BZ55
Edulf Rd., Borwd. 28 BM23
Edward Amey Clo., Wat. 27 BD21
Edward Ave. E4 39 CE29
Edward Ave., Mord. 86 BT53
Edward Clo. N9 39 CA26
Edward Clo., Abb.L. 17 BB19
Edward Clo., Hmptn. 74 BG49
Edward Clo., Nthlt. 54 BD37
Edward Clo., Rom. 51 CV31
Edward Clo., St.Alb. 9 BH14
Edward Ct. E16 58 CH39
Alexandra St.
Edward Ct., Hem.H. 8 AX15
King Edward St.
Edward Ct., Stai. 73 AX50
Elizabeth Ave.
Edward Ct., Wal.Abb. 22 CG20
Ninefields
Edward Gro., Barn. 29 BT25

Edward Ms. NW1 1 K1
Edward Pl. SE8 67 CD43
Edward Rd. E17 48 CC31
Edward Rd. SE20 77 CC50
Edward Rd., Barn. 29 BT24
Edward Rd., Brom. 78 CH50
Edward Rd., Chis. 78 CL49
Edward Rd., Couls. 104 BW61
Edward Rd., Croy. 87 CA54
Edward Rd., Felt. 73 BA46
Edward Rd., Hmptn. 74 BG49
Edward Rd., Har. 45 BG31
Edward Rd., Nthlt. 54 BD37
Edward Rd., Rom. 50 CQ32
Edward Rd., West. 106 CK62
Edward II Ave., Wey. 92 AY60
Edward Sq. N1 56 BX37
Edward St. E16 58 CH38
Edward St. SE8 67 CD43
Edward St. SE14 67 CD43
Edward Temme Ave. E15 58 CG36
Edward Way, Ashf. 73 AY48
Edwardes Sq. W8 65 BR41
Edwards Ave., Ruis. 53 BC36
Edwards Clo., Brwd. 122 DF25
Edwards Clo., Wor.Pk. 85 BQ55
Edwards Cotts. N1 56 BY36
Compton Ave.
Edwards Ct., Slou. 62 AP41
Chalvey Pk.
Edwards Dr. N11 38 BW29
Edwards Gdns., Swan. 89 CS52
Edwards La. N16 48 BZ34
Edwards Ms. W1 1 G9
Kensal Rd.
Edwards Rd., Belv. 69 CR42
Edwards Ter., Ong. 24 CY19
Edwards Way, Brwd. 122 DF25
Edwin Ave. E6 58 CL38
Edwin Clo., Bexh. 69 CQ43
Edwin Clo., Rain. 59 CT38
Edwin Rd., Dart. 79 CU48
Edwin Rd., Edg. 37 BN29
Edwin Rd., Lthd. 110 BA66
Edwin Rd., Twick. 74 BH47
Edwin St. E1 57 CC38
Edwin St. E16 58 CH39
Edwin St., Grav. 81 DG47
Edwina Gdns., Ilf. 49 CK32
Edwins Mead E9 48 CD35
Kings Mead Est.
Edwyn Clo., Barn. 28 BQ25
Effie Pl. SW6 66 BS43
Effie Rd. SW6 66 BS43
Effingham Clo., Sutt. 95 BS57
Effingham Ct., Wok. 100 AS62
Constitution Hill
Effingham Rd. N8 47 BY32
Effingham Rd. SE12 78 CG46
Effingham Rd., Croy. 86 BX54
Effingham Rd., Reig. 121 BS71
Effingham Rd., Surb. 84 BJ54
Effort St. SW17 76 BU49
Effra Clo. SW19 76 BS50
Effra Par. SW2 76 BY46
Effra Rd. SW2 66 BY45
Effra Rd. SW19 76 BS50
Egan Way SE16 67 CB42
Bonamy Est. E.
Egan Way, Hayes 53 BB40
Egbert St. NW1 56 BV36
Egdean Wk., Sev. 108 CV65
Egerton Ave., Swan. 79 CT50
Egerton Clo., Dart. 79 CU47
Egerton Clo., Pnr. 44 BC31
Egerton Cres. SW3 3 D8
Egerton Cres. SW3 66 BU42
Egerton Dr. SE10 67 CE44
Egerton Gdns. NW4 46 BP31
Egerton Gdns. NW10 55 BQ37
Egerton Gdns. SW3 3 C7
Egerton Gdns. SW3 66 BU41
Egerton Gdns. W13 54 BJ39
Egerton Gdns., Ilf. 49 CN34
Egerton Gdns. Ms. SW3 3 D7
Egerton Gdns. Ms. SW3 66 BU41
Egerton Pl. SW3 3 D7
Egerton Pl. SW3 66 BU41
Egerton Pl., Wey. 92 BA57
Egerton Rd. N16 48 CA33
Egerton Rd. SE25 87 CA52
Egerton Rd., Berk. 7 AQ12
Egerton Rd., Guil. 118 AP70
Egerton Rd., N.Mal. 85 BO52
Egerton Rd., Twick. 74 BH46
Egerton Rd., Wem. 55 BL36
Egerton Rd., Wey. 92 BA57
Egerton Ter. SW3 3 D7
Egerton Ter. SW3 66 BU41
Egg Hall, Epp. 23 CO18
Eggpie La., Sev. 117 CV70
Eggpie La., Ton. 117 CV70
Egham By-pass, Egh. 72 AS49
Egham Clo. SW19 75 BR48
Frimley Clo.
Egham Clo. SW19 75 BR48
Winterfold Clo.
Egham Clo., Sutt. 85 BR55
Egham Cres., Sutt. 85 BQ55
Egham Hill, Egh. 72 AR50
Egham Rd. E13 58 CH39
Eglantine La., Hort.K. 90 CX54
Eglantine Rd. SW18 76 BT46
Egleston Rd., Mord. 86 BS53
Egley Dr., Wok. 100 AR64
Egley Rd., Wok. 100 AR64
Eglington Ct. SE17 67 BZ43
Carter St.
Eglington Rd. E4 39 CF26
Eglington Rd., Swans. 81 DC48
Eglinton Hill SE18 68 CL43
Eglinton Rd. SE18 68 CL43
Eglise Rd., Warl. 105 CD62
Egliston Ms. SW15 65 BQ45
Egliston Rd. SW15 65 BQ45

Eglon Ms. NW1 56 BU36
Berkley Rd.
Egmont Ave., Surb. 85 BL54
Egmont Pk. Rd., Tad. 112 BP66
Egmont Rd., N.Mal. 85 BO52
Egmont Rd., Surb. 85 BL54
Egmont Rd., Sutt. 95 BT57
Egmont Rd., Walt. 83 BC54
Egmont St. SE14 67 CC43
Egmont Way, Tad. 103 BR63
Egremont Rd. SE27 76 BY48
Eighth Ave. E12 49 CK35
Eighth Ave., Hayes 53 BC40
Eileen Rd. SE25 87 BZ53
Eisenhower Dr. E6 58 CK39
Elaine Gro. NW5 47 BV35
Elam Clo. SE5 66 BY44
Elam St. SE5 66 BY44
Elan Rd., S.Ock. 60 DA39
Eland Rd. SW11 66 BU45
Eland Rd., Croy. 86 BY55
Elba Pl. SE17 4 J8
Elba Pl. SE17 67 BZ42
Rodney Pl.
Elbe St. SW6 66 BT44
Elberon Ave., Croy. 86 BW53
Elborough Rd. SE25 87 CB53
Elborough St. SW18 76 BS47
Elbow La., Hert. 12 CB11
Elbow Meadow, Slou. 62 AV44
Elbury Dr. E16 58 CH39
Elcho St. SW11 66 BU43
Elcom St. W10 55 BR39
Elcot Ave. SE15 67 CB43
Elder Ave. N8 47 BX32
Elder Clo., Guil. 118 AT69
Sutherland Dr.
Elder Ct., Bush. 36 BH27
Elder Oak Clo. SE20 87 CB51
Elder Rd. SE27 77 BZ49
Elder St. E1 2 P5
Elder St. E1 57 CA39
Elder Wk. N1 56 BY37
Essex Rd.
Elder Way, Dor. 119 BK73
Elder Way, Rain. 60 CV38
Elder Way, Slou. 62 AS41
Waterside Dr.
Elderbeck, Chsnt. 21 CB18
Elderberry Gro. SE27 77 BZ49
Linton Gro.
Elderberry Rd. W5 65 BL41
Elderberry Way, Wat. 26 BC21
Elderfield, Harl. 6 CP9
Elderfield Rd. E5 48 CC35
Elderfield Rd., Slou. 52 AP36
Elderfield Wk. E11 49 CH32
Eldersley Clo., Red. 121 BU69
Elderslie Clo., Beck. 87 CE53
Elderslie Rd. SE9 78 CL46
Elderton Rd. SE26 77 CD49
Eldertree Pl., Mitch. 86 BV51
Eldertree Way, Mitch. 86 BV51
Elderwood Pl. SE27 77 BZ49
Eldon Ave., Borwd. 28 BM23
Eldon Ave., Croy. 87 CC55
Eldon Ave., Houns. 64 BF43
Eldon Gro. NW3 47 BT35
Eldon Pk. SE25 87 CB52
Eldon Rd. E17 48 CD31
Eldon Rd. N9 39 CC27
Eldon Rd. N22 38 BY30
Eldon Rd. W8 66 BS41
Eldon Rd., Cat. 105 BZ64
Eldon Rd., Hodd. 12 CF13
Eldon St. EC2 2 L7
Eldon St. EC2 57 BZ39
Eldon Way NW10 55 BM37
Eldred Dr., Orp. 89 CP54
Eldred Gdns., Upmin. 51 CZ33
Eldred Rd., Bark. 58 CM37
Eldridge Clo., Felt. 73 BC47
Eleanor Ave., Epsom 94 BN58
Eleanor Ave., St.Alb. 9 BG12
Eleanor Clo. SE16 67 CC41
Eleanor Cres. NW7 37 BQ28
Eleanor Cross Rd., Wal.Cr. 21 CD20
Eleanor Gdns., Barn. 28 BQ25
Chesterfield Rd.
Eleanor Gdns., Dag. 50 CQ34
Eleanor Gro. SW13 65 BO45
Eleanor Gro., Uxb. 44 AZ34
Eleanor Rd. E8 57 CB36
Eleanor Rd. E15 58 CG36
Eleanor Rd. N11 38 BX29
Eleanor Rd., Ger.Cr. 34 AR30
Eleanor Rd., Wal.Cr. 21 CD20
Eleanor St. E3 57 CE38
Eleanor Wk. SE18 68 CK42
Samuel St.
Eleanor Way, Brwd. 42 DB28
Eleanor Way, Wal.Cr. 21 CD20
Electric Ave. SW9 66 BY45
Electric La. SW9 66 BY45
Electric Par., Surb. 84 BK53
Elephant & Castle SE1 4 G8
Elephant & Castle SE1 66 BY42
Elephant La. SE16 67 CC41
Elephant Rd. SE17 4 H8
Elephant Rd. SE17 67 BZ42
Elers Rd. W13 64 BK41
Elers Rd., Hayes 63 BA42
Eleven Acre Ri., Loug. 31 CK24
Eley Rd. N18 39 CC28
Eleys Est. N18 39 CC28
Elf Row E1 57 CC40
Elfin Gro., Tedd. 74 BH49
Elfindale Rd. SE24 77 BZ46
Elford Clo. SE3 68 CJ45
Elfort Rd. N5 47 BY34
Elfrida Cres. SE6 77 CE49
Elfrida Rd., Wat. 27 BD25
Elfwine Rd. W7 54 BH39

Elgal Clo., Orp. 97 CL56
Orchard Rd.
Elgar Ave. NW10 55 BN36
Mitchellbrook Way
Elgar Ave. SW16 86 BX52
Elgar Ave. W5 65 BL41
Elgar Ave., Surb. 85 BM54
Elgar Clo. SE8 67 CE43
Elgar Clo., Borwd. 36 BK26
Sullivan Way
Elgar Clo., Buck.H. 40 CJ27
Elgar Clo., Uxb. 44 AZ34
Elgar Gdns., Til. 71 DG44
Elgar St. SE16 67 CD41
Elgin Ave. W9 56 BS38
Elgin Ave., Ashf. 73 BA50
Elgin Ave., Har. 36 BJ30
Elgin Ave., Rom. 42 CX29
Elgin Clo., Nthwd. 35 BB29
Elgin Cres. W11 55 BR40
Elgin Cres., Cat. 105 CB64
Elgin Cres., Houns. 63 BB44
Eastern Perimeter Rd.
Elgin Gdns., Guil. 118 AT70
Bladon Clo.
Elgin Ms. W11 55 BR39
Elgin Ms. N. W9 56 BS38
Elgin Ms. S. W9 56 BS38
Elgin Rd. N22 38 BW30
Elgin Rd., Brox. 12 CD15
Elgin Rd., Chsnt. 21 CC18
Elgin Rd., Croy. 87 CA55
Elgin Rd., Ilf. 49 CN33
Elgin Rd., Sutt. 86 BT55
Elgin Rd., Wall. 95 BW57
Elgin Rd., Wey. 92 AZ56
Elgood Ave., Nthwd. 35 BB29
Elgood Clo. W11 55 BR40
Avondale Pk. Rd.
Elham Clo., Brom. 78 CJ50
Romney Dr.
Elia Ms. N1 2 F1
Elia Ms. N1 56 BY37
Elia St. N1 2 F1
Elia St. N1 56 BY37
Elias Pl. SW8 66 BY43
Elibank Rd. SE9 68 CK45
Elim Est. SE1 4 M6
Elim Est. SE1 67 CA41
Elim Way E13 58 CG38
Eliot Bank SE23 77 CB48
Eliot Cotts. SE3 68 CG44
Eliot Dr., Har. 45 BF34
Eliot Gdns. SW15 65 BP45
Eliot Hill SE13 67 CF44
Eliot Pk. SE13 67 CF44
Eliot Pl. SE3 68 CG44
Eliot Rd., Dag. 50 CP35
Eliot Rd., Dart. 80 CX46
Eliot Vale SE3 67 CF44
Elizabeth Ave. N1 57 BZ37
Elizabeth Ave., Amer. 25 AQ23
Elizabeth Ave., Enf. 29 BY24
Elizabeth Ave., Ilf. 49 CM34
Elizabeth Ave., Stai. 73 AX50
Elizabeth Bri. SW1 3 J9
Elizabeth Bri. SW1 66 BV42
Elizabeth Clo. E14 57 CE39
Grundy St.
Elizabeth Clo., Barn. 28 BQ24
Elizabeth Clo., Rom. 41 CR30
Elizabeth Clo., Til. 71 DG44
London Rd.
Elizabeth Clo., Wal.Abb. 12 CF15
Nazeing Rd.
Elizabeth Clo., Welw.G.C. 5 BT8
Elizabeth Clyde Clo. N15 48 CA31
Lawrence Rd.
Elizabeth Cotts., Rich. 65 BL44
Elizabeth Ct. SW1 3 P7
Elizabeth Ct., Mord. 85 BR54
Dudley Dr.
Elizabeth Ct., St.Alb. 9 BK12
Villiers Cres.
Elizabeth Ct., Wat. 26 BB22
Elizabeth Dr., Epp. 31 CN21
Elizabeth Est. SE17 67 BZ43
Elizabeth Gdns. W3 55 BO40
Elizabeth Gdns., Stan. 36 BK29
Elizabeth Gdns., Sun. 83 BC52
Elizabeth Ms. NW3 56 BU36
Elizabeth Pl. N15 48 BZ31
Elizabeth Ride N9 39 CB26
Elizabeth Rd. E6 58 CJ37
Elizabeth Rd. N15 48 CA32
Elizabeth Rd., Brwd. 33 DA25
Elizabeth Rd., Grays 71 DC41
Elizabeth St. SW1 3 H8
Elizabeth St. SW1 66 BV42
Elizabeth St., Green. 80 CZ46
Elizabeth Ter. SE9 78 CK46
Elizabeth Way SE19 87 BZ51
Elizabeth Way, Felt. 74 BD49
Elizabeth Way, Harl. 13 CK11
Elizabeth Way, Orp. 89 CP53
Elizabeth Way, Slou. 52 AP37
Elizabethan Clo., Stai. 73 AX47
Elizabethan Way, Stai. 73 AX47
Elkington Rd. E13 58 CH38
Elkins, The, Rom. 41 CT30
Elkins Gdns., Guil. 118 AT69
Elkins Rd., Slou. 43 AP34
Elkstone Rd. W10 55 BR39
Ella Rd. N8 47 BX33
Ellaline Rd. W6 65 BQ43
Ellanby Cres. N18 39 CB28
Elland Rd. SE15 67 CC45
Ellement Clo., Pnr. 45 BD32
Ellen Clo., Brom. 88 CJ52
Ellen Ct. N9 39 CC27
Densworth Gro.
Ellen St. E1 57 CB39
Ellenborough Pl. SW15 65 BP45
Ellenborough Rd. N22 38 BY30

Ellenborough Rd., Sid. 79 C
Ellenbridge Way, S.Croy. 96 C
Ellenbrook Cres., Hat. 10 BI
Ellenbrook La., Hat. 10 BI
Elleray Rd., Tedd. 74 B
Ellerby St. SW6 65 B
Ellerdale Clo. NW3 47 B
Ellerdale Rd. NW3 47 B
Ellerdale St. SE13 67 C
Ellerdine Rd., Houns. 64 B
Ellerker Gdns., Rich. 75 B
Ellerman Ave., Twick. 74 B
Ellerman Rd., Til. 71 D
Church Rd.
Ellerslie, Grav. 81 D
Ellerslie Gdns. NW10 55 B
Ellerslie Rd. W12 55 B
Ellerton Gdns., Dag. 59 C
Ellerton Rd. SW13 65 B
Ellerton Rd. SW18 76 B
Ellerton Rd. SW20 75 B
Ellerton Rd., Dag. 59 C
Ellerton Rd., Surb. 85 B
Ellery Rd. SE19 77 B
Ellery St. SE15 67 C
Elles Ave., Guil. 118 A
Ellesborough Clo., Wey. 36 B
Ellesmere Ave. NW7 37 B
Ellesmere Ave., Beck. 87 C
Ellesmere Clo. E11 49 C
Ellesmere Clo., Ruis. 44 B
Ellesmere Dr., S.Croy. 96 C
Ellesmere Gdns., Ilf. 49 C
Ellesmere Gro., Barn. 28 B
Ellesmere Rd. E3 57 C
Ellesmere Rd. NW10 46 B
Ellesmere Rd. W4 65 B
Ellesmere Rd., Berk. 7 A
Ellesmere Rd., Grnf. 54 B
Ellesmere Rd., Twick. 74 B
Ellesmere Rd., Wey. 92 B
Ellesmere St. E14 57 C
Ellice Rd., Oxt. 115 C
Elliman Ave., Slou. 52 A
Ellingfort Rd. E8 57 C
Ellingham Clo., Hem.H. 8 A
Ellingham Rd. E15 48 C
Ellingham Rd. W12 65 B
Ellingham Rd., Chess. 93 B
Ellingham Rd., Hem.H. 8 A
Ellington Rd. N10 47 B
Ellington Rd., Felt. 73 B
Ellington Rd., Houns. 64 B
Ellington St. N7 56 B
Elliot Clo. E15 58 C
Elliot Rd. NW4 46 B
Elliot Rd., Stan. 36 B
Elliott Clo., Wem. 46 B
Elliott Gdns., Rom. 41 C
Elliott Gdns., Shep. 83 A
Elliott Rd. SW9 66 B
Elliott Rd. W4 65 B
Elliott Rd., Brom. 88 C
Elliott Rd., Th.Hth. 86 B
Elliott St., Grav. 81 D
Elliotts Ct. EC4 56 B
Old Bailey
Elliotts Pl. N1 56 B
St. Peters St.
Elliotts Row SE11 4
Elliotts Row SE11 66 B
Ellis Ave., Ger.Cr. 34 A
Ellis Ave., Guil. 118 A
Ellis Ave., Rain. 59 C
Ellis Ave., Slou. 62 A
Ellis Clo. SE9 78 C
Ellis Clo., Couls. 104 B
Ellis Fm. Clo., Wok. 100 A
Ellis Ms. SE7 68 C
Ellis Rd., Couls. 104 B
Ellis Rd., Mitch. 86 B
Ellis St. SW1 3
Ellis St. SW1 66 B
Elliscombe Rd. SE7 68 C
Ellisfield Dr. SW15 75 B
Ellison Clo., Wind. 61 A
Ellison Gdns., Sthl. 64 B
Ellison Rd. SW13 65 B
Ellison Rd. SW16 76 B
Ellison Rd., Sid. 78 C
Ellmore Clo., Rom. 41 C
Ellora Rd. SW16 76 B
Ellsworth St. E2 57 C
Ellwood Gdns., Wat. 17 B
Ellwood Ri., Ch.St.G. 34 A
Elm Ave. W5 55 B
Elm Ave., Ruis. 44 B
Elm Ave., Upmin. 51 C
Elm Ave., Wat. 36 B
Elm Bank Ave., Guil. 118 A
Elm Bank Dr., Brom. 88 C
Sundridge Ave.
Elm Bank Gdns. SW13 65 B
Elm Clo. E11 49 C
Elm Clo. N19 47 B
Hargrave Pk.
Elm Clo. NW4 46 B
Elm Clo. SW20 85 B
Elm Clo., Amer. 25 A
Elm Clo., Buck.H. 40 C
Elm Clo., Cars. 86 B
Elm Clo., Dart. 80 C
Elm Clo., Epp. 13 C
Elm Clo., Har. 45 B
Elm Clo., Hayes 53 B
Elm Clo., Lthd. 102 B
Elm Clo., Rom. 41 C
Elm Clo., S.Croy. 96 B
Elm Clo., Stai. 73 A
Diamedes Ave.
Elm Clo., Stai. 73 A
Diamedes Ave.
Elm Clo., Surb. 85 B

Clo., Twick.	74	BF48	Elm Ter., Grays	70	DA43	Elmington Clo., Bex.	79	CR46	Elsinore Rd. SE23	77	CD47	Embankment Pl. WC2	56	BX40
Clo., Wal.Abb.	21	CF20	Elm Ter., Har.	36	BG29	Elmington Est. SE5	67	BZ43	Elsinore Way, Rich.	65	BM45	*Villiers St.*		
Clo., Warl.	105	CC62	**Elm Tree Clo. NW8**	**1**	**A2**	Elmington Rd. SE5	67	BZ44	Elsley Rd. SW11	66	BU45	Embassy Ct., Sid.	79	CO48
Clo., Wok.	100	AR61	Elm Tree Clo. NW8	56	BT38	Elmira St. SE13	67	CE45	Elspeth Rd. SW11	66	BU45	Ember Clo., Orp.	88	CM54
Clo. (Sendmarsh),	101	AW65	Elm Tree Clo., Ashf.	73	AZ49	Elmlea Dr., Hayes	53	BB39	Elspeth Rd., Wem.	46	BL35	Ember Clo., Wey.	92	AX56
Vok.			Elm Tree Clo., Cher.	82	AV55	*Grange Rd.*			Elsrick Ave., Mord.	86	BS53	Ember Fm. Ave., E.Mol.	84	BG53
Ct. EC4	**2**	**D10**	Elm Tree Gdns., Nthlt.	54	BE37	Elmlee Clo., Chis.	78	CK50	Elstan Way, Croy.	87	CD54	Ember Fm. Way, E.Mol.	84	BG53
Ct. N3	37	BR30	**Elm Tree Rd. NW8**	**1**	**A2**	Elmley Clo. E6	58	CK39	**Elsted St. SE17**	**4**	**L9**	Ember Gdns., T.Ditt.	84	BH53
Ct., Mitch.	86	BU51	Elm Tree Rd. NW8	56	BT38	*Northumberland Rd.*			Elsted St. SE17	67	BZ42	Ember La., E.Mol.	84	BG54
Ct., Wok.	100	AO62	Elm Wk. NW3	47	BS34	Elmley St. SE18	68	CM42	Elstow Clo. SE9	78	CL46	Ember La., Esher	84	BG54
eechwood Rd.			Elm Wk. SW20	85	BQ52	Elmore Clo., Wem.	55	BL37	Elstow Clo., Ruis.	45	BD33	Ember Rd., Slou.	62	AT41
Cres. W5	55	BL40	Elm Wk., Orp.	88	CK55	Elmore Rd. E11	48	CF34	Elstow Gdns., Dag.	59	CQ37	Embercourt Rd., T.Ditt.	84	BH53
Cres., Kings.T.	85	BL51	Elm Wk., Rad.	27	BH21	Elmore Rd., Couls.	104	BU64	Elstow Rd., Dag.	59	CQ36	Emberson Way, Epp.	23	CR16
Cft., Slou.	62	AR44	Elm Wk., Rom.	50	CU31	Elmore Rd., Enf.	30	CC22	Elstree Gdns. N9	39	CB26	Embleton Rd. SE13	67	CE45
Cft. Dr., Ashf.	73	AZ49	Elm Way N11	38	BV29	Elmore St. N1	57	BZ36	Elstree Gdns., Belv.	69	CO42	Embleton Rd., Wat.	35	BC27
Dr., Chsnt.	21	CD17	Elm Way NW10	46	BO35	Elmores, Loug.	31	CL24	Elstree Gdns., Ilf.	49	CM35	Embley Pt. E5	48	CB34
Dr., Har.	45	BF32	Elm Way, Brwd.	42	DA28	Elmroyd Ave., Pot.B.	19	BR20	Elstree Hill, Brom.	78	CG50	*Downs Est.*		
Dr., Hat.	10	BP13	Elm Way, Epsom	94	BN56	Elmroyd Clo., Pot.B.	19	BR20	Elstree Hill N., Borwd.	27	BK25	Embry Clo., Stan.	36	BJ28
Dr., Lthd.	102	BF32	Elm Way, Rick.	35	AW26	Elms, The SW13	65	BO45	Elstree Hill S., Borwd.	36	BK26	Embry Dr., Stan.	36	BJ29
Dr., St.Alb.	9	BK13	Elm Way, Wor.Pk.	85	BQ55	Elms, The, Mord.	85	BO45	Elstree Rd., Borwd.	27	BJ25	Embry Way, Stan.	36	BJ28
Dr., Sun.	84	BU55	Elmar Rd. N15	48	BZ31	Elms, The, Ong.	24	CX18	Elstree Rd., Bush.	36	BQ26	Emden St. SW6	66	BS44
Dr., Swan.	89	CS51	Elmbank N14	38	BX26	*Coopers Hill*			Elstree Rd., Hem.H.	8	AZ10	Emden St. E16	58	CJ39
Dr., Wok.	91	AP58	Elmbank Ave., Barn.	28	BQ24	Elms, The, Slou.	62	AV44	Elstree Rd., Stan.	36	BK27	Emerald Ct., Slou.	62	AP41
Fld., Lthd.	102	BF65	Elmbank Ave., Egh.	72	AQ50	Elms Ave. N10	47	BV31	Elstree Rd., Wat.	27	BH23	*Chalvey Rd. E.*		
Friars Wk. NW1	56	BW36	Elmbank Way W7	54	BG39	Elms Ave. NW4	46	BQ32	Elstree Way, Borwd.	28	BM23	Emerald Clo. E16	58	CJ39
Maiden La.			Elmbourne Dr., Belv.	69	CR42	Elms Ct., Wem.	45	BJ35	Elswick Rd. SE13	67	CE44	Emerald St. WC1	2	B6
Gdns. N2	47	BT31	Elmbourne Rd. SW17	76	BV48	Elms Cres. SW4	76	BW46	Elswick St. SW6	66	BT44	Emerald St. WC1	56	BX39
Gdns., Epp.	30	BZ22	Elmbridge Ave., Surb.	85	BM53	Elms Fm. Rd., Horn.	51	CV35	Elsworthy, T.Ditt.	84	BH53	Emerson Dr., Horn.	51	CV33
Gdns., Epsom	103	BQ63	Elmbridge Clo., Ruis.	44	BC32	Elms Gdns., Dag.	50	CQ35	Elsworthy Ri. NW3	56	BU36	Emerson Gdns., Har.	46	BL32
Gdns., Esher	93	BH57	Elmbridge Dr., Ruis.	44	BB32	Elms Gdns., Wem.	45	BJ35	Elsworthy Rd. NW3	56	BT37	Emerson Rd., Ilf.	49	CL33
Gdns., Mitch.	86	BW52	Elmbridge La., Wok.	100	AS63	Elms Rd., Ger.Cr.	34	AS29	Elsworthy Ter. NW3	56	BU36	**Emerson St. SE1**	**4**	**H2**
Gdns., Welw.G.C.	5	BP8	Elmbridge Rd., Ilf.	41	CO29	Elms Rd., Har.	36	BH29	Elsynge Rd. SW18	76	BT46	Emerson St. SE1	57	BZ40
Grn. W3	55	BO39	Elmbridge Wk. E8	57	CB36	Elms Rd., Wdf.Grn.	102	BE65	Eltham Grn. SE9	78	CJ46	Emersons Ave., Swan.	79	CT50
Grn., Hem.H.	7	AV12	*Wilman Gro.*			**Elms Ms. W2**	**1**	**A10**	Eltham Grn. Rd. SE9	78	CJ45	Emerton Clo., Bexh.	69	CQ45
Gro. N8	47	BX32	Elmbrook Clo., Sun.	83	BC51	Elms Ms. W2	56	BT40	Eltham High St. SE9	78	CK46	Emerton Ct., Berk.	7	AP11
Gro. NW2	46	BQ35	*The Ave.*			Elms Pk. Ave., Wem.	45	BJ35	Eltham Hill SE9	78	CJ46	*Emerton Garth*		
Gro. SE15	67	CA44	Elmbrook Gdns. SE9	68	CK45	Elms Rd. SW4	76	BW46	Eltham Palace Rd. SE9	78	CJ46	Emerton Garth, Berk.	7	AP11
Gro. SW19	75	BR50	Elmbrook Rd., Sutt.	94	BR56	Elms Rd., Ger.Cr.	34	AS29	Eltham Pk. Gdns. SE9	68	CL45	Emerton Rd., Lthd.	102	BG64
Gro., Berk.	7	AR13	Elmcote, Rick.	26	AY25	Elms Rd., Har.	36	BH29	Eltham Pl., Guil.	118	AP69	**Emery Hill St. SW1**	**3**	**M7**
Gro., Cat.	105	CA64	Elmcourt Rd. SE27	76	BY48	Elms Rd., Wal. Lthd.	102	BE65	Eltham Rd. SE9	78	CG46	Emery Hill St. SW1	66	BW41
Gro., Epsom	94	BN60	Elmcroft Ave. E11	49	CH32	Elmscott Gdns. N21	30	BZ25	Eltham Rd. SE12	78	CG46	**Emery St. SE1**	**4**	**E6**
Gro., Erith	69	CS43	Elmcroft Ave. N9	30	CB25	Elmscott Rd., Brom.	68	CF50	Elthiron Rd. SW6	66	BS44	Emery St. SE1	66	BY41
Gro., Har.	45	BF33	Elmcroft Ave. NW11	46	BR33	Elmshaw Rd. SW15	75	BP46	Elthorne Ave. W7	64	BH41	*Morley St.*		
Gro., Horn.	51	CW32	Elmcroft Ave., Sid.	78	CN46	Elmshorn, Epsom	103	BQ61	Elthorne Ct., Felt.	74	BD47	Emes Rd., Erith	69	CS43
Gro., Kings.T.	85	BL51	Elmcroft Clo. E11	49	CH31	Elmshott La., Slou.	61	AM40	Elthorne Pk. Rd. W7	64	BH41	Emily Pl. N7	47	BY35
Gro., Orp.	88	CN54	Elmcroft Clo. W5	54	BK39	Elmside, Croy.	96	CE57	Elthorne Rd. N19	47	BW34	Emily Rd., Wey.	83	AW55
Gro., Sutt.	95	BS56	Elmcroft Clo., Chess.	85	BL55	Elmside, Guil.	118	AQ71	Elthorne Rd. NW9	46	BN33	Emily St. E16	58	CG39
High St.			Elmcroft Clo., Felt.	73	BB46	Elmside Rd., Wem.	46	BM34	Elthorne Rd., Uxb.	53	AX37	*Jude St.*		
Gro., Wat.	26	BC22	Elmcroft Cres. NW11	46	BQ33	Elmsleigh Ave., Har.	45	BJ31	Elthorne Way NW9	46	BN32	Emlyn Gdns. W12	65	BO41
Gro., West Dr.	53	AY40	Elmcroft Cres., Har.	45	BF31	Elmsleigh Ct., Sutt.	86	BS55	Elthruda Rd. SE13	77	CF46	Emlyn La., Lthd.	102	BJ64
Gro. Clo., Wok.	100	AO63	Elmcroft Dr., Chess.	85	BL55	Elmsleigh Rd., Stai.	72	AV49	Eltisley Rd., Ilf.	49	CL35	Emlyn Rd. W12	65	BO41
Gro. Par., Wall.	86	BV55	Elmcroft Gdns. NW9	46	BM32	Elmsleigh Rd., Twick.	74	BG48	Elton Ave., Barn.	28	BR25	Emlyn Rd., Red.	121	BV71
Gro. Rd. SW13	65	BP44	Elmcroft Rd., Orp.	89	CO54	Elmsleigh Rd., Wem.	45	BJ35	Elton Ave., Grnf.	54	BH36	Emma Rd. E13	58	CG37
Gro. Rd. W5	65	BL41	Elmcroft St. E5	48	CC35	Elmslie Clo., Epsom	94	BN60	Elton Ave., Wem.	45	BJ35	Emma St. E2	57	CB37
La. SE6	77	CD48	Elmdale Rd. N13	38	BX28	Elmslie Clo., Wdf.Grn.	40	CK29	Elton Clo., Kings.T.	74	BK50	Emmanuel Clo., Guil.	118	AQ69
La. (Ripley), Wok.	101	AX63	Elmdene, Surb.	85	BN54	Elmstead Ave., Chis.	78	CK49	*Normansfield Ave.*			*Shepherds Hill*		
Lawn Clo., Uxb.	53	AY36	Elmdene Ave., Horn.	51	CW32	Elmstead Ave., Wem.	46	BL33	Elton Clo., Tedd.	74	BK50	Emmanuel Rd. Nthwd.	35	BB29
Ms. W2	66	BT41	Elmdene Clo., Beck.	87	CD53	Elmstead Clo. N20	38	BS27	Elton Pk., Wat.	26	BC23	Emmanuel Rd. SW12	76	BW47
Ms., Rich.	75	BL46	Elmdene Est., Rain.	59	CU36	Elmstead Clo., Epsom	94	BO56	*Langley Rd.*			Emmanuel Rd., Nthwd.	35	BB29
Grove Rd.			Elmdene Rd. SE18	68	CL42	Elmstead Clo., Sev.	107	CT64	Elton Pl. N16	48	CA35	Emmaus Way, Chig.	40	CL28
Nursery Est., Mitch.	86	BV51	Elmdon Rd. (Hatton	63	BB45	Elmstead Cres., Well.	69	CP43	Elton Rd., Kings.T.	85	BL51	Emmott Ave., Ilf.	49	CM32
Pk. SW2	76	BX46	Cross), Felt.			Elmstead Gdns., Wor.Pk.	85	BP55	Elton Rd., Pur.	95	BW59	Emmott Clo. E1	57	CD38
Pk., Stan.	36	BJ28	Elmdon Rd., Houns.	64	BE44	Elmstead Glade, Chis.	78	CK50	Elton Way, Bush.	27	BF23	Emmott Clo. NW11	47	BT32
Pk. Ave. N15	48	CA32	Elmer Ave., Hav.	41	CT27	Elmstead La., Chis.	78	CK50	Eltringham St. SW18	66	BT45	Emnetts Clo., Wok.	100	AR52
Pk. Ave., Horn.	50	CU35	Elmer Clo., Enf.	29	BX24	Elmstead Rd., Erith	69	CT44	*Petergate*			*Kirby Rd.*		
Pk. Ct., Pnr.	45	BD31	Elmer Clo., Rain.	59	CU36	Elmstead Rd., Ilf.	49	CN34	Elvaston Ms. SW7	66	BT41	Emperors Gate SW7	66	BS41
Pk. Gdns. NW4	46	BQ32	Elmer Cotts., Lthd.	102	BJ64	Elmstead Rd., Wey.	92	AW60	Elvaston Pl. SW7	66	BT41	Empire Ave. N18	39	BZ28
Pk. Gdns. SW10	66	BT42	Elmer Gdns., Edg.	37	BM29	Elmswav. Ashf.	73	AY49	Elveden Clo., Wok.	101	AW62	Empire Cen., Wat.	27	BD23
Pk. Gdns. S.Croy.	96	CC58	Elmer Gdns., Islw.	64	BG45	Elmsworth Ave., Houns.	64	BF44	Elveden Pl. NW10	55	BM37	Empire Par. N18	39	BZ29
Pk. La. SW3	66	BT42	Elmer Gdns., Rain.	59	CU36	Elmton Way E5	48	CB34	Elveden Rd. NW10	55	BM37	Empire Rd., Grnf.	54	BJ37
Pk. Mans. SW10	66	BT43	Elmer Rd. SE6	77	CF47	Elmtree Ave., Brwd.	33	CZ22	Elvendon Rd. N13	38	BX29	**Empire Way, Wem.**	46	BL35
Pk. Rd. E10	48	CD33	Elmers Dr., Tedd.	74	BJ50	Elmtree Ave., Esher	84	BG54	Elver Gdns. E2	57	CB38	Empire Wf. Rd. E14	67	CF42
Pk. Rd. N3	37	BR29	Elmers End Rd. SE20	87	CC51	Elmtree Rd., Tedd.	74	BH49	*Avebury Rd.*			Empire Yd. N7	47	BX34
Pk. Rd. N21	39	BZ26	Elmers End Rd., Beck.	87	CC51	Elmway, Grays	71	DE40	Elverson Rd. SE8	67	CE44	Empress Ave. E4	39	CE29
Pk. Rd. SE25	87	CA52	Elmers Rd. SE25	87	CB54	Elmwood, Saw.	6	CQ6	Elverton St. SW1	66	BW42	Empress Ave. E12	49	CJ34
Pk. Rd. SW3	66	BT43	Elmerside Rd., Beck.	87	CD52	Elmwood, Welw.G.C.	5	BP8	Elvet Ave., Rom.	51	CV31	Empress Ave., Ilf.	49	CK34
Pl. SW7	**3**	**A10**	Elmfield Ave. N8	47	BX32	Elmwood Ave. N13	38	BX28	Elvino Rd. SE26	77	CC49	Empress Ave., Wdf.Grn.	40	CG29
Pl. SW7	66	BT42	Elmfield Ave., Mitch.	86	BV51	Elmwood Ave., Borwd.	28	BM24	Elvis Rd. NW2	55	BQ36	Empress Dr., Chis.	78	CL50
Rd. E7	58	CG36	Elmfield Ave., Tedd.	74	BH49	Elmwood Ave., Felt.	73	BC48	Elwell Clo., Egh.	72	AT50	Empress Pl. SW6	66	BS42
Rd. E11	48	CF34	Elmfield Clo., Grav.	81	DG47	Elmwood Ave., Har.	45	BJ32	Elwick Rd., S.Ock.	60	DB39	Empress Rd., Grav.	81	DJ47
Rd. E17	48	CF32	Elmfield Clo., Har.	45	BG34	Elmwood Clo., Ash.	102	BK62	Elwill Way, Beck.	87	CF52	Empress St. SE17	67	BZ43
Rd. N22	38	BY30	*Mount Pk. Ave.*			*Woodfield*			Elwill Way, Grav.	81	DF51	Empson St. E3	57	CE38
Rd. SW14	65	BN45	Elmfield Pk., Brom.	88	CH52	Elmwood Clo., Epsom	94	BP57	Elwin St. E2	57	CA38	Emsworth Clo. N9	39	CC26
Rd., Barn.	28	BR24	Elmfield Rd. E4	39	CF27	Elmwood Clo., Wall.	86	BV55	Elwood St. N5	47	BY34	Emsworth Rd., Ilf.	40	CL30
Rd., Beck.	87	CD51	Elmfield Rd. E17	48	CC32	Elmwood Ct., Wem.	45	BJ34	Elwyn Gdns. SE12	78	CH47	Emsworth St. SW2	76	BX48
Rd., Chess.	93	BK56	Elmfield Rd. N2	47	BT31	Elmwood Cres. NW9	46	BN31	Ely Clo., Amer.	25	AP23	Emu Rd. SW8	66	BV44
Rd., Dart.	80	CV47	Elmfield Rd. SW17	76	BV48	Elmwood Dr., Bex.	79	CQ47	Ely Clo., Erith	69	CT44	Ena Rd. SW16	86	BX52
Rd., Epsom	94	BO57	Elmfield Rd., Brom.	88	CH51	Elmwood Dr., Epsom	94	BP57	Ely Clo., Hat.	10	BO12	Enborne Grn., S.Ock.	60	DA39
Rd., Erith	69	CU44	Elmfield Rd., Pot.B.	19	BR19	Elmwood Gdns. W7	54	BH39	Ely Clo., N.Mal.	85	BO51	Endale Clo., Cars.	86	BU55
Rd., Esher	93	BH57	Elmfield Rd., Sthl.	64	BE41	Elmwood Pk., Ger.Cr.	43	AS33	**Ely Ct. EC1**	**2**	**E7**	Endeavour Rd., Chsnt.	21	CD17
Rd., Felt.	73	BA47	Elmfield Way W9	65	BR38	Elmwood Rd. SE24	77	BZ46	Ely Gdns., Borwd.	28	BN25	Endeavour Way SW19	76	BS49
Rd., Grav.	81	DH48	Elmfield Way, S.Croy.	96	CA58	Elmwood Rd. W4	65	BN43	Ely Gdns., Dag.	50	CS34	Endeavour Way, Bark.	59	CO37
Rd., Grays	71	DE43	Elmgate Ave., Felt.	73	BC48	Elmwood Rd., Croy.	86	BY54	**Ely Pl. EC1**	**2**	**E7**	Endeavour Way, Croy.	86	BW54
Rd., Green.	80	CZ46	Elmgate Gdns., Edg.	37	BN28	Elmwood Rd., Mitch.	86	BU52	Ely Pl. EC1	56	BY39	**Endell St. WC2**	**1**	**Q8**
Rd., Hodd.	12	CE12	Elmgreen Clo. E15	58	CG37	Elmwood Rd., Red.	121	BV69	Ely Pl., Welw.G.C.	5	BR8	Endell St. WC2	56	BX39
Rd., Kings.T.	85	BL51	*Church St. N.*			Elmwood Rd., Slou.	52	AQ40	Ely Pl., Wdf.Grn.	40	CL29	Enderley Clo., Har.	36	BH30
Rd., Lthd.	102	BJ64	Elmgrove Cres., Har.	45	BH32	Elmwood Rd., Wok.	100	AO63	Ely Rd. E10	48	CF32	Enderley Rd., Har.	36	BH30
Rd., N.Mal.	85	BN52	Elmgrove Gdns., Har.	45	BJ32	Elmworth Gro. SE21	77	BZ48	Ely Rd., Croy.	87	BZ53	Enderley St. SE10	68	CG42
Rd., Orp.	98	CO57	Elmgrove Rd., Cob.	102	BD61	Elnathan Ms. W9	56	BS38	Ely Rd., Houns.	63	BB44	Enderby Rd., Barn.	28	BQ25
Rd., Pur.	95	BY60	Elmgrove Rd., Croy.	87	CB54	Elphinstone Rd. E17	39	CD30	*Eastern Perimeter Rd.*			Endersleigh Gdns.	46	BP31
Rd., Red.	121	BU70	Elmgrove Rd., Har.	45	BH32	Elphinstone St. N5	47	BY34	Ely Rd., Houns.	64	BD45	NW4		
Rd., Rom.	41	CR30	Elmgrove Rd., Wey.	83	AZ55	Elrick Clo., Erith	69	CT43	Ely Rd., St.Alb.	9	BJ14	Endlebury Rd. E4	39	CE27
Rd., Sid.	79	CO49	Elmhall Gdns. E11	49	CH32	*Queen St.*			Elyne Rd. N4	47	BY32	Endlesham Rd. SW12	76	BV47
Rd., S.Ock.	60	CY40	Elmhurst, Belv.	69	CQ43	Elrington Rd. E8	57	CB36	Elysian Ave., Orp.	88	CN53	Endsleigh Clo., S.Croy.	96	CC58
Rd., Th.Hth.	87	BZ52	Elmhurst Ave. N2	47	BT31	Elruge Clo., West Dr.	63	AX41	**Elysian Pl. SW6**	65	BR44	**Endsleigh Gdns. WC1**	**1**	**N4**
Rd., Wall.	86	BV54	Elmhurst Ave., Mitch.	76	BV50	Elsa Rd., Well.	69	CO44	*Fulham Pk. Rd.*			Endsleigh Gdns. WC1	56	BW38
Rd., Warl.	105	CC62	Elmhurst Ct., Guil.	118	AS71	Elsa St. E1	57	CD39	Elysium St. SW6	65	BR44	Endsleigh Gdns., Ilf.	49	CK34
Rd., Wem.	46	BL35	*Lower Edgeborough Rd.*			Elsdale St. E9	57	CC36	*Fulham Pk. Gdns.*			Endsleigh Gdns., Surb.	84	BK53
Rd., West.	115	CM66	Elmhurst Dr. E18	40	CH30	Elsden Ms. E2	57	CC37	Elystan Clo., Wall.	95	BV57	Endsleigh Gdns., Walt.	92	BC56
Rd., Wind.	61	AN45	Elmhurst Dr., Dor.	119	BJ72	*Old Ford Rd.*			**Elystan Pl. SW3**	**3**	**D10**	**Endsleigh Pl. WC1**	**1**	**P4**
Rd., Wok.	100	AR62	Elmhurst Dr., Horn.	51	CV33	Elsden Rd. N17	39	CA30	Elystan Pl. SW3	66	BU42	Endsleigh Pl. WC1	56	BW38
Rd. (Horsell), Wok.	100	AS61	Elmhurst Est. N2	47	BT31	Elsdon Rd., Wok.	100	AQ62	**Elystan St. SW3**	**3**	**C9**	Endsleigh Rd. W13	64	BJ40
Rd. W., Sutt.	85	BR54	Elmhurst Gdns. E18	40	CH30	Elsenham Rd. E12	49	CK35	Elystan St. SW3	66	BU42	Endsleigh Rd., Red.	113	BW68
Row NW3	47	BT34	Elmhurst Rd. E7	58	CH36	Elsenham St. SW18	75	BR47	Elystan Wk. N1	56	BY37	Endsleigh Rd., Sthl.	64	BE42
St. WC1	**2**	**C5**	Elmhurst Rd. N17	39	CA30	Elsham Rd. E11	49	CG34	**Endsleigh St. WC1**	**1**	**P4**			
St. WC1	56	BX38	Elmhurst Rd. SE9	78	CK48	Elsham Rd. W14	65	BR41	Emanuel Ave. W3	55	BN39	Endsleigh St. WC1	56	BW38
Ter. NW2	47	BS34	Elmhurst Rd., Enf.	30	CC22	Elsham Ter. W14	65	BR41	Emba St. SE16	67	CB41	Endway, Surb.	85	BM54
Hermitage La.			Elmhurst Rd., Slou.	62	AT41	Elsie Rd. SE22	67	CA45	**Embankment, The SW15**	65	BQ44	Endwell Rd. SE4	67	CD44
Ter. NW3	47	BU35	Elmhurst St. SW4	66	BW45	Elsiedene Rd. N21	39	BZ26	Embankment, The, Stai.	72	AR47	Endymion Rd. N4	47	BY33
South End Grn.			Elmhurst Way, Loug.	40	CK26	Elsiemaud Rd. SE4	77	CD46	Embankment, The, Twick.	74	BJ47	Endymion Rd. SW2	76	BX46
Ter. SE9	78	CL46				Elsinge Rd., Enf.	30	CB22	**Embankment Gdns. SW3**	66	BU43	Endymion Rd., Hat.	10	BQ12
						Elsinore Ave., Stai.	73	AY47	**Embankment Pl. WC2**	**4**	**A2**	Enfield Clo., Uxb.	53	AX37

Enfield Rd. N1 57 CA36
Enfield Rd. W3 65 BM41
Enfield Rd., Brent. 64 BK42
Enfield Rd., Enf. 29 BW24
Enfield Rd., Houns. 63 BB44
Eastern Perimeter Rd.
Enfield Rd. E., Brent. 64 BK42
Enfield Wk., Brent. 64 BK42
Enfield Rd.
Enford St. W1 1 E6
Enford St. W1 56 BU39
Engadine Clo., Croy. 87 CA55
Engadine St. SW18 75 BR47
Engate St. SE13 67 CF45
Engayne Gdns., Upmin. 51 CX33
Engel Pk. NW7 37 BQ29
Engineer Clo. SE18 68 CL43
Engineers Dr., Bush. 27 BF24
Engineers Way, Wem. 46 BM35
Englands La. NW3 56 BU36
Englands La., Loug. 31 CL23
Englefield Clo., Croy. 87 BZ53
Queens Rd.
Englefield Clo., Enf. 29 BY23
Englefield Clo., Orp. 88 CN53
Englefield Cres., Orp. 88 CN52
Englefield Path, Orp. 88 CN52
Englefield Rd. N1 57 BZ36
Englefield Rd., Wok. 100 AO62
Englefield Wk., Egh. 72 AR50
Alexandra Rd.
Engleheart Dr., Felt. 73 BB46
Engleheart Rd. SE6 77 CE47
Englehurst, Egh. 72 AR50
Englewood Rd. SW12 76 BV46
Engliff La., Wok. 100 AV61
English Gdns., Stai. 72 AR46
English Grds. SE1 4 M3
English Grds. SE1 57 CA40
English St. E3 57 CD38
Enid Clo., St.Alb. 18 BE19
Enid St. SE16 4 Q6
Enid St. SE16 67 CA41
Enkel St. N7 47 BX34
Enmore Ave. SE25 87 CB53
Enmore Gdns. SW14 75 BN46
Enmore Rd. SE25 87 CB53
Enmore Rd. SW15 65 BQ45
Enmore Rd., Sthl. 54 BF38
Ennerdale Ave., Horn. 50 CU35
Ennerdale Ave., Stan. 45 BK31
Ennerdale Clo., Felt. 73 BB47
Westmacott Dr.
Ennerdale Clo., St.Alb. 9 BJ14
Ennerdale Clo. (Cheam), Sutt. 94 BR56
Elmbrook Rd.
Ennerdale Dr. NW9 46 BN32
Ennerdale Gdns., Wem. 45 BK33
Ennerdale Rd., Bexh. 69 CR44
Ennerdale Rd., Rich. 65 BL44
Ennersdale Rd. SE13 77 CF46
Ennis Rd. N4 47 BY33
Ennis Rd. SE18 68 CM43
Ennismore Ave. W4 65 BO42
Ennismore Ave., Grnf. 54 BH36
Ennismore Ave., Guil. 118 AS70
Ennismore Gdns. SW7 3 C6
Ennismore Gdns. SW7 66 BU41
Ennismore Gdns., T.Ditt. 84 BH53
Ennismore Gdns. Ms. SW7 3 C6
Ennismore Gdns. Ms. SW7 66 BU41
Ennismore Ms. SW7 3 C6
Ennismore Ms. SW7 66 BU41
Ennismore St. SW7 3 C6
Ennismore St. SW7 66 BU41
Ennismore Gdns.
Ensign Clo., Pur. 95 BY58
Ensign Clo., Stai. 73 AX47
Ensign Dr. N13 39 BZ27
Ensign St. E1 57 CB40
Ensign Way, Stai. 73 AX47
Enslin Rd. SE9 78 CL46
Ensor Ms. SW7 3 A10
Ensor Ms. SW7 66 BT42
Cranley Gdns.
Enstone Rd., Enf. 30 CD24
Enstone Rd., Uxb. 44 AY34
Enterprise Clo., Croy. 86 BY54
Enterprise Way NW10 55 BP38
Hythe Rd.
Enterprise Way SW18 66 BS45
Enterprise Way, Tedd. 74 BJ50
Station Rd.
Enterprize Way SE8 67 CD42
Envis Way, Guil. 118 AO69
Envis Way, Guil. 118 AQ69
Epirus Ms. SW6 66 BS43
Epirus Rd. SW6 65 BR43
Epping Clo. E14 67 CE42
Charnwood Gdns.
Epping Clo., Rom. 50 CR31
Epping Glade E4 30 CF25
Epping Grn., Hem.H. 8 AZ11
Epping La., Rom. 32 CO23
Epping New Rd., Buck.H. 40 CH27
Epping New Rd., Loug. 31 CH25
Epping Pl. N1 56 BY36
Liverpool Rd.
Epping Rd., Epp. 22 CM19
Epping Rd. (Colliers Hatch), Epp. 23 CS18
Epping Rd. (Epping Forest), Epp. 23 CP17
Epping Rd. (Epping Grn.), Epp. 13 CL14
Epping Rd. (Theydon Bois), Epp. 31 CL21
Epping Rd., Harl. 13 CJ12
Epping Rd., Ong. 14 CT15
Epping Way E4 30 CE25
Epple Rd. SW6 65 BR44
Epsom Clo., Bexh. 69 CR45
Epsom Clo., Nthlt. 45 BE35
Epsom Gap, Lthd. 102 BJ61
Epsom La., Epsom 103 BP63
Epsom La. S., Tad. 103 BQ64
Epsom Rd. E10 48 CF32
Epsom Rd., Ash. 103 BL62
Epsom Rd., Croy. 95 BY56
Epsom Rd., Epsom 94 BO59
Epsom Rd., Guil. 118 AS71
Epsom Rd. (East Clandon), Guil. 110 AX69
Epsom Rd., Ilf. 49 CN32
Epsom Rd., Lthd. 102 BJ64
Epsom Rd., Mord. 85 BR54
Epsom Rd., Sutt. 85 BR54
Epsom Sq., Houns. 63 BB44
Eastern Perimeter Rd.
Epsom Way, Horn. 51 CW35
Epstein Rd. SE28 59 CO40
Epworth Pl. EC2 57 BZ38
Epworth St.
Epworth Rd., Islw. 64 BJ43
Epworth St. EC2 2 L5
Epworth St. EC2 57 BZ38
Erasmus St. SW1 3 P9
Erasmus St. SW1 66 BW42
Erconwald St. W12 55 BO39
Eresby Dr., Beck. 87 CE54
Eresby Pl. NW6 56 BS36
Kingsgate Rd.
Eric Clo. E7 49 CH35
Eric Rd. E7 49 CH35
Eric Rd., Rom. 50 CP33
Eric St. E3 57 CD38
Erica Ct., Wok. 100 AR62
Erica Gdns., Croy. 87 CE55
Erica St. W12 55 BP40
Ericcson Clo. SW18 76 BS46
Eridge Rd. W4 65 BN41
Erin Clo., Brom. 78 CG50
Erindale SE18 68 CM43
Erindale Ter. SE18 68 CM43
Eriswell Cres., Walt. 92 BB57
Eriswell Rd., Walt. 92 BB56
Erith Ct., Grays 70 CX42
Erith Cres., Rom. 41 CS30
Erith Rd., Belv. 69 CR42
Erith Rd., Bexh. 69 CR45
Erith Rd., Erith 69 CR44
Erkenwald Clo., Cher. 82 AV53
Erlanger Rd. SE14 67 CC44
Erlesmere Gdns. W13 64 BJ41
Ermine Clo., Chsnt. 21 CB19
Ermine Clo., Houns. 64 BD45
Ermine Clo., St.Alb. 9 BF14
Ermine Rd. N15 48 CA32
Ermine Rd. SE13 67 CE45
Ermine Side, Enf. 30 CB25
Ermington Rd. SE9 78 CM48
Ermyn Clo., Lthd. 102 BK64
Ermyn Way, Lthd. 102 BK64
Ernald Ave. E6 58 CK37
Ernan Clo., S.Ock. 60 DA39
Ernan Rd., S.Ock. 60 DA39
Erncroft Way, Twick. 74 BH46
Ernest Ave. SE27 76 BY49
Ernest Clo., Beck. 87 CE53
Ernest Gdns. W4 65 BM43
Ernest Gro., Beck. 87 CD53
Ernest Rd., Horn. 51 CW32
Ernest Rd., Kings.T. 85 BM51
Ernest Sq., Kings.T. 85 BM51
Ernest St. E1 57 CC38
Ernle Rd. SW20 75 BP50
Ernshaw Pl. SW15 75 BR46
Carlton Dr.
Erpingham Rd. SW15 65 BQ45
Erridge Rd. SW19 86 BS51
Erriff Dr., S.Ock. 60 CZ39
Errington Clo., Grays 71 DG41
Cedar Rd.
Errington Dr., Wind. 61 AN44
Errington Rd. W9 55 BR38
Errol Gdns., Hayes 53 BC38
Errol Gdns., N.Mal. 85 BP52
Errol St. EC1 2 J5
Errol St. EC1 57 BZ38
Erroll Rd., Rom. 50 CT31
Erskine Clo., Sutt. 86 BU55
Erskine Cres. N17 48 CB31
Erskine Hill NW11 47 BS32
Erskine Ms. NW3 56 BU36
Ainger Rd.
Erskine Rd. E17 48 CD31
Erskine Rd. NW3 56 BU36
Erskine Rd., Sutt. 95 BT56
Erwood Rd. SE7 68 CK42
Esam Way SW16 76 BY49
Escombe Dr., Guil. 109 AQ68
Escot Way, Barn. 28 BQ25
Escott Gdns. SE9 78 CK49
Escott Pl., Cher. 91 AU57
Escreet Gro. SE18 68 CL42
Esdaile Gdns., Upmin. 51 CY33
Esdaile La., Hodd. 12 CE12
Esher Ave., Rom. 50 CS32
Esher Ave., Sutt. 85 BQ55
Esher Ave., Walt. 83 BC54
Esher Clo., Bex. 79 CQ47
Esher Clo., Esher 93 BF56
Esher Cres., Houns. 63 BB44
Eastern Perimeter Rd.
Esher Gdns. SW19 75 BQ48
Esher Grn., Esher 93 BF56
Esher Ms., Mitch. 86 BU52
Esher Pk. Ave., Esher 93 BF56
Esher Pl. Ave., Esher 93 BF56
Esher Rd., E.Mol. 84 BG53
Esher Rd., Ilf. 49 CN34
Esher Rd., Walt. 93 BE56
Esk Rd. E13 58 CH38
Esk Way, Rom. 41 CS29
Eskdale, Hem.H. 8 AY12
Lonsdale
Eskdale, St.Alb. 19 BL17
Thamesdale
Eskdale Ave., Chesh. 16 AO18
Eskdale Ave., Nthlt. 54 BE37
Eskdale Clo., Dart. 80 CY47
Eskdale Clo., Wem. 45 BK34
Eskdale Gdns., Maid. 61 AG42
Eskdale Gdns., Pur. 96 BZ60
Eskdale Rd., Bexh. 69 CR44
Eskdale Rd., Uxb. 53 AW37
Eskley Gdns., S.Ock. 60 DA39
Eskmont Ridge SE19 77 CA50
Esmar Cres. NW9 46 BP33
Esmeralda Rd. SE1 67 CB42
Esmond Clo., Rain. 59 CU36
Esmond Gdns. W5 64 BK41
St. Marys Rd.
Esmond Rd. NW6 55 BR37
Esmond Rd. W4 65 BN42
Esmond St. SW15 65 BR45
Esparto St. SW18 76 BS47
Essenden Clo., Belv. 69 CR42
Essenden Rd., Belv. 69 CR42
Essenden Rd., S.Croy. 96 BZ57
Essendene Rd., Cat. 105 CA65
Essendine Rd. W9 56 BS38
Essendon Clo., Hat. 11 BU12
Essendon Gdns., Welw.G.C. 5 BR8
Essendon Hill, Hat. 11 BU12
Essendon Rd., Hert. 11 BV11
Essex Ave., Islw. 64 BH45
Essex Ave., Slou. 52 AO39
Essex Clo. E17 48 CC31
Essex Clo., Mord. 85 BQ54
Essex Clo., Rom. 50 CR31
Essex Clo., Ruis. 45 BD33
Essex Clo., Wey. 92 AX56
Garfield Rd.
Essex Ct. EC4 2 D9
Essex Ct. EC4 56 BY39
Middle Temple La.
Essex Ct. SW13 65 BO44
Essex Gdns. N4 47 BY32
Rutland Gdns.
Essex Gdns., Horn. 51 CX32
Essex Gdns., S.le H. 71 DK41
Somerset Rd.
Essex Gro. SE19 77 BZ50
Essex La., Kings L. 17 BA20
Essex Mead, Hem.H. 8 AY10
Essex Pk. N3 38 BS29
Essex Pk. Ms. W3 55 BO40
Essex Pl. W4 65 BN42
Essex Rd. E4 40 CG26
Essex Rd. E10 48 CF32
Essex Rd. E12 49 CK35
Essex Rd. E17 48 CD32
Essex Rd. E18 40 CH30
Essex Rd. N1 56 BY37
Essex Rd. NW10 55 BO36
Essex Rd. W3 55 BN40
Essex Rd. W4 65 BN42
Belmont Rd.
Essex Rd., Bark. 58 CM36
Essex Rd., Borwd. 28 BM24
Essex Rd., Dag. 50 CS35
Essex Rd., Dart. 80 CV46
Essex Rd., Enf. 30 BZ24
Essex Rd., Grav. 81 DG47
Essex Rd., Grays 70 DA43
Essex Rd., Hodd. 12 CE11
Essex Rd., Long. 90 DB51
Essex Rd., Rom. 50 CR31
Essex Rd. (Chadwell Heath), Rom. 50 CP33
Essex Rd., Wat. 26 BC23
Essex Rd. S. E11 48 CF33
Essex St. E7 49 CH35
Essex St. WC2 2 D10
Essex St. WC2 56 BY39
Essex St., St.Alb. 9 BH13
Essex Vill. W8 66 BS41
Essex Way, Brwd. 42 DB29
Essex Wf. E5 48 CC34
Essian St. E1 57 CD39
Essoldo Way, Edg. 46 BL31
Queensbury Sta. Par.
Estate Way E10 48 CE33
Estcourt Rd. SE25 87 CB53
Estcourt Rd. SW6 65 BR43
Estcourt Rd., Wat. 27 BD24
Este Rd. SW11 66 BU45
Estella Ave., N.Mal. 85 BP52
Estelle Rd. NW3 47 BU35
Esterbrooke St. SW1 3 N9
Esterbrooke St. SW1 66 BW42
Esther Clo. N21 38 BY26
Esther Rd. E11 49 CG33
Estreham Rd. SW16 76 BW50
Estridge Clo., Houns. 64 BF45
Eswyn Rd. SW17 76 BU49
Etchingham Ct. N12 38 BS29
Etchingham Pk. Rd. N3 38 BS29
Etchingham Rd. E15 48 CF35
Eternit Wk. SW6 65 BQ44
Etfield Gro., Sid. 79 CO49
Ethel Rankin Ct. SW6 65 BR44
Fulham Rd.
Ethel Rd. E16 58 CH39
Ethel Rd., Ashf. 73 AY49
Ethel St. SE17 4 J9
Ethel Ter., Orp. 98 CP58
Ethelbert Clo., Brom. 88 CH52
Ethelbert Gdns., Ilf. 49 CK32
Ethelbert Rd. SW20 85 BQ51
Ethelbert Rd., Brom. 88 CH52
Ethelbert Rd., Dart. 80 CW49
Ethelbert Rd., Erith 69 CS43
Hengist Rd.
Ethelbert Rd., Orp. 89 CP52
Ethelbert St. SW12 76 BV47
Fernlea Rd.
Ethelburga Rd., Rom. 42 CW30
Ethelburga St. SW11 66 BU44
Ethelden Rd. W12 55 BP40
Etheldene Ave. N10 47 BW31
Ethelred Clo., Welw.G.C. 5 BR8
Etheridge Grn., Loug. 31 CM24
Etheridge Rd. NW4 46 BQ33
Prince Charles Dr.
Etheridge Rd., Loug. 31 CL23
Etherley Rd. N15 48 BZ32
Etherow St. SE22 77 CB46
Etherstone Grn. SW16 76 BX49
Etherstone Rd. SW16 76 BY49
Ethnard Rd. SE15 67 CB43
Ethorpe Clo., Ger.Cr. 43 AS32
Ethronvi Rd., Bexh. 69 CQ45
Etloe Rd. E10 48 CE34
Wiseman Rd.
Etna Rd., St.Alb. 9 BG13
Eton Ave. N12 38 BT29
Eton Ave. NW3 56 BT36
Eton Ave., Barn. 29 BU25
Eton Ave., Houns. 64 BE43
Eton Ave., N.Mal. 85 BN53
Eton Ave., Wem. 45 BJ35
Eton Clo., Slou. 62 AQ43
Eton College Rd. NW3 56 BU36
Eton Ct., Stai. 72 AV49
Eton Ct., Wem. 45 BK35
Eton Ct. (Eton), Wind. 61 AO43
Eton Garages NW3 56 BU36
Lambolle Pl.
Eton Gro. NW9 46 BM31
Eton Gro. SE13 68 CG45
Eton Ho. SW11 66 BT44
Eton Pl. NW3 56 BU36
Eton Rd. NW3 56 BU36
Eton Rd., Hayes 63 BB43
Eton Rd., Ilf. 49 CM35
Eton Rd., Orp. 98 CO56
Eton Rd., Slou. 62 AP42
Eton Sq. (Eton), Wind. 61 AO43
Eton St., Rich. 75 BL46
Eton Vill. NW3 56 BU36
Eton Wick Rd. (Eton Wick), Wind. 61 AN42
Etta St. SE8 67 CD43
Etton Clo., Horn. 51 CW34
Ettrick St. E14 57 CF39
Etwell Pl., Surb. 85 BL53
Euclid Way, Grays 70 CZ42
Eugene Clo., Rom. 51 CV31
Eugenia Rd. SE16 67 CC42
Eunice Gro., Chesh. 16 AO19
Eureka Rd., Kings.T. 85 BM51
Europa Pl. EC1 2 H3
Europa Pl. EC1 57 BZ38
Lever St.
Europa Rd., Hem.H. 8 AY12
Europe Rd. SE18 68 CK41
Eustace Pl. SE18 68 CK42
Eustace Rd. E6 58 CK38
Eustace Rd. SW6 66 BS43
Eustace Rd., Guil. 118 AU69
Eustace Rd., Rom. 50 CP33
Euston Ave., Wat. 26 BB25
Euston Gro. NW1 1 N3
Euston Gro. NW1 56 BW38
Euston Rd. NW1 1 K5
Euston Rd. NW1 56 BW38
Euston Rd., Croy. 86 BX54
Euston Sq. NW1 1 N3
Euston Sq. NW1 56 BW38
Euston Sta. Colonnade NW1 1 N3
Euston St. NW1 1 M3
Euston St. NW1 56 BW38
Eva Rd., Rom. 50 CP33
Evandale Rd. SW9 66 BY44
Evangelist Rd. NW5 47 BV35
Evans Ave., Wat. 26 BB21
Evans Clo. E8 57 CA36
Forest Rd.
Evans Clo., Green. 80 DA46
Evans Clo., Rick. 26 AZ25
Evans Dale, Rain. 59 CT38
Evans Gro., Felt. 74 BF48
Evans Gro., St.Alb. 9 BK11
Evans Rd. SE6 78 CG48
Evanston Ave. E4 39 CF29
Evanston Gdns., Ilf. 49 CK32
Eve Rd. E11 49 CG35
Eve Rd. E15 58 CG37
Eve Rd. N17 48 CA31
Eve Rd., Islw. 64 BJ45
Eve Rd., Wok. 100 AT61
Evelina Rd. SE15 67 CC45
Evelina Rd. SE20 77 CC50
Eveline Rd., Mitch. 86 BU51
Evelyn Ave. NW9 46 BN31
Evelyn Ave., Ruis. 44 BB33
Evelyn Clo., Twick. 74 BF47
Evelyn Clo., Wok. 100 AR63
Evelyn Ct. N1 2 K1
Evelyn Ct. N1 57 BZ37
Evelyn Cres., Sun. 83 BB51
Evelyn Dennington Rd. E6 58 CK39
Evelyn Dr., Pnr. 36 BD29
Evelyn Gdns. SW7 66 BT42
Evelyn Gdns., Gdse. 114 CC68
Evelyn Gdns., Rich. 65 BL45
Kew Rd.
Evelyn Gro. W5 55 BL40
Evelyn Gro., Sthl. 54 BE39
Evelyn Rd. E16 58 CH40
Evelyn Rd. E17 48 CF31
Evelyn Rd. SW19 76 BS49
Evelyn Rd. W4 65 BN41
Evelyn Rd., Barn. 29 BU24
Evelyn Rd., Rich. 65 BL45
Evelyn Rd. (Ham), Rich. 74 BK48
Evelyn Rd., Sev. 108 C
Evelyn Sharp Clo., Rom. 51 C
Evelyn St. SE8 67 C
Evelyn Ter., Rich. 65 B
Evelyn Wk. N1 2
Evelyn Wk. N1 57 B
Evelyn Wk., Brwd. 42 D
Evelyn Way, Cob. 102 B
Evelyn Way, Sun. 83 B
Evelyn Way, Wall. 95 BV
Evelyn Yd. W1 1
Evelyns Clo., Uxb. 53 A
Evening Hill, Beck. 77 C
Evenwood Clo. SW15 75 B
Everard Ave., Brom. 88 C
Everard Ave., Slou. 62 A
Everard Clo., St.Alb. 9 B
Everard La., Cat. 105 C
Everard Way, Wem. 46 B
Everatt Clo. SW18 75 B
Amerland Rd.
Everdon Rd. SW13 65 B
Everest Clo., Grav. 81 D
Everest Ct., Wok. 100 A
Everest Pl. E14 57 C
Everest Pl., Swan. 89 C
Everest Rd. SE9 78 C
Everest Rd., Stai. 73 A
Everest Way, Hem.H. 8 A
Everett Clo., Pnr. 44 B
Wiltshire La.
Everett Wk., Belv. 69 C
Osborne Rd.
Everglade, West. 106 C
Everglade Strand NW9 37 BC
Evergreen Oak Ave., Wind. 62 AC
Evergreen Way, Hayes 53 B
Evergreen Way, Stai. 73 A
Diamedes Ave.
Everilda St. N1 56 B
Evering Rd. E5 48 C
Evering Rd. N16 48 C
Everington Rd. N10 38 B
Everington St. W6 65 BC
Everitt Rd. NW10 55 B
Everlands Clo., Wok. 100 A
Everlasting La., St.Alb. 9 BC
Everleigh St. N4 47 B
Eversfield Gdns. NW7 37 BC
Eversfield Rd., Reig. 121 B
Eversfield Rd., Rich. 65 B
Eversham Wk. SW9 66 B
Myatts Flds. Dev.
Eversholt St. NW1 56 BW
Evershot Rd. N4 47 B
Eversleigh Gdns., Upmin. 51 C
Eversleigh Rd. E6 58 C
Eversleigh Rd. N3 37 B
Eversleigh Rd. SW11 66 B
Eversleigh Rd., Barn. 29 B
Eversley Ave., Bexh. 69 C
Eversley Ave., Wem. 46 B
Eversley Clo. N21 29 BX
Eversley Clo., Egh. 82 A
Eversley Cres. N21 29 BX
Eversley Cres., Islw. 64 BG
Eversley Cres., Ruis. 44 BB
Eversley Cross, Bexh. 69 C
Eversley Mt. N21 29 B
Eversley Pk. SW19 75 B
Eversley Pk. Rd. N21 29 B
Eversley Rd. SE7 68 CH
Eversley Rd. SE19 77 BZ
Eversley Rd., Surb. 85 BL
Eversley Way, Croy. 87 CE
Everthorpe Rd. SE15 67 C
Everton Bldgs. NW1 1
Everton Bldgs. NW1 56 BW
Stanhope St.
Everton Dr., Stan. 46 BL
Everton Rd., Croy. 87 CB
Evesham Ave. E17 39 CE
Evesham Clo., Grnf. 54 BF
Evesham Clo., Reig. 120 BR
Evesham Clo., Sutt. 95 BS
Evesham Grn., Mord. 86 BS
Evesham Rd. E15 58 CG
Evesham Rd. N11 38 BW
Evesham Rd., Felt. 74 BD
Evesham Rd., Grav. 81 DH
Evesham Rd., Mord. 86 BS
Evesham Rd., Reig. 120 BR
Evesham Rd. N., Reig. 120 BR
Evesham St. W11 55 BO
Evesham Wk. SE5 66 BY
Love Wk.
Evesham Way SW11 66 BV
Evesham Way, Ilf. 49 CL
Evreham Rd., Iver 52 AV
Evry Rd., Sid. 79 CP
Ewald Rd. SW6 65 BR
Ewanrigg Ter., Wdf.Grn. 40 CJ
Ewart Gro. N22 38 BX
Ewart Rd. SE23 77 CC
Ewe Clo. N7 56 BX
Ewell By-pass, Epsom 94 BP
Ewell Ct. Ave., Epsom 94 BO
Ewell Downs Rd., Epsom 94 BP
Ewell Ho. Gro., Epsom 94 BO
Ewell Pk. Way, Epsom 94 BP
Ewell Rd., Surb. 85 BL
Ewell Rd. (Long Ditton), Surb. 84 BJ
Ewell Rd., Sutt. 94 BQ
Ewellhurst Rd., Ilf. 40 CK
Ewelme Rd. SE23 77 CC
Ewen Cres. SW2 76 BY
Ewer St. SE1 4
Ewer St. SE1 57 BZ
Ewhurst Ave., S.Croy. 96 CA
Ewhurst Clo., Sutt. 94 BQ
Ewhurst Rd. SE4 77 CD

:bury Rd. SE6 77 CD48
xcel Ct. WC2 3 P1
:celsior Clo., Kings.T. 85 BM51
Washington Rd.
:celsior Gdns. SE13 67 CF44
Lewisham Rd.
xchange Arc. EC2 2 N6
xchange Bldgs. E1 57 CA39
Cutler St.
xchange Ct. WC2 4 A1
xchange Pl. EC2 2 M6
xchange Rd., Wat. 26 BC24
xchange St., Rom. 50 CT32
xedown Rd., Sev. 108 DB61
xeforde Ave., Ashf. 73 AZ49
xeter Clo. E6 58 CK39
xeter Gdns., Ilf. 49 CK33
xeter Ho. SW15 75 BQ46
xeter Pl., Guil. 118 AP69
xeter Rd. E16 58 CH39
xeter Rd. E17 48 CE32
xeter Rd. N9 39 CC27
xeter Rd. N14 38 BV26
xeter Rd. NW2 46 BR35
xeter Rd. SE15 67 CA44
xeter Rd., Croy. 87 CA54
xeter Rd., Dag. 59 CR36
xeter Rd., Enf. 30 CC24
xeter Rd., Felt. 74 BE48
xeter Rd., Grav. 81 DH48
xeter Rd., Har. 45 BE34
xeter Rd., Well. 68 CN44
xeter St. WC2 2 A10
xeter St. WC2 56 BX40
xeter Way SE14 67 CD43
New Cross Sta.
xford Gdns. SE12 78 CH47
xford Rd. SE12 78 CH48
xhibition Clo. W12 55 BQ40
White City Clo.
xhibition Rd. SW7 3 B6
xhibition Rd. SW7 66 BT41
xmoor Clo., Ilf. 40 CM30
xmoor St. W10 55 BQ39
xmouth Mkt. EC1 2 D4
xmouth Mkt. EC1 56 BY38
xmouth Ms. NW1 1 M3
xmouth Rd. E17 48 CD32
xmouth Rd., Brom. 88 CH52
xmouth Rd., Grays 71 DD43
xmouth Rd., Hayes 53 BB38
xmouth Rd., Ruis. 45 BD34
xmouth Rd., Well. 69 CO43
xmouth St. E1 57 CC39
xning Rd. E16 58 CG38
xon St. SE17 4 M9
xon St. SE17 67 CA42
xplorer Ave., Stai. 73 AY47
xton Cres. NW10 55 BN36
xton Gdns., Dag. 50 CP35
xton St. SE1 4 D3
xton St. SE1 56 BY40
yebright Clo., Croy. 87 CC54
Primrose La.
yethorne Rd. SW9 66 BY44
yhurst Ave., Horn. 50 CU34
yhurst Clo. NW2 46 BP34
yhurst Clo., Tad. 103 BR65
yhurst Spur, Tad. 103 BR65
ylewood Rd. SE27 77 BZ49
ynella Rd. SE22 77 CA47
ynham Rd. W12 55 BQ39
ynsford Clo., Orp. 88 CN54
ynsford Cres., Bex. 79 CP47
ynsford Ri., Eyns. 99 CV56
ynsford Rd., Farn. 90 CW54
ynsford Rd., Green. 80 DB46
ynsford Rd., Ilf. 49 CN34
ynsford Rd., Sev. 98 CU59
ynsford Rd., Swan. 89 CS53
ynsford Ter., West Dr. 53 AY39
Royal La.
ynsham Bri. SE2 69 CO42
ynsham Dr. SE2 69 CO41
ynswood Dr., Sid. 79 CO49
yot Gdns. W6 65 BO42
yre Clo. NW8 56 BT37
yre Clo., Rom. 51 CV31
yre St. Hill EC1 2 D5
yre St. Hill EC1 56 BY38
ythorne Rd. SW9 66 BY44
ywood Rd., St.Alb. 9 BG14
zra St. E2 2 Q2
zra St. E2 57 CA38

F

aber Gdns. NW4 46 BP32
abian Rd. SW6 65 BR43
abian St. E6 58 CK38
ackenden La., Sev. 98 CU60
actory La. N17 39 CA30
actory La., Croy. 86 BY54
actory Path, Stai. 72 AV49
actory Pl. E14 67 CF42
actory Rd. E16 58 CK40
actory Rd., Grav. 81 DE46
actory Sq. SW16 76 BX50
actory Yd. W7 54 BH40
aesten Way, Bex. 79 CT48
aggoters La., Harl. 6 CS9
aggoters La., Ong. 14 CT11
aggots Clo., Rad. 27 BJ21
aggs Rd., Felt. 63 BB45
agus Ave., Rain. 60 CV38
air Acre, Hem.H. 8 AY15
air Acres, Brom. 88 CH53
air Acres, Wind. 61 AL44
air Clo., Bush. 36 BF26

Fair Grn., Saw. 6 CQ6
Fair La., Couls. 113 BT66
Fair Lawn, Lthd. 102 BE65
Fair Lawns, Wey. 91 AV59
Fair St. SE1 4 N4
Fair St. SE1 67 CA41
Fair St., Houns. 64 BG45
Fair Vw., Cob. 102 BD61
Fairacre, Islw. 64 BG44
Fairacre, N.Mal. 85 BO52
Fairacres SW15 65 BP45
Fairacres, Cob. 93 BD59
Fairacres, Croy. 96 CD58
Fairacres, Ruis. 44 BB33
Fairacres, Tad. 103 BQ64
Fairacres Clo., Pot.B. 19 BR20
Fairbairn Clo., Pur. 95 BY60
Beaumont Rd.
Fairbairn Grn. SW9 66 BY44
Fairbank Ave., Orp. 88 CL55
Fairbank Clo., Ong. 24 CW18
Fairbanks Rd. N17 48 CA31
Fairbourne, Cob. 93 BD60
Fairbourne Clo., Wok. 100 AQ62
Shilburn Way
Fairbourne La., Cat. 105 BZ64
Fairbourne Rd. N17 48 CA31
Fairbridge Rd. N19 47 BW34
Fairbrook Clo. N13 38 BY28
Fairbrook Rd. N13 38 BY29
Tottenhall Rd.
Fairburn Clo., Borwd. 28 BM23
Fairby La., Hartley 90 DC53
Fairby Rd. SE12 78 CH46
Fairchild Pl. EC2 2 N5
Fairchild St. EC2 2 N5
Fairchildes, Warl. 97 CG60
Fairchildes Ave., Croy. 96 CF59
Fairchildes Rd., Warl. 96 CF60
Fairclough St. E1 57 CB39
Faircross Ave., Bark. 58 CM36
Faircross Ave., Rom. 41 CS29
Faircross Way, St.Alb. 9 BJ12
Fairdale Gdns. SW15 65 BP45
Fairdale Gdns., Hayes 53 BC40
Fairdene Rd., Couls. 104 BW62
Fairey Ave., Hayes 63 BB42
Fairfax Ave., Epsom 94 BP58
Fairfax Ave., Red. 121 BU70
Fairfax Clo., Walt. 83 BC54
Fairfax Gdns. SE3 68 CJ44
Fairfax Pl. NW6 56 BT36
Fairfax Rd. N8 47 BY31
Fairfax Rd. NW6 56 BT36
Fairfax Rd. W4 65 BO41
Fairfax Rd., Grays 71 DD42
Fairfax Rd., Tedd. 74 BJ50
Fairfax Rd., Til. 71 DF44
Fairfax Rd., Wok. 100 AT63
Fairfax Ter., Sthl. 64 BE42
Fairfield, Lthd. 111 BF66
Fairfield App., Stai. 72 AR46
Fairfield Ave. NW4 46 BP32
Fairfield Ave., Edg. 37 BM29
Fairfield Ave., Grays 71 DE40
Fairfield Ave., Ruis. 44 BA33
Fairfield Ave., Slou. 62 AR43
Fairfield Ave., Stai. 72 AV49
Fairfield Ave., Twick. 74 BF47
Fairfield Ave., Upmin. 51 CY35
Fairfield Ave., Wat. 36 BD27
Fairfield Clo. N12 38 BT28
Fairfield Clo., Dor. 119 BJ70
Fairfield Clo., Enf. 30 CD25
Scotland Grn. Rd. N.
Fairfield Clo., Epsom 94 BO56
Fairfield Clo., Hat. 10 BQ11
Lockley Cres.
Fairfield Clo., Mitch. 76 BU50
Fairfield Clo., Nthwd. 35 BA29
Rickmansworth Rd.
Fairfield Clo., Rad. 27 BH22
Fairfield Clo., Rom. 50 CU33
Fairfield Clo., Sev. 108 CX62
Fairfield Clo., Sid. 78 CN46
Fairfield Clo., Slou. 62 AR43
Fairfield Cotts., Lthd. 111 BF66
Fairfield Ct. NW10 55 BP37
Longstone Ave.
Fairfield Ct., Wdf.Grn. 40 CH29
Fairfield Rd.
Fairfield Cres., Edg. 37 BM29
Fairfield Dr. SW18 76 BS46
Fairfield Dr., Brox. 12 CD15
Fairfield Dr., Dor. 119 BJ70
Fairfield Dr., Grnf. 54 BK37
Fairfield Dr., Har. 45 BG31
Fairfield E., Kings.T. 85 BL51
Fairfield Gdns. N8 47 BX32
Elder Ave.
Fairfield Gro. SE7 68 CJ43
Fairfield N., Kings.T. 85 BL51
Fairfield Path, Croy. 87 CA55
Fairfield Pl., Kings.T. 85 BL52
Fairfield Ri., Guil. 118 AP70
Fairfield Rd. E3 57 CE37
Fairfield Rd. E17 39 CD30
Fairfield Rd. N8 47 BX32
Fairfield Rd. N18 39 CB28
Fairfield Rd. W7 64 BJ41
Fairfield Rd., Beck. 87 CE51
Fairfield Rd., Bexh. 69 CQ44
Fairfield Rd., Brwd. 42 DB27
Fairfield Rd., Brom. 78 CH50
Fairfield Rd., Croy. 87 BZ55
Fairfield Rd., Epp. 23 CO18
Fairfield Rd., Hodd. 12 CE11
Fairfield Rd., Ilf. 58 CL36
Fairfield Rd., Kings.T. 85 BL51
Fairfield Rd., Lthd. 102 BJ64
Fairfield Rd., Ong. 24 CW18
Fairfield Rd., Orp. 88 CM54
Fairfield Rd., Sev. 108 DC63
Fairfield Rd., Sthl. 54 BE39

Fairfield Rd., Stai. 72 AR46
Fairfield Rd., Uxb. 53 AX36
Fairfield Rd., West Dr. 53 AY40
Fairfield Rd., Wdf.Grn. 40 CH29
Fairfield S., Kings.T. 85 BL52
Fairfield St. SW18 76 BS46
Fairfield Wk., Chsnt. 21 CD17
Fairfield Way, Barn. 29 BS25
Fairfield Way, Couls. 95 BW60
Fairfield Way, Epsom 94 BO56
Fairfield W., Kings.T. 85 BL51
Fairfields Clo. NW9 46 BN32
Fairfields Cres. NW9 46 BN31
Fairfields Rd., Houns. 64 BG45
Fairfolds, Wat. 27 BE21
Fairfoot Rd. E3 57 CE38
Fairford Ave., Bexh. 69 CS44
Fairford Ave., Croy. 87 CC53
Fairford Clo., Croy. 87 CC53
Fairford Clo., Reig. 121 BT69
Fairford Clo., Rom. 42 CX29
Fairford Clo., Wey. 91 AV60
Fairford Gdns., Wor.Pk. 85 BO55
Fairford Way, Rom. 42 CX29
Fairgreen, Barn. 29 BU24
Fairgreen E., Barn. 29 BU24
Fairgreen Rd., Th.Hth. 86 BY53
Fairham Ave., S.Ock. 60 DA40
Fairhaven, Egh. 72 AS49
Fairhaven Ave., Croy. 87 CC53
Fairhaven Cres., Wat. 35 BC27
Fairhaven Rd., Red. 113 BV68
Fairhazel Gdns. NW6 56 BS36
Fairholme, Felt. 73 BA47
Fairholme Ave., Rom. 50 CU32
Fairholme Clo. N3 46 BR31
Fairholme Cres., Ash. 102 BK62
Fairholme Cres., Hayes 53 BB38
Fairholme Gdns. N3 46 BR31
Fairholme Gdns., Upmin. 51 CZ33
Fairholme Rd. W14 65 BR42
Fairholme Rd., Ashf. 73 AY49
Fairholme Rd., Croy. 86 BY54
Fairholme Rd., Har. 45 BH32
Fairholme Rd., Ilf. 49 CK32
Fairholme Rd., Sutt. 94 BR57
Fairholt Clo. N16 48 CA33
Fairholt Rd. N16 48 BZ33
Fairholt St. SW7 3 D6
Fairholt St. SW7 66 BU41
Montpelier Wk.
Fairkytes Ave., Horn. 51 CV33
Fairland Rd. E15 58 CG36
Fairlands Ave., Buck.H. 40 CH27
Fairlands Ave., Sutt. 86 BS55
Fairlands Ave., Th.Hth. 86 BX52
Fairlands Rd., Guil. 109 AO68
Fairlawn SE7 68 CJ43
Fairlawn, Lthd. 111 BE66
Fairlawn, Wat. 26 BB22
Langley Rd.
Fairlawn, Wey. 92 BB56
Fairlawn, Wdf.Grn. 40 CK29
Vicarage Rd.
Fairlawn Ave. N2 47 BU31
Fairlawn Ave. W4 65 BN42
Fairlawn Ave., Bexh. 69 CP44
Fairlawn Clo. N14 29 BW25
Fairlawn Clo., Esher 93 BH57
Fairlawn Clo., Felt. 74 BE49
Fairlawn Clo., Kings.T. 75 BN50
Fairlawn Ct. W4 65 BN42
Cunnington St.
Fairlawn Dr., Red. 121 BJ71
Fairlawn Dr., Wdf.Grn. 40 CH29
Fairlawn Gdns., Sthl. 54 BE40
Fairlawn Gro. W4 65 BN42
Fairlawn Gro., Bans. 95 BT60
Fairlawn Pk. SE26 77 CD49
Fairlawn Pk., Wind. 61 AM45
Fairlawn Rd. SW19 75 BR50
Fairlawn Rd., Sutt. 95 BT59
Fairlawns SW15 75 BQ46
Putney Hill
Fairlawns, Pnr. 36 BD30
Fairlawns, Sun. 83 BC52
Fairlawns, Twick. 74 BK46
Fairlawns Clo., Horn. 51 CW33
Herbert Rd.
Fairlawns Clo., Stai. 73 AW50
Kingston Rd.
Fairlea Pl. W5 54 BK38
Fairley Way, Chsnt. 21 CB17
Fairlie Gdns. SE23 77 CC47
Fairlight Ave. E4 39 CF27
Fairlight Ave. NW10 55 BO37
Fairlight Ave., Wind. 61 AO44
Fairlight Ave., Wdf.Grn. 40 CH29
Fairlight Clo. E4 39 CF27
Fairlight Clo., Wor.Pk. 94 BQ56
Fairlight Dr., Uxb. 53 AX36
Fairlight Rd. SW17 76 BT49
Fairlop Clo., Horn. 59 CU36
Fairlop Gdns., Ilf. 40 CM29
Fairlop Pl. NW8 56 BT38
Fairlop Rd. E11 48 CF33
Fairlop Rd., Ilf. 40 CM30
Fairmark Dr., Uxb. 53 AZ36
Fairmead, Brom. 88 CK52
Fairmead, Surb. 85 BM54
Fairmead, Wok. 100 AR62
Fairmead Clo., Brom. 88 CK52
Fairmead Clo., Houns. 64 BD43
Fairmead Clo., N.Mal. 85 BN52
Fairmead Cres., Edg. 37 BN27
Fairmead Gdns., Ilf. 49 CJ32
Fairmead Rd. N19 47 BW34
Fairmead Rd., Croy. 86 BX54
Fairmead Rd., Loug. 31 CH25
Fairmead Side, Loug. 31 CJ25
Fairmeads, Cob. 93 BE60
Fairmile Ave. SW16 76 BW49
Fairmile Ave., Cob. 93 BE60
Fairmile La., Cob. 93 BD59

Fairmile Pk. Rd., Cob. 93 BE59
Fairmont Clo., Belv. 69 CQ43
Albany Rd.
Fairmount Rd. SW2 76 BX46
Fairoak Clo., Ken. 104 BY61
Fairoak Clo., Lthd. 93 BG59
Fairoak Clo., Orp. 88 CL54
Fairoak Dr. SE9 78 CM46
Fairoak Gdns., Rom. 41 CT30
Fairoak La., Lthd. 93 BG59
Fairs Rd., Lthd. 102 BJ63
Fairseat Clo., Bush. 36 BH27
Hive Rd.
Fairshot Ct., St.Alb. 9 BK10
Fairstead Wk. N1 57 BZ37
Fairthorn Rd. SE7 68 CH42
Fairtrough Rd., Orp. 98 CO60
Fairview, Epsom 94 BR57
Fairview, Erith 69 CT43
Fairview, Pot.B. 20 BS18
Fairview Ave., Brwd. 122 DF26
Fairview Ave., Rain. 60 CV37
Fairview Ave., Wem. 54 BK36
Fairview Clo. E17 39 CD30
Fairview Clo., Chig. 40 CN28
Fairview Clo., Epsom 94 BQ59
Fairview Cres., Har. 45 BF33
Fairview Dr., Chig. 40 CN28
Fairview Dr., Orp. 97 CM56
Fairview Dr., Shep. 83 AY53
Fairview Dr., Wat. 26 BB21
Fairview Gdns., Wdf.Grn. 40 CH30
Fairview Pl. SW2 76 BX47
Holmewood Gdns.
Fairview Rd. N15 48 CA32
Fairview Rd. SW16 86 BX51
Fairview Rd., Chig. 40 CN28
Fairview Rd., Enf. 29 BX23
Fairview Rd., Epsom 94 BO59
Fairview Rd., Grav. 81 DE50
Fairview Rd., Sutt. 95 BT56
Fairview Way, Edg. 37 BM28
Fairwall Ho. SE5 67 CA44
Glebe Est.
Fairwater Ave., Well. 69 CO45
Fairwater Dr., Wey. 92 AX58
Fairway SW20 85 BQ52
Fairway, Bexh. 79 CQ46
Fairway, Cars. 95 BT59
Fairway, Cher. 83 AW54
Fairway, Grays 71 DD40
Fairway, Guil. 118 AU70
Fairway, Hem.H. 8 AY15
Fairway, Orp. 88 CM53
Fairway, Saw. 6 CQ6
Fairway, Vir.W. 82 AR53
Fairway, Wdf.Grn. 40 CJ28
Fairway, The N13 39 BZ27
Fairway, The N14 29 BV25
Fairway, The NW7 37 BN27
Fairway, The W3 55 BO39
Fairway, The, Abb.L. 17 BA19
Fairway, The, Barn. 29 BS25
Fairway, The, Brom. 88 CK53
Fairway, The, E.Mol. 84 BF52
Fairway, The, Grav. 81 DG48
Fairway, The, Lthd. 102 BJ62
Fairway, The, N.Mal. 85 BN51
Fairway, The, Nthlt. 54 BG36
Fairway, The, Nthwd. 35 BB28
Fairway, The, Ruis. 45 BD35
Fairway, The, Upmin. 51 CY33
Fairway, The, Uxb. 53 AY37
Fairway, The, Wem. 45 BJ34
Fairway, The, Wey. 92 AZ59
Fairway Ave. NW9 46 BM31
Fairway Ave., Borwd. 28 BM23
Fairway Ave., West Dr. 53 AX40
Fairway Clo. NW11 47 BT33
Fairway Clo., Croy. 87 CD53
Fairway Clo., Epsom 85 BN55
Riverview Rd.
Fairway Clo., Houns. 74 BD46
Fairway Clo., St.Alb. 18 BG17
Fairway Clo., West Dr. 53 AX40
Fairway Clo., Wok. 100 AQ63
Fairway Ct., Hem.H. 8 AY15
Fairway
Fairway Dr., Dart. 80 CX47
Fairway Dr., Grnf. 54 BG36
Fairway Gdns., Ilf. 49 CM35
Fairways, Ashf. 73 AZ50
Fairways, Ken. 105 BZ62
Hayes La.
Fairways, Stai. 73 AW49
Knowle Grn.
Fairways, Stan. 37 BL30
Fairways, Tedd. 74 BK50
Fairways, Wal.Abb. 22 CG20
Fairways, Wal.Cr. 21 CC16
Fairways, The, Harl. 14 CO12
Fairweather Clo. N15 48 CA31
Lawrence Rd.
Fairweather Rd. N16 48 CB32
Fairwell La., Lthd. 110 AZ67
Fairwood Ct. E11 48 CF33
Fairwyn Rd. SE26 77 CD49
Falaise, Egh. 72 AS49
Falcon Ave., Brom. 88 CK52
Falcon Ave., Grays 71 DD43
Falcon Clo. SE1 4 G2
Falcon Clo., Dart. 80 CW46
Falcon Clo., Hat. 10 BP13
Falcon Clo., Nthwd. 35 BB29
Falcon Clo., Saw. 6 CP6
Falcon Clo., Wal.Abb. 22 CH20
Falcon Ct., Wok. 91 AU60
Blackmore Cres.
Falcon Cres., Enf. 30 CC25
Falcon Dr., Stai. 73 AX46
Falcon Gro. SW11 66 BU45
Falcon La. SW11 66 BU45
Falcon Ms., Grav. 81 DF47
Falcon Ridge, Berk. 7 AR13

Falcon Rd. SW11 66 BU44
Falcon Rd., Enf. 30 CC25
Falcon Rd., Guil. 118 AR71
Falcon Rd., Hmptn. 74 BE50
Falcon St. E13 58 CG38
Falcon Ter. SW11 66 BU45
Falcon Trd. Est. NW10 46 BO35
Falcon Way E11 49 CH31
Falcon Way E14 67 CE42
Undine Rd.
Falcon Way, Felt. 73 BC46
Falcon Way, Har. 46 BL32
Falcon Way, Rain. 59 CU36
Falcon Way, Sun. 83 BB51
Falcon Way, Wat. 18 BE20
Falcon Way, Welw.G.C. 5 BR7
Falconberg Ct. W1 1 P8
Falconberg Ms. W1 1 N8
Falconberg Ms. W1 56 BW39
Sutton Row
Falconer Rd., Bush. 27 BE25
Falconer Rd., Ilf. 41 CO28
Falconer Wk. N7 47 BX34
Andover Est.
Falconers Pk., Saw. 6 CP6
Falconhurst, Lthd. 102 BG61
Falconwood Ave., Well. 68 CM44
Falconwood Par., Well. 68 CN45
Falconwood Rd., Croy. 96 CD58
Falcourt Clo., Sutt. 95 BS56
Robin Hood La.
Falkirk Clo., Horn. 51 CX34
Falkirk Gdns., Wat. 36 BD28
Falkirk St. N1 2 N1
Falkirk St. N1 57 CA37
Falkland Ave. N3 38 BS29
Falkland Ave. N11 38 BV28
Falkland Gdns., Dor. 119 BJ72
Falkand Gro.
Falkland Gro., Dor. 119 BJ71
Vincents La.
Falkland Pk. Ave. SE25 87 CA52
Falkland Pl. NW5 47 BW35
Falkland Rd.
Falkland Rd. N8 47 BY31
Falkland Rd. NW5 47 BW35
Falkland Rd., Barn. 28 BR23
Falkland Rd., Dor. 119 BJ72
Fallaize Ave., Ilf. 49 CL35
Riverdene Rd.
Falling La., West Dr. 53 AY40
Falloden Way NW11 47 BS31
Fallow Clo., Chig. 40 CN28
Fallow Ct. Ave. N12 38 BT29
Fallow Hurst Path N3 38 BT29
Park Cres.
Fallowfield, Stan. 36 BJ27
Fallowfield, Welw.G.C. 5 BR6
Fallowfield Clo., Uxb. 35 AX30
Northwood Rd.
Fallowfield Ct., Stan. 36 BJ27
Fallowfield Wk., Hem.H. 8 AW12
Fallsbrook Rd. SW16 76 BV50
Falmer Rd. E17 48 CE31
Falmer Rd. N15 48 BZ32
Falmer Rd., Enf. 30 CA24
Falmouth Ave. E4 39 CF28
Falmouth Clo. N22 38 BX29
Falmouth Clo. SE12 78 CG46
Taunton Rd.
Falmouth Gdns., Ilf. 49 CJ31
Falmouth Rd. SE1 4 J7
Falmouth Rd. SE1 67 BZ41
Falmouth Rd., Walt. 93 BD56
Falmouth St. E15 48 CF35
Falstaff Gdns., St.Alb. 9 BG15
Falstaff Ho. N1 57 CA37
Purcell St.
Falstone, Wok. 100 AQ62
Fambridge Clo. SE26 77 CD49
Fambridge Rd., Dag. 50 CR33
Famet Ave., Pur. 96 BZ60
Famet Clo., Pur. 96 BZ60
Famet Wk., Pur. 96 BZ60
Fane St. W14 65 BR43
Fann St. EC1 2 H5
Fann St. EC1 57 BZ38
Fanns Ri., Grays 70 CX42
Fanshaw St. N1 2 M2
Fanshaw St. N1 57 CA38
Fanshawe Ave., Bark. 58 CM36
Fanshawe Cres., Dag. 50 CQ35
Fanshawe Cres., Horn. 51 CV32
Fanshawe Rd., Grays 71 DG41
Fanshawe Rd., Rich. 74 BK49
Fanshaws La., Hert. 12 BZ12
Fanthorpe St. SW15 65 BQ45
Far End, Hat. 10 BP14
Faraday Ave., Sid. 79 CO48
Faraday Clo. N7 56 BX36
Faraday Clo., Wat. 26 BB25
Faraday Rd. E15 58 CG36
Faraday Rd. SE18 68 CJ41
Faraday Rd. SW19 76 BS50
Faraday Rd. W3 55 BN40
Faraday Rd. W10 55 BR39
Faraday Rd., E.Mol. 84 BF52
Faraday Rd., Sthl. 54 BF39
Faraday Rd., Well. 69 CO45
Faraday Way, Croy. 86 BX54
Faraday Way, Orp. 89 CO52
Fareham Rd., Felt. 74 BD46
Fareham St. W1 1 N8
Farewell Pl., Mitch. 86 BT51
Faringdon Ave., Brom. 88 CL54
Faringdon Ave., Rom. 42 CV30
Faringford Clo., Pot.B. 20 BT19
Penshurst Rd.
Faringford Clo., St.Alb. 18 BF16
Faringford Rd. E15 58 CG36
Farington Acres, Wey. 83 BA55
Faris La., Wey. 91 AV59
Farisbarn Dr., Wey. 91 AV59
Farjeon Rd. SE3 68 CJ44

Far–Fer

Farland Rd., Hem.H. 8 AZ13
Farleigh Ave., Brom. 88 CG53
Farleigh Ct. Rd., Warl. 96 CD60
Farleigh Dean Cres., Croy. 96 CE59
Farleigh Pl. N16 48 CA35
Farleigh Rd. N16 48 CA35
Farleigh Rd., Warl. 105 CC62
Farleigh Rd., Wey. 92 AW59
Farleton Clo., Wey. 92 BA57
Farley Cft., West. 115 CM66
Farley Dr., Ilf. 49 CN33
Farley Pk., Oxt. 114 CF68
Farley Pl. SE25 87 CB52
Farley Rd. SE6 77 CE46
Farley Rd., Grav. 81 DJ47
Farley Rd., S.Croy. 96 CB58
Farleys Clo., Lthd. 110 BA66
Farlington Pl. SW15 75 BP47
Farlow Clo., Grav. 81 DF48
Grieves Rd.
Farlow Rd. SW15 65 BQ45
Farlton Rd. SW18 76 BS47
Farm, The SW19 75 BQ47
Princes Way
Farm Ave. NW2 46 BR34
Farm Ave. SW16 76 BX49
Farm Ave., Har. 45 BE33
Farm Ave., Orp. 88 CM54
Farm Ave., Swan. 89 CS52
Farm Ave., Wem. 54 BK36
Farm Clo., Amer. 25 AR23
Farm Clo., Barn. 28 BP25
Farm Clo., Borwd. 27 BK22
Farm Clo., Brwd. 122 DE26
Farm Clo., Buck.H. 40 CJ27
Farm Clo., Cher. 82 AT53
Farm Clo., Chsnt. 21 CC18
Great Cambridge Rd.
Farm Clo., Cuffley 20 BW17
Farm Clo., Dag. 59 CS36
Farm Clo., Guil. 118 AR69
Farm Clo. (East Horsley), Lthd. 110 BB67
Farm Clo. (Fetcham), Lthd. 102 BG65
Farm Clo., Maid. 61 AH42
Farm Clo., Shep. 83 AZ54
Farm Clo., Sthl. 54 BF40
Farm Clo., Stai. 72 AV49
Farm Clo., Sutt. 95 BT57
Farm Clo., Wall. 95 BW58
Farm Clo., Welw.G.C. 5 BQ8
Farm Clo., W.Wick. 88 CG55
Farm Ct. NW4 46 BP31
Farm Ct., Uxb. 44 AZ34
Farm Cres., Slou. 52 AR39
Farm Dr., Croy. 87 CD55
Farm Dr., Pur. 95 BW59
Farm End E4 31 CG25
Farm End, Nthwd. 35 AZ30
Farm Fld., Wat. 26 BB22
Farm Flds., S.Croy. 96 CA59
Farm Hill Rd., Wal.Abb. 21 CF20
Farm Ho. Clo., Brox. 21 CD16
Farm Ho. Clo., Wok. 100 AU61
Farm La. SW6 66 BS43
Farm La., Ash. 103 BM61
Farm La., Beac. 34 AO29
Farm La., Croy. 87 CD55
Farm La., Lthd. 110 BB67
Farm La., Pur. 95 BW58
Farm La., Rick. 26 AX24
Farm La., Slou. 52 AO40
Farm La., Wok. 100 AU65
Farm Pl. W8 56 BS40
Farm Pl., Berk. 7 AP12
Farm Pl., Dart. 69 CU45
Farm Rd. N21 38 BY26
Farm Rd., Edg. 37 BM29
Farm Rd., Esher 84 BF54
Farm Rd., Grays 71 DF41
Farm Rd., Hmptn. 74 BE47
Farm Rd., Houns. 74 BE47
Farm Rd., Mord. 86 BS53
Farm Rd., Nthwd. 35 BA28
Farm Rd., Rain. 60 CV38
Farm Rd., Rick. 25 AT24
Farm Rd., St.Alb. 9 BJ13
Farm Rd., Sev. 108 CV63
Farm Rd., Stai. 73 AW50
Farm Rd. (Wraysbury), Stai. 72 AU46
Farm Rd., Sutt. 95 BT57
Farm Rd., Warl. 105 CD63
Farm Rd., Wok. 100 AT63
Farm St. W1 3 J1
Farm St. W1 56 BV40
Farm Vale, Bex. 79 CR46
Farm Wk. NW11 46 BR32
Farm Wk., Guil. 118 AP71
Farm Way, Buck.H. 40 CJ28
Farm Way, Bush. 27 BF24
Farm Way, Horn. 50 CU35
Farm Way, Nthwd. 35 BB28
Farm Way, Stai. 72 AV46
Farm Way, Wor.Pk. 85 BQ55
Farman Gro., Nthlt. 54 BD38
Wayfarer Rd.
Farmborough Clo., Har. 45 BG33
Pool Rd.
Farmcote Rd. SE12 78 CH47
Farmcroft, Grav. 81 DG48
Farmdale Rd. SE10 68 CH42
Farmdale Rd., Cars. 95 BU57
Farmer Ct., Wal.Abb. 22 CH20
Winters Way
Farmer Rd. E10 48 CE33
Farmer St. W8 56 BS40
Farmers Clo., Wat. 17 BC20
Farmers Rd. SE5 66 BY43
Farmers Rd., Stai. 72 AV49
Farmers Way, Beac. 34 AO29
Farmfield Clo. N12 38 BS28
Farmfield Rd., Brom. 77 CF49
Farmhouse Rd. SW16 76 BW50
Farmilo Rd. E17 48 CD33
Farmington Ave., Sutt. 86 BT55
Farmland Wk., Chis. 78 CL49
Farmlands, Enf. 29 BY23
Farmlands, Pnr. 44 BC31
Farmlands, The, Nthlt. 54 BE36
Farmleigh N14 38 BW26
Farmleigh Gro., Walt. 92 BB56
Farmstead Rd. SE6 77 CE49
Farmstead Rd., Har. 36 BG30
Farmway, Dag. 50 CP34
Farn Yd., Wind. 61 AO43
Farnaby Dr., Sev. 116 CU66
Farnaby Rd. SE9 68 CJ45
Farnaby Rd., Brom. 77 CF50
Farnan Ave. E17 39 CE30
Farnan Rd. SW16 76 BX49
Farnborough Ave. E17 48 CD31
Farnborough Ave., S.Croy. 96 CE58
Farnborough Clo., Wem. 46 BM34
Farnborough Common, Orp. 88 CK55
Farnborough Cres., Brom. 88 CG54
Saville Row
Farnborough Cres., S.Croy. 96 CD58
Farnborough Hill, Orp. 97 CM56
Farnborough Way SE15 67 CA43
Farnborough Way, Orp. 97 CL56
Farncombe St. SE16 67 CB41
Farndale Ave. N13 38 BY27
Farndale Cres, Grnf. 54 BG38
Farndon Mill La., Harl. 6 CL9
Farnell Ms. SW5 66 BS42
Farnell Pt. E5 48 CB34
Downs Est.
Farnell Rd., Islw. 64 BG45
Farnell Rd., Stai. 73 AW48
Farnes Dr., Rom. 42 CV30
Farnham Clo. N20 38 BT26
Farnham Clo., Hem.H. 16 AT17
Farnham Gdns. SW20 85 BP51
Farnham Pk. La., Slou. 52 AO37
Farnham Pl. SE1 4 G3
Farnham Pl. SE1 56 BY40
Farnham Rd., Guil. 118 AO72
Farnham Rd., Ilf. 49 CN33
Farnham Rd., Rom. 42 CV28
Farnham Rd., Slou. 61 AO40
Farnham Rd., Well. 69 CP44
Farnham Royal SE11 66 BX43
Farningham Cres., Cat. 105 CB65
Farningham Hill Rd., Farn. 90 CV53
Farningham Rd. N17 39 CB29
Farningham Rd., Cat. 105 CB65
Farnley, Wok. 100 AP62
Clifton Way
Farnley Rd. E4 40 CG26
Farnley Rd. SE25 87 BZ52
Farnol Rd., Dart. 80 CX46
Faro Clo., Brom. 88 CL51
Faroe Rd. W14 65 BQ41
Farorna Wk., Enf. 29 BY23
Farquhar Rd. SE19 77 CA49
Farquhar Rd. SW19 76 BS48
Farquharson Rd., Croy. 87 BZ54
Farr Ave., Bark. 59 CO37
Maybury Rd.
Farr Rd., Enf. 30 BZ23
Farraday Clo., St.Alb. 9 BH11
Darwin Clo.
Farraline Rd., Wat. 26 BC24
Farrance Est. E14 57 CE39
Farrance Rd., Rom. 50 CQ32
Farrance St. E14 57 CE39
Farrans Ct., Har. 45 BJ33
Farrant Ave. N22 38 BY30
Farrant Clo., Orp. 97 CN57
Farrant Way, Borwd. 28 BL23
Farren Rd. SE23 77 CD48
Farrer Rd. N8 47 BW31
Farrer Rd., Har. 46 BL32
Farrier Clo., Sun. 83 BC52
Anvil Rd.
Farrier Rd., Nthlt. 54 BF37
Farrier St. NW1 56 BW36
Farriers Clo., Epsom 94 BO59
Farriers Clo., Grav. 81 DJ47
Lower Higham Rd.
Farriers Ct., Wat. 17 BC19
Horseshoe La.
Farriers End, Brox. 21 CD16
Tarpan Way
Farriers Rd., Epsom 94 BO59
Farriers Way, Borwd. 28 BN25
Farringdon La. EC1 2 E5
Farringdon La. EC1 56 BY38
Farringdon Rd. EC1 56 BY38
Farringdon St. EC4 2 F8
Farringdon St. EC4 56 BY39
Farrington Ave., Orp. 89 CO52
Farrington Pl., Chis. 78 CM50
Farrins Rents SE16 57 CD40
Farrow Gdns., Grays 71 DD40
Farrow Pl. SE16 67 CD41
Farthing All. SE1 67 CB41
Wolseley St.
Farthing Barn La., Orp. 97 CK58
Farthing Clo., Dart. 70 CW45
Farthing Flds. E1 57 CB40
Raine St.
Farthing Grn. La., Slou. 52 AQ37
Farthing St., Orp. 97 CK57
Farthingale La., Wal.Abb. 22 CH20
Farthings, Wok. 100 AP61
Mead Ct.
Farthings, The, Kings.T. 85 BM51
Brunswick Rd.
Farthings Clo. E4 40 CG27
Farthings Clo., Pnr. 44 BC32
Farwell Rd., Sid. 79 CO48
Farwig La., Brom. 88 CG51
Fashion St. E1 2 Q7
Fashion St. E1 57 CA39
Fashoda Rd., Brom. 88 CJ52
Fassett Rd. E8 57 CB36
Fassett Rd., Kings.T. 85 BL52
Fassett Sq. E8 57 CB36
Fauconberg Rd. W4 65 BN43
Faulkner Clo., Dag. 50 CP33
Palmer Rd.
Faulkner St. SE14 67 CC44
Kender St.
Faulkners All. EC1 2 F6
Faulkners Rd., Walt. 93 BD56
Fauna Clo., Rom. 50 CP32
Faunce St. SE17 66 BY42
Favart Rd. SW6 66 BS44
Faversham Ave. E4 40 CG26
Faversham Ave., Enf. 30 BZ25
Faversham Clo., Chig. 41 CO27
Faversham Rd. SE6 77 CD47
Faversham Rd., Beck. 87 CD51
Croydon Rd.
Faversham Rd., Mord. 86 BS53
Fawcett Clo. SW11 66 BT44
Wye St.
Fawcett Est. E5 48 CB33
Fawcett Rd. NW10 55 BO37
Fawcett Rd., Croy. 87 BZ55
Fawcett Rd., Wind. 61 AN44
Fawcett St. SW10 66 BT43
Fawcus Clo., Esher 93 BH57
Fawe Pk. Rd. SW15 65 BR45
Fawe St. E14 57 CE39
Fawke Common Rd., Sev. 117 CX66
Fawkham Grn. Rd., Fawk. 90 DA55
Fawkham Rd., Sev. 99 CZ57
Fawkham Rd., S.Dnth. 90 DB52
Fawkon Wk., Hodd. 12 CE12
Fawley Rd. NW6 47 BS35
Fawn Ct., Hat. 10 BQ11
Fawn Rd. E13 58 CJ37
Fawn Rd., Chig. 40 CN28
Fawnbrake Ave. SE24 76 BY46
Fawns Manor Clo., Felt. 73 BA47
Bedfont Rd.
Fawns Manor Rd., Felt. 73 BA47
Fawood Ave. NW10 55 BN36
Fawsley Clo., Slou. 62 AV44
Coleridge Cres.
Fawters Clo., Brwd. 122 DE25
Fay Grn., Abb.L. 17 BA20
Fayerfield, Pot.B. 20 BT19
Blunesfield
Faygate Cres., Bexh. 79 CR46
Faygate Rd. SW2 76 BX48
Fayland Ave. SW16 76 BW49
Fayland Est. SW16 76 BW49
Faymore Gdns., S.Ock. 60 DA39
Feacey Down, Hem.H. 8 AW12
Fearn Clo., Lthd. 110 BB68
Fearney Mead, Rick. 35 AW26
Hall Clo.
Fearnley Cres., Hmptn. 74 BE49
Fearnley Rd., Welw.G.C. 5 BQ8
Fearnley St., Wat. 26 BC24
Fearns Mead, Brwd. 42 DB28
Fearon St. SE10 68 CH42
Feather Dell, Hat. 10 BO12
Featherbed La., Abb.L. 17 BC16
Featherbed La., Croy. 96 CD57
Featherbed La., Hem.H. 17 AW16
Featherbed La., Rom. 41 CQ26
Feathers La., Stai. 72 AT48
Feathers Pl. SE10 67 CF43
Featherstone Ave. SE23 77 CB48
Featherstone Clo., Pot.B. 20 BT19
Featherstone Ct. EC1 57 BZ38
Featherstone St.
Featherstone Gdns., Borwd. 28 BN24
Featherstone Rd. NW7 37 BP29
Featherstone Rd., Sthl. 64 BE41
Featherstone St. EC1 2 K4
Featherstone St. EC1 57 BZ38
Featherstone Ter., Sthl. 64 BE41
Featley Rd. SW9 66 BY45
Angell Rd.
Federal Rd., Grnf. 54 BK37
Federal Way, Wat. 27 BD22
Federation Rd. SE2 69 CO42
Fee Fm. Rd., Esher 93 BH57
Feenan Highway, Til. 71 DG43
Felbridge Ave., Stan. 36 BJ30
Felbridge Clo. SW16 76 BY49
Felbridge Clo., Sutt. 95 BS58
Felbrigge Rd., Ilf. 49 CN34
Felcott Clo., Walt. 84 BD55
Felcott Rd., Walt. 84 BD55
Felday Rd. SE13 77 CE46
Felden Clo., Pnr. 36 BE29
Felden Clo., Wat. 18 BD20
Felden Dr., Hem.H. 8 AW15
Felden La., Hem.H. 8 AW15
Felden Rd., Hem.H. 8 AX15
Felden St. SW6 65 BR44
Feldman Clo. N16 48 CB33
Oldhill St.
Feldwick Pl., Red. 121 BV70
Ladbroke Rd.
Felgate Ms. W6 65 BP42
Felhampton Rd. SE9 78 CL48
Felhurst Cres., Dag. 50 CR35
Felicia Way, Grays 71 DG42
Felix Ave. N8 47 BX32
Felix Dr., Guil. 110 AW67
Felix La., Shep. 83 BB53
Felix Rd. W13 54 BJ40
Felix Rd., Walt. 83 BD53
Felixstowe Rd. N9 39 CB27
Felixstowe Rd. N17 48 CA31
Felixstowe Rd. NW10 55 BP38
Felixstowe Rd. SE2 69 CO41
Fell Path, Borwd. 28 BN25
Fell Rd., Croy. 87 BZ55
Fell Wk., Edg. 37 BN30
East Rd.
Felland Way, Reig. 121 BT72
Fellbrigg Rd. SE22 77 CA46
Fellbrigg St. E1 57 CB38
Headlam St.
Fellbrook, Rich. 74 BJ48
Fellowes Clo., Hayes 54 BD38
Fellowes La., St.Alb. 10 BO15
Fellowes Rd., Cars. 86 BU55
Fellows Ct. E2 2 P1
Fellows Ct. E2 57 CA37
Fellows Rd. NW3 56 BT36
Felltram Way SE7 68 CH42
Felmersham Clo. SW4 66 BW45
Haselrigge Rd.
Felmingham Rd. SE20 87 CC51
Felmongers, Harl. 6 CO10
Felnex Est. NW10 55 BN38
Fels Clo., Dag. 50 CR34
Fels Fm. Ave., Dag. 50 CS34
Felsberg Rd. SW2 76 BX46
Felsham Rd. SW15 65 BQ45
Felspar Clo. SE18 68 CN42
Felstead Ave., Ilf. 40 CL30
Felstead Clo., Brwd. 122 DE25
Bannister Dr.
Felstead Gdns. E14 67 CF42
Ferry St.
Felstead Rd. E11 49 CH33
Felstead Rd., Epsom 94 BN59
Felstead Rd., Loug. 40 CK26
Felstead Rd., Orp. 89 CO55
Felstead Rd., Rom. 41 CS29
Felstead Rd., Wal.Cr. 21 CD19
Felstead St. E9 57 CD36
Felsted Rd. E16 58 CJ39
Feltham Ave., E.Mol. 84 BH52
Feltham Hill Rd., Ashf. 73 AZ49
Feltham Rd., Ashf. 73 AZ49
Feltham Rd., Mitch. 86 BV51
Feltham Rd., Red. 121 BU73
Feltham Wk., Red. 121 BU73
Felthambrook Way, Felt. 73 BC49
Felthamhill Rd., Felt. 73 BC49
Felton Clo., Borwd. 28 BL22
Felton Clo., Brox. 21 CD16
Felton Clo., Orp. 88 CL53
Felton Gdns., Bark. 58 CN37
Felton Rd.
Felton Lea, Sid. 78 CN49
Felton Rd. W13 64 BK41
Camborne Ave.
Felton Rd., Bark. 58 CN37
Felton St. N1 57 BZ37
Fen Clo., Brwd. 122 DE24
Fen Ct. EC3 2 M10
Fen Ct. EC3 57 CA39
Fen Gro., Sid. 78 CN46
Fen La., Upmin. 51 DB35
Fen La., Upmin. 123 DD35
Fen Pond Rd., Sev. 108 DB62
Fen St. E16 58 CG40
Caxton St. N.
Fencepiece Rd., Chig. 40 CM28
Fencepiece Rd., Ilf. 40 CM30
Fenchurch Ave. EC3 2 M9
Fenchurch Ave. EC3 57 CA39
Fenchurch Bldgs. EC3 2 N9
Fenchurch Bldgs. EC3 57 CA39
Fenchurch Pl. EC3 2 N10
Fenchurch St. EC3 2 M10
Fenchurch St. EC3 57 BZ40
Fendall Rd., Epsom 94 BN56
Fendall St. SE1 4 N7
Fendall St. SE1 67 CA41
Fendt Clo. E16 58 CG40
Bowman Ave.
Fendyke Rd., Belv. 69 CP42
Fenelon Pl. W14 65 BR42
Fengates Rd., Red. 121 BU70
Fenham Rd. SE15 67 CB43
Fenman Ct. N17 39 CB30
Shelbourne Rd.
Fenn Clo., Brom. 78 CH50
Fenn St. E9 48 CC35
Fennel Clo., Croy. 87 CC54
Primrose La.
Fennel Clo., Guil. 118 AT69
Fennel St. SE18 68 CL43
Fennells Mead, Epsom 94 BO58
Fennels, Harl. 13 CM13
Fenner Sq. SW11 66 BT45
Thomas Baines Rd.
Fenning St. SE1 4 M4
Fenning St. SE1 67 CA41
St. Thomas St.
Fennings, The, Amer. 25 AO21
Fenns Way, Wok. 100 AS61
Fennycroft Rd., Hem.H. 7 AV12
Fens Way, Swan. 79 CU50
Fensomes All., Hem.H. 8 AX13
Fenstanton Ave. N12 38 BT29
Fentiman Rd. SW8 66 BX43
Fentiman Way, Horn. 51 CW33
Fenton Ave., Stai. 73 AX50
Fenton Clo. SW9 66 BX44
Stockwell La.
Fenton Clo., Chis. 78 CK49
Fenton Clo., Red. 121 BV70
Fenton Ho. Est. NW3 47 BT34
Fenton Rd. N17 39 BZ29
Fenton Rd., Red. 121 BV70
Fenton St. E1 57 CB39
Commercial Rd.
Fentons Ave. E13 58 CH37
Fentum Rd., Guil. 118 AQ69
Fenwick Clo. SE18 68 CL43
Ritter St.
Fenwick Clo., Wok. 100 AQ62
Fenwick Gro. SE15 67 CB45
Fenwick Path, Borwd. 28 BL22
Berwick Rd.
Fenwick Pl. SW9 66 BX
Fenwick Rd. SE15 67 CB
Ferdinand Est. NW1 56 BV
Ferdinand Pl. NW1 56 BV
Ferdinand St.
Ferdinand St. NW1 56 BV
Fergus Rd. N5 47 BY
Calabria Rd.
Ferguson Ave., Grav. 81 DH
Ferguson Ave., Rom. 42 CV
Ferguson Ave., Surb. 85 BL
Ferguson Clo., Brom. 87 CF
Ferguson Ct., Rom. 42 CV
Ferguson Cres., Rom. 42 CV
Ferguson Dr. W3 55 BN
Ferme Pk. Rd. N4 47 BX
Ferme Pk. Rd. N8 47 BX
Fermor Rd. SE23 77 CD
Fermoy Rd. W9 55 BR
Fermoy Rd., Grnf. 54 BF
Fern Ave., Mitch. 86 BW
Fern Clo., Brox. 12 CD
Cozens La. E.
Fern Clo., Warl. 105 CD
Fern Ct., Berk. 7 AQ
Charles St.
Fern Cft., St.Alb. 9 BG
Fern Dale, Guil. 118 AP
Fern Dells, Hat. 10 BO
Fern Dene W13 54 BJ
Templewood
Fern Dr., Felt. 73 BC
Fern Dr., Hem.H. 8 AY
Fern Gro., Felt. 73 BC
Fern Gro., Welw.G.C. 5 BC
Fern Hill, Lthd. 93 BG
Fern Hill La., Wok. 100 AR6
Fern La., Houns. 64 BE4
Fern Leys, St.Alb. 9 BK1
Fern St. E3 57 CE3
Fern Wk., Ashf. 73 AX4
Fern Way, Wat. 26 BC2
Fernbank, Buck.H. 40 CH2
Fernbank Ave., Horn. 51 CV3
Fernbank Ave., Walt. 84 BE5
Fernbank Ave., Wem. 45 BH3
Fernbank Rd., Wey. 92 AW5
Fernbrook Ave., Sid. 78 CN4
Fernbrook Cres. SE13 78 CG4
Fernbrook Dr., Har. 45 BF3
Fernbrook Rd. SE13 78 CG4
Ferncliff Rd. E8 48 CB3
Ferncroft Ave. N12 38 BU2
Ferncroft Ave. NW3 47 BS3
Ferncroft Ave., Ruis. 45 BD3
Ferndale, Brom. 88 CJ5
Ferndale Ave. E17 48 CF3
Ferndale Ave., Cher. 82 AV5
Ferndale Ave., Houns. 64 BE4
Ferndale Ct. SE3 68 CG4
Ferndale Ct. SW9 66 BX4
Ferndale Cres., Uxb. 53 AX3
Ferndale Rd. E7 58 CH3
Ferndale Rd. E11 49 CG3
Ferndale Rd. N15 48 CA3
Ferndale Rd. SE25 87 CB5
Ferndale Rd. SW4 66 BX4
Ferndale Rd. SW9 66 BX4
Ferndale Rd., Ashf. 73 AX4
Ferndale Rd., Bans. 103 BR6
Ferndale Rd., Enf. 30 CD2
Ferndale Rd., Grav. 81 DG4
Ferndale Rd., Rom. 41 CS3
Ferndale Rd., Wok. 100 AS6
Ferndale St. E6 58 CL4
Ferndale Ter., Har. 45 BH3
Ferndale Way, Orp. 97 CM5
Ferndell Ave., Bex. 79 CS4
Fernden Way, Rom. 50 CR3
Ferndene, St.Alb. 18 BE1
Ferndene Rd. SE24 67 BZ4
Ferndown, Horn. 51 CW3
Ferndown Ave., Orp. 88 CN5
Ferndown Clo., Guil. 118 AT7
Ferndown Clo., Pnr. 36 BE2
Ferndown Clo., Sutt. 95 BF5
Ferndown Ct., Guil. 118 AR7
Stocton Clo.
Ferndown Gdns., Cob. 93 BD6
Ferndown Rd. SE9 78 CJ4
Ferndown Rd., Nthwd. 35 BC3
Ferndown Rd., Wat. 36 BD2
Fernecroft, St.Alb. 9 BG1
Fernery, The, Stai. 72 AV4
Fernes Clo., Uxb. 53 AX3
Ferney Clo. (Byfleet), Wey. 92 AX5
Ferney Rd.
Ferney Rd., Barn. 38 BV2
Ferney Rd., Wey. 92 AX5
Fernhall Dr., Ilf. 49 CJ3
Fernhall La., Wal.Abb. 22 CJ1
Fernham Rd., Th.Hth. 87 BZ5
Fernhead Rd. W9 55 BR3
Fernhead Yd. W9 55 BR3
Fernhead Rd.
Fernheath Way, Dart. 79 CS4
Fernhill, Harl. 13 CN1
Fernhill Clo., Wok. 100 AR6
Fernhill Ct. E17 39 CF3
Fernhill Ct., Kings.T. 74 BK4
Fernhill Gdns., Kings.T. 74 BK4
Fernhill La., Harl. 13 CN1
Fernhill Pk., Wor.Pk. 100 AR6
Fernhill St. E16 58 CK4
Fernhills, Kings L. 17 BA2
Fernholme Rd. SE15 77 CC4
Fernhurst Gdns., Edg. 37 BM2
Fernhurst Rd. SW6 65 BR4
Fernhurst Rd., Ashf. 73 BA4
Fernhurst Rd., Croy. 87 CB5
Fernie Clo., Chig. 41 CO2
Fernihouch Clo., Wey. 92 AZ5
Kaye Don Way
Fernlands Clo., Cher. 82 AV5

rnlea, Lthd. 102 BF65
rnlea Rd. SW12 76 BV47
rnlea Rd., Mitch. 86 BV51
rnleigh Clo., Croy. 95 BY56
Stafford Rd.
rnleigh Ct., Har. 36 BF30
rnleigh Ct., Wem. 46 BL34
rnleigh Rd. N21 38 BY27
rns Clo., Enf. 30 CD21
rns Clo., S.Croy. 96 CB58
rns Rd E15 58 CG36
rnsbury St. WC1 2 D3
Margery St.
rnsbury St. WC1 56 BY38
rnshaw Rd. SW10 66 BT43
rnside NW11 47 BS34
rnside, Buck.H. 40 CH26
rnside Ave. NW7 37 BN27
rnside Ave., Felt. 73 BC49
rnside La., Sev. 117 CV68
rnside Rd. SW12 76 BW50
rnsleigh Clo., Ger.Cr. 34 AS29
rnthorpe Rd. SW16 76 BW50
rntower Rd. N5 48 BZ35
rntville La., Hem.H. 8 AX13
rnways, Ilf. 49 CL35
Cecil Ave.
rnwood Ave. SW16 76 BW49
rnwood Ave., Wem. 54 BK36
rnwood Clo., Brom. 88 CJ51
rnwood Cres. N20 38 BU27
rny Hill, Barn. 29 BU22
rranti Clo. SE18 68 CJ42
rrers Ave., Wall. 95 BW56
rrers Ave., West Dr. 63 AX41
rrers Rd. SW16 76 BW49
rrestone Rd. N8 47 BX31
Glebe Rd.
rriby Clo. N1 56 BY36
Bewdley St.
rrier St. SW18 66 BS45
rriers Way, Epsom 103 BQ63
rring Clo., Har. 45 BG33
rrings SE21 77 CA48
rris Ave., Croy. 87 CD55
rris Rd. SE22 67 CB45
rro Rd., Rain. 59 CU38
rron Rd. E5 48 CB34
rry App. SE18 68 CL41
rry Ave., Stai. 72 AV50
rry La. N17 48 CB31
rry La. SW13 65 BO43
rry La., Brent. 65 BL43
rry La., Guil. 118 AR72
rry La., Rain. 59 CT39
rry La., Rich. 65 BL43
rry La., Shep. 83 AZ54
rry La. (Hythe End), 72 AT48
Stai.
rry Path, Cher. 83 AW53
rry Pl. SE18 68 CL41
rry Rd. SW13 65 BP43
rry Rd., E.Mol. 84 BF52
rry Rd., Maid. 61 AH41
rry Rd., Surb. 84 BJ53
rry Rd., Tedd. 74 BJ49
rry Rd., Til. 71 DG45
rry Rd., Twick. 74 BJ47
rry Sq., Brent. 64 BK43
rry Sq., Shep. 83 AZ54
Church Sq.
rry St. E14 67 CF42
rryhills Clo., Wat. 36 BD27
rrymead Ave., Grnf. 54 BF38
rrymead Dr., Grnf. 54 BF37
rrymead Gdns., Grnf. 54 BF37
rrymoor, Rich. 74 BJ48
ryby Rd., Grays 71 DG41
ryrings Clo., Harl. 6 CP9
rsants Cft., Harl. 6 CO9
sting Rd. SW15 65 BQ45
stival Clo., Bex. 79 CP47
stival Clo., Erith 69 CT43
stival Clo., Uxb. 53 AZ37
tcham Common La., 102 BF64
Lthd.
tcham Pk. Dr., Lthd. 102 BH65
tter La. EC4 2 E9
tter La. EC4 56 BY39
inch St. SE8 67 CE43
ddle Bri. La., Hat. 10 BO12
dler Pl., Bush. 36 BF26
Ashfield Ave.
eld Clo. E4 39 CE29
eld Clo., Brom. 88 CJ51
eld Clo., Buck.H. 40 CJ27
eld Clo., Chesh. 16 AP17
eld Clo., Chess. 93 BK57
eld Clo., E.Mol. 84 BF53
eld Clo., Guil. 118 AU69
eld Clo., Hayes 63 BA43
eld Clo., Houns. 63 BC44
eld Clo., Rom. 32 CO24
eld Clo., Ruis. 44 BA33
eld Clo., St.Alb. 9 BJ11
eld Clo., S.Croy. 96 CB60
eld Clo., Uxb. 44 AZ34
eld Ct. WC1 2 C7
eld Ct., Oxt. 115 CG67
eld End, Barn. 28 BP24
eld End, Couls. 95 BD60
eld End, Nthlt. 54 BD36
Arnold Rd.
eld End, Ruis. 54 BD36
eld End, Twick. 74 BH49
eld End, Wat. 36 BE26
eld End Clo., Wat. 36 BC32
eld End Rd., Pnr. 44 BD33
eld End Rd., Ruis. 45 BD33
eld Gate La., Mitch. 86 BU52
eld La., Brent. 64 BK43

Field La., Tedd. 74 BJ49
Field Mead NW9 37 BO29
Field Pk. Cres., Rom. 50 CP32
Field Pl. EC1 56 BY37
St. John St.
Field Pl., N.Mal. 85 BO53
Field Rd. E7 49 CG35
Field Rd. E17 48 CE31
Field Rd. N17 48 BZ31
Field Rd. W6 65 BR42
Field Rd., Felt. 73 BC46
Field Rd., Hem.H. 8 AZ14
Field Rd., S.Ock. 60 CY40
Field Rd., Uxb. 43 AV35
Field Rd., Wat. 27 BE25
Field St. WC1 2 B2
Field St. WC1 56 BX38
Field Vw., Egh. 72 AU49
Field Vw., Felt. 73 BA49
Field Vw. Ri., St.Alb. 18 BE18
Field Vw. Rd., Pot.B. 20 BS20
Field Way NW10 55 BN36
Field Way, Berk. 7 AS14
Field Way, Croy. 96 CE57
Field Way, Dag. 50 CO35
Field Way, Ger.Cr. 34 AR29
Field Way, Grnf. 54 BF37
Field Way, Hem.H. 16 AT17
Field Way, Rick. 35 AW26
Field Way, Ruis. 44 BA33
Field Way, Wok. 109 AV66
Burntcommon La.
Field Waye, Uxb. 53 AX38
Fieldcommon La., Walt. 84 BE54
Fieldend Rd. SW16 86 BW51
Fielders Clo., Har. 45 BG33
Dudley Gdns.
Fielders Grn., Guil. 118 AT70
Springhaven Clo.
Fieldfare Rd. SE28 59 CP40
Fieldgate St. E1 57 CB39
Fieldhouse Rd. SW12 76 BW47
Fieldhurst, Slou. 62 AS42
The Briars
Fieldhurst Clo., Wey. 92 AW56
Fielding Ave., Til. 71 DG44
Fielding Ave., Twick. 74 BG48
Fielding Rd. W4 65 BN41
Fielding Rd. W14 65 BQ41
Fielding St. SE17 67 BZ43
Fielding Ter. W5 55 BL40
Uxbridge Rd.
Fielding Way, Brwd. 122 DE25
Fieldings, The SE23 77 CC47
Fieldings, The, Wok. 100 AP61
Fieldings Rd., Chsnt. 21 CD18
Fields Ct., Pot.B. 20 BT20
Fields End La., Hem.H. 7 AU12
Fields Est. E8 57 CB36
Fieldsend Rd., Sutt. 94 BR56
Fieldside Clo., Orp. 97 CL56
State Fm. Ave.
Fieldside Rd., Brom. 77 CF49
Fieldview SW18 76 BT47
Fieldway, Grays 71 DD40
Fieldway, Orp. 88 CM53
Fieldway, Wok. 109 AV66
Fieldway Cres. N5 47 BY35
Fiennes Clo., Dag. 50 CP33
Fife Ct. W3 55 BM39
Links Rd.
Fife Rd. E16 58 CH39
Fife Rd. N22 38 BY29
Fife Rd. SW14 75 BN46
Fife Rd., Kings.T. 85 BL51
Fife Ter. N1 56 BX37
Wynford Rd.
Fife Way, Brom. 88 CH51
White Hart Slip
Fifehead Clo., Ashf. 73 AY50
Fifeway, Lthd. 111 BF66
Fifield La., Wind. 61 AH45
Fifield Path SE23 77 CC48
Bampton Rd.
Fifield Rd., Maid. 61 AH43
Fifield Rd., Wind. 61 AH44
Fifth Ave. E12 49 CK35
Fifth Ave. W10 55 BR38
Fifth Ave., Enf. 30 CA25
Fifth Ave., Grays 70 DA43
Fifth Ave., Harl. 6 CM9
Fifth Ave., Hayes 53 BB40
Fifth Ave., Wat. 27 BD21
Fifth Cross Rd., Twick. 74 BG48
Fifth Way, Wem. 46 BM35
Fig St., Sev. 116 CT67
Fig Tree Hill, Hem.H. 8 AX13
Figges Rd., Mitch. 76 BV50
Filby Rd., Chess. 93 BL57
Filey Ave. N16 48 CB33
Filey Clo., Sutt. 95 BT57
Filey Clo., West. 106 CH63
Filey Rd., Slou. 61 AN41
Scarborough Way
Filey Wave, Ruis. 44 BC34
Fillebrook Ave., Enf. 30 CA23
Fillebrook Rd. E11 48 CF33
Filmer La., Sev. 108 CW64
Filmer Rd. SW6 65 BR44
Filmer Rd., Wind. 61 AL44
Filston La., Sev. 107 CS61
Filston Rd., Erith 69 CR42
Riverdale Rd.
Finborough Rd. SW10 66 BS42
Finborough Rd. SW17 76 BU50
Finch Ave. SE27 77 BZ49
Finch Clo. NW10 55 BN36
Brentfield Rd.
Finch Clo., Barn. 29 BS25
Finch Clo., Hat. 10 BP13
Finch Clo., Wok. 100 AO62
Finch Dr., Felt. 74 BD47
Finch La. EC3 2 L9
Finch La. EC3 57 BZ39

Finch La., Amer. 25 AP24
Finch La., Bush. 27 BE24
Finch Rd., Berk. 7 AQ12
Finch Rd., Guil. 118 AR70
Finchale Rd. SE2 69 CO41
Fincham Clo., Uxb. 44 BA34
Aylsham Dr.
Finchdale, Hem.H. 8 AW14
Finchdean Way SE15 67 CA43
Finches Ri., Guil. 118 AU69
Finchingfield Ave., 40 CJ29
Wdf.Grn.
Finchley Clo., Dart. 80 CX46
Finchley Ct. N3 38 BS29
Finchley La. NW4 46 BQ31
Finchley Pk. N12 38 BT28
Finchley Pl. NW8 56 BT37
Finchley Rd. NW2 47 BS34
Finchley Rd. NW3 47 BS35
Finchley Rd. NW8 56 BT37
Finchley Rd. NW11 46 BR31
Finchley Rd., Grays 71 DD43
Finchley Way N3 38 BS29
Finchmoor, Harl. 13 CM12
Finck St. SE1 66 BX41
Finden Rd. E7 49 CH35
Findhorn St. E14 57 CF39
Aberfeldy St.
Findlay Dr., Guil. 109 AP68
Findhorne Ave., Hayes 53 BC39
Findon Clo. SW18 76 BS46
Findon Clo., Har. 45 BF34
Findon Gdns., Rain. 59 CU39
Findon Rd. N9 39 CB26
Findon Rd. W12 65 BP41
Fine Bush La., Uxb. 44 AZ32
Fingal St. SE10 68 CG42
Fingrith Hall La., Ing. 24 DC17
Finians Clo., Uxb. 53 AY36
Finland Pl. SE16 67 CD41
Finland Rd. SE4 67 CD45
Finland St. SE16 67 CD41
Finlay Gdns., Wey. 92 AX56
Finlay St. SW6 65 BQ44
Finlays Clo., Chess. 94 BM56
Finnart Clo., Wey. 92 BA56
Meadows Leigh Clo.
Finnis St. E2 57 CB38
Finnymore Rd., Dag. 59 CQ36
Finsbury Ave. EC2 2 L7
Finsbury Circ. EC2 2 L7
Finsbury Circ. EC2 57 BZ39
Finsbury Cotts. N22 38 BX29
Finsbury Est. EC1 2 E3
Finsbury Mkt. EC2 2 M5
Finsbury Mkt. EC2 57 CA38
Finsbury Pk. Rd. N4 47 BY34
Finsbury Pavement EC2 2 L6
Finsbury Pavement EC2 57 BZ39
Finsbury Rd. N22 38 BX29
Finsbury Sq. EC2 2 L5
Finsbury Sq. EC2 57 BZ38
Finsbury St. EC2 2 K6
Finsbury St. EC2 57 BZ39
Finsen Rd. SE5 67 BZ45
Finstock Rd. W10 55 BQ39
Finucane Dr., Orp. 89 CP54
Finucane Gdns., Rain. 59 CU36
Finucane Ri., Bush. 36 BG27
Finway Rd., Hem.H. 8 AZ11
Fiona Clo., Lthd. 102 BF65
Fir Clo., Walt. 83 BC54
Fir Dene, Orp. 88 CK55
Fir Gra. Ave., Wey. 92 AZ56
Fir Gro., N.Mal. 85 BO53
Fir Gro., Wok. 100 AQ63
Fir Pk., Harl. 13 CL12
Fir Rd., Felt. 74 BD49
Fir Rd., Sutt. 85 BR54
Fir Tree Ave., Slou. 52 AP38
Fir Tree Clo. SW16 76 BW49
Fir Tree Clo. W5 55 BL39
Fir Tree Clo., Epsom 103 BO61
Fir Tree Clo. 94 BO56
(Stoneleigh), Epsom
Fir Tree Clo., Esher 93 BG56
Fir Tree Clo., Grays 71 DE43
Lawn Cres.
Fir Tree Clo., Hem.H. 8 AZ14
Fir Tree Clo., Lthd. 102 BK65
Fir Tree Clo., Rom. 50 CT31
Fir Tree Ct., Brwd. 28 BL24
Fir Tree Gdns., Croy. 96 CE56
Fir Tree Hill, Rick. 26 AY22
Fir Tree Pl., Ashf. 73 AZ49
Fir Tree Rd., Bans. 94 BR60
Fir Tree Rd., Epsom 103 BP61
Fir Tree Rd., Guil. 118 AR69
Fir Tree Rd., Houns. 64 BE45
Fir Tree Rd., Lthd. 102 BK65
Fir Tree Wk., Enf. 30 BZ24
Fir Tree Wk., Reig. 121 BT70
Fir Trees, Epp. 23 CO18
Tidys La.
Fir Wk., Sutt. 94 BQ57
Firbank Clo. E16 58 CJ39
Firbank Clo., Enf. 30 BZ24
Gladbeck Way
Firbank Dr., Wat. 36 BE26
Firbank Dr., Wok. 100 AQ63
Firbank La., Wok. 100 AQ63
Firbank Pl., Egh. 72 AQ50
Firbank Rd. SE15 67 CB44
Firbank Rd., Rom. 41 CR28
Firbank Rd., St.Alb. 9 BH11
Fircroft Ave., Chess. 94 BL56
Fircroft Clo., Slou. 52 AQ36
Fircroft Clo., Wok. 100 AS62
Ockenden Rd.
Fircroft Gdns., Har. 45 BH34
Fircroft Rd. SW17 76 BU48
Firdene, Surb. 85 BN54
Fire Bell All., Surb. 85 BL53
Firecrest Dr. NW3 47 BS34

Firefly Clo., Wall. 95 BX57
Firfield Rd., Wey. 92 AW56
Firham Pk. Ave., Rom. 42 CX29
Firhill Rd. SE6 77 CE49
Firlands, Wey. 92 BB57
Firmin Rd., Dart. 80 CV46
Firs, The N20 38 BT26
Athenaeum Rd.
Firs, The SW20 75 BP50
Firs, The W5 54 BK39
Firs, The, Bex. 79 CS47
Dartford Rd.
Firs, The, Brwd. 33 DA25
Ongar Rd.
Firs, The, Cat. 105 BZ64
Chatfield Ct.
Firs, The, Grays 71 DE40
Firs, The, Guil. 118 AQ72
Firs, The, St.Alb. 9 BJ15
Firs, The, Welw.G.C. 5 BQ6
Firs Ave. N10 47 BV31
Firs Ave. N11 38 BV29
Firs Ave. SW14 65 BN45
Firs Ave., Wind. 61 AM45
Firs Clo. N10 47 BV31
Firs Ave.
Firs Clo. SE23 77 CD47
Firs Clo., Dor. 119 BJ72
Firs Clo., Esher 93 BH57
Firs Clo., Hat. 10 BP13
Firs Clo., Mitch. 86 BV51
Firs Dr., Houns. 63 BC44
Firs Dr., Loug. 31 CK23
Firs Dr., Slou. 52 AS40
Firs End, Ger.Cr. 43 AS31
Firs La. N13 39 BZ27
Firs La. N21 39 BZ27
Firs La., Pot.B. 20 BS20
Firs Pk. Ave. N21 39 BZ26
Firs Pk. Gdns. N21 39 BZ26
Firs Rd., Ken. 104 BY61
Firs Wk., Nthwd. 35 BA29
Firs Wk., Wdf.Grn. 40 CH28
Firs Way, Guil. 118 AQ70
Firs Wd. Clo., Pot.B. 20 BU19
Firsby Ave., Croy. 87 CC54
Firsby Rd. N16 48 CA33
Firscroft N13 39 BZ27
Firsdene Clo., Cher. 91 AU57
Firsgrove Cres., Brwd. 42 DA28
Firsgrove Rd., Brwd. 42 DA28
Firside Gro., Sid. 78 CN47
First Ave. E12 49 CK35
First Ave. E13 58 CH38
First Ave. E17 48 CE32
First Ave. N18 39 CC28
First Ave. NW4 46 BQ31
First Ave. SW14 65 BO45
First Ave. W3 55 BO40
First Ave. W10 55 BR38
First Ave., Amer. 25 AO23
First Ave., Bexh. 69 CP43
First Ave., Brwd. 24 DB20
First Ave., Dag. 59 CR37
First Ave., E.Mol. 84 BE52
First Ave., Enf. 30 CA25
First Ave., Epsom 94 BO58
First Ave., Grav. 81 DF47
First Ave., Grays 70 DA43
First Ave., Harl. 6 CM10
First Ave., Hayes 53 BB40
First Ave., Rom. 50 CP32
First Ave., Walt. 83 BC53
First Ave., Wat. 27 BD21
First Ave., Wem. 45 BK34
First Clo., E.Mol. 84 BG52
First Cross Rd., Twick. 74 BH48
First St. SW3 3 D8
First St. SW3 66 BU42
First Way SW20 85 BQ51
First Way, Wem. 46 BM35
Firswood Ave., Epsom 94 BO56
Firth Gdns. SW6 65 BR44
Firtree Ave., Mitch. 86 BV51
Firtree Ave., West Dr. 63 AZ41
Firtree Clo. SE16 57 CD40
Firtree Clo., Orp. 97 CN56
Firtree Gro., Cars. 95 BU57
Firtree Rd., Dag. 50 CS34
Firwood Ave., St.Alb. 10 BL13
Firwood Clo., Wok. 100 AP63
Firwood Rd., Vir.W. 82 AP53
Fish St. Hill EC3 4 L1
Fish St. Hill EC3 57 BZ40
Lower Thames St.
Fisher Clo., Croy. 87 CA54
Lower Addiscombe Rd.
Fisher Clo., Grnf. 54 BF38
Fisher Clo., Kings L. 17 AZ18
Fisher Clo., Wal.Cr. 21 CE20
Fisher Clo., Walt. 92 BC56
Fisher Rd., Har. 36 BH30
Fisher St. E16 58 CH39
Fisher St. WC1 2 B7
Fisher St. WC1 56 BX39
Fisherman Clo., Rich. 74 BK49
Fishermans Dr. SE16 57 CC41
Fishermans Hill, Grav. 81 DD46
Fishers Ct. SE14 67 CC44
Fishers Hatch, Harl. 6 CN10
Fishers Hill, Wok. 100 AP64
Fishers La. W4 65 BN42
Fishers La., Epp. 22 CN19
Fishers Way, Belv. 59 CS40
Fishersdene, Esher 93 BJ57
Kilnside
Fisherton St. NW8 1 A4
Fisherton St. NW8 56 BT38
Fisherton St. Est. NW8 56 BT38
Fishery Pl., Hem.H. 8 AW14
Fishery Rd., Hem.H. 8 AW14
Fishery Rd., Maid. 61 AH40
Fishmongers Hall St. EC4 57 BZ40
Wharfside

Fishponds Rd. SW17 76 BU49
Fishponds Rd., Kes. 97 CJ56
Fishpool St., St.Alb. 9 BF13
Fisons Rd. E16 58 CH40
Fitzalan Rd. N3 46 BR31
Fitzalan Rd., Esher 93 BH57
Fitzalan St. SE11 4 D8
Fitzalan St. SE11 66 BY42
Fitzgeorge Ave. W14 65 BR42
Fitzgeorge Ave., N.Mal. 85 BN51
Fitzgerald Ave. SW14 65 BO45
Fitzgerald Rd. E11 49 CH32
Fitzgerald Rd. SW14 65 BN45
Fitzgerald Rd., T.Ditt. 84 BJ53
Fitzhardinge St. W1 1 G8
Fitzhardinge St. W1 56 BV39
Fitzhugh Gro. SW18 76 BT46
Fitzilian Ave., Rom. 42 CW30
Fitzjames Ave. W14 65 BR42
Fitzjames Ave., Croy. 87 CG55
Fitzjohn Ave., Barn. 28 BR25
Fitzjohn Clo., Guil. 109 AU69
Fitzjohns Ave. NW3 47 BS35
Fitzmaurice Pl. W1 3 K2
Fitzmaurice Pl. W1 56 BV40
Curzon St.
Fitzneal St. W12 55 BO39
Fitzrobert Pl., Egh. 72 AT50
Fitzroy Clo. N6 47 BU33
Fitzroy Cres. W4 65 BN43
Fitzroy Ct. W1 1 M5
Fitzroy Cres. W4 65 BN43
Fitzroy Gdns. SE19 77 CA50
Fitzroy Ms. W1 1 L5
Fitzroy Ms. W1 56 BW38
Cleveland St.
Fitzroy Pk. N6 47 BU33
Fitzroy Rd. NW1 56 BV37
Fitzroy Sq. W1 1 L5
Fitzroy Sq. W1 56 BW38
Fitzroy St. W1 1 L5
Fitzroy St. W1 56 BW38
Fitzstephen Rd., Dag. 50 CO35
Fitzwarren Gdns. N19 47 BW33
Fitzwilliam Ave., Rich. 65 BL44
Fitzwilliam Ct., Harl. 6 CQ9
Sheering Rd.
Fitzwilliam Rd. SW4 66 BW45
Fitzwygram Clo., Hmptn. 74 BG49
Five Acre NW9 37 BO30
Five Acre Wk., Welw.G.C. 5 BR8
Salisbury Rd.
Five Acres, Chesh. 16 AO20
Five Acres, Harl. 13 CN12
Five Acres, Kings L. 17 AY18
Five Acres, St.Alb. 18 BE18
Five Acres Ave., St.Alb. 18 BE18
Five Elms Rd., Brom. 88 CJ55
Five Elms Rd., Dag. 50 CO34
Five Oaks, Wey. 91 AV47
Five Oaks Clo., Wok. 100 AP63
Five Oaks La., Chig. 41 CQ29
Five Ways Rd. SW9 66 BY44
Fiveacre Clo., Th.Hth. 86 BY53
Fiveash Rd., Grav. 81 CF47
Fivewents, Swan. 89 CU51
Fladbury Rd. N15 48 BZ32
Fladgate Rd. E11 49 CG32
Flag Clo., Croy. 87 CC54
Primrose La.
Flag Wk., Pnr. 44 BC32
Flags, The, Hem.H. 8 AZ14
Flagstaff Rd., Wal.Abb. 21 CE20
Flambard Rd., Har. 45 BJ32
Flamborough Clo., 106 CH63
West.
Flamborough Rd., Ruis. 44 BC34
Flamborough Spur, Slou. 61 AN41
Flamborough St. E14 57 CD39
Flamborough Wk. E14 57 CD39
Flamborough St.
Flamingo Gdns., Nthlt. 54 BE38
Jetstar Way
Flamingo Wk., Rain. 59 CU36
Fulmar Rd.
Flamstead End Relief Rd., 21 CA18
Wal.Cr.
Flamstead End Rd., 21 CB17
Chsnt.
Flamstead Gdns., Dag. 59 CP36
Flamstead Rd. SE7 68 CK42
Flamstead Rd., Dag. 59 CP36
Flamsted Ave., Wem. 55 BM36
Flanchford Rd. W12 65 BO41
Flanchford Rd., Reig. 120 BP73
Flanders, Egh. 72 AU49
Mullens Rd.
Flanders Cres. SW17 76 BU50
Flanders Rd. E6 58 CK37
Flanders Rd. W4 65 BO42
Flanders Wk., Egh. 72 AU49
Mullens Rd.
Flanders Way E9 57 CC36
Flank St. E1 57 CB40
Dock St.
Flash La., Enf. 29 BY22
Flask Wk. NW3 47 BT35
Flatfield Rd., Hem.H. 8 AZ14
Flaunden Bottom, Chesh. 25 AS21
Flaunden Bottom, Hem.H. 16 AS20
Flaunden Hill, Hem.H. 16 AS20
Flaunden La., Hem.H. 16 AT19
Flaunden La., Rick. 16 AU20
Flaunden Pk., Hem.H. 16 AS20
Flavian Clo., St.Alb. 9 BE15
Flaxley Rd., Mord. 86 BS54
Flaxman Ct. W1 1 N9
Flaxman Ct. W1 56 BW39
Wardour St.
Flaxman Rd. SE5 66 BY45
Flaxman Ter. WC1 1 P3
Flaxman Ter. WC1 56 BW38

Flaxmore Pl., Beck. 87 CF53
Flaxton Rd. SE18 68 CM44
Flecker Clo., Stan. 36 BH28
Fleece Dr., Surb. 84 BK54
Fleece Wk. N7 56 BX36
Fleeming Clo. E17 39 CD30
Pennant Ter.
Fleeming Rd. E17 39 CD30
Fleet Ave., Dart. 80 CY47
Fleet Ave., Upmin. 51 CY32
Fleet Clo., E.Mol. 84 BF53
Fleet Clo., Upmin. 51 CY32
Fleet La. EC4 2 F8
Fleet La. EC4 56 BY39
Fleet La., E.Mol. 84 BE53
Fleet Rd. NW3 47 BU35
Fleet Rd., Dart. 80 CY47
Fleet Rd., Grav. 81 DE48
Fleet Side, E.Mol. 84 BE53
Fleet Sq. WC1 2 C3
Fleet St. EC4 2 E9
Fleet St. EC4 56 BY39
Fleet St. Hill E1 57 CB38
Weaver St.
Fleet Way, Egh. 82 AU52
Fleetdale Par., Dart. 80 CY47
Swaledale Rd.
Fleethall Gro., Grays 71 DD40
Fleetwood Clo. E16 58 CJ39
Fleetwood Clo., Ch.St.G. 34 AQ28
Fleetwood Clo., Chess. 93 BK57
Fleetwood Clo., Croy. 87 CA55
Chepstow Ri.
Fleetwood Clo., Tad. 103 BQ63
Fleetwood Ct. E6 58 CK39
Pembroke Rd.
Fleetwood Ct., Wey. 92 AW60
Madeira Rd.
Fleetwood Rd. NW10 46 BP35
Fleetwood Rd., Kings.T. 85 BM52
Fleetwood Rd., Slou. 52 AP40
Fleetwood Sq., Kings.T. 85 BM52
Fleetwood St. N16 48 CA34
Fleetwood Way, Wat. 36 BD28
Fleming Clo. E17 39 CD30
Pennant Ter.
Fleming Clo., Chsnt. 21 CB17
Spicersfield
Fleming Ct. W2 1 A6
Fleming Ct. W2 56 BT39
St. Marys Ter.
Fleming Ct., Croy. 95 BY56
Fleming Gdns., Til. 71 DH44
Fielding Ave.
Fleming Mead, Mitch. 76 BU50
Fleming Rd. SE17 66 BY43
Fleming Rd., Sthl. 54 BF39
Fleming Way SE28 59 CP40
Fleming Way, Islw. 64 BH45
Flemings, Brwd. 42 DA28
Flemish Flds., Cher. 83 AW54
Flempton Rd. E10 48 CD33
Fletcher Clo., Cher. 91 AV57
Fletcher La. E10 48 CF33
Fletcher Path SE8 67 CE43
New Butt La.
Fletcher Rd. W4 65 BN41
Fletcher Rd., Cher. 91 AU57
Fletcher Rd., Chig. 40 CN28
Fletcher St. E1 57 CB40
Fletcher Way, Hem.H. 8 AX12
Fletchers Clo., Brom. 88 CH52
Fletching Rd. E5 48 CC34
Fletching Rd. SE7 68 CJ42
Lansdowne La.
Fletton Rd. N11 38 BX29
Fleur de Lis St. E1 2 N5
Fleur de Lis St. E1 57 CA38
Fleur Gates SW19 75 BQ47
Princes Way
Flexley Wd., Welw.G.C. 5 BR6
Flexmere Rd. N17 39 BZ30
Flimwell Clo., Brom. 78 CG49
Flinder Clo., St.Alb. 9 BJ14
Flint Clo., Lthd. 111 BF66
Flint Clo., Red. 121 BU70
Flint Hill, Dor. 119 BJ73
Flint Hill Clo., Dor. 119 BJ73
Flint St. SE17 4 L9
Flint St. SE17 67 BZ42
Flint St., Grays 70 DA43
Flint Way, St.Alb. 9 BG11
Flintlock Clo., Stai. 63 AW45
Flintmill Cres. SE3 68 CK44
Flinton St. SE17 4 N10
Flinton St. SE17 67 CA42
Flitcroft St. WC2 1 P9
Flitcroft St. WC2 56 BW39
Flockton St. SE16 67 CB41
George Row
Flodden Rd. SE5 67 BZ44
Flood La., Twick. 74 BJ47
Church La.
Flood Pas. SE18 68 CK42
Samuel St.
Flood St. SW3 66 BU42
Flood Wk. SW3 66 BU43
Flora Clo. E14 57 CE39
Flora Clo., Croy. 96 CF59
Flora Gdns., Rom. 50 CP32
Flora Gdns. Est. W6 65 BP42
Flora Gro., St.Alb. 9 BH14
Flora St., Belv. 69 CQ42
Floral Ct., Ash. 102 BK62
Floral Dr., St.Alb. 18 BK16
Floral St. WC2 1 Q10
Floral St. WC2 56 BX40
Florence Ave., Enf. 30 BZ24
Florence Ave., Mord. 86 BT53
Florence Ave., Wey. 92 AW59
Florence Clo., Grays 71 DC43
Florence Clo., Harl. 14 CP12
London Rd.
Florence Clo., Horn. 51 CW34

Florence Clo., Walt. 84 BD54
Florence Clo., Wat. 26 BC21
Florence Dr., Enf. 30 BZ24
Florence Gdns. W4 65 BN43
Florence Gdns., Stai. 73 AW50
Florence Rd. E6 58 CJ37
Florence Rd. E13 58 CG38
Florence Rd. N4 47 BX33
Florence Rd. SE2 69 CP42
Florence Rd. SE14 67 CD44
Florence Rd. SW19 76 BS50
Florence Rd. W4 65 BN41
Florence Rd. W5 55 BL40
Florence Rd., Beck. 87 CC51
Florence Rd., Brom. 88 CH51
Florence Rd., Felt. 73 BC47
Florence Rd., Kings.T. 75 BL50
Florence Rd., S.Croy. 96 BZ58
Florence Rd., Sthl. 64 BD42
Florence Rd., Walt. 83 BC54
Florence St. E16 58 CG38
Florence St. N1 56 BY36
Florence St. NW4 46 BQ31
Florence Ter. SE14 67 CD44
Florian Ave., Sutt. 95 BT56
Florian Rd. SW15 65 BR45
Florida Clo., Bush. 36 BG27
Florida Rd., Guil. 118 AS73
Florida Rd., Th.Hth. 86 BY51
Florida St. E2 57 CB38
Floriston Ave., Uxb. 53 BA36
Floriston Clo., Stan. 36 BJ30
Floriston Gdns., Stan. 36 BJ30
Florys Ct. SW19 75 BR47
Floss St. SW15 65 BQ44
Flower & Dean Wk. E1 2 Q7
Flower Cres., Cher. 91 AT57
Flower La. NW7 37 BQ28
Flower La., Gdse. 114 CC68
Flower Wk., Guil. 118 AR72
Flowerfield, Sev. 107 CT62
Flowerhill Way, Grav. 81 DF50
Flowers Ms. N19 47 BW34
St. Johns Way
Flowersmead SW17 76 BV48
Floyd Rd. SE7 68 CJ42
Floyds La., Wok. 101 AW61
Fludyer St. SE13 68 CG45
Fluys La., Epp. 23 CO20
Brook Rd.
Folair Way SE16 67 CB42
Bonamy Est. W.
Fold Cft., Harl. 6 CL10
Fold Rd., Red. 121 BV71
Foley Ms., Esher 93 BH57
Foley Rd.
Foley Rd., Esher 93 BH57
Foley Rd., West. 106 BQ53
Foley St. W1 1 L7
Foley St. W1 56 BW39
Folgate St. E1 2 N6
Folgate St. E1 57 CA39
Foliot St. W12 55 BO39
Folkes La., Upmin. 51 CZ31
Folkestone Rd. E6 58 CL37
Folkestone Rd. E17 48 CE31
Folkestone Rd. N18 39 CB28
Folkingham La. NW9 37 BO30
Folkington Cor. N12 37 BR28
Follett Clo., Wind. 72 AQ46
Follett Dr., Abb.L. 17 BB19
Follett St. E14 57 CF39
Folly Ave., St.Alb. 9 BG13
Folly Clo., Rad. 27 BH21
Folly La. E17 39 CD30
Folly La., St.Alb. 9 BG13
Folly Ms. W11 55 BR39
Kensington Pk.
Folly Pathway, Rad. 27 BH21
Folly Wall E14 67 CF41
Follyfield Rd., Bans. 95 BS60
Font Hills N2 38 BT30
Fontaine Rd. SW16 76 BX50
Fontarabia Rd. SW11 66 BV45
Fontayne Ave., Chig. 40 CM28
Fontayne Ave., Rain. 59 CT36
Fontayne Ave., Rom. 41 CT30
Fontenoy Rd. SW12 76 BV48
Fonteyne Gdns., Wdf.Grn. 40 CJ30
Fonthill Clo. SE20 87 CB51
Selby Rd.
Fonthill Ms. N4 47 BX34
Lennox Rd.
Fonthill Rd. N4 47 BX33
Fontley Way SW15 75 BP47
Fontmell Clo., Ashf. 73 AZ49
Fontmell Clo., St.Alb. 9 BH12
Fontmell Pk., Ashf. 73 AY49
Fontwell Clo., Har. 36 BH29
Fontwell Clo., Nthlt. 54 BF36
Fontwell Dr., Brom. 88 CK53
Fontwell Pk. Gdns., Horn. 51 CW35
Football La., Har. 45 BH33
Footbury Hill Rd., Orp. 89 CO54
Foots Cray High St., Sid. 79 CP50
Foots Cray La., Sid. 79 CP47
Footscray Rd. SE9 78 CL46
Forbes Ave., Pot.B. 20 BT20
Forbes Clo., Horn. 50 CU33
Forbes St. E1 57 CB39
Forburg Rd. N16 48 CB33
Ford Bri. Clo., Cher. 83 AW54
Ford Clo., Ashf. 73 AY50
Ford Clo., Bush. 27 BG24
Ford Clo., Har. 45 BG33
Ford Clo., Rain. 59 CT36
Ford Clo., Shep. 83 AZ52
Ford Clo., Th.Hth. 86 BY53
Ford End, Wdf.Grn. 40 CH29
Ford La., Iver 53 AW39
Ford La., Rain. 59 CT36
Ford Rd. E3 57 CD37
Ford Rd., Ashf. 73 AY49

Ford Rd., Cher. 83 AW54
Ford Rd., Dag. 59 CQ36
Ford Rd., Grav. 81 DD46
Ford Rd., Wok. 100 AT63
Ford Sq. E1 57 CB39
Cavell St.
Ford St. E3 57 CD37
Ford St. E16 58 CG39
Fordbridge Rd., Ashf. 73 AY50
Fordbridge Rd., Shep. 83 BB53
Fordbridge Rd., Sun. 83 BB53
Fordcroft Rd., Orp. 89 CO53
Forde Ave., Brom. 88 CJ52
Fordel Rd. SE6 77 CF47
Fordham Clo., Barn. 29 BU24
Fordham Clo., Horn. 51 CX33
Fordham Clo., West Dr. 53 AY39
Fordham Rd., Barn. 29 BT24
Fordham St. E1 57 CB39
Fordhook Ave. W5 55 BL40
Fordingley Rd. W9 55 BR38
Fordington Rd. N6 47 BU32
Fordland St. SE18 68 CM42
Fordmill Rd. SE6 77 CE48
Fords Gro. N21 39 BZ26
Fords Pk. Rd. E16 58 CH39
Fordwater Rd., Cher. 83 AW54
Fordwich Clo., Orp. 88 CN54
Fordwich Rd., Welw.G.C. 5 BQ8
Fordwych Cres. NW2 46 BR35
Fordwych Rd. NW2 46 BR35
Fordyce Clo., Horn. 51 CX33
Fordyce Rd. SE13 77 CF46
Fordyke Rd., Dag. 50 CQ34
Fore St. EC2 2 J7
Fore St. EC2 57 BZ39
Fore St. N9 39 CA29
Fore St. N18 39 CA29
Fore St., Harl. 6 CP9
Fore St., Hat. 10 BQ12
Fore St., Pnr. 44 BB31
Fore St. Ave. EC2 2 K7
Fore St. Ave. EC2 57 BZ39
Forebury, The, Saw. 6 CQ6
Forebury Ave., Saw. 6 CQ6
Forebury Cres., Saw. 6 CQ6
Forefield, St.Alb. 18 BF17
Foreland Ct. NW4 37 BR30
Foreland St. SE18 68 CM42
Plumstead Rd.
Foreman Ct. W6 65 BQ42
Foremark Clo., Ilf. 40 CN28
Foreshore SE8 67 CD42
Forest, The E11 49 CG31
Forest App., Wdf.Grn. 40 CG29
Forest Ave. E4 40 CG26
Forest Ave., Chig. 40 CL28
Forest Ave., Hem.H. 8 AY14
Forest Clo. E11 49 CG32
Forest Clo., Chis. 88 CL51
Caveside Clo.
Forest Clo., Lthd. 110 BB66
Forest Clo., Wal.Abb. 31 CH22
Forest Clo., Wok. 100 AU61
Forest Clo., Wdf.Grn. 40 CH28
Forest Ct. E4 40 CG26
Forest Ct. E11 49 CG31
Forest Cres., Ash. 103 BM61
Forest Dr. E12 49 CJ34
Forest Dr., Epp. 31 CN21
Forest Dr., Kes. 97 CK56
Forest Dr., Sun. 73 BB50
Forest Dr., Tad. 104 BS64
Forest Dr., Wdf.Grn. 39 CF29
Forest Dr. E. E11 48 CF33
Forest Dr. W. E11 48 CF33
Forest Edge, Buck.H. 40 CJ28
Forest Gdns. N17 39 CA30
Bruce Gro.
Forest Gate NW9 46 BO32
Forest Glade E4 40 CG28
Forest Glade E11 49 CG32
Forest Glade, Epp. 23 CQ17
Forest Grn. Rd., Maid. 61 AG44
Forest Gro. E8 57 CA36
Forest Hill Rd. SE22 77 CB46
Forest Hill Rd. SE23 77 CB46
Forest La. E7 49 CG35
Forest La. E15 49 CH35
Forest La., Chig. 40 CL28
Forest La., Lthd. 101 BB65
Forest Mt. Rd., Wdf.Grn. 39 CF29
Forest Ridge, Beck. 87 CE52
Forest Ridge, Kes. 97 CK56
Forest Ri. E17 48 CF31
Forest Rd. E7 49 CH35
Forest Rd. E8 57 CA36
Forest Rd. E11 48 CF33
Forest Rd. E17 48 CC31
Forest Rd. N9 39 CB26
Forest Rd. N17 48 CC31
Forest Rd., Chsnt. 21 CC18
Forest Rd., Enf. 30 CD21
Forest Rd., Erith 69 CU44
Forest Rd., Felt. 74 BD48
Forest Rd., Ilf. 40 CM30
Forest Rd., Lthd. 110 BB66
Forest Rd., Loug. 31 CJ24
Forest Rd., Rich. 65 BM43
Forest Rd., Rom. 50 CR31
Forest Rd., Sutt. 86 BS54
Forest Rd., Wat. 17 BC20
Forest Rd., Wind. 61 AL44
Forest Rd., Wok. 100 AU61
Forest Rd., Wdf.Grn. 40 CH27
Forest Side E4 40 CG26
Forest Side E7 49 CH35
Capel Rd.
Forest Side, Buck.H. 40 CJ26
Forest Side, Epp. 22 CM20
Forest Side, Wal.Abb. 31 CJ21
Forest Side, Wor.Pk. 85 BO54
Forest St. E7 49 CH35
Forest Vw. E4 30 CF25

Forest Vw. E11 49 CG33
Forest Vw. Ave. E10 48 CF32
Forest Vw. Rd. E12 49 CK35
Forest Vw. Rd. E17 39 CF30
Forest Vw. Rd., Loug. 31 CJ24
Forest Wk., Bush. 27 BE23
Forest Wk., Wey. 92 AZ56
Hanger Hill
Forest Way N19 47 BW34
Hargrave Pk.
Forest Way, Ash. 103 BL62
Forest Way, Loug. 31 CK24
Forest Way, Orp. 88 CN53
Forest Way, Sid. 78 CM47
Forest Way, Wdf.Grn. 40 CH28
Forestdale N14 38 BW28
Forester Rd. SE15 67 CB45
Foresters Clo., Wall. 95 BW57
Foresters Clo., Wok. 100 AP62
Foresters Cres., Bexh. 69 CR45
Foresters Dr. E17 48 CF31
Foresters Dr., Wall. 95 BW57
Forestholme Clo. SE23 77 CC48
Taymount Ri.
Forfar Rd. N22 38 BY30
Forfar Rd. SW11 66 BV44
Forge Ave., Couls. 104 BY63
Forge Clo., Brom. 88 CH54
Forge Clo., Hayes 63 BA43
Forge Clo., Kings L. 17 AW19
Forge Dr., Esher 93 BJ57
Forge End, St.Alb. 18 BF16
Forge End, Wok. 100 AS62
Forge La., Felt. 74 BE49
Forge La., Grav. 81 DJ48
Forge La., Hort.K. 90 CY52
Forge La., Nthwd. 35 BB29
Forge La., Sev. 99 DA58
Forge La., Sun. 83 BC52
Forge La., Sutt. 94 BR57
Forge Pl. NW1 56 BV36
Forge Way, Sev. 98 CT59
Forgefield, West. 106 CJ61
Forlong Path, Nthlt. 54 BE36
Ridgeway Wk.
Forman Pl. N16 48 CA35
Farleigh Rd.
Formby Ave., Stan. 45 BK31
Formosa St. W9 56 BS38
Formunt Clo. E16 58 CG39
Forres Clo., Hodd. 12 CE11
Forres Ct. SE19 77 CA49
Forres Gdns. NW11 47 BS32
Forrest Gdns. SW16 86 BX52
Forrester Path SE26 77 CC49
Queensthorpe Rd.
Forresters Dr., Welw.G.C. 5 BT8
Forris Ave., Hayes 53 BB40
Forset St. W1 1 D8
Forset St. W1 56 BU39
Forstal Clo., Brom. 88 CG52
Forster Rd. E17 48 CD32
Forster Rd. N17 48 CA31
Forster Rd. SW2 76 BX47
Forster Rd., Beck. 87 CD52
Forster Rd., Croy. 87 BZ53
Windmill Rd.
Forsters Clo., Rom. 50 CQ32
Forsters Way, Hayes 53 BC39
Forston St. N1 57 BZ37
Forsyte Cres. SE19 87 CA51
Forsyth Gdns. SE17 66 BY43
Forsyth Path, Wok. 91 AU60
Forsyth Pl., Enf. 30 CA25
Forsyth Rd., Wok. 100 AU61
Forsythe Ave., Hodd. 12 CE11
Forsythia Clo., Ilf. 49 CL35
Lavender Pl.
Fort La., Reig. 113 BS68
Fort Pas. SE16 67 CA42
Fort Pas. SE18 68 CL42
Sandy Hill Rd.
Fort Rd. SE1 4 Q9
Fort Rd. SE1 67 CA42
Fort Rd., Guil. 118 AS72
Fort Rd., Nthlt. 54 BF36
Fort Rd., Sev. 107 CS61
Fort Rd., Tad. 120 BM69
Fort Rd., Til. 71 DG45
Fort St. E1 2 N7
Fort St. E16 58 CH40
Forterie Gdns., Ilf. 50 CO34
Fortescue Ave. E8 57 CB36
Mentmore Ter.
Fortescue Ave., Twick. 74 BG48
Fortescue Rd. SW19 76 BT50
Fortescue Rd., Edg. 37 BN30
Fortescue Rd., Wey. 92 AY56
Fortess Gro. NW5 47 BW35
Fortess Rd.
Fortess Rd. NW5 47 BW35
Fortess Wk. NW5 47 BV35
Fortess Rd.
Forth Rd., Upmin. 51 CY32
Forthbridge Rd. SW11 66 BV45
Fortin Clo., S.Ock. 60 DA40
Fortin Path, S.Ock. 60 DA40
Fortin Way
Fortin Way, S.Ock. 60 DA40
Fortis Clo. E16 58 CJ39
Fortis Grn. N2 47 BU31
Fortis Grn. Ave. N2 47 BU31
Fortis Grn. Rd. N10 47 BV31
Fortismere Ave. N10 47 BV31
Fortnam Rd. N19 47 BW34
Fortnums Acre, Stan. 36 BH29
Fortrose Gdns. SW2 76 BX47
New Pk. Rd.
Fortuna Clo. N7 56 BX36
Roman Way
Fortune Gate Rd. NW10 55 BO37
Fortune Grn. Rd. NW6 47 BS35
Fortune La., Borwd. 28 BL25
Fortune St. EC1 2 J5

Fortune St. EC1 57 BZ
Fortune Wk. SE28 68 CM
Garrick Dr.
Fortune Way NW10 55 BF
Fortunes, The, Harl. 13 CN
Fortunes Mead, Nthlt. 54 BE
Forty Acre La. E16 58 CH
Forty Ave., Wem. 46 BL
Forty Clo., Wem. 46 BL
Forty Hall Est., Enf. 30 CA
Forty Hill, Enf. 30 CA
Forty La., Wem. 46 BM
Fortyfoot Rd., Lthd. 102 BK
Forum, The, E.Mol. 84 BF
Forum, The, Edg. 37 BM
Forum Pl., Hat. 10 BC
Fiddle Bri. La.
Forval Clo., Mitch. 86 BU
Forward Dr., Har. 45 BJ
Fosbury Ms. W2 56 BS
Inverness Ter.
Foscote Ms. W9 56 BS
Amberley Rd.
Foscote Rd. NW4 46 BP
Foskett Rd. SW6 65 BR
Foss Ave., Croy. 95 BY
Foss Rd. SW17 76 BT
Fossdene Rd. SE7 68 CH
Fossdyke Clo., Hayes 54 BE
Telford Way
Fosse, The, St.Alb. 9 BE
Fosse Way W13 54 BJ
Fossil Rd. SE13 67 CE
Fossington Rd., Belv. 69 CP
Fossway, Dag. 50 CP
Foster Ave., Wind. 61 AM
Foster La. EC2 2
Foster La. EC2 57 BZ
Foster La., Wok. 100 AO
Foster Rd. E13 58 CH
Foster Rd. W3 55 BO
Foster Rd. W4 65 BN
Foster Rd., Hem.H. 8 AW
Foster St. NW4 46 BQ
Foster St., Harl. 14 CQ
Foster Wk. NW4 46 BQ
Fosterdown, Gdse. 114 CB
Fosters Clo. E18 40 CH
Latchett Rd.
Fosters Clo., Chis. 78 CK
Fothergill Clo. E13 58 CG
Fotheringham Rd., Enf. 30 CA
Fotherley Rd., Rick. 34 AV
Fouberts Pl. W1 1
Fouberts Pl. W1 56 BW
Foulden Rd. N16 48 CA
Foulis Ter. SW7 3 B
Foulis Ter. SW7 66 BT
Foulser Rd. SW17 76 BU
Foulsham Rd., Th.Hth. 87 BZ
Founders Ct. EC2 2
Founders Dr., Uxb. 43 AV
Queen Mother Dr.
Founders Gdns. SE19 77 BZ
Hermitage Rd.
Foundry Clo. SE16 57 CD
Foundry La., Slou. 62 AT
Foundry Ms. NW1 1 M
Fount St. SW8 66 BW
Fountain Clo., Uxb. 53 BA
Fountain Ct. EC4 2 D1
Fountain Ct. EC4 56 BY
Fountain Ct. SE26 77 CC
Fountain Dr. SE19 77 CA
Fountain Fm., Harl. 13 CN
Fountain Gdns., Wind. 61 AO
Fountain La., Sev. 108 CZ
Fountain Ms. N5 48 BZ
Kelross Rd.
Fountain Pl. SW9 66 BY
Fountain Pl., Wal.Abb. 21 CF
Fountain Rd. SW17 76 BT
Fountain Rd., Red. 121 BU
Fountain Rd., Th.Hth. 87 BZ
Fountain Sq. SW1 3
Fountain St. E2 57 CA
Columbia Rd.
Fountain Wk., Grav. 81 DF
Fountains Ave., Felt. 74 BE
Fountains Clo., Felt. 74 BE
Fountains Cres. N14 38 BX
Fountayne Rd. N15 48 CB
Fountayne Rd. N16 48 CB
Four Acres, Cob. 93 BE
Four Acres, Guil. 118 AU
Four Acres, Saw. 6 CQ
Four Acres, Welw.G.C. 5 BR
Four Acres Dr., Hem.H. 8 AY
Four Acres Wk., Hem.H. 8 AY
Four Seasons Cres., Sutt. 85 BR
Four Tubs, Bush. 36 BG
Fouracres, Enf. 30 CD
Fouracres, Kings.T. 75 BN
Fourfield Clo., Epsom 103 BN
Fourland Wk., Edg. 37 BN
Fournier St. E1 2 C
Fournier St. E1 57 CA
Fourth Ave. E12 49 CK
Fourth Ave. W10 55 BR
Fourth Ave., Enf. 30 CA
Fourth Ave., Grays 70 DA
Fourth Ave., Harl. 13 CK
Fourth Ave., Hayes 53 BB
Fourth Ave., Rom. 50 CS
Fourth Ave., Wat. 27 BD
Fourth Cross Rd., Twick. 74 BG
Fourth Dr., Couls. 104 BW
Fourth Way, Wem. 46 BN
Fourways, Hat. 10 BQ
Fourways, St.Alb. 10 BL
Fourwents, Cob. 93 BD
Fowell St. W11 55 BQ
Fowey Ave., Ilf. 49 CJ

wey Clo. E1 57 CB40
Kennet St.
wler Clo., Sid. 79 CQ49
wler Rd. E7 49 CH35
wler Rd., Ilf. 41 CO28
wler Rd., Mitch. 86 BV51
Priestley Rd.
wlers Clo. SW11 66 BT45
Plough Rd.
wlers Mead, Wok. 91 AP58
wlers Wk. W5 54 BK38
wley Clo., Wal.Cr. 21 CE20
Longcroft Dr.
wnes St. SW11 66 BU45
x and Knot St. EC1 2 G6
x Burrow Rd., Chig. 41 CP28
x Clo. E1 57 CC38
Colebert Ave.
x Clo. E16 58 CH39
x Clo., Borwd. 27 BK25
Rodgers Clo.
x Clo., Orp. 98 CO56
x Clo., Rom. 41 CR28
x Clo., Wey. 92 BA56
x Clo., Wok. 100 AU61
x Covert, Lthd. 105 BG65
High Flds.
x Dell, Nthwd. 35 BA29
x Hatch, Brwd. 33 CZ22
x Hill SE19 77 CA50
x Hill, Kes. 97 CJ56
x Hill Gdns. SE19 77 CA50
x Hills, Wok. 100 AR62
Parley Dr.
x Hills Clo., Cher. 91 AT57
x Hollows, Hat. 10 BP11
x Ho. Rd., Belv. 69 CR42
x La. N13 38 BX27
x La. W5 55 BL38
x La., Cat. 104 BY64
x La., Kes. 97 CH56
x La., Lthd. 111 BE66
x La. N., Cher. 82 AV54
x La. S., Cher. 82 AV54
x Rd. E16 58 CG39
x Rd., Slou. 62 AR42
xberry Rd. SE4 67 CD45
xborough Clo., Slou. 62 AT42
xborough Gdns. SE4 77 CE46
xbourne Rd. SW17 76 BV48
xburrows Ave., Guil. 118 AP70
xburrows Ct., Guil. 118 AP70
Foxburrows Ave.
oxbury Ave., Chis. 78 CM50
oxbury Clo., Brom. 78 CH50
oxbury Clo., Orp. 98 CO56
oxbury Dr., Orp. 98 CO57
oxbury Rd., Brom. 78 CH50
oxcombe, Croy. 96 CE57
oxcombe Clo. E6 58 CJ37
Boleyn Rd.
oxcombe Rd. SW15 75 BP47
oxcroft, St.Alb. 9 BJ14
oxcroft Rd. SE18 68 CL44
oxdell Way, Ger.Cr. 34 AS28
oxearth Clo., West. 107 CK62
oxearth Rd., S.Croy. 96 CB58
oxearth Spur, S.Croy. 96 CC58
oxenden Rd., Guil. 118 AS71
oxes Dale SE3 68 CH45
oxes Dale, Brom. 87 CF52
oxes Dr., Wal.Cr. 21 CA18
Hornbeam Way
oxes Grn., Grays 71 DG41
oxfield Clo., Nthwd. 35 BB29
oxfield Rd., Orp. 88 CM55
oxglove Clo., Hat. 10 BP13
oxglove Clo., Stai. 73 AX47
Diamedes Ave.
oxglove Cres., Ilf. 58 CL36
Bluebell Way
oxglove Gdns., Guil. 118 AU69
oxglove Gdns., Pur. 95 BX59
oxglove La., Chess. 94 BM56
oxglove Rd., S.Ock. 60 DB39
oxglove St. W12 55 BO40
oxglove Way, Wall. 86 BV54
oxgloves, The, Hem.H. 7 AV14
oxgrove N14 38 BX27
oxgrove Ave., Beck. 77 CE50
oxgrove Dr., Wok. 100 AT61
oxgrove Path, Wat. 36 BD28
oxgrove Rd., Beck. 77 CE50
oxhall Rd., Upmin. 51 CY35
oxham Rd. N19 47 BW34
oxherne, Slou. 62 AR41
oxhill, Wat. 26 BC21
oxhills Rd., Cher. 91 AT56
oxhills Rd., Grays 71 DE40
Brookmans Ave.
oxhole Rd. SE9 78 CK46
oxholes, Wey. 92 BA56
oxhollow Dr., Bexh. 69 CP45
oxholt Gdns. NW10 55 BN36
oxhome Clo., Chis. 78 CL50
oxhounds La., Grav. 81 DD48
oxlake Rd., Wey. 92 AY59
oxlands Cres., Dag. 50 CS35
oxlands Rd., Dag. 50 CS35
oxlees, Wem. 45 BJ35
oxley Clo. E8 48 CB35
oxley Clo., Loug. 31 CL24
oxley Clo., Red. 121 BV73
oxley Gdns., Pur. 95 BY60
oxley Hill Rd., Pur. 95 BY59
oxley La., Pur. 95 BW59
oxley Rd. SW9 66 BY43
oxley Rd., Ken. 95 BY60
oxley Rd., Th.Hth. 86 BY52
oxleys, Wat. 36 BE27
oxmanor Way, Grays 70 DA43
oxmead Clo., Enf. 29 BX24
oxmore St. SW11 66 BU44
oxoak Hill, Walt. 92 BB58
Foxon Clo., Cat. 105 CA64
Foxon La., Cat. 105 BZ64
Foxon La. Gdns., Cat. 105 CA64
Foxs La., Hat. 10 BQ15
Foxs Path, Mitch. 86 BT51
Foxton Rd., Grays 70 DB43
Foxton Rd., Hodd. 12 CE12
Foxwarren, Esher 93 BH58
Foxwell St. SE4 67 CD45
Foxwood Clo., Felt. 73 BC48
Foxwood Dr., Dart. 80 DA48
Foxwood Rd. SE3 68 CG45
Foyle Dr., S.Ock. 60 DA39
Foyle Rd. N17 39 CB30
Foyle Rd. SE3 68 CG43
Frailey Clo., Wok. 100 AT61
Frailey Hill, Wok. 100 AT61
Framewood Rd., Slou. 52 AR36
Framfield Clo. N12 38 BS27
Framfield Rd. N5 47 BY35
Framfield Rd. W7 54 BH39
Framfield Rd., Mitch. 76 BV50
Framlingham Clo. E5 48 CB34
Southwold Rd.
Framlingham Cres. SE9 78 CK49
Frampton Clo., Sutt. 95 BS57
Frampton Pk. Est. E9 57 CC36
Frampton Pk. Rd. E9 57 CC36
Frampton Rd., Epp. 23 CO17
Frampton Rd., Houns. 64 BE45
Frampton Rd., Pot.B. 20 BT18
Frampton St. NW8 1 B5
Frampton St. NW8 56 BT38
Francemary Rd. SE4 77 CE46
Frances Gdns., S.Ock. 60 CZ39
Frances Rd. E4 39 CE29
Frances Rd., Wind. 61 AO44
Frances St. SE18 68 CK42
Frances St., Chesh. 16 AO18
Franche Ct. Rd. SW17 76 BT48
Francis Ave., Bexh. 69 CR44
Francis Ave., Felt. 73 BC48
Francis Ave., Har. 45 BJ32
Francis Ave., Ilf. 49 CM34
Francis Ave., St.Alb. 9 BG12
Francis Barber Clo. SW16 76 BX49
Valley Rd.
Francis Chichester Way SW11 66 BV44
Francis Clo. E14 67 CF42
Saunders Ness Rd.
Francis Clo., Epsom 94 BN56
Francis Clo., Shep. 83 AZ52
Francis Gro. SW19 75 BR50
Francis Rd. E10 48 CF33
Francis Rd. N2 47 BU31
Lynmouth Rd.
Francis Rd., Cat. 105 BZ64
Francis Rd., Croy. 86 BY53
Francis Rd., Dart. 80 CV46
Francis Rd., Grnf. 54 BJ37
Francis Rd., Har. 45 BJ32
Francis Rd., Houns. 64 BD44
Francis Rd., Ilf. 49 CM34
Francis Rd., Orp. 89 CP52
Francis Rd., Pnr. 45 BD32
Francis Rd., Wall. 95 BW57
Francis Rd., Wat. 26 BC24
Francis St. E15 49 CG35
Francis St. SW1 3 L8
Francis St. SW1 66 BW42
Francis St., Ilf. 49 CM34
Francis Ter. N19 47 BW34
Franciscan Rd. SW17 76 BU49
Francklyn Gdns., Edg. 37 BM27
Francombe Gdns., Rom. 50 CU32
Franconia Rd. SW4 76 BW46
Frank Bailey Wk. E12 49 CK35
Gainsborough Ave.
Frank Dixon Clo. SE21 77 CA47
Frank Dixon Way SE21 77 CA47
Frank St. E13 58 CH38
Frankfurt Rd. SE24 77 BZ46
Frankham St. SE8 67 CE43
Frankland Clo. SE16 67 CB41
Wardale Clo.
Frankland Clo., Rick. 35 AZ26
Frankland Clo., Wdf.Grn. 40 CJ28
Frankland Rd. E4 39 CE28
Frankland Rd. SW7 3 A7
Frankland Rd., Rick. 26 AZ25
Franklands Dr., Wey. 92 AW57
Franklin Ave., Chsnt. 21 CB18
Franklin Clo. N20 38 BT26
Franklin Clo. SE27 76 BY48
Franklin Clo., Hem.H. 8 AY15
Franklin Clo., Kings.T. 85 BM52
Willingham Way
Franklin Clo., St.Alb. 10 BO14
Franklin Cres., Mitch. 86 BW52
Franklin Pas. SE9 68 CK45
Franklin Rd. SE20 77 CC50
Franklin Rd., Bexh. 69 CQ44
Franklin Rd., Grav. 81 DH49
Franklin Rd., Horn. 60 CV36
Franklin Rd., Wat. 26 BC23
Franklin Sq. SW5 65 BR42
Marchbank Rd.
Franklin St. E3 57 CE38
Bromley High St.
Franklin St. N15 48 CA32
Franklins Ms., Har. 45 BG34
Franklins Row SW3 3 F10
Franklins Row SW3 66 BU42
Franklyn Clo., Dag. 59 CS36
Franklyn Cres., Wind. 61 AL45
Franklyn Gdns., Ilf. 40 CM29
Franklyn Rd. NW10 55 BO36
Franklyn Rd., Walt. 83 BC53
Franklyns, Harl. 13 CM11
Franks Ave., N.Mal. 85 BN52
Franks La., Hort.K. 90 CX53
Franks Rd., Guil. 118 AQ69
Franks Wd. Ave., Orp. 88 CL53
Frankswood Ave., West Dr. 53 AY39
Franlaw Cres. N13 39 BZ28
Franmil Rd., Horn. 50 CU33
Fransfield Gro. SE26 77 CB48
Frant Clo. SE20 77 CC50
Frant Rd., Th.Hth. 86 BY53
Franthorne Way SE6 77 CE48
Randlesdown Rd.
Fraser Clo. E6 58 CK39
Linton Gdns.
Fraser Clo., Bex. 79 CS48
Dartford Rd.
Fraser Gdns., Dor. 119 BJ71
Fraser Rd. E17 48 CE32
Fraser Rd. N9 39 CB27
Fraser Rd., Chsnt. 21 CD17
Fraser Rd., Erith 69 CS42
Fraser Rd., Grnf. 54 BJ37
Fraser St. W4 65 BO42
Frating Cres., Wdf.Grn. 40 CH29
Frays Ave., West Dr. 63 AX41
Frays Clo., West Dr. 63 AX41
Frays Lea, Uxb. 53 AX37
Frays Waye, Uxb. 53 AX37
Frazer Ave., Ruis. 45 BD35
Frazer Clo., Rom. 50 CT33
Frazier St. SE1 4 D5
Frazier St. SE1 66 BY41
Frean St. SE16 67 CB41
Frederic Ms. SW1 3 F5
Frederic St. E17 48 CD32
Frederica Rd. E4 39 CF26
Frederica St. N7 56 BX36
Caledonian Rd.
Frederick Andrews Ct., Grays 71 DE43
Silverlocke Rd.
Frederick Clo. W2 1 D10
Frederick Clo. W2 56 BU39
Frederick Clo., Sutt. 94 BR56
Frederick Cres. SW9 66 BY43
Frederick Cres., Enf. 30 CC23
Frederick Gdns., Sutt. 94 BR56
Frederick Pl. SE18 68 CL42
Frederick Rd. SE17 66 BY43
Frederick Rd., Rain. 59 CS37
Frederick Rd., Sutt. 94 BR56
Frederick Sanger Rd., Guil. 118 AO70
Frederick St. WC1 2 B3
Frederick St. WC1 56 BX38
Frederick Ter. E8 57 CA36
Fredericks Pl. EC2 2 K9
Fredericks Pl. EC2 57 BZ39
Old Jewry
Fredericks Pl. N12 38 BT28
Fredericks Row EC1 2 F2
Fredora Ave., Hayes 53 BB38
Free Prae Rd., Cher. 83 AW54
Freeborne Gdns., Rain. 59 CU36
Mungo Pk. Rd.
Freedom St. SW11 66 BU44
Freedown La., Sutt. 95 BT60
Freegrove Rd. N7 47 BX35
Freeland Pk. NW4 37 BR30
Freeland Rd. W5 55 BL40
Freeland Way, Erith 69 CU44
Freelands Ave., S.Croy. 96 CC58
Freelands Gro., Brom. 88 CH51
Freelands Rd., Brom. 88 CH51
Freelands Rd., Cob. 92 BC60
Freeman Clo., Nthlt. 54 BE36
Freeman Clo., Shep. 83 BB52
The Cfts.
Freeman Ct., Chesh. 16 AO18
Barnes Ave.
Freeman Rd., Grav. 81 DJ48
Freeman Rd., Mord. 86 BT53
Freeman Way, Horn. 51 CW32
Freemans Clo., Slou. 52 AQ36
Freemans La., Hayes 53 BB40
Freemantle Ave., Enf. 30 CC25
Freemasons Rd. E16 58 CH39
Freemasons Rd., Croy. 87 CA54
Freesia Clo., Orp. 97 CN56
Briarswood Way
Freethorpe Clo. SE19 77 BZ50
Freke Rd. SW11 66 BV45
Fremantle Ho., Til. 71 DG44
Leicester Rd.
Fremantle Rd., Belv. 69 CR42
Fremantle Rd., Ilf. 40 CM30
Fremantle St. SE17 4 M10
Fremantle St. SE17 67 CA42
Fremont St. E9 57 CC37
French Gdns., Cob. 93 BD60
French Horn La., Hat. 10 BP12
French Pl. E1 2 N4
French Row, St.Alb. 9 BG13
Market Pl.
French St., Sun. 84 BD51
French Wells, Wok. 100 AQ62
Frencham Ct., Mitch. 86 BT52
Belgrave Rd.
Frenchaye, Wey. 92 AX56
Frenches, The, Red. 121 BV69
Frenches Dr., Red. 121 BV69
The Frenches
Frenches Rd., Red. 121 BV69
Frenchlands Hatch, Lthd. 110 BB67
Frenchum Gdns., Slou. 61 AM40
Frendsbury Rd. SE4 67 CC45
Frensham, Chsnt. 21 CA17
Frensham Clo., Sthl. 54 BE38
Frensham Dr. SW15 75 BO48
Frensham Dr., Croy. 96 CF57
Frensham Rd. SE9 78 CM48
Frensham Rd., Ken. 95 BY60
Frensham St. SE15 67 CB43
Frensham Way, Epsom 103 BQ61
Frere St. SW11 66 BU44
Fresh Wf. Est., Bark. 58 CL37
Fresh Wf. Rd., Bark. 58 CL37
Freshborough Ct., Guil. 118 AS71
Lower Edgeborough Rd.
Freshfield Clo. SE13 67 CF45
Marischal Rd.
Freshfield Dr. N14 38 BV26
Freshfields, Croy. 87 CD54
Freshfields Ave., Upmin. 51 CX35
Freshford St. SW18 76 BT48
Freshmount Gdns., Epsom 94 BM59
Freshwater Clo. SW17 76 BV50
Freshwater Rd. SW17 76 BV50
Freshwater Rd., Dag. 50 CP33
Freshwaters, Harl. 6 CN10
Freshwell Ave., Rom. 50 CP31
Freshwell Gdns., Brwd. 123 DE32
Freshwood Clo., Beck. 87 CE51
Freshwood Way, Wall. 95 BV57
Freston Gdns., Barn. 29 BV25
Freston Pk. N3 37 BR30
Freston Rd. W10 55 BQ40
Freta Rd., Bexh. 79 CQ46
Fretherne Rd., Welw.G.C. 5 BQ8
Frewin Rd. SW18 76 BT47
Friar Ms. SE27 76 BY48
Prioress Rd.
Friar Rd., Hayes 54 BD38
Friar Rd., Orp. 89 CO53
Friar St. EC4 2 G9
Friar St. EC4 56 BY39
Carter La.
Friars, The, Chig. 40 CN28
Friars, The, Harl. 13 CL12
Friars Ave. N20 38 BU27
Friars Ave. SW15 75 BO48
Friars Ave., Brwd. 122 DD26
Friars Clo. N2 47 BT31
Friars Clo., Brwd. 122 DD26
Friars Clo., Nthlt. 54 BD38
Broomcroft Ave.
Friars Fld., Berk. 7 AP11
Herons Elm
Friars Gdns. W3 55 BN40
St. Dunstans Ave.
Friars Gate, Guil. 118 AQ71
Friars Gate Clo., Wdf.Grn. 40 CH28
Friars La., Rich. 74 BK46
Friars Mead E14 67 CF41
Friars Ms. SE9 78 CL46
Friars Orchard, Lthd. 102 BG64
Friars Pl. La. W3 55 BN40
Friars Ri., Wok. 100 AT62
Friars Rd. E6 58 CJ37
Friars Rd., Vir.W. 82 AR52
Friars Stile Pl., Rich. 75 BL46
Friars Stile Rd.
Friars Stile Rd., Rich. 75 BL46
Friars Wk. N14 38 BV26
Friars Wk. SE2 69 CP42
Friars Wk., Har. 36 BH29
Friars Way W3 55 BN39
Friars Way, Bush. 27 BE23
Friars Way, Cher. 82 AV53
Friars Way, Kings L. 17 AZ18
Friars Wd., Croy. 96 CD58
Friarscroft, Brox. 12 CE13
Friary, The, Wind. 72 AR46
Friary Bri., Guil. 118 AR71
Friary Clo. N12 38 BU28
Friary Ct. SW1 3 M3
Friary Est. SE15 67 CB43
Friary La., Wdf.Grn. 40 CH28
Friary Rd. N12 38 BT28
Friary Rd. SE15 67 CB43
Friary Rd. W3 55 BN39
Friary Rd., Stai. 72 AR47
Friary St., Guil. 118 AR71
Friary Way N12 38 BU28
Friday Hill E4 40 CG27
Friday Hill, Belv. 69 CR42
Friday Hill W. E4 40 CG27
Friday Rd., Erith 69 CS42
Friday Rd., Mitch. 76 BU50
Friday St. EC4 2 H10
Friday St. EC4 57 BZ39
Cannon St.
Frideswide Pl. NW5 47 BW35
Islip St.
Friend St. EC1 2 F2
Friend St. EC1 56 BY38
Friendly St. SE8 67 CE44
Friendly St. Ms. SE8 67 CE44
Friends Rd., Croy. 87 BZ55
Friends Rd., Pur. 95 BY59
Friendship Wk., Nthlt. 54 BD38
Wayfarer Rd.
Friern Barnet La. N11 38 BT27
Friern Barnet La. N20 38 BT27
Friern Barnet Rd. N11 38 BU28
Friern Ct. N20 38 BT27
Friern Mt. Dr. N20 38 BT26
Friern Pk. N12 38 BT28
Friern Rd. SE22 77 CB47
Friern Watch Ave. N12 38 BT28
Frieze Hill, Brwd. 42 CX26
Frigate Ms. SE8 67 CE43
Watergate St.
Frimley Ave., Horn. 51 CX33
Frimley Clo. SW19 75 BR48
Frimley Clo., Croy. 96 CF57
Frimley Ct., Sid. 79 CP49
Frimley Cres., Croy. 96 CF57
Frimley Gdns., Mitch. 86 BU52
Frimley Rd., Chess. 94 BL56
Frimley Rd., Hem.H. 7 AV13
Frimley Rd., Ilf. 49 CN34
Frimley St. E1 57 CC38
Frimley Way
Frimley Vw., Wind. 61 AL44
Frimley Way E1 57 CC38
Fringewood Clo., Nthwd. 35 AZ30
Frinsted Clo., Orp. 89 CP52
Frinsted Rd., Erith 69 CS43
Frinton Clo., Wat. 35 BC27
Frinton Dr., Wdf.Grn. 39 CF29
Frinton Ms., Ilf. 49 CL32
Bramley Cres.
Frinton Rd. E6 58 CJ38
Frinton Rd. N15 48 CA32
Frinton Rd. SW17 76 BV50
Frinton Rd., Rom. 41 CQ29
Frinton Rd., Sid. 79 CQ48
Friston Path, Chig. 40 CN28
Manford Way
Friston St. SW6 66 BS44
Frith Ct. NW7 37 BR29
Frith Knowle, Walt. 92 BC57
Frith La. NW7 37 BR29
Frith Rd. E11 48 CF35
Frith Rd., Croy. 87 BZ55
Frith St. W1 1 N9
Frith St. W1 56 BW39
Fritham Clo., N.Mal. 85 BO53
Frithe, The, Slou. 52 AR40
Friths Dr., Reig. 121 BS69
Raglan Rd.
Frithsden Copse, Berk. 7 AS11
Frithville Gdns. W12 55 BQ40
Frithwald Rd., Cher. 82 AV54
Frithwood Ave., Nthwd. 35 BB28
Frizlands La., Dag. 50 CR35
Frobisher Clo., Ken. 105 BZ62
Hayes La.
Frobisher Clo., Pnr. 45 BD33
Frobisher Ct. SE23 77 CB48
Sydenham Ri.
Frobisher Cres., Stai. 73 AY47
Frobisher Gdns., Guil. 118 AT70
Frobisher Gdns., Stai. 73 AY47
Frobisher Rd. E6 58 CK39
Frobisher Rd. N8 47 BY31
Frobisher Rd., Erith 69 CU43
Frobisher Rd., St.Alb. 9 BK14
Frobisher St. SE10 68 CG43
Frobisher Way, Grav. 81 DJ49
Frog La., Guil. 109 AS66
Frog St., Brwd. 33 CZ23
Froggy La., Uxb. 43 AU34
Froghall La., Chig. 40 CM28
Froghole La., Eden. 115 CN70
Frogley Rd. SE22 67 CA45
Frogmoor La., Rick. 35 AX27
Frogmore SW18 76 BS46
Frogmore Ave., Hayes 53 BB38
Frogmore Clo., Slou. 61 AN41
Frogmore Clo., Sutt. 85 BQ55
Frogmore Ct., Rick. 35 AX27
Frogmore La.
Frogmore Ct., Sthl. 64 BF42
Norwood Rd.
Frogmore Dr., Wind. 62 AP44
Frogmore Fm. Est., Hayes 53 BA38
Frogmore Gdns., Hayes 53 BB38
Frogmore Gdns., Sutt. 94 BQ56
Frogmore Rd., Hem.H. 8 AX15
Frognal NW3 47 BT35
Frognal Ave., Har. 45 BH31
Frognal Ave., Sid. 79 CO50
Frognal Clo. NW3 47 BT35
Frognal Ct. NW3 56 BT36
Frognal Gdns. NW3 47 BT35
Frognal La. NW3 47 BS35
Frognal Par. NW3 56 BT36
Frognal Ct.
Frognal Pl., Sid. 79 CO50
Frognal Ri. NW3 47 BT34
Frognal Way NW3 47 BT35
Froissart Rd. SE9 78 CJ46
Frome Sq., Hem.H. 8 AY11
Frome St. N1 57 BZ37
Fromondes Rd., Sutt. 94 BR56
Front, The, Berk. 7 AT11
Front La., Upmin. 51 CZ33
Frostic Pl. E1 57 CA39
Hopetown
Frostic Wk. E1 57 CA39
Chicksand St.
Froude St. SW8 66 BW44
Robertson St.
Frowick Clo., Hat. 10 BP15
Frowyke Cres., Pot.B. 19 BP19
Fruen Rd., Felt. 73 BB47
Fry Clo., Rom. 41 CR28
Fry Rd. E6 58 CJ36
Fry Rd. NW10 55 BO37
Fry Rd., Ashf. 73 AX49
Fryatt Rd. N17 39 BZ29
Fryatt St. E14 58 CG39
Fryent Clo. NW9 46 BM32
Fryent Cres. NW9 46 BO32
Fryent Flds. NW9 46 BO32
Fryent Gro. NW9 46 BO32
Fryent Way NW9 46 BM32
Fryer Clo., Chesh. 16 AO20
Fryern Wd., Cat. 105 BZ64
Frying Pan All. E1 2 P7
Frying Pan All. E1 57 CA39
Bell La.
Fryston Ave., Couls. 95 BV60
Fryston Ave., Croy. 87 CB55
Fryth Mead, St.Alb. 9 BF13
Fuchsia St. SE2 69 CO42
Fulbeck Dr. NW9 37 BO30
Fulbeck Way, Har. 36 BG30
Fulbourne Est. E1 57 CB38
Fulbourne Rd. E17 39 CF30
Fulbourne St. E1 57 CB39
Durward St.
Fulbrook La., S.Ock. 60 CZ40
Fulbrook Rd. N19 47 BW35
Junction Rd.
Fuley Rd., West. 106 CJ62
Fulford Gro., Wat. 35 BC27
Fulford Rd., Cat. 105 BZ64
Fulford Rd., Epsom 94 BN57
Fulford St. SE16 67 CB41
Fulham Bdy. SW6 66 BS43

Fulham Clo., Uxb. 53 BA38
Fulham Ct. SW6 66 BS44
Fulham Est. SW6 65 BR43
Fulham High St. SW6 65 BR44
Fulham Palace Rd. SW6 65 BQ43
Fulham Palace Rd. W6 65 BQ42
Fulham Pk. Gdns. SW6 65 BR44
Fulham Pk. Rd. SW6 65 BR44
Fulham Rd. SW3 65 BR44
Fulham Rd. SW6 65 BR44
Fulham Rd. SW8 65 BR44
Fulham Rd. SW10 65 BR44
Fullarton Cres., S.Ock. 60 DA40
Fullbrook Ave., Wey. 92 AW59
Fullbrooks Ave., Wor.Pk. 85 BO54
Fuller Clo., Orp. 97 CN56
Fuller Gdns., Wat. 26 BC22
Fuller Rd., Dag. 50 CO34
Fuller Rd., Wat. 26 BC22
Fuller St. E2 57 CB38
Cheshire St.
Fuller St. NW4 46 BQ31
Fuller Way, Hayes 63 BB42
Fuller Way, Rick. 26 AZ25
Fullers Ave., Surb. 85 BL55
Fullers Ave., Wdf.Grn. 40 CG29
Fullers Clo., Rom. 41 CS29
Fullers Clo., Wal.Abb. 22 CH20
Fullers Hill, West. 115 CM66
High St.
Fullers La., Rom. 41 CS29
Fullers Mead, Harl. 14 CP11
Fullers Rd. E18 40 CG30
Fullers St., Sev. 108 CX63
Fullers Way N., Surb. 85 BL55
Fullers Way S., Chess. 94 BL56
Fullers Wd., Croy. 96 CE56
Fullers Wd. La., Red. 121 BW71
Fullerton Clo., Wey. 92 AY60
Fullerton Dr., Wey. 92 AY60
Fullerton Rd. SW18 76 BT46
Fullerton Rd., Cars. 95 BU58
Fullerton Rd., Croy. 87 CA54
Fullerton Rd., Wey. 92 AY60
Fullerton Way, Wey. 92 AY60
Fullmer Way, Wey. 91 AV58
Fullwell Ave., Ilf. 40 CK30
Fullwoods Ms. N1 2 L2
Fullwoods Ms. N1 57 BZ38
Bevenden St.
Fulmar Cres., Hem.H. 8 AW14
Fulmar Rd., Rain. 59 CU36
Fulmead St. SW6 66 BS44
Fulmer Clo., Hmptn. 74 BE49
Fulmer Common Rd., Iver 52 AR36
Fulmer Common Rd., Slou. 52 AR36
Fulmer Dr., Ger.Cr. 43 AR34
Fulmer La., Ger.Cr. 43 AS34
Fulmer Rd. E15 58 CJ39
Fulmer Rd., Ger.Cr. 43 AS33
Fulmer Way W13 64 BJ41
Fulmer Way, Ger.Cr. 43 AS32
Fulready Rd. E10 48 CF32
Fulstone Clo., Houns. 64 BE45
Fulthorp Rd. SE3 68 CG44
Fulton Ms. W2 56 BT40
Porchester Ter.
Fulton Rd., Wem. 46 BM34
Fulwell Pk. Ave., Twick. 74 BF48
Fulwell Rd., Tedd. 74 BG49
Fulwich Rd., Dart. 80 CW46
Fulwood Ave., Wem. 55 BL37
Fulwood Clo., Hayes 53 BB39
Fulwood Gdns., Twick. 74 BJ46
Fulwood Pl. WC1 2 C7
Fulwood Pl. WC1 56 BX39
Fulwood Wk. SW19 75 BR47
Furber St. W6 65 BP41
Furham Feild, Pnr. 36 BF29
Furley Rd. SE15 67 CB44
Furlong Clo., Wall. 86 BV54
Furlong Rd. N7 56 BY36
Furlong Rd., Dor. 119 BG72
Furlongs, Hem.H. 8 AW13
Furmage St. SW18 76 BS47
Furmingers Rd., Orp. 98 CR56
Furneaux Ave. SE27 76 BY49
Furner Clo., Dart. 69 CT45
Furness, Wind. 61 AL44
Furness Clo., Grays 71 DG42
St. Johns Rd.
Furness Pl., Wind. 61 AL44
Furness
Furness Rd. NW10 55 BP37
Furness Rd. SW6 66 BS44
Furness Rd., Har. 45 BF33
Furness Rd., Mord. 86 BS54
Furness Row, Wind. 61 AL44
Furness
Furness Sq., Wind. 61 AL44
Furness
Furness Wk., Wind. 61 AL44
Furness
Furness Way, Horn. 50 CU35
Furness Way, Wind. 61 AL44
Furnival Clo., Vir.W. 82 AR53
Furnival St. EC4 2 D8
Furnival St. EC4 56 BY39
Furrow La. E9 48 CC35
Furrowfield, Hat. 10 BP11
Crop Common
Furrows, The, Uxb. 44 AX32
Furrows, The, Walt. 84 BD55
Furrows Pl., Cat. 105 CA65
Fursby Ave. N3 38 BS29
Furse Ave., St.Alb. 9 BJ11
Further Acre NW9 37 BO37
Further Grn. Rd. SE6 78 CG47
Furtherfield, Abb.L. 17 BB19
Furtherfield Clo., Croy. 86 BY53
Boston Rd.
Furtherground, Hem.H. 8 AY13
Wood Fm. Rd.
Furze Clo., Red. 121 BU70
Furze Clo., Wat. 36 BD28
Furze Fm. Clo., Rom. 41 CQ30
Furze Fld., Lthd. 93 BH60
Furze Gro., Tad. 103 BR64
Furze Hill, Pur. 95 BX59
Furze Hill, Red. 121 BU70
Furze Hill, Tad. 103 BR64
Furze La., Pur. 95 BX59
Furze Rd., Hem.H. 7 AV14
Furze Rd., Th.Hth. 87 BZ52
Furze Rd., Wey. 91 AV57
Furze St. E3 57 CE39
Furze Vw., Rick. 25 AU25
Furze Wd., Sun. 83 BC51
Furzebushes La., St.Alb. 18 BE16
Furzedown Dr. SW17 76 BV49
Furzedown Rd. SW17 76 BV49
Furzedown Rd., Sutt. 95 BT59
Furzefield, Chsnt. 21 CB17
Flamstead End Rd.
Furzefield Clo., Chis. 78 CL50
Furzefield Cres., Reig. 121 BT71
Furzefield Rd. SE3 68 CH43
Furzefield Rd., Reig. 121 BT71
Furzefield Rd., Welw.G.C. 5 BR8
Furzeground Way, West Dr. 53 BA40
Furzeham Rd., West Dr. 63 AY41
Furzehill Par., Borwd. 28 BM24
Furzehill Rd.
Furzehill Rd., Borwd. 28 BM24
Furzen Cres., Hat. 10 BO14
Fusedale Way, S.Ock. 60 CZ40
Fyfe Way, Brom. 88 CH51
Lownds Ave.
Fyfield Clo., Brwd. 123 DE32
Fyfield Clo., Brom. 87 CF52
Fyfield Ct. E7 58 CH36
Fyfield Rd. E17 48 CF31
Fyfield Rd. SW9 66 BY45
Fyfield Rd., Enf. 30 CA24
Fyfield Rd., Ong. 24 CX16
Fyfield Rd. (Moreton), Ong. 15 CW13
Fyfield Rd. (Willingale), Ong. 15 DA13
Fyfield Rd., Rain. 59 CT37
Fyfield Rd., Wdf.Grn. 40 CJ29
Fynes St. SW1 3 N8
Fynes St. SW1 66 BW42
Regency St.

G

Gabion Ave., Grays 70 CY42
Gable Clo., Abb.L. 17 BB19
Gable Clo., Dart. 79 CU46
Gable Clo., Pnr. 36 BF29
Gable Ct. SE26 77 CB49
Gables, The, Bans. 103 BR62
Gables, The, Grays 71 DC42
Gables, The, Lthd. 93 BG59
Gables Ave., Ashf. 73 AY49
Gables Ave., Borwd. 28 BL24
Gables Clo. SE12 78 CH47
Gables Clo., Ger.Cr. 34 AS28
Gables Clo., Slou. 62 AQ43
Gables Clo., Wok. 100 AS63
Gabriel Clo., Felt. 74 BD49
Gabriel Clo., Rom. 41 CS29
Gabriel Spring Rd., Dart. 90 CZ55
Gabriel St. SE23 77 CC47
Gabrielle Clo., Wem. 46 BL34
Gabriels Gdns., Grav. 81 DJ49
Gadbrook Rd., Bet. 120 BN73
Gaddesden Ave., Wem. 55 BL36
Gaddesden Cres., Wat. 18 BD20
Gaddesdon Gro., Welw.G.C. 5 BT8
Chilton Grn.
Gade Ave., Wat. 26 BB24
Gade Bank, Rick. 26 BA24
Gade Clo., Hayes 53 BC40
Gade Clo., Hem.H. 8 AW12
Gade Clo., Wat. 26 BB24
Gade Valley Clo., Kings L. 17 AZ17
Gade Vw. Gdns., Kings L. 17 BA19
Gade Vw. Rd., Hem.H. 8 AX15
Gadebridge La., Hem.H. 8 AW12
Gadebridge Rd., Hem.H. 8 AW12
Gadesden Rd., Epsom 94 BN57
Gadeside, Wat. 26 BA21
Gadsbury Clo. NW9 46 BO32
Gadsden Clo., Upmin. 51 CZ32
Gadwall Way SE28 68 CM41
Gadwell Clo., Wat. 27 BE21
Gage Rd. E16 58 CG39
Gage St. WC1 2 A6
Gage St. WC1 56 BX39
Boswell St.
Gainford St. N1 56 BY37
Gains Sq., Bexh. 69 CP45
Gainsborough Ave. E12 49 CL35
Gainsborough Ave., Dart. 80 CV46
Gainsborough Ave., St.Alb. 9 BH13
Gainsborough Ave., Til. 71 DG44
Gainsborough Clo., Beck. 77 CD50
Brackley Rd.
Gainsborough Clo., Esher 84 BH54
Gainsborough Ct., Walt. 83 BC55
Gainsborough Dr., Grav. 81 DE48
Gainsborough Dr., S.Croy. 96 CB60
Gainsborough Gdns. NW3 47 BT34
Gainsborough Gdns. NW11 46 BR33
Gainsborough Gdns., Edg. 37 BL30
Gainsborough Gdns., Grnf. 45 BH35
Gainsborough Gdns., Islw. 74 BG46
Gainsborough Ms. SE26 77 CB48
Panmure Rd.
Gainsborough Rd. E11 49 CG33
Gainsborough Rd. E15 58 CG38
Gainsborough Rd. N12 38 BS28
Gainsborough Rd. W4 65 BO42
Gainsborough Rd., Dag. 50 CO35
Gainsborough Rd., Epsom 94 BN58
Gainsborough Rd., Hayes 53 BA37
Gainsborough Rd., N.Mal. 85 BN53
Gainsborough Rd., Rain. 59 CU37
Gainsborough Rd., Rich. 65 BL44
Gainsborough Rd., Wdf.Grn. 40 CK29
Gainsborough Sq., Bexh. 69 CP45
Regency Way
Gainsford Rd. E17 48 CD31
Gainsford St. SE1 4 P4
Gainsford St. SE1 67 CA41
Gainsthorpe Rd., Ong. 15 CV15
Gainswood, Welw.G.C. 5 BR8
Gairloch Rd. SE5 67 CA44
Gaisford St. NW5 56 BW36
Gaist Ave., Cat. 105 CB64
Gaitskell Rd. SE9 78 CM47
Galahad Clo., Slou. 61 AN41
Mitchell Clo.
Galahad Rd., Brom. 78 CH48
Galata Rd. SW13 65 BP43
Galatia Sq. SE15 67 CB45
Scylla Rd.
Galbraith St. E14 67 CF41
Galdana Ave., Barn. 29 BT24
Gale Clo., Hmptn. 74 BE50
Gale Clo., Mitch. 86 BT52
Gale Cres., Bans. 104 BS62
Gale Grn., S.Ock. 60 DA39
Gale St. E3 57 CE39
Gale St., Dag. 59 CP37
Galeborough Ave., Wdf.Grn. 39 CF29
Galen Pl. WC1 2 A7
Galen Pl. WC1 56 BX39
Bury Pl.
Galena Rd. W6 65 BP42
Gales Clo., Guil. 118 AU69
Gilliat Dr.
Gales Gdns. E2 57 CB38
Bethnal Grn. Rd.
Gales Way, Wdf.Grn. 40 CK29
Galesbury Rd. SW18 76 BT46
Galey Grn., S.Ock. 60 DA39
Galgate Clo. SW19 75 BR47
Gallants Fm. Rd., Barn. 38 BU26
Galleon Boul., Dart. 70 CY45
Galleon Clo. SE16 67 CC41
Kinburn St.
Gallery Gdns., Nthlt. 54 BD37
Gallery Rd. SE21 77 BZ47
Galley Hill, Hem.H. 7 AV12
Galley Hill Rd., Grav. 81 DC46
Galley La., Barn. 28 BP23
Galleyhill Rd., Wal.Abb. 22 CG19
Galleymead Rd., Slou. 62 AV44
Galleywall Rd. SE16 67 CB42
Galleywood Cres., Rom. 41 CS29
Gallia Rd. N5 47 BY35
Calabria Rd.
Galliard Clo. N9 30 CC25
Galliard Rd. N9 39 CB26
Gallions Clo., Bark. 59 CO38
Gallions La., Slou. 52 AR38
Gallions Rd. E16 58 CL40
Gallions Rd. SE7 68 CH42
Gallon Clo. SE7 68 CJ42
Gallop, The, S.Croy. 96 CB57
Gallop, The, Sutt. 95 BT58
Gallop, The, Wind. 72 AO47
Gallosson Rd. SE18 68 CN42
Galloway Clo., Brox. 21 CD16
Galloway Rd. W12 55 BP40
Gallows Cor., Rom. 42 CV30
Gallows Hill, Kings L. 17 BA19
Gallows Hill La., Abb.L. 17 BA19
Gallows Wd., Fawk. 99 DA56
Gallus Clo. N21 29 BX25
Gallus Sq. SE3 68 CH45
Gallys Rd., Wind. 61 AL44
Galpins Rd., Th.Hth. 86 BX53
Galsworthy Ave., Rom. 50 CO33
Galsworthy Clo. SE28 59 CO40
Galsworthy Cres. SE3 68 CJ44
Merriman Rd.
Galsworthy Rd. NW2 46 BR35
Galsworthy Rd., Cher. 83 AW54
Galsworthy Rd., Kings.T. 75 BM50
Galsworthy Rd., Til. 71 DH44
Galsworthy Ter. N16 48 CA34
Galton St. W10 55 BR38
Galva Clo., Barn. 29 BV24
Galvani Way, Croy. 86 BX54
Galveston Rd. SW15 75 BR46
Galvins Clo., Guil. 118 AQ69
Galway St. EC1 2 J3
Gambetta St. SW8 66 BV44
Gambia St. SE1 4 G3
Gambia St. SE1 56 BY40
Gambles La., Wok. 101 AX65
Gambole Rd. SW17 76 BU49
Games Rd., Barn. 29 BU24
Gamlen Rd. SW15 65 BQ45
Gammon Clo., Hem.H. 8 AZ14
Bennets End Rd.
Gammons Fm. Clo., Wat. 26 BB21
Gammons La., Brox. 21 CA16
Gammons La., Wat. 26 BB21
Gander Grn. La., Sutt. 94 BR56
Ganders Ash, Wat. 17 BC20
Gandhi Clo. E17 48 CE32
Gane Clo., Wall. 95 BX57
Gangers Hill, Gdse. 114 CD67
Ganghill, Guil. 118 AT69
Gant Ct., Wal.Abb. 22 CG20
Ganton St. W1 1 L10
Ganton St. W1 56 BW40
Kingly St.
Gantshill Cres., Ilf. 49 CL32
Gantshill Cross, Ilf. 49 CL32
Ganymede Pl., Hem.H. 8 AY12
Gap Rd. SW19 76 BS49
Garage Rd. W3 55 BM39
Garbrand Wk., Epsom 94 BO58
Lyncroft Gdns.
Garbutt Pl. W1 1 H6
Garbutt Pl. W1 56 BV39
Garbutt Rd., Upmin. 51 CY34
Gard St. EC1 2 G2
Gard St. EC1 56 BY38
Masons Pl.
Garden Ave., Bexh. 69 CR45
Garden Ave., Hat. 10 BP14
Garden Ave., Mitch. 76 BV50
Garden City, Edg. 37 BM29
Garden Clo. E4 39 CE28
Garden Clo. SE12 78 CH48
Garden Clo. SW15 75 BP47
Garden Clo., Ashf. 73 BA50
Garden Clo., Bans. 104 BS61
Garden Clo., Barn. 28 BQ24
Garden Clo., Hmptn. 74 BE49
Garden Clo., Lthd. 111 BK66
Garden Clo., Nthlt. 54 BE37
Garden Clo., Ruis. 44 BB34
Garden Clo., St.Alb. 9 BJ13
Garden Clo., Wall. 95 BX56
Garden Clo., Wat. 26 BB23
Garden Clo., Wey. 92 AX56
Garden Cotts., Epsom 94 BO59
East St.
Garden Ct. EC4 2 D10
Garden Ct. EC4 56 BY40
Fountain Ct.
Garden Ct. SE15 67 CA44
Sumner Est.
Garden Ct., Rich. 65 BL44
Garden Ct., Welw.G.C. 5 BR7
Garden End, Amer. 25 AP22
Garden Fld. La., Berk. 7 AS13
Garden Flds., Ong. 24 CW20
Garden La. SW2 76 BX47
Garden La., Brom. 78 CH50
Garden Ms. W2 56 BS40
Linden Gdns.
Garden Pl., Dart. 80 CV48
Garden Reach, Ch.St.G. 25 AR24
Garden Rd. NW8 56 BT38
Garden Rd. SE20 87 CC51
Garden Rd., Abb.L. 17 BB19
Garden Rd., Brom. 78 CH50
Garden Rd., Rich. 65 BM45
Garden Rd., Sev. 108 CV64
Garden Rd., Walt. 83 BC53
Garden Row SE1 4 F7
Garden Row SE1 66 BY41
Garden Row, Grav. 81 DF48
Haynes Rd.
Garden St. E1 57 CC39
Garden Ter. SW1 3 N10
Garden Ter. SW1 66 BW42
Moreton St.
Garden Ter. Rd., Harl. 6 CP9
Garden Wk. EC2 2 M3
Garden Wk. EC2 57 CA38
Rivington St.
Garden Wk., Beck. 87 CP51
Hayne Rd.
Garden Wk., Couls. 104 BV65
Garden Way NW10 55 BN36
Garden Way, Cat. 105 BZ64
Garden Way, Loug. 31 CL22
Gardeners Rd. E3 57 CC37
Gardeners Rd., Croy. 86 BY54
Albion St.
Gardenia Rd., Enf. 30 CA25
Gardens, The N8 47 BX31
Rectory Gdns.
Gardens, The N16 48 CA33
Gardens, The SE22 67 CB45
Gardens, The, Beck. 87 CF51
Gardens, The, Brwd. 33 DA21
Gardens, The, Esher 93 BF56
Gardens, The, Felt. 73 BA46
Gardens, The, Har. 45 BG32
Gardens, The, Hat. 19 BR17
Gardens, The, Pnr. 45 BE32
Gardens, The, Wat. 26 BB23
Gardiner Ave. NW2 46 BQ35
Gardiner Clo., Orp. 89 CP51
Gardner Clo. E11 49 CH32
Gardner Gro., Felt. 74 BE48
Gardner Rd. E13 58 CH38
Gardner Rd., Guil. 118 AR70
Gardners Wk., Lthd. 111 BF66
Gardnor Rd. NW3 47 BT35
Flask Wk.
Garendon Gdns., Mord. 86 BS54
Garendon Rd., Mord. 86 BS54
Gareth Clo., Wor.Pk. 85 BW55
Burnham Dr.
Gareth Gro., Brom. 78 CH49
Garfield Pl., Wind. 61 AO44
Albany Rd.
Garfield Rd. E4 39 CF26
Garfield Rd. E13 58 CG38
Garfield Rd. SW11 66 BV45
Garfield Rd. SW19 76 BT49
Garfield Rd., Enf. 30 CC24
Garfield Rd., Twick. 74 BJ
York St.
Garfield Rd., Wey. 92 AX
Garfield St., Wat. 26 BC
Garford St. E14 57 CE
Garganey Wk. SE28 59 CP
Garibaldi Rd., Red. 121 BU
Garibaldi St. SE18 68 CN
Garland Clo., Hem.H. 8 AX
Allandale
Garland Rd. SE18 68 CM
Garland Rd., Stan. 37 BL
Garland Way, Horn. 51 CW
Garlands, Ton. 117 CY
Garlands Rd., Lthd. 102 BJ
Garlands Rd., Red. 121 BU
Garlichill Rd., Epsom 103 BP
Garlick Hill EC4 2 J
Garlick Hill EC4 57 BZ
Queen Victoria St.
Garlies Rd. SE23 77 CD
Garlinge Rd. NW2 55 BR
Garman Rd. N17 39 CC
Garnault Ms. EC1 2
Garnault Ms. EC1 56 BY
Hardwick St.
Garnault Pl. EC1 2
Garnault Pl. EC1 56 BY
Myddleton St.
Garnault Rd., Enf. 30 CA
Garner Dr., Brox. 21 CD
Garner Rd. E17 39 CF
Garner St. E2 57 CB
Coate St.
Garners Clo., Ger.Cr. 34 AS
Garners End, Ger.Cr. 34 AS
Garners Rd., Ger.Cr. 34 AS
Garnet Clo., Slou. 61 AN
Garnet Rd. NW10 55 BO
Garnet Rd., Th.Hth. 87 BZ
Garnet St. E1 57 CC
Garnet Wk. E6 58 CK
Kingfisher St.
Garnet Way E17 39 CD
McEntee Ave.
Garnett Clo. SE9 68 CK
Garnett Clo., Wat. 27 BD
Garnett Dr., St.Alb. 18 BF
Garnett Rd. NW3 47 BU
Garnham Clo. N16 48 CA
Smalley Rd.
Garnham St. N16 48 CA
High St.
Garnies Clo. SE15 67 CA
Thruxton Rd.
Garnon Mead, Epp. 23 CP
Garrads Rd. SW16 76 BW
Garrard Clo., Bexh. 69 CR
Garrard Clo., Chis. 78 CL
Garrard Rd., Bans. 104 BS
Garratt Clo., Croy. 95 BX
Croydon Rd.
Garratt La. SW17 76 BT
Garratt La. SW18 76 BS
Garratt Rd., Edg. 37 BM
Garratt Ter. SW17 76 BU
Garratts La., Bans. 103 BR
Garratts Rd., Bush. 36 BG
Garrett Clo. W3 55 BN
Jenner Ave.
Garrett St. EC1 2 J
Garrett St. EC1 57 BZ
Garrick Ave. NW11 46 BR
Garrick Clo. SW18 66 BT
Garrick Clo. W5 55 BL
Garrick Clo., Rich. 74 BK
The Grn.
Garrick Clo., Stai. 73 AW
Garrick Clo., Walt. 92 BC
Garrick Cres., Croy. 86 CB
Garrick Dr. NW4 37 BQ
Garrick Dr. SE18 68 CM
Garrick Gdns., E.Mol. 84 BF
Garrick Pk. NW4 37 BQ
Garrick Rd. NW9 46 BO
Garrick Rd., Grnf. 54 BF
Garrick Rd., Rich. 65 BM
Garrick St. WC2 1 Q1
Garrick St. WC2 56 BX
Garrick Way NW4 46 BQ
Garrison Clo. SE18 68 CL
Red Lion La.
Garrison La., Chess. 93 BK
Garrod St., Grav. 81 DG
New Rd.
Garron La., S.Ock. 60 CZ
Garry Clo., Rom. 41 CT2
Garry Way, Rom. 41 CT2
Garside Clo. SE28 68 CM
Goosander Way
Garside Clo., Hmptn. 74 BF
Garsington Ms. SE4 67 CD
Garsmouth Way, Wat. 27 BD2
Garson La., Stai. 72 AR
Garson Rd., Esher 93 BE
Garston Cres., Wat. 18 BD2
Garston Dr., Wat. 18 BD2
Garston La., Ken. 96 BZ6
Garston La., Wat. 18 BD2
Garston Pk. Par., Wat. 18 BD2
Garstons, The, Lthd. 111 BF6
Garth, The, Abb.L. 17 BA2
Garth, The, Cob. 93 BE6
Garth, The, Hmptn. 74 BF5
Garth, The, Har. 46 BL3
Garth Clo., Kings.T. 75 BL4
Garth Clo., Mord. 85 BQ5
Garth Clo., Ruis. 45 BD3
Garth Ct. W4 65 BO4
Garth Rd.
Garth Ms. W5 55 BL3
Greystoke Gdns.
Garth Rd. NW2 46 BR3
Garth Rd. W4 65 BN4

Street	Page	Grid
:h Rd., Kings.T.	75	BL49
:h Rd., Mord.	85	BQ53
:h Rd., Sev.	117	CV67
:h Rd., S.Ock.	60	DB38
:hland Dr., Barn.	28	BP25
:thorne Rd. SE23	77	CC47
:thside, Rich.	75	BL49
:thway N12	38	BU29
:lett Rd., Wat.	27	BD25
:tmoor Gdns. SW19	75	BR47
:tmore Rd., Ilf.	49	CN34
:ton Pl. SW18	76	BT46
:tons Clo., Enf.	30	CC24
:rfield Rd.		
:tons Way SW11	66	BT45
:vary Rd. E16	58	CH39
:vock Dr., Sev.	116	CU66
:ppington Rd.		
:way Rd. W2	56	BS39
La., Maid.	61	AG41
bbert Rd.		
Wks. La., Brox.	12	CE13
Wks. Rd., Sthl.	64	BE41
coigne Gdns.,	40	CG29
:df.Grn.		
coigne Pl. E2	**2**	**P2**
coigne Pl. E2	57	CA38
coigne Rd., Bark.	58	CM37
coigne Rd., Croy.	96	CF58
coigne Rd., Wey.	83	AZ55
cony Ave. NW6	56	BS36
coyne Clo., Pot.B.	19	BP19
coyne Clo., Rom.	42	CV29
coyne Dr., Dart.	69	CT45
coyne Est. E9	57	CD36
coyne Rd. E9	57	CC36
elee St. E14	57	CF40
holder Pl. SE11	66	BX42
karth Rd. SW12	76	BV46
karth Rd., Edg.	37	BN30
kell Rd. N6	47	BU32
kell St. SW4	66	BX44
kin St. N1	56	BY37
par Ms. SW5	66	BS42
ourtfield Gdns.		
siot Rd. SW17	76	BU49
ssiot Way, Sutt.	86	BT55
sson Rd., Swans.	81	DC46
tein Rd. W6	65	BQ43
ston Bell Clo., Rich.	65	BL45
ston Bri. Rd., Shep.	83	BA53
ston Rd., Mitch.	86	BV52
ston Way, Shep.	83	BA53
aker St. SE16	67	CB41
combe Rd. N19	47	BW34
e Clo., Borwd.	28	BN23
anziger Way		
e End, Nthwd.	35	BC29
e Ms. SW7	**3**	**D5**
e St. WC2	**2**	**B8**
e St. WC2	56	BX39
'ngsway		
eforth St. NW8	**1**	**C5**
eforth St. NW8	56	BU38
ehill Rd., Nthwd.	35	BB29
ehope Dr., S.Ock.	60	CZ39
ehouse Clo., Kings.T.	85	BN51
ely Rd. SW9	66	BX45
es Grn. Rd., W.Wick.	88	CG55
esborough St. EC2	**2**	**M4**
esborough St. EC2	57	CA38
hipp St.		
esden Rd., Lthd.	102	BG65
eshead Rd., Borwd.	28	BL23
eside Rd. SW17	76	BU48
estone Rd. SE19	77	CA50
eway SE17	67	BZ43
eway, Wey.	83	AZ55
alace Dr.		
eway, The, Wok.	91	AU60
eway Clo., Nthwd.	35	BA29
eway Trd. Est. NW10	55	BO38
eways, Guil.	118	AT70
eways, Surb.	85	BL53
urbiton Hill Rd.		
teways, The SW3	**3**	**D9**
eways, The SW3	66	BU42
/hiteheads Gro.		
ewick Clo., Slou.	52	AP40
tfield Gro., Felt.	74	BF48
thorne Rd. N22	38	BY30
thorne St. E2	57	CC37
ley Ave., Epsom	94	BM56
liff Rd. SW1	66	BV42
ling Rd. SE2	69	CO42
ting Clo., Edg.	37	BM29
avilion Way		
tting Way, Uxb.	53	AY36
ton Bottom, Red.	113	BU67
ton Clo., Reig.	121	BT69
ton Clo., Sutt.	95	BS58
ton Pk. Rd., Red.	121	BT69
ton Pk. Rd., Reig.	121	BT69
ton Rd. SW17	76	BU49
ton Rd., Reig.	121	BT69
tons Way, Sid.	79	CQ49
ward Clo. N21	29	BY25
ward Grn. N9	39	CA27
wick Rd. SW18	75	BR47
wick Rd., Grav.	81	DG48
wick Way, Horn.	51	CW34
uden Clo. SW4	66	BW44
uden Rd. SW4	66	BW44
umont App., Wat.	26	BC24
unt St. SE1	**4**	**G6**
unt St. SE1	67	BZ41
'ewington Causeway		
untlet Clo., Nthlt.	54	BE36
untlet Cres., Ken.	105	BZ63
untlett Ct., Wem.	45	BJ35
untlett Rd., Sutt.	95	BT56
utrey Rd. SE15	67	CC44
utrey Sq. E6	58	CK39
ruesdale Rd.		
Gavel St. SE17	**4**	**L8**
Gavel St. SE17	67	BZ42
Mason St.		
Gavell Rd., Cob.	92	BC60
Gavenny Path, S.Ock.	60	CZ39
Gaveston Dr., Berk.	7	AQ12
Gaveston Rd., Lthd.	102	BJ63
Gavestone Clo., Wey.	92	AY60
Gavestone Rd. SE12	78	CH47
Gavin St. SE18	68	CN42
Gavina Clo., Mord.	86	BT53
Gaviots Clo., Ger.Cr.	43	AS33
Gaviots Grn., Ger.Cr.	43	AS33
Gaviots Way, Ger.Cr.	43	AS33
Gawber St. E2	57	CC38
Gawsworth Clo. E15	49	CG35
Gawthorne Ave. NW7	37	BR28
Gay Clo. NW2	46	BP35
Gay Gdns., Dag.	50	CS35
Gay Rd. E15	57	CF37
Gay St. SW15	65	BQ45
Gaydon La. NW9	37	BO30
Gayfere Rd., Epsom	94	BP56
Gayfere Rd., Ilf.	49	CK31
Gayfere St. SW1	**3**	**Q7**
Gayfere St. SW1	66	BX41
Great Peter St.		
Gayford Rd. W12	65	BO41
Gayhurst Rd. E8	57	CB36
Gaylor Rd., Nthlt.	45	BE35
Gaylor Rd., Til.	71	DF44
Gaynes Ct., Upmin.	51	CX35
Gaynes Hill Rd., Wdf.Grn.	40	CK29
Gaynes Pk. Rd., Upmin.	51	CX35
Gaynes Parkway, Upmin.	51	CW34
Gaynes Rd., Upmin.	51	CX34
Gaynesford Rd. SE23	77	CC48
Gaynesford Rd., Cars.	95	BU57
Gays La., Maid.	61	AG43
Gaysham Ave., Ilf.	49	CL32
Gayton Clo., Amer.	25	AP21
Gayton Cres. NW3	47	BT35
Gayton Rd. NW3	47	BT35
Gayton Rd. SE2	69	CP42
Wilton Rd.		
Gayton Rd., Har.	45	BH32
Gayville Rd. SW11	76	BU46
Gaywood Ave., Chsnt.	21	CC18
Gaywood Clo. SW2	76	BY47
Gaywood Est. SE1	**4**	**G7**
Gaywood Est. SE1	66	BY41
Gaywood Rd. E17	48	CE31
Gaywood Rd., Ash.	103	BL62
Gaywood St. SE1	**4**	**G7**
Gaywood St. SE1	66	BY41
Gaza St. SE17	66	BY42
Gazelda Vill., Wat.	27	BD25
Gazelle Glade, Grav.	81	DJ49
Gean Wk., Hat.	10	BP14
Southdown Rd.		
Geariesville Gdns., Ilf.	49	CL31
Geary Ct., Brwd.	42	DB26
Geary Dr.		
Geary Dr., Brwd.	42	DB26
Geary Rd. NW10	46	BP35
Geary St. N7	47	BX35
Geddes Rd., Bush.	27	BG24
Geddings Rd., Hodd.	12	CE12
Gedeney Rd. N17	39	BZ30
Gedling Pl. SE1	**4**	**Q6**
Gedling Pl. SE1	67	CA41
Abbey St.		
Gee St. EC1	**2**	**H4**
Gee St. EC1	56	BY38
Geere Rd. E15	58	CG37
Gees Ct. W1	**1**	**H9**
Gees Ct. W1	56	BV39
Barrett St.		
Geffrye Ct. N1	**2**	**N1**
Geffrye Ct. N1	57	CA37
Geffrye St. E2	**2**	**P1**
Geffrye St. E2	57	CA37
Geisthorp Ct., Wal.Abb.	22	CH20
Winters Way		
Geldart Rd. SE15	67	CB43
Geldeston Rd. E5	48	CB34
Gell Clo., Uxb.	44	AY35
Gellatly Rd. SE14	67	CC44
Gelsthorpe Rd., Rom.	41	CR29
Gemini Gro., Nthlt.	54	BD38
Javelin Way		
General Gordon Pl. SE18	68	CL42
General Wolfe Rd. SE10	67	CF44
Generals Wk., The, Enf.	30	CD22
Genesta Glade, Grav.	81	DJ49
Genesta Rd. SE18	68	CL43
Geneva Clo., Shep.	83	BB51
Haslett Rd.		
Geneva Ct. N16	48	BZ33
Geneva Dr. SW9	66	BY45
Geneva Gdns., Rom.	50	CQ32
Geneva Rd., Kings.T.	85	BL52
Geneva Rd., Th.Hth.	87	BZ53
Genever Clo. E4	39	CE28
Genista Rd. N18	39	CB28
Angel Rd.		
Genoa Ave. SW15	75	BQ46
Genoa Rd. SE20	87	CC51
Genotin Rd., Enf.	30	BZ24
Genotin Ter., Enf.	30	BZ24
Genotin Rd.		
Gentian Row SE13	67	CF44
Sparta St.		
Gentlemans Row, Enf.	30	BZ24
Gentry Gdns. E13	58	CH38
Genyn Rd., Guil.	118	AQ71
Geoffrey Ave., Rom.	42	CX29
Geoffrey Clo. SE5	67	BZ44
Lilford Rd.		
Geoffrey Gdns. E6	58	CK37
Geoffrey Rd. SE4	67	CD45
George Avey Cft., Epp.	23	CR16
Church La.		
George Beard Rd. SE8	67	CD42
George Comberton Wk. E12	49	CL35
Gainsborough Ave.		
George Ct. WC2	**4**	**A1**
George Ct. WC2	56	BX40
Strand		
George Cres. N10	38	BV29
George Crooks Ho., Grays	71	DD43
New Rd.		
George Downing Est. N16	48	CA34
George V Ave., Pnr.	36	BE30
George V Clo., Pnr.	45	BF31
George V Way, Grnf.	54	BJ37
George IV Way, Rick.	26	AW21
George Grn. Rd., Slou.	52	AS39
George Gros. Rd. SE20	87	CB51
George Inn Yd. SE1	**4**	**K3**
George Inn Yd. SE1	57	BZ40
Borough High St.		
George Lands (Ripley), Wok.	101	AW64
George La. E18	40	CH30
George La. SE13	77	CE46
George La., Brom.	88	CH54
George Loveless Ho. E2	**2**	**Q2**
George Ms. NW1	**1**	**L3**
George Ms., Enf.	30	BZ24
Sydney Rd.		
George Rd. E4	39	CE29
George Rd., Guil.	118	AR70
George Rd., Kings.T.	75	BM50
George Rd., N.Mal.	85	BO52
George Row SE16	67	CB41
George Sq. SW19	85	BR52
George Sq., Uxb.	53	AX36
George St. E16	58	CG39
George St. EC4	**2**	**K9**
George St. W1	**1**	**E8**
George St. W1	56	BU39
George St. W7	54	BH40
George St., Bark.	58	CM36
George St., Berk.	7	AR13
George St., Chesh.	16	AO18
George St., Croy.	87	BZ55
George St., Grays	71	DD43
George St., Hem.H.	8	AX13
George St., Houns.	64	BE44
George St., Rich.	74	BK46
George St., Rom.	50	CT32
George St., St.Alb.	9	BG13
George St., Sthl.	64	BE42
George St., Stai.	72	AV49
George St., Sutt.	95	BS56
High St.		
George St., Uxb.	53	AX36
George St., Wat.	27	BD24
George Tilbury Ho., Grays	71	DG41
George Wyver Clo. SW19	75	BR47
Beaumont Rd.		
George Yd. EC3	**2**	**L9**
George Yd. EC3	57	BZ39
Lombard St.		
George Yd. W1	**1**	**H10**
George Yd. W1	56	BV40
Georges Clo., Orp.	89	CP52
Georges Dr., Brwd.	33	CZ25
Georges Mead, Borwd.	28	BL25
Georges Rd. N7	47	BX35
Georges Rd., West.	106	CJ63
Georges Sq. SW6	65	BR43
Georges Ter., Cat.	105	BZ64
Georges Wd. Rd., Hat.	20	BS16
Georgetown Clo. SE19	77	CA49
St. Kitts Ter.		
Georgette Pl. SE10	67	CF43
Georgeville Gdns., Ilf.	49	CL31
Georgewood Rd., Hem.H.	17	AY16
Georgia Rd., N.Mal.	85	BN52
Georgia Rd., Th.Hth.	86	BY51
Georgian Clo., Brom.	88	CH54
Georgian Clo., Nthwd.	35	BB28
Georgian Clo., Stai.	73	AW49
Georgian Clo., Stan.	36	BJ29
Georgian Clo., Uxb.	44	AX35
Georgian Ct. NW4	46	BP32
Foscote Rd.		
Georgian Ct., Wem.	55	BM36
Georgian Way, Har.	45	BG34
Georgiana St. NW1	56	BW37
Georgina Gdns. E2	**2**	**Q2**
Georgina Gdns. E2	57	CA38
Columbia Rd.		
Geraint Rd., Brom.	78	CH48
Gerald Clo., Grav.	81	DJ47
Gerald Ms. SW1	**3**	**H8**
Gerald Rd. E16	58	CG38
Gerald Rd. SW1	**3**	**H8**
Gerald Rd. SW1	66	BV42
Gerald Rd., Dag.	50	CQ34
Geraldine Rd. SW18	76	BT46
Geraldine Rd. W4	65	BM43
Geraldine St. SE11	**4**	**F7**
Geraldine St. SE11	66	BY41
St. Georges Rd.		
Geralds Gro., Bans.	94	BQ60
Gerard Ave., Houns.	74	BF47
Gerard Gdns., Rain.	59	CT37
Gerard Rd. SW13	65	BO44
Gerard Rd., Har.	45	BJ32
Gerards Clo. SE16	67	CB42
Varcoe Rd.		
Gerda Rd. SE9	78	CL48
Gerdview Dr., Dart.	80	CV49
Germander Way E15	58	CG38
Gernon Clo., Rain.	60	CV37
Gernon Rd. E3	57	CD37
Geron Way NW2	46	BP33
Gerpins La., Upmin.	60	CW37
Gerrard Cres., Brwd.	42	DB27
Gerrard Gdns., Pnr.	44	BC32
Gerrard Pl. W1	**1**	**P10**
Gerrard Pl. W1	56	BW40
Gerrard St.		
Gerrard Rd. N1	56	BY37
Gerrard St. W1	**1**	**P10**
Gerrard St. W1	56	BW40
Gerrards Clo. N14	29	BW25
Gerrards Cross Rd., Slou.	52	AQ36
Gerrards Mead, Bans.	103	BR61
Garratts La.		
Gerridge St. SE1	**4**	**E6**
Gerridge St. SE1	66	BY41
Gerry Raffles Sq. E15	57	CF36
Salway Rd.		
Gertrude Rd., Belv.	69	CR42
Gertrude St. SW10	66	BT43
Gervase Clo., Wem.	46	BN34
Chalkhill Rd.		
Gervase Rd., Edg.	37	BN30
Gervase St. SE15	67	CB43
Gews Cor., Chsnt.	21	CC18
Ghent St. SE6	77	CE48
Ghent Way E8	57	CA36
Ramsgate St.		
Giant Tree Hill, Bush.	36	BG26
Gibbins Rd. E15	57	CF36
Gibbon Rd. SE15	67	CC45
Gibbon Rd. W3	55	BN40
Gibbon Rd., Kings.T.	85	BL51
Gibbon Wk. SW15	65	BP45
Swinburne Rd.		
Gibbons Clo., Borwd.	28	BL23
Gibbons Rd. NW10	55	BN36
Gibbs Ave. SE19	77	BZ49
Gibbs Brook La., Oxt.	114	CF71
Gibbs Clo. SE19	77	BZ49
Gibbs Clo., Chsnt.	21	CC18
Gibbs Couch, Wat.	36	BD27
Gibbs Grn. W14	65	BR42
Gibbs Grn., Edg.	37	BN28
Gibbs Rd. N18	39	CC28
Gibbs Sq. SE19	77	BZ49
Gibons Clo., St.Alb.	9	BK10
Gibraltar Clo., Brwd.	42	DA28
Gibraltar Cres., Epsom	94	BO58
Gibraltar Gdns. E2	57	CA38
Bethnal Grn. Rd.		
Gibraltar Wk. E2	**2**	**Q3**
Gibraltar Wk. E2	57	CA38
Gibson Clo. E1	57	CC38
Colebert Ave.		
Gibson Clo., Chess.	93	BK56
Mansfield Rd.		
Gibson Clo., Epp.	23	CS16
Gibson Clo., Islw.	64	BH45
Gibson Ct., Slou.	62	AS42
Gibson Gdns. N16	48	CA34
Gibson Pl., Stai.	73	AX46
Gibson Rd. SE11	**4**	**C9**
Gibson Rd. SE11	66	BX42
Gibson Rd., Dag.	50	CP33
Gibson Rd., Sutt.	95	BS56
Robin Hood Rd.		
Gibson Rd., Uxb.	44	AY35
Gibson Sq. N1	56	BY37
Gibson St. SE10	68	CG42
Gibsons Hill SW16	76	BY50
Gidd Hill, Couls.	104	BV61
Gidea Ave., Rom.	50	CU31
Gidea Clo., Rom.	50	CU31
Gidea Clo., S.Ock.	60	DB37
Gidean Ct., St.Alb.	8	BG17
Gideon Clo., Belv.	69	CR42
Gideon Rd. SW11	66	BV45
Giesbach Rd. N19	47	BW34
Giffard Rd. N18	39	CA28
Giffin St. SE8	67	CE43
Gifford Gdns. W7	54	BG39
Gifford Pl., Brwd.	42	DB28
Blackthorn Way		
Gifford St. N1	56	BX36
Giffordside, Grays	71	DG42
Gift La. E15	58	CG37
Giggs Hill, Orp.	89	CO51
Giggs Hill Gdns., T.Ditt.	84	BJ54
Giggs Hill Rd., T.Ditt.	84	BJ54
Gilbert Clo., Swans.	80	DB46
Gilbert Gro., Edg.	37	BN30
Gilbert Ho. SE8	67	CE43
Gilbert Pl. WC1	**1**	**Q7**
Gilbert Pl. WC1	56	BX39
Gilbert Rd. SE11	**4**	**E9**
Gilbert Rd. SE11	66	BY42
Gilbert Rd. SW19	76	BT50
Gilbert Rd., Belv.	69	CR41
Gilbert Rd., Brom.	78	CH50
Gilbert Rd., Pnr.	45	BD31
Gilbert Rd., Rom.	50	CT31
Gilbert Rd., Uxb.	35	AX30
Gilbert St. E15	49	CG35
Gilbert St. W1	**1**	**H9**
Gilbert St. W1	56	BV39
Gilbert St., Enf.	30	CC22
Gilbert St., Houns.	64	BG45
High St.		
Gilbert Way, Berk.	7	AQ13
Gilbey Clo., Uxb.	44	AZ35
Gilbey Rd. SW17	76	BU49
Gilbourne Rd. SE18	68	CN43
Gilda Ave., Enf.	30	CD25
Gilda Ct. NW7	37	BP30
Gilda Cres. N16	48	CB33
Gildea St. W1	**1**	**K7**
Gildea St. W1	56	BV39
Great Portland St.		
Gilden Clo., Harl.	6	CQ9
Sheering Rd.		
Gilden Cres. NW5	47	BV35
Gilden Way, Harl.	6	CP9
Gildenhill Rd., Swan.	80	CV50
Gilder St. W1	56	BV39
Portland St.		
Gilders, Saw.	6	CP6
Gilders Rd., Chess.	94	BL57
Giles Clo., Rain.	60	CV37
Giles Coppice SE19	77	CA49
Giles Travers Clo., Egh.	82	AU52
Gilfrid Clo., Uxb.	53	AZ39
Craig Dr.		
Gilhams Ave., Bans.	94	BQ59
Gilkes Cres. SE21	77	CA46
Gilkes Pl. SE21	77	CA46
Gill Ave. E16	58	CH39
Gill Ave., Guil.	118	AP71
Gill Cres., Grav.	81	CD48
Packham Rd.		
Gill St. E14	57	CD40
Gillam Way, Rain.	59	CU36
Gillan Grn., Bush.	36	BG27
Gillender St. E3	57	CF38
Gillender St. E14	57	CF38
Gillespie Rd. N5	47	BY34
Gillett Ave. E6	58	CK37
Gillett Pl. N16	48	CA35
Gillett St.		
Gillett Rd., Th.Hth.	87	BZ52
Gillett St. N16	48	CA35
Gillfoot NW1	**1**	**L1**
Gillham Ter. N17	39	CB29
Gilliam Clo., Pur.	95	BY58
Gillian Ave., St.Alb.	9	BG15
Gillian Cres., Rom.	42	CV30
Gillian Pk. Rd., Sutt.	85	BR54
Gillian St. SE13	77	CE46
Gilliat Dr., Guil.	118	AU69
Gilliat Rd., Slou.	52	AP40
Gilliatt Clo., Iver	52	AV39
Dutton Way		
Gillies Rd., Sev.	99	CZ57
Gillies St. NW5	47	BV35
Gilling Ct. NW3	56	BU36
Gillingham Ms. SW1	**3**	**L8**
Gillingham Ms. SW1	66	BV42
Gillingham St.		
Gillingham Rd. NW2	46	BR34
Gillingham Row SW1	**3**	**L8**
Gillingham Row SW1	66	BW42
Vauxhall Bri. Rd.		
Gillingham St. SW1	**3**	**K8**
Gillingham St. SW1	66	BW42
Gillman Dr. E15	58	CG37
Gillmans Rd., Orp.	89	CO54
Gills Hill, Rad.	27	BH21
Gills Hill La., Rad.	27	BH21
Gills Hollow, Rad.	27	BH21
Gillum Clo., Barn.	38	BU26
Gilmais, Lthd.	111	BG66
Gilman Cres., Wind.	61	AL45
Gilmore Clo., Slou.	62	AR41
Gilmore Clo., Uxb.	44	AZ34
Gilmore Cres., Ashf.	73	AZ49
Gilmore Rd. SE13	67	CF45
Gilmour Clo., Enf.	30	CB21
Gilpin Ave. SW14	65	BN45
Gilpin Clo., Mitch.	86	BU51
Lowry Cres.		
Gilpin Cres. N18	39	CA28
Gilpin Cres., Twick.	74	BF47
Gilpin Rd. E5	48	CD35
Gilpin Way, Hayes	63	BA43
Gilpins Ride, Berk.	7	AR12
Gilroy Clo., Rain.	59	CT36
Gilroy Way, Orp.	89	CO54
Gilsand, Wal.Abb.	31	CG21
Gilsland Rd., Th.Hth.	87	BZ52
Gilstead Rd. SW6	66	BS44
Gilston Rd. SW10	66	BT42
Gilton Rd. SE6	78	CG48
Giltspur St. EC1	**2**	**G8**
Giltspur St. EC1	56	BY39
Gilwell Clo. E4	30	CE25
Antlers Hill		
Gilwell La. E4	30	CF24
Gimcrack Hill, Lthd.	102	BJ64
Gippeswyck Clo., Pnr.	36	BD30
Uxbridge Rd.		
Gipsy Hill SE19	77	CA49
Gipsy La. SW15	65	BP45
Gipsy La., Grays	71	DE43
Gipsy Rd. SE27	77	BZ49
Gipsy Rd., Well.	69	CP44
Gipsy Rd. Gdns. SE27	77	BZ49
Giralda Clo. E16	58	CJ39
Fulmer Rd.		
Giraud St. E14	57	CE39
Girdlers Rd. W14	65	BQ42
Girdlestone Est. N19	47	BW34
Girdlestone Wk. N19	47	BW34
Girdwood Rd. SW18	75	BR47
Girling Way, Felt.	63	BC45
Gironde Rd. SW6	65	BR43
Girtin Rd., Bush.	27	BF24
Girton Ave. NW9	46	BM31
Girton Clo., Nthlt.	54	BF36
Girton Gdns., Croy.	87	CE55
Girton Ms. N1	56	BY36
Lofting Rd.		
Girton Rd. SE26	77	CC49
Girton Rd., Nthlt.	54	BG36
Girton Way, Rick.	26	BA25
Gisborne Gdns., Rain.	59	CT38
Gisburn Rd. N8	47	BX31
Gissing Wk. N1	56	BY36
Lofting Rd.		
Given Wilson Wk. E13	58	CG37
Stride Rd.		
Givons Gro., Lthd.	111	BK66
Gladbeck Way, Enf.	30	BZ24
Gladding Rd. E12	49	CJ35
Glade, The N21	38	BX26
Glade, The SE7	68	CJ43
Glade, The, Brwd.	122	DD26
Glade, The, Brom.	88	CJ51
Glade, The, Couls.	104	BY63
Glade, The, Croy.	87	CC53

Glade, The, Enf. 29 BY24
Glade, The, Epsom 94 BP57
Glade, The, Ger.Cr. 43 AR33
Glade, The, Ilf. 40 CK30
Glade, The, Lthd. 102 BF64
Glade, The, Sev. 107 CU65
Glade, The, Stai. 73 AW50
Glade, The, Sutt. 94 BR58
Glade, The, Tad. 104 BS64
Glade, The, Upmin. 51 CY35
Glade, The, Welw.G.C. 5 BQ7
Glade, The, Wok. 91 AV60
Glade, The, W.Wick. 87 CE55
Glade, The, Wdf.Grn. 40 CH27
Glade Clo., Surb. 84 BK55
Glade Ct., Ilf. 40 CK30
Glade Gdns., Croy. 87 CD54
Glade La., Sthl. 64 BF41
Glade Spur, Tad. 104 BS64
Glades, The, Brom. 88 CH51
Glades, The, Grav. 81 BH50
Glades, The, Hem.H. 7 AV13
The Shrubbery
Gladeside N21 29 BX25
Gladeside, Croy. 87 CC53
Gladeside, St.Alb. 9 BK12
Gladeside Clo., Chess. 93 BK57
Gladeside Ct., Warl. 105 CB63
Gladesmore Rd. N15 48 CA32
Gladeswood Rd., Belv. 69 CR42
Gladeway, The, Wal.Abb. 21 CF20
Gladiator St. SE23 77 CD47
Glading Ter. N16 48 CA34
Gladioli Clo., Hmptn. 74 BF50
Gresham Rd.
Gladsdale Dr., Pnr. 44 BC31
Gladsmuir Clo., Walt. 84 BD55
Gladsmuir Rd. N19 47 BW33
Gladsmuir Rd., Barn. 28 BR23
Gladstone Ave. E12 58 CK36
Gladstone Ave. N22 38 BY30
Gladstone Ave., Felt. 73 BC46
Gladstone Ave., Twick. 74 BG47
Gladstone Ms. N22 38 BY30
Pelham Rd.
Gladstone Ms. SE20 77 CC50
Graveney Gro.
Gladstone Pk. Gdns. NW2 46 BP35
Gladstone Pl. E3 57 CD37
Roman Rd.
Gladstone Pl., Barn. 28 BQ24
Gladstone Rd. SW19 76 BS50
Gladstone Rd. W4 65 BN41
Gladstone Rd., Ash. 102 BK62
Gladstone Rd., Buck.H. 40 CH26
Gladstone Rd., Croy. 87 BZ54
Gladstone Rd., Dart. 80 CW46
Gladstone Rd., Hodd. 12 CE11
Gladstone Rd., Kings.T. 85 BM52
Gladstone Rd., Orp. 97 CM56
Gladstone Rd., Sthl. 64 BE41
Gladstone Rd., Surb. 84 BK55
Gladstone Rd., Wat. 27 BD24
Gladstone St. SE1 4 F6
Gladstone St. SE1 66 BY41
Gladstone Ter. SE27 77 BZ49
Gladstone Ter. SW8 66 BV44
Gladstone Way, Har. 45 BH31
Palmerston Rd.
Gladstone Way, Slou. 61 AN41
Gladwell Rd. N8 47 BX32
Gladwell Rd., Brom. 78 CH50
Gladwyn Rd. SW15 65 BQ45
Gladys Rd. NW6 56 BS36
Glaisyer Way, Iver 52 AU37
Glamis Clo., Chsnt. 21 CB18
Glamis Clo., Hem.H. 8 AZ10
Dunster Rd.
Glamis Cres., Hayes 63 BA41
Glamis Dr., Horn. 51 CW33
Glamis Pl. E1 57 CC40
Glamis Rd. E1 57 CC40
Glamis Way, Nthlt. 54 BG36
Glamorgan Clo., Mitch. 86 BX52
Glamorgan Rd., Kings.T. 74 BK50
Glanfield, Hem.H. 8 AY12
Glanfield Rd., Beck. 87 CD52
Glanleam Rd., Stan. 36 BK28
Glanmead, Brwd. 122 DC26
Glanmor Rd., Slou. 52 AQ40
Glanthams Clo., Brwd. 122 DC27
Glanthams Rd., Brwd. 122 DC27
Glanty, The, Egh. 72 AT49
Glanville Dr., Horn. 51 CW34
Glanville Rd. SW2 76 BX46
Glanville Rd., Brom. 88 CH52
Glasbrook Ave., Twick. 74 BE47
Glasbrook Rd. SE9 78 CJ47
Glaserton Rd. N16 48 CA33
Glasford St. SW17 76 BU50
Glasgow Rd. E13 58 CH37
Glasgow Rd. N18 39 CB28
Glasgow Ter. SW1 66 BW42
Lupus St.
Glass Ho. Yd. EC1 57 BZ39
Aldersgate St.
Glass St. E2 57 CB38
Coventry Rd.
Glass Yd. SE18 68 CL41
Glasse Clo. W13 54 BJ40
Glasshill St. SE1 4 G4
Glasshill St. SE1 66 BY41
Glasshouse All. EC4 2 E9
Glasshouse Flds. E1 57 CC40
Glasshouse St. W1 3 M1
Glasshouse St. W1 56 BW40
Glasshouse Wk. SE11 4 A10
Glasshouse Wk. SE11 66 BX42
Glasshouse Yd. EC1 2 H5
Glasslyn Rd. N8 47 BW32
Glassmill La., Brom. 88 CG51
Glasson Clo., West Dr. 63 AY41

Glastonbury Ave., Wdf.Grn. 40 CJ29
Glastonbury Rd. N9 39 CB26
Chichester Rd.
Glastonbury Rd., Mord. 86 BS54
Glastonbury St. NW6 46 BR35
Glaucus St. E3 57 CE39
Glazbury Rd. W14 65 BR42
Glazebrook Clo. SE21 77 BZ48
Glazebrook Rd., Tedd. 74 BH50
Gleave Clo., St.Alb. 9 BJ13
Glebe, The SE3 68 CG45
Glebe, The SW16 76 BW49
Prentis Rd.
Glebe, The, Chis. 88 CM51
Glebe, The, Kings L. 17 AZ18
Glebe, The, Reig. 120 BP74
Glebe, The, Wat. 18 BD20
Glebe, The, West Dr. 63 AY42
Glebe, The, Wor.Pk. 85 BO54
Glebe Ave., Enf. 29 BY24
Glebe Ave., Har. 46 BL31
Glebe Ave., Mitch. 86 BU51
Glebe Ave., Ruis. 53 BC36
Glebe Ave., Uxb. 44 BA35
Glebe Ave., Wdf.Grn. 40 CH29
Glebe Clo. W4 69 CO42
Glebe St.
Glebe Clo., Ger.Cr. 34 AR29
Glebe Clo., Hat. 11 BU12
Glebe Clo., Hem.H. 8 AY15
Glebe Clo., Lthd. 111 BF66
Glebe Clo., Maid. 61 AJ41
Glebe Clo., S.Croy. 96 CA59
Glebe Clo., Uxb. 44 BA35
Glebe Cotts., Felt. 74 BF48
Glebe Cotts., Guil. 110 AW69
Glebe Cotts., Hat. 11 BU12
Glebe Ct. W7 54 BG40
Glebe Ct., Guil. 118 AS70
Glebe Ct., Hat. 10 BP12
Brian Clo.
Glebe Ct., Mitch. 86 BU52
Glebe Ct., Stan. 36 BK28
Glebe Cres. NW4 46 BQ31
Glebe Cres., Har. 46 BL31
Glebe Est. SE5 67 CA44
Glebe Gdns., N.Mal. 85 BO54
Glebe Gdns., Wey. 92 AY60
Glebe Ho. Dr., Brom. 88 CH54
Glebe Hyrst SE19 77 CA49
Giles Coppice
Glebe Hyrst, S.Croy. 96 CA59
Glebe La., Barn. 28 BP25
Glebe La., Har. 146 BL31
Glebe La., Sev. 116 CU66
Glebe Path, Mitch. 86 BU52
Glebe Pl. SW3 66 BU43
Glebe Pl., Hort.K. 90 CY52
Glebe Rd. E8 57 CA36
Glebe Rd. N3 38 BT30
Glebe Rd. N8 47 BX31
Glebe Rd. NW10 55 BP36
Glebe Rd. SW13 65 BP44
Glebe Rd., Ash. 102 BK62
Glebe Rd., Brom. 88 CH51
Glebe Rd., Cars. 95 BU57
Glebe Rd., Dag. 59 CR36
Church St.
Glebe Rd., Dor. 119 BH71
Glebe Rd., Egh. 72 AU49
Glebe Rd., Ger.Cr. 34 AR30
Glebe Rd., Grav. 81 DF47
Glebe Rd., Hayes 53 BB40
Glebe Rd., Maid. 61 AG40
Glebe Rd., Ong. 24 CW18
Glebe Rd., Rain. 59 CU38
Glebe Rd., Red. 104 BV65
Glebe Rd., Sev. 116 CU69
Glebe Rd., Stai. 73 AW49
Glebe Rd., Stan. 36 BK28
Glebe Rd., Sutt. 94 BR58
Glebe Rd., Uxb. 53 AX37
Glebe Rd., Warl. 105 CC62
Glebe Rd., Wind. 72 AQ46
Glebe Side, Twick. 74 BH46
Glebe St. W4 65 BN42
Glebe Ter. E3 57 CE38
Glebe Way, Amer. 25 AO21
Glebe Way, Erith 69 CT43
Glebe Way, Felt. 74 BF48
Glebe Way, S.Croy. 96 CA59
Glebe Way, W.Wick. 87 CF55
Glebefields, The, Sev. 107 CT64
Shoreham La.
Glebeland, Hat. 10 BQ12
Glebeland Gdns., Shep. 83 BA53
Glebelands, Chig. 41 CO27
Glebelands, Dart. 69 CT45
Glebelands, E.Mol. 84 BF53
Glebelands, Esher 93 BH58
Glebelands, Harl. 13 CN11
Glebelands Ave. E18 40 CH30
Glebelands Ave., Ilf. 49 CM33
Glebelands Clo. SE5 67 CA45
Grove Hill Rd.
Glebelands Rd., Felt. 73 BC47
Glebeway, Horn. 51 CW33
Glebeway, Wdf.Grn. 40 CJ28
Gledhow Gdns. SW5 66 BT42
Gledhow Wd., Tad. 104 BS64
Gledstanes Rd. W14 65 BR42
Gledwood Ave., Hayes 53 BB39
Gledwood Cres., Hayes 53 BB39
Gledwood Dr., Hayes 53 BB39
Gledwood Gdns., Hayes 53 BB39
Gleed Ave., Bush. 36 BG27
Gleeson Dr., Orp. 97 CN56
Glegg Pl. SW15 65 BQ45
Glen, The, Brom. 88 CG51
Glen, The, Croy. 87 CC55
Glen, The, Enf. 29 BY24
Glen, The, Hem.H. 8 AY11
Glen, The, Nthwd. 35 BA29

Glen, The, Orp. 88 CK55
Glen, The, Pnr. 45 BE33
Glen, The (Eastcote), Pnr. 44 BC32
Glen, The, Rain. 60 CV38
Glen, The, Slou. 62 AR42
Glen, The, Sthl. 64 BE42
Glen, The, Wem. 45 BK35
Glen, The, Wey. 91 AV56
Glen Albyn Rd. SW19 75 BQ48
Glen Ave., Ashf. 73 AZ49
Glen Clo., Shep. 83 AZ52
Glen Clo., Tad. 103 BR64
Glen Cres., Wdf.Grn. 40 CH29
Glen Dale Rd., Grav. 81 DF49
Glen Faba Rd., Harl. 13 CG12
Glen Gdns., Croy. 86 BY55
Glen Hazel, Brwd. 33 DB21
Glen Mill, Hmptn. 74 BE49
Glen Ri., Wdf.Grn. 40 CH29
Glen Rd. E13 58 CJ38
Glen Rd. E17 48 CD32
Glen Rd., Chess. 85 BL55
Glen Rd. End, Wall. 95 BV58
Glen Vw., Grav. 81 DH47
Glen Wk., Islw. 74 BG46
Glen Way, Wat. 26 BB22
Glen Wd., Dor. 119 BK72
Glena Mt., Sutt. 95 BT56
Glenaffric Ave. E14 67 CF42
Glenalla Rd., Ruis. 44 BB33
Glenalmond Rd., Har. 46 BL31
Glenalyon Way SE18 68 CK42
Glenarm Rd. E5 48 CC35
Glenavon Clo., Esher 93 BJ57
Glenavon Gdns., Slou. 62 AR42
Glenavon Rd. E15 58 CG36
Glenbarr Clo. SE9 68 CL45
Glenbow Rd., Brom. 78 CG50
Glenbrook N., Enf. 29 BX24
Glenbrook Rd. NW6 47 BS35
Glenbrook S., Enf. 29 BX24
Glenbuck Ct., Surb. 85 BL53
Glenbuck Rd., Surb. 84 BK53
Glenburnie Rd. SW17 76 BU48
Glencairn Dr. W5 54 BJ38
Glencairn Rd. SW16 86 BX51
Glencairne Clo. E16 58 CJ39
Glencoe Ave., Ilf. 49 CM33
Glencoe Dr., Dag. 50 CR35
Glencoe Rd., Bush. 27 BF25
Glencoe Rd., Hayes 54 BD39
Glencoe Rd., Wey. 83 AZ55
Glencourse Grn., Wat. 36 BD28
Coldwell Rd.
Glendale, Swan. 89 CT53
Glendale Ave. N22 38 BY29
Glendale Ave., Edg. 37 BM28
Glendale Ave., Rom. 50 CP33
Glendale Clo. SE9 68 CL45
Glendale Clo., Brwd. 122 DC26
Glendale Clo., Wok. 100 AR62
Glendale Dr. SW19 75 BR49
Glendale Dr., Guil. 109 AU68
Glendale Gdns., Hem.H. 8 AW13
Glendale Gdns., Wem. 45 BK33
Glendale Ms., Beck. 87 CE51
Westgate Rd.
Glendale Ri., Pur. 104 BY61
Glendale Rd., Erith 69 CS42
Glendale Wk., Chsnt. 21 CD18
Glendale Way SE28 59 CP40
Glendall St. SW9 66 BX45
Glendarvon St. SW15 65 BQ45
Glendene Ave., Lthd. 110 BB66
Glendish Rd. N17 39 CB30
Glendor Gdns. NW7 37 BN28
Glendower Cres., Orp. 89 CO53
Glendower Gdns. SW14 65 BN45
Glendower Rd.
Glendower Pl. SW7 3 A8
Glendower Pl. SW7 66 BT42
Harrington Rd.
Glendower Rd. E4 39 CF26
Glendower Rd. SW14 65 BN45
Glendown Rd. SE2 69 CO42
Glendun Ct. W3 55 BO40
Glendun Rd.
Glendun Rd. W3 55 BO40
Gleneagle Ms. SW16 76 BW49
Ambleside Ave.
Gleneagle Rd. SW16 76 BW50
Gleneagles, Stan. 36 BJ29
Gordon Ave.
Gleneagles Clo., Orp. 88 CM54
Gleneagles Clo., Rom. 42 CW29
Gleneagles Clo., Stai. 73 AX46
Park Rd.
Gleneagles Clo., Stan. 36 BJ29
Gleneagles Clo., Wat. 36 BD28
Gleneagles Grn., Orp. 88 CM54
Gleneagles Clo.
Gleneldon Ms. SW16 76 BX49
Gleneldon Rd. SW16 76 BX49
Glenelg Rd. SW2 76 BX46
Glenesk Rd. SE9 68 CL45
Glenester Clo., Hodd. 12 CE10
Glenfarg Rd. SE6 77 CF47
Glenferrie Rd., St.Alb. 9 BJ13
Glenfield Clo., Bet. 120 BM72
Glenfield Cres., Ruis. 44 BA33
Glenfield Rd. SW12 76 BW47
Glenfield Rd. W13 64 BJ41
Glenfield Rd., Ashf. 73 AZ50
Glenfield Rd., Bans. 104 BS61
Glenfield Rd., Bet. 120 BM72
Glenfield Ter. W13 54 BJ40
Glenfinlas Way SE5 66 BY43
Glenforth St. SE10 68 CG42
Glengall Causeway E14 67 CE41
Glengall Gro. E14 67 CE41
Glengall Rd. NW6 55 BR37
Glengall Rd. SE15 67 CA42
Glengall Rd., Bexh. 69 CQ45
Glengall Rd., Edg. 37 BM27

Glengall Rd., Wdf.Grn. 40 CH29
Glengall Ter. SE15 67 CA43
Glengarnock Ave. E14 67 CF42
Glengarry Rd. SE22 77 CA46
Glenham Dr., Ilf. 49 CL32
Glenhaven Ave., Borwd. 28 BM24
Glenhead Clo. SE9 68 CL45
Glenhill Clo. N3 38 BS30
Glenhouse Rd. SE9 78 CL46
Glenhurst Ave. NW5 47 BV35
Glenhurst Ave., Bex. 79 CQ47
Glenhurst Ave., Ruis. 44 BA33
Glenhurst Ri. SE19 77 BZ50
Glenhurst Rd. N12 38 BT28
Glenhurst Rd., Brent. 64 BK43
Glenilla Rd. NW3 56 BU36
Glenister Pk. Rd. SW16 76 BW50
Glenister Rd. SE10 68 CG42
Glenister St. E16 58 CL40
Glenlea Rd. SE9 78 CK46
Glenloch Rd. NW3 56 BU36
Glenloch Rd., Enf. 30 CC23
Glenluce Rd. SE3 68 CH43
Glenlyn Ave., St.Alb. 9 BJ14
Glenlyon Rd. SE9 78 CL46
Glenmere Ave. NW7 37 BP29
Glenmore Clo., Wey. 83 AW55
Glenmore Rd. NW3 56 BU36
Glenmore Rd., Well. 68 CN43
Glenmore Way, Bark. 59 CO37
Glenmount Path SE18 68 CM42
Raglan Rd.
Glenn Ave., Pur. 95 BY59
Glennie Rd. SE27 76 BY48
Glenny Rd., Bark. 58 CM36
Glenorchy Clo., Hayes 54 BE39
Kilpatrick Way
Glenparke Rd. E7 58 CH36
Glenrosa Gdns., Grav. 81 DK49
Glenrosa St. SW6 66 BT44
Glenrose Ct., Sid. 79 CO49
Sidcup Hill
Glenroy St. W12 55 BQ39
Glensdale Rd. SE4 67 CD45
Glenshee Clo., Nthwd. 35 BA29
Merrows Clo.
Glenshiel Rd. SE9 78 CL46
Glenside, Chig. 40 CM29
Glenside Cotts., Slou. 62 AP41
Upton Clo.
Glenside Rd. SE18 68 CN42
Glentanner Way SW17 76 BT48
Aboyne Rd.
Glentham Gdns. SW13 65 BP43
Glentham Rd.
Glentham Rd. SW13 65 BP43
Glenthorne Ave., Croy. 87 CB54
Glenthorne Clo., Sutt. 86 BS54
Glenthorne Gdns., Ilf. 49 CL31
Glenthorne Gdns., Sutt. 86 BS54
Glenthorne Rd. E17 48 CD32
Glenthorne Rd. N11 38 BU28
Glenthorne Rd. W6 65 BP42
Glenthorne Rd., Kings.T. 85 BL52
Glenthorpe Rd., Mord. 85 BQ53
Glenton Clo., Rom. 41 CT29
Glenton Rd. SE13 68 CG45
Glenton Way, Rom. 41 CT29
Glentrammon Ave., Orp. 97 CN57
Glentrammon Clo., Orp. 97 CN56
Glentrammon Gdns., Orp. 97 CN57
Glentrammon Rd., Orp. 97 CN57
Glentworth Pl., Slou. 61 AO40
Glentworth St. NW1 1 F5
Glentworth St. NW1 56 BU38
Glenure Rd. SE9 78 CL46
Glenview SE2 69 CP43
Glenview Rd., Brom. 88 CJ51
Glenview Rd., Hem.H. 8 AW13
Glenville Ave., Enf. 30 BZ22
Glenville Clo., Surb. 85 BN54
Glenville Gro. SE8 67 CD43
Glenville Ms. SW18 76 BS47
Glenville Rd., Kings.T. 85 BM51
Glenwood, Brox. 12 CD13
Glenwood, Welw.G.C. 5 BT8
Glenwood Ave. NW9 46 BN33
Glenwood Ave., Rain. 59 CU38
Glenwood Clo., Har. 45 BH32
Glenwood Dr., Rom. 50 CU31
Glenwood Gdns., Ilf. 49 CL32
Glenwood Gro. NW9 46 BN33
Glenwood Rd. N15 47 BY32
Glenwood Rd. NW7 37 BO27
Glenwood Rd. SE6 77 CD47
Glenwood Rd., Epsom 94 BP57
Glenwood Rd., Houns. 64 BG45
Glenwood Way, Croy. 87 CC53
Glenworth Ave. E14 67 CF42
Glevum Clo., St.Alb. 9 BE14
Gliddon Rd. W14 65 BR42
Glimpsing Grn., Belv. 69 CQ41
Glisson Rd., Uxb. 53 AZ37
Gload Cres., Orp. 89 CP55
Global App. E3 57 CF38
Globe La. SE18 68 CL41
Globe Pond Rd. SE16 57 CD40
Globe Rd. E1 57 CC38
Globe Rd. E2 57 CC38
Globe Rd. E15 49 CG35
Globe Rd., Horn. 50 CU32
Globe Rd., Wdf.Grn. 40 CJ29
Globe St. SE1 4 K5
Globe St. SE1 67 BZ41
Globe Ter. E2 57 CC38
Globe Rd.
Globe Yd. W1 1 J9
Glory Mead, Dor. 119 BJ73
Glossop Rd., S.Croy. 96 BZ58
Gloster Rd., N.Mal. 85 BO52
Gloster Rd., Wok. 100 AT63
Gloucester Ave. NW1 56 BV36
Gloucester Ave., Grays 71 DE41

Gloucester Ave., Horn. 51 C
Gloucester Ave., Sid. 78 C
Gloucester Ave., Slou. 52 A
Gloucester Ave., Wal.Cr. 21 C
Gloucester Ave., Well. 68 C
Gloucester Circ. SE10 67
Gloucester Clo. NW10 55 B
Gloucester Clo., S.Ock. 60 D
South Rd.
Gloucester Clo., T.Ditt. 84
Gloucester Ct. EC3 4
Gloucester Ct. EC3 57 C
Tower Hill
Gloucester Ct. W3 55 B
Links Rd.
Gloucester Ct., Rich. 65 B
Gloucester Cres. NW1 56
Gloucester Cres., Stai. 73 A
Gloucester Dr. N4 47 B
Gloucester Dr. NW11 47 B
Gloucester Dr., Stai. 72 A
Gloucester Gdns. NW11 46 B
Gloucester Gdns. W2 56
Gloucester Gdns., Barn. 29 B
Gloucester Gdns., Ilf. 49 C
Gloucester Gdns., Sutt. 86 B
Gloucester Gate NW1 56 B
Gloucester Gate Ms. NW1 56 B
Gloucester Gate
Gloucester Gro., Edg. 37 B
Gloucester Ms. NW1 56 B
Albany St.
Gloucester Ms. W2 56
Gloucester Ms. W. W2 56
Gloucester Par., Sid. 79 C
Gloucester Pl. NW1 1
Gloucester Pl. NW1 56 B
Gloucester Pl. W1 1
Gloucester Pl., Wind. 61 A
Gloucester Pl. Ms. W1 1
Gloucester Pl. Ms. W1 56 B
Gloucester Rd. E10 48 C
Gloucester Rd. E11 49 C
Gloucester Rd. E12 49 C
Gloucester Rd. E17 39 C
Gloucester Rd. N17 39 B
Gloucester Rd. N18 39 C
Gloucester Rd. SW7 66 B
Gloucester Rd. W3 65 B
Gloucester Rd. W5 64 B
Gloucester Rd., Barn. 29 B
Gloucester Rd., Belv. 69 C
Gloucester Rd., Brwd. 33 D
Gloucester Rd., Croy. 87 B
Gloucester Rd., Dart. 79 C
Gloucester Rd., Enf. 30 B
Gloucester Rd., Felt. 74 B
Gloucester Rd., Grav. 81 D
Gloucester Rd., Guil. 118 A
Gloucester Rd., Hmptn. 74 B
Gloucester Rd., Har. 45 B
Gloucester Rd., Houns. 64 B
Gloucester Rd., Kings.T. 85 B
Gloucester Rd., Red. 121 B
Gloucester Rd., Rich. 65 B
Gloucester Rd., Rom. 50 C
Gloucester Rd., Tedd. 74 B
Gloucester Rd., Twick. 74 B
Gloucester Sq. W2 1
Gloucester Sq. W2 56 B
Gloucester Sq., Wok. 100 A
Civic Way
Gloucester St. SW1 66 B
Gloucester Ter. W2 56 B
Gloucester Wk. W8 66 B
Gloucester Way EC1 2
Gloucester Way EC1 56 B
Glover Rd., Pnr. 45 B
Glovers Fld., Brwd. 33 C
Glovers Gro., Ruis. 44 A
Glovers La., Harl. 14 C
Glovers Rd., Reig. 121 B
Gloxinia Rd., Grav. 81 D
Gloxinia Wk., Hmptn. 74 B
The Ave.
Glycena Rd. SW11 66 B
Glyn Ave., Barn. 29 B
Glyn Clo. SE25 87 C
Grange Hill
Glyn Clo., Epsom 94 B
Glyn Ct. SW16 76 B
Glyn Dr., Sid. 79 C
Glyn Rd. E5 48 C
Glyn Rd., Enf. 30 C
Glyn Rd., Wor.Pk. 85 B
Glyn St. SE11 66 B
Glynde Ms. SW3 3
Glynde Ms. SW3 66 B
Yeomans Row
Glynde Rd., Bexh. 69 C
Glynde St. SE4 77 C
Glyndebourne Pk., Orp. 88 C
Glyndon Rd. SE18 68 C
Glynfield Rd. NW10 55 B
Glynswood, Ger.Cr. 34 A
Glynwood Ct. SE26 77 C
Glynwood Dr.
Glynwood Dr. SE23 77 C
Goat Ho. Bri. SE25 87 C
Goat La., Enf. 30 C
Goat La., Surb. 84 B
Goat Rd., Mitch. 86 B
Goat St. SE1 67 C
Lafone St.
Goat Wf., Brent. 65 B
Goatsfield Rd., West. 106 C
Gobions, Rom. 41 C
Gobions Ave., Rom. 41 C
Gobions Way, Pot.B. 20 B
Goblins Grn., Welw.G.C. 5 B
Godalming Ave., Wall. 95 B
Godalming By-pass, Guil. 118 A

alming Rd. E14 57 CE39
rrisp St.
bold Rd. E15 58 CG38
dard Clo., Shep. 83 AY52
agdalene Rd.
dard Rd., Beck. 87 CC52
dard Rd., Grays 71 DD40
dards Clo., Hert. 11 BW13
dington Chase, Orp. 98 CO56
dington La., Orp. 89 CO55
dfrey Ave., Nthlt. 54 BE37
dfrey Ave., Twick. 74 BG47
dfrey Hill SE18 68 CK42
dfrey Rd. SE18 68 CK42
dfrey St. E15 57 CF37
dfrey St. SW3 3 D10
dfrey St. SW3 66 BU42
dfrey Way, Houns. 74 BE47
dfries Clo., Welw. 5 BU5
ding St. SE11 66 BX42
dley Rd. SW18 76 BT47
dley Rd., Wey. 92 AY60
dliman St. EC4 2 H9
dliman St. EC4 56 BY39
dman Rd. SE15 67 CB44
dman Rd., Grays 71 DG41
dolphin Clo., Sutt. 94 BR58
dolphin Rd. W12 55 BP40
dolphin Rd., Beac. 34 AO29
dolphin Rd., Slou. 52 AO40
dolphin Rd., Wey. 92 BA57
dric Cres., Croy. 96 CF58
dsafe, Harl. 6 CQ9
dson Rd., Croy. 86 BY55
dson St. N1 56 BY37
dstone By-pass, 114 CD69
dse.
dstone Hill, Gdse. 114 CB67
dstone Rd., Cat. 105 CB65
dstone Rd., Oxt. 114 CE69
dstone Rd., Pur. 95 BY59
dstone Rd., Red. 114 CA70
dstone Rd., Sutt. 95 BT56
dstone Rd., Twick. 74 BJ46
dstow Rd. SE2 69 CO41
dwin Clo., Epsom 94 BN57
dwin Ct. NW1 56 BW37
halton St.
dwin Rd. E7 49 CH35
dwin Rd., Brom. 88 CJ52
ffers Rd. SE3 68 CG44
ffs Cres., Chsnt. 21 BZ18
ffs La., Chsnt. 21 BZ18
ffs Oak Ave., Chsnt. 21 BZ17
ffs Rd., Ashf. 73 BA50
gmore Fm. Clo., Cher. 82 AV53
gmore La., Cher. 83 AW54
idel Clo., Wall. 95 BW56
lborne Gdns. W10 55 BR38
olborne Rd.
lborne Ms. W10 55 BR39
ortobello Rd.
lborne Rd. W10 55 BR39
ld Cft., Hem.H. 8 AZ14
ld Hill, Edg. 37 BN29
ld Hill E., Ger.Cr. 34 AR30
ld Hill N., Ger.Cr. 34 AR30
ld Hill W., Ger.Cr. 34 AR30
ld La., Edg. 37 BN29
lda Clo., Barn. 28 BQ25
ldbeaters Gro., Edg. 37 BO29
ldcliff Clo., Mord. 86 BS54
ldcrest Clo. E16 58 CJ39
ldcrest Clo. SE28 59 CP40
ldcrest Ms. W5 54 BK39
Montpelier Rd.
ldcrest Way, Bush. 36 BG26
ldcrest Way, Croy. 96 CF58
ldcrest Way, Pur. 95 BW58
Great Woodcote Dr.
lden Ct., Rich. 74 BK46
George St.
lden Cres., Hayes 53 BB40
lden Dell, Welw.G.C. 5 BR10
lden La. EC1 2 H5
lden La. EC1 57 BZ38
lden La. Est. EC1 2 H5
lden La. Est. EC1 57 BZ38
lden Manor W7 54 BH40
lden Sq. W1 1 M10
lden Sq. W1 56 BW40
lders Clo., Edg. 37 BM28
lders Gdns. NW11 46 BR33
lders Grn. Cres. 46 BR33
NW11
lders Grn. Rd. NW11 46 BR32
lders Manor Dr. NW11 46 BQ32
lders Pk. Clo. NW11 47 BS33
lders Ri. NW4 46 BQ32
lders Way NW11 46 BR33
ldfinch Clo., Orp. 98 CO56
ldfinch Gdns., Guil. 118 AU70
ldfinch Rd. SE28 68 CM41
ldfinch Rd., S.Croy. 96 CC58
ldfinch Way, Borwd. 28 BM24
ldfort Wk., Wok. 100 AP61
Langmans Way
ldhawk Rd. W6 65 BO42
ldhawk Rd. W12 65 BP41
ldhaze Clo., Wdf.Grn. 40 CJ29
ldhurst Ter. NW6 56 BS36
lding Rd., Sev. 108 CV64
lding St. E1 57 CB39
ldingham Ave., Loug. 31 CM23
ldings Cres., Hat. 10 BP12
ldings Hill, Loug. 31 CK21
ldings Ri., Loug. 31 CL23
ldings Rd., Loug. 31 CL23
ldington Clo., Hodd. 12 CD10
ldington Cres. NW1 56 BW37
ldington St. NW1 56 BW37
ldman Clo. E2 57 CB38
ldney Rd. W9 56 BS38
ldrings Rd., Lthd. 93 BF60

Goldsborough Cres. E4 39 CE27
Goldsborough Rd. SW8 66 BW44
Goldsdown Clo., Enf. 30 CD23
Goldsdown Rd., Enf. 30 CC23
Goldsell Rd., Swan. 89 CS53
Goldsmid St. SE18 68 CN42
Sladedale Rd.
Goldsmith Ave. E12 58 CK36
Goldsmith Ave. NW9 46 BO32
Goldsmith Ave. W3 55 BN40
Goldsmith Ave., Rom. 50 CR33
Goldsmith Clo. W3 55 BN40
East Acton La.
Goldsmith Clo., Har. 45 BF33
Goldsmith La. NW9 46 BM31
Goldsmith Rd. E10 48 CE33
Goldsmith Rd. E17 39 CC30
Goldsmith Rd. N11 38 BU28
Goldsmith Rd. SE15 67 CB44
Goldsmith Rd. W3 55 BN40
Goldsmith St. EC2 2 J8
Goldsmith St. EC2 57 BZ39
Gutter La.
Goldsmiths Clo., Wok. 100 AR62
Goldsmiths Row E2 57 CB37
Goldsmiths Sq. E2 57 CB37
Goldsworth Orchard, Wok. 100 AQ62
Goldsworth Relief Rd., Wok. 100 AR62
Goldsworth Rd., Wok. 100 AR62
Goldsworthy Gdns. SE16 67 CC42
Goldwell Rd., Th.Hth. 86 BX52
Goldwin Clo. SE14 67 CC44
Pomeroy St.
Golf Clo., Bush. 27 BD23
Golf Clo., Stan. 36 BK29
Golf Clo., Wok. 91 AV60
Golf Club Dr., Kings.T. 75 BN50
Golf Club Rd., Wey. 92 AZ58
Golf Club Rd., Wok. 100 AQ63
Golf Links Ave., Grav. 81 DG49
Golf Ride, Enf. 29 BY21
Golf Rd. W5 55 BL39
Boileau Rd.
Golf Rd., Brom. 88 CL52
Golf Rd., Ken. 105 BZ62
Golf Side, Sutt. 94 BR59
Golf Side, Twick. 74 BG48
Golfe Rd., Ilf. 49 CM34
Golfside Clo. N20 38 BU27
Golfside Clo., N.Mal. 85 BO51
Goliath Clo., Wall. 95 BX57
Gollogly Ter. SE7 68 CJ42
Nadine St.
Gombards, St.Alb. 9 BG13
Gombards All., St.Alb. 9 BG13
Gomer Gdns., Tedd. 74 BJ50
Gomer Pl., Tedd. 74 BJ49
Gomm Rd. SE16 67 CC41
Gomshall Ave., Wall. 95 BX56
Gomshall Gdns., Ken. 105 BZ61
Gomshall Rd., Sutt. 94 BQ58
Gondar Gdns. NW6 46 BR35
Gonnerston, St.Alb. 9 BF13
Kings Rd.
Gonson Pl. SE8 67 CE43
Gonson St. SE8 67 CE43
Gonston Clo. SW19 75 BR48
Bodicott Clo.
Gonville Ave., Rick. 26 AZ25
Gonville Cres., Nthlt. 54 BF36
Gonville Rd., Th.Hth. 86 BX53
Gonville St. SW6 65 BR45
Putney Bri. App.
Good Clo., Couls. 104 BY63
Goodall Rd. E11 48 CF35
Goodbury Rd., Sev. 99 CX60
Gooden Ct., Har. 45 BH34
Goodenough Rd. SW19 75 BR50
Goodenough Way, Couls. 104 BX63
Gooderham Ho., Grays 71 DG41
Goodge Pl. W1 1 M7
Goodge Pl. W1 56 BW39
Goodge St.
Goodge St. W1 1 M7
Goodge St. W1 56 BW39
Goodhall St. NW10 55 BO38
Goodhart Way, W.Wick. 88 CG54
Goodhew Rd., Croy. 87 CB53
Gooding Ho. SE7 68 CJ42
Goodinge Clo. N7 47 BX35
North Rd.
Goodinge Rd. N7 56 BX36
Goodlake Ct., Uxb. 43 AV33
Goodlake Ct., Uxb. 43 AV33
Goodley Stock Rd., West. 115 CL67
Goodman Cres. SW2 76 BW48
Goodman Pk., Slou. 52 AR40
Goodman Pl., Stai. 72 AV49
High St.
Goodman Rd. E10 48 CF33
Goodmans Ct., Wem. 45 BK35
Lancelot Rd.
Goodmans Flds. E1 57 CB39
Goodmans Stile E1 57 CB39
Commercial Rd.
Goodmans Yd. E1 2 P10
Goodmans Yd. E1 57 CA40
Goodmayes Ave., Ilf. 50 CO33
Goodmayes La., Ilf. 50 CO35
Goodmayes Rd., Ilf. 50 CO33
Goodmead Rd., Orp. 89 CO54
Goodrich Clo., Wat. 26 BC21
Goodrich Rd. SE22 77 CA46
Goods Way NW1 56 BW37
Goodson Rd. NW10 55 BO36
Goodstone Rd., Whyt. 105 CA62
Goodway Gdns. E14 57 CF39
Goodwin Clo., Mitch. 86 BT52
Phipps Bri. Rd.
Goodwin Dr., Sid. 79 CP48
Goodwin Gdns., Croy. 95 BY57

Goodwin Rd. N9 39 CC26
Goodwin Rd. W12 65 BP41
Goodwin Rd., Croy. 95 BY57
Goodwin St. N4 47 BY34
Goodwins Ct. WC2 1 Q10
Goodwins Ct. WC2 56 BX40
St. Martins La.
Goodwood Ave., Enf. 30 CC22
Goodwood Ave., Horn. 51 CW35
Goodwood Ave., Wat. 26 BB21
Goodwood Clo., Hodd. 12 CE11
Goodwood Clo., Mord. 86 BS52
Goodwood Clo., Stan. 36 BK28
Marsh La.
Goodwood Cres., Grav. 81 DH50
Goodwood Dr., Nthlt. 54 BF36
Goodwood Par., Wat. 26 BB21
Goodwood Path, Borwd. 28 BM23
Stratfield Rd.
Goodwood Rd. SE14 67 CD43
Goodwood Rd., Red. 121 BU69
Goodwyn Ave. NW7 37 BO28
Goodwyns Fm. Est., Dor. 119 BJ73
Goodwyns Rd., Dor. 119 BJ73
Goodwyns Vale N10 38 BV30
Goodyear Pl. SE5 67 BZ43
Addington Sq.
Goodyear Ter., Grays 70 DA43
Goodyers Ave., Rad. 18 BH20
Goodyers Gdns. NW4 46 BQ32
Brent Grn.
Goosander Way SE28 68 CM41
Goose Acre, Chesh. 16 AQ18
Goose Acre, Welw.G.C. 5 BR9
Goose Cft., Hem.H. 7 AV13
Goose Grn., Cob. 101 BC63
Goose Grn. Clo., Orp. 89 CO51
Goose La., Wok. 100 AQ64
Goose Rye Rd., Guil. 109 AO66
Goose Sq. E6 58 CK39
Harper Rd.
Goose Yd. EC1 56 BY37
St. John St.
Gooseacre La., Har. 45 BK32
Goosefield, E.Mol. 84 BF52
Gooseley La. E6 58 CL38
Gooshays Dr., Rom. 42 CW28
Gooshays Gdns., Rom. 42 CW29
Goossens Clo., Sutt. 95 BT56
Turnpike La.
Gophir La. EC4 2 K10
Gophir La. EC4 57 BZ40
Bush La.
Gopsall St. N1 57 BZ37
Goral Mead, Rick. 35 AX26
Gordon Ave. E4 40 CG29
Gordon Ave. SW14 65 BO45
Gordon Ave., Horn. 50 CT34
Gordon Ave., S.Croy. 96 BZ58
Gordon Ave., Stan. 36 BH29
Gordon Ave., Twick. 74 BJ46
Gordon Clo. E17 48 CE32
Lennox Rd.
Gordon Clo. N19 47 BW33
Highgate Hill
Gordon Clo., Cher. 82 AV55
Gordon Clo., St.Alb. 9 BJ14
Gordon Clo., Stai. 73 AW50
Gordon Ct. W12 55 BP39
Du Cane Rd.
Gordon Cres., Croy. 87 CA54
Gordon Cres., Hayes 63 BC41
Gordon Dr., Cher. 82 AV55
Gordon Dr., Shep. 83 BA53
Gordon Gdns., Edg. 37 BM30
Gordon Gro. SE5 66 BY44
Gordon Hill, Enf. 30 BZ23
Gordon Ho. Rd. NW5 47 BV35
Gordon Pl. W8 66 BS41
Gordon Prom., Grav. 81 DH46
Gordon Rd. E4 40 CG26
Gordon Rd. E11 49 CH32
Gordon Rd. E12 49 CL34
Gordon Rd. E15 48 CF35
Gordon Rd. E18 40 CH30
Gordon Rd. N3 37 BR29
Gordon Rd. N9 39 CB27
Gordon Rd. N11 38 BW29
Gordon Rd. SE15 67 CB44
Gordon Rd. W4 65 BM43
Gordon Rd. W5 54 BK40
Gordon Rd. W13 54 BJ40
Gordon Rd., Ashf. 73 AY48
Gordon Rd., Bark. 58 CN37
Gordon Rd., Beck. 87 CC51
Gordon Rd., Beck. 87 CD52
Gordon Rd., Belv. 69 CS42
Gordon Rd., Brwd. 122 DD26
Gordon Rd., Cars. 95 BU57
Gordon Rd., Cat. 105 BZ64
Gordon Rd., Chesh. 16 AO19
Gordon Rd., Dart. 80 CV47
Gordon Rd., Enf. 30 BZ23
Gordon Rd., Esher 93 BH57
Gordon Rd., Grav. 81 DF47
Gordon Rd., Grays 71 DF41
Gordon Rd., Har. 45 BH31
Gordon Rd., Houns. 64 BG45
Gordon Rd., Ilf. 49 CM34
Gordon Rd., Kings.T. 85 BL51
Gordon Rd., Red. 121 BV69
Gordon Rd., Rich. 65 BL44
Gordon Rd., Rom. 50 CQ32
Gordon Rd., Sev. 116 CU66
Gordon Rd., Shep. 83 BA53
Gordon Rd., Sid. 78 CM46
Gordon Rd., Sthl. 64 BE42
Gordon Rd., Stai. 72 AU49
Gordon Rd., Surb. 85 BL54
Gordon Rd., Wal.Abb. 21 CE20
Gordon Rd., West Dr. 53 AY40
Gordon Rd., Wind. 61 AM44
Gordon Sq. WC1 1 N4

Gordon Sq. WC1 56 BW38
Gordon St. E13 58 CH38
Gordon St. WC1 1 N4
Gordon St. WC1 56 BW38
Gordon St., Twick. 74 BJ46
Gordon Way, Barn. 28 BR24
Gordon Way, Ch.St.G. 34 AQ27
Gordonbrock Rd. SE4 77 CE46
Gordondale Rd. SW19 76 BS48
Gordons Way, Oxt. 114 CF67
Gore Cotts., Dart. 80 CX49
Gore Ct. NW9 46 BM32
Gore Rd. E9 57 CC37
Gore Rd. SW20 85 BQ51
Gore Rd., Dart. 80 CY47
Gore St. SW7 66 BT41
Gorefield Pl. NW6 56 BS37
Gorelands La., Ch.St.G. 34 AR26
Goresbrook Rd., Dag. 59 CO37
Gorham Dr., St.Alb. 9 BH15
Gorham Pl. W11 55 BR40
Mary Pl.
Gorhambury Dr., St.Alb. 9 BE12
Goring Clo., Rom. 41 CS30
Goring Gdns., Dag. 50 CP35
Goring Rd. N11 38 BX29
Goring Rd., Dag. 59 CS36
Goring Rd., Stai. 72 AV49
Goring Rd. N., Dag. 59 CS36
Goring St. EC3 2 N8
Goring St. EC3 57 CA39
Houndsditch
Goring Way, Grnf. 54 BG37
Gorings Sq., Stai. 72 AV49
Gorle Clo., Wat. 26 BC21
Gorleston Rd. N15 48 BZ32
Gorleston St. W14 65 BR42
Gorman Rd. SE18 68 CK42
Gorringe Ave., S.Dnth. 90 CY51
Gorringe Pk. Ave., Mitch. 76 BU50
Gorse Clo., Hat. 10 BO14
Gorse Ct., Guil. 118 AU69
Gorse Hill, Farn. 90 CX54
Gorse Hill La., Vir.W. 82 AR52
Gorse Hill Rd., Vir.W. 82 AR52
Gorse La., Wok. 91 AP57
Windsor Rd.
Gorse Mead, Slou. 61 AN40
Weekes Dr.
Gorse Ri. SW17 76 BV49
Gorse Rd., Croy. 96 CE56
Gorse Rd., Orp. 89 CQ54
Gorse Wk., West Dr. 53 AY39
Gorselands Clo., Wey. 92 AX59
Gorseway, Rom. 50 CT33
Gorsewood Rd., Wok. 100 AO63
Gorst Rd. NW10 55 BN38
Gorst Rd. SW11 76 BU46
Gorsuch Pl. E2 2 P2
Gorsuch St. E2 2 P2
Gorsuch St. E2 57 CA38
Gosberton Rd. SW12 76 BU47
Gosbury Hill, Chess. 94 BL56
Gosden Hill Rd., Guil. 109 AU68
Gosfield Rd., Dag. 50 CR34
Gosfield Rd., Epsom 94 BN59
Gosfield St. W1 1 L6
Gosfield St. W1 56 BW39
Gosford Gdns., Ilf. 49 CK32
Gosforth La., Wat. 35 BC27
Goshawk Gdns., Hayes 53 BB38
Goslar Way, Wind. 61 AN44
Goslett Yd. WC2 1 P9
Goslett Yd. WC2 56 BW39
Charing Cross Rd.
Gosling Clo., Grnf. 54 BF38
Gosling Grn., Slou. 62 AS41
Gosling Rd.
Gosling Rd., Slou. 62 AS41
Gosling Way SW9 66 BY44
Gospatrick Rd. N17 39 BZ29
Gospel Oak Est. NW5 47 BU35
Gosport Dr., Horn. 60 CV36
Gosport Rd. E17 48 CD32
Gosport Way SE15 67 CA43
Goss Hill, Swan. 80 CV50
Gossage Rd. SE18 68 CM42
Ancona Rd.
Gossage Rd., Uxb. 53 AY36
Gossamers, The, Wat. 27 BE21
Gosset St. E2 2 Q3
Gosset St. E2 57 CA38
Gosshill Rd., Chis. 88 CL51
Gossington Clo., Chis. 78 CL49
Beechwood Ri.
Gossoms End, Berk. 7 AQ12
Gossoms Ryde, Berk. 7 AQ12
Victory Rd.
Gosterwood St. SE8 67 CD43
Gostling Rd., Twick. 74 BF47
Goston Gdns., Th.Hth. 86 BY52
Goswell Hill, Wind. 61 AO44
Goswell Pl. EC1 56 BY38
Goswell Rd.
Goswell Rd. EC1 2 F1
Goswell Rd. EC1 56 BY37
Goswell Rd., Wind. 61 AO44
Gothic Clo., Dart. 80 CW48
Gothic Ct., Hayes 63 BA43
Sipson La.
Gothic Rd., Twick. 74 BG48
Goudhurst Rd., Brom. 78 CG49
Gouge Ave., Grav. 81 DF47
Gough Rd. E15 49 CG35
Gough Rd., Enf. 30 CB23
Gough Sq. EC4 2 E8
Gough Sq. EC4 56 BY39
Gough St. WC1 2 C4
Gough St. WC1 56 BX38
Gough Wk. E14 57 CE39
Gould Clo., Hat. 10 BP15
Gould Ct. SE19 77 CA49
Gould Ct., Guil. 109 AU69
Eustace Rd.

Gould Rd., Felt. 73 BB47
Gould Rd., Twick. 74 BH47
Goulds Grn., Uxb. 53 AZ40
Goulston St. E1 2 P8
Goulston St. E1 57 CA39
Goulton Rd. E5 48 CB35
Gourley Pl. N15 48 CA32
Gourley St.
Gourley St. N15 48 CA32
Gourock Rd. SE9 78 CL46
Govan St. E2 57 CB37
Whiston Rd.
Government Row, Enf. 30 CE22
Governors Ave., Uxb. 43 AV32
Govett Ave., Shep. 83 BA53
Govier Clo. E15 58 CG36
Gowan Ave. SW6 65 BR44
Gowan Rd. NW10 55 BP36
Gowar Fld., Pot.B. 19 BP19
Gower, The, Egh. 82 AT52
Gower Ct. WC1 1 N4
Gower Ct. WC1 56 BW38
Gower St.
Gower Ms. WC1 1 P7
Gower Ms. WC1 56 BW39
Gower Pl. WC1 1 M4
Gower Pl. WC1 56 BW38
Gower Rd. E7 58 CH36
Gower Rd., Islw. 64 BH43
Gower Rd., Wey. 92 BA57
Gower St. WC1 1 N5
Gower St. WC1 56 BW38
Gowers, The, Amer. 25 AP22
Gowers, The, Harl. 6 CO10
Gowers La., Grays 71 DF41
Gowers Wk. E1 57 CB39
Gowland Pl., Beck. 87 CD51
Gowlett Rd. SE15 67 CB45
Gowrie Rd. SW11 66 BV45
Graburn Way, E.Mol. 84 BG52
Grace Ave., Bexh. 69 CQ44
Grace Clo. SE9 78 CJ49
Dunkery Rd.
Grace Clo., Edg. 37 BM29
Pavilion Way
Grace Clo., Ilf. 40 CN29
Grace Jones Clo. E8 57 CB36
Parkholme Rd.
Grace Path SE26 77 CC49
Silverdale Rd.
Grace Rd., Croy. 87 BZ53
Grace St. E3 57 CE38
Gracechurch St. EC3 2 L10
Gracechurch St. EC3 57 BZ40
Gracedale Rd. SW16 76 BV49
Gracefield Gdns. SW16 76 BX48
Graces All. E1 57 CB40
Ensign St.
Graces Ms. SE5 67 BZ44
Graces Rd. SE5 67 CA44
Gracious La., Sev. 116 CU68
Gracious Pond Rd., Wok. 91 AQ57
Gradient, The SE26 77 CB49
Graeme Rd., Enf. 30 BZ23
Graemes Dyke Rd., Berk. 7 AQ13
Graemesdyke Ave. SW14 65 BM45
Grafton Clo. W13 54 BJ39
Grafton Clo., Houns. 74 BE47
Grafton Clo., Slou. 52 AS39
Grafton Clo., Wey. 91 AV60
Grafton Clo., Wor.Pk. 85 BO55
Grafton Cres. NW1 56 BV36
Grafton Gdns. N4 48 CB32
Rutland Gdns.
Grafton Gdns., Dag. 50 CQ34
Grafton Ms. W1 1 L5
Grafton Ms. W1 56 BW38
Grafton Pk. Rd., Wor.Pk. 85 BO55
Grafton Pl. NW1 1 N3
Grafton Pl. NW1 56 BW38
Grafton Rd. NW5 47 BV35
Grafton Rd. W3 55 BN40
Grafton Rd., Croy. 86 BY54
Grafton Rd., Dag. 50 CQ34
Grafton Rd., Enf. 29 BX24
Grafton Rd., Har. 45 BG32
Grafton Rd., N.Mal. 85 BO52
Grafton Rd., Wor.Pk. 85 BN55
Grafton Sq. SW4 66 BW45
Grafton St. W1 3 K1
Grafton St. W1 56 BV40
Grafton Ter. NW5 47 BU35
Grafton Way W1 1 L5
Grafton Way W1 56 BW38
Grafton Way WC1 1 M5
Grafton Way WC1 56 BW38
Grafton Way, E.Mol. 84 BE52
Grafton Yd. NW5 56 BV36
Prince of Wales Rd.
Graham Ave. W13 64 BJ41
Graham Ave., Brox. 12 CD14
Graham Ave., Mitch. 86 BV51
Graham Clo., Brwd. 122 DE25
Graham Clo., Croy. 87 CE55
Graham Clo., St.Alb. 9 BG15
Graham Gdns., Surb. 85 BL54
Graham Rd. E8 57 CB36
Graham Rd. E13 58 CH38
Graham Rd. N15 47 BY31
Graham Rd. NW4 46 BP32
Graham Rd. SW19 75 BR50
Graham Rd. W4 65 BN41
Graham Rd., Bexh. 69 CQ45
Graham Rd., Hmptn. 74 BF49
Graham Rd., Har. 45 BG31
Graham Rd., Mitch. 86 BV51
Graham Rd., Pur. 95 BY60
Graham St. N1 2 G1
Graham St. N1 56 BY37
Graham Ter. SW1 3 G9
Graham Ter. SW1 66 BV42
Grahame Pk. Est. NW9 37 BO30
Grahame Pk. Way NW7 37 BO29
Grahame Pk. Way NW9 37 BO30

Grainger Clo., Nthlt. 45 BG35
Grainger Rd. N22 39 BZ30
Grainger Rd., Islw. 64 BH44
Grainges Yd., Uxb. 53 AX36
Windsor St.
Gramer Clo. E11 48 CF34
Norman Rd.
Grampian Clo., Orp. 89 CN53
Cotswold Ri.
Grampian Gdns. NW2 46 BR33
Grampian Way, Hayes 63 BA43
Pennine Way
Grampian Way, Slou. 62 AT42
Granada St. SW17 76 BU49
Granard Ave. SW15 75 BP46
Granard Rd. SW12 76 BU47
Turin Rd.
Granary Clo. N9 39 CC26
Granary Meadow, Brwd. 33 DC21
Granary Way NW1 56 BW37
Granby Bldgs. SE11 4 B9
Granby Pk. Rd., Chsnt. 21 CB17
Granby Rd. SE9 68 CK44
Granby Rd., Grav. 81 DE46
Granby St. E2 57 CA38
Granby Ter. NW1 1 L1
Granby Ter. NW1 56 BW37
Granbys Bldgs. SE11 66 BX42
Salamanca St.
Grand Ave. EC1 2 G6
Grand Ave. EC1 56 BY39
Charterhouse St.
Grand Ave. N10 47 BV31
Grand Ave., Surb. 85 BM53
Grand Ave., Wem. 46 BM35
Grand Ave. E., Wem. 46 BM35
Grand Depot Rd. SE18 68 CL42
Grand Dr. SW20 85 BQ52
Grand Par., Surb. 85 BM54
Grand Par., Wem. 46 BM34
Grand Par. Ms. SW15 75 BR46
Upper Richmond Rd.
Grand Stand Rd., Epsom 103 BO62
Grand Union Ind. Est. NW10 55 BM37
Grand Vw. Ave., West. 106 CJ62
Grand Wk. E1 57 CD38
Solebay St.
Granden Rd. SW16 86 BX51
Grandfield Ave., Wat. 26 BC23
Grandis Cotts., Wok. 101 AW64
Grandison Rd. SW11 66 BU45
Grandison Rd., Wor.Pk. 85 BQ55
Granfield St. SW11 66 BT44
Grange, The N20 38 BT26
Grange, The NW3 47 BS34
Grange, The SE1 4 P6
Grange, The SE1 67 CA41
Grange, The SW19 75 BQ49
Grange, The, Croy. 87 CD55
Grange, The, Dart. 90 CY51
Grange, The, N.Mal. 85 BP53
Grange, The, Sev. 99 CZ58
Grange, The, Walt. 83 BC55
Grange, The, Wem. 55 BM36
Grange, The, Wind. 72 AQ46
Grange, The, Wok. 91 AP58
Grange, The, Wor.Pk. 85 BN55
Grange Ave. N12 38 BT28
Grange Ave. N20 37 BR26
Grange Ave. SE25 87 CA51
Grange Ave., Barn. 38 BU26
Grange Ave., Stan. 36 BJ30
Grange Ave., Twick. 74 BH48
Grange Ave., Wdf.Grn. 40 CH29
Grange Clo., Brwd. 122 DE28
Grange Clo., E.Mol. 84 BF52
Grange Clo., Edg. 37 BN28
Grange Clo., Ger.Cr. 34 AS30
Grange Clo., Guil. 109 AQ68
Grange Clo., Hayes 53 BB39
Grange Clo., Hem.H. 8 AZ14
Grange Clo., Houns. 64 BE43
Grange Clo., Lthd. 102 BK63
Grange Clo., N.Mal. 85 BP53
Grange Clo., Red. 113 BV67
Grange Clo., Sid. 79 CO48
Grange Clo., Stai. 72 AS46
Grange Clo., West. 115 CM66
Grange Clo., Wdf.Grn. 40 CH29
Grange Ct. WC2 2 C9
Grange Ct. WC2 56 BX39
Grange Ct., Chig. 40 CM27
Grange Ct., Loug. 31 CJ25
Grange Ct., Nthlt. 54 BD37
Grange Ct., St.Alb. 9 BG13
Grange St.
Grange Ct., Shep. 83 AZ52
Watersplash Rd.
Grange Ct., Wal.Abb. 21 CE20
Grange Ct., Walt. 83 BC55
Grange Cres. SE28 59 CP39
Grange Cres., Chig. 40 CM28
Grange Dr., Chis. 78 CK50
Grange Dr., Orp. 98 CP59
Grange Dr., Red. 113 BV67
Grange Dr., Wok. 100 AS61
Grange Est. N2 38 BT30
Grange Fm. Clo., Har. 45 BG34
Grange Flds., Ger.Cr. 34 AS30
Grange Gdns. N14 38 BW26
Grange Gdns. NW3 47 BS34
Templewood Ave.
Grange Gdns. SE25 87 CA51
Grange Gdns., Bans. 95 BS60
Grange Gdns., Pnr. 45 BE31
Grange Gdns., Slou. 43 AO35
Grange Gro. N1 56 BY36
Grange Hill SE25 87 CA51
Grange Hill, Edg. 37 BN28
Grange La. SE21 77 CA48
Grange La., Harl. 13 CJ11
Grange Meadow, Bans. 95 BS60
Grange Mt., Lthd. 102 BK63

Grange Par., Hayes 53 BB39
Grange Pk. W5 55 BL40
Grange Pk., Wok. 100 AS61
Grange Pk. Ave. N21 30 BZ25
Grange Pk. Pl. SW20 75 BP50
Thurstan Rd.
Grange Pk. Rd. E10 48 CE33
Grange Pk. Rd., Th.Hth. 87 BZ52
Grange Pl. NW6 56 BS37
Grange Pl. SE16 67 CB41
Yalding Rd.
Grange Pl., Stai. 83 AW51
Grange Rd. E10 48 CE33
Grange Rd. E13 58 CG38
Grange Rd. E17 48 CD32
Grange Rd. N6 47 BU32
Grange Rd. N17 39 CB29
Grange Rd. NW10 55 BP36
Grange Rd. SE1 4 N7
Grange Rd. SE1 67 CA41
Grange Rd. SE19 87 BZ51
Grange Rd. SW13 65 BP44
Grange Rd. W4 65 BM42
Grange Rd. W5 54 BK40
Grange Rd., Borwd. 28 BL25
Grange Rd., Bush. 27 BE25
Grange Rd., Cat. 114 CA66
Grange Rd., Chess. 85 BL55
Grange Rd., E.Mol. 84 BF53
Grange Rd., Edg. 37 BN29
Grange Rd., Egh. 72 AS49
Grange Rd., Ger.Cr. 34 AS30
Grange Rd., Grav. 81 DG47
Grange Rd., Grays 71 DD43
Grange Rd., Guil. 109 AQ68
Grange Rd., Har. 45 BG34
Grange Rd., Har. 45 BJ32
Grange Rd., Hayes 53 BB39
Grange Rd., Ilf. 49 CL35
Grange Rd., Kings.T. 85 BL52
Grange Rd., Lthd. 102 BK63
Grange Rd., Orp. 88 CM55
Grange Rd., Rom. 41 CU29
Grange Rd., Sev. 116 CU67
Grange Rd., S.Croy. 96 BZ58
Grange Rd., S.Ock. 60 CY40
Grange Rd., Sthl. 64 BE41
Grange Rd., Sutt. 95 BS57
Grange Rd., Th.Hth. 87 BZ52
Grange Rd., Walt. 93 BE56
Grange Rd., Wey. 92 AW58
Grange Rd., Wok. 91 AS60
Grange St., St.Alb. 9 BG13
Grange Vale, Sutt. 95 BS57
Grange Vw. Rd. N20 38 BT26
Grange Wk. SE1 4 N6
Grange Wk. SE1 67 CA41
Grange Way, Erith 69 CU43
Grange Way, Iver 52 AV39
Grange Yd. SE1 4 P7
Grange Yd. SE1 67 CA41
Grangecliffe Gdns. SE25 87 CA51
Grangecourt Rd. N16 48 CA33
Grangedale Clo., Nthwd. 35 BB29
Grangefields Rd., Guil. 109 AR67
Grangehill Pl. SE9 68 CK45
Grangehill Rd. SE9 68 CK45
Grangemill Rd. SE6 77 CE48
Grangemill Way SE6 77 CE48
Granger Way, Rom. 50 CU32
Grangeway N12 38 BS28
Grangeway NW6 56 BS36
Messina Ave.
Grangeway, Wdf.Grn. 40 CJ28
Grangeway, The N21 29 BY25
Grangeway Gdns., Ilf. 49 CK32
Grangeways Clo., Grav. 81 DF49
Grangewood, Bex. 79 CQ47
Hurst Rd.
Grangewood, Pot.B. 20 BS18
Grangewood, Slou. 52 AR39
Grangewood Ave., Grays 71 DF41
Grangewood Ave., Rain. 60 CV38
Grangewood Clo., Brwd. 122 DD27
Grangewood Clo., Pnr. 44 BC32
Grangewood Dr., Sun. 73 BB50
Forest Dr.
Grangewood La., Beck. 77 CD50
Grangewood St. E6 58 CJ37
Granham Gdns. N9 39 CA27
Granite St. SE18 68 CN42
Granleigh Rd. E11 49 CG34
Gransden Ave. E8 57 CB36
London La.
Gransden Rd. W12 65 BO41
Wendell Rd.
Grant Ave., Slou. 52 AP39
Grant Clo. N14 38 BW26
Grant Clo., Shep. 83 AZ53
Grant Pl., Croy. 87 CA54
Grant Rd. SW11 66 BT45
Grant Rd., Croy. 87 CA54
Grant Rd., Har. 45 BH31
Grant St. E13 58 CH38
Grant St. N1 56 BY37
Chapel Mkt.
Grant Way, Islw. 64 BJ43
Grant Way, Islw. 64 BJ43
Grantbridge St. N1 56 BY37
Grantchester Clo., Har. 45 BH34
Grantham Clo., Edg. 37 BL27
Grantham Gdns., Rom. 50 CQ32
Grantham Grn., Borwd. 28 BN25
Grantham Pl. W1 3 J3
Grantham Pl. W1 56 BV40
Old Pk. La.
Grantham Rd. E12 49 CL34
Grantham Rd. SW9 66 BX44
Grantham Rd. W4 65 BO43
Grantham Way, Grays 71 DD40
Grantley Gdns., Guil. 118 AQ70
Grantley Rd., Guil. 118 AQ70
Grantley Rd., Houns. 63 BC44
Grantley St. E1 57 CC38

Grantock Rd. E17 39 CF30
Granton Ave., Upmin. 51 CW34
Granton Rd. SW16 86 BW51
Granton Rd., Ilf. 50 CO33
Granton Rd., Sid. 79 CP50
Grants Clo. NW7 37 BQ29
Grants La., Oxt. 115 CJ70
Grantully Rd. W9 56 BS38
Grantwood Clo., Red. 121 BV73
Granville Ave. N9 39 CC27
Granville Ave., Felt. 73 BC48
Granville Ave., Houns. 74 BF46
Granville Ave., Slou. 52 AO39
Granville Clo., Croy. 87 CB55
Granville Clo., Wey. 92 AY60
Church Rd.
Granville Clo., Wey. 92 BA57
Granville Dene, Hem.H. 16 AT17
Granville Gdns. SW16 86 BX51
Granville Gdns. W5 55 BL40
Granville Gro. SE13 67 CF45
Granville Ms. NW2 46 BR34
Granville Pk. SE13 67 CF45
Granville Pl. N12 38 BT29
High Rd. N. Finchley
Granville Pl. W1 1 G9
Granville Pl. W1 56 BV39
Granville Rd. E17 48 CE32
Granville Rd. E18 40 CH30
Granville Rd. N4 47 BX32
Granville Rd. N12 38 BS29
Granville Rd. N13 38 BX29
Granville Rd. N22 38 BY30
Granville Rd. NW2 46 BR34
Granville Rd. NW6 56 BS37
Granville Rd. SW18 75 BR47
Granville Rd. SW19 76 BS50
Granville Rd., Barn. 28 BQ24
Granville Rd., Berk. 7 AP12
Granville Rd., Epp. 23 CO18
Granville Rd., Grav. 81 DF47
Granville Rd., Hayes 63 BB42
Granville Rd., Ilf. 49 CL33
Granville Rd., Oxt. 115 CG68
Granville Rd., St.Alb. 9 BH13
Granville Rd., Sev. 107 CU65
Granville Rd., Sid. 79 CO49
Granville Rd., Uxb. 53 AZ36
Granville Rd., Wat. 27 BD24
Granville Rd., Well. 69 CP45
Granville Rd., West. 115 CM66
Granville Rd., Wey. 92 BA57
Granville Rd., Wok. 100 AS63
Granville Sq. SE15 67 CA43
Blakes Rd.
Granville Sq. WC1 2 C3
Granville Sq. WC1 56 BX38
Granville St. WC1 2 C3
Granville St. WC1 56 BX38
Wharton St.
Grape St. WC2 1 Q8
Grape St. WC2 56 BX39
High Holborn
Graphite Sq. SE11 4 B10
Grasdene Rd. SE18 69 CO43
Grasmere Ave. SW15 75 BN49
Grasmere Ave. SW19 86 BS51
Grasmere Ave. W3 55 BN40
Grasmere Ave., Houns. 74 BF46
Grasmere Ave., Orp. 88 CL55
Grasmere Ave., Ruis. 44 BA33
Grasmere Ave., Slou. 52 AQ40
Grasmere Ave., Wem. 45 BK33
Grasmere Clo., Egh. 72 AT50
Keswick Way
Grasmere Clo., Felt. 73 BB47
Derwent Clo.
Grasmere Clo., Guil. 118 AT70
Grasmere Clo., Hem.H. 8 AZ14
Grasmere Clo., Loug. 31 CK23
Grasmere Clo., Wat. 17 BC19
Grasmere Ct. N22 38 BX29
Palmerston Rd.
Grasmere Gdns., Har. 36 BJ30
Grasmere Gdns., Ilf. 49 CK32
Grasmere Gdns., Orp. 88 CL55
Grasmere Rd. E13 58 CH37
Grasmere Rd. N10 38 BV30
Grasmere Rd. N17 39 CB29
Grasmere Rd. SE25 87 CB53
Grasmere Rd. SW16 76 BX49
Grasmere Rd., Bexh. 69 CS44
Grasmere Rd., Brom. 88 CG51
Grasmere Rd., Horn. 51 CW31
Grasmere Rd., Orp. 88 CL55
Grasmere Rd., Pur. 95 BY59
Grasmere Rd., St.Alb. 9 BJ14
Grasmere Way, Wey. 92 AY59
Grass Mt. SE23 77 CB48
Grass Pk. N3 37 BR30
Grass Warren, Welw. 5 BU6
Grassfield Clo., Couls. 104 BW63
Grassingham End, Ger.Cr. 34 AS29
Grassingham Rd., Ger.Cr. 34 AS29
Grassington Clo., St.Alb. 18 BF18
West Riding
Grassington Rd., Sid. 79 CO49
Grassmount SE23 77 CB48
Grassmount, Pur. 95 BW58
Grassway, Wall. 95 BW56
Grassy Clo., Hem.H. 8 AW13
Grassy La., Sev. 116 CU66
Grasvenor Ave., Barn. 29 BS25
Grateley Way SE15 67 CA43
Hordle Prom. N.
Gratton Bottom, Reig. 113 BT68
Gratton Dr., Wind. 61 AM45
Gratton Rd. W14 65 BR41
Gratton Ter. NW2 46 BQ34
Gravel Clo., Chig. 41 CO27
Gravel Hill N3 37 BR30
The Bdy.
Gravel Hill, Bexh. 79 CR46

Gravel Hill, Ger.Cr. 34 AS29
Gravel Hill, Hem.H. 8 AW13
Gravel Hill, Lthd. 102 BJ64
Kingston Ave.
Gravel Hill, Loug. 31 CH23
Gravel Hill, S.Croy. 96 CC57
Gravel Hill, Uxb. 44 AX35
Gravel Hill Clo., Bexh. 79 CR46
Gravel Hill Ter., Hem.H. 8 AW14
Gravel La. E1 2 P8
Gravel La. E1 57 CA39
Gravel La., Chig. 41 CO26
Gravel La., Hem.H. 8 AW13
Gravel Path, Berk. 7 AR13
Gravel Path, Hem.H. 8 AW13
Gravel Pit La. SE9 78 CM46
Gravel Pit Way, Orp. 89 CO55
Gravel Rd., Brom. 88 CK55
Gravel Rd., Twick. 74 BH47
Graveley Ave., Borwd. 28 BN24
Graveley Ct., Hem.H. 8 BA14
Graveley Dell, Welw.G.C. 5 BS8
Waterford Grn.
Gravelly Hill, Cat. 114 CA67
Gravelly Ride SW19 75 BP49
Gravelwood Clo., Chis. 78 CM48
Graveney Gro. SE20 77 CC50
Graveney Rd. SW17 76 BU49
Gravesend Rd. W12 55 BP40
Gravetts La., Guil. 109 AP68
Gray Ave., Dag. 50 CQ33
Gray Gdns., Rain. 59 CU36
Gray St. SE1 4 E5
Gray St. SE1 66 BY41
Grayburn Clo., Ch.St.G. 34 AQ27
Grayburne, Grav. 80 DB49
Graydon St. SE18 68 CL43
Grayford Clo. E6 58 CJ39
Neatscourt Rd.
Grayham Cres., N.Mal. 85 BN52
Grayham Rd., N.Mal. 85 BN52
Grayland Clo., Brom. 88 CJ51
Graylands, Epp. 31 CM22
Graylands, Wok. 100 AS61
Graylands Clo., Wok. 100 AS61
Horsell Pk.
Graylands La., Swans. 60 DB46
Graylands Sq., Swans. 60 DB46
Grayling Rd. N16 48 BZ34
Grayling Sq. E2 57 CB38
Avebury Est.
Graylings, The, Abb.L. 17 BA20
Grays End Clo., Grays 71 DD41
Grays Fm. Rd., Orp. 89 CO51
Grays Inn Pl. WC1 2 C7
Grays Inn Rd. WC1 2 A2
Grays Inn Rd. WC1 56 BX38
Grays Inn Sq. WC1 2 D6
Grays Inn Sq. WC1 56 BY39
Grays La., Ashf. 73 AZ49
Grays La., Ash. 103 BL63
Grays Pk. Rd., Slou. 52 AQ37
Grays Pl., Slou. 52 AP40
Grays Rd., Slou. 52 AP40
Grays Rd., Uxb. 53 AY36
Grays Rd., West. 106 CL64
Grays Wk., Brwd. 122 DE26
Grays Yd. W1 1 H8
Grayscroft Rd. SW16 76 BW50
Graysfield, Welw.G.C. 5 BS9
Grayshot Rd. SW11 66 BU44
Grayswood Gdns. SW20 85 BP51
Graywood Ct. N12 38 BT29
Grazebrook Rd. N16 48 BZ34
Grazeley Clo., Bexh. 79 CS46
Grazings, The, Hem.H. 8 AZ12
Great Acre Ct. SW4 66 BW45
Clapham Pk. Rd.
Great Bell All. EC2 2 K8
Great Bell All. EC2 57 BZ39
Moorgate
Great Benty, West Dr. 63 AY42
Great Braitch La., Hat. 5 BO10
Great Brays, Harl. 14 CO11
Great Break, Welw.G.C. 5 BS8
Great Brownings SE21 77 CA29
Great Bushey Dr. N20 38 BS26
Great Cambridge Rd. N9 39 BZ28
Great Cambridge Rd. N17 39 BZ30
Great Cambridge Rd. N18 39 BZ28
Great Cambridge Rd., Chsnt. 21 CC19
Great Cambridge Rd., Enf. 30 CB25
Great Castle St. W1 1 K8
Great Castle St. W1 56 BV39
Great Cen. Ave., Ruis. 45 BD35
Great Cen. St. NW1 56 BU39
Melcombe Sq.
Great Cen. Way NW10 46 BN35
Great Cen. St. NW1 1 E6
Great Chapel St. W1 1 N8
Great Chapel St. W1 56 BW39
Great Chertsey Rd. W4 65 BN44
Great Chertsey Rd., Felt. 74 BE48
Great Ch. La. W6 65 BQ42
Great College St. SW1 3 Q6
Great College St. SW1 66 BX41
Great Conduit, Welw.G.C. 5 BT7
Great Cross Ave. SE10 68 CG43
Great Cullings, Rom. 50 CT34
Great Cumberland Ms. W1 1 E9
Great Cumberland Ms. W1 56 BU39
Seymour Pl.
Great Cumberland Pl. W1 1 F8
Great Cumberland Pl. W1 56 BU39
Great Dell, Welw.G.C. 7 BQ7
Great Dover St. SE1 4 K5
Great Dover St. SE1 67 BZ41
Great Eastern Rd. E15 57 CF36

Great Eastern Rd., Brwd. 42 D
Great Eastern St. EC2 2
Great Eastern St. EC2 57 C
Great Eastern Wk. EC2 2
Great Ellshams, Bans. 104 B
Great Elms Rd., Brom. 88 C
Great Elms Rd., Hem.H. 8 A
Great Fld. NW9 37 B
Great Fox Meadow, Brwd. 33 C
Great Ganett, Welw.G.C. 5
Great Gdns. Rd., Horn. 50 C
Great George St. SW1 3
Great George St. SW1 66 BV
Great Goodwin Dr., Guil. 118 A
Great Gro., Bush. 27 B
Great Guildford St. SE1 4
Great Harry Dr. SE9 78 C
Great Heath, Hat. 10 B
Great Hurstend, Lthd. 102 B
Great James St. WC1 2
Great James St. WC1 56 BX
Great Lawn, Ong. 24 CX
Great Ley, Welw.G.C. 5
Great Leylands, Harl. 14 CC
Great Marlborough St. W1 1
Great Marlborough St. W1 56 BW
Great Maze Pond SE1 4
Great Maze Pond SE1 67 BZ
St. Thomas St.
Great Meadow, Brox. 12 CE
Great Nelmes Chase, Horn. 51 CW
Great New St. EC4 2
Great New St. EC4 56 BY
East Harding St.
Great Newport St. WC2 1 P
Great Newport St. WC2 56 BX
Upper St. Martins La.
Great N. Rd. N2 47 BU
Great N. Rd. N6 47 BU
Great N. Rd., Barn. 29 BS
Great N. Rd., Hat. 10 BF
Great N. Rd., Pot.B. 20 BT
Great N. Way NW4 37 BP
Great Oaks, Brwd. 122 DD
Great Oaks, Chig. 40 CM
Great Oaks Pk., Guil. 109 AT
Great Ormond St. WC1 2
Great Ormond St. WC1 56 BX
Great Owl Rd., Chig. 40 CL
Great Palmers, Hem.H. 8 AY
Great Pk., Kings L. 17 AY
Great Parndon, Harl. 13 CL
Great Percy St. WC1 2
Great Percy St. WC1 56 BX
Great Peter St. SW1 3
Great Peter St. SW1 66 BX
Great Plumtree, Harl. 6 CN
Great Portland St. W1 1
Great Portland St. W1 56 BV
Great Pulteney St. W1 1 M
Great Pulteney St. W1 56 BW
Great Quarry, Guil. 118 AR
Great Queen St. WC2 2
Great Queen St. WC2 56 BX
Great Queen St., Dart. 80 CW
Great Rd., Hem.H. 8 AY
Great Ropers La., Brwd. 42 DA
Great Russell St. WC1 1
Great Russell St. WC1 56 BW
Great St. Helens EC3 2 N
Great St. Helens EC3 57 CA
Great St. Thomas Apostle EC4 2 J
Great St. Thomas Apostle EC4 57 BZ
Queen St.
Great Scotland Yd. SW1 3
Great Scotland Yd. SW1 56 BX
Great Slades, Pot.B. 19 BR
Great Smith St. SW1 3
Great Smith St. SW1 66 BW
Great S. W. Rd., Felt. 73 BA
Great Spilmans SE22 77 CA
Great Strand NW9 37 BO
Great Sturgess Rd., Hem.H. 7 AV
Great Suffolk St. SE1 4
Great Suffolk St. SE1 56 BY
Great Sutton St. EC1 2
Great Sutton St. EC1 56 BY
Great Swan All. EC2 2
Great Swan All. EC2 57 BZ
Great Tattenhams, Epsom 103 BP
Great Thrift, Orp. 88 CM
Great Titchfield St. W1 1
Great Titchfield St. W1 56 BV
Great Twr. St. EC3 2 M
Great Twr. St. EC3 57 CA
Great Trinity La. EC4 2 J
Great Trinity La. EC4 57 BZ
Queen Victoria St.
Great Turnstile WC1 2
Great Turnstile WC1 56 BX
High Holborn
Great Warley St., Brwd. 42 DA
Great W. Rd. W4 65 BM
Great W. Rd. W6 65 BO
Great W. Rd., Houns. 64 BE
Great Western Rd. W9 55 BR
Great Western Rd. W11 55 BR
Great Whites Rd., Hem.H. 8 AY
Great Winchester St. EC2 2
Great Winchester St. EC2 57 BZ
Great Windmill St. W1 1 N
Great Windmill St. W1 56 BW
Great Woodcote Dr., Pur. 95 BW
Great Woodcote Pk., Pur. 95 BW

at Yd. SE1 4 N4
atdown Rd. W7 54 BH38
atfield Ave. E6 58 CK38
atfield Clo. N19 47 BW34
arrender Rd.
atfield Clo. SE4 67 CE45
atfields Dr., Uxb. 53 AZ39
atfields Rd., Bark. 58 CM37
atford Dr., Guil. 118 AU70
atham Rd., Bush. 27 BD24
atham Wk. SW15 75 BP47
essborough Rd.
atheart, Hem.H. 8 AY12
atness La., Sev. 108 CV64
atness Rd., Sev. 108 CV64
atorex St. E1 57 CB39
atwood, Chis. 78 CL50
atwood Clo., Cher. 91 AU58
aves Clo., Bark. 58 CN36
orfolk Rd.
aves Pl. SW17 76 BU49
be Crest, Grays 70 DA42
cian Cres. SE19 76 BY50
ding Wk., Brwd. 122 DD27
ek Ct. W1 1 P9
ek Ct. W1 56 BW39
ld Compton St.
ek St. W1 1 P9
ek St. W1 56 BW39
ek Yd. WC2 1 Q10
en, The E4 39 CF26
en, The E11 49 CH32
en, The E15 58 CG36
en, The N9 39 CB27
een, The N14 38 BW27
een, The N21 38 BY26
een, The W3 55 BO39
een, The W5 54 BK40
een, The, Amer. 25 AO22
een, The, Bexh. 69 CR44
een, The, Brom. 78 CH48
een, The, Brom. 88 CH54
een, The, Cat. 105 CE65
een, The, Chsnt. 21 CC17
een, The, Croy. 96 CD58
een, The, Epp. 31 CM21
een, The, Epsom 94 BP59
een, The, Felt. 73 BC48
rowells La.
een, The, Gdse. 114 CB69
een, The, Hem.H. 16 AT18
een, The, Houns. 64 BF43
eston Rd.
een, The, Ing. 24 DC19
een, The, Lthd. 102 BG65
een, The, Mord. 85 BR52
een, The, N.Mal. 85 BN52
een, The, Orp. 79 CO50
een, The, Orp. 98 CP58
een, The, Rain. 60 CW40
een, The, Rich. 74 BK46
een, The, Rick. 26 AW21
een, The, Rick. 26 AY25
een, The, St.Alb. 18 BK17
een, The, Sev. 108 CV64
een, The, Shep. 83 BB52
he Cfts.
een, The, Sid. 79 CO49
een, The, Slou. 61 AO41
een, The, Slou. 62 AQ43
een, The, Sthl. 64 BE41
een, The, Stai. 72 AS46
een, The, Sutt. 86 BS55
een, The, Tad. 103 BR63
een, The, Twick. 74 BH47
een, The, Wal.Abb. 21 CF20
lile Rd.
een, The, Walt. 92 BB58
een, The, Wat. 26 BC22
een, The, Well. 68 CN45
een, The, Wem. 45 BJ34
een, The, West Dr. 63 AX41
een, The, West. 115 CM66
een, The, Wdf.Grn. 40 CH28
een Acre, Wind. 61 AM44
een Acre, Wok. 100 AP61
lead Ct.
een Acre Clo., Barn. 28 BR22
een Acres, Croy. 87 CA55
een Acres, Hem.H. 8 BA14
een Acres, Lthd. 102 BF65
een Acres, Welw.G.C. 5 BR9
een Arbour Ct. EC1 2 F8
een Arbour Ct. EC4 56 BY39
ld Bailey
een Ave. NW7 37 BN28
een Ave. W13 64 BJ41
een Bank E1 57 CB40
een Bank N12 38 BS28
een Bank Clo., Rom. 42 CV27
een Banks, Upmin. 51 CZ34
een Clo. NW9 46 BN32
een Clo. NW11 47 BT33
een Clo., Brom. 88 CG52
een Clo., Cars. 86 BU55
een Clo., Chsnt. 21 CD19
een Clo., Epp. 13 CL15
een Clo., Felt. 74 BE49
een Clo., Hat. 19 BR16
een Ct., Edg. 37 BM29
een Ct. Rd., Swan. 89 CS53
een Cft., Hat. 10 BP11
een Curve, Bans. 94 BR60
een Dale NW7 37 BO28
een Dale SE22 67 BZ45
een Dale Clo. SE22 77 CA46
reen Dale
een Dell Way, Hem.H. 8 AZ13
een Dene, Lthd. 110 BA70
een Dragon Ct. SE1 4 K2
een Dragon La. N21 29 BY25
een Dragon La., Brent. 65 BL42
een Dragon Yd. E1 57 CB39
ld Montague St.
Green Dr., Slou. 62 AS42
Green Dr., Sthl. 54 BF40
Green Dr., Wok. 100 AV65
Green E. Rd., Beac. 34 AP29
Green End N21 38 BY27
Green End, Chess. 93 BK56
Green End La., Hem.H. 7 AV13
Green End Rd., Hem.H. 8 AW14
Green Fld. Rd., Berk. 7 AR13
Green Gdns., Orp. 97 CM56
Green Glade, Epp. 31 CN22
Green Hayes Clo., Reig. 121 BT70
Green Hill SE18 68 CK42
Green Hill, Buck.H. 40 CJ26
Green Hill, Orp. 97 CK59
Green Hill La., Warl. 105 CD62
Green Hill Ter. SE18 68 CK42
Green Hundred Rd. SE15 67 CB43
Green La. E4 30 CF24
Green La. NW4 46 BQ31
Green La. SE9 78 CL47
Green La. SE20 77 CC50
Green La. SW16 76 BX50
Green La. W7 64 BH41
Green La., Amer. 25 AO21
Green La., Amer. 25 AP22
Green La., Ash. 102 BK62
Green La., Brwd. 33 CY23
Green La., Brwd. 42 DA26
Green La., Brwd. 33 DB25
Green La. (Warley), Brwd. 42 DA29
Green La., Brox. 12 CE15
Green La., Cat. 105 BZ64
Green La., Cher. 82 AV55
Green La., Chesh. 16 AQ20
Green La., Chess. 93 BK58
Green La., Chig. 40 CM26
Green La., Chis. 78 CL49
Green La., Cob. 93 BE59
Green La., Dag. 49 CM34
Green La., Dag. 50 CP34
Green La., E.Mol. 84 BF53
Green La., Edg. 37 BL28
Green La., Egh. 72 AT49
Green La. (Thorpe), Egh. 82 AU51
Green La., Felt. 74 BE49
Green La., Guil. 118 AT70
Green La., Guil. 110 AW67
Green La., Harl. 14 CR11
Green La., Har. 45 BH34
Green La., Hem.H. 8 BA14
Green La. (Bovingdon), Hem.H. 16 AT17
Green La., Houns. 63 BC45
Green La., Ilf. 49 CM34
Green La., Ing. 24 DB19
Green La., Lthd. 102 BK64
Green La., Maid. 61 AG40
Green La. (Fifield), Maid. 61 AG44
Green La., Mord. 86 BS53
Green La., N.Mal. 85 BN53
Green La., Nthwd. 35 BA29
Green La., Pur. 95 BW59
Green La., Red. 121 BU69
Green La., Red. 121 BV73
Green La., Red. 114 CA68
Green La., Reig. 120 BR70
Green La., Rick. 26 AY25
Green La., St.Alb. 9 BG12
Green La., Shep. 83 BA53
Green La. (Datchet), Slou. 62 AQ44
Green La., Stan. 36 BJ28
Green La., Sun. 73 BB50
Green La., Tad. 112 BR66
Green La., Th.Hth. 76 BX50
Green La., Upmin. 60 CY37
Green La., Uxb. 53 BA39
Green La., Wal.Abb. 22 CJ20
Green La., Walt. 92 BC57
Green La., Warl. 105 CD62
Green La., Wat. 36 BD26
Green La., West. 106 CM65
Green La., Wey. 92 AY59
Green La., Wind. 61 AN44
Green La., Wok. 91 AP58
Green La., Wok. 100 AQ64
Green La., Wok. 100 AR62
Green La., Wok. 101 AZ65
Green La., Wor.Pk. 85 BP54
Green La. Ave., Walt. 93 BD56
Green La. Clo., Amer. 25 AO21
Green La. Clo., Cher. 82 AV55
Green La. Clo., Wey. 92 AY56
Green La. Gdns., Th.Hth. 87 BZ51
Green La. W., Wok. 100 AZ66
Green Las. N4 47 BY33
Green Las. N8 47 BY31
Green Las. N13 38 BX29
Green Las. N16 48 BZ34
Green Las. N21 38 BY27
Green Las., Epsom 94 BO58
Green Las., Welw.G.C. 5 BO9
Green Lawns, Ruis. 45 BD33
Green Leas, Sun. 73 BB50
Green Leas, Wal.Abb. 21 CF20
Green Man Gdns. W13 54 BJ40
Green Man La. W13 54 BJ40
Green Man La., Felt. 63 BC45
Green Manor Way, Grav. 71 DC45
Green Mead, Esher 93 BE57
Green Meadow, Pot.B. 20 BS18
Green Moor Link N21 38 BY26
Green N. Rd., Beac. 34 AP29
Green Pk., Stai. 72 AV48
Vicarage Rd.
Green Pl., Dart. 79 CT46
Green Pond Rd. E17 48 CD31
Green Ride, Epp. 22 CM20
Green Ride, Loug. 31 CH25
Green Rd. N14 29 BV25
Green Rd. N20 38 BT27
Green Rd., Egh. 82 AT52
Green Slade Ave., Ash. 103 BM63
Green St. E7 58 CH36
Green St. E13 58 CJ37
Green St. W1 1 F10
Green St. W1 56 BV40
Green St., Enf. 30 CC23
Green St., Hat. 11 BS13
Green St., Rad. 28 BM21
Green St., Rick. 25 AU24
Green St., Sun. 83 BC51
Green St. Grn. Rd., Dart. 80 CX48
Green Ter. EC1 56 BY38
Green Vale W5 55 BL39
Green Vale, Bexh. 79 CP46
Green Vale Rd., Wok. 100 AO62
Southwood Ave.
Green Verges, Stan. 36 BK29
Green Vw., Chess. 94 BL57
Green Vw. Clo., Hem.H. 16 AT18
Green Wk. E4 39 CF26
Green Wk. NW4 46 BQ31
Green Wk. SE1 4 M7
Green Wk. SE1 67 CA41
Green Wk., Dart. 79 CT46
Green Wk., Hmptn. 74 BE50
Orpwood Clo.
Green Wk., Ong. 24 CW18
Green Wk., Ruis. 44 BB33
Green Wk., S.Croy. 96 CD57
Green Wk., Sthl. 64 BF42
Green Wk., Wdf.Grn. 40 CK29
Green Way SE9 78 CJ46
Green Way, Brom. 88 CK53
Green Way, Hartley 90 DC53
Green Way, Red. 121 BU69
Green Way, Sun. 83 BC52
Green Way, The, Houns. 64 BE45
Green W. Rd., Beac. 34 AP29
Green Wrythe La., Cars. 86 BT53
Green Yd., Wal.Abb. 21 CF21
Greenacre, Dart. 80 CV48
Greenacre Clo., Rain. 60 CW38
Greenacre Clo., Swan. 89 CT52
Greenacre Gdns. E17 48 CF31
Greenacre Sq. SE16 67 CC41
Fishermans Dr.
Greenacre Wk. N14 38 BX27
Cannon Hill
Greenacres SE9 78 CL46
Greenacres, Bush. 36 BG27
Greenacres, Epp. 22 CN17
Lindsey St.
Greenacres, Oxt. 115 CG67
Greenacres Ave., Uxb. 44 AY34
Greenacres Clo., Orp. 97 CL56
State Fm. Ave.
Greenacres Ct., Egh. 72 AR50
South Rd.
Greenacres Dr., Stan. 36 BJ29
Greenall Clo., Chsnt. 21 CD18
Roundmoor Dr.
Greenaway Gdns. NW3 47 BS35
Greenbank, Chsnt. 21 CB17
Greenbank Ave., Wem. 45 BJ35
Greenbank Clo. E4 39 CF27
Greenbank Cres. NW4 46 BR31
Greenbank Rd., Wat. 26 BA21
Greenbanks, Dart. 80 CW48
Greenbanks, St.Alb. 9 BH14
Colindale Ave.
Greenbay Rd. SE7 68 CJ43
Greenberry St. NW8 1 C1
Greenberry St. NW8 56 BU37
Greenbrook Ave., Barn. 29 BT23
Greenbury Clo., Rick. 25 AU24
Greencoat Pl. SW1 3 M8
Greencoat Pl. SW1 66 BW42
Greencoat Row SW1 3 M7
Greencoat Row SW1 66 BW41
Francis St.
Greencourt Ave., Croy. 87 CB55
Greencourt Ave., Edg. 37 BM30
Greencourt Gdns., Croy. 87 CB54
Greencourt Rd., Orp. 88 CM53
Greencrest Pl. NW2 46 BP34
Dollis Hill La.
Greencroft, Guil. 118 AT70
Greencroft Ave., Ruis. 45 BD34
Greencroft Clo. E6 58 CJ39
Neatscourt Rd.
Greencroft Gdns. NW6 56 BS36
Greencroft Gdns., Enf. 30 CA24
Greencroft Rd., Houns. 64 BE44
Greendale Ms., Slou. 52 AQ40
St. Pauls Ave.
Greendale Wk., Grav. 81 DF48
Greene Wk., Berk. 7 AR13
Greenefielde End, Stai. 73 AX50
Greenend Rd. W4 65 BO41
Greenfarm Clo., Orp. 97 CN57
Greenfell St. SE10 68 CG41
Greenfield, Welw.G.C. 5 BQ6
Greenfield Ave., Surb. 85 BM54
Greenfield Ave., Wat. 36 BE27
Greenfield End, Ger.Cr. 34 AS29
Greenfield Gdns. NW2 46 BR34
Greenfield Gdns., Dag. 59 CP37
Greenfield Gdns, Orp. 88 CM54
Greenfield Link, Couls. 104 BX61
Greenfield Rd. E1 57 CB39
Greenfield Rd. N15 48 CA32
Greenfield Rd., Dag. 59 CP37
Greenfield Rd., Dart. 79 CS49
Greenfield St., Wal.Abb. 21 CF20
Greenfield Way, Har. 45 BF31
Greenfields NW7 37 BO27
Lawrence St.
Greenfields, Hat. 10 BQ11
Greenfields, Loug. 31 CL24
Greenfields, Sthl. 54 BF40
Greenfields Clo., Brwd. 42 DA28
Greenfields Clo., Loug. 31 CL24
Greenford Ave. W7 54 BH38
Greenford Ave., Sthl. 54 BE40
Greenford Gdns., Grnf. 54 BF38
Greenford Rd., Har. 45 BH35
Greenford Rd., Sthl. 54 BG40
Greenford Rd., Sutt. 95 BS56
St. Nicholas Way
Greengate, Grnf. 54 BJ36
Greengate St. E13 58 CH37
Greenglades, Horn. 51 CW32
Greenhalgh Wk. N2 47 BT31
Greenham Clo. SE1 4 D5
Greenham Clo. SE1 66 BY41
Frazier St.
Greenham Rd. N10 38 BV30
Greenham Wk., Wok. 100 AR62
Greenhayes Ave., Bans. 95 BS60
Greenhayes Gdns., Bans. 104 BS61
Greenheys Clo., Nthwd. 35 BB30
Greenheys Dr. E18 49 CG31
Greenheys Pl., Wok. 100 AS62
Greenhill NW3 47 BT35
Hampstead High St.
Greenhill, Sutt. 86 BT55
Greenhill, Wem. 46 BM34
Greenhill Ave., Cat. 105 CB64
Greenhill Cres., Wat. 26 BB25
Greenhill Gdns., Guil. 118 AU69
Greenhill Gdns., Nthlt. 54 BE37
Greenhill Gro. E12 49 CK35
Greenhill Pk. NW10 55 BO37
Greenhill Pk., Barn. 29 BS25
Greenhill Rd. NW10 55 BO37
Greenhill Rd., Grav. 81 DF48
Greenhill Rd., Har. 45 BH32
Greenhill Rd., Sev. 108 CV61
Greenhill Ter., Nthlt. 54 BE37
Greenhill Way, Har. 45 BH32
Greenhill Way, Wem. 46 BM34
Greenhills, Harl. 13 CN11
Greenhills Clo., Rick. 26 AW25
Greenhills Rents EC1 2 F6
Greenhills Rents EC1 56 BY39
Cowcross St.
Greenhills Ter. N1 57 BZ36
Baxter Rd.
Greenhithe Clo., Sid. 78 CN47
Greenholm Rd. SE9 78 CL46
Greenhurst La., Oxt. 115 CH69
Greenhurst Rd. SE27 76 BY49
Greening St. SE2 69 CP42
Greenland Cres., Sthl. 64 BD41
Greenland Ms. SE8 67 CC42
Trundleys Rd.
Greenland Pl. NW1 56 BV37
Greenland Rd.
Greenland Quay SE16 67 CC42
Greenland Rd. NW1 56 BV37
Greenland Rd., Barn. 28 BQ25
Greenland St. NW1 56 BV37
Camden High St.
Greenlands Rd., Sev. 108 CX63
Greenlands Rd., Stai. 73 AW49
Greenlands Rd., Wey. 83 AZ55
Greenlaw Gdns., N.Mal. 85 BO54
Greenlaw St. SE18 68 CK41
Greenleaf Rd. E6 58 CJ37
Greenleaf Rd. E17 48 CD31
Greenleafe Dr., Ilf. 49 CL31
Greenman St. N1 57 BZ36
Greenmeads, Wok. 100 AS64
Greenmoor Rd., Enf. 30 CC23
Greeno Cres., Shep. 83 AZ53
Greenoak Ri., West. 106 CJ62
Greenoak Way SW19 75 BQ50
Greenock Rd. SW16 86 BW51
Greenock Rd. W3 65 BM41
Corville Rd.
Greenock Way, Rom. 41 CT29
Greenpark Ct., Wem. 54 BK36
Greens Clo., The, Loug. 31 CL23
Greens Ct. W1 1 N10
Greens End SE18 68 CL42
Greensand Rd., Red. 121 BV69
Noke Dr.
Greenshank Clo. E17 39 CD29
Banbury Rd.
Greenshaw, Brwd. 42 DA26
Greenside, Bex. 79 CQ47
Greenside, Borwd. 28 BM22
Greenside, Dag. 50 CP33
Greenside, Rich. 74 BK46
Greenside, Swan. 89 CS51
Greenside Clo., Guil. 118 AU69
Foxglove Gdns.
Greenside Rd. W12 65 BP41
Greenside Rd., Croy. 86 BY54
Greenside Rd., Wey. 83 AZ55
Kings Rd.
Greenside Wk., West. 106 CJ62
Kings Rd.
Greenstead, Saw. 6 CQ6
Greenstead Ave., Wdf.Grn. 40 CJ29
Greenstead Clo., Brwd. 122 DF26
Greenstead Clo., Wdf.Grn. 40 CJ29
Greenstead Gdns. SW15 75 CP46
Greenstead Gdns., Wdf.Grn. 40 CJ29
Greensted Rd., Loug. 40 CK26
Greensted Rd., Ong. 23 CU17
Greenstone Ms. E11 49 CH32
Voluntary Pl.
Greensward, Bush. 36 BF26
Ashfield Ave.
Greentiles La., Uxb. 43 AV33
Greenvale, Wat. 36 BD26
Greenvale, Welw.G.C. 5 BS8
Greenvale Rd. SE9 68 CK45
Greenvale Rd., Wok. 100 AO62
Greenview Ave., Croy. 87 CD53
Greenview Ct., Ashf. 73 AY49
Greenville Clo., Cob. 93 BD60
Greenway N14 38 BX27
Greenway N20 38 BS27
Greenway SW20 85 CQ52
Greenway, Berk. 7 AQ13
Greenway, Brwd. 122 DD26
Greenway, Chis. 78 CL49
Greenway, Dag. 50 CP34
Greenway, Har. 46 BL32
Greenway, Hayes 53 BC38
Greenway, Hem.H. 8 AZ13
Greenway, Lthd. 102 BF64
Greenway, Pnr. 35 BC30
Greenway, Rom. 42 CX29
Greenway, Wall. 95 BW56
Greenway, West. 106 CJ63
Greenway, Wdf.Grn. 40 CJ28
Greenway, The NW9 37 BN30
Greenway, The, Enf. 30 CC21
Greenway, The, Epsom 103 BM61
Greenway, The, Ger.Cr. 43 AR31
Greenway, The, Har. 36 BH30
Greenway, The, Orp. 89 CO53
Greenway, The, Oxt. 115 CH70
Greenway, The, Pnr. 45 BE32
Greenway, The, Pot.B. 20 BS20
Greenway, The, Rick. 35 AW26
Greenway, The, Slou. 61 AL40
Greenway, The, Uxb. 53 AX37
Greenway, The, Uxb. 44 AZ34
Greenway Ave. E17 48 CF31
Greenway Clo. N4 48 BZ34
Greenway Clo. N11 38 BV29
Poplar Gro.
Greenway Clo. N20 38 BS27
Greenway Clo. NW9 37 BN30
Greenway Clo., Wey. 92 AW60
Greenway Dr., Stai. 83 AX51
Greenway Gdns. NW9 37 BN30
Greenway Gdns., Croy. 87 CD55
Greenway Gdns., Grnf. 54 BF38
Greenway Gdns., Har. 36 BH30
Greenways, Abb.L. 17 BB19
Greenways, Beck. 87 CE52
Greenways, Chsnt. 20 BY18
Greenways, Egh. 72 AS50
Greenways, Esher 93 BH56
Greenways, Tad. 112 BP66
Greenways Est. E2 57 CC38
Greenwell St. W1 1 K5
Greenwell St. W1 56 BV38
Greenwich Ch. St. SE10 67 CF43
Greenwich Cres. E6 58 CK39
Swann App.
Greenwich High Rd. SE10 67 CE44
Greenwich Mkt. SE10 67 CF43
Greenwich Pk. St. SE10 67 CF42
Greenwich S. St. SE10 67 CE44
Greenwich Vw. Pl. E14 67 CE41
Greenwood, The, Guil. 118 AT70
Greenwood Ave., Chsnt. 21 CB19
Greenwood Ave., Dag. 50 CR35
Greenwood Ave., Enf. 30 CD23
Greenwood Clo., Amer. 25 AP22
Greenwood Clo., Beac. 34 AO29
Farmers Way
Greenwood Clo., Bush. 36 BH26
Langmead Dr.
Greenwood Clo., Chsnt. 21 CB19
Greenwood Clo., Mord. 85 BR52
Greenwood Clo., Orp. 88 CN53
Greenwood Clo., Sid. 79 CO48
Greenwood Clo., T.Ditt. 84 BJ54
Greenwood Clo., Wey. 91 AV59
Greenwood Dr. E4 39 CF28
Avril Way
Greenwood Dr., Red. 121 BV73
Greenwood Dr., Wat. 17 BC20
Greenwood Gdns. N13 38 BY27
Greenwood Gdns., Cat. 114 CB66
Greenwood Gdns., Ilf. 40 CM29
Greenwood Ho., Grays 71 DD43
Hawkes Clo.
Greenwood La., Hmptn. 74 BF49
Greenwood Pk., Kings.T. 75 BO50
Greenwood Pl. NW5 47 BV35
Highgate Rd.
Greenwood Rd. E8 57 CB36
Greenwood Rd. E13 58 CG37
Maud Rd.
Greenwood Rd., Bex. 79 CS49
Greenwood Rd., Chig. 41 CO28
Greenwood Rd., Croy. 86 BY53
Greenwood Rd., Islw. 64 BH45
Greenwood Rd., Mitch. 86 BW52
Greenwood Rd., T.Ditt. 84 BJ54
Greenwood Rd., Wok. 100 AP63
Greenwood Ter. NW10 55 BN37
Greenwood Way, Sev. 116 CT66
Greenwrythe Cres., Cars. 86 BU54
Greer Rd., Har. 36 BG30
Greet St. SE1 4 E3
Greet St. SE1 66 BY41
Gregor Ms. SE3 68 CH43
Gregory Ave., Pot.B. 20 BT20
Gregory Cres. SE9 78 CJ47
Gregory Dr., Wind. 72 AQ46
Gregory Pl. W8 66 BS41
Gregory Rd., Rom. 50 CP31
Gregory Rd., Slou. 43 AO34
Gregory Rd., Sthl. 64 BF41
Gregson Clo., Borwd. 28 BN23
Greig Clo. N8 47 BX32
Greig Ter. SE17 66 BY43
Lorrimore Sq.
Grena Gdns., Rich. 65 BL45
Grena Rd., Rich. 65 BL45
Grenaby Ave., Croy. 87 BZ54
Grenaby Rd., Croy. 87 BZ54
Grenada Rd. SE7 68 CJ43
Grenade St. E14 57 CD40
Grenadier St. E16 58 CK40
Grendon Gdns., Wem. 46 BM34
Grendon St. NW8 1 C4
Grendon St. NW8 56 BU38
Grenfell Ave., Horn. 50 CT33

Grenfell Clo., West. 97 CJ59
Grenfell Gdns., Har. 46 BL33
Grenfell Rd. W11 55 BQ40
Grenfell Rd., Mitch. 76 BU50
Grenfell Wk. W11 55 BQ40
Lancaster Rd.
Grennell Clo., Sutt. 86 BT55
Grennell Rd., Sutt. 86 BT55
Grenoble Gdns. N13 38 BY29
Grenville Ave., Brox. 12 CD14
Grenville Clo. N3 37 BR30
Grenville Clo., Wal.Cr. 21 CC19
Grenville Ct., Rick. 25 AU24
Grenville Gdns., Wdf.Grn. 40 CJ30
Grenville Ms. SW7 66 BT42
Grenville Ms., Hmptn. 74 BF49
Grenville Pl. NW7 37 BN28
Grenville Pl. SW7 66 BT41
Grenville Rd. N19 47 BX33
Grenville Rd., Croy. 96 CG58
Grenville St. WC1 2 A5
Grenville St. WC1 56 BX38
Guilford St.
Gresford Clo., St.Alb. 9 BK13
Gresham Ave. N20 38 BU28
Gresham Ave., Warl. 105 CD62
Gresham Clo., Bex. 79 CQ46
Gresham Clo., Enf. 30 BZ24
Gladbeck Way
Gresham Ct., Berk. 7 AQ13
Ashlyns Rd.
Gresham Dr., Rom. 50 CO32
Gresham Gdns. NW11 46 BR33
Gresham Ms. W4 65 BN41
Reynolds Rd.
Gresham Rd. E6 58 CK37
Gresham Rd. E16 58 CH39
Gresham Rd. NW10 46 BN35
Gresham Rd. SE25 87 CB52
Gresham Rd. SW9 66 BY45
Gresham Rd., Beck. 87 CD51
Gresham Rd., Brwd. 42 DB27
Gresham Rd., Edg. 37 BL29
Gresham Rd., Hmptn. 74 BF50
Gresham Rd., Houns. 64 BG44
Gresham Rd., Oxt. 115 CG68
Gresham Rd., Stai. 72 AV49
Gresham Rd., Uxb. 53 AZ37
Gresham St. EC2 2 J8
Gresham St. EC2 57 BZ39
Gresham Way SW19 76 BS48
Gresley Clo., Welw.G.C. 5 BR7
Gresley Ct., Pot.B. 20 BS18
Heathfield Clo.
Gresley Rd. N19 47 BW33
Gresse St. W1 1 N8
Gresse St. W1 56 BW39
Gressenhall Rd. SW18 75 BR46
Gresswell Clo., Sid. 79 CO48
Greswell St. SW6 65 BQ44
Greta Bank, Lthd. 110 BA66
Gretton Rd. N17 39 CA29
Beaufoy Rd.
Greville Ave., S.Croy. 96 CC58
Greville Clo., Ash. 103 BL63
Greville Clo., Guil. 118 AP70
Greville Clo., Hat. 10 BQ15
Greville Clo., Twick. 74 BJ47
Greville Ct., Lthd. 111 BF66
Greville Hall NW6 56 BS37
Greville Ms. NW6 56 BS37
Greville Rd.
Greville Pk. Ave., Ash. 103 BL62
Greville Pk. Rd., Ash. 103 BL62
Greville Pl. NW6 56 BS37
Greville Rd. E17 48 CF31
Greville Rd. NW6 56 BS37
Greville Rd., Rich. 75 BL46
Greville St. EC1 2 E7
Greville St. EC1 56 BY39
Grey Alders, Bans. 94 BQ60
High Beeches
Grey Clo. NW11 47 BT32
Grey Eagle St. E1 2 Q5
Grey Eagle St. E1 57 CA39
Grey Twrs. Ave., Horn. 51 CV33
Grey Twrs. Gdns., Horn. 51 CV33
Greycaine Rd., Wat. 27 BD22
Greycoat Pl. SW1 3 N7
Greycoat Pl. SW1 66 BW41
Greycoat St. SW1 3 N7
Greycoat St. SW1 66 BW41
Greycot Rd., Beck. 77 CE49
Greyfell Clo., Stan. 36 BJ28
Coverdale Clo.
Greyfields Clo., Pur. 95 BY60
Partridge Knoll
Greyfriars, Brwd. 122 DD26
Greyfriars Pas. EC1 2 G8
Greyfriars Pas. EC1 56 BY39
Newgate St.
Greyfriars Rd., Wok. 101 AW65
Greygoose Pk., Harl. 13 CL12
Greyhound Ct. WC2 56 BX40
Milford La.
Greyhound Hill NW4 46 BP31
Greyhound La. SW16 76 BW50
Greyhound La., Grays 71 DG41
Greyhound La., Pot.B. 19 BP20
Greyhound Rd. N17 48 CA31
Greyhound Rd. NW10 55 BP38
Greyhound Rd. W6 65 BQ43
Greyhound Rd., Sutt. 95 BT56
Greyhound Ter. SW16 86 BW51
Greyhound Way, Dart. 79 CT46
Stadium Way
Greyladies Gdns. SE10 67 CF44
Wat Tyler Rd.
Greys Pk. Clo., Kes. 97 BJ56
Greystead Rd. SE23 77 CC47
Greystoke Ave., Pnr. 45 BF31
Greystoke Clo., Berk. 7 AQ13
Greystoke Dr., Ruis. 44 AZ33
Greystoke Gdns. W5 55 BL38
Greystoke Gdns., Enf. 29 BW24
Greystoke Lo. W5 55 BL38
Hanger La.
Greystoke Pk. Ter. W5 54 BK38
Greystoke Pl. EC4 2 D8
Greystoke Pl. EC4 56 BY39
Cursitor St.
Greystone Clo., Croy. 96 CC59
Greystone Gdns., Har. 45 BK32
Greystone Gdns., Ilf. 40 CM30
Greystone Pk., Sev. 116 CQ66
Greystones Clo., Red. 121 BT71
Hardwicke Rd.
Greystones Clo., Sev. 108 CW62
Greystones Dr., Reig. 121 BT69
Greyswood St. SW16 76 BV50
Greythorne Rd., Wok. 100 AQ62
Grice Ave., West. 97 CH60
Grid Iron Pl., Upmin. 51 CX34
Grierson Rd. SE23 77 CC47
Grieves Rd., Grav. 81 DF48
Griffin Ave., Upmin. 51 CZ32
Griffin Clo. NW10 46 BP35
Griffin Clo., Slou. 61 AN41
Griffin Manor Way SE28 68 CM41
Griffin Rd. N17 39 CA30
Griffin Rd. SE18 68 CM42
Griffin Way, Lthd. 111 BF66
Griffin Way, Sun. 83 BC51
Griffins, The, Grays 71 DD41
Griffith Clo., Dag. 50 CP33
Gibson Rd.
Griffiths Clo., Wor.Pk. 85 BP55
Griffiths Rd. SW19 76 BS50
Griffiths Way, St.Alb. 9 BG14
Griggs App., Ilf. 49 CM34
Griggs Pl. SE1 4 N6
Griggs Pl. SE1 67 CA41
Grange Rd.
Griggs Rd. E10 48 CF32
Grilse Clo. N9 39 CB28
Parr Clo.
Grimsby St. E2 2 Q5
Grimsby St. E2 57 CA38
Grimsdells La., Amer. 25 AO22
Grimsdyke Cres., Barn. 28 BQ24
Grimsdyke Rd., Pnr. 36 BE29
Grimsel Path SE5 66 BY43
Brandon Est.
Grimshaw Clo. N6 47 BV33
Grimston Rd. SW6 65 BR44
Grimston Rd., St.Alb. 9 BH14
Grimstone Clo., Rom. 41 CR29
Grimthorpe Clo., St.Alb. 9 BG12
Grimwade Ave., Croy. 87 CB55
Grimwood Rd., Twick. 74 BH47
Grindal St. SE1 4 D5
Grindal St. SE1 66 BY41
Lower Marsh
Grindall Clo., Croy. 95 BY56
Hillside Rd.
Grinling Pl. SE8 67 CE43
Grinstead Rd. SE8 67 CD42
Grisedale Clo., Pur. 96 CA60
Grisedale Gdns., Pur. 96 CA60
Grittleton Ave., Wem. 55 BM36
Grittleton Rd. W9 56 BS38
Grizedale Ter. SE23 77 CB48
Grocers Hall Ct. EC2 2 K9
Grocers Hall Ct. EC2 57 BZ39
Poultry
Grogan Clo., Hmptn. 74 BE50
Groom Cres. SW18 76 BT47
Groom Pl. SW1 3 H6
Groom Pl. SW1 66 BV41
Chapel St.
Groom Rd., Brox. 21 CD16
Groom Wk., Guil. 118 AR69
Groombridge Clo., Walt. 92 BC56
Groombridge Clo., Well. 79 CO46
Groombridge Rd. E9 57 CC36
Groomfield Clo. SW17 76 BV49
Grooms Cotts., Chesh. 16 AQ18
Grooms Dr., Pnr. 44 BC32
Fore St.
Grosmont Rd. SE18 68 CN43
Grosse Way SW15 75 BP46
Dover Pk. Dr.
Grosvenor Ave. N5 48 BZ35
Grosvenor Ave. SW14 65 BO45
Grosvenor Ave., Cars. 95 BU57
Grosvenor Ave., Har. 45 BF33
Grosvenor Ave., Hayes 53 BB37
Grosvenor Ave., Kings L. 17 BA17
Grosvenor Ave., Rich. 75 BL46
Grosvenor Rd.
Grosvenor Clo., Iver 52 AU38
Grosvenor Clo., Loug. 31 CL23
Grosvenor Cotts. SW1 3 G8
Grosvenor Ct. N14 38 BW26
Grosvenor Ct., Guil. 118 AT69
Grosvenor Ct., Mord. 86 BS52
Grosvenor Ct., Rick. 26 BA25
Mayfare
Grosvenor Ct., Wey. 92 BA57
Grosvenor Cres. NW9 46 BM31
Grosvenor Cres. SW1 3 H5
Grosvenor Cres. SW1 66 BV41
Grosvenor Cres., Dart. 80 CV46
Grosvenor Cres., Uxb. 53 AZ36
Grosvenor Cres. Ms. SW1 3 G5
Grosvenor Cres. Ms. SW1 66 BV41
Grosvenor Dr., Horn. 51 CV33
Grosvenor Dr., Loug. 31 CL23
Grosvenor Est. SW1 3 P8
Grosvenor Est. SW1 66 BW42
Grosvenor Gdns. E6 58 CJ38
Grosvenor Gdns. N10 47 BW31
Grosvenor Gdns. N14 29 BW24
Grosvenor Gdns. NW2 55 BQ36
Grosvenor Gdns. NW11 46 BR32
Grosvenor Gdns. SW1 3 K7
Grosvenor Gdns. SW1 66 BV41
Grosvenor Gdns. SW14 65 BO45
Grosvenor Gdns., Kings.T. 74 BK50
Grosvenor Gdns., Upmin. 51 CY33
Grosvenor Gdns., Wall. 95 BW57
Grosvenor Gdns., Wdf.Grn. 40 CH29
Grosvenor Gdns. Ms. E. SW1 3 K6
Grosvenor Gdns. Ms. N. SW1 3 J7
Grosvenor Gdns. Ms. N. SW1 66 BV41
Ebury St.
Grosvenor Gdns. Ms. S. SW1 3 K7
Grosvenor Gdns. Ms. S. SW1 66 BV41
Ebury St.
Grosvenor Gate W1 3 F1
Grosvenor Hill SW19 75 BR50
Grosvenor Hill W1 1 J10
Grosvenor Hill W1 56 BV40
Grosvenor Ms., St.Alb. 9 BG13
Lower Dagnall St.
Grosvenor Pk. SE5 67 BZ43
Grosvenor Pk. Rd. E17 48 CE32
Grosvenor Path, Loug. 31 CM23
Grosvenor Pl. SW1 3 H5
Grosvenor Pl. SW1 66 BV41
Grosvenor Ri. E. E17 48 CE32
Grosvenor Rd. E6 58 CJ37
Grosvenor Rd. E7 58 CH36
Grosvenor Rd. E10 48 CF33
Grosvenor Rd. E11 49 CH32
Grosvenor Rd. N3 37 BR29
Grosvenor Rd. N9 39 CB26
Grosvenor Rd. N10 38 BV30
Grosvenor Rd. SE25 87 CB52
Grosvenor Rd. SW1 66 BV43
Grosvenor Rd. W4 65 BM42
Grosvenor Rd. W7 54 BJ40
Grosvenor Rd., Belv. 69 CQ43
Grosvenor Rd., Bexh. 79 CP46
Grosvenor Rd., Borwd. 28 BM24
Grosvenor Rd., Brent. 64 BK43
Grosvenor Rd., Brox. 12 CD13
Grosvenor Rd., Dag. 50 CQ33
Grosvenor Rd., Epsom 103 BN63
Grosvenor Rd., Houns. 64 BE45
Grosvenor Rd., Ilf. 49 CM34
Grosvenor Rd., Nthwd. 35 BB28
Grosvenor Rd., Orp. 88 CN53
Grosvenor Rd., Rich. 75 BL46
Grosvenor Rd., Rom. 50 CS33
Grosvenor Rd., St.Alb. 9 BH14
Grosvenor Rd., Sthl. 64 BE41
Grosvenor Rd., Stai. 73 AW50
Grosvenor Rd., Twick. 74 BJ47
Grosvenor Rd., Wall. 95 BV57
Grosvenor Rd., Wat. 27 BD24
Grosvenor Rd., W.Wick. 87 CE55
Grosvenor Rd., Wok. 91 AO60
Grosvenor Sq. W1 1 H10
Grosvenor Sq. W1 56 BV40
Grosvenor Sq., Long. 90 DC52
Bramblefield Clo.
Grosvenor St. W1 1 J10
Grosvenor St. W1 56 BV40
Grosvenor Ter., Hem.H. 8 AW14
Grosvenor Vale, Ruis. 44 BB34
Grosvenor Wf. Rd. E14 67 CF42
Grotes Bldgs. SE3 68 CG44
Grotes Pl. SE3 68 CG44
Groton Rd. SW18 76 BS48
Grotto Pas. W1 1 H6
Grotto Pas. W1 56 BV39
Paddington St.
Grotto Rd., Twick. 74 BH48
Grotto Rd., Wey. 83 AZ55
Ground La., Hat. 10 BP11
Grove, The E15 58 CG36
Grove, The N3 38 BS30
Grove, The N4 47 BX33
Grove, The N6 47 BV33
Grove, The N8 47 BW32
Grove, The N13 38 BY28
Grove, The N14 29 BW25
Chase Rd.
Grove, The NW9 46 BN32
Grove, The NW11 46 BR33
Grove, The SW16 76 BW49
Grove, The W5 54 BK40
Grove, The, Amer. 25 AO21
Grove, The, Bexh. 69 CP45
Grove, The, Brwd. 42 CZ28
Grove, The, Cat. 105 BZ64
Grove, The, Chesh. 25 AR21
Grove, The, Couls. 104 BW61
Grove, The, Edg. 37 BM28
Grove, The, Egh. 72 AT49
Grove, The, Enf. 29 BY23
Grove, The, Epsom 94 BO60
Grove, The (Ewell), Epsom 94 BO58
Grove, The, Esher 84 BF54
Grove, The, Grav. 81 DH47
Grove, The, Grnf. 54 BG39
Grove, The, Hat. 20 BS17
Grove, The, Islw. 64 BH44
Grove, The, Pot.B. 20 BT19
Grove, The, Rad. 18 BJ20
Grove, The, Sev. 99 CZ58
Grove, The, Sid. 79 CQ49
Grove, The, Slou. 62 AQ41
Grove, The, Swans. 81 DC46
Grove, The, Tedd. 74 BJ49
Grove, The, Upmin. 51 CX35
Grove, The, Uxb. 44 AZ35
Grove, The, Walt. 83 BC53
Grove, The, W.Wick. 87 CE55
Grove, The, West. 106 CJ62
Grove, The, Wey. 92 AW56
Grove, The, Wok. 100 AS61
Grove Ave. N3 38 BS29
Grove Ave. N10 38 BW30
Grove Ave. W7 54 BH39
Grove Ave., Epsom 94 BO60
Grove Ave., Pnr. 45 BE32
Grove Ave., Sutt. 95 BS57
Grove Ave., Twick. 74 BH47
Grove Bldgs. SW3 66 BU43
Grove Clo. N14 38 BW26
Grove Clo. SE23 77 CD47
Grove Clo., Brom. 88 CH55
Grove Clo., Felt. 74 BE49
Grove Clo., Ger.Cr. 34 AR30
Grove Clo., Kings.T. 85 BL52
Grove Clo., Lthd. 111 BF67
Groveside Clo.
Grove Clo., Slou. 62 AQ41
Grove Clo., Uxb. 44 AZ35
Grove Clo., Wind. 72 AQ47
Grove Cor., Lthd. 111 BF66
Lower Shott
Grove Ct. SE3 68 CH44
Grove Ct., E.Mol. 84 BG53
Grove Ct., Tedd. 74 BJ49
Cambridge Rd.
Grove Ct., Wal.Abb. 21 CE20
Grove Cres. E18 40 CG30
Grove Cres. NW9 46 BN31
Grove Cres. SE5 67 CA44
Grove Cres., Felt. 74 BE49
Grove Cres., Kings.T. 85 BL52
Grove Cres., Rick. 26 AZ24
Grove Cres., Walt. 83 BC54
Grove Cres. Rd. E15 57 CF36
Grove End, Ger.Cr. 34 AR30
Grove End La., Esher 84 BG54
Grove End Rd. NW8 1 A2
Grove End Rd. NW8 56 BT38
Grove Est. SE5 67 CA44
Grove Est., Pnr. 45 BE32
Grove Fm. Pk., Nthwd. 35 BA28
Grove Footpath, Surb. 85 BL52
Grove Gdns. E15 58 CG36
Grove Gdns. NW4 46 BP31
Grove Gdns. NW8 1 D3
Grove Gdns. NW8 56 BU38
Grove Gdns., Dag. 50 CS34
Grove Gdns., Enf. 30 CC23
Grove Gdns., Tedd. 74 BJ49
Grove Grn., Nthwd. 35 BA28
Grove Grn. Rd. E11 48 CF34
Grove Hall Ct. NW8 56 BT38
Grove Heath N., Wok. 101 AW64
Grove Heath Rd. (Ripley), Wok. 101 AW65
Grove Hill E18 40 CG30
Grove Hill, Ger.Cr. 34 AR29
Grove Hill, Har. 45 BH33
Grove Hill Rd. SE5 67 CA45
Grove Hill Rd., Har. 45 BH33
Grove Hill Rd., Red. 121 BU70
Grove Ho. Rd. N8 47 BX31
Grove La. SE5 67 BZ44
Grove La., Chesh. 16 AQ17
Grove La., Chig. 40 CN27
Grove La., Couls. 95 BU59
Grove La., Ger.Cr. 34 AQ30
Grove La., Kings.T. 85 BL52
Grove La., Uxb. 53 AY38
Grove Lea, Hat. 10 BP14
Grove Mkt. Pl. SE9 78 CK46
Grove Mead, Hat. 10 BO12
Grove Meadow, Welw.G.C. 5 BS8
Grove Ms. W6 65 BQ41
Grove Mill La., Wat. 26 BA22
Grove Pk. E11 49 CH32
Grove Pk. NW9 46 BN31
Grove Pk. SE5 67 CA44
Grove Pk. Ave. E4 39 CE29
Grove Pk. Bri. W4 65 BN43
Grove Pk. Gdns. W4 65 BM43
Grove Pk. Ms. W4 65 BN43
Grove Pk. Bri.
Grove Pk. Rd. N15 48 CA31
Grove Pk. Rd. SE9 78 CJ48
Grove Pk. Rd. W4 65 BM43
Grove Pk. Rd., Rain. 59 CU37
Grove Pk. Ter. W4 65 BM43
Grove Pas. E2 57 CB37
Grove Pas., Tedd. 74 BJ49
Grove Path, Chsnt. 21 CB19
Grove Pl. NW3 47 BT34
Christchurch Hill
Grove Pl. W3 55 BN40
Grove Pl. W5 54 BK40
Grove Pl., Bark. 58 CM36
Clockhouse Ave.
Grove Pl., Hat. 10 BQ15
Dixons Hill Rd.
Grove Pl., Wat. 27 BF23
Grove Pl., Wey. 92 BA56
Grove Rd. E3 57 CD37
Grove Rd. E4 39 CE28
Grove Rd. E9 57 CC37
Grove Rd. E11 49 CG33
Grove Rd. E17 48 CE32
Grove Rd. N11 38 BV28
Grove Rd. N12 38 BT28
Grove Rd. N15 48 CA32
Grove Rd. NW2 55 BQ36
Grove Rd. SW13 65 BO44
Grove Rd. SW19 76 BT50
Grove Rd. W3 55 BN40
Grove Rd. W5 54 BK40
Grove Rd., Amer. 25 AP22
Grove Rd., Ash. 103 BL62
Grove Rd., Barn. 29 BU24
Grove Rd., Belv. 69 CQ43
Grove Rd., Bexh. 69 CS45
Grove Rd., Borwd. 28 BM23
Grove Rd., Brent. 64 B
Grove Rd., Cher. 82 A
Grove Rd., E.Mol. 84 B
Grove Rd., Edg. 37 BN
Grove Rd., Epsom 94 B
Grove Rd., Grav. 81 D
Grove Rd., Grays 71 D
Grove Rd., Guil. 118 A
Grove Rd., Hem.H. 8 AV
Grove Rd., Houns. 64 B
Grove Rd., Islw. 64 B
Grove Rd., Mitch. 86 B
Grove Rd., Nthwd. 35 B
Grove Rd., Oxt. 114 C
Grove Rd., Pnr. 45 B
Grove Rd., Rich. 75 B
Grove Rd., Rick. 35 AV
Grove Rd., Rom. 50 CC
Grove Rd., St.Alb. 9 BC
Grove Rd., Sev. 108 C
Grove Rd. (Seal), Sev. 108 C
Grove Rd., Shep. 83 B
Grove Rd., Surb. 84 B
Grove Rd., Sutt. 95 B
Grove Rd., Th.Hth. 86 B
Grove Rd., Twick. 74 B
Grove Rd., Uxb. 53 A
Grove Rd., West. 106 C
Grove Rd., Wind. 61 A
Grove Rd., Wok. 100 A
Grove Rd. W., Enf. 30 C
Grove Shaw, Tad. 103 B
Grove Side, Lthd. 111 B
Grove Stile Waye, Felt. 73 B
Grove St. N18 39 C
Grove St. SE8 67 C
Grove Ter. NW5 47 B
Highgate Rd.
Grove Ter., Tedd. 74 B
Grove Vale SE22 67 C
Grove Vale, Chis. 78 C
Grove Vill. E14 57 C
Grove Way, Dag. 50 C
Grove Way, Esher 84 BC
Grove Way, Rick. 25 A
Grove Waye, Uxb. 53 A
Grove Wd. Clo., Rick. 25 A
Grove Wd. Hill, Couls. 95 BV
Grovebarns, Stai. 73 AV
Grovebury Clo., Erith 69 C
Grovebury Ct. N14 38 BV
Grovebury Rd. SE2 69 CC
Grovedale Clo., Chsnt. 21 C
Grovedale Rd. N19 47 BV
Grovehall Rd., Bush. 27 B
Groveland Ave. SW16 76 B
Groveland Ct. EC4 2
Groveland Ct. EC4 57 B
Bow La.
Groveland Rd., Beck. 87 C
Groveland Way, N.Mal. 85 B
Grovelands, St.Alb. 18 B
Grovelands, E.Mol. 84 B
Grovelands Clo. SE5 67 C
Grovelands Clo., Har. 45 B
Grovelands Ct. N14 38 BV
Grovelands Rd. N13 38 B
Grovelands Rd. N15 48 C
Grovelands Rd., Orp. 79 C
Grovelands Rd., Pur. 95 B
Grovelands Way, Grays 71 D
Groveley Rd., Sun. 73 B
Grover Clo., Hem.H. 8 A
Grover Rd., Wat. 36 B
Groveside Clo. W3 55 B
Groveside Clo., Cars. 86 B
Groveside Clo., Lthd. 111 B
Grove Side
Groveside Rd. E4 40 C
Groveway SW9 66 B
Groveway, Wem. 46 B
Grovewood, Rich. 65 B
Sandycombe Rd.
Grubb St., Oxt. 115 C
Grubbs La., Hat. 11 B
Grummant Rd. SE15 67 C
Grundy St. E14 57 C
Gruneisen Rd. N3 38 B
Guardian Clo., Horn. 50 C
Guards Rd., Wind. 61 A
Guards Wk., Wind. 61 A
Guardsman Clo., Brwd. 42 D
Woodman Rd.
Gubbins La., Rom. 42 CV
Gubyon Ave. SE24 76 B
Guerin Sq. E3 58 C
Malmesbury Rd.
Guernsey Clo., Guil. 109 AT
Cotts Wd. Dr.
Guernsey Clo., Houns. 64 B
Guernsey Fm. Dr., Wok. 100 A
Guernsey Gro. SE24 77 B
Guernsey Rd. E11 48 C
Guessens Ct., Welw.G.C. 5 B
Guessens Gro., Welw.G.C. 5 B
Guessens Rd., Welw.G.C. 5 B
Guessens Wk., Welw.G.C. 5 B
Guibal Rd. SE12 78 C
Guild Cft., Guil. 118 A
Guild Rd. SE7 68 C
Guild Rd., Erith 69 C
Guildables La., Eden. 115 C
Guildersfield Rd. SW16 76 B
Guildford & Godalming By-pass, Guil. 118 A
Guildford Ave., Felt. 73 B
Guildford Gdns., Rom. 42 C
Guildford Gro. SE10 67 C
Guildford La., Guil. 118 A
Guildford Lo. Ri., Lthd. 110 B
Guildford Pk. Ave., Guil. 118 A
Guildford Pk. Rd., Guil. 118 A
Guildford Pl., Wok. 100 A
Guildford Rd. E6 58 C

ildford Rd. E17 39 CF30
ildford Rd. SW8 66 BX44
ildford Rd., Cher. 91 AU57
ildford Rd., Cher. 82 AV54
ildford Rd., Croy. 87 BZ53
ildford Rd., Dor. 119 BC73
ildford Rd., Dor. 119 BF72
ildford Rd., Guil. 109 AR66
ildford Rd., Ilf. 49 CN34
ildford Rd., Lthd. 102 BH65
ildford Rd. 111 BE67
3ookham), Lthd.
ildford Rd. (East 110 BB68
orsley), Lthd.
ildford Rd., Rom. 42 CW29
ildford Rd., St.Alb. 9 BJ14
ildford Rd., Wok. 100 AS63
ildford Rd., Wok. 100 AR65
ildford St., Cher. 82 AV54
ildford St., Stai. 73 AW50
ildford Vill., Surb. 85 BL53
ildford Way, Wall. 95 BX56
ildhall Bldgs. EC2 2 K8
ildhall Bldgs. EC2 57 BZ39
ildhall Yd. EC2 57 BZ39
iresham St.
ildhouse St. SW1 3 L8
ildhouse St. SW1 66 BW42
ildown Ave. N12 38 BS28
ildown Ave., Guil. 118 AQ72
ildown Rd., Guil. 118 AQ72
ildsway E17 39 CD30
ileshill La., Wok. 101 AY65
ilford Ave., Surb. 85 BL53
ilford Pl. WC1 2 B5
ilford Pl. WC1 56 BX38
ilford St. WC1 2 A5
ilford St. WC1 56 BX38
ilfords, Harl. 6 CP9
ilsborough Clo. NW10 55 BO36
inevere Gdns., Wal.Cr. 21 CC18
King Arthur Ct.
inne Clo., Hayes 63 BA41
inness Bldgs. SE1 4 M7
inness Bldgs. SE1 67 CA42
inness Bldgs. SE11 66 BY42
inness Bldgs. SW3 66 BU42
inness Bldgs. W6 65 BQ42
Fulham Palace Rd.
inness Clo. E9 57 CD36
inness Clo., Hayes 63 BA41
Bourne Ave.
inness Ct., Wok. 100 AP62
vergh Rd.
inness Sq. SE1 4 M8
inness Sq. SE1 67 CA42
Pages Wk.
inness Trust SE24 66 BY45
inness Trust Bldgs. 4 F10
SE11
inness Trust Bldgs. 3 E9
SW3
inness Trust Bldgs. 68 CN44
SW10
inness Trust Dws. N16 48 CA33
ion Rd. SW6 65 BR44
ll Clo., Wall. 95 BX57
ll Wk., Rain. 59 CU36
Fulmar Rd.
lland Clo., Bush. 27 BG25
lland Wk. N1 57 BZ36
llbrook, Hem.H. 8 AW13
llet Wd. Rd., Wat. 17 BC21
Rushton Ave.
lliver Clo., Nthlt. 54 BE37
lliver Rd., Sid. 78 CN48
lliver St. SE16 67 CD41
mleigh Rd. W5 64 BK42
mley Gdns., Islw. 64 BJ45
mley Rd., Grays 70 DB43
mping Rd., Orp. 88 CM55
n Hill, Til. 71 DH43
un St. E1 2 P7
ndulph Rd., Brom. 88 CJ52
nfleet Clo., Grav. 81 DJ47
Roehampton Clo.
nmakers La. E3 57 CD37
nn Rd., Swans. 81 DC46
nner La. SE18 68 CL42
nners Gro. E4 39 CF27
nners Rd. SW18 76 BT48
nnersbury Ave. W5 55 BL40
nnersbury Ct. W3 65 BM41
Bollo La.
nnersbury Cres. W3 65 BM41
nnersbury Dr. W5 65 BL41
nnersbury Gdns. W3 65 BM41
nnersbury La. W3 65 BM41
nnersbury Ms., Brent. 65 BM42
nning St. SE18 68 CN42
unpowder Sq. EC4 2 E8
nstor Rd. N16 48 CA35
nter Gro. SW10 66 BT43
nter Gro., Edg. 37 BN30
nterstone Rd. W14 65 BR42
unthorpe St. E1 2 Q7
nthorpe St. E1 57 CA39
Wentworth St.
nton Rd. E5 48 CB34
nton Rd. SW17 76 BV50
nwhale Clo. SE16 57 CC40
Surrey Water Rd.
rdon Rd. SE7 68 CH42
rnard Clo., West Dr. 53 AX40
Trout Rd.
rnell Gro. W13 54 BH38
rney Clo. E15 49 CG35
Gurney Rd.
rney Clo. E17 39 CC30
rney Clo., Bark. 58 CL36
rney Ct. Rd., St.Alb. 9 BH12
rney Cres., Croy. 86 BX54
rney Dr. N2 47 BT31
rney Rd. E15 49 CG35
Gurney Rd., Cars. 95 BU56
Gurney Rd., Nthlt. 53 BC38
Gurneys Clo., Red. 121 BU71
Brook Rd.
Guthrie St. SW3 3 C10
Guthrie St. SW3 66 BU42
Cale St.
Gutter La. EC2 2 J8
Gutter La. EC2 57 BZ39
Guy Rd., Wall. 86 BW55
Guy St. SE1 4 L4
Guy St. SE1 67 BZ41
Guyatt Gdns., Mitch. 86 BV51
Ormerod Gdns.
Guyscliff Rd. SE13 77 CF46
Guysfield Clo., Rain. 59 CU37
Guysfield Dr., Rain. 59 CU37
Gwalior Rd. SW15 65 BQ45
Felsham Rd.
Gwendolen Ave. SW15 65 BQ45
Gwendolen Clo. SW15 75 BO46
Gwendoline Ave. E13 58 CH37
Gwendwr Rd. W14 65 BR42
Gwent Clo., Wat. 18 BD20
Gwillim Clo., Sid. 79 CO46
Gwydor Rd., Beck. 87 CC52
Gwydyr Rd., Brom. 88 CG52
Gwyn Clo. SW6 66 BT43
Gwynn Rd., Grav. 81 DE48
Gwynne Ave., Croy. 87 CC54
Gwynne Clo., Wind. 61 AM44
Cawcott Dr.
Gwynne Pk. Ave., 40 CK29
Wdf.Grn.
Gwynne Pl. WC1 2 C3
Gwynne Pl. WC1 56 BX38
Kings Cross Rd.
Gwynne Rd. SW11 66 BT44
Gwynne Vaughan Ave., 109 AQ68
Guil.
Gyfford Wk., Wal.Cr. 21 CB19
Hawthorne Clo.
Gylcote Clo. SE5 67 BZ45
Gyles Pk., Stan. 36 BK29
Gyllyngdune Gdns., Ilf. 49 CN34
Gypsy La., Kings L. 17 BA20
Gypsy La., Slou. 43 AP35
Gypsy La., Welw.G.C. 5 BR10
Gypsy La., Wey. 83 AZ55

H

Ha-Ha Rd. SE18 68 CK43
Haarlem Rd. W14 65 BQ41
Haberdasher Pl. N1 2 L2
Haberdasher St. N1 2 L2
Haberdasher St. N1 57 BZ38
Habgood Rd., Loug. 31 CK24
Haccombe Rd. SW19 76 BT50
Hackbridge Pk. Gdns., 86 BU55
Cars.
Hackbridge Rd., Wall. 86 BV55
Hacketts La., Wok. 91 AV60
Hackford Rd. SW9 66 BX44
Hackforth Clo., Barn. 28 BP25
Hackington Cres., Beck. 77 CE50
Hackney Clo., Borwd. 28 BN25
Hackney Gro. E8 57 CB36
Hackney Rd. E2 2 P2
Hackney Rd. E2 57 CA38
Hacton Dr., Horn. 51 CV35
Hacton La., Horn. 51 CW34
Hacton Parkway, Upmin. 51 CW35
Hadden Rd. SE28 68 CN41
Hadden Way, Grnf. 54 BG36
Haddington Rd., Brom. 77 CF48
Haddo St. SE10 67 CE43
Haddon Clo., Borwd. 28 BM23
Haddon Clo., Enf. 30 CB25
Haddon Clo., Hem.H. 8 AZ14
Haddon Clo., N.Mal. 85 BO53
Cromwell Ave.
Haddon Clo., Wey. 83 BA55
Haddon Gro., Sid. 78 CN47
Haddon Rd., Orp. 89 CP53
Haddon Rd., Rick. 25 AU25
Haddon Rd., Sutt. 95 BS56
Thorncroft Rd.
Haden Ct. N4 47 BY34
Hadfield Rd., Stai. 73 AX47
Hadleigh Clo. E1 57 CC38
Martus Rd.
Hadleigh Ct., Brox. 12 CD14
Hadleigh Rd. N9 39 CB26
Hadleigh St. E2 57 CC38
Hadleigh Wk. E6 58 CK39
Dunnock Rd.
Hadley Clo. N21 29 BY25
Hadley Clo., Borwd. 28 BL25
Hadley Common, Barn. 29 BS23
Hadley Gdns. W4 65 BN42
Hadley Gdns., Sthl. 64 BE42
Hadley Grn. Rd., Barn. 28 BR23
Hadley Grn. W., Barn. 28 BR23
Hadley Gro., Barn. 28 BR23
Hadley Highstone, Barn. 28 BR23
Hadley Ridge, Barn. 28 BR24
Hadley Rd., Barn. 29 BS24
Hadley Rd., Belv. 69 CQ42
Hadley Rd., Enf. 29 BW22
Hadley Rd., Mitch. 86 BW52
Hadley St. NW1 56 BV36
Hadley Way N21 29 BY25
Hadley Wd. Ri., S.Croy. 104 BY61
Hadlow Ct., Slou. 61 AO40
Hadlow Pl. SE19 77 CB50
Hadlow Rd., Sid. 79 CO49
Hadlow Rd., Well. 69 CP43
Hadlow Way, Grav. 81 DF50
Hadrian Clo., Stai. 73 AY47
Hadrian Clo., Wall. 95 BX57
Hadrian Est. E2 57 CB37
Hadrian St. SE10 68 CG42
Hadrian Way, Stai. 73 AX47
Hadrians Clo., St.Alb. 9 BE15
Hadrians Ride, Enf. 30 CA25
Hadyn Pk. Rd. W12 65 BP41
Hafer Rd. SW11 66 BU45
Hafton Rd. SE6 78 CG47
Hagden La., Wat. 26 BB25
Haggard Rd., Twick. 74 BJ47
Haggerston Est. E8 57 CA37
Haggerston Rd. E8 57 CA36
Haggerston Rd., Borwd. 28 BL22
Hague St. E2 57 CB38
Derbyshire St.
Haig Clo., St.Alb. 9 BJ14
Haig Dr., Slou. 61 AN41
Haig Rd., Grays 71 DG41
Haig Rd., Stan. 36 BK28
Haig Rd., Uxb. 53 AZ39
Haig Rd., West. 106 CK62
Haig Rd. E. E13 58 CJ38
Haig Rd. W. E13 58 CJ38
Haigh Cres., Red. 121 BV71
Haigville Gdns., Ilf. 49 CL31
Hailes Clo. SW19 76 BT50
North Rd.
Hailey Rd., Erith 69 CR41
Haileybury Ave., Enf. 30 CA25
Haileybury Rd., Orp. 98 CO56
Hailsham Ave. SW2 76 BX48
Hailsham Clo., Rom. 42 CV28
Hailsham Clo., Surb. 84 BK54
Hailsham Dr., Har. 45 BH31
Hailsham Gdns., Rom. 42 CV28
Hailsham Rd. SW17 76 BV50
Hailsham Rd., Rom. 42 CV28
Hailsham Ter. N18 39 BZ28
Haimo Rd. SE9 78 CJ46
Hainault Ct. E17 48 CF31
Hainault Gore, Rom. 50 CQ32
Hainault Gro., Chig. 40 CM28
Hainault Rd. E11 48 CF33
Hainault Rd., Chig. 40 CL27
Hainault Rd., Rom. 41 CO29
Hainault Rd., Rom. 50 CQ32
Hainault Rd., Rom. 41 CS30
Hainault St. SE9 78 CL47
Hainault St., Ilf. 49 CM34
Haines Ct., Wey. 92 BA56
Haines Way, Wat. 17 BC20
Hainford Clo. SE4 67 CD45
Frendsbury Rd.
Haining Clo., Brent. 65 BM42
Wellesley Rd.
Hainthorpe Rd. SE27 76 BY48
Hainton Path E1 57 CB39
Watney Mkt.
Halberd Ms. E5 48 CB34
Knightland Rd.
Halbutt Gdns., Dag. 50 CQ34
Halbutt St., Dag. 50 CQ34
Halcomb St. N1 57 CA37
Orsman Rd.
Halcot Ave., Bexh. 79 CR46
Halcrow St. E1 57 CB39
Halcyon Way, Horn. 51 CW33
Haldan Rd. E4 39 CF29
Haldane Clo. N10 38 BV29
Haldane Pl. SW18 76 BS47
Haldane Rd. E6 58 CJ38
Haldane Rd. SE28 59 CP40
Haldane Rd. SW6 65 BR43
Haldane Rd., Sthl. 54 BG40
Haldens, Welw.G.C. 5 BR6
Haldon Clo., Chig. 40 CN28
Arrowsmith Rd.
Haldon Rd. SW18 75 BR46
Hale, The E4 39 CF30
Hale, The N17 48 CB31
Hale Clo. E4 39 CF27
Hale Clo., Edg. 37 BN28
Hale Clo., Orp. 97 CM56
Broadwater Gdns.
Hale Ct., Edg. 37 BN28
Hale Dr. NW7 37 BN29
Hale End, Rom. 41 CU29
Hale End Clo., Ruis. 44 BC32
Hale End Rd. E4 39 CF29
Hale End Rd. E17 39 CF30
Hale End Rd., Wdf.Grn. 39 CF30
Hale Gdns. N17 48 CB31
High Cross Rd.
Hale Gdns. W3 55 BM40
Hale Gro. Gdns. NW7 37 BN28
Hale La. NW7 37 BN28
Hale La., Edg. 37 BM28
Hale La., Sev. 107 CT62
Hale Oak Rd., Sev. 116 CU70
Hale Path SE27 76 BY49
Hale Pit Rd., Lthd. 111 BG66
Hale Rd. E6 58 CK38
Hale Rd. N17 48 CB31
The Hale
Hale St. E14 57 CE40
Hale St., Stai. 72 AV49
Hale Wk. W7 54 BH39
Halefield Rd. N17 39 CB30
Hales Oak, Lthd. 111 BG66
Hales Pk., Hem.H. 8 BA13
Hales Pk. Clo., Hem.H. 8 BA13
Hales St. SE8 67 CE43
Halesowen Rd., Mord. 86 BS54
Haleswood, Cob. 83 BC60
Haleswood Rd., Hem.H. 8 AZ13
Halesworth Clo. E5 48 CB34
Southwold Rd.
Halesworth Clo., Rom. 42 CW29
Halesworth Rd. SE13 67 CE45
Halesworth Rd., Rom. 42 CW29
Haley Rd. NW4 46 BQ32
Half Acre, Brent. 64 BK43
Half Acre Hill, Ger.Cr. 34 AS30
Half Acre Rd. W7 54 BH40
Half Moon Ct. EC1 2 H7
Half Moon Ct. EC1 57 BZ39
Bartholomew Clo.
Half Moon Cres. N1 56 BX37
Half Moon La. SE24 77 BZ46
Half Moon Meadow, 8 AZ11
Hem.H.
Half Moon Pas. E1 2 Q9
Half Moon Pas. E1 57 CA39
Braham St.
Half Moon St. W1 3 K2
Half Moon St. W1 56 BV40
Halfhide La., Chsnt. 21 CC16
Halfhides, Wal.Abb. 21 CF20
Halford Rd. E10 48 CF32
Halford Rd. SW6 66 BS43
Halford Rd., Rich. 75 BL46
Halford Rd., Uxb. 44 AZ35
Halfpenny Clo., Guil. 118 AU73
Halfpenny La., Guil. 118 AU71
Halfway Ct., Grays 70 CX42
Halfway Grn., Walt. 83 BC55
Halfway St., Sid. 78 CM47
Haliburton Rd., Twick. 74 BJ46
Haliday Wk. N1 57 BZ36
Mildmay St.
Halidon Clo. E9 48 CC35
Halidon Ri., Rom. 42 CX29
Halifax Rd., Enf. 30 BZ23
Halifax Rd., Grnf. 54 BF37
Halifax Rd., Rick. 34 AU26
Halifax St. SE26 77 CB49
Halifax Way, Welw.G.C. 5 BU7
Halifield Dr., Belv. 69 CQ41
Haling Gro., S.Croy. 96 BZ57
Haling Pk. Gdns., S.Croy. 95 BY57
Haling Pk. Rd., S.Croy. 95 BY57
Haling Rd., S.Croy. 96 BZ57
Halings La., Uxb. 43 AU31
Halkin Arc. SW1 3 G6
Halkin Arc. SW1 66 BV41
Motcomb St.
Halkin Ms. SW1 3 G6
Halkin Ms. SW1 66 BV41
Motcomb St.
Halkin Pl. SW1 3 G6
Halkin Pl. SW1 66 BV41
Halkin St. SW1 3 H5
Halkin St. SW1 66 BV41
Halkingcroft, Slou. 62 AR41
Hall, The SE3 68 CH45
Hall Ave., S.Ock. 60 CY40
Hall Clo. W5 54 BK39
Regal Clo.
Hall Clo. W5 55 BL39
Hall Clo., Rick. 35 AW26
Hall Ct., Slou. 62 AQ43
Hall Cres., S.Ock. 70 CY41
Hall Dene Clo., Guil. 118 AU70
Hall Dr. SE26 77 CB49
Hall Dr. W7 54 BH39
Hall Dr., Uxb. 35 AX29
Hall Fm. Clo., Stan. 36 BJ27
Hall Fm. Dr., Twick. 74 BG47
Hall Gdns. E4 39 CD28
Hall Gdns., St.Alb. 10 BN15
Hall Gate NW8 56 BT38
Hall Rd.
Hall Grn. La., Brwd. 122 DE26
Hall Gro., Welw.G.C. 5 BS9
Hall Heath Clo., St.Alb. 9 BJ12
Hall Hill, Oxt. 114 CF69
Hall Hill, Sev. 108 CX65
Hall La. E4 39 CD28
Hall La. NW4 37 BP30
Hall La., Brwd. 122 DC25
Hall La., Hayes 63 BA43
Hall La., S.Ock. 60 DB37
Hall La., Upmin. 42 CY30
Hall Oak Wk. NW6 55 BR36
Maygrove Rd.
Hall Pk., Berk. 7 AS13
Hall Pk. Gate, Berk. 7 AS14
Hall Pk. Hill, Berk. 7 AS14
Hall Pk. Rd., Upmin. 51 CY35
Hall Pl. W2 1 A5
Hall Pl. W2 56 BT38
Hall Pl., Wok. 100 AT61
North Rd.
Hall Pl. Cres., Bex. 79 CS46
Hall Pl. Dr., Wey. 92 BB56
Hall Pl. Gdns., St.Alb. 9 BH13
Hall Rd. E6 58 CK37
Hall Rd. E15 48 CF35
Hall Rd. NW8 56 BT38
Hall Rd., Dart. 70 CW45
Hall Rd., Grav. 81 DE48
Hall Rd., Hem.H. 8 AZ12
Hall Rd., Islw. 74 BG46
Hall Rd., Rom. 50 CP32
Hall Rd., Rom. 51 CV31
Hall Rd., S.Ock. 70 CY41
Hall Rd., Wall. 95 BV58
Hall St. EC1 2 G2
Hall St. EC1 56 BY38
Hall St. N12 38 BT28
Hall Ter., S.Ock. 70 CY41
Hall Vw. SE9 78 CJ48
Hall Way, Pur. 95 BY60
Hallam Clo., Brwd. 33 DA22
Hallam Clo., Chis. 78 CK49
Hallam Gdns., Pnr. 36 BE29
Hallam Ms. W1 1 K6
Hallam Ms. W1 56 BV39
Hallam St.
Hallam Rd. N15 47 BY31
Hallam St. W1 1 K5
Hallam St. W1 56 BV38
Halland Way, Nthwd. 35 BA29
Halley Gdns. SE13 67 CF45
Halley Rd. E7 58 CJ36
Halley Rd. E12 58 CJ36
Halley St. E14 57 CD39
Halleys App., Wok. 100 AQ62
Halleys Wk., Wey. 92 AX57
Hallfield Est. W2 56 BT39
Hallford Way, Dart. 80 CV46
Halliards, The, Walt. 83 BC53
Felix Rd.
Halliford Clo., Shep. 83 BB52
Halliford Rd., Shep. 83 BB53
Halliford Rd., Sun. 83 BB52
Halliford St. N1 57 BZ36
Halling Hill, Harl. 6 CN10
Hallingbury Rd., Saw. 6 CR5
Hallington Clo., Wok. 100 AQ62
Halliwell Rd. SW2 76 BX46
Halliwick Rd. N10 38 BV30
Hallmead, Sutt. 86 BS55
Hallmores, Brox. 12 CE13
Hallowell Ave., Croy. 95 BX56
Hallowell Clo., Mitch. 86 BV52
Hallowell Cres., Wat. 35 BC27
Hayling Rd.
Hallowell Rd., Nthwd. 35 BB29
Halls Fm. Clo., Wok. 100 AO62
Hallside Rd., Enf. 30 CA22
Hallsville Rd. E16 58 CG39
Hallswelle Rd. NW11 46 BR32
Hallwood Cres., Brwd. 122 DC26
Hallywell Cres. E6 58 CK39
Halons Rd. SE9 78 CL47
Halpin Pl. SE17 4 L9
Halpin Pl. SE17 67 BZ42
Halsbrook Rd. SE3 68 CJ45
Halsbury Clo., Stan. 36 BJ28
Halsbury Rd. W12 55 BP40
Halsbury Rd. E., Nthlt. 45 BG35
Halsbury Rd. W., Nthlt. 45 BF35
Halsend, Hayes 63 BC41
Halsey Ms. SW3 3 E8
Halsey Pl., Wat. 26 BC22
Halsey Rd., Wat. 26 BC24
Halsey St. SW3 3 E8
Halsey St. SW3 66 BU42
Halsham Cres., Bark. 49 CN35
Halsmere Rd. SE5 66 BY44
Halstead Ct. N1 2 L1
Halstead Gdns. N21 39 BZ26
Halstead Hill, Chsnt. 21 CA18
Halstead Rd. E11 49 CH32
Halstead Rd. N21 39 BZ26
Halstead Rd., Enf. 30 CA24
Halstead Rd., Erith 69 CT44
Halstead Way, Brwd. 122 DE25
Halston Clo. SW11 76 BU46
Northcote Rd.
Halstow Rd. NW10 55 BQ38
Halstow Rd. SE10 68 CH42
Halsway, Hayes 53 BC40
Halt Dr., S.le H. 71 DK42
Halt Robin La., Belv. 69 CR42
Halt Robin Rd.
Halt Robin Rd., Belv. 69 CR42
Halter Clo., Borwd. 28 BN25
Clydesdale Clo.
Halton Cross St. N1 56 BY36
Halton Rd.
Halton Pl. N1 57 BZ37
Dibden St.
Halton Rd. N1 56 BY36
Halton Rd., Grays 71 DG41
Haltside, Hat. 10 BO13
Crossbrook
Halyons, The, Shep. 83 BA53
Gordon Rd.
Ham, The, Brent. 64 BK43
Ham Clo., Rich. 74 BK48
Ham Fm. Rd., Rich. 74 BK49
Ham Gate Ave., Rich. 74 BK48
Ham La., Egh. 72 AQ49
Ham La., Wind. 62 AR45
Ham La. (Old Windsor), 72 AQ46
Wind.
Ham Pk. Rd. E15 58 CG36
Ham Ridings, Rich. 75 BL49
Ham Shades Clo., Sid. 79 CO48
Ham St., Rich. 74 BK47
Ham Vw., Croy. 87 CD53
Ham Yd. W1 1 N10
Ham Yd. W1 56 BW40
Windmill St.
Hambalt Rd. SW4 76 BW46
Hamberlins La., Berk. 7 AO11
Hamble Clo., Ruis. 44 BB34
Hamble Clo., Wok. 100 AQ62
Denton Way
Hamble La., S.Ock. 60 CZ39
Hamble St. SW6 66 BS45
Hamble Wk., Nthlt. 54 BF37
Leander Rd.
Hamble Wk., Wok. 100 AQ62
Denton Way
Hambleden Pl. SE21 77 CA47
Hambledon Clo., Uxb. 53 AZ38
Aldenham Dr.
Hambledon Gdns. SE25 87 CA52
Hambledon Hill, Epsom 103 BN61
Hambledon Rd. SW18 75 BR47
Hambledon Vale, Epsom 103 BN61
Hambledown Rd., Sid. 78 CM47
Hambro Ave., Brom. 88 CH54
Hambro Rd. SW16 76 BW50
Hambro Rd., Brwd. 42 DB27
Ingrave Rd.
Hambrook Rd. SE25 87 CB52
Hambrough Rd., Sthl. 54 BE40
Hamden Cres., Dag. 50 CR34
Hamelin St. E14 57 CF39
Hamerton Rd., Grav. 81 DD46
Hameway E6 58 CL38
Hamfield Clo., Oxt. 114 CF67
Hamfrith Rd. E15 58 CG36
Hamilton Ave. N9 39 CB26
Hamilton Ave., Cob. 92 BC60
Hamilton Ave., Hodd. 12 CE11

Hamilton Ave., Ilf. 49 CL31
Hamilton Ave., Rom. 41 CS30
Hamilton Ave., Surb. 85 BM55
Hamilton Ave., Sutt. 85 BR54
Hamilton Ave., Wok. 100 AV61
Hamilton Clo. N17 48 CA31
Hamilton Clo. NW8 1 A3
Hamilton Clo. NW8 56 BT38
Hamilton Clo. SE16 67 CD41
Somerford Rd.
Hamilton Clo., Barn. 29 BU24
Hamilton Clo., Cher. 82 AV54
Hamilton Clo., Epsom 94 BN59
Hamilton Clo., Felt. 73 BB49
Hamilton Clo., Guil. 109 AQ68
Oregano Way
Hamilton Clo., Pot.B. 19 BP20
Hamilton Clo., Pur. 95 BY59
Hamilton Clo., St.Alb. 18 BF19
Hamilton Clo., Stan. 36 BH27
Hamilton Ct. W5 55 BL40
Hamilton Rd.
Hamilton Ct. W9 56 BT38
Hamilton Ct., Lthd. 111 BF66
Hamilton Cres. N13 38 BY28
Hamilton Cres., Brwd. 42 DB28
Hamilton Cres., Har. 45 BE34
Hamilton Cres., Houns. 74 BF46
Hamilton Dr., Guil. 109 AQ68
Hamilton Dr., Rom. 42 CW30
Hamilton Gdns. NW8 56 BT38
Hamilton Gordon Ct., Guil. 118 AR70
Josephs Rd.
Hamilton La. N5 47 BY35
Hamilton Mead, Hem.H. 16 AT17
Hamilton Ms. W1 3 J4
Hamilton Pk. N5 47 BY35
Hamilton Pk. W. N5 47 BY35
Hamilton Pl. W1 3 H3
Hamilton Pl. W1 56 BV40
Hamilton Pl., Guil. 109 AQ68
Oregano Way
Hamilton Pl., Sun. 73 BC50
Hamilton Rd. E15 58 CG38
Hamilton Rd. E17 39 CD30
Hamilton Rd. N2 47 BT31
Hamilton Rd. N9 39 CB26
Hamilton Rd. NW10 46 BP35
Hamilton Rd. NW11 46 BQ33
Hamilton Rd. SE27 77 BZ49
Hamilton Rd. SW19 76 BS50
Hamilton Rd. W4 65 BO41
Hamilton Rd. W5 55 BL40
Hamilton Rd., Barn. 29 BU24
Hamilton Rd., Berk. 7 AQ13
Hamilton Rd., Bexh. 69 CQ44
Hamilton Rd., Brent. 64 BK43
Hamilton Rd., Felt. 73 BB49
Hamilton Rd., Har. 45 BH32
Hamilton Rd., Hayes 53 BC40
Hamilton Rd., Ilf. 49 CL35
Hamilton Rd., Kings L. 17 BA20
Hamilton Rd., Rom. 50 CU32
Hamilton Rd., St.Alb. 9 BJ13
Hamilton Rd., Sid. 79 CO49
Hamilton Rd., Sthl. 54 BE40
Hamilton Rd., Th.Hth. 87 BZ52
Hamilton Rd., Twick. 74 BH47
Hamilton Rd., Uxb. 53 AX38
Hamilton Rd., Wat. 35 BC27
Hamilton Sq. SE1 4 L4
Hamilton Sq. SE1 67 BZ41
Kipling St.
Hamilton St. SE8 67 CE43
Deptford High St.
Hamilton St., Wat. 27 BD25
Hamilton Ter. NW8 56 BS37
Hamilton Wk., Erith 69 CT43
Hamilton Way N3 38 BS29
Hamilton Way N13 38 BY28
Hamilton Cres.
Hamilton Way, Wall. 95 BW58
Hamish St. SE11 66 `BX42
Lambeth Wk.
Hamlea Clo. SE12 78 CH46
Hamlet, The SE5 67 BZ45
Hamlet, The, Berk. 7 AT11
Hamlet Clo., Rom. 41 CR29
Hamlet Clo., Wdf.Grn. 40 CH29
Hamlet Gdns. W6 65 BP42
Hamlet Hill, Harl. 13 CH13
Hamlet Rd. SE19 77 CA50
Hamlet Rd., Rom. 41 CQ29
Hamlet Sq. NW2 46 BQ34
Cricklewood Trd. Est.
Hamlets Way E3 57 CD38
Hamlin Cres., Pnr. 45 BD32
Hamlin Rd., Sev. 107 CT64
Hamlyn Clo., Edg. 37 BL27
Hamlyn Gdns. SE19 77 CA50
Hamm Moor La., Wey. 92 AY56
Hammarskjold Rd., Harl. 6 CM10
Hammelton Rd., Brom. 88 CG51
Hammer La., Hem.H. 8 AY13
Hammers Gate, St.Alb. 18 BF16
Hammers La. NW7 37 BP28
Hammersmith Bri. Rd. W6 65 BQ42
Hammersmith Gro. W6 65 BQ41
Hammersmith Rd. W6 65 BQ42
Hammersmith Ter. W6 65 BP42
Hammet Clo., Hayes 54 BD39
Hammett St. EC3 2 P10
Hammett St. EC3 57 CA40
Minories
Hammond Ave., Mitch. 86 BV51
Hammond Clo., Barn. 28 BR25
Hammond Clo., Chsnt. 21 CA16
Hammond Clo., Hmptn. 84 BF51
Hammond Clo., Har. 45 BG35
Lilian Board Way
Hammond Clo., Wok. 100 AR61
Hammond Rd., Enf. 30 CS23
Hammond Rd., Sthl. 64 BE41
Hammond Rd., Wok. 100 AR61
Hammond St. NW5 56 BW36
Hammond St. Rd., Chsnt. 21 BZ16
Hammond Way SE28 59 CO40
Hammonds La., Brwd. 42 DA29
Hammonds La., Hat. 5 BM9
Hamonde Clo., Edg. 37 BM27
Hampden Ave., Beck. 87 CD51
Hampden Clo. NW1 1 P1
Hampden Clo. NW1 56 BW37
Hampden Clo., Epp. 23 CR17
Wellington Rd.
Hampden Clo., Slou. 52 AQ38
Hampden Ct. N10 38 BV29
Hampden Cres., Brwd. 42 DB28
Hampden Cres., Chsnt. 21 CB19
Hampden Gurney St. W1 1 E9
Hampden Gurney St. W1 56 BU39
Seymour Pl.
Hampden La. N17 39 CA30
Hampden Rd. N8 47 BY31
Hampden Rd. N10 38 BV29
Hampden Rd. N17 39 CB30
Hampden Rd. N19 47 BW34
Holloway Rd.
Hampden Rd., Beck. 87 CD51
Hampden Rd., Ger.Cr. 34 AR30
Hampden Rd., Grays 71 DD42
Hampden Rd., Har. 36 BG30
Hampden Rd., Kings.T. 85 BM51
Hampden Rd., Rom. 41 CR29
Hampden Rd., Slou. 62 AS41
Hampden Sq. N14 38 BV26
Hampden Way N14 38 BV26
Hampden Way, Wat. 26 BB21
Hampdon Pl., St.Alb. 18 BH18
Hamper Mill La., Wat. 35 BC26
Hampshire Ave., Slou. 52 AO39
Hampshire Clo. N18 39 CB28
Berkshire Gdns.
Hampshire Gdns., S.le H. 71 DK41
Somerset Rd.
Hampshire Rd. N22 38 BX29
Hampshire Rd., Horn. 51 CX31
Hampshire St. NW5 56 BW36
Torriano Ave.
Hampson Way SW8 66 BX44
Hampstead Clo. SE28 59 CO40
Hampstead Gdns. NW11 47 BS32
Hampstead Gro. NW3 47 BT34
Hampstead High St. NW3 47 BT35
Hampstead Hill Gdns. NW3 47 BT35
Hampstead La. N6 47 BT33
Hampstead La. NW3 47 BT33
Hampstead La., Dor. 119 BH72
Hampstead Rd. NW1 1 L1
Hampstead Rd. NW1 56 BW37
Hampstead Rd., Dor. 119 BJ72
Hampstead Sq. NW3 47 BT34
Hampstead Way NW11 47 BS32
Hampton Clo. NW6 56 BS38
Hampton Clo. SW20 75 BQ50
Hampton Ct. N1 56 BY36
Upper St.
Hampton Ct. Ave., E.Mol. 84 BG53
Hampton Ct. Rd., Hmptn. 84 BG51
Hampton Ct. Rd., Kings.T. 84 BH53
Hampton Ct. Way, E.Mol. 84 BH53
Hampton Cres., Grav. 81 DJ48
Hampton Gro., Epsom 94 BO59
Hampton La., Felt. 74 BE49
Hampton Mead, Loug. 31 CL24
Hampton Pl. NW6 56 BS39
Hampton Ri., Har. 46 BL32
Hampton Rd. E4 39 CD28
Hampton Rd. E7 49 CH35
Hampton Rd. E11 48 CF33
Hampton Rd., Croy. 87 BZ53
Hampton Rd., Ilf. 49 CL35
Hampton Rd., Red. 121 BU73
Hampton Rd., Tedd. 74 BG49
Hampton Rd., Twick. 74 BG48
Hampton Rd., Wor.Pk. 85 BP55
Hampton Rd. E., Felt. 74 BE48
Hampton Rd. W., Felt. 74 BE48
Hampton St. SE1 4 G9
Hampton St. SE17 4 G9
Hampton St. SE17 66 BY42
Hamsey Grn. Gdns., Warl. 105 CB61
Hamsey Way, S.Croy. 105 CB61
Hamshades Clo., Sid. 78 CN48
Hamstel Rd., Harl. 6 CM10
Hanameel St. E16 58 CH40
Hanbury Clo., Chsnt. 21 CC18
Hanbury Dr., West. 97 CH60
Hanbury La., Hat. 11 BU12
Hanbury Ms. N1 57 BZ37
Mary St.
Hanbury Path, Wok. 91 AU60
Hanbury Rd. N17 39 CB30
Hanbury Rd. W3 65 BM41
Hanbury St. E1 2 Q6
Hanbury St. E1 57 CB39
Hanbury Wk., Bex. 79 CS48
Hancock Ct., Borwd. 28 BN23
Hancock Rd. E3 57 CF38
Hancock Rd. SE19 77 BZ50
Hand Ct. WC1 2 C7
Hand Ct. WC1 56 BX39
Sandland St.
Hand La., Saw. 6 CP6
Handa Clo., Hem.H. 8 AZ15
Handa Wk. N1 57 BZ36
Handcroft Rd., Croy. 86 BY54
Handel Clo., Edg. 37 BL29
Handel Cres., Til. 71 DG43
Handel Pl. NW10 55 BN36
Mitchellbrook Way
Handel St. WC1 1 Q4
Handel St. WC1 56 BX38
Handel Way, Edg. 37 BM29
Handen Rd. SE12 78 CG46
Handforth Rd. SW9 66 BY43
Handforth Rd., Ilf. 49 CL34
Winston Way
Handley Rd. E9 57 CC37
Victoria Pk. Rd.
Handowe Clo. NW4 46 BP31
Handpost Hill, Cuffley 20 BV17
Hands Wk. E16 58 CH39
Butchers Rd.
Handside Clo., Welw.G.C. 5 BQ8
Handside Clo., Wor.Pk. 85 BQ54
Handside Grn., Welw.G.C. 5 BQ7
Handside La., Welw.G.C. 5 BP9
Handsworth Ave. E4 39 CF29
Handsworth Clo., Wat. 35 BC27
Handsworth Rd. N17 48 BZ31
Handtrough Way, Bark. 58 CL37
Fresh Wf. Rd.
Hanford Clo. SW18 76 BS47
Hanford Rd., S.Ock. 60 CY40
Hanford Row SW19 75 BQ50
Hangar Ruding, Wat. 36 BE27
Hanger Ct. W5 55 BL38
Heathcroft
Hanger Grn. W5 55 BM38
Hanger Hill, Wey. 92 AZ57
Hanger La. W5 55 BL37
Hanger Vale La. W5 55 BL39
Hanger Vw. Way W3 55 BL39
Hanger Vale La.
Hanging Hill La., Brwd. 122 DD27
Hangrove Hill, Orp. 97 CL60
Hankey Pl. SE1 4 L5
Hankey Pl. SE1 67 BZ41
Hankins La. NW7 37 BO27
Hanks Vw., Cob. 93 BE60
Hanley Clo., Wind. 61 AL44
Hanley Rd. N4 47 BX33
Hanmer Wk. N7 47 BX34
Newington Way
Hannah Clo. NW10 46 BN35
Hannah Ms., Wall. 95 BW57
Blenheim Gdns.
Hannards Way, Chig. 41 CO28
Hannell Rd. SW6 65 BR43
Hannen Rd. SE27 76 BY48
Hannibal Rd. E1 57 CC39
Hannibal Rd., Stai. 73 AX47
Hannibal Way, Croy. 95 BX56
Hannington Rd. SW4 66 BV45
Hanover Ave., Felt. 73 BC47
Hanover Circ., Hayes 53 BA39
Hanover Clo., Egh. 72 AQ50
Blays La.
Hanover Clo., Red. 113 BW67
Hanover Clo., Rich. 65 BM43
Hanover Clo., Slou. 62 AQ41
Yew Tree Rd.
Hanover Clo., Sutt. 94 BR56
Hanover Ct. W12 55 BP40
Hanover Ct., Dor. 119 BH71
Hanover Dr., Chis. 78 CL49
Beechwood Ri.
Hanover Gdns. SE11 66 BY43
Hanover Gdns., Ilf. 40 CM29
Hanover Gate NW1 1 D3
Hanover Gate NW1 56 BU38
Hanover Grn., Hem.H. 8 AW14
Hanover Mead, Maid. 61 AH41
Hanover Pk. SE15 67 CB44
Hanover Pl. WC2 2 A9
Hanover Pl. WC2 56 BX40
Long Acre
Hanover Pl., Egh. 72 AR50
Blays La.
Hanover Rd. N15 48 CA31
Hanover Rd. NW10 55 BQ36
Hanover Rd. SW19 76 BT50
Hanover Sq. W1 1 K9
Hanover Sq. W1 56 BV39
Hanover St. W1 1 K9
Hanover St. W1 56 BV39
Hanover St., Croy. 86 BY55
Latimer Rd.
Hanover Ter. NW1 1 D3
Hanover Ter. NW1 56 BU38
Hanover Ter. Ms. NW1 1 D3
Hanover Ter. Ms. NW1 56 BU38
Hanover Wk., Hat. 10 BO14
Tudor Clo.
Hanover Wk., Wey. 83 BB55
Hanover Way, Bexh. 69 CP45
Hanover Way, Wind. 61 AM44
Hanover W. Ind. Est. NW10 55 BN38
Hanover Yd. N1 56 BY37
Noel Rd.
Hans Cres. SW1 3 E6
Hans Cres. SW1 66 BU41
Hans Pl. SW1 3 F6
Hans Pl. SW1 66 BU41
Hans Rd. SW3 3 E6
Hans Rd. SW3 66 BU41
Hans St. SW1 3 F7
Hans St. SW1 66 BU41
Pavilion Rd.
Hansard Ms. W14 65 BQ41
Hansart Way, Enf. 29 BY23
Hanselin Clo., Stan. 36 BH28
Chenduit Way
Hansells Mead, Harl. 13 CH11
Hanshaw Dr., Edg. 37 BN30
Hansler Gro., E.Mol. 84 BG53
Hansler Rd. SE22 77 CA46
Hansol Rd., Bexh. 79 CQ46
Hanson Clo. SW12 76 BV47
Hanson Clo., Guil. 118 AS69
Hanson Clo., Loug. 31 CM23
Hanson Dr., Loug. 31 CM23
Hanson Gdns., Sthl. 64 BE41
Hanson Grn., Loug. 31 CM23
Hanson St. W1 1 L6
Hanson St. W1 56 BW39
Hanway Pl. W1 1 N8
Hanway Pl. W1 56 BW39
Hanway St.
Hanway Rd. W7 54 BG39
Hanway St. W1 1 N8
Hanway St. W1 56 BW39
Hanworth Clo., Felt. 74 BE49
Hanworth La., Cher. 82 AV54
Hanworth Rd., Felt. 73 BC47
Hanworth Rd., Hmptn. 74 BE49
Hanworth Rd., Houns. 74 BE47
Hanworth Rd., Red. 121 BU73
Hanworth Rd., Sun. 73 BC50
Hanworth Ter., Houns. 64 BF45
Whitton Rd.
Hanworth Trd. Est., Cher. 82 AV54
Hanworth Trd. Est., Felt. 74 BE48
Hanyards End, Cuffley 20 BW17
Hill Ri.
Hanyards La., Cuffley 20 BW17
Hapgood Clo., Grnf. 45 BG35
Harads Pl. E1 57 CB40
Ensign St.
Harben Rd. NW6 56 BT36
Harberson Rd. E15 58 CG37
Harberson Rd. SW12 76 BV47
Harberton Rd. N19 47 BW33
Harberts Rd., Harl. 13 CL11
Harbet Rd. N18 39 CC28
Harbet Rd. W2 1 B7
Harbet Rd. W2 56 BT39
Harbex Clo., Bex. 79 CR47
Harbinger Rd. E14 67 CE42
Harbledown Pl., Orp. 89 CP52
Okemore Gdns.
Harbledown Rd. SW6 66 BS44
Harbledown Rd., S.Croy. 96 CB59
Harbord St. SW6 65 BQ44
Harborough Ave., Sid. 78 CN47
Harborough Clo., Slou. 61 AL40
Harborough Rd. SW16 76 BX49
Harbour Ave. SW10 66 BT44
Harbour Ex. Sq. E14 67 CE41
Harbour Rd. SE5 67 BZ45
Harbourer Clo., Ilf. 41 CO28
Harbourer Rd., Ilf. 41 CO28
Harbourfield Rd., Bans. 104 BS61
Harbridge Ave. SW15 75 BO47
Harbury Rd., Cars. 95 BU58
Harbut Rd. SW11 66 BT45
Harcombe Rd. N16 48 CA34
Harcourt Ave. E12 49 CK35
Harcourt Ave., Edg. 37 BN27
Harcourt Ave., Sid. 79 CP46
Harcourt Ave., Wall. 95 BV56
Harcourt Clo., Egh. 72 AU50
Harcourt Clo., Islw. 64 BJ45
Silverhall St.
Harcourt Fld., Wall. 95 BV56
Harcourt La., Maid. 61 AJ41
Harcourt Rd. E15 58 CG37
Harcourt Rd. N22 38 BW30
Harcourt Rd. SE4 67 CD45
Harcourt Rd. SW19 76 BS50
Russell Rd.
Harcourt Rd., Bexh. 69 CQ45
Harcourt Rd., Bush. 27 BF25
Harcourt Rd., Maid. 61 AJ41
Harcourt Rd., Th.Hth. 86 BX53
Harcourt Rd., Wall. 95 BV56
Harcourt Rd., Wind. 61 AM44
Harcourt St. W1 1 D7
Harcourt St. W1 56 BU39
Harcourt Ter. SW10 66 BS42
Hardcastle Clo., Croy. 87 CA53
Adams Way
Hardcourts Clo., W.Wick. 87 CE55
Hardel Ri. SW2 76 BY47
Hardell Clo., Egh. 72 AT49
Harden Rd., Grav. 81 DF48
Harden St. SE18 68 CK42
Hardens Manor Way SE7 68 CJ41
Harders Rd. SE15 67 CB44
Harders Rd. Ms. SE15 67 CB44
Hardess St. SE24 67 BY45
Herne Hill Rd.
Hardess St. SE24 67 BZ45
Herne Hill Rd.
Hardie Clo. NW10 46 BN35
Hardie Rd., Dag. 50 CS34
Harding Clo., Wat. 18 BD20
Harding Rd., Bexh. 69 CQ44
Harding Rd., Chesh. 16 AO18
Harding Rd., Epsom 103 BO63
Harding Rd., Grays 71 DG41
Hardinge Clo., Uxb. 53 AZ39
Hardinge Rd. N18 39 CA29
Hardinge Rd. NW10 55 BP37
Hardinge St. E1 57 CC39
Hardings, Welw.G.C. 5 BT7
Hardings La. SE20 77 CC50
Hardings Row, Iver 52 AU38
Hardley Cres., Horn. 51 CV31
Hardman Rd. SE7 68 CH42
Hardman Rd., Kings.T. 85 BL51
Hardwick Clo., Stan. 36 BK28
Marsh La.
Hardwick Grn. W13 54 BJ39
Templewood
Hardwick La., Cher. 82 AU54
Hardwick Rd., Red. 121 BT71
Hardwick St. EC1 2 E3
Hardwick St. EC1 56 BY38
Hardwicke Ave., Houns. 64 BF44
Hardwicke Clo., Cob. 102 BG61
Hardwicke Gdns., Amer. 25 AP22
Green La.
Hardwicke Pl., St.Alb. 18 BK17
Hardwicke Rd. N13 38 BX29
Hardwicke Rd. W4 65 BN42
Hardwicke Rd., Reig. 121 BS70
Hardwicke Rd., Rich. 74 BK49
Hardwicke St., Bark. 58 CM37
Hardwicks Way SW18 76 BS
Hardwidge St. SE1 4
Hardwidge St. SE1 67 CA
Snows Flds.
Hardy Ave., Grav. 81 DF
Hardy Ave., Ruis. 44 BC
Hardy Clo. SE16 67 CC
Middleton Dr.
Hardy Clo., Dor. 119 B
Hardy Clo., Pnr. 45 BD
Hardy Clo., Slou. 61 AN
Hardy Gro., Dart. 70 CX
Hardy Pas. N22 38 BY
Cranbrook Pk.
Hardy Rd. SE3 68 CG
Hardy Rd. SW19 76 BS
Hardy Rd., Hem.H. 8 AY
Hardy Way, Enf. 29 BY
Hare & Billet Rd. SE3 67 CF
Hare Ct. EC4 2
Hare Ct. EC4 56 BY
Middle Temple La.
Hare Cres., Wat. 17 BC
Hare Hall La., Rom. 50 CU
Hare Hill, Wey. 91 AV
Hare Hill Clo., Wok. 101 AW
Hare La., Esher 93 BH
Hare La., Hat. 10 BP
Hare Marsh E2 57 CB
Cheshire St.
Hare Pk. Clo., Hem.H. 7 AV
Hare Pl. EC4 2
Hare Pl. EC4 56 BY
Fleet St.
Hare Row E2 57 CB
Cambridge Heath Rd.
Hare St. SE18 68 CL
Hare St. Springs, Harl. 13 CL
Hare Wk. N1 2
Hare Wk. N1 57 CA
Harebell, Welw.G.C. 5 B
Harebell Hill, Cob. 93 BD
Harebell Way, Rom. 42 CV
Harebreaks, The, Wat. 26 BC
Harecastle Clo., Hayes 54 BE
Braunston Dr.
Harecourt Rd. N1 57 BZ
Harecroft, Dor. 119 BK
Harecroft, Lthd. 102 BF
Haredale Rd. SE24 67 BZ
Haredon Clo. SE23 77 CC
Harefield, Esher 84 BH
Harefield, Harl. 6 CO
Harefield Ave., Sutt. 94 BQ
Harefield Clo., Enf. 29 BY
Hunters Way
Harefield Grn. NW7 37 BQ
Harefield Ms. SE4 67 CD
Harefield Pl., St.Alb. 9 BK
Harefield Pl. Est., Uxb. 44 AY
Harefield Rd. N8 47 BW
Harefield Rd. SE4 67 CD
Harefield Rd. SW16 76 BX
Harefield Rd., Rick. 35 AX
Harefield Rd., Sid. 79 CP
Harefield Rd., Uxb. 53 AX
Harelands Clo., Wok. 100 AR
Harelands La., Wok. 100 AQ
Harendon, Tad. 103 BQ
Hares Bank, Croy. 96 CF
Haresfield Rd., Dag. 59 CR
Harestone Dr., Cat. 105 CA
Harestone Hill, Cat. 114 CA
Harestone La., Cat. 114 CA
Harestone Valley Rd., Cat. 114 CA
Hareward Rd., Guil. 109 AU
Harewood, Rick. 26 AX
Harewood Ave. NW1 1 D
Harewood Ave. NW1 56 BU
Harewood Ave., Nthlt. 54 BE
Harewood Clo., Nthlt. 54 BE
Harewood Clo., Reig. 121 BT
Harewood Dr., Ilf. 40 CK
Harewood Gdns., S.Croy. 105 CB
Harewood Hill, Epp. 31 CN
Harewood Pl. W1 1 K
Harewood Pl. W1 56 BV
Hanover Sq.
Harewood Pl., Slou. 62 AQ
Harewood Rd. SW19 76 BU
Harewood Rd., Brwd. 33 DA
Harewood Rd., Ch.St.G. 25 AR
Harewood Rd., Islw. 64 BH
Harewood Rd., S.Croy. 96 CA
Harewood Rd., Wat. 35 BC
Harewood Row NW1 1 D
Harewood Row NW1 56 BU
Harewood Ave.
Harewood Ter., Sthl. 64 BE
Harfield Gdns. SE5 67 CA
Harfield Rd., Sun. 84 BD
Harford Clo. E4 39 CE
Harford Dr., Wat. 26 BB
Harford Rd. E4 39 CE
Harford St. E1 57 CD
Harford Wk. N2 47 BT
Harfst Way, Swan. 89 CS
Hargood Clo., Har. 46 BL
Hargood Rd. SE3 68 CJ
Hargrave Pk. N19 47 BW
Hargrave Pl. N7 47 BW
Brecknock Rd.
Hargrave Rd. N19 47 BW
Hargreaves Ave., Chsnt. 21 CB
Hargreaves Clo., Chsnt. 21 CB
Hargwyne St. SW9 66 BX
Haringey Pk. N8 47 BX
Haringey Pas. N4 47 BY
Haringey Rd. N8 47 BX
Harington Ter. N18 39 BZ
Harkett Clo., Har. 36 BH
Church La.
Harkness, Chsnt. 21 CB

kness Clo., Epsom 103 BQ61
kness Clo., Rom. 42 CW28
land Ave., Croy. 87 CA55
land Ave., Sid. 78 CM48
land Rd. SE12 78 CH47
lands Gro., Orp. 97 CL56
inecrest Gdns.
lech Gdns., Houns. 64 BD43
lech Rd. N14 38 BX27
lequin Ave., Brent. 64 BJ43
lequin Rd., Tedd. 74 BJ50
lescott Rd. SE15 67 CC45
lesden Clo., Rom. 42 CW29
lesden Gdns. NW10 55 BO37
lesden La. NW10 55 BP37
lesden Rd. NW10 55 BP36
lesden Rd., Rom. 42 CW29
lesden Rd., St.Alb. 9 BJ13
lesden Wk., Rom. 42 CW29
leston Clo. E5 48 CB34
outhwold Rd.
ley Clo., Wem. 54 BK36
ley Ct., Har. 45 BG31
ley Ct., St.Alb. 9 BK11
illiers Cres.
ley Cres., Har. 45 BG31
ley Gdns. SW10 66 BT42
ley Gdns., Orp. 97 CN56
ley Gro. E3 57 CD38
ley Pl. W1 1 J7
ley Pl. W1 56 BV39
ley Rd. NW3 56 BT36
ley Rd. NW10 55 BO37
ley Rd., Har. 45 BG31
ley St. W1 1 J5
ley St. W1 56 BV38
leyford, Brom. 88 CJ51
leyford Rd. SE11 66 BX43
leyford St. SE11 66 BY43
lington Clo., Hayes 63 BA43
lington High St., 63 BA43
ayes
lington Rd., Bexh. 69 CQ45
lington Rd., Hayes 53 AZ38
lington Rd., Uxb. 53 AZ38
lington Rd. E., Felt. 73 BC47
lington Rd. W., Felt. 73 BC46
low Common Rd., 14 CP12
arl.
low Gdns., Rom. 41 CS29
low Rd. N13 39 BZ27
low Rd., Bish. 6 CR7
low Rd., Ong. 15 CV13
low Rd., Rain. 59 CT37
low Rd., Saw. 6 CP7
low St., Hem.H. 8 AZ11
lowe Clo. E8 57 CB37
rougham Rd.
lton Ct., Wal.Abb. 22 CG20
lyn Dr., Pnr. 44 BC31
man Ave., Grav. 81 DG49
man Ave., Wdf.Grn. 40 CG29
man Clo. E4 39 CF28
man Clo. NW2 46 BR35
man Dr. NW2 46 BR35
man Dr., Sid. 78 CN46
man Est. N1 57 CA37
man Pl., Pur. 95 BY59
man Rd., Enf. 30 CA25
mer Grn. La., 5 BR5
Velw.G.C.
rmer Rd., Swans. 81 DC46
rmer St., Grav. 81 DH46
rmondsworth La., 63 AY43
Vest Dr.
rmondsworth Rd., 63 AY42
Vest Dr.
rmony Clo. NW11 46 BR32
rmony Clo., Wall. 95 BX58
rmood Gro. NW1 56 BV36
Clarence Way
rmood St. NW1 56 BV36
rms Gro., Guil. 109 AU69
rmsworth St. SE17 66 BY42
rmsworth Way N20 37 BR26
rnage Rd., Brent. 65 BL42
rness Rd. SE28 69 CO41
rness Way, St.Alb. 9 BK12
rold Ave., Belv. 69 CQ42
rold Ave., Hayes 63 BB41
rold Ct. Rd., Rom. 42 CX29
rold Cres., Wal.Abb. 21 CF19
rold Est. SE1 4 N7
rold Est., Wal.Abb. 21 CF19
rold Gibbons Ct. SE7 68 CJ43
rold Hill Ind. Est., Rom. 42 CV29
rold Rd. E4 39 CF27
rold Rd. E11 49 CG33
rold Rd. E13 58 CH37
rold Rd. N8 47 BX32
rold Rd. N15 48 CA32
rold Rd. NW10 55 BN38
rold Rd. SE19 77 BZ50
rold Rd., Dart. 80 CW49
rold Rd., Sutt. 95 BT56
rold Rd., Wdf.Grn. 40 CH30
rold Vw., Rom. 42 CW30
Heath Rd.
rolds Clo., Harl. 13 CK11
Harolds Rd.
rolds Rd., Harl. 13 CK11
roldstone Rd. E17 48 CC32
rp All. EC4 2 F8
rp All. EC4 56 BY39
St. Bride St.
rp La. EC3 4 M1
rp La. EC3 57 CA40
ower Thames St.
rp Rd. W7 54 BH38
rpenden Rd. E12 49 CJ34
rpenden Rd. SE27 76 BY48
rpenden Rd., St.Alb. 9 BG11
rper La., Rad. 18 BJ19
rper Rd. E6 58 CK39

Harper Rd. SE1 4 J6
Harper Rd. SE1 67 BZ41
Harpers La., Borwd. 33 DB22
Harpers Yd. N17 39 CA30
Ruskin Rd.
Harpesford Ave., Vir.W. 82 AQ53
Harpley Sq. E1 57 CC38
Harpour Rd., Bark. 58 CM36
Harps Oak La., Red. 113 BU66
Harpsden St. SW11 66 BV44
Harpsfield Bdy., Hat. 10 BO12
Harptree Way, St.Alb. 9 BJ12
Harpur Ms. WC1 2 B6
Harpur St. WC1 2 B6
Harpur St. WC1 56 BX39
Dombey St.
Harpurs, Tad. 103 BQ64
Harraden Rd. SE3 68 CJ44
Harrap Chase, Grays 71 DC42
Harrier Clo., Rain. 59 CU36
Harrier Ms. SE28 68 CM41
Harrier Way E6 58 CK39
Harriers Clo. W5 55 BL40
Harries Rd., Hayes 54 BD38
Harriescourt, Wal.Abb. 22 CH19
Harriet Clo. E8 57 CB37
Harriet Gdns., Croy. 87 CB55
Harriet St. SW1 3 F5
Harriet St. SW1 66 BU41
Sloane St.
Harriet Wk. SW1 3 F5
Harriet Wk. SW1 66 BU41
Harriet Way, Bush. 36 BG26
Harringay Gdns. N8 47 BY31
Harringay Rd. N15 47 BY32
Harrington Clo., Croy. 86 BX55
Harrington Clo., Reig. 120 BP74
Harrington Clo., Wind. 61 AM45
Harrington Gdns. SW7 66 BS42
Harrington Hill E5 48 CB33
Harrington Pl., Reig. 121 BS69
Reigate Hill
Harrington Rd. E11 49 CG33
Harrington Rd. SE25 87 CB52
Harrington Rd. SW7 3 B8
Harrington Rd. SW7 66 BT42
Harrington Sq. NW1 1 L1
Harrington Sq. NW1 56 BW37
Harrington St. NW1 1 L1
Harrington St. NW1 56 BW38
Harrington Way SE18 68 CJ41
Harriott Clo. SE10 68 CG42
Tunnel Ave.
Harriotts Clo., Ash. 102 BK63
Harriotts La., Ash. 102 BK63
Harris Clo., Enf. 29 BY23
Harris Clo., Grav. 81 DF48
Harris Clo., Houns. 64 BF44
Willow Gdns.
Harris La., Rad. 19 BM20
Harris Rd., Bexh. 69 CQ44
Harris Rd., Dag. 50 CQ35
Harris Rd., Wat. 26 BC21
Harris St. E17 48 CD33
Harris St. SE5 67 BZ43
Harris Way, Sun. 83 BB51
Harrison Clo., Brwd. 122 DE25
Harrison Clo., Nthwd. 35 BA29
Harrison Clo., Reig. 121 BS71
Harrison Ct., Shep. 83 AZ53
Harrison Dr., Epp. 23 CR16
High Rd.
Harrison Rd., Dag. 59 CR36
Harrison St. WC1 2 A3
Harrison St. WC1 56 BX38
Harrison Wk., Chsnt. 21 CC18
Harrison Way, Sev. 107 CU64
Harrison Way, Slou. 61 AL40
Harrisons Ri., Croy. 86 BY55
Harrogate Ct., Slou. 62 AT42
Harrogate Rd., Wat. 36 BD27
Harrold Rd., Dag. 50 CO35
Harrow Ave., Enf. 30 CA25
Harrow Bottom Rd., 82 AS53
Vir.W.
Harrow Clo., Chess. 93 BK57
Harrow Clo., Dor. 119 BJ72
Harrow Clo., Wey. 83 AW55
Harrow Cotts., Felt. 73 AZ48
Harrow Cres., Rom. 41 CU29
Harrow Dr. N9 39 CA26
Harrow Dr., Horn. 50 CU33
Harrow Flds. Gdns., Har. 45 BH34
Harrow Gdns., Orp. 98 CO56
Harrow Gdns., Warl. 105 CD61
Harrow La. E14 57 CF40
Harrow Manorway SE2 59 CP40
Harrow Pk., Har. 45 BH34
Harrow Pl. E1 2 P8
Harrow Pl. E1 57 CA39
Harrow Rd. E6 58 CK37
Harrow Rd. E11 49 CG34
Harrow Rd. NW10 55 BP38
Harrow Rd. W10 55 BR38
Harrow Rd., Bark. 58 CN37
Harrow Rd., Cars. 95 BU57
Harrow Rd., Felt. 73 AZ48
Harrow Rd., Ilf. 49 CM35
Harrow Rd., Sev. 107 CQ61
Harrow Rd., Slou. 62 AS41
Harrow Rd., Warl. 105 CD61
Harrow Rd., Wem. 55 BM35
Harrow Rd. E., Dor. 119 BJ72
Harrow Rd. W., Dor. 119 BJ72
Harrow Vw., Har. 45 BG31
Harrow Vw., Hayes 53 BC39
Harrow Vw., Uxb. 53 BA38
Harrow Vw. Rd. W5 54 BJ38
Harrow Way, Shep. 83 BA51
Harrow Way, Wat. 36 BE27
Harrow Weald, Har. 36 BG29
Harrow Weald Pk., Har. 36 BG29
Harroway Rd. SW11 66 BT44
Harrowby Gdns., Grav. 81 DF48

Harrowby St. W1 1 D8
Harrowby St. W1 56 BU39
Harrowdene Clo., Wem. 45 BK35
Harrowdene Gdns., 74 BJ50
Tedd.
Harrowdene Rd., Wem. 45 BK34
Harrowes Meade, Edg. 37 BM27
Harrowfields Gdns., Har. 45 BH34
Sudbury Hill
Harrowgate Rd. E9 57 CD36
Hart Cres., Chig. 40 CN28
Hart Dyke Cres., Swan. 89 CS52
Hart Dyke Rd., Orp. 89 CP54
Hart Dyke Rd., Swan. 89 CS52
Hart Gro. W5 55 BM40
Hart Gro., Sthl. 54 BF39
Hart Gro. Clo. W5 55 BM40
Hart Gro.
Hart Rd., Dor. 119 BJ71
Hart Rd., Harl. 6 CP8
Hart Rd., St.Alb. 9 BG14
Hart Rd., Wey. 92 AY60
Hart St. EC3 2 N10
Hart St. EC3 57 CA40
Mark La.
Hart St., Brwd. 42 DB27
Harte Rd., Houns. 64 BE44
Hartfield Ave., Borwd. 28 BM25
Hartfield Ave., Nthlt. 53 BC37
Hartfield Clo., Borwd. 28 BM25
Hartfield Cres. SW19 75 BR50
Hartfield Cres., W.Wick. 88 CH55
Hartfield Gro. SE20 87 CB51
Hartfield Rd. SW19 75 BR50
Hartfield Rd., Chess. 93 BK56
Hartfield Rd., W.Wick. 97 CH56
Hartfield Ter. E3 57 CE37
Hartford Ave., Har. 45 BJ31
Hartford Pl., Grav. 81 DE47
Hartford Rd., Bex. 79 CR46
Hartford Rd., Epsom 94 BM57
Hartforde Rd., Borwd. 28 BM23
Harthall La., Hem.H. 17 AZ17
Hartham Clo. N7 47 BX35
Hartham Clo., Islw. 64 BJ44
Hartham Rd. N7 47 BX35
Hartham Rd. N17 39 CA30
Hartham Rd., Islw. 64 BH44
Hartin Clo., Uxb. 53 AY37
Harting Rd. SE9 78 CK49
Hartington Clo., Har. 45 BH35
Hartington Ct. W4 65 BM43
Hartington Pl., Reig. 121 BS69
Reigate Hill Rd.
Hartington Rd. E16 58 CH39
Hartington Rd. E17 48 CD32
Hartington Rd. SW8 66 BX44
Hartington Rd. W4 65 BM43
Hartington Rd. W13 54 BJ40
Hartington Rd., Sthl. 64 BE41
Hartington Rd., Twick. 74 BJ46
Hartismere Rd. SW6 65 BR43
Hartlake Rd. E9 57 CC36
Hartland Clo., Edg. 37 BM27
Hartland Clo., Slou. 52 AO40
Bath Rd.
Hartland Clo., Wey. 92 AX58
Hartland Dr., Edg. 37 BM27
Hartland Dr., Ruis. 44 BC34
Hartland Gro. NW1 56 BV36
Hartland Rd.
Hartland Rd. E15 58 CG36
Hartland Rd. N11 38 BU28
Hartland Rd. NW1 56 BV36
Hartland Rd. NW6 55 BR37
Hartland Rd., Chsnt. 21 CC18
Hartland Rd., Epp. 23 CO19
Hartland Rd., Hmptn. 74 BF49
Hartland Rd., Horn. 50 CU34
Hartland Rd., Islw. 64 BJ45
Hartland Rd., Mord. 86 BS54
Hartland Rd., Wey. 92 AW57
Hartland St. NW1 56 BV36
Hartland Way, Croy. 87 CD55
Hartland Way, Mord. 85 BR54
Hartley Ave. E6 58 CK37
Hartley Ave. NW7 37 BO28
Hartley Clo. NW7 37 BO28
Hartley Clo., Brom. 88 CK51
Hartley Clo., Slou. 52 AR37
Hartley Down Rd., Pur. 104 BX61
Hartley Fm. Est., Pur. 104 BX61
Hartley Hill, Pur. 104 BX61
Hartley Old Rd., Pur. 104 BX61
Hartley Rd. E11 49 CG33
Hartley Rd., Croy. 86 BY54
Hartley Rd., Long. 90 DC51
Hartley Rd., Well. 69 CP43
Hartley Rd., West. 115 CM66
Hartley St. E2 57 CC38
Hartley Way, Pur. 104 BX61
Hartmann Rd. E16 58 CJ40
Hartnoll St. N7 47 BX35
Eden Gro.
Harton Clo., Brom. 88 CJ51
Harton Rd. N9 39 CB27
Harton St. SE8 67 CE44
Harts Clo., Bush. 27 BF23
Harts Gdns., Guil. 118 AQ69
Harts Hill Clo., Uxb. 53 AZ36
Harts La. SE14 67 CC43
Harts La., Bark. 58 CL36
Hartsbourne Ave., Bush. 36 BG27
Hartsbourne Clo., Bush. 36 BG27
Hartsbourne Rd., Bush. 36 BG27
Hartsbourne Way, Hem.H. 8 BA14
Hartscroft, Croy. 96 CD58
Hartshill, Guil. 118 AO70
Hartshill Rd., Grav. 81 DF48
Hartshill Wk., Wok. 100 AQ61
Hartshorn All. EC3 2 N9
Hartshorn All. EC3 57 CA39
Leadenhall St.
Hartshorn Gdns. E6 58 CL38

Hartslands Rd., Sev. 108 CV65
Hartslock Dr. SE2 69 CP41
Hartsmead Rd. SE9 78 CK48
Hartspiece Rd., Red. 121 BV71
Hartspring La., Bush. 27 BF23
Hartsway, Enf. 30 CC24
Hartswood, Dor. 119 BK73
Hartswood Ave., Reig. 121 BS72
Hartswood Clo., Brwd. 42 DB28
Hartswood Rd. W12 65 BO41
Hartswood Rd., Brwd. 122 DC28
Hartsworth Clo. E13 58 CG37
Rudolph Rd.
Hartville Rd. SE18 68 CN42
Hartwell Dr. E4 39 CF29
Hartwell St. E8 57 CA36
Dalston La.
Harty Clo., Grays 71 DD40
Harvard Ct. NW6 47 BS35
West End La.
Harvard Hill W4 65 BM43
Wolseley Gdns.
Harvard La. W4 65 BN42
Harvard Rd.
Harvard Rd. SE13 77 CF46
Harvard Rd. W4 65 BM42
Harvard Rd., Islw. 64 BH44
Harvard Wk., Horn. 50 CU35
Harvel Cres. SE2 69 CP42
Harvest Bank Rd., 88 CG55
W.Wick.
Harvest End, Wat. 27 BD21
Harvest La., T.Ditt. 84 BJ53
Harvest Mead, Hat. 10 BP12
Crop Common
Harvest Rd., Bush. 27 BF24
Harvest Rd., Egh. 72 AR49
Harvest Rd., Felt. 73 BC48
Harvest Way, Swan. 89 CS54
Harvester Rd., Epsom 94 BN58
Harvesters, St.Alb. 9 BK11
Harvesters Clo., Islw. 74 BG46
Harvey, Grays 71 DD41
Harvey Cen., Harl. 13 CM11
Harvey Flds., Wal.Abb. 21 CF20
Harvey Gdns. E11 49 CG33
Harvey Rd.
Harvey Gdns. SE7 68 CJ42
Harvey Gdns., Loug. 31 CL24
Harvey Rd. E11 49 CG33
Harvey Rd. N8 47 BX32
Harvey Rd. SE5 67 BZ44
Harvey Rd., Guil. 118 AS71
Harvey Rd., Houns. 74 BE47
Harvey Rd., Ilf. 49 CL35
Harvey Rd., Nthlt. 54 BD36
Harvey Rd., Rick. 26 AZ25
Harvey Rd., St.Alb. 18 BK16
Harvey Rd., Slou. 62 AX41
Harvey Rd., Uxb. 53 AZ37
Harvey Rd., Walt. 83 BC54
Harvey St. N1 57 BZ37
Harveys La., Rom. 50 CS34
Harvil Rd., Uxb. 44 AX31
Harvill Rd., Sid. 79 CP49
Harvington Wk. E8 57 CB36
Wilman Gro.
Harvist Rd. NW6 55 BQ37
Harwater Dr., Loug. 31 CK23
Harwell Clo., Ruis. 44 BA33
Harwell Pas. N2 47 BU31
Harwich La. EC2 2 N6
Harwood Ave., Brom. 88 CH51
Harwood Ave., Horn. 51 CW31
Harwood Ave., Mitch. 86 BU52
Harwood Clo., Welw.G.C. 5 BR6
Harwood Clo., Welw.G.C. 5 BU6
Harwood Clo., Wem. 45 BK34
Harrowdene Rd.
Harwood Ct. SW15 65 BQ45
Upper Richmond Rd.
Harwood Dr., Uxb. 53 AY37
Harwood Gdns., Wind. 72 AQ47
Harwood Hall La., Upmin. 60 CX36
Harwood Hill, Welw.G.C. 5 BR6
Harwood Rd. SW6 66 BS43
Harwood Ter. SW6 66 BS44
Harwoods Rd., Wat. 26 BC24
Harwoods Yd. N21 38 BY26
Wades Hill
Hascombe Ter. SE5 67 BZ44
Hasedines Rd., Hem.H. 8 AW13
Haselbury Rd. N18 39 CA28
Haseldene Rd., St.Alb. 18 BK16
Haseldine Meadows, Hat. 10 BO13
Haseley End SE23 77 CC47
Tyson Rd.
Haselmere Ave., Houns. 64 BD44
Haselrigge Rd. SW4 66 BW45
Haseltine Rd. SE26 77 CD49
Green La.
Haselwood Dr., Enf. 29 BY24
Haskard Rd., Dag. 50 CP35
Hasker St. SW3 3 D8
Hasker St. SW3 66 BU42
Haslam Ave., Sutt. 85 BR54
Haslam Clo. N1 56 BY36
Haslam Clo., Uxb. 44 BA34
Haslemere Ave. NW4 46 BQ32
Haslemere Ave. SW18 76 BS48
Haslemere Ave. W7 64 BJ41
Haslemere Ave. W13 64 BJ41
Haslemere Ave., Barn. 38 BU26
Haslemere Ave., Houns. 64 BD44
Haslemere Ave., Mitch. 86 BT51
Haslemere Clo., Hmptn. 74 BE49
Haslemere Clo., Wall. 95 BX56
Haslemere Gdns. N3 46 BR31
Haslemere Rd. N8 47 BW33
Haslemere Rd. N21 38 BY27
Haslemere Rd., Bexh. 69 CQ44
Haslemere Rd., Ilf. 49 CN34
Haslemere Rd., Th.Hth. 86 BY53
Haslemere Rd., Wind. 61 AN44

Hasler Clo. SE28 59 CP40
Haslet Rd., Wat. 26 BC24
Haslett Rd., Shep. 83 BB51
Haslewood Ave., Hodd. 12 CE12
Hasluck Gdns., Barn. 29 BT25
Hassard St. E2 2 Q1
Hassard St. E2 57 CA37
Hassendean Rd. SE3 68 CH43
Hassett Rd. E9 57 CC36
Hassock Wd., Kes. 97 CJ56
Hassocks Clo. SE26 77 CB48
Hassocks Rd. SW16 86 BW51
Hassop Rd. NW2 46 BQ35
Hassop Wk. SE9 78 CK49
Hasted Clo., Green. 80 DB46
Hasted Rd. SE7 68 CJ42
Hastings Ave., Ilf. 49 CL31
Hastings Clo. SE15 67 CB43
Bells Gdns.
Hastings Clo., Barn. 29 BT24
Leicester Rd.
Hastings Clo., Maid. 61 AH42
Hastings Rd. N11 38 BW28
Hastings Rd. W13 54 BJ40
Hastings Rd., Brom. 88 CK54
Hastings Rd., Croy. 87 CA54
Hastings Rd., Rom. 50 CU32
Hastings St. WC1 1 Q3
Hastings St. WC1 56 BX38
Hastings Way, Bush. 27 BE24
Hastings Way, Rick. 26 BA24
Hastingwood Rd., Harl. 14 CP13
Hastoe Clo., Hayes 54 BD38
Kingsash Dr.
Hat and Mitre Ct. EC1 2 G5
Hatch, The, Enf. 30 CC23
Hatch, The, Wind. 61 AL43
Hatch Clo., Wey. 83 AW55
Hatch End, Pnr. 36 BE29
Hatch Gdns., Tad. 103 BQ63
Hatch Gro., Rom. 50 CQ31
Hatch La. E4 39 CF28
Hatch La., Bans. 104 BU61
Hatch La., West Dr. 63 AX43
Hatch La., Wind. 61 AN45
Hatch La., Wok. 101 AZ63
Hatch Pl., Kings.T. 75 BL49
Hatch Rd. SW16 86 BX51
Hatch Rd., Brwd. 33 DA25
Hatch Side, Chig. 40 CL28
Hatcham Pk. Ms. SE14 67 CC44
Hatcham Pk. Rd.
Hatcham Pk. Rd. SE14 67 CC44
Hatcham Rd. SE15 67 CC43
Hatchard Rd. N19 47 BW34
Hatchcroft NW4 46 BP31
Hatchett Rd., Felt. 73 BA47
Hatchlands Rd., Red. 121 BU70
Hatchwood Clo., Wdf.Grn. 40 CG28
Sunset Ave.
Hatcliffe Clo. SE3 68 CG45
Hatcliffe St. SE10 68 CG42
Hatfield Clo. SE14 67 CC43
Hatfield Clo., Brwd. 122 DE26
Hutton Dr.
Hatfield Clo., Horn. 51 CV35
Hatfield Clo., Ilf. 49 CL31
Hatfield Clo., Mitch. 86 BT52
Hatfield Cres., Hem.H. 8 AY11
Hatfield Mead, Mord. 86 BS53
Hatfield Rd. E15 49 CG35
Hatfield Rd. W4 65 BN41
Hatfield Rd. W13 54 BJ40
Hatfield Rd., Ash. 103 BL62
Hatfield Rd., Dag. 59 CQ36
Hatfield Rd., Hat. 5 BU10
Hatfield Rd., Pot.B. 20 BT19
Hatfield Rd., St.Alb. 9 BH13
Hatfield Rd., St.Alb. 10 BL13
Hatfield Rd., Slou. 62 AQ41
Hatfield Rd., Wat. 26 BC23
Hatfields SE1 4 E2
Hatfields SE1 56 BY40
Hatfields, Loug. 31 CL24
Hatham Grn. La., Sev. 99 DB58
Hatham Rd., Grays 71 DH41
Hathaway Clo., Brom. 88 CK54
Seymour Dr.
Hathaway Clo., Ruis. 44 BB35
Stafford Rd.
Hathaway Clo., Stan. 36 BJ28
Uxbridge Rd.
Hathaway Ct., St.Alb. 10 BL13
Hatfield Rd.
Hathaway Cres. E12 58 CK36
Hathaway Gdns. W13 54 BJ39
Hathaway Gdns., Grays 71 DD41
Hathaway Rd.
Hathaway Gdns., Rom. 50 CP32
Hathaway Rd., Croy. 86 BY54
Hathaway Rd., Grays 71 DD41
Hatherleigh Clo., Chess. 93 BK56
Hatherleigh Clo., Mord. 86 BS52
Hatherleigh Gdns., Pot.B. 20 BT19
Hatherleigh Rd., Ruis. 44 BC34
Hatherleigh Way, Rom. 42 CV30
Hatherley Cres., Sid. 79 CO48
Hatherley Gdns. E6 58 CJ37
Hatherley Gdns. N8 47 BX32
Hatherley Gro. W2 56 BS39
Hatherley Ms. E17 48 CE31
Hatherley Rd.
Hatherley Rd. E17 48 CD31
Hatherley Rd., Rich. 65 BL44
Hatherley Rd., Sid. 79 CO49
Hatherley St. SW1 3 M9
Hatherley St. SW1 66 BW42
Vincent Sq.
Hathern Gdns. SE9 78 CL49
Hatherop Rd., Hmptn. 74 BE50
Hatherwood, Ash. 102 BK64
Hathorne Clo. SE15 67 CC44
Hathway St. SE15 67 CC44
Gibbon Rd.

Hathway Ter. SE14 67 CC44
Gibbon Rd.
Hatley Ave., Ilf. 49 CM31
Hatley Clo. N11 38 BU28
Hatley Rd. N4 47 BX34
Hatteraick St. SE16 67 CC41
Church St.
Hatters La., Wat. 26 BA25
Hattersfield Clo., Belv. 69 CQ42
Hatton Ave., Slou. 52 AO38
Hatton Clo. SE18 68 CM43
Hatton Clo., Grav. 81 DF48
Hatton Ct. E5 48 CC35
Clapton Pk. Est.
Hatton Gdn. EC1 2 **E6**
Hatton Gdn. EC1 56 BY39
Hatton Gdns., Mitch. 86 BU53
Hatton Grn., Felt. 63 BC45
Hatton Pl. EC1 56 BY39
Hatton Wall
Hatton Rd., Chsnt. 21 CC18
Hatton Rd., Croy. 86 BY54
Hatton Rd., Felt. 73 BA47
Hatton Rd. N., Houns. 53 BA44
Hatton Rd. N., West Dr. 53 AX40
Hatton Rd. S., Felt. 63 BB45
Hatton Cres.
Hatton Row NW8 1 **B5**
Hatton St. NW8 1 **B5**
Hatton St. NW8 56 BT38
Hatton Wall EC1 2 **D6**
Hatton Wall EC1 56 BY39
Haunch of Venison Yd. W1 1 **J9**
Haunch of Venison Yd. 56 BV39
W1
Brook St.
Havana Clo., Rom. 50 CT32
Havana Rd. SW19 76 BS48
Havannah St. E14 67 CE41
Havant Rd. E17 48 CF31
Havant Way SE15 67 CA43
Landport Way
Havelius Clo. SE10 68 CG42
Flamstead Est.
Havelock Ct., Sthl. 64 BE41
Havelock Pl. SE18 68 CL42
Anglesea Rd.
Havelock Pl., Har. 45 BH32
Havelock Rd. N17 39 CB30
Havelock Rd. SW19 76 BT49
Havelock Rd., Belv. 69 CQ42
Havelock Rd., Brom. 88 CJ52
Havelock Rd., Croy. 87 CA55
Havelock Rd., Dart. 79 CU46
Havelock Rd., Grav. 81 DF47
Havelock Rd., Har. 45 BH31
Havelock Rd., Kings L. 17 AY17
Havelock Rd., Sthl. 64 BE41
Havelock St. N1 56 BX37
Havelock St., Ilf. 49 CL34
Havelock Ter. SW8 66 BV43
Havelock Wk. SE23 77 CC47
Haven, The, Grays 71 DG42
Haven, The, Rich. 65 BM45
Haven Clo. SE9 78 CK48
Mottingham Rd.
Haven Clo. SW19 75 BQ48
Haven Clo., Grav. 81 CF50
Haven Clo., Hat. 10 BP12
Haven Clo., Hayes 53 BB39
Haven Clo., Sid. 79 CP50
Haven Clo., Swan. 89 CT51
Haven Grn. W5 54 BK39
Haven Grn. Ct. W5 54 BK39
Haven Grn.
Haven La. W5 54 BK39
Haven Pl. W5 54 BK40
The Bdy.
Haven Pl., Grays 71 DE41
Haven Rd., Ashf. 73 AZ49
Reedsfield Rd
Haven St. NW1 56 BV36
Castlehaven Rd.
Haven Ter. W5 54 BK40
The Bdy.
Havengore Ave., Grav. 81 DJ47
Havenhurst Ri., Enf. 29 BY23
Havensfield, Kings L. 17 AW19
Nunfield
Havenwood, Wem. 46 BM34
Havenwood Clo., Brwd. 42 DA28
Havercroft Clo., St.Alb. 9 BF14
Haverfield Gdns., Rich. 65 BM43
Haverfield Rd. E3 57 CD38
Haverford Way, Edg. 37 BL30
Haverhill Rd. E4 39 CF26
Pretoria Rd.
Haverhill Rd. SW12 76 BW47
Havering Dr., Rom. 50 CT31
Havering Gdns., Rom. 50 CP32
Havering Pl., Hav. 41 CS27
Havering Rd., Rom. 41 CS30
Havering St. E1 57 CC39
Havering Way, Bark. 59 CO38
Havers Ave., Walt. 93 BD56
Haversham Clo., Twick. 74 BK46
Haversham Gra., Twick. 74 BK46
Haverstock Hill NW3 47 BU35
Haverstock Rd. NW5 47 BU35
Haverstock St. N1 2 **G1**
Haverstock St. N1 56 BY37
Haverthwaite Rd., Orp. 88 CM55
Havil St. SE5 67 CA43
Havisham Pl. SE19 76 BY50
Havisham Rd., Grav. 81 DK48
Haward Rd., Hodd. 12 CF11
Hawarden Ave., Wal.Cr. 21 CC20
Hawarden Gro. SE24 77 BZ47
Hawarden Hill NW2 46 BP34
Hawarden Rd. E17 48 CC31
Hawarden Rd., Cat. 105 BZ64
Hawbridge Rd. E11 48 CF33
Hawes Clo., Nthwd. 35 BB29
Hawes La. E4 30 CF22

Hawes La., W.Wick. 87 CF54
Hawes Rd. N18 39 CB29
Hawes Rd., Brom. 88 CH51
Hawes Rd., Tad. 103 BQ63
Hawes St. N1 56 BY36
Hawfield Bank, Orp. 89 CP55
Hawfield Gdns., St.Alb. 18 BG16
Hawgood St. E3 57 CE39
Hawk Clo., Wal.Abb. 22 CH20
Hawkdene E4 30 CE25
Hawke Pk. Rd. N22 47 BY31
Hawke Pl. SE16 67 CC41
Middleton Dr.
Hawke Rd. SE19 77 BZ50
Hawkenbury, Harl. 13 CL12
Hawker Clo., Wall. 95 BX57
Hawkes Clo., Grays 71 DD43
Hawkes Ms. SE10 67 CF43
Luton Pl.
Hawkes Rd., Mitch. 86 BU51
Hawkesbury Rd. SW15 75 BP46
Hawkesfield Rd. SE23 77 CD48
Hawkesley Clo., Twick. 74 BJ49
Hawkewood Rd., Sun. 83 BA52
Hawkfield Ct., Islw. 64 BH44
Hawkhirst Rd., Ken. 105 BZ61
Hawkhurst, Cob. 93 BF60
Hawkhurst Gdns., Chess. 94 BL56
Orchard St.
Hawkhurst Gdns., Rom. 41 CS29
Hawkhurst Rd. SW16 86 BW51
Hawkhurst Way, N.Mal. 85 BN53
Hawkhurst Way, W.Wick. 87 CE55
Hawkinge Wk., Orp. 89 CO52
Robin Way
Hawkinge Way, Horn. 60 CV36
Hawkins Ave., Grav. 81 DH49
Hawkins Clo., Borwd. 28 BN23
Hawkins Clo., Har. 45 BG33
Hawkins Rd., Tedd. 74 BJ50
Hawkley Gdns. SE27 76 BY48
Hawkridge Clo., Rom. 50 CP32
Hawks Hill, Lthd. 102 BH65
Hawks Hill Clo., Lthd. 102 BH64
Hawks Ms. SE10 67 CF43
Luton Pl.
Hawks Nest, The, Wok. 100 AR65
Hawks Rd., Kings.T. 85 BL51
Hawkshaw Clo. SW2 76 BX47
Coniston Rd.
Hawkshead La., Hat. 19 BQ17
Hawkshead Rd. NW10 55 BO36
Hawkshead Rd. W4 65 BO41
Hawkshead Rd., Pot.B. 20 BS18
Hawkshill, St.Alb. 9 BJ14
Hawkshill Clo., Esher 93 BF57
Hawkshill Dr., Hem.H. 7 AV15
Hawkshill Way, Esher 93 BF57
Hawkslade Rd. SE15 77 CC46
Hawksley Rd. N16 48 BZ34
Hawksmead Clo., Enf. 30 CC21
Hawksmoor, Rad. 19 BM20
Hawksmoor Clo. E6 58 CK39
Allhallows Rd.
Hawksmoor Grn., Brwd. 122 DE25
Hawksmoor Ms. E1 57 CB40
Cable St.
Hawksmoor St. W6 65 BQ43
Hawksmouth E4 39 CF26
Hawkstone Rd. SE16 67 CC42
Hawksway, Stai. 72 AV48
Hawkswell Clo., Wok. 100 AP62
Hawkswell Wk. N1 57 BZ37
Basire St.
Hawkswood Est., Chis. 88 CM52
Hawkswood Gro., Slou. 52 AS36
Hawkswood La., Ger.Cr. 43 AS35
Hawksworth Clo., Nthwd. 35 BB29
Hawkwell Wk. N1 57 BZ37
Basire St.
Hawkwood Cres. E4 30 CE25
Hawkwood Dell, Kes. 111 BF66
Hawkwood La., Chis. 88 CM51
Hawkwood Mt. E5 48 CB33
Hawkwood Ri., Lthd. 111 BF66
Hawlands Dr., Pnr. 45 BE33
Hawley Clo., Hmptn. 74 BE50
Hawley Cres. NW1 56 BV36
Hawley Ms. NW1 56 BV36
Hawley St.
Hawley Rd. NW1 56 BV36
Hawley Rd., Dart. 80 CW48
Hawley St. NW1 56 BV36
Hawley Way, Ashf. 73 AZ49
Haws La., Stai. 73 AW46
Hawstead La., Orp. 98 CQ56
Hawstead Rd. SE6 77 CE46
Hawsted, Buck.H. 40 CH26
Hawthorn Ave. N13 38 BX28
Hawthorn Ave., Brwd. 122 DC27
Hawthorn Ave., Cars. 95 BV57
Hawthorn Ave., Rain. 59 CU38
Hawthorn Ave., Th.Hth. 86 BY51
Hawthorn Clo., Hmptn. 74 BF49
Hawthorn Clo., Orp. 88 CM53
Hawthorn Clo., Oxt. 115 CH70
Holland La.
Hawthorn Clo., Red. 121 BV73
Hawthorn Clo., Wat. 28 BB22
Hawthorn Clo., Wok. 100 AS63
Hawthorn Ct., Sutt. 95 BS56
Hawthorn Cres. SW17 76 BV49
Hawthorn Cres., Croy. 96 CC59
Hawthorn Dr., Har. 45 BE32
Hawthorn Dr., Uxb. 53 AX36
Hawthorn Dr., W.Wick. 97 CG56
Hawthorn Gdns. W5 64 BK41
Hawthorn Gro. SE20 87 CB51
Hawthorn Gro., Barn. 28 BO25
Hawthorn Gro., Enf. 30 BZ22
Hawthorn Hatch, Brent. 64 BJ43
Hawthorn La., Hem.H. 7 AV13
Hawthorn La., Sev. 107 CT64

Hawthorn Ms. NW7 37 BQ30
Holders Hill Rd.
Hawthorn Pl., Erith 69 CS42
Hawthorn Pl., Hayes 53 BB40
Hawthorn Rd. N8 47 BW31
Hawthorn Rd. N18 39 CA29
Hawthorn Rd. NW10 55 BP36
Hawthorn Rd., Bexh. 79 CQ46
Hawthorn Rd., Brent. 64 BJ43
Hawthorn Rd., Buck.H. 40 CJ28
Hawthorn Rd., Dart. 80 CV47
Hawthorn Rd., Hodd. 12 CE11
Hawthorn Rd., Stai. 72 AU49
Hawthorn Rd., Sutt. 95 BT56
Hawthorn Rd., Wall. 95 BV57
Hawthorn Rd., Wok. 100 AR63
Hawthorn Rd. 100 AV65
(Sendmarsh), Wok.
Hawthorn Wk. W10 55 BR38
Droop St.
Hawthorn Way N9 39 CA27
Hawthorn Way, Chesh. 16 AO18
Hawthorn Way, St.Alb. 18 BF16
Hawthorn Way, Shep. 83 BA52
Hawthorn Way, Stai. 73 AX47
Diamedes Ave.
Hawthorn Way, Wey. 92 AW58
Hawthorndene Clo., 88 CG55
Brom.
Hawthorndene Rd., Brom. 88 CG55
Hawthorne Ave., Chsnt. 21 CB19
Hawthorne Ave., Har. 45 BJ32
Hawthorne Ave., Mitch. 86 BT51
Hawthorne Ave., Ruis. 44 BC33
Hawthorne Ave., West. 106 CJ61
Hawthorne Clo. N1 57 CA36
Hawthorne Clo., Brom. 88 CK52
Hawthorne Clo., Chsnt. 21 CB19
Hawthorne Clo., Sutt. 86 BT55
Hawthorne Cres., Slou. 52 AP39
Hawthorne Cres., S.Croy. 96 CC58
Hawthorne Cres., West 63 AY41
Dr.
Hawthorne Fm. Ave., 54 BE37
Nthlt.
Hawthorne Gro. NW9 46 BN33
Hawthorne Ms., Grnf. 54 BG39
Hawthorne Pl., Epsom 94 BO59
Hawthorne Rd. E17 48 CE31
Hawthorne Rd., Brom. 88 CK52
Hawthorne Rd., Rad. 18 BJ20
Hawthorne Way, Guil. 109 AT69
Hawthornes, Hat. 10 BO13
Hawthornes, Rick. 34 AU28
Hawthorns, Welw.G.C. 5 BQ7
Hawthorns, Wdf.Grn. 40 CH27
Hawthorns, The, Berk. 7 AQ12
Hawthorns, The, Epsom 94 BP57
Hawthorns, The, Hem.H. 7 AV15
Beechwood Pk.
Hawthorns, The, Loug. 31 CL24
Hawthorns, The, Slou. 62 AV44
Raymond Clo.
Hawtrees, Rad. 27 BH21
Hawtrey Ave., Nthlt. 54 BD37
Hawtrey Clo., Slou. 62 AQ41
Hawtrey Dr., Ruis. 44 BC33
Hawtrey Rd. NW3 56 BT36
Hawtrey Rd., Wind. 61 AO44
Haxtead Rd., Brom. 88 CH51
Hay Clo. E15 58 CG36
Hay Clo., Borwd. 28 BN23
Hay Currie St. E14 57 CE39
Hay Hill W1 3 **K1**
Hay Hill W1 56 BV40
Hay La. NW9 46 BN31
Hay La., Slou. 43 AR35
Haybourn Mead, Hem.H. 8 AW14
Haycroft Clo., Ken. 104 BZ62
Haycroft Gdns. NW10 55 BP37
Haycroft Rd. SW2 76 BX46
Haycroft Rd., Surb. 84 BK55
Hayday Rd. E16 58 CH39
Hayden Ct., Wey. 92 AW59
Hayden Pl., Guil. 118 AR71
Hayden Way, Rom. 41 CS30
Haydens Clo., Orp. 89 CP54
Haydens Pl. W11 55 BR39
Haydens Rd., Harl. 13 CM11
Haydn Ave., Pur. 95 BY60
Haydns Ms. W3 55 BN39
Haydock Ave., Nthlt. 54 BE36
Haydock Grn., Horn. 51 CW35
Haydock Grn., Nthlt. 54 BF36
Haydon Clo. NW9 46 BN31
Haydon Clo., Enf. 30 BZ25
Mortimer Dr.
Haydon Dr., Pnr. 44 BC31
Haydon Pk. Rd. SW19 76 BS49
Haydon Rd., Dag. 50 CP34
Haydon Rd., Wat. 27 BE25
Haydon Sq. E1 57 CA39
Haydon St. EC3 2 **P10**
Haydon St. EC3 57 CA40
Haydon Wk. E1 2 **Q10**
Haydons Rd. SW19 76 BS49
Hayes, The, Epsom 103 BN63
Hayes Barton, Wok. 100 AV61
Hayes Chase, W.Wick. 87 CF53
Hayes Clo., Brom. 88 CH55
Hayes Clo., Grays 70 DB43
Hayes Ct. SW2 76 BX47
Hayes Cres. NW11 46 BR32
Hayes Cres., Sutt. 94 BQ56
Hayes Dr., Rain. 59 CU36
Hayes End Clo., Hayes 53 BA38
Hayes End Dr., Hayes 53 BA38
Hayes End Rd., Hayes 53 BA38
Hayes Gdns., Brom. 88 CH55
Hayes Hill, Brom. 88 CG54
Hayes Hill Rd., Brom. 88 CG54
Hayes La., Beck. 87 CF52

Hayes La., Brom. 88 CH54
Hayes La., Ken. 104 BY61
Hayes Mead, Brom. 88 CG54
Hayes Pl. NW1 1 **D5**
Hayes Pl. NW1 56 BU39
Hayes Rd., Brom. 88 CH52
Hayes Rd., Green. 80 CZ47
Hayes Rd., Sthl. 63 BC42
Hayes St., Brom. 88 CH54
Hayes Wk., Brox. 21 CD16
Hayes Way, Beck. 87 CF52
Hayes Wd. Ave., Brom. 88 CH54
Hayesford Pk. Dr., Brom. 88 CG53
Hayesford Pk. Est., Brom. 88 CH53
Hayfield Clo., Bush. 27 BF24
Hayfield Pas. E1 57 CC38
Hayfield Rd., Orp. 89 CO53
Haygarth Pl. SW19 75 BU49
Haygreen Clo., Kings.T. 75 BN50
Hayland Clo. NW9 46 BN31
Hayles St. SE11 4 **F8**
Hayles St. SE11 66 BY42
Hayling Ave., Felt. 73 BC48
Hayling Rd., Wat. 35 BC27
Haymaker Clo., Uxb. 53 AY36
Honey Hill
Hayman Cres., Hayes 53 BA37
Haymarket SW1 3 **N1**
Haymarket SW1 56 BW40
Haymarket Arc. SW1 3 **N1**
Haymeads, Welw.G.C. 5 BR6
Haymeads Dr., Esher 93 BG57
Haymeads Hill, Welw.G.C. 5 BS8
Haymer Gdns., Wor.Pk. 85 BP55
Haymerle Rd. SE15 67 CB43
Hayne Rd., Beck. 87 CD51
Hayne St. EC1 2 **G6**
Hayne St. EC1 56 BY39
Haynes Clo. N11 38 BU27
Haynes Clo. N17 39 CB29
Haynes Clo. SE3 68 CG45
Haynes Clo., Slou. 62 AS42
Haynes Clo., Welw.G.C. 5 BS8
Haynes La. SE19 77 CA50
Haynes Mead, Berk. 7 AQ12
Haynes Rd., Grav. 81 DF48
Haynes Rd., Horn. 51 CV32
Haynt Wk. SW20 85 BR52
Hays La. SE1 4 **M3**
Hays La. SE1 57 CA40
Hays Ms. W1 3 **J2**
Hays Ms. W1 56 BV40
Hays Wk., Sutt. 94 BQ58
Hayse Hill, Wind. 61 AL44
Haysleigh Gdns. SE20 87 CB51
Haysoms Clo., Rom. 50 CT31
Ingrave Rd.
Haystall Clo., Hayes 53 BB37
Hayter Rd. SW2 76 BX46
Hayton Clo. E8 57 CA36
Forest Rd.
Haywains, Oxt. 114 CF68
Hayward Clo. SW19 86 BS51
Hayward Clo., Bex. 79 CS46
Bourne Rd.
Hayward Gdns. SW15 75 BQ46
Hayward Rd. N20 38 BT27
Haywards Clo., Brwd. 122 DF25
Haywards Clo., Dart. 79 CS46
Haywards Mead (Eton 61 AN42
Wick), Wind.
Haywards Pl. EC1 2 **F5**
Haywards Pl. EC1 56 BY38
Sekforde St.
Haywood Clo., Pnr. 36 BD30
Haywood Ct., Wal.Abb. 22 CG20
Haywood Pk., Rick. 25 AV25
Haywood Ri., Orp. 97 CN56
Haywood Rd., Brom. 88 CJ52
Hayworth Clo., Enf. 30 CD23
Hazel Ave., Guil. 109 AR68
Hazel Ave., West Dr. 63 AZ41
Hazel Bank, Surb. 85 BN54
Hazel Clo. N13 39 BZ27
Hazel Clo. N19 47 BW34
Hargrave Pk.
Hazel Clo. SE15 67 CB44
Hazel Clo., Brent. 64 BJ43
Hazel Clo., Croy. 87 CC54
Hazel Clo., Egh. 72 AQ50
Hazel Clo., Horn. 50 CU34
Hazel Clo., Mitch. 86 BW52
Hazel Clo., Reig. 121 BT71
Hazel Clo., Twick. 74 BG47
Hazel Clo., Welw.G.C. 5 BR5
Hazel Clo., Wem. 55 BL37
Carlyon Rd.
Hazel Cft., Pnr. 36 BF29
Hazel Dr., Erith 69 CU44
Hazel Dr., Wok. 100 AV65
Hazel End, Swan. 89 CT53
Hazel Gdns., Edg. 37 BM28
Hazel Gdns., Grays 71 DF41
Hazel Gro. SE26 77 CC49
Hazel Gro., Enf. 30 CB25
Dimsdale Dr.
Hazel Gro., Hat. 10 BO14
Hazel Gro., Orp. 88 CL55
Hazel Gro., Rom. 50 CQ31
Hazel Gro., Stai. 73 AW50
Hazel Gro., Wat. 26 BC21
Hazel Gro., Welw.G.C. 5 BS7
Hazel Gro., Wem. 55 BL37
Carlyon Rd.
Hazel La., Rich. 75 BL48
Hazel Mead, Barn. 28 BP25
Hazel Mead, Epsom 94 BP58
Hazel Ri., Horn. 51 CV32
Hazel Rd. E15 49 CG35
Wingfield Rd.
Hazel Rd. NW10 55 BQ38
Hazel Rd., Berk. 7 AR13

Hazel Rd., Dart. 80 CV…
Hazel Rd., Erith 69 CL…
Hazel Rd., Reig. 121 BT…
Hazel Rd., St.Alb. 18 BC…
Hazel Rd., Wey. 91 AV…
Hazel Tree Rd., Wat. 26 BC…
Hazel Wk., Brom. 88 CL…
Hazel Wk., Dor. 119 BK…
Homesdale Rd.
Hazel Way E4 39 CD…
Hazel Way SE1 4
Hazel Way SE1 67 CA…
Alscot Rd.
Hazel Way, Lthd. 102 BG…
Hazel Way, Slou. 52 AF…
Hazelbank Rd. SE6 77 CF…
Hazelbank Rd., Cher. 83 BD…
Hazelbourne Rd. SW12 76 BV…
Hazelbrouck Gdns., Ilf. 40 CM…
Hazelbury Ave., Abb.L. 17 BA…
Hazelbury Grn. N9 39 CA…
Hazelbury La. N9 39 CA…
Hazelcroft Clo., Uxb. 53 AY…
Hazeldean Rd. NW10 55 BN…
Hazeldell Link, Hem.H. 7 AV…
Lindlings
Hazelden Clo., Sev. 99 DA…
Hazeldene, Wey. 92 AX…
Crockford Pk. Rd.
Hazeldene, Wey. 92 AX…
Hazeldene Clo., Wey. 92 AX…
Crockford Pk. Rd.
Hazeldene Ct., Ken. 105 BZ…
Hazeldene Dr., Pnr. 45 BD…
Hazeldene Gdns., Uxb. 53 BA…
Hazeldene Rd., Ilf. 50 CO…
Hazeldene Rd., Well. 69 CP…
Hazeldon Rd. SE4 77 CD…
Hazeleigh, Brwd. 122 DD…
Hazeleigh Gdns., 40 CK…
Wdf.Grn.
Hazelgreen Clo. N21 38 BY…
Hazelhurst, Beck. 87 CF…
Hazelhurst Clo., Guil. 109 AT…
Weybrook Dr.
Hazelhurst Rd. SW17 76 BT…
Hazell Cres., Rom. 41 CR…
Hazells Rd., Grav. 81 DD…
Hazellville Rd. N19 47 BW…
Hazelmere Clo., Felt. 73 BA…
Hazelmere Clo., Lthd. 102 BJ…
Hazelmere Clo., Nthlt. 54 BE…
Hazelmere Dr., Nthlt. 54 BE…
Hazelmere Rd.
Hazelmere Gdns., Horn. 51 CU…
Hazelmere Rd. NW6 55 BT…
Hazelmere Rd., Nthlt. 54 BE…
Hazelmere Rd., Orp. 88 CM…
Hazelmere Rd., St.Alb. 9 BK…
Hazelmere Wk., Nthlt. 54 BE…
Hazelmere Way, Brom. 88 CH…
Hazeltree La., Nthlt. 54 BE…
Hazelwood, S.le H. 71 DK…
Hazelwood Ave., Mord. 86 BS…
Hazelwood Clo. W5 65 BL…
Hazelwood Clo., Chesh. 16 AO…
Hazelwood Clo., Har. 45 BF…
Hazelwood Ct., Surb. 85 BL…
Hazelwood Cres. N13 38 BY…
Hazelwood Cres. W10 55 BR…
Hazelwood Dr., Pnr. 35 BC…
Hazelwood Dr., St.Alb. 9 BK…
Hazelwood Gdns., Brwd. 33 DA…
Hazelwood Ho. SE8 67 CD…
Hazelwood La. N13 38 BY…
Hazelwood La., Abb.L. 17 BA…
Hazelwood La., Couls. 104 BU…
Hazelwood Pk. Clo., Chig. 40 CN…
Hazelwood Rd. E17 48 CD…
Hazelwood Rd., Enf. 30 CA…
Hazelwood Rd., Oxt. 115 CH…
Hazelwood Rd., Rick. 26 BA…
Hazelwood Rd., Sev. 97 CM…
Hazelwood Rd., Wok. 100 AO…
Southwood Ave.
Hazlebury Rd. SW6 66 BS…
Hazledean Rd., Croy. 87 BZ…
Hazledene, Wal.Cr. 21 CC…
Eastfield Rd.
Hazledene Rd. W4 65 BN…
Hazlemere Clo., Lthd. 102 BJ…
Hazlemere Gdns., 85 BP…
Wor.Pk.
Hazlemere Rd., Slou. 52 AQ…
Hazlewell Rd. SW15 75 BP…
Hazlewood, Loug. 31 CJ…
Hazlewood Cres. W10 55 BR…
Hazlewood Gro., S.Croy. 96 CB…
Hazlitt Rd. W14 65 BR…
Hazon Way, Epsom 94 BN…
Heacham Ave., Uxb. 44 BA…
Head St. E1 57 CC…
Headcorn Pl., Th.Hth. 86 BX…
Headcorn Rd. N17 39 CA…
Tenterden Rd.
Headcorn Rd., Brom. 78 CG…
Headcorn Rd., Th.Hth. 86 BX…
Headfort Pl. SW1 3 **H…**
Headfort Pl. SW1 66 BV…
Heading St. N4 47 BV…
Headingley Clo., Chsnt. 21 CA…
Holbeck La.
Headingley Clo., Ilf. 40 CN…
Wickets Way
Headington Rd. SW18 76 BT…
Headlam Rd. SW4 76 BW…
Headlam St. E1 57 CB…
Headley App., Ilf. 49 CL…
Headley Ave., Wall. 95 BX…
Headley Chase, Brwd. 42 DB…
Headley Clo., Epsom 94 BM…

adley Common Rd., 112 BN67
psom
adley Dr., Croy. 96 CE57
adley Dr., Epsom 103 BP63
adley Dr., Ilf. 49 CL32
adley Gro., Tad. 103 BP63
adley Heath App., 112 BM69
ad.
adley Rd., Dor. 111 BK68
adley Rd., Epsom 103 BM62
adley Rd., Epsom 103 BN64
adley Rd., Lthd. 102 BK64
ads Ms. W2 56 BS39
rtesian Rd.
adstone Dr., Har. 45 BG31
adstone Gdns., Har. 45 BG31
adstone La., Har. 45 BF31
adstone Rd., Har. 45 BG32
adway, The, Epsom 94 BO58
ald St. SE14 67 CE44
aley Dr., Orp. 97 CN56
aley Rd., Wat. 26 BB25
aley St. NW1 56 BV36
anor Ct. E5 48 CC35
lapton Pk. Est.
ards La., Brwd. 122 DC23
arn Ri., Nthlt. 54 BD37
arn Rd., Rom. 50 CT32
arn St. EC2 2 N5
arn St. EC2 57 CA38
urtain Rd.
arne Ct., Ch.St.G. 34 AQ27
Gordon Way
arne Rd. W4 65 BM42
arnes Clo., Beac. 34 AO28
arnes Mead, Beac. 34 AO28
arns Bldgs. SE17 4 L9
arns Bldgs. SE17 67 BZ42
lsted St.
arns Clo., Orp. 89 CP52
arns Ri., Orp. 89 CP52
arns Rd., Orp. 89 CP52
arnville Rd. SW12 76 BV47
ath, The W7 54 BH40
ower Boston Rd.
ath, The, Cat. 105 BZ65
ath, The, Rad. 18 BJ20
ath Ave., Bexh. 69 CP43
ath Ave., St.Alb. 9 BG12
ath Brow NW3 47 BT34
North End Way
ath Brow, Hem.H. 8 AX14
Heath La.
ath Clo. NW11 47 BS33
ath Clo. W5 55 BL38
ath Clo., Bans. 95 BS60
ath Clo., Hayes 63 BA43
ath Clo., Hem.H. 8 AX14
ath Clo., Orp. 89 CP54
ath Clo., Pot.B. 20 BS18
ath Clo., Rom. 50 CU31
ath Clo., Stai. 73 AX46
ath Clo., Vir.W. 82 AR52
ath Ct. W5 55 BL38
ath Cft. NW11 47 BS33
ath Dr. NW3 47 BS35
ath Dr. SW20 85 BQ52
ath Dr., Epp. 31 CN21
ath Dr., Pot.B. 20 BS18
ath Dr., Rom. 41 CU30
ath Dr., Sutt. 95 BT58
ath Dr., Tad. 112 BP66
ath Dr., Wok. 100 AT64
ath End Rd., Bex. 79 CT47
ath Fm. Ct., Wat. 26 BA22
Grove Mill La.
ath Fm. La., St.Alb. 9 BH12
ath Gdns., Twick. 74 BH47
ath Gro. SE20 77 CC50
ath Hill, Dor. 119 BJ71
ath Ho. La., Wok. 100 AO64
ath Hurst Rd. NW3 47 BT35
Keats Gro.
ath La. SE3 67 CF44
ath La., Dart. 79 CU48
ath La., Hem.H. 8 AX14
ath La. Lower, Dart. 80 CV47
ath La. Upper, Dart. 79 CU47
ath Mead SW19 75 BQ48
ath Pk. Ct., Rom. 50 CU32
ath Pk. Dr., Brom. 88 CK52
ath Pk. Rd., Rom. 50 CU32
ath Ridge Grn., Cob. 93 BF60
ath Ri. SW15 75 BQ46
ath Ri., Brom. 88 CG53
ath Ri., Dor. 119 BG72
ath Ri., Vir.W. 82 AR52
ath Ri., Wok. 101 AW65
ath Rd. SW8 66 BV44
ath Rd., Bex. 79 CS47
ath Rd., Cat. 105 BZ65
ath Rd., Dart. 79 CT46
ath Rd., Grays 71 DF40
ath Rd., Har. 45 BG33
ath Rd., Houns. 64 BF45
ath Rd., Lthd. 93 BG59
ath Rd., Pot.B. 20 BS18
ath Rd., Rom. 50 CP33
ath Rd., St.Alb. 9 BH12
ath Rd., Th.Hth. 87 BZ52
ath Rd., Twick. 74 BH47
ath Rd., Uxb. 53 BA38
ath Rd., Wat. 36 BD26
ath Rd., Wey. 92 AZ56
ath Rd., Wok. 100 AS61
ath Side NW3 47 BT35
ath Side, Houns. 74 BE47
ath Side, Orp. 88 CM54
ath St. NW3 47 BT34
ath St., Bark. 58 CM37
ath St., Dart. 80 CV47
ath Vw. N2 47 BT31
ath Vw., Lthd. 110 BB66
ath Vw. Clo. N2 47 BT31

Heath Vw. Gdns., Grays 71 DE41
Heath Vw. Rd., Grays 71 DE41
Heath Vill. SE18 68 CN42
Heath Way, Erith 69 CS44
Heath Way, West Dr. 53 AX40
Heatham Pk., Twick. 74 BH47
Heathbourne Rd., Bush. 36 BH26
Heathclose Rd., Dart. 79 CU47
Heathcote, Tad. 103 BQ64
Heathcote Ave., Hat. 10 BP11
Heathcote Ave., Ilf. 40 CK30
Heathcote Gro. E4 39 CF27
Heathcote Rd., Epsom 94 BN60
Heathcote Rd., Twick. 74 BJ46
Heathcote St. WC1 2 B4
Heathcote St. WC1 56 BX38
Heathcote Way, West Dr. 53 AX40
Tavistock Rd.
Heathcroft W5 55 BL38
Heathcroft Ave., Sun. 73 BB50
Heathcroft Grn., Sun. 73 BB50
Heathdale Ave., Houns. 64 BE45
Heathdene, Tad. 103 BR62
Canons La.
Heathdene Dr., Belv. 69 CR42
Heathdene Rd. SW16 76 BX50
Heathdene Rd., Wall. 95 BV57
Heathdown Rd., Wok. 100 AU61
Heathedge SE26 77 CB48
Heathend Rd., Bex. 79 CT47
Heather Ave., Rom. 41 CS30
Heather Clo. E6 58 CL39
Heather Clo. SW8 66 BV45
Heather Clo., Brwd. 42 DB25
Heather Clo., Brwd. 33 DA25
Heather Clo., Guil. 118 AQ69
Heather Clo., Hmptn. 84 BE51
Heather Clo., Islw. 74 BG46
Heather Clo., Rom. 41 CS30
Heather Clo., Tad. 103 BR64
Heather Clo., Uxb. 53 AY39
Heather Clo., Wey. 92 AW58
Heather Clo., Wok. 100 AR61
Heather Dr., Dart. 79 CU47
Heather Dr., Enf. 29 BY23
Chasewood Ave.
Heather Dr., Rom. 41 CS30
Heather Gdns. NW11 46 BR32
Heather Gdns., Rom. 41 CS30
Heather Gdns., Sutt. 95 BS57
Heather Glen, Rom. 41 CS30
Heather La., West Dr. 53 AY39
Heather Mt., Guil. 118 AP69
Heather Pk. Dr., Wem. 55 BM36
Heather Pl., Esher 93 BF56
Heather Ri., Bush. 27 BE23
Heather Rd. NW2 46 BO34
Heather Rd. SE12 78 CH48
Heather Rd., Welw.G.C. 5 BQ9
Heather Wk. W10 55 BR38
Droop St.
Heather Wk., Edg. 37 BM28
Heather Wk., Houns. 74 BF47
Stephenson Rd.
Heather Wk., Walt. 92 BB58
Heather Way, Hem.H. 8 AX13
Heather Way, Pot.B. 19 BR19
Heather Way, Rom. 41 CS30
Heather Way, S.Croy. 96 CC58
Heather Way, Stan. 36 BH29
Heather Way, Wok. 91 AP57
Heatherbank SE9 68 CK44
Heatherbank, Chis. 88 CL51
Heatherdale Clo., Kings.T. 75 BM50
Heatherdean Clo., Mitch. 86 BT52
Heatherden Grn., Iver 52 AU37
Heatherdene, Lthd. 110 BA66
Heatherlands, Sun. 73 BC50
Heatherley Dr., Ilf. 49 CK31
Heathers, The, Stai. 73 AY47
Heathers Land, Dor. 119 BK73
Heatherset Gdns. SW16 76 BX50
Heatherside Dr., Vir.W. 82 AQ53
Heatherside Gdns., Slou. 43 AO34
Heatherside Rd., Epsom 94 BN57
Heatherside Rd., Sid. 79 CP48
Bexley La.
Heatherton Ter. N3 38 BS30
Squires La.
Heathervale Rd., Wey. 92 AW58
Heatherwood Clo. E12 49 CJ34
Heatherwood Dr., Hayes 53 BA37
Heathfield E4 39 CF27
Heathfield, Chis. 78 CM50
Heathfield, Cob. 93 BF60
Heathfield Ave. SW18 76 BT47
Heathfield Clo. E16 58 CJ39
Heathfield Clo., Hert. 20 BS18
Church Rd.
Heathfield Clo., Kes. 97 CJ56
Heathfield Clo., Pot.B. 20 BS18
Heathfield Clo., Wok. 100 AT62
Heathfield Ct. W4 65 BN42
Heathfield Ter.
Heathfield Ct., St.Alb. 9 BH13
Avenue Rd.
Heathfield Dr., Mitch. 86 BU51
Heathfield Dr., Red. 121 BU73
Heathfield Gdns. NW11 46 BQ32
Heathfield Gdns. SW18 76 BT46
Heathfield Gdns. W4 65 BN42
Heathfield Gdns., Croy. 96 BZ56
Heathfield Rd.
Heathfield La., Chis. 78 CL50
Heathfield N., Twick. 74 BH47
Heathfield Pk. NW2 55 BQ36
Heathfield Ri., Ruis. 44 BA33
Heathfield Rd. SW18 76 BT46
Heathfield Rd. W3 65 BM41
Heathfield Rd., Bexh. 69 CQ45
Heathfield Rd., Brom. 78 CG50
Heathfield Rd., Bush. 27 BE24
Heathfield Rd., Croy. 96 BZ56
Heathfield Rd., Kes. 97 CJ56

Heathfield Rd., Sev. 107 CT64
Heathfield Rd., Walt. 93 BE56
Heathfield Rd., Wok. 100 AT62
Heathfield S., Twick. 74 BH47
Heathfield Sq. SW18 76 BT47
Heathfield St. W11 55 BR40
Portland Rd.
Heathfield Ter. SE18 68 CN43
Heathfield Ter. W4 65 BN42
Heathfield Vale, S.Croy. 96 CC58
Heathfield Way, Ger.Cr. 43 AR32
Heathfields Ct., Houns. 74 BE46
Heathlands Way
Heathgate NW11 47 BS32
Heathland Clo., Wok. 91 AS60
Heathland Rd. N16 48 CA33
Heathlands, The, Tad. 103 BR64
Heathlands Clo., Sun. 83 BC51
Heathlands Clo., Twick. 74 BH47
Heathlands Dr., St.Alb. 9 BH12
Heathlands Ri., Dart. 79 CU46
Heathlands Way, Houns. 74 BE46
Heathlee Rd. SE3 68 CG45
Heathlee Rd., Dart. 79 CT46
Heathley End, Chis. 78 CM50
Heathrow Clo., West Dr. 63 AW44
Heaths Clo., Enf. 30 CA23
Heathside, Esher 84 BH55
Heathside, Wey. 92 AZ56
Heathside Ave., Bexh. 69 CQ44
Heathside Clo., Esher 84 BH55
Heathside Clo., Nthwd. 35 BA28
Heathside Cres., Wok. 100 AS62
Heathside Gdns., Wok. 100 AT62
Heathside Pk. Rd., Wok. 100 AS62
Heathside Rd., Nthwd. 35 BA28
Heathside Rd., Wok. 100 AS62
Heathstan Rd. W12 55 BP39
Heathurst Rd., S.Croy. 96 BZ58
Heathview Ave., Dart. 79 CT47
Heathview Cres., Dart. 79 CU47
Heathview Dr. SE2 69 CP43
Heathview Gdns. SW15 75 BQ47
Heathview Rd., Th.Hth. 86 BT52
Heathville Rd. N19 47 BX33
Heathwall St. SW11 66 BU45
Heathway SE3 68 CH43
Heathway, Cat. 114 BZ66
Heathway, Croy. 87 CD55
Heathway, Dag. 50 CQ34
Heathway, Iver 52 AU37
Heathway, Lthd. 101 BB65
Heathway, Wdf.Grn. 40 CJ28
Heathwood Gdns. SE7 68 CK42
Heathwood Gdns., Swan. 89 CS51
Heathwood Wk., Bex. 79 CT47
Heaton Ave., Rom. 41 CU29
Heaton Clo., Rom. 42 CV29
Heaton Gra. Rd., Rom. 41 CT30
Heaton Rd. SE15 67 CB45
Heaton Rd., Mitch. 76 BV50
Heaton Way, Rom. 42 CV29
Heaver Rd. SW11 66 BT45
Wye St.
Heaverham Rd., Sev. 108 CX62
Heavitree Rd. SE18 68 CM42
Heayfield, Welw.G.C. 5 BT7
Hebdon Rd. SW17 76 BU48
Heber Rd. NW2 46 BQ35
Heber Rd. SE22 77 CA46
Hebron Rd. W6 65 BP41
Hecham Clo. E17 39 CD30
Heckfield Pl. SW6 66 BS43
Fulham Rd.
Heckford St. E1 57 CC40
The Highway
Hector St. SE18 68 CN42
Heddington Gro. N7 47 BX35
Heddon Clo., Islw. 64 BJ45
Heddon Ct. Ave., Barn. 29 BU25
Heddon Rd., Barn. 29 BU25
Heddon St. W1 1 L10
Heddon St. W1 56 BW40
Hedge Brooms, Welw.G.C. 5 BT7
New Wd.
Hedge Hill, Enf. 29 BY23
Hedge La. N13 38 BY27
Hedge Pl. Rd., Green. 80 CZ46
Hedge Row, Ger.Cr. 34 AS29
Hedge Wk. SE6 77 CE49
Lushington Rd.
Hedgeley, Ilf. 49 CK31
Hedgeley St. SE12 78 CG46
Hedgemans Rd., Dag. 59 CP36
Hedgemans Way, Dag. 59 CQ36
Hedgerley Ct., Wok. 100 AR62
Hedgerley Gdns., Grnf. 54 BG37
Hedgerley Hill, Slou. 43 AO34
Hedgerley La., Slou. 43 AP32
Hedgerows, Saw. 6 CQ6
Hedgers Gro. E9 57 CD36
Hedges Clo., Hat. 10 BP12
Stonecross Rd.
Hedgeside, Berk. 7 AT11
Hedgeside Rd., Nthwd. 35 BA28
Hedgeway, Guil. 118 AQ71
Hedgewood Gdns., Ilf. 49 CL31
Hedingham Clo. N1 57 BZ36
Poplar Rd.
Hedingham Clo. N1 57 BZ37
Popham Rd.
Hedingham Rd., Dag. 50 CO35
Hedingham Rd., Horn. 51 CX33
Hedley Ave., Grays 70 DB43
Hedley Rd., St.Alb. 9 BJ13
Hedley Rd., Twick. 74 BF47
Hedley Row N5 48 BZ35
Poets Rd.
Hedworth Ave., Wal.Cr. 21 CC20
Heenan Clo., Bark. 58 CM36
Glenny Rd.
Heene Rd., Enf. 30 BZ23
Heideck Gdns., Brwd. 122 DD27
Victors Cres.

Heigham Rd. E6 58 CJ36
Heighams, Harl. 13 CK12
Heighton Gdns., Croy. 95 BY56
Heights, The SE7 68 CJ42
Heights, The, Beck. 77 CF50
Heights, The, Hem.H. 8 AY12
Saturn Way
Heights, The, Loug. 31 CK23
Heights, The, Nthlt. 45 BE35
Heights Clo. SW20 75 BP50
Heights Clo., Bans. 103 BR61
Heiron St. SE17 67 BZ43
John Ruskin St.
Helby Rd. SW4 76 BW46
Helder Gro. SE12 78 CG47
Helder St., S.Croy. 96 BZ57
Heldmann Clo., Islw. 64 BG45
Helen Ave., Felt. 73 BC47
Helen Clo. N2 47 BT31
Thomas More Way
Helen Clo., Dart. 79 CU47
Havelock Rd.
Helen Clo., E.Mol. 84 BF52
Helen Rd., Horn. 51 CV31
Helen St. SE18 68 CL42
Helena Clo., Barn. 29 BT22
Helena Clo., Wall. 95 BX57
Helena Ct. W5 54 BK39
Eaton Ri.
Helena Rd. E13 58 CG37
Helena Rd. E17 48 CE32
Helena Rd. NW10 46 BP35
Helena Rd. W5 54 BK39
Helena Rd., Wind. 61 AO44
Helens Pl. E2 57 CC38
Roman Rd.
Helenslea Ave. NW11 46 BR33
Helford Clo., Ruis. 44 BB34
Chichester Ave.
Helford Ct., S.Ock. 60 DA40
Cample La.
Helford Wk., Wok. 100 AQ62
Muirfield Rd.
Helford Way, Upmin. 51 CY32
Helgiford Gdns., Sun. 73 BB50
Helions Rd., Harl. 13 CL11
Helix Gdns. SW2 76 BX46
Helix Rd. SW2 76 BX46
Helleborine, Grays 71 DC42
Helling St. E1 57 CB40
Hermitage Wall
Helme Clo. SW19 75 BR49
Helmet Row EC1 2 J4
Helmet Row EC1 57 BZ38
Helmsdale, Wok. 100 AQ62
Winnington Way
Helmsdale Clo., Hayes 54 BE38
Berrydale Rd.
Helmsdale Clo., Rom. 41 CT29
Helmsdale Rd. SW16 86 BW51
Helmsdale Rd., Rom. 41 CT29
Helmsley Pl. E8 57 CB36
Helston Clo., Pnr. 36 BE29
Helston Dene, Hem.H. 8 AX11
Washington Ave.
Helston Gro., Hem.H. 8 AX11
Helston La., Wind. 61 AN44
Helston Pl., Abb.L. 17 BB19
Helvellyn Clo., Egh. 72 AU50
Helvetia St. SE6 77 CD48
Hemans St. SW8 66 BX43
Wandsworth Rd.
Hemberton Rd. SW9 66 BX45
Hemel Hempstead Rd., Hem.H. 8 BB14
Hemel Hempstead Rd., St.Alb. 9 BD14
Hemel Hempstead Rd., Wat. 26 BA21
Heming Rd., Edg. 37 BM29
Hemingford Rd. N1 56 BX37
Hemingford Rd., Sutt. 94 BQ56
Hemingford Rd., Wat. 26 BB21
Hemington Ave. N11 38 BU28
Hemlock Clo., Tad. 103 BR65
Hemlock Rd. W12 55 BO40
Hemmen La., Hayes 53 BB39
Hemming Clo., Hmptn. 84 BF51
Hemming St. E1 57 CB38
Hemming Way, Wat. 26 BC21
Hemmings, The, Berk. 7 AP13
Hemnall St., Epp. 22 CN19
Hemp Wk. SE17 4 L8
Hemp Wk. SE17 67 BZ42
Chatham St.
Hempshaw Ave., Bans. 104 BU61
Hempson Ave., Slou. 62 AR41
Hempstall, Welw.G.C. 5 BS9
Hempstead Clo., Buck.H. 40 CH27
Hempstead Rd. E17 48 CF31
Hempstead Rd., Berk. 7 AT12
Hempstead Rd., Hem.H. 16 AT16
Hempstead Rd., Kings L. 17 AY16
Hemsby Rd., Chess. 94 BL57
Hemstal Rd. NW6 56 BS36
Hemsted Rd., Erith 69 CT43
Hemswell Dr. NW9 37 BO30
Hemsworth Ct. N1 57 CA37
Hemsworth St.
Hemsworth St. N1 57 CA37
Hemus Pl. SW3 66 BU42
Chelsea Manor St.
Hemwood Rd., Wind. 61 AL45
Hen & Chickens Ct. EC4 56 BY39
Fleet St.
Hen Gro. Cres., Ashf. 73 AX48
Henbane Path, Rom. 42 CV29
Clematis Clo.
Henbit Clo., Tad. 103 BP63
Henbury Way, Wat. 36 BD27
Henchley Dene, Guil. 118 AU69
Henchman St. W12 55 BO39
Hencroft St., Slou. 62 AP41
Hendale Ave. NW4 46 BP31

Henderson Ave., Guil. 109 AQ68
Henderson Clo. NW10 55 BN36
Henderson Clo., Horn. 50 CU34
Henderson Clo., St.Alb. 9 BG11
Henderson Dr. NW8 1 A4
Henderson Dr. NW8 56 BT38
Henderson Dr., Dart. 70 CW45
Henderson Pl., Abb.L. 17 BB17
Henderson Rd. E7 58 CJ36
Henderson Rd. N9 39 CB26
Henderson Rd. SW18 76 CU47
Henderson Rd., Croy. 87 BZ53
Henderson Rd., West. 97 CJ59
Hendham Rd. SW17 76 BU48
Hendon Ave. N3 37 BR30
Hendon Gdns., Rom. 41 CS29
Hendon La. N3 46 BR31
Hendon Pk. Mans. NW4 46 BQ32
Hendon Pk. Row NW11 46 BR32
Hendon Rd. N9 39 CB27
Hendon Way NW2 46 BR33
Hendon Way NW4 46 BP32
Hendon Way, Stai. 73 AX46
Hendon Wd. La. NW7 37 BO25
Hendons Way, Maid. 61 AG42
Hendre Rd. SE1 4 N9
Hendre Rd. SE1 67 CA42
Hendren Clo., Grnf. 45 BG35
Dimmock Dr.
Hendrick Ave. SW12 76 BU47
Hendricks Ter. N17 48 CB31
Heneage Cres., Croy. 96 CF58
Heneage La. EC3 2 N9
Heneage La. EC3 57 CA39
Bevis Marks
Heneage St. E1 2 Q6
Heneage St. E1 57 CA39
Henfield Clo. N19 47 BW33
Henfield Clo., Bex. 79 CR46
Henfield Rd. SW19 85 BR51
Hengelo Gdns., Mitch. 86 BT52
Hengist Rd. SE12 78 CH47
Hengist Rd., Erith 69 CR43
Hengist Way, Brom. 87 CF52
Hengrave Rd. SE23 77 CC46
Hengrove Ct., Bex. 79 CQ47
Hurst Rd.
Henhurst Rd., Grav. 81 DJ50
Henley Ave., Sutt. 85 BR55
Henley Bank, Guil. 118 AQ71
Henley Clo., Green. 54 BG37
Henley Clo., Islw. 64 BH44
Henley Ct. N14 38 BW26
Henley Deane, Grav. 81 DF49
Henley Dr. SE1 4 Q8
Henley Dr., Kings.T. 75 BO50
Henley Gdns., Pnr. 44 BC31
Henley Gdns., Rom. 50 CQ32
Henley Rd. E16 68 CK41
Henley Rd. N18 39 CA28
Henley Rd. NW10 55 BQ37
Henley Rd., Ilf. 49 CM35
Henley St. SW11 66 BV44
Henley Way, Felt. 74 BD49
Hennel Clo. SE23 77 CC48
Henniker Gdns. E6 58 CJ38
Henniker Ms. SW3 66 BT44
Callow St.
Henniker Rd. E15 48 CF35
Henning St. SW11 66 BU44
Shuttleworth Rd.
Henningham Rd. N17 39 BZ30
Henrietta Ms. WC1 2 A4
Henrietta Ms. WC1 56 BX38
Brunswick Sq.
Henrietta Pl. W1 1 J8
Henrietta Pl. W1 56 BV39
Henrietta St. E15 48 CF35
Henrietta St. WC2 2 A10
Henrietta St. WC2 56 BX40
Henriques St. E1 57 CB39
Henry Cooper Way SE9 78 CJ49
Dunkery Rd.
Henry Darlot Dr. NW7 37 BQ28
Henry Dickens Ct. W11 55 BQ40
Henry Jackson Rd. SW15 65 BQ45
Henry Rd. E6 58 CK37
Henry Rd. N4 47 BY33
Henry Rd., Barn. 29 BT25
Henry Rd., Slou. 61 AO41
Henry St., Brom. 88 CH51
Henry St., Hem.H. 8 AX15
Henry Wells Sq., Hem.H. 8 AY11
Henrys Ave., Wdf.Grn. 40 CG28
Henrys Ter., Brwd. 24 DA20
Henrys Wk., Ilf. 40 CM29
Henryson Rd. SE4 77 CD46
Hensford Gdns. SE26 77 CB48
Wells Pk. Rd.
Henshall St. N1 57 BZ36
Henshaw St. SE17 4 K8
Henshaw St. SE17 67 BZ42
Henshawe Rd., Dag. 50 CP34
Henslow Way, Wok. 91 AU60
Henslowe Rd. SE22 77 CB46
Henson Ave. NW2 46 BQ35
Henson Clo., Orp. 88 CL55
Henson Path, Har. 45 BK31
Henson Pl., Nthlt. 54 BD37
Henstridge Pl. NW8 56 BU37
Hensworth Rd., Ashf. 73 AX49
Henty Clo. SW11 66 BU43
Henty Wk. SW15 75 BP46
Henville Rd., Brom. 88 CH51
Henwick Rd. SE9 68 CJ45
Henwood Rd. SE16 67 CC41
Henwood Side, Wdf.Grn. 40 CK29
Hepburn Gdns., W.Wick. 88 CG54
Hepburn Ms. SW11 76 BU46
Webbs Rd.
Hepple Clo., Islw. 64 BJ44
Hepplestone Clo. SW15 75 BP46
Dover Pk. Dr.
Hepscott Rd. E9 57 CE36

Hepworth Gdns., Bark. 50 CO35
Hepworth Rd. SW16 76 BX50
Hepworth Way, Walt. 83 BB54
Heracles Clo., Wall. 95 BX57
Herald Gdns., Wall. 86 BV55
Wandle Rd.
Herald St. E2 57 CB38
Herald Wk., Dart. 80 CW46
Heralds Ct. SE11 4 F9
Heralds Pl. SE11 4 E8
Heralds Pl. SE11 66 BY42
Gilbert Rd.
Herbal Hill EC1 2 E5
Herbal Hill EC1 56 BY38
Ray St.
Herbert Cres. SW1 3 F6
Herbert Cres. SW1 66 BU41
Pavilion Rd.
Herbert Cres., Wok. 100 AP62
Herbert Gdns. NW10 55 BP37
Herbert Gdns. W4 65 BM43
Magnolia Rd.
Herbert Gdns., Rom. 50 CP33
Herbert Rd. E12 49 CK35
Herbert Rd. E17 48 CD33
Herbert Rd. N11 38 BX29
Herbert Rd. N15 48 CA32
Herbert Rd. NW9 46 BP32
Herbert Rd. SE18 68 CL43
Herbert Rd. SW19 75 BR50
Herbert Rd., Bexh. 69 CQ44
Herbert Rd., Brom. 88 CJ53
Herbert Rd., Horn. 51 CW33
Herbert Rd., Ilf. 49 CN34
Herbert Rd., Kings.T. 85 BL52
Herbert Rd., Sthl. 54 BE40
Herbert Rd., Swan. 79 CU50
Herbert Rd., Swans. 81 DC46
Herbert St. E13 58 CH37
Herbert St. NW5 47 BV35
Herbert St., Hem.H. 8 AX13
Herbert St., Wat. 27 BD24
Herbrand St. WC1 1 Q4
Herbrand St. WC1 56 BX38
Hercies Rd., Uxb. 53 AY36
Hercules Pl. N7 47 BX34
Hercules St.
Hercules Rd. SE1 4 C7
Hercules Rd. SE1 66 BX41
Hercules St. N7 47 BX34
Hercules Yd. N7 47 BX34
Hercules St.
Hereford Ave., Barn. 38 BU26
Hereford Clo., Epsom 94 BN60
Hereford Clo., Guil. 118 AP69
Hereford Clo., Stai. 83 AW51
Hereford Clo., Wok. 100 AQ63
Hereford Gdns. SE13 77 CF46
Longhurst Rd.
Hereford Gdns., Ilf. 49 CK33
Hereford Gdns., Pnr. 45 BE32
Hereford Gdns., Twick. 74 BG47
Hereford Ms. W2 56 BS39
Hereford Rd.
Hereford Retreat SE15 67 CB43
Bird-in-Bush Rd.
Hereford Rd. E11 49 CH32
Hereford Rd. W2 56 BS39
Hereford Rd. W3 55 BM40
Hereford Rd. W5 64 BK41
Hereford Rd., Felt. 74 BD47
Hereford Sq. SW7 66 BT42
Hereford St. E2 57 CB38
Hereford Way, Chess. 93 BK56
Herent Dr., Ilf. 49 CK31
Hereward Ave., Pur. 95 BY59
Hereward Clo., Wal.Abb. 21 CF19
Hereward Gdns. N13 38 BY28
Hereward Rd. SW17 76 BU49
Herga Ct., Har. 45 BH34
Herga Ct., Wat. 26 BC23
Herga Rd., Har. 45 BH31
Herington Gro., Brwd. 122 DD26
Heriot Ave. E4 39 CD27
Heriot Rd. NW4 46 BQ32
Heriot Rd., Cher. 83 AW54
Heriots Clo., Stan. 36 BJ28
Heritage Clo., St.Alb. 9 BG13
High St.
Heritage Clo., Uxb. 53 AX38
Heritage Ct., Egh. 72 AT49
Station Rd.
Heritage Hill, Kes. 97 CJ56
Heritage Vw., Har. 45 BH34
Herkomer Clo., Bush. 27 BF25
Herkomer Rd., Bush. 27 BF25
Herlwyn Ave., Ruis. 45 BB34
Herlwyn Gdns. SW17 76 BU49
Hermes St. N1 2 D1
Hermes St. N1 56 BY37
Hermes Wk., Nthlt. 54 BF37
Leander Rd.
Hermes Way, Wall. 95 BW57
Hermiston Ave. N8 47 BX32
Hermit Rd. E16 58 CG39
Hermit St. EC1 2 F2
Hermit St. EC1 56 BY38
Hermitage, The SE23 77 CC47
Hermitage, The SW13 65 BO44
Hermitage, The, Felt. 73 BB48
St. Dunstans Rd.
Hermitage, The, Rich. 75 BL46
Hermitage, The, Uxb. 53 AX36
Hermitage Clo. E18 49 CG31
Hermitage Clo., Enf. 29 BY23
Hermitage Clo., Esher 93 BJ57
Hermitage Clo., Pot.B. 20 BT20
Hermitage Clo., Shep. 83 AZ52
Hermitage Clo., Slou. 62 AR41
Hermitage Ct. E18 49 CH31
Hermitage Ct., Pot.B. 20 BT20
Southgate Rd.
Hermitage Gdns. NW2 47 BS34
Hermitage Gdns. SE19 77 BZ50

Hermitage La. N18 39 BZ28
Hermitage La. NW2 47 BS34
Hermitage La. SE25 87 CB53
Hermitage La. SW16 76 BX50
Hermitage La., Wind. 61 AN45
Hermitage Path SW16 86 BX51
Acacia Rd.
Hermitage Rd. N4 48 BZ33
Hermitage Rd. N15 48 BZ32
Hermitage Rd. SE19 77 BZ50
Hermitage Rd., Ken. 105 BZ61
Hermitage Rd., Wok. 100 AO63
Hermitage St. W2 1 A7
Hermitage Wk. E18 49 CG31
Hermitage Wall E1 57 CB40
Hermitage Way, Stan. 36 BJ30
Hermitage Wds. Cres., 100 AO63
Wok.
Hermon Clo., Wok. 100 AS62
Hermon Gro., Hayes 53 BC40
Mount Hermon Rd.
Hermon Hill E11 49 CH32
Hermon Hill E18 49 CH32
Herndon Clo., Egh. 72 AT49
Herndon Rd. SW18 76 BT46
Herne Clo. NW10 46 BN35
Herne Hill SE24 77 BZ46
Herne Hill Rd. SE24 67 BZ45
Herne Ms. N18 39 CB28
Herne Pl. SE24 76 BY46
Herne Rd., Bush. 27 BF25
Herne Rd., Surb. 84 BK55
Herneshaw, Hat. 10 BO13
Herns La., Welw.G.C. 5 BS7
Herns Way, Welw.G.C. 5 BS7
Heron Clo. E17 39 CD30
Heron Clo. NW10 55 BO36
Heron Clo., Buck.H. 40 CH26
Heron Clo., Guil. 118 AQ69
Heron Clo., Rick. 35 AX27
Heron Clo., Saw. 6 CP6
Heron Clo., Uxb. 53 AX36
Heron Ct., Brom. 88 CJ52
Heron Ct., Rich. 74 BK46
Bridge St.
Heron Cres., Sid. 78 CN48
Heron Dale, Wey. 92 AX56
Heron Flight Ave., Rain. 59 CU36
Heron Hill, Belv. 69 CQ42
Heron Ms., Ilf. 49 CL34
Heron Quay E14 57 CE40
Heron Rd. SE24 67 BZ45
Heron Rd., Croy. 87 CA54
Heron Rd., Twick. 64 BJ45
Heron Sq., Rich. 74 BK46
Whittaker Ave.
Heron Wk., Wok. 91 AU60
Blackmore Cres.
Heron Way, Brwd. 122 DD26
Heron Way, Grays 70 DA42
Heron Way, Hat. 10 BP13
Heron Way, Upmin. 51 CZ33
Herondale, S.Croy. 96 CC58
Herondale Ave. SW18 76 BT47
Heronfield, Egh. 72 AQ50
Heronfield, Pot.B. 20 BT18
Herongate Rd. E12 49 CJ34
Herongate Rd., Chsnt. 21 CD17
Herongate Rd., Swan. 79 CT50
Heronry, The, Walt. 92 BC57
Herons, The E11 49 CG32
Herons Cft., Wey. 92 BA57
Herons Elm, Berk. 7 AP11
Herons La., Ong. 15 CY14
Herons Pl., Islw. 64 BJ45
Herons Ri., Barn. 29 BU24
Herons Way, St.Alb. 9 BJ15
Herons Wd., Harl. 6 CL10
Heronsforde W13 54 BK39
Heronsgate, Edg. 37 BM28
Heronsgate, Rick. 25 AT25
Heronslea, Wat. 27 BD21
Heronslea Dr., Stan. 37 BL28
Heronswood, Wal.Abb. 22 CG20
Roundhills
Heronswood Pl., 5 BS8
Welw.G.C.
Heronswood Rd., 5 BS8
Welw.G.C.
Heronway, Brwd. 122 DD26
Heronway, Wdf.Grn. 40 CJ28
Herrick Rd. N5 48 BZ34
Herrick St. SW1 3 P9
Herrick St. SW1 66 BW42
Herries St. W10 55 BR37
Herring St. SE5 67 CA43
Herringham Rd. SE7 68 CJ41
Herrings La., Cher. 83 AW53
Herrongate Clo., Enf. 30 CA23
Hersant Clo. NW10 55 BP37
Herschel Pk. Dr., Slou. 62 AP41
Albert Rd.
Herschel St., Slou. 62 AP41
Herschell Rd. SE23 77 CC47
Hersham By-pass, Walt. 92 BC56
Hersham Clo. SW15 75 BP47
Hersham Rd., Walt. 83 BC55
Hersham Trd. Est., Walt. 84 BE55
Hertford Ave. SW14 75 BN46
Hertford Pl. W1 1 L5
Hertford Pl. W1 56 BW38
Whitfield St.
Hertford Rd. N1 57 CA37
Hertford Rd. N2 47 BU31
Hertford Rd. N9 39 CB27
Hertford Rd., Bark. 58 CL36
Hertford Rd., Barn. 29 BT24
Hertford Rd., Enf. 30 CC24
Hertford Rd., Hat. 10 BQ11
Hertford Rd., Hodd. 12 CC10
Hertford Rd., Ilf. 49 CN32
Hertford Rd. (Tewin), 5 BU6
Welw.

Hertford Rd., Welw.G.C. 5 BR5
Hertford Sq., Mitch. 86 BX52
Hertford St. W1 3 H3
Hertford St. W1 56 BV40
Hertford Wk., Belv. 69 CR42
Hood Rd.
Hertford Way, Mitch. 86 BX52
Hertslet Rd. N7 47 BX34
Hervey Clo. N3 38 BS30
Hervey Pk. Rd. E17 48 CD31
Hervey Rd. SE3 68 CH44
Hervey Rd. N3 38 BS30
Hervey Clo.
Hesa Rd., Hayes 53 BC39
Hesham Rd., Berk. 7 AP15
Hesiers Hill, Warl. 106 CG62
Hesiers Rd., Warl. 106 CG61
Hesketh Ave., Dart. 80 CX47
Hesketh Pl. W11 55 BR40
Hesketh Rd. E7 49 CH34
Heslop Rd. SW12 76 BU47
Hesper Ms. SW5 66 BS42
Hessel Rd. W13 64 BJ41
Hessel St. E1 57 CB39
Hesselyn Dr., Rain. 59 CU36
Hessle Gro., Epsom 94 BO59
Hester Rd. N18 39 CB28
Hester Rd. SW11 66 BU43
Hestercombe Ave. SW6 65 BR44
Heston Ave., Houns. 64 BE43
Heston Gra. La., Houns. 64 BE43
Heston Gro., Houns. 64 BE43
Walnut Tree Rd.
Heston Ho. SE8 67 CD44
Heston Rd., Houns. 64 BF43
Heston Rd., Red. 121 BU72
Heston St. SE14 67 CD44
Heston Wk., Red. 121 BU72
Hetchleys, Hem.H. 8 AW12
Hetherington Rd. SW4 66 BX45
Hetherington Rd., Shep. 83 BA51
Hetherington Way, Uxb. 44 AY35
Hetley Gdns. SE19 77 CA50
Fox Hill
Hetley Rd. W12 55 BP40
Hetton St. W6 65 BQ42
Glenthorne Rd.
Heusden Way, Ger.Cr. 43 AS33
Hevelius Clo. SE10 68 CG42
Hever Ave., Sev. 99 CU57
Hever Ct. Rd., Grav. 81 DH50
Hever Cft. SE9 78 CL49
Hever Rd., Brom. 88 CL51
Hever Rd., Sev. 99 CZ57
Hever Wd. Rd., Sev. 99 CZ57
Heverham Rd. SE18 68 CN42
Heversham Rd., Bexh. 69 CR44
Hewens Rd., Uxb. 53 BA38
Hewer St. W10 55 BQ39
Hewers Way, Tad. 103 BQ63
Hewett Clo., Stan. 36 BJ28
Hewett Pl., Swan. 89 CS52
Hewett St. EC2 2 N5
Hewett St. EC2 57 CA38
Curtain Rd.
Hewish Rd. N18 39 CA28
Hewitt Ave. N22 38 BY30
Hewitt Rd. N8 47 BY32
Hewitts, Orp. 98 CQ57
Hewlett Rd. E3 57 CD37
Hexagon, The N6 47 BU33
Hexal Rd. SE6 78 CG48
Hexham Gdns., Islw. 64 BJ43
Hexham Rd. SE27 77 BZ48
Hexham Rd., Barn. 29 BS24
Hexham Rd., Mord. 86 BS54
Hextalls La., Red. 114 BZ67
Heybourne Rd. N17 39 CB29
Heybridge Ave. SW16 76 BX50
Heybridge Dr., Ilf. 49 CM31
Heybridge Way E10 48 CD33
Heydons Clo., St.Alb. 9 BG12
Heyford Ave. SW8 66 BX43
Heyford Ave. SW20 85 BR52
Heyford Rd., Mitch. 86 BU51
Heyford Rd., Rad. 27 BJ21
Heygate St. SE17 4 H9
Heygate St. SE17 67 BZ42
Heylyn Sq. E3 58 CE37
Malmesbury Rd.
Heymede, Lthd. 102 BK65
Heynes Rd., Dag. 50 CP35
Heysham Dr., Wat. 36 BD28
Heysham Rd. N15 48 BZ32
Heythorp St. SW18 75 BR47
Heythorpe Clo., Wok. 100 AP62
Kenton Way
Heywood Ave. NW9 37 BO30
Heyworth Rd. E5 48 CB35
Heyworth Rd. E15 49 CG35
Hibbert Ave., Wat. 27 BD22
Hibbert Rd. E17 48 CD33
Hibbert Rd., Har. 36 BH30
Hibbert Rd., Maid. 61 AG41
Hibbert St. SW11 66 BT45
Hibberts All., Wind. 61 AO44
Peascod St.
Hibberts Way, Ger.Cr. 43 AS31
Hibernia Dr., Grav. 81 DJ48
Hibernia Gdns., Houns. 64 BF45
Hibernia Rd., Houns. 64 BF45
Hichisson Rd. SE15 77 CC46
Hickin Clo. SE7 68 CJ42
Hickin St. E14 67 CF41
Plevna St.
Hickling Rd., Ilf. 49 CL35
Hickman Ave. E4 39 CF28
Hickman Clo. E16 58 CJ39
Hickman Rd., Rom. 50 CP33
Hickmans Clo., Gdse. 114 CC69
Hickmore Wk. SW4 66 BW45
Belmont Clo.

Hicks Ave., Grnf. 54 BG37
Hicks Clo. SW11 66 BU45
Hicks St. SE8 67 CD42
Hidalgo Ct., Hem.H. 8 AY12
Hide Pl. SW1 3 N9
Hide Pl. SW1 66 BW42
Hide Rd., Har. 45 BG31
Hides, The, Harl. 6 CM10
Hides St. N7 56 BX36
Sheringham Rd.
High Acres, Abb.L. 17 BA19
High Banks Rd., Pnr. 36 BF29
High Beech, S.Croy. 96 CA57
High Beech Rd., Loug. 31 CK24
High Beeches, Bans. 94 BQ60
High Beeches, Ger.Cr. 43 AR33
High Beeches, Orp. 98 CO57
High Beeches, Sid. 79 CQ49
High Bois La., Amer. 25 AO21
High Bri. SE10 67 CF42
High Bri. St., Wal.Abb. 21 CE20
High Broom Cres., 87 CE54
W.Wick.
High Canons, Borwd. 28 BN22
High Cedar Dr. SW20 75 BQ50
High Clo., Rick. 26 AX25
High Coombe Pl., 75 BN50
Kings.T.
High Ct., Wdf.Grn. 40 CH29
High Cross, Wat. 27 BG22
High Cross Rd. N17 48 CB31
High Cross Rd., Sev. 117 DA66
High Dells, Hat. 10 BO13
High Dr., Cat. 105 CE64
High Dr., Lthd. 93 BG60
High Dr., N.Mal. 85 BN51
High Elms, Chig. 40 CN28
High Elms, Upmin. 51 CZ33
High Elms, Wdf.Grn. 40 CH28
High Elms Clo., Nthwd. 35 BA29
High Elms Rd., Orp. 97 CL59
High Fld., Bans. 104 BU62
High Fld., Wind. 61 AM45
High Firs, Rad. 27 BJ21
High Firs, Swan. 89 CT52
High Foleys, Esher 93 BJ57
High Gables, Loug. 31 CJ25
High Garth, Esher 93 BG57
High Gro. SE18 68 CM43
High Gro., Brom. 88 CJ51
High Gro., Welw.G.C. 5 BQ7
High Hill Est. E5 48 CB33
High Hill Rd., Warl. 96 CF60
High Holborn WC1 1 Q8
High Holborn WC1 56 BX39
High Ho. La., Grays 71 DH41
High La. W7 54 BG39
High La., Warl. 105 CD62
High Laver La., Ong. 14 CU12
High Lawns, Har. 45 BH34
Sudbury Hill
High Level Dr. SE26 77 CB49
High Mead, Chig. 40 CL27
High Mead, Har. 45 BH33
High Mead, W.Wick. 87 CF55
High Meadow Clo., Dor. 119 BJ72
High Meadow Clo., Pnr. 44 BC31
High Meadow Cres. NW9 46 BN32
High Meadows, Chig. 40 CM28
High Meads Rd. E16 58 CJ39
Alestan Beck Rd.
High Moor, Amer. 25 AO23
High Mt. NW4 46 BP32
High Oaks, Enf. 29 BX22
High Oaks, St.Alb. 9 BG11
High Oaks Rd., Welw.G.C. 5 BP7
High Ongar Rd., Ong. 24 CX17
High Pk. Ave., Rich. 110 BB66
High Pk. Rd., Rich. 65 BM44
High Pastures, Bish. 6 CS7
High Path SW19 86 BS51
High Path Rd., Guil. 118 AU70
High Pewley, Guil. 118 AS71
High Pine Clo., Wey. 92 BA56
High Pines, Warl. 105 CC63
High Pt. SE9 78 CL48
High Pt., Wey. 92 AZ56
High Ridge N10 38 BV30
High Ridge, Cuffley 20 BX17
High Ridge Clo., Epsom 94 BO60
High Ridge Rd., Hem.H. 17 AX16
High Rd. E11 49 CG34
High Rd. E18 40 CG29
High Rd. N11 38 BV28
High Rd. N12 38 BT27
High Rd. N15 48 CA32
High Rd. N17 39 CA30
High Rd. N20 38 BT26
High Rd. N22 38 BX29
High Rd. NW10 55 BP36
High Rd. (Willesden Grn.) 55 BO36
NW10
High Rd., Brox. 12 CD15
High Rd., Buck.H. 40 CH27
High Rd., Bush. 36 BG26
High Rd., Chig. 40 CL28
High Rd. (Wilmington), 80 CV48
Dart.
High Rd., Epp. 14 CO15
High Rd., Epp. 23 CO17
High Rd., Epp. 23 CR16
High Rd., Grays 71 DC40
High Rd. (Harrow Weald), 36 BH29
Har.
High Rd., Hat. 10 BU12
High Rd., Ilf. 49 CL34
High Rd., Loug. 31 CJ25
High Rd., Reig. 113 BY67
High Rd., Rom. 50 CO33
High Rd., Uxb. 53 AX39

High Rd. (Ickenham), Uxb. 44 A?
High Rd. (Leavesden), 17 B?
Wat.
High Rd., Wem. 45 B?
High Rd., Wey. 92 A?
High Rd., Wdf.Grn. 40 C?
High Rd. E. Finchley N2 38 B?
High Rd. Leyton E10 48 C?
High Rd. Leyton E15 48 C?
High Rd. Leytonstone E11 49 C?
High Rd. Leytonstone E15 49 C?
High Rd. N. Finchley N12 38 B?
High Silver, Loug. 31 C?
High St. E11 49 C?
High St. E13 58 C?
High St. E15 57 C?
High St. E17 48 C?
High St. N8 47 B?
High St. N14 38 B?
High St. (Southgate) N14 38 B?
High St. NW7 37 B?
High St. NW10 55 B?
High St. SE20 77 C?
High St. SW6 65 B?
High St. (Colliers Wd.) 76 B?
SW19
High St. (Wimbledon) 75 B?
SW19
High St. W3 55 B?
High St. W5 54 B?
High St. (Abbots 17 B?
Langley), Abb.L.
High St. (Bedmond), 17 B?
Abb.L.
High St., Bans. 104 B?
High St., Barn. 28 B?
High St., Beck. 87 C?
High St., Berk. 7 A?
High St., Bex. 79 C?
High St. (Elstree), Borwd. 27 B?
Borwd
High St., Brent. 64 B?
High St., Brwd. 122 D?
High St., Brom. 88 D?
High St., Bush. 27 B?
High St., Cars. 95 B?
High St., Ch.St.G. 34 A?
High St., Chsnt. 21 C?
High St., Chsnt. 21 C?
High St., Chis. 78 C?
High St., Cob. 101 B?
High St., Croy. 87 B?
High St., Dart. 80 C?
High St. (Bean), Dart. 80 D?
High St. (Crayford), Dart. 79 C?
High St., Dor. 119 B?
High St., E.Mol. 84 B?
High St., Edg. 37 B?
High St., Egh. 72 A?
High St., Enf. 30 C?
High St. (Ponders End), 30 C?
Enf.
High St., Epp. 22 C?
High St., Epsom 94 B?
High St. (Ewell), Epsom 94 B?
High St., Erith 69 C?
High St., Esher 93 B?
High St. (Claygate), 93 B?
Esher
High St., Eyns. 90 C?
High St., Farn. 90 C?
High St., Felt. 73 B?
High St., Ger.Cr. 34 A?
High St., Grav. 81 D?
High St. (Northfleet), 81 D?
Grav.
High St., Grays 71 D?
High St., Green. 70 D?
High St., Guil. 118 A?
High St., Hmptn. 84 B?
High St., Harl. 6 C?
High St. (Roydon), Harl. 13 C?
High St., Har. 45 B?
High St. (Wealdstone), 36 B?
Har.
High St., Hem.H. 8 A?
High St. (Bovingdon), 16 A?
Hem.H.
High St., Hodd. 12 C?
High St., Horn. 51 C?
High St., Houns. 64 B?
High St. (Cranford), 63 B?
Houns.
High St. (Barkingside), Ilf. 49 C?
High St., Iver 52 A?
High St., Kings L. 17 A?
High St., Kings.T. 84 B?
High St. (Hampton Wick), 84 B?
Kings.T.
High St., Lthd. 102 B?
High St. (Bookham), 111 B?
Lthd.
High St. (Oxshott), 93 B?
Lthd.
High St. (Bray), Maid. 61 A?
High St., N.Mal. 85 B?
High St., Nthwd. 35 B?
High St., Ong. 24 C?
High St., Orp. 89 C?
High St. (Downe), Orp. 97 C?
High St. (Farnborough), 97 C?
Orp.
High St. (Green St. Grn.), 97 C?
Orp.
High St. (St. Mary Cray), 89 C?
Orp.
High St., Oxt. 114 C?
High St. (Limpsfield), 115 C?
Oxt.
High St., Pnr. 45 B?
High St., Pot.B. 20 B?
High St., Pur. 95 B?
High St., Red. 114 B?
High St. (Bletchingley), 121 B?
Red.

gh St. (Merstham), 121 BU70
Red.
gh St. (Nutfield), Red. 113 BV67
gh St., Reig. 121 BS70
gh St., Rick. 35 AX26
gh St., Rom. 50 CT32
gh St., Ruis. 44 BB33
gh St., St.Alb. 9 BG13
gh St. (Colney Heath), 10 BN14
St.Alb.
gh St. (London Colney), 18 BK16
St.Alb.
gh St., Sev. 117 CV66
gh St. (Chipstead), 107 CS64
Sev.
gh St. (Kemsing), Sev. 108 CX62
gh St. (Otford), Sev. 107 CU61
gh St. (Plaxtol), Sev. 117 DC67
gh St. (Seal), Sev. 108 CW64
gh St. (Shoreham), 98 CT58
Sev.
gh St., Shep. 83 AZ54
gh St., Sid. 79 CP50
gh St., Slou. 62 AP41
gh St. (Chalvey), Slou. 61 AO41
gh St. (Colnbrook), 62 AU43
Slou.
gh St. (Datchet), Slou. 62 AQ44
gh St., S.Ock. 60 DB38
gh St. (Aveley), S.Ock. 60 CY40
gh St., Sthl. 54 BE40
gh St., Stai. 72 AV49
gh St. (Stanwell), Stai. 73 AX46
gh St., Sutt. 95 BS56
gh St. (Cheam), Sutt. 94 BR57
gh St., Swan. 89 CT52
gh St., Swans. 81 DC46
gh St., Tad. 103 BQ65
gh St., Tedd. 74 BJ49
gh St., T.Ditt. 84 BJ53
gh St., Th.Hth. 87 BZ52
gh St. (Whitton), Twick. 74 BG47
gh St., Uxb. 53 AX36
gh St. (Cowley), Uxb. 53 AX39
gh St. (Harefield), Uxb. 35 AX30
gh St., Walt. 83 BC54
gh St., Wat. 27 BD24
gh St., Well. 69 CO45
gh St., Wem. 46 BL35
gh St., West Dr. 63 AX43
gh St. (Yiewsley), 53 AX40
West Dr.
gh St., W.Wick. 87 CE54
gh St., West. 115 CM67
gh St., Wey. 92 AZ56
gh St. (Addlestone), 92 AW56
Wey.
gh St., Wind. 61 AO44
gh St. (Eton), Wind. 61 AO43
gh St., Wok. 100 AS62
gh St. (Chobham), 91 AP59
Wok.
gh St. (Horsell), Wok. 100 AR61
gh St. (Old Woking), 100 AT64
Wok.
gh St. (Ripley), Wok. 101 AW64
gh St. (Wraysbury), 72 AS46
Wraysbury
gh St. Grn., Hem.H. 8 AZ12
gh St. Ms. SW19 75 BR49
Courthope Rd.
gh St. N. E6 58 CK36
gh St. N. E12 49 CK35
gh St. S. E6 58 CK37
gh St. S. (Norwood) 87 CA52
SE25
gh Timber St. EC4 57 BZ40
Upper Thames St.
gh Tor Clo., Brom. 78 CH50
Babbacombe Rd.
gh Tree Clo., Wey. 92 AW56
gh Tree Ct. W7 54 BH40
gh Trees SW2 76 BY47
gh Trees, Barn. 29 BU25
gh Trees, Croy. 87 CD54
gh Trees Clo., Cat. 105 CA64
gh Trees Rd., Reig. 121 BT71
gh Vw., Hat. 10 BO13
gh Vw., Rick. 26 AW24
gh Vw., Sutt. 94 BR59
gh Vw., Wat. 26 BB25
gh Vw. Ave., Grays 71 DE42
gh Vw. Clo. SE19 87 CA51
gh Vw. Clo., Loug. 31 CJ25
gh Vw. Clo., Pot.B. 20 BT20
High Vw. Gdns.
gh Vw. Gdns., Pot.B. 20 BT20
gh Vw. Rd. E18 49 CG31
gh Vw. Rd., Guil. 118 AO72
gh Vw. Rd., Orp. 97 CL58
gh Vw. Rd., Sid. 79 CO49
gh Wickfield, Welw.G.C. 5 BT8
gh Worple, Har. 45 BE33
gh Wych La., Saw. 6 CO6
gh Wych Rd., Harl. 6 CN7
gham Ave., Hem.H. 8 AX14
gham Hill Rd. E17 39 CD30
gham La., Ton. 117 DC70
gham Pl. E17 48 CD31
gham Rd. N17 48 BZ31
gham Rd., Wdf.Grn. 40 CH29
gham Sta. Ave. E4 39 CE29
gham St. E17 48 CD31
gham Vw., Epp. 23 CR16
ghams Hill, Warl. 97 CH59
ghams Pk., The, 40 CG28
Wdf.Grn.
ghash Clo., S.le H. 71 DK42
ghbanks Clo., Well. 69 CO43
ghbarn Rd., Lthd. 111 BD68
ghbarns Rd., Hem.H. 17 AZ16
ghbarrow Rd., Croy. 87 CA54
ghbridge Rd., Bark. 58 CL37
ghbrook Rd. SE3 68 CJ45

Highbury Ave., Hodd. 12 CE11
Highbury Ave., Th.Hth. 86 BY51
Highbury Clo., W.Wick. 87 CE55
Highbury Cor. N5 56 BY36
Highbury Cres. N5 47 BY35
Highbury Gdns., Ilf. 49 CN34
Highbury Gra. N5 47 BY35
Highbury Gro. N5 56 BY36
Highbury Gro., N.Mal. 85 BN52
Highbury Hill N5 47 BY35
Highbury Ms. N5 47 BY35
Ronalds Rd.
Highbury New Pk. N5 48 BZ34
Highbury Pk. N5 47 BY35
Highbury Pl. N5 56 BY36
Highbury Quad. N5 47 BY34
Highbury Quad. Est. N5 48 BZ34
Highbury Rd. SW19 75 BR49
Highbury Sta. Rd. N1 56 BY36
Highbury Ter. N5 47 BY35
Highbury Ter. Ms. N5 47 BY35
Ronalds Rd.
Highclere, Guil. 118 AT69
Highclere Clo., Ken. 105 BZ61
Highclere Ct., St.Alb. 9 BH13
Avenue Rd.
Highclere Dr., Hem.H. 8 AZ15
Highclere Gdns., Wok. 100 AO62
Highclere Rd., N.Mal. 85 BN52
Highclere Rd., Wok. 100 AO62
Highclere St. SE26 77 CD49
Highcliffe Dr. SW15 75 BO46
Highcliffe Gdns., Ilf. 49 CK32
Highcombe SE7 68 CH43
Highcombe Clo. SE9 78 CJ47
Highcotts La., Wok. 109 AV66
Highcroft NW9 46 BO32
Highcroft Ave., Wem. 55 BL36
Highcroft Gdns. NW11 46 BR32
Highcroft Rd. N19 47 BX33
Highcroft Rd., Hem.H. 17 AW16
Highcross Rd., Grav. 80 DB49
Highcross Way SW15 75 BP47
Bessborough Rd.
Highdaun Dr. SW16 86 BX52
Highdown, Wor.Pk. 85 BO55
Highdown Rd. SW15 75 BP46
Highelms La., Wat. 17 BC18
Higher Dr., Bans. 94 BQ59
Higher Dr., Lthd. 110 BB67
Higher Dr., Pur. 95 BY60
Higher Grn., Epsom 94 BP60
Highfield, Ch.St.G. 34 AR26
Highfield, Harl. 14 CO11
Highfield, Kings L. 17 AY17
Highfield, Rom. 41 CS29
Highfield Ave. NW9 46 BN32
Highfield Ave. NW11 46 BQ33
Highfield Ave., Erith 69 CR43
Highfield Ave., Grnf. 45 BH35
Highfield Ave., Orp. 97 CN56
Highfield Ave., Pnr. 45 BE32
Highfield Ave., Wem. 46 BL34
Highfield Clo. NW9 46 BN32
Highfield Clo., Amer. 25 AO22
Highfield Clo., Egh. 72 AR50
Highfield Clo., Lthd. 93 BG59
Highfield Clo., Nthwd. 35 BB30
Highfield Clo., Rom. 41 CS29
Highfield Clo., Surb. 84 BK54
Highfield Clo., Wey. 92 AW60
Highfield Ct. N14 29 BW25
Highfield Cres., Horn. 51 CW34
Highfield Cres., Nthwd. 35 BB30
Highfield Dr., Brom. 88 CG52
Highfield Dr., Brox. 12 CD14
Highfield Dr., Epsom 94 BO57
Highfield Dr., Uxb. 44 AY34
Highfield Dr., W.Wick. 87 CE55
Highfield Gdns. NW11 46 BR32
Highfield Gdns., Grays 71 DE41
Highfield Grn., Epp. 22 CN19
Highfield Hill SE19 77 BZ50
Highfield La., Hem.H. 8 AY12
Highfield La., St.Alb. 9 BK14
Highfield Link, Rom. 41 CS29
Highfield Pl., Epp. 22 CN19
Highfield Rd. N21 38 BY26
Highfield Rd. NW11 46 BR32
Highfield Rd. W3 55 BM39
Highfield Rd., Berk. 7 AR13
Highfield Rd., Bexh. 79 CQ46
Highfield Rd., Brom. 88 CK52
Highfield Rd., Bush. 27 BE25
Highfield Rd., Cat. 105 CB64
Highfield Rd., Cher. 83 AW54
Highfield Rd., Chsnt. 21 CA16
Highfield Rd., Chis. 88 CN52
Highfield Rd., Dart. 80 CV47
Highfield Rd., Felt. 73 BC47
Highfield Rd., Horn. 51 CW34
Highfield Rd., Islw. 64 BH44
Highfield Rd., Nthwd. 35 BB30
Highfield Rd., Pur. 95 BX58
Highfield Rd., Rom. 41 CS29
Highfield Rd., St.Alb. 9 BJ10
Highfield Rd., Sev. 108 CW61
Highfield Rd., Sun. 83 BB53
Highfield Rd., Surb. 85 BN54
Highfield Rd., Sutt. 95 BU56
Highfield Rd., Walt. 83 BC54
Highfield Rd., West. 106 CJ62
Highfield Rd., Wey. 92 AW60
Highfield Rd., Wdf.Grn. 40 CK29
Highfield Rd. S., Dart. 80 CV47
Highfield Way, Horn. 51 CW34
Highfield Way, Pot.B. 20 BS19
Highfield Way, Rick. 26 AW25
Highfields, Ash. 102 BK63
Highfields, Cuffley 20 BX17
Highfields, Lthd. 102 BG65
Highfields (East Horsley), 110 BB67
Lthd.
Highfields Gro. NW3 47 BV33

Highgate Ave. N6 47 BV33
Highgate Clo. N6 47 BV33
Highgate Gro, Saw. 6 CP6
White Post Fld.
Highgate High St. N6 47 BV33
Highgate Hill N19 47 BV33
Highgate Rd. NW5 47 BV33
Highgate W. Hill N6 47 BV33
Highgrove Clo., Chis. 88 CK51
Logs Hill
Highgrove Rd., Dag. 50 CP35
Highgrove Way, Ruis. 44 BC33
Highland Ave. W7 54 BH39
Highland Ave., Brwd. 42 DB26
Highland Ave., Dag. 50 CS34
Highland Ave., Loug. 31 CK25
Highland Cotts., Wall. 95 BV56
Highland Cft., Beck. 77 CE50
Highland Dr., Bush. 36 BG26
Highland Dr., Hem.H. 8 AZ13
Highland Pk., Felt. 73 BB49
Highland Rd. SE19 77 CA50
Highland Rd., Amer. 25 AO23
Highland Rd., Bexh. 79 CR46
Highland Rd., Brom. 88 CG51
Highland Rd., Nthwd. 44 BB31
Highland Rd., Pur. 95 BY60
Highland Rd., Sev. 98 CR59
Highland Rd., Wal.Abb. 13 CG14
Highlands, Hat. 10 BQ11
Highlands, Wat. 36 BD26
Highlands, Wok. 100 AS64
Highlands, The, Edg. 37 BM30
Highlands, The, Lthd. 110 BB66
Highlands, The, Pot.B. 20 BT18
Highlands, The, Rick. 35 AW26
Highlands Ave. W3 55 BN40
Highlands Ave., Lthd. 102 BK64
Highlands Clo. N4 47 BX33
Mount Vw. Rd.
Highlands Clo., Ger.Cr. 34 AS29
Highlands Clo., Houns. 64 BF44
Highlands Clo., Lthd. 102 BJ64
Highlands End, Ger.Cr. 34 AS29
Highlands Gdns., Ilf. 49 CK33
Highlands Hill, Swan. 89 CU51
Highlands La., Ger.Cr. 34 AS29
Highlands Pk., Lthd. 102 BK65
Highlands Pk., Sev. 108 CW64
Highlands Rd., Barn. 29 BS25
Highlands Rd., Beac. 34 AO28
Highlands Rd., Lthd. 102 BJ64
Highlands Rd., Orp. 89 CO54
Highlands Rd., Reig. 121 BT70
Highlea Clo. NW9 37 BO30
Highlever Rd. W10 55 BQ39
Highmead SE18 68 CN43
Highmead Cres., Wem. 55 BL36
Highmore Rd. SE3 68 CG43
Highover Pk., Amer. 25 AO23
Highridge La., Bet. 120 BM73
Highridge Pl., Enf. 29 BY23
The Ridgeway
Highshore Rd. SE15 67 CA44
Highstead Cres., Erith 69 CT43
Highstone Ave. E11 49 CH32
Highview, Pnr. 45 BD31
Highview Ave., Edg. 37 BN28
Highview Ave., Wall. 95 BX56
Highview Cres., Brwd. 122 DE25
Highview Gdns. N3 46 BR31
Highview Gdns. N11 38 BW28
Highview Gdns., Edg. 37 BN28
Highview Gdns., St.Alb. 9 BK11
Highview Gdns., Upmin. 51 CX34
Highview Pk., Bans. 104 BS61
Highview Rd. SE19 77 BZ50
Highview Rd. W13 54 BJ39
Highway, The E1 57 CB40
Highway, The, Orp. 98 CO56
Highway, The, Stan. 36 BH30
Highway, The, Sutt. 95 BT58
Highwold, Couls. 104 BV62
Highwood Ave. N12 38 BT28
Highwood Ave., Bush. 27 BE23
Highwood Clo., Brwd. 42 DA26
Highwood Clo., Ken. 105 BZ62
Highwood Clo., Orp. 88 CM55
Highwood Dr., Orp. 88 CM55
Highwood Gdns., Ilf. 49 CK32
Highwood Gro. NW7 37 BN28
Highwood Hill NW7 37 BO27
Highwood La., Loug. 31 CL25
Highwood Rd. N19 47 BX34
Highwood Rd., Hodd. 12 CD10
Highwoods, Cat. 114 CA66
Highwoods, Lthd. 102 BK64
Highworth Rd. N11 38 BW29
Highwych Way, Hem.H. 8 AZ10
Elstree Rd.
Hilary Ave., Mitch. 86 BV52
Hilary Clo. SW6 66 BS43
Hilary Clo., Erith 69 CR44
Hilary Clo., Horn. 51 CV35
Hilary Rd. W12 55 BO39
Hilary Rd., Slou. 62 AS41
Hilbert Rd., Sutt. 85 BQ55
Hilborough Way, Orp. 97 CM56
Hilda May Ave., Swan. 89 CT52
Hilda Rd. E6 58 CJ36
Hilda Rd. E16 58 CG38
Hilda Ter. SW9 66 BY44
Myatts Flds. Dev.
Hilda Vale Clo., Orp. 97 CL56
Hilda Vale Rd., Orp. 97 CL56
Hilden Dr., Erith 69 CU43
Hildenborough Gdns., 78 CG50
Brom.
Hildenlea Pl., Brom. 88 CG51
Hildenley Clo., Red. 113 BW67
Malmstone Ave.
Hildens, The, Dor. 119 BG72
Hilders, The, Ash. 103 BM62
Hildreth St. SW12 76 BV47

Hildyard Rd. SW6 66 BS43
Hiley Rd. NW10 55 BQ38
Hilfield La., Wat. 27 BF23
Hilfield La. S., Bush. 27 BH25
Hilgrove Rd. NW6 56 BT36
Hiliard Rd., Nthwd. 35 BC30
Hiliary Gdns., Stan. 36 BK30
Hiljon Cres., Ger.Cr. 34 AS30
Hill, The, Cat. 105 CA65
Hill, The, Grav. 81 DE46
Hill, The, Harl. 6 CP9
Hill Barn, S.Croy. 96 CA59
Hill Brow, Brom. 88 CJ51
Hill Brow, Dart. 79 CT46
Hill Clo. NW2 46 BP34
Hill Clo. NW11 47 BS32
Hill Clo., Barn. 28 BQ25
Hill Clo., Chis. 78 CL49
Hill Clo., Grav. 81 DF50
Hill Clo., Har. 45 BH34
Hill Clo., Pur. 96 BZ60
Hill Clo., Rom. 42 CV28
Hill Clo., Stan. 36 BJ28
Hill Clo., Wok. 100 AR61
Hill Common, Hem.H. 8 AZ15
Hill Ct. SW15 75 BQ46
Putney Hill
Hill Ct. W5 55 BL38
The Ridings
Hill Cres. N20 38 BS27
Hill Cres., Bex. 79 CS47
Hill Cres., Har. 45 BJ32
Hill Cres., Horn. 51 CV32
Hill Cres., Surb. 85 BL53
Hill Cres., Wor.Pk. 85 BQ55
Hill Crest, Pot.B. 20 BT20
Hill Crest, Sev. 107 CU64
Hill Crest, Sid. 79 CO47
Hill Crest Dr., Green. 80 DA46
Hill Crest Gdns. N3 46 BR31
Hill Dr. NW9 46 BN33
Hill Dr. SW16 86 BX52
Hill End, Orp. 88 CN55
Hill End La., St.Alb. 9 BK14
Hill End Rd., Uxb. 35 AX29
Hill Fm. Ave., Wat. 17 BC20
Hill Fm. Clo., Wat. 17 BC20
Hill Fm. La., Ch.St.G. 34 AQ26
Hill Fm. Rd. W10 55 BQ39
Hill Fm. Rd., Chesh. 16 AO20
Hill Fm. Rd., Uxb. 44 BA35
Hill Gdns., Wey. 91 AV56
Hill Gro., Rom. 50 CT31
Hill Ho. Ave., Stan. 36 BH29
Hill Ho. Clo. N21 38 BY26
Hill Ho. Clo., Ger.Cr. 34 AS29
Rickmansworth La.
Hill Ho. Dr., Reig. 121 BS71
Hill Ho. Rd. SW16 76 BX49
Hill La., Ruis. 44 BA33
Hill La., Tad. 103 BR64
Hill Ley, Hat. 10 BO12
Bishops Ri.
Hill Leys, Cuffley 20 BX17
Homewood Ave.
Hill Path SW16 76 BX49
Hill Ri. N9 30 CB25
Hill Ri. NW11 47 BS31
Hill Ri. SE23 77 CB47
Hill Ri., Cuffley 20 BW17
Hill Ri., Dart. 80 CY49
Hill Ri., Dor. 119 BJ70
Hill Ri., Esher 84 BJ55
Hill Ri., Ger.Cr. 34 AR30
Hill Ri., Grnf. 54 BG36
Hill Ri., Pot.B. 20 BT20
Hill Ri., Rich. 74 BK46
Hill Ri., Rick. 35 AW26
Hill Ri., Ruis. 44 BA33
Hill Ri., Slou. 62 AT43
Hill Ri., Upmin. 51 CX34
Hill Ri., Walt. 83 BB54
Hill Ri. Cres., Ger.Cr. 34 AS30
Hill Rd. N10 38 BU30
Hill Rd. NW8 56 BT38
Hill Rd., Amer. 25 AO22
Hill Rd., Brwd. 42 DA27
Hill Rd., Cars. 95 BU57
Hill Rd., Dart. 80 CW48
Hill Rd., Epp. 31 CN22
Hill Rd., Har. 45 BJ32
Hill Rd., Hem.H. 7 AV14
Hill Rd., Lthd. 102 BF64
Hill Rd., Mitch. 86 BV51
Hill Rd., Nthwd. 35 BA29
Hill Rd., Pnr. 45 BE32
Hill Rd., Pur. 95 BX59
Hill Rd., Sutt. 95 BS56
Hill Rd., Wem. 45 BJ34
Hill Side, Surb. 84 BK54
Hill Side Rd., Sev. 108 CV65
Hill St. W1 3 H2
Hill St. W1 56 BV40
Hill St., Rich. 74 BK46
Hill St., St.Alb. 9 BG13
Hill Ter., Abb.L. 17 BB19
Hill Top NW11 47 BS31
Hill Top, Loug. 31 CL24
Hill Top, Sutt. 85 BR54
Hill Top Clo., Berk. 7 AR13
Hill Top Clo., Guil. 109 AP68
Hill Top Clo., Loug. 31 CL24
Hill Top Rd., Berk. 7 AR13
Hill Top Vw., Chig. 40 CK29
Hill Vw., Wok. 100 AS62
Hill Vw. Rd.
Hill Vw. Clo., Pnr. 36 BE29
Hill Vw. Clo., Tad. 103 BQ64
Shelvers Way
Hill Vw. Cres., Guil. 118 AP69
Hill Vw. Cres., Ilf. 49 CK32
Hill Vw. Cres., Orp. 88 CN54
Hill Vw. Dr., Well. 68 CN44
Hill Vw. Gdns. NW9 46 BN32

Hill Vw. Rd. NW7 37 BQ28
Hill Vw. Rd., Esher 93 BJ57
Hill Vw. Rd., Orp. 88 CN54
Hill Vw. Rd., Pnr. 36 BE29
Hill Vw. Rd., Stai. 72 AR46
Hill Vw. Rd., Twick. 74 BJ46
Hill Vw. Rd., Wok. 100 AS62
Hill Waye, Ger.Cr. 43 AS32
Hillars Heath Rd., Couls. 104 BX61
Hillary Ave., Grav. 81 DF48
Hillary Cres., Walt. 84 BD54
Hillary Ri., Barn. 29 BS24
Hillary Rd., Hem.H. 8 AZ13
Hillary Rd., Sthl. 64 BF41
Hillbeck Clo. SE15 67 CC43
Hillbeck Way, Grnf. 54 BG37
Hillborne Clo., Hayes 63 BC42
Hillborough Ave., Sev. 108 CV64
Hillborough Clo. SW19 76 BT50
Hillbrook Rd. SW17 76 BU48
Hillbrow, N.Mal. 85 BO52
Hillbrow Clo., Bex. 79 CS49
Hillbrow Ct., Gdse. 114 CC69
Hickmans Clo.
Hillbrow Rd., Brom. 78 CG50
Hillbrow Rd., Esher 93 BG56
Hillbury, Hat. 10 BO13
Hillbury Ave., Har. 45 BJ32
Hillbury Clo., Warl. 105 CC62
Hillbury Rd. SW17 76 BV48
Hillbury Rd., Whyt. 105 CB62
Hillcote Ave. SW16 76 BY50
Hillcourt Ave. N12 38 BS29
Hillcourt Est. N16 48 BZ33
Hillcourt Rd. SE22 77 CB46
Hillcrest N6 47 BV33
Hillcrest N21 38 BY26
Hillcrest, Hat. 10 BO12
Hillcrest, St.Alb. 9 BF14
Hillcrest, Wey. 92 AZ56
Hillcrest Ave. NW11 46 BR32
Hillcrest Ave., Cher. 82 AV55
Hillcrest Ave., Edg. 37 BM28
Hillcrest Ave., Grays 70 DA43
Hillcrest Ave., Pnr. 45 BD31
Hillcrest Clo. SE26 77 CB49
Hillcrest Clo., Beck. 87 CD53
Hillcrest Clo., Epsom 103 BO61
Treadwell Rd.
Hillcrest Gdns. NW2 46 BP34
Hillcrest Gdns., Esher 84 BH55
Hillcrest Gdns., Ruis. 45 BD34
Hillcrest Rd. E17 39 CF30
Hillcrest Rd. E18 40 CG30
Hillcrest Rd. W3 55 BM40
Hillcrest Rd. W5 55 BL39
Hillcrest Rd., Brom. 78 CH49
Hillcrest Rd., Dart. 79 CT47
Hillcrest Rd., Epp. 23 CT18
Hillcrest Rd., Guil. 118 AP70
Hillcrest Rd., Horn. 50 CU33
Hillcrest Rd., Loug. 31 CJ25
Hillcrest Rd., Orp. 89 CO55
Hillcrest Rd., Pur. 95 BX58
Hillcrest Rd., Rad. 19 BM20
Hillcrest Rd., West. 106 CJ61
Hillcrest Rd., Whyt. 105 CA62
Hillcrest Vw., Beck. 87 CD53
Hillcrest Way, Epp. 23 CO19
Bower Hill
Hillcrest Waye, Ger.Cr. 43 AS32
Hillcroft, Loug. 31 CL23
Hillcroft Ave., Pnr. 45 BE32
Hillcroft Ave., Pur. 95 BW60
Hillcroft Cres. W5 54 BK39
Hillcroft Cres., Ruis. 45 BD34
Hillcroft Cres., Wat. 35 BC26
Hillcroft Cres., Wem. 46 BL35
Hillcroft Rd. E6 58 CL39
Hillcroft Rd., Chesh. 16 AO18
Hillcroome Rd., Sutt. 95 BT57
Hillcross Ave., Mord. 85 BQ53
Hilldale Rd., Sutt. 94 BR56
Hilldene Ave., Rom. 42 CV29
Hilldene Clo., Rom. 42 CV28
Hilldene Ave.
Hilldown Rd. SW16 76 BX50
Hilldown Rd., Brom. 88 CG54
Hilldown Rd., Hem.H. 8 AW12
Hilldrop Cres. N7 47 BW35
Hilldrop Est. N7 47 BW35
Hilldrop La. N7 47 BW35
Hilldrop Rd. N7 47 BW35
Hilldrop Rd., Brom. 78 CH50
Hillend SE18 68 CL44
Hillers Ave., Uxb. 53 AZ38
Hillersdon, Slou. 52 AQ39
Hillersdon Ave. SW13 65 BP44
Hillersdon Ave., Edg. 37 BL28
Hillery Clo. SE17 4 L9
Hillery Clo. SE17 67 BZ42
Catesby St.
Hilley Fld. La., Lthd. 102 BG64
Hillfarm Rd., Ger.Cr. 34 AS29
Hillfield, Hat. 10 BQ11
Hillfield Ave. N8 47 BX32
Hillfield Ave. NW9 46 BO32
Hillfield Ave., Mord. 86 BU53
Hillfield Ave., Wem. 55 BL36
Hillfield Clo., Guil. 118 AU69
Hillfield Clo., Har. 45 BG31
Hillfield Clo., Red. 121 BV70
Hillfield Ct. NW3 47 BU35
Belsize Ave.
Hillfield Ct., Esher 93 BF56
Hillfield Pk. N10 47 BV31
Hillfield Pk. N21 38 BY27
Hillfield Pk. Ms. N10 47 BV31
Hillfield Pk.
Hillfield Rd. NW6 46 BR35
Hillfield Rd., Ger.Cr. 34 AS29
Hillfield Rd., Hmptn. 74 BE50
Hillfield Rd., Hem.H. 8 AX13
Hillfield Rd., Red. 121 BV70

Hillfield Rd., Sev. 107 CT63
Hillfield Sq., Ger.Cr. 34 AS29
Hillfoot Ave., Rom. 41 CS30
Hillfoot Rd., Rom. 41 CS30
Hillford Pl., Red. 121 BV73
Hillgate Pl. SW12 76 BV46
Hillgate Pl. W8 56 BS40
Hillgate St. W8 56 BS40
Hillgay Clo., Guil. 118 AS70
Hillgay Ct., Guil. 118 AS70
Hillgrove, Ger.Cr. 34 AS30
Hillhouse, Wal.Abb. 22 CG20
Hillhouse La., Wey. 92 AZ58
Hillhouse Rd., Dart. 80 CY47
Hillhurst Gdns., Cat. 105 CA63
Hilliard Rd., Nthwd. 35 BB30
Hilliards Ct. E1 57 CC40
Hilliards Rd., Uxb. 53 AX39
Hillier Clo., Barn. 29 BS25
Hillier Rd. SW11 76 BU46
Hillier Rd., Guil. 118 AT70
Hilliers La., Croy. 86 BX55
Hillingdale, West. 106 CH62
Hillingdon Ave., Sev. 108 CV64
Hillingdon Ave., Stai. 73 AY47
Hillingdon Circ., Uxb. 53 AZ36
Hillingdon Hill, Uxb. 53 AY37
Hillingdon Ri., Sev. 108 CV64
Hillingdon Rd., Bexh. 69 CS44
Hillingdon Rd., Grav. 81 DG48
Hillingdon Rd., Uxb. 53 AX37
Hillingdon Rd., Wat. 17 BC20
Hillingdon St. SE17 66 BY43
Hillington Gdns., Wdf.Grn. 40 CJ30
Hillman Clo., Horn. 51 CV31
Stafford Ave.
Hillman Clo., Uxb. 44 AY35
Hillman St. E8 57 CB36
Hillmarton Rd. N7 47 BX35
Hillmay Dr., Hem.H. 8 AW14
Hillmead, Berk. 7 AQ13
Hillmead Dr. SW9 66 BY45
Hillmont Rd., Esher 84 BH55
Hillmore Gro. SE26 77 CC49
Hillreach SE18 68 CK42
Hillrise Ave., Wat. 27 BD22
Hillrise Est. N19 47 BX33
Hillrise Rd.
Hillrise Rd. N19 47 BX33
Hillrise Rd., Rom. 41 CS29
Hills Chace, Brwd. 42 DB28
Hills La., Nthwd. 35 BB30
Hills Ms. W5 55 BL40
Hills Pl. W1 1 L9
Hills Pl. W1 56 BW39
Ramillies Pl.
Hills Rd., Buck.H. 40 CH26
Hillsborough Grn., Wat. 35 BC27
Ashburnham Dr.
Hillsborough Rd. SE22 77 CA46
Hillside NW9 46 BN31
Hillside NW10 55 BN37
Hillside SW19 75 BQ50
Hillside, Bans. 103 BR61
Hillside, Barn. 29 BT25
Hillside, Dart. 80 CY49
Hillside, Erith 69 CS42
Hillside, Farn. 90 CW54
Hillside, Grays 71 DE42
Hillside, Harl. 14 CP12
Hillside, Hat. 10 BP12
Hillside, Hodd. 12 CD11
Hillside, Slou. 62 AP41
Hillside, Slou. 62 AR41
Hillside, Uxb. 44 AX32
Hillside, Vir.W. 82 AR53
Hillside, Welw.G.C. 5 BS9
Hillside, Wok. 100 AR63
Hillside, The, Orp. 98 CO58
Hillside Ave. N11 38 BU29
Hillside Ave., Borwd. 28 BM24
Hillside Ave., Chsnt. 21 CC19
Hillside Ave., Grav. 81 DH48
Hillside Ave., Pur. 95 BY60
Hillside Ave., Wem. 46 BL35
Hillside Ave., Wdf.Grn. 40 CJ28
Hillside Clo. NW8 56 BT37
Carlton Hill
Hillside Clo., Abb.L. 17 BB19
Hillside Clo., Bans. 103 BR61
Hillside Clo., Bet. 120 BM71
Hillside Clo., Ch.St.G. 34 AQ27
Hillside Clo., Ger.Cr. 34 AS29
Hillside Clo., Mord. 85 BR52
Hillside Clo., Wok. 100 AO62
Hillside Clo., Wdf.Grn. 40 CJ28
Hillside Ct. NW4 37 BQ30
Hillside Ct., Guil. 118 AS71
Hillside Ct., St.Alb. 9 BH13
Hillside Rd.
Hillside Cres., Chsnt. 21 CC19
Hillside Cres., Enf. 30 BZ22
Hillside Cres., Har. 45 BG33
Hillside Cres., Nthwd. 35 BC30
Hillside Cres., Wat. 27 BD25
Hillside Dr., Edg. 37 BM28
Hillside Dr., Grav. 81 DH48
Hillside Est. N15 48 CA32
Hillside Gdns. E17 48 CF31
Hillside Gdns. N6 47 BV32
Hillside Gdns. N11 38 BW29
Hillside Gdns. SW2 76 BY48
Hillside Gdns., Barn. 28 BR25
Hillside Gdns., Berk. 7 AR13
Hillside Gdns., Bet. 120 BM70
Hillside Gdns., Edg. 37 BL28
Hillside Gdns., Har. 46 BL33
Hillside Gdns., Nthwd. 35 BC29
Hillside Gdns., Wall. 95 BW57
Hillside Gdns., Wey. 91 AV56
Hillside Gro. N14 38 BW26
Hillside Gro. NW7 37 BP29
Hillside La., Brom. 88 CG55
Hillside Ri., Nthwd. 35 BC29
Hillside Rd. N15 48 CA33
Hillside Rd. W5 55 BL39
Hillside Rd., Ash. 103 BL62
Hillside Rd., Brom. 88 CG52
Hillside Rd., Bush. 27 BE25
Hillside Rd., Couls. 104 BX62
Hillside Rd., Croy. 95 BY56
Hillside Rd., Dart. 79 CT46
Hillside Rd., Epsom 94 BQ58
Hillside Rd., Nthwd. 35 BC29
Hillside Rd., Rad. 27 BJ21
Hillside Rd., Rick. 25 AU25
Hillside Rd., St.Alb. 9 BH13
Hillside Rd., Sev. 108 CV65
Hillside Rd., Sthl. 54 BE38
Hillside Rd., Surb. 85 BM52
Hillside Rd., Sutt. 94 BR57
Hillside Rd., West. 106 CK63
Hillside Rd., Whyt. 105 CB62
Hillside Wk., Brwd. 42 CZ27
Hillsleigh Rd. W8 55 BR40
Hillsmead Way, S.Croy. 96 CB60
Hillspur Clo., Guil. 118 AP70
Hillspur Rd., Guil. 118 AP70
Hillstowe St. E5 48 CC34
Hilltop, Loug. 31 CL24
Hilltop, Mord. 86 BS53
Hilltop Clo., Chsnt. 21 CA16
Hilltop Clo., Lthd. 102 BK65
Hilltop Clo., Loug. 31 CL24
Hilltop Gdns. NW4 37 BP30
Hilltop Gdns., Dart. 80 CW46
Hilltop Gdns., Orp. 88 CN55
Hilltop La., Cat. 113 BY66
Hilltop Ri., Lthd. 111 BG66
Hilltop Rd. NW6 56 BS36
Hilltop Rd., Grays 70 DA43
Hilltop Rd., Kings L. 17 BA17
Hilltop Rd., Reig. 121 BS71
Hilltop Rd., Whyt. 105 CA62
Hilltop Way, Stan. 36 BJ27
Hillview SW20 75 BP50
Heights Clo.
Hillview, Whyt. 105 CB62
Hillview Ave., Har. 46 BL32
Hillview Ave., Horn. 51 CV32
Hillview Clo., Pur. 95 BY59
Hillview Dr., Red. 121 BV71
Hillview Gdns. NW4 46 BQ31
Hillview Gdns., Chsnt. 21 CD17
Hillview Gdns., Har. 45 BF31
Hillview Rd., Chis. 78 CL49
Hillview Rd., Sutt. 86 BT55
Hillway N6 47 BV34
Hillway NW9 46 BO33
Hillwood Clo., Brwd. 122 DD26
Hillwood Gro., Brwd. 122 DD26
Hillworth Rd. SW2 76 BY47
Hilly Fld., Harl. 14 CO13
Hilly Flds. Cres. SE4 67 CE45
Hillyard Rd. W7 54 BH39
Hillyard St. SW9 66 BX44
Hillydeal Rd., Sev. 108 CV61
Hillyfield E17 39 CD30
Hillyfields, Loug. 31 CL23
Hillyfields, Welw.G.C. 5 BT7
Hillyfields Est., Loug. 31 CL23
Hilperton Rd., Slou. 62 AP41
Burlington Ave.
Hilsea St. E5 48 CC35
Hilton Ave. N12 38 BT28
Hilton Clo., Uxb. 53 AW37
Hilton Way, S.Croy. 105 CB61
Hilversum Cres. SE22 77 CA46
Dulwich Gro.
Himley Rd. SW17 76 BU49
Hinchcliffe Clo., Wall. 95 BX57
Hinchley Clo., Esher 84 BH55
Hinchley Dr., Esher 84 BH55
Hinchley Way, Esher 84 BJ55
Hinckler Clo., Wall. 95 BX57
Hinckley Rd. SE15 67 CB45
Hind Clo., Chig. 40 CN28
Hind Ct. EC4 2 E9
Hind Ct. EC4 56 BY39
Gough Sq.
Hind Cres., Erith 69 CS43
Hind Gro. E14 57 CE39
Hinde St. W1 1 H8
Hinde St. W1 56 BV39
Hindes Rd., Har. 45 BG32
Hindhead Clo. N16 48 CA33
Hindhead Clo., Uxb. 53 AZ38
Aldenham Dr.
Hindhead Gdns., Nthlt. 54 BE37
Hindhead Grn., Wat. 36 BD28
Hindhead Way, Wall. 95 BX56
Hindmans Rd. SE22 77 CB46
Hindmans Way, Dag. 59 CQ38
Hindmarsh Clo. E1 57 CB40
Cable St.
Hindrey Rd. E5 48 CB35
Hindrey Rd. Est. E5 48 CB35
Pembury Rd.
Hindsley Pl. SE23 77 CC48
Hinkler Rd., Har. 45 BK31
Hinkley Clo., Uxb. 44 AX31
Hinksey Clo., Slou. 62 AT41
Hinksey Path SE2 69 CP41
Hinstock Rd. SE18 68 CM43
Hinton Ave., Houns. 64 BD45
Hinton Clo. SE9 78 CK47
Hinton Rd. N18 39 CA28
Hinton Rd. SE24 67 BZ45
Hinton Rd., Uxb. 53 AX37
Hinton Rd., Wall. 95 BW57
Hintons, Harl. 13 CL13
Hipley Ct., Guil. 118 AT71
Hipley St., Wok. 100 AT63
Hippodrome Pl. W11 55 BR40
Portland Rd.
Hiroshima Wk. SE7 68 CH41
Hitcham Rd. E17 48 CD33
Hitchcock Clo., Shep. 83 AY52
Studios Rd.
Hitchen Hatch La., Sev. 107 CU65
Hitchens Clo., Hem.H. 7 AV13
Hitchin Clo., Rom. 42 CV28
Hitchin Sq. E3 57 CD37
Hitchings Way, Reig. 121 BS72
Hither Grn. La. SE13 77 CF46
Hither Meadow, Ger.Cr. 34 AS30
Hither Way, Welw.G.C. 5 BQ6
Hitherbaulk, Welw.G.C. 5 BR9
Hitherbroom Rd., Hayes 53 BC40
Hitherbury Clo., Guil. 118 AR72
Hitherfield Rd. SW16 76 BX48
Hitherfield Rd., Dag. 50 CQ34
Hithermoor Rd., Stai. 72 AV46
Hitherwell Dr., Har. 36 BG30
Hitherwood Clo., Horn. 51 CV35
Swanbourne Dr.
Hitherwood Clo., Reig. 121 BU69
Hitherwood Dr. SE19 77 CA49
Hive Clo., Bush. 36 BG27
Hive La., Grav. 81 DD46
Hive Rd., Bush. 36 BG27
Hixberry La., St.Alb. 10 BL14
Hoadly Rd. SW16 76 BW48
Hobart Clo. N20 38 BU27
Hobart Gdns., Th.Hth. 87 BZ52
Hobart Pl. SW1 3 J6
Hobart Pl. SW1 66 BV41
Belgrave St.
Hobart Pl., Rich. 75 BL47
Chisholm Rd.
Hobart Rd., Dag. 50 CP35
Hobart Rd., Hayes 54 BD38
Hobart Rd., Ilf. 40 CM30
Hobart Rd., Til. 71 DF44
Hobart Rd., Wor.Pk. 85 BP55
Hobart Wk., St.Alb. 9 BH11
Hobarts Dr., Uxb. 43 AV32
Queen Mothers Dr.
Hobbayne Rd. W7 54 BG39
Hobbes Wk. SW15 75 BP46
Sunnymead Rd.
Hobbs Clo., Chsnt. 21 CC18
Hobbs Clo., St.Alb. 10 BL13
Hobbs Clo., Wey. 92 AW60
Hobbs Cross Rd., Epp. 32 CP21
Hobbs Cross Rd., Harl. 6 CQ9
Hobbs Grn. N2 47 BT31
Hobbs Rd. SE27 77 BZ49
Hobbs Way, Welw.G.C. 5 BQ8
Hobbshill Rd., Hem.H. 8 AY15
Hobday St. E14 57 CE39
Hobhouse Ct. SW1 56 BW40
Suffolk St.
Hobill Wk., Surb. 85 BL53
Hoblands End, Chis. 78 CN50
Hobletts Rd., Hem.H. 8 AY13
Hobsons Clo., Hodd. 12 CD10
Hobtoe Rd., Harl. 6 CL10
Hobury St. SW10 66 BT43
Hockenden La., Swan. 89 CR52
Hocker St. E2 2 P3
Hocker St. E2 57 CA38
Arnold Circ.
Hockering Clo., Wok. 100 AT62
Hockering Gdns., Wok. 100 AT62
Hockering Rd., Wok. 100 AT62
Hockett Clo. SE8 67 CD42
Hocklands, Welw.G.C. 5 BT7
Hockley Ave. E6 58 CK37
Hockley Dr., Rom. 41 CU30
Hockley La., Slou. 52 AQ36
Hocroft Ave. NW2 46 BR34
Hocroft Rd. NW2 46 BR35
Hodder Dr., Grnf. 54 BH37
Hoddesdon By-pass, Brox. 12 CC14
Hoddesdon Rd., Belv. 69 CR42
Hodds Wd. Rd., Chesh. 16 AO20
Hodford Rd. NW11 46 BR33
Hodgkin Clo. SE28 59 CP40
Fleming Way
Hodgson Gdns., Guil. 118 AS69
Hodings Rd., Harl. 6 CL10
Hodnet Gro. SE16 67 CC42
Suffolk Gro.
Hodsoll Ct., Orp. 89 CP53
Hodson Clo., Har. 45 BE34
Hodson Cres., Orp. 89 CP53
Hoe, The, Wat. 36 BD27
Hoe Cft., Wal.Abb. 13 CG14
Hoe La., Enf. 30 CB22
Hoe La., Rom. 32 CO24
Hoe La., Wal.Abb. 13 CG14
Hoe St. E17 48 CE31
Hoestock Rd., Saw. 6 CP6
Hofland Rd. W14 65 BR41
Hog Hill Rd., Rom. 41 CQ29
Hog La., Chesh. 7 AO14
Hogans Ms. W2 1 A6
Hogarth Ave., Ashf. 73 BA50
Hogarth Ave., Brwd. 122 DC27
Hogarth Clo. E16 58 CJ39
Hogarth Clo. W5 55 BL39
Hillcrest Rd.
Hogarth Ct. EC3 2 N10
Hogarth Ct. EC3 57 CA40
Fenchurch St.
Hogarth Ct. SE19 77 CA49
Fountain Dr.
Hogarth Ct., Bush. 36 BF26
Steeplands
Hogarth Cres. SW19 86 BT51
Hogarth Cres., Croy. 87 BZ54
Hogarth Est. W4 65 BO42
Hogarth Gdns., Houns. 64 BF43
Hogarth Hill NW11 46 BR31
Hogarth La. W4 65 BO43
Hogarth Pl. SW5 66 BS42
Hogarth Rd.
Hogarth Reach, Loug. 31 CK25
Hogarth Rd. SW5 66 BS42
Hogarth Rd., Edg. 37 BM30
Hogarth Way, Hmptn. 84 BG51
Hogarths Rd., Grays 71 DD40
Hogden Clo., Tad. 112 BR66
Hogden La., Dor. 119 BE70
Hogden La., Dor. 111 BF68
Hogg End La., Hem.H. 8 BB12
Hogg End La., St.Alb. 8 BB12
Hogg La., Borwd. 27 BJ24
Hogg La., Grays 71 DD41
Hogpits Bottom, Hem.H. 16 AT19
Hogs Back, Guil. 118 AO72
Hogscross La., Couls. 104 BU65
Hogsden Clo. N1 57 BZ37
Forston St.
Hogshead Pas. E1 57 CB40
Pennington St.
Hogshill La., Cob. 92 BC60
Hogsmill Way, Epsom 94 BN56
Hogtrough Hill, West. 106 CN64
Hogtrough La., Oxt. 114 CE67
Hogtrough La., Red. 121 BW71
Holbeach Gdns., Sid. 78 CN46
Holbeach Ms. SW12 76 BV47
Harberson Rd.
Holbeach Rd. SE6 77 CE47
Holbeck La., Chsnt. 21 CA16
Holbeck Row SE15 67 CB43
Holbein Ms. SW1 3 G10
Holbein Ms. SW1 66 BV42
Holbein Pl. SW1 3 G9
Holbein Pl. SW1 66 BV42
Holberton Gdns. NW10 55 BP38
Holborn EC1 2 D7
Holborn EC1 56 BY39
Holborn Circ. EC1 2 E7
Holborn Circ. EC1 56 BY39
Holborn Clo., St.Alb. 9 BK11
Holborn Pl. WC1 2 B7
Holborn Rd. E13 58 CH38
Holborn Viaduct EC1 2 E7
Holborn Viaduct EC1 56 BY39
Holbrook Clo. N19 47 BV33
Dartmouth Pk. Hill
Holbrook Clo., Enf. 30 CA23
Holbrook La., Chis. 78 CM50
Holbrook Rd. E15 58 CG37
Holbrook Way, Brom. 88 CK53
Holbrooke Ct. N7 47 BX35
Holbrooke Pl., Rich. 74 BK46
Hill Ri.
Holburne Clo. SE3 68 CJ44
Holburne Gdns. SE3 68 CJ44
Holburne Rd. SE3 68 CJ44
Holcombe Dale NW7 37 BP27
Holcombe Hill NW7 37 BP27
Holcombe Rd. N17 48 CA31
Holcombe Rd., Ilf. 49 CL33
Holcombe St. W6 65 BP42
Holcon Ct., Red. 121 BV69
Holcote Clo., Belv. 69 CQ41
Blakemore Way
Holcroft Rd. E9 57 CC36
Holdbrook, Wal.Cr. 21 CD20
Holdbrook N., Wal.Cr. 21 CD20
Holdbrook S., Wal.Cr. 21 CD20
Holdbrook Way, Rom. 42 CW30
Gubbins La.
Holden Ave. N12 38 BS28
Holden Ave. NW9 46 BN33
Holden Gdns., Brwd. 42 DB28
Holden Rd. N12 38 BS28
Holden Rd., Dag. 50 CO34
Holden St. SW11 66 BV44
Holden Way, Upmin. 51 CY33
Holdenby Rd. SE4 77 CD46
Holdenhurst Ave. N12 38 BT29
Holderness Way SE27 76 BY49
Holdernesse Rd. SW17 76 BU48
Holders Hill Ave. NW4 37 BQ30
Holders Hill Circ. NW4 37 BR29
Holders Hill Cres. NW4 37 BQ30
Holders Hill Dr. NW4 46 BQ31
Holders Hill Gdns. NW4 37 BR30
Holders Hill Rd. NW4 37 BQ30
Holders Hill Rd. NW7 37 BR29
Holdgate St. SE7 68 CJ41
Westmoor St.
Holdings, The, Hat. 10 BQ11
Hole Cft., Wal.Abb. 22 CG20
Roundhills
Hole Fm. La., Brwd. 42 DA30
Holehill La., Dor. 119 BF71
Holford Pl. WC1 2 C2
Holford Pl. WC1 56 BY38
Holford Rd. NW3 47 BT34
Hampstead Sq.
Holford Rd., Guil. 118 AU70
Holford Rd., S.le H. 71 DH42
Holford St. WC1 2 D2
Holford St. WC1 56 BY38
Holgate Ave. SW11 66 BT45
Holgate Ct., Edg. 37 BL28
Holgate Gdns., Dag. 50 CR35
Holgate Rd., Dag. 50 CR35
Holland Ave. SW20 85 BO51
Holland Ave., Sutt. 95 BS57
Holland Clo., Barn. 38 BT26
Holland Clo., Brom. 88 CG55
Holland Clo., Red. 121 BU70
Holland Clo., Stan. 36 BJ28
Holland Cres., Oxt. 115 CH70
Holland Dr. SE23 77 CD48
Queenswood Rd.
Holland Gdns. W14 65 BR41
Holland Gdns., Egh. 82 AV51
Holland Gdns., Wat. 27 BD21
Holland Gro. SW9 66 BY43
Holland Gro., Barn. 29 BT25
Holland La. W14 65 BR41
Holland La., Oxt. 115 CH70
Holland Pk. W11 55 BR40
Holland Pk. Ave. W11 55 BR40
Holland Pk. Ave., Ilf. 49 CN32
Holland Pk. Gdns. W14 65 BR
Holland Pk. Ms. W11 55 BR
Holland Pk. Rd. W14 65 BR
Holland Pas. N1 57 BZ
Basire St.
Holland Rd. E6 58 CK
Holland Rd. E15 58 CG
Holland Rd. NW10 55 BP
Holland Rd. SE25 87 CB
Holland Rd. W14 65 BQ
Holland Rd., Oxt. 115 CH
Holland Rd., Wem. 54 BK
Holland St. SE1 4 C
Holland St. SE1 56 BY
Holland St. W8 66 BS
Holland Vill. Rd. W14 65 BR
Holland Wk. N19 47 BW
Holland Wk. W8 66 BS
Holland Wk., Stan. 36 BJ
Holland Way, Brom. 88 CG
Hollands, The, Wor.Pk. 85 BO
Hollar Rd. N16 48 CA
Stoke Newington High St.
Hollen St. W1 1 N
Hollen St. W1 56 BW
Wardour St.
Holles Clo., Hmptn. 74 BF
Holles St. W1 1 H
Holles St. W1 56 BV
Cavendish Sq.
Holley Rd. W3 65 BO
Hollickwood Ave. N12 38 BU
Holliday St., Berk. 7 AR
Hollidge Way, Dag. 59 CR
Hollier Ct., Hat. 10 BP
Holliers Way, Hat. 10 BP
Hollies, The E11 49 CH
New Wanstead
Hollies, The, Grav. 81 DH
Hollies, The, Hem.H. 16 AT
Hollies Ave., Sid. 78 CN
Hollies Ave., Wey. 91 AV
Hollies Clo. SW16 76 BY
Hollies Clo., Twick. 74 BH
Hollies Ct., Wey. 92 AX
Hollies End NW7 37 BP
Hollies Rd. W5 64 BK
Hollies St. W1 56 BV
Cavendish Sq.
Hollies Way SW12 76 BV
Bracken Ave.
Hollies Way, Pot.B. 20 BT
Holligrave Rd., Brom. 88 CH
Hollingbourne Ave., Bexh. 69 CQ
Hollingbourne Gdns. W13 54 BJ
Hollingbourne Rd. SE24 77 BZ
Hollingsworth Rd., Croy. 96 CB
Hollington Cres., N.Mal. 85 BO
Hollington Rd. E6 58 CK
Hollington Rd. N17 39 CB
Sherringham Ave.
Hollingworth Rd., Orp. 88 CL
Hollingworth Way, West. 115 CM
Quebec Ave.
Hollis Pl., Grays 71 DD
Hollman Gdns. SW16 76 BY
Hollow, The, Wdf.Grn. 40 CG
Hollow Cotts., Grays 70 CX
Hollow Hill La., Iver 52 AT
Hollow La., Dor. 119 BD
Hollow La., Vir.W. 82 AR
Hollow Way La., Amer. 25 AP
Holloway Arc. N7 47 BX
Holloway Rd.
Holloway Clo., West Dr. 63 AY
Holloway Hill, Cher. 82 AU
Holloway La., Rick. 25 AU
Holloway La., West Dr. 63 AY
Holloway Rd. E6 58 CK
Holloway Rd. E11 48 CF
Holloway Rd. N7 47 BX
Holloway Rd. N19 47 BW
Holloway St., Houns. 64 BF
Holloways La., Hat. 10 BQ
Hollowfield Ave., Grays 71 DE
Hollowfield Wk., Nthlt. 54 BE
Hollows, The, Brent. 65 BL
Holly Acre, Wok. 100 AR
Holly Ave., Stan. 37 BL
Holly Ave., Walt. 84 BD
Holly Ave., Wey. 92 AW
Holly Bank Rd., Wok. 100 AQ
Holly Bush Clo., Sev. 108 CV
Holly Bush Hill NW3 47 BT
Holly Bush Hill, Berk. 7 AU
Holly Bush La., Hmptn. 74 BE
Holly Bush La., Sev. 108 CV
Holly Bush Vale NW3 47 BT
Heath St.
Holly Bush Wk. SW9 66 BY
Holly Clo. NW10 55 BO
Holly Clo., Buck.H. 40 CJ
Holly Clo., Cher. 82 AQ
Holly Clo., Egh. 72 AQ
Holly Clo., Felt. 74 BE
Holly Clo., Hat. 10 BO
Holly Clo., Wall. 95 BV
Holly Clo., Wok. 100 AQ
Holly Cres., Beck. 87 CD
Holly Cres., Wind. 61 AL
Holly Cres., Wdf.Grn. 39 CF
Holly Dr. E4 39 CE
Holly Dr., Berk. 7 AR
Holly Dr., Pot.B. 20 BS
Holly Dr., Wind. 72 AP
Holly Fm. Rd., Sthl. 64 BE
North Hyde La.
Holly Fld., Harl. 13 CM
Holly Gdns., West Dr. 63 AY
Holly Grn., Wey. 92 BA
Holly Gro. NW9 46 BN
Holly Gro. SE15 67 CA
Holly Gro., Bush. 36 BG

olly Hedge Ter. SE13 77 CF46
Dermody Rd.
olly Hedges La., Hem.H. 16 AU18
olly Hill N21 29 BX25
olly Hill NW3 47 BT35
olly Hill Dr., Bans. 104 BS61
olly Hill Rd., Belv. 69 CR42
olly La., Bans. 104 BS61
olly La., Guil. 109 AO68
olly La. E., Bans. 104 BS61
olly La. W., Bans. 104 BS62
olly Lea, Guil. 109 AR67
olly Lo. Gdns. N6 47 BV33
olly Ms. SW10 66 BT42
Drayton Gdns.
olly Mt. NW3 47 BT35
Holly Bush Hill
olly Pk. N3 46 BR31
olly Pk. N4 47 BX33
olly Pk. Gdns. N3 47 BS31
olly Pk. Rd. N11 38 BV28
olly Pk. Rd. W7 54 BH40
olly Rd. E11 49 CG33
olly Rd., Dart. 80 CV47
olly Rd., Enf. 30 CC21
olly Rd., Hmptn. 74 BG50
olly Rd., Houns. 64 BF45
olly Rd., Orp. 98 CO57
olly Rd., Reig. 121 BS71
olly Rd., Twick. 74 BH47
olly St. E1 57 CB39
olly St. E8 57 CA36
olly St. Est. E8 57 CA36
olly Ter. N20 38 BT27
olly Tree Clo., Chesh. 16 AQ19
olly Vw. Clo. NW4 46 BP32
olly Wk. NW3 47 BT35
olly Wk., Enf. 30 BZ24
olly Wk., Welw.G.C. 5 BQ6
olly Way, Mitch. 86 BW52
ollybank Clo., Hmptn. 74 BF49
ollybank Rd., Wey. 92 AW60
ollyberry, Hem.H. 16 AU19
ollyberry La. NW3 47 BT35
Holly Wk.
ollybrake Clo., Chis. 78 CM50
ollybush Ave., St.Alb. 9 BF15
ollybush Clo. E11 49 CH32
Woodford Rd.
ollybush Clo., Berk. 7 AU11
ollybush Clo., Har. 36 BH30
ollybush Clo., Wat. 36 BD26
ollybush Gdns. E2 57 CB38
ollybush Hill E11 49 CG33
ollybush Hill, Slou. 52 AQ36
ollybush La., Amer. 25 AO21
ollybush La., Hem.H. 7 AV12
ollybush La., Iver 52 AT39
ollybush La., Orp. 98 CR57
ollybush La., Uxb. 43 AU34
ollybush La., Welw.G.C. 5 BR10
ollybush La., Wok. 101 AX63
ollybush Pl. E2 57 CB38
Bethnal Grn. Rd.
ollybush Rd., Grav. 81 DH48
ollybush Rd., Kings.T. 75 BL49
ollybush St. E13 58 CH37
ollybush Wk. SW9 66 BY45
Somerleyton Rd. Dev.
ollybush Way, Wal.Cr. 21 CB17
ollycombe, Egh. 72 AR49
ollycroft Ave. NW3 47 BS34
ollycroft Ave., Wem. 46 BL34
ollycroft Clo., West Dr. 63 AZ43
ollycroft Gdns., West Dr. 63 AZ43
ollydale Dr., Brom. 88 CK55
ollydale Rd. SE15 67 CC44
ollydene SE15 67 CB44
ollydown Way E11 48 CF34
ollyfield, Hat. 10 BP14
ollyfield Ave. N11 38 BU28
ollyfield Rd., Surb. 85 BL54
ollyfields, Brox. 21 CD16
ollyhedge Rd., Cob. 92 BC60
ollymead, Cars. 95 BU56
ollymead Rd., Couls. 104 BV62
ollymeoak Rd., Couls. 104 BV62
ollymoor La., Epsom 94 BN58
ollymount Clo. SE10 67 CF44
ollytree, Ger.Cr. 34 AS28
Monument La.
ollytree Ave., Swan. 89 CT51
ollytree Clo. SW19 75 BQ47
ollytree Clo., Ger.Cr. 34 AS28
ollywood Gdns., Hayes 53 BC39
ollywood La., Sev. 99 CZ59
ollywood Rd. E4 39 CD28
ollywood Rd. SW10 66 BT43
ollywood Way, Wdf.Grn. 39 CF29
ollywoods, Croy. 96 CD58
olm Clo., Wey. 91 AV59
olm Gro., Uxb. 53 AZ36
olm Oak Clo. SW15 75 BR46
West Hill
olm Oak Ms. SW4 76 BX46
Kings Ave.
olm Wk. SE3 68 CH44
Blackheath Pk.
olman Ct., Epsom 94 BP58
olman Hunt Ho. W14 65 BR42
Field Rd.
olman Rd. SW11 66 BT44
olman Rd., Epsom 94 BN56
olmbank Dr., Shep. 83 BB52
olmbridge Gdns., Enf. 30 CC24
olmbrook Dr. NW4 46 BQ32
olmbury Ct. SW17 76 BU48
olmbury Ct. SW19 76 BU50
Cavendish Rd.
olmbury Dr., Dor. 119 BK73
olmbury Gdns., Hayes 53 BB40
olmbury Gro., Croy. 96 CD57
olmbury Pk., Brom. 78 CK50
olmbury Vw. E5 48 CB33
Holmbush Rd. SW15 75 BR46
Holmcote Gdns. N5 48 BZ35
Highbury New Pk.
Holmcroft, Tad. 112 BP66
Holmcroft Way, Brom. 88 CK53
Holmdale Clo., Borwd. 28 BL23
Holmdale Gdns. NW4 46 BQ32
Holmdale Rd. NW6 47 BS35
Holmdale Rd., Chis. 78 CM49
Holmdale Ter. N15 48 CA33
Holmdene Ave. NW7 37 BP29
Holmdene Ave. SE24 77 BZ46
Holmdene Ave., Har. 45 BF31
Holmdene Clo., Beck. 87 CF51
Holme Chase, Mord. 85 BR53
Holme Chase, Wey. 92 BA57
Holme Clo., Chsnt. 21 CD19
Holme Clo., Hat. 10 BO11
Holme Lacey Rd. SE12 78 CG46
Holme Lea, Wat. 18 BD20
Holme Pk., Borwd. 28 BL23
Holme Rd. E6 58 CK37
Holme Rd., Hat. 10 BO11
Holme Rd., Horn. 51 CX33
Holmead Rd. SW6 66 BS43
Holmebury Clo., Bush. 36 BH27
Holmecote Gdns. N5 48 BZ35
Holmedale, Slou. 52 AR40
Holmes Ave. E17 48 CD31
Holmes Ave. NW7 37 BR28
Holmes Meadow, Harl. 13 CL14
Holmes Rd. NW5 56 BV36
Holmes Rd. SW19 76 BT50
Holmes Rd., Twick. 74 BH48
Holmes Ter. SE1 4 D4
Holmes Ter. SE1 66 BY41
Waterloo Rd.
Holmes Way, Stan. 36 BH29
Holmesdale, Wal.Cr. 30 CC21
Holmesdale Ave. SW14 65 BM45
Holmesdale Clo. SE25 87 CA52
Holmesdale Clo., Guil. 118 AT70
Holmesdale Hill, S.Dnth. 90 CY51
Holmesdale Rd. N6 47 BV32
Holmesdale Rd. SE25 87 BZ53
Holmesdale Rd., Bexh. 69 CP44
Holmesdale Rd., Croy. 87 BZ53
Holmesdale Rd., Dor. 119 BK73
Holmesdale Rd., Red. 121 BX71
Holmesdale Rd., Reig. 121 BS70
Holmesdale Rd., Rich. 65 BL44
Holmesdale Rd., S.Dnth. 90 CY51
Holmesdale Rd., Tedd. 74 BK50
Holmesley Rd. SE23 77 CD46
Holmethorpe Ave., Red. 121 BV69
Holmewood Gdns. SW2 76 BX47
Holmewood Rd. SE25 87 CA52
Holmewood Rd. SW2 76 BX47
Holmfield Ave. NW4 46 BQ32
Holmfield Ct. NW3 47 BU35
Holmhurst Rd., Belv. 69 CR42
Holmlea Rd., Slou. 62 AR44
Holmlea Wk., Slou. 62 AR44
Holmleigh Ave., Dart. 70 CV45
Holmleigh Rd. N16 48 CA33
Holmsdale Clo., Iver 52 AV40
Thorney La. N.
Holmsdale Gro., Bexh. 69 CT44
Holmsdale Rd. N11 38 BV28
Holmsdale Rd., Sev. 108 CV65
Holmshaw Clo. SE26 77 CD49
Holmshill La., Borwd. 28 BO21
Holmside Ri., Wat. 35 BC27
Holmside Rd. SW12 76 BV46
Holmsley Clo., N.Mal. 85 BO53
Holmstall Ave., Edg. 37 BN30
Holmwood Ave., Brwd. 122 DD25
Holmwood Ave., S.Croy. 96 CA60
Holmwood Clo., Har. 45 BG31
Holmwood Clo., Lthd. 110 BB67
Holmwood Clo., Nthlt. 54 BF36
Holmwood Clo., Sutt. 94 BQ58
Holmwood Clo., Wey. 92 AW56
Holmwood Gdns. N3 38 BS30
Holmwood Gdns., Wall. 95 BV57
Holmwood Gro. NW7 37 BN28
Holmwood Rd., Chess. 94 BL56
Holmwood Rd., Enf. 30 CC21
Holmwood Rd., Ilf. 49 CN34
Holmwood Rd., Sutt. 94 BQ58
Holne Chase N2 47 BT32
Holness Rd. E15 58 CG36
Holroyd Clo., Esher 93 BJ58
Holroyd Rd. SW15 65 BQ45
Holroyd Rd., Lthd. 93 BH58
Holstein Ave., Wey. 92 AZ56
Holstein Way, Erith 69 CP41
Holstock Rd., Ilf. 49 CM34
Holsworth Clo., Har. 45 BG32
Holsworthy Sq. WC1 2 C5
Holsworthy Way, Chess. 93 BK56
Holt, The, Hem.H. 8 AY14
Holt, The, Ilf. 40 CM29
Holt, The, Wall. 95 BW56
Holt, The, Welw.G.C. 5 BT8
Sylvandale
Holt Clo. N10 47 BV31
Holt Clo. SE28 59 CO40
Holt Clo., Borwd. 28 BL24
Holt Clo., Chig. 40 CN28
Holt Ct. E15 48 CE35
Holt Rd. E16 58 CK40
Holt Rd., Wem. 45 BJ34
Holt Way, Chig. 40 CN28
Holton St. E1 57 CC38
Holtsmere Clo., Wat. 27 BD21
Holtwhites Ave., Enf. 30 BZ23
Holtwhites Hill, Enf. 29 BY23
Holtwood Rd., Lthd. 93 BG60
Holwell Ct., Hat. 11 BU10
Holwell Hyde, Welw.G.C. 5 BT8
Holwell Hyde La., Welw.G.C. 5 BT9
Holwell La., Hat. 5 BU10
Holwell Pl., Pnr. 45 BE31
Holwell Rd., Welw.G.C. 5 BR8
Holwood Clo., Walt. 84 BD55
Holwood Pk. Ave., Orp. 97 CK56
Holwood Pl. SW4 66 BW45
Holy Cross Hill, Brox. 12 CB15
Holy Wk., Brox. 12 CE13
St. Catharines Rd.
Holybourne Ave. SW15 75 BP47
Holyfield Rd., Wal.Abb. 21 CF18
Holyhead Clo. E3 57 CE38
Campbell Rd.
Holyoak Rd. SE11 4 F8
Holyoak Rd. SE11 66 BY42
Holyoake Ave., Wok. 100 AR62
Holyoake Cres., Wok. 100 AR62
Holyoake Ter., Sev. 107 CU65
Holyoake Wk. N2 47 BT31
Holyoake Wk. W5 54 BK38
Holyport Rd. SW6 65 BQ43
Holyport Rd., Maid. 61 AG43
Holyport St., Maid. 61 AG43
Holyrood Ave., Har. 45 BE35
Holyrood Cres., St.Alb. 9 BG15
Holyrood Gdns., Edg. 46 BM31
Holyrood Gdns., Grays 71 DH42
Holyrood Rd., Barn. 29 BT25
Holyrood St. SE1 4 M3
Holyrood St. SE1 67 CA41
Bermondsey St.
Holywell Clo. SE3 68 CH43
Holywell Clo., Stai. 73 AY47
Holywell Hill, St.Alb. 9 BG14
Holywell La. EC2 2 N4
Holywell La. EC2 57 CA38
Holywell Rd., Wat. 26 BC25
Holywell Row EC2 2 M5
Holywell Row EC2 57 CA38
Scrutton St.
Holywell Way, Stai. 73 AY47
Home Clo., Brox. 12 CD15
Home Clo., Cars. 86 BU55
Home Clo., Harl. 13 CN11
Home Clo., Lthd. 102 BG64
Home Clo., Nthlt. 54 BE38
Home Ct., Felt. 73 BC47
Home Fm. Clo., Bet. 120 BO71
Home Fm. Clo., Epsom 103 BQ62
Home Fm. Clo., Esher 93 BF57
Home Fm. Clo., Shep. 83 BB52
Home Fm. Clo., T.Ditt. 84 BH54
Home Fm. Gdns., Walt. 84 BD55
Home Fm. Rd., Berk. 7 AO11
Home Fm. Rd., Brwd. 42 DC30
Home Fm. Rd., Rick. 35 AZ28
Home Fm. Way, Slou. 52 AR37
Home Gdns., Dag. 50 CS34
Home Gdns., Dart. 80 CW46
Home Hill, Swan. 79 CT50
Home Lea, Orp. 97 CN56
Osgood Ave.
Home Ley, Welw.G.C. 5 BR8
Peartree La.
Home Mead, Stan. 36 BK30
Home Mead Clo., Grav. 81 DG47
Home Meadow, Bans. 104 BS61
Home Meadow, Welw.G.C. 5 BR8
Peartree La.
Home Orchard, Dart. 80 CW46
Home Pk., Oxt. 115 CH69
Home Pk. Rd. SW19 75 BR49
Home Pk. Wk., Kings.T. 84 BK52
Home Rd. SW11 66 BU44
Home Way, Rick. 34 AV26
Home Wd. La., Pot.B. 20 BW17
Homecroft Gdns., Loug. 31 CL24
Homecroft Rd. N22 38 BY30
Homecroft Rd. SE26 77 CC49
Homedean Rd., Sev. 107 CS64
Homefarm Clo., Cher. 91 AT57
Homefarm Rd. W7 54 BH39
Homefield, Berk. 7 AT11
Homefield, Hem.H. 16 AT17
Homefield, Wal.Abb. 22 CH19
Homefield, Walt. 93 BD56
Homefield Ave., Ilf. 49 CN32
Homefield Clo. NW10 55 BN36
Homefield Clo., Epp. 23 CO18
Homefield Clo., Hem.H. 8 AZ13
Homefield Clo., Lthd. 102 BK64
Homefield Clo., Swan. 89 CT52
Homefield Clo., Wey. 91 AV59
Homefield Gdns. N2 47 BT31
Stanley Rd.
Homefield Gdns., Mitch. 86 BT51
Homefield Gdns., Tad. 103 BQ63
Homefield Pk., Sutt. 95 BS57
Sutton Pk. Rd.
Homefield Ri., Orp. 89 CO54
Homefield Rd. SW19 75 BQ50
Homefield Rd. W4 65 BO42
Homefield Rd., Brom. 88 CJ51
Homefield Rd., Bush. 27 BF25
Homefield Rd., Couls. 104 BY63
Homefield Rd., Edg. 37 BN29
Homefield Rd., Rad. 27 BH22
Homefield Rd., Rick. 25 AU24
Homefield Rd., Sev. 107 CT64
Homefield Rd., Walt. 84 BE54
Homefield Rd., Warl. 105 CC63
Homefield Rd., Wem. 45 BJ35
Homefield St. N1 2 M1
Homefield St. N1 57 CA37
Regan Way
Homeland Dr., Sutt. 95 BS58
Homelands, Lthd. 102 BK64
Homelands Dr. SE19 77 CA50
Homeleigh Rd. SE15 77 CC46
Homemead, Hat. 10 BP11
Homemead Rd., Brom. 88 CK53
Homemead Rd., Croy. 86 BW53
Homer Clo., Bexh. 69 CS44
Homer Dr. E14 67 CE42
Homer Rd. E9 57 CD36
Homer Rd., Croy. 87 CC53
Homer Row W1 1 D7
Homer Row W1 56 BU39
Homer St. W1 1 D7
Homer St. W1 56 BU39
Homerfield, Welw.G.C. 5 BQ7
Homers Rd., Wind. 61 AL44
Homersham Rd., Kings.T. 85 BM51
Homerswood La., Welw. 5 BP6
Homerton Gro. E9 48 CC35
Homerton High St. E9 48 CC35
Homerton Rd. E9 48 CD35
Homerton Row E9 48 CC35
Homerton Ter. E9 57 CC36
Homesdale Clo. E11 49 CH32
New Wanstead
Homesdale Rd., Brom. 88 CJ52
Homesdale Rd., Cat. 105 BZ65
London Rd.
Homesdale Rd., Orp. 88 CN54
Homesfield NW11 47 BS32
Homestall, Guil. 118 AO70
Homestall Rd. SE22 77 CC46
Homestead, The, Dart. 80 CV46
Homestead Ct., Welw.G.C. 5 BR9
Homestead Gdns., Esher 93 BH56
Homestead La., Welw.G.C. 5 BR9
Homestead Paddock N14 29 BV25
Homestead Pk. NW2 46 BO34
Homestead Rd. SW6 65 BR43
Homestead Rd., Cat. 105 BZ65
Homestead Rd., Dag. 50 CQ34
Homestead Rd., Hat. 10 BP11
Homestead Rd., Orp. 98 CO57
Homestead Rd., Rick. 35 AX26
Homestead Rd., Stai. 73 AW50
Homestead Way, Croy. 96 CF59
Homewater Ave., Sun. 83 BB51
Homeway, Rom. 42 CX29
Homewillow Clo. N21 29 BY25
Homewood, Slou. 52 AR39
Homewood Ave., Cuffley 20 BX17
Homewood Clo., Hmptn. 74 BE49
Fearnley Cres.
Homewood Cres., Chis. 78 CN50
Homewood Rd., St.Alb. 9 BJ12
Honduras St. EC1 2 H4
Honduras St. EC1 57 BZ38
Baltic St.
Hone Par. SE11 66 BX42
Lambeth Wk.
Honey Clo., Borwd. 33 DB21
Honey Cft., Welw.G.C. 5 BQ8
Honey Hill, Uxb. 53 AY36
Honey La. EC2 2 J9
Honey La. EC2 57 BZ39
Cheapside
Honey La., Wal.Abb. 22 CG20
Honeybourne Rd. NW6 47 BS35
Honeybourne Way, Orp. 88 CM54
Honeybrook, Wal.Abb. 22 CG20
Honeybrook Rd. SW12 76 BW47
Honeycrock La., Red. 121 BV74
Honeycroft, Loug. 31 CL24
Honeycroft Hill, Uxb. 53 AY36
Honeycross Rd., Hem.H. 7 AV14
Honeyden Rd., Sid. 79 CQ50
Honeyhill, Harl. 13 CN13
Honeyman Clo. NW6 55 BQ36
Honeymeade, Saw. 6 CP7
Honeypot Clo. NW9 46 BL31
Honeypot La. NW9 46 BL31
Honeypot La., Brwd. 42 DA27
Honeypot La., Sev. 108 CX63
Honeypot La., Stan. 36 BK29
Honeypots Rd., Wok. 100 AR64
Honeysett Rd. N17 39 CA30
Reform Row
Honeysuckle Bottom, Lthd. 110 BB70
Honeysuckle Clo., Brwd. 33 DA25
Honeysuckle Clo., Rom. 42 CV29
Cloudberry Rd.
Honeysuckle Gdns., Croy. 87 CC54
Primrose La.
Honeysuckle Gdns., Hat. 10 BP13
Honeysuckle La. N22 39 BZ30
Crawley Rd.
Honeysuckle La., Dor. 119 BK73
Honeywell Rd. SW11 76 BU46
Honeywood Clo., Pot.B. 20 BT20
Honeywood Rd. NW10 55 BO37
Honeywood Rd., Islw. 64 BJ45
Honeywood Wk., Cars. 95 BU56
Honister Clo., Stan. 36 BJ29
Honister Gdns., Stan. 36 BJ29
Honister Heights, Pur. 96 BZ60
Honister Pl., Stan. 36 BJ30
Honiton Rd. NW6 55 BR37
Honiton Rd., Rom. 50 CS32
Honiton Rd., Well. 68 CN44
Honley Rd. SE6 77 CE47
Honnor Rd., Stai. 73 AX50
Bingham Dr.
Honor Oak Est. SE4 67 CD45
Honor Oak Pk. SE23 77 CC46
Honor Oak Ri. SE23 77 CC46
Honor Oak Rd. SE23 77 CC47
Hoo, The, Harl. 6 CP8
Hood Ave. N14 29 BW25
Hood Ave. SW14 75 BN46
Hood Ave., Orp. 89 CO53
Hood Clo., Croy. 86 BY54
Parsons Mead
Hood Ct. EC4 2 E9
Hood Rd. SW20 75 BO50
Hood Rd., Rain. 59 CT37
Hood Wk., Rom. 41 CR30
Hoodcote Gdns. N21 38 BY26
Hook, The, Barn. 29 BT25
Hook End La., Borwd. 24 DB20
Hook End Rd., Borwd. 33 DA21
Hook Fm. Rd., Brom. 88 CJ53
Hook Flds., Grav. 81 DF48
Hook Gate, Enf. 30 CB21
Hook Grn. La., Dart. 79 CT48
Hook Grn. Rd., Grav. 81 DC50
Hook Heath Ave., Wok. 100 AQ63
Hook Heath Gdns., Wok. 100 AQ64
Hook Heath Rd., Wok. 100 AP64
Hook Hill, S.Croy. 96 CA58
Hook Hill La., Wok. 100 AQ64
Hook Hill Pk., Wok. 100 AQ64
Hook La., Pot.B. 20 BU19
Hook La., Rom. 32 CQ25
Hook La., Well. 78 CN46
Hook Ri. N., Surb. 85 BL55
Hook Ri. S., Surb. 85 BL55
Hook Rd., Chess. 93 BK56
Hook Rd., Epsom 94 BN57
Hook Wk., Edg. 37 BN29
Hooke Rd., Lthd. 110 BB66
Hookers Rd. E17 48 CC31
Hookfield, Epsom 94 BN60
Hookfield, Harl. 13 CN12
Hooking Grn., Har. 45 BF32
Hooks Clo. SE15 67 CB44
Wood Rd.
Hooks Hall Dr., Dag. 50 CS34
Hooks Way SE22 77 CB47
Dulwich Common
Hookstone Way, Wdf.Grn. 40 CJ29
Hookwood Rd., Orp. 98 CP59
Hooley La., Red. 121 BU71
Hoop La. NW11 46 BR33
Hooper Rd. E16 58 CH39
Hooper St. E1 57 CB39
Hoopers Ct. SW3 3 E5
Hoopers Ct. SW3 66 BU41
Basil St.
Hoopers Ms. W3 55 BM40
Churchfield Rd.
Hoopers Yd., Sev. 117 CV66
Hop Flds., Wok. 100 AS61
Hop Gdns. WC2 3 Q1
Hop Gdns. WC2 56 BX40
Bedfordbury
Hope Clo. SE12 78 CH48
Hope Clo., Sutt. 95 BT56
Hope Clo., Wdf.Grn. 40 CJ29
West Gro.
Hope Grn., Wat. 17 BC20
Hope Pk., Brom. 78 CG50
Hope Rd., Swans. 81 DC46
High St.
Hope St. SW11 66 BT45
Hopedale Rd. SE7 68 CH43
Hopefield Ave. NW6 55 BR37
Hopetown St. E1 2 Q7
Hopetown St. E1 57 CA39
Hopewell Dr., Grav. 81 DJ49
Hopewell St. SE5 67 BZ43
Hopfield Ave., Wey. 92 AY59
Hopgarden La., Sev. 116 CU67
Hopgood St. W12 55 BQ40
Macfarlane Rd.
Hopground Clo., St.Alb. 9 BJ14
Hopkins Cres., St.Alb. 9 BJ10
Hopkins St. W1 1 M9
Hopkins St. W1 56 BW39
Hopkinsons Pl. NW1 56 BV37
Fitzroy Rd.
Hoppers Rd. N13 38 BY27
Hoppers Rd. N21 38 BY27
Hoppett Rd. E4 40 CG27
Hoppety, The, Tad. 103 BQ64
Hopping La. N1 56 BY36
St. Marys Gro.
Hoppingwood Ave., N.Mal. 85 BO52
Hoppit Rd., Wal.Abb. 21 CE19
Hoppitt, The, Ong. 15 CV13
Hoppner Rd., Hayes 53 BA37
Hopton Gdns. SE1 4 G2
Hopton Gdns., N.Mal. 85 BP53
Hopton Rd. SW16 76 BX49
Hopton St. SE1 4 G2
Hopton St. SE1 56 BY40
Hopwood Rd. SE17 67 BZ43
Hopwood Wk. E8 57 CB36
Wilman Gro.
Horace Ave., Rom. 50 CS33
Horace Rd. E7 49 CH35
Horace Rd., Ilf. 49 CM31
Horace Rd., Kings.T. 85 BL52
Horatio St. E2 2 Q1
Horatio St. E2 57 CA37
Horatius Way, Croy. 95 BX57
Horbury Cres. W11 56 BS40
Horbury Ms. W11 55 BR40
Horder Rd. SW6 65 BR44
Hordle Gdns., St.Alb. 9 BH14
Hordle Prom. E. SE15 67 CA43
Hordle Prom. N. SE15 67 CA43
Hordle Prom. S. SE15 67 CA43
Hordle Prom. W. SE15 67 CA43
Horizon Way SE7 68 CH42
Horksley Gdns., Brwd. 122 DE25
Horley Clo., Bexh. 79 CR46
Horley Rd. SE9 78 CK49
Horley Rd., Red. 121 BU71
Hormead Rd. W9 55 BR38
Horn Hill La., Ger.Cr. 34 AS28
Horn La. SE10 68 CH42
Horn La. W3 55 BN40
Horn La., Bexh. 69 CS44
Horn La., Wdf.Grn. 40 CH29
Horn Pk. Clo. SE12 78 CH46
Horn Pk. La. SE12 78 CH46
Hornbeam Ave., Upmin. 51 CX35
Hornbeam Clo. SE11 4 D8
Hornbeam Clo., Borwd. 28 BM23
Hornbeam Clo., Brwd. 122 DD27
Hornbeam Clo., Buck.H. 40 CJ27
Hornbeam Rd.
Hornbeam Clo., Nthlt. 45 BE35
Dabbs Hill La.

Hornbeam Cres., Brent. 64 BJ43
Hornbeam Gdns., Slou. 62 AQ41
Upton Rd.
Hornbeam Gro. E4 40 CG27
Hornbeam La. E4 31 CG25
Hornbeam La., Bexh. 69 CS44
Hornbeam La., Hat. 11 BU14
Hornbeam Rd., Buck.H. 40 CJ27
Hornbeam Rd., Epp. 31 CM22
Hornbeam Rd., Guil. 118 AR69
Hornbeam Rd., Hayes 54 BD39
Hornbeam Rd., Reig. 121 BS71
Hornbeam Wk., Walt. 92 BB58
Hornbeam Way, Brom. 88 CL53
Hornbeam Way, Wal.Cr. 21 CA18
Hornbeams, St.Alb. 18 BE18
Hornbeams, The, Harl. 6 CM10
Hornbeams Ave., Enf. 30 CC21
Hornbeams Ri. N11 38 BV29
Hornbill Clo., Uxb. 53 AX39
Hornbuckle Clo., Har. 45 BG34
Hornby Clo. NW3 56 BT36
Horncastle Clo. SE12 78 CH47
Horncastle Rd. SE12 78 CH47
Hornchurch Hill, Whyt. 105 CA62
Hornchurch Rd., Horn. 50 CT33
Horndean Clo. SW15 75 BP47
Bessborough Rd.
Horndon Clo., Rom. 41 CS30
Horndon Grn., Rom. 41 CS30
Horndon Rd., Rom. 41 CS30
Horne Rd., Shep. 83 AZ52
Horne Way SW15 65 BQ44
Horner La., Mitch. 86 BT51
Hornets, The, Wat. 26 BC24
Hornfair Rd. SE7 68 CJ43
Hornford Way, Rom. 50 CT33
Hornhatch, Guil. 118 AT73
Hornhatch Clo., Guil. 118 AT73
Hornhill Rd., Rick. 34 AU28
Horniman Dr. SE23 77 CB47
Horning Clo. SE9 78 CK49
Hornminster Glen, Horn. 51 CX34
Horns End Pl., Pnr. 45 BD32
Horns Fld., Welw.G.C. 5 BT7
Horns Rd., Ilf. 49 CM32
Hornsby La., Grays 71 DG41
Hornsey La. N6 47 BV33
Hornsey La. Est. N19 47 BW33
Hornsey La. Gdns. N6 47 BW33
Hornsey Pk. Rd. N8 47 BX31
Hornsey Ri. N19 47 BW33
Hornsey Ri. Gdns. N19 47 BW33
Hornsey Rd. N7 47 BX34
Hornsey Rd. N19 47 BX33
Hornsey St. N7 47 BX35
Hornshay St. SE15 67 CC43
Hornton Pl. W8 66 BS41
Hornton St.
Hornton St. W8 66 BS41
Horsa Rd. SE12 78 CJ47
Horsa Rd., Erith 69 CR43
Horscroft, Bans. 104 BS62
Horse and Dolphin Yd. W1 1 P10
Horse Fair, Kings.T. 84 BK51
Horse Fair, Kings.T. 85 BL51
Wood St.
Horse Guards Ave. SW1 3 Q3
Horse Guards Ave. SW1 56 BX40
Horse Guards Rd. SW1 3 P3
Horse Guards Rd. SW1 56 BW40
Horse Hill, Chesh. 16 AR19
Horse Ride SW1 3 N3
Horse Shoe Cres., Nthlt. 54 BF37
Horse Shoe Yd. W1 1 K10
Horse Yd. N1 56 BY37
Essex Rd.
Horsebridge Clo., Dag. 59 CQ37
Horsecroft Clo., Harl. 13 CK11
Horsecroft Clo., Orp. 89 CO54
Horsecroft Rd., Edg. 37 BN29
Horsecroft Rd., Harl. 13 CK11
Horsecroft Rd., Hem.H. 8 AW14
Horseferry Pl. SE10 67 CF43
Horseferry Rd. SW1 3 N7
Horseferry Rd. SW1 66 BW41
Horselers, Hem.H. 8 AY15
Horsell Birch, Wok. 100 AQ61
Horsell Common Rd., Wok. 91 AR60
Horsell Ct., Cher. 83 AW54
Horsell Moor, Wok. 100 AR62
Horsell Pk., Wok. 100 AS61
Horsell Pk. Clo., Wok. 100 AR61
Horsell Ri., Wok. 100 AR61
Horsell Ri. Clo., Wok. 100 AR61
Horsell Rd. N5 47 BY35
Horsell Rd., Orp. 89 CO51
Horsell Vale, Wok. 100 AS61
Horsell Way, Wok. 100 AR61
Horselydown La. SE1 4 P4
Horselydown La. SE1 67 CA41
Horseman Side, Borwd. 33 CV25
Horsemonden Clo., Orp. 88 CN54
Horsemoor Clo., Slou. 62 AT42
Parlaunt Rd.
Horsenden Ave., Grnf. 45 BH35
Horsenden Cres., Grnf. 45 BH35
Horsenden La. N., Grnf. 54 BH36
Horsenden La. S., Grnf. 54 BJ3
Horseshoe, The, Bans. 103 BR61
Horseshoe, The, Couls. 95 BW60
Horseshoe, The, Hem.H. 8 BA14
Horseshoe All. SE1 57 BZ40
Bankside
Horseshoe Clo. E14 67 CF42
Ferry St.
Horseshoe Clo. NW2 46 BP34
Horseshoe Grn., Sutt. 86 BS55
Horseshoe Hill, Wal.Abb. 22 CJ19
Horseshoe La. N20 37 BQ26
Horseshoe La., Enf. 30 BZ24
Chase Side

Horseshoe La., Guil. 118 AT70
Horseshoe La., Wat. 17 BC19
Horsfeld Gdns. SE9 78 CK46
Horsfeld Rd. SE9 78 CJ46
Horsford Rd. SW2 76 BX46
Horsham Ave. N12 38 BU28
Horsham Rd., Bexh. 79 CR46
Horsham Rd., Dor. 119 BJ72
Horsham Rd., Felt. 73 BA46
Horsham Rd., Guil. 118 AS74
Horsley Clo., Epsom 94 BN60
Horsley Dr., Croy. 96 CF57
Horsley Rd. E4 39 CF27
Horsley Rd., Brom. 88 CH51
Horsley Rd., Cob. 101 BC64
Horsley St. SE17 67 BZ43
Horsleys, Rick. 34 AU28
Long Cft. Rd.
Horsmonden Rd. SE4 77 CD46
Hortensia Rd. SW10 66 BT43
Horticultural Pl. W4 65 BN42
Heathfield Ter.
Horton Ave. NW2 46 BR35
Horton Bri. Rd., West Dr. 53 AY40
Horton Clo., West Dr. 53 AY40
Horton Gdns., Hem.H. 8 AZ10
Elstree Rd.
Horton Hill, Epsom 94 BN59
Horton La., Epsom 94 BM59
Horton La., West Dr. 53 AY40
Horton Rd. E8 57 CB36
Horton Rd., Hort.K. 90 CY52
Horton Rd., Slou. 62 AT44
Horton Rd., Slou. 62 AU45
Horton Rd. (Datchet), Slou. 62 AQ43
Horton Rd., Stai. 73 AW46
Horton Rd., West Dr. 53 AY40
Horton St. SE13 67 CE45
Horton Way, Farn. 90 CW54
Hortons Way, West. 115 CM66
Hortus Rd. E4 39 CF26
Hortus Rd., Sthl. 64 BE41
Horvath Clo., Wey. 92 BA56
Rosslyn Pk.
Hosack Rd. SW17 76 BU47
Hoselands Vw., Hartley 90 DC52
Hoser Ave. SE12 78 CH48
Hosey Common La., Eden. 115 CM70
Hosey Common Rd., West. 115 CM67
Hosier La. EC1 2 F7
Hosier La. EC1 56 BY39
Hoskins Clo. E16 58 CJ39
Hoskins Clo., Hayes 63 BB42
Hoskins Rd., Oxt. 115 CG68
Hoskins St. SE10 67 CF42
Hospital Bri. Rd., Twick. 74 BF47
Hospital Hill, Chesh. 16 AO19
Hospital La., Islw. 74 BH46
Hospital Rd., Houns. 64 BF45
Hospital Rd., Sev. 108 CV64
Hotham Clo., E.Mol. 84 BF52
Hotham Clo., S.at H. 80 CX50
Hotham Rd. SW15 65 BQ45
Hotham Rd. SW19 76 BT50
Hotham St. E15 58 CG37
Hothfield Pl. SE16 67 CC41
Hotspur Rd., Nthlt. 54 BF37
Hotspur St. SE11 4 D10
Hotspur St. SE11 66 BY42
Hottsfield, Hartley 90 DC52
Houblon Rd., Rich. 75 BL46
Houblons Hill, Epp. 23 CP19
Houchin Dr., Ong. 15 CY14
Hough St. SE18 68 CL41
Houghton Clo. E8 57 CA36
Forest Rd.
Houghton Clo., Hmptn. 74 BE50
Houghton Rd. N15 48 CA31
Houghton St. WC2 2 C9
Houghton St. WC2 56 BX39
Houlder Cres., Croy. 95 BY57
Houndsden Rd. N21 29 BX25
Houndsditch EC3 2 N8
Houndsditch EC3 57 CA39
Houndsfield Rd. N9 39 CB26
Hounslow Ave., Houns. 74 BF46
Hounslow Gdns., Houns. 74 BF46
Hounslow Rd., Felt. 73 BC47
Hounslow Rd., Felt. 74 BE48
Hounslow Rd., Twick. 74 BF46
House La., St.Alb. 9 BK10
Houseman Way SE5 67 BZ43
Bantry St.
Housewood End, Hem.H. 8 AW12
Houston Rd. SE23 77 CD48
Hove Ave. E17 48 CD32
Hove Clo., Brwd. 122 DE27
Hove Gdn., Sutt. 86 BS54
Hoveden Rd. NW2 46 BQ35
Hoveton Rd. SE28 59 CP40
How La., Couls. 104 BU63
How Wd., St.Alb. 18 BF17
Howard Agne Clo., Hem.H. 16 AT17
Howard Ave., Bex. 79 CP47
Howard Ave., Epsom 94 BP58
Howard Ave., Slou. 52 AO39
Howard Clo. N11 38 BV27
Howard Clo. NW2 46 BR35
Marnham Ave.
Howard Clo. W3 55 BM39
Howard Clo., Ash. 103 BL62
Howard Clo., Bush. 36 BH26
Howard Clo., Hmptn. 74 BG50
Howard Clo., Lthd. 102 BK65
Howard Clo. (Horsley), Lthd. 110 BA66
Howard Clo., St.Alb. 9 BK14
Howard Clo., Sun. 73 BB50
Howard Clo., Tad. 112 BO66
Howard Clo., Wal.Abb. 21 CF20

Howard Clo., Wat. 26 BC22
Howard Cres., Beac. 34 AO28
Howard Dr., Borwd. 28 BN24
Howard Gdns. SE25 87 CB53
Howard Gdns., Guil. 118 AT70
Howard Lo. Rd., Borwd. 33 CY22
Howard Ms. N5 47 BY35
Hamilton Pk.
Howard Pl. SW1 3 L7
Howard Pl. SW1 66 BW41
Vauxhall Bri. Rd.
Howard Ridge, Guil. 109 AT68
Howard Rd. E6 58 CK37
Howard Rd. E11 49 CG34
Howard Rd. E17 48 CE31
Howard Rd. N15 48 CA32
Howard Rd. N16 48 BZ35
Howard Rd. NW2 46 BQ35
Howard Rd. SE20 87 CC51
Howard Rd. SE25 87 CB53
Howard Rd., Ashf. 73 AX49
Howard Rd., Bark. 58 CM37
Howard Rd., Beac. 34 AO28
Howard Rd., Brom. 78 CG50
Howard Rd., Couls. 104 BW61
Howard Rd., Dart. 80 CX46
Howard Rd., Dor. 119 BJ71
Howard Rd., Ilf. 49 CL35
Howard Rd., Islw. 64 BH45
Howard Rd., Lthd. 101 BC64
Howard Rd. (Bookham), Lthd. 111 BF67
Howard Rd., N.Mal. 85 BO52
Howard Rd., Reig. 121 BS71
Howard Rd., Sthl. 54 BF39
Howard Rd., Surb. 85 BL53
Howard Rd., Upmin. 51 CY34
Howard St., T.Ditt. 84 BJ54
Howard Wk. N2 47 BT31
Howard Way SE2 77 CB47
Wilkie Way
Howard Way, Harl. 6 CN9
Howards Clo., Pnr. 35 BC30
Howards Crest Clo., Beck. 87 CF51
Howards Dr., Hem.H. 8 AW12
Howards La. SW15 65 BP45
Howards La., Wey. 91 AV57
Howards Rd. E13 58 CH38
Howards Rd., Wok. 100 AS63
Howards Thicket, Ger.Cr. 43 AR33
Howards Wd. Dr., Ger.Cr. 43 AR34
Howards Yd. SE18 68 CL41
Powis St.
Howardsgate, Welw.G.C. 5 BQ8
Howarth Ct. E15 48 CE35
Howarth Rd. SE2 69 CO42
Howberry Clo., Edg. 36 BK29
Howberry Rd., Edg. 36 BK29
Howberry Rd., Th.Hth. 87 BZ51
Howbury La., Erith 69 CT44
Howbury Rd. SE15 67 CC45
Howcroft Cres. N3 38 BS29
Howcroft La., Grnf. 54 BG37
Cowgate Rd.
Howden Clo. SE28 59 CP40
Howden Rd. SE25 87 CA51
Howden St. SE15 67 CB45
Howe Clo., Rom. 41 CR30
Howe Dell, Hat. 10 BP12
Howe Dr., Cat. 105 BZ64
Howe Rd., Hem.H. 8 AZ15
Howell Clo., Rom. 50 CP32
Howell Hill Clo., Epsom 94 BQ59
Howell Hill Gro., Epsom 94 BQ58
Howell Wk. SE1 4 G9
Howell Wk. SE1 66 BY42
Howells Clo., Sev. 99 CZ57
Howes Clo. N3 47 BS31
Mountfield Rd.
Howfield Grn., Hodd. 12 CD10
Howgate Rd. SW14 65 BN45
Howick Pl. SW1 3 M7
Howick Pl. SW1 66 BW41
Howicks Grn., Welw.G.C. 5 BS9
Howie St. SW11 66 BU43
Howitt Rd. NW3 56 BU36
Howland Garth, St.Alb. 9 BG15
Howland Ms. E. W1 1 M6
Howland Ms. E. W1 56 BW39
Howland St.
Howland St. W1 1 L6
Howland St. W1 56 BW39
Howland Way SE16 67 CD41
Howlands, Welw.G.C. 5 BQ9
Howletts La., Ruis. 44 BA32
Howletts Rd. SE24 77 BZ46
Howley Pl. W2 56 BT39
Howley Rd., Croy. 86 BY55
Hows Clo., Uxb. 53 AX37
Hows Mead, Epp. 14 CS15
Hows Rd., Uxb. 53 AX37
Hows St. E2 57 CA37
Howsman Rd. SW13 65 BP43
Howson Rd. SE4 67 CD45
Howson Ter., Rich. 75 BL46
Howton Pl., Bush. 36 BG26
Hoxton Mkt. N1 2 M3
Hoxton Mkt. N1 57 CA38
Boot St.
Hoxton Sq. N1 2 M3
Hoxton Sq. N1 57 CA38
Hoxton St. N1 57 CA37
Hoy St. E16 58 CG40
Caxton St. N.
Hoylake Cres., Uxb. 44 AZ34
Hoylake Gdns., Mitch. 86 BW52
Hoylake Gdns., Rom. 42 CW30
Hoylake Gdns., Ruis. 44 BC33
Hoylake Gdns., Wat. 36 BD28
Hoylake Rd. W3 55 BO39
Hoyland Clo. SE15 67 CB43
Commercial Way
Hoyle Rd. SW17 76 BU49
Hubbard Rd. SE27 77 BZ49

Hubbard St. E15 58 CG37
Hubbards Chase, Horn. 51 CX32
Hubbards Clo., Horn. 51 CX32
Hubbards Hill, Sev. 116 CU68
Hubbards Rd., Rick. 25 AU25
Hubert Gro. SW9 66 BX45
Hubert Rd. E6 58 CJ38
Hubert Rd., Brwd. 42 DA27
Hubert Rd., Rain. 59 CT38
Hubert Rd., Slou. 62 AR42
Hucknall Clo., Rom. 42 CW29
Petersfield Ave.
Huddart St. E3 57 CD39
Huddleston Rd. N7 47 BW34
Huddlestone Cres., Red. 113 BW67
Huddlestone Rd. E7 49 CG35
Huddlestone Rd. NW2 55 BP36
Hudson Clo., St.Alb. 9 BG15
Hudson Clo., Wat. 26 BB21
Hudson Pl. SE18 68 CM42
Hudson Pl. SW1 66 BW42
Hudson Rd., Bexh. 69 CQ44
Hudson Rd., Hayes 63 BA43
Hudsons, Tad. 103 BQ64
Hudsons Pl. SW1 3 L8
Huggin Ct. EC4 2 J10
Huggin Hill EC4 2 J10
Huggin Hill EC4 57 BZ40
Queen Victoria St.
Huggins La., Hat. 10 BQ15
Hugh Ms. SW1 3 K9
Hugh Ms. SW1 66 BV42
Hugh St.
Hugh Pl. SW1 3 N8
Hugh St. SW1 3 K9
Hugh St. SW1 66 BV42
Hughan Rd. E15 48 CF35
Hughenden Ave., Har. 45 BJ32
Hughenden Gdns., Nthlt. 54 BD38
Hughenden Rd., St.Alb. 9 BK12
Hughenden Rd., Slou. 52 AO39
Hughenden Rd., Wor.Pk. 85 BP54
Hughendon Ter. E15 48 CF35
Hughes Rd., Ashf. 73 BA50
Hughes Rd., Grays 71 DG41
Hughes Rd., Hayes 53 BC40
Hughes Wk., Croy. 87 BZ54
St. Saviours Rd.
Hugo Gdns., Rain. 59 CU36
Hugo Rd. N19 47 BW35
Hugon Rd. SW6 65 BS45
Huguenot Pl. SW18 76 BT46
Huguenot Sq. SE15 67 CB45
Scylla Rd.
Huitt Sq. SW11 66 BT45
Winstanley Rd.
Hull Clo. SE16 57 CC40
Hull Gro., Harl. 13 CL13
Hull Pl. SE18 68 CN42
Hull Rd., Rom. 50 CQ32
Hull St. EC1 2 H3
Hull St. EC1 57 BZ38
Hulletts La., Brwd. 33 CZ24
Hulse Ave., Bark. 58 CM36
Hulse Ave., Rom. 41 CR30
Hulsewood Clo., Dart. 79 CU48
Hulton Clo., Lthd. 102 BK65
Hulverston Clo., Sutt. 95 BS58
Humber Ave., S.Ock. 60 CZ39
Humber Dr., Upmin. 51 CY32
Humber Rd. NW2 46 BP34
Humber Rd. SE3 68 CG43
Humber Rd., Dart. 80 CV46
Humber Way, Slou. 62 AT42
Humberstone Rd. E13 58 CJ38
Humberton Clo. E9 48 CD35
Swinnerton St.
Humbolt Clo., Guil. 118 AP70
Humbolt Rd. W6 65 BR43
Hume Ave., Til. 71 DG44
Hume Way, Ruis. 44 BC32
Humes Ave. W7 64 BH41
Hummer Rd., Egh. 72 AT49
Humphrey Clo., Ilf. 40 CK30
Humphrey Clo., Lthd. 102 BG64
Humphrey St. SE1 4 P10
Humphrey St. SE1 67 CA42
Humphries Clo., Dag. 50 CQ35
Hundred Acre NW9 37 BO30
Hundred Acres La., Amer. 25 AO23
Hungerdown E4 39 CF26
Hungerford Ave., Slou. 52 AP39
Hungerford Bri. SE1 4 B3
Hungerford Bri. WC2 4 B3
Hungerford La. WC2 4 A2
Hungerford La. WC2 56 BX40
Craven St.
Hungerford Rd. N7 56 BW36
Hungerford Sq., Wey. 92 BA56
Rosslyn Pk.
Hungerford St. E1 57 CB39
Commercial Rd.
Hungry Hill, Wok. 110 AX66
Hunsdon, Welw.G.C. 5 BT8
Hunsdon Clo., Dag. 59 CQ36
Hunsdon Dr., Sev. 107 CU65
Hunsdon Est. E5 48 CB34
Hunsdon Rd. SE14 67 CC43
Hunslett St. E2 57 CC37
Royston St.
Hunston Rd., Mord. 86 BS54
Hunt Clo., St.Alb. 9 BK12
Hunt Rd., Grav. 81 DF48
Hunt Rd., Sthl. 64 BF41
Hunt St. W11 55 BQ40
Hunt Way SE22 77 CB47
Hunter Ave., Brwd. 122 DD25
Hunter Clo. SE1 4 L7
Hunter Clo. SE1 67 BZ41
Hunter Clo., Borwd. 28 BN25
Hunter Clo., Pot.B. 20 BS20
Hunter Dr., Horn. 51 CV35
Hunter Rd. SW20 85 BQ51
Hunter Rd., Guil. 118 AS71

Hunter Rd., Ilf. 49 CL
Hunter Rd., Th.Hth. 87 BZ
Hunter St. WC1 2
Hunter St. WC1 56 BX
Hunter Wk. E13 58 CH
Hunter Wk., Borwd. 28 BN
Huntercombe La., Maid. 61 AK
Huntercrombe Gdns., Wat. 36 BD
Hunters, The, Beck. 77 CE
Foxgrove Rd.
Hunters Clo. SW12 76 BV
Balham Pk. Rd.
Hunters Clo. SW12 76 BV
Balham Pk. Rd.
Hunters Clo., Epsom 94 BN
Burnet Gro.
Hunters Clo., Hem.H. 16 AT
Hunters Gro., Har. 45 BK
Hunters Gro., Hayes 53 BC
Hunters Gro., Orp. 97 CL
State Fm. Ave.
Hunters Gro., Rom. 41 CR
Hunters Hall Rd., Dag. 50 CR
Hunters Hill, Ruis. 45 BD
Hunters La., Wat. 17 BB
Hunters Meadow SE19 77 CA
Dulwich Wd. Ave.
Hunters Oak, Hem.H. 8 AZ
Hunters Pk., Berk. 7 AS
Hunters Reach, Wal.Cr. 21 CB
Hunters Ride, St.Alb. 18 BF
Hunters Rd., Chess. 85 BL
Hunters Sq., Dag. 50 CR
Hunters Wk., Sev. 98 CO
Hunters Way, Enf. 29 BY
Hunters Way, Welw.G.C. 5 B
Huntersfield Clo., Reig. 121 BS
Hunting Clo., Esher 93 BF
Hunting Gate, Hem.H. 8 AY
Hunting Gate Clo., Enf. 29 BY
Slades Ri.
Hunting Gate Dr., Chess. 94 BL
Hunting Gate Ms., Sutt. 86 BS
Hunting Gate Ms., Twick. 74 BH
Colne Rd.
Huntingdon Clo., Brox. 12 CD
Huntingdon Clo., Mitch. 86 BX
Huntingdon Gdns. W4 65 BN
Crofton Ave.
Huntingdon Gdns., Wor.Pk. 85 BQ
Huntingdon Rd. N2 47 BU
Huntingdon Rd. N9 39 CC
Huntingdon Rd., Red. 121 BU
Cromwell Rd.
Huntingdon Rd., Wok. 100 AP
Huntingdon St. E16 58 CG
Huntingdon St. N1 56 BX
Huntingdon Way, Croy. 96 CA
Huntingfield, Croy. 96 CD
Huntingfield Rd. SW15 65 BP
Huntingfield Way, Egh. 72 AU
Huntings Rd., Dag. 59 CR
Huntland Clo., Rain. 59 CU
Beechwood Gdns.
Huntley Ave., Grav. 81 DD
Huntley Dr. N3 38 BS
Nether St.
Huntley St. WC1 1 M
Huntley St. WC1 56 BW
Huntley Way SW20 85 BP
Huntly Rd. SE25 87 CA
Hunton St. E1 57 CB
Huntonbridge Hill, Kings L. 17 BA
Hunts Clo. SE3 68 CH
Hunts Clo., Guil. 118 AO
Hunts Ct. WC2 3
Hunts Ct. WC2 56 BW
Charing Cross Rd.
Hunts La. E15 57 CF
Hunts Mill Rd., Hem.H. 7 AV
Hunts Slip Rd. SE21 77 CA
Huntsman Clo., Warl. 105 CC
Huntsman Dr., Upmin. 51 CY
Huntsman Rd., Ilf. 41 CO
Huntsman St. SE17 4 L
Huntsman St. SE17 67 BZ
Barlow St.
Huntsmans Clo., Felt. 73 BC
Huntsmans Clo., Lthd. 102 BG
The Grn.
Huntsmead, Enf. 30 CC
Huntsmead Clo., Chis. 78 CK
Bullerswood Dr.
Huntsmoor Rd., Epsom 94 BN
Huntspill St. SW17 76 BT
Huntsworth Ms. NW1 1 E
Huntsworth Ms. NW1 56 BU
Hurley Clo., Walt. 83 BC
Hurley Cres. SE16 67 CC
Marlow Way
Hurley Gdns., Guil. 109 AT
Hurley Rd., Grnf. 54 BF
Hurlfield, Dart. 80 CV
Hurlford, Wok. 100 AQ
Hurlingham Ct. SW6 65 BR
Hurlingham Gdns. SW6 65 BR
Hurlingham Rd. SW6 65 BR
Hurlingham Rd., Bexh. 69 CQ
Hurlock St. N5 47 BY
Hurlstone Rd. SE25 87 BZ
Hurn Ct. Rd., Houns. 64 BD
Hurnford Clo., S.Croy. 96 CA
Huron Rd. SW17 76 BV
Hurren Clo. SE3 68 CG
Hurry Clo. E15 58 CG
Hursley Rd., Chig. 40 CN
Hart Cres.
Hurst Ave. E4 39 CE
Hurst Ave. N6 47 BW
Hurst Clo, Brom. 88 CG
Hurst Clo. E4 39 CE
Hurst Clo. NW11 47 BS

rst Clo., Chess. 94 BM56
rst Clo., Nthlt. 45 BE35
rst Clo., Welw.G.C. 5 BT8
ylvandale
rst Clo., Wok. 100 AR63
rst Cft., Guil. 118 AS72
rst Dr., Tad. 112 BP66
rst Dr., Wal.Cr. 21 CC20
rst Fm. Rd., Sev. 116 CU69
rst Grn., Oxt. 115 CG69
rst Grn. Rd., Oxt. 115 CG69
rst Gro., Walt. 83 BB54
rst La. SE2 69 CP42
rst La., E.Mol. 84 BG52
rst La., Egh. 82 AT51
rst La., Epsom 103 BH65
rst Pk. Ave., Horn. 51 CW35
rst Pl., Nthwd. 35 AZ30
rst Pl. Est. SE2 69 CP42
rst Ri., Barn. 29 BS24
rst Rd. E17 48 CE31
rst Rd. N21 38 BY26
rst Rd., Bex. 79 CP47
rst Rd., Buck.H. 40 CJ26
rst Rd., E.Mol. 84 BF52
rst Rd., Epsom 94 BN59
rst Rd., Erith 69 CS44
rst Rd., Orp. 96 BZ56
rst Rd., Sid. 79 CO48
rst Rd., S.Croy. 96 BZ56
rst Rd., Tad. 103 BP65
rst Rd., Walt. 84 BD53
rst Springs, Bex. 79 CQ47
rst St. SE24 76 BY46
rst Vw. Rd., S.Croy. 96 CA57
rst Way, Sev. 117 CV57
rst Way, S.Croy. 96 CA57
rst Way, Wok. 91 AV60
rstbourne, Esher 93 BH57
rstbourne Gdns., 58 CN36
ark.
rstbourne Rd. SE23 77 CD47
rstcourt Rd., Sutt. 86 BS55
rstdene Ave., Brom. 88 CG54
rstdene Ave., Stai. 73 AW50
rstdene Gdns. N15 48 CA32
rstfield, Brom. 88 CH53
rstfield Cres., Hayes 53 BB39
rstfield Rd., E.Mol. 84 BF52
rstlands, Oxt. 115 CH69
rstlands Clo., Horn. 51 CV32
rstleigh Clo., Red. 121 BU69
rstleigh Dr., Red. 121 BU69
rstleigh Gdns., Ilf. 40 CK30
rstlings, Welw.G.C. 5 BS8
rstmead Ct., Edg. 37 BM28
rstway Wk. W11 55 BQ40
ancaster Rd.
rstwood Ave. E18 49 CH31
rstwood Ave., Bex. 79 CQ47
rstwood Ave., Brwd. 42 DA26
rstwood Ave., Erith 69 CT44
rstwood Ct. N12 38 BU29
Voodleigh Ave.
rstwood Ct. NW11 46 BR31
rstwood Dr., Brom. 88 CK52
rstwood Rd. NW11 46 BR31
rtwood Rd., Walt. 84 BE54
rworth Rd., Slou. 62 AR41
son Clo. NW3 56 BU36
sseywell Cres., Brom. 88 CH54
tchings St. E14 67 CE41
tchings Wk. NW11 47 BS31
tchingsons Rd., Croy. 96 CF59
tchins Clo. E15 58 CG36
ibbins Rd.
tchinson Ter., Wem. 45 BK34
tton Clo., Har. 45 BG35
lary Peters Dr.
tton Clo., Wdf.Grn. 40 CH28
tton Dr., Brwd. 122 DE26
tton Gdns., Har. 36 BG29
tton Gate, Brwd. 122 DD26
tton Gro. N12 38 BS28
tton La., Har. 36 BG29
tton Rd., Brwd. 122 DC26
tton Row, Edg. 37 BM29
avilion Way
tton St. EC4 2 E9
tton St. EC4 56 BY39
orset Ri.
tton Vill., Brwd. 122 DF26
tton Wk., Har. 36 BG29
xbear St. SE4 77 CD46
xley Clo. E10 48 CF34
xley Clo., Nthlt. 54 BE37
xley Clo., Uxb. 53 AX38
xley Dr., Rom. 50 CO33
xley Gdns. NW10 55 BL38
xley Par. N18 39 BZ28
xley Pl. N13 38 BY27
xley Rd. E10 48 CF34
xley Rd. N18 39 BZ28
xley Rd., Guil. 118 AP71
xley Rd., Well. 68 CN45
xley Sayze N18 39 BZ28
xley S. N18 39 BZ28
xley St. W10 55 BR38
acinth Clo., Hmptn. 74 BF50
resham Rd.
acinth Clo., Ilf. 58 CL36
luebell Way
acinth Ct., Pnr. 45 BD31
ursery Rd.
acinth Dr., Uxb. 53 AY36
acinth Rd. SW15 75 BP47
ourn Clo., St.Alb. 18 BE18
cliffe Gdns., Chig. 40 CM28
de, The NW9 46 BO31
de Ave., Pot.B. 20 BS20
de Clo. E13 58 CH37
urpin Est.
de Clo., Ashf. 73 BB50
yde Ter.

Hyde Clo., Barn. 28 BR24
Hyde Cres. NW9 46 BO32
Hyde La. SW11 66 BU44
Battersea Bri. Rd.
Hyde La., Hem.H. 17 AZ17
Hyde La. (Bovingdon), 16 AT17
Hem.H.
Hyde La., St.Alb. 18 BG17
Hyde La., Wok. 101 AZ63
Hyde Mead, Wal.Abb. 13 CG15
Hyde Meadows, Hem.H. 16 AT17
Hyde Pk. W2 3 C2
Hyde Pk. Ave. N21 39 BZ26
Hyde Pk. Cor. W1 3 H4
Hyde Pk. Cor. W1 66 BV41
Hyde Pk. Cres. W2 1 C9
Hyde Pk. Cres. W2 56 BU39
Hyde Pk. Gdns. N21 39 BZ26
Hyde Pk. Gdns. W2 1 B10
Hyde Pk. Gdns. W2 56 BT40
Hyde Pk. Gdns. Ms. W2 1 B10
Hyde Pk. Gdns. Ms. W2 56 BT40
Hyde Pk. Gate SW7 66 BT41
Hyde Pk. Gate Ms. SW7 66 BT41
Hyde Pk. Mans. NW1 56 BU39
Edgeware Rd.
Hyde Pk. Pl. W2 1 D10
Hyde Pk. Pl. W2 56 BU40
Bayswater Rd.
Hyde Pk. Sq. W2 1 C9
Hyde Pk. Sq. W2 56 BU39
Hyde Pk. Sq. Ms. W2 1 C9
Hyde Pk. St. W2 1 C9
Hyde Pk. St. W2 56 BU39
Hyde Rd. N1 57 BZ37
Hyde Rd., Bexh. 69 CQ44
Hyde Rd., Rich. 75 BL46
Albert Rd.
Hyde Rd., S.Croy. 96 BZ60
Hyde Rd., Wat. 26 BC23
Hyde St. SE8 67 CE43
Deptford High St.
Hyde Ter., Ashf. 73 BB50
Hyde Vale SE10 67 CF43
Hyde Valley, Welw.G.C. 5 BR9
Hyde Wk., Mord. 86 BS54
Hyde Way N9 39 CA27
Hyde Way, Hayes 63 BB42
Hyde Way, Welw.G.C. 5 BR8
Hydefield Clo. N21 39 BZ26
Hydefield Ct. N9 39 CA27
Hyder Rd., Grays 71 DH41
Hydes Pl. N1 56 BY36
Compton Ave.
Hydeside Gdns. N9 39 CA27
Hydethorpe Ave. N9 39 CA27
Hydethorpe Rd. SW12 76 BW47
Hyland Clo., Horn. 50 CU33
Hyland Way, Horn. 50 CU33
Hylands Clo., Epsom 103 BN61
Hylands Ms., Epsom 103 BN61
Hylands Rd. E17 39 CF30
Hylands Rd., Epsom 103 BN61
Hylle Clo., Wind. 61 AM44
Cawcott Dr.
Hylton St. SE18 68 CN42
Hyndewood SE23 77 CC48
Bampton Rd.
Hyndman St. SE15 67 CB43
Hynton Rd., Dag. 50 CP34
Hyperion Ct., Hem.H. 8 AY12
Hyperion Pl., Epsom 94 BN58
Hyrons Clo., Amer. 25 AP22
Hyrons La., Amer. 25 AO22
Hyrst Dene, S.Croy. 95 BY56
Hyson Rd. SE16 67 CB42
Hythe, The, Stai. 72 AV49
Hythe Ave., Bexh. 69 CQ43
Hythe Clo. N18 39 CB28
Hythe Clo., Orp. 89 CP52
Hythe End Rd., Stai. 72 AT48
Hythe Fld. Ave., Egh. 72 AU50
Hythe Pk. Rd., Egh. 72 AV49
Hythe Rd. NW10 55 BP38
Hythe Rd., Stai. 72 AU49
Hythe Rd., Th.Hth. 87 BZ51
Hythe St., Dart. 80 CW46
Hyver Hill NW7 37 BN26

I

Ian Sq., Enf. 30 CC23
Ibbetson Path, Loug. 31 CL24
Ibbotson Ave. E16 58 CG39
Ibbott St. E1 57 CC38
Mantus Rd.
Iberian Ave., Wall. 95 BW56
Ibis La. W4 65 BN44
Ibscott Clo., Dag. 59 CS36
Ibsley Gdns. SW15 75 BP47
Ibsley Way, Barn. 29 BU24
Icehouse Wd., Oxt. 115 CG69
Iceland Rd. E3 57 CE37
Ickburgh Est. E5 48 CB34
Ickburgh Rd. E5 48 CB34
Ickenham Clo., Ruis. 44 BA34
Ickenham Rd., Ruis. 44 BA33
Ickenham Rd., Uxb. 44 BA34
Ickleton Rd. SE9 78 CK49
Icklingham Rd., Cob. 93 BD59
Icknield Clo., St.Alb. 9 BE15
Icknield Dr., Ilf. 49 CL32
Ickworth Pk. Rd. E17 48 CD31
Ida Rd. N15 48 BZ32
Ida St. E14 57 CF39
Ide Hill, Sev. 107 CS65
Ide Hill Rd., Sev. 116 CQ69
Ide Hill Rd., Sev. 116 CS67
Iden Clo., Brom. 88 CG52

Idlecombe Rd. SW17 76 BV50
Idmiston Rd. E15 49 CG35
Idmiston Rd. SE27 77 BZ48
Idmiston Rd., Wor.Pk. 85 BO54
Idmiston Sq., Wor.Pk. 85 BO54
Idol La. EC3 4 M1
Idol La. EC3 57 CA40
Idonia St. SE8 67 CD43
Iffley Clo., Uxb. 53 AX36
Iffley Rd. W6 65 BP41
Ifield Rd. SW10 66 BS43
Ifield Ter., Green. 80 DA46
Ifield Way, Grav. 81 DH50
Ightham By-pass, Sev. 108 DB64
Ightham Mote, Sev. 117 DA67
Ightham Rd., Erith 69 CR43
Ightham Rd., Sev. 108 DB64
Ikea Way, Croy. 86 BX54
Ikona Ct., Wey. 92 BA56
Ilbert St. W10 55 BQ38
Ilchester Gdns. W2 56 BS40
Ilchester Pl. W14 65 BR41
Ilchester Rd., Dag. 50 CO35
Ildersley Gro. SE21 77 BZ48
Ilderton Rd. SE15 67 CC43
Ilderton Rd. SE16 67 CB42
Ilex Clo., Egh. 72 AQ50
Ilex Clo., Sun. 83 BD51
Ilex Ct., Berk. 7 AQ13
Angle Pl.
Ilex Rd. NW10 55 BO36
Ilex Way SW16 76 BY49
Ilford Hill, Ilf. 49 CL34
Ilford La., Ilf. 49 CL34
Ilfracombe Cres., Horn. 51 CV35
Ilfracombe Gdns., Rom. 50 CO33
Ilfracombe Rd., Brom. 78 CG48
Iliffe St. SE17 4 G10
Iliffe St. SE17 66 BY42
Iliffe Yd. SE17 4 G10
Iliffe Yd. SE17 66 BY42
Amelia St.
Ilkeston Ct. E5 48 CC35
Clapton Pk. Est.
Ilkley Clo. SE19 77 BZ50
Rockmount Rd.
Ilkley Rd. E16 58 CJ39
Ilkley Rd., Wat. 36 BD28
Illingworth, Wind. 61 AM45
Illingworth Clo., Mitch. 86 BT52
Illingworth Way, Enf. 30 CA25
Ilmington Rd., Har. 45 BK32
Ilminster Gdns. SW11 66 BU45
Imber Clo. N14 38 BW26
Imber Ct., E.Mol. 84 BG54
Imber Gro., Esher 84 BG54
Imber Pk. Rd., Esher 84 BG54
Imber St. N1 57 BZ37
Poole St.
Imperial Ave. N16 48 CA35
Imperial Clo., Har. 45 BF32
Imperial College Rd. SW7 3 A6
Imperial Dr., Grav. 81 DJ49
Imperial Dr., Har. 45 BF33
Imperial Gdns., Mitch. 86 BV52
Imperial Ms. E6 58 CJ37
Imperial Rd. N22 38 BX30
Imperial Rd. SW6 66 BS44
Imperial Rd., Felt. 73 BB47
Imperial Rd., Wind. 61 AN45
Imperial Sq. SW6 66 BS44
Imperial St. E3 57 CF38
Imperial Way SE18 68 CK43
Imperial Way, Chis. 78 CM48
Imperial Way, Croy. 95 BY57
Imperial Way, Har. 46 BL32
Imperial Way, Wat. 27 BD23
Inca Dr. SE9 78 CL47
Ince Rd., Wat. 92 BB57
Inchmery Rd. SE6 77 CE48
Inchwood, Croy. 96 CE56
Indells, Hat. 10 BO13
Independents Rd. SE3 68 CG45
Inderwick Rd. N8 47 BX32
Indescon Ct. E14 67 CE41
India Rd., Slou. 62 AQ41
India St. EC3 2 P9
India St. EC3 57 CA39
Jewry St.
India Way W12 55 BP40
Indus Rd. SE7 68 CJ43
Industrial Est., Grnf. 54 BF37
Industrial Est., Iver 52 AV40
Industrial Est., Mitch. 86 BU53
Ingal Rd. E13 58 CH38
Ingate Pl. SW8 66 BV44
Ingatestone Rd. E12 49 CJ33
Ingatestone Rd. SE25 87 CB52
Ingatestone Rd., Ing. 24 DC19
Ingatestone Rd., Wdf.Grn. 40 CH29
Ingelow Rd. SW8 66 BV44
Ingels Mead, Epp. 22 CN18
Ingersoll Rd. W12 55 BP40
Ingersoll Rd., Enf. 30 CC22
Ingestre Pl. W1 1 M9
Ingestre Pl. W1 56 BW39
Ingestre Rd. E7 49 CH35
Ingestre Rd. NW5 47 BV35
Ingham Clo., S.Croy. 96 CC58
Ingham Rd. NW6 47 BS35
Ingham Rd., S.Croy. 96 CC56
Ingle Clo., Pnr. 45 BE31
Inglebert St. EC1 2 D2
Inglebert St. EC1 56 BY38
Ingleboro Dr., Pur. 96 BZ60
Ingleby Clo., Dag. 59 CR36
Ingleby Dr., Har. 45 BG34
Ingleby Gdns., Chig. 41 CO27
Ingleby Rd. N7 47 BX34
Ingleby Rd., Dag. 59 CR36
Ingleby Rd., Grays 71 DG41
Ingleby Rd., Ilf. 49 CL33
Ingleby Way, Chis. 78 CL49
Ingleby Way, Wall. 95 BW57

Ingledew Rd. SE18 68 CM42
Ingleglen, Horn. 51 CX33
Inglehurst, Wey. 92 AW58
Inglehurst Gdns., Ilf. 49 CK32
Inglemere Rd. SE23 77 CC48
Inglemere Rd., Mitch. 76 BU50
Ingles, Welw.G.C. 5 BQ6
Inglesham Wk. E9 57 CD36
Trowbridge Est.
Ingleside, Slou. 62 AV44
Bath Rd.
Ingleside Clo., Beck. 77 CE50
Ingleside Gro. SE3 68 CG43
Inglethorpe St. SW6 65 BQ44
Ingleton Ave., Well. 79 CO46
Ingleton Rd. N18 39 CB29
Ingleton Rd., Cars. 95 BU58
Ingleway N12 38 BT29
Inglewood, Cher. 82 AV55
Inglewood, Wok. 100 AQ62
Inglewood Clo. E14 67 CE42
Barnsdale Ave.
Inglewood Clo., Horn. 51 CV35
Inglewood Clo., Ilf. 40 CN29
Inglewood Copse, Brom. 88 CK51
Inglewood Rd. NW6 47 BS35
Inglewood Rd., Bexh. 69 CS45
Inglis Rd. W5 55 BL40
Inglis Rd., Croy. 87 CA54
Inglis St. SE5 66 BY44
Knatchbull Rd.
Ingoldsby Rd., Grav. 81 DJ47
Ingram Ave. NW11 47 BT33
Ingram Clo. SE11 4 C8
Ingram Clo. SE11 66 BX42
Juxon St.
Ingram Clo., Stan. 36 BK28
Ingram Rd. N2 47 BU31
Ingram Rd., Dart. 80 CW47
Ingram Rd., Grays 71 DE42
Ingram Rd., Th.Hth. 87 BZ51
Ingram Way, Grnf. 54 BG37
Ingrams Clo., Walt. 93 BD56
Ingrave Rd., Brwd. 42 DB27
Ingrave Rd., Rom. 50 CS31
Ingrave St. SW11 66 BT45
Ingrebourne Gdns., 51 CY33
Upmin.
Ingrebourne Rd., Rain. 59 CU38
Ingress Gdns., Green. 80 DB46
Ingreway, Rom. 42 CX29
Inholms La., Dor. 119 BJ73
Inigo Jones Rd. SE7 68 CJ43
Inigo Pl. WC2 1 Q10
Inkerman Rd. NW5 56 BV36
Inkerman Rd., St.Alb. 9 BH14
Inkerman Rd. (Eton Wick), 61 AM42
Wind.
Inkerman Rd., Wok. 100 AP62
Inkerman Ter., Chesh. 16 AO20
Inkerman Way, Wok. 100 AP62
Inks Grn. E4 39 CE28
Inman Rd. NW10 55 BO37
Inman Rd. SW18 76 BT47
Inmans Row, Wdf.Grn. 40 CH28
Inner Circle NW1 1 G3
Inner Circ. NW1 56 BV38
Inner Pk. Rd. SW19 75 BQ47
Inner Ring E., Houns. 63 AZ45
Conway Rd.
Inner Ring W., Houns. 63 AZ45
Chester Rd.
Inner Staithe W4 65 BN43
Upper Staithe
Inner Temple La. EC4 2 D9
Inner Temple La. EC4 56 BY39
Fleet St.
Innes Clo. SW20 85 BR51
Innes Ct., Hem.H. 8 AX15
Seaton Rd.
Innes Gdns. SW15 75 BP46
Innes Lo. SE23 77 CC48
Innes Yd., Croy. 87 BZ55
Whitgift St.
Inniskilling Rd. E13 58 CJ37
Inskip Clo. E10 48 CE34
Inskip Dr., Horn. 51 CW33
Inskip Rd., Dag. 50 CP33
Institute Pl. E8 48 CB35
Amhurst Rd.
Institute Rd., Epp. 23 CP18
Institution Rd., Dor. 119 BG72
Instone Clo., Pur. 95 BY58
Instone Clo., Wall. 95 BX57
Instone Rd., Dart. 80 CV47
Insurance St. WC1 2 D3
Insurance St. WC1 56 BY38
Margery St.
Integer Gdns. E11 48 CF33
Forest Rd.
International Ave., Houns. 64 BD42
Inver Clo. E5 48 CB34
Southwold Rd.
Inverarey Pl. SE18 68 CM43
Inverclyde Gdns., Rom. 50 CP31
Inveresk Gdns., Wor.Pk. 85 BO55
Inverforth Clo. NW3 47 BT34
North End Way
Inverforth Rd. N11 38 BV28
Inverine Rd. SE7 68 CH42
Invermore Pl. SE18 68 CM42
Inverness Ave., Enf. 30 CA23
Inverness Ct. W3 55 BM39
Links Rd.
Inverness Dr., Ilf. 40 CN29
Inverness Gdns. W8 56 BS40
Inverness Ms. W2 56 BS40
Inverness Ter.
Inverness Pl. W2 56 BS40
Inverness Ter.
Inverness Rd. N18 39 CB28
Inverness Rd., Houns. 64 BE45
Inverness Rd., Sthl. 64 BE42
Inverness Rd., Wor.Pk. 85 BQ54

Inverness St. NW1 56 BV37
Inverness Ter. W2 56 BS39
Inverton Rd. SE15 67 CC45
Invicta Clo., Chis. 78 CL49
Invicta Gro., Nthlt. 54 BE38
Invicta Rd. SE3 68 CH43
Invicta Rd., Dart. 80 CX46
Inville Rd. SE1 67 BZ42
Inwood Ave., Couls. 104 BY63
Inwood Ave., Houns. 64 BG45
Inwood Clo., Croy. 87 CD55
Inwood Ct., Walt. 84 BD55
Inwood Rd., Houns. 64 BF45
Inworth St. SW11 66 BU44
Inworth Wk. N1 57 BZ37
Popham St.
Ion Sq. E2 57 CB37
Hackney Rd.
Iona Clo. SE6 77 CD47
Ionian Way, Hem.H. 8 AY12
Ipswich Rd. SW17 76 BV50
Ireland Pl. N22 38 BX29
Whittington Rd.
Ireland Yd. EC4 2 G9
Ireland Yd. EC4 56 BY39
St. Andrews Hill
Irene Rd. SW6 66 BS44
Irene Rd., Cob. 102 BF61
Irene Rd., Orp. 88 CN54
Ireton Ave., Walt. 83 BB55
Ireton Pl., Grays 71 DD42
Irford Clo. SE4 67 CD45
St. Norbert Rd.
Iris Ave., Bex. 79 CQ46
Iris Clo., Brwd. 33 DA25
Iris Clo., Croy. 87 CC54
Iris Clo., Surb. 95 BL54
Iris Ct., Pnr. 45 BD31
Nursery Rd.
Iris Cres., Bexh. 69 CQ43
Iris Path, Rom. 42 CV29
Iris Rd., Epsom 94 BM56
Iris Way E4 39 CD29
Irkdale Ave., Enf. 30 CA23
Iron Bri. Rd., West Dr. 53 AZ40
Iron Mill La., Dart. 69 CT45
Iron Mill Pl. SW18 76 BS46
Garratt La.
Iron Mill Pl., Dart. 69 CT45
Iron Mill Rd. SW18 76 BS46
Ironmonger La. EC2 2 K9
Ironmonger La. EC2 57 BZ39
Ironmonger Pas. EC1 2 J3
Ironmonger Row EC1 2 J3
Ironmonger Row EC1 57 BZ38
Ironmongers Pl. E14 67 CE42
Spindrift Ave.
Irons Bottom Rd., Reig. 121 BS74
Irons Way, Rom. 41 CS29
Ironside Clo. SE16 67 CC41
Kinburn St.
Irvine Ave., Har. 45 BJ31
Irvine Clo. N20 38 BU27
Irvine Gdns., S.Ock. 60 CZ39
Irvine Way, Orp. 88 CN54
Irving Ave., Nthlt. 54 BD37
Irving Gro. SW9 66 BX44
Irving Rd. W14 65 BQ41
Irving St. WC2 3 P1
Irving St. WC2 56 BW40
Leicester Sq.
Irving Wk., Swans. 81 DC47
Irving Way NW9 46 BO32
Irving Way, Swan. 89 CS51
Irwin Ave. SE18 68 CN43
Irwin Gdns. NW10 55 BP37
Irwin Rd., Guil. 118 AQ71
Isabel St. SW9 66 BX44
Isabella Dr., Orp. 97 CM56
Isabella Rd. E9 48 CC35
Isabella St. SE1 4 F3
Isabella St. SE1 56 BY40
Joan St.
Isambard Clo., Uxb. 53 AX38
Isambard Ms. E14 67 CF41
Isambard Pl. SE16 67 CC41
Rotherhithe St.
Isbell Gdns., Rom. 41 CT29
Isbells Dr., Reig. 121 BS71
Isel Way SE22 77 CA46
Dulwich Gro.
Isenburg Way, Hem.H. 8 AX11
Isham Rd. SW16 86 BX51
Isis Clo. SW15 65 BQ45
Isis Clo., Ruis. 44 BA32
Thames Dr.
Isis Dr., Upmin. 51 CZ32
Isis St. SW18 76 BT48
Isla Rd. SE18 68 CM43
Island, The, Stai. 72 AT48
Island Clo., Stai. 72 AV49
Island Fm. Ave., E.Mol. 84 BF53
Island Fm. Rd., E.Mol. 84 BE53
Island Rd., Mitch. 76 BU50
Island Row E14 57 CD39
Islay Gdns., Houns. 74 BD46
Islay Wk. N1 57 BZ36
Isledon Rd. N7 47 BY34
Islehurst Clo., Chis. 88 CL51
Summer Hill
Islington Grn. N1 56 BY37
Upper St.
Islington High St. N1 56 BY37
Islington Pk. St. N1 56 BY36
Islip Gdns., Edg. 37 BN29
Islip Gdns., Nthlt. 54 BE36
Islip Manor Rd., Nthlt. 54 BE36
Islip St. NW5 47 BW35
Ismailia Rd. E7 58 CH36
Ismay Ct., Slou. 52 AP39
Ismays Rd., Sev. 117 DA66
Isom Clo. E13 58 CJ38
Belgrave Rd.
Istead Ri., Grav. 81 DF50

Itchingwood Common Rd., Oxt. 115 CJ70
Ivanhoe Clo., Uxb. 53 AX39
Ivanhoe Dr., Har. 45 BJ31
Ivanhoe Rd. SE5 67 CA45
Ivanhoe Rd., Houns. 64 BD45
Ivatt Pl. W14 65 BR42
Ivatt Way N17 48 BZ31
Ive Fm. Clo. E10 48 CE34
Ive Fm. La. E10 48 CE34
Iveagh Ave. NW10 55 BM37
Iveagh Clo. E9 57 CC37
Iveagh Clo. NW10 55 BM37
Iveagh Clo., Nthwd. 35 AZ30
Iveagh Rd., Guil. 118 AQ71
Iveagh Rd., Wok. 100 AP62
Ivedon Rd., Well. 69 CP44
Iveley Rd. SW4 66 BW44
Iver La., Iver 53 AW39
Iver La., Uxb. 53 AW39
Iver Rd., Brwd. 33 DA25
Harewood Rd.
Iverdale Clo., Iver 52 AU40
Ivere Dr., Barn. 29 BS25
Iverhurst Clo., Bexh. 79 CP46
Iverna Ct. W8 66 BS41
Iverna Gdns.
Iverna Gdns. W8 66 BS41
Iverna Gdns., Felt. 73 BA46
Ivers Way, Croy. 96 CE57
Iverson Rd. NW6 55 BR36
Ives Gdns., Rom. 50 CT31
Ives Rd. E16 58 CG39
Ives Rd., Slou. 62 AS41
Ives St. SW3 3 D8
Ives St. SW3 66 BU42
Ivestor Ter. SE23 77 CC47
Ivimey St. E2 57 CB38
Barnet Gro.
Ivinghoe Clo., Enf. 30 BZ23
Ivinghoe Clo., St.Alb. 9 BK11
Highview Gdns.
Ivinghoe Clo., Wat. 27 BD21
Ivinghoe Rd., Bush. 36 BG26
Ivinghoe Rd., Dag. 50 CO35
Ivinghoe Rd., Rick. 34 AV26
Ivor Clo., Guil. 118 AT71
Ivor Gro. SE9 78 CL47
Ivor Pl. NW1 1 E5
Ivor Pl. NW1 56 BU38
Ivor St. NW1 56 BW36
Ivory Sq. SW11 66 BT45
Gartons Way
Ivorydown, Brom. 78 CH49
Ivy Bower Clo., Green. 80 DA46
Riverview Rd.
Ivy Clo., Dart. 80 CX47
Ivy Clo., Grav. 81 DH49
Ivy Clo., Har. 45 BE35
Ivy Clo., Pnr. 45 BD33
Ivy Clo., Sun. 84 BD51
Ivy Cotts. E14 57 CE40
Grove Vill.
Ivy Cres. W4 65 BN42
Ivy Dene Clo., Red. 121 BV73
Ivy Gdns. N8 47 BX32
Ivy Gdns., Mitch. 86 BW52
Ivy Ho. La., Berk. 7 AR13
Ivy Ho. La., Sev. 107 CS62
Ivy La., Houns. 64 BE45
Ivy La., Wok. 100 AT62
Ivy Lea, Rick. 35 AW27
Springwell Ave.
Ivy Lo. La., Rom. 42 CX30
Ivy Mill Clo., Gdse. 114 CB69
Ivy Mill La., Gdse. 114 CB69
Ivy Pl., Surb. 85 BL53
Ivy Rd. E16 58 CH39
Ivy Rd. E17 48 CE32
Ivy Rd. N14 38 BW26
Ivy Rd. NW2 46 BQ35
Ivy Rd. SE4 67 CD45
Ivy Rd., Houns. 64 BF45
Ivy Rd., Surb. 85 BM54
Ivy St. N1 57 CA37
Ivy Ter., Hodd. 12 CF11
Ivy Wk., Dag. 59 CQ36
Ivybridge, Brox. 12 CE13
Ivybridge Clo., Twick. 74 BJ46
Ivybridge La. W2 56 BX40
Savoy Pl.
Ivybridge La. WC2 4 A1
Ivychimneys Rd., Epp. 22 CN20
Ivychurch Clo. SE20 77 CB50
Laurel Gro.
Ivychurch La. SE17 4 N10
Ivychurch La. SE17 67 CA42
Kinglake St.
Ivydale Rd. SE15 77 CC46
Ivydale Rd., Cars. 86 BU55
Ivyday Gro. SW16 76 BX48
Ivydene, E.Mol. 84 BE53
Ivydene Clo., Sutt. 95 BT56
Ivydene Rd. E8 57 CB36
Ivyhouse Rd., Dag. 59 CP36
Ivyhouse Rd., Uxb. 44 AZ34
Ivymount Rd. SE27 76 BY48
Ixworth Pl. SW3 3 C10
Ixworth Pl. SW3 66 BU42
Izane Rd., Bexh. 69 CQ45

J

Jack Barnett Way N22 38 BX30
Mayes Rd.
Jack Cornwell St. E12 49 CL35
Jack Stevens Clo., Harl. 14 CP12
Hillside
Jack Walker Ct. N5 47 BY35
Jackass La., Kes. 97 CH57
Jackass La., Oxt. 114 CD69
Jackdaws, Welw.G.C. 5 BT8
Grove Meadow
Jackets La., Nthwd. 35 AZ29
Jacketts Fld., Abb.L. 17 BB18
Jacklin Grn., Wdf.Grn. 40 CH28
Jackman Ms. NW10 46 BO34
North Circular Rd.
Jackman St. E8 57 CB37
Jackmans La., Wok. 100 AQ63
Jacks La., Uxb. 35 AW30
Jackson Clo., Epsom 94 BN60
Jackson Clo., Uxb. 53 AY36
St. Lukes Rd.
Jackson Rd. N7 47 BX35
Jackson Rd., Bark. 58 CM37
Jackson Rd., Barn. 29 BU25
Jackson Rd., Brom. 88 CK55
Jackson Rd., Grnf. 54 BJ37
Sindall Rd.
Jackson Rd., Uxb. 53 AY36
St. Lukes Rd.
Jackson St. SE18 68 CL43
Jackson Way, Sthl. 64 BF41
Jacksons Clo., Ong. 24 CW18
Jacksons Dr., Wal.Cr. 21 CB17
Jacksons La. N6 47 BV33
Jacksons Pl., Croy. 87 BZ54
Jacob St. SE1 67 CB41
Jacobs Clo., Wind. 61 AM44
Jacobs Ladder, Hat. 10 BQ12
The Bdy.
Jacobs Ladder, Warl. 105 CB63
Jacobs Well Ms. W1 1 H8
Jacobs Well Ms. W1 56 BV39
George St.
Jacobs Well Rd., Guil. 109 AR68
Jacqueline Clo., Nthlt. 54 BE37
Jade Clo. E16 58 CJ39
Jade Clo., Dag. 50 CP33
Jaffray Pl. SE27 76 BY49
Jaffray Rd., Brom. 88 CJ52
Jaggard Way SW12 76 BU47
Nightingale La.
Jago Clo. SE18 68 CM43
Jago Wk. SE5 67 BZ43
Lomond Gro.
Jail La. (Biggin Hill), West. 106 CJ61
Jamaica Rd. SE1 4 Q5
Jamaica Rd. SE1 67 CA41
Jamaica Rd. SE16 67 CB41
Jamaica Rd., Th.Hth. 86 BY53
Jamaica St. E1 57 CC39
James Ave. NW2 46 BQ35
James Ave., Dag. 50 CQ33
James Bedford Clo., Pnr. 36 BD30
James Boswell Clo. SW16 76 BX49
Curtis Fld. Rd.
James Clo. E13 58 CH37
Turpin Est.
James Clo. NW11 46 BR32
James Clo., Bush. 27 BE25
James Clo., Rom. 50 CU32
James Collins Clo. W9 55 BR38
Fermoy Rd.
James Cotts., Rich. 65 BM43
Kew Rd.
James Ct. N1 57 BZ36
Morton Rd.
James Ct. N1 57 BZ36
Morton Rd.
James Gdns. N22 38 BY29
James Hammett Ho. E2 2 Q2
James La. E10 48 CF33
James La. E11 48 CF33
James Martin Clo., Uxb. 44 AW32
James Newman Ct. SE9 78 CL49
James Rd., Dart. 79 CT47
James St. W1 1 H8
James St. W1 56 BV39
James St. WC2 2 A10
James St. WC2 56 BX40
Long Acre
James St., Bark. 58 CM36
James St., Enf. 30 CA25
James St., Epp. 23 CO17
James St., Houns. 64 BG45
James St., Wind. 61 AO44
Peascod St.
Jameson Ct., St.Alb. 9 BH13
Avenue Rd.
Jameson St. W8 56 BS40
James's Cotts., Rich. 65 BM43
Kew Rd.
Jamestown Rd. NW1 56 BV37
Jamnagar Clo., Stai. 72 AV50
Jan Mead, Brwd. 122 DD26
Jane Clo., Hem.H. 8 AZ11
Jane Pl., Uxb. 53 AX36
Vine St.
Jane St. E1 57 CB39
Commercial Rd.
Janet St. E14 67 CE41
Janeway Pl. SE16 67 CB41
Janeway St.
Janeway St. SE16 67 CB41
Janice Ms., Ilf. 49 CL34
Oakfield Rd.
Janoway Hill La., Wok. 100 AR63
Jansen Wk. SW11 66 BT45
Wayland Rd.
Janson Clo. E15 49 CG35
Janson Rd.
Janson Clo. NW10 46 BN34
Janson Rd. E15 49 CG35
Jansons Rd. N15 48 CA31
Japan Cres. N4 47 BX33
Japan Rd., Rom. 50 CP32
Japonica Clo., Wok. 100 AR62
Silversmiths Way
Jarman Clo., Hem.H. 8 AY14
Jarrah Cotts., Grays 70 CY43
Jarrett Clo. SW2 76 BY47
Abbess Clo.
Jarrow Clo., Mord. 86 BS53
Jarrow Rd. N17 48 CB31
Jarrow Rd. SE16 67 CC42
Jarrow Rd., Rom. 50 CP32
Jarrow Way E9 48 CD35
Jarvis Cleys, Chsnt. 21 CA16
Jarvis Clo., Barn. 28 BQ25
Jarvis Rd. SE22 67 CA45
Melbourne Gro.
Jarvis Rd., S.Croy. 96 BZ57
Jasmin Clo., Nthwd. 35 BB30
Pinner Rd.
Jasmin Rd., Epsom 94 BM57
Jasmine Clo., Ilf. 49 CL35
Lavender Pl.
Jasmine Clo., Orp. 88 CL55
Jasmine Clo., Red. 121 BV73
Jasmine Clo., Wok. 100 AP61
Jasmine Gdns., Croy. 87 CE55
Jasmine Gdns., Har. 45 BF34
Sandringham Cres.
Jasmine Gdns., Hat. 10 BP11
Lemsford Rd.
Jasmine Gro. SE20 87 CB51
Jasmine Ter., West Dr. 63 AZ41
Jasmine Way, E.Mol. 84 BH52
Jason Clo., Brwd. 42 CZ27
Jason Clo., Red. 121 BU73
Jason Clo., Wey. 92 BA56
Jason Wk. SE9 78 CL49
Jasons Dr., Guil. 118 AU69
Jasons Hill, Chesh. 16 AQ18
Jasper Clo., Enf. 30 CC22
Jasper Pas. SE19 77 CA50
Jasper Rd. E16 58 CJ39
Jasper Rd. SE19 77 CA50
Jasper Wk. N1 2 K1
Javelin Way, Nthlt. 54 BD38
Jay Bldgs. W1 56 BX37
Rodney St.
Jay Gdns., Chis. 78 CK49
Jay Ms. SW7 66 BT41
Jaycroft, Enf. 29 BY23
Hansart Way
Jebb Ave. SW2 76 BX46
Jebb St. E3 57 CE37
Jedburgh Rd. E13 58 CJ38
Jedburgh St. SW11 66 BV45
Jeddo Rd. W12 65 BO41
Jefferson Clo. W13 64 BJ41
Jefferson Clo., Ilf. 49 CL32
Jefferson Clo., Slou. 62 AT42
Swabey Rd.
Jefferson Wk. SE18 68 CL43
Kempt St.
Jeffreys Pl. NW1 56 BW36
Jeffreys St.
Jeffreys Rd. SW4 66 BX44
Jeffreys Rd., Enf. 30 CD24
Jeffreys St. NW1 56 BW36
Jeffreys Wk. SW4 66 BX44
Jeffries Rd., Lthd. 110 BA68
Jeffs Clo., Hmptn. 74 BF50
Uxbridge Rd.
Jeffs Rd., Sutt. 94 BR56
Jeken Rd. SE9 68 CJ45
Jelf Rd. SW2 76 BY46
Jellicoe Ave., Grav. 81 DH48
Jellicoe Clo., Slou. 61 AN41
Jellicoe Gdns., Stan. 36 BJ29
Jellicoe Rd. E13 58 CH38
Jutland Rd.
Jellicoe Rd. N17 39 BZ29
Jengar Clo., Sutt. 95 BS56
Jenkins Ave., St.Alb. 18 BE18
Jenkins La., Bark. 58 CL37
Jenkins Rd. E13 58 CH38
Jenner Ave. W3 55 BN39
Jenner Pl. SW13 65 BP43
Jenner Rd. N16 48 CA34
Jenner Rd., Guil. 118 AS71
Jennett Rd., Croy. 86 BY55
Jennifer Rd., Brom. 78 CG48
Jenningham Dr., Grays 71 DD40
Jennings Clo., Wey. 92 AX58
Jennings Rd. SE22 77 CA46
Jennings Rd., St.Alb. 9 BH13
Jennings Way, Barn. 28 BQ24
Jenningtree Rd., Erith 69 CU43
Jenningtree Way, Belv. 69 CS41
Jenny Hammond Clo. E11 49 CG34
Newcomen Rd.
Jenny Path, Rom. 42 CV29
Jenson Way SE19 77 CA50
Fox Hill
Jenton Ave., Bexh. 69 CQ44
Jephson Rd. E7 58 CJ36
Jephson St. SE5 67 BZ44
Grove La.
Jephtha Rd. SW18 76 BS46
Jeppos La., Mitch. 86 BU52
Jerdan Pl. SW6 66 BS43
Fulham Bdy.
Jeremiah St. E14 57 CE39
Jeremys Grn. N18 39 CB28
Jericho Pl., Ing. 24 DC19
Jermyn St. SW1 3 M2
Jermyn St. SW1 56 BW40
Jerningham Ave., Ilf. 40 CL30
Jerningham Rd. SE14 67 CD44
Jerome Cres. NW8 1 C4
Jerome Cres. NW8 56 BU38
Jerome Dr., St.Alb. 9 BF15
Jerome Pl. SE17 67 BZ43
Hillingdon St.
Jerome St. E1 2 P5
Jerome St. E1 57 CA38
Calvin St.
Jerounds, Harl. 13 CL12
Jerrard St. N1 2 N1
Jerrard St. N1 57 CA37
Stanway St.
Jerrard St. SE13 67 CE45
Jersey Ave., Stan. 36 BJ30
Jersey Clo., Cher. 82 AV55
Jersey Clo., Guil. 109 AT68
Weybrook Dr.
Jersey Clo., Hodd. 12 CE11
Jersey Dr., Orp. 88 CM53
Jersey La., St.Alb. 9 BJ12
Jersey Rd. E11 48 CF33
Jersey Rd. E16 58 CH39
Jersey Rd. SW17 76 BV50
Jersey Rd. W7 64 BJ41
Jersey Rd., Houns. 64 BF44
Jersey Rd., Ilf. 49 CL35
Jersey Rd., Rain. 59 CU36
Jersey St. E2 57 CB38
Bethnal Grn. Rd.
Jerusalem Pas. EC1 2 F5
Jerusalem Pas. EC1 56 BY38
Aylesbury St.
Jervis Ave., Enf. 30 CD21
Jervis Ct. W1 1 K9
Jerviston Gdns. SW16 76 BY50
Jesmond Ave., Wem. 55 BL36
Jesmond Rd., Croy. 87 CA54
Jesmond Rd., Grays 71 DE40
Jesmond Way, Stan. 37 BL28
Jessam Ave. E5 48 CB33
Jessamine Pl., Dart. 80 CW48
Jessamine Rd., Dart. 80 CY47
Jessamine Rd. W7 54 BH40
Jessamy St., Wey. 83 AZ55
Jesse Rd. E10 48 CF33
Jessel Dr., Loug. 31 CM23
Jessica Rd. SW18 76 BT46
Jessiman Ter., Shep. 83 AZ53
Jessop Ave., Sthl. 64 BE42
Jessop Rd. SE24 67 BZ45
Jessopp Ct., Wal.Abb. 22 CG20
Shernbroke Rd.
Jessops Way, Mitch. 86 BW53
Jessup Clo. SE18 68 CM42
Jetstar Way, Nthlt. 54 BD38
Jetty Wk., Grays 71 DD43
Jevington Way SE12 78 CH47
Jewel Rd. E17 48 CE31
Jewels Hill, West. 97 CH60
Jewry St. EC3 2 P9
Jewry St. EC3 57 CA39
Jews Row SW18 66 BS45
Jews Wk. SE26 77 CB49
Jeymer Ave. NW2 46 BP35
Jeymer Dr., Grnf. 54 BG37
Jeypore Rd. SW18 76 BT46
Jillian Clo., Hmptn. 74 BF50
Jim Bradley Clo. SE18 68 CL42
John Wilson St.
Jinnings, The, Welw.G.C. 5 BS9
Joan Cres. SE9 78 CJ47
Joan Gdns., Dag. 50 CQ34
Joan Rd., Dag. 50 CQ34
Joan St. SE1 4 F3
Joan St. SE1 56 BY40
Jocelyn Rd., Rich. 65 BL45
Jocelyns, Harl. 6 CP9
Jocketts Hill, Hem.H. 7 AV14
Jocketts Rd., Hem.H. 7 AV14
Jockeys Flds. WC1 2 C6
Jockeys Flds. WC1 56 BX39
Jodrell Rd. E3 57 CD37
Jodrell Way, Grays 70 CZ42
Joe Hunt Ct. SE27 76 BY49
Cedar Tree Gro.
Joel St., Nthwd. 44 BC31
Johanna St. SE1 4 D5
Johanna St. SE1 66 BY41
John Adam St. WC2 4 A1
John Adam St. WC2 56 BX40
Villiers St.
John Aird Ct. W2 56 BT39
Howley Pl.
John Ashby Clo. SW2 76 BX46
John Barnes Wk. E15 58 CG36
John Bradshaw Rd. N14 38 BW26
John Burns Dr., Bark. 58 CN36
John Campbell Rd. N16 48 CA35
John Carpenter St. EC4 2 E10
John Carpenter St. EC4 56 BY40
John Clay Gdns., Grays 71 DD40
Whitmore Ave.
John Clynes Ct. SW15 65 BP45
Woodborough Rd.
John Cobb Rd., Wey. 92 AZ57
John Ct., Hodd. 12 CE10
Molesworth
John Dwight Ho. SW6 66 BS45
John Eliot Clo., Wal.Abb. 13 CG14
John Felton Rd. SE16 67 CB41
John Fisher St. E1 57 CB40
John Gooch Dr., Enf. 29 BY23
John Islip St. SW1 3 P10
John Islip St. SW1 66 BW42
John Parker Clo., Dag. 59 CR36
John Parker Sq. SW11 66 BT45
Thomas Baines Rd.
John Penn St. SE13 67 CE44
John Perrin Pl., Har. 46 BL33
John Princes St. W1 1 K8
John Princes St. W1 56 BV39
John Rennie Wk. E1 57 CB40
John Ruskin St. SE5 66 BY43
John Russell Clo., Guil. 118 AQ69
John Spencer Sq. N1 56 BY36
John St. E15 58 CG37
John St. SE25 87 CB52
John St. WC1 2 C5
John St. WC1 56 BX38
John St., Enf. 30 CA25
John St., Grays 71 DE43
John St., Houns. 64 BE44
John Taylor Ct., Slou. 61 AO40
Tuns La.
John Wilson St. SE18 68 CL41
John Woolley Clo. SE13 67 CF45
Johnby Clo., Enf. 30 CI
Manly Dixon Dr.
Johns, The, Ong. 24 CX
Johns Ave. NW4 46 BC
Johns Clo., Ashf. 73 BA
Johns Gro., Rich. 65 B
Kew Foot Rd.
Johns La., Chesh. 7 A
Johns La., Mord. 86 B
Johns Ms. WC1 2
Johns Ms. WC1 56 BX
Johns Pl. E1 57 CE
Nelson St.
Johns Rd., West. 106 C
Johns Ter., Croy. 87 CA
Johns Wk., Whyt. 105 CE
Johnsdale, Oxt. 115 CC
Johnson Clo., Grav. 81 DE
Johnson Ct., Hem.H. 8 AY
Woodman Rd.
Johnson Rd., Brom. 88 C
Johnson Rd., Croy. 87 BZ
Johnson Rd., Houns. 64 BD
Johnson St. E1 57 CC
Johnson St., Sthl. 64 BD
Johnsons Ave., Sev. 98 CF
Johnsons Clo., Cars. 86 BU
Johnsons Ct., Sev. 108 CW
School La.
Johnsons Dr., Hmptn. 84 BG
Johnsons Pl. SW1 66 BW
Claverton St.
Johnsons Way NW10 55 BM
Johnsons Way, Green. 80 DE
Johnston Grn., Guil. 109 AC
Johnston Rd., Wdf.Grn. 40 CH
Johnston Ter. NW2 46 BC
Johnston Wk., Guil. 109 AC
Johnstone Rd. E6 58 CK
Joiner St. SE1 4
Joiner St. SE1 57 BZ
Joiners Clo., Chesh. 16 AC
Joiners Clo., Ger.Cr. 34 AS
Joiners La., Ger.Cr. 34 AS
Joiners Way, Ger.Cr. 34 AS
Joinville Pl., Wey. 92 AX
Jolliffe Rd., Red. 113 BW
Jollys La., Har. 45 BG
Jollys La., Hayes 54 BD
Jonathan St. SE11 4 E
Jonathan St. SE11 66 BX
Jones Rd. E13 58 CH
Holborn Rd.
Jones Rd., Chsnt. 20 BY
Jones St. W1 3
Jones St. W1 56 BV
Bourdon St.
Jones Wk., Rich. 75 BL
Ryland Rd.
Jones Way, Slou. 43 AC
Jonquil Clo., Welw.G.C. 5 B
Jonquil Gdns., Hmptn. 74 BF
Partridge Rd.
Jonson Clo., Hayes 53 BC
Jonson Clo., Mitch. 86 BV
Joram Way SE16 67 CE
The Bonamy Est. E.
Jordan Clo., Dag. 50 CF
Muggeridge Rd.
Jordan Clo., Har. 45 BE
Jordan Clo., Islw. 64 BH
Jordan Rd., Grnf. 54 BJ
Jordans, Welw.G.C. 5 B
Jordans Clo., Guil. 118 AT
Beatty Ave.
Jordans Clo., Red. 121 BV
Jordans Clo., S.Croy. 96 CA
Jordans Clo., Stai. 73 AX
Jordans Clo., Wat. 26 BB
Jordans La., Beac. 34 AP
Jordans Way, Beac. 34 AP
Jordans Way, Rain. 60 CV
Jordans Way, St.Alb. 18 BE
Jordon Dr., Red. 121 BV
Joseph Ave. W3 55 BN
Joseph Powell Clo. SW12 76 BW
Hazelbourne Rd.
Joseph St. E3 57 CD
Josephine Ave. SW2 76 BX
Josephine Ave., Tad. 112 BF
Josephs Rd., Guil. 118 AR
Joshua St. E14 57 CF
Joslin Rd., Grays 70 CY
Joubert St. SW11 66 BU
Journeys End, Slou. 52 AF
Jowett St. SE15 67 CA
Joy Rd., Grav. 81 DH
Joyce Ave. N18 39 CA
Joyce Ct., Wal.Abb. 21 CF
Joyce Dawson Way SE28 59 CC
Joyce Grn. La., Dart. 70 CW
Joyce Grn. Wk., Dart. 80 CW
Joyce Page Clo. SE7 68 CJ
Lansdowne La.
Joycroft, Enf. 29 BY
Hansart Way
Joydens Wd. Rd., Bex. 79 CS
Joydon Dr., Rom. 50 CO
Joyes Clo., Rom. 42 CV
Troopers Dr.
Joyners Clo., Dag. 50 CC
Connor Rd.
Joyners Fld., Harl. 13 CM
Jubilee Ave. E4 39 CF
Jubilee Ave., Rom. 50 CR
Jubilee Ave., Twick. 74 BG
Jubilee Clo. NW9 46 BN
Jubilee Clo., Green. 80 DB
Jubilee Clo., Pnr. 36 BD
Jubilee Clo., Rom. 50 CR
Jubilee Clo., Stai. 73 AX
Lauser Rd.
Jubilee Ct., Hat. 10 BF
Northfield

lee Ct., Th.Hth. 86 BY52
lee Cres. E14 67 CF41
anchester Rd.
lee Cres. N9 39 CB26
ilee Cres., Grav. 81 DJ48
ilee Cres., Sev. 108 DB64
ilee Cres., Wey. 92 AX56
ilee Dr., Ruis. 45 BD35
ilee Gdns., Sthl. 54 BF39
ilee Pl. SW3 3 D10
ilee Pl. SW3 66 BU42
ilee Ri., Sev. 108 CW46
ilee Rd., Grays 70 DA43
ilee Rd., Grnf. 54 BJ37
ilee Rd., Orp. 98 CQ57
ilee Rd., St.Alb. 18 BK16
ilee Rd., Sutt. 94 BQ57
ilee Rd., Wat. 26 BC22
ilee St. E1 57 CC39
ilee Ter., Bet. 120 BN72
ilee Ter., Dor. 119 BJ71
ilee Way SW19 86 BS51
ilee Way, Chess. 94 BM56
ilee Way, Sid. 79 CO48
d St. WC1 1 Q3
d St. WC1 56 BX38
e St. E16 58 CG39
eth Gdns., Grav. 81 DJ49
ge Heath La., Hayes 53 BA39
ge St., Wat. 26 BC22
ge Wk., Esher 93 BH57
ges Hill, Pot.B. 20 BU18
ges Wk. NW3 47 BT34
ith Ann Ct., Upmin. 51 CZ34
ith Ave., Rom. 41 CR29
r St. SW11 66 BU43
Hill, West. 106 CG61
lans Rd., Orp. 89 CO54
a Gdns., Bark. 59 CP37
a St. NW5 47 BV35
ak Village
an Ave. W3 55 BM40
an Clo., Barn. 29 BS24
an Clo., Wok. 100 AR62
ilversmiths Way
an Clo., Wok. 100 AR62
an Hill, Har. 45 BH34
an Hill, Wey. 92 AZ57
an Pl. E14 67 CE42
an Rd., Orp. 98 CO57
an Taylor Path SE23 77 CB48
iot Bank
ans Clo., Sev. 116 CU67
ians Way, Sev. 116 CU67
ien Rd. W5 64 BK42
ien Rd., Couls. 104 BW61
iet Ho. N1 57 CA37
urcell St.
iet Way, Grays 70 CW41
nction App. SE13 67 CF45
nction App. SW11 66 BU45
nction Ms. W2 1 C8
nction Ms. W2 56 BU39
ale Pl
nction Pl. W2 1 B8
nction Rd. E13 58 CH37
nction Rd. N9 39 CB26
nction Rd. N17 48 CB31
nction Rd. N19 47 BW34
nction Rd. W5 64 BK42
nction Rd., Ashf. 73 BA49
nction Rd., Brwd. 42 DB28
nction Rd., Dart. 80 CV46
nction Rd., Dor. 119 BJ71
nction Rd., Har. 45 BG32
nction Rd., Rom. 50 CT31
nction Rd., S.Croy. 96 BZ57
nction Rd. E., Rom. 50 CQ33
enneth Rd.
nction Rd. W., Rom. 50 CQ33
nction Wf. N1 2 H1
ne Clo., Couls. 95 BV60
ne La., Red. 121 BV74
newood Clo., Wey. 91 AV59
niper Ave., St.Alb. 18 BF19
niper Clo., Brox. 21 CD16
niper Clo., Guil. 109 AR68
niper Clo., Reig. 121 BT71
niper Clo., Rick. 35 AX27
niper Clo., Wem. 46 BM35
niper Clo., West. 106 CK62
niper Ct., Slou. 62 AQ41
Nixey Clo.
niper Gdns. SE16 86 BW51
eonard Rd.
niper Gdns., Sun. 73 BB50
Vicarage Rd.
niper Gate, Rick. 35 AX27
niper Grn., Hem.H. 7 AV13
niper Gro., Wat. 26 BC22
niper La. E6 58 CK39
Northumberland Rd.
niper Rd., Ilf. 49 CL35
Riverdene Rd.
niper Rd., Reig. 121 BT71
niper St. E1 57 CC40
niper Wk., Bet. 120 BN71
niper Way, Hayes 53 BA40
niper Way, Rom. 42 CW30
no Rd., Hem.H. 8 AY12
no Way SE14 67 CC43
piter Dr., Hem.H. 8 AY12
piter Way N7 56 BX36
pp Rd. E15 57 CF36
pp Rd. W. E15 57 CF37
rgens Rd., Grays 70 CY43
ry St., Grav. 81 DG46
Church St.
stice Wk. SW3 66 BU43
Lawrence St.
stin Clo., Brent. 64 BK43
stin Rd. E4 39 CD29
te La., Enf. 30 CD24
tland Gdns., Couls. 104 BX63

Jutland Pl., Egh. 72 AU49
Mullens Rd.
Jutland Rd. E13 58 CH38
Jutland Rd. SE6 77 CF47
Jutsums Ave., Rom. 50 CR32
Jutsums La., Rom. 50 CR32
Juxon Clo., Har. 36 BF30
Juxon St. SE11 4 C8
Juxon St. SE11 66 BX42

K

Kaduna Clo., Pnr. 44 BC32
Kale Rd., Erith 69 CQ41
Kambala Rd. SW11 66 BT44
Kandlewood, Brwd. 122 DD26
Kangley Bri. Rd. SE26 77 CD49
Karen Clo., Brwd. 42 DB26
Karen Clo., Rain. 59 CT37
Karen Ct. SE4 67 CD44
Karen Ct., Brom. 88 CG51
Karen Ter. E11 49 CG34
Montague Rd.
Karl Ho., Harl. 13 CN13
Karoline Gdns., Grnf. 54 BG37
Kashgar Rd. SE18 68 CN42
Kashmir Clo., Wey. 92 AX58
Kashmir Rd. SE7 68 CJ43
Kassala Rd. SW11 66 BU44
Kates Clo., Barn. 28 BP25
Kates Cft., Welw.G.C. 5 BR10
Katharine Rd., Twick. 74 BJ47
London Rd.
Katharine St., Croy. 87 BZ55
Katherine Clo., Hem.H. 8 AY15
Newell Rd.
Katherine Clo., Wey. 92 AW57
Katherine Gdns. SE9 68 CJ45
Katherine Gdns., Ilf. 40 CM29
Katherine Rd. E6 58 CJ36
Katherine Rd. E7 49 CJ35
Katherine Sq. W11 55 BQ40
Wilsham St.
Katherines Way, Harl. 13 CL12
Kathleen Ave. W3 55 BN39
Kathleen Ave., Wem. 55 BL36
Kathleen Rd. SW11 66 BU45
Katrine Sq., Hem.H. 8 AX11
Kavanaghs Rd., Brwd. 42 DA27
Kavanaghs Ter., Brwd. 42 DA27
Kavanaghs Rd.
Kavanaghs Ter., Brwd. 42 DA27
Kay Rd. SW9 66 BX44
Kay St. E2 57 CB37
Kay St. E15 57 CF36
New Mkt. St.
Kay St., Well. 69 CO44
Kaye Ct., Guil. 118 AR69
Kaye Don Way, Wey. 92 AZ59
Kayemoor Rd., Sutt. 95 BT57
Kaywood Clo., Slou. 62 AR41
Kean St. WC2 2 B9
Kean St. WC2 56 BX39
Kearton Clo., Ken. 105 BZ62
Keary Rd., Swans. 81 DC47
Keatings, The, Brwd. 33 CZ22
Mill La.
Keats Ave., Rom. 41 CU30
Keats Clo. E11 49 CH32
Nightingale La.
Keats Clo. NW3 47 BU35
Keats Gro.
Keats Clo. SE1 4 P9
Keats Clo. SE1 67 CA42
Milton Clo.
Keats Clo. SW19 76 BT50
North Rd.
Keats Clo., Chig. 40 CM29
Keats Clo., Hayes 53 BC39
Keats Clo., Hem.H. 8 AZ10
Bronte Cres.
Keats Gdns., Til. 71 DG44
Keats Gro. NW3 47 BT35
Keats La., Wind. 61 AO43
Keats Pl. EC2 2 K7
Keats Rd., Belv. 69 CS41
Keats Rd., Well. 68 CN44
Keats Wk., Brwd. 122 DE26
Keats Way, Croy. 87 CC53
Keats Way, Grnf. 54 BF39
Keats Way, West Dr. 63 AY42
Keble Clo., Nthlt. 45 BG35
Keble Clo., Wor.Pk. 85 BO54
Keble St. SW17 76 BT49
Keble Ter., Abb.L. 17 BB19
Kechill Gdns., Brom. 88 CH54
Kedeston Ct., Sutt. 86 BS55
Kedleston Ct. E5 48 CC35
Clapton Pk. Est.
Kedleston Dr., Orp. 88 CN53
Kedleston Wk. E2 57 CB38
Kedward Rd., Rom. 50 CT32
Victoria Rd.
Keedonwood Rd., Brom. 78 CG49
Keefield, Harl. 13 CL13
Keel Clo. SE16 57 CC40
Hull Clo.
Keel Dr., Slou. 61 AN40
Keeler Clo., Wind. 61 AM45
Keeley Rd., Croy. 87 BZ55
Keeley St. WC2 2 B9
Keeley St. WC2 56 BX39
Keeling Rd. SE9 78 CJ46
Keely Clo., Barn. 29 BU25
Keemor Clo. SE18 68 CL43
Llanover St.
Keens La., Guil. 109 AP68
Keens Pk. Rd., Guil. 109 AP68
Keens Rd., Croy. 96 BZ56

Keens Yd. N1 56 BY36
St. Pauls Rd.
Keensacre, Iver 52 AU37
Keep, The SE3 68 CH44
Keep, The, Kings.T. 75 BL50
Keepers Clo., Guil. 118 AU69
Keepers Fm. Clo., Wind. 61 AM44
Keepers Wk., Vir.W. 82 AR53
Keetons Rd. SE16 67 CB41
Keevil Dr. SW19 75 BQ47
Keighley Clo. N7 47 BX35
Penn Rd.
Keighley Rd., Rom. 42 CW29
Keightley Dr. SE9 78 CK47
Keilder Clo., Chig. 40 CN29
Keilder Clo., Uxb. 53 AZ37
Charnwood Rd.
Keildon Rd. SW11 66 BU45
Keir, The SW19 75 BQ49
Keir Hardie Est. E5 48 CB33
Keir Hardie Ho. W6 65 BQ43
Keir Hardie Way, Bark. 59 CO36
Keir Hardie Way, Hayes 53 BC38
Keith Ave., S.at H. 80 CX50
Keith Connor Clo. SW8 66 BV45
Heath Rd.
Keith Gro. W12 65 BP41
Keith Pk. Cres., West. 97 CH59
Keith Pk. Rd., Uxb. 53 AY36
Keith Rd. E17 39 CD30
Keith Rd., Bark. 58 CM37
Keith Rd., Hayes 63 BB41
Keiths Rd., Hem.H. 8 AZ14
Keithway, Horn. 51 CW33
Kelbrook Rd. SE3 68 CK44
Kelburn Way, Rain. 59 CT38
Kelby Path SE9 78 CL48
Kelbys, Welw.G.C. 5 BT7
Kelceda Clo. NW2 46 BP34
Kelf Gro., Hayes 53 BB39
Kelfield Gdns. W10 55 BQ39
Kell St. SE1 4 G6
Kell St. SE1 66 BY41
Borough Rd.
Kelland Clo. N8 47 BW32
Kelland Rd. E13 58 CH38
Kellaway Rd. SE3 68 CJ44
Kellerton Rd. SE13 78 CG46
Kellett Rd. SW2 66 BY45
Kelling Gdns., Croy. 86 BY54
Kellino St. SW17 76 BU49
Kellner Rd. SE28 68 CN41
Kelly Clo., Shep. 83 BB51
Geneva Clo.
Kelly Rd. NW7 37 BR29
Kelly St. NW1 56 BV36
Kelly Way, Rom. 50 CQ32
Kelman Clo. SW4 66 BW44
Kelman Clo., Wal.Cr. 21 CD19
Kelmore Gro. SE22 67 CB45
Kelmscott Clo. E17 39 CD30
Kelmscott Clo., Wat. 26 BC25
Kelmscott Cres., Wat. 26 BC25
Kelmscott Gdns. W12 65 BP41
Kelmscott Rd. SW11 76 BU46
Kelross Pas. N5 48 BZ35
Kelross Rd.
Kelross Rd. N5 47 BY35
Kelsall Clo. SE3 68 CH44
Kelsey La., Beck. 87 CE52
Kelsey Pk. Ave., Beck. 87 CE51
Kelsey Pk. Rd., Beck. 87 CE51
Kelsey Rd., Orp. 89 CO51
Kelsey St. E2 57 CB38
Kelsey Way, Beck. 87 CE52
Kelshall, Wat. 27 BE21
Kelshall Ct. N4 48 BZ34
Kings Cres. Est.
Kelsie Way, Ilf. 40 CN29
Kelsmore La., Chsnt. 21 CC18
Kelso Dr., Grav. 81 DJ49
Kelso Pl. W8 65 BS41
Kelso Rd., Cars. 86 BT54
Kelston Rd., Ilf. 40 CL30
Kelvedon Ave., Wat. 92 BB57
Kelvedon Clo., Brwd. 122 DF26
Lambourne Dr.
Kelvedon Clo., Kings.T. 75 BM50
Kelvedon Grn., Borwd. 33 CZ22
Kelvedon Hall La., Borwd. 33 CX21
Kelvedon Rd. SW6 65 BR43
Kelvedon Wk., Rain. 59 CT37
Kelvedon Way, Wdf.Grn. 40 CK29
Kelvin Ave. N13 38 BX29
Kelvin Ave., Lthd. 102 BH63
Kelvin Ave., Tedd. 74 BH50
Kelvin Clo., Epsom 94 BM57
Kelvin Cres., Har. 36 BH29
Kelvin Dr., Twick. 74 BJ46
Kelvin Gdns., Sthl. 54 BF39
Kelvin Gro. SE26 77 CB48
Kelvin Gro., Chess. 84 BK55
Kelvin Par., Orp. 88 CN54
Kelvin Rd. N5 48 BZ35
Kelvin Rd., Til. 71 DG44
Kelvin Rd., Well. 69 CO45
Kelvinbrook, E.Mol. 84 BF52
Kelvington Clo., Croy. 87 CD53
Kelvington Rd. SE15 77 CC46
Kember St. N1 56 BX36
Carnoustie Dr.
Kemble Clo., Pot.B. 20 BT20
Kemble Clo., Wey. 92 BA56
Kemble Dr., Brom. 88 CK55
Kemble Par., Pot.B. 20 BT19
High St.
Kemble Rd. N17 39 CB30
Kemble Rd. SE23 77 CC47
Kemble Rd., Croy. 86 BY55
Kemble St. WC2 2 B9
Kemble St. WC2 56 BX39
Kembleside Rd., West. 106 CJ62
Kings Rd.
Kemerton Rd. SE5 67 BZ45

Kemerton Rd., Beck. 87 CE51
Kemerton Rd., Croy. 87 CA54
Kemeys St. E9 48 CD35
Kemnal Rd., Chis. 78 CM50
Kemp Gdns., Croy. 87 BZ53
St. Saviours Rd.
Kemp Pl., Bush. 27 BF25
Kemp Rd., Dag. 50 CP33
Kempe Clo., St.Alb. 9 BG15
Kempe Rd. NW6 55 BQ37
Kempe Rd., Enf. 30 CB21
Kempis Way SE22 77 CA46
Dulwich Gro.
Kemplay Rd. NW3 47 BT35
Kempley Ct., Grays 71 DE43
Dock Rd.
Kemps Ct. W1 1 M9
Kemps Dr. E14 57 CE40
Morant St.
Kemps Dr., Nthwd. 35 BB29
Kemps Gdns. SE13 77 CF46
Thornford Rd.
Kempsford Gdns. SW5 66 BS42
Kempsford Rd. SE11 4 F9
Kempshott Rd. SW16 76 BW50
Kempson Rd. SW6 66 BS43
Kempt St. SE18 68 CL43
Kempthorne Rd. SE8 67 CD42
Kempton Ave., Horn. 51 CW35
Kempton Ave., Nthlt. 54 BF36
Kempton Ave., Sun. 83 BC51
Kempton Clo., Erith 69 CS43
Kempton Clo., Uxb. 44 BA35
Lawrence Dr.
Kempton Ct., Sun. 83 BC51
Kempton Ave.
Kempton Rd. E6 58 CK37
Kempton Rd., Hmptn. 84 BE51
Kempton Wk., Croy. 87 CD53
Kemsing Clo., Bex. 79 CQ47
Kemsing Clo., Brom. 88 CG55
Bourne Way
Kemsing Clo., Th.Hth. 87 BZ52
Kemsing Rd. SE10 68 CH42
Kemsing Rd., Sev. 108 DA62
Kemsley Clo., Grav. 81 DF49
Kemsley Clo., Green. 80 DA46
Kemsley Rd., West. 106 CJ63
Ken Way, Wem. 46 BN34
Kenbury Clo., Uxb. 44 AZ34
Kenbury St. SE5 67 BZ44
Kenchester Clo. SW8 66 BX43
Kencot Way, Erith 69 CQ41
Kendal Ave. N18 39 BZ28
Kendal Ave. W3 55 BM39
Kendal Ave., Bark. 58 CN37
Kendal Ave., Epp. 23 CO19
Kendal Clo. SW9 66 BY43
Foxley Rd.
Kendal Clo., Felt. 73 BB47
Ambleside Dr.
Kendal Clo., Reig. 121 BT70
Kendal Clo., Slou. 52 AQ40
Kendal Clo., Wdf.Grn. 40 CG27
Kendal Cft., Horn. 50 CU35
Kendal Dr., Slou. 52 AQ40
Kendal Gdns. N18 39 BZ28
Kendal Gdns., Sutt. 86 BT55
Kendal Par. N18 39 BZ28
Kendal Pl. SW15 75 BR46
Upper Richmond Rd.
Kendal Rd. NW10 46 BP35
Kendal St. W2 1 D9
Kendal St. W2 56 BU39
Kendale, Grays 71 DG41
Godman Rd.
Kendale, Hem.H. 8 AZ14
Kendale Clo., Hayes 53 BB37
Kendale Rd., Brom. 78 CG49
Kendall Ave., Beck. 87 CD51
Kendall Ave., S.Croy. 96 BZ58
Kendall Ave. S., S.Croy. 96 BZ58
Kendall Clo., Welw.G.C. 5 BR10
Boundary La.
Kendall Pl. W1 1 G7
Kendall Pl. W1 56 BV39
George St.
Kendall Rd., Beck. 87 CD51
Kendall Rd., Islw. 64 BJ44
Kendals Clo., Rad. 27 BH21
Kender Est. SE14 67 CC44
Kender St. SE14 67 CC44
Kendoa Rd. SW4 66 BW45
Kendon Clo. E11 49 CH32
The Ave.
Kendor Ave., Epsom 94 BN59
Kendra Hall Rd., S.Croy. 95 BY57
Kendrey Gdns., Twick. 74 BH46
Kendrick Ms. SW7 3 A8
Kendrick Ms. SW7 66 BT42
Reece Ms.
Kendrick Pl. SW7 3 A9
Kendrick Pl. SW7 66 BT42
Reece Ms.
Kendrick Rd., Slou. 62 AQ41
Kenelm Clo., Har. 45 BJ34
Kenerne Dr., Barn. 28 BR25
Kenford Clo., Wat. 17 BC19
Kenia Wk., Grav. 81 DJ48
Cervia Way
Kenilford Rd. SW12 76 BV47
Kenilworth Ave. E17 39 CE30
Kenilworth Ave. SW19 76 BS49
Kenilworth Ave., Cob. 93 BF60
Kenilworth Ave., Har. 45 BE35
Kenilworth Ave., Rom. 42 CX29
Kenilworth Clo., Bans. 104 BS61
Kenilworth Clo., Borwd. 28 BN24
Kenilworth Clo., Slou. 62 AP41
Kenilworth Clo., Wal.Cr. 21 CC20
Kenilworth Ct. SW15 65 BQ45
Kenilworth Ct., Twick. 74 BG48
Kenilworth Ct., Wat. 26 BC23
Kenilworth Cres., Enf. 30 CA23

Kenilworth Dr., Borwd. 28 BN24
Kenilworth Dr., Rick. 26 AZ24
Kenilworth Dr., Walt. 84 BD55
Kenilworth Gdns. SE18 68 CL44
Kenilworth Gdns., Hayes 53 BB39
Kenilworth Gdns., Horn. 51 CV34
Kenilworth Gdns., Ilf. 49 CN34
Kenilworth Gdns., Loug. 31 CK25
Kenilworth Gdns., Sthl. 54 BE38
Kenilworth Gdns., Stai. 73 AX49
Kenilworth Gdns., Wat. 36 BD28
Kenilworth Rd. E3 57 CD37
Kenilworth Rd. NW6 55 BR37
Kenilworth Rd. SE20 87 CC51
Kenilworth Rd. W5 55 BL40
Kenilworth Rd., Ashf. 73 AX48
Kenilworth Rd., Edg. 37 BN27
Kenilworth Rd., Epsom 94 BP56
Kenilworth Rd., Orp. 88 CM53
Kenilworth Way, Slou. 62 AP41
Mere Rd.
Kenley Ave. NW9 37 BO30
Kenley Clo., Bex. 79 CR47
Kenley Clo., Cat. 105 BZ63
Kenley Clo., Chis. 88 CN52
Kenley Gdns., Horn. 51 CW34
Kenley Gdns., Th.Hth. 86 BY52
Kenley La., Ken. 105 BZ61
Kenley Rd. SW19 85 BR51
Kenley Rd., Kings.T. 85 BM51
Kenley Rd., Twick. 74 BJ46
Kenley Wk. W11 55 BR40
Kenley Wk., Sutt. 94 BQ56
Kenlor Rd. SW17 76 BT49
Kenmare Dr., Mitch. 76 BU50
Kenmare Gdns. N13 39 BZ28
Kenmare Rd., Th.Hth. 86 BX53
Kenmere Gdns., Wem. 55 BM37
Kenmere Rd., Well. 69 CP44
Kenmont Gdns. NW10 55 BP38
Kenmore Ave., Har. 45 BJ32
Kenmore Clo., Rich. 65 BM43
Kent Rd.
Kenmore Cres., Hayes 53 BB38
Kenmore Gdns., Edg. 37 BM30
Kenmore Rd., Har. 45 BK31
Kenmore Rd., Ken. 95 BY60
Kenmure Rd. E8 48 CB35
Kennal La., Lthd. 102 BF64
Kennard Rd. E15 57 CF36
Kennard Rd. N11 38 BU28
Kennard St. E16 58 CK40
Kennard St. SW11 66 BV44
Kenneally, Wind. 61 AL44
Kenneally Clo., Wind. 61 AL44
Kenneally
Kenneally Pl., Wind. 61 AL44
Kenneally
Kenneally Wk., Wind. 61 AL44
Kenneally
Kennedy Ave., Enf. 30 CC25
Kennedy Ave., Hodd. 12 CD12
Kennedy Clo. E13 58 CH37
Kennedy Clo., Chsnt. 21 CD17
High St.
Kennedy Clo., Orp. 88 CM54
Kennedy Clo., Pnr. 36 BE29
Kennedy Gdns., Sev. 108 CV65
Kennedy Rd. W7 54 BH39
Kennedy Rd., Bark. 58 CN37
Kennel Clo., Lthd. 102 BG65
Kennel La., Borwd. 33 CY23
Kennel Wd. La., Hat. 10 BP12
Kennelwood Cres., Croy. 96 CF59
Kenners La., Wal.Abb. 13 CK13
Kennet Cl SW11 66 BT45
Maysoule Rd.
Kennet Clo., Upmin. 51 CZ32
Kennet Grn., S.Ock. 60 DA40
Cawdor Ave.
Kennet Rd. W9 55 BR38
Kennet Rd., Dart. 69 CU45
Kennet Rd., Islw. 64 BH45
Kennet Sq., Mitch. 86 BU51
Mortlake Dr.
Kennet St. E1 57 CB40
Kennet Wf. La. EC4 2 J10
Kennet Wf. La. EC4 57 BZ40
Upper Thames St.
Kenneth Ave., Ilf. 49 CL35
Kenneth Cres. NW2 46 BP35
Kenneth Gdns., Stan. 36 BJ29
Kenneth More Rd., Ilf. 49 CL34
Oakfield Rd.
Kenneth Rd., Bans. 104 BT61
Kenneth Rd., Rom. 50 CP33
Kennett Dr., Hayes 54 BE39
Kennett Rd., Slou. 62 AT41
Kenning Rd., Hodd. 12 CE11
Kenning St. SE16 67 CC41
Kenning Ter. N1 57 CA37
Branch Pl.
Kenninghall Rd. E5 48 CB34
Kenninghall Rd. N18 39 CC28
Kennings Est. SE11 66 BY42
Kennings Way SE11 4 F10
Kennings Way SE11 66 BY42
Kennington Gro. SE11 66 BX43
Kennington La. SE11 66 BX42
Kennington Oval SE11 66 BX43
Kennington Pk. Est. SE11 66 BY43
Kennington Pk. Gdns. SE11 66 BY43
Kennington Pk. Pl. SE11 66 BY43
Kennington Pk. Rd. SE11 66 BY43
Kennington Rd. SE1 4 D6
Kennington Rd. SE1 66 BY41
Kennington Rd. SE11 4 D8
Kenny Rd. NW7 37 BR29
Kennyland Ct. NW4 46 BP32
Kenrick Pl. W1 1 G7
Kenrick Pl. W1 56 BV39
Dorset St.
Kenrick Sq., Red. 114 CA70

Kensal Rd. W10 55 BQ38
Kensington Ave. E12 58 CK36
Kensington Ave., Th.Hth. 86 BY51
Kensington Ave., Wat. 26 BB24
Kensington Ch. St. W8 56 BS40
Kensington Ch. Wk. W8 66 BS41
Holland St.
Kensington Ct. W8 66 BS41
Kensington Ct. Ms. W8 66 BS41
Kensington Ct. Pl.
Kensington Ct. Pl. W8 66 BS41
Kensington Dr., Wdf.Grn. 40 CJ30
Kensington Gdns., Ilf. 49 CK33
Kensington Gdns. Sq. W2 56 BS39
Kensington Gate W8 66 BT41
Kensington Gore SW7 3 A5
Kensington Gore SW7 66 BT41
Kensington High St. W8 65 BR41
Kensington Mall W8 56 BS40
Kensington Palace Gdns. W8 56 BS40
Kensington Pk. Gdns. W11 55 BR40
Kensington Pk. Ms. W11 55 BR39
Kensington Pk. Rd. W11 55 BR39
Kensington Pl. W8 56 BS40
Kensington Rd. SW7 66 BT41
Kensington Rd. W8 66 BT41
Kensington Rd., Brwd. 33 DA25
Kensington Rd., Nthlt. 54 BF38
Kensington Rd., Rom. 50 CS32
Kensington Sq. W8 66 BS41
Kensington Ter., S.Croy. 96 BZ57
Kent Ave. W13 54 BJ39
Kent Ave., Dag. 59 CR39
Kent Ave., Slou. 52 AO39
Kent Ave., Well. 78 CN46
Kent Clo., Borwd. 28 BN22
Kent Clo., Mitch. 86 BX52
Kent Clo., Orp. 97 CN57
Kent Clo., Stai. 73 AX50
Kent Clo., Uxb. 53 AX36
Kent Dr., Barn. 29 BV24
Kent Dr., Horn. 51 CV35
Kent Dr., Tedd. 74 BH49
Kent Gdns. W13 54 BJ39
Kent Gdns., Ruis. 44 BC32
Kent Gate Way, Croy. 96 CD57
Kent Hatch Rd., Oxt. 115 CJ68
Kent Ho. La., Beck. 77 CD50
Kent Ho. Rd. SE26 77 CD49
Kent Ho. Rd., Beck. 77 CD50
Kent Pas. NW1 1 E4
Kent Pas. NW1 56 BU38
Kent Rd. N15 48 CA32
Kent Rd. N21 39 BZ26
Kent Rd. W4 65 BN41
Kent Rd., Dag. 50 CR35
Kent Rd., Dart. 80 CV46
Kent Rd., E.Mol. 84 BG52
Kent Rd., Grav. 81 DG47
Kent Rd., Grays 71 DE43
Kent Rd., Kings.T. 84 BK52
Kent Rd., Long. 90 DB51
Kent Rd., Orp. 89 CO53
Kent Rd., Rich. 65 BM43
Kent Rd., W.Wick. 87 CE54
Kent Rd., Wok. 100 AT61
Kent St. E2 57 CA37
Kent St. E13 58 CH38
Kent Ter. NW1 2 Q3
Kent Ter. NW1 56 BU38
Kent Vw., S.Ock. 70 CY41
Kent Vw. Gdns., Ilf. 49 CN34
Kent Wk. SW9 66 BY45
Kent Way SE15 67 CA44
Sumner Est.
Kent Way, Surb. 85 BL55
Kent Yd. SW7 3 D5
Kent Yd. SW7 66 BU41
Rutland Gdns.
Kentford Way, Nthlt. 54 BE37
Kentish Bldgs. SE1 4 K4
Kentish Bldgs. SE1 67 BZ41
Borough High St.
Kentish La., Hat. 20 BT16
Kentish Rd., Belv. 69 CR42
Kentish Town Rd. NW1 56 BV36
Kentish Town Rd. NW5 56 BV36
Kentish Way, Brom. 88 CH51
Kentmere Rd. SE18 68 CN42
Kenton Ave., Har. 45 BH33
Kenton Ave., Sthl. 54 BF40
Kenton Ave., Sun. 84 BD51
Kenton Ct., Har. 45 BJ32
Kenton Gdns., Har. 45 BK32
Kenton Gdns., St.Alb. 9 BH14
Kenton La., Har. 36 BH29
Kenton Pk. Ave., Har. 45 BK31
Kenton Pk. Clo., Har. 45 BK32
Kenton Pk. Cres., Har. 45 BK31
Kenton Pk. Rd., Har. 45 BK31
Kenton Rd. E9 57 CC36
Kenton Rd., Har. 45 BH33
Kenton St. WC1 1 Q4
Kenton St. WC1 56 BX38
Kenton Way, Hayes 53 BB38
Kenton Way, Wok. 100 AP61
Kentons La., Wind. 61 AM44
Kents Ave., Hem.H. 8 AX15
Kents La., Epp. 14 CS14
Kents Pas., Hmptn. 84 BE51
Kentwell Clo. SE4 77 CD46
Turnham Rd.
Kentwode Grn. SW13 65 BP43
Kentwyns Ri., Red. 121 BX71
Kenver Ave. N12 38 BT29
Kenward Rd. SE9 78 CJ46
Kenway, Rain. 60 CV38
Kenway, Rom. 41 CS30
Kenway Clo., Rain. 60 CV38
Kenway Dr., Amer. 25 AQ23
Kenway Rd. SW5 66 BS42
Kenway Wk., Rain. 60 CV38
Kenwood Ave. N14 29 BW25
Kenwood Ave. SE14 67 CC44
Briant St.
Kenwood Clo. NW3 47 BT33
Kenwood Clo., West Dr. 63 AZ43
Kenwood Dr., Beck. 87 CF52
Kenwood Dr., Rick. 34 AV27
Kenwood Dr., Walt. 92 BC57
Kenwood Gdns. E18 49 CH31
Kenwood Gdns., Ilf. 49 CL31
Kenwood Pk., Wey. 92 BA57
Kenwood Ridge, Ken. 104 BY62
Kenwood Rd. N6 47 BU32
Kenwood Rd. N9 39 CB26
Malmstone Ave.
Kenworthy Rd. E9 48 CD35
Kenwyn Dr. NW2 46 BO34
Kenwyn Rd. SW4 66 BW45
Kenwyn Rd. SW20 85 BQ51
Kenwyn Rd., Dart. 70 CV45
Kenya Rd. SE7 68 CJ43
Kenyngton Dr., Sun. 73 BC49
Kenyngton Pl., Har. 45 BK32
Kenyon St. SW6 65 BQ44
Kenyons, Lthd. 110 AZ67
Keogh Rd. E15 58 CG36
Kepler Rd. SW4 66 BX45
Keppel Rd. E6 58 CK36
Keppel Rd., Dag. 50 CQ35
Keppel Row SE1 4 H3
Keppel Row SE1 57 BZ40
Great Guildford St.
Keppel Spur, Wind. 72 AQ47
Keppel St. WC1 1 P6
Keppel St. WC1 56 BW39
Malet St.
Keppel St., Wind. 61 AO44
Helena Rd.
Keppell Rd., Dor. 119 BJ70
Kerbela St. E2 57 CB38
Kerbey St. E14 57 CE39
Kerdistone Clo., Pot.B. 20 BS18
Kerfield Cres. SE5 67 BZ44
Grove La.
Kerfield Pl. SE5 67 BZ44
Kernel Ct., Guil. 118 AR70
Kernow Clo., Horn. 51 CW34
Kerrill Ave., Couls. 104 BY63
Kerrison Pl. W5 54 BK40
Kerrison Rd. E15 57 CF37
Kerrison Rd. SW11 66 BU45
Kerrison Rd. W5 54 BK40
Kerry Ave., Grays 70 CW41
Kerry Ave., Stan. 36 BK28
Kerry Clo. E16 58 CH39
Kerry Clo., Barn. 28 BQ24
Kerry Clo., Upmin. 51 CZ33
Kerry Dr., Upmin. 51 CZ33
Kerry Path SE14 67 CD43
Kerry Rd., Grays 71 DE40
Kerry Ter., Wok. 100 AT61
Kersey Dr., S.Croy. 96 CC59
Kersey Gdns. SE9 78 CK49
Kersey Gdns., Rom. 42 CW29
Kersfield Rd. SW15 75 BQ46
Kershaw Clo. SW18 76 BT46
Kershaw Rd., Dag. 50 CR34
Kersley Ms. SW11 66 BU44
Kersley Rd. N16 48 CA34
Kersley St. SW11 66 BU44
Kerstin Clo., Hayes 53 BB40
Kerswell Clo. N15 48 CA32
Kerwick Clo. N7 56 BX36
Blundell St.
Keslake Rd. NW6 55 BQ37
Kessock Clo. N17 48 CB32
Kesters Rd., Chesh. 16 AO19
Kesteven Clo., Ilf. 40 CN29
Keston Ave., Couls. 104 BY63
Keston Ave., Kes. 97 CJ56
Keston Ave., Wey. 92 AW59
Keston Clo. N18 39 BZ27
Keston Clo., Well. 69 CP43
Keston Gdns., Kes. 97 CJ56
Keston Ms., Wat. 26 BC23
Keston Pk. Clo., Kes. 88 CK55
Keston Rd. N17 48 BZ31
Keston Rd. SE15 67 CB45
Keston Rd., Th.Hth. 86 BX53
Kestrel Ave. E6 58 CK39
Swann App.
Kestrel Ave. SE24 77 BZ46
Kestrel Ave., Stai. 72 AV48
Kestrel Clo. NW10 55 BN36
Kingfisher Way
Kestrel Clo., Berk. 7 AR13
Kestrel Clo., Guil. 118 AV69
Kestrel Clo., Ilf. 41 CP28
Kestrel Clo., Rain. 59 CU36
Kestrel Clo., Wat. 18 BE20
Kestrel Ct. E17 39 CC30
Kestrel Grn., Hat. 10 BP13
Kestrel Ho. EC1 2 H2
Kestrel Rd., Wal.Abb. 22 CH20
Kestrel Way, Croy. 96 CF58
Kestrel Way, Welw.G.C. 5 BR7
Keswick Ave. SW15 75 BO49
Keswick Ave. SW19 86 BS51
Keswick Ave., Horn. 51 CV33
Keswick Ave., Shep. 83 BB52
Grange Fm. Caravan Site
Keswick Clo., St.Alb. 9 BJ14
Keswick Clo., Sutt. 95 BT56
Keswick Ct., Slou. 52 AP40
Stoke Rd.
Keswick Dr., Enf. 30 CC22
Keswick Gdns., Ilf. 49 CK31
Keswick Gdns., Ruis. 44 BA32
Keswick Gdns., Wem. 46 BL35
Keswick Ms. W5 54 BK40
Keswick Rd. SW15 75 BR46
Keswick Rd., Bexh. 69 CR44
Keswick Rd., Egh. 72 AT50
Keswick Rd., Lthd. 111 BF66
Keswick Rd., Orp. 88 CN54
Keswick Rd., Twick. 74 BG46
Keswick Rd., W.Wick. 88 CG55
Kett Gdns. SW2 76 BX46
Kettering Rd., Enf. 30 CC22
Kettering Rd., Rom. 42 CW29
Kettering St. SW16 76 BV50
Kettlebaston Rd. E10 48 CD33
Kettlebury Way, Ong. 24 CW18
Kettlewell Clo., Swan. 89 CT51
Kettlewell Clo., Wok. 100 AR61
Kettlewell Dr., Wok. 91 AS60
Kettlewell Hill, Wok. 91 AS60
Ketton Grn., Red. 113 BW67
Malmstone Ave.
Kevan Dr., Wok. 100 AV65
Kevelioc Rd. N17 39 BZ30
Kevin Clo., Houns. 64 BD44
Kevington Clo., Orp. 89 CO52
Kevington Dr., Brom. 88 CN52
Kevington Dr., Chis. 88 CN52
Kevington Dr., Orp. 88 CN52
Kew Bri. Ct. W4 65 BM42
Kew Bri. Rd., Brent. 65 BL43
Kew Cres., Sutt. 85 BR55
Kew Foot Rd., Rich. 65 BL45
Kew Gdns. Rd., Rich. 65 BL43
Kew Grn., Rich. 65 BL43
Kew Meadows Path, Rich. 65 BM44
Kew Palace, Rich. 65 BL43
Kew Rd., Rich. 65 BL45
Keway Ct., Berk. 7 AQ13
Cross Oak Rd.
Kewferry Dr., Nthwd. 35 AZ28
Kewferry Rd., Nthwd. 35 BA29
Key Clo. E1 57 CC38
Keyes Rd. NW2 46 BQ35
Keyes Rd., Dart. 70 CW45
Keyfield Ter., St.Alb. 9 BG14
Keymer Clo., West. 106 CJ61
Keymer Rd. SW2 76 BX48
Keynes Clo. N2 47 BU31
Keynsham Ave., Wdf.Grn. 40 CG28
Keynsham Gdns. SE9 78 CK46
Keynsham Rd. SE9 78 CJ46
Keynsham Rd., Mord. 86 BS54
Keynsham Wk., Mord. 86 BS54
Keys, The, Brwd. 42 DB29
Eagle Way
Keyse Rd. SE1 4 P7
Keyse Rd. SE1 67 CA41
Grange Rd.
Keysers Rd., Brox. 12 CE14
Keysham Ave., Houns. 63 BC43
Keystone Cres. N1 2 A1
Keystone Cres. N1 56 BX37
Caledonian Rd.
Keywood Dr., Sun. 73 BC50
Keyworth Pl. SE1 4 G6
Keyworth St. SE1 4 G6
Keyworth St. SE1 66 BY41
Kezia St. SE8 67 CC42
Trundleys Rd.
Khama Rd. SW17 76 BU49
Khartoum Rd. E13 58 CH38
Khartoum Rd. SW17 76 BT49
Khartoum Rd., Ilf. 49 CL35
Khyber Rd. SW11 66 BU44
Kibworth St. SW8 66 BX43
Dorset Rd.
Kidborough Down, Lthd. 111 BF67
Kidbrooke Gdns. SE3 68 CH44
Kidbrooke Gro. SE3 68 CH44
Kidbrooke La. SE9 68 CK45
Kidbrooke Pk. Clo. SE3 68 CH44
Kidbrooke Pk. Rd. SE3 68 CH44
Kidbrooke Way SE3 68 CH44
Kidd Pl. SE7 68 CK42
Kidderminster Rd., Croy. 86 BY54
Kidderpore Ave. NW3 47 BS35
Kidderpore Gdns. NW3 47 BS35
Kidlington Way NW9 37 BO30
Kidron Way E9 57 CC37
Cleremont Rd.
Kielder Clo., Ilf. 40 CN29
New N. Rd.
Kiffen St. EC2 2 L4
Kiffen St. EC2 57 BZ38
Clere St.
Kilberry Clo., Islw. 64 BG44
Kilbride Ct., Hem.H. 8 AY11
Kilburn Bldgs. NW6 56 BS37
Kilburn High St.
Kilburn Gate NW6 56 BS37
Kilburn High Rd. NW6 55 BR36
Kilburn La. W9 55 BQ38
Kilburn La. W10 55 BQ38
Kilburn Pk. Rd. NW6 56 BS38
Kilburn Pl. NW6 56 BS37
Kilburn Priory NW6 56 BS37
Kilburn Sq. NW6 56 BS37
Kilburn Vale NW6 56 BS37
Belsize Rd.
Kilby Clo., Wat. 18 BD20
Kilcorral Clo., Epsom 94 BP60
Kildare Clo., Ruis. 45 BD33
Kildare Gdns. W2 56 BS39
Kildare Rd. E16 58 CH39
Kildare Ter. W2 56 BS39
Kildare Wk. E14 58 CE39
Farrance St.
Kildonan Clo., Wat. 26 BB23
Kildoran Rd. SW2 76 BX46
Kildowan Rd., Ilf. 50 CO33
Kilfillan Gdns., Berk. 7 AQ13
Kilgour Rd. SE23 77 CD46
Kilgowan Rd., Ilf. 50 CO33
Kilkie St. SW6 66 BT44
Killarney Rd. SW18 76 BT46
Killearn Rd. SE6 77 CF47
Killester Gdns., Wor.Pk. 94 BP56
Killewarren Way, Orp. 89 CP54
Killick St. N1 56 BX37
Killieser Ave. SW2 76 BX48
Killip Clo. E16 58 CG39
Killowen Ave., Nthlt. 45 BG35
Killowen Rd. E9 57 CC36
Killy Hill, Wok. 91 AP57
Killyon Rd. SW8 66 BW44
Kilmaine Rd. SW6 65 BR43
Kilmarnock Gdns., Dag. 50 CP34
Lindsey Rd.
Kilmarnock Pk., Reig. 121 BS70
Kilmarnock Rd., Wat. 36 BD28
Woodhall La.
Kilmarsh Rd. W6 65 BQ42
Kilmartin Ave. SW16 86 BX52
Kilmartin Rd., Ilf. 50 CO34
Kilmartin Way, Horn. 50 CU35
Kilmeston Way SE15 67 CA43
Kilmington Clo., Brwd. 122 DD27
Kilmington Rd. SW13 65 BP43
Kilmiston Ave., Shep. 83 BA53
Kilmorey Gdns., Twick. 74 BJ46
Kilmorey Rd., Twick. 64 BJ45
Kilmorie Rd. SE23 77 CD47
Kiln Ave., Amer. 25 AR22
Kiln Clo., Hayes 63 BA43
Kiln Fld., Brwd. 33 DB21
Kiln Fld., Welw.G.C. 5 BR6
Kiln Grd., Hem.H. 8 AZ14
Kiln La., Bet. 120 BN70
Kiln La., Chesh. 16 AQ19
Kiln La., Epsom 94 BO59
Kiln La., Slou. 43 AO33
Kiln La., Wok. 109 AO68
Kiln Meadows, Guil. 109 AO68
Kiln Pl. NW5 47 BV35
Kiln Rd., Epp. 23 CR17
Kiln Way, Grays 71 DC42
Kilncroft, Hem.H. 8 AZ14
Kilndown, Grav. 81 DH50
Kilner St. E14 57 CE39
Kilnfield, Ong. 24 CW18
Greenstead Rd.
Kilnside, Esher 93 BJ57
Kilnway Clo., Nthwd. 35 BB29
Kilnwood, Sev. 98 CQ60
Kilpatrick Way, Hayes 54 BE39
Kilravock St. W10 55 BR38
Kilrue La., Walt. 92 BB56
Kilrush Ter., Wok. 100 AT61
Kilsby Wk., Dag. 59 CO36
Rugby Rd.
Kilsha Rd., Walt. 84 BD53
Kilvinton Dr., Enf. 30 BZ22
Kilworth Ave., Brwd. 122 DD25
Kilworth Clo., Welw.G.C. 5 BS9
Kimbell Gdns. SW6 65 BR44
Kimber Clo., Wind. 61 AN45
Kimber Ct., Guil. 118 AU69
Gilliat Dr.
Kimber Rd. SW18 76 BS47
Kimberley Ave. E6 58 CK37
Kimberley Ave. SE15 67 CB44
Kimberley Ave., Ilf. 49 CM33
Kimberley Ave., Rom. 50 CS32
Kimberley Clo., Slou. 62 AS42
Kimberley Dr., Sid. 79 CP48
Kimberley Gdns. N4 47 BY32
Kimberley Gdns., Enf. 30 CA24
Kimberley Pl., Pur. 95 BY59
Brighton Rd.
Kimberley Ride, Cob. 93 BF60
Kimberley Rd. E4 40 CG26
Kimberley Rd. E11 48 CF34
Kimberley Rd. E16 58 CG38
Kimberley Rd. E17 39 CD30
Kimberley Rd. N17 39 CB30
Kimberley Rd. N18 39 CB29
Kimberley Rd. NW6 55 BR37
Kimberley Rd. SW9 66 BX44
Kimberley Rd., Beck. 87 CC51
Kimberley Rd., Croy. 86 BY53
Kimberley Rd., St.Alb. 9 BG13
Kimberley Way E4 40 CG26
Kimble Clo., Wat. 35 BB26
Chenies Way
Kimble Cres., Bush. 36 BG26
Kimble Rd. SW19 76 BT50
Kimbolton Clo. SE12 78 CG46
Kimbolton Grn., Brwd. 28 BN24
Kimbolton Row SW3 3 C9
Kimbolton Row SW3 66 BU42
Fulham Rd.
Kimmeridge Gdns. SE9 78 CK49
Kimmeridge Rd. SE9 78 CK49
Kimps Way, Hem.H. 8 AZ15
Kimpton Ave., Brwd. 42 DA26
Kimpton Clo., Hem.H. 8 AZ11
Kimpton Clo., Wat. 18 BD20
Kimpton Rd. SE5 67 BZ44
Kimpton Rd., Sutt. 85 BR55
Kimptons Clo., Ong. 24 CW16
Kimptons Clo., Pot.B. 19 BQ19
Kimptons Mead, Pot.B. 19 BQ19
Kinburn St. SE16 67 CC41
Kincaid Rd. SE15 67 CB43
Kinch Gro., Har. 46 BL33
Kincraig Dr., Sev. 107 CU65
Kinder Clo. SE28 59 CP40
Kinder Scout, Hem.H. 8 AZ14
Crofts Path
Kinder St. E1 57 CB39
Kindersley Way, Abb.L. 17 BA19
Kinfauns Ave., Horn. 51 CV32
Kinfauns Rd. SW2 76 BY48
Kinfauns Rd., Ilf. 50 CO33
King Acre Ct., Stai. 72 AV48
King Alfred Ave. SE6 77 CE49
King Alfred Rd., Rom. 42 CW30
King & Queen St. SE17 4 J10
King & Queen St. SE17 67 BZ42
King Arthur Clo. SE15 67 CC43
King Arthur Ct., Wal.Cr. 21 CC18
King Charles Cres., Surb. 85 BL54
King Charles Rd., Surb. 85 BL53
King Charles St. SW1 3
King Charles St. SW1 66 B
King Charles Wk. SW19 75 B
Princes Way
King Craig Dr., Sev. 107 C
King David La. E1 57 C
King Edward Ave., Dart. 80 C
King Edward Ave., Rain. 60 C
King Edward Ct., Wind. 61 A
King Edward Dr., Chess. 84 B
King Edward Dr., Grays 71 D
King Edward Ms. SW13 65 B
Byfield Gdns.
King Edward Rd. E10 48 C
King Edward Rd. E17 48 C
King Edward Rd., Barn. 29 B
King Edward Rd., Brwd. 42 D
King Edward Rd., Green. 80 D
King Edward Rd., Rad. 19 B
King Edward Rd., Rom. 50 C
King Edward Rd., Wal.Cr. 21 C
King Edward Rd., Wat. 27 B
King Edward VII Ave., Wind. 61 A
King Edward St. EC1 2
King Edward St. EC1 57 B
King Edward St., Hem.H. 8 A
King Edward St., Slou. 61 A
King Edward Wk. SE1 4
King Edward Wk. SE1 66 B
King Edwards Gdns. W3 55 BM
King Edwards Gro., Tedd. 74 B
King Edwards Rd. E9 57 C
King Edwards Rd. N9 39 C
King Edwards Rd., Bark. 58 CN
King Edwards Rd., Enf. 30 C
King Edwards Rd., Rom. 50 C
Victoria Rd.
King Edwards Rd., Ruis. 44 B
King Gdns., Croy. 95 B
King George Ave. E16 58 C
King George Ave., Bush. 27 B
King George Ave., Walt. 84 B
King George Clo., Rom. 50 C
King George Clo., Sun. 73 B
King George V Rd., Amer. 25 A
King George Rd., Wal.Abb. 21 C
King George VI Ave., Mitch. 86 B
King George VI Ave., West. 106 C
King George Sq., Rich. 75 B
King George St. SE10 67 C
King Georges Ave., Wat. 26 B
King Georges Dr., Sthl. 54 B
Lady Margaret Rd.
King Georges Dr., Wey. 92 AW
King Georges Rd., Brwd. 33 D
King Harolds Way, Bexh. 69 C
King Harry La., St.Alb. 9 B
King Harry St., Hem.H. 8 A
King Henry Ms., Orp. 97 CN
Osgood Ave.
King Henry St. N16 48 CA
King Henrys Dr., Croy. 96 C
King Henrys Ms., Enf. 30 C
King Henrys Rd. NW3 56 BU
King Henrys Rd., Kings.T. 85 BM
King Henrys Wk. N1 57 CA
King James Ave., Cuffley 20 BX
King James St. SE1 4
King James St. SE1 66 BY
King John Ct. EC2 2
King John Ct. EC2 57 CA
New Inn Yd.
King John St. E1 57 CC
King Johns Clo., Stai. 72 AR
King Johns Wk. SE9 78 CJ
King Sq. EC1 2
King Sq. EC1 57 BZ
Lever St.
King Sq. Est. EC1 56 BY
King Stairs Clo. SE16 67 CC
Elephant La.
King St. E13 58 CH
King St. EC2 2
King St. EC2 57 BZ
King St. N2 47 BT
King St. SW1 3
King St. SW1 56 BW
King St. W3 55 BM
King St. W6 65 BO
King St. WC2 1
King St. WC2 56 BX
King St., Cher. 82 AV
King St., Grav. 81 DG
King St., Ong. 24 CZ
King St., Rich. 74 BK
King St., Sthl. 64 BE
King St., Twick. 74 BJ
King St., Wat. 27 BD
King St. Wk., Grays 71 DD
Argent St.
King William IV Gdns. SE20 77 CC
St. Johns Rd.
King William La. SE10 68 CG
Orlop St.
King William St. EC4 4
King William St. EC4 57 BZ
King William Wk. SE10 67 CF
Kingaby Gdns., Rain. 59 CU
Kingcup Clo., Croy. 87 CC
Primrose La.
Kingdon Rd. NW6 56 BS
Kingfield Clo., Wok. 100 AS
Kingfield Dr., Wok. 100 AS
Kingfield Gdns., Wok. 100 AS
Kingfield Rd. W5 54 BK
Kingfield Rd., Wok. 100 AS
Kingfield St. E14 67 CF
Kingfisher Clo. SE28 59 CP
Kingfisher Clo., Brwd. 122 DD

ɡfisher Clo., Nthwd. 35 AZ30
ɡfisher Clo., Orp. 89 CP52
ndpiper Way
ɡfisher Clo., Walt. 93 BE56
ɡfisher Ct., Wok. 91 AU60
ackmore Cres.
ɡfisher Dr., Guil. 118 AU69
ɡfisher Dr., Red. 121 BV69
ɡfisher Dr., Rich. 74 BK49
ɡfisher Dr., Stai. 72 AV49
ɡfisher Gdns., S.Croy. 96 CC59
ɡfisher Lure, Kings L. 17 AZ18
ɡfisher Lure, Rick. 26 AW24
ɡfisher Rd., Upmin. 51 CZ33
ɡfisher Sq. SE8 67 CD43
orking Clo.
ɡfisher St. E6 58 CK39
ɡfisher Way NW10 55 BN36
ɡham Clo. SW18 76 BT47
ɡham Clo. W14 65 BR41
ghorn St. EC1 2 H7
ɡlake Ct., Wok. 100 AP62
'illiam Russel Ct.
glake Est. SE17 4 N10
ɡlake Est. SE17 67 CA42
ɡlake St. SE17 67 CA42
gly Ct. W1 1 M10
ɡly Ct. W1 56 BW40
eak St.
gly St. W1 1 L10
ɡly St. W1 56 BW39
ɡs Arbour, Sthl. 64 BE42
'ngway
ɡs Arms Ct. E1 57 CB39
gs Arms Yd. EC2 2 K8
ɡs Arms Yd. EC2 57 BZ39
ɡs Arms Yd., Rom. 50 CT32
uadrant Arc.
ɡs Ave. N10 47 BV31
ɡs Ave. N21 38 BY26
ɡs Ave. SW4 76 BW47
ɡs Ave. SW12 76 BW47
ɡs Ave. W5 54 BK39
ɡs Ave., Brom. 78 CG50
ɡs Ave., Buck.H. 40 CJ27
ɡs Ave., Cars. 95 BU57
ɡs Ave., Grnf. 54 BF39
ɡs Ave., Hem.H. 8 AY15
ɡs Ave., Houns. 64 BF44
ɡs Ave., N.Mal. 85 BO52
ɡs Ave., Red. 121 BU71
ɡs Ave., Rom. 50 CQ32
ɡs Ave., Sun. 73 BB49
ɡs Ave., Wat. 26 BB25
ɡs Ave., Wey. 92 AX59
ɡs Ave., Wdf.Grn. 40 CH29
gs Bench St. SE1 4 G4
ɡs Bench St. SE1 66 BY41
gs Bench Wk. EC4 2 E9
ɡs Brook, Lthd. 102 BJ62
ingston Rd.
ɡs Chase, Brwd. 42 DB27
ɡs Chase, E.Mol. 84 BG52
ɡs Clo. E10 48 CE33
ɡs Clo. NW4 46 BQ31
ɡs Clo., Ch.St.G. 34 AR27
ɡs Clo., Dart. 69 CT45
ɡs Clo., Kings L. 17 AW19
ɡs Clo., Nthwd. 35 BB29
ɡs Clo., Stai. 73 AX50
ɡs Clo., Walt. 83 BC54
ɡs Clo., Wat. 27 BD24
xchange Rd.
ɡs College Rd. NW3 56 BT36
ɡs College Rd., Ruis. 44 BB32
ɡs Ct. E13 58 CH37
ɡs Ct. SE1 67 BZ41
ireat Suffolk St.
ɡs Ct. SW19 76 BS50
ɡs Ct. W5 54 BK39
'astlebar Pk.
ɡs Ct. W6 65 BP42
ɡs Ct., Berk. 7 AR12
ower Kings Rd.
ɡs Ct., Har. 45 BF34
ɡs Ct., Tad. 103 BP64
ɡs Ct., Wem. 46 BM34
ɡs Cres. N4 48 BZ34
ɡs Cres. Est. N4 48 BZ34
ɡs Cft., Welw.G.C. 5 BS7
Hazel Gro.
gs Cross Rd. WC1 2 B2
ɡs Cross Rd. WC1 56 BX38
ɡs Dr., Edg. 37 BL28
ɡs Dr., Grav. 81 DG48
ɡs Dr., Surb. 85 BM54
ɡs Dr., Tedd. 74 BG49
ɡs Dr., T.Ditt. 84 BJ53
ɡs Dr., Walt. 92 BB58
ɡs Dr., Wem. 46 BM34
ɡs Fm. Ave., Rich. 65 BM45
ɡs Fm. Rd., Rick. 25 AU25
ɡs Gdns., Ilf. 49 CM33
ɡs Gdns., Upmin. 51 CZ33
ɡs Grn., Loug. 31 CK24
ɡs Gro. SE15 67 CB44
ɡs Gro., Rom. 50 CU32
ɡs Hall Rd., Beck. 77 CD50
ɡs Head Ct. EC3 57 BZ40
'ish St. Hill
ɡs Head Ct., Saw. 6 CQ6
London Rd.
ɡs Head Hill E4 39 CE26
ɡs Head Pas. SW4 66 BW45
Clapham Pk. Rd.
gs Head Yd. SE1 4 K3
ɡs Head Yd. SE1 57 BZ40
Borough High St.
ɡs Henrys Ms., Enf. 30 CE22
ɡs Highway SE18 68 CN43
ɡs Hill, Loug. 31 CK23
ɡs La., Egh. 72 AQ49
ɡs La., Kings L. 17 AW19
ɡs La., Sutt. 95 BT56
Kings Lynn Clo., Rom. 42 CV29
Kings Lynn Dr., Rom. 42 CV29
Kings Lynn Path, Rom. 42 CV29
Kings Lynn Dr.
Kings Mead Est. E9 48 CD35
Kings Mead Pk., Esher 93 BH57
Kings Mead Way E9 48 CD35
Kings Meadow, Kings L. 17 AZ17
Kings Ms. SW4 76 BX46
Kings Ms. WC1 2 C5
Kings Ms. WC1 56 BX38
Kings Mill La., Red. 121 BW73
Kings Orchard SE9 78 CK46
Kings Pk., Wok. 100 AP62
Kings Pas., Kings.T. 84 BK51
Kings Pl. SE1 4 H5
Kings Pl. SE1 67 BZ41
Kings Pl. W4 65 BN42
Kings Pl., Buck.H. 40 CJ27
Kings Reach Twr. SE1 4 E2
Kings Ride Gate, Rich. 65 BM45
Kings Rd. E4 39 CF26
Kings Rd. E6 58 CJ37
Kings Rd. E11 49 CG33
Kings Rd. N17 39 CA30
Kings Rd. N18 39 CB28
Kings Rd. N22 38 BX30
Kings Rd. NW10 55 BP36
Kings Rd. SE25 87 CB52
Kings Rd. SW1 3 H8
Kings Rd. SW1 66 BV42
Kings Rd. SW3 66 BS43
Kings Rd. SW6 66 BS44
Kings Rd. SW10 66 BT43
Kings Rd. SW14 65 BN45
Kings Rd. SW19 76 BS50
Kings Rd. W5 54 BK39
Kings Rd., Bark. 58 CM36
North St.
Kings Rd., Barn. 28 BQ24
Kings Rd., Berk. 7 AQ13
Kings Rd., Brwd. 42 DB27
Kings Rd., Ch.St.G. 34 AR27
Kings Rd., Egh. 72 AT49
Kings Rd., Felt. 74 BD47
Kings Rd., Guil. 118 AR70
Kings Rd., Har. 45 BE34
Kings Rd., Kings.T. 85 BL51
Kings Rd., Mitch. 86 BV52
Kings Rd., Orp. 97 CN56
Kings Rd., Rich. 75 BL46
Kings Rd., Rom. 50 CU32
Kings Rd., St.Alb. 9 BF13
Kings Rd., St.Alb. 18 BK16
Kings Rd., Slou. 62 AP41
Kings Rd., Surb. 84 BK54
Kings Rd., Sutt. 95 BS58
Kings Rd., Tedd. 74 BG49
Kings Rd., Twick. 74 BJ46
Kings Rd., Uxb. 53 AX37
Kings Rd., Wal.Cr. 21 CD20
Kings Rd., Walt. 83 BC55
Kings Rd., West Dr. 63 AY41
Kings Rd., West. 106 CJ62
Kings Rd., Wey. 92 AW58
Kings Rd., Wind. 61 AO45
Kings Rd., Wok. 100 AT61
Kings Scholars Pas. SW1 66 BW41
Carlisle Pl.
Kings Scholars Pas. SW1 3 L7
Kings Ter. NW1 56 BW37
Plender St.
Kings Ter., Islw. 64 BJ45
Kings Wk., Grays 71 DD43
West St.
Kings Wk., Kings.T. 84 BK51
Kings Wk., S.Croy. 96 CB60
Kings Way, Har. 45 BH31
Kingsand Rd. SE12 78 CH48
Kingsash Dr., Hayes 54 BD38
Kingsbridge Ave. W3 65 BL41
Kingsbridge Circ., Rom. 42 CW29
Kingsbridge Clo., Rom. 42 CW29
Kingsbridge Cres., Sthl. 54 BE39
Kingsbridge Rd. W10 55 BQ39
Kingsbridge Rd., Bark. 58 CM37
Kingsbridge Rd., Mord. 85 BQ53
Kingsbridge Rd., Rom. 42 CW29
Kingsbridge Rd., Sthl. 64 BE42
Kingsbridge Rd., Walt. 83 BC54
Kingsbridge Way, Hayes 53 BB38
Weymouth Dr.
Kingsbury Ave., St.Alb. 9 BG13
Kingsbury Circ. NW9 46 BM32
Kingsbury Cres., Stai. 72 AU49
The Causeway
Kingsbury Dr., Wind. 72 AQ47
Kingsbury Rd. N1 57 CA36
Kingsbury Rd. NW9 46 BM32
Kingsbury Ter. N1 57 CA36
Kingsclere Clo. SW15 75 BP47
Kingscliffe Gdns. SW19 75 BR47
Kingscote Rd. W4 65 BN41
Kingscote Rd., Croy. 87 CB54
Kingscote Rd., N.Mal. 85 BN52
Kingscote St. EC4 2 F10
Kingscote St. EC4 56 BY40
Tudor St.
Kingscourt Rd. SW16 76 BW48
Kingscroft, Welw.G.C. 5 BS7
Hazel Gro.
Kingscroft Rd. NW2 55 BR36
Kingscroft Rd., Bans. 104 BT61
Kingscroft Rd., Lthd. 102 BJ63
Kingscross La., Red. 121 BW71
Kingsdale Est. SE18 68 CN43
Kingsdale Gdns. W11 55 BQ40
Kingsdale Rd. SE18 68 CN43
Kingsdale Rd. SE20 77 CC50
Kingsdale Rd., Berk. 7 AQ13
Kingsdene, Tad. 103 BP64
Kingsdon La., Harl. 14 CP11
Kingsdown Ave. W3 55 BO40
Kingsdown Ave. W13 64 BJ41
Kingsdown Ave., S.Croy. 95 BY58
Kingsdown Clo. W10 55 BQ39
Kingsdown Clo., Grav. 81 DJ47
Farley Rd.
Kingsdown Rd. E11 49 CG34
Kingsdown Rd. N19 47 BX34
Kingsdown Rd., Epsom 94 BP60
Kingsdown Rd., Sutt. 94 BR56
Kingsdown Way, Brom. 88 CH53
Kingsdowne Rd., Surb. 85 BL54
Kingsend, Ruis. 44 BA33
Kingsfield, Hodd. 12 CE11
Kingsfield, Wind. 61 AL44
Kingsfield Ave., Har. 45 BF31
Kingsfield Dr., Enf. 30 CC21
Kingsfield Rd., Har. 45 BG33
Kingsfield Rd., Wat. 36 BD26
Kingsfield Ter., Dart. 80 CV46
Kingsfield Ter., Har. 45 BG33
Kingsfield Way, Enf. 30 CC21
Kingsford Ave., Wall. 95 BX57
Kingsford St. NW5 47 BU35
Southampton Rd.
Kingsgate, Wem. 46 BM34
Kingsgate Ave. N3 47 BS31
Kingsgate Clo., Bexh. 69 CQ44
Kingsgate Clo., Orp. 89 CP52
Main Rd.
Kingsgate Pl. NW6 56 BS36
Kingsgate Rd. NW6 56 BS36
Kingsgate Rd., Kings.T. 85 BL51
Kingsground SE9 78 CK47
Kingshead La., Wey. 92 AX59
Kingshill Ave., Har. 45 BJ31
Kingshill Ave., Hayes 53 BB38
Kingshill Ave., Nthlt. 54 BD38
Kingshill Ave., Rom. 41 CS29
Kingshill Ave., St.Alb. 9 BJ11
Kingshill Ave., Wor.Pk. 85 BP54
Kingshill Dr., Har. 36 BK30
Kingshill Way, Berk. 7 AQ14
Kingshold Est. E9 57 CC37
Kingshold Rd. E9 57 CC36
Kingsholm Gdns. SE9 68 CJ45
Kingshurst Rd. SE12 78 CH47
Kingsingfield Clo., Sev. 99 CZ57
Kingsingfield Rd., Sev. 99 CZ58
Kingsland NW8 56 BU37
Kingsland, Harl. 13 CM12
Kingsland Est. E2 57 CA37
Kingsland Grn. N16 57 CA36
Kingsland High St. E8 57 CA36
Kingsland Pas. E8 57 CA36
Kingsland Grn.
Kingsland Rd. E2 2 N2
Kingsland Rd. E2 57 CA38
Kingsland Rd. E13 58 CJ38
Kingsland Rd., Hem.H. 8 AW14
Kingslawn Clo. SW15 75 BP46
Kingslea, Lthd. 102 BJ63
Kingsleigh Pl., Mitch. 86 BU52
Whitford Gdns.
Kingsleigh Wk., Brom. 88 CG52
Stamford Dr.
Kingsley Ave. W13 54 BJ39
Kingsley Ave., Bans. 104 BS61
Kingsley Ave., Brwd. 28 BL23
Kingsley Ave., Chsnt. 21 CB18
Kingsley Ave., Dart. 80 CX46
Kingsley Ave., Houns. 64 BG44
Kingsley Ave., Sthl. 54 BF40
Kingsley Ave., Sutt. 95 BT56
Kingsley Clo. N2 47 BT32
Kingsley Clo., Dag. 50 CR35
Kingsley Ct., Welw.G.C. 5 BR10
Kingsley Dr., Egh. 72 AQ50
Kingsley Dr., Wor.Pk. 85 BO55
Badgers Copse
Kingsley Gdns. E4 39 CE28
Kingsley Gdns., Horn. 51 CV31
Kingsley Gro., Reig. 121 BS72
Kingsley Ms. E1 57 CB40
Wapping La.
Kingsley Ms. W8 66 BS41
Stanford Rd.
Kingsley Pl. N6 47 BV33
Kingsley Rd. E7 58 CH36
Kingsley Rd. E17 39 CF30
Kingsley Rd. N13 38 BY28
Kingsley Rd. NW6 55 BR37
Kingsley Rd. SW19 76 BS49
Kingsley Rd., Brwd. 122 DE26
Kingsley Rd., Croy. 86 BY54
Kingsley Rd., Har. 45 BG35
Kingsley Rd., Houns. 64 BF44
Kingsley Rd., Ilf. 40 CM30
Kingsley Rd., Loug. 31 CM24
Kingsley Rd., Orp. 97 CN57
Kingsley Rd., Pnr. 45 BE31
Kingsley St. SW11 66 BU45
Kingsley Wk., Grays 71 DG42
Kingsley Way N2 47 BT32
Kingsley Wd. Dr. SE9 78 CK48
Kingslyn Cres. SE19 87 CA51
Kingsman St. SE18 68 CK41
Kingsmead, Barn. 29 BS24
Kingsmead, Cuffley 20 BX17
Kingsmead, Rich. 75 BL46
Kingsmead, St.Alb. 9 BK12
Kingsmead, Saw. 6 CQ6
Kingsmead, Wal.Cr. 21 CC17
Kingsmead, West. 106 CJ61
Kingsmead Ave. N9 39 CB26
Kingsmead Ave. NW9 46 BN33
Kingsmead Ave., Mitch. 86 BW52
Kingsmead Ave., Rom. 50 CT32
Kingsmead Ave., Sun. 84 BD51
Kingsmead Ave., Surb. 85 BM55
Kingsmead Ave., Wor.Pk. 85 BP55
Kingsmead Clo., Epsom 94 BN57
Kingsmead Clo., Harl. 13 CH11
Kingsmead Clo., Sid. 79 CO48
Kingsmead Clo., Tedd. 74 BJ50
Kingsmead Dr., Nthlt. 54 BE36
Kingsmead Rd. SW2 76 BY48
Kingsmere Clo. SW15 65 BR45
Weimar St.
Kingsmere Pk. NW9 46 BM33
Kingsmere Rd. SW19 75 BQ48
Kingsmill Gdns., Dag. 50 CQ35
Kingsmill Rd., Dag. 50 CQ35
Kingsmill Ter. NW8 56 BT37
Kingsmoor Rd., Harl. 13 CL12
Kingsnympton Pk., Kings.T. 75 BM50
Kingspark Ct. E18 49 CH31
Kingspark Ct., Ilf. 49 CK33
The Dr.
Kingsridge SW19 75 BR48
Kingsridge Gdns., Dart. 80 CV46
Kingstable St., Wind. 61 AO43
Kingstable St. (Eton), Wind. 61 AO43
Kingsthorpe Rd. SE26 77 CC49
Kingston Ave., Felt. 73 BB46
Kingston Ave., Lthd. 110 BB66
Kingston Ave., Lthd. 102 BJ64
Kingston Ave., Sutt. 85 BR55
Kingston Ave., West Dr. 53 AY40
Kingston Bri., Kings.T. 84 BK51
Kingston By-pass SW15 75 BO49
Kingston By-pass SW20 85 BP51
Kingston By-pass, Esher 84 BH55
Kingston By-pass, N.Mal. 83 BO53
Kingston By-pass, Surb. 85 BL55
Kingston Clo., Nthlt. 54 BE36
Kingston Clo., Rom. 50 CQ31
Kingston Clo., Tedd. 74 BJ50
Kingston Ct. N4 48 BZ32
Wiltshire Gdns.
Kingston Ct., Grav. 81 DD46
Kingston Cres., Ashf. 73 AX49
Kingston Cres., Beck. 87 CD51
Kingston Gdns., Croy. 86 BX55
Wandle Rd.
Kingston Hall Rd., Kings.T. 84 BK52
Kingston Hill, Kings.T. 85 BM51
Kingston Hill Ave., Rom. 41 CQ30
Kingston Ho. Gdns., Lthd. 102 BJ64
Upper Fairfield Rd.
Kingston La., Lthd. 110 AZ67
Kingston La., Tedd. 74 BJ49
Kingston La., Uxb. 53 AY38
Kingston La., West Dr. 63 AY41
Kingston Pk. Est., Kings.T. 75 BM50
Kingston Pl., Har. 36 BH29
Richmond Gdns.
Kingston Ri., Wey. 92 AW58
Kingston Rd. N9 39 CB27
Kingston Rd. SW15 75 BP48
Kingston Rd. SW19 75 BP48
Kingston Rd. SW20 85 BQ51
Kingston Rd., Ashf. 73 AY50
Kingston Rd., Ashf. 73 AW49
Kingston Rd., Barn. 29 BT25
Kingston Rd., Epsom 94 BO57
Kingston Rd., Ilf. 49 CL35
Kingston Rd., Kings.T. 85 BM52
Kingston Rd., Lthd. 102 BJ62
Kingston Rd., N.Mal. 85 BN52
Kingston Rd., Rom. 50 CT31
Kingston Rd., Sthl. 64 BE41
Kingston Rd., Stai. 73 AW49
Kingston Rd., Surb. 85 BM55
Kingston Rd., Tedd. 74 BJ49
Kingston Sq. SE19 77 BZ49
Kingston Vale SW15 75 BN49
Kingstown St. NW1 56 BV37
Kingswater Pl. SW11 66 BT44
Battersea Ch. Rd.
Kingsway N12 38 BT29
Kingsway SW14 65 BM45
Kingsway WC2 2 B8
Kingsway WC2 56 BX39
Kingsway, Croy. 95 BX56
Kingsway, Cuffley 20 BX18
Kingsway, Enf. 30 CB25
Kingsway, Ger.Cr. 34 AS30
Kingsway, Hayes 53 BA39
Kingsway, Iver 52 AV39
Kingsway, N.Mal. 85 BQ52
Kingsway, Orp. 88 CM53
Kingsway, Stai. 73 AX47
Kingsway, Wat. 26 BB21
Kingsway, Wat. 18 BD20
Kingsway, Wem. 46 BL35
Kingsway, W.Wick. 88 CG55
Kingsway, Wok. 100 AR62
Kingsway, Wdf.Grn. 40 CJ28
Kingsway, The, Epsom 94 BP59
Kingsway Ave., S.Croy. 96 CC58
Kingsway Ave., Wok. 100 AR62
Kingsway Cres., Har. 45 BG31
Kingsway Ind. Est. N18 39 CC29
Kingsway Rd., Sutt. 94 BR57
Kingsway Rd., Sutt. 94 BR57
Kingswear Rd. NW5 47 BV34
Kingswear Rd., Ruis. 44 BC34
Kingswell Ride, Cuffley 20 BX18
Kingswood Ave. NW6 55 BR37
Kingswood Ave., Belv. 69 CQ42
Kingswood Ave., Brom. 88 CG52
Kingswood Ave., Hmptn. 74 BF50
Kingswood Ave., Houns. 64 BE44
Kingswood Ave., S.Croy. 105 CB61
Kingswood Ave., Swan. 89 CT52
Kingswood Ave., Th.Hth. 86 BY53
Kingswood Clo. N20 38 BT26
Kingswood Clo. SW8 66 BX43
Kenchester Clo.
Kingswood Clo., Dart. 80 CV46
Kingswood Clo., Egh. 72 AR49
Kingswood Clo., Guil. 118 AU70
Kingswood Clo., N.Mal. 85 BO53
Motspur Pk.
Kingswood Clo., Orp. 88 CM54
Woodcote Rd.
Kingswood Clo., Surb. 85 BL54
Kingswood Clo., Wey. 92 AZ57
Kingswood Ct., Rich. 75 BL46
Marchmont Rd.
Kingswood Ct., Tad. 103 BR65
Kingswood Creek, Stai. 72 AR46
Kingswood Dr. SE19 77 CA49
Kingswood Dr., Cars. 86 BU54
Kingswood Dr., Sutt. 95 BS58
Kingswood Est. SE21 77 CA49
Kingswood La., Warl. 105 CC61
Kingswood Pk. N3 37 BR30
Kingswood Pl. SE13 68 CG45
Kingswood Ri., Egh. 72 AR49
Kingswood Rd. SE20 77 CC50
Kingswood Rd. SW2 76 BX46
Kingswood Rd. SW19 75 BR50
Kingswood Rd. W4 65 BN41
Kingswood Rd., Brom. 87 CF52
Kingswood Rd., Ilf. 50 CO33
Kingswood Rd., Sev. 107 CT64
Kingswood Rd., Tad. 103 BP64
Kingswood Rd., Wat. 17 BC20
Kingswood Way, Croy. 96 CC60
Kingswood Way, Wall. 95 BX56
Kingsworth Clo., Beck. 87 CD52
Shirley Cres.
Kingsworthy Clo., Kings.T. 85 BL52
Dawson Rd.
Kingthorpe Rd. NW10 55 BN36
Kingthorpe Ter. NW10 55 BN36
Kingwell Rd., Barn. 29 BT22
Kingwood Rd. SW6 65 BR44
Kinlet Clo. SE18 68 CM44
Kinlet Rd.
Kinlet Rd. SE18 68 CL44
Kinloch Dr. NW9 46 BN33
Kinloch St. N7 47 BX34
Kinloss Ct. N3 46 BR31
Kinloss Gdns.
Kinloss Gdns. N3 46 BR31
Kinloss Rd., Cars. 86 BT54
Kinnaird Ave. W4 65 BN43
Kinnaird Ave., Brom. 78 CG50
Kinnaird Clo., Brom. 78 CG50
Kinnaird Way, Wdf.Grn. 40 CK29
Kinnear Rd. W12 65 BO41
Kinnersley Wk., Reig. 121 BS72
Castle Dr.
Kinnerton Pl. N. SW1 3 F5
Kinnerton Pl. N. SW1 66 BU41
Kinnerton St.
Kinnerton Pl. S. SW1 3 F5
Kinnerton Pl. S. SW1 66 BU41
Kinnerton St.
Kinnerton St. SW1 3 G5
Kinnerton St. SW1 66 BV41
Kinnerton Yd. SW1 3 F5
Kinnoul Rd. W6 65 BR43
Kinross Ave., Wor.Pk. 85 BP55
Kinross Clo., Har. 46 BL32
Kinross Clo., Sun. 73 BB49
Kinross Dr., Sun. 73 BB49
Kinross St. SE1 67 CA41
Tanner St.
Kinsale Rd. SE15 67 CB45
Kinsfield, Hodd. 12 CE11
Kintore Way SE1 4 P8
Kintore Way SE1 67 CA42
Alscot Rd.
Kintyre Clo. SW16 86 BX51
Kinveachy Gdns. SE7 68 CK42
Kinver Rd. N. SE26 77 CC49
Kinver Rd. S. SE26 77 CC49
Kipings, Tad. 103 BQ64
Kipling Ave., Til. 71 DG44
Kipling Dr. SW19 76 BT50
Kipling Est. SE1 4 L5
Kipling Gro., Hem.H. 8 AZ10
Kipling Pl., Stan. 36 BH29
Kipling Rd., Bexh. 69 CQ44
Kipling Rd., Dart. 80 CX46
Kipling St. SE1 4 L5
Kipling St. SE1 67 BZ41
Kipling Ter. N9 38 BZ30
Kippington Clo., Sev. 107 CT65
Kippington Dr. SE9 78 CJ47
Kippington Rd., Sev. 107 CU65
Kirby Clo., Epsom 94 BO56
Kirby Clo., Ilf. 40 CN29
Kirby Clo., Loug. 40 CK26
Kirby Clo., Nthwd. 35 BB29
Kirby Est. SE16 67 CB41
Kirby Gro. SE1 4 M4
Kirby Gro. SE1 67 CA41
Kirby Rd., Dart. 80 CY47
Kirby Rd., Wok. 100 AR61
Kirby St. EC1 2 E6
Kirby St. EC1 56 BY39
Kirby Way, Walt. 84 BD53
Kircaldy Grn., Wat. 36 BD27
Trevose Way
Kirchen Rd. W13 54 BJ40
Kirk Ct., Sev. 107 CU65
Kirk La. SE18 68 CM43
Kirk Ri., Sutt. 86 BS55
Kirk Rd. E17 48 CD32
Kirkdale SE26 77 CB48
Kirkdale Rd. E11 49 CG33
Kirkham Rd. E6 58 CK39
Kirkham St. SE18 68 CN43
Kirkland Ave., Ilf. 40 CL30
Kirkland Ave., Wok. 100 AP61
Kirkland Clo., Sid. 78 CN46
Kirkland Wk. E8 57 CA36
Laurel St.
Kirkland Way, Orp. 89 CP52
Kirklands, Welw.G.C. 5 BQ6
Kirklees Rd., Surb. 85 BL54
Kirklees Rd., Th.Hth. 86 BX52
Kirkley Rd. SW19 76 BS50

Kirkly Clo., S.Croy. 96 CA58
Kirkman Pl. W1 1 N7
Kirkmichael Rd. E14 57 CF39
Kirks Pl. E14 57 CD39
Rhodeswell Rd.
Kirkside Rd. SE3 68 CH43
Kirkstall Ave. N17 48 BZ31
Kirkstall Gdns. SW2 76 BW47
Kirkstall Rd. SW2 76 BW47
Kirkstead Ct. E5 48 CC35
Clapton Pk. Est.
Kirksted Rd., Mord. 86 BS54
Kirkstone Way, Brom. 78 CG50
Kirkton Clo. W4 65 BN42
Dolman Rd.
Kirkton Gdns. E2 57 CA38
Chambord St.
Kirkton Rd. N15 48 CA32
Kirkwall Pl. E2 57 CC38
Kirkwood Rd. SE15 67 CB44
Kirn Rd. W13 54 BJ40
Kirchen Rd.
Kirtley Rd. SE26 77 CD49
Kirtling St. SW8 66 BW43
Kirton Clo. W4 65 BN42
Dolman Rd.
Kirton Clo., Horn. 60 CV36
Sarre Ave.
Kirton Gdns. E2 2 Q3
Kirton Rd. E13 58 CJ37
Kirton Wk., Edg. 37 BN29
Kirwyn Way SE5 67 BZ43
Kitchener Ave., Grav. 81 DH48
Kitchener Clo., St.Alb. 9 BJ14
Kitchener Rd. E7 58 CH36
Kitchener Rd. E17 39 CE30
Kitchener Rd. N2 47 BU31
Kitchener Rd. N17 48 BZ31
Kitchener Rd., Dag. 59 CR36
Kitchener Rd., Th.Hth. 87 BZ52
Kitcheners La., Red. 114 CA70
Kite Fld., Berk. 7 AP12
Kitkat Ter. E3 57 CE38
Kitley Gdns. SE19 87 CA51
Kitsbury Rd., Berk. 7 AQ13
Kitsbury Ter., Berk. 7 AQ13
Kitsmead La., Cher. 82 AR54
Kitson Rd. SE5 67 BZ43
Kitson Rd. SW13 65 BP44
Kitson Way, Harl. 6 CM10
Kitswell Way, Rad. 18 BH20
Kittiwake Clo., S.Croy. 96 CD58
Kittiwake Rd., Nthlt. 54 BD38
Kitto Rd. SE14 67 CC44
Kitts End Rd., Barn. 28 BQ21
Kiver Rd. N19 47 BW34
Klea Ave. SW4 76 BW46
Knapdale Clo. SE23 77 CB48
Knapmill Rd. SE6 77 CE48
Knapmill Way SE6 77 CE48
Knapp Clo. NW10 55 BO36
Knapp Rd. E3 57 CE38
Knappe Rd., Ashf. 73 AY49
Knaresborough Pl. SW5 66 BS42
Knatchbull Rd. NW10 55 BN37
Knatchbull Rd. SE5 66 BY44
Knatts La., Sev. 99 CY59
Knatts Valley Rd., Sev. 99 CY59
Knavewood Rd., Sev. 108 CW62
Knavewood Rd., Sev. 108 CW62
Knebworth Ave. E17 39 CE30
Knebworth Path, Brwd. 28 BN24
Knebworth Rd. N16 48 CA35
Knee Hill SE2 69 CP42
Knee Hill Cres. SE2 69 CP42
Knella Grn., Welw.G.C. 5 BS8
Knella Rd., Welw.G.C. 5 BR8
Kneller Gdns., Islw. 74 BG46
Kneller Rd. SE4 67 CD45
Kneller Rd., N.Mal. 85 BN54
Kneller Rd., Twick. 74 BG46
Knight St., Saw. 6 CQ6
Knighten St. E1 57 CB40
Knightland Rd. E5 48 CB34
Knighton Clo., Rom. 50 CS32
Knighton Clo., S.Croy. 95 BY57
Knighton Clo., Wdf.Grn. 40 CH28
Knighton Dr., Wdf.Grn. 40 CH28
Knighton La., Buck.H. 40 CH27
Knighton Pk. Rd. SE26 77 CC49
Knighton Rd. E7 49 CH34
Knighton Rd., Red. 121 BV71
Knighton Rd., Rom. 50 CS32
Knighton Rd., Sev. 107 CT61
Knighton Way La., Uxb. 53 AW36
Knightrider Ct. EC4 57 BZ40
Knightrider St.
Knightrider St. EC4 2 G10
Knightrider St. EC4 57 BZ39
Godliman St.
Knights Arc. SW1 3 E5
Knights Ave. W5 65 BL41
Knights Clo. E9 48 CC35
Churchill Wk.
Knights Clo., Egh. 72 AU50
Knights Clo., Wind. 61 AL44
Knights Ct., Kings.T. 85 BL52
Knights Hill SE27 76 BY49
Knights Hill Sq. SE27 76 BY49
Knights Hill
Knights La. N9 39 CB27
Knights Manor Way, Dart. 80 CW46
Knights Pk., Kings.T. 85 BL52
Knights Ridge, Orp. 98 CO56
Stirling Dr.
Knights Rd. E16 68 CH41
Knights Rd., Stan. 36 BK28
Knights Wk. SE11 4 F9
Knights Wk., Rom. 32 CO24
Knights Way, Brwd. 122 DD27
Knights Way, Ilf. 40 CM29
Knightsbridge SW1 3 F4
Knightsbridge SW7 3 D5
Knightsbridge SW7 66 BU41
Knightsbridge Cres., Stai. 73 AW50
Knightsbridge Gdns., Rom. 50 CS32
Knightsbridge Grn. SW1 3 E5
Knightsbridge Grn. SW1 66 BU41
Knightsbridge
Knightsbridge Way, Hem.H. 8 AY13
Knightsfield, Welw.G.C. 5 BQ5
Knightswood, Wok. 100 AP62
Knightwood Clo., Edg. 37 BN27
Knightwood Clo., Reig. 121 BS71
Knightwood Cres., N.Mal. 85 BO53
Knipp Hill, Cob. 93 BE60
Knivet Rd. SW6 66 BS43
Knobs Hill Rd. E15 57 CE37
Knockhall Chase, Green. 80 DB46
Knockhall Rd., Green. 80 DB46
Knockholt Main Rd., Sev. 106 CN63
Knockholt Rd. SE9 78 CJ46
Knockholt Rd., Sev. 107 CO61
Knole, The SE9 78 CL49
Knole, The, Grav. 81 DF50
Knole Clo., Croy. 87 CC53
Knole Gate, Sid. 78 CN48
Woodside Cres.
Knole La., Sev. 117 CV66
Knole Rd., Dart. 79 CU47
Knole Rd., Sev. 108 CV65
Knole Way, Sev. 117 CV66
Knoll, The W13 54 BK39
Knoll, The, Beck. 87 CE51
Knoll, The, Brom. 88 CH55
Knoll, The, Cob. 93 BF60
Knoll Cres., Nthwd. 35 BB30
Knoll Dr. N14 38 BV26
Knoll Ri., Orp. 88 CN54
Knoll Rd. SW18 76 BT46
Knoll Rd., Bex. 79 CR47
Knoll Rd., Dor. 119 BJ72
Knoll Rd., Sid. 79 CO49
Knolles Cres., Hat. 10 BP15
Knollmead, Surb. 85 BN54
Knolls, The, Epsom 103 BQ61
Knolls Clo., Wor.Pk. 85 BP55
Knollys Clo. SW16 76 BY48
Knollys Rd. SW16 76 BX48
Knolton Way, Slou. 52 AQ39
Knottisford St. E2 57 CC38
Knotts Grn. Rd. E10 48 CE32
Knotts Pl., Sev. 107 CU65
Knowl Hill, Wok. 100 AT63
Knowl Way, Borwd. 28 BL24
Knowland Way, Uxb. 43 AV32
Knowle, The, Hodd. 12 CE12
Cock La.
Knowle, The, Tad. 103 BQ64
Knowle Ave., Bexh. 69 CQ43
Knowle Clo. SW9 66 BY45
Knowle Gdns., Wey. 91 AV60
Madeira Rd.
Knowle Grn., Stai. 73 AW49
Knowle Gro., Vir.W. 82 AR54
Knowle Gro. Clo., Vir.W. 82 AR54
Knowle Hill, Vir.W. 82 AR54
Knowle Pk., Cob. 102 BE61
Knowle Pk. Ave., Stai. 73 AW50
Knowle Rd., Brom. 88 CK55
Knowle Rd., Twick. 74 BH47
Knowles Clo., West Dr. 53 AY40
Knowles Hill Cres. SE13 77 CF46
Knowles Wk. SW4 66 BW45
Knowlton Grn., Brom. 88 CG53
Knowsley Ave., Sthl. 54 BF40
Knowsley Rd. SW11 66 BU44
Knox Rd. E7 58 CG36
Knox Rd., Guil. 109 AQ68
Knox St. W1 1 E6
Knox St. W1 56 BU39
Knoyle St. SE14 67 CD43
Chubworthy St.
Knutsford Ave., Wat. 27 BD22
Koh-i-noor Ave., Bush. 27 BF25
Kohat Rd. SW19 76 BS49
Koonowla Clo., West. 106 CJ61
Dowding Rd.
Korda Clo., Shep. 83 AY52
Kossuth St. SE10 68 CG42
Kramer Ms. SW5 66 BS42
Kreisel Wk., Rich. 65 BL43
Kuala Gdns. SW16 86 BX51
Bush Rd.
Kuhn Way E7 49 CH35
Kydbrook Clo., Orp. 88 CM54
Kylemore Clo. E6 58 CJ37
Parr Rd.
Kylemore Rd. NW6 56 BS36
Kymberley Rd., Har. 45 BH32
Kyme Rd., Horn. 50 CT32
Kynance Clo., Rom. 42 CV28
Kynance Gdns., Stan. 36 BK29
Kynance Ms. SW7 66 BS41
Kynance Pl. SW7 66 BT41
Kynaston Ave. N16 48 CA34
Dynevor Rd.
Kynaston Ave., Th.Hth. 87 BZ53
Kynaston Clo., Har. 36 BG29
Kynaston Cres., Th.Hth. 87 BZ53
Kynaston Rd. N16 48 CA34
Kynaston Rd., Brom. 78 CH49
Kynaston Rd., Enf. 30 BZ23
Kynaston Rd., Orp. 89 CO54
Kynaston Rd., Th.Hth. 87 BZ53
Kynaston Wd., Har. 36 BG29
Kynnersley Clo., Cars. 86 BU55
William St.
Kynock Rd. N18 39 CC28
Kyrle Rd. SW11 76 BU46
Kytes Dr., Wat. 18 BD20
Kyverdale Rd. N16 48 CA33

L

La Plata Gro., Brwd. 42 DA27
La Roche Clo., Slou. 62 AR41
Hempson Ave.
La Tourne Gdns., Orp. 88 CM55
Labour-in-Vain Rd., Sev. 99 DB60
Laburnham Ave., West Dr. 53 AY40
Laburnham Clo., Upmin. 51 DA33
Laburnham Ct., Stan. 36 BK28
Laburnham Gdns., Croy. 87 CC54
Primrose La.
Laburnham Gdns., Upmin. 51 CZ33
Laburnham Rd., Epp. 23 CP18
Laburnum Ave. N9 39 CA27
Laburnum Ave. N17 39 BZ29
Laburnum Ave., Dart. 80 CV47
Laburnum Ave., Horn. 50 CT34
Laburnum Ave., Sutt. 86 BU55
Laburnum Ave., Swan. 89 CS52
Laburnum Clo. E4 39 CD29
Maple Ave.
Laburnum Clo. N11 38 BV29
Laburnum Clo. SE15 67 CC43
Clifton Way
Laburnum Clo., Chsnt. 21 CC19
Laburnum Clo., Guil. 118 AR69
Laburnum Ct. E2 57 CA37
Laburnum St.
Laburnum Cres., Sun. 83 BC51
Laburnum Gdns. N21 39 BZ27
Laburnum Gro. N21 39 BZ27
Laburnum Gro. NW9 46 BN33
Laburnum Gro., Grav. 81 DE47
Laburnum Gro., Houns. 64 BE45
Laburnum Gro., N.Mal. 85 BN51
Laburnum Gro., Ruis. 44 BA32
Laburnum Gro., St.Alb. 18 BF16
Laburnum Gro., Slou. 62 AT43
Laburnum Gro., Sthl. 54 BE38
Laburnum Pl. SE9 78 CL46
Laburnum Pl., Egh. 72 AQ50
Laburnum Rd. SW19 76 BT50
Laburnum Rd., Cher. 83 AW54
Laburnum Rd., Epsom 94 BO60
Laburnum Rd., Hayes 63 BB42
Laburnum Rd., Hodd. 12 CE11
Laburnum Rd., Mitch. 86 BV51
Laburnum Rd., Wok. 100 AR63
Laburnum St. E2 57 CA37
Laburnum Wk., Horn. 51 CV35
Laburnum Way, Brom. 88 CL54
Laburnum Way, Chsnt. 20 BY17
Laburnum Way, Stai. 73 AY47
Lacebark Clo., Sid. 78 CN47
Lacey Ave., Couls. 104 BY63
Lacey Clo. N9 39 CB27
Lacey Clo. N9 39 CB27
Lacey Clo., Egh. 72 AU50
Lacey Dr., Edg. 37 BL28
Lacey Dr., Hmptn. 84 BE51
Lacey Grn., Couls. 104 BY63
Lacey Wk. E3 57 CE37
Lackford Rd., Couls. 104 BU62
Lackington St. EC2 2 L6
Lackington St. EC2 57 BZ39
Lackmore Rd., Enf. 30 CC21
Lacock Clo. SW19 76 BT50
Lacock Ct. W13 54 BJ40
Lacon Rd. SE22 67 CB45
Lacy Dr., Couls. 104 BY63
Lacy Rd. SW15 65 BQ45
Ladas Rd. SE27 77 BZ49
Ladbroke Clo. W11 55 BR39
Ladbroke Gro.
Ladbroke Cres. W11 55 BR39
Ladbroke Gro.
Ladbroke Gdns. W11 55 BR40
Ladbroke Gro. W10 55 BQ38
Ladbroke Gro., Red. 121 BV70
Ladbroke Ms. W11 55 BR40
Ladbroke Rd.
Ladbroke Rd. W11 55 BR40
Ladbroke Rd., Enf. 30 CA25
Ladbroke Rd., Epsom 94 BN60
Ladbroke Rd., Red. 121 BV70
Ladbroke Sq. W11 55 BR40
Ladbroke Ter. W11 55 BR40
Ladbroke Wk. W11 55 BR40
Ladbrook Clo., Pnr. 45 BE32
Ladbrook Rd. SE25 87 BZ52
Ladbrooke Clo., Pot.B. 20 BS19
Strafford Gate
Ladbrooke Cres., Sid. 79 CP48
Ladbrooke Dr., Pot.B. 20 BS19
Ladbrooke Rd., Slou. 61 AO41
Ladderstile Ride, Kings.T. 75 BN49
Ladderswood Way N11 38 BW28
Palmers Rd.
Ladds Way, Swan. 89 CS52
Ladenhatch La., Swan. 89 CS51
Ladies Gro., St.Alb. 9 BF13
Lady Amhersts Dr., Sev. 116 CR69
Lady Booth Rd., Kings.T. 85 BL51
Eden St.
Lady Gro., Welw.G.C. 5 BR9
Lady Hay, Wor.Pk. 85 BO55
Lady Margaret Rd. N19 47 BW35
Lady Margaret Rd. NW5 47 BW35
Lady Margaret Rd., Sthl. 54 BE40
Lady Shaw Ct. N13 38 BX27
St. Georges Rd.
Lady Somerset Rd. NW5 47 BV35
Lady Spencer Gro., St.Alb. 9 BG14
Lady Vane Clo., Ton. 117 DB68
Ladybower Ct. E5 48 CC35
Clapton Pk. Est.
Ladycroft Gdns., Orp. 97 CM56
Ladycroft Rd. SE13 67 CE45
Ladycroft Wk., Stan. 36 BK30
Ladycroft Way, Orp. 97 CM56
Ladyday Pl., Slou. 61 AO40
Glentworth Pl.
Ladyegate Clo., Dor. 119 BK71
Ladyegate Rd., Dor. 119 BK71
Ladyfield Clo., Loug. 31 CL24
Ladyfields
Ladyfields, Grav. 81 DF49
Ladyfields, Loug. 31 CL24
Ladygate La., Ruis. 44 AZ32
Ladygrove, Croy. 96 CD58
Ladygrove Dr., Guil. 109 AT68
Ladymead Parkway, Guil. 118 AR70
Ladymeadow, Kings L. 17 AX17
Ladys Clo., Wat. 27 BD24
Ladyshot, Harl. 6 CO10
Ladysmith Ave. E6 58 CK37
Ladysmith Ave., Ilf. 49 CM33
Ladysmith Rd. E16 58 CG38
Ladysmith Rd. N17 39 CB30
Ladysmith Rd. N18 39 CB28
Ladysmith Rd. SE9 78 CL46
Ladysmith Rd., Enf. 30 CA24
Ladysmith Rd., Har. 36 BH30
Ladysmith Rd., St.Alb. 9 BG13
Ladythorne Clo., Wey. 92 AW56
Church Rd.
Ladywalk, Rick. 34 AV28
Ladywell Prospect, Bish. 6 CR6
Ladywell Rd. SE13 77 CE46
Ladywell St. E15 58 CG37
Ladywood Ave., Orp. 88 CN53
Ladywood Clo., Rick. 26 AX24
Ladywood Rd., Dart. 80 CZ49
Ladywood Rd., Surb. 85 BM55
Lafone Ave., Felt. 74 BD48
Lafone St. SE1 4 P4
Lafone St. SE1 67 CA41
Lagado Ms. SE16 57 CC40
Lagger, The, Ch.St.G. 34 AQ27
Lagger Clo., Ch.St.G. 34 AQ27
Laglands Clo., Reig. 121 BT69
Lagonda Ave., Ilf. 40 CN29
Lagonda Clo., Wey. 92 AY59
Viscount Gdns.
Lagonda Way, Dart. 70 CV45
Arundel Rd.
Lagoon Rd., Orp. 89 CO53
Lahore Rd., Croy. 87 BZ53
Sydenham Rd.
Laidon Sq., Hem.H. 8 AX11
Laing Clo., Ilf. 40 CM29
Laing Dene, Nthlt. 54 BD37
Laings Ave., Mitch. 86 BU51
Lainlock Pl., Houns. 64 BF44
Spring Gro. Rd.
Lainson St. SW18 76 BS47
Laird Ave., Grays 71 DE41
Lairdale Clo. SE21 77 BZ47
Lairs Clo. N7 47 BX35
Laitwood Rd. SW12 76 BV47
Lake, The, Bush. 36 BG26
Lake Ave., Brom. 78 CH50
Lake Ave., Rain. 60 CV37
Lake Ave., Slou. 52 AO40
Lake Clo. SW19 75 BR49
Lake Rd.
Lake Clo., Wey. 92 AX59
Lake End Rd., Maid. 61 AK40
Lake Gdns., Dag. 50 CR35
Lake Gdns., Rich. 74 BJ48
Lake Gdns., Wall. 86 BV55
Lake Ho. Rd. E11 49 CH34
Lake Ri., Grays 70 DA42
Lake Ri., Rom. 41 CT30
Lake Rd. SW19 75 BR49
Lake Rd., Croy. 87 CD55
Lake Rd., Rom. 50 CP31
Lake Rd., Vir.W. 82 AQ52
Lake Rd., Wal.Abb. 13 CG14
Lake Vw., Dor. 119 BK73
Lake Vw., Edg. 37 BL28
Lake Vw., Pot.B. 20 BT20
Lakedale Rd. SE18 68 CN43
Lakefield Rd. N22 38 BY30
Lakefields Clo., Rain. 60 CV37
Lakehall Gdns., Th.Hth. 86 BY53
Lakehall Rd., Th.Hth. 86 BY53
Lakehurst Rd., Epsom 94 BO56
Lakeland Clo., Chig. 41 CO28
Lakeland Clo., Har. 36 BG29
Lakenheath N14 29 BW25
Laker Pl. SW15 75 BR46
Lakers Ri., Bans. 104 BU61
Lakes Clo., Guil. 118 AT73
Lakes Rd., Kes. 97 CJ56
Lakeside W13 54 BK39
Edge Hill Rd.
Lakeside, Beck. 87 CE52
Lakeside, Enf. 29 BW24
Lakeside, Rain. 60 CW37
Lakeside, Red. 121 BV69
Kingfisher Dr.
Lakeside, Wall. 95 BV56
Lakeside, Wey. 83 BB55
Lakeside, Wok. 100 AP63
Lakeside Ave., Ilf. 49 CJ31
Lakeside Clo. SE25 87 CA51
Lakeside Clo., Ruis. 44 BA31
Lakeside Clo., Sid. 79 CP46
Lakeside Clo., Wok. 100 AP63
Lakeside Ct., Borwd. 28 BM24
Lakeside Cres., Barn. 29 BU25
Lakeside Cres., Brwd. 42 DB27
Lakeside Dr., Brom. 88 CK55
Lakeside Dr., Esher 93 BG57
Lakeside Dr., Slou. 52 AP37
Lakeside Pl., St.Alb. 18 BK17
Lakeside Rd. N13 38 BX28
Lakeside Rd. W14 65 BQ41
Lakeside Rd., Chsnt. 21 CC17
Lakeside Rd., Slou. 63 AW43
Lakeside Way, Wem. 46 BM35
Lakeswood Rd., Orp. 88 C
Lakeview Rd. SE27 76 B
Lakeview Rd., Sev. 107 C
Lakeview Rd., Well. 69 C
Lakis Clo. NW3 47 B
Flask Wk.
Laleham Ave. NW7 37 B
Laleham Ct., Wok. 100 A
Chobham Rd.
Laleham Rd. SE6 77 C
Laleham Rd., Shep. 83 A
Laleham Rd., Stai. 72 A
Lalor St. SW6 65 B
Lamb Clo., Hat. 10 B
Lamb Clo., Til. 71 D
Coleridge Rd.
Lamb Clo., Wat. 18 B
Lamb La. E8 57 C
Lamb Ms. N1 56 B
Camden Wk.
Lamb St. E1 2
Lamb St. E1 57 C
Lamb Wk. SE1 4
Lamb Wk. SE1 67 C
Lamb Yd., Wat. 27 B
Lambarde Ave. SE9 78 C
Lambarde Dr., Sev. 107 C
Lambarde Rd., Sev. 107 C
Lambardes Clo., Orp. 98 C
The Grn.
Lamberhurst Clo., Orp. 89 C
Lamberhurst Rd. SE27 76 B
Lamberhurst Rd., Dag. 50 C
Lambert Ave., Rich. 65 B
Lambert Ave., Slou. 62 A
Lambert Clo., West. 106 C
Sunningvale Ave.
Lambert Ct., Bush. 27 B
Lambert Rd. E16 58 C
Lambert Rd. N12 38 B
Lambert Rd. SW2 76 B
Lambert Rd., Bans. 95 B
Lambert St. N1 56 B
Lambert Wk., Wem. 45 B
Hutchinson Ter.
Lambert Way N12 38 B
Lamberton Ct., Borwd. 28 B
Lamberts Pl., Croy. 87 B
Lamberts Rd., Surb. 85 B
Lambeth Bri. SE1 4
Lambeth Bri. SW1 4
Lambeth High St. SE1 4
Lambeth High St. SE1 66 BX
Lambeth Hill EC4 2 H
Lambeth Hill EC4 57 BZ
Upper Thames St.
Lambeth Ms. SE11 66 BX
Lambeth Palace Rd. SE1 4
Lambeth Palace Rd. SE1 66 BX
Lambeth Rd. SE1 4
Lambeth Rd. SE1 66 BX
Lambeth Rd., Croy. 86 BY
Lambeth St. E1 57 CB
Lambeth Wk. N1 56 BX
Outram St.
Lambeth Wk. SE11 4
Lambeth Wk. SE11 66 BX
Lamble St. NW5 47 BV
Lambley Rd., Dag. 59 CO
Lambolle Ms. NW3 56 BU
Lambolle Rd.
Lambolle Pl. NW3 56 BU
Lambolle Rd. NW3 56 BU
Lambourn Chase, Rad. 27 BH
Lambourn Clo. W7 64 BH
Lambourn Rd. SW4 66 BV
Lambourne Ave. SW19 75 BR
Lambourne Clo., Chig. 41 CO
Lambourne Cres., Chig. 41 CO
Lambourne Cres., Wok. 91 AU
Lambourne Dr., Brwd. 122 DF
Lambourne Gdns. E4 39 CE
Lambourne Gdns., Bark. 58 CN
Lambourne Rd.
Lambourne Gdns., Enf. 30 CA
Lambourne Gdns., Horn. 51 CV
Lambourne Gro., Kings.T. 85 BM
Gloucester Rd.
Lambourne Pl. SE3 68 CH
Shooters Hill Rd.
Lambourne Rd. E11 48 CF
Lambourne Rd., Bark. 58 CN
Lambourne Rd., Chig. 40 CN
Lambourne Rd., Ilf. 49 CN
Lambrook Ter. SW6 65 BR
Lambs Bldgs. EC1 2
Lambs Bldgs. EC1 57 BZ
Errol St.
Lambs Clo. N9 39 CB
Winchester Rd.
Lambs Clo., Cuffley 20 BX
Lambs Conduit Pas. WC1 2
Lambs Conduit Pas. WC1 56 BX
Red Lion Sq.
Lambs Conduit St. WC1 2
Lambs Conduit St. WC1 56 BX
Lambs Cft. Way, Ger.Cr. 34 AS
Lambs La., Rain. 59 CU
Lambs Meadow, Wdf.Grn. 40 CJ
Lambs Ms. N1 56 BY
Colebrook Row
Lambs Pas. EC1 2
Lambs Pas. EC1 57 BZ
Lambs Pas., Brent. 65 BL
Lambs Ter. N9 39 BZ
Lambs Wk., Enf. 30 BZ
Lambscroft Ave. SE9 78 CJ
Lambton Ave., Wal.Cr. 21 CC
Lambton Pl. W11 56 BS
Lambton Rd. N19 47 BX
Lambton Rd. SW20 85 BQ
Lamerock Rd., Brom. 78 CG
Lamerton Rd., Ilf. 40 CL
Lamerton St. SE8 67 CE

ıford Clo. N17 39 BZ29
ıington St. W6 65 BP42
ılash St. SE11 4 F8
ılash St. SE11 66 BY42
ayles St.
ımas Ave., Mitch. 86 BV51
ımas Ct., Stai. 72 AU48
ımas Ct., Wind. 61 AO44
ımas Dr., Stai. 72 AU49
ımas Grn. SE26 77 CB48
ımas Hill, Esher 93 BF56
ımas La., Esher 93 BF56
ımas Mead, Brox. 12 CD15
ımas Pk. Gdns. W5 54 BK40
ımas Pk. Rd. W5 54 BK40
ımas Rd. E9 57 CC36
ımas Rd. E10 48 CD33
ımas Rd., Rich. 74 BK49
ımas Rd., Wat. 27 BD25
ımermoor Rd. SW12 76 BV47
ıont Rd. SW10 66 BT43
ıorbey Clo., Sid. 78 CN47
ıorna Ave., Grav. 81 DH48
ıorna Clo., Orp. 89 CO54
ıorna Clo., Rad. 18 BJ20
ıorna Gro., Stan. 36 BK30
ıpard Gro. N16 48 CA33
ıpern Sq. E2 57 CB38
'elson Gdns.
ıpeter Clo., Wok. 100 AS62
ıpeter Sq. W6 65 BR43
umbolt Rd.
ıpits, Hodd. 12 CE12
ıplighter Clo. E1 57 CC38
leveland Way
ıplighters Clo., Dart. 80 CW46
ufnail Rd.
ıpmead Rd. SE12 78 CG46
ıport Clo. SE18 68 CK42
ıpton Ave., Houns. 64 BF44
ıpton Ho. Clo. SW19 75 BQ49
ıpton Pk. Rd., Houns. 64 BF44
ıpton Rd., Houns. 64 BF44
ısey Rd., Hem.H. 8 AX14
ıson Rd., Rain. 59 CT39
ıacre Ave. NW9 37 BO30
ıark Clo. W5 54 BK39
ıark Pl. W9 56 BT38
ıark Rd. W9 56 BS37
ıark Sq. E14 67 CE41
elsdon Way
ıark Sq. E14 67 CE41
'epper St.
ıata Wk., Hayes 54 BD38
'amulis Dr.
ıbury Rd. SE15 67 CC45
ıcashire Ct. W1 1 K10
ıcashire Ct. W1 56 BV40
very Row
ıcashire Rd. E17 39 CD30
ıcaster Ave. E18 49 CH31
ıcaster Ave. SE27 76 BY48
ıcaster Ave. SW19 75 BQ49
ıcaster Ave., Bark. 58 CN36
ıcaster Ave., Barn. 29 BT22
ıcaster Ave., Mitch. 86 BX53
ıcaster Clo. N17 39 CB29
'ark La.
ıcaster Clo. SE27 77 BZ48
ıcaster Clo., Brwd. 33 DA25
ıcaster Clo., Brom. 88 CG52
ıcaster Clo., Kings.T. 74 BK49
ıcaster Clo., Wall. 86 BX55
Beddington La.
ıcaster Cotts., Rich. 75 BL46
ancaster Pk.
ıcaster Ct. SW6 65 BR43
ıcaster Ct. W2 56 BT40
ıcaster Ct., Bans. 94 BR60
ıcaster Ct., Walt. 83 BC54
ıcaster Dr. E14 57 CF40
'restons Rd.
ıcaster Dr. NW3 56 BU36
ıcaster Dr., Hem.H. 16 AS17
ıcaster Dr., Horn. 50 CU35
ıcaster Gdns. NW3 56 BU36
.ambolle Pl.
ıcaster Gdns. SW19 75 BR49
ıcaster Gdns. W13 54 BJ40
ıcaster Gdns., Kings.T. 74 BK49
ıcaster Gate W2 56 BT40
ıcaster Gro. NW3 56 BT36
ıcaster Ms. W2 56 BT40
ıcaster Ms., Rich. 75 BL46
Richmond Hill
ıcaster Pk., Rich. 75 BL46
ıcaster Pl. SW19 75 BQ49
ıcaster Pl. WC2 2 B10
ıcaster Pl. WC2 56 BX40
ıcaster Pl., Houns. 64 BD44
ıcaster Pl., Twick. 74 BJ47
ıcaster Rd. E7 58 CH36
ıcaster Rd. E11 48 CG34
ıcaster Rd. N4 47 BY33
ıcaster Rd. N11 38 BW29
ıcaster Rd. N18 39 CA28
ıcaster Rd. NW10 46 BP35
ıcaster Rd. SE25 87 CA51
ıcaster Rd. SW19 75 BQ49
ıcaster Rd. W11 55 BR39
ıcaster Rd., Barn. 29 BT24
ıcaster Rd., Enf. 30 BZ23
ıcaster Rd., Epp. 23 CR16
ıcaster Rd., Har. 45 BF32
ıcaster Rd., Nthlt. 54 BG36
ıcaster Rd., St.Alb. 9 BH12
ıcaster Rd., Sthl. 54 BE40
ıcaster Rd., Uxb. 53 AX36
ıcaster Stables NW3 56 BU36
Lambolle Pl.
ıcaster St. SE1 4 G5
ıcaster St. SE1 66 BY41
ıcaster Ter. W2 1 A10
ıcaster Ter. W2 56 BT40

Lancaster Wk., Hayes 53 BA39
Lancaster Way, Abb.L. 17 BB19
Wadham Rd.
Lancaster Way, Welw. 5 BQ5
Lance Rd., Har. 45 BG33
Lancefield St. W10 55 BR38
Lancell St. N16 48 CA34
Lancelot Ave., Wem. 45 BK35
Lancelot Clo., Slou. 61 AN41
Mitchell Clo.
Lancelot Ct., Wem. 45 BK35
Lancelot Rd.
Lancelot Cres., Wem. 45 BK35
Lancelot Gdns., Barn. 38 BV26
Lancelot Pl. SW7 3 E5
Lancelot Pl. SW7 66 BU41
Lancelot Rd., Ilf. 40 CN29
Lancelot Rd., Well. 69 CO45
Lancelot Rd., Wem. 45 BK35
Lancey Clo. SE7 68 CJ42
Cleveley Clo.
Lanchester Rd. N6 47 BU32
Lancing Gdns. N9 39 CA26
Lancing Rd. W13 54 BJ40
Drayton Grn. Rd.
Lancing Rd., Croy. 86 BX54
Lancing Rd., Felt. 73 BB48
Lancing Rd., Ilf. 49 CM32
Lancing Rd., Orp. 89 CO55
Lancing Rd., Rom. 42 CW29
Lancing St. NW1 1 N3
Lancing St. NW1 56 BW38
Lancing Way, Rick. 26 AZ25
Lancresse Clo., Uxb. 53 AX36
Landau Way, Brox. 21 CD16
Landau Way, Erith 70 CV43
Landcroft Rd. SE22 77 CA46
Landells Rd. SE22 77 CA46
Lander Rd., Grays 71 DE42
Landfold Clo., Rick. 35 AY27
Landford Rd. SW15 65 BQ45
Landgrove Rd. SW19 76 BS49
Landguard, Saw. 6 CQ6
Landmann Way SE14 67 CC42
Landmead Rd., Chsnt. 21 CD18
Landon Pl. SW1 3 E6
Landon Pl. SW1 66 BU41
Landon Wk. E14 57 CE40
Cottage St.
Landon Way, Ashf. 73 BA50
Landons Clo. E14 57 CF40
Landor Ct. N16 48 CA35
Arundel Gro.
Landor Rd. SW9 66 BX45
Landor Wk. W12 65 BP41
Landport Way SE15 67 CA43
Landra Gdns. N21 29 BY25
Landridge Rd. SW6 65 BR44
Landrock Rd. N8 47 BX32
Lands End, Bush. 27 BK25
Landsbury Dr., Hayes 53 BC38
Landscape Rd., Warl. 105 CB63
Landscape Rd., Wdf.Grn. 40 CH29
Landseer Ave. E12 49 CL35
Landseer Ave., Grav. 81 DE48
Landseer Clo. SW19 86 BT51
Brangwyn Cres.
Landseer Clo., Edg. 37 BM30
Landseer Clo., Horn. 50 CU33
Landseer Rd. N19 47 BX34
Landseer Rd., Enf. 30 CB25
Landseer Rd., N.Mal. 85 BN54
Landseer Rd., Sutt. 95 BS57
Landstead Rd. SE18 68 CM43
Landview Gdns., Ong. 24 CX18
Landway, The, Orp. 89 CP52
Landway, The, Sev. 108 CW63
Landway, The, Sev. 108 CX62
Lane, The NW8 56 BT37
Lane, The SE3 68 CH45
Lane, The, Cher. 83 AW52
Lane, The, Vir.W. 82 AS52
Lane App. NW7 37 BR28
Lane Ave., Green. 80 DB46
Lane Clo. NW2 46 BP34
Lane Clo., Wey. 92 AW56
Lane Ct. SW11 76 BU46
Thurleigh Rd.
Lane End, Bexh. 69 CR45
Lane End, Epsom 94 BN60
Lane End, Hat. 10 BO14
Lane Gdns., Bush. 36 BH26
Lanefield Wk., Welw.G.C. 5 BQ8
Lanercost Clo. SW2 76 BY48
Lanercost Gdns. N14 38 BX26
Lanercost Rd. SW2 76 BY48
Lanes Ave., Grav. 81 DF48
Laneside, Chis. 78 CL49
Laneside, Edg. 37 BN28
Laneside Ave., Dag. 50 CQ33
Laneway SW15 75 BP46
Sunnymead Rd.
Lanewood Clo., Amer. 25 AP23
Lanfranc Rd. E3 57 CD37
Lanfrey Pl. W14 65 BR42
North End Rd.
Lang Clo., Lthd. 102 BF65
Lang St. E1 57 CC38
Langafel Clo., Long. 90 DC51
Langaller La., Lthd. 102 BF64
Langbourne Ave. N6 47 BV34
Langbourne Way, Esher 93 BJ56
Langbrook Rd. SE3 68 CJ45
Langcroft Clo., Cars. 86 BU55
Langdale Ave., Mitch. 86 BU52
Langdale Clo. SE17 66 BY44
Olney St.
Langdale Clo. SW14 65 BM45
Clifford Ave.
Langdale Clo., Orp. 88 CL55
Grasmere Gdns.
Langdale Clo., Wok. 100 AR61
Langdale Ct., Hem.H. 8 AY12
Langdale Cres., Bexh. 69 CR43

Langdale Dr., Hayes 53 BB37
Langdale Gdns., Grnf. 54 BJ38
Langdale Gdns., Horn. 50 CU35
Langdale Gdns., Wal.Cr. 30 CC21
Langdale Rd. SE10 67 CE43
Langdale Rd., Th.Hth. 86 BY52
Langdale St. E1 57 CB39
Langdale Wk., Grav. 81 DF48
Langdon Ct. NW10 55 BO37
Langdon Cres. E6 58 CL37
Langdon Dr. NW9 46 BN33
Langdon Pk. Rd. N6 47 BW33
Langdon Pl. SW14 65 BN45
Rosemary La.
Langdon Rd. E6 58 CL37
Langdon Rd., Brom. 88 CH52
Langdon Rd., Mord. 86 BT53
Langdon Shaw, Sid. 78 CN49
Langford Clo. E8 48 CB35
Ferncliffe Est.
Langford Clo. E8 48 CB35
Ferncliff Rd.
Langford Clo. N15 48 CA32
Langford Clo. NW8 56 BT37
Langford Ct. NW8 56 BT37
Langford Cres., Barn. 29 BU24
Langford Grn. SE5 67 CA45
Champion Hill
Langford Grn., Brwd. 122 DE25
Langford Pl. NW8 56 BT37
Langford Pl., Sid. 79 CO48
Langford Rd. SW6 66 BS44
Langford Rd., Barn. 29 BU24
Langford Rd., Wdf.Grn. 40 CJ29
Langfords, Buck.H. 40 CJ27
Langham Clo. N15 47 BY31
Langham Rd.
Langham Clo., St.Alb. 9 BK11
Langham Ct., Horn. 51 CV33
Langham Dene, Ken. 104 BY61
Langham Dr., Rom. 50 CO32
Langham Gdns. N21 29 BY25
Langham Gdns. W13 54 BJ40
Langham Gdns., Edg. 37 BN29
Langham Gdns., Rich. 74 BK49
Langham Gdns., Wem. 45 BK34
Langham Ho. Clo., Rich. 74 BK49
Langham Pl. N15 47 BY31
Langham Pl. W1 1 K7
Langham Pl. W1 56 BV39
Langham Pl. W4 65 BO43
Hogarth Roundabout
Langham Pl., Egh. 72 AS49
Langham Rd. N15 47 BY31
Langham Rd. SW20 85 BQ51
Langham Rd., Edg. 37 BN29
Langham Rd., Tedd. 74 BJ49
Langham St. W1 1 K7
Langham St. W1 56 BV39
Langhedge Clo. N18 39 CA29
Langhedge La. N18 39 CA28
Langholme, Bush. 38 BG26
Sparrows Herne
Langhorne Rd., Dag. 59 CR36
Langland Ct., Nthwd. 35 BA29
Langland Cres. E., Stan. 36 BK30
Langland Cres. N., Stan. 36 BK30
Langland Cres. S., Stan. 46 BL31
Langland Cres. W., Stan. 36 BK30
Langland Dr., Pnr. 36 BE29
Langland Gdns. NW3 47 BS35
Langland Gdns., Croy. 87 CD55
Langland Ri., Epsom 94 BN60
Langlands Dr., Dart. 80 CZ49
Langler Rd. NW10 55 BQ37
Langley Ave., Hem.H. 8 AY15
Langley Ave., Ruis. 44 BC34
Langley Ave., Surb. 84 BK54
Langley Ave., Wor.Pk. 85 BQ54
Langley Broom, Slou. 62 AS42
Langley Clo., Epsom 103 BN63
Langley Clo., Guil. 118 AR70
Langley Clo., Rom. 42 CV29
Faringdon Ave.
Langley Ct. SE9 78 CL46
Langley Ct. WC2 1 Q10
Langley Ct. WC2 56 BX40
Long Acre
Langley Ct., Beck. 87 CE53
Langley Ct., W.Wick. 87 CF54
Langley Cres. E11 49 CH33
Langley Cres., Dag. 59 CP36
Langley Cres., Edg. 37 BN27
Langley Cres., Hayes 63 BB43
Langley Cres., Kings L. 17 AZ18
Langley Cres., St.Alb. 9 BG12
Langley Dr. E11 49 CH33
Langley Dr. W3 65 BM41
Langley Dr., Brwd. 42 DA27
Langley Gdns., Brom. 88 CJ52
Langley Gdns., Dag. 59 CP36
Langley Gdns., Orp. 88 CL53
Langley Gro., N.Mal. 85 BO51
Langley High St., Slou. 62 AT42
Langley Hill, Kings L. 17 AY18
Langley Hill Clo., Kings L. 17 AZ18
Langley La. SW8 66 BX43
Langley La., Abb.L. 17 BB19
Langley La., Epsom 112 BM66
Langley Lo. La., Kings L. 17 AZ19
Langley Meadows, Loug. 31 CM23
Langley Oaks Ave., S.Croy. 96 CB58
Langley Pk. NW7 37 BO29
Langley Pk. Rd., Iver 52 AT40
Langley Pk. Rd., Slou. 52 AT40
Langley Pk. Rd., Sutt. 95 BT56
Langley Quay, Slou. 62 AS41
Waterside Dr.
Langley Rd. SW19 85 BR51
Langley Rd., Abb.L. 17 BB19
Langley Rd., Beck. 87 CC52
Langley Rd., Islw. 64 BH44

Langley Rd., Kings L. 17 AW18
Langley Rd., Slou. 62 AR41
Langley Rd., S.Croy. 96 CC58
Langley Rd., Stai. 72 AV50
Langley Rd., Surb. 85 BL54
Langley Rd., Wat. 26 BB22
Langley Rd., Well. 69 CP43
Langley St. WC2 1 Q9
Langley St. WC2 56 BX39
Langley Vale Rd., Epsom 103 BN63
Langley Vale Rd., Epsom 103 BO62
Langley Wk., Wok. 100 AS63
Midhope Rd.
Langley Way, Wat. 26 BB23
Langley Way, W.Wick. 87 CF54
Langleybury La., Kings L. 26 AZ22
Langmans Way, Wok. 100 AP61
Langmead Dr., Bush. 36 BH26
Langmead St. SE27 76 BY49
Langport Ct., Walt. 84 BD54
Langroyd Rd. SW17 76 BU48
Langshott Clo., Wey. 91 AV59
Langside Ave. SW15 65 BP45
Langside Cres. N14 38 BW27
Langston Rd., Loug. 31 CM25
Langthorn Ct. EC2 2 L8
Langthorn Ct. EC2 57 BZ39
Copthall Ave.
Langthorne Cres., Grays 71 DE42
Langthorne Rd. E11 48 CF34
Langthorne St. SW6 65 BQ43
Langton Ave. E6 58 CL38
Langton Ave. N20 38 BT26
Langton Ave., Epsom 94 BO59
Langton Clo. WC1 2 C4
Langton Clo. WC1 56 BX38
Wren St.
Langton Clo., Wey. 83 AW55
Langton Clo., Wok. 100 AP62
Langton Gro., Nthwd. 35 BA28
Langton Ri. SE23 77 CB47
Langton Rd. NW2 46 BQ34
Langton Rd. SW9 66 BY43
Langton Rd., E.Mol. 84 BG53
Langton Rd., Har. 36 BG29
Langton Rd., Hodd. 12 CD12
Langton St. SW10 66 BT43
Langton Way SE3 68 CG44
Langton Way, Croy. 87 CA55
Langton Way, Egh. 72 AU50
Langton Way, Grays 71 DH42
Langtry Rd. NW8 56 BS37
Langtry Rd., Nthlt. 54 BD37
Langtry Wk. NW8 56 BT37
Ainsworth Est.
Langwood Chase, Tedd. 74 BK50
Langwood Gdns., Wat. 26 BC23
Langworth Clo., Dart. 80 CV48
Langworth Dr., Hayes 53 BC39
Langworthy End, Maid. 61 AG43
Langworthy La., Maid. 61 AG43
Lanhill Rd. W9 56 BS38
Lanier Rd. SE13 77 CF46
Lankaster Gdns. N2 38 BT30
Lankers Dr., Har. 45 BE32
Lankton Clo., Beck. 87 CF51
Lannock Rd., Hayes 53 BB40
Lannoy Rd. SE9 78 CM47
Lanrick Copse, Berk. 7 AS12
Lanrick Rd. E14 57 CF39
Lanridge Rd. SE2 69 CP41
Lansbury Ave. N18 39 BZ28
Lansbury Ave., Bark. 59 CO36
Lansbury Ave., Felt. 73 BC46
Lansbury Ave., Rom. 50 CQ32
Lansbury Clo. NW10 46 BN35
Lansbury Cres., Dart. 80 CX46
Lansbury Dr., Hayes 53 BB37
Lansbury Est. E14 57 CE39
Lansbury Gdns. E14 57 CF39
Lansbury Gdns., Til. 71 DG44
Central Ave.
Lansbury Rd., Enf. 30 CC23
Lansbury Way N18 39 CA28
Lansbury Ave.
Lansdell Rd., Mitch. 86 BV51
Lansdown, Guil. 118 AT70
Lansdown Clo., Walt. 84 BD54
St. Johns
Lansdown Clo., Wok. 100 AP63
Lansdown Pl., Grav. 81 DF47
Lansdown Rd. E7 58 CJ36
Lansdown Rd., Ger.Cr. 34 AR30
Lansdown Rd., Sid. 79 CO48
Lansdowne Ave., Bexh. 69 CP43
Lansdowne Ave., Orp. 88 CL54
Lansdowne Ave., Slou. 52 AP40
Lansdowne Clo. SW20 75 BQ50
Lansdowne Clo., Twick. 74 BH47
Lansdowne Clo., Wat. 27 BD21
Lansdowne Ct., Pur. 95 BY58
Lansdowne Ct., Slou. 52 AP40
Lansdowne Ave.
Lansdowne Ct., Wor.Pk. 85 BP55
Lansdowne Cres. W11 55 BR40
Lansdowne Dr. E8 57 CB36
Lansdowne Gdns. SW8 66 BX44
Lansdowne Grn. Est. SW8 66 BX44
Lansdowne Gro. NW10 46 BO35
Lansdowne Hill SE27 76 BY48
Lansdowne La. SE7 68 CJ43
Lansdowne Ms. SE7 68 CJ42
Lansdowne Ms. W11 55 BR40
Lansdowne Rd.
Lansdowne Pl. SE1 4 L6
Lansdowne Pl. SE1 67 BZ41
Lansdowne Pl. SE19 77 CA50
Lansdowne Ri. W11 55 BR40
Lansdowne Rd. E4 39 CE27
Lansdowne Rd. E11 49 CG34
Lansdowne Rd. E17 48 CE32
Lansdowne Rd. E18 49 CH31
Lansdowne Rd. N3 37 BR29

Lansdowne Rd. N10 38 BW30
Lansdowne Rd. N17 39 CB30
Lansdowne Rd. SW20 75 BQ50
Lansdowne Rd. W11 55 BR40
Lansdowne Rd., Brom. 78 CH50
Lansdowne Rd., Croy. 87 BZ55
Lansdowne Rd., Epsom 94 BN57
Lansdowne Rd., Har. 45 BH33
Lansdowne Rd., Houns. 64 BF45
Lansdowne Rd., Ilf. 49 CN33
Lansdowne Rd., Pur. 95 BX59
Lansdowne Rd., Stai. 73 AW50
Lansdowne Rd., Stan. 36 BK29
Lansdowne Rd., Til. 71 DF44
Lansdowne Rd., Uxb. 53 AZ39
Lansdowne Row W1 3 K2
Lansdowne Row W1 56 BV40
Berkeley St.
Lansdowne Ter. WC1 2 A5
Lansdowne Ter. WC1 56 BX38
Lansdowne Wk. W11 55 BR40
Lansdowne Way SW8 66 BW44
Lansdowne Wd. Clo. SE27 76 BY48
Lansdowne Hill
Lansfield Ave. N18 39 CB28
Lant St. SE1 4 H4
Lant St. SE1 67 BZ41
Lantern Clo. SW15 65 BP45
Lantern Clo., Wem. 45 BK35
Lanterns Ct. E14 67 CE41
Lanvanor Rd. SE15 67 CC44
Lapford Clo. W9 55 BR38
Lapponum Wk., Hayes 54 BD39
Jollys La.
Lapse Wd. Wk. SE23 77 CB48
Lapstone Gdns., Har. 45 BK32
Lapwing Clo., Hem.H. 8 AY11
Lapwing Clo., S.Croy. 96 CD58
Lapwing Gro., Guil. 118 AU69
Lapwings, The, Grav. 81 DH48
Lapworth Clo., Orp. 89 CP55
Woodley Rd.
Lara Clo. SE13 77 CF46
Lara Clo., Chess. 94 BL57
Larbert Rd. SW16 76 BW50
Larby Pl., Epsom 94 BO58
Larch Ave. W3 55 BO40
Larch Ave., Guil. 118 AR69
Larch Ave., St.Alb. 18 BE18
Larch Clo. N11 38 BV29
Larch Clo. SE8 67 CD43
Clyde St.
Larch Clo. SW12 76 BV47
Larch Clo., Red. 121 BT71
Larch Clo., Tad. 104 BT64
Larch Clo., Warl. 105 CD63
Larch Cres., Epsom 94 BM57
Larch Cres., Hayes 54 BD38
Larch Grn. NW9 37 BO29
Clayton Fld.
Larch Gro., Sid. 78 CN47
Larch Ms. N19 47 BW34
Bredgar Rd.
Larch Rd. NW2 46 BQ35
Larch Rd., Dart. 80 CV47
Larch Tree Way, Croy. 87 CE55
Larch Way, Brom. 88 CL54
Larchdene, Orp. 88 CL55
Larches, The N13 39 BZ27
Larches, The, Berk. 7 AO12
Larches, The, Uxb. 53 AZ38
Larches, The, Wat. 27 BE25
Larches Ave. SW14 65 BN45
Larches Ave., Enf. 30 CC21
Larchwood, Wey. 92 AY56
Bridge Rd.
Larchwood Ave., Rom. 41 CR29
Larchwood Clo., Bans. 103 BR61
Larchwood Clo., Rom. 41 CS29
Larchwood Dr., Egh. 72 AQ50
Larchwood Gdns., Brwd. 33 DA25
Larchwood Rd. SE9 78 CL48
Larchwood Rd., Hem.H. 8 AY12
Larchwood Rd., Wok. 100 AO63
Gorsewood Rd.
Larcom St. SE17 4 J9
Larcom St. SE17 67 BZ42
Larcombe Clo., Croy. 96 CA56
Larden Rd. W3 55 BO40
Largewood Ave., Surb. 85 BL55
Largo Wk., Erith 69 CT44
Drummond Clo.
Larissa St. SE17 4 L10
Larissa St. SE17 67 BZ42
Tisdall Pl.
Lark Ave., Stai. 72 AV48
Lark Fld., Cob. 92 BC60
Lark Flds., Grav. 81 DF48
Lark Ri., Hat. 10 BP13
Lark Ri., Lthd. 100 BB69
Lark Row E2 57 CC37
Larkbere Rd. SE26 77 CD49
Larken Dr., Bush. 36 BG26
Larkfield Ave., Har. 45 BJ31
Larkfield Clo., Brom. 88 CH55
Station Hill
Larkfield Rd., Rich. 65 BL45
Larkfield Rd., Sev. 107 CS65
Larkfield Rd., Sid. 78 CN48
Larkhall Clo., Walt. 93 BD56
Larkhall Est. SW8 66 BW44
Larkhall La. SW4 66 BW44
Larkhall Ri. SW4 66 BW44
Larkin Clo., Brwd. 122 DE26
Grays Wk.
Larkings La., Slou. 52 AR37
Larkins Clo., Brwd. 122 DE26
Grays Wk.
Larks Fld., Hartley 90 DC52
Larks Gro., Bark. 58 CN36
Larks Ri., Chesh. 16 AO20
Larksfield, Egh. 72 AR50
Larksfield Gro., Enf. 30 CB23

Larkshall Cres. E4 39 CF28
Larkshall Rd. E4 39 CF28
Larkspur Clo. E6 58 CK39
Larkspur Clo. N17 39 BZ29
Larkspur Clo., Orp. 89 CP55
Berrylands
Larkspur Clo., S.Ock. 60 DB38
Larkspur Way, Dor. 119 BK73
Larkspur Way, Epsom 94 BN56
Larkswood, Harl. 14 CP12
Larkswood Ri., Pnr. 45 BD31
Larkswood Ri., St.Alb. 9 BK11
Sandringham Cres.
Larkswood Rd. E4 39 CE28
Larkway Clo. NW9 46 BN31
Larmans Rd., Enf. 30 CC21
Larnach Rd. W6 65 BQ43
Larne Rd., Ruis. 44 BB33
Larner Rd., Erith 69 CT43
Larpent Ave. SW15 65 BQ45
Larsen Dr., Wal.Abb. 21 CF20
Larwood Clo., Grnf. 45 BG35
Lascelles Ave., Har. 45 BG33
Lascelles Clo. E11 48 CF34
Lascelles Clo., Brwd. 33 DA25
Lascelles Rd., Slou. 62 AQ42
Lascotts Rd. N22 38 BX29
Lassa Rd. SE9 78 CK46
Lassell St. SE10 67 CF42
Lasswade Rd., Cher. 82 AV54
Latchett Rd. E18 40 CH30
Latchford Pl., Chig. 41 CO28
Latching Clo., Rom. 42 CV28
Troopers Dr.
Latchingdon Gdns., Wdf.Grn. 40 CK29
Latchmere Clo., Rich. 75 BL49
Latchmere Ho., Kings.T. 75 BL49
Latchmere La., Kings.T. 75 BL50
Latchmere Pas. SW11 66 BU44
Cabul Rd.
Latchmere Rd. SW11 66 BU44
Latchmere Rd., Kings.T. 75 BL50
Latchmere St. SW11 66 BU44
Burns Rd.
Latchmoor Ave., Ger.Cr. 43 AR31
Latchmoor Way, Ger.Cr. 43 AR31
Late Braxton Rd. SW16 76 BX50
Westwell Rd.
Lateward Rd., Brent. 64 BK43
Latham Clo., Twick. 74 BJ47
Latham Clo., West. 106 CJ61
Latham Rd., Bexh. 79 CR46
Latham Rd., Twick. 74 BH47
Lathams Way, Croy. 86 BX54
Lathkill Clo., Enf. 39 CA26
Lathom Clo. E6 58 CK39
Oliver Gdns.
Lathom Rd. E6 58 CK36
Latima Clo., Wok. 100 AT61
Alpha Rd.
Latimer Ave. E6 58 CK37
Latimer Clo., Amer. 25 AR23
Latimer Clo., Hem.H. 8 AZ11
Latimer Clo., Pnr. 36 BD30
Latimer Clo., Wat. 35 BB26
Chenies Way
Latimer Clo., Wor.Pk. 94 BP56
Latimer Gdns., Pnr. 36 BD30
Latimer Ms., Chesh. 25 AS22
Latimer Pl. W10 55 BQ39
Latimer Rd. E7 49 CH35
Latimer Rd. N15 48 CA32
Latimer Rd. SW19 76 BS50
Latimer Rd. W10 55 BQ39
Latimer Rd. W11 55 BO40
Latimer Rd., Barn. 29 BS24
Latimer Rd., Chesh. 16 AP20
Latimer Rd., Tedd. 74 BH49
Latimer St. E1 57 CC39
Latona Dr., Grav. 81 DJ49
Latona Rd. SE15 67 CA43
Lattimore Rd., St.Alb. 9 BH14
Latton Clo., Esher 93 BF56
Latton Clo., Walt. 84 BE54
Latton Common Rd., Harl. 14 CO12
Latton Grn., Harl. 13 CN13
Latton Hall Clo., Harl. 6 CO10
Burgoyne Hatch
Latton Ho., Harl. 14 CO12
Latymer Clo., Wey. 92 BA56
Latymer Ct. W6 65 BQ42
Latymer Rd. N9 39 CA26
Latymer Way N9 39 CA27
Laud St. SE11 4 B10
Laud St. SE11 66 BX42
Laud St., Croy. 87 BZ55
Lauder Clo., Nthlt. 54 BD37
Lauderdale Dr., Rich. 74 BK48
Lauderdale Rd. W9 56 BS38
Laudersdale Rd., Kings L. 17 BA20
Laughton Rd., Nthlt. 54 BD37
Launcelot Rd., Brom. 78 CH49
Launcelot St. SE1 4 D5
Launceston Clo., Rom. 42 CV30
Launceston Gdns., Grnf. 54 BK37
Launceston Pl. W8 66 BT41
Launceston Rd., Grnf. 54 BK37
Launch St. E14 67 CF41
Launders La., Rain. 60 CW39
Laundry La., Wal.Abb. 13 CG15
Laundry Rd. E4 39 CF26
Station Rd.
Laundry Rd. W6 65 BR43
Laundry Rd., Guil. 118 AR71
Laura Clo. E11 49 CJ32
Laura Clo., Enf. 30 CA25
Private Rd.
Laura Dr., Swan. 79 CU50
Laura Pl. E5 48 CC35
Lauradale Rd. N2 47 BU31
Laurel Ave., Egh. 72 AQ49
Laurel Ave., Grav. 81 DH48
Laurel Ave., Pot.B. 19 BR19
Laurel Ave., Slou. 62 AS41
Laurel Ave., Twick. 74 BH47
Laurel Bank Gdns. SW6 65 BR44
New Kings Rd.
Laurel Bank Rd., Enf. 30 BZ23
Laurel Clo. N19 47 BW34
Hargrave Pk.
Laurel Clo., Brwd. 122 DD25
Laurel Clo., Dart. 80 CV47
Laurel Clo., Hem.H. 8 AY13
Laurel Clo., Ilf. 40 CM29
Laurel Clo., Sid. 79 CO48
Laurel Clo., Slou. 62 AV44
Laurel Cres., Croy. 87 CE55
Laurel Cres., Rom. 50 CT33
Laurel Cres., Wok. 91 AU60
Laurel Dene, Tedd. 74 BG49
Laurel Dr. N21 38 BY26
Laurel Dr., Oxt. 115 CG69
Laurel Fld., Pot.B. 19 BR19
Laurel Gdns. E4 39 CE26
Laurel Gdns. NW7 37 BN27
Laurel Gdns. W7 54 BH40
Laurel Gdns., Houns. 64 BE45
Laurel Gro. SE20 77 CB50
Laurel Gro. SE26 77 CC49
Laurel La., West Dr. 63 AY42
Laurel Lo. La., Barn. 28 BQ21
Laurel Pk., Har. 36 BH29
Kenton La.
Laurel Rd. SW13 65 BP44
Laurel Rd. SW20 85 BP51
Laurel Rd., Ger.Cr. 34 AR30
Laurel Rd., St.Alb. 9 BH13
Laurel Rd., Tedd. 74 BG49
Laurel St. E8 57 CA36
Laurel Vw. N12 38 BS27
Laurel Way E18 49 CG31
Laurel Way N20 38 BS27
Laurels, The, Berk. 7 AU12
Laurels, The, Cob. 102 BE61
Laurels, The, Dart. 80 CV49
Stock La.
Laurels, The, Har. 36 BH29
Kenton La.
Laurels, The, Wey. 83 BA55
Laurels Rd., Iver 52 AU37
Laurelsfield, St.Alb. 9 BF15
Laurence Ms. W12 65 BP41
Askew Rd.
Laurence Pountney Hill EC4 2 K10
Laurence Pountney Hill EC4 57 BZ40
Cannon St.
Laurence Pountney La. EC4 2 K10
Laurence Pountney La. EC4 57 BZ40
Laurie Gdns. W7 54 BH39
Laurie Gro. SE14 67 CD44
Laurie Rd. W7 54 BH39
Laurie Wk., Rom. 50 CT32
Laurier Rd. NW5 47 BV34
Laurier Rd., Croy. 87 CA54
Lauries La., Hem.H. 7 AU14
Laurimel Clo., Stan. 36 BJ29
September Way
Lauriston Clo., Wok. 100 AO62
Victoria Rd.
Lauriston Rd. E9 57 CC36
Lauriston Rd. SW19 75 BQ50
Lausanne Rd. N8 47 BY31
Lausanne Rd. SE15 67 CC44
Lauser Rd., Stai. 73 AX47
Laustan Clo., Guil. 118 AU70
Lavell St. N16 48 BZ35
Albion Rd.
Lavender Ave. NW9 46 BN33
Lavender Ave., Brwd. 33 DA25
Lavender Ave., Mitch. 86 BU51
Lavender Ave., Wor.Pk. 85 BQ55
Lavender Clo. SW3 66 BU43
Danvers St.
Lavender Clo., Cars. 95 BV56
Lavender Rd.
Lavender Clo., Chsnt. 21 CA17
Peakes Way
Lavender Clo., Couls. 104 BW63
Starrock Rd.
Lavender Clo., Red. 121 BV73
Lavender Clo., Rom. 42 CV29
Lavender Gdns. SW11 66 BU45
Lavender Gdns., Enf. 29 BY22
Lavender Gro. E8 57 CA36
Lavender Gro., Mitch. 86 BU51
Lavender Hill SW11 66 BU45
Lavender Hill, Enf. 29 BY23
Lavender Hill, Swan. 89 CS52
Lavender Pk. Rd., Wey. 92 AW60
Lavender Pl., Ilf. 49 CL35
Lavender Ri., West Dr. 63 AZ41
Lavender Rd. SE16 57 CD40
Lavender Rd. SW11 66 BT45
Lavender Rd., Cars. 95 BV56
Lavender Rd., Croy. 86 BX53
Lavender Rd., Enf. 30 BZ23
Lavender Rd., Epsom 94 BM57
Lavender Rd., Sutt. 95 BT56
Parkhurst Rd.
Lavender Rd., Uxb. 53 AY39
Lavender Rd., Wok. 100 AT61
Lavender St. E15 58 CG36
Lavender Sweep SW11 66 BU45
Lavender Ter. SW11 66 BU45
Falcon Rd.
Lavender Vale, Wall. 95 BW57
Lavender Wk. SW11 66 BU45
Lavender Hill
Lavender Wk., Mitch. 86 BV52
Lavender Way, Croy. 87 CC53
Lavengro Rd. SE27 77 BZ48
Lavenham Rd. SW18 75 BR48
Lavernock Rd., Bexh. 69 CR44
Lavers Rd. N16 48 CA34
Laverstoke Gdns. SW15 75 BO47
Laverton Pl. SW5 66 BS42
Courtfield Gdns.
Lavidge Rd. SE9 78 CK48
Lavie Ms. W10 55 BR38
Portobello Rd.
Lavina Gro. N1 56 BX37
Wharfdale Rd.
Lavington Rd. W13 54 BJ40
Lavington Rd., Croy. 86 BX55
Lavington St. SE1 4 G3
Lavington St. SE1 56 BY40
Lavinia Ave., Wat. 18 BD20
Lavinia Rd., Dart. 80 CW46
Lavrock La., Rick. 35 AY26
Law St. SE1 4 L6
Law St. SE1 67 BZ41
Lawdons Gdns., Croy. 95 BY56
Lawford Ave., Rick. 25 AU25
Lawford Clo., Horn. 51 CV35
Lawford Clo., Wall. 95 BX58
Lawford Gdns., Dart. 80 CV46
Lawford Gdns., Ken. 105 BZ61
Lawford Rd. N1 57 CA36
Lawford Rd. NW5 56 BW36
Lawford Rd. W4 65 BN43
Lawford Rd. Clo., Rick. 25 AU25
Lawless St. E14 57 CE40
Lawley Rd. N14 38 BV26
Lawley St. E5 48 CC35
Lawn, The, Harl. 6 CO9
Lawn, The, Houns. 64 BF44
Lawn, The, Sthl. 64 BF42
Lawn Ave., West Dr. 63 AX41
Lawn Clo. N9 39 CA26
Lawn Clo., Brom. 78 CH50
Lawn Clo., N.Mal. 85 BO51
Lawn Clo., Ruis. 44 BB34
Lawn Clo., Slou. 62 AR43
Lawn Clo., Swan. 89 CS51
Lawn Ct., Wem. 46 BM34
The Ave.
Lawn Cres., Rich. 65 BL44
Lawn Fm. Gro., Rom. 50 CQ31
Lawn Gdns. W7 54 BH40
Lawn La. SW8 66 BX43
Lawn La., Hem.H. 8 AX14
Lawn Pl. SE15 67 CA44
Sumner Est.
Lawn Rd. NW3 47 BU35
Lawn Rd., Beck. 77 CD50
Lawn Rd., Grav. 81 DE46
Lawn Rd., Guil. 118 AR72
Lawn Rd., Uxb. 53 AX36
Lawn Ter. SE3 68 CG45
Lawn Vale, Pnr. 36 BD30
Lawnfield NW2 55 BQ36
Lawns, The E4 39 CE28
Lawns, The SE3 68 CG45
Lawns, The SE19 87 BZ51
Lawns, The, Brwd. 122 DC28
Uplands Rd.
Lawns, The, Hem.H. 7 AV13
Lawns, The, Pnr. 36 BF29
Lawns, The, St.Alb. 9 BG13
Lawns, The, Sid. 79 CO49
Lawns, The, Slou. 62 AV44
Bath Rd.
Lawns, The, Sutt. 94 BR57
Lawns, The, Welw.G.C. 5 BQ6
Lawns Cres., Grays 71 DE43
Lawns Dr., The, Brox. 12 CD14
High Rd.
Lawns Est., The SE19 87 BZ51
Lawnside SE3 68 CG45
Lawnsway, Rom. 41 CS29
Lawrance Rd., St.Alb. 9 BG11
Lawrance Sq., Grav. 81 DF48
Lawrence Ave. E12 49 CL35
Lawrence Ave. E17 39 CC30
Lawrence Ave. N13 38 BY28
Lawrence Ave. NW7 37 BO28
Lawrence Ave., N.Mal. 85 BN53
Lawrence Ave., N.Mal. 85 BO54
Lawrence Bldgs. N16 48 CA34
Brook Rd.
Lawrence Campe Clo. N20 38 BT27
Friern Barnet La.
Lawrence Clo. E3 57 CE37
Malmesbury Rd.
Lawrence Clo. N15 48 CA31
Lawrence Clo., Guil. 109 AT68
Ladygrove Dr.
Lawrence Ct. NW7 37 BO28
Lawrence Cres., Dag. 50 CR34
Lawrence Cres., Edg. 37 BM30
Lawrence Dr., Uxb. 44 BA35
Lawrence Gdns. NW7 37 BO27
Lawrence Gdns., Chsnt. 21 CC17
Lawrence Gdns., Ken. 105 BZ61
Lawrence Gdns., Til. 71 DG43
Lawrence Hill E4 39 CE27
Lawrence Hill Gdns., Dart. 80 CV46
Lawrence Hill Rd., Dart. 80 CV46
Lawrence La. EC2 2 J9
Lawrence La. EC2 57 BZ39
Trump St.
Lawrence La., Bet. 120 BP69
Lawrence Moorings, Saw. 6 CQ6
Lawrence Pl. N1 56 BX37
Delhi St.
Lawrence Rd. E6 58 CK37
Lawrence Rd. E13 58 CH37
Lawrence Rd. N15 48 CA31
Lawrence Rd. N18 39 CB28
Lawrence Rd. SE25 87 CA52
Lawrence Rd. W5 64 BK42
Lawrence Rd., Hmptn. 74 BE50
Lawrence Rd., Hayes 53 BA37
Lawrence Rd., Houns. 64 BD45
Lawrence Rd., Pnr. 45 BD32
Lawrence Rd., Rich. 74 BK49
Lawrence Rd., Rom. 50 CU32
Lawrence Rd., W.Wick. 97 CH56
Lawrence St. E16 58 CG39
Lawrence St. NW7 37 BO28
Lawrence St. SW3 66 BU43
Lawrence Way, Grnf. 54 BJ37
Lawrie Pk. Ave. SE26 77 CB49
Lawrie Pk. Cres. SE26 77 CB49
Lawrie Pk. Gdns. SE26 77 CB49
Lawrie Pk. Rd. SE26 77 CB50
Lawson Clo. SW19 75 BQ48
Lawson Est. SE1 4 K7
Lawson Gdns., Pnr. 44 BC31
Tolcarne Dr.
Lawson Rd., Dart. 70 CV45
Lawson Rd., Enf. 30 CC23
Lawson Rd., Sthl. 54 BE38
Lawsons Clo. E16 58 CJ39
Lawton Rd. E3 57 CD38
Lawton Rd. E10 48 CF33
Lawton Rd., Barn. 29 BT24
Lawton Rd., Loug. 31 CL23
Laxcon Clo. NW10 46 BN35
Laxey Rd., Orp. 97 CN57
Laxley Clo. SE5 66 BY43
Laxton Gdns., Red. 113 BW67
Laxton Pl. NW1 1 K4
Layard Rd. SE16 67 CB42
Layard Rd., Enf. 30 CA23
Layard Rd., Th.Hth. 87 BZ51
Layard Sq. SE16 67 CB41
Laybrook Clo., St.Alb. 9 BJ11
Layburn Cres., Slou. 62 AT43
Laycock St. N1 56 BY36
Layer Gdns. W3 55 BM40
Layfield Clo. NW4 46 BP33
Layfield Cres. NW4 46 BP33
Layfield Rd. NW4 46 BP33
Layhams Rd., Kes. 97 CG59
Laymarsh Clo., Belv. 69 CQ41
Laymead Clo., Nthlt. 54 BE36
Laystall St. EC1 2 D5
Laystall St. EC1 56 BY38
Layters Ave., Ger.Cr. 34 AR30
Layters Ave. S., Ger.Cr. 34 AR30
Layters Clo., Ger.Cr. 34 AR30
Layters End, Ger.Cr. 34 AR30
Layters Grn. La., Ger.Cr. 34 AQ30
Layters Way, Ger.Cr. 43 AR32
Layton Cotts., Brent. 65 BL43
Kew Bri. Rd.
Layton Ct., Wey. 92 AZ56
Layton Cres., Croy. 95 BY56
Layton La., Sun. 83 BB51
Layton Rd. N1 56 BY37
Layton Rd., Brent. 64 BK42
Layton Rd., Houns. 64 BF45
Laytons Bldgs. SE1 4 K4
Layzell Wk. SE9 78 CJ47
Mottingham La.
Lazar Wk. N7 47 BX34
Briset Way
Le May Ave. SE12 78 CH48
Le Personne Rd., Cat. 105 BZ64
Lea, The, Egh. 82 AV51
Lea Bri. Rd. E5 48 CB34
Lea Bri. Rd. E10 48 CE33
Lea Bri. Rd. E17 48 CE33
Lea Bushes, Wat. 27 BE21
Lea Clo., Bush. 27 BF25
Lea Cres., Ruis. 44 BB35
Lea Gdns., Wem. 46 BL35
Lea Hall Rd. E10 48 CE33
Lea Rd., Beck. 87 CD51
Lea Rd., Enf. 30 BZ23
Lea Rd., Grays 71 DG42
Lea Rd., Hodd. 12 CF11
Lea Rd., Sev. 117 CV67
Lea Rd., Sthl. 64 BE42
Lea Rd., Wal.Abb. 21 CE20
Lea Side, Lthd. 102 BF65
Lea Vale, Dart. 69 CS45
Lea Valley Rd., Enf. 30 CD25
Lea Vw., Wal.Abb. 21 CE20
Lea Vw. Ho. E5 48 CB33
Leabank Clo., Har. 45 BH34
Leabank Vw. N15 48 CB32
Leabourne Rd. N16 48 CB32
Leachcroft, Ger.Cr. 34 AQ30
Leacroft, Stai. 73 AW49
Leacroft Ave. SW12 76 BU47
Leacroft Clo., Ken. 105 BZ61
Leacroft Clo., Stai. 73 AW49
Leacroft Clo., West Dr. 53 AY39
Leacroft Rd., Iver 52 AV39
Leadale Ave. E4 39 CD27
Leadale Rd. N15 48 CB32
Leadale Rd. N16 48 CB32
Leadenhall Mkt. EC3 2 M9
Leadenhall Pl. EC3 2 M9
Leadenhall Pl. EC3 57 CA39
Lime St.
Leadenhall St. EC3 2 M9
Leadenhall St. EC3 57 CA39
Leadenham Ct. E3 57 CE38
Campbell Rd.
Leader Ave. E12 49 CL35
Leadings, The, Wem. 46 BN34
Leaf Clo., E.Mol. 84 BH53
Leaf Clo., Nthwd. 35 BA29
Leaf Gro. SE27 76 BY49
Leafield Clo. SW16 76 BY50
Leafield Clo., Wok. 100 AQ62
Winnington Way
Leafield La., Sid. 79 CQ49
Leafield Rd. SW20 85 BR52
Leafield Rd., Sutt. 86 BS55
Leaford Cres., Wat. 26 BB22
Leaforis Rd., Wal.Cr. 21 CB17
Leafy Gro., Kes. 97 CJ56
Leafy Oak Rd. SE12 78 C
Leafy Way, Brwd. 122 D
Leafy Way, Croy. 87 C
Leagrave St. E5 48 C
Leaholme Waye, Ruis. 44 B
Leahurst Rd. SE13 77 C
Leake Ct. SE1 4
Leake Ct. SE1 66 B
Addington St.
Leake St. SE1 4
Leake St. SE1 66 B
Lealand Rd. N15 48 C
Leamead Ave., Nthlt. 54 B
Leamington Ave. E17 48 C
Leamington Ave., Brom. 78 C
Leamington Ave., Mord. 85 B
Leamington Ave., Orp. 97 C
Leamington Clo. E12 49 C
Leamington Clo., Brom. 78 C
Leamington Clo., Houns. 74 B
Leamington Clo., Rom. 42 C
Leamington Cres., Har. 45 B
Leamington Gdns., Ilf. 49 C
Leamington Pk. W3 55 B
Leamington Pl., Hayes 53 B
Leamington Rd., Rom. 42 C
Leamington Rd., Sthl. 64 B
Leamington Rd. Vill. W11 55 B
Leamore St. W6 65 B
Leamouth Rd. E6 58 C
Leamouth Rd. E14 57 C
Leander Dr., Grav. 81 D
Leander Gdns., Wat. 27 B
Eastlea Ave.
Leander Rd. SW2 76 B
Leander Rd., Nthlt. 54 B
Leander Rd., Th.Hth. 86 B
Leapale La., Guil. 118 A
Leapale Rd., Guil. 118 A
Learoyd Gdns. E6 58 C
Leas, The, Bush. 27 B
Leas, The, Hem.H. 17 A
Leas, The, Upmin. 51 C
Leas Clo., Chess. 94 B
Leas Dale SE9 78 C
Leas Dr., Iver 52 A
Leas Grn., Chis. 78 C
Leas La., Warl. 105 C
Leas Rd., Guil. 118 A
Leas Rd., Warl. 105 C
Leaside, Hem.H. 8 B
Leaside Ave. N10 47 B
Leaside Rd. E5 48 C
Leasowes Rd. E10 48 C
Leasway, Brwd. 42 D
Leasway, Grays 71 D
Leasway, Upmin. 51 C
Leat Clo., Saw. 6 C
Leather Bottle La., Belv. 69 C
Leather Clo., Mitch. 86 B
Leather Gdns. E15 58 C
Leather La. EC1 2
Leather La. EC1 56 B
Leather La., Horn. 51 C
Leatherbottle Grn., Erith 69 C
Leatherdale St. E1 57 C
Portelet Rd.
Leatherhead By-pass, Lthd. 102 B
Leatherhead Clo. N16 48 C
Leatherhead Rd., Ash. 102 B
Leatherhead Rd., Chess. 93 B
Leatherhead Rd., Cob. 102 B
Leatherhead Rd., Lthd. 111 B
Leatherhead Rd., Lthd. 93 B
Leatherhead Rd., Lthd. 102 B
Leathermarket St. SE1 4
Leathermarket St. SE1 67 C
Leathsail Rd., Har. 45 B
Leathwaite Rd. SW11 66 B
Leathwell Rd. SE8 67 C
Leaveland Clo., Beck. 87 C
Leaver Gdns., Grnf. 54 B
Leaves Grn. Cres., Kes. 97 C
Leaves Grn. Rd., Kes. 97 C
Leavesden Rd., Stan. 36 B
Leavesden Rd., Wat. 26 B
Leavesden Rd., Wey. 92 A
Leaway E10 48 C
Leazes Ave., Cat. 104 B
Lebanon Ave., Felt. 74 B
Lebanon Clo., Wat. 26 B
Lebanon Ct., Twick. 74 B
Lebanon Dr., Cob. 93 B
Lebanon Gdns. SW18 76 B
Lebanon Gdns., West. 106 C
Lebanon Pk., Twick. 74 B
Lebanon Rd. SW18 76 B
Lebanon Rd., Croy. 87 C
Lebrun Sq. SE3 68 C
Lechmere Ave., Chig. 40 C
Lechmere Ave., Wdf.Grn. 40 C
Lechmere Rd. NW2 55 B
Leckford Rd. SW18 76 B
Leckwith Ave., Bexh. 69 C
Lecky St. SW7 3
Lecky St. SW7 66 B
Leconfield Ave. SW13 65 B
Leconfield Rd. N5 48 B
Leconfield Wk., Horn. 60 C
Airfield Way
Lectern La., St.Alb. 9 B
Creighton Ave.
Leda Ave., Enf. 30 C
Leda Rd. SE18 68 C
Ledbury Ms. N. W11 56 B
Ledbury Ms. W. W11 56 B
Ledbury Pl., Croy. 96 B
Ledbury Rd. W11 55 B
Ledbury Rd., Croy. 96 B
Ledbury Rd., Reig. 121 B
Ledbury St. SE15 67 C
Ledger Clo., Guil. 118 A
Ledger Dr., Wey. 91 A

dger La., Maid. 61 AH44
dgers Rd., Slou. 61 AO41
dgers Rd., Warl. 105 CE62
drington Rd. SE19 77 CA50
dway Dr., Wem. 46 BL33
e Ave., Rom. 50 CQ32
e Bri. SE13 67 CF45
e Ch. St. SE13 68 CG45
e Clo. E17 39 CC30
e Conservancy Rd. E9 48 CD35
e Fm. Clo., Chesh. 16 AQ18
e Gdns. Ave., Horn. 51 CX33
e Grn. SE12 68 CG45
e Grn., Orp. 89 CO53
e Grn. La., Epsom 103 BM65
e Gro., Chig. 40 CL27
e High Rd. SE12 68 CG45
e High Rd. SE13 67 CF45
e Pk. SE3 68 CG45
e Pk. Way N18 39 CC28
e Rd. NW7 37 BQ29
e Rd. SE3 68 CG45
e Rd. SW19 86 BS51
e Rd., Enf. 30 CB25
e Rd., Grnf. 54 BK37
e St. E8 57 CA37
e Ter. SE3 68 CG45
e Valley Trd. Est. N18 39 CC28
e Vw., Enf. 29 BY23
ech La., Lthd. 112 BM66
echcroft Ave., Sid. 78 CN46
echcroft Ave., Swan. 89 CT52
echcroft Rd., Wall. 86 BV55
ecroft Rd., Barn. 28 BR24
eds Clo., Orp. 89 CP55
eds Pl. N4 47 BX33
eds Rd., Ilf. 49 CM33
eds Rd., Slou. 52 AP40
eds St. N18 39 CB28
efern Rd. W12 65 BP41
egate Ho. SE12 78 CG46
eke St. WC1 2 **B2**
eke St. WC1 56 BX38
eland Rd. W13 54 BJ40
Broadway
eland Ter. W13 54 BJ40
eland Way NW10 46 BO35
eming Rd., Borwd. 28 BL22
emount Clo. NW4 46 BQ31
erdam Dr. E14 67 CF41
es, The, Croy. 87 CD55
es Ave., Nthwd. 35 BB30
es Pl. W1 1 **G10**
es Pl. W1 56 BV40
es Rd., Uxb. 53 AZ38
eside, Barn. 28 BR25
eside Cres. NW11 46 BR32
eside Rd. N17 39 CC29
eson Rd. SE24 66 BY45
Mayall Rd.
esons Hill, Chis. 88 CN52
esons Way, Orp. 88 CN51
eward Gdns. SW19 75 BR49
eway SE8 67 CD42
eway Clo., Pnr. 36 BE29
Wood Ridings Clo.
ewood Pl., Swan. 89 CS52
ewood Way, Lthd. 111 BD67
efevre Wk. E3 57 CD37
efroy Rd. W12 65 BO41
egard Rd. N5 47 BY34
egatt Rd. SE9 78 CJ46
eggatt Rd. E15 57 CF37
eggatts Clo., Wat. 26 BB21
eggatts Ri., Wat. 26 BC21
eggatts Way, Wat. 26 BB21
eggatts Wd. Ave., Wat. 26 BC21
egge St. SE13 77 CF46
eggfield Ter., Hem.H. 7 AV13
eghorn Rd. NW10 55 BO37
eghorn Rd. SE18 68 CM42
egion Clo. N1 56 BY36
egion Ct., Mord. 86 BS53
egion Rd., Grnf. 54 BG37
egon Ave., Rom. 50 CS33
egrace Ave., Houns. 64 BD44
eicester Ave., Mitch. 86 BX52
eicester Clo., Wor.Pk. 94 BQ56
eicester Ct. WC2 1 **P10**
eicester Ct. WC2 56 BW40
Cranbourn St.
eicester Gdns., Ilf. 49 CN33
eicester Pl. WC2 1 **P10**
eicester Pl. WC2 56 BW40
Lisle St.
eicester Rd. E11 49 CH32
eicester Rd. N2 47 BU31
eicester Rd. NW10 55 BN36
eicester Rd., Barn. 29 BS25
eicester Rd., Croy. 87 CA54
eicester Rd., Til. 71 DF44
eicester Sq. WC2 3 **P1**
eicester Sq. WC2 56 BW40
eicester St. WC2 1 **P10**
eicester St. WC2 56 BW40
Lisle St.
eigh Ave., Ilf. 49 CJ31
eigh Clo., N.Mal. 85 BN52
eigh Clo., Wey. 91 AV57
eigh Common, Welw.G.C. 5 BR9
eigh Cor., Cob. 102 BD61
eigh Ct., Har. 45 BH33
eigh Ct. Clo., Cob. 93 BD60
eigh Cres., Croy. 96 CE57
eigh Dr., Rom. 42 CV28
eigh Gdns. NW10 55 BQ37
eigh Hill Rd., Cob. 93 BD60
eigh Hunt St. SE1 4 **H4**
eigh Hunt St. SE1 67 BZ41
Lant La.
eigh Orchard Clo. SW16 76 BX48
Ivyday Gro.
eigh Pk., Slou. 62 AQ43
Leigh Pl., Cob. 102 BD61
Leigh Pl., Well. 69 CO44
Leigh Pl. La., Gdse. 114 CC69
Leigh Pl. Rd., Reig. 120 BP73
Leigh Rd. E6 58 CL36
Leigh Rd. E10 48 CF33
Leigh Rd. N5 47 BY35
Leigh Rd., Cob. 92 BC60
Leigh Rd., Grav. 81 DG48
Leigh Rd., Houns. 64 BG45
Leigh Rood, Wat. 36 BE27
Leigh Sq., Wind. 61 AL44
Leigh St. WC1 1 **Q4**
Leigh St. WC1 56 BX38
Leigh Ter., Orp. 89 CO52
Leigham Ave. SW16 76 BX48
Leigham Ct. Rd. SW16 76 BX48
Leigham Dr., Islw. 64 BH43
Leigham Vale SW2 76 BX48
Leigham Vale SW16 76 BX48
Leighton Ave. E12 49 CL35
Leighton Ave., Pnr. 45 BE31
Leighton Buzzard Rd., Hem.H. 8 AW10
Leighton Clo., Edg. 37 BM30
Leighton Cres. NW5 47 BW35
Leighton Gro.
Leighton Gdns. NW10 55 BP37
Leighton Gdns., S.Croy. 96 CB60
Leighton Gdns., Til. 71 DG43
Leighton Gro. NW5 47 BW35
Leighton Ho. W14 65 BR41
Leighton Pl. NW5 47 BW35
Leighton Rd.
Leighton Rd. NW5 47 BW35
Leighton Rd. W13 64 BJ41
Leighton Rd., Enf. 30 CA25
Leighton Rd., Har. 36 BG30
Leighton St. E., Croy. 86 BY54
Leighton St. W., Croy. 86 BY54
Leighton Way, Epsom 94 BN60
Leinster Ave. SW14 65 BN45
Leinster Gdns. W2 56 BT39
Leinster Ms. W2 56 BT40
Leinster Pl. W2 56 BT39
Leinster Rd. N10 47 BV31
Leinster Sq. W2 56 BS40
Leinster Ter. W2 56 BT40
Leiston Spur, Slou. 52 AP39
Leisure La., Wey. 92 AW59
Leith Clo. NW9 46 BN33
Leith Hill, Orp. 88 CN51
Leith Hill Grn., Orp. 89 CO51
Leith Hill
Leith Pk. Rd., Grav. 81 DG47
Leith Rd. N22 38 BY30
Leith Rd., Epsom 94 BO59
Leith Vw., Dor. 119 BK73
Leithcote Gdns. SW16 76 BX49
Leithcote Path SW16 76 BX48
Ivyday Gro.
Lela Ave., Houns. 64 BD44
Leman St. E1 2 **Q9**
Leman St. E1 57 CA39
Lemark Clo., Stan. 36 BK28
Lemmon Rd. SE10 68 CG43
Lemna Rd. E11 49 CG33
Lemonfield Dr., Wat. 18 BE20
Lemonwell Ct. SE9 78 CM46
Lemsford Clo. N15 48 CB32
Lemsford Ct. N4 48 BZ34
Kings Cres. Est.
Lemsford Ct., Borwd. 28 BN24
Lemsford La., Welw.G.C. 5 BP8
Lemsford Rd., Hat. 10 BP11
Lemsford Rd., St.Alb. 9 BH13
Lemsford Village, Welw.G.C. 5 BO8
Lena Gdns. W6 65 BQ41
Lena Kennedy Clo. E4 39 CE29
Lena Kennedy Clo. E4 39 CE29
Lendal Ter. SW4 66 BX45
Lenelby Rd., Surb. 85 BM54
Lenham Rd. SE12 68 CG45
Lenham Rd., Bexh. 69 CQ43
Lenham Rd., Sutt. 95 BS56
Lenham Rd., Th.Hth. 87 BZ51
Lenmore Ave., Grays 71 DE41
Lennard Ave., W.Wick. 88 CG55
Lennard Clo., W.Wick. 88 CG55
Lennard Rd. SE20 77 CC50
Lennard Rd., Beck. 77 CD50
Lennard Rd., Brom. 88 CK54
Lennard Rd., Croy. 87 BZ54
Lennard Rd., Sev. 107 CT63
Lennard Row, S.Ock. 60 CY40
Lennon Rd. NW2 55 BQ36
Lennox Ave., Grav. 81 DF47
Lennox Clo., Rom. 50 CT32
Lennox Gdns. NW10 46 BO35
Lennox Gdns. SW1 3 **E7**
Lennox Gdns. SW1 66 BU41
Lennox Gdns., Croy. 95 BY56
Violet La.
Lennox Gdns., Ilf. 49 CK33
Lennox Gdns. Ms. SW1 3 **E7**
Lennox Gdns. Ms. SW1 66 BU41
Lennox Rd. E17 48 CD32
Lennox Rd. N4 47 BX34
Lennox Rd., Grav. 81 DF46
Lennox Rd. E., Grav. 81 DG47
Lenor Clo., Bex. 69 CQ45
Lens Rd. E7 58 CJ36
Lensbury Clo., Chsnt. 21 CD17
Lensbury Way SE2 69 CP41
Lenthall Ave., Grays 71 DD41
Lenthall Pl. SW7 66 BT42
Gloucester Rd.
Lenthall Rd. E8 57 CA36
Lenthall Rd., Loug. 31 CM24
Lenthorp Rd. SE10 68 CG42
Lentmead Rd., Brom. 78 CG48
Lenton Ri., Rich. 65 BL45
Evelyn Ter.
Lenton St. SE18 68 CM42
Lenville Way SE16 67 CB42
The Bonamy Est. W.
Leo St. SE15 67 CB43
Leo Yd. EC1 2 **G5**
Leo Yd. EC1 56 BY38
St. John St.
Leof Cres. SE6 77 CE49
Leominster Rd., Mord. 86 BT53
Leominster Wk., Mord. 86 BT53
Leonard Ave., Mord. 86 BT53
Leonard Ave., Rom. 50 CS33
Leonard Ave., Sev. 107 CU61
Leonard Ave., Swans. 81 DC47
Leonard Rd. E4 39 CE29
Leonard Rd. E7 49 CH35
Leonard Rd. N9 39 CA27
Leonard Rd. SW16 86 BW51
Leonard Rd., Sthl. 64 BD41
Leonard Robbins Path SE28 59 CO40
Tawney Rd.
Leonard St. E16 58 CK40
Leonard St. EC2 2 **L4**
Leonard St. EC2 57 BZ38
Leonard Way, Brwd. 42 CZ28
Leontine Clo. SE15 67 CB43
Leopards Ct. EC1 2 **D6**
Leopold Ave. SW19 75 BR49
Leopold Rd. E17 48 CE32
Leopold Rd. N2 47 BT31
Leopold Rd. N18 39 CB28
Albany Rd.
Leopold Rd. NW10 55 BO36
Leopold Rd. SW19 75 BR49
Leopold Rd. W5 55 BL40
Leopold St. E3 57 CD39
Lepe Clo., Brom. 78 CG49
Leppoc Rd. SW4 76 BW46
Leret Way, Lthd. 102 BJ64
Leroy St. SE1 4 **M7**
Leroy St. SE1 67 CA42
Lesbourne Rd., Reig. 121 BS71
Lescombe Clo. SE23 77 CD48
Lescombe Rd. SE23 77 CD48
Lesley Clo., Bex. 79 CR47
Lesley Clo., Grav. 81 DF50
Lesley Clo., Swan. 89 CS52
Leslie Gdns., Sutt. 95 BS57
Leslie Gro., Croy. 87 BZ54
Leslie Pk. Rd., Croy. 87 CA54
Leslie Rd. E11 48 CF35
Leslie Rd. E16 58 CH39
Leslie Rd. N2 47 BT31
Leslie Rd., Dor. 119 BK70
Leslie Rd., Wok. 91 AP58
Leslie Smith Sq. SE18 68 CL43
Nightingale Vale
Lesney Fm. Est., Erith 69 CT43
Lesney Pk., Erith 69 CS43
Lesney Pk. Rd., Erith 69 CS43
Lessar Ave. SW4 76 BV46
Lessing St. SE23 77 CD47
Lessingham Ave. SW17 76 BU49
Lessingham Ave., Ilf. 49 CL31
Lessington Ave., Rom. 50 CS32
Lessness Ave., Bexh. 69 CP43
Lessness Pk., Belv. 69 CQ42
Lessness Rd., Belv. 69 CR43
Stapley Rd.
Lessness Rd., Mord. 86 BT53
Lester Ave. E15 58 CG38
Leston Clo., Rain. 59 CU38
Leswin Pl. N16 48 CA34
Leswin Rd.
Leswin Rd. N16 48 CA34
Letchfield, Chesh. 16 AQ19
Letchford Cotts., Har. 36 BF30
Letchford Gdns. NW10 55 BP38
Letchford Ms. NW10 55 BP38
Letchford Gdns.
Letchmore Heath Rd., Wat. 27 BG22
Letchmore Rd., Rad. 27 BJ21
Letchworth Ave., Felt. 73 BB47
Letchworth Clo., Brom. 88 CH53
Letchworth Clo., Wat. 36 BD29
Letchworth Dr., Brom. 88 CH53
Letchworth St. SW17 76 BU49
Lethbridge Clo. SE13 67 CF44
Lett Rd. E15 57 CF36
Letter Box La., Sev. 117 CV68
Letterstone Rd. SW6 65 BR43
Varna Rd.
Lettice St. SW6 65 BR44
Lettsom St. SE5 67 CA44
Lettsom Wk. E13 58 CH37
Hunter Wk.
Leucha Rd. E17 48 CD32
Levana Clo. W19 75 BQ47
Victoria Dr.
Levehurst Way SW4 66 BX44
Paradise Rd.
Leven Clo., Wat. 36 BD28
Leven Dr., Wal.Cr. 21 CC20
Leven Rd. E14 57 CF39
Leven Way, Hayes 53 BB39
Leven Way, Hem.H. 8 AX11
Lomond Rd.
Levendale Rd. SE23 77 CD48
Lever Sq., Grays 71 DF42
Lever St. EC1 2 **G3**
Lever St. EC1 56 BY38
Leveret Clo., Croy. 96 CF58
Leveret Clo., Wat. 17 BC20
Leverett Pl. SW3 66 BU42
Denyer St.
Leverett St. SW3 3 **D8**
Leverett St. SW3 66 BU42
Denyer St.
Leverholme Gdns. SE9 78 CL49
Leverington Pl. N1 57 BZ38
Charles Sq.
Leverson St. SW16 76 BW50
Leverstock Grn., Hem.H. 8 AZ13
Leverstock Grn. Rd., Hem.H. 8 AZ13
Leverstock Grn. Way, Hem.H. 8 BA13
Leverton Pl. NW5 47 BW35
Leverton St.
Leverton St. NW5 47 BW35
Leverton Way, Wal.Abb. 21 CF20
Leveson Rd., Grays 71 DG41
Levett Gdns., Ilf. 49 CN35
Levett Rd., Bark. 58 CN36
Levett Rd., Lthd. 102 BJ63
Levine Gdns., Bark. 59 CP37
Levison Way N19 47 BW33
Ashbrook Rd.
Levylsdene, Guil. 118 AU70
Lewes Clo., Nthlt. 54 BF36
Lewes Rd. N12 38 BU28
Lewes Rd., Brom. 88 CJ51
Lewes Rd., Rom. 42 CV28
Lewes Way, Rick. 26 BA24
Lewesdon Clo. SW19 75 BQ47
Leweston Pl. N16 48 CA33
Lewgars Ave. NW9 46 BN32
Lewin Rd. SW14 65 BN45
Lewin Rd. SW16 76 BW50
Lewin Rd., Bexh. 79 CQ46
Lewins Rd., Epsom 94 BM60
Lewins Rd., Ger.Cr. 43 AR31
Lewis Ave. E17 39 CE30
Lewis Clo., Brwd. 122 DC26
Lewis Clo., Wey. 92 AX56
Cabbell Pl.
Lewis Cres. NW10 46 BN35
Lewis Gdns. N2 38 BT30
Lewis Gro. SE13 67 CF45
Lewis La., Ger.Cr. 34 AS30
Lewis Rd., Grav. 81 DF51
Lewis Rd., Horn. 51 CV32
Lewis Rd., Mitch. 86 BT51
Lewis Rd., Rich. 74 BK46
Red Lion St.
Lewis Rd., Sid. 79 CP48
Lewis Rd., Sthl. 64 BE41
Lewis Rd., Sutt. 86 BS55
Lewis Rd., Swans. 81 DC46
Lewis Rd., Well. 69 CP45
Lewis St. NW1 56 BV36
Lewis Trust Bldgs. SW3 66 BU42
Lewisham High St. SE13 77 CE46
Lewisham Hill SE13 67 CF44
Lewisham Pk. SE13 77 CE46
Lewisham Rd. SE13 67 CE44
Lewisham St. SW1 3 **P5**
Lewisham St. SW1 66 BW41
Lewisham Way SE4 67 CD44
Lewisham Way SE14 67 CD44
Lexden Dr., Rom. 50 CO32
Lexden Rd. W3 55 BM40
Lexden Rd., Mitch. 86 BW52
Lexham Clo., Nthlt. 54 BE36
Lexham Gdns. W8 66 BS42
Lexham Gdns., Amer. 25 AO22
Lexham Gdns. Ms. W8 66 BS41
Lexham Ms. W8 66 BS42
Lexham Wk. W8 66 BS41
Lexington Clo., Borwd. 28 BL23
Lexington Clo., Pur. 96 BZ58
Lexington St. W1 1 **M10**
Lexington St. W1 56 BW39
Lexington Way, Barn. 28 BQ24
Lexington Way, Upmin. 51 CZ32
Lexton Gdns. SW12 76 BW47
Ley Hill Rd., Hem.H. 16 AR18
Ley St., Ilf. 49 CL34
Ley Wk., Welw.G.C. 5 BT8
Leyborne Ave. W13 64 BJ41
Leyborne Pk., Rich. 65 BM44
Leybourne Ave., Wey. 92 AY60
Leybourne Clo., Brom. 88 CH53
Leybourne Clo., Wey. 92 AY60
Leybourne Rd. E11 49 CG33
Leybourne Rd. NW1 56 BV36
Leybourne Rd. NW9 46 BM32
Leybourne Rd., Uxb. 53 BA37
Leybourne St. NW1 56 BV36
Hawley St.
Leybridge Ct. SE12 78 CH46
Leyburn Clo. E17 48 CE31
Leyburn Cres., Rom. 42 CW29
Leyburn Gdns., Croy. 87 CA55
Leyburn Gro. N18 39 CB29
Leyburn Rd. N18 39 CB29
Leyburn Rd., Rom. 42 CW29
Leycroft Clo., Loug. 31 CL25
Leycroft Gdns., Erith 69 CU44
Leyden St. E1 2 **P7**
Leyden St. E1 57 CA39
Leydon Clo. SE16 57 CC40
Lagado Ms.
Leyes Rd. E16 58 CJ39
Leyfield, Wor.Pk. 85 BO54
Leyhill Clo., Swan. 89 CT53
Leyland Ave., Enf. 30 CD23
Leyland Ave., St.Alb. 9 BG14
Leyland Clo., Chsnt. 21 CC17
Leyland Gdns., Wdf.Grn. 40 CJ28
Leyland Rd. SE12 78 CG46
Leylands La., Slou. 62 AV45
Leylang Rd. SE14 67 CC43
Leys, The N2 47 BT31
Leys, The, Har. 46 BL32
Leys, The, St.Alb. 9 BK12
Leys Ave., Dag. 59 CS37
Leys Clo., Dag. 59 CS36
Leys Clo., Har. 45 BG32
Leys Clo., Uxb. 35 AX30
Leys Gdns., Barn. 29 BV25
Leys Rd., Hem.H. 8 AY14
Leys Rd., Lthd. 93 BG59
Leys Rd. E., Enf. 30 CD23
Leys Rd. W., Enf. 30 CD23
Leysdown, Welw.G.C. 5 BT8
Leysdown Ave., Bexh. 69 CS45
Leysdown Rd. SE9 78 CK48
Leysfield Rd. W12 65 BP41
Leyspring Rd. E11 49 CG33
Leyswood Dr., Ilf. 49 CN32
Leythe Rd. W3 65 BN41
Leyton Cross Rd., Dart. 79 CT48
Leyton Gra. E10 48 CE34
Leyton Grn. Rd. E10 48 CF32
Leyton Pk. Rd. E10 48 CF34
Leyton Rd. E15 48 CF35
Leyton Rd. SW19 76 BT50
Leyton Way E11 49 CG33
Leytonstone Rd. E15 58 CG36
Leywick St. E15 58 CG37
Leywood Clo., Amer. 25 AO23
Lezayre Rd., Orp. 97 CN57
Liardet St. SE14 67 CD43
Liberia Rd. N5 56 BY36
Liberty, The, Rom. 50 CT32
Liberty Ave. SW19 86 BT51
Liberty Hall Rd., Wey. 92 AW56
Liberty La., Wey. 92 AW57
Liberty Ms. SW12 76 BV46
Liberty Ri., Wey. 92 AW57
Liberty St. SW9 66 BX44
Libra Rd. E3 57 CD37
Libra Rd. E13 58 CH37
Library Hill, Brwd. 42 DB27
Queens Rd.
Library Pl. E1 57 CB40
Library St. SE1 4 **F5**
Library St. SE1 66 BY41
Lichfield Clo., Upmin. 51 CZ34
Lichfield Gdns., Rich. 75 BL45
Lichfield Gro. N3 38 BS30
Lichfield Rd. E3 57 CD38
Lichfield Rd. E6 58 CJ38
Lichfield Rd. N9 39 CB27
Winchester Rd.
Lichfield Rd. NW2 46 BR35
Lichfield Rd., Dag. 50 CO35
Lichfield Rd., Houns. 64 BD45
Lichfield Rd., Nthwd. 44 BC31
Lichfield Rd., Rich. 65 BL44
Lichfield Rd., Wdf.Grn. 40 CG28
Lichfield Ter., Upmin. 51 CZ34
Lichfield Way, Brox. 12 CD14
Lichfield Way, S.Croy. 96 CC58
Lichlade Clo., Orp. 97 CN56
Lidbury Rd. NW7 37 BR29
Liddall Way, West Dr. 53 AY40
Liddell, Wind. 61 AL45
Liddell Clo., Har. 45 BK31
Liddell Gdns. NW10 55 BQ37
Liddell Pl., Wind. 61 AL45
Liddell
Liddell Rd. NW6 56 BS36
Liddell Sq., Wind. 61 AL45
Liddell
Liddell Way, Wind. 61 AL45
Liddell
Lidding Rd., Har. 45 BK32
Liddington Hall Dr., Guil. 118 AP69
Liddington New Rd., Guil. 118 AP69
Liddington Rd. E15 58 CG37
Liddon Rd. E13 58 CH38
Liddon Rd., Brom. 88 CJ52
Liden Clo. E17 48 CD33
Lidfield Rd. N16 48 BZ35
Lidiard Rd. SW18 76 BT48
Lidlington Pl. NW1 1 **M1**
Lidlington Pl. NW1 56 BW37
Lidstone Clo., Wok. 100 AQ62
Lidyard Rd. N19 47 BW33
Liffler Rd. SE18 68 CM42
Lifford St. SW15 65 BQ45
Liffords Pl. SW13 65 BO44
Barnes High St.
Lightcliffe Rd. N13 38 BY28
Lightermans Rd. E14 67 CE41
Lightfoot Rd. N8 47 BX31
Lightley Clo., Wem. 55 BL36
Stanley Ave.
Ligonier St. E2 2 **P4**
Ligonier St. E2 57 CA38
Lila Pl., Swan. 89 CS52
Azalea Dr.
Lilac Ave., Wok. 100 AR63
Lilac Clo. E4 39 CD29
Lilac Clo., Brwd. 33 DB25
Magnolia Way
Lilac Clo., Chsnt. 21 CB19
Greenwood Ave.
Lilac Clo., Guil. 109 AR68
Lilac Gdns. W5 64 BK41
Lilac Gdns., Croy. 87 CE55
Lilac Gdns., Hayes 53 BB39
Lilac Gdns., Ilf. 49 CL35
Lilac Gdns., Rom. 50 CT33
Lilac Gdns., Swan. 89 CS52
Lilac Pl. SE11 4 **B9**
Lilac Pl. SE11 66 BX42
Lilac Rd., Hodd. 12 CE11
Lilac St. W12 55 BP40
Lilacs Ave., Enf. 30 CC21
Lilburne Gdns. SE9 78 CK46
Lilburne Rd. SE9 78 CK46
Lilburne Wk. NW10 55 BN36
Lile Cres. W7 54 BH39
Lilestone Est. NW8 56 BT38
Lilestone St. NW8 1 **C4**
Lilestone St. NW8 56 BU38
Lilford Rd. SE5 66 BY44
Lilian Board Way, Grnf. 45 BG35
Lilian Clo. N16 48 CA34
Barbauld Rd.
Lilian Cres., Brwd. 122 DE27
Lilian Rd. SW16 86 BW51
Lillechurch Rd., Dag. 59 CO36
Lilleshall Rd., Mord. 86 BT53
Lilley Clo., Brwd. 42 CZ28
Lilley Dr., Tad. 104 BS64

Lil–Lit

Lilley La. NW7 37 BN28
Lillian Ave. W3 65 BM41
Lillian Gdns., Wdf.Grn. 40 CH30
Lillian Rd. SW13 65 BP43
Lillie Bri. Ms. SW6 66 BS43
Lillie Rd. SW6 65 BQ43
Lillie Rd., West. 106 CJ62
Lillie Yd. SW6 66 BS43
Lillieshall Rd. SW4 66 BV45
Lillington Gdns. Est. SW1 3 M9
Lilliput Ave., Nthlt. 54 BE37
Lilliput Rd., Rom. 50 CS33
Lily Clo. W14 65 BR42
Lily Gdns., Wem. 54 BK37
Lily Pl. EC1 2 E6
Lily Rd. E17 48 CE32
Lily Wk., Grnf. 54 BK37
Lilyville Rd. SW6 65 BR44
Limbourne Ave., Dag. 50 CQ33
Limburg Rd. SW11 66 BU45
Lime Ave., Brwd. 122 DC27
Lime Ave., Grav. 81 DE47
Lime Ave., Upmin. 51 CX35
Lime Ave., West Dr. 53 AY40
Lime Clo. E1 57 CB40
Lime Clo., Brom. 88 CK52
Lime Clo., Buck.H. 40 CJ27
Lime Clo., Cars. 86 BU55
Lime Clo., Guil. 110 AW67
Lime Clo., Pnr. 44 BB31
Lime Clo., Reig. 121 BS72
Lime Clo., Rom. 50 CS31
Lime Clo., S.Ock. 60 DB38
Lime Clo., Wat. 36 BD26
Lime Ct., Mitch. 86 BT51
Lewis Rd.
Lime Cres., Sun. 84 BD51
Lime Gro. N20 37 BR26
Lime Gro. W12 65 BQ41
Lime Gro., Borwd. 33 DB22
Lime Gro., Guil. 109 AR68
Lime Gro., Hayes 53 BA40
Lime Gro., Ilf. 40 CN29
Lime Gro., N.Mal. 85 BN52
Lime Gro., Orp. 88 CL55
Lime Gro., Ruis. 44 BC33
Lime Gro., Sid. 78 CN46
Lime Gro., Twick. 74 BH46
Lime Gro., Warl. 105 CD62
Lime Gro., Wey. 92 AW56
Lime Gro., Wok. 100 AS64
Lime Gro. Rd., Guil. 110 AW67
Lime Meadow Ave., S.Croy. 96 CB60
Lime Pit La., Sev. 107 CS62
Lime Rd., Epp. 22 CN19
Lime Rd., Erith 69 CQ41
Northwood Pl.
Lime Rd., Rich. 65 BL45
St Marys Gro.
Lime Rd., Swan. 89 CS52
Lime Row, Erith 69 CQ41
Northwood Pl.
Lime St. E17 48 CD31
Lime St. EC3 2 M10
Lime St. EC3 57 CA40
Lime St. Pas. EC3 2 M10
Lime St. Pas. EC3 57 CA39
Lime St.
Lime Ter. W7 54 BH40
Lime Tree Clo., Lthd. 102 BE65
Lime Tree Gro., Croy. 87 CD55
Lime Tree Pl., Mitch. 86 BV51
Lime Tree Wk., Amer. 25 AP23
Lime Tree Wk., Bush. 36 BH26
Lime Tree Wk., Enf. 30 BZ22
Lime Tree Wk., Rick. 26 AW25
Lime Tree Wk., Sev. 116 CU66
Lime Tree Wk., W.Wick. 97 CG56
Lime Wk. E15 58 CG37
Church St. N.
Lime Wk., Hem.H. 8 AY14
Lime Wk., Uxb. 44 AX35
Lime Way Ter., Dor. 119 BJ70
Lime Wks. Rd., Red. 113 BW66
Limebush Clo., Wey. 92 AX58
Limecroft Clo., Epsom 94 BN57
Limedene Clo., Pnr. 36 BD30
Limeharbour E14 67 CE41
Limehouse Causeway E14 57 CD40
Limehouse Flds. Est. E14 57 CD39
Limerick Clo. SW12 76 BW47
Limerick Gdns., Upmin. 51 CZ33
Limerston St. SW10 66 BT43
Limes, The, Brwd. 122 DC27
Limes, The, Brom. 88 CK55
Limes, The, Grays 70 CX42
Limes, The, St.Alb. 9 BH12
Limes, The, Welw.G.C. 5 BS9
Limes Ave. E11 49 CH31
Limes Ave. N12 38 BT28
Limes Ave. NW7 37 BO29
Limes Ave. NW11 46 BR33
Limes Ave. SE20 77 CB50
Limes Ave. SW13 65 BO44
Limes Ave., Cars. 86 BU54
Limes Ave., Chig. 40 CM28
Limes Ave., Croy. 86 BX55
Limes Ave., The N11 38 BW28
Limes Clo., Ashf. 73 AZ49
Limes Gdns. SW18 76 BS46
Limes Gro. SE13 67 CF45
Limes Pl., Croy. 87 BZ53
Limes Rd., Beck. 87 CE51
Limes Rd., Chsnt. 21 CC19
Limes Rd., Croy. 87 BZ53
Limes Rd., Egh. 72 AS49
Limes Rd., Wey. 92 AZ56
Limes Row, Orp. 97 CL56
Orchard Rd.
Limes Wk. SE15 67 CC45
Limes Wk. W5 65 BM41
Chestnut Gro.
Limesdale Gdns., Edg. 37 BN30
Limesfield Rd. SW14 65 BO45
White Hart La.
Limesford Rd. SE15 67 CC45
Limestone Wk., Erith 69 CP41
Yarnton Way
Limetree Ave. SE20 87 CB51
Limetree Ave., T.Ditt. 84 BG54
Limetree Clo. SW2 76 BX47
Limetree Rd., Houns. 64 BF44
Limetree Wk. SW17 76 BV49
Limewood Clo. W13 54 BJ39
St. Stephens Rd.
Limewood Clo., Wok. 100 AO63
Limewood Ct., Ilf. 49 CK32
Limewood Rd., Erith 69 CS43
Limpsfield Ave. SW19 75 BQ47
Limpsfield Ave., Th.Hth. 86 BX53
Limpsfield Rd., S.Croy. 96 CB59
Limpsfield Rd., Warl. 105 CC62
Linacre Ct. W6 65 BQ42
Colet Gdns.
Linacre Rd. NW2 55 BP36
Linberry Wk. SE8 67 CD42
Carteret Way
Lince La., Dor. 119 BG71
Linces Way, Welw.G.C. 5 BS9
Linchfield Rd., Slou. 62 AR44
Linchmere Rd. SE12 78 CG47
Lincoln Ave. N14 38 BW27
Lincoln Ave. SW19 75 BQ48
Lincoln Ave., Rom. 50 CT34
Lincoln Ave., Twick. 74 BG48
Lincoln Clo. SE25 87 CB53
Lincoln Clo., Erith 69 CT44
Lincoln Clo., Grnf. 54 BG37
Lincoln Clo., Har. 45 BE32
Lincoln Clo., Horn. 51 CX32
Lincoln Clo., St.Alb. 9 BK11
Lincoln Clo., Welw.G.C. 5 BT7
Lincoln Ct. N16 48 BZ33
Lincoln Ct., Borwd. 28 BN25
Lincoln Cres., Enf. 30 CA25
Lincoln Dr., Rick. 26 AZ24
Lincoln Dr., Wat. 36 BD27
Lincoln Dr., Wok. 100 AV61
Lincoln Est. E3 57 CE38
Lincoln Gdns., Ilf. 49 CK33
Lincoln Grn. Rd., Orp. 88 CN53
Lincoln Ms. NW6 55 BR37
Lincoln Ms. SE21 77 BZ47
Lincoln Pk., Amer. 25 AP23
Lincoln Rd. E7 58 CJ36
Lincoln Rd. E13 58 CH38
Lincoln Rd. E18 40 CH30
Lincoln Rd. N2 47 BU31
Lincoln Rd. SE25 87 CB52
Lincoln Rd., Dor. 119 BK70
Lincoln Rd., Enf. 30 CA24
Lincoln Rd., Erith 69 CT44
Lincoln Rd., Felt. 74 BE48
Lincoln Rd., Ger.Cr. 34 AS30
Lincoln Rd., Guil. 118 AP69
Lincoln Rd., Har. 45 BE32
Lincoln Rd., Mitch. 86 BX53
Lincoln Rd., N.Mal. 85 BN52
Lincoln Rd., Nthwd. 44 BB31
Lincoln Rd., Sid. 79 CO49
Lincoln Rd., Wem. 54 BK36
Lincoln Rd., Wor.Pk. 85 BP54
Lincoln St. E11 49 CG34
Lincoln St. SW3 3 E9
Lincoln St. SW3 66 BU42
Lincoln Wk., Epsom 94 BN58
Hollymoor La.
Lincoln Way, Enf. 30 CB25
Lincoln Way, Rick. 26 AZ24
Lincoln Way, Sun. 83 BB51
Lincolns, The NW7 37 BO27
Lincolns Fld., Epp. 22 CN18
Lincolns Inn Flds. WC2 2 B8
Lincolns Inn Flds. WC2 56 BX39
Lincolns La., Brwd. 42 CY26
Lincombe Rd., Brom. 78 CG48
Lind Rd., Sutt. 95 BT56
Lind St. SE8 67 CE44
Lindal Cres., Enf. 29 BX24
Lindal Rd. SE4 77 CD46
Lindale Clo., Vir.W. 82 AP52
Lindales, The N17 39 CA29
Brantwood Rd.
Lindbergh, Welw.G.C. 5 BT8
Wellington Dr.
Lindbergh Rd., Wall. 95 BX57
Linden Ave. NW10 55 BQ37
Linden Ave., Couls. 104 BV61
Linden Ave., Dart. 80 CV47
Linden Ave., Enf. 30 CB23
Linden Ave., Houns. 74 BF46
Linden Ave., Ruis. 44 BC33
Linden Ave., Th.Hth. 86 BY52
Linden Ave., Wem. 46 BL35
Linden Chase Rd., Sev. 107 CU64
Linden Clo. N14 29 BW25
Linden Clo., Grays 70 CY42
Linden Clo., Maid. 61 AG43
Linden Clo., Orp. 98 CO56
Linden Clo., Ruis. 44 BC33
Linden Clo., Stan. 36 BJ28
Linden Clo., T.Ditt. 84 BJ54
Linden Clo., Wey. 92 AW59
Linden Ct. W12 55 BQ40
Linden Ct., Egh. 72 AQ50
Linden Ct., Lthd. 102 BJ64
Linden Rd.
Linden Cres., Grnf. 54 BH36
Linden Cres., Kings.T. 85 BL51
Linden Cres., St.Alb. 9 BK13
Linden Cres., Wdf.Grn. 40 CH29
Linden Dr., Cat. 105 BZ65
Linden Dr., Ger.Cr. 34 AS30
Linden Gdns. W2 56 BS40
Linden Gdns. W4 65 BO42
Linden Gdns. W9 56 BS40
Linden Gdns., Enf. 30 CB23
Linden Gdns., Lthd. 102 BK64
Linden Glade, Hem.H. 8 AW14
Wrensfield
Linden Gro. SE15 67 CB45
Linden Gro. SE26 77 CC50
Linden Gro., N.Mal. 85 BO52
Linden Gro., Tedd. 74 BH49
Linden Gro., Walt. 83 BB55
Linden Gro., Warl. 105 CD62
Linden Gro. Est. SE15 67 CB45
Linden Lawns, Wem. 46 BL35
Linden Lea N2 47 BT32
Linden Lea, Dor. 119 BK72
Linden Lea, Wat. 17 BC20
Linden Leas, W.Wick. 87 CF55
Linden Ms. N1 48 BZ35
Linden Ms. W2 56 BS40
Linden Gdns.
Linden Pas. W4 65 BN42
Linden Gdns.
Linden Pit Path, Lthd. 102 BJ64
Linden Ri., Brwd. 42 DB28
Blackthorn Way
Linden Rd. E17 48 CD32
Linden Rd. N10 47 BV31
Linden Rd. N11 38 BV27
Linden Rd. N15 48 BZ31
Linden Rd., Guil. 118 AR70
Linden Rd., Hmptn. 74 BF50
Linden Rd., Lthd. 102 BJ64
Linden Rd., Wey. 92 BA58
Linden Sq., Sev. 107 CT64
London Rd.
Linden St., Rom. 50 CS31
Linden Way N14 29 BW25
Linden Way, Pur. 95 BW58
Linden Way, Shep. 83 BA53
Linden Way, Wok. 100 AS64
Linden Way, Wok. 100 AV65
Lindenfield, Chis. 88 CL51
Lindens, The N12 38 BT28
Lindens, The W4 65 BN44
Hartington Rd.
Lindens, The, Croy. 96 CF57
Lindens, The, Hem.H. 7 AV15
Lindens, The, Loug. 31 CL25
Lindens Clo., Lthd. 111 BE67
Mount Pleasant
Lindfield Gdns. NW3 47 BT35
Lindfield Gdns., Guil. 118 AS70
Lindfield Rd. W5 54 BK38
Lindfield Rd., Croy. 87 CA53
Lindfield Rd., Rom. 42 CW28
Lindfield St. E14 57 CE39
Lindisfarne SW20 75 BP50
Lindisfarne Clo., Grav. 81 DJ48
St. Benedicts Ave.
Lindisfarne Rd. SW20 75 BP50
Lindisfarne Rd., Dag. 50 CP34
Lindisfarne Way E9 48 CD35
Lindley Est. SE15 67 CB43
Lindley Rd. E10 48 CE34
Lindley Rd., Gdse. 114 CC68
Lindley Rd., Walt. 84 BE55
Lindley St. E1 57 CC39
Lindlings, Hem.H. 7 AV14
Lindore Rd. SW11 66 BU45
Lindores Rd., Cars. 86 BT54
Lindores Rd., Maid. 61 AG43
Lindrop St. SW6 66 BT44
Lindsay Clo., Chess. 94 BL57
Hunting Gate Dr.
Lindsay Clo., Epsom 94 BN60
Lindsay Clo., Stai. 73 AX46
Lindsay Dr., Har. 46 BL32
Lindsay Dr., Shep. 83 BA53
Lindsay Rd., Hmptn. 74 BF49
Lindsay Rd., Wey. 92 AW58
Lindsay Rd., Wor.Pk. 85 BP55
Lindsell St. SE10 67 CF44
Lindsey Clo., Brwd. 42 DA28
Lindsey Clo., Brom. 88 CK52
Clarence Rd.
Lindsey Clo., Mitch. 86 BX52
Lindsey Dr. W5 54 BK39
Regal Clo.
Lindsey Gdns., Felt. 73 BA47
Natalie Clo.
Lindsey Ms. N1 57 BZ36
Elmore St.
Lindsey Rd., Dag. 50 CP35
Lindsey Rd., Uxb. 44 AW34
Lindsey St. EC1 2 G6
Lindsey St. EC1 56 BY39
Lindsey St., Epp. 22 CN17
Lindsey Way, Horn. 51 CW32
Lindum Pl., St.Alb. 9 BF14
Lindum Rd., Tedd. 74 BK50
Lindway SE27 76 BY49
Lindwood Clo. E6 58 CK39
Northumberland Rd.
Linfield Clo., Walt. 92 BC56
Linfields, Amer. 25 AR23
Linford Clo., Harl. 13 CL12
Linford End, Harl. 13 CM12
Linford Rd. E17 48 CF31
Linford Rd., Grays 71 CD42
Linford St. SW8 66 BW44
Ling Rd. E16 58 CH39
Ling Rd., Erith 69 CS43
Lingards Rd. SE13 67 CF45
Lingey Clo., Sid. 78 CN48
Lingfield Ave., Dart. 80 CX47
Lingfield Ave., Kings.T. 85 BL52
Lingfield Ave., Upmin. 51 CW34
Lingfield Clo., Enf. 30 CA25
Lingfield Clo., Nthwd. 35 BB29
Lingfield Cres. SE9 68 CM45
Lingfield Gdns. N9 39 CB26
Lingfield Gdns., Couls. 104 BY63
Lingfield Rd. SW19 75 BQ49
Lingfield Rd., Grav. 81 DG48
Lingfield Rd., Wor.Pk. 85 BQ55
Lingham St. SW9 66 BX44
Lingholm Way, Barn. 28 BQ24
Lingmere Clo., Chig. 40 CM27
Lingrove Gdns., Wdf.Grn. 40 CH27
Beech La.
Lings Coppice SE21 77 BZ48
Lingwell Rd. SW17 76 BU48
Lingwood Gdns., Islw. 64 BH43
Lingwood Rd. E5 48 CB33
Linhope St. NW1 1 E4
Linhope St. NW1 56 BU38
Link, The W3 55 BM40
Saxon Dr.
Link, The, Enf. 30 CD23
Link, The, Pnr. 45 BD33
Link, The, Slou. 52 AQ39
Link, The, Wem. 45 BK33
Nathans Rd.
Link Ave., Wok. 100 AU61
Link Dr., Hat. 10 BP12
Link Fld., Welw.G.C. 5 BR10
Link La., Wall. 95 BW57
Link Rd. N11 38 BV28
Link Rd., Bush. 27 BD23
Link Rd., Dag. 59 CR37
Link Rd., Felt. 73 BB47
Link Rd., Slou. 62 AR44
Link Rd., Wall. 86 BV54
Link Rd., Wey. 92 AY56
Link St. E9 48 CC35
Link Way, Brom. 88 CK53
Link Way, Dag. 50 CP35
Link Way, Guil. 118 AP70
Link Way, Pnr. 36 BD30
Link Way, Stai. 73 AW50
Link Way, Uxb. 44 AW32
Link Way, Wok. 100 AU62
Linkfield, Brom. 88 CH53
Linkfield, E.Mol. 84 BF52
Linkfield Gdns., Red. 121 BU70
Linkfield La., Red. 121 BU70
Linkfield Rd., Islw. 64 BH44
Linkfield St., Red. 121 BU70
Linklea Clo. NW9 37 BO29
Links, The E17 48 CD31
Links, The, Chsnt. 21 CC16
Links, The, Walt. 83 BC55
Links, The, Welw.G.C. 5 BP8
Valley Rd.
Links Ave., Mord. 86 BS45
Links Ave., Rom. 41 CU30
Links Brow, Lthd. 102 BH65
Links Clo., Ash. 102 BK62
Links Dr. N20 38 BS26
Links Dr., Borwd. 28 BL24
Links Dr., Rad. 18 BH20
Links Gdns. SW16 76 BY50
Links Grn. Way, Cob. 93 BE60
Links Pl., Ash. 102 BK62
Links Rd. NW2 46 BO34
Links Rd. SW17 76 BU50
Links Rd. W3 55 BM39
Links Rd., Ashf. 73 AY49
Links Rd., Ash. 102 BK62
Links Rd., Epsom 94 BP60
Links Rd., W.Wick. 87 CF54
Links Rd., Wdf.Grn. 40 CH28
Links Side, Enf. 29 BX24
Links Vw. N2 47 BU31
Great N. Rd.
Links Vw. N3 37 BR29
Links Vw., Dart. 79 CU47
Links Vw., St.Alb. 9 BF12
Links Vw. Ave., Bet. 120 BM70
Links Vw. Clo., Stan. 36 BJ29
Links Vw. Rd., Croy. 87 CE55
Links Vw. Rd., Hmptn. 74 BG49
Links Way, Beck. 87 CE53
Links Way, Lthd. 111 BE67
Links Way, Nthwd. 35 BA29
Links Way, Rick. 26 BA24
Linkscroft Ave., Ashf. 73 AZ50
Linkside N12 37 BR29
Linkside, Chig. 40 CM28
Linkside, N.Mal. 85 BO51
Linkside Clo., Enf. 29 BX24
Linkside Gdns., Enf. 29 BX24
Linksway NW4 37 BQ30
Linksway, Stan. 36 BJ29
May Tree La.
Linkway N4 48 BZ33
Vale Rd.
Linkway SW20 85 BP52
Linkway, Horn. 51 CW33
Linkway, Rich. 74 BJ48
Linkway, The, Barn. 29 BS25
Linkway, The, Sutt. 95 BT58
Linkway Rd., Brwd. 42 CZ27
Linley Cres., Rom. 50 CR31
Linley Rd. N17 39 CA30
Linnell Clo. NW11 47 BS32
Linnell Dr. NW11 47 BS32
Linnell Rd. N18 39 CB28
Linnell Rd. SE5 67 CA44
Linnell Rd., Red. 121 BV71
Linnet Clo. SE28 59 CP40
Linnet Clo., Bush. 36 BG26
Linnet Clo., S.Croy. 96 CC58
Mallard Rd.
Linnet Gro., Guil. 118 AU69
Linnet Ms. SW12 76 BV47
Linnet Wk., Hat. 10 BP13
Lark Ri.
Linnet Way, Grays 70 CX42
Linnett Clo. E4 39 CF28
Linnington Ave., Chesh. 16 AQ18
Linom Rd. SW4 66 BX45
Linscott Rd. E5 48 CC35
Linsdell Rd., Bark. 58 CM37
Linsey Clo., Hem.H. 8 AZ15
Linsey St. SE16 67 CB42
Linslade Clo., Houns. 74 BE46
Heathlands Way
Linslade Clo., Pnr. 44 BC31
Linslade Rd., Orp. 98 CC
Linstead Ct. SE9 78 CN
Linstead St. NW6 56 BS
Linstead Way SW18 75 BR
Linster Gro., Borwd. 28 BN
Lintaine Clo. W6 65 BR
Moylan Rd.
Linthorpe Ave., Wem. 54 BK
Linthorpe Rd. N16 48 CA
Linthorpe Rd., Barn. 29 BU
Linton Ave., Borwd. 28 BL
Linton Clo., Well. 69 CO
Anthony Rd.
Linton Ct., Rom. 41 CT
Rise Pk. Par.
Linton Ct., Stai. 73 AX
High St.
Linton Gdns. E6 58 CK
Linton Glade, Croy. 96 CD
Linton Gro. SE27 77 BZ
Linton Rd., Bark. 58 CM
Linton St. N1 57 BZ
Lintons La., Epsom 94 BO
Lintott Ct., Stai. 73 AX
Stanwell Clo.
Linver Rd. SW6 66 BS
Linwood, Saw. 6 C
Linwood Clo. E6 58 CK
Northumberland Rd.
Linwood Way SE15 67 CA
Linx Hill, Lthd. 110 BB
Linzee Rd. N8 47 BX
Lion Ave., Twick. 74 BH
Lion Clo. SE4 77 CE
Lion Clo., Shep. 83 AY
Lion Ct., Borwd. 28 BN
Lion Gate Gdns., Rich. 65 BL
Lion Grn. Rd., Couls. 104 BW
Lion Rd. E6 58 CK
Lion Rd. N9 39 CB
Lion Rd., Bexh. 69 CQ
Lion Rd., Croy. 87 BZ
Lion Rd., Twick. 74 BH
Lion Way, Brent. 64 BK
Lion Wf. Rd., Islw. 64 BJ
Lionel Gdns. SE9 78 CJ
Lionel Ms. W10 55 BR
Telford Rd.
Lionel Oxley Ho., Grays 71 DD
New Rd.
Lionel Rd. SE9 78 CJ
Lionel Rd., Brent. 65 BL
Lions Clo. SE9 78 CJ
Liphook Clo., Horn. 50 CT
Petworth Way
Liphook Cres. SE23 77 CC
Liphook Rd., Wat. 36 BD
Lippitts Hill, Loug. 31 CG
Lipsham Clo., Bans. 95 BT
Lipton Clo. SE28 59 CP
Lipton Rd. E1 57 CC
Lisbon Ave., Twick. 74 BG
Lisburne Rd. NW3 47 BU
Lisford St. SE15 67 CA
Lisgar Ter. W14 65 BR
Liskeard Clo., Chis. 78 CM
Liskeard Ct., Cat. 114 CB
Liskeard Gdns. SE3 68 CH
Lisle Pl., Grays 71 DD
Lisle St. WC2 1 P
Lisle St. WC2 56 BW
Lismore, Hem.H. 8 BA
Lismore Circ. NW5 47 BV
Lismore Clo., Islw. 64 BJ4
Lismore Rd. N17 48 BZ
Lismore Rd., S.Croy. 96 CA
Lismore Wk. N1 57 BZ
Marquess Est.
Liss Way SE15 67 CA
Hordle Prom. S.
Lissenden Gdns. NW5 47 BV3
Lissoms Rd., Couls. 104 BV6
Lisson Grn. Est. NW8 1 C
Lisson Grn. Est. NW8 56 BT
Lisson Gro. NW1 1 D
Lisson Gro. NW1 56 BT
Lisson Gro. NW8 1 B
Lisson St. NW1 1 C
Lisson St. NW1 56 BU
Lister Clo. W3 55 BN
Jenner Ave.
Lister Clo., Mitch. 86 BU5
Longfield Dr.
Lister Ct. N16 48 CA3
Lister Gdns. N18 39 BZ2
Lister Ms. N7 47 BX3
Lister Rd. E11 49 CG3
Lister Rd., Til. 71 DG4
Lister St. E13 58 CH3
Sewell St.
Lister Wk. SE28 59 CP4
Haldane Rd.
Liston Rd. N17 39 CB3
Liston Rd. SW4 66 BW4
Liston Way, Wdf.Grn. 40 CJ2
Listowel Rd., Dag. 50 CR3
Listria Pk. N16 48 CA3
Litcham Spur, Slou. 52 AO3
Litchfield Ave. E15 58 CG3
Litchfield Ave., Mord. 85 BR5
Litchfield Gdns. NW10 55 BP3
Litchfield Rd., Sutt. 95 BT5
Litchfield St. WC2 1 P1
Litchfield St. WC2 56 BW4
Litchfield Way NW11 47 BS3
Litchfield Way, Guil. 118 AP7
Lithgows Rd., Felt. 63 BB4
Lithos Rd. NW3 56 BS3
Litlington St. SE16 67 CB4
Little Acre, Beck. 87 CE5
Little Acre, St.Alb. 9 BG1
Little Albany St. NW1 1 K
Little Albany St. NW1 56 BV3
Little Argyll St. W1 1 L

tle Argyll St. W1 — 56 BW39
argyll St.
le Aston Rd., Rom. — 42 CW30
le Belhus Clo., S.Ock. — 60 DA38
le Birch Clo., Wey. — 92 AX56
le Birches, Sid. — 78 CN48
le Boltons, The SW10 — 66 BS42
le Bookham St., Lthd. — 111 BE66
le Bornes SE21 — 77 CA49
le Borough, Bet. — 120 BM71
le Brays, Harl. — 14 CO11
le Bri. Rd., Berk. — 7 AR13
tle Britain EC1 — 2 G7
tle Britain EC1 — 56 BY39
le Brownings SE23 — 77 CB48
le Buntings, Wind. — 61 AM45
le Burrow, Welw.G.C. — 5 BQ9
le Bury St. N9 — 39 BZ26
le Bushey La., Bush. — 27 BF23
le Cattins, Harl. — 13 CK13
le Cedars N12 — 38 BT28
Woodside Ave.
tle Chester St. SW1 — 3 J6
tle Chester St. SW1 — 66 BV41
Wilton Ms.
tle College La. EC4 — 57 BZ40
College St.
tle College St. SW1 — 3 Q6
tle College St. SW1 — 66 BX41
tle Common La., Red. — 121 BY69
tle Ct., W.Wick. — 88 CG55
tle Ct. Rd., Sev. — 107 CU65
tle Cranmore La., Lthd. — 110 AZ67
tle Deans Yd. SW1 — 3 Q6
tle Dell, Welw.G.C. — 5 BQ7
tle Dimocks SW12 — 76 BV48
tle Dorrit Ct. SW1 — 4 J4
tle Dorrit Ct. SE1 — 67 BZ41
tle Ealing La. W5 — 64 BK42
tle Edward St. NW1 — 1 K2
tle Edward St. NW1 — 56 BV38
Redhill St.
tle Elms, Hayes — 63 BA43
tle Essex St. WC2 — 2 D10
tle Ferry Rd., Twick. — 74 BJ47
Ferry Rd.
tle Friday Hill E4 — 40 CG27
tle Friday Rd. E4 — 40 CG27
tle Ganett, Welw.G.C. — 5 BS9
tle Gaynes Gdns., Upmin. — 51 CX35
tle Gaynes La., Upmin. — 51 CX35
tle Gearies, Ilf. — 49 CL31
tle George St. SW1 — 3 Q5
tle George St. SW1 — 66 BX41
Great George St.
tle Gerpins La., Upmin. — 60 CV36
tle Graylings, Abb.L. — 17 BB20
tle Grn., Rich. — 64 BK45
tle Grn., Rick. — 26 AZ24
tle Grn. La., Cher. — 82 AV55
tle Grn. La., Rick. — 26 AZ24
tle Grn. St. NW5 — 47 BV35
College La.
tle Gregories La., Epp. — 31 CM21
tle Gro., Bush. — 27 BF24
tle Gro. Fld., Harl. — 13 CM11
tle Halliards, Walt. — 83 BC53
Felix La.
tle Hardings, Welw.G.C. — 5 BT7
tle Hayes, Kings L. — 17 AZ18
High St.
tle Heath SE7 — 68 CK43
tle Heath, Rom. — 50 CO31
tle Heath La., Berk. — 7 AT14
tle Heath Rd., Bexh. — 69 CQ44
tle Heath Rd., Wok. — 91 AP58
tle Hide, Guil. — 118 AT69
tle Hill, Rick. — 25 AU25
tle Holt E11 — 49 CH32
tle How Cft., Abb.L. — 17 BA19
tle Ilford La. E12 — 49 CK35
tle John Rd. W7 — 54 BH39
tle Julian Hill, Sev. — 116 CU67
tle Lake, Welw.G.C. — 5 BS9
tle Laver Rd., Ong. — 15 CW11
tle Ley, Welw.G.C. — 5 BR9
tle Marlborough St. W1 — 1 L9
tle Marlborough St. W1 — 56 BW39
Kingly St.
tle Martins, Bush. — 27 BF25
tle Mead, Hat. — 10 BP11
tle Moss La., Pnr. — 36 BE30
ttle New St. EC4 — 2 E8
tle New St. EC4 — 56 BY39
ttle Newport St. WC2 — 1 P10
tle Newport St. WC2 — 56 BW40
Charing Cross Rd.
tle Orchard, Wey. — 91 AV59
tle Orchard Clo., Pnr. — 36 BE30
tle Orchard, Wok. — 91 AT60
tle Oxhey La., Wat. — 36 BE28
tle Pk., Hem.H. — 16 AT17
tle Pk. Dr., Felt. — 74 BD48
tle Pk. Gdns., Enf. — 30 BZ24
tle Pastures, Brwd. — 42 CZ28
River Rd.
tle Pipers Clo., Chsnt. — 21 BZ18
tle Platt, Guil. — 118 AU57
tle Plucketts Way, Buck.H. — 40 CJ26
tle Port Spur, Slou. — 52 AP39
ttle Portland St. W1 — 1 K8
tle Portland St. W1 — 56 BW39
tle Potters, Bush. — 36 BG26
tle Pynchons, Harl. — 13 CN12
tle Queen St., Dart. — 80 CW47
tle Queens Rd., Tedd. — 74 BH50
tle Redlands, Brom. — 88 CK51
tle Reeves Ave., Amer. — 25 AP23

Little Ridge, Welw.G.C. — 5 BS8
Little Rivers, Welw.G.C. — 5 BS7
Little Rd., Hayes — 63 BB41
Little Rd., Hem.H. — 8 AY13
Little Rogues La. SE16 — 67 CC41
Lower Rd.
Little Roke Ave., Ken. — 95 BY60
Little Roke Rd., Ken. — 96 BZ60
Little Russell St. WC1 — 1 Q7
Little Russell St. WC1 — 56 BX39
Little St. James's St. SW1 — 3 L3
Little St. Leonards SW14 — 65 BN45
Little Sanctuary SW1 — 66 BX41
Broad Sanctuary
Little Smith St. SW1 — 3 P6
Little Smith St. SW1 — 66 BW41
Great Smith St.
Little Somerset St. E1 — 2 P9
Little Somerset St. E1 — 57 CA39
Little St. James's St. SW1 — 56 BW40
Little Stream Clo., Nthwd. — 35 BB28
Eastbury Ave.
Little St., Guil. — 109 AQ68
Little Sutton La., Slou. — 62 AU42
Little Thistle, Welw.G.C. — 5 BT9
Little Thrift, Orp. — 88 CM52
Little Titchfield St. W1 — 1 L7
Little Titchfield St. W1 — 56 BW39
Great Titchfield St.
Little Trinity La. EC4 — 2 J10
Little Trinity La. EC4 — 57 BZ40
Queen Victoria St.
Little Turnstile WC1 — 2 B7
Little Turnstile WC1 — 56 BX39
High Holborn
Little Wade, Welw.G.C. — 5 BR9
Little Warley Hall La., Borwd. — 123 DC30
Little Warren Clo., Guil. — 118 AT71
Little Windmill Hill, Kings L. — 16 AV19
Little Woodcote La., Cars. — 95 BV59
Little Youngs, Welw.G.C. — 5 BQ8
Littlebrook Clo., Croy. — 87 CC53
Littlebrook Gdns., Chsnt. — 21 CC18
Littlebrook Manor Way, Dart. — 80 CX46
Littlebury Ct., Borwd. — 33 CZ22
Kelvedon Grn.
Littlebury Rd. SW4 — 66 BW45
Littlecombe SE7 — 68 CH43
Littlecombe Clo. SW15 — 75 BQ46
Lytton Gro.
Littlecote Clo. SW19 — 75 BR47
Littlecote Pl., Pnr. — 36 BE30
Littlecroft SE9 — 68 CL45
Littlecroft, Grav. — 81 DF50
Littlecroft Rd., Egh. — 72 AS49
Littledale SE2 — 69 CO43
Littledown Rd., Slou. — 52 AP40
Junction Rd.
Littlefield Clo. N19 — 47 BW35
Littlefield Clo., Guil. — 109 AO68
Littlefield Ct., West Dr. — 63 AX43
Littlefield Rd., Edg. — 37 BN29
Littlefield Way, Guil. — 109 AO68
Littlegrove, Barn. — 29 BU25
Littleheath La., Cob. — 93 BF60
Littleheath Rd., S.Croy. — 96 CB58
Littlejohn Rd., Orp. — 69 CO53
Littlemead, Esher — 93 BG56
Littlemede SE9 — 78 CK48
Littlemoor Rd., Ilf. — 49 CM34
Littlemore Rd. SE2 — 69 CO41
Littlestone Clo., Beck. — 77 CE50
Abbey La.
Littleton Ave. E4 — 40 CG26
Valance Ave.
Littleton Cres., Har. — 45 BH34
Littleton Gdns., Ashf. — 73 BA50
Littleton La., Guil. — 118 AQ73
Littleton La., Reig. — 120 BQ71
Littleton La., Shep. — 83 AX54
Littleton Rd., Ashf. — 73 BA50
Littleton Rd., Har. — 45 BH34
Littleton St. SW18 — 76 BT48
Littlewick Rd., Wok. — 100 AP61
Littlewick Rd., Wok. — 91 AR60
Littlewood SE13 — 67 CF46
Littlewood Clo. W13 — 64 BJ41
Littlewood, Sev. — 108 CV64
Littleworth Ave., Esher — 93 BG56
Littleworth Common Rd., Esher — 84 BG55
Littleworth La., Esher — 93 BG56
Littleworth Pl., Esher — 93 BG56
Littleworth Rd., Esher — 93 BG56
Liverpool Gro. SE17 — 67 BZ42
Liverpool Rd. E10 — 48 CF32
Liverpool Rd. E16 — 58 CG38
Liverpool Rd. N1 — 56 BY36
Liverpool Rd. N7 — 47 BX35
Liverpool Rd. W5 — 64 BK41
Liverpool Rd., Kings.T. — 75 BM50
Liverpool Rd., St.Alb. — 9 BH13
Liverpool Rd., Th.Hth. — 87 BZ52
Liverpool Rd., Wat. — 26 BC25
Liverpool St. EC2 — 2 M7
Liverpool St. EC2 — 57 CA39
Livesey Pl. SE15 — 67 CB43
Peckham Pk. Rd.
Livingstone Clo., Ong. — 24 CX18
Livingstone Gdns., Grav. — 81 DH49
Livingstone Pl. E14 — 57 CF42
Ferry St.
Livingstone Rd. E15 — 57 CF37
Livingstone Rd. E17 — 48 CE32
Livingstone Rd. N13 — 38 BX29

Livingstone Rd. SW11 — 66 BT45
Winstanley Rd.
Livingstone Rd., Cat. — 105 BZ64
Livingstone Rd., Grav. — 81 DH49
Livingstone Rd., Houns. — 64 BG45
Livingstone Rd., Sthl. — 54 BD40
Livingstone Rd., Th.Hth. — 87 BZ51
Livingstone Ter., Rain. — 59 CT37
Livingstone Wk. SW11 — 66 BT45
Plough Rd.
Livingstone Wk., Hem.H. — 8 AY11
Livonia St. W1 — 1 M9
Livonia St. W1 — 56 BW39
Berwick St.
Lizard St. EC1 — 2 J3
Lizard St. EC1 — 57 BZ38
Lizban St. SE3 — 68 CH43
Llanbury Clo., Ger.Cr. — 34 AS29
Llanelly La. NW2 — 46 BR34
Llanelly Rd. NW2 — 46 BR34
Crewys Rd.
Llanover Rd. SE18 — 68 CL43
Llanover Rd., Wem. — 45 BK34
Llanthony Rd., Mord. — 86 BT53
Llanvanor Rd. NW2 — 46 BR34
Llewellyn St. SE16 — 67 CA41
Chambers St.
Lloyd Ave. SW16 — 86 BX51
Lloyd Ave., Couls. — 95 BV60
Lloyd Baker St. WC1 — 2 C3
Lloyd Baker St. WC1 — 56 BX38
Lloyd Ct., Pnr. — 45 BD32
Lloyd Pk. Ave., Croy. — 96 CA56
Lloyd Rd. E6 — 58 CK37
Lloyd Rd. E17 — 48 CC31
Lloyd Rd., Dag. — 59 CQ36
Lloyd Rd., Wor.Pk. — 85 BQ55
Lloyd Sq. WC1 — 2 D2
Lloyd Sq. WC1 — 56 BY38
Lloyd St. WC1 — 2 D2
Lloyd St. WC1 — 56 BY38
Lloyds Ave. EC3 — 2 N9
Lloyds Ave. EC3 — 57 CA39
Lloyds Pl. SE3 — 68 CG44
Lloyds Row EC1 — 2 F3
Lloyds Row EC1 — 56 BY38
Lloyds Way, Beck. — 87 CD53
Loampit Hill SE13 — 67 CE44
Loampit Vale SE13 — 67 CE45
Loanda Clo. E8 — 57 CA37
Clarissa St.
Loates La., Wat. — 27 BD24
Loats Rd. SW2 — 76 BX46
Lobelia Clo. E6 — 58 CK39
Sorrell Gdns.
Local Board Rd., Wat. — 27 BD25
Locarno Rd. W3 — 65 BO41
High St.
Locarno Rd., Grnf. — 54 BG38
Lochaber Rd. SE13 — 68 CG45
Lochaline St. W6 — 65 BQ43
Lochinvar Clo., Slou. — 61 AN41
Lochinvar St. SW12 — 76 BV47
Lochmere Clo., Erith — 69 CR43
Lochnagar St. E14 — 57 CF39
Lochnell Rd., Berk. — 7 AP12
Lock Chase SE3 — 68 CG45
Lock La., Wok. — 101 AW61
Lock Path, Wind. — 61 AL43
Lock Rd., Guil. — 118 AR69
Lock Rd., Rich. — 74 BK49
Locke Clo., Rain. — 59 CT36
Locke Gdns., Slou. — 62 AR41
Locke King Clo., Wey. — 92 AZ57
Locke King Rd., Wey. — 92 AZ57
Lockers Pk. La., Hem.H. — 8 AW13
Lockesfield Pl. E14 — 67 CE42
Lockesley Dr., Orp. — 88 CN53
Lockesley Sq., Surb. — 84 BK53
Locket Rd., Har. — 36 BH30
Lockets Clo., Wind. — 61 AL44
Lockfield Ave., Enf. — 30 CD23
Lockfield Dr., Wok. — 100 AP61
Lockhart Clo. N7 — 56 BX36
Lockhart Clo., Cob. — 93 BD60
Lockhart St. E3 — 57 CD38
Lockhurst St. E5 — 48 CC35
Lockie Pl. SE25 — 87 CB52
Lockier Wk., Wem. — 45 BK34
Hutchinson Ter.
Lockington Rd. SW8 — 66 BV44
Lockley Cres., Hat. — 10 BP11
Lockmead Rd. N15 — 48 CB32
Lockmead Rd. SE13 — 67 CF45
Locks La., Mitch. — 86 BU51
Locksley Est. E14 — 57 CD39
Locksley St. E14 — 57 CD39
Locksmeade Rd., Rich. — 74 BK49
Lockwood Clo. SE26 — 77 CC49
Mayow Rd.
Lockwood Path, Wok. — 91 AV60
Lockwood Rd., Ilf. — 49 CM34
Lockwood Sq. SE16 — 67 CB41
Southwark Pk. Rd.
Lockwood Wk., Rom. — 50 CT32
Lockwood Way E17 — 39 CC30
Lockwood Way, Chess. — 94 BM56
Lockyer Est. SE1 — 4 M4
Lockyer St., Grays — 70 CY43
Lockyer St. SE1 — 4 L5
Lockyer St. SE1 — 67 BZ41
Kipling St.
Locton Est. E3 — 57 CD37
Loddiges Rd. E9 — 57 CC36
Loddon Spur, Slou. — 52 AO39
Oatlands Dr.
Loder Clo., Wok. — 91 AU60
Loder St. SE15 — 67 CC43
Lodge Ave. SW14 — 65 BN45
South Worple Way
Lodge Ave., Borwd. — 28 BL25
Lodge Ave., Croy. — 86 BX55
Lodge Ave., Dag. — 59 CO37

Lodge Ave., Dart. — 80 CV46
Lodge Ave., Hartley — 46 BL31
Lodge Ave., Rom. — 50 CT32
Lodge Clo. N18 — 39 BZ28
Lodge Clo., Chig. — 41 CO27
Lodge Clo., Cob. — 102 BE61
Lodge Clo., Dor. — 119 BK73
Lodge Clo., Edg. — 37 BL29
Lodge Clo., Egh. — 72 AR49
Lodge Clo., Epsom — 94 BW58
Lodge Clo., Islw. — 65 BJ44
London Rd.
Lodge Clo., Lthd. — 102 BG64
Lodge Clo., Orp. — 89 CO54
Lodge Clo., Slou. — 61 AO41
Lodge Clo., Uxb. — 53 AX38
Lodge Ct., Horn. — 51 CW34
Lodge Cres., Orp. — 89 CO54
Lodge Cres., Wal.Abb. — 21 CC20
Lodge Dr. N13 — 38 BY28
Lodge Dr., Hat. — 10 BQ11
Lodge Dr., Rick. — 26 AX24
Lodge End, Rad. — 18 BJ20
Lodge Fld., Welw.G.C. — 5 BR6
Lodge Gdns., Beck. — 87 CD53
Lodge Hall, Harl. — 13 CN13
Lodge Hill, Ilf. — 49 CK31
Lodge Hill, Pur. — 104 BY61
Lodge Hill, Well. — 69 CO43
Lodge La. N12 — 38 BT28
Lodge La., Bex. — 79 CP46
Lodge La., Ch.St.G. — 25 AS23
Lodge La., Croy. — 96 CE57
Lodge La., Grays — 71 DD41
Lodge La., Rom. — 41 CR29
Lodge La., Wal.Abb. — 30 CF21
Lodge La., West. — 115 CM67
Aberdeen La.
Lodge Pl., Sutt. — 95 BS56
Lodge Rd. NW4 — 46 BQ31
Lodge Rd. NW8 — 1 B3
Lodge Rd. NW8 — 56 BT38
Lodge Rd., Brom. — 78 CH50
Lodge Rd., Croy. — 86 BY53
Lodge Rd., Epp. — 22 CL20
Lodge Rd., Lthd. — 102 BG64
Lodge Rd., Sutt. — 95 BS56
Throwley Way
Lodge Rd., Wall. — 95 BV56
Lodge Vill., Wdf.Grn. — 40 CG29
Lodge Way, Ashf. — 73 AY48
Lodge Way, Shep. — 83 BA51
Lodge Way, Wind. — 61 AM45
Lodgebottom Rd., Lthd. — 112 BL67
Lodgehill Pk. Clo., Har. — 45 BF34
Lodore Gdns. NW9 — 46 BN32
Lodore Grn., Uxb. — 44 AY34
Lodore St. E14 — 57 CF39
Loewen Rd., Grays — 71 DG41
Loftie St. SE16 — 67 CB41
Chambers St.
Lofting Rd. N1 — 56 BX36
Loftus Rd. W12 — 55 BP40
Logan Clo., Enf. — 30 CC23
Logan Clo., Houns. — 64 BE45
Logan Ms. W8 — 66 BS42
Logan Pl. W8 — 66 BS42
Logan Rd. N9 — 39 CB27
Logan Rd., Wem. — 45 BK34
Loggetts, The SE21 — 77 CA48
Alleyn Pk.
Logmore La., Dor. — 119 BF72
Logs Hill, Chis. — 88 CK51
Logs Hill Clo., Chis. — 88 CK51
Lois Dr., Shep. — 83 BA53
Lolesworth Clo. E1 — 2 Q7
Lolesworth Clo. E1 — 57 CA39
Commercial Rd.
Lollard St. SE11 — 4 C8
Lollard St. SE11 — 66 BX42
Lollards Clo., Lthd. — 110 BA66
Loman Path, S.Ock. — 60 CZ39
Loman St. SE1 — 4 G4
Loman St. SE1 — 66 BY41
Lomas Clo., Croy. — 96 CF57
Lomas St. E1 — 57 CB39
Lombard Ave., Enf. — 30 CC23
Lombard Ave., Ilf. — 49 CN33
Lombard Ct. EC3 — 2 L10
Lombard Ct. EC3 — 57 BZ40
Gracechurch St.
Lombard La. EC4 — 2 E9
Lombard La. EC4 — 56 BY39
Lombard Rd. N11 — 38 BW28
Lombard Rd. SW11 — 66 BT44
Lombard Rd. SW19 — 86 BS51
Lombard St. EC3 — 2 L9
Lombard St. EC3 — 57 BZ39
Lombard Wall SE7 — 68 CH41
Lombards, The, Horn. — 51 CW33
Lombards Chase, Brwd. — 123 DE32
Station La.
Lombardy Clo., Hem.H. — 8 BA14
Lombardy Clo., Wok. — 100 AP62
Nethercote Ave.
Lombardy Dr., Berk. — 7 AR13
Lombardy Pl. W2 — 56 BS40
Bark Pl.
Lombardy Way, Borwd. — 28 BL23
Lomond Clo. N15 — 48 CA31
Lomond Clo., Wem. — 55 BL36
Lomond Gdns., S.Croy. — 96 CD57
Lomond Gro. SE5 — 67 BZ43
Lomond Rd., Hem.H. — 8 AX11
Loncin Mead Ave., Wey. — 92 AX58
Londesborough Rd. N16 — 48 CA35
London Bri. EC4 — 4 L2
London Bri. EC4 — 57 BZ40
London Bri. SE1 — 4 L2
London Bri. St. SE1 — 4 L3
London Bri. St. SE1 — 57 BZ40

London Bri. Wk. SE1 — 57 BZ40
Tooley St.
London Colney By-pass, St.Alb. — 19 BL16
London Flds. E8 — 57 CB37
London Flds. E. Side E8 — 57 CB36
London Flds. W. Side E8 — 57 CB36
London La. E8 — 57 CB36
London La., Brom. — 78 CG50
London La., Lthd. — 110 BC68
London La., Uxb. — 53 AZ38
London Ms. W2 — 1 B9
London Ms. W2 — 56 BT39
London St.
London Rd. E13 — 58 CH37
London Rd. SE1 — 4 F6
London Rd. SE1 — 66 BY41
London Rd. SE23 — 77 CB47
London Rd. SW16 — 86 BX51
London Rd. SW17 — 86 BU53
London Rd., Ashf. — 73 AW49
London Rd., Bark. — 58 CL36
London Rd., Berk. — 7 AS13
London Rd., Brwd. — 42 CZ28
London Rd., Brom. — 78 CG50
London Rd., Bush. — 27 BE25
London Rd., Cat. — 105 BZ65
London Rd., Ch.St.G. — 34 AR27
London Rd., Croy. — 86 BY52
London Rd., Croy. — 86 BX51
London Rd., Dart. — 80 CX47
London Rd., Dart. — 79 CS46
London Rd., Dor. — 119 BJ71
London Rd., Enf. — 30 BZ25
London Rd., Epsom — 94 BP58
London Rd., Felt. — 73 AW49
London Rd., Grav. — 81 DE46
London Rd., Grays — 70 DB42
London Rd., Green. — 80 DB46
London Rd., Guil. — 118 AS71
London Rd., Harl. — 6 CP9
London Rd., Harl. — 14 CP11
London Rd., Harl. — 14 CP14
London Rd., Har. — 45 BH34
London Rd., Hem.H. — 8 AX15
London Rd., Houns. — 64 BG45
London Rd., Islw. — 64 BH44
London Rd., Kings.T. — 85 BL51
London Rd., Mitch. — 86 BU53
London Rd., Mitch. — 86 BV53
London Rd., Mord. — 86 BS53
London Rd., Ong. — 24 CV20
London Rd., Purfleet — 70 CX42
London Rd., Rad. — 12 BL20
London Rd., Red. — 121 BU70
London Rd., Reig. — 121 BS70
London Rd., Rick. — 35 AY27
London Rd., Rom. — 50 CR22
London Rd., Rom. — 32 CS23
London Rd., St.Alb. — 9 BH14
London Rd., Saw. — 6 CP6
London Rd., Sev. — 98 CO58
London Rd., Sev. — 99 CR59
London Rd., Sev. — 107 CS62
London Rd., Sev. — 116 CU66
London Rd., Sev. — 99 CY56
London Rd., Sev. — 117 CW70
London Rd., Slou. — 62 AQ43
London Rd., Slou. — 62 AR41
London Rd., Stai. — 73 AW49
London Rd., Stan. — 36 BK28
London Rd., Sutt. — 85 BQ55
London Rd., Swan. — 89 CS51
London Rd., Swan. — 89 CU52
London Rd., Swans. — 81 DC46
London Rd., Th.Hth. — 86 BX51
London Rd., Til. — 71 DG44
London Rd., Ton. — 117 CW70
London Rd., Twick. — 74 BJ47
London Rd., Vir.W. — 82 AQ51
London Rd., Wall. — 86 BV55
London Rd., Welw. — 5 BQ5
London Rd., Wem. — 55 BL35
London Rd., West. — 115 CM66
London Rd., Wok. — 109 AU67
London Rd. E., Amer. — 25 AP24
London Rd. N., Red. — 113 BW67
London Rd. S., Red. — 113 BV68
London Rd. W., Amer. — 25 AO23
London Stile W4 — 65 BM42
Wellesley Rd.
London St. EC3 — 2 N10
London St. EC3 — 57 CA39
London St. W2 — 1 A8
London St. W2 — 56 BT39
London St., Cher. — 83 AW54
London Tilbury Rd., Rain. — 60 CV38
London Wall EC2 — 2 J7
London Wall EC2 — 57 BZ39
Londons Clo., Upmin. — 51 CY35
Londrina Ter., Berk. — 7 AR13
Lonesome La., Reig. — 121 BS72
Lonfield, Saw. — 6 CP9
Brook Rd.
Long Acre WC2 — 1 Q10
Long Acre WC2 — 56 BX40
Long Acre, Hem.H. — 16 AT18
Long Acre, Orp. — 89 CP55
Long Arrotts, Hem.H. — 8 AU12
Long Banks, Harl. — 13 CM12
Long Barn Clo., Wat. — 17 BC19
Long Barn La., Sev. — 116 CU70
Long Chaulden, Hem.H. — 7 AV13
Long Copse Clo., Lthd. — 102 BF65
Long Ct. WC2 — 3 P1
Long Ct., Grays — 70 CX42
Long Cft., Wat. — 35 BC26
Long Cft. Rd., Rick. — 34 AU18
Long Deacon Rd. E4 — 40 CG26
Long Dr. W3 — 55 BO39
Long Dr., Grnf. — 54 BF37

Long Dr., Ruis. 45 BD35
Long Dyke, Guil. 118 AT69
Long Elmes, Har. 36 BF30
Long Elms, Abb.L. 17 BA20
Long Elms Clo., Abb.L. 17 BA20
Long Elms
Long Fallow, St.Alb. 18 BF17
Long Fld. NW9 37 BO30
Long Grn., Chig. 40 CN28
Long Gro., Beac. 34 AO29
Long Gro. Rd., Epsom 94 BM58
Long Hill, Cat. 105 CC64
Long John, Hem.H. 8 AY14
Long La. EC1 2 G6
Long La. EC1 56 BY39
Long La. N2 38 BT30
Long La. N3 38 BS30
Long La. SE1 4 K5
Long La. SE1 67 BZ41
Long La., Bexh. 69 CP43
Long La., Croy. 87 CB53
Long La., Grays 71 DD41
Long La., Hem.H. 16 AS19
Long La., Rick. 25 AU25
Long La., Rick. 34 AV27
Long La., Stai. 73 AY48
Long La., Uxb. 44 AZ35
Long Ley, Harl. 14 CO11
Long Ley, Welw.G.C. 5 BT8
Long Leys E4 39 CE29
Long Lo. Dr., Walt. 84 BD55
Long Mark Rd. E16 58 CJ39
Long Mead NW9 37 BO30
Long Mead, Hat. 10 BP11
Long Meadow NW5 47 BW35
Long Meadow, Brwd. 122 DE27
Long Meadow, Lthd. 111 BE66
Long Moor, Wal.Cr. 21 CD18
Long Pk., Amer. 25 AO21
Long Pond Rd. SE3 68 CG44
Long Reach, Wok. 101 AZ65
Long Reach Rd., Bark. 58 CN38
Long Ride, The, Hat. 10 BR11
Long Ridings Ave., Brwd. 122 DD25
Long Rd. SW4 66 BV45
Long Shaw, Lthd. 102 BJ63
Long Spring, St.Alb. 9 BH11
Long St. E2 2 P2
Long St. E2 57 CA38
Long St., Wal.Abb. 22 CK19
Long Vw., Berk. 7 AQ12
Long Wk. SE1 4 N6
Long Wk. SE1 67 CA41
Long Wk. SE18 68 CL43
Long Wk. SW13 65 BO44
The Ter.
Long Wk., Ch.St.G. 25 AR24
Long Wk., Epsom 103 BQ63
Long Wk., Grav. 81 DF51
Long Wk., Guil. 110 AY68
Long Wk., N.Mal. 85 BN52
Long Wk., Wal.Abb. 21 CE18
Long Wk., The, Wind. 72 AO47
Long Wall E15 57 CF38
Long Wd. Dr., Beac. 34 AP29
Long Yd. WC1 2 B5
Long Yd. WC1 56 BX38
Longacre Pl., Cars. 95 BV57
Longacre Rd. E17 39 CF30
Longacres, St.Alb. 9 BK13
Longaford Way, Brwd. 122 DE26
Longbeach Rd. SW11 66 BU45
Longberrys NW2 46 BR34
Longbottom La., Beac. 34 AO29
Longbourne Way, Cher. 82 AV53
Longboyds, Cob. 101 BC61
Longbridge Rd., Bark. 58 CM36
Longbridge Way SE13 77 CF46
Longbridge Way, Uxb. 53 AW37
Longbury Clo., Orp. 89 CO52
Longbury Dr., Orp. 89 CO52
Longcliffe Path, Wat. 35 BC27
Gosforth La.
Longcroft SE9 78 CK48
Longcroft Ave., Bans. 95 BT60
Longcroft Dr., Wal.Cr. 21 CD20
Longcroft Grn., Welw.G.C. 5 BQ9
Stanborough La.
Longcroft La., Hem.H. 16 AU17
Longcroft La., Welw.G.C. 5 BQ8
Longcroft Ri., Loug. 31 CL25
Longcroft Rd. SE5 67 CA43
Longcrofte Rd., Edg. 36 BK29
Longcrofts, Wal.Abb. 22 CG20
Roundhills
Longcross Rd., Cher. 82 AP55
Longdean Pk., Hem.H. 17 AZ16
Longdon Wd., Kes. 97 CK56
Longdown La. N., Epsom 94 BP60
Longdown La. S., Epsom 103 BP61
Longdown Rd. SE6 77 CE49
Longdown Rd., Epsom 94 BP60
Longdown Rd., Guil. 118 AT72
Longfellow Dr., Brwd. 122 DE26
Longfellow Rd. E17 48 CD32
Longfellow Rd., Wor.Pk. 85 BP54
Longfellow Way SE1 4 Q9
Longfield, Brom. 88 CG51
Longfield, Harl. 14 CO12
Longfield, Hem.H. 8 AZ14
Longfield, Loug. 31 CJ25
Longfield, Slou. 43 AO34
Longfield Ave. E17 48 CD31
Longfield Ave. NW7 37 BP29
Longfield Ave. W5 54 BK40
Longfield Ave., Enf. 30 CC22
Longfield Ave., Horn. 50 CT33
Longfield Ave., Wall. 86 BV54
Longfield Ave., Wem. 46 BL33
Longfield Cres. SE26 77 CC48
Longfield Cres., Tad. 103 BQ63
Longfield Dr. SW14 75 BM46
Longfield Dr., Mitch. 86 BU51
Longfield Est. SE1 4 Q9
Longfield Est. SE1 67 CA42
Longfield La., Chsnt. 21 CB17
Longfield Rd. W5 54 BK40
Longfield Rd., Dor. 119 BH72
Longfield St. SW18 76 BS47
Longfield Wk. W5 54 BK39
Longfields, Ong. 24 CX18
Longford Ave., Felt. 73 BB46
Longford Ave., Sthl. 54 BF40
Longford Ave., Stai. 73 AY47
Longford Clo., Hmptn. 74 BF49
Longford Clo., Hayes 54 BD40
Longford Ct. E5 48 CC35
Clapton Pk. Est.
Longford Ct., Epsom 94 BN56
Watersedge
Longford Gdns., Hayes 54 BD40
Longford Gdns., Sutt. 86 BT55
Longford Rd., Twick. 74 BF47
Longford St. NW1 1 K4
Longford St. NW1 56 BV38
Longford Way, Stai. 73 AY47
Longhayes Ave., Rom. 50 CP31
Longheath Gdns., Croy. 87 CC53
Longhedge St. SW11 66 BV44
Rowditch La.
Longhill Rd. SE6 77 CF48
Longhook Gdns., Nthlt. 53 BC38
Longhouse Rd., Grays 71 DG41
Longhurst Rd. SE13 77 CF46
Longhurst Rd., Croy. 87 CB53
Longhurst Rd., Lthd. 110 BB68
Longland Dr. N20 38 BS27
Longlands, Hem.H. 8 AY13
Longlands Ave., Couls. 95 BV60
Longlands Clo., Chsnt. 21 CC19
Longlands Ct. W11 55 BR40
Westbourne Gro.
Longlands Pk. Cres., Sid. 78 CN48
Longlands Rd., Sid. 78 CN48
Longlands Rd., Welw.G.C. 5 BR8
Longleat Ms., Orp. 89 CP52
Star La.
Longleat Rd., Enf. 30 CA25
Longleat Way, Felt. 73 BA47
Longlees, Rick. 34 AU28
Long Cft. Rd.
Longleigh Ho. SE5 67 CA44
Glebe Est.
Longleigh La. SE2 69 CP43
Longley Ave., Wem. 55 BL37
Longley Rd. SW17 76 BU50
Longley Rd., Croy. 86 BY54
Longley Rd., Har. 45 BG32
Longley St. SE1 67 CB42
Longley Way NW2 46 BQ34
Longmarsh Vw., S.at H. 90 CX51
Longmead, Chis. 88 CL51
Longmead, Guil. 118 AU70
Longmead, Wind. 61 AM44
Longmead Clo., Brwd. 122 DC26
Longmead Clo., Cat. 105 CA64
Longmead Dr., Sid. 79 CP48
Longmead Rd. SW17 76 BU49
Longmead Rd., Epsom 94 BN59
Longmead Rd., Hayes 53 BB40
Longmead Rd., T.Ditt. 84 BH54
Longmeadow Rd., Sid. 78 CN47
Longmere Gdns., Tad. 103 BQ63
Longmoor, Chsnt. 21 CD18
Longmoore St. SW1 3 L9
Longmoore St. SW1 66 BW42
Longmore Ave., Barn. 29 BT25
Longmore Clo., Rick. 34 AV28
Longmore Gdns., Welw.G.C. 5 BR8
Longmore Rd., Walt. 93 BE56
Longnor Rd. E1 57 CC38
Longport Clo., Ilf. 41 CO29
Longreach Rd., Erith 69 CU43
Longridge Gro., Wok. 91 AV60
Woking Rd.
Longridge La., Sthl. 54 BF40
Longridge Rd. SW5 66 BS42
Longs Clo., Wok. 101 AW61
Longshaw Rd. E4 39 CF27
Longshore SE8 67 CD42
Longside Clo., Egh. 82 AU51
Longspring, Wat. 26 BC22
Longstaff Cres. SW18 76 BS46
Longstaff Rd. SW18 76 BS46
Longstone Ave. NW10 55 BO36
Longstone Rd. SW17 76 BV49
Longstone Rd., Iver 52 AU37
Longthornton Rd. SW16 86 BW51
Longton Ave. SE26 77 CB49
Longton Gro. SE26 77 CB49
Longtown Clo., Rom. 42 CV28
Longtown Rd., Rom. 42 CV28
Longview Way, Rom. 41 CS30
Longville Rd. SE11 4 G8
Longville Rd. SE11 66 BY42
Longwalk Rd., West Dr. 53 AZ40
Longways, Stai. 82 AV51
Longwood Clo., Upmin. 51 CY35
Longwood Dr. SW15 75 BP46
Longwood Gdns., Ilf. 49 CK31
Longwood La., Amer. 25 AO23
Longwood Rd., Ken. 105 BZ61
Longworth Clo. SE28 59 CP39
Loning, The NW9 46 BO31
Loning, The, Enf. 30 CC22
Lonsdale, Hem.H. 8 AY12
Lonsdale Ave. E6 58 CJ38
Lonsdale Ave., Brwd. 122 DE25
Lonsdale Ave., Rom. 50 CS32
Lonsdale Ave., Wem. 46 BL35
Lonsdale Clo. E6 58 CK38
Lonsdale Clo. SE9 78 CJ49
Lonsdale Clo., Edg. 37 BL28
Lonsdale Clo., Pnr. 36 BE29
Lonsdale Clo., Uxb. 53 BA39
Lonsdale Cres., Dart. 80 CY47
Lonsdale Cres., Ilf. 49 CL32
Lonsdale Dr., Enf. 29 BW24
Lonsdale Dr. N., Enf. 29 BX25
Lonsdale Gdns., Th.Hth. 86 BX52
Lonsdale Ms. W11 55 BR39
Lonsdale Rd.
Lonsdale Ms., Rich. 65 BL44
Lonsdale Pl. N1 56 BY36
Lonsdale Rd. E11 49 CG33
Lonsdale Rd. NW6 55 BR37
Lonsdale Rd. SE25 87 CB52
Lonsdale Rd. SW13 65 BO44
Lonsdale Rd. W4 65 BO42
Lonsdale Rd. W11 55 BR39
Lonsdale Rd., Bexh. 69 CQ44
Lonsdale Rd., Dor. 119 BJ71
Lonsdale Rd., Sthl. 64 BD41
Lonsdale Rd., Wey. 92 AZ57
Lonsdale Sq. N1 56 BY36
Lonsdale Way, Maid. 61 AH42
Springfield Pk.
Loobert Rd. N15 48 CA31
Looe Gdns., Ilf. 49 CL31
Loom La., Rad. 27 BH22
Loom Pl., Rad. 27 BJ21
Loop Rd., Chis. 78 CL50
Loop Rd., Epsom 103 BN61
Loop Rd., Wal.Abb. 21 CE19
Loop Rd., Wok. 100 AS64
Lopen Rd. N18 39 CA28
Loraine Clo., Enf. 30 CC25
Loraine Gdns., Ash. 103 BL62
Loraine Rd. N7 47 BX35
Loraine Rd. W4 65 BM43
Lord Ave., Ilf. 49 CK31
Lord Chancellor Wk., Kings.T. 85 BN51
Lord Gdns., Ilf. 49 CK31
Lord Hills Bri. W2 56 BS39
Lord Hills Rd. W2 56 BS39
Lord Holland La. SW9 66 BY44
Myatts Flds. Dev.
Lord Knyvett Clo., Stai. 73 AX46
Lord Napier Pl. W6 65 BP42
Upper Mall
Lord N. St. SW1 3 Q7
Lord N. St. SW1 66 BX41
Lord Roberts Ms. SW6 66 BS43
Moore Pk. Rd.
Lord Roberts Ter. SE18 68 CL42
Lord St. E16 58 CK40
Lord St., Grav. 81 DG47
Lord St., Hodd. 12 CB12
Lord St., Wat. 27 BD24
Loates La.
Lord Warwick St. SE18 68 CK41
Lorden Wk. E2 57 CB38
Lords Clo. SE21 77 BZ47
Lords Clo., Felt. 74 BE48
Lords Vw. NW8 1 C3
Lords Wd., Welw.G.C. 5 BT8
Lordsbury Fld., Wall. 95 BW58
Lordship Clo., Brwd. 122 DE26
Lordship Gro. N16 48 BZ34
Lordship La. N17 39 BZ30
Lordship La. N22 38 BY30
Lordship La. SE22 77 CA46
Lordship Pk. N16 48 BZ34
Lordship Pl. SW3 66 BU43
Cheyne Row
Lordship Rd. N16 48 BZ33
Lordship Rd., Chsnt. 21 CB18
Lordship Rd., Nthlt. 54 BE36
Lordship Ter. N16 48 BZ34
Lordsmead Rd. N17 39 CA30
Lordswood Clo., Dart. 80 CZ49
Coombfield Dr.
Lorenzo St. WC1 2 B1
Lorenzo St. WC1 56 BX38
Loretto Gdns., Har. 46 BL31
Lorian Clo. N12 38 BS28
Guildown Ave.
Lorian Dr., Reig. 121 BT70
Loring Rd. N20 38 BU27
Loring Rd., Berk. 7 AR13
Loring Rd., Islw. 64 BH44
Loring Rd., Wind. 61 AM44
Loris Rd. W6 65 BQ41
Lorn Rd. SW9 66 BX44
Lorne, The, Lthd. 111 BF66
Lorne Ave., Croy. 87 CC54
Lorne Clo. NW8 1 D3
Lorne Clo. NW8 56 BU38
Park Rd.
Lorne Clo., Slou. 61 AN41
Lorne Gdns. E11 49 CJ31
Lorne Gdns. W11 65 BQ41
Lorne Gdns. W14 46 BQ32
Lorne Gdns., Croy. 87 CC54
Lorne Rd. E7 49 CH35
Lorne Rd. E17 48 CE32
Lorne Rd. N4 47 BX33
Lorne Rd., Brwd. 42 DB28
Lorne Rd., Har. 36 BH30
Lorne Rd., Rich. 75 BL46
Albert Rd.
Lorraine Clo., Grays 70 CX41
Lorraine Pk., Har. 36 BH29
Lorrimore Rd. SE17 66 BY43
Lorrimore Sq. SE17 66 BY43
Lorton Clo., Grav. 81 DJ48
Losberne Way SE16 67 CB42
Bonamy Est. W.
Loseberry Rd., Esher 93 BG56
Losfield Rd., Wind. 61 AM44
Lossie Dr., Iver 52 AU40
Lothair Rd. W5 64 BK41
Lothair Rd. N. N4 47 BY32
Lothair Rd. S. N4 47 BY33
Lothbury EC2 2 K8
Lothbury EC2 57 BZ39
Lothian Ave., Hayes 53 BC39
Lothian Clo., Wem. 45 BJ35
St. Andrews Clo.
Lothian Ms. SW9 66 BY44
Lothian Rd.
Lothian Rd. SW9 66 BY44
Lothian Wd., Tad. 103 BP64
Lothrop St. W10 55 BR38
Lots Rd. SW10 66 BT43
Lotus Rd., West. 106 CK62
Loubet St. SW17 76 BU50
Loudhams Rd., Amer. 25 AR23
Loudhams Wd. La., Ch.St.G. 25 AR23
Loudoun Ave., Ilf. 49 CL32
Loudoun Rd. NW8 56 BT36
Loudwater Clo., Sun. 83 BC52
Loudwater Dr., Rick. 26 AX24
Loudwater Heights, Rick. 26 AW24
Loudwater Hill, Rick. 26 AX25
Loudwater La., Rick. 26 AX24
Loudwater Ridge, Rick. 26 AX24
Loudwater Rd., Sun. 83 BC52
Lough Rd. N7 47 BX35
Loughborough Est. SW9 66 BY44
Loughborough Pk. SW9 66 BY45
Loughborough Rd. SW9 66 BY44
Loughborough St. SE11 66 BX42
Loughton Ct., Wal.Abb. 22 CH20
Loughton La., Epp. 31 CM22
Loughton Way, Buck.H. 40 CJ26
Louis Fld., Guil. 109 AO68
Louisa Gdns. E1 57 CC38
Louisa St.
Louisa St. E1 57 CC38
Louise Gdns., Rain. 59 CT38
Louise Rd. E15 58 CG36
Louisville Rd. SW17 76 BV48
Lourdon Rd. Ms. NW8 56 BT37
Lourdon Rd.
Lousehall La., Wal.Abb. 21 CF16
Louvain Rd., Green. 80 CZ47
Louvain Way, Wat. 17 BC19
Louvaine Rd. SW11 66 BT45
Lovage App. E6 58 CK39
Lovat Clo. NW2 46 BO34
Lovat La. EC3 4 M1
Lovat La. EC3 57 CA40
Lovat Wk., Houns. 64 BE43
Cranford La.
Lovatt Clo., Edg. 37 BM29
Lovatt Dr., Ruis. 44 BB32
Lovatts, Rick. 26 AZ24
Love Grn. La., Iver 52 AV39
Love Hill La., Slou. 52 AT40
Love La. EC2 2 J8
Love La. EC2 57 BZ39
Love La. N17 39 CA29
Love La. SE18 68 CL42
Love La. SE25 87 CB52
Love La., Abb.L. 17 BB18
Love La., Bex. 79 CQ46
Love La., Brom. 88 CH51
Love La., Gdse. 114 CC69
Love La., Grav. 81 CH47
Love La., Hat. 19 BP17
Love La., Iver 52 AU39
Love La., Kings L. 17 AY18
Love La., Mitch. 86 BU52
Love La., Mord. 86 BS54
Love La., Ong. 24 CX17
Love La., Pnr. 45 BE31
Love La., S.Ock. 60 CY40
Love La., Surb. 84 BK55
Love La., Sutt. 94 BR57
Love La., Tad. 112 BO67
Love La., Wdf.Grn. 40 CK29
Love Wk. SE5 67 BZ44
Loveday Rd. W13 54 BJ40
Lovegrove St. SE1 67 CB43
Lovegrove Wk. E14 57 CF40
Lovejoy La., Wind. 61 AL44
Lovekyn Clo., Kings.T. 85 BL51
Lovel Ave., Well. 69 CO44
Lovel Clo., Hem.H. 8 AW13
Lovel End, Ger.Cr. 34 AR29
Lovel Mead, Ger.Cr. 34 AR29
Lovel Rd., Ger.Cr. 34 AR29
Lovelace Ave., Brom. 88 CL53
Lovelace Clo., Lthd. 101 BC65
Lovelace Clo., Sev. 99 CZ57
Lovelace Dr., Wok. 100 AV61
Lovelace Gdns., Bark. 50 CO35
Lovelace Gdns., Surb. 84 BK54
Lovelace Gdns., Walt. 93 BD56
Lovelace Grn. SE9 68 CK45
Lovelace Rd. SE21 77 BZ48
Lovelace Rd., Barn. 38 BU26
Lovelace Rd., Surb. 84 BK54
Lovelands La., Tad. 113 BS67
Lovelands La., Wok. 91 AO60
Lovelinch Clo. SE15 67 CC43
Lovell Pl. SE16 67 CD41
Lovell Rd., Enf. 30 CB21
Lovell Rd., Rich. 74 BK48
Lovell Rd., Sthl. 54 BF39
Lovell Wk., Rain. 59 CT36
Lovelock Clo., Ken. 105 BZ62
Loveridge Ms. NW6 55 BR36
Loveridge Rd.
Loveridge Rd. NW6 55 BR36
Lovers La., Green. 70 DB45
Lovers Wk. N3 38 BS29
Lovers Wk. SE10 67 CF43
Lovers Wk. W1 3 G2
Lovers Wk., Rom. 41 CS28
Lovet Rd., Harl. 13 CL11
Lovett Dr., Cars. 86 BT54
Lovett Rd., Egh. 72 AT49
Lovett Rd., Uxb. 44 AX31
Lovett Way NW10 46 BN35
Lovetts Pl. SW18 66 BS45
York Rd.
Lovibonds Ave., Orp. 97 CL56
Lovibonds Ave., West Dr. 53 AY39
Low Clo., Green. 80 DA46
Low Cross Wd. La. SE21 77 CA48
Low Hall Clo. E4 39 C
Low Hall La. E17 48 CL
Low Hill, Harl. 13 CC
Low Hill Rd., Harl. 13 CC
Low Rd., Hat. 11 BL
Low St. La., Til. 71 D
Lowbell La., St.Alb. 19 BI
Lowbrook Rd., Ilf. 49 CI
Lowburys, Dor. 119 B
Lowdell Clo., West Dr. 53 AY
Lowden Rd. N9 39 CE
Lowden Rd. SE24 66 BY
Lowden Rd., Sthl. 54 BE
Lowe, The, Chig. 41 CC
Lowe Ave. E16 58 CH
Watford Rd.
Lowe Clo., Chig. 41 CC
Lowell St. E14 57 CD
Lowen Rd., Rain. 59 CS
Lower Addiscombe Rd., Croy. 87 CA
Lower Addison Gdns. W14 65 BF
Lower Barn, Hem.H. 8 AY
Lower Barn Rd., Pur. 96 BZ
Lower Bedfords Rd., Rom. 41 CT
Lower Belgrave St. SW1 3
Lower Belgrave St. SW1 66 BV
Lower Boston Rd. W7 54 BH
Lower Bri. Rd., Red. 121 BU
Lower Broad St., Dag. 59 CR
Lower Bury La., Epp. 22 CN
Lower Camden, Chis. 78 CK
Lower Ch. Hill, Green. 80 CZ
Lower Ch. St., Croy. 86 BY
Waddon New Rd.
Lower Cippenham La., Slou. 61 AM
Lower Clapton Rd. E5 48 CB
Lower Clarendon Wk. W11 55 BO
Lancaster Rd.
Lower Common S. SW15 65 BP
Lower Coombe St., Croy. 96 BZ
Lower Ct. Rd., Epsom 94 BN
Lower Cres., S.le H. 71 DK
Lower Cft., Swan. 89 CT
Lower Dagnal St., St.Alb. 9 BG
Lower Derby Rd., Wat. 27 BD
Lower Downs Rd. SW20 85 BC
Lower Drayton Pl., Croy. 86 BY
Drayton Rd.
Lower Dunnymans Ms., Bans. 94 BR
Basing Rd.
Lower Edgeborough Rd., Guil. 118 AS
Lower Emms, Hem.H. 8 AZ
Hunters Oak
Lower Fm. Rd., Lthd. 101 BC
Lower George St., Rich. 74 BK
George St.
Lower Gravel Rd., Brom. 88 CK
Lower Grn. Rd., Esher 84 BF
Lower Grn. W., Mitch. 86 BU
Lower Grosvenor Pl. SW1 3
Lower Grosvenor Pl. SW1 66 BV
Lower Gro. Rd., Rich. 75 BL
Lower Guildford Rd., Wok. 100 AO
Lower Hall La. E4 39 CD
Lower Ham Rd., Kings.T. 74 BK
Lower Hampton Rd., Sun. 84 BD
Lower Hatfield Rd., Hert. 11 BX
Lower Higham Rd., Grav. 81 DJ
Lower Hill Rd., Epsom 94 BM
Lower Hythe St., Dart. 80 CW
Lower Island Way, Wal.Abb. 30 CE
Lower James St. W1 1 M
Lower James St. W1 56 BW
Brewer St.
Lower John St. W1 1 M
Lower John St. W1 56 BW
Brewer St.
Lower Kenwood Ave., Enf. 29 BW
Lower Kings Rd., Berk. 7 AR
Lower Lea Crossing E14 58 CG
Lower Maidstone Rd. N11 38 BW
Lower Mall W6 65 BP
Lower Mardyke Ave., Rain. 59 CS
Lower Marsh SE1 4
Lower Marsh SE1 66 BY
Lower Marsh La., Kings.T. 85 BL
Lower Mead, Iver 52 AU
Lower Meadow, Harl. 13 CN
Lower Merton Ri. NW3 56 BU
Lower Morden La., Mord. 85 BQ
Lower Mortlake Rd., Rich. 65 BL
Lower Noke Clo., Rom. 42 CW
Lower Northfield Rd., Bans. 94 BR
Basing Rd.
Lower Paddock Rd., Wat. 27 BE
Lower Pk. Rd. N11 38 BW
Lower Pk. Rd., Bans. 104 BU
Lower Pk. Rd., Belv. 69 CR
Lower Pk. Rd., Loug. 31 CJ
Lower Paxton Rd., St.Alb. 9 BH
Paxton Rd.
Lower Peryers, Lthd. 110 BB
Lower Pillory Downs, Cars. 95 BV
Lower Plantation, Rick. 26 AX
Lower Pyrford Rd., Wok. 101 AW
Lower Queens Rd., Buck.H. 40 CJ
Lower Range Rd., Grav. 81 DJ

ower Richmond Rd. SW14 65 BM45
ower Richmond Rd. SW15 65 BP45
ower Richmond Rd., Rich. 65 BM45
ower Rd. SE8 67 CC41
ower Rd. SE16 67 CC41
ower Rd., Belv. 69 CR41
ower Rd., Brwd. 122 DE23
ower Rd., Erith 69 CS42
ower Rd., Ger.Cr. 43 AS31
ower Rd., Grav. 71 DC45
ower Rd., Grav. 81 DK47
ower Rd., Har. 45 BG34
ower Rd., Hem.H. 17 AZ16
ower Rd., Ken. 95 BY60
ower Rd., Lthd. 111 BD67
ower Rd., Lthd. 102 BG65
ower Rd., Loug. 31 CL23
ower Rd., Orp. 89 CO54
ower Rd., Red. 121 BT71
ower Rd., Rick. 25 AU24
ower Rd., Sutt. 95 BT56
ower Rd., Swan. 79 CT50
ower Rd., Uxb. 43 AU33
ower Robert St. WC2 4 A1
ower Sales, Hem.H. 7 AV14
ower Sandfields, Wok. 100 AU65
ower Sawley Wd., Bans. 94 BR60
Basing Rd.
ower Shott, Chsnt. 21 CA16
Adamsfield
ower Shott, Lthd. 111 BF66
ower Shott Clo., Lthd. 111 BF66
Lower Shott
ower Sloane St. SW1 3 G9
ower Sloane St. SW1 66 BV42
ower Sq., Islw. 64 BJ45
ower Staithe W4 65 BN44
ower Sta. Rd. (Crayford), Dart. 79 CT46
ower Strand NW9 37 BO30
ower Sunbury Rd., Hmptn. 84 BE51
ower Swaines, Epp. 22 CN18
ower Tail, Wat. 36 BE27
ower Teddington Rd., Kings.T. 74 BK50
ower Ter. NW3 47 BT34
ower Thames St. EC3 4 L1
ower Thames St. EC3 57 BZ40
ower Tub, Bush. 36 BG26
ower Wd. Rd., Esher 93 BJ57
ower Yott, Hem.H. 8 AY13
owerfield, Welw.G.C. 5 BS8
owestoft Clo. E5 48 CB34
Southwold Rd.
owestoft Rd., Wat. 26 BC23
oweswater Clo., Wem. 45 BK34
Carlton Ave. E.
owfield, Saw. 6 CQ6
Brook Rd.
owfield La., Hodd. 12 CE12
owfield Rd. NW6 56 BS36
owfield Rd. W3 55 BM39
owfield St., Dart. 80 CW48
owick Rd., Har. 45 BH31
owlands, Hat. 10 BQ11
owlands Dr., Stai. 73 AX46
Oaks Rd.
owlands Gdns., Rom. 50 CR32
owlands Rd., Har. 45 BH33
owlands Rd., Pnr. 45 BD33
owlands Rd., S.Ock. 60 CX40
owman Rd. N7 47 BX35
owndes Clo. SW1 3 H7
owndes Clo. SW1 66 BV41
owndes Pl. SW1 3 G7
owndes Pl. SW1 66 BV41
owndes Sq. SW1 3 F5
owndes Sq. SW1 66 BU41
owndes St. SW1 3 F6
owndes St. SW1 66 BU41
owood St. E1 57 CB40
owry Cres., Mitch. 86 BU51
owshoe La., Rom. 41 CR30
owson Gro., Wat. 36 BE26
owswood Clo., Nthwd. 35 BA30
owth Rd. SE5 67 BZ44
owther Clo., Borwd. 28 BL25
owther Dr., Enf. 29 BX24
owther Gdns. SW7 3 A5
owther Hill SE23 77 CD47
owther Rd. E17 39 CD30
owther Rd. N7 47 BY35
Mackenzie Rd.
owther Rd. SW13 65 BO44
owther Rd., Kings.T. 85 BL51
owther Rd., Stan. 46 BL31
owthorpe, Wok. 100 AQ62
Shilburn Way
oxford Ave. E6 58 CJ37
oxford La., Ilf. 49 CM35
oxford Rd., Bark. 58 CL36
oxham Rd. E4 39 CE29
oxham St. WC1 2 A3
oxham St. WC1 56 BX38
Cromer St.
oxley Clo. SE26 77 CC49
Trewsbury Rd.
oxley Rd. SW18 76 BT47
oxley Rd., Berk. 7 AP12
oxley Rd., Hmptn. 74 BE49
oxton Rd. SE23 77 CC47
oxwood Clo., Orp. 89 CP55
Chelsfield La.
oxwood Rd. N17 48 CA31
ubbock Rd., Chis. 78 CK50
ubbock St. SE14 67 CC43
ucan Dr., Stai. 73 AX50
Bingham Dr.
ucan Pl. SW3 3 C9
ucan Pl. SW3 66 BU42
Lucan Rd., Barn. 28 BR24
Lucas Ave. E13 58 CH37
Lucas Ave., Har. 45 BF34
Lucas Ct., Har. 45 BF34
Lucas Ct., Wal.Abb. 22 CG20
Lucas Rd. SE20 77 CC50
Lucas Rd., Grays 71 DD41
Lucas St. SE8 67 CD44
Lucerne Clo. N13 38 BX27
Lucerne Clo., Wok. 100 AS63
Claremont Ave.
Lucerne Ct., Erith 69 CQ41
Middle Way
Lucerne Gro. E17 48 CF31
Lucerne Ms. W8 56 BS40
Kensington Mall
Lucerne Rd. N5 47 BY35
Lucerne Rd., Orp. 88 CN54
Lucerne Rd., Th.Hth. 86 BY52
Lucerne Way, Rom. 42 CV29
Lucey Rd. SE16 67 CB41
Lucey Way SE16 67 CB41
Linsey St.
Lucie Ave., Ashf. 73 AZ50
Lucien Rd. SW17 76 BV49
Lucien Rd. SW19 76 BS48
Lucknow St. SE18 68 CN43
Lucks Hill, Hem.H. 7 AV13
Lucorn Clo. SE12 78 CG46
Luctons Ave., Buck.H. 40 CJ26
Lucy Cres. W3 55 BN39
Lucy Gdns., Dag. 50 CQ34
Luddesdon Rd., Erith 69 CR43
Luddington Ave., Vir.W. 82 AS51
Ludford Clo. NW9 37 BO30
Ludford Clo., Croy. 86 BY55
Warrington Rd.
Ludgate Bdy. EC4 2 F9
Ludgate Bdy. EC4 56 BY39
Pilgrim St.
Ludgate Circ. EC4 2 F9
Ludgate Circ. EC4 56 BY39
Ludgate Ct. EC4 2 F9
Ludgate Ct. EC4 56 BY39
Ludgate Hill
Ludgate Hill EC4 2 F9
Ludgate Hill EC4 56 BY39
Ludgate Sq. EC4 2 G9
Ludgate Sq. EC4 56 BY39
Creed La.
Ludham Clo. SE28 59 CP40
Rollesby Way
Ludlow Clo., Brom. 88 CH52
Aylesbury Rd.
Ludlow Clo., Har. 45 BE35
Ludlow Mead, Wat. 35 BC27
Ludlow Pl., Grays 71 DD41
Ludlow Rd. W5 54 BK38
Ludlow Rd., Felt. 73 BB48
Ludlow Rd., Guil. 118 AQ71
Ludlow St. EC1 2 H4
Ludlow St. EC1 57 BZ38
Gee St.
Ludlow Way N2 47 BT31
Ludlow Way, Rick. 26 BA24
Ludovic Wk. SW15 65 BO45
Ludwick Grn., Welw.G.C. 5 BR8
Ludwick Ms. SE14 67 CD43
Ludwick Way, Welw.G.C. 5 BR8
Luff Clo., Wind. 61 AM45
Luffield Rd. SE2 69 CO41
Luffman Rd. SE12 78 CH48
Lugard Rd. SE15 67 CB44
Lugg App. E12 49 CL34
Luke St. EC2 2 M4
Luke St. EC2 57 CA38
Lukin Cres. E4 39 CF27
Lukin St. E1 57 CC39
Lullarook Clo., West. 106 CJ61
Lullingstone Ave., Swan. 89 CT52
Lullingstone Clo., Orp. 79 CO50
Lullingstone Cres., Orp. 79 CO50
Lullingstone La., Eyns. 90 CV55
Lullingstone Rd., Belv. 69 CQ43
Barnfield Rd.
Lullington Garth N12 37 BR28
Lullington Garth, Borwd. 28 BM25
Lullington Garth, Brom. 78 CG50
Lullington Rd. SE20 77 CB50
Lullington Rd., Dag. 59 CQ36
Lulot Gdns. N19 47 BV34
Lulworth SE17 4 K10
Lulworth Ave., Chsnt. 20 BY18
Lulworth Ave., Houns. 64 BF44
Lulworth Ave., Wem. 45 BK33
Lulworth Clo., Har. 45 BE34
Lulworth Dr., Pnr. 45 BD33
Lulworth Dr., Rom. 41 CR28
Lulworth Gdns., Har. 45 BE34
Lulworth Rd. SE9 78 CK48
Lulworth Rd. SE15 67 CB44
Lulworth Rd., Well. 68 CN44
Lulworth Waye, Hayes 53 BC39
Lumbards, Welw.G.C. 5 BS6
Lumley Clo., Belv. 69 CR43
Lumley Ct. WC2 4 A1
Lumley Ct. WC2 56 BX40
Strand
Lumley Gdns., Sutt. 94 BR56
Lumley Rd., Sutt. 94 BR57
Lumley St. W1 1 H9
Lumley St. W1 56 BV39
Luna Rd., Th.Hth. 87 BZ52
Lunar Clo., West. 106 CJ61
Lundin Wk., Wat. 36 BD28
Lundy Dr., Hayes 63 BB42
Lundy St. W6 65 BR43
Field Rd.
Lundy Wk. N1 57 BZ36
Marquess Est.
Lunedale Rd., Dart. 80 CX47
Lunghurst Rd., Cat. 105 CD63
Lunham Rd. SE19 77 CA50
Luntly Pl. E1 57 CA39
Chicksand St.
Lupin Clo. SW2 76 BY48
Palace Rd.
Lupin Clo., Croy. 87 CC54
Lupin Clo., West Dr. 63 AX42
Lupin Gdns., Ilf. 58 CL36
Luppit Clo., Brwd. 122 DD26
Lupton Clo. SE12 78 CH49
Lupton St. NW5 47 BW35
Lupus St. SW1 66 BV42
Luralda Gdns. E14 67 CF42
Lurgan Ave. W6 65 BQ43
Lurline Gdns. SW11 66 BV44
Luscombe Way SW8 66 BX43
Lushes Rd., Loug. 31 CL25
Lushington Dr., Cob. 92 BC60
Lushington Rd. NW10 55 BP37
Lushington Rd. SE6 77 CE49
Lusted Hall La., West. 106 CH63
Lusted Rd., Sev. 107 CT63
Lusteds Clo., Dor. 119 BK73
Luther Clo., Edg. 37 BN27
Luther King Clo. E17 48 CD32
Luther King Rd., Harl. 13 CM11
Luther Rd., Tedd. 74 BH49
Luthers Clo., Brwd. 33 CZ22
Luton Pl. SE10 67 CF43
Luton Rd. E17 48 CD31
Luton Rd., Sid. 79 CP48
Luton St. NW8 1 B5
Luton St. NW8 56 BT38
Lutton Ter. NW3 47 BT35
Flask Wk.
Luttrell Ave. SW15 75 BP46
Lutwyche Rd. SE6 77 CD48
Luxborough La., Chig. 40 CK27
Luxborough St. W1 1 G5
Luxborough St. W1 56 BV39
Luxemburg Gdns. W6 65 BQ42
Luxfield Rd. SE9 78 CK47
Luxford St. SE16 67 CC42
Luxmore Gdns. SE4 67 CD44
Luxmore St. SE4 67 CC44
Luxor St. SE5 67 BZ44
Luxted Rd., Orp. 97 CL59
Lyal Rd. E3 57 CD37
Lyall Ave. SE21 77 CA48
Lyall Ms. SW1 3 G7
Lyall Ms. E. SW1 66 BV41
Lyall Ms. W. SW1 3 G7
Lyall Ms. W. SW1 66 BV41
Lyall St.
Lyall St. SW1 3 G7
Lyall St. SW1 66 BV41
Lycaste Clo., St.Alb. 9 BJ14
Dellfield
Lycett Pl. W12 65 BP41
Becklow Rd.
Lych Gate, Wat. 18 BD20
Lych Gate Rd., Orp. 89 CO54
Lych Gate Wk., Hayes 53 BB40
Lych Way, Wok. 100 AR61
Lyconby Gdns., Croy. 87 CD54
Lycrome La., Chesh. 16 AO17
Lycrome Rd., Chesh. 16 AP17
Lydd Clo., Sid. 78 CN48
Lydd Rd., Bexh. 69 CQ43
Lydden Ct. SE9 78 CN46
Lydden Gro. SW18 76 BS47
Lydden Rd. SW18 76 BS47
Lydeard Rd. E6 58 CK36
Lydele Clo., Wok. 100 AS61
Lydford Ave., Slou. 52 AO38
Lydford Rd. N15 48 BZ32
Lydford Rd. NW2 55 BQ36
Lydford Rd. W9 55 BR38
Lydhurst Ave. SW2 76 BX48
Lydia Ms., Hat. 10 BQ15
Lydia Rd., Erith 69 CT43
Lydney Clo. SE15 67 CA43
Blakes Rd.
Lydney Clo. SW19 75 BR48
Princes Way
Lydon Rd. SW4 66 BW45
Lydstep Rd., Chis. 78 CL49
Lye, The, Tad. 103 BQ65
Lye Grn. Rd., Chesh. 16 AP18
Lye La., St.Alb. 18 BF17
Lye Rd., Wok. 100 AO63
Lyell, Wind. 61 AL45
Lyell Pl. E., Wind. 61 AL45
Lyell
Lyell Pl. W., Wind. 61 AL45
Lyell
Lyell Wk. E., Wind. 61 AL45
Lyell
Lyell Wk. W., Wind. 61 AL45
Lyell
Lyfield, Cob. 93 BF60
Lyford Rd. SW18 76 BT47
Lyford St. SE18 68 CK42
Lygon Pl. SW1 3 J7
Lyham Clo. SW2 76 BX46
Lyham Rd. SW2 76 BX46
Lyle Clo., Mitch. 86 BV54
Lyle Pk., Sev. 107 CU65
Lymbourne Clo., Sutt. 95 BS58
Lymden Gdns., Reig. 121 BS71
Lyme Ave., Berk. 7 AO11
Lyme Fm. Rd. SE12 68 CH45
Lyme Regis Rd., Bans. 103 BR62
Lyme Rd., Well. 69 CO44
Lyme St. NW1 56 BW36
Lyme Ter. NW1 56 BW36
Royal College St.
Lymer Ave. SE19 77 CA49
Lymescote Gdns., Sutt. 86 BS55
Lyminge Clo., Sid. 78 CN48
Lyminge Gdns. SW18 76 BU47
Lymington Ave. N22 38 BY30
Lymington Clo. SW16 86 BW51
Lymington Dr., Ruis. 44 BA34
Lymington Gdns., Epsom 94 BO56
Lymington Rd. NW6 56 BS36
Lymington Rd., Dag. 50 CP33
Lympstone Gdns. SE15 67 CB43
Lyn Rd., Vir.W. 82 AS53
Lynbridge Gdns. N13 38 BY28
Lynbrook Clo. SE15 67 CA43
Blakes Rd.
Lynbrook Clo., Rain. 59 CS37
Lynceley Gra., Epp. 23 CO18
Lynch, The, Uxb. 53 AX36
Lynch Clo., Uxb. 53 AX36
The Lynch
Lynch Pl., The, Uxb. 53 AX36
Lynchen Clo., Houns. 63 BC44
Lyncott Cres. SW4 66 BV45
Cedars Rd.
Lyncroft Ave., Pnr. 45 BE32
Lyncroft Gdns. NW6 47 BS35
Lyncroft Gdns. W13 64 BK41
Lyncroft Gdns., Epsom 94 BO58
Lyncroft Gdns., Houns. 74 BG46
Lyncross Clo., Rom. 42 CW30
Lyndale NW2 46 BR35
Lyndale, Brwd. 33 CZ22
Stock Fld.
Lyndale Ave. NW2 46 BR34
Lyndale Clo. SE3 68 CG43
Lyndale Ct., Wey. 92 AW60
Parvis Rd.
Lyndale Rd., Red. 121 BU69
Lynden Way, Swan. 89 CS52
Lyndhurst Ave. N12 38 BU29
Lyndhurst Ave. NW7 37 BO29
Lyndhurst Ave. SW16 86 BW51
Lyndhurst Ave., Pnr. 35 BC30
Lyndhurst Ave., Sthl. 54 BF40
Lyndhurst Ave., Sun. 83 BC52
Lyndhurst Ave., Surb. 85 BM54
Lyndhurst Ave., Twick. 74 BE47
Lyndhurst Clo. NW10 46 BN34
Lyndhurst Clo., Bexh. 69 CR45
Lyndhurst Clo., Croy. 87 CA55
Selborne Rd.
Lyndhurst Clo., Orp. 97 CL56
Broadwater Gdns.
Lyndhurst Clo., Wok. 100 AR61
Lyndhurst Ct. E18 40 CH30
Lyndhurst Dr. E10 48 CF33
Lyndhurst Dr., Horn. 51 CV33
Lyndhurst Dr., N.Mal. 85 BO53
Lyndhurst Dr., Sev. 107 CT65
Lyndhurst Gdns. N3 37 BR30
Lyndhurst Gdns. NW3 47 BT35
Lyndhurst Gdns., Bark. 58 CN36
Lyndhurst Gdns., Enf. 30 CA24
Lyndhurst Gdns., Ilf. 49 CM32
Lyndhurst Gdns., Pnr. 35 BC30
Lyndhurst Gro. SE15 67 CA44
Lyndhurst Ri., Chig. 40 CL28
Lyndhurst Rd. E4 39 CF29
Lyndhurst Rd. N18 39 CB28
Lyndhurst Rd. N22 38 BX29
Lyndhurst Rd. NW3 47 BT35
Lyndhurst Rd., Bexh. 69 CR45
Lyndhurst Rd., Couls. 104 BV61
Lyndhurst Rd., Grnf. 54 BF38
Lyndhurst Rd., Reig. 121 BS72
Lyndhurst Rd., Th.Hth. 86 BY52
Lyndhurst Sq. SE15 67 CA44
Lyndhurst Ter. NW3 47 BT35
Lyndhurst Way SE15 67 CA44
Lyndhurst Way, Brwd. 122 DE26
Lyndhurst Way, Cher. 82 AV55
Lyndhurst Way, Grav. 81 DF51
Lyndhurst Way, Sutt. 95 BS58
Lyndon Ave., Pnr. 36 BE29
Lyndon Ave., Sid. 78 CN46
Lyndon Ave., Wall. 86 BV55
Lyndon Rd., Belv. 69 CR42
Lyndwood Dr., Wind. 72 AQ46
Lyne Clo., Vir.W. 82 AS53
Lyne Cres. E17 39 CD30
Lyne Crossing Rd., Cher. 82 AT53
Lyne La., Vir.W. 82 AT53
Lyne Way, Hem.H. 7 AV12
Lynegrove Ave., Ashf. 73 BA49
Lyneham Wk. E5 48 CD35
Durrington Rd.
Lyneham Wk. E5 48 CD35
Boscombe Clo.
Lyneham Wk., Pnr. 44 BB31
Lynett Rd., Dag. 50 CP34
Lynette Ave. SW4 76 BV46
Lynford Clo., Edg. 37 BN29
Lynford Gdns., Edg. 37 BM27
Lynford Gdns., Ilf. 49 CN34
Lynford Ter. N9 39 CA26
Lynhurst Cres., Uxb. 53 BA36
Lynhurst Rd., Uxb. 53 BA36
Lynmere Rd., Well. 69 CO44
Lynmouth Ave., Enf. 30 CA25
Lynmouth Ave., Mord. 85 BQ53
Lynmouth Dr., Ruis. 44 BC34
Lynmouth Gdns., Grnf. 54 BJ37
Lynmouth Gdns., Houns. 64 BD43
Lynmouth Ri., Orp. 89 CO52
Lynmouth Rd. E17 48 CD32
Lynmouth Rd. N2 47 BU31
Lynmouth Rd. N16 48 CA33
Lynmouth Rd., Grnf. 54 BJ37
Lynn Clo., Ashf. 73 BA49
Lynn Clo., Har. 36 BG30
Lynn Ms. E11 49 CG34
Lynn Rd.
Lynn Rd. E11 49 CG34
Lynn Rd. SW12 76 BV47
Lynn Rd., Ilf. 49 CM33
Lynn St., Enf. 30 BZ23
Lynn Wk., Reig. 120 BS72
Lynne Clo., Orp. 97 CN57
Lynne Clo., S.Croy. 96 CC58
Lynne Wk., Esher 93 BG56
Lynne Way NW10 55 BO36
Lynne Way, Nthlt. 54 BD37
Lynscott Way, S.Croy. 95 BY58
Lynsted Clo., Bexh. 79 CR46
Lynsted Clo., Brom. 88 CJ51
Lynsted Gdns. SE9 68 CJ45
Lynton Ave. N12 38 BT28
Lynton Ave. NW9 46 BO31
Lynton Ave. W13 54 BJ39
Lynton Ave., Orp. 89 CO52
Lynton Ave., Rom. 41 CR30
Lynton Ave., St.Alb. 9 BK14
Lynton Clo., Chess. 94 BL56
Lynton Clo., Islw. 64 BH45
Lynton Cres., Ilf. 49 CL32
Lynton Crest, Pot.B. 20 BS19
Strafford Gate
Lynton Gdns. N11 38 BW29
Lynton Gdns., Enf. 39 CA26
Lynton Mead N20 38 BS27
Lynton Par., Wal.Cr. 21 CC18
Turners Crossbrook St.
Lynton Rd. E4 39 CE28
Lynton Rd. N8 47 BW32
Lynton Rd. NW6 55 BR37
Lynton Rd. SE1 4 Q9
Lynton Rd. SE1 67 CA42
Lynton Rd. W3 55 BM40
Lynton Rd., Croy. 86 BY53
Lynton Rd., Dag. 50 CP34
Lynton Rd., Grav. 81 DG47
Lynton Rd., Har. 45 BE34
Lynton Rd., N.Mal. 85 BN53
Lynton Rd. S., Grav. 81 DG47
Lynton Wk., Hayes 53 BB38
Exmouth Rd.
Lynwood, Guil. 118 AQ71
Lynwood Ave., Couls. 104 BV61
Lynwood Ave., Egh. 72 AS50
Lynwood Ave., Epsom 94 BO60
Lynwood Ave., Slou. 62 AR41
Lynwood Clo. E18 40 CJ30
Lynwood Clo., Har. 45 BE34
Lynwood Clo., Rom. 41 CR29
Lynwood Clo., Wok. 91 AU60
Lynwood Dr., Nthwd. 35 BB30
Lynwood Dr., Rom. 41 CR29
Lynwood Dr., Wor.Pk. 85 BP55
Lynwood Gdns., Croy. 95 BX56
Lynwood Gdns., Sthl. 54 BE39
Lynwood Gro. N21 38 BY26
Lynwood Gro., Orp. 88 CN54
Lynwood Heights, Rick. 26 AW25
Lynwood Rd. SW17 76 BU49
Lynwood Rd. W5 54 BK38
Lynwood Rd., Epsom 94 BO60
Lynwood Rd., Red. 121 BV69
Lynwood Rd., T.Ditt. 84 BH55
Lyon Meade, Stan. 36 BK30
Lyon Pk. Ave., Wem. 55 BL36
Lyon Rd. SW19 86 BT51
Lyon Rd., Har. 45 BH32
Lyon Rd., Rom. 50 CT33
Lyon Rd., Walt. 84 BE55
Lyon St. N1 56 BX36
Caledonian Rd.
Lyon Way, Grnf. 54 BH37
Lyon Way, St.Alb. 10 BM13
Lyons Ct., Dor. 119 BJ71
High St.
Lyons Dene, Tad. 112 BR67
Lyons Dr., Guil. 109 AQ68
Lyons Pl. NW8 1 A5
Lyons Pl. NW8 56 BT38
Lyons Wk. W14 65 BR42
Blythe Rd.
Lyonsdown Ave., Barn. 29 BT25
Lyonsdown Rd., Barn. 29 BT25
Lyoth Rd., Orp. 88 CM55
Lyric Dr., Grnf. 54 BF38
Lyric Rd. SW13 65 BO44
Lysander Clo., Hem.H. 16 AS17
Lancaster Dr.
Lysander Gro. N19 47 BW33
Lysander Rd., Croy. 95 BX57
Lysander Rd., Ruis. 44 BA34
Lysander Way, Orp. 88 CM55
Lysander Way, Welw.G.C. 5 BT7
Lysia St. SW6 65 BQ43
Lysias Rd. SW12 76 BV46
Lysons Wk. SW15 75 BP46
Swinburne Rd.
Lytchet Rd., Brom. 78 CH50
Lytchet Way, Enf. 30 CC23
Lytchgate Clo., S.Croy. 96 CA57
Lytcott Gro. SE22 77 CA46
Lytham Ave., Wat. 36 BD28
Lytham Gro. W5 55 BL38
Lytham St. SE17 67 BZ42
Lyttelton Clo. NW3 56 BU36
Lyttelton Ct. N2 47 BT32
Lyttelton Rd. E10 48 CE34
Lyttelton Rd. N2 47 BT32
Lyttleton Rd. N8 47 BY31
Lytton Ave. N13 38 BY27
Lytton Ave., Enf. 30 CD22
Lytton Clo. N2 47 BT32
Lytton Clo., Loug. 31 CM24
Lytton Clo., Nthlt. 54 BE36
Lytton Gdns., Wall. 95 BW56
Lytton Gdns., Welw.G.C. 5 BQ8
Lytton Gro. SW15 75 BQ46
Lytton Rd. E11 49 CG33
Lytton Rd., Barn. 29 BT24
Lytton Rd., Grays 71 DG42
Lytton Rd., Pnr. 36 BE29
Lytton Rd., Rom. 50 CU32
Lytton Rd., Wok. 100 AT61
Lytton Strachey Path SE28 59 CO40
Curtis Way
Lytton Way, Hodd. 12 CE10
Bridleway S.
Lyveden Rd. SE3 68 CH43
Lyvedon Rd. SW17 76 BU50

Lywood Clo., Tad. 103 BQ64

M

Mabbits Clo., St.Alb. 18 BE18
Jenkins Ave.
Mabbotts, Tad. 103 BQ64
Mabel Rd., Swan. 79 CU50
Mabel St., Wok. 100 AR62
Maberley Cres. SE19 77 CB50
Maberley Rd. SE19 87 CA51
Maberley Rd., Beck. 87 CC52
Mabeys Wk., Saw. 6 CO6
Mabledon Pl. WC1 1 P3
Mabledon Pl. WC1 56 BW38
Mablethorpe Rd. SW6 65 BR43
Mabley St. E9 48 CD35
Mabyn Rd. SE18 68 CN42
Macaret Clo. N20 38 BT26
Macarthur Ter. SE7 68 CJ43
Charlton La.
Macaulay Ct. SW4 66 BV45
Macaulay Rd. E6 58 CJ37
Macaulay Rd. SW4 66 BV45
Macaulay Rd., Cat. 105 CA64
Macaulay Sq. SW4 66 BV45
Macaulay Way SE28 59 CO40
Macauley Ave., Esher 84 BH55
Macauley Ms. SE13 67 CF44
Macbean St. SE18 68 CL41
Macbeth Ho. N1 57 CA37
Purcell St.
Macbeth St. W6 65 BP42
Macclesfield Bri. NW1 56 BU37
Macclesfield Rd. EC1 2 H2
Macclesfield Rd. EC1 57 BZ38
Macclesfield Rd. SE25 87 CB53
Macclesfield St. W1 1 P10
Macclesfield St. W1 56 BW40
Gerrard St.
Macdonald Ave., Dag. 50 CR34
Macdonald Ave., Horn. 51 CW31
Macdonald Clo., Amer. 25 AO21
Macdonald Clo., Horn. 51 CW31
Macdonald Rd. E7 49 CH35
Macdonald Rd. E17 39 CF30
Macdonald Rd. N11 38 BU28
Macdonald Rd. N19 47 BW34
Macdonald Way, Horn. 51 CW31
Macdonell Gdns., Wat. 26 BB21
High Rd.
Macduff Rd. SW11 66 BV44
Mace Clo. E1 57 CB40
Kennet St.
Mace Ct., Grays 71 DF43
Medlar Rd.
Mace La., Sev. 97 CM60
Mace St. E2 57 CC37
Macers Ct., Brox. 12 CD15
Macers La., Brox. 12 CD15
Macfarlane Rd. W12 55 BQ40
Macfarren Pl. NW1 1 H5
Macgregor Rd. E16 58 CJ39
Machell Rd. SE15 67 CC45
Mackay Rd. SW4 66 BV45
Mackennal St. NW8 56 BU37
Mackenzie Mall, Slou. 62 AP41
Mackenzie Rd. N7 56 BX36
Mackenzie Rd., Beck. 87 CC51
Mackenzie St., Slou. 62 AP41
High St.
Mackenzie Way, Grav. 81 DH50
Mackeson Rd. NW3 47 BU35
Mackie Rd. SW2 76 BY47
Mackintosh La. E9 48 CC35
High St.
Macklin St. WC2 2 A8
Macklin St. WC2 56 BX39
Mackrells Rd., Red. 121 BT72
Mackrow Wk. E14 57 CF40
Macks Rd. SE16 67 CB42
Mackworth St. NW1 1 L2
Mackworth St. NW1 56 BW38
Maclean Rd. SE23 77 CD46
Maclennan Ave., Rain. 60 CV38
Macleod Clo., Grays 71 DE42
Palmers Dr.
Macleod St. SE17 67 BZ42
Maclise Rd. W14 65 BR41
Macmillan Gdns., Dart. 70 CX45
Macoma Rd. SE18 68 CM43
Macoma Ter. SE18 68 CM43
Macon Way, Upmin. 51 CZ32
Maconochies Rd. E14 67 CE42
Macquarie Way E14 67 CE42
Macready Pl. N7 47 BX35
Macroom Rd. W9 55 BR38
Mada Rd., Orp. 88 CL55
Madan Rd., West. 115 CM66
Madans Wk., Epsom 103 BN61
Maddams St. E3 57 CE38
Maddells, Epp. 22 CN19
Madden Clo., Swans. 80 DB46
Maddison Clo., Tedd. 74 BH50
Maddison Way, Sev. 107 CT65
Maddock Way SE17 66 BY43
Maddocks Clo., Sid. 79 CQ49
Maddox La., Lthd. 102 BE65
Maddox Pk., Lthd. 102 BF65
Maddox Rd., Harl. 6 CN10
Maddox Rd., Hem.H. 8 AZ13
Maddox St. W1 1 K10
Maddox St. W1 56 BV40
Madeira Ave., Brom. 78 CG50
Madeira Clo., Wey. 92 AW60
Brantwood Gdns.
Madeira Cres., Wey. 92 AW60
Brantwood Gdns.
Madeira Gro., Wdf.Grn. 40 CJ29
Madeira Rd. E11 48 CF33
Madeira Rd. N13 38 BY28
Madeira Rd. SW16 76 BX49
Madeira Rd., Mitch. 86 BU52
Madeira Rd., Wey. 91 AV60
Madeira Wk., Brwd. 122 DC27
Madeira Wk., Reig. 121 BT70
Madeira Wk., Wind. 61 AO44
Madeley Clo., Amer. 25 AO21
Madeley Rd. W5 54 BK39
Madeline Rd. SE20 77 CB50
Madewell Lo., Borwd. 28 BL23
Theobald St.
Madison Cres., Bexh. 69 CP43
Madison Gdns., Bexh. 69 CP43
Madison Gdns., Brom. 88 CG52
Madras Pl. N7 56 BY36
Madras Rd., Ilf. 49 CL35
Madrid Rd. SW13 65 BP44
Madrid Rd., Guil. 118 AQ71
Madron St. SE17 4 N10
Madron St. SE17 67 CA42
Maesmaur Rd., West. 106 CJ64
Mafeking Ave. E6 58 CK37
Mafeking Ave., Brent. 64 BK43
Mafeking Ave., Ilf. 49 CM33
Mafeking Rd. E16 58 CG38
Mafeking Rd. N17 39 CB30
Mafeking Rd., Enf. 30 CA24
Mafeking Rd., Stai. 72 AT48
Magazine Pl., Lthd. 102 BJ64
Magazine Rd., Cat. 104 BY64
Magdala Ave. N19 47 BV34
Magdala Rd., Islw. 64 BJ45
Magdala Rd., S.Croy. 96 BZ57
Magdalen Clo., Wey. 92 AY60
Magdalen Cres., Wey. 92 AY60
Magdalen Gdns., Brwd. 122 DF26
Hutton Dr.
Magdalen Gro., Orp. 98 CO56
Magdalen Pas. E1 2 Q10
Magdalen Rd. SW18 76 BT47
Magdalen St. SE1 4 M3
Magdalen St. SE1 57 CA40
Magdalene Clo. SE15 67 CB44
Heaton Rd.
Magdalene Gdns. E6 58 CL38
Homeway
Magdalene Rd., Shep. 83 AZ52
Magee St. SE11 66 BY43
Maggie Blakes Cause SE1 4 P3
Magna Carta La., Stai. 72 AR47
Magna Rd., Egh. 72 AQ50
Magnaville Rd., Bush. 36 BH26
Magnet Rd., Grays 70 DB43
Magnolia Clo., Kings.T. 75 BM50
Magnolia Ct., Har. 46 BL33
Magnolia Dr., West. 106 CJ61
Magnolia Gdns., Slou. 62 AR41
Appletree La.
Magnolia Pl. SW4 66 BX45
Kings Ave.
Magnolia Pl., Guil. 118 AR69
Magnolia Rd. W4 65 BM43
Magnolia St., West Dr. 63 AX42
Magnolia Way, Brwd. 33 DA25
Magnolia Way, Dor. 119 BK73
Magnolia Way, Epsom 94 BN56
Magnum Clo., Rain. 60 CV39
The Glen
Magpie All. EC4 2 E9
Magpie All. EC4 56 BY39
Whitefriars St.
Magpie Clo., Couls. 104 BW62
Magpie Clo., Enf. 30 CB22
Magpie Hall Clo., Brom. 88 CK53
Magpie Hall La., Brom. 88 CK54
Magpie Hall Rd., Bush. 36 BH27
Magpie La., Brwd. 42 DB30
Magpie La., Sev. 99 CW60
Magpie Wk., Hat. 10 BP13
Lark Ri.
Magpies, The, Epp. 13 CL15
Magri Wk. E1 57 CC39
Ashfield St.
Maguire Dr., Rich. 74 BK49
Maguire St. SE1 4 Q4
Maguire St. SE1 67 CA41
Mahlon Ave., Ruis. 44 BC35
Mahogany Clo. SE16 57 CD40
Mahon Clo., Enf. 30 CA23
Maid of Honour Row, Rich. 74 BK46
The Grn.
Maida Ave. E4 39 CE26
Maida Ave. W2 56 BT39
Maida Rd., Belv. 69 CR41
Maida Vale W9 56 BS37
Maida Vale Rd., Dart. 79 CU46
Maida Way E4 39 CE26
Maiden Erlegh Ave., Bex. 79 CQ47
Maiden La. N7 56 BW36
Maiden La. NW1 56 BW36
Maiden La. SE1 4 J2
Maiden La. WC2 2 A10
Maiden La. WC2 56 BX40
Bedford St.
Maiden La., Dart. 69 CU45
Maiden Rd. E15 58 CG36
Maidenhead Rd., Wind. 61 AL44
Maidenshaw Rd., Epsom 94 BN59
Maidenstone Hill SE10 67 CF44
Maidstone Ave., Rom. 41 CS30
Maidstone Bldgs. SE1 4 K3
Maidstone Bldgs. SE1 57 BZ40
Maidstone Rd. N11 38 BW29
Maidstone Rd., Grays 71 DD43
Maidstone Rd., Sev. 107 CT64
Maidstone Rd., Sid. 79 CP50
Mail Coach Yd. N1 2 N2
Mail Coach Yd. N1 57 CA38
Kingsland Rd.
Main Ave., Enf. 30 CA25
Main Ave., Nthwd. 35 BA27
Main Dr., Ger.Cr. 43 AR32
Main Dr., Houns. 64 BG43
Main Par., Rick. 25 AU24
Main Rd., Eden. 115 CM70
Main Rd., Farn. 90 CW53
Main Rd., Long. 90 DB51
Main Rd., Orp. 89 CP51
Main Rd., Rom. 50 CT31
Main Rd., Sev. 107 CP65
Main Rd., Sid. 78 CM48
Main Rd., S.at H. 80 CX50
Main Rd., Swan. 79 CT50
Main Rd., West. 106 CJ62
Main St., Felt. 74 BD49
Mainridge Rd., Chis. 78 CL49
Maisemore St. SE15 67 CB43
Peckham Pk. Rd.
Maisie Webster Clo., Stai. 73 AX47
Lauser Rd.
Maitland Clo. SE10 67 CE43
Maitland Clo., Houns. 64 BE45
Maitland Clo., Wey. 92 AW60
Maitland Pk. Est. NW3 56 BU36
Maitland Pk. Rd. NW3 56 BU36
Maitland Pk. Vill. NW3 56 BU35
Maitland Pl. E5 48 CB35
Clarence Rd.
Maitland Rd. E15 58 CG36
Maitland Rd. SE26 77 CC50
Maize Row E14 57 CD40
Maizey Ct., Brwd. 33 DA25
Danes Way
Majendie Rd. SE18 68 CM42
Majestic Way, Mitch. 86 BU51
St. Marks Rd.
Major Rd. E15 48 CF35
Major Rd. SE16 67 CB41
Majors Fm. Rd., Slou. 62 AR43
Makepeace Ave. N6 47 BV34
Makepeace Rd., Nthlt. 54 BE37
Makins St. SW3 3 D9
Makins St. SW3 66 BU42
Malabar St. E14 67 CE41
Malacca Fm. Rd., Guil. 110 AW67
Malam Gdns. E14 57 CE40
Wades Pl.
Malan Clo., West. 106 CK62
Malan Sq., Rain. 59 CU36
Malbrook Rd. SW15 65 BP45
Malby Ct., Borwd. 29 BL23
Leeming Rd.
Malcolm Ct. W5 55 BL38
Malcolm Ct., Stan. 36 BK28
Malcolm Cres. NW4 46 BP32
Malcolm Dr., Surb. 84 BK54
Malcolm Ho. N1 57 CA37
Purcell St.
Malcolm Pl. E2 57 CC38
Malcolm Rd. E1 57 CC38
Malcolm Rd. SE20 77 CC50
Malcolm Rd. SE25 87 CB53
Malcolm Rd. SW19 75 BR50
Malcolm Rd., Couls. 104 BW61
Malcolm Rd., Uxb. 44 AY35
Malcolm Way E11 49 CH31
Malden Ave. SE25 87 CB52
Malden Ave., Grnf. 45 BH35
Malden Ct., N.Mal. 85 BP52
Malden Cres. NW1 56 BV36
Malden Grn. Ave., Wor.Pk. 85 BO54
Malden Hill, N.Mal. 85 BO52
Malden Hill Gdns., N.Mal. 85 BO52
Malden Manor, The, N.Mal. 85 BO54
Malden Pk., N.Mal. 85 BO53
Malden Pl. NW5 47 BV35
Grafton Ter.
Malden Rd. NW5 47 BV35
Malden Rd., Borwd. 28 BM24
Malden Rd., N.Mal. 85 BO53
Malden Rd., Sutt. 94 BO56
Malden Rd., Wat. 26 BC23
Malden Rd., Wor.Pk. 85 BO54
Malden Way, N.Mal. 85 BN53
Maldon Clo. N1 57 BZ37
Popham St.
Maldon Clo. SE5 67 CA45
Maldon Ct., N.Mal. 85 BP52
Maldon Rd. N9 39 CA27
Maldon Rd. W3 55 BN40
Maldon Rd., Rom. 50 CS33
Maldon Rd., Wall. 95 BV56
Maldon Wk., Wdf.Grn. 40 CJ29
Malet Clo., Egh. 72 AU50
Malet Pl. WC1 1 N5
Malet Pl. WC1 56 BW38
Malet St. WC1 1 N5
Malet St. WC1 56 BW38
Maley Ave. SE27 76 BY48
Malford Ct. E18 40 CH30
Malford Gro. E18 49 CG31
Malfort Rd. SE5 67 CA45
Malham Rd. SE23 77 CC47
Malins Clo., Barn. 28 BP25
Mall, The E15 57 CF36
Mall, The N14 38 BX27
Mall, The SW1 3 M4
Mall, The SW1 66 BW41
Mall, The SW14 75 BN46
Mall, The W5 54 BK40
Mall, The, Brom. 88 CH52
Mall, The, Dag. 59 CR36
Mall, The, Har. 46 BL33
Mall, The, St.Alb. 18 BG17
Mall, The, Surb. 84 BK53
Mall Rd. W6 65 BP42
Mallams Ms. SW9 66 BY45
St. James Cres.
Mallard Clo. E9 57 CD36
Mallard Clo., Barn. 29 BT25
Mallard Clo., Dart. 80 CW46
Mallard Clo., Red. 121 BV69
Mallard Clo., Twick. 74 BF47
Mallard Clo., Upmin. 51 CZ33
Mallard Ct. NW9 46 BN33
Mallard Path SE28 68 CM41
Tom Cribb Rd.
Mallard Pl., Twick. 74 BJ48
Mallard Rd., S.Croy. 96 CC58
Mallard Wk., Sid. 79 CP50
Cray Rd.
Mallard Way NW9 46 BN33
Mallard Way, Brwd. 122 DD26
Mallard Way, Cars. 95 BW58
Mallard Way, Nthwd. 35 BA29
Ducks Hill Rd.
Mallard Way, Wat. 27 BE21
Mallards, The, Stai. 83 AW51
Beech Tree La.
Mallards Reach, Wey. 83 BA55
Mallards Rd., Wdf.Grn. 40 CH29
Mallet Dr., Nthlt. 45 BE35
Mallet Rd. SE13 77 CF46
Malling Clo., Croy. 87 CC53
Stockbury Rd.
Malling Gdns., Mord. 86 BT53
Malling Way, Brom. 88 CG54
Mallinson Rd. SW11 76 BU46
Mallinson Rd., Croy. 86 BW55
Mallion Ct., Wal.Abb. 22 CG20
Mallord St. SW3 66 BT43
Mallory Clo. SE4 67 CD45
Mallory Gdns., Barn. 38 BV26
Mallory St. NW8 1 C5
Mallory St. NW8 56 BU38
Mallow Clo., Croy. 87 CC54
Primrose La.
Mallow Clo., Grav. 81 DF49
Sorrel Way
Mallow Ct., Grays 71 DE43
Mallow Mead NW7 37 BR29
Mallow St. EC1 2 K4
Mallow St. EC1 57 BZ38
Mallows, The, Uxb. 44 AZ34
Mallows Grn., Harl. 13 CL13
Malm Clo., The, Rick. 35 AX27
Malmains Clo., Beck. 87 CF53
Malmains Way, Beck. 87 CF52
Malmesbury Clo., Pnr. 44 BB31
Malmesbury Rd. E3 57 CD38
Malmesbury Rd. E16 58 CG39
Malmesbury Rd. E18 40 CG30
Malmesbury Rd., Mord. 86 BT54
Malmesbury Ter. E16 58 CG39
Malmescroft, Hem.H. 8 BA14
Malmsdale, Welw.G.C. 5 BQ6
Malmstone Ave., Red. 113 BW67
Malpas Dr., Pnr. 45 BD32
Malpas Rd. E8 57 CB36
Malpas Rd. SE4 67 CD44
Malpas Rd., Dag. 59 CP36
Malpas Rd., Grays 71 DH41
Malpas Rd., Slou. 52 AQ40
Malt Hill, Egh. 72 AS49
Malt Ho. Clo., Wind. 72 AQ47
Malt Ho. Pas. SW13 65 BO44
The Ter.
Malt La., Rad. 27 BJ21
Malt St. SE1 67 CB43
Malta Rd. E10 48 CE33
Malta Rd., Til. 71 DF44
Malta St. EC1 2 G4
Malta St. EC1 56 BY38
Maltby Clo., Orp. 89 CO54
Vinson Clo.
Maltby Dr., Enf. 30 CB22
Maltby Rd., Chess. 94 BM57
Maltby St. SE1 4 P5
Maltby St. SE1 67 CA41
Malthouse Ct., Guil. 118 AS73
The St.
Malthouse Ct., St.Alb. 9 BG14
Sopwell La.
Malthouse Dr., Felt. 74 BD49
Malthus Path SE28 59 CP40
Owen Clo.
Malting La., Epp. 23 CO18
Maltings, The, Kings L. 17 BA20
Maltings, The, Orp. 88 CN54
Elm Gro.
Maltings, The, Oxt. 115 CG69
Maltings, The, St.Alb. 9 BG13
Maltings, The, Stai. 72 AV49
Maltings, The, Wey. 92 AY60
Brewery La.
Maltings Clo. SW13 65 BO44
Cleveland Gdns.
Maltings Dr., Epp. 23 CO18
High St.
Maltings Hill, Ong. 15 CV13
Maltings Ms., Sid. 79 CO48
Station Rd.
Maltings Pl. SW6 66 BS44
Maltmans La., Ger.Cr. 43 AR31
Maltmans Pk., Grnf. 54 BG38
Malton Ms. W10 55 BR39
Cambridge Gdns.
Malton Rd. W10 55 BR39
Malton St. SE18 68 CN43
Maltravers St. WC2 2 C10
Maltravers St. WC2 56 BX40
Arundel St.
Malus Clo., Hem.H. 8 AZ13
Malus Clo., Wey. 91 AV57
Malus Dr., Wey. 91 AV57
Malva Clo. SW18 76 BS46
Malva Rd.
Malva Rd. SW18 76 BS46
Malvern Ave. E4 39 CF29
Malvern Ave., Bexh. 69 CQ43
Malvern Ave., Har. 45 BE34
Malvern Clo. SE20 87 CB51
Derwent Rd.
Malvern Clo. W10 55 BR39
Malvern Clo., Cher. 91 AU
Chobham Rd.
Malvern Clo., Hat. 10 BC
Malvern Clo., Mitch. 86 BW
Malvern Clo., St.Alb. 9 BK
Malvern Clo., Surb. 85 BL
Malvern Clo., Uxb. 44 AZ
Malvern Ct. SW7 3
Malvern Ct. SW7 66 BT
Malvern Ct., Slou. 62 AT
Malvern Dr., Felt. 74 BD
Malvern Dr., Ilf. 49 CN
Malvern Dr., Wdf.Grn. 40 CJ
Malvern Gdns. NW2 46 BR
Malvern Gdns. NW6 55 BR
Canterbury Rd.
Malvern Gdns., Har. 46 BL
Malvern Gdns., Loug. 31 CK
Malvern Ms. NW6 56 BS
Malvern Pl. NW6 55 BR
Malvern Rd. E6 58 CK
Malvern Rd. E8 57 CB
Malvern Rd. E11 49 CG
Malvern Rd. N8 47 BX
Malvern Rd. N17 48 CB
Malvern Rd. NW6 56 BS
Malvern Rd., Enf. 30 CD
Malvern Rd., Grays 71 DF
Malvern Rd., Hmptn. 74 BF
Malvern Rd., Hayes 63 BB
Malvern Rd., Horn. 50 CU
Malvern Rd., Orp. 98 CO
Malvern Rd., Surb. 85 BL
Malvern Rd., Th.Hth. 86 BY
Malvern Ter. N1 56 BY
Malvern Ter. N9 39 CA
Malvern Way W13 54 BJ
Malvern Way, Hem.H. 8 AY
Malvern Way, Rick. 26 AZ
Malvina Ave., Grav. 81 DG
Malwood Rd. SW12 76 BV
Malyons Rd. SE13 77 CE
Malyons Rd., Swan. 79 CT
Malyons Ter. SE13 77 CE
Managers St. E14 57 CF
Manan Clo., Hem.H. 8 BA
Manaton Clo. SE15 67 CB
Manaton Clo. W., Borwd. 27 BK
Manaton Cres., Sthl. 54 BF
Manbey Gro. E15 58 CG
Manbey Pk. Rd. E15 58 CG
Manbey Rd. E15 58 CG
Manbey St. E15 58 CG
Manborough Ave. E6 58 CK
Manbre Rd. W6 65 BQ
Manchester Dr. W10 55 BR
Manchester Est. E14 67 CF
Manchester Gro. E14 67 CF
Manchester Ms. W1 1 C
Manchester Ms. W1 56 BV
Manchester St.
Manchester Rd. E14 67 CF
Manchester Rd. N15 48 BZ
Manchester Rd., Th.Hth. 87 BZ
Manchester Row, Dart. 69 CT
Manchester Sq. W1 1 C
Manchester Sq. W1 56 BV
Manchester St. W1 1 C
Manchester St. W1 56 BV
Manchester Way, Dag. 50 CR
Manchuria Rd. SW11 76 BV
Manciple St. SE1 4
Manciple St. SE1 67 BZ
Mancroft Rd., Hem.H. 8 AY
Mandalay Rd. SW4 76 BW
Mandarin St. E14 57 CE
Salter St.
Mandela Clo. NW10 55 BN
Mandela Rd. E16 58 CH
Mandela St. NW1 56 BW
Mandela St. SW9 66 BY
Mandela Way SE1 4 N
Mandela Way SE1 67 CA
Mandelyns, Berk. 7 AP1
Mandeville Clo. SE3 68 CG
Vanbrugh Pk.
Mandeville Clo. SW20 85 BR
Mandeville Clo., Brox. 12 CD
Mandeville Clo., Guil. 118 AQ
Mandeville Clo., Harl. 14 CP
Mandeville Clo., Wat. 26 BB
Mandeville Ct. E4 39 CD
Lower Hall La.
Mandeville Ct., Egh. 72 AT
Mandeville Dr., St.Alb. 9 BG
Mandeville Dr., Surb. 84 BK
Mandeville Hos. N1 56 BY
Mandeville Pl. W1 1 H
Mandeville Pl. W1 56 BV
Mandeville Ri., Welw.G.C. 5 BQ
Mandeville Rd. N14 38 BV
Mandeville Rd., Enf. 30 CC
Mandeville Rd., Islw. 64 BJ
Mandeville Rd., Nthlt. 54 BE
Mandeville Rd., Pot.B. 20 BT1
Mandeville Rd., Shep. 83 AZ
Mandeville St. E5 48 CD
Mandeville Wk., Brwd. 122 DF
Hutton Dr.
Mandrake Rd. SW17 76 BU
Mandrell Rd. SW2 76 BX
Manette St. W1 1 F
Manette St. W1 56 BW
Charing Cross Rd.
Manford Clo., Chig. 41 CO
Manford Cross, Chig. 41 CO
Manford Way, Chig. 40 CN
Manfred Ct. SW15 75 BR
Manfred Rd.
Manfred Rd. SW15 75 BR
Manger Rd. N7 56 BX
Mangles Rd., Guil. 118 AR
Mangold Way, Erith 69 CP

angrove La., Hert. 12 CA10
anilla St. E14 67 CE41
anister Rd. SE2 69 CO41
anley Ct. N16 48 CA34
Stoke Newington High St.
anley Rd., Hem.H. 8 AY13
anley St. NW1 56 BV37
anly Dixon Dr., Enf. 30 CD22
annicotts, Welw.G.C. 5 BP8
annin Rd., Rom. 50 CO33
anning Gdns., Har. 45 BK33
anning Rd. E17 48 CC32
anning Rd., Dag. 59 CR36
anning Rd., Orp. 89 CP53
anning St., S.Ock. 60 CY40
anningford Clo. EC1 2 F2
anningford Clo. EC1 56 BY38
anningtree Clo. SW19 75 BR47
anningtree Rd., Ruis. 44 BC35
anningtree St. E1 57 CB39
annock Dr., Loug. 31 CM23
annock Rd. N22 47 BY31
anns Clo., Islw. 74 BH46
anns Rd., Edg. 37 BM29
anoel Rd., Twick. 74 BG48
anor All. W4 65 BO42
Devonshire Rd.
anor Ave. SE4 67 CD44
anor Ave., Cat. 105 CA65
anor Ave., Hem.H. 8 AX15
anor Ave., Horn. 51 CV32
anor Ave., Houns. 64 BD45
anor Ave., Nthlt. 54 BE36
anor Ave. Par., Chig. 40 CM28
Grange Cres.
anor Chase, Wey. 92 AZ56
anor Clo. NW7 37 BN28
Manor Dr.
anor Clo. NW9 46 BM31
anor Clo. SE28 59 CP39
anor Clo., Barn. 28 BR24
Wood St.
anor Clo., Berk. 7 AR13
anor Clo., Dag. 59 CS36
anor Clo. (Crayford), 69 CS45
Dart.
anor Clo. (Wilmington), 79 CU48
Dart.
anor Clo., Hat. 10 BO11
anor Clo., Lthd. 110 BB67
anor Clo., Rom. 50 CU32
Manor Rd.
anor Clo., Ruis. 44 BB33
anor Clo., S.Ock. 60 CY40
anor Clo., Warl. 105 CD62
anor Clo., Wok. 100 AV61
anor Clo., Wor.Pk. 85 BO54
anor Clo. S., S.Ock. 60 CY40
Manor Clo.
anor Cotts., Nthwd. 35 BB30
anor Cotts. App. N2 38 BT30
anor Ct. N2 47 BU32
anor Ct. N14 38 BW27
anor Ct. SW16 76 BX48
Streatham Ct.
anor Ct., Enf. 30 CB21
anor Ct., Wey. 92 AZ56
anor Ct. Rd. W7 54 BH40
anor Cres., Beac. 34 AO28
anor Cres., Guil. 118 AQ69
anor Cres., Horn. 51 CV32
anor Cres., Surb. 85 BM53
anor Cres., Wey. 92 AY60
anor Dr. N14 38 BV26
anor Dr. N20 38 BU28
anor Dr. NW7 37 BN28
anor Dr., Epsom 94 BO57
anor Dr., Esher 84 BH55
anor Dr., Felt. 74 BD49
anor Dr., St.Alb. 18 BF17
anor Dr., Sun. 83 BC51
anor Dr., Surb. 85 BL53
anor Dr., Wem. 46 BL35
anor Dr., Wey. 92 AW58
anor Dr., The, Wor.Pk. 85 BO54
anor Dr. N., N.Mal. 85 BN54
anor Dr. N., Wor.Pk. 85 BO54
anor Fm., Farn. 90 CW54
anor Fm. Ave., Shep. 83 AZ53
anor Fm. Clo., Wind. 61 AM45
anor Fm. Dr. E4 40 CG27
anor Fm. Dr., Enf. 30 CB21
anor Fm. Est., Stai. 72 AR46
anor Fm. La., Egh. 72 AT49
anor Fm. Rd., Enf. 30 CB21
anor Fm. Rd., Th.Hth. 86 BY51
anor Fm. Rd., Wem. 54 BK37
anor Fm. Way, Beac. 34 AO29
anor Flds. SW15 75 BQ46
anor Gdns. N7 47 BX34
anor Gdns. SW20 85 BR51
anor Gdns. W3 65 BM42
anor Gdns., Guil. 118 AQ69
anor Gdns., Hmptn. 74 BF50
anor Gdns., Lthd. 111 BD67
anor Gdns., Rich. 65 BL45
anor Gdns., Ruis. 45 BD35
anor Gdns., S.Croy. 96 CA57
anor Gdns., Sun. 83 BC51
anor Gate, Nthlt. 54 BE36
anor Grn. Rd., Epsom 94 BM60
anor Gro. SE15 67 CC43
anor Gro., Beck. 87 CE51
anor Gro., Lthd. 110 BB67
anor Gro., Maid. 61 AH43
anor Gro., Rich. 65 BM45
anor Hall Ave. NW4 37 BQ30
anor Hall Dr. NW4 37 BQ30
anor Hatch, Harl. 14 CO12
anor Hatch Clo., Harl. 14 CO11
Tumbler Rd.
anor Hill, Bans. 95 BU60
anor Ho., Chis. 88 CM51
anor Ho., Surb. 84 BK55

Manor Ho., Wor.Pk. 85 BN54
Manor Ho. Ct., Epsom 94 BN60
Manor Ho. Ct., Shep. 83 AZ54
Church Rd.
Manor Ho. Dr. NW6 55 BQ36
Manor Ho. Gdns., Abb.L. 17 BA19
Manor Ho. La., Slou. 62 AQ43
Manor Ho. Way, Islw. 64 BJ45
Church St.
Manor La. SE12 78 CG46
Manor La. SE13 68 CG45
Manor La., Fawk. 90 DB54
Manor La., Felt. 73 BC48
Manor La., Ger.Cr. 43 AR33
Manor La., Hayes 63 BA43
Manor La., Sun. 83 BC51
Manor La., Sutt. 95 BS56
Manor La., Tad. 113 BS68
Manor La. Ter. SE13 68 CG45
Manor Leaze, Egh. 72 AT49
Manor Ms. NW6 56 BS37
Cambridge Ave.
Manor Ms. SE4 67 CD44
Lewisham Way
Manor Mt. SE23 77 CC47
Manor Par., Hat. 10 BO11
Manor Par., Hayes 63 BA43
Manor Pk. SE13 67 CF45
Manor Pk., Chis. 88 CM51
Manor Pk., Hat. 10 BO11
Manor Pk., Rich. 65 BL45
Manor Pk. Clo., W.Wick. 87 CE54
Manor Pk. Cres., Edg. 37 BM29
Manor Pk. Dr., Har. 45 BF31
Manor Pk. Gdns., Edg. 37 BM28
Manor Pk. Par. SE13 67 CF45
Lee High Rd.
Manor Pk. Rd. E12 49 CJ35
Manor Pk. Rd. N2 47 BT31
Manor Pk. Rd. NW10 55 BO37
Manor Pk. Rd., Chis. 88 CM51
Manor Pk. Rd., Sutt. 95 BT56
Manor Pk. Rd., W.Wick. 87 CE54
Manor Pl. SE17 4 H10
Manor Pl. SE17 66 BY42
Manor Pl., Chis. 88 CM51
Manor Pl., Dart. 80 CV47
Manor Pl., Felt. 73 BC47
Manor Pl., Mitch. 86 BW52
Manor Pl., Stai. 73 AW49
Manor Pl., Sutt. 95 BS56
Manor Rd. E10 48 CE33
Manor Rd. E15 58 CG37
Manor Rd. E16 58 CG38
Manor Rd. E17 39 CD30
Manor Rd. N16 48 BZ34
Manor Rd. N17 39 CB30
Manor Rd. N22 38 BX29
Manor Rd. SE25 87 CB52
Manor Rd. SW20 85 BR51
Manor Rd. W13 54 BJ40
Manor Rd., Ashf. 73 AY49
Manor Rd., Bark. 58 CN36
Manor Rd., Barn. 28 BR25
Manor Rd., Beac. 34 AO28
Manor Rd., Beck. 87 CE51
Manor Rd., Bex. 79 CR47
Manor Rd., Chig. 40 CK29
Manor Rd., Dag. 59 CS36
Manor Rd., Dart. 69 CT45
Manor Rd., E.Mol. 84 BG52
Manor Rd., Enf. 30 BZ23
Manor Rd., Erith 69 CT43
Manor Rd., Grays 71 DE43
Manor Rd. (West 70 DB43
Thurrock), Grays
Manor Rd., Guil. 118 AQ69
Manor Rd., Harl. 6 CP8
Manor Rd., Har. 45 BJ32
Manor Rd., Hat. 5 BM10
Manor Rd., Hayes 53 BC39
Manor Rd., Hodd. 12 CE11
Manor Rd., Loug. 31 CH25
Manor Rd. (High Beech), 31 CH22
Loug.
Manor Rd., Mitch. 86 BW52
Manor Rd., Pot.B. 19 BR19
Manor Rd., Red. 113 BW68
Manor Rd., Reig. 120 BR69
Manor Rd., Rich. 65 BL45
Manor Rd., Rom. 50 CU32
Manor Rd. (Chadwell 50 CP32
Heath), Rom.
Manor Rd. (Lambourne 41 CP27
End), Rom.
Manor Rd., Ruis. 44 BA33
Manor Rd., St.Alb. 9 BH13
Manor Rd. (London 18 BK16
Colney), St.Alb.
Manor Rd., Sev. 107 CP65
Manor Rd., Sid. 78 CN48
Manor Rd., Sutt. 94 BR57
Manor Rd., Swans. 80 DB46
Manor Rd., Tedd. 74 BJ49
Manor Rd., Til. 71 DG44
Manor Rd., Twick. 74 BR48
Manor Rd., Wall. 95 BV56
Manor Rd., Wal.Abb. 21 CF20
Manor Rd., Walt. 83 BB54
Manor Rd., Wat. 26 BC23
Manor Rd., W.Wick. 87 CE55
Manor Rd., West. 106 CK63
Manor Rd., Wind. 61 AM44
Manor Rd., Wok. 100 AR61
Manor Rd. (Sendmarsh), 100 AV65
Wok.
Manor Rd., Wdf.Grn. 40 CK29
Manor Rd. N., Esher 84 BH55
Manor Rd. N., T.Ditt. 84 BJ54
Manor Rd. N., Wall. 95 BV56
Manor Rd. S., Esher 93 BH55
Manor Sq., Dag. 50 CP34
Manor St., Berk. 7 AR13
Manor Vale, Brent. 64 BK42

Manor Vw. N3 38 BS30
Manor Vw., Beck. 87 CE51
High St.
Manor Wk., Wey. 92 AZ56
Manor Way E4 39 CF28
Manor Way NW9 46 BO31
Manor Way SE3 68 CG45
Manor Way, Bans. 104 BU61
Manor Way, Beck. 87 CE51
Manor Way, Bex. 79 CR47
Manor Way, Bexh. 69 CS45
Manor Way, Borwd. 28 BN23
Manor Way, Brwd. 42 DA27
Manor Way, Brom. 88 CK53
Manor Way, Chesh. 16 AO18
Manor Way, Chsnt. 21 CD18
Manor Way, Egh. 72 AS50
Manor Way (Bridge Rd.), 71 DD43
Grays
Manor Way (Manor Rd.), 71 DE43
Grays
Manor Way, Guil. 118 AO72
Manor Way, Har. 45 BF31
Manor Way, Lthd. 102 BG61
Manor Way, Maid. 61 AG43
Manor Way, Mitch. 86 BW52
Manor Way, Orp. 88 CM53
Manor Way, Pot.B. 20 BS18
Manor Way, Rain. 59 CT39
Manor Way, Rick. 26 AZ24
Manor Way, Ruis. 44 BB33
Manor Way, S.Croy. 96 CA57
Manor Way, Sthl. 64 BD42
Manor Way, Swans. 70 DB45
Manor Way, Wok. 100 AT64
Manor Way, Wor.Pk. 85 BO54
Manor Way, The, Pur. 95 BX59
Manor Way, The, Wall. 95 BV56
Manor Waye, Uxb. 53 AX37
Manor Wd. Rd., Pur. 95 BX60
Manorbrook SE3 68 CH45
Manorcroft Rd., Egh. 72 AT50
Manordene Clo., T.Ditt. 84 BJ54
Manordene Rd. SE28 59 CP39
Manorfield Clo. N19 47 BW35
Tufnell Pk. Rd.
Manorgate Rd., Kings.T. 85 BM51
Manorhall Gdns. E10 48 CE33
Manorhouse La., Lthd. 111 BE66
Manorside, Barn. 28 BR24
Manorside Clo. SE2 69 CP42
New Rd.
Manorville Rd., Hem.H. 8 AX15
Manorway, Enf. 39 CA26
Manorway, Grays 71 DD43
Manorway, Wdf.Grn. 40 CJ28
Manresa Rd. SW3 66 BU42
Mansard Beeches SW17 76 BV49
Mansard Clo., Horn. 50 CU34
Mansard Clo., Pnr. 45 BD31
Manscroft Rd., Hem.H. 8 AW12
Manse Clo., Hayes 63 BA43
Manse Rd. N16 48 CA34
Manse Way, Swan. 89 CU52
Mansel Clo., Guil. 109 AQ68
Mansel Clo., Slou. 52 AQ39
Mansel Gro. E17 39 CE30
Mansel Rd. SW19 75 BR50
Mansell Clo., Wind. 61 AM44
Mansell Rd. W3 65 BN41
Mansell Rd., Grnf. 54 BF39
Mansell St. E1 2 Q9
Mansell St. E1 57 CA39
Mansell Way, Cat. 105 BZ64
Manser Rd., Rain. 59 CT38
Mansfield, Saw. 6 CO6
Mansfield Ave. N15 48 BZ31
Mansfield Ave., Barn. 29 BU25
Mansfield Clo. N9 30 CB25
Mansfield Clo., Orp. 89 CP54
Mansfield Clo., Wey. 92 AZ56
Mansfield Dr., Hayes 53 BB38
Mansfield Dr., Red. 113 BW67
Mansfield Gdns., Horn. 51 CV34
Mansfield Hill E4 39 CE26
Mansfield Ms. W1 1 J7
Mansfield Ms. W1 56 BV39
Duchess St.
Mansfield Pl. NW3 47 BT35
Streatley Pl.
Mansfield Pl., S.Croy. 96 BZ57
Mansfield Rd. E11 49 CH32
Mansfield Rd. E17 48 CD31
Mansfield Rd. NW3 47 BU35
Mansfield Rd. W3 55 BM38
Mansfield Rd., Chess. 93 BK56
Mansfield Rd., Ilf. 49 CL33
Mansfield Rd., S.Croy. 96 BZ57
Mansfield Rd., Swan. 79 CT50
Mansfield St. W1 1 J7
Mansfield St. W1 56 BV39
Mansford St. E2 57 CB37
Manship Rd., Mitch. 76 BV50
Mansion Gdns. NW3 47 BS34
Firecrest Dr.
Mansion Ho. Pl. EC4 2 K9
Mansion La., Iver 52 AU40
Manson Ms. SW7 3 A9
Manson Ms. SW7 66 BT42
Manson Pl. SW7 3 A9
Manson Pl. SW7 66 BT42
Manstead Clo., Rain. 59 CU39
Mansted Gdns., Rom. 50 CP33
Manston Ave., Sthl. 64 BF42
Manston Clo. SE20 87 CC51
Manston Clo., Chsnt. 21 CC18
Elgin Rd.
Manston Rd., Guil. 109 AT68
Manston Rd., Harl. 13 CN11
Manston Way, Horn. 59 CU36
Manstone Rd. NW2 46 BR35
Manthorp Rd. SE18 68 CM42
Mantilla Rd. SW17 76 BV49
Mantle Rd. SE4 67 CD45

Manton Ave. W7 64 BH41
Manton Clo., Hayes 53 BB40
Manton Rd. SE2 69 CO42
Mantus Clo. E1 57 CC38
Mantus Rd.
Mantus Rd. E1 57 CC38
Manus Way N20 38 BT27
Manville Gdns. SW17 76 BV48
Manville Rd. SW17 76 BV48
Manwood Rd. SE4 77 CD46
Manwood St. E16 58 CK40
Manygate La., Shep. 83 BA54
Manygates SW12 76 BV48
Maori Rd., Guil. 118 AS70
Mape St. E2 57 CB38
Mapesbury Rd. NW2 55 BR36
Maple Ave. E4 39 CD28
Maple Ave. W3 55 BO40
Maple Ave., Har. 45 BF34
Maple Ave., St.Alb. 9 BG11
Maple Ave., Upmin. 51 CX35
Maple Ave., West Dr. 53 AY40
Maple Clo. N16 48 CB32
Maple Clo. SW4 76 BW46
Maple Clo., Brwd. 122 DC27
Maple Clo., Buck.H. 40 CJ27
Maple Clo., Bush. 27 BE23
Maple Clo., Hat. 10 BP13
Maple Clo., Horn. 50 CU34
Maple Clo., Mitch. 86 BV51
Maple Clo., Orp. 88 CM53
Maple Clo., Ruis. 44 BC32
Maple Clo., Swan. 89 CT51
Maple Clo., Whyt. 105 CA62
Maple Ct., Egh. 72 AQ50
Maple Ct., N.Mal. 85 BO52
Maple Ct., Wok. 100 AR61
Maple Cres., Sid. 79 CO46
Maple Cres., Slou. 52 AQ40
Maple Dr., Red. 121 BU73
Maple Gdns., Edg. 37 BO29
Maple Gdns., Stai. 73 AY48
Maple Grn., Hem.H. 7 AV12
Maple Gro. NW9 46 BN33
Maple Gro. W5 64 BK41
Maple Gro., Brent. 64 BJ43
Maple Gro., Guil. 118 AR69
Maple Gro., Sthl. 54 BE39
Maple Gro., Wat. 26 BC23
Maple Gro., Welw.G.C. 5 BR6
Maple Gro., Wok. 100 AS64
Maple Hill, Hem.H. 16 AR18
Maple Ho. SE8 67 CD43
Idonia St.
Maple Leaf Dr., Sid. 78 CN47
Maple Leaf Sq. SE16 67 CC41
St. Elmos Rd.
Maple Ms. NW6 56 BS37
Kilburn Pk. Rd.
Maple Ms. SW16 76 BX49
Maple Pl. W1 1 M5
Maple Pl. W1 56 BW38
Maple St.
Maple Pl., Bans. 94 BQ60
Maple Pl., West Dr. 53 AY40
Maple Rd. E11 49 CG32
Maple Rd. SE20 87 CB51
Maple Rd., Ash. 102 BK63
Maple Rd., Dart. 80 CV47
Maple Rd., Grav. 81 DH49
Maple Rd., Grays 71 DE43
Maple Rd., Hayes 54 BD38
Maple Rd., Red. 121 BU72
Maple Rd., Surb. 84 BK53
Maple Rd., Whyt. 105 CA62
Maple Rd., Wok. 100 AV65
Maple Springs, Wal.Abb. 22 CH20
Maple St. W1 1 L6
Maple St. W1 56 BW39
Maple St., Rom. 50 CS31
Maple Ter., Rick. 34 AV28
Maple Wk. W10 55 BR38
Droop St.
Maple Wk., Sutt. 95 BS58
Cotswold Rd.
Maple Way, Couls. 104 BV64
Maple Way, Felt. 73 BC48
Maplecroft Clo. E6 58 CK39
Allhallows Rd.
Maplecroft La., Wal.Abb. 13 CG14
Mapledale Ave., Croy. 87 CB55
Mapledene, Chis. 78 CM50
Mapledene Rd. E8 57 CA36
Maplefield, St.Alb. 18 BF18
Maplefield La., Ch.St.G. 25 AQ24
Maplehurst Clo., Kings.T. 85 BL52
Surbiton Rd.
Mapleleafe Gdns., Ilf. 49 CL31
Maplelodge Clo., Rick. 34 AV28
Maples, The, Bans. 95 BS60
Maples, The, Cher. 91 AU57
Maples, The, Harl. 13 CL13
Maples Pl. E1 57 CB39
Raven Row
Maplescombe La., Farn. 90 CX55
Maplestead Rd. SW2 76 BX47
Maplestead Rd., Dag. 59 CO37
Maplethorpe Rd., Th.Hth. 86 BY52
Mapleton Clo., Brom. 88 CH53
Mapleton Cres. SW18 76 BS46
Mapleton Rd.
Mapleton Cres., Enf. 30 CC22
Mapleton Rd. E4 39 CF27
Mapleton Rd. SW18 76 BS46
Mapleton Rd., Enf. 30 CB23
Mapleton Rd., West. 115 CN68
Maplin Clo. N21 29 BX25
Maplin Pk., Slou. 62 AV41
Maplin Rd. E16 58 CH39
Maplin St. E3 57 CD38
Mapperley Dr., Wdf.Grn. 40 CG29
Forest Dr.
Mar Rd., S.Ock. 60 DB38
Maran Way, Erith 69 CP41

Marban Rd. W9 55 BR38
Marbeck Clo., Wind. 61 AL44
Marble Arch W1 1 E10
Marble Arch W1 56 BU40
Marble Clo. W3 55 BM40
Gunnersbury La.
Marble Hill Clo., Twick. 74 BJ47
Marble Hill Gdns., Twick. 74 BJ47
Marble Hill River Path, 74 BK47
Twick.
Orleans Rd.
Marbles Way, Tad. 103 BQ63
Marbrook Ct. SE12 78 CJ48
Marcellina Way, Orp. 88 CN55
Marcet Rd., Dart. 80 CV46
March Rd., Twick. 74 BJ47
March Rd., Wey. 92 AZ56
Marchant Rd. E11 48 CF34
Marchant St. SE14 67 CD43
Sanford St.
Marchbank Rd. SW5 65 BR43
Marchmant Clo., Horn. 51 CV34
Connaught Rd.
Marchmont Rd., Rich. 75 BL46
Marchmont Rd., Wall. 95 BW57
Marchmont St. WC1 1 Q4
Marchmont St. WC1 56 BX38
Marchside Clo., Houns. 64 BD44
Springwell Rd.
Marchwood Clo. SE5 67 CA43
Marchwood Cres. W5 54 BK39
Marcia Rd. SE1 4 N9
Marcia Rd. SE1 67 CA42
Marcilly Rd. SW18 76 BT46
Marco Rd. W6 65 BP41
Marcon Pl. E8 48 CB35
Marconi Rd., Grav. 81 DE48
Marconi Way, Sthl. 54 BF39
Marcus Ct. E15 58 CG37
Marcus Garvey Way SE24 66 BY45
Marcus Rd., Dart. 79 CU47
Marcus St. E15 58 CG37
Marcus St. SW18 76 BS46
Marcus Ter. SW18 76 BS46
Denton St.
Mardale Dr. NW9 46 BN32
Mardell Rd., Croy. 87 CC53
Marden Ave., Brom. 88 CG53
Marden Clo., Chig. 41 CO27
Marden Cres., Bex. 79 CS46
Marden Cres., Croy. 86 BX53
Marden Rd. N17 39 CA30
The Ave.
Marden Rd., Croy. 86 BX53
Marden Rd., Rom. 50 CT32
Marden Sq. SE16 67 CB41
Marder Rd. W13 64 BJ41
Mardyke Rd., Harl. 6 CO10
Mardyke St. SE17 67 BZ42
Townsend St.
Mare St. E8 57 CB37
Marechal Niel Ave., Sid. 78 CM48
Mares Fld., Croy. 87 CA55
Mareschal Rd., Guil. 118 AR71
Maresfield Gdns. NW3 47 BT35
Marfield Ct., N.Mal. 85 BO54
Marfleet Clo., Cars. 86 BU55
Brooklyn Clo.
Marford Rd., Welw.G.C. 5 BN8
Margaret Ave. E4 30 CE25
Margaret Ave., Brwd. 122 DC26
Margaret Ave., St.Alb. 9 BG12
Margaret Bondfield Ave., 59 CO36
Bark.
Margaret Bldgs. N16 48 CA33
Margaret Rd.
Margaret Clo., Abb.L. 17 BB19
Margaret Clo., Epp. 22 CN18
Margaret Rd.
Margaret Clo., Pot.B. 20 BT20
Margaret Clo., Rom. 50 CU32
Margaret Clo., Stai. 73 AX50
Margaret Clo., Wal.Abb. 21 CF20
Moremead
Margaret Ct. W1 1 L8
Margaret Ct. W1 56 BW39
Margaret St.
Margaret Dr., Horn. 51 CW33
Margaret Rd. N16 48 CA33
Margaret Rd., Barn. 29 BT24
Margaret Rd., Bex. 79 CP46
Margaret Rd., Epp. 23 CO18
Margaret Rd., Guil. 118 AR71
Margaret Rd., Rom. 50 CU32
Margaret St. W1 1 K8
Margaret St. W1 56 BV39
Margaret St., Uxb. 53 AX36
Cross St.
Margaret Way, Couls. 104 BY62
Margaret Way, Ilf. 49 CJ32
Margaretta Ter. SW3 66 BU43
Margaretting Rd. E12 49 CJ34
Margate Rd. SW2 76 BX46
Margeholes, Wat. 36 BE27
Margery Gro., Tad. 112 BR68
Margery La., Tad. 112 BR68
Margery Pk. Rd. E7 58 CH36
Margery Rd., Dag. 50 CP34
Margery St. WC1 2 D3
Margery St. WC1 56 BY38
Margery Wd., Welw.G.C. 5 BS6
Margin Dr. SW19 75 BQ49
Margravine Gdns. W6 65 BQ42
Margravine Rd. W6 65 BQ42
Marham Gdns. SW18 76 BU47
Marham Gdns., Mord. 86 BT53
Maria Clo. SE1 67 CB42
Beatrice Rd.
Maria Ter. E1 57 CC38
Maria Theresa Clo., 85 BN53
N.Mal.
Mariam Gdns., Horn. 51 CW34
Marian Clo., Grays 60 DC40
Marian Clo., Hayes 54 BD38

Mar–Mas

Marian Ct., Sutt. 95 BS56
Marian Pl. E2 57 CB37
Marian Rd. SW16 86 BW51
Marian Sq. E2 57 CB37
Marian Way NW10 55 BO36
Maricas Ave., Har. 36 BG29
Marie Lloyd Wk. E8 57 CA36
Forest Rd.
Mariette Way, Wall. 95 BX58
Marigold All. SE1 4 F1
Marigold La. SE28 59 CP40
Marigold Rd. N17 39 CC29
Marigold St. SE16 67 CB41
Marigold Way, Croy. 87 CC54
Marina App., Hayes 54 BE39
West Quay Dr.
Marina Ave., N.Mal. 85 BP53
Marina Clo., Brom. 88 CG52
Marina Dr., Dart. 80 CW47
Marina Dr., Grav. 81 DF47
Marina Dr., Well. 68 CN44
Marina Gdns., Chsnt. 21 CC18
Marina Gdns., Rom. 50 CS32
Marina Way, Iver 52 AV40
Marina Way, Tedd. 74 BK50
Fairways
Marine Dr. SE18 68 CK42
Marine St. SE16 67 CB41
Enid St.
Marinefield Rd. SW6 66 BS44
Mariner Gdns., Rich. 74 BJ48
Ashburnham Rd.
Mariner Rd. E12 49 CL35
Mariner Way, Hem.H. 8 AZ14
Mariners Ms. E14 67 CF42
Sextant Ave.
Mariners Wk., Erith 69 CU43
Frobisher Rd.
Marion Ave., Shep. 83 AZ53
Marion Clo., Bush. 27 BE23
Marion Clo., Ilf. 40 CM29
Marion Cres., Orp. 89 CO53
Marion Gro., Wdf.Grn. 40 CG28
Marion Rd. NW7 37 BP28
Marion Rd., Th.Hth. 87 BZ53
Marischal Rd. SE13 67 CF45
Marisco Clo., Grays 71 DG42
Marish La., Uxb. 43 AU31
Maritime St. E3 57 CD38
Marius Pas. SW17 76 BV48
Marius Rd.
Marius Rd. SW17 76 BV48
Marjorams Ave., Loug. 31 CL23
Marjorie Gro. SW11 66 BU45
Mark Ave. E4 30 CE25
Mark Clo., Bexh. 69 CQ44
Mark Clo., Sthl. 54 BF40
Mark Dr., Ger.Cr. 34 AR28
Mark Grn., Wat. 36 BD28
Mark Hall Moors, Harl. 6 CO9
Mark La. EC3 2 N10
Mark La. EC3 57 CA40
Mark La., Grav. 81 DJ47
Mark Oak La., Lthd. 102 BF64
Mark Pl., Sthl. 54 BF40
Mark Rd. N22 38 BY30
Mark Rd., Hem.H. 8 AZ12
Mark St. E15 58 CG36
Mark St. EC2 2 M4
Mark St. EC2 57 CA38
Mark St., Reig. 121 BS70
Mark Way, Swan. 89 CU53
Markab Rd., Nthwd. 35 BB28
Marke Clo., Kes. 97 CK56
Markedge La., Couls. 104 BU65
Markedge La., Red. 113 BU66
Markenfield Rd., Guil. 118 AR70
Market, The, Cars. 86 BT54
Market Ct. W1 1 L8
Market Ct. W1 56 BW39
Market Pl.
Market Hill SE18 68 CL41
Market La., Slou. 62 AU42
Market Link, Rom. 50 CT31
Market Meadow Pl., Orp. 89 CP52
Market Ms. W1 3 J3
Market Ms. W1 56 BV40
Market Oak La., Hem.H. 8 AZ15
Market Par. SE15 67 CB44
Market Pl. N2 47 BU31
Market Pl. NW11 47 BS31
Market Pl. SE16 67 CB42
Southwark Pk. Rd.
Market Pl. W1 1 L8
Market Pl. W1 56 BW39
Market Pl. W3 55 BN40
Market Pl., Brent. 64 BK43
Market Pl., Dart. 80 CW47
Market St.
Market Pl., Dor. 119 BJ71
Market Pl., Enf. 30 BZ24
Market Pl., Ger.Cr. 34 AR30
Market Pl., Grav. 81 DH47
Market Pl., Grays 71 DD43
Market Pl., Hat. 10 BP12
Market Pl., Kings.T. 84 BK51
Market Pl., Rom. 50 CT32
Market Pl. (Abridge), Rom. 32 CO24
Market Pl., St.Alb. 9 BG13
Market Pl., Wat. 27 BD24
Market Rd. N7 56 BX36
Market Rd., Rich. 65 BM45
Market Row SW9 66 BY45
Atlantic Rd.
Market Sq., Brom. 88 CH51
Market Sq., Hem.H. 8 AX13
Market Sq., Stai. 72 AV49
Clarence St.
Market Sq., Uxb. 53 AX36
High St.
Market Sq., Wal.Abb. 21 CF20
Market Sq., Wok. 100 AS62
Market St. E6 58 CK37
Market St. SE18 68 CL42
Market St., Dart. 80 CW47
Market St., Guil. 118 AR71
Market St., Harl. 6 CP9
Market St., Wat. 26 BC24
Market Way E14 57 CE39
Market Way, West. 115 CM66
Costells Meadows
Markfield, Croy. 96 CB58
Markfield Gdns. E4 39 CE26
Markfield Rd. N15 48 CB31
Markfield Rd., Cat. 114 CB66
Markham Pl. SW3 3 E10
Markham Sq. SW3 3 E10
Markham Sq. SW3 66 BU42
Markham St. SW3 3 D10
Markham St. SW3 66 BU42
Markhole Clo., Hmptn. 74 BE50
Markhouse Ave. E17 48 CD32
Markhouse Rd. E17 48 CD32
Markmanor Ave. E17 48 CD33
Marks Ave., Ong. 24 CW17
Marks Rd., Rom. 50 CS32
Marks Rd., Warl. 105 CD62
Marks Sq., Grav. 81 DF49
Marks St. E1 57 CA39
Marksbury Ave., Rich. 65 BM45
Markville Gdns., Cat. 114 CB66
Markway, Sun. 84 BD51
Markwell Clo. SE26 77 CB49
Taylors La.
Markyate Rd., Dag. 50 CO35
Marl Rd. SW18 66 BS45
Marlands Rd., Ilf. 49 CK31
Marlborough Ave. E8 57 CB37
Marlborough Ave. N14 38 BW27
Marlborough Ave., Edg. 37 BM27
Marlborough Ave., Ruis. 44 BA32
Marlborough Bldgs. SW3 3 D8
Marlborough Bldgs. SW3 66 BU42
Marlborough Clo. N20 38 BU27
Marlborough Clo. SE17 4 H9
Marlborough Clo. SE17 66 BY42
Marlborough Clo. SW19 76 BU50
Marlborough Clo., Grays 71 DE41
Marlborough Clo., Orp. 88 CN54
Marlborough Clo., Upmin. 51 CZ33
Marlborough Clo., Walt. 84 BD55
Marlborough Ct. W8 66 BS42
Marlborough Cres. W4 65 BN41
Marlborough Cres., Sev. 107 CT65
Marlborough Dr., Ilf. 49 CK31
Marlborough Dr., Wey. 83 BA55
Marlborough Gdns. N20 38 BU27
Marlborough Gdns., Surb. 84 BK54
Marlborough Gdns., Upmin. 51 CY33
Marlborough Gate, St.Alb. 9 BH13
Marlborough Gate Ho. W2 1 A10
Marlborough Gro. SE1 67 CB42
Marlborough Hill NW8 56 BT37
Marlborough Hill, Dor. 119 BJ71
Marlborough Hill, Har. 45 BG32
Marlborough La. SE7 68 CJ43
Marlborough Pk. Ave., Sid. 79 CO47
Marlborough Pl. NW8 56 BT37
Marlborough Ri., Hem.H. 8 AY12
Marlborough Rd. E4 39 CE29
Marlborough Rd. E7 58 CJ36
Marlborough Rd. E15 49 CG35
Borthwick Rd.
Marlborough Rd. E18 49 CH31
Marlborough Rd. N9 39 CA26
Marlborough Rd. N19 47 BW34
Marlborough Rd. N22 38 BX29
Marlborough Rd. SW1 3 M3
Marlborough Rd. SW1 56 BW40
Marlborough Rd. SW19 76 BT50
Marlborough Rd. W4 65 BN42
Marlborough Rd. W5 64 BK41
Marlborough Rd., Ashf. 73 AX49
Marlborough Rd., Bexh. 69 CP45
Marlborough Rd., Brwd. 33 DA25
Marlborough Rd., Brom. 88 CJ52
Marlborough Rd., Dag. 50 CO35
Marlborough Rd., Dart. 80 CV46
Marlborough Rd., Dor. 119 BJ71
Marlborough Rd., Felt. 74 BD48
Marlborough Rd., Hmptn. 74 BF50
Marlborough Rd., Har. 45 BH31
Marlborough Rd., Islw. 64 BJ44
Marlborough Rd., Rich. 75 BL46
Marlborough Rd., Rom. 50 CR31
Marlborough Rd., St.Alb. 9 BH13
Marlborough Rd., Slou. 62 AR42
Marlborough Rd., S.Croy. 96 BZ57
Marlborough Rd., Sthl. 64 BD41
Marlborough Rd., Sutt. 86 BS55
Marlborough Rd., Uxb. 53 AZ38
Marlborough Rd., Wat. 26 BC24
Marlborough Rd., Wok. 100 AT61
Marlborough St. SW3 3 C9
Marlborough St. SW3 66 BU42
Marlborough Yd. N19 47 BW34
Marlborough Rd.
Marld, The, Ash. 103 BL62
Marle Gdns., Wal.Abb. 21 CF19
Marler Rd. SE23 77 CD47
Marlescroft Way, Loug. 31 CL25
Marley Ave., Bexh. 69 CP43
Marley Clo., Grnf. 54 BF37
Marley Clo., Wey. 91 AV57
Marley Rd., Welw.G.C. 5 BS9
Marlin Clo., Berk. 7 AP12
Marlin Sq., Abb.L. 17 BB19
Marling Way, Grav. 81 DJ49
Marlingdene Clo., Hmptn. 74 BF50
Marlings Clo., Chis. 88 CN52
Marlings Clo., Whyt. 105 CA62
Marlings Pk. Ave., Chis. 88 CN52
Marlins, The, Nthwd. 35 BB28
Eastbury Ave.
Marlins Clo., Rick. 25 AV23
Marlins Clo., Sutt. 95 BT56
Turnpike La.
Marlins Meadow, Wat. 26 BA25
Marlins Turn, Hem.H. 8 AW12
Marloes Clo. W8 66 BS41
Marloes Clo., Wem. 45 BK35
Marloes Rd. W8 66 BS41
Marlow Ave., Grays 70 CX42
Marlow Clo. SE20 87 CB52
Marlow Ct. NW6 55 BQ36
Marlow Cres., Twick. 74 BH46
Marlow Dr., Sutt. 85 BQ55
Marlow Gdns., Hayes 63 BA41
Marlow Gdns., Rom. 42 CV30
Marlow Rd. E6 58 CK38
Marlow Rd. SE20 87 CB52
Marlow Rd., Sthl. 64 BE41
Marlow Way SE16 67 CC41
Marlowe Clo., Chis. 78 CM50
Marlowe Clo., Ilf. 40 CM30
Marlowe Gdns. SE9 78 CL46
Footscray Rd.
Marlowe Gdns., Rom. 43 CV30
Shenstone Gdns.
Marlowe Rd. E17 48 CF31
Marlowe Sq., Mitch. 86 BV52
Marlowe Way, Croy. 86 BX55
Marlowes, Hem.H. 8 AX14
Marlowes, The NW8 56 BT37
Marlowes, The, Dart. 69 CS45
Marlpit Ave., Couls. 104 BX62
Marlpit La., Couls. 104 BW61
Marlton St. SE10 68 CG42
Marlyns Clo., Guil. 109 AT68
Marlyns Dr., Guil. 109 AT68
Marlyon Rd., Ilf. 41 CO28
Marmadon Rd. SE18 68 CN42
Marmion App. E4 39 CE28
Marmion Clo.
Marmion App. E4 39 CD28
Marmion Ave. E4 39 CD28
Marmion Clo. E4 39 CE28
Marmion Ms. SW11 66 BV45
Taybridge Rd.
Marmion Rd. SW11 66 BV45
Marmont Rd. SE15 67 CB44
Marmora Rd. SE22 77 CC46
Marmot Rd., Houns. 64 BD45
Marne Ave. N11 38 BV28
Marne Ave., Well. 69 CO45
Marne St. W10 55 BR38
Marnell Way, Houns. 64 BD45
Marney Rd. SW11 66 BV45
Marneys Clo., Epsom 103 BM61
Marnham Ave. NW2 46 BR35
Marnham Cres., Grnf. 54 BF37
Marnham Ri., Hem.H. 8 AW12
Marnock Rd. SE4 77 CD46
Maroon St. E14 57 CD39
Maroons Way SE6 77 CE49
Marquess Gro. N1 57 BZ36
Marquess Rd.
Marquess Rd. N1 57 BZ36
Marquis Clo., Wem. 55 BL36
Marquis Rd. N4 47 BX33
Marquis Rd. N22 38 BX29
Marquis Rd. NW1 56 BW36
Marram Ct., Grays 71 DF43
Medlar Rd.
Marrick Clo. SW15 65 BP45
Marrilyne Ave., Enf. 30 CD22
Marriot Rd., Barn. 28 BQ24
Marriots, The, Harl. 6 CP8
Marriott Clo. NW9 46 BO32
Marriott Clo., Felt. 73 BA46
Marriott Lo. Clo., Wey. 92 AX56
Marriott Rd. E15 38 CG37
Marriott Rd. N4 47 BX33
Marriott Rd. N10 38 BU30
Marriott Rd., Dart. 80 CW47
Waldeck Rd.
Marrowells, Wey. 83 BB55
Marryat Pl. SW19 75 BR49
Marryat Rd. SW19 75 BQ49
Marryat Rd., Enf. 30 CB21
Marsala Rd. SE13 67 CE45
Marsden Clo., Welw.G.C. 5 BP9
Marsden Grn., Welw.G.C. 5 BP8
Marsden Rd. N9 39 CB27
Marsden Rd. SE15 67 CA45
Marsden Rd., Welw.G.C. 5 BP8
Marsden St. NW5 56 BV36
Marsden Way, Orp. 88 CN55
Stapleton Rd.
Marsh Ave., Epsom 94 BO58
Marsh Ave., Loug. 31 CM23
Marsh Ave., Mitch. 86 BU51
Marsh Clo. NW7 37 BO27
Marsh Clo., Wal.Cr. 21 CD20
Marsh Dr. NW9 46 BO32
Marsh Fm. Rd., Twick. 74 BH47
Marsh Grn. Rd., Dag. 59 CR37
Marsh Hill E9 48 CD35
Marsh Hill, Wal.Abb. 22 CG17
Marsh La. E10 48 CE34
Marsh La. N17 39 CB30
Marsh La. NW7 37 BN28
Marsh La., Harl. 6 CQ8
Marsh La., Maid. 61 AJ40
Marsh La., Stan. 36 BK28
Marsh La., Wey. 92 AW56
Marsh Rd., Pnr. 45 BE31
Marsh Rd., Wem. 54 BK37
Marsh St. E14 67 CE42
Marsh St., Dart. 70 CX45
Marsh Wall E14 67 CE41
Marsh Way, Rain. 59 CS39
Marshall Ave., St.Alb. 9 BH12
Marshall Clo. SW18 76 BT46
Allfarthing La.
Marshall Clo., Houns. 74 BE46
Marshall Dr., Hayes 53 BB39
Marshall Gdns. SE1 66 BY41
London Rd.
Marshall Path SE28 59 CO40
Titmuss Ave.
Marshall Rd. N17 39 BZ30
Marshall St. W1 1 M9
Marshall St. W1 56 BW39
Marshalls Clo. N11 38 BV28
Marshalls Clo., Epsom 94 BN60
Marshalls Dr., Rom. 50 CT31
Marshalls Gro. SE18 68 CK42
Marshalls Pl. SE16 4 Q7
Marshalls Pl. SE16 67 CA41
Marshalls Rd., Rom. 50 CS31
Marshalls Rd., Sutt. 95 BS56
High St.
Marshals Dr., St.Alb. 9 BJ12
Marshalsea Rd. SE1 4 J4
Marshalsea Rd. SE1 67 BZ41
Marshalswick La., St.Alb. 9 BJ12
Marsham Clo., Chis. 78 CL49
Marsham La., Ger.Cr. 43 AS32
Marsham St. SW1 3 P7
Marsham St. SW1 66 BW41
Marsham Way, Ger.Cr. 43 AS32
Marshbrooke Clo. SE3 68 CJ45
Marshcroft Dr., Chsnt. 21 CD18
Southmead Cres.
Marshe Clo., Pot.B. 20 BT19
Marshfield St. E14 67 CF41
Marshfoot Rd., Grays 71 DF42
Marshgate, Harl. 6 CN9
Marshgate La. E15 57 CE37
Marshgate Path SE28 68 CM41
Tom Cribb Rd.
Marshmoor Cres., Hat. 10 BQ15
Marshmoor La., Hat. 10 BQ14
Marsland Clo. SE17 66 BY42
Marston, Epsom 94 BN58
Marston Ave., Chess. 94 BL57
Marston Ave., Dag. 50 CR34
Marston Clo. NW6 56 BT36
Marston Clo., Dag. 50 CR34
Marston Clo., Hem.H. 8 AZ14
Marston Ct., Walt. 84 BD54
St. Johns Dr.
Marston Dr., Warl. 105 CD62
Marston Rd., Hodd. 12 CE11
Marston Rd., Ilf. 40 CK30
Marston Rd., Tedd. 74 BJ49
Marston Rd., Wok. 100 AQ62
Marston Way SE19 76 BY50
Marsworth Ave., Pnr. 36 BD30
Marsworth Clo., Wat. 35 BB26
Chenies Way
Mart St. WC2 2 A10
Mart St. WC2 56 BX40
Floral St.
Martaban Rd. N16 48 CA34
Listria Pk.
Martell Rd. SE21 77 BZ48
Martello St. E8 57 CB36
Marten Gate, St.Alb. 9 BJ11
Marten Rd. E17 39 CE30
Martens Ave., Bexh. 69 CR45
Martens Clo., Bexh. 69 CS45
Martha Ct. E2 57 CB37
Cambridge Heath Rd.
Martha Rd. E15 58 CG36
Martha St. E1 57 CB39
Martham Clo. SE28 59 CP40
Surlingham Clo.
Marthorne Cres., Har. 36 BG30
Martian Ave., Hem.H. 8 AZ12
Martin Bowes Rd. SE9 68 CK45
Martin Clo., Hat. 10 BP13
Martin Clo., S.Croy. 96 CC59
Martin Clo., Warl. 105 CB61
Martin Clo., Wind. 61 AL44
Martin Cres., Croy. 86 BY54
Martin Dene, Bexh. 79 CQ46
Martin Dr., Nthlt. 45 BE35
Martin Dr., Rain. 59 CU38
Martin Gdns., Dag. 50 CP35
Martin Gro., Mord. 86 BS52
Martin La. EC4 2 L10
Martin La. EC4 57 BZ40
Martin Ri., Bexh. 79 CQ46
Martin Rd., Dag. 50 CP35
Martin Rd., Dart. 80 CV48
Martin Rd., Guil. 118 AQ69
Martin Rd., Slou. 62 AP41
Martin Rd., S.Ock. 60 CY40
Martin Way SW20 85 BR52
Martin Way, Mord. 85 BR52
Martin Way, Wok. 100 AQ62
Martindale SW14 75 BN46
Martindale Ave., Orp. 97 CN56
Martindale Clo., Guil. 109 AU69
Gilliat Dr.
Martindale Rd. SW12 76 BV47
Martindale Rd., Hem.H. 7 AV13
Martindale Rd., Houns. 64 BE45
Martindale Rd., Wok. 100 AQ62
Martineau Clo., Esher 93 DG56
Martineau Dr., Dor. 119 BJ72
Martineau Est. E1 57 CC40
Martineau Rd. N5 47 BY35
Martineau St. E1 57 CC39
Lukin St.
Martinfield, Welw.G.C. 5 BR8
Martingale Clo., Sun. 83 BC52
Martingales Clo., Rich. 74 BK48
Martins Clo., Guil. 118 AU70
Martins Clo., Orp. 89 CP52
Martins Ct., St.Alb. 9 BJ15
Swallow La.
Martins Dr., Chsnt. 21 CD17
Martins Mt., Barn. 29 BS24
Martins Rd., Brom. 88 CG51
Martins Shaw, Sev. 107 CT64
Martins Wk. M10 38 BV30
Martins Wk., Borwd. 28 BM24
Goldfinch Way
Martlesham, Welw.G.C. 5 BU8
Martlesham Clo., Horn. 51 CV35
Martlet Gro., Nthlt. 54 BS
Javelin Way
Martlett Ct. WC2 2
Martlett Ct. WC2 56 BX
Drury La.
Martley Dr., Ilf. 49 CL
Martock Clo., Har. 45 BJ
Marton Clo. SE6 77 CE
Martyr Clo., St.Alb. 9 BG
Creighton Ave.
Martyr Rd., Guil. 118 AR
Martyrs La., Wok. 91 AT
Martys Yd. NW3 47 BT
Hampstead High St.
Marvell Ave., Hayes 53 BC
Marvels Clo. SE12 78 CH
Marvels La. SE12 78 CH
Marville Rd. SW6 65 BR
Marvin St. E8 57 CB
Sylvester Rd.
Marwell, West. 115 CM
Farley Cft.
Marwell Clo., Rom. 50 CU
Marwell Clo., W.Wick. 88 CG
Deer Pk. Way
Marwood Clo., Kings L. 17 AY
Marwood Clo., Well. 69 CO
Marwood Way SE16 67 CB
Bonamy Est. W.
Mary Adelaide Clo. SW15 75 BO
Kingston Vale
Mary Ann Gdns. SE8 67 CE
Mary Burrows Gdn., Sev. 108 CX
Church La.
Mary Clo., Stan. 46 BL
Mary Datchelor Clo. SE5 67 BZ
Vicarage Gro.
Mary Hill Clo., Ken. 105 BZ
Mary Lawrenson Pl. SE3 68 CH
Heathway
Mary Macarthur Ho. W14 65 BR
Mary Peters Dr., Grnf. 45 BG
Mary Pl. W11 55 BR
Mary Rd., Guil. 118 AR
Mary Rose Clo., Hmptn. 84 BF
Ashley Rd.
Mary Rose Mall E6 58 CK
Frobisher Rd.
Mary Rose Way N20 38 BT
Mary Seacole Clo. E8 57 CA
Clarissa St.
Mary St. N1 57 BZ
Mary Ter. NW1 56 BV
Maryatt Ave., Har. 45 BF
Marybank SE18 68 CK
Frances St.
Maryfield Clo., Bex. 79 CT
Maryland, Hat. 10 BO
Maryland Pk. E15 49 CG
Maryland Rd. E15 48 CF
Maryland Rd. N22 38 BX
Maryland Rd., Th.Hth. 86 BY
Maryland Sq. E15 49 CG
Maryland St. E15 48 CF
Maryland Wk. N1 57 BZ
Popham St.
Maryland Way, Sun. 83 BC
Marylands Rd. W9 56 BS
Marylebone Circ. NW1 56 BU
Marylebone Flyover NW1 1
Marylebone Flyover W2 1
Marylebone High St. W1 1
Marylebone High St. W1 56 BV
Marylebone La. W1 1
Marylebone La. W1 56 BV
Marylebone Ms. W1 1
Marylebone Ms. W1 56 BV
Marylebone Pas. W1 1
Marylebone Rd. NW1 1
Marylebone Rd. NW1 56 BU
Marylebone St. W1 1
Marylebone St. W1 56 BV
Marylee Way SE11 4 C
Marylee Way SE11 66 BX
Maryon Gro. SE7 68 CK
Maryon Ms. NW3 47 BU
South End Rd.
Maryon Rd. SE7 68 CK
Maryon Rd. SE18 68 CK
Marys Ter., Twick. 74 BJ
Maryside, Slou. 62 AS
Masbro Rd. W14 65 BQ
Mascalls Ct. SE7 68 CJ
Victoria Way
Mascalls Gdns., Brwd. 42 CZ
Mascalls La., Brwd. 42 CZ
Mascalls Rd. SE7 68 CJ
Mascotte Rd. SW15 65 BQ
Felsham Rd.
Mascotts Clo. NW2 46 BP
Masefield Ave., Borwd. 28 BM
Masefield Ave., Sthl. 54 BF
Masefield Ave., Stan. 36 BH
Masefield Clo., Erith 69 CT
Masefield Clo., Rom. 41 CU
Masefield Cres. N14 29 BV
Masefield Cres., Rom. 42 CV
Masefield Dr., Upmin. 51 CY
Masefield Gdns. E6 58 CL
Masefield La., Hayes 53 BC
Masefield Rd., Dart. 80 CX
Masefield Rd., Grav. 81 DE
Masefield Rd., Grays 71 DF
Masefield Rd., Hmptn. 74 BE
Masefield Vw., Orp. 88 CM
Masefield Way, Stai. 73 AY
Chesterton Dr.
Mashie Rd. W3 55 BO
Mashiters Hill, Rom. 41 CS
Mashiters Wk., Rom. 50 CT
Maskall Clo. SW2 76 BY
Maskell Rd. SW17 76 BT
Maskelyn Clo. SW11 66 BU
Mason Clo. E16 58 CH

ason Clo., Bexh. 69 CR45
ason Clo., Borwd. 28 BN23
ason Clo., Hmptn. 84 BE51
ason Rd., Wdf.Grn. 40 CG28
ason St. SE17 4 L8
ason St. SE17 67 BZ42
ason Way, Wal.Abb. 22 CG20
asonic Hall Rd., Cher. 82 AV53
asons Arms Ms. W1 1 K10
asons Arms Ms. W1 56 BV40
Maddox St.
asons Ave. EC2 2 K8
asons Ave. EC2 57 BZ39
asons Ave., Croy. 87 BZ55
asons Ave., Har. 45 BH31
asons Bri. Rd., Red. 121 BV73
asons Ct., Wem. 46 BM34
asons Grn. La. W3 55 BM38
asons Hill SE18 68 CL42
asons Hill, Brom. 88 CH52
asons Paddock, Dor. 119 BJ70
asons Pl. EC1 2 H2
asons Pl. EC1 56 BY38
asons Pl., Mitch. 86 BU51
asons Rd., Enf. 30 CB21
asons Rd., Hem.H. 8 AZ13
asons Yd. SW1 3 M2
asons Yd. SW1 56 BW40
Duke St.
assey Clo. N11 38 BV28
Grove Rd.
assie Rd. E8 57 CB36
Graham Rd.
assinger St. SE17 4 M9
assinger St. SE17 67 CA42
assingham St. E1 57 CC38
asson Ave., Ruis. 54 BD36
ast Ho. Ter. E14 67 CE42
aster Gunner Pl. SE18 68 CK43
asterman Rd. E6 58 CK38
asters St. E1 57 CC39
asthead Clo., Dart. 70 CY45
astmaker Rd. E14 67 CE41
aswell Pk. Cres., Houns. 74 BG46
aswell Pk. Rd., Houns. 74 BF46
atcham Rd. E11 49 CG34
atching Rd., Harl. 6 CR9
atchless Dr. SE18 68 CL44
Red Lion La.
atfield Clo., Brom. 88 CH53
atfield Rd., Belv. 69 CR43
atham Gro. SE22 67 CA45
atham Rd., E.Mol. 84 BG53
atheson Rd. W14 65 BR42
athews La., Stai. 72 AV49
athews Pk. Ave. E15 58 CG36
athews Yd. WC2 56 BX39
Short Gdns.
athias Clo., Epsom 94 BN60
athon Ct., Guil. 118 AS70
atilda St. N1 56 BX37
atlock Clo. SE24 67 BZ45
atlock Ct. SE5 67 BZ45
atlock Cres., Sutt. 85 BR55
atlock Cres., Wat. 36 BD27
atlock Gdns., Horn. 51 CW34
atlock Gdns., Sutt. 94 BR56
atlock Pl., Sutt. 94 BR56
atlock Rd. E10 48 CF32
atlock Rd., Cat. 105 CA64
atlock St. E14 57 CD39
atlock Way, N.Mal. 85 BN51
atrimony Pl. SW8 66 BW44
Wandsworth Rd.
atthew Arnold Clo., Cob. 92 BC60
atthew Clo. W10 55 BQ38
atthew Parker St. SW1 3 P5
atthew Parker St. SW1 66 BW41
atthew St., Reig. 121 BS72
atthews Ave. E6 58 CL37
Folkestone Rd.
atthews Clo., Hav. 42 CW30
Oak Rd.
atthews Gdns., Croy. 96 CF59
atthews Rd., Grnf. 45 BG35
atthews St. SW11 66 BU44
atthews Yd. WC2 1 Q9
atthias Rd. N16 48 BZ35
attingley Way SE15 67 CA43
attison Rd. N4 47 BY32
attock La. W5 54 BK40
attock La. W13 54 BJ40
attock Rd. W5 54 BK40
Mattock La.
aud Gdns. E13 58 CG37
aud Gdns., Bark. 58 CN37
aud Rd. E10 48 CF34
aud Rd. E13 58 CG37
aud St. E16 58 CG39
aude Cres., Wat. 26 BC22
aude Rd. E17 48 CD32
aude Rd. SE5 67 CA44
aude Rd., Swan. 79 CU50
aude Ter. E17 48 CD31
audesville Cotts. W7 54 BH40
audlins Grn. E1 57 CB40
Burr Clo.
audslay Rd. SE9 68 CK45
auleverer Rd. SW2 76 BX46
aunder Rd. W7 54 BH40
aunsel St. SW1 3 N8
aunsel St. SW1 66 BW42
aurice Ave. N22 38 BY30
aurice Ave., Cat. 105 BZ64
aurice Brown Clo. NW7 37 BQ28
aurice St. W12 55 BP39
aurice Wk. NW11 47 BT31
aurier Clo., Nthlt. 54 BD37
auritius Rd. SE10 68 CG42
aury Rd. N16 48 CB34
auve St. E14 57 CF39
St. Leonards Ave.
avelstone Clo., Brom. 88 CK51
avelstone Rd., Brom. 88 CJ51

Maverton Rd. E3 57 CE37
Mavis Ave., Epsom 94 BO56
Mavis Clo., Epsom 94 BO56
Mavis Gro., Horn. 51 CW34
Mavis Wk. E6 58 CK39
Tollgate Rd.
Mawbey Est. SE1 67 CB42
Mawbey Pl. SE1 67 CA42
Mawbey Rd.
Mawbey Rd. SE1 67 CA42
Mawbey Rd., Cher. 91 AU57
Mawbey St. SW8 66 BX43
Mawney Clo., Rom. 41 CR30
Mawney Rd., Rom. 41 CR30
Mawson Clo. SW20 85 BR51
Mawson Ho. EC1 56 BY39
Baldwins Gdns.
Mawson La. W4 65 BO43
Maxey Gdns., Dag. 50 CQ35
Maxey Rd. SE18 68 CM42
Maxey Rd., Dag. 50 CQ35
Maxilla Wk. W10 55 BQ39
Bartle Rd.
Maxim Rd. N21 29 BY25
Maxim Rd., Dart. 79 CT46
Roman Way
Maxim Rd., Erith 69 CS42
Maximfeldt Rd., Erith 69 CT42
Maxted Clo., Hem.H. 8 AZ12
Maxted Pk., Har. 45 BH33
Maxted Rd. SE15 67 CA45
Maxted Rd., Hem.H. 8 AZ12
Maxwell Clo., Rick. 35 AW27
Maxwell Dr., Wey. 92 AX59
Maxwell Gdns., Orp. 88 CN55
Maxwell Ri., Wat. 36 BE26
Maxwell Rd. SW6 66 BS43
Maxwell Rd., Ashf. 73 BA50
Maxwell Rd., Borwd. 28 BN23
Maxwell Rd., Nthwd. 35 BA29
Maxwell Rd., St.Alb. 9 BJ14
Maxwell Rd., Well. 69 CO45
Maxwell Rd., West Dr. 63 AY42
Maxwelton Ave. NW7 37 BN28
Maxwelton Clo. NW7 37 BN28
May Ave., Grav. 81 DF47
May Ave., Orp. 89 CO53
May Clo., Chess. 94 BL57
May Clo., St.Alb. 9 BG12
May Ct., Grays 71 DE43
Medlar Rd.
May Ct., Hem.H. 8 AX13
May Gdns., Wem. 54 BK37
May Pl. La. SE18 68 CL43
May Rd. E4 39 CE29
May Rd. E13 58 CH37
May Rd., Dart. 80 CW49
May Rd., Twick. 74 BH47
May Tree La., Stan. 36 BJ29
May Wk. E13 58 CH37
Maya Rd. N2 47 BT31
Mayall Rd. SE24 76 BY46
Maybank Ave. E18 40 CH30
Maybank Ave., Horn. 50 CU35
Maybank Ave., Wem. 45 BH35
Maybank Gdns., Pnr. 44 BC32
Maybank Rd. E18 40 CH30
Maybank Vill., Ilf. 50 CO33
Mayberry Pl., Surb. 85 BL54
Maybourne Clo. SE26 77 CB49
Maybourne Ri., Wok. 100 AR65
Maybrick Rd., Horn. 51 CV32
Maybrook Meadow Est., Bark. 59 CO36
Maybury Ave., Chsnt. 21 CB17
Maybury Ave., Dart. 80 CY47
Maybury Clo., Orp. 88 CL53
Maybury Clo., Tad. 103 BR63
Maybury Gdns. NW10 55 BP36
Maybury Hill, Wok. 100 AT61
Maybury Ms. N6 47 BW33
Maybury Rd. E13 58 CJ38
Maybury Rd., Bark. 58 CN37
Maybury Rd., Wok. 100 AS62
Maybury St. SW17 76 BU49
Maybush Rd., Horn. 51 CW33
Maychurch Clo., Stan. 36 BK29
Maycock Gro., Nthwd. 35 BB29
Carew Rd.
Maycroft, Pnr. 35 BC30
Maycroft Ave., Grays 71 DE42
Maycroft Gdns., Grays 71 DE42
Maycroft Rd., Chsnt. 21 CA16
Maycross Ave., Mord. 85 BR52
Mayday Gdns. SE3 68 CK44
Mayday Rd., Th.Hth. 86 BY53
Mayell Clo., Lthd. 102 BK65
Mayerne Rd. SE9 78 CJ46
Mayes Clo., Swan. 89 CU52
Mayes Clo., Warl. 105 CC62
Mayes Rd. N22 38 BX30
Mayesbrook Rd., Bark. 58 CN37
Mayesbrook Rd., Dag. 50 CO34
Mayesbrook Rd., Ilf. 50 CO34
Mayesford Rd., Rom. 50 CP33
Mayeswood Rd. SE12 78 CJ48
Mayfair Ave., Bexh. 69 CP44
Mayfair Ave., Ilf. 49 CK34
Mayfair Ave., Rom. 50 CP32
Mayfair Ave., Twick. 74 BG47
Mayfair Ave., Wor.Pk. 85 BP54
Mayfair Clo., Beck. 87 CE51
Mayfair Clo., St.Alb. 9 BK11
Mayfair Clo., Surb. 85 BL54
Mayfair Ct., Beck. 87 CE51
Mayfair Gdns. N17 39 BZ29
Mayfair Gdns., Wdf.Grn. 40 CH29
Mayfair Pl. W1 3 K2
Mayfair Pl. W1 56 BV40
Mayfair Rd., Dart. 80 CV46
Mayfair Ter. N14 38 BW26
Mayfare, Rick. 26 BA25
Mayfield, Bexh. 69 CQ45
Church Rd.

Mayfield, Wal.Abb. 21 CF20
Roundhills
Mayfield, Welw.G.C. 5 BQ6
Mayfield Ave. N12 38 BT28
Mayfield Ave. N14 38 BW27
Mayfield Ave. W4 65 BO42
Mayfield Ave. W13 64 BJ41
Mayfield Ave., Ger.Cr. 43 AR31
Mayfield Ave., Har. 45 BJ32
Mayfield Ave., Orp. 88 CN54
Mayfield Ave., Wey. 92 AW58
Mayfield Ave., Wdf.Grn. 40 CH29
Mayfield Clo. E8 57 CA36
Forest Rd.
Mayfield Clo. SE20 87 CB51
Anerley Rd.
Mayfield Clo. SW4 76 BW46
Mayfield Clo., Ashf. 73 AZ50
Mayfield Clo., Harl. 6 CQ9
Mayfield Clo., Red. 121 BV73
Brookfield Clo.
Mayfield Clo., T.Ditt. 84 BJ54
Mayfield Clo., Uxb. 53 AZ38
Mayfield Clo., Walt. 92 BC56
Mayfield Clo., Wey. 92 AW58
Mayfield Cres. N9 30 CB25
Mayfield Cres., Th.Hth. 86 BX52
Mayfield Dr., Pnr. 45 BE31
Mayfield Gdns. NW4 46 BQ32
Mayfield Gdns. W7 54 BG39
Mayfield Gdns., Brwd. 42 DA26
Mayfield Gdns., Stai. 72 AV50
Mayfield Gdns., Walt. 92 BC56
Mayfield Rd. E4 39 CF27
Mayfield Rd. E8 57 CA36
Mayfield Rd. E13 58 CG38
Mayfield Rd. E17 39 CD30
Mayfield Rd. N8 47 BX32
Mayfield Rd. SW19 85 BR51
Mayfield Rd. W3 55 BM40
Mayfield Rd. W12 65 BO41
Mayfield Rd., Belv. 69 CS42
Mayfield Rd., Brom. 88 CK53
Mayfield Rd., Dag. 50 CP33
Mayfield Rd., Enf. 30 CC23
Mayfield Rd., Grav. 81 DF47
Mayfield Rd., S.Croy. 96 BZ58
Mayfield Rd., Sutt. 95 BT57
Mayfield Rd., Th.Hth. 86 BX52
Mayfield Rd., Walt. 92 BC56
Mayfield Rd., Wey. 92 AZ56
Mayfields, Grays 71 DE41
Mayfields, Wem. 46 BM34
Mayfields Clo., Wem. 46 BM34
Mayflower Ave., Hem.H. 8 AX13
Mayflower Clo., Ruis. 44 BA32
Mayflower Clo., S.Ock. 60 DB38
Mayflower Clo., Wal.Abb. 13 CG15
Crooked Way
Mayflower Path, Brwd. 42 DB29
Mayflower Rd. SW9 66 BX44
Mayflower Rd., St.Alb. 18 BF17
Mayflower St. SE16 67 CC41
St. Mary Ch. St.
Mayflower Way, Ong. 24 CX17
Mayflower Way, Slou. 43 AO35
Mayfly Gdns., Nthlt. 54 BD38
Valliant Clo.
Mayford, Wok. 100 AR64
Mayford Clo. SW12 76 BU47
Mayford Clo., Beck. 87 CC52
Gwydor Rd.
Mayford Clo., Wok. 100 AR64
Mayford Rd. SW12 76 BU47
Maygold Wk., Amer. 25 AR23
Maygood St. N1 56 BY37
Maygoods Clo., Uxb. 53 AX39
Maygoods Grn., Uxb. 53 AX39
Maygoods La., Uxb. 53 AX39
Maygoods Vw., Uxb. 53 AX39
Maygreen Cres., Horn. 50 CU33
Maygrove Rd. NW6 55 BR36
Mayhew Clo. E4 39 CE27
Mayhill Rd. SE7 68 CH43
Mayhill Rd., Barn. 28 BR25
Mayhurst Ave., Wok. 100 AU61
Mayhurst Clo., Wok. 100 AU61
Mayhurst Ave.
Mayhurst Cres., Wok. 100 AU61
Mayhurst Ave.
Maylands Ave., Hem.H. 8 AZ12
Maylands Ave., Horn. 50 CU35
Maylands Dr., Sid. 79 CP48
Maylands Dr., Uxb. 53 AX36
Maylands Rd., Wat. 36 BD28
Maylands Way, Rom. 42 CY29
Maylins Dr., Saw. 6 CP6
Maynard Clo. N15 48 CA31
Brunswick Rd.
Maynard Clo. SW6 66 BS43
Cambria St.
Maynard Clo., Erith 69 CT43
Maynard Ct., Wal.Abb. 22 CG20
Maynard Dr., St.Alb. 9 BG15
Maynard Pl., Cuffley 20 BX18
Station Rd.
Maynard Rd. E17 48 CE32
Maynard Rd., Hem.H. 8 AX14
Maynards, Horn. 51 CW33
Clairvale
Maynards Quay E1 57 CC40
Garnet St.
Mayne Ave., St.Alb. 9 BF14
Mayo Clo., Chsnt. 21 CC17
Mayo Rd. NW10 55 BO36
Mayo Rd., Croy. 87 BZ53
Mayo Rd., Walt. 83 BB54
Mayola Rd. E5 48 CC35
Mayors La., Dart. 80 CV49
Mayow Rd. SE23 77 CC49
Mayow Rd. SE26 77 CC49
Mayplace Ave., Dart. 69 CU45
Mayplace Clo., Bexh. 69 CR45

Mayplace Rd. E., Bexh. 69 CR45
Mayplace Rd. W., Bexh. 69 CR45
Maypole Cres., Erith 70 CV43
Maypole Cres., Ilf. 40 CM29
Maypole Dr., Chig. 41 CO27
Maypole Rd., Grav. 81 DJ47
Maypole Rd., Orp. 98 CQ56
Mayroyd Ave., Surb. 85 BM55
Mays Bldgs. Ms. SE10 67 CF43
Crooms Hill
Mays Ct. WC2 3 Q1
Mays Ct. WC2 56 BX40
St. Martins La.
Mays Gro., Wok. 100 AU65
Mays Hill Rd., Brom. 88 CG51
Mays La. E4 39 CF27
Mays La., Barn. 37 BP26
Mays Rd., Tedd. 74 BG49
Maysfield Rd., Wok. 100 AU65
Maysgrove, Wok. 100 AU65
Maysfield Rd.
Maysoule Rd. SW11 66 BT45
Mayswood Gdns., Dag. 59 CS36
Maythorn Clo., Wat. 26 BB24
Mayton St. N7 47 BX34
Maytree Clo., Edg. 37 BN27
Maytree Clo., Guil. 109 AR68
Maytree Clo., Rain. 59 CT37
Maytree Cres., Wat. 26 BB23
Maytree Wk. SW2 76 BY48
Maytrees, Rad. 27 BJ22
Mayville Est. N16 48 CA35
Mayville Rd. E11 49 CG34
Mayville Rd., Ilf. 49 CL35
Mayville St. N16 48 CD35
Woodville Rd.
Maywards Ho. SE5 67 CA44
Glebe Est.
Maywater Clo., S.Croy. 96 BZ59
Maywin Dr., Horn. 51 CW33
Maywood Clo., Beck. 77 CE50
Maze Hill SE3 68 CG43
Maze Hill SE10 68 CG43
Maze Rd., Rich. 65 BM43
Mazenod Ave. NW6 56 BS36
McAdam Clo., Hodd. 12 CE11
McAdam Dr., Enf. 29 BY23
McAll Clo. SW4 66 BX44
McAuley Clo. SE1 4 D6
McAuley Clo. SE1 66 BY41
McAuley Clo. SE9 78 CL46
McCall Cres. SE7 68 CK42
McCarthy Rd., Felt. 74 BD49
McCoid Wk. SE1 67 BZ41
Scovell Rd.
McCoid Way SE1 4 H5
McCrone Ms. NW3 56 BT36
Belsize La.
McDermott Clo. SW11 66 BU45
McDermott Rd. SE15 67 CB45
McDonough Clo., Chess. 94 BL56
Hook Rd.
McDowall Rd. SE5 67 BZ44
McDowell Clo. E16 58 CH39
McEntee Ave. E17 39 CD30
McEwan Way E15 57 CF37
McGrath Rd. E15 49 CG35
McGredy, Chsnt. 21 CB18
McGregor Rd. W11 55 BR39
McIntosh Clo., Rom. 50 CT31
McIntosh Clo., Wall. 95 BX57
Redford Ave.
McIntosh Rd., Rom. 50 CT31
McKay Rd. SW20 75 BP50
McKellar Clo., Bush. 36 BG27
McKenzie Rd., Brox. 12 CD13
McKerrell Rd. SE15 67 CB44
McLeod Rd. SE2 69 CO42
McLeods Ms. SW7 66 BS41
McMillan St. SE8 67 CE43
McNeil Rd. SE5 67 CA44
Mead, The N2 38 BT30
Mead, The W13 54 BJ39
Templewood
Mead, The, Ash. 103 BL63
Mead, The, Beck. 87 CF51
Mead, The, Chsnt. 21 CC18
Mead, The, Rom. 32 CO24
Mead, The, Uxb. 44 AZ34
Mead, The, Wall. 95 BW57
Mead, The, Wat. 36 BE27
Mead, The, W.Wick. 87 CF54
Mead Ave., Slou. 62 AT41
Mead Clo., Egh. 72 AT50
Mead Clo., Grays 71 DD41
Mead Clo., Har. 36 BG30
Mead Clo., Red. 121 BU69
Mead Clo., Rom. 41 CU30
Mead Clo., Slou. 62 AT41
Mead Clo., Swan. 89 CU53
Mead Clo., Uxb. 44 AW34
Mead Ct. NW9 46 BN32
Mead Ct., Wal.Abb. 21 CE20
Mead Ct., Wok. 100 AP61
Mead Cres. E4 39 CF28
Mead Cres., Dart. 80 CV47
Mead Cres., Lthd. 111 BF66
Mead Cres., Sutt. 95 BU56
Mead End, Ash. 103 BL62
Mead Gro., Rom. 50 CP31
Mead Ho. Rd., Hayes 53 BA38
Mead La., Cher. 83 AW54
Mead Path SW17 76 BT49
Mead Pl. E9 57 CC36
Mead Pl., Croy. 86 BY54
Mead Pl., Rick. 35 AW26
Mead Plat NW10 55 BN36
Mead Rd., Cat. 105 CA65
Mead Rd., Chis. 78 CM50
Mead Rd., Dart. 80 CV47
Mead Rd., Edg. 37 BM29
Mead Rd., Grav. 81 DG48
Mead Rd., Rich. 74 BK48
Mead Rd., Uxb. 53 AX36

Mead Rd., Walt. 93 BE56
Mead Row SE1 4 D6
Mead Row SE1 66 BY41
Westminster Bri. Rd.
Mead Wk., Ong. 24 CW18
Mead Wk., Slou. 62 AT41
Mead Way, Brom. 88 CG53
Mead Way, Bush. 27 BE23
Mead Way, Croy. 87 CD55
Mead Way, St.Alb. 10 BN15
Mead Way, Warl. 105 CC61
Mead Way, The, Sev. 107 CT64
Meadcroft Rd. SE11 66 BY43
St. Agnes Pl.
Meade Clo. W4 65 BM43
Meades, The, Wey. 92 BA57
Old Ave.
Meadfield, Edg. 37 BM27
Meadfield Ave., Slou. 62 AT41
Meadfield Grn., Edg. 37 BM27
Meadfield Rd., Slou. 62 AT41
Meadfoot Rd. SW16 76 BW50
Meadgate Ave., Wdf.Grn. 40 CK28
Meadgate Rd., Epp. 12 CF13
Meadhurst Rd., Cher. 83 AW54
Meadlands Dr., Rich. 74 BK48
Meadow, The, Chis. 78 CM50
Meadow Ave., Croy. 87 CC53
Meadow Bank N21 29 BX25
Meadow Bank, Lthd. 110 BB67
Meadow Bank, Oxt. 114 CF68
Meadow Bank, Sev. 99 CZ58
Ash Tree Dr.
Meadow Bank, Wat. 36 BD26
Meadow Clo. E4 39 CE26
Meadow Clo. SE6 77 CE49
Meadow Clo. SW20 85 BQ52
Meadow Clo., Barn. 28 BR25
Meadow Clo., Brwd. 122 DE29
The Meadows
Meadow Clo., Chis. 78 CL49
Meadow Clo., Enf. 30 CD22
Meadow Clo., Esher 84 BH55
Meadow Clo., Hat. 10 BQ15
Meadow Clo., Houns. 74 BF46
Meadow Clo., Nthlt. 54 BF37
Meadow Clo., Pur. 95 BW60
Meadow Clo., Rich. 75 BL47
Meadow Clo., Ruis. 44 BB32
Meadow Clo., St.Alb. 18 BK17
Meadow Clo. (Bricket Wd.), St.Alb. 18 BF18
Meadow Clo. (London Colney), St.Alb. 9 BK11
Meadow Clo., S.le H. 71 DK41
Lower Cres.
Meadow Clo., Sutt. 86 BT55
Meadow Clo., Walt. 93 BE56
Meadow Clo., Wind. 72 AQ46
Meadow Ct., Epsom 94 BN60
Meadow Ct., Harl. 13 CN13
Meadow Ct., Stai. 72 AV48
Moor La.
Meadow Cft., Hat. 10 BO12
Meadow Cross, Wal.Abb. 22 CG20
Meadow Dell, Hat. 10 BO12
Meadow Dr. N10 47 BV31
Meadow Dr. NW4 37 BQ30
Meadow Dr., Amer. 25 AP22
Meadow Dr., Sev. 107 CU65
Lambarde Rd.
Meadow Dr., Wok. 100 AV65
Meadow Gdns., Edg. 37 BM29
Meadow Gdns., Stai. 72 AU49
Meadow Garth NW10 55 BN36
Meadow Grn., Welw.G.C. 5 BQ8
Meadow Hill, N.Mal. 85 BO53
Meadow Hill, Pur. 95 BW60
Meadow La., Lthd. 102 BG64
Meadow La. (Eton), Wind. 61 AO43
Meadow Mead, Rad. 18 BH20
Meadow Ms. SW8 66 BX43
Meadow Pl. SW8 66 BX43
Meadow Ri., Couls. 95 BW60
Meadow Ri., Ing. 24 DC19
Meadow Rd. SW8 66 BX43
Meadow Rd. SW19 76 BT50
Meadow Rd., Ashf. 73 BA49
Meadow Rd., Ash. 103 BL62
Meadow Rd., Bark. 58 CN36
Meadow Rd., Berk. 7 AQ12
Meadow Rd., Borwd. 28 BM23
Meadow Rd., Brom. 88 CG51
Meadow Rd., Bush. 27 BF25
Meadow Rd., Dag. 59 CQ36
Meadow Rd., Epp. 22 CN18
Meadow Rd., Esher 93 BH57
Meadow Rd., Felt. 74 BE48
Meadow Rd., Grav. 81 DG48
Meadow Rd. (Northfleet), Grav. 81 DE47
Meadow Rd., Grays 71 DD40
Meadow Rd., Guil. 109 AT68
Meadow Rd., Hem.H. 17 AZ16
Meadow Rd., Loug. 31 CK25
Meadow Rd., Pnr. 45 BE31
Meadow Rd., Rom. 50 CS33
Meadow Rd., Slou. 62 AS42
Meadow Rd., Sthl. 54 BE40
Meadow Rd., Sutt. 95 BU56
Meadow Rd., Vir.W. 82 AP53
Meadow Rd., Wat. 17 BC20
Meadow Row SE1 4 H7
Meadow Row SE1 67 BZ41
Meadow Stile, Croy. 87 BZ55
High St.
Meadow Vw., Ch.St.G. 34 AQ27
Meadow Vw., Orp. 89 CP52
Meadow Vw., Sid. 79 CO47
Meadow Vw., Stai. 72 AV46
Meadow Vw. Rd., Hayes 53 BA38
Meadow Vw. Rd., Th.Hth. 86 BY53
Meadow Wk. E18 49 CH31

Mea–Mer

Meadow Wk., Dag. 59 CQ36
Meadow Wk., Dart. 80 CV49
Meadow Wk., Epsom 94 BO57
Meadow Wk., Tad. 103 BP65
Meadow Wk., Wall. 86 BV55
Meadow Way NW9 46 BN32
Meadow Way, Abb.L. 17 BB17
Meadow Way, Chess. 94 BL56
Meadow Way, Chig. 40 CM27
Meadow Way, Dart. 80 CY47
Meadow Way, Hem.H. 8 AW15
Meadow Way, Kings L. 17 AZ18
Meadow Way (Bookham), Lthd. 102 BF65
Meadow Way (Horsley), Lthd. 110 BA66
Meadow Way (Dorney Reach), Maid. 61 AJ41
Meadow Way (Fifield), Maid. 61 AH44
Meadow Way, Orp. 88 CL55
Meadow Way, Pot.B. 20 BS20
Meadow Way, Reig. 121 BS72
Meadow Way, Rick. 35 AX26
Meadow Way, Ruis. 44 BC33
Meadow Way, Saw. 6 CR6
Meadow Way, Tad. 103 BR62
Meadow Way, Upmin. 51 CY35
Meadow Way, Wem. 45 BK35
Meadow Way, Wey. 92 AW56
Meadow Way, Wind. 72 AQ46
Meadow Way, The, Har. 36 BH30
Meadow Waye, Houns. 64 BE43
Meadowbank NW3 56 BU36
Meadowbank SE3 68 CG45
Meadowbank, Surb. 85 BL53
Meadowbank, Twick. 74 BK47
Meadowbank Clo. SW6 65 BQ43
Meadowbank Gdns., Houns. 63 BC44
Meadowbank Rd. NW9 46 BN33
Meadowbanks, Barn. 28 BP25
Meadowbrook Clo., Slou. 62 AV44
Meadowbrook Rd., Dor. 119 BJ71
Meadowcourt Rd. SE3 68 CG45
Meadowcroft, Brom. 88 CK52
Meadowcroft, Bush. 27 BF25
Clay Hill
Meadowcroft, Ger.Cr. 34 AR30
Meadowcroft, St.Alb. 9 BJ15
Meadowcroft Clo. N13 38 BY27
Meadowcroft Rd. N13 38 BY27
Meadowlands, Cob. 92 BC60
Meadowlands, Guil. 110 AW68
Meadowlands, Horn. 51 CW33
Meadowlands, Oxt. 115 CH70
Meadowlands, Sev. 108 CW63
Meadows, The, Amer. 25 AP23
Meadows, The, Brwd. 122 DE29
Meadows, The, Guil. 118 AR72
Meadows, The, Orp. 98 CP57
Meadows, The, Saw. 6 CR6
Meadows, The, Sev. 98 CQ60
Meadows, The, Welw.G.C. 5 BT8
Meadows Clo. E10 48 CE34
Meadows Clo., Brwd. 122 DE29
The Meadows
Meadows End, Sun. 83 BC51
Meadows Leigh Clo., Wey. 83 BA55
Meadowside SE9 68 CJ45
Meadowside, Beac. 34 AP29
Meadowside, Dart. 80 CW47
Meadowside, Lthd. 102 BF65
Meadowside, Twick. 74 BK47
Meadowside, Walt. 84 BD55
Meadowside Rd., Sutt. 94 BR58
Meadowside Rd., Upmin. 51 CY35
Meadowsweet Clo. E16 58 CJ39
Monarch Dr.
Meadowview, Shep. 83 BA54
Russell Rd.
Meadowview Rd. SE6 77 CD49
Meadowview Rd., Bex. 79 CQ46
Meadowview Rd., Epsom 94 BO58
Meads, The, Berk. 7 AP12
Meads, The, Edg. 37 BN29
Meads, The, St.Alb. 18 BF18
Meads, The, Sutt. 85 BQ55
Meads, The, Upmin. 51 CZ34
Meads, The, Uxb. 53 AY38
Meads La., Ilf. 49 CN33
Meads Rd. N22 38 BY30
Meads Rd., Enf. 30 CD23
Meads Rd., Guil. 118 AT70
Meadsway, Brwd. 42 DA28
Meadvale Rd. W5 54 BJ38
Meadvale Rd., Croy. 87 CA54
Meadway N14 38 BW27
Meadway NW11 47 BS32
Meadway SW20 85 BQ52
Meadway, Ashf. 73 AZ49
Meadway, Barn. 28 BR24
Meadway, Beck. 87 CF51
Meadway, Berk. 7 AS12
Meadway, Couls. 104 BX62
Meadway, Enf. 30 CC21
Meadway, Epsom 94 BM59
Meadway, Esher 93 BF58
Meadway, Grays 71 DE42
Meadway, Guil. 109 AU68
Meadway, Hodd. 12 CE13
Meadway, Ilf. 49 CN35
Meadway (Bookham), Lthd. 111 BE67
Meadway (Oxshott), Lthd. 93 BH60
Meadway, Rich. 74 BG47
Meadway, Rom. 41 CT30
Meadway, Ruis. 44 BA32
Meadway, Sev. 98 CQ60
Meadway, Stai. 73 AW50
Meadway, Surb. 85 BN54
Meadway, Welw.G.C. 5 BR9
Meadway, Wdf.Grn. 40 CJ28
Meadway, The SE3 67 CF44
Meadway, The, Buck.H. 40 CJ26
Meadway, The, Cuffley 20 BX18
Meadway, The, Loug. 31 CK25
Meadway, The, Orp. 98 CO56
Meadway Clo. NW11 47 BS32
Meadway Clo., Barn. 29 BS24
Meadway Clo., Pnr. 36 BF29
High Banks Rd.
Meadway Clo., Stai. 73 AW50
Meadway Clo., Twick. 74 BK49
Meadway Ct. NW11 47 BS32
Meadway Dr., Wey. 92 AX57
Meadway Dr., Wok. 100 AR61
Meadway Gdns., Ruis. 44 BA32
Meadway Gate NW11 47 BS32
Meadway Pk., Ger.Cr. 43 AR33
Meaford Way SE20 77 CB50
Meakin Est. SE1 4 M6
Meakin Est. SE1 67 CA41
Meanley Rd. E12 49 CK35
Meard St. W1 1 N9
Meard St. W1 56 BW39
Meare Clo., Tad. 103 BQ65
Meath Clo., Orp. 89 CO53
Meath Rd. E15 58 CG37
Meath Rd., Ilf. 49 CM34
Meath St. SW11 66 BV44
Meautys, St.Alb. 9 BF15
Mechanics Pas. SE8 67 CE43
Mecklenburgh Pl. WC1 2 B4
Mecklenburgh Pl. WC1 56 BX38
Guilford St.
Mecklenburgh Sq. WC1 2 B4
Mecklenburgh Sq. WC1 56 BX38
Mecklenburgh St. WC1 2 B4
Medburn St. NW1 56 BW37
Medcalf Rd., Enf. 30 CD22
Medcroft Gdns. SW14 65 BN45
Mede Clo., Stai. 72 AR47
Mede Fld., Lthd. 102 BG65
Highfields
Medebourne Clo. SE3 68 CH45
Medesenge Way N13 38 BY29
Wolves La.
Medewar Rd., Guil. 118 AO71
Medfield St. SW15 75 BP47
Medhurst Clo. E3 57 CD37
Medhurst Cres., Grav. 81 DJ48
Medhurst Gdns., Grav. 81 DJ48
Medhurst Rd. E3 57 CD37
Arbery Rd.
Median Rd. E5 48 CC35
Medick Ct., Grays 71 DF43
Medlar Rd.
Medina Ave., Esher 84 BH55
Medina Gro. N7 47 BY34
Medina Rd. N7 47 BY34
Medina Rd., Grays 71 DE42
Medlake Rd., Egh. 72 AU50
Medland Clo., Wall. 86 BV54
Medlar Clo., Guil. 118 AR69
Medlar Clo., Nthlt. 54 BD37
Medlar Rd., Grays 71 DF43
Medlar St. SE5 67 BZ44
Medley Rd. NW6 56 BS36
Medman Clo., Uxb. 53 AX37
Chiltern Vw. Rd.
Medora Rd. SW2 76 BX47
Medora Rd., Rom. 50 CS31
Medusa Rd. SE6 77 CE47
Medway, Wat. 18 BD20
Medway Bldgs. E3 57 CD37
Medway Rd.
Medway Clo., Croy. 87 CC53
Medway Clo., Ilf. 49 CM35
Loxford La.
Medway Dr., Grnf. 54 BH37
Medway Gdns., Wem. 45 BJ35
Medway Ms. E3 57 CD37
Medway Rd.
Medway Par., Grnf. 54 BH37
Welland Gdns.
Medway Rd. E3 57 CD37
Medway Rd., Dart. 69 CU45
Medway Rd., Hem.H. 8 AY11
Medway St. SW1 3 P7
Medway St. SW1 66 BW41
Medwick Ms., Hem.H. 8 AZ11
Hunters Oak
Medwin St. SW4 66 BX45
Meek St. SW10 66 BT43
Ulverdale Rd.
Meerbrook Rd. SE3 68 CJ45
Meeson Rd. E15 58 CG37
Meeson St. E5 48 CD35
Meesons La., Grays 71 DC42
Meeting Flds. Path E9 57 CC36
Homerton Ter.
Meeting Ho. La. SE15 67 CB44
Meetinghouse All. E1 57 CB40
Chandler St.
Megg La., Kings L. 17 AW18
Mehetabel Rd. E9 48 CC35
Melanda Clo., Chis. 78 CK49
Melanie Clo., Bexh. 69 CQ44
Melba Gdns., Til. 71 DG43
Melba Way SE13 67 CE44
Melbourne Ave. N13 38 BX29
Melbourne Ave. W13 54 BJ40
Melbourne Ave., Pnr. 45 BF31
Melbourne Clo. E5 48 CC35
Clapton Pk. Est.
Melbourne Clo., Orp. 88 CN54
Melbourne Clo., St.Alb. 9 BH11
Melbourne Clo., Uxb. 44 AZ35
Melbourne Clo., Wall. 95 BW56
Melbourne Ct. SE20 77 CB50
Melbourne Ct., Welw.G.C. 5 BP8
Melbourne Gdns., Rom. 50 CQ31
Melbourne Gro. SE22 67 CA45
Melbourne Ms. SE6 77 CF47
Laleham Rd.
Melbourne Ms. SW9 66 BY44
Melbourne Pl. WC2 2 C9
Melbourne Pl. WC2 56 BX40
Melbourne Rd. E6 58 CK37
Melbourne Rd. E10 48 CE33
Melbourne Rd. E17 48 CD31
Melbourne Rd. SW19 86 BS51
Melbourne Rd., Bush. 27 BF25
Melbourne Rd., Ilf. 49 CL33
Melbourne Rd., Tedd. 74 BK50
Melbourne Rd., Til. 71 DF44
Melbourne Rd., Wall. 95 BV56
Melbourne Sq. SW9 66 BY44
Brixton Rd.
Melbourne Ter. SW6 66 BS43
Britannia Rd.
Melbourne Way, Enf. 30 CA25
Melbury Ave., Sthl. 64 BF41
Melbury Clo., Cher. 83 AW54
London St.
Melbury Clo., Chis. 78 CK50
Melbury Clo., Esher 93 BJ57
Melbury Clo., Wey. 92 AW60
Melbury Ct. W8 65 BR41
Melbury Dr. SE5 67 CA43
Sedgmoor Pl.
Melbury Gdns. SW20 85 BP51
Melbury Rd. W14 65 BR41
Melbury Rd., Har. 46 BL32
Melbury Ter. NW1 1 D5
Melbury Ter. NW1 56 BU38
Harewood Ave.
Melcombe Gdns., Har. 46 BL32
Melcombe Pl. NW1 1 E6
Melcombe Pl. NW1 56 BU39
Melcombe St. NW1 1 F5
Melcombe St. NW1 56 BU38
Meldon Clo. SW6 66 BS44
Meldrum Clo., Orp. 89 CP54
Killewarren Way
Meldrum Clo., Oxt. 115 CG69
Meldrum Rd., Ilf. 50 CO34
Melfield Gdns. SE6 77 CF49
Melford Ave., Bark. 58 CN36
Melford Rd. E6 58 CK38
Melford Rd. E11 49 CG34
Melford Rd. E17 48 CD31
Melford Rd. SE22 77 CB47
Melford Rd., Ilf. 49 CM34
Melfort Ave., Th.Hth. 86 BY52
Melfort Rd., Th.Hth. 86 BY52
Melgund Rd. N5 47 BY35
Melina Clo., Hayes 53 BA39
Middleton Rd.
Melina Pl. NW8 1 A3
Melina Pl. NW8 56 BT38
Melina Rd. W12 65 BP41
Melior Pl. SE1 4 M4
Melior St. SE1 4 M4
Melior St. SE1 67 BZ41
Weston St.
Meliot Rd. SE6 77 CF48
Melksham Clo., Rom. 42 CW29
Melksham Dr., Rom. 42 CW29
Melksham Gdns., Rom. 42 CW29
Melksham Grn., Rom. 42 CW29
Mell St. SE10 68 CG42
Meller Clo., Croy. 86 BX55
Melling St. SE18 68 CN43
Mellings, The, Hem.H. 8 AZ11
Mellish Clo., Bark. 58 CN37
Mellish St. E14 67 CE41
Mellison Rd. SW17 76 BU49
Mellitus St. W12 55 BO39
Mellor Clo., Walt. 84 BE54
Mellow Clo., Bans. 95 BS60
Mellow La., Uxb. 53 BA38
Mellow La. E., Hayes 53 BA38
Mellows Rd., Ilf. 49 CK31
Mellows Rd., Wall. 95 BW56
Mells Cres. SE9 78 CK49
Melody Rd. SW18 76 BT46
Melody Rd., West. 106 CH62
Melon Pl. W8 66 BS41
Kensington Ch. St.
Melon Rd. SE15 67 CA44
Melrose Ave. N22 38 BY30
Melrose Ave. NW2 46 BP35
Melrose Ave. SW16 86 BX52
Melrose Ave. SW19 75 BR48
Melrose Ave., Borwd. 28 BM25
Melrose Ave., Grnf. 54 BF37
Melrose Ave., Mitch. 76 BV50
Melrose Ave., Pot.B. 20 BS19
Melrose Ave., Twick. 74 BF47
Melrose Clo. SE12 78 CH47
Melrose Clo., Grnf. 54 BF37
Melrose Clo., Hayes 53 BC39
Melrose Ct. W13 54 BJ40
Broadway
Melrose Cres., Orp. 97 CM56
Melrose Dr., Sthl. 54 BF40
Melrose Gdns. W6 65 BQ41
Melrose Gdns., Edg. 37 BM30
Melrose Gdns., N.Mal. 85 BN52
Melrose Gdns., Walt. 93 BD56
Melrose Pl., Wat. 26 BB22
Melrose Rd. SW13 65 BO44
Melrose Rd. SW18 75 BR46
Melrose Rd. SW19 86 BS51
Melrose Rd. W3 65 BM41
Melrose Rd., Couls. 104 BV61
Melrose Rd., Pnr. 45 BE31
Melrose Rd., West. 106 CJ61
Melrose Rd., Wey. 92 AZ56
Melrose Ter. W6 65 BQ41
Melsa Rd., Mord. 86 BT53
Melsted Rd., Hem.H. 8 AW13
Melstock Ave., Upmin. 51 CY35
Meltham Way SE16 67 CB42
Egan Way
Melthorne Dr., Ruis. 45 BD34
Melthorpe Gdns. SE3 68 CJ44
Melton Clo., Ruis. 45 BD33
Melton Ct. SW7 3 B9
Melton Ct. SW7 66 BT42
Melton Flds., Epsom 94 BN58
Melton Pl.
Melton Gdns., Rom. 50 CT33
Melton Pl., Epsom 94 BN58
Melton Rd., Red. 113 BW68
Melton St. NW1 1 M3
Melton St. NW1 56 BW38
Melville Ave. SW20 75 BP50
Melville Ave., Grnf. 45 BH35
Melville Ave., S.Croy. 96 CA56
Melville Clo., Uxb. 44 BA34
Melville Ct. W12 65 BP41
Melville Gdns. N13 38 BY28
Melville Rd. E17 48 CD31
Melville Rd. NW10 55 BN36
Melville Rd. SW13 65 BP44
Melville Rd., Rain. 59 CU38
Melville Rd., Rom. 41 CR29
Melville Rd., Sid. 79 CP48
Melville St. N1 57 BZ36
Essex Rd.
Melville Vill. Rd. W3 55 BO40
Melvin Rd. SE20 87 CC51
Melvin Shaw, Lthd. 102 BK64
Melvyn Clo., Chsnt. 20 BY17
Melyn Clo. N7 47 BW35
Anson Rd.
Memel Ct. EC1 2 H5
Memel St. EC1 2 H5
Memel St. EC1 57 BZ38
Baltic St.
Memess Path SE18 68 CL43
Engineer Clo.
Memorial Ave. E15 58 CG38
Memorial Clo., Houns. 64 BF43
Mendip Clo. SE26 77 CC49
Peak Hill Ave.
Mendip Clo. SW19 75 BR48
Queensmere Rd.
Mendip Clo., Hayes 63 BA43
Pennine Way
Mendip Clo., St.Alb. 9 BK11
Chiltern Rd.
Mendip Clo., Slou. 62 AT42
Mendip Cres. SW11 66 BT45
Mendip Dr. NW2 46 BQ34
Mendip Rd. SW11 66 BT45
Mendip Rd., Bexh. 69 CT44
Mendip Rd., Bush. 27 BG25
Mendip Rd., Horn. 50 CU33
Mendip Rd., Ilf. 49 CN32
Mendip Way, Hem.H. 8 AY12
Mendlesham, Welw.G.C. 5 BU8
Mendora Rd. SW6 65 BR43
Mendoza Clo., Horn. 51 CW32
Menelik Rd. NW2 46 BR35
Menlo Gdns. SE19 77 BZ50
Menotti St. E2 57 CB38
Dunbridge St.
Menthone Pl., Horn. 51 CV33
North St.
Mentmore Clo., Har. 45 BK32
Mentmore Rd., St.Alb. 9 BG14
Mentmore Ter. E8 57 CB36
Meon Clo., Tad. 103 BP64
Meon Rd. W3 65 BN41
Meopham Rd., Mitch. 86 BW51
Mepham Cres., Har. 36 BG29
Mepham Gdns., Har. 36 BG29
Mepham St. SE1 4 D3
Mepham St. SE1 56 BX40
Mera Dr., Bexh. 69 CR45
Merantun Way SW19 86 BY51
Merbury Clo. SE13 77 CF46
Hither Grn. La.
Merbury Rd. SE28 68 CM41
Mercator Rd. SE13 67 CF45
Mercer Clo., T.Ditt. 84 BJ54
Mercer Pl., Pnr. 36 BD30
Mercer St. WC2 1 Q9
Mercer St. WC2 56 BX39
Mercer Wk., Uxb. 53 AX36
High St.
Merceron St. E1 57 CB38
Mercers, Harl. 13 CL12
Mercers, Hem.H. 8 AY12
Mercers Clo. SE10 68 CG42
Tunnel Ave.
Mercers Pl. W6 65 BQ42
Mercers Rd. N19 47 BW34
Mercers Row, St.Alb. 9 BG14
Merchant St. E3 57 CD38
Merchiston Rd. SE6 77 CF48
Merchland Rd. SE9 78 CM47
Mercia Gro. SE13 67 CF45
Mercia Wk., Wok. 100 AS62
Church St. W.
Mercian Way, Slou. 61 AL40
Mercier Rd. SW15 75 BR46
Mercury Gdns., Rom. 50 CT31
Mercury Rd., Brent. 64 BK42
Mercury Wk., Hem.H. 8 AY12
Mercury Way SE14 67 CC43
Mercy Ter. SE13 67 CE45
Mere, The, Slou. 62 AP41
Mere Rd.
Mere Clo. SW15 75 BQ47
Mere Clo., Orp. 88 CL55
Mere End, Croy. 87 CC54
Mere Rd., Shep. 83 AZ53
Mere Rd., Slou. 62 AP41
Mere Rd., Tad. 103 BP65
Mere Rd., Wey. 83 BA55
Mere Side, Orp. 88 CL55
Merebank La., Wall. 95 BX56
Meredith Ave. NW2 46 BQ35
Meredith Clo., Pnr. 36 BD29
Meredith Rd., Grays 71 DG42
Meredith St. E13 58 CH38
Meredith St. EC1 2 F3
Meredith St. EC1 56 BY38
Meredyth Rd. SW13 65 BP44
Merefield, Saw. 6 C
Brook Rd.
Merefield Gdns., Tad. 103 BC
Mereside, Vir.W. 82 A
Mereside Pl., Vir.W. 82 AC
Meretone Clo. SE4 67 CI
Meretune Ct., Mord. 85 B
Merevale Cres., Mord. 86 B
Mereway Rd., Twick. 74 BC
Merewood Clo., Brom. 88 C
Merewood Rd., Bexh. 69 CS
Mereworth Clo., Brom. 88 CC
Mereworth Dr. SE18 68 C
Merganser Gdns. SE28 68 CM
Avocet Ms.
Meriden Clo., Brom. 88 C
Meriden Clo., Ilf. 40 CM
Meriden Way, Wat. 27 BE
Meridian Est. SE7 68 CH
Meridian Rd. SE7 68 C
Meridian Wk. N17 39 CA
Meridian Way N18 39 CC
Merifield Rd. SE9 68 C
Merino Pl., Sid. 79 CC
Merivale Rd. SW15 65 BF
Merivale Rd., Har. 45 BG
Merland Clo., Bans. 103 BC
Merland Ri.
Merland Grn., Tad. 103 BC
Merland Ri., Epsom 103 BC
Merle Ave., Uxb. 35 AW
Merlewood, Sev. 107 CL
Merlewood Clo., Cat. 105 BZ
Ninehams Rd.
Merlewood Dr., Chis. 88 CK
Merley Ct. NW9 46 BN
Merlin Clo., Croy. 87 CA
Merlin Clo., Ilf. 41 CF
Merlin Clo., Rom. 41 CS
Merlin Clo., Slou. 62 AT
Merlin Clo., Wal.Abb. 22 CH
Peregrine Rd.
Merlin Ct., Wok. 91 AU
Blackmore Cres.
Merlin Cres., Edg. 37 BL
Merlin Gdns., Brom. 78 CH
Merlin Gdns., Rom. 41 CS
Merlin Gro., Beck. 87 CD
Merlin Gro., Ilf. 40 CL
Merlin Rd. E12 49 CJ
Merlin Rd., Rom. 41 CS
Merlin Rd., Well. 69 CO
Merlin Rd. N., Well. 69 CO
Merlin St. WC1 2
Merlin St. WC1 56 BY
Wilmington St.
Merling Cft., Berk. 7 AF
Kite Fld.
Merling Cft., Berk. 7 AF
Kite Fld.
Merlins Ave., Har. 45 BE
Mermagen Dr., Rain. 59 CU
Mermaid Ct. SE1 4
Mermaid Ct. SE1 67 BZ
Mermers Gdns., Grav. 81 DJ
Merredene St. SW2 76 BX
Merrick Rd., Sthl. 64 BE
Merrick Sq. SE1 4
Merrick Sq. SE1 67 BZ
Merridene N21 29 BY
Merrielands Cres., Dag. 59 CO
Merrilands Rd., Wor.Pk. 85 BO
Merrilees Rd., Sid. 78 CN
Merrilyn Clo., Esher 93 BJ
Merriman Rd. SE3 68 CJ
Merrington Rd. SW6 66 BS
Merrion Ave., Stan. 36 BK
Merritt Rd. SE4 77 CD
Merritt Wk., Hat. 10 BP
Dellsome La.
Merrivale N14 29 BW
Merrivale Ave., Ilf. 49 CJ
Merrivale Gdns., Wok. 100 AR
Merrivale Ms., West Dr. 53 AX
Merrow Chase, Guil. 118 AU
Merrow Common Rd., Guil. 118 AU
Merrow Copse, Guil. 118 AT
Boxgrove La.
Merrow Ct., Guil. 118 AU
Merrow Cft., Guil. 118 AU
Merrow Dr., Hem.H. 7 AV
Merrow La., Guil. 109 AU
Merrow Rd., Sutt. 94 BA
Merrow St. SE17 67 BZ
Merrow St., Guil. 118 AU
Merrow Wk. SE17 4 L
Merrow Way, Croy. 96 CF
Merrow Way, Guil. 118 AU
Merrow Wds., Guil. 109 AT
Merrows Clo., Nthwd. 35 BA
Rickmansworth Rd.
Merry Hill Mt., Bush. 36 BF
Merry Hill Rd., Bush. 27 BE
Merrydown Way, Chis. 88 CK
Merryfield SE3 68 CG
Merryfield Gdns., Stan. 36 BK
Merryfields, Uxb. 53 AX
Merryhill Clo. E4 39 CE
Merryhills Clo., West. 106 CJ
Merryhills Dr., Enf. 29 BW
Merrylands, Cher. 82 AV
Merrylands Ct., Lthd. 102 BE
Merrylands Rd.
Merrylands Rd., Lthd. 102 BE
Merrymeet, Bans. 95 BU
Merrywood Pk., Reig. 121 BS
Mersey Ave., Upmin. 51 CY
Mersey Pl., Hem.H. 8 AY
Mersey Rd. E17 48 CD
Mersey Wk., Nthlt. 54 BF
Leander Rd.
Mersham Dr. NW9 46 BM
Mersham Pl. SE20 87 CB

-sham Rd., Th.Hth. 87 BZ52
-stham Rd., Red. 113 BY68
-ten Rd., Rom. 50 CQ33
-thyr Ter. SW13 65 BP43
-ton Ave. W4 65 BQ42
-ton Ave., Hartley 90 DC52
-ton Ave., Nthlt. 45 BG35
-ton Ave., Uxb. 53 AZ36
-ton Gdns., Orp. 88 CL53
-ton Gdns., Tad. 103 BQ63
-ton Hall Gdns. SW20 85 BR51
-ton Hall Rd. SW19 75 BR50
-ton High St. SW19 76 BT50
-ton La. N6 47 BU34
-ton Mans. SW20 85 BQ51
-ton Pl., Grays 71 DG42
-ton Ri. NW3 56 BU36
-ton Rd. E17 48 CF32
-ton Rd. SE25 87 CB53
-ton Rd. SW18 76 BS46
-ton Rd. SW19 76 BS50
-ton Rd., Bark. 58 CN36
-ton Rd., Enf. 30 BZ22
-ton Rd., Har. 45 BG33
-ton Rd., Ilf. 49 CN33
-ton Rd., Slou. 62 AQ41
-ton Rd., Wat. 26 BC24
rton Spur SW20 85 BP52
ushey Rd.
rton Wk., Lthd. 102 BJ62
lerton Way
rton Way, E.Mol. 84 BF52
rton Way, Lthd. 102 BJ63
rton Way, Uxb. 53 AZ36
rttins Rd. SE15 77 CC46
rvan Rd. SW2 66 BY45
rvyn Ave. SE9 78 CM48
rvyn Rd. W13 64 BJ41
rvyn Rd., Shep. 83 AZ54
rwin Way, Wind. 61 AL45
ryfield Clo., Borwd. 28 BL23
sne Way, Sev. 98 CT59
ssaline Ave. W3 55 BN39
ssent Rd. SE9 78 CJ46
sseter Pl. SE9 78 CL46
ssina Ave. NW6 56 BS36
tcalf Rd., Ashf. 73 AZ49
tcalf Wk., Felt. 74 BE49
reswell Clo.
teor St. SW11 66 BV45
teor Way, Wall. 95 BX57
theringham Way NW9 37 BO30
thley St. SE11 66 BY42
thuen Clo., Edg. 37 BM29
thuen Pk. N10 38 BV30
thuen Rd., Belv. 69 CR42
thuen Rd., Bexh. 69 CQ45
thuen Rd., Edg. 37 BM29
thwold Rd. W10 55 BQ39
ux Clo., Chsnt. 21 CB19
ws, The N1 57 BZ37
it Paul St.
ws, The, Harl. 13 CN13
Commonside Rd.
ws, The, Ilf. 49 CJ32
ws, The, Long. 90 DC52
Bramblefield Clo.
ws, The, Rom. 50 CT31
ws, The, Saw. 6 CQ5
ws, The, Slou. 62 AP41
ws, The, Twick. 74 BJ46
Bridge Rd.
ws End, West. 106 CJ62
ws Pl., Wdf.Grn. 40 CH28
xfield Rd. SW15 75 BR46
yer Gro., Enf. 30 CB22
yer Rd., Erith 69 CS43
eymott St. SE1 4 F3
eymott St. SE1 56 BY40
eynell Cres. E9 57 CC36
eynell Rd. E9 57 CC36
eynell Rd., Rom. 41 CU29
eyrick Clo., Wok. 100 AP61
Creston Ave.
eyrick Rd. NW10 55 BP36
eyrick Rd. SW11 66 BT45
ezen Clo., Nthwd. 35 BA29
all Wk. SE26 77 CD49
Dillwyn Clo.
cawber Ave., Uxb. 53 AZ39
cawber St. N1 2 J2
cawber St. N1 57 BZ38
chael Faraday Ho. 67 BZ42
SE17
chael Gdns., Grav. 81 DJ49
chael Gdns., Horn. 51 CV31
chael Gaynor Clo. W7 54 BH40
chael Rd. E11 49 CG33
chael Rd. SE25 87 CA52
chael Rd. SW6 66 BS44
chaels Clo. SE13 68 CG45
cheldever Rd. SE12 78 CG46
chelham Gdns., Tad. 103 BQ63
chelham Gdns., Twick. 74 BJ48
chels Row, Rich. 65 BL45
Kew Foot Rd.
chigan Ave. E12 49 CK35
chleham Down N12 37 BR28
cholls Ave., Ger.Cr. 34 AS28
ckelfield Rd., Hem.H. 8 BA13
cklefield Way, Borwd. 28 BL22
ckleham By-pass, 111 BJ67
Dor.
ckleham Clo., Orp. 88 CN51
Mickleham Rd.
ckleham Dr., Lthd. 111 BK66
ckleham Gdns., Sutt. 94 BR57
ckleham Rd., Orp. 88 CN51
ckleham Way, Croy. 96 CF57
cklem Dr., Hem.H. 7 AV13
cklethwaite Rd. SW6 66 BS43
id Cft., Ruis. 44 BB33
id Cross La., Ger.Cr. 34 AS28
id St., Red. 121 BX72

Midcot Way, Berk. 7 AP12
Middle Boy, Rom. 32 CP24
Middle Clo., Amer. 25 AP22
Middle Clo., Couls. 104 BY63
Middle Clo., Epsom 94 BO59
Middle Cres., Uxb. 43 AU33
Middle Dene NW7 37 BN27
Middle Fld. NW8 56 BT37
Middle Furlong, Bush. 27 BF24
Middle Grn., Brwd. 33 DB22
Middle Grn., Slou. 52 AS40
Middle Grn., Stai. 73 AX50
Middle Grn. La., Surb. 85 BL54
Alpha Rd.
Middle Hill, Egh. 72 AR49
Middle Hill, Hem.H. 7 AV13
Middle La. N8 47 BX32
Middle La., Epsom 94 BO59
Middle La., Hem.H. 16 AT18
Middle La., Tedd. 74 BH50
Middle La. Ms. N8 47 BX32
Middle La.
Middle Meadow, 34 AR27
Ch.St.G.
Middle Ope, Wat. 26 BC22
Middle Pk. Ave. SE9 78 CJ46
Middle Path, Har. 45 BG33
Middle Rd. E13 58 CH37
London Rd.
Middle Rd. SW16 86 BW51
Middle Rd., Barn. 29 BU25
Middle Rd., Berk. 7 AQ13
Middle Rd., Brwd. 122 DE28
Middle Rd., Har. 45 BG34
Middle Rd., Lthd. 102 BJ64
Upper Fairfield Rd.
Middle Rd., Uxb. 43 AU33
Middle Rd., Wal.Abb. 21 CE19
Middle Row W10 55 BR38
Middle Row Pl. WC1 56 BY39
High Holborn
Middle St. EC1 2 H6
Middle St. EC1 57 BZ39
Bartholomew Clo.
Middle St., Bet. 120 BM71
Middle St., Croy. 87 BZ55
Middle St., Wal.Abb. 13 CG14
Middle Temple La. EC4 2 D9
Middle Temple La. EC4 56 BY39
Middle Wk., Wok. 100 AS62
Church St. W.
Middle Way SW16 86 BW51
Middle Way, Erith 69 CQ41
Middle Way, Hayes 54 BD38
Middle Way, Wat. 26 BC22
Middle Way, The, Har. 36 BH30
Middle Yd. SE1 4 M2
Middlefield NW8 56 BT37
Boundary Rd.
Middlefield, Hat. 10 BP12
Lemsford Rd.
Middlefield, Welw.G.C. 5 BR9
Middlefield Ave., Hodd. 12 CE11
Middlefield Clo., St.Alb. 9 BK12
Middlefield Gdns., Ilf. 49 CL32
Middlefield Rd., Hodd. 12 CE11
Middlefielde W13 54 BJ39
Templewood
Middlefields, Croy. 96 CD58
Middlegreen Rd., Slou. 62 AR41
Middleham Gdns. N18 39 CB29
Middleham Rd. N18 39 CB29
Middleknights Hill, 8 AW12
Hem.H.
Middlemead Clo., Lthd. 111 BE66
Middlemead Rd., Lthd. 111 BE66
Middlesborough Rd. N18 39 CB29
Middlesex Pas. EC1 2 G7
Middlesex Rd., Mitch. 86 BX53
Middlesex St. E1 2 N7
Middlesex St. E1 57 CA39
Middlesex Wf. E5 48 CC34
Middleton, Guil. 118 AP71
Middleton Ave. E4 39 CD28
Middleton Ave., Grnf. 54 BG37
Middleton Ave., Sid. 79 CO50
Middleton Bldgs. W1 1 L7
Middleton Bldgs. W1 56 BW39
Langham St.
Middleton Clo. E4 39 CD27
Middleton Dr. SE16 67 CC41
Middleton Dr., Pnr. 44 BC31
Middleton Gdns., Ilf. 49 CL32
Middleton Gro. N7 47 BX35
Middleton Hall La., 122 DC27
Brwd.
Middleton Ind. Est. Rd., 118 AQ70
Guil.
Middleton Ms. N7 47 BX35
Middleton Gro.
Middleton Rd. E8 57 CA36
Middleton Rd. NW11 47 BS33
Middleton Rd., Brwd. 122 DC26
Middleton Rd., Cob. 102 BD63
Middleton Rd., Epsom 94 BN58
Eleanor Ave.
Middleton Rd., Hayes 53 BA39
Middleton Rd., Mord. 86 BS53
Middleton Rd., Rick. 35 AW26
Middleton St. E2 57 CB38
Canrobert St.
Middleton Way SE13 67 CF45
Middleway NW11 47 BS32
Middlings, The, Sev. 116 CT66
Middlings Ri., Sev. 116 CT66
Middlings Wd., Sev. 116 CT66
Midfield Ave., Bexh. 69 CS45
Midfield Way, Orp. 89 CO51
Midford Pl. W1 1 M5
Midford Pl. W1 56 BW38
Tottenham Ct. Rd.
Midholm NW11 47 BS31
Midholm, Wem. 46 BM33
Midholm Clo. NW11 47 BS31

Midholm Rd., Croy. 87 CD55
Midhope Clo., Wok. 100 AS63
Midhope Rd.
Midhope Gdns., Wok. 100 AS63
Midhope Rd.
Midhope Rd., Wok. 100 AS63
Midhope St. WC1 2 A3
Midhope St. WC1 56 BX38
Argyle Wk.
Midhurst Ave. N10 47 BV31
Midhurst Ave., Croy. 86 BY54
Midhurst Clo., Horn. 50 CU35
Cowdray Way
Midhurst Gdns., Uxb. 53 BA37
Midhurst Hill, Bexh. 79 CR46
Midhurst Rd. W13 64 BJ41
Midland Pl. E14 67 CF42
Ferry St.
Midland Rd. E10 48 CF33
Midland Rd. NW1 1 P1
Midland Rd. NW1 56 BW37
Midland Rd., Hem.H. 8 AX13
Midland Ter. NW2 46 BQ34
Midland Ter. NW10 55 BO38
Midleton Rd., N.Mal. 85 BN51
Midlothian Rd. E3 57 CD38
Burdett Rd.
Midmoor Rd. SW12 76 BW47
Midmoor Rd. SW19 75 BQ50
Midship Clo. SE16 57 CC40
Surrey Water Rd.
Midstrath Rd. NW10 46 BO35
Balnacraig Ave.
Midsummer Ave., Houns. 64 BE45
Midway, St.Alb. 9 BF15
Midway, Sutt. 85 BR54
Midway, Walt. 83 BC55
Midway Ave., Cher. 83 AW52
Midway Ave., Egh. 82 AT52
Midwood Clo. NW2 46 BP34
Miena Way, Ash. 102 BK62
Miers Clo. E6 58 CL37
Mighell Ave., Ilf. 49 CJ32
Milberry Grn., Warl. 105 CF62
Milborne Gro. SW10 66 BT42
Gilston Rd.
Milborne St. E9 57 CC36
Well St.
Milborough Cres. SE12 78 CG46
Milbourne La., Esher 93 BG57
Milbrook, Esher 93 BG57
Milburn Dr., West Dr. 53 AY40
Milburn Wk., Epsom 103 BO61
Milburn Way, Green. 80 CZ46
Milcombe Clo., Wok. 100 AQ62
Inglewood
Milcote St. SE1 4 F5
Milcote St. SE1 66 BY41
Mildenhall Rd. E5 48 CB35
Mildenhall Rd., Slou. 52 AP39
Mildmay Ave. N1 57 BZ36
Mildmay Gro. N1 48 BZ35
Mildmay Pk. N1 48 BZ35
Mildmay Pl., Sev. 98 CT59
Mildmay Rd. N1 48 BZ35
Mildmay Rd., Ilf. 49 CL34
Mildmay Rd., Rom. 50 CS32
Mildmay St. N1 57 BZ36
Mildred Ave., Borwd. 28 BM24
Mildred Ave., Hayes 63 BA42
Mildred Ave., Nthlt. 45 BF35
Mildred Ave., Wat. 26 BB24
Mildred Clo., Dart. 80 CX46
Mildred Rd., Erith 69 CS42
Mile Clo., Wal.Abb. 21 CF19
Mile End, The E17 39 CC30
Mile End Pl. E1 57 CC38
Mile End Rd. E1 57 CC38
Mile End Rd. E3 57 CD38
Mile Ho. Clo., St.Alb. 9 BJ15
Mile Ho. La., St.Alb. 9 BJ15
Mile Path, Wok. 100 AQ63
Mile Rd., Wall. 86 BV54
Miles Clo., Harl. 13 CL11
Miles La. EC4 57 BZ40
Arthur St.
Miles La., Cob. 93 BE60
Miles Pl. NW1 1 C6
Miles Pl. NW1 56 BT39
Miles Pl., Surb. 85 BL52
Miles Rd. N8 47 BX31
Miles Rd., Epsom 94 BN59
Miles Rd., Mitch. 86 BT52
Miles St. SW8 66 BX43
Miles Way N20 38 BU27
Milespit Hill NW7 37 BP28
Milestone Clo., Sutt. 95 BT57
Milestone Clo., Wok. 101 AW64
Milestone Rd. SE19 77 CA50
Milestone Rd., Dart. 80 CX47
Milfoil St. W12 55 BP40
Milford Clo. SE2 69 CQ43
Milford Clo., St.Alb. 9 BK11
Milford Ct., Slou. 62 AQ41
Wexham Rd.
Milford Gdns., Edg. 37 BM29
Milford Gdns., Wem. 45 BK35
Milford Gro., Sutt. 95 BT56
Milford La. WC2 2 D10
Milford La. WC2 56 BX40
Milford Ms. SW16 76 BX49
Milford Rd. W13 54 BJ40
Milford Rd., Grays 71 DE40
Milford Rd., Sthl. 54 BF40
Milford Way SE15 67 CA44
Sumner Est.
Milk St. E16 58 CL40
Milk St. EC2 2 J8
Milk St. EC2 57 BZ39
Milk St., Brom. 78 CH50
Milk Yd. E1 57 CC40
Milking La., Kes. 97 CJ59
Milkwell Gdns., 40 CH29
Wdf.Grn.

Milkwell Yd. SE5 67 BZ44
Denmark Hill
Milkwood Rd. SE24 76 BY46
Mill Ave., Uxb. 53 AX37
Mill Brook Rd., Orp. 89 CP52
Mill Clo., Cars. 86 BV55
Mill Clo., Chesh. 16 AP20
Mill Clo. (Apsley End), 17 AZ16
Hem.H.
Mill Clo. (Piccotts End), 8 AW11
Hem.H.
Mill Clo., Lthd. 102 BF65
Mill Clo., Wal.Cr. 21 CD17
Mill Clo., Welw.G.C. 5 BP8
Mill Clo., West Dr. 63 AX41
Mill Cor., Barn. 28 BR23
Mill Ct. E10 48 CF34
Mill Fm. Clo., Pnr. 36 BD30
Mill Fm. Cres., Houns. 74 BE47
Mill Fld., Berk. 7 AR12
Mill Fld., Harl. 6 CP9
Mill Fld., Welw.G.C. 5 BT7
Mill Flds., Saw. 6 CQ5
Mill Gdns. SE26 77 CB49
Mill Grn. La., Hat. 10 BR11
Mill Grn. Rd., Mitch. 86 BU54
Mill Grn. Rd., Welw.G.C. 5 BR8
Mill Hedge Clo., Cob. 102 BE61
Mill Hill, Brwd. 122 DC26
Mill Hill Circ. NW7 37 BO28
Mill Hill Gro. W3 55 BN40
Mill Hill Rd. SW13 65 BP44
Mill Hill Rd. W3 65 BM41
Mill Hill Ter. W3 55 BM40
Mill Ho. Clo., Farn. 90 CW54
Mill Ho. La., Cher. 82 AT52
Mill La. E4 30 CE24
Mill La. NW6 46 BR35
Mill La. SE18 68 CL42
Mill La. (Doddinghurst), 33 DB21
Brwd.
Mill La. (Kelvedon Hatch), 33 CZ22
Brwd.
Mill La., Brox. 12 CD14
Mill La., Cars. 95 BU56
Mill La., Ch.St.G. 34 AQ27
Mill La., Chsnt. 40 CG28
Mill La., Croy. 86 BX55
Mill La., Dor. 119 BJ71
Mill La., Egh. 82 AU52
Mill La., Epsom 94 BO58
Mill La., Eyns. 90 CW54
Mill La., Ger.Cr. 43 AS32
Mill La., Grays 70 DB41
Mill La., Guil. 118 AR71
Millbrook
Mill La. (Chilworth), 118 AV73
Guil.
Mill La., Harl. 6 CQ9
Mill La., Kings L. 17 AZ18
Mill La., Kings.T. 85 BL52
Mill La., Lthd. 102 BJ64
Mill La. (Longham), 107 CT64
Longham
Mill La., Ong. 24 CY18
Mill La. (Moreton), Ong. 15 CV12
Mill La. (Toot Hill), Ong. 23 CT18
Mill La. (Downe), Orp. 97 CL58
Mill La. (St. Mary Cray), 89 CO52
Orp.
Mill La., Oxt. 115 CG69
Mill La. (The Chart), Oxt. 115 CK69
Mill La., Red. 121 BW69
Mill La., Rick. 26 BA25
Mill La. (Chadwell Heath), 50 CQ32
Rom.
Mill La. (Navestock), Rom. 32 CU23
Mill La., Saw. 6 CQ6
Mill La., Sev. 108 CV64
Mill La. (Ightham), Sev. 108 DB64
Mill La. (Shoreham), Sev. 98 CT58
Mill La. (Underriver), 117 CY69
Sev.
Mill La., Slou. 62 AT45
Mill La., Ton. 117 CX71
Mill La., Wal.Cr. 21 CD17
Mill La., West. 115 CM67
Mill La., Wey. 92 AY60
Mill La., Wind. 61 AN43
Mill La., Wok. 101 AX63
Mill La. Clo., Brox. 12 CD14
Mill Mead, Stai. 72 AV49
Mill Mead, Wey. 92 AY59
Mill Mead Rd. N17 48 CB31
Mill Pk. Ave., Horn. 51 CW34
Mill Pl. E14 57 CD39
Mill Pl., Chis. 88 CL51
Mill Pl., Dart. 69 CU45
Mill Pl., Kings.T. 85 BL52
Mill Pl., Slou. 62 AR44
Mill Plat, Islw. 64 BJ44
Mill Plat Ave., Islw. 64 BJ44
Mill Pond Ct., Wey. 92 AX56
Bourneside Rd.
Mill Pond Rd., Dart. 80 CW46
Mill Ridge, Edg. 37 BL28
Mill Rd. E16 58 CH40
Mill Rd. SE13 67 CF45
Loampit Vale
Mill Rd. SW19 76 BT50
Mill Rd., Dart. 80 CW49
Mill Rd., Epsom 94 BO59
Mill Rd., Erith 69 CS43
Mill Rd., Esher 84 BF55
Mill Rd., Grav. 81 DF47
Mill Rd., Grays 70 CX43
Mill Rd., Ilf. 49 CL34
Mill Rd., S.Ock. 60 CY40
Mill Rd., Tad. 103 BQ65
Mill Rd., Twick. 74 BG48
Mill Rd., West Dr. 63 AX41
Mill Row N1 57 CA37
Mill Shaw, Oxt. 115 CG69
Mill Shot Clo. SW6 65 BQ44

Mill St. SE1 4 Q5
Mill St. SE1 67 CA41
Mill St. W1 1 L10
Mill St. W1 56 BV40
Mill St., Berk. 7 AR13
Mill St., Harl. 14 CQ12
Mill St., Hem.H. 8 AX15
Mill St., Kings.T. 85 BL52
Mill St., Red. 121 BU71
Mill St., Slou. 52 AP40
Mill St. (Colnbrook), 62 AU43
Slou.
Mill St., West. 115 CM67
Mill Vale, Brom. 88 CG51
Mill Vw. Gdns., Croy. 87 CC55
Mill Way, Bush. 27 BE23
Mill Way, Felt. 73 BC46
Mill Way, Rick. 34 AV26
Millais Ave. E12 49 CL35
Millais Gdns., Edg. 37 BM30
Millais Pl., Til. 71 DG43
Millais Rd. E11 48 CF35
Millais Rd., Enf. 30 CA25
Millais Rd., N.Mal. 85 BO53
Millais Way, Epsom 94 BN56
Millan Clo., Wey. 92 AW58
Millard Ter., Dag. 59 CR36
Millbank SW1 3 Q6
Millbank SW1 66 BW42
Millbank Ave., Ong. 24 CW18
Millbank Twr. SW1 3 Q9
Millbank Way SE12 78 CH46
Osberton Rd.
Millbourne Rd., Felt. 74 BE49
Millbro, Swan. 89 CU51
Millbrook, Guil. 118 AR71
Millbrook, Wey. 92 BB56
Millbrook Ave., Well. 68 CM45
Millbrook Ct. SW15 75 BR46
Keswick Rd.
Millbrook Gdns., Rom. 41 CT30
Millbrook Gdns. 50 CQ32
(Chadwell Heath), Rom.
Millbrook Gdns., Wey. 92 AZ57
Millbrook Rd. N9 39 CB26
Millbrook Rd. SW9 66 BY45
Millbrook Rd., Bush. 27 BE23
Millbrook Way, Slou. 62 AV44
Mathisen Way
Millcrest Rd., Chsnt. 20 BY17
Millender Wk. SE16 67 CC42
Miller Clo., Pnr. 36 BD30
Miller Rd. SW19 76 BT50
Miller Rd., Croy. 86 BX54
Miller Rd., Grav. 81 DK48
Miller Rd., Guil. 118 AU69
Miller St. NW1 56 BW37
Millers Ave. E8 48 CA35
Millers Clo. NW7 37 BP28
Millers Clo., Chig. 41 CO27
Millers Clo., Stai. 73 AW49
Millers Copse, Epsom 103 BN63
Millers Ct. W4 65 BO42
Chiswick Mall
Millers Grn. Clo., Enf. 29 BY24
Millers Grn. Rd., Ong. 15 DA13
Millers La., Chig. 41 CO26
Millers La., Wind. 72 AP46
Millers Ri., St.Alb. 9 BH14
Millers Ter. E8 48 CA35
Millers Way W12 65 BQ41
Millersdale, Harl. 13 CL13
Millet Rd., Grnf. 54 BF38
Millfarm Ave., Sun. 73 BB50
Millfield, Berk. 7 AR12
Millfield, Sun. 83 BA51
Millfield Ave. E17 39 CD30
Millfield La. N6 47 BU34
Millfield La., New A.G. 90 DC55
Millfield La., Tad. 112 BR66
Millfield Pl. N6 47 BV34
Millfield Rd., Edg. 37 BN30
Millfield Rd., Houns. 74 BE47
Millfield Rd., Sev. 99 CY57
Millfield Wk., Hem.H. 8 AZ15
Millfields, Ong. 24 CY17
Millfields Clo., Orp. 89 CO52
Millfields Rd. E5 48 CC35
Millford, Wok. 100 AQ62
Millgrove St. SW11 66 BV44
Millharbour E14 67 CE41
Millhaven Clo., Rom. 50 CO32
Millhill La., Bet. 120 BM70
Millhoo Ct., Wal.Abb. 22 CG20
Millhouse La., Abb.L. 17 BB17
Millhouse Pl. SE27 76 BY49
Millicent Rd. E10 48 CD33
Milligan St. E14 57 CD40
Milling Rd., Edg. 37 BN29
Millman Ms. WC1 2 B5
Millman St. WC1 2 B5
Millman St. WC1 56 BX38
Millmans Ms. WC1 56 BX38
Millmark Gro. SE14 67 CD44
Millmarsh La., Enf. 30 CD23
Millmead, Guil. 118 AR71
Millmead Ter., Guil. 118 AR71
Millmead Way, Loug. 31 CK23
Millpond Est. SE16 67 CB41
Mills Clo., Uxb. 53 AZ37
Mills Ct. E11 49 CG34
Harrow Rd.
Mills Ct. EC2 2 M4
Mills Cres., Sev. 108 CW62
Mills Gro. E14 57 CF39
Mills Gro. NW4 46 BQ31
Mills Rd., Walt. 93 BD56
Mills Row W4 65 BN42
Bridge St.
Mills Spur, Wind. 72 AQ47
Mills Way, Brwd. 122 DE26
Millshot Dr., Amer. 25 AO23
Millside, Cars. 86 BU55
Millside Pl., Islw. 64 BJ44

Millson Clo. N20 38 BT27
Damville Clo.
Millstead Clo., Tad. 103 BP65
Spindlewoods
Millstone Clo., S.at H. 90 CY51
Millstream La., Slou. 61 AM40
Millstream Rd. SE1 4 P5
Millstream Rd. SE1 67 CA41
Millthorn Clo., Rick. 26 AY25
Millview Clo., Reig. 121 BT69
Millwall Dock Rd. E14 67 CE41
Tiller St.
Millwards, Hat. 10 BP14
Millway NW7 37 BQ28
Millway, Reig. 121 BT70
Millway Gdns., Nthlt. 54 BE36
Millwell Cres., Chig. 40 CM28
Millwood Rd., Houns. 74 BG46
Millwood Rd., Orp. 89 CP52
Millwood St. W10 55 BQ39
Chesterton Rd.
Milman Clo., Pnr. 36 BD30
Milman Rd. NW6 55 BQ37
Milmans St. SW10 66 BT43
Milne Est. SE18 68 CK42
Milne Fld., Pnr. 36 BF29
Milne Gdns. SE9 78 CK46
Milne Pk. E., Croy. 96 CF59
Milne Pk. W., Croy. 96 CF59
Milne Way, Uxb. 35 AW30
Milner App., Cat. 105 CB64
Milner Clo., Cat. 105 CA64
Milner Clo., Wat. 17 BC20
Milner Ct., Bush. 36 BF26
Bridgewater Way
Milner Dr., Cob. 93 BE59
Milner Dr., Twick. 74 BR47
Milner Pl. N1 56 BY37
Milner Rd. E15 58 CG38
Milner Rd. SW19 86 BS51
Milner Rd., Cat. 105 CA64
Milner Rd., Dag. 50 CP34
Milner Rd., Kings.T. 84 BK52
Milner Rd., Mord. 86 BT53
Milner Rd., Th.Hth. 87 BZ52
Milner Sq. N1 56 BY36
Milner St. SW3 3 E8
Milner St. SW3 66 BU42
Milnthorpe Rd. W4 65 BN43
Milo Rd. SE22 77 CA46
Milroy Ave., Grav. 81 DF48
Milroy Wk. SE1 4 F2
Milroy Wk. SE1 56 BY40
Stamford St.
Milson Rd. W14 65 BQ41
Milstead Clo., Tad. 103 BP64
The Ave.
Milton Ave. E6 58 CJ36
Milton Ave. N6 47 BW33
Milton Ave. NW9 46 BM31
Milton Ave. NW10 55 BN37
Milton Ave., Barn. 28 BR25
Milton Ave., Croy. 87 BZ54
Milton Ave., Dor. 119 BG72
Milton Ave., Ger.Cr. 43 AR31
Milton Ave., Grav. 81 DH47
Milton Ave., Horn. 50 CT34
Milton Ave., Sev. 98 CR58
Milton Ave., Sutt. 86 BT55
Milton Clo. N2 47 BT32
Milton Clo. SE1 4 P9
Milton Clo., Hayes 53 BC39
Milton Clo., Pnr. 36 BE29
Milton Clo., Slou. 62 AT45
Milton Clo., Sutt. 86 BT55
Milton Ct. EC2 2 K6
Milton Ct. EC2 57 BZ39
Milton St.
Milton Ct., Kings.T. 75 BL49
Milton Ct., Uxb. 44 AZ34
Milton Ct., Wal.Abb. 21 CF20
Milton St.
Milton Ct. Rd. SE14 67 CD43
Milton Cres., Ilf. 49 CM33
Milton Dene, Hem.H. 8 AZ10
Coleridge Cres.
Milton Dr., Borwd. 28 BM25
Milton Dr., Shep. 83 AY52
Milton Flds., Ch.St.G. 34 AQ27
Milton Gdns., Epsom 94 BO60
Milton Gdns., Stai. 73 AY47
Chesterton Dr.
Milton Gdns., Til. 71 DG44
Milton Gro. N11 38 BW28
Milton Gro. N16 48 BZ35
Milton Hall Rd., Grav. 81 DH47
Milton Hill, Ch.St.G. 34 AQ27
Milton Lawns, Amer. 25 AO21
Milton Pk. N6 47 BW33
Milton Pl. N7 47 BY35
Georges Rd.
Milton Pl., Grav. 81 DH46
Milton Rd. E17 48 CE31
Milton Rd. N6 47 BW33
Milton Rd. N15 47 BY31
Milton Rd. NW7 37 BP28
Milton Rd. NW9 46 BP33
Milton Rd. SE24 76 BY46
Milton Rd. SW14 65 BN45
Milton Rd. SW19 76 BT50
Milton Rd. W3 55 BN40
Milton Rd. W7 54 BH40
Milton Rd., Belv. 69 CR42
Milton Rd., Brwd. 42 DA28
Milton Rd., Cat. 105 BZ64
Milton Rd., Croy. 87 BZ54
Milton Rd., Egh. 72 AS49
Milton Rd., Grav. 81 DG46
Milton Rd., Grays 71 DD42
Milton Rd., Hmptn. 74 BF50
Milton Rd., Har. 45 BH31
Milton Rd., Mitch. 76 BV50
Milton Rd., Rom. 50 CU32
Milton Rd., Sev. 107 CT64
Milton Rd., Slou. 52 AO38
Milton Rd., Sutt. 86 BS55
Milton Rd., Swans. 81 DC46
Milton Rd., Uxb. 44 AZ35
Milton Rd., Wall. 95 BW57
Milton Rd., Walt. 84 BD55
Lindley Rd.
Milton Rd., Well. 68 CN44
Milton Rd., Wey. 92 AW57
Milton St. EC2 2 K6
Milton St. EC2 57 BZ39
Milton St., Dor. 119 BG72
Milton St., Swans. 80 DB46
Milton St., Wal.Abb. 21 CF20
Woollard St.
Milton St., Wat. 26 BC22
Milton Way, West Dr. 63 AY42
Miltoncourt La., Dor. 119 BH71
Milverton Dr., Uxb. 44 BA35
Milverton Gdns., Ilf. 49 CN34
Milverton Rd. NW6 55 BQ36
Milverton St. SE11 66 BY42
Milverton Way SE9 78 CL49
Milward St. E1 57 CB39
Milward Wk. SE18 68 CL43
Spearman St.
Milwards, Harl. 13 CL13
Mimas Rd., Hem.H. 8 AY12
Mimms Hall Rd., Pot.B. 19 BQ19
Mimms La., Pot.B. 19 BN19
Mimms La., Rad. 19 BM20
Mimosa Clo., Brwd. 33 DA25
Mimosa Clo., Orp. 89 CP55
Berrylands
Mimosa Clo., Rom. 42 CV29
Mimosa Rd., Hayes 54 BD39
Mimosa Rd., Rom. 42 CV29
Mimosa St. SW6 65 BR44
Mina Ave., Slou. 62 AR41
Mina Rd. SE17 67 CA42
Mina Rd. SW19 86 BS51
Minard Rd. SE6 78 CG47
Minchen Rd., Harl. 6 CO10
Minchenden Cres. N14 38 BW27
Minchin Clo., Lthd. 102 BJ64
Mincing La. EC3 2 M10
Mincing La. EC3 57 CA40
Mincing La., Wok. 91 AP58
Minden Rd. SE20 87 CB51
Minden Rd., Sutt. 85 BR55
Minehead Ct., Har. 45 BF34
Minehead Rd. SW16 76 BX49
Minehead Rd., Har. 45 BF34
Minera Ms. SW1 3 H8
Minera Ms. SW1 66 BV42
Mineral St. SE18 68 CM42
Minerva Clo. SW9 66 BY43
Minerva Clo., Sid. 78 CN49
Minerva Dr., Wat. 26 BB21
Minerva Est. E2 57 CB37
Minerva Rd. E4 39 CE29
Minerva Rd. NW10 55 BN38
Minerva Rd., Kings.T. 85 BL51
Minerva St. E2 57 CB37
Minet Ave. NW10 55 BO37
Minet Dr., Hayes 53 BC40
Minet Gdns. NW10 55 BO37
Minet Gdns., Hayes 53 BC40
Minet Rd. SW9 66 BY44
Minford Gdns. W14 65 BQ41
Minford Ho. W14 65 BQ41
Ming St. E14 57 CE40
Mingard Wk. N7 47 BX34
Ministry Way SE9 78 CK48
Miniver Pl. EC4 57 BZ40
Queen Victoria St.
Mink Ct., Houns. 64 BD45
Minnersley Wk., Reig. 121 BS73
Castle Dr.
Minniedale, Surb. 85 BL53
Minnow Wk. SE17 4 N9
Minnow Wk. SE17 67 CA42
Minorca Rd., Wey. 92 AZ56
Minories EC3 2 P9
Minories EC3 57 CA39
Minshull Pl., Beck. 77 CD50
Park Rd.
Minshull St. SW8 66 BW44
Wandsworth Rd.
Minson Rd. E9 57 CC37
Minstead Gdns. SW15 75 BO46
Minstead Way, N.Mal. 85 BO53
Minster Ave., Sutt. 86 BS55
Minster Clo., Hat. 10 BP13
Minster Dr., Croy. 96 CA56
Minster Gdns., E.Mol. 84 BE52
Minster Rd. NW2 46 BR35
Minster Rd., Brom. 78 CH50
Minster Wk. N8 47 BX31
Minster Way, Horn. 51 CW33
Minster Way, Slou. 62 AS41
Minsterley Ave., Shep. 83 BB53
Minstrel Gdns., Surb. 85 BL52
Mint Gdns., Dor. 119 BJ71
Mint Rd., Bans. 104 BT61
Mint Rd., Wall. 95 BV56
Mint St. SE1 4 H4
Mint St. SE1 67 BZ41
Mint Wk., Croy. 87 BZ55
High St.
Mint Wk., Warl. 105 CC62
Mint Wk., Wok. 100 AP62
Staveley Way
Mintern Clo. N13 38 BY27
Mintern St. N1 57 BZ37
Minterne Ave., Sthl. 64 BF42
Minterne Rd., Har. 46 BL32
Minterne Way, Hayes 54 BD39
Minton Ms. NW6 56 BS36
Lymington Rd.
Mirabel Rd. SW6 65 BR43
Mirador Cres., Slou. 52 AQ40
Miramar Way, Horn. 51 CV35
Chevington Way
Miranda Ct. W3 55 BL39
Queens Dr.
Miranda Ho. N1 57 CA37
Purcell St.
Miranda Rd. N19 47 BW33
Mirfield St. SE7 68 CJ41
Miriam Rd. SE18 68 CN42
Mirrie La., Uxb. 43 AU32
Mirror Path SE9 78 CJ48
Charlesfield
Misbourne Ave., Ger.Cr. 34 AR28
Misbourne Clo., Ger.Cr. 34 AS28
Misbourne Rd., Uxb. 53 AZ37
Misbourne Vale, Ger.Cr. 34 AR28
Miskin Rd., Dart. 80 CV47
Miskin Way, Grav. 81 DH50
Missden Dr., Hem.H. 8 BA14
Missenden Gdns., Mord. 86 BT53
Mission Gro. E17 48 CD32
Mission Pl. SE15 67 CB44
Mission Sq., Brent. 65 BL43
Pottery Rd.
Mistletoe Clo., Croy. 87 CC54
Marigold Way
Mistley Rd., Harl. 6 CO10
Mistys Fld., Walt. 84 BD54
Mitcham Gdn. Vill., 86 BV53
Mitch.
Mitcham Ind. Est., Mitch. 86 BV51
Mitcham La. SW16 76 BV50
Mitcham Pk., Mitch. 86 BU52
Mitcham Rd. E6 58 CK38
Mitcham Rd. SW17 76 BU49
Mitcham Rd., Croy. 86 BW53
Mitcham Rd., Ilf. 49 CN33
Mitchell Ave., Grav. 81 DE48
Mitchell Clo. SE2 69 CP42
Mitchell Clo., Belv. 69 CS41
Mitchell Clo., Dart. 80 CW48
Mitchell Clo., Hem.H. 16 AS17
Lancaster Dr.
Mitchell Clo., Orp. 88 CN55
Stapleton Rd.
Mitchell Clo., St.Alb. 9 BG15
Mitchell Clo., Slou. 61 AN41
Mitchell Clo., Welw.G.C. 5 BT8
Wellington Dr.
Mitchell Rd. N13 38 BY28
Mitchell Rd., Orp. 97 CN56
Mitchell St. EC1 2 H4
Mitchell St. EC1 57 BZ38
Mitchell Wk. E6 58 CK39
Oliver Gdns.
Mitchell Wk., Amer. 25 AP22
Mitchell Wk., Swans. 81 DC47
Manor Rd.
Mitchell Way NW10 55 BN36
Mitchell Way, Brom. 88 CH51
Tweedy Rd.
Mitchellbrook Way NW10 55 BN36
Mitchells Clo., Guil. 118 AS73
Station Rd.
Mitchem Clo., Sev. 99 CZ57
Mitcheners La., Red. 114 CA70
Mitchison Rd. N1 57 BZ36
Mitchley Ave., Pur. 96 BZ60
Mitchley Gro., S.Croy. 96 CB60
Mitchley Hill, S.Croy. 96 CA60
Mitchley Rd. N17 48 CB31
Mitchley Vw., S.Croy. 96 CB60
Mitford Rd. N19 47 BX34
Mitre, The E14 57 CD40
Mitre Clo., Shep. 83 BA53
Gordon Dr.
Mitre Clo., Sutt. 95 BT57
Mitre Ct. EC2 2 J8
Mitre Ct. EC2 57 BZ39
Wood St.
Mitre Ct. EC4 2 E9
Mitre Rd. E15 58 CG37
Mitre Rd. SE1 4 E4
Mitre Rd. SE1 66 BY41
Mitre Sq. EC3 2 N9
Mitre St. EC3 2 N9
Mitre St. EC3 57 CA39
Mitre Way NW10 55 BP39
Mixbury Gro., Wey. 92 BA57
Bridgewater Rd.
Mixnams La., Cher. 83 AW52
Mizen Clo., Cob. 102 BD61
Mizen Way, Cob. 102 BD61
Moat, The, N.Mal. 85 BO51
Moat, The, Ong. 23 CT18
Moat Clo., Brwd. 33 DB21
Moat Clo., Bush. 27 BF25
Moatfield Rd.
Moat Clo., Orp. 97 CN57
Moat Ct., Ash. 103 BL62
Moat Cres. N3 47 BS31
Basing Way
Moat Dr. E13 58 CJ37
Boundary Rd.
Moat Dr., Har. 45 BG31
Moat Dr., Ruis. 44 BB33
Moat Dr., Slou. 52 AR39
Moat Fm. Rd., Nthlt. 54 BE36
Moat Gdns. SE28 59 CP40
Moat La., Erith 69 CU44
Moat Pl. SW9 66 BX45
Moat Pl. W3 55 BM39
Moat Side, Enf. 30 CC24
Durants Pk.
Moatfield Rd., Bush. 27 BF25
Moats La., Red. 121 BY73
Moatside, Felt. 74 BD49
Moatwood Grn., 5 BR8
Welw.G.C.
Moberley Rd. SW4 76 BW47
Modbury Gdns. NW5 56 BV36
Queens Cres.
Modder Pl. SW15 65 BQ45
Cardinal Pl.
Model Cotts. SW14 65 BN45
Upper Richmond Rd.
Model Cotts. W13 64 BJ41
Glenfield Rd.
Model Fm. Clo. SE9 78 CK48
Modena St. W10 55 BR39
Kensal Rd.
Modern Ct. EC4 56 BY39
Farringdon St.
Moelyn Ms., Har. 45 BJ32
Moffat Gdns., Mitch. 86 BT52
Moffat Rd. N13 38 BX29
Moffat Rd. SW17 76 BU49
Moffat Rd., Th.Hth. 87 BZ51
Moffats Clo., Hat. 20 BS16
Moffats La., Hat. 19 BR17
Moffatt Ct. SW19 76 BS49
Gap Rd.
Mogador Rd., Tad. 112 BR67
Mogden La., Islw. 74 BH46
Moiety Rd. E14 67 CE41
Moir Clo., S.Croy. 96 CB58
Moira Clo. N17 39 CA30
Moira Rd. SE9 68 CK45
Moiravale, Kings.T. 84 BK51
Moland Mead SE16 67 CC42
Crane Mead
Molash Rd., Orp. 89 CP52
Molasses Row SW18 66 BT45
Clove Hitch Quay
Mole Abbey Gdns., E.Mol. 84 BF52
Mole Ct., Epsom 94 BN56
Mole Rd., Walt. 93 BD56
Mole Valley Pl., Ash. 102 BK63
Molember Ct., E.Mol. 84 BH52
Molember Rd., E.Mol. 84 BH53
Moles Hill, Lthd. 93 BG59
Molescroft SE9 78 CM48
Molesey Ave., E.Mol. 84 BE53
Molesey Clo., Walt. 93 BE56
Molesey Dr., Sutt. 85 BR55
Molesey Pk. Ave., E.Mol. 84 BF53
Molesey Pk. Clo., E.Mol. 84 BG53
Molesey Pk. Rd., E.Mol. 84 BF53
Molesey Rd., E.Mol. 84 BE53
Molesey Rd., Walt. 93 BD56
Molesford Rd. SW6 66 BS44
Molesham Clo., E.Mol. 84 BF52
Molesham Way, E.Mol. 84 BF52
Molesworth, Hodd. 12 CE10
Molesworth Rd., Cob. 92 BC60
Pennyfield
Molesworth St. SE13 67 CF45
Mollands La., S.Ock. 60 DB38
Mollison Ave., Enf. 30 CD25
Mollison Dr., Wall. 95 BW57
Mollison Way, Edg. 37 BM30
Molly Huggins Clo. SW12 76 BW47
Molteno Rd., Wat. 26 BC23
Molyneaux Ave., Hem.H. 16 AS17
Molyneux Rd., Wey. 92 AZ56
Molyneux St. W1 1 D7
Molyneux St. W1 56 BU39
Momples Rd., Harl. 6 CO10
Mona Rd. SE15 67 CC44
Mona St. E16 58 CG39
Monahan Ave., Pur. 95 BX59
Monarch Clo., Felt. 73 BB47
Monarch Clo., Til. 71 DG44
Monarch Clo., W.Wick. 97 CG56
Monarch Ct. N2 47 BT32
Monarch Dr. E16 58 CJ39
Monarch Ms. SW16 76 BY49
Monarch Rd., Belv. 69 CR41
Ambrooke Rd.
Monarchs Way, Ruis. 44 BA33
Monarchs Way, Wal.Cr. 21 CD20
Monastery Clo., St.Alb. 9 BG14
Monastery Gdns., Enf. 30 BZ23
Monaveen Gdns., E.Mol. 84 BF52
Monck St. SW1 3 P7
Monck St. SW1 66 BW41
Monclar Rd. SE5 67 BZ45
Moncorvo Clo. SW7 3 C5
Moncorvo Clo. SW7 66 BU41
Ennismore Gdns.
Moncrieff Clo. E6 58 CK39
Linton Gdns.
Moncrieff St. SE15 67 CB44
Monega Rd. E7 58 CJ36
Monega Rd. E12 58 CJ36
Money Ave., Cat. 105 BZ64
Money Hill Rd., Rick. 35 AX26
Money Hole La., 5 BU7
Welw.G.C.
Money La., West Dr. 63 AX41
Money Rd., Cat. 105 BZ64
Mongers La., Epsom 94 BO58
Monica Clo., Wat. 27 BD23
Monier Rd. E3 57 CE36
Monivea Rd., Beck. 77 CD50
Monk Dr. E16 58 CG39
Monk St. SE18 68 CL42
Monkchester Clo., Loug. 31 CK23
Monkey Island La., Maid. 61 AJ42
Monkfrith Ave. N14 29 BV25
Monkfrith Clo. N14 38 BV26
Monkfrith Way N14 38 BV26
Monkhams Ave., 40 CH28
Wdf.Grn.
Monkhams Dr., Wdf.Grn. 40 CH28
Monkhams La., Wdf.Grn. 40 CH28
Monkleigh Rd., Mord. 85 BR52
Monks Ave., Barn. 29 BT25
Monks Ave., E.Mol. 84 BE53
Monks Chase, Brwd. 122 DE28
Monks Clo. SE2 69 CP42
New Rd.
Monks Clo., Brox. 12 CE13
Monks Clo., Enf. 30 BZ23
Monks Clo., Har. 45 BF34
Priest Pk. Ave.
Monks Clo., Ruis. 45 BD35
Monks Clo., St.Alb. 9 BH14
Monks Cres., Walt. 83 BC54
Monks Cres., Wey. 92 AW56
Monks Dr. W3 55 B
Monks Grn., Lthd. 102 B
Monks Gro., Loug. 31 C
Monks Horton Way, 9 E
St.Alb.
Monks Orchard, Dart. 80 C
Monks Orchard Rd., Beck. 87 C
Monks Pk., Wem. 55 B
Monks Pk. Gdns., Wem. 55 B
Monks Pk. Par., Wem. 55 B
Monks Pl., Cat. 105 C
Monks Ri., Welw.G.C. 5
Monks Rd., Bans. 104 B
Monks Rd., Enf. 29 B
Monks Rd., Vir.W. 82 A
Monks Rd., Wind. 61 A
Monks Wk., Egh. 82 A
Monks Wk., Egh. 72 A
Mullens Rd.
Monks Wk., Grav. 81 D
Rectory Meadow
Monks Wk., Reig. 121 B
Monks Wk., Welw.G.C. 5 E
Monks Way, Beck. 87 C
Monks Way, Orp. 88 CN
Monks Way, Stai. 73 A
Bingham Dr.
Monks Way, West Dr. 63 A
Monksdene Gdns., Sutt. 86 B
Monksmead, Borwd. 28 B
Monkswell Ct. N10 38 B
Monkswell La., Couls. 104 B
Monkswick Rd., Harl. 6 C
Monkswood, Welw.G.C. 5 E
Monkswood Ave., 21 C
Wal.Abb.
Monkswood Gdns., 28 B
Borwd.
Monkswood Gdns., Ilf. 49 C
Monkton Rd., Well. 68 C
Monkton St. SE11 4
Monkton St. SE11 66 B
Monkville Ave. NW11 46 B
Monkwell Sq. EC2 2
Monkwell Sq. EC2 57 BZ
Monmouth Ave. E18 49 CH
Monmouth Ave., Kings.T. 74 BK
Monmouth Clo., Mitch. 86 BX
Monmouth Clo., Well. 69 CC
Monmouth Gro. W5 65 BL
Sterling Pl.
Monmouth Pl. W2 56 BS
Monmouth Rd. E6 58 CK
Monmouth Rd. N9 39 CB
Monmouth Rd. W2 56 BS
Monmouth Rd., Dag. 50 CC
Monmouth Rd., Hayes 63 BE
Monmouth Rd., Wat. 26 BC
Monmouth St. WC2 1 O
Monmouth St. WC2 56 BX
Monnery Rd. N19 47 BW
Monnow Grn., S.Ock. 60 CY
Monnow Rd.
Monnow Rd. SE1 67 CB
Monnow Rd., S.Ock. 60 CY
Monnow Ter., Wok. 100 AO
Mono La., Felt. 73 BC
Monoux Gro. E17 39 CD
Monro Gdns., Har. 36 BH
Monroe Cres., Enf. 30 CB
Monroe Dr. SW14 75 BM
Mons Way, Brom. 88 CK
Monsal Ct. E5 48 CC
Clapton Pk. Est.
Monsell Gdns., Stai. 72 AV
Monsell Rd. N4 47 BY
Monson Rd. NW10 55 BP
Monson Rd. SE14 67 CC
Monson Rd., Brox. 12 CD
Monson Rd., Red. 121 BU
Montacute Rd. SE6 77 CD
Montacute Rd., Bush. 36 BH
Montacute Rd., Croy. 96 CF
Montacute Rd., Mord. 86 BT
Montagu Cres. N18 39 CB
Montagu Gdns. N18 39 CB
Montagu Gdns., Wall. 95 BW
Montagu Mans. W1 1
Montagu Mans. W1 56 BU
Montagu Ms. N. W1 1
Montagu Ms. S. W1 1
Montagu Ms. W. W1 1
Montagu Pl. W1 1
Montagu Pl. W1 56 BU
Montagu Rd. N9 39 CC
Montagu Rd. N18 39 CB
Montagu Rd. NW4 46 BP
Montagu Row W1 1
Montagu Row W1 56 BU
Montagu Sq. W1 1
Montagu Sq. W1 56 BU
Montagu St. W1 1
Montagu St. W1 56 BU
Montague Ave. SE4 67 CD
Montague Ave. W7 54 BH
Montague Ave., S.Croy. 96 CA
Montague Clo. SE1 4 K
Montague Clo. SE1 57 BZ
Montague Clo., Walt. 83 BC
Montague Gdns. W3 55 BM
Montague Ind. Est. N18 39 CC
Montague Pl. WC1 1 F
Montague Pl. WC1 56 BW
Montague Rd. E8 48 CB
Montague Rd. E11 49 CG
Montague Rd. N8 47 BX
Montague Rd. N15 48 CB
Montague Rd. SW19 76 BS
Montague Rd. W7 54 BH
Montague Rd. W13 54 BJ
Montague Rd., Berk. 7 AQ
Montague Rd., Croy. 86 BY
Montague Rd., Houns. 64 BF
Montague Rd., Rich. 75 BL

ntague Rd., Slou. 52 AP40
ntague Rd. (Datchet), 62 AQ44
ou.
ntague Rd., Sthl. 64 BE42
ntague Rd., Swan. 89 CT52
ntague Rd., Uxb. 53 AX36
ntague Sq. SE15 67 CC43
ntague St. EC1 2 H7
ntague St. WC1 1 Q6
ntague St. WC1 56 BX39
ntague Waye, Sthl. 64 BE41
ntalt Rd., Wdf.Grn. 40 CG28
ntana Clo., Croy. 96 BZ58
ntana Rd. SW17 76 BV49
ntana Rd. SW20 85 BQ51
ntayne Rd., Chsnt. 21 CC19
ntbelle Rd. SE9 78 CL48
ntcalm Clo., Brom. 88 CH53
ntcalm Clo., Hayes 53 BC38
yles Rd.
ntcalm Rd. SE7 68 CJ43
ntclare St. E2 2 P4
ntclare St. E2 57 CA38
nteagle Ave., Bark. 58 CM36
nteagle Way E5 48 CB34
owns Est.
nteagle Way SE15 67 CB45
ntefiore St. SW8 66 BV44
nteith Rd. E3 57 CD37
ntem La., Slou. 61 AO40
ntem Rd. SE23 77 CD47
ntem Rd., N.Mal. 85 BO52
ntem St. N4 47 BX33
ntenotte Rd. N8 47 BW32
nterey Clo., Bex. 79 CS48
ntesole Ct., Pnr. 36 BD30
ntford Pl. SE11 66 BY42
ntford Rd., Sev. 108 CW62
ntford Rd., Sun. 83 BC52
ntfort Gdns., Ilf. 40 CM29
ntfort Pl. SW19 75 BQ47
ntgolfier Wk., Nthlt. 54 BD38
ntgomerie Clo., Berk. 7 AQ12
lortain Dr.
ntgomerie Dr., Guil. 109 AQ68
ntgomery Ave., Esher 84 BH55
ntgomery Ave., 8 AZ13
em.H.
ntgomery Clo., Grays 71 DE41
ntgomery Clo., Mitch. 86 BX52
ntgomery Clo., Sid. 78 CN46
ntgomery Cres., Rom. 42 CV28
ntgomery Dr., Chsnt. 21 CD17
ntgomery Pl., Slou. 52 AR40
ntgomery Rd. W4 65 BN42
ntgomery Rd., Edg. 37 BL29
ntgomery Rd., S.Dnth. 90 CY51
ntgomery Rd., Wok. 100 AS62
ntholme Rd. SW11 76 BU46
ntolieu Gdns. SW15 75 BP46
ntpelier Ave. W5 54 BK39
ntpelier Ave., Bex. 79 CP47
ntpelier Clo., Uxb. 53 AZ37
ntpelier Gdns. E6 58 CJ38
ntpelier Gdns., Rom. 50 CP33
ntpelier Gro. NW5 47 BW35
ntpelier Ms. SW7 3 D6
ntpelier Pl. SW7 3 D6
ntpelier Pl. SW7 66 BU41
ntpelier Ri. NW11 46 BR33
ntpelier Ri., Wem. 45 BK33
ntpelier Rd. N3 38 BT30
ntpelier Rd. SE15 67 CB44
ntpelier Rd. W5 54 BK39
ntpelier Rd., Pur. 95 BY58
ntpelier Rd., Sutt. 95 BT56
ntpelier Row SE3 68 CG44
ntpelier Row, Twick. 74 BK47
ntpelier Sq. SW7 3 D6
ntpelier Sq. SW7 66 BU41
ntpelier St. SW7 3 D5
ntpelier St. SW7 66 BU41
ntpelier Ter. SW7 3 D5
ntpelier Ter. SW7 66 BU41
ntpelier Vale SE3 68 CG44
ntpelier Wk. SW7 3 C6
ntpelier Wk. SW7 66 BU41
ntpelier Way NW11 46 BR33
ntrave Rd. SE20 77 CC50
ntreal Pl. WC2 2 B10
ntreal Pl. WC2 56 BX40
ldwych
ntreal Rd., Ilf. 49 CM33
ntreal Rd., Sev. 107 CT65
ntreal Rd., Til. 71 DG45
ntrell Rd. SW2 76 BX47
ntrose Ave. NW6 55 BR37
ntrose Ave., Edg. 37 BN30
ntrose Ave., Rom. 42 CV30
ntrose Ave., Sid. 79 CO47
ntrose Ave., Slou. 62 AR43
ntrose Ave., Twick. 74 BF47
ntrose Ave., Well. 68 CM45
ntrose Clo., Ash. 73 BA50
ntrose Clo., Well. 68 CN45
ntrose Clo., Wdf.Grn. 40 CH28
ntrose Ct. NW9 37 BN30
ntrose Ct. NW11 46 BR31
ddison Way
ntrose Ct. SW7 3 B5
ntrose Cres. N12 38 BT29
ntrose Cres., Wem. 55 BL36
ntrose Gdns., Lthd. 93 BH59
ntrose Gdns., Mitch. 86 BU51
ntrose Gdns., Sutt. 86 BS55
ntrose Pl. SW1 3 H5
ntrose Pl. SW1 66 BV41
ntrose Rd., Felt. 73 BA46
ntrose Rd., Har. 36 BH30
ntrose Wk., Wey. 83 AZ55
ntrose Way SE23 77 CC47
Rockbourne Rd.
ntrose Way, Slou. 62 AR43
ntrouge Cres., Epsom 103 BQ61

Montserrat Ave., 39 CF29
Wdf.Grn.
Montserrat Clo. SE19 77 BZ49
Berridge Rd.
Montserrat Rd. SW15 65 BR45
Monument Gdns. SE13 77 CF46
Monument Grn., Wey. 83 AZ55
Monument Hill, Wey. 92 AZ56
Monument La., Ger.Cr. 34 AS29
Monument Rd., Wey. 92 AZ56
Monument Rd., Wok. 91 AT60
Monument St. EC3 2 L10
Monument St. EC3 57 BZ40
Monument Way N17 48 CA31
Monument Way E., Wok. 100 AT61
Monument Way W., Wok. 100 AT61
Monza St. E1 57 CC40
Moodkee St. SE16 67 CC41
Moody La., Dart. 80 CX46
Moody St. E1 57 CC38
Moon Ct. SE12 68 CH45
Lyme Fm. Rd.
Moon La., Barn. 28 BR24
Moon St. N1 56 BY37
Moonrakers, St.Alb. 10 BN14
High St.
Moor End, Maid. 61 AH42
Moor End Rd., Hem.H. 8 AX14
Moor Hall Rd., Harl. 6 CQ9
Moor Holme, Wok. 100 AS63
Moor La. EC2 2 K7
Moor La. EC2 57 BZ39
Moor La., Chess. 94 BL56
Moor La., Rick. 35 AY27
Moor La. (Sarratt), St.Alb. 25 AV21
Moor La., Stai. 72 AV48
Moor La., Upmin. 51 CZ33
Moor La., West Dr. 63 AX43
Moor La., Wok. 100 AS64
Moor Mead Rd., Twick. 74 BJ46
Moor Mill La., St.Alb. 18 BH18
Moor Pk. Est., Nthwd. 35 BA28
Moor Pk. Rd., Nthwd. 35 BA29
Moor Pl. EC2 2 K7
Moor Rd., Chesh. 16 AO20
Moor St. W1 1 P9
Moor St. W1 56 BW39
Old Compton St.
Moor Vw., Wat. 26 BC25
Moorcroft La., Uxb. 53 AZ39
Moorcroft Rd. SW16 76 BW48
Moorcroft Way, Pnr. 45 BE32
Moordown SE18 68 CL43
Moore Ave., Grays 71 DC42
Moore Ave., Til. 71 DG44
Moore Clo. SW14 65 BN45
Little St. Leonards
Moore Clo., Mitch. 86 BV51
Moore Clo., Slou. 61 AN41
Moore Clo., Wall. 95 BX57
Moore Clo., Wey. 92 AW56
Moore Cres., Dag. 59 CO37
Moore Gro. Cres., Egh. 72 AS50
Moore Pk. Rd. SW6 66 BS43
Moore Rd. SE19 76 BY50
Moore Rd., Berk. 7 AP12
Moore Rd., Swans. 81 DC46
Moore St. SW3 3 E8
Moore St. SW3 66 BU42
Moore Wk. E7 49 CH35
Stracey Rd.
Moore Way SE22 77 CB47
Wilkie Way
Moore Way, Sutt. 95 BS58
Moorefield Rd. N17 39 CA30
Moorehead Way SE3 68 CH45
Mooreland Rd., Brom. 78 CG50
Moorend, Welw.G.C. 5 BS9
Moores La. (Eton 61 AM42
Wick), Wind.
Moores Pl., Brwd. 42 DB27
High St.
Moores Rd., Dor. 119 BJ71
Moorescroft, Brwd. 33 CZ22
Moorey Clo. E15 58 CG37
Stephens Rd.
Moorfield, Harl. 13 CM13
Moorfield Ave. W5 54 BK38
Moorfield Highbank EC2 57 BZ39
St. Alphages Gdns.
Moorfield Rd., Chess. 94 BL56
Moorfield Rd., Enf. 30 CC23
Moorfield Rd., Guil. 109 AR68
Moorfield Rd., Orp. 89 CO54
Moorfield Rd., Uxb. 53 AX39
Moorfield Rd. (Denham), 44 AW33
Uxb.
Moorfields EC2 2 K7
Moorfields EC2 57 BZ39
Moorfields Clo., Stai. 82 AV51
Moorgate EC2 2 K7
Moorgate EC2 57 BZ39
Moorgate Pl. EC2 2 K8
Moorhall Rd., Uxb. 44 AW32
Moorhayes Dr., Stai. 83 AX52
Moorhouse Rd. W2 56 BS39
Moorhouse Rd., Har. 45 BK31
Moorhouse Rd., Oxt. 115 CK69
Moorhurst Ave., Chsnt. 20 BY18
Moorland Clo., Mitch. 86 BU52
Church Rd.
Moorland Clo., Rom. 41 CR29
Moorland Clo., Twick. 74 BF47
Moorland Rd. SW9 66 BY45
Moorland Rd., Har. 46 BL32
Moorland Rd., Hem.H. 8 AW14
Moorland Rd., West Dr. 63 AX43
Moorlands, St.Alb. 18 BH17
Radlett Rd.
Moorlands, Welw.G.C. 5 BS9
Moorlands, The, Wok. 100 AS64
Moorlands Ave. NW7 37 BP29
Moormead Dr., Epsom 94 BO56
Moormede Cres., Stai. 72 AV49

Moors, The, Welw.G.C. 5 BS7
Moors La., Sev. 107 CU63
Moors Wk., Welw.G.C. 5 BS7
Moorside, Welw.G.C. 5 BS9
Moorside Rd., Brom. 78 CG48
Moorsom Way, Couls. 104 BW62
Moortown Rd., Wat. 36 BD28
Moot Ct. NW9 46 BM32
Mora Rd. NW2 46 BQ35
Mora St. EC1 2 J3
Mora St. EC1 57 BZ38
Morant Gdns., Rom. 41 CR28
Morant Pl. N22 38 BX30
Morant Rd., Grays 71 DG41
Morant St. E14 57 CE40
Morants Ct. Rd., Sev. 107 CS62
Morat St. SW9 66 BX44
Moravian Pl. SW10 66 BT43
Milmans St.
Moravian St. E2 57 CC38
Gawber St.
Moray Ave., Hayes 53 BB40
Moray Clo., Rom. 41 CT29
Moray Ms. N7 47 BX34
Durham Rd.
Moray Rd. N4 47 BX34
Moray Way, Rom. 41 CS29
Morcote Clo., Guil. 118 AS74
Mordaunt Gdns., Dag. 59 CQ36
Mordaunt Rd. NW10 55 BN37
Mordaunt St. SW9 66 BX45
Morden Clo. SE13 67 CF44
Morden Clo., Tad. 103 BQ63
Morden Ct., Mord. 86 BS52
Morden Gdns., Grnf. 45 BH35
Morden Gdns., Mitch. 86 BT52
Morden Hall Rd., Mord. 86 BS52
Morden Hill SE13 67 CF44
Morden La. SE13 67 CF44
Morden Lo., Mord. 86 BT52
Morden Rd. SE3 68 CH44
Morden Rd. SW19 86 BS51
Morden Rd., Mitch. 86 BT52
Morden Rd., Rom. 50 CQ33
Morden Rd. Ms. SE3 68 CH44
Morden St. SE13 67 CE44
Morden Way, Sutt. 86 BS54
Morden Wf. Rd. SE10 68 CG41
Mordon Rd., Ilf. 49 CN33
Mordred Rd. SE6 78 CG48
More Clo. E16 58 CG39
More Clo. W14 65 BQ42
More Clo., Pur. 95 BY59
More La., Esher 84 BF55
Moreau Wk., Slou. 52 AS39
Alan Way
Morecambe Clo. E1 57 CC39
Morecambe Clo., Horn. 50 CU35
Morecambe Gdns., Stan. 36 BK28
Morecambe St. SE17 4 J9
Morecambe St. SE17 67 BZ42
Morecambe Ter. N18 39 BZ28
Morecombe Clo., Kings.T. 75 BM50
Kingston Hill
Moree Way N18 39 CB28
Moreland Ave., Grays 71 DE41
Victoria Ave.
Moreland Ave., Slou. 62 AU43
Moreland Clo. NW11 47 BS33
Moreland St. EC1 2 G2
Moreland St. EC1 56 BY38
Moreland Way E4 39 CE27
Morelands Dr., Ger.Cr. 43 AS32
Morell Clo., Barn. 29 BT24
Galdana Ave.
Morella Clo., Vir.W. 82 AR52
Morella Rd. SW12 76 BU47
Morello Ave., Uxb. 53 AZ39
Morello Dr., Slou. 52 AS40
Moremead, Wal.Abb. 21 CF20
Moremead Rd. SE6 77 CD49
Morena St. SE6 77 CE47
Mores La., Brwd. 33 CY25
Moresby Ave., Surb. 85 BM54
Moresby Rd. E5 48 CB33
Moresby Wk. SW8 66 BV45
Heath Rd.
Moretaine Rd., Ashf. 73 AX48
Moreton Ave., Islw. 64 BG44
Moreton Bri., Ong. 15 CV14
Moreton Clo. E5 48 CC34
Moreton Clo. N15 48 BZ32
Moreton Clo. NW7 37 BQ29
Moreton Clo., Chsnt. 21 CB17
Moreton Clo., Swan. 89 CT51
Moreton Gdns., Wdf.Grn. 40 CK28
Moreton Pl. SW1 3 M10
Moreton Pl. SW1 66 BW42
Moreton Rd. N15 48 BZ32
Moreton Rd., Ong. 15 CW15
Moreton Rd. (Fyfield), 15 CX13
Ong.
Moreton Rd., S.Croy. 96 BZ56
Moreton Rd., Wor.Pk. 85 BP55
Moreton St. SW1 3 M10
Moreton St. SW1 66 BW42
Moreton Ter. SW1 3 M10
Moreton Ter. SW1 66 BW42
Moreton Ter. Ms. N. SW1 3 M10
Moreton Ter. Ms. S. SW1 3 M10
Moreton Way, Slou. 61 AL40
Morewood Clo., Sev. 107 CT65
Morford Clo., Ruis. 44 BC33
Morford Way, Ruis. 44 BC33
Morgan Ave. E17 48 CF31
Morgan Clo., Bark. 59 CR36
Morgan Clo., Nthwd. 35 BB28
Morgan Cres., Epp. 31 CM21
Morgan Dr., Green. 80 CZ47
Morgan Rd. N7 47 BY35
Morgan Rd. W10 55 BR39
Morgan Rd., Brom. 78 CG50
Morgan St. E3 57 CD38
Morgan St. E16 58 CG39

Morgan Way, Rain. 60 CV38
Morgan Way, Wdf.Grn. 40 CK29
Morgans La. SE1 4 M3
Morgans La. SE1 57 CA40
Morgans La., Hayes 53 BA39
Morgans Wk. SW11 66 BU43
Moriatri Clo. N7 47 BX35
Morice Rd., Hodd. 12 CD11
Morie St. SW18 66 BS45
Ferrier St.
Morieux Rd. E10 48 CD33
Moring Rd. SW17 76 BV49
Morkyns Wk. SE21 77 CA48
Morland Ave., Croy. 87 CA54
Morland Ave., Dart. 79 CU46
Morland Clo., Hmptn. 74 BE49
Morland Clo., Mitch. 86 BU52
Morland Gdns. NW10 55 BN36
Morland Gdns., Sthl. 51 BF40
Morland Ms. N1 56 BY36
Lofting Rd.
Morland Rd. E17 48 CC32
Morland Rd. SE20 77 CC50
Morland Rd., Croy. 87 CA54
Morland Rd., Dag. 59 CR36
Morland Rd., Ilf. 49 CL34
Morland Rd., Sutt. 95 BT56
Morland Way, Chsnt. 21 CD17
Morley Ave. E4 39 CF29
Morley Ave. N18 39 CB28
Morley Ave. N22 38 BY30
Morley Clo., Orp. 88 CL55
Morley Clo., Slou. 62 AS41
Morley Cres., Edg. 37 BN27
Morley Cres., Ruis. 45 BD34
Morley Cres. E., Stan. 36 BK30
Morley Cres. W., Stan. 36 BK30
Morley Gro., Harl. 6 CM10
Morley Hill, Enf. 30 BZ22
Morley Ho. E5 48 CB34
Morley Rd. E10 48 CF33
Morley Rd. E15 58 CG37
Morley Rd. SE13 67 CF45
Morley Rd., Bark. 58 CM37
Morley Rd., Chis. 88 CM51
Morley Rd., Rom. 50 CQ32
Morley Rd., S.Croy. 96 CA58
Morley Rd., Sutt. 85 BR54
Morley Rd., Twick. 74 BK46
Morley Sq., Grays 71 DG42
Morley St. SE1 4 E6
Morley St. SE1 66 BY41
Morleys Rd., Sev. 117 CV70
Morna Rd. SE5 67 BZ44
Morning La. E9 57 CC36
Morning Ri., Rick. 26 AX24
Morningside Est. E9 57 CC36
Morningside Rd., Wor.Pk. 85 BP55
Mornington Ave. W14 65 BR42
Mornington Ave., Brom. 88 CJ52
Mornington Ave., Ilf. 49 CL33
Mornington Clo., West. 106 CJ62
Mount Pleasant
Mornington Clo., Wdf.Grn. 40 CH28
Mornington Ct., Bex. 79 CS47
Mornington Cres. NW1 56 BW37
Mornington Cres., Houns. 63 BC44
Mornington Gro. E3 57 CE38
Mornington Ms. SE5 67 BZ44
County Gro.
Mornington Pl. NW1 56 BV37
Mornington Ter.
Mornington Rd. E4 39 CF26
Mornington Rd. E11 49 CG33
Mornington Rd. SE8 67 CD43
Mornington Rd., Ashf. 73 BA49
Mornington Rd., Grnf. 54 BF39
Mornington Rd., Loug. 31 CM24
Mornington Rd., Rad. 18 BJ20
Mornington Rd., Wdf.Grn. 40 CG28
Mornington St. NW1 56 BV37
Mornington Ter. NW1 56 BV37
Mornington Wk., Rich. 74 BK49
Morningtons, Harl. 13 CM13
Morocco St. SE1 4 M5
Morocco St. SE1 67 CA41
Morpeth Ave., Borwd. 28 BL22
Morpeth Gro. E9 57 CC37
Morpeth Rd. E9 57 CC37
Morpeth St. E2 57 CC38
Morpeth Ter. SW1 3 L7
Morpeth Ter. SW1 66 BW41
Morrab Gdns., Ilf. 49 CN34
Morrice Clo., Slou. 62 AS42
Morris Ave. E12 49 CK35
Morris Clo., Ger.Cr. 34 AS30
Morris Clo., Orp. 88 CN55
Morris Ct., Wal.Abb. 22 CG20
Morris Gdns. SW18 76 BS47
Morris Gdns., Dart. 80 CX46
Morris Pl. N4 47 BY34
Morris Rd. E14 57 CE39
Morris Rd. E15 49 CG35
Morris Rd., Dag. 50 CQ34
Morris Rd., Islw. 64 BH45
Morris Rd., Red. 121 BX71
Morris Rd., Rom. 41 CU29
Morris St. E1 57 CB39
Morris Way, St.Alb. 18 BK16
Morrish Rd. SW2 76 BX47
Morrison Ave. N17 48 CA31
Morrison Rd., Bark. 59 CQ37
Morrison Rd., Hayes 53 BC38
Morrison St. SW11 66 BV45
Morriston Clo., Wat. 36 BD28
Morse Clo. E13 58 CH38
Morshead Rd. W9 56 BS38
Morston Clo., Tad. 103 BP63
Morston Gdns. SE9 78 CK49
Mortain Dr., Berk. 7 AP12
Morten Clo. SW4 76 BW46
Morten Gdns., Uxb. 44 AW33
Mortens Wd., Amer. 25 AO23
Morteyne Rd. N17 39 BZ30

Mortgramit Sq. SE18 68 CL41
Hare St.
Mortham St. E15 58 CG37
Mortimer Clo. NW2 46 BR34
Cricklewood La.
Mortimer Clo. SW16 76 BW48
Mortimer Clo., Bush. 36 BF26
Ashfield Ave.
Mortimer Cres. NW6 56 BS37
Mortimer Cres., Wor.Pk. 85 BN55
Mortimer Dr., Enf. 30 BZ25
Mortimer Est. NW6 56 BS37
Mortimer Mkt. WC1 1 M5
Mortimer Mkt. WC1 56 BW38
Mortimer Pl. NW6 56 BS37
Mortimer Rd. E6 58 CK38
Mortimer Rd. N1 57 CA36
Mortimer Rd. NW10 55 BQ38
Mortimer Rd. W13 54 BK39
Mortimer Rd., Erith 69 CS43
Mortimer Rd., Mitch. 86 BU51
Mortimer Rd., Orp. 89 CO55
Mortimer Rd., Slou. 62 AR41
Stile Rd.
Mortimer Rd., West. 97 CJ59
Mortimer Sq. W11 55 BQ40
St. Anns Rd.
Mortimer St. W1 1 L8
Mortimer St. W1 56 BW39
Mortimer Ter. NW5 47 BV35
Mortlake Clo., Croy. 86 BX55
Mortlake Dr., Mitch. 86 BU51
Mortlake High St. SW14 65 BN45
Mortlake Rd. E16 58 CH39
Mortlake Rd., Ilf. 49 CM35
Mortlake Rd., Rich. 65 BM43
Mortlock Clo. SE15 67 CB44
Morton, Tad. 103 BQ64
Morton Clo., Wok. 100 AR61
Morton Cres. N14 38 BW28
Morton Gdns., Wall. 95 BW56
Morton Pl. SE1 4 D7
Morton Pl. SE1 66 BY41
Morton Rd. E15 58 CG36
Morton Rd. N1 57 BZ36
Morton Rd., Mord. 86 BT53
Morton Rd., Wok. 100 AR61
Morton Way N14 38 BW27
Morval Rd. SW2 76 BY46
Morvale Clo., Belv. 69 CQ42
Morven Clo., Pot.B. 20 BT19
Morven Rd. SW17 76 BU48
Morville St. E3 57 CE37
Morwell St. WC1 1 P7
Morwell St. WC1 56 BW39
Mosbach Gdns., Brwd. 122 DD27
Moscow Pl. W2 56 BS40
Moscow Rd.
Moscow Rd. W2 56 BS40
Mosedale St. SE5 67 BZ44
Moselle Ave. N22 38 BY30
Moselle Clo. N8 47 BX31
Moselle Pl. N17 39 CA29
High Rd.
Moselle Rd., West. 106 CK62
Moselle St. N17 39 CA29
Mospey Cres., Epsom 103 BO61
Moss Clo. E1 57 CB39
Moss Clo., Pnr. 36 BE30
Moss Clo., Rick. 35 AX27
Heron Clo.
Moss Gdns., Felt. 73 BC48
Rose Gdns.
Moss Gdns., S.Croy. 96 CC57
Warren Ave.
Moss Grn., Welw.G.C. 5 BR9
Moss Hall Cres. N12 38 BS29
Moss Hall Gro. N12 38 BS29
Moss La., Pnr. 36 BE30
Moss La., Rom. 50 CT32
Moss Rd., Dag. 59 CR36
Moss Rd., S.Ock. 60 DB39
Moss Rd., Wat. 17 BC20
Moss Side, St.Alb. 18 BE18
Mossborough Clo. N12 38 BS29
Mossbury Rd. SW11 66 BU45
Mossdown Clo., Belv. 69 CR42
Mossendew Clo., Uxb. 35 AX30
Mossfield, Cob. 92 BC60
Mossford Grn., Ilf. 49 CL31
Mossford La., Ilf. 40 CL30
Mossford St. E3 57 CD38
Mossington Gdns. SE16 67 CC42
Abbeyfield Rd.
Mosslea Rd. SE20 77 CC50
Mosslea Rd., Brom. 88 CJ53
Mosslea Rd., Orp. 88 CL55
Mosslea Rd., Whyt. 105 CA61
Mossop St. SW3 3 D8
Mossop St. SW3 66 BU42
Mossville Gdns., Mord. 85 BR52
Moston Clo., Hayes 63 BB42
Mostyn Ave., Wem. 46 BL35
Mostyn Gdns. NW10 55 BQ37
Mostyn Gro. E3 57 CD37
Mostyn Rd. SW9 66 BY44
Mostyn Rd. SW19 85 BR51
Mostyn Rd., Bush. 27 BG25
Mostyn Rd., Edg. 37 BN29
Mostyn Ter., Red. 121 BV71
Mosul Way, Brom. 88 CK53
Mosyer Dr., Orp. 89 CP55
Motcomb St. SW1 3 F6
Motcomb St. SW1 66 BV41
Mote Rd., Lthd. 102 BG64
Mote Rd., Sev. 117 CZ68
Motherwell Way, Grays 70 DA42
Motspur Pk., N.Mal. 85 BO53
Mott St. E4 30 CF22
Mott St., Loug. 31 CG23
Mottingham Gdns. SE9 78 CJ47
Mottingham La. SE9 78 CJ47
Mottingham La. SE12 78 CJ47
Mottingham Rd. N9 39 CC26

Mottingham Rd. SE9 78 CK48
Mottisfont Rd. SE2 69 CO41
Motts Hill La., Tad. 103 BP65
Mottscroft Clo., Loug. 31 CL25
Mouchotte Clo., West. 97 CH59
Moulins Rd. E9 57 CC36
Moultain Hill, Swan. 89 CU52
Moulton Ave., Houns. 64 BE44
Moultrie Way, Upmin. 51 CZ33
Mound, The SE9 78 CL48
William Barefoot Dr.
Moundfield Rd. N16 48 CB32
Mount, The N20 38 BT27
Mount, The NW3 47 BT34
Heath St.
Mount, The, Brwd. 42 DB27
St. James Rd.
Mount, The, Chsnt. 21 BZ16
Pear Tree Wk.
Mount, The, Couls. 104 BV61
Mount, The (Ewell), Epsom 94 BO58
Mount, The (Stoneleigh), Epsom 94 BP56
Mount, The, Esher 93 BF57
Mount, The, Guil. 118 AR72
Mount, The, Lthd. 102 BH65
Mount, The, N.Mal. 85 BO52
Mount, The, Pot.B. 20 BS18
Mount, The, Rick. 26 AX25
Mount, The, Rom. 42 CV27
Mount, The, Tad. 112 BR66
Mount, The, Wem. 46 BN34
Mount, The, Wey. 83 BB55
Mount, The, Wok. 100 AR62
Elm Rd.
Mount Adon Pk. SE22 77 CB47
Mount Angelus Rd. SW15 75 BO47
Mount Ararat SW20 75 BQ50
Mount Ararat Rd., Rich. 75 BL46
Mount Ash Rd. SE26 77 CB48
Mount Ave. E4 39 CE27
Mount Ave. W5 54 BK39
Mount Ave., Brwd. 122 DD25
Mount Ave., Rom. 42 CY29
Mount Ave., Sthl. 54 BF39
Mount Clo. W5 55 BM39
Mount Ave.
Mount Clo., Barn. 29 BV24
Mount Clo., Brom. 88 CK51
Mount Clo., Cars. 95 BV58
Mount Clo., Hem.H. 7 AV13
Mount Clo., Ken. 105 BZ61
Mount Clo., Lthd. 102 BH65
Mount Clo., Sev. 107 CT65
Mount Clo., Wok. 100 AQ64
Mount Clo., The, Vir.W. 82 AR53
Mount Ct., W.Wick. 88 CG55
Mount Cres., Brwd. 42 DB28
Mount Culver Ave., Sid. 79 CP50
Mount Culver Par., Sid. 79 CP50
Maidstone Rd.
Mount Dr., Bexh. 79 CQ46
Mount Dr., Har. 45 BE32
Mount Dr., Reig. 121 BT69
Mount Dr., St.Alb. 18 BG16
Mount Dr., Wem. 46 BN34
Mount Echo Ave. E4 39 CE26
Mount Echo Dr. E4 39 CE26
Mount Ephraim La. SW16 76 BW48
Mount Ephraim Rd. SW16 76 BW48
Mount Est., The E5 48 CB34
Mount Felix, Walt. 83 BB54
Mount Gdns. SE26 77 CB48
Mount Gro., Edg. 37 BN27
Mount Harry Rd., Sev. 107 CU65
Mount Hermon Clo., Wok. 100 AS62
Mount Hermon Rd.
Mount Hermon Rd., Wok. 100 AR63
Mount Hill, Sev. 107 CO62
Mount Hill La., Ger.Cr. 43 AQ33
Mount La., Uxb. 43 AU34
Mount Lee, Egh. 72 AS49
Mount Mills EC1 2 G3
Mount Mills EC1 56 BY38
Seward St.
Mount Nod Rd. SW16 76 BX48
Mount Pk., Cars. 95 BV57
Mount Pk. Ave., Har. 45 BG34
Mount Pk. Ave., S.Croy. 95 BY58
Mount Pk. Cres. W5 54 BK39
Mount Pk. Rd. W5 54 BK39
Mount Pk. Rd., Har. 45 BG34
Mount Pk. Rd., Pnr. 44 BC32
Mount Pleasant SE27 77 BZ49
Hubbard Rd.
Mount Pleasant WC1 2 D5
Mount Pleasant WC1 56 BY38
Mount Pleasant, Barn. 29 BU24
Mount Pleasant, Epsom 94 BO58
Mount Pleasant, Guil. 118 AR71
Mount Pleasant (Effingham), Lthd. 111 BE67
Mount Pleasant (Horsley), Lthd. 110 AZ68
Mount Pleasant, Ruis. 45 BD34
Mount Pleasant, St.Alb. 9 BF13
Mount Pleasant, Uxb. 35 AW30
Mount Pleasant, Wem. 55 BL37
Mount Pleasant, West. 106 CJ62
Mount Pleasant, Wey. 83 AZ55
Mount Pleasant Ave., Brwd. 122 DF25
Mount Pleasant Clo., Hat. 10 BQ11
Mount Pleasant Cres. N4 47 BX33
Mount Pleasant Hill E5 48 CB34
Mount Pleasant La. E5 48 CB33
Mount Pleasant La., Hat. 10 BQ11
Mount Pleasant La., St.Alb. 18 BE18
Mount Pleasant Rd. E17 39 CD30
Mount Pleasant Rd. N17 39 CA30
Mount Pleasant Rd. NW10 55 BQ36
Mount Pleasant Rd. SE13 77 CE46
Mount Pleasant Rd. W5 54 BK38
Mount Pleasant Rd., Cat. 105 CB65
Mount Pleasant Rd., Chig. 40 CM28
Mount Pleasant Rd., Dart. 80 CW46
Mount Pleasant Rd., N.Mal. 85 BN52
Mount Pleasant Rd., Rom. 41 CS29
Mount Pleasant Rd., Sev. 116 CU70
Mount Pleasant Vill. N4 47 BX33
Mount Pleasant Wk., Bex. 79 CS46
Mount Ri., Red. 121 BT71
Cotland Acres
Mount Rd. NW2 46 BP34
Mount Rd. NW4 46 BP32
Mount Rd. SE19 77 BZ50
Mount Rd. SW19 76 BS48
Mount Rd., Barn. 29 BU25
Mount Rd., Bexh. 79 CP46
Mount Rd., Chess. 94 BL56
Mount Rd., Dag. 50 CQ33
Mount Rd., Dart. 79 CT46
Mount Rd., Epp. 23 CP19
Mount Rd., Felt. 74 BE48
Mount Rd., Hayes 63 BC41
Mount Rd., Ilf. 49 CL35
Mount Rd., Mitch. 86 BT51
Mount Rd., N.Mal. 85 BN52
Mount Rd., Wok. 100 AQ64
Mount Rd. (Chobham), Wok. 91 AQ59
Mount Row W1 3 J1
Mount Row W1 56 BV40
Mount Side, Guil. 118 AQ71
Mount Sq., The NW3 47 BT34
Heath St.
Mount Stewart Ave., Har. 45 BK33
Mount St. W1 3 G1
Mount St. W1 56 BV40
Mount St., Dor. 119 BJ71
Mount Ter. E1 57 CB39
Mount Vernon NW3 47 BT35
Mount Vw. NW7 37 BN27
Mount Vw. W5 54 BK38
Mount Vw., Enf. 29 BX22
Mount Vw., Rick. 35 AW26
Mount Vw., St.Alb. 19 BL17
Mount Vw. Rd. E4 39 CF26
Mount Vw. Rd. N4 47 BX33
Mount Vw. Rd. NW9 46 BN32
Mount Vill. SE27 76 BY48
Canterbury Gro.
Mount Way, Cars. 95 BV58
Mountacre Clo. SE26 77 CB49
Mountague Pl. E14 57 CF40
Mountbatten Clo. SE18 68 CN43
Mountbatten Clo. SE19 77 CA49
Mountbatten Clo., Buck.H. 40 CJ27
Lower Queens Rd.
Mountbatten Clo., St.Alb. 9 BJ15
Mountbatten Clo., Slou. 62 AQ41
Yew Tree Rd.
Mountbatten Ct., Buck.H. 40 CJ27
Lower Queens Rd.
Mountbatten Ms. SW18 76 BT47
Inman Rd.
Mountbatten Sq., Wind. 61 AO44
Ward Royal
Mountbel Rd., Stan. 36 BJ30
Mountcombe Clo., Surb. 85 BL54
Mountearl Gdns. SW16 76 BX48
Mountfield Rd. E6 58 CK37
Mountfield Rd. N3 47 BS31
Mountfield Rd. W5 54 BK39
Mountfield Rd., Hem.H. 8 AY13
Mountfield Way, Orp. 89 CP52
Mountford St. E1 57 CB39
Adler St.
Mountfort Ter. N1 56 BY36
Barnsbury Sq.
Mountgrace Rd., Pot.B. 20 BS19
Mountgrove Rd. N5 47 BY34
Mounthurst Rd., Brom. 88 CG54
Mountington Pk. Clo., Har. 45 BK32
Donnington Rd.
Mountjoy Clo. SE2 69 CO41
Mountnessing La., Brwd. 33 DB22
Mounts Pond Rd. SE3 67 CF44
Mounts Rd., Green. 80 DA46
Mountsfield Clo., Stai. 73 AW46
Benenstock Rd.
Mountsfield Ct. SE13 77 CF46
Mountside, Felt. 74 BE48
Mountside, Stan. 36 BH30
Mountview, Nthwd. 35 BB29
Mountview Ct. N8 47 BY31
Mountview Dr., Red. 121 BU71
Mountview Rd., Chsnt. 21 CA16
Mountview Rd., Esher 93 BJ57
Mountview Rd., Orp. 89 CO54
Mountway, Pot.B. 20 BS18
Mountway, Welw.G.C. 5 BR9
Mountway Clo., Welw.G.C. 5 BR9
Mountwood, E.Mol. 84 BF52
Mountwood Clo., S.Croy. 96 CB58
Movers La., Bark. 58 CM37
Mowatt Clo. N19 47 BW33
Mowbray Ave., Wey. 92 AY60
Mowbray Cres., Egh. 72 AT49
Mowbray Gdns., Dor. 119 BJ70
Mowbray Rd. NW6 55 BR36
Mowbray Rd. SE19 87 CA51
Mowbray Rd., Barn. 29 BT24
Mowbray Rd., Edg. 37 BM28
Mowbray Rd., Harl. 6 CN10
Mowbray Rd., Rich. 74 BK48
Mowbrays Clo., Rom. 41 CS30
Mowbrays Rd., Rom. 41 CS30
Mowbrey Gdns., Loug. 31 CM23
Mowlem St. E2 57 CB37
Mowll St. SW9 66 BY43
Moxon Clo. E13 58 CG37
Whitelegg Rd.
Moxon St. W1 1 G7
Moxon St. W1 56 BV39
Moxon St., Barn. 28 BR24
Moye Clo. E2 57 CB37
Moyers Rd. E10 48 CF33
Moylan Rd. W6 65 BR43
Moyne Ct., Wok. 100 AP62
Iveagh Rd.
Moyne Pl. NW10 55 BM37
Moyser Rd. SW16 76 BV49
Mozart Sq. SW1 66 BV42
Ebury Bri. Rd.
Mozart St. W10 55 BR38
Mozart Ter. SW1 3 H9
Muchelney Rd., Mord. 86 BT53
Muckhatch La., Egh. 82 AT52
Muckingford Rd., Til. 71 DJ42
Mud La. W5 54 BK39
Muddy La., Slou. 52 AP39
Mudlarks Way SE4 68 CH41
Mudlarks Way SE10 68 CH41
Muggeridge Rd., Dag. 50 CR35
Muir Rd. E5 48 CB35
Muir St. E16 58 CK40
Muirdown Ave. SW14 65 BN45
Muirfield W3 55 BO39
Muirfield Clo., Wat. 36 BD28
Muirfield Grn., Wat. 35 BC28
Muirfield Rd., Wat. 36 BD28
Muirfield Rd., Wok. 100 AP62
Muirkirk Rd. SE6 77 CF47
Mulberry Ave., Stai. 73 AY47
Mulberry Clo. E4 39 CE27
Mulberry Clo. NW3 47 BT35
Hampstead High St.
Mulberry Clo. NW4 46 BQ31
Mulberry Clo. SE7 68 CJ43
Mulberry Clo. SW16 76 BW49
Mulberry Clo., Barn. 29 BT24
Margaret Rd.
Mulberry Clo., Brox. 12 CD15
Mulberry Clo., Nthlt. 54 BD37
Mulberry Clo., Rom. 51 CV31
Mulberry Clo., St.Alb. 18 BF17
Mulberry Clo., Wey. 83 AZ55
Mulberry Clo., Wok. 91 AS60
Mulberry Ct., Bark. 58 CN36
Westrow Dr.
Mulberry Cres., Brent. 64 BJ43
Mulberry Cres., West Dr. 63 AZ41
Mulberry Dr., Grays 70 CW42
Mulberry Dr., Slou. 62 AS42
Mulberry Hill, Brwd. 122 DC26
Mulberry La., Croy. 87 CA54
Mulberry Ms., Wall. 95 BW57
Clarendon Rd.
Mulberry Rd., Grav. 81 DF48
Mulberry St. E1 57 CB39
Mulberry Trees, Shep. 83 BA54
Mulberry Wk. SW3 66 BT43
Mulberry Way E18 40 CH30
Mulberry Way, Belv. 69 CS41
Mulberry Way, Ilf. 49 CM31
Mulgrave Rd. NW10 46 BO35
Mulgrave Rd. SW6 65 BR43
Mulgrave Rd. W5 54 BK38
Mulgrave Rd., Croy. 87 BZ55
Mulgrave Rd., Har. 45 BJ34
Mulgrave Rd., Sutt. 94 BR57
Mulgrave Way, Wok. 100 AP62
Mulholland Clo., Mitch. 86 BV51
Mulkern Rd. N19 47 BW33
Mull Wk. N1 57 BZ36
Marquess Est.
Mullein Ct., Grays 71 DE43
Mullender Ct., Grav. 81 DK47
Mullens Rd., Egh. 72 AT49
Muller Rd. SW4 76 BW46
Mullet Gdns. E2 57 CB38
St. Peters Clo.
Mullins Path SW14 65 BN45
North Worple Way
Mullion Clo., Har. 36 BF30
Mullion Wk., Wat. 36 BD28
Mulready St. NW8 1 C5
Mulready St. NW8 56 BU38
Multi Way W3 65 BO41
Valetta Rd.
Multon Rd. SW18 76 BT47
Multon Rd., Sev. 99 CZ57
Mulvaney Way SE1 4 L5
Mumford Ct. EC2 2 J8
Mumford Ct. EC2 57 BZ39
Milk St.
Mumford Rd. SE24 76 BY46
Mumfords La., Ger.Cr. 43 AQ31
Muncaster Clo., Ashf. 73 AZ49
Muncaster Rd. SW11 66 BU45
Muncaster Rd., Ashf. 73 AZ49
Muncies Ms. SE6 77 CF48
Mund St. W14 65 BR42
Mundania Rd. SE22 77 CB46
Munday Rd. E16 58 CH40
Mundells, Wal.Cr. 21 CB17
Rumsley
Mundells, Welw.G.C. 5 BR7
Mundells Ct., Welw.G.C. 5 BR7
Munden Gro., Wat. 27 BD22
Munden Pl. W14 65 BR42
Munden St.
Munden St. W14 65 BR42
Mundesley Spur, Slou. 52 AP39
Mundford Rd. E5 48 CC34
Mundon Gdns., Ilf. 49 CM33
Mundy St. N1 2 N2
Mundy St. N1 57 CA38
Hoxton Sq.
Munford Dr., Swans. 81 DC47
Mungo Pk. Clo., Bush. 36 BG27
Mungo Pk. Rd., Grav. 81 DH49
Mungo Pk. Rd., Rain. 59 CU36
Mungo Pk. Way, Orp. 89 CP54
Munnery Way, Orp. 88 CL55
Munnings Gdns., Islw. 74 BG46
Munro Dr. N11 38 BW29
Munro Ms. W10 55 BR39
Munro Rd., Bush. 27 BF25
Munro Ter. SW10 66 BT43
Riley St.
Munstead Vw., Guil. 118 AQ72
Munster Ave., Houns. 64 BE45
Munster Ct., Tedd. 74 BK50
Munster Gdns. N13 38 BY28
Munster Rd. SW6 65 BR43
Munster Rd., Tedd. 74 BJ50
Munster Sq. NW1 1 K3
Munster Sq. NW1 56 BV38
Munton Rd. SE17 4 J8
Munton Rd. SE17 67 BZ42
Murchison Ave., Bex. 79 CP47
Murchison Rd. E10 48 CF34
Murchison Rd., Hodd. 12 CE10
Murdoch Clo., Stai. 73 AW49
Cherry Orchard
Murdock Clo. E16 58 CG39
Rogers Rd.
Murdock St. SE15 67 CB43
Murfett Clo. SW19 75 BR48
Victoria Dr.
Murfitt Way, Upmin. 51 CX35
Muriel Ave., Wat. 27 BD25
Muriel St. N1 56 BX37
Murillo Rd. SE13 67 CF45
Murphy St. SE1 4 D5
Murphy St. SE1 66 BY41
Murray Ave., Brom. 88 CH52
Murray Ave., Houns. 74 BF46
Murray Cres., Pnr. 36 BD30
Murray Grn., Wok. 91 AU60
Murray Gro. N1 2 J1
Murray Gro. N1 57 BZ37
Murray Ms. NW1 56 BW36
Murray Rd. SW19 75 BQ50
Murray Rd. W5 64 BK42
Murray Rd., Berk. 7 AR12
Murray Rd., Cher. 91 AU57
Murray Rd., Nthwd. 35 BB29
Murray Rd., Orp. 89 CO52
Murray Rd., Rich. 74 BJ48
Murray Sq. E16 58 CH39
Murray St. NW1 56 BW36
Murray Ter. NW3 47 BT35
Flash Wk.
Murray Yd. SE18 68 CL42
Powis St.
Murrells Wk., Lthd. 102 BF65
Murreys, The, Ash. 102 BK62
Murthering La., Rom. 32 CT25
Murton Clo., St.Alb. 9 BH13
Hillside Rd.
Murton Ct., St.Alb. 9 BH13
Althorp Rd.
Murton St. EC1 57 BZ38
Lever St.
Murtwell Dr., Chig. 40 CM29
Musard Rd. W6 65 BR43
Musbury St. E1 57 CC39
Muscatel Pl. SE5 67 CA44
Dalwood St.
Muschamp Rd. SE15 67 CA45
Muschamp Rd., Cars. 86 BT55
Muscovy St. EC3 4 N1
Muscovy St. EC3 57 CA40
Seething La.
Museum Pas. E2 57 CC38
Victoria Pk. Sq.
Museum St. WC1 1 Q7
Museum St. WC1 56 BX39
Musgrave Clo., Barn. 29 BT23
Musgrave Cres. SW6 66 BS43
Musgrave Rd., Islw. 64 BH44
Musgrove Rd. SE14 67 CC44
Musjid Rd. SW11 66 BT44
Musk Hill, Hem.H. 7 AV14
Muskalls Clo., Chsnt. 21 CB17
Spicersfield
Muskham Rd., Harl. 6 CO9
Musquash Way, Houns. 64 BD44
Mussenden La., Hort.K. 90 CY53
Mustard Mill Rd., Stai. 72 AV49
Muston Rd. E5 48 CB34
Muswell Ave. N10 38 BV30
Muswell Hill N10 47 BV31
Muswell Hill Bdy. N10 47 BV31
Muswell Hill Est. N10 38 BU30
Muswell Hill Pl. N10 47 BV31
Muswell Hill Rd. N6 47 BV32
Muswell Hill Rd. N10 47 BV32
Muswell Ms. N10 47 BV31
Muswell Rd.
Muswell Rd. N10 47 BV31
Mutchetts Clo., Wat. 18 BE20
Mutrix Rd. NW6 56 BS37
Mutton La., Pot.B. 19 BQ19
Mutton Pl. NW1 56 BV36
Harmood St.
Mutton Row, Ong. 24 CV18
Muybridge Rd., N.Mal. 85 BN51
Myatt Rd. SW9 66 BY44
Myatts Flds. Dev. SW9 66 BY44
Myburn Clo., Hem.H. 8 AZ14
Mycenae Rd. SE3 68 CH43
Myddelton Av, Enf. 30 CA22
Myddelton Clo., Enf. 30 CA22
Myddelton Ave.
Myddelton Gdns. N21 38 BY26
Myddelton Pk. N20 38 BT27
Myddelton Pas. EC1 2 E2
Myddelton Pas. EC1 56 BY38
Myddelton Rd. N8 47 BX31
Myddelton Sq. EC1 2 E2
Myddelton Sq. EC1 56 BY38
Myddelton St. EC1 2
Myddelton St. EC1 56 B
Myddleton Path, Chsnt. 21 C
Myddleton Rd. N22 38 B
Myddleton Rd., Uxb. 53 A
Mygrove Clo., Rain. 60 C
Mygrove Gdns., Rain. 60 C
Mygrove Rd., Rain. 60 C
Mylis Clo. SE26 77 C
Mylne St. EC1 2
Mylor Clo., Wok. 91 A
Grange Rd.
Mymms Dr., Hat. 20 B
Mynns Clo., Epsom 94 BN
Myra St. SE2 69 CC
Myrdle St. E1 57 CE
Myrke, The, Slou. 62 A
Myrna Clo., Mitch. 76 BL
Myron Pl. SE13 67 C
Myrtle All. SE18 68 C
Hare St.
Myrtle Ave., Houns. 63 B
Myrtle Ave., Ruis. 44 B
Myrtle Clo., Barn. 38 B
Myrtle Clo., Erith 69 C
Myrtle Clo., Slou. 62 A
Coleridge Cres.
Myrtle Clo., Slou. 62 A
Coleridge Cres.
Myrtle Clo., Uxb. 53 A
Myrtle Clo., West Dr. 63 A
Myrtle Cres., Slou. 52 A
Myrtle Gdns. W7 54 B
Myrtle Grn., Hem.H. 7 A
Myrtle Gro., Enf. 30 B
Myrtle Gro., N.Mal. 85 BN
Myrtle Gro., S.Ock. 70 C
Myrtle Pass, Dor. 119 B
Church St.
Myrtle Pl., Dart. 80 C
Myrtle Rd. E6 58 C
Myrtle Rd. E17 48 CL
Myrtle Rd. N13 39 B
Myrtle Rd. W3 55 BN
Myrtle Rd., Brwd. 42 DE
Myrtle Rd., Croy. 87 CE
Myrtle Rd., Dart. 80 CV
Myrtle Rd., Dor. 119 B
Myrtle Rd., Hmptn. 74 BC
Myrtle Rd., Houns. 64 BF
Myrtle Rd., Ilf. 49 CL
Myrtle Rd., Rom. 42 CV
Myrtle Rd., Sutt. 95 BT
Myrtle Wk. N1 2
Myrtleberry Clo. E8 57 CA
Rhodes Dev.
Myrtledene Rd. SE2 69 CC
Myrtleside Clo., Nthwd. 35 BA
Mysore Rd. SW11 66 BU
Myton Rd. SE21 77 BZ

N

Nadine St. SE7 68 CJ
Nagasaki Wk. SE7 68 CJ
Nagle Clo. E17 39 CF
Nags Head Ct. EC1 2
Nags Head Est. E2 57 CA
Nags Head La., Brwd. 42 CZ
Nags Head La., Upmin. 42 CY
Nags Head La., Well. 69 CO
Nags Head Rd., Enf. 30 CC
Nailsworth Cres., Red. 113 BW
Nailzee Clo., Ger.Cr. 43 AS
Nairn Grn., Wat. 35 BC
Nairn Rd., Ruis. 45 BD
Nairn St. E14 57 CF
Nairne Gro. SE24 67 BZ
Naish Ct. N1 56 BX
Nalders Rd., Chesh. 16 AC
Nallhead Rd., Felt. 74 BD
Namton Dr., Th.Hth. 86 BX
Nan-Clarks La. NW7 37 BC
Nancy Downs, Wat. 36 BD
Nankin St. E14 57 CE
Nansen Rd. SW11 66 BV
Nansen Rd., Grav. 81 DH
Nant Rd. NW2 46 BR
Nant St. E2 57 CB
Nantes Clo. SW18 66 BT
Nantes Pas. E1 2
Nantes Pas. E1 57 CA
Lamb St.
Nap, The, Kings L. 17 AZ
Napier Ave. E14 67 CE
Napier Ave. SW6 65 BR
Napier Clo. SE8 67 CD
Amersham Vale
Napier Clo. W14 65 BR
Napier Rd.
Napier Clo., Horn. 50 CU
Napier Clo., West Dr. 63 AY
Napier Ct. SW6 65 BR
Napier Dr., Bush. 27 BE
Napier Gdns., Guil. 118 AT
Napier Gro. N1 57 BZ
Napier Lo., Ashf. 73 BA
Napier Rd.
Napier Pl. W14 65 BR
Napier Rd. E6 58 CL
Napier Rd. E11 49 CG
Napier Rd. E15 58 CG
Napier Rd. N17 48 CA
Napier Rd. NW10 55 BP
Victor Rd.
Napier Rd. SE25 87 CB
Napier Rd. W14 65 BR
Napier Rd., Ashf. 73 BA
Napier Rd., Belv. 69 CO

pier Rd., Brom. 88 CH52
pier Rd., Enf. 30 CC25
pier Rd., Grav. 81 DF47
pier Rd., Houns. 63 AX44
pier Rd., Islw. 64 BJ45
pier Rd., S.Croy. 96 BZ57
pier Rd., Wem. 45 BK35
pier Ter. N1 56 BY36
poleon Rd. E5 48 CB34
poleon Rd., Twick. 74 BJ47
psbury Ave., St.Alb. 18 BK16
psbury La., St.Alb. 9 BJ15
pton Clo., Hayes 54 BD38
Kingsash Dr.
rbonne Ave. SW4 76 BW46
rborough Clo., Uxb. 44 BA34
rborough St. SW6 66 BS44
rcissus Rd. NW6 47 BS35
rcot La., Ch.St.G. 34 AQ27
rcot Rd., Ch.St.G. 34 AQ27
rcot Way, Ch.St.G. 34 AQ28
re Rd., S.Ock. 60 CY40
rford Rd. E5 48 CB34
rrow La., Warl. 105 CB63
rrow St. E14 57 CD40
rrow St. W3 55 BM40
Steyne Rd.
rrow Way, Brom. 88 CK53
scot Pl., Wat. 26 BC23
scot Rd., Wat. 26 BC23
scot St. W12 55 BQ39
scot St., Wat. 26 BC23
scot Wd. Rd., Wat. 26 BB22
seby Clo. NW6 56 BT36
seby Clo., Islw. 64 BH44
seby Ct., Walt. 84 BD55
seby Rd. SE19 77 BZ50
seby Rd., Dag. 50 CR34
seby Rd., Ilf. 40 CK30
sh Clo., Borwd. 28 BL24
sh Clo., Hat. 10 BQ15
sh Cft., Grav. 81 DF49
Henley Deane
sh Dr., Red. 121 BU69
sh Gdns., Red. 121 BU70
sh Grn., Brom. 78 CH50
sh Grn., Hem.H. 17 AZ16
sh La., Kes. 97 CH57
sh Mills La., Hem.H. 17 AY16
sh Rd. N9 39 CC27
sh Rd. SE4 67 CD45
sh Rd., Rom. 50 CP31
sh Rd., Slou. 62 AS42
sh St. NW1 1 K2
sh St. NW1 56 BV38
shleigh Hill, Chesh. 16 AO17
smyth St. W6 65 BP41
ssau Path SE28 59 CP40
Disraeli Clo.
ssau Rd. SW13 65 BO44
ssau St. W1 1 L7
ssau St. W1 56 BW39
ssington Rd. NW3 47 BU35
tal Rd. N11 38 BW29
tal Rd. SW16 76 BW50
tal Rd., Ilf. 49 CL35
tal Rd., Th.Hth. 87 BZ52
talie Clo., Felt. 73 BA47
than Way SE28 69 CO41
thaniel Clo. E1 2 Q7
thans Rd., Wem. 45 BK33
val Row E14 57 CF40
val Wk., Brom. 88 CH51
High St.
varino Gro. E8 57 CB36
varino Rd. E8 57 CB36
varre Gdns., Rom. 41 CR28
varre Rd. E6 58 CK37
varre St. E2 2 P4
varre St. E2 57 CA38
venby Wk. E3 57 CE38
Rounton Rd.
vestock Clo. E4 39 CF27
Mapleton Rd.
vestock Cres., Wdf.Grn. 40 CJ29
vestock Side, Brwd. 33 CY23
vy St. SW4 66 BW45
ylor Gro., Enf. 30 CC25
South St.
ylor Rd. N20 38 BT27
ylor Rd. SE15 67 CB43
zeing Common, 13 CJ15
Wal.Abb.
zeing New Rd., Brox. 12 CE14
zeing Rd., Wal.Abb. 12 CF14
zeing Wk., Rain. 59 CT37
zrul St. E2 2 P2
agle Clo., Borwd. 28 BN23
al Ave., Sthl. 54 BE38
al Clo., Ger.Cr. 43 AT33
al Clo., Nthwd. 35 BB30
al Rd., Sev. 99 CZ57
al St. WC2 1 Q9
al St. WC2 56 BX39
al St., Wat. 27 BD25
alden St. SW9 66 BX45
ale Clo. N2 47 BT31
als Rd., Erith 69 CS43
Brook St.
als Yd. WC2 1 Q9
ar Acre NW9 37 BO30
asden Clo. NW10 46 BO35
asden La. NW10 46 BO35
asden La. N. NW10 46 BN34
asham Rd., Dag. 50 CO35
at Clo., Wal.Abb. 22 CG20
Hillhouse
ate St. SE5 67 CA43
ath Gdns., Mord. 86 BT53
athouse Pl. SW1 3 L8
athouse Pl. SW1 66 BW42
Vauxhall Bri. Rd.
ats Acre, Ruis. 44 BA33
atscourt Rd. E6 58 CJ39

Neave Cres., Rom. 42 CV30
Neb Cor. Rd., Oxt. 114 CF69
Nebraska St. SE1 4 K5
Nebraska St. SE1 67 BZ41
Neckinger SE16 4 Q6
Neckinger SE16 67 CA41
Neckinger Est. SE16 4 Q6
Neckinger Est. SE16 67 CA41
Neckinger St. SE1 4 Q6
Nectarine Way SE13 67 CE44
Needham Clo., Wind. 61 AM44
Needham Rd. W11 56 BS39
Artesian Rd.
Needham Ter. NW2 46 BQ34
Needleman St. SE16 67 CC41
Neela Clo., Uxb. 44 AZ35
Neeld Cres. NW4 46 BP32
Neeld Cres., Wem. 46 BM35
Neil Clo., Ashf. 73 BA49
Nelgarde Rd. SE6 77 CE47
Nell Gwynne Ave., Shep. 83 BA53
Green La.
Nella Rd. W6 65 BQ43
Nelldale Rd. SE16 67 CC42
Nellgrove Rd., Uxb. 53 AZ38
Nello James Gdns. SE27 77 BZ49
Hamilton Rd.
Nelmes Clo., Horn. 51 CW32
Nelmes Cres., Horn. 51 CW32
Nelmes Rd., Horn. 51 CW33
Nelmes Way, Horn. 51 CV31
Nelson Ave., St.Alb. 9 BJ15
Nelson Clo., Brwd. 42 DB28
Nelson Clo., Croy. 86 BY54
Nelson Clo., Rom. 41 CR30
Lynton Ave.
Nelson Clo., Slou. 62 AR42
Nelson Clo., Uxb. 53 AZ38
Nelson Clo., Walt. 83 BC54
Nelson Clo., West. 106 CK62
Nelson Gdns. E2 57 CB38
Nelson Gdns., Guil. 118 AT70
Nelson Gdns., Houns. 74 BF46
Nelson Gro. Rd. SW19 86 BW51
Nelson La., Uxb. 53 AZ38
Nelson Mandela Clo. N10 38 BV30
Nelson Mandela Rd. SE3 68 CJ45
Nelson Pas. EC1 2 J3
Nelson Pl. N1 2 G1
Nelson Pl. N1 56 BY37
Nelson Pl. W3 55 BM40
Steyne Rd.
Nelson Pl., Sid. 79 CO49
Nelson Rd. E4 39 CE29
Nelson Rd. E11 49 CH31
Nelson Rd. N8 47 BX32
Nelson Rd. N9 39 CB27
Nelson Rd. N15 48 CA31
Nelson Rd. SE10 67 CF43
Nelson Rd. SW19 76 BS50
Nelson Rd., Ashf. 73 AY49
Nelson Rd., Belv. 69 CQ42
Nelson Rd., Brom. 88 CJ52
Nelson Rd., Cat. 105 BZ65
Nelson Rd., Dart. 80 CV46
Nelson Rd., Enf. 30 CC25
Nelson Rd., Grav. 81 DF48
Nelson Rd., Har. 45 BH33
Nelson Rd., Houns. 74 BF46
Nelson Rd. (Heathrow), 63 AY44
Houns.
Nelson Rd., N.Mal. 85 BN53
Nelson Rd., Rain. 59 CT37
Nelson Rd., Sid. 79 CO49
Nelson Rd., S.Ock. 60 DB37
Nelson Rd., Stan. 36 BK29
Nelson Rd., Uxb. 53 AZ38
Nelson Rd., Wind. 61 AM45
Nelson Sq. SE1 4 F4
Nelson Sq. SE1 66 BY41
Nelson St. E1 57 CB39
Nelson St. E6 58 CK37
Nelson St. E16 58 CG40
Caxton St. N.
Nelson Ter. N1 2 G1
Nelson Wk. SE16 57 CD40
Nelsons Row SW4 66 BW45
Nelwyn Ave., Horn. 51 CW32
Nemoure Rd. W3 55 BN40
Nene Gdns., Felt. 74 BE48
Nene Rd., Houns. 63 AZ44
Nepaul Rd. SW11 66 BU44
Nepean St. SW15 75 BP46
Neptune Dr., Hem.H. 8 AY12
Neptune Rd., Har. 45 BG32
Neptune St. SE16 67 CC41
Nesbit Clo. SE3 68 CG45
Hurren Clo.
Nesbit Rd. SE9 68 CJ45
Nesham St. E1 57 CB40
Ness Rd., Erith 70 CV43
Ness St. SE16 67 CB41
Spa Rd.
Nesta Rd., Wdf.Grn. 40 CG29
Nestles Ave., Hayes 63 BB41
Neston Rd., Wat. 27 BD22
Nestor Ave. N21 29 BY25
Nethan Dr., S.Ock. 60 CY40
Nether Clo. N3 38 BS29
Nether Mt., Guil. 118 AQ71
Nether St. N3 38 BS30
Nether St. N12 38 BS29
Netheravon Rd. W4 65 BO42
Netheravon Rd. W7 54 BH40
Netheravon Rd. S. W4 65 BO42
Netherbury Rd. W5 64 BK41
Netherby Gdns., Enf. 29 BX24
Netherby Rd. SE23 77 CC47
Nethercote Ave., Wok. 100 AP62
Clifton Way
Nethercourt Ave. N3 38 BS29
Netherfield Gdns., Bark. 58 CM36
Netherfield Rd. N12 38 BS28
Netherfield Rd. SW17 76 BV48

Netherfield St. W11 55 BR40
Portland Rd.
Netherford Rd. SW4 66 BW44
Netherhall Gdns. NW3 56 BT36
Netherhall Rd., Harl. 13 CG12
Netherhall Way NW3 47 BT35
Netherhall Gdns.
Netherland Rd., Barn. 29 BT25
Netherlands, The, Couls. 104 BW63
Netherleigh Clo. N6 47 BW33
Netherleigh Pk., Red. 121 BX72
Nethern Ct. Rd., Cat. 105 CE65
Netherne La., Couls. 104 BW65
Netherpark Dr., Rom. 41 CT30
Netherton Gro. SW10 66 BT43
Netherton Rd., Twick. 74 BJ46
Netherway, St.Alb. 9 BF15
Netherwood Rd. W14 65 BQ41
Netherwood St. NW6 55 BR36
Netherwood St. Est. 55 BR36
NW6
Netley Clo., Croy. 96 CF57
Netley Clo., Sutt. 94 BQ56
Netley Dr., Walt. 84 BE54
Netley Gdns., Mord. 86 BT54
Netley Rd. E17 48 CD32
Netley Rd., Brent. 65 BL43
Netley Rd., Ilf. 49 CM32
Netley Rd., Mord. 86 BT54
Netley Rd. W., Houns. 63 BA44
Netley St. NW1 1 L3
Nettle Cft., Welw.G.C. 5 BS7
Hazel Gro.
Nettlecombe Clo., Sutt. 95 BS58
Nettlecroft, Hem.H. 8 AW14
Nettleden Ave., Wem. 55 BM36
Nettleden Rd., Berk. 7 AS12
Nettlefold Pl. SE27 76 BY48
Nettles Ter., Guil. 118 AR70
Nettlestead Clo., Beck. 77 CD50
Nettleton Rd. SE14 67 CC44
Nettleton Rd., Houns. 63 AZ44
Nettleton Rd., Uxb. 44 AY35
Nettlewood Rd. SW16 76 BW50
Neuchatel Rd. SE6 77 CD48
Nevada Clo., N.Mal. 85 BN52
Georgia Rd.
Nevada St. SE10 67 CF43
Nevell Rd., Grays 71 DG41
Brentwood Rd.
Nevern Pl. SW5 66 BS42
Nevern Rd. SW5 66 BS42
Nevern Sq. SW5 66 BS42
Nevill Gro., Wat. 26 BC23
Nevill Rd. N16 48 CA34
Nevill Way, Loug. 40 CK26
Neville Ave., N.Mal. 85 BN51
Neville Clo. E11 49 CG34
Cobbold Rd.
Neville Clo. NW1 1 P1
Neville Clo. NW1 56 BW37
Neville Clo. NW6 55 BR37
Neville Clo. SE15 67 CB43
Neville Clo. W3 65 BN41
Acton La.
Neville Clo., Bans. 95 BS60
Neville Clo., Esher 93 BE57
Neville Clo., Houns. 64 BF44
Neville Clo., Pot.B. 19 BR19
Neville Clo., Sid. 78 CN49
Neville Clo., Slou. 52 AP36
Neville Dr. N2 47 BT32
Neville Gdns., Dag. 50 CP34
Neville Rd.
Neville Gill Clo. SW18 76 BS46
Neville Rd. E7 58 CH36
Neville Rd. NW6 55 BR37
Neville Rd. W5 54 BK38
Neville Rd., Croy. 87 BZ54
Neville Rd., Dag. 50 CP34
Neville Rd., Ilf. 40 CM30
Neville Rd., Kings.T. 85 BM51
Neville Rd., Rich. 74 BK48
Neville St. SW7 3 A10
Neville St. SW7 66 BT42
Neville Ter. SW7 3 A10
Neville Ter. SW7 66 BT42
Neville Wk., Cars. 86 BU54
Green Wrythe La.
Neville Way, Houns. 64 BF44
Nevilles Ct. NW2 46 BP34
Nevin Dr. E4 39 CE26
Nevis Clo., Rom. 41 CT30
Nevis Rd. SW17 76 BV48
New Ash Clo. N2 47 BT31
Oakridge Dr.
New Barn La., Sev. 106 CM62
New Barn La., West. 106 CM62
New Barn La., Whyt. 105 CA61
New Barn Rd., Grav. 81 DD49
New Barn Rd., Swan. 89 CT51
New Barn St. E13 58 CH39
New Barnes Ave., St.Alb. 9 BJ15
New Barns Ave., Mitch. 86 BW52
New Barns Way, Chig. 40 CL27
New Battlebridge La., 113 BV68
Red.
New Bond St. W1 1 J9
New Bond St. W1 56 BV39
New Brent St. NW4 46 BQ32
New Bri., Erith 69 CS42
New Bri. St. EC4 2 F9
New Bri. St. EC4 56 BY39
New Broad St. EC2 2 M7
New Broad St. EC2 57 BZ39
New Bdy. W5 54 BK40
New Burlington Ms. W1 1 L10
New Burlington Ms. W1 56 BW40
Regent St.
New Burlington Pl. W1 1 L10
New Burlington St. W1 1 L10
New Burlington St. W1 56 BW40
New Bury La., Walt. 93 BD56
New Butt La. SE8 67 CE43

New Causeway, Reig. 121 BS72
New Cavendish St. W1 1 H7
New Cavendish St. W1 56 BV39
New Change EC4 2 H9
New Change EC4 57 BZ39
New Chapel Sq., Felt. 73 BC47
New Charles St. EC1 2 G2
New Ch. Rd. SE5 67 BZ43
New City Rd. E13 58 CJ38
New Clo. SW19 86 BT51
New Clo., Felt. 74 BE49
New Clo. Est., Mitch. 86 BT51
New College Ms. N1 56 BY36
College Cross
New Compton St. WC2 1 P9
New Compton St. WC2 56 BW39
New Ct. EC4 2 D10
New Ct., Dart. 80 CW46
New Ct., Nthlt. 45 BF35
Dorchester Clo.
New Ct., Uxb. 53 AX39
New Ct., Wey. 83 AX55
New Coventry St. W1 3 P1
New Coventry St. W1 56 BW40
Coventry St.
New Crane Pl. E1 57 CC40
Garnet St.
New Cross Rd. SE14 67 CC43
New Cross Rd., Guil. 118 AQ69
New End NW3 47 BT35
New End Sq. NW3 47 BT35
New England St., St.Alb. 9 BG13
New Fm. Ave., Brom. 88 CH52
New Fm. Dr., Rom. 32 CP24
New Fm. La., Nthwd. 35 BB30
New Fetter La. EC4 2 E8
New Fetter La. EC4 56 BY39
New Ford Rd., Wal.Cr. 21 CD20
New Forest La., Chig. 40 CL29
New Goulston St. E1 2 P8
New Goulston St. E1 57 CA39
Middlesex St.
New Grns. Ave., St.Alb. 9 BG11
New Hall Clo., Hem.H. 16 AT17
High St.
New Hall Dr., Rom. 42 CW30
New Haw Rd., Wey. 92 AX56
New Heston Rd., Houns. 64 BE43
New Hill Rd., Orp. 97 CK58
New Ho. La., Epp. 23 CS16
New Ho. La., Grav. 81 DF48
New Ho. La., Sev. 108 DC61
New Inn (Broadway) EC2 57 CA38
New Inn Yd.
New Inn Bdy. EC2 2 N4
New Inn La., Guil. 109 AT68
New Inn Pas. WC2 2 C9
New Inn St. EC2 2 N4
New Inn Yd. EC2 2 N4
New Inn Yd. EC2 57 CA38
New James Ct. SE15 67 CB45
New James St. SE15 67 CB45
Scylla Rd.
New Kent Rd. SE1 4 H7
New Kent Rd. SE1 67 BZ41
New Kent Rd., St.Alb. 9 BG13
New King St. SE8 67 CE43
New Kings Rd. SW6 65 BR44
New La., Guil. 109 AS66
New La., Guil. 100 AS64
New La., Wok. 100 AS64
New Lo. Dr., Oxt. 115 CG67
New London St. EC3 2 N10
New London St. EC3 57 CA40
Hart St.
New Lyndenburgh St. 68 CJ41
SE7
New Meadows Path, 65 BM44
Rich.
Townmead Rd.
New Mill Rd., Orp. 89 CP51
New Mt. St. E15 57 CF36
New N. Pl. EC2 2 M5
New N. Pl. EC2 57 CA38
Luke St.
New N. Rd. N1 57 BZ36
New N. Rd., Ilf. 40 CM29
New N. Rd., Reig. 120 BR72
New N. St. WC1 2 B6
New N. St. WC1 56 BX39
New Oak Rd. N2 38 BT30
New Orleans Wk. N19 47 BW33
New Oxford St. WC1 1 P8
New Oxford St. WC1 56 BW39
New Par., Ashf. 73 AY49
Church Rd.
New Pk. Ave. N13 39 BZ27
New Pk. Clo., Nthlt. 54 BE36
New Pk. Ct. SW2 76 BX47
New Pk. Dr., Hem.H. 8 AZ13
New Pk. Rd. SW2 76 BW47
New Pk. Rd., Ashf. 73 BA49
New Pk. Rd., Hert. 11 BW15
New Pk. Rd., Uxb. 35 AX30
New Peachey La., Uxb. 53 AX39
New Peachey La. Clo., 53 AX39
Uxb.
New Pl. Gdns., Upmin. 51 CY34
New Pl. Sq. SE16 67 CB41
Southwark Pk. Rd.
New Plaistow Rd. E15 58 CG37
New Pond Rd., Guil. 118 AO74
New Quebec St. W1 1 F9
New Quebec St. W1 56 BU39
New Ride SW7 3 C4
New River Clo., Hodd. 12 CE11
New River Ct. N5 48 BZ35
New River Ct., Wal.Cr. 21 CB19
New River Cres. N13 38 BY28
New River Wk. N1 57 BZ36
New Rd. E1 57 CB39
New Rd. E4 39 CE28
New Rd. N8 47 BX32
New Rd. N9 39 CB27

New Rd. N17 39 CA30
New Rd. N22 39 BZ30
New Rd. (Hendon Wd. La.) 37 BO26
NW7
New Rd. (Mill Hill E.) 37 BR29
NW7
New Rd. SE2 69 CP42
New Rd., Amer. 25 AP22
New Rd., Berk. 7 AS11
New Rd. (Northchurch), 7 AP12
Berk.
New Rd., Borwd. 27 BK25
High St.
New Rd. (South Mimms), 19 BM20
Borwd.
New Rd., Brent. 64 BK43
New Rd., Brwd. 42 DB27
Coptfold Rd.
New Rd., Brox. 12 CD13
New Rd., Ch.St.G. 25 AS24
New Rd., Dag. 59 CR37
New Rd., Dor. 119 BK72
New Rd., E.Mol. 84 BF52
New Rd., Epp. 23 CR19
New Rd., Esher 84 BG55
New Rd., Felt. 73 BC47
New Rd. (East Bedfont), 73 BA46
Felt.
New Rd. (Hanworth), 74 BE49
Felt.
New Rd., Grav. 81 DG46
New Rd., Grays 71 DD43
New Rd., Guil. 110 AY69
New Rd., Harl. 6 CP9
New Rd., Har. 45 BH35
New Rd., Hayes 63 BA43
New Rd., Houns. 64 BF45
New Rd., Ilf. 49 CN34
New Rd., Kings L. 16 AV18
New Rd., Kings.T. 75 BM50
New Rd., Lthd. 93 BH59
New Rd., Maid. 61 AG43
New Rd., Mord. 86 BU54
New Rd., Orp. 89 CO54
New Rd., Oxt. 115 CH68
New Rd., Pot.B. 19 BP20
New Rd., Rad. 27 BH21
New Rd., Rain. 59 CS37
New Rd., Rich. 74 BK49
New Rd., Rick. 26 AZ25
New Rd. (Church End), 25 AV23
Rick.
New Rd., Rom. 32 CP25
New Rd., Shep. 83 AZ52
New Rd. (Datchet), Slou. 62 AR44
New Rd. (Langley), Slou. 62 AT41
New Rd., S.Dnth. 90 CY51
New Rd., Stai. 72 AU49
New Rd., Swan. 89 CT52
New Rd. (Hextable), 79 CT50
Swan.
New Rd., Tad. 103 BQ65
New Rd., Uxb. 53 BA38
New Rd., Wat. 27 BD24
New Rd. (Letchmore 27 BH23
Heath), Wat.
New Rd., Well. 69 CO44
New Rd., Welw.G.C. 5 BP9
New Rd. (High Welwyn), 5 BR5
Welw.G.C.
New Rd., Wey. 92 BA56
New Row WC2 1 Q10
New Row WC2 56 BX40
New Spring Gdns., Brent. 64 BK43
Albany Rd.
New Sq. WC2 2 C8
New Sq. WC2 56 BX39
New Sq., Slou. 62 AP41
New St. EC2 2 N7
New St. EC2 57 CA39
New St., Berk. 7 AR13
New St., Saw. 6 CQ5
New St., Stai. 73 AW49
New St., Wat. 27 BD24
Church St.
New St., West. 115 CM67
New St. Hill EC4 56 BY39
Little New St.
New St. Hill, Brom. 78 CH49
New St. Sq. EC4 2 E8
New St. Sq. EC4 56 BY39
New Trinity Rd. N2 47 BT31
New Turnstile WC1 2 B7
New Union Clo. E14 67 CF41
New Union St. EC2 2 K7
New Wk., Sev. 108 DC61
Battlefields Rd.
New Wanstead E11 49 CG32
New Way La., Harl. 14 CR11
New Way Rd. NW9 46 BO31
New Wf. Rd. N1 56 BX37
New Wickham La., Egh. 72 AT50
New Windsor St., Uxb. 53 AX37
New Wd., Welw.G.C. 5 BT7
New Years La., Sev. 106 CN61
New Zealand Ave., Walt. 83 BB54
New Zealand Way W12 55 BP40
New Zealand Way, Rain. 59 CT38
Newall Rd., Houns. 63 BA44
Newark Clo., Guil. 109 AT68
Dairymans Wk.
Newark Ct., Walt. 84 BD54
Stratton Clo.
Newark Cres. NW10 55 BN38
Newark Grn., Borwd. 28 BN24
Newark La., Wok. 100 AV63
Newark Pl., Wok. 101 AW64
Newark Rd., S.Croy. 96 BZ57
Newark St. E1 57 CB39
Newark Way NW4 46 BP31
Newbarn La., Beac. 34 AP28
Newberries Ave., Rad. 27 BJ21
Newberry Cres., Wind. 61 AL44
Newberry Est. N1 57 BZ36

Newbery Rd., Erith 69 CT44
Newbery Way, Slou. 61 AO41
Newbiggin Path, Wat. 36 BD28
Newbolt Ave., Sutt. 94 BQ56
Newbolt Rd., Stan. 36 BH28
Newborough Grn., N.Mal. 85 BN52
Newburgh Rd. W3 55 BN40
Newburgh St. W1 1 L9
Newburgh St. W1 56 BW39
Fouberts Pl.
Newburn St. SE11 66 BX42
Newbury Ave., Enf. 30 CD22
Newbury Clo., Nthlt. 54 BE36
Newbury Clo., Rom. 42 CV29
Newbury Ct. E11 49 CH31
Newbury Gdns., Epsom 94 BO56
Newbury Gdns., Rom. 42 CV29
Newbury Gdns., Upmin. 51 CW34
Newbury Ms. NW5 56 BV36
Malden Rd.
Newbury Rd. E4 39 CF29
Newbury Rd., Brom. 88 CH52
Newbury Rd., Houns. 63 AY44
Newbury Rd., Ilf. 49 CN32
Newbury Rd., Rom. 42 CV28
Newbury St. EC1 2 H6
Newbury St. EC1 57 BZ39
Newbury Wk., Rom. 42 CV28
Newbury Way, Nthlt. 54 BE36
Newby Clo., Enf. 30 CA23
Newby Pl. E14 57 CF40
Newby St. SW8 66 BV45
Newcastle Ave., Ilf. 41 CO29
Newcastle Clo. EC4 2 F8
Newcastle Clo. EC4 56 BY39
Farringdon St.
Newcastle Pl. W2 1 B7
Newcastle Pl. W2 56 BT39
Newcastle Row EC1 2 E5
Newcastle St. W8 66 BS41
Newcombe Pk. NW7 37 BO28
Newcombe Pk., Wem. 55 BL37
Newcombe Ri., West Dr. 53 AY39
Newcombe Rd., Rad. 19 BM20
Newcombe St. W8 56 BS40
Newcome Path, Rad. 19 BM20
Newcomen Rd. E11 49 CG34
Newcomen Rd. SW11 66 BT45
Newcomen St. SE1 4 K4
Newcomen St. SE1 67 BZ41
Newcourt St. NW8 1 C1
Newcourt St. NW8 56 BU37
Newcroft Clo., Uxb. 53 AY39
Newdales Clo. N9 39 CB27
Balham Rd.
Newdene Ave., Nthlt. 54 BD37
Newdigate Grn., Uxb. 35 AX30
Newdigate Rd., Uxb. 35 AX30
Newdigate Rd. E., Uxb. 35 AX30
Newell Rd., Hem.H. 8 AY15
Newell St. E14 57 CD39
Newenham Rd., Lthd. 111 BF66
Newent Clo. SE15 67 CA43
Newent Clo., Cars. 86 BU54
Newfield Clo., Hmptn. 84 BF51
Newfield La., Hem.H. 8 AY13
Newfield Ri. NW2 46 BP34
Newfields, Welw.G.C. 5 BP8
Newford Clo., Hem.H. 8 AZ13
Newgale Gdns., Edg. 37 BL30
Newgate, Croy. 87 BZ54
Newgate Clo., Felt. 74 BE48
Newgate Clo., St.Alb. 9 BK12
Newgate St. E4 40 CG27
Newgate St. EC1 2 G8
Newgate St. EC1 56 BY39
Newgate St., Hert. 11 BW15
Newgate St. Rd., Chsnt. 20 BY16
Newgate St. Village, Hert. 20 BX16
Newhall Ct., Wal.Abb. 22 CG20
Newham Rd., Houns. 63 BA44
Newall Rd.
Newham Way E6 58 CL38
Newham Way E16 58 CJ39
Newham Way, Har. 46 BL31
Newhams Clo., Brom. 88 CK52
Newhams Row SE1 4 N5
Newhams Row SE1 67 CA41
Newhaven Clo., Hayes 63 BB42
Newhaven Cres., Ashf. 73 BA49
Newhaven Gdns. SE9 68 CJ45
Newhaven Rd. SE25 87 BZ53
Newhouse Ave., Rom. 50 CP31
Newhouse Clo., N.Mal. 85 BO54
Newhouse Cres., Wat. 17 BC19
Newhouse La., Ong. 15 CV14
Newhouse Pk., St.Alb. 9 BJ15
Newhouse Rd., Hem.H. 16 AT16
Newhouse Wk., Mord. 86 BT54
Newick Clo., Bex. 79 CR46
Newick Rd. E5 48 CB34
Newing Grn., Brom. 78 CJ50
Newington Barrow Way N7 47 BX34
Andover Est.
Newington Butts SE1 4 G9
Newington Butts SE1 66 BY42
Newington Butts SE11 4 G9
Newington Butts SE11 66 BY42
Newington Causeway SE1 4 G7
Newington Causeway SE1 66 BY41
Newington Grn. N16 48 BZ35
Newington Grn. Rd. N1 48 BZ35
Newington Way N7 47 BX34
Newland Clo., Pnr. 36 BE29
Newland Clo., St.Alb. 9 BJ15
Mile Ho. Clo.
Newland Dr., Enf. 30 CB23
Newland Gdns. W13 64 BJ41
Newland Rd. N8 47 BX31
Newland St. E16 58 CK40
Newlands, Hat. 10 BQ11
Old Hertford Rd.
Newlands, The, Wall. 95 BW57
Newlands Ave., Rad. 18 BH20
Newlands Ave., T.Ditt. 84 BH54
Newlands Ave., Wok. 100 AS64
Newlands Clo., Brwd. 122 DE26
Newlands Clo., Edg. 37 BL27
Newlands Clo., Sthl. 64 BE42
Newlands Clo., Walt. 93 BE56
Newlands Clo., Wem. 54 BK36
Newlands Ct., Wem. 46 BM34
Newlands Dr., Slou. 62 AV45
Newlands Est. SW17 76 BV49
Newlands Pk. SE26 77 CC50
Newlands Pl., Barn. 28 BQ25
Newlands Quay E1 57 CC40
Newlands Rd. SW16 86 BX51
Newlands Rd., Hem.H. 7 AV13
Newlands Rd., Wdf.Grn. 40 CG27
Newlands Wk., Wat. 18 BD20
Newlands Way, Chess. 93 BK56
Newlands Way, Pot.B. 20 BS18
Osborne Rd.
Newlands Wd., Croy. 96 CD58
Newling Clo. E6 58 CK39
Newling Est. E2 57 CA38
Newlyn Clo., St.Alb. 18 BE18
Newlyn Clo., Uxb. 53 AZ39
Newlyn Gdns., Har. 45 BE33
Newlyn Rd. N17 39 CA30
Newlyn Rd. NW2 46 BQ33
Newlyn Rd., Barn. 28 BR24
Newlyn Rd., Well. 68 CN44
Newman Clo., Horn. 51 CW32
Newman Pas. W1 1 M7
Newman Pas. W1 56 BW39
Newman St.
Newman Rd. E13 58 CH38
Newman Rd. E17 48 CC32
Newman Rd., Brom. 88 CH51
Newman Rd., Croy. 86 BX54
Newman Rd., Hayes 53 BC40
Newman Rd., Houns. 63 AZ44
Nimrod Rd.
Newman St. W1 1 M7
Newman St. W1 56 BW39
Newman Yd. W1 1 M8
Newmans Clo., Loug. 31 CL24
Newmans Ct. EC3 2 L9
Newmans Dr., Brwd. 122 DE26
Newmans La., Loug. 31 CL24
Newmans Rd., Grav. 81 DF48
Newmans Row WC2 2 C7
Newmans Row WC2 56 BX39
Great Turnstile
Newmans Way, Barn. 29 BT23
Newmarket Ave., Nthlt. 45 BF35
Newmarket Grn. SE9 78 CJ47
Newmarket Way, Horn. 51 CW35
Newminster Rd., Mord. 86 BT53
Newnes Path SW15 65 BP45
Newnham Ave., Ruis. 45 BD33
Newnham Clo., Loug. 31 CJ25
Newnham Clo., Nthlt. 54 BG36
Newnham Clo., Slou. 52 AQ40
Newnham Clo., Th.Hth. 87 BZ51
Newnham Gdns., Nthlt. 54 BG36
Newnham Ms. N22 38 BX30
Newnham Rd.
Newnham Par., Wal.Cr. 21 CC18
Newnham Pl., Grays 71 DG42
Newnham Rd. N22 38 BX30
Newnham Ter. SE1 4 D6
Newnham Ter. SE1 66 BY41
Newnhams Clo., Brom. 88 CK52
Newnton Clo. N4 48 BZ33
Newpiece, Loug. 31 CL24
Newport Ave. E13 58 CH38
Palmer Rd.
Newport Clo., Enf. 30 CD21
Mandeville Rd.
Newport Ct. WC2 1 P10
Newport Ct. WC2 56 BW40
Charing Cross Rd.
Newport Mead, Wat. 36 BD28
Newport Pl. WC2 1 P10
Newport Pl. WC2 56 BW40
Shaftesbury Ave.
Newport Rd. E10 48 CF34
Newport Rd. E17 48 CD31
Newport Rd. SW13 65 BP44
Newport Rd., Hayes 53 BA39
Newport Rd., Houns. 63 AY44
Newbury Rd.
Newport St. SE11 4 B9
Newport St. SE11 66 BX42
Newports, Saw. 6 CP6
Newports, Swan. 89 CS54
Newquay Cres., Har. 45 BE34
Newquay Gdns., Wat. 35 BC27
Newquay Rd. SE6 77 CE48
Newry Rd., Twick. 74 BJ46
Newsam Ave. N15 48 BZ32
Newsham Rd., Wok. 100 AP62
Newstead, Hat. 10 BO14
Newstead Ave., Orp. 88 CM65
Newstead Ri., Cat. 114 CB66
Newstead Rd. SE12 78 CG47
Newstead Rd., Cat. 114 CB66
Newstead Wk., Cars. 86 BT54
Newstead Way SW19 75 BQ49
Newteswell Dr., Wal.Abb. 21 CF19
Newton Abbot Rd., Grav. 81 DF48
Newton Ave. N10 38 BV30
Newton Ave. W3 65 BN41
Newton Clo., Slou. 62 AS41
Newton Ct., Stai. 72 AQ46
Newton Dr., Saw. 6 CP6
Newton Gro. N1 57 BZ37
Northport St.
Newton Gro. W4 65 BO41
Newton La., Wind. 72 AQ46
Newton Rd. E15 48 CF35
Newton Rd. N15 48 CA32
Newton Rd. NW2 46 BQ35
Newton Rd. SW19 75 BR50
Newton Rd. W2 56 BS39
Newton Rd., Chig. 41 CO28
Newton Rd., Har. 36 BH30
Newton Rd., Houns. 63 AY44
Newton Rd., Islw. 64 BH44
Newton Rd., Pur. 95 BW59
Newton Rd., Til. 71 DG44
Newton Rd., Well. 69 CO45
Newton Rd., Wem. 55 BL36
Newton St. WC2 2 A8
Newton St. WC2 56 BX39
Newton Wk., Edg. 37 BM30
North Rd.
Newton Way N18 39 BZ28
Newton Wd. Rd., Ash. 103 BL61
Newtons Clo., Rain. 59 CT36
Newtons Cor., Rain. 59 CT36
Newtons Yd. SW18 76 BS46
Wandsworth High St.
Newtown Rd., Uxb. 53 AW36
Newtown St. SW11 66 BV44
Strasburg Rd.
Newyears Grn. La., Uxb. 44 AY32
Niagara Ave. W5 64 BK42
Niagara Clo., Chsnt. 21 CC18
Forest Rd.
Nibthwaite Rd., Har. 45 BH32
Nichol Clo. N14 38 BW26
Nichol La., Brom. 78 CH50
Nicholas Clo., Grnf. 54 BF37
Nicholas Clo., St.Alb. 9 BG11
Nicholas Clo., S.Ock. 60 DB38
Nicholas Clo., Wat. 26 BC22
Nicholas Dr., Sev. 117 CV66
Nicholas Gdns. W5 54 BK40
Nicholas Gdns., Wok. 100 AV61
Nicholas La. EC4 2 L10
Nicholas La. EC4 57 BZ40
Nicholas Rd. E1 57 CC38
Nicholas Rd., Borwd. 28 BL25
Nicholas Rd., Croy. 95 BX56
Nicholas Rd., Dag. 50 CQ34
Nicholas Way, Hem.H. 8 AY12
Nicholas Way, Nthwd. 35 BA30
Nicholay Rd. N19 47 BW33
Calverley Gro.
Nicholes Rd., Houns. 64 BF45
Nicholl Rd., Epp. 22 CN19
Nicholls, Wind. 61 AL45
Nicholls Ave., Uxb. 53 AZ38
Nicholls Fld., Harl. 14 CO11
Nichollsfield Wk. N7 47 BX35
Nichols Grn. W5 54 BK39
Montpelier Rd.
Nicholson Dr., Bush. 36 BG26
Nicholson Dr., Egh. 72 AT49
Nicholson Ms., Egh. 72 AT49
Nicholson Dr.
Nicholson Rd., Croy. 87 CA54
Nicholson St. SE1 4 F3
Nicholson St. SE1 56 BY40
Nicholson Way, Sev. 108 CV64
Nickelby Clo. SE28 59 CP39
Nickelby Clo., Uxb. 53 AZ39
Thackeray Clo.
Nickelby Rd., Grav. 81 DK47
Nicol Clo., Ger.Cr. 34 AR30
Nicol Rd.
Nicol Clo., Twick. 74 BJ46
Nicol End, Ger.Cr. 34 AR30
Nicol Rd., Ger.Cr. 34 AR30
Nicola Clo., Har. 36 BG30
Nicola Clo., S.Croy. 96 BZ57
Nicolas Wk., Grays 71 DG41
Godman Rd.
Nicoll Pl. NW4 46 BP32
Nicoll Rd. NW10 55 BO37
Nicoll Way, Borwd. 28 BN24
Nicolson Rd., Orp. 89 CP54
Nicosia Rd. SW18 76 BU47
Niddersdale, Hem.H. 8 AY12
Niederwald Rd. SE26 77 CD49
Nield Rd., Hayes 63 BB41
Nigel Clo., Nthlt. 54 BE37
Church Rd.
Nigel Ms., Ilf. 49 CL35
Nigel Playfair Ave. W6 65 BP42
Nigel Rd. E7 49 CJ35
Nigel Rd. SE15 67 CB45
Nigeria Rd. SE7 68 CJ43
Nightingale Ave. E4 40 CG28
Nightingale Ave., Lthd. 101 BA65
Nightingale Ave., Upmin. 51 CZ33
Nightingale Clo. E4 39 CF28
Nightingale Clo. W4 65 BN43
Nightingale Clo., Cars. 86 BV55
Nightingale Clo., Cob. 93 BD59
Nightingale Clo., Grav. 81 DF49
Mulberry Rd.
Nightingale Clo., Ruis. 45 BD32
Nightingale Cres., Lthd. 101 BA65
Nightingale Dr., Epsom 94 BM57
Nightingale Gro. SE13 77 CF46
Nightingale Gro., Dart. 70 CX45
Nightingale La. E11 49 CH32
Nightingale La. N6 47 BU33
Nightingale La. N8 47 BX31
Nightingale La. SW4 76 BV46
Nightingale La. SW12 76 BV47
Nightingale La., Brom. 88 CJ51
Nightingale La., Rich. 75 BL47
Nightingale La., St.Alb. 9 BK15
Nightingale La., Sev. 116 CR68
Nightingale Pl. SE18 68 CL43
Nightingale Pl., Rick. 35 AX26
Nightingale Rd.
Nightingale Rd. E5 48 CB34
Nightingale Rd. N9 39 CC26
Nightingale Rd. N22 38 BX29
Nightingale Rd. NW10 55 BO37
Nightingale Rd. W7 54 BH40
Nightingale Rd., Bush. 27 BF25
Nightingale Rd., Cars. 86 BU55
Nightingale Rd., Croy. 96 CC59
Nightingale Rd., E.Mol. 84 BF53
Nightingale Rd., Esher 93 BE56
Nightingale Rd., Guil. 118 AR70
Nightingale Rd., Hmptn. 74 BF49
Nightingale Rd., Lthd. 110 BB66
Nightingale Rd., Orp. 88 CM53
Nightingale Rd., Rick. 35 AX26
Nightingale Rd., Sev. 108 CW62
Nightingale Rd., S.Croy. 96 CC58
Nightingale Rd., Walt. 84 BD54
Nightingale Sq. SW12 76 BV47
Nightingale Vale SE18 68 CL43
Nightingale Wk. SW4 76 BV46
Nightingale Wk., Hem.H. 8 BA10
Nightingale Way E6 58 CK39
Nightingale Way, Swan. 89 CT52
London Rd.
Nightingale Way, Uxb. 43 AV33
Nightingales, Wal.Abb. 22 CG20
Roundhills
Nightingales, The, Stai. 73 AY47
Nightingales La., Ch.St.G. 25 AR24
Nile Path SE18 68 CL43
Jackson St.
Nile Rd. E13 58 CJ37
Nile St. N1 2 J2
Nile St. N1 57 BZ38
Nile Ter. SE15 67 CA42
Nimbus Rd., Epsom 94 BN58
Nimegen Way SE22 77 CA46
Dulwich Gro.
Nimmo Dr., Bush. 36 BG26
Nimrod Clo., Nthlt. 54 BD38
Britannia Clo.
Nimrod Rd. SW16 76 BV50
Nimrod Rd., Houns. 63 AZ44
Nimrod Way, Houns. 63 AZ44
Nimrod Rd.
Nine Acres Clo. E12 49 CK35
Nine Ashes Rd., Brwd. 24 DA20
Nine Ashes Rd., Ing. 24 DC18
Nine Elms Ave., Uxb. 53 AX39
Nine Elms Clo., Uxb. 53 AX39
Nine Elms Gro., Grav. 81 DG47
Nine Elms La. SW8 66 BW43
Nine Stiles Clo., Uxb. 53 AW36
Nineacres Way, Couls. 104 BX61
Ninefields, Wal.Abb. 22 CG20
Ninehams Clo., Cat. 105 BZ63
Ninehams Gdns., Cat. 105 BZ63
Ninehams Rd.
Ninehams Rd., Cat. 105 BZ64
Ninehams Rd., West. 106 CH64
Nineteenth Rd., Mitch. 86 BX52
Carisbrooke Rd.
Ninhams Wd., Orp. 97 CK56
Ninian Rd., Hem.H. 8 AY11
Ninnings Rd., Ger.Cr. 34 AS29
Ninnings Way, Ger.Cr. 34 AS29
Ninth Ave., Hayes 53 BC40
Nisbet Ho. E9 48 CC35
Nita Rd., Brwd. 42 DB28
Nithdale Rd. SE18 68 CL43
Nithsdale Gro., Uxb. 44 BA34
Tweeddale Gro.
Niton Clo., Barn. 28 BQ25
Niton Rd., Rich. 65 BM45
Niton St. SW6 65 BQ43
Nixey Clo., Slou. 62 AQ41
Nizels La., Ton. 117 CW71
Nizels Rd., Ton. 117 CW70
Noahs Ark, Sev. 108 CX62
Noak Hill Rd., Rom. 42 CV28
Nobel Dr., Hayes 63 BA43
Nobel Rd. N18 39 CC28
Noble Cor., Houns. 64 BF44
Noble St. EC2 2 H8
Noble St. EC2 57 BZ39
Nobles Way, Egh. 72 AS50
Noel Pk. Rd. N22 38 BY30
Noel Rd. E6 58 CK38
Noel Rd. N1 56 BY37
Noel Rd. W3 55 BM40
Noel Sq., Dag. 50 CP35
Noel St. W1 1 M9
Noel St. W1 56 BW39
Noel Ter. SE23 77 CC48
Dartmouth Rd.
Noke Dr., Red. 121 BV70
Noke La., St.Alb. 18 BE16
Noke Side, St.Alb. 18 BF17
Nokes, The, Hem.H. 8 AW12
Nolan Way E5 48 CB35
Nolton Pl., Edg. 37 BL30
Nonsuch Clo., Ilf. 40 CL29
Nonsuch Ct. Ave., Epsom 94 BP58
Nonsuch Wk., Sutt. 94 BQ58
Nora Gdns. NW4 46 BQ31
Nora Ter., Har. 45 BH33
Norbiton Ave., Kings.T. 85 BM51
Norbiton Common Rd., Kings.T. 85 BM52
Norbiton Hall, Kings.T. 85 BL51
Norbiton Rd. E14 57 CD39
Norbreck Gdns. NW10 55 BL38
Norbreck Par. NW10 55 BL38
Norbroke St. W12 55 BO40
Norburn St. W10 55 BR39
Chesterton Rd.
Norbury Ave. SW16 86 BX51
Norbury Ave., Houns. 64 BG45
Norbury Ave., Th.Hth. 86 BY51
Norbury Ave., Wat. 27 BD23
Norbury Clo. SW16 86 BY51
Norbury Ct. E5 48 CC35
Clapton Pk. Est.
Norbury Ct. Rd. SW16 86 BX52
Norbury Cres. SW16 86 BX51
Norbury Cross SW16 86 BX52
Norbury Gdns., Rom. 50 CP32
Norbury Gro. NW7 37 BO27
Norbury Hill SW16 76 BY50
Norbury Ms. SW16 86 BX
Norbury Cres.
Norbury Ri. SW16 86 BX
Norbury Rd. E4 39 CE
Norbury Rd., Reig. 120 BR
Norbury Rd., Th.Hth. 87 BZ
Norbury Way, Lthd. 111 BG
Norcombe Gdns., Har. 45 BK
Norcott Clo., Hayes 54 BD
Norcott Rd. N16 48 CB
Norcroft Gdns. SE22 77 CB
Norcutt Rd., Twick. 74 BH
Nordenfeldt Rd., Erith 69 CS
Norfield Rd., Bex. 79 CS
Norfolk Ave. N13 38 BY
Norfolk Ave. N15 48 CA
Norfolk Ave., Slou. 52 AO
Norfolk Ave., S.Croy. 96 CA
Norfolk Ave., Wat. 27 BD
Norfolk Clo. N2 47 BU
Park Rd.
Norfolk Clo. N13 38 BY
Norfolk Clo., Barn. 29 BV
Norfolk Clo., Twick. 74 BJ
Norfolk Cres. W2 1
Norfolk Cres. W2 56 BU
Norfolk Cres., Sid. 78 CN
Norfolk Est. E1 57 CC
Norfolk Fm. Clo., Wok. 100 AU
Norfolk Fm. Rd., Wok. 100 AU
Norfolk Gdns., Bexh. 69 CQ
Norfolk Gdns., Borwd. 28 BN
Norfolk Ho. Rd. SW16 76 BW
Norfolk Pl. W2 1
Norfolk Pl. W2 56 BT
Norfolk Pl., Well. 69 CO
Norfolk Rd. E6 58 CK
Norfolk Rd. E17 39 CC
Norfolk Rd. NW8 56 BT
Norfolk Rd. NW10 55 BO
Norfolk Rd. SW19 76 BU
Norfolk Rd., Bark. 58 CN
Norfolk Rd., Barn. 29 BS
Norfolk Rd., Dag. 50 CR
Norfolk Rd., Dor. 119 BJ
Norfolk Rd., Enf. 30 CB
Norfolk Rd., Esher 93 BH
Norfolk Rd., Felt. 74 BD
Norfolk Rd., Grav. 81 DH
Norfolk Rd., Har. 45 BF
Norfolk Rd., Ilf. 49 CN
Norfolk Rd., Rick. 35 AY
Norfolk Rd., Rom. 50 CS
Norfolk Rd., Th.Hth. 87 BZ
Norfolk Rd., Upmin. 51 CX
Norfolk Rd., Uxb. 53 AX
Norfolk Row SE1 4
Norfolk Sq. W2 1
Norfolk Sq. W2 56 BT
Norfolk Sq. Ms. W2 1
Norfolk St. E7 49 CH
Norfolk Ter. W6 65 BR
Norgrove Pk., Ger.Cr. 43 AS
Norgrove St. SW12 76 BV
Norheads, West. 106 CH
Norheads La., West. 106 CJ
Norhyrst Ave. SE25 87 CA
Nork Gdns., Bans. 94 BR
Nork Ri., Bans. 103 BQ
Nork Way, Bans. 103 BQ
Norland Pl. W11 55 BR
Princedale Rd.
Norland Rd. W11 55 BQ
Norland Sq. W11 55 BR
Norlands Cres., Chis. 88 CL
Norlands La., Egh. 82 AV
Norley Vale SW15 75 BP
Norlington Rd. E10 48 CF
Norlington Rd. E11 48 CF
Norman Ave. N22 38 BY
Norman Ave., Epsom 94 BO
Norman Ave., Felt. 74 BE
Norman Ave., S.Croy. 96 BZ
Norman Ave., Sthl. 54 BE
Norman Ave., Twick. 74 BJ
Norman Clo. N22 39 BZ
Norman Ave.
Norman Clo., Dart. 80 CW
Norman Clo., Orp. 88 CM
Norman Clo., Rom. 41 CR
Norman Clo., Wal.Abb. 21 CF
Norman Ct. N4 47 BY
Norman Ct., Pot.B. 20 BT
Norman Cres., Brwd. 122 DD
Norman Cres., Houns. 64 BD
Norman Cres., Pnr. 36 BD
Norman Gro. E3 57 CD
Norman Ho., Felt. 74 BE
Norman Hurst, Ashf. 73 AZ
Norman Rd. E6 58 CK
Norman Rd. E11 48 CF
Norman Rd. N15 48 CA
Norman Rd. SE10 67 CE
Norman Rd. SW19 76 BT
Norman Rd., Ashf. 73 BA
Norman Rd., Belv. 69 CR
Norman Rd., Dart. 80 CW
Norman Rd., Horn. 50 CU
Norman Rd., Ilf. 49 CL
Norman Rd., Sutt. 95 BS
Norman Rd., Th.Hth. 86 BY
Norman Rd., Welw.G.C. 5 B
Norman St. EC1 2
Norman St. EC1 57 BZ
Norman Way N14 38 BX
Norman Way W3 55 BM
Normanby Clo. SW15 75 BR
Manfred Rd.
Normanby Rd. NW10 46 BO
Normand Ms. W14 65 BR
Normand Rd. W14 65 BR
Normandy Ave., Barn. 28 BR
Normandy Dr., Berk. 7 AQ
Normandy Dr., Hayes 53 BA

rmandy Pl., Egh. 72 AU49
rmandy Rd. SW9 66 BY44
rmandy Rd., St.Alb. 9 BG12
rmandy Ter. E16 58 CH39
Coolfin Rd.
rmandy Way, Erith 69 CT44
rmanhurst Ave., Bexh. 69 CP44
rmanhurst Dr., Twick. 74 BJ46
St. Margarets Rd.
rmanhurst Rd. SW2 76 BX48
rmanhurst Rd., Orp. 89 CO51
rmanhurst Rd., Walt. 84 BD55
rmans, The, Slou. 52 AQ39
rmans Bldgs. EC1 57 BZ38
Norman St.
rmans Clo. NW10 55 BN36
rmans Clo., Grav. 81 DG47
rmans Clo., Uxb. 53 AY39
rmans Mead NW10 55 BN36
rmansfield, Tedd. 74 BK50
rmansfield Ave., Tedd. 74 BK50
rmansfield Clo., Bush. 36 BF26
rmanshire Ave. E4 39 CF28
rmanshire Dr. E4 39 CE28
rmanton Ave. SW19 76 BS48
rmanton Pk. E4 40 CG27
rmanton Rd., S.Croy. 96 CA57
rmanton St. SE23 77 CC48
rmington Clo. SW16 76 BY49
rrels Dr., Lthd. 110 BB66
rrels Ride, Lthd. 110 BB66
rrice Lea N2 47 BT32
rris Gro., Brox. 12 CD13
rris La., Hodd. 12 CE11
rris Ri., Hodd. 12 CD11
rris Rd., Hodd. 12 CE12
rris Rd., Stai. 72 AV49
rris St. SW1 3 N1
rris St. SW1 56 BW40
Haymarket
rris Way, Dart. 69 CT45
rroy Rd. SW15 65 BQ45
rrys Clo., Barn. 29 BU24
rrys Rd., Barn. 29 BU24
rseman Ct., Brwd. 33 CZ22
Kelvedon Grn.
rseman Way, Grnf. 54 BF37
Olympic Way
rstead Pl. SW15 75 BP48
rsted La., Orp. 98 CO59
rth Access Rd. E17 48 CC32
rth Acre NW9 37 BO30
rth Acre, Bans. 103 BR61
rth Acton Rd. NW10 55 BN37
rth Albert Rd., Reig. 120 BR70
rth App., Nthwd. 35 BA27
rth App., Wat. 17 BC20
rth Ash Rd., New A.G. 90 DC55
rth Audley St. W1 1 G9
rth Audley St. W1 56 BV39
rth Ave. N18 39 CB28
rth Ave. W13 54 BJ39
rth Ave., Cars. 95 BU57
rth Ave., Har. 45 BF32
rth Ave., Hayes 53 BC40
rth Ave., Rich. 65 BM44
Sandycombe Rd.
rth Ave., Sthl. 54 BE40
rth Ave., Walt. 92 BB58
rth Bank NW8 1 C3
rth Bank NW8 56 BU38
rth Barns, Brox. 12 CE14
rth Birkbeck Rd. E11 48 CF34
rth Bri. Rd., Berk. 7 AP12
rth Carriage Dr. W2 1 C10
rth Circular Rd. E4 39 CD28
rth Circular Rd. E18 40 CG30
rth Circular Rd. N3 47 BS31
rth Circular Rd. N12 38 BU29
rth Circular Rd. N13 38 BY28
rth Circular Rd. NW2 46 BO34
rth Circular Rd. NW10 55 BL38
rth Circular Rd. NW11 46 BQ32
rth Clo., Barn. 28 BQ25
rth Clo., Bexh. 69 CP45
rth Clo., Chig. 41 CO28
rth Clo., Dag. 59 CR37
rth Clo., Dor. 119 BK73
rth Clo., Felt. 73 BA46
North Rd.
rth Clo., Mord. 85 BR52
rth Clo., St.Alb. 18 BF16
rth Clo., Wind. 61 AM44
rth Common, Wey. 92 BA56
rth Common Rd. W5 55 BL40
rth Common Rd., Uxb. 44 AX35
rth Countess Rd. E17 39 CD30
rth Ct. W1 1 N5
rth Ct. W1 56 BW39
Chitty St.
rth Cray Rd., Bex. 79 CR48
rth Cray Rd., Sid. 79 CQ50
rth Cres. N3 37 BR30
rth Cres. WC1 1 N6
rth Cres. WC1 56 BW39
Store St.
rth Cross Rd. SE22 77 CA46
rth Cross Rd., Ilf. 49 CM31
rth Dene NW7 37 BN27
rth Dene, Houns. 64 BF44
rth Down, S.Croy. 96 CA59
rth Down La., Guil. 118 AS72
rth Down Rd., Ger.Cr. 34 AS29
rth Down Rd., Sutt. 95 BS58
rth Downs Cres., Croy. 96 CE58
rth Downs Rd., Croy. 96 CE58
rth Downs Way, Bet. 112 BP68
rth Downs Way, Dor. 119 BD72
rth Downs Way, Red. 113 BW67
rth Downs Way, Sev. 108 DB61
rth Downs Way, Tad. 113 BS68
rth Downs Way, West. 106 CL65

North Dr. SW11 66 BU43
North Dr. SW16 76 BW49
North Dr., Houns. 64 BG44
North Dr., Orp. 97 CN56
North Dr., Rom. 51 CV31
North Dr., Ruis. 44 BB33
North Dr., Vir.W. 82 AP53
North End NW3 47 BT34
North End, Buck.H. 40 CJ26
North End, Croy. 87 BZ54
North End Ave. NW3 47 BT34
North End Cres. W14 65 BR42
North End Ho. W14 65 BR42
North End La., Orp. 97 CL58
North End Par. W14 65 BR42
North End Rd.
North End Rd. NW11 47 BS33
North End Rd. SW6 65 BR43
North End Rd. W14 65 BR42
North End Rd., Wem. 46 BM34
North End Way NW3 47 BT34
North Eyot Gdns. W6 65 BO42
Berestead Rd.
North Feltham Trd. Est., Felt. 73 BC46
North Gdns. SW19 76 BT50
North Gate, Harl. 6 CM10
North Gate Path, Borwd. 28 BL22
North Glade, The, Bex. 79 CQ47
North Gower St. NW1 1 M3
North Gower St. NW1 56 BW38
North Grn. NW9 37 BO29
Clayton Fld.
North Grn., Slou. 52 AP40
North Gro. N6 47 BV33
North Gro. N15 48 BZ32
North Gro., Cher. 82 AV53
North Gro., Harl. 14 CO11
North Harrow Est., Har. 45 BF31
North Hill N6 47 BU32
North Hill, Rick. 25 AV23
North Hill Ave. N6 47 BU32
North Hill Dr., Rom. 42 CV27
North Hill Grn., Rom. 42 CV28
North Hyde Gdns., Hayes 63 BC42
North Hyde La., Houns. 64 BE42
North Hyde La., Sthl. 64 BD42
North Hyde Rd., Hayes 63 BB41
North Kent Ave., Grav. 81 DE46
North Kent Rd., St.Alb. 9 BG13
North La., Tedd. 74 BH50
North Lo. W5 54 BK40
North Lo. Clo. SW15 75 BQ46
Westleigh Ave.
North Mall N9 39 CB27
North Mead, Reig. 121 BU69
North Ms. WC1 2 C5
North Ms. WC1 56 BX38
North Moors, Guil. 109 AS68
North Ockham Rd. S., Lthd. 110 BA66
North Orbital Rd., Hat. 5 BP10
North Orbital Rd., St.Alb. 18 BE18
North Orbital Rd., Uxb. 43 AV33
North Orbital Rd., Wat. 17 BC20
North Par., Chess. 94 BL56
North Pk. SE9 78 CK46
North Pk., Ger.Cr. 43 AS31
North Pk., Iver 62 AU41
North Pk. La., Gdse. 114 CB68
North Pas. SW18 76 BS46
North Pl., Mitch. 76 BU50
North Pl., Tedd. 74 BH50
North Pl., Wal.Abb. 21 CE20
North Pole La., Kes. 97 CG57
North Pole Rd. W10 55 BQ39
North Ride W2 3 C1
North Ride W2 56 BU40
North Riding, St.Alb. 18 BF18
North Rd. N6 47 BV33
North Rd. N7 56 BX36
North Rd. N9 39 CB26
North Rd. SE18 68 CN42
North Rd. SW19 76 BT50
North Rd. W5 64 BK41
North Rd., Amer. 25 AO21
North Rd., Belv. 69 CR41
North Rd., Berk. 7 AQ13
North Rd., Brent. 65 BL43
North Rd., Brwd. 42 DB26
North Rd., Brom. 88 CH51
North Rd., Dart. 79 BT46
North Rd., Edg. 37 BM30
North Rd., Felt. 73 BA46
North Rd., Grays 70 CY42
North Rd., Guil. 118 AQ69
North Rd., Hav. 41 CT27
North Rd., Hayes 53 BA39
North Rd., Hodd. 12 CE11
North Rd., Ilf. 49 CN34
North Rd., Reig. 120 BR72
North Rd., Rich. 65 BM45
North Rd., Rick. 25 AU25
North Rd., Rom. 50 CQ32
North Rd., S.Ock. 60 DA37
North Rd., Sthl. 54 BF40
North Rd., Surb. 84 BK53
North Rd., Wal.Cr. 21 CD20
North Rd., Walt. 93 BD56
North Rd., West Dr. 63 AY41
North Rd., W.Wick. 87 CE54
North Rd., Wok. 100 AT61
North Rd. Ave., Brwd. 42 DB26
North Row W1 1 F10
North Row W1 56 BU40
North Service Rd., Brwd. 42 DB27
North Several SE3 67 CF44
North Side SW18 76 BT46
North Sq. N9 39 CB27
North Sq. NW11 47 BS32
North Sta. App., Red. 121 BX71
North St. E13 58 CH37
North St. NW4 46 BQ32
Heriot Rd.

North St. SW4 66 BW45
North St., Bark. 58 CL36
North St., Bexh. 69 CR45
North St., Brom. 88 CH51
North St., Cars. 86 BU55
North St., Dart. 80 CV47
Heath St.
North St., Dor. 119 BJ71
North St. (Westcott), Dor. 119 BG72
North St., Egh. 72 AS49
North St., Guil. 118 AR71
North St., Horn. 51 CV33
North St., Islw. 64 BJ45
North St., Lthd. 102 BJ64
North St., Red. 121 BU70
North St., Rom. 50 CS31
North St., Rom. 50 CT32
North St., Wal.Abb. 13 CG14
North St. Pas. E13 58 CH37
North Tenter St. E1 2 Q9
North Tenter St. E1 57 CA39
North Ter. SW3 3 C7
North Ter. SW3 66 BU41
North Verbena Gdns. W6 65 BP42
St. Peters Sq.
North Vw. SW19 75 BP49
North Vw. W5 54 BK38
North Vw., Ilf. 41 CO29
North Vw., Pnr. 45 BD33
North Vw. Ave., Til. 71 DG44
North Vw. Cres. NW10 46 BO35
North Vw. Cres., Epsom 103 BP62
North Vw. Dr., Wdf.Grn. 40 CJ30
North Vw. Rd. N8 47 BW31
North Vill. NW1 56 BW36
North Wk., Croy. 96 CF57
North Wk., Sutt. 94 BQ59
North Way N9 39 CC27
North Way N11 38 BW29
North Way NW9 46 BM31
North Way, Mord. 85 BR52
North Way, Pnr. 45 BD31
North Way, Uxb. 53 AY36
North Way, Welw.G.C. 5 BR6
North Western Ave., Wat. 26 BB21
North Western Ave., Wat. 27 BD21
North Wf. Rd. W2 1 A7
North Wf. Rd. W2 56 BT39
North Woolwich Rd. E16 58 CH40
North Worple Way SW14 65 BN45
Northall Rd., Bexh. 69 CS44
Northallerton Way, Rom. 42 CV28
Northampton Gro. N1 48 BZ35
St. Pauls Pl.
Northampton Pk. N1 57 BZ36
Northampton Rd. EC1 2 E4
Northampton Rd. EC1 56 BY38
Northampton Rd., Croy. 87 CB55
Northampton Rd., Enf. 30 CD25
Northampton Sq. EC1 2 F3
Northampton Sq. EC1 56 BY38
Northampton St. N1 57 BZ36
Northanger Rd. SW16 76 BX50
Northaw Clo., Hem.H. 8 AZ11
Northaw Rd. E., Cuffley 20 BW19
Northaw Rd. W., Pot.B. 20 BU18
Northbank Rd. E17 39 CF30
Northborough Rd. SW16 86 BW52
Northbourne, Brom. 88 CH54
Northbourne Rd. SW4 66 BW45
Northbrook Dr., Nthwd. 35 BB30
Northbrook Rd. N22 38 BX29
Northbrook Rd. SE13 77 CF46
Northbrook Rd., Barn. 28 BR25
Northbrook Rd., Croy. 87 BZ53
Northbrook Rd., Ilf. 49 CL34
Northbrooks, Harl. 13 CM11
Northburgh St. EC1 2 G5
Northburgh St. EC1 56 BY38
Northchurch SE17 4 L10
Northchurch Rd. N1 57 BZ36
Northchurch Rd., Wem. 55 BM36
Northchurch Ter. N1 57 CA36
De Beauvoir Rd.
Northcliffe Clo., Wor.Pk. 85 BO55
Auriol Pk. Rd.
Northcliffe Dr. N20 37 BR26
Northcliffe Rd., Grav. 81 DF47
Northcote, Lthd. 93 BG60
Northcote, Wey. 92 AX56
Northcote Ave. W5 55 BL40
Northcote Ave., Islw. 74 BJ46
Northcote Ave., Sthl. 54 BE40
Northcote Ave., Surb. 85 BM54
Northcote Clo., Lthd. 110 BA66
Northcote Cres., Lthd. 110 BA66
Northcote Rd. E17 48 CD31
Northcote Rd. NW10 55 BO36
Northcote Rd. SW11 76 BU46
Northcote Rd., Croy. 87 BZ53
Northcote Rd., Lthd. 110 BA66
Northcote Rd., N.Mal. 85 BN52
Northcote Rd., Sid. 78 CN49
Northcote Rd., Twick. 74 BJ46
Northcott Ave. N22 38 BX30
Northcourt, Rick. 35 AW27
Springwell Ave.
Northcroft Clo., Egh. 72 AQ49
Northcroft Gdns., Egh. 72 AQ49
Northcroft Rd. W13 64 BJ41
Northcroft Rd., Egh. 72 AQ49
Northcroft Rd., Epsom 94 BN57
Northcroft Vill., Egh. 72 AQ49
Northdene, Chig. 40 CM28
Northdene Gdns. N15 48 CA32
Northdon Clo., Ruis. 44 BB34
Northdown Gdns., Ilf. 49 CN32
Northdown Rd., Cat. 105 CE65
Northdown Rd., Hat. 10 BP14
Northdown Rd., Horn. 50 CU33
Northdown Rd., Long. 90 DB51
Northdown Rd., Sev. 108 CW62
Northdown Rd., Well. 69 CO44

Northdown St. N1 56 BX37
Northeast Pl. N1 56 BY37
Chapel Mkt.
Northend, Brwd. 42 DB28
Northend, Hem.H. 8 AZ14
Northend Rd., Erith 69 CT44
Northern Ave. N9 39 CA27
Northern Perimeter Rd., Houns. 63 AX44
Northern Prec., Grays 70 CZ42
Northern Relief Rd., Bark. 58 CL36
Northern Rd. E13 58 CH37
Northern Rd., Slou. 52 AO38
Northernhay Wk., Mord. 85 BR52
Northey Ave., Sutt. 94 BQ58
Northey St. E14 57 CD40
Northfield, Hat. 10 BP11
Northfield Ave. W5 64 BK41
Northfield Ave. W13 54 BJ40
Northfield Ave., Orp. 89 CP53
Northfield Ave., Pnr. 45 BD31
Northfield Clo., Brom. 88 CK51
Logs Hill
Northfield Clo., Hayes 63 BB41
Northfield Ct., Stai. 83 AW51
Northfield Cres., Sutt. 94 BR56
Abbotts Rd.
Northfield Gdns., Dag. 50 CQ35
Northfield Gdns., Wat. 27 BD22
Northfield Ind. Est., Wem. 55 BM37
Northfield Pk., Hayes 63 BB41
Northfield Path, Dag. 50 CQ34
Northfield Pl., Wey. 92 AZ57
Northfield Rd. E6 58 CK36
Northfield Rd. N16 48 CA33
Northfield Rd. W13 64 BJ41
Northfield Rd., Barn. 29 BU24
Northfield Rd., Borwd. 28 BM23
Northfield Rd., Cob. 92 BC60
Northfield Rd., Dag. 50 CQ35
Northfield Rd., Enf. 30 CB25
Northfield Rd., Houns. 64 BD43
Northfield Rd., Stai. 83 AW51
Northfield Rd., Wal.Cr. 21 CD19
Northfield Rd. (Eton Wick), Wind. 61 AM42
Northfields SW18 66 BS45
Northfields, Ash. 103 BL63
Northfields, Grays 71 DE42
Northfields Rd. W3 55 BM39
Northfleet Grn. Rd., Grav. 81 DE50
Northgate, Nthwd. 35 BA29
Northgate Dr. NW9 46 BO32
Snowdon Dr.
Northiam N12 38 BS28
Northiam St. E8 57 CB37
Northington St. WC1 2 C5
Northington St. WC1 56 BX38
Northlands, Pot.B. 20 BT19
Northlands Ave., Orp. 97 CM56
Northlands St. SE5 67 BZ44
Northolm, Edg. 37 BN28
Northolme Clo., Grays 71 DE41
Premier Ave.
Northolme Gdns., Edg. 37 BM30
Northolme Ri., Orp. 88 CN55
Northolme Rd. N5 47 BY35
Northolt Ave., Ruis. 44 BC35
Northolt Gdns., Grnf. 45 BH35
Northolt Rd., Har. 45 BF35
Northolt Rd., Houns. 63 AX44
Northolt Way, Horn. 60 CV36
Northover, Brom. 78 CG48
Northport St. N1 57 BZ37
Northridge Rd., Grav. 81 DH48
Northridge Way, Hem.H. 7 AV14
Northrop Rd., Houns. 63 BB44
Northside Rd., Brom. 88 CH51
Tweedy Rd.
Northspur Rd., Sutt. 86 BS55
Northstead Rd. SW2 76 BY48
Northumberland All. EC3 2 N9
Northumberland All. EC3 57 CA39
Northumberland Ave. E12 49 CJ33
Northumberland Ave. WC2 3 Q2
Northumberland Ave. WC2 56 BX40
Northumberland Ave., Enf. 30 CB22
Northumberland Ave., Horn. 51 CV32
Northumberland Ave., Islw. 64 BH44
Northumberland Ave., Well. 68 CM45
Northumberland Clo., Erith 69 CS43
Northumberland Clo., Stai. 73 AY46
Northumberland Cres., Felt. 73 BB46
Northumberland Gdns. N9 39 CA27
Northumberland Gdns., Mitch. 86 BW53
Northumberland Gro. N17 39 CB29
Northumberland Pk. N17 39 CA29
Northumberland Pk., Erith 69 CR43
Northumberland Pl. W2 56 BS39
Northumberland Pl., Rich. 74 BK46
Hill Ri.
Northumberland Rd. E6 58 CK39
Northumberland Rd. E17 48 CE33
Northumberland Rd., Barn. 38 BT26
Northumberland Rd., Grav. 81 DF50
Northumberland Rd., Har. 45 BE32
Northumberland Rd., S.le H. 71 DJ41

Northumberland Row, Twick. 74 BH47
Colne Rd.
Northumberland St. WC2 3 Q2
Northumberland St. WC2 56 BX40
Northumberland Way, Erith 69 CS44
Northumbria St. E14 57 CE39
Northview, Swan. 89 CT51
Northview Rd., Sev. 108 CV64
Northway NW11 47 BS32
Northway, Guil. 118 AQ69
Northway, Rick. 35 AX26
Northway, Wall. 95 BW56
Northway Circ. NW7 37 BN28
Northway Cres. NW7 37 BN28
Northway Rd. SE5 67 BZ45
Northway Rd., Croy. 87 CA53
Northways NW3 56 BT36
College Cres.
Northwest Pl. N1 56 BY37
Chapel Mkt.
Northwick Ave., Har. 45 BJ32
Northwick Circle, Har. 45 BK32
Northwick Clo. NW8 1 A4
Northwick Clo. NW8 56 BT38
Norwood Cres.
Northwick Pk. Rd., Har. 45 BH32
Northwick Rd., Wat. 36 BD28
Northwick Rd., Wem. 54 BK37
Northwick Sq., Houns. 63 BA44
Northwick Ter. NW8 1 A4
Northwick Ter. NW8 56 BT38
Northwick Wk., Har. 45 BH33
Northwold Dr., Pnr. 36 BD30
Northwold Est. E5 48 CB34
Northwold Rd. E5 48 CB34
Northwold Rd. N16 48 CA34
Northwood, Grays 71 DG41
Northwood, Welw.G.C. 5 BT8
Shackleton Way
Northwood Ave., Horn. 50 CU35
Northwood Ave., Pur. 95 BY59
Northwood Ave., Wok. 100 AO62
Northwood Gdns. N12 38 BT28
Northwood Gdns., Grnf. 45 BH35
Northwood Gdns., Ilf. 49 CL31
Northwood Hills, Nthwd. 35 BC30
Northwood Hills Circ., Nthwd. 35 BC30
Northwood Pl., Erith 69 CQ41
Northwood Rd. N6 47 BV33
Northwood Rd. SE23 77 CD47
Northwood Rd., Cars. 95 BV57
Northwood Rd., Houns. 63 AX44
Northwood Rd., Th.Hth. 86 BY51
Northwood Rd., Uxb. 35 AX30
Northwood Way SE19 77 CA50
Central Hill Est.
Northwood Way, Nthwd. 35 BB29
Northwood Way, Uxb. 35 AX30
Nortoft Rd., Ger.Cr. 34 AS29
Norton Ave., Surb. 85 BM54
Norton Clo. E4 39 CE28
Norton Clo., Borwd. 28 BM23
Norton Clo., Enf. 30 CB23
Norton Folgate E1 2 N6
Norton Folgate E1 57 CA39
Norton Gdns. SW16 86 BX51
Norton Heath Rd., Ong. 15 DB15
Norton La., Cob. 101 BB63
Norton La., Ong. 24 DA16
Norton Rd. E10 47 BX33
Dagenham Rd.
Norton Rd., Dag. 59 CS36
Norton Rd., Uxb. 53 AX38
Norton Rd., Wem. 54 BK36
Norval Grn. SW9 66 BY44
Myatts Flds. Dev.
Norval Rd., Wem. 45 BJ34
Norway Dr., Slou. 52 AQ39
Norway Gate SE16 67 CD41
Norway Pl. E14 57 CD39
Norway St. SE10 67 CE43
Norway Wk., Rain. 60 CV39
The Glen
Norwich Ms., Ilf. 50 CO33
Ashgrove Rd.
Norwich Rd. E7 49 CH35
Norwich Rd., Dag. 59 CR37
Norwich Rd., Grnf. 54 BF37
Norwich Rd., Nthwd. 44 BB31
Norwich Rd., Th.Hth. 87 BZ52
Norwich St. EC4 2 D8
Norwich St. EC4 56 BY39
Norwich Wk., Edg. 37 BN29
Norwich Way, Rick. 26 AZ24
Norwood Ave., Rom. 50 CT33
Norwood Ave., Wem. 55 BL37
Norwood Clo., Lthd. 111 BE67
Norwood Clo., Sthl. 64 BF42
Norwood Cres., Houns. 63 BA44
Norwood Dr., Har. 45 BE32
Norwood End, Ong. 15 CX11
Norwood Gdns., Hayes 54 BD38
Norwood Gdns., Sthl. 64 BE42
Norwood Grn. Rd., Sthl. 64 BF42
Norwood High St. SE27 76 BY48
Norwood La., Iver 52 AU38
Norwood Pk. Rd. SE27 77 BZ49
Norwood Rd. SE24 76 BY47
Norwood Rd. SE27 76 BY47
Norwood Rd., Lthd. 111 BE67
Norwood Rd., Sthl. 64 BE41
Norwood Ter., Sthl. 64 BF42
Notley End, Egh. 72 AR50
Notley St. SE5 67 BZ43
Notre Dame Est. SW4 76 BW46
Notson Rd. SE25 87 CB52
Notting Barn Rd. W10 55 BQ38
Notting Hill Gate W11 56 BS40
Nottingham Ave. E16 58 CJ39
Nottingham Clo., Wat. 17 BC20
Nottingham Clo., Wok. 100 AP62

Nottingham Ct. WC2 1 Q9
Nottingham Ct. WC2 56 BX39
Shorts Gdns.
Nottingham Pl. W1 1 G5
Nottingham Pl. W1 56 BV38
Nottingham Rd. E10 48 CF32
Nottingham Rd. SW17 76 BU47
Nottingham Rd., Islw. 64 BH44
Nottingham Rd., Rick. 34 AU26
Nottingham Rd., S.Croy. 96 BZ56
Nottingham St. W1 1 G6
Nottingham St. W1 56 BV39
Nottingham Ter. NW1 1 G5
Nottingham Ter. NW1 56 BV38
Allsop Pl.
Nottingsdale Sq. W11 55 BR40
Wilsham St.
Nova Ms., Sutt. 85 BR54
Nova Rd., Croy. 86 BY54
Novar Clo., Orp. 88 CN54
Novar Rd. SE9 78 CM47
Novello St. SW6 66 BS44
Nowell Rd. SW13 65 BP43
Nower, The, Sev. 106 CN63
Nower Hill, Pnr. 45 BE31
Nower Rd., Dor. 119 BJ71
Noyna Rd. SW17 76 BU48
Nuding Clo. SE13 67 CE45
Nuffield Rd., Swan. 79 CU50
Nugent Rd. N19 47 BX33
Nugent Rd. SE25 87 CA52
Nugent Rd., Guil. 118 AO71
Nugent Ter. NW8 56 BT38
Nugents Ct., Pnr. 36 BE30
Nugents Pk., Pnr. 36 BE30
Nun Ct. EC2 2 K8
Nunappleton Way, Oxt. 115 CH69
Nuneaton Rd., Dag. 59 CP36
Nunfield, Kings L. 17 AW19
Nunhead Cres. SE15 67 CB45
Nunhead Grn. SE15 67 CB45
Nunhead Gro. SE15 67 CB45
Nunhead La. SE15 67 CB45
Nunhead Pas. SE15 67 CB45
Peckham Rye
Nunnery Clo., St.Alb. 9 BH14
Nunnery Stables, St.Alb. 9 BG14
Nunnington Clo. SE9 78 CK48
Nunns Rd., Enf. 30 BZ23
Nunns Wk., Egh. 72 AU49
Nunns Way, Grays 71 DE42
Nuns La., St.Alb. 9 BH15
Nuns Wk., Vir.W. 82 AR53
Nunsbury Dr., Brox. 21 CD16
Nupton Dr., Barn. 28 BQ25
Nursery, The, Erith 69 CT43
Nursery, The, West. 115 CM67
Nursery Ave. N3 38 BT30
Nursery Ave., Bexh. 69 CQ45
Nursery Ave., Croy. 87 CC55
Nursery Clo. SW15 65 BQ45
Nursery Clo., Amer. 25 AP23
Nursery Clo., Croy. 87 CC55
Nursery Clo., Dart. 80 CV47
Nursery Clo., Enf. 30 CC23
Nursery Clo., Epsom 94 BO58
Nursery Clo., Felt. 73 BC47
Nursery Clo., Orp. 89 CO54
Nursery Clo., Rom. 50 CP32
Nursery Clo., Sev. 108 CV64
Nursery Clo., S.Ock. 60 DB38
Nursery Clo., Swan. 89 CS51
Nursery Clo., Tad. 112 BP66
Nursery Clo., Wey. 91 AV58
Nursery Clo., Wok. 100 AR61
Nursery Clo., Wdf.Grn. 40 CH28
Nursery Gdns., Enf. 30 CC23
Nursery Gdns., Guil. 118 AT73
Nursery Gdns., Stai. 73 AW50
Nursery Gdns., Sun. 83 BB51
Nursery Gdns., Welw.G.C. 5 BR6
Nursery Hill, Welw.G.C. 5 BR6
Nursery La. E7 58 CH36
Nursery La. W10 55 BQ39
Highlever Rd.
Nursery La., Uxb. 53 AX38
Nursery La. Rd., Slou. 52 AR40
Nursery Pl., Sev. 107 CS65
Nursery Rd. N2 38 BT30
Nursery Rd. N14 38 BW26
Nursery Rd. SW9 66 BX45
Nursery Rd. SW19 75 BR50
Nursery Rd., Brwd. 24 DB20
Nursery Rd., Brox. 21 CD16
Nursery Rd., Hodd. 12 CE10
Nursery Rd., Loug. 31 CJ25
Nursery Rd. (High Beech), Loug. 31 CH23
Nursery Rd., Pnr. 45 BD31
Nursery Rd., Sun. 83 BB51
Nursery Rd., Sutt. 95 BT56
Nursery Rd., Tad. 112 BP66
Nursery Rd., Th.Hth. 87 BZ52
Nursery Rd., Wal.Abb. 12 CF14
Nursery Rd., Wok. 100 AO62
Nursery St. N17 39 CA29
Nursery Wk. NW4 46 BP31
Nursery Wk., Rom. 50 CS32
Nursery Way, Stai. 72 AR46
Nursery Waye, Uxb. 53 AX37
Nurstead Rd., Erith 69 CR43
Nut Gro., Welw.G.C. 5 BQ6
Nut Tree Clo., Orp. 89 CP55
Nutberry Ave., Grays 71 DD41
Nutberry Clo., Grays 71 DD41
Nutbourne St. W10 55 BR38
Nutbrook St. SE15 67 CA45
Nutbrowne Rd., Dag. 59 CQ37
Nutcombe La., Dor. 119 BH71
Nutcroft Gro., Lthd. 102 BH64
Nutcroft Rd. SE15 67 CB43
Nutfield, Welw.G.C. 5 BS6
Nutfield Clo. N18 39 CB29
Fore St.
Nutfield Clo., Cars. 86 BT54
Wrythe La.
Nutfield Gdns., Ilf. 50 CO34
Nutfield Gdns., Nthlt. 54 BD37
Nutfield Marsh Rd., Red. 121 BW69
Nutfield Pl., Th.Hth. 86 BY52
Nutfield Rd. E15 48 CF35
Nutfield Rd. NW2 46 BP34
Nutfield Rd. SE22 67 CA45
Nutfield Rd., Couls. 104 BV61
Nutfield Rd., Red. 121 BV70
Nutfield Rd. (South Merstham), Red. 113 BW68
Nutfield Rd., Th.Hth. 86 BY52
Nutfield Way, Orp. 88 CL55
Nutford Pl. W1 1 D8
Nutford Pl. W1 56 BU39
Nuthatch Clo., Stai. 73 AY47
Nuthatch Gdns. SE28 68 CM41
Nuthurst Ave. SW2 76 BX48
Nutley Clo., Swan. 89 CT51
Nutley Gro., Reig. 120 BR70
Nutley La., Reig. 120 BR70
Nutley Ter. NW3 56 BT36
Nutmead Clo., Bex. 79 CS47
Nutmeg La. E14 57 CF39
Nutt Gro., Edg. 36 BK27
Nutt St. SE15 67 CA43
Sumner Rd.
Nuttall St. N1 57 CA37
Nutter La. E11 49 CH32
Nuttfield Clo., Rick. 26 AZ25
Nutty La., Shep. 83 BA52
Nutwell St. SW17 76 BU49
Nutwood Ave., Bet. 120 BN71
Nutwood Clo., Bet. 120 BN71
Nuxley Rd., Belv. 69 CQ43
Nyanza St. SE18 68 CM43
Nye Bevan Est. E5 48 CC34
Nye Way, Hem.H. 16 AT17
Nyefield Pk., Tad. 112 BP66
Nylands Ave., Rich. 65 BM44
Nymans Gdns. SW20 85 BP51
Nynehead St. SE14 67 CD43
Nyon Gro. SE6 77 CD48
Nyssa Clo., Wdf.Grn. 40 CK29
Nyth Clo., Upmin. 51 CY32
Nyton Clo. N19 47 BX33

O

Oak Ave. N8 47 BX31
Oak Ave. N10 38 BV29
Oak Ave. N17 39 BZ29
Oak Ave., Croy. 87 CE54
Oak Ave., Egh. 72 AU50
Oak Ave., Enf. 29 BX22
Oak Ave., Hmptn. 74 BE49
Oak Ave., Houns. 64 BE43
Oak Ave., St.Alb. 18 BF18
Oak Ave., Sev. 116 CU67
Oak Ave., Upmin. 51 CX35
Oak Ave., Uxb. 44 AZ34
Oak Ave., West Dr. 63 AZ41
Oak Bank, Croy. 96 CF57
Oak Bank, Wok. 100 AS63
Oak Clo. N14 38 BV26
Oak Clo., Dart. 69 CT45
Oak Clo., Hem.H. 8 AY15
Oak Clo., Sutt. 86 BT55
Oak Clo., Wal.Abb. 21 CF20
Oak Clo., West Dr. 63 AZ41
Oak Cor., Berk. 7 AO13
Oak Cottage Clo. SE6 78 CG47
Verdant La.
Oak Ct., Barn. 29 BU25
Oak Cres. E16 58 CG39
Oak Dene W13 54 BJ39
The Dene
Oak Dene, Tad. 103 BR63
Oak Dr., Berk. 7 AR13
Oak Dr., Saw. 6 CP7
Oak End, Harl. 13 CN12
Oak End Way, Wey. 91 AV59
Oak Fm., Borwd. 28 BN25
Oak Gdns., Croy. 87 CE54
Oak Gdns., Edg. 37 BN30
Oak Glade, Nthwd. 35 BA30
Oak Glen, Horn. 51 CW31
Oak Gra. Rd., Guil. 110 AW68
Oak Grn., Abb.L. 17 BB19
Oak Grn. Way, Abb.L. 17 BB19
Oak Gro. NW2 46 BQ35
Oak Gro., Hat. 10 BO12
Oak Gro., Ruis. 44 BC33
Oak Gro., Sun. 73 BC50
Oak Gro., W.Wick. 87 CF55
Oak Gro. Rd. SE20 87 CC51
Oak Hall Rd. E11 49 CH32
Oak Hill, Epsom 103 BN61
Oak Hill, Guil. 109 AU68
Oak Hill, Wdf.Grn. 39 CF29
Oak Hill Ave. NW3 47 BS35
Oak Hill Clo., Wdef.Grn. 39 CF29
Oak Hill Ct., Wdf.Grn. 39 CF29
Oak Hill Cres., Wdf.Grn. 39 CF29
Oak Hill Pk. NW3 47 BS35
Oak Hill Pk. Ms. NW3 47 BS35
Oak Hill Rd., Orp. 88 CN54
Oak Hill Rd., Rom. 41 CS26
Oak Hill Rd., Sev. 107 CU65
Oak Hill Way NW3 47 BT35
Oak La. E14 57 CD40
Oak La. N2 38 BT30
Oak La. N11 38 BW29
Oak La., Cuffley 20 BX17
Oak La., Egh. 72 AR48
Oak La., Islw. 64 BH45
Oak La., Sev. 116 CT68
Oak La., Twick. 74 BJ47
Oak La., Wind. 61 AN44
Oak La., Wok. 100 AT61
Oak La., Wdf.Grn. 40 CG28
Oak Lo. Ave., Chig. 40 CM28
Oak Lo. Clo., Stan. 36 BK28
Oak Lo. Clo., Walt. 93 BD56
Oak Lo. Dr., W.Wick. 87 CE54
Oak Pk., Wey. 91 AV60
Oak Pk. Gdns. SW19 75 BQ47
Oak Path, Bush. 36 BF26
Ashfield Ave.
Oak Piece, Epp. 23 CS16
Oak Ridge, Dor. 119 BJ73
Oak Ri., Buck.H. 40 CJ27
Oak Rd. W5 54 BK40
Oak Rd., Cat. 105 CA64
Oak Rd., Cob. 102 BE61
Oak Rd., Epp. 22 CN18
Oak Rd., Erith 69 CS43
Oak Rd. (Slade Grn.), Erith 69 CU44
Oak Rd., Grav. 81 DH48
Oak Rd., Grays 71 DE43
Oak Rd., Green. 80 CZ46
Oak Rd., Lthd. 102 BJ63
Oak Rd., N.Mal. 85 BN51
Oak Rd., Orp. 98 CO57
Oak Rd., Reig. 121 BS70
Oak Rd., Rom. 42 CW30
Oak Rd., West. 115 CM66
Oak Row SW16 86 BW51
Oak Side, Uxb. 53 AW36
Oak St., Hem.H. 8 AY15
Oak St., Rom. 50 CS31
Oak Stubbs La., Maid. 61 AJ41
Oak Tree Clo. W5 54 BK39
Pinewood Gro.
Oak Tree Clo., Brwd. 122 DC28
Oak Tree Clo. (Burpham), Guil. 109 AU68
Oak Tree Clo. (Stringers Common), Guil. 109 AR67
Oak Tree Clo., Hat. 10 BP12
Oak Tree Clo., Stan. 36 BK29
Oak Tree Clo., Vir.W. 82 AR53
Oak Tree Clo., Wal.Cr. 20 BY17
Oak Tree Ct., Borwd. 27 BK25
Oak Tree Dell NW9 46 BN32
Oak Tree Dr. N20 38 BS26
Oak Tree Dr., Egh. 72 AR49
Oak Tree Dr., Guil. 109 AR68
Oak Tree Gdns., Brom. 78 CH49
Oak Tree Rd. NW8 1 B3
Oak Tree Rd. NW8 56 BT38
Oak Village NW5 47 BV35
Oak Wk., Saw. 6 CP7
Oak Way N14 38 BV26
Oak Way W3 55 BO40
Oak Way, Ash. 103 BM61
Oak Way, Croy. 87 CC53
Oak Way, Felt. 73 BB47
Oak Way, Reig. 121 BT71
Oak Wd., Berk. 7 AP13
Oak Wd. Chase, Horn. 51 CW32
Oak Wd. Dr., Lthd. 110 BB67
Oakapple Clo., S.Croy. 96 CB60
Cherry Tree Grn.
Oakbank, Brwd. 122 DF25
Oakbank Ave., Walt. 84 BE54
Oakbank Gro. SE24 67 BZ45
Oakbrook Clo., Brom. 78 CH49
Ridgeway Dr.
Oakbury Rd. SW6 66 BS44
Oakcombe Clo., N.Mal. 85 BO51
Traps La.
Oakcroft Clo., Wey. 91 AV60
Oakcroft Rd. SE13 67 CF44
Oakcroft Rd., Chess. 94 BL56
Oakcroft Rd., Wey. 91 AV60
Oakcroft Vill., Chess. 94 BL56
Oakdale N14 38 BV26
Oakdale, Welw.G.C. 5 BQ6
Oakdale Ave., Har. 46 BL32
Oakdale Ave., Nthwd. 35 BC30
Oakdale Clo., Wat. 36 BD28
Oakdale Ct. E4 39 CF28
Oakdale La., Eden. 115 CM70
Oakdale Rd. E7 58 CH36
Oakdale Rd. E11 48 CF34
Oakdale Rd. E18 40 CH30
Oakdale Rd. N4 48 BZ32
Oakdale Rd. SE15 67 CC45
Ivydale Rd.
Oakdale Rd. SW16 76 BX49
Oakdale Rd., Epsom 94 BN57
Oakdale Rd., Wat. 36 BD27
Oakdale Rd., Wey. 83 AZ55
Oakdale Way, Mitch. 86 BV54
Wolseley Rd.
Oakden St. SE11 4 E8
Oakden St. SE11 66 BY42
Oakdene, Chsnt. 21 CD18
Oakdene, Wok. 91 AP58
Oakdene Ave., Chis. 78 CL49
Oakdene Ave., Erith 69 CS43
Oakdene Ave., T.Ditt. 84 BJ54
Oakdene Clo., Bet. 120 BN71
Oakdene Clo., Horn. 50 CU32
Oakdene Clo., Lthd. 111 BF67
Oakdene Clo., Pnr. 36 BE29
Oakdene Dr., Surb. 85 BN54
Oakdene Ms., Sutt. 85 BR54
Ash Rd.
Oakdene Pk. N3 37 BR29
Oakdene Rd., Bet. 120 BM72
Oakdene Rd., Cob. 92 BC60
Oakdene Rd., Hem.H. 8 AY15
Oakdene Rd., Lthd. 102 BE65
Oakdene Rd., Orp. 88 CN53
Oakdene Rd., Red. 121 BU70
Oakdene Rd., Sev. 107 CU64
Oakdene Rd., Uxb. 53 AZ37
Oakdene Rd., Wat. 26 BC21
Oakdene Way, St.Alb. 9 BK13
Oaken Coppice La., Ash. 103 BM63
Oaken Dr., Esher 93 BH57
Oaken Gro., Welw.G.C. 5 BR9
Oaken La., Esher 93 BH56
Oakend Way, Ger.Cr. 43 AS32
Oakenshaw Clo., Surb. 85 BL54
Oakes Clo. E6 58 CK39
Savage Gdns.
Oakeshott Ave. N6 47 BV34
Oakey La. SE1 4 D6
Oakey La. SE1 66 BY41
Oakfield, Rick. 34 AV26
Oakfield, Wok. 100 AP61
Oakfield Ave., Har. 45 BJ31
Oakfield Ave., Slou. 61 AN40
Oakfield Clo., N.Mal. 85 BO53
Oakfield Ct. N8 47 BX33
Oakfield Ct. NW2 46 BQ33
Oakfield Dr., Reig. 121 BS69
Reigate Hill Rd.
Oakfield Gdns. N18 39 CA28
Oakfield Gdns. SE19 77 CA49
Oakfield Gdns., Beck. 87 CE53
Oakfield Gdns., Cars. 86 BU54
Oakfield Gdns., Grnf. 54 BG38
Oakfield Glade, Wey. 92 BA56
Oakfield La., Dart. 80 CV48
Oakfield La., Kes. 97 CJ56
Oakfield Pk. Rd., Dart. 80 CV48
Oakfield Pl., Dart. 80 CV48
Oakfield Rd. E6 58 CK37
Oakfield Rd. E17 39 CD30
Oakfield Rd. N3 38 BS30
Oakfield Rd. N4 47 BY32
Oakfield Rd. N14 38 BX27
Oakfield Rd. SE20 87 CB51
Oakfield Rd. SW19 75 BQ48
Oakfield Rd., Ashf. 73 AZ49
Oakfield Rd., Ash. 103 BL62
Oakfield Rd., Croy. 87 BZ54
Oakfield Rd., Ilf. 49 CL34
Oakfield Rd., Orp. 89 CO54
Oakfield St. SW10 66 BT43
Oakfields, Guil. 118 AP69
Oakfields, Sev. 116 CU66
Oakfields, Walt. 83 BC54
Oakfields, Wey. 92 AW60
Oakfields Rd. NW11 46 BR32
Oakford Rd. NW5 47 BW35
Oakhall Ct. E11 49 CH32
Eastern Ave.
Oakhall Dr., Sun. 73 BB49
Oakham Clo. SE6 77 CD48
Rutland Wk.
Oakham Dr., Brom. 88 CG52
Oakhampton Rd. NW7 37 BQ29
Oakhill, Esher 93 BJ57
Oakhill, Surb. 85 BL54
Oakhill Ave., Pnr. 36 BE30
Oakhill Clo., Ash. 102 BK62
Oakhill Cres., Surb. 85 BL54
Oakhill Dr., Surb. 85 BL54
Oakhill Gdns., Wey. 83 BB55
Oakhill Gdns., Wdf.Grn. 40 CG30
Oakhill Gro., Surb. 85 BL53
Oakhill Path, Surb. 85 BL53
Oakhill Pl. SW15 76 BS46
Oakhill Rd.
Oakhill Rd. SW15 75 BR46
Oakhill Rd. SW16 86 BX51
Oakhill Rd., Ash. 102 BK62
Oakhill Rd., Beck. 87 CF51
Oakhill Rd., Grays 70 CX42
Oakhill Rd., Reig. 121 BS71
Oakhill Rd., Rick. 34 AU28
Oakhill Rd., Surb. 85 BL53
Oakhill Rd., Sutt. 86 BS55
Oakhill Rd., Wey. 91 AV57
Oakhouse Rd., Bexh. 79 CR46
Oakhurst, Wok. 91 AP58
Oakhurst Ave., Barn. 38 BU26
Oakhurst Ave., Bexh. 69 CQ44
Oakhurst Clo. E17 49 CG31
Oakhurst Clo., Ilf. 40 CM30
Oakhurst Gdns. E4 40 CG26
Oakhurst Gdns. E17 49 CG31
Oakhurst Gdns., Bexh. 69 CQ43
Oakhurst Gro. SE22 67 CB45
Oakhurst Ri., Cars. 95 BU58
Oakhurst Rd., Enf. 30 CC21
Oakhurst Rd., Epsom 94 BN57
Oakington, Welw.G.C. 5 BT7
Oakington Ave., Amer. 25 AS23
Oakington Ave., Har. 45 BF33
Oakington Ave., Hayes 63 BA42
Oakington Ave., Wem. 46 BL34
Oakington Dr., Sun. 84 BD51
Oakington Manor Dr., Wem. 46 BM35
Oakington Rd. W9 56 BS38
Oakington Way N8 47 BX32
Oakland Gdns., Brwd. 122 DE25
Oakland Way, Epsom 94 BN57
Oaklands N21 38 BX27
Oaklands, Ken. 105 BZ61
Oaklands, Lthd. 102 BG65
Oaklands, Twick. 74 BG47
Oaklands Ave. N9 30 CB25
Oaklands Ave., Esher 84 BG54
Oaklands Ave., Hat. 19 BR17
Oaklands Ave., Islw. 64 BH43
Oaklands Ave., Rom. 50 CT31
Oaklands Ave., Sid. 78 CN47
Oaklands Ave., Th.Hth. 86 BY52
Oaklands Ave., Wat. 35 BC26
Oaklands Ave., W.Wick. 87 CE55
Oaklands Clo., Bexh. 79 CQ46
Oaklands Clo., Esher 93 BK56
Oaklands Clo., Orp. 88 CN53
Oaklands Clo., Sev. 99 CZ57
Oaklands Ct. SE26 77 CB49
Oaklands Ct., Wat. 26 BC23
Oaklands Ct., Wem. 45 BH
Oaklands Ct., Wey. 83 AW
Oaklands Dr., Red. 121 BV
Oaklands Dr., S.Ock. 60 DE
Oaklands Est. SW4 76 BW
Oaklands Gdns., Ken. 96 BZ
Oaklands Gate, Nthwd. 35 BA
Green La.
Oaklands Gro. W12 55 BP
Oaklands La., Barn. 28 BP
Oaklands La., St.Alb. 10 BM
Oaklands La., West. 97 CH
Oaklands Pk. Ave., Ilf. 49 CM
Oaklands Pl. SW4 66 BW
Oaklands Rd. N20 37 BP
Oaklands Rd. NW2 46 BC
Oaklands Rd. SW14 65 BN
Oaklands Rd. W7 64 BH
Oaklands Rd., Bexh. 69 CQ
Oaklands Rd., Brom. 78 CG
Oaklands Rd., Chsnt. 21 CA
Oaklands Rd., Dart. 80 CX
Oaklands Rd., Grav. 81 DF
Oaklands Way, Tad. 103 BQ
Oaklands Way, Wall. 95 BW
Oaklawn Rd., Lthd. 102 BH
Oaklea Pas., Kings.T. 84 BK
Oakleafe Gdns., Ilf. 49 CL
Oakleigh Ave. N20 38 BT
Oakleigh Ave., Edg. 37 BM
Oakleigh Ave., Surb. 85 BM
Oakleigh Clo. N20 38 BU
Oakleigh Clo., Swan. 89 CT
Oakleigh Ct., Edg. 37 BN
Oakleigh Cres. N20 38 BU
Oakleigh Dr., Rick. 26 BA
Oakleigh Gdns. N20 38 BT
Oakleigh Gdns., Edg. 37 BL
Oakleigh Gdns., Orp. 97 CN
Oakleigh Pk. Ave., Chis. 88 CL
Oakleigh Pk. N. N20 38 BT
Oakleigh Pk. S. N20 38 BU
Oakleigh Ri., Epp. 23 CP
Oakleigh Rd., Pnr. 36 BE
Oakleigh Rd., Uxb. 53 BA
Oakleigh Rd. N. N20 38 BT
Oakleigh Rd. S. N11 38 BV
Oakleigh Way, Mitch. 86 BV
Oakleigh Way, Surb. 85 BM
Oakley Ave. W5 55 BM
Oakley Ave., Bark. 58 CN
Oakley Ave., Croy. 95 BX
Oakley Clo. E4 39 CF
Mapleton Rd.
Oakley Clo. E6 58 CK
Northumberland Rd.
Oakley Clo. W7 54 BH
Oakley Clo., Grays 70 DB
Oakley Clo., Islw. 64 BG
Oakley Clo., Wey. 92 AX
Oakley Ct., Mitch. 86 BV
Oakley Cres. EC1 2
Oakley Cres. N1 56 BY
City Rd.
Oakley Cres., Slou. 52 AP
Oakley Dell, Guil. 118 AU
Oakley Dr. SE9 78 CM
Oakley Dr., Brom. 88 CK
Oakley Dr., Rom. 42 CX
Oakley Gdns. N8 47 BX
Oakley Gdns. SW3 66 BU
Oakley Gdns., Bans. 104 BS
Oakley Grn. Rd., Wind. 61 AK
Oakley Ho. W5 55 BM
Oakley Pk., Bex. 79 CP
Oakley Pl. SE1 67 CA
Oakley Rd. N1 57 BZ
Oakley Rd. SE25 87 CB
Oakley Rd., Brom. 88 CK
Oakley Rd., Har. 45 BH
Oakley Rd., Warl. 105 CB
Oakley Sq. NW1 56 BW
Oakley St. SW3 66 BU
Oakmead Ave., Brom. 88 CH
Oakmead Gdns., Edg. 37 BN
Oakmead Grn., Epsom 103 BM
Oakmead Pl., Mitch. 86 BU
Oakmead Rd. SW12 76 BV
Oakmead Rd., Croy. 86 BW
Oakmeade, Pnr. 36 BF
Oakmere Ave., Pot.B. 20 BT
Oakmere Clo., Pot.B. 20 BT
Oakmere La., Pot.B. 20 BT
Oakmere Rd. SE2 69 CO
Oakmoor Way, Chig. 40 CN
Parkes Rd.
Oakmount Pl., Orp. 88 CM
Oakridge, St.Alb. 18 BE
Oakridge Ave., Rad. 18 BH
Oakridge La., Rad. 18 BH
Oakridge La., Wat. 27 BG
Oakridge Rd., Brom. 77 CF
Oakroyd Ave., Pot.B. 19 BR
Oakroyd Clo., Pot.B. 19 BR
Oaks, The SE18 68 CM
Oaks, The, Berk. 7 AQ
Oaks, The, Epsom 94 BO
Oaks, The, Hayes 53 BA
Oaks, The, Ruis. 44 BB
Oaks, The, Stai. 72 AV
Moormede Cres.
Oaks, The, Swan. 89 CT
The Spinney
Oaks, The, Wey. 92 AW
Oaks, The, Wdf.Grn. 40 CG
Oaks Ave. SE19 77 BZ
Oaks Ave., Felt. 74 BE
Oaks Ave., Rom. 41 CS
Oaks Ave., Wor.Pk. 85 BP
Oaks Clo., Lthd. 102 BJ
Oaks Clo., Rad. 27 BH
Oaks Est. (West Byfleet), Wey. 92 AW
Oaks Gro. E4 40 CG

‹s La., Croy. 96 CB56
‹s La., Croy. 87 CC55
‹s La., Ilf. 49 CN31
‹s Rd., Croy. 96 CB56
‹s Rd., Ken. 95 BY60
‹s Rd., Reig. 121 BT70
‹s Rd., Stai. 73 AX46
‹s Rd., Wok. 100 AS62
‹s Way, Cars. 95 BU57
‹s Way, Epsom 103 BP63
‹s Way, Ken. 96 BZ60
‹s Way, Surb. 84 BK55
‹sford Ave. SE26 77 CB49
‹shade Rd., Brom. 77 CF49
‹shade Rd., Lthd. 93 BG60
‹shaw, Oxt. 114 CF67
‹shaw Rd. SW18 76 BS47
‹side, Uxb. 44 AW35
‹thorpe Rd. N13 38 BY28
‹tree Ave. N13 38 BY27
‹tree Clo., Brwd. 122 DC28
‹tree Garth, Welw.G.C. 5 BR8
‹view Clo., Wal.Cr. 21 CB17
‹view Gdns. N2 47 BT31
‹view Gro., Croy. 87 CD54
‹view Rd. SE6 77 CE49
‹way SW20 85 BQ52
‹way, Brom. 87 CF51
‹way, Grays 71 DD40
‹way, Wok. 100 AP63
‹way Clo., Bex. 79 CQ46
‹ways SE9 78 CL46
‹wood, Guil. 109 AQ68
Tarragon Dr.
‹kwood, Wall. 95 BV58
‹kwood, Wal.Abb. 21 CF20
‹kwood Ave. N14 38 BW26
‹kwood Ave., Beck. 87 CF51
‹kwood Ave., Borwd. 28 BM24
‹kwood Ave., Brwd. 122 DF25
‹kwood Ave., Brom. 88 CH52
‹kwood Ave., Mitch. 86 BT51
‹kwood Ave., Pur. 95 BY59
‹kwood Ave., Sthl. 54 BF40
‹kwood Clo. N14 29 BW25
‹kwood Clo., Chis. 78 CK50
‹kwood Clo., Dart. 80 CX47
‹kwood Clo., Lthd. 110 BB67
‹kwood Clo., Red. 121 BV70
‹kwood Clo. (South Nutfield), Red. 121 BX71
‹kwood Clo., Wdf.Grn. 40 CK29
‹kwood Ct. W14 65 BR41
‹kwood Cres. N21 29 BX25
‹kwood Cres., Grnf. 54 BJ36
‹kwood Dr. SE19 77 BZ50
‹kwood Dr., Bexh. 69 CS45
‹kwood Dr., Edg. 37 BN29
‹kwood Dr., Lthd. 110 BB67
‹kwood Dr., St.Alb. 9 BK13
‹kwood Gdns., Ilf. 49 CN34
‹kwood Gdns., Orp. 88 CM55
‹kwood Gdns., Sutt. 86 BS55
‹kwood Hill, Loug. 31 CK25
‹kwood La. W14 65 BR41
‹kwood Par., Enf. 30 CA25
Queen Annes Pl.
‹kwood Pk. Rd. N14 38 BW26
‹kwood Pl., Croy. 86 BY53
‹kwood Ri., Long. 90 DC52
‹kwood Rd. NW11 47 BS31
‹kwood Rd. SW20 85 BP51
‹kwood Rd., Croy. 86 BY53
‹kwood Rd., Orp. 88 CM55
‹kwood Rd., Pnr. 35 BC30
‹kwood Rd., Red. 113 BY68
‹kwood Rd., St.Alb. 18 BE18
‹kwood Rd., Vir.W. 82 AR53
‹kwood Rd., Wok. 100 AP63
‹kwood Vw. N14 29 BW25
‹kworth Rd. W10 55 BQ39
‹st Ho. Clo., Stai. 72 AS47
‹st Rd., Oxt. 115 CG69
‹st Way, Hartley 90 DC53
‹sthouse Way, Orp. 89 CO52
‹at La. EC2 2 J8
‹at La. EC2 57 BZ39
‹ates Clo., Brom. 87 CF52
‹ates Rd., Rom. 41 CR28
‹atfield Rd., Orp. 88 CN54
‹atfield Rd., Tad. 103 BP64
‹atland Ri. E17 39 CD30
‹atlands Ave., Wey. 92 BA56
‹atlands Chase, Wey. 83 BB55
‹atlands Clo., Wey. 92 BA56
‹atlands Dr., Slou. 52 AO39
‹atlands Dr., Wey. 92 AZ56
‹atlands Grn., Wey. 83 BA55
‹atlands Mere, Wey. 83 BA55
‹atlands Rd., Enf. 30 CC23
‹atlands Rd., Tad. 103 BR63
‹ban Ct., Slou. 61 AO41
‹ban Ho. E14 57 CF39
‹ban Rd. E13 58 CJ38
‹ban Rd. SE25 87 BZ52
‹ban St. E14 57 CF39
‹belisk Par. SE13 67 CF45
Loampit Vale
‹belisk Ride, Egh. 72 AP50
‹beron Ho. N1 57 CA37
Purcell St.
‹beron Way, Shep. 82 AY52
‹berstein Rd. SW11 66 BT45
‹borne Clo. SE24 76 BY46
‹bservatory Gdns. W8 65 BS41
‹bservatory Rd. SW14 65 BN45
‹ccam Rd., Guil. 118 AO70
‹ccupation La. SE18 68 CL44
‹ccupation La. W5 64 BK42
‹ccupation Rd. SE17 4 H10
‹ccupation Rd. SE17 67 BZ42
Manor Pl.
‹ccupation Rd. W7 64 BJ42
‹ccupation Rd., Belv. 69 CQ41
Occupation Rd., Wat. 26 BC25
Ocean Est. E1 57 CC38
Ocean St. E1 57 CC39
Masters St.
Ockenden Clo., Wok. 100 AS62
Ockenden Rd.
Ockenden Rd. N1 57 BZ36
Ockenden Rd., Upmin. 51 CY35
Ockenden Rd., Wok. 100 AS62
Ockham Dr., Orp. 79 CO50
Ockham La., Cob. 101 BA63
Ockham Rd. N., Wok. 101 AZ64
Ockham Rd. N. (Ripley), Wok. 101 AY63
Ockham Rd. S., Lthd. 110 BB67
Ockley Rd. SW16 76 BX49
Ockley Rd., Croy. 86 BX54
Ockleys Mead, Gdse. 114 CC68
Octagon Arc. EC2 2 M7
Octagon Rd., Walt. 92 BB58
Octavia Clo., Mitch. 86 BU53
Octavia Rd., Islw. 64 BH45
Octavia St. SW11 66 BU44
Octavia Way SE28 59 CO40
Octavia Way, Stai. 73 AW50
Octavius St. SE8 67 CE43
Odard Rd., E.Mol. 84 BF52
Oddesey Rd., Borwd. 28 BM23
Odeon Par. N7 47 BX34
Holloway Rd.
Odessa Rd. E7 49 CG35
Odessa Rd. NW10 55 BP37
Odessa St. SE16 67 CD41
Odger St. SW11 66 BU44
Odhams Wk. WC2 1 Q9
Offa Rd., St.Alb. 9 BG13
Offas Mead E9 48 CD35
Kings Mead Est.
Offenham Rd. SE9 78 CK49
Offerton Rd. SW4 66 BW45
Offham Slope N12 37 BR28
Offley Rd. SW9 66 BY43
Offord Clo. N17 39 CB29
Offord Rd. N1 56 BX36
Offord St. N1 56 BX36
Ogard Rd., Hodd. 12 CF11
Ogilby St. SE18 68 CK42
Oglander Rd. SE15 67 CA45
Ogle St. W1 1 L6
Ogle St. W1 56 BW39
Oglethorpe Rd., Dag. 50 CQ34
Ohio Rd. E13 58 CG38
Oil Mill La. W6 65 BP42
Okeburn Rd. SW17 76 BV49
Okehampton Clo. N12 38 BT28
Okehampton Cres., Well. 69 CO43
Okehampton Rd. NW10 55 BQ37
Okehampton Rd., Rom. 42 CV29
Okehampton Sq., Rom. 42 CV29
Okemore Gdns., Orp. 89 CP52
Olaf St. W11 55 BQ40
Old Acre, Wey. 92 AW60
Old Ave., Wey. 92 BA57
Old Ave. (West Byfleet), Wey. 91 AV60
Old Ave. Clo., Wey. 91 AV60
Old Bailey EC4 2 G9
Old Bailey EC4 56 BY39
Old Barge Ho. All. SE1 4 E2
Old Barn Clo., Sutt. 94 BR57
Old Barn La., Rick. 26 AY25
Old Barn La., Whyt. 105 CA61
Old Barn Rd., Epsom 103 BN62
Old Barn Way, Bexh. 69 CS45
Old Barrack Yd. SW1 3 G5
Old Barrowfield E15 58 CG37
New Plaistow Rd.
Old Bethnal Grn. Rd. E2 57 CB38
Old Bexley La., Bex. 79 CS48
Old Bexley La., Dart. 79 CT47
Old Bond St. W1 3 L1
Old Bond St. W1 56 BW40
Old Brewers Yd. WC2 1 Q9
Old Brewery Ms. NW3 47 BT35
Hampstead High St.
Old Bri. Clo., Nthlt. 54 BF37
Old Bri. St., Kings.T. 84 BK51
Thames St.
Old Broad St. EC2 2 L9
Old Broad St. EC2 57 BZ39
Old Bromley Rd., Brom. 77 CF49
Old Brompton Rd. SW5 66 BS42
Old Brompton Rd. SW7 66 BT42
Old Bldgs. WC2 2 D8
Old Burlington St. W1 1 L10
Old Burlington St. W1 56 BW40
Old Carriageway, The, Sev. 107 CS64
High St.
Old Castle St. E1 2 P8
Old Castle St. E1 57 CA39
Old Cavendish St. W1 1 J8
Old Cavendish St. W1 56 BV39
Old Change Ct. EC4 57 BZ39
Peters Hill
Old Chapel Rd., Swan. 89 CS54
Old Charlton Rd., Shep. 83 BA53
Old Chertsey La., Stai. 72 AV49
Old Chertsey Rd., Wok. 91 AQ58
Old Chestnut Ave., Esher 93 BF57
Old Ch. La. NW9 46 BN34
Old Ch. La., Brwd. 122 DF24
Old Ch. La., Grnf. 54 BJ38
Perivale La.
Old Ch. La., Stan. 36 BJ28
Old Ch. Path, Esher 93 BF56
Old Ch. Rd. E1 57 CC39
Old Ch. Rd. E4 39 CE28
Old Ch. St. SW3 66 BT42
Old Claygate La., Esher 93 BJ57
Old Clem Sq. SE18 68 CL43
Kempt St.
Old Coach Rd., Cher. 82 AV53
Old Coach Rd., Sev. 99 DC60
Old Common Rd., Cob. 92 BC60
Old Compton St. W1 1 N10
Old Compton St. W1 56 BW40
Old Cote Dr., Houns. 64 BF43
Old Ct. W5 55 BL39
Hillcrest Rd.
Old Ct., Ash. 103 BL63
Old Ct. Pl. W8 66 BS41
Old Ct. Rd., Guil. 118 AQ71
Old Crabtree La., Hem.H. 8 AY14
Old Crown La., Brwd. 33 CY23
Old Crown Rd., Brwd. 33 CY23
Old Dartford Rd., Farn. 90 CW53
Old Dean, Hem.H. 16 AT17
Old Deer Pk. Gdns., Rich. 65 BL45
Old Devonshire Rd. SW12 76 BV47
Old Dock App. Rd., Grays 71 DF42
Old Dock Clo., Rich. 65 BM43
Old Dock Ct., Rich. 65 BM43
Bushwood Rd.
Old Dover Rd. SE3 68 CH43
Old Downs, Hartley 90 DC53
Old Dr., The, Welw.G.C. 5 BP8
Old Esher Clo., Walt. 93 BD56
Old Esher Rd., Walt. 93 BD56
Old Farleigh Rd., S.Croy. 96 CC58
Old Farleigh Rd., Warl. 105 CD62
Old Fm. Ave. N14 38 BW26
Old Fm. Ave., Sid. 78 CM47
Old Fm. Clo., Houns. 64 BE45
Old Fm. Gdns., Swan. 89 CT52
Old Fm. Pas., Hmptn. 84 BG51
Old Fm. Rd. N2 38 BT30
Old Fm. Rd., Guil. 118 AR69
Old Fm. Rd., Hmptn. 74 BE50
Old Fm. Rd., West Dr. 63 AX41
Old Fm. Rd. E., Sid. 79 CO48
Old Fm. Rd. W., Sid. 78 CN48
Old Farmhouse Dr., Lthd. 93 BG61
Old Ferry Dr., Stai. 72 AR46
Old Fish St. Hill EC4 2 H10
Old Fishery Cut, Hem.H. 7 AV15
Old Fishery La., Hem.H. 7 AV14
Old Fold Clo., Barn. 28 BR23
Old Fold La., Barn. 28 BR23
Old Fold Vw., Barn. 28 BQ24
Old Ford Rd. E2 57 CC37
Old Ford Rd. E3 57 CD37
Old Forge Clo., Stan. 36 BJ28
Old Forge Clo., Wat. 17 BC20
Old Forge Clo., Welw.G.C. 5 BR6
Old Forge Ct., Guil. 118 AS73
Station Rd.
Old Forge Cres., Shep. 83 AZ53
Old Forge Ms. W12 65 BP41
Goodwin Rd.
Old Forge Rd., Enf. 30 CA22
Old Forge Way, Sid. 79 CO49
Old Fox Clo., Cat. 104 BY64
Old Fox Footpath, S.Croy. 96 CA58
Old French Horn La., Hat. 10 BP12
Old Gannon Clo., Nthwd. 35 BA28
Old Gdn., The, Sev. 107 CS65
Old Gdn. Ct., St.Alb. 9 BG13
Mount Pleasant
Old Gloucester St. WC1 2 A6
Old Gloucester St. WC1 56 BX39
Old Hall Clo., Pnr. 36 BE30
Old Hall Dr., Pnr. 36 BE30
Old Harpenden Rd., St.Alb. 9 BH12
Old Harrow La., West. 106 CM63
Old Hatch Manor, Ruis. 44 BB33
Old Hertford Rd., Hat. 10 BQ11
Old Highway, Hodd. 12 CE10
Old Hill, Chis. 88 CL51
Old Hill, Orp. 97 CM57
Old Hill, Wok. 100 AR63
Old Homesdale Rd., Brom. 88 CJ52
Old Ho. Clo. SW19 75 BR49
Old Ho. Clo., Epsom 94 BO58
Old Ho. Ct., Hem.H. 8 AY13
Old Ho. Cft., Harl. 6 CN10
Old Ho. La., Wal.Abb. 13 CG15
Old Ho. Rd., Hem.H. 8 AY13
Old Jamaica Rd. SE16 67 CB41
Old James St. SE15 67 CB45
Old Jewry EC2 2 K9
Old Jewry EC2 57 BZ39
Old Kent Rd. SE1 4 M8
Old Kent Rd. SE1 67 CA42
Old Kent Rd. SE15 67 CB43
Old Kenton La. NW9 46 BM32
Old Kingston Rd., Wor.Pk. 85 BN55
Old La., Cob. 101 AZ62
Old La., Sev. 108 DA65
Old La., West. 106 CJ64
Old La. Gdns., Cob. 101 BB64
Old Leys, Hat. 10 BP14
Old Lo. La., Pur. 95 BX60
Old Lo. Pl., Twick. 74 BJ46
Old Lo. Way, Stan. 36 BJ28
Old London Rd., Dor. 111 BK67
Old London Rd., Epsom 103 BP62
Old London Rd., Harl. 6 CP10
Old London Rd., Lthd. 110 BC66
Old London Rd., St.Alb. 9 BH14
Old London Rd., Sev. 107 CQ61
Old Maidstone Rd., Sid. 79 CQ50
Old Malden La., Wor.Pk. 85 BN55
Old Malt Way, Wok. 100 AR62
Old Manor Dr., Islw. 74 BG46
Old Manor Gdns., Guil. 118 AU73
Old Manor La., Guil. 118 AU73
Old Manor Rd., Til. 71 DG45
Old Manor Way, Bexh. 69 CS44
Old Manor Way, Chis. 78 CK49
Old Manor Yd. SW5 66 BS42
Earls Ct. Rd.
Old Maple, Hem.H. 8 AY10
Old Marsh La., Maid. 61 AJ41
Old Marylebone Rd. NW1 1 D7
Old Marylebone Rd. NW1 56 BU39
Old Mead, Ger.Cr. 34 AS29
Old Merrow St., Guil. 118 AU69
Old Ms., Har. 45 BH32
Old Mill Clo., Eyns. 90 CW54
Old Mill Ct. E18 49 CJ31
Old Mill Gdns., Berk. 7 AR13
London Rd.
Old Mill La. W6 65 BP42
Upper Mall
Old Mill La., Maid. 61 AH41
Old Mill La., Red. 113 BV67
Old Mill La., Uxb. 53 AW39
Old Mill Rd. SE18 68 CM43
Old Mill Rd., Kings L. 17 BA20
Old Mill Rd., Uxb. 44 AW34
Old Montague St. E1 57 CA39
Old Nazeing Rd., Brox. 12 CE14
Old Nichol St. E2 2 P4
Old Nichol St. E2 57 CA38
Old N. St. WC1 2 B6
Old N. St. WC1 56 BX39
Theobalds Rd.
Old Oak Ave., Couls. 104 BU63
Old Oak Common La. NW10 55 BO39
Old Oak Common La. W3 55 BO39
Old Oak Common Way W3 55 BO40
Old Oak Est. W12 55 BO40
Old Oak La. NW10 55 BO38
Old Oak Rd. W3 55 BO40
Old Orchard, Harl. 13 CM12
Old Orchard, St.Alb. 18 BG16
Old Orchard, Sun. 84 BD51
Old Orchard, Wey. 92 AY59
Old Orchard, The NW3 47 BU35
Nassington Rd.
Old Otford Rd., Sev. 107 CU62
Old Palace La., Rich. 74 BK46
Old Palace Rd., Croy. 86 BY55
Old Palace Rd., Guil. 118 AQ71
Old Palace Rd., Wey. 83 AZ55
Old Palace Yd. SW1 3 Q6
Old Palace Yd., Rich. 74 BK46
Old Paradise St. SE11 4 B8
Old Paradise St. SE11 66 BX42
Old Pk. Ave. SW12 76 BV46
Old Pk. Ave., Enf. 30 BZ24
Old Pk. Gro., Enf. 30 BZ24
Old Pk. La. W1 3 H3
Old Pk. La. W1 56 BV40
Old Pk. Ms., Houns. 64 BE43
Old Pk. Ride, Wal.Cr. 20 BY19
Old Pk. Ridings N21 29 BY25
Old Pk. Rd. N13 38 BX28
Old Pk. Rd. SE2 69 CO42
Old Pk. Rd., Enf. 29 BY24
Old Pk. Rd. S., Enf. 29 BY24
Old Pk. Vw., Enf. 29 BY24
Old Parkbury La., St.Alb. 18 BH18
Old Parvis Rd., Wey. 92 AX59
Old Perry St., Chis. 78 CN50
Old Perry St., Grav. 81 DF47
Old Portsmouth Rd., Guil. 118 AR74
Old Pottery Clo., Reig. 121 BS71
Old Pye St. SW1 3 N6
Old Pye St. SW1 66 BW41
Old Quebec St. W1 1 F9
Old Quebec St. W1 56 BU39
Old Queen St. SW1 3 P5
Old Queen St. SW1 66 BW41
Old Rectory Clo., Tad. 103 BP65
Old Rectory Dr., Hat. 10 BP12
Old Rectory Gdns., Edg. 37 BM29
Old Rectory Ho. SW19 75 BR49
Old Rectory La., Lthd. 110 BB66
Old Rectory La., Uxb. 43 AV33
Old Rectory Rd., Ong. 24 CV20
Old Redding, Har. 36 BF28
Old Redstone Dr., Red. 121 BV71
Old Reigate Rd., Bet. 120 BM70
Old Reigate Rd., Dor. 120 BL70
Old Rd. SE13 68 CG45
Old Rd., Brwd. 33 CV24
Old Rd., Dart. 79 CS46
Old Rd., Enf. 30 CC23
Old Rd., Harl. 6 CP8
Old Rd., Rom. 33 CV23
Old Rd., Wey. 91 AV57
Old Rd. E., Grav. 81 DG47
Old Rd. W., Grav. 81 DF47
Old Rope Wk., Sun. 83 BC52
Old Ruislip Rd., Nthlt. 54 BD37
Old Sch. Clo. SW19 86 BS51
Old Sch. Clo., Beck. 87 CD51
Old Sch. Ct., Stai. 72 AS47
Old Sch. La., Bet. 120 BM72
Old Sch. Ms., Wey. 92 BA56
Old Schools La., Epsom 94 BO58
Old Seacoal La. EC4 2 F9
Old Shire La., Rick. 25 AT25
Old Shire La., Wal.Abb. 31 CH21
Old Slade La., Iver 62 AV41
Old Sopwell Gdns., St.Alb. 9 BG14
Cottonmill La.
Old S. Clo., Pnr. 36 BD30
Old S. Lambeth Rd. SW8 66 BX43
Old Sq. WC2 2 C8
Old Sta. App., Lthd. 102 BJ64
Old Sta. La., Stai. 72 AS46
Old Sta. Rd., Hayes 63 BB41
Old Sta. Rd., Loug. 31 CK25
Old Sta. Rd. (Knockholt), Sev. 98 CQ58
Old Stockley Rd., West Dr. 63 AZ41
Old St. E13 58 CH37
Old St. EC1 2 H5
Old St. EC1 57 BZ38
Old Swan Yd., Cars. 95 BU56
Old Terrys Lo. Rd., Sev. 108 CZ61
Old Town SW4 66 BW45
Old Town, Croy. 86 BY55
Old Tye Ave., West. 106 CK61
Old Uxbridge Rd., Rick. 34 AV29
Old Wk., The, Sev. 108 CV62
Old Watford Rd., St.Alb. 18 BE18
Old Watling St., Grav. 81 DG49
Old Westhall Clo., Warl. 105 CC63
Old Woking Rd., Wok. 100 AT63
Old Woolwich Rd. SE10 67 CF43
Oldacre Ms. SW12 76 BV47
Balham Gro.
Oldberry Rd., Edg. 37 BN29
Oldborough Rd., Wem. 45 BK34
Oldbury Clo., Cher. 82 AV54
Oldbury Rd
Oldbury Clo., Orp. 89 CP52
Oldbury Clo., Sev. 108 DA64
Oldbury La., Sev. 108 DA64
Oldbury Pl. W1 1 H6
Oldbury Pl. W1 56 BV38
Oldbury Rd., Cher. 82 AV54
Oldbury Rd., Enf. 30 CB23
Oldchurch Gdns., Rom. 50 CS33
Oldchurch Ri., Rom. 50 CT33
Oldchurch Rd., Rom. 50 CS33
Olden La., Pur. 95 BY59
Oldfield Circ., Nthlt. 54 BG36
Oldfield Clo., Amer. 25 AS23
Oldfield Clo., Brom. 88 CK52
Oldfield Clo., Chsnt. 21 CD17
Oldfield Clo., Grnf. 45 BH35
Oldfield Clo., Stan. 36 BJ28
Oldfield Dr., Chsnt. 21 CD17
Oldfield Fm. Gdns., Grnf. 54 BG37
Oldfield Gdns., Ash. 102 BK63
Oldfield Gro. SE16 67 CC42
Oldfield La. N., Grnf. 54 BG36
Oldfield La. S., Grnf. 54 BG38
Oldfield Ms. N6 47 BW33
Oldfield Pk., Brom. 88 CL52
Oldfield Rd. N16 48 CA34
Oldfield Rd. NW10 55 BO36
Oldfield Rd. SW19 75 BR50
Oldfield Rd., Bexh. 69 CQ44
Oldfield Rd., Brom. 88 CK52
Oldfield Rd., Hmptn. 84 BE51
Oldfield Rd., Hem.H. 7 AV14
Oldfield Rd., St.Alb. 18 BK16
Oldfields Rd., Sutt. 85 BR55
Oldhams Ter. W3 55 BN40
Oldhill St. N16 48 CB33
Oldhouse La., Harl. 13 CJ12
Oldhouse La., Kings L. 26 AY21
Oldridge Rd. SW12 76 BV47
Olds App., Wat. 35 BA26
Oldstead Rd., Brom. 77 CF49
Oldway La., Slou. 61 AL40
Oleander Clo., Orp. 97 CM56
O'Leary Sq. E1 57 CC39
Adelina Gro.
Oley Pl. E1 57 CC39
Olga St. E3 57 CD37
Conyer St.
Olinda Rd. N16 48 CA32
Oliphant St. W10 55 BQ38
Olive Rd. E13 58 CJ38
Olive Rd. NW2 46 BQ35
Olive Rd. SW19 76 BT50
Olive Rd. W5 64 BK41
Olive Rd., Dart. 80 CV47
Olive St., Rom. 50 CS31
Olive Taylor Ct., Hem.H. 8 AY11
Stevenage Ri.
Oliver Ave. SE25 87 CA52
Oliver Clo. E10 48 CE34
Oliver Clo. W4 65 BM43
Oliver Clo., Grays 70 CZ43
Oliver Clo., Hem.H. 8 AY15
Oliver Clo., St.Alb. 18 BG17
Oliver Clo., Wey. 92 AW56
Oliver Cres., Farn. 90 CW54
Oliver Gdns. E6 58 CK39
Oliver Goldsmith Est. SE15 67 CB44
Oliver Gro. SE25 87 CA52
Oliver Rd. E10 48 CE34
Oliver Rd. E17 48 CF32
Oliver Rd., Brwd. 122 DD25
Oliver Rd., Grays 70 DA43
Oliver Rd., Hem.H. 8 AY15
Oliver Rd., N.Mal. 85 BN51
Oliver Rd., Rain. 59 CT37
Oliver Rd., Sutt. 95 BT56
Oliver Rd., Swan. 89 CS52
Olivers Ave., Berk. 7 AU11
Olivers Mill, Dart. 90 DC55
Olivers Yd. EC1 2 L4
Olivers Yd. EC2 57 BZ38
City Rd.
Olivette St. SW15 65 BW45
Felsham Rd.
Ollards Gro., Loug. 31 CJ24
Olleberrie La., Rick. 16 AU19
Ollerton Grn. E3 57 CD37
Ollerton Rd. N11 38 BW28
Olley Clo., Wall. 95 BX57
Redford Ave.
Ollgar Clo. W12 55 BP40
Olliffe St. E14 67 CF41
Olmar St. SE1 67 CB43
Olney Rd. SE17 66 BY43
Olron Cres., Bexh. 79 CP46
Olven Rd. SE18 68 CM43
Olveston Wk., Cars. 86 BT53
Olyffe Ave., Well. 69 CO44
Olyffe Dr., Beck. 87 CF51
Olympic Way, Grnf. 54 BF37
Olympic Way, Wem. 46 BM34
Olympus Sq. E5 48 CB34
Downs Est.
Oman Ave. NW2 46 BP35
O'Meara St. SE1 4 J3

O'Meara St. SE1 57 BZ40
Omega Pl. N1 2 A1
Omega Pl. N1 56 BX37
Caledonian Rd.
Omega Rd., Wok. 100 AT61
Omega St. SE14 67 CD44
Ommaney Rd. SE14 67 CC44
On The Hill, Wat. 36 BE27
Ondine Rd. SE15 67 CA45
One Pin La., Slou. 43 AO35
One Tree Clo. SE23 77 CC46
One Tree Hill Rd., Guil. 118 AT71
Onega Gate SE16 67 CD41
O'Neill Path SE18 68 CL43
Kempt St.
Ongar Clo., Rom. 50 CP32
Ongar Clo., Wey. 91 AV56
Ongar Hill, Wey. 92 AW57
Ongar Pl., Brwd. 42 DB27
Ongar Pl., Wey. 92 AW57
Ongar Rd. SW6 66 BS43
Ongar Rd., Brwd. 42 DA26
Ongar Rd. (Pilgrims Hatch), Brwd. 33 CY24
Ongar Rd. (Stondon Massey), Brwd. 24 CZ20
Ongar Rd., Epp. 23 CO18
Ongar Rd., Ong. 15 CY14
Ongar Rd., Rom. 32 CO24
Ongar Rd., Wey. 92 AW56
Ongar Way, Rain. 59 CT37
Onra Rd. E17 48 CE33
Onslow Ave., Rich. 75 BL46
Onslow Ave., Sutt. 94 BR58
Onslow Clo. E4 39 CF27
Onslow Clo., Hat. 10 BP12
Onslow Clo., Surb. 84 BH54
Onslow Way
Onslow Clo., Wok. 100 AT62
Onslow Cres., Chis. 88 CL51
Onslow Cres., Wok. 100 AT62
Onslow Dr., Sid. 79 CP48
Onslow Gdns. E18 49 CH31
Onslow Gdns. N10 47 BV32
Onslow Gdns. N21 29 BY25
Onslow Gdns. SW7 3 A10
Onslow Gdns. SW7 66 BT42
Onslow Gdns., Ong. 24 CX17
Onslow Gdns., S.Croy. 96 CB59
Onslow Gdns., T.Ditt. 84 BH54
Onslow Gdns., Wall. 95 BW57
Onslow Ms. E. SW7 3 A9
Onslow Ms. W. SW7 3 A9
Onslow Ms. W. SW7 66 BT42
Cranley Pl.
Onslow Rd., Croy. 86 BX54
Onslow Rd., Guil. 118 AR70
Onslow Rd., N.Mal. 85 BP52
Onslow Rd., Rich. 75 BL46
Onslow Rd., Walt. 92 BB56
Onslow Sq. SW7 3 B9
Onslow Sq. SW7 66 BT42
Onslow St. EC1 2 E5
Onslow St. EC1 56 BY38
Clerkenwell Rd.
Onslow St., Guil. 118 AR71
Onslow Way, T.Ditt. 84 BH54
Onslow Way, Wok. 100 AV61
Ontario St. SE1 4 G7
Ontario St. SE1 66 BY41
Opal Clo. E16 58 CJ39
Opal Ct., Slou. 52 AQ38
Opal Ms., Ilf. 49 CL34
Ley St.
Opal St. SE11 4 F10
Opal St. SE11 66 BY42
Openshaw Rd. SE2 69 CO42
Openview SW18 76 BT47
Ophelia Gdns. NW2 46 BQ34
Cricklewood Trd. Est.
Ophir Ter. SE15 67 CB44
Opossum Way, Houns. 64 BD45
Oppidans Ms. NW3 56 BU36
Oppidans Rd. NW3 56 BU36
Oram Pl., Hem.H. 8 AX15
Orange Ct. E1 57 CB40
Hermitage Wall
Orange Ct. La., Orp. 97 CL58
Orange Hill Rd., Edg. 37 BN29
Orange Pl. SE16 67 CC41
Orange St. WC2 3 P1
Orange St. WC2 56 BW40
Orange Tree Hill, Hav. 41 CS28
Orange Yd. W1 1 P9
Orangery, The, Rich. 74 BK48
Orangery La. SE9 78 CK46
Oratory La. SW3 3 B10
Orb St. SE17 4 K9
Orb St. SE17 67 BZ42
Orbain Rd. SW6 65 BR43
Orbel St. SW11 66 BU44
Orbital 1, Dart. 80 CX48
Orbital Cres., Wat. 26 BB21
Orchard, The N21 30 BZ25
Orchard, The NW11 47 BS32
Orchard, The SE3 67 CF44
Orchard, The W4 65 BN42
Orchard, The W5 54 BK39
Orchard, The, Bans. 104 BS61
Orchard, The, Dor. 119 BK73
Orchard, The, Epsom 94 BO57
Orchard, The, Houns. 64 BG44
Orchard, The, Kings L. 17 AZ18
Orchard, The, Sev. 107 CT64
Milton Rd.
Orchard, The, Swan. 89 CS51
Orchard, The, Vir.W. 82 AS53
Orchard, The, Welw.G.C. 5 BQ7
Orchard, The, Wok. 100 AS64
Orchard Ave. N3 47 BS31
Orchard Ave. N14 38 BW26
Orchard Ave. N20 38 BT27
Orchard Ave., Ashf. 73 BA50
Orchard Ave., Belv. 69 CQ43
Orchard Ave., Berk. 7 AQ13
Orchard Ave., Brwd. 122 DC27
Orchard Ave., Croy. 87 CD54
Orchard Ave., Dart. 79 CU47
Orchard Ave., Felt. 73 BA46
Orchard Ave., Grav. 81 DG49
Orchard Ave., Houns. 64 BE43
Orchard Ave., Mitch. 86 BV54
Orchard Ave., N.Mal. 85 BO51
Orchard Ave., Rain. 60 CV38
Orchard Ave., Sthl. 54 BE40
Orchard Ave., T.Ditt. 84 BJ54
Orchard Ave., Wat. 17 BC19
Orchard Ave., Wey. 91 AV59
Orchard Ave., Wind. 61 AN44
Orchard Clo. NW2 46 BP34
Orchard Clo. SE23 67 CC46
Brenchley Gdns.
Orchard Clo. SW20 85 BQ52
Orchard Clo. W10 55 BR39
Wornington Rd.
Orchard Clo., Ashf. 73 BA50
Orchard Clo., Bans. 95 BS60
Orchard Clo., Bexh. 69 CQ44
Orchard Clo., Bish. 6 CS7
Orchard Clo., Borwd. 28 BL24
Orchard Clo., Bush. 36 BG26
Orchard Clo., Cuffley 20 BX17
Orchard Clo., Edg. 37 BL29
Orchard Clo., Egh. 72 AT49
Orchard Clo., Epsom 94 BM57
Orchard Clo., Guil. 118 AT70
Orchard Clo., Hem.H. 8 AZ12
Orchard Clo., Hert. 11 BW13
Orchard Clo. (Effingham), Lthd. 101 BB65
Orchard Clo. (Fetcham), Lthd. 102 BG64
Orchard Clo., Nthlt. 54 BG36
Newnham Gdns.
Orchard Clo., Rad. 27 BH22
Orchard Clo., Rick. 25 AU24
Orchard Clo., Ruis. 44 BA33
Orchard Clo., St.Alb. 9 BH14
Orchard Clo., Sev. 108 CV63
Orchard Clo., S.Ock. 60 DB38
Orchard Clo., Surb. 84 BJ54
Orchard Clo., Uxb. 53 AW36
Orchard Clo., Walt. 83 BC53
Garden Rd.
Orchard Clo., Wat. 26 BB23
Orchard Clo., Wem. 55 BL36
Orchard Clo., Wok. 100 AT61
Orchard Cotts., Brwd. 123 DC32
Orchard Ct., Edg. 37 BL28
Orchard Ct., Hem.H. 16 AT17
Apple Cotts.
Orchard Ct., Islw. 64 BG44
Thornbury Ave.
Orchard Ct., Wor.Pk. 85 BP54
Orchard Cres., Edg. 37 BN28
Orchard Cres., Enf. 30 CA23
Orchard Cft., Harl. 6 CO10
Orchard Dr. SE3 67 CF44
Orchard Dr., Ash. 102 BK63
Orchard Dr., Edg. 37 BL28
Orchard Dr., Epp. 31 CN21
Orchard Dr., Grays 71 DD41
Orchard Dr., Rick. 25 AU24
Orchard Dr., St.Alb. 18 BF17
Orchard Dr., Shep. 83 BB52
Orchard Dr., Uxb. 53 AX38
Orchard Dr., Wat. 26 BB23
Orchard Dr., Wok. 100 AS61
Orchard End, Cat. 105 CA64
Town End Clo.
Orchard End, Lthd. 102 BG65
Orchard End, Ong. 24 CW16
Springfield Clo.
Orchard End, Wey. 83 BB55
Orchard End Ave., Amer. 25 AP23
Orchard Est. SE13 67 CE44
Orchard Gdns., Chess. 94 BL56
Orchard Gdns., Epsom 94 BN60
Orchard Gdns., Lthd. 111 BE67
Orchard Gdns., Sutt. 95 BS56
Orchard Gdns., Wal.Abb. 21 CF20
Orchard Gate NW9 46 BO31
Orchard Gate, Esher 84 BG54
Orchard Gate, Grnf. 54 BJ36
Orchard Grn., Orp. 88 CN55
Orchard Gro. SE20 77 CB50
Orchard Gro., Croy. 87 CD54
Orchard Gro., Edg. 37 BM30
Orchard Gro., Ger.Cr. 34 AR30
Orchard Gro., Har. 46 BL32
Orchard Gro., Orp. 88 CN55
Orchard Hill SE13 67 CE44
Coldbath St.
Orchard Hill, Cars. 95 BU56
Orchard Hill, Dart. 79 CT46
Orchard La. SW20 85 BP51
Orchard La., Amer. 25 AO22
Orchard La., Brwd. 33 CZ25
Orchard La., E.Mol. 84 BG53
Orchard La., Harl. 6 CQ9
Orchard La., Wdf.Grn. 40 CJ28
Orchard Lea Clo., Wok. 100 AV61
Orchard Leigh, Chesh. 16 AQ17
Orchard Mains, Wok. 100 AR63
Orchard Mead, Hat. 10 BO12
Orchard Ms. N1 57 BZ36
Southgate Gro.
Orchard Ms., Beac. 34 AO28
Orchard Rd.
Orchard Par., Pot.B. 19 BQ19
Mutton La.
Orchard Piece, Ing. 24 DC18
Orchard Pl. E14 58 CG40
Orchard Pl. N17 39 CA29
Orchard Pl., Brom. 88 CH51
Orchard Ri., Croy. 87 CD54
Orchard Ri., Kings.T. 85 BN51
Orchard Ri., Pnr. 44 BB31
Orchard Ri., Rich. 75 BM46
Orchard Ri. E., Sid. 78 CN46
Orchard Ri. W., Sid. 68 CN45
Orchard Rd. N6 47 BV33
Orchard Rd. SE3 68 CG44
Orchard Rd. SE18 68 CM42
Orchard Rd., Barn. 28 BR24
Orchard Rd., Beac. 34 AO28
Orchard Rd., Belv. 69 CR42
Orchard Rd., Brent. 64 BK43
Orchard Rd., Brom. 88 CJ51
Orchard Rd., Ch.St.G. 34 AR27
Orchard Rd., Chess. 94 BL56
Orchard Rd., Dag. 59 CR37
Orchard Rd., Dor. 119 BJ72
Orchard Rd., Enf. 30 CC25
Orchard Rd., Grav. 81 DE48
Orchard Rd., Guil. 118 AP71
Orchard Rd. (Burpham), Guil. 109 AT68
Orchard Rd. (Shalford), Guil. 118 AS73
Orchard Rd., Hmptn. 74 BE50
Orchard Rd., Hayes 53 BC40
Orchard Rd., Houns. 74 BE46
Orchard Rd., Kings.T. 85 BL52
Orchard Rd., Mitch. 86 BV54
Orchard Rd. (Farnborough), Orp. 97 CL56
Orchard Rd. (Pratts Bottom), Orp. 98 CP58
Orchard Rd., Reig. 121 BS70
Orchard Rd., Rich. 65 BM45
Orchard Rd., Rom. 41 CR30
Orchard Rd. (Otford), Sev. 107 CT61
Orchard Rd. (Riverhead), Sev. 107 CT64
Orchard Rd., Sid. 78 CN49
Orchard Rd., S.Croy. 96 CB60
Orchard Rd., S.Ock. 60 DB38
Orchard Rd., Sun. 73 BC50
Orchard Rd., Sutt. 95 BS56
Orchard Rd., Swans. 81 DC46
Orchard Rd., Twick. 74 BJ46
Orchard Rd., Well. 69 CO45
Orchard Rd., Wind. 72 AQ46
Orchard Sq. W14 65 BR42
Sun Rd.
Orchard Sq., Brox. 12 CD15
Orchard St. E17 48 CD31
Orchard St. W1 1 G9
Orchard St. W1 56 BV39
Orchard St., Dart. 80 CW46
Orchard St., Hem.H. 8 AX15
Orchard St., St.Alb. 9 BG14
Orchard Ter., Enf. 30 CB25
Orchard Vw., Uxb. 53 AX38
Orchard Way, Ashf. 73 AY48
Orchard Way, Chsnt. 20 BY17
Orchard Way, Chig. 41 CO27
Orchard Way, Croy. 87 CD54
Orchard Way, Dart. 80 CV48
Orchard Way, Dor. 119 BJ72
Orchard Way, Enf. 30 CA24
Orchard Way, Esher 93 BG57
Orchard Way, Hem.H. 16 AT17
Orchard Way, Oxt. 115 CH70
Orchard Way, Pot.B. 20 BS18
Orchard Way, Reig. 121 BS72
Orchard Way, Rick. 35 AW26
Orchard Way, Sev. 108 CX62
Orchard Way, Slou. 52 AS40
Firs Dr.
Orchard Way, Sutt. 95 BT56
Orchard Way, Tad. 112 BR66
Orchard Way, Wey. 92 AW56
Orchard Way, Wok. 109 AU66
Orchard Waye, Uxb. 53 AX37
Orchardleigh, Lthd. 102 BJ64
St Nicholas Hill
Orchardleigh Ave., Enf. 30 CC23
Orchardmede N21 30 BZ25
Orchards, The, Saw. 6 CQ6
Orchards N., The, Epp. 23 CO19
Orchards S., The, Epp. 23 CO19
Orchardson St. NW8 1 A5
Orchardson St. NW8 56 BT38
Orchehill Ave., Ger.Cr. 43 AR31
Orchehill Ri., Ger.Cr. 43 AS32
Orchid Clo. E6 58 CK38
Orchid Ct., Egh. 72 AT49
Orchid Rd. N14 38 BW26
Orchid St. W12 55 BP40
Orchis Gro., Grays 71 DC42
Orchis Way, Rom. 42 CW29
Orde Hall St. WC1 2 B6
Orde Hall St. WC1 56 BX39
Ordell Rd. E3 57 CD37
Ordnance Clo., Felt. 73 BC48
Ordnance Cres. SE10 68 CG41
Ordnance Hill NW8 56 BT37
Ordnance Rd. E16 58 CG39
Ordnance Rd. SE18 68 CL43
Ordnance Rd., Enf. 30 CC22
Ordnance Rd., Grav. 81 DH46
Oregano Way, Guil. 109 AQ68
Oregon Ave. E12 49 CK35
Oregon Clo., N.Mal. 85 BN52
Georgia Rd.
Oregon Sq., Orp. 88 CM54
Orestan La., Lthd. 110 BC67
Orestes Ms. NW6 47 BS35
Aldred Rd.
Oreston Rd., Rain. 60 CV38
Orewell Gdns., Reig. 121 BS71
Orford Ct. SE27 76 BY48
Orford Gdns., Twick. 74 BH48
Orford Rd. E17 48 CE32
Orford Rd. E18 49 CH31
Organ Hall Rd., Borwd. 27 BK23
Organ La. E4 39 CF27
Oriel Clo., Mitch. 86 BW52
Holly Way
Oriel Ct., Mitch. 86 BW52
Oriel Gdns., Ilf. 49 CK31
Oriel Pl. NW3 47 BT35
Oriel Rd. E9 57 CC36
Oriel Way, Nthlt. 54 BF36
Orient Rd., Til. 71 DG45
Orient St. SE11 4 F8
Orient St. SE11 66 BY42
West Sq.
Orient Way E5 48 CC34
Oriental Clo., Wok. 100 AS62
Oriental Rd. E16 58 CJ40
Oriental Rd., Wok. 100 AS62
Oriole Way SE28 59 CO40
Orion Pk. W7 64 BJ41
Orion Way, Nthwd. 35 BB28
Orissa Rd. SE18 68 CN42
Orkney St. SW11 66 BV44
Orlando Gdns., Epsom 94 BN58
Ormonde Ave.
Orlando Rd. SW4 66 BW45
Orleans Rd. SE19 77 BZ50
Orleans Rd., Twick. 74 BJ47
Orleston Ms. N7 56 BY36
Orleston Rd. N7 56 BY36
Orlestone Gdns., Orp. 98 CQ56
Orley Fm. Rd., Har. 45 BH34
Orlick Rd., Grav. 81 DK48
Orlop St. SE10 68 CG42
Ormanton Rd. SE26 77 CB49
Orme Ct. W2 56 BS40
Orme Ct. Ms. W2 56 BS40
Orme La.
Orme La. W2 56 BS40
Orme Rd., Kings.T. 85 BM51
Orme Sq. W2 56 BS40
Ormeley Rd. SW12 76 BV47
Ormerod Gdns., Mitch. 86 BV51
Ormesby Clo. SE28 59 CP40
Wroxham Rd.
Ormesby Dr., Pot.B. 19 BQ19
Ormesby Way, Har. 46 BL32
Ormiston Gro. W12 55 BP40
Ormiston Rd. SE10 68 CH42
Ormond Ave., Hmptn. 84 BF51
Ormond Ave., Rich. 74 BK46
Ormond Rd.
Ormond Clo. WC1 2 A6
Ormond Cres., Hmptn. 84 BF51
Ormond Dr., Hmptn. 74 BF50
Ormond Ms. WC1 2 A5
Ormond Ms. WC1 56 BX38
Guilford St.
Ormond Rd. N19 47 BX33
Ormond Rd., Rich. 74 BK46
Ormond Yd. SW1 3 M2
Ormond Yd. SW1 56 BW40
Duke of York St.
Ormonde Ave., Epsom 94 BN58
Ormonde Ave., Orp. 88 CM55
Ormonde Ct. SW15 65 BQ45
Upper Richmond Rd.
Ormonde Gate SW3 66 BU42
Ormonde Pl. SW1 3 G9
Ormonde Pl. SW1 66 BV42
Bourne St.
Ormonde Ri., Buck.H. 40 CJ26
Ormonde Rd. SW14 65 BM45
Ormonde Rd., Nthwd. 35 BA28
Ormonde Rd., Wok. 100 AR61
Ormonde Ter. NW8 56 BU37
Ormsby Gdns., Grnf. 54 BG37
Ormsby Pl. N16 48 CD34
Victorian Gro.
Ormsby St. E2 2 P1
Ormsby St. E2 57 CA37
Ormside St. SE15 67 CC43
Ormside Way, Red. 121 BV69
Ormskirk Rd., Wat. 36 BD28
Ornan Rd. NW3 47 BU35
Oronsay, Hem.H. 8 AZ14
Oronsay Wk. N1 57 BZ36
Orphanage Rd., Wat. 27 BD23
Orpheus St. SE5 67 BZ44
Orpin Rd., Red. 113 BV68
Orpington By-Pass, Orp. 98 CP56
Orpington Gdns. N18 39 CA27
Orpington Rd. N21 38 BY26
Orpington Rd., Chis. 88 CN51
Orpwood Clo., Hmptn. 74 BE50
Orris Ms. W6 65 BQ42
Beadon Rd.
Orsett Heath Cres., Grays 71 DG41
Orsett Rd., Grays 71 DD42
Orsett St. SE11 4 C10
Orsett St. SE11 66 BX42
Orsett Ter. W2 56 BS39
Orsett Ter., Wdf.Grn. 40 CJ29
Orsman Rd. N1 57 CA37
Orton Clo., St.Alb. 9 BJ11
Runcie Clo.
Orton St. E1 57 CB40
Hermitage Wall
Orville Rd. SW11 66 BT44
Orwell Clo., Rain. 59 CS39
Orwell Clo., Wind. 61 AO45
Orwell Ct. N5 48 BZ35
Orwell Rd. E13 58 CJ37
Osbaldeston Rd. N16 48 CA34
Osbert St. SW1 3 N9
Osbert St. SW1 66 BW42
Vincent Sq.
Osberton Rd. SE12 78 CH46
Osborn Clo. E8 57 CB37
Osborn Gdns. NW7 37 BQ29
Osborn La. SE23 77 CD47
Brockley Pk.
Osborn St. E1 2 Q7
Osborn St. E1 57 CA39
Osborn Ter. SE3 68 CG45
Osborn Way, Welw.G.C. 5 BQ8
Osborne Ave., Stai. 73 AY47
Osborne Clo., Beck. 87 CD52
Osborne Clo., Felt. 74 BD49
Osborne Clo., Horn. 50 CU
Osborne Clo., Sutt. 95 BT
Albert Rd.
Osborne Gdns., Pot.B. 20 BS
Osborne Rd.
Osborne Gdns., Th.Hth. 87 BZ
Osborne Gro. E17 48 CD
Osborne Ms., Wind. 61 AC
Osborne Pl., Sutt. 95 BT
Albert Rd.
Osborne Rd. E7 49 CH
Osborne Rd. E9 57 CD
Osborne Rd. E10 48 CE
Osborne Rd. N4 47 BY
Osborne Rd. N13 38 BY
Osborne Rd. NW2 55 BP
Osborne Rd. W3 65 BM
Osborne Rd., Belv. 69 CC
Osborne Rd., Brwd. 33 DA
Osborne Rd., Brox. 12 CE
Osborne Rd., Buck.H. 40 CH
Osborne Rd., Dag. 50 CC
Osborne Rd., Egh. 72 AS
Osborne Rd., Enf. 30 CD
Osborne Rd., Horn. 50 CU
Osborne Rd., Houns. 64 BE
Osborne Rd., Kings.T. 75 BL
Osborne Rd., Pot.B. 20 BS
Osborne Rd., Red. 121 BV
Osborne Rd., Sthl. 54 BF
Osborne Rd., Th.Hth. 87 BZ
Osborne Rd., Uxb. 53 AX
Oxford Rd.
Osborne Rd., Wal.Cr. 21 CD
Osborne Rd., Walt. 83 BC
Osborne Rd., Wat. 27 BD
Osborne Rd., Wind. 61 AC
Osborne Sq., Dag. 50 CQ
Osborne St. SE17 67 BZ
Osborne St., Slou. 62 AP
Osbourne Ave., Kings L. 17 AY
Oscar St. SE8 67 CE
Oseney Cres. NW5 47 BW
Osgood Ave., Orp. 97 CN
Osgood Gdns., Orp. 97 CN
O'Shea Gro. E3 57 CD
Osidge La. N14 38 BV
Osier St. E1 57 CC
Cephas Ave.
Osier Way E10 48 CE
Osier Way, Bans. 94 BP
Osier Way, Mitch. 86 BU
Osiers Rd. SW18 66 BS
Oslac Rd. SE6 77 CE
Oslo Ct. NW8 1
Oslo Ct. NW8 56 BU
Osman Clo. N15 48 BZ
Tewkesbury Rd.
Osman Rd. N9 39 CB
Osmond Clo., Har. 45 BG
Osmond Gdns., Wall. 95 BW
Osmund St. W12 55 BO
Braybrook St.
Osnaburgh St. NW1 1
Osnaburgh St. NW1 56 BV
Osnaburgh Ter. NW1 1
Osnaburgh Ter. NW1 56 BV
Osnaburgh St.
Osney Wk., Cars. 86 BT
Osney Way, Grav. 81 DJ
Osprey Clo. E6 58 CK
Dove App.
Osprey Clo. E11 49 CH
Osprey Clo., Lthd. 102 BG
Osprey Clo., Wat. 18 BE
Osprey Clo., West Dr. 63 AY
Osprey Gdns., S.Croy. 96 CC
Osprey Ms., Enf. 30 CB
Derby Rd.
Ospringe Clo. SE20 87 CC
Ospringe Ct. SE9 78 CM
Ospringe Rd. NW5 47 BW
Osric Path N1 2 N
Osric Path N1 57 CA
Ossian Rd. N4 47 BX
Ossington Bldgs. W1 1
Ossington Bldgs. W1 56 BV
Moxon St.
Ossington Clo. W2 56 BS
Ossington St.
Ossington St. W2 56 BS
Ossory Rd. SE1 67 CB
Ossulston St. NW1 1
Ossulston St. NW1 56 BW
Ossulton Pl. N2 47 BT
Ossulton Way
Ossulton Way N2 47 BT
Ostade Rd. SW2 76 BX
Osten Ms. SW7 66 BS
Oster St., St.Alb. 9 BG
Osterberg Rd., Dart. 70 CW
Osterley Ave., Islw. 64 BG
Osterley Clo., Orp. 88 CO
Leith Hill
Osterley Ct., Islw. 64 BG
Osterley Cres., Islw. 64 BH
Osterley Gdns., Th.Hth. 87 BZ
Osterley La., Sthl. 64 BF
Osterley Pk. Rd., Sthl. 64 BE
Osterley Pk. Vw. Rd. W7 64 BH
Osterley Rd. N16 48 CA
Osterley Rd., Islw. 64 BH
Ostliffe Rd. N13 39 BZ
Oswald Clo., Lthd. 102 BG
Oswald Rd., Lthd. 102 BG
Oswald Rd., St.Alb. 9 BH1
Oswald Rd., Sthl. 54 BE
Oswald St. E5 48 CC
Oswalds Mead E9 48 CD
Kings Mead Est.
Osward, Croy. 96 CD
Osward Pl. N9 39 CB
Osward Rd. SW17 76 BU
Oswin St. SE11 4 G

win St. SE11 66 BY42
wyth Rd. SE5 67 CA44
ford Clo., Bex. 79 CR46
ford Clo., Brom. 88 CL52
ford Cres. SE4 77 CD46
ford La., Sev. 98 CQ59
ford Rd., Sev. 107 CU63
hello Clo. SE11 4 F10
hello Clo. SE11 66 BY42
s St. E3 57 CF38
ey App., Ilf. 49 CL32
ey Dr., Ilf. 49 CL32
ey Rd. E16 58 CJ39
ey Rd., Chesh. 16 AP18
ey Ter. E5 48 CC34
ey Way, Wat. 36 BD27
inge Clo., Orp. 89 CP52
tawa Gdns., Dag. 59 CS36
tawa Rd., Til. 71 DG44
taway St. E5 48 CB34
ter Gdns., Hat. 10 BP13
ter Rd., Grnf. 54 BG38
terbourne Rd. E4 39 CF27
terbourne Rd., Croy. 86 BY55
uskin Rd.
terburn Gdns., Islw. 64 BJ43
terburn St. SW17 76 BU50
terden Clo., Orp. 97 CN56
terden St. SE6 77 CE49
terfield Rd., West Dr. 53 AY40
termead La., Cher. 91 AU57
terspool La., Wat. 27 BE22
terspool Way, Wat. 27 BE23
to Clo. SE26 77 CB48
to St. SE17 66 BY43
toman Ter., Wat. 27 BD24
bury Rd.
tways Ave., Ash. 102 BK63
tways La., Ash. 102 BK63
ways Clo., Pot.B. 20 BS19
ilton Clo. E5 48 CB34
Southwold Rd.
ilton Clo. SE28 59 CP40
ollesby Way
ilton Cres, Bark. 49 CN35
ilton Cres., Pot.B. 19 BQ19
ilton Rd. N15 48 BZ32
ilton Way, Wat. 36 BE28
undle Ave., Bush. 27 BG25
usden Clo., Chsnt. 21 CD18
usden Dr., Chsnt. 21 CD18
useley Rd. SW12 76 BU47
useley Rd., Wind. 72 AR47
uter Circle NW1 56 BV38
utfield Rd., Ger.Cr. 34 AR29
utgate Rd. NW10 55 BO36
utings La., Brwd. 33 DA21
utlook Dr., Ch.St.G. 34 AR27
utram Pl. N1 56 BX37
utram Pl., Wey. 92 BA56
St. Georges Ave.
utram Rd. E6 58 CK37
utram Rd. N22 38 BW30
utram Rd., Croy. 87 CA55
utram St. N1 56 BX37
utwich St. EC3 2 N8
utwich St. EC3 57 CA39
Houndsditch
utwood La., Couls. 104 BU63
utwood La., Red. 114 BZ71
utwood La., Tad. 104 BS64
val, The E2 57 CB37
val, The, Bans. 95 BS60
val, The, Brox. 12 CD15
val, The, Guil. 118 AQ71
val, The, Sid. 79 CO47
val Ct., Edg. 37 BM29
Pavilion Way
val Gdns., Grays 71 DE41
val Pl. SW8 66 BX43
val Rd. NW1 56 BV37
val Rd., Croy. 87 BZ55
val Rd. N., Dag. 59 CR37
val Rd. S., Dag. 59 CR37
val Way SE11 66 BX42
val Way, Ger.Cr. 43 AS31
venden Rd., Sev. 107 CP63
ver The Misbourne, Ger.Cr. 43 AT32
verbrae, Beck. 77 CE50
verbrook, Lthd. 110 AZ68
verbrook Wk., Edg. 37 BM29
Chandos Cres.
verbury Ave., Beck. 87 CE52
verbury Cres., Croy. 96 CF58
verbury Rd. N15 48 BZ32
verbury St. E5 48 CC35
vercliff Rd. SE13 67 CE45
vercliff Rd., Grays 71 DE42
vercliffe, Grav. 81 DF46
vercourt Clo., Sid. 79 CO46
Blackfen Rd.
verdale, Ash. 103 BL61
verdale, Dor. 119 BK71
verdale, Red. 114 BZ70
verdale Ave., N.Mal. 85 BN51
verdale Rd. W5 64 BK41
verdown Rd. SE6 77 CE49
verhill, Whyt. 105 CC63
verhill Gdns. SE22 77 CB47
verhill Rd. SE22 77 CB47
verhill Rd., Pur. 95 BY58
verhill Way, Beck. 87 CF53
verlea Rd. E5 48 CB33
vermead, Sid. 78 CM47
vermead, Swan. 89 CT53
verstand Clo., Beck. 87 CE53
verstone Gdns., Croy. 87 CD54
verstone Rd. W6 65 BQ41
verstream, Rick. 26 AW24
verthorpe Clo., Wok. 100 AP62
verton Clo. NW10 55 BN36
verton Clo., Islw. 64 BH44

Overton Dr. E11 49 CH33
Overton Dr., Rom. 50 CP33
Overton Rd. E10 48 CD33
Overton Rd. N14 29 BX25
Overton Rd. SE2 69 CP41
Overton Rd. SW9 66 BY44
Overton Rd., Sutt. 95 BS57
Overton Rd. E. SE2 69 CP41
Overton Rd.
Overtons Yd., Croy. 87 BZ55
Overy Liberty, Dart. 80 CW47
Overy St., Dart. 80 CW46
Ovesdon Ave., Har. 45 BE33
Oveton Way, Lthd. 111 BF66
Ovett Clo. SE19 77 CA50
Westow St.
Ovex Clo. E14 67 CF41
Ovington Ct., Wok. 100 AP61
Roundthorne Way
Ovington Gdns. SW3 3 D7
Ovington Gdns. SW3 66 BU41
Ovington Ms. SW3 3 D7
Ovington Ms. SW3 66 BU41
Ovington Sq. SW3 3 D7
Ovington Sq. SW3 66 BU41
Ovington St. SW3 3 D7
Ovington St. SW3 66 BU42
Owen Clo. SE28 59 CP40
Owen Clo., Hayes 53 BC38
Owen Gdns., Wdf.Grn. 40 CK29
Owen Pl., Lthd. 102 BJ64
Church Rd.
Owen Rd. N13 39 BZ28
Owen Rd., Hayes 53 BC38
Owen St. EC1 2 E1
Owen Wk. SE20 87 CB51
Sycamore Gro.
Owen Way NW10 46 BN35
Owenite St. SE2 69 CO42
Owens Ct. EC1 2 F2
Owens Ct. EC1 56 BY38
Goswell Rd.
Owens Row EC1 2 F2
Owens Way SE23 77 CD47
Brockley Pk.
Owens Way, Rick. 26 AZ24
Owgan Clo. SE5 67 BZ43
Benhill Rd.
Owl Clo., S.Croy. 96 CC58
Kingfisher Gdns.
Owlets Hall Clo., Rom. 51 CW31
Ownstead Gdns., S.Croy. 96 CA59
Ownstead Hill, Croy. 96 CF58
Ox La., Epsom 94 BP58
Oxberry Ave. SW6 65 BR44
Oxdowne Clo., Cob. 93 BF60
Oxenden Dr., Hodd. 12 CE12
Oxenden Wd. Rd., Orp. 98 CO57
Oxendon St. SW1 3 N1
Oxendon St. SW1 56 BW40
Oxenford St. SE15 67 CA45
Oxenhill Rd., Sev. 108 CW62
Oxenholme NW1 1 M1
Oxenpark Ave., Wem. 46 BL33
Oxestalls Rd. SE8 67 CD42
Oxfield Clo., Berk. 7 AQ13
Oxford Ave. SW20 85 BR51
Oxford Ave., Grays 71 DG42
Oxford Ave., Hayes 63 BB43
Oxford Ave., Horn. 51 CX31
Oxford Ave., Houns. 64 BF43
Oxford Ave., St.Alb. 9 BK14
Oxford Circ. Ave. W1 1 L9
Oxford Clo. N9 39 CB27
Oxford Clo., Ashf. 73 BA50
Oxford Clo., Chsnt. 21 CC18
Oxford Clo., Grav. 81 DJ48
Oxford Clo., Mitch. 86 BW52
Oxford Ct. EC4 2 K10
Oxford Ct., Brwd. 42 DB28
Oxford Ct., Felt. 74 BD49
Oxford Cres., N.Mal. 85 BN53
Oxford Dr., Ruis. 45 BD34
Oxford Gdns. N20 38 BT26
Oxford Gdns. N21 39 BZ26
Oxford Gdns. W4 65 BM42
Oxford Gdns. W10 55 BQ39
Oxford Gdns., Uxb. 44 AW34
Oxford La., Guil. 118 AR71
Oxford Ms., Bex. 79 CR47
Bexley High St.
Oxford Rd. E15 57 CF36
Oxford Rd. N4 47 BY33
Oxford Rd. N9 39 CB27
Oxford Rd. NW6 56 BS37
Oxford Rd. SE19 77 BZ50
Oxford Rd. SW15 65 BR45
Oxford Rd. W5 54 BK40
Oxford Rd., Cars. 95 BU57
Oxford Rd., Cat. 114 CA66
Oxford Rd., Enf. 30 CB25
Oxford Rd., Ger.Cr. 43 AO31
Oxford Rd., Guil. 118 AR71
Oxford Rd., Har. 45 BG32
Oxford Rd., Ilf. 49 CM35
Oxford Rd., Red. 121 BU70
Oxford Rd., Rom. 42 CW29
Oxford Rd., Sid. 79 CO49
Oxford Rd., Tedd. 74 BG49
Oxford Rd., Uxb. 53 AX36
Oxford Rd. (Denham), Uxb. 44 AW34
Oxford Rd., Wall. 95 BW56
Oxford Rd., Wdf.Grn. 40 CJ28
Oxford Rd. N. W4 65 BM42
Oxford Rd. S. W4 65 BM42
Oxford Sq. W2 1 D9
Oxford Sq. W2 56 BU39
Oxford St. W1 1 G9
Oxford St. W1 56 BV39
Oxford St., Bark. 58 CL36
Oxford St., Wat. 26 BC25
Oxford Way, Cat. 114 CA66
Oxford Way, Felt. 74 BD49

Oxgate Gdns. NW2 46 BP34
Oxgate La. NW2 46 BP34
Oxhawth Cres., Brom. 88 CL53
Oxhey Ave., Wat. 36 BD26
Oxhey Dr., Nthwd. 35 BC28
Oxhey La., Wat. 36 BE26
Oxhey Ridge Clo., Nthwd. 35 BC28
Oxhey Rd., Wat. 27 BD25
Oxleas Clo., Well. 68 CM44
Oxlease Dr., Hat. 10 BP13
Oxleay Ct., Har. 45 BF33
Oxleay Rd., Har. 45 BF33
Oxleigh Clo., N.Mal. 85 BO53
Oxley Clo. SE1 4 Q10
Oxley Clo., Rom. 42 CV30
Oxleys, The, Harl. 6 CQ9
Oxleys Rd. NW2 46 BP34
Oxleys Rd., Wal.Abb. 22 CH20
Oxlip Clo., Croy. 87 CC54
Marigold Way
Oxlow La., Dag. 50 CQ35
Oxonian St. SE22 67 CA45
Oxshott Ave., Cob. 102 BF61
Oxshott Ri., Cob. 93 BE60
Oxshott Way, Cob. 102 BE61
Oxted Clo., Mitch. 86 BT52
Oxted Rd., Gdse. 114 CC68
Oxtoby Way SW16 86 BW51
Oyster Hill, Epsom 103 BN65
Oyster La., Wey. 92 AY59
Oyster Row E1 57 CC39
Ozolins Way E16 58 CG39

P

Pace Pl. E1 57 CB39
Paceheath Clo., Rom. 41 CS29
Pachesham Dr., Lthd. 102 BH61
Pachesham Pk., Lthd. 102 BJ61
Pacific Rd. E16 58 CH39
Packe Cres., Ruis. 44 BA32
Bury St.
Packet Boat La., Uxb. 53 AX39
Packham Clo., Orp. 89 CP55
Berrylands
Packham Rd., Grav. 81 DF48
Packhorse Clo., St.Alb. 9 BK11
Packhorse La., Borwd. 19 BN20
Packhorse La., Borwd. 28 BO22
Packhorse La., Pot.B. 19 BN18
Packhorse Path, Stai. 72 AV49
South St.
Packhorse Rd., Ger.Cr. 43 AS31
Packhorse Rd., Sev. 107 CS65
Packington Sq. N1 57 BZ37
Packington St. N1 56 BY37
Packmores Rd. SE9 78 CM46
Padbrook, Oxt. 115 CH68
Padbury Ct. E2 2 Q3
Padbury Ct. E2 57 CA38
Padcroft Rd., West Dr. 53 AX40
Paddenswick Ct. W6 65 BP41
Paddenswick Rd.
Paddenswick Rd. W6 65 BP41
Paddick Clo., Hodd. 12 CD11
Paddington Clo., Hayes 54 BD38
Paddington Grn. W2 1 B6
Paddington Grn. W2 56 BT39
Paddington St. W1 1 G6
Paddington St. W1 56 BV39
Paddock, The, Brox. 12 CE13
Paddock, The, Dor. 119 BG72
Paddock, The, Ger.Cr. 34 AS28
Paddock, The, Guil. 118 AU70
Paddock, The, Hat. 10 BP11
Lemsford Rd.
Paddock, The, Slou. 62 AQ44
Paddock, The, Uxb. 44 AZ35
Paddock, The, West. 115 CM66
Paddock Clo. SE3 68 CH44
Paddock Clo. SE26 77 CC49
Paddock Clo., Har. 45 BF35
Paddock Clo., Nthlt. 54 BF37
Paddock Clo., Orp. 97 CL56
State Fm. Ave.
Paddock Clo., Oxt. 115 CG69
Paddock Clo., S.Dnth. 90 CY51
Paddock Clo., Wor.Pk. 85 BO54
Paddock Gdns. SE19 77 CA50
Paddock Mead, Harl. 13 CM13
Paddock Rd. NW2 46 BP34
Paddock Rd., Bexh. 69 CQ45
Paddock Rd., Ruis. 45 BD34
Paddock Wk., Warl. 105 CB63
Paddock Way, Chis. 78 CM50
Paddock Way, Hem.H. 7 AV13
Paddock Way, Oxt. 115 CG69
Paddock Way, Wok. 91 AT60
Paddocks, Cob. 93 BD60
Paddocks, The, Barn. 29 BU24
Paddocks, The, Croy. 96 CE56
Addington Village Rd.
Paddocks, The, Lthd. 111 BF66
Leatherhead Rd.
Paddocks, The, Lthd. 111 BF66
Paddocks, The, Rick. 25 AV24
Paddocks, The, Welw.G.C. 5 BS7
Brooksfield
Paddocks, The, Wem. 46 BM34
Paddocks, The, Wey. 83 BB55
Paddocks Clo., Ash. 103 BL62
Paddocks Clo., Orp. 89 CP55
Paddocks Mead, Wok. 100 AP61
Paddocks Rd., Guil. 109 AT68
Paddocks Way, Ash. 103 BL62
Paddocks Way, Cher. 83 AW54
Padfield Rd. SE5 67 BZ45
Padgets, The, Wal.Abb. 22 CG20
Honey La.

Padnall Rd., Rom. 50 CP31
Padstow Clo., Slou. 62 AS41
St. Marys Rd.
Padstow Rd., Enf. 29 BY23
Padua Rd. SE20 87 CC51
Pagden St. SW8 66 BV44
Page Clo., Dag. 50 CQ35
Page Clo., Dart. 80 DB48
Page Clo., Hmptn. 74 BE50
Page Clo., Har. 46 BL32
Page Cres., Croy. 95 BY57
Page Cres., Erith 69 CT43
Page Gdns., Chis. 88 CL51
Page Grn. Rd. N15 48 CB32
Page Grn. Ter. N15 48 CA32
Page Heath La., Brom. 88 CJ52
Page Heath Vill., Brom. 88 CJ52
Page Meadow NW7 37 BP29
Page Rd., Felt. 73 BA46
Page St. NW7 37 BP29
Page St. SW1 3 P8
Page St. SW1 66 BW42
Pageant Clo., Til. 71 DG44
Pageant Rd., St.Alb. 9 BG14
Pageant Wk., Croy. 87 CA55
Pagehurst Rd., Croy. 87 CB54
Pages Cft., Berk. 7 AQ12
Pages Hill N10 38 BV30
Pages La. N10 38 BV30
Pages La., Rom. 42 CX30
Pages La., Uxb. 53 AX36
Pages Wk. SE1 4 M8
Pages Wk. SE1 67 CA42
Pages Yd. W4 65 BO43
Church St.
Paget Ave., Sutt. 86 BT55
Paget Clo., Hmptn. 74 BG49
Paget La., Islw. 64 BH45
Paget Pl., Kings.T. 75 BN50
Paget Ri. SE18 68 CL43
Paget Rd. N16 48 BZ33
Paget Rd., Ilf. 49 CL35
Paget Rd., Slou. 62 AS42
Paget Rd., Uxb. 53 BA38
Paget St. EC1 2 F2
Paget St. EC1 56 BY38
Paget Ter. SE18 68 CL43
Pagette Way, Grays 71 DD42
Pagitts Gro., Barn. 29 BS23
Paglesfield, Brwd. 122 DE25
Rayleigh Rd.
Pagnell St. SE14 67 CD43
Pagoda Ave., Rich. 65 BL45
Pagoda Gdns. SE3 67 CF44
Paignton Rd. N15 48 CA32
Paignton Rd., Ruis. 44 BC34
Paines Brook Rd., Rom. 42 CW29
Paines Brook Way, Rom. 42 CW29
Paines Clo., Pnr. 45 BE31
Paines Hill, Oxt. 115 CJ69
Paines La., Pnr. 36 BE30
Pains Clo., Mitch. 86 BV51
Painsthorpe Rd. N16 48 CA34
Oldfield Rd.
Painters Ash La., Grav. 81 DE48
Painters La., Enf. 30 CD21
Painters Rd., Ilf. 49 CN31
Paisley Rd. N22 38 BY30
Paisley Rd., Cars. 86 BT54
Pakeman St. N7 47 BX34
Pakenham Clo. SW12 76 BV47
Balham Pk. Rd.
Pakenham St. WC1 2 C3
Pakenham St. WC1 56 BX38
Pakes Way, Epp. 31 CN22
Palace Ave. W8 56 BS40
Palace Clo., Kings L. 17 AY18
Palace Ct. W2 56 BS40
Palace Ct., Brom. 88 CH51
Palace Ct., Har. 46 BL32
Palace Ct. Gdns. N10 38 BW30
Palace Dr., Wey. 83 AZ55
Palace Gdn. Ms. W8 56 BS40
Palace Gdns., Buck.H. 40 CJ26
Palace Gdns., Enf. 30 BZ24
Palace Gdns. Ter. W8 56 BS40
Palace Gate W8 66 BT41
Palace Gates Rd. N22 38 BW30
Palace Grn., Croy. 96 CD57
Palace Gro. SE19 77 CA50
Palace Gro., Brom. 88 CH51
Palace Ms. SW1 3 H9
Palace Ms., Enf. 30 BZ24
Palace Gdns.
Palace Pl. SW1 3 L6
Palace Pl. SW1 66 BW41
Palace St.
Palace Rd. N8 47 BW32
Palace Rd. N11 38 BW29
Palace Rd. SE19 77 CA50
Palace Rd. SW2 76 BX47
Palace Rd., Brom. 88 CH51
Palace Rd., E.Mol. 84 BG52
Palace Rd., Kings.T. 84 BK52
Palace Rd., Ruis. 45 BE35
Palace Rd., West. 106 CL64
Palace Sq. SE19 77 CA50
Palace St. SW1 3 L6
Palace St. SW1 66 BW41
Palace Vw. SE12 78 CH48
Palace Vw., Brom. 88 CH52
Palace Vw., Croy. 87 CD55
Palace Vw. Rd. E4 39 CE28
Palace Way, Wey. 83 BA55
Palace Dr.
Palamos Rd. E10 48 CE33
Palatine Rd. N16 48 CA35
Palermo Rd. NW10 55 BP37
Palestine Gro. SW19 86 BT51
Palewell Clo., Orp. 89 CO51
Palewell Common Dr. SW14 75 BN46
Palewell Pk. SW14 75 BN46
Paley Gdns., Loug. 31 CL24

Palfrey Clo., St.Alb. 9 BG12
Palfrey Pl. SW8 66 BX43
Palgrave Ave., Sthl. 54 BF40
Palgrave Rd. W12 65 BO41
Palins Way, Grays 71 DD40
Palissy St. E2 2 P3
Palissy St. E2 57 CA38
Pall Mall SW1 3 M3
Pall Mall SW1 56 BW40
Pall Mall E. SW1 3 P2
Pall Mall E. SW1 56 BW40
Pall Mall Pl. SW1 3 M3
Pall Mall Pl. SW1 56 BW40
Pallas Rd., Hem.H. 8 AY12
Paller Way SE18 68 CJ44
Tellson Ave.
Palliser Rd. W14 65 BR42
Palliser Rd., Ch.St.G. 34 AQ27
Palm Ave., Sid. 79 CP50
Palm Gro. W5 65 BL41
Palm Gro., Guil. 109 AR68
Palm Rd., Rom. 50 CS32
Palmar Cres., Bexh. 69 CR45
Palmar Rd., Bexh. 69 CR44
Palmarsh Clo., Orp. 89 CP52
Palmeira Rd., Bexh. 69 CP45
Palmer Ave., Bush. 27 BF25
Palmer Ave., Grav. 81 DH49
Palmer Ave., Sutt. 94 BQ56
Palmer Clo., Houns. 64 BF44
Palmer Clo., Red. 121 BV71
Palmer Cres., Cher. 91 AU57
Palmer Cres., Kings.T. 85 BL52
Palmer Pl. N7 47 BY35
Palmer Rd. E13 58 CH38
Palmer Rd., Dag. 50 CP33
Palmer St. SW1 3 N6
Palmer St. SW1 66 BW41
Palmers Ave., Grays 71 DE42
Palmers Dr., Grays 71 DE42
Palmers Gdns., Barn. 28 BQ25
Palmers Gro., E.Mol. 84 BF52
Palmers Gro., Wal.Abb. 13 CG14
Palmers La., Enf. 30 CB23
Palmers Moor La., Iver 53 AW38
Palmers Orchard, Sev. 98 CT59
Palmers Pas. SW14 65 BN45
Palmers Rd.
Palmers Rd. E2 57 CC37
Palmers Rd. N11 38 BW28
Palmers Rd. SW14 65 BN45
Palmers Rd. SW16 86 BX51
Palmers Rd., Borwd. 28 BM23
Palmers Way, Chsnt. 21 CD18
Palmersfield Rd., Bans. 95 BS60
Palmerston Ave., Slou. 62 AQ41
Palmerston Clo., Welw.G.C. 5 BQ8
Palmerston Clo., Wok. 91 AS60
Palmerston Cres. N13 38 BX28
Palmerston Cres. SE18 68 CM43
Palmerston Gdns., Grays 70 DB42
Grays
Palmerston Gro. SW19 76 BS50
Palmerston Rd. E7 49 CH35
Palmerston Rd. E17 48 CD31
Palmerston Rd. N22 38 BX29
Palmerston Rd. NW6 56 BS36
Palmerston Rd. SE18 68 CM43
Palmerston Rd. SW14 65 BN45
Palmerston Rd. SW19 76 BS50
Palmerston Rd. W3 65 BN41
Palmerston Rd., Buck.H. 40 CH27
Palmerston Rd., Cars. 95 BU56
Palmerston Rd., Grays 70 DB43
Palmerston Rd., Har. 45 BH31
Palmerston Rd., Orp. 97 CM56
Palmerston Rd., Rain. 60 CV37
Palmerston Rd., Sutt. 95 BT56
Palmerston Rd., Th.Hth. 87 BZ53
Palmerston Rd., Twick. 74 BH46
Palmerston Way SW8 66 BV43
Bradmead
Pamber St. W10 55 BQ39
Pamela Ave., Hem.H. 8 AY15
Pamela Gdns., Pur. 44 BC32
Pampisford Rd., Pur. 95 BY59
Pams Way, Epsom 94 BN56
Pancake La., Hem.H. 8 BA14
Pancras La. EC4 2 J9
Pancras La. EC4 57 BZ39
Queen Victoria St.
Pancras Rd. NW1 56 BW37
Pancroft, Rom. 32 CO24
Pandora Rd. NW6 56 BS36
Panfield Ms., Ilf. 49 CL32
Panfield Rd. SE2 69 CO41
Pangbourne Ave. W10 55 BQ39
Pangbourne Dr., Stan. 37 BL28
Pankhurst Clo. SE14 67 CC44
Briant St.
Pankhurst Rd., Walt. 84 BD54
Panmuir Rd. SW20 85 BP51
Panmure Clo. N5 47 BY35
Panmure Rd. SE26 77 CB48
Pannard Pl., Sthl. 54 BF40
Panshanger Dr., Welw.G.C. 5 BS8
Pansy Gdns. W12 55 BP40
Panters, Swan. 79 CT50
Pantile Rd., Wey. 92 BA56
Pantile Row, Slou. 62 AT42
Pantile Wk., Uxb. 53 AX36
High St.
Pantiles, The NW11 46 BR31
Pantiles, The, Bexh. 69 CQ43
Pantiles, The, Brom. 88 CJ52
Pantiles, The, Bush. 36 BG26
The Butts
Pantiles Clo., Wok. 100 AQ62
Panton St. SW1 3 N1
Panton St. SW1 56 BW40
Haymarket
Panxworth Rd., Hem.H. 8 AX14

Panyer All. EC4 2 H8
Panyer All. EC4 56 BY39
Newgate St.
Paper Ms., Dor. 119 BJ71
Papercourt La., Wok. 100 AU64
Papillons Wk. SE3 68 CH45
Papworth Gdns. N7 47 BX35
Chill Rd.
Papworth Way SW2 76 BY47
Parade, The N4 47 BY33
Stroud Grn. La.
Parade, The NW6 56 BS37
Kilburn High Rd.
Parade, The, Brwd. 42 DB27
King Edward Rd.
Parade, The, Dart. 79 CT46
Crayford Way
Parade, The, Epsom 94 BN60
Parade, The, Esher 93 BH57
Parade, The, Guil. 109 AQ68
Parade, The, Hat. 10 BQ11
Parade, The, S.Ock. 70 CY41
Parade, The, Sun. 73 BB50
Parade, The, Wind. 61 AL44
Parade Mans. NW4 46 BP32
Parade Ms. SE27 76 BY48
Norwood Rd.
Paradise Clo. W8 66 BS41
Adam & Eve Ms.
Paradise Clo., Chsnt. 21 CB17
Paradise Cotts., Rich. 75 BL46
Paradise Rd.
Paradise Hill, Brox. 21 CB16
Paradise Pas. N7 47 BY35
Paradise Pl. SE18 68 CK42
Samuel St.
Paradise Rd. SW4 66 BX44
Paradise Rd., Rich. 74 BK46
Paradise Row E2 57 CB38
Bethnal Grn. Rd.
Paradise Row, Wal.Abb. 21 CF20
Paradise St. SE16 67 CB41
Paradise Wk. SW3 66 BU43
Paradise Wd. La., Hem.H. 8 AX14
Paragon, The SE3 68 CG44
Paragon Gro., Surb. 85 BL53
Paragon Ms. SE1 4 L8
Paragon Pl. SE3 68 CG44
Paragon Pl., Surb. 85 BL53
Paragon Rd. E9 57 CB36
Paragon Row SE17 67 BZ42
Parbury Ri., Chess. 94 BL57
Parbury Rd. SE23 77 CD46
Parchment Clo., Amer. 25 AP22
Chestnut La.
Parchmore Rd., Th.Hth. 86 BY51
Parchmore Way, Th.Hth. 86 BY51
Pardon St. EC1 2 G4
Pardon St. EC1 56 BY38
Dallington St.
Pardoner St. SE1 4 L6
Pardoner St. SE1 67 BZ41
Pares Clo., Wok. 100 AR61
Parfett St. E1 57 CB39
Parfour Dr., Ken. 105 BZ61
Abbots La.
Parfrey St. W6 65 BQ43
Parham Dr., Ilf. 49 CL32
Parham Way N10 38 BW30
Paringdon Rd., Harl. 13 CL13
Paris Gdn. SE1 4 F2
Paris Gdn. SE1 56 BY40
Parish Clo., Horn. 50 CU34
Steed Clo.
Parish Gate Dr., Sid. 78 CN46
Parish La. SE20 77 CC50
Parish La., Slou. 43 AO34
Parish Ms. SE20 77 CC50
Parish La.
Park, The N6 47 BV32
Park, The NW11 47 BS33
Park, The SE19 77 CA50
Park, The W5 54 BK40
Park, The, Cars. 95 BU56
Park, The, Lthd. 102 BF65
Park, The, St.Alb. 9 BJ12
Park, The, Sid. 79 CO49
Park App., Well. 69 CO45
Park Ave. E6 58 CL37
Park Ave. E15 58 CG36
Park Ave. N3 38 BS30
Park Ave. N13 38 BY27
Park Ave. N18 39 CB28
Park Ave. N22 38 BX30
Park Ave. NW2 55 BP36
Park Ave. NW10 55 BL37
Park Ave. NW11 47 BS33
Park Ave. SW14 65 BN45
Park Ave., Bark. 58 CM36
Park Ave., Barn. 29 BT25
Park Ave., Brwd. 122 DE26
Park Ave., Brom. 78 CG50
Park Ave., Bush. 27 BD24
Park Ave., Cars. 95 BV57
Park Ave., Cat. 105 CA65
Park Ave., Egh. 72 AU50
Park Ave., Enf. 30 BZ25
Park Ave., Grav. 81 DH47
Park Ave. (Perry St.), Grav. 81 DF47
Park Ave., Grays 70 DA43
Park Ave., Harl. 14 CP12
Park Ave., Houns. 74 BF46
Park Ave., Ilf. 49 CL33
Park Ave., Mitch. 76 BV50
Park Ave., Orp. 89 CO55
Park Ave. (Farnborough), Orp. 88 CK55
Park Ave., Pot.B. 20 BT20
Park Ave., Rad. 18 BJ20
Park Ave., Rick. 26 AW25
Park Ave., Ruis. 44 BA32
Park Ave., St.Alb. 9 BJ13
Park Ave., Sthl. 64 BE41
Park Ave., Stai. 72 AV50
Park Ave. (Sunnymeads), Stai. 72 AR46
Park Ave., Upmin. 51 CZ33
Park Ave., Wat. 26 BC24
Park Ave., W.Wick. 87 CF55
Park Ave., Wdf.Grn. 40 CH28
Park Ave. E., Epsom 94 BP57
Park Ave. Ms., Mitch. 76 BV50
Park Ave.
Park Ave. N. N8 47 BW31
Park Ave. N. NW10 46 BP35
Park Ave. Rd. N17 39 CB29
Park Ave. S. N8 47 BW31
Park Ave. W., Epsom 94 BP57
Park Barn Dr., Guil. 118 AP69
Park Barn E., Guil. 118 AP70
Park Boul., Rom. 41 CT30
Park Chase, Guil. 118 AS70
Park Chase, Wem. 46 BL35
Park Clo. NW2 46 BP34
Park Clo. NW10 55 BL38
Park Clo. SW1 3 E5
Park Clo. SW1 66 BU41
Park Clo. W14 65 BR41
Park Clo., Bet. 120 BM73
Park Clo., Bush. 27 BD24
Park Clo., Cars. 95 BU57
Park Clo., Epp. 23 CR17
Park Clo., Esher 93 BF57
Park Clo., Hmptn. 84 BG51
Park Clo., Har. 36 BH30
Park Clo., Hat. 10 BQ12
Park Clo. (Brookmans Pk.), Hat. 20 BS16
Park Clo., Houns. 74 BG46
Park Clo., Lthd. 102 BG65
Park Clo., Rick. 35 AZ28
Park Clo., Walt. 83 BB55
Park Clo., Wey. 92 AW58
Park Clo., Wind. 61 AO44
Park Copse, Dor. 119 BK71
Park Cor., Wind. 61 AM45
Park Cor. Dr., Lthd. 110 BB67
Park Cor. Rd., Grav. 81 DC49
Park Ct. N12 38 BT28
Park Ct. SE21 77 BZ48
Park Ct., Beck. 87 CF52
Park Ct., Harl. 6 CN10
Park Ct., Kings.T. 84 BK51
Park Ct., Lthd. 111 BF66
Church Rd.
Park Ct., N.Mal. 85 BN52
Park Ct., Wall. 95 BX56
Park Ct., Wem. 46 BL35
Park Ct., Wok. 100 AS62
Park Cres. N3 38 BS29
Park Cres. W1 1 J5
Park Cres. W1 56 BV38
Park Cres., Borwd. 28 BL24
Park Cres., Enf. 30 BZ24
Park Cres., Erith 69 CS43
Park Cres., Har. 36 BH30
Park Cres., Hem.H. 8 AZ11
Park Cres., Horn. 50 CU33
Park Cres., Twick. 74 BG47
Park Cres. Ms. E. W1 1 K5
Park Cres. Ms. E. W1 56 BV38
Great Portland St.
Park Cres. Ms. W. W1 1 J5
Park Cres. Ms. W. W1 56 BV38
Park Cres. Rd., Erith 69 CS43
Park Cft., Edg. 37 BN30
Park Dr. N21 30 BZ25
Park Dr. NW11 47 BS33
Park Dr. SE7 68 CK42
Park Dr. SW14 65 BN45
Park Dr. W3 65 BM41
Park Dr., Dag. 50 CS34
Park Dr., Har. 45 BF33
Park Dr. (Harrow Weald), Har. 36 BH29
Park Dr., Long. 90 DC52
Park Dr., Pot.B. 20 BS19
Park Dr., Rom. 50 CS33
Park Dr., Upmin. 51 CX35
Park Dr., Wey. 92 AZ56
Park Dr., Wok. 100 AS62
Park Dr. Clo. SE7 68 CK42
Park End NW3 47 BU35
Park End, Brom. 88 CG51
Park End Rd., Rom. 50 CT31
Park Fm. Clo. N2 47 BT31
Park Fm. Clo., Pnr. 44 BC32
Park Fm. Rd., Brom. 88 CJ51
Park Fm. Rd., Kings.T. 75 BL50
Park Fm. Rd., Upmin. 51 CW35
Park Flds., Harl. 13 CH11
Park Gdn. Pl. W2 1 B9
Park Gdns. E10 48 CE33
Park Gdns. NW9 46 BM31
Park Gdns., Erith 69 CS42
Park Gdns., Kings.T. 75 BL50
Park Gate N2 47 BT31
Park Gate N21 38 BX26
Park Gate SE3 68 CG45
Park Gate W5 54 BK39
Mount Ave.
Park Grn., Lthd. 102 BF65
Park Gro. E15 58 CH37
Park Gro. N11 38 BW29
Park Gro., Bexh. 69 CS45
Park Gro., Brom. 88 CH51
Park Gro., Ch.St.G. 25 AR24
Park Gro., Edg. 37 BL28
Park Gro. Rd. E11 49 CG34
Park Hall Rd. N2 47 BU31
Park Hall Rd. SE21 77 BZ48
Park Hall Rd., Reig. 121 BS69
Park Hill SE23 77 CB48
Park Hill SW4 76 BW46
Park Hill W5 54 BK39
Park Hill, Brom. 88 CK52
Park Hill, Cars. 95 BU57
Park Hill, Harl. 6 CO9
Park Hill, Loug. 31 CJ25
Park Hill, Rich. 75 BL46
Park Hill Clo., Cars. 95 BU56
Park Hill Ct. SW17 76 BU48
Beeches Rd.
Park Hill Gdns., Croy. 87 CA55
Park Hill Rd.
Park Hill Ri., Croy. 87 CA55
Park Hill Rd., Brom. 87 CF51
Park Hill Rd., Croy. 87 CA55
Park Hill Rd., Hem.H. 8 AW13
Park Hill Rd., Sev. 108 CW62
Park Hill Rd., Sid. 78 CM48
Park Hill Rd., Wall. 95 BV57
Park Horsley, Lthd. 110 BC68
Park Ho. N21 38 BX26
Park Ho. Dr., Reig. 120 BR71
Park Ho. Gdns., Twick. 74 BK46
Park Ho. Pas. N6 47 BV33
Park La. E15 57 CF37
High St.
Park La. N9 39 CA27
Park La. N17 39 CB29
Park La. N18 39 CA27
Park La. W1 1 F10
Park La. W1 56 BU40
Park La., Brox. 12 CD13
Park La. (Wormley), Brox. 12 CB14
Park La., Cars. 95 BV56
Park La., Chsnt. 21 CB17
Park La., Couls. 104 BW64
Park La., Croy. 87 BZ55
Park La., Guil. 118 AU69
Park La., Harl. 6 CM10
Park La., Har. 45 BF34
Park La., Hayes 53 BB39
Park La., Hem.H. 8 AX14
Park La., Horn. 59 CU36
Park La., Houns. 63 BC43
Park La. (Cranford), Houns. 63 BC43
Park La., Reig. 120 BR71
Park La., Rich. 64 BK45
Park La., Rom. 50 CT32
Park La. (Chadwell Heath), Rom. 50 CP32
Park La., St.Alb. 10 BM15
Park La., Sev. 108 CV65
Park La. (Kemsing), Sev. 108 CX62
Park La. (Seal), Sev. 108 CX64
Park La., Slou. 62 AQ41
Park La. (Horton), Slou. 62 AT45
Park La., S.Ock. 60 CY40
Park La., Stan. 36 BJ27
Park La., Sutt. 94 BR57
Park La., Swan. 90 CV51
Park La., Tedd. 74 BH50
Park La., Uxb. 35 AW29
Park La., Wal.Cr. 21 CC20
Park La., Wem. 46 BL35
Park La. Clo. N17 39 CB29
Park La.
Park La. Paradise, Ash. 103 BL62
Park La. Paradise, Chsnt. 21 CB16
Park Lawn Ave., Epsom 94 BM60
Park Lawn Rd., Wey. 92 AZ56
Park Lawns, Wem. 46 BL35
Park Ley Rd., Cat. 105 CC63
Park Mans. NW4 46 BP32
Park Mead, Harl. 6 CL10
Park Mead, Har. 45 BF34
Park Mead, Sid. 79 CO46
Park Meadow, Brwd. 33 DB22
Park Meadow, Hat. 10 BQ12
Park Ms., Hmptn. 74 BG49
Park Ms., Hat. 10 BQ11
Park Nook Gdns., Enf. 30 BZ22
Park Par. NW10 55 BO37
Park Par. W3 65 BM41
Park Par., Pnr. 36 BE29
Park Pl. SW1 3 L3
Park Pl. SW1 56 BW40
Park Pl. W3 65 BM42
Park Pl. W5 54 BK40
Park Pl., Amer. 25 AP22
Park Pl., Hmptn. 74 BG50
Park Pl., Mitch. 86 BU52
Park Pl., St.Alb. 18 BG17
Park Pl., Sev. 107 CS65
Bessels Grn. Rd.
Park Pl., Wem. 46 BL35
Park Pl., Wind. 61 AO44
Kings Rd.
Park Pl. Gdns. W2 56 BT39
Park Pl. Vill.
Park Pl. Vill. W2 56 BT39
Park Ridings N8 47 BY31
Park Ri. SE23 77 CD47
St. Germans Rd.
Park Ri., Berk. 7 AP12
Park Ri., Har. 36 BH30
Park Ri., Lthd. 102 BJ64
Park Ri. Clo., Lthd. 102 BJ64
Park Ri. Rd. SE23 77 CD47
Park Rd. E6 58 CJ37
Park Rd. E10 48 CE33
Park Rd. E12 49 CH33
Park Rd. E15 58 CH37
Park Rd. E17 48 CD32
Park Rd. N2 47 BT31
Park Rd. N8 47 BW31
Park Rd. N11 38 BW29
Park Rd. N14 38 BW26
Park Rd. N15 47 BY31
Park Rd. N18 39 CA28
Park Rd. NW1 1 E4
Park Rd. NW1 56 BU38
Park Rd. NW4 46 BP33
Park Rd. NW8 1 C2
Park Rd. NW8 56 BU38
Park Rd. NW9 46 BN33
Park Rd. NW10 55 BN37
Park Rd. SE25 87 CA52
Park Rd. SW19 76 BT50
Park Rd. SW20 75 BP50
Park Rd. W4 65 BN43
Park Rd. W7 54 BH40
Park Rd., Amer. 25 AP22
Park Rd., Ashf. 73 AZ49
Park Rd., Ash. 103 BL62
Park Rd., Bans. 104 BS61
Park Rd., Barn. 28 BR24
Park Rd. (New Barnet), Barn. 29 BT24
Park Rd., Beck. 77 CD50
Park Rd., Brwd. 42 DA27
Park Rd., Brom. 88 CH51
Park Rd., Bush. 27 BF25
Park Rd., Cat. 105 CA65
Park Rd., Chis. 78 CL50
Park Rd., Dart. 80 CX47
Park Rd., E.Mol. 84 BG52
Park Rd., Egh. 72 AT49
Park Rd., Enf. 30 CD21
Park Rd., Esher 93 BF56
Park Rd., Felt. 74 BD49
Park Rd., Grav. 81 DG48
Park Rd., Grays 71 DD42
Park Rd., Guil. 118 AR70
Park Rd., Hmptn. 74 BF49
Park Rd., Hayes 53 BB39
Park Rd., Hem.H. 8 AX14
Park Rd., Hodd. 12 CE12
Park Rd., Houns. 74 BF46
Park Rd., Ilf. 49 CM34
Park Rd., Islw. 64 BJ44
Park Rd., Ken. 104 BY61
Park Rd., Kings.T. 75 BL49
Park Rd. (Hampton Wick), Kings.T. 84 BK51
Park Rd., Long. 90 DC52
Park Rd., N.Mal. 85 BN52
Park Rd., Orp. 89 CP53
Park Rd., Oxt. 115 CG67
Park Rd., Pot.B. 20 BV18
Park Rd., Rad. 27 BJ21
Park Rd., Red. 121 BU69
Park Rd., Rich. 75 BL46
Park Rd., Rick. 35 AY26
Park Rd., Shep. 83 AZ54
Park Rd., Slou. 52 AO37
Park Rd., Stai. 73 AW46
Park Rd., Sun. 73 BC50
Park Rd., Surb. 85 BL53
Park Rd., Sutt. 94 BR57
Park Rd., Swan. 89 CT52
Park Rd., Swans. 81 DC46
Park Rd., Tedd. 74 BH50
Park Rd., Twick. 74 BK46
Park Rd., Uxb. 53 AY36
Park Rd., Wall. 95 BV56
Park Rd. (Hackbridge), Wall. 86 BV55
Park Rd., Wal.Cr. 21 CC20
Park Rd., Warl. 97 CG60
Park Rd., Wat. 26 BC23
Park Rd., Wem. 55 BL36
Park Rd., Wok. 100 AS62
Park Rd. E. W3 65 BM41
Park Rd. E., Kings.T. 75 BL49
Park Rd. E., Uxb. 53 AX37
Park Rd. N. W3 65 BM41
Park Rd. N. W4 65 BN42
Park Rd. W., Kings.T. 75 BL49
Park Row SE10 67 CF42
Park Royal Rd. NW10 55 BN38
Park Royal Rd. W3 55 BN38
Park Side, Sutt. 94 BR57
Park Side, Wey. 92 AW58
Park Spring Gro., Iver 52 AT36
Park Sq., Esher 93 BF56
Park Rd.
Park Sq. E NW1 56 BV38
Park Sq. E. NW1 1 J4
Park Sq. Ms. NW1 1 J5
Park Sq. Ms. NW1 56 BV38
Park Sq. W. NW1 1 J4
Park Sq. W. NW1 56 BV38
Park St. SE1 4 H2
Park St. SE1 57 BZ40
Park St. W1 1 G10
Park St. W1 56 BV40
Park St., Berk. 7 AQ12
Park St., Croy. 87 BZ55
Park St., Guil. 118 AR71
Park St., Hat. 10 BQ12
Park St., St.Alb. 18 BG16
Park St., Slou. 62 AP41
Park St. (Colnbrook), Slou. 62 AU44
Park St., Tedd. 74 BH50
Park St., Wind. 61 AO44
Park St. La., St.Alb. 18 BF18
Park Ter., Green. 80 DB46
Park Ter., Wor.Pk. 85 BP54
Park Vw. N21 38 BX26
Park Vw. W3 55 BN39
Park Vw., Hat. 10 BQ11
Park Vw., Hodd. 12 CE12
Park Vw., Lthd. 111 BF66
Park Vw., N.Mal. 85 BO52
Park Vw., Pnr. 36 BE30
Park Vw., Pot.B. 20 BT20
Park Vw., Sev. 107 CP65
Park Vw., S.Ock. 60 CY40
Park Vw., Wem. 46 BM35
Park Vw. Cres. N11 38 BV28
Park Vw. Est. E2 57 CC37
Park Vw. Gdns. N22 38 BY30
Dunbar Rd.
Park Vw. Gdns. NW4 46 BQ32
Park Vw. Gdns., Bark. 58 CN37
Park Vw. Gdns., Grays 71 DD42
Park Vw. Gdns., Ilf. 49 CK31
Woodford Ave.
Park Vw. Rd. N3 38 BS30
Park Vw. Rd. N17 48 CB31
Park Vw. Rd. NW10 46 BO35
Park Vw. Rd. W5 55 BL
Park Vw. Rd., Berk. 7 AC
Park Vw. Rd., Cat. 105 CD
Park Vw. Rd., Pnr. 35 BC
Park Vw. Rd., Sthl. 54 BF
Park Vw. Rd., Well. 69 CO
Park Vill., Rom. 50 CF
Park Village E. NW1 56 BV
Park Village W. NW1 56 BV
Park Vista SE10 67 CF
Park Wk. SW10 66 BT
Park Wk., Ash. 103 BL
Rectory La.
Park Wk., Barn. 29 BT
Park Way N20 38 BU
Park Way NW11 46 BP
Park Way, Bex. 79 CT
Park Way, Brwd. 122 DC
Park Way, E.Mol. 84 BF
Park Way, Edg. 37 BM
Park Way, Enf. 29 BY
Park Way, Felt. 73 BC
Park Way, Ilf. 49 CN
Park Way, Lthd. 102 BF
Park Way, Rain. 59 CU
Park Way, Rick. 35 AX
Park Way, Ruis. 44 BC
Park W. W2 1
Park W. W2 56 BU
Park W. Pl. W2 1
Park W. Pl. W2 56 BU
Park Wd. Clo., Bans. 103 BO
Park Wd. Vw., Bans. 103 BO
Park Wks. Rd., Red. 121 BX
Parkcroft Rd. SE12 78 CG
Parkdale N11 38 BW
Parkdale Cres., Wor.Pk. 85 BN
Parkdale Rd. SE18 68 CN
Parke Rd. SW13 65 BP
Parke Rd., Sun. 83 BC
Parker Ave., Til. 71 DH
Parker Clo. E16 58 CK
Parker St.
Parker Ms. WC2 2
Parker Rd., Croy. 96 BZ
Parker Rd., Grays 71 DC
Parker St. E16 58 CK
Parker St. WC2 2
Parker St. WC2 56 BX
Parker St., Wat. 26 BC
Parkers Clo., Ash. 103 BL
Parkers Hill, Ash. 103 BL
Parkers La., Ash. 103 BL
Parkers Row SE1 4
Parkers Row SE1 67 CA
Parkes Rd., Chig. 40 CN
Parkfield, Long. 90 DC
Parkfield, Rick. 25 AV
Parkfield, Sev. 108 CW
Parkfield Ave. SW14 65 BO
Parkfield Ave., Amer. 25 AO
Parkfield Ave., Felt. 73 BC
Parkfield Ave., Har. 36 BG
Parkfield Ave., Nthlt. 54 BD
Parkfield Ave., Uxb. 53 AZ
Parkfield Clo., Edg. 37 BM
Parkfield Clo., Nthlt. 54 BE
Parkfield Cres., Felt. 73 BC
Parkfield Cres., Har. 36 BG
Parkfield Cres., Ruis. 45 BE
Parkfield Dr., Nthlt. 54 BD
Parkfield Gdns., Har. 45 BF
Parkfield Rd. NW10 55 BP
Parkfield Rd. SE14 67 CD
Parkfield Rd., Felt. 73 BC
Parkfield Rd., Har. 45 BG
Parkfield Rd., Nthlt. 54 BE
Parkfield Rd., Uxb. 44 AZ
Parkfield St. N1 56 BY
Parkfield Way, Brom. 88 CK
Parkfields SW15 65 BQ
Parkfields, Croy. 87 CD
Parkfields, Welw.G.C. 5 BC
Parkfields Ave. NW9 46 BN
Parkfields Ave. SW20 85 BP
Parkfields Clo., Cars. 95 BV
Devonshire Rd.
Parkfields Rd., Kings.T. 75 BL
Parkgate Ave., Barn. 29 BT
Parkgate Clo., Kings.T. 75 BM
Warboys App.
Parkgate Cres., Barn. 29 BT
Parkgate Gdns. SW14 75 BN
Parkgate Rd. SW11 66 BU
Parkgate Rd., Reig. 121 BS
Parkgate Rd., Wall. 95 BV
Parkgate Rd., Wat. 27 BD
Parkham St. SW11 66 BT
Parkhill Clo., Horn. 51 CV
Parkhill Rd. E4 39 CF
Parkhill Rd. NW3 47 BU
Parkhill Rd., Bex. 79 CQ
Parkhill Rd., Epsom 94 BO
Parkhill Wk. NW3 47 BU
Parkholme Rd. E8 57 CA
Parkhouse St. SE5 67 BZ
Parkhurst, Epsom 94 BN
Parkhurst Gdns., Bex. 79 CQ
Parkhurst Rd. E12 49 CL
Parkhurst Rd. E17 48 CD
Parkhurst Rd. N7 47 BX
Parkhurst Rd. N11 38 BV
Parkhurst Rd. N17 39 CB
Parkhurst Rd. N22 38 BX
Parkhurst Rd., Bex. 79 CR
Parkhurst Rd., Guil. 118 AQ
Parkhurst Rd., Sutt. 95 BT
Parkland Ave., Rom. 41 CT
Parkland Ave., Slou. 62 AR
Parkland Ave., Upmin. 51 CX
Parkland Clo., Hodd. 12 CE
Parkland Clo., Sev. 117 CV
Parkland Gdns. SW19 75 BQ
Inner Pk. Rd.

kland Gro., Ashf. 73 AZ49
kland Rd. N22 38 BX30
kland Rd., Ashf. 73 AZ49
kland Rd., Wdf.Grn. 40 CH29
kland Wk. N6 47 BW33
kland Way, Ong. 24 CW18
klands, Chig. 40 CM27
klands, Epp. 23 CP18
klands, Oxt. 115 CG69
klands, Surb. 85 BL53
klands, Wal.Abb. 21 CF19
klands, Wey. 92 AX56
berty La.
klands, Wey. 92 AX57
klands Clo. SW14 75 BN46
klands Clo., Chig. 40 CM27
klands Ct., Houns. 64 BD44
klands Dr. N3 46 BR31
klands Pl., Guil. 118 AT70
klands Rd. SW16 76 BV49
klands Way, Wor.Pk. 85 BO55
afton Pk. Rd.
klea Clo. NW9 37 BO30
kleigh Rd. SW19 86 BS51
kleys, Rich. 74 BK49
kmead SW15 75 BP46
kmead, Loug. 31 CL25
kmead Gdns. NW7 37 BO29
kmore Clo., Wdf.Grn. 40 CH28
kpale La., Bet. 120 BM73
ksend Rd. SW11 66 BV44
attersea Pk. Rd.
kshot, Rich. 64 BK45
kside N3 38 BS30
kside NW2 46 BP34
kside NW7 37 BO29
kside SE3 68 CG43
kside SW19 75 BQ47
kside, Buck.H. 40 CH27
kside, Grays 71 DE41
kside, Hmptn. 74 BG49
kside, Pot.B. 20 BT19
kside, Sev. 98 CQ60
kside, Sid. 79 CO48
kside Ave. SW19 75 BQ49
kside Ave., Bexh. 69 CS44
kside Ave., Brom. 88 CK52
kside Ave., Rom. 50 CS31
kside Ave., Til. 71 DG44
kside Clo., Lthd. 110 BB66
kside Cres., Surb. 85 BN53
kside Cross, Bexh. 69 CT44
kside Dr., Edg. 37 BM27
kside Dr., Wat. 26 BB23
kside Est. E9 57 CC37
kside Gdns. SW19 75 BQ49
kside Gdns., Barn. 38 BU26
kside Gdns., Couls. 104 BV62
kside Pl., Lthd. 110 BB66
kside Rd. SW11 66 BV44
kside Rd., Belv. 69 CS42
kside Rd., Houns. 74 BF46
kside Rd., Nthwd. 35 BB28
kside Ter. N18 39 BZ28
kside Way, Har. 45 BF31
kstead Rd. SW15 75 BP46
kstone Ave. N18 39 CA29
kstone Ave., Horn. 51 CW32
kstone Rd. SE15 67 CB44
ye La.
kthorne Clo., Har. 45 BF32
kthorne Dr., Har. 45 BF32
kthorne Rd. SW12 76 BW47
kview Rd. SE9 78 CL47
kview Rd., Croy. 87 CB54
kview Vale, Guil. 118 AU69
kville Rd. SW6 65 BR43
rkway N14 38 BX27
rkway NW1 56 BV37
rkway SW20 85 BQ52
rkway, Croy. 96 CE58
rkway, Dor. 119 BJ71
rkway, Erith 69 CQ41
rkway, Rom. 41 CT30
rkway, Saw. 6 CQ6
rkway, Uxb. 53 AZ36
rkway, Welw.G.C. 5 BQ8
rkway, Wey. 92 BA56
rkway, Wdf.Grn. 40 CJ28
rkway, The (Cranford), Houns. 63 BC42
rkway, The, Iver 52 AU37
rkway Clo., Welw.G.C. 5 BQ8
rkway Ct., St.Alb. 9 BJ15
Drakes Dr.
rkway Ms., Croy. 76 BV50
Park Ave.
rkwood N20 38 BU27
rkwood, Beck. 77 CE50
rkwood Ave., Esher 84 BG54
rkwood Clo., Hodd. 12 CD13
rkwood Dr., Hem.H. 7 AV13
rkwood Gro., Sun. 83 BC52
rkwood Ms. N6 47 BV32
Wood La.
rkwood Rd. SW19 75 BR49
rkwood Rd., Bans. 103 BQ61
rkwood Rd., Bex. 79 CQ47
rkwood Rd., Islw. 64 BH44
rkwood Rd., Red. 121 BX70
rkwood Rd., West. 106 CK64
rlaunt Rd., Slou. 62 AT42
rley Dr., Wok. 100 AR62
rliament Hill NW3 47 BU35
rliament Ms. SW14 65 BN44
rliament Sq. SW1 3 Q5
rliament Sq. SW1 66 BX41
rliament St. SW1 3 Q5
rliament St. SW1 66 BX41
rma Cres. SW11 66 BU45
rmiter St. E2 57 CB37
rnall Rd., Harl. 13 CM12
rndon Wd. Rd., Harl. 13 CM13
rnell Clo., Abb.L. 17 BB18

Parnell Clo., Edg. 37 BM27
Parnell Rd. E3 57 CD37
Parnham St. E14 57 CD39
Parolles Rd. N19 47 BW33
Paroma Rd., Belv. 69 CR41
Parr Ave., Epsom 94 BP58
Parr Clo. N9 39 CB28
Parr Clo., Lthd. 102 BH63
Parr Ct., Felt. 74 BD49
Parr Rd. E6 58 CJ37
Parr Rd., Stan. 36 BK30
Parris Cft., Dor. 119 BK73
Parrock Ave., Grav. 81 DH47
Parrock Rd., Grav. 81 DH47
Parrock St., Grav. 81 DG46
Parrots Clo., Rick. 26 AZ25
Parrotts Fld., Hodd. 12 CE11
Essex Rd.
Parrs Clo., S.Croy. 94 BZ58
Parrs Pl., Hmptn. 74 BF50
Tudor Rd.
Parry Ave. E6 58 CK39
Parry Clo., Epsom 94 BP57
Parry Dr., Wey. 92 AZ59
Parry Grn., Slou. 62 AS42
Parry Pl. SE18 68 CL42
Parry Rd. SE25 87 CA52
Parry St. SW8 66 BX43
Parsifal Rd. NW6 46 BS35
Parsley Gdns., Croy. 87 CC54
Primrose La.
Parsloe Rd., Epp. 13 CL14
Parsloes Ave., Dag. 50 CP35
Parson St. NW4 46 BQ31
Parsonage Clo., Abb.L. 17 BB18
Parsonage Clo., Dor. 119 BG72
Parsonage La.
Parsonage Clo., Hayes 53 BB39
Parsonage Clo., Warl. 105 CD61
Parsonage Fld., Brwd. 33 DB22
Parsonage Gdns., Enf. 30 BZ23
Parsonage La., Dor. 119 BG72
Parsonage La., Enf. 30 BZ23
Parsonage La., Hat. 10 BP15
Parsonage La., Sid. 79 CQ49
Parsonage La., Slou. 52 AO36
Parsonage La., S.Dnth. 80 CX50
Parsonage La., Wind. 61 AN44
Parsonage Leys, Harl. 13 CN11
Parsonage Manorway, Belv. 69 CR43
Parsonage Rd., Ch.St.G. 34 AQ27
Parsonage Rd., Egh. 72 AR49
Parsonage Rd., Grays 70 DB43
Parsonage Rd., Hat. 10 BP15
Parsonage Rd., Rain. 60 CV37
Parsonage Rd., Rick. 35 AX26
Parsonage St. E14 67 CF42
Parsons Cres., Edg. 37 BM27
Parsons Grn. SW6 66 BS44
Parsons Grn., Guil. 109 AR69
Parsons Grn. La. SW6 66 BS44
Parsons Gro., Edg. 37 BM27
Parsons Hill SE18 68 CL41
Powis St.
Parsons La., Dart. 79 CU48
Parsons Mead, Croy. 86 BY54
Parsons Mead, E.Mol. 84 BG52
Parsons Pightle, Couls. 104 BY63
Parsons Rd. E13 58 CJ37
Parsons Wd. La., Slou. 52 AO36
Parsonsfield Clo., Bans. 103 BQ61
Parsonsfield Rd., Bans. 103 BQ61
Parthenia Rd. SW6 66 BS44
Parthia Clo., Tad. 103 BP63
Partingdale La. NW7 37 BQ28
Partington Clo. N19 47 BW33
Partridge Clo. E16 58 CJ39
Partridge Clo., Bush. 36 BF26
Partridge Clo., Chesh. 16 AP17
Partridge Dr., Orp. 88 CM55
Partridge Grn. SE9 78 CL48
Partridge Knoll, Pur. 96 BY60
Partridge Mead, Bans. 103 BQ61
Partridge Rd., Hmptn. 74 BF50
Partridge Rd., Harl. 13 CM12
Partridge Rd., St.Alb. 9 BG11
Partridge Rd., Sid. 78 CN48
Partridge Sq. E6 58 CK39
Nightingale Way
Partridge Vill., Uxb. 53 AX37
Cricket Fld. Rd.
Partridge Way N22 38 BX30
Partridge Way, Guil. 118 AV69
Parvills Rd., Wal.Abb. 21 CF19
Parvin St. SW8 66 BW44
Deeley Rd.
Parvis Rd., Wey. 92 AW60
Pasadena Clo., Hayes 63 BC41
Pascal St. SW8 66 BW43
Pascoe Rd. SE13 77 CF46
Pasfield Clo., Wal.Abb. 21 CF19
Parvills Rd.
Pasquier Rd. E17 48 CD31
Passage, The, Rich. 65 BL45
The Quad.
Passey Pl. SE9 78 CK46
Passfield Dr. E14 57 CE39
St. Leonards Rd.
Passfield Path SE28 59 CO40
Booth Clo.
Passfields W14 65 BR42
Passing All. EC1 2 F5
Passmore Gdns. N11 38 BW29
Passmore St. SW1 3 G9
Passmore St. SW1 66 BV42
Pastens Rd., Oxt. 115 CJ69
Pasteur Clo. NW9 37 BO30
Pasteur Gdns. N18 38 BY28
Paston Clo. E5 48 CC34
Millfields Rd.
Paston Cres. SE12 78 CH47
Paston Rd., Hem.H. 8 AX12
Pastor St. SE11 4 G8

Pastor St. SE11 66 BY42
Pasture, The, St.Alb. 9 BF15
Pasture Clo., Bush. 36 BG26
Pasture Clo., Wem. 45 BJ34
Pasture Rd. SE6 78 CG47
Pasture Rd., Dag. 50 CQ35
Pasture Rd., Wem. 45 BJ34
Pastures, The N20 37 BR26
Pastures, The, Hat. 10 BP13
Pastures, The, Hem.H. 7 AV13
Pastures, The, Wat. 36 BD26
Pastures, The, Welw.G.C. 5 BS9
Pastures Mead, Uxb. 53 AZ36
Hercies Rd.
Pat More La., Walt. 92 BB57
Patch, The, Sev. 107 CT64
Patcham Ct., Sutt. 95 BT57
Patcham Ter. SW8 66 BV44
Pater St. W8 66 BS41
Paternoster Clo., Wal.Abb. 22 CG20
Paternoster Hill, Wal.Abb. 22 CG19
Paternoster Row EC4 2 H9
Paternoster Row EC4 56 BY39
St. Pauls Chyd.
Paternoster Row, Hav. 42 CV26
Paternoster Sq. EC4 2 G8
Paternoster Sq. EC4 56 BY39
Warwick La.
Paterson Rd., Ashf. 73 AX49
Pates Manor Dr., Felt. 73 BA47
Path, The SW19 86 BS51
Pathfield Rd. SW16 76 BW50
Pathway, The, Rad. 27 BH21
Pathway, The, Wat. 36 BD26
Pathway, The, Wok. 109 AV66
Patience Rd. SW11 66 BU44
Patio Clo. SW4 76 BW46
Patmore Link, Hem.H. 8 BA13
Patmore Rd., Wal.Abb. 22 CG20
Patmore St. SW8 66 BW44
Patmore Way, Rom. 41 CR28
Patmos Rd. SW9 66 BY43
Paton Clo. E3 57 CE38
Paton St. EC1 2 H3
Paton St. EC1 57 BZ38
Patricia Ct., Well. 69 CO43
Wickham La.
Patricia Dr., Horn. 51 CW33
Patricia Gdns., Sutt. 95 BS59
Patrick Connolly Gdns. E3 57 CE38
Talwin St.
Patrick Pas. SW11 66 BU44
Winders Rd.
Patrick Rd. E13 58 CJ38
Patrington Clo., Uxb. 53 AX38
Patriot Sq. E2 57 CB37
Patrol Pl. SE6 77 CE46
Patrons Dr., Uxb. 43 AV32
Patrons Dr., Uxb. 43 AV32
Patrons Way, Uxb. 43 AV32
Patshull Pl. NW5 56 BW36
Patshull Rd.
Patshull Rd. NW5 56 BW36
Patten All., Rich. 74 BK46
Ormond Rd.
Patten Ave., Rich. 74 BK46
Ormond Rd.
Patten Rd. SW18 76 BU47
Pattenden Rd. SE6 77 CD47
Patterdale Clo., Brom. 78 CG50
Patterdale Rd. SE15 67 CC43
Patterdale Rd., Dart. 80 CY47
Patterson Ct. SE19 77 CA50
Patterson Ct., Dart. 80 CX46
Farnol Rd.
Patterson Rd. SE19 77 CA50
Pattison Rd. NW2 47 BS34
Pattison Wk. SE18 68 CM42
Sandbach Pl.
Paul Clo. E15 58 CG37
Paul St.
Paul Gdns., Croy. 87 CA55
Paul St. E15 57 CF37
Paul St. EC2 2 L5
Paul St. EC2 57 BZ38
Paulet Rd. SE5 66 BY44
Paulhan Rd., Har. 45 BK31
Paulin Dr. N21 38 BY26
Pauline Cres., Twick. 74 BG47
Paulinus Clo., Orp. 89 CP51
Pauls Grn., Wal.Cr. 21 CC20
Eleanor Rd.
Pauls La., Hodd. 12 CE12
Pauls Pl., Ash. 103 BM62
Paultons Sq. SW3 66 BT43
Paultons St. SW3 66 BT43
Old Ch. St.
Pauntley St. N19 47 BW33
Paved Ct., Rich. 74 BK46
King St.
Paveley Dr. SW11 66 BU43
Paveley St. NW8 1 D3
Paveley St. NW8 56 BU38
Pavement, The SW4 66 BW45
Pavement Ms., Rom. 50 CP33
Pavement Sq., Croy. 87 CA54
Teevan Rd.
Pavet Clo., Dag. 59 CR36
Pavilion Gdns., Stai. 73 AW50
Pavilion Rd. SW1 3 F5
Pavilion Rd. SW1 66 BU41
Pavilion Rd., Ilf. 49 CK33
Pavilion St. SW1 3 F7
Pavilion Ter., Ilf. 49 CN32
South Down Cres.
Pavilion Way, Amer. 25 AR23
Pavilion Way, Edg. 37 BM29
Pavilion Way, Ruis. 45 BD34
Pawleyne Clo. SE20 77 CC50
Pawsey Clo. E13 58 CH37
Plashet Rd.
Pawsons Rd., Croy. 87 BZ53
Paxford Rd., Wem. 45 BJ34

Paxton Ave., Slou. 61 AO41
Paxton Clo., Rich. 65 BL44
Paxton Clo., Walt. 84 BD54
Paxton Gdns., Wok. 91 AU59
Paxton Pl. SE27 77 CA49
Paxton Rd. N17 39 CA29
Paxton Rd. SE23 77 CD48
Paxton Rd. W4 65 BO43
Paxton Rd., Berk. 7 AR13
Paxton Rd., Brom. 78 CH50
College Rd.
Paxton Rd., St.Alb. 9 BH14
Paxton Ter. SW1 66 BV42
Churchill Gdns. Rd.
Paycock Rd., Harl. 13 CL12
Payne Rd. E3 57 CE38
Bow Rd.
Payne St. SE8 67 CD43
Paynes La., Wal.Abb. 12 CF15
Paynesfield Ave. SW14 65 BN45
Paynesfield Rd., Bush. 36 BH26
Paynesfield Rd., West. 106 CJ63
Pea La., Berk. 7 AO12
Pea La., Upmin. 60 DA36
Peabody Ave. SW1 66 BV42
Peabody Bldgs. WC1 56 BX38
Peabody Clo. SE10 67 CE44
Devonshire Dr.
Peabody Dws. WC1 1 Q4
Peabody Est. EC1 2 J5
Peabody Est. EC1 57 BZ38
Peabody Est. N17 39 CA30
Peabody Est. SE1 56 BY40
Peabody Est. SE24 76 BY47
Peabody Est. SW11 66 BU45
Peabody Est. W6 65 BQ42
Peabody Hill SE21 76 BY47
Peabody Hill Est. SE21 77 BZ47
Peabody Sq. SE1 4 F5
Peabody Trust SW3 66 BU43
Chelsea Manor St.
Peabody Yd. N1 57 BZ36
Greenman St.
Peace Clo. N14 29 BV25
Peace Clo., Wal.Cr. 21 CB18
Peace Gro., Wem. 46 BM34
Chalkhill Rd.
Peach Cft., Grav. 81 DE48
Peach Tree Ave., West Dr. 53 AY39
Peaches Clo., Sutt. 94 BR57
Peachey La., Uxb. 53 AX39
Peachum Rd. SE3 68 CG43
Peacock Ave., Felt. 73 BA47
Peacock Clo., Horn. 51 CW31
Peacock Gdns., S.Croy. 96 CD58
Peacock St. SE17 4 G9
Peacock St. SE17 66 BY42
Peacock St., Grav. 81 DH47
Peacock Wk. N6 47 BV33
Cholmeley Cres.
Peacock Wk., Dor. 119 BJ72
Rose Hill
Peacock Yd. SE17 4 G9
Peacocks, Harl. 13 CK12
Peahen Ct. EC2 57 CA39
Bishopsgate
Peak, The SE26 77 CC49
Peak Clo., Guil. 118 AQ69
Peak Hill SE26 77 CC49
Peak Hill Ave. SE26 77 CC49
Peak Hill Gdns. SE26 77 CC49
Spring Hill
Peakes La., Chsnt. 21 CA17
Peakes Way, Chsnt. 21 CA17
Peaketon Ave., Ilf. 49 CJ31
Peaks Hill, Pur. 95 BW58
Peaks Hill Ri., Pur. 95 BX58
Peal Gdns. W13 54 BJ38
Peall Rd., Croy. 86 BX53
Pear Ave., Shep. 83 BB52
Grange Fm. Caravan Site
Pear Clo. NW9 46 BN31
Pear Clo. SE14 67 CD43
Southerngate Way
Pear Pl. SE1 4 D4
Pear Tree Ave., West Dr. 53 AY39
Pear Tree Clo., Beac. 34 AO29
Pear Tree Clo., Swan. 89 CS51
Pear Tree Clo., Wey. 92 AW56
Pear Tree Rd.
Pear Tree Ct. EC1 2 E5
Pear Tree Ct. EC1 56 BY38
Pear Tree Mead, Harl. 14 CO12
Pear Tree Rd., Ashf. 73 BA49
Pear Tree Rd., Wey. 92 AW56
Pear Tree St. EC1 2 G4
Pear Tree St. EC1 56 BY38
Pear Tree Wk., Chsnt. 21 BZ16
Pear Trees, Brwd. 122 DE29
Pearcefield Ave. SE23 77 CC47
Pearcroft Rd. E11 48 CF34
Peardon St. SW8 66 BV44
Silverthorne Rd.
Peareswood Gdns., Stan. 36 BK30
Peareswood Rd., Erith 69 CT44
Pearfield Rd. SE23 77 CD48
Pearl Clo. E6 58 CL39
Pearl Ct., Wok. 100 AP61
Langmans Way
Pearl Gdns., Slou. 61 AN40
Pearl Rd. E17 48 CE31
Pearl St. E1 57 CB40
Penang St.
Pearle Rd., E.Mol. 84 BF51
Pearmain Clo., Shep. 83 AZ53
Laleham Rd.
Pearman St. SE1 4 E6
Pearman St. SE1 66 BY41
Pears Rd., Houns. 64 BG45
Pearscroft Ct. SW6 66 BS44
Pearscroft Rd. SW6 66 BS44
Pearson St. E2 57 CA37
Pearsons Ave. SE14 67 CD44
Tanners Hill

Peartree Ave., Ashf. 73 BA49
Peartree Clo., Brwd. 33 DB22
Peartree Clo., Erith 69 CS44
Peartree Clo., Hem.H. 8 AW13
Peartree Clo., Mitch. 86 BU51
Peartree Clo., S.Croy. 96 CB60
Orchard Rd.
Peartree Clo., S.Ock. 60 DB37
Peartree Clo., Welw.G.C. 5 BR8
Peartree Ct., Welw.G.C. 5 BR8
Peartree Fm., Welw.G.C. 5 BR8
Peartree Gdns., Dag. 50 CO35
Peartree Gdns., Rom. 41 CR30
Peartree La. E1 57 CC40
Glamis Rd.
Peartree La., Brwd. 33 DB22
Peartree La., Welw.G.C. 5 BR8
Peartree Rd., Enf. 30 CA24
Peartree Rd., Hem.H. 8 AW13
Peary Pl. E2 57 CC38
Kirkwall Pl.
Peascod Pl., Wind. 61 AO44
Peascod St.
Peascod St., Wind. 61 AO44
Peascroft Rd., Hem.H. 8 AZ15
Pease Hill, Sev. 99 DC57
Peatmore Ave., Wok. 101 AW61
Pebble Hill, Lthd. 110 BA70
Pebble La., Epsom 103 BL64
Pebble La., Lthd. 103 BL65
Pebblehill Rd., Bet. 120 BO69
Pebblehill Rd., Tad. 112 BO68
Pebworth Rd., Har. 45 BJ34
Peckarmans Wd. SE26 77 CB48
Peckett Sq. N5 48 BZ35
Peckford Pl. SW9 66 BY44
Peckham Gro. SE15 67 CA43
Peckham High St. SE15 67 CA44
Peckham Hill St. SE15 67 CB43
Peckham Pk. Rd. SE15 67 CB43
Peckham Rd. SE5 67 CA44
Peckham Rd. SE15 67 CA44
Peckham Rye SE15 67 CB45
Peckham Rye SE22 67 CB45
Peckham Wk. Ave., Sev. 117 DC67
Peckham Wk. Ave., Ton. 117 DC67
Pecks Hill, Wal.Abb. 13 CG14
Peckwater St. NW5 47 BW35
Islip St.
Peckwater St. Est. NW5 47 BW35
Pedlars End, Ong. 14 CU14
Pedlars Wk. N7 56 BX36
Pedley Rd., Dag. 50 CP33
Pedley St. E1 2 Q5
Pedley St. E1 57 CA38
Pedro St. E5 48 CC34
Pedworth Gdns. SE16 67 CC42
Rotherhithe New Rd.
Peek Cres. SW19 75 BQ49
Peel Clo. E4 39 CE27
Peel Clo., Wind. 61 AN45
Peel Dr. NW9 46 BP31
Peel Dr., Ilf. 49 CK31
Peel Gro. E2 57 CC37
Peel Pl., Ilf. 40 CK30
Peel Prec. NW6 56 BS37
Peel Rd. E18 40 CG30
Peel Rd. NW6 56 BS38
Peel Rd. NW9 46 BP31
Peel Rd., Har. 45 BH31
Peel Rd., Orp. 97 CM56
Peel Rd., Wem. 45 BK34
Peel St. W8 56 BS40
Peel Way, Rom. 42 CW30
Peel Way, Uxb. 53 AY39
Peerage Way, Horn. 51 CW33
Peerless Dr., Uxb. 44 AX32
Peerless St. EC1 2 K3
Peerless St. EC1 57 BZ38
Pegamoid Rd. N18 39 CC27
Pegasus Pl. SE11 66 BY43
Clayton St.
Pegasus Rd., Croy. 95 BY57
Pegelm Gdns., Horn. 51 CW33
Pegg Rd., Houns. 64 BD43
Peggotty Waye, Uxb. 53 AZ39
Pegley Gdns. SE12 78 CH48
Pegmire La., Wat. 27 BG23
Pegrams Rd., Harl. 13 CM12
Pegwell St. SE18 68 CN43
Peket Clo., Stai. 82 AV51
Pekin Clo. E14 57 CE39
Pekin St.
Pekin St. E14 57 CE39
Peldon Ct., Rich. 65 BL45
Peldon Pas., Rich. 65 BL45
Sheen Rd.
Peldon Rd., Harl. 13 CL12
Peldon Wk. N1 57 BZ37
Popham St.
Pelham Ave., Bark. 58 CN37
Pelham Clo. SE5 67 CA45
Pelham Ct. SW3 66 BU42
Fulham Rd.
Pelham Ct., Hem.H. 8 BA13
Pelham Ct., Stai. 73 AW49
Pelham Ct., Welw.G.C. 5 BT8
Pelham Cres. SW7 3 C9
Pelham Cres. SW7 66 BU42
Pelham Pl. SW7 3 C8
Pelham Pl. SW7 66 BU42
Pelham Rd. E18 49 CH31
Pelham Rd. N15 48 CA31
Pelham Rd. N22 38 BY30
Pelham Rd. SW19 76 BS50
Pelham Rd., Beck. 87 CC51
Pelham Rd., Bexh. 69 CR45
Pelham Rd., Grav. 81 DF47
Pelham Rd., Ilf. 49 CM34
Pelham St. SW7 3 B8
Pelham St. SW7 66 BT42
Pelham Way, Lthd. 111 BF66
Pelhams, The, Wat. 27 BD21
Pelhams Clo., Esher 93 BF56

Pelhams Wk., Esher 84 BF55
Pelican Wk. SW9 66 BY45
Loughborough Pk.
Pelier St. SE17 67 BZ43
Pelinore Rd. SE6 78 CG48
Pellant Rd. SW6 65 BR43
Pellatt Gro. N22 38 BY30
Pellatt Rd. SE22 77 CA46
Pellerin Rd. N16 48 CA35
Pelling Hill, Wind. 72 AQ47
Pelling St. E14 57 CE39
Pellipar Clo. N13 38 BY27
Pellipar Clo. SE18 68 CK42
Hillreach
Pellipar Gdns. SE18 68 CK42
Ogilby St.
Pellipar Rd. SE18 68 CK42
Pells La., Sev. 99 DA59
Pelly Rd. E13 58 CH37
Pelter St. E2 2 P2
Pelter St. E2 57 CA38
Pelton Ave., Sutt. 95 BS58
Pelton Rd. SE10 68 CG42
Pembar Ave. E17 48 CD31
Pember Rd. NW10 55 BQ38
Pemberton Ave., Rom. 51 CV31
Pemberton Clo., St.Alb. 9 BG15
Pemberton Gdns. N19 47 BW34
Pemberton Gdns., Rom. 50 CQ32
Pemberton Gdns., Swan. 89 CT51
Bonney Way
Pemberton Pl. E8 57 CB36
Mare St.
Pemberton Rd. N4 47 BY32
Pemberton Rd., E.Mol. 84 BG52
Pemberton Row EC4 2 E8
Pemberton Row EC4 56 BY39
East Harding St.
Pemberton Ter. N19 47 BW34
Pembrey Way, Horn. 60 CV36
Pembridge Ave., Twick. 74 BE47
Pembridge Chase, Hem.H. 16 AT17
Pembridge Clo.
Pembridge Clo., Hem.H. 16 AS17
Pembridge Cres. W11 56 BS40
Pembridge Gdns. W2 56 BS40
Pembridge La., Hert. 12 BZ13
Pembridge Ms. W11 56 BS40
Pembridge Pl. W2 56 BS40
Pembridge Rd. W11 56 BS40
Pembridge Rd., Hem.H. 16 AT17
Pembridge Sq. W2 56 BS40
Pembridge Vill. W11 56 BS40
Pembroke Ave., Enf. 30 CB23
Pembroke Ave., Har. 45 BJ31
Pembroke Ave., Surb. 85 BM53
Pembroke Ave., Walt. 93 BD56
Pembroke Clo. SW1 3 H5
Pembroke Clo. SW1 66 BV41
Pembroke Clo., Bans. 104 BS62
Pembroke Clo., Brox. 12 CD15
Church La.
Pembroke Clo., Horn. 51 CW31
Pembroke Clo., S.at H. 90 CX51
Main Rd.
Pembroke Dr., Chsnt. 20 BY18
Pembroke Gdns W8 65 BR42
Pembroke Gdns., Dag. 50 CR34
Pembroke Gdns., Wok. 100 AT62
Pembroke Rd.
Pembroke Gdns. Clo. W8 66 BS41
Pembroke Ms. E3 57 CD38
Morgan St.
Pembroke Ms. N10 38 BV30
Pembroke Rd.
Pembroke Ms. W8 66 BS41
Earls Ct. Rd.
Pembroke Pl. W8 66 BS41
Pembroke Pl., Edg. 37 BM29
Pembroke Pl., Islw. 64 BH44
Clifton Rd.
Pembroke Pl., S.at H. 90 CX51
Main Rd.
Pembroke Rd. E6 58 CK39
Pembroke Rd. E17 48 CE32
Pembroke Rd. N8 47 BX31
Pembroke Rd. N10 38 BV30
Pembroke Rd. N13 39 BZ27
Pembroke Rd. N15 48 CA32
Pembroke Rd. SE25 87 CA52
Pembroke Rd. W8 65 BR42
Pembroke Rd., Brom. 88 CJ51
Pembroke Rd., Erith 69 CS42
Pembroke Rd., Grnf. 54 BF38
Pembroke Rd., Ilf. 49 CN33
Pembroke Rd., Mitch. 86 BV51
Pembroke Rd., Nthwd. 35 BA27
Pembroke Rd., Ruis. 44 BB33
Pembroke Rd., Sev. 116 CU66
Pembroke Rd., Wem. 45 BK34
Pembroke Rd., Wok. 100 AT62
Pembroke Sq. W8 66 BS41
Pembroke St. N1 56 BX36
Pembroke Studios W8 65 BR41
Pembroke Vill. W8 66 BS41
Pembroke Vill., Rich. 64 BK45
Pembroke Wk. W8 66 BS42
Pembroke Vill.
Pembroke Way, Hayes 63 BA41
Pembury Ave., Wor.Pk. 85 BP54
Pembury Clo., Brom. 88 CG54
Pembury Clo., Couls. 95 BV60
Pembury Ct., Hayes 63 BA43
Pembury Cres., Sid. 79 CQ48
Pembury Est. E5 48 CB35
Pembury Pl. E5 48 CB35
Pembury Rd. E5 48 CB35
Pembury Rd. N17 39 CA30
Pembury Rd. SE25 87 CB52
Pembury Rd., Bexh. 69 CQ43
Pemdevon Rd., Croy. 86 BY54
Pemell Clo. E1 57 CC38
Colebert Ave.
Pemerich Clo., Hayes 63 BB42
Pempath Pl., Wem. 45 BK34
Strathcona Rd.
Pemsel Ct., Hem.H. 8 AX14
Crabtree La.
Pen Dr., Uxb. 43 AV32
Penally Pl. N1 57 BZ37
Penang St. E1 57 CB40
Penarth St. SE15 67 CC43
Penates, Esher 93 BG56
Littleworth Common Rd.
Penberth Rd. SE6 77 CF47
Penbury Rd., Sthl. 64 BE42
Pencombe Ms. W11 56 BS40
Ledbury Ms. W.
Pencraig Way SE15 67 CB43
Penda Rd., Erith 69 CS43
Pendarves Rd. SW20 85 BQ51
Pendas Mead E9 48 CD35
Kings Mead Est.
Pendell Ave., Hayes 63 BB43
Pendell Rd., Red. 121 BY69
Pendennis Clo., Wey. 92 AW60
Pendennis Rd. N17 48 BZ31
Pendennis Rd. SW16 76 BX49
Pendennis Rd., Orp. 89 CP55
Pendennis Rd., Sev. 107 CU65
Penderel Rd., Houns. 74 BF46
Penderry Ri. SE6 77 CF48
Penderyn Way N7 47 BW35
Carleton Rd.
Pendle Rd. SW16 76 BV50
Pendlestone Rd. E17 48 CE32
Pendleton Rd., Red. 121 BU71
Sandpit Rd.
Pendleton Rd., Red. 121 BT72
Pendleton Rd., Reig. 121 BT72
Pendragon Rd., Brom. 78 CG48
Pendragon Wk. NW9 46 BO32
Fryent Gro.
Pendrell Rd. SE4 67 CD44
Pendrell St. SE18 68 CM43
Pendula Dr., Hayes 54 BD38
Penerley Rd. SE6 77 CE47
Penerley Rd., Rain. 59 CU39
Penfold Clo., Croy. 95 BY56
Epsom Rd.
Penfold La., Bexh. 79 CP48
Penfold Pl. NW1 1 C6
Penfold Pl. NW1 56 BU39
Penfold Rd. N9 39 CC26
Penfold St. NW1 1 C6
Penfold St. NW1 56 BT38
Penfold St. NW8 1 B5
Penfold St. NW8 56 BT38
Penford Gdns. SE9 68 CJ45
Penford St. SE5 66 BY44
Pengarth Rd., Bex. 79 CP46
Penge La. SE20 77 CC50
Penge Rd. E13 58 CJ37
Penge Rd. SE20 87 CB51
Penge Rd. SE25 87 CB52
Pengelly Clo., Chsnt. 21 CB18
Burygreen Rd.
Penhall Rd. SE7 68 CJ42
Penhill Rd., Bex. 79 CP47
Penhurst, Wok. 91 AS60
Penhurst Rd., Ilf. 40 CL29
Penifather La., Grnf. 54 BG38
Peninsular Clo., Felt. 73 BA46
Penistone Rd. SW16 76 BX50
Penistone Wk., Rom. 42 CV29
Okehampton Rd.
Penketh Dr., Har. 45 BG34
Penlow Rd., Harl. 13 CM12
Penman Clo., St.Alb. 18 BF17
Penmon Rd. SE2 69 CO41
Penn Clo., Grnf. 54 BF37
Penn Clo., Har. 45 BK31
Penn Clo., Rick. 25 AU25
Penn Clo., Uxb. 53 AX38
Penn Gdns., Chis. 88 CL51
Penn Gdns., Rom. 41 CR29
Penn Gaskell La., Ger.Cr. 34 AS28
Penn La., Bexh. 79 CP46
Penn Meadow, Slou. 52 AP37
Penn Pl., Rick. 35 AX26
Northway
Penn Rd. N7 47 BX35
Penn Rd., Ger.Cr. 34 AR30
Penn Rd., Rick. 34 AV26
Penn Rd., St.Alb. 18 BG17
Penn Rd., Slou. 52 AO38
Penn Rd. (Datchet), Slou. 62 AR44
Penn Rd., Wat. 26 BC23
Penn St. N1 57 BZ37
Penn Way, Rick. 25 AU25
Pennack Rd. SE15 67 CA43
Pennant Ms. W8 66 BS42
Pennant Ter. E17 39 CD30
Pennard Rd. W12 65 BQ41
Pennards, The, Sun. 84 BD52
Penner Clo. SW19 75 BR48
Victoria Dr.
Pennethorne Clo. E9 57 CC37
Victoria Pk. Rd.
Pennethorne Rd. SE15 67 CB43
Penney Clo., Dart. 80 CV47
Pennine Dr. NW2 46 BQ34
Pennine La. NW2 46 BQ34
Pennine Dr.
Pennine Way, Bexh. 69 CT44
Pennine Way, Grav. 81 DF48
Pennine Way, Hayes 63 BA43
Pennine Way, Hem.H. 8 AY12
Pennings Ave., Guil. 118 AP69
Pennington Clo. SE27 77 BZ49
Pennington Clo., Rom. 41 CR28
Pennington Dr., Wey. 83 BB55
Pennington Rd., Ger.Cr. 34 AR29
Pennington St. E1 57 CB40
Penningtons, The, Amer. 25 AP22
Penny Clo., Rain. 59 CU38
Stirling Clo.
Penny La., Shep. 83 BB54
Penny Rd. NW10 55 BM38
Pennycroft, Croy. 96 CC58
Pennyfield, Cob. 92 BC60
Pennyfields E14 57 CE40
Pennyfields, Brwd. 42 DB28
Junction Rd.
Pennylets Grn., Slou. 52 AP36
Pennymead, Harl. 14 CO11
Pennymead Dr., Lthd. 110 BB67
Pennymead Ri., Lthd. 110 BB67
Pennymore Wk. W9 55 BR38
Ashmore Rd.
Pennypot La., Wok. 91 AO59
Pennyroyal Ave. E6 58 CL39
Penpoll Rd. E8 57 CB36
Wilton Way
Penpool La., Well. 69 CO45
Penrhyn Ave. E17 39 CD30
Penrhyn Cres. E17 39 CE30
Penrhyn Cres. SW14 65 BN45
Penrhyn Gdns., Kings.T. 84 BK52
Penrhyn Gro. E17 39 CE30
Penrhyn Rd., Kings.T. 85 BL52
Penrith Clo. SW15 75 BR46
Penrith Clo., Beck. 87 CE51
Albemarle Rd.
Penrith Clo., Red. 121 BU70
Penrith Clo., Uxb. 53 AX37
High St.
Penrith Cres., Horn. 50 CU35
Penrith Pl. SE27 76 BY48
Penrith Rd. N15 48 BZ32
Penrith Rd., Ilf. 40 CN29
Penrith Rd., N.Mal. 85 BN52
Penrith Rd., Rom. 42 CX29
Penrith Rd., Th.Hth. 87 BZ51
Penrith St. SW16 76 BW50
Penrose Ave., Wat. 36 BE27
Penrose Ct., Hem.H. 8 AY11
Penrose Gro. SE17 67 BZ42
Penrose Ho. SE17 67 BZ42
Penrose Rd., Lthd. 102 BG64
Penrose St. SE17 67 BZ42
Penry St. SE1 4 N9
Penry St. SE1 67 CA42
Marcia Rd.
Penryn St. NW1 56 BW37
Pensbury Pl. SW8 66 BW44
Pensbury St. SW8 66 BW44
Penscroft Gdns., Borwd. 28 BN24
Pensford Ave., Rich. 65 BM44
Pensh St., Orp. 89 CP52
Penshurst, Harl. 6 CP9
Penshurst Ave., Sid. 79 CO46
Penshurst Clo., Ger.Cr. 34 AR30
Penshurst Clo., Sev. 99 CZ57
Penshurst Gdns., Edg. 37 BM28
Penshurst Grn., Brom. 88 CG53
Penshurst Rd. E9 57 CC36
Penshurst Rd. N17 39 CA29
Penshurst Rd., Bexh. 69 CQ44
Penshurst Rd., Pot.B. 20 BT19
Penshurst Rd., Th.Hth. 86 BY53
Penshurst Way, Sutt. 95 BS57
Pensmead Ter. E4 39 CF28
Mead Cres.
Pensons La., Ong. 23 CU17
Penstock Footpath N22 47 BX31
Pentelowe Gdns., Felt. 73 BC46
Pentire Clo., Upmin. 51 CZ32
Pentire Rd. E17 39 CF30
Pentland, Hem.H. 8 AY12
Mendip Way
Pentland Ave., Shep. 83 AZ53
Pentland Clo. NW11 46 BR34
Pentland Gdns. SW18 76 BT46
St. Annes Hill
Pentland Pl., Nthlt. 54 BE37
Pentland Rd., Bush. 27 BG25
Pentland St. SW18 76 BT46
Pentland Way, Uxb. 44 BA34
Pentlands Clo., Mitch. 86 BV52
Pentley Clo., Welw.G.C. 5 BQ6
Pentley Pk., Welw.G.C. 5 BQ6
Pentlow St. SW15 65 BQ45
Pentlow Way, Buck.H. 40 CK26
Pentney Rd. E4 39 CF26
Pretoria Rd.
Pentney Rd. SW12 76 BW47
Pentney Rd. SW19 85 BR51
Midmoor Rd.
Penton Ave., Stai. 72 AV50
Penton Dr., Chsnt. 21 CC18
Penton Gro. N1 2 D1
Penton Hall Dr., Stai. 83 AW51
Penton Hook Rd., Stai. 83 AW51
Penton Pl. SE17 4 G10
Penton Pl. SE17 66 BY42
Penton Ri. WC1 2 C2
Penton Ri. WC1 56 BX38
Penton Rd., Stai. 72 AV50
Penton St. N1 2 D1
Penton St. N1 56 BY37
Pentonville Rd. N1 2 B1
Pentonville Rd. N1 56 BX37
Pentreath Ave., Guil. 118 AP71
Pentrich Ave., Enf. 30 CB22
Pentridge St. SE15 67 CA43
Pentyre Ave. N18 39 BZ28
Penwerris Ave., Islw. 64 BG43
Penwith Rd. SW18 76 BS48
Penwood End, Wok. 100 AQ64
Penwortham Rd. SW16 76 BV50
Penwortham Rd., S.Croy. 96 BA58
Penylan Pl., Edg. 37 BM29
Penywern Rd. SW5 66 BS42
Penzance Clo., Uxb. 35 AX30
Penzance Gdns., Rom. 42 CX29
Penzance Pl. W11 55 BR40
Penzance Rd., Rom. 42 CX29
Penzance St. W11 55 BR40
Peony Clo., Brwd. 33 DA25
Lavender Ave.
Peony Gdns. W12 55 BP40
The Curve
Peplins Clo., Hat. 19 BR16
Peplins Way, Hat. 19 BR16
Peploe Rd. NW6 55 BQ37
Peplow Clo., West Dr. 53 AX40
Pepper All., Loug. 31 CG23
Pepper Clo. E6 58 CK39
Hallywell Cres.
Pepper Hill, Grav. 81 DE48
Pepper St. E14 67 CE41
Pepper St. SE1 4 H4
Pepper St. SE1 67 BZ41
Peppercroft St., Grav. 81 DG47
Peppermint Clo., Croy. 86 BX54
Alfriston Ave.
Pepys Clo., Ash. 103 BL62
Pepys Clo., Dart. 70 CX45
Pepys Clo., Grav. 81 DE48
Pepys Clo., Slou. 62 AT43
Pepys Clo., Til. 71 DH44
Pepys Clo., Uxb. 44 AZ35
Pepys Cres., Barn. 28 BQ25
Pepys Ri., Orp. 88 CN54
Pepys Rd. SE14 67 CC44
Pepys Rd. SW20 85 BQ51
Pepys St. EC3 2 N10
Pepys St. EC3 57 CA40
Perceval Ave. NW3 47 BU35
Perch St. E8 48 CA35
Percheron Rd., Borwd. 28 BN25
Percival Ct. N17 39 CA29
High Rd.
Percival Gdns., Rom. 50 CP32
Percival Rd. SW14 75 BN46
Percival Rd., Enf. 30 CA24
Percival Rd., Felt. 73 BB48
Percival Rd., Horn. 51 CV32
Percival Rd., Orp. 88 CL55
Percival St. EC1 2 F4
Percival St. EC1 56 BY38
Percival St. SE2 69 CP41
Harrow Manorway
Percival Way, Epsom 94 BN56
Percy Ave., Ashf. 73 AZ49
Percy Bryant Rd., Sun. 73 BB50
Percy Circ. WC1 2 C2
Percy Circ. WC1 56 BX38
Percy Gdns., Enf. 30 CC25
Percy Gdns., Hayes 53 BB38
Percy Gdns., Islw. 64 BJ45
Percy Gdns., Wor.Pk. 85 BN54
Percy Ms. W1 1 N7
Percy Ms. W1 56 BW39
Rathbone Pl.
Percy Pas. W1 1 M7
Percy Pl., Slou. 62 AQ44
Percy Rd. E11 49 CG33
Percy Rd. E16 58 CG38
Percy Rd. N12 38 BT28
Percy Rd. N21 39 BZ26
Percy Rd. NW6 56 BS38
Percy Rd. SE20 87 CC51
Percy Rd. SE25 87 CA53
Percy Rd. W12 65 BP41
Percy Rd., Bexh. 69 CQ44
Percy Rd., Guil. 118 AQ69
Percy Rd., Hmptn. 74 BF50
Percy Rd., Ilf. 50 CO33
Percy Rd., Islw. 64 BJ45
Percy Rd., Mitch. 86 BV54
Percy Rd., Rom. 50 CR31
Percy Rd., Twick. 74 BF47
Percy Rd., Wat. 26 BC24
Percy St. W1 1 N7
Percy St. W1 56 BW39
Percy St., Grays 71 DE43
Percy Ter., Ch.St.G. 34 AQ27
Percy Way, Twick. 74 BG47
Percy Yd. WC1 2 C2
Peregrin Rd., Wal.Abb. 22 CH20
Peregrine Clo. NW10 55 BN36
Kingfisher Way
Peregrine Clo., Wat. 18 BE20
Peregrine Ct. SW16 76 BX49
Leithcote Gdns.
Peregrine Gdns., Croy. 87 CD55
Peregrine Ho. EC1 2 G2
Peregrine Rd., Ilf. 41 CO28
Peregrine Rd., Sun. 83 BB51
Peregrine Wk., Rain. 59 CU36
Heron Flight Ave.
Peregrine Way SW19 75 BQ50
Perham Rd. W14 65 BR42
Peridot St. E6 58 CK39
Perifield SE21 77 BZ47
Perimeade Rd., Grnf. 54 BK37
Perimeter Rd., Red. 121 BW73
Periton Rd. SE9 68 CJ45
Perivale Gdns. W13 54 BJ38
Bellevue Rd.
Perivale Gdns., Wat. 17 BC20
Perivale La., Grnf. 54 BJ38
Perkins Clo., Wem. 45 BJ35
Perkins Ct., Ashf. 73 AY49
Fairholme Rd.
Perkins Rents SW1 3 N6
Perkins Rents SW1 66 BW41
Old Pye St.
Perkins Rd., Ilf. 49 CM32
Perks Clo. SE3 68 CG45
Hurren Clo.
Perpins Rd. SE9 78 CM46
Perram Clo., Brox. 21 CD16
Garner Dr.
Perran Clo., Hartley 90 DC52
Perran Rd. SW2 76 BY47
Perran Wk., Brent. 65 BL42
Burford Rd.
Perren St. NW5 56 BV36
Ryland Rd.
Perrers Rd. W6 65 BP42
Perrin Clo., Ashf. 73 AY49
Perrin Rd., Wem. 45 BJ35
Perring Est. E3 57 C
Perrins Ct. NW3 47 B
Hampstead High St.
Perrins La. NW3 47 B
Perrins Wk. NW3 47 B
Perriors Clo., Chsnt. 21 C
Adamsfield
Perry Clo., Rain. 59 C
Perry Clo., Uxb. 53 A
Perry Cft., Wind. 61 AN
Perry Gdns. N9 39 B
Perry Garth, Nthlt. 54 BD
Perry Grn., Hem.H. 8 A
Perry Gro., Dart. 70 CX
Perry Hall Clo., Orp. 89 CC
Perry Hall Rd., Orp. 88 CN
Perry Hill SE6 77 CD
Perry Hill, Wal.Abb. 13 CG
Perry Hill Est. SE23 77 C
Perry How, Wor.Pk. 85 BC
Perry Mead, Bush. 36 B
Perry Mead, Enf. 29 BY
Perry Ri. SE23 77 CD
Perry Rd., Harl. 13 CM
Perry Spring, Harl. 14 CF
Perry St., Chis. 78 CM
Perry St., Dart. 69 CT
Perry St., Grav. 81 DF
Perry St. Gdns., Chis. 78 CN
Perry St. Shaw, Chis. 78 CN
Perry Vale SE23 77 CC
Perry Way, S.Ock. 60 CY
Perrycoste Ct., St.Alb. 9 BJ
Taylor Clo.
Perryfield La., Ong. 15 CY
Perryfield Way NW9 46 BC
Perryfield Way, Rich. 74 B
Perrymans Fm. Rd., Ilf. 49 CM
Perrymead St. SW6 66 BS
Perryn Rd. SE16 67 CE
Perryn Rd. W3 55 BN
Perrys La., Orp. 98 CC
Perrys Pl. W1 1
Perrysfield Rd., Chsnt. 21 CD
Persant Rd. SE6 78 CG
Perseverance Pl. SW9 66 BY
Mandela St.
Perseverance Pl., Rich. 65 BL
Kew Rd.
Persfield Clo., Epsom 94 BO
Pershore Clo., Ilf. 49 CL
Pershore Gro., Cars. 86 BT
Pert Clo. N10 38 BV
Perth Ave. NW9 46 BN
Perth Ave., Hayes 54 BD
Perth Clo. SW20 85 BP
Perth Rd. E10 48 CD
Perth Rd. E13 58 CH
Perth Rd. N4 47 BY
Perth Rd. N22 38 BY
Perth Rd., Bark. 58 CM
Perth Rd., Beck. 87 CF
Perth Rd., Ilf. 49 CL
Perth Ter., Ilf. 49 CM
Perwell Ave., Har. 45 BE
Perwell Ct., Har. 45 BE
Perystreete SE23 77 CC
Perry Vale
Pescot Hill, Hem.H. 8 AW
Peter Ave. NW10 55 BP
Peter Ave., Oxt. 114 CF
Peter St. W1 1 N
Peter St. W1 56 BW
Peterboat Clo. SE10 68 CG
Peterborough Ave., Upmin. 51 CZ
Peterborough Gdns., Ilf. 49 CK
Peterborough Ms. SW6 66 BS
Peterborough Rd. E10 48 CF
Peterborough Rd. SW6 66 BS
Peterborough Rd., Cars. 86 BT
Peterborough Rd., Guil. 118 AP
Peterborough Rd., Har. 45 BH
Peterborough Vill. SW6 66 BS
Petergate SW11 66 BT
Peterhill Clo., Ger.Cr. 34 AS
Peterlee Ct., Hem.H. 8 AY
Peters Ave., St.Alb. 18 BK
Peters Clo., Dag. 50 CP
Peters Clo., Stan. 36 BK
Peters Hill EC4 2 H1
Peters Hill EC4 57 BZ
Carter La.
Peters La. EC1 2 F
Peters La. EC1 56 BY
Cowcross St.
Peters La., Maid. 61 AG
Peters Path SE26 77 CB
Peters Pl., Berk. 7 AP1
Petersfield Ave., Rom. 42 CW2
Petersfield Ave., Slou. 52 AQ4
Petersfield Ave., Stai. 73 AX4
Petersfield Clo. N18 39 BZ2
Petersfield Clo., Rom. 42 CX2
Petersfield Cres., Couls. 104 BX6
Petersfield Ri. SW15 75 BP4
Petersfield Rd. W3 65 BN4
Petersfield Way, Brwd. 123 DE
Petersham Ave., Wey. 92 AY5
Petersham Clo., Rich. 74 BK4
Petersham Clo., Sutt. 95 BS5
Petersham Clo., Wey. 92 AY5
Petersham Dr., Orp. 88 CN5
Petersham Gdns., Orp. 88 CN5
Petersham Dr.
Petersham La. SW7 66 BT4
Petersham Ms. SW7 66 BT4
Petersham Pl. SW7 66 BT4
Petersham Rd., Rich. 74 BK4
Petersham Ter., Croy. 86 BX5
Richmond Grn.
Petersham Way, Orp. 89 CO5
Peterstone Rd. SE2 69 CO4

terstow Clo. SW19 75 BR48
Princes Way
terswood, Harl. 13 CM13
therton Rd. N5 48 BZ35
tley Rd. W6 65 BQ43
to Pl. NW1 1 K4
to Pl. NW1 56 BV38
to St. N. E16 58 CG40
to St. S. E16 58 CG40
tre Clo., Brwd. 123 DE32
tridge Rd., Red. 121 BU73
trie Clo. NW2 55 BR36
tt St. SE18 68 CK42
tten Clo., Orp. 89 CP54
tten Gro., Orp. 89 CP54
tters Rd., Ash. 103 BL61
tticoat Sq. E1 2 P8
ttits Boul., Rom. 41 CT30
ttits Clo., Rom. 41 CT30
ttits La., Brwd. 33 DC22
ttits La., Rom. 41 CT30
ttits La. N., Rom. 41 CS30
ttits Pl., Dag. 50 CR35
ttits Rd., Dag. 50 CR35
ttiward Clo. SW15 65 BP45
Colinette Rd.
ttley Gdns., Rom. 50 CS32
ttman Cres. SE28 68 CM41
tts Hill, Nthlt. 45 BF35
tts La., Shep. 83 AZ52
tts Wd. Rd., Orp. 88 CM53
ttsgrove Ave., Wem. 45 BK35
tty France SW1 3 M6
tty France SW1 66 BW41
tty La., Brom. 88 CH51
Church Rd.
tworth Clo., Couls. 104 BW63
Starrock Rd.
tworth Clo., Nthlt. 54 BE36
tworth Gdns. SW20 85 BP52
tworth Gdns., Uxb. 53 BA37
tworth Rd. N12 38 BU28
tworth Rd., Bexh. 79 CR46
tworth St. SW11 66 BU44
tworth Way, Horn. 50 CT35
tyt Pl. SW3 66 BU43
tyward SW3 3 D9
tyward SW3 66 BU42
vensey Ave. N11 38 BW28
vensey Ave., Enf. 30 BZ23
vensey Clo., Islw. 64 BG43
vensey Rd. E7 49 CG35
vensey Rd. SW17 76 BT49
vensey Rd., Felt. 74 BE47
veril Dr., Tedd. 74 BG49
wley Bank, Guil. 118 AS71
wley Hill, Guil. 118 AR71
wley Pt., Guil. 118 AS71
wley Way, Guil. 118 AS71
wsey Clo. E4 39 CE28
yton Pl. SE10 67 CF43
ytons Cotts., Red. 113 BX69
easant Clo., Berk. 7 AR13
easant Clo., Pur. 95 BY60
Partridge Knoll
easant Hill, Ch.St.G. 34 AR27
easant Ri., Chesh. 16 AO20
easant Wk., Ger.Cr. 34 AR28
easants Way, Rick. 35 AW26
elips Rd., Harl. 13 CL13
elp St. SE17 67 BZ42
elps Clo., Sev. 99 CZ57
elps Way, Hayes 63 BB42
ene St. SW3 66 BU43
il Brown Pl. SW8 66 BV45
Heath Rd.
ilan Way, Rom. 41 CS29
ilanthropic Rd., Red. 121 BV71
ilbeach Gdns. SW5 66 BS42
ilchurch Pl. E1 57 CB39
Ellen St.
ilip Ave., Rom. 50 CS33
ilip Clo., Brwd. 33 DA25
ilip Clo., Rom. 50 CS33
Philip Ave.
ilip Gdns., Croy. 87 CD55
ilip La. N15 48 BZ31
ilip Rd., Rain. 59 CT38
ilip Rd., Stai. 73 AX50
ilipot Path SE9 78 CK46
ilipp St. E13 58 CH38
ilipp Wk. SE15 67 CB45
ilippa Gdns. SE9 78 CJ46
ilippa Way, Grays 71 DG42
illida Rd., Rom. 42 CX30
illimore Clo., Rad. 27 BH21
illimore Gdns. NW10 55 BQ37
illimore Gdns. W8 66 BS41
illimore Gdns. Clo. W8 66 BS41
illimore Pl. W8 66 BS41
illimore Pl., Rad. 27 BH21
illimore Wk. W8 66 BS41
illip Ave., Swan. 89 CS52
illipers, Wat. 27 BD21
illipp St. N1 57 CA37
illips Clo., Dart. 79 CU46
ilpot La. EC3 2 M10
ilpot La. EC3 57 CA40
ilpot La., Wok. 91 AR59
ilpot Path, Ilf. 49 CM34
ilpot Sq., Surb. 66 BS45
Peterborough Rd.
ilpot St. E1 57 CB39
ineas Pett Rd. SE9 68 CK45
ipp St. EC2 2 M4
ipp St. EC2 57 CA38
ipps Bri. Rd. SW19 86 BT51
ipps Bri. Rd., Mitch. 86 BT52
ipps Hatch La., Enf. 30 BZ22
ipps Ms. SW1 3 J7
obe Rd., Hem.H. 8 AY12
oebeth Rd. SE4 77 CE46
oenix Clo. E8 57 CA37
Stean St.

Phoenix Clo., Nthwd. 35 BB28
Phoenix Clo., W.Wick. 87 CF55
Phoenix Dr., Kes. 88 CJ55
Phoenix Lo. Mans. W6 65 BQ42
Brook Grn.
Phoenix Pl. WC1 2 C4
Phoenix Pl. WC1 56 BX38
Phoenix Pl., Dart. 80 CV47
Phoenix Rd. NW1 1 N2
Phoenix Rd. NW1 56 BW38
Phoenix Rd. SE20 77 CC50
Phoenix St. WC2 1 P9
Phoenix St. WC2 56 BW39
Stacey St.
Phoenix Way, Houns. 64 BD43
Phygtle, The, Ger.Cr. 34 AS29
Phyllis Ave., N.Mal. 85 BP53
Picardy Manorway, Belv. 69 CR41
Picardy Rd., Belv. 69 CR42
Picardy St., Belv. 69 CR41
Piccadilly W1 3 K3
Piccadilly W1 56 BV40
Piccadilly Arc. SW1 3 L2
Piccadilly Circ. W1 3 N1
Piccadilly Pl. W1 3 M1
Piccadilly Pl. W1 56 BW40
Piccadilly
Piccards, The, Guil. 118 AR72
Piccotts End La., Hem.H. 8 AX12
Piccotts End Rd., Hem.H. 8 AW11
Pick Hill, Wal.Abb. 22 CG19
Pickard St. EC1 2 G2
Pickard St. EC1 56 BY38
Moreland St.
Pickering Ave. E6 58 CL37
Pickering Ms. W2 56 BS39
Bishops Bri. Rd.
Pickering Pl. SW1 3 M3
Pickering Pl. SW1 56 BW40
St. James St.
Pickering St. N1 56 BY37
Essex Rd.
Pickets Clo., Bush. 36 BH26
Pickets St. SW12 76 BV47
Pickett Cft., Stan. 36 BK30
Picketts, Welw.G.C. 5 BQ6
Picketts Lock La. N9 39 CC27
Pickford Clo., Bexh. 69 CQ44
Pickford Dr., Slou. 52 AS40
Pickford La., Bexh. 69 CQ45
Pickford Rd., Bexh. 69 CQ45
Pickford Rd., St.Alb. 9 BJ14
Sutton Rd.
Pickford Wf. N1 2 H1
Pickhurst Grn., Brom. 88 CG54
Pickhurst La., Brom. 88 CG54
Pickhurst La., W.Wick. 88 CG53
Pickhurst Mead, Brom. 88 CG54
Pickhurst Pk., Brom. 88 CG53
Pickhurst Ri., W.Wick. 87 CF54
Pickins Piece, Slou. 62 AT44
Pickmoss La., Sev. 107 CU61
Pickwick Clo., Houns. 74 BE46
Dorney Way
Pickwick Gdns., Grav. 81 DE48
Pickwick Ms. N18 39 CA28
Pickwick Pl., Har. 45 BH33
Pickwick Rd. SE21 77 BZ47
Pickwick St. SE1 4 H5
Pickwick St. SE1 67 BZ41
Pickwick Way, Chis. 78 CM50
Dickens Dr.
Pickworth Clo. SW8 66 BX43
Kenchester Clo.
Picquets Way, Bans. 103 BR61
Picton Pl. W1 1 H9
Picton Pl. W1 56 BV39
Picton St. SE5 67 BZ43
Piedmont Rd. SE18 68 CM42
Pield Heath Ave., Uxb. 53 AZ38
Pield Heath Rd., Uxb. 53 AY38
Pier Rd. E16 58 CL40
Pier Rd., Erith 69 CT43
Pier Rd., Felt. 73 BC46
Pier Rd., Grav. 81 DF46
Pier Rd., Green. 70 DA45
High St.
Pier Rd. Est. E16 68 CL41
Pier St. E14 67 CF42
Pier Ter. SW18 66 BS45
Jews Row
Pier Wk., Grays 71 DD43
Pier Way SE28 68 CM41
Piercing Hill, Epp. 31 CM21
Piermont Grn. SE22 77 CB46
Peckham Rye
Piermont Pl., Brom. 88 CK51
Piermont Rd. SE22 77 CB46
Upland Rd.
Pierrepoint Rd. W3 55 BM40
Pierrepoint Row Arc. N1 56 BY37
Charlton Pl.
Pierson Rd., Wind. 61 AL44
Pigeon La., Hmptn. 74 BF49
Pigeonhouse La., Couls. 113 BT66
Piggot St. E14 57 CE39
Pike Clo., Brom. 78 CH49
Pike Gdns. SE1 56 BY40
Pike La., Upmin. 51 CZ35
Pike Rd. NW7 37 BN28
Ellesmere Ave.
Pike Way, Epp. 23 CR17
Pikes End, Pnr. 44 BC31
Pikes Hill, Epsom 94 BO60
Pikestone Clo., Hayes 54 BE38
Berrydale Rd.
Pilgrim Clo., Brwd. 33 CZ25
Pilgrim Clo., St.Alb. 18 BG17
Pilgrim Hill SE27 77 BZ49
Pilgrim Hill, Orp. 89 CQ51
Pilgrim St. EC4 2 F9
Pilgrim St. EC4 56 BY39
Pilgrimage St. SE1 4 K5
Pilgrimage St. SE1 67 BZ41

Pilgrims Clo. N13 38 BX28
Pilgrims Clo., Brwd. 33 CZ25
Pilgrims Clo., Dor. 119 BJ69
Pilgrims Clo., Nthlt. 45 BG35
Pilgrims Clo., Wat. 18 BD20
Kytes Dr.
Pilgrims Ct. SE3 68 CH44
Pilgrims La. NW3 47 BT35
Pilgrims La., Brwd. 33 CY24
Pilgrims La., Cat. 113 BY66
Pilgrims La., Grays 60 DB40
Pilgrims La., Oxt. 115 CH66
Pilgrims Pl. NW3 47 BT35
Hampstead High St.
Pilgrims Pl., Reig. 121 BS69
Pilgrims Ri., Barn. 29 BU25
Pilgrims Rd., Swans. 71 DC45
Pilgrims Way N19 47 BW33
Pilgrims Way, Bet. 120 BL70
Pilgrims Way, Dart. 80 CX47
Pilgrims Way, Dor. 119 BG70
Pilgrims Way, Dor. 120 BL70
Pilgrims Way (West Humble), Dor. 119 BJ69
Pilgrims Way, Guil. 118 AO73
Pilgrims Way, Guil. 118 AR72
Pilgrims Way, Reig. 120 BR69
Pilgrims Way, Sev. 108 CY61
Pilgrims Way, S.Croy. 96 CA57
Pilgrims Way, Wem. 46 BM33
Pilgrims Way, West. 106 CL65
Pilgrims Way E., Sev. 108 CV61
Pilgrims Way W., Sev. 107 CS61
Pilkington Rd. SE15 67 CB44
Pilkington Rd., Orp. 88 CL55
Pillions, The, Hayes 53 BA38
Pillmans Clo., Sid. 79 CO50
Pilot Ind. Est. NW10 55 BN38
Pilots Pl., Grav. 81 DH46
East Ter.
Pilsdon Clo. SW19 75 BQ47
Inner Pk. Rd.
Piltdown Rd., Wat. 36 BD28
Pilton Est., Croy. 86 BY55
Pimlico Rd. SW1 3 G10
Pimlico Rd. SW1 66 BV42
Pimlico Wk. N1 2 M2
Pimlico Wk. N1 57 CA38
Pimms Clo., Guil. 109 AT68
Pimpernel Way, Rom. 42 CV29
Pinceybrook Rd., Harl. 13 CM13
Pinchbeck Rd., Orp. 97 CN57
Pinchfield, Rick. 34 AU28
Pinchin St. E1 57 CB40
Pincott La., Lthd. 110 AZ68
Pincott Rd. SW19 76 BT50
Pincott Rd., Bexh. 79 CR46
Pindar Rd., Hodd. 12 CF11
Pindar St. EC2 2 M6
Pindock Ms. W9 56 BS38
Pine Ave. E15 48 CF35
Ashlin Rd.
Pine Ave., Grav. 81 DH47
Pine Ave., W.Wick. 87 CE54
Pine Clo. N14 38 BW26
Pine Clo. N19 47 BW34
Hargrave Pk.
Pine Clo., Berk. 7 AQ13
Pine Clo., Chsnt. 21 CC17
Pine Clo., Ken. 105 BZ62
Pine Clo., Stan. 36 BJ28
Pine Clo., Swan. 89 CT52
Pine Clo., Wey. 92 AW59
Pine Clo., Wok. 100 AR61
Pine Coombe, Croy. 96 CC56
Pine Ct., Upmin. 51 CX35
Pine Cres., Brwd. 122 DE25
Pine Cres., Cars. 95 BT59
Pine Cft., Brwd. 122 DD26
Pine Dean, Lthd. 111 BF66
Pine Gdns., Ruis. 44 BC33
Pine Gdns., Surb. 85 BM53
Pine Glade, Orp. 97 CK56
Pine Gro. N4 47 BX34
Pine Gro. N20 37 BR26
Pine Gro. SW19 75 BR49
Pine Gro., Bush. 27 BE23
Pine Gro., Hat. 20 BS16
Pine Gro., St.Alb. 18 BE18
Pine Gro., Wey. 92 AZ56
Pine Gro. Mt., Wey. 92 BA56
Pine Hill, Epsom 103 BN61
Pine Needles La., Sev. 107 CU65
Pine Pl., Bans. 94 BQ60
Pine Pl., Hayes 53 BB38
Pine Ridge, Cars. 95 BV57
Pine Rd. N11 38 BV27
Pine Rd. NW2 46 BQ35
Pine Rd., Wok. 100 AR63
Pine St. EC1 2 D4
Pine St. EC1 56 BY38
Pine Tree Clo., Houns. 63 BC44
Pine Tree Hill, Wok. 100 AU61
Pine Trees Dr., Uxb. 44 AY35
Pine Wk., Bans. 104 BU62
Pine Wk., Cat. 105 CA64
Pine Wk., Cob. 93 BD60
Pine Wk. (Bookham), Lthd. 111 BF66
Pine Wk. (East Horsley), Lthd. 110 BB67
Pine Wk., Surb. 85 BM53
Pine Wk. E., Cars. 95 BT59
Pine Wk. W., Cars. 95 BT58
Pine Way, Egh. 72 AQ50
Pine Wd., Sun. 83 BC51
Pineapple Ct. SW1 3 L6
Pineapple Rd., Amer. 25 AP23
Pinecrest Gdns., Orp. 97 CL56
Pinecroft, Brwd. 122 DD26
Pinecroft, Hem.H. 8 AY15
Pinecroft, Pnr. 36 BF29
Pinecroft Cres., Barn. 28 BR25
Hillside Gdns.

Pinefield Clo. E14 57 CE40
Pinehurst, Sev. 108 CW64
Pinehurst Clo., Abb.L. 17 BB19
Pinehurst Clo., Tad. 104 BS64
Pinehurst Wk, Orp. 88 CN54
Pinelands Clo. SE3 68 CG43
St. Johns Pk.
Pines, The N14 29 BW25
Chase Rd.
Pines, The, Dor. 119 BJ72
South Ter.
Pines, The, Grays 71 DD40
Pines, The, Pur. 95 BY60
Pines, The, Sun. 83 BC52
Pines, The, Wdf.Grn. 40 CH27
Pines Ave., Enf. 30 CC21
Pines Clo., Nthwd. 35 BB29
Pines Rd., Brom. 88 CK51
Pinetree Clo., Ger.Cr. 34 AR29
Pinetree Clo., Hem.H. 8 AX13
Christchurch Rd.
Pinetree La., Sev. 117 DA66
Pineview Clo., Guil. 118 AV73
Pinewood, Welw.G.C. 5 BR9
Pinewood Ave., Pnr. 36 BF29
Pinewood Ave., Rain. 59 CU38
Pinewood Ave., Sev. 108 CV64
Pinewood Ave., Sid. 78 CN47
Pinewood Ave., Uxb. 53 AY39
Pinewood Ave., Wey. 92 AX58
Pinewood Clo., Borwd. 28 BN23
Pinewood Clo., Croy. 87 CD55
Pinewood Clo., Ger.Cr. 43 AS33
Pinewood Clo., Harl. 14 CP11
London Rd.
Pinewood Clo., Iver 52 AU36
Pinewood Clo., Orp. 88 CM54
Pinewood Clo., St.Alb. 9 BK13
Pinewood Clo., S.le H. 71 DK42
Pinewood Clo., Wok. 100 AT61
Pinewood Dr., Orp. 97 CM56
Pinewood Dr., Stai. 73 AW49
Pinewood Gdns., Hem.H. 8 AW13
Pinewood Grn., Iver 52 AU36
Pinewood Gro. W5 54 BK39
Pinewood Gro., Wey. 92 AW58
Pinewood Pk., Wey. 92 AW59
Pinewood Rd. SE2 69 CP43
Pinewood Rd., Brom. 88 CH52
Pinewood Rd., Felt. 73 BC48
Pinewood Rd., Hav. 41 CS28
Pinewood Rd., Iver 52 AT36
Pinewood Rd., Vir.W. 82 AQ52
Pinewood Way, Brwd. 122 DE25
Pinfold Rd. SW16 76 BX49
Pinfold Rd., Bush. 27 BE23
Pinkcoat Clo., Felt. 73 BC48
Tanglewood Way
Pinkerton Pl. SW16 76 BW49
Riggindale Rd.
Pinks Hill, Swan. 89 CT53
Pinkwell Ave., Hayes 63 BA42
Pinkwell La., Hayes 63 BA42
Pinley Gdns., Dag. 59 CO37
Pinn Clo., Uxb. 53 AX39
Pinn Way, Ruis. 44 BA33
Pinnacle Hill, Bexh. 69 CR45
Pinnacle Hill N., Bexh. 69 CR45
Pinnacles, Wal.Abb. 22 CG20
Pinnate Pl., Welw.G.C. 5 BR10
Pinnell Pl. SE9 68 CJ45
Pinnell Rd. SE9 68 CJ45
Pinner Ct., Pnr. 45 BF31
Pinner Cres., Pnr. 45 BE32
Pinner Grn., Pnr. 36 BD30
Pinner Hill, Pnr. 36 BD30
Pinner Hill Rd., Pnr. 36 BD30
Pinner Pk. Ave., Har. 36 BG30
Pinner Pk. Gdns., Har. 36 BG30
Pinner Rd., Nthwd. 35 BB30
Pinner Rd., Pnr. 45 BE31
Pinner Rd., Wat. 27 BD25
Pinner Vw., Har. 45 BG32
Pinnicks Ave., Grav. 81 DG47
Pintail Clo. E6 58 CK39
Swann App.
Pintail Rd., Wdf.Grn. 40 CH29
Pinto Clo., Borwd. 28 BN25
Pinto Way SE3 68 CH45
Pioneer Pl., Croy. 96 CE58
Pioneer Way W12 55 BP39
Piper Clo. N7 47 BX35
Piper Rd., Kings.T. 85 BM52
Pipers Clo., Cob. 102 BD61
Pipers End, Vir.W. 82 AR52
Pipers Gdns., Croy. 87 CD54
Pipers Grn. NW9 46 BN32
Pipers Grn. La., Edg. 37 BL27
Pipers Grn. Rd., West. 116 CO67
Pipers La., West. 116 CO67
Pipewell Rd., Cars. 86 BU53
Pippbrook Gdns., Dor. 119 BJ71
Pippens, Welw.G.C. 5 BR6
Pippin Clo., Croy. 87 CO54
Pippins, The, Slou. 52 AS40
Pickford Dr.
Pippins Clo., West Dr. 63 AX41
Pippins Ct., Ashf. 73 AZ50
Piquet Rd. SE20 87 CC51
Pirbright Cres., Croy. 96 CF57
Pirbright Rd. SW18 75 BR47
Pirie St. E16 58 CH40
Pirrip Clo., Grav. 81 DK48
Pirton Clo., St.Alb. 9 BK11
Pishiobury Dr., Saw. 6 CP7
Pishiobury Ms., Saw. 6 CP7
Pit Fm. Rd., Guil. 118 AT70
Pit Wd. Grn., Tad. 103 BQ63
Pitcairn Clo., Rom. 50 CR31
Pitcairn Rd., Mitch. 76 BU50
Pitchfont La., Oxt. 115 CH66
Pitchford St. E15 57 CF36
Pitfield Cres. SE28 59 CO40
Pitfield Est. N1 2 M2

Pitfield Est. N1 57 CA38
Pitfield St. N1 2 M3
Pitfield St. N1 57 CA38
Pitfield Way NW10 55 BN36
Pitfield Way, Enf. 30 CC23
Pitfold Clo. SE12 78 CH46
Pitfold Rd. SE12 78 CH46
Pitlake, Croy. 86 BY55
Pitman St. SE5 67 BZ43
Pitmans Fld., Harl. 6 CN10
Pitsea Pl. E1 57 CC39
Pitsea St.
Pitsea St. E1 57 CC39
Pitsfield, Welw.G.C. 5 BQ6
Pitshanger La. W5 54 BJ38
Pitson Clo., Wey. 92 AX56
Pitstone Clo., St.Alb. 9 BK11
Highview Gdns.
Pitt Cres. SW19 76 BS49
Pitt Pl., Epsom 94 BO60
Pitt Rd., Epsom 94 BO60
Pitt Rd., Har. 45 BG34
Pitt Rd., Orp. 97 CM56
Pitt Rd., Th.Hth. 87 BZ53
Pitt St. SE15 67 CA44
Pitt St. W8 66 BS41
Pittman Clo., Brwd. 122 DE28
Brentwood Rd.
Pittman Gdns., Ilf. 49 CM35
Pitts Head Ms. W1 3 H3
Pitts Head Ms. W1 56 BV40
Pitts Rd., Slou. 61 AO40
Pittsmead Ave., Brom. 88 CH54
Pittville Gdns. SE25 87 CB52
Pittwood, Brwd. 122 DD26
Pix Fm. La., Berk. 7 AT14
Pixfield Ct., Brom. 88 CG51
Pixham La., Dor. 119 BK70
Pixholme Gro., Dor. 119 BK70
Pixie Cres., Hem.H. 7 AV14
Pixley St. E14 57 CD39
Pixton Way, Croy. 96 CD58
Place Fm. Rd., Brwd. 33 DA21
Place Fm. Rd., Red. 114 BZ68
Place Ho. La., Couls. 104 BX63
Placket Way, Slou. 61 AL40
Plain, The, Epp. 23 CP18
Plaistow Grn., Brom. 78 CH50
Plaistow Gro. E15 58 CG37
Plaistow Gro., Brom. 78 CH50
Plaistow La., Brom. 78 CH50
Plaistow Pk. Rd. E13 58 CH37
Plaistow Rd. E15 58 CG37
Plaitford Clo., Rick. 35 AY27
Plane Ave., Grav. 81 DE47
Plane St. SE26 77 CB48
Plane Tree Cres., Felt. 73 BC48
Plane Tree Wk. SE19 77 CA50
Central Hill Est.
Planes, The, Cher. 83 AX54
Bridge Rd.
Plantagenet Clo., Wor.Pk. 94 BN56
Plantagenet Gdns., Rom. 50 CP33
Plantagenet Pl., Rom. 50 CP33
Broomfield Rd.
Plantagenet Rd., Barn. 29 BT24
Plantain Pl. SE1 4 K4
Plantation, The SE3 68 CH44
Plantation Dr., Orp. 89 CP54
Plantation La., Warl. 105 CD63
Plantation Rd., Amer. 25 AP22
Plantation Rd., Erith 69 CU44
Plantation Rd., Swan. 79 CO50
Plantation Wk., Hem.H. 8 AW12
Plantation Way, Amer. 25 AP22
Plasel Ct. E13 58 CH37
Plashet Gdns., Brwd. 122 DD28
Plashet Gro. E6 58 CJ36
Plashet Rd. E13 58 CH37
Plashetts, Bish. 6 CS7
Plassy Rd. SE6 77 CE47
Platford Grn., Horn. 51 CW31
Platina St. EC1 57 BZ38
Tabernacle St.
Platina St. EC2 2 L4
Plato Rd. SW2 66 BX45
Platt, The SW15 65 BQ45
Platt Meadow, Guil. 109 AU69
Eustace Rd.
Platt St. NW1 56 BW37
Platts La. NW3 47 BS35
Platts Rd., Enf. 30 CC23
Plawsfield Rd., Beck. 87 CC51
Plaxdale Grn. Rd., Sev. 99 DB59
Plaxtol Clo., Brom. 88 CJ51
Plaxtol Pl. SE10 68 CH42
Westcombe Hill
Plaxtol Rd., Erith 69 CR43
Playfield Ave., Rom. 41 CS30
Playfield Cres. SE22 77 CA46
Playfield Rd., Edg. 37 BN30
Playford Rd. N4 47 BX34
Playgreen Way SE6 77 CE48
Playground Clo., Beck. 87 CC51
Playhouse Yd. EC4 2 F9
Playhouse Yd. EC4 56 BY39
Pleasance, The SW15 65 BP45
Pleasance Rd.
Pleasance Rd. SW15 65 BP45
Pleasance Rd., Orp. 89 CO51
Pleasant Gro., Croy. 87 CD55
Pleasant Pl. N1 56 BY36
Pleasant Pl., Har. 45 BG33
Pleasant Pl., Walt. 93 BD57
Pleasant Ri., Hat. 10 BQ11
Pleasant Rd., Kings.T. 85 BN52
Pleasant Row NW1 56 BV37
Camden High St.
Pleasant Vw., Erith 69 CT42
Pleasant Vw. Pl., Orp. 97 CM56
Pleasant Way, Wem. 54 BK37
Pleasure Pit Rd., Ash. 103 BM62
Plender Pl. NW1 56 BW37
Plender St.

Plender St. NW1 56 BW37
Plender St. Est. NW1 56 BW37
Pleshey Rd. N7 47 BW35
Plesman Way, Wall. 95 BX57
Plevna Cres. N15 48 CA32
Plevna Rd. N9 39 CB27
Plevna Rd., Hmptn. 84 BF51
Plevna St. E14 67 CF41
Pleydell Ave. SE19 77 CA50
Pleydell Ave. W6 65 BO42
Pleydell Ct. EC4 56 BY39
Fleet St.
Pleydell St. EC4 2 E9
Plimsoll Clo. E14 57 CE39
Grundy St.
Plimsoll Rd. N4 47 BY34
Plough All. E1 57 CB40
Hermitage Wall
Plough Ct. EC3 2 L10
Plough Est. SE8 67 CC42
Plough Fm. Clo., Ruis. 44 BA32
Plough Hill, Cuffley 20 BX18
Plough La. SE22 77 CA46
Plough La. SW17 76 BS49
Plough La. SW19 76 BS49
Plough La., Berk. 7 AT11
Plough La., Cob. 101 BC62
Plough La., Pur. 95 BX58
Plough La., Rick. 16 AV20
Plough La., Slou. 52 AQ37
Plough La., Uxb. 35 AX29
Plough La., Wall. 95 BX56
Plough La. Clo., Wall. 95 BX56
Plough Pl. EC4 2 E8
Plough Pl. EC4 56 BY39
New Fetter La.
Plough Ri., Upmin. 51 CZ33
Plough Rd. SW11 66 BT45
Plough Rd., Brent. 64 BK43
Brent Way
Plough Rd., Epsom 94 BN58
Plough Ter. SW11 66 BT45
Plough Way SE16 67 CC42
Plough Yd. EC2 2 N5
Plough Yd. EC2 57 CA38
Hearn St.
Ploughlees La., Slou. 52 AP40
Ploughmans End, Islw. 74 BG46
Crofters Clo.
Ploughmans End, Welw.G.C. 5 BT8
Forresters Dr.
Plover Clo., Berk. 7 AR13
Plover Clo., Stai. 72 AV48
Plover Gdns., Upmin. 51 CZ33
Plovers Baron, Brwd. 33 DB21
Plovers Mead, Brwd. 33 DB21
Plowman Way, Dag. 50 CP33
Ployters Rd., Harl. 13 CM13
Pluckington Pl., Sthl. 64 BE41
Plum Garth, Brent. 64 BK42
Plum La. SE18 68 CL43
Plumbers Row E1 57 CB39
Plumbridge St. SE10 67 CE44
Plummer La., Mitch. 86 BU51
Plummer Rd. SW4 76 BW46
Plumpton Ave., Horn. 51 CW35
Plumpton Clo., Nthlt. 54 BF36
Plumpton Rd., Hodd. 12 CF11
Plumpton Way, Cars. 86 BU55
Plumstead Common Rd. SE18 68 CL43
Plumstead High St. SE18 68 CN42
Plumstead Rd. SE18 68 CL42
Plumtree Clo., Wall. 95 BW57
Plumtree Ct. EC4 2 F8
Plumtree Ct. EC4 56 BY39
Shoe La.
Plumtree Mead, Loug. 31 CL24
Pluto Ri., Hem.H. 8 AY12
Plymouth Dr., Sev. 108 CV65
Plymouth Pk., Sev. 108 CV65
Plymouth Rd. E16 58 CH39
Plymouth Rd., Brom. 88 CH51
Plymouth Wf. E14 67 CF42
Plympton Ave. NW6 55 BR36
Plympton Clo., Belv. 69 CQ41
Halifield Dr.
Plympton Pl. NW8 1 C5
Plympton Rd. NW6 55 BR36
Plympton St. NW8 1 C5
Plympton St. NW8 56 BU38
Plymstock Rd., Well. 69 CP43
Pocketsdell La., Hem.H. 16 AR17
Pocklington Clo. NW9 37 BO30
Pocock St. SE1 4 F4
Pocock St. SE1 66 BY41
Pococks La. (Eton), Wind. 62 AP42
Podmore Rd. SW18 66 BT45
Poets Rd. N5 48 BZ35
Poets Way, Har. 45 BH31
Point, The, Ruis. 44 BB35
Point Clo. SE10 67 CF44
Point Hill
Point Hill SE10 67 CF43
Point Pleasant SW18 66 BS45
Pointalls Clo. N3 38 BT30
Pointer Clo. SE28 59 CP39
Pointers Clo. E14 67 CE42
Pointers Cotts., Rich. 74 BK48
Pointers Hill, Dor. 119 BG72
Pointers Rd., Cob. 101 BA61
Poland St. W1 1 M8
Poland St. W1 56 BW39
Polayn Garth, Welw.G.C. 5 BQ7
Pole Cat All., Brom. 88 CG55
Pole Hanger La., Hem.H. 7 AV12
Pole Hill Rd. E4 39 CF26
Pole Hill Rd., Uxb. 53 AZ38
Pole La., Ong. 14 CT12
Polebrook Rd. SE3 68 CJ45
Polecroft La. SE6 77 CD48
Poles Hill, Rick. 16 AV20
Polesden Gdns. SW20 85 BP51
Polesden La., Wok. 100 AV65
Polesden Rd., Dor. 111 BF68
Polesden Vw., Lthd. 111 BF67
Polesteeple Hill, West. 106 CJ62
Polesworth Rd., Dag. 59 CP36
Polhill, Sev. 107 CS61
Police Sta. La., Bush. 36 BF26
School La.
Police Sta. Rd., Walt. 93 BD57
Pollard Ave., Ger.Cr. 43 AV32
Pollard Clo. E16 58 CH40
Munday Rd.
Pollard Clo. N7 47 BX35
Pollard Clo., Chig. 41 CO28
Pollard Clo., Wind. 72 AO46
Pollard Hatch, Harl. 13 CL12
Pollard Rd. N20 38 BU27
Pollard Rd. NW9 46 BO33
The Bdy.
Pollard Rd., Mord. 86 BT53
Pollard Rd., Wok. 100 AT61
Pollard Row E2 57 CB38
Pollard St. E2 57 CB38
Pollard Wk., Sid. 79 CP50
Evry Rd.
Pollards, Loug. 31 CJ25
Pollards, Rick. 34 AU28
Pollards Clo., Chsnt. 21 BZ18
Pollards Cres. SW16 86 BX52
Pollards Hill E. SW16 86 BX52
Pollards Hill N. SW16 86 BX52
Pollards Hill S. SW16 86 BX52
Pollards Hill W. SW16 86 BX52
Pollards Oak Cres., Oxt. 115 CH69
Pollards Oak Rd., Oxt. 115 CH69
Pollards Wd. Hill, Oxt. 115 CH68
Pollards Wd. Rd. SW16 86 BX52
Pollards Wd. Rd., Oxt. 115 CH69
Pollen St. W1 1 L9
Pollen St. W1 56 BW39
Hanover St.
Pollicot Clo., St.Alb. 9 BK11
Pirton Clo.
Pollitt Dr. NW8 1 B4
Polls La., Sev. 99 DA60
Pollyhaugh, Eyns. 90 CV55
Polperro Clo., Orp. 89 CN53
Cotswold Ri.
Polsted La., Guil. 118 AO73
Polsted Rd. SE6 77 CD47
Polthorne Gro. SE18 68 CM42
Poltimore Rd., Guil. 118 AQ71
Polworth Rd. SW16 76 BX49
Polygon Rd. NW1 1 N1
Polygon Rd. NW1 56 BW37
Polytechnic St. SE18 68 CL42
Pomell Way E1 2 Q8
Pomeroy Clo., Amer. 25 AO23
Pomeroy Cres., Wat. 26 BC21
Pomeroy St. SE14 67 CC44
Pomfret Rd. SE5 67 BZ45
Flaxman Rd.
Pompadour Clo., Brwd. 42 DB28
Queen St.
Pond Clo. SE3 68 CG44
Pond Clo., Uxb. 35 AX30
Pond Clo., Walt. 92 BB57
Pond Cottage La., W.Wick. 87 CE54
Pond Cotts. SE21 77 CA47
Pond Cft., Hat. 10 BO12
Pond Grn., Ruis. 44 BB34
Pond Hill, Sutt. 94 BR57
Pond Hill Gdns., Sutt. 94 BR57
Pond Ho. SW3 66 BU42
Pond La., Ger.Cr. 34 AQ30
Pond La., Sev. 117 CZ66
Pond Mead SE21 77 BZ46
Pond Meadow, Guil. 118 AP70
Pond Piece, Lthd. 93 BF60
Pond Pl. SW3 3 C9
Pond Pl. SW3 66 BU42
Pond Rd. E15 58 CG37
Pond Rd. SE3 68 CG44
Pond Rd., Egh. 72 AU50
Pond Rd., Hem.H. 17 AZ16
Pond Rd., Wok. 100 AQ63
Pond Sq. N6 47 BV33
Pond St. NW3 47 BU35
Pond Wk., Upmin. 51 CZ34
Pond Way, Tedd. 74 BK50
Pondcroft, Welw.G.C. 5 BR8
Ponder St. N7 56 BX36
Pondfield, Welw.G.C. 5 BS6
Lumbards
Pondfield Cres., St.Alb. 9 BJ11
Pondfield La., Brwd. 122 DD27
Pondfield Rd., Brom. 88 CG54
Pondfield Rd., Dag. 50 CR35
Pondfield Rd., Ken. 104 BY61
Pondfield Rd., Orp. 88 CL55
Ponds, The, Wey. 92 BA57
Ellesmere Rd.
Pondside Clo., Hayes 63 BA43
Pondwicks Clo., St.Alb. 9 BG14
Pondwood Ri., Orp. 88 CN54
Ponler St. E1 57 CB39
Ponsard Rd. NW10 55 BP38
Ponsford St. E9 57 CC36
Ponsonby Pl. SW1 3 P10
Ponsonby Pl. SW1 66 BW42
Ponsonby Rd. SW15 75 BP47
Ponsonby Ter. SW1 3 P10
Ponsonby Ter. SW1 66 BW42
Pont St. SW1 3 E7
Pont St. SW1 66 BU41
Pont St. Ms. SW1 3 E7
Pont St. Ms. SW1 66 BU41
Pontefract Rd., Brom. 78 CG49
Ponton Rd. SW8 66 BW43
Pontosie Clo., Sev. 107 CT64
Pontypool Pl. SE1 4 F4
Pontypool Wk., Rom. 42 CV29
Saddleworth Rd.
Pony Chase, Cob. 93 BE60
Pool Clo., Beck. 77 CE49
Pool Clo., E.Mol. 84 BF53
Pool Rd., E.Mol. 84 BE53
Pool Rd., Har. 45 BG33
Poole Clo., Ruis. 44 BB34
Poole Ct. Rd., Houns. 64 BE44
Vicarage Ct. Rd.
Poole Ho., Grays 71 DG41
Poole Rd. E9 57 CC36
Poole Rd., Epsom 94 BN57
Poole Rd., Horn. 51 CX33
Poole Rd., Wok. 100 AS62
Poole St. N1 57 BZ37
Poole Way, Hayes 53 BB38
Pooles Bldgs. EC1 2 D5
Pooles Cotts., Rich. 74 BK48
Clifford Rd.
Pooles La. SW10 66 BT43
Lots Rd.
Pooles La., Dag. 59 CQ37
Pooles Pk. N4 47 BY34
Pooley Ave., Egh. 72 AT49
Pooley Grn. Clo., Egh. 72 AV49
Pooley Grn. Rd., Egh. 72 AT49
Pooleys La., Hat. 10 BP15
Poolmans Rd., Wind. 61 AL45
Poolmans St. SE16 67 CC41
Poolsford Rd. NW9 46 BO31
Poonah St. E1 57 CC39
Hardinge St.
Pootings Rd., Eden. 115 CM70
Pope Clo. SW19 76 BT50
Shelley Way
Pope Clo., Felt. 73 BB47
Pope Rd., Brom. 88 CJ53
Pope St. SE1 4 N5
Pope St. SE1 67 CA41
Popes Ave., Twick. 74 BH48
Popes Clo., Amer. 25 AP22
Popes Clo., Slou. 62 AT43
Popes Dr. N3 38 BS30
Popes Gro., Croy. 87 CD55
Popes Gro., Twick. 74 BH48
Popes La. W5 64 BK41
Popes La., Oxt. 115 CG70
Popes La., Wat. 26 BC22
Popes Rd. SW9 66 BY45
Popes Rd., Abb.L. 17 BB19
Popham Clo., Felt. 74 BE48
Popham Gdns., Rich. 65 BM45
Marksbury Ave.
Popham Rd. N1 57 BZ37
Popham St. N1 57 BZ37
Essex Rd.
Poplar Ave., Amer. 25 AP23
Poplar Ave., Grav. 81 DH49
Poplar Ave., Lthd. 102 BJ64
Poplar Ave., Mitch. 86 BU51
Poplar Ave., Orp. 88 CL55
Poplar Ave., Sthl. 64 BF41
Poplar Ave., West Dr. 53 AY40
Poplar Bath St. E14 57 CE40
Lawless St.
Poplar Clo., Ing. 24 DC19
Poplar Clo., Pnr. 36 BD30
Poplar Clo., Slou. 62 AV44
Poplar Clo., Wat. 17 BC19
Poplar Cotts., Guil. 118 AP69
Poplar Ct. SW19 76 BS49
Poplar Cres., Epsom 94 BN57
Poplar Dr., Bans. 94 BQ60
High Beeches
Poplar Dr., Brwd. 122 DE25
Poplar Fm. Clo., Epsom 94 BN57
Poplar Gdns., N.Mal. 85 BN51
Poplar Gro. N11 38 BV29
Poplar Gro. W6 65 BQ41
Poplar Gro., N.Mal. 85 BN52
Poplar Gro., Wem. 46 BN34
Poplar Gro., Wok. 100 AS63
Poplar High St. E14 57 CE40
Poplar Mt., Belv. 69 CR42
Poplar Pl. SE28 59 CP40
Poplar Pl. W2 56 BS40
Poplar Pl., Hayes 53 BC40
Poplar Rd. SE24 67 BZ45
Poplar Rd. SW19 86 BS51
Poplar Rd., Ashf. 73 BA49
Poplar Rd., Guil. 118 AS74
Poplar Rd., Lthd. 102 BJ64
Poplar Rd., Sutt. 85 BR54
Poplar Rd., Uxb. 44 AX35
Poplar Rd. S. SW19 86 BS52
Poplar Row, Epp. 31 CN22
Poplar Shaw, Wal.Abb. 22 CG20
Poplar St., Rom. 50 CS31
Poplar Wk. SE24 67 BZ45
Poplar Wk., Croy. 87 BZ54
Poplar Way, Felt. 73 BC48
Poplar Way, Ilf. 49 CM31
Poplars, Welw.G.C. 5 BS7
Poplars, The N14 29 BV25
Poplars, The, Borwd. 28 BM23
Grove Rd.
Poplars, The, Hem.H. 8 AW14
Poplars, The, Rom. 32 CO24
Poplars, The, St.Alb. 9 BJ15
Poplars Ave. NW2 55 BQ36
Poplars Ave., Hat. 10 BN12
Poplars Clo., Hat. 10 BN12
Poplars Clo., Ruis. 44 BB33
Poplars Rd. E17 48 CE32
Poppins Ct. EC4 2 F9
Poppins Ct. EC4 56 BY39
St. Bride St.
Poppleton Rd. E11 49 CG32
Poppy Clo., Brwd. 33 DA25
Poppy Clo., Wall. 86 BV54
Clover Way
Poppy La., Croy. 87 CC54
Poppyfields, Welw.G.C. 5 BT8
Forresters Dr.
Porch Way N20 38 BU27
Porchester Clo., Horn. 51 CW32
Porchester Gdns. W2 56 BS40
Porchester Mead, Beck. 77 CE50
Porchester Pl. W2 1 D9
Porchester Pl. W2 56 BU39
Porchester Rd. W2 56 BS39
Porchester Rd., Kings.T. 85 BM51
Porchester Sq. W2 56 BS39
Porchester Ter. W2 56 BT39
Porchester Ter. N. W2 56 BS39
Porchfield Clo., Grav. 81 DH48
Porchfield Clo., Sutt. 95 BS58
Hulverston Clo.
Porcupine Clo. SE9 78 CK48
Porden Rd. SW2 66 BX45
Porlock Ave., Har. 45 BG33
Porlock Rd., Enf. 39 CA26
Porlock St. SE1 4 L4
Porlock St. SE1 67 BZ41
Porrington Clo., Chis. 88 CL51
Lubbock Rd.
Port Ave., Green. 80 DA46
Port Cres. E13 58 CH38
Port Hill, Orp. 98 CO59
Portal Clo. SE27 76 BY48
Portal Clo., Ruis. 44 BC35
Portal Clo., Uxb. 53 AY36
Portbury Clo. SE15 67 CB44
Clayton Rd.
Portchester Clo. SE5 67 BZ45
Portcullis Lo. Rd., Enf. 30 BZ24
Silver St.
Portelet Rd. E1 57 CC38
Porten Rd. W14 65 BR41
Porter Clo., Grays 70 DB43
Porter Rd. E6 58 CK39
Porter St. SE1 4 J2
Porter St. W1 1 F6
Porter St. W1 56 BU39
Baker St.
Porters Ave., Dag. 59 CO36
Porters Clo., Brwd. 42 DA26
Greenshaw
Porters Wk. E1 57 CB40
Pennington St.
Porters Way, West Dr. 63 AY41
Porters Wd., St.Alb. 9 BH11
Porteus Rd. W2 56 BT39
Portgate Clo. W9 55 BR38
Ashmore Rd.
Porthcawe Rd. SE26 77 CD49
Porthkerry Ave., Well. 69 CO45
Portia Way E3 57 CD38
Portinscale Rd. SW15 75 BR46
Portland Ave. N16 48 CA33
Portland Ave., Grav. 81 DG48
Portland Ave., N.Mal. 85 BO54
Portland Ave., Sid. 79 CO46
Portland Clo., Rom. 50 CP32
Portland Gdns.
Portland Cres. SE9 78 CK48
Portland Cres., Felt. 73 BA49
Portland Cres., Grnf. 54 BF38
Portland Cres., Stan. 36 BK30
Portland Dr., Chsnt. 21 CB19
Portland Dr., Red. 113 BW68
Portland Gdns. N4 47 BY32
Portland Gdns., Rom. 50 CP32
Portland Gro. SW8 66 BX44
Lansdowne Way
Portland Ms. W1 1 M9
Portland Pl. SE25 87 CB52
Portland Rd.
Portland Pl. W1 1 J5
Portland Pl. W1 56 BV38
Portland Pl., Epsom 94 BO59
Portland Ri. N4 47 BY33
Portland Ri. Est. N4 47 BY33
Portland Rd. N15 48 CA31
Portland Rd. SE9 78 CK48
Portland Rd. SE25 87 CB52
Portland Rd. W11 55 BR40
Portland Rd., Ashf. 73 AY49
Portland Rd., Brom. 78 CJ49
Portland Rd., Dor. 119 BJ71
Portland Rd., Grav. 81 DE46
Portland Rd., Grav. 81 DG47
Portland Rd., Hayes 53 BB38
Portland Rd., Kings.T. 85 BL52
Portland Rd., Mitch. 86 BU51
Portland Rd., Sthl. 64 BE41
Portland Sq. E1 57 CB40
Vinegar St.
Portland St. SE17 4 K10
Portland St. SE17 67 BZ42
Portland St., St.Alb. 9 BG13
Portland Ter., Rich. 64 BK45
Portley La., Cat. 105 CA64
Portley Wd. Rd., Cat. 105 CA63
Portman Ave. SW14 65 BN45
Portman Bldgs. NW1 56 BU38
Portman Clo. W1 1 F8
Portman Clo. W1 56 BU39
Portman Clo., Bex. 79 CS47
Portman Clo., Bexh. 69 CP45
Glynde Rd.
Portman Clo., St.Alb. 9 BK11
Portman Dr., Wdf.Grn. 40 CJ30
Portman Gdns. NW9 37 BN30
Portman Ms. S. W1 1 G9
Portman Ms. S. W1 56 BV39
Portman Pl. E2 57 CC38
Portman Rd., Kings.T. 85 BL51
Portman Sq. W1 1 G8
Portman Sq. W1 56 BV39
Portman St. W1 1 G9
Portman St. W1 56 BV39
Portmeadow Wk. SE2 69 CP41
Portmeers Clo. E17 48 CD32
Lennox Rd.
Portmore Gdns., Rom. 41 CR28
Portmore Pk. Rd., Wey. 92 AY56
Portmore Way, Wey. 83 AZ55
Portnall Dr., Vir.W. 82 AP53
Portnall Ri., Vir.W. 82 AP53
Portnall Rd. W9 55 BF
Portnall Rd., Vir.W. 82 AF
Portnalls Clo., Couls. 104 BV
Portnalls Ri., Couls. 104 BV
Portnalls Rd., Couls. 104 BV
Portnoi Clo., Rom. 41 CS
Portobello Ct. W11 55 BR
Portobello Ms. W11 56 BS
Portobello Rd.
Portobello Rd. W10 55 BR
Portobello Rd. W11 55 BR
Portpool La. EC1 2
Portpool La. EC1 56 BY
Portree Clo. N22 38 BX
Portree St. E14 57 CF
Portsdown Ave. NW11 46 BR
Portsdown La., Edg. 37 BM
Portsea Ms. W2 1
Portsea Ms. W2 56 BU
Kendal St.
Portsea Pl. W2 1
Portsea Pl. W2 56 BU
Kendal St.
Portsea Rd., Til. 71 DH
Portslade Rd. SW8 66 BW
Portsmouth Ave., Surb. 84 BJ
Portsmouth Bldgs. NW1 56 BU
Portsmouth Ct., Slou. 52 AP
Portsmouth Rd. SW15 75 BQ
Portsmouth Rd., Cob. 92 BA
Portsmouth Rd., Cob. 92 BC
Portsmouth Rd., Esher 93 BG
Portsmouth Rd. (Esher Common), Esher 93 BE
Portsmouth Rd. (Hinchley Wd.), Esher 84 BH
Portsmouth Rd., Guil. 118 AR
Portsmouth Rd., Kings.T. 84 BK
Portsmouth Rd., Surb. 84 BK
Portsmouth Rd., T.Ditt. 84 BH
Portsmouth Rd. (Ripley), Wok. 101 AW
Portsmouth Rd. (Sendmarsh), Wok. 109 AV
Portsmouth Rd. (Wisley), Wok. 101 AZ
Portsmouth St. WC2 2
Portsmouth St. WC2 56 BX
Portugal St.
Portsoken St. E1 2 P
Portsoken St. E1 57 CA
Portswood Pl. SW15 75 BO
Danebury Ave.
Portugal Gdns., Twick. 74 BG
Portugal Rd., Wok. 100 AS
Portugal St. WC2 2
Portugal St. WC2 56 BX
Portway E15 58 CG
Portway, Epsom 94 BP
Portway Cres., Epsom 94 BP
Portway Gdns. SE18 68 CJ
Post Ho. La., Lthd. 111 BF
Post La., Twick. 74 BG
Post Meadow, Iver 52 AU
Post Office All., Hmptn. 84 BF
Thames St.
Post Office App. E7 49 CH
Post Office Ct. EC3 2
Post Office La., Slou. 52 AR
Post Office Way SW8 66 BW
Postern Grn., Enf. 29 BY
Postfield, Welw.G.C. 5 B
Lumbards
Postway Ms., Ilf. 49 CL
Clements Rd.
Potier St. SE1 4
Potier St. SE1 67 BZ
Potkiln La., Beac. 34 AO
Pott St. E2 57 CB
Bethnal Grn. Rd.
Potten End, Berk. 7 AT
Potter Clo., Mitch. 86 BV
Potter Heights Clo., Pnr. 35 BC
Potter St., Harl. 14 CO
Potter St., Nthwd. 35 BC
Potter St., Pnr. 35 BC
Potter St. Hill, Pnr. 35 BC
Potterne Clo. SW19 75 BO
Castlecombe Dr.
Potters Clo., Croy. 87 CD
Potters Clo., Loug. 31 CK
Potters Cross, Iver 52 AV
Potters Fld., Harl. 14 CP
Potters Fld., St.Alb. 9 BH
Potters Flds. SE1 57 CA
Potters Gro., N.Mal. 85 BN
Potters La. SW16 76 BW
Potters La., Barn. 29 BS
Potters La., Borwd. 28 BN
Potters La., Guil. 109 AT
Potters La., Wok. 100 AT
Potters Rd., Barn. 29 BS
Potters Way, Reig. 121 BT
Pottery La. W11 55 BR
Portland Rd.
Pottery Rd., Bex. 79 CS
Whenman Ave.
Pottery Rd., Brent. 65 BL
Pottery St. SE16 67 CB
Wilson Gro.
Pouchen End La., Hem.H. 7 AU
Pouchen Hill La., Hem.H. 7 AU
Poulcott, Stai. 72 AS
Poulett Gdns., Twick. 74 BJ
Poulett Rd. E6 58 CK
Poulner Way SE15 67 CA
Poulters Wd., Kes. 97 CJ
Poulton Ave., Sutt. 86 BT
Poulton Clo. E8 48 CB
Spurstowe Ter.
Poultry EC2 2
Poultry EC2 57 BZ
Cheapside

nd Bank Clo., Sev. 99 CZ58
sh Tree Dr.
nd Clo., Orp. 88 CM55
nd Clo., Surb. 84 BK54
nd Clo., Wal.Abb. 13 CG15
nd Ct., Ash. 103 BL62
e Marld
nd Ct. Dr., Orp. 88 CM55
nd Cres., Lthd. 102 BG64
nd Fld., Wat. 26 BB21
shfields
nd La. NW10 55 BP36
nd La., Epsom 94 BN59
nd La., Rad. 19 BL20
nd La., Sev. 108 CV65
nd La. (Knockholt 107 CP61
und), Sev.
nd Pk. Rd. SE7 68 CJ42
nd Pl. SE9 78 CL46
nd Pl., Guil. 118 AS73
nd Pl. Clo., Guil. 118 AS73
nd Rd., Bans. 103 BR62
nd Rd., Cher. 83 AW54
nd St., Cars. 95 BU56
ndfield, Guil. 118 AR70
ndfield Gdns., Wok. 100 AU63
ndfield Rd., Loug. 31 CL25
ndwell, Welw.G.C. 5 BS8
nsley Rd., Sev. 107 CT64
ntney Rd. SW11 66 BV45
erest Rd., Orp. 88 CN53
vder Mill La., Dart. 80 CW48
vder Mill La., Twick. 74 BE47
vderham Ct., Wok. 100 AO62
vdermill La., Wal.Abb. 21 CE20
vell Clo., Edg. 37 BL29
vell Clo., Guil. 118 AP71
vell Gdns., Dag. 50 CR35
vell Rd. E5 48 CB34
vell Rd., Buck.H. 40 CJ26
vells Clo., Dor. 119 BJ73
vells Wk. W4 65 BO43
ver Rd. W4 65 BM42
ver Rd. N., Houns. 65 BM42
vers Ct., Twick. 74 BK47
verscroft Rd. E5 48 CC35
verscroft Rd., Sid. 79 CP50
vis Ct., Pot.B. 20 BT20
vis Gdns. NW11 46 BR33
vis Gdns. W11 55 BR39
vis Ms. W11 55 BR39
vis Pl. WC1 2 A5
vis Pl. WC1 56 BX38
vis Rd. E3 57 CE38
vis Sq. W11 55 BR39
wis St. SE18 68 CL41
wis Ter. W11 55 BR39
wlett Pl. NW1 56 BV36
armood St.
wnall Gdns., Houns. 64 BF45
wnall Rd. E8 57 CA37
wnall Rd., Houns. 64 BF45
wster Rd., Brom. 78 CH49
wys Clo., Bexh. 69 CP43
wys La. N13 38 BX28
wys La. N14 38 BX28
yle New Cotts., Slou. 62 AV44
yle Rd., Guil. 118 AS71
yle Rd., Slou. 62 AV45
ynder Rd., Til. 71 DG44
ynders Ct. SW4 76 BW46
ynders Gdns. SW4 76 BW47
ynders Hill, Hem.H. 8 BA14
ynders Rd. SW4 76 BW46
Plummer Rd.
ynings, The, Iver 62 AV42
ynings Clo., Orp. 89 CO55
ynings Rd. N19 47 BW34
ynings Way N12 38 BS28
ynings Way, Rom. 42 CW30
yntell Cres., Chis. 78 CM50
ynter Rd., Enf. 30 CA25
ynton Rd. N17 39 CB30
yntz Rd. SW11 66 BU44
yser St. E2 57 CB37
Old Bethnal Grn. Rd.
ae Clo., St.Alb. 9 BF13
aed Ms. W2 1 B8
aed Ms. W2 56 BT39
Norfolk Pl.
aed St. W2 1 B8
aed St. W2 56 BT39
aetorian Ct., St.Alb. 9 BG15
agel St. E13 58 CJ37
agnell Rd. SE12 78 CH48
ague Pl. SW2 76 BX46
ah Rd. N4 47 BY34
airie Clo., Wey. 83 AW55
airie Rd., Wey. 83 AW55
airie St. SW8 66 BV44
att Ms. NW1 56 BW37
Pratt St.
att St. NW1 56 BW37
att Wk. SE11 4 C8
att Wk. SE11 66 BX42
atts La., Walt. 93 BD56
ayle Gro. NW2 46 BQ33
ebend Gdns. W4 65 BO42
ebend Gdns. W6 65 BO42
ebend St. N1 57 BZ37
ecinct, The, E.Mol. 84 BF52
ecinct Rd., Hayes 53 BC40
emier Ave., Grays 71 DE41
emier Pl. SW15 65 BQ45
Putney High St.
endergast Rd. SE3 68 CG45
entice Pl., Harl. 14 CP12
entis Rd. SW16 76 BW49
entiss Ct. SE7 68 CJ42
esburg Rd., N.Mal. 85 BO53
escelly Pl., Edg. 37 BL30
escot Rd., Slou. 62 AV44
escot St. E1 2 Q10
escot St. E1 57 CA40

Prescott Ave., Orp. 88 CL53
Prescott Clo. SW16 76 BX50
Prescott Grn., Loug. 31 CM24
Prescott Pl. SW4 66 BW45
Prescott Rd., Chsnt. 21 CD17
President Dr. E1 57 CB40
President St. EC1 2 H2
Press Rd. NW10 46 BN34
Press Rd., Uxb. 53 AX36
Pressland St. W10 55 BR39
Kensal Rd.
Prestbury Ct., Wok. 100 AQ62
Muirfield Rd.
Prestbury Cres., Bans. 104 BU61
Prestbury Rd. E7 58 CJ36
Prestbury Sq. SE9 78 CK49
Prested Rd. SW11 66 BU45
St. Johns Hill
Preston Ave. E4 39 CF29
Preston Clo. SE1 4 M8
Preston Clo. SE1 67 CA42
Preston Clo., Twick. 74 BH48
Preston Ct., Shep. 83 AZ53
Preston Rd.
Preston Ct., Walt. 84 BD54
St. Johns Dr.
Preston Dr. E11 49 CJ32
Preston Dr., Bexh. 69 CP44
Preston Dr., Epsom 94 BO57
Preston Gdns., Enf. 30 CD22
Preston Gdns., Ilf. 49 CK32
Preston Gro., Ash. 102 BK62
Preston Hill, Chesh. 16 AO18
Preston Hill, Har. 46 BL32
Preston La., Tad. 103 BQ63
Preston Pl. NW2 55 BP36
Preston Pl., Rich. 75 BL46
Preston Rd. E11 49 CG32
Preston Rd. SE19 76 BY50
Preston Rd. SW20 75 BO50
Preston Rd., Grav. 81 DF47
Preston Rd., Har. 46 BL33
Preston Rd., Rom. 42 CV28
Preston Rd., Shep. 83 AZ53
Preston Rd., Slou. 52 AR40
Preston Rd., Wem. 46 BL33
Preston Waye, Har. 46 BL33
Prestons Rd. E14 57 CF40
Prestons Rd., Brom. 88 CH55
Prestwick Clo., Sthl. 64 BE42
Prestwick Rd., Wat. 35 BC28
Prestwood, Slou. 52 AQ39
Prestwood Ave., Har. 45 BJ31
Prestwood Clo., Har. 45 BJ31
Prestwood Dr., Rom. 41 CS28
Prestwood Gdns., Croy. 87 BZ54
Queens Rd.
Prestwood St. N1 2 J1
Prestwood St. N1 57 BZ37
Wenlock Rd.
Pretoria Ave. E17 48 CD31
Pretoria Clo. N17 39 CA29
Pretoria Cres. E4 39 CF26
Pretoria Rd. E4 39 CF26
Pretoria Rd. E11 48 CF33
Pretoria Rd. E16 58 CG38
Pretoria Rd. N17 39 CA29
Pretoria Rd. SW16 76 BV50
Pretoria Rd., Cher. 82 AV54
Pretoria Rd., Ilf. 49 CL35
Pretoria Rd., Rom. 50 CS31
Pretoria Rd., Wat. 26 BC24
Pretoria Rd. N. N18 39 CA29
Prevost Rd. N11 38 BV27
Prey Heath Clo., Wok. 100 AR65
Prey Heath Rd., Wok. 100 AQ65
Price Clo. NW7 37 BR29
Price Clo. SW17 76 BU48
Price Clo., Hem.H. 8 AZ13
Price Rd., Croy. 95 BY56
Price Way, Hmptn. 74 BE50
Victors Dr.
Prices La., Reig. 121 BS72
Prices St. SE1 4 G3
Prices St. SE1 56 BY40
Prices Yd. N1 56 BX37
Caledonian Rd.
Pricklers Hill, Barn. 29 BS25
Prickley Wd., Brom. 88 CG54
Prideaux Pl. W3 55 BN40
Friars Pl. La.
Prideaux Pl. WC1 2 C2
Prideaux Pl. WC1 56 BX38
Prideaux Rd. SW9 66 BX45
Pridham Rd., Th.Hth. 87 BZ52
Priest Ct. EC2 2 H8
Priest Hill, Egh. 72 AR48
Priest Hill, Wind. 72 AR48
Priest Pk. Ave., Har. 45 BF34
Priest Wk., Grav. 81 DK48
Priestfield Rd. SE23 77 CD48
Priestlands Pk. Rd., Sid. 78 CN48
Priestley Clo. N16 48 CA33
Priestley Ct., Grays 71 DE42
Palmers Dr.
Priestley Gdns., Rom. 50 CO32
Priestley Rd., Guil. 118 AO71
Priestley Rd., Mitch. 86 BV51
Priestley Way E17 48 CC31
Priestley Way NW2 46 BP33
Priests Ave., Rom. 41 CS30
Priests Bri. SW14 65 BO45
Priests Ct. EC2 57 BZ39
Foster La.
Priests Fld., Brwd. 122 DE28
Priests La., Brwd. 122 DC26
Prima Rd. SW9 66 BY43
Primley La., Bish. 6 CS6
Primmett Clo., Sev. 99 CZ57
Hever Rd.
Primrose Ave., Enf. 30 BZ23
Primrose Ave., Rom. 50 CO33
Primrose Clo. SE6 77 CF49
Primrose Clo., Har. 45 BE34

Primrose Clo., Hat. 10 BP13
Primrose Clo., Hem.H. 7 AV14
Campion Rd.
Primrose Clo., Wall. 86 BV54
Primrose Fld., Harl. 13 CN12
Primrose Gdns. NW3 56 BU36
Primrose Gdns., Bush. 36 BF26
Primrose Gdns., Ruis. 45 BD35
Primrose Glen, Horn. 51 CW31
Primrose Hill EC4 2 E9
Primrose Hill EC4 56 BY39
Primrose Hill NW3 56 BU36
Primrose Hill, Brwd. 42 DB27
Primrose Hill, Kings L. 17 AZ17
Primrose Hill, Orp. 97 CN58
Primrose Hill Ct. NW3 56 BU36
Primrose Hill Rd. NW3 56 BU36
Primrose La., Croy. 87 CC54
Primrose La., Maid. 61 AG43
Primrose Path, Chsnt. 21 CB19
Primrose Rd. E10 48 CE33
Primrose Rd. E18 40 CH30
Primrose Rd., Walt. 93 BD56
Primrose St. EC2 2 M6
Primrose St. EC2 57 CA39
Primrose Way, Wem. 54 BK37
Primula St. W12 55 BP39
Prince Albert Rd. NW1 1 D1
Prince Albert Rd. NW1 56 BU37
Prince Albert Rd. NW8 1 D1
Prince Albert Rd. NW8 56 BU38
Prince Albert Sq., Red. 121 BU73
Prince Alberts Rd., Wind. 62 AP43
Prince Alberts Wk., Wind. 62 AP43
Prince Arthur Ms. NW3 47 BT35
Perrins La.
Prince Arthur Rd. NW3 47 BT35
Prince Charles Ave., 90 CY51
S.Dnth.
Prince Charles Dr. NW4 46 BQ33
Prince Charles Rd. SE3 68 CG44
Prince Charles Way, Wall. 86 BV55
Prince Consort Cotts., 61 AO44
Wind.
Prince Consort Dr., Chis. 88 CM51
Prince Consort Rd. SW7 3 A6
Prince Consort Rd. SW7 66 BT41
Prince Edward Rd. E9 57 CD36
Prince Edward St., Berk. 7 AR13
Prince George Ave. N14 29 BW24
Prince George Rd. N16 48 CA35
Prince Georges Ave. 85 BQ51
SW20
Prince Georges Rd. 86 BT51
SW19
Prince Henry Rd. SE7 68 CJ43
Prince Imperial Rd., Chis. 78 CL50
Prince Imperial Way 68 CL43
SE18
Prince John Rd. SE9 78 CK46
Prince of Wales Clo. NW4 46 BP31
Church Ter.
Prince of Wales Dr. SW11 66 BU44
Prince of Wales Gate SW7 3 C5
Prince of Wales Pas. NW1 1 L3
Prince of Wales Rd. E16 58 CJ39
Prince of Wales Rd. NW5 56 BV36
Prince of Wales Rd. SE3 68 CG44
Prince of Wales Rd., Red. 121 BY74
Prince of Wales Rd., Sutt. 86 BT55
Prince of Wales Ter. W4 65 BO42
Devonshire Rd.
Prince of Wales Ter. W8 66 BS41
Prince Pk., Hem.H. 8 AW14
Prince Philip Ave., Grays 71 DD40
Prince Regent Rd., 64 BG45
Houns.
Prince Regents La. E13 58 CH38
Prince Regents La. E16 58 CJ39
Prince Rd. SE25 87 CA53
Prince Rupert Rd. SE9 68 CK45
Prince St. SE8 67 CD43
Prince St., Wat. 27 BD24
Princedale Rd. W11 55 BR40
Princelet St. E1 2 Q6
Princelet St. E1 57 CA39
Princes Arc. SW1 3 M2
Princes Ave. N3 38 BS30
Princes Ave. N10 47 BV31
Princes Ave. N13 38 BY28
Princes Ave. N22 38 BW30
Princes Ave. NW9 46 BM31
Princes Ave. W3 65 BM41
Princes Ave., Cars. 95 BU57
Princes Ave., Dart. 80 CX47
Princes Ave., Enf. 30 CD21
Princes Ave., Grnf. 54 BF39
Princes Ave., Orp. 88 CN53
Princes Ave., S.Croy. 105 CB61
Princes Ave., Surb. 85 BM54
Princes Ave., Wat. 26 BB25
Princes Ave., Wdf.Grn. 40 CH28
Princes Clo. NW9 46 BM31
Princes Clo. SW4 66 BW45
Old Town
Princes Clo., Berk. 7 AQ12
Princes Clo., Edg. 37 BM28
Princes Clo., Epp. 23 CS16
Princes Clo., Sid. 79 CP48
Princes Clo., S.Croy. 105 CB61
Princes Clo., Tedd. 74 BG49
Princes Ct., Hem.H. 8 AW15
Roughdown Rd.
Princes Ct., Wem. 46 BL35
Princes Dr., Har. 45 BH31
Princes Dr., Lthd. 93 BH59
Princes Gdns. SW7 3 B6
Princes Gdns. SW7 66 BT41
Princes Gdns. W3 55 BM39
Princes Gdns. W5 54 BK38
Princes Gate SW7 3 B5
Princes Gate SW7 66 BT41
Princes Gate, Harl. 6 CN9
Princes Gate Ct. SW7 3 B5

Princes Gate Ct. SW7 66 BT41
Exhibition Rd.
Princes Gate Ms. SW7 3 B6
Princes Gate Ms. SW7 66 BT41
Princes La. N10 47 BV31
Princes Ms. SW7 66 BT41
Exhibition Rd.
Princes Ms. W2 56 BS40
Princes Par., Pot.B. 20 BS20
High St.
Princes Pk., Rain. 59 CU36
Princes Pk. Ave. NW11 46 BR32
Princes Pk. Ave., Hayes 53 BA40
Princes Pk. Circ., Hayes 53 BA40
Princes Pk. Clo., Hayes 53 BA40
Princes Pk. La., Hayes 53 BA40
Princes Pk. Par., Hayes 53 BA40
Princes Pl. SW1 3 M2
Princes Pl. W11 55 BR40
Princes Plain, Brom. 88 CK54
Princes Ri. SE13 67 CF44
Princes Rd. N18 39 CC28
Princes Rd. SE20 77 CC50
Princes Rd. SW14 65 BN45
Princes Rd. SW19 76 BS50
Princes Rd. W13 54 BJ40
Mattock La.
Princes Rd., Ashf. 73 AY49
Princes Rd., Buck.H. 40 CJ27
Princes Rd., Dart. 79 CU47
Princes Rd., Dart. 80 CY47
Princes Rd., Egh. 72 AS50
Princes Rd., Felt. 73 BB48
Princes Rd., Grav. 81 DG49
Princes Rd., Ilf. 49 CM31
Princes Rd., Kings.T. 75 BM50
Princes Rd., Red. 121 BU71
Princes Rd., Rich. 75 BL46
Princes Rd. (Kew), Rich. 65 BL44
Princes Rd., Rom. 50 CU32
Princes Rd. (Navestock), 33 CW23
Rom.
Princes Rd., Tedd. 74 BG49
Princes Rd., Wey. 92 AZ56
Princes Rd. N., Dart. 79 CU46
Princes Sq. W2 56 BS40
Princes St. EC2 2 K9
Princes St. EC2 57 BZ39
Princes St. N17 39 CA29
Queen St.
Princes St. W1 1 K9
Princes St. W1 56 BV39
Princes St., Bexh. 69 CQ45
Princes St., Rich. 65 BL45
Princes St., Slou. 62 AQ41
Princes St., Sutt. 95 BT56
Princes Ter. E13 58 CH37
Princes Vw., Dart. 80 CX47
Princes Way SW19 75 BQ47
Princes Way, Brwd. 122 DD27
Princes Way, Buck.H. 40 CJ27
Princes Way, Croy. 95 BX57
Princes Way, Ruis. 45 BE35
Princes Way, W.Wick. 97 CG56
Princesfield Rd., Wal.Abb. 22 CH20
Princess Ave., Wem. 46 BL34
Princess Ave., Wind. 61 AN45
Princess Cres. N4 47 BY34
Princess Gdns., Wok. 100 AT61
Princess La., Ruis. 44 BB33
Princess Margaret Rd., 71 DK41
S.le H.
Princess Marys Rd., Wey. 83 AX55
Princess May Rd. N16 48 CA35
Princess Ms. NW3 47 BT35
Princess Par., Dag. 59 CR37
Whitebarn La.
Princess Par., Orp. 88 CL55
Princess Rd. NW1 56 BV37
Princess Rd. NW6 56 BS37
Princess Rd., Croy. 87 BZ53
Princess Rd., Swan. 79 CU50
Princess Rd., Wok. 100 AT61
Princess St. SE1 4 G7
Princess St. SE1 66 BY41
Princess St., Grav. 81 DG46
Church St.
Princess Way, Red. 121 BU70
Princethorpe Rd. SE26 77 CC49
Princeton St. WC1 2 B7
Princeton St. WC1 56 BX39
Pring St. W10 55 BQ40
Freston Rd.
Pringle Gdns. SW16 76 BW49
Printer St. EC4 2 E8
Printers Way, Harl. 6 CO8
Printing Ho. La., Hayes 63 BB41
Printing Ho. Yd. E2 2 N3
Printing Ho. Yd. E2 57 CA38
Hackney Rd.
Priolo Rd. SE7 68 CJ42
Prior Ave., Sutt. 95 BT57
Prior Boulton St. N1 56 BY36
Compton Rd.
Prior Chase, Grays 71 DC42
Bersham La.
Prior Gro., Chesh. 16 AO18
Prior Rd., Ilf. 49 CL34
Prior St. SE10 67 CF43
Prioress Rd. SE27 76 BY48
Prioress St. SE1 4 L7
Prioress St. SE1 67 BZ41
Priors, The, Ash. 102 BK63
Priors Clo., Slou. 62 AQ41
Priors Cft. E17 39 CD30
Priors Cft., Wok. 100 AT64
Priors Fld., Nthlt. 54 BE36
Arnold Rd.
Priors Gdns., Ruis. 45 BD35
Priors Mead, Enf. 30 CA23
Priors Mead, Lthd. 111 BF66
Priors Pk., Horn. 51 CV34
Priors Rd., Wind. 61 AL45
Priors Way, Maid. 61 AG42

Priorsford Ave., Orp. 89 CO52
Priory, The SE3 68 CG45
Priory, The, Gdse. 114 CB69
Priory Ave. E4 39 CD27
Priory Ave. E17 48 CE32
Priory Ave. N8 47 BW31
Priory Ave. W4 65 BO42
Priory Ave., Harl. 6 CP8
Priory Ave., Orp. 88 CM53
Priory Ave., Sutt. 94 BQ56
Priory Ave., Uxb. 44 AX31
Priory Ave., Wem. 45 BH35
Priory Clo. E4 39 CD27
Priory Clo. E18 40 CH30
Priory Clo. N3 37 BR30
Priory Clo. N14 29 BU25
Priory Clo. N20 37 BR26
Priory Clo., Beck. 87 CD52
Priory Clo., Brwd. 33 DA25
Priory Clo., Brox. 12 CD15
Priory Clo., Chis. 88 CK51
Priory Clo., Dart. 80 CV46
Priory Clo., Dor. 119 BJ72
Harrow Rd. W.
Priory Clo., Hmptn. 84 BE51
Priory Clo., Hodd. 12 CE12
Priory Clo., Ruis. 44 BB33
Priory Clo., Stan. 36 BH27
Priory Clo., Sun. 73 BC50
Priory Clo. (Denham), Uxb. 44 AW34
Priory Clo. (Harefield), 44 AX31
Uxb.
Priory Clo. (Sudbury), 45 BH35
Wem.
Priory Clo., Wok. 91 AU60
Priory Cotts., Uxb. 44 AX31
Priory Ct. E6 58 CJ37
Priory Rd.
Priory Ct. E17 39 CD30
Priory Ct. SW8 66 BW44
Priory Ct., Berk. 7 AR13
Priory Gdns.
Priory Ct., Guil. 118 AR72
Priory Ct., Harl. 14 CO12
Priory Ct., St.Alb. 9 BH14
Old London Rd.
Priory Ct. Est. E17 39 CD30
Priory Cres. SE19 77 BZ50
Priory Cres., Sutt. 94 BQ56
Priory Cres., Wem. 45 BJ34
Priory Dr. SE2 69 CP42
Priory Dr., Reig. 121 BS71
Priory Dr., Stan. 36 BH27
Priory Fld. Dr., Edg. 37 BM28
Priory Flds., Farn. 90 CW54
Priory Gdns. N6 47 BV32
Priory Gdns. SW13 65 BO45
Priory Gdns. W5 55 BL38
Priory Gdns., Berk. 7 AR13
Priory Gdns., Dart. 80 CV46
Priory Gdns., Hmptn. 74 BE50
Priory Gdns., Uxb. 44 AX31
Priory Gdns., Walt. 83 BC55
Priory Grn., Stai. 73 AW49
Priory Grn. Est. N1 56 BX37
Priory Gro. SW8 66 BX44
Priory Gro., Rom. 42 CW27
Priory Hill, Dart. 80 CV46
Priory Hill, Wem. 45 BJ35
Priory La. SW15 75 BO46
Priory La., E.Mol. 84 BF52
Priory La., Farn. 90 CW54
Priory La., Rich. 65 BM43
Forest Rd.
Priory Mead, Brwd. 33 DB21
Priory Ms. SW8 66 BW44
Priory Ms., Stai. 73 AW49
Chestnut Manor Clo.
Priory Par., Wem. 45 BH35
Priory Pk. SE3 68 CG45
Priory Pk. Rd. NW6 55 BR37
Priory Pk. Rd., Wem. 45 BJ35
Priory Path, Rom. 42 CW27
Priory Pl., Dart. 80 CV46
Priory Rd.
Priory Pl., Walt. 83 BC55
Priory Clo.
Priory Rd. E6 58 CJ37
Priory Rd. N8 47 BW31
Priory Rd. NW6 56 BS37
Priory Rd. SW19 76 BT50
Priory Rd. W4 65 BN41
Priory Rd., Bark. 58 CM36
Priory Rd., Chess. 85 BL55
Priory Rd., Croy. 86 BY54
Priory Rd., Dart. 80 CV46
Priory Rd., Ger.Cr. 43 AR31
Priory Rd., Hmptn. 74 BE50
Priory Rd., Houns. 74 BG46
Priory Rd., Loug. 31 CK24
Priory Rd., Reig. 121 BS71
Priory Rd., Rich. 65 BM43
Priory Rd., Rom. 42 CW27
Priory Rd., Sutt. 94 BQ56
Priory St. E3 57 CE38
Bromley High St.
Priory Ter. NW6 56 BS37
Priory Ter., Sun. 73 BC50
Priory Vw., Bush. 36 BH26
Priory Wk. SW10 66 BT42
Priory Wk., St.Alb. 9 BH15
Priory Way, Ger.Cr. 43 AR31
Priory Way, Har. 45 BF31
Priory Way, Slou. 62 AQ43
Priory Way, Sthl. 64 BD41
Western Rd.
Priory Way, West Dr. 63 AY43
Pritchards Rd. E2 57 CB37
Priter Rd. SE16 67 CB41
St. James Rd.
Priter Way SE16 67 CB41
Private Rd., Enf. 30 BZ25
Private Rd., Grav. 81 DD47
Private Rd., S.Ock. 70 CX41

Private Rd., Wal.Cr. 21 BZ19
Probert Rd. SW2 66 BY45
Probyn Rd. SW2 76 BY48
Procter St. WC1 2 B7
Procter St. WC1 56 BX39
High Holborn
Proctor Gdns., Lthd. 111 BF66
Proctors Clo., Felt. 73 BC47
Profumo Rd., Walt. 93 BD56
Progress Way N22 38 BY30
Progress Way, Croy. 86 BX55
Progress Way, Enf. 30 CB25
Promenade, The W4 65 BO44
Promenade App. Rd. W4 65 BO43
Promenade de Verdun, Pur. 95 BW59
Prospect Clo. SE26 77 CB49
Wells Pk. Rd.
Prospect Clo., Belv. 69 CR42
Prospect Clo., Grav. 81 DH47
Prospect Clo., Houns. 64 BE44
Prospect Clo., Ruis. 45 BD33
Prospect Cotts. SW18 66 BS45
Point Pleasant
Prospect Cres., Twick. 74 BG46
Prospect Hill E17 48 CE31
Prospect La., Egh. 72 AQ49
Prospect Pl. E1 57 CC40
Prospect Pl. N2 47 BT31
Prospect Pl. N17 39 CA29
Prospect Pl. NW2 46 BR34
Prospect Rd.
Prospect Pl. W4 65 BN42
Chiswick High Rd.
Prospect Pl., Brom. 88 CH52
Prospect Pl., Dart. 80 CW46
Prospect Pl., Epsom 94 BO60
Prospect Pl., Grav. 81 DH47
Prospect Pl., Grays 71 DD43
Prospect Pl., Rom. 41 CS30
Prospect Pl., Stai. 72 AV49
Prospect Ring N2 47 BT31
Prospect Rd. NW2 46 BR34
Prospect Rd., Barn. 29 BS24
Prospect Rd., Chsnt. 21 CC18
Prospect Rd., Horn. 51 CW31
Prospect Rd., St.Alb. 9 BG14
Prospect Rd., Sev. 108 CV65
Prospect Rd., Surb. 84 BK53
Prospect Rd., Wdf.Grn. 40 CJ29
Prospect St. SE16 67 CB41
Jamaica Rd.
Prospect Vale SE18 68 CK42
Prospect Way, Brwd. 122 DF24
Prospero Rd. N19 47 BW33
Prossers, Tad. 103 BQ64
Prothero Gdns. NW4 46 BP32
Protheroe Rd. SW6 65 BR43
Prout Gro. NW10 46 BO35
Prout Rd. E5 48 CB34
Provence St. N1 57 BZ37
Providence Ct. W1 1 H10
Providence Ct. W1 56 BV40
Providence La., Hayes 63 BA43
Providence Pl. N1 56 BY37
Upper St.
Providence Pl., Epsom 94 BO59
Providence Pl., Rom. 41 CQ30
Providence Rd., West Dr. 53 AY40
Providence Row N1 2 B1
Providence Row N1 56 BX37
Northdown St.
Providence St., Green. 80 DA46
Provost Dws. N1 57 BZ37
Provost Est. N1 2 K2
Provost Rd. NW3 56 BU36
Provost St. N1 2 K1
Provost St. N1 57 BZ37
Prowse Ave., Bush. 36 BG27
Prowse Pl. NW1 56 BW36
Bonny St.
Pruden Clo. N14 38 BW27
Prudent Pas. EC2 2 K8
Prune Hill, Egh. 72 AR50
Prusom St. E1 57 CB40
Pryor Clo., Abb.L. 17 BB19
Pryors, The NW3 47 BT34
Puck La., Wal.Abb. 21 CF18
Puckshill, Wok. 100 AO62
Beechwood Rd.
Pudding La. EC3 4 L1
Pudding La. EC3 57 BZ40
Pudding La., Chig. 40 CN26
Pudding La., Hem.H. 8 AW12
Pudding La., Sev. 108 CX64
Church Rd.
Pudding Mill La. E15 57 CE37
Puddle Dock EC4 2 G10
Puddle Dock EC4 56 BY40
Upper Thames St.
Puddledock La., Dart. 79 CT49
Puddledock La., West. 115 CN70
Puers La., Beac. 34 AP29
Pulborough Rd. SW18 75 BR47
Pulborough Way, Houns. 64 BD45
Pulford Rd. N15 48 BZ32
Pulham Ave. N2 47 BT31
Puller Rd., Barn. 28 BR23
Puller Rd., Hem.H. 8 AW14
Pulleyns Ave. E6 58 CK38
Pulleys Clo., Hem.H. 7 AV13
Pulleys La., Hem.H. 7 AV12
Pullman Ct. SW2 76 BX47
Pullman Gdns. SW15 75 BQ46
Pulross Rd. SW9 66 BX45
Pulteney Clo. E3 57 CD37
Pulteney Rd. E18 49 CH31
Pulteney Ter. N1 56 BX37
Pulton Rd. SW6 66 BS43
Puma Ct. E1 2 P6
Puma Ct. E1 57 CA39
Commercial St.
Pump All., Brent. 64 BK53
High St.
Pump Ct. EC4 2 D9
Pump Hill, Loug. 31 CK23
Pump La., Chesh. 16 AP20
Pump La., Epp. 13 CL15
Pump La., Hayes 63 BB41
Pump La., Orp. 98 CR56
Pump Pail N., Croy. 87 BZ55
Pump Pail S., Croy. 87 BZ55
Pumping Sta. Rd. W4 65 BO43
Punch Bowl La., Hem.H. 8 BA12
Punch Bowl La., St.Alb. 8 BA12
Punchbowl La., Dor. 119 BK71
Pundersons Gdns. E2 57 CB38
Purbeck Ave., N.Mal. 85 BO53
Purbeck Dr. NW2 46 BQ34
Purbeck Dr., Wok. 91 AS60
Purbeck Rd., Horn. 50 CU33
Purberry Gro., Epsom 94 BO58
Purbrock Ave., Wat. 27 BD21
Purbrook Clo., Red. 113 BW67
Purbrook Est. SE1 4 N5
Purbrook Est. SE1 67 CA41
Purbrook St. SE1 4 N6
Purbrook St. SE1 67 CA41
Purcell Clo., Borwd. 27 BK23
Stainer Rd.
Purcell Cres. SW6 65 BR43
Purcell Ms. NW10 55 BO36
Suffolk Rd.
Purcell Rd., Grnf. 54 BF39
Purcell St. N1 57 CA37
Purcells Ave., Edg. 37 BM28
Purcells Clo., Ash. 103 BL62
Purcers Rd. SW6 65 BR45
Purchese St. NW1 56 BW37
Purdy St. E3 57 CE38
Purex Rd., Grnf. 54 BG37
Purfleet Arterial Rd., S.Ock. 70 CX41
Purfleet By-pass, S.Ock. 70 CX42
Purfleet Rd., S.Ock. 70 CX41
Purford Grn., Harl. 14 CO11
Purland Clo., Dag. 50 CQ33
Purland Rd. SE28 68 CN41
Purleigh Ave., Wdf.Grn. 40 CK29
Purley Ave. NW2 46 BR34
Purley Bury Ave., Pur. 96 BZ59
Purley Bury Clo., Pur. 96 BZ59
Purley Clo., Ilf. 40 CL30
Purley Ct., Pur. 95 BY58
Purley Downs Rd., Pur. 96 BZ58
Purley Hill, Pur. 95 BY59
Purley Knoll, Pur. 95 BX59
Purley Oaks Rd., S.Croy. 96 BZ58
Purley Pk. Rd., Pur. 95 BY58
Purley Pl. N1 56 BY36
Islington Pk. St.
Purley Ri., Pur. 95 BX59
Purley Rd. N9 39 BZ27
Purley Rd., Pur. 95 BY59
Purley Rd., S.Croy. 96 BZ57
Purley Vale, Pur. 95 BY60
Purley Way, Croy. 86 BX54
Purlieu Way, Epp. 31 CN21
Purlings Rd., Bush. 27 BF25
Purneys Rd. SE9 68 CJ45
Purrett Rd. SE18 68 CN42
Pursers Cross Rd. SW6 65 BR44
Pursewardens Clo. W13 54 BK40
Pursley Gdns., Borwd. 28 BM22
Pursley Rd. NW7 37 BP29
Purves Rd. NW10 55 BP38
Putney Bri. App. SW6 65 BR45
Putney Bri. Rd. SW15 65 BR45
Putney Bri. Rd. SW18 76 BS46
Putney Common SW15 65 BQ45
Putney Heath SW15 75 BP47
Putney Heath La. SW15 75 BQ46
Putney High St. SW15 65 BQ45
Putney Hill SW15 75 BQ46
Tibbets Ride
Putney Pk. Ave. SW15 65 BP45
Putney Pk. La. SW15 65 BP45
Putney Rd., Enf. 30 CC21
Puttenham Clo., Wat. 36 BD27
Putters Cft., Hem.H. 8 AY11
Puttocks Clo., Hat. 10 BQ15
Puttocks Dr., Hat. 10 BQ15
Pycroft Way N9 39 CB28
Pyecombe Cor. N12 37 BR28
Pyenest Rd., Harl. 13 CL12
Pyghtle, The, Uxb. 44 AW33
Pylbrook Rd., Sutt. 86 BS55
Pyle Hill, Guil. 109 AS66
Pyle Hill, Wok. 100 AR65
Pym Clo., Barn. 29 BT25
Pym Pl., Grays 71 DD42
Pymers Mead SE21 77 BZ47
Pymmes Clo. N13 38 BX28
Pymmes Clo. N17 39 CB30
Pymmes Gdns. N. N9 39 CA27
Pymmes Gdns. S. N9 39 CA27
Pymmes Grn. Rd. N11 38 BV28
Pymmes Rd. N13 38 BX29
Pymms Gdns., Barn. 29 BU24
Pynchester Clo., Uxb. 44 AZ34
Pyne Rd., Surb. 85 BM54
Pynestgreen La., Wal.Abb. 31 CH22
Pynham Clo. SE2 69 CO41
Pynnacles Clo., Stan. 36 BJ28
Pypers Hatch, Harl. 13 CN11
Pyrcroft La., Wey. 92 AZ56
Hanger Hill
Pyrcroft Rd., Cher. 82 AV54
Pyrford Common Rd., Wok. 100 AU61
Pyrford Heath, Wok. 100 AV61
Pyrford Rd., Wey. 92 AW60
Pyrford Rd., Wok. 101 AW61
Pyrford Wds., Wok. 100 AV61
Pyrford Wds. Clo., Wok. 100 AV61
Pyrford Wds. Rd., Wok. 100 AV61
Pyrland Rd. N5 48 BZ35
Pyrland Rd., Rich. 75 BL46
Pyrles Grn., Loug. 31 CL23
Pyrles La., Loug. 31 CL23
Pyrmont Gro. SE27 76 BY48
Pyrmont Rd. W4 65 BM43
Pyrmont Rd., Ilf. 49 CM34
High Rd.
Pytchley Cres. SE19 77 BZ50
Pytchley Rd. SE22 67 CA45
Pytt Fld., Harl. 14 CO11

Q

Quadrangle, The, Guil. 118 AQ71
Quadrangle, The, Welw.G.C. 5 BQ7
Quadrant, The SE24 77 BZ46
Quadrant, The SW20 85 BR51
Quadrant, The, Bexh. 69 CP43
Quadrant, The, Grays 70 CY42
Quadrant, The, Rich. 74 BK46
Quadrant, The, St.Alb. 9 BJ12
Quadrant, The, Sutt. 95 BT57
Wellesley Rd.
Quadrant, The, Wey. 92 AZ56
Quadrant Arc. W1 3 M1
Quadrant Arc., Rom. 50 CT32
Quadrant Clo. NW4 46 BP32
Quadrant Gro. NW5 47 BU35
Quadrant Rd. N1 57 BZ36
Essex Rd.
Quadrant Rd., Rich. 64 BK45
Quadrant Rd., Th.Hth. 86 BY52
Quaggy Wk. SE3 68 CH45
Quail Gdns., S.Croy. 96 CD58
Quainton St. NW10 46 BN34
Quaker Clo., Sev. 108 CV65
Quaker La., Sthl. 64 BF41
Quaker La., Wal.Abb. 21 CF20
Quaker St. E1 2 P5
Quaker St. E1 57 CA38
Quakers Clo., Hartley 90 DC52
Quakers Course NW9 37 BO30
Quakers Hall La., Sev. 108 CV64
Quakers La., Islw. 64 BJ44
Quakers La., Pot.B. 20 BS18
Quakers Wk. N21 30 BZ25
Quality Ct. WC2 2 D8
Quality Ct. WC2 56 BY39
Chancery La.
Quality St., Red. 113 BV67
Quantock Clo., Hayes 63 BA43
Quantock Clo., St.Alb. 9 BK11
Chiltern Rd.
Quantock Clo., Slou. 62 AT42
Quantock Gdns. NW2 46 BQ34
Quantock Rd., Bexh. 69 CT44
Quantocks, Hem.H. 8 AY12
Quarles Clo., Rom. 41 CR29
Quarley Way SE15 67 CA43
Quarr Rd., Cars. 86 BT53
Quarrendon Rd., Amer. 25 AO23
Quarrendon St. SW6 66 BS44
Quarry Clo., Couls. 104 BX61
Quarry Clo., Oxt. 115 CG68
Quarry Hill, Grays 71 DD42
Quarry Hill, Sev. 108 CV65
Quarry Hill Pk. Rd., Reig. 121 BY69
Quarry Hill Rd., Sev. 108 DC64
Quarry Ms., Grays 70 CX42
Fanns Ri.
Quarry Pk. Rd., Sutt. 94 BR57
Quarry Ri., Sutt. 94 BR57
Quarry Rd. SW18 76 BT46
Quarry Rd., Gdse. 114 CC67
Quarry Rd., Oxt. 115 CG68
Quarry Spring, Harl. 14 CO11
Quarry St., Guil. 118 AR71
Quarry Way, Grays 70 CZ43
Quarter Mile La. E10 48 CE35
Quarter Mile La. E15 48 CE35
Quartermaine Ave., Wok. 100 AS64
Quartermass Clo., Hem.H. 8 AW13
Quartermass Rd., Hem.H. 8 AW13
Quaves Rd., Slou. 62 AQ41
Quay W., Tedd. 74 BJ49
Quebec Ave., West. 115 CM66
Quebec Ms. W1 1 F9
Quebec Ms. W1 56 BU39
Quebec Rd., Hayes 54 BD39
Quebec Rd., Ilf. 49 CL33
Quebec Rd., Til. 71 DG44
Quebec Sq., West. 115 CM66
Quebec Way SE16 67 CC41
Queen Adelaide Rd. SE20 77 CC50
Queen Alexandras Ct. SW19 75 BR49
Queen Anne Ave., Brom. 88 CG52
Queen Anne Clo., Esher 93 BH58
Queen Anne Gate, Bexh. 69 CP45
Glynde Rd.
Queen Anne Ms. W1 1 K7
Queen Anne Ms. W1 56 BV39
Chandos St.
Queen Anne Rd. E9 57 CC36
Queen Anne St. W1 1 J8
Queen Anne St. W1 56 BV39
Queen Annes Clo., Twick. 74 BG48
Queen Annes Gdns. W4 65 BO41
Queen Annes Gdns. W5 65 BL41
Queen Annes Gdns., Enf. 30 CA25
Queen Annes Gdns., Lthd. 102 BJ64
Upper Fairfield Rd.
Queen Annes Gdns., Mitch. 86 BU52
Queen Annes Gate SW1 3 N5
Queen Annes Gate SW1 66 BW41
Queen Annes Gate, Bexh. 69 CP45
Regency Way
Queen Annes Gro. W4 65 BO41
Bedford Rd.
Queen Annes Gro. W5 65 BL41
Queen Annes Gro., Enf. 39 BZ26
Queen Annes Pl., Enf. 30 CA25
Queen Annes Rd., Wind. 61 AO45
Queen Annes Ter., Lthd. 102 BJ64
Upper Fairfield Rd.
Queen Annes Wk. WC1 2 A5
Queen Annes Wk. WC1 56 BX39
Guilford St.
Queen Caroline Est. W6 65 BQ42
Queen Caroline St. W6 65 BQ42
Queen Clo., Wey. 92 BB57
Queen Dale Ct., Wok. 100 AP61
Queen Eleanor Clo., Ash. 103 BL63
Queen Eleanor Rd., Guil. 118 AP71
Queen Elizabeth Gdns., Mord. 86 BS52
Hatherleigh Clo.
Queen Elizabeth Pl., Til. 71 DG45
Queen Elizabeth Rd. E17 48 CD31
Queen Elizabeth Rd., Kings.T. 85 BL51
Queen Elizabeth St. SE1 4 P4
Queen Elizabeth St. SE1 67 CA41
Queen Elizabeth Wk. SW13 65 BP44
Queen Elizabeth Wk., Wall. 95 BW56
Queen Elizabeth Way, Wok. 100 AS63
Queen Elizabeths Clo. N16 48 BZ34
Queen Elizabeths Dr. N14 38 BX26
Queen Elizabeths Dr., Croy. 96 CF58
Queen Elizabeths Gdns., Croy. 96 CF58
Queen Elizabeth Dr.
Queen Elizabeths Wk. N16 48 BZ33
Queen Hythe Rd., Guil. 109 AR67
Queen Margarets Gro. N1 48 CA35
Queen Mary Ave., Mord. 85 BQ53
Queen Mary Clo., Rom. 50 CT32
Richmond Rd.
Queen Mary Clo., Wok. 100 AU61
Queen Mary Rd. SE19 76 BY50
Queen Mary Rd., Shep. 83 BA51
Queen Marys Ave., Cars. 95 BU57
Queen Marys Ave., Wat. 26 BB24
Queen Marys Dr., Wey. 91 AV58
Queen Mothers Dr., Uxb. 43 AV32
Queen Sq. WC1 2 A6
Queen Sq. WC1 56 BX38
Queen Sq. Pl. WC1 2 A5
Queen St. EC4 2 J10
Queen St. EC4 57 BZ40
Queen St. N17 39 CA29
Queen St. W1 3 J2
Queen St., Bexh. 69 CQ45
Queen St., Brwd. 42 DB28
Queen St., Cher. 83 AW54
Queen St., Croy. 87 BZ55
Queen St., Erith 67 CT43
Queen St., Grav. 81 DG46
Queen St., Kings L. 17 AW19
Queen St., Ong. 15 CZ14
Queen St., Rom. 50 CS32
Queen St., St.Alb. 9 BG13
Queen St. Mayfair W1 56 BV40
Queen St. Pl. EC4 4 J1
Queen St. Pl. EC4 57 BZ40
Queen Victoria Ave., Wem. 54 BK36
Queen Victoria St. EC4 2 G10
Queen Victoria St. EC4 56 BY40
Queenborough Gdns., Chis. 78 CM50
Queenborough Gdns., Ilf. 49 CL31
Queenhill Rd., S.Croy. 96 CB58
Queenhithe EC4 2 J10
Queenhithe EC4 57 BZ40
Queens Acre, Sutt. 94 BQ57
Queens Acre, Wind. 61 AO45
Queens All., Epp. 22 CN19
Hemnall St.
Queens Ave. N3 38 BT29
Queens Ave. N10 47 BV31
Queens Ave. N20 38 BT27
Queens Ave. N21 38 BY26
Queens Ave., Felt. 74 BD49
Queens Ave., Grnf. 54 BF39
Queens Ave., Stan. 45 BK31
Queens Ave., Wat. 26 BB24
Queens Ave., Wey. 92 AX59
Queens Ave., Wdf.Grn. 40 CH28
Queens Circ. SW8 66 BV43
Queens Clo., Dag. 37 BM28
Queens Clo., Tad. 103 BP65
Queens Clo., Wind. 72 AQ46
Queens Club Gdns. W14 65 BR43
Queens Ct. NW11 46 BR32
Queens Ct. SE23 77 CC48
Queens Ct. W5 54 BK39
Queens Wk.
Queens Ct., St.Alb. 9 BJ13
Queens Ct., Slou. 52 AP40
Queens Rd.
Queens Ct. Ride, Cob. 92 BC60
Queens Cres. NW5 56 BV36
Queens Cres., Rich. 75 BL46
Queens Cres., St.Alb. 9 BJ12
Queens Dr. E10 48 CE33
Queens Dr. N4 47 BY34
Queens Dr. W3 55 BL39
Queens Dr., Abb.L. 17 BB19
Queens Dr., Guil. 118 AQ69
Queens Dr., Lthd. 93 BG59
Queens Dr., Sev. 108 CV63
Queens Dr., Slou. 52 AS37
Queens Dr., Surb. 85 BM54
Queens Dr., T.Ditt. 84
Queens Dr., Wal.Cr. 21
Queens Dr., The, Rick. 34
Queens Elm Sq. SW3 66
Queens Gdns. NW4 46
Queens Gdns. W2 56
Queens Gdns. W5 54
Queens Gdns., Dart. 80
Queens Gdns., Houns. 64
Queens Gdns., Rain. 59
Queens Gdns., Upmin. 51
Queens Gate SW7 66
Queens Gate Gdns. SW7 66
Queens Gate Ms. SW7 66
Queens Gate Pl. SW7 66
Queens Gate Pl. Ms. SW7 66
Queens Gate Ter. SW7 66
Queens Gro. NW8 56
Queens Gro. Rd. E4 39
Queens Head St. N1 56
Queens Head Wk., Brox. 12
High Rd.
Queens Head Yd. SE1 4
Queens Ho., Tedd. 74
Queens La. N10 47
Queens La., Ashf. 73
Clarendon Rd.
Queens Mans. NW4 46
Queens Mkt. E13 58
Queens Mead Rd., Brom. 88
Queens Ms. W2 56
Salem Rd.
Queens Par. Clo. N12 38
Hollyfield Ave.
Queens Pk. Ct. W10 55
Queens Pk. Gdns., Felt. 73
Queens Pk. Rd., Cat. 105
Queens Pk. Rd., Rom. 42
Queens Pl., Mord. 86
Queens Pl., Walt. 92
Queens Pl., Wat. 27
Queens Prom., Kings.T. 84
Queens Reach, E.Mol. 84
Creek Rd.
Queens Ride SW13 65
Queens Ri., Rich. 75
Queens Rd. E11 48
Queens Rd. E13 58
Queens Rd. E17 48
Queens Rd. N3 38
Queens Rd. N9 39
Queens Rd. N11 38
Queens Rd. NW4 46
Queens Rd. SE15 67
Queens Rd. SW14 65
Queens Rd. SW19 75
Queens Rd. W5 55
Queens Rd., Bark. 58
Queens Rd., Barn. 28
Queens Rd., Beck. 87
Queens Rd., Berk. 7
Queens Rd., Brwd. 42
Queens Rd., Brom. 88
Queens Rd., Buck.H. 40
Queens Rd., Chis. 78
Queens Rd., Croy. 86
Queens Rd., Egh. 72
Queens Rd., Enf. 30
Queens Rd., Epp. 23
Queens Rd., Erith 69
Queens Rd., Felt. 73
Queens Rd., Grav. 81
Queens Rd., Guil. 118
Queens Rd., Hmptn. 74
Queens Rd., Hayes 53
Queens Rd., Houns. 64
Queens Rd., Ilf. 49
Queens Rd., Kings.T. 75
Queens Rd., Loug. 31
Queens Rd., Mitch. 86
Queens Rd., Mord. 86
Queens Rd., N.Mal. 85
Queens Rd., Rich. 75
Queens Rd., Slou. 52
Queens Rd. (Datchet), Slou. 62
Queens Rd., Sthl. 64
Queens Rd., Sutt. 95
Queens Rd., Tedd. 74
Queens Rd., T.Ditt. 84
Queens Rd., Twick. 74
Queens Rd., Uxb. 53
Queens Rd., Wall. 95
Queens Rd., Wal.Cr. 21
Queens Rd., Walt. 92
Queens Rd., Wat. 27
Queens Rd., Well. 69
Queens Rd., West Dr. 63
Queens Rd., Wey. 92
Queens Rd., Wind. 61
Queens Rd. (Eton Wick), Wind. 61
Queens Rd., Wok. 100
Queens Rd. W. E13 58
Queens Row SE17 67
Queens Sq, The, Hem.H. 8
Queens Ter. E13 58
Queens Ter. NW8 56
Queens Ter., Islw. 64
Queens Ter., Wind. 61
Queens Wk. E4 39
Green Wk.
Queens Wk. NW9 46
Queens Wk. SW1 3
Queens Wk. SW1 56
Queens Wk. W5 54
Queens Wk., Ashf. 73
Queens Wk., Har. 45
Queens Wk., Ruis. 45
Queens Way NW4 46
Queens Way, Felt. 74
Queens Way, Rad. 19
Queens Way, Wal.Cr. 21

eens Wd. Rd. N10 47 BV32
eens Yd. WC1 1 M5
eensberry Ms. W. SW7 3 A8
eensberry Ms. W. SW7 66 BT42
ueens Gate
eensberry Pl. SW7 3 A8
eensberry Pl. SW7 66 BT42
eensberry Way SW7 3 A8
eensborough Pas. W2 56 BT40
ueensborough Ter.
eensborough Ter. W2 56 BT40
eensbridge Ms., Islw. 74 BH46
eensbridge Pk., Islw. 74 BH46
eensbridge Rd. E2 2 Q1
eensbridge Rd. E2 57 CA36
eensbridge Rd. E8 57 CA36
eensbury Pl., Rich. 74 BK46
etreat Rd.
eensbury Rd. NW9 46 BN33
eensbury Rd., Wem. 55 BL37
eensbury Sta. Par., 46 BL31
dg.
eensbury St. N1 57 BZ36
lorton Rd.
eenscourt, Wem. 46 BL35
eenscroft Rd. SE9 78 CJ46
eensdale Cres. W11 55 BQ40
eensdale Pl. W11 55 BR40
eensdale Rd. W11 55 BQ40
eensdale Wk. W11 55 BR40
eensdown Rd. E5 48 CB35
eensgate, Cob. 93 BD59
eensgate Gdns. SW15 65 BP45
eensgate Gdns., Chis. 88 CM51
rince Consort Dr.
eensgate Pl. NW6 56 BS36
ingsgate Rd.
eensgate Pl. NW6 56 BS37
ingsgate Pl.
eensland Ave. N18 39 BZ29
eensland Ave. SW19 86 BS51
eensland Pl. N7 47 BY35
ueensland Rd.
eensland Rd. N7 47 BY35
eensmead NW8 56 BT37
eensmead, Slou. 62 AQ44
ueens Rd.
eensmead Ave., Epsom 94 BP58
eensmere, Slou. 62 AP41
eensmere Clo. SW19 75 BQ48
eensmere Rd. SW19 75 BQ48
eensmere Rd., Slou. 62 AQ41
eensmill Rd. SW6 65 BQ43
eensthorpe Rd. SE26 77 CC49
eenstown Gdns., Rain. 59 CT38
eenstown Rd. SW8 66 BV45
eensville Rd. SW12 76 BW47
eensway W2 56 BS39
eensway, Croy. 95 BX57
eensway, Enf. 30 CB25
eensway, Hat. 10 BP12
eensway, Hem.H. 8 AX13
eensway, Ong. 24 CW16
eensway, Orp. 88 CM53
eensway, Red. 121 BU70
eensway, Sun. 83 BC51
eensway, Wal.Cr. 21 CD20
ongcroft Dr.
eensway, Walt. 93 BD56
eensway, W.Wick. 97 CG56
eensway, The, Ger.Cr. 43 AR31
eensway N., Walt. 93 BD56
eech Clo.
eensway S., Walt. 93 BD56
eenswell Ave. N20 38 BU28
eenswood Ave. E17 39 CF30
eenswood Ave., 122 DE25
rwd.
eenswood Ave., 74 BF50
mptn.
eenswood Ave., Houns. 64 BE44
eenswood Ave., Th.Hth. 86 BY53
eenswood Ave., Wall. 95 BW56
eenswood Ct. SW4 76 BX46
eenswood Cres., Wat. 17 BC20
eenswood Gdns. E11 49 CH33
eenswood Pk. N3 37 BR30
eenswood Rd. SE23 77 CC48
eenswood Rd., Sid. 78 CN46
eenswood Rd., Wok. 100 AO63
emerford Rd. N7 47 BX35
endon Dr., Wal.Abb. 21 CF20
ennel Way, Brwd. 122 DE26
entin Pl. SE13 68 CG45
entin Rd. SE13 68 CG45
entin Way, Vir.W. 82 AQ52
ernmore Clo., Brom. 78 CH50
ernmore Rd. N4 47 BY32
ernmore Rd., Brom. 78 CH50
errin St. SW6 66 BT44
ex Ms. NW6 56 BS37
ex Rd. NW6 56 BS37
ick Pl. N1 56 BY37
ssex Rd.
ick Rd. W4 65 BO42
ick St. N1 2 G1
ick St. N1 56 BY37
ickbeams, Welw.G.C. 5 BS6
owans
ickberry Pl., Amer. 25 AO23
ickley Brow, Rick. 25 AT25
ickley La., Rick. 25 AU25
ickley Ri., Rick. 25 AU25
ickmoor La., Kings L. 17 AW20
icks Rd. SW19 76 BS50
icksilver Pl. N22 38 BX30
ickswood NW3 56 BU36
ickwood Clo., Rick. 25 AV25
iet Clo., Wey. 92 AW56
iet Nook, Kes. 88 CJ55
ill Hall La., Amer. 25 AP22
ill La. SW15 65 BQ45
ardinal Pl.
illot, The, Walt. 92 BB56

Quilp St. SE1 4 H4
Quilp St. SE1 67 BZ41
Redcross Way
Quilter Gdns., Orp. 89 CP54
Quilter Rd., Orp. 89 CP54
Quilter St. E2 57 CA38
Quinbrookes, Slou. 52 AR39
Quince Tree Clo., S.Ock. 60 DB38
Quinces Cft., Hem.H. 8 AW12
Quincy Rd., Egh. 72 AT49
Quinta Dr., Barn. 28 BP25
Quintin Clo., Pnr. 44 BC32
High Road, Eastcote
Quinton Ave. SW20 85 BR51
Quinton Clo., Beck. 87 CF52
Quinton Clo., Houns. 63 BC43
Quinton Clo., Wall. 95 BV56
Quinton Rd., T.Ditt. 84 BJ54
Quinton St. SW18 76 BT48
Quinton Way, Wal.Abb. 30 CF21
Quintrell Clo., Wok. 100 AQ62
Quixley St. E14 57 CF40
Naval Row
Quorn Rd. SE22 67 CA45

R

Raans Rd., Amer. 25 AP22
Rabbit La., Walt. 92 BC57
Rabbit Row W8 56 BS40
Kensington Mall
Rabbits Rd. E12 49 CK35
Rabbits Rd., S.Dnth. 90 CZ51
Rabbs Mill, Uxb. 53 AX37
Rabies Heath Rd., Red. 114 CA70
Rabournmead Dr., Nthlt. 45 BE35
Raby Rd., N.Mal. 85 BN52
Raby St. E14 57 CD39
Raccoon Way, Houns. 64 BD44
Rachel Pt. E5 48 CB34
Downs Est.
Rachels Way, Chesh. 16 AO20
Cresswell Rd.
Rackham Ms. SW16 76 BW49
Westcote Rd.
Racquet Ct. EC4 56 BY39
Fleet St.
Racton Rd. SW6 66 BS43
Radbourne Ave. W5 64 BK42
Radbourne Clo. E5 48 CC35
Glyn Rd.
Radbourne Ct. E5 48 CC35
Clapton Pk. Est.
Radbourne Cres. E17 48 CF31
Radbourne Rd. SW12 76 BW47
Radburn Clo., Harl. 14 CO13
Radcliffe Ave. NW10 55 BP37
Radcliffe Ave., Enf. 30 BZ23
Radcliffe Gdns., Cars. 95 BU57
Radcliffe Path SW8 66 BW44
St. Rule St.
Radcliffe Rd. N21 38 BY26
Radcliffe Rd., Croy. 87 CA55
Radcliffe Rd., Har. 36 BJ30
Radcliffe Sq. SW15 75 BQ46
Radcliffe Way, Nthlt. 54 BD38
Radcot Ave., Slou. 62 AU41
Radcot St. SE11 66 BY42
Raddington Rd. W10 55 BR39
Radfield Way, Sid. 78 CM47
Radford Rd. SE13 77 CF46
Radford Way, Bark. 58 CN38
Radipole Rd. SW6 65 BR44
Radland Rd. E16 58 CG39
Radlet Ave. SE26 77 CB48
Radlett Clo. E7 58 CH36
Radlett La., Rad. 27 BK21
Radlett Pk. Rd., Rad. 18 BJ20
Radlett Pl. NW8 56 BU37
Radlett Rd., St.Alb. 18 BH18
Radlett Rd., Wat. 27 BD24
Radlett Rd. (Aldenham), 27 BG22
Wat.
Radley Ave., Ilf. 50 CO35
Radley Ct. SE16 67 CC41
Thame Rd.
Radley Gdns., Har. 46 BL31
Radley Ms. W8 66 BS41
Radley Rd. N17 39 CA30
Radleys La. E18 40 CH30
Radleys Mead, Dag. 59 CR36
Radlix Rd. E10 48 CE33
Radnor Ave., Har. 45 BH32
Radnor Ave., Well. 79 CO46
Radnor Clo., Chis. 88 CN50
Homewood Cres.
Radnor Clo., Mitch. 86 BX52
Radnor Ct., Red. 121 BU70
Linkfield St.
Radnor Cres., Ilf. 49 CK32
Radnor Gdns., Enf. 30 CA23
Radnor Gdns., Twick. 74 BH48
Radnor Gro., Uxb. 53 AZ37
Charnwood Rd.
Radnor Ho., Twick. 74 BJ48
Radnor Ms. W2 1 B9
Radnor Ms. W2 56 BT39
Radnor Pl. W2 1 C9
Radnor Pl. W2 56 BU39
Radnor Rd. NW6 55 BR37
Radnor Rd. SE15 67 CB43
Radnor Rd., Har. 45 BG32
Radnor Rd., Twick. 74 BH47
Radnor Rd., Wey. 83 AZ55
Radnor St. EC1 2 J3
Radnor St. EC1 57 BZ38
Radnor Ter. SW8 66 BX43
South Lambeth Rd.
Radnor Ter. W14 65 BR42

Radnor Wk. E14 67 CE42
Barnsdale Ave.
Radnor Wk. SW3 66 BU42
Radnor Wk., Croy. 87 CD53
Radnor Way NW10 55 BM38
Radnor Way, Slou. 62 AS42
Radolphs, Tad. 103 BQ64
Radstock Ave., Har. 45 BJ31
Radstock St. SW11 66 BU43
Parkgate Rd.
Radstock Way, Red. 113 BW67
Radstone Ct., Wok. 100 AS62
Hill Vw. Rd.
Radwell Path, Borwd. 28 BL23
Cromwell Rd.
Raebarn Gdns., Barn. 28 BP25
Raeburn Ave., Dart. 79 CU46
Raeburn Ave., Surb. 85 BM54
Raeburn Clo. NW11 47 BS32
Raeburn Clo., Kings.T. 74 BK50
Raeburn Rd., Edg. 37 BM30
Raeburn Rd., Hayes 53 BA37
Raeburn Rd., Sid. 78 CN46
Raeburn St. SW2 66 BX45
Raeside Clo., Beac. 34 AO28
Rafford Way, Brom. 88 CH51
Raft Rd. SW18 76 BS46
Rag Hill Clo., West. 106 CK64
Rag Hill Rd., West. 106 CJ64
Ragge Way, Sev. 108 CW63
The Landway
Ragged Hall La., 9 BE15
St.Alb.
Raggleswood, Chis. 88 CL51
Raglan Ave., Wal.Cr. 21 CC20
Raglan Clo., Houns. 74 BE46
Frampton Rd.
Raglan Clo., Reig. 121 BT69
Raglan Ct., S.Croy. 95 BY56
Raglan Ct., Wem. 46 BL35
Raglan Gdns., Wat. 35 BC26
Raglan Rd. E17 48 CF32
Raglan Rd. SE18 68 CL42
Raglan Rd., Belv. 69 CQ42
Raglan Rd., Brom. 88 CJ52
Raglan Rd., Enf. 39 CA26
Raglan Rd., Reig. 121 BS69
Raglan Rd., Wok. 100 AP62
Raglan St. NW5 56 BV36
Raglan Ter., Har. 45 BF35
Stroud Gate
Raglan Way, Nthlt. 54 BG36
Ragley Clo. W3 65 BM41
Avenue Rd.
Ragley Clo. W3 55 BN40
Church Rd.
Rags La., Chsnt. 21 CA17
Ragstone Rd., Slou. 61 AO41
Rahn Rd., Epp. 22 CN19
Raider Clo., Rom. 41 CR30
Raikes La., Dor. 119 BC74
Railey Ms. NW5 47 BW35
Leverton St.
Railpit La., Warl. 106 CG61
Railshead Rd., Twick. 64 BJ45
Richmond Rd.
Railton Rd. SE24 66 BY45
Railway App. SE1 4 L3
Railway App. SE1 57 BZ40
Railway App., Cher. 82 AV54
Railway App., Har. 45 BH31
Railway App., Twick. 74 BJ47
Railway App., Wall. 95 BV56
Railway Ave. SE16 67 CC41
Railway Cotts., Hat. 10 BO13
Railway Cotts., Ilf. 40 CM29
Railway Cotts, St.Alb. 9 BH10
Railway Ms. W10 55 BR39
Ladbroke Gro.
Railway Pas., Tedd. 74 BJ50
Clarence Rd.
Railway Pl. SW19 75 BR50
Hartfield Rd.
Railway Pl., Belv. 69 CR41
Railway Ri. SE22 67 CA45
Derwent Rd.
Railway Rd., Tedd. 74 BH49
Railway Rd., Wal.Cr. 21 CD20
Railway Side SW13 65 BO45
White Hart La.
Railway Sq., Brwd. 42 DB27
Railway St. N1 2 A1
Railway St. N1 56 BX37
Railway St., Grav. 81 DD46
Railway St., Rom. 50 CP33
Railway Ter. SE13 77 CE46
Railway Ter., Felt. 73 BC47
Railway Ter., Slou. 52 AP40
Railway Ter., Stai. 72 AU49
Railway Ter., West. 115 CN66
Rainborough Clo. NW10 55 BN36
Rainbow Ave. E14 67 CE42
Rainbow Ct., Wat. 36 BD26
Oxhey Rd.
Rainbow Ct., Wok. 100 AP61
Langmans Way
Rainbow St. SE5 67 CA43
Raine St. E1 57 CB40
Rainer Clo., Chsnt. 21 CC18
Rainham Clo. SE9 78 CN46
Rainham Clo. SW11 76 BU46
Rainham Rd. NW10 55 BQ38
Rainham Rd., Rain. 59 CT36
Rainham Rd. N., Dag. 50 CR34
Rainham Rd. S., Dag. 50 CR35
Rainhill Way E3 57 CE38
Rainsborough Ave. SE8 67 CD42
Rainsford Rd. NW10 55 BM37
Rainsford St. W2 1 C8
Rainsford St. W2 56 BU39
Sale Pl.
Rainsford Way, Horn. 50 CU33
Rainton Rd. SE7 68 CH42
Rainville Rd. W6 65 BQ43

Raisins Hill, Pnr. 44 BC31
Raith Ave. N14 38 BW27
Raleana Rd. E14 57 CF40
Prestons Rd.
Raleigh Ave., Hayes 53 BC39
Raleigh Ave., Wall. 95 BW56
Raleigh Clo. NW4 46 BQ32
Raleigh Clo., Erith 69 CU43
Frobisher Rd.
Raleigh Clo., Pnr. 45 BD33
Raleigh Clo., Ruis. 44 BB34
Raleigh Clo., Slou. 61 AN40
Raleigh Ct., Beck. 87 CE51
Raleigh Ct., Stai. 73 AW49
Raleigh Ct., Wall. 95 BV57
Raleigh Dr. N20 38 BU27
Raleigh Dr., Esher 93 BG56
Raleigh Dr., Surb. 85 BN54
Raleigh Gdns., Mitch. 86 BU51
Raleigh Ms., Orp. 97 CN56
Osgood Ave.
Raleigh Rd. N8 47 BY31
Raleigh Rd. SE20 77 CC50
Raleigh Rd., Enf. 30 BZ24
Raleigh Rd., Felt. 73 BB48
Raleigh Rd., Rich. 65 BL45
Raleigh Rd., Sthl. 64 BE42
Raleigh St. N1 56 BY37
Raleigh Way N14 38 BW26
Raleigh Way, Felt. 74 BD49
Ralliwood Rd., Ash. 103 BM63
Ralph St. SE1 67 BZ41
Ralston St. SW3 66 BU42
Tedworth Sq.
Ralston Way, Wat. 36 BD27
Ram Gorse, Harl. 6 CL10
Ram Pl. E9 57 CC36
Chatham Pl.
Ram St. SW18 76 BS46
Rama Ct., Har. 45 BH34
Ramac Way SE7 68 CH42
Rambler Clo. SW16 76 BW49
Rambler La., Slou. 62 AR41
Ramblers Way, Welw.G.C. 5 BT8
Rambling Way, Berk. 7 AU12
Ramilles Clo. SW2 76 BX46
Ramillies Pl. W1 1 L9
Ramillies Pl. W1 56 BW39
Ramillies Rd. NW7 37 BO27
Ramillies Rd. W4 65 BN42
Ramillies Rd., Sid. 79 CO46
Ramillies St. W1 1 L9
Ramillies St. W1 56 BW39
Great Marlborough St.
Ramin Ct., Guil. 118 AR69
Rowan Clo.
Ramney Dr., Enf. 30 CD22
Ramorne Clo., Walt. 93 BE56
Rampart St. E1 57 CB39
Commercial Rd.
Ramparts, The, St.Alb. 9 BF14
Rampayne St. SW1 3 N10
Rampayne St. SW1 66 BW42
Rampton Clo. E4 39 CE27
Rams Gro., Rom. 50 CQ31
Ramsay Clo., Brox. 12 CD14
Ramsay Gdns., Rom. 42 CV30
Ramsay Pl., Har. 45 BG33
West St.
Ramsay Rd. E7 49 CG35
Ramsay Rd. W3 65 BN41
Ramsbury Rd., St.Alb. 9 BH14
Ramscroft Clo. N9 39 CA26
Ramsdale Rd. SW17 76 BV49
Ramsden Clo., Orp. 89 CP54
Ramsden Rd.
Ramsden Dr., Rom. 41 CR29
Ramsden Ri., Hem.H. 7 AV14
The Foxgloves
Ramsden Rd. N11 38 BU28
Ramsden Rd. SW12 76 BV46
Ramsden Rd., Erith 69 CS43
Ramsden Rd., Orp. 89 CO54
Ramsey Clo. NW9 46 BO32
Ramsey Clo., Grnf. 45 BG35
Ramsey Clo., Hat. 20 BT17
Ramsey Clo., St.Alb. 9 BJ14
Ramsey Ct. N8 47 BW32
Ramsey Rd., Th.Hth. 86 BX53
Ramsey St. E2 57 CB38
Ramsey Wk. N1 57 BZ36
Marquess Est.
Ramsey Way N14 38 BW26
Windsor Ct.
Ramsgate St. E8 57 CA36
Ramsgill App., Ilf. 49 CN31
Ramsgill Dr., Ilf. 49 CN32
Ramson Ri., Hem.H. 7 AV14
The Foxgloves
Ramulis Dr., Hayes 54 BE38
Ramus Wd. Ave., Orp. 97 CN56
Rancliffe Gdns. SE9 68 CK45
Rancliffe Rd. E6 58 CK38
Randal Cres., Reig. 121 BS71
Randall Ave. NW2 46 BO34
Randall Clo. SW11 66 BU44
Randall Clo., Erith 69 CS43
Randall Clo., Slou. 62 AS42
Randall Cres., Lthd. 102 BJ63
Randall Dr., Horn. 51 CV35
Randall Pl. SE10 67 CF43
Randall Rd. SE11 4 B9
Randall Rd. SE11 66 BX42
Randall Row SE11 4 B9
Randall Row SE11 66 BX42
Randalls Dr., Brwd. 122 DF25
Randalls Fm. La., Lthd. 102 BJ63
Randalls Pk. Ave., Lthd. 102 BJ63
Randalls Pk. Dr., Lthd. 102 BJ64
Randalls Ride, Hem.H. 8 AY12
Randalls Rd., Lthd. 102 BH63
Randalls Way, Lthd. 102 BJ64
Randell Hill Rd., Sev. 108 DC61
Battlefields Rd.

Randells Rd. N1 56 BX37
Randisbourne Gdns. SE6 77 CE47
Bromley Rd.
Randle Rd., Rich. 74 BK49
Randles La., Sev. 98 CP60
Randlesdown Rd. SE6 77 CE49
Randolph App. E16 58 CJ39
Baxter Rd.
Randolph Ave. W9 56 BS38
Randolph Clo., Bexh. 69 CS45
Randolph Clo., Cob. 102 BF61
Randolph Clo., Kings.T. 75 BN49
Randolph Clo., Wok. 100 AP62
Randolph Cres. W9 56 BT38
Randolph Gdns. NW6 56 BS37
Randolph Gro., Rom. 50 CP32
Donald Dr.
Randolph Ms. W9 56 BT38
Randolph Rd. E17 48 CE32
Randolph Rd. W9 56 BT38
Randolph Rd., Epsom 94 BO60
Randolph Rd., Slou. 62 AS42
Randolph Rd., Sthl. 64 BE41
Randolph St. NW1 56 BW36
Randon Clo., Har. 36 BF30
Ranelagh Ave. SW6 65 BR45
Ranelagh Ave. SW13 65 BP44
Ranelagh Bri. W2 56 BS39
Ranelagh Clo., Edg. 37 BM28
Ranelagh Dr., Edg. 37 BM28
Ranelagh Dr., Twick. 64 BJ45
Ranelagh Est. SW15 65 BQ44
Ranelagh Gdns. E11 49 CJ32
Ranelagh Gdns. SW6 65 BR45
Ranelagh Gdns. W4 65 BN43
Grove Pk. Gdns.
Ranelagh Gdns., Grav. 81 DF47
Ranelagh Gdns., Ilf. 49 CK33
Ranelagh Gro. SW1 3 H10
Ranelagh Gro. SW1 66 BV42
Ranelagh Ms. W5 64 BK41
Ranelagh Rd.
Ranelagh Pl., N.Mal. 85 BO53
Ranelagh Rd. E6 58 CL37
Ranelagh Rd. E11 49 CG35
Ranelagh Rd. E15 58 CG37
Ranelagh Rd. N17 48 CA31
Ranelagh Rd. N22 38 BX30
Ranelagh Rd. NW10 55 BO37
Ranelagh Rd. SW1 66 BW42
Lupus St.
Ranelagh Rd. W5 64 BK41
Ranelagh Rd., Hem.H. 8 AZ13
Ranelagh Rd., Red. 121 BU70
Ranelagh Rd., Sthl. 54 BD40
Ranelagh Rd., Wem. 45 BK35
Ranfurly Rd., Sutt. 86 BS55
Range Rd., Grav. 81 DJ47
Range Way, Shep. 83 AZ54
Rangefield Rd., Brom. 78 CG49
Rangemoor Rd. N15 48 CA32
Rangers Rd. E4 40 CG26
Rangers Sq. SE10 67 CF44
Rangeworth Pl., Sid. 78 CN48
Priestlands Pk. Rd.
Rangoon St. EC3 57 CA39
Northumberland All.
Rankin Clo. NW9 46 BO31
Ranleigh Gdns., Bexh. 69 CQ43
Ranmere St. SW12 76 BV47
Ranmoor Clo., Har. 45 BG31
Ranmoor Gdns., Har. 45 BG31
Ranmore Ave., Croy. 87 CA55
Ranmore Clo., Red. 121 BV69
Ranmore Common Rd. 119 BD70
(Dogkennel Grn.), Dor.
Ranmore Common Rd. 119 BH69
(West Humble), Dor.
Ranmore Path, Orp. 89 CO52
Ranmore Rd., Couls. 104 BX62
Ranmore Rd., Dor. 119 BG70
Ranmore Rd., Sutt. 94 BQ58
Rannoch Rd. W6 65 BQ43
Rannoch Wk., Hem.H. 8 AX11
Rannock Ave. NW9 46 BN33
Ranskill Rd., Borwd. 28 BM23
Ransom Clo., Wat. 36 BD26
Ransom Rd. SE7 68 CJ42
Ranston Clo., Uxb. 43 AV32
Ranston St. NW1 1 C6
Ranston St. NW1 56 BU39
Rant Meadow, Hem.H. 8 AZ14
Ranulf Rd. NW2 46 BR35
Ranworth Clo., Erith 69 CT44
Ranworth Clo., Hem.H. 8 AX14
Ranworth Rd. N9 39 CC27
Raphael Ave., Rom. 41 CT30
Raphael Ave., Til. 71 DG44
Raphael Dr., Wat. 27 BD23
Raphael Rd., Grav. 81 DH47
Raphael St. SW7 3 E5
Raphael St. SW7 66 BU41
Rapier Clo., Grays 70 CX42
Rasehill Clo., Rick. 26 AX25
Rashleigh St. SW8 66 BV44
Rashleigh Way, Hort.K. 90 CY52
Rasper Rd. N20 38 BT27
Rastell Ave. SW2 76 BW48
Ratcliff Rd. E7 49 CJ35
Ratcliffe Cross St. E1 57 CC39
Ratcliffe La. E14 57 CD39
Ratcliffe Orchard E1 57 CC40
Ratcliffe Rd., Uxb. 53 AX38
Rathbone Mkt. E16 58 CG39
Rathbone Pl. W1 1 N7
Rathbone Pl. W1 56 BW39
Rathbone Pt. E5 48 CB34
Downs Est.
Rathbone St. E16 58 CG39
Rathbone St. W1 1 M7
Rathbone St. W1 56 BW39
Rathcoole Ave. N8 47 BX31
Rathcoole Gdns. N8 47 BX32
Rathfern Rd. SE6 77 CD47

Rathgar Ave. W13 54 BJ40
Rathgar Clo. N3 37 BR30
Rathgar Clo., Red. 121 BV73
Rathlin, Hem.H. 8 AZ14
Rathlin Wk. N1 57 BZ36
Marquess Est.
Rathmell Dr. SW4 76 BW46
Rathmore Rd. SE7 68 CH42
Rathmore Rd., Grav. 81 DG47
Rats La., Loug. 31 CH22
Rattray Rd. SW2 66 BY45
Rattys La., Hodd. 12 CF12
Raul Rd. SE15 67 CB44
Ravel Gdns., S.Ock. 60 CY39
Ravel Rd., S.Ock. 60 CY39
Raveley St. NW5 47 BW35
Raven Clo., Rick. 35 AX26
Raven Ct., Hat. 10 BP13
Raven Rd. E18 40 CJ30
Raven Row E1 57 CB39
Ravencroft, Grays 71 DG41
Alexandra Clo.
Ravendale Rd., Sun. 83 BB51
Ravenet St. SW11 66 BV44
Strasburg Rd.
Ravenfield, Egh. 72 AR50
Ravenfield Rd. SW17 76 BU48
Ravenfield Rd., Welw.G.C. 5 BR8
Ravenhill Rd. E13 58 CJ37
Ravenna Rd. SW15 65 BQ45
Ravenor Pk. Rd., Grnf. 54 BF38
Ravens Clo., Brom. 88 CG51
Ravens Clo., Enf. 30 CA23
Ravens Clo., Red. 121 BU70
Ravens Clo., Wok. 100 AO61
Ravens Ct., Sun. 83 BB51
Ravens La., Berk. 7 AR13
Ravens Mead, Ger.Cr. 34 AS28
Ravens Way SE12 78 CH46
Ravensbourne Ave., Brom. 77 CF50
Ravensbourne Ave., Ilf. 40 CL30
Ravensbourne Ave., Stai. 73 AY47
Ravensbourne Cres., Rom. 51 CW31
Ravensbourne Est., Brom. 77 CF49
Ravensbourne Gdns. W13 54 BJ39
Ravensbourne Gdns., Ilf. 40 CL30
Ravensbourne Pk. SE6 77 CD47
Ravensbourne Pk. Cres. SE6 77 CD47
Ravensbourne Rd. SE6 77 CD47
Ravensbourne Rd., Brom. 88 CH52
Ravensbourne Rd., Dart. 69 CU45
Ravensbourne Rd., Twick. 74 BK46
Ravensbury Ave., Mord. 86 BT53
Ravensbury Gro., Mitch. 86 BT52
Ravensbury La., Mitch. 86 BT52
Ravensbury Path, Mitch. 86 BT52
Ravensbury Rd. SW18 76 BS48
Ravensbury Rd., Orp. 88 CN52
Ravensbury Ter. SW18 76 BS47
Ravensbury Rd.
Ravenscar Rd., Brom. 78 CG49
Ravenscar Rd., Surb. 85 BL55
Ravenscourt Ave. W6 65 BP42
Ravenscourt Clo., Horn. 51 CW34
Ravenscourt Dr.
Ravenscourt Clo., Ruis. 44 BA33
Ravenscourt Dr., Horn. 51 CW34
Ravenscourt Gdns. W6 65 BP42
Ravenscourt Gro., Horn. 51 CW34
Ravenscourt Pk. W6 65 BP42
Ravenscourt Pl. W6 65 BP42
King St.
Ravenscourt Rd. W6 65 BP41
Ravenscourt Rd., Orp. 89 CO51
Ravenscourt Sq. W6 65 BP41
Ravenscraig Rd. N11 38 BW28
Ravenscroft, Wat. 27 BE21
Ravenscroft, Wat. 27 BE21
Ravenscroft Ave. NW11 46 BR33
Ravenscroft Ave., Wem. 46 BL33
Ravenscroft Clo. E16 58 CH39
Ravenscroft Cres. SE9 78 CK48
Ravenscroft Pk., Barn. 28 BQ24
Ravenscroft Pk. Rd., Barn. 28 BQ24
Ravenscroft Rd. E16 58 CH39
Ravenscroft Rd. W4 65 BN42
Ravenscroft Rd., Beck. 87 CC51
Ravenscroft Rd., Wey. 92 BA59
Ravenscroft St. E2 2 Q1
Ravenscroft St. E2 57 CA37
Ravensdale Ave. N12 38 BT28
Ravensdale Gdns. SE19 77 BZ50
Ravensdale Ms., Stai. 73 AW50
Worple Rd.
Ravensdale Rd. N16 48 CA33
Ravensdale Rd., Houns. 64 BE45
Ravensdell, Hem.H. 7 AV13
Ravensdon St. SE11 66 BY42
Ravensfield, Slou. 62 AR41
Ravensfield Clo., Dag. 50 CP35
Ravensfield Gdns., Epsom 94 BO56
Ravenshaw St. NW6 46 BR35
Ravenshead Clo., S.Croy. 96 CC59
Ravenshill, Chis. 88 CL51
Ravenshurst Ave. NW4 46 BQ31
Ravenslea Rd. SW12 76 BU47
Ravensmead Rd., Brom. 77 CF50
Ravensmede Way W4 65 BO42
Ravensmere, Epp. 23 CO19
Ravenstone Rd. N8 47 BY31
Ravenstone Rd. NW9 46 BO32
Ravenstone St. SW12 76 BV47
Ravenswold, Ken. 105 BZ61
Ravenswood, Bex. 79 CQ47
Ravenswood Ave., Surb. 85 BL55
Ravenswood Ave., W.Wick. 87 CF54
Ravenswood Clo., Cob. 102 BD61
Ravenswood Clo., Croy. 86 BY55
Ravenswood Rd.
Ravenswood Clo., Rom. 41 CR28
Ravenswood Ct., Kings.T. 75 BM50
Ravenswood Ct., Wok. 100 AS62
Hill Vw. Rd.
Ravenswood Cres., Har. 45 BE34
Ravenswood Cres., W.Wick. 87 CF54
Ravenswood Gdns., Islw. 64 BH44
Ravenswood Pk., Nthwd. 35 BC29
Ravenswood Rd. E17 48 CE31
Ravenswood Rd. SW12 76 BV47
Ravenswood Rd., Croy. 86 BY55
Ravensworth Rd. NW10 55 BP38
Ravensworth Rd. SE9 78 CK48
Ravent Rd. SE11 4 C8
Ravent Rd. SE11 66 BX42
Ravey St. EC2 2 M4
Ravey St. EC2 57 CA38
Ravine Gro. SE18 68 CN43
Rawchester Clo. SW18 75 BR47
Rawdon Dr., Hodd. 12 CE12
Rawlings Clo., Orp. 97 CN56
Rawlings La., Beac. 34 AO27
Rawlings St. SW3 3 E8
Rawlings St. SW3 66 BU42
Rawlins Clo. N3 37 BR30
Rawlins Clo., S.Croy. 96 CD57
Rawlinson Ter. N17 48 CA31
Rawnsley Ave., Mitch. 86 BU53
Rawreth Wk. N1 57 BZ37
Basire St.
Rawson St. SW11 66 BV44
Strasburg Rd.
Rawstone Wk. E13 58 CH37
Grasmere Rd.
Rawstorne Pl. EC1 2 F2
Rawstorne Pl. EC1 56 BY38
Rawstorne St.
Rawstorne St. EC1 2 F2
Rawstorne St. EC1 56 BY38
Ray Fld., Welw.G.C. 5 BQ6
Ray Gdns., Bark. 59 CO37
Ray Gdns., Stan. 36 BJ28
Ray Lo. Rd., Wdf.Grn. 40 CJ29
Ray Rd., E.Mol. 84 BF53
Ray Rd., Rom. 41 CR28
Ray St. EC1 2 E5
Ray St. EC1 56 BY38
Ray St. Bri. EC1 2 E5
Ray Wk. N7 47 BX34
Andover Rd.
Raybarn Rd., Hem.H. 8 AW12
Rayburn Rd., Horn. 51 CX33
Raydean Rd., Barn. 29 BS25
Raydon Rd., Chsnt. 21 CC19
Theobalds La.
Raydon St. N19 47 BV34
Raydons Gdns., Dag. 50 CO35
Raydons Rd., Dag. 50 CQ35
Rayfield, Epp. 22 CN18
Rayfield Clo., Brom. 88 CK53
Rayford Ave. SE12 78 CG47
Rayford Clo., Dart. 80 CV46
Raylands Mead, Ger.Cr. 43 AR32
Rayleas Clo. SE18 68 CL44
Rayleigh Ave., Tedd. 74 BH50
Rayleigh Clo. N13 39 BZ27
Rayleigh Clo., Brwd. 122 DE25
Rayleigh Ct. N22 39 BZ30
Rayleigh Ct., Kings.T. 85 BM51
Cambridge Rd.
Rayleigh Ri., S.Croy. 96 CA57
Rayleigh Rd. N13 39 BZ27
Rayleigh Rd. SW19 85 BR51
Rayleigh Rd., Brwd. 122 DD25
Rayleigh Rd., Wdf.Grn. 40 CJ29
Rayley La., Epp. 14 CR15
Raymead NW4 46 BQ31
Raymead Ave., Th.Hth. 86 BY53
Raymead Clo., Lthd. 102 BH64
Raymead Clo., Loug. 31 CM25
Raymead Way, Lthd. 102 BH64
Raymer Clo., St.Alb. 9 BH13
Raymere Gdns. SE18 68 CM43
Raymond Ave. E18 49 CG31
Raymond Ave. W13 64 BJ41
Raymond Bldgs. WC1 2 C6
Raymond Bldgs. WC1 56 BX39
Raymond Clo. SE26 77 CC49
Raymond Clo., Abb.L. 17 BA19
Raymond Clo., Slou. 62 AV44
Raymond Cres., Guil. 118 AP71
Raymond Gdns., Chig. 41 CO27
Raymond Rd. E13 58 CJ36
Raymond Rd. SW19 75 BR50
Raymond Rd., Beck. 87 CD52
Raymond Rd., Ilf. 49 CM33
Raymond Rd., Slou. 62 AT42
Raymond Way, Esher 93 BJ57
Raymonds Clo., Welw.G.C. 5 BR9
Raymonds Plain, Welw.G.C. 5 BR9
Raymouth Rd. SE16 67 CB42
Rayne Ct. E18 49 CG31
Rayners Clo., Slou. 62 AU43
Rayners Ct., Har. 45 BF33
Rayners Cres., Nthlt. 53 BC38
Rayners Gdns., Nthlt. 53 BC38
Rayners La., Har. 45 BF33
Rayners La., Pnr. 45 BE32
Rayners Rd. SW15 75 BQ46
Raynes Ave. E11 49 CJ33
Raynham Ave. N18 39 CB29
Raynham Rd. N18 39 CB28
Raynham Rd. W6 65 BP42
Raynham Ter. N18 39 CB28
Raynor Clo., Sthl. 54 BE40
Raynors Clo., Wem. 45 BK35
Raynton Clo., Har. 45 BE33
Raynton Clo., Hayes 53 BB38
Raynton Dr., Hayes 53 BB38
Raynton Rd., Enf. 30 CC22
Rays Ave. N18 39 CC28
Rays Ave., Wind. 61 AM43
Rays Hill, Dart. 90 CY53
Rays Rd. N18 39 CB28
Rays Rd., W.Wick. 87 CF54
Raywood Clo., Hayes 63 BA43
Raywood St. SW8 66 BV44
Read Ct., Wal.Abb. 22 CH20
Read Rd., Ash. 102 BK62
Read Way, Grav. 81 DH49
Reade Wk. NW10 55 BO36
Denbigh Clo.
Readens, The, Bans. 104 BU61
Reading Arch Rd., Red. 121 BU70
Reading La. E8 57 CB36
Reading Rd., Nthlt. 45 BF35
Reading Rd., Sutt. 95 BT56
Reading Way NW7 37 BR28
Readings, The, Harl. 13 CN12
Readings, The, Rick. 25 AV24
Reads Clo., Ilf. 49 CL34
Roden St.
Reads Rest La., Tad. 104 BS63
Reapers Way, Islw. 74 BG46
Reardon Path E1 57 CB40
Reardon St. E1 57 CB40
Reaston St. SE14 67 CC43
Rebecca Ter. SE16 67 CC41
Reckingham Rd., Guil. 118 AQ69
Reckitt Rd. W4 65 BO42
Record St. SE15 67 CC43
Recovery St. SW17 76 BU49
Recreation Ave., Rom. 50 CS32
Recreation Ave. (Harold Wd.), Rom. 42 CW35
Recreation Rd. SE26 77 CC49
Recreation Rd., Brom. 88 CG51
Recreation Rd., Guil. 118 AR70
Recreation Rd., Sthl. 64 BE42
Recreation Way, Mitch. 86 BW52
Rector St. N1 57 BZ37
Rectory Chase, Brwd. 51 DB31
Rectory Chase (Doddinghurst), Brwd. 33 DB22
Rectory Clo. E4 39 CE27
Rectory Clo. E4 39 CE27
Brindwood Rd.
Rectory Clo. N3 37 BR30
Rectory Clo. SW20 85 BQ52
Rectory Clo., Ash. 103 BL63
Rectory Clo., Dart. 69 CT45
Rectory Clo., Guil. 118 AU69
Rectory Clo., Hat. 11 BU12
Rectory Clo., Shep. 83 AZ52
Rectory Clo., Sid. 79 CO49
Rectory Clo., Stan. 36 BJ28
Rectory Clo., Surb. 84 BK54
Rectory Clo., Wey. 92 AY60
Rectory Clo., Wind. 61 AN44
Rectory Cres. E11 49 CJ32
Rectory Fld., Harl. 13 CL12
Rectory Fld. Cres. SE7 68 CJ43
Rectory Gdns. N8 47 BX31
Rectory Gdns. SW4 66 BW45
Rectory Gro.
Rectory Gdns., Hat. 10 BP12
Rectory Gdns., Hayes 63 BA42
Rectory Gdns., Nthlt. 54 BE37
Rectory Gdns., Upmin. 51 CZ34
Rectory Grn., Beck. 87 CD51
Rectory Grn. La., Bet. 120 BO69
Rectory Gro. SW4 66 BW45
Rectory Gro., Croy. 86 BY55
Rectory Gro., Hmptn. 74 BE49
Rectory La. SW17 76 BV50
Rectory La., Ash. 103 BL62
Rectory La., Bans. 95 BU60
Rectory La., Berk. 7 AR13
Rectory La., Edg. 37 BM29
Rectory La., Kings L. 17 AZ17
Rectory La., Lthd. 111 BE66
Rectory La., Loug. 31 CL23
Rectory La., Rad. 19 BM19
Rectory La., Rick. 35 AX26
Rectory La., Sev. 117 CV66
Rectory La. (Ightham), Sev. 108 BD64
Rectory La., Sid. 79 CO49
Rectory La., Stan. 36 BJ28
Rectory La., Surb. 84 BJ54
Rectory La., Wall. 86 BW55
Rectory La., West. 107 CP65
Rectory La., Wey. 92 AY60
Rectory Meadow, Grav. 81 DD50
Rectory Pk., S.Croy. 96 CA60
Rectory Pk. Ave., Nthlt. 54 BE38
Rectory Pl. SE18 68 CL42
Rectory Rd. E12 49 CK35
Rectory Rd. E17 48 CE31
Rectory Rd. N16 48 CA34
Rectory Rd. SW13 65 BP44
Rectory Rd. W3 55 BM40
Rectory Rd., Beck. 87 CE51
Rectory Rd., Couls. 113 BS66
Rectory Rd., Dag. 59 CR36
Rectory Rd., Grays 71 DE41
Rectory Rd., Green. 80 CZ46
Church Rd.
Rectory Rd., Hayes 53 BC39
Rectory Rd., Houns. 63 BC44
Rectory Rd., Kes. 97 CJ57
Rectory Rd., Rick. 35 AX26
Rectory Rd., Sthl. 64 BE41
Rectory Rd., Sutt. 86 BS55
Rectory Rd., Swans. 81 DC47
Rectory Rd., Til. 71 DH43
Rectory Rd., Welw.G.C. 5 BP6
Rectory Rd., West. 106 CK65
Rectory Sq. E1 57 CC39
Rectory Way, Uxb. 44 AZ34
Rectory Wd., Harl. 6 CM10
Reculver Ms. N18 39 CB28
Reculver Rd. SE16 67 CC42
Red Anchor Clo. SW3 66 BU43
Old Ch. St.
Red Barracks Rd. SE18 68 CK42
Red Bull Yd. EC4 57 BZ40
Upper Thames St.
Red Cedars Rd., Orp. 88 CN54
Red Cottage Ms., Slou. 62 AR41
London Rd.
Red Ct., Slou. 52 AP40
Stoke Poges La.
Red Cross, Reig. 121 BS70
Red Hall La., Rick. 26 AY23
Red Hill, Chis. 78 CL49
Red Hill, Cob. 101 BA61
Red Ho. La., Bexh. 69 CP45
Red Ho. La., Walt. 83 BC55
Red Ho. Rd., Croy. 86 BW53
Red La., Dor. 120 BL74
Red La., Esher 93 BJ57
Red La., Oxt. 115 CH69
Red Law Way SE16 67 CB42
Red Leaf Clo., Slou. 52 AS40
Pickford Dr.
Red Lion Clo. SE17 67 BZ42
Red Lion Row
Red Lion Clo., Orp. 89 CP53
Red Lion Ct. EC4 2 E9
Red Lion Ct. EC4 56 BY39
Fleet St.
Red Lion Cres., Harl. 14 CP12
Red Lion Hill N2 38 BT30
Red Lion La. SE18 68 CL44
Red Lion La., Harl. 14 CP12
Red Lion La., Hem.H. 17 AZ16
Red Lion La., Rick. 26 AW21
Red Lion La., Wok. 91 AP58
Red Lion Rd., Surb. 85 BL55
Red Lion Rd., Wok. 91 AP58
Red Lion Row SE17 67 BZ43
Red Lion Sq. WC1 2 B7
Red Lion Sq. WC1 56 BX39
Red Lion Sq., Hmptn. 84 BF51
Red Lion St. WC1 2 B6
Red Lion St. WC1 56 BX39
Theobalds Rd.
Red Lion St., Rich. 74 BK46
Red Lion Yd. W1 3 H2
Red Lion Yd., Wat. 27 BD24
Red Lo. Cres., Bex. 79 CS48
Red Lo. Gdns., Berk. 7 AQ13
Red Lo. Rd., Bex. 79 CS48
Red Lo. Rd., W.Wick. 87 CF54
Red Oak Clo., Orp. 88 CL55
Red Oaks Mead, Epp. 31 CM22
Red Pl. W1 1 G10
Red Pl. W1 56 BV40
Park St.
Red Post Hill SE21 67 BZ46
Red Post Hill SE24 67 BZ45
Red Rd., Bet. 120 BN69
Red Rd., Borwd. 28 BL24
Red Rd., Brwd. 42 DA28
Red Rose La., Ing. 24 DC18
Red St., Grav. 81 DD50
Red Willow, Harl. 13 CK12
Red Wd. Mt., Reig. 121 BS69
Redan Pl. W2 56 BS39
Redan St. W14 65 BQ41
Redan Ter. SE5 67 BZ44
Flaxman Rd.
Redbarn Clo., Pur. 95 BY59
Redberry Gro. SE26 77 CC48
Redbourn Rd., Hem.H. 8 AZ11
Redbourn Rd., St.Alb. 9 BE12
Redbourne Ave. N3 38 BS30
Redbridge Gdns. SE5 67 CA44
Dalwood St.
Redbridge La. E., Ilf. 49 CJ32
Redbridge La. W. E11 49 CH32
Redburn St. SW3 66 BU43
Redburn Ter., Enf. 30 CC25
South St.
Redbury Clo., Rain. 60 CV39
Redcar Clo., Nthlt. 54 BF36
Redcar Rd., Rom. 42 CW28
Redcar St. SE5 67 BZ43
Redcastle Clo. E1 57 CC40
Redchurch St. E2 2 P4
Redchurch St. E2 57 CA38
Redcliffe Gdns. SW10 66 BS42
Redcliffe Gdns., Ilf. 49 CL33
Redcliffe Ms. SW10 66 BS42
Redcliffe Pl. SW10 66 BT43
Redcliffe Rd. SW10 66 BT42
Redcliffe Sq. SW10 66 BS42
Redcliffe St. SW10 66 BS43
Redclose Ave., Mord. 86 BS53
Redclyffe Rd. E6 58 CJ37
Redcourt, Wok. 100 AU61
Redcroft Rd., Sthl. 54 BG40
Redcross Pl. SE1 67 BZ41
Redcross Way
Redcross Way SE1 4 J4
Redcross Way SE1 67 BZ41
Redden Ct. Rd., Horn. 51 CW31
Reddings, Hem.H. 8 AY14
Reddings, Welw.G.C. 5 BQ7
Reddings, The NW7 37 BO27
Reddings, The, Borwd. 28 BL24
Red Rd.
Reddings Ave., Bush. 27 BF25
Reddings Clo. NW7 37 BO28
Reddington Clo., S.Croy. 96 CA58
Reddington Dr., Slou. 62 AS42
Reddins Rd. SE15 67 CB43
Redditch Ct., Hem.H. 8 AY11
Reddons Rd., Beck. 77 CD50
Reddown Rd., Couls. 104 BW62
Reddy Rd., Erith 69 CT43
Rede Ct., Wey. 83 AZ55
Rede Pl. W2 56 BS39
Redesdale Gdns., Islw. 64 BJ43
Redesdale St. SW3 66 BU42
Redfern Ave., Houns. 74 BF47
Redfern Clo., Uxb. 53 AX37
Redfern Gdns., Rom. 42 CV30
Redfern Rd. NW10 55 BO36
Redfern Rd. SE6 77 CF
Brownhill Rd.
Redfield La. SW5 66 BS
Redford Ave., Couls. 95 BV
Redford Ave., Th.Hth. 86 BX
Redford Ave., Wall. 95 BX
Redford Rd., Wind. 61 AI
Redford Wk. N1 57 BZ
Popham St.
Redford Way, Uxb. 53 AX
Redgate Dr., Brom. 88 CH
Redgate Ter. SW15 75 BC
Lytton Gro.
Redgrave Clo., Croy. 87 CA
Redgrave Rd. SW15 65 BC
Redhall Clo., Hat. 10 BC
Redhall Dr., Hat. 10 BC
Redheath Clo., Wat. 17 BC
Redhill, Uxb. 43 AU
Redhill Dr., Edg. 37 BN
Redhill Rd., Cob. 92 AZ
Redhill St. NW1 1
Redhill St. NW1 56 BV
Redholm Vill. N16 48 BZ
Winston Rd.
Redhouse Rd., West. 106 CJ
Redington Gdns. NW3 47 BS
Redington Rd. NW3 47 BS
Redlands, Couls. 104 BX
Redlands Gdns., E.Mol. 84 BE
Redlands Rd., Enf. 30 CD
Redlands Rd., Sev. 107 CT
Redlands Way SW2 76 BX
Redlaw Way SE16 67 CB
Bonamy Est. W.
Redleaf Clo., Belv. 69 CR
Redleaves Ave., Ashf. 73 AZ
Redlees Clo., Islw. 64 BJ
Redmans La., Sev. 98 CT
Redmans Pl., Sev. 117 CV
Redmans Rd. E1 57 CC
Redmead La. E1 57 CE
Redmead Rd., Hayes 63 BE
Redmore Rd. W6 65 BF
Redpoll Way, Erith 69 CF
Maran Way
Redrick La., Harl. 6 CI
Redriff Est. SE16 67 CD
Redriff Rd. SE16 67 CC
Redriff Rd., Rom. 41 CR
Redriffe Rd. E13 58 CG
Redroofs Clo., Beck. 87 CE
The Ave.
Redruth Clo. N22 38 BX
Redruth Clo., Rom. 42 CW
Redruth Gdns., Rom. 42 CW
Redruth Rd. E9 57 CC
Redruth Rd., Rom. 42 CW
Redruth Wk., Rom. 42 CW
Redstart Clo. E6 58 CK
Columbine Ave.
Redstart Clo. SE14 67 CD
Southerngate Way
Redstart Clo., Croy. 96 CF
Redston Rd. N8 47 BW
Redstone Hill, Red. 121 BV
Redstone Hollow, Red. 121 BV
Redstone Mans., Red. 121 BV
Redstone Pk., Red. 121 BV
Redstone Rd., Red. 121 BV
Redvers Rd. N22 38 BY
Redvers Rd., Warl. 105 CC
Redvers St. N1 2
Redwald Rd. E5 48 CC
Redway Dr., Twick. 74 BG
Redwell La., Sev. 108 DA
Redwing Clo., S.Croy. 96 CC
Redwing Path SE28 68 CM
Whinchat Rd.
Redwing Ri., Guil. 118 AU
Redwood, Egh. 82 AV
Redwood Clo. N14 38 BW
The Vale
Redwood Clo. SE16 57 CD
Redwood Clo., Guil. 118 AU
Redwood Clo., Ken. 96 BZ
Redwood Clo., Uxb. 53 AZ
Redwood Clo., Wat. 36 BD
Redwood Dr., Hem.H. 8 AY
Redwood Gdns., Chig. 41 CO
Redwood Gdns., Slou. 52 AO
Godolphin Rd.
Redwood Ri., Borwd. 28 BM
Redwood Way, Barn. 28 BQ
Redwoods SW15 75 BP
Redwoods, Welw.G.C. 5 B
Redwoods Clo., Buck.H. 40 CH
Beech La.
Reece Ms. SW7 3
Reece Ms. SW7 66 BT
Reed Ave., Orp. 88 CM
Reed Clo. E16 58 CH
Plymouth Rd.
Reed Clo. SE12 78 CH
Reed Clo., Iver 52 AV
Dutton Way
Reed Holm Vill. N16 48 BZ
Reed Pl., Wey. 91 AV
Reed Pond Wk., Rom. 41 CT
Reed Rd. N17 39 CA
Reedan Clo., St.Alb. 18 BF
Reede Gdns., Dag. 50 CR
Reede Rd., Dag. 59 CR
Reede Way, Dag. 59 CR
Reedham Clo. N17 48 CB
Reedham Dr., Pur. 95 BX
Reedham Pk. Ave., Pur. 104 BY
Reedham St. SE15 67 CB
Reeds Cres., Wat. 27 BD
Reeds La., Ton. 117 DC
Reeds Pl. NW1 56 BW
Rochester Pl.
Reedsfield Rd., Ashf. 73 AZ
Reedworth St. SE11 4

edworth St. SE11 66 BY42
nglass Rd., Stan. 36 BK28
s Gdns., Croy. 87 CA53
s Rd., Red. 121 BU70
gh St.
s St. N1 57 BZ37
sland Clo. E12 49 CL35
ts Fm. Clo. NW9 46 BO32
ve Rd., Maid. 61 AG43
ve Rd., Reig. 121 BT72
ves Ave. NW9 46 BN33
ves Clo., Brwd. 24 DA20
ves Cres., Swan. 89 CS52
ves La., Harl. 13 CJ13
ves Ms. W1 3 G1
ves Ms. W1 56 BV40
ves Rd. E3 57 CE38
ves Rd. SE18 68 CL43
orm Row N17 39 CA30
orm St. SW11 66 BU44
al Clo. E1 57 CB39
al Clo. W5 54 BK39
al Ct. N18 39 CA28
al Cres., Wall. 86 BV55
ince Charles Way
al Fld. Clo., Guil. 109 AP68
al La. NW1 56 BV37
egents Pk. Rd.
al Way, Har. 45 BK32
al Way, Wat. 27 BD22
an Clo., Guil. 109 AQ68
gan Way N1 2 M1
gan Way N1 57 CA37
garder Rd., Chig. 41 CO28
garth Ave., Rom. 50 CT32
gency Clo. W5 55 BL39
gency Clo., Chig. 40 CM28
gency Clo., Hmptn. 74 BE49
gency Clo., Sev. 99 CZ57
gency Ct., Brwd. 42 DB27
rown St.
gency Ct., Harl. 14 CO12
gency Dr., Ruis. 44 BB33
gency Dr., Wey. 91 AV60
gency Gdns., Horn. 51 CV33
gency Gdns., Walt. 84 BD54
gency Ms. NW10 55 BO36
igh Rd.
gency Ms., Beck. 77 CE50
oxgrove Rd.
gency Ms., Islw. 74 BH46
gency Pl. SW1 3 P8
gency St. SW1 3 P8
gency St. SW1 66 BW42
gency Wk., Croy. 87 CD53
gency Wk., Rich. 75 BL46
he Vineyard
gency Way, Bexh. 69 CP45
gent Ave., Uxb. 53 AZ36
gent Clo., Grays 71 DE41
gent Clo., Har. 46 BL32
gent Clo., Houns. 63 BC44
gent Clo., St.Alb. 9 BK11
ortman Clo.
gent Clo., Wey. 92 AX58
gent Ct., Slou. 52 AP39
toke Poges La.
gent Cres., Red. 121 BU69
inkfield La.
gent Gdns., Ilf. 50 CO32
gent Ho., Surb. 85 BL53
gent Pl. W1 1 M10
gent Pl. W1 56 BW40
Varwick St.
gent Pl., Croy. 87 CA54
gent Rd. SE24 76 BY46
gent Rd., Epp. 22 CN18
gent Rd., Surb. 85 BL53
gent Sq. E3 57 CE38
gent Sq. WC1 2 A3
gent Sq. WC1 56 BX38
gent Sq., Belv. 69 CR42
gent St. NW10 55 BQ38
ilburn La.
gent St. SW1 3 N1
gent St. SW1 56 BW40
gent St. W1 1 K8
gent St. W1 56 BV39
gent St. W4 65 BM42
gent St., Wat. 26 BC22
gents Ave. N13 38 BY28
gents Bri. Gdns. SW8 66 BX43
gents Clo., Hayes 53 BB39
range Par.
gents Clo., Rad. 18 BJ20
gents Clo., S.Croy. 96 CA57
gents Clo., Whyt. 105 CA62
gents Dr., Kes. 97 CJ56
gents Pk. NW1 1 E1
gents Pk. Est. NW1 1 L3
gents Pk. Est. NW1 56 BV38
gents Pk. Rd. N3 46 BR31
gents Pk. Rd. NW1 56 BU37
gents Pk. Ter. NW1 56 BY37
val Rd.
gents Pl. SE3 68 CH44
gents Row E8 57 CB37
gina Clo., Barn. 28 BQ24
gina Rd. N4 47 BX33
gina Rd. SE25 87 CB52
gina Rd. W13 54 BJ40
gina Rd., Sthl. 64 BE42
ginald Rd. E7 58 CH36
ginald Rd. SE8 67 CE43
ginald Rd., Nthwd. 35 BB30
ginald Rd., Rom. 42 CX30
ginald Sq. SE8 67 CE43
gis Rd. NW5 47 BV35
gis Way SE17 66 BY43
gnart Bldgs. NW1 1 M4
gnart Bldgs. NW1 56 BW38
uston St.
id Ave., Cat. 105 BZ64
id Clo., Pnr. 44 BC31

Reidhaven Rd. SE18 68 CN42
Reigate Ave., Sutt. 86 BS55
Reigate Hill, Reig. 113 BS68
Reigate Hill Clo., Reig. 121 BS69
Reigate Hill Rd., Reig. 121 BS70
Reigate Rd., Bet. 120 BN70
Reigate Rd., Brom. 78 CG48
Reigate Rd., Dor. 119 BK71
Reigate Rd., Epsom 94 BP58
Reigate Rd., Ilf. 49 CN34
Reigate Rd., Lthd. 102 BK65
Reigate Rd., Reig. 121 BS70
Reigate Rd. (Sidlow Bri.), Reig. 121 BS74
Reigate Way, Wall. 95 BX56
Reighton Rd. E5 48 CB34
Relay Rd. W12 55 BQ40
Relf Rd. SE15 67 CB45
Relko Ct., Epsom 94 BN59
Blakeney Clo.
Relko Gdns., Sutt. 95 BT56
Sutton Gro.
Relton Ms. SW7 3 D6
Rembrandt Clo. E14 67 CF41
Amsterdam Rd.
Rembrandt Clo. SW1 3 G9
Rembrandt Dr., Grav. 81 DE48
Rembrandt Rd. SE13 68 CG45
Rembrandt Rd., Edg. 37 BM30
Rembrandt Way, Walt. 83 BC55
Remington Rd. E6 58 CK39
Remington Rd. N15 48 BZ32
Remington St. N1 2 G1
Remington St. N1 56 BY37
Remnant St. WC2 2 B8
Remnant St. WC2 56 BX39
Kingsway
Remus Rd. E3 57 CE36
Monier Rd.
Rendlesham Ave., Rad. 27 BH22
Rendlesham Clo., Brom. 88 CJ51
Rendlesham Rd. E5 48 CB35
Rendlesham Rd., Enf. 29 BY23
Rendlesham Way, Rick. 25 AU25
Renforth St. SE16 67 CC41
Renfree Way, Shep. 83 AZ54
Renfrew Clo. E6 58 CL40
Renfrew Rd. SE11 4 F8
Renfrew Rd. SE11 66 BY42
Renfrew Rd., Houns. 64 BD44
Renfrew Rd., Kings.T. 75 BN50
Renmans, The, Ash. 103 BL61
Renmuir St. SW17 76 BU50
Rennell St. SE13 67 CF45
Rennels Way, Islw. 64 BH44
Renness Rd. E17 47 CD31
Rennets Clo. SE9 78 CM46
Rennets Wd. Rd. SE9 78 CM46
Rennie Clo., Ashf. 73 AX48
Rennie St. SE1 4 F2
Rennie St. SE1 56 BY40
Rennie Ter., Red. 121 BV71
Renown Clo., Croy. 86 BY54
Renown Clo., Rom. 41 CR30
Rensburg Rd. E17 48 CC32
Renters Ave. NW4 46 BQ32
Renton Dr., Orp. 89 CP54
Renwick Clo., Orp. 89 CP52
Renwick Rd., Bark. 59 CO38
Repens Way, Hayes 54 BD38
Stipularis Dr.
Rephidim St. SE1 4 L7
Replingham Rd. SW18 75 BR47
Reporton Rd. SW6 65 BR43
Repository Rd. SE18 68 CK43
Repton Ave., Hayes 63 BA42
Repton Ave., Rom. 50 CU31
Repton Ave., Wem. 45 BK35
Repton Clo., Cars. 95 BU56
Repton Ct. E5 48 CC35
Clapton Pk. Est.
Repton Ct., Beck. 87 CE51
Repton Dr., Rom. 50 CU31
Repton Gdns., Rom. 50 CU31
Repton Grn., St.Alb. 9 BG12
Repton Gro., Ilf. 40 CK30
Repton Rd., Har. 46 BL31
Repton Rd., Orp. 98 CO56
Repton St. E14 57 CD39
Repton Way, Rick. 26 AZ25
Repulse Clo., Rom. 41 CR30
Reservoir Rd. N14 29 BW25
Reservoir Rd. SE4 67 CD44
Reservoir Rd., Loug. 31 CH23
Reservoir Rd., Ruis. 44 BA32
Resolution Wk. SE18 68 CK41
Venus Rd.
Reson Way, Hem.H. 8 AW14
Ressland Clo. E12 49 CL35
Restell Clo. SE3 68 CG43
Reston Clo., Borwd. 28 BM22
Reston Path, Borwd. 28 BM22
Reston Pl. SW7 66 BT41
Palace Gate
Restons Cres. SE9 78 CM46
Restormel Clo., Houns. 74 BF46
Retcar Clo. N19 47 BV34
Retford Clo., Rom. 42 CX29
Retford Path, Rom. 42 CX29
Retford Rd., Rom. 42 CX29
Retford St. N1 2 N1
Retingham Way E4 39 CE27
Retreat, The NW9 46 BN32
Retreat, The SW14 65 BO45
South Worple Way
Retreat, The, Amer. 25 AS23
Retreat, The, Brwd. 42 DA26
Costead Manor Rd.
Retreat, The, Brwd. 122 DD25
Retreat, The, Egh. 72 AR49
Retreat, The, Grays 71 DD43
Retreat, The, Har. 45 BF33
Retreat, The, Maid. 61 AJ43
Retreat, The, Orp. 98 CO57

Retreat, The, Surb. 85 BL53
Retreat, The, Th.Hth. 87 BZ52
Retreat, The, Wor.Pk. 85 BP55
Retreat Clo., Har. 45 BK32
Retreat Pl. E9 57 CC36
Retreat Rd., Rich. 74 BK46
Retreat Ter., Brent. 64 BK43
Brickfield Clo.
Retreat Way, Chig. 41 CO27
Reubens Rd., Brwd. 122 DD25
Reunion Row E1 57 CB40
Pennington St.
Reveley Sq. SE16 67 CD41
Howland Way
Revell Clo., Lthd. 102 BF64
Revell Dr., Lthd. 102 BF64
Revell Ri. SE18 68 CN43
Revell Rd., Kings.T. 85 BM51
Revell Rd., Sutt. 94 BR57
Revelon Rd. SE4 67 CD45
Revelstoke Rd. SW18 75 BR48
Reventlow Rd. SE9 78 CM47
Reverdy Rd. SE1 67 CB42
Reverend Clo., Har. 45 BF34
Revesby Rd., Cars. 86 BT53
Review Rd. NW2 46 BO34
Review Rd., Dag. 59 CR37
Rewell St. SW6 66 BT43
Rewley Rd., Cars. 86 BT53
Rex Ave., Ashf. 73 AZ50
Rex Clo., Rom. 41 CR29
Rex Pl. W1 3 H1
Rex Pl. W1 56 BV40
Reydon Ave. E11 49 CJ32
Reynard Clo., Brom. 88 CL52
Blackbrook La.
Reynard Dr. SE19 77 CA50
Reynards Way, St.Alb. 18 BE18
Reynardson Rd. N17 39 BZ29
Reynolds Ave. E12 49 CL35
Reynolds Ave., Chess. 94 BL57
Reynolds Ave., Rom. 50 CP33
Reynolds Clo. NW11 47 BS33
Reynolds Clo. SW19 86 BT51
Reynolds Clo., Cars. 86 BU54
Reynolds Clo., Hem.H. 8 AW13
Reynolds Ct. E11 49 CG34
Reynolds Cres., St.Alb. 9 BJ11
Reynolds Dr., Edg. 46 BL31
Reynolds Pl. SE3 68 CH43
Reynolds Pl., Rich. 75 BL46
Cambrian Rd.
Reynolds Rd. SE15 67 CC45
Reynolds Rd. W4 65 BN41
Reynolds Rd., Hayes 54 BD38
Reynolds Rd., N.Mal. 85 BN54
Reynolds Way, Croy. 96 CA56
Rheidol Ter. N1 56 BY37
Rheingold Way, Wall. 95 BX58
Rheola Clo. N17 39 CA30
Rhoda St. E2 2 Q4
Rhoda St. E2 57 CA38
Rhodes Ave. N22 38 BW30
Rhodes Clo., Egh. 72 AU49
Mullens Rd.
Rhodes Moorhouse Ct., Mord. 86 BS53
Rhodes St. N7 47 BX35
Mackenzie Rd.
Rhodes St. Est. E8 57 CA36
Rhodes Way, Wat. 27 BD23
Rhodesia Rd. E11 48 CF34
Rhodesia Rd. SW9 66 BX44
Rhodeswell Rd. E14 57 CD39
Rhododendron Ride, Egh. 72 AP49
Rhodrons Ave., Chess. 94 BL56
Rhondda Gro. E3 57 CD38
Rhyl Rd., Grnf. 54 BH37
Rhyl St. NW5 56 BV36
Rhys Ave. N11 38 BW29
Rialto Rd., Mitch. 86 BV51
Ribble Clo., Wdf.Grn. 40 CJ29
Prospect Rd.
Ribblesdale, St.Alb. 19 BL17
Thamesdale
Ribblesdale, Dor. 119 BJ72
Roman Rd.
Ribblesdale, Hem.H. 8 AY12
Wharfedale
Ribblesdale Ave., Nthlt. 54 BF36
Ribblesdale Rd. N8 47 BX31
Ribblesdale Rd. SW16 76 BV50
Ribblesdale Rd., Dart. 80 CY47
Ribchester Ave., Grnf. 54 BH38
Ribston Clo., Brom. 88 CK54
Ricardo Path SE28 59 CP40
Byron Clo.
Ricardo Rd., Wind. 72 AQ46
Ricardo St. E14 57 CE39
Ricards Rd. SW19 75 BR49
Ricebridge La., Reig. 120 BP72
Rich Clo., West. 106 CH62
Rich La. SW5 66 BS42
Earls Ct. Rd.
Rich St. E14 57 CD40
Richard Clo. SE18 68 CK42
Godfrey Hill
Richard Foster Clo. E17 48 CD33
Verulam Ave.
Richard Stagg Clo., St.Alb. 9 BK14
Richard St. E1 57 CB39
Richards Ave., Rom. 50 CS32
Richards Clo., Har. 45 BJ32
Richards Clo., Uxb. 53 AZ37
Richards Clo., Wat. 36 BG26
Richards Cotts. W3 55 BN40
Churchfield Rd.
Richards Pl. E17 48 CE31
Richards Pl. SW3 3 D8
Richards Pl. SW3 66 BU42
Richards Rd., Cob. 93 BF60
Richardson Clo. E8 57 CA37
Clarissa St.
Richardson Clo., Hayes 63 BA43

Richardson Clo., St.Alb. 19 BL17
Richardson Ms. W1 56 BW39
Warren St.
Richardson Pl., St.Alb. 10 BM14
Richardson Rd. E15 58 CG37
Richardsons Ms. W1 1 L5
Richbell Clo., Ash. 102 BK62
Richbell Pl. WC1 2 B6
Richbell Pl. WC1 56 BX39
Emerald St.
Richborne Ter. SW8 66 BX43
Richborough Clo., Orp. 89 CP52
Richborough Rd. NW2 46 BQ35
Riches Rd., Ilf. 49 CM34
Richfield Rd., Bush. 36 BG26
Richford Rd. E15 58 CG37
Richford St. W6 65 BQ41
Richings Way, Iver 62 AV41
Richland Ave., Couls. 95 BV60
Richlands Ave., Epsom 94 BP56
Richmer Rd., Erith 69 CT43
Richmond Ave. E4 39 CF28
Richmond Ave. N1 56 BX37
Richmond Ave. NW10 55 BQ36
Richmond Ave. SW20 85 BR51
Richmond Ave., Felt. 73 BB46
Richmond Ave., Uxb. 53 AZ36
Richmond Bri., Rich. 74 BK46
Richmond Bri., Twick. 74 BK46
Richmond Bldgs. W1 1 N9
Richmond Bldgs. W1 56 BW39
Dean St.
Richmond Clo. E17 48 CD32
Richmond Clo., Chsnt. 21 CC18
Dewhurst Rd.
Richmond Clo., Epsom 94 BO60
Richmond Clo., Lthd. 102 BF65
Richmond Ct. N4 48 BZ32
Wiltshire Gdns.
Richmond Ct. SW20 85 BP51
Richmond Rd.
Richmond Ct., Brox. 12 CD13
Richmond Ct., Pot.B. 20 BT19
Hatfield Rd.
Richmond Cres. E4 39 CF28
Richmond Cres. N1 56 BY37
Richmond Cres. N9 39 CB26
Richmond Cres., Slou. 52 AQ40
Richmond Cres., Stai. 72 AV49
Richmond Dr., Shep. 83 BA53
Richmond Dr., Wat. 26 BB23
Richmond Gdns. NW4 46 BP31
Richmond Gdns., Har. 36 BH29
Richmond Grn., Croy. 86 BX55
Richmond Gro. N1 56 BY36
Halton Rd.
Richmond Gro., Surb. 85 BL53
Richmond Hill, Rich. 75 BL46
Richmond Hill Ct., Rich. 75 BL46
Richmond Ms. W1 1 N9
Richmond Ms. W1 56 BW39
Dean St.
Richmond Pk. Heights, Kings.T. 75 BN49
Richmond Pk. Rd. SW14 75 BN46
Richmond Pk. Rd., Kings.T. 85 BL51
Richmond Pl. SE18 68 CM42
Richmond Rd. E4 39 CF26
Richmond Rd. E7 49 CH35
Richmond Rd. E8 57 CA36
Richmond Rd. E11 48 CF34
Richmond Rd. N2 38 BT30
Brighton Rd.
Richmond Rd. N11 38 BX29
Richmond Rd. N15 48 CA32
Richmond Rd. SW20 85 BP51
Richmond Rd. W5 65 BL41
Richmond Rd., Barn. 29 BT25
Richmond Rd., Couls. 104 BV61
Richmond Rd., Croy. 86 BX55
Richmond Rd., Grays 71 DE43
Richmond Rd., Ilf. 49 CM34
Richmond Rd., Islw. 64 BJ45
Richmond Rd., Kings.T. 74 BK49
Richmond Rd., Pot.B. 20 BT19
Richmond Rd., Rom. 50 CT32
Richmond Rd., Stai. 72 AV49
Richmond Rd., Th.Hth. 86 BY52
Richmond Rd., Twick. 74 BJ47
Richmond St. E13 58 CH37
Richmond Ter. SW1 3 Q4
Richmond Ter. SW1 66 BX41
Richmond Ter. Ms. SW1 66 BX41
Parliament St.
Richmond Way E11 49 CH34
Richmond Way W12 65 BQ41
Richmond Way W14 65 BQ41
Richmond Way, Lthd. 102 BF65
Richmond Way, Rick. 26 BA24
Richmount Gdns. SE3 68 CH45
Rickard Clo. NW4 46 BP31
Rickard Clo. SW2 76 BX47
Rickard Clo., West Dr. 63 AX41
Rickards Clo., Surb. 85 BL54
Ricketts Hill Rd., West. 106 CJ62
Ricketts St. SW6 66 BS43
Rickfield Clo., Hat. 10 BP13
Woods Ave.
Rickford Hill, Guil. 109 AO66
Rickman Cres., Wey. 83 AW55
Rickman Hill, Couls. 104 BV62
Rickman Hill Rd., Couls. 104 BV62
Rickman St. E1 57 CC38
Mantos Rd.
Rickmans La., Slou. 43 AP35
Rickmansworth By-pass, Rick. 35 AX26
Rickmansworth La., Ger.Cr. 34 AS29
Rickmansworth Rd., Amer. 25 AO22
Rickmansworth Rd., Nthwd. 35 AZ28

Rickmansworth Rd., Pnr. 35 BC30
Rickmansworth Rd., Rick. 25 AV24
Rickmansworth Rd., Uxb. 35 AX30
Rickmansworth Rd., Wat. 26 BB24
Ricksons La., Lthd. 110 AZ67
Rickthorne Rd. N19 47 BX34
Rickyard, Guil. 118 AO70
Rickyard Path SE9 68 CK45
Riddell Pk. Ms., Enf. 29 BY23
Bycullah Rd.
Ridding La., Grnf. 45 BH35
Riddings La., Harl. 14 CO13
Riddlesdown Ave., Pur. 96 BZ59
Riddlesdown Rd., Pur. 96 BZ59
Riddons Rd. SE12 78 CJ48
Ride, The, Brent. 64 BJ42
Ride, The, Enf. 30 CC24
Ride, The, Lthd. 110 BB66
Rider Clo., Sid. 78 CN46
Riders Way, Gdse. 114 CC69
Ridgdale St. E3 57 CE37
Ridge, The, Bex. 79 CQ47
Ridge, The, Cat. 114 CE66
Ridge, The, Couls. 95 BX60
Ridge, The, Epsom 103 BN62
Ridge, The, Orp. 88 CM55
Ridge, The, Pur. 95 BW58
Ridge, The, Surb. 85 BM53
Ridge, The, Twick. 74 BG47
Ridge, The, Wok. 100 AT62
Ridge Ave. N21 39 BZ26
Ridge Ave., Dart. 79 CT46
Ridge Clo. NW4 37 BQ30
Ridge Clo. NW9 46 BN31
Ridge Clo., Bet. 120 BM72
Ridge Clo., Houns. 64 BF45
Ridge Clo., Wok. 100 AQ64
Ridge Crest, Enf. 29 BX23
Ridge Grn., Red. 121 BX72
Ridge Grn. Clo., Red. 121 BX72
Ridge Hill NW11 46 BR33
Ridge Hill, Pot.B. 19 BN18
Ridge La., Wat. 26 BB21
Ridge Langley, S.Croy. 96 CB58
Ridge Lea, Hem.H. 7 AV13
Ridge Pk., Pur. 95 BW58
Ridge Pl. SW4 66 BW45
Ridge Rd. N8 47 BX32
Ridge Rd. N21 39 BZ26
Ridge Rd. NW2 46 BR34
Ridge Rd., Mitch. 76 BV50
Ridge Rd., Sutt. 85 BR54
Ridge St., Wat. 26 BC22
Ridge Vw. Clo., Barn. 28 BQ25
Ridge Way SE19 77 CA50
Central Hill Est.
Ridge Way, Dart. 79 CT46
Ridge Way, Iver 52 AV40
Ridgebrook Rd. SE3 68 CJ45
Ridgecroft Clo., Bex. 79 CS47
Ridgegate Clo., Reig. 121 BT69
Ridgehurst Ave., Wat. 17 BB20
Ridgelands, Lthd. 102 BG65
Ridgemead Rd., Egh. 72 AQ48
Ridgemont Gdns., Edg. 37 BN28
Ridgemount, Guil. 118 AQ71
Ridgemount, Wey. 83 BB55
Ridgemount Ave., Couls. 104 BV62
Ridgemount Ave., Croy. 87 CC55
Ridgemount Clo. SE20 77 CB50
Ridgemount End, Ger.Cr. 34 AS28
Ridgemount Gdns., Enf. 29 BY23
Ridges, The, Guil. 118 AR73
Ridgeview Rd. N20 38 BS27
Ridgeway N14 38 BX27
Ridgeway, Berk. 7 AP13
Ridgeway, Brwd. 122 DD26
Ridgeway, Brom. 88 CH55
Ridgeway, Dart. 80 CZ49
Ridgeway, Epsom 94 BN59
Ridgeway, Felt. 74 BE48
Ridgeway, Grays 71 DF42
Ridgeway, Rick. 35 AW26
Ridgeway, Walt. 83 BB54
Ridgeway, Welw.G.C. 5 BS8
Ridgeway, Wok. 100 AR61
Ridgeway, Wdf.Grn. 40 CJ28
Ridgeway, The E4 39 CE27
Ridgeway, The N3 38 BS29
Ridgeway, The N11 38 BU28
Ridgeway, The N14 38 BX27
Ridgeway, The NW7 37 BP27
Ridgeway, The NW9 46 BN31
Ridgeway, The NW11 46 BR33
Ridgeway, The W3 65 BM41
Ridgeway, The, Amer. 25 AO23
Ridgeway, The, Croy. 86 BX55
Ridgeway, The, Cuffley 20 BV17
Ridgeway, The, Enf. 29 BV21
Ridgeway, The, Ger.Cr. 43 AR31
Ridgeway, The, Guil. 118 AT71
Ridgeway, The (Kenton), Har. 45 BK32
Ridgeway, The (North Harrow), Har. 45 BE32
Ridgeway, The, Lthd. 102 BG65
Ridgeway, The (Oxshott), Lthd. 93 BG60
Ridgeway, The, Pot.B. 29 BU21
Ridgeway, The, Rad. 27 BH22
Ridgeway, The (Gidea Pk.), Rom. 50 CU31
Ridgeway, The (Harold Wd.), Rom. 42 CW30
Ridgeway, The, Ruis. 44 BC33
Ridgeway, The, St.Alb. 9 BJ11
Ridgeway, The, S.Croy. 96 CA58
Ridgeway, The, Stan. 36 BK29
Ridgeway, The, Wat. 26 BB22
Ridgeway Ave., Barn. 29 BU25
Ridgeway Ave., Grav. 81 DG48
Ridgeway Clo., Dor. 119 BJ72
Ridgeway Rd.
Ridgeway Clo., Lthd. 93 BG60

Rid–Roc

Ridgeway Clo., Wok. 100 AR61
Ridgeway Ct., Red. 121 BU71
Ridgeway Cres., Orp. 88 CN55
Ridgeway Cres. Gdns., Orp. 88 CN55
Ridgeway Dr., Brom. 78 CH49
Ridgeway Dr., Dor. 119 BJ73
Ridgeway E., Sid. 78 CN46
Ridgeway Gdns. N6 47 BW33
Hornsey La.
Ridgeway Gdns., Ilf. 49 CK32
Ridgeway Gdns., Wok. 100 AR61
Ridgeway Rd. E4 39 CF26
Ridgeway Rd., Dor. 119 BJ72
Ridgeway Rd., Islw. 64 BH43
Ridgeway Rd., Red. 121 BU70
Ridgeway Rd. N., Islw. 64 BH43
Ridgeway Wk., Nthlt. 54 BE36
Ridgeway W., Sid. 78 CN46
Ridgewell Clo. N1 57 BZ37
Basire St.
Ridgewell Clo., Dag. 59 CR37
Ridgewell Rd. E16 58 CJ39
Ridgewick Ct., Guil. 118 AS71
Chesham Rd.
Ridgmont Rd., St.Alb. 9 BH14
Ridgmount Gdns. WC1 1 N6
Ridgmount Gdns. WC1 56 BW38
Ridgmount Pl. WC1 1 N6
Ridgmount Rd. SW18 76 BS46
Ridgmount St. WC1 1 N6
Ridgmount St. WC1 56 BW39
Store St.
Ridgway SW19 75 BQ50
Ridgway, Wok. 101 AW61
Ridgway, The, Sutt. 95 BT57
Ridgway Clo., Wok. 100 AR61
Ridgway Gdns. SW19 75 BQ50
Ridgway Pl. SW19 75 BR50
Ridgway Rd. SW9 66 BY45
Riding, The NW11 46 BR33
Golders Grn. Rd.
Riding, The, Wok. 91 AT60
Riding Ct. Rd., Slou. 62 AR43
Riding Hill, S.Croy. 96 CB60
Riding Ho. St. W1 1 K7
Riding Ho. St. W1 56 BV39
Riding La., Sev. 117 CY71
Riding La., Ton. 117 CY71
Ridings, The W5 55 BL38
Ridings, The, Amer. 25 AO21
Ridings, The, Ash. 102 BK62
Ridings, The, Chesh. 25 AR21
Ridings, The, Cob. 93 BF59
Ridings, The, Epsom 103 BO61
Ridings, The, Iver 62 AV42
Ridings, The, Lthd. 110 BB66
Ridings, The, Loug. 31 CJ24
Ridings, The, Reig. 121 BT69
Ridings, The, Sun. 83 BC51
Ridings, The, Surb. 85 BM53
Ridings, The, Tad. 103 BR63
Ridings, The, West. 106 CK62
Ridings, The, Wey. 91 AV57
Ridings, The, Wok. 101 AW65
Ridings Ave. N21 29 BY24
Ridings Clo. N6 47 BW33
Ridings La., Wok. 101 AZ65
Ridlands Clo., Oxt. 115 CK68
Ridlands Gro., Oxt. 115 CK68
Ridlands Ri., Oxt. 115 CK68
Ridler Rd., Enf. 30 CA22
Ridley Ave. W13 64 BJ41
Ridley Clo., Brom. 88 CG52
Ridley Clo., Rom. 41 CU30
Ridley Rd. E7 49 CJ35
Ridley Rd. E8 48 CA35
Ridley Rd. NW10 55 BP37
Ridley Rd. SW19 76 BS50
Ridley Rd., Brom. 88 CG52
Ridley Rd., Warl. 105 CC62
Ridley Rd., Well. 69 CO44
Ridley Several SE3 68 CH44
Blackheath Pk.
Ridout St. SE18 68 CK42
Ridsdale Rd. SE20 87 CB51
Ridsdale Rd., Wok. 100 AQ62
Riefield Rd. SE9 78 CM46
Riesco Dr., Croy. 96 CC57
Riffel Rd. NW2 46 BQ35
Riffhams, Brwd. 122 DD27
Rifle Butts All., Epsom 94 BO60
Rifle Pl. W11 55 BQ40
Rifle St. E14 57 CE39
Rigault Rd. SW6 65 BR44
Rigby Clo., Croy. 86 BY55
Rigby Gdns., Grays 71 DG42
Rigby La., Hayes 63 BA41
Rigby Ms., Ilf. 49 CL34
Rigden St. E14 57 CE39
Duff St.
Rigeley Rd. NW10 55 BP38
Rigg App. E10 48 CC33
Riggindale Rd. SW16 76 BW49
Riley Rd. SE1 4 P6
Riley Rd. SE1 67 CA41
Riley Rd., Enf. 30 CC22
Riley St. SW10 66 BT43
Rinaldo Rd. SW12 76 BV47
Ring, The W2 1 C10
Ring, The W2 56 BT40
Ring Clo., Brom. 77 CH50
Ring Rd., Hayes 53 BC40
Ring Way Rd., St.Alb. 18 BG17
Ringcroft St. N7 47 BY35
Madras Pl.
Ringers Rd., Brom. 88 CH52
Ringford Rd. SW18 75 BR46
Ringlestone Clo., West Dr. 63 AY43
Ringlewell Clo., Enf. 30 CB23
Bishops Clo.
Ringley Pk. Ave., Reig. 121 BT71
Ringley Pk. Rd., Reig. 121 BT70
Ringmer Ave. SW6 65 BR44
Ringmer Gdns. N19 47 BX34
Ringmer Pl. N21 30 BZ25
Ringmer Way, Brom. 88 CK53
Ringmore Dr., Guil. 118 AU69
Ringmore Ri. SE23 77 CB47
Ringmore Rd., Walt. 84 BD55
Ringshall Rd., Orp. 89 CO52
Ringslade Rd. N22 38 BX30
Ringstead Rd. SE6 77 CE47
Ringstead Rd., Sutt. 95 BT56
Ringway N11 38 BW29
Ringway, Sthl. 64 BE42
Ringwold Clo., Beck. 77 CD50
Aldersmead Rd.
Ringwood Ave. N2 38 BU30
Ringwood Ave., Croy. 86 BX54
Ringwood Ave., Horn. 51 CV34
Ringwood Ave., Orp. 98 CP58
Ringwood Ave., Red. 121 BU69
Ringwood Clo., Pnr. 45 BD31
Ringwood Gdns. SW15 75 BP46
Ringwood Rd. E17 48 CD32
Ringwood Way N21 38 BY26
Ringwood Way, Hmptn. 74 BF49
Ripley Ave., Egh. 72 AS50
Ripley By-pass, Wok. 109 AV66
Ripley Clo., Brom. 88 CK53
Ringmer Way
Ripley Clo., Croy. 96 CF57
Ripley Clo., Slou. 62 AS42
Ripley Gdns. SW14 65 BN45
Ripley Gdns., Sutt. 95 BT56
Ripley La., Lthd. 110 AZ66
Ripley La., Wok. 101 AY65
Ripley Rd. E16 58 CJ39
Ripley Rd., Belv. 69 CR42
Ripley Rd., Enf. 30 BZ22
Ripley Rd., Guil. 110 AW67
Ripley Rd., Hmptn. 74 BF50
Ripley Rd., Ilf. 49 CN34
Ripley Vw., Loug. 31 CL22
Ripley Way, Chsnt. 21 CB18
Ripley Way, Hem.H. 7 AV13
Riplington Ct. SW15 75 BP47
Ripon Clo., Guil. 118 AP69
Ripon Clo., Nthlt. 54 BF36
Ripon Gdns., Chess. 93 BK56
Ripon Gdns., Ilf. 49 CK32
Ripon Rd. N9 39 CB26
Ripon Rd. N17 48 BZ31
Ripon Rd. SE18 68 CL43
Ripon Way, Borwd. 28 BN24
Ripon Way, St.Alb. 9 BK11
Rippersley Rd., Well. 69 CO44
Ripple Rd., Bark. 58 CM36
Ripplevale Gro. N1 56 BX36
Rippolson Rd. SE18 68 CN42
Ripston Rd., Ashf. 73 BA49
Risborough Dr., Wor.Pk. 85 BP54
Risborough St. SE1 4 G4
Risborough St. SE1 66 BY41
Risdon St. SE16 67 CC41
Rise, The E11 49 CH32
Rise, The N13 38 BY28
Rise, The NW7 37 BO29
Rise, The NW10 46 BN35
Rise, The, Amer. 25 AO22
Rise, The, Bex. 79 CP47
Rise, The, Borwd. 28 BL25
Rise, The, Buck.H. 40 CJ26
Rise, The, Couls. 95 BW60
Rise, The, Dart. 69 CT45
Rise, The, Edg. 37 BM28
Rise, The, Epsom 94 BO58
Rise, The, Grav. 81 DJ49
Rise, The, Grnf. 45 BJ35
Rise, The, St.Alb. 18 BG16
Rise, The, Sev. 117 CV67
Rise, The, Sid. 79 CP47
Rise, The, S.Croy. 96 CC58
Rise, The, Tad. 103 BQ64
Fairacres
Rise, The, Uxb. 53 AY37
Rise Pk. Boul., Rom. 41 CT30
Rise Pk. Par., Rom. 41 CT30
Risebridge Chase, Rom. 41 CT29
Risebridge Rd., Rom. 41 CT30
Risedale Clo., Hem.H. 8 AY15
Risedale Hill, Hem.H. 8 AY15
Risedale Rd., Bexh. 69 CR45
Risedale Rd., Hem.H. 8 AY15
Riseldine Rd. SE23 77 CD46
Riseway, Brwd. 122 DC27
Rising Hill Clo., Nthwd. 35 BA29
Rising Sun Ct. EC1 2 G7
Risinghill St. N1 56 BX37
Risingholme Clo., Bush. 36 BF26
Risingholme Clo., Har. 36 BH30
Risingholme Rd., Har. 36 BH30
Risings, The E17 48 CF31
Risley Ave. N17 39 BZ30
Rita Rd. SW8 66 BX43
Ritches Rd. N15 48 BZ32
Ritchie Rd., Croy. 87 CB53
Ritchie St. N1 56 BY37
Ritchings Ave. E17 48 CD31
Ritcroft Clo., Hem.H. 8 AZ14
Ritcroft Dr., Hem.H. 8 AZ14
Ritcroft St.
Ritcroft St., Hem.H. 8 AZ14
Ritherdon Rd. SW17 76 BV48
Ritson Rd. E8 57 CB36
Ritter St. SE18 68 CL43
Ritz Ct., Pot.B. 20 BS19
Rivaz Pl. E9 57 CC36
Rivenhall End, Welw.G.C. 5 BT8
Rivenhall Gdns. E18 49 CG31
River Ave. N13 38 BY27
River Ave., Hodd. 12 CE11
River Ave., T.Ditt. 84 BJ54
River Bank N21 39 BZ26
River Bank, T.Ditt. 84 BH52
River Barge Clo. E14 67 CF41
Stewart St.
River Clo. E11 49 CJ32
River Clo., Rain. 59 CU39
River Clo., Ruis. 44 BB32
River Clo., Surb. 84 BK53
River Clo., Wal.Cr. 21 CE20
River Dr., Upmin. 51 CY32
River Front, Enf. 30 BZ24
River Gdns., Cars. 86 BV55
River Gdns., Felt. 74 BD46
River Gdns., Maid. 61 AH41
River Gro. Pk., Beck. 87 CD51
River Hill, Sev. 117 CW68
River La., Lthd. 102 BG64
River La., Rich. 74 BK47
River Mead Ct. SW6 65 BR45
Ranelagh Gdns.
River Meads Ave., Twick. 74 BF48
River Meads Est., Twick. 74 BF48
River Nook Clo., Walt. 84 BD53
River Pk., Hem.H. 8 AW14
River Pk. Gdns., Brom. 77 CF50
River Pk. Rd. N22 38 BX30
River Pl. N1 57 BZ36
River Reach, Tedd. 74 BK49
Broom Water
River Rd., Bark. 58 CN37
River Rd., Brwd. 42 CZ28
River Rd., Buck.H. 40 CK26
River Rd., Stai. 82 AV51
River St. EC1 2 D2
River St. EC1 56 BY38
River St., Wind. 61 AO43
River Ter. W6 65 BQ42
Crisp Rd.
River Ter., Berk. 7 AQ12
River Vw., Enf. 30 BZ24
River Vw., Welw.G.C. 5 BR6
River Vw. Gdns., Twick. 74 BH48
River Wk., Uxb. 44 AX35
River Wk., Walt. 83 BC53
River Way SE10 68 CG41
River Way, Epsom 94 BN56
River Way, Loug. 31 CK25
River Way, Twick. 74 BF48
Riverbank, E.Mol. 84 BH52
Riverbank Way, Brent. 64 BK43
Rivercourt Rd. W6 65 BP42
Riverdale SE13 67 CF45
Riverdale Dr., Wok. 100 AS64
Riverdale Gdns., Twick. 74 BK46
Riverdale Rd. SE18 68 CN42
Riverdale Rd., Bex. 79 CQ47
Riverdale Rd., Erith 69 CR42
Riverdale Rd., Felt. 74 BE49
Riverdale Rd., Twick. 74 BK46
Riverdell Clo., Cher. 82 AV54
Riverdene, Edg. 37 BN27
Riverdene Rd., Ilf. 49 CL34
Riverfield La., Saw. 6 CQ5
Riverfield Rd., Stai. 72 AV50
Riverhead Clo. E17 39 CC30
Riverholme Dr., Epsom 94 BN58
Rivermead, Wey. 92 AY60
Rivermead Clo., Tedd. 74 BJ49
Rivermead Clo., Wey. 92 AX57
Rivermill, Harl. 6 CM10
Rivermount, Walt. 83 BB54
Rivermount Gdns., Guil. 118 AR72
Riverpark Ave., Egh. 72 AU49
Rivers End Rd., Hem.H. 8 AX15
Riversdale, Grav. 81 DF48
Riversdale Rd. N5 47 BY34
Riversdale Rd., Rom. 41 CR29
Riversdale Rd., Surb. 84 BJ53
Riversdell Clo., Cher. 82 AV54
Riversfield Rd., Enf. 30 CA24
Riverside NW4 46 BP33
Riverside SE7 68 CH41
Riverside, Dor. 119 BK70
Riverside (Runnymede), Egh. 72 AT48
Riverside, Eyns. 90 CV55
Riverside, Guil. 118 AR69
Riverside, Shep. 83 BB54
Riverside, Stai. 82 AV51
Riverside (Wraysbury), Stai. 72 AR47
Riverside, Twick. 74 BJ47
Riverside Ave., Brox. 12 CE14
Riverside Ave., E.Mol. 84 BG53
Riverside Clo. W7 54 BH38
Riverside Clo., Kings L. 17 AZ18
Riverside Clo., Kings.T. 84 BK52
Riverside Clo., Orp. 89 CP51
Riverside Clo., St.Alb. 9 BH14
Riverside Clo., Stai. 72 AV50
Riverside Clo., Wall. 86 BV55
Riverside Dr. W4 65 BN43
Riverside Dr., Esher 93 BF56
Riverside Dr., Mitch. 86 BU53
Riverside Dr., Rich. 74 BJ48
Riverside Dr., Rick. 35 AX26
Riverside Dr., Stai. 82 AV51
Riverside Dr. (Egham Hythe), Stai. 72 AV49
Riverside Gdns. W6 65 BP42
Riverside Gdns., Berk. 7 AQ12
Riverside Gdns., Enf. 30 BZ23
Riverside Gdns., Wem. 55 BL37
Riverside Gdns., Wok. 100 AT64
High St.
Riverside Path, Chsnt. 21 CC18
Riverside Pl., Stai. 73 AX46
Riverside Rd. E15 57 CF37
Riverside Rd. N15 48 CB32
Riverside Rd. SW17 76 BS49
Riverside Rd., St.Alb. 9 BH14
Riverside Rd., Sid. 79 CQ48
Riverside Rd., Stai. 72 AV50
Riverside Rd. (Stanwell), Stai. 73 AX46
Riverside Rd., Walt. 93 BE56
Riverside Rd., Wat. 26 BC25
Riverside Wk. E5 48 CC34
Riverside Wk. SE1 4 C2
Riverside Wk. SE1 66 BX41
Riverside Wk., Bex. 79 CP47
Riverside Wk., Dart. 80 CW48
Riverside Wk., Islw. 64 BH45
Riverside Way, Dart. 80 CW46
Riverside Way, Uxb. 53 AW37
Riversmead, Hodd. 12 CE12
Riverton Clo. W9 55 BR38
Riverview, Grays 71 DF42
Riverview, Guil. 118 AR70
Riverview Gdns. SW13 65 BP43
Riverview Gro. W4 65 BM43
Riverview Pk. SE6 77 CE48
Riverview Rd. W4 65 BM43
Riverview Rd., Epsom 94 BN56
Riverview Rd., Green. 80 DA46
Riverway N13 38 BY28
Riverway, Harl. 6 CO9
Riverway, Stai. 83 AW51
Riverwood La., Chis. 88 CM51
Rivett Drake Rd., Guil. 109 AQ58
Rivey Clo., Wey. 91 AV60
Rivington Ave., Wdf.Grn. 40 CJ30
Rivington Ct. NW10 55 BP37
Longstone Ave.
Rivington Cres. NW7 37 BO29
Rivington Pl. EC2 2 N3
Rivington St. EC2 2 M3
Rivington St. EC2 57 CA38
Rivington Wk. E8 57 CB37
Wilde Clo.
Rivulet Rd. N17 39 BZ29
Rixon Clo., Slou. 52 AS39
Rixon Ho. SE18 68 CL43
Rixsen Rd. E12 49 CK35
Roach Rd. E3 57 CE36
Roads Pl. N19 47 BX34
Roakes Ave., Wey. 83 AW55
Roan St. SE10 67 CE43
Roasthill La., Wind. 61 AL43
Robart Ho. E11 49 CG33
Robarts Clo., Ruis. 44 BC32
Field End Rd.
Robb Rd., Stan. 36 BJ29
Robbs Clo., Hem.H. 8 AW12
Robe End, Hem.H. 7 AV12
Robert Adam St. W1 1 G8
Robert Adam St. W1 56 BV39
Robert Ave., St.Alb. 9 BF15
Robert Clo. W9 56 BT38
Robert Clo., Chig. 40 CN28
Robert Clo., Pot.B. 19 BR20
Robert Clo., Walt. 92 BC56
Robert Dashwood Way SE17 4 H9
Robert Gentry Ho. W14 65 BR42
Robert Keen Clo. SE15 67 CB44
Cicely Rd.
Robert Lowe Clo. SE14 67 CC43
Robert Ms. NW1 56 BW38
Hampstead Rd.
Robert Owen Ho. SW6 65 BQ44
Robert Rd., Slou. 43 AO34
Robert St. E16 58 CL40
Robert St. NW1 1 K3
Robert St. NW1 56 BV38
Robert St. SE18 68 CM42
Robert St. WC2 4 A1
Robert St. WC2 56 BX40
Savoy Pl.
Robert St., Croy. 87 BZ55
High St.
Roberta St. E2 57 CB38
Roberton Dr., Brom. 88 CJ51
Roberts All. W5 64 BK41
Church Gdns.
Roberts Clo. SE9 78 CM47
Beaverbank Rd.
Roberts Clo., Orp. 89 CP53
Sholden Gdns.
Roberts Clo., Rom. 41 CU30
Roberts Clo., Stai. 73 AX46
Park Rd.
Roberts Clo., Sutt. 94 BQ57
Roberts Clo., West Dr. 53 AY40
Roberts La., Ger.Cr. 34 AT28
Roberts Ms. SW1 3 G7
Roberts Pl. EC1 2 E4
Roberts Rd. E17 39 CE30
Roberts Rd. NW7 37 BR29
Roberts Rd., Belv. 69 CR42
Roberts St., Wat. 27 BD25
Roberts Way, Egh. 72 AR50
Roberts Way, Hat. 10 BO13
Roberts Wd. Dr., Ger.Cr. 34 AS28
Robertsbridge Rd., Cars. 86 BT54
Robertson Clo., Brox. 21 CD16
Robertson Rd. E15 57 CF37
Robertson St. SW8 66 BV45
Robeson St. E3 57 CD39
Ackroyd Dr.
Robin Clo. NW7 37 BO27
Robin Clo., Hmptn. 74 BE49
Robin Clo., Rom. 41 CS29
Robin Clo., Wey. 92 AW56
Robin Cres. E6 58 CJ39
Robin Gdns., Red. 121 BV69
Kingfisher Dr.
Robin Gro. N6 47 BV34
Robin Gro., Brent. 64 BK43
Robin Gro., Har. 46 BL32
Robin Hill, Berk. 7 AR13
St. Edmunds
Robin Hill Dr., Chis. 78 CK50
Wood Dr.
Robin Hood Clo., Slou. 61 AM40
Robin Hood Clo., Wok. 100 AP62
Robin Hood Cres., Wok. 100 AP62
Robin Hood Dr., Bush. 27 BE23
Robin Hood Dr., Har. 36 BH29
Robin Hood Grn., Orp. 89 CO53
Robin Hood La. E14 57 CF39
Robin Hood La. SW15 75 BO48
Robin Hood La., Bexh. 79 C
Robin Hood La., Guil. 100 A
Robin Hood La., Hat. 10 E
The Common
Robin Hood La., Sutt. 95 E
Robin Hood Meadow, Hem.H. 8 A
Robin Hood Rd. SW19 75 B
Robin Hood Rd., Brwd. 42 D
Robin Hood Rd., Wok. 100 A
Robin Hood Way SW15 75 B
Robin Hood Way SW20 75 B
Robin Hood Way, Grnf. 54 B
Robin Hood Yd. EC1 56 B
Leather La.
Robin Mead, Welw.G.C. 5
Robin Rd., Hem.H. 8 A
Robin St. SW3 66 B
Flood St.
Robin Way, Cuffley 20 B
Robin Way, Guil. 109 A
Robin Way, Orp. 89 C
Robin Way, Stai. 72 A
Robina Clo., Bexh. 69 C
Brunswick Rd.
Robinhood Clo., Mitch. 86 BV
Robinhood La., Mitch. 86 BV
Robinia Ave., Grav. 81 D
Robinia Clo., Chig. 40 C
Robins, The, Brwd. 33 D
Robins Clo., Uxb. 53 A
Robins Ct. SE12 78 C
Robins Ct., Beck. 87 C
Robins Dale, Wok. 100 A
Robins Gro., Kes. 88 C
Robins La., Epp. 31 CN
Robins Nest Hill, Hert. 11 BV
Robins Orchard, Ger.Cr. 34 A
Robins Way, Hat. 10 B
Robinsfield, Hem.H. 8 AV
Robinson Ave., Chsnt. 20 B
Robinson Cres., Bush. 36 B
Robinson Rd. E2 57 C
Robinson Rd. SW17 76 B
Robinson Rd., Dag. 50 C
Robinson St. SW3 66 B
Christchurch St.
Robinsons Clo. W13 54 B
Robinsway, Wal.Abb. 22 C
Roundhills
Robinsway, Walt. 93 B
Robinwood Gro., Uxb. 53 A
Robinwood Pl. SW15 75 B
Robsart St. SW9 66 B
Robson Ave. NW10 55 B
Robson Clo. E6 58 C
Linton Gdns.
Robson Clo., Enf. 29 BY
Robson Clo., Ger.Cr. 34 A
Robson Rd. SE27 76 BY
Robsons Clo., Chsnt. 21 C
Robsons Clo., Wal.Cr. 21 C
Robyns Cft., Grav. 81 D
Peach Cft.
Robyns Way, Sev. 107 C
Roch Ave., Edg. 37 B
Rochdale Rd. E17 48 C
Rochdale Rd. SE2 69 C
Rochdale Way SE8 67 C
Idonia St.
Roche Rd. SW16 86 B
Roche Wk., Cars. 86 B
Rochelle Clo. SW11 66 B
Nantes Clo.
Rochelle St. E2 2
Rochelle St. E2 57 C
Swanfield St.
Rochemont Wk. E8 57 C
Broadway Mkt. Est.
Rochester Ave. E13 58 C
Rochester Ave., Brom. 88 C
Rochester Ave., Felt. 73 B
Rochester Clo. SW16 76 B
Rochester Clo., Enf. 30 C
Rochester Clo., Sid. 79 C
Rochester Dr., Bex. 79 C
Rochester Dr., Pnr. 45 B
Rochester Gdns., Croy. 87 C
Rochester Gdns., Ilf. 49 C
Rochester Ms. NW1 56 B
Rochester Rd.
Rochester Pl. NW1 56 B
Rochester Rd. NW1 56 B
Rochester Rd., Cars. 95 B
Rochester Rd., Dart. 80 C
Rochester Rd., Grav. 81 D
Rochester Rd., Nthwd. 44 B
Rochester Row SW1 3
Rochester Row SW1 66 B
Rochester Sq. NW1 56 B
Rochester St. SW1 3
Rochester St. SW1 66 B
Rochester Row
Rochester Ter. NW1 56 B
Rochester Wk. SE1 4
Rochester Wk., Reig. 121 BS
Castle Dr.
Rochester Way SE3 68 C
Rochester Way SE9 68 CK
Rochester Way, Dart. 79 CT
Rochester Way, Rick. 26 AZ
Rochester Way Relief Rd. SE9 68 CL
Rochford Ave., Brwd. 122 DD
Rochford Ave., Loug. 31 CM
Rochford Ave., Rom. 50 CP
Rochford Ave., Wal.Abb. 21 CF
Rochford Clo. E6 58 CJ
Boleyn Rd.
Rochford Clo., Brox. 21 CD
Rochford Clo., Horn. 59 CU
Rochford Grn., Loug. 31 CM
Rochford St. NW5 47 BU

chford Wk. E8 57 CB36
Vilman Gro.
chford Way, Croy. 86 BX53
chfords Gdns., Slou. 52 AR40
ck Ave. SW14 65 BN45
South Worple Way
ck Gdns., Dag. 50 CR35
ck Gro. Way SE16 67 CB42
Blue Anchor La.
ck Hill SE26 77 CA49
ck Hill, Orp. 98 CR57
ck La., Dag. 59 CR36
ck St. N4 47 BY34
ckbourne Rd. SE23 77 CC47
ckchase Gdns., Horn. 51 CW32
ckcliffe Ave., Kings L. 17 AZ18
ckdale Rd., Sev. 116 CU66
ckells Pl. SE22 77 CB46
ckfield Clo., Oxt. 115 CG69
ckfield Rd., Oxt. 115 CG68
ckford Ave., Grnf. 54 BJ37
ckhall Rd. NW2 46 BQ35
ckhampton Rd. SE27 76 BY49
ckhampton Rd., S.Croy. 96 BZ57
ckingham Ave., Horn. 50 CU32
ckingham Clo. SW15 65 BO45
ckingham Clo., Uxb. 53 AX37
ckingham Est. SE1 4 H7
ckingham Est. SE1 67 BZ41
ckingham Par., Uxb. 53 AX36
ckingham Rd., Uxb. 53 AX37
ckingham St. SE1 4 H7
ckingham St. SE1 67 BZ41
ckland Rd. SW15 65 BR45
cklands Dr., Stan. 36 BJ30
ckley Rd. W14 65 BQ41
ckmount Rd. SE18 68 CN42
ckmount Rd. SE19 77 BZ50
cks La. SW13 65 BP44
ckshaw Rd., Red. 113 BW67
ckware Ave., Grnf. 54 BH37
ckways, Barn. 28 BO25
ckwell Gdns., Dag. 50 CR35
ckwell Rd., Dag. 50 CR35
ckwells Ct. SE19 77 CA49
ckwells Gdns. SE19 77 CA49
ckwood Gdns., Wdf.Grn. 40 CH27
Whitehall La.
ckwood Pl. W12 65 BQ41
Shepherds Bush Grn.
cky La., Reig. 113 BU67
cliffe St. N1 2 G1
cliffe St. N1 56 BY37
combe Cres. SE23 77 CC47
cque La. SE3 68 CG45
dborough Rd. NW11 47 BS33
den Clo., Harl. 6 CQ9
den Gdns., Croy. 87 CA53
den St. N7 47 BX34
den St., Ilf. 49 CL34
den Way, Ilf. 49 CL34
Roden St.
denhurst Rd. SW4 76 BW46
derick Rd. NW3 47 BU35
dgers Clo., Borwd. 27 BK25
ding Ave., Wdf.Grn. 40 CK29
ding Clo., Ong. 15 CY14
ding Dr., Brwd. 33 CZ22
ding Ho., Wdf.Grn. 40 CK29
ding La., Buck.H. 40 CJ27
ding La. N., Wdf.Grn. 40 CJ30
ding La. S., Ilf. 49 CJ31
ding Ms. E1 57 CB40
Kennet St.
ding Rd. E5 48 CC35
ding Rd. E6 58 CL39
ding Rd., Loug. 31 CK25
ding Trd. Est., Bark. 58 CL36
ding Vw., Buck.H. 40 CJ26
ding Vw., Ong. 24 CX17
ding Way, Rain. 60 CV37
Briscoe Rd.
dings, The, Upmin. 51 CY32
dings, The, Wdf.Grn. 40 CJ29
Snakes La.
dings Clo., Ong. 15 CY14
Ongar Rd.
dmarton St. W1 1 F7
dmarton St. W1 56 BU39
dmell Clo., Hayes 54 BE38
Ditchfield Rd.
dmell Slope N12 37 BR28
dmere St. SE10 68 CG42
dmill La. SW2 76 BX47
dney Ave., St.Alb. 9 BJ14
dney Clo., Croy. 86 BY54
dney Clo., N.Mal. 85 BO52
dney Clo., Pnr. 45 BE33
dney Clo., Walt. 84 BD55
Rodney Rd.
dney Cres., Hodd. 12 CE11
dney Gdns., Pnr. 44 BC32
dney Gdns., W.Wick. 97 CH56
dney Grn., Walt. 84 BD55
Rodney Rd.
dney Pl. E17 39 CD30
dney Pl. SE17 4 J8
dney Pl. SE17 67 BZ42
dney Pl. SW19 86 BT51
dney Rd. E11 49 CH31
dney Rd. SE17 4 J8
dney Rd. SE17 67 BZ42
dney Rd., Mitch. 86 BU51
dney Rd., N.Mal. 85 BO53
dney Rd., Ong. 24 CW18
dney Rd., Twick. 74 BF46
dney Rd., Walt. 83 BC55
dney St. N1 56 BX37
dney St. SE18 68 CL41
dney Way, Guil. 118 AT70
dney Way, Rom. 41 CR30
dney Way, Slou. 62 AV44
dona Rd., Wey. 92 BA59
Rodsley Pl. SE15 67 CB44
Commercial Way
Rodsley St. SE1 67 CB43
Old Kent Rd.
Rodway Rd. SW15 75 BP47
Rodwell Clo., Ruis. 45 BD33
Rodwell Pl., Edg. 37 BM29
Rodwell Rd. SE22 77 CA46
Roe End NW9 46 BN31
Roe Flds. Clo., Hem.H. 8 AW15
Roe Grn. NW9 46 BN32
Roe Grn. Clo., Hat. 10 BO13
Roe Grn. La., Hat. 10 BO12
Roe Hill Clo., Hat. 10 BO13
Roe La. NW9 46 BM31
Roe Way, Wall. 95 BX57
Roebourne Way E16 58 CL40
Pier Rd.
Roebuck Clo., Ash. 103 BL63
Roebuck Clo., Felt. 73 BC49
Roebuck Clo., Reig. 121 BS70
Roebuck Grn., Slou. 61 AM40
Roebuck La. N17 39 CA29
High Rd.
Roebuck La., Buck.H. 40 CJ26
Roebuck Rd., Chess. 94 BM56
Roebuck Rd., Ilf. 41 CO28
Roedean Ave., Enf. 30 CC23
Roedean Clo., Enf. 30 CC23
Roedean Clo., Orp. 98 CO56
Roedean Cres. SW15 75 BO46
Roehampton Clo. SW15 65 BP45
Roehampton Clo., Grav. 81 DJ47
Roehampton Dr., Chis. 78 CM50
Roehampton Gate SW15 75 BO46
Roehampton High St. SW15 75 BP47
Roehampton La. SW15 65 BP45
Roehampton Vale SW15 75 BO48
Roestock Gdns., St.Alb. 10 BO14
Roestock La., St.Alb. 10 BN15
Rofant Rd., Nthwd. 35 BB29
Roffes La., Cat. 114 BZ66
Roffey Clo., Pur. 104 BY61
Roffey St. E14 67 CF41
Roffords, Wok. 100 AQ62
Marston Rd.
Roffords Clo., Wok. 100 AQ62
Rogate Ho. E5 48 CB34
Downs Est.
Roger Simmons Ct., Lthd. 102 BE65
Roger St. WC1 2 C5
Roger St. WC1 56 BX38
Rogers Clo., Cat. 105 CB64
Rogers Clo., Couls. 104 BY62
Rogers Ct., Swan. 89 CU52
London Rd.
Rogers Gdns., Dag. 50 CR35
Rogers La., Slou. 52 AP36
Rogers Mead, Gdse. 114 CB69
Rogers Rd. E16 58 CG39
Rogers Rd. SW17 76 BT49
Rogers Rd., Dag. 50 CR35
Rogers Rd., Grays 71 DE42
Rogers Ruff, Nthwd. 35 BA30
Rogers Wk. N12 38 BS27
Brook Meadow
Rogers Wd. La., Fawk. 99 DA56
Rojack Rd. SE23 77 CC47
Roke Clo., Ken. 96 BZ60
Roke Lo. Rd., Ken. 95 BY60
Roke Rd., Ken. 104 BY61
Rokeby Ct., Wok. 100 AP62
Rokeby Gdns., Wdf.Grn. 40 CH30
Rokeby Pl. SW20 75 BP50
Rokeby Rd. SE4 67 CD44
Rokeby St. E15 57 CF37
Roker Pk. Ave., Uxb. 44 AY35
Rokesby Clo., Well. 68 CM44
Rokesby Clo., Wem. 45 BK35
Rokesby Pl., Wem. 45 BK35
Rokesly Ave. N8 47 BX32
Roland Gdns. SW7 66 BT42
Roland Gdns., Felt. 74 BE48
Roland Ms. E1 57 CC39
Stepney Grn.
Roland Rd. E17 48 CF32
Roland St., St.Alb. 9 BJ13
Roland Way SE17 67 BZ42
Roland Way SW7 66 BT42
Roland Way, Wor.Pk. 85 BO55
Roles Gro., Rom. 50 CP31
Rolfe Clo., Barn. 29 BU24
Rolinsden Way, Kes. 97 CJ56
Roll Gdns., Ilf. 49 CL32
Rollesby Rd., Chess. 94 BM57
Rollesby Way SE28 59 CP40
Rolleston Ave., Orp. 88 CL53
Rolleston Clo., Orp. 88 CL54
Rolleston Rd., S.Croy. 96 BZ57
Rollins St. SE15 67 CC43
Rollit Cres., Houns. 74 BF46
Rollit St. N7 47 BY35
Rollo Rd., Swan. 79 CT50
Rolls Bldgs. EC4 2 D8
Rolls Bldgs. EC4 56 BY39
Fetter La.
Rolls Pk. Ave. E4 39 CE28
Rolls Pk. Rd. E4 39 CE28
Rolls Pas. EC4 2 D8
Rolls Pas. EC4 56 BY39
Chancery La.
Rolls Rd. SE1 4 Q10
Rolls Rd. SE1 67 CA42
Rollscourt Ave. SE24 77 BZ46
Rollswood, Welw.G.C. 5 BR9
Rolt St. SE8 67 CD43
Rolvenden Gdns., Brom. 78 CJ50
Rom Cres., Rom. 50 CT33
Rom Valley Way, Rom. 50 CT33
Roma Read Clo. SW15 75 BP47
Roma Rd. E17 48 CD31
Roman Clo. W3 65 BM41
Roman Clo., Felt. 74 BD46
Roman Clo., Green. 80 CZ46
Thamesview Clo.
Roman Clo., Rain. 59 CS37
Roman Clo., Uxb. 35 AW30
Roman Gdns., Kings L. 17 AZ18
Roman Ri. SE19 77 BZ50
Roman Rd. E2 57 CC38
Roman Rd. E3 57 CC38
Roman Rd. E6 58 CK38
Roman Rd. N10 38 BV29
Roman Rd. W4 65 BO42
Roman Rd., Dor. 119 BJ72
Roman Rd., Epsom 103 BL65
Roman Rd., Grav. 81 DE48
Roman Rd., Ilf. 58 CL36
Roman Sq. SE28 59 CO40
Roman St., Hodd. 12 CE11
Roman Vale, Harl. 6 CP8
Roman Vill. Rd., S.Dnth. 80 CY50
Roman Way N7 56 BX36
Roman Way SE15 67 CC43
Clifton Way
Roman Way, Croy. 86 BY55
Roman Way, Dart. 79 CT46
Roman Way, Enf. 30 CA25
Romanhurst Ave., Brom. 88 CG52
Romanhurst Gdns., Brom. 88 CG52
Romans End, St.Alb. 9 BG14
Romans Way, Wok. 101 AW61
Romany Gdns. E17 39 CD30
McEntee Ave.
Romany Gdns., Sutt. 86 BS54
Romany Ri., Orp. 88 CM54
Romany Rd., Grav. 81 DF48
Romany Rd., Wok. 91 AO60
Romberg Rd. SW17 76 BV48
Romborough Gdns. SE13 77 CF46
Romborough Way SE13 77 CE46
Romeland, Borwd. 27 BK25
Romeland, Wal.Abb. 21 CF20
Romeland Hill, St.Alb. 9 BG13
Romero Clo. SW9 66 BX45
Stockwell Rd.
Romero Sq. SE3 68 CJ45
Romeyn Rd. SW16 76 BX48
Romford Cres., Rom. 50 CT33
Romford Rd. E7 58 CG36
Romford Rd. E12 58 CG36
Romford Rd. E15 58 CG36
Romford Rd., Chig. 41 CO27
Romford Rd., Ong. 24 CW19
Romford Rd., Rom. 41 CQ29
Romford Rd., S.Ock. 60 CW39
Romford St. E1 57 CB39
Romilly Dr., Wat. 36 BE28
Romilly Rd. N4 47 BY34
Romilly St. W1 1 N10
Romilly St. W1 56 BW40
Rommany Rd. SE27 77 BZ49
Romney Chase, Horn. 51 CX32
Romney Clo. N17 39 CB30
Romney Clo. NW11 47 BT33
Romney Clo. SE14 67 CC43
Romney Clo., Ashf. 73 BA49
Romney Clo., Chess. 94 BL56
Romney Clo., Har. 45 BF33
Romney Dr., Brom. 78 CJ50
Romney Dr., Har. 45 BF33
Romney Gdns., Bexh. 69 CQ44
Romney Lock Rd., Wind. 62 AP43
Romney Rd. SE10 67 CF43
Romney Rd., Hayes 53 BA37
Romney Rd., N.Mal. 85 BN53
Romney St. SW1 3 Q7
Romney St. SW1 66 BW41
Romola Rd. SE24 76 BY47
Romsey Clo., Orp. 97 CL56
Broadwater Gdns.
Romsey Clo., Slou. 62 AS41
Romsey Dr., Slou. 43 AO34
Romsey Gdns., Dag. 59 CP37
Romsey Rd. W13 54 BJ40
Romsey Rd., Dag. 59 CP37
Rona Rd. NW3 47 BV35
Rona Wk. N1 57 BZ36
Marquess Est.
Ronald Ave. E15 58 CG38
Ronald Clo., Beck. 87 CD52
Ronald Rd., Rom. 42 CX30
Ronald St. E1 57 CC39
Devonport St.
Ronalds Rd. N5 47 BY35
Ronalds Rd., Brom. 88 CH51
Ronaldstone Rd., Sid. 78 CN46
Ronart St., Har. 45 BH31
Rondu Rd. NW2 46 BR35
Ronelean Rd., Surb. 85 BL55
Roneo Cor., Horn. 50 CT33
Roneo Link, Horn. 50 CT33
Ronfearn Ave., Orp. 89 CP53
Ronneby Clo., Wey. 83 BB55
Ronson Way, Lthd. 102 BJ64
Ronver Rd. SE12 78 CG47
Rood La. EC3 2 M10
Rood La. EC3 57 CA40
Rook Clo., Rain. 59 CU37
Rook Dean, Sev. 107 CS64
Rook Hill, Cat. 104 BY65
Rook La., Cat. 104 BX65
Rook Wk. E6 58 CK39
Allhallows Rd.
Rooke Way SE10 68 CG42
Glenister Rd.
Rookeries Clo., Felt. 73 BC48
Rookery, The, Dor. 119 BF72
Rookery, The, Grays 70 DA43
Rookery, The, Wat. 35 BC26
Rookery Clo. NW9 46 BO32
Rookery Clo., Grays 70 DA43
The Rookery
Rookery Clo., Lthd. 102 BG65
Rookery Ct., Grays 70 DA43
The Rookery
Rookery Cres., Dag. 59 CR36
Rookery Dr., Chis. 88 CL51
Rookery Dr., Dor. 119 BF72
Rookery Gdns., Orp. 89 CP53
Rookery Hill, Ash. 103 BM62
Rookery La., Brom. 88 CJ53
Rookery La., Grays 71 DE42
Rookery La., Wal.Abb. 21 CF18
Rookery Rd. SW4 66 BW45
Rookery Rd., Ing. 24 DB17
Rookery Rd., Orp. 97 CK58
Rookery Rd., Stai. 73 AW49
Rookery Vw., Grays 71 DE42
Rookery Way NW9 46 BO32
Rookery Way, Tad. 112 BR67
Rookesley Rd., Orp. 89 CP54
Rookfield Ave. N10 47 BW31
Rookfield Clo. N10 47 BW31
Cranmore Way
Rookley Clo., Sutt. 95 BS58
Hulveston Clo.
Rooks Hill, Rick. 26 AX24
Rooks Hill, Sev. 117 CY68
Rooks Hill, Welw.G.C. 5 BQ8
Rooksmead Rd., Sun. 83 BB51
Rookstone Rd. SW17 76 BU49
Rookwood Ave., Loug. 31 CM24
Rookwood Ave., N.Mal. 85 BP52
Rookwood Ave., Wall. 95 BW56
Rookwood Clo., Grays 71 DD42
Rookwood Clo., Red. 113 BV68
Rookwood Ct., Guil. 118 AR72
Rookwood Gdns. E4 40 CG27
Whitehall Rd.
Rookwood Gdns., Ilf. 41 CO29
Rookwood Gdns., Loug. 31 CM24
Rookwood Rd. N16 48 CA32
Roosevelt Way, Dag. 59 CS36
Roothill La., Bet. 120 BM73
Rope Maker Rd. SE16 67 CD41
Rope St. SE16 67 CD41
Rope Wk., Sun. 84 BD52
Rope Wk. Gdns. E1 57 CB39
Commercial Rd.
Rope Yd. Rails SE18 68 CL41
Ropemaker St. EC2 2 K6
Ropemaker St. EC2 57 BZ39
Ropemakers Flds. E14 57 CD40
Roper La. SE1 4 N5
Roper La. SE1 67 CA41
Roper St. SE9 78 CK46
Roper Way, Mitch. 86 BV51
Ropers Ave. E4 39 CE28
Ropery St. E3 57 CD38
Ropley St. E2 57 CB37
Shipton St.
Rosa Alba Ms. N5 48 BZ35
Kelross Rd.
Rosa Ave., Ashf. 73 AZ49
Rosalind Franklin Clo., Guil. 118 AP71
Rosaline Rd. SW6 65 BR43
Rosamond St. SE26 77 CB48
Rosary, The, Egh. 82 AV51
Rosary Clo., Houns. 64 BE44
Rosary Ct., Pot.B. 20 BS18
Rosary Gdns. SW7 66 BT42
Rosary Gdns., Ashf. 73 AZ49
Rosaville Rd. SW6 65 BR43
Roscoe Dr., Wok. 100 AT62
Pembroke Rd.
Roscoe St. EC1 2 J5
Roscoe St. EC1 57 BZ38
Roscoff Clo., Edg. 37 BM30
East Rd.
Rose Acre, Saw. 6 CP5
Rose All. SE1 4 J2
Rose All. SE1 57 BZ40
Rose & Crown Ct. EC2 2 H8
Rose & Crown Ct. EC2 57 BZ39
Foster La.
Rose & Crown La. W6 65 BQ42
Talgarth Rd.
Rose & Crown Yd. SW1 3 M2
Rose & Crown Yd. SW1 56 BW40
King St.
Rose Ave. E18 40 CH30
Rose Ave., Grav. 81 DJ47
Rose Ave., Mitch. 86 BU51
Rose Ave., Mord. 86 BT53
Rose Bank SE20 77 CB50
Rose Bank, Brwd. 42 DB27
Rose Bates Dr. NW9 46 BM31
Rose Briar Clo., Wok. 101 AW61
Pyrford Rd.
Rose Cotts. W5 54 BK40
Western Rd.
Rose Ct. SE26 77 CB48
Rose Ct., Pnr. 45 BD31
Nursery Rd.
Rose Dr., Chesh. 16 AO19
Rose End, Wor.Pk. 85 BQ54
Rose Gdn. Clo., Edg. 37 BL29
Rose Gdns. W5 64 BK41
Rose Gdns., Felt. 73 BC48
Rose Gdns., Sthl. 54 BF38
Rose Gdns., Stai. 73 AX47
Rose Gdns., Stai. 73 AX47
Diamedes Ave.
Rose Gdns., Wat. 26 BC25
Rose Glen NW9 46 BN31
Rose Glen, Rom. 50 CT33
Rose Hill, Dor. 119 BJ71
Rose Hill, Hmptn. 84 BF51
Rose Hill, Sutt. 86 BS55
Rose Hill Ave., Wok. 100 AR61
Rose La., Rom. 50 CP31
Rose La., Wok. 101 AX64
Rose Lawn, Bush. 36 BG26
Rose Mary Cres., Guil. 109 AP68
Rose Mead, Pot.B. 20 BT18
Rose St. WC2 1 Q10
Rose St. WC2 56 BX40
Floral St.
Rose St., Grav. 81 DD46
Rose Vale, Hodd. 12 CE12
Rose Valley, Brwd. 42 DB27
Rose Wk., Pur. 95 BW59
Rose Wk., Rad. 27 BJ22
Rose Wk., St.Alb. 9 BK12
Rose Wk., Surb. 85 BM53
Rose Wk., W.Wick. 87 CF55
Rose Way SE12 78 CH46
Rose Wd. Gdns., Wall. 95 BV57
Roseacre, Oxt. 115 CH70
Roseacre Clo. W13 54 BJ39
Roseacre Clo., Horn. 51 CW33
Roseacre Gdns., Guil. 118 AV73
Roseacre Gdns., Welw.G.C. 5 BT8
Sylvan Way
Roseacre Rd., Well. 69 CO45
Roseary Clo., West Dr. 63 AX42
Rosebank, Epsom 94 BN60
Rosebank, Wal.Abb. 22 CG20
Rosebank Ave., Horn. 51 CV35
Rosebank Ave., Wem. 45 BH35
Rosebank Cotts., Wok. 100 AS64
Rosebank Gdns. E3 57 CD37
St. Stephens Rd.
Rosebank Gdns. W3 55 BN39
York Rd.
Rosebank Gro. E17 48 CD31
Rosebank Rd. E17 48 CE32
Rosebank Rd. W7 64 BH41
Rosebank Vill. E17 48 CE31
High St.
Rosebank Wk. NW1 56 BW36
Maiden La.
Rosebank Wk. SE18 68 CK42
Samuel St.
Rosebank Way W3 55 BN39
Roseberry Ave. EC1 56 BY38
Roseberry Clo., Upmin. 51 CZ32
Roseberry Ct., Wat. 26 BC23
Roseberry Gdns. N4 47 BY32
Roseberry Gdns., Dart. 80 CV47
Roseberry Gdns., Orp. 88 CN55
Roseberry Gdns., Upmin. 51 CZ32
Roseberry Pl. E8 57 CA36
Roseberry St. SE16 67 CB42
Rosebery Ave. E12 58 CK36
Rosebery Ave. EC1 2 D4
Rosebery Ave. N17 39 CB30
Rosebery Ave., Epsom 94 BO60
Rosebery Ave., Har. 45 BE35
Rosebery Ave., N.Mal. 85 BO51
Rosebery Ave., Sid. 78 CN47
Rosebery Ave., Th.Hth. 87 BZ51
Rosebery Clo., Mord. 85 BQ53
Rosebery Cres., Wok. 100 AS64
Rosebery Gdns. N8 47 BX32
Rosebery Gdns. W13 54 BJ39
Rosebery Gdns., Sutt. 95 BS56
Lewis Rd.
Rosebery Ms. N10 38 BW30
Rosebery Rd.
Rosebery Rd. N9 39 CB27
Rosebery Rd. N10 38 BW30
Rosebery Rd. SW2 76 BX46
Rosebery Rd., Bush. 36 BF26
Rosebery Rd., Epsom 103 BN63
Rosebery Rd., Grays 71 DC43
Rosebery Rd., Houns. 74 BG46
Rosebery Rd., Kings.T. 85 BM51
Rosebery Rd., Sutt. 94 BR57
Rosebery Sq. EC1 2 D5
Rosebery Sq., Kings.T. 85 BM51
Rosebine Ave., Twick. 74 BG47
Rosebriar Wk., Wat. 26 BB21
Rosebriars, Cat. 105 CA63
Salmons La. W.
Rosebury Rd. SW6 66 BS44
Rosebury Vale, Ruis. 44 BB33
Rosebushes, Epsom 103 BP61
Rosecourt Rd., Croy. 86 BX53
Rosecroft Ave. NW3 47 BS34
Rosecroft Clo., Orp. 89 CP53
Rosecroft Dr., Wat. 26 BB22
Rosecroft Gdns. NW2 46 BP34
Rosecroft Gdns., Twick. 74 BG47
Rosecroft Rd., Sthl. 54 BF38
Rosecroft Wk., Pnr. 45 BD32
Rosecroft Wk., Wem. 45 BK35
Rosedale, Ash. 102 BK62
Rosedale, Chsnt. 21 CA17
Rosedale, Orp. 88 CL55
Rosedale, Welw.G.C. 5 BR6
Rosedale Ave., Chsnt. 21 CA18
Rosedale Ave., Hayes 53 BA39
Rosedale Clo. SE2 69 CO41
Finchale Rd.
Rosedale Clo. W7 64 BH41
Boston Rd.
Rosedale Clo., Dart. 80 CX47
Rosedale Clo., St.Alb. 18 BE18
Rosedale Clo., Stan. 36 BJ29
Rosedale Ct. N5 47 BY35
Leigh Rd.
Rosedale Gdns., Dag. 59 CO36
Rosedale Rd. E7 49 CJ35
Rosedale Rd., Dag. 59 CO36
Rosedale Rd., Epsom 94 BP56
Rosedale Rd., Grays 71 DE42
Rosedale Rd., Rich. 65 BL45
Rosedale Rd., Rom. 41 CS30
Rosedale Way, Chsnt. 21 CB17
Rosedene NW6 55 BQ37
Rosedene Ave. SW16 76 BX48
Rosedene Ave., Croy. 86 BX54
Rosedene Ave., Grnf. 54 BF38
Rosedene Ave., Mord. 86 BS53
Rosedene Ct., Dart. 80 CV47
Shepherds La.
Rosedene Ct., Ruis. 44 BB33
Rosedene Gdns., Ilf. 49 CL31

Rosedene Ter. E10 48 CE34
Rosedew Rd. W6 65 BQ43
Rosefield, Sev. 107 CU65
Rosefield Gdns. E14 57 CE40
Morant St.
Rosefield Gdns., Cher. 91 AU57
Rosefield Rd., Stai. 73 AW49
Rosehart Ms. W11 56 BS39
Westbourne Gro.
Rosehatch Ave., Rom. 50 CP31
Roseheath, Hem.H. 7 AV13
Roseheath Rd., Houns. 74 BE46
Rosehill, Esher 93 BJ57
Rosehill Ave., Sutt. 86 BT54
Rosehill Clo., Hodd. 12 CD12
Rosehill Ct., Slou. 62 AQ41
Yew Tree Rd.
Rosehill Fm. Meadow, Bans. 104 BS61
The Tracery
Rosehill Gdns., Abb.L. 17 BA19
Rosehill Gdns., Grnf. 45 BH35
Rosehill Gdns., Sutt. 86 BS55
Rosehill Pk. W., Sutt. 86 BS54
Rosehill Rd. SW18 76 BT46
Rosehill Rd., West. 106 CJ62
Roseland Clo. N17 39 BZ29
Roselands Ave., Hodd. 12 CD11
Roseleigh Ave. N5 47 BY35
Roseleigh Clo., Twick. 74 BK46
Rosemary Ave. N3 38 BS30
Rosemary Ave. N9 39 CB26
Rosemary Ave., E.Mol. 84 BF52
Rosemary Ave., Enf. 30 BZ23
Rosemary Ave., Houns. 64 BD44
Rosemary Ave., Rom. 50 CT31
Rosemary Clo., Harl. 6 CP9
Garden Ter. Rd.
Rosemary Clo., Oxt. 115 CH70
Holland La.
Rosemary Clo., S.Ock. 60 DB38
Rosemary Clo., Uxb. 53 AZ39
Rosemary Dr. E14 57 CF39
Coriander Ave.
Rosemary Dr., Ilf. 49 CJ32
Rosemary Gdns. SW14 65 BN45
Rosemary La.
Rosemary Gdns., Chess. 94 BL56
Rosemary Gdns., Dag. 50 CQ33
Rosemary La. SW14 65 BN45
Rosemary La., Egh. 82 AT52
Rosemary Rd. SE15 67 CA43
Rosemary Rd. SW17 76 BT48
Rosemary Rd., Well. 68 CN44
Rosemead NW9 46 BO33
Rosemead Ave., Felt. 73 BB48
Rosemead Ave., Mitch. 86 BW52
Rosemead Ave., Wem. 46 BL35
Rosemead Clo., Red. 121 BT71
Rosemead Gdns., Brwd. 122 DE24
Rosemont Ave. N12 38 BT29
Rosemont Rd. NW3 56 BT36
Rosemont Rd. W3 55 BM40
Rosemont Rd., N.Mal. 85 BN52
Rosemont Rd., Rich. 75 BL46
Rosemont Rd., Wem. 55 BL37
Rosemoor St. SW3 3 E9
Rosemoor St. SW3 66 BU42
Rosemount, Harl. 13 CL12
Rosemount Ave., Wey. 92 AW60
Rosemount Clo., Wdf.Grn. 40 CK29
Chapelmount Rd.
Rosemount Dr., Brom. 88 CK52
Rosemount Rd. W13 54 BJ39
Rosenau Cres. SW11 66 BU44
Rosenau Rd. SW11 66 BU44
Rosendale Rd. SE21 77 BZ47
Rosendale Rd. SE24 77 BZ47
Roseneath St. E5 48 CB34
Roseneath Ave. N21 38 BY26
Roseneath Clo., Orp. 98 CP57
Roseneath Rd. SW11 76 BV46
Roseneath Wk., Enf. 30 BZ24
Rosens Wk., Edg. 37 BM27
Rosenthal Rd. SE6 77 CE46
Rosenthorpe Rd. SE15 77 CC46
Roserton St. E14 67 CF41
Rosery, The, Croy. 87 CC53
Roses, The, Wdf.Grn. 40 CG29
Bunces La.
Roses La., Wind. 61 AL44
Rosethorn Clo. SW12 76 BW47
Rosetrees, Guil. 118 AT71
Roseveare Rd. SE12 78 CJ49
Roseville Ave., Houns. 74 BF46
Roseville Rd., Hayes 63 BC42
Rosevine Rd. SW20 85 BQ51
Rosewarne Clo., Wok. 100 AQ62
Roseway SE21 77 BZ46
Rosewood, Bex. 79 CT49
Rosewood, Cars. 95 BT58
Bawtree Clo.
Rosewood Ave., Grnf. 45 BJ35
Rosewood Ave., Horn. 50 CU35
Rosewood Clo., Sid. 79 CP48
Rosewood Ct., Brom. 88 CJ51
Rosewood Ct., Hem.H. 7 AV13
The Shrubbery
Rosewood Dr., Enf. 29 BY21
Rosewood Dr., Shep. 83 AY53
Rosewood Gdns. SE13 67 CF44
Lewisham Rd.
Rosewood Gro., Sutt. 86 BT55
Rosewood Sq. W12 55 BP39
Primula St.
Rosher Clo. E15 57 CF36
Rosherville Way, Grav. 81 DF47
Rosina St. E9 48 CC35
Roskell Rd. SW15 65 BQ45
Roslin Rd. W3 65 BM41
Roslin Way, Brom. 78 CH49
Roslyn Clo., Brox. 12 CD14
Roslyn Clo., Mitch. 86 BT51
Roslyn Gdns., Rom. 41 CT30
Roslyn Ms. N15 48 BZ32
Roslyn Rd.
Roslyn Rd. N15 48 BZ32
Rosmead Rd. W11 55 BR40
Rosoman Pl. EC1 2 E4
Rosoman St. EC1 2 E3
Rosoman St. EC1 56 BY38
Ross Ave. NW7 37 BR28
Ross Ave., Dag. 50 CQ34
Ross Clo. E4 39 CF27
Ross Clo., Har. 36 BG29
Ross Clo., Hat. 10 BP11
Ross Clo., Hayes 63 BA42
Ross Ct. SW15 75 BQ47
Ross Cres., Wat. 26 BC21
Ross Par., Wall. 95 BV57
Ross Rd. SE25 87 BZ52
Ross Rd., Cob. 93 BD60
Ross Rd., Dart. 79 CU46
Ross Rd., Twick. 74 BG47
Ross Rd., Wall. 95 BW56
Ross Way SE9 68 CK45
Ross Way, Nthwd. 35 BB28
Rossall Clo., Horn. 50 CU32
Rossall Cres. NW10 55 BL38
Rossdale, Sutt. 95 BU56
Rossdale Dr. N9 30 CC25
Rossdale Dr. NW9 46 BN33
Rossdale Rd. SW15 65 BQ45
Rosse Ms. SE3 68 CH44
Rossendale St. E5 48 CB34
Rossendale Way NW1 56 BW36
Rossgate, Hem.H. 8 AW12
Galley Hill
Rossindel Rd., Houns. 74 BF46
Rossington Ave., Borwd. 28 BL22
Rossington St. E5 48 CB34
Rossiter Clo., Slou. 62 AS42
Rossiter Rd. SW12 76 BV47
Rossland Clo., Bexh. 79 CR46
Rosslyn Ave. E4 40 CG27
Rosslyn Ave. SW13 65 BO45
Rosslyn Ave., Barn. 29 BU25
Rosslyn Ave., Dag. 50 CQ33
Rosslyn Ave., Felt. 73 BC46
Rosslyn Ave., Rom. 42 CW30
Rosslyn Clo., Hayes 53 BA39
Rosslyn Clo., Sun. 73 BB50
Cadbury Rd.
Rosslyn Clo., W.Wick. 88 CG55
Rosslyn Ct., Wok. 100 AQ62
St. Johns Rd.
Rosslyn Cres., Har. 45 BH31
Rosslyn Cres., Wem. 46 BL35
Rosslyn Cres. N., Har. 45 BH31
Rosslyn Cres. S., Har. 45 BH32
Rosslyn Hill NW3 47 BT35
Rosslyn Ms. NW3 47 BT35
Rosslyn Hill
Rosslyn Pk., Wey. 92 BA56
Rosslyn Pk. Ms. NW3 47 BT35
Rosslyn Rd. E17 48 CF31
Rosslyn Rd., Bark. 58 CM36
Rosslyn Rd., Twick. 74 BK46
Rosslyn Rd., Wat. 26 BC24
Rossmore Rd. NW1 1 D5
Rossmore Rd. NW1 56 BU38
Rossway Dr., Bush. 27 BG25
Rossway La., Berk. 7 AO13
Rosswood Gdns., Wall. 95 BW57
Rostrevor Ave. N15 48 CA32
Rostrevor Gdns., Hayes 53 BB40
Rostrevor Gdns., Iver 52 AU37
Rostrevor Gdns., Sthl. 64 BE42
Rostrevor Ms. SW6 65 BR44
Rostrevor Rd. SW6 65 BR44
Rostrevor Rd. SW19 76 BS49
Roswell Clo., Chsnt. 21 CD18
Rotary St. SE1 4 F6
Rotary St. SE1 66 BY41
Roth Dr., Brwd. 122 DD27
Roth Wk. N7 47 BX34
Durham Rd.
Rothbury Ave., Rain. 59 CU39
Rothbury Gdns., Islw. 64 BJ43
Rothbury Rd. E9 57 CD36
Rothbury Wk. N17 39 CB29
Rother Clo., Wat. 18 BD20
Rotherfield Rd., Cars. 95 BV56
Rotherfield Rd., Enf. 30 CC22
Rotherfield St. N1 57 BZ36
Rotherham Wk. SE1 4 F3
Rotherhill Ave. SW16 76 BW50
Rotherhithe New Rd. SE16 67 CB42
Rotherhithe Old Rd. SE16 67 CC42
Rotherhithe St. SE16 67 CB41
Rotherhithe Tunnel App. E14 57 CD40
Rothermere Rd., Croy. 95 BX56
Rotherwick Hill W5 55 BL38
Rotherwick Rd. NW11 47 BS33
Rotherwood Clo. SW20 85 BR51
Rotherwood Rd. SW15 65 BQ45
Rothery St. N1 56 BY37
Gaskin St.
Rothes Rd., Dor. 119 BJ71
Rothesay Ave. SW20 85 BR51
Rothesay Ave., Grnf. 54 BG36
Rothesay Ave., Rich. 65 BM45
Rothesay Rd. SE25 87 BZ52
Rothsay Rd. E7 58 CJ36
Rothsay St. SE1 4 M6
Rothsay St. SE1 67 CA41
Rothsay Wk. E14 67 CE42
Charnwood Gdns.
Rothschild Rd. W4 65 BN41
Rothschild St. SE27 76 BY49
Rothwell Gdns., Dag. 59 CP37
Rothwell Rd., Dag. 59 CP37
Rothwell St. NW1 56 BU36
Rotten Row SE3 68 CG44
Rotten Row SW1 3 E4
Rotten Row SW7 3 D4
Rotten Row SW7 66 BU41
Rotten Row SW11 66 BU43
Rotterdam Dr. E14 67 CF41
Rouel Rd. SE16 67 CB41
Rougemont Ave., Mord. 86 BS53
Rough Rew, Dor. 119 BJ73
Rough Rd., Wok. 100 AO64
Rough Wd. Clo., Wat. 26 BB22
Roughdown Ave., Hem.H. 8 AW15
Roughdown Rd., Hem.H. 8 AW15
Roughdown Vill. Rd., Hem.H. 8 AW15
Roughetts La., Red. 114 CA68
Roughlands, Wok. 100 AV60
Roughs, The, Nthwd. 35 BB27
Roughwood La., Ch.St.G. 34 AS26
Round Ash Way, Hartley 90 DC53
Round Gro., Croy. 87 CC54
Round Hill SE26 77 CB48
Round Oak Rd., Wey. 83 AY55
Round Way, Egh. 72 AU49
Round Wd. Rd., Amer. 25 AP22
Round Wd. Vw., Bans. 103 BQ61
Round Wd. Way, Bans. 103 BQ61
Roundabouts, The, Dor. 119 BE71
Roundacre Est. SW19 75 BQ48
Roundaway Rd., Ilf. 40 CK30
Roundcroft, Chsnt. 21 CA16
Roundhay Clo. SE23 77 CC48
Roundhedge Way, Enf. 29 BX22
Roundhill Clo., Wok. 100 AT62
Roundhill Dr., Enf. 29 BX24
Roundhill Dr., Wok. 100 AT63
Roundhill Way, Cob. 93 BF59
Roundhill Way, Guil. 118 AP70
Roundhills, Wal.Abb. 22 CG20
Roundmead Ave., Loug. 31 CL24
Roundmead Clo., Loug. 31 CL24
Roundmoor Dr., Chsnt. 21 CD18
Roundtable Rd., Brom. 78 CG48
Roundthorne Way, Wok. 100 AP61
Roundtree Rd., Wem. 45 BJ35
Roundway, West. 106 CJ61
Sunningvale Ave.
Roundway, The N17 39 BZ30
Roundway, The, Esher 93 BH57
Roundway, The, Wat. 26 BB25
Roundways, The, Ruis. 44 BB34
Roundwood, Chis. 88 CL51
Roundwood, Kings L. 17 AY17
Roundwood Ave., Brwd. 122 DD26
Roundwood Ave., West Dr. 53 BA40
Roundwood Clo., Ruis. 44 BA33
Roundwood Dr., Welw.G.C. 5 BQ7
Roundwood Gro., Brwd. 122 DD26
Roundwood Rd. NW10 55 BO36
Rounton Dr., Wat. 26 BB22
Rounton Rd. E3 57 CE38
Rounton Rd., Wal.Abb. 22 CG20
Roupel Pk. Est. SW2 76 BX47
Roupell Rd. SW2 76 BX47
Roupell St. SE1 4 E3
Roupell St. SE1 56 BY40
Rous Rd., Buck.H. 40 CK26
Rousden St. NW1 56 BW36
Camden Rd.
Rouse Gdns. SE21 77 CA49
Rousebarn La., Rick. 26 AY22
Rousebarn La., Wat. 26 BA24
Routh Rd. SW18 76 BU47
Routh St. E6 58 CK39
Rover Ave., Ilf. 40 CN29
Row Cft., Hem.H. 7 AV14
Rowallan Rd. SW6 65 BR43
Rowan Ave. E4 39 CD29
Rowan Ave., Egh. 72 AU49
Rowan Clo. SW16 86 BW51
Rowan Clo. W5 65 BL41
Rowan Clo., Guil. 118 AR69
Rowan Clo., N.Mal. 85 BO51
Rowan Clo., Reig. 121 BT71
Rowan Clo., St.Alb. 10 BL13
Cranbrook Dr.
Rowan Clo. (Bricket Wd.), St.Alb. 18 BF19
Rowan Clo., Stan. 36 BH29
Woodlands Dr.
Rowan Clo., Wem. 45 BJ34
Rowan Ct. SE12 78 CG47
Rowan Cres. SW16 86 BW51
Rowan Cres., Dart. 80 CV47
Rowan Dr. NW9 46 BP31
Rowan Dr., Brox. 21 CD16
Rowan Gdns. W6 65 BQ42
Bute Gdns.
Rowan Gdns., Croy. 87 CA55
Rowan Grn., Brwd. 122 DC27
Rowan Grn., Couls. 104 BV64
Rowan Grn., Wey. 92 BA56
Rowan Pl., Hayes 53 BB40
Rowan Rd. SW16 86 BW51
Rowan Rd. W6 65 BQ42
Rowan Rd., Bexh. 69 CQ45
Rowan Rd., Brent. 64 BJ43
Rowan Rd., Swan. 89 CS52
Rowan Rd., West Dr. 63 AX42
Rowan Wk. N2 47 BT32
Rowan Wk. N19 47 BW34
Bredgar Rd.
Rowan Wk. W10 55 BR38
Droop St.
Rowan Wk., Brom. 88 CK55
Rowan Wk., Hat. 10 BP14
Southdown Rd.
Rowan Wk., Horn. 51 CV31
Rowan Way, Rom. 50 CP31
Rowanhurst Dr., Slou. 43 AO35
Rowans, Welw.G.C. 5 BS6
Rowans, The N13 38 BY27
Rowans, The, Ger.Cr. 43 AR31
Rowans, The, Hem.H. 8 AW13
Rowans, The, Sun. 73 BB49
Rowans, The, Wok. 100 AS62
Montgomery Rd.
Rowantree Clo. N21 39 BZ26
Rowantree Rd. N21 39 BZ26
Rowantree Rd., Enf. 29 BY23
Rowanwood Ave., Sid. 79 CO47
Rowbarns Way, Lthd. 110 BB68
Rowben Clo. N20 38 BS26
Rowberry Clo. SW6 65 BQ44
Rowcross St. SE1 4 Q10
Rowcross St. SE1 67 CA42
Rowdell Rd., Nthlt. 54 BF37
Rowden Pk. Gdns. E4 39 CE29
Rowden Rd.
Rowden Rd. E4 39 CE29
Rowden Rd., Beck. 87 CD51
Rowden Rd., Epsom 94 BM56
Rowditch La. SW11 66 BV44
Rowdon Ave. NW10 55 BP36
Rowdow La., Sev. 99 CV60
Rowdow La., Sev. 108 CV61
Rowdown Cres., Croy. 96 CF58
Rowdowns Rd., Dag. 59 CQ37
Rowe Gdns., Bark. 58 CN37
Rowe La. E9 48 CC35
Urswick Rd.
Rowe Wk., Har. 45 BF34
Rowena Cres. SW11 66 BU44
Rowfant Rd. SW17 76 BV47
Rowhedge, Brwd. 122 DD27
Rowhill, Wey. 91 AV57
Rowhill Rd. E5 48 CB35
Rowhill Rd., Dart. 79 CT50
Rowhurst Ave., Lthd. 102 BH62
Rowhurst Ave., Wey. 92 AW57
Rowington Clo. W2 56 BS39
Rowland Ave., Har. 45 BK31
Rowland Clo., Wind. 61 AL45
Rowland Cres., Chig. 40 CN28
Fairview Dr.
Rowland Gro. SE26 77 CB48
Dallas Rd.
Rowland Hill Ave. N17 39 BZ29
Rowland Hill St. NW3 47 BU35
Rowland Wk., Hav. 41 CT27
Rowland Way SW19 86 BS51
Hayward Clo.
Rowland Way, Ashf. 73 BA50
Rowlands Ave., Pnr. 36 BF28
Rowlands Clo. NW7 37 BP29
Rowlands Clo., Chsnt. 21 CC18
Rowlands Flds., Chsnt. 21 CC18
Clarendon Rd.
Rowlands Rd., Dag. 50 CQ34
Rowlatt Clo., Dart. 80 CV49
Rowlatt Dr., St.Alb. 9 BF14
Rowlatt Rd., Dart. 80 CV49
Rowley Ave., Sid. 79 CO47
Rowley Clo., Wat. 27 BE25
Rowley Clo., Wem. 55 BL36
Rowley Ct., Cat. 105 BZ64
Fairbourne La.
Rowley Gdns. N4 48 BZ33
Rowley Gdns., Chsnt. 21 CC17
Davison Dr.
Rowley Grn. Rd., Barn. 28 BO25
Rowley La., Borwd. 28 BN23
Rowley La., Slou. 52 AR37
Rowley Mead, Epp. 23 CP16
Rowley Rd. N15 48 BZ32
Rowley Way NW8 56 BS37
Rowlheys Pl., West Dr. 63 AY41
Rowlls Rd., Kings.T. 85 BL52
Rowney Gdns., Dag. 59 CO36
Rowney Gdns., Saw. 6 CP7
Rowney Rd., Dag. 59 CO36
Rowney Wd., Saw. 6 CP6
Rowns Way, Loug. 31 CK24
Rowntree Path SE28 59 CO40
MacAuley Way
Rowntree Rd., Twick. 74 BH47
Rowse Clo. E15 57 CF37
Rowsley Ave. NW4 46 BQ31
Rowstock Gdns. N7 47 BW35
Rowton Rd. SE18 68 CM43
Rowtown, Wey. 91 AV57
Rowzill Rd., Swan. 79 CT50
Roxborough Ave., Har. 45 BG33
Roxborough Ave., Islw. 64 BH43
Roxborough Pk., Har. 45 BH33
Roxborough Rd., Har. 45 BG32
Roxbourne Clo., Nthlt. 54 BE36
Arnold Rd.
Roxburgh Ave., Upmin. 51 CY35
Roxburgh Rd. SE27 76 BY49
Roxburn Way, Ruis. 44 BB34
Roxby Pl. SW6 66 BS43
Roxeth Ct., Ashf. 73 AZ49
Roxeth Grn. Ave., Har. 45 BF34
Roxeth Gro., Har. 45 BF35
Roxeth Hill, Har. 45 BG34
Roxford Clo., Shep. 83 BB53
Roxley Rd. SE13 77 CE46
Roxton Gdns., Croy. 96 CE56
Roxwell Clo., Slou. 61 AM40
Roxwell Rd. W12 65 BP41
Roxwell Rd., Bark. 59 CO37
Roxwell Way, Wdf.Grn. 40 CJ29
Roxy Ave., Rom. 50 CP33
Roy Gdns., Ilf. 49 CN31
Roy Gro., Hmptn. 74 BF50
Roy Rd., Nthwd. 35 BB29
Roy Sq. E14 57 CD40
Royal Albert Dock Spine Rd. E16 58 CK40
Royal Arc. W1 3 L1
Royal Ave. SW3 3 E10
Royal Ave. SW3 66 BU42
Royal Ave., Wal.Cr. 21 CD20
Royal Ave., Wor.Pk. 85 BO55
Royal Circ. SE27 76 BY48
Royal Clo., Ilf. 50 CO33
Royal Clo., Uxb. 53 AY39
Royal Clo., Wor.Pk. 85 BO55
Royal College St. NW1 56 BW
Royal Ct., Hem.H. 8 AY
Royal Cres. W11 55 BC
Royal Cres., Ruis. 45 BE
Royal Dr., Epsom 103 BF
Royal Ex. EC3 2
Royal Ex. Ave. EC3 2
Royal Ex. Bldgs. EC3 2
Royal Ex. Bldgs. EC3 57 BZ
Cornhill
Royal Hill SE10 67 CF
Royal Hospital Rd. SW3 66 BU
Royal La., Uxb. 53 AY
Royal La., West Dr. 53 AY
Royal London Ind. Est. NW10 55 BN
Royal Mint Pl. E1 2 C
Royal Mint Pl. E1 57 CA
Royal Mint St.
Royal Mint St. E1 2 C
Royal Mint St. E1 57 CA
Royal Naval Pl. SE14 67 CD
Hereford Pl.
Royal Oak Ct. N1 57 CA
Royal Oak Pl. SE22 77 CE
Royal Oak Rd. E8 57 CE
Wilton Way
Royal Oak Rd., Bexh. 79 CC
Royal Oak Rd., Wok. 100 AF
Royal Opera Arc. SW1 3
Royal Par. SE3 68 CG
Royal Par. W5 55 BL
Western Ave.
Royal Par., Chis. 78 CM
Royal Par. Ms., Chis. 78 CM
Royal Par.
Royal Pier Ms., Grav. 81 DG
Royal Pier Rd.
Royal Pier Rd., Grav. 81 DG
Royal Pl. SE10 67 CF
Royal Rd. E16 58 CJ
Royal Rd. SE17 66 BY
Royal Rd., Dart. 80 CX
Royal Rd., St.Alb. 9 BJ
Royal Rd., Sid. 79 CP
Royal Rd., Tedd. 74 BG
Royal Route, Wem. 46 BL
Royal St. SE1 4
Royal St. SE1 66 BX
Royal Victor Pl. E3 57 CC
Old Ford Rd.
Royal Wk., Wall. 86 BV
Prince Charles Way
Royalty Ms. W1 1
Royalty Ms. W1 56 BW
Dean St.
Royce Clo., Brox. 12 CD
Roycraft Ave., Bark. 58 CN
Roycraft Clo., Bark. 58 CN
Roycroft Clo. E18 40 CH
Roycroft Clo. SW2 76 BY
High Trees
Roydene Rd. SE18 68 CN
Roydon Clo. SW11 66 BU
Reform St.
Roydon Clo., Loug. 40 CK
Roydon Ct., Hem.H. 8 AZ
Elstree Rd.
Roydon Rd., Harl. 13 CJ
Roydon St. SW11 66 BV
Royle Clo., Ger.Cr. 34 AS
Royle Clo., Rom. 50 CU
Royle Cres. W13 54 BJ
Roymount Ct., Twick. 74 BH
Royston Ave. E4 39 CE
Royston Ave., Sutt. 86 BT
Royston Ave., Wall. 95 BW
Royston Ave., Wey. 92 AY
Royston Clo., Houns. 63 BC
Royston Clo., Walt. 83 BC
Royston Ct., Rich. 65 BL
Royston Ct., Surb. 85 BM
Royston Gdns., Ilf. 49 CJ
Royston Gro., Pnr. 36 BE
Royston Pk. Rd., Pnr. 36 BE
Royston Rd. SE20 87 CC
Royston Rd., Dart. 79 CT
Royston Rd., Rich. 75 BL
Royston Rd., Rom. 42 CX
Royston Rd., St.Alb. 9 BJ
Royston Rd., Wey. 92 AY
Royston St. E2 57 CC
Roystons, The, Surb. 85 BM
Rozel Rd. SW4 66 BW
Rubastic Rd., Sthl. 64 BD
Rubens Rd., Nthlt. 54 BD
Rubens St. SE6 77 CD
Ruberoid Rd., Enf. 30 CD
Ruby Clo., Slou. 61 AN
Ruby Rd. E17 48 CE
Ruby St. SE15 67 CB
Ruckholt Clo. E10 48 CE
Ruckholt Rd. E10 48 CE
Rucklers La., Kings L. 17 AW
Ruckles Way, Amer. 25 AO
Station Rd.
Rucklidge Ave. NW10 55 BO
Rudall Cres. NW3 47 BT
Willoughby Rd.
Rudd St. SE18 68 CL
Ruddles Way, Wind. 61 AL
Ruden Way, Epsom 103 BP
Rudge Rd., Wey. 91 AV
Rudland Rd., Bexh. 69 CR
Rudloe Rd. SW12 76 BW
Rudolph Rd. E13 58 CG
Rudolph Rd. NW6 56 BS
Rudolph Rd., Bush. 27 BF
Rudwick Clo., Wal.Cr. 21 CD
Ashdown Cres.
Rudyard Gro. NW7 37 BN
Rue de St. Laurence, Wal.Abb. 21 CF
Quaker La.

ffets Wd., Grav. 81 DH50
ffetts, The, S.Croy. 96 CB57
ffetts Clo., S.Croy. 96 CB57
ffetts Way, Tad. 103 BR62
fford Clo., Har. 45 BJ32
fford St. N1 56 BX37
fus Clo., Ruis. 45 BE34
fus St. EC1 57 CA38
Old St.
fus St. N1 2 M3
gby Ave. N9 39 CA26
gby Ave., Grnf. 54 BG36
gby Ave., Wem. 45 BJ35
gby Clo., Har. 45 BH31
gby Gdns., Dag. 59 CP36
gby La., Sutt. 94 BQ58
gby Rd. NW9 46 BM31
gby Rd. W4 65 BO41
gby Rd., Dag. 59 CO36
gby Rd., Twick. 74 BH46
ugby St. WC1 2 B5
gby St. WC1 56 BX38
gby Way, Rick. 26 AZ25
gg St. E14 57 CE40
gged La., Wal.Abb. 22 CJ20
ggles-Brise Rd., Ashf. 73 AX49
islip Clo., Grnf. 54 BF38
islip Rd., Grnf. 54 BE38
islip Rd., Nthlt. 54 BD37
islip Rd. E. W7 54 BG38
islip Rd. E. W13 54 BG38
islip Rd. E., Grnf. 54 BG38
islip St. SW17 76 BU49
m Clo. E1 57 CB40
mania Wk., Grav. 81 DJ48
Cervia Way
mballs Clo., Hem.H. 8 AZ15
mballs Rd., Hem.H. 8 AZ15
mbold Rd. SW6 66 BS43
mbold Rd., Hodd. 12 CF11
msey Clo., Hmptn. 74 BE50
msley, Wal.Cr. 21 CB17
msley Rd. SW9 66 BX45
nbury Circ. NW9 46 BN34
ncie Clo., St.Alb. 9 BJ11
nciman Clo., Orp. 98 CP58
ncorn Clo. N17 48 CB31
Yarmouth Cres.
ncorn Cres., Hem.H. 8 AY11
ncorn Pl. W11 55 BR40
ndell Cres. NW4 46 BP32
ndells, Harl. 14 CO13
nham Rd., Hem.H. 8 AY14
nnelfield, Har. 45 BH34
nnemede Ct., Egh. 72 AT49
nnemede Rd., Egh. 72 AS49
nning Horse Yd., Brent. 65 BL43
Pottery Rd.
nning Waters, Brwd. 122 DD28
nnymede SW19 86 BT51
nnymede Clo., Twick. 74 BF46
nnymede Cres. SW16 86 BW51
nnymede Gdns., Grnf. 54 BG37
nnymede Gdns., Twick. 74 BF46
nnymede Rd., Twick. 74 BF46
nrig Hill, Amer. 25 AP21
nsley, Welw.G.C. 5 BR6
ntley Wd. La., Guil. 109 AS66
nway, The, Ruis. 45 BD35
pack St. SE16 67 CC41
St. Mary Ch. St.
pert Ave., Wem. 46 BL35
upert Ct. W1 1 N10
pert Gdns. SW9 66 BY44
pert Rd. N19 47 BW34
pert Rd. NW6 55 BR37
pert Rd. W4 65 BO41
pert Rd., Guil. 118 AQ71
upert St. W1 1 N10
pert St. W1 56 BW40
ral Clo., Horn. 50 CU34
ral Vale, Grav. 81 DF47
ral Way SW16 76 BV50
ral Way, Red. 121 BV70
scoe Dr., Wok. 100 AT62
Pembroke Rd.
scoe Rd. E16 58 CG39
scombe Dr., St.Alb. 18 BG16
scombe Gdns., Slou. 62 AQ43
scombe Way, Felt. 73 BB47
sh Grn. Gdns., Rom. 50 CS33
sh Grn. Rd., Rom. 50 CR33
sh Gro. St. SE18 68 CK42
sh Hill Ms. SW11 66 BV45
Rush Hill Rd.
sh Hill Rd. SW11 66 BV45
sham Pk. Ave., Egh. 72 AS50
sham Rd. SW12 76 BU46
sham Rd., Egh. 72 AS50
shbrook Cres. E17 39 CD30
shbrook Rd. SE9 78 CM48
shcroft Rd. E4 39 CE29
shcroft Rd. SW2 66 BY45
shden Clo. SE19 77 BZ50
shden Gdns. NW7 37 BQ29
shden Gdns., Ilf. 49 CL31
shdene SE2 69 CP41
shdene Ave., Barn. 38 BU26
shdene Clo., Nthlt. 54 BD37
shdene Cres., Nthlt. 54 BD37
shdene Gdns., Ilf. 40 CL30
shdene Rd., Brwd. 42 DB26
shdene Rd., Pnr. 45 BD32
shdene Wk., West. 106 CJ62
shdon Clo., Grays 71 DD41
shen Wk., Cars. 86 BT54
shes Mead, Harl. 13 CN12
shes Mead, Uxb. 53 AX37
shet Rd., Orp. 89 CO51
shett Clo., T.Ditt. 84 BJ54
shett Dr., Dor. 119 BJ73
shett Gdns., Surb. 84 BJ54
shett La., Chess. 93 BK59
shett Rd., T.Ditt. 84 BJ54

Rushetts Rd., Reig. 121 BT72
Rushetts Rd., Sev. 99 CZ57
Rushey Clo., N.Mal. 85 BN52
Rushey Grn. SE6 77 CE47
Rushey Hill, Enf. 29 BX24
Rushey Mead SE4 77 CE46
Rushfield, Pot.B. 19 BQ20
Rushfield, Saw. 6 CQ6
Rushford Rd. SE4 77 CD46
Rushgrove Ave. NW9 46 BO32
Rushleigh Ave., Chsnt. 21 CC18
Rushley Clo., Grays 71 DE40
Rushley Clo., Kes. 97 CJ56
Rushmead E2 57 CB38
Florida St.
Rushmead, Rich. 74 BJ48
Rushmead Clo., Croy. 96 CA56
Rushmead Clo., Edg. 37 BM27
Rushmere Ave., Upmin. 51 CY35
Rushmere La., Chesh. 16 AQ17
Rushmoor Clo., Guil. 118 AP69
Rushmoor Clo., Pnr. 44 BC31
Rushmoor Clo., Rick. 35 AX27
Rushmoor Ct., Wor.Pk. 85 BP55
Rushmore Clo., Brom. 88 CK52
Rushmore Cres. E5 48 CC35
Rushmore Hill, Orp. 98 CP58
Rushmore Hill Rd., Sev. 98 CP60
Rushmore Rd. E5 48 CC35
Rusholme Ave., Dag. 50 CR34
Rusholme Gro. SE19 77 CA49
Rusholme Rd. SW15 75 BQ46
Rushout Ave., Har. 45 BJ32
Rushton Ave., Wat. 26 BC21
Rushton St. N1 57 BZ37
Rushworth Gdns. NW4 46 BP31
Rushworth Rd., Reig. 121 BS70
Rushworth St. SE1 4 G4
Rushworth St. SE1 66 BY41
Rushymead, Sev. 108 CX62
Ruskin Ave. E12 58 CK36
Ruskin Ave., Felt. 73 BB46
Ruskin Ave., Rich. 65 BM43
Ruskin Ave., Upmin. 51 CY33
Ruskin Ave., Wal.Abb. 22 CG20
Ruskin Ave., Well. 69 CO45
Ruskin Clo. NW11 47 BS32
Ruskin Clo., Chsnt. 21 CA16
Hammond St. Rd.
Ruskin Dr., Orp. 88 CN55
Ruskin Dr., Well. 69 CO45
Ruskin Dr., Wor.Pk. 85 BP55
Ruskin Gdns. W5 54 BK38
Ruskin Gdns., Har. 46 BL31
Ruskin Gdns., Rom. 41 CU30
Ruskin Gro., Dart. 80 CX46
Ruskin Gro., Well. 69 CO44
Ruskin Pk. Ho. SE5 67 BZ45
Ruskin Rd. N17 39 CA30
Ruskin Rd., Belv. 69 CR42
Ruskin Rd., Cars. 95 BU56
Ruskin Rd., Croy. 86 BY55
Ruskin Rd., Grays 71 DG42
Ruskin Rd., Islw. 64 BH45
Ruskin Rd., Sthl. 54 BE40
Ruskin Rd., Stai. 72 AV50
Ruskin Wk. N9 39 CB27
Ruskin Wk. SE24 77 BZ46
Ruskin Wk., Brom. 88 CK53
Ruskin Way SW19 86 BT51
Brangwyn Cres.
Rusland Ave., Orp. 88 CM55
Rusland Pk. Rd., Har. 45 BH31
Rusper Clo. NW2 46 BQ34
Rusper Clo., Stan. 36 BK28
Rusper Ct. SW9 66 BX44
Clapham Rd.
Rusper Rd. N22 38 BY30
Rusper Rd., Dag. 59 CP36
Russelcroft Rd., WelwG.C. 5 BQ7
Russell Ave. N22 38 BY30
Russell Ave., St.Alb. 9 BG13
Russell Clo. NW10 55 BN36
Russell Clo. SE7 68 CJ43
Russell Clo., Amer. 25 AR23
Russell Clo., Beck. 87 CE52
Russell Clo., Bexh. 69 CR45
Russell Clo., Brwd. 42 DA26
Russell Clo., Dart. 69 CU45
Russell Clo., Nthwd. 35 BA28
Russell Clo., Ruis. 45 BD34
Russell Clo., Tad. 112 BP66
Russell Clo., Wok. 100 AR61
Russell Ct. SW1 3 M3
Russell Ct. SW1 56 BW40
Cleveland Row
Russell Ct., Chesh. 16 AO18
Russell Ct., Guil. 118 AR69
Rowan Clo.
Russell Ct., Lthd. 102 BJ64
Russell Ct., St.Alb. 18 BF18
Black Boy Wd.
Russell Cres., Wat. 26 BB21
Russell Dr., Stai. 73 AX46
Russell Gdns. N20 38 BU27
Russell Gdns. NW11 46 BR32
Russell Gdns. W14 65 BR41
Russell Gdns., Rich. 74 BK48
Russell Gdns., West Dr. 63 AZ43
Russell Gdns. Ms. W14 65 BR41
Russell Grn. Clo., Pur. 95 BY58
Russell Gro. NW7 37 BO28
Russell Gro. SW9 66 BY43
Russell Hill, Pur. 95 BX58
Russell Hill Pl., Pur. 95 BY59
Russell Hill Rd., Pur. 95 BY58
Russell Kerr Clo. W4 65 BN43
Burlington La.
Russell La. N20 38 BU27
Russell La., Wat. 26 BA21
Russell Mead, Har. 36 BH29
Russell Pl. NW3 47 BU35
Aspern Rd.

Russell Pl. SE16 67 CD41
Onega Gate
Russell Pl. SW1 66 BW42
Vauxhall Bri. Rd.
Russell Pl., Hem.H. 8 AW15
Russell Pl., S.at H. 90 CX51
Russell Rd. E4 39 CD28
Russell Rd. E10 48 CE32
Russell Rd. E16 58 CH39
Russell Rd. E17 48 CD31
Russell Rd. N8 47 BW32
Russell Rd. N13 38 BX29
Russell Rd. N15 48 CA32
Russell Rd. N20 38 BU27
Russell Rd. NW9 46 BO32
Russell Rd. SW19 76 BS50
Russell Rd. W14 65 BR41
Russell Rd., Buck.H. 40 CH26
Russell Rd., Enf. 30 CA22
Russell Rd., Grav. 81 DH46
Russell Rd., Grays 71 DD42
Russell Rd., Mitch. 86 BU52
Russell Rd., Nthlt. 45 BG35
Russell Rd., Nthwd. 35 BA27
Russell Rd., Shep. 83 AZ54
Russell Rd., Til. 71 DF44
Russell Rd., Twick. 74 BH46
Russell Rd., Walt. 83 BC53
Russell Rd., Wok. 100 AR61
Russell Sq. WC1 1 Q5
Russell Sq. WC1 56 BX38
Russell St. WC2 2 A10
Russell St. WC2 56 BX40
Russell St., Wind. 61 AO44
Russell Wk., Rich. 75 BL46
Pyrland Rd.
Russell Way, Sutt. 95 BS56
Russells Footpath SW16 76 BX49
Russells Ride, Chsnt. 21 CD19
Russels, Tad. 103 BQ64
Russet Ave., Shep. 83 BB52
Russet Clo., Stai. 72 AV46
Russet Clo., Uxb. 53 BA38
Russet Clo., Walt. 84 BE55
Broad Clo.
Russet Cres. N7 47 BX35
Stock Orchard Cres.
Russet Dr., Croy. 87 CD54
Russet Way SE13 67 CE44
Conington Rd.
Russet Way, Dor. 119 BK73
Russets, The, Ger.Cr. 34 AR30
Russets Clo., Wok. 100 AS61
Russett Clo., Cat. 114 CB66
Russett Clo., Orp. 98 CO56
Russett Way, Swan. 89 CS51
Russett Wd., Welw.G.C. 5 BT8
Russetts, Horn. 51 CW31
Russetts Clo. E4 39 CF28
Larkshall Rd.
Russia Ct. EC2 2 J9
Russia Dock Rd. SE16 57 CD40
Russia La. E2 57 CC37
Russia Row EC2 2 J9
Russia Row EC2 57 BZ39
Milk St.
Russington Rd., Shep. 83 BA53
Rust Sq. SE5 67 BZ43
Rusthall Ave. W4 65 BN42
Rusthall Clo., Croy. 87 CC53
Rustic Ave. SW16 76 BV50
Rustic Clo., Upmin. 51 CZ33
Rustic Pl., Wem. 45 BK35
Rustington Wk., Mord. 85 BR54
Ruston Ave., Surb. 85 BM54
Ruston Ms. W11 55 BR39
Ruston St. E3 57 CD37
Rutford Rd. SW16 76 BX49
Ruth Clo., Stan. 46 BL31
Ruthen Clo., Epsom 94 BM60
Rutherford Clo., Sutt. 95 BT57
Rutherford St. SW1 3 N8
Rutherford Way, Bush. 36 BG26
Rutherford Way, Wem. 46 BM35
Rutherglen Rd. SE2 69 CO43
Rutherwick Ri., Couls. 104 BX62
Rutherwyk Rd., Cher. 82 AV54
Rutherwyke Clo., Epsom 94 BP57
Ruthin Clo. NW9 46 BO32
Ruthin Rd. SE3 68 CH43
Ruthven Ave., Wal.Cr. 21 CC20
Ruthven St. E9 57 CC37
Lauriston Rd.
Rutland App., Horn. 51 CX32
Rutland Ave., Sid. 79 CO47
Rutland Ave., Slou. 52 AO39
Rutland Clo. SW14 65 BN45
Rutland Clo. SW19 76 BU50
Rutland Rd.
Rutland Clo., Bex. 79 CP47
Rutland Clo., Chess. 94 BL57
Rutland Clo., Dart. 80 CV46
Rutland Clo., Epsom 94 BN58
Rutland Clo., Red. 121 BU70
Rutland Ct. SE5 67 BZ45
Denmark Hill
Rutland Dr., Horn. 51 CX32
Rutland Dr., Mord. 85 BR53
Rutland Dr., Rich. 74 BK47
Rutland Gdns. N4 47 BY32
Rutland Gdns. SW7 3 D5
Rutland Gdns. SW7 66 BU41
Rutland Gdns. W13 54 BJ39
Rutland Gdns., Croy. 96 CA56
Rutland Gdns., Dag. 50 CP35
Rutland Gdns., Hem.H. 8 AY13
Rutland Gdns., Rich. 74 BK47
Rutland Gdns. Ms. SW7 3 D5
Rutland Gate SW7 3 D5
Rutland Gate SW7 66 BU41
Rutland Gate, Belv. 69 CR42
Rutland Gate, Brom. 88 CG52
Rutland Gate Ms. SW7 3 C5
Rutland Gate Ms. SW7 66 BU41

Rutland Gro. W6 65 BP42
Rutland Ms. NW8 56 BS37
Rutland Ms. E. SW7 3 C6
Rutland Ms. S. SW7 3 C6
Rutland Pk. NW2 55 BQ36
Rutland Pk. SE6 77 CD48
Rutland Pl. EC1 2 G6
Rutland Pl., Bush. 36 BG26
The Butts
Rutland Rd. E7 58 CJ36
Rutland Rd. E9 57 CC37
Rutland Rd. E11 49 CH32
Rutland Rd. E17 48 CE32
Rutland Rd. SW19 76 BU50
Rutland Rd., Har. 45 BG32
Rutland Rd., Hayes 63 BA42
Rutland Rd., Ilf. 49 CL35
Rutland Rd., Sthl. 54 BF38
Rutland Rd., Twick. 74 BG48
Rutland St. SW7 3 D6
Rutland St. SW7 66 BU41
Rutland Wk. SE6 77 CD48
Rutland Way, Orp. 89 CP53
Rutley Clo. SE17 66 BY43
Royal Rd.
Rutlish Rd. SW19 86 BS51
Rutson Rd., Wey. 92 AY60
Rutter Gdns., Mitch. 86 BT52
Rutters Clo., West Dr. 63 AZ41
Ruttesland St. N1 57 CA37
Hoxton St.
Rutts, The, Bush. 36 BG26
Rutts Ter. SE14 67 CC44
Ruvigny Gdns. SW15 65 BQ45
Ruxbury Rd., Cher. 82 AU53
Ruxley Clo., Epsom 94 BM56
Ruxley Clo., Sid. 79 CP50
Ruxley Cres., Esher 93 BJ57
Ruxley La., Epsom 94 BM57
Ruxley Ms., Epsom 94 BM56
Ruxley Ridge, Esher 93 BJ57
Ruxton Clo., Swan. 89 CT52
Ryall Clo., St.Alb. 18 BE18
Ryan Clo. SE3 68 CJ45
Ryan Way, Wat. 27 BD23
Ryarsh Cres., Orp. 97 CN56
Rycott Path SE22 77 CB47
Lordship La.
Rycroft Cres., Barn. 28 BP25
Rycroft La., Sev. 116 CT68
Rycroft Way N17 48 CA31
Ryculff Sq. SE3 68 CG44
Rydal Clo. NW4 37 BR30
Rydal Clo., Pur. 96 BZ60
Rydal Cres., Grnf. 54 BJ37
Rydal Dr., Bexh. 69 CQ44
Rydal Dr., W.Wick. 88 CG55
Rydal Gdns. NW9 46 BO32
Rydal Gdns. SW15 75 BO49
Rydal Gdns., Houns. 74 BF46
Rydal Gdns., Wem. 45 BK33
Rydal Rd. SW16 76 BW49
Rydal Way, Egh. 72 AT50
Rydal Way, Enf. 30 CC25
Rydal Way, Ruis. 45 BD35
Ryde, The, Hat. 10 BQ11
Ryde, The, Stai. 83 AW51
Ryde Clo., Wok. 101 AX64
Ryde Heron, Wok. 100 AP62
Ryde Pl., Twick. 74 BK46
Ryde Vale Rd. SW12 76 BV48
Rydens Ave., Walt. 83 BC55
Rydens Clo., Walt. 84 BD55
Rydens Gro., Walt. 93 BD56
Rydens Rd., Walt. 83 BC55
Rydens Way, Wok. 100 AT63
Ryder Clo., Brom. 78 CH49
Ryder Clo., Bush. 27 BF25
Ryder Clo., Hem.H. 16 AT17
Ryder Ct. SW1 3 M2
Ryder Gdns., Rain. 59 CT36
Ryder St. SW1 3 M2
Ryder St. SW1 56 BW40
Ryder Yd. SW1 3 M2
Ryders Ave., Hat. 10 BO13
Ryders Ter. NW8 56 BT37
Rydes Ave., Guil. 118 AP69
Rydes Clo., Wok. 100 AY63
Rydes Hill Cres., Guil. 109 AP68
Rydes Hill Rd., Guil. 118 AP69
Rydings, Wind. 61 AM45
Rydon St. N1 57 BZ37
St Paul St.
Rydons Clo. SE9 68 CK45
Rydons La., Couls. 105 BZ63
Rydons Pk., Walt. 84 BD55
Rydons Wd. Clo., Couls. 105 BZ63
Rydston Clo. N7 56 BX36
Sutterton St.
Rye, The N14 38 BW26
Rye Clo., Bex. 79 CR46
Rye Clo., Guil. 118 AP69
Rye Clo., Horn. 51 CV35
Rye Cres., Orp. 89 CP54
Rye Hill Est. SE15 67 CC45
Rye Hill Pk. SE15 67 CC45
Rye Hill Rd., Epp. 14 CO15
Rye Hill Rd., Harl. 13 CM13
Rye La. SE15 67 CB44
Rye La. (Longford), Sev. 107 CT63
Rye La. (Otford), Sev. 107 CU61
Rye Pas. SE15 67 CB45
Rye Rd. SE15 67 CC45
Rye Rd., Hodd. 12 CE11
Rye Wk. SW15 75 BQ46
Rye Way, Edg. 37 BL29
Ryebrook Clo., Lthd. 102 BJ62
Ryebrook Rd., Lthd. 102 BJ62
Ryecotes Mead SE21 77 CA47
Ryecroft, Harl. 13 CL11
Ryecroft, Hat. 10 BO13
Ryecroft, Wind. 61 AM45
Ryecroft Ave., Ilf. 40 CL30
Ryecroft Ave., Twick. 74 BF47

Ryecroft Clo., Hem.H. 8 BA14
Poynders Hill
Ryecroft Ct., St.Alb. 10 BL13
Fourways
Ryecroft Rd. SE13 77 CF46
Ryecroft Rd. SW16 76 BY50
Ryecroft Rd., Orp. 88 CM53
Ryecroft Rd., Sev. 107 CU61
Ryecroft St. SW6 66 BS44
Ryedale SE22 77 CB46
Ryefield, Orp. 89 CP55
Ryefield Ave., Uxb. 53 AZ36
Ryefield Cres., Pnr. 35 BC30
Ryefield Path SW15 75 BP47
Bessborough Rd.
Ryefield Rd. SE19 77 BZ50
Ryefield Rd., Croy. 96 CC60
Ryehill Ct., N.Mal. 85 BO54
Ryeland Clo., West Dr. 53 AY39
Ryelands, Welw.G.C. 5 BR9
Ryelands Clo., Cat. 105 CA64
Ryelands Ct., Lthd. 102 BJ62
Kingston Rd.
Ryelands Cres. SE12 78 CJ46
Ryfold Rd. SW19 76 BS48
Ryhope Rd. N11 38 BV28
Ryhkill, Grays 71 DG41
Ryland Clo., Felt. 73 BB49
Ryland Rd. NW5 56 BV36
Rylandes Rd. NW2 46 BP34
Rylandes Rd., S.Croy. 96 CD58
Rylett Cres. W12 65 BO41
Rylett Rd. W12 65 BO41
Rylston Rd. N13 39 BZ27
Rylston Rd. SW6 65 BR43
Ryman Ct., Rick. 25 AU25
Stag La.
Rymer Rd. SW18 66 BT45
Alma Rd.
Rymer Rd., Croy. 87 CA54
Rymer St. SE24 76 BY46
Rymill Clo., Hem.H. 16 AT17
Rymill St. E16 58 CL40
Rysbrack St. SW3 3 E6
Rysbrack St. SW3 66 BU41
Rysted La., West. 115 CM66
Rythe Ct., T.Ditt. 84 BJ54
Rythe Rd., Esher 93 BH56
Ryvers Rd., Slou. 62 AS41

S

Sabah Ct., Ashf. 73 AZ49
Sabbarton St. E16 58 CG39
Victoria Dock Rd.
Sabella Ct. E3 57 CE37
Mostyn Gro.
Sabina Rd., Grays 71 DH42
Sabine Rd. SW11 66 BU45
Sabines Rd., Rom. 33 CV23
Sable Clo., Houns. 64 BD45
Sable St. N1 56 BY36
Sach Rd. E5 48 CB34
Sackville Ave., Brom. 88 CH54
Sackville Clo., Har. 45 BG34
Sackville Clo., Sev. 107 CU64
Sackville Cres., Rom. 42 CW30
Sackville Est. SW16 76 BX48
Sackville Gdns., Ilf. 49 CK33
Sackville Rd., Dart. 80 CV48
Sackville Rd., Sutt. 95 BS57
Sackville St. W1 3 M1
Sackville St. W1 56 BW40
Sackville Way SE22 77 CB47
Wilkie Way
Sacombe Rd., Hem.H. 7 AV12
Saddington St., Grav. 81 DH47
Saddlers Clo., Borwd. 28 BN25
Farriers Way
Saddlers Clo., Pnr. 36 BF29
Saddlers Mead, Harl. 14 CO11
Saddlers Ms., Wem. 45 BH35
The Boltons
Saddlers Pk., Eyns. 90 CV55
Saddlers Way, Epsom 103 BN63
Saddlescombe Way N12 38 BS28
Saddleworth Rd., Rom. 42 CV29
Saddleworth Sq., Rom. 42 CV29
Sadler Clo., Mitch. 86 BU51
Sadlers Clo., Guil. 118 AU70
Sadlers Ride, E.Mol. 84 BG51
Sadlier Rd., St.Alb. 9 BH14
Saffron Clo. NW11 46 BR32
Saffron Clo., Brwd. 123 DE32
Saffron Clo., Hodd. 12 CD11
Saffron Clo., Slou. 62 AQ44
Saffron Hill EC1 2 E6
Saffron Hill EC1 56 BY38
Saffron La., Hem.H. 8 AW13
Saffron Platt, Guil. 109 AQ68
Saffron Rd., Rom. 41 CS30
Saffron St. EC1 2 E6
Saffron St. EC1 56 BY39
Saffron Hill
Sage St. E1 57 CC40
Cable St.
Sage Way WC1 2 B3
Saigasso Clo. E16 58 CJ39
Royal Rd.
Sail St. SE11 4 C8
Sail St. SE11 66 BX42
Sainfoin Rd. SW17 76 BV48
Sainsbury Rd. SE19 77 BZ49
St. Agathas Dr., Kings.T. 75 BL50
St. Agathas Gro., Cars. 86 BU54
St. Agathas Wk., Kings.T. 75 BM50
Alexandra Rd.
St. Agnells Ct., Hem.H. 8 AZ11
St. Agnells La., Hem.H. 8 AY11

Street	Page	Grid
St. Agnes Clo. E9	57	CC37
Gore Rd.		
St. Agnes Pl. SE11	66	BY43
St. Aidans Rd. SE22	77	CB46
St. Aidans Rd. W13	64	BJ41
St. Aidans Way, Grav.	81	DJ48
St. Albans Ave. E6	58	CK38
St. Albans Ave. W4	65	BN42
St. Albans Ave., Felt.	74	BD49
St. Albans Ave., Upmin.	51	CZ34
St. Albans Ave., Wey.	83	AZ55
St. Albans Clo. NW11	47	BS33
North End Rd.		
St. Albans Clo., Grav.	81	DH48
St. Albans Cres. N22	38	BY30
St. Albans Gdns., Grav.	81	DH48
St. Albans Gdns., Tedd.	74	BJ49
St. Albans Gro. W8	66	BS41
St. Albans Gro., Cars.	86	BU54
St. Albans Hill, Hem.H.	8	AY15
St. Albans La. NW11	47	BS33
West Heath Bri.		
St. Albans La., Abb.L.	17	BC16
St. Albans Ms. W2	**1**	**B6**
St. Albans Ms. W2	56	BT39
Edgware Rd.		
St. Albans Rd. NW5	47	BV34
St. Albans Rd. NW10	55	BO37
St. Albans Rd., Barn.	28	BQ22
St. Albans Rd., Dart.	80	CW47
St. Albans Rd., Epp.	23	CP18
St. Albans Rd., Hat.	10	BP12
St. Albans Rd., Hem.H.	8	AX14
St. Albans Rd., Ilf.	49	CN33
St. Albans Rd., Kings.T.	75	BL50
St. Albans Rd., Kings.T.	75	BL50
St. Albans Rd., Pot.B.	19	BO19
St. Albans Rd., Reig.	121	BS70
St. Albans Rd., St.Alb.	9	BJ11
St. Albans Rd., Sutt.	94	BR56
St. Albans Rd., Wat.	26	BC23
St. Albans Rd. (Garston), Wat.	18	BD20
St. Albans Rd., Wdf.Grn.	40	CH29
St. Albans Rd. E., Hat.	10	BP12
St. Albans Rd. W., Hat.	10	BN12
St. Albans St. SW1	**3**	**N1**
St. Albans St. SW1	56	BW40
Jermyn St.		
St. Albans St., Wind.	61	AO44
St. Albans Ter. W6	65	BR43
St. Alfege Pas. SE10	67	CF43
Roan St.		
St. Alfege Rd. SE7	68	CJ43
St. Alphage Ct. NW9	46	BN31
St. Alphage Gdns. EC2	**2**	**J7**
St. Alphage Gdns. EC2	57	BZ39
St. Alphege Rd. N9	39	CC26
St. Alphonsus Rd. SW4	66	BW45
St. Amunds Clo. SE6	77	CE49
St. Andrew St. EC4	**2**	**E7**
St. Andrew St. EC4	56	BY39
St. Andrews Ave., Horn.	50	CU35
St. Andrews Ave., Wem.	45	BJ35
St. Andrews Ave., Wind.	61	AM44
St. Andrews Clo. N12	38	BT28
Woodside Ave.		
St. Andrews Clo. NW2	46	BP34
St. Andrews Clo., Epp.	14	CS15
St. Andrews Clo., Islw.	64	BH44
St. Andrews Clo., Reig.	121	BS71
St. Marys Rd.		
St. Andrews Clo., Ruis.	45	BD34
St. Andrews Clo., Shep.	83	BA52
St. Andrews Clo., Stai.	72	AS47
St. Andrews Clo., Stan.	36	BK30
St. Andrews Clo., Wind.	72	AQ46
St. Andrews Ct. SW18	76	BT48
Waynflete St.		
St. Andrews Cres., Wind.	61	AM44
St. Andrews Dr., Orp.	89	CO53
St. Andrews Dr., Stan.	36	BK30
St. Andrews Gro. N16	48	BZ33
St. Andrews Hill EC4	**2**	**G10**
St. Andrews Hill EC4	56	BY39
St. Andrews Ms. N16	48	CA33
Dunsmure Rd.		
St. Andrews Pl. NW1	**1**	**K4**
St. Andrews Pl. NW1	56	BV38
St. Andrews Pl., Brwd.	122	DC27
St. Andrews Rd. E11	49	CG32
St. Andrews Rd. E13	58	CH38
St. Andrews Rd. E17	39	CC30
St. Andrews Rd. N9	39	CC26
St. Andrews Rd. NW9	46	BN33
St. Andrews Rd. NW10	55	BP36
St. Andrews Rd. NW11	46	BR32
St. Andrews Rd. W3	55	BO40
St. Andrews Rd. W7	64	BH41
St. Andrews Rd. W14	65	BR43
St. Andrews Rd., Cars.	86	BU55
St. Andrews Rd., Couls.	104	BV61
St. Andrews Rd., Croy.	96	BZ56
St. Andrews Rd., Enf.	30	BZ24
St. Andrews Rd., Hem.H.	8	AX15
St. Andrews Rd., Ilf.	49	CK33
St. Andrews Rd., Rom.	50	CS32
St. Andrews Rd., Sid.	79	CP48
St. Andrews Rd., Surb.	84	BK53
St. Andrews Rd., Til.	71	DF44
St. Andrews Rd., Uxb.	53	AY37
St. Andrews Rd., Wat.	36	BD27
St. Andrews Sq. W11	55	BR39
St. Marks Rd.		
St. Andrews Sq., Surb.	84	BK53
St. Andrews Wk., Cob.	101	BC61
St. Andrews Way E3	57	CE38
St. Andrews Way, Oxt.	115	CK69
St. Andrews Way, Slou.	61	AL40
St. Anne St. E14	57	CD39
St. Annes Ave., Stai.	73	AX47
St. Annes Clo. N6	47	BV34
St. Annes Clo., Chsnt.	21	CA17
St. Annes Clo., Grays	71	DD40

Street	Page	Grid
St. Annes Clo., Wat.	36	BD28
St. Annes Ct. W1	**1**	**N9**
St. Annes Ct. W1	56	BW39
Wardour St.		
St. Annes Gdns. NW10	55	BL38
St. Annes Pas. E14	57	CD39
Newell St.		
St. Annes Rd. E11	48	CF34
St. Annes Rd., Brwd.	122	DE23
St. Annes Rd., Cher.	82	AV53
St. Annes Rd., St.Alb.	18	BK17
St. Annes Rd., Uxb.	44	AX31
St. Annes Rd., Wem.	45	BK35
St. Annes Row E14	57	CD39
St. Anne St.		
St. Anns, Bark.	58	CM37
St. Anns Clo., Cher.	82	AV53
St. Anns Cres. SW18	76	BT46
St. Anns Gdns. NW5	56	BV36
Queens Cres.		
St. Anns Hill SW18	76	BS46
St. Anns Hill Rd., Cher.	82	AU53
St. Anns La. SW1	**3**	**P6**
St. Anns La. SW1	66	BW41
Old Pye St.		
St. Anns Pk. Rd. SW18	76	BT46
St. Anns Pas. SW13	65	BO45
Cross St.		
St. Anns Rd. N9	39	CA27
St. Anns Rd. N15	47	BY32
St. Anns Rd. SW13	65	BO44
St. Anns Rd. W11	55	BQ40
St. Anns Rd., Cher.	82	AV53
St. Anns Rd., Har.	45	BH32
St. Anns St. SW1	**3**	**P6**
St. Anns St. SW1	66	BW41
St. Anns St., Bark.	58	CM37
Morley Rd.		
St. Anns Ter. NW8	56	BT37
St. Anns Vill. W11	55	BQ40
St. Anns Way, S.Croy.	95	BY57
St. Anselms Pl. W1	**1**	**J9**
St. Anselms Pl. W1	56	BV40
Davies St.		
St. Anselms Rd., Hayes	63	BB41
St. Anthonys Ave., Hem.H.	8	AZ14
St. Anthonys Ave., Wdf.Grn.	40	CJ29
St. Anthonys Clo. E1	57	CB40
St. Anthonys Clo. SW17	76	BU48
College Gdns.		
St. Anthonys Rd. E7	58	CH36
St. Anthonys Way, Felt.	63	BB45
St. Arvans Clo., Croy.	87	CA55
St. Asaph Rd. SE4	67	CC45
St. Aubyns Ave. SW19	75	BR49
St. Aubyns Ave., Houns.	74	BF46
St. Aubyns Clo., Orp.	88	CN55
St. Aubyns Gdns., Orp.	88	CN55
St. Aubyns Rd. SE19	77	CA50
St. Audrey Ave., Bexh.	69	CR44
St. Audreys Clo., Hat.	10	BP13
St. Audreys Grn., Welw.G.C.	5	BR8
St. Augustine Rd., Grays	71	DG42
St. Augustines Ave. W5	55	BL37
St. Augustines Ave., Brom.	88	CK53
St. Augustines Ave., S.Croy.	96	BZ57
St. Augustines Ave., Wem.	46	BL34
St. Augustines Clo., Brox.	12	CD13
St. Augustines Dr., Brox.	12	CD13
St. Augustines Rd. NW1	56	BW36
St. Augustines Rd., Belv.	69	CQ42
St. Austell Clo., Edg.	37	BL30
St. Austell Rd. SE13	67	CF44
St. Awdrys Rd., Bark.	58	CM36
St. Awdrys Wk., Bark.	58	CM36
St. Barnabas Clo., Beck.	87	CF51
St. Barnabas Rd. E17	48	CE32
St. Barnabas Rd., Mitch.	76	BV50
St. Barnabas Rd., Sutt.	95	BT56
St. Barnabas Rd., Wdf.Grn.	40	CH30
St. Barnabas St. SW1	**3**	**H10**
St. Barnabas St. SW1	66	BV42
St. Barnabas Ter. E9	48	CC35
Wardle St.		
St. Barnabas Vill. SW8	66	BX44
Guildford Rd.		
St. Bartholomews Clo. SE26	77	CB49
St. Bartholomews Rd. E6	58	CK37
St. Benedicts Ave., Grays	81	DJ48
St. Benedicts Clo. SW17	76	BV49
Church La.		
St. Benets Clo. SW17	76	BU48
College Gdns.		
St. Benets Gro., Cars.	86	BT54
St. Benets Pl. EC3	**2**	**L10**
St. Bernards, Croy.	87	CA55
St. Bernards Clo. SE27	77	BZ49
St. Gothard Rd.		
St. Bernards Rd. E6	58	CJ37
St. Bernards Rd., St.Alb.	9	BH13
St. Bernards Rd., Slou.	62	AR41
St. Blaise Ave., Brom.	88	CH51
St. Botolph Rd., Grav.	81	DE48
Pepper Hill		
St. Botolph Row EC3	**2**	**P9**
St. Botolph Row EC3	57	CA39
Houndsditch		
St. Botolph St. EC3	**2**	**P8**
St. Botolph St. EC3	57	CA39
St. Botolphs Ave., Sev.	107	CU65
St. Botolphs Rd., Sev.	107	CU65
St. Brelades Clo., Dor.	119	BJ72
St. Bride St. EC4	**2**	**F8**
St. Bride St. EC4	56	BY39
St. Brides Ave., Edg.	37	BL30
St. Brides Clo., Erith	69	CP41
St. Katherines Rd.		
St. Brides Pas. EC4	**2**	**F9**

Street	Page	Grid
St. Brides Pas. EC4	56	BY39
Dorset Ri.		
St. Catharines Rd., Brox.	12	CE13
St. Catherines Clo. SW17	76	BU48
College Gdns.		
St. Catherines Clo., Wok.	100	AR63
St. Catherines Ct. W4	65	BO42
Newton Gro.		
St. Catherines Cross, Red.	114	CA70
St. Catherines Dr. SE14	67	CC44
Kitto Rd.		
St. Catherines Dr., Guil.	118	AQ72
St. Catherines Est., Wok.	100	AR63
St. Catherines Fm. Ct., Ruis.	44	BA32
Howletts La.		
St. Catherines Ms. SW3	**3**	**E8**
St. Catherines Rd. E4	39	CE27
St. Catherines Rd., Ruis.	44	BA32
St. Cecilia Rd., Grays	71	DG42
St. Chads Dr., Grav.	81	DJ48
St. Chads Gdns., Rom.	50	CQ33
St. Chads Pl. WC1	**2**	**A2**
St. Chads Pl. WC1	56	BX38
St. Chads Rd., Rom.	50	CQ32
St. Chads Rd., Til.	71	DG44
St. Chads St. WC1	**2**	**A2**
St. Chads St. WC1	56	BX38
St. Charles Pl. W10	55	BR39
Chesterton Rd.		
St. Charles Pl., Wey.	92	AZ56
St. Charles Rd., Brwd.	42	DA26
St. Charles Sq. W10	55	BQ39
St. Christopher Rd., Uxb.	53	AX39
St. Christophers Clo., Islw.	64	BG44
St. Christophers Gdns., Th.Hth.	86	BY52
Warwick Rd.		
St. Christophers Ms., *Wall.*	95	BW56
Bute Rd.		
St. Christophers Pl. W1	**1**	**H8**
St. Christophers Pl. W1	56	BV39
Barrett St.		
St. Clair Clo., Ilf.	40	CK30
St. Clair Clo., Oxt.	114	CF68
St. Clair Clo., Reig.	121	BT70
St. Clair Dr., Wor.Pk.	85	BP55
St. Clair Rd. E13	58	CH37
St. Clairs Rd., Croy.	87	CA55
St. Clare St. EC3	**2**	**P9**
St. Clare St. EC3	57	CA39
Minories		
St. Clement St. N7	56	BY36
Offord Rd.		
St. Clement Way, Uxb.	53	AX39
St. Clements Ave., Grays	70	DA43
St. Clements Ct. N7	56	BY36
Arundel Sq.		
St. Clements Ct., Grays	70	CX42
Thamley		
St. Clements Heights SE26	77	CB48
Wells Pk. Rd.		
St. Clements La. WC2	**2**	**C9**
St. Clements La. WC2	56	BX39
Portugal St.		
St. Clements Rd., Grays	70	DB43
St. Clere Hill Rd., Sev.	99	CY60
St. Cloud Rd. SE27	77	BZ49
St. Columbas Clo., Grav.	81	DJ48
St. Crispins Clo. NW3	47	BU35
St. Crispins Clo., Sthl.	54	BE39
St. Crispins Way, Cher.	91	AU58
St. Cross St. EC1	**2**	**E6**
St. Cross St. EC1	56	BY39
St. Cuthberts Gdns., Pnr.	36	BE29
Westfield Pk.		
St. Cuthberts Rd. N13	38	BY29
St. Cuthberts Rd. NW2	55	BR36
St. Cuthberts Rd., Hodd.	12	CF10
St. Cyprians St. SW17	76	BU49
St. David Clo., Uxb.	53	AX39
St. Davids, Pur.	104	BX62
St. Davids Clo., Hem.H.	8	BA14
St. Davids Clo., Iver	52	AU37
St. Davids Clo., Reig.	121	BT70
St. Davids Clo., Wem.	46	BN34
St. Davids Clo., W.Wick.	87	CE54
St. Davids Cres., Grav.	81	DH49
St. Davids Dr., Brox.	12	CD13
St. Davids Dr., Edg.	37	BL30
St. Davids Pl. NW4	46	BP33
St. Davids Rd., Swan.	79	CT50
St. Denis Rd. SE27	77	BZ49
St. Denys Clo., Wok.	100	AO62
St. Dionis Rd. SW6	65	BR44
St. Donatts Rd. SE14	67	CD44
St. Dunstans All. EC3	**4**	**M1**
St. Dunstans All. EC3	57	CA40
Idol La.		
St. Dunstans Ave. W3	55	BN40
St. Dunstans Clo., Hayes	63	BB42
St. Dunstans Dr., Grav.	81	DJ49
St. Dunstans Gdns. W3	55	BN40
St. Dunstans Ave.		
St. Dunstans Hill EC3	**4**	**M1**
St. Dunstans Hill EC3	57	CA40
St. Dunstans Hill, Sutt.	94	BR57
St. Dunstans La. EC3	**4**	**M1**
St. Dunstans La. EC3	57	CA40
Idol La.		
St. Dunstans La., Beck.	87	CF53
St. Dunstans Rd. E7	58	CJ36
St. Dunstans Rd. SE25	87	CA52
St. Dunstans Rd. W6	65	BQ42
St. Dunstans Rd. W7	64	BH41
St. Dunstans Rd., Felt.	73	BB48
St. Dunstans Rd., Houns.	63	BC44
St. Ediths Rd., Sev.	108	CX62
St. Edmunds, Berk.	7	AR13
St. Edmunds Ave., Ruis.	44	BA32

Street	Page	Grid
St. Edmunds Clo. NW8	56	BU37
St. Edmunds Ter.		
St. Edmunds Clo. SW17	76	BU48
College Gdns.		
St. Edmunds Clo., Erith	69	CP41
St. Katherines Rd.		
St. Edmunds Dr., Stan.	36	BJ30
St. Edmunds La., Twick.	74	BF47
St. Edmunds Rd. N9	39	CB26
St. Edmunds Rd., Dart.	70	CX45
St. Edmunds Rd., Ilf.	49	CK32
St. Edmunds Ter. NW8	56	BU37
St. Edmunds Way, Harl.	6	CP9
St. Edwards Clo. NW11	47	BS32
Finchley Rd.		
St. Edwards Clo., Croy.	96	CF59
St. Edwards Way, Rom.	50	CT31
St. Egberts Way E4	39	CF26
St. Elmo Clo., Slou.	52	AO38
St. Elmo Cres.		
St. Elmo Cres., Slou.	52	AO38
St. Elmo Rd. W12	55	BO40
St. Elmos Rd. SE16	67	CC41
St. Erkenwald Rd., Bark.	58	CM37
St. Ermins Hill SW1	**3**	**N6**
St. Ermins Hill SW1	66	BW41
Broadway		
St. Ervans Rd. W10	55	BR39
St. Ethelredas Dr., Hat.	10	BQ12
St. Faiths Clo., Enf.	30	BZ23
St. Faiths Rd. SE21	76	BY47
St. Fidelis Rd., Erith	69	CS42
St. Fillans Rd. SE6	77	CF47
St. Francis Ave., Grav.	81	DJ49
St. Francis Clo., Orp.	88	CN53
St. Francis Clo., Pot.B.	20	BT20
St. Vincents Way		
St. Francis Clo., Wat.	35	BC26
St. Francis Rd. SE22	67	CA45
St. Francis Rd., Erith	69	CS42
West St.		
St. Francis Rd., Uxb.	43	AV32
St. Francis Way, Grays	71	DH42
St. Gabriels Clo. E11	49	CH33
St. Gabriels Rd. NW2	46	BQ35
St. George St. W1	**1**	**K10**
St. George St. W1	56	BV39
St. Georges Ave. E7	58	CH36
St. Georges Ave. N7	47	BW35
St. Georges Ave. NW9	46	BN31
St. Georges Ave. W5	64	BK41
St. Georges Ave., Grays	71	DE42
St. Georges Ave., Horn.	51	CW33
St. Georges Ave., Sthl.	54	BE40
St. Georges Ave., Wey.	92	AZ57
St. Georges Circ. SE1	**4**	**F6**
St. Georges Circ. SE1	66	BY41
St. Georges Clo. NW11	46	BR32
St. Georges Clo., Brwd.	33	DA21
St. Georges Clo., Wem.	45	BJ34
St. Georges Clo., Wey.	92	BA56
St. Georges Clo., Wind.	61	AM44
St. Georges Ct. E6	58	CK38
St. Georges Cres., Grav.	81	DH49
St. Georges Dr. SW1	**3**	**K9**
St. Georges Dr. SW1	66	BV42
St. Georges Dr., Uxb.	44	AY34
St. Georges Dr., Wat.	36	BE27
St. Georges Est., Amer.	25	AQ23
St. Georges Flds. W2	**1**	**D9**
St. Georges Flds. W2	56	BU39
Albion St.		
St. Georges Gdns., Epsom	94	BO60
St. Georges Gdns., Surb.	85	BM55
Hamilton Ave.		
St. Georges Gro. SW17	76	BT48
St. Georges La. EC3	**2**	**L10**
St. Georges La. EC3	57	BZ40
Pudding La.		
St. Georges Lo., Wey.	92	BA56
St. Georges Ms. NW1	56	BU36
Regents Pk. Rd.		
St. Georges Pl., Twick.	74	BJ47
Church St.		
St. Georges Rd. E7	58	CH36
St. Georges Rd. E10	48	CF34
St. Georges Rd. N9	39	CB27
St. Georges Rd. N13	38	BX27
St. Georges Rd. N21	38	BX27
St. Georges Rd. NW11	46	BR32
St. Georges Rd. SE1	**4**	**E6**
St. Georges Rd. SE1	66	BY41
St. Georges Rd. SW19	75	BR50
St. Georges Rd. W4	65	BN41
St. Georges Rd. W7	54	BH40
St. Georges Rd., Beck.	87	CE51
St. Georges Rd., Brom.	88	CK51
St. Georges Rd., Dag.	50	CQ35
St. Georges Rd., Enf.	30	CA22
St. Georges Rd., Felt.	74	BD49
St. Georges Rd., Hem.H.	8	AX15
St. Georges Rd., Ilf.	49	CK33
St. Georges Rd., Kings.T.	75	BM50
St. Georges Rd., Mitch.	86	BV52
St. Georges Rd., Orp.	88	CM53
St. Georges Rd., Rich.	65	BL45
St. Georges Rd., Sev.	107	CU64
St. Georges Rd., Sid.	79	CP50
St. Georges Rd., Swan.	89	CT52
St. Georges Rd., Twick.	74	BJ46
St. Georges Rd., Wall.	95	BV56
St. Georges Rd., Wat.	26	BC22
St. Georges Rd., Wey.	92	BA57
St. Georges Rd. (Addlestone), Wey.	92	AX56
St. Georges Rd. W., Brom.	88	CK51
St. Georges Sq. E7	58	CH36
St. Georges Sq. E14	57	CD40
Narrow St.		
St. Georges Sq. SE8	67	CD42
St. Georges Sq. SW1	66	BW42
St. Georges Sq., Long.	90	DC52
Bramblefield Clo.		
St. Georges Wk., Croy.	87	BZ55

Street	Page	Grid
St. Georges Way SE15	67	CA
St. Gerards Clo. SW4	76	BW
St. Germans Pl. SE3	68	CH
St. Germans Rd. SE23	77	CD
St. Giles Ave., Dag.	59	CF
St. Giles Ave., Pot.B.	19	BF
St. Giles Ave., Uxb.	44	BA
St. Giles Clo., Dag.	59	CH
St. Giles Clo., Orp.	97	CM
St. Giles High St. WC2	**1**	
St. Giles High St. WC2	56	BW
St. Giles Pas. WC2	**1**	
St. Giles Rd. SE5	67	CA
St. Gothard Rd. SE27	77	BZ
St. Gregory Clo., Ruis.	45	BD
St. Gregorys Cres., Grav.	81	DJ
St. Helena Rd. SE16	67	CC
St. Helena St. WC1	**2**	
St. Helena Ter., Rich.	74	BK
Friars La.		
St. Helens Clo., Uxb.	53	AX
St. Helens Ct., Epp.	23	CC
St. Helens Ct., Rain.	59	CU
St. Helens Cres. SW16	86	BX
St. Helens Gdns. W10	55	BQ
St. Helens Pl. EC3	**2**	
St. Helens Pl. EC3	57	CA
Bishopgate		
St. Helens Rd. SW16	86	BX
St. Helens Rd. W13	54	BJ
Dane Rd.		
St. Helens Rd., Erith	69	CF
St. Helens Rd., Ilf.	49	CK
St. Helier Ave., Mord.	86	BT
St. Heliers Ave., Houns.	74	BF
St. Heliers Rd. E10	48	CF
St. Heliers Rd., St.Alb.	9	BJ
St. Hildas Ave., Ashf.	73	AY
St. Hildas Clo. NW6	55	BQ
St. Hildas Clo. SW17	76	BU
St. Hildas Clo., Ashf.	73	AY
St. Hildas Clo., Wok.	100	AO
St. Hildas Rd. SW13	65	BP
St. Hildas Way, Grav.	81	DJ
St. Huberts Clo., Ger.Cr.	43	AS
St. Huberts La., Ger.Cr.	43	AS
St. Hughes Clo. SW17	76	BU
College Gdns.		
St. Hughs Rd. SE20	87	CB
Ridsdale Rd.		
St. Ives Clo., Welw.G.C.	5	B
St. Ivians Dr., Rom.	50	CU
St. James Ave. E2	57	CC
St. James Ave. N20	38	BU
St. James Ave. W13	54	BJ
St. James Ave., Beck.	87	CD
St. James Ave., Epsom	94	CO
St. James Ave., Ong.	24	CW
St. James Ave., Sutt.	95	BS
St. James Clo. N20	38	BU
St. James Clo. SE18	68	CM
Congleton Gro.		
St. James Clo., Epsom	94	BO
St. James Clo., Ruis.	45	BD
St. James Gdns., Wem.	54	BK
St. James La., Green.	80	CZ
St. James Ms. E14	67	CF
St. James Pl., Dart.	80	CV
St. James Pl., Enf.	30	CC
South St.		
St. James Rd. E15	49	CG
St. James Rd. N9	39	CB
St. James Rd., Mitch.	76	BV
St. James Rd., Pur.	95	BY
St. James Rd., Surb.	84	BK
St. James Rd., Sutt.	95	BS
St. James Wk. SE15	67	CA
Sumner Est.		
St. James Wk., Iver	62	AV
St. James Way, Sid.	79	CQ4
St. James's SE14	67	CD4
St. James's Ave., Grav.	81	DG4
St. James's Ave., Hmptn.	74	BG4
St. James's Clo. SW17	76	BU
St. James's Dr.		
St. James's Clo., N.Mal.	85	BO5
St. James's Cotts., Rich.	75	BL
Paradise Rd.		
St. James's Ct. SW1	**3**	**M**
St. James's Cres. SW9	66	BY
St. James's Dr. SW17	76	BU
St. James's Gdns. W11	55	BR
St. James's Gro. SW11	66	BU
Reform St.		
St. James's La. N10	47	BV3
St. James's Mkt. SW1	**3**	**N**
St. James's Pk. SW1	**3**	**N**
St. James's Pk., Croy.	87	BZ5
St. James's Pas. EC3	**2**	**N**
St. James's Pas. EC3	57	CA3
Dukes Pl.		
St. James's Path E17	48	CD3
St. James's Pl. SW1	**3**	**L**
St. James's Pl. SW1	56	BW4
St. James's Rd. SE1	67	CB4
St. James's Rd. SE16	67	CB4
St. James's Rd., Brwd.	42	DB2
St. James's Rd., Cars.	86	BU5
St. James's Rd., Chsnt.	21	BZ1
St. James's Rd., Croy.	86	BY5
St. James's Rd., Grav.	81	DG4
St. James's Rd., Hmptn.	74	BF4
St. James's Rd., Kings.T.	84	BK5
St. James's Rd., Sev.	107	CU6
St. James's Rd., Wat.	26	BC2
St. James's Row EC1	**2**	**F**
St. James's Row EC1	56	BY3
Clerkenwell Clo.		
St. James's Sq. SW1	**3**	**M**
St. James's Sq. SW1	56	BW4
St. James's St. E17	48	CD3
St. James's St. SW1	**3**	**L**
St. James's St. SW1	56	BW4
St. James's St. W6	65	BQ4

James's St., Grav. 81 DG46
James's Ter. Ms. NW8 56 BU37
James's Wk. EC1 2 F4
James's Wk. EC1 56 BY38
Sekforde St.
Jeromes Gro., Hayes 53 BA39
Joans Rd. N9 39 CA27
John Fisher Rd., Erith 69 CQ41
John St. EC1 2 F2
John St. EC1 56 BY37
Johns, Dor. 119 BK73
Johns Ave. N11 38 BU28
Johns Ave. NW10 55 BO37
Johns Ave. SW15 75 BQ46
Johns Ave., Brwd. 42 DB28
Johns Ave., Epsom 94 BO59
Johns Ave., Harl. 6 CP9
Johns Ave., Lthd. 102 BJ64
Johns Ch. Rd. E9 48 CC35
Urswick Rd.
Johns Ch. Rd., Dor. 119 BE73
Johns Clo., Guil. 118 AQ71
Johns Clo., Lthd. 102 BK64
Johns Clo., Pot.B. 20 BT20
Johns Clo., Rain. 59 CU36
Johns Clo., Wem. 46 BL35
Johns Cotts. SE20 77 CC50
Maple Rd.
Johns Cotts., Rich. 65 BL45
Kew Foot Rd.
Johns Ct. N4 47 BY34
Johns Ct., Buck.H. 40 CJ26
Johns Ct., Egh. 72 AT49
Johns Ct., Islw. 64 BH44
Johns Ct., Nthwd. 35 BB29
Murray Rd.
Johns Ct., St.Alb. 9 BJ12
Beaumont Ave.
Johns Cres. SW9 66 BY45
Johns Cres. SW9 66 BY45
Johns Cres., Islw. 64 BH44
Johns Cres., Islw. 64 BH44
Johns Dr. SW18 76 BS47
Johns Dr., Walt. 84 BD54
Johns Dr., Wind. 61 AM44
Johns Est. N1 2 L1
Johns Est. N1 57 BZ37
Johns Est. SE1 4 P5
Johns Est. SE1 67 CA41
Johns Est. SW11 66 BT44
Johns Gdns. W11 55 BR40
Johns Gro. N19 47 BW34
Johns Gro. SW13 65 BO44
Terrace Gdns.
Johns Gro., Rich. 65 BL45
Kew Foot Rd.
Johns Hill SW11 66 BT45
Johns Hill, Couls. 104 BY62
Johns Hill, Pur. 104 BY61
Johns Hill, Sev. 108 CV64
Johns Hill Gro. SW11 66 BT45
Johns Hill Rd., Wok. 100 AQ63
Johns La. EC1 2 F5
Johns La. EC1 56 BY38
Johns Ms., Wok. 100 AQ62
St. Johns Rd.
Johns Par., Sid. 79 CO49
Johns Pk. SE3 68 CG43
Johns Pas. SW19 75 BR50
Johns Path EC1 2 F5
Johns Pathway SE23 77 CC47
Devonshire Rd.
Johns Pl. EC1 2 F5
Johns Ri., Wok. 100 AQ62
Johns Rd. E4 39 CE28
Johns Rd. E6 58 CK37
Johns Rd. E16 58 CH39
Johns Rd. E17 39 CE30
Johns Rd. N15 48 CA32
Johns Rd. NW11 46 BR32
Johns Rd. SE20 77 CC50
Johns Rd. SW11 66 BU45
Johns Rd. SW19 75 BR50
Johns Rd., Bark. 58 CN37
Johns Rd., Cars. 86 BU55
Johns Rd., Croy. 86 BY55
Sylverdale Rd.
Johns Rd., Dart. 80 CY47
Johns Rd., Dor. 119 BG72
Johns Rd., E.Mol. 84 BG52
Johns Rd., Epp. 22 CN18
Johns Rd., Erith 69 CS42
Johns Rd., Felt. 74 BE49
Johns Rd., Grav. 81 DH47
Johns Rd., Grays 71 DG42
Johns Rd., Guil. 118 AQ71
Johns Rd., Har. 45 BH32
Johns Rd., Hem.H. 8 AW14
Johns Rd., Ilf. 49 CM33
Johns Rd., Islw. 64 BH44
Johns Rd., Kings.T. 84 BK51
Johns Rd., Lthd. 102 BK64
Johns Rd., Loug. 31 CK23
Johns Rd., N.Mal. 85 BN52
Johns Rd., Orp. 88 CM53
Johns Rd., Red. 121 BU71
Johns Rd., Rich. 65 BL45
Johns Rd., Rom. 41 CS28
Johns Rd., Sev. 107 CU64
Johns Rd., Sid. 79 CO49
Johns Rd., Slou. 52 AQ40
Johns Rd., Sthl. 64 BE41
Johns Rd., Sutt. 86 BS55
Johns Rd., Uxb. 53 AW37
Johns Rd., Wat. 26 BC23
Johns Rd., Well. 69 CO45
Johns Rd., Wem. 45 BK35
Johns Rd., Wind. 61 AN44
Johns Rd., Wok. 100 AQ62
Johns Sq. EC1 2 F5
Johns Sq. EC1 56 BY38
Clerkenwell Rd.
Johns Ter. E7 58 CH36

St. Johns Ter. SE18 68 CM43
St. Johns Ter. W10 55 BQ39
Harrow Rd.
St. Johns Ter., Enf. 30 BZ22
St. Johns Ter. Rd., Red. 121 BU71
St. Johns Vale SE8 67 CE44
St. Johns Vill. N19 47 BW34
St. Johns Way N19 47 BW34
St. Johns Well La., Berk. 7 AQ12
St. Johns Wd. Ct. NW8 1 B3
St. Johns Wd. Ct. NW8 56 BT38
St. Johns Wd. Rd.
St. Johns Wd. High St. NW8 1 B1
St. Johns Wd. High St. NW8 56 BT37
St. Johns Wd. Pk. NW8 56 BT37
St. Johns Wd. Rd. NW8 1 A4
St. Johns Wd. Rd. NW8 56 BT38
St. Johns Wd. Ter. NW8 1 B1
St. Johns Wd. Ter. NW8 56 BT37
St. Joseph St. SW8 66 BV44
St. Josephs Clo. W10 55 BR39
Bevington Rd.
St. Josephs Clo., Orp. 97 CN56
Stapleton Rd.
St. Josephs Dr., Sthl. 54 BE40
St. Josephs Gro. NW4 46 BP31
St. Josephs Rd. N9 39 CB26
St. Josephs Rd., Wal.Cr. 21 CD20
Swanfield Rd.
St. Josephs Vale SE3 67 CF45
St. Jude St. N16 48 CA35
St. Judes Clo., Egh. 72 AR49
St. Judes Rd. E2 57 CB37
St. Judes Rd., Egh. 72 AR49
St. Julians Clo. SW16 76 BY49
St. Julians Fm. Rd. SE27 76 BY49
St. Julians Hill, St.Alb. 9 BG15
St. Julians Rd. NW6 55 BR37
St. Julians Rd., St.Alb. 9 BG14
St. Julians Rd., Sev. 117 CW68
St. Justin Clo., Orp. 89 CP52
St. Katharines Prec. NW1 56 BV37
Outer Circle
St. Katharines Way E1 4 Q2
St. Katharines Way E1 57 CB40
St. Katherines Rd., Cat. 114 CB66
St. Katherines Rd., Erith 69 CP41
St. Katherines Row EC3 2 N10
St. Katherines Way, Berk. 7 AP11
St. Keverne Rd. SE9 78 CK49
St. Kilda Rd. W13 54 BJ40
St. Kilda Rd., Orp. 88 CN54
St. Kildas Rd. N16 48 BZ33
St. Kildas Rd., Brwd. 42 DA26
St. Kildas Rd., Har. 45 BH32
St. Kitts Rd. Ter. SE19 77 CA49
St. Laurence Clo. NW6 55 BQ37
St. Laurence Clo., Orp. 89 CP52
St. Laurence Dr., Brox. 12 CD15
St. Lawrence Clo., Abb.L. 17 BB18
St. Lawrence Clo., Edg. 37 BL29
Whitchurch La.
St. Lawrence Clo., Hem.H. 16 AT17
St. Lawrence Clo., St.Alb. 18 BE18
St. Lawrence Dr., Pnr. 44 BC32
St. Lawrence Gdns., Ing. 24 DC19
St. Lawrence Rd., Upmin. 51 CY34
St. Lawrence St. E14 57 CF40
St. Lawrence Ter. W10 55 BR39
St. Lawrence Way SW9 66 BY44
St. Lawrence Way, St.Alb. 18 BE18
St. Lawrence Way, Slou. 62 AQ41
St. Lawrences Way, Reig. 121 BS70
Church St.
St. Leonards Ave. E4 39 CF29
St. Leonards Ave., Har. 45 BK32
St. Leonards Ave., Wind. 61 AO44
St. Leonards Clo., Bush. 27 BE24
St. Leonards Clo., Well. 69 CO45
Hook La.
St. Leonards Ct. N1 2 L2
St. Leonards Ct. SW14 65 BN45
St. Leonards Rd.
St. Leonards Cres., St.alb. 9 BK10
St. Leonards Gdns., Houns. 64 BE44
St. Leonards Gdns., Ilf. 49 CM35
St. Leonards Hill, Wind. 61 AM45
St. Leonards Ri., Orp. 97 CM56
St. Leonards Rd. E14 57 CE39
St. Leonards Rd. NW10 55 BN38
St. Leonards Rd. SW14 65 BM45
St. Leonards Rd. W13 54 BK40
St. Leonards Rd., Amer. 25 AP21
St. Leonards Rd., Croy. 86 BY55
St. Leonards Rd., Epsom 103 BQ63
St. Leonards Rd., Esher 93 BH57
St. Leonards Rd., Surb. 84 BJ53
St. Leonards Rd., T.Ditt. 84 BK53
St. Leonards Rd., . Wal.Abb. 12 CF15
St. Leonards Rd., Wind. 61 AN45
St. Leonards Sq. NW5 56 BV36
St. Leonards Sq., Surb. 84 BK53
St. Leonards St. E3 57 CE38
St. Leonards Ter. SW3 66 BU42
St. Leonards Wk. SW16 76 BX50
St. Leonards Wk., Iver 62 AV41
St. Leonards Way, Horn. 50 CU34
St. Loo Ave. SW3 66 BU43
St. Louis Rd. SE27 77 BZ49
St. Loys Rd. N17 39 CA30
St. Luke Clo., Uxb. 53 AX39
St. Lukes Ave. SW4 66 BW45
St. Lukes Ave., Enf. 30 BZ22
St. Lukes Ave., Ilf. 49 CL35
St. Lukes Clo. EC1 57 BZ38
Old St.
St. Lukes Clo. SE25 87 CB53

St. Lukes Clo., Swan. 89 CS51
The Orchard
St. Lukes Est. EC1 2 K3
St. Lukes Ms. W11 55 BR39
St. Lukes Pas., Kings.T. 85 BL51
St. Lukes Pl., St.Alb. 9 BJ14
St. Lukes Rd. W11 55 BR39
St. Lukes Rd., Uxb. 53 AY36
Thompson Rd.
St. Lukes Rd., Whyt. 105 CA62
St. Lukes Rd., Wind. 72 AQ46
St. Lukes Sq. E16 58 CG39
St. Lukes St. SW3 3 D10
St. Lukes St. SW3 66 BU42
St. Lukes Yd. W9 55 BR38
St. Malo Ave. N9 39 CC27
St. Margarets, Bark. 58 CM37
St. Margarets, Guil. 118 AS70
St. Margarets Ave. N15 47 BY31
St. Margarets Ave. N20 38 BT27
St. Margarets Ave., Ashf. 73 AZ49
St. Margarets Ave., Har. 45 BG34
St. Margarets Ave., Sid. 78 CM48
St. Margarets Ave., Sutt. 85 BR55
St. Margarets Ave., Uxb. 53 AZ38
St. Margarets Clo. SE7 68 CJ43
St. Margarets Clo., Berk. 7 AR13
St. Margarets Clo., Iver 52 AU37
St. Margarets Clo., Orp. 89 CO55
St. Margarets Ct. SE1 4 K3
St. Margarets Cres. SW15 75 BP46
St. Margarets Cres., Grav. 81 DJ48
St. Margarets Dr., Twick. 74 BJ46
St. Margarets Gate, Iver 52 AU37
St. Margarets Gro. SE18 68 CM43
St. Margarets Gro., Twick. 74 BJ46
St. Margarets Pas. SE13 68 CG45
St. Margarets Path SE18 68 CM42
St. Margarets Pl. SW1 66 BW41
Artillery Row
St. Margarets Rd. E12 49 CJ34
St. Margarets Rd. N17 48 CA31
St. Margarets Rd. NW10 55 BQ38
St. Margarets Rd. SE4 67 CD45
St. Margarets Rd. W7 64 BH41
St. Margarets Rd., Beck. 87 CC52
St. Margarets Rd., Couls. 104 BV64
St. Margarets Rd., Edg. 37 BM28
St. Margarets Rd., Grav. 81 DF47
Perry St.
St. Margarets Rd., Ruis. 44 BA32
St. Margarets Rd., S.Dnth. 80 CZ50
St. Margarets Rd., Twick. 64 BJ45
St. Margarets Sq. SE4 67 CD45
Adelaide Ave.
St. Margarets St. SW1 3 Q5
St. Margarets St. SW1 66 BX41
St. Margarets Ter. SE18 68 CM42
St. Margarets Way, Hem.H. 8 BA13
St. Mark St. E1 2 Q9
St. Marks Ave., Grav. 81 DF47
St. Marks Clo. SE10 67 CF43
Ashburnham Pl.
St. Marks Clo. W11 55 BQ40
Lancaster Rd.
St. Marks Clo., Barn. 29 BS24
St. Marks Clo., St.Alb. 10 BM14
St. Marks Cres. NW1 56 BV37
St. Marks Gate E9 57 CD36
St. Marks Gro. SW10 66 BS43
St. Marks Hill, Surb. 85 BL53
St. Marks Pl. SW19 75 BR50
Wimbledon Hill Rd.
St. Marks Pl. W11 55 BR39
St. Marks Pl., Wind. 61 AO44
St. Marks Ri. E8 48 CA35
St. Marks Rd. SE25 87 CB52
Coventry Rd.
St. Marks Rd. W5 55 BL40
The Common
St. Marks Rd. W7 64 BH41
St. Marks Rd. W10 55 BQ39
St. Marks Rd. W11 55 BR39
St. Marks Rd., Brom. 88 CH52
St. Marks Rd., Enf. 30 CA25
St. Marks Rd., Epsom 103 BQ62
St. Marks Rd., Mitch. 86 BU51
St. Marks Rd., Tedd. 74 BJ50
St. Marks Rd., Wind. 61 AO44
St. Marks Sq. NW1 56 BV37
Regents Pk. Rd.
St. Marthas Ave., Wok. 100 AS64
St. Martin Clo., Uxb. 53 AX39
St. Martins App., Ruis. 44 BB33
St. Martins Ave. E6 58 CJ37
St. Martins Ave., Epsom 94 BO60
St. Martins Clo., Brwd. 122 DE26
St. Martins Clo., Enf. 30 CB23
St. Martins Clo., Epsom. 94 BO60
St. Martins Clo., Erith 69 CP41
St. Helens Rd.
St. Martins Clo., Lthd. 110 BB69
St. Martins Clo., Wat. 36 BD28
Muirfield Rd.
St. Martins Clo., West Dr. 63 AX41
St. Martins Ct. WC2 1 Q10
St. Martins Ct. WC2 56 BX40
St. Martins La.
St. Martins Ct., Ashf. 73 AX49
St. Martins Dr., Eyns. 99 CV56
St. Martins Dr., Walt. 84 BD55
St. Martins Est. SW2 76 BY47
St. Martins La. WC2 1 Q10
St. Martins La. WC2 56 BX40
St. Martins le Grand EC1 2 H8

St. Martins le Grand EC1 57 BZ39
St. Martins Meadow, West. 107 CP65
St. Martins Ms. WC2 56 BX40
Adelaide St.
St. Martins Pl. WC2 3 Q1
St. Martins Rd. N9 39 CB27
St. Martins Rd. SW9 66 BX44
St. Martins Rd., Dart. 80 CW46
St. Martins Rd., West Dr. 63 AX41
St. Martins St. WC2 3 P1
St. Martins St. WC2 56 BW40
Whitcomb St.
St. Martins Way SW17 76 BT48
St. Mary Abbots Pl. W8 65 BR41
St. Mary Abbots Ter. W14 65 BR41
St. Mary at Hill EC3 4 M1
St. Mary at Hill EC3 57 CA40
Lower Thames St.
St. Mary Ave., Wall. 86 BV55
St. Mary Axe EC3 2 M9
St. Mary Axe EC3 57 CA39
St. Mary Rd. E17 48 CE32
St. Mary St. SE18 68 CK42
St. Marychurch St. SE16 67 CC41
St. Marys, Bark. 58 CM37
St. Marys App. E12 49 CK35
Church Rd.
St. Marys Ave. E11 49 CH32
St. Marys Ave. N3 37 BR30
St. Marys Ave., Berk. 7 AO12
St. Marys Ave., Brwd. 122 DD25
St. Marys Ave., Brom. 88 CG52
St. Marys Ave., Nthwd. 35 BB28
St. Marys Ave., Sthl. 64 BF42
St. Marys Ave., Stai. 73 AX47
St. Marys Ave., Tedd. 74 BH50
St. Marys Clo. N17 39 CB30
Kemble Rd.
St. Marys Clo., Chess. 94 BL57
St. Marys Clo., Epsom 94 BO57
St. Marys Clo., Grav. 81 DH48
St. Marys Clo., Grays 71 DE43
Dock Rd.
St. Marys Clo., Lthd. 102 BG65
St. Marys Clo., Orp. 89 CO51
St. Marys Clo., Oxt. 115 CG68
St. Marys Clo., Stai. 73 AX47
St. Marys Clo., Sun. 83 BC52
St. Marys Clo., Uxb. 44 AW31
St. Marys Clo., Wat. 27 BD24
St. Marys Ct. E6 58 CK38
St. Marys Cres. NW4 46 BP31
St. Marys Cres., Hayes 53 BC40
St. Marys Cres., Islw. 64 BG43
St. Marys Cres., Stai. 73 AX47
St. Marys Dr., Felt. 73 BA47
St. Marys Dr., Sev. 107 CT65
St. Marys Gdns. SE11 4 E8
St. Marys Gdns. SE11 66 BY42
St. Marys Grn. N2 47 BT31
Thomas More Way
St. Marys Grn., West. 106 CJ62
St. Marys Gro.
St. Marys Gro. N1 56 BY36
St. Marys Gro. SW13 65 BP45
St. Marys Gro. W4 65 BM43
St. Marys Gro., Rich. 65 BL45
St. Marys Gro., West. 106 CJ62
St. Marys La. (West Horndon), Brwd. 123 DC33
St. Marys La., Upmin. 51 CX34
St. Marys Mans. W2 1 A6
St. Marys Mans. W2 56 BT39
St. Marys Ms. NW6 56 BS36
Priory Rd.
St. Marys Path N1 56 BY37
Gaskin St.
St. Marys Pl. SE9 78 CK46
Eltham High St.
St. Marys Pl. W5 64 BK41
St. Marys Rd.
St. Marys Rd. E10 48 CF34
St. Marys Rd. E13 58 CH37
St. Marys Rd. N8 47 BX31
High St.
St. Marys Rd. N9 39 CB26
St. Marys Rd. NW10 55 BO37
St. Marys Rd. NW11 46 BR33
St. Marys Rd. SE15 67 CC44
St. Marys Rd. SE25 87 CA52
St. Marys Rd. (Wimbledon) SW19 75 BR49
St. Marys Rd. W5 54 BK40
St. Marys Rd., Barn. 38 BU26
St. Marys Rd., Bex. 79 CS47
St. Marys Rd., Chsnt. 21 CC18
St. Marys Rd., E.Mol. 84 BG53
St. Marys Rd., Grays 71 DG42
St. Marys Rd., Green. 70 CZ45
St. Marys Rd., Hayes 53 BB40
St. Marys Rd., Hem.H. 8 AX13
St. Marys Rd., Ilf. 49 CM34
St. Marys Rd., Lthd. 102 BJ64
St. Marys Rd., Reig. 121 BS71
St. Marys Rd., Slou. 52 AS40
St. Marys Rd., S.Croy. 96 BZ58
St. Marys Rd., Surb. 84 BK53
St. Marys Rd. (Long Ditton), Surb. 84 BK54
St. Marys Rd., Swan. 89 CS52
St. Marys Rd. (Denham), Uxb. 43 AV32
St. Marys Rd. (Harefield), Uxb. 44 AW31
St. Marys Rd., Wat. 26 BC24
St. Marys Rd., Wey. 92 BA56
St. Marys Rd., Wok. 100 AR62
St. Marys Rd., Wor.Pk. 85 BO55
St. Marys Sq. W2 1 A6

St. Marys Sq. W2 56 BT39
St. Marys Ter.
St. Marys Ter. W2 1 A6
St. Marys Ter. W2 56 BT39
St. Marys Vw., Har. 45 BK32
St. Leonards Ave.
St. Marys Wk. SE11 4 E8
St. Marys Wk. SE11 66 BY42
St. Marys Wk., Hayes 53 BB40
St. Marys Wk., St.Alb. 9 BJ11
St. Marys Way, Ger.Cr. 34 AR30
St. Marys Way, Long. 90 DC52
St. Marys Way, Wdf.Grn. 40 CL28
St. Matthew Clo., Uxb. 53 AX39
St. Matthew Rd., Red. 121 BU70
St. Matthew St. SW1 3 N7
St. Matthew St. SW1 66 BW41
Old Pye St.
St. Matthews Ave., Surb. 85 BL54
St. Matthews Clo., Rain. 59 CU36
St. Matthews Dr., Brom. 88 CK52
St. Matthews Rd. SW2 66 BX45
St. Matthews Rd. W5 55 BL40
The Common
St. Matthews Row E2 57 CB38
St. Matthias Clo. NW9 46 BO32
St. Maur Rd. SW6 65 BR44
St. Merryn Clo. SE18 68 CM43
St. Meryl Est., Wat. 36 BE27
St. Michaels All. EC3 2 L9
St. Michaels All. EC3 57 BZ39
Cornhill
St. Michaels Ave. N9 39 CC26
St. Michaels Ave., H Hem.H. 8 AZ14
St. Michaels Ave., Wem. 55 BM36
St. Michaels Clo. E16 58 CJ39
Long Mark Rd.
St. Michaels Clo. N3 37 BR30
Hendon La.
St. Michaels Clo. N12 38 BU28
St. Michaels Clo., Belv. 69 BP41
St. Helens Rd.
St. Michaels Clo., Brom. 88 CK52
St. Michaels Clo., Harl. 6 CN10
School La.
St. Michaels Clo., Pot.B. 20 BS18
Church Rd.
St. Michaels Clo., Walt. 84 BD55
St. Michaels Cres., Pnr. 45 BE32
St. Michaels Dr., Sev. 108 CV61
St. Michaels Gdns. W10 55 BR39
Ladbroke Gro.
St. Michaels Rd. NW2 46 BQ35
St. Michaels Rd. SW9 66 BX44
St. Michaels Rd., Ashf. 73 AZ49
St. Michaels Rd., Brox. 12 CD13
St. Michaels Rd., Cat. 105 BZ64
St. Michaels Rd., Croy. 87 BZ54
St. Michaels Rd., Grays 71 DG42
St. Michaels Rd., Wall. 95 BW56
St. Michaels Rd., Well. 69 CO45
St. Michaels Rd., Wok. 91 AU60
St. Michaels St. W2 1 B8
St. Michaels St. W2 56 BT39
St. Michaels St., St.Alb. 9 BF13
St. Michaels Ter. N22 38 BX30
St. Michaels Vw., Hat. 10 BP11
Drovers Way
St. Michaels Way, Pot.B. 20 BS18
Church Rd.
St. Mildreds Ct. EC2 2 K9
St. Mildreds Ct. EC2 57 BZ39
Poultry
St. Mildreds Rd. SE12 78 CG47
St. Mildreds Rd., Guil. 118 AS70
St. Monicas Rd., Tad. 103 BR64
St. Nazaire Clo., Egh. 72 AU49
Mullens Rd.
St. Neots Clo., Borwd. 28 BM22
The Campions
St. Neots Rd., Rom. 42 CW29
St. Nicholas Ave., Horn. 50 CU34
St. Nicholas Ave., Lthd. 111 BF66
St. Nicholas Clo., Amer. 25 AQ23
St. Nicholas Clo., Borwd. 27 BK25
Elstree Hill N.
St. Nicholas Clo., Uxb. 53 AX39
St. Nicholas Dr., Shep. 83 AZ54
St. Nicholas Glebe SW17 76 BV49
St. Nicholas Gro., Brwd. 122 DE28
St. Nicholas Hill, Lthd. 102 BJ64
St. Nicholas La., Chis. 88 CK51
St. Nicholas Mt., Hem.H. 7 AV13
St. Nicholas Rd. SE18 68 CN42
St. Nicholas Rd., Sutt. 95 BS56
St. Nicholas Rd., T.Ditt. 84 BH53
St. Nicholas St. SE8 67 CE44
Lucas St.
St. Nicholas Way, Sutt. 95 BS56
Robin Hood Rd.
St. Norbert Grn. SE4 67 CD45

St. Norbert Rd. SE4 77 CC46
St. Normans Way, Epsom 94 BP58
St. Olafs Rd. SW6 65 BR43
St. Olaves Clo., Twick. 72 AV50
St. Olaves Ct. EC2 2 K9
St. Olaves Est. SE1 4 N4
St. Olaves Est. SE1 67 CA41
St. Olaves Gdns. SE11 4 D8
St. Olaves Rd. E6 58 CL37
St. Olaves Wk. SW16 86 BW51
St. Omer Ridge, Guil. 118 AT71
St. Omer Rd., Guil. 118 AT71
St. Oswalds Pl. SE11 66 BX42
St. Oswalds Rd. SW16 86 BT51
St. Oswulf St. SW1 3 P9
St. Oswulf St. SW1 66 BW42
Erasmus St.
St. Pancras Ct. N2 38 BT30
St. Pancras Way NW1 56 BW36
St. Patricks Gdns., Grav. 81 DH48
St. Patricks Pl., Grays 71 DG42
St. Paul Clo., Uxb. 53 AX39
St. Paul St. N1 57 BZ37
St. Pauls All. EC4 56 BY39
St. Pauls Chyd.
St. Pauls Ave. NW2 55 BP36
St. Pauls Ave. SE16 57 CC40
St. Pauls Ave., Har. 46 BL32
St. Pauls Ave., Slou. 52 AP40
St. Pauls Chyd. EC4 2 G9
St. Pauls Chyd. EC4 56 BY39
St. Pauls Clo. SE7 68 CJ42
St. Pauls Clo. W5 65 BL41
St. Pauls Clo., Ashf. 73 BA49
St. Pauls Clo., Cars. 86 BU54
St. Pauls Clo., Chess. 93 BK56
St. Pauls Clo., Hayes 63 BA42
St. Pauls Clo., Houns. 64 BE44
St. Pauls Clo., S.Ock. 60 CY40
St. Pauls Clo., Wey. 92 AW56
School La.
St. Pauls Ctyd. SE8 67 CE43
Deptford High St.
St. Pauls Cray Est., Chis. 88 CN52
St. Pauls Cray Rd., Chis. 78 CM50
St. Pauls Cres. NW1 56 BW36
St. Pauls Dr. E15 48 CF35
St. Pauls Est. W14 65 BQ42
St. Pauls Pl. N1 57 BZ36
St. Pauls Pl., St.Alb. 9 BJ13
St. Pauls Pl., S.Ock. 60 CY40
St. Pauls Clo.
St. Pauls Rd. N1 56 BY36
St. Pauls Rd. N17 39 CB29
St. Pauls Rd., Bark. 58 CM37
St. Pauls Rd., Brent. 64 BK43
St. Pauls Rd., Erith 69 CS43
St. Pauls Rd., Hem.H. 8 AX13
St. Pauls Rd., Rich. 65 BL45
St. Pauls Rd., Stai. 72 AU50
St. Pauls Rd., Th.Hth. 87 BZ52
St. Pauls Rd., Wok. 100 AT62
St. Pauls Rd. E., Dor. 119 BJ71
St. Pauls Rd. W., Dor. 119 BJ72
St. Pauls Shrubbery N1 57 BZ36
St. Pauls Sq., Brom. 88 CG51
Church Rd.
St. Pauls St. E3 57 CD39
St. Pauls Ter. SE17 66 BY43
St. Pauls Way E3 57 CD39
St. Pauls Way N3 38 BS29
St. Pauls Way, Wal.Abb. 21 CF20
Rochford Ave.
St. Pauls Way, Wat. 27 BD23
St. Pauls Wd. Hill, Orp. 88 CN51
St. Peters All. EC3 2 L9
St. Peters Ave. E2 57 CB37
St. Peters Clo.
St. Peters Ave. E17 49 CG31
St. Peters Ave. N18 39 CB28
St. Peters Ave., Ong. 24 CW16
St. Peters Clo. E2 57 CB37
St. Peters Clo. SW17 76 BU48
College Gdns.
St. Peters Clo. W5 54 BK39
Regal Clo.
St. Peters Clo., Barn. 28 BP25
St. Peters Clo., Bush. 36 BG26
St. Peters Clo., Chis. 78 CM50
St. Peters Clo., Ger.Cr. 34 AS30
St. Peters Clo., Hat. 10 BP12
St. Albans Rd.
St. Peters Clo., Ilf. 49 CN31
St. Peters Clo., Rick. 35 AW26
St. Peters Clo., Ruis. 45 BD34
St. Peters Clo., St.Alb. 9 BG13
St. Peters Clo., Wind. 72 AQ46
St. Peters Clo., Wok. 100 AU63
St. Peters Ct. NW4 46 BQ32
Queens Rd.
St. Peters Ct. SE3 68 CG45
St. Peters Ct., Ger.Cr. 34 AS30
St. Peters Gdns. SE27 76 BY49
St. Peters Gro. W6 65 BP42
St. Peters La., Orp. 89 CO51
St. Peters Rd. N9 39 CB26
St. Peters Rd. W6 65 BP42
St. Peters Rd., Brwd. 42 DA28
St. Peters Rd., Croy. 96 BZ56
St. Peters Rd., E.Mol. 84 BF52
St. Peters Rd., Grays 71 DG42
St. Peters Rd., Kings.T. 85 BM51
Cambridge Rd.
St. Peters Rd., St.Alb. 9 BH13
St. Peters Rd., Sthl. 54 BF39
St. Peters Rd., Stai. 72 AV50
St. Peters Rd., Twick. 74 BJ46
St. Peters Rd., Uxb. 53 AX39
St. Peters Rd., Wok. 100 AT63
St. Peters Sq. E2 57 CB37
St. Peters Clo.
St. Peters Sq. W6 65 BP42
St. Peters St. N1 56 BY37
St. Peters St., St.Alb. 9 BG13
St. Peters St., S.Croy. 96 BZ56
St. Peters St. Ms. N1 56 BY37
St. Peters St.
St. Peters Ter. SW6 65 BR43
Filmer Rd.
St. Peters Vill. W6 65 BP42
St. Peters Way N1 57 CA36
De Beauvoir Sq.
St. Peters Way W5 54 BK39
St. Peters Way, Cher. 91 AU55
St. Peters Way, Hayes 63 BA42
St. Peters Way, Rick. 25 AT24
St. Petersburgh Ms. W2 56 BS40
St. Petersburgh Pl. W2 56 BS40
St. Philip Sq. SW8 66 BV44
St. Philip St. SW8 66 BV44
St. Philips Ave., Wor.Pk. 85 BP55
St. Philips Rd. E8 57 CB36
St. Philips Rd., Surb. 84 BK53
St. Philips Way N1 57 BZ37
Linton St.
St. Pinnocks Ave., Stai. 83 AW51
St. Quentin Rd., Well. 68 CN45
St. Quintin Ave. W10 55 BQ39
St. Quintin Gdns. W10 55 BQ39
St. Quintin Rd. E13 58 CH37
St. Raphaels Way NW10 55 BN36
St. Regis Clo. N10 38 BV30
St. Ronans Clo., Barn. 29 BT22
St. Ronans Cres., Wdf.Grn. 40 CH29
St. Rule St. SW8 66 BW44
St. Saviours Est. SE1 4 P6
St. Saviours Est. SE1 67 CA41
St. Saviours Rd. SW2 76 BX46
St. Saviours Rd., Croy. 86 BY53
St. Silas Pl. NW5 56 BV36
St. Simons Ave. SW15 75 BQ46
St. Stephens Ave. E17 48 CF32
St. Stephens Ave. W12 55 BP40
St. Stephens Ave. W13 54 BJ39
St. Stephens Ave., Ash. 103 BL61
St. Stephens Ave., St.Alb. 9 BF14
St. Stephens Clo. E17 48 CE32
St. Stephens Clo. NW8 56 BU37
St. Stephens Clo., Grays 70 CX42
St. Stephens Clo., St.Albs. 9 BF15
St. Stephens Clo., Sthl. 54 BF39
St. Stephens Cres. W2 56 BS39
St. Stephens Cres., Brwd. 122 DD28
St. Stephens Cres., Th.Hth. 86 BY52
St. Stephens Gdn. Est. W2 56 BS39
St. Stephens Gdns. SW15 75 BR46
Normanby Clo.
St. Stephens Gdns. W2 56 BS39
St. Stephens Gdns., Twick. 74 BK46
St. Stephens Gro. SE13 67 CF45
St. Stephens Hill, St.Alb. 9 BG14
St. Stephens Ms. W2 56 BS39
Chepstow Rd.
St. Stephens Pas., Twick. 74 BK46
St. Stephens Rd. E6 58 CJ36
St. Stephens Rd. E17 48 CE32
St. Stephens Rd. W13 54 BJ39
St. Stephens Rd., Barn. 28 BQ25
St. Stephens Rd., Enf. 30 CC22
St. Stephens Rd., Houns. 74 BF46
St. Stephens Rd., West Dr. 53 AX40
St. Stephens Row EC4 2 K10
St. Stephens Row EC4 57 BZ39
Walbrook
St. Stephens Ter. SW8 66 BX43
St. Stephens Wk. SW7 66 BT42
Southwell Gdns.
St. Swithins La. EC4 2 K10
St. Swithins La. EC4 57 BZ40
St. Swithuns Rd. SE13 77 CF46
St. Teresa Wk., Grays 71 DG42
St. Theodores Way, Welw.G.C. 5 BQ7
Wigmores N.
St. Theresas Rd., Felt. 63 BB45
St. Thomas Ct., Bex. 79 CR47
St. Thomas Dr., Orp. 88 CM54
St. Thomas Dr., Pnr. 36 BE30
St. Thomas Pl., Grays 71 DE43
East Thurrock Rd.
St. Thomas Rd. E16 58 CH39
St. Thomas Rd. N14 38 BW26
St. Thomas Rd., Belv. 69 CS41
St. Thomas Rd., Brwd. 42 DB27
St. Thomas St. SE1 4 L3
St. Thomas St. SE1 57 BZ40
St. Thomas's Ave., Grav. 81 DG48
St. Thomas's Clo., Wal.Abb. 22 CH20
St. Thomas's Dr., Guil. 110 AY69
St. Thomas's Gdns. NW5 56 BV36
Queens Cres.
St. Thomas's Gdns., Ilf. 58 CM36
St. Thomas's Pl. E9 57 CC36
St. Thomas's Rd. N4 47 BY34
St. Thomas's Rd. NW10 55 BO37
St. Thomas's Rd. W4 65 BN43
St. Thomas's Sq. E9 57 CB36
St. Thomas's Way SW6 65 BR43
St. Ursula Gro., Pnr. 45 BD32
St. Ursula Rd., Sthl. 54 BF39
St. Vincent Clo. SE27 76 BY49
Knights Hill
St. Vincent Dr., St.Alb. 9 BJ15
St. Vincent Est. E14 57 CD40
St. Vincent Rd., Twick. 74 BG46
St. Vincent Rd., Walt. 83 BC55
St. Vincent St. W1 1 H7
St. Vincent St. W1 56 BV39
Aybrook St.
St. Vincents Ave., Dart. 80 CX46
St. Vincents Rd., Dart. 80 CX46
St. Vincents Way, Pot.B. 20 BT20
St. Wilfrids Clo., Barn. 29 BT25
St. Wilfrids Rd.
St. Wilfrids Rd., Barn. 29 BT25
St. Winifreds, Ken. 105 BZ61
St. Winifreds Ave. E12 49 CK35
St. Winifreds Clo., Chig. 40 CM28
St. Winifreds Rd., Tedd. 74 BJ50
St. Winifreds Rd., West. 106 CK62
St. Winifrids Wk. SE17 66 BY43
Lorrimore Rd.
St. Yon Ct., St.Alb. 10 BL13
Saints, The, Wat. 18 BD20
Saints Dr. E7 49 CJ35
Saints Wk., Grays 71 DH42
Sakins Cft., Harl. 13 CN12
Saladin Dr., Grays 70 CX42
Chieftan Dr.
Salamanca Pl. SE11 4 B9
Salamanca Pl. SE11 66 BX42
Salamanca St.
Salamanca St. SE11 4 B9
Salamanca St. SE11 66 BX42
Salamons Way, Rain. 59 CT39
Salcombe Dr., Mord. 85 BQ54
Salcombe Dr., Rom. 50 CQ32
Salcombe Gdns. NW7 37 BQ29
Salcombe Rd. E17 48 CD33
Salcombe Rd., Ashf. 73 AY49
Salcombe Way, Hayes 53 BB38
Salcombe Waye, Ruis. 44 BC34
Salcot Cres., Croy. 96 CF58
Salcote Rd., Grav. 81 DJ49
Salcott Rd. SW11 76 BU46
Salcott Rd., Croy. 86 BX55
Sale, The E4 40 CG28
Sale Pl. W2 1 C7
Sale Pl. W2 56 BU39
Salehurst Clo., Har. 46 BL32
Salehurst Rd. SE4 77 CD46
Salem Pl., Croy. 87 BZ55
Salem Rd. W2 56 BS40
Porchester Gdns.
Salford Rd. SW2 76 BW47
Salhouse Clo. SE28 59 CP40
Rollesby Way
Salisbury Ave. N3 46 BR31
Salisbury Ave., Bark. 58 CM36
Salisbury Ave., St.Alb. 9 BJ13
Salisbury Ave., Sutt. 94 BR57
Salisbury Ave., Swan. 89 CU52
Salisbury Clo. SE17 4 K8
Salisbury Clo. SE17 67 BZ42
Chatham St.
Salisbury Clo., Amer. 25 AP23
Salisbury Clo., Pot.B. 20 BT19
Salisbury Clo., Upmin. 51 CZ34
Salisbury Clo., Wor.Pk. 85 BO55
Salisbury Ct. EC4 2 E9
Salisbury Ct. EC4 56 BY39
Salisbury Cres., Chsnt. 21 CC19
Theobalds La.
Salisbury Gdns. SW19 75 BR50
Salisbury Gdns., Buck.H. 40 CJ27
Victoria Rd.
Salisbury Gdns., Welw.G.C. 5 BR8
Salisbury Pl. SW9 66 BY43
Langton Rd.
Salisbury Pl. W1 1 E6
Salisbury Pl. W1 56 BU39
Salisbury Plain NW4 46 BQ32
Brent St.
Salisbury Rd. E4 39 CE27
Salisbury Rd. E7 58 CH36
Salisbury Rd. E10 48 CF34
Salisbury Rd. E12 49 CJ35
Salisbury Rd. E17 48 CF32
Salisbury Rd. N4 47 BY32
Salisbury Rd. N9 39 CB27
Salisbury Rd. N22 38 BY30
Salisbury Rd. SE25 87 CB53
Salisbury Rd. SW19 75 BR50
Salisbury Rd. W13 64 BJ41
Salisbury Rd., Bans. 95 BS60
Salisbury Rd., Barn. 28 BR24
Salisbury Rd., Bex. 79 CR47
Salisbury Rd., Brom. 88 CK53
Salisbury Rd., Cars. 95 BU57
Salisbury Rd., Dag. 59 CR36
Salisbury Rd., Dart. 80 CY47
Salisbury Rd., Enf. 30 CD22
Salisbury Rd., Felt. 74 BD47
Salisbury Rd., Gdse. 114 CC69
Salisbury Rd., Grav. 81 DF47
Salisbury Rd., Grays 71 DE43
Salisbury Rd., Har. 45 BG32
Salisbury Rd., Hodd. 12 CF11
Salisbury Rd., Houns. 64 BD45
Salisbury Rd., Ilf. 49 CN34
Salisbury Rd., N.Mal. 85 BN52
Salisbury Rd., Pnr. 44 BC31
Salisbury Rd., Rich. 65 BL45
Salisbury Rd., Rom. 50 CU32
Salisbury Rd., Sthl. 64 BE42
Salisbury Rd., Uxb. 53 AW37
Salisbury Rd., Wat. 27 BD23
Salisbury Rd., Welw.G.C. 5 BR8
Salisbury Rd., Wok. 100 AS63
Salisbury Rd., Wor.Pk. 94 BN56
Salisbury Sq. EC4 2 E9
Salisbury Sq. EC4 56 BY39
Salisbury Sq., Hat. 10 BQ12
Salisbury St. NW8 1 C5
Salisbury St. NW8 56 BU38
Salisbury St. W3 65 BN41
Salisbury Ter. SE15 67 CC45
Salisbury Wk. N19 47 BW34
Magdala Ave.
Salix Clo., Sun. 73 BC50
Salix Rd., Grays 71 DE43
Salliesfield, Twick. 74 BG46
Kneller Rd.
Salmen Rd. E13 58 CG37
Salmon La. E14 57 CD39
Salmon Rd., Belv. 69 CR42
Salmon St. E14 57 CD39
Salmon La.
Salmon St. NW9 46 BM33
Salmond Clo., Stan. 36 BJ29
Salmonds Gro., Brwd. 122 DE28
St. Nicholas Gro.
Salmons La., Whyt. 105 CA63
Salmons La. W., Cat. 105 CA63
Salmons Rd. N9 39 CB26
Salmons Rd., Chess. 94 BL57
Salmons Rd., Lthd. 111 BD68
Salomons Rd. E13 58 CJ39
Salop Rd. E17 48 CC32
Salt Box Hill, West. 97 CH60
Salt Box Rd., Guil. 109 AP68
Salt Hill Ave., Slou. 61 AO40
Salt Hill Clo., Uxb. 44 AY35
Salt Hill Dr., Slou. 61 AO40
Salt Hill Way, Slou. 61 AO40
Saltash Clo., Sutt. 94 BR56
Saltash Rd., Ilf. 40 CM29
Saltash Rd., Well. 69 CP44
Saltcoats Rd. W4 65 BO41
Greenend Rd.
Saltcroft Clo., Wem. 46 BM33
Salter Rd. SE16 57 CD40
Salter St. E14 57 CE40
Salter St. NW10 55 BP38
Salterford Rd. SW17 76 BV50
Salters Clo., Berk. 7 AP12
Salters Gdns., Wat. 26 BC23
Salters Hall Ct. EC4 2 K10
Salters Hill SE19 77 BZ49
Salters Rd. E17 48 CF31
Salters Rd. W10 55 BQ38
Salterton Rd. N7 47 BX34
Saltford Clo., Erith 69 CT42
Saltoun Rd. SW2 66 BY45
Saltram Clo. N15 48 CA31
Saltram Cres. W9 55 BR38
Saltwell St. E14 57 CE40
Saltwood Clo., Orp. 98 CP56
Salusbury Rd. NW6 55 BR37
Salvador SW17 76 BU49
Salvia Gdns., Grnf. 54 BJ37
Salvin Rd. SW15 65 BQ45
Salway Clo., Wdf.Grn. 40 CG29
Salway Pl. E15 57 CF36
Broadway
Salway Rd. E15 57 CF36
Salwey Cres., Brox. 12 CD13
Sam Bartram Clo. SE7 68 CJ42
Samantha Clo. E17 48 CD33
Samantha Ms., Hav. 41 CT27
Sambruck Ms. SE6 77 CE47
Samels Ct. W6 65 BP42
South Black Lion La.
Samford St. NW8 1 C5
Samian Gate, St.Alb. 9 BE15
Samos Rd. SE20 87 CB51
Samphire Ct., Grays 71 DE43
Salix Rd.
Sampleoak La., Guil. 118 AV73
Sampson Ave., Barn. 28 BQ25
Sampson Clo., Belv. 69 CP41
Carrill Way
Sampson St. E1 57 CB40
Samson St. E13 58 CJ37
Samuel Clo. SE18 68 CK42
Samuel Johnson Clo. SW16 76 BX49
Curtis Fld. Rd.
Samuel Lewis Bldgs. SE5 67 BZ44
Samuel Lewis Dws. SW6 66 BS43
Vanston Pl.
Samuel Lewis Trust Bldgs. E8 48 CB35
Samuel Lewis Trust Dws. N1 56 BY36
Samuel Lewis Trust Dws. SW3 3 C9
Samuel St. SE18 68 CK42
Sancroft Clo. NW2 46 BP34
Sancroft Rd., Stan. 36 BJ30
Sancroft St. SE11 4 C10
Sancroft St. SE11 66 BX42
Sanctuary, The SW1 3 P6
Sanctuary, The, Bex. 79 CP46
Sanctuary, The, Mord. 86 BS53
Sanctuary Clo., Dart. 80 CV46
Sanctuary Clo., Uxb. 35 AX29
Sanctuary Rd., Houns. 73 AZ46
Beacon Rd.
Sanctuary St. SE1 4 J5
Sanctuary St. SE1 67 BZ41
Sandal Rd. N18 39 CB28
Sandal Rd., N.Mal. 85 BN53
Sandal St. E15 58 CG37
Sandal Wd., Guil. 118 AQ71
Sandale Clo. N16 48 BZ34
Stoke Newington St.
Sandall Clo. W5 55 BL38
Sandall Rd. NW5 56 BW36
Sandall Rd. W5 55 BL38
Sandalwood Clo. E1 57 CD38
Solebay St.
Sandalwood Rd., Felt. 73 BC48
Sanday Clo., Hem.H. 8 AZ
Sandbach Pl. SE18 68 CM
Sandbanks Hill, Dart. 80 DA
Sandbourne Ave. SW19 86 BS
Sandbourne Rd. SE4 67 CD
Sandbrook Clo. NW7 37 BN
Sunnyvale Gro.
Sandbrook Rd. N16 48 CA
Sandby Grn. SE9 68 CK
Sandcliff Rd., Erith 69 CS
Sandcross La., Reig. 120 BR
Sandell St. SE1 4
Sandell St. SE1 66 BY
Sandells Ave., Ashf. 73 BA
Sanders Clo., Hmptn. 74 BG
Sanders Clo., Hem.H. 8 AY
Sanders Clo., St.Alb. 18 BK
Sanders La. NW7 37 BQ
Sanders La., Wok. 100 AQ
Sanders Rd., Hem.H. 8 AY
Sanders Way N19 47 BW
Sussex Way
Sandersfield Gdns., Bans. 104 BS
Sandersfield Rd., Bans. 104 BS
Sanderson Clo. NW5 47 BV
Highgate Rd.
Sanderson Clo., Brwd. 123 DE
Sanderson Cres., Grnf. 54 BJ
Clausen Way
Sanderstead Ave. NW2 46 BR
Sanderstead Clo. SW12 76 BW
Sanderstead Ct. Ave., S.Croy. 96 CB
Sanderstead Hill, S.Croy. 96 CA
Sanderstead Rd. E10 48 CD
Sanderstead Rd., Orp. 89 CO
Sanderstead Rd., S.Croy. 96 BZ
Sandes Pl., Lthd. 102 BJ
Sandfield, Hat. 10 BP
Sandfield Gdns., Th.Hth. 86 BY
Sandfield Pas., Th.Hth. 87 BZ
Sandfield Rd., St.Alb. 9 BJ
Sandfield Rd., Th.Hth. 86 BY
Sandfield Ter., Guil. 118 AR
Sandfields, Wok. 100 AU
Sandford Ave. N22 39 BZ
Sandford Ave., Loug. 31 CM
Sandford Clo. E6 58 CK
Sandford Rd.
Sandford Ct. N16 48 CA
Sandford Rd. E6 58 CK
Sandford Rd., Bexh. 69 CQ
Sandford Rd., Brom. 88 CH
Sandford Row SE17 67 BZ
Sandford St. SW6 66 BS
Kings Rd.
Sandford Wk. SE14 67 CC
Sandford St.
Sandgate La. SW18 76 BU
Sandgate Rd., Well. 69 CP
Sandgate St. SE15 67 CB
Sandhills, Wall. 95 BW
Sandhills Ct., Vir.W. 82 AS
Sandhills La., Vir.W. 82 AS
Sandhills Rd., Reig. 121 BS
Sandhurst Ave., Har. 45 BF
Sandhurst Ave., Surb. 85 BM
Sandhurst Clo. NW9 46 BM
Sandhurst Clo., S.Croy. 96 CA
Sandhurst Ct. SW2 66 BX
Sandhurst Dr., Ilf. 49 CN
Sandhurst Rd. N9 30 CC
Sandhurst Rd. NW9 46 BM
Sandhurst Rd. SE6 77 CF
Sandhurst Rd., Bex. 79 CP
Sandhurst Rd., Orp. 89 CO
Sandhurst Rd., Sid. 78 CN
Sandhurst Rd., Til. 71 DH
Sandhurst Way, S.Croy. 96 CA
Sandiford Rd., Sutt. 85 BR
Sandiland Cres., Brom. 88 CG
Sandilands, Croy. 87 CB
Sandilands, Sev. 107 CS
Sandilands Rd. SW6 66 BS
Sandison St. SE15 67 CA
Sandland St. WC1 2 C
Sandland St. WC1 56 BX
Sandlands Gro., Tad. 103 BP
Sandlands Rd., Tad. 103 BP
Sandlewood Ave., Cher. 82 AV
Sandling Ri. SE9 78 CL
Sandlings, The N22 38 BY
Sandmere Clo., Hem.H. 8 AZ
St. Albans Rd.
Sandmere Rd. SW4 66 BX
Sandon Clo., Esher 84 BG
Sandon Pl., Ong. 24 CX
Sandon Rd., Chsnt. 21 CC
Sandow Ave., Horn. 51 CV
Sandown Ave., Dag. 59 CS
Sandown Ave., Esher 93 BG
Sandown Clo., Houns. 63 BC
Sandown Ct., Esher 93 BF
Sandown Cres., Hayes 63 BB
Sandown Dr., Cars. 95 BV
Southdown Rd.
Sandown Rd. SE25 87 CB
Sandown Rd., Couls. 104 BV
Sandown Rd., Esher 93 BG
Sandown Rd., Grav. 81 DH
Sandown Rd., Wat. 27 BD
Sandown Way, Nthlt. 54 BE
Sandpiper Clo. E17 39 CC
Sandpiper Rd., S.Croy. 96 CC
Sandpiper Way, Orp. 89 CP
Sandpipers, The, Grav. 81 DH
Sandpit Cres., St.Alb. 9 BJ1
Sandpit Gro., Hert. 11 BV1
Sandpit Hall Rd., Wok. 91 AQ5
Sandpit La., Brwd. 33 CZ2
Sandpit La., St.Alb. 9 BH1
Sandpit Pl. SE7 68 CK4
Maryon Rd.

ndpit Rd., Brom. 78 CG49
ndpit Rd., Dart. 70 CV45
ndpit Rd., Red. 121 BU71
ndpit Rd., Welw.G.C. 5 BR9
ndpits Head, Guil. 109 AO68
ndpits Rd., Croy. 96 CC56
ndpits Rd., Rich. 74 BK48
ndra Clo. N22 39 BZ30
iew Rd.
ndra Clo., Houns. 74 BF46
ndridge Clo., Har. 45 BH31
ndridge Clo., Hem.H. 8 AZ10
lstree Rd.
ndridge Ct. N4 48 BZ34
ings Cres. Est.
ndridge Rd., St.Alb. 9 BH12
ndridge St. N19 47 BW34
rchway
ndridgebury La., St.Alb. 9 BH11
ndringham Ave. SW20 85 BR51
ndringham Clo., Enf. 30 CA23
ndringham Clo., Ilf. 49 CM31
andringham Gdns.
ndringham Ct. W9 56 BT38
ndringham Ct., Har. 45 BF34
ndringham Cres., Har. 45 BF34
ndringham Cres., t.Alb. 9 BJ11
ndringham Dr., Ashf. 73 AX49
ndringham Dr., Well. 68 CN44
ndringham Gdns. N8 47 BX32
ndringham Gdns. N12 38 BT29
ndringham Gdns., ouns. 63 BC43
ndringham Gdns., Ilf. 49 CM31
ndringham Ms. W5 54 BK40
igh St.
ndringham Rd. E7 49 CJ35
ndringham Rd. E8 48 CA35
ndringham Rd. E10 48 CF32
ndringham Rd. N22 48 BZ31
ndringham Rd. NW2 55 BP36
ndringham Rd. NW11 46 BR33
ndringham Rd., Bark. 49 CN35
ndringham Rd., Brwd. 33 DA25
ndringham Rd., Brom. 78 CH49
ndringham Rd., Houns. 73 AY46
ndringham Rd., Nthlt. 54 BF36
ndringham Rd., Pot.B. 20 BS18
ndringham Rd., Th.Hth. 87 BZ53
ndringham Rd., Wat. 27 BD22
ndringham Rd., Vor.Pk. 85 BP55
ndringham Way, Val.Cr. 21 CC20
ndrock Pl., Croy. 96 CC56
ndrock Rd. SE13 67 CE45
ndrock Rd., Dor. 119 BF72
ndroyd Way, Cob. 93 BF60
nds Way, Wdf.Grn. 40 CK29
ndsend La. SW6 66 BS44
ndstone Pl. N19 47 BV34
ndstone Rd. SE12 78 CH48
ndtoft Rd. SE7 68 CH43
ndway, Orp. 89 CP52
ndway Rd., Orp. 89 CP52
ndwell Cres. NW6 47 BS35
Sumatra Rd.
ndwich St. WC1 1 Q3
ndwich St. WC1 56 BX38
ndy Bank Rd., Grav. 81 DG47
ndy Bury, Orp. 88 CM55
ndy Clo., Twick. 74 BJ47
ndy Clo., Wok. 100 AU62
ndy Dr., Cob. 93 BF59
ndy Dr., Felt. 73 BB47
ndy Hill Ave. SE18 68 CL42
ndy Hill Rd. SE18 68 CL42
ndy Hill Rd., Wall. 95 BW58
ndy La., Bet. 120 BO71
ndy La., Bush. 27 BG24
ndy La., Cob. 93 BE59
ndy La., Dart. 80 DB48
ndy La. (Chadwell St. Mary), Grays 71 DG43
ndy La. (West Thurrock), Grays 70 DA42
ndy La., Guil. 118 AO73
ndy La., Har. 46 BL32
ndy La., Mitch. 86 BV51
ndy La., Nthwd. 35 BB27
ndy La., Orp. 89 CO54
ndy La. (St. Pauls Cray), Orp. 89 CP51
ndy La., Oxt. 114 CF68
ndy La. (Limpsfield), Oxt. 115 CH67
ndy La., Rain. 60 CW40
ndy La. (Bletchingley), Red. 121 BY69
ndy La. (Nutfield), Red. 121 BW71
ndy La., Reig. 120 BP71
ndy La., Rich. 74 BK48
ndy La., Sev. 108 CV65
ndy La. (Ivy Hatch), Sev. 117 DA66
ndy La., Sid. 79 CP50
ndy La., Sutt. 94 BR58
ndy La., Tad. 103 BR65
ndy La., Tedd. 74 BJ50
ndy La., Vir.W. 82 AS52
ndy La., Walt. 83 BS53
ndy La., West. 115 CM66
ndy La., Wok. 100 AU61
ndy La. (Chobham), Wok. 91 AP58
ndy La. (Send), Wok. 100 AU65
andy La. Est., Rich. 74 BK48
andy La. N., Wall. 95 BW56
andy La. S., Wall. 95 BW58
andy Lo. La., Nthwd. 35 BB27
andy Lo. Rd., Rick. 35 AZ27
andy Lo. Way, Nthwd. 35 BB29

Sandy Mead, Maid. 61 AH42
Moor End
Sandy Ridge, Chis. 78 CK50
Sandy Ri., Ger.Cr. 34 AS30
Sandy Rd. NW3 47 BS34
Sandy Rd., Wey. 92 AW57
Sandy Way, Cob. 93 BF59
Sandy Way, Croy. 87 CD55
Sandy Way, Walt. 83 BB54
Sandy Way, Wok. 100 AU62
Sandycombe Rd., Felt. 73 BC47
Sandycombe Rd., Rich. 65 BL45
Sandycombe Rd., Twick. 74 BK46
Sandycroft SE2 69 CO43
Sandycroft, Epsom 94 BQ58
Birchfield Gro.
Sandycroft Rd., Amer. 25 AR22
Sandyhill Rd., Ilf. 49 CL35
Sandymount Ave., Stan. 36 BK28
Sandys Row E1 2 N7
Sandys Row E1 57 CA39
Sanfoin End, Hem.H. 8 AZ12
Sanford La. N16 48 CA34
High St.
Sanford St. SE14 67 CD43
Sanford Ter. N16 48 CA34
Sanford Wk. N16 48 CA34
Smalley Rd.
Sanford Wk. SE14 67 CD43
Coldblow La.
Sanger Ave., Chess. 94 BL56
Sangley Rd. SE6 77 CE47
Sangley Rd. SE25 87 CA52
Sangora Rd. SW11 66 BT45
Strathblaine Rd.
Sans Wk. EC1 2 E4
Sans Wk. EC1 56 BY38
Woodbridge St.
Sansom Rd. E11 49 CG34
Sansom St. SE5 67 BZ43
Santers La., Pot.B. 19 BR20
Santley St. SW4 66 BX45
Santos Rd. SW18 76 BS46
Santway, The, Stan. 36 BH28
Sanway Clo., Wey. 92 AY60
Sanway Rd., Cob. 101 AY61
Sanway Rd., Wey. 92 AY60
Sapho Pk., Grav. 81 DJ49
Saphora Clo., Orp. 97 CM56
Sappers Clo., Saw. 6 CQ6
Sapphire Clo. E6 58 CL39
Sapphire Clo., Dag. 50 CP33
Crystal Way
Sapphire Rd. SE8 67 CD42
Sara Pk., Grav. 81 DJ49
Saracen Clo., Croy. 87 BZ53
Saracen St. E14 57 CE39
Saracens Head, Hem.H. 8 AZ13
Saracens Head Yd. EC3 2 P9
Sarah St. N1 2 N2
Sarah St. N1 57 CA38
Saratoga Rd. E5 48 CC35
Sardinia St. WC2 2 B9
Sardinia St. WC2 56 BX39
Kingsway
Sargeant Clo., Uxb. 53 AX38
Sarita Clo., Har. 36 BG30
Sarjant Path SW19 75 BR48
Queensmere Rd.
Sark Clo., Houns. 64 BF44
Sark Wk. E16 58 CH39
Sarnesfield Rd., Enf. 30 BZ24
Sarratt Ave., Hem.H. 8 AZ10
Sarratt La., Rick. 26 AW23
Sarratt Rd., Rick. 26 AW22
Sarre Ave., Horn. 60 CV36
Sarre Rd. NW2 46 BR35
Sarre Rd., Orp. 89 CP53
Sarsby Dr., Stai. 72 AT48
Feathers La.
Sarsen Ave., Houns. 64 BE44
Sarsfeld Rd. SW12 76 BU47
Sarsfield Rd., Grnf. 54 BJ37
Sartor Rd. SE15 67 CC45
Sarum Grn., Wey. 83 BB55
Sarum Pl., Hem.H. 8 AY11
Satanita Clo. E16 58 CJ39
Satchell Mead NW9 37 BO30
Satchwell Rd. E2 2 Q3
Satchwell St. E2 2 Q3
Saturn Way, Hem.H. 8 AY12
Sauls Grn. E11 49 CG34
Napier Rd.
Saunders Clo., Grav. 81 DF48
Saunders Copse, Wok. 100 AQ64
Saunders La., Wok. 100 AP64
Saunders Ness Rd. E14 67 CF42
Saunders Rd. SE18 68 CN42
Saunders Rd., Uxb. 53 AY36
Saunders St. SE11 66 BY42
Saunders Way SE28 59 CO40
Saunderton Rd., Wem. 45 BJ35
Saunton Ave., Hayes 63 BB43
Saunton Rd., Horn. 50 CU34
Savage Gdns. E6 58 CK39
Savage Gdns. EC3 2 N10
Savage Gdns. EC3 57 CA40
Savay Clo., Uxb. 44 AW33
Savay La., Uxb. 44 AW32
Savernake Rd. N9 30 CB25
Savernake Rd. NW3 47 BU35
Savile Clo., N.Mal. 85 BO53
Savile Gdns., Croy. 87 CA55
Savile Row W1 1 L10
Savile Row W1 56 BW40
Savill Gdns. SW20 85 BP52
Saville Cres., Ashf. 73 BA50
Saville Gdns., Croy. 87 CA55
Saville Rd. E16 58 CK40
Saville Rd. W4 65 BN41
Saville Rd., Rom. 50 CQ32
Saville Rd., Twick. 74 BK47
Saville Row, Brom. 88 CG54
Saville Row, Enf. 30 CC23

Saville Row, Wdf.Grn. 40 CH29
Savona Clo. SW19 75 BQ50
Savona Est. SW8 66 BW43
Savona St. SW8 66 BW43
Savoy Ave., Hayes 63 BB42
Savoy Bldgs. WC2 4 B1
Savoy Clo. E15 58 CG37
Savoy Clo., Edg. 37 BM28
Savoy Clo., Uxb. 35 AX30
Savoy Ct. WC2 4 A1
Savoy Ct. WC2 56 BX40
Strand
Savoy Hill WC2 4 B1
Savoy Pl. WC2 4 A1
Savoy Pl. WC2 56 BX40
Savoy Rd., Dart. 80 CV46
Savoy Row WC2 4 B1
Savoy Steps WC2 4 B1
Savoy St. WC2 4 B1
Savoy St. WC2 56 BX40
Savoy Way WC2 4 B1
Savoy Way WC2 56 BX40
Carting La.
Savoy Wd., Harl. 13 CL13
Sawells, Brox. 12 CD14
Sawkins Clo. SW19 75 BQ48
Thursley Gdns.
Sawley Rd. W12 55 BP40
Sawpit La., Guil. 110 AY69
Sawtry Clo., Cars. 86 BT54
Sawyer Clo. N9 39 CB27
Lion Rd.
Sawyer St. SE1 4 H4
Sawyer St. SE1 67 BZ41
Sawyers Clo., Dag. 59 CS36
Sawyers Clo., Wind. 61 AM43
Sawyers Hall La., Brwd. 42 DB26
Sawyers La., Borwd. 27 BJ23
Sawyers La., Pot.B. 19 BQ20
Sawyers Lawn W13 54 BJ39
Sawyers Way, Hem.H. 8 AY13
Saxby Rd. SW2 76 BX47
Saxbys Rd., Sev. 108 CY64
Saxham Rd., Bark. 58 CN37
Saxlingham Rd. E4 39 CF27
Saxon Ave., Felt. 74 BE48
Saxon Clo., Brwd. 122 DD27
Saxon Clo., Grav. 81 DE48
Saxon Clo., Rom. 42 CW30
Saxon Clo., Slou. 62 AS41
Saxon Clo., Surb. 84 BK53
Saxon Clo., Uxb. 53 AY39
Saxon Ct., Borwd. 28 BL23
Saxon Dr. W3 55 BM39
Saxon Gdns., Sthl. 54 BE40
Saxon Ho., Felt. 74 BE48
Saxon Pl., Hort.K. 90 CY53
Saxon Rd. E3 57 CD37
Saxon Rd. E6 58 CK38
Saxon Rd. N22 38 BY30
Saxon Rd. SE25 87 BZ53
Saxon Rd., Ashf. 73 BA50
Saxon Rd., Brom. 78 CG50
Saxon Rd., Dart. 80 CW49
Saxon Rd., Ilf. 58 CL36
Saxon Rd., Sthl. 54 BE40
Saxon Rd., Walt. 84 BD55
Linley Dr.
Saxon Rd., Welw. 5 BP5
Saxon Rd., Wem. 46 BM34
Saxon Wk., Sid. 79 CP50
Cray Rd.
Saxon Way N14 29 BW25
Saxon Way, Reig. 120 BR70
Saxon Way, Wal.Abb. 21 CF20
Saxon Way, West Dr. 63 AX43
Saxon Way, Wind. 72 AQ46
Saxonbury Ave., Sun. 83 BC51
Saxonbury Clo., Mitch. 86 BT52
Saxonbury Gdns., Surb. 84 BK54
Saxons, Tad. 103 BQ64
Saxony Par., Hayes 53 BA39
Saxton Clo. SE13 67 CF45
Saxville Rd., Orp. 89 CO52
Sayer Ct., Wok. 100 AP62
Sayers Clo., Lthd. 102 BG65
Sayers Gdns., Berk. 7 AQ11
Sayers Wk., Rich. 75 BL47
Stafford Pl.
Sayes Ct., Wey. 92 AW56
Sayes Ct. Est. SE8 67 CD42
Sayes Ct. Fm. Dr., Wey. 92 AW56
Sayes Ct. Rd., Orp. 89 CO52
Sayes Ct. St. SE8 67 CD43
Sayesbury Ave., Saw. 6 CP5
Sayward Clo., Chesh. 16 AO18
Scabharbour Rd., Sev. 117 CV70
Scads Hill Clo., Orp. 88 CN53
Scala St. W1 1 M6
Scala St. W1 56 BW39
Scales Rd. N17 48 CA31
Scampston Ms. W10 55 BQ39
Scampton Rd., Houns. 73 AY46
Southampton Rd.
Scandrett St. E1 57 CB40
Wapping High St.
Scarba Wk. N1 57 BZ36
Scarborough Clo., Sutt. 94 BR59
Scarborough Clo., West. 106 CJ62
Scarborough Rd. E11 48 CF33
Scarborough Rd. N4 47 BY33
Scarborough Rd. N9 39 CC26
Scarborough St. E1 2 Q9
Scarborough Way, Slou. 61 AN41
Scarbrook Rd., Croy. 87 BZ55
Scarbrook St., Croy. 86 BZ55
Scarbrook Rd.
Scarle Rd., Wem. 54 BK36
Scarlet Rd. SE6 78 CG48
Scarlett Clo., Wok. 100 AP62
Scarsbrook Rd. SE3 68 CJ45
Scarsdale Pl. W8 66 BS41
Wrights La.

Scarsdale Rd., Har. 45 BG34
Scarsdale Vill. W8 66 BS41
Scarth Rd. SW13 65 BO45
Scatterdells La., Kings L. 16 AV18
Scawen Rd. SE8 67 CD42
Scawfell St. E2 2 Q1
Scaynes Link N12 38 BS28
Sceaux Est. SE5 67 CA44
Sceptre Rd. E2 57 CC38
Schofield Wk. SE3 68 CH43
Dornbergh Clo.
Scholars Ct., St.Alb. 10 BN15
High St.
Scholars Rd. E4 39 CF26
Scholars Rd. SW12 76 BW47
Scholars Wk., Ger.Cr. 34 AS29
Scholars Wk., Hat. 10 BP13
Scholefield Rd. N19 47 BW33
Scholes Cres. SW2 76 BY47
School All., Twick. 74 BJ47
Bell La.
School Bell Ms. E3 57 CD38
Arbery Rd.
School Clo., Guil. 118 AR69
Bellfields Rd.
School Gdns., Berk. 7 AT12
School Grn. La., Epp. 23 CS16
School Hill, Red. 113 BW67
School Ho. La., Tedd. 74 BJ50
School La. SE23 77 CB48
Eliot Bank
School La., Beac. 34 AO29
School La., Brwd. 122 DE29
School La., Bush. 36 BF26
School La., Cat. 114 CA66
School La., Ch.St.G. 34 AQ27
School La., Dart. 80 DB49
School La., Dor. 119 BG72
School La. (Mickleham), Dor. 111 BK67
School La., Egh. 72 AT49
School La., Ger.Cr. 34 AR30
School La., Guil. 110 AY69
School La. (West Horsley), Guil. 110 AZ68
School La., Harl. 6 CN10
School La., Hat. 10 BQ12
School La. (Essenden), Hat. 11 BU12
School La., Hort.K. 90 CY52
School La., Kings.T. 84 BK51
Park Rd.
School La., Lthd. 102 BG65
School La., Ong. 15 CZ10
School La. (Tilegate Grn.), Ong. 14 CS12
School La., Pnr. 45 BE31
School La., St.Alb. 18 BF19
School La. (Plaxtol), Sev. 117 DC67
School La. (Seal), Sev. 108 CW64
School La., Shep. 83 AZ53
School La., Slou. 52 AQ36
School La., Surb. 85 BM54
School La., Swan. 89 CU51
School La., Tad. 112 BP66
School La. (West Kingsdown), Ton. 99 CZ59
School La., Well. 69 CO45
School La. (Ayot St. Peter), Welw. 5 BO5
School La. (Tewin), Welw. 5 BU6
School La., Wey. 92 AW56
School La., Wok. 101 AZ64
School Mead, Abb.L. 17 BA19
School Pas., Kings.T. 85 BL51
School Pas., Sthl. 54 BE40
School Pl. E1 57 CB38
Buckhurst St.
School Rd. E12 49 CK35
School Rd. NW10 55 BN38
School Rd., Ashf. 73 AZ49
School Rd., Brwd. 33 CZ22
School Rd., Chis. 88 CM51
School Rd., Dag. 59 CR37
School Rd., E.Mol. 84 BG52
School Rd., Grav. 81 DH48
School Rd., Hmptn. 74 BG50
School Rd., Houns. 64 BG45
School Rd., Kings.T. 84 BK51
Park Rd.
School Rd., Ong. 23 CT18
School Rd., Pot.B. 20 BT18
School Rd., West Dr. 63 AX43
School Rd. Ave., Hmptn. 74 BG50
School Row, Hem.H. 7 AV14
School Wk., Sun. 83 BC52
School Way N12 38 BT28
School Way, Dag. 50 CP34
Schoolbell Ms. E3 57 CD37
Arbery Rd.
Schoolfield Rd., Grays 70 DA43
Schoolhouse La. E1 57 CC40
Schooner Clo. SE16 67 CC41
Kinburn St.
Schroder Ct., Egh. 72 AQ49
Schubert Rd. SW15 75 BR46
Schubert Rd., Borwd. 27 BK25
Scilla Ct., Grays 71 DE43
Scillonian Rd., Guil. 118 AQ71
Sclater St. E1 2 P4
Sclater St. E1 57 CA38
Scoble Pl. N16 48 CA35
Amhurst Rd.
Scoresby St. SE1 4 F3
Scoresby St. SE1 56 BY40
Scorton Ave., Grnf. 54 BJ37
Scot Gro., Pnr. 36 BD29
Scotch Common W13 54 BJ39
Scoter Clo., Wdf.Grn. 40 CH29
Scotland Bri. Rd., Wey. 92 AW59
Scotland Grn. N17 39 CA30
Scotland Grn. Rd., Enf. 30 CC25
Scotland Grn. Rd. N., Enf. 30 CC24
Scotland Pl. SW1 3 Q3

Scotland Rd., Buck.H. 40 CJ26
Scotney Wk., Horn. 51 CV35
Bonnington Rd.
Scots Hill, Rick. 26 AY25
Scots Hill Clo., Rick. 26 AY25
Scotscraig, Rad. 27 BH21
Scotsdale Clo., Orp. 88 CN52
Scotsdale Clo., Sutt. 94 BR57
Scotsdale Rd. SE12 78 CH46
Scotshall La., Warl. 105 CF61
Scotswood St. EC1 2 E4
Scotswood Wk. N17 39 CB29
Northumberland Pk.
Scott Clo. SW16 86 BX51
Fairview Rd.
Scott Clo., Epsom 94 BN56
Scott Clo., Guil. 118 AQ69
Scott Clo., West Dr. 63 AY42
Scott Cres., Erith 69 CT44
Scott Cres., Har. 45 BF33
Scott Ellis Gdns. NW8 1 A3
Scott Ellis Gdns. NW8 56 BT38
Scott Fm. Clo., E.Mol. 84 BJ54
Scott Gdns., Houns. 64 BD43
Scott Lidgett Cres. SE16 67 CB41
Scott Rd., Grav. 81 DH49
Scott Rd., Grays 71 DG42
Scott St. E1 57 CB38
Scottes Rd., Dag. 50 CP33
Valence Ave.
Scotts Ave., Brom. 87 CF51
Scotts Ave., Sun. 73 BB50
Scotts Clo., Horn. 51 CV35
Rye Clo.
Scotts Clo., Stai. 73 AX47
Scotts Dr., Hmptn. 74 BF50
Scotts Fm. Rd., Epsom 94 BN57
Scotts Gro. Clo., Wok. 91 AO60
Scotts Gro. Rd., Wok. 91 AO60
Scotts La., Brom. 87 CF52
Scotts Mill Rd., Rick. 26 AY25
Scotts Rd. E10 48 CF33
Scotts Rd. W12 65 BP41
Scotts Rd., Brom. 78 CH50
Scotts Rd., Sthl. 64 BD41
Scotts Way, Sev. 107 CT64
Scotts Way, Sun. 73 BB50
Scotts Yd EC4 2 K10
Scottswood Clo., Bush. 27 BE23
Scottswood Rd., Bush. 27 BE23
Scoulding Rd. E16 58 CG39
Rogers Rd.
Scout App. NW10 46 BN35
Scout La. SW4 66 BW45
Scout Way NW7 37 BN28
Scovell Cres. SE1 4 H5
Scovell Cres. SE1 67 BZ41
Great Suffolk St.
Scovell Rd. SE1 4 H5
Scovell Rd. SE1 67 BZ41
Scovell Wk. SE1 67 BZ41
Scovell Rd.
Scrafton Rd., Ilf. 49 CL34
Scratchers La., Farn. 90 CY55
Scrattons Ter., Bark. 59 CP37
Scriven St. E8 57 CA37
Scrooby St. SE6 77 CE46
Scrubbits Pk. Rd., Rad. 27 BJ21
Scrubbits Sq., Rad. 27 BJ21
The Dell
Scrubs La. NW10 55 BP38
Scrubs La. W10 55 BP39
Scrutton Clo. SW12 76 BW47
Scrutton St. EC2 2 M5
Scrutton St. EC2 57 CA38
Scudamore La. NW9 46 BN31
Scudders Hill, Fawk. 90 DA53
Scutari Rd. SE22 77 CB46
Scylla Rd. SE15 67 CB45
Scylla Rd., Houns. 73 AZ46
Seaborough Rd., Grays 71 DH41
Seabright St. E2 57 CB38
Bethnal Grn. Rd.
Seabrook Dr., W.Wick. 87 CF55
Seabrook Gdns., Rom. 50 CR33
Seabrook Rd., Dag. 50 CP34
Seabrook Rd., Kings L. 17 BA17
Seabrooke Ri., Grays 71 DD43
Seaburn Clo., Rain. 59 CT38
Seacoal La. EC4 2 F9
Seacoal La. EC4 56 BY39
Seacole Clo. W3 55 BN39
Seacourt Rd. SE2 69 CP41
Seacourt Rd., Slou. 62 AT42
Seacroft Gdns., Wat. 36 BD27
Seafield Rd. N11 38 BW28
Seaford Clo., Ruis. 44 BA34
Seaford Rd. E17 48 CE31
Seaford Rd. N15 48 BZ31
Seaford Rd. W13 54 BJ40
Seaford Rd., Enf. 30 CA24
Seaford Rd., Stai. 73 AX46
Sandringham Rd.
Seaford St. WC1 2 A3
Seaford St. WC1 56 BX38
Seaforth Ave., N.Mal. 85 BP53
Seaforth Clo., Rom. 41 CT29
Seaforth Cres. N5 48 BZ35
Seaforth Dr., Wal.Cr. 21 CC20
Seaforth Gdns. N21 38 BX26
Seaforth Gdns., Epsom 94 BO56
Seaforth Gdns., Wdf.Grn. 40 CJ28
Seaforth Pl. SW1 3 M6
Seaforth Pl. SW1 66 BW41
Buckingham Gate
Seager Pl. E3 57 CD39
Burdett Rd.
Seagrave Clo., Wey. 92 AZ57
Seagrave Rd. SW6 66 BS43
Seagry Rd. E11 49 CH32
Seal Chart, Sev. 108 CY64
Seal Dr., Sev. 108 CW64
Seal Hill, Sev. 108 CX64
Seal Hollow Rd., Sev. 108 CV65

Seal Rd., Sev. 108 CV64
Seal St. E8 48 CA35
Sealand Rd., Houns. 73 AZ46
Sealand Wk., Nthlt. 54 BD38
Wayfarer Rd.
Seale Hill, Reig. 121 BS71
Seaman Clo., St.Alb. 18 BG16
Searches La., Abb.L. 17 BC17
Searchwood Rd., Warl. 105 CB62
Searle Pl. N4 47 BX33
Evershot Rd.
Searles Clo. SW11 66 BU43
Searles Rd. SE1 4 L8
Searles Rd. SE1 67 BZ42
Sears St. SE5 67 BZ43
Seasprite Clo., Nthlt. 54 BD38
Seaton Ave., Ilf. 49 CN35
Seaton Clo. E13 58 CH38
New Barn St.
Seaton Clo. SE11 4 E10
Seaton Clo. SW15 75 BP47
Seaton Clo., Twick. 74 BG46
Seaton Dr., Ashf. 73 AY48
Seaton Gdns., Ruis. 44 BC34
Seaton Pl. NW1 1 L4
Seaton Pl. NW1 56 BW38
Seaton Pt. E5 48 CB34
Downs Est.
Seaton Rd., Dart. 79 CU47
Seaton Rd., Hayes 63 BA42
Seaton Rd., Hem.H. 8 AX15
Seaton Rd., Mitch. 86 BU51
Seaton Rd., St.Alb. 18 BK17
Seaton Rd., Twick. 74 BG46
Seaton Rd., Well. 69 CP43
Seaton Rd., Wem. 55 BL37
Seaton St. N18 39 CB28
Sebastian Ave., Brwd. 122 DD25
Sebastian St. EC1 2 G3
Sebastian St. EC1 56 BY38
Sebastopol Rd. N9 39 CB28
Sebbon St. N1 56 BY36
Sebert Rd. E7 49 CH35
Sebright Pas. E2 57 CB37
Sebright Rd., Barn. 28 BQ23
Sebright Rd., Hem.H. 8 AW14
Secker Cres., Har. 36 BG30
Secker St. SE1 4 D3
Secker St. SE1 56 BY40
Second Ave. E12 49 CK35
Second Ave. E13 58 CH38
Second Ave. E17 48 CE32
Second Ave. N18 39 CC28
Second Ave. NW4 46 BQ31
Second Ave. SW14 65 BQ45
Second Ave. W3 55 BO40
Second Ave. W10 55 BR38
Second Ave., Brwd. 24 DB20
Second Ave., Dag. 59 CR37
Second Ave., Enf. 30 CA25
Second Ave., Grays 70 DA43
Second Ave., Harl. 13 CN11
Second Ave., Hayes 53 BB40
Second Ave., Rom. 50 CP32
Second Ave., Walt. 83 BC53
Second Ave., Wat. 27 BD21
Second Ave., Wem. 45 BK34
Second Clo., E.Mol. 84 BG52
Second Cross Rd., Twick. 74 BG48
Second Way, Wem. 46 BM35
Sedan Way SE17 4 M10
Sedan Way SE17 67 CA42
Sedcombe Clo., Sid. 79 CO49
Knoll Rd.
Sedcote Rd., Enf. 30 CC25
Sedding St. SW1 3 G8
Sedding St. SW1 66 BV42
Seddon Rd., Mord. 86 BT53
Seddon St. WC1 2 C3
Sedge Ct., Grays 71 DE43
Sedge Grn., Harl. 12 CF13
Sedge Rd. N17 39 CC29
Sedgebrook Rd. SE3 68 CJ44
Sedgecombe Ave., Har. 45 BK32
Sedgefield Clo., Rom. 42 CW28
Sedgefield Cres., Rom. 42 CW28
Sedgeford Rd. W12 55 BO40
Sedgehill Rd. SE6 77 CE49
Sedgemere Ave. N2 47 BT31
Sedgemere Rd. SE2 69 CP41
Sedgemoor Dr., Dag. 50 CR35
Sedgeway SE6 78 CG47
Sedgewick Ave., Uxb. 53 AZ36
Sedgewood Clo., Brom. 88 CG54
Sedgmoor Pl. SE5 67 CA43
Sedgwick Rd. E10 48 CF34
Sedgwick St. E9 48 CC35
Sedleigh Rd. SW18 75 BR46
Sedlescombe Rd. SW6 66 BS43
Sedley, Grav. 81 DD49
Sedley Gro., Uxb. 44 AX31
Sedley Pl. W1 1 J9
Sedley Pl. W1 56 BV39
Oxford St.
Sedley Ri., Loug. 31 CK23
Seeley Dr. SE21 77 CA49
Seeleys, Harl. 6 CP9
Seelig Ave. NW9 46 BP33
Seely Rd. SW17 76 BV50
Seer Grn. La., Beac. 34 AP29
Seer Mead, Beac. 34 AO29
Seething La. EC3 2 N10
Seething La. EC3 57 CA40
Seething Wells La., Surb. 84 BK53
Sefton Ave. NW7 37 BN28
Sefton Ave., Har. 36 BG30
Sefton Clo., Orp. 88 CN52
Sefton Clo., St.Alb. 9 BH13
Blenheim Rd.
Sefton Clo., Slou. 52 AP37
Sefton Paddock, Slou. 52 AQ36
Sefton Rd., Croy. 87 CB54
Sefton Rd., Epsom 94 BN58
Sefton Rd., Orp. 88 CN52
Sefton St. SW15 65 BQ45
Sefton Way, Uxb. 53 AX39
Segal Clo. SE23 77 CD47
Brockley Pk.
Sekforde St. EC1 2 F5
Sekforde St. EC1 56 BY38
Selah Dr., Swan. 89 CS51
Selan Gdns., Hayes 53 BC39
Selbie Ave. NW10 46 BO35
Selborne Ave. E12 49 CL35
Selborne Ave., Bex. 79 CQ47
Selborne Gdns. NW4 46 BP31
Selborne Gdns., Grnf. 54 BJ37
Selborne Rd. E17 48 CD32
Selborne Rd. N14 38 BX27
Selborne Rd. N22 38 BX30
Selborne Rd. SE5 67 BZ44
Denmark Hill
Selborne Rd., Croy. 87 CA55
Selborne Rd., Ilf. 49 CL34
Selborne Rd., N.Mal. 85 BO51
Selborne Rd., Sid. 79 CO49
Selbourne Ave., Surb. 85 BL55
Selbourne Ave., Wey. 92 AW58
Selbourne Clo., Wey. 92 AW58
Selbourne Rd., Guil. 118 AT69
Sutherland Dr.
Selbourne Sq., Gdse. 114 CC68
Selby Ave., St.Alb. 9 BG13
Selby Chase, Ruis. 44 BC34
Selby Clo. E6 58 CK39
Linton Gdns.
Selby Clo., Chess. 94 BL57
Selby Clo., Chis. 78 CL50
Selby Gdns., Sthl. 54 BF38
Selby Grn., Cars. 86 BU54
Selby Rd. E11 49 CG34
Selby Rd. E13 58 CH39
Selby Rd. N17 39 CA29
Selby Rd. SE20 87 CB51
Selby Rd. W5 54 BJ38
Selby Rd., Ashf. 73 BA50
Selby Rd., Cars. 86 BU54
Selby St. E1 57 CB38
Selby Wk., Wok. 100 AQ62
Wyndham Rd.
Selcroft Rd., Pur. 95 BY59
Selden Hill, Hem.H. 8 AX14
Selden Rd. SE15 67 CC44
Selden Wk. N7 47 BX34
Durham Rd.
Selhurst Clo., Wok. 100 AS61
Selhurst New Rd. SE25 87 CA53
Selhurst Pl. SE25 87 CA53
Selhurst Rd. N9 39 BZ27
Selhurst Rd. SE25 87 CA53
Selinas La., Dag. 50 CQ33
Selkirk Dr., Erith 69 CT44
Selkirk Rd. SW17 76 BU49
Selkirk Rd., Twick. 74 BG48
Sellers Hall Clo. N3 38 BS29
Sellincourt Rd. SW17 76 BU49
Sellindge Clo., Beck. 77 CD50
Sellon Ms. SE11 4 C9
Sellon Ms. SE11 66 BX42
Newport St.
Sellons Ave. NW10 55 BO37
Sellwood Dr., Barn. 28 BQ25
Selma Ho. W12 55 BP39
Du Cane Rd.
Selsdon Ave., S.Croy. 96 BZ57
Selsdon Clo., Rom. 41 CS30
Selsdon Clo., Surb. 85 BL53
Selsdon Cres., S.Croy. 96 CC58
Selsdon Pk. Rd., S.Croy. 96 CC58
Selsdon Rd. E11 49 CH33
Selsdon Rd. E13 58 CJ37
Selsdon Rd. NW2 46 BO34
Selsdon Rd. SE27 76 BY48
Selsdon Rd., S.Croy. 96 BZ56
Selsdon Rd., Wey. 92 AW59
Selsdon Way E14 67 CE41
Selsea Pl. N16 48 CA35
Crossway
Selsey Cres., Well. 69 CP44
Selsey St. E14 57 CE39
Selvage La. NW7 37 BN28
Selway Clo., Pnr. 44 BC31
Selwood Clo., Stai. 73 AX46
Selwood Gdns., Stai. 73 AX46
Selwood Pl. SW7 3 A10
Selwood Pl. SW7 66 BT42
Selwood Rd., Brwd. 42 CZ27
Selwood Rd., Chess. 93 BK56
Selwood Rd., Croy. 87 CB55
Selwood Rd., Sutt. 85 BR54
Selwood Rd., Wok. 100 AT63
Selwood Ter. SW7 3 A10
Selwood Ter. SW7 66 BT42
Selworthy Clo. E11 49 CH32
Selworthy Rd. SE6 77 CD48
Selwyn Ave. E4 39 CF29
Selwyn Ave., Hat. 10 BN13
Selwyn Ave., Ilf. 49 CN32
Selwyn Ave., Rich. 65 BL45
Selwyn Clo., Houns. 64 BE45
Cambridge Rd.
Selwyn Ct. SE3 68 CG45
Selwyn Ct., Edg. 37 BM29
Selwyn Cres., Hat. 10 BO12
Selwyn Cres., Well. 69 CO45
Selwyn Dr., Hat. 10 BN12
Selwyn Grn., Walt. 84 BD54
Cromwell Rd.
Selwyn Pl., Orp. 89 CO52
Selwyn Rd. E3 57 CD37
Selwyn Rd. E13 58 CH37
Selwyn Rd. NW10 55 BN36
Selwyn Rd., N.Mal. 85 BN53
Selwyn Rd., Til. 71 DF44
Selwyn Rd., Walt. 84 BD54
St. Johns Dr.
Semaphore Rd., Guil. 118 AS71
Semley Pl. SW1 3 H9
Semley Pl. SW1 66 BV42
Semley Rd. SW16 86 BX51
Semper Clo., Wok. 100 AP62
Semper Rd., Grays 71 DH41
Semphill Rd., Hem.H. 8 AY15
Senate St. SE15 67 CC44
Gibbon Rd.
Senator Wk. SE28 68 CM41
Garrick Dr.
Send Barns La., Wok. 100 AU65
Send Clo., Wok. 100 AU65
Send Hill Rd., Wok. 100 AU65
Send Par. Clo., Wok. 100 AU65
Send Rd., Wok. 100 AT65
Sendbarns La., Wok. 100 AU65
Sendmarsh Rd., Wok. 100 AU65
Seneca Rd., Th.Hth. 87 BZ52
Senga Rd., Wall. 86 BV54
Senhouse Rd., Sutt. 85 BQ55
Senior St. W2 56 BS39
Senlac Rd. SE12 78 CH47
Sennen Rd., Enf. 39 CA26
Sennen Wk. SE9 78 CK48
Nunnington Clo.
Senrab St. E1 57 CC39
Sentinel Clo., Nthlt. 54 BE38
Sentinel Sq. NW4 46 BQ31
Sentis Ct., Nthwd. 35 BB29
Carew Rd.
September Way, Stan. 36 BJ29
Septimus Pl., Enf. 30 CB25
Ermine Side
Sequoia Clo., Bush. 36 BG26
Sequoia Gdns., Orp. 88 CN54
Sequoia Pk., Pnr. 36 BF29
Serbin Clo. E10 48 CF33
Sergeants Grn. La., Wal.Abb. 22 CJ20
Sergehill La., Abb.L. 17 BC16
Serjeants Inn EC4 2 E9
Serle St. WC2 2 C8
Serle St. WC2 56 BX39
Sermon Dr., Swan. 89 CS52
Sermon La. EC4 57 BZ39
Carter La.
Serpentine Ct., Sev. 108 CV65
Serpentine Rd.
Serpentine Grn., Red. 113 BW68
Malmstone Ave.
Serpentine Rd. W2 3 E3
Serpentine Rd. W2 56 BU40
Serpentine Rd., Sev. 108 CV65
Service La., Ing. 24 DB19
Service Rd., Brwd. 42 DB27
Service Rd., Wind. 61 AL44
Service Rd., The, Pot.B. 20 BS19
Byng Dr.
Serviden Dr., Brom. 88 CJ51
Setchell Rd. SE1 4 P8
Setchell Rd. SE1 67 CA42
Setchell Way SE1 4 P8
Seth St. SE16 67 CC41
Swan Rd.
Seton Gdns., Dag. 59 CP36
Settle Rd. E13 58 CH37
Settle Rd., Rom. 42 CX28
Settles St. E1 57 CB39
Settrington Rd. SW6 66 BS44
Seven Acres, Cars. 86 BU55
Brooklyn Clo.
Seven Acres (New Ash Grn.), Dart. 90 DC55
Seven Acres, Swan. 89 CS53
Seven Arches (New Ash Grn.), Dart. 90 DC55
Seven Arches Rd., Brwd. 42 DB27
Seven Hills Clo., Walt. 92 BB58
Seven Hills Rd., Cob. 92 BB59
Seven Hills Rd., Iver 43 AT35
Seven Hills Rd., Walt. 92 BB57
Seven Kings Rd., Ilf. 49 CN33
Seven Sisters Rd. N4 48 BZ33
Seven Sisters Rd. N7 47 BX34
Seven Sisters Rd. N15 48 BZ33
Sevenoaks By-pass, Sev. 117 CV69
Sevenoaks By-pass, Ton. 117 CV69
Sevenoaks Clo., Bexh. 69 CR45
Sevenoaks Clo., Rom. 42 CV28
Sevenoaks Rd. SE4 77 CD46
Sevenoaks Rd., Orp. 97 CN56
Sevenoaks Rd. (Green St. Grn.), Orp. 97 CN57
Sevenoaks Rd., Sev. 108 DA65
Sevenoaks Rd. (Otford), Sev. 107 CU62
Sevenoaks Rd., West. 115 CM66
Sevenoaks Way, Sid. 79 CO50
Seventh Ave. E12 49 CK35
Seventh Ave., Enf. 30 CB25
Seventh Ave., Hayes 53 BC40
Severalls Ave., Chesh. 16 AO18
Severn Ave., Rom. 50 CU31
Severn Cres., Slou. 62 AT43
Severn Dr., Enf. 30 CB22
Severn Dr., Esher 84 BJ55
Severn Dr., Upmin. 51 CY32
Severn Dr., Walt. 84 BD55
Severn Mead, Hem.H. 8 AY12
Severn Rd., S.Ock. 60 CY39
Severn Way NW10 46 BO35
Severn Way, Wat. 18 BD20
Severnake Clo. E14 67 CE42
Charnwood Gdns.
Severns Fld., Epp. 23 CO18
Severnvale, St.Alb. 19 BL17
Thamesdale
Severus Rd. SW11 66 BU45
Seville St. SW1 3 F5
Seville St. SW1 66 BU41
Sevington Rd. NW4 46 BP32
Sevington St. W9 56 BS38
Seward Rd. W7 64 BJ41
Seward Rd., Beck. 87 CC51
Seward St. EC1 2 G3
Seward St. EC1 56 BY38
Sewardstone Gdns. E4 30 CE25
Sewardstone Rd. E2 57 CC37
Sewardstone Rd. E4 39 CE26
Sewardstone St, Wal.Abb. 21 CF20
Sewardstone Way, Wal.Abb. 30 CF21
Sewdley St. E5 48 CC34
Sewell Clo., St.Alb. 10 BL13
Sewell Harris Clo., Harl. 6 CN10
Minchen Rd.
Sewell Rd. SE2 69 CO41
Sewell St. E13 58 CH38
Sewells, Welw.G.C. 5 BR6
Sextant Ave. E14 67 CF42
Sexton Clo., Rain. 59 CT37
Sexton Rd., Til. 71 DF44
Seymer Rd., Rom. 50 CS31
Seymour Ave. N17 39 CB30
Seymour Ave., Epsom 94 BP58
Seymour Ave., Mord. 85 BQ53
Seymour Clo., E.Mol. 84 BG53
Seymour Clo., Pnr. 36 BE30
Seymour Ct. E4 40 CG27
Seymour Ct. N10 38 BV30
Seymour Ct. NW2 46 BP34
Seymour Cres., Hem.H. 8 AY13
Seymour Dr., Brom. 88 CK54
Seymour Gdns. SE4 67 CD45
Seymour Gdns., Felt. 74 BD49
Seymour Gdns., Ilf. 49 CK33
Seymour Gdns., Ruis. 45 BD33
Seymour Gdns., Surb. 85 BL53
Seymour Gdns., Twick. 74 BJ47
Seymour Ms. W1 1 G8
Seymour Ms. W1 56 BV39
Seymour Ms., Saw. 6 CQ7
Seymour Pl. SE25 87 CB52
Seymour Pl. W1 1 D6
Seymour Pl. W1 56 BU39
Seymour Rd. E4 39 CE26
Seymour Rd. E6 58 CJ37
Seymour Rd. E10 48 CD33
Seymour Rd. N3 38 BS29
Seymour Rd. N8 47 BY32
Seymour Rd. N9 39 CB27
Seymour Rd. SW18 75 BR46
Seymour Rd. SW19 75 BQ48
Seymour Rd. W4 65 BN42
Seymour Rd., Berk. 7 AP12
Seymour Rd., Cars. 95 BV56
Seymour Rd., Ch.St.G. 34 AR28
Seymour Rd., E.Mol. 84 BG53
Seymour Rd., Grav. 81 DF48
Seymour Rd., Hmptn. 74 BG49
Seymour Rd., Kings.T. 84 BK51
Seymour Rd., Mitch. 86 BV54
Seymour Rd., St.Alb. 9 BH12
Seymour Rd., Slou. 61 AO41
Seymour Rd., Til. 71 DF44
Seymour St. W1 1 E9
Seymour St. W1 56 BU39
Seymour St. W2 1 E9
Seymour St. W2 56 BU39
Seymour Ter. SE20 87 CB51
Selby Rd.
Seymour Vill. SE20 87 CB51
Seymour Wk. SW10 66 BT42
Seymour Way, Sun. 73 BB50
Seymours, Harl. 13 CK12
Seymours, Loug. 31 CL23
Seyssel St. E14 67 CF42
Shaa Rd. W3 55 BN40
Shacklands Rd., Sev. 98 BR59
Shackleford Rd., Wok. 100 AT64
Shacklegate La., Tedd. 74 BH49
Shackleton Clo. SE23 77 CB48
Featherstone Ave.
Shackleton Rd., Slou. 52 AP40
Shackleton Rd., Sthl. 54 BE40
Shackleton Wk., Guil. 118 AP70
Humbolt Clo.
Shackleton Way, Welw.G.C. 5 BT8
Shacklewell Grn. E8 48 CA35
Shacklewell La.
Shacklewell La. E8 48 CA35
Shacklewell Rd. N16 48 CA35
Shacklewell St. E2 2 Q4
Shacklewell St. E2 57 CA38
Shad Thames SE1 4 P3
Shad Thames SE1 57 CA40
Shadbolt Clo., Wor.Pk. 85 BO55
Shadwell Dr., Nthlt. 54 BE38
Shadwell Pl. E1 57 CC40
Shady Bush Clo., Bush. 36 BG26
Shady La., Wat. 26 BC23
Shaef Way, Tedd. 74 BJ50
Shafter Rd., Dag. 59 CS36
Shaftesbury, Loug. 31 CJ24
Shaftesbury Ave. W1 1 N10
Shaftesbury Ave. W1 56 BW40
Shaftesbury Ave. WC2 3 N1
Shaftesbury Ave. WC2 56 BW40
Shaftesbury Ave., Barn. 29 BT24
Shaftesbury Ave., Enf. 30 CC23
Shaftesbury Ave., Felt. 73 BC46
Shaftesbury Ave., Har. 45 BF33
Shaftesbury Ave. (Kenton), Har. 45 BK32
Shaftesbury Ave., Sthl. 64 BF42
Shaftesbury Ct. N1 57 BZ37
Shaftesbury Cres., Stai. 73 AX50
Shaftesbury La., Dart. 70 CX45
Shaftesbury Rd. E4 39 CF26
Shaftesbury Rd. E7 58 CJ36
Shaftesbury Rd. E10 48 CE33
Shaftesbury Rd. E17 48 CE32
Shaftesbury Rd. N18 39 CA29
Shaftesbury Rd. N19 47 BX33
Shaftesbury Rd., Beck. 87 CD51
Shaftesbury Rd., Cars. 86 BT54
Shaftesbury Rd., Epp. 22 CN18
Shaftesbury Rd., Rich. 65 BL45
Shaftesbury Rd., Rom. 50 C
Shaftesbury Rd., Wat. 27 BD
Shaftesbury Rd., Wok. 100 A
Shaftesbury St. N1 2
Shaftesbury St. N1 57 B
Shaftesbury Way, Twick. 74 BH
Shaftesbury Waye, Hayes 54 BD
Shaftesburys, The, Bark. 58 CN
Shafto Ms. SW1 3
Shafto Ms. SW1 66 BU
Cadogan Sq.
Shafton Rd. E9 57 CC
Shafts Ct. EC3 57 CA
Shaftsbury Rd., Beck. 87 CD
Croydon Rd.
Shaftsbury Way, Kings L. 17 BA
Shaggy Calf La., Slou. 52 AC
Shakespeare Ave. N11 38 BW
Shakespeare Ave. NW10 55 BN
Shakespeare Ave., Felt. 73 BC
Shakespeare Ave., Hayes 53 BC
Shakespeare Ave., Til. 71 DG
Shakespeare Cres. E12 58 CK
Shakespeare Cres. NW10 55 BN
Shakespeare Dr., Har. 46 BL
Shakespeare Gdns. N2 47 BU
Shakespeare Ho. N14 38 BW
Shakespeare Rd. E17 39 CC
Shakespeare Rd. NW7 37 BC
Shakespeare Rd. SE24 76 BY
Shakespeare Rd. W3 55 BN
Shakespeare Rd. W7 54 BH
Shakespeare Rd., Bexh. 69 CO
Shakespeare Rd., Dart. 70 CX
Shakespeare Rd., Rom. 50 CT
Shakespeare Rd., Wey. 92 AX
Shakespeare Sq., Ilf. 40 CM
Shakespeare St., Wat. 26 BC
Shakespeare Wk. N16 48 CA
Shakespeare Way, Felt. 74 BD
Shakletons, Ong. 24 CX
Shalcomb St. SW10 66 BT
Shalcross Dr., Chsnt. 21 CD
Shaldon Dr., Mord. 85 BR
Shaldon Dr., Ruis. 45 BD
Shaldon Rd., Edg. 37 BL
Shaldon Way, Walt. 84 BD
Shale Grn., Red. 113 BW
Shalfleet Dr. W10 55 BO
Shalford Clo., Orp. 97 CM
Shalford Rd., Guil. 118 AR
Shalimar Gdns. W3 55 BN
Shalimar Rd. W3 55 BM
Hereford Rd.
Shallcross Cres., Hat. 10 BO
Shallons Rd. SE9 78 CL
Shalston Rd. SW14 65 BM
Shalston Vill., Surb. 85 BL
Shamrock Clo., Lthd. 102 BG
Shamrock Rd., Croy. 86 BX
Shamrock Rd., Grav. 81 DJ
Shamrock St. SW4 66 BW
Clapham Manor St.
Shamrock Way N14 38 BV
Shand St. SE1 4
Shand St. SE1 67 CA
Shandon Rd. SW4 76 BW
Shandy St. E1 57 CC
Shanklin Clo., Wal.Cr. 21 CA
Hornbeam Way
Shanklin Gdns., Wat. 36 BD
Shanklin Rd. N8 47 BW
Shanklin Rd. N15 48 CB
Shanklin Way SE15 67 CA
Hordle Prom. S.
Shannon Clo. NW2 46 BQ
Shannon Clo., Sthl. 64 BE
Ringway
Shannon Gro. SW9 66 BX
Shannon Pl. NW8 56 BU
Shannon Way, Beck. 77 CE
Shannon Way, S.Ock. 60 CY
Shantock Hall La., Hem.H. 16 AS
Shantock La., Hem.H. 16 AS
Shap Cres., Cars. 86 BU
Shardcroft Ave. SE24 76 BY
Shardeloes Rd. SE14 67 CD
Shards Sq. SE15 67 CB
Sharland Rd., Grav. 81 DH
Sharman Ct., Sid. 79 CO
Carlton Rd.
Sharnbrooke Clo., Well. 69 CP
Sharney Ave., Slou. 62 AT
Sharon Clo., Epsom 94 BN
Sharon Clo., Lthd. 102 BF
Sharon Clo., Surb. 84 BK
Sharon Gdns. E9 57 CC
Sharon Rd. W4 65 BN
Sharon Rd., Enf. 30 CD
Sharp Way, Dart. 70 CW
Sharpe Cft., Harl. 13 CM
Sharpes La., Berk. 7 AT
Sharples Hall St. NW1 56 BU
Regents Pk. Rd.
Sharpness Clo., Hayes 54 BE
Kennett Dr.
Sharps La., Ruis. 44 BA
Sharratt St. SE15 67 CC
Sharsted St. SE17 66 BY
Sharvel La., Nthlt. 53 BC
Shavers Pl. SW1 3 N
Shaw Ave., Bark. 59 CQ
Shaw Clo. SE28 59 CO4
Shaw Clo., Bush. 36 BH2
Shaw Clo., Cher. 91 AU5
Shaw Clo., Chsnt. 21 CC1
Shaw Clo., Epsom 94 BO5
Shaw Clo., Horn. 50 CU3
Shaw Clo., S.Croy. 96 CA5
Shaw Cres., Brwd. 122 DE2
Shaw Cres., S.Croy. 96 CA5
Shaw Cres., Til. 71 DG4
Shaw Dr., Walt. 84 BD5
Shaw Gdns., Bark. 59 CQ3

aw Rd., Brom. 78 CG48
aw Rd., Enf. 30 CC23
aw Rd., West. 106 CJ63
aw Sq. E17 39 CD30
aw Way, Wall. 95 BX57
awbridge, Harl. 13 CM12
awbrooke Rd. SE9 78 CJ46
awbury Rd. SE22 77 CA46
awbury Rd., Grnf. 54 BF38
awfield Pk., Brom. 88 CJ51
awfield St. SW3 66 BU42
awford Ct. SW15 75 BP47
awford Rd., Epsom 94 BN57
awley Cres., Epsom 103 BQ62
awley Way, Epsom 103 BP62
awline Cres. E17 39 CD30
aws, The, Welw.G.C. 5 BT8
aws Cotts. SE23 77 CD48
axton Cres., Croy. 96 CF58
earing Dr., Cars. 86 BT54
'tavordale Rd.
earling Way N7 56 BX36
earman Rd. SE3 68 CG45
ears Grn. Ct., Grav. 81 DG48
earwood Cres., Dart. 69 CU45
eaths La., Lthd. 93 BF60
eaveshill Ave. NW9 46 BO31
eehy Way, Slou. 52 AQ40
een Common Dr., Rich. 65 BM45
een Ct., Rich. 65 BM45
een Ct. Rd., Rich. 65 BM45
een Gate Gdns. SW14 65 BN45
een La. SW14 75 BN46
een Pk., Rich. 65 BL45
een Rd., Orp. 88 CN52
een Rd., Rich. 75 BL46
een Way, Wall. 95 BX56
een Wd. SW14 75 BN46
eendale Rd., Rich. 65 BL45
eenewood SE26 77 CB49
eep Hill, Sev. 117 DB66
eep La. E8 57 CB37
eep Wk., Epsom 103 BN64
eep Wk., Reig. 120 BP69
eep Wk., Shep. 83 AY54
eep Wk., The, Wok. 100 AU62
eepbarn La., Warl. 97 CG59
eepcot Dr., Wat. 18 BD20
eepcot La., Wat. 17 BC20
eepcote, Welw.G.C. 5 BS9
eepcote Clo., Houns. 63 BC43
eepcote Gdns., Uxb. 43 AV32
)enham Grn. La.
eepcote La. SW11 66 BU44
eepcote La., Orp. 89 CQ53
eepcote Rd., Har. 45 BH32
eepcote Rd., Hem.H. 8 AY13
eepcote Rd. (Eton Vick), Wind. 61 AN42
eepcotes Rd., Rom. 50 CP31
eepfold, Twick. 74 BK47
eepfold La., Amer. 25 AO23
eepfold Rd., Guil. 118 AP69
eephouse Grn., Dor. 119 BE73
eephouse La., Dor. 119 BE73
eephouse Rd., Hem.H. 8 AY14
eephouse Way, N.Mal. 85 BN54
eeplands Ave., Guil. 118 AU69
eepwalk La., Lthd. 110 BB70
eering Lower Rd., 'aw. 6 CR6
eering Mill La., Saw. 6 CQ6
eering Rd., Harl. 6 CP9
eerwater Ave., Wey. 91 AV59
eerwater Rd. E16 58 CJ39
eerwater Rd., Wey. 91 AV60
eet Hill, Sev. 117 DC66
eet St., Wind. 61 AO44
eet St. Rd., Wind. 61 AO46
eethanger La., Hem.H. 8 AW15
effield Dr., Rom. 42 CX28
effield Gdns., Rom. 42 CX28
effield Sq. E3 58 CE37
Malmesbury Rd.
effield St. WC2 2 B9
effield St. WC2 56 BX39
'ortugal St.
effield Ter. W8 66 BS41
efton Ri., Nthwd. 35 BC29
eila Clo., Rom. 41 CR29
eila Rd., Rom. 41 CR29
eilings, The, Horn. 51 CW32
eilings, The, Sev. 108 CW63
elbourne Clo., Pnr. 45 BE31
elbourne Rd. N17 39 CB30
elburne Rd. N7 47 BX35
elbury Clo., Sid. 79 CO48
elbury Rd. SE22 77 CB46
elden Ct., Guil. 118 AS71
eldon Ave. N6 47 BU33
eldon Ave., Ilf. 40 CL30
eldon Clo. SE12 78 CH46
eldon Clo. SE20 77 CB51
eldon Clo., Chsnt. 21 CA16
eldon Clo., Reig. 121 BS71
ymden Gdns.
eldon Ct., Guil. 118 AS71
ower Edgeborough Rd.
eldon Rd. N18 39 CA28
eldon Rd. NW2 46 BQ35
eldon Rd., Bexh. 69 CQ44
eldon Rd., Dag. 59 CQ36
eldon St., Croy. 87 BZ55
eldrake Pl. W8 66 BS41
eldrick Clo. SW19 86 BT51
eldwick Ter., Brom. 88 CK53
elford Pl. N16 48 BZ34
elford Ri. SE19 77 CA50
elford Rd., Barn. 28 BQ25
elgate Rd. SW11 76 BU46
ell Clo., Brom. 88 CK53
Manor Way
ell Rd. SE13 67 CE45
ellbank La., Dart. 80 DA49

Shelley Ave. E12 58 CK36
Shelley Ave., Grnf. 54 BG38
Shelley Ave., Horn. 50 CT34
Shelley Clo., Bans. 103 BQ61
Shelley Clo., Edg. 37 BM28
Shelley Clo., Grnf. 54 BG38
Shelley Clo., Hayes 53 BC39
Shelley Clo., Nthwd. 35 BB28
Shelley Clo., Ong. 24 CW16
Shelley Clo., Orp. 88 CN55
Shelley Clo., Slou. 62 AT42
Shelley Cres., Houns. 64 BD44
Shelley Cres., Sthl. 54 BE39
Shelley Dr., Well. 68 CN44
Shelley Gdns., Wem. 45 BK34
Shelley Gro., Loug. 31 CK24
Shelley Rd., Brwd. 122 DE26
Shelley Rd., Har. 45 BH31
Shelley Way SW19 76 BT50
Shelleys La., Sev. 107 CO61
Shellfield Clo., Stai. 73 AW46
Shellgrove Est. N16 48 CA35
Shellness Rd. E5 48 CB35
Shellow Rd., Ong. 15 DB13
Shellwood Dr., Dor. 119 BK73
Shellwood Rd. SW11 66 BU44
Shellwood Rd., Reig. 120 BN74
Shelmerdine Clo. E3 57 CE39
Shelson Ave., Felt. 73 BB48
Shelton Ave., Warl. 105 CC62
Shelton Clo., Guil. 109 AQ68
Montgomerie Dr.
Shelton Clo., Warl. 105 CC62
Shelton Ct., Slou. 62 AR41
St. Bernards Rd.
Shelton Rd. SW19 86 BS51
Shelton St. WC2 1 Q9
Shelton St. WC2 56 BX39
Shelvers Grn., Tad. 103 BQ64
Shelvers Spur, Tad. 103 BQ64
Shelvers Way, Tad. 103 BQ64
Shen Clo., Sev. 117 CV67
Shenden Way, Sev. 117 CV67
Shenfield Cres., Brwd. 122 DC27
Shenfield Gdns., Brwd. 122 DD25
Shenfield Grn., Brwd. 122 DD26
Shenfield Pl., Brwd. 122 DC26
Shenfield Rd., Brwd. 42 DB27
Shenfield Rd., Wdf.Grn. 40 CH29
Shenfield St. N1 2 N1
Shenfield St. N1 57 CA37
Shenley Ave., Ruis. 44 BB34
Shenley Hill, Rad. 27 BJ21
Shenley La., St.Alb. 18 BJ16
Shenley Rd. SE5 67 CA44
Shenley Rd., Borwd. 28 BM24
Shenley Rd., Dart. 80 CX47
Shenley Rd., Hem.H. 8 AZ10
Shenley Rd., Houns. 64 BE44
Shenley Rd., Rad. 18 BK20
Shenstone Clo., Dart. 69 CS45
Shenstone Gdns., Rom. 42 CV30
Shenstone Hill, Berk. 7 AS12
Shepherd Mkt. W1 3 J3
Shepherd Mkt. W1 56 BV40
Shepherd St. W1 3 J3
Shepherd St. W1 56 BV40
Shepherd St., Grav. 81 DE47
Shepherdess Pl. N1 2 J2
Shepherdess Pl. N1 57 BZ38
Shepherdess Wk.
Shepherdess Wk. N1 2 J1
Shepherdess Wk. N1 57 BZ37
Shepherds Bush Grn. W12 65 BQ41
Shepherds Bush Mkt. W12 65 BQ41
Shepherds Bush Pl. W12 65 BQ41
Shepherds Bush Rd. W6 65 BQ42
Shepherds Clo. N6 47 BV32
Shepherds Clo., Rom. 50 CP32
Shepherds Clo., Shep. 83 AZ53
Shepherds Clo., Uxb. 53 AX38
Shepherds Grn., Chis. 78 CM50
Shepherds Grn., Hem.H. 7 AV14
Shepherds Hill N6 47 BV32
Shepherds Hill, Guil. 118 AQ69
Shepherds Hill, Red. 113 BW66
Shepherds Hill, Rom. 42 CX30
Shepherds La. E9 48 CC35
Shepherds La., Dart. 79 CU47
Shepherds La., Guil. 118 AP69
Shepherds La., Rick. 25 AU25
Shepherds Path NW3 47 BT35
Lyndhurst Ter.
Shepherds Path, Nthlt. 54 BE36
Ridgeway Wk.
Shepherds Pl. W1 1 G10
Shepherds Pl. W1 56 BV40
Lees Pl.
Shepherds Rd., Wat. 26 BB24
Shepherds Wk. NW2 46 BP34
Shepherds Wk. NW3 47 BT35
Hampstead High St.
Shepherds Wk., Epsom 103 BM64
Shepherds Way, Chesh. 16 AO20
Shepherds Way, Guil. 118 AS72
Shepherds Way, Hat. 20 BT17
Shepherds Way, Rick. 35 AW26
Shepherds Way, S.Croy. 96 CC57
Shepiston La., Hayes 63 AZ42
Shepley Clo., Cars. 86 BV55
Shepley Clo., Horn. 51 CV35
Chevington Way
Shepley Dr., Ascot 82 AO53
Shepley End, Ascot 82 AO53
Shepley Ms., Enf. 30 CE22
Sheppard Clo., Enf. 30 CB22
Sheppard Clo., Kings.T. 85 BL52
Beaufort Rd.
Sheppard St. E16 58 CG38
Sheppards, Harl. 13 CK12
Sheppards Clo., St.Alb. 9 BH12
Shepperton Clo., Borwd. 28 BN23

Shepperton Ct. Dr., Shep. 83 AZ53
Shepperton Rd. N1 57 BZ37
Shepperton Rd., Orp. 88 CM53
Shepperton Rd., Shep. 83 AY52
Shepperton Rd., Stai. 83 AX52
Sheppey Clo., Erith 69 CU43
Sheppey Gdns., Dag. 59 CP36
Sheppey Rd.
Sheppey Rd., Dag. 59 CO36
Sheppey Wk. N1 57 BZ36
Marquess Est.
Sheppeys La., Kings L. 17 BA18
Sheppy Pl., Grav. 81 DG47
Sherard Rd. SE9 78 CK46
Sheraton Clo., Borwd. 28 BL25
Sheraton Dr., Epsom 94 BN59
Sheraton Ms., Wat. 26 BB24
Sheraton St. W1 1 N9
Sheraton St. W1 56 BW39
Wardour St.
Sherborne Ave., Enf. 30 CC23
Sherborne Ave., Sthl. 64 BF42
Sherborne Clo., Epsom 103 BQ62
Sherborne Gdns. NW9 46 BM31
Sherborne Gdns. W13 54 BJ39
Sherborne Gdns., Rom. 41 CR28
Sherborne La. EC4 2 K10
Sherborne La. EC4 57 BZ40
King William St.
Sherborne Rd., Chess. 94 BL56
Sherborne Rd., Felt. 73 BA47
Sherborne Rd., Orp. 88 CN53
Sherborne Rd., Sutt. 86 BS55
Sherborne St. N1 57 BZ37
Sherborne Wk., Lthd. 102 BK64
Windfield
Sherbourne Clo., Sev. 99 CZ57
Sherbourne Clo., Slou. 62 AV44
Sherbourne Cres., Cars. 86 BU54
Sherbourne Dr., Vir.W. 82 AO53
Sherbourne Dr., Wind. 61 AM45
Sherbourne Way, Bexh. 69 CQ45
Sherbourne Way, Rick. 26 AZ24
Sherbrook Gdns. N21 38 BY26
Sherbrooke Clo., Bexh. 69 CR45
Graham Rd.
Sherbrooke Rd. SW6 65 BR43
Shere Ave., Sutt. 94 BQ58
Shere Clo., Dor. 119 BK73
Holmbury Dr.
Shere Rd., Guil. 110 AW70
Shere Rd., Ilf. 49 CL32
Shere Rd., Lthd. 110 BA71
Shere Rd. (West Horsley), Lthd. 110 AZ68
Shereboro Rd. N15 48 CA32
Ermine Rd.
Sheredan Rd. E4 39 CF28
Sheredes Dr., Hodd. 12 CD13
Sherfield Ave., Rick. 35 AX27
Sherfield Gdns. SW15 75 BO46
Sherfield Rd., Grays 71 DD43
Sheridan Clo., Rom. 42 CV29
Sheridan Clo., Swan. 89 CT52
Sheridan Clo., Uxb. 53 BA38
Alpha Rd.
Sheridan Ct., Dart. 70 CW45
Keyes Rd.
Sheridan Ct., Houns. 74 BE46
Frampton Rd.
Sheridan Cres., Chis. 88 CL51
Penn Gdns.
Sheridan Dr., Reig. 121 BS69
Sheridan Gdns., Har. 45 BK32
Sheridan Ms. E11 49 CH32
Woodbine Pl.
Sheridan Pl. SW13 65 BO44
Brookwood Ave.
Sheridan Pl., Hmptn. 84 BG51
Sheridan Rd. E7 49 CG34
Sheridan Rd. E12 49 CK35
Sheridan Rd. SW19 85 BR51
Sheridan Rd., Belv. 69 CR42
Sheridan Rd., Bexh. 69 CQ45
Sheridan Rd., Rich. 74 BK48
Sheridan Rd., Wat. 36 BD26
Sheridan St. E1 57 CB39
Watney St.
Sheridan Ter., Nthlt. 45 BF35
Sheridan Wk. NW11 47 BS32
Sheridan Wk., Cars. 95 BU56
Park Hill
Sheridan Way, Beck. 87 CD51
Turners Meadow Way
Sheridans Rd., Lthd. 111 BG66
Sheriff Way, Wat. 17 BC20
Sheringham Ave. E12 49 CK35
Sheringham Ave. N14 29 BW25
Sheringham Ave., Felt. 73 BC48
Sheringham Ave., Rom. 50 CS32
Sheringham Ave., Twick. 74 BE47
Sheringham Dr., Bark. 49 CN35
Sheringham Rd. N7 56 BX36
Sheringham Rd. SE10 87 CC51
Sherington Ave., Pnr. 36 BF29
Sherington Rd. SE7 68 CH43
Sherland Rd., Twick. 74 BH47
Sherlies Ave., Orp. 88 CN55
Sherlock Ms. W1 1 G6
Sherman Rd., Brom. 88 CH51
Sherman Rd., Slou. 52 AP39
Shermanbury Pl., Erith 69 CT43
Shernbroke Rd., Wal.Abb. 22 CG20
Shernhall St. E17 48 CF31
Sherpa Rd., Houns. 73 AZ46
Sherrard Rd. E7 58 CJ36
Sherrard Rd. E12 58 CJ36
Sherrards Pk. Rd., Welw.G.C. 5 BQ7
Sherrards Way, Barn. 29 BS25
Sherrick Grn. Rd. NW10 46 BP35
Sherriff Rd. NW6 56 BS36
Sherringham Ave. N17 39 CB30
Sherrock Gdns. NW4 46 BP31

Sherwin Rd. SE14 67 CC44
Sherwood, Grays 71 DC40
Sherwood Ave. E18 49 CH31
Sherwood Ave. SW16 76 BW50
Sherwood Ave., Grnf. 54 BH36
Sherwood Ave., Hayes 53 BC38
Sherwood Ave., Pot.B. 19 BR19
Sherwood Ave., Ruis. 44 BB32
Sherwood Ave., St.Alb. 9 BJ12
Sherwood Clo. SW13 65 BP45
Sherwood Clo. W13 54 BJ40
Sherwood Clo., Bex. 79 CP46
Sherwood Clo., Lthd. 102 BG65
Sherwood Clo., Slou. 62 AS42
Sherwood Clo., Wok. 100 AP62
Sherwood Cres., Reig. 121 BS72
Sherwood Gdns. E14 67 CE42
Barnsdale Ave.
Sherwood Gdns., Bark. 58 CM36
Sherwood Pk. Ave., Sid. 79 CO47
Sherwood Pk. Rd., Mitch. 86 BW52
Sherwood Pk. Rd., Sutt. 95 BS56
Sherwood Pl., Hem.H. 8 AY11
Henry Wells Sq.
Sherwood Rd. NW4 46 BQ31
Sherwood Rd. SW19 75 BR50
Sherwood Rd., Couls. 104 BW61
Sherwood Rd., Croy. 87 CH54
Sherwood Rd., Hmptn. 74 BG49
Sherwood Rd., Har. 45 BG34
Sherwood Rd., Ilf. 49 CM31
Sherwood Rd., Well. 68 CN44
Sherwood St. N20 38 BT27
Sherwood St. W1 1 M10
Sherwood St. W1 56 BW40
Brewer St.
Sherwood Ter. N20 38 BT27
Sherwood Way, W.Wick. 87 CE55
Sherwoods Rd., Wat. 36 BE26
Shetland Clo., Borwd. 28 BN25
Percheron Rd.
Shetland Clo., Guil. 109 AT68
Weybrook Dr.
Shetland Rd. E3 57 CD37
Shevon Way, Brwd. 42 CZ28
Shewins Rd., Wey. 92 BA56
St. Marys Rd.
Shey Copse, Wok. 100 AU62
Shield Dr., Brent. 64 BJ43
Shield Rd., Ashf. 73 BA49
Shieldhall St. SE2 69 CP42
Shifford Path SE23 77 CC48
Shilburn Way, Wok. 100 AQ62
Shillibeer Pl. W1 1 D7
Shillibeer Wk., Chig. 40 CN27
Shillingford St. N1 56 BY36
Cross St.
Shillitoe Ave., Pot.B. 19 BQ19
Shillitoe Rd. N13 38 BY28
Shimmings, The, Guil. 118 AT70
Shinfield St. W12 55 BQ39
Shingle Ct., Wal.Abb. 22 CH20
Winters Way
Shinglewell Rd., Erith 69 CR43
Shinners Clo. SE25 87 CB52
Stanger Rd.
Ship All. E1 57 CB40
Wellclose Sq.
Ship & Half Moon Pas. SE18 68 CL41
Ship and Mermaid Row SE1 4 L4
Ship Hill, West. 106 CJ64
Ship La. SW14 65 BN45
Ship La., S.Ock. 60 CW40
Ship La., S.at H. 90 CV51
Ship St. SE8 67 CE44
Ship Tavern Pas. EC3 2 M10
Ship Tavern Pas. EC3 57 CA39
Lime St.
Shipbourne Rd., Sev. 117 CY69
Shipbourne Rd., Ton. 117 CY69
Shipfield Clo., West. 106 CJ64
Shipka Rd. SW12 76 BV47
Shipman Rd. E16 58 CH39
Shipman Rd. SE23 77 CC48
Shipton Clo., Dag. 50 CP34
Shipton Rd., Uxb. 44 AY35
Shipton St. E2 2 Q2
Shipton St. E2 57 CA38
Shipway Ter. N16 48 CA34
Victorian Rd.
Shipwright Rd. SE16 67 CD41
Shirburn Clo. SE23 77 CC47
Shirbutt St. E14 57 CE40
Shire Clo., Brox. 21 CD16
Groom Rd.
Shire La., Ger.Cr. 34 AT27
Shire La., Orp. 97 CK57
Shire La., Rick. 25 AT25
Shirebrook Rd. SE3 68 CJ45
Shirehall Clo. NW4 46 BQ32
Shirehall Gdns. NW4 46 BQ32
Shirehall La. NW4 46 BQ32
Shirehall Pk. NW4 46 BQ32
Shirehall Rd., Dart. 80 CV49
Shiremeade, Borwd. 28 BL25
Shires, The, Rich. 75 BL49
Shires Ho., Wey. 92 AY60
Shirland Ms. W9 55 BR38
Shirley Ave., Bex. 79 CP47
Shirley Ave., Couls. 104 BY63
Shirley Ave., Croy. 87 CC54
Shirley Ave., Red. 121 BU73
Shirley Ave., Sutt. 95 BT56
Shirley Ave. (Cheam), Sutt. 94 BR58
Shirley Ave., Wind. 61 AM44
Shirley Ch. Rd., Croy. 87 CC55
Shirley Clo. E17 48 CE32
Addison Rd.
Shirley Clo., Brox. 12 CD15
Westlea Rd.
Shirley Clo., Chsnt. 21 CB18

Shirley Clo., Dart. 70 CV45
Shirley Clo., Houns. 74 BG46
Shirley Cres., Beck. 87 CC52
Shirley Dr., Houns. 74 BG46
Shirley Gdns. W7 54 BH40
Shirley Gdns., Bark. 58 CN36
Shirley Gdns., Horn. 51 CV34
Shirley Gro. N9 39 CC26
Shirley Gro. SW11 66 BV45
Shirley Heights, Wall. 95 BW58
Shirley Rd.
Shirley Hills Rd., Croy. 96 CC56
Shirley Ho. Dr. SE7 68 CJ43
Shirley Oak Rd., Croy. 87 CC54
Shirley Pk. Rd., Croy. 87 CB54
Shirley Pl., Wok. 100 AO62
Shirley Rd. E15 58 CG36
Shirley Rd. W4 65 BN41
Shirley Rd., Abb.L. 17 BB19
Shirley Rd., Croy. 87 CB54
Shirley Rd., Enf. 30 BZ24
Shirley Rd., St.Alb. 9 BH14
Shirley Rd., Sid. 78 CN48
Shirley Rd., Wall. 95 BW58
Shirley St. E16 58 CG39
Shirley Way, Croy. 87 CD55
Shirlock Rd. NW3 47 BU35
Shobden Rd. N17 39 BZ30
Shoe La. EC4 2 E8
Shoe La. EC4 56 BY39
Shoe La., Harl. 14 CQ11
Shoebury Rd. E6 58 CK36
Sholden Gdns., Orp. 89 CP53
Shonks Mill Rd., Rom. 32 CU22
Shoot Up Hill NW2 46 BR35
Shooters Ave., Har. 45 BK31
Shooters Dr., Wal.Abb. 13 CG14
Shooters Hill SE18 68 CK44
Shooters Hill, Well. 68 CK44
Shooters Hill Rd. SE3 67 CF44
Shooters Hill Rd. SE18 67 CF44
Shooters Rd., Enf. 29 BY22
Shootersway, Berk. 7 AO12
Shootersway La., Berk. 7 AP13
Shootersway Pk., Berk. 7 AP13
Shoplands, Welw.G.C. 5 BQ6
Shord Hill, Ken. 105 BZ61
Shore, The, Grav. 81 DE46
Shore Clo., Felt. 73 BB47
Shore Clo., Hmptn. 74 BE50
Stewart Clo.
Shore Gro., Felt. 74 BF48
Shore Pl. E9 57 CC36
Shore Rd. E9 57 CC36
Shorediche Clo., Uxb. 44 AY34
Shoreditch High St. E1 2 N5
Shoreditch High St. E1 57 CA38
Shoreham Clo. SW18 76 BS46
Ram St.
Shoreham Clo., Bex. 79 CP47
Stansted Cres.
Shoreham Clo., Croy. 87 CC53
Shoreham La., Orp. 98 CR57
Shoreham La., Sev. 107 CT64
Shoreham La. (Halstead), Sev. 98 CQ59
Shoreham Pl., Sev. 98 CU59
Shoreham Rd., Orp. 89 CO51
Shoreham Rd., Sev. 98 CU59
Shoreham Rd. E., Houns. 73 AY46
Shoreham Rd. W., Houns. 73 AY46
Shoreham Way, Brom. 88 CH53
Shorehill La., Sev. 108 CW61
Shores Rd., Wok. 91 AS60
Shorncliffe Rd. SE1 4 P10
Shorncliffe Rd. SE1 67 CA42
Shorndean St. SE6 77 CF47
Shorne Clo., Orp. 89 CP52
Shorne Clo., Sid. 79 CO46
Park Mead
Shornefield Clo., Brom. 88 CL52
Shornells Way SE2 69 CO42
Shorrolds Rd. SW6 65 BR43
Short Cft., Brwd. 33 CZ22
Short Gate N12 37 BR28
Short Hill, Har. 45 BH33
High St.
Short La., Oxt. 115 CH69
Short La., St.Alb. 18 BE18
Short La., Stai. 73 AY47
Short Path SE18 68 CL43
Westdale Rd.
Short Rd. E11 49 CG34
Short Rd. E15 57 CF37
Short Rd. W4 65 BO43
Short Rd., Houns. 73 AY46
Short St. NW4 46 BQ31
Short St. SE1 4 E4
Short St. SE1 66 BY41
Short Wall E15 57 CF38
Short Way N12 38 BU29
Short Way SE9 68 CK45
Short Way, Amer. 25 AO22
Short Way, Twick. 74 BG47
Shortcroft Rd., Epsom 94 BO57
Shortcrofts Rd., Dag. 59 CQ36
Shorter Ave., Brwd. 122 DC26
Shorter St. E1 2 Q10
Shortfern, Slou. 52 AR39
Knolton Way
Shortland Rd. E10 48 CE33
Shortlands W6 65 BQ42
Shortlands, Hayes 63 BA43
Shortlands Ave., Ong. 24 CW16
Shortlands Clo. N18 39 BZ27
Shortlands Gdns., Brom. 88 CG51
Shortlands Grn., Welw.G.C. 5 BR8
Shortlands Gro., Brom. 87 CF51
Shortlands Rd., Brom. 87 CF52
Shortlands Rd., Kings.T. 75 BL50
Shortmead Dr., Chsnt. 21 CD19
Shorts Cft. NW9 46 BM31
Shorts Gdns. WC2 1 Q9

Shorts Gdns. WC2 56 BX39
Shorts Rd., Cars. 95 BU56
Shortwood Ave., Stai. 73 AW48
Shotfield, Wall. 95 BV57
Shothanger Way, Hem.H. 16 AU16
Shott Clo., Sutt. 95 BT56
Turnpike La.
Shottendane Rd. SW6 66 BS44
Shottery Clo. SE9 78 CK48
Shottfield Ave. SW14 65 BO45
Shouldam St. W1 56 BU39
Shoulder of Mutton All. E14 57 CD40
Narrow St.
Shouldham St. W1 1 D7
Showers Way, Hayes 53 BC40
Shrapnel Clo. SE18 68 CK43
Stadium Rd.
Shrapnel Rd. SE9 68 CK45
Shrewsbury Ave. SW14 65 BN45
Shrewsbury Ave., Har. 46 BL31
Shrewsbury Clo., Surb. 84 BK55
Shrewsbury Cres. NW10 55 BN37
Shrewsbury Ho. SW3 66 BU43
Shrewsbury La. SE18 68 CL44
Shrewsbury Ms. W2 56 BS39
Chepstow Rd.
Shrewsbury Rd. E7 49 CJ35
Shrewsbury Rd. N11 38 BW29
Shrewsbury Rd. W2 56 BS39
Shrewsbury Rd., Beck. 87 CD52
Shrewsbury Rd., Cars. 86 BU53
Shrewsbury Rd., Red. 121 BU70
Shrewsbury Wk., Islw. 64 BJ45
South St.
Shrewton Rd. SW17 76 BU50
Shroffold Rd., Brom. 78 CG49
Shropshire Clo., Mitch. 86 BX52
Shropshire Pl. WC1 1 M5
Shropshire Rd. N22 38 BX29
Shroton St. NW1 1 C6
Shroton St. NW1 56 BU39
Shrubberies, The E18 40 CH30
Shrubberies, The, Chig. 40 CM28
Shrubbery, The, Hem.H. 7 AV13
Shrubbery, The, Upmin. 51 CY34
Shrubbery Gdns. N21 38 BY26
Shrubbery Rd. N9 39 CB27
Shrubbery Rd. SW16 76 BX49
Shrubbery Rd., Grav. 81 DH47
Shrubbery Rd., S.Dnth. 90 CY51
Shrubbery Rd., Sthl. 54 BF40
Shrubbs Hill, Wok. 91 AO58
Shrubhill Rd., Hem.H. 7 AV14
Shrubland Est. E8 57 CA36
Shrubland Gro., Wor.Pk. 85 BQ55
Shrubland Rd. E8 57 CA37
Shrubland Rd. E10 48 CE33
Shrubland Rd. E17 48 CE32
Shrubland Rd., Bans. 103 BR61
Shrublands, Hat. 20 BS16
Shrublands, The, Pot.B. 19 BR20
Shrublands Ave., Berk. 7 AQ13
Shrublands Ave., Croy. 87 CE55
Shrublands Clo. N20 38 BT26
Shrublands Clo., Chig. 40 CM29
Shrublands Rd., Berk. 7 AQ12
Shrubs Rd., Rick. 35 AY28
Shuna Wk. N1 57 BZ36
Clephane Rd.
Shurland Ave., Barn. 29 BT25
Shurland Gdns. SE15 67 CA43
Rosemary Rd.
Shurlock Ave., Swan. 89 CS51
Shurlock Dr., Orp. 97 CM56
Broadwater Gdns.
Shuter Sq. W14 65 BR42
Sun Rd.
Shuttle Clo., Sid. 78 CN47
Shuttle Rd., Dart. 69 CU45
Shuttle St. E1 57 CA38
Buxton St.
Shuttlemead, Bex. 79 CQ47
Shuttleworth Rd. SW11 66 BU44
Sibella Rd. SW4 66 BW44
Sibley Clo., Bexh. 79 CQ46
Mount Rd.
Sibley Gro. E12 58 CK36
Sibthorp Rd., Mitch. 86 BU51
Sibthorpe Rd. SE12 78 CH47
Sibthorpe Rd., Hat. 10 BQ15
Sibton Rd., Cars. 86 BU54
Sicilian Ave. WC1 2 A7
Sickert Ct. N1 57 BZ36
Sickle Cor., Dag. 59 CR38
Sicklefield Clo., Chsnt. 21 CA16
Sidbury St. SW6 65 BR44
Sidcup By-pass, Sid. 78 CM48
Sidcup High St., Sid. 79 CO49
Sidcup Hill, Sid. 79 CO49
Sidcup Hill Gdns., Sid. 79 CP49
Sidcup Pl., Sid. 79 CO49
Sidcup Rd. SE9 78 CJ47
Sidcup Rd. SE12 78 CJ47
Siddons Clo., S.le H. 71 DK41
Lower Cres.
Siddons La. NW1 1 F5
Siddons La. NW1 56 BU38
Siddons Rd. N17 39 CB30
Siddons Rd. SE23 77 CC48
Siddons Rd., Croy. 86 BY55
Side Rd. E17 48 CD32
South Gro.
Side Rd., Uxb. 43 AU33
Sidewood Rd. SE9 78 CM47
Sidford Clo., Hem.H. 7 AV13
Sidford Pl. SE1 4 C7
Sidford Pl. SE1 66 BX41
Sidings, The E11 48 CF33
Sidings, The, Hat. 10 BO13
Crossbrook
Sidmouth Ave., Islw. 64 BH44
Sidmouth Clo., Wat. 35 BC27
Sidmouth Dr., Ruis. 44 BC34
Sidmouth Rd. E10 48 CF34
Sidmouth Rd. NW2 55 BQ36
Sidmouth Rd. SE15 67 CA44
Sidmouth Rd., Orp. 89 CO53
Sidmouth Rd., Well. 69 CP43
Sidmouth St. WC1 2 A3
Sidmouth St. WC1 56 BX38
Sidney Ave. N13 38 BX28
Sidney Elson Way E6 58 CL38
Edwin Ave.
Sidney Est. E1 57 CC39
Sidney Gdns., Brent. 64 BK43
Boston Manor Rd.
Sidney Gdns., Sev. 108 CV62
Sidney Gro. EC1 2 F1
Sidney Gro. EC1 56 BY38
Wakley St.
Sidney Rd. E7 49 CH34
Sidney Rd. N22 38 BX29
Sidney Rd. SE25 87 CB53
Sidney Rd. SW9 66 BX44
Sidney Rd., Beck. 87 CD51
Sidney Rd., Epp. 31 CM21
Sidney Rd., Har. 45 BG31
Sidney Rd., Sutt. 95 BS56
Sidney Rd., Twick. 74 BJ46
Sidney Rd., Walt. 83 BC54
Sidney Sq. E1 57 CC39
Sidney St. E1 57 CB39
Sidney St., Stai. 73 AW49
Sidworth St. E8 57 CB36
Siebert Rd. SE3 68 CH43
Siemens Rd. SE18 68 CJ41
Sifford Pl., Brwd. 42 DB28
Blackthorn Way
Sigdon Rd. E8 48 CB35
Sigers, The, Pnr. 44 BC32
Sigismund St. SE10 68 CG41
Silas St. Est. NW5 56 BV36
Silbury Ave., Mitch. 86 BU51
Silbury St. N1 2 K2
Silbury St. N1 57 BZ38
East Rd.
Silchester Ct., Th.Hth. 86 BY52
Silchester Ms. W10 55 BQ40
Walmer Rd.
Silchester Rd. W10 55 BQ39
Silecroft Rd., Bexh. 69 CR44
Silesia Bldgs. E8 57 CB36
London La.
Silex St. SE1 4 G5
Silex St. SE1 66 BY41
Silk Clo. SE12 78 CH46
Silk Mill Rd., Wat. 35 BC26
Silk Mills Path SE13 67 CF44
Silk St. EC2 2 J6
Silk St. EC2 57 BZ39
Silkfield Rd. NW9 46 BO32
Silkham Rd., Oxt. 114 CF67
Silkins, The, Rom. 41 CT30
Silkmore La., Lthd. 110 AZ66
Silkstream Rd., Edg. 37 BN30
Silsden Cres., Ch.St.G. 34 AR27
Silsoe Rd. N22 38 BX30
Silver Birch Ave. E4 39 CD29
Silver Birch Ave., Epp. 23 CQ17
Silver Birch Clo. N11 38 BV29
Poplar Gro.
Silver Birch Clo., Dart. 79 CT49
Silver Birch Clo., Uxb. 44 AY35
Silver Birch Clo., Wey. 91 AV59
Silver Birches, Brwd. 122 DD26
Silver Clo. SE14 67 CD43
Southerngate Way
Silver Clo., Har. 36 BG29
Silver Clo., Sutt. 94 BR56
Silver Clo., Tad. 103 BP63
Silver Cres. W4 65 BM42
Silver Dell, Wat. 26 BB21
Silver Hill, Ch.St.G. 34 AQ27
Silver Jubilee Way, Houns. 63 BC44
Silver La., Pur. 95 BW59
Silver La., W.Wick. 87 CF55
Silver Pl. W1 1 M10
Silver Pl. W1 56 BW40
Lexington St.
Silver Rd. W12 55 BQ40
Silver Rd., Grav. 81 DJ48
Silver Spring Clo., Erith 69 CR43
Silver St. EC2 57 BZ39
Wood St.
Silver St. N18 39 BZ28
Silver St., Chsnt. 21 BZ18
Silver St., Enf. 30 BZ24
Silver St., Rom. 32 CO24
Silver St., Wal.Abb. 21 CF20
Silver Wk. SE16 57 CD40
Silver Way, Rom. 50 CR31
Silverbirch Wk. NW3 56 BU36
Maitland Pk. Vw.
Silvercliffe Gdns., Barn. 29 BU24
Silverdale SE26 77 CC49
Silverdale, Enf. 29 BX24
Silverdale, Stai. 73 AW49
Leacroft
Silverdale Ave., Ilf. 49 CN32
Silverdale Ave., Lthd. 93 BG60
Silverdale Ave., Walt. 83 BB55
Silverdale Clo. W7 54 BH40
Cherington Rd.
Silverdale Clo., Bet. 120 BM72
Silverdale Clo., Har. 45 BE35
Silverdale Ct., Stai. 73 AW49
Silverdale Dr. SE9 78 CK48
Silverdale Dr., Horn. 50 CU35
Silverdale Dr., Sun. 83 BC51
Silverdale Gdns., Hayes 63 BC41
Silverdale Rd. E4 39 CF29
Silverdale Rd., Bexh. 69 CR44
Silverdale Rd., Bush. 27 BE25
Silverdale Rd., Hayes 63 BB41
Silverdale Rd. (Petts Wd.), Orp. 88 CM52
Silverdale Rd. (St. Mary Cray), Orp. 89 CO52
Silverfield, Brox. 12 CD14
Silverhall St., Islw. 64 BJ45
Silverholme Clo., Har. 46 BL33
Silverland St. E16 58 CK40
Silverleigh Rd., Th.Hth. 86 BX52
Silverlocke Rd., Grays 71 DE43
Silvermere Ave., Rom. 41 CR28
Silvermere Rd. SE6 77 CE47
Silversmiths Way, Wok. 100 AR62
Silverst Clo., Nthlt. 54 BF36
Silverstead La., West. 106 CM64
Silverston Way, Stan. 36 BK29
Silverstone Clo., Red. 121 BU69
Goodwood Rd.
Silverthorn Dr., Hem.H. 8 AZ15
Silverthorne Gdns. E4 39 CE27
Silverthorne Rd. SW8 66 BV44
Silverton Rd. W6 65 BQ43
Silvertown By-pass E16 58 CJ40
Silvertown Way E16 58 CG39
Silvertree Clo., Walt. 83 BC55
Silvertree La., Grnf. 54 BG38
Silvertrees, St.Alb. 18 BE18
Silverwood Clo., Beck. 77 CE50
Brackley Rd.
Silverwood Clo., Croy. 96 CD58
Silverwood Clo., Nthwd. 35 BA30
Silvester Rd. SE22 77 CA46
Silvester St. SE1 4 K5
Silvester St. SE1 67 BZ41
Silvesters, Harl. 13 CK12
Silwood Est. SE16 67 CC42
Silwood St. SE16 67 CC42
Simla Clo. SE14 67 CD43
Chubworthy St.
Simla Ho. SE1 4 L5
Simmil Rd., Esher 93 BH56
Simmonds Ri., Hem.H. 8 AX14
Lamsey Rd.
Simmons Clo. N20 38 BU27
Simmons Clo., Slou. 62 AT42
Simmons La. E4 39 CF27
Simmons Pl., Grays 71 DD40
Simmons Rd. SE18 68 CL42
Brookhill Rd.
Simmons Way N20 38 BU27
Simms Clo., Cars. 86 BU55
Simms Rd. SE1 67 CB42
Simnel Rd. SE12 78 CH47
Simon Clo. W11 56 BS40
Portobello Rd.
Simon Dean, Hem.H. 16 AT17
Simonds Rd. E10 48 CE34
Simone Clo., Brom. 88 CJ51
Simone Dr., Ken. 105 BZ62
Simons Clo., Cher. 91 AU57
Simons Wk. E15 57 CF36
Alma St.
Simons Wk., Egh. 72 AR50
Simplemarsh Rd., Wey. 92 AW56
Simpson Dr. W3 55 BN39
Ferguson Dr.
Simpson Rd., Houns. 74 BE46
Simpson Rd., Rain. 59 CT36
Simpson Rd., Rich. 74 BK49
Simpson St. SW11 66 BU44
Simpsons Rd. E14 57 CE40
Simpsons Rd., Brom. 88 CH52
Simrose Ct. SW18 76 BS46
Wandsworth High St.
Sims Clo., Rom. 50 CT31
Sims Wk. SE3 68 CG45
Lee Rd.
Sinclair Dr., Sutt. 95 BS58
Sinclair Dr., Sutt. 95 BS58
Sinclair Gdns. W14 65 BQ41
Sinclair Gro. NW11 46 BQ32
Sinclair Rd. E4 39 CD28
Sinclair Rd. W14 65 BQ41
Sinclair Way, Dart. 80 CY49
Sinclare Clo., Enf. 30 CA23
Sincots Rd., Red. 121 BU70
Lower Bri. Rd.
Sindall Rd., Grnf. 54 BJ37
Sinderby Clo., Brwd. 28 BL23
Singapore Rd. W13 54 BJ40
Singer St. EC2 2 L3
Singer St. EC2 57 BZ38
Cowper St.
Single St., Orp. 97 CL60
Singles Cross La., Sev. 98 CP60
Singleton Clo. SW17 76 BU50
Singleton Clo., Croy. 87 BZ54
St. Saviours Rd.
Singleton Clo., Horn. 50 CU35
Cowdray Way
Singleton Rd., Dag. 50 CQ35
Singleton Scarp N12 38 BS28
Singlewell Rd., Grav. 81 DG48
Singret Pl., Uxb. 53 AX38
Sinnott Rd. E17 39 CC30
Sion Rd., Twick. 74 BJ47
Sipson Clo., West Dr. 63 AZ43
Sipson La., West Dr. 63 AZ43
Sipson Rd., West Dr. 63 AY41
Sipson Way, West Dr. 63 AZ44
Sir Alexander Clo. W3 55 BO40
Sir Alexander Rd.
Sir Alexander Rd. W3 55 BO40
Sir Francis Way, Brwd. 42 DA27
Sir Theodores Way, Welw.G.C. 5 BQ7
Stonehills
Sir Thomas More Est. SW3 66 BT43
Sirdar Rd. N22 47 BY31
Sirdar Rd. W11 55 BQ40
Sirdar Rd., Mitch. 76 BU50
Sirdar Strand, Grav. 81 DJ49
Sirus Rd., Nthwd. 35 BC28
Sise La. EC4 2 K9
Siskin Clo., Borwd. 28 BM24
Goldfinch Way
Sisley Rd., Bark. 58 CN37
Sispara Gdns. SW18 75 BR46
Sissinghurst Rd., Croy. 87 CB54
Sisters Ave. SW11 66 BU45
Sistova Rd. SW12 76 BV47
Sisulu Pl. SW9 66 BY45
Wiltshire Rd.
Sittingbourne Ave., Enf. 30 BZ25
Sitwell Gro., Stan. 36 BH28
Siverst Clo., Nthlt. 54 BF36
Sivill Ho. E2 2 Q2
Siviter Way, Dag. 59 CR36
Siward Rd. N17 39 BZ30
Siward Rd. SW17 76 BT48
Siward Rd., Brom. 88 CH52
Six Acres, Hem.H. 8 AZ15
Six Bells La., Sev. 117 CV66
Sixth Ave. E12 49 CL35
Sixth Ave. W10 55 BR38
Sixth Ave., Enf. 30 CA25
Sixth Ave., Hayes 53 BB40
Sixth Ave., Wat. 27 BD21
Sixth Cross Rd., Twick. 74 BG48
Skardu Rd. NW2 46 BR35
Skarnings Ct., Wal.Abb. 22 CH20
Skeena Hill SW18 75 BR47
Skeet Hill La., Orp. 89 CQ54
Skeffington Rd. E6 58 CK37
Skelbrook St. SW18 76 BS48
Skelgill Rd. SW15 65 BR45
Skelley Rd. E15 58 CG36
Skelton Clo. E8 57 CA36
Rhodes Dev.
Skelton Rd. E7 58 CH36
Skeltons La. E10 48 CE33
Skelwith Rd. W6 65 BQ43
Skerries Ct., Slou. 62 AT42
Blacksmith Row
Sketchley Gdns. SE16 67 CC42
Sketty Rd., Enf. 30 CA24
Skibbs La., Orp. 98 CQ56
Skid Hill La., Warl. 97 CG60
Skidmore Way, Rick. 35 AY26
Skiers St. E15 57 CF37
Skiffington Clo. SW2 76 BY47
Skillet Hill, Wal.Abb. 31 CH21
Skimpans Clo., Hat. 10 BQ15
Skin Mkt. Pl. SE1 57 BZ40
Skinner Ct. E2 57 CB37
Parmiter St.
Skinner Pl. SW1 3 G9
Skinner Pl. SW1 66 BV42
Bourne St.
Skinner St. EC1 2 E3
Skinner St. EC1 56 BY38
Skinners La. EC4 2 J10
Skinners La. (Garlick Hill) EC4 57 BZ40
Queen Victoria St.
Skinners La., Ash. 102 BK62
Skinners La., Houns. 64 BF44
Skips Cor., Epp. 23 CS16
Skipsey Ave. E6 58 CK38
Skipton Dr., Hayes 63 BA42
Skipton St. SE1 4 G7
Skipton St. SE1 66 BY41
Keyworth St.
Skipworth Rd. E9 57 CC37
Skomer Wk. N1 57 BZ36
Sky Peals Rd., Wdf.Grn. 39 CF30
Skylark Rd., Uxb. 43 AU33
Skyport Dr., West Dr. 63 AX43
Skys Wd. Rd., St.Alb. 9 BJ11
Slackesbury Hatch, Harl. 13 CL11
Slade, The SE18 68 CN43
Slade Ct., Cher. 91 AU57
Slade Ct., Rad. 27 BJ21
Slade End, Epp. 31 CN21
Slade Gdns., Erith 69 CT44
Slade Grn. Rd., Erith 69 CU43
Slade Oak La., Ger.Cr. 43 AU31
Slade Rd., Cher. 91 AU57
Slade Wk. SE17 67 BZ43
Sladebrook Rd. SE3 68 CJ45
Sladedale Rd. SE18 68 CN42
Slades Clo., Enf. 29 BY24
Slades Cotts., Chis. 78 CL49
Slades Dr., Chis. 78 CM48
Slades Gdns., Enf. 29 BY23
Slades Hill, Enf. 29 BY24
Slades Ri., Enf. 29 BY24
Slagrove Pl. SE13 77 CE46
Slaidburn St. SW10 66 BT43
Slaithwaite Rd. SE13 67 CF45
Slaney Pl. N7 47 BY35
Rolitt St.
Slapleys, Wok. 100 AS63
Sleaford Grn., Wat. 36 BD27
Sleaford St. SW8 66 BW43
Sleap Cross Gdns., St.Alb. 10 BM14
Sleapshyde La., St.Alb. 10 BM14
Sleddale, Hem.H. 8 AY12
Wharfedale
Sleepers Fm. Rd., Grays 71 DG41
Sleets End, Hem.H. 8 AW12
Slewins Clo., Horn. 51 CV32
Slewins La., Horn. 51 CV32
Slievemore Clo. SW4 66 BW45
Voltaire Rd.
Slimmons Dr., St.Alb. 9 BJ11
Slines New Rd., Cat. 105 CB63
Slines Oaks Rd., Cat. 105 CE64
Slingsby Pl. WC2 1 Q10
Slingsby Pl. WC2 56 BX40
Long Acre
Slipe La., Brox. 12 CD15
Slippers Pl. SE16 67 CB41
Slipshatch Rd., Reig. 120 BQ72
Slipshoe St., Reig. 120 BR70
Sloane Ave. SW3 3 D9
Sloane Ave. SW3 66 BU42
Sloane Ct. E. SW3 3
Sloane Ct. E. SW3 66 B
Sloane Ct. W. SW3 3
Sloane Ct. W. SW3 66 B
Sloane Gdns. SW1 3
Sloane Gdns. SW1 66 B
Sloane Gdns., Orp. 88 C
Sloane Sq. SW1 3
Sloane Sq. SW1 66 B
Sloane Sq., Long. 90 D
Bramblefield Clo.
Sloane St. SW1 3
Sloane St. SW1 66 B
Sloane Ter. SW1 3
Sloane Ter. SW1 66 B
Sloane Wk., Croy. 87 C
Sloansway, Welw.G.C. 5
Slocock Hill, Wok. 100 A
Slocum Clo. SE28 59 C
Woodpecker Rd.
Slough La. NW9 46 B
Slough La., Bet. 120 B
Slough La., Epsom 112 B
Slough Rd., Iver 52 A
Slough Rd., Slou. 62 A
Slough Rd. (Eton), Wind. 61 A
Sly St. E1 57 C
Cannon St. Rd.
Slyfield Grn., Guil. 109 A
Small Acre, Hem.H. 7 A
Small Cft., Welw.G.C. 5
Brooksfield
Small Grains, Fawk. 90 D
Smallbrook Ms. W2 1
Smallbrook Ms. W2 56 B
Craven Rd.
Smallbury Ave., Islw. 64 B
Smallcroft, Welw.G.C. 5
Brooksfield
Smalley Clo. N16 48 C
Smalley Rd.
Smalley Rd. N16 48 C
Smallford La., St.Alb. 10 BN
Smalls Hill Rd., Reig. 120 B
Smallwood Rd. SW17 76 B
Smardale Rd. SW18 76 B
Alma Rd.
Smarden Clo., Belv. 69 C
Essenden Rd.
Smarden Gro. SE9 78 C
Prestbury Sq.
Smart Clo., Rom. 41 CL
Smart St. E2 57 C
Smarts Grn., Chsnt. 21 C
Adamsfield
Smarts Heath La., Wok. 100 A
Smarts Heath Rd., Wok. 100 A
Smarts La., Loug. 31 C
Smarts Pl. N18 39 C
Fore St.
Smarts Pl. WC2 2
Smarts Pl. WC2 56 B
Stukeley St.
Smarts Rd., Grav. 81 D
Smeaton Rd. SW18 76 B
Smeaton Rd., Wdf.Grn. 40 C
Smeaton St. E1 57 C
Smedley St. SW4 66 BW
Smedley St. SW8 66 BW
Smeed Rd. E3 57 C
Smith Clo. SE16 57 C
Smith Ct., Wok. 91 AL
Smith Hill, Brent. 65 BL
High St.
Smith Rd., Reig. 120 B
Smith Sq. SW1 3
Smith Sq. SW1 66 B
Smith St. SW3 3
Smith St. SW3 66 BL
Smith St., Surb. 85 B
Smith St., Wat. 27 BD
Smith Ter. SW3 66 BL
Smithambottom La., Pur. 95 BW
Smithamdowns Rd., Pur. 95 BW
Smithers, The, Bet. 120 BM
Smithfield St. EC1 2
Smithfield St. EC1 56 B
Smithies Ct. E15 48 C
Smithies Rd. SE2 69 CC
Smiths Ct. W1 1 M
Smiths Cres., St.Alb. 10 BM
Smiths La., Chsnt. 21 BZ
Smiths La., Eden. 115 CM
Smiths La., Wind. 61 AM
Smiths Yd. SW18 76 BS
Summerley St.
Smithson Rd. N17 39 BZ
Smithwood Clo. SW19 75 BR
Smithy Clo., Tad. 112 BF
Smithy La., Tad. 112 BF
Smithy St. E1 57 CC
Smock Wk., Croy. 87 BZ
Beulah Gro.
Smoke La., Reig. 121 BS
Smoothfield, Houns. 64 BF
Smug Oak La., St.Alb. 18 BF
Smugglers Way SW18 66 BS
Smyrks Rd. SE17 67 CA
Smyrna Rd. NW6 56 BS
Smythe Rd., S.at H. 90 CX
Smythe St. E14 57 CE
Snag La., Sev. 97 CM
Snakes Hill, Brwd. 33 CY
Snakes La., Wdf.Grn. 40 CH
Snape Spur, Slou. 52 AF
Snaresbrook Dr., Stan. 36 BK
Snaresbrook Rd. E11 49 CG
Snarsgate St. W10 55 BO
Snatts Hill, Oxt. 115 CG
Sneath Ave. NW11 46 BR
Snelling Ave., Grav. 81 DF
Snellings Rd., Walt. 93 BD
Snells La., Amer. 25 AO
Snells Pk. N18 39 CA

ells Wd. Ct., Amer. 25 AR23
eyd Rd. NW2 46 BQ35
odland Clo., Orp. 97 CL58
ow Hill EC1 2 F7
ow Hill EC1 56 BY39
ow Hill Cotts., Chesh. 7 AP15
ow Hill Ct. EC1 2 G8
owbury Rd. SW6 66 BS44
owden Ave., Uxb. 53 AZ37
owden St. EC2 2 M5
owden St. EC2 57 CA39
owdon Clo., Wind. 61 AL45
owdon Cres., Hayes 63 BA41
owdon Dr. NW9 46 BO32
owdown Clo. SE20 87 CC51
venue Rd.
owdrop Clo., Hmptn. 74 BF50
resham Rd.
owdrop Path, Rom. 42 CV29
owerhill Rd., Bet. 120 BO71
ows Flds. SE1 67 BZ41
owsfields SE1 4 L4
owshill Rd. E12 49 CK35
owy Fielder Way, Islw. 64 BJ44
ames Mead, Brwd. 24 DA20
ames St. SE15 67 CA45
ames Wk., N.Mal. 85 BO51
cket La., Brom. 88 CH53
ham Rd., Enf. 30 CD22
ho Sq. W1 1 N8
ho Sq. W1 56 BW39
ho St. W1 1 N8
lander Gdns. Est. E1 57 CC40
le Fm. Ave., Lthd. 111 BE66
le Fm. Clo., Lthd. 102 BE65
le Fm. Rd., Lthd. 111 BE66
lebay St. E1 57 CD38
lecote, Lthd. 111 BF66
lefelds Rd., Sev. 116 CU67
lent Rd. NW6 47 BS35
lent Rd., Houns. 73 AY46
leoak, Sev. 117 CV67
lesbridge Clo., Rick. 25 AV24
lesbridge La., Rick. 25 AV24
ley Ms. WC1 2 D2
lid La., Brwd. 33 CZ23
lna Ave. SW15 75 BQ46
lna Rd. N21 39 BZ26
lomon Hill, Rick. 35 AX26
lomons Pas. SE15 67 CB45
lomons Ter. N20 38 BT26
loms Ct. Rd., Bans. 104 BT62
lon New Rd. SW4 66 BX45
lon Rd. SW2 66 BX45
loway Clo. E8 57 CA36
Rhodes Dev.
lway, Hem.H. 8 AY12
lway Clo., Houns. 64 BE45
lway Rd. N22 38 BY30
lway Rd. SE22 67 CB45
maford Gro., Barn. 29 BT25
mali Rd. NW2 46 BR35
merby Clo., Brox. 12 CE14
merby Rd., Bark. 58 CM36
mercoates Clo., Barn. 29 BU24
merden Rd., Orp. 89 CP54
merfield Clo., Pnr. 44 BC31
merfield Clo., Tad. 103 BR63
merfield Rd. N4 47 BY34
merford Est. N16 48 CA35
merford Gro. N16 48 CA35
merford Gro. N17 39 CB29
merford St. E1 57 CB38
Brady St.
merford Way SE16 67 CD41
merhill Ave., Sid. 79 CO47
merhill Rd., Well. 69 CO44
meries Rd., Hem.H. 7 AV12
merleyton Pas. SW9 66 BY45
Mayall Rd.
merleyton Rd. SW9 66 BY45
mers Clo., Reig. 121 BS70
mers Cres. W2 1 C9
mers Cres. W2 56 BU39
mers Ms. W2 1 C9
mers Ms. W2 56 BU39
Radnor Pl.
omers Pl. SW2 76 BX47
omers Rd. E17 48 CD31
omers Rd. SW2 76 BX46
omers Rd., Hat. 10 BQ15
omers Rd., Reig. 121 BS70
omers Sq., Hat. 10 BQ15
omers Way, Bush. 36 BG26
omersby Gdns., Ilf. 49 CK32
omerset Ave. SW20 85 BP51
omerset Ave., Chess. 93 BK56
omerset Ave., Well. 78 CN46
omerset Clo., Epsom 94 BN58
Hollymoor La.
omerset Clo., N.Mal. 85 BO53
omerset Clo., Walt. 92 BC56
Queens Rd.
omerset Clo., Wdf.Grn. 40 CH30
Harold Rd.
omerset Est. SW11 66 BT44
omerset Gdns. N6 47 BV33
omerset Gdns. SE13 67 CE44
omerset Gdns. SW16 86 BX52
omerset Gdns., Horn. 51 CX33
omerset Gdns., Tedd. 74 BH49
omerset Rd. E17 48 CE32
omerset Rd. N17 48 CA31
omerset Rd. N18 39 CA28
omerset Rd. NW4 46 BQ31
omerset Rd. SW19 75 BQ48
omerset Rd. W4 65 BN41
omerset Rd. W13 54 BJ40
omerset Rd., Barn. 29 BS25
omerset Rd., Brent. 64 BK43
omerset Rd., Dart. 79 CU46
omerset Rd., Enf. 30 CE22
omerset Rd., Har. 45 BG32
omerset Rd., Kings.T. 85 BL51
Somerset Rd., Orp. 89 CO54
Somerset Rd., Red. 121 BT71
Somerset Rd., Sthl. 54 BE39
Somerset Rd., S.le H. 71 DK41
Somerset Rd., Tedd. 74 BH49
Somerset Sq. W14 65 BR41
Somerset Way, Iver 62 AV41
Somerset Waye, Houns. 64 BE43
Somersham, Welw.G.C. 5 BU8
Somersham Rd., Bexh. 69 CQ44
Somerton Ave., Rich. 65 BM45
Somerton Clo., Pur. 104 BY61
Somerton Rd. NW2 46 BQ34
Somerton Rd. SE15 67 CB45
Somertons Clo., Guil. 118 AQ69
Somertrees Ave. SE12 78 CH48
Somervell Ct., Har. 45 BF35
Somervell Rd., Har. 45 BE35
Somerville Rd. SE20 77 CC50
Somerville Rd., Cob. 93 BF60
Somerville Rd., Dart. 80 CW46
Somerville Rd., Rom. 50 CP32
Somerville Rd. (Eton), Wind. 61 AO42
Sonderburg Rd. N7 47 BX34
Seven Sisters Rd.
Sondes Pl. Dr., Dor. 119 BH71
Sondes St. SE17 67 BZ43
Sonia Clo., Wat. 36 BD26
Sonia Ct., Har. 45 BH32
Sonia Gdns. N12 38 BT28
Sonia Gdns. NW10 46 BO35
Sonia Gdns., Houns. 64 BF43
Sonnet Wk., West. 106 CJ62
Kings Rd.
Sonning Gdns., Hmptn. 74 BE50
Sonning Rd. SE25 87 CB53
Soothouse Spring, St.Alb. 9 BH11
Sopers Rd., Cuffley 20 BX18
Sophia Clo. N7 56 BX36
Mackenzie Rd.
Sophia Rd. E10 48 CE33
Sophia Rd. E16 58 CH39
Sopwell La., St.Alb. 9 BG14
Sopwith Ave., Chess. 93 BL56
Sopwith Clo., West. 106 CJ61
Hillcrest Rd.
Sopwith Dr., Wey. 92 AY59
Sopwith Rd., Houns. 64 BD43
Sopwith Way, Kings.T. 85 BL51
Kingsgate Rd.
Sorbie Clo., Wey. 92 BA57
Sorrel Bank, Croy. 96 CD58
Sorrel Clo. SE28 59 CO40
Sorrel Ct., Grays 71 DE43
Salix Rd.
Sorrel Wk., Rom. 50 CT31
Sorrel Way, Grav. 81 DF49
Sorrell Clo. SE14 67 CD43
Southerngate Way
Sorrell Clo. SW9 66 BY44
Myatts Flds. Dev.
Sorrell Gdns. E6 58 CK39
Sorrento Rd., Sutt. 86 BS55
Sotheby Rd. N5 47 BY34
Sotheran Clo. E8 57 CB37
Sotheron Rd. SW6 66 BS43
Sotheron Rd., Wat. 27 BD24
Soudan Rd. SW11 66 BU44
Souldern Rd. W14 65 BQ41
Souldern St., Wat. 26 BC25
Sounds Lo., Swan. 89 CS53
South Access Rd. E17 48 CD33
South Acre NW9 37 BO30
South Africa Rd. W12 55 BP40
South Albert Rd., Reig. 120 BR70
South App., Nthwd. 35 BA27
South Ash Rd., Sev. 99 DB58
South Audley St. W1 3 H1
South Audley St. W1 56 BV40
South Ave. E4 39 CE26
South Ave., Cars. 95 BU57
South Ave., Egh. 72 AU50
South Ave., Rich. 65 BM44
Sandycombe Rd.
South Ave., Sthl. 54 BE40
South Ave. Gdns., Sthl. 54 BE40
South Bank, Chis. 78 CM49
South Bank, Surb. 85 BL53
South Bank, West. 115 CM66
South Bank Lo., Surb. 85 BL53
South Bank Rd., Berk. 7 AP12
South Bank Ter., Surb. 85 BL53
South Birkbeck Rd. E11 48 CF34
South Black Lion La. W6 65 BP42
South Bolton Gdns. SW5 66 BS42
South Border, The, Pur. 95 BX59
South Carriage Dr. SW7 3 C4
South Ch. Ct. N13 38 BX28
Palmerston Cres.
South Circular Rd. SE23 77 CC47
South Circular Rd., Rich. 65 BM43
South Clo. N6 47 BV32
South Clo., Barn. 28 BR24
South Clo., Bexh. 69 CP45
South Clo., Dag. 59 CR37
South Clo., Epsom 94 BN58
South Clo., Mord. 86 BS53
South Clo., Pnr. 45 BE33
South Clo., St.Alb. 18 BF16
South Clo., Twick. 74 BF48
South Clo., West Dr. 63 AY41
South Clo., Wok. 100 AR61
South Clo. Grn., Red. 113 BV67
South Common Rd., Uxb. 53 AY36
South Consort Way, Uxb. 43 AV32
South Cottage Dr., Rick. 25 AV25
South Cottage Gdns., Rick. 25 AV25
South Countess Rd. E17 48 CD31
South Cres. WC1 1 N7
South Cres. WC1 56 BW39
South Cross Rd., Ilf. 49 CM32
South Croxted Rd. SE21 77 BZ48
South Dagenham Rd., Dag. 59 CS36
South Dene NW7 37 BN27
South Dr., Bans. 95 BU60
South Dr., Brwd. 42 DB28
South Dr., Couls. 104 BW61
South Dr., Cuffley 20 BX18
South Dr., Dor. 119 BK71
South Dr., Orp. 97 CN56
South Dr., Rom. 51 CV31
South Dr., Ruis. 44 BB33
South Dr., Sutt. 94 BR58
South Dr., Vir.W. 82 AQ54
South Ealing Rd. W5 64 BK41
South Eastern Ave. N9 39 CA27
South Eaton Pl. SW1 3 H8
South Eaton Pl. SW1 66 BV42
South Eden Pk. Rd., Beck. 87 CE53
South Edwardes Sq. W8 65 BR41
South Emmwood Clo., Hem.H. 8 AZ13
South End W8 66 BS41
St. Albans Gro.
South End, Croy. 96 BZ56
South End, Lthd. 111 BF66
South End Clo. NW3 47 BU35
South End Rd.
South End Grn. NW3 47 BU35
South End Rd. NW3 47 BU35
South End Rd., Rain. 59 CU37
South End Row W8 66 BS41
South Esk Rd. E7 58 CJ36
South Gdns. SW19 76 BT50
South Gate, Harl. 13 CM11
South Gipsy Rd., Well. 69 CP45
South Glade, The, Bex. 79 CQ47
South Grn. NW9 37 BO29
Clayton Fld.
South Grn., Slou. 52 AP40
South Gro. E17 48 CD32
South Gro. N6 47 BV33
South Gro. N15 48 BZ32
South Gro., Cher. 82 AV53
South Gro. Ho. N6 47 BV33
South Hall Clo., Farn. 90 CW43
Eynsford Rd.
South Hall Dr., Rain. 59 CU39
South Hill, Chis. 78 CK50
South Hill, Guil. 118 AR71
South Hill Ave., Har. 45 BG34
South Hill Gro., Har. 45 BH35
South Hill Pk. NW3 47 BU35
South Hill Pk. Gdns. NW3 47 BU35
South Hill Rd., Brom. 88 CG52
South Hill Rd., Grav. 81 DH47
South Hill Rd., Hem.H. 8 AX13
South Island Pl. SW9 66 BX43
South Kent Ave., Grav. 81 DE46
South Lambeth Pl. SW8 66 BX43
South Lambeth Rd.
South Lambeth Rd. SW8 66 BX43
South La., Kings.T. 84 BK52
South La., N.Mal. 85 BN52
South La. W., N.Mal. 85 BN52
South Ley, Welw.G.C. 5 BR9
South Lo. W5 54 BK40
Webster Gdns.
South Lo. Ave., Mitch. 86 BX52
South Lo. Cres., Enf. 29 BW24
South Lo. Dr. N14 29 BW24
South Mall N9 39 CB27
South Mead NW9 37 BO30
South Mead, Epsom 94 BO57
South Mead, Red. 121 BU69
South Meadow La., Wind. 61 AO43
South Meadows, Wem. 46 BL35
Park Lawns
South Mimms By-pass, Pot.B. 19 BO19
South Molton La. W1 1 J9
South Molton La. W1 56 BV39
South Molton Rd. E16 58 CH39
South Molton St. W1 1 J9
South Molton St. W1 56 BV39
South Mundells, Welw.G.C. 5 BR7
South Norwood Hill SE25 87 CA51
South Oak Rd. SW16 76 BX49
South Par. SW3 3 B10
South Par. SW3 66 BT42
South Par. W4 65 BN42
South Pk., Ger.Cr. 43 AS32
South Pk., Sev. 116 CU66
South Pk. Ave., Rick. 25 AV25
South Pk. Ct., Beck. 77 CE50
South Pk. Cres. SE6 78 CG47
South Pk. Cres., Ger.Cr. 43 AS31
South Pk. Cres., Ilf. 49 CM34
South Pk. Dr., Ger.Cr. 43 AS31
South Pk. Dr., Ilf. 49 CN34
South Pk. Est. SE16 67 CB41
South Pk. Gdns., Berk. 7 AQ12
South Pk. Gro., N.Mal. 85 BN52
South Pk. Hill Rd., S.Croy. 96 BZ56
South Pk. La., Red. 114 CB71
South Pk. Ley Rd., Cat. 105 CC63
South Pk. Ms. SW6 66 BS45
South Pk. Rd. SW19 75 BR50
South Pk. Rd., Ilf. 49 CM34
South Pk. Ter., Ilf. 49 CM34
South Pk. Vw., Ger.Cr. 43 AS31
South Pk. Way, Ruis. 54 BD36
South Path, Wind. 61 AO44
South Pl. EC2 2 L7
South Pl. EC2 57 BZ39
South Pl., Enf. 30 CC25
South St.
South Pl., Harl. 6 CO9
South Pl., Surb. 85 BL54
South Pl. Ms. EC2 2 L7
South Pl. Ms. EC2 57 BZ39
South Pl.
South Ridge, Wey. 92 AZ58
South Riding, St.Alb. 18 BF18
South Ri., Cars. 95 BU58
South Rd. N9 39 CB26
South Rd. SE23 77 CC48
South Rd. SW19 76 BT50
South Rd. W5 64 BK42
South Rd., Amer. 25 AO21
South Rd., Edg. 37 BM30
South Rd., Egh. 72 AR50
South Rd., Erith 69 CT43
South Rd., Felt. 74 BD49
South Rd., Guil. 118 AQ69
South Rd., Hmptn. 74 BE50
South Rd., Harl. 6 CO9
South Rd., Reig. 121 BS71
South Rd., Rick. 25 AU25
South Rd., Rom. 50 CQ32
South Rd. (Little Heath), Rom. 50 CP32
South Rd., S.Ock. 60 DB39
South Rd., Sthl. 54 BE40
South Rd., Twick. 74 BG48
South Rd., West Dr. 63 AY41
South Rd., Wey. 92 BA56
South Rd. (St. Georges Hill), Wey. 92 AZ58
South Rd., Wok. 100 AR61
South Row SE3 68 CG44
South Sea St. SE16 67 CD41
South Side W6 65 BO41
South Side Common SW19 75 BQ50
South Sq. NW11 47 BS32
South Sq. WC1 2 D7
South Sta. App., Red. 121 BX71
South St. W1 3 H2
South St. W1 56 BV40
South St., Brwd. 42 DB27
South St., Brom. 88 CH51
South St., Dor. 119 BJ72
South St., Enf. 30 CC25
South St., Epsom 94 BN60
South St., Guil. 118 AR71
South St., Islw. 64 BJ45
South St., Rain. 59 CS37
South St., Rom. 50 CT32
South St., Stai. 72 AV49
South Tenter St. E1 2 Q9
South Tenter St. E1 57 CA40
South Ter. SW7 3 C8
South Ter. SW7 66 BU42
South Ter., Dor. 119 BJ72
South Ter., Surb. 85 BL53
South Vale SE19 77 CA50
South Vale, Har. 45 BH35
South Vw., Brom. 88 CJ51
South Vw., Dart. 79 CT46
South Vw. Ave. NW10 46 BO35
South Vw. Ave., Til. 71 DG44
South Vw. Ct., Wok. 100 AS62
Constitution Hill
South Vw. Dr. E18 49 CH31
South Vw. Rd. N8 47 BW31
South Vw. Rd., Ash. 102 BK63
South Vw. Rd., Dart. 80 CV48
South Vw. Rd., Ger.Cr. 43 AR31
South Vw. Rd., Grays 70 DB43
South Vw. Rd., Loug. 31 CK25
South Vw. Rd., Pnr. 35 BC29
South Vw. Rd., Warl. 105 CB63
South Vill. NW1 56 BW36
South Ville St. W. SW8 66 BW44
Wandsworth Rd.
South Wk., Hayes 53 BA39
South Wk., Reig. 121 BS70
South Wk., W.Wick. 88 CG55
South Way N9 39 CC27
South Way N11 38 BW29
South Way, Abb.L. 17 BA20
South Way, Brom. 88 CH54
South Way, Cars. 95 BT58
South Way, Croy. 87 CD55
South Way, Har. 45 BF31
South Way, Wal.Abb. 30 CE21
South Way, Wem. 46 BL35
South Weald Rd., Brwd. 42 DA27
South Western Rd., Twick. 74 BJ46
South Wf. Rd. W2 1 A8
South Wf. Rd. W2 56 BT39
South Worple Ave. SW14 65 BO45
South Worple Way
South Worple Way SW14 65 BN45
Southacre Way, Pnr. 36 BD30
Southall La., Houns. 63 BC43
Southall Pl. SE1 4 K5
Southall Way, Brwd. 42 CZ28
Southam St. W10 55 BR38
Southampton Bldgs. WC2 2 D7
Southampton Bldgs. WC2 56 BY39
Southampton Gdns., Mitch. 86 BX53
Southampton Pl. WC1 2 A7
Southampton Pl. WC1 56 BX39
Southampton Rd. NW5 47 BU35
Southampton Rd., Houns. 73 AY46
Southampton Row WC1 2 A6
Southampton Row WC1 56 BX39
Southampton St. WC2 2 A10
Southampton St. WC2 56 BX40
Southampton Way SE5 67 BZ43
Southbank, T.Ditt. 84 BJ54
Southborough Clo., Surb. 84 BK54
Southborough La., Brom. 88 CK53
Southborough Rd. E9 57 CC37
Southborough Rd., Brom. 88 CK53
Southborough Rd., Surb. 85 BL54
Southbourne, Brom. 88 CH54
Southbourne Ave. NW9 37 BN30
Southbourne Clo., Pnr. 45 BE33
Southbourne Cres. NW4 46 BR31
Southbourne Gdns. SE12 78 CH46
Southbourne Gdns., Ilf. 49 CM35
Southbourne Gdns., Ruis. 44 BC33
Southbridge Pl., Croy. 96 BZ56
Southbridge Rd., Croy. 87 BZ55
Southbridge Way, Sthl. 64 BE41
Southbrook, Saw. 6 CQ6
Southbrook Dr., Chsnt. 21 CC17
Southbrook Ms. SE12 78 CG46
Southbrook Rd.
Southbrook Rd. SE12 78 CG48
Southbrook Rd. SW16 86 BX51
Southbury Ave., Enf. 30 CB25
Southbury Clo., Horn. 51 CV35
Southbury Rd., Enf. 30 CA24
Southchurch Rd. E6 58 CK37
Southcliffe Dr., Ger.Cr. 34 AS28
Southcombe St. W14 65 BR42
Southcote, Wok. 100 AR61
Southcote Ave., Felt. 73 BB48
Southcote Ave., Surb. 85 BM54
Southcote Ri., Ruis. 44 BA33
Southcote Rd. E17 48 CC32
Southcote Rd. N19 47 BW35
Southcote Rd. SE25 87 CB53
Southcote Rd., Red. 113 BW68
Southcote Rd., S.Croy. 96 CA58
Southcroft Ave., Well. 68 CN45
Southcroft Ave., W.Wick. 87 CF55
Southcroft Rd. SW16 76 BV50
Southcroft Rd. SW17 76 BV50
Southcroft Rd., Orp. 88 CN55
Southdale, Chig. 40 CM29
Southdean Gdns. SW19 75 BR48
Southdene, Sev. 98 CQ60
Southdene Ct. N11 38 BW27
Pymmes Grn. Rd.
Southdown Ave. W7 64 BJ41
Southdown Ct., Hat. 10 BP14
Southdown Rd.
Southdown Cres., Har. 45 BF33
Southdown Cres., Ilf. 49 CN32
Southdown Dr. SW20 75 BQ50
Crescent Rd.
Southdown Rd. SW20 85 BQ51
Southdown Rd., Cars. 95 BV58
Southdown Rd., Cat. 105 CD64
Southdown Rd., Hat. 10 BP14
Southdown Rd., Horn. 50 CU33
Southdown Rd., Walt. 93 BE56
Southdowns, S.Dnth. 90 CY51
Southend Arterial Rd., Brwd. 51 DA32
Southend Arterial Rd., Rom. 42 CV30
Southend Clo. SE9 78 CL46
Southend Cres. SE9 78 CL46
Southend La. SE6 77 CD49
Southend La. SE26 77 CD49
Southend Rd. E6 58 CK36
Southend Rd. E17 39 CF30
Southend Rd. E18 40 CH30
Southend Rd., Beck. 77 CE50
Southend Rd., Grays 71 DE42
Southend Rd., Wdf.Grn. 40 CH30
Southern Ave. SE25 87 CA52
Southern Ave., Felt. 73 BC47
Southern Dr., Loug. 31 CK25
Southern Gro. E3 57 CD38
Southern Perimeter Rd., Houns. 73 AY46
Southern Pl., Swan. 89 CS52
Southern Rd. E13 58 CH37
Southern Rd. N2 47 BU31
Southern Row W10 55 BR38
Southern St. N1 56 BX37
Southern Way, Harl. 13 CL12
Southern Way, Rom. 50 CR32
Southerngate Way SE14 67 CD43
Southernhay, Loug. 31 CJ24
Southerns La., Couls. 104 BT65
Southerton Rd. W6 65 BQ41
Southey Rd. N15 48 CA32
Southey Rd. SW9 66 BY44
Southey Rd. SW19 76 BS50
Southey St. SE20 77 CC50
Southey Wk., Til. 71 DG44
Southfield, Barn. 28 BQ25
Southfield, Welw.G.C. 5 BQ9
Southfield Ave., Wat. 27 BD22
Southfield Clo., Uxb. 53 AZ38
Southfield Clo., Wind. 61 AL42
Southfield Gdns., Twick. 74 BH49
Southfield Pk., Har. 45 BF31
Southfield Pl., Wey. 92 AZ58
Southfield Rd. N17 39 CA30
The Ave.
Southfield Rd. W4 65 BN41
Southfield Rd., Chis. 88 CN52
Southfield Rd., Enf. 30 CB25
Southfield Rd., Hodd. 12 CE11
Southfield Rd., Sev. 99 CZ57
Southfield Rd., Wal.Cr. 21 CD19
Southfield Way, St.Alb. 9 BK12
Southfields NW4 37 BP30
Southfields, E.Mol. 84 BH53
Southfields Ave., Ashf. 73 AZ50
Southfields Cotts. W7 64 BH41
Southfields Pas. SW18 76 BS46
Southfields Rd.
Southfields Rd. SW18 76 BS46
Southfields Rd., Cat. 105 CE64
Southfleet Rd., Dart. 80 DA49
Southfleet Rd., Grav. 81 DF47
Milroy Ave.
Southfleet Rd., Orp. 88 CN55
Southfleet Rd., Swans. 81 DC47
Southgate Ave., Felt. 73 BA49
Southgate Circ. N14 38 BW26
Southgate Gro. N1 57 BZ36
Southgate Rd. N1 57 BZ37
Southgate Rd., Grays 70 CY42
Southgate Rd., Pot.B. 20 BT20

Southholme Clo. SE19 87 CA51
Sylvan Hill
Southill La., Pnr. 44 BC31
Southill Rd., Chis. 78 CK50
Southill St. E14 57 CE39
Chrisp St.
Southland Rd. SE18 68 CN43
Southland Way, Houns. 74 BG46
Southlands Ave., Orp. 97 CM56
Southlands Clo., Pur. 104 BX61
Southlands Gro., Brom. 88 CK52
Southlands La., Oxt. 114 CE70
Southlands Rd., Brom. 88 CJ53
Southlands Rd., Uxb. 43 AV35
Southlea Rd., Slou. 62 AQ44
Southly Clo., Sutt. 86 BS55
Southmead Cres., Chsnt. 21 CD18
Southmead Rd. SW19 75 BR47
Southmont Rd., Esher 84 BH55
Southmoor Way E9 57 CD36
Trowbridge Est.
Southold Ri. SE9 78 CK48
Southolm St. SW11 66 BV44
Southover N12 38 BS27
Southover, Brom. 78 CH49
Southport Rd. SE18 68 CM42
Southridge Pl. SW20 75 BQ50
Southsea Ave., Wat. 26 BC24
Southsea Rd., Kings.T. 85 BL52
Southside, Ger.Cr. 43 AR31
Southspring, Sid. 78 CM47
Southvale Rd. SE3 68 CG44
Southview Ave. NW10 46 BO35
Southview Clo., Bex. 79 CQ46
Southview Clo., Chsnt. 21 CA16
Southview Clo., Swan. 89 CT52
West Vw. Rd.
Southview Cres., Ilf. 49 CL32
Southview Dr., Upmin. 51 CX34
Southview Gdns., Wall. 95 BW57
Southview Rd., Brom. 77 CF49
Southview Rd., Cat. 105 CE65
Southview Rd., Dart. 80 CV48
Southviews, S.Croy. 96 CC58
Southville Clo., Epsom 94 BN57
Southville Clo., Felt. 73 BB47
Southville Cres., Felt. 73 BB47
Southville Rd., Felt. 73 BB47
Southville Rd., T.Ditt. 84 BJ54
Southwark Bri. EC4 4 J1
Southwark Bri. EC4 57 BZ40
Southwark Bri. SE1 4 J1
Southwark Bri. SE1 57 BZ40
Southwark Bri. Rd. SE1 4 H5
Southwark Bri. Rd. SE1 66 BY41
Southwark Gro. SE1 4 H3
Southwark Gro. SE1 57 BZ40
Southwark Pk. Rd. SE16 4 Q8
Southwark Pk. Rd. SE16 67 CA42
Southwark Pl., Brom. 88 CK52
St. Georges Rd.
Southwark St. SE1 4 G2
Southwark St. SE1 56 BY40
Southwater Clo. E14 57 CD39
Southwater Clo., Beck. 77 CE50
Southway N20 38 BS27
Southway NW11 47 BS32
Southway SW20 85 BQ52
Southway, Guil. 118 AP70
Southway, Hat. 10 BP14
Southway, Wall. 95 BW56
Southway Clo. W12 65 BP41
Scotts Rd.
Southway Ct., Guil. 118 AP70
Southway
Southweald Dr., Wal.Abb. 21 CF19
Southwell Ave., Nthlt. 54 BF36
Southwell Gdns. SW7 66 BT41
Southwell Gro. Rd. E11 49 CG34
Southwell Rd. SE5 67 BZ45
Southwell Rd., Croy. 86 BY53
Southwell Rd., Har. 45 BK32
Southwest Rd. E11 48 CF33
Southwick Ms. W2 1 B8
Southwick Ms. W2 56 BT39
Southwick St.
Southwick Pl. W2 1 C9
Southwick Pl. W2 56 BU39
Southwick St. W2 1 C8
Southwick St. W2 56 BU39
Southwold Dr., Bark. 50 CO35
Southwold Rd. E5 48 CB34
Southwold Rd., Bex. 79 CR46
Southwold Rd., Wat. 27 BD22
Southwold Spur, Slou. 62 AU41
Southwood Ave. N6 47 BV33
Southwood Ave., Cher. 91 AU57
Southwood Ave., Couls. 104 BW61
Southwood Ave., Kings.T. 85 BN51
Southwood Ave., Wok. 100 AO62
Southwood Clo., Brom. 88 CK52
Southwood Clo., Wor.Pk. 85 BQ54
Southwood Ct. NW11 47 BS32
Southwood Dr., Surb. 85 BN54
Southwood Gdns., Esher 84 BJ55
Southwood Gdns., Ilf. 49 CL31
Southwood La. N6 47 BV33
Southwood Lawn Rd. N6 47 BV33
Southwood Rd. SE9 78 CL48
Southwood Rd. SE28 59 CO40
Sovereign Clo. E1 57 CB40
Wapping La.
Sovereign Clo. W5 54 BK39
Sovereign Clo., Ruis. 44 BB33
Sovereign Ms. E2 57 CA37
Pearson St.
Sovereign Pk. W3 55 BM38
Sovereign Way, St.Alb. 9 BG13
Chequer St.
Sowerby Clo. SE9 78 CK46
Sowrey Ave., Rain. 59 CT36
Spa Clo. SE25 87 CA51
Spa Dr., Epsom 94 BM60
Spa Grn. Est. EC1 2 E2
Spa Grn. Est. EC1 56 BY38
Spa Hill SE19 87 BZ51
Spa Rd. SE16 4 P7
Spa Rd. SE16 67 CA41
Spacewaye, Felt. 73 BC46
Spackmans Way, Slou. 61 AO41
Spafield St. EC1 2 D4
Spains Hall Rd., Ong. 15 DB13
Spalding Rd. NW4 46 BQ33
Spalding Rd. SW17 76 BV49
Spalt Clo., Brwd. 122 DD27
Spanby Rd. E3 57 CE38
Spangate SE3 68 CG45
Spaniards Clo. NW11 47 BT33
Spaniards End NW3 47 BT33
Spaniards Rd. NW3 47 BT34
Spanish Pl. W1 1 H8
Spanish Pl. W1 56 BV39
Spanish Rd. SW18 76 BT46
Spareleaze Hill, Loug. 31 CK25
Sparepenny La., Eyns. 90 CV54
Sparkbridge Rd., Har. 45 BH31
Sparks Clo. W3 55 BN39
Joseph Ave.
Sparks Clo., Hmptn. 74 BE50
Victors Dr.
Sparrow Clo., Hmptn. 74 BE49
Sparrow Dr., Orp. 88 CM54
Sparrow Fm. Dr., Felt. 74 BD47
Sparrow Fm. Rd., Epsom 94 BP56
Sparrow Fm. Rd., Felt. 74 BD47
Sparrow Fm. Dr.
Sparrow Grn., Dag. 50 CR34
Sparrows Herne, Bush. 36 BF26
Sparrows La. SE9 78 CM47
Sparrows Mead, Red. 121 BV69
Kingfisher Dr.
Sparrows Way, Bush. 36 BG26
Sparrows Herne
Sparrowswick Ride, St.Alb. 9 BG11
Sparsholt Rd. N19 47 BX33
Sparsholt Rd., Bark. 58 CN37
Sparta St. SE10 67 CE44
Spear Ms. SW5 66 BS42
Spearman St. SE18 68 CL43
Spearpoint Gdns., Ilf. 49 CN31
Spears Rd. N19 47 BX33
Speart La., Houns. 64 BE43
Spedan Clo. NW3 47 BT34
Speedgate Hill, Fawk. 90 DA55
Speedwell Clo., Guil. 109 AU69
Speedwell Clo., Hem.H. 7 AV14
Campion Rd.
Speedwell Ct., Grays 71 DE43
Speedwell St. SE8 67 CE43
Comet St.
Speedy Pl. WC1 1 Q3
Speer Rd., T.Ditt. 84 BH53
Speke Hill SE9 78 CK48
Speke Rd., Th.Hth. 87 BZ51
Speldhurst Clo., Brom. 88 CG53
Speldhurst Rd. E9 57 CC36
Speldhurst Rd. W4 65 BN41
Spellbrook Wk. N1 57 BZ37
Basire St.
Spelman St. E1 57 CA39
Spelthorne Gro., Sun. 73 BB50
Spelthorne La., Ashf. 83 BA51
Spence Ave. (Byfleet), Wey. 92 AY60
Spencer Ave. N13 38 BX29
Spencer Ave., Chsnt. 21 CA16
Spencer Ave., Hayes 53 BC39
Spencer Clo. N3 38 BS30
Spencer Clo. NW10 55 BL38
Spencer Clo., Epsom 103 BO65
Spencer Clo., Orp. 88 CN55
Spencer Clo., Uxb. 53 AX38
Spencer Clo., Wok. 91 AU60
Spencer Clo., Wdf.Grn. 40 CJ28
Spencer Ct. SW20 85 BP51
Spencer Rd.
Spencer Ct., Rich. 74 BK49
Spencer Cres., Upmin. 51 CY33
Spencer Dr. N2 47 BT32
Spencer Gdns. SE9 78 CK46
Spencer Gdns. SW14 75 BN46
Spencer Gdns., Egh. 72 AR49
Spencer Gate, St.Alb. 9 BH12
Spencer Hill SW19 75 BR50
Spencer Hill Rd. SW19 75 BR50
Spencer Ms. W6 65 BR43
Greyhound Rd.
Spencer Pk. SW18 76 BT46
Spencer Pas. E2 57 CB37
Dinmont St.
Spencer Pl. SW1 66 BW41
Greycoat Pl.
Spencer Pl., Croy. 87 BZ54
Spencer Ri. NW5 47 BV34
Spencer Rd. E6 58 CJ37
Spencer Rd. E17 39 CF30
Spencer Rd. N11 38 BV28
Spencer Rd. N17 39 CB30
Spencer Rd. SW18 66 BT45
Spencer Rd. SW20 85 BP51
Spencer Rd. W3 55 BN40
Spencer Rd. W4 65 BN43
Spencer Rd., Brom. 78 CG50
Spencer Rd., Cat. 105 BZ64
Spencer Rd., Cob. 101 BC61
Spencer Rd., E.Mol. 84 BG53
Spencer Rd., Har. 36 BH30
Spencer Rd., Ilf. 49 CN33
Spencer Rd., Islw. 64 BG44
Spencer Rd., Mitch. 86 BV52
Spencer Rd. (Beddington), Mitch. 86 BU54
Spencer Rd., Rain. 59 CS38
Spencer Rd., Slou. 62 AS42
Spencer Rd., S.Croy. 96 CA56
Spencer Rd., Twick. 74 BH48
Spencer Rd., Wem. 45 BK34
Spencer St. EC1 2 F3
Spencer St. EC1 56 BY38
Spencer St., Grav. 81 DG47
Spencer St., St.Alb. 9 BG13
Spencer St., Sthl. 64 BD41
Spencer Wk. NW3 47 BT35
Hampstead High St.
Spencer Wk. SW15 65 BQ45
Spencer Wk., Rick. 26 AW25
Spencer Wk., Til. 71 DG44
Spencer Way, Hem.H. 8 AW12
Spencer Way, Red. 121 BV73
Spencers Cft., Harl. 14 CO12
Spenser Ave., Wey. 92 AZ58
Spenser Cres., Upmin. 51 CY33
Spenser Gro. N16 48 CA35
Spenser Rd. SE24 76 BY46
Spenser St. SW1 3 M6
Spenser St. SW1 66 BW41
Spensley Wk. N16 48 BZ34
Speranza St. SE18 68 CN42
Sperling Rd. N17 39 CA30
Spert St. E14 57 CD40
Spey St. E14 57 CF39
Spey Way, Rom. 41 CT29
Speyside N14 29 BW25
Spezia Rd. NW10 55 BP37
Spicer Clo. SW9 66 BY44
Spicer Clo., Walt. 84 BD53
Spicers Fld., Lthd. 93 BG60
Spicers St., St.Alb. 9 BG13
Spicersfield, Chsnt. 21 CB17
Spices Yd., Croy. 96 BZ56
South End
Spielman Rd., Dart. 70 CW45
Spiers Clo., N.Mal. 85 BO53
Spigurnell Rd. N17 39 BZ30
Spikes Bri. Rd., Sthl. 54 BE39
Spillbutters, Brwd. 33 DA21
Spilsby Clo. NW9 37 BO30
Spilsby Rd., Rom. 42 CV29
Spindles, Til. 71 DG43
Spindlewood Gdns., Croy. 87 CA55
Coombe Rd.
Spindlewoods, Tad. 103 BP65
Spindrift Ave. E14 67 CE42
Spinel Clo. SE18 68 CN42
Spingate Clo., Horn. 51 CV35
Tylers Cres.
Spinnells Rd., Har. 45 BE33
Spinners Wk., Wind. 61 AO44
Spinney, Slou. 61 AN41
Spinney, The N21 38 BY26
Spinney, The SW16 76 BW48
Spinney, The, Barn. 29 BS23
Spinney, The, Brwd. 122 DE25
Spinney, The, Brox. 12 CD13
Glenwood
Spinney, The, Chesh. 16 AO18
Spinney, The, Epsom 103 BP63
Spinney, The, Guil. 110 AX67
Spinney, The, Lthd. 93 BG59
Spinney, The (Great Bookham), Lthd. 102 BF65
Spinney, The, Ong. 24 CX18
Spinney, The, Pot.B. 20 BT19
Bearwood Clo.
Spinney, The, Pur. 95 BY59
Spinney, The, Sid. 79 CQ49
Spinney, The, Stan. 37 BL28
Spinney, The, Sun. 83 BC51
Spinney, The, Sutt. 94 BQ56
Spinney, The, Swan. 89 CT51
Spinney, The, Wat. 26 BC23
Spinney, The, Welw.G.C. 5 BR8
Peartree La.
Spinney, The, Wem. 45 BJ34
Spinney Clo., Cob. 93 BF59
Spinney Clo., N.Mal. 85 BO53
Spinney Clo., Rain. 59 CT37
Spinney Clo., West Dr. 53 AY40
Yew Ave.
Spinney Dr., Felt. 73 BA47
Spinney Gdns. SE19 77 CA49
Spinney Gdns., Dag. 50 CQ35
Spinney Hill, Wey. 91 AV56
Spinney Oak, Brom. 88 CK51
Spinney Way, Sev. 97 CM59
Spinneycroft, Lthd. 102 BG61
Spinneys, The, Brom. 88 CK51
Spinning Wheel Mead, Harl. 14 CO12
Spire Clo., Grav. 81 DG47
Spring Gro.
Spires, The, Dart. 80 CV48
Spirit Quay E1 57 CB40
Vaughan Way
Spital Heath, Dor. 119 BK71
Spital La., Brwd. 42 CZ27
Spital Sq. E1 2 N6
Spital Sq. E1 57 CA39
Spital St. E1 57 CA39
Spital St., Dart. 80 CV46
Spital Yd. E1 2 N6
Spitalfields Mkt. E1 2 P6
Spitfire Way, Houns. 64 BD42
Spode Wk. NW6 56 BS36
Lymington Rd.
Spondon Rd. N15 48 CB31
Spook Hill, Dor. 119 BJ73
Spooner Wk., Wall. 95 BW56
Spooners Dr., St.Alb. 18 BG17
Sportsbank St. SE6 77 CF47
Spottons Gro. N17 39 BZ30
Spout Hill, Croy. 96 CE56
Spout La., Stai. 73 AW46
Spout La. N., Stai. 63 AW45
Spratt Hall Rd. E11 49 CH32
Spratts All., Cher. 91 AV57
Spratts La., Cher. 91 AV57
Spray St. SE18 68 CL42
Spreighton Rd., E.Mol. 84 BF53
Sprimont Pl. SW3 3 E10
Sprimont Pl. SW3 66 BU42
Spring Ave., Egh. 72 AS50
Spring Bottom La., Red. 113 BY67
Spring Bri. Ms. W5 54 BK40
Spring Bri. Rd.
Spring Bri. Rd. W5 54 BK40
Spring Clo., Barn. 28 BQ25
Spring Clo., Borwd. 28 BM23
Spring Clo., Chesh. 25 AR21
Spring Clo., Dag. 50 CP33
Spring Clo., Uxb. 35 AX30
Spring Clo. La., Sutt. 94 BR57
Spring Cotts., Surb. 84 BK53
St. Leonards Rd.
Spring Ct., Guil. 109 AQ68
Spring Ct., Sid. 79 CO48
Spring Ct. Rd., Enf. 29 BY22
Spring Cfts., Bush. 27 BF25
Spring Dr., Pnr. 44 BC32
Spring Gdns. N5 48 BZ35
Spring Gdns. SW1 3 P2
Spring Gdns. SW1 56 BW40
Spring Gdns., Dor. 119 BJ71
Spring Gdns., E.Mol. 84 BG53
Spring Gdns., Horn. 50 CU35
Spring Gdns., Orp. 98 CO57
Spring Gdns., Rom. 50 CS32
Spring Gdns., Wall. 95 BW56
Spring Gdns., Wat. 27 BD21
Spring Gdns., Wdf.Grn. 40 CJ29
Spring Glen, Hat. 10 BO13
Spring Gro. W4 65 BM42
Spring Gro., Grav. 81 DG47
Spring Gro., Hmptn. 84 BF51
Spring Gro., Lthd. 102 BF65
Spring Gro., Loug. 31 CJ25
Spring Gro., Mitch. 86 BV51
Spring Gro. Cres., Houns. 64 BG44
Spring Gro. Rd., Houns. 64 BF44
Spring Gro. Rd., Rich. 75 BL46
Spring Hill E5 48 CB33
Spring Hill SE26 77 CC49
Sydenham Rd.
Spring Hills, Harl. 6 CL10
Spring Lake, Stan. 36 BJ28
Spring La. E5 48 CB33
Spring La. SE25 87 CB53
Spring La., Hem.H. 8 AW12
Spring La., Oxt. 114 CF69
Spring La., Sev. 108 DA64
Spring La., Slou. 61 AM40
Spring Ms. W1 1 F6
Spring Ms. W1 56 BU39
Crawford St.
Spring Ms., Epsom 94 BO58
Old Schools La.
Spring Pk. Ave., Croy. 87 CC55
Spring Pk. Dr. N4 48 BZ33
Spring Pk. Rd., Croy. 87 CC55
Spring Pas. SW15 65 BQ45
The Embk.
Spring Pl. NW5 47 BV35
Spring Pond Meadow, Brwd. 33 DB21
Spring Ri., Egh. 72 AS50
Spring Rd., Felt. 73 BB48
Spring Shaw Clo., Sev. 107 CS65
Spring St. W2 1 A9
Spring St. W2 56 BT39
Spring St., Epsom 94 BO58
Spring St., Harl. 6 CM9
Spring Vale, Bexh. 69 CR45
Spring Vale, Dart. 80 CV47
Spring Vale, Green. 80 DB46
Spring Vale Clo., Swan. 79 CT50
Egerton Ave.
Spring Vill. Rd., Edg. 37 BM29
Spring Wk., Brox. 12 CC14
Spring Wds., Vir.W. 82 AQ52
Springall St. SE15 67 CB43
Springate Fld., Slou. 62 AS41
Springbank N21 29 BX25
Springbank Ave., Horn. 51 CV35
Springbank Rd. SE13 77 CF46
Springbank Wk. NW1 56 BW36
Agar Gro.
Springbourne Ct., Beck. 87 CF51
Springclose La., Sutt. 94 BR57
Springcopse Rd., Reig. 121 BT71
Springcroft Ave. N2 47 BU31
Springdale Rd. N16 48 BZ35
Springett Pl., Amer. 25 AP22
Springfarm Clo., Rain. 60 CV38
Springfield E5 48 CB33
Springfield, Bush. 36 BG26
Springfield, Epp. 22 CN19
Springfield, Oxt. 114 CF68
Springfield, Wal.Abb. 22 CG20
Springfield Ave. N10 47 BW31
Springfield Ave. SW20 85 BR52
Springfield Ave., Brwd. 122 DF26
Springfield Ave., Hmptn. 74 BF50
Springfield Ave., Swan. 89 CT52
Springfield Clo. N12 38 BS28
Springfield Clo., Chesh. 16 AO20
Springfield Clo., Ong. 24 CW16
Springfield Clo., Pot.B. 20 BT19
Springfield Clo., Rick. 26 AZ25
Springfield Clo., Stan. 36 BJ27
Springfield Clo., Wind. 61 AN44
Springfield Clo., Wok. 100 AP62
Springfield Dr., Ilf. 49 CM32
Springfield Est. SW8 66 BW44
Springfield Gdns. E5 48 CB33
Springfield Gdns. NW9 46 BN32
Springfield Gdns., Brom. 88 CK52
Springfield Gdns., Ruis. 44 BC33
Springfield Gdns., Upmin. 51 CY34
Springfield Gdns., W.Wick. 87 CE55
Springfield Gdns., Wdf.Grn. 40 CJ29
Springfield Gro. SE7 68 C
Springfield Gro., Sun. 83 B
Springfield La. NW6 56 B
Springfield La., Wey. 92 A
Springfield Meadows, Wey. 92 A
Springfield Mt. NW9 46 B
Springfield Orchard, Ong. 24 CV
Springfield Clo.
Springfield Pk., Maid. 61 A
Springfield Ri. SE26 77 C
Springfield Rd. E4 40 C
Springfield Rd. E6 58 C
Springfield Rd. E15 58 C
Springfield Rd. E17 48 C
Springfield Rd. N11 38 B
Springfield Rd. N15 48 C
Springfield Rd. NW8 56 B
Springfield Rd. SE26 77 C
Springfield Rd. SW19 75 B
Springfield Rd. W7 54 B
Springfield Rd., Ashf. 73 A
Springfield Rd., Berk. 7 A
Springfield Rd., Bexh. 69 C
Springfield Rd., Brom. 88 C
Springfield Rd., Chesh. 16 A
Springfield Rd., Chsnt. 21 C
Springfield Rd., Dor. 119 B
Springfield Rd., Epsom 94 B
Springfield Rd., Grays 71 D
Springfield Rd., Guil. 118 A
Springfield Rd., Har. 45 B
Springfield Rd., Hayes 54 B
Springfield Rd., Hem.H. 8 A
Springfield Rd., Kings.T. 85 B
Springfield Rd., St.Alb. 9 B
Springfield Rd. (Colney Heath), St.Alb. 10 BN
Springfield Rd., Slou. 62 A
Springfield Rd., Tedd. 74 B
Springfield Rd., Th.Hth. 87 B
Springfield Rd., Twick. 74 B
Springfield Rd., Wall. 95 B
Springfield Rd., Wat. 17 B
Haines Way
Springfield Rd., Well. 69 CC
Springfield Rd., Wind. 61 AN
Springfield Wk. NW6 56 BS
Springfield Wk., Orp. 88 CM
Farm Ave.
Springfields, Brox. 12 CD
Springfields, Welw.G.C. 5 B
Springhall La., Saw. 6 C
Springhall Rd., Saw. 6 C
Springhaven Clo., Guil. 118 A
Springhead Rd., Erith 69 C
Springhead Rd., Grav. 81 DE
Springhead Rd., Sev. 108 CW
Springhill Clo. SE5 67 BZ
Springholm Clo., West. 106 C
Upper Dr.
Springpark Dr., Beck. 87 C
Springpond Rd., Dag. 50 CQ
Springrice Rd. SE13 77 CF
Springs, The, Brox. 21 CD
Springside Ct., Guil. 118 AF
Springvale Ave., Brent. 65 BL
Springvale Est. W14 65 BF
Springvale Ter. W14 65 BQ
Springvale Way, Orp. 89 CP
Springwater Clo. SE18 68 CL
Springwell Ave. NW10 55 BC
Springwell Ave., Rick. 35 AW
Springwell Clo. SW16 76 BX
Springwell Ct., Houns. 64 BD
Springwell La., Rick. 35 AW
Springwell Rd. SW16 76 BX
Springwell Rd., Houns. 64 BD
Springwood, Chsnt. 21 CB
Springwood Clo., Uxb. 35 AX
Springwood Cres., Edg. 37 BM
Springwood Wk., St.Alb. 9 BK
Springwood Way, Rom. 50 CU
Manor Rd.
Sprowston Ms. E7 49 CH
Sprowston Rd. E7 49 CH
Spruce Ct. W5 65 BL
Spruce Dale Gdns., Wall. 95 BX
Spruce Hill, Harl. 13 CN
Spruce Hills Rd. E17 39 CE
Spruce Pk., Brom. 88 CG
Cumberland Rd.
Spruce Rd., West. 106 CK
Acer Rd.
Spruce Way, St.Alb. 18 BF
Sprucedale Clo., Swan. 89 CT
The Spinney
Sprucedale Gdns., Croy. 96 CC
Sprules Rd. SE4 67 CD
Spur Clo., Abb.L. 17 BA
Fay Grn.
Spur Clo., Rom. 32 CO
Spur Rd. N15 48 BZ
Philip La.
Spur Rd. SW1 3
Spur Rd. SW1 66 BW
Spur Rd., Bark. 58 CM
Spur Rd., Edg. 37 BL
Spur Rd., Felt. 73 BC
Spur Rd., Islw. 64 BJ
Spur Rd., Orp. 89 CO
Spur Rd. Est., Edg. 37 BL
Spurfield, E.Mol. 84 BF
Spurgate, Brwd. 122 DD
Spurgeon Ave. SE19 87 BZ
Spurgeon Rd. SE19 87 BZ
Spurgeon St. SE1 4
Spurgeon St. SE1 67 BZ
Spurling Rd. SE22 67 CA
Spurling Rd., Dag. 59 CQ
Spurrell Ave., Bex. 79 CS
Spurstowe Rd. E8 57 CB
Cottrill Rd.
Spurstowe Ter. E8 48 CB

uadrons App., Horn. 60 CV36
uare, The, Berk. 7 AT11
uare, The, Cars. 95 BV56
uare, The, Guil. 118 AP71
)rchard Rd.
uare, The, Ilf. 49 CL33
uare, The, Rich. 65 BL45
'he Quad.
uare, The, Saw. 6 CQ6
uare, The, Wat. 26 BC22
uare, The, West Dr. 63 AW44
uare, The, West. 106 CJ63
uare, The, Wey. 92 BA56
uare, The, Wok. 101 AY61
uare, The, Wdf.Grn. 40 CH28
uare Rigger Row SW11 66 BT45
'ork Pl.
uarey St. SW17 76 BT48
uerryes Mead, West. 115 CM67
uirel Chase, Hem.H. 7 AV13
uires Bri. Rd., Shep. 83 AY52
uires Ct. SW19 76 BS49
uires La. N3 38 BS30
uires Mt. NW3 47 BT34
:ast Heath Rd.
uires Ride, Hem.H. 8 AY10
uires Rd., Shep. 83 AZ52
uires Wk., Ashf. 73 BA50
Vapier Rd.
uires Way, Dart. 79 CS49
uires Wd. Dr., Chis. 78 CK50
3ullerswood Dr.
uirrel Clo., Houns. 64 BD45
uirrel Wd., Wey. 92 AW59
uirrels, The SE13 67 CF45
uirrels, The, Bush. 27 BG25
uirrels, The, Pnr. 45 BE31
uirrels, The, Welw.G.C. 5 BT8
:orresters Dr.
uirrels Chase, Grays 71 DG41
Hornsby La.
uirrels Clo. N12 38 BT28
Voodside Ave.
uirrels Clo., Uxb. 53 AZ36
uirrels Grn., Lthd. 102 BF65
uirrels Grn., Wor.Pk. 85 BO55
uirrels Heath Ave., Rom. 50 CU31
uirrels Heath La., Rom. 51 CV31
uirrels Heath Rd., Rom. 51 CW31
uirrels La., Buck.H. 40 CJ27
uirrels Ms. W13 54 BJ40
Felix Rd.
uirrels Way, Epsom 103 BN61
uirries St. E2 57 CB38
able Clo., Nthlt. 54 BF37
able La., Beac. 34 AO29
able Wk. N2 38 BT30
able Way W10 55 BQ39
Latimer Rd.
able Yd. SW1 3 **L4**
able Yd. SW9 66 BX44
Broomgrove Rd.
able Yd. Rd. SW1 3 **M4**
able Yd. Rd. SW1 56 BW40
ables, The, Buck.H. 40 CJ26
ables, The, Guil. 118 AR69
ables End, Orp. 88 CM55
ables Ms. SE27 77 BZ49
Elder Rd.
ables Way SE11 4 **D10**
ables Way SE11 66 BY42
acey Ave. N18 39 CC28
acey Clo. E10 48 CF32
Halford Rd.
acey Clo., Grav. 81 DJ49
acey St. WC2 1 **P9**
acey St. WC2 56 BW39
ack Fld., Harl. 6 CO9
ack La., Hartley 90 DC53
ack Rd., Dart. 90 CY52
ackhouse St. SW3 3 **E6**
ackhouse St. SW3 66 BU41
Pavilion Rd.
acklands Clo., Sev. 99 CZ57
acklands Rd., Welw.G.C. 5 BP9
acy Path SE5 67 BZ43
Elmington Est.
adium Rd. NW2 46 BQ33
adium Rd. SE18 68 CK43
adium St. SW10 66 BT43
adium Way, Wem. 46 BL35
aff St. EC1 2 **L3**
aff St. EC1 57 BZ38
Cranwood St.
affa Rd. E10 48 CC33
afford Ave., Horn. 51 CV31
afford Ave., Wall. 95 BX56
afford Clo. N14 29 BW25
afford Clo. NW6 56 BS38
afford Clo., Chsnt. 21 CB18
afford Clo., Sutt. 94 BR57
afford Ct. W8 66 BS41
afford Cripps Est. EC1 57 BZ38
afford Dr., Brox. 12 CE13
afford Pl. SW1 3 **L6**
afford Pl. SW1 66 BW41
afford Pl., Rich. 75 BL47
Queens Rd.
afford Rd. E3 57 CD37
afford Rd. E7 58 CJ36
afford Rd. NW6 56 BS38
afford Rd., Cat. 105 CA65
afford Rd., Croy. 95 BX56
afford Rd., Har. 36 BG30
afford Rd., N.Mal. 85 BN52
afford Rd., Ruis. 44 BB35
afford Rd., Sid. 78 CN49
afford Rd., Wall. 95 BW57
afford Sq., Wey. 92 BA56
Rosslyn Pk.
afford St. W1 3 **L2**
afford St. W1 56 BW40
afford Ter. W8 66 BS41

Stafford Way, Sev. 117 CV67
Staffords, Harl. 6 CQ9
Staffordshire St. SE15 67 CB44
Stag Clo., Edg. 37 BM30
Stag Grn. Ave., Hat. 10 BQ11
Stag La. NW9 37 BN30
Stag La. SW15 75 BO48
Stag La., Buck.H. 40 CH27
Stag La., Edg. 37 BN30
Stag La., Rick. 25 AU25
Stag Leys, Ash. 103 BL63
Stag Pl. SW1 3 **L6**
Stag Pl. SW1 66 BW41
Stag Ride SW19 75 BP48
Stagbury Ave., Couls. 104 BU62
Stagbury Clo., Couls. 104 BU63
Stagg Hill, Barn. 29 BU21
Staggart Grn., Chig. 41 CO29
Staghill, Guil. 118 AQ71
Stags Way, Islw. 64 BH43
Stahlton La., Brwd. 123 DC30
Stainash Cres., Stai. 73 AW49
Stainbank Rd., Mitch. 86 BV52
Stainby Clo., West Dr. 63 AY41
Stainby Rd. N15 48 CA31
Stainer Rd., Borwd. 27 BK22
Stainer St. SE1 4 **L3**
Stainer St. SE1 57 BZ40
Staines Ave., Sutt. 85 BQ55
Staines By-pass, Ashf. 73 AW49
Staines By-pass, Egh. 72 AU48
Staines By-pass, Stai. 72 AU48
Staines Clo., Cher. 82 AV53
Staines La., Cher. 82 AV53
Staines Rd., Cher. 82 AV52
Staines Rd., Felt. 73 AZ47
Staines Rd., Houns. 64 BE45
Staines Rd., Ilf. 49 CM35
Staines Rd., Stai. 73 AW50
Staines Rd. (Wraysbury), Stai. 72 AS47
Staines Rd., Twick. 74 BF48
Staines Rd. E., Sun. 73 BC50
Staines Rd. W., Ashf. 73 AZ50
Staines Rd. W., Sun. 73 AZ50
Staines Wk., Sid. 79 CP50
Evry Rd.
Stainford Clo., Ashf. 73 BA49
Stainforth Rd. E17 48 CE31
Stainforth Rd., Ilf. 49 CM33
Staining La. EC2 2 **J8**
Staining La. EC2 57 BZ39
Gresham St.
Stainmore Clo., Chis. 78 CM50
Stains Clo., Chsnt. 21 CD17
Stainsbury St. E2 57 CC37
Royston St.
Stainsby Pl. E14 57 CE39
Stainsby Rd. E14 57 CE39
Stainton Rd. SE6 77 CF46
Stainton Rd., Enf. 30 CC23
Stainton Wk., Wok. 100 AQ62
Inglewood
Stairfoot La., Sev. 107 CS64
Staithes Way, Tad. 103 BP63
Headley Gro.
Stalbridge St. NW1 1 **D6**
Staleys Rd., Sev. 108 DC63
Stalham St. SE16 67 CB41
Stalisfield Pl., Orp. 97 CL58
Stambourne Way SE19 77 CA50
Stambourne Way, W.Wick. 87 CF55
Stamford Brook Ave. W6 65 BO41
Stamford Brook Rd. W6 65 BO41
Stamford Clo. N15 48 CB31
Stamford Rd.
Stamford Clo., Har. 36 BH29
Stamford Clo., Pot.B. 20 BT19
Stamford Clo., Sthl. 54 BF40
Stamford Ct. W6 65 BO42
Stamford Dr., Brom. 88 CG52
Stamford Gdns., Dag. 59 CP36
Stamford Grn. Rd., Epsom 94 BM60
Stamford Gro. E. N16 48 CB33
Oldhill St.
Stamford Gro. W. N16 48 CB33
Oldhill St.
Stamford Hill N16 48 CA34
Stamford Hill Est. N16 48 CA33
Stamford Ho. W12 65 BP41
Stamford Rd. E6 58 CK37
Stamford Rd. N1 57 CA36
Stamford Rd. N15 48 CB32
Stamford Rd., Dag. 59 CO37
Stamford Rd., Walt. 84 BD55
Stamford Rd., Wat. 26 BC23
Stamford St. SE1 4 **D3**
Stamford St. SE1 56 BY40
Stamp Pl. E2 2 **P2**
Stamp Pl. E2 57 CA38
Stanard Clo. N16 48 CA33
Stanborough Ave., Borwd. 28 BM22
Stanborough Clo., Borwd. 28 BM22
Stanborough Ave.
Stanborough Clo., Hmptn. 74 BE50
Stanborough Clo., Welw.G.C. 5 BQ8
Stanborough Grn., Welw.G.C. 5 BQ9
Stanborough La., Welw.G.C. 5 BP9
Stanborough Pas. E8 57 CA36
Abbot St.
Stanborough Rd., Islw. 64 BG45
Stanborough Rd., Welw.G.C. 5 BP9
Stanbridge Rd. SW15 65 BQ45
Stanbrook Rd. SE2 69 CO41
Stanbrook Rd., Grav. 81 DF47
Stanbury Ave., Wat. 26 BB22
Stanbury Rd. SE15 67 CB44

Stancroft NW9 46 BO32
Standale Gro., Ruis. 44 BA32
Standard Pl. EC2 2 **N3**
Standard Rd. NW10 55 BN38
Standard Rd., Belv. 69 CR42
Standard Rd., Bexh. 69 CQ45
Standard Rd., Enf. 30 CD22
Standard Rd., Houns. 64 BE45
Standard Rd., Orp. 97 CL58
Standen Ave., Horn. 51 CW34
Standen Rd. SW18 75 BR47
Standfield, Abb.L. 17 BB19
Standfield Gdns., Dag. 59 CR36
Standfield Rd., Dag. 50 CR35
Standingford, Harl. 13 CL13
Standish Rd. W6 65 BP42
Standring Ri., Hem.H. 8 AW15
Stane Clo. SW19 76 BS50
Hayward Clo.
Stane Pass SW16 76 BX49
Streatham High Rd.
Stane St., Dor. 119 BJ74
Stane St., Lthd. 112 BL66
Stane Way SE18 68 CJ43
Staneway, Epsom 94 BP58
Stanfield Rd. E3 57 CD37
Stanford Clo., Hmptn. 74 BE50
Stanford Clo., Rom. 50 CR32
Stanford Clo., Ruis. 44 BA32
Stanford Clo., Wdf.Grn. 40 CK28
Stanford Ct., Wal.Abb. 22 CH20
Stanford Gdns., S.Ock. 60 CZ40
Stanford Pl. SE17 4 **M9**
Stanford Pl. SE17 67 CA42
Old Kent Rd.
Stanford Rivers Rd., Ong. 24 CW19
Stanford Rd. N11 38 BU28
Stanford Rd. SW16 86 BW51
Stanford Rd. W8 66 BS41
Stanford Rd., Grays 71 DE41
Stanford St. SW1 3 **N9**
Stanford St. SW1 66 BW42
Vincent Sq.
Stanford Way SW16 86 BW51
Stangate Cres., Borwd. 28 BN24
Stangate Gdns., Stan. 36 BJ28
Stangate Rd., Sev. 108 DC63
Stanger Rd. SE25 87 CB52
Stanham Pl., Dart. 69 CU45
Stanham Rd., Dart. 79 CU46
Stanhope Ave. N3 46 BR31
Stanhope Ave., Brom. 88 CG54
Stanhope Ave., Har. 36 BG30
Stanhope Bldgs. SE1 67 BZ41
Redcross Way
Stanhope Clo. SE16 67 CC41
Middleton Dr.
Stanhope Gdns. N4 47 BY32
Stanhope Gdns. N6 47 BV32
Stanhope Gdns. NW7 37 BO28
Stanhope Gdns. SW7 66 BT42
Stanhope Gdns., Dag. 50 CQ34
Stanhope Gdns., Ilf. 49 CK33
Stanhope Gate W1 3 **H2**
Stanhope Gate W1 56 BV40
Stanhope Gro., Beck. 87 CD53
Stanhope Heath, Stai. 73 AX46
Stanhope Ms. E. SW7 66 BT42
Stanhope Gdns.
Stanhope Ms. S. SW7 66 BT42
Gloucester Rd.
Stanhope Ms. W. SW7 66 BT42
Stanhope Par. NW1 1 **L2**
Stanhope Pk. Rd., Grnf. 54 BG38
Stanhope Pl. W2 1 **E9**
Stanhope Pl. W2 56 BU39
Stanhope Rd. E17 48 CE32
Stanhope Rd. N6 47 BW32
Stanhope Rd. N11 38 BV28
Stanhope Rd. N12 38 BT28
Stanhope Rd., Barn. 28 BQ25
Stanhope Rd., Bexh. 69 CQ44
Stanhope Rd., Cars. 95 BV57
Stanhope Rd., Croy. 87 CA55
Stanhope Rd., Dag. 50 CQ34
Stanhope Rd., Grnf. 54 BG38
Stanhope Rd., Rain. 59 CU37
Stanhope Rd., St.Alb. 9 BH13
Stanhope Rd., Sid. 79 CO49
Stanhope Rd., Swans. 81 DC46
Stanhope Rd., Wal.Cr. 21 CD20
Stanhope Row W1 3 **J3**
Stanhope St. NW1 1 **L2**
Stanhope St. NW1 56 BW37
Stanhope Ter. W2 1 **B10**
Stanhope Ter. W2 56 BT40
Stanhope Way, Sev. 107 CS64
Stanhope Way, Stai. 73 AX46
Stanhopes, Oxt. 115 CH67
Stanier Clo. SW5 65 BR42
Aisgill Ave.
Stanier Ri., Berk. 7 AQ11
Stanlake Ms. W12 55 BQ40
Stanlake Vill.
Stanlake Rd. W12 55 BQ40
Stanlake Vill. W12 55 BQ40
Stanley Ave., Bark. 58 CN37
Stanley Ave., Beck. 87 CF51
Stanley Ave., Dag. 50 CQ33
Stanley Ave., Grnf. 54 BG37
Stanley Ave., N.Mal. 85 BP53
Stanley Ave., Rom. 50 CU31
Stanley Ave., St.Alb. 18 BF16
Stanley Ave., Wem. 55 BL36
Stanley Clo., Couls. 104 BX62
Stanley Clo., Green. 80 CZ46
Stanley Clo., Horn. 51 CV34
Stanley Clo., Rom. 50 CU31
Stanley Clo., Uxb. 53 AX37
Stanley Clo., Wem. 55 BL36
Stanley Cotts., Slou. 52 AP40
Stanley Cres. W11 55 BR40
Stanley Cres., Grav. 81 DH49
Stanley Gdns. NW2 46 BQ35

Stanley Gdns. SW17 76 BV50
Ashbourne Rd.
Stanley Gdns. W3 55 BO40
Stanley Gdns. W11 55 BN38
Stanley Gdns., Borwd. 28 BL23
Stanley Gdns., S.Croy. 96 CB59
Stanley Gdns., Wall. 95 BW57
Stanley Gdns., Walt. 93 BD57
Burwood Rd.
Stanley Gdns. Ms. W11 55 BR40
Kensington Pk. Rd.
Stanley Gdns. Rd., Tedd. 74 BH49
Stanley Grn., Slou. 62 AS42
Stanley Gro. SW8 66 BV44
Stanley Gro., Croy. 86 BY53
Stanley Hill, Amer. 25 AO23
Stanley Hill Ave., Amer. 25 AO23
Stanley Pk. Dr., Wem. 55 BL36
Stanley Pk. Rd., Cars. 95 BU57
Stanley Pas. NW1 1 **Q1**
Stanley Pas. NW1 56 BX37
Stanley Pl., Ong. 24 CX18
Stanley Rd. E4 39 CF26
Stanley Rd. E10 48 CE32
Stanley Rd. E12 49 CK35
Stanley Rd. E15 57 CF37
Stanley Rd. E18 40 CG30
Stanley Rd. N2 47 BT31
Stanley Rd. N9 39 CA26
Stanley Rd. N10 38 BV29
Stanley Rd. N11 38 BW29
Stanley Rd. N15 47 BY31
Stanley Rd. NW9 46 BP33
Stanley Rd. SW14 65 BM45
Stanley Rd. SW19 76 BS50
Stanley Rd. W3 65 BN41
Stanley Rd., Ashf. 73 AY49
Stanley Rd., Brom. 88 CH52
Stanley Rd., Cars. 95 BV57
Stanley Rd., Croy. 86 BY54
Stanley Rd., Enf. 30 CA24
Stanley Rd. (Ponders End), Enf. 30 CC25
Stanley Rd., Grav. 81 DF47
Coopers Rd.
Stanley Rd., Grays 71 DD42
Stanley Rd., Har. 45 BG34
Stanley Rd., Horn. 51 CV34
Stanley Rd., Houns. 64 BG45
Stanley Rd., Ilf. 49 CM34
Stanley Rd., Mitch. 76 BV50
Stanley Rd., Mord. 86 BS52
Stanley Rd., Nthwd. 35 BC30
Stanley Rd., Orp. 88 CN54
Stanley Rd., Sid. 79 CO48
Stanley Rd., Sthl. 54 BE40
Stanley Rd., Sutt. 95 BS57
Stanley Rd., Swans. 81 DC46
Stanley Rd., Twick. 74 BG48
Stanley Rd., Wat. 27 BD24
Stanley Rd., Wem. 55 BL36
Stanley Rd., Wok. 100 AS61
Stanley Rd. N., Rain. 59 CT37
Stanley Rd. S., Rain. 59 CT37
Stanley Sq., Cars. 95 BU58
Stanley St. SE8 67 CD43
Stanley St., Cat. 105 BZ64
Stanley Ter. N19 47 BX34
Kingsdown Rd.
Stanley Way, Orp. 89 CO53
Stanley Wd., Amer. 25 AP23
Stanleycroft Clo., Islw. 64 BG44
Thornbury Rd.
Stanleycroft Clo., Islw. 64 BH44
Stanmer St. SW11 66 BU44
Stanmore Gdns., Rich. 65 BL45
Stanmore Gdns., Sutt. 86 BT55
Stanmore Hill, Stan. 36 BJ27
Stanmore Pl. NW1 56 BV37
Arlington Rd.
Stanmore Rd. E11 49 CG33
Stanmore Rd. N15 47 BY31
Stanmore Rd., Belv. 69 CS42
Stanmore Rd., Rich. 65 BL45
Stanmore Rd., Wat. 26 BC23
Stanmore St. N1 56 BX37
Stanmore Ter., Beck. 87 CE51
Stanmore Way, Loug. 31 CL23
Stanmount Rd., St.Alb. 18 BF16
Stannard Cres. E6 58 CL39
Stannard Rd. E8 57 CB36
Stannary St. SE11 66 BY43
Stannington Path, Borwd. 28 BM23
Warenford Way
Stansfeld Rd. E6 58 CJ39
Stansfield Rd. SW9 66 BX45
Stansfield Rd., Houns. 63 BC44
Stansgate Rd., Dag. 50 CR34
Stanstead Clo., Brom. 88 CG53
Stanstead Dr., Hodd. 12 CE11
Stanstead Gro. SE6 77 CD47
Stanstead Rd.
Stanstead Rd. E11 49 CH32
Stanstead Rd. SE6 77 CC47
Stanstead Rd. SE23 77 CC47
Stanstead Rd., Cat. 105 CA65
Stanstead Rd., Hodd. 12 CE11
Stanstead Rd., Houns. 73 AY46
Stansted Clo., Horn. 60 CV36
Stansted Cres., Bex. 79 CP47
Stansted La., Sev. 99 DA58
Stanswood Gdns. SE5 67 CA43
Sedgmoor Pl.
Stanthorpe Clo. SW16 76 BX49
Stanthorpe Rd. SW16 76 BX49
Stanton Ave., Sun. 73 BB50
Stanton Ave., Tedd. 74 BH50
Stanton Clo., Chig. 40 CN28
Tine Rd.
Stanton Clo., Epsom 94 BM56
Stanton Clo., Orp. 89 CP54
Finucane Dr.
Stanton Clo., St.Alb. 9 BK11
Stanton Clo., Wor.Pk. 85 BQ55

Stanton Rd. SE26 77 CD49
Stanton Way
Stanton Rd. SW13 65 BO44
Stanton Rd. SW20 85 BQ51
Stanton Rd., Croy. 87 BZ54
Stanton Sq. SE26 77 CD49
Stanton Way
Stanton St. SE15 67 CB44
Stanton Way SE26 77 CD49
Stanton Way, Slou. 62 AS42
Stantons, Harl. 13 CL11
Stanway Ct. N1 57 CA37
Hoxton St.
Stanway Gdns. W3 55 BM40
Stanway Gdns., Edg. 37 BN29
Stanway Rd., Wal.Abb. 22 CH20
Ninefields
Stanway St. N1 57 CA37
Stanwell Clo., Stai. 73 AX46
Stanwell Gdns., Stai. 73 AX46
Stanwell Moor Rd., Stai. 73 AW48
Stanwell Moor Rd., West Dr. 63 AW43
Stanwell New Rd., Stai. 73 AW48
Stanwell Rd., Ashf. 73 AY48
Stanwell Rd., Felt. 73 AZ47
Stanwell Rd., Slou. 62 AT45
Stanwick Rd. W14 65 BR42
Stanworth St. SE1 4 **P5**
Stanworth St. SE1 67 CA41
Stanwyck Dr., Chig. 40 CM28
Stanwyck Gdns., Rom. 41 CU28
Stapenhill Rd., Wem. 45 BJ34
Staple Clo., Bex. 79 CS48
Tile Kiln La.
Staple Hill Rd., Wok. 91 AO57
Staple Inn Bldgs. WC1 2 **D7**
Staple Inn Bldgs. WC2 56 BY39
Holborn
Staple La., Guil. 110 AX69
Staple St. SE1 4 **L5**
Staple St. SE1 67 BZ41
Staple Tye, Harl. 13 CM12
Staplefield Clo. SW2 76 BX47
Staplefield Clo., Pnr. 36 BE29
Stapleford, Welw.G.C. 5 BT8
Tempsford
Stapleford Ave., Ilf. 49 CN32
Stapleford Clo. E4 39 CF27
Stapleford Clo. SW19 75 BR47
Beaumont Rd.
Stapleford Clo., Kings.T. 85 BM52
Vincent Rd.
Stapleford Ct., Sev. 107 CT65
Stapleford Gdns., Rom. 41 CR29
Stapleford Rd., Rom. 32 CR25
Stapleford Rd., Wem. 54 BK36
Stapleford Tawney Rd., Rom. 32 CS22
Stapleford Way, Bark. 59 CO38
Bastable Ave.
Staplehurst Dr., Reig. 121 BT72
Staplehurst Rd. SE13 77 CF46
Staplehurst Rd., Cars. 95 BU57
Staplehurst Rd., Reig. 121 BT72
Staples Clo. SE16 57 CD40
Staples Cor. NW2 46 BP33
Staples Rd., Loug. 31 CJ24
Stapleton Clo., Pot.B. 20 BU19
Coopers La. Rd.
Stapleton Cres., Rain. 59 CU36
Stapleton Gdns., Croy. 95 BY56
Stapleton Hall Rd. N4 47 BX33
Stapleton Pl., Pot.B. 20 BU19
Coopers La. Rd.
Stapleton Rd. SW17 76 BV48
Stapleton Rd., Bexh. 69 CQ43
Stapleton Rd., Borwd. 28 BM22
Stapleton Rd., Orp. 88 CN55
Sevenoaks Rd.
Stapley Rd., Belv. 69 CR42
Stapley Rd., St.Alb. 9 BG13
Stapylton Rd., Barn. 28 BR24
Star & Garter Hill, Rich. 75 BL47
Star Hill, Dart. 79 CT46
Star Hill, Wok. 100 AR63
Star Hill Rd., Sev. 107 CQ61
Star La. E16 58 CG38
Star La., Couls. 104 BV64
Star La., Epp. 23 CO18
Star La., Orp. 89 CP52
Star La., Wok. 100 AR63
College La.
Star Path, Nthlt. 54 BF37
Leander Rd.
Star Rd. W14 65 BR43
Star Rd., Islw. 64 BG44
Star Rd., Uxb. 53 BA38
Star St. E16 58 CG39
Star St. W2 1 **B8**
Star St. W2 56 BT39
Star Yd. WC2 2 **D8**
Star Yd. WC2 56 BY39
Starboard Ave., Green. 80 DA46
Starboard Way E14 67 CE41
Tiller St.
Starch Ho. La., Ilf. 40 CM30
Starcross St. NW1 1 **M3**
Starcross St. NW1 56 BW38
Starfield Rd. W12 65 BP41
Starkleigh Way SE16 67 CB42
Egan Way
Starling Clo., Buck.H. 40 CH26
Starling Clo., Pnr. 45 BD31
Starling La., Cuffley 20 BX17
Starlings, The, Lthd. 93 BG60
Starrock La., Couls. 104 BU63
Starrock Rd., Couls. 104 BV63
Startfield Rd., Slou. 62 AQ41
Wellesley Rd.
Starts Clo., Orp. 88 CL55
Starts Hill Ave., Orp. 97 CL56
Starts Hill Rd., Orp. 97 CL56
Starts Rd., Orp. 88 CL55

Starvecrow Clo., Ton. 117 DB71
Starwood Clo., Wey. 92 AX59
Starwood Ct., Slou. 62 AR41
  London Rd.
State Fm. Ave., Orp. 97 CL56
Staten Gdns., Twick. 74 BH47
Statham Gro. N16 48 BZ34
Statham Gro. N18 39 CA28
Station App. E7 49 CH35
  Woodford Rd.
Station App. N11 38 BV28
Station App. (Southgate) 38 BW26
  N14
Station App. SE3 68 CH45
Station App. (Eltham) SE9 78 CK46
Station App. (Mottingham) 78 CK47
  SE9
Station App. SE26 77 CC49
Station App. SW6 65 BR45
Station App. W7 54 BH40
  Station St.
Station App., Ashf. 73 AY49
Station App., Bark. 58 CM36
Station App., Bex. 79 CR47
  High St.
Station App., Bexh. 69 CQ44
  Pickford La.
Station App. (Barnehurst), 69 CS44
  Bexh.
  Barnehurst Rd.
Station App., Buck.H. 40 CJ28
Station App., Chsnt. 21 CD18
Station App., Chis. 58 CL51
Station App. (Elmstead 78 CK50
  Wds.), Chis.
Station App., Couls. 104 BW61
Station App. (Chipstead), 104 BU62
  Couls.
Station App., Dart. 80 CW46
Station App. (Crayford), 79 CT46
  Dart.
  Station Rd.
Station App., Dor. 119 BK70
Station App., Epsom 94 BN60
Station App. (Ewell E.), 94 BP58
  Epsom
Station App. (Ewell W.), 94 BO58
  Epsom
Station App. (Stoneleigh), 94 BO56
  Epsom
Station App. (Hinchley 84 BH55
  Wd.), Esher
Station App., Ger.Cr. 43 AS32
Station App., Grays 71 DD43
Station App., Grnf. 54 BJ36
Station App., Guil. 118 AS71
Station App., Hmptn. 84 BF51
  Milton Rd.
Station App., Har. 45 BH33
Station App. (Kent), 88 CG54
  Hayes
Station App. (Middlesex), 63 BB41
  Hayes
Station App., Hem.H. 8 AW15
Station App. (Elm Pk.), 50 CU35
  Horn.
Station App. (Norbiton), 85 BM51
  Kings.T.
Station App., Lthd. 110 BB66
Station App., Loug. 31 CK25
Station App. (Debden), 31 CM24
  Loug.
Station App., Nthwd. 35 BB29
Station App., Orp. 88 CN55
Station App. (Chelsfield), 98 CO56
  Orp.
Station App. (St. Mary 89 CO52
  Cray), Orp.
Station App., Pnr. 45 BE31
Station App. (Hatch End), 36 BE29
  Pnr.
Station App., Pot.B. 19 BR19
Station App., Purfleet 70 CX42
Station App., Pur. 95 BY59
  Whytecliffe Rd.
Station App., Rich. 65 BM44
Station App., Rick. 25 AU24
Station App., Ruis. 44 BB33
Station App., Shep. 83 BA53
Station App., Sid. 79 CO48
Station App., Sthl. 64 BE41
Station App., Stai. 73 AW49
Station App., Sun. 83 BC51
Station App. (Cheam), 94 BR57
  Sutt.
Station App., Swan. 89 CT52
Station App. (Denham), 44 AW33
  Uxb.
Station App. (Denham 43 AU33
  Golf Club), Uxb.
Station App., Vir.W. 82 AR52
Station App., Wal.Cr. 21 CD20
Station App. (Upper), 105 CA62
  Warl.
Station App., Wat. 26 BB24
Station App., Well. 69 CO44
Station App., Wem. 54 BJ36
Station App., West Dr. 63 AY40
Station App., Wey. 92 AW59
Station App., Wok. 100 AS62
Station App. E., Croy. 87 BZ55
Station App. E., Red. 121 BU71
Station App. N., Sid. 79 CO48
  Station Rd.
Station App. Rd. W4 65 BM43
  Grove Pk. Rd.
Station App. Rd., Tad. 103 BQ64
Station App. Rd., Til. 71 DG45
Station App. S., Sid. 79 CO48
  Station Rd.
Station App. W., Red. 121 BU71
Station Ave., Cat. 105 CB65

Station Ave. (Ewell W.), 94 BO58
  Epsom
Station Ave., N.Mal. 85 BO52
Station Ave., Rich. 65 BM44
  Station Par.
Station Ave., Walt. 92 BB56
Station Bldgs., Hayes 88 CG54
Station Clo. N3 38 BS30
Station Clo., Hmptn. 84 BF51
Station Clo., Hat. 19 BR16
Station Clo., Pot.B. 19 BR19
Station Cres. N15 48 BZ31
Station Cres. SE3 68 CH42
Station Cres., Ashf. 73 AX49
Station Cres., Wem. 54 BJ36
Station Dr. NW1 56 BW38
Station Est. (Elmers End), 87 CC52
  Beck.
Station Est. Rd., Felt. 73 BC47
Station Garage Ms. 76 BW50
  SW16
  Estreham Rd.
Station Gdns. W4 65 BN43
Station Gro., Wem. 55 BL36
Station Hill, Hayes 88 CH55
Station La., Brwd. 123 DE32
Station La., Edg. 37 BM29
Station La., Horn. 51 CV34
Station Par. E11 49 CH32
  High St.
Station Par. NW2 55 BQ36
Station Par. W3 55 BM39
Station Par., Horn. 50 CU35
Station Par., Sev. 107 CU65
Station Par., Uxb. 53 AZ36
Station Par., Vir.W. 82 AR52
Station Pas. E18 40 CH30
  Maybank Rd.
Station Pas. SE15 67 CB44
  Asylum Rd.
Station Path, Stai. 72 AV49
Station Pl. N4 47 BY34
Station Ri. SE27 76 BY48
  Norwood Rd.
Station Rd. (Chingford) 39 CF26
  E4
Station Rd. E7 49 CH35
Station Rd. E10 48 CF34
Station Rd. E12 49 CJ35
Station Rd. E17 48 CD32
Station Rd. N3 38 BS30
Station Rd. N11 38 BV28
Station Rd. N17 48 CB31
Station Rd. N18 39 CA28
  Silver St.
Station Rd. N19 47 BW34
Station Rd. N21 38 BY26
Station Rd. (Winchmore 38 BY26
  Hill) N21
Station Rd. N22 38 BX30
Station Rd. NW4 46 BP32
Station Rd. NW7 37 BO28
Station Rd. NW10 55 BO37
Station Rd. SE20 77 CC50
Station Rd. (Norwood 87 CC52
  Junct.) SE25
Station Rd. SW13 65 BO44
Station Rd. SW19 86 BY51
Station Rd. W5 55 BL39
Station Rd. (Hanwell) 54 BH40
  W7
Station Rd., Amer. 25 AO23
Station Rd., Ashf. 73 AY49
  Station App.
Station Rd., Ash. 103 BL62
Station Rd., Barn. 29 BS25
Station Rd., Belv. 69 CR41
Station Rd., Berk. 7 AR12
Station Rd., Bet. 120 BO69
Station Rd., Bexh. 69 CQ45
Station Rd., Borwd. 28 BM24
Station Rd., Brom. 88 CH51
Station Rd. (Shortlands), 88 CG51
  Brom.
Station Rd., Brox. 12 CD13
Station Rd., Cars. 95 BU56
Station Rd., Cat. 105 CD64
Station Rd., Cher. 82 AV54
Station Rd., Chess. 94 BL56
Station Rd., Chig. 40 CL27
Station Rd., Cob. 102 BE62
Station Rd. (West 87 BX54
  Croydon), Croy.
Station Rd., Cuffley 20 BX16
Station Rd., Dag. 50 CP33
Station Rd. (Crayford), 79 CT47
  Dart.
Station Rd., Dor. 119 BJ71
Station Rd., Edg. 37 BM29
Station Rd., Egh. 72 AS49
Station Rd., Epp. 23 CO19
Station Rd. (North 23 CR17
  Weald), Epp.
Station Rd., Esher 84 BG55
Station Rd. (Claygate), 93 BH56
  Esher
Station Rd., Eyns. 90 CV55
Station Rd., Ger.Cr. 43 AS32
Station Rd. (Northfleet), 81 DD46
  Grav.
Station Rd. (Southfleet), 81 DD49
  Grav.
Station Rd., Green. 80 DA46
Station Rd., Guil. 118 AS73
Station Rd., Hmptn. 84 BF51
Station Rd., Harl. 6 CP8
Station Rd., Har. 45 BH31
Station Rd. (North 45 BF32
  Harrow), Har.
Station Rd., Hat. 10 BQ15
Station Rd., Hayes 63 BB42
Station Rd., Hem.H. 8 AW14
Station Rd., Houns. 64 BF45
Station Rd., Ilf. 49 CL34

Station Rd. (Barkingside), 49 CM31
  Ilf.
Station Rd., Ken. 96 BZ60
Station Rd., Kings L. 17 AZ18
Station Rd., Kings.T. 85 BM51
Station Rd. (Hampton 84 BK51
  Wick), Kings.T.
Station Rd. (Knockholt), 98 CQ58
  Knockholt
Station Rd., Lthd. 102 BJ64
Station Rd., Long. 90 DC52
Station Rd., Loug. 31 CK24
Station Rd. (Motspur Pk.), 85 BP53
  N.Mal.
Station Rd., Orp. 88 CN55
Station Rd. (St. Mary 89 CP52
  Cray), Orp.
Station Rd., Pnr. 45 BE31
Station Rd., Rad. 27 BJ21
Station Rd., Red. 121 BU70
Station Rd. (Merstham), 113 BW67
  Red.
Station Rd., Rick. 35 AX26
Station Rd., Rom. 50 CU31
Station Rd. (Gidea Pk.), 50 CU31
  Rom.
Station Rd. (Harold Wd.), 42 CW30
  Rom.
Station Rd. (Bricket Wd.), 18 BF19
  St.Alb.
Station Rd. (Colney 10 BM13
  Heath), St.Alb.
Station Rd., Saw. 6 CQ5
Station Rd. (Dunton 107 CT63
  Grn.), Sev.
Station Rd. (Halstead), 98 CQ59
  Sev.
Station Rd. (Shoreham), 98 CU59
  Sev.
Station Rd., Shep. 83 BA53
Station Rd., Sid. 79 CO49
Station Rd. (Langley), 62 AT41
  Slou.
Station Rd. (Poyle), Slou. 62 AV44
Station Rd., S.Dnth. 90 CX51
Station Rd., S.Ock. 60 DB38
Station Rd. (Wraysbury), 72 AS46
  Stai.
Station Rd., Sun. 73 BC50
Station Rd., Sutt. 95 BS58
Station Rd. (Belmont), 95 BS58
  Sutt.
Station Rd., Swan. 89 CT52
Station Rd., Tedd. 74 BJ50
Station Rd., T.Ditt. 84 BH54
Station Rd., Til. 71 DJ43
Station Rd., Twick. 74 BH47
Station Rd., Upmin. 51 CY34
Station Rd., Uxb. 53 AX38
Station Rd., Wal.Cr. 21 CE20
Station Rd. (Upper), 105 CA62
  Warl.
Station Rd., Wat. 26 BC23
Station Rd., Welw.G.C. 5 BR5
Station Rd., West Dr. 63 AY41
Station Rd., W.Wick. 87 CF54
Station Rd., West. 107 CO65
Station Rd. (Addlestone), 92 AX56
  Wey.
Station Rd. (West 92 AW59
  Byfleet), Wey.
Station Rd., Whyt. 105 CA62
Station Rd., Wok. 91 AP59
Station Rd. E., Oxt. 115 CG67
Station Rd. N., Belv. 69 CR41
Station Rd. N., Red. 113 BW67
Station Rd. S., Red. 113 BW67
Station Rd. W., Oxt. 115 CG68
Station Row, Guil. 118 AS73
Station Sq. (Petts Wd.), 88 CM53
  Orp.
Station Sq. (St. Mary 89 CO52
  Cray), Orp.
Station St. E15 57 CF36
Station St. E16 58 CL40
Station Ter. NW10 55 BQ37
Station Ter. SE5 67 BZ44
  Station Rd.
Station Vw., Grnf. 54 BG37
Station Vill. NW7 37 BO29
  Bittacy Hill
Station Way (Roding 40 CJ28
  Valley), Buck.H.
Station Way (Claygate), 93 BH57
  Esher
Station Way, St.Alb. 9 BH13
Station Way (Cheam), 94 BR57
  Sutt.
Station Way, Welw.G.C. 5 BQ7
Station Yd., Twick. 74 BJ47
Staunton Rd., Kings.T. 75 BL50
Staunton Rd., Slou. 52 AO39
Staunton St. SE8 67 CD43
Stave Yd. Rd. SE16 57 CD40
Staveley Clo. E9 48 CC35
  Churchill Wk.
Staveley Clo. N7 47 BX35
  Penn Rd.
Staveley Clo. SE15 67 CC44
Staveley Gdns. W4 65 BN44
Staveley Rd. W4 65 BN43
Staveley Rd., Ashf. 73 BA50
Staveley Way, Wok. 100 AP62
Staverton Rd. NW2 55 BQ36
Staverton Rd., Horn. 51 CV32
Stavordale Rd. N5 47 BY35
Stavordale Rd., Cars. 86 BT54
Stayne End, Vir.W. 82 AQ52
Stayners Rd. E1 57 CC38
Stayton Rd., Sutt. 86 BS55
Stead St. SE17 4 K9
Stead St. SE17 67 BZ42
Steadfast Rd., Kings.T. 84 BK51
Steam Fm. La., Felt. 63 BB45

Stean St. E8 57 CA37
Stebbing Way, Bark. 59 CO37
Stebondale St. E14 67 CF42
Stedham Pl. WC1 1 Q8
Stedman Clo., Bex. 79 CT48
Stedman Clo., Uxb. 44 AZ34
Steed Clo., Horn. 50 CU34
Steedman St. SE17 4 H9
Steedman St. SE17 67 BZ42
Steeds Rd. N10 38 BU30
Steeds Way, Loug. 31 CK24
Steele Ave., Green. 80 DA46
Steele Rd. E11 49 CG35
Steele Rd. N17 48 CA31
Steele Rd. NW10 55 BN37
Steele Rd. W4 65 BN41
Steele Rd., Islw. 64 BJ45
Steeles Ms. NW3 56 BU36
Steeles Rd. NW3 56 BU36
Steels La. E1 57 CC39
  Devonport St.
Steels La., Lthd. 93 BF60
Steen Way SE22 77 CA46
  Dulwich Gro.
Steep Clo., Orp. 97 CN57
Steep Hill SW16 76 BW48
Steep Hill, Croy. 96 CA56
Steep Hill, Wok. 91 AO57
Steeplands, Bush. 36 BF26
Steeple Clo. SW6 65 BR45
Steeple Clo. SW19 75 BR49
Steeple Heights Dr., 106 CJ62
  West.
Steeple Wk. N1 57 BZ37
  Basire St.
Steeple Way, Brwd. 33 DA22
Steeplestone Clo. N18 39 BZ28
Steerforth St. SW18 76 BS48
Steers Mead, Mitch. 86 BU51
Steers Way SE16 57 CD41
Stella Rd. SW17 76 BU50
Stelling Rd., Erith 69 CS43
Stellman Clo. E5 48 CB34
Stembridge Rd. SE20 87 CB51
Stenning Ave., S.le H. 71 DK42
Stents La., Cob. 102 BE63
Stepgates Mead La., 83 AW54
  Cher.
Stephan Clo. E8 57 CB37
Stephen Ave., Rain. 59 CU36
Stephen Clo., Egh. 72 AU50
Stephen Clo., Orp. 88 CN55
Stephen Ms. W1 1 N7
Stephen Ms. W1 56 BW39
  Gresse St.
Stephen Rd., Bexh. 69 CS45
Stephen St. W1 1 N7
Stephen St. W1 56 BW39
Stephendale Rd. SW6 66 BS45
Stephens Clo., Pnr. 45 BD32
Stephens Clo., Rom. 42 CV28
Stephens Rd. E15 58 CG37
Stephenson Dr., Wind. 61 AN43
  Clewer Ct. Rd.
Stephenson Rd. W7 54 BH39
Stephenson Rd., Houns. 74 BF47
Stephenson St. E16 58 CG38
Stephenson St. NW10 55 BO38
Stephenson Way NW1 1 M4
Stephenson Way NW1 56 BW38
Stepney Causeway E1 57 CC39
Stepney Grn. E1 57 CC39
Stepney Grn. Dws. E1 57 CC39
Stepney High St. E1 57 CC39
Stepney Way E1 57 CB39
Sterling Ave., Edg. 37 BL28
Sterling Ave., Wal.Cr. 21 CC20
Sterling Pl. W5 65 BL42
Sterling Rd., Enf. 30 BZ22
Sterling St. SW7 3 D5
Sterling St. SW7 66 BU41
  Montpelier Pl.
Sterling Way N18 39 BZ28
Sterndale Rd. W14 65 BQ41
Sterndale Rd., Dart. 80 CW47
Sterne St. W12 65 BQ41
Sternhall La. SE15 67 CB44
Sternhold Ave. SW2 76 BW48
Sterry Cres., Dag. 50 CR35
Sterry Dr., Epsom 94 BO56
Sterry Dr., T.Ditt. 84 BH53
Sterry Gdns., Dag. 59 CR36
Sterry Rd., Bark. 58 CN37
Sterry Rd., Dag. 50 CR35
Sterry St. SE1 4 K5
Sterry St. SE1 67 BZ41
Steucers La. SE23 77 CD47
  St. Germans Rd.
Steve Biko La. SE6 77 CE49
Steve Biko Way, Houns. 64 BF45
  Staines Rd.
Stevedale Rd., Well. 69 CP44
Stevenage Cres., Borwd. 28 BL23
Stevenage Ri., Hem.H. 8 AY11
Stevenage Rd. E6 58 CL36
Stevenage Rd. SW6 65 BQ43
Stevens Ave. E9 57 CC36
Stevens Clo., Beck. 77 CE50
  Stumps Hill La.
Stevens Clo., Bex. 79 CS49
Stevens Clo., Epsom 94 BO60
  High St.
Stevens Clo., Hmptn. 74 BE49
Stevens Cotts. NW2 55 BP36
  High St.
Stevens Grn., Bush. 36 BG26
Stevens La., Esher 93 BJ57
Stevens Rd., Dag. 50 CO34
Stevens St. SE1 4 N6
Stevens St. SE1 67 CA41
  Riley Rd.
Stevens Way, Chig. 40 CN28
Stevenson Clo., Erith 69 CU43

Stevenson Rd., Slou. 43 AO
Steventon Rd. W12 55 BO
Steward St. E1 2 C
Steward St. E1 57 CA
Stewards Clo., Epp. 23 CO
Stewards Grn. La., Epp. 23 CP
Stewards Grn. Rd., Epp. 23 CP
Stewards Wk., Rom. 50 CT
  South St.
Stewart, Tad. 103 BO
Stewart Ave., Shep. 83 BO
Stewart Ave., Slou. 52 AP
Stewart Clo. NW9 46 BN
Stewart Clo., Abb.L. 17 AX
Stewart Clo., Chsnt. 21 CD
Stewart Clo., Chis. 78 CL
Stewart Clo., Hmptn. 74 BE
Stewart Clo., Maid. 61 AH
Stewart Clo., Wok. 100 AP
  Nethercote Ave.
Stewart Rd. E15 48 CF
Stewart St. E14 67 CF
Stewarts Gro. SW3 3 C
Stewarts Rd. SW8 66 BW
Stewarts Wk., S.Croy. 96 BU
Stewartsby Clo. N18 39 BZ
Steyne Rd. W3 55 BM
Steyning Clo., Ken. 104 BY
Steyning Gro. SE9 78 CK
Steyning Way, Houns. 64 BD
Steynings Way N12 38 BT
Steynton Ave., Bex. 79 CP
Stickland Rd., Belv. 69 CR
Stickleton Clo., Grnf. 54 BF
Stifford Clays Rd., Grays 71 DC
Stifford Est. E1 57 CC
Stifford Hill, S.Ock. 60 DB
Stifford Rd., S.Ock. 60 CZ
Stile Hall Gdns. W4 65 BM
Stile Path, Sun. 83 BC
Stile Rd., Slou. 62 AR
Stilecroft, Harl. 14 CO
Stilecroft Gdns., Wem. 45 BJ
Stiles Clo., Brom. 88 CK
Stillingfleet Rd. SW13 65 BP
Stillington St. SW1 3 G
Stillington St. SW1 66 BW
Stillness Rd. SE23 77 CD
Stilton Cres. NW10 55 BN
Stilton Path, Borwd. 28 BM
  Stapleton Rd.
Stipularis Dr., Hayes 54 BD
Stirling Ave., Shep. 83 BR
Stirling Clo., Bans. 103 BR
Stirling Clo., Rain. 59 CU
Stirling Clo., Uxb. 53 AX
Stirling Clo., Wind. 61 AL
Stirling Dr., Orp. 98 CO
Stirling Rd. E13 58 CH
Stirling Rd. E17 48 CC
Stirling Rd. N17 39 CB
Stirling Rd. N22 38 BY
Stirling Rd. SW9 66 BX
Stirling Rd. W3 65 BM
Stirling Rd., Guil. 118 AO
Stirling Rd., Har. 45 BH
Stirling Rd., Hayes 53 BC
Stirling Rd., Houns. 73 AY
  Southampton Rd.
Stirling Rd., Twick. 74 BF
Stirling Rd. Path E17 48 CD
Stirling Wk., Surb. 85 BM
Stirling Way, Borwd. 28 BN
Stirling Way, Croy. 86 BX
Stirling Way, Welw.G.C. 5 BU
Stites Hill Rd., Cat. 104 BY
Stiven Cres., Har. 45 BE
Stoats Nest Rd., Couls. 95 BX
Stoats Nest Village, 104 BX
  Couls.
Stock Hill, West. 106 CJ
Stock La., Dart. 80 CV
Stock Orchard Cres. N7 47 BX
Stock Orchard St. N7 47 BX
Stock St. E13 58 CH
Stockbreach Clo., Hat. 10 BP
Stockbreach Rd., Hat. 10 BP
Stockbury Rd., Croy. 87 CC
Stockdale Rd., Dag. 50 CQ
Stockdales Rd. (Eton 61 AM
  Wick), Wind.
Stockdove Way, Grnf. 54 BH
Stockers Fm. Rd., Rick. 35 AX
Stockers La., Wok. 100 AT
Stockfield Ave., Hodd. 12 CE
Stockfield Rd. SW16 76 BX
Stockfield Rd., Esher 93 BH
Stockhams Clo., S.Croy. 96 BZ
Stockholm Rd. SE16 67 CC
Stockhurst Clo. SW15 65 BQ
  Ashlone Rd.
Stocking La., Hert. 11 BW
Stocking La. (Bayford), 11
  Hert.
Stockingswater La., Enf. 30 CD
Stockland Rd., Rom. 50 CS
Stockley Clo., West Dr. 63 AZ
Stockley Fm. Rd., West 63 AZ
  Dr.
Stockley Rd., West Dr. 63 AZ
Stockport Rd. SW16 86 BW
Stockport Rd., Rick. 34 AU
Stocks La., Brwd. 33 CZ
Stocks Pl. E14 57 CE
  Grenade St.
Stocksfield, Brwd. 33 CZ
Stocksfield Rd. E17 48 CF
Stockton Gdns. N17 39 BZ
Stockton Gdns. NW7 37 BN
Stockton Rd. N17 39 BZ
Stockton Rd. N18 39 CB
Stockton Rd., Reig. 121 BS
Stockwell Ave. SW9 66 BX

ockwell Clo., Brom. 88 CH51
Kentish Way
ockwell Clo., Chsnt. 21 CB17
ockwell Gdns. SW9 66 BX44
ockwell Grn. SW9 66 BX44
ockwell La. SW9 66 BX44
ockwell La., Chsnt. 21 CB17
ockwell Pk. SW9 66 BX45
ockwell Pk. Cres. SW9 66 BX44
ockwell Pk. Rd. SW9 66 BX44
ockwell Rd. SW9 66 BX44
ockwell St. SE10 67 CF43
octon Clo., Guil. 118 AR70
octon Rd., Guil. 118 AR70
odart Rd. SE20 87 CC51
ofield Gdns. SE9 78 CJ48
oford Clo. SW19 75 BR47
Southmead Rd.
oke Ave., Ilf. 41 CO29
oke Clo., Cob. 102 BE61
oke Common Rd., 43 AQ35
Slou.
oke Ct. Dr., Slou. 52 AP37
oke Flds., Guil. 118 AR71
oke Gdns., Slou. 52 AP40
oke Grn., Slou. 52 AQ38
oke Gro., Guil. 118 AR71
Stoke Flds.
oke Newington Ch. 48 BZ34
St. N16
oke Newington 48 CA34
Common N16
oke Newington High 48 CA34
St. N16
oke Newington Rd. 48 CA35
N16
oke Pl. NW10 55 BO38
oke Poges La., Slou. 52 AP40
oke Rd., Cob. 102 BD61
oke Rd., Guil. 118 AR70
oke Rd., Kings.T. 75 BN50
oke Rd., Rain. 60 CV37
oke Rd., Slou. 52 AP40
oke Rd., Walt. 84 BD55
oke St., Cob. 102 BD61
oke Wd. La., Slou. 43 AP35
okenchurch St. SW6 66 BS44
okes Rd. E6 58 CK38
okes Rd., Croy. 87 CC53
okesay, Slou. 52 AQ40
okesby Rd., Chess. 94 BL57
okesheath Rd., Lthd. 93 BG59
okesley St. W12 55 BO39
oll Clo. NW2 46 BQ34
ompits Rd., Maid. 61 AG43
ompond La., Walt. 83 BC55
oms Path SE6 77 CE49
onard Rd. N13 38 BY27
onard Rd., Dag. 50 CO35
onards Hill, Epp. 23 CO18
onards Hill, Loug. 31 CK25
ondon Pk. SE23 77 CD46
ondon Rd., Ong. 24 CX18
ondon Wk. E6 58 CJ37
Abbots Rd.
one Bldgs. WC2 2 **C7**
one Bldgs. WC2 56 BX39
one Clo., Dag. 50 CQ34
one Clo., West Dr. 53 AY40
one Cres., Felt. 73 BB47
Westmacott Dr.
one Cross, Harl. 6 CM10
one Cross Rd., Swan. 89 CS53
one Hall Rd. N21 38 BX26
one Ho. Ct. EC3 2 **N8**
one Ho. Ct. EC3 57 CA39
Houndsditch
one Pk. Ave., Beck. 87 CE52
one Pl., Wor.Pk. 85 BP55
one Pl. Rd., Green. 80 CZ46
one Rd., Brom. 88 CG53
one St., Croy. 95 BY56
one St., Grav. 81 DG47
one St., Sev. 108 CY65
one St. Rd., Sev. 117 CZ66
one Yd. La. E14 57 CE40
onebank, Welw.G.C. 5 BQ8
onebanks, Walt. 83 BC54
onebridge Est. E8 57 CA37
onebridge Pk. NW10 55 BN36
onebridge Rd. N15 48 CA32
onebridge Rd., Grav. 81 DD46
onebridge Way, Wem. 55 BM36
onechat Sq. E6 58 CK39
Peridot St.
onecot Clo., Sutt. 85 BR54
onecot Hill, Sutt. 85 BR54
onecourt Way, Green. 80 CZ46
onecroft Ave., Iver 52 AV39
onecroft Rd., Erith 69 CS43
onecroft Way, Croy. 86 BX54
onecrop Rd., Guil. 118 AU69
onecross, St.Alb. 9 BH13
onecross Clo., St.Alb. 9 BH12
onecross Rd., Hat. 10 BP12
onecutter St. EC4 2 **F8**
onecutter St. EC4 56 BY39
Shoe La.
onefield Clo., Bexh. 69 CR45
onefield Clo., Ruis. 45 BE35
onefield St. N1 56 BY37
onefield Way SE7 68 CJ43
Green Bay Rd.
onefield Way, Ruis. 45 BE35
onegate Clo., Orp. 89 CP52
Main Rd.
onegrove, Edg. 37 BL28
onegrove Ct., Edg. 37 BL28
onegrove Gdns., Edg. 37 BL28
onehall Ave., Ilf. 49 CK32
oneham Rd. E5 48 CB34
oneham Rd. N11 38 BW28
onehams Hill, Dart. 69 CT45
onehill Clo. SW14 75 BN46
Stonehill Clo., Lthd. 111 BF66
The Garstons
Stonehill Cres., Wok. 91 AS57
Stonehill Grn. Rd., Dart. 79 CS50
Stonehill Rd. SW14 75 BN46
Stonehill Rd. W4 65 BM42
Wellesley Rd.
Stonehill Rd., Wok. 91 AR58
Stonehills, Welw.G.C. 5 BQ7
Stonehills Ct. SE21 77 CA48
Stonehorse Rd., Enf. 30 CC25
Stonehouse Gdns., Cat. 114 CA66
Stonehouse La., Grays 70 CZ42
Stonehouse La., Sev. 98 CP58
Stonehouse Rd., Sev. 98 CP58
Stoneings La., Sev. 106 CN62
Stonelea Rd., Hem.H. 8 AY14
Stoneleigh, Saw. 6 CQ5
Stoneleigh Ave., Enf. 30 CB22
Stoneleigh Ave., Wor.Pk. 85 BP55
Stoneleigh Clo., Wal.Cr. 21 CC20
Stoneleigh Ct., Ilf. 49 CK31
Stoneleigh Cres., Epsom 94 BQ56
Stoneleigh Dr., Hodd. 12 CE10
Stoneleigh Pk., Wey. 92 BA57
Stoneleigh Pk. Ave., Croy. 87 CC53
Stoneleigh Pk. Rd., 94 BO57
Epsom
Stoneleigh Pl. W11 55 BQ40
Stoneleigh Rd. N17 48 CA31
Stoneleigh Rd., Cars. 86 BU54
Stoneleigh Rd., Ilf. 49 CK31
Stoneleigh Rd., Oxt. 115 CK68
Stoneleigh St. W11 55 BQ40
Stoneleigh Ter. N19 47 BV34
Dartmouth Pk. Hill
Stonells Rd. SW11 76 BU46
Chatham Rd.
Stonemead, Welw.G.C. 5 BQ5
Stoneness Rd., Grays 70 DA43
Stonenest St. N4 47 BX33
Evershot Rd.
Stones All., Wat. 26 BC24
Stones End St. SE1 4 **H5**
Stones End St. SE1 67 BZ41
Stones La., Dor. 119 BG72
Stones Rd., Epsom 94 BO59
Stoneswood Rd., Oxt. 115 CH68
Stonewood, Dart. 80 DB48
Stonewood Rd., Erith 69 CT42
Stoney Brook, Guil. 118 AP70
Stoney Ct., Welw.G.C. 5 BS7
Stoney Gro., Chesh. 16 AO18
Stoney La. E1 2 **P8**
Stoney La. E1 57 CA39
Stoney La. SE19 77 CA50
Stoney La., Hem.H. 16 AT17
Stoney La., Kings L. 16 AV18
Stoney Meade, Slou. 61 AN40
Stoney St. SE1 4 **K2**
Stoney St. SE1 57 BZ40
Stoneycroft, Hem.H. 8 AW13
Long Chaulden
Stoneycroft Clo. SE12 78 CG47
Stoneycroft Rd., Wdf.Grn. 40 CK29
Stoneydown E17 48 CD31
Stoneydown Ave. E17 48 CC31
Stoneyfield Rd., Couls. 104 BX62
Stoneyfields Gdns., Edg. 37 BN28
Stoneyfields La., Edg. 37 BN28
Stoneylands Ct., Egh. 72 AS49
Stoneylands Rd., Egh. 72 AS49
Stonhouse St. SW4 66 BW45
Stonny Cft., Ash. 103 BL62
Stonor Rd. W14 65 BR42
Stony Hill, Esher 93 BE57
Stony La., Amer. 25 AS22
Stony La., Ong. 14 CU15
Stony Path, Loug. 31 CK23
Stonyshotts, Wal.Abb. 22 CG20
Stopford Rd. E13 58 CH37
Store Gdns., Brwd. 122 DE25
Store Rd. E16 68 CL41
Store St. E15 48 CF35
Store St. WC1 1 **N7**
Store St. WC1 56 BW39
Storers Quay E14 67 CF42
Storey Rd. E17 48 CD31
Storey Rd. N6 47 BU32
Storey St. E16 58 CL40
Storey St., Hem.H. 8 AX15
Storeys Gate SW1 3 **P5**
Storeys Gate SW1 66 BW41
Stories Ms. SE5 67 CA44
Stories Rd. SE5 67 CA45
Stork Rd. E7 58 CG36
Storks Rd. SE16 67 CB41
Storksmead Rd., Edg. 37 BO29
Stormont Rd. N6 47 BU33
Stormont Rd. SW11 66 BV45
Stormont Way, Chess. 93 BK56
Stormount Dr., Hayes 63 BA41
Stornaway Strand, Grav. 81 DJ49
Stornoway, Hem.H. 8 AZ14
Northend
Storr Gdns., Brwd. 122 DE25
Storrington Rd., Croy. 87 CA54
Stort Mill, Harl. 6 CO8
Stortford Rd., Hodd. 12 CE11
Story St. N1 2 BX36
Stothard Pl. EC2 2 **N6**
Stothard St. E1 57 CC38
Colebert Ave.
Stoughton Ave., Sutt. 94 BQ56
Stoughton Clo. SE11 4 **C9**
Stoughton Clo. SW15 75 BP47
Bessborough Rd.
Stoughton Rd., Guil. 118 AQ69
Stour Ave., Sthl. 64 BF41
Stour Clo., Kes. 97 CJ56
Stour Clo., Slou. 61 AN41
Stour Rd. E3 57 CE36
Stour Rd., Dart. 69 CU45
Stour Rd., Grays 71 DG42
Stour Way, Upmin. 51 CZ32
Stourcliffe St. W1 1 **E9**
Stourcliffe St. W1 56 BU39
Stourhead Clo. SW19 75 BQ47
Stourhead Gdns. SW20 85 BP51
Stourton Ave., Felt. 74 BE49
Stovell Rd., Wind. 61 AN43
Stow, The, Harl. 6 CN10
Stow Ct., Dart. 80 CY47
Nursery Clo.
Stow Cres. E17 39 CD29
Stowage, The SE8 67 CE43
Stowe Cres., Ruis. 44 BA32
Stowe Gdns. N9 39 CA28
Stowe Pl. N15 48 CA31
Stowe Rd. W12 65 BP41
Stowe Rd., Orp. 98 CO56
Stowell Ave., Croy. 96 CF58
Stowting Rd., Orp. 97 CN56
Stox Mead, Har. 36 BG30
Stracey Rd. E7 49 CH35
Stracey Rd. NW10 55 BN37
Strachan Pl. SW19 75 BQ50
Stradbroke Dr., Chig. 40 CL29
Stradbroke Gro., Buck.H. 40 CJ26
Stradbroke Gro., Ilf. 49 CK31
Stradbroke Rd. N5 48 BZ35
Balfour Rd.
Stradella Rd. SE24 77 BZ46
Strafford Ave., Ilf. 40 CL30
Strafford Clo., Pot.B. 20 BS19
Strafford Gate
Strafford Gate, Pot.B. 20 BS19
Strafford Rd. W3 65 BN41
Bollo Bri. Rd.
Strafford Rd., Barn. 28 BR24
Strafford Rd., Houns. 64 BE45
Strafford Rd., Twick. 74 BJ47
Strafford St. E14 67 CE41
Strahan Rd. E3 57 CD38
Straight, The, Sthl. 64 BE41
Straight Rd., Rom. 41 CU28
Straight Rd., Wind. 72 AQ46
Straightsmouth SE10 67 CF43
Strait Rd. E6 58 CK40
Straits, The, Wal.Abb. 21 CE19
Strakers Rd. SE22 67 CB45
Strand WC2 3 **Q1**
Strand WC2 56 BX40
Strand Clo., Epsom 103 BN63
Strand La. WC2 2 **C10**
Strand La. WC2 56 BX40
Temple Pl.
Strand on the Grn. W4 65 BM43
Strand Pl. N18 39 CA28
Strand Sch. App. W4 65 BM43
Thames Rd.
Strandfield Clo. SE18 68 CN42
Strangeways, Wat. 26 BB21
Strangways Ter. W14 65 BR41
Melbury Rd.
Stranraer Rd., Houns. 73 AY46
Southampton Rd.
Stranraer Way N1 56 BX36
Strasburg Rd. SW11 66 BV44
Stratfield Dr., Brox. 12 CD13
Stratfield Pk. Clo. N21 38 BY26
Stratfield Rd., Borwd. 28 BL24
Stratfield Rd., Slou. 62 AQ41
Stratford Ave. W8 66 BS41
Stratford Ave., Uxb. 53 AY37
Stratford Clo., Bark. 59 CO36
Stratford Clo., Dag. 59 CS36
Stratford Ct., N.Mal. 85 BN52
Kingston Rd.
Stratford Gro. SW15 65 BQ45
Stratford Pl. W1 1 **J9**
Stratford Pl. W1 56 BV39
Stratford Pl., Guil. 118 AS72
Stratford Rd. E13 58 CG37
Stratford Rd. W3 65 BN41
Stratford Rd. W8 66 BS41
Stratford Rd., Hayes 53 BC38
Stratford Rd., Sthl. 64 BE42
Stratford Rd., Th.Hth. 86 BY52
Stratford Rd., Wat. 26 BC23
Stratford Vill. NW1 56 BW36
Stratford Way, Hem.H. 8 AW15
Stratford Way, St.Alb. 18 BE18
Stratford Way, Wat. 26 BB23
Strath Ter. SW11 66 BU45
Strathan Clo. SW18 75 BR46
Strathaven Rd. SE12 78 CH46
Strathblaine Rd. SW11 66 BT45
Strathbrook Rd. SW16 76 BX50
Strathcona Ave., Lthd. 111 BE67
Strathcona Rd., Wem. 45 BK34
Strathdale SW16 76 BX49
Strathdon Dr. SW17 76 BT48
Strathearn Ave., Hayes 63 BB43
Strathearn Ave., Twick. 74 BF47
Strathearn Pl. W2 1 **C10**
Strathearn Pl. W2 56 BU40
Strathearn Rd. SW19 76 BS49
Strathearn Rd., Sutt. 95 BS56
Stratheden Rd. SE3 68 CH44
Strathfield Gdns., Bark. 58 CM36
Strathleven Rd. SW2 66 BX45
Strathmore Clo., Cat. 105 CA64
Strathmore Gdns. N3 38 BS30
Hervey Clo.
Strathmore Gdns. W8 56 BS40
Strathmore Gdns., Edg. 37 BM30
Strathmore Gdns., 50 CT33
Horn.
Strathmore Rd. SW19 76 BS48
Strathmore Rd., Croy. 87 BZ54
Strathmore Rd., Tedd. 74 BH49
Strathnairn St. SE1 67 CB42
Strathray Gdns. NW3 56 BU36
Strathville Rd. SW18 76 BS48
Strathyre Ave. SW16 86 BX52
Stratton Ave., Enf. 30 BZ22
Stratton Ave., Wall. 95 BW58
Stratton Chase Dr., 34 AQ26
Ch.St.G.
Stratton Clo. SW19 86 BS51
Stratton Clo., Bexh. 69 CQ45
Stratton Clo., Edg. 37 BL29
Stratton Clo., Houns. 64 BF44
Stratton Clo., Walt. 84 BD54
Stratton Ct., Guil. 118 AQ69
Worplesdon Rd.
Stratton Dr., Bark. 49 CN35
Stratton Gdns., Sthl. 54 BE39
Stratton Rd. SW19 86 BS51
Stratton Rd., Bexh. 69 CQ45
Stratton Rd., Rom. 42 CX28
Stratton Rd., Sun. 83 BB51
Stratton St. W1 3 **K2**
Stratton St. W1 56 BV40
Stratton Wk., Rom. 42 CX28
Strattondale St. E14 67 CF41
Strauss Rd. W4 65 BN41
Straw Mead, Hat. 10 BP11
Strawberry Fld., Hat. 10 BP14
Strawberry Flds., Swan. 89 CT51
Strawberry Hill Clo., 74 BH48
Twick.
Strawberry Hill Rd., 74 BH48
Twick.
Strawberry La., Cars. 86 BU55
Strawberry Vale N2 38 BT30
Strawberry Vale, Twick. 74 BJ48
Strawfields, Welw.G.C. 5 BS7
Strayfield Rd., Enf. 29 BY21
Streakes Fld. Rd. NW2 46 BP33
Stream La., Edg. 37 BM28
Streamdale SE2 69 CO43
Streamside Clo., Brom. 88 CH52
Sandford Rd.
Streamway, Belv. 69 CQ43
Streatfield Ave. E6 58 CK37
Streatfield Rd., Har. 45 BK31
Streatham Clo. SW16 76 BX48
Leigham Ct. Rd.
Streatham Common N. 76 BX49
SW16
Streatham Common S. 76 BX50
SW16
Streatham Ct. SW16 76 BX48
Streatham High Rd. 76 BX49
SW16
Streatham Hill SW2 76 BX48
Streatham Hill Est. 76 BX48
SW16
Streatham Pl. SW2 76 BX47
Streatham Rd. SW16 86 BU51
Streatham Rd., Mitch. 86 BU51
Streatham St. WC1 1 **Q8**
Streatham St. WC1 56 BX39
Streatham Vale SW16 86 BW51
Streathbourne Rd. SW17 76 BV48
Streatley Pl. NW3 47 BT35
Streatley Rd. NW6 55 BR36
Street, The, Ash. 103 BL62
Street, The, Bet. 120 BP70
Street, The, Bish. 6 CS7
Street, The, Dart. 90 CY52
Street, The, Guil. 118 AR73
Street, The (West 110 AW69
Clandon), Guil.
Street, The, Kings L. 17 AW19
Street, The, Lthd. 102 BG64
Street, The 111 BD67
(Effingham), Lthd.
Street, The (West 110 AZ67
Horsley), Lthd.
Street, The, New A.G. 99 DB56
Street, The, Ong. 24 CY17
Street, The (Ightham), 108 DB64
Sev.
Streeters Pit Rd., Wall. 86 BW55
Streetfield Ms. SE3 68 CH45
Streimer Rd. E15 57 CF37
Strelley Way W3 55 BO40
Stretton Rd., Croy. 87 CA54
Stretton Rd., Rich. 74 BK48
Stretton Way, Borwd. 28 BL22
Strickland Ave., Dart. 70 CW45
Strickland Rd., Belv. 69 CR42
Picardy Rd.
Strickland Row SW18 76 BT47
Strickland St. SE8 67 CE44
Strickland Way, Orp. 97 CM56
Stride Rd. E13 58 CG37
Stringer Ave., Guil. 109 AR67
Stringhams Copse, Wok. 100 AV65
Tuckey Gro.
Strode Clo. N10 38 BV29
Strode Rd. E7 49 CH35
Strode Rd. N17 39 CA30
Strode Rd. NW10 55 BP36
Strode Rd. SW6 65 BR43
Strode St., Egh. 72 AT49
Strodes Cres., Stai. 73 AX49
Stroma Clo., Hem.H. 8 BA14
Strone Rd. E7 58 CJ36
Strone Rd. E12 58 CJ36
Strone Way, Hayes 54 BE38
Strongbow Cres. SE9 78 CK46
Strongbow Rd. SE9 78 CK46
Strongbridge Clo., Har. 45 BF33
Stronsa Rd. W12 65 BO41
Stronsay Clo., Hem.H. 8 AZ14
Strood Ave., Rom. 50 CS33
Stroud Clo., Wind. 61 AL45
Stroud Cres. SW15 75 BP48
Stroud Fm. Rd., Maid. 61 AG43
Stroud Fld., Nthlt. 54 BE36
Stroud Gate, Har. 45 BF35
Stroud Grn. Gdns., Croy. 87 CC54
Stroud Grn. Rd. N4 47 BX33
Stroud Grn. Way, Croy. 87 CB54
Stroud Rd. SE25 87 CB53
Stroud Rd. SW19 76 BS48
Stroud Way, Ashf. 73 AZ50
Stroude Rd., Egh. 72 AT50
Stroude Rd., Vir.W. 82 AS52
Stroudes Clo., Wor.Pk. 85 BO54
Stroudley Wk. E3 57 CE38
Devons Rd.
Stroudwater Pk., Wey. 92 AZ57
Strouts Pl. E2 2 **P2**
Strouts Pl. E2 57 CA38
Pelter St.
Strutton Ave., Grav. 81 DF48
Strutton Grd. SW1 3 **N6**
Strutton Grd. SW1 66 BW41
Strype St. E1 2 **P7**
Strype St. E1 57 CA39
Leyden St.
Stuart Ave. NW9 46 BP33
Stuart Ave. W5 55 BL40
Stuart Ave., Brom. 88 CH54
Stuart Ave., Har. 45 BE34
Stuart Ave., Walt. 83 BC54
Stuart Clo., Brwd. 33 DA25
Stuart Clo., Swan. 89 CU51
Victoria Hill Rd.
Stuart Clo., Uxb. 53 AZ36
Stuart Clo., Wind. 61 AM44
Stuart Ct. (Elstree), Borwd. 27 BK25
High St.
Stuart Cres. N22 38 BX30
Stuart Cres., Croy. 87 CD55
Stuart Cres., Hayes 53 BA39
Stuart Cres., Reig. 121 BS72
Stuart Evans Clo., Well. 69 CP45
Stuart Gro., Tedd. 74 BH49
Stuart Mantle Way, 69 CS43
Erith
Stuart Pl., Mitch. 86 BU51
Stuart Rd. NW6 56 BS38
Stuart Rd. SE15 67 CC45
Stuart Rd. SW19 76 BS48
Stuart Rd. W3 55 BN40
Stuart Rd., Bark. 58 CN36
Dawson Ave.
Stuart Rd., Barn. 38 BU26
Stuart Rd., Grav. 81 DG46
Stuart Rd., Grays 71 DD42
Stuart Rd., Har. 45 BH31
Stuart Rd., Reig. 121 BS72
Stuart Rd., Rich. 74 BJ48
Stuart Rd., Th.Hth. 87 BZ52
Stuart Rd., Warl. 105 CB63
Stuart Rd., Well. 69 CO44
Stuart Rd., Welw. 5 BP5
Stuart Way, Chsnt. 21 CB19
Stuart Way, Stai. 73 AW50
Stuart Way, Vir.W. 82 AQ52
Stuart Way, Wind. 61 AM44
Stubbers La., Upmin. 60 CZ36
Stubbings Hall La., 21 CF17
Wal.Abb.
Stubbs Clo., Dor. 119 BK72
Stubbs End Clo., Amer. 25 AP21
Stubbs Hill, Dor. 119 BK72
Stubbs Hill, Sev. 98 CP60
Stubbs La., Tad. 112 BR67
Stubbs Way SW19 86 BT51
Brangwyn Cres.
Stubbs Wd., Amer. 25 AP21
Stucley Rd., Houns. 64 BG43
Stud Grn., Wat. 17 BC19
Studdridge St. SW6 66 BS44
Studholm St. SE15 67 CB43
Studholme Ct. NW3 47 BS35
Studio, The, Bush. 27 BF25
Studio Dr., Wem. 46 BM34
Empire Way
Studio Pl. SW1 3 **F5**
Studio Way, Borwd. 28 BN23
Studios Rd., Shep. 83 AZ52
Studland SE17 4 **K10**
Studland Clo., Sid. 78 CN48
Studland Rd. SE26 77 CC49
Studland Rd. W7 54 BG39
Studland Rd., Kings.T. 75 BL50
Studland Rd., Wey. 92 AY60
Studland St. W6 65 BP42
Studley Ave. E4 39 CF29
Studley Clo. E5 48 CD35
Studley Ct., Sid. 79 CO49
Studley Dr., Ilf. 49 CJ32
Studley Gra. Rd. W7 64 BH41
Studley Rd. E7 58 CH36
Studley Rd. SW4 66 BX44
Studley Rd., Dag. 59 CP36
Stukeley Rd. E7 58 CH36
Stukeley St. WC2 2 **A8**
Stukeley St. WC2 56 BX39
Stumble Hill, Ton. 117 DB68
Stump Rd., Epp. 23 CP17
Stumps Hill La., Beck. 77 CE50
Stumps La., Whyt. 105 CA62
Sturdy Rd. SE15 67 CB44
Sturge Ave. E17 39 CE30
Sturge St. SE1 4 **H4**
Sturge St. SE1 67 BZ41
Sturges Fld., Chis. 78 CM50
Sturgess Ave. NW4 46 BP33
Sturlas Way, Wal.Cr. 21 CC20
Sturmer Way N7 47 BX35
Stock Orchard Cres.
Sturrock Clo. N15 48 BZ31
Ida Rd.
Sturry St. E14 57 CE39
Sturt Ct., Guil. 118 AT69
Ashbury Cres.
Sturt St. N1 2 **J1**
Sturt St. N1 57 BZ37
Sturts La., Tad. 112 BO67
Stutfield St. E1 57 CB39
Styants Bottom Rd., 108 CZ64
Sev.
Stychens Clo., Red. 114 BZ70
Stychens La., Red. 114 BZ69
Style Rd., Slou. 62 AR41
Stylecroft Rd., Ch.St.G. 34 AR27
Styles End, Lthd. 111 BF67

Styles Gdns. SW9 66 BY44
Styles Way, Beck. 87 CF52
Styventon Pl., Cher. 82 AV54
Cowley Ave.
Succombs Hill, Warl. 105 CN63
Succombs Pl., Warl. 105 CB62
View Rd.
Sudbourne Rd. SW2 76 BX46
Sudbrook Gdns., Rich. 74 BK48
Sudbrook La., Rich. 75 BL47
Sudbrooke Rd. SW12 76 BU46
Sudbury Ave., Wem. 45 BK34
Sudbury Ct. E5 48 CC35
Clapton Pk. Est.
Sudbury Ct. Dr., Har. 45 BH34
Sudbury Ct. Rd., Har. 45 BH34
Sudbury Cres., Brom. 78 CH50
Sudbury Cres., Wem. 45 BJ35
Sudbury Cft., Wem. 45 BH35
Sudbury Gdns., Croy. 87 CA55
Sudbury Heights Ave., Grnf. 45 BH35
Sudbury Hill, Har. 45 BH34
Sudbury Hill Clo., Wem. 45 BH35
Sudbury Par., Wem. 45 BJ35
Sudbury Rd., Bark. 49 CN35
Sudeley St. N1 2 G1
Sudeley St. N1 56 BY37
Sudicamps Ct., Wal.Abb. 22 CH20
Winters Way
Sudlow Rd. SW18 76 BS46
Sudrey St. SE1 4 H5
Sudrey St. SE1 67 BZ41
Suez Ave., Grnf. 54 BH37
Suez Rd., Enf. 30 CD24
Suffield Clo., S.Croy. 96 CC59
Suffield Rd. E4 39 CE28
Suffield Rd. N15 48 CA32
Suffield Rd. SE20 87 CC51
Suffolk Clo., Borwd. 28 BN25
Suffolk Clo., St.Alb. 18 BK16
Suffolk Ct. E10 48 CE33
Suffolk Ct., Ilf. 49 CN32
Suffolk Dr., Guil. 109 AT68
Suffolk La. EC4 2 K10
Suffolk La. EC4 57 BZ40
Suffolk Pk. Rd. E17 48 CD31
Suffolk Pl. SW1 3 P2
Suffolk Pl. SW1 56 BW40
Suffolk St.
Suffolk Rd. E13 58 CG38
Suffolk Rd. N15 48 BZ32
Suffolk Rd. NW10 55 BO36
Suffolk Rd. SE25 87 CA52
Suffolk Rd. SW13 65 BO43
Suffolk Rd., Bark. 58 CM36
Suffolk Rd., Dag. 50 CS35
Suffolk Rd., Dart. 80 CW46
Suffolk Rd., Enf. 30 CB25
Suffolk Rd., Grav. 81 DH46
Suffolk Rd., Har. 45 BE32
Suffolk Rd., Ilf. 49 CN32
Suffolk Rd., Pot.B. 19 BR19
Suffolk Rd., Sid. 79 CP50
Suffolk Rd., Wor.Pk. 85 BO55
Suffolk St. E7 49 CH35
Suffolk St. SW1 3 P1
Suffolk St. SW1 56 BW40
Suffolk Way, Horn. 51 CX31
Suffolk Way, Sev. 117 CV66
Buckhurst La.
Sugar Bakers Ct. EC3 2 N9
Sugar Ho. La. E15 57 CF37
Sugar La., Berk. 7 AT14
Sugar Loaf Wk. E2 57 CC38
Sugden Rd. SW11 66 BV45
Sugden Rd., T.Ditt. 84 BJ54
Sugden St. SE5 67 BZ43
Sugden Way, Bark. 58 CN37
Sulgrave Rd. W6 65 BQ41
Sulina Rd. SW2 76 BX47
Sulivan Ct. SW6 66 BS44
Sulivan Rd. SW6 66 BS45
Sullivan Ave. E16 58 CJ39
Sullivan Clo. SW11 66 BU45
Sullivan Clo., Dart. 79 CU47
Sullivan Cres., Uxb. 35 AX30
Sullivan Rd. SE11 4 E8
Sullivan Rd. SE11 66 BY42
Brook Dr.
Sullivan Rd., E.Mol. 84 BH52
Sullivan Rd., Til. 71 DG44
Sullivan Way, Brwd. 27 BK25
Sullivans Reach, Walt. 83 BB54
Sultan Rd. E11 49 CH31
Sultan St. SE5 67 BZ43
Sultan St., Beck. 87 CC51
Sumatra Rd. NW6 47 BS35
Sumburgh Rd. SW12 76 BV46
Summer Ave., E.Mol. 84 BH53
Summer Clo., Lthd. 102 BG65
The Grn.
Summer Ct., Hem.H. 8 AX12
Townsend
Summer Ct. Rd. E1 57 CC39
West Arbour St.
Summer Dale, Welw.G.C. 5 BQ6
Summer Gdns., E.Mol. 84 BH53
Summer Gro., Borwd. 27 BK25
Summer Hill, Borwd. 28 BM25
Hartfield Ave.
Summer Hill, Chis. 88 CL51
Summer Hill Vill., Chis. 88 CL51
Summer Ho. Rd. N16 48 CA34
Summer Rd., E.Mol. 84 BH53
Summer Rd., T.Ditt. 84 BH53
Summerfield, Hat. 10 BP14
Summerfield Ave. NW6 55 BR37
Summerfield Clo., St.Alb. 18 BK16
Summerfield Clo., Wey. 92 AW56
Summerfield La., Surb. 84 BK55
Summerfield Rd. W5 54 BJ38
Summerfield Rd., Loug. 31 CJ25
Summerfield Rd., Wat. 26 BC21
Summerfield St. SE12 78 CG47
Summerhayes Clo., Wok. 91 AS60
Summerhays, Cob. 93 BD60
Summerhill Clo., Orp. 97 CN56
Summerhill Ct., St.Alb. 9 BH13
Avenue Rd.
Summerhill Gro., Enf. 30 CA25
Summerhill Rd. N15 48 BZ31
Summerhill Rd., Dart. 80 CV47
Summerhill Way, Mitch. 86 BV51
Summerhouse Ave., Houns. 64 BE44
Summerhouse Dr., Bex. 79 CS49
Summerhouse Dr., Dart. 79 CS48
Summerhouse La., Uxb. 35 AW29
Summerhouse La., Wat. 27 BG23
Summerhouse La., West Dr. 63 AX43
Summerhouse Way, Abb.L. 17 BB18
Summerland Gdns. N10 47 BV31
Muswell Hill Bdy.
Summerlands Ave. W3 55 BN40
Summerlands Rd., St.Alb. 9 BK11
The Ridgeway
Summerlay Clo., Tad. 103 BR63
Summerlea, Slou. 61 AN41
Summerlee Ave. N2 47 BU31
Summerlee Gdns. N2 47 BU31
Summerley St. SW18 76 BS48
Summerly Ave., Reig. 121 BS70
Summers Clo., Sutt. 95 BS57
Overton Rd.
Summers Clo., Wem. 46 BM33
Summers Clo., Wey. 92 AZ59
Summers La. N12 38 BT29
Summers Row N12 38 BU29
Summers St. EC1 2 D5
Summers St. EC1 56 BY38
Back Hill
Summersby Rd. N6 47 BV32
Summerstown SW17 76 BT48
Summerswood Clo., Ken. 105 BZ61
Longwood Rd.
Summerswood La., Borwd. 19 BO10
Summerton Way SE28 59 CP39
Summertrees, Sun. 83 BC51
Summerville Gdns., Sutt. 94 BR57
Summerwood Rd., Islw. 74 BH46
Summit, The, Loug. 31 CK23
Summit Ave. NW9 46 BN32
Summit Clo. N14 38 BW27
Summit Clo. NW2 46 BR35
Summit Clo. NW9 46 BN31
Summit Clo., Edg. 37 BM29
Summit Clo., Wey. 91 AV56
Summit Dr., Wdf.Grn. 40 CJ30
Summit Est. N16 48 CB33
Summit Rd. E17 48 CE31
Summit Rd., Nthlt. 54 BF36
Summit Rd., Pot.B. 19 BR18
Summit Way N14 38 BV27
Summit Way SE19 77 CA50
Sumner Ave. SE15 67 CA44
Sumner Rd.
Sumner Bldgs. SE1 57 BZ40
Sumner St.
Sumner Clo., Orp. 97 CM56
Isabella Dr.
Sumner Est. SE15 67 CA44
Sumner Gdns., Croy. 86 CY54
Sumner Pl. SW7 3 B9
Sumner Pl. SW7 66 BT42
Sumner Pl., Wey. 92 AW56
Lime Gro.
Sumner Pl. Ms. SW7 3 B9
Sumner Pl. Ms. SW7 66 BT42
Sumner Pl.
Sumner Rd. SE15 67 CA43
Sumner Rd., Croy. 86 BY54
Sumner Rd., Har. 45 BG33
Sumner Rd., S.Croy. 86 BY54
Sumner St. SE1 4 G2
Sumner St. SE1 56 BY40
Sumners Fm. Clo., Harl. 13 CL13
Sumpter Clo. NW3 56 BT36
Sumpter Yd., St.Alb. 9 BG13
Sun All., Rich. 65 BL45
Sun Ct. EC3 2 L9
Sun Hill, Fawk. 90 CZ55
Sun La. SE3 68 CH43
Sun La., Grav. 81 DH48
Sun Pas., Wind. 61 AO44
Peascod St.
Sun Ray Ave., Brwd. 122 DF25
Sun Rd. W14 65 BR42
Sun Rd., Swans. 81 DC46
Sun Sq., Hem.H. 8 AX13
High St.
Sun St. EC2 2 L6
Sun St. EC2 57 BZ39
Sun St., Wal.Abb. 21 CF20
Sun St. Pas. EC2 2 M7
Sun St. Pas. EC2 57 CA39
Sunbeam Rd. NW10 55 BN38
Sunbury Ave. NW7 37 BN28
Sunbury Ave. SW14 65 BN45
Sunbury Ct. Rd., Sun. 84 BD51
Sunbury Cres., Felt. 73 BB49
Ryland Clo.
Sunbury Gdns. NW7 37 BN28
Sunbury La. SW11 66 BT44
Sunbury La., Walt. 83 BC53
Sunbury Rd., Felt. 73 BB48
Sunbury Rd., Sutt. 85 BQ55
Sunbury Rd. (Eton), Wind. 61 AO43
Sunbury St. SE18 68 CK41
Sunbury Way, Felt. 74 BD49
Suncourt, Erith 69 CT44
Suncroft Pl. SE26 77 CC48
Sundale Ave., S.Croy. 96 CC58
Sunderland Ave., St.Alb. 9 BJ13
Sunderland Ct. SE22 77 CB47
Sunderland Rd. SE23 77 CC48
Sunderland Rd. W5 64 BK41
Sunderland Rd., Houns. 73 AY46
Southampton Rd.
Sunderland Ter. W2 56 BS39
Sunderland Way E12 49 CJ34
Sundew Ave. W12 55 BP40
Sundew Ct., Grays 71 DE43
Salix Rd.
Sundew Rd., Hem.H. 7 AV14
Sundial Ave. SE25 87 CA52
Sundon Cres., Vir.W. 82 AQ53
Sundorne Rd. SE7 68 CH42
Sundown Ave., S.Croy. 96 CA59
Sundown Pl., Ilf. 49 CL34
Ilford Hill
Sundown Rd., Ashf. 73 BA49
Sundra Wk. E1 57 CC38
Beaumont Gro.
Sundridge Ave., Brom. 88 CJ51
Sundridge Ave., Well. 68 CM44
Sundridge Clo., Dart. 80 CX46
Sundridge Hill, Sev. 107 CP62
Sundridge Ho., Brom. 78 CH49
Sundridge La., Sev. 107 CO62
Sundridge Pl., Croy. 87 CB54
Sundridge Rd.
Sundridge Rd., Croy. 87 CA54
Sundridge Rd., Sev. 107 CQ64
Sundridge Rd., Wok. 100 AT63
Sunfields Pl. SE3 68 CH43
Sunflower Way, Rom. 42 CV30
Sunkist Way, Wall. 95 BX58
Sunland Ave., Bexh. 69 CQ45
Sunleigh Rd., Wem. 55 BL37
Sunley Gdns., Grnf. 54 BJ37
Sunmead Clo., Lthd. 102 BH64
Sunmead Rd., Hem.H. 8 AX13
Sunmead Rd., Sun. 83 BC52
Sunna Gdns., Sun. 83 BC51
Sunning Hill, Grav. 81 DF48
Sunningdale N14 38 BW28
Wilmer Way
Sunningdale Ave. W3 55 BO39
Sunningdale Ave., Bark. 58 CM37
Sunningdale Ave., Felt. 74 BE48
Sunningdale Ave., Rain. 59 CU38
Sunningdale Ave., Ruis. 45 BD33
Sunningdale Clo. E6 58 CK38
Ascot Rd.
Sunningdale Clo., Stan. 36 BJ29
Sunningdale Gdns. NW9 46 BN32
Sunningdale Gdns. W8 66 BS42
Lexham Ms.
Sunningdale Ms., Welw.G.C. 5 BR6
Viaduct Way
Sunningdale Rd., Brom. 88 CK52
Sunningdale Rd., Rain. 59 CU36
Sunningdale Rd., Sutt. 85 BR55
Sunningfields Cres. NW4 37 BP30
Sunningfields Rd. NW4 37 BP30
Sunninghill Rd. SE13 67 CE44
Sunnings La., Upmin. 60 CY36
Sunningvale Ave., West. 106 CJ61
Sunningvale Clo., West. 106 CJ61
Sunny Bank SE25 87 CB52
Sunny Bank, Epsom 103 BN61
Sunny Bank, Warl. 105 CD62
Sunny Cres. NW10 55 BN36
Sunny Gdns. Rd. NW4 37 BP30
Sunny Hill NW4 46 BP31
Sunny Hill Rd., Ger.Cr. 34 AU29
Sunny Nook Gdns., S.Croy. 96 BZ57
Selsdon Rd.
Sunny Ri., Cat. 105 BZ65
Sunny Rd., The, Enf. 30 CC23
Sunny Side, Wal.Abb. 13 CG14
Hoe La.
Sunny Side, Walt. 84 BD53
Sunny Vw. NW9 46 BN32
Sunny Way N12 38 BU29
Sunnybank Rd., Pot.B. 20 BS20
Sunnycroft Gdns., Upmin. 51 CZ33
Sunnycroft Rd. SE25 87 CB52
Sunnycroft Rd., Houns. 64 BF44
Sunnycroft Rd., Sthl. 54 BF39
Sunnydale, Orp. 88 CL55
Sunnydale Gdns. NW7 37 BN29
Sunnydale Rd. SE12 78 CH46
Sunnydell, St.Alb. 18 BF16
Sunnydene, Wem. 54 BK36
Sunnydene Ave. E4 39 CF28
Sunnydene Ave., Ruis. 44 BC33
Sunnydene Clo., Rom. 42 CW29
Sunnydene Rd., Pur. 95 BY60
Sunnydene St. SE26 77 CD49
Sunnyfield NW7 37 BO27
Sunnyfield, Hat. 10 BQ11
Sunnyfield Rd., Chis. 89 CO52
Sunnyhill Rd. SW16 76 BX49
Sunnyhill Rd., Hem.H. 8 AW13
Sunnyhurst Clo., Sutt. 86 BS55
Sunnymead Ave., Chesh. 16 AP17
Sunnymead Ave., Mitch. 86 BW52
Sunnymead Rd. NW9 46 BN33
Sunnymead Rd. SW15 75 BP46
Sunnymede Ave., Cars. 95 BT59
Sunnymede Ave., Epsom 94 BO58
Sunnymede Dr., Ilf. 49 CL32
Sunnyside NW2 46 BR34
Sunnyside SW19 75 BR50
Sunnyside Cotts., Chesh. 16 AP16
Sunnyside Dr. E4 39 CF26
Sunnyside Gdns., Upmin. 51 CY34
Sunnyside Pas. SW19 75 BR50
Sunnyside Rd. E10 48 CE33
Sunnyside Rd. N19 47 BW33
Sunnyside Rd. W5 54 BK40
Sunnyside Rd., Epp. 22 CN19
Sunnyside Rd., Ilf. 49 CM34
Sunnyside Rd., Tedd. 74 BG49
Sunnyside Rd. E. N9 39 CB27
Sunnyside Rd. N. N9 39 CB27
Sunnyside Rd. S. N9 39 CA27
Sunray Ave. SE24 67 BZ45
Sunray Ave., Brom. 88 CK53
Sunray Ave., Surb. 85 BM55
Sunray Ave., West Dr. 63 AX41
Sunrise Ave., Horn. 51 CV34
Sunrise Clo., Felt. 74 BE48
Sunrise Cres., Hem.H. 8 AY15
Sunset Ave. E4 39 CE26
Sunset Ave., Wdf.Grn. 40 CG28
Sunset Dr., Hav. 41 CU28
Sunset Gdns. SE25 87 CA51
Sunset Rd. SE5 67 BZ45
Sunset Vw., Barn. 28 BR23
Sunshine Way, Mitch. 86 BU51
Sunstone Grn., Red. 113 BX68
Sunwell Clo. SE15 67 CB44
Surbiton Ct., Surb. 84 BK53
Surbiton Cres., Kings.T. 85 BL52
Surbiton Hall Clo., Kings.T. 85 BL52
Surbiton Hill Pk., Surb. 85 BL53
Surbiton Hill Rd., Surb. 85 BL52
Surbiton Pk. Ter., Kings.T. 85 BL52
Surbiton Rd., Kings.T. 84 BK52
Surlingham Clo. SE28 59 CP40
Surly Hall Wk., Wind. 61 AM44
Surman Cres., Brwd. 122 DE26
Surr St. N7 47 BX35
Surrendale Pl. W9 56 BS38
Surrey Ave., Slou. 52 AO39
Surrey Canal Rd. SE15 67 CC43
Surrey Cres. W4 65 BM42
Surrey Dr., Horn. 51 CX31
Surrey Gdns. N4 48 BZ32
Surrey Gdns., Lthd. 101 BB64
Surrey Gro. SE17 67 CA42
Surrey Gro., Sutt. 86 BT55
Surrey La. SW11 66 BU44
Surrey Lo. SE1 4 D7
Surrey Ms. SE27 77 CA49
Hamilton Rd.
Surrey Mt. SE23 77 CB47
Surrey Quays Rd. SE16 67 CC41
Surrey Rd. SE15 77 CC46
Surrey Rd., Bark. 58 CN36
Surrey Rd., Dag. 50 CR35
Surrey Rd., Har. 45 BG32
Surrey Rd., W.Wick. 87 CE54
Surrey Row SE1 4 F4
Surrey Row SE1 66 BY41
Surrey Sq. SE17 4 M10
Surrey Sq. SE17 67 CA42
Surrey St. E13 58 CH38
Surrey St. WC2 2 C10
Surrey St. WC2 56 BX40
Temple Pl.
Surrey St., Croy. 87 BZ55
Surrey Ter. SE17 4 N10
Surrey Ter. SE17 67 CA42
Surrey Sq.
Surrey Water Rd. SE16 57 CC40
Surridge Clo., Rain. 60 CV38
Surridge Gdns. SE19 77 BZ50
Susan Clo., Rom. 50 CS31
Susan Rd. SE3 68 CH44
Susan Wd., Chis. 88 CL51
Susannah St. E14 57 CE39
Sussex Ave., Islw. 64 BH45
Sussex Ave., Rom. 42 CW29
Sussex Clo. N19 47 BX34
Sussex Clo., Ch.St.G. 34 AQ27
Sussex Clo., Hodd. 12 CE11
Roman St.
Sussex Clo., Ilf. 49 CK32
Sussex Clo., N.Mal. 85 BO52
Sussex Clo., Reig. 121 BT71
Sussex Clo., Slou. 62 AQ41
Sussex Keep
Sussex Clo., Twick. 74 BJ46
Cumberland Clo.
Sussex Cres., Nthlt. 54 BF36
Sussex Gdns. N4 48 BZ32
Rosebery Gdns.
Sussex Gdns. N6 47 BU32
Sussex Gdns. W2 1 A10
Sussex Gdns. W2 56 BT39
Sussex Gdns., Chess. 93 BK57
Sussex Keep, Slou. 62 AQ41
Sussex Ms. NW1 56 BU38
Sussex Pl.
Sussex Ms. E. W2 1 B9
Sussex Ms. E. W2 56 BT40
Clifton Pl.
Sussex Ms. W. W2 1 B10
Sussex Pl. NW1 1 E3
Sussex Pl. NW1 56 BU38
Sussex Pl. W2 1 B9
Sussex Pl. W2 56 BT39
Sussex Pl. W6 65 BQ42
Sussex Pl., Erith 69 CR43
Sussex Pl., N.Mal. 85 BO52
Sussex Rd.
Sussex Pl., Slou. 62 AQ41
Sussex Rd. E6 58 CL37
Sussex Rd., Brwd. 42 DA28
Sussex Rd., Cars. 95 BU57
Sussex Rd., Dart. 80 CX47
Sussex Rd., Erith 69 CR43
Sussex Rd., Har. 45 BF32
Sussex Rd., N.Mal. 85 BO52
Sussex Rd., Orp. 89 CP53
Sussex Rd., Sid. 79 CO49
Sussex Rd., S.Croy. 96 BZ57
Sussex Rd., Sthl. 64 BD41
Sussex Rd., Uxb. 44 BA35
Sussex Rd., Wat. 26 BC22
Sussex Rd., W.Wick. 87 CE54
Sussex Sq. W2 1 B10
Sussex Sq. W2 56 BT40
Sussex St. E13 58 CH
Sussex St. SW1 66 BV
Sussex Wk. SW9 66 BY
Sussex Way N7 47 BX
Sussex Way, Barn. 29 BV
Sussex Way, Uxb. 43 AV
Sutcliffe Clo. NW11 47 BS
Sutcliffe Clo., Bush. 27 BG
Sutcliffe Rd. SE18 68 CN
Sutcliffe Rd., Well. 69 CP
Sutherland Ave. W9 56 BS
Sutherland Ave. W13 54 BJ
Sutherland Ave., Cuffley 20 BW
Sutherland Ave., Guil. 109 AS
Sutherland Ave., Hayes 63 BC
Sutherland Ave., Orp. 88 CN
Sutherland Ave., Sun. 83 BB
Sutherland Ave., Well. 68 CN
Sutherland Ave., West. 106 CJ
Sutherland Clo., Barn. 28 BR
Sutherland Clo., Wey. 92 BA
Vaillant Rd.
Sutherland Ct. NW9 46 BM
Sutherland Ct., Welw.G.C. 5 B
Sutherland Dr. SW19 86 BT
Brangwyn Cres.
Sutherland Dr., Guil. 109 AS
Sutherland Gdns. SW14 65 BO
Sutherland Gdns., Sun. 83 BB
Sutherland Gdns., Wor.Pk. 85 BP
Sutherland Gro. SW18 75 BR
Sutherland Gro., Tedd. 74 BH
Sutherland Pl. W2 56 BS
Sutherland Pt. E5 48 CB
Downs Est.
Sutherland Rd. E17 39 CC
Sutherland Rd. N9 39 CB
Sutherland Rd. N17 39 CB
Sutherland Rd. W4 65 BO
Sutherland Rd. W13 54 BJ
Sutherland Rd., Belv. 69 CR
Sutherland Rd., Croy. 86 BY
Sutherland Rd., Enf. 30 CC
Sutherland Rd., Sthl. 54 BE
Sutherland Rd. Path E17 48 CC
Sutherland Rd.
Sutherland Row SW1 3 K1
Sutherland Row SW1 66 BV4
Sutherland St.
Sutherland Sq. SE17 67 BZ4
Sutherland St. E3 57 CD3
Sutherland St. SW1 3 J1
Sutherland St. SW1 66 BV4
Sutherland Wk. SE17 67 BZ4
Sutherland Way, Cuffley 20 BW1
Sutlej Rd. SE7 68 CJ4
Sutterton St. N7 56 BX3
Sutton Ave., Slou. 62 AR4
Sutton Ave., Wok. 100 AP6
Sutton Clo., Beck. 87 CE5
Albemarle Rd.
Sutton Clo., Brox. 12 CD1
Sutton Clo., Loug. 40 CK2
Sutton Clo., Pnr. 44 BC3
Sutton Common Rd., Sutt. 85 BR5
Sutton Ct. W4 65 BN4
Sutton Ct., Guil. 118 AQ6
Barrack Rd.
Sutton Ct. Rd. E13 58 CJ3
Sutton Ct. Rd. W4 65 BN4
Sutton Ct. Rd., Sutt. 95 BT5
Sutton Ct. Rd., Uxb. 53 AZ3
Sutton Cres., Barn. 28 BQ2
Sutton Dene, Houns. 64 BF4
Sutton Dws. N1 56 BY3
Sutton Dws. SE8 67 CC4
Sutton Dws. SW3 66 BU4
Sutton Dws. W10 55 BQ3
Sutton Est. SW3 3 D1
Sutton Gdns., Bark. 58 CN3
Felton Rd.
Sutton Gdns., Croy. 87 CA5
Sutton Gdns., Red. 113 BW6
Sutton Grn., Bark. 58 CN3
Saxham Rd.
Sutton Grn. Rd., Guil. 109 AS6
Sutton Gro., Sutt. 95 BT5
Sutton Hall Rd., Houns. 64 BF4
Sutton La. W4 65 BN4
Sutton La., Houns. 64 BE4
Sutton La., Slou. 62 AT4
Sutton La., Sutt. 95 BS5
Sutton La. S. W4 65 BN4
Sutton Pk. Rd., Sutt. 95 BS5
Sutton Path, Borwd. 28 BM2
Sutton Pl. E9 48 CC3
Sutton Pl., Slou. 62 AT4
Sutton Rd. E13 58 CG3
Sutton Rd. E17 39 CC3
Sutton Rd. N10 38 BV3
Sutton Rd., Bark. 58 CN3
Sutton Rd., Houns. 64 BF4
Sutton Rd., St.Alb. 9 BJ1
Sutton Rd., Wat. 27 BD2
Sutton Row W1 1 P
Sutton Row W1 56 BW3
Sutton Sq. E9 48 CC3
Urswick Rd.
Sutton Sq., Houns. 64 BE4
Sutton St. E1 57 CC4
Sutton Way W10 55 BQ3
Sutton Way, Houns. 64 BE4
Suttons Ave., Horn. 51 CV3
Suttons Gdns., Horn. 51 CV3
Suttons La., Horn. 51 CV3
Suttons Parkway, Upmin. 51 CW3
Suttons Way EC1 2
Swabey Rd., Slou. 62 AT4
Swaby Rd. SW18 76 BT4
Swaffham Way N22 38 BY2
Swaffield Rd. SW18 76 BS4

waffield Rd., Sev. 108 CV64
wain Rd., Th.Hth. 87 BZ53
wains Clo., West Dr. 63 AY41
wains La. N6 47 BV34
wains Rd. SW17 76 BU50
wainson Rd. W3 65 BO41
waisland Dr., Dart. 79 CT46
Crayford Rd.
waisland Rd., Dart. 79 CU46
wakeleys Dr., Uxb. 44 AZ35
wakeleys Rd., Uxb. 44 AY35
wale Clo., S.Ock. 60 CY39
wale Rd., Dart. 69 CU45
waledale Rd., Dart. 80 CY47
wallands Rd. SE6 77 CE48
wallow Clo. SE14 67 CC44
wallow Clo., Bush. 36 BF26
wallow Clo., Rick. 35 AX26
Nightingale Rd.
wallow Clo., Stai. 72 AV49
wallow Ct., Ruis. 45 BD33
Dollis Cres.
wallow Dr. NW10 55 BN36
Kingfisher Way
wallow Dr., Nthlt. 54 BE37
Hazelmere Rd.
wallow End, Welw.G.C. 5 BR8
wallow Flds., Welw.G.C. 5 BR8
wallow Gdns., Hat. 10 BP13
wallow La., St.Alb. 9 BJ15
wallow Pas. W1 1 K9
wallow Pl. W1 1 K9
wallow St. E6 58 CK39
wallow St. W1 3 M1
wallow St. W1 56 BW40
Piccadilly
wallow St., Iver 52 AU38
wallow Wk., Rain. 59 CU36
Heron Flight Ave.
wallowdale, Iver 52 AU38
wallowdale, S.Croy. 96 CC58
wallowdale Est., Iver 52 AU38
wallowdale La., Hem.H. 8 AZ12
wallowfield, Egh. 72 AQ50
Heronfield
wallowfield Rd. SE7 68 CH42
wallowfield Way, Hayes 63 BA41
wallowfields, Grav. 81 DF48
Hillary Ave.
wallows, Harl. 6 CP9
wallows, The, Welw.G.C. 5 BR6
wan & Pike Rd., Enf. 30 CE22
wan App. E6 58 CK39
wan Ave., Upmin. 51 CZ33
wan Clo. E17 39 CD29
Banbury Rd.
wan Clo., Croy. 87 CA54
wan Clo., Felt. 74 BE49
wan Clo., Orp. 89 CO52
wan Ct. N20 38 BT27
wan Ct. SW3 66 BU42
wan La. EC4 4 K1
wan La. EC4 57 BZ40
Wharfside
wan La. N20 38 BT27
wan La., Brwd. 33 CZ22
wan La., Dart. 79 CT47
wan La., Guil. 118 AR71
wan Mead SE1 4 M7
wan Mead SE1 67 CA41
wan Ms. SW9 66 BX44
Stockwell Pk. Rd.
wan Mill Gdns., Dor. 119 BK70
wan Paddock, Brwd. 42 DB27
Chestnut Gro.
wan Pas. E1 57 CA40
Royal Mint St.
wan Pl. SW13 65 BO44
wan Rd. SE16 67 CC41
wan Rd. SE18 68 CJ41
wan Rd., Felt. 74 BE49
wan Rd., Iver 52 AV39
wan Rd., Sthl. 54 BF39
wan Rd., West Dr. 63 AX41
wan St. SE1 4 J6
wan St. SE1 67 BZ41
wan St., Islw. 64 BJ45
wan Ter., Wind. 61 AN43
wan Wk. SW3 66 BU43
wan Wk., Rom. 50 CT32
wan Way, Enf. 30 CC23
wan Wf. EC4 57 BZ40
Wharfside
wan Yd. N1 56 BY36
Highbury Sta. Rd.
wanage Rd. E4 39 CF29
wanage Rd. SW18 76 BT46
wanage Waye, Hayes 54 BD39
wanbourne Dr., Horn. 51 CV35
wanbridge Rd., Bexh. 69 CR44
wandon Way SW18 66 BS45
wanfield Rd., Wal.Cr. 21 CD20
wanfield St. E2 2 P3
wanfield St. E2 57 CA38
wanhill, Welw.G.C. 5 BS6
wanland Rd., Hat. 19 BP16
wanland Rd., Pot.B. 19 BP20
wanley Bar La., Pot.B. 20 BS17
wanley By-pass, Swan. 89 CS52
wanley Cres., Pot.B. 20 BS18
wanley La., Swan. 89 CT52
wanley Rd., Well. 69 CP44
wanley Vill. Rd., Swan. 89 CU51
wanns Meadow, Lthd. 111 BF66
wans Clo., St.Alb. 10 BL14
wanscombe Rd. W4 65 BO42
wanscombe Rd. W11 55 BQ40
wanscombe St., Swans. 81 DC46
wansea Rd., Enf. 30 CC24
wanshope, Loug. 31 CL23
wansland Gdns. E17 39 CD30
McEntee Ave.
wanston Path, Wat. 36 BD27

Swanton Gdns. SW19 75 BQ47
Swanton Rd., Erith 69 CR43
Swanwick Clo. SW15 75 BO47
Swanworth La., Dor. 111 BJ67
Swanzy Rd., Sev. 108 CV63
Sward Rd., Orp. 89 CO53
Swaton Rd. E3 57 CE38
Swaylands Rd., Belv. 69 CR43
Swaynes La., Guil. 118 AV70
Swaynesland Rd., Eden. 115 CK70
Sweden Gate SE16 67 CD41
Swedenborg Gdns. E1 57 CB40
Sweeney Cres. SE1 4 Q5
Sweeney Cres. SE1 67 CA41
Sweeps La., Egh. 72 AS49
Sweeps La., Orp. 89 CP53
Sweet Briar, Welw.G.C. 5 BS8
Sweet Briar Grn. N9 39 CA27
Briary La.
Sweet Briar Gro. N9 39 CA27
Sweet Briar Wk. N18 39 CA28
Sweetbriar Clo., Hem.H. 8 AW12
Sweetbriar La., Epsom 94 BN60
Sweetcroft La., Uxb. 53 AY36
Sweetenham Wk. SE18 68 CM42
Sandbach Pl.
Sweetmans Ave., Pnr. 45 BD31
Sweets Way N20 38 BT27
Swete St. E13 58 CH37
Sweyn Pl. SE3 68 CH44
Sweyn Rd., Green. 80 DB46
Sweyne Rd., Swans. 81 DC46
Sweyns, Harl. 14 CP12
Swievelands Hill Rd., West. 106 CH63
Swift Clo. E17 39 CD29
Banbury Rd.
Swift Clo., Har. 45 BF34
Swift Clo., Hayes 53 BB39
Swift Clo., Upmin. 51 CZ33
Swift Rd., Felt. 74 BD49
Swift Rd., Sthl. 64 BF41
Swift St. SW6 65 BR44
Swiftfields, Welw.G.C. 5 BR7
Swiftsden Way, Brom. 78 CG50
Swinbourne Gdns., Til. 71 DG44
Swinbrook Rd. W10 55 BQ38
Swinburn Cres., Croy. 87 CC53
Swinburne Ct. SE5 67 BZ45
Basingdon Way
Swinburne Rd. SW15 65 BP45
Swinderby Rd., Wem. 55 BL36
Swindon Clo., Ilf. 49 CN34
Salisbury Rd.
Swindon Clo., Rom. 42 CW28
Swindon Gdns., Rom. 42 CW28
Swindon La., Rom. 42 CW28
Swindon St. W12 55 BP40
Swinfield Clo., Felt. 74 BE48
Swinford Gdns. SW9 66 BY45
Swing Gate La., Berk. 7 AR14
Swingate La. SE18 68 CN43
Swinnerton St. E9 48 CD35
Swinton Clo., Wem. 46 BM33
Swinton Pl. WC1 2 B2
Swinton Pl. WC1 56 BX38
Swinton St.
Swinton St. WC1 2 B2
Swinton St. WC1 56 BX38
Swires Shaw, Kes. 97 BJ56
Swiss Ave., Wat. 26 BB24
Swiss Clo., Wat. 26 BB24
Swiss Cottage Pl., Loug. 31 CJ25
High Rd.
Swithland Gdns. SE9 78 CK49
Swyncombe Ave. W5 64 BJ42
Swynford Gdns. NW4 46 BP31
Handowe Clo.
Sybourn St. E17 48 CD33
Sycamore App., Rick. 26 BA25
Sycamore Ave. W5 64 BK41
Sycamore Ave., Hat. 10 BP13
Sycamore Ave., Hayes 53 BB40
Sycamore Ave., Sid. 78 CN46
Sycamore Ave., Upmin. 51 CX34
Sycamore Clo. E16 58 CG38
Clarence Rd.
Sycamore Clo. N9 39 CB28
Sycamore Clo. SE9 78 CK48
Sycamore Clo., Amer. 25 AO22
Sycamore Clo., Barn. 29 BT25
Sycamore Clo., Bush. 27 BE23
Sycamore Clo., Cars. 95 BU56
Sycamore Clo., Ch.St.G. 34 AQ27
Sycamore Clo., Felt. 73 BC48
Sycamore Clo., Grav. 81 DH47
Sycamore Clo., Lthd. 102 BH64
Sycamore Clo., Nthlt. 54 BE37
Sycamore Clo., Wat. 26 BC21
Sycamore Clo., West Dr. 53 AY40
Sycamore Dean, Chesh. 16 AO17
Sycamore Dr., Brwd. 42 DB26
Mayfield Gdns.
Sycamore Dr., St.Alb. 18 BG17
Sycamore Dr., Swan. 89 CT32
Sycamore Fld., Harl. 13 CL12
Sycamore Gdns. W6 65 BP41
Sycamore Gdns., Mitch. 86 BT51
Sycamore Gro. NW9 46 BN33
Sycamore Gro. SE20 77 CB51
Sycamore Gro., N.Mal. 85 BN52
Sycamore Hill N11 38 BV29
Sycamore Ri., Bans. 94 BQ60
High Beeches
Sycamore Ri., Berk. 7 AR13
Sycamore Ri., Ch.St.G. 34 AQ27
Sycamore Rd. SW19 75 BQ50
Sycamore Rd., Amer. 25 AO22
Sycamore Rd., Ch.St.G. 34 AQ27
Sycamore Rd., Dart. 80 CV47
Sycamore Rd., Guil. 118 AR70
Sycamore Rd., Rick. 26 BA25
Sycamore Rd., Tedd. 74 BK50
Sycamore St. EC1 2 H5

Sycamore St. EC1 57 BZ38
Baltic St.
Sycamore Wk. W10 55 BR38
Droop St.
Sycamore Wk., Egh. 72 AQ50
Sycamore Wk., Ilf. 49 CM31
Civic Way
Sycamore Wk., Slou. 52 AS39
Sycamore Way, Th.Hth. 86 BY53
Sycamores, The, Hem.H. 7 AV15
Sycamores, The, Rad. 18 BJ20
Sycamores, The, S.Ock. 60 CY40
Dacre Ave.
Sydenham Ave. SE26 77 CB49
Sydenham Clo., Rom. 50 CT31
Sydenham Hill SE23 77 CB47
Sydenham Hill SE26 77 CB47
Sydenham Pk. SE26 77 CC49
Sydenham Pk. Rd. SE26 77 CC48
Sydenham Ri. SE23 77 CC48
Sydenham Rd. SE26 77 CC49
Sydenham Rd., Croy. 87 BZ54
Sydenham Rd., Guil. 118 AR71
Sydmons Ct. SE23 77 CC47
Sydner Ms. N16 48 CA35
Sydner Rd.
Sydner Rd. N16 48 CA35
Sydney Ave., Pur. 95 BX59
Sydney Clo. SW3 3 B9
Sydney Clo. SW3 66 BT42
Sydney Cres., Ashf. 73 AZ50
Sydney Gro. NW4 46 BQ32
Sydney Gro., Slou. 52 AO39
Sydney Ms. SW3 3 B9
Sydney Ms. SW3 66 BT42
Sydney Pl. SW7 3 B9
Sydney Pl. SW7 66 BU42
Sydney Rd. E11 49 CH32
Sydney Rd. N8 47 BY31
Sydney Rd. N10 38 BV30
Sydney Rd. SE2 69 CP41
Sydney Rd. SW20 85 BQ51
Sydney Rd. W13 54 BJ40
Sydney Rd., Bexh. 69 CP45
Sydney Rd., Enf. 30 BZ24
Sydney Rd., Felt. 73 BC47
Sydney Rd., Guil. 118 AS71
Sydney Rd., Ilf. 40 CM30
Sydney Rd., Rich. 65 BL45
Sydney Rd., Sid. 78 CN49
Sydney Rd., Tedd. 74 BH49
Sydney Rd., Til. 71 DG44
Sydney Rd., Wat. 26 BB25
Sydney Rd., Wdf.Grn. 40 CH28
Sydney Sq. SE15 67 CB43
Latona Rd.
Sydney St. SW3 3 C10
Sydney St. SW3 66 BU42
Sykecluan, Iver 62 AV41
Sykeings, Iver 62 AV41
Sykes Dr., Stai. 73 AW49
Sylvan Ave. N3 38 BS30
Sylvan Ave. N22 38 BX29
Sylvan Ave. NW7 37 BO29
Sylvan Ave., Horn. 51 CW32
Sylvan Ave., Rom. 50 CQ32
Sylvan Clo., Grays 71 DC42
Sylvan Clo., Hem.H. 8 AZ14
Sylvan Clo., Oxt. 115 CH68
Sylvan Clo., S.Croy. 96 CB58
Sylvan Clo., Wok. 100 AT62
Sylvan Gdns., Surb. 84 BK54
Sylvan Gro. SE15 67 CB43
Sylvan Hill SE19 87 CA51
Sylvan Rd. E7 58 CH36
Sylvan Rd. E11 49 CH32
Sylvan Rd. E17 48 CE32
Sylvan Rd. SE19 87 CA51
Sylvan Rd., Ilf. 49 CM34
Sylvan Way, Chig. 41 CO27
Sylvan Way, Dag. 50 CO34
Sylvan Way, Red. 121 BV71
Sylvan Way, Welw.G.C. 5 BT8
Sylvan Way, W.Wick. 97 CG56
Sylvana Clo., Uxb. 53 AY37
Sylvandale, Welw.G.C. 5 BT8
Sylverdale Rd., Croy. 86 BY55
Sylverdale Rd., Ken. 95 BY60
Sylvester Ave., Chis. 78 CK50
Sylvester Gdns., Ilf. 41 CO28
Sylvester Rd. E8 57 CB36
Sylvester Rd. E17 48 CD33
Sylvester Rd. N2 38 BT30
Sylvester Rd., Wem. 45 BK35
Sylvestrus Clo., Kings.T. 85 BM51
Sylvia Ave., Brwd. 122 DE27
Sylvia Ave., Pnr. 36 BE29
Sylvia Ct., Wem. 55 BM36
Sylvia Gdns., Wem. 55 BM36
Symes Ms. NW1 56 BW37
Symonds Clo., Sev. 99 CZ56
Symonds Hyde La., Welw.G.C. 5 BN9
Symons St. SW3 3 F9
Symons St. SW3 66 BU42
Syon Gate Way, Brent. 64 BJ43
Syon Gate Way, Islw. 64 BJ43
Syon La.
Syon La., Islw. 64 BH43
Syon Pk. Gdns., Islw. 64 BH43
Syracuse Ave., Rain. 60 CV38
Syringa Ct., Grays 71 DE43
Sythwood, Wok. 100 AQ61

T

Tabard Gdn. Est. SE1 4 L5
Tabard Gdn. Est. SE1 67 BZ41
Tabard St. SE1 4 K5

Tabard St. SE1 67 BZ41
Tabarin Way, Epsom 103 BQ61
Tabernacle Ave. E13 58 CH38
Tabernacle St. EC2 2 L5
Tabernacle St. EC2 57 BZ38
Tableer Ave. SW4 76 BW46
Tabley Rd. N7 47 BX35
Tabor Gdns., Sutt. 94 BR57
Tabor Gro. SW19 75 BR50
Tabor Rd. W6 65 BP41
Tabrums Way, Upmin. 51 CZ33
Tachbrook Ms. SW1 3 L8
Tachbrook Ms. SW1 66 BW42
Longmore St.
Tachbrook Rd., Felt. 73 BB47
Tachbrook Rd., Sthl. 64 BD41
Tachbrook Rd., Uxb. 53 AX37
Tachbrook St. SW1 3 M9
Tachbrook St. SW1 66 BW42
Tack Ms. SE4 67 CE45
Tadema Rd. SW10 66 BT43
Tadlows Clo., Upmin. 51 CX35
Tadmor Clo., Sun. 83 BB52
Tadmor St. W12 55 BQ40
Tadorne Rd., Tad. 103 BQ64
Tadworth Ave., N.Mal. 85 BO53
Tadworth Lo. Est., Mitch. 86 BV52
Tadworth Par., Horn. 50 CU35
Tadworth Rd. NW2 46 BP34
Tadworth St., Tad. 103 BQ65
Taeping St. E14 67 CE42
Taffys How, Mitch. 86 BU51
Taft Way E3 57 CE38
St. Leonards St.
Tait Rd., Croy. 87 CA54
Takeley Clo., Rom. 41 CS30
Takeley Clo., Wal.Abb. 21 CF20
Talacre Rd. NW5 56 BV36
Talbot Ave. N2 47 BT31
Talbot Ave., Slou. 62 AS41
Talbot Ave., Wat. 36 BE26
Talbot Clo. N15 48 CA31
Talbot Rd.
Talbot Clo., Reig. 121 BS71
Lymden Gdns.
Talbot Ct. EC3 2 L10
Talbot Ct. EC3 57 BZ40
Gracechurch St.
Talbot Ct., Hem.H. 8 AX14
Crabtree La.
Talbot Cres. NW4 46 BP32
Talbot Gdns., Ilf. 50 CO34
Talbot Pl. SE3 68 CG44
Talbot Pl., Slou. 62 AR44
Talbot Rd. E6 58 CK37
Talbot Rd. E7 49 CH35
Talbot Rd. N6 47 BV32
Talbot Rd. N15 48 CA31
Talbot Rd. N22 38 BW30
Talbot Rd. W2 56 BS39
Talbot Rd. W11 55 BR39
Talbot Rd. W13 54 BJ40
Talbot Rd., Ashf. 73 AY49
Talbot Rd., Brom. 88 CH52
Talbot Rd., Cars. 95 BV56
Talbot Rd., Dag. 59 CQ36
Talbot Rd., Har. 36 BH30
Talbot Rd., Hat. 10 BP11
Talbot Rd., Islw. 64 BJ45
Talbot Rd., Rick. 35 AY26
Talbot Rd., Sthl. 64 BE42
Talbot Rd., Th.Hth. 87 BZ52
Talbot Rd., Twick. 74 BH47
Talbot Rd., Wem. 54 BK36
Talbot Sq. W2 1 B9
Talbot Sq. W2 56 BT39
Talbot Wk. W11 55 BQ40
Lancaster Rd.
Talbot Yd. SE1 4 K3
Talbot Yd. SE1 57 BZ40
Borough High St.
Talbrook, Brwd. 42 CZ27
Talents Clo., Dart. 80 CX49
Taleworth Clo., Ash. 102 BK63
Taleworth Rd., Ash. 102 BK63
Talfourd Pl. SE15 67 CA44
Talfourd Rd. SE15 67 CA44
Talgarth Rd. W6 65 BQ42
Talgarth Wk. NW9 46 BO32
Talisman Sq. SE26 77 CB49
Talisman Way, Epsom 103 BQ61
Talisman Way, Wem. 46 BL34
Tall Elms Clo., Brom. 88 CG53
Tall Oaks, Amer. 25 AO22
Tall Trees SW16 86 BX52
Tall Trees, Slou. 62 AU44
Park St.
Tall Trees Clo., Horn. 51 CW32
Tallack Clo., Har. 36 BH29
Tallack Rd. E10 48 CD33
Tallents Clo., S.at H. 80 CX50
Tallis Gro. SE7 68 CH43
Tallis St. EC4 2 E10
Tallis St. EC4 56 BY40
Tallis Way, Brwd. 27 BK23
Tallon Rd., Brwd. 122 DF25
Tally Ho Cor. N12 38 BT28
Tally Rd., Oxt. 115 CK69
Talma Gdns., Twick. 74 BH46
Talma Rd. SW2 66 BY45
Talmage Clo. SE23 77 CC47
Talman Gro., Stan. 36 BK29
Talus Clo., Grays 70 CY42
Brimfield Rd.
Talwin St. E3 57 CE38
Tamar Clo., Upmin. 51 CZ32
Tamar Dr., S.Ock. 60 CY39
Tamar Grn., Hem.H. 8 AY11
Tamar Sq., Wdf.Grn. 40 CH29
Tamar St. SE7 68 CK42
Tamar Way N17 48 CA31
Tamar Way, Slou. 62 AT42
Tamarind Clo., Guil. 109 AQ68

Tamarind Yd. E1 57 CB40
Asher Way
Tamarisk Clo., St.Alb. 9 BG11
New Grns. Ave.
Tamarisk Rd., S.Ock. 60 DB38
Tamarisk Sq. W12 55 BO40
Tamesis Gdns., Wor.Pk. 85 BO55
Tamesis Strand, Grav. 81 DJ49
Tamian Way, Houns. 64 BD45
Tamplin Ms. W9 56 BS38
Warlock Rd.
Tamworth Ave., Wdf.Grn. 40 CG29
Tamworth Gdns., Pnr. 36 BD30
Tamworth La., Mitch. 86 BV51
Tamworth Pk., Mitch. 86 BV52
Tamworth Pl., Croy. 87 BZ55
Tamworth Rd., Croy. 86 BY55
Tamworth St. SW6 66 BS43
Tan Ho. La., Brwd. 33 CX24
Tancred Rd. N4 47 BY32
Tandridge Dr., Orp. 88 CM54
Tandridge Gdns., Gdse. 114 CD68
Tandridge La., Oxt. 114 CE69
Tandridge Rd., Warl. 105 CC63
Tanfield Ave. NW2 46 BO35
Tanfield Clo., Chsnt. 21 CB17
Spicersfield
Tanfield Rd., Croy. 96 BZ56
Tangent Rd., Rom. 42 CV30
Tangier La. (Eton), Wind. 61 AO43
Tangier Rd., Guil. 118 AT71
Tangier Rd., Rich. 65 BM45
Tangier Way, Tad. 103 BR62
Tangier Wd., Tad. 103 BR62
Tanglebury Clo., Brom. 88 CK52
Oldfield Rd.
Tangles Clo., Uxb. 53 AZ38
Tanglewood Clo., Cher. 82 AQ55
Tanglewood Clo., Croy. 87 CC55
Tanglewood Clo., Stan. 36 BH27
Tanglewood Clo., Wok. 100 AU61
Tanglewood Way, Felt. 73 BC48
Tangley Gro. SW15 75 BO46
Tangley La., Guil. 109 AP68
Tangley Pk. Rd., Hmptn. 74 BE49
Tanglyn Ave., Shep. 83 AZ53
Tangmere Cres., Horn. 59 CU36
Tangmere Gdns., Nthlt. 54 BD37
Tangmere Way NW9 37 BO30
Tanhouse Rd., Oxt. 114 CF69
Tanhurst Wk. SE2 69 CP41
Alsike Rd.
Tank Hill Rd., Grays 70 CX42
Tank La., Grays 70 CX42
Tankerfield Pl., St.Alb. 9 BG13
Romeland Hill
Tankerton Rd., Surb. 85 BL55
Tankerton St. WC1 2 A3
Tankerton St. WC1 56 BX38
Cromer St.
Tankerville Rd. SW16 76 BW50
Tankridge Rd. NW2 46 BP34
Tanner St. SE1 4 N5
Tanner St. SE1 67 CA41
Tanner St., Bark. 58 CM36
Tanners Clo., Walt. 83 BC53
Tanners Dean, Lthd. 102 BK64
Tanners End La. N18 39 CA28
Tanners Hill SE8 67 CD44
Tanners Hill, Abb.L. 17 BB19
Tanners Hill, Bet. 120 BM71
Tanners La., Ilf. 49 CM31
Tanners Wd. La., Abb.L. 17 BB19
Tannery, The, Red. 121 BU70
Oakdene Rd.
Tannery Clo., Beck. 87 CC52
Tannery Clo., Dag. 50 CR34
Tannery La., Wok. 100 AU65
Tannington Ter. N4 47 BY34
Tannsfeld Rd. SE26 77 CC49
Tannsfield Clo., Hem.H. 8 AY12
Tannsmore Clo., Hem.H. 8 AY12
Tanrides Rd., Orp. 88 CM54
Tansley Clo. N7 47 BW35
Hilldrop Rd.
Tanswell Est. SE1 4 E5
Tanswell Est. SE1 66 BY41
Tanswell St. SE1 4 D5
Tanswell St. SE1 66 BY41
Tansy Clo. E6 58 CL39
Tansy Clo., Guil. 118 AU69
Tansy Clo., Rom. 42 CW29
Tansycroft, Welw.G.C. 5 BS7
Tant Ave. E16 58 CG39
Tantallon Rd. SW12 76 BV47
Tantony Gro., Rom. 50 CP31
Tanworth Clo., Nthwd. 35 BA29
Thirlmere Gdns.
Tanys Dell, Harl. 6 CO9
Tanza Rd. NW3 47 BU35
Tapestry Clo., Sutt. 95 BS57
Taplow SE17 4 L10
Taplow Rd. N13 39 BZ28
North Circular Rd.
Taplow St. N1 2 J1
Taplow St. N1 57 BZ37
Tapners Rd., Reig. 120 BO73
Tapp St. E1 57 CB38
Tappesfield Rd. SE15 67 CC45
Tapster St., Barn. 28 BR24
Tara Pk., Couls. 104 BU63
Taransay, Hem.H. 8 AZ14
Tarbay La., Wind. 61 AK45
Tarbert Rd. SE22 77 CA46
Tarbert Wk. E1 57 CC39
Juniper St.
Target Clo., Felt. 73 BB46
Tariff Rd. N17 39 CB29
Tarleton Gdns. SE23 77 CB48
Tarling Clo., Sid. 79 CO48
Tarling Est. E1 57 CB40
Tarling Rd. E16 58 CG39
Tarling Rd. N2 38 BT30

Tarling St. E1 57 CC39
Tarmac Way, Houns. 63 AW43
Tarn St. SE1 4 H7
Tarn St. SE1 67 BZ41
Tarnbank, Enf. 29 BX25
Tarnwood Pk. SE9 78 CK47
Tarnwood Pk. Est. SE9 78 CK47
Tarnworth Rd., Rom. 42 CX28
Tarpan Way, Brox. 21 CD16
Tarragon Dr., Guil. 109 AQ68
Tarragon Gro. SE26 77 CC50
Tarrant Ct., Guil. 109 AQ68
Grange Rd.
Tarrant Pl. W1 1 E7
Tarrington Clo. SW16 76 BW49
Tarry La. SE8 67 CD42
Yeoman St.
Tartar Rd., Cob. 93 BD60
Tarver Rd. SE17 66 BY42
Tarves Way SE10 67 CE43
Tash Pl. N11 38 BV28
Woodland Rd.
Tasker Clo., Hayes 63 BA43
Tasker Rd. NW3 47 BU35
Tasker Rd., Grays 71 DG41
Tasman Ct., Ashf. 73 BB50
Warren Rd.
Tasman Ho., Til. 71 DG44
Leicester Rd.
Tasman Rd. SW9 66 BX45
Tasman Wk. E16 58 CJ39
Royal Rd.
Tasmania Ter. N18 39 BZ29
Tasso Rd. W6 65 BR43
Tatam Rd. NW10 55 BN36
Tate Clo., Lthd. 102 BK65
Tate Rd. E16 58 CK40
Tate Rd., Ger.Cr. 34 AS28
Tate Rd., Sutt. 95 BS56
Tatnell Rd. SE23 77 CD46
Tatsfield App. Rd., West. 106 CH65
Tatsfield Ave., Wal.Abb. 12 CF15
Tatsfield La., West. 106 CK64
Tattenham Cor. Rd., Epsom 103 BO62
Tattenham Cres., Epsom 103 BP62
Tattenham Gro., Epsom 103 BP62
Tattenham Way, Tad. 103 BQ62
Tattersall Clo. SE9 78 CK46
Tattershall Dr., Hem.H. 8 AZ10
Tatum St. SE17 4 L9
Tatum St. SE17 67 BZ42
Taunton Ave. SW20 85 BP51
Taunton Ave., Cat. 105 CA65
Taunton Ave., Couls. 104 BY63
Taunton Ave., Houns. 64 BG44
Taunton Clo., Bexh. 69 CS44
Taunton Clo., Ilf. 40 CN29
Wickets Way
Taunton Clo., Sutt. 86 BS54
Taunton Dr., Enf. 29 BY24
Taunton La., Couls. 104 BY63
Taunton Ms. NW1 1 E5
Taunton Ms. NW1 56 BU38
Gloucester Pl.
Taunton Pl. NW1 1 E4
Taunton Pl. NW1 56 BU38
Taunton Rd. SE12 78 CG46
Taunton Rd., Grav. 81 DD46
Taunton Rd., Grnf. 54 BF37
Taunton Rd., Rom. 42 CV28
Taunton Vale, Grav. 81 DH48
Taunton Way, Stan. 46 BL31
Tavern La. SW9 66 BY44
Myatts Flds. Dev.
Taverner Sq. N5 48 BZ35
Taverners, Hem.H. 8 AY12
Taverners Clo. W11 55 BR40
Addison Ave.
Taverners Way E4 40 CG26
Douglas Rd.
Tavistock Ave. E17 48 CC31
Tavistock Ave., Grnf. 54 BJ37
Tavistock Ave., St.Alb. 9 BG15
Tavistock Clo., Pot.B. 20 BT19
Tavistock Clo., Rom. 42 CV30
Tavistock Clo., St.Alb. 9 BG15
Tavistock Clo., Stai. 73 AX50
Shaftesbury Cres.
Tavistock Cres. W11 55 BR39
Tavistock Cres., Mitch. 86 BX52
Tavistock Gdns., Ilf. 49 CN35
Tavistock Gro., Croy. 87 BZ54
Tavistock Ms. E18 49 CH31
Avon Way
Tavistock Pl. N14 29 BV25
Tavistock Pl. WC1 1 Q4
Tavistock Pl. WC1 56 BX38
Tavistock Pl., Ilf. 49 CH31
Tavistock Rd. E7 49 CG35
Tavistock Rd. E15 58 CG36
Tavistock Rd. E18 49 CH31
Tavistock Rd. N4 48 BZ32
Tavistock Rd. NW10 55 BO37
Tavistock Rd. W11 55 BR39
Tavistock Rd., Brom. 88 CG52
Tavistock Rd., Cars. 86 BT54
Tavistock Rd., Croy. 87 BZ54
Tavistock Rd., Edg. 37 BL30
Tavistock Rd., Uxb. 44 BA35
Tavistock Rd., Wat. 27 BD23
Tavistock Rd., Well. 69 CP44
Tavistock Rd., West Dr. 53 AX40
Tavistock Sq. WC1 1 P4
Tavistock Sq. WC1 56 BW38
Tavistock St. WC2 2 A10
Tavistock St. WC2 56 BX40
Tavistock Ter. N19 47 BW34
Tavistock Wk., Cars. 86 BY54
Taviton St. WC1 1 N4
Taviton St. WC1 56 BW38
Tavy Bri. SE2 69 CP41
Tavy Clo. SE11 4 E10
Tavy Clo. SE11 66 BY42
White Hart St.
Tawney Common, Epp. 23 CR18
Tawney Rd. SE28 59 CO40
Tawneys Rd., Harl. 13 CN12
Tawny Ave., Upmin. 51 CX35
Tawny Clo., Felt. 73 BC48
Tawny Way SE16 67 CC42
Tay Way, Rom. 41 CT30
Tayben Ave., Twick. 74 BH46
Taybridge Rd. SW11 66 BV45
Tayburn Clo. E14 57 CF39
St. Leonards Rd.
Tayfield Clo., Uxb. 44 BA34
Tayles Hill, Epsom 94 BO58
Taylifers, Harl. 13 CL13
Taylor Ave., Rich. 65 BM44
Taylor Clo. N17 39 CB29
Northumberland Pk.
Taylor Clo., Hmptn. 74 BG49
Taylor Clo., Orp. 97 CM56
Strickland Way
Taylor Clo., Rom. 41 CR29
Taylor Clo., St.Alb. 9 BJ11
Taylor Rd., Ash. 102 BK62
Taylor Rd., Mitch. 76 BU50
Taylor Rd., Wall. 95 BV56
Taylor St. SE18 68 CL42
Taylors Ave., Hodd. 12 CE12
Taylors Bldgs. SE18 68 CL42
Spray St.
Taylors Clo., Sid. 78 CN49
Taylors Ct. E15 48 CF35
Taylors Grn. W3 55 BO39
Long Dr.
Taylors La. NW10 55 BO36
Taylors La. SE26 77 CB49
Taylors La., Barn. 28 BR23
Taylors Rd., Chesh. 16 AO18
Taymount Gra. SE23 77 CC48
Taymount Ri. SE23 77 CC48
Taynton Dr., Red. 113 BW68
Tayport Clo. N1 56 BX36
Taywood Rd., Nthlt. 54 BE38
Teak Clo. SE16 57 CD40
Teal Clo. E16 58 CJ39
Fulmer Rd.
Teal Clo., S.Croy. 96 CC59
Teal Dr., Nthwd. 35 BA29
Teale St. E2 57 CB37
Tealing Dr., Epsom 94 BN56
Teasel Clo., Croy. 87 CC54
Teasel Way E15 58 CG38
Memorial Ave.
Teazlewood Pk., Lthd. 102 BJ62
Tebworth Rd. N17 39 CA29
Church Rd.
Tedder Clo., Esher 93 BK56
Mansfield Rd.
Tedder Clo., Hayes 63 BA43
West End La.
Tedder Clo., Ruis. 44 BC35
Tedder Clo., Uxb. 53 AY36
Tedder Rd., Hem.H. 8 AZ13
Tedder Rd., S.Croy. 96 CC57
Teddington Clo., Epsom 94 BN58
Teddington Pk., Tedd. 74 BH49
Teddington Pk. Rd., Tedd. 74 BH49
Tedworth Gdns. SW3 66 BU42
Tedworth Sq. SW3 66 BU42
Tee, The W3 55 BO39
Tees Ave., Grnf. 54 BH37
Tees Clo., Upmin. 51 CY32
Tees Dr., Rom. 42 CV27
Teesdale, Hem.H. 8 AY12
Teesdale Ave., Islw. 64 BJ44
Teesdale Clo. E2 57 CB37
Claredale St.
Teesdale Est. E2 57 CB38
Teesdale Gdns., Islw. 64 BJ44
Teesdale Rd. E11 49 CG32
Teesdale Rd., Dart. 80 CY47
Teesdale St. E2 57 CB37
Teevan Clo., Croy. 87 CB54
Teevan Rd., Croy. 87 CB54
Teggs La., Wok. 100 AV61
Teignmouth Clo. SW4 66 BW45
Teignmouth Clo., Edg. 37 BL30
Teignmouth Gdns., Grnf. 54 BJ37
Teignmouth Rd. NW2 46 BQ35
Teignmouth Rd., Well. 69 CP44
Telcote Way, Ruis. 45 BD33
Telegraph Hill NW3 47 BS34
Telegraph La., Esher 93 BJ57
Telegraph Ms., Ilf. 50 CO33
Eastwood Rd.
Telegraph Rd. SW15 75 BP46
Telegraph St. EC2 2 K8
Telegraph St. EC2 57 BZ39
Telemann Sq. SE3 68 CH45
Telephone Pl. SW6 65 BR43
Telferscot Rd. SW12 76 BW47
Telford Ave. SW2 76 BW47
Telford Clo. SE19 77 CA50
Aubyns Rd.
Telford Clo., Wat. 27 BD21
Telford Ct., St.Alb. 9 BH14
Alma Rd.
Telford Dr., Slou. 61 AN41
Telford Dr., Walt. 84 BD54
Telford Rd. N11 38 BW29
Telford Rd. NW9 46 BO33
The Bdy.
Telford Rd. SE9 78 CM48
Telford Rd. W10 55 BR39
Telford Rd., St.Alb. 18 BK17
Telford Rd., Sthl. 54 BF39
Telford Rd., Twick. 74 BF47
Telford Ter. SW1 66 BW43
Churchill Gdns. Rd.
Telford Way W3 55 BO39
Telford Way, Hayes 54 BE39
Telfords Yd. E1 57 CB40
The Highway
Telham Rd. E6 58 CL37
Tell Gro. SE22 67 CA45
Tellisford, Esher 93 BF56
Tellson Ave. SE18 68 CJ44
Telscombe Clo., Orp. 88 CN55
Telston La., Sev. 107 CT62
Temeraire St. SE16 67 CC41
Swan Rd.
Temperance St., St.Alb. 9 BG13
Temperley Rd. SW12 76 BV47
Tempest Ave., Pot.B. 20 BT19
Tempest Rd., Egh. 72 AU50
Tempest Way, Rain. 59 CU36
Templar Dr. SE28 59 CP39
Templar Ho. NW2 55 BR36
Templar Pl., Hmptn. 74 BF50
Templar St. SE5 66 BY44
Templars Ave. NW11 46 BR32
Templars Cres. N3 38 BS30
Templars Dr., Har. 36 BG29
Temple EC4 2 D10
Temple, The EC4 56 BY40
Temple Ave. EC4 2 E10
Temple Ave. EC4 56 BY40
Temple Ave. N20 38 BT26
Temple Ave., Croy. 87 CD55
Temple Ave., Dag. 50 CR33
Temple Bank, Harl. 6 CO8
Temple Bar Rd., Wok. 100 AP63
Temple Clo. E11 49 CG33
Wadley Rd.
Temple Clo. N3 37 BR30
Cyprus Rd.
Temple Clo. SE28 68 CM41
Temple Clo., Chsnt. 21 CB19
Temple Clo., Wat. 26 BB23
Temple Ct., Pot.B. 19 BQ19
Temple Cft., Ashf. 73 BA50
Temple Fld. Clo., Wey. 92 AW57
Temple Fortune Hill NW11 47 BS32
Temple Fortune La. NW11 46 BR32
Temple Gdns. NW11 46 BR32
Temple Gdns., Dag. 50 CP34
Bennetts Castle La.
Temple Gdns., Rick. 35 AZ28
Temple Gdns., Stai. 82 AV51
Temple Gdns EC4 56 BY40
Middle Temple La.
Temple Gro. NW11 47 BS32
Temple Gro., Enf. 29 BY24
Temple Hill, Dart. 80 CW46
Temple Hill Sq., Dart. 80 CW46
Temple La. EC4 2 E9
Temple La. EC4 56 BY39
Temple Mead, Harl. 13 CH10
Temple Mead, Hem.H. 8 AX12
Temple Mead Clo., Stan. 36 BJ29
Temple Mill La. E15 48 CE35
Temple Mill Rd. E15 48 CE35
Temple Pk., Uxb. 53 AZ38
Temple Pl. WC2 2 C10
Temple Pl. WC2 56 BX40
Temple Rd. E6 58 CK37
Temple Rd. N8 47 BX31
Temple Rd. NW2 46 BQ35
Temple Rd. W4 65 BN41
Temple Rd. W5 64 BK41
Temple Rd., Croy. 96 BZ56
Temple Rd., Epsom 94 BN59
Temple Rd., Houns. 64 BF45
Temple Rd., Rich. 65 BL45
Temple Rd., West. 106 CJ61
Hillcrest Rd.
Temple Rd., Wind. 61 AO44
Temple Sheen SW14 65 BN45
Temple Sheen Rd. SW14 65 BM45
Temple St. E2 57 CB37
Temple Way, Sutt. 86 BT55
Temple W. Ms. SE11 4 F7
Temple Wd. La., Slou. 43 AO35
Templecombe Ms., Wok. 100 AT61
Templecombe Rd. E9 57 CC37
Templecombe Way, Mord. 85 BR53
Templedene Ave., Stai. 73 AW50
Templehof Ave. NW2 46 BQ33
Templeman Clo., Pur. 104 BY61
Templeman Rd. W7 54 BH39
Templemead Clo. W3 55 BO39
Carlisle Ave.
Templemere, Wey. 83 BA55
Templepan La., Rick. 26 AY22
Templer Ave., Grays 71 DG42
Templer Dr., Grav. 81 DG49
Templeton Ave. E4 39 CE27
Templeton Clo. SE19 87 BZ51
Templeton Pl. SW5 66 BS42
Templeton Rd. N15 48 BZ32
Templewood W13 54 BJ39
Templewood, Welw.G.C. 5 BQ6
Templewood Ave. NW3 47 BS34
Templewood Gdns. NW3 47 BS34
Tempsford, Welw.G.C. 5 BT8
Tempsford Ave., Borwd. 28 BN24
Tempsford Clo., Enf. 30 BZ24
Gladbeck Way
Temsford Clo., Har. 36 BG30
Ten Acre, Wok. 100 AQ62
Abercorn Way
Ten Acre La., Egh. 82 AU51
Ten Acres, Lthd. 102 BG65
The Grn.
Ten St. EC2 57 BZ39
Tenbury Clo. E7 49 CJ35
Tenbury Ct. SW2 76 BW47
Tenby Ave., Har. 36 BJ30
Tenby Clo. N15 48 CA31
Tenby Clo., Rom. 50 CQ32
Tenby Gdns., Nthlt. 54 BF36
Tenby Rd. E17 48 CD32
Tenby Rd., Edg. 37 BL30
Tenby Rd., Enf. 30 CC24
Tenby Rd., Rom. 50 CQ32
Tenby Rd., Well. 69 CP44
Tench St. E1 57 CB40
Tenchleys La., Oxt. 115 CJ69
Tenda Rd. SE16 67 CB42
Tendring Rd., Harl. 13 CM12
Tendring Way, Rom. 50 CP32
Tenham Ave. SW2 76 BW48
Tenison Ct. W1 1 L10
Tenison Ct. W1 56 BW40
Kingly St.
Tenison Way SE1 4 C3
Tenison Way SE1 56 BX40
Tennand Clo., Chsnt. 21 CA16
Tenniel Clo. W2 58 CJ40
Porchester Gdns.
Tennis St. SE1 4 K4
Tennis St. SE1 67 BZ41
Tennison Ave., Borwd. 28 BM25
Tennison Clo., Couls. 104 BY63
Tennison Rd. SE25 87 CA52
Tenniswood Rd., Enf. 30 CA23
Tennyson Ave. E11 49 CH33
Tennyson Ave. E12 58 CK36
Tennyson Ave. NW9 46 BN31
Tennyson Ave., Grays 71 DD41
Tennyson Ave., N.Mal. 85 BP53
Tennyson Ave., Twick. 74 BH47
Tennyson Ave., Wal.Abb. 22 CG20
Tennyson Clo., Felt. 73 BC46
Tennyson Clo., Well. 68 CN44
Tennyson Ct., Rich. 74 BK49
Tennyson Rd. E10 48 CE34
Tennyson Rd. E15 58 CG36
Tennyson Rd. E17 48 CD32
Tennyson Rd. NW6 55 BR37
Tennyson Rd. NW7 37 BP28
Tennyson Rd. SE20 77 CC50
Tennyson Rd. SW19 76 BT50
Tennyson Rd. W7 54 BH40
Tennyson Rd., Ashf. 73 AY49
Tennyson Rd., Brwd. 122 DE26
Tennyson Rd., Dart. 80 CX46
Tennyson Rd., Houns. 64 BG44
Tennyson Rd., Rom. 41 CU29
Tennyson Rd., St.Alb. 18 BF16
Tennyson Rd., Well. 68 CN44
Shelley Dr.
Tennyson Rd., Wey. 92 AY56
Tennyson St. SW8 66 BV44
Tennyson Wk., Grav. 81 DE48
Tennyson Wk., Til. 71 DG44
Tennyson Way, Horn. 50 CU34
Tensing Ave., Grav. 81 DF48
Tensing Rd., Sthl. 64 BF41
Tent St. E1 57 CB38
Tentelow La., Sthl. 64 BF42
Tenter Grd. E1 2 P7
Tenter Gro. E1 57 CA39
Brune St.
Tenterden Clo. NW4 46 BQ31
Tenterden Clo. SE9 78 CK49
Framlingham Cres.
Tenterden Dr. NW4 46 BQ31
Tenterden Gdns. NW4 46 BQ31
Tenterden Gdns., Croy. 87 CB54
Tenterden Gro. NW4 46 BQ31
Tenterden Rd. N17 39 CA29
Tenterden Rd., Croy. 87 CB54
Tenterden Rd., Dag. 50 CQ34
Tenterden St. W1 1 K9
Tenterden St. W1 56 BV39
Tenzing Rd., Hem.H. 8 AZ13
Terborch Way SE22 77 CA46
Dulwich Gro.
Tercel Path, Chig. 41 CO28
Terence Clo., Grav. 81 DJ48
Teresa Gdns., Wal.Cr. 21 CC20
Teresa Ms. E17 48 CE31
Cairo Rd.
Teresa Wk. N10 47 BV32
Terling Clo. E11 49 CG34
Terling Rd., Dag. 50 CR34
Terling Wk. N1 57 BZ37
Popham St.
Terlings, The, Brwd. 42 DA27
Kavanagh Rd.
Terminus Pl. SW1 3 K7
Terminus Pl. SW1 66 BV41
Terminus St., Harl. 6 CM10
Tern Gdns., Upmin. 51 CZ33
Tern Way, Brwd. 42 CZ28
River Rd.
Terrace, The N3 37 BR30
Hendon La.
Terrace, The NW6 56 BS37
Terrace, The SW13 65 BO44
Terrace, The, Dor. 119 BK72
Terrace, The, Grav. 81 DG46
Terrace, The, Kings.T. 84 BK51
Church Gro.
Terrace, The, Maid. 61 AH41
Terrace, The, Rich. 75 BL46
Terrace, The, Sev. 107 CS64
Terrace, The, Wey. 92 AY56
Terrace Gdns. SW13 65 BO44
Terrace Gdns., Wat. 26 BC23
Terrace La., Rich. 75 BL46
Friars Stile Rd.
Terrace Rd. E9 57 CC36
Terrace Rd. E13 58 CH37
Terrace Rd., Walt. 83 BC54
Terrace St., Grav. 81 DG46
Terrace Wk., Dag. 50 CQ35
Terraces, The, Dart. 80 CY47
Terrapin Rd. SW17 76 BV48
Terretts Pl. N1 56 BY36
Upper St.
Terrick Rd. N22 38 BX30
Terrick St. W12 55 BP39
Terrilands, Pnr. 45 BE31
Terront Rd. N15 48 BZ32
Terry Way, Brom. 88 CH51
Church Rd.
Tessa Sanderson Pl. SW8 66 BV
Heath Rd.
Testard Rd., Guil. 118 AR
Testers Clo., Oxt. 115 CH
Testerton Wk. W11 55 BQ
Lancaster Rd.
Testwood Rd., Wind. 61 AL
Tetbury Pl. N1 56 BY
Upper St.
Tetcott Rd. SW10 66 BT
Tetherdown N10 38 BV
Tethys Rd., Hem.H. 8 AY
Tetterby Way SE16 67 CB
The Bonamy Est. W.
Teversham La. SW8 66 BX
Teviot Ave., S.Ock. 60 CW
Teviot Clo., Well. 69 CO
Stuart Rd.
Teviot St. E14 57 CF
Tewin Clo., St.Alb. 9 BK
Tewin Ct., Welw.G.C. 5 B
Tewin Hill, Welw.G.C. 5 B
Tewin Rd., Hem.H. 8 BA
Tewin Rd., Welw.G.C. 5 B
Tewkesbury Ave. SE23 77 CB
Tewkesbury Ave., Pnr. 45 BE
Tewkesbury Clo. N15 48 BZ
Tewkesbury Rd.
Tewkesbury Clo., Wey. 92 AX
Tewkesbury Gdns. NW9 46 BM
Tewkesbury Rd. N15 48 BZ
Tewkesbury Rd. W13 54 BJ
Talbot Rd.
Tewkesbury Rd., Cars. 86 BT
Tewkesbury Ter. N11 38 BW
Tewson Rd. SE18 68 CN
Teynham Ave., Enf. 30 BZ
Teynham Grn., Brom. 88 CH
Teynton Ter. N17 39 BZ
Thackeray Ave. N17 39 CB
Thackeray Ave., Til. 71 DG
Thackeray Clo. SW19 75 BQ
Thackeray Clo., Uxb. 53 AZ
Thackeray Dr., Rom. 50 CO
Thackeray Rd. E6 58 CJ
Thackeray Rd. SW8 66 BV
Thackeray St. W8 66 BS
Thackery Clo., Har. 45 BF
Thakeham Clo. SE26 77 CB
Thakrah Clo. N2 38 BT
Thalia Clo. SE10 67 CF
Feathers Pl.
Thalmassing Clo., Brwd. 122 DD
Roth Dr.
Thame Rd. SE16 67 CC4
Thames Ave. SW10 66 BT4
Thames Ave., Cher. 83 AW
Eastern Ave.
Thames Ave., Dag. 59 CS
Thames Ave., Grnf. 54 BH3
Thames Ave., Hem.H. 8 AY1
Thames Ave., Wind. 61 AO4
Thames Bank SW14 65 BN4
Thames Clo., Cher. 83 AX
Thames Clo., Hmptn. 84 BF5
Thames Clo., Rain. 59 CU
Thames Dr., Grays 71 DG4
Thames Dr., Ruis. 44 BA3
Thames Mead, Walt. 83 BC5
Thames Mead, Wind. 61 AM4
Thames Meadow, E.Mol. 84 BF5
Thames Pl. E14 57 CD4
Thames Prom., Twick. 64 BJ4
Thames Rd. E16 58 CJ4
Thames Rd. W4 65 BM4
Thames Rd., Bark. 58 CN3
Thames Rd., Dart. 69 CT4
Thames Rd., Grays 71 DD4
Thames Rd., Slou. 62 AT4
Thames Side, Cher. 83 AX5
Thames Side, Kings.T. 84 BK5
Thames Side, Stai. 83 AW5
Thames Side, Tedd. 74 BK5
Thames Side, Wind. 61 AO4
Thames St. SE10 67 CE4
Thames St., Hmptn. 84 BF5
Thames St., Kings.T. 84 BK5
Thames St., Stai. 72 AV4
Thames St., Sun. 83 BC5
Thames St., Walt. 83 BB5
Thames St., Wey. 83 AZ5
Thames St., Wind. 61 AO4
Thames Vw., Grays 71 DG4
Thames Vw. Est., Bark. 58 CN3
Thames Vill. W4 65 BN4
Thames Way, Grav. 81 DG4
Thamesbank Pl. SE28 59 CP3
Thamesdale, St.Alb. 19 BL1
Thamesfield Ct., Shep. 83 BA5
Russell Rd.
Thamesgate Clo., Rich. 74 BJ4
Thameshill Ave., Rom. 41 CS3
Thameside, Tedd. 74 BK5
Thamesmead, Walt. 83 BC5
Thamesmere Dr. SE28 59 CO4
Thamesvale Clo., Houns. 64 BF4
Lampton Rd.
Thamesview Clo., Green. 80 CZ4
Thamley, Grays 70 CX4
Thane Vill. N7 47 BX3
Thanescroft Gdns., Croy. 87 CA5
Thanet Pl., Croy. 96 BZ5
Thanet Rd., Bex. 79 CR4
Thanet Rd., Erith 69 CT4
Thanet St. WC1 1 Q
Thanet St. WC1 56 BX3
Thanington Ct. SE9 78 CN4
Thant Clo. E10 48 CE3
Tharp Rd., Wall. 95 BW5
Thatcham Gdns. N20 38 BT2
Thatcher Clo., West Dr. 63 AY4
Thatchers Clo., Loug. 31 CM2
Mannock Dr.

atchers Cft., Hem.H. 8 AY11
atchers La., Guil. 109 AO67
atchers Way, Islw. 74 BG46
eapers Way
atches Gro., Rom. 50 CQ31
avies Inn EC1 2 E8
avies Inn EC1 56 BY39
t. Andrew St.
axted Grn., Brwd. 122 DE25
axted Pl. SW20 75 BQ50
axted Rd. SE9 78 CM48
axted Rd., Buck.H. 40 CJ26
axted Wk., Rain. 59 CT37
axted Way, Wal.Abb. 21 CF20
axton Rd. W14 65 BR43
ayer St. W1 1 H7
ayer St. W1 56 BV39
ayers Fm. Rd., Beck. 87 CD51
aynesfield, Pot.B. 20 BT19
eatre St. SW11 66 BU45
eberton St. N1 56 BY37
eed St. SE1 4 E3
eed St. SE1 56 BY40
elma Clo., Grav. 81 DJ49
elma Gdns. SE3 68 CK44
elma Gdns., Felt. 74 BE48
elma Gro., Tedd. 74 BJ50
eobald Clo., Borwd. 28 BL23
heobald St.
eobald Cres., Har. 36 BF30
eobald Rd. E17 48 CD33
eobald Rd., Croy. 86 BY55
eobald St. SE1 4 K7
eobald St. SE1 67 BZ41
eobald St., Borwd. 28 BL23
eobald St., Rad. 27 BJ21
eobalds Ave. N12 38 BT28
eobalds Ave., Grays 71 DE42
eobalds Clo., Cuffley 20 BX18
eobalds Ct. N4 48 BZ34
ings Cres. Est.
eobalds La., Chsnt. 21 CB19
eobalds Pk. Rd., Enf. 29 BY21
eobalds Rd. WC1 2 A7
eobalds Rd. WC1 56 BX39
eobalds Rd., Cuffley 20 BX18
eodore Rd. SE13 77 CF46
epps Clo., Red. 121 BX72
erapia La., Croy. 86 BW54
erapia La., Croy. 86 BX53
erapia Rd. SE22 77 CB46
eresa Rd. W6 65 BP42
eresas Wk., Croy. 96 BZ58
erfield Ct. N4 48 BZ34
ings Cres. Est.
erfield Rd., St.Alb. 9 BG12
ermopylae Gate E14 67 CE42
eseus Wk. N1 2 G1
eseus Wk. N1 56 BY37
elson Pl.
esiger Rd. SE20 77 CC50
essaly Rd. SW8 66 BW43
etford Clo. N13 38 BY29
etford Gdns., Dag. 59 CQ37
etford Rd., Ashf. 73 AY49
etford Rd., Dag. 59 CP37
etford Rd., N.Mal. 85 BN53
eydon Ct., Wal.Abb. 22 CH20
bbots Dr.
eydon Gdns., Rain. 59 CT36
eydon Gro., Epp. 23 CO18
eydon Gro., Wdf.Grn. 40 CJ29
eydon Pk. Rd., Epp. 31 CN22
eydon Pl., Epp. 22 CN19
eydon Rd. E5 48 CC34
eydon Rd., Epp. 22 CM20
eydon St. E17 48 CD33
icket, The, West Dr. 53 AY39
icket Cres., Sutt. 95 BT56
icket Gro. SE19 77 CB50
nerley Rd.
icket Gro., Dag. 59 CP36
icket Rd. SE20 77 CB50
icket Rd., Sutt. 95 BT56
icketts, Sev. 108 CV65
ickhorne La., Stai. 73 AX50
ird Ave. E12 49 CK35
ird Ave. E13 58 CH38
ird Ave. E17 48 CE32
ird Ave. W3 55 BO40
ird Ave. W10 55 BR38
ird Ave., Dag. 59 CR37
ird Ave., Enf. 30 CA25
ird Ave., Grays 70 DA43
ird Ave., Harl. 13 CK11
ird Ave., Hayes 53 BB40
ird Ave., Rom. 50 CP32
ird Ave., Wat. 27 BD21
ird Ave., Wem. 45 BK34
ird Clo., E.Mol. 84 BG52
ird Cross Rd., Twick. 74 BG48
ird Way, Wem. 46 BM35
irkleby Clo., Slou. 61 AO40
irleby Rd. SW1 3 M7
irleby Rd. SW1 66 BW41
irleby Rd., Edg. 37 BN30
irlmere Ave., Grnf. 54 BJ38
irlmere Dr., St.Alb. 9 BJ14
irlmere Gdns., Nthwd. 35 BA29
irlmere Gdns., Wem. 45 BK33
irlmere Ri., Brom. 78 CG50
irlmere Rd. N10 38 BV30
irlmere Rd. SW16 76 BW49
irlmere Rd., Bexh. 69 CS44
irlstane, St.Alb. 9 BH13
emsford Rd.
irsk Clo., Nthlt. 54 BF36
irsk Rd. SE25 87 BZ52
irsk Rd. SW11 66 BV45
irsk Rd., Borwd. 28 BM22
irsk Rd., Mitch. 76 BV50
irza Rd., Dart. 80 CW46
istle Clo., Hem.H. 7 AV14
The Foxgloves

Thistle Cft., Hem.H. 7 AV14
The Foxgloves
Thistle Gro. SW10 66 BT42
Thistle Gro., Welw.G.C. 5 BT9
Thistle Mead, Loug. 31 CL24
Thistle Rd., Grav. 81 DJ47
Thistle Wd. Cres., Croy. 96 CF59
Thistlebrook SE2 69 CP41
Thistlecroft, Hem.H. 8 AW14
Thistlecroft Gdns., Stan. 36 BK30
Thistlecroft Rd., Walt. 93 BD56
Thistledene, T.Ditt. 84 BH53
Thistledene, Wey. 91 AV60
Thistledene Ave., Har. 45 BE34
Thistledene Ave., Rom. 41 CR28
Thistledown, Grav. 81 DH50
Thistlemead, Chis. 88 CL51
Thistles, The, Hem.H. 8 AW13
Thistlewaite Rd. E5 48 CB34
Thistlewood Clo. N7 47 BX34
Durham Rd.
Thistleworth Clo., Islw. 64 BG43
Thomas a Beckett Clo., Wem. 45 BH35
Thomas Baines Rd. SW11 66 BT45
Thomas Clo., Brwd. 122 DC27
Thomas Derby Ct. W11 55 BR39
Thomas Doyle St. SE1 4 G6
Thomas Doyle St. SE1 66 BY41
London Rd.
Thomas Dr., Grav. 81 DH48
Thomas La. SE6 77 CE47
Thomas More St. E1 57 CB40
Thomas More Way N2 47 BT31
Thomas Rd. E14 57 CD39
Thomas Rochford Way, Wal.Cr. 21 CD17
Thomas Sims Ct., Horn. 59 CU36
South End Rd.
Thomas St. SE18 68 CL42
Thomas Wall Clo., Sutt. 95 BS56
Robin Hood La.
Thompson Ave. SE5 67 BZ43
Thompson Ave., Rich. 65 BM45
Thompson Clo., Ilf. 49 CM34
Thompson Clo., Slou. 62 AS42
Thompson Rd. SE22 77 CA46
Thompson Rd., Dag. 50 CQ34
Thompson Rd., Uxb. 53 AY36
Thompson Way, Ilf. 49 CM34
Thompsons La., Loug. 31 CG23
Thomson Cres., Croy. 86 BY54
Thomson Rd., Har. 45 BH31
Thong La., Grav. 81 DJ49
Thong La., Sev. 108 DC64
Thorburn Way SW19 86 BT51
Phipps Bri. Rd.
Thoresby St. N1 2 J2
Thoresby St. N1 57 BZ38
Thorkhill Gdns., T.Ditt. 84 BJ54
Thorkhill Rd., T.Ditt. 84 BJ54
Thorley Clo., Wey. 92 AW60
Thorley Gdns., Wok. 92 AW60
Thorley Rd., Grays 71 DD40
Thorn Ave., Bush. 36 BG26
Thorn Ave., Cat. 105 BZ64
Thorn Bank, Edg. 37 BM29
Thorn Bank, Guil. 118 AQ71
Thorn Clo., Brom. 88 CL53
Thorn Clo., Nthlt. 54 BE38
Thorn Dr., Slou. 52 AS39
Thorn La., Rain. 60 CV37
Thornaby Gdns. N18 39 CB29
Thornash Clo., Wok. 100 AR61
Thornash Rd., Wok. 100 AR61
Thornash Way, Wok. 100 AR61
Thornbank Clo., Stai. 73 AW46
Thornbridge Rd., Iver 52 AU37
Thornbury Ave., Islw. 64 BG43
Thornbury Gdns., Borwd. 28 BN24
Thornbury Rd. SW2 76 BX46
Thornbury Rd., Islw. 64 BG43
Thornbury Sq. N6 47 BW33
Thornby Rd. E5 48 CC34
Thorncliffe Rd. SW2 76 BX46
Thorncliffe Rd., Sthl. 64 BE42
Thorncombe Rd. SE22 77 CA46
Thorncroft, Egh. 72 AR50
Thorncroft, Hem.H. 8 AZ14
Thorncroft, Horn. 50 CU32
Thorncroft Clo., Couls. 104 BY63
Waddington Ave.
Thorncroft Dr., Lthd. 102 BJ65
Dorking Rd.
Thorncroft Rd., Sutt. 95 BS56
Thorncroft St. SW8 66 BX43
Thorndales, Brwd. 42 DB28
Thorndean St. SW18 76 BT48
Thorndene Ave. N11 38 BV26
Thorndike Clo. SW10 66 BT43
Thorndike St. SW1 3 N9
Thorndike St. SW1 66 BW42
Thorndon Ave., Brwd. 123 DE31
Thorndon Clo., Orp. 88 CN51
Thorndon Gdns., Epsom 94 BO56
Thorndon Gate, Brwd. 122 DE28
Thorndon Rd., Orp. 88 CN51
Thorndyke Ave., Nthlt. 54 BD37
Thorne Clo. E11 49 CG35
Thorne Clo. E16 58 CG39
Thorne Clo., Ashf. 73 BA50
Thorne Clo., Erith 69 CS43
Thorne Pas. SW13 65 BO44
White Hart La.
Thorne Rd. SW8 66 BX43
Thorne St. SW13 65 BO45
Thorneloe Gdns., Croy. 95 BY56
Thornes Clo., Beck. 87 CF52
Thornet Wd. Rd., Brom. 88 CL52
Thorney Hedge Rd. W4 65 BM42
Thorney La. N., Iver 52 AV40
Thorney La. S., Iver 62 AV41
Thorney Mill Rd., Iver 63 AW41

Thorney St. SW1 3 Q8
Thorney St. SW1 66 BX42
Thorneycroft Clo., Walt. 84 BD53
Thornfield Ave. NW7 37 BR30
Thornfield Rd. W12 65 BP41
Thornfield Rd., Bans. 104 BS62
Thornford Rd. SE13 77 CF46
Thorngate Rd. W9 56 BS38
Thorngrove Rd. E13 58 CH37
Thornham Gro. E15 48 CF35
Thornham St. SE10 67 CE43
Thornhaugh Ms. WC1 1 P5
Thornhaugh St. WC1 1 P6
Thornhaugh St. WC1 56 BW38
Thornhill, Epp. 23 CS16
Thornhill Ave. SE18 68 CN43
Thornhill Ave., Surb. 85 BL55
Thornhill Bri. Wf. N1 56 BX37
Caledonian Rd.
Thornhill Cres. N1 56 BX36
Thornhill Gdns. E10 48 CE34
Thornhill Gdns., Bark. 58 CN36
Thornhill Gro. N1 56 BX36
Lofting Rd.
Thornhill Rd. E10 48 CE34
Thornhill Rd. N1 56 BY36
Thornhill Rd., Croy. 87 BZ54
Thornhill Rd., Nthwd. 35 BA28
Thornhill Rd., Surb. 85 BL55
Thornhill Rd., Uxb. 44 AZ35
Thornhill Sq. N1 56 BX36
Thornhill Way, Shep. 83 AZ53
Sheep Wk.
Thornlaw Rd. SE27 76 BY49
Thornley Clo. N17 39 CB29
Thornley Cres. SW11 66 BT43
Thornley Dr., Har. 45 BF34
Thornley Pl. SE10 68 CG42
Caradoc St.
Thornridge, Brwd. 42 DA26
Greenshaw
Thorns Meadow, West. 107 CP65
Thornsbeach Rd. SE6 77 CF47
Thornsett Pl. SE20 87 CB51
Thornsett Rd. SE20 87 CB51
Thornsett Rd. SW18 76 BS47
Thornton Ave. SW2 76 BW47
Thornton Ave. W4 65 BO42
Thornton Ave., Croy. 86 BX53
Thornton Ave., West Dr. 63 AY41
Thornton Clo., Guil. 118 AQ69
Thornton Clo., West Dr. 63 AY41
Thornton Ct. SW20 85 BQ53
Thornton Dene, Beck. 87 CE51
Thornton Gdns. SW12 76 BW47
Thornton Gro., Pnr. 36 BF29
Thornton Hill SW19 75 BR50
Thornton Pl. W1 1 E6
Thornton Pl. W1 56 BU39
Thornton Rd. E11 48 CF34
Thornton Rd. SW12 76 BW47
Thornton Rd. SW14 65 BN45
Thornton Rd. SW19 75 BQ50
Thornton Rd., Barn. 28 BR24
Thornton Rd., Belv. 69 CR42
Thornton Rd., Brom. 78 CH49
Thornton Rd., Cars. 86 BT54
Thornton Rd., Croy. 86 BX54
Thornton Rd., Ilf. 49 CL35
Thornton Rd., Pot.B. 20 BT18
Thornton Rd. E. SW19 75 BQ50
Thornton Rd.
Thornton Row, Th.Hth. 86 BY53
Thornton St. SW9 66 BT44
Robsart St.
Thornton St., St.Alb. 9 BG13
Thornton Way NW11 47 BS32
Thorntons, Brwd. 122 DE29
Brentwood Rd.
Thorntons Fm. Ave., Rom. 50 CS33
Thorntree Rd. SE7 68 CJ42
Thornville St. SE8 67 CE44
Thornwood Clo. E18 40 CH30
Thornwood Rd. SE13 78 CG46
Thornwood Rd., Epp. 23 CO18
Thorogood Gdns. E15 49 CG35
Thorogood Way, Rain. 59 CT37
Thorold Clo., S.Croy. 96 CC58
Thorold Rd. N22 38 BX29
Thorold Rd., Ilf. 49 CL34
Thoroughfare, The, Tad. 103 BP65
Thorparch Rd. SW8 66 BW44
Thorpe By-pass, Egh. 82 AT52
Thorpe Clo. SE26 77 CC49
Silverdale
Thorpe Clo. W10 55 BR39
Cambridge Gdns.
Thorpe Clo., Croy. 96 CF59
Thorpe Clo., Nthlt. 54 BE36
Thorpe Clo., Orp. 88 CN55
Thorpe Cres. E17 39 CD30
Thorpe Cres., Wat. 36 BD26
Thorpe Hall Ms. W5 54 BK39
Eaton Ri.
Thorpe Hall Rd. E17 39 CF30
Thorpe Lea Rd., Egh. 72 AT50
Thorpe Lo., Horn. 51 CW33
Thorpe Rd. E6 58 CK37
Thorpe Rd. E7 49 CG35
Thorpe Rd. E17 39 CF30
Thorpe Rd. N15 48 CA32
Thorpe Rd., Bark. 58 CM36
Thorpe Rd., Cher. 82 AU52
Thorpe Rd., Kings.T. 75 BL50
Thorpe Rd., St.Alb. 9 BG14
Thorpe Rd., Stai. 72 AU50
Thorpebank Rd. W12 55 BP40
Thorpedale Gdns., Ilf. 49 CL31
Thorpedale Rd. N4 47 BX33
Thorpefield Clo., St.Alb. 9 BK12
Thorpes Clo., Guil. 118 AQ69
Thorpewood Ave. SE26 77 CB48
Thorpland Ave., Uxb. 44 BA34

Thorsden Clo., Wok. 100 AS63
Thorsden Ct., Wok. 100 AS62
Guildford Rd.
Thorsden Way SE19 77 CA49
Oaks Ave.
Thorton Cres., Couls. 104 BX63
Thorverton Rd. NW2 46 BR34
Thoydon Rd. E3 57 CD37
Thrale Rd. SW16 76 BW49
Thrale St. SE1 4 J3
Thrale St. SE1 57 BZ40
Thrasher Clo. E8 57 CA37
Stean St.
Thrawl St. E1 2 Q7
Thrawl St. E1 57 CA39
Threadneedle St. EC2 2 L9
Threadneedle St. EC2 57 BZ39
Three Arch Rd., Red. 121 BU72
Three Cherrytrees La., Hem.H. 8 AZ11
Three Clo. La., Berk. 7 AR13
Three Colts La. E2 57 CB38
Three Colts St. E14 57 CD39
Three Cors., Bexh. 69 CR44
Three Cors., Hem.H. 8 AZ14
Three Cups Yd. WC1 2 C7
Three Gates, Guil. 118 AU69
Three Gates Rd., Fawk. 90 DA54
Three Horseshoes Rd., Harl. 13 CL12
Three Households, Ch.St.G. 34 AP28
Three Kings Ct. EC4 56 BY39
Gough Sq.
Three Kings Rd., Mitch. 86 BU52
Three Kings Yd. W1 1 J10
Three Kings Yd. W1 56 BV40
Three Mill La. E3 57 CF38
Three Nun Ct. EC2 57 BZ39
Aldermanbury
Three Oak La. SE1 4 P4
Three Oak La. SE1 67 CA41
Three Oaks Clo., Uxb. 44 AY34
Three Pears Rd., Guil. 118 AU70
Threshers Pl. W11 55 BR40
Thriffwood SE26 77 CC48
Thrift, The, Dart. 80 DB48
Beacon Dr.
Thrift Fm. La., Borwd. 28 BN23
Thrift Grn., Brwd. 122 DD27
Thrift La., West. 106 CM62
Thrifts Mead, Epp. 31 CN22
Thriftvale, Guil. 118 AU69
Thrigby Rd., Chess. 94 BL57
Throckmorten Rd. E16 58 CH39
Throgmorton Ave. EC2 2 L8
Throgmorton Ave. EC2 57 BZ39
Throgmorton St. EC2 2 L8
Throgmorton St. EC2 57 BZ39
Throwley Clo. SE2 69 CP41
Throwley Rd., Sutt. 95 BS56
Throwley Way
Throwley Way, Sutt. 95 BS56
Thrums, The, Wat. 26 BC22
Thrupp Clo., Mitch. 86 BV51
Thrupps Ave., Walt. 93 BD56
Thrupps La., Walt. 93 BD56
Thrush Ave., Hat. 10 BP13
Thrush Grn., Har. 45 BF31
Woodlands
Thrush Grn., Har. 45 BF31
Thrush Grn., Rick. 35 AX26
Thrush La., Cuffley 20 BX17
Thrush St. SE17 4 H10
Thrush St. SE17 67 BZ42
Thruxton Way SE15 67 CA43
Thumbswood, Welw.G.C. 5 BS9
Thumpers, Hem.H. 8 AY12
Thundridge Clo., Welw.G.C. 5 BS8
Thurbarn Rd. SE6 77 CE49
Thurgood Rd., Hodd. 12 CE11
Thurland Rd. SE16 67 CB41
Thurlastone Par., Shep. 83 BA53
High St.
Thurlby Clo., Har. 45 BJ32
Gayton Rd.
Thurlby Clo., Wdf.Grn. 40 CK28
Thurlby Rd. SE27 76 BY49
Thurlby Rd., Wem. 54 BK36
Thurleigh Ave. SW12 76 BV46
Thurleigh Rd. SW12 76 BU46
Thurleston Ave., Mord. 85 BR53
Thurlestone Ave. N12 38 BU29
Thurlestone Ave., Ilf. 49 CN35
Thurlestone Rd. SE27 76 BY48
Thurloe Clo. SW7 3 C8
Thurloe Clo. SW7 66 BU42
Thurloe Pl. SW7 3 B8
Thurloe Pl. SW7 66 BT42
Thurloe Pl. Ms. SW7 3 B8
Thurloe Pl. Ms. SW7 66 BT42
Thurloe Pl.
Thurloe Sq. SW7 3 C8
Thurloe Sq. SW7 66 BU42
Thurloe St. SW7 3 B8
Thurloe St. SW7 66 BT42
Thurloe Wk., Grays 71 DD41
Thurlow Clo. E4 39 CE29
Higham Sta. Ave.
Thurlow Ct. SW3 66 BU42
Fulham Rd.
Thurlow Gdns., Ilf. 40 CN29
Thurlow Gdns., Wem. 45 BK35
Thurlow Hill SE21 77 BZ47
Thurlow Pk. Rd. SE21 76 BY47
Thurlow Rd. NW3 47 BT35
Thurlow Rd. W7 64 BJ41
Elthorne Pk. Rd.
Thurlow St. SE17 4 L10
Thurlow St. SE17 67 BZ42
Thurlow Ter. NW5 47 BU35
Thurlston Rd., Ruis. 44 BC34
Thurlstone Clo., Shep. 83 BA53

Thurlstone Rd. SE27 76 BY48
Thurlton Ct., Wok. 100 AS61
Thurnby Ct., Twick. 74 BH48
Thurnham Way, Tad. 103 BQ63
Thurrock Pk. Way, Grays 71 DE43
Thursby Rd., Wok. 100 AQ62
Thursland Rd., Sid. 79 CQ49
Thursley Cres., Croy. 96 CF57
Thursley Gdns. SW19 75 BQ48
Thursley Rd. SE9 78 CK48
Thurso Clo., Rom. 42 CX29
Thurso St. SW17 76 BT49
Thurstan Rd. SW20 75 BP50
Thurstans, Harl. 13 CM13
Thurston Path, Borwd. 28 BL23
Linton Ave.
Thurston Rd. SE13 67 CE44
Thurston Rd., Slou. 52 AP39
Thurston Rd., Sthl. 54 BE39
Thurtle Rd. E2 57 CA37
Thwaite Clo., Erith 69 CS43
Thyer Clo., Orp. 97 CM56
Thyra Gro. N12 38 BS29
Tibbatts Rd. E3 57 CE38
Tibbenham Wk. E13 58 CG37
Tibberton Sq. N1 57 BZ36
Popham Rd.
Tibbets Clo. SW19 75 BQ47
Tibbets Cor. SW19 75 BQ47
Tibbets Ride SW15 75 BQ47
Tibbles Clo., Wat. 27 BE21
Tibbs Hill Rd., Abb.L. 17 BB18
Tiber Gdns. N1 56 BX37
Treaty St.
Ticehurst Clo., Orp. 79 CO50
Grovelands Rd.
Ticehurst Rd. SE23 77 CD48
Tichborne Row W2 56 BU39
Hyde Pk. Cres.
Tichborne Wd., Rick. 34 AU28
Tichmarsh, Epsom 94 BN58
Tickford Clo. SE2 69 CP41
Tidal Basin Rd. E16 58 CG40
Tidenham Gdns., Croy. 87 CA55
Tideswell Rd. SW15 65 BQ45
Tideswell Rd., Croy. 87 CE55
Tideway Clo., Rich. 74 BJ49
Tidey St. E3 57 CE39
Tidford Rd., Well. 68 CN44
Tidys La., Epp. 23 CO18
Tiepigs La., W.Wick. 88 CG55
Tierney Rd. SW2 76 BX47
Tiger La., Brom. 88 CH52
Tiger Way E5 48 CB35
Tilbrook Rd. SE3 68 CJ45
Tilburstow Hill Rd., Gdse. 114 CC69
Tilbury Clo. SE15 67 CA43
Willowbrook Rd.
Tilbury Clo., Orp. 89 CO51
Tilbury Gdns., Til. 71 DG45
Tilbury Hotel Rd., Til. 71 DG45
Tilbury Mead, Harl. 14 CO12
Tilbury Rd. E6 58 CK37
Tilbury Rd. E10 48 CF33
Tilbury Rd., Brwd. 123 DF31
Tildesley Rd. SW15 75 BQ46
Tile Fm. Rd., Orp. 88 CM55
Tile Gate Rd., Harl. 13 CN12
Tile Gate Rd., Ong. 14 CS13
Tile Kiln Clo., Hem.H. 8 AZ14
Tile Kiln Cres., Hem.H. 8 AZ14
Tile Kiln La. N6 47 BW33
Tile Kiln La. N13 39 BZ28
Tile Kiln La., Bex. 79 CS48
Tile Kiln La., Hem.H. 8 AZ14
Tile Kiln La., Uxb. 44 AZ33
Tile Yd. E14 57 CD39
St. Anne St.
Tilecroft, Welw.G.C. 5 BQ6
Tilehouse Clo., Borwd. 28 BL24
Tilehouse La., Ger.Cr. 34 AV30
Tilehouse Rd., Guil. 118 AS72
Tilehouse Way, Uxb. 43 AV33
Tilehurst La., Bet. 120 BL72
Tilehurst La., Dor. 120 BL72
Tilehurst Rd. SW18 76 BT47
Tilehurst Rd., Sutt. 94 BR56
Tilers Way, Reig. 121 BT72
Tileyard Rd. N7 56 BX36
Tilford Ave., Croy. 96 CF58
Tilford Gdns. SW19 75 BQ47
Tilia Rd. E5 48 CB35
Till Ave., Farn. 90 CW54
Tiller Rd. E14 67 CE41
Tillett Clo. NW10 55 BN36
Tillett Sq. SE16 67 CD41
Howland Way
Tillett Way E2 57 CB38
Gosset St.
Tilley La., Epsom 103 BM65
Tillgate Common, Red. 114 BZ70
Tilling Rd. NW2 46 BQ33
Tillingbourne Gdns. N3 46 BR31
Tillingbourne Grn., Orp. 88 CN52
Tillingbourne Rd., Guil. 118 AS73
Tillingbourne Way N3 46 BR31
Tillingbourne Gdns.
Tillingdown Hill, Cat. 105 CB64
Tillingdown La., Cat. 105 CB65
Tillingham Ct., Wal.Abb. 22 CH20
Tillingham Way N12 38 BS28
Tillman St. E1 57 CB39
Tilloch St. N1 56 BX36
Carnoustie Dr.
Tillotson Rd. N9 39 CA27
Tillotson Rd., Har. 36 BF29
Tillotson Rd., Ilf. 49 CL33
Tillwicks Rd., Harl. 14 CO11
Tillys La., Stai. 72 AV49
Tilmans Mead, Farn. 90 CW54
Tilney Ct. EC1 2 J4
Tilney Ct. EC1 57 BZ38
Old St.
Tilney Dr., Buck.H. 40 CH27

Street	Page	Grid
Tilney Gdns. N1	57	BZ36
Baxter Rd.		
Tilney Rd., Dag.	59	CQ36
Tilney Rd., Sthl.	64	BD42
Tilney St. W1	**3**	**H2**
Tilney St. W1	56	BV40
Tilson Gdns. SW2	76	BW47
Tilson Ho. SW2	76	BX47
Tilson La., Wind.	61	AM42
Tilson Rd. N17	39	CB30
Tilstone Ave. (Eton Wick), Wind.	61	AM42
Tilstone Clo. (Eton Wick), Wind.	61	AM42
Tilsworth Wk., St.Alb.	9	BK11
Sandringham Cres.		
Tilt Clo., Cob.	102	BE61
Tilt Meadows, Cob.	102	BE61
Tilt Rd., Cob.	102	BD61
Tilt Yd. App. SE9	78	CK46
Tilton Rd., Sev.	108	DC63
Tilton St. SW6	65	BR43
Tiltwood, The W3	55	BN40
Acacia Rd.		
Timber Clo., Chis.	88	CL51
Timber Clo., Lthd.	111	BG67
Timber Clo., Wok.	91	AV60
Timber Mill Way SW4	66	BW45
Timber Pond Rd. SE16	67	CC41
Timber Ridge, Rick.	26	AX24
Timber Slip Dr., Wall.	95	BW58
Timber St. EC1	**2**	**H4**
Timber St. EC1	57	BZ38
Baltic St.		
Timbercroft, Epsom	94	BN56
Timbercroft, Welw.G.C.	5	BR6
Timbercroft La. SE18	68	CN43
Timberdene NW4	37	BQ30
Timberdene Ave., Ilf.	40	CM30
Timberhill Rd., Cat.	105	CB65
Timberland Rd. E1	57	CB39
Watney Mkt.		
Timberling Gdns., Croy.	96	BZ58
White Hill		
Timbertop Rd., West.	106	CJ62
Timberwharf Rd. N16	48	CB32
Times Sq., Sutt.	95	BS56
High St.		
Timothy Clo. SW4	76	BW46
Elms Rd.		
Timperley Gdns., Red.	121	BU69
Timplings Row, Hem.H.	8	AW12
Tims Way, Stai.	72	AV49
Timsbury Wk. SW15	75	BP47
Foxcombe Rd.		
Tindal St. SW9	66	BY44
Tindale Clo., S.Croy.	96	BZ59
Tindall Clo., Rom.	42	CW30
Rosslyn Ave.		
Tinderbox All. SW14	65	BN45
North Worple Way		
Tine Rd., Chig.	40	CN28
Tingeys Top La., Enf.	29	BY21
Tinglefield, Pot.B.	20	BS18
Tinkerpot La., Sev.	99	CY60
Tinkerpot Ri., Sev.	99	CY60
Tinkers La., Wind.	61	AL44
Tinsby Wk. SW15	75	BP47
Alton Rd.		
Tinsey Clo., Egh.	72	AT49
Tinsley Rd. E1	57	CC39
Tintagel Clo., Epsom	94	BO60
College Rd.		
Tintagel Clo., Hem.H.	8	AY11
Helston Gro.		
Tintagel Cres. SE22	67	CA45
Tintagel Dr., Stan.	36	BK28
Tintagel Gdns. SE22	67	CA45
Oxonian St.		
Tintagel Rd., Orp.	89	CP55
Tintagel Way, Wok.	100	AT61
Tintells La., Lthd.	110	AZ67
Tintern Ave. NW9	46	BM31
Tintern Clo. SW15	75	BR46
Tintern Clo. SW19	76	BT50
Tintern Clo., Slou.	61	AO41
Tintern Ct. W13	54	BJ40
Tintern Gdns. N14	38	BX26
Tintern Path NW9	46	BO32
Ruthin Clo.		
Tintern Rd. N22	39	BZ30
Tintern Rd., Cars.	86	BT54
Tintern St. SW4	66	BX45
Tintern Way, Har.	45	BF33
Tinto Rd. E16	58	CH38
Tinworth Ho. SE11	66	BX42
Tinworth St.		
Tinworth St. SE11	**4**	**A10**
Tinworth St. SE11	66	BX42
Tippendell La., St.Alb.	18	BF16
Tippetts Clo., Enf.	30	BZ23
Tipps Cross La., Brwd.	24	DA20
Tipps Cross Mead, Brwd.	33	DA21
Tipthorpe Rd. SW11	66	BV45
Tipton Dr., Croy.	96	CA56
Tiptree Clo. E4	39	CF27
Tiptree Clo., Horn.	51	CX33
Tiptree Cres., Ilf.	49	CL31
Tiptree Dr., Enf.	30	BZ24
Tiptree Rd., Ruis.	44	BC35
Tiree Clo., Hem.H.	8	AZ14
Tirlemont Rd., S.Croy.	96	BZ57
Tirrell Rd., Croy.	87	BZ53
Tisbury Ct. W1	**1**	**N10**
Tisbury Ct. W1	56	BW40
Rupert St.		
Tisbury Rd. SW16	86	BX51
Tisdall Pl. SE17	**4**	**L9**
Tisdall Pl. SE17	67	BZ42
Titan Rd., Grays	71	DD42
Orsett Rd.		
Titan Rd., Hem.H.	8	AY12
Titan Way, Grays	71	DD42
Titchborne Row W2	**1**	**D9**
Titchfield Rd. NW8	56	BU37
Titchfield Rd., Cars.	86	BT54
Titchfield Rd., Enf.	30	CD22
Titchfield Wk., Cars.	86	BT54
Titchwell Rd. SW18	76	BT47
Tite Hill, Egh.	72	AR49
Tite St. SW3	66	BU42
Tithe Barn Clo., Kings.T.	85	BL51
Birkenhead Ave.		
Tithe Barn Clo., St.Alb.	9	BG15
Tithe Barn Dr., Maid.	61	AJ42
Tithe Barn Way, Nthlt.	53	BC37
Tithe Clo. NW7	37	BP30
Tithe Clo., Maid.	61	AH42
Tithe Ct. NW4	37	BP30
Tithe Ct., Slou.	62	AT42
Tithe Fm. Ave., Har.	45	BF34
Tithe Fm. Clo., Har.	45	BF34
Tithe La., Stai.	72	AT46
Tithe Meadow, Vir.W.	82	AR53
Tithe Meadow, Wat.	26	BA25
Tithe Wk. NW7	37	BP30
Tithebarns La., Wok.	110	AW66
Tithelands, Harl.	13	CK12
Tithepit Shaw La., Warl.	105	CB62
Titian Ave., Bush.	36	BH26
Titley Clo. E4	39	CE28
Titmus Clo., Uxb.	53	BA39
Titmuss Ave. SE28	59	CO40
Titmuss St. W12	65	BQ41
Titsey Hill, Oxt.	106	CH65
Titsey Rd., Oxt.	115	CH67
Tiverton Ave., Ilf.	49	CL31
Tiverton Dr. SE9	78	CM47
Tiverton Gro., Rom.	42	CX28
Tiverton Rd. N15	48	BZ32
Tiverton Rd. N18	39	CA28
Tiverton Rd. NW10	55	BQ37
Tiverton Rd., Edg.	37	BL30
Tiverton Rd., Houns.	64	BF44
Tiverton Rd., Pot.B.	20	BT19
Tiverton Rd., Ruis.	44	BC34
Tiverton Rd., Wem.	55	BL37
Tiverton St. SE1	**4**	**H6**
Tiverton St. SE1	67	BZ41
Tiverton Way, Chess.	93	BK56
Tivoli Gdns. SE18	68	CK42
Tivoli Rd. N8	47	BW32
Tivoli Rd. SE27	77	BZ49
Tivoli Rd., Houns.	64	BE45
Tobacco Quay E1	57	CB40
Wapping La.		
Tobago St. E14	67	CE41
Manilla St.		
Tobin Clo. NW3	56	BU36
Toby La. E1	57	CD38
Solebay St.		
Todd Brook, Harl.	13	CL11
Todd Clo., Rain.	60	CV38
Todds Wk. N7	47	BX34
Andover Rd.		
Toft Ave., Grays	71	DE42
Tokenhouse Yd. EC2	**2**	**K8**
Tokenhouse Yd. EC2	57	BZ39
Tokyngton Ave., Wem.	55	BL36
Toland Sq. SW15	75	BP46
Tolavaddon, Wok.	100	AQ62
Cardingham		
Tolcarne Dr., Pnr.	35	BC30
Toley Ave., Wem.	46	BL33
Tollbridge Clo. W10	55	BR38
Kensal Rd.		
Tolldene Clo., Wok.	100	AP62
Tollers La., Couls.	104	BX63
Tollesbury Gdns., Ilf.	49	CM31
Tollet St. E1	57	CC38
Tollgate, Guil.	118	AU70
Tollgate Ave., Red.	121	BU73
Tollgate Clo., Rick.	25	AV24
Tollgate Dr. SE21	77	CA48
Tollgate Gdns. NW6	56	BS37
Tollgate Rd. E6	58	CK39
Tollgate Rd. E16	58	CJ39
Tollgate Rd., Dart.	80	CY47
Tollgate Rd., Dor.	119	BJ73
Tollgate Rd., St.Alb.	10	BN15
Tollgate Rd., Wal.Cr.	30	CC21
Tollhouse La., Wall.	95	BW58
Tollhouse Way N19	47	BW34
Tollington Pk. N4	47	BX34
Tollington Pl. N4	47	BX34
Tollington Rd. N7	47	BX35
Tollington Way N7	47	BX34
Tollpit End, Hem.H.	8	AW12
Tolmers Ave., Cuffley	20	BX17
Tolmers Gdns., Cuffley	20	BX18
Tolmers Ms., Hert.	20	BX16
Tolmers Rd., Cuffley	20	BW16
Tolmers Sq. NW1	**1**	**M4**
Tolmers Sq. NW1	56	BW38
Tolpits Clo., Wat.	26	BB25
Tolpits La., Wat.	35	BA26
Tolpuddle St. N1	56	BY37
Tolsford Rd. E5	48	CB35
Tolson Rd., Islw.	64	BJ45
Tolver Ct., Brwd.	42	DB27
Tower Hill		
Tolverne Rd. SW20	85	BQ51
Tolworth Clo., Surb.	85	BM54
Tolworth Gdns., Rom.	50	CP32
Tolworth Pk. Rd., Surb.	85	BL55
Tolworth Ri. N., Surb.	85	BM54
Tolworth Ri. S., Surb.	85	BM54
Tolworth Rd., Surb.	85	BL55
Tom Coombs Clo. SE9	68	CK45
Westhorne Ave.		
Tom Cribb Rd. SE28	68	CM41
Tom Mann Clo., Bark.	58	CN37
Tomahawk Gdns., Nthlt.	54	BD38
Javelin Way		
Tomkins Clo., Borwd.	27	BK23
Organ Hall Rd.		
Tomkyns La., Upmin.	42	CY30
Tomlins Gro. E3	57	CE38
Tomlins Orchard, Bark.	58	CM37
Tomlins Ter. E14	57	CD39
Tomlins Wk. N7	47	BX34
Briset Way		
Tomlinson Clo. E2	**2**	**Q3**
Tomlinson Clo. E2	57	CA38
Tomlinson Clo. W4	65	BM42
Oxford Rd.		
Tomlyns Clo., Brwd.	122	DF25
Tompion Ho. EC1	56	BY38
Percival St.		
Tompion St. EC1	**2**	**F3**
Tompion St. EC1	56	BY38
Northampton Sq.		
Toms Cft., Hem.H.	8	AY14
Toms Fld., Hat.	10	BO13
College La.		
Toms Hill, Rick.	26	AY21
Toms La., Kings L.	17	AZ18
Tomswood Hill, Ilf.	40	CL29
Tomswood Rd., Chig.	40	CL29
Tonbridge & Sevenoaks By-pass, Sev.	117	CV69
Tonbridge Clo., Bans.	95	BU60
Merrymeet		
Tonbridge Cres., Har.	46	BL31
Tonbridge Rd., E.Mol.	84	BE53
Tonbridge Rd., Rom.	42	CV29
Tonbridge Rd., Sev.	117	CV67
Tonbridge Rd., Sev.	117	DB67
Tonbridge Rd., Ton.	117	DB67
Tonbridge St. WC1	**1**	**Q2**
Tonbridge St. WC1	56	BX38
Tonbridge Wk. WC1	**1**	**Q2**
Tonbridge Wk. WC1	56	BX38
Tonbridge St.		
Tonfield Rd., Sutt.	85	BR54
Tonge Clo., Beck.	87	CE53
Tonsley Hill SW18	76	BS46
Tonsley Pl. SW18	76	BS46
Tonsley Rd. SW18	76	BS46
Tonsley St. SW18	76	BS46
Tonstall Rd., Epsom	94	BN59
Tonstall Rd., Mitch.	86	BV51
Tooke Clo., Pnr.	36	BE30
Tooks Ct. EC4	**2**	**D8**
Tooks Ct. EC4	56	BY39
Cursitor St.		
Toolands Rd., Islw.	64	BJ44
Tooley St. SE1	**4**	**L2**
Tooley St. SE1	57	BZ40
Tooley St., Grav.	81	DE47
Toorack Rd., Har.	36	BG30
Toot Hill Rd., Ong.	23	CT18
Tooting Bec Gdns. SW16	76	BW49
Tooting Bec Rd. SW17	76	BV48
Tooting Gro. SW17	76	BU49
Tooting High St. SW17	76	BU49
Toots Wd. Rd., Brom.	88	CG53
Tooveys Mill Clo., Kings L.	17	AZ18
Mill La.		
Top Dartford Rd., Swan.	79	CT50
Top Ho. Ri. E4	39	CF26
Top La., Rick.	16	AV20
Top Pk., Beck.	87	CF53
Top Pk., Ger.Cr.	43	AR32
Top Wk., Cat.	105	CD64
Topaz Clo., Slou.	61	AN40
Pearl Gdns.		
Topcliffe Dr., Orp.	97	CM56
Topham Sq. N17	39	BZ30
Topham St. EC1	**2**	**D4**
Topham St. EC1	56	BY38
Topiary Sq., Rich.	65	BL45
Topland Rd., Ger.Cr.	34	AR29
Toplands Ave., S.Ock.	60	CX40
Topley St. SE9	68	CJ45
Topp Wk. NW2	46	BQ34
Topsfield Rd. N8	47	BX32
Topsham Rd. SW17	76	BU48
Tor Gdns. W8	66	BS41
Tor La., Wey.	92	BA59
Tor Rd., Well.	69	CP44
Torbay Rd. NW6	55	BR36
Torbay Rd., Har.	45	BE34
Torbay St. NW1	56	BV36
Hawley Rd.		
Torbridge Clo., Edg.	37	BL29
Torbrook Clo., Bex.	79	CQ46
Torcross Dr. SE23	77	CC48
Torcross Rd., Ruis.	44	BC34
Torin Ct., Egh.	72	AR49
Torland Dr., Lthd.	93	BG60
Tormead Clo., Sutt.	95	BS57
Tormead Rd., Guil.	118	AS70
Tormount Rd. SE18	68	CN43
Toronto Ave. E12	49	CK35
Toronto Rd. E11	48	CF35
Toronto Rd., Ilf.	49	CL33
Toronto Rd., Til.	71	DG44
Torquay Gdns., Ilf.	49	CJ31
Torquay St. W2	56	BS39
Harrow Rd.		
Torr Rd. SE20	77	CC50
Torrance Clo., Horn.	51	CV33
Torrans Wk., Grav.	81	DJ49
Torre Wk., Cars.	86	BU54
Torrens Rd. E15	58	CG36
Torrens Rd. SW2	76	BX46
Torrens Sq. E15	58	CG36
Torrens St. N1	**2**	**E1**
Torrens St. N1	56	BY37
Torriano Ave. NW5	47	BW35
Torriano Cotts. NW5	47	BW35
Torriano Ave.		
Torriano Est. NW5	47	BW35
Torridge Gdns. SE15	67	CC45
Torridge Rd., Slou.	62	AT43
Torridge Rd., Th.Hth.	86	BY53
Torridge Wk., Hem.H.	8	AY11
Torridon Clo., Wok.	100	AQ62
Torridon Rd. SE6	77	CF47
Torridon Rd. SE13	77	CF47
Torrington Ave. N12	38	BT28
Torrington Clo. N12	38	BT28
Torrington Pk.		
Torrington Clo., Esher	93	BH57
Torrington Dr., Har.	45	BF35
Torrington Dr., Loug.	31	CM24
Torrington Dr., Pot.B.	20	BT19
Torrington Gdns. N11	38	BW29
Torrington Gdns., Grnf.	54	BK37
Torrington Gdns., Loug.	31	CM24
Torrington Gro. N12	38	BU28
Torrington Pk. N12	38	BT28
Torrington Pl. E1	57	CB40
Torrington Pl. WC1	**1**	**M6**
Torrington Pl. WC1	56	BW38
Torrington Rd. E18	49	CH31
Torrington Rd., Berk.	7	AQ13
Torrington Rd., Dag.	50	CQ33
Torrington Rd., Esher	93	BH57
Torrington Rd., Grnf.	54	BK37
Torrington Rd., Ruis.	44	BB34
Torrington Sq. WC1	**1**	**P5**
Torrington Sq., Croy.	87	BZ54
Tavistock Gro.		
Torrington Way, Mord.	86	BS54
Torver Rd., Har.	45	BH31
Torver Way, Orp.	88	CM55
Torwood Clo., Berk.	7	AP13
Torwood La., Whyt.	105	CA63
Torwood Rd. SW15	75	BP46
Torworth Rd., Borwd.	28	BL22
Totham Lo. SW20	85	BP51
Richmond Rd.		
Tothill St. SW1	**3**	**N5**
Tothill St. SW1	66	BW41
Totnes Rd., Well.	69	CO43
Totnes Wk. N2	47	BT31
Tottenhall Rd. N13	38	BY29
Tottenham Ct. Rd. W1	**1**	**M5**
Tottenham Ct. Rd. W1	56	BW38
Tottenham Grn. E. N15	48	CA31
Tottenham La. N8	47	BX32
Tottenham Ms. W1	**1**	**M6**
Tottenham Ms. W1	56	BW39
Tottenham St.		
Tottenham Rd. N1	57	BZ36
Tottenham Sq. N1	57	CA36
Tottenham St. W1	**1**	**M7**
Tottenham St. W1	56	BW39
Totterdown St. SW17	76	BU49
Totteridge Clo. N20	38	BS27
Totteridge Common N20	37	BP27
Totteridge La. N20	38	BS27
Totteridge Rd., Enf.	30	CC22
Totteridge Village N20	37	BR26
Totternhoe Clo., Har.	45	BK32
Totton Rd., Th.Hth.	86	BY52
Toulmin Dr., St.Alb.	9	BG11
Toulmin St. SE1	**4**	**H5**
Toulmin St. SE1	67	BZ41
Toulon St. SE5	67	BZ43
Wyndham Rd.		
Tournay Rd. SW6	65	BR43
Tovey Ave., Hodd.	12	CE11
Tovey Clo., Wal.Abb.	13	CG15
Tovil Clo. SE20	87	CB51
Towcester Rd. E3	57	CE38
Tower Bri. E1	**4**	**P3**
Tower Bri. SE1	**4**	**P3**
Tower Bri. SE1	57	CA40
Tower Bri. App. E1	**4**	**P2**
Tower Bri. App. E1	57	CA40
Tower Bri. Rd. E1	67	CA41
Tower Bri. Rd. SE1	**4**	**M7**
Tower Bri. Rd. SE1	67	CA41
Tower Cen., Hodd.	12	CE12
Tower Clo. NW3	47	BT35
Lyndhurst Rd.		
Tower Clo. SE20	77	CB50
Tower Clo., Berk.	7	AQ13
Tower Clo., Epp.	14	CS15
Tower Clo., Grav.	81	DJ49
Tower Clo., Ilf.	40	CM29
Tower Clo., Orp.	88	CN55
Tower Clo., Wok.	100	AR62
Tower Ct. N16	48	CA33
Tower Ct. WC2	**1**	**Q9**
Tower Ct., Brwd.	42	DA27
Tower Ct., Ong.	24	CX18
Stanley Pl.		
Tower Gdns. Rd. N17	39	BZ30
Tower Gro., Wey.	83	BB54
Tower Hamlets Rd. E7	49	CG35
Tower Hamlets Rd. E17	48	CE31
Tower Hill EC3	**4**	**P1**
Tower Hill EC3	57	CA40
Tower Hill, Brwd.	42	DB27
Tower Hill, Dor.	119	BJ72
Tower Hill, Kings L.	16	AV18
Tower Hill Rd., Dor.	119	BJ72
Tower La., Reig.	113	BT68
Tower Ms. E17	48	CE31
High St.		
Tower Pl. EC3	**4**	**N1**
Tower Pl. EC3	57	CA40
Tower Ri., Rich.	65	BL45
Tower Rd. NW10	55	BP36
Tower Rd., Belv.	69	CS42
Tower Rd., Bexh.	69	CR45
Tower Rd., Dart.	80	CV47
Tower Rd., Epp.	22	CN18
Tower Rd., Orp.	88	CN55
Tower Rd., Tad.	103	BQ65
Tower Rd., Twick.	74	BH48
Tower Royal EC4	**2**	**J10**
Tower Royal EC4	57	BZ40
Cannon St.		
Tower St. WC2	**1**	**P9**
Tower St. WC2	56	BW39
Tower Ter. N22	38	BX30
Mayes Rd.		
Tower Vw., Croy.	87	CD54
Towers, The, Ken.	105	BZ61
Towers Ave., Uxb.	53	BA38
Towers Pl., Rich.	75	BL
Eton St.		
Towers Rd., Grays	71	DE
Towers Rd., Hem.H.	8	AY
Towers Rd., Pnr.	36	BE
Towers Rd., Sthl.	54	BF
Towers Wk., Wey.	92	AZ
Towers Wd., Dart.	90	CY
Towerscroft, Eyns.	90	CW
Towfield Rd., Felt.	74	BE
Town, The, Enf.	30	BZ
Town Ct. La., Orp.	88	CM
Town Ct. Path N4	48	BZ
Town End Clo., Cat.	105	CA
Town End High St., Cat.	105	CA
Town Fm. Way, Stai.	73	AX
Town La.		
Town Fld. La., Ch.St.G.	34	AR
Town Flds., Hat.	10	BP
Town Hall App. N16	48	CA
Milton Gro.		
Town Hall App. Rd. N15	48	CA
Town Hall Ave. W4	65	BN
Town Hall Rd. SW11	66	BU
Town La., Stai.	73	AX
Town Meadow, Brent.	64	BK
Town Quay, Bark.	58	CL
Town Quay, Stai.	83	AW
Blacksmiths La.		
Town Rd. N9	39	CB
Town Tree Rd., Ashf.	73	AZ
Town Wf., Islw.	64	BJ
Towncourt Cres., Orp.	88	CM
Towney Mead, Nthlt.	54	BE
Townfield, Rick.	35	AX
Townfield Rd., Hayes	53	BB
Townfield Sq., Hayes	53	BB
Townford Rd., Dor.	119	BJ
Townholm Cres. W7	64	BH
Townley Ct. E15	58	CG
Faraday Rd.		
Townley Rd. SE22	77	CA
Townley Rd., Bexh.	79	CQ
Townley St. SE17	**4**	**K**
Townley St. SE17	67	BZ
Townmead, Red.	114	BZ
Townmead Est. SW6	66	BS
Townmead Rd. SW6	66	BS
Townmead Rd., Rich.	65	BM
Townmead Rd., Wal.Abb.	21	CF
Townsend, Hem.H.	8	AX
Townsend Ave. N14	38	BW
Townsend Ave., St.Alb.	9	BH
Townsend Dr., St.Alb.	9	BG
Townsend Ind. Est. NW10	55	BN
Townsend La. NW9	46	BN
Townsend La., Wok.	100	AT
St. Peters Rd.		
Townsend Rd. N15	48	CA
Townsend Rd., Ashf.	73	AY
Townsend Rd., Sthl.	54	BE
Townsend St. SE17	**4**	**N**
Townsend St. SE17	67	BZ
Townsend Way, Nthwd.	35	BB
Townsends Yd. N6	47	BV
Townshend Est. NW8	56	BU
Townshend Rd. NW8	56	BU
Townshend Rd., Chis.	78	CL
Townshend Rd., Rich.	65	BL
Townshend Ter., Rich.	65	BL
Townshott Clo., Lthd.	111	BF
Townside, Harl.	14	CP
Townslow La., Wok.	101	AX
Townson Ave., Nthlt.	53	BC
Townson Way, Nthlt.	53	BC
Towpath, Shep.	83	AY
Towton Rd. SE27	77	BZ
Toynbec Clo., Chis.	78	CL
Beechwood Ri.		
Toynbee Rd. SW20	85	BQ
Toynbee St. E1	**2**	
Toynbee St. E1	57	CA
Toyne Way N6	47	BU
Gaskell Rd.		
Toys Hill, West.	116	CO
Tozer Wk., Wind.	61	AL
Tinkers La.		
Tracery, The, Bans.	104	BS
Tracey Ave. NW2	46	BP
Tracey St. SE11	66	BY
Tracious Clo., Wok.	100	AQ
Tracious La., Wok.	100	AQ
Tracy Ct., Stan.	36	BK
Tracyes Rd., Harl.	14	CO
Tradescant Rd. SW8	66	BX
Trading Est. Rd. NW10	55	BN
Trafalgar Ave. N17	39	CA
Trafalgar Ave. SE15	67	CA
Trafalgar Ave., Brox.	12	CD
Trafalgar Ave., Wor.Pk.	85	BQ
Trafalgar Ct., Cob.	92	BC
Trafalgar Dr., Walt.	83	BC
Trafalgar Gdns. E1	57	CC
Trafalgar Gro. SE10	67	CF
Trafalgar Pl. E11	49	CH
Trafalgar Pl. N18	39	CB
Trafalgar Rd. SE10	67	CF
Trafalgar Rd. SW19	76	BS
Trafalgar Rd., Dart.	80	CW
Trafalgar Rd., Grav.	81	DG
Trafalgar Rd., Rain.	59	CT
Trafalgar Rd., Twick.	74	BG
Trafalgar Sq. WC2	**3**	
Trafalgar Sq. WC2	56	BW
Trafalgar St. SE17	**4**	**K**
Trafalgar St. SE17	67	BZ
Trafalgar Ter., Har.	45	BG
Nelson Rd.		
Trafalgar Way, Croy.	86	BX
Trafford Clo. E15	48	CE
Trafford Clo., Ilf.	40	CN
Trent Bri. Clo.		
Trafford Rd., Th.Hth.	86	BX

orn St. E1 57 CB39
odeham St.
nway Ave. E15 57 CG36
oadway
nway Ave. N9 39 CB26
nway Path, Mitch. 86 BU53
nby Pl. E9 48 CC35
nley Ms. NW3 47 BU35
et Rd.
mere Rd. N9 39 CA26
mere Rd. SW18 76 BT47
mere Rd., Twick. 74 BF47
quil Dale, Bet. 120 BO69
quil Pas. SE3 68 CG44
anquil Vale
quil Ri., Erith 69 CT42
quil Vale SE3 68 CG44
nsay Wk. N1 57 BZ36
ephane Rd.
nsept St. NW1 1 D7
nsept St. NW1 56 BU39
nsmere Clo., Orp. 88 CM53
nsom Sq. E14 67 CE42
estferry Rd.
nsport Ave., Brent. 64 BJ43
nton Rd. SE16 67 CB41
ops La., Chesh. 16 AO19
ops La., Chesh. 16 AO20
os Hill, Loug. 31 CK24
os La., N.Mal. 85 BO51
sher Mead, Dor. 119 BK73
vellers Clo., Hat. 10 BQ15
vellers La., Hat. 10 BP13
vellers La. (North 10 BQ14
ymms), Hat.
vellers Way, Houns. 64 BD44
vers Rd. N7 47 BY34
acy Clo., Bush. 36 BG27
adgold St. W11 55 BQ40
adway St. E2 57 CB37
adwell Rd., Epsom 103 BO61
aty Rd., Houns. 64 BF45
aty St. N1 56 BX37
oble Rd., Swans. 81 DC46
beck St. W1 3 J2
beck St. W1 56 BV40
urzon St.
bellan Dr., Hem.H. 8 AY13
bovir Rd. SW5 66 BS42
by St. E3 57 CD38
castle Way N7 47 BW35
arleton Rd.
degar Ms. E3 57 CD37
redegar Ter.
degar Ms. E3 57 CD38
edegar Ter.
degar Rd. E3 57 CD37
degar Rd. N11 38 BW29
degar Rd., Dart. 79 CU48
degar Sq. E3 57 CD38
degar Ter. E3 57 CD38
derwen Rd. E8 57 CB37
down Rd. SE26 77 CC49
dwell Rd. SE27 76 BY49
e Bourne Rd., West. 106 CJ62
e Clo., Rich. 74 BK47
e Mt. Ct., Epsom 94 BO60
e Rd. E16 58 CJ39
e Tops, Brwd. 42 DB26
e Tops, Grav. 81 DG49
e Tops Clo. SE2 69 CQ42
e Tops Clo., Nthwd. 35 BA28
ebys Ave., Guil. 109 AR67
elands, Dor. 119 BK73
en Ave. SW13 65 BO45
eside Clo., West Dr. 63 AX42
eview Clo. SE19 87 CA51
ylvan Hill
ewall Gdns., Brom. 78 CH49
eway, Reig. 121 BS69
fgarne Rd., Dag. 50 CR34
fil Wk. N7 47 BX35
Villiamson St.
foil Rd. SW18 76 BT46
fusis Wk., Wat. 26 BB23
garon Ave. N8 47 BX32
garon Gdns., N.Mal. 85 BO52
venue Rd.
garth Pl., Wok. 100 AP62
garvon Rd. SW11 66 BV45
gelles Rd., Hodd. 12 CE11
genna Ave., Har. 45 BE35
genna Clo. N14 29 BW25
go Rd. E9 57 CD36
gothnan Rd. SW9 66 BX45
gunter Rd. SW10 66 BS43
haven Par., Reig. 121 BS72
Hornbeam Rd.
hearn Rd., Ilf. 40 CM29
hern Rd. SW14 65 BN45
herne Ct. SW17 76 BV49
hurst St. E5 48 CD35
lawn Clo., Cher. 91 AU57
lawn Rd. E10 48 CF34
lawn Rd. SW2 76 BY46
lawney Ave., Slou. 62 AS41
lawney Est. E9 57 CC36
lawney Gro., Wey. 92 AZ57
Elgin Rd.
lawney Rd., Ilf. 40 CM29
llis Sq. E3 58 CE37
Malmesbury Sq.
loar Gdns. SE19 77 BZ50
madoc Rd. SW4 66 BW45
maine Clo. SE4 67 CE44
maine Gro., Hem.H. 8 AY11
maine Rd. SE20 87 CB51
maton, Tedd. 74 BK50
mlett Gro. N19 47 BW34
mlett Ms. N19 47 BW34
Junction Rd.
enance, Wok. 100 AQ62
Cardingham
enance Gdns., Ilf. 50 CO34

Trenchard Ave., Ruis. 44 BC35
Trenchard Clo., Stan. 36 BJ29
Trenchard Clo., Walt. 93 BD56
Trenchard Ct., Mord. 86 BS53
Trenchard Rd., Maid. 61 AG43
Trenchard St. SE10 67 CF42
Trenches La., Slou. 52 AT40
Trenchold St. SW8 66 BX43
Trenham Dr., Warl. 105 CC61
Trenholme Clo. SE20 77 CB50
Trenholme Rd. SE20 77 CB50
Trenmar Gdns. NW10 55 BP38
Trent Ave. W5 64 BK41
Trent Ave., Upmin. 51 CY32
Trent Gdns. N14 29 BV25
Trent Rd. SW2 76 BX46
Trent Rd., Buck.H. 40 CH26
Trent Rd., Slou. 62 AT43
Trent Way, Hayes 53 BB37
Trent Way, Wor.Pk. 85 BQ55
Trentbridge Clo., Ilf. 40 CN29
Trentham Cres., Wok. 100 AT64
Trentham Dr., Orp. 89 CO53
Trentham Rd., Red. 121 BV71
Trentham St. SW18 76 BS47
Trentwood Side, Enf. 29 BX24
Treport St. SW18 76 BS47
Tresco Clo., Brom. 78 CG50
Hillbrow Rd.
Tresco Gdns., Ilf. 50 CO34
Tresco Rd. SE15 67 CB45
Tresco Rd., Berk. 7 AP12
Trescoe Gdns., Har. 45 BE33
Trescoe Gdns., Rom. 41 CS28
Tresham Cres. NW8 1 C4
Tresham Cres. NW8 56 BU38
Tresham Rd., Bark. 58 CN36
Tresham Wk. E9 48 CC35
Churchill Wk.
Tresilian Sq., Hem.H. 8 AY11
Tresillian Way, Wok. 100 AQ62
Tressell Clo. N1 56 BY36
Sebbon St.
Tressillian Cres. SE4 67 CE45
Tressillian Rd. SE4 67 CD45
Tresta Wk., Wok. 100 AQ61
Trestis Clo., Hayes 54 BD39
Jollys La.
Treswell Rd., Dag. 59 CQ37
Tretawn Gdns. NW7 37 BO28
Tretawn Pk. NW7 37 BO28
Trevanion Rd. W14 65 BR42
Treve Ave., Har. 45 BG33
Trevelga Way, Hem.H. 8 AY11
Tremaine Gro.
Trevellance Way, Wat. 18 BD20
Trevelyan Ave. E12 49 CK35
Trevelyan Clo., Dart. 70 CW45
Trevelyan Cres., Har. 46 BL33
Trevelyan Gdns. NW10 55 BQ37
Trevelyan Rd. E15 49 CG35
Trevelyan Rd. SW17 76 BU49
Trevelyan Way, Berk. 7 AQ12
Trevelyn Ct., N.Mal. 85 BO54
Trevereux Hill, Oxt. 115 CK69
Treveris St. SE1 4 G3
Treveris St. SE1 56 BY40
Bear La.
Treverton St. W10 55 BQ38
Ladbroke Gro.
Treville St. SW15 75 BP47
Treviso Rd. SE23 77 CC47
Farren Rd.
Trevithick Dr., Dart. 70 CW45
Trevithick St. SE8 67 CE42
Watergate St.
Trevone Gdns., Pnr. 45 BE32
Trevor Clo., Bans. 29 BT25
Trevor Clo., Brom. 88 CG54
Trevor Clo., Islw. 74 BH46
Trevor Clo., Nthlt. 54 BD37
Trevor Clo., Stan. 36 BH29
Trevor Ct., Stai. 73 AW46
Horton Rd.
Trevor Cres., Ruis. 44 BB35
Trevor Gdns., Edg. 37 BN30
Trevor Gdns., Nthlt. 54 BD37
Trevor Pl. SW7 3 D5
Trevor Pl. SW7 66 BU41
Trevor Rd. SW19 75 BR50
Trevor Rd., Edg. 37 BN30
Trevor Rd., Hayes 63 BB41
Trevor Rd., Wdf.Grn. 40 CH29
Trevor Sq. SW7 3 E5
Trevor Sq. SW7 66 BU41
Trevor St. SW7 3 D5
Trevor St. SW7 66 BU41
Trevose Ave., Wey. 91 AV60
Trevose Rd. E17 39 CF30
Trevose Way, Wat. 36 BD27
Trewenna Dr., Chess. 93 BK56
Hook Rd.
Trewenna Dr., Pot.B. 20 BT19
Trewince Rd. SW20 85 BQ51
Trewint St. SW18 76 BT48
Trewsbury Rd. SE26 77 CC49
Triandra Way, Hayes 54 BD39
Triangle, Wok. 100 AR62
Triangle, The, Bark. 58 CM36
Park Ave.
Triangle, The, Hmptn. 84 BG51
Triangle, The, 85 BN51
Kings.T.
Triangle Ct. E16 58 CJ39
Tollgate Rd.
Triangle Pl. SW4 66 BW45
Triangle Rd. E8 57 CB37
Trident Gdns., Nthlt. 54 BD38
Jetstar Way
Trident Rd., Wat. 17 BB20
Trident St. SE16 67 CC42
Trident Way, Sthl. 63 BK41
Triggs Clo., Wok. 100 AR63
Triggs La., Wok. 100 AR63

Trigo Ct., Epsom 94 BN59
Blakeney Clo.
Trigon Rd. SW8 66 BX43
Trilby Rd. SE23 77 CC48
Trimmer Wk., Brent. 65 BL43
Netley Rd.
Trinder Gdns. N19 47 BX33
Trinder Rd. N19 47 BX33
Trinder Rd., Barn. 28 BQ25
Trindles Rd., Red. 121 BX71
Tring Ave. W5 55 BL40
Tring Ave., Sthl. 54 BE39
Tring Ave., Wem. 55 BM36
Tring Clo., Ilf. 49 CM32
Tring Clo., Rom. 42 CW28
Tring Gdns., Rom. 42 CW28
Tring Grn., Rom. 42 CW28
Tring Rd., Berk. 7 AO11
Tring Wk., Rom. 42 CW28
Tringham Clo., Cher. 91 AU56
Trinidad Gdns., Dag. 59 CS36
Trinidad St. E14 57 CD40
Trinity Ave. N2 47 BT31
Trinity Ave., Enf. 30 CA25
Trinity Ch. Rd. SW13 65 BP43
Trinity Ch. Sq. SE1 4 J6
Trinity Ch. Sq. SE1 67 BZ41
Trinity Clo. E11 49 CG34
Trinity Clo. NW3 47 BT35
Hampstead High St.
Trinity Clo. SE13 67 CF45
Wisteria Rd.
Trinity Clo., Brom. 88 CK54
Trinity Clo., Houns. 64 BE45
Trinity Clo., Nthwd. 35 BB29
Trinity Clo., S.Croy. 96 CA58
Trinity Clo., Stai. 73 AX46
Trinity Cotts., Rich. 65 BL45
Trinity Rd.
Trinity Ct. N1 57 CA37
Trinity Cres. SW17 76 BU48
Trinity Est. SE8 67 CD42
Trinity Gdns. E16 58 CG39
Trinity Gdns. SW9 66 BX45
Trinity Gro. SE10 67 CF44
Trinity La., Wal.Cr. 21 CD19
Trinity Ms. W10 55 BQ39
Cambridge Gdns.
Trinity Ms., Hem.H. 8 BA14
Pancake La.
Trinity Pl. EC3 57 CA40
Trinity Sq.
Trinity Pl., Bexh. 69 CQ45
Trinity Pl., Wind. 61 AO44
Trinity Ri. SW2 76 BY47
Trinity Rd. N2 47 BT31
Trinity Rd. N22 38 BX29
Trinity Rd. SW18 76 BT46
Trinity Rd. SW19 76 BS50
Trinity Rd., Grav. 81 DH47
Trinity Rd., Ilf. 49 CM31
Trinity Rd., Rich. 65 BL45
Trinity Rd., Sthl. 54 BE40
Trinity Sq. EC3 4 N1
Trinity Sq. EC3 57 CA40
Trinity St. E16 58 CG39
Trinity St. SE1 4 J5
Trinity St. SE1 67 BZ41
Trinity St., Enf. 30 BZ23
Trinity Wk. NW3 56 BT36
College Cres.
Trinity Wk., Hem.H. 8 BA14
Pancake La.
Trinity Way E4 39 CD29
Trinity Way W3 55 BO40
Trio Pl. SE1 4 J5
Trio Pl. SE1 67 BZ41
Tripps Hill Clo., Ch.St.G. 34 AQ27
Tripton Rd., Harl. 13 CN11
Tristan Sq. SE3 68 CG45
Tristram Clo. E17 48 CF31
Tristram Rd., Brom. 78 CG49
Triton Sq. NW1 1 L4
Triton Sq. NW1 56 BW38
Triton Way, Hem.H. 8 AY12
Tritton Ave., Croy. 95 BX56
Tritton Rd. SE21 77 BZ48
Trittons, Tad. 103 BQ64
Triumph Clo., Hayes 63 BA43
Triumph Rd. E6 58 CK39
Trodds La., Guil. 118 AU70
Trojan Way, Croy. 86 BX55
Trolling Down Hill, Dart. 80 CY48
Troon St. E1 57 CD39
Troopers Dr., Rom. 42 CV28
Trosley Ave., Grav. 81 DG48
Trosley Rd., Belv. 69 CR43
Trossachs Rd. SE22 77 CA46
Trothy Rd. SE1 67 CB42
Trots La., West. 115 CM67
Trotsworth Ave., Vir.W. 82 AS52
Trott Rd. N10 38 BU29
Trott St. SW11 66 BT44
Trotters Bottom, Barn. 28 BP22
Trotters La., Wok. 91 AQ59
Trotters Rd., Harl. 14 CO12
Trotwood, Brwd. 122 DC26
Trotwood, Chig. 40 CM28
Troughton Rd. SE7 68 CH42
Trout La., West Dr. 53 AX40
Trout Ri., Rick. 26 AW24
Trout Rd., West Dr. 53 AX40
Troutbeck Rd. SE14 67 CD44
Troutstream Way, Rick. 26 AW24
Trouville Rd. SW4 76 BW46
Trowbridge Est. E9 48 CD35
Trowbridge Rd. E9 57 CD36
Trowbridge Rd., Rom. 42 CV29
Trowers Way, Red. 121 BV69
Trowley Ri., Abb.L. 17 BB19
Trowlock Ave., Tedd. 74 BK50
Trowlock Way, Tedd. 74 BK50
Troy Clo., Tad. 103 BP63
Troy Ct. SE18 68 CL42

Troy Ct. W8 66 BS41
Troy Rd. SE19 77 BZ50
Troy Town SE15 67 CB45
Nutbrook St.
Trucks All., Swan. 89 CR51
Truesdale Dr., Uxb. 44 AX31
Truesdale Rd. E6 58 CK39
Trulock Ct. N17 39 CB29
Trulock Rd. N17 39 CB29
Truman Clo., Edg. 37 BM29
Pavilion Way
Trumans Rd. N16 48 CA35
Trump St. EC2 2 J9
Trump St. EC2 57 BZ39
King St.
Trumper Way, Uxb. 53 AX37
Trumpers Way W7 64 BH41
Trumpetshill Rd., Reig. 120 BP71
Trumpington Dr., St.Alb. 9 BG15
Trumpington Rd. E7 49 CG35
Trumps Grn. Clo., Vir.W. 82 AS53
Trumpsgreen Rd.
Trumps Mill La., Vir.W. 82 AS53
Trumpsgreen Ave., 82 AR53
Vir.W.
Trumpsgreen Rd., Vir.W. 82 AR53
Trundle St. SE1 4 H4
Trundle St. SE1 67 BZ41
Weller St.
Trundlers Way, Bush. 36 BH26
Trundleys Rd. SE8 67 CC42
Trundleys Ter. SE8 67 CC42
Truro Gdns., Ilf. 49 CK33
Truro Rd. E17 48 CD31
Truro Rd. N22 38 BX29
Truro Rd., Grav. 81 DH48
Truro St. NW5 56 BV36
Truro Wk., Rom. 42 CV29
Truro Way, Hayes 53 BB38
Truslove Rd. SE27 76 BY49
Trussley Rd. W6 65 BQ41
Trust Rd., Wal.Cr. 21 CD20
Trustees Way, Uxb. 43 AV32
Trustings Clo., Esher 93 BJ57
Trustons Gdns., Horn. 50 CU33
Trycewell La., Sev. 108 DB64
Tryfan Clo., Ilf. 49 CJ32
Tryon St. SW3 3 E10
Tryon St. SW3 66 BU42
Trys Hill, Cher. 82 AT55
Tuam Rd. SE18 68 CM43
Tubbenden Clo., Orp. 88 CN55
Tubbenden Dr., Orp. 97 CM56
Tubbenden La., Orp. 97 CM56
Tubbenden La. S., Orp. 97 CM56
Tubbs Rd. NW10 55 BO37
Tubs Hill, Sev. 107 CU65
Tubwell Rd., Slou. 52 AQ37
Tuck Rd., Rain. 59 CU36
Tucker Rd., Cher. 91 AU57
Tucker St., Wat. 27 BD25
Tuckey Gro., Wok. 100 AV65
Tuckton Wk. SW15 75 BO47
Tudor Ave., Chsnt. 21 CB19
Tudor Ave., Hmptn. 74 BF50
Tudor Ave., Rom. 50 CU31
Tudor Ave., Wat. 27 BD22
Tudor Ave., Wor.Pk. 85 BP55
Tudor Clo. N6 47 BW33
Tudor Clo. NW3 47 BU35
Tudor Clo. NW7 37 BP29
Tudor Clo. NW9 46 BN34
Tudor Clo. SW2 76 BX46
Tudor Clo., Ashf. 73 AY49
Tudor Clo., Bans. 103 BR61
Tudor Clo., Brwd. 122 DD25
Tudor Clo., Chsnt. 21 CB19
Tudor Clo., Chess. 94 BL56
Tudor Clo., Chig. 40 CL28
Tudor Clo., Chis. 88 CK51
Tudor Clo., Cob. 93 BE60
Tudor Clo., Couls. 104 BY62
Tudor Clo., Dart. 79 CU46
Tudor Clo., Hat. 10 BO14
Tudor Clo., Lthd. 102 BE65
Tudor Clo., Pnr. 44 BC32
Tudor Clo., S.Croy. 105 CB61
Tudor Clo., Sutt. 94 BQ57
Tudor Clo., Wall. 95 BW57
Tudor Clo., Wdf.Grn. 40 CH28
Tudor Ct. SE9 68 CK45
Tudor Ct., Borwd. 28 BL23
Tudor Ct., Felt. 74 BD49
Tudor Ct., Saw. 6 CQ5
West Rd.
Tudor Ct. N., Wem. 46 BM45
Tudor Ct. S., Wem. 46 BM45
Tudor Cres., Enf. 30 BZ23
Tudor Cres., Ilf. 40 CL29
Tudor Cres., Sev. 108 CV61
Tudor Dr., Kings.T. 74 BK49
Tudor Dr., Mord. 85 BQ53
Tudor Dr., Rom. 50 CU31
Tudor Dr., Sev. 108 CV61
Tudor Dr., Walt. 84 BD54
Tudor Dr., Wat. 27 BD22
Tudor Est. NW10 55 BM38
Tudor Gdns. NW9 46 BN34
Tudor Gdns. SW13 65 BO45
Treen Ave.
Tudor Gdns. W3 55 BM39
Tudor Gdns., Rom. 50 CU31
Tudor Gdns., Twick. 74 BH47
Tudor Gdns., Upmin. 51 CY34
Tudor Gdns., W.Wick. 87 CF55
Tudor Gro. E9 57 CC36
Tudor Gro. N20 38 BU27
Church Cres.
Tudor Hill, Hem.H. 8 AX14
Tudor Manor Gdns., Wat. 18 BD19
Tudor Par., Rick. 35 AW26
Berry La.
Tudor Pk., Amer. 25 AO22
Tudor Pl. W1 1 N8

Tudor Pl. W1 56 BW39
Gresse St.
Tudor Pl., Mitch. 76 BU50
Tudor Ri., Brox. 12 CD14
Tudor Rd. E4 39 CE29
Tudor Rd. E6 58 CJ37
Tudor Rd. E9 57 CB37
Tudor Rd. N9 39 CB26
Tudor Rd. SE19 77 CA50
Tudor Rd. SE25 87 CB53
Tudor Rd., Ashf. 73 BA50
Tudor Rd., Bark. 58 CN37
Tudor Rd., Barn. 29 BS24
Tudor Rd., Beck. 87 CE52
Tudor Rd., Hmptn. 74 BF50
Tudor Rd., Har. 36 BG30
Tudor Rd., Hayes 53 BA39
Tudor Rd., Houns. 64 BG45
Tudor Rd., Kings.T. 75 BM50
Tudor Rd., Pnr. 36 BD30
Tudor Rd., St.Alb. 9 BH11
Tudor Rd., Sthl. 54 BE40
Tudor Sq., Welw. 5 BP5
Tudor Sq., Hayes 53 BA39
Tudor St. EC4 2 E10
Tudor St. EC4 56 BY39
Tudor Wk., Bex. 79 CQ46
Tudor Wk., Lthd. 102 BH63
Tudor Wk., Wat. 27 BD22
Tudor Wk., Wey. 83 AZ55
Palace Dr.
Tudor Way N14 38 BW26
Tudor Way W3 65 BM41
Tudor Way, Orp. 88 CM53
Tudor Way, Rick. 35 AW26
Tudor Way, Uxb. 53 AZ36
Tudor Way, Wal.Abb. 21 CF20
Tudor Way, West Dr. 63 AY42
Tudor Way, Wind. 61 AM44
Tudor Well Clo., Stan. 36 BJ28
Tudors, The, Reig. 121 BT69
Tudway Rd. SE3 68 CJ45
Tufnail Rd., Dart. 80 CW46
Tufnell Pk. Rd. N7 47 BW35
Tufter Rd., Chig. 40 CN28
Tufton Gdns., E.Mol. 84 BF51
Tufton Rd. E4 39 CE28
Tufton St. SW1 4 A7
Tufton St. SW1 66 BW41
Tugela Rd., Croy. 87 BZ53
Tugela St. SE6 77 CD48
Tugmutton Clo., Orp. 97 CL56
Starts Hill Rd.
Tuilerie St. E2 57 CB37
Tulip Clo., Brwd. 33 DA25
Poppy Clo.
Tulip Clo., Croy. 87 CC54
Primrose La.
Tulip Clo., Hmptn. 74 BF50
Partridge Rd.
Tulip Clo., Rom. 42 CV29
Cloudberry Rd.
Tulip Ct., Pnr. 45 BD31
Nursery Rd.
Tulip Dr., Ilf. 49 CL35
Tulse Clo., Beck. 87 CF52
Tulse Hill SW2 76 BY46
Tulse Hill Est. SW2 76 BY46
Tulsemere Rd. SE27 77 BZ48
Tulyar Clo., Tad. 103 BP63
Tumber St., Epsom 112 BN66
Tumblefield Rd., Sev. 99 DC60
Tumbler Rd., Harl. 14 CO11
Tumblewood Rd., Bans. 103 BR61
Tumbling Bay, Walt. 83 BC53
Tummons Gdns. SE25 87 CA51
Tuncombe Rd. N18 39 CA28
Tunfield Rd., Hodd. 12 CE10
Tunis Rd. W12 55 BP40
Tunley Rd. NW10 55 BO37
Tunley Rd. SW17 76 BV47
Tunmarsh La. E13 58 CJ38
Tunmers End, Ger.Cr. 34 AR30
Tunnel Ave. SE10 68 CG42
Tunnel Cotts., Grays 70 DA43
The Rookery
Tunnel Gdns. N11 38 BW29
Tunnel Rd. SE16 67 CC41
Church St.
Tunnel Wd. Clo., Wat. 26 BB22
Tunnel Wd. Rd., Wat. 26 BB22
Tunnmeade, Harl. 6 CO10
Tuns La., Slou. 61 AO40
Tunsgate, Guil. 118 AR71
Tunstall Ave., Ilf. 41 CO29
Tunstall Clo., Orp. 97 CN56
Tunstall Rd. SW9 66 BX45
Tunstall Rd., Croy. 87 CA54
Tunstall Wk., Brent. 64 BK42
Ealing Rd.
Tunstock Way, Belv. 69 CQ41
Tunworth Clo. NW9 46 BN32
Tunworth Cres. SW15 75 BO46
Tupwood La., Cat. 114 CB66
Tupwood Scrubbs Rd., 114 CB67
Cat.
Turenne Clo. SW18 66 BT45
Turfhouse La., Wok. 91 AP58
Turin Rd. N9 39 CC26
Turin St. E2 57 CB38
Turkey Oak Clo. SE19 87 CA51
Hamlyn Gdns.
Turkey St., Enf. 30 CB21
Turks Clo., Uxb. 53 AZ38
Turks Head Ct. (Eton), 61 AO43
Wind.
High St.
Turks Head Yd. EC1 2 F6
Turks Head Yd. EC1 56 BY38
Turnhill St.
Turks Row SW3 3 F10
Turks Row SW3 66 BU42
Turle Rd. N4 47 BX33
Turle Rd. SW16 86 BW51

Turlewray Clo. N4 47 BX33
Turley Clo. E15 58 CG37
Turmore Dale, Welw.G.C. 5 BQ8
Turnagain La. EC4 2 F8
Turnagain La. EC4 56 BY39
Farringdon St.
Turnagain La., Dart. 79 CU48
Turnage Rd., Dag. 50 CQ33
Turnant Rd. N17 39 BZ30
Lordship La.
Turnberry Dr., St.Alb. 18 BE18
Turnberry Quay E14 67 CE41
Pepper St.
Turnberry Way, Orp. 88 CM54
Turnbull Clo., Green. 80 CZ47
Turner Ave. N15 48 CA31
Turner Ave., Mitch. 86 BU51
Turner Ave., Twick. 74 BG48
Turner Clo. NW11 47 BS32
Turner Clo., Hayes 53 BA37
Turner Dr. NW11 47 BS32
Turner Rd. E17 48 CF31
Turner Rd., Bush. 27 BG24
Turner Rd., Dart. 80 DA48
Turner Rd., Edg. 37 BL30
Turner Rd., N.Mal. 85 BN54
Turner Rd., Slou. 62 AR41
Turner Rd., West. 97 CJ59
Turner St. E1 57 CB39
Turner St. E16 58 CG39
Turners All. EC3 57 CA40
Eastcheap
Turners Clo., Ong. 24 CW18
Turners Clo., Stai. 73 AW49
Turners Gdns., Sev. 117 CV67
Turners Hill, Chsnt. 21 CC18
Turners Hill, Hem.H. 8 AY14
Turners La., Walt. 92 BC57
Turners Meadow Way, Beck. 87 CD51
Turners Rd. E3 57 CD39
Turners Way, Croy. 86 BY55
Turners Wd. NW11 47 BT33
Wildwood Rd.
Turners Wd. Dr., Ch.St.G. 34 AR27
Turneville Rd. W14 65 BR43
Turney Rd. SE21 77 BZ47
Turneys Orchard, Rick. 25 AU25
Turnham Grn. Ter. W4 65 BO42
Turnham Grn. Ter. Ms. W4 65 BO42
Turnham Grn. Ter.
Turnham Rd. SE4 77 CD46
Turnmill St. EC1 2 E5
Turnmill St. EC1 56 BY38
Turnoak Ave., Wok. 100 AS63
Turnoak La., Wok. 100 AS63
Turnoak Pk., Wind. 61 AM45
St. Leonards Hill
Turnpike Clo. SE8 67 CD43
Amersham Vale
Turnpike Ct., Bexh. 69 CP45
Crook Log
Turnpike Dr., Orp. 98 CP58
Turnpike Grn., Hem.H. 8 AY11
Turnpike Ho. EC1 2 G3
Turnpike La. N8 47 BX31
Turnpike La., Sutt. 95 BT56
Turnpike La., Til. 71 DH42
Turnpike La., Uxb. 53 AY37
Turnpike Link, Croy. 87 CA55
Turnpin La. SE10 67 CF43
King William Wk.
Turnstone Clo. E13 58 CH38
Turnstone Clo., S.Croy. 96 CC58
Turnstones, The, Grav. 81 DH48
Turnstones, The, Wat. 27 BE21
Turp Ave., Grays 71 DE41
Turpentine La. SW1 66 BV42
Sutherland St.
Turpin Ave., Rom. 41 CR29
Turpin Est. E13 58 CH37
Turpin Rd., Felt. 73 BB46
Staines Rd.
Turpin Way N19 47 BW33
Ashbrook Rd.
Turpin Way, Wall. 95 BV57
Turpington Clo., Brom. 88 CK54
Turpington La., Brom. 88 CK54
Turpins La., Wdf.Grn. 40 CK28
Turquand St. SE17 4 J9
Turquand St. SE17 67 BZ42
Turret Ct., Ong. 24 CX18
Turret Gro. SW4 66 BW45
Turton Mkt., Wem. 46 BL35
Turton Rd.
Turton Rd., Wem. 46 BL35
Turton Way, Slou. 61 AO41
Turville Ct., Lthd. 111 BF66
Turville St. E2 2 Q4
Turville St. E2 57 CA38
Old Nichol St.
Tuscan Rd. SE18 68 CM42
Tuskar St. SE10 68 CG42
Tustin Est. SE15 67 CC43
Tuttlebee La., Buck.H. 40 CH27
Tuxford Clo., Borwd. 28 BL22
Tweedwell Clo., Brom. 88 CK52
Tweed Glen, Rom. 41 CS29
Tweed Grn., Rom. 41 CS29
Tweed La., Bet. 120 BM72
Tweed Rd., Slou. 62 AT43
Tweed Way, Rom. 41 CS29
Tweedale Ct. E15 48 CE35
Tweedale Gro., Uxb. 44 BA34
Tweedale Rd., Cars. 86 BT54
Tweedmouth Rd. E13 58 CH37
Tweedy Rd., Brom. 88 CH51
Tweenways, Chesh. 16 AP18
Tweezers All. WC2 2 D10
Twelve Acre Clo., Lthd. 102 BE65
Twelve Acres, Welw.G.C. 5 BR9
Twelve Trees Cres. E3 57 CF38
Devas St.
Twelvetrees Cres. E3 57 CF38
Twentyman Clo., Wdf.Grn. 40 CH28
Twickenham Bri., Rich. 74 BK46
Twickenham Bri., Twick. 74 BK46
Twickenham Clo., Croy. 86 BX55
Twickenham Gdns., Grnf. 45 BJ35
Twickenham Gdns., Har. 36 BH29
Twickenham Rd. E11 48 CF34
Twickenham Rd., Felt. 74 BE48
Twickenham Rd., Islw. 74 BJ46
Twickenham Rd., Rich. 64 BK45
Twickenham Rd., Tedd. 74 BJ49
Twigg Clo., Erith 69 CT43
Twilley St. SW18 76 BS47
Twinches La., Slou. 61 AN40
Twine Ct. E1 57 CC40
Cable St.
Twineham Grn. N12 38 BS28
Twining Ave., Twick. 74 BG48
Twinn Rd. NW7 37 BR29
Twinoaks, Cob. 93 BF60
Twisden Rd. NW5 47 BV35
Twitchells La., Beac. 34 AP29
Twitton Bungalows, Sev. 107 CA52
Twitton La., Sev. 107 CS61
Two Acres, Welw.G.C. 5 BR9
Two Dells La., Chesh. 16 AP16
Two Waters Rd., Hem.H. 8 AX15
Twybridge Way NW10 55 BN36
Twyford Abbey Rd. NW10 55 BL38
Twyford Ave. N2 47 BU31
Twyford Ave. W3 55 BM40
Twyford Cres. W3 55 BM40
Twyford Pl. WC2 2 B8
Twyford Pl. WC2 56 BX39
Kingsway
Twyford Rd., Cars. 86 BT54
Twyford Rd., Har. 45 BF33
Twyford Rd., Ilf. 49 CM35
Twyford Rd., St.Alb. 9 BK11
Twyford St. N1 56 BX37
Twysdens Ter., Hat. 10 BQ15
Station Rd.
Tyas Rd. E16 58 CG38
Tybenham Rd. SW19 85 BR52
Tyberry Rd., Enf. 30 CB24
Tyburn La., Har. 45 BH33
Tyburn Way W1 1 F10
Tyburns, The, Brwd. 122 DE27
Tycehurst Hill, Loug. 31 CK24
Tychbourne Dr., Guil. 118 AU69
Tydcombe Rd., Warl. 105 CC63
Tye Grn. Village, Harl. 13 CN12
Tye La., Epsom 112 BN67
Tye La., Orp. 97 CM56
Tyers Est. SE1 4 M4
Tyers Est. SE1 67 CA41
Tyers Gate SE1 4 M5
Tyers Gate SE1 67 CA41
Tyers St. SE11 66 BX42
Tyers Ter. SE11 66 BX42
Tyeshurst Clo. SE2 69 CQ42
Tyfield Clo., Chsnt. 21 CC18
Tykeswater La., Borwd. 27 BK23
Tyle Grn., Horn. 51 CW31
Tyle Pl., Wind. 72 AQ46
Tylecroft Rd. SW16 86 BX51
Tylehost, Guil. 109 AQ68
Tylehurst Gdns., Ilf. 49 CM35
Tyler Clo. E2 57 CA37
Hows St.
Tyler Gdns., Wey. 92 AX56
Tyler Gro., Dart. 70 CW45
Tyler St. SE10 68 CG42
Tylers Causeway, Hert. 11 BW14
Tylers Clo., Gdse. 114 CB68
Tylers Clo., Kings L. 17 AY18
Tylers Clo., Loug. 40 CK26
Tylers Ct. W1 1 N9
Tylers Cres., Horn. 51 CV35
Tylers Gate, Har. 46 BL32
Tylers Grn. Rd., Swan. 89 CS53
Tylers Hill Rd., Chesh. 16 AP18
Tylers Rd., Harl. 13 CJ13
Tylers Way, Wat. 27 BG24
Tylersfield, Abb.L. 17 BC19
Tylney Ave. SE19 77 CA49
Tylney Cft., Harl. 13 CM12
Tylney Rd. E7 49 CJ35
Tylney Rd., Brom. 88 CJ51
Tylsworth Clo., Amer. 25 AO22
King George V Rd.
Tynan Clo., Felt. 73 BC47
Tyndale Clo., Dart. 80 CY47
Princes Rd.
Tyndale La. N1 56 BY36
Upper St.
Tyndale Ter. N1 56 BY36
Tyndale La.
Tyndall Rd. E10 48 CF34
Tyndall Rd., Well. 68 CN45
Tyne Clo., Upmin. 51 CY32
Tyne Gdns., S.Ock. 60 CY40
Tyne Rd., Ilf. 49 CM34
Tyne St. E1 2 Q8
Tyne St. E1 57 CA39
Old Castle St.
Tynedale, St.Alb. 19 BL17
Thamesdale
Tynedale Rd., Bet. 120 BM72
Tyneham Rd. SW11 66 BV44
Tynemouth Dr., Enf. 30 CB22
Tynemouth Rd. N15 48 CA31
Tynemouth Rd., Mitch. 76 BV50
Tynemouth St. SW6 66 BT44
Tynley Gro., Guil. 109 AR67
Type St. E2 57 CC37
Tyrawley Rd. SW6 66 BS44
Tyrell Clo., Har. 45 BH35
Tyrell Ct., Cars. 95 BU56
Tyrell Gdns., Wind. 61 AM45
Tyrell Ri., Brwd. 42 DB28
Chindits La.
Tyrell Sq., Mitch. 86 BU51
Mortlake Dr.
Tyrells Clo., Upmin. 51 CX34
Tyron Way, Sid. 78 CN49
Tyrone Rd. E6 58 CK37
Tyrrel Way NW9 46 BO33
Tyrrell Ave., Well. 79 CO46
Tyrrell Rd. SE22 67 CB45
Tyrrells Hall Clo., Grays 71 DE42
Tyrrells Wd. Dr., Lthd. 103 BL65
Tyrwhitt Ave., Guil. 109 AQ68
Tyrwhitt Rd. SE4 67 CE45
Tysea Clo., Harl. 13 CN12
Tysea Hill, Rom. 41 CT26
Tysea Rd., Harl. 13 CN12
Tysoe Ave., Enf. 30 CD22
Tysoe St. EC1 2 D3
Tysoe St. EC1 56 BY38
Tyson Gdns. SE23 77 CC47
Devonshire Rd.
Tyson Rd. SE23 77 CC47
Tyssen Pl., S.Ock. 60 DB37
Gidea Clo.
Tyssen Rd. N16 48 CA34
Stoke Newington High St.
Tyssen St. E8 57 CA36
Tyssen St. N1 2 N1
Tythebarn Clo., Guil. 109 AT68
Dairymans Wk.
Tytherton Rd. N19 47 BW34
Tyttenhanger Grn., St.Alb. 10 BL15
Tyttenhanger La., St.Alb. 9 BK14

U

Uamvar St. E14 57 CE39
Uckfield Gro., Mitch. 86 BV51
Uckfield Rd., Enf. 30 CC22
Udall Gdns., Rom. 41 CR29
Udall St. SW1 3 M9
Udall St. SW1 66 BW42
Vincent Sq.
Udney Hall, Tedd. 74 BJ49
Udney Pk. Rd., Tedd. 74 BJ50
Uffington Rd. NW10 55 BP37
Uffington Rd. SE27 76 BY49
Ufford Clo., Har. 36 BF29
Ufford Rd., Har. 36 BF29
Ufford St. SE1 4 E4
Ufford St. SE1 66 BY41
Ufton Gro. N1 57 BZ36
Ufton Rd. N1 57 BZ36
Ujima Ct. SW16 76 BX49
Sunnyhill Rd.
Ullathorne Rd. SW16 76 BW49
Ulleswater Rd. N14 38 BX28
Ullin St. E14 57 CF39
St. Leonards Rd.
Ullswater Clo. SW15 75 BN49
Ullswater Clo., Brom. 78 CG50
Ullswater Clo., Hayes 53 BB37
Ullswater Cres. SW15 75 BN49
Ullswater Cres., Couls. 104 BW61
Ullswater Rd. SE27 76 BY48
Ullswater Rd. SW13 65 BP43
Ullswater Rd., Hem.H. 8 AZ14
Ullswater Way, Horn. 50 CU35
Ulstan Clo., Cat. 105 CE65
Ulster Gdns. N13 39 BZ28
Ulster Pl. NW1 1 J5
Ulster Pl. NW1 56 BV38
Ulster Ter. NW1 1 J4
Ulundi Rd. SE3 68 CG43
Ulva Rd. SW15 65 BQ45
Ravenna Rd.
Ulverscroft Rd. SE22 77 CA46
Ulverston Rd. E17 39 CF30
Ulverstone Rd. SE27 76 BY48
Ulwin Ave., Wey. 92 AY60
Ulysses Rd. NW6 46 BR35
Umberston St. E1 57 CB39
Umbria St. SW15 75 BP46
Umfreville Rd. N4 47 BY32
Underacres Clo., Hem.H. 8 AZ13
Undercliff Rd. SE13 67 CE45
Underhill, Barn. 29 BS25
Underhill Pk. Rd., Reig. 121 BS69
Underhill Rd. SE22 77 CB46
Underhill St. NW1 56 BV37
Camden High St.
Underne Ave. N14 38 BV27
Underriver Ho. Rd., Sev. 117 CX68
Undershaft EC3 2 M9
Undershaft EC3 57 CA39
St. Mary Axe
Undershaw Rd., Brom. 78 CG48
Underwood, Croy. 96 CF57
Underwood, The SE9 78 CK48
Underwood Rd. E1 57 CB38
Underwood Rd. E4 39 CE28
Underwood Rd., Cat. 114 CA66
Underwood Rd., Wdf.Grn. 40 CJ29
Underwood Row N1 2 J2
Underwood Row N1 57 BZ38
Underwood St. E1 57 CB38
Underwood Rd.
Underwood St. N1 2 J2
Underwood St. N1 57 BZ38
Undine Rd. E14 67 CE41
Undine St. SW17 76 BU49
Uneeda Dr., Grnf. 54 BG37
Union Cotts. E15 58 CG36
Union Ct. EC2 2 M8
Union Ct. EC2 57 CA39
Old Broad St.
Union Ct., Ilf. 49 CL34
Ilford Hill
Union Ct., Rich. 75 BL46
Eton St.
Union Dr. E1 57 CD38
Solebay St.
Union Gro. SW8 66 BW44
Union La., Islw. 64 BJ44
Park Rd.
Union Rd. N11 38 BW29
Union Rd. SW8 66 BW44
Union Rd., Brom. 88 CJ53
Union Rd., Croy. 87 BZ54
Union Rd., Nthlt. 54 BF37
Union Rd., Wem. 55 BL36
Union Sq. N1 57 BZ37
Union St. E15 57 CF37
Union St. SE1 4 G3
Union St. SE1 66 BY41
Union St., Barn. 28 BR24
Union St., Hem.H. 8 AX13
Union St., Kings.T. 84 BK51
Union Wk. E2 2 N2
Union Wk. E2 57 CA38
Union Yd. W1 56 BV39
Dering St.
Unity Clo., Croy. 96 CE58
Castle Hill Ave.
Unity Rd., Enf. 30 CC22
Unity Way SE18 68 CJ41
University Clo. NW7 37 BO30
Rivington Cres.
University Pl., Erith 69 CS43
Belmont Rd.
University Rd. SW19 76 BT50
University St. WC1 1 M5
University St. WC1 56 BW38
Unwin Ave., Felt. 73 BA46
Unwin Clo. SE15 67 CB43
Unwin Rd. SW7 3 A6
Unwin Rd., Islw. 64 BH45
Upbrook Ms. W2 56 BT39
Upcerne Rd. SW10 66 BT43
Burnaby St.
Upchurch Clo. SE20 77 CB50
Woodbine Gro.
Upcroft, Wind. 61 AN45
Upcroft Ave., Edg. 37 BN28
Updale Clo., Pot.B. 19 BQ20
Updale Rd., Sid. 78 CN49
Upfield, Croy. 87 CB55
Upfield Rd. W7 54 BH38
Upfolds Grn., Guil. 109 AU68
Uphall Rd., Ilf. 49 CL35
Upham Pk. Rd. W4 65 BO42
Uphill Dr. NW7 37 BO28
Uphill Dr. NW9 46 BN32
Uphill Gro. NW7 37 BO28
Uphill Rd. NW7 37 BO28
Upland Ct. Rd., Rom. 42 CW30
Upland Rd. E13 58 CG38
Upland Rd. SE22 77 CB46
Upland Rd., Bexh. 69 CQ45
Upland Rd., Cat. 105 CE63
Upland Rd., Epp. 22 CM16
Upland Rd., S.Croy. 96 BZ56
Upland Rd., Sutt. 95 BT57
Upland Way, Epsom 103 BQ62
Uplands SW16 76 BY49
Uplands, Ash. 102 BK63
Uplands, Beck. 87 CE51
Uplands, Rick. 26 AY25
Uplands, Welw.G.C. 5 BQ6
Uplands, The, Ger.Cr. 43 AS33
Uplands, The, Loug. 31 CK24
Uplands, The, Ruis. 44 BC33
Uplands, The, St.Alb. 18 BE18
Uplands Ave. E17 39 CC30
Uplands Clo. SW14 75 BM46
Uplands Clo., Ger.Cr. 43 AS33
Uplands Clo., Sev. 107 CT65
Uplands Ct. N21 38 BY26
Uplands Dr., Hat. 20 BS16
Uplands Dr., Lthd. 93 BG60
Uplands End, Wdf.Grn. 40 CK29
Uplands Pk. Rd., Enf. 29 BY24
Uplands Rd. N8 47 BX32
Uplands Rd., Barn. 38 BV26
Uplands Rd., Brwd. 122 DC28
Uplands Rd., Ken. 105 BZ61
Uplands Rd., Orp. 89 CO54
Uplands Rd., Rom. 50 CP31
Uplands Rd., Wdf.Grn. 40 CK29
Uplands Way N21 29 BY25
Uplands Way, Sev. 107 CT65
Upminster Rd., Horn. 51 CW34
Upminster Rd. N., Rain. 60 CV38
Upminster Rd. S., Rain. 59 CU38
Upney Clo., Horn. 51 CV35
Tylers Cres.
Upney La., Bark. 49 CN35
Upnor Way SE17 4 N10
Upnor Way SE17 67 CA42
Uppark Dr., Ilf. 49 CM32
Upper Abbey Rd., Belv. 69 CQ42
Upper Addison Gdns. W14 65 BR41
Upper Ashlyns Rd., Berk. 7 AQ13
Upper Austin Lo. Rd., Eyns. 99 CV56
Upper Ave., Grays 81 DF51
Upper Bardsey Wk. N1 57 BZ36
Marquess Est.
Upper Barn, Hem.H. 8 AY15
Upper Belgrave St. SW1 3 H6
Upper Belgrave St. SW1 66 BV41
Upper Berenger Wk. SW10 66 BT43
Worlds End
Upper Berkeley St. W1 1 E9
Upper Berkeley St. W1 56 BU39
Upper Beulah Hill SE19 87 CA51
Upper Blantyre Wk. SW10 66 BT43
Worlds End
Upper Bray Rd., Maid. 61 AH42
Upper Brentwood Rd., Rom. 51 CV
Upper Bri. Rd., Red. 121 BU
Upper Brighton Rd., Surb. 84 BK
Upper Brockley Rd. SE4 67 CD
Upper Brook St. W1 3 C
Upper Brook St. W1 56 BV
Upper Butts, Brent. 64 BK
Upper Caldy Wk. N1 57 BZ
Marquess Est.
Upper Camelford Wk. W11 55 BQ
Lancaster Rd.
Upper Cavendish Ave. N3 47 BS
Upper Cheyne Row SW3 66 BU
Upper Ch. Hill, Green. 80 CZ
Upper Clapton Rd. E5 48 CB
Upper Clarendon Wk. W11 55 BQ
Lancaster Rd.
Upper Cor. Clo., Ch.St.G. 34 AQ
Upper Cornsland, Brwd. 42 DB
Upper Ct. Rd., Cat. 105 CE
Upper Ct. Rd., Epsom 94 BN
Upper Culver Rd., St.Alb. 9 BH
Upper Dagnal St., St.Alb. 9 BG1
Upper Dartrey Wk. SW10 66 BT
Worlds End
Upper Dengie Wk. N1 57 BZ
Popham St.
Upper Drayton Pl., Croy. 86 BY
Drayton Rd.
Upper Dr., West. 106 CJ
Upper Dunnymans Ms., Bans. 94 BR
Basing Rd.
Upper Edgeborough Rd., Guil. 118 AS
Upper Elmers End Rd., Beck. 87 CD
Upper End Rd., Beck. 87 CE
Upper Fairfield Rd., Lthd. 102 BJ
Upper Fm. Rd., E.Mol. 84 BE
Upper Fld. Rd., Welw.G.C. 5 BF
Upper Fosters NW4 46 BQ
Upper George St., Chesh. 16 AO
Upper Grn., Welw.G.C. 5 BL
Upper Grn. E., Mitch. 86 BU
Upper Grn. La., Ton. 117 DB
Upper Grn. Rd., Welw.G.C. 5 BL
Upper Grn. W., Mitch. 86 BU
Upper Grenfell Wk. W11 55 BQ
Lancaster Rd.
Upper Grosvenor St. W1 3 G
Upper Grosvenor St. W1 56 BV
Upper Grotto Rd., Twick. 74 BH
Upper Grd. SE1 4 D
Upper Grd. SE1 56 BY
Upper Gro. SE25 87 CA
Upper Gro. Rd., Belv. 69 CQ
Upper Guildown Rd., Guil. 118 AQ
Upper Gulland Wk. N1 57 BZ
Marquess Est.
Upper Hall Pk., Berk. 7 AR1
Upper Halliford Rd., Shep. 83 BB
Upper Ham Rd., Rich. 74 BK
Upper Handa Wk. N1 57 BZ
Marquess Est.
Upper Harley St. NW1 1 H
Upper Harley St. NW1 56 BV
Upper Hawkwell Wk. N1 57 BZ
Popham St.
Upper Heath Rd., St.Alb. 9 BH1
Upper High St., Epsom 94 BO
Upper Highway, Abb.L. 17 BA
Upper Highway, Kings L. 17 BA
Upper Hill Ri., Rick. 26 AW
Upper Hill Vw. Rd., Pnr. 36 BE
Upper Hitch, Wat. 36 BE
Upper Holly Hill Rd., Belv. 69 CR
Upper James St. W1 1 M1
Upper James St. W1 56 BW
Beak St.
Upper John St. W1 1 M1
Upper John St. W1 56 BW
Beak St.
Upper Lattimore Rd., St.Alb. 9 BH1
Upper Lismore Wk. N1 57 BZ
Marquess Est.
Upper Mall W6 65 BP
Upper Marlborough Rd., St.Alb. 9 BH1
Upper Marsh SE1 4 C
Upper Marsh SE1 66 BX
Upper Marsh La., Hodd. 12 CE1
Upper Mealines, Harl. 14 CO1
Upper Montagu St. W1 1 E
Upper Montagu St. W1 56 BU
Upper Mulgrave Rd., Sutt. 94 BR
Upper N. St. E14 57 CE
Upper Paddock Rd., Wat. 27 BE
Upper Palace Rd., E.Mol. 84 BG
Upper Pk., Harl. 6 CL1
Upper Pk., Loug. 31 CJ
Upper Pk. Rd. N11 38 BV
Upper Pk. Rd. NW3 47 BU
Upper Pk. Rd., Belv. 69 CR
Upper Pk. Rd., Brom. 88 CH
Upper Pk. Rd., Kings.T. 75 BM
Upper Phillimore Gdns. W8 66 BS
Upper Pillory Downs, Cars. 95 BV
Upper Pines, Bans. 104 BU
Upper Rainham Rd., Horn. 50 CT
Upper Ramsey Wk. N1 57 BZ
Marquess Est.

Vicarage La. E15 58 CG36
Vicarage La., Chig. 40 CM27
Vicarage La., Epp. 14 CS15
Vicarage La., Epsom 94 BP58
Vicarage La., Grav. 81 DK48
Vicarage La., Hem.H. 16 AT17
Vicarage La., Ilf. 49 CM33
Vicarage La., Kings L. 17 AY18
Vicarage La., Lthd. 102 BJ64
Vicarage La., Sev. 107 CS63
Vicarage La. (Laleham), Stai. 83 AX52
Vicarage La. (Wraysbury), Stai. 72 AS47
Vicarage La., Wok. 109 AU66
Vicarage Pk. SE18 68 CM42
Vicarage Path N8 47 BW33
Vicarage Pl., Slou. 62 AQ41
Vicarage Rd. E10 48 CE33
Vicarage Rd. E15 58 CG36
Vicarage Rd. N17 39 CB30
Vicarage Rd. NW4 46 BP32
Vicarage Rd. SE18 68 CM42
Vicarage Rd. SW14 75 BN46
Vicarage Rd., Berk. 7 AT11
Vicarage Rd., Bex. 79 CR47
Vicarage Rd., Croy. 86 BY55
Vicarage Rd., Dag. 59 CR36
Vicarage Rd., Egh. 72 AT50
Vicarage Rd., Epp. 23 CP18
Vicarage Rd., Horn. 50 CU33
Vicarage Rd., Kings.T. 84 BK51
Vicarage Rd. (Hampton Wick), Kings.T. 84 BK51
Vicarage Rd., Stai. 72 AV48
Vicarage Rd., Sun. 73 BB49
Vicarage Rd., Sutt. 95 BS56
Vicarage Rd., Tedd. 74 BJ49
Vicarage Rd., Twick. 74 BH48
Vicarage Rd. (Whitton), Twick. 74 BG46
Vicarage Rd., Wat. 26 BC25
Vicarage Rd., Wok. 100 AS64
Vicarage Rd. (Chobham), Wok. 91 AO59
Vicarage Rd., Wdf.Grn. 40 CK29
Vicarage Sq., Grays 71 DD43
West St.
Vicarage Wk. SW11 66 BT44
Battersea Ch. Rd.
Vicarage Wk., Maid. 61 AH41
Vicarage Wk., Walt. 83 BC54
Vicarage Way NW10 46 BN34
Vicarage Way, Ger.Cr. 43 AS32
Vicarage Way, Har. 45 BF33
Vicarage Wd., Harl. 6 CO10
Vicars Bri. Clo., Wem. 55 BL37
Vicars Clo. E9 57 CC37
Pennethorpe Clo.
Vicars Clo. E15 58 CH37
Vicars Clo., Enf. 30 CA23
Vicars Hill SE13 67 CE45
Vicars Moor La. N21 38 BY26
Vicars Oak Rd. SE19 77 CA50
Vicars Rd. NW5 47 BV35
Vicars Wk., Dag. 50 CO34
Viceroy Ct. NW8 56 BU37
Viceroy Rd. SW8 66 BX44
Hartington Rd.
Vickers Dr. N., Wey. 92 AY58
Vickers Dr. S., Wey. 92 AY59
Vickers Rd., Erith 69 CS42
Victor App., Horn. 51 CV33
Victor Clo., Horn. 51 CV33
Abbs Cross Gdns.
Victor Gdns., Horn. 51 CV33
Victor Gro., Wem. 55 BL36
Victor Rd. NW10 55 BP38
Victor Rd. SE20 77 CC50
Victor Rd., Har. 45 BG31
Victor Rd., Tedd. 74 BH49
Victor Rd., Wind. 61 AO45
Victor Vill. N9 39 BZ27
Victor Wk., Horn. 51 CV33
Victoria Arc., Sthl. 54 BE40
Victoria Ave. E6 58 CJ37
Victoria Ave. EC2 2 N7
Victoria Ave. EC2 57 CA39
Bishopsgate
Victoria Ave. N3 37 BR30
Victoria Ave., Barn. 29 BT24
Victoria Ave., E.Mol. 84 BF52
Victoria Ave., Grav. 81 DG47
Victoria Ave., Grays 71 DE41
Victoria Ave., Houns. 74 BF46
Victoria Ave., Rom. 41 CR29
Victoria Ave., S.Croy. 96 BZ58
Victoria Ave., Surb. 84 BK54
Victoria Ave., Uxb. 53 AZ36
Victoria Ave., Wall. 86 BV55
Victoria Ave., Wem. 55 BM36
Victoria Clo., Barn. 29 BT24
Victoria Clo., Grays 71 DE41
Victoria Ave.
Victoria Clo., Hayes 53 BA39
Victoria Clo., Rick. 35 AX26
Nightingale Rd.
Victoria Clo., Wey. 83 BA55
Victoria Cotts. N10 38 BV30
Victoria Cotts., Rich. 65 BL44
Victoria Ct. W3 65 BM41
Victoria Ct., Wem. 55 BM36
Victoria Cres. N15 48 CA32
Victoria Cres. SE19 77 CA50
Victoria Cres. SW19 75 BR50
Victoria Cres., Hayes 53 AW40
Victoria Dock Rd. E16 58 CG39
Victoria Dr. SW19 75 BQ47
Victoria Dr., S.Dnth. 90 CY51
Victoria Embk. EC4 2 D10
Victoria Embk. SW1 4 A4
Victoria Embk. SW1 66 BX41
Victoria Embk. WC2 4 C1
Victoria Gdns. W11 56 BS40
Victoria Gdns., Houns. 64 BE44
Victoria Gdns., West. 106 CJ61
Victoria Gro. N12 38 BT28
Victoria Gro. W8 66 BT41
Victoria Gro. Ms. W2 56 BS40
Victoria Hill Rd., Swan. 89 CT51
Victoria La., Barn. 28 BR24
Victoria La., Hayes 63 BA42
Victoria Ms. NW6 56 BS37
Victoria Ms. SW4 66 BV45
Victoria Ri.
Victoria Pk. Rd. E9 57 CB37
Victoria Pk. Sq. E2 57 CC38
Victoria Pl., Epsom 94 BO59
Victoria Pl., Rich. 74 BK46
Victoria Ri. SW4 66 BV45
Victoria Rd. E4 40 CG26
Victoria Rd. E13 58 CH37
Victoria Rd. E17 39 CF30
Victoria Rd. E18 40 CH30
Victoria Rd. N4 47 BX33
Victoria Rd. N9 39 CA27
Victoria Rd. N15 48 CB31
Victoria Rd. N18 39 CA28
Victoria Rd. N22 38 BW30
Victoria Rd. NW4 46 BQ31
Victoria Rd. NW6 55 BR37
Victoria Rd. NW7 37 BO28
Victoria Rd. NW10 55 BN39
Victoria Rd. SW14 65 BN45
Victoria Rd. W3 55 BN39
Victoria Rd. W5 54 BJ39
Victoria Rd. W8 66 BT41
Victoria Rd., Bark. 58 CL36
Victoria Rd., Barn. 29 BT24
Victoria Rd., Berk. 7 AR13
Victoria Rd., Bexh. 79 CR46
Victoria Rd., Brwd. 42 DB28
Victoria Rd., Brom. 88 CJ53
Victoria Rd., Buck.H. 40 CJ27
Victoria Rd., Bush. 36 BF26
Victoria Rd., Chis. 78 CL49
Victoria Rd., Couls. 104 BW61
Victoria Rd., Dag. 50 CR35
Victoria Rd., Dart. 80 CV46
Victoria Rd., Erith 69 CT43
Victoria Rd., Felt. 73 BC47
Victoria Rd., Grav. 81 DF47
Victoria Rd., Guil. 118 AS71
Victoria Rd., Kings.T. 85 BL51
Victoria Rd., Mitch. 76 BU50
Victoria Rd., Red. 121 BV71
Victoria Rd., Rom. 50 CT32
Victoria Rd., Ruis. 44 BC33
Victoria Rd., Sev. 116 CU66
Victoria Rd., Sid. 78 CN48
Victoria Rd., Slou. 52 AQ40
Victoria Rd., Sthl. 64 BE41
Victoria Rd., Stai. 72 AV48
Victoria Rd., Surb. 84 BK53
Victoria Rd., Sutt. 95 BY56
Victoria Rd., Tedd. 74 BJ50
Victoria Rd., Twick. 74 BJ47
Victoria Rd., Uxb. 53 AX36
Victoria Rd., Wal.Abb. 21 CF20
Victoria Rd., Wat. 26 BC22
Victoria Rd., Wey. 83 BA55
Victoria Rd. (Addlestone), Wey. 92 AX56
Victoria Rd. (Eton Wick), Wind. 61 AM42
Victoria Rd., Wok. 100 AS62
Victoria Rd. (Knaphill), Wok. 100 AO62
Victoria Sq. SW1 3 K6
Victoria Sq. SW1 66 BV41
Beeston Pl.
Victoria Sta. SW1 3 K8
Victoria St. E15 58 CG36
Victoria St. SW1 3 L7
Victoria St. SW1 66 BV41
Victoria St., Belv. 69 CQ42
Victoria St., Egh. 72 AR50
Victoria St., St.Alb. 9 BG13
Victoria St., Slou. 62 AP41
Victoria St., Wind. 61 AO44
Victoria Ter. N4 47 BY33
Victoria Ter., Dor. 119 BJ71
Victoria Ter., Har. 45 BG33
Victoria Vill., Rich. 65 BL45
Victoria Way SE7 68 CH42
Victoria Way, Wey. 83 BA55
Victoria Way, Wok. 100 AS62
Victorian Gro. N16 48 CA34
Victorian Rd. N16 48 CA34
Victors Cres., Brwd. 122 DD27
Victors Dr., Hmptn. 74 BE50
Victors Way, Barn. 28 BR24
Victory Ave., Mord. 86 BT53
Victory Pk. Rd., Wey. 83 AX55
Victory Pl. SE17 4 J8
Victory Pl. SE17 67 BZ42
Victory Pl. SE19 77 CA50
Victory Rd. SW19 76 BT50
Victory Rd., Berk. 7 AQ12
Victory Rd., Cher. 83 AW54
Victory Rd., Rain. 59 CU37
Victory Sq. SE5 67 BZ43
Victory Wk. SE8 67 CE44
Ship St.
Victory Way, Houns. 64 BD42
Victory Way, Rom. 41 CR30
Vienna Clo., Ilf. 40 CK30
Coburg Gdns.
View, The SE2 69 CQ42
View Clo. N6 47 BU32
View Clo., Chig. 40 CM28
View Clo., Har. 45 BG31
View Clo., West. 106 CJ61
View Rd. N6 47 BU33
View Rd., Grays 71 DD43
View Rd., Pot.B. 20 BT19
Viewfield Clo., Har. 46 BL33
Viewfield Rd. SW18 75 BR46
Viewfield Rd., Bex. 79 CP47
Viewland Rd. SE18 68 CN42
Viewlands Ave., Sev. 106 CN63
Viga Rd. N21 29 BY25
Vigerons Way, Grays 71 DG42
Viggory La., Wok. 100 AR61
Vigilant Clo. SE26 77 CB49
Vigilant Way, Grav. 81 DJ49
Vignoles Rd., Rom. 50 CR33
Vigo St. W1 3 L1
Vigo St. W1 56 BW40
Vigors Cft., Hat. 10 BO13
Viking Clo. E3 57 CD37
Selwyn Rd.
Viking Rd., Grav. 81 DE48
Viking Rd., Sthl. 54 BE40
Viking Way, Brwd. 33 DA25
Viking Way, Sev. 99 CZ57
Villa Clo., Grav. 81 DK48
Villa Ct., Dart. 80 CW48
Greenbanks
Villa Rd. SW9 66 BY45
Villa St. SE17 67 BZ42
Villacourt Rd. SE18 69 CO43
Village, The SE7 68 CJ43
Village, The, Ong. 15 DB13
Village Clo. E4 39 CF28
Village Gdns., Epsom 94 BO58
Village Grn. Ave., West. 106 CK62
Village Grn. Rd., Dart. 69 CU45
Village Grn. Way, West. 106 CK62
Village La., Slou. 43 AO33
Village Ms. NW9 46 BN34
Village Rd. N3 37 BR30
Village Rd., Egh. 82 AU52
Village Rd., Enf. 39 BZ26
Village Rd., Uxb. 43 AV34
Village Rd., Wind. 61 AK41
Village Row, Sutt. 95 BS57
Village Way NW10 46 BN35
Village Way SE21 77 BZ46
Village Way, Amer. 25 AR23
Village Way, Ashf. 73 AY49
Village Way, Beck. 87 CE52
Village Way, Pnr. 45 BE33
Village Way, S.Croy. 96 CB60
Village Way E., Har. 45 BE33
Villas Rd. SE18 68 CM42
Villier St., Uxb. 53 AX37
Villiers Ave., Surb. 85 BL53
Villiers Ave., Twick. 74 BE47
Villiers Clo. E10 48 CE34
Villiers Clo., Surb. 85 BL52
Villiers Ct. N20 38 BT26
Villiers Cres., St.Alb. 9 BK12
Villiers Gro., Sutt. 94 BQ58
Villiers Path, Surb. 85 BL53
Villiers Rd. NW2 55 BP36
Villiers Rd., Beck. 87 CC51
Villiers Rd., Islw. 64 BH44
Villiers Rd., Kings.T. 85 BL52
Villiers Rd., Slou. 52 AO39
Villiers Rd., Sthl. 54 BE40
Villiers Rd., Wat. 27 BE25
Villiers St. WC2 4 A2
Villiers St. WC2 56 BX40
Vincam Clo., Twick. 74 BF47
Vince St. EC1 2 L3
Vince St. EC1 57 BZ38
Vincent Ave., Cars. 95 BT59
Vincent Ave., Surb. 85 BM54
Vincent Clo. SE16 67 CD41
Vincent Clo., Barn. 29 BS24
Vincent Clo., Brom. 88 CH52
Vincent Clo., Cher. 82 AV54
Vincent Clo., Chsnt. 21 CD17
Vincent Clo., Couls. 104 BU63
Vincent Clo., Esher 84 BF55
Vincent Clo., Ilf. 40 CM29
Vincent Clo., Lthd. 102 BF65
Vincent Clo., Sid. 79 CN47
Valliers Wd. Rd.
Vincent Clo., West Dr. 63 AZ43
Vincent Ct. NW4 46 BQ31
Vincent Dr., Shep. 83 BB52
Vincent Gdns. NW2 46 BO34
Vincent Grn., Couls. 104 BU63
Vincent La., Dor. 119 BJ71
Vincent Par. N4 47 BX33
Hanley Rd.
Vincent Rd. E4 39 CF29
Vincent Rd. N15 48 BZ31
Vincent Rd. N22 38 BY30
Vincent Rd. SE18 68 CL42
Vincent Rd. W3 65 BN41
Palmerston Rd.
Vincent Rd., Cher. 82 AV54
Vincent Rd., Cob. 102 AM52
Vincent Rd., Couls. 104 BW61
Vincent Rd., Croy. 87 CA54
Vincent Rd., Dag. 59 CQ36
Vincent Rd., Dor. 119 BJ71
Vincent Rd., Houns. 64 BD44
Vincent Rd., Islw. 64 BG44
Vincent Rd., Kings.T. 85 BM52
Vincent Rd., Rain. 60 CV38
Vincent Rd., Wem. 55 BL36
Vincent Row, Hmptn. 74 BG50
Vincent Sq. SW1 3 N8
Vincent Sq. SW1 66 BW42
Vincent Sq., West. 97 CJ60
Vincent St. E16 58 CG39
Vincent St. SW1 3 N8
Vincent St. SW1 66 BW42
Vincent Ter. N1 56 BY37
Vincent Wk., Dor. 119 BJ71
Arundel Rd.
Vincents Dr., Dor. 119 BJ72
Vincents Path, Nthlt. 54 BE36
Arnold Rd.
Vincenzo Clo., Hat. 10 BQ15
Vine Ave., Sev. 107 CU65
Vine Clo., Stai. 73 AW46
Vine Clo., Surb. 85 BL53
Vine Clo., Sutt. 86 BT55
Vine Clo., Welw.G.C. 5 BR7
Vine Clo., West Dr. 63 AZ42
Vine Ct. E1 57 CB39
Vine Ct., Har. 46 BL32
Vine Ct. Rd., Sev. 108 CV65
Vine Gdns., Ilf. 49 CM35
Vine Gro., Uxb. 53 AZ36
Vine Hill EC1 2 D5
Vine Hill EC1 56 BY38
Vine La. SE1 4 N3
Vine La. SE1 57 CA40
Vine La., Uxb. 53 AY37
Vine Pl., Houns. 64 BF45
Vine Rd. E15 58 CG36
Vine Rd. SW13 65 BO45
Vine Rd., E.Mol. 84 BG52
Vine Rd., Orp. 97 CN57
Vine Rd., Slou. 52 AP36
Vine Sq. W14 65 BR42
Vine St. EC3 2 P9
Vine St. EC3 57 CA39
Vine St. W1 3 M1
Vine St. W1 56 BW40
Swallow St.
Vine St., Rom. 50 CS31
Vine St., Uxb. 53 AX37
Vine St. Bri. EC1 2 E5
Vine St. Bri. EC1 56 BY38
Farringdon Rd.
Vine Way, Brwd. 42 DB26
Vine Yd. SE1 4 J5
Vine Yd. SE1 67 BZ41
Sanctuary St.
Vine Yd. Path SW14 65 BN45
North Worple Way
Vinegar All. E17 48 CE31
Vinegar St. E1 57 CB40
Vinegar Yd. SE1 4 M4
Vinegar Yd. SE1 67 CA41
St. Thomas St.
Viner Clo., Walt. 84 BD53
Vineries, The N14 29 BW25
Vineries, The, Enf. 30 CA24
Vineries Bank NW7 37 BP28
Vineries Clo., Dag. 59 CR36
Heath Way
Vineries Clo., West Dr. 63 AZ43
Vinery Vill. NW8 56 BU38
Park Rd.
Vines Ave. N3 38 BS30
Vines La., Ton. 117 CY70
Viney Bank, Croy. 96 CD58
Viney Rd. SE13 67 CE45
Vineyard, The, Rich. 74 BK46
Vineyard, The, Welw.G.C. 5 BR7
Vineyard Ave. NW7 37 BR29
Vineyard Clo. SE6 77 CE47
Vineyard Hill, Pot.B. 20 BV18
Vineyard Hill Rd. SW19 75 BR49
Vineyard Pas., Rich. 75 BL46
Vineyard Rd., Felt. 73 BC48
Vineyard Rd., Pot.B. 20 BV18
Vineyard Row, Kings.T. 84 BK51
Vineyard Wk. EC1 2 D4
Vineyard Wk. EC1 56 BY38
Pine St.
Vining St. SW9 66 BY45
Vinlake Ave., Uxb. 44 AZ34
Vinson Clo., Orp. 89 CO54
Vintners Pl. EC4 2 J10
Vintners Pl. EC4 57 BZ40
Viola Ave. SE2 69 CO42
Viola Ave., Felt. 74 BD46
Viola Ave., Stai. 73 AY47
Viola Clo., S.Ock. 60 DB38
Viola Sq. W12 55 BO40
Violet Ave., Enf. 30 BZ22
Violet Ave., Uxb. 53 AY39
Violet Clo., Wall. 86 BV54
Clover Way
Violet Gdns., Croy. 95 BY56
Violet Hill NW8 56 BT37
Violet La., Croy. 95 BY56
Violet Rd. E3 57 CE38
Violet Rd. E17 48 CE32
Violet Rd. E18 40 CH30
Violet St. E2 57 CB38
Three Colts La.
Violet Way, Rick. 26 AX24
Virgil Dr., Brox. 12 CD15
Virgil Pl. W1 1 E7
Virgil Pl. W1 56 BU39
Seymour Pl.
Virgil St. SE1 4 C6
Virgil St. SE1 66 BX41
Virginia Ave., Vir.W. 82 AR53
Virginia Beeches, Vir.W. 82 AR52
Virginia Clo., Ash. 102 BK62
Skinners La.
Virginia Clo., N.Mal. 85 BN52
Willow Rd.
Virginia Clo., Stai. 83 AX52
Blacksmiths La.
Virginia Clo., Wey. 92 BA57
Virginia Dr., Vir.W. 82 AR53
Virginia Gdns., Ilf. 40 CM30
Virginia Rd. E2 2 P3
Virginia Rd. E2 57 CA38
Virginia Rd., Th.Hth. 86 BY51
Virginia St. E1 57 CB40
Virginia Wk. SW2 76 BX46
Beechdale Rd.
Virginia Wk., Grav. 81 DH50
Viscount Dr. E6 58 CK39
Viscount Gdns., Wey. 92 AY59
Viscount Gro., Nthlt. 54 BD38
Wayfarer Rd.
Viscount Rd., Stai. 73 AX47
Viscount St. EC1 2 H6
Viscount St. EC1 57 BZ38
Viscount Way, Houns. 63 BB45
Vista, The SE9 78 CJ46
Vista, The, Sid. 78 C
Langdon Shaw
Vista Ave., Enf. 30 C
Vista Dr., Ilf. 49 C
Vista Way, Har. 46 B
Vivash Clo., Hayes 63 B
Vivian Ave. NW4 46 B
Vivian Ave., Wem. 46 B
Vivian Clo., Wat. 35 B
Vivian Gdns., Wat. 35 B
Vivian Gdns., Wem. 46 B
Vivian Rd. E3 57 C
Vivian Sq. SE15 67 C
Vivian Way N2 47 B
Vivien Clo., Chess. 94 B
Hunting Gate Dr.
Vivienne Clo., Twick. 74 B
Voce Rd. SE18 68 C
Voewood Clo., N.Mal. 85 B
Vogan Clo., Reig. 121 B
Volta Way, Croy. 86 B
Voltaire Rd. SW4 66 B
Voltaire Way, Hayes 53 B
Voluntary Pl. E11 49 C
Vorley Rd. N19 47 B
Voss Ct. SW16 76 B
Voss St. E2 57 C
Vulcan Clo., Wall. 95 B
Vulcan Gate, Enf. 29 B
Uplands Pk. Rd.
Vulcan Rd. SE4 67 C
Vulcan Ter. SE4 67 C
Vulcan Way N7 56 B
Vulcan Way, Croy. 97 C
Vyne, The, Bexh. 69 C
Vyner Rd. W3 55 B
Vyner St. E2 57 C
Vyners Way, Uxb. 44 A
Vyse Clo., Barn. 28 B

W

Waborne Cres., Ruis. 44 B
Thames Dr.
Wacketts, Chsnt. 21 C
Wadding St. SE17 4
Wadding St. SE17 67 B
Waddington Ave., Couls. 104 B
Waddington Clo., Couls. 104 B
Waddington Rd. E15 48 C
Waddington Rd., St.Alb. 9 B
Waddington St. E15 57 C
Waddington Ter., Bexh. 79 C
Waddington Way SE19 77 B
Waddon Clo., Croy. 86 B
Waddon Ct. Rd., Croy. 95 B
Waddon Ind. Est., Croy. 95 B
Waddon Marsh Way, Croy. 86 B
Waddon New Rd., Croy. 86 BY
Waddon Pk. Ave., Croy. 95 BY
Waddon Rd., Croy. 86 BY
Waddon Way, Croy. 95 BY
Wade, The, Welw.G.C. 5 B
Wade Ave., Orp. 89 C
Wade Dr., Slou. 61 AN
Wade Rd. E16 58 C
Leyes Rd.
Wades, The, Hat. 10 B
Wades Gro. N21 38 BY
Wades Hill N21 29 BY
Wades La., Tedd. 74 B
Wades Pl. E14 57 C
Wadeson St. E2 57 CB
Wadeville Ave., Rom. 50 C
Wadeville Clo., Belv. 69 C
Wadham Ave. E17 39 C
Wadham Clo., Shep. 83 BA
Wadham Gdns. NW3 56 BU
Wadham Gdns., Grnf. 54 BG
Wadham Rd. E17 39 C
Wadham Rd. SW15 65 B
Wadham Rd., Abb.L. 17 BB
Wadhurst Clo. SE20 87 CB
Wadhurst Rd. SW8 66 B
Wadhurst Rd. W4 65 BN
Wadley Clo., Hem.H. 8 AY
Wadley Rd. E11 49 CG
Wadsworth Clo., Enf. 30 CC
Falcon Rd.
Wadsworth Clo., Grnf. 54 BK
Wadsworth Rd., Grnf. 54 BJ
Wager St. E3 57 CD
Waggon Clo., Guil. 118 AP
Waggon La. N17 39 CB
Waggon Ms. N14 38 BV
Chase Side
Waghorn Rd. E13 58 CJ
Waghorn Rd., Har. 45 BK
Waghorn St. SE15 67 CB
Wagner St. SE15 67 CC
Ilderton Rd.
Wagon Rd., Barn. 29 BS
Wagon Way, Rick. 26 AX
Wagtail Gdns., S.Croy. 96 CC
Waid Clo., Dart. 80 CW
Wain Clo., Pot.B. 20 BS
Wainfleet Ave., Rom. 41 CS
Wainford Clo. SW19 75 BQ
Windlesham Gro.
Wainwright Ave., Brwd. 122 DE
Wainwright Gro., Islw. 64 BG
Waite Davies Rd. SE12 78 CG
Waite St. SE15 67 CA
Waitham St. EC4 56 BY
Pilgrim St.
Waithman St. EC4 2
Wake Rd., Loug. 31 CJ

efield Cres., Slou. 52 AP36
efield Gdns. SE19 77 CA50
efield Gdns., Ilf. 49 CK32
efield Ms. WC1 2 A3
efield Rd. N11 38 BW28
efield Rd. N15 48 CA32
efield Rd., Rich. 74 BK46
efield St. E6 58 CJ37
efield St. N18 39 CB28
efield St. WC1 2 A3
efield St. WC1 56 BX38
efield Wk., Wal.Cr. 21 CD19
ownfield Rd.
ehams Hill, Pnr. 45 BE31
ehurst Path, Wok. 91 AU60
ehurst Rd. SW11 76 BU46
elin Rd. E15 58 CG37
eling Rd. W7 54 BH39
eling St. E14 57 CD39
ely Clo., West. 106 CJ62
eman Rd. NW10 55 BQ38
emans Hill Ave. NW9 46 BN32
enham St. N1 57 BZ36
erfield Clo., Horn. 51 CW32
ering Rd., Bark. 58 CM36
erley Clo. E6 58 CK39
uesdale Rd.
kley St. EC1 2 F2
kley St. EC1 56 BY38
berswick St. SW8 66 BX43
outh Lambeth Rd.
brook EC4 2 K10
brook EC4 57 BZ40
burgh St. E1 57 CB39
burton Rd., Pur. 95 BW60
corde Ave. SE17 4 J9
corde Ave. SE17 67 BZ42
rowning St.
cot Rd., Enf. 30 CD23
cot Sq. SE11 4 E8
cot Sq. SE11 66 BY42
cott St. SW1 3 M8
cott St. SW1 66 BW42
ochester Row
deck Gro. SE27 76 BY48
deck Rd. N15 47 BY31
deck Rd. SW14 65 BN45
ower Richmond Rd.
deck Rd. W4 65 BM43
deck Rd. W13 54 BJ39
ldeck Rd., Dart. 80 CW47
ldeck Ter. SW14 65 BN45
ower Richmond Rd.
ldegrave Ave., Tedd. 74 BH49
ldegrave Gdns., Twick. 74 BH48
ldegrave Gdns., 51 CX34
pmin.
ldegrave Pk., Twick. 74 BH49
ldegrave Rd. N8 47 BY31
ldegrave Rd. SE19 77 CA50
ldegrave Rd. W5 55 BL39
ldegrave Rd., Brom. 88 CK52
ldegrave Rd., Dag. 50 CP34
ldegrave Rd., Twick. 74 BH49
ldegrove, Croy. 87 CA55
elborne Rd.
ldemar Ave. SW6 65 BR44
ldemar Ave. W13 54 BK40
ldemar Rd. SW19 76 BS49
lden Ave. N13 39 BZ28
lden Ave., Chis. 78 CK49
lden Ave., Rain. 59 CS37
lden Clo., Belv. 69 CQ42
lden Gdns., Th.Hth. 86 BX52
lden Pl., Welw.G.C. 5 BQ7
lden Rd. N17 39 BZ30
ordship La.
lden Rd., Chig. 78 CK50
lden Rd., Horn. 51 CV32
lden Rd., Welw.G.C. 5 BQ7
lden St. E1 57 CB39
ew Rd.
lden Way NW7 37 BQ29
lden Way, Horn. 51 CV32
lden Way, Ilf. 40 CN29
ldenhurst Rd., Orp. 89 CP54
ldens Clo., Orp. 89 CP54
ldens Pk. Rd., Wok. 100 AR61
ldens Rd., Orp. 89 CQ54
ldens Rd., Wok. 100 AR62
ldenshaw Rd. SE23 77 CC47
ldo Clo. SW4 76 BW46
ms Rd.
ldo Pl., Mitch. 76 BU50
ldo Rd. NW10 55 BP38
ldo Rd., Brom. 88 CJ52
ldorf Clo., S.Croy. 95 BY57
ldram Cres. SE23 77 CC47
ldram Pk. Rd. SE23 77 CC47
ldram Pl. SE23 77 CC47
aldram Cres.
ldrist Way, Erith 69 CQ41
ldron Gdns., Brom. 87 CF52
ldron Ms. SW3 66 BU43
ld Ch. St.
ldron Rd. SW18 76 BT48
ldron Rd., Har. 45 BH33
ldron Yd., Har. 45 BG34
ldronhyrst, Croy. 95 BY56
ldrons, The, Croy. 95 BY56
ldrons, The, Oxt. 115 CG69
ldrons Path, Croy. 95 BY56
leran Bldgs. SE1 67 CA42
ld Kent Rd.
leran Clo., Stan. 36 BH28
henduit Way
lerand Rd. SE13 67 CF44
les Ave., Cars. 95 BU56
les Fm. Rd. W3 55 BN39
ley St. E1 57 CC39
lfield Ave. N20 38 BS26
lford Rd. N16 48 CA35
lford Rd., Dor. 119 BK73
lford Rd., Uxb. 53 AX37
Walfords Clo., Harl. 6 CP9
Walfrey Gdns., Dag. 59 CQ36
Walham Gro. SW6 66 BS43
Walham Ri. SW19 75 BR49
Walham Yd. SW6 66 BS43
Walham Gro.
Walk, The, Horn. 51 CW34
Walk, The, Oxt. 114 CE70
Tanridge La.
Walk, The, Pot.B. 20 BS19
Walk, The, Sun. 73 BB50
Walk, The (Eton Wick), 61 AN42
Wind.
Walkden Rd., Chis. 78 CL49
Walker Ave., Ong. 15 CY14
Walker Clo. SE18 68 CM42
Walker Clo. W7 54 BH40
Walker Clo., Dart. 69 CT45
Walker Clo., Hmptn. 74 BE50
Fearnley Ct.
Walkers Ct. W1 1 N10
Walkers Ct. W1 56 BW40
Peter St.
Walkerscroft Mead SE21 77 BZ47
Walkfield Dr., Epsom 103 BP62
Walkford Way SE15 67 CA43
Walkley Rd., Dart. 79 CU46
Walks, The N2 47 BT31
Wall End Rd. E6 58 CK36
Wall St. N1 57 BZ36
Wallace Clo. SE28 59 CP40
Haldane Rd.
Wallace Clo., Horn. 50 CU34
Wallace Clo., Shep. 83 BA52
Hawthorn Way
Wallace Clo., Uxb. 53 AY37
Wallace Cres., Cars. 95 BU56
Wallace Flds., Epsom 94 BO59
Wallace Gdns., Swans. 80 DB46
Milton St.
Wallace Rd. N1 57 BZ36
Wallace Rd., Grays 71 DD41
Wallace Wk., Wey. 92 AX56
Wallasey Cres., Uxb. 44 AZ34
Wallbutton Rd. SE4 67 CD44
Wallcote Ave. NW2 46 BQ33
Walled Gdn., The, Bet. 120 BN71
Walled Gdn., The, Tad. 103 BQ64
Heathcote
Wallenger Ave., Rom. 50 CU31
Waller Dr., Nthwd. 35 BC30
Waller La., Cat. 105 CA65
Waller Rd. SE14 67 CC44
Wallers Clo., Wdf.Grn. 40 CK29
Wallers Hoppit, Loug. 31 CK23
Wallers Way, Hodd. 12 CE10
Wallflower St. W12 55 BO40
Wallgrave Rd. SW5 66 BS42
Wallgrave Rd. W8 66 BS43
Wallhouse Rd., Erith 69 CU43
Wallingford Ave. W10 55 BQ39
Wallingford Rd., Uxb. 53 AW38
Wallingford Wk., St.Alb. 9 BG15
Wallington Clo., Ruis. 44 BA32
Wallington Ct., Wall. 95 BV57
Wallington Rd., Ilf. 49 CN33
Wallington Sq., Wall. 95 BV57
Wallis All. SE1 4 J5
Wallis Clo. SW11 66 BT45
Hope St.
Wallis Clo., Dart. 79 CT48
Wallis Ct., Slou. 62 AQ41
Nixey Clo.
Wallis Pk., Grav. 81 DD46
Wallis Rd. E9 57 CD36
Wallis Rd., Sthl. 54 BF39
Walliss Cotts. SW2 76 BX47
Wallorton Gdns. SW14 65 BN45
Wallwood Rd. E11 48 CF33
Wallwood St. E14 57 CD39
Walm La. NW2 55 BQ36
Walmar Clo., Barn. 29 BT22
Walmer Clo. E4 39 CE27
Wellington Ave.
Walmer Clo., Rom. 41 CR30
Walmer Gdns. W13 64 BJ41
Walmer Pl. W1 1 E6
Walmer Rd. W11 55 BR40
Walmer St. W1 1 E6
Walmer Ter. SE18 68 CM42
Walmgate Rd., Grnf. 54 BJ37
Walmington Fold N12 38 BS29
Walney Wk. N1 57 BZ36
Clephane Rd.
Walnut Ave., West Dr. 63 AZ41
Walnut Clo. SE8 67 CD43
Clyde St.
Walnut Clo., Cars. 95 BU56
Park Hill
Walnut Clo., Epsom 103 BO61
Walnut Clo., Hayes 53 BB40
Walnut Clo., Ilf. 49 CM31
Civic Way
Walnut Clo., St.Alb. 18 BF17
Walnut Ct., Welw.G.C. 5 BR9
Walnut Dr., Tad. 103 BR65
Walnut Flds., Epsom 94 BO58
Walnut Gdns. E15 48 CF35
Ashlin Rd.
Walnut Grn., Bush. 27 BE23
Walnut Gro., Bans. 94 BQ60
Walnut Gro., Enf. 30 BZ25
Walnut Gro., Hem.H. 8 AX13
Walnut Gro., Welw.G.C. 5 BR9
Walnut Ms., Sutt. 95 BT57
Christchurch Pk.
Walnut Tree Ave., Dart. 80 CW48
Walnut Tree Clo. SW13 65 BO44
Lonsdale Rd.
Walnut Tree Clo., Bans. 94 BR59
Walnut Tree Clo., Chsnt. 21 CC19
Turners Hill
Walnut Tree Clo., Chis. 88 CM51
Walnut Tree Clo., Guil. 118 AR70
Walnut Tree Clo., Hodd. 12 CE12
Walnut Tree Cotts. 75 BR49
SW19
Church Rd.
Walnut Tree Cres., Saw. 6 CQ5
Walnut Tree La., Wey. 92 AX59
Chertsey La.
Walnut Tree Pk., Guil. 118 AR70
Walnut Tree Rd. SE10 68 CG42
Walnut Tree Rd., 65 BL43
Brent.
Walnut Tree Rd., Dag. 50 CQ34
Walnut Tree Rd., Erith 69 CT42
Walnut Tree Rd., Houns. 64 BE43
Walnut Tree Rd., Shep. 83 BA52
Walnut Tree Wk. SE11 4 D8
Walnut Tree Wk. SE11 66 BY42
Walnut Way, Buck.H. 40 CJ27
Walnut Way, Ruis. 54 BD36
Walnut Way, Swan. 89 CS51
Walnuts Rd., Orp. 89 CO54
Walpole Ave., Couls. 104 BU62
Walpole Ave., Rich. 65 BL44
Walpole Clo. W13 64 BK41
Walpole Clo., Grays 71 DE42
Palmer Dr.
Walpole Clo., Pnr. 36 BF29
Walpole Ct., Twick. 74 BH48
Walpole Cres., Tedd. 74 BH49
Walpole Gdns. W4 65 BN42
Walpole Gdns., Twick. 74 BH48
Walpole Pk., Wey. 92 AZ57
Walpole Pl., Tedd. 74 BH49
Walpole Rd. E6 58 CJ36
Walpole Rd. E17 48 CD31
Walpole Rd. E18 40 CG30
Walpole Rd. N17 39 BZ30
Walpole Rd. SW19 76 BT50
Walpole Rd., Brom. 88 CJ53
Walpole Rd., Croy. 87 BZ55
Walpole Rd., Surb. 85 BL54
Walpole Rd., Tedd. 74 BH49
Walpole Rd., Twick. 74 BH48
Walpole Rd., Wind. 72 AQ47
Walpole St. SW3 3 E10
Walpole St. SW3 66 BU42
Walpole Way, Barn. 28 BQ25
Walrond Ave., Wem. 46 BL35
Walsh Cres., Croy. 97 CG59
Walsham Clo. N16 48 CB33
Braydon Rd.
Walsham Clo. SE28 59 CP40
Walsham Rd. SE14 67 CC44
Walsham Rd., Felt. 73 BC47
Walshford Way, Borwd. 28 BM22
Walsingham Clo., Hat. 10 BP11
Lemsford Rd.
Walsingham Gdns., 94 BO56
Epsom
Walsingham Pk., Chis. 88 CM51
Walsingham Rd. E5 48 CB34
Walsingham Rd. W13 54 BJ40
Walsingham Rd., Croy. 96 CF58
Walsingham Rd., Enf. 30 BZ24
Walsingham Rd., Mitch. 86 BU53
Walsingham Rd., Orp. 89 CO51
Walsingham Wk., Belv. 69 CR43
Walsingham Way, St.Alb. 18 BK17
Walter St. E2 57 CC38
Walter St., Kings.T. 85 BL51
Canbury Pas.
Walter Ter. E1 57 CC39
Walter Wk., Edg. 37 BN29
Walters Mead, Ash. 103 BL62
Walters Rd. SE25 87 CA52
Walters Rd., Enf. 30 CC25
Walters Way SE23 77 CC46
Walters Yd., Brom. 88 CH51
Walterton Rd. W9 55 BR38
Waltham Ave. NW9 46 BM32
Waltham Ave., Guil. 109 AQ68
Waltham Ave., Hayes 63 BA41
Waltham Clo., Dart. 79 CU46
Waltham Clo., Orp. 89 CP54
Waltham Ct., Har. 36 BF30
Waltham Dr., Edg. 37 BM30
Waltham Gdns., Enf. 30 CC22
Waltham Pk. Way E17 39 CE30
Waltham Rd., Cars. 86 BT54
Waltham Rd., Cat. 105 CB64
Waltham Rd., Sthl. 64 BE41
Waltham Rd., Wal.Abb. 22 CG16
Waltham Rd., Wdf.Grn. 40 CK29
Waltham Way E4 39 CD28
Walthamstow Ave. E4 39 CD29
Waltheof Ave. N17 39 BZ30
Waltheof Gdns. N17 39 BZ30
Walthorne Gdns., Dag. 59 CR36
Acre Rd.
Walton Ave., Har. 45 BE35
Walton Ave., N.Mal. 85 BO52
Walton Ave., Sutt. 85 BR55
Walton Bri. Rd., Shep. 83 BA53
Walton Clo. E5 48 CC34
Millfields Rd.
Walton Clo. NW2 46 BP34
Walton Clo. SW8 66 BX43
South Lambeth Rd.
Walton Clo., Har. 45 BG31
Walton Ct., Wok. 100 AT61
Boundary Rd.
Walton Cres., Har. 45 BE35
Walton Dr. NW10 55 BN36
Mitchellbrook Way
Walton Dr., Har. 45 BG31
Walton Gdns. W3 55 BM39
Walton Gdns., Brwd. 122 DE25
Walton Gdns., Felt. 73 BB49
Walton Gdns., Grnf. 45 BH35
Walton Gdns., Wal.Abb. 21 CE20
Walton Gdns., Wem. 46 BL34
Walton Grn., Croy. 96 CE58
Walton La., Shep. 83 BA54
Walton La., Wey. 83 AZ55
Walton Pk., Walt. 84 BD55
Walton Pk. La., Walt. 84 BD55
Walton Pl. SW3 3 E6
Walton Pl. SW3 66 BU41
Walton Rd. E12 49 CL34
Walton Rd. E13 58 CJ37
Walton Rd., Bush. 27 BD24
Walton Rd., E.Mol. 84 BE52
Walton Rd. (Epsom 103 BO62
Downs), Epsom
Walton Rd. (Headley), 103 BN64
Epsom
Walton Rd., Har. 45 BG31
Walton Rd., Hodd. 12 CE11
Walton Rd., Rom. 41 CQ29
Walton Rd., Sid. 79 CO48
Walton Rd., Walt. 84 BD53
Walton Rd., Wok. 100 AS61
Walton St. SW3 3 D8
Walton St. SW3 66 BU42
Walton St., Enf. 30 BZ23
Walton St., St.Alb. 9 BH12
Walton St., Tad. 103 BP65
Walton Ter. SW8 66 BX43
South Lambeth Rd.
Walton Ter., Wok. 100 AT61
Walton Way W3 55 BM39
Walton Way, Mitch. 86 BW52
Waltons Hall Rd., S.le H. 71 DK41
Walverns Clo., Wat. 27 BD25
Walworth Pl. SE17 67 BZ42
Walworth Rd. SE1 4 H9
Walworth Rd. SE17 4 H9
Walworth Rd. SE17 67 BZ42
Walwyn Ave., Brom. 88 CJ52
Wambrook Clo., Brwd. 122 DE26
Wanborough Dr. SW15 75 BP47
Wandle Bank SW19 76 BT50
Wandle Bank, Croy. 86 BX55
Wandle Ct., Epsom 94 BN56
Wandle Ct. Gdns., Croy. 86 BX55
Wandle Pk. Trd. Est., 86 BY54
Croy.
Wandle Rd. SW17 76 BU48
Wandle Rd., Croy. 87 BZ55
Wandle Rd. (Waddon), 86 BX55
Croy.
Wandle Rd., Mord. 86 BT52
Wandle Rd., Wall. 86 BV55
Wandle Side, Croy. 86 BX55
Wandle Side, Wall. 86 BV55
Wandle Way SW18 76 BS47
Wandle Way, Mitch. 86 BU53
Wandon Rd. SW6 66 BS43
Wandsworth Bri. SW6 66 BS45
Wandsworth Bri. SW18 66 BS45
Wandsworth Bri. Rd. 66 BS44
SW6
Wandsworth High St. 76 BS46
SW18
Wandsworth Plain SW18 76 BS46
Wandsworth Rd. SW8 66 BV45
Wangey Rd., Rom. 50 CP33
Wanless Rd. SE24 67 BZ45
Wanley Rd. SE5 67 BZ45
Wanlip Rd. E13 58 CH38
Wannions Clo., Chesh. 16 AQ18
Wannock Gdns., Ilf. 40 CL29
Wansbeck Rd. E9 57 CD36
Wansbury Way, Swan. 89 CU53
Wansey St. SE17 4 J9
Wansey St. SE17 67 BZ42
Wansford Clo., Brwd. 42 CZ27
Wansford Grn., Wok. 100 AP62
Kenton Way
Wansford Pk., Borwd. 28 BN24
Wansford Rd., Wdf.Grn. 40 CJ30
Wanstead Clo., Brom. 88 CJ51
Wanstead La., Ilf. 49 CJ32
Wanstead Pk. Ave. E12 49 CJ33
Wanstead Pk. Rd., Ilf. 49 CJ32
Wanstead Pl. E11 49 CH32
Wanstead Rd., Brom. 88 CJ51
Wansunt Rd., Bex. 79 CS47
Wantage Rd. SE12 78 CG46
Wantz La., Rain. 59 CU38
Wantz Rd., Dag. 50 CR35
Waplings, The, Tad. 103 BP65
Wapping Dock St. E1 57 CB40
Cinnamon St.
Wapping High St. E1 57 CB40
Wapping La. E1 57 CB40
Wapping Wall E1 57 CC40
Wapseys La., Slou. 43 AP32
Wapshott Rd., Stai. 72 AV50
War Coppice Rd., Cat. 114 BZ67
Warbank Clo., Croy. 97 CG58
Warbank Cres., Croy. 97 CG58
Warbank La., Kings.T. 75 BO50
Warbeck Rd. W12 55 BP40
Warberry Rd. N22 38 BX30
Warblers Grn., Cob. 93 BE60
Warboys App., Kings.T. 75 BM50
Warboys Cres. E4 39 CF28
Warboys Rd., Kings.T. 75 BM50
Warburton Clo., Har. 36 BG29
Warburton Rd., Twick. 74 BF47
Warburton Ter. E17 39 CE30
Ward Ave., Grays 71 DD42
Ward Clo., Chsnt. 21 CB17
Spicersfield
Ward Clo., Erith 69 CS43
Ward Gdns., Slou. 61 AM40
Ward Hatch, Harl. 6 CO9
Ward La., Warl. 105 CC61
Ward Rd. E15 57 CF37
Ward Rd. N19 47 BW34
Ward Royal, Wind. 61 AO44
Ward St., Guil. 118 AR71
Wardale Clo. SE16 67 CB41
Wardell Clo. NW7 37 BO29
Wardell Fld. NW9 37 BO30
Warden Ave., Har. 45 BE33
Warden Ave., Rom. 41 CS28
Warden Ct., Har. 45 BE33
Warden Rd. NW5 56 BV36
Wardens Gro. SE1 4 H3
Wardens Gro. SE1 57 BZ40
Wardle St. E9 48 CC35
Wardley St. SW18 76 BS47
Wardo Ave. SW6 65 BR44
Wardour Ms. W1 1 M9
Wardour St. W1 1 M8
Wardour St. W1 56 BW39
Wardrobe, The, Rich. 74 BK46
Old Palace Yd.
Wardrobe Pl. EC4 2 G9
Wardrobe Ter. EC4 2 G10
Wards La., Borwd. 27 BH23
Wards Rd., Ilf. 49 CM33
Ware Rd., Hodd. 12 CE10
Wareham Clo., Houns. 64 BF45
Waremead Rd., Ilf. 49 CL32
Warenford Way, Borwd. 28 BM23
Warenne Rd., Lthd. 102 BG64
Warepoint Dr. SE28 68 CM41
Warescot Clo., Brwd. 42 DA26
Warescot Rd., Brwd. 42 DA26
Wareside, Hem.H. 8 AZ10
Wareside Clo., Welw.G.C. 5 BS8
Waterford Grn.
Warfield Rd. NW10 55 BQ38
Warfield Rd., Felt. 73 BB47
Warfield Rd., Hmptn. 84 BF51
Wargrave Ave. N15 48 CA32
Wargrave Rd., Har. 45 BG34
Warham Rd. N4 47 BY32
Warham Rd., Har. 36 BH30
Warham Rd., Sev. 107 CU61
Warham Rd., S.Croy. 95 BY56
Warham St. SE5 66 BY43
Waring Clo., Orp. 97 CN57
Waring Dr., Orp. 97 CN57
Waring Rd., Sid. 79 CP50
Waring St. SE27 77 BZ49
Warkworth Gdns., Islw. 64 BJ43
Warkworth Rd. N17 39 BZ29
Warland Rd. SE18 68 CM43
Warland Rd., Sev. 99 CZ58
Warland Rd. E., Sev. 99 CZ58
Warley Ave., Dag. 50 CQ33
Warley Ave., Hayes 53 BC39
Warley Gap, Brwd. 42 DA29
Warley Hall La., Upmin. 123 DC33
Warley Hill, Brwd. 42 DA29
Warley Mt., Brwd. 42 DB28
Warley Rd. N9 39 CC27
Warley Rd., Brwd. 42 DA29
Warley Rd., Hayes 53 BC39
Warley Rd., Ilf. 40 CL30
Warley Rd., Upmin. 42 CY30
Warley Rd., Wdf.Grn. 40 CH29
Warley St. E2 57 CC38
Warley St., Brwd. 51 DB32
Warley St., Upmin. 51 DB33
Warlingham Rd., Th.Hth. 86 BY52
Warlock Rd. W9 55 BR38
Warlters Clo. N7 47 BX35
Warlters Rd. N7 47 BX35
Warltersville Rd. N19 47 BX33
Warmark Rd., Hem.H. 7 AV12
Warmington Clo. E5 48 CC34
Denton Way
Warmington Rd. SE24 77 BZ46
Warmington St. E13 58 CH38
Warminster Gdns. SE25 87 CB51
Warminster Rd. SE25 87 CA51
Warminster Sq. SE25 87 CB51
Warminster Way, Mitch. 86 BV51
Warndon St. SE16 67 CC42
Warneford Pl., Wat. 27 BE25
Warneford Rd., Har. 45 BK31
Warneford St. E9 57 CB37
Warner Ave., Sutt. 85 BR55
Warner Clo. E15 49 CG35
Warner Clo. NW9 46 BO33
Warner Clo., Hayes 63 BA43
Warner Clo., Slou. 61 AM40
Warner Par., Hayes 63 BA43
Warner Pl. E2 57 CB37
Warner Rd. E17 48 CD31
Warner Rd. N8 47 BW31
Warner Rd. SE5 67 BZ44
Warner Rd., Brom. 78 CG50
Warner St. EC1 2 D5
Warner St. EC1 56 BY38
Warner Yd. EC1 2 D5
Warners Ave., Hodd. 12 CD13
Warners Clo., Wdf.Grn. 40 CH28
Warners End Rd., Hem.H. 8 AW13
Warners La., Kings.T. 74 BK49
Warnford Rd., Orp. 97 CN56
Warnham Ct. Rd., Cars. 95 BU57
Warnham Rd. N12 38 BU28
Warnsford Grn., Wok. 100 AP62
Kenton Way
Warple Way W3 55 BO40
Warren, The E12 49 CK35
Warren, The, Ash. 103 BL63
Warren, The, Cars. 95 BT58
Warren, The, Ger.Cr. 34 AS30
Warren, The, Grav. 81 DH49
Warren, The, Hayes 53 BC39
Warren, The, Houns. 64 BE43
Warren, The, Lthd. 93 BG59
Warren, The (East 110 BB68
Horsley), Lthd.
Warren, The, Rad. 18 BJ20
Warren, The, Tad. 103 BR65
Warren, The, Wor.Pk. 94 BN56
Warren Ave. E10 48 CF34
Warren Ave., Brom. 78 CG50
Warren Ave., Orp. 97 CN56
Warren Ave., Rich. 65 BM45
Warren Ave., S.Croy. 96 CC57
Warren Ave., Sutt. 94 BR58
Warren Clo. N9 39 CC26
Warren Clo. SE21 77 BZ46

Warren Clo., Bexh. 79 CR46
Warren Clo., Esher 93 BF56
Warren Clo., Hat. 10 BP11
Warren Clo., Slou. 62 AS41
Warren Clo., Wem. 45 BK34
Warren Ct., Beck. 77 CD50
Warren Ct., Chig. 40 CM28
Warren Ct., Sev. 117 CV66
Warren Ct., Wey. 92 AZ56
Heath Rd.
Warren Cres. N9 39 CA26
Warren Cutting, Kings.T. 75 BN50
Warren Dale, Welw.G.C. 5 BQ6
Warren Dr., Grnf. 54 BF38
Warren Dr., Horn. 50 CU35
Warren Dr., Orp. 98 CO56
Warren Dr., Ruis. 45 BD33
Warren Dr., Tad. 103 BR64
Warren Dr., The E11 49 CJ33
Warren Dr. N., Surb. 85 BM54
Warren Dr. S., Surb. 85 BN54
Warren Fld., Epp. 23 CO19
Charles St.
Warren Fld., Iver 52 AU37
Warren Flds., Stan. 36 BK28
Warren Gdns. E15 48 CF35
Warren Gdns., Orp. 98 CO56
Warren Grn., Hat. 10 BP11
Warren Gro., Borwd. 28 BN24
Warren Hill, Epsom 103 BN61
Warren Hill, Loug. 31 CJ25
Warren Hill Ho., Loug. 31 CH25
Warren Ho., Kings.T. 75 BN50
Warren Hyrst, Guil. 118 AT71
Warren La. SE18 68 CL41
Warren La., Brwd. 33 CZ23
Warren La., Grays 70 DB42
Warren La., Lthd. 93 BG59
Warren La., Oxt. 115 CG70
Warren La., Stan. 36 BH27
Warren La., Wok. 101 AW62
Warren Lo. Dr., Tad. 103 BR65
Warren Mead, Bans. 103 BQ61
Warren Ms. W1 1 L5
Warren Pk., Kings.T. 75 BN50
Warren Pk., Warl. 105 CC62
Warren Pk. Rd., Sutt. 95 BU57
Warren Pl. E1 57 CC39
Pitsea St.
Warren Pond Rd. E4 40 CG26
Warren Ri., N.Mal. 85 BN51
Warren Rd. E4 39 CF27
Warren Rd. E10 48 CF34
Warren Rd. E11 49 CJ32
Warren Rd. NW2 46 BO34
Warren Rd. SW19 76 BU50
Warren Rd., Ashf. 73 BB50
Warren Rd., Bans. 94 BQ60
Warren Rd., Bexh. 79 CR46
Warren Rd., Brom. 88 CH55
Warren Rd., Bush. 36 BG26
Warren Rd., Croy. 87 CA54
Warren Rd., Dart. 80 CW48
Warren Rd., Grav. 81 DD49
Warren Rd., Guil. 118 AS71
Warren Rd., Ilf. 49 CM32
Warren Rd., Kings.T. 75 BN50
Warren Rd., Orp. 97 CN56
Warren Rd., Pur. 95 BY59
Warren Rd., Reig. 121 BS70
Warren Rd., St.Alb. 9 BG15
Warren Rd., Sid. 79 CP48
Warren Rd., Twick. 74 BG46
Warren Rd., Uxb. 44 AY35
Warren Rd., Wey. 92 AW58
Warren St. W1 1 K5
Warren St. W1 56 BW38
Warren St. Ms. W1 56 BW38
Warren St.
Warren Ter., Grays 70 DB41
Warren Ter., Rom. 50 CP31
Warren Wk. SE7 68 CJ43
Warren Way NW7 37 BR29
Warren Way, Welw.G.C. 5 BR5
Warren Way, Wey. 92 BA56
Warren Wd. Clo., Brom. 88 CG55
Warren Wd. Rd., Brom. 88 CG55
Warrender Rd. N19 47 BW34
Warrender Rd., Chesh. 16 AP18
Warrender Way, Ruis. 44 BC33
Warreners La., Wey. 92 BA57
Warrenfield Clo., Chsnt. 21 CB19
Portland Dr.
Warrengate La., Pot.B. 19 BQ19
Warrengate Rd., Hat. 19 BQ17
Warrenne Rd., Bet. 120 BN71
Warrens, The, Hartley 90 DC53
Warrens Shawe La., Edg. 37 BM26
Warriner Ave., Horn. 51 CV34
Warriner Gdns. SW11 66 BU44
Warrington Ave., Slou. 52 AO39
Warrington Cres. W9 56 BT38
Warrington Gdns. W9 56 BS39
Warwick Ave.
Warrington Gdns., Horn. 51 CV32
Warrington Pl. E14 57 CF40
Yabsley St.
Warrington Rd., Croy. 86 BY55
Warrington Rd., Dag. 50 CP34
Warrington Rd., Har. 45 BH32
Warrington Rd., Rich. 75 BL46
The Hermitage
Warrington Spur, Wind. 72 AQ47
Warrington Sq., Dag. 50 CP34
Warrington St. E13 58 CH38
Warrior Ave., Grav. 81 DH49
Warrior Sq. E12 49 CL35
Warsaw Clo., Ruis. 53 BC36
Warspite Rd. SE18 68 CK41
Warton Rd. E15 57 CF37
Warwick Ave. W2 56 BS38
Warwick Ave. W9 56 BS38
Warwick Ave., Cuffley 20 BW17
Warwick Ave., Edg. 37 BM27
Warwick Ave., Egh. 82 AU51
Warwick Ave., Har. 45 BE35
Warwick Ave., Slou. 52 AO38
Warwick Ave., Stai. 73 AX50
Warwick Clo., Barn. 29 BT25
Warwick Clo., Bush. 36 BH26
Warwick Clo., Cuffley 20 BW17
Warwick Clo., Hmptn. 74 BG50
Warwick Clo., Orp. 89 CO55
Warwick Ct. SE15 67 CB44
Warwick Ct. WC1 2 C7
Warwick Ct. WC1 56 BX39
Warwick Ct., Surb. 85 BL55
Warwick Cres. W2 56 BT39
Warwick Cres., Hayes 53 BB38
Warwick Deeping Pl., Cher. 91 AU56
Warwick Dene W5 55 BL40
Warwick Dr. SW15 65 BP45
Warwick Dr., Chsnt. 21 CC17
Warwick Est. W2 56 BS39
Warwick Gdns. N4 48 BZ32
Warwick Gdns. W14 65 BR41
Warwick Gdns., Ash. 102 BK62
Warwick Gdns., Ilf. 49 CL33
Warwick Gdns., Rom. 51 CV31
Warwick Gdns., T.Ditt. 84 BH53
Warwick Gro. E5 48 CB33
Warwick Gro., Surb. 85 BL54
Warwick Ho. St. SW1 3 P2
Warwick Ho. St. SW1 56 BW40
Warwick La. EC4 2 G9
Warwick La. EC4 56 BY39
Warwick La., Upmin. 60 CW38
Warwick La., Wok. 100 AQ63
Warwick Pl. W5 64 BK41
Warwick Rd.
Warwick Pl. W9 56 BT39
Warwick Pl., Brwd. 33 CY24
Warwick Pl., Grav. 81 DD46
Warwick Pl., Uxb. 53 AX36
Warwick Pl. N. SW1 3 L9
Warwick Pl. N. SW1 66 BW42
Warwick Rd. E4 39 CE28
Warwick Rd. E11 49 CH32
Warwick Rd. E12 49 CK35
Warwick Rd. E15 58 CG36
Warwick Rd. E17 39 CD30
Warwick Rd. N11 38 BW29
Warwick Rd. N18 39 CA28
Warwick Rd. SE20 87 CB52
Warwick Rd. SW5 66 BS42
Warwick Rd. W5 64 BK41
Warwick Rd. W14 65 BR42
Warwick Rd., Ashf. 73 AY49
Warwick Rd., Barn. 29 BS24
Warwick Rd., Borwd. 28 BN24
Warwick Rd., Couls. 95 BW60
Warwick Rd., Enf. 30 CD22
Warwick Rd., Houns. 63 BC45
Warwick Rd., Kings.T. 84 BK51
Warwick Rd., N.Mal. 85 BN52
Warwick Rd., Rain. 60 CV38
Warwick Rd., Red. 121 BU70
Warwick Rd., St.Alb. 9 BH12
Warwick Rd., Sid. 79 CO49
Warwick Rd., Sthl. 64 BE41
Warwick Rd., Sutt. 95 BT56
Warwick Rd., T.Ditt. 84 BH53
Warwick Rd., Th.Hth. 86 BY52
Warwick Rd., Twick. 74 BH47
Warwick Rd., Well. 69 CP45
Warwick Rd., West Dr. 53 AY40
Warwick Row SW1 3 K6
Warwick Row SW1 66 BV41
Warwick Sq. EC4 2 G8
Warwick Sq. EC4 56 BY39
Warwick Sq. SW1 3 L10
Warwick Sq. SW1 66 BW42
Warwick Sq. Ms. SW1 3 N9
Warwick St. W1 1 M10
Warwick St. W1 56 BW40
Warwick Ter. SE18 68 CM43
Warwick Way SW1 3 K10
Warwick Way SW1 66 BV42
Warwick Way, Rick. 26 BA24
Warwick Wold Rd., Red. 113 BY68
Warwick Yd. EC2 2 J5
Warwicks Bench, Guil. 118 AS72
Warwicks Bench La., Guil. 118 AS72
Warwicks Bench Rd., Guil. 118 AS72
Warwickshire Path SE8 67 CD43
Payne St.
Wash La., Pot.B. 19 BP20
Wash Rd., Brwd. 122 DE25
Washington Ave. E12 49 CK35
Washington Ave., Hem.H. 8 AY11
Washington Clo., Reig. 121 BS69
Washington Dr., Wind. 61 AM45
Washington Rd. E6 58 CJ36
St. Stephens Rd.
Washington Rd. E18 40 CG30
Washington Rd. SW13 65 BP43
Washington Rd., Kings.T. 85 BM51
Washington Rd., Wor.Pk. 85 BP55
Washington Row, Amer. 25 AO23
Washneys La., Orp. 98 CO60
Washpond La., Warl. 105 CF62
Wastdale Ms. SE23 77 CC47
Wastdale Rd.
Wastdale Rd. SE23 77 CC47
Wat Tyler Rd. SE10 67 CF44
Watch Mead, Welw.G.C. 5 BS7
Watchfield Ct. W4 65 BN42
Watchgate, Dart. 80 CY49
Watchlytes, Welw.G.C. 5 BT8
Watcombe Cotts., Rich. 65 BM43
Rushwood Rd.
Watcombe Rd. SE25 87 CB53
Water End Rd., Berk. 7 AT12
Water Fld., Welw.G.C. 5 BS7
Water Gdns., Stan. 36 BJ29
Gordon Ave.
Water La. E15 58 CG36
Water La., Berk. 7 AR13
Water La., Brwd. 33 CY23
Water La., Cob. 102 BE61
Water La., Grays 70 CX42
Water La., Harl. 13 CK12
Water La., Hem.H. 16 AT18
Water La., Ilf. 49 CN34
Water La., Kings L. 17 AZ18
Water La., Kings.T. 84 BK51
Water La., Lthd. 111 BD66
Water La., Oxt. 115 CH66
Water La., Red. 114 BZ69
Water La., Rich. 74 BK46
Water La., Sev. 98 CT60
Water La., Sid. 79 CQ48
Water La., Twick. 74 BJ47
Water La., Wat. 27 BD24
Water Mead, Tad. 103 BP63
Water Mill Way, S.Dnth. 90 CX51
Water Rd., Wem. 55 BL37
Water St. WC2 2 C10
Water St. WC2 56 BY40
Maltravers St.
Water St., Kings.T. 85 BL51
Canbury Pas.
Water Twr. Clo., Uxb. 44 AY35
Water Twr. Hill, Croy. 96 BZ56
Waterbank Rd. SE6 77 CE48
Waterbeach, Welw.G.C. 5 BT8
Waterbeach Rd., Dag. 50 CP35
Waterbeach Rd., Slou. 52 AO39
Waterbrook La. NW4 46 BQ32
Brent Grn.
Watercress Clo., Sev. 108 CV63
Watercress Dr.
Watercress Dr., Sev. 108 CV63
Watercress Way, Wok. 100 AQ62
Watercroft Rd., Sev. 98 CQ58
Waterdale Rd. SE2 69 CO43
Waterdale St., Grav. 81 DE48
Waterden Clo., Guil. 118 AS71
Waterden Rd. E15 48 CE35
Waterden Rd., Guil. 118 AS71
Waterend La., St.Alb. 5 BN7
Waterer Gdns., Tad. 103 BR62
Waterer Ri., Wall. 95 BW57
Waterer Rd. N20 38 BT27
Waterers Ri., Wok. 100 AO62
Waterfall Clo. N14 38 BW27
Waterfall Rd.
Waterfall Clo., Vir.W. 82 AQ52
Waterfall Cotts. SW19 76 BT50
Waterfall Rd. N11 38 BV28
Waterfall Rd. N14 38 BV28
Waterfall Rd. SW19 76 BT50
Waterfall Ter. SW17 76 BU50
Waterfield, Tad. 103 BP63
Waterfield Clo. SE28 59 CO40
Waterfield Dr., Warl. 105 CC63
Waterfield Gdns. SE25 87 BZ53
Holmesdale
Waterfield Grn., Tad. 103 BP63
Waterfields, Lthd. 102 BJ63
Waterford Grn., Welw.G.C. 5 BS8
Waterford Rd. SW6 66 BS43
Watergate EC4 2 F10
Watergate EC4 56 BY40
Tudor St.
Watergate, Wat. 36 BD27
Watergate St. SE8 67 CE43
Watergate Wk. WC2 4 A1
Watergate Wk. WC2 56 BX40
Waterhall Ave. E4 40 CG28
Waterhall Clo. E17 39 CC30
Waterhead Clo., Erith 69 CT43
Waterhouse Clo. E16 58 CJ39
Waterhouse Clo. NW3 47 BT35
Lyndhurst Rd.
Waterhouse Clo. W6 65 BQ42
Great Ch. La.
Waterhouse La., Ken. 105 BZ63
Waterhouse La., Red. 114 CA69
Waterhouse La., Tad. 103 BR64
Waterhouse Moor, Harl. 13 CN11
Waterhouse St., Hem.H. 8 AX13
Wateringbury Clo., Orp. 89 CO52
Waterloo Bri. SE1 4 B1
Waterloo Bri. SE1 56 BX40
Waterloo Bri. WC2 4 B1
Waterloo Bri. WC2 56 BX40
Waterloo Clo. E9 48 CC35
Waterloo Est. E2 57 CC37
Waterloo Gdns. E2 57 CC37
Waterloo Gdns., Rom. 50 CT32
Waterloo Ms. SE5 67 BZ43
Elmington Rd.
Waterloo Pas. NW6 55 BR36
Willesden La.
Waterloo Pl. SW1 3 N2
Waterloo Pl. SW1 56 BW40
Waterloo Pl., Rich. 65 BL45
The Quad.
Waterloo Pl., Rich. 65 BM43
Waterloo Rd. E6 58 CJ36
Waterloo Rd. E7 49 CG35
Wellington Rd.
Waterloo Rd. E10 48 CE33
Waterloo Rd. NW2 46 BP33
Waterloo Rd. SE1 4 D4
Waterloo Rd. SE1 56 BX40
Waterloo Rd., Brwd. 42 DB26
Waterloo Rd., Epsom 94 BN59
Waterloo Rd., Ilf. 40 CM30
Waterloo Rd., Rom. 50 CT32
Waterloo Rd., Sutt. 95 BT56
Waterloo Rd., Uxb. 53 AX37
Waterloo St. EC1 57 BZ38
Lever St.
Waterloo Ter. N1 56 BY36
Waterlow Ct. NW11 47 BS33
Waterlow Rd. N19 47 BW33
Waterlow Rd., Reig. 121 BT71
Waterman Clo., Wat. 26 BC25
Waterman St. SW15 65 BQ45
Waterman Way E1 57 CB40
Waterman Way, Epp. 23 CR17
Watermans Wk. SE16 57 CD40
Watermead, Felt. 73 BB47
Watermead, Wok. 100 AP61
Watermead La., Cars. 86 BU53
Watermead Rd. SE6 77 CE49
Watermead Way N17 39 CB30
Watermill Clo., Rich. 74 BK48
Watermill La. N18 39 CA28
Watermill Way SW19 86 BY51
Watermill Way, Felt. 74 BE48
Watermint Quay N16 48 CB32
Craven Wk.
Waterpetty La., Wok. 91 AP58
Waters Dr., Rick. 35 AY26
Norfolk Rd.
Waters Dr., Stai. 72 AV48
Waters Gdns., Dag. 50 CR35
Waters Meet, Harl. 13 CL13
Waters Rd. SE6 78 CG48
Waters Rd., Kings.T. 85 BM51
Waters Side Way, Wok. 100 AQ62
Winnington Way
Waters Sq., Kings.T. 85 BM52
Watersedge, Epsom 94 BN56
Watersfield Way, Edg. 36 BK29
Waterside, Beck. 87 CD51
Waterside, Berk. 7 AR13
Waterside, Chesh. 16 AO20
Waterside, Dart. 79 CT46
Waterside, Kings L. 17 AZ18
Waterside, St.Alb. 19 BL17
Waterside, Uxb. 53 AX39
Waterside, Welw.G.C. 5 BS7
Waterside Clo. SE16 67 CB41
Bevington St.
Waterside Clo., Bark. 50 CO35
Waterside Clo., Nthlt. 54 BE38
Waterside Dr., Walt. 83 BC53
Waterside Ms., Guil. 118 AR69
Waterside Pl. NW1 56 BV37
Princess Rd.
Waterside Rd., Guil. 118 AR69
Waterside Rd., Sthl. 64 BF41
Waterside Way SW17 76 BT49
Watersmeet Clo., Guil. 109 AT68
Cotts Wd. Dr.
Watersmeet Way SE28 59 CP39
Waterson Rd., Grays 71 DG42
Waterson St. E2 2 N2
Waterson St. E2 57 CA38
Watersplash, Houns. 63 BC42
Watersplash Ct., St.Alb. 19 BL17
Barnet Rd.
Watersplash La., Hayes 63 BC42
Watersplash Rd., Shep. 83 AZ52
Waterton Ave., Grav. 81 DJ47
Waterway Rd., Lthd. 102 BJ64
Waterworks La. E5 48 CC34
Lea Bri. Rd.
Waterworks Rd. SW2 76 BX46
Waterworks Yd., Croy. 87 BZ55
Surrey St.
Watery La. SW20 85 BR51
Watery La., Brox. 21 CD16
Watery La., Cher. 82 AU54
Watery La., Hat. 10 BO13
Watery La., Hayes 63 BB42
Watery La., Nthlt. 54 BD37
Watery La. (High Laver), Ong. 15 CV11
Watery La. (Willingale), Ong. 15 DA13
Watery La., St.Alb. 18 BK17
Watery La., Sev. 108 CY64
Watery La., Sid. 79 CO50
Watery La., Wok. 91 AO58
Wates Way, Mitch. 86 BU53
Wateville Rd. N17 39 BZ30
Watford By-pass, Borwd. 36 BJ26
Watford Clo. SW11 66 BU44
Petworth St.
Watford Clo., Guil. 118 AS70
Watford Fld. Rd., Wat. 27 BD25
Watford Heath, Wat. 36 BD26
Watford Rd. E16 58 CH39
Watford Rd., Borwd. 27 BK25
Watford Rd., Har. 45 BJ33
Watford Rd., Kings L. 17 AZ20
Watford Rd., Nthwd. 35 BB29
Watford Rd., Rad. 27 BH21
Watford Rd., Rick. 26 AZ25
Watford Rd., St.Alb. 18 BF17
Watford Way NW4 37 BN28
Watford Way NW7 37 BN28
Wathen Rd., Dor. 119 BJ71
Watkin Rd., Wem. 46 BM34
Watkinson Rd. N7 56 BX36
Watling Ave., Edg. 37 BN30
Watling Clo., Hem.H. 8 AY11
Watling Ct. EC4 2 J9
Watling Ct. EC4 57 BZ39
Watling St.
Watling Ct., Bush. 27 BK25
Watling Fm. Clo., Stan. 36 BJ26
Watling Gdns. NW2 55 BR36
Watling Knoll, Rad. 18 BH20
Watling St. EC4 2 H9
Watling St. EC4 57 BZ39
Watling St., Bexh. 69 CR45
Watling St., Borwd. 27 BK23
Watling St., Dart. 80 CX47
Watling St., Grav. 81 DE48
Watling St., Rad. 18 BH19
Watling St., St.Alb. 9 BD10
Watling Vw., St.Alb. 9 BG15
Watlings Clo., Croy. 87 CD53
Watlington Gro. SE26 77 CD49
Watlington Rd., Harl. 6
Watney Mkt. E1 57 C
Watney Rd. SW14 65 B
Watney St. E1 57 C
Watneys Rd., Mitch. 86 B
Watson Ave. E6 58 C
Watson Ave., Sutt. 85 B
Watson Clo. N16 48 B
Matthias Rd.
Watson Clo. SW19 76 B
Watson Clo., Grays 70 D
Watson Ms. W1 1
Watson Rd., Dor. 119 B
Watson St. E13 58 C
Watson Way, Grnf. 54 B
Sindall Dr.
Watsons Ave., St.Alb. 9 B
Watsons Ms. W1 56 B
Crawford Pl.
Watsons Rd. N22 38 B
Watsons St. SE8 67 C
Watsons Wk., St.Alb. 9 B
Watsons Yd. NW2 46 B
Wattendon Rd., Ken. 104 B
Wattisfield Rd. E5 48 C
Watts Bri. Rd., Erith 69 C
Watts Cres., Grays 70 C
Watts Fm. Par., Wok. 91 A
Watts Gro. E3 57 C
Watts La., Chis. 88 C
Watts La., Tad. 103 B
Watts La., Tedd. 74 B
Watts Mead, Tad. 103 B
Watts Rd., T.Ditt. 84 B
Watts St. E1 57 C
Watts Way SW7 3
Watts Way SW7 66 BT
Wauthier Clo. N13 38 BY
Wavel Ms. N8 47 BW
Park Ave. S.
Wavel Ms. NW6 56 BS
Wavel Pl. SE26 77 CA
Sydenham Hill
Wavell Clo., Chsnt. 21 CD
Wavell Dr., Sid. 78 CN
Wavendene Ave., Egh. 72 AT
Wavendon Ave. W4 65 BN
Waveney, Hem.H. 8 AY
Waveney Ave. SE15 67 CB
Waveney Clo. E1 57 CB
Kennet St.
Waverley Ave. E4 39 CD
Waverley Ave. E17 48 CF
Waverley Rd.
Waverley Ave., Ken. 105 CA
Waverley Ave., Surb. 85 BM
Waverley Ave., Sutt. 86 BS
Waverley Ave., Twick. 74 BE
Waverley Ave., Wem. 55 BL
Waverley Clo. E18 40 CJ
Waverley Clo., Brom. 88 CJ
Waverley Clo., Hayes 63 BA
Waverley Cres. SE18 68 CM
Waverley Cres., Rom. 42 CV
Waverley Dr., Cher. 82 AU
Waverley Dr., Vir.W. 82 AC
Waverley Gdns. E6 58 CK
Oliver Gdns.
Waverley Gdns. NW10 55 BL
Waverley Gdns., Bark. 58 CN
Waverley Gdns., Grays 71 DD
Waverley Gdns., Ilf. 40 CM
Waverley Gdns., Nthwd. 35 BC
Waverley Gro. N3 46 BO
Waverley Pl. N4 47 BY
Adolphus Rd.
Waverley Pl. NW8 56 BT
Waverley Pl., Lthd. 102 BK
Church Rd.
Waverley Rd. E17 48 CF
Waverley Rd. E18 40 CJ
Waverley Rd. N8 47 BW
Waverley Rd. N17 39 CB
Waverley Rd. SE18 68 CM
Waverley Rd. SE25 87 CB
Waverley Rd., Cob. 93 BF
Waverley Rd., Enf. 29 BY
Waverley Rd., Epsom 94 BP
Waverley Rd., Har. 45 BE
Waverley Rd., Rain. 59 CU
Waverley Rd., St.Alb. 9 BG
Waverley Rd., Sthl. 54 BF
Waverley Rd., Wey. 92 AZ
Waverley Wk. W2 56 BS
Waverley Way, Cars. 95 BU
Waverton Rd. SW18 76 BT
Waverton St. W1 3
Waverton St. W1 65 BV
Wavertree Ct. SW2 76 BX
Wavertree Rd. E18 40 CH
Wavertree Rd. SW2 76 BX
Waxhouse Gate, St.Alb. 9 BG
High St.
Waxlow Cres., Sthl. 54 BF
Waxlow Rd. NW10 55 BN
Waxwell Clo., Pnr. 36 BD
Waxwell La., Pnr. 36 BD
Waxwell Ter. SE1 66 BX
Way, The, Reig. 121 BT
Way Side, Kings L. 17 AW
Way Volante, Grav. 81 DJ
Waycross Rd., Upmin. 51 CZ
Waye Ave., Houns. 63 BC
Wayfarer Rd., Nthlt. 54 BD
Wayfaring Grn., Grays 71 DC
Curling La.
Wayford St. SW11 66 BU
Wayland Ave. E8 48 CB
Waylands, Swan. 89 CT
Waylands Clo., Sev. 107 CQ
Waylands Mead, Beck. 87 CE
Waylett Pl. SE27 76 BY
Waylett Pl., Wem. 45 BK
Wayne Clo., Orp. 88 CN

Way–Wes

ɣneflete Twr. Ave., 84 BF55
sher
ɣnflete Ave., Croy. 86 BY55
ɣnflete Sq. W10 55 BQ40
ɣnflete St. SW18 76 BT48
ɣre Rd., Harl. 6 CP9
yside NW11 46 BR33
yside SW14 75 BN46
yside, Pot.B. 20 BT20
yside, The, Hem.H. 8 AZ14
yside Ave., Bush. 27 BG25
yside Ave., Horn. 51 CV34
yside Clo. N14 29 BW25
yside Clo., Rom. 50 CT31
yside Ct., Twick. 74 BK46
yside Gdns. SE9 78 CK49
/ayside Gro.
yside Gdns., Dag. 50 CR35
yside Gdns., Ger.Cr. 43 AR33
yside Gro. SE9 78 CK49
yside Ms., Ilf. 49 CL32
aysham Ave.
yville Rd., Dart. 80 CX47
ald, The, Chis. 78 CK50
ald, The, Grav. 81 DF50
ald Bri. Rd., Epp. 14 CS15
ald Clo., Brwd. 42 DA27
ald Clo., Brom. 88 CK55
ald Clo., Guil. 118 AS73
tation Rd.
ald Clo., Sev. 116 CU70
ald Hall La., Epp. 23 CP16
ald La., Har. 36 BG30
ald Pk. Way, Brwd. 42 CZ27
ald Ri., Har. 36 BH29
ald Rd., Brwd. 42 CX26
ald Rd., Sev. 116 CU67
ald Rd., Uxb. 53 AZ37
ald Sq. E5 48 CB34
'ossington St.
ald Way, Cat. 114 CA67
ald Way, Hayes 53 BB38
ald Way, Reig. 121 BT72
ald Way, Rom. 50 CR32
aldstone Rd., Sutt. 85 BR55
aldwood Gdns., Pnr. 36 BF29
ligh Banks Rd.
ale Rd. E4 39 CF27
all Grn., Wat. 17 BC19
ar Pl. E2 57 CB38
ar St. E2 57 CB38
'eesdale St.
ardale Ave., Dart. 80 CY47
ardale Gdns., Enf. 30 BZ23
ardale Rd. SE13 67 CF45
arside Rd. SE13 67 CE45
asdale Ct., Wok. 100 AP61
atherall Clo., Wey. 92 AW56
atherley Clo. E3 57 CD39
aver St. E1 57 CB38
aver Wk. SE27 76 BY49
avers Clo., Grav. 81 DG47
avers Clo., Islw. 64 BH45
avers La. SE1 57 CA40
avers La., Sev. 108 CV64
avers Ter. SW6 66 BS43
Micklethwaite Rd.
bb Clo., Slou. 62 AR42
bb Est. E5 48 CB33
bb Gdns. E13 58 CH38
Kelland Rd.
bb Rd. SE3 68 CG43
bb St. SE1 4 M7
bb St. SE1 67 CA41
ebber Clo., Borwd. 27 BK25
ebber Clo., Erith 69 CU43
ebber Row SE1 4 E5
ebber Row SE1 66 BY41
ebber St. SE1 4 F5
ebber St. SE1 66 BY41
ebbs All., Sev. 117 CV66
ebbs Rd. SW11 66 BU45
ebbs Rd., Hayes 53 BC38
ebbscroft Rd., Dag. 50 CR35
ebster Clo., Cob. 93 BF60
ebster Clo., Uxb. 53 AX38
ebster Clo., Wal.Abb. 22 CG20
ebster Gdns. W5 54 BK40
ebster Rd. E11 48 CF34
ebster Rd. SE16 67 CB41
ebster Vill. W5 54 BK40
Webster Gdns.
ebsters Clo., Wok. 100 AQ63
edderburn Rd. NW3 47 BT35
edderburn Rd., Bark. 58 CM37
edgewood Clo., Epp. 23 CO18
Theydon Clo.
edgewood Clo., Nthwd. 35 BA29
edgewood Wk. NW6 56 BS36
Lymington Rd.
edgewood Way SE19 77 BZ50
Beulah Hill
edgewoods, West. 106 CJ64
Westmore Rd.
edgwood Ms. W1 1 P9
edhey, Harl. 13 CM11
edlake Clo., Horn. 51 CW33
edlake St. W10 55 BR38
Kensal Rd.
edmore Ave., Ilf. 40 CL30
edmore Gdns. N19 47 BW34
edmore Ms. N19 47 BW34
Wedmore St.
edmore Rd., Grnf. 54 BG38
edmore St. N19 47 BW34
ednesbury Gdns., Rom. 42 CW29
ednesbury Grn., Rom. 42 CW29
ednesbury Rd., Rom. 42 CW29
eech Rd. NW6 47 BS35
eedington Rd. NW5 47 BV35
eedon Clo., Ger.Cr. 34 AQ30
eekes Dr., Slou. 61 AN40
eekley Sq. SW11 66 BT45
Thomas Baines Rd.

Weigall Rd. SE12 78 CH46
Weighouse St. W1 1 H9
Weighouse St. W1 56 BV39
Weighton Ms. SE20 87 CB51
Weighton Rd.
Weighton Rd. SE20 87 CB51
Weighton Rd., Har. 36 BG30
Weihurst Gdns., Sutt. 95 BT56
Weimar St. SW15 65 BR45
Weind, The, Epp. 31 CN21
Weint, The, Slou. 62 AU43
Weir Hall Ave. N18 39 BZ29
Weir Hall Gdns. N18 39 BZ28
Weir Hall Rd. N17 39 BZ29
Weir Hall Rd. N18 39 BZ29
Weir Pl., Stai. 82 AV51
Weir Rd. SW12 76 BW47
Weir Rd. SW19 76 BS49
Weir Rd., Bex. 79 CR47
Weir Rd., Cher. 83 AW54
Weir Rd., Walt. 83 BC53
Weirdale Ave. N20 38 BU27
Weirs Pas. NW1 1 P2
Weirs Pas. NW1 56 BW38
Chalton St.
Weiss Rd. SW15 65 BQ45
Welbeck Ave., Brom. 78 CH49
Welbeck Ave., Hayes 53 BC38
Welbeck Ave., Sid. 79 CO47
Welbeck Clo. N12 38 BT28
Welbeck Clo., Borwd. 28 BM24
Welbeck Clo., Epsom 94 BP57
Welbeck Clo., N.Mal. 85 BO53
Welbeck Rd. E6 58 CJ38
Welbeck Rd., Barn. 29 BT25
Welbeck Rd., Cars. 86 BU54
Welbeck Rd., Har. 45 BF33
Welbeck Rd., Sutt. 86 BT55
Welbeck St. W1 1 H7
Welbeck St. W1 56 BV39
Welbeck Wk., Cars. 86 BT54
Welbeck Rd.
Welbeck Way W1 1 J8
Welbeck Way W1 56 BV39
Welby St. SE5 66 BY44
Welch Pl., Pnr. 35 BC30
Welclose St., St.Alb. 9 BG13
Welcomes Rd., Ken. 105 BZ61
Welcote Dr., Nthwd. 35 BA29
Weld Pl. N11 38 BV28
Welden, Slou. 52 AR39
Knolton Way
Welders La., Beac. 34 AP29
Weldon Clo., Ruis. 53 BC36
Weldon Dr., E.Mol. 84 BE52
Weldon Way, Red. 113 BW68
Welfare Rd. E15 58 CG36
Welford Clo. E5 48 CC34
Denton Way
Welford Pl. SW19 75 BR49
Welham Clo., Hat. 10 BQ15
Welham Ct., Hat. 10 BQ15
Dixons Hill Rd.
Welham Manor, Hat. 10 BQ15
Welham Rd. SW17 76 BV49
Welhouse Rd., Cars. 86 BU54
Well App., Barn. 28 BQ25
Well Clo. SW16 76 BX49
Valley Rd.
Well Clo., Ruis. 45 BE34
Well Clo., Wok. 100 AR62
Well Cottage Clo. E11 49 CJ32
Well Ct. EC4 2 J9
Well Ct. EC4 57 BZ39
Queen St.
Well Ct. NW8 56 BT37
Well Cft., Hem.H. 8 AW13
Well End Rd., Borwd. 28 BN22
Well Fld., Hartley 90 DC52
Well Garth, Welw.G.C. 5 BR8
Peartree La.
Well Gro. N20 38 BT26
Well Hall Rd. SE9 68 CK45
Well Hill, Orp. 98 CR57
Well Hill La., Orp. 98 CR57
Well Hill Rd., Sev. 98 CS57
Well La. SW14 75 BN46
Well La., Brwd. 33 CZ24
Well La., Grays 60 DC40
Well La., Harl. 6 CL10
Well La., Wok. 100 AR62
Well Pas. NW3 47 BT34
Well Path, Wok. 100 AR62
Well Rd. NW3 47 BT34
Well Rd., Barn. 28 BQ25
Well Rd., Pot.B. 20 BU17
Well Rd., Sev. 108 CV62
Well Row, Hert. 11 BX12
Well St. E9 57 CC36
Well St. E15 58 CG36
Well Wk. NW3 47 BT35
Well Way, Epsom 103 BM61
Wellacre Rd., Har. 45 BJ32
Wellan Clo., Well. 79 CO46
Welland Clo., Slou. 62 AT43
Welland Gdns., Grnf. 54 BH37
Welland Ms. E1 57 CB40
Kennet St.
Welland St. SE10 67 CF43
Wellands, Hat. 10 BP11
Wellands Clo., Brom. 88 CK51
Wellbrook Rd., Orp. 97 CL56
Wellbury Ter., Hem.H. 8 BA13
Wellclose Sq. E1 57 CB40
Wellcome Ave., Dart. 70 CW45
Wellcroft Clo., Welw.G.C. 5 BS9
Wellcroft Rd., Slou. 61 AN40
Wellcroft Rd., Welw.G.C. 5 BS9
Welldon Cres., Har. 45 BH32
Wellen Ri., Hem.H. 8 AY15
Weller Clo., Amer. 25 AP22
Weller Rd., Amer. 25 AP22
Weller St. SE1 4 H4
Weller St. SE1 67 BZ41

Wellers Clo., West. 115 CM67
Wellers Ct. NW1 56 BX37
Wellers Ct NW1 1 Q1
Wellers Gro., Chsnt. 21 CB17
Wellesford Clo., Bans. 103 BR62
Wellesley, Harl. 13 CL13
Wellesley Ave. W6 65 BP41
Wellesley Ave., Iver 62 AV41
Wellesley Ave., Nthwd. 35 BB28
Wellesley Ct. W9 56 BT38
Wellesley Ct. Rd., Croy. 87 BZ55
Wellesley Gro.
Wellesley Cres., Pot.B. 19 BR20
Wellesley Cres., Twick. 74 BH48
Wellesley Gro., Croy. 87 BZ55
Wellesley Path, Slou. 62 AQ41
Wellesley Rd.
Wellesley Pl. NW1 1 N3
Wellesley Pl. NW5 47 BV35
Wellesley Rd. E11 49 CH32
Wellesley Rd. E17 48 CE32
Wellesley Rd. N22 38 BY30
Redvers Rd.
Wellesley Rd. NW5 47 BV35
Wellesley Rd. W4 65 BM42
Wellesley Rd., Brwd. 42 DB26
Wellesley Rd., Croy. 87 BZ55
Wellesley Rd., Har. 45 BH32
Wellesley Rd., Ilf. 49 CL34
Wellesley Rd., Slou. 62 AQ41
Wellesley Rd., Sutt. 95 BT57
Wellesley Rd., Twick. 74 BG48
Wellesley St. E1 57 CC39
Wellesley Ter. N1 2 J2
Welley Ave., Stai. 62 AS45
Welley Rd., Stai. 72 AS46
Wellfarm Rd., Whyt. 105 CB63
Wellfield Ave. N10 47 BV31
Wellfield Clo., Hat. 10 BP12
Wellfield Rd. SW16 76 BX49
Wellfield Rd., Hat. 10 BP11
Wellfield Wk. SW16 76 BX49
Wellfields Rd., Loug. 31 CL24
Wellfit St. SE24 66 BY45
Hinton Rd.
Wellgarth, Welw.G.C. 5 BR8
Peartree La.
Wellgarth Gdns., Grnf. 54 BJ36
Wellgarth Rd. NW11 47 BS33
Wellhouse La., Barn. 28 BQ24
Wellhouse La., Bet. 120 BN72
Wellhouse Rd., Beck. 87 CD52
Welling Way SE9 68 CM45
Welling Way, Well. 68 CM45
Wellington Arc. SW1 66 BV41
Wellington Ave. E4 39 CE27
Wellington Ave. N9 39 CB27
Wellington Ave. N15 48 CA32
Wellington Ave., Houns. 74 BF46
Wellington Ave., Pnr. 36 BE30
Wellington Ave., Sid. 79 CO46
Wellington Ave., Vir.W. 82 AQ52
Wellington Ave., Wor.Pk. 94 BQ56
Wellington Clo. E4 39 CE27
Wellington Ave.
Wellington Clo. SE14 67 CC44
Wild Goose Dr.
Wellington Clo. W11 56 BS39
Wellington Clo., Dag. 59 CS36
Wellington Clo., Walt. 83 BB54
Wellington Cotts, Lthd. 110 BB68
Wellington Ct. NW8 1 A1
Wellington Cres., N.Mal. 85 BN52
Wellington Dr., Dag. 59 CS36
Wellington Dr., Welw.G.C. 5 BT8
Wellington Gdns. SE7 68 CJ42
Wellington Gdns., Hmptn. 74 BG49
Wellington Hill, Loug. 31 CH22
Wellington Ms. SE22 67 CB45
Peckham Rye
Wellington Pas. E11 49 CH32
Wellington Rd.
Wellington Pl. N2 47 BU32
Wellington Pl. NW8 1 B2
Wellington Pl. NW8 56 BT38
Wellington Pl., Brwd. 42 DB28
Britannia Rd.
Wellington Rd. E6 58 CK37
Wellington Rd. E7 49 CG35
Wellington Rd. E10 48 CD33
Wellington Rd. E11 49 CH32
Wellington Rd. E17 48 CD31
Wellington Rd. NW8 56 BT37
Wellington Rd. NW10 55 BQ39
Wellington Rd. SW19 76 BS48
Wellington Rd. W5 64 BK41
Wellington Rd., Ashf. 73 AY49
Wellington Rd., Belv. 69 CQ42
Wellington Rd., Bex. 79 CP46
Wellington Rd., Brom. 88 CJ52
Wellington Rd., Cat. 105 BZ64
Wellington Rd., Croy. 86 BY54
Wellington Rd., Dart. 80 CV46
Wellington Rd., Enf. 30 CA25
Wellington Rd., Epp. 23 CR17
Wellington Rd., Felt. 73 BB46
Wellington Rd., Hmptn. 74 BG49
Wellington Rd., Har. 45 BH31
Wellington Rd., Orp. 89 CO53
Wellington Rd., Pnr. 36 BE29
Wellington Rd., St.Alb. 9 BJ14
Wellington Rd. (London Colney), St.Alb. 18 BK16
Wellington Rd., Til. 71 DG45
Wellington Rd., Uxb. 53 AX37
Wellington Rd., Wat. 26 BC23
Wellington Rd. N., Houns. 64 BE45
Wellington Rd. S., Houns. 64 BE45
Wellington Row E2 2 Q2
Wellington Row E2 57 CA38
Wellington Sq. SW3 3 E10
Wellington Sq. SW3 66 BU42
Wellington St. SE18 68 CL42
Wellington St. WC2 2 A10

Wellington St. WC2 56 BX40
Wellington St., Bark. 58 CM37
Axe St.
Wellington St., Grav. 81 DH47
Wellington St., Slou. 62 AQ41
Wellington Ter. E1 57 CB40
Wellington Ter., Har. 45 BG33
Wellington Way E3 57 CE38
Wellington Way, Wey. 92 AY59
Wellington Yd., Rich. 74 BK46
George St.
Wellingtonia Ave., Hav. 41 CS27
Wellmeade Dr., Sev. 116 CU67
Wellmeadow Rd. SE6 78 CG46
Wellmeadow Rd. SE13 78 CG46
Wellmeadow Rd. W7 64 BJ42
Wellow Wk., Cars. 86 BT54
Wells, The N14 38 BW26
Wells Clo., Lthd. 102 BF65
Wells Clo., Nthlt. 54 BD38
Yeading La.
Wells Clo., Wind. 61 AN44
Wells Dr. NW9 46 BN33
Wells Gdns., Dag. 50 CR35
Wells Gdns., Ilf. 49 CK33
Wells Gdns., Rain. 59 CT36
Wells Ho. Rd. NW10 55 BO39
Wells Ms. W1 1 M7
Wells Ms. W1 56 BW39
Wells Pk. Rd. SE26 77 CB48
Wells Pl. W5 54 BK40
Wells Pl., Red. 113 BV68
Wells Ri. NW8 56 BU37
Wells Rd. W12 65 BQ41
Wells Rd., Brom. 88 CK51
Wells Rd., Epsom 94 BM60
Wells Rd., Guil. 118 AU69
Wells Sq. WC1 2 B3
Wells St. W1 1 L7
Wells St. W1 56 BW39
Wells Ter. N4 47 BY34
Wells Way SE5 67 BZ43
Wells Way SW7 3 A6
Wells Yd. N7 47 BY35
Holloway Rd.
Wellside Clo., Barn. 28 BQ24
Wellside Gdns. SW14 75 BN46
Wellsmoor Gdns., Brom. 88 CL52
Wellsprings Cres., Wem. 46 BM34
Wellstead Ave. N9 39 CC26
Wellstead Rd. E6 58 CL37
Wellstones, Wat. 26 BC24
Market St.
Wellswood Clo., Hem.H. 8 AZ13
Wellwood Clo., Couls. 95 BX60
Wellwood Rd., Ilf. 50 CO33
Welsford St. SE1 67 CB42
Welsh Clo. E13 58 CH38
Welsh Side NW9 46 BO32
Fryent Gro.
Welsh Side Wk. NW9 46 BO32
Fryent Gro.
Welshpool St. E8 57 CB37
Weltje Rd. W6 65 BP42
Welton Rd. SE18 68 CN43
Welwyn Ave., Felt. 73 BB46
Welwyn Ct., Hem.H. 8 AY11
Welwyn St. E2 57 CC38
Globe Rd.
Welwyn Way, Hayes 53 BB38
Wembley Hill Rd., Wem. 46 BL34
Wembley Pk. Dr., Wem. 46 BL35
Wembley Rd., Hmptn. 84 BF51
Wembley Way, Wem. 55 BM36
Wemborough Rd., Stan. 36 BK30
Wembury Rd. N6 47 BV33
Wemyss Rd. SE3 68 CG44
Wend, The, Couls. 95 BW60
Wendela Clo., Wok. 100 AS62
Wendela Ct., Har. 45 BH34
Wendell Rd. W12 65 BO41
Wendley Dr., Wey. 91 AV58
Wendling Rd., Sutt. 86 BT55
Wendon St. E3 37 CD37
Wendover SE17 4 M10
Wendover Clo., Hayes 54 BD38
Kingsash Dr.
Wendover Clo., St.Alb. 9 BK11
Wendover Dr., N.Mal. 85 BO53
Wendover Pl., Stai. 72 AU49
Wendover Rd. NW10 55 BO37
Wendover Rd. SE9 68 CJ45
Wendover Rd. SE17 67 CA42
Wendover Rd., Brom. 88 CH52
Wendover Rd., Stai. 72 AU49
Wendover Wk. SE17 67 CA42
Wendover Way, Bush. 27 BG25
Wendover Way, Horn. 51 CV35
Springbank Ave.
Wendover Way, Orp. 89 CO53
Wendover Way, Well. 79 CO46
Wendron Clo., Wok. 100 AQ62
Shilburn Way
Wendy Clo., Enf. 30 CA25
First Ave.
Wendy Cres., Guil. 118 AQ69
Wendy Way, Wem. 55 BL37
Wenham Gdns., Brwd. 122 DE25
Bannister Dr.
Wenlack Clo., Uxb. 44 AW34
Wenlock Ct. N1 2 L1
Wenlock Edge, Dor. 119 BK72
Wenlock Gdns. NW4 46 BP31
Rickard Clo.
Wenlock Rd. N1 2 H1
Wenlock Rd. N1 57 BZ37
Wenlock Rd., Edg. 37 BM29
Wenlock St. N1 2 J1
Wenlock St. N1 57 BZ37
Wenlocks La., Ing. 24 DB20
Wennington Rd. E3 57 CC37
Grove Rd.
Wennington Rd., Rain. 59 CU38
Wensley Ave., Wdf.Grn. 40 CG29

Wensley Clo. SE9 78 CK46
Court Rd.
Wensley Clo., Rom. 41 CR28
Wensley Rd. N18 39 CB29
Wensleydale, Hem.H. 8 AY12
Wensleydale Ave., Ilf. 40 CK30
Wensleydale Gdns., Hmptn. 74 BF50
Wensleydale Pas., Hmptn. 84 BF51
Wensleydale Rd., Hmptn. 74 BF50
Wensum Way, Rick. 35 AX26
Wentbridge Path, Borwd. 28 BL22
Wentland Clo. SE6 77 CF48
Wentland Rd.
Wentland Rd. SE6 77 CF48
Wentworth Ave. N3 38 BS29
Wentworth Ave., Borwd. 28 BL25
Wentworth Clo. N3 38 BS29
Wentworth Clo., Ashf. 73 AZ49
Reedsfield Rd.
Wentworth Clo., Grav. 81 DG49
Chalky Bank
Wentworth Clo., Mord. 86 BS54
Wentworth Clo., Orp. 97 CN56
Wentworth Clo., Pot.B. 20 BS19
Strafford Gate
Wentworth Clo., Surb. 84 BK55
Wentworth Clo., Wat. 26 BB22
Wentworth Clo., Wok. 101 AW64
Wentworth Cotts., Brox. 12 CD14
Wentworth Cres. SE15 67 CB43
Wentworth Cres., Hayes 63 BA41
Wentworth Dr., Dart. 79 CU46
Wentworth Dr., Pnr. 44 BC32
Wentworth Dr., Vir.W. 82 AP52
Wentworth Gdns. N13 38 BY28
Wentworth Hill, Wem. 46 BL33
Wentworth Ms. E3 57 CD38
Eric St.
Wentworth Pk. N3 38 BS29
Wentworth Pl., Grays 71 DE41
Wentworth Pl., Stan. 36 BJ29
Wentworth Rd. E12 49 CJ35
Wentworth Rd. NW11 46 BR32
Wentworth Rd., Barn. 28 BQ24
Wentworth Rd., Croy. 86 BY54
Wentworth Rd., Sthl. 64 BD42
Wentworth St. E1 2 P8
Wentworth St. E1 57 CA39
Wentworth Way, Pnr. 45 BD31
Wentworth Way, Rain. 59 CU38
Wentworth Way, S.Croy. 96 CB60
Wenvoe Ave., Bexh. 69 CR44
Wernbrook St. SE18 68 CM43
Werndee Rd. SE25 87 CB52
Werneth Hall Rd., Ilf. 49 CK31
Werrington St. NW1 1 M1
Werrington St. NW1 56 BW37
Werter Rd. SW15 65 BR45
Wesley Ave. NW10 55 BN38
Wesley Ave., Houns. 64 BE44
Wesley Clo. N7 47 BX34
Wesley Clo. SE17 4 G9
Wesley Clo., Chsnt. 21 BZ17
Wesley Clo., Har. 45 BG34
Wesley Clo., Orp. 89 CP52
Main Rd.
Wesley Clo., Reig. 120 BR72
Wesley Dr., Egh. 72 AT50
Wesley Rd. E10 48 CF33
Wesley Rd. NW10 55 BN37
Wesley Rd., Hayes 53 BC40
Wesley Sq. W11 55 BQ39
Lancaster Rd.
Wesley St. W1 1 H7
Wesley St. W1 56 BV39
Weymouth St.
Wesleyan Pl. NW5 47 BV35
Mortimer Ter.
Wessels, Tad. 103 BQ64
Wessex Ave. SW19 86 BS52
Wessex Clo., Ilf. 49 CN32
Wessex Clo., Kings.T. 85 BM51
Gloucester Rd.
Wessex Dr., Erith 69 CT44
Wessex Dr., Pnr. 36 BE29
Wessex Gdns. NW11 46 BR33
Wessex La., Grnf. 54 BG37
Wessex Rd., Houns. 63 AW45
Wessex St. E2 57 CC38
Wessex Way NW11 46 BR33
West Acres, Amer. 25 AO23
West App., Orp. 88 CM53
West Arbour St. E1 57 CC39
West Ave. E17 48 CE31
West Ave. N3 38 BS29
West Ave. NW4 46 BQ32
West Ave., Hayes 53 BB40
West Ave., Pnr. 45 BE32
West Ave., Red. 121 BV73
West Ave., St.Alb. 18 BF16
West Ave., Sthl. 54 BE40
West Ave., Wall. 95 BX56
West Ave., Wat. 92 BB58
West Ave. Rd. E17 48 CE31
West Bank N16 48 CA33
West Bank, Bark. 58 CL37
West Bank, Dor. 119 BH72
West Bank, Enf. 30 BZ23
West Barnes La. SW20 85 BP52
West Barnes La., N.Mal. 85 BP53
West Brook, Harl. 13 CK12
West Burrow Fld., Welw.G.C. 5 BQ9
West Carriage Dr. W2 3 C1
West Cen. St. WC1 56 BX39
New Oxford St.
West Cen. St. WC1 1 Q8
West Clo. N9 39 CA27
West Clo., Ashf. 73 AY49
West Clo., Barn. 28 BP25
West Clo. (Cockfosters), Barn. 29 BV24
West Clo., Grnf. 54 BG37

Wes–Wes

West Clo., Hmptn. 74 BE49
Oak Ave.
West Clo., Hodd. 12 CE11
West Clo., Rain. 59 CU38
West Clo., Wem. 46 BL33
West Common, Ger.Cr. 43 AR32
West Common Clo., Ger.Cr. 43 AS32
West Common Rd., Brom. 88 CH55
West Common Rd., Uxb. 53 AX36
West Cotts. NW6 47 BS35
West Ct. SE18 68 CL43
Prince Imperial Way
West Ct., Wem. 45 BK34
West Cres., Wind. 61 AM44
West Cres. Rd., Grav. 81 DG46
West Cromwell Rd. SW5 65 BR42
West Cromwell Rd. W14 65 BR42
West Cross Route W11 55 BQ40
West Cross Way, Brent. 64 BJ43
West Dean, Sutt. 94 BR57
Park La.
West Dene, Sutt. 94 BR57
Park La.
West Dene Way, Wem. 83 BB55
West Drayton Pk. Ave., West Dr. 63 AY41
West Drayton Rd., Uxb. 53 AY39
West Dr. SW16 76 BW49
West Dr., Ascot 82 AO53
West Dr., Cars. 95 BT58
West Dr., Har. 36 BG29
West Dr., Sutt. 94 BQ58
West Dr., Tad. 103 BQ62
West Dr., Vir.W. 82 AO53
West Dr., Wat. 26 BC21
West Dr. Gdns., Har. 36 BG29
West Eaton Pl. SW1 3 G8
West Eaton Pl. SW1 66 BV42
West Eaton Pl. Ms. SW1 3 G7
West Ella Rd. NW10 55 BO36
West End, Sev. 108 CW62
West End, West. 116 CO66
West End Ave. E10 48 CF32
West End Ave., Pnr. 45 BD31
West End Ct., Pnr. 45 BD31
West End Ct., Slou. 52 AP37
West End Gdns., Esher 93 BE56
West End Gdns., Nthlt. 54 BD37
West End La. NW6 47 BS35
West End La., Barn. 28 BQ24
West End La., Esher 93 BE57
West End La., Hat. 11 BT12
West End La., Hayes 63 BA43
West End La., Pnr. 45 BD31
West End La., Slou. 52 AP37
West End Rd., Brox. 12 CA15
West End Rd., Nthlt. 54 BD36
West End Rd., Ruis. 44 BB33
West End Rd., Sthl. 54 BE40
West Fm. Ave., Ash. 102 BK62
West Fm. Clo., Ash. 102 BK63
West Fm. Dr., Ash. 102 BK63
West Gdns. E1 57 CB40
West Gdns. SW17 76 BU50
West Gdns., Epsom 94 BO58
West Gate W5 55 BL38
West Gate, Harl. 13 CM11
West Gate Ms. W10 55 BQ38
West Row
West Grn. Rd. N15 47 BY31
West Gro. SE10 67 CF44
West Gro., Walt. 92 BC56
West Gro., Wdf.Grn. 40 CJ29
West Halkin St. SW1 3 G6
West Halkin St. SW1 66 BV41
West Hall Rd., Rich. 65 BM44
West Hallowes SE9 78 CJ47
West Ham La. E15 58 CG36
West Hampstead Ms. NW6 56 BS36
West Harding St. EC4 2 E8
West Harding St. EC4 56 BY39
Fetter La.
West Hatch Manor, Ruis. 44 BB33
West Heath Ave. NW11 47 BS33
West Heath Clo. NW3 47 BS34
West Heath Clo., Dart. 79 CT46
West Heath Rd.
West Heath Ct. NW11 47 BS33
West Heath Dr. NW11 47 BS33
West Heath Gdns. NW3 47 BS34
West Heath La., Sev. 116 CU67
West Heath Rd. NW3 47 BS34
West Heath Rd. SE2 69 CP43
West Heath Rd., Dart. 79 CT46
West Hendon Bdy. NW9 46 BP33
West Hill SW15 75 BQ47
West Hill SW18 75 BQ47
West Hill, Ash. 103 BL63
West Hill, Dart. 80 CV46
West Hill, Epsom 94 BN60
West Hill, Har. 45 BH34
West Hill, Orp. 97 CK59
West Hill, S.Croy. 96 CA58
West Hill, Wem. 46 BL33
West Hill Ave., Epsom 94 BM60
West Hill Bank, Oxt. 114 CF68
West Hill Ct. N6 47 BV34
West Hill Ct. SW18 75 BR46
West Hill Rd.
West Hill Dr., Dart. 80 CV46
West Hill Pk. N6 47 BU34
West Hill Ri., Dart. 80 CV46
West Hill Rd. SW18 75 BR46
West Hill Rd., Wok. 100 AR63
West Hill Way N20 38 BS26
West Holme, Erith 69 CS44
West Ho. Clo. SW19 75 BR47
West Hyde La., Ger.Cr. 34 AS29
West India Dock Rd. E14 57 CE40
West Kent Ave., Grav. 81 DE46
West Kentish Town Est. NW5 47 BV35

West La. SE16 67 CB41
West La., Dor. 119 BD73
West Lo. Ave. W3 55 BM40
West Mall W8 56 BS40
West Malling Way, Horn. 51 CV35
West Mead, Epsom 94 BO57
West Mead, Welw.G.C. 5 BS9
West Mead, Wok. 100 AQ62
West Meads, Guil. 118 AP71
West Mede, Chig. 40 CM29
West Ms. N18 39 CB29
West Ms. SW1 3 L9
West Mill, Grav. 81 DF46
West Mt. Ave., Amer. 25 AO23
West Oak, Beck. 87 CF51
West Palace Gdns., Wey. 83 AZ55
West Pk. SE9 78 CK48
West Pk. Ave., Rich. 65 BM44
West Pk. Clo., Rom. 50 CQ32
West Pk. Hill, Brwd. 42 DA27
West Pk. Rd., Epsom 94 BL59
West Pk. Rd., Rich. 65 BM44
West Pl. SW19 75 BQ49
West Pt., Slou. 61 AL40
West Poultry Ave. EC1 2 F7
West Poultry Ave. EC1 56 BY39
Charterhouse St.
West Quarters W12 55 BP39
Du Cane Rd.
West Quay Dr., Hayes 54 BE39
West Ramp, Houns. 63 AZ44
West Ridge Clo., Hem.H. 7 AV13
West Ridge Gdns., Grnf. 54 BG37
West Riding, St.Alb. 18 BE18
West Rd. E15 58 CG37
West Rd. N17 39 CB29
West Rd. SW3 66 BU42
West Rd. SW4 76 BW46
West Rd. SW14 65 BN45
West Rd. W5 55 BL39
West Rd., Barn. 38 BV26
West Rd., Berk. 7 AQ12
West Rd., Chess. 93 BK59
West Rd., Felt. 73 BA46
West Rd., Guil. 118 AS71
West Rd., Harl. 6 CO9
West Rd., Kings.T. 85 BN51
West Rd., Reig. 121 BS71
West Rd. (Chadwell Heath), Rom. 50 CQ32
West Rd. (Rush Grn.), Rom. 50 CS33
West Rd., Saw. 6 CO5
West Rd., S.Ock. 60 DA38
West Rd., West Dr. 63 AY41
West Rd., Wey. 92 AZ58
West Row W10 55 BQ38
West Shaw, Long. 90 DB51
West Sheen Vale, Rich. 65 BL45
West Side SW18 76 BT46
West Side, Brox. 12 CD15
West Side Common SW19 75 BQ49
West Smithfield EC1 2 F7
West Smithfield EC1 56 BY39
West Sq. SE1 66 BY41
West Sq. SE11 4 F7
West Sq. SE11 66 BY41
West Sq. SE18 68 CK42
West Sq., Iver 52 AV39
West St. E2 57 CB37
Clare St.
West St. E11 49 CG34
West St. E17 48 CE32
West St. EC2 57 BZ39
Moorgate
West St. WC2 1 P10
West St. WC2 56 BW39
Lichfield St.
West St., Bexh. 69 CQ45
West St., Brent. 64 BK43
West St., Brom. 88 CH51
West St., Cars. 86 BU55
West St., Croy. 96 BZ56
West St., Dor. 119 BJ71
West St., Epsom 94 BN60
West St. (Ewell), Epsom 94 BO58
West St., Erith 69 CS42
West St., Grav. 81 DG46
West St., Grays 71 DD43
West St., Har. 45 BG33
West St., Reig. 120 BR70
West St., Sutt. 95 BS56
West St., Wat. 26 BC23
West St. La., Cars. 95 BU56
West Temple Sheen SW14 65 BM45
West Tenter St. E1 2 Q9
West Tenter St. E1 57 CA40
West Thurrock Arterial Rd., Grays 70 DA41
West Thurrock Way, Grays 70 CZ42
West Twrs., Pnr. 45 BD32
West Valley Rd., Hem.H. 17 AX16
West Vw. NW4 46 BQ31
West Vw., Chesh. 16 AO18
West Vw., Felt. 73 BA47
West Vw., Loug. 31 CK24
West Vw. Ave., Whyt. 105 CA62
Station Rd.
West Vw. Dr., Wdf.Grn. 40 CJ30
West Vw. Ri., Hem.H. 8 AX13
West Vw. Rd., Dart. 80 CW46
West Vw. Rd., St.Alb. 9 BG13
West Vw. Rd., Swan. 89 CU52
West Vw. Rd. (Crockenhill), Swan. 89 CS53
West Vw. Rd., Warl. 105 CB63
West Wk. W5 55 BL39
West Wk., Barn. 38 BV26
West Wk., Harl. 13 CM11
West Wk., Hayes 53 BC40
West Wk. Way, Sutt. 95 BS56
Robin Hood Rd.

West Warwick Pl. SW1 3 L9
West Warwick Pl. SW1 66 BW42
West Way N18 39 BZ28
West Way NW10 46 BN35
West Way, Brwd. 42 DA27
West Way, Cars. 95 BT58
West Way, Croy. 87 CD55
West Way, Edg. 37 BM29
West Way, Houns. 64 BE44
West Way, Pnr. 45 BD31
West Way, Rick. 35 AW26
West Way, Ruis. 44 BB33
West Way, Sev. 107 CT64
West Way, Shep. 83 BA53
West Way, Wal.Abb. 30 CE21
West Way, W.Wick. 88 CG53
West Way, West. 115 CM66
West Way Gdns., Croy. 87 CC55
West Woodside, Bex. 79 CQ47
Westacott, Hayes 53 BB39
Westacott Clo. N19 47 BW33
Hazelville Rd.
Westacres, Esher 93 BE57
Westall Rd., Loug. 31 CL24
Westanley Ave., Amer. 25 AO23
Westbank Rd., Hmptn. 74 BG50
Westbeech Rd. N22 47 BY31
Westbere Dr., Stan. 36 BK28
Westbere Rd. NW2 46 BR35
Westbourne Ave. N9 39 CB27
Eastbournia Ave.
Westbourne Ave. W3 55 BN39
Westbourne Ave., Sutt. 85 BR55
Westbourne Bri. W2 56 BT39
Westbourne Clo., Hayes 54 BD38
Westbourne Cres. W2 1 A10
Westbourne Cres. W2 56 BT40
Westbourne Cres. Ms. W2 1 A10
Westbourne Dr. SE23 77 CC48
Westbourne Dr., Brwd. 42 CZ28
Westbourne Gdns. W2 56 BS39
Westbourne Gro. W2 56 BS39
Westbourne Gro. W11 55 BR40
Westbourne Gro. Ms. W11 56 BS39
Westbourne Gro.
Westbourne Gro. Ter. W2 56 BS39
Westbourne Pk. Ms. W2 56 BS39
Westbourne Gdns.
Westbourne Pk. Pas. W2 56 BS39
Westbourne Pk. Rd. W2 55 BR39
Westbourne Pk. Rd. W11 55 BR39
Westbourne Pk. Vill. W2 56 BS39
Westbourne Pl. N9 39 CB27
Eastbournia Ave.
Westbourne Rd. N7 56 BX36
Westbourne Rd. SE26 77 CC50
Westbourne Rd., Bexh. 69 CP43
Westbourne Rd., Croy. 87 CA53
Westbourne Rd., Felt. 73 BB48
Westbourne Rd., Stai. 73 AW50
Westbourne Rd., Uxb. 53 AZ38
Westbourne St. W2 1 A10
Westbourne St. W2 56 BT40
Westbourne Ter. W2 56 BT39
Westbourne Ter. Ms. W2 56 BT39
Westbourne Ter. Rd. W2 56 BT39
Westbridge Rd. SW11 66 BT44
Westbrook, Maid. 61 AJ42
Westbrook Ave., Hmptn. 74 BE50
Westbrook Clo., Barn. 29 BT24
Westbrook Cres., Barn. 29 BT24
Westbrook Dr., Orp. 89 CP54
Westbrook Rd. SE3 68 CH44
Westbrook Rd., Houns. 64 BE43
Westbrook Rd., Stai. 72 AV49
Westbrook Rd., Th.Hth. 87 BZ51
Westbrook Sq., Barn. 29 BT24
Westbrooke Cres., Well. 69 CP45
Westbrooke Rd., Sid. 78 CM48
Westbrooke Rd., Well. 69 CO45
Westbury Ave. N22 47 BY31
Westbury Ave., Esher 93 BH57
Westbury Ave., Sthl. 54 BF38
Westbury Ave., Wem. 55 BL36
Westbury Clo., Ruis. 44 BC33
Westbury Clo., Shep. 83 AZ53
Burchetts Way
Westbury Clo., Whyt. 105 CA62
Station App.
Westbury Dr., Brwd. 42 DA27
Westbury Gro. N12 38 BS29
Westbury La., Buck.H. 40 CH27
Westbury Lo. Clo., Pnr. 45 BD31
Westbury Pl., Brent. 64 BK43
Hamilton Rd.
Westbury Rd. E7 49 CH35
Westbury Rd. E17 48 CD31
Westbury Rd. N11 38 BX29
Westbury Rd. N12 38 BS29
Westbury Rd. SE20 87 CC51
Westbury Rd. W5 55 BL39
Westbury Rd., Bark. 58 CM37
Westbury Rd., Beck. 87 CD52
Westbury Rd., Brwd. 42 DB27
Westbury Rd., Brom. 88 CJ51
Westbury Rd., Buck.H. 40 CJ27
Westbury Rd., Croy. 87 BZ53
Westbury Rd., Felt. 74 BD47
Westbury Rd., Ilf. 49 CK34
Westbury Rd., N.Mal. 85 BN52
Westbury Rd., Nthwd. 35 BA28
Westbury Rd., Wat. 26 BC25
Westbury Rd., Wem. 55 BL36
Westbury St. SW8 66 BW44
Westbury Ter. E7 58 CH36
Westbury Ter., Upmin. 51 CZ34
Westbury Ter., West. 115 CM66
Westbush Clo., Hodd. 12 CD10
Westcar La., Walt. 92 BC57
Westchester Dr. NW4 46 BQ31
Westcombe Ave., Croy. 86 BX53
Westcombe Ct. SE3 68 CG43

Westcombe Dr., Barn. 29 BS25
Westcombe Hill SE3 68 CH42
Westcombe Lo. Dr., Hayes 53 BA39
Westcombe Pk. Rd. SE3 68 CG43
Westcoombe Ave. SW20 85 BO51
Westcote Ri., Ruis. 44 BA33
Westcote Rd. SW16 76 BW49
Westcott, Welw.G.C. 5 BT7
Westcott Clo. N15 48 CA32
Ermine Rd.
Westcott Clo., Brom. 88 CK53
Ringmer Way
Westcott Clo., Croy. 96 CE58
Westcott Cres. W7 54 BH39
Westcott Rd. SE17 66 BY43
Westcott Rd., Dor. 119 BH72
Westcott St., Dor. 119 BF72
Westcott Way, Sutt. 94 BQ58
Westcott Waye, Uxb. 53 AX37
Westcourt Ave., Grav. 81 DG48
Westcroft Clo. NW2 46 BR35
Westcroft Clo., Enf. 30 CC22
Westcroft Est. NW2 46 BR35
Westcroft Gdns., Mord. 85 BR52
Westcroft Rd., Cars. 95 BV56
Westcroft Sq. W6 65 BO42
Westcroft Way NW2 46 BR35
Westdale Rd. SE18 68 CL43
Westdean Ave. SE12 78 CH47
Westdean Clo. SW18 76 BS46
Denton St.
Westdene Dr., Rom. 42 CV28
Westdown, Lthd. 111 BF67
Westdown Rd. E15 48 CF35
Westdown Rd. SE6 77 CE47
Wested La., Swan. 89 CU54
Westerdale, Hem.H. 8 AY12
Westerdale Ct. N5 47 BY35
Leigh Rd.
Westerdale Rd. SE10 68 CH42
Westerfield Rd. N15 48 CA32
Westerfolds Clo., Wok. 100 AU62
Westergate Rd. SE2 69 CQ43
Westerham Ave. N9 39 BZ27
Westerham Clo., Wey. 92 AX57
Westerham Dr., Sid. 79 CO46
Westerham Rd. E10 48 CE32
Westerham Rd., Kes. 97 CJ58
Westerham Rd., Oxt. 115 CG68
Westerham Rd., Sev. 107 CR65
Westerham Rd., West. 97 CJ60
Westerley Cres. SE26 77 CD49
Western Ave. NW11 46 BQ32
Western Ave. W3 54 BJ38
Western Ave. W5 54 BJ38
Western Ave., Brwd. 42 DB26
Western Ave., Cher. 83 AW52
Western Ave., Dag. 59 CS36
Western Ave., Egh. 82 AT52
Western Ave., Epp. 22 CN19
Western Ave., Grnf. 54 BJ38
Western Ave., Rom. 42 CV30
Western Ave., Ruis. 53 BC36
Western Ave., Uxb. 53 BA36
Western Ave. (Denham), Uxb. 44 AX35
Western Clo., Cher. 83 AW52
Western Ave.
Western Ct. N3 38 BS29
Western Ct. W3 55 BN39
York Rd.
Western Cross Clo., Green. 80 DB46
Johnsons Way
Western Dr., Shep. 83 BA53
Western Gdns. W5 55 BM40
Western Gdns., Brwd. 42 DB27
Western Gateway E16 58 CH40
Western La. SW12 76 BV47
Western Par., Barn. 29 BS25
Western Perimeter Rd., Houns. 63 AW45
Western Pl. SE16 67 CC41
Canon Beck Rd.
Western Rd. E13 58 CJ37
Western Rd. E17 48 CF32
Western Rd. N2 47 BU31
Western Rd. N22 38 BX30
Western Rd. NW10 55 BN38
Western Rd. SW9 66 BY45
Western Rd. SW19 86 BT51
Western Rd. W5 54 BK40
Western Rd., Brwd. 42 DB27
Western Rd., Epp. 22 CN19
Western Rd., Mitch. 86 BT51
Western Rd., Rom. 50 CT32
Western Rd., Sthl. 64 BD42
Western Rd., Sutt. 95 BS56
Western Rd., Wal.Abb. 13 CG14
Western Trd. Est. NW10 55 BN38
Western Vw., Hayes 63 BB41
Western Way SE28 68 CM41
Western Way, Barn. 29 BS25
Westernville Gdns., Ilf. 49 CM33
Westferry Rd. E14 57 CE40
Westfield, Ash. 103 BL62
Westfield, Harl. 13 CN11
Westfield, Hat. 10 BR15
Westfield, Loug. 31 CJ25
Longfield
Westfield, Reig. 121 BS69
Westfield, Sev. 108 CV64
Westfield, Welw.G.C. 5 BS7
Daniells
Westfield Ave., S.Croy. 96 BZ60
Westfield Ave., Wat. 27 BD22
Westfield Ave., Wok. 100 AS64
Westfield Clo., Enf. 30 CD24
Westfield Clo., Grav. 81 DH49
Westfield Clo., Sutt. 94 BR56
Westfield Clo., Wal.Cr. 21 CD19
Westfield Ct., St.Alb. 9 BK12
Southfield Way

Westfield Dr., Har. 45 B
Westfield Dr., Lthd. 102 B
Westfield Gdns., Har. 45 B
Westfield Gro., Wok. 100 A
Westfield La., Har. 45 B
Westfield La., Slou. 52 A
Westfield Par., Wey. 92 A
Westfield Pk., Pnr. 36 B
Westfield Rd. NW7 37 B
Westfield Rd. W13 54 B
Westfield Rd., Beck. 87 C
Westfield Rd., Berk. 7 A
Westfield Rd., Bexh. 69 C
Westfield Rd., Croy. 86 B
Westfield Rd., Dag. 50 C
Westfield Rd., Guil. 109 A
Westfield Rd., Hodd. 12 C
Westfield Rd., Mitch. 86 B
Westfield Rd., Surb. 84 B
Westfield Rd., Sutt. 94 B
Westfield Rd., Walt. 84 B
Westfield Rd., Wok. 100 A
Westfield St. SE18 68 C
Westfield Wk., Wal.Cr. 21 C
Westfield Way, Ruis. 44 B
Westfield Way, Wok. 100 A
Westfields SW13 65 BC
Westfields, St.Alb. 9 B
Westfields Ave. SW13 65 BC
Westfields Rd. W3 55 BM
Westgate Clo., Epsom 103 BN
Chalk La.
Westgate Ct., Wal.Cr. 30 CC
Holmesdale
Westgate Rd. SE25 87 CB
Westgate Rd., Beck. 87 CE
Westgate Rd., Dart. 80 CV
Westgate St. E8 57 CE
Westgate Ter. SW10 66 BS
Westglade Ct., Har. 45 BK
Westgrove La. SE10 67 CF
Westhall Pk. Rd., Warl. 105 CC
Westhall Rd., Warl. 105 CB
Westharold, Swan. 89 CS
Westhay Gdns. SW14 75 BM
Westhill Clo., Grav. 81 DG
Leith Pk. Rd.
Westhill Rd., Hodd. 12 CD
Westholm NW11 47 BS
Westholme, Orp. 88 CN
Westholme Gdns., Ruis. 44 BC
Westhorne Ave. SE9 78 CH
Westhorne Ave. SE12 78 CH
Westhorpe Gdns. NW4 46 BO
Westhorpe Rd. SW15 65 BC
Westhumble St., Dor. 119 BJ
Westhurst Dr., Chis. 78 CL
Westlake Clo. N13 38 BY
Westlake Clo., Hayes 54 BE
Lochan Clo.
Westlake Rd., Bex. 79 CP
Blendon Rd.
Westland Ave., Horn. 51 CW
Westland Clo., Stai. 73 AX
Douglas Rd.
Westland Clo., Stai. 73 AX
De Havilland Way
Westland Dr., Brom. 88 CG
Westland Dr., Hat. 19 BR
Westland Pl. N1 2
Westland Pl. N1 57 BZ
Westland Rd., Wat. 26 BC
Westland Vw., Grays 71 DD
Westlands Clo., Hayes 63 BC
Westlands Ct., Epsom 103 BN
Dorking Rd.
Westlands Ter. SW12 76 BW
Gaskarth Rd.
Westlands Way, Oxt. 114 CF
Westlea, St.Alb. 10 BM
Westlea Ave., Wat. 27 BE
Westlea Clo., Brox. 12 CD
Westlea Rd. W7 64 BJ
Westlea Rd., Brox. 12 CD
Westlees Clo., Dor. 119 BK
Westleigh Ave. SW15 75 BP
Westleigh Ave., Couls. 104 BV
Westleigh Dr., Brom. 88 CK
Westleigh Gdns., Egh. 37 BM
Westley Wd., Welw.G.C. 5 B
Westlyn Clo., Rain. 60 CV
Westmacott Dr., Felt. 73 BB
Westmead SW15 75 BP
Westmead, Ruis. 45 BD
Westmead, Wind. 61 AN
Westmead Rd., Sutt. 95 BT
Westmeade Clo., Chsnt. 21 CB
Westmere Dr. NW7 37 BN
Westmill Ct. N4 48 BZ
Kings Cres. Est.
Westminster Ave., Th.Hth. 86 BY
Westminster Bri. SE1 4
Westminster Bri. SE1 66 BX
Westminster Bri. SW1 4
Westminster Bri. SW1 66 BX
Westminster Bri. Rd. SE1 4
Westminster Bri. Rd. SE1 66 BX
Westminster Cathedral Piazza SW1 3
Westminster Clo., Ilf. 40 CM
Westminster Clo., Tedd. 74 BJ
Cambridge Rd.
Westminster Ct., St.Alb. 9 BG
Westminster Dr. N13 38 BX
Westminster Gdns. E4 40 CG
Westminster Gdns., Bark. 58 CN
Westminster Gdns., Ilf. 40 CM
Westminster Ms. W2 56 BS
Shrewsbury Rd.
Westminster Rd. N9 39 CB
Westminster Rd. W7 54 BH
Westminster Rd., Sutt. 86 BT
Westmoat Clo., Beck. 77 CF

stmont Rd., Esher 84 BH55
stmoor Gdns., Enf. 30 CC23
stmoor Rd., Enf. 30 CC23
stmoor St. SE7 68 CJ41
stmore Rd., West. 106 CJ64
stmoreland, Epsom 94 BN58
ollymoor La.
stmoreland Ave., 51 CV32
rn.
stmoreland Ave., Well. 68 CN45
stmoreland Bldgs. 57 BZ39
:1
dersgate St.
stmoreland Dr., Sutt. 95 BS57
stmoreland Pl. SW1 66 BV42
stmoreland Pl. W5 54 BK39
ount Ave.
stmoreland Rd. NW9 46 BL31
stmoreland Rd. SE17 67 BZ43
stmoreland Rd. SW13 65 BO44
stmoreland Rd., Brom. 88 CG53
stmoreland Rd., Har. 45 BF32
stmoreland St. W1 1 H7
stmoreland St. W1 56 BV39
stmoreland Ter. SW1 66 BV42
stmorland Clo. E12 49 CJ33
stmorland Clo., 94 BO58
som
ngmead Rd.
stmorland Clo., Twick. 74 BJ46
mberland Clo.
stmorland Rd. E17 48 CE32
stmorland Way, Mitch. 86 BW52
stmount, Guil. 118 AR71
stmount Rd. SE9 68 CK44
stoe Rd. N9 39 CB27
ston Ave., E.Mol. 84 BE52
ston Ave., Grays 70 CZ42
ston Ave., T.Ditt. 84 BH54
ston Ave., Wey. 92 AW56
ston Clo., Brwd. 122 DE26
ston Clo., Couls. 104 BX53
ston Ct. N4 48 BZ34
ngs Cres. Est.
ston Dr., Stan. 36 BJ30
ston Gdns., Islw. 64 BH44
ston Grn., Dag. 50 CQ35
ston Grn., T.Ditt. 84 BH54
ston Grn. Rd., Esher 84 BG54
ston Grn. Rd., T.Ditt. 84 BH54
ston Gro., Brom. 78 CG50
ston Gro., Wok. 100 AV61
ston Lea, Lthd. 110 BA66
ston Pk. N8 47 BX32
ston Pk., Kings.T. 85 BL51
airfield W.
ston Pk., T.Ditt. 84 BH54
ston Pk. Clo., T.Ditt. 84 BH54
ston Ri. WC1 2 C1
ston Ri. WC1 56 BX38
ston Rd. W4 65 BN41
ston Rd., Brom. 78 CG50
ston Rd., Dag. 50 CQ35
ston Rd., Enf. 30 BZ23
ston Rd., Epsom 94 BO59
ston Rd., Guil. 109 AQ70
ston Rd., T.Ditt. 84 BH54
ston St. SE1 4 L4
ston St. SE1 67 BZ41
ston Way, Wok. 100 AV61
ston Yd. SE1 67 BZ41
eston St.
stover Clo., Sutt. 95 BS58
ulverston Clo.
stover Hill NW3 47 BS34
stover Rd. SW18 76 BT47
stow Hill SE19 77 CA50
stow St. SE19 77 CA50
stpole Ave., Barn. 29 BV24
stport Rd. E13 58 CH38
stport St. E1 57 CC39
stray, Hem.H. 8 AZ14
strow SW15 75 BQ46
strow Dr., Bark. 50 CO35
strow Gdns., Ilf. 49 CN34
stside NW4 37 BP30
stview, Hat. 10 BP11
stview Clo. NW10 46 BO35
stview Clo. W7 54 BH39
stview Ct., Borwd. 27 BK25
estview Gdns.
stview Cres. N9 39 CA26
stview Gdns., Borwd. 27 BK25
stville Rd. W12 65 BP41
stville Rd., T.Ditt. 84 BJ54
stward Dr., Amer. 25 AR23
stward Ho., Guil. 118 AS69
stward Rd. E4 39 CD28
stward Way, Har. 46 BL32
stway SW20 85 BP52
stway W10 55 BQ39
stway W12 55 BO40
stway, Cat. 105 BZ64
stway, Guil. 118 AP69
stway, Orp. 88 CM53
stway Clo. SW20 85 BP52
stway Gdns., Red. 121 BV69
stways, Epsom 94 BO56
stwell App. SW16 76 BX50
estwell Rd.
stwell Clo., Orp. 89 CP54
stwell Rd. SW16 76 BX50
stwick Clo., Hem.H. 8 BA14
stwick Gdns. W14 65 BQ41
stwick Gdns., Houns. 63 BC44
stwick Pl., Wat. 18 BD20
stwick Row, Hem.H. 8 BA13
stwood Ave. SE19 87 BZ51
stwood Ave., Brwd. 42 DA28
stwood Ave., Har. 45 BF35
stwood Ave., Wey. 91 AV59
stwood Clo., Amer. 25 AR23
stwood Clo., Brom. 88 CJ51
stwood Clo., Esher 84 BG55
Westwood Clo., Pot.B. 20 BS18
Westwood Clo., Ruis. 44 AZ32
Westwood Ct., Guil. 118 AP70
Hillcrest Rd.
Westwood Gdns. SW13 65 BO45
Westwood Hill SE26 77 CB49
Westwood La., Sid. 79 CO46
Westwood La., Well. 68 CN45
Westwood Pk. SE23 77 CB47
Westwood Rd. E16 58 CH40
Westwood Rd. SW13 65 BO45
Westwood Rd., Couls. 104 BW62
Westwood Rd., Grav. 81 DC50
Westwood Rd., Ilf. 49 CN33
Westyoke Rd., Fawk. 90 DA55
Wetheral Dr., Stan. 36 BJ30
Wetherby Clo., Nthlt. 54 BF36
Wetherby Gdns. SW5 66 BT42
Wetherby Ms. SW5 66 BS42
Bolton Gdns.
Wetherby Pk., Wey. 92 BB56
Wetherby Pl. SW7 66 BT42
Gloucester Rd.
Wetherby Rd., Borwd. 28 BL23
Wetherby Rd., Enf. 30 BZ22
Wetherby Way, Chess. 94 BL57
Wetherden St. E17 48 CD33
Wetherell Rd. E9 57 CC37
Wetherill Rd. N10 38 BV30
Wettern Clo., S.Croy. 96 BZ58
Purley Oaks Rd.
Wetton Pl., Egh. 72 AS49
High St.
Wexfenne Gdns., Wok. 101 AW61
Wexford Rd. SW12 76 BU47
Wexham Pk. La., Slou. 52 AR38
Wexham Rd., Slou. 52 AQ40
Wexham St., Slou. 52 AQ38
Wexham Wds., Slou. 52 AR39
Wey Ave., Cher. 83 AW52
Eastern Ave.
Wey Barton, Wey. 92 AY60
Wey Clo., Wey. 92 AW60
Wey Ct., Epsom 94 BN56
Wey Ct., Wey. 92 AX58
Wey Manor Rd., Wey. 92 AX58
Wey Rd., Wey. 83 AY55
Wey Side Clo., Wey. 92 AY59
Weybank, Wok. 101 AY61
Weybourne Pl., S.Croy. 96 BZ58
Weybourne St. SW18 76 BT48
Weybridge Pk., Wey. 92 AZ56
Weybridge Rd., Th.Hth. 86 BY52
Weybridge Rd., Wey. 83 AX55
Weybrook Dr., Guil. 109 AT68
Weydown Clo. SW19 75 BR47
Weydown Clo., Guil. 109 AQ68
Weydown La., Guil. 109 AQ68
Cumberland Ave.
Weyhill Rd. E1 57 CB39
Holly St.
Weylands Pk., Wey. 92 BA57
Weylea Ave., Guil. 118 AT69
Weylond Rd., Dag. 50 CQ34
Weyman Rd. SE3 68 CJ44
Weymarks, The N17 39 BZ29
Weymead Clo., Cher. 83 AX54
Weymede, Wey. 92 AY59
Weymouth Ave. NW7 37 BO28
Weymouth Ave. W5 64 BK41
Weymouth Ct., Sutt. 95 BS57
Weymouth Dr., Hayes 53 BB38
Weymouth Ms. W1 1 J6
Weymouth Ms. W1 56 BV39
Weymouth St. W1 1 H7
Weymouth St. W1 56 BV39
Weymouth St., Hem.H. 8 AX15
Weymouth Ter. E2 57 CA37
Weymouth Wk., Stan. 36 BJ29
Weyside Gdns., Guil. 118 AR69
Weyside Rd., Guil. 118 AQ70
Weystone Rd., Wey. 92 AY56
Whadcote St. N4 47 BY34
Whalebone Ave., Rom. 50 CQ32
Whalebone Ct. EC2 2 L8
Whalebone Gro., Rom. 50 CQ32
Whalebone La. E15 58 CG36
Whalebone La. N., Rom. 41 CQ29
Whalebone La. S., Dag. 50 CQ32
Whalebone La. S., Rom. 50 CQ32
Whaley Rd., Pot.B. 20 BT20
Wharf La., Berk. 7 AO11
Wharf La., Rick. 35 AY26
Wharf La., Twick. 74 BJ47
Wharf La. (Ripley), Wok. 101 AX62
Wharf La. (Send), Wok. 100 AU65
Wharf Pl. E2 57 CB37
Wharf Rd. E15 57 CF37
Wharf Rd. N1 2 H1
Wharf Rd. N1 57 BZ37
Wharf Rd., Brwd. 42 DB27
Wharf Rd., Brox. 12 CD15
Wharf Rd., Enf. 30 CD25
Wharf Rd., Grav. 81 CJ46
Wharf Rd., Grays 71 DC43
Wharf Rd., Guil. 118 AR70
Wharf Rd., Hem.H. 8 AW14
Wharf Rd., Stai. 72 AR47
Wharf Rd. S., Grays 71 DC43
Wharf St. E16 58 CG39
Wharfdale Rd. N1 56 BX37
Wharfedale, Hem.H. 8 AY12
Wharfedale Ct. E5 48 CC35
Clapton Pk. Est.
Wharfedale Gdns., 86 BX52
Th.Hth.
Wharfedale Rd., Dart. 80 CY47
Teesdale Rd.
Wharfedale St. SW10 66 BS42
Wharfside Rd. E16 58 CG39
Barking Rd.
Wharley Hook, Harl. 13 CN12
Wharncliffe Dr., Sthl. 54 BG40
Wharncliffe Gdns. SE25 87 CA51
Wharncliffe Rd. SE25 87 BZ51
Wharton Clo. NW10 55 BO36
Wharton Ms., Brom. 88 CH51
Wharton Rd.
Wharton Rd., Brom. 88 CH51
Wharton St. WC1 2 C3
Wharton St. WC1 56 BX38
Whateley Rd. SE20 77 CC50
Whateley Rd. SE22 77 CA46
Whateley Rd., Guil. 109 AQ68
Whatley Ave. SW20 85 BQ52
Whatman Rd. SE23 77 CC47
Whatmore Clo., Houns. 73 AW46
Wheat Barn, Welw.G.C. 5 BS7
Wheat Clo., St.Alb. 9 BJ11
Wheat Knoll, Ken. 105 BZ61
Hayes La.
Wheat Leys, St.Alb. 9 BK12
Wheat St. W1 56 BV39
Marylebone St.
Wheatash Rd., Wey. 83 AW55
Wheatbutts, The (Eton 61 AM42
Wick), Wind.
Common Rd.
Wheatcroft, Chsnt. 21 CB17
Wheatfield, Hat. 10 BP12
Crop Common
Wheatfield Way, Kings.T. 85 BL51
Wheatfields, Enf. 30 CD23
Wheathill Rd. SE20 87 CB51
Wheatland Rd., Slou. 62 AQ41
Wheatlands, Houns. 64 BF43
Wheatlands Rd. SW17 76 BV48
Wheatley Clo. NW4 37 BP30
Wheatley Clo., Saw. 6 CP6
Wheatley Clo., Welw.G.C. 5 BS9
Wheatley Cres., Hayes 53 BC40
Wheatley Gdns. N9 39 CA27
Wheatley Rd., Islw. 64 BH45
Wheatley Rd., Welw.G.C. 5 BR8
Wheatley St. W1 1 H7
Wheatley St. W1 56 BV39
Marylebone St.
Wheatley Ter. Rd., Erith 69 CT43
Wheatley Way, Ger.Cr. 34 AS29
Wheatsheaf Clo., Cher. 91 AU57
Wheatsheaf Clo., Nthlt. 45 BE35
Wheatsheaf Clo., Wok. 100 AS61
Wheatsheaf Hill 98 CQ58
(Halstead), Sev.
Wheatsheaf Hill (Ide 116 CQ69
Hill), Sev.
Wheatsheaf La. SW6 65 BQ43
Holyport Rd.
Wheatsheaf La. SW8 66 BX43
Wheatsheaf La., Stai. 72 AV50
Wheatsheaf Rd., Rom. 50 CT32
Wheatstone Clo., Mitch. 86 BU51
Longfield Dr.
Wheatstone Rd. W10 55 BR39
Wheel Fm. Dr., Dag. 50 CS34
Wheeler Ave., Oxt. 114 CF68
Wheelers, Epp. 22 CN18
Wheelers Clo., Wal.Abb. 13 CG14
Wheelers Cross, Bark. 58 CM37
Wheelers Dr., Ruis. 44 BA32
Wheelers Fm. Gdns., 23 CR16
Epp.
Wheelers La., Bet. 120 BM71
Wheelers La., Brwd. 33 CX24
Wheelers La., Epsom 94 BM60
Wheelers La., Hem.H. 8 AY14
Wheelers Orchard, 34 AS29
Ger.Cr.
Wheelwright Clo., Bush. 36 BF26
Fidler Pl.
Wheelwright St. N7 56 BX36
Whelan Way, Wall. 86 BW55
Wheler St. E1 2 P5
Wheler St. E1 57 CA38
Whellock Rd. W4 65 BO41
Whenman Ave., Bex. 79 CS48
Whernside Clo. SE28 59 CP40
Wherwell Rd., Guil. 118 AR71
Whetstone Clo. N20 38 BT27
Whetstone Pk. WC2 2 B8
Whetstone Pk. WC2 56 BX39
Gate St.
Whetstone Rd. SE3 68 CJ44
Whewell Rd. N19 47 BX34
Whichcote Gdns., Chesh. 16 AO20
Whichcote St. SE1 4 B3
Whichcote St. SE1 56 BY40
Mepham St.
Whidborne Clo. SE8 67 CE44
Cliff Ter.
Whidborne St. WC1 2 A3
Whidborne St. WC1 56 BX38
Whimbrel Clo. SE28 59 CP40
Whinchat Rd. SE28 68 CM41
Whinfell Clo. SW16 76 BW49
Whinfell Way, Grav. 81 DJ49
Whinyates Rd. SE9 68 CK45
Whipley Clo., Guil. 109 AT68
Weybrook Dr.
Whippendale Clo., Orp. 89 CO51
Whippendell Hill, Kings L. 17 AX18
Whippendell Rd., Wat. 26 BB25
Whippendell Way, Orp. 89 CO51
Whipps Cross Rd. E11 48 CF32
Whiskin St. EC1 2 F3
Whiskin St. EC1 56 BY38
Gloucester Way
Whisper Wd., Rick. 26 AW24
Whisperwood Clo., Har. 36 BH29
College Hill Rd.
Whistler Gdns., Edg. 37 BL30
Whistler St. N5 47 BY35
Whistler Wk. SW10 66 BT43
Worlds End
Whistlers Ave. SW11 66 BT43
Whiston Rd. E2 57 CA37
Whitakers Way, Loug. 31 CK23
Whitbread Clo. N17 39 CB30
Whitbread Rd. SE4 67 CD45
Whitburn Rd. SE13 67 CE45
Whitby Ave. NW10 55 BM38
Whitby Ave., Brwd. 122 DE29
Whitby Clo., West. 106 CH62
Whitby Ct. N7 47 BX35
Parkhurst Rd.
Whitby Gdns. NW9 46 BM31
Whitby Gdns., Sutt. 86 BT55
Whitby Rd. SE18 68 CK42
Whitby Rd., Har. 45 BG34
Whitby Rd., Ruis. 44 BC34
Whitby Rd., Slou. 52 AO40
Whitby Rd., Sutt. 86 BT55
Whitby St. E1 2 P4
Whitcher Clo. SE14 67 CD43
Chubworthy St.
Whitcher Pl. NW1 56 BW36
Rochester Rd.
Whitchurch Ave., Edg. 37 BL29
Whitchurch Clo., Edg. 37 BL29
Whitchurch Gdns., Edg. 37 BL29
Whitchurch La., Edg. 36 BK29
Whitchurch Rd. W11 55 BQ40
Whitchurch Rd., Rom. 42 CV28
Whitcomb St. WC2 3 P1
Whitcomb St. WC2 56 BW40
White Acre NW9 37 BO30
White Adder Way E14 67 CE42
Spindrift Ave.
White Ave., Grav. 81 DF48
White Beam Way, Tad. 103 BP64
White Beams, Hat. 10 BP14
Southdown Rd.
White Beams, St.Alb. 18 BG17
White Bear Clo. NW3 47 BT35
New End Sq.
White Ch. La. E1 57 CB39
White City Clo. W12 55 BQ40
South Africa Rd.
White City Est. W12 55 BP40
White City Rd. W12 55 BP40
White Clo., Slou. 61 AO40
White Conduit St. N1 56 BY37
White Craig Clo., Pnr. 36 BF28
White Craig Clo., Stan. 46 BL31
Everton Dr.
White Cft., Swan. 89 CT51
White Cross Row, Rich. 74 BK46
Water La.
White Downs, Dor. 119 BC73
White Friars, Sev. 116 CU67
White Gdns., Dag. 59 CR36
White Gate Gdns., Har. 36 BH29
White Gates, Warl. 105 CB63
White Gates Clo., Rick. 26 AZ24
White Hands Clo., Hodd. 12 CD12
White Hart Clo., Ch.St.G. 34 AQ27
Back La.
White Hart Clo., Hayes 63 BA43
White Hart Clo., Sev. 117 CV68
White Hart Dr., Hem.H. 8 AY14
White Hart La. N17 38 BX30
White Hart La. N22 39 BZ30
White Hart La. NW10 55 BO36
Church Rd.
White Hart La. SW13 65 BO44
White Hart La., Brwd. 42 DB27
Chestnut Gro.
White Hart La., Hem.H. 16 AS17
White Hart La., Rom. 41 CR30
White Hart Meadows, 101 AX64
Wok.
White Hart Rd. SE18 68 CN42
White Hart Rd., Hem.H. 8 AZ14
White Hart Rd., Slou. 61 AO41
White Hart St. SE11 4 E10
White Hart St. SE11 66 BY42
White Hart Wd., Sev. 117 CV68
White Hart Yd. SE1 4 K3
White Hart Yd. SE1 57 BZ40
Borough High St.
White Heart Ave., Uxb. 53 BA39
White Hedge Dr., St.Alb. 9 BG12
White Hill, Berk. 7 AR15
White Hill, Chesh. 16 AO18
White Hill, Couls. 104 BU65
White Hill, Croy. 96 BZ58
White Hill, Hem.H. 7 AV14
White Hill, Rick. 35 AZ29
White Hill, Welw. 5 BP5
White Hill Clo., Chesh. 16 AO18
White Hill La., Red. 114 BZ67
White Hill Rd., Berk. 7 AQ14
White Horse All. EC1 56 BY39
Cowcross St.
White Horse Dr., Epsom 94 BN60
White Horse Dr., Guil. 118 AT70
White Horse Hill, Chis. 78 CK49
White Horse La. E1 57 CC38
White Horse La., Wok. 101 AX63
White Horse Rd. E1 57 CD39
White Horse Rd. E6 58 CK38
White Horse Rd., Wind. 61 AL45
White Horse St. W1 3 K3
White Horse St. W1 56 BV40
White Horse Yd. EC2 57 BZ39
Coleman St.
White Ho. SW11 66 BT44
White Ho. Dr., Stan. 36 BK28
White Ho. La., Guil. 109 AR68
White Ho. Rd., Sev. 116 CT68
White Kennet St. E1 2 N8
White Kennett St. E1 57 CA39
White Knights Rd., 92 BA57
Wey.
White Knobs Way, Cat. 114 CB66
White La., Guil. 118 AU71
White La., Oxt. 106 CH65
White Lion Clo., Amer. 25 AQ23
White Lion Ct. EC3 2 M9
White Lion Hill EC4 2 G10
White Lion Hill EC4 56 BY40
White Lion Rd., Amer. 25 AP23
White Lion Sq., Hat. 10 BP12
The Common
White Lion St. N1 2 D1
White Lion St. N1 56 BY37
White Lion St., Hem.H. 8 AX15
White Lion Yd. W1 1 J10
White Lo. Clo. N2 47 BT32
White Lo. Clo., Sutt. 95 BT57
White Lo. Est. SE19 77 BZ50
White Lyons Rd., Brwd. 42 DB27
Kings Rd.
White Oak Dr., Beck. 87 CF51
White Orchards N20 37 BR26
White Orchards, Stan. 36 BJ28
White Post Fld., Saw. 6 CP6
White Post Hill, Farn. 90 CX54
White Post La. E9 57 CD36
White Post La. SE13 67 CE45
Overcliff Rd.
White Post St. SE15 67 CC43
White Rd. E15 58 CG36
White Rd., Bet. 120 BM70
White Rd., Tad. 120 BM70
White Rose La., Wok. 100 AS62
White Shack La., Wat. 26 AY22
White St., Sthl. 64 BD41
White Stubbs La., Brox. 12 BZ14
White Stubbs La., Hert. 11 BX13
White Swan Ms. W4 65 BO43
Bennett St.
White Way, Lthd. 111 BF66
White Wd. Rd., Berk. 7 AQ13
Whiteadder Way E14 67 CE42
Spindrift Ave.
Whitear Wk. E15 57 CF36
Whitebarn La., Dag. 59 CR37
Whitebeam Ave., Brom. 88 CL54
Whitebeam Clo. SW9 66 BX43
Whitebeam Twr. E17 48 CD31
Oatland Ri.
Whitebeams, Hat. 10 BP14
Southdown Rd.
Whitebridge Clo., Felt. 73 BB46
Whitebroom Rd., Hem.H. 7 AV12
Whitebutts Rd., Ruis. 45 BD34
Whitechapel High St. E1 2 Q8
Whitechapel High St. E1 57 CA39
Whitechapel Rd.
Whitechapel Rd. E1 57 CB39
Whitecote Rd., Sthl. 54 BF39
Whitecroft, St.Alb. 9 BJ15
Whitecroft Clo., Beck. 87 CF52
Whitecroft Way, Beck. 87 CF53
Whitecross Pl. EC2 2 L6
Whitecross Pl. EC2 57 BZ39
Whitecross St. EC1 2 J4
Whitecross St. EC1 57 BZ38
Whitecross St. EC2 2 J6
Whitecross St. EC2 57 BZ39
Whitefield Ave. NW2 46 BQ33
Whitefield Ave., Pur. 104 BY61
Whitefield Clo. SW15 75 BR46
Whitefield Clo., Orp. 89 CP52
Whitefields Rd., Chsnt. 21 CC17
Whitefoot La., Brom. 77 CF49
Whitefoot Ter., Brom. 78 CG48
Whiteford Rd., Slou. 52 AP39
Whitefriars Ave., Har. 36 BG30
Whitefriars St. EC4 2 E9
Whitefriars St. EC4 56 BY39
Whitegates, Wok. 100 AS63
Loop Rd.
Whitegates Ave., Sev. 99 CZ57
Whitehall SW1 3 Q2
Whitehall SW1 56 BX40
Whitehall Clo., Chig. 41 CO27
Whitehall Clo., Uxb. 53 AX37
Whitehall Clo., Wal.Abb. 13 CG14
Whitehall Ct. SW1 4 A3
Whitehall Ct. SW1 56 BX40
Whitehall Cres., Chess. 93 BK56
Whitehall Fm. La., Vir.W. 82 AS52
Whitehall Gdns. E4 40 CG26
Whitehall Gdns. SW1 3 Q3
Whitehall Gdns. W3 55 BM40
Whitehall Gdns. W4 65 BM43
Whitehall La., Buck.H. 40 CH27
Whitehall La., Egh. 72 AS50
Whitehall La., Erith 69 CT44
Whitehall La., Grays 71 DE43
Whitehall La., Reig. 120 BR72
Whitehall La., Stai. 72 AT46
Whitehall Pk. N19 47 BW33
Whitehall Pk. Rd. W4 65 BM43
Whitehall Pl. E7 3 Q3
Whitehall Pl. E7 49 CH35
Kuhn Way
Whitehall Pl. SW1 56 BX40
Whitehall Rd. E4 40 CG27
Whitehall Rd. W7 64 BJ41
Whitehall Rd., Brom. 88 CJ53
Whitehall Rd., Grays 71 DE42
Whitehall Rd., Har. 45 BH33
Whitehall Rd., Th.Hth. 86 BY53
Whitehall Rd., Uxb. 53 AX37
Whitehall Rd., Wdf.Grn. 40 CG27
Whitehall St. N17 39 CA29
Whitehart Rd., Orp. 89 CO54
Whitehart Slip, Brom. 88 CH51
Whitehaven, Slou. 52 AP40
Montague Rd.
Whitehaven Clo., Brom. 88 CH52
Whitehaven St. NW8 1 C5
Whitehaven St. NW8 56 BU38
Whitehead Clo. SW18 76 BT47
Whitehead Clo., Dart. 80 CV48
Whiteheads Gro. SW3 3 D10
Whiteheads Gro. SW3 66 BU42
Whiteheath Ave., Ruis. 44 BA33
Whitehill, Berk. 7 AR12
Whitehill Ct., Berk. 7 AR12
Whitehill
Whitehill La., Grav. 81 DH48
Whitehill La., Wok. 101 BA65

Whitehill Pl., Vir.W. 82 AS53
The Orchard
Whitehill Rd., Dart. 79 CU46
Whitehill Rd., Grav. 81 DH48
Whitehill Rd., Loug. 90 DB51
Whitehills Rd., Long. 31 CL24
Whitehorn Gdns., Croy. 87 CB55
Whitehorn Gdns., Enf. 30 BZ25
Whitehorse La. SE25 87 BZ52
Whitehorse La., St.Alb. 18 BK16
Whitehorse Rd. SE1 4 E6
Whitehorse Rd., Croy. 87 BZ54
Whitehouse Ave., Borwd. 28 BM24
Whitehouse Clo., Ger.Cr. 34 AS29
Whitehouse Ct. N14 38 BW27
Whitehouse Est. E10 48 CF32
Whitehouse La., Abb.L. 17 BC16
Whitehouse La., Enf. 30 BZ23
Whitehouse Way N14 38 BV27
Whitehouse Way, Iver 52 AU38
Whiteland Ave., Rick. 25 AT24
Whitelands, Brwd. 33 DB21
Whitelands Way, Rom. 42 CV30
Whiteleaf Rd., Hem.H. 8 AX15
Whiteledges W13 54 BK39
Whitelegg Rd. E13 58 CG37
Whiteley, Wind. 61 AM43
Whiteley Rd. SE19 77 BZ49
Whiteleys Cotts. W14 65 BR42
Whiteleys Way, Felt. 74 BF48
Whitemore Rd., Guil. 109 AR68
Whiteoak Gdns., Sid. 78 CN47
Whiteoaks, Bans. 95 BS60
Beechfield
Whiteoaks La., Grnf. 54 BG38
Whitepost Hill, Red. 121 BU70
Whites Ave., Ilf. 49 CN32
Whites Clo., Green. 80 DB46
Whites Grds. SE1 4 N5
Whites Grds. SE1 67 CA41
Whites Grds. Est. SE1 4 N4
Whites Grds. Est. SE1 67 CA41
Whites La., Slou. 62 AQ43
Whites Row E1 2 P7
Whites Row E1 57 CA39
Whites Sq. SW4 66 BW45
Nelsons Row
Whitestile Rd., Brent. 64 BK42
Whitestone La. NW3 47 BT34
Heath St.
Whitestone Wk. NW3 47 BT34
North End Way
Whitestone Wk., Hem.H. 8 AW12
Whitethorn, Welw.G.C. 5 BS8
Whitethorn Ave., Couls. 104 BV61
Whitethorn Ave., West Dr. 53 AY40
Whitethorn Gdns., Enf. 30 BZ25
Whitethorn Gdns., Horn. 51 CV32
Whitethorn Pl., West Dr. 53 AY40
Whitethorn Ave.
Whitethorn St. E3 57 CE38
Whitewaits, Harl. 6 CN10
Whiteways Ct., Stai. 73 AW50
Pavilion Gdns.
Whitewebbs La., Enf. 30 CA21
Whitewebbs Rd., Enf. 29 BY21
Whitewebbs Way, Orp. 88 CN51
Whitewood Cotts., West. 106 CJ63
Whitfield Pl. W1 1 L5
Whitfield Pl. W1 56 BW38
Whitfield St.
Whitfield Rd. E6 58 CJ36
Whitfield Rd. SE3 67 CF44
Whitfield Rd., Bexh. 69 CQ43
Whitfield St. W1 1 L5
Whitfield St. W1 56 BW38
Whitfield Way, Rick. 34 AV26
Whitford Gdns., Mitch. 86 BU52
Whitgift Ave., S.Croy. 95 BY56
Whitgift St. SE11 4 B8
Whitgift St. SE11 66 BX42
Whitgift St., Croy. 87 BZ55
Whiting Ave., Bark. 58 CL36
Whiting Hill Est., Barn. 28 BP25
Whitings Rd., Barn. 28 BQ25
Whitings Way E6 58 CL39
Whitland Rd., Cars. 86 BT54
Whitlars Dr., Kings L. 17 AY17
Whitley Clo., Stai. 73 AY46
Whitley Rd. N17 39 CA30
Whitley Rd., Hodd. 12 CE11
Whitlock Dr. SW19 75 BR47
Whitman Rd. E3 57 CD38
Whitmoor La., Guil. 109 AR66
Whitmore Ave., Grays 71 DD40
Whitmore Clo. N11 38 BV28
High Rd.
Whitmore Gdns. NW10 55 BQ37
Whitmore Rd. N1 57 CA37
Whitmore Rd., Beck. 87 CD52
Whitmore Rd., Har. 45 BF33
Whitmores Clo., Epsom 103 BN61
Whitnell Way SW15 75 BQ46
Whitney Ave., Ilf. 49 CJ31
Whitney Rd. E10 48 CE33
Whitney Wk., Sid. 79 CQ50
Maidstone Rd.
Whitstable Clo., Beck. 87 CD51
Whitstable Clo., Ruis. 44 BB34
Chichester Ave.
Whitta Rd. E12 49 CJ35
Whittaker Ave., Rich. 74 BK46
Whittaker Rd. E6 58 CJ36
Whittaker Rd., Sutt. 85 BR55
Whittaker St. SW1 3 G9
Whittaker St. SW1 66 BV42
Bourne St.
Whittell Gdns. SE26 77 CC48
Whittenham Clo., Slou. 52 AQ40
Whittingstall Rd. SW6 65 BR44
Whittingstall Rd., Hodd. 12 CE11
Whittington Ave. EC3 2 M9
Whittington Ave., Hayes 53 BB39
Whittington Ct. N2 47 BU32
Whittington Rd. N22 38 BX29
Whittington Rd., Brwd. 122 DE25
Whittington Way, Pnr. 45 BE32
Whittle Clo., Sthl. 54 BF39
Whittle Rd., Houns. 64 BD43
Whittlebury Clo., Cars. 95 BU57
Whittlesea Path, Har. 36 BG30
Whittlesea Rd., Har. 36 BG29
Whittlesey St. SE1 4 E3
Whittlesey St. SE1 56 BY40
Whitton Ave. E., Grnf. 45 BH35
Whitton Ave. W., Grnf. 45 BF35
Whitton Ave. W., Nthlt. 45 BF35
Whitton Clo., Grnf. 54 BJ36
Whitton Dene, Houns. 74 BF46
Whitton Dr., Grnf. 54 BJ36
Whitton Manor Rd., Islw. 74 BG46
Whitton Rd., Houns. 64 BF45
Whitton Rd., Twick. 74 BH46
Whitton Wk. E3 58 CE37
Whitton Waye, Houns. 74 BF46
Whitwell Rd. E13 58 CH38
Whitwell Rd., Wat. 27 BD21
Whitworth Rd. SE18 68 CL43
Whitworth Rd. SE25 87 CA52
Whitworth St. SE10 68 CG42
Whopshot Ave., Wok. 100 AR61
Whopshot Clo., Wok. 100 AR61
Whopshot Dr., Wok. 100 AR61
Whorlton Rd. SE15 67 CB45
Whybridge Clo., Rain. 59 CT37
Whymark Ave. N22 47 BY31
Whytecliffe Rd. N., Pur. 95 BY59
Whytecliffe Rd. S., Pur. 95 BY59
Whytecroft, Houns. 64 BD43
Whyteleafe Hill, Whyt. 105 CA63
Whyteleafe Rd., Cat. 105 CA63
Whyteville Rd. E7 58 CH36
Wick La. E3 57 CD36
Wick La., Egh. 72 AP50
Wick Rd. E9 57 CC36
Wick Rd., Egh. 82 AQ51
Wick Rd., Tedd. 74 BJ50
Wickenden Rd., Sev. 108 CV64
Wicker St. E1 57 CB39
Wickers Oake SE19 77 CA49
Wickersley Rd. SW11 66 BV44
Wicket, The, Croy. 96 CE56
Wicket Rd., Grnf. 54 BJ38
Wickets Way, Ilf. 40 CN29
Wickford Clo., Rom. 42 CW28
Wickford Dr., Rom. 42 CW28
Wickford St. E1 57 CC38
Wickford Way E17 48 CC31
Wickham Ave., Croy. 87 CD55
Wickham Ave., Sutt. 94 BQ56
Wickham Chase, W.Wick. 87 CF54
Wickham Clo., Enf. 30 CB24
Wickham Clo., N.Mal. 85 BO53
Wickham Clo., Uxb. 35 AX30
Wickham Ct. Rd., W.Wick. 87 CF55
Wickham Cres., W.Wick. 87 CF55
Wickham Fld., Sev. 107 CT61
Wickham Gdns. SE4 67 CD45
Wickham La. SE2 69 CO42
Wickham La., Egh. 72 AT50
Wickham Rd. E4 39 CF29
Wickham Rd. SE4 67 CD45
Wickham Rd., Beck. 87 CE51
Wickham Rd., Croy. 87 CC55
Wickham Rd., Grays 71 DH41
Wickham Rd., Har. 36 BG30
Wickham St. SE11 4 B10
Wickham St. SE11 66 BX42
Wickham St., Well. 68 CN44
Wickham Way, Beck. 87 CF52
Wickhurst Rd., Sev. 116 CT69
Wickliffe Ave. N3 37 BR30
Wickliffe Gdns., Wem. 46 BM34
Wicklow St. WC1 2 B2
Wicklow St. WC1 56 BX38
Wicks Clo. SE9 78 CJ49
Dunkery Rd.
Wicks Rd., Rick. 34 AU28
Wicksteed Clo., Bex. 79 CS48
Wickwood Ct., St.Alb. 9 BJ13
Woodstock Rd. N.
Wickwood St. SE5 66 BY44
Wid Clo., Brwd. 122 DE25
Widdecombe Ave., Har. 45 BE34
Widdenham Rd. N7 47 BX35
Widdial Grn., Welw.G.C. 5 BS8
Widford Rd.
Widdin St. E15 57 CF36
Wide Way, Mitch. 86 BW52
Widecombe Clo., Rom. 42 CV30
Widecombe Ct. N2 47 BT32
Widecombe Gdns., Ilf. 49 CK31
Widecombe Rd. SE9 78 CK48
Widecombe Way N2 47 BT32
Widecroft Rd., Iver 52 AV39
Widegate St. E1 2 N7
Widegate St. E1 57 CA39
Sandys Row
Widenham Clo., Pnr. 45 BD32
Widford Rd., Welw.G.C. 5 BS8
Widford Ter., Hem.H. 8 AZ10
Elstree Rd.
Widgeon Way, Wat. 27 BE22
Widley Rd. W9 56 BS38
Widmore Dr., Hem.H. 8 AZ12
Widmore Lo. Rd., Brom. 88 CJ51
Widmore Rd., Brom. 88 CH51
Widmore Rd., Uxb. 53 AZ38
Widworthy Hayes, Brwd. 122 DD26
Wieland Rd., Nthwd. 35 BC29
Wigan Ho. E5 48 CB33
Wigeon Path SE28 68 CM41
Whinchat Rd.
Wiggenhall Rd., Wat. 26 BC24
Wiggie La., Red. 121 BV69
Wiggington Ave., Wem. 55 BM36
Wiggins La., Rich. 74 BK48
Wiggins Mead NW9 37 BO30
Wightman Rd. N4 47 BY31
Wightman Rd. N8 47 BY31
Wigley Bush La., Brwd. 42 CZ27
Wigley Rd., Felt. 74 BD48
Wigmore Pl. W1 1 J8
Wigmore Pl. W1 56 BV39
Wigmore Rd., Cars. 86 BT55
Wigmore St. W1 1 G9
Wigmore St. W1 56 BV39
Wigmore Wk., Cars. 86 BT55
Wigmores N., Welw.G.C. 5 BQ7
Wigmores S., Welw.G.C. 5 BQ8
Wigram Rd. E11 49 CJ32
Wigram Sq. E17 48 CF31
Wigston Rd. E13 58 CH38
Wigton Gdns., Stan. 37 BL30
Wigton Pl. SE11 66 BY42
Milver St.
Wigton Rd. E17 39 CD30
Wigton Rd., Rom. 42 CW28
Wigton Way, Rom. 42 CW28
Wilberforce Rd. N4 47 BY34
Wilberforce Rd. NW9 46 BP32
Wilberforce Way SW19 75 BQ50
Wilberforce Way, Grav. 81 DH49
Wilbraham Pl. SW1 3 F8
Wilbraham Pl. SW1 66 BV42
Wilbury Ave., Sutt. 94 BR58
Wilbury Rd., Wok. 100 AR62
Wilbury Way N18 39 BZ28
Wilby Ms. W11 55 BR40
Wilcot Ave., Wat. 36 BE26
Wilcox Clo., Borwd. 28 BN23
Wilcox Gdns., Shep. 83 AY52
Wilcox Pl. SW1 3 M7
Wilcox Pl. SW1 66 BW41
Victoria St.
Wilcox Rd. SW8 66 BX43
Wilcox Rd., Sutt. 95 BS56
Brandon Rd.
Wilcox Rd., Tedd. 74 BG49
Wild Acres, Wey. 92 AX59
Wild Ct. WC2 2 B8
Wild Ct. WC2 56 BX39
Wild Goose Dr. SE14 67 CC44
Wild Grn. N., Slou. 62 AT42
Verney Rd.
Wild Grn. S., Slou. 62 AT42
Swabey Rd.
Wild Hatch NW11 47 BS32
Wild Oaks Clo., Nthwd. 35 BB29
Wild St. WC2 2 A9
Wild St. WC2 56 BX39
Wildcroft Dr., Dor. 119 BK73
Wildcroft Gdns., Edg. 36 BK29
Wildcroft Manor SW15 75 BQ47
Wildcroft Rd.
Wildcroft Rd. SW15 75 BQ47
Wilde Clo. E8 57 CB37
Wilde Clo., Til. 71 DH44
Coleridge Rd.
Wilde Pl. N13 38 BY29
Medesenge Way
Wilde Pl. SW18 76 BT47
Wilderness, The, Berk. 7 AR13
Wilderness, The, Hmptn. 74 BF49
Park Rd.
Wilderness Rd., Chis. 78 CL50
Wilderness Rd., Guil. 118 AP71
Wilderness Rd., Oxt. 115 CG68
Wildernesse Ave., Sev. 108 CW64
Wildernesse Mt., Sev. 108 CV64
Wilders Clo., Wok. 100 AR62
Wilderton Rd. N16 48 CA33
Wildfell Rd. SE6 77 CE47
Wildhill Rd., Hat. 11 BS14
Wilds Rents SE1 4 M6
Wilds Rents SE1 67 CA41
Wildwood, Nthwd. 35 BA29
Wildwood Ave., St.Alb. 18 BE18
Wildwood Clo. SE12 78 CG47
Wildwood Clo., Lthd. 110 BB66
Wildwood Clo., Wok. 100 AV61
Wildwood Ct., Ken. 105 BZ61
Hawkhirst Rd.
Wildwood Gro. NW3 47 BT33
North End Rd.
Wildwood Ri. NW11 47 BT33
Wildwood Rd. NW11 47 BT33
Wilford Clo., Enf. 30 BZ24
Little Pk. Gdns.
Wilford Clo., Nthwd. 35 BA29
Wilford Rd., Slou. 62 AS42
Wilfred Ave., Rain. 59 CU39
Wilfred Owen Clo. SW19 76 BT50
Tennyson Rd.
Wilfred St. SW1 3 L6
Wilfred St. SW1 66 BW41
Wilfred St., Wok. 100 AR62
Wilfred Turney Est. W6 65 BQ41
Wilfrid Gdns. W3 55 BN39
Wilhelmina Ave., Couls. 104 BW63
Wilk Pl. N13 38 BY29
Wolves La.
Wilkes Rd., Brwd. 122 DE25
Wilkes St. E1 2 Q6
Wilkie Way SE22 77 CB47
Wilkin St. NW5 56 BV36
Wilkin St. Ms. NW5 56 BV36
Wilkin St.
Wilkins Clo., Hayes 63 BB42
Wilkins Clo., Mitch. 86 BU51
Wilkins Grn. La., Hat. 10 BN13
Wilkins Grn. La., St.Alb. 10 BM13
Wilkins Way, West. 107 CO65
Wilkinson Clo., Dart. 70 CW45
Wilkinson Rd. E16 58 CJ39
Wilkinson St. SW8 66 BX43
Wilkinson Way W4 65 BN41
Wilks Pl. N1 2 N1
Wilks Pl. N1 57 CA37
Hoxton St.
Will Crooks Gdns. SE9 68 CJ45
Willan Rd. N17 39 BZ30
Willan Wall E16 58 CG40
Peto St. N.
Willard Est. SW8 66 BV45
Willcocks Clo., Chess. 85 BL55
Willcott Rd. W3 55 BM40
Willenhall Ave., Barn. 29 BT25
Willenhall Dr., Hayes 53 BB40
Willenhall Rd. SE18 68 CL42
Willersley Ave., Orp. 88 CM55
Willersley Ave., Sid. 78 CN47
Willersley Clo., Sid. 78 CN47
Willes Rd. NW5 56 BV36
Willesden Grn. NW2 55 BQ36
Willesden La. NW2 55 BQ36
Willesden La. NW6 55 BQ36
Willet Way SE16 67 CB42
Egan Way
Willets La., Uxb. 43 AV35
Willett Clo., Nthlt. 54 BD38
Broomcroft Ave.
Willett Clo., Orp. 88 CN53
Willett Clo., Th.Hth. 86 BY53
Willett Rd., Th.Hth. 86 BY53
Willett Way, Orp. 88 CM53
Willey Broom La., Cat. 113 BY66
Willey Fm. La., Cat. 114 BZ66
Willey La., Cat. 114 BZ66
William Barefoot Dr. SE9 78 CK49
William Bonney Est. SW4 66 BW45
William Booth Rd. SE20 77 CB51
William Carey Way, Har. 45 BH32
William Clo., Rom. 41 CS30
William Cory Prom., Erith 69 CT42
High St.
William Ct., Hem.H. 8 AX15
King Edward St.
William Covell Clo., Enf. 29 BX22
William Ellis Clo., Wind. 72 AQ46
William IV St. WC2 3 Q1
William IV St. WC2 56 BX40
William Gdns. SW15 75 BP46
William Hayne Gdns., Wor.Pk. 85 BQ55
William Margrie Clo. SE15 67 CB44
Moncrieff Est.
William Ms. SW1 3 F5
William Ms. SW1 66 BU41
William Morley Clo. E6 58 CJ37
William Morris Clo. E17 48 CD31
William Morris Ho. W6 65 BQ43
William Parnell Ho. SW6 66 BS44
William Rd. NW1 1 L3
William Rd. NW1 56 BV38
William Rd. SW19 75 BR50
William Rd., Cat. 105 BZ64
William Rd., Guil. 118 AR70
William Rd., Sutt. 95 BT56
William Russell Ct., Wok. 100 AP62
William St. E10 48 CE32
William St. N17 39 CA29
William St. SW1 3 F5
William St. SW1 66 BU41
William St., Bark. 58 CM36
William St., Berk. 7 AR13
William St., Bush. 27 BD24
William St., Cars. 86 BU55
William St., Grav. 81 DG47
William St., Grays 71 DD43
William St., Slou. 52 AP40
William St., Wind. 61 AO44
William Willison Est. SW19 75 BR47
Williams Ave. E17 39 CD30
Williams Bldgs. E2 57 CC38
Malcolm Pl.
Williams Gro. N22 38 BY30
Williams La. SW14 65 BN45
Williams La., Mord. 86 BT53
Williams Rd. W13 54 BJ40
Williams Rd., Sthl. 64 BE42
Williams Ter., Croy. 95 BY57
Williams Ter., Well. 68 CN44
Williams Wk., Guil. 109 AQ68
Williams Way, Rad. 27 BJ21
Williamson Clo. SE10 68 CG42
Lenthorpe Rd.
Williamson Rd. N4 47 BY32
Williamson St. N7 47 BX35
Williamson Way NW7 37 BR29
Willifield Way NW11 46 BR31
Willingale Clo., Brwd. 122 DF25
Fairview Ave.
Willingale Clo., Loug. 31 CM23
Willingale Clo., Wdf.Grn. 40 CJ29
Willingale Rd., Ing. 24 DC16
Willingale Rd., Loug. 31 CM24
Willingale Rd. (Fyfield), Ong. 15 CZ14
Willingale Rd. (Willingale), Ong. 15 DB15
Willingdon Rd. N22 38 BY30
Willinghall Clo., Wal.Abb. 21 CF19
Southweald Dr.
Willingham Clo. NW5 47 BW35
Leighton Rd.
Willingham Ter. NW5 47 BW35
Willingham Way, Kings.T. 85 BM52
Willington Ct. E5 48 CC35
Clapton Pk. Est.
Willington Rd. SW9 66 BX45
Willis Ave., Sutt. 95 BU57
Willis Clo., Epsom 94 BM60
Willis Rd. E15 58 CG37
Willis Rd., Croy. 87 BZ54
Willis Rd., Erith 69 CS42
Willis St. E14 57 CE39
Willmore End SW19 86 BS51
Willoughby Ave., Croy. 95 B
Willoughby Clo., Brox. 12 C
Willoughby Ct., St.Alb. 18 B
Willoughby Dr., Rain. 59 C
Willoughby Gro. N17 39 C
Willoughby La. N17 39 C
Willoughby Pk. Rd. N17 39 C
Willoughby Rd. N8 47 B
Willoughby Rd. NW3 47 B
Willoughby Rd., Kings.T. 85 B
Willoughby Rd., Slou. 62 A
Willoughby Rd., Twick. 74 B
Willoughby St. WC1 1
Willoughby Way SE7 68 C
Willow Ave. SW13 65 B
Willow Ave., Sid. 79 C
Willow Ave., Swan. 89 C
Willow Ave., Uxb. 44 A
Willow Ave., West Dr. 53 A
Willow Bank SW6 65 B
Willow Bank, Rich. 74 B
Willow Bri. Rd. N1 57 B
Willow Clo. W5 54 B
Willow Clo., Bex. 79 C
Willow Clo., Brent. 64 B
Willow Clo., Brwd. 122 D
Willow Clo. (Doddinghurst), Brwd. 33 D
Willow Clo., Brom. 88 C
Willow Clo., Buck.H. 40 C
Willow Clo., Chsnt. 21 C
Willow Clo., Erith 69 C
Willow Clo., Horn. 50 C
Willow Clo., Orp. 89 C
Willow Clo., Slou. 62 A
Willow Clo., Th.Hth. 86 B
Willow Clo., Wey. 91 A
Willow Cotts. Rd., Cars. 86 B
Willow Cotts, Rich. 65 B
Waterloo Pl.
Willow Ct., Edg. 37 B
Willow Cres., St.Alb. 9 B
Willow Cres. E., Uxb. 44 A
Willow Cres. W., Uxb. 44 A
Willow Dene, Pnr. 36 B
Willow Dr., Barn. 28 B
Willow Dr., Maid. 61 A
Willow Edge, Kings L. 17 A
Blackwell Rd.
Willow End N20 38 B
Willow End, Surb. 85 B
Willow Gdns., Houns. 64 B
Willow Gdns., Ruis. 44 B
Willow Grn. NW9 37 B
Clayton Fld.
Willow Grn., Borwd. 28 B
Ashley Dr.
Willow Grn., Dor. 119 B
Willow Gro. E13 58 C
Willow Gro., Chis. 78 C
Willow Gro., Ruis. 44 B
Willow Gro., Welw.G.C. 5 B
Willow Hayne Dr., Walt. 83 B
Willow La., Amer. 25 A
Willow La., Mitch. 86 B
Willow La., Wat. 26 B
Willow Mead, Chig. 41 C
Willow Mt., Croy. 87 C
Langton Way
Willow Pk., Sev. 107 C
Willow Pk., Slou. 52 A
Willow Path, Epsom 94 B
Willow Path, Wal.Abb. 22 C
Willow Pl. SW1 3
Willow Pl. SW1 66 B
Francis St.
Willow Rd. NW3 47 B
Willow Rd. W5 65 B
Willow Rd., Dart. 80 C
Willow Rd., Enf. 30 C
Willow Rd., Erith 69 C
Willow Rd., N.Mal. 85 B
Willow Rd., Red. 121 B
Willow Rd., Rom. 50 C
Willow Rd., Slou. 62 A
Willow Rd., Wall. 95 B
Willow Side, St.Alb. 19 B
Willow St. E4 39 C
Willow St. EC2 2
Willow St. EC2 57 C
Willow St., Rom. 50 C
Willow Tree Clo. SW18 76 B
Willow Tree Clo., Hayes 54 B
Willow Tree La., Hayes 54 B
Willow Tree Wk., Brom. 88 C
Willow Vale W12 55 B
Willow Vale, Chis. 78 C
Willow Vale, Lthd. 102 B
Willow Vw. SW19 86 B
Palestine Gro.
Willow Wk. E17 48 C
Willow Wk. N2 38 B
Willow Wk. N15 47 B
Willow Wk. N21 29 B
Willow Wk. SE1 4
Willow Wk. SE1 67 C
Willow Wk., Cher. 83 A
Willow Wk., Dart. 70 C
Willow Wk., Egh. 72 A
Willow Wk., Ilf. 49 C
Station Rd.
Willow Wk., Orp. 88 C
Willow Wk., Sutt. 85 B
Willow Wk., Upmin. 51 C
Willow Way N3 38 B
Willow Way SE26 77 C
Willow Way W11 55 B
St. Anns Rd.
Willow Way, Epsom 94 B
Willow Way, Gdse. 114 C
Willow Way, Guil. 109 A
Willow Way, Hat. 10 B
Willow Way, Hem.H. 8 A
Willow Way, Pot.B. 20 B

ow Way, Rad. 27 BH21
ow Way, Rom. 42 CX29
ow Way, St.Alb. 18 BF17
ow Way, Sun. 83 BC52
ow Way, Twick. 74 BF48
ow Way, Wem. 45 BJ34
ow Way, Wey. 92 AX59
ow Way, Wok. 100 AR64
ow Wd. Cres. SE25 87 CA53
owbrook (Eton), Wind. 61 AO42
owbrook Rd. SE15 67 CA43
owbrook Rd., Sthl. 64 BF41
owbrook Rd., Stai. 73 AY48
owcourt Ave., Har. 45 BJ32
owdene N6 47 BU33
enewood Rd.
owdene, Brwd. 33 CZ25
owdene, Bush. 36 BH26
owdene, Wal.Cr. 21 CD17
owdene Clo., Twick. 74 BG47
owdene Ct., Brwd. 42 DB28
arley Mt.
owfield, Harl. 13 CM12
owfield, Saw. 6 CQ6
ringham Rd.
owhayne Gdns., 85 BQ55
or.Pk.
owherb Wk., Rom. 42 CV29
ematis Clo.
owmead, Saw. 6 CQ6
ringhall Rd.
owmead, Stai. 83 AW51
owmead Clo. W5 54 BK38
entham Way
owmead Clo., Wok. 100 AQ61
owmere, Esher 93 BG56
ows, The, Esher 93 BH57
ows, The, Grays 71 DE43
ows, The, Rick. 35 AW27
xbridge Rd.
ows, The, St.Alb. 9 BJ15
ows, The, Wat. 35 BC26
ookside
ows, The, Wey. 92 AY60
ows Ave., Mord. 86 BS53
ows Clo., Pnr. 36 BD30
ows Path, Wind. 61 AL44
owtree Clo., Uxb. 44 BA34
rose Cres. SE2 69 CO42
s Cres., Houns. 74 BF46
s Gro. NW7 37 BP28
son Rd., Egh. 72 AQ49
y St. WC1 56 BX39
reat Russell St.
man Gro. E8 57 CB36
mar Clo., Hayes 53 BA38
mar Clo., Uxb. 53 AX36
mar Gdns., W.Wick. 87 CE54
mar Way, Sev. 108 CW63
ne Landway
mer Clo., Kings.T. 75 BL49
mer Cres., Kings.T. 75 BL49
mer Gdns. N1 57 CA37
mer Ho., Kings.T. 75 BL49
mer Lea Clo. E15 57 CF36
mer Way N14 38 BW28
merhatch La., 103 BM62
psom
mington Ave. W4 65 BN43
mington Ave., Orp. 89 CP55
mington Ct. Rd., Dart. 79 CU48
mington Gdns., Bark. 58 CM36
mington Sq. WC1 2 D3
mington Sq. WC1 56 BY38
mington St. WC1 2 D3
mington St. WC1 56 BY38
mot Clo. N2 38 BT30
mot Clo. SE15 67 CB43
mot Grn., Brwd. 42 DA28
mot Pl. NW1 56 BW36
mot Pl. W7 54 BH40
mot Rd. E10 48 CE34
mot Rd. N17 48 BZ31
mot Rd., Dart. 79 CU46
mot Rd., Pur. 95 BY59
mot St. E2 57 CB38
mot Way, Bans. 95 BS60
mots Clo., Reig. 121 BT70
mount St. SE18 68 CL42
na Rd. SW18 76 BT47
sham St. W11 55 BQ40
shaw St. SE14 67 CE44
eptford Bdy.
shere Ave., St.Alb. 9 BG15
sman Rd., S.Ock. 60 DB37
smere Dr., Har. 36 BH29
smere Dr., Nthlt. 54 BE36
son Ave., Mitch. 76 BU50
son Clo., Dag. 59 CS36
son Clo., Wem. 46 BL33
Wilson Dr.
son Dr., Cher. 91 AT56
son Dr., Wem. 46 BL33
son Gdns., Har. 45 BG33
son Gro. SE16 67 CB41
son Rd. E6 58 CJ38
son Rd. SE5 67 BZ44
son Rd., Chess. 94 BL57
son Rd., Har. 45 BG33
son Rd., Ilf. 49 CK33
son St. E17 48 CF32
son St. EC2 2 L6
son St. EC2 57 BZ39
son St. N21 38 BY26
son Way, Wok. 100 AR61
sons, Tad. 103 BQ64
sons Pl. E14 57 CD39
almon La.
sons Rd. W6 65 BQ42
stone Clo., Hayes 54 BD38
ingsash Dr.
stone Dr., St.Alb. 9 BK11
lthorne Gdns., Dag. 59 CR36
cre Rd.

Wilton Ave. W4 65 BO42
Wilton Ct., West Dr. 63 AX43
Hatch La.
Wilton Ct. N10 38 BV30
Wilton Cres. SW1 3 G5
Wilton Cres. SW1 66 BV41
Wilton Cres. SW19 85 BR51
Wilton Cres., Wind. 61 AL45
Wilton Dr., Rom. 41 CS29
Wilton Gdns., E.Mol. 84 BF52
Wilton Gdns., Walt. 84 BD54
Wilton Gro. SW19 75 BR50
Wilton Gro., N.Mal. 85 BO53
Wilton La., Beac. 34 AO29
Wilton Ms. SW1 3 H6
Wilton Ms. SW1 66 BV41
Wilton Par., Felt. 73 BC48
Wilton Pk. Ct. SE18 68 CL43
Prince Imperial Rd.
Wilton Pl. SW1 3 G5
Wilton Pl. SW1 66 BV41
Wilton Pl., Wey. 92 AX58
Wilton Rd. N10 38 BV30
Wilton Rd. SE2 69 CP42
Wilton Rd. SW1 3 K7
Wilton Rd. SW1 66 BV41
Wilton Rd. SW19 76 BU50
Wilton Rd., Barn. 29 BU24
Wilton Rd., Houns. 64 BD45
Wilton Rd., Ilf. 49 CL35
Cecil Rd.
Wilton Rd., Red. 121 BU71
Wilton Row SW1 3 G5
Wilton Row SW1 66 BV41
Wilton Sq. N1 57 BZ37
Wilton St. SW1 3 J6
Wilton St. SW1 66 BV41
Wilton Ter. SW1 3 G6
Wilton Ter. SW1 66 BV41
Wilton Way E8 57 CB36
Wilton Yd. W10 55 BQ40
Bard Rd.
Wiltshire Ave., Horn. 51 CW31
Wiltshire Clo. SW3 3 E9
Wiltshire Clo. SW3 66 BU42
Wiltshire Gdns. N4 48 BZ32
Wiltshire Gdns., Twick. 74 BG47
Wiltshire La., Pnr. 44 BB31
Wiltshire Rd. N1 57 BZ37
Wiltshire Rd. SW9 66 BY45
Wiltshire Rd., Orp. 89 CO54
Wiltshire Rd., Th.Hth. 86 BY52
Wilverley Cres., N.Mal. 85 BO53
Wimbart Rd. SW2 76 BX47
Wimbledon Clo. SW20 75 BQ50
Wimbledon Hill Rd. 75 BR50
SW19
Wimbledon Pk. Est. 75 BR47
SW19
Wimbledon Pk. Rd. SW18 75 BR47
Wimbledon Pk. Rd. SW19 75 BR48
Wimbledon Pk. Side 75 BQ48
SW19
Wimbledon Rd. SW17 76 BT49
Wimbolt St. E2 57 CB38
Wimborne Ave., Hayes 53 BC39
Wimborne Ave., Orp. 88 CN52
Wimborne Ave., Sthl. 64 BF42
Wimborne Clo. SE12 78 CG46
Wimborne Clo., Epsom 94 BO60
Wimborne Clo., Saw. 6 CP6
Wimborne Clo., Wor.Pk. 85 BQ54
Dorchester Rd.
Wimborne Dr. NW9 46 BM31
Wimborne Dr., Pnr. 45 BD33
Wimborne Gdns. W13 54 BJ39
Wimborne Gro., Wat. 26 BB22
Wimborne Rd. N9 39 CB27
Wimborne Rd. N17 39 CA30
Wimborne Way, Beck. 87 CC52
Wimbourne Ave., Red. 121 BU73
Wimbourne Clo., Buck.H. 40 CH27
Wimbourne Ct. N1 57 BZ37
Wimbourne St. N1 57 BZ37
Wimbrel Clo., S.Croy. 96 BZ59
Wimpole Clo., Brom. 88 CJ52
Wimpole Clo., Kings.T. 85 BL51
Wimpole Ms. W1 1 J6
Wimpole Ms. W1 56 BV39
Wimpole Rd., West Dr. 53 AX40
Wimpole St. W1 1 J7
Wimpole St. W1 56 BV39
Winans Wk. SW9 66 BY44
Wincanton Cres., Nthlt. 45 BF35
Wincanton Gdns., Ilf. 40 CL30
Wincanton Rd. SW18 75 BR47
Wincanton Rd., Rom. 42 CV27
Winch Dells, Hem.H. 8 AZ15
Winchcomb Gdns. SE9 68 CJ45
Winchcombe Rd., Cars. 86 BT54
Winchelsea Ave., Bexh. 69 CQ43
Winchelsea Clo. SW15 75 BQ46
Winchelsea Cres., E.Mol. 84 BG51
Winchelsea Rd. E7 49 CH34
Winchelsea Rd. N17 48 CA31
Winchelsea Rd. NW10 55 BN37
Winchelsey Rd., S.Croy. 96 CA57
Winchendon Rd. SW6 65 BR44
Winchendon Rd., Tedd. 74 BG49
Winchester Ave. NW6 55 BR37
Winchester Ave. NW9 46 BM31
Winchester Ave., Houns. 64 BE43
Winchester Ave., Upmin. 51 CZ33
Winchester Clo. E6 58 CK39
Winchester Clo. SE17 4 G9
Winchester Clo., Amer. 25 AP23
Winchester Clo., Brom. 88 CG52
Winchester Clo., Enf. 30 CA25
Winchester Clo., Esher 93 BF56
Winchester Clo., Kings.T. 75 BM50
Winchester Clo., Slou. 62 AV44
Rodney Way
Winchester Cres., Grav. 81 DH48
Winchester Dr., Pnr. 45 BD32

Winchester Gro., Sev. 107 CU65
Winchester Ms. NW3 56 BT36
Winchester Rd.
Winchester Pk., Brom. 88 CG52
Winchester Pl. E8 48 CA35
Kingsland High St.
Winchester Pl. N6 47 BV33
Winchester Pl. W3 65 BN41
Winchester Rd. E4 39 CF29
Winchester Rd. N6 47 BV33
Winchester Rd. N9 39 CA26
Winchester Rd. NW3 56 BT36
Winchester Rd., Bexh. 69 CP44
Winchester Rd., Brom. 88 CG52
Winchester Rd., Felt. 74 BE48
Winchester Rd., Har. 46 BL31
Winchester Rd., Hayes 63 BB43
Winchester Rd., Ilf. 49 CM34
Winchester Rd., Nthwd. 44 BB31
Winchester Rd., Orp. 98 CO56
Winchester Rd., Twick. 74 BJ46
Winchester Rd., Walt. 83 BC54
Winchester Sq. SE1 4 K2
Winchester St. SW1 3 K10
Winchester St. SW1 66 BV42
Winchester St. W3 65 BN41
Winchester Wk. SE1 4 K2
Winchester Wk. SE1 57 BZ40
Winchester Way, Rick. 26 AZ25
Winchet Wk., Croy. 87 CC53
Long La.
Winchfield Clo., Har. 45 BK32
Winchfield Rd. SE26 77 CD49
Winchfield Way, Rick. 35 AX26
Winchmore Hill Rd. N14 38 BW26
Winchmore Hill Rd. N21 38 BW26
Winchstone Clo., Shep. 83 AY52
Winckley Clo., Har. 46 BL32
Wincott St. SE11 4 E9
Wincott St. SE11 66 BY42
Wincrofts Dr. SE9 68 CM45
Wind Hill, Ong. 14 CU13
Wind Hill, Welw.G.C. 5 BS7
Windborough Rd., Cars. 95 BV57
Windermere Ave. N3 47 BS31
Windermere Ave. NW6 55 BR37
Windermere Ave. SW19 86 BS52
Windermere Ave., Horn. 50 CU35
Windermere Ave., Ruis. 45 BD33
Windermere Ave., St.Alb. 9 BJ14
Windermere Ave., Wem. 45 BK33
Windermere Clo., Dart. 79 CU47
Windermere Clo., Egh. 72 AT50
Derwent Rd.
Windermere Clo., Felt. 73 BB47
Ambleside Dr.
Windermere Clo., Hem.H. 8 BA14
Windermere Clo., Orp. 88 CL55
Grasmere Gdns.
Windermere Clo., Rick. 25 AU25
Copmans Wick
Windermere Clo., Stai. 73 AY47
Viola Ave.
Windermere Ct. SW13 65 BO43
Windermere Gdns., Ilf. 49 CK32
Windermere Gro., Wem. 45 BK33
Windermere Ave.
Windermere Rd. N10 38 BV30
Windermere Rd. N19 47 BW34
Holloway Rd.
Windermere Rd. SW15 75 BO49
Windermere Rd. SW16 86 BW51
Windermere Rd. W5 64 BK41
Windermere Rd., Bexh. 69 CS44
Windermere Rd., Couls. 104 BX61
Windermere Rd., Croy. 87 CA54
Windermere Rd., Sthl. 54 BE39
Windermere Rd., W.Wick. 88 CG55
Windermere Way, Red. 121 BU70
Windermere Way, West 53 AY40
Dr.
Providence Rd.
Winders Rd. SW11 66 BU44
Windfield, Lthd. 102 BJ64
Windfield Clo. SE26 77 CC49
Windgates, Guil. 118 AU69
Windham Ave., Croy. 96 CF58
Windham Rd., Rich. 65 BL45
Windhover Way, Grav. 81 DJ49
Winding Shot, Hem.H. 8 AW13
Winding Way, Dag. 50 CP34
Winding Way, Har. 45 BH35
Windings, The, S.Croy. 96 CA59
Windlass Pl. SE8 67 CD42
Windlesham Gro. SW19 75 BQ47
Windlesham Rd., Wok. 91 AO58
Windley Clo. SE23 77 CC48
Windmill Ave., Epsom 94 BO59
Windmill Ave., St.Alb. 9 BK11
Windmill Clo. SE1 67 CB42
Beatrice Rd.
Windmill Clo., Cat. 105 BZ64
Coulsdon Rd.
Windmill Clo., Epsom 94 BO59
Windmill Clo., Sun. 73 BB50
Windmill Clo., Surb. 84 BK54
Windmill Clo., Upmin. 51 CX34
Windmill Clo., Wal.Abb. 22 CG20
Windmill Clo., Wind. 61 AN44
Windmill Dr. SW4 76 BV46
Windmill Dr., Kes. 97 CJ56
Lakes Rd.
Windmill Dr., Lthd. 102 BK65
Windmill Dr., Reig. 121 BT69
Windmill Dr., Rick. 26 AY25
Windmill End, Epsom 94 BO59
Windmill Gdns., Enf. 29 BY23
Windmill Gro., Croy. 87 BZ53
Queens Rd.
Windmill Hill NW3 47 BT34
Windmill Hill, Enf. 29 BY24
Windmill Hill, Kings L. 16 AV19
Windmill Hill, Ruis. 44 BB33
Windmill La. E15 57 CF36

Windmill La., Barn. 28 BO25
Windmill La., Bush. 36 BG26
Windmill La., Chsnt. 21 CD18
Windmill La., Epsom 94 BO59
Windmill La., Grnf. 54 BG38
Windmill La., Islw. 64 BH42
Windmill La., Sthl. 64 BG41
Windmill La., Surb. 84 BJ53
Windmill Ms., Brent. 65 BO42
Windmill Rd.
Windmill Ri., Kings.T. 75 BM50
Windmill Rd. N18 39 BZ28
Windmill Rd. SW18 76 BT46
Windmill Rd. SW19 75 BQ48
Windmill Rd. W4 65 BO42
Windmill Rd. W5 64 BK42
Windmill Rd., Brent. 64 BK42
Windmill Rd., Croy. 87 BZ54
Windmill Rd., Ger.Cr. 34 AR29
Windmill Rd., Hmptn. 74 BF49
Windmill Rd., Hem.H. 8 AY13
Windmill Rd., Mitch. 86 BW53
Windmill Rd., Sev. 116 CU68
Windmill Rd. 116 CU70
(Sevenoaks Weald), Sev.
Windmill Rd., Slou. 61 AO40
Windmill Rd. (Fulmer), 43 AR35
Slou.
Windmill Rd., Sun. 83 BB51
Windmill Rd. W., Sun. 83 BB51
Windmill Row SE11 66 BY42
Windmill St. W1 1 N7
Windmill St. W1 56 BW39
Windmill St., Bush. 36 BH26
Windmill St., Grav. 81 DG47
Windmill Wk. SE1 4 E3
Windmill Wk. SE1 56 BY40
Windmill Way, Brwd. 33 CZ22
Windmill Way, Reig. 121 BT69
Windmill Way, Ruis. 44 BB33
Windmore Ave., Pot.B. 19 BQ19
Windover Ave. NW9 46 BN31
Windridge Clo., St.Alb. 9 BF15
Windridge Rd., St.Alb. 9 BD15
Windrose Clo. SE16 67 CC41
Kinburn St.
Windrush Ave., Slou. 62 AT42
Windrush Clo. SW11 66 BT45
Maysoule Rd.
Windrush Clo. W4 65 BN44
Windrush Clo., Uxb. 44 AY35
Windrush La. SE23 77 CC48
Winds End Clo., Hem.H. 8 AZ12
Winds Pt. Dr. SE15 67 CB43
Ethna Rd.
Winds Ridge, Wok. 109 AU66
Windsland Ms. W2 56 BT39
London St.
Windsor Ave. E17 39 CD30
Windsor Ave. SW19 86 BT51
Windsor Ave., E.Mol. 84 BF52
Windsor Ave., Edg. 37 BM28
Windsor Ave., Grays 71 DD41
Windsor Ave., N.Mal. 85 BN53
Windsor Ave., Rick. 35 AW26
Windsor Ave., Sutt. 85 BR55
Windsor Ave., Uxb. 53 AZ37
Windsor Clo. N3 37 BR30
Windsor Rd.
Windsor Clo. SE27 77 BZ49
Windsor Clo., Borwd. 28 BM23
Windsor Clo., Brent. 64 BJ43
Amalgamated Dr.
Windsor Clo., Chsnt. 21 CB18
Windsor Clo., Chis. 78 CL49
Windsor Clo., Guil. 118 AP71
Powell Clo.
Windsor Clo., Har. 45 BF34
Windsor Clo., Hem.H. 16 AT17
Pembridge Rd.
Windsor Clo., Nthwd. 35 BC30
Windsor Clo., Welw.G.C. 5 BP5
Windsor Ct. N14 38 BW26
Windsor Ct., Sun. 73 BC50
Windsor Ct. Rd., Wok. 91 AP58
Windsor Cres., Har. 45 BF35
Windsor Cres., Wem. 46 BM34
Windsor Dr., Ashf. 73 AX49
Windsor Dr., Barn. 29 BU25
Windsor Dr., Dart. 79 CU46
Windsor Dr., Orp. 98 CO57
Windsor Gdns. W9 56 BS39
Windsor Gdns., Croy. 86 BX55
Richmond Rd.
Windsor Gdns., Hayes 63 BA41
Windsor Gro. SE27 77 BZ49
Windsor Pk. Rd., Hayes 63 BB43
Windsor Pl. SW1 3 M7
Windsor Pl. SW1 66 BW42
Francis St.
Windsor Rd. E4 39 CE28
Chivers Rd.
Windsor Rd. E7 49 CH35
Windsor Rd. E10 48 CE34
Windsor Rd. E11 49 CH33
Windsor Rd. N3 37 BR30
Windsor Rd. N7 47 BX34
Windsor Rd. N13 38 BY27
Windsor Rd. N17 39 CB30
Windsor Rd. NW2 55 BP36
Windsor Rd. W5 54 BK40
Windsor Rd., Barn. 28 BQ25
Windsor Rd., Bexh. 69 CQ45
Windsor Rd., Brwd. 33 DA25
Windsor Rd., Dag. 50 CQ34
Windsor Rd., Egh. 72 AR47
Windsor Rd., Enf. 30 CC21
Windsor Rd., Ger.Cr. 43 AQ35
Windsor Rd., Grav. 81 DG48
Windsor Rd., Har. 36 BG30
Windsor Rd., Horn. 51 CV33
Windsor Rd., Houns. 63 BC44
Windsor Rd., Ilf. 49 CL35
Windsor Rd., Kings.T. 75 BL50

Windsor Rd., Maid. 61 AG41
Windsor Rd., Rich. 65 BL44
Windsor Rd., Sid. 79 CO50
Windsor Rd., Slou. 62 AP41
Windsor Rd. (Datchet), 62 AQ43
Slou.
Windsor Rd., Sthl. 64 BE41
Windsor Rd., Stai. 72 AS46
Windsor Rd., Sun. 73 BC50
Windsor Rd., Tedd. 74 BG49
Windsor Rd., Th.Hth. 86 BY51
Windsor Rd., Wat. 27 BD22
Windsor Rd., Welw. 5 BP5
Windsor Rd., Wind. 61 AO42
Windsor Rd., Wok. 91 AO56
Windsor Rd., Wor.Pk. 85 BP55
Windsor St. N1 56 BY37
Windsor St., Cher. 83 AW53
Windsor St., Uxb. 53 AX36
Windsor Ter. N1 2 J2
Windsor Ter. N1 57 BZ38
Windsor Wk. SE5 67 BZ44
Windsor Wk., Wey. 92 AZ56
Windsor Way W6 65 BQ42
Windsor Way, Wok. 100 AU61
Windsors, The, Buck.H. 40 CK27
Windspoint Dr. SE15 67 CB43
Green Hundred Rd.
Windus Rd. N16 48 CA33
Windus Wk. N16 48 CA33
Alkham Rd.
Windward Clo., Enf. 30 CC21
Windy Hill, Brwd. 122 DE26
Windy Ridge, Brom. 88 CK51
Windyridge Clo. SW19 75 BQ49
Wine Clo. E1 57 CC40
Wine Office Ct. EC4 2 E9
Wine Office Ct. EC4 56 BY39
Winern Glebe, Wey. 92 AX60
Winford Dr., Brox. 12 CD14
Winforton St. SE10 67 CF44
Winfrith Rd. SW18 76 BT47
Wing Way, Brwd. 42 DB26
Wingate Cres., Croy. 86 BW53
Wingate Rd. W6 65 BP41
Wingate Rd., Ilf. 49 CL35
Wingate Rd., Sid. 79 CP49
Sidcup Hill
Wingate Way, St.Alb. 9 BJ14
Wingfield, Grays 71 DC42
Wingfield Clo., Brwd. 122 DD27
Wingfield Clo., Wey. 92 AW58
Wingfield Gdns., Upmin. 51 CZ32
Wingfield Ms. SE15 67 CB45
Wingfield St.
Wingfield Rd. E15 49 CG35
Wingfield Rd. E17 48 CE32
Wingfield Rd., Grav. 81 DG47
Wingfield Rd., Kings.T. 75 BL50
Wingfield St. SE15 67 CB45
Wingfield Way, Ruis. 44 BC35
Wingford Rd. SW2 76 BX46
Wingletye La., Horn. 51 CW33
Wingmore Rd. SE24 67 BZ45
Wingrave Cres., Brwd. 42 CZ28
Wingrave Rd. W6 65 BQ43
Wingrove Rd. SE6 78 CG48
Winifred Ave., Horn. 51 CV35
Winifred Gro. SW11 66 BU45
Marjorie Gro.
Winifred Rd. SW19 86 BS51
Winifred Rd., Couls. 104 BV61
Winifred Rd., Dag. 50 CQ34
Winifred Rd., Dart. 79 CU46
Winifred Rd., Erith 69 CT42
Winifred Rd., Hmptn. 74 BF49
Winifred Rd., Hem.H. 8 AX15
Winifred St. E16 58 CK40
Winifred Ter. E13 58 CH37
High St.
Winifred Ter., Enf. 39 CA26
Winkers Clo., Ger.Cr. 34 AS30
Winkers La., Ger.Cr. 34 AS30
Winkfield Rd. E13 58 CH37
Winkfield Rd. N22 38 BY30
Winkfield Rd., Wind. 61 AM46
Winkley St. E2 57 CB38
Canrobert St.
Winkwell, Hem.H. 7 AU14
Winkworth Pl., Bans. 95 BS60
Winkworth Rd., Bans. 95 BS60
Winlaton Rd., Brom. 77 CF49
Winmill Rd., Dag. 50 CQ34
Winn Common Rd. 68 CN43
SE18
Winn Rd. SE12 78 CH47
Winnett St. W1 1 N10
Winnings Wk., Nthlt. 54 BE36
Arnold Rd.
Winnington Clo. N2 47 BT32
Winnington Rd. N2 47 BT32
Winnington Rd., Enf. 30 CC22
Winnington Way, Wok. 100 AQ62
Winnock Rd., West Dr. 53 AX40
Winns Ave. E17 48 CD31
Winns Ms. N15 48 CA31
Grove Pk. Rd.
Winns Ter. E17 39 CE30
Winsbeach E17 48 CF31
Winscombe Cres. W5 54 BK38
Winscombe St. N19 47 BV34
Winscombe Way, Stan. 36 BJ28
Winsford Rd. SE6 77 CD48
Winsford Ter. N18 39 BZ28
Winsham Gro. SW11 76 BV46
Winslade Rd. SW2 76 BX46
Winslade Way SE26 77 CE47
Winsland Ms. W2 1 A8
Winsland Ms. W2 56 BT39
Winsland St.
Winsland St. W2 1 A8
Winsland St. W2 56 BT39
Winsley St. W1 1 L8
Winsley St. W1 56 BW39

Winslow Clo. NW10 46 BO34
Neasden La. N.
Winslow Clo., Pnr. 44 BC32
Winslow Rd. W6 65 BQ43
Winslow Way, Felt. 74 BE48
Winslow Way, Walt. 84 BD55
Winsor Est. W9 56 BS39
Winsor Ter. E6 58 CL39
Winstanley Clo., Cob. 92 BC60
Winstanley Rd. SW11 66 BT45
Winstead Gdns., Dag. 50 CS35
Winston Ave. NW9 46 BO33
Winston Clo., Har. 36 BH29
Winston Clo., Rom. 50 CR31
Winston Ct., Har. 36 BF29
Winston Dr., Cob. 102 BE62
Winston Gdns., Berk. 7 AP13
Winston Rd. N16 48 BZ35
Winston Wk. W4 65 BN41
Winston Way, Ilf. 49 CL34
Winston Way, Pot.B. 20 BS20
Winston Way, Wok. 100 AT63
Winstone Clo., Rom. 50 CR31
Marlborough Rd.
Winstre Rd., Borwd. 28 BM23
Winter Ave. E6 58 CK37
Winter Box Wk., Rich. 75 BL46
Kings Rd.
Winterborne Ave., Orp. 88 CM55
Winterbourne Gro., Wey. 92 BA57
Winterbourne Rd. SE6 77 CD47
Winterbourne Rd., Dag. 50 CP34
Winterbourne Rd., Th.Hth. 86 BY52
Winterbrook Rd. SE24 77 BZ46
Winterdown Gdns., Esher 93 BE57
Winterdown Rd., Esher 93 BE57
Winterfold Clo. SW19 75 BR48
Wintergreen Clo. E6 58 CK39
Yarrow Cres.
Winterhill Way, Guil. 109 AT68
Winters Cft., Grav. 81 DH50
Winters Rd., T.Ditt. 84 BJ54
Winters Way, Wal.Abb. 22 CH20
Winterscroft Rd., Hodd. 12 CD11
Wintersells Rd., Wey. 92 AX58
Winterstoke Gdns. NW7 37 BP28
Winterstoke Rd. SE6 77 CD47
Winterton Pl. SW10 66 BT43
Winterwell Rd. SW2 76 BX46
Winthorpe Rd. SW15 65 BR45
Winthrop St. E1 57 CB39
Winthrop Wk., Wem. 45 BK34
Hutchinson Ter.
Winton App., Rick. 26 BA25
Winton Ave. N11 38 BW29
Winton Clo. N9 39 CC26
Winton Cres., Rick. 26 AZ25
Winton Dr., Chsnt. 21 CD18
Winton Dr., Rick. 26 AZ25
Winton Gdns., Edg. 37 BL29
Winton Rd., Orp. 97 CL56
Winton Way SW16 76 BY49
Winvale, Slou. 62 AP41
Winwood, Slou. 52 AR39
Winyatt St. EC1 56 BY38
Wisbeach Rd., Croy. 87 BZ53
Wisborough Rd., S.Croy. 96 CA58
Wisdons Clo., Dag. 50 CR34
Wise La. NW7 37 BP28
Wise La., West Dr. 63 AX41
Wise Rd. E15 57 CF37
Wisemans Gdns., Saw. 6 CP6
Wises La., Hat. 19 BQ17
Wises La., Sev. 99 DC57
Wiseton Rd. SW17 76 BU47
Wishart Rd. SE3 68 CJ44
Wishbone Way, Wok. 100 AP61
Wishford Ct., Ash. 103 BL62
Wisley La., Wok. 101 AX61
Wisley Rd. SW11 76 BU46
Wisley Rd., Orp. 79 CO50
Wissants, Harl. 13 CL13
Wisteria Clo., Brwd. 33 DB25
Lavender Ave.
Wisteria Clo., Ilf. 49 CL35
Wisteria Clo., Orp. 88 CL55
Wisteria Gdns., Swan. 89 CS51
Wisteria Rd. SE13 67 CF45
Witan St. E2 57 CB38
Coventry Rd.
Witches La., Sev. 107 CT65
Witchford, Welw.G.C. 5 BT8
Witham Clo., Loug. 31 CK25
Witham Rd. SE20 87 CC52
Witham Rd. W13 54 BJ40
Green Man La.
Witham Rd., Dag. 50 CR35
Witham Rd., Horn. 50 CU32
Witham Rd., Islw. 64 BG44
Withens Clo., Orp. 89 CP52
Witherby Clo., Croy. 96 CA56
Witherfield Way SE16 67 CB42
Egan Way
Witherings, The, Horn. 51 CW32
Witherington Rd. N5 47 BY35
Withers Mead NW9 37 BO30
Withers Pl. EC1 57 BZ38
Old St.
Witherston Way SE9 78 CL48
Withey Clo., Wind. 61 AM44
Witheygate Ave., Stai. 73 AW50
Withies, The, Lthd. 102 BJ63
Withy La., Ruis. 44 BA32
Withy Mead E4 39 CF27
Withybed Cor., Tad. 103 BP65
Withycombe Rd. SW19 75 BQ47
Victoria Dr.
Withycroft, Slou. 52 AS39
Witley Ct., Sthl. 64 BE42
Witley Cres., Croy. 96 CF57
Witley Gdns., Sthl. 64 BE42
Witley Rd. N19 47 BW34
Holloway Rd.

Witmore Clo. N11 38 BV28
Witney Clo., Pnr. 36 BE29
Witney Clo., Uxb. 44 AY35
Witney Path SE23 77 CC48
Wittenham Way E4 39 CF27
Wittersham Rd., Brom. 78 CG49
Wivenhoe Clo. SE15 67 CB45
Wivenhoe Ct., Houns. 64 BE45
Staines Rd.
Wivenhoe Rd., Bark. 59 CO37
Wiverton Rd. SE26 77 CC50
Wix Hill, Lthd. 110 AZ68
Wix Rd., Dag. 59 CP37
Wixs La. SW4 66 BV45
Woburn Ave., Epp. 31 CN22
Woburn Ave., Horn. 50 CU35
Woburn Ave., Pur. 95 BY59
Woburn Clo. SW19 76 BT50
Tintern Clo.
Woburn Clo., Bush. 27 BG25
Woburn Pl. WC1 1 P4
Woburn Pl. WC1 56 BW38
Woburn Rd., Cars. 86 BU54
Woburn Rd., Croy. 87 BZ54
Woburn Sq. WC1 1 P5
Woburn Sq. WC1 56 BW38
Woburn Wk. WC1 1 P3
Woburn Wk. WC1 56 BW38
Wodeham St. E1 57 CB39
Wodeland Ave., Guil. 118 AQ71
Woffington Clo., Kings.T. 84 BK51
Wokindon Rd., Grays 71 DG41
Woking Clo. SW15 65 BO45
Woking Rd., Guil. 109 AR67
Woking Rd., Wey. 91 AV60
Wold, The, Cat. 105 CE64
Woldham Rd., Brom. 88 CJ52
Woldingham Rd., Cat. 105 CB63
Woldingham Rd. (Woldingham), Cat. 114 CF66
Wolds Dr., Orp. 97 CL56
Wolf La., Wind. 61 AL45
Wolfe Clo., Brom. 88 CH53
Wolfe Clo., Hayes 53 BC38
Ayles Rd.
Wolfe Cres. SE7 68 CJ42
Wolfe Cres. SE16 67 CC41
Canada St.
Wolferton Rd. E12 49 CK35
Wolffe Gdns. E15 58 CG36
Wolffram Clo. SE13 78 CG46
Wolfington Rd. SE27 76 BY49
Wolfs Hill, Oxt. 115 CH69
Wolfs Row, Oxt. 115 CH68
Wolfs Wd., Oxt. 115 CH69
Wolftencroft Clo. SW11 66 BT45
Wollaston Clo. SE1 4 H8
Wollaston Clo. SE1 67 BZ42
Wolmer Clo., Edg. 37 BM28
Wolmer Gdns., Edg. 37 BM27
Wolseley Ave. SW19 76 BS48
Wolseley Gdns. W4 65 BM43
Wolseley Rd. E7 58 CH36
Wolseley Rd. N8 47 BW32
Wolseley Rd. N22 38 BX30
Wolseley Rd. W4 65 BN42
Wolseley Rd., Har. 45 BH31
Wolseley Rd., Mitch. 86 BV54
Wolseley Rd., Rom. 50 CS33
Wolseley St. SE1 4 Q5
Wolseley St. SE1 67 CA41
Wolsey Ave. E6 58 CL38
Wolsey Ave. E17 48 CD31
Wolsey Ave., Chsnt. 21 CB18
Wolsey Ave., T.Ditt. 84 BH53
Wolsey Clo. SW20 75 BP50
Wolsey Clo., Houns. 74 BG46
Wolsey Clo., Kings.T. 85 BM51
Wolsey Clo., Sthl. 64 BG41
Wolsey Clo., Wor.Pk. 94 BO56
Wolsey Cres., Croy. 96 CF58
Wolsey Cres., Mord. 85 BR54
Wolsey Dr., Kings.T. 75 BL49
Wolsey Dr., Walt. 84 BD54
Wolsey Gdns., Ilf. 40 CL29
Wolsey Gro., Edg. 37 BN29
Wolsey Gro., Esher 93 BF56
Wolsey Ms. NW5 56 BW36
Caversham Rd.
Wolsey Ms., Orp. 97 CN56
Osgood Ave.
Wolsey Rd. N1 48 BZ35
Wolsey Rd., Ashf. 73 AY49
Wolsey Rd., E.Mol. 84 BG52
Wolsey Rd., Enf. 30 CB23
Wolsey Rd., Esher 93 BF56
Wolsey Rd., Hmptn. 74 BF50
Wolsey Rd., Nthwd. 35 BA27
Wolsey Rd., Sun. 73 BB50
Wolsey St. E1 57 CC39
Sidney St.
Wolsey Wk., Wok. 100 AS62
Church St. W.
Wolsey Way, Chess. 94 BM56
Wolsley Clo., Dart. 79 CT46
Wolstonbury N12 37 BR28
Wolvens La., Dor. 119 BF73
Wolvercote Rd. SE2 69 CP41
Wolverley St. E2 57 CB38
Bethnal Grn. Rd.
Wolverton SE17 4 M10
Wolverton Ave., Kings.T. 85 BM51
Wolverton Gdns. W5 55 BL40
Wolverton Gdns. W6 65 BQ42
Wolverton Rd., Stan. 36 BK29
Wolverton Way N14 29 BW25
Wolves La. N13 38 BY29
Wolves La. N22 38 BY29
Womersley Rd. N8 47 BX32
Wonersh Way, Sutt. 94 BQ58
Wonford Clo., Kings.T. 85 BO51
Wonford Clo., Tad. 112 BP66
Wonham La., Bet. 120 BO71
Wontford Rd., Pur. 104 BY61

Wontner Rd. SW17 76 BU48
Wood, The, Surb. 85 BL53
Wood Ave., Grays 70 CY42
Wood Ch. Dr., Brom. 78 CJ50
Wood Clo. NW9 46 BN33
Wood Clo., Bex. 79 CT48
Wood Clo., Har. 45 BG33
Wood Clo., Hat. 10 BP12
Wood Clo., Wind. 61 AO45
Wood Common, Hat. 10 BP11
Wood Cres., Hem.H. 8 AX14
Wood Dene, Lthd. 93 BG59
Wood Dr., Chis. 78 CK50
Wood Dr., Sev. 116 CT66
Wood End, Esher 84 BG55
Wood End, Hayes 53 BB39
Wood End, Lthd. 111 BK66
Wood End, St.Alb. 18 BG17
Wood End Ave., Har. 45 BF35
Wood End Clo., Nthlt. 45 BG35
Wood End Clo., Slou. 43 AO34
Wood End Gdns., Nthlt. 45 BG35
Wood End Grn. Rd., Hayes 53 BA39
Wood End La., Nthlt. 54 BF36
Wood End Rd., Har. 45 BG35
Wood End Way, Nthlt. 45 BG35
Wood Fm. Rd., Hem.H. 8 AY14
Wood Gate, Wat. 17 BC20
Wood Grn. Way, Chsnt. 21 CD19
Wood La. N6 47 BV32
Wood La. NW9 46 BN33
Wood La. W12 55 BQ39
Wood La., Cat. 105 BZ65
Wood La., Dag. 50 CP35
Wood La., Dart. 80 CY49
Wood La., Horn. 50 CU35
Wood La., Islw. 64 BH43
Wood La., Iver 52 AU38
Wood La., Ong. 15 DC13
Wood La., Ruis. 44 BA33
Wood La., Slou. 61 AN41
Wood La., Stan. 36 BJ27
Wood La., Tad. 103 BR62
Wood La., Wey. 92 BA58
Wood La., Wok. 100 AO62
Wood La., Wdf.Grn. 40 CG28
Wood La. Clo., Iver 52 AU38
Wood La. End, Hem.H. 8 AZ13
Wood Lo. Gdns., Brom. 78 CK50
Wood Lo. La., W.Wick. 87 CF55
Wood Meads, Epp. 23 CO18
Wood Pond Clo., Beac. 34 AO29
Drovers Way
Wood Ride, Barn. 29 BT23
Wood Ride, Orp. 88 CM52
Wood Riding, Wok. 100 AV61
Wood Ri., Guil. 118 AP69
Wood Ri., Pnr. 44 BC32
Wood Rd., Sev. 99 CZ57
Wood Rd., Shep. 83 AZ52
Wood Rd., West. 106 CJ62
Wood St. E16 58 CH39
Ethel Rd.
Wood St. E17 48 CF31
Wood St. EC2 2 J9
Wood St. EC2 57 BZ39
Wood St. W4 65 BO42
Wood St., Barn. 28 BQ24
Wood St., Grays 71 DE43
Wood St., Kings.T. 84 BK51
Wood St., Mitch. 86 BU54
Wood St., Red. 113 BW68
Wood St., Swan. 90 CV51
Wood Vale N10 47 BW32
Wood Vale SE23 77 CB47
Wood Vale, Hat. 10 BP12
Wood Vale Est. SE23 77 CB47
Wood Vw., Chess. 93 BK59
Wood Vw., Cuffley 20 BW17
Wood Vw., Grays 71 DE41
Wood Vw., Hem.H. 8 AW12
Wood Way, Orp. 88 CL55
Wood Way, Sev. 107 CT64
Wood Wf. SE10 67 CF43
Woodall Rd., Enf. 30 CC25
Woodbank Dr., Ch.St.G. 34 AR27
Woodbank Rd., Brom. 78 CG48
Woodbarn Way, Wal.Cr. 21 CD19
Woodbastwick Rd. SE26 77 CC50
Woodberry Ave. N21 38 BY27
Woodberry Ave., Har. 45 BF31
Woodberry Clo., Sun. 73 BC50
Woodberry Cres. N10 47 BV31
Woodberry Down N4 48 BZ33
Woodberry Down, Epp. 23 CO17
Woodberry Down Est. N4 48 BZ33
Woodberry Gdns. N12 38 BT29
Woodberry Gro. N4 48 BZ33
Woodberry Gro. N12 38 BT29
Woodberry Gro., Bex. 79 CS48
Briar Rd.
Woodberry Way E4 39 CF26
Woodberry Way N12 38 BT29
Woodbine Clo., Harl. 13 CM12
Linford End
Woodbine Clo., Twick. 74 BG48
Woodbine Clo., Wal.Abb. 31 CJ21
Woodbine Cotts., Guil. 118 AS74
Chinthurst La.
Woodbine Gro. SE20 77 CB50
Woodbine Gro., Enf. 30 BZ22
Woodbine La., Wor.Pk. 85 BP55
Woodbine Pl. E11 49 CH32
Woodbine Rd., Sid. 78 CN47
Woodbine Ter. E9 57 CC36
Homerton Ter.
Woodbines Ave., Kings.T. 84 BK52
Woodborough Rd. SW15 65 BP45
Woodbourne Ave. SW16 76 BW48
Woodbourne Clo. SW16 76 BW48
Woodbourne Dr., Esher 93 BH57
Woodbourne Gdns., Wall. 95 BV57

Woodbridge Ave., Lthd. 102 BJ62
Woodbridge Clo. N7 47 BX34
Durham Rd.
Woodbridge Clo. NW2 46 BP34
Newfield Ri.
Woodbridge Clo., Rom. 42 CV28
Woodbridge Ct., Wdf.Grn. 40 CK29
Vicarage Rd.
Woodbridge Gdns., Lthd. 102 BJ62
Woodbridge Hill, Guil. 118 AQ70
Woodbridge Hill Gdns., Guil. 118 AQ70
Woodbridge La., Rom. 42 CV27
Woodbridge Meadows, Guil. 118 AQ70
Woodbridge Rd., Bark. 49 CN35
Woodbridge Rd., Guil. 118 AR70
Woodbridge St. EC1 2 F4
Woodbridge St. EC1 56 BY38
Woodbrook Clo., Wal.Abb. 22 CG20
Woodbrook Rd. SE2 69 CO43
Woodburn Clo. NW4 46 BQ32
Woodburn Clo., Uxb. 53 AZ38
Aldenham Dr.
Woodbury Clo. E11 49 CH31
Woodbury Clo., Croy. 87 CA55
Woodbury Clo., West. 106 CK62
Belvedere Rd.
Woodbury Dr., Sutt. 95 BT58
Woodbury Gro., Brwd. 33 DB22
Peartree Clo.
Woodbury Hill, Loug. 31 CK23
Woodbury Pk. Rd. W13 54 BJ38
Woodbury Rd. E17 48 CE31
Woodbury Rd., West. 106 CK62
Woodbury St. SW17 76 BU49
Woodchester Sq. W2 56 BS39
Woodchurch Clo., Sid. 78 CM48
Woodchurch Rd. NW6 56 BS36
Woodclyffe Dr., Chis. 88 CL51
Woodcock Dell Ave., Har. 45 BK33
Woodcock Hill, Borwd. 28 BM25
Woodcock Hill, Har. 45 BK32
Woodcock Hill, Rick. 35 AX28
Woodcock Hill, St.Alb. 9 BK10
Woodcombe Cres. SE23 77 CC47
Woodcote, Guil. 118 AQ72
St. Catherines Dr.
Woodcote Ave. NW7 37 BQ29
Woodcote Ave., Horn. 50 CU35
Woodcote Ave., Th.Hth. 86 BY52
Woodcote Ave., Wall. 95 BV58
Woodcote Clo., Chsnt. 21 CC18
Woodcote Clo., Enf. 30 CC25
Woodcote Clo., Epsom 94 BN60
Woodcote Clo., Kings.T. 75 BL50
Woodcote Dr., Pur. 95 BW58
Woodcote End, Epsom 103 BN61
Woodcote Grn. Rd., Epsom 103 BN61
Woodcote Grn. Rd., Wall. 95 BW58
Woodcote Gro., Cars. 95 BV59
Woodcote Gro. Rd., Couls. 104 BW61
Woodcote Hurst, Epsom 103 BN61
Woodcote La., Pur. 95 BW59
Woodcote Pk. Ave., Pur. 95 BW59
Woodcote Pk. Rd., Epsom 103 BN61
Woodcote Pl. SE27 76 BY49
Woodcote Rd. E11 49 CH33
Woodcote Rd., Epsom 94 BN60
Woodcote Rd., Orp. 88 CN54
Woodcote Rd., Wall. 95 BV57
Woodcote Side, Epsom 103 BM61
Woodcote Valley Rd., Pur. 95 BW60
Woodcourt Clo., Wal.Cr. 21 CC18
Woodcraft Ave., Stan. 36 BJ30
Woodcrest Rd., Pur. 95 BX60
Woodcrest Wk., Reig. 121 BU69
Woodcroft N21 38 BX26
Woodcroft SE9 78 CK48
Woodcroft, Grnf. 54 BJ36
Woodcroft, Harl. 13 CM12
Woodcroft Ave. NW7 37 BO29
Woodcroft Cres., Uxb. 53 AZ37
Woodcroft Rd., Chesh. 16 AO17
Woodcroft Rd., Th.Hth. 86 BY53
Woodcutters Ave., Grays 71 DE41
Woodedge Clo. E4 40 CG26
Forest Side
Woodend SE19 77 BZ50
Woodend, Sutt. 86 BT55
Woodend, The, Wall. 95 BV58
Woodend Clo., Wok. 100 AQ63
Woodend Gdns., Enf. 29 BX24
Woodend Pk., Cob. 102 BD61
Woodend Rd. E17 39 CF30
Wooder Gdns. E7 49 CG35
Wooderson Clo. SE25 87 CA52
Clifton Rd.
Woodfall Ave., Barn. 28 BR25
Woodfall Dr., Dart. 69 CT45
Woodfall Rd. N4 47 BY33
Woodfall St. SW3 66 BU42
Woodfarrs SE5 67 BZ45
Woodfield Ave. NW9 46 BO31
Woodfield Ave. SW16 76 BW48
Woodfield Ave. W5 54 BK38
Woodfield Ave., Cars. 95 BV57
Woodfield Ave., Grav. 81 DG48
Woodfield Ave., Nthwd. 35 BB28
Woodfield Ave., Wem. 45 BK34
Woodfield Clo. SE19 77 BZ50
Woodfield Clo., Ash. 102 BK62
Woodfield Clo., Couls. 104 BW63
Woodfield Clo., Red. 121 BU70
Woodfield Cres. W5 54 BK38
Woodfield Dr., Barn. 38 BV26
Woodfield Dr., Hem.H. 8 BA14
Woodfield Dr., Rom. 50 CU31

Woodfield Gdns. W9 55 E
Woodfield Rd.
Woodfield Gdns., Hem.H. 8 B
Woodfield Dr.
Woodfield Gdns., N.Mal. 85 B
Woodfield Gro. SW16 76 B
Woodfield Hill, Couls. 104 B
Woodfield La. SW16 76 B
Woodfield La., Ash. 103 E
Woodfield La., Hat. 11 B
Woodfield Pl. W9 55 B
Woodfield Ri., Bush. 36 B
Woodfield Rd. W5 54 B
Woodfield Rd. W9 55 E
Woodfield Rd., Ash. 102 E
Woodfield Rd., Houns. 63 B
Woodfield Rd., Rad. 27 B
Woodfield Rd., T.Ditt. 84 B
Woodfield Rd., Welw.G.C. 5
Woodfield Way N11 38 B
Woodfield Way, Horn. 51 C
Woodfield Way, Red. 121 B
Woodfield Way, St.Alb. 9 B
Woodfields, Sev. 107 C
Woodfields, The, S.Croy. 96 C
Woodfines, The, Horn. 51 C
Burntwood Ave.
Woodford Ave., Ilf. 49 C
Woodford Bri. Rd., Ilf. 49 C
Woodford Ct., Wal.Abb. 22 C
Abbots Dr.
Woodford Cres., Pnr. 35 B
Woodford New Rd. E17 49 C
Woodford New Rd. E18 49 C
Woodford New Rd., Wdf.Grn. 49 C
Woodford Pl., Wem. 46 B
Woodford Rd. E7 49 C
Woodford Rd. E18 49 C
Woodford Rd., Wat. 27 B
Woodford Trd. Est., Wdf.Grn. 40 C
Woodgate Ave., Chess. 93 B
Woodgate Cres., Nthwd. 35 B
Woodgavil, Bans. 103 B
Woodger Clo., Guil. 118 A
Woodger Rd. W12 65 B
Goldhawk Rd.
Woodgers Gro., Swan. 89 C
Swanley La.
Woodget Clo. E6 58 C
Remington Rd.
Woodgrange Ave. N12 38 B
Woodgrange Ave. W5 55 BN
Woodgrange Ave., Enf. 30 C
Woodgrange Ave., Har. 45 B
Woodgrange Clo., Har. 45 B
Woodgrange Gdns., Enf. 30 C
Woodgrange Rd. E7 49 C
Woodgrange Ter., Enf. 30 C
Woodgreen La., Wal.Abb. 22 C
Woodgreen Rd., Wal.Abb. 22 C
Woodhall Ave. SE21 77 C
Woodhall Ave., Pnr. 36 B
Woodhall Clo., Uxb. 44 A
Woodhall Ct., Welw.G.C. 5 E
Woodhall Cres., Horn. 51 CV
Woodhall Dr. SE21 77 C
Woodhall Dr., Pnr. 36 B
Woodhall Gate, Pnr. 36 B
Woodhall La., Hem.H. 8 A
Woodhall La., Rad. 28 B
Woodhall La., Wat. 36 B
Woodhall La., Welw.G.C. 5 E
Woodhall Par., Welw.G.C. 5 E
Woodhall Rd., Pnr. 36 B
Woodham Ct. E18 49 C
Woodham La., Wey. 91 A
Woodham La., Wok. 91 A
Woodham Pk. Rd., Wey. 91 A
Woodham Pk. Way, Wey. 91 A
Woodham Ri., Wok. 100 A
Woodham Rd. SE6 77 C
Woodham Rd., Wok. 100 AS
Woodham Waye, Wok. 91 A
Woodhatch Clo. E6 58 CK
Leamouth Rd.
Woodhatch Rd., Red. 121 BT
Woodhatch Rd., Reig. 121 BT
Woodhatch Spinney, Couls. 104 B
Woodhaven Gdns., Ilf. 49 CM
Brandville Gdns.
Woodhaw, Egh. 72 A
Woodhayes Rd. SW19 75 BC
Woodhead Dr., Orp. 88 C
Woodheyes Rd. NW10 46 B
Woodhill SE18 68 CK
Woodhill, Harl. 13 C
Woodhill, Wok. 109 A
Woodhill Ave., Ger.Cr. 43 AS
Woodhill Cres., Har. 45 BK
Woodhouse Ave., Grnf. 54 BH
Woodhouse Clo., Grnf. 54 BH
Woodhouse Clo., Hayes 63 BB
Woodhouse Eaves, Nthwd. 35 BC
Eastbury Ave.
Woodhouse Gro. E12 58 CK
Woodhouse Rd. E11 49 CG
Woodhouse Rd. N12 38 BT
Woodhurst Ave., Orp. 88 CL
Woodhurst Ave., Wat. 27 BD
Woodhurst Dr., Uxb. 43 AV
Woodhurst La., Oxt. 115 CG
Woodhurst Pk., Oxt. 115 CG
Woodhurst Rd. SE2 69 CO
Woodhurst Rd. W3 55 BN
Woodhyrst Gdns., Ken. 104 BY
Wooding Gro., Harl. 13 CL
Woodington Clo. SE9 78 CL
Woodison St. E3 57 CD
Woodknoll Dr., Chis. 88 CK

Woodland App., Grnf. 54 BJ36
Whitton Dr.
Woodland Ave., Brwd. 122 DD25
Woodland Ave., Hem.H. 8 AW14
Woodland Ave., Slou. 52 AO40
Woodland Ave., Wind. 61 AM45
Woodland Clo. NW9 46 BN32
Woodland Clo., Brwd. 122 DE25
Woodland Clo., Epsom 94 BO57
Woodland Clo., Lthd. 110 BB67
Woodland Clo., Uxb. 44 AZ34
Woodland Clo., Wdf.Grn. 40 CH27
Woodland Ct., Oxt. 114 CF67
Woodland Cres. SE10 68 CG43
Woodland Dr., Lthd. 110 BB67
Woodland Dr., St.Alb. 9 BK13
Woodland Dr., Wat. 26 BB23
Woodland Gdns. N10 47 BV32
Woodland Gdns., Croy. 96 CC59
Woodland Gdns., Islw. 64 BH45
Woodland Gdns., S.Croy. 96 CC58
Woodland Gro. SE10 68 CG42
Woodland Gro., Wey. 92 BA56
Woodland Hill SE19 77 CA50
Woodland La., Rick. 25 AU24
Woodland Pl., Hem.H. 8 AW14
Woodland Ri. N10 47 BV31
Woodland Ri., Grnf. 54 BJ36
Woodland Ri., Oxt. 115 CG68
Woodland Ri., Sev. 108 CW65
Woodland Ri., Welw.G.C. 5 BQ7
Woodland Rd. E4 39 CF26
Woodland Rd. N11 38 BV28
Woodland Rd. SE19 77 CA49
Woodland Rd., Loug. 31 CK24
Woodland Rd., Rick. 34 AU28
Woodland Rd., Th.Hth. 86 BY52
Woodland St. E8 57 CA36
Dalston La.
Woodland Ter. SE7 68 CK42
Woodland Ter. SE18 68 CK42
Woodland Vw., Chesh. 16 AO20
Woodland Wk. NW3 47 BU35
Aspern Rd.
Woodland Wk. SE10 68 CG42
Woodland Gro.
Woodland Way N21 38 BY27
Woodland Way NW7 37 BO29
Woodland Way SE2 69 CP42
Woodland Way, Cat. 114 CA67
Woodland Way, Chsnt. 20 BY17
Woodland Way, Croy. 87 CD54
Woodland Way, Epp. 31 CM21
Woodland Way, Mitch. 76 BV50
Woodland Way, Mord. 85 BR52
Woodland Way, Ong. 24 CW18
Woodland Way, Orp. 88 CM52
Woodland Way, Pur. 95 BY60
Woodland Way, Surb. 85 BM55
Woodland Way, Tad. 103 BR64
Woodland Way, W.Wick. 96 CE56
Woodland Way, Wey. 92 BA56
Woodland Way, Wdf.Grn. 40 CH27
Woodlands NW11 46 BR32
Woodlands SW20 85 BQ52
Woodlands, Har. 45 BF31
Woodlands, Hat. 20 BS17
Woodlands, Rad. 18 BJ20
Woodlands, The N14 38 BV26
Woodlands, The SE13 77 CF47
Woodlands, The SE19 77 BZ50
Woodlands, The, Amer. 25 AO21
Woodlands, The, Esher 84 BG55
Woodlands, The, Ger.Cr. 43 AS32
Woodlands, The, Islw. 64 BH44
Woodlands, The, Orp. 98 CO57
Woodlands, The, Wall. 95 BV58
Woodlands, The, Wind. 61 AM45
Nelson Rd.
Woodlands Ave. E11 49 CH33
Woodlands Ave. N3 38 BT29
Woodlands Ave. W3 55 BM40
High St.
Woodlands Ave., Berk. 7 AR13
Woodlands Ave., Horn. 51 CV32
Woodlands Ave., N.Mal. 85 BN51
Woodlands Ave., Red. 121 BU71
Woodlands Ave., Rom. 50 CQ32
Woodlands Ave., Ruis. 45 BD33
Woodlands Ave., Sid. 78 CN47
Woodlands Ave., Wey. 91 AV60
Woodlands Ave., Wor.Pk. 85 BO55
Woodlands Clo. NW11 46 BR32
Woodlands Clo., Borwd. 28 BM24
Woodlands Clo., Brom. 88 CK51
Woodlands Clo., Cher. 91 AT58
Woodlands Clo., Esher 93 BH57
Woodlands Clo., Ger.Cr. 43 AT32
Woodlands Clo., Grays 71 DF41
Woodlands Clo., Hem.H. 8 AW14
Woodlands Clo., Hodd. 12 CE12
Woodlands Clo., Swan. 89 CT52
Woodlands Clo., Wey. 92 BA56
Woodlands Ct., Wok. 100 AS63
Constitution Hill
Woodlands Dr., Har. 36 BH29
Woodlands Dr., Hodd. 12 CE13
Woodlands Dr., Kings L. 17 BA17
Woodlands Dr., Sun. 84 BD51
Woodlands Dr., Wat. 26 BC23
Woodlands Gdns. E17 49 CG31
Woodford New Rd.
Woodlands Gro., Couls. 104 BV62
Woodlands Gro., Islw. 64 BH44
Woodlands La., Cob. 104 BF62
Woodlands Par., Ashf. 73 BA50
Hogarth Ave.
Woodlands Pk., Bex. 79 CS49
Woodlands Pk., Guil. 118 AT70
Woodlands Pk., Tad. 120 BM69
Woodlands Pk., Wey. 91 AV56
Woodlands Pk. Rd. N15 47 BY32
Woodlands Pk. Rd. SE10 68 CG43
Woodlands Ri., Swan. 89 CT51
Woodlands Rd. E11 49 CG34
Woodlands Rd. E17 48 CF31
Woodlands Rd. N9 39 CC26
Woodlands Rd. SW13 65 BO45
Woodlands Rd., Bexh. 69 CQ45
Woodlands Rd., Brom. 88 CK51
Woodlands Rd., Bush. 27 BE25
Woodlands Rd., Enf. 30 BZ23
Woodlands Rd., Epsom 103 BM61
Woodlands Rd., Guil. 109 AR68
Woodlands Rd., Har. 45 BH32
Woodlands Rd., Hem.H. 17 AZ17
Woodlands Rd., Ilf. 49 CM34
Woodlands Rd., Islw. 64 BG45
Woodlands Rd., Lthd. 102 BG62
Woodlands Rd. (Effingham), Lthd. 111 BE67
Woodlands Rd., Orp. 98 CO57
Woodlands Rd., Red. 121 BU71
Woodlands Rd., Rom. 50 CT31
Woodlands Rd. (Harold Wd.), Rom. 42 CX30
Woodlands Rd., Sthl. 54 BD40
Woodlands Rd., Surb. 84 BK54
Woodlands Rd., Vir.W. 82 AR52
Woodlands Rd., Wey. 91 AV60
Woodlands Rd. E., Vir.W. 82 AR52
Woodlands Rd. W., Vir.W. 82 AR52
Woodlands St. SE13 77 CF47
Woodlands Way SW15 75 BR46
Woodlands Way, Ash. 103 BM61
Woodlawn Clo. SW15 75 BR46
Woodlawn Cres., Twick. 74 BF48
Woodlawn Dr., Felt. 74 BD48
Woodlawn Gro., Wok. 100 AS61
Woodlawn Rd. SW6 65 BQ43
Woodlea Dr., Brom. 88 CG53
Woodlea Est., Brom. 88 CG53
Woodlea Gro., Nthwd. 35 BA29
Woodlea Rd. N16 48 CA34
Woodleigh Ave. N12 38 BU29
Woodleigh Gdns. SW16 76 BX48
Woodley Clo. SW17 76 BU50
Woodley Hill, Chesh. 16 AO20
Woodley La., Cars. 86 BU55
Woodley Rd., Orp. 89 CP55
Woodman La. E4 31 CG25
Woodman Path, Chig. 40 CN29
Woodman Rd., Brwd. 42 DB28
Woodman Rd., Couls. 104 BW61
Woodman Rd., Hem.H. 8 AY14
Woodman St. E16 58 CL40
Woodmancote Gdns., Wey. 92 AW60
Elmstead Rd.
Woodmans Ct., Stan. 37 BL30
Woodmans Gro. NW10 46 BO35
Broadfields Way
Woodmans Ms. W12 55 BP39
Woodmansterne La., Bans. 104 BS61
Woodmansterne La., Cars. 95 BU59
Woodmansterne Rd. SW16 76 BW50
Woodmansterne Rd., Cars. 76 BU58
Woodmansterne Rd., Couls. 104 BW61
Woodmansterne St., Bans. 104 BU61
Woodmere SE9 78 CK47
Woodmere Ave., Croy. 87 CC54
Woodmere Ave., Wat. 27 BD22
Woodmere Clo. SW11 66 BV45
Lavender Hill
Woodmere Clo., Croy. 87 CC54
Woodmere Gdns., Croy. 87 CC54
Woodmere Way, Beck. 87 CF53
Woodmount, Swan. 89 CS54
Woodnook Rd. SW16 76 BV49
Woodpecker Clo. N9 30 CB25
Woodpecker Clo., Bush. 36 BG26
Woodpecker Clo., Cob. 93 BE59
Green La.
Woodpecker Clo., Hat. 10 BO14
Tudor Clo.
Woodpecker Mt., Croy. 96 CD58
Woodpecker Rd. SE14 67 CD43
Woodpecker Rd. SE28 59 CP40
Woodpecker Way, Wok. 100 AR65
Woodplace Clo., Couls. 104 BW63
Woodplace La., Couls. 104 BW64
Woodquest Ave. SE24 77 BZ46
Woodredon Clo., Harl. 13 CH11
Woodridden Hill, Wal.Abb. 31 CJ21
Woodridge Clo., Enf. 29 BY23
Woodridge Way, Nthwd. 35 BB29
Woodridings Ave., Pnr. 36 BE30
Woodridings Clo., Pnr. 36 BE29
Woodriffe Rd. E11 48 CF33
Woodrow SE18 68 CK42
Woodrow Ave., Hayes 53 BB39
Woodrow Clo., Grnf. 54 BJ36
Woodruff Ave., Guil. 118 AT69
Woodrush Clo. SE14 67 CD43
Southerngate Way
Woodrush Way, Rom. 50 CP31
Woods, The, Nthwd. 35 BC28
Woods, The, Uxb. 44 AZ35
Woods Ave., Hat. 10 BP12
Woods Bldgs. E1 57 CB39
Durward St.
Woods Clo. SE19 77 CA50
Woodland Hill
Woods Ms. W1 1 G10
Woods Ms. W1 56 BV40
Woods Pl. SE1 4 N7
Woods Pl. SE1 67 CA41
Woods Rd. SE15 67 CB44
Woods Way, Lthd. 93 BH60
Woodseer St. E1 2 Q6
Woodseer St. E1 57 CA39
Woodsford Sq. W14 65 BR41
Woodshire Rd., Dag. 50 CR34
Woodshore Clo., Vir.W. 82 AQ53
Woodshots Meadow, Wat. 26 BA25
Woodside NW11 47 BS32
Woodside SW19 75 BR50
Woodside, Borwd. 28 BL24
Woodside, Buck.H. 40 CJ27
Woodside, Chsnt. 21 CB19
Woodside, Epp. 23 CP16
Woodside, Lthd. 102 BF64
Woodside (Horsley), Lthd. 110 BA66
Woodside, Orp. 98 CO56
Woodside, Tad. 112 BR67
Woodside, Wat. 26 BC22
Woodside Ave. N6 47 BU32
Woodside Ave. N10 47 BU32
Woodside Ave. N12 38 BS28
Woodside Ave. SE25 87 CB53
Woodside Ave., Amer. 25 AO21
Woodside Ave., Chis. 78 CL49
Woodside Ave., Esher 84 BH54
Woodside Ave., Walt. 92 BC56
Woodside Ave., Wem. 55 BL37
Woodside Clo., Amer. 25 AO22
Woodside Clo., Bexh. 69 CS45
Woodside Clo., Brwd. 122 DE25
Woodside Clo., Cat. 105 CA65
Woodside Clo., Ger.Cr. 34 AS30
Woodside Clo., Rain. 60 CV38
Woodside Clo., Stan. 36 BJ28
Woodside Clo., Surb. 85 BN54
Woodside Clo., Wem. 55 BL37
Woodside Clo., Wok. 100 AO62
Woodside Ct. Rd., Croy. 87 CB54
Woodside Cres., Sid. 78 CN48
Woodside Dr., Dart. 79 CT49
Woodside End, Wem. 55 BL37
Woodside Gdns. E4 39 CE28
Woodside Gdns. N17 39 CA30
Woodside Gra. Rd. N12 38 BS28
Woodside Grn. SE25 87 CB53
Woodside Gro. N12 38 BT27
Woodside Hill, Ger.Cr. 34 AS30
Woodside La. N12 38 BS27
Woodside La., Bex. 79 CP46
Woodside La., Hat. 11 BS15
Woodside Pk. SE25 87 CB53
Woodside Pk. Ave. E17 48 CF32
Woodside Pk. Rd. N12 38 BS28
Woodside Pl., Wem. 55 BL37
Woodside Rd. E13 58 CJ38
Woodside Rd. N22 38 BX29
Woodside Rd. SE25 87 CB53
Woodside Rd., Amer. 25 AO22
Woodside Rd., Bexh. 69 CS45
Woodside Rd., Brom. 88 CK53
Woodside Rd., Cob. 93 BF60
Woodside Rd., Guil. 118 AP70
Woodside Rd., Kings.T. 75 BL50
Woodside Rd., N.Mal. 85 BN51
Woodside Rd., Nthwd. 35 BB29
Woodside Rd., Pur. 95 BW60
Woodside Rd., St.Alb. 18 BE18
Woodside Rd., Sev. 107 CU65
Woodside Rd., Sid. 78 CN48
Woodside Rd., Sutt. 86 BT55
Woodside Rd., Wat. 17 BC19
Woodside Rd., Welw.G.C. 5 BR5
Woodside Rd. (Brasted), West. 107 CP65
Woodside Rd., Wdf.Grn. 40 CH28
Woodside Vw., Sev. 98 CR58
Woodside Way, Croy. 87 CC53
Woodside Way, Mitch. 86 BV51
Woodside Way, Red. 121 BV73
Woodside Way, Reig. 121 BV71
Woodside Way, Vir.W. 82 AQ52
Woodsome Clo., Wey. 92 BA57
Woodsome Rd. NW5 47 BV34
Woodspring Rd. SW19 75 BR48
Woodstead Gro., Edg. 37 BL29
Woodstock, Guil. 110 AW67
Woodstock, Surb. 84 BK55
Woodstock Ave. NW11 46 BR33
Woodstock Ave. W13 64 BJ41
Woodstock Ave., Islw. 74 BJ46
Woodstock Ave., Rom. 42 CX28
Woodstock Ave., Slou. 62 AR42
Woodstock Ave., Sthl. 54 BE38
Woodstock Ave., Sutt. 85 BR54
Woodstock Clo., Bex. 79 CQ47
Woodstock Clo., Stan. 37 BL30
Woodstock Clo., Wok. 100 AR61
Horsell Pk.
Woodstock Ct. SE12 78 CH46
Woodstock Cres. N9 30 CB25
Woodstock Dr., Uxb. 44 AY35
Woodstock Gdns., Beck. 77 CE50
Woodstock Gdns., Hayes 53 BB39
Woodstock Gdns., Ilf. 50 CO34
Woodstock Gro. W12 65 BQ41
Woodstock La., Esher 93 BJ57
Woodstock Ms. W1 1 H7
Woodstock Ri., Sutt. 85 BR54
Woodstock Rd. E7 58 CJ36
Woodstock Rd. E17 39 CF30
Woodstock Rd. N4 47 BY33
Woodstock Rd. NW11 46 BR33
Woodstock Rd. W4 65 BO42
Woodstock Rd., Brox. 12 CD13
Woodstock Rd., Bush. 36 BH26
Woodstock Rd., Cars. 95 BV56
Woodstock Rd., Couls. 104 BV61
Woodstock Rd., Croy. 87 BZ55
Woodstock Rd., Wem. 55 BL37
Woodstock Rd. N., St.Alb. 9 BJ12
Woodstock Rd. S., St.Alb. 9 BJ13
Woodstock St. E16 58 CG39
Woodstock St. W1 1 J9
Woodstock St. W1 56 BV39
Oxford St.
Woodstock Ter. E14 57 CE40
Woodstock Way, Mitch. 86 BV51
Woodstone Ave., Epsom 94 BP56
Woodsyre Est. SE26 77 CA49
Woodthorpe Rd. SW15 65 BP45
Woodthorpe Rd., Ashf. 73 AX50
Woodtree Clo. NW4 37 BQ30
Ashley La.
Woodvale Ave. SE25 87 CA52
Woodview Ave. E4 39 CF28
Woodview Clo. N4 47 BY33
Woodview Clo., Kings.T. 75 BN49
Woodview Clo., Orp. 88 CL55
Crofton Rd.
Woodview Clo., Sev. 99 CZ57
Woodview Clo., S.Croy. 96 CB60
Woodview Rd., Swan. 89 CS51
Woodville SE3 68 CH44
Woodville Clo. SE12 78 CH46
Woodville Clo., Tedd. 74 BJ49
Woodville Ct., Wat. 26 BC23
Woodville Gdns. NW11 46 BQ33
Hendon Way
Woodville Gdns. W5 55 BL39
Woodville Gdns., Ilf. 49 CL31
Woodville Gdns., Ruis. 44 BA33
Woodville Gro., Well. 69 CO45
Ruskin Ave.
Woodville Pl., Cat. 105 BZ64
Woodville Rd. E11 49 CG33
Woodville Rd. E17 48 CD31
Woodville Rd. E18 40 CH30
Woodville Rd. N16 48 CA35
Woodville Rd. NW6 55 BR37
Woodville Rd. NW11 46 BQ33
Woodville Rd. W5 54 BK39
Woodville Rd., Barn. 29 BS24
Woodville Rd., Lthd. 102 BJ63
Woodville Rd., Mord. 86 BS52
Woodville Rd., Rich. 74 BJ48
Woodville Rd., Th.Hth. 87 BZ52
Woodville St. SE18 68 CK42
Woodward Ave. NW4 46 BP32
Woodward Clo., Grays 71 DD42
Woodward Gdns., Dag. 59 CO36
Woodward Rd.
Woodward Gdns., Stan. 36 BJ29
May Tree La.
Woodward Heights, Grays 71 DD42
Woodward Clo.
Woodward Rd., Dag. 59 CO36
Woodward Ter., Green. 80 CZ46
Woodwarde Rd. SE22 77 CA46
Woodwards, Harl. 13 CM12
Woodway, Brwd. 122 DD26
Woodway, Guil. 118 AT70
Woodway Cres., Harl. 45 BJ32
Woodwaye, Wat. 36 BD26
Woodwell St. SW18 76 BT46
Huguenot Pl.
Woodyard Clo. NW5 47 BV35
Gillies St.
Woodyard La. SE21 77 CA47
Woodyates Rd. SE12 78 CG46
Wool Rd. SW20 75 BP50
Woolacombe Rd. SE3 68 CH44
Woolacombe Way, Hayes 63 BB42
Wooler St. SE17 67 BZ42
Woolf Clo. SE28 59 CO40
Woolf Wk., Til. 71 DH44
Coleridge Rd.
Woolhampton Way, Chig. 41 CO27
Woollam Cres., St.Alb. 9 BG11
Woollard St., Wal.Abb. 21 CF20
Woollard Way, Ing. 24 DC19
Woollaston Rd. N4 47 BY32
Umfreville Rd.
Woolmans Clo., Brox. 12 CD14
Woolmead Ave. NW9 46 BP33
Woolmer Clo., Borwd. 28 BM22
Woolmer Dr., Hem.H. 8 BA13
Woolmer Gdns. N18 39 CB29
Woolmer Rd. N18 39 CB28
Woolmongers La., Ing. 24 DA19
Woolmore St. E14 57 CF40
Woolnams, Cat. 114 CA66
Woolneigh St. SW6 66 BS45
Woolsey Rd., Hem.H. 8 AX14
Woolstan Clo., Uxb. 44 AW34
Woolston Clo. E17 39 CC30
Woolstone Rd. SE23 77 CD48
Woolwich Ch. St. SE18 68 CK41
Woolwich Common SE18 68 CL43
Woolwich High St. SE18 68 CK41
Woolwich Ind. Est. SE28 68 CN41
Woolwich Manor Way E16 58 CL40
Woolwich New Rd. SE18 68 CL42
Woolwich Rd. SE2 69 CP43
Woolwich Rd. SE7 68 CG42
Woolwich Rd. SE10 68 CG42
Woolwich Rd., Belv. 69 CP43
Woolwich Rd., Bexh. 69 CR45
Wooster Gdns. E14 57 CF39
Woosters Ms., Har. 45 BG31
Fairfield Dr.
Wooton Dr., Hem.H. 8 AY11
Wootton Clo., Epsom 103 BO61
Wootton Clo., Horn. 51 CV32
Wootton Gro. N3 38 BS30
Station Rd.
Wootton St. SE1 4 E3
Wootton St. SE1 66 BY41
Worbeck Rd. SE20 87 CB51
Worcester Ave. N17 39 CB29
Worcester Ave., Upmin. 51 CZ34
Worcester Clo., Croy. 87 CD55
Worcester Clo., Green. 70 DA45
Worcester Clo., Mitch. 86 BV51
Worcester Ct., Walt. 84 BD54
Worcester Cres. NW7 37 BO27
Worcester Cres., Wdf.Grn. 40 CH28
Worcester Gdns., Grnf. 54 BG36
Worcester Gdns., Ilf. 49 CK33
Worcester Gdns., Wor.Pk. 85 BO55
Worcester Ms. NW6 56 BS36
Lymington Rd.
Worcester Pk. Rd., Wor.Pk. 85 BN55
Worcester Pl. EC4 2 J10
Worcester Rd. E12 49 CK35
Worcester Rd. E17 39 CC30
Worcester Rd. SW19 75 BR49
Worcester Rd., Guil. 118 AP69
Worcester Rd., Hat. 10 BO12
Worcester Rd., Reig. 121 BS70
Worcester Rd., Sutt. 95 BS57
Worcester Rd., Uxb. 53 AX39
Worcesters Ave., Enf. 30 CB22
Wordsworth Ave. E12 58 CK36
Wordsworth Ave. E18 49 CG31
Wordsworth Ave., Grnf. 54 BG38
Wordsworth Ave., Pur. 105 BZ61
Valley Rd.
Wordsworth Clo., Rom. 42 CV30
Wordsworth Clo., Til. 71 DH44
Coleridge Rd.
Wordsworth Dr., Sutt. 94 BQ56
Wordsworth Par. N8 47 BY31
Alfoxton Ave.
Wordsworth Rd. N16 48 CA35
Wordsworth Rd. SE1 4 P9
Wordsworth Rd. SE20 77 CC50
Wordsworth Rd., Hmptn. 74 BE49
Wordsworth Rd., Har. 45 BH31
Wordsworth Rd., Wall. 95 BW57
Wordsworth Rd., Well. 68 CN44
Wordsworth Rd., Wey. 92 AX56
Wordsworth Wk. NW11 47 BS31
Wordsworth Way, Dart. 70 CX45
Wordsworth Way, West Dr. 63 AY42
Worfield St. SW11 66 BU43
Worgan St. SE11 4 B10
Worgan St. SE11 66 BX42
Worland Rd. E15 58 CG36
World Trade Cen. E1 4 Q1
Worlds End SW10 66 BT43
Worlds End, Cob. 92 BC60
Worlds End La. N21 29 BX25
Worlds End La., Enf. 29 BX25
Worlds End La., Orp. 97 CN57
Worlds End Pas. SW10 66 BT43
Worlds End Pl. SW10 66 BT43
Worlds End
Worley Rd., St.Alb. 9 BG13
Worlidge St. W6 65 BQ42
Worlingham Rd. SE22 67 CA45
Wormholt Est. W12 55 BO40
Wormholt Rd. W12 55 BP40
Wormingford Ct., Wal.Abb. 22 CH20
Ninefields
Wormley Ct., Wal.Abb. 22 CH20
Winters Way
Wormley Lo. Clo., Brox. 12 CD15
Wormwood St. EC2 2 M8
Wormwood St. EC2 57 CA39
Wornington Rd. W10 55 BR38
Wornington Yd. W10 55 BR38
Wornington Rd.
Woronzow Rd. NW8 56 BT37
Worple, The, Stai. 72 AS46
Worple Ave. SW19 75 BQ50
Worple Ave., Islw. 74 BJ46
Worple Ave., Stai. 73 AW50
Worple Clo., Har. 45 BE33
Worple Rd. SW19 85 BQ51
Worple Rd. SW20 85 BQ51
Worple Rd., Epsom 103 BN61
Worple Rd., Islw. 64 BJ45
Worple Rd., Lthd. 102 BJ64
Worple Rd., Stai. 73 AW50
Worple Rd. Ms. SW19 75 BR50
Worple St. SW14 65 BN45
Worple Way, Har. 45 BE33
Worple Way, Rich. 75 BL46
Worplesdon Rd., Guil. 109 AP67
Worrin Clo., Brwd. 122 DC26
Worrin Rd., Brwd. 122 DC26
Worship St. EC2 2 L5
Worship St. EC2 57 BZ38
Worships Hill, Sev. 107 CT65
Worslade Rd. SW17 76 BT49
Worsley Bri. Rd. SE26 77 CD49
Worsley Bri. Rd., Beck. 77 CD49
Worsley Rd. E11 49 CG35
Worsopp Dr. SW4 66 BW45
Worsted Grn., Red. 113 BW68
Worthfield Clo., Epsom 94 BN57
Worthing Clo. E15 58 CG37
Worthing Rd., Houns. 64 BE43
Worthington Rd., Surb. 85 BL54
Worthydown Ct. SE18 68 CL43
Prince Imperial Rd.
Wortley Rd. E6 58 CJ36
Wortley Rd., Croy. 86 BY54
Worton Gdns., Islw. 64 BG44
Worton Rd., Islw. 64 BG45
Worton Way, Islw. 64 BG44
Wotton Dr., Dor. 119 BD73
Wotton Grn., Orp. 89 CP52
Wotton Rd. NW2 46 BQ35
Wotton Rd. SE8 67 CD43
Wotton Way, Sutt. 94 BQ58
Wouldham Rd. E16 58 CG39
Wouldham Rd., Grays 71 DC43
Wrabness Way, Stai. 83 AW51
Wragby Rd. E11 49 CG34
Wrampling Pl. N9 39 CB26
Croyland Rd.
Wrangley Ct., Wal.Abb. 22 CH20
Winters Way
Wrangthorn Wk., Croy. 95 BY56
Epsom Rd.
Wray Ave., Ilf. 49 CL31
Wray Clo., Horn. 51 CV33
Wray Common Rd., Reig. 121 BT70
Wray Cres. N4 47 BX34
Wray La., Reig. 113 BT68
Wray Pk. Rd., Reig. 121 BS70
Wray Rd., Sutt. 94 BR58

Wrayfield Ave., Reig. 121 BT70
Wrayfield Rd., Sutt. 85 BQ55
Wraylands Dr., Reig. 121 BT69
Wrays Way, Hayes 53 BB38
Wraysbury Clo., Houns. 74 BE46
Dorney Way
Wraysbury Rd., Stai. 72 AT48
Wrekin Rd. SE18 68 CM43
Wren Ave. NW2 46 BQ35
Wren Ave., Sthl. 64 BE42
Wren Clo. E16 58 CG39
Wren Clo., Orp. 89 CP52
Sandpiper Way
Wren Clo., S.Croy. 96 CC58
Wren Ct., Slou. 62 AT41
Wren Cres., Bush. 36 BG26
Wren Cres., Wey. 92 AX56
Wren Dr., West Dr. 63 AX41
Wren Gdns., Dag. 50 CP35
Wren Gdns., Horn. 50 CT33
Wren Path SE28 68 CM41
Whinchat Rd.
Wren Pl., Brwd. 42 DB27
Wren Rd. SE5 67 BZ44
Wren Rd., Dag. 50 CP35
Wren Rd., Sid. 79 CP49
Wren St. WC1 2 C4
Wren St. WC1 56 BX38
Grays Inn Rd.
Wren Wk., Til. 71 DG44
Poynder Rd.
Wren Wd., Welw.G.C. 5 BS7
Wrens Ave., Ashf. 73 BA49
Wrens Cft., Grav. 81 DF49
Henley Deane
Wrens Hill, Lthd. 102 BG61
Wrensfield, Hem.H. 8 AW13
Wrentham Ave. NW10 55 BQ37
Wrenthorpe Rd., Brom. 78 CG49
Wrenwood Way, Pnr. 44 BC31
Wrestlers Clo., Hat. 10 BQ11
Lockley Cres.
Wrexham Rd. E3 57 CE37
Wrexham Rd., Rom. 42 CV27
Wricklemarsh Rd. SE3 68 CH44
Wrigglesworth St. SE14 67 CC43
Wright, Wind. 61 AL45
Wright Clo., Swans. 80 DB46
Milton St.
Wright Rd. N1 57 CA36
Pond Rd.
Wright Rd., Houns. 64 BD43
Wright Sq., Wind. 61 AL45
Wright
Wright Way, Wind. 61 AL45
Wright
Wrights All. SW19 75 BQ50
Wrights Clo. SE13 67 CF45
Wisteria Rd.
Wrights Clo., Dag. 50 CR35
Webbscroft Rd.
Wrights Grn. SW4 66 BW45
Wrights La. W8 66 BS41
Wrights La., Brwd. 33 DB21
Wrights Pl. NW10 55 BN36
Mitchell Way
Wrights Rd. E3 57 CD37
Wrights Rd. SE25 87 CA52
Wrights Row, Wall. 95 BV56
Wrights Wk. SW14 65 BN45
North Worple Way
Wrightsbridge Rd., Rom. 42 CX26
Wrigley Clo. E4 39 CF28
The Ave.
Wriotsley Way, Wey. 92 AW57
Writtle Wk., Rain. 59 CT37
Wrotham Rd. NW1 56 BW36
Agar Pl.
Wrotham Rd. W13 54 BJ40
Mattock La.
Wrotham Rd., Barn. 28 BR23
Wrotham Rd., Grav. 81 DF51
Wrotham Rd., Well. 69 CP44
Wroths Path, Loug. 31 CK23
Wrottesley Rd. NW10 55 BP37
Wrottesley Rd. SE18 68 CL43
Wroughton Rd. SW11 76 BU46
Wroughton Ter. NW4 46 BP31
Babington Rd.
Wroxall Rd., Dag. 59 CP36
Wroxham Ave., Hem.H. 8 AX14
Wroxham Gdns. N11 38 BW29
Wroxham Gdns., Enf. 29 BY21
Wroxham Gdns., Pot.B. 19 BQ19
Wroxham Rd. SE28 59 CP40
Wroxton Rd. SE15 67 CB44
Wrythe Grn., Cars. 86 BU55
Wrythe Grn. Rd.
Wrythe Grn. Rd., Cars. 86 BU55
Wrythe La., Cars. 86 BT54
Wulfred Way, Sev. 108 CX62
Wulfstan St. W12 55 BO39
Wyatt Clo., Hayes 53 BC39
Wyatt Clo., Nthlt. 54 BE36
Wyatt Clo., Sev. 108 DC63
Wyatt Pk. Rd. SW2 76 BX48
Wyatt Rd. E7 58 CH36
Wyatt Rd. N5 48 BZ34
Wyatt Rd., Dart. 69 CT45
Wyatt Rd., Stai. 73 AW49
Wyatt Rd., Wind. 61 AL45
Wyatts Clo., Rick. 26 AW24
Wyatts Grn. La., Brwd. 33 DB21
Wyatts Grn. Rd., Brwd. 33 DB21
Wyatts La. E17 48 CF31
Wyatts Rd., Rick. 25 AV24
Wybert St. NW1 1 L4
Wybert St. NW1 56 BV38
Munster Sq.
Wyborne Way NW10 55 BN36
Wyburn Ave., Barn. 28 BR24
Wych Elm, Harl. 6 CM10
Wych Elm Clo., Horn. 51 CX32
Wych Elm Pas., Kings.T. 75 BL50
Wych Elm Ri., Guil. 118 AS72
Wych Elm Rd., Horn. 51 CX32
Wych Hill, Wok. 100 AR63
Wych Hill La., Wok. 100 AS63
Wych Hill Pk., Wok. 100 AR63
Wych Hill Ri., Wok. 100 AR63
Wych Hill Waye, Wok. 100 AR63
Wyche Gro., S.Croy. 96 BZ57
Wychelms, St.Alb. 18 BF17
Wycherley Clo. SE3 68 CG43
Vanbrugh Pk. Rd. W.
Wycherley Cres., Barn. 29 BS25
Wychford Dr., Saw. 6 CP6
Wychling Clo., Orp. 89 CP54
Wychwood Ave., Edg. 36 BK29
Wychwood Ave., Th.Hth. 87 BZ52
Wychwood Clo., Edg. 36 BK29
Wychwood End N6 47 BW33
Wychwood Gdns., Ilf. 49 CK31
Wychwood Wk., Edg. 36 BK29
Wychwood Way SE19 77 CA50
Central Hill Est.
Wychwood Way, Nthwd. 35 BB29
Wyclif St. EC1 2 F3
Wyclif St. EC1 56 BY38
Wycliffe Clo., Well. 68 CN44
Wycliffe Gdns., Red. 113 BW68
Wycliffe Rd. SW11 66 BV44
Wycliffe Rd. SW19 76 BS50
Wycliffe Row, Grav. 81 DF47
Alfred Pl.
Wycliffe Way, Grav. 81 DF47
Dover Rd. E.
Wycombe Gdns. NW11 47 BS34
Wycombe Pl. SW18 76 BT46
St. Anns Cres.
Wycombe Rd. N17 39 CB30
Wycombe Rd., Ilf. 49 CK32
Wycombe Rd., Wem. 55 BM37
Wycombe Way, St.Alb. 9 BK12
Wyddial Grn., Welw.G.C. 5 BS8
Widford Rd.
Wydehurst Rd., Croy. 87 CB54
Wydell Clo., Mord. 85 BQ53
Wydeville Manor Rd. SE12 78 CH49
Wye, The, Hem.H. 8 AZ11
Wye Clo., Ashf. 73 AZ49
Wye Clo., Orp. 88 CN54
Wye Clo., Ruis. 44 BA32
Thames Dr.
Wye Rd., Grav. 81 DH48
Wye St. SW11 66 BT44
Wyedale, St.Alb. 19 BL17
Thamesdale
Wyemead Cres. E4 40 CG27
Normanton Pk.
Wyeths Rd., Epsom 94 BO60
Wyevale Clo., Pnr. 44 BC31
Wyfields, Ilf. 40 CL30
Wyfold Rd. SW6 65 BR44
Wyhill Wk., Dag. 59 CS36
Wyke Clo., Islw. 64 BH43
Wyke Est. E9 57 CD36
Wyke Gdns. W7 64 BJ41
Wyke Rd. E3 57 CE36
Wyke Rd. SW20 85 BQ51
Wykeham Ave., Dag. 59 CP36
Wykeham Ave., Horn. 51 CV32
Wykeham Clo., West Dr. 63 AZ43
Wykeham Grn., Dag. 59 CP36
Wykeham Hill, Wem. 46 BL33
Wykeham Ri. N20 37 BR26
Wykeham Rd. NW4 46 BQ31
Wykeham Rd., Guil. 118 AU70
Wykeham Rd., Har. 45 BJ31
Wylands Rd., Slou. 62 AT42
Wylchin Clo., Pnr. 44 BB31
Fore St.
Wyld Way, Wem. 55 BM36
Wyldes Clo. NW11 47 BT33
Wildwood Rd.
Wyldfield Gdns. N9 39 CA27
Latymer Rd.
Wyldwood Clo., Harl. 6 CP8
Wyleu St. SE23 77 CD47
Wylie Rd., Sthl. 64 BF41
Wyllen Clo. E1 57 CC38
Wyllyotts Clo., Pot.B. 19 BR19
Wylo Dr., Barn. 28 BO25
Wymering Rd. W9 56 BS38
Wymond St. SW15 65 BQ45
Wynan Rd. E14 67 CE42
Wynaud Ct. N22 38 BX29
Palmerston Rd.
Wyncham Ave., Sid. 78 CN47
Wynchgate N14 38 BW26
Wynchgate N21 38 BX26
Wynchgate, Har. 36 BH29
Wynchlands Cres., St.Alb. 9 BK13
Wyncote Way, S.Croy. 96 CC58
Wyncroft Clo., Brom. 88 CK52
Wyndale Ave. NW9 46 BM32
Wyndcliff Rd. SE7 68 CH42
Wyndcroft Clo., Enf. 29 BY24
Wyndham Ave., Barn. 38 BU26
Wyndham Ave., Cob. 92 BC60
Wyndham Clo., Orp. 88 CM54
Wyndham Clo., Sutt. 95 BS57
Sackville Rd.
Wyndham Cres. N19 47 BW34
Wyndham Cres., Houns. 74 BF46
Wyndham Est. SE5 67 BZ43
Wyndham Ms. W1 1 E7
Wyndham Ms. W1 56 BU39
Upper Montagu St.
Wyndham Pl. W1 1 E7
Wyndham Pl. W1 56 BU39
Wyndham Rd. E6 58 CJ36
Wyndham Rd. SE5 66 BY43
Wyndham Rd. W13 64 BJ41
Wyndham Rd., Kings.T. 75 BL50
Wyndham Rd., Wok. 100 AQ62
Wyndham St. W1 1 E6
Wyndham St. W1 56 BU39
Wyndham Yd. W1 1 E7
Wyndhams End, Welw.G.C. 5 BR10
Wyneham Rd. SE24 77 BZ46
Wynell Rd. SE23 77 CC48
Wynford Gro., Orp. 89 CO52
Wynford Rd. N1 56 BX37
Wynford Way SE9 78 CK48
Wynlie Gdns., Pnr. 35 BC30
Wynndale Rd. E18 40 CH30
Wynne Rd. SW9 66 BY44
Wynns Ave., Sid. 79 CO46
Lyndon Ave.
Wynnstay Gdns. W8 66 BS41
Wynnstow Pk., Oxt. 115 CG69
Wynter St. SW11 66 BT45
Wynton Gdns. SE25 87 CA52
Wynton Gro., Walt. 83 BC55
Wynton Pl. W3 55 BM39
Wynyard Clo., Rick. 26 AW21
Wynyard Ter. SE11 4 C10
Wynyard Ter. SE11 66 BX42
Aveline St.
Wynyatt St. EC1 2 F3
Wyre Gro., Edg. 37 BM27
Wyre Gro., Hayes 63 BC42
Wyresdale Cres., Grnf. 54 BH38
Wyte Leaf Clo., Ruis. 44 BA32
Wythburn Pl. W1 1 E9
Wythburn Pl. W1 56 BU39
Seymour Pl.
Wythens Wk. SE9 78 CL46
Southend Cres.
Wythenshawe Rd., Dag. 50 CR34
Wythes Clo., Brom. 88 CK51
Wythes Rd. E16 58 CK40
Wythfield Rd. SE9 78 CK46
Wyton, Welw.G.C. 5 BT8
Wyvenhoe Rd., Har. 45 BG34
Wyver Ct., St.Alb. 9 BH13
Avenue Rd.
Wyvern Clo., Dart. 80 CV47
Wyvern Clo., Orp. 89 CO55
Wyvern Rd., Pur. 95 BY58
Wyvil Est. SW8 66 BX43
Wyvil Rd. SW8 66 BX43
Wyvis St. E14 57 CE39

Y

Yabsley St. E14 57 CF40
Yaffle Rd., Wey. 92 BA58
Yalding Clo., Orp. 89 CP52
Yalding Rd. SE16 67 CB41
Yale, Houns. 74 BE46
Yale Way, Horn. 50 CU35
Yarborough Rd. SW19 86 BT51
Runnymede
Yard Mead, Stai. 72 AT48
Yardbridge Clo., Sutt. 95 BS58
Hulverston Clo.
Yardley Clo. E4 30 CE25
Yardley Clo., Reig. 121 BS69
Yardley La. E4 30 CE25
Yardley St. WC1 2 D3
Yardley St. WC1 56 BY38
Yarm Clo., Lthd. 102 BK65
Yarm Ct. Rd., Lthd. 102 BK65
Yarm Way, Lthd. 102 BK65
Yarmouth Cres. N17 48 CB32
Yarmouth Pl. W1 3 J3
Yarmouth Pl. W1 56 BV40
Brick St.
Yarmouth Rd., Wat. 27 BD22
Yarnton Way SE2 69 CP41
Yarnton Way, Erith 69 CP41
Yarrow Cres. E6 58 CK39
Yarrow Fld., Wok. 100 AR65
Yarrow Side, Amer. 25 AQ23
Yateley St. SE18 68 CJ41
Yates Ct. NW2 55 BQ36
Yeading Ave., Har. 45 BE34
Yeading Gdns., Hayes 53 BC39
Yeading La., Hayes 53 BC39
Yeading La., Nthlt. 54 BD38
Yeading La. Fork, Hayes 54 BD38
Yeading Wk., Har. 45 BE32
Yeate St. N1 57 BZ36
Yeatman Rd. N6 47 BU32
Yeats Clo. SE13 67 CF44
Eliot Pk.
Yeats Clo., Red. 121 BT72
Yeldham Rd. W6 65 BQ42
Yellowpine Way, Ilf. 41 CO28
Yelverton Clo., Rom. 42 CV30
Neave Cres.
Yelverton Rd. SW11 66 BT44
Yens, The, Ashf. 73 AZ49
Reedsfield Rd.
Yenston Clo., Mord. 86 BS53
Yeo St. E3 57 CE39
Yeoman Clo. SE27 76 BY48
Canterbury Gro.
Yeoman Rd., Nthlt. 54 BE36
Yeoman St. SE8 67 CD42
Yeoman Way, Red. 121 BV73
Spencer Way
Yeomans Acre, Ruis. 44 BC32
Yeomans Meadow, Sev. 116 CU66
Yeomans Ms., Islw. 74 BG46
Yeomans Rd., Hem.H. 8 AZ10
Yeomans Row SW3 3 D7
Yeomans Row SW3 66 BU41
Yeomans Way, Enf. 30 CB23
Yeomans Yd. E1 2 Q10
Yeomans Yd. E1 57 CA40
Chamber St.
Yeomen Way, Ilf. 40 CM29
Yeoveney Clo., Stai. 72 AU48
Yeovil Clo., Orp. 88 CN55
Yerbury Rd. N19 47 BW34
Yester Dr., Chis. 78 CK50
Yester Pk., Chis. 78 CK50
Yester Rd., Chis. 78 CL50
Yevele Way, Horn. 51 CW33
Yew Ave., West Dr. 53 AY40
Yew Clo., Buck.H. 40 CJ27
Yew Gro. NW2 46 BQ35
Yew Gro., Welw.G.C. 5 BT8
Forresters Dr.
Yew Tree Bottom Rd., Epsom 103 BP61
Yew Tree Clo. N21 38 BY26
Yew Tree Clo., Brwd. 122 DD25
Yew Tree Clo., Chesh. 16 AQ18
Yew Tree Clo., Couls. 104 BU63
Yew Tree Clo., Hem.H. 8 AW14
Yew Tree Clo., Sev. 107 CS65
Yew Tree Clo., Well. 69 CO44
Yew Tree Clo., Wor.Pk. 85 BO54
Yew Tree Dr., Cat. 114 CA66
Yew Tree Dr., Guil. 109 AR68
Yew Tree Dr., Hem.H. 16 AT17
Yew Tree Gdns., Rom. 50 CS32
Yew Tree La., Reig. 121 BS69
Yew Tree Rd. W12 55 BO40
Yew Tree Rd., Dor. 119 BJ70
Yew Tree Rd., Slou. 62 AQ41
Yew Tree Rd., Uxb. 53 AY37
Yew Tree Wk., Houns. 74 BE46
Yew Tree Wk., Lthd. 111 BO67
Yew Tree Wk., S.Croy. 96 BZ58
Yew Trees, Egh. 82 AU52
Yew Trees, Shep. 83 AY52
Laleham Rd.
Yew Wk., Har. 45 BH33
Yew Wk., Hodd. 12 CE12
Yewbank Clo., Ken. 105 BZ61
Church Rd.
Yewdale Clo., Brom. 78 CG50
Yewfield Rd. NW10 55 BO36
Yewlands, Hodd. 12 CE12
Yewlands, Saw. 6 CQ6
Yewlands Clo., Bans. 104 BT61
Yews, The, Grav. 81 DH47
Yews Ave., Enf. 30 CB21
Yewtree Clo. N22 38 BW30
Yewtree End, St.Alb. 18 BG17
Yewtree Gdns., Epsom 103 BM61
Yewtree La., Dor. 119 BF69
Yewtree Rd., Beck. 87 CD52
Yewtree Wk., Pur. 96 BZ58
Yiewsley By-pass, Uxb. 53 AZ39
Yiewsley By-pass, West Dr. 53 AZ39
Yiewsley Sta. Rd., West Dr. 53 AY40
Yoakley Rd. N16 48 CA34
Yoke Clo. N7 56 BX36
Yolande Gdns. SE9 78 CK46
Yonge Pk. N4 47 BY34
York Ave. SE17 67 BZ42
Browning St.
York Ave. SW14 75 BN46
York Ave. W7 54 BH40
York Ave., Hayes 53 BA39
York Ave., Sid. 78 CN48
York Ave., Slou. 52 AO39
York Ave., Stan. 36 BJ30
York Ave., Wind. 61 AN44
York Bri. NW1 1 G4
York Bldgs. WC2 4 A1
York Bldgs. WC2 56 BX40
Watergate Wk.
York Clo. E6 58 CK39
Boultwood Rd.
York Clo. SE5 67 BZ44
Lilford Rd.
York Clo. W7 54 BH40
York Clo., Amer. 25 AP23
York Clo., Brwd. 122 DC26
York Clo., Kings L. 17 AZ18
York Clo., Wey. 92 AY59
York Ct., Mord. 86 BS52
York Cres., Borwd. 28 BN23
York Cres., Loug. 31 CK24
York Gdns., Walt. 84 BD55
York Gate N14 38 BX26
York Gate NW1 1 G5
York Gate NW1 56 BV38
York Gate, Cat. 105 BZ64
York Gro. SE15 67 CC44
York Hill SE27 76 BY48
York Hill, Loug. 31 CK24
York Ho. Pl. W8 66 BS41
York Ms. NW5 47 BV35
York Ms., Ilf. 49 CL34
York Rd.
York Pl. SW11 66 BT45
York Pl. W7 54 BH40
York Pl. WC2 4 A1
York Pl. WC2 56 BX40
Villiers St.
York Pl., Grays 71 DD43
York Pl., Ilf. 49 CL34
York Rd.
York Pl., Wind. 61 AO44
York Ri. NW5 47 BV34
York Ri., Orp. 88 CN55
York Rd. E4 39 CD28
York Rd. E7 58 CH36
York Rd. E10 48 CF34
York Rd. E17 48 CC32
York Rd. N11 38 BW29
York Rd. N18 39 CB29
York Rd. N21 39 BZ26
York Rd. SE1 4 C4
York Rd. SE1 66 BX41
York Rd. SW11 66 BT45
York Rd. SW19 76 BS50
York Rd. W3 55 BN39
York Rd. W5 64 BK41
York Rd., Barn. 29 BT
York Rd., Brent. 64 BK
York Rd., Brwd. 122 DC
York Rd., Croy. 86 BY
York Rd., Dart. 80 CW
York Rd., Epp. 23 CR
York Rd., Grav. 81 DH
York Rd. (Northfleet), Grav. 81 DE
York Rd., Guil. 118 AR
York Rd., Houns. 64 BF
York Rd., Ilf. 49 CL
York Rd., Kings.T. 75 BL
York Rd., Nthwd. 35 BC
York Rd., Rain. 59 CT
York Rd., Rich. 75 BL
Albert Rd.
York Rd., St.Alb. 9 BH
York Rd., S.Croy. 96 CC
York Rd., Sutt. 95 BS
York Rd., Tedd. 74 BH
York Rd., Uxb. 53 AX
York Rd., Wal.Cr. 21 CD
York Rd., Wat. 27 BD
York Rd., West. 106 CH
York Rd., Wey. 92 BA
York Rd. (Byfleet), Wey. 92 AX
York Rd., Wind. 61 AN
York Rd., Wok. 100 AR
York Sq. E14 57 CD
York St. W1 1 E
York St. W1 56 BU
York St., Bark. 58 CL
Abbey Rd.
York St., Mitch. 86 BV
York St., Twick. 74 BJ
York Ter., Enf. 30 BZ
York Ter., Erith 69 CS
York Ter. E. NW1 1 H
York Ter. E. NW1 56 BV
York Ter. W. NW1 1 G
York Ter. W. NW1 56 BV
York Way N1 56 BW
York Way N7 56 BW
York Way N20 38 BU
York Way, Borwd. 28 BN
York Way, Chess. 94 BL
York Way, Felt. 74 BE
York Way, Wat. 27 BD
York Way, Welw. 5 BP
York Way Ct. N1 56 BX
Yorke Gdns., Reig. 121 BS
Yorke Rd., Reig. 121 BS
Yorke Rd., Rick. 26 AZ
Yorkland Ave., Well. 68 CN
Yorks Hill, Sev. 116 CR
Yorkshire Clo. N16 48 CA
Yorkshire Gdns. N18 39 CB
Yorkshire Grey Pl. NW3 47 BY
Heath St.
Yorkshire Grey Yd. WC1 2 B
Yorkshire Rd. E14 57 CD
Yorkshire Rd., Mitch. 86 BX
Yorkton St. E2 57 CB
Young Rd. E16 58 CJ
Young St. W8 66 BS
Young St., Lthd. 102 BH
Youngfield, Hem.H. 7 AV
Youngmans Clo., Enf. 30 BZ
Youngs Bldgs. EC1 2 J
Youngs Bldgs. EC1 57 BZ
Old St.
Youngs Ri., Welw.G.C. 5 BP
Youngs Rd., Ilf. 49 CM
Youngstroat La., Wok. 91 AS
Yoxley App., Ilf. 49 CM
Yoxley Dr., Ilf. 49 CM
Yukon Rd. SW12 76 BV
Yule Clo., St.Alb. 18 BE
St. Lawrence Way
Yuletide Clo. NW10 55 BO
Yunus Khan Clo. E17 48 CE

Z

Zambra Way, Sev. 108 CW63
Zampa Rd. SE16 67 CC42
Zander Ct. E2 57 CB38
St. Peters Clo.
Zangwill Rd. SE3 68 CJ44
Zealand Ave., West Dr. 63 AX43
Zealand Clo. NW2 46 BQ33
Zealand Rd. E3 57 CD37
Zelah Rd., Orp. 89 CO54
Zennor Rd. SW12 76 BV47
Zenoria St. SE22 67 CA45
Zermatt Rd., Th.Hth. 87 BZ52
Zetland St. E14 57 CE39
Zig Zag Rd., Dor. 111 BK68
Zig-Zag Rd., Ken. 105 BZ61
Zig-Zag Rd., Tad. 120 BL69
Zion Pl., Th.Hth. 87 BZ52
Zion Rd., Th.Hth. 87 BZ52
Zion St., Grav. 81 DG47
Zoar St. SE1 4 H2
Zoar St. SE1 57 BZ40
Zoffany St. N19 47 BW34
Ashbrook Rd.

The following is a comprehensive listing of the places of interest which appear on map pages 1-123.

Acton Town *Dist & Picc* BM41 **65**
Aldgate *Met & Circle* CA39 **57**
Aldgate East *Dist & Ham* CA39 **57**
Aldwych *Picc* BX40 **56**
All Saints *Dock* CF40 **57**
Alperton *Picc* BL37 **55**
Amersham *Met* AO22 **25**
Angel *N'thn* BY37 **56**
Archway *N'thn* BW34 **57**
Arnos Grove *Picc* BW28 **38**
Arsenal *Piccc* BY34 **47**

Baker Street *B'loo,Met,Ham Circle & J'lee* BU38 **56**
Balham *N'thn* BV47 **76**
Bank *N'thn, Cent & Dock* BZ39 **57**
Barbican *Met, Circle & Ham* RZ39 **57**
Barking *Dist & Ham* CM36 **58**
Barkingside *Cent* CM31 **49**
Barons Court *Dist & Picc* BR42 **65**
Bayswater *Dist & Circle* BS40 **56**
Becontree *Dist* CP36 **59**
Belsize Park *N'thn* BU35 **47**
Bethnal Green *Cent* CC38 **57**
Blackfriars *Dist & Circle* BY40 **56**
Blackhorse Road *Vic* CC31 **48**
Bond Street *Cent & J'lee* BV39 **56**
Borough *N'thn* BZ41 **67**
Boston Manor *Picc* BJ42 **64**
Bounds Green *Picc* BW29 **38**
Bow Church *Dock* CE38 **57**
Bow Road *Ham & Dist* CE38 **57**
Brent Cross *N'thn* BO33 **46**
Brixton *Vic* BY45 **66**
Bromley by Bow *Met & Dist* CF38 **57**
Buckhurst Hill *Cent* CJ27 **40**
Burnt Oak *N'thn* BN30 **37**

Caledonian Road *Picc* BX35 **47**
Camden Town *N'thn* BV37 **56**
Canary Wharf *Dock* CE40 **57**
Cannon Street *Dist & Circle* BZ40 **57**
Cannons Park *J'lee* BL29 **37**
Chalfont & Latimer *Met* AR23 **25**
Chalk Farm *N'thn* BV36 **56**
Chancery Lane *Cent* BY39 **56**
Charing Cross *B'loo, N'thn & J'lee* BW40 **56**
Chesham *Met* OUTSIDE ATLAS AREA
Chigwell *Cent* CL27 **40**
Chiswick Park *Dist* BN42 **65**
Chorleywood *Met* AU24 **25**
Clapham Common *N'thn* BW45 **66**
Clapham North *N'thn* BX45 **66**
Clapham South *N'thn* BV46 **76**
Cockfosters *Picc* BV24 **29**
Colindale *N'thn* BO31 **46**
Colliers Wood *N'thn* BT50 **76**
Covent Garden *Picc* BX40 **56**
Crossharbour *Dock* CE41 **67**
Croxley *Met* AZ25 **26**

Dagenham East *Dist* CS36 **59**
Dagenham Heathway *Dist* CO36 **59**
Debden *Cent* CM24 **31**
Devons Road *Dock* CE38 **57**

Dollis Hill *J'lee* BP35 **46**

Ealing Broadway *Dist & Cent* BK39 **54**
Ealing Common *Dist & Picc* BL40 **55**
Earl's Court *Dist & Picc* BS42 **66**
East Acton *Cent* BO39 **55**
Eastcote *Met & Picc* BO33 **45**
East Finchley *N'thn* BU31 **47**
East Ham *Dist & Ham* CK36 **58**
East Putney *Dist* BR46 **75**
Edgware *N'thn* BM29 **37**
Edgware Road *Ham, Dist, B'loo & Circle* BU39 **56**
Elephant and Castle *N'thn & B'loo* BY41 **66**
Elm Park *Dist* CU35 **50**
Embankment *B'loo, N'thn, Dist & Circle* BX40 **56**
Epping *Cent* CO19 **23**
Euston *N'thn & Vic* BW38 **56**
Euston Square *Circle, Ham & Met* BW38 **56**

Fairlop *Cent* CM30 **40**
Farringdon *Met, Circle & Ham* BY39 **56**
Finchley Central *N'thn* BS30 **38**
Finchley Road *Met & J'lee* BT36 **56**
Finsbury Park *Picc & Vic* BY34 **47**
Fulham Broadway *Dist* BS43 **66**

Gants Hill *Cent* CL32 **49**
Gloucester Road *Picc, Dist & Circle* BT42 **66**
Golders Green *N'thn* BS33 **47**
Goldhawk Road *Ham* BO41 **65**
Goodge Street *N'thn* BW39 **56**
Grange Hill *Cent* CM28 **40**
Great Portland Street *Met, Ham & Circle* BV38 **56**
Greenford *Cent* BG37 **54**
Green Park *Picc, Vic & J'lee* BV40 **56**
Gunnersbury *Dist* BM42 **65**

Hainault *Cent* CN29 **40**
Hammersmith *Ham, Picc & Dist* BO42 **65**
Hampstead *N'thn* BT35 **47**
Hanger Lane *Cent* BL38 **55**
Harlesden *B'loo* BN37 **55**
Harrow & Wealdstone *B'loo* BH31 **46**
Harrow-on-the-Hill *Met* BH32 **45**
Hatton Cross *Picc* BB45 **63**
Heathrow Central (Terminals 1,2 & 3) *Picc* AZ45 **63**
Heathrow (Terminal 4) *Picc* BA46 **73**
Hendon Central *N'thn* BO32 **46**
Heron Quays *Dock* CE40 **57**
High Barnet *N'thn* BS24 **29**
Highbury and Islington *Vic* BY36 **56**
Highgate *N'thn* BV32 **47**
High Street Kensington *Dist & Circle* BS41 **66**
Hilligdon *Met & Picc* AZ35 **44**
Holborn *Cent & Picc* BX39 **56**
Holland Park *Cent* BR40 **55**
Holloway Road *Picc* BX35 **47**
Hornchurch *Dist* CV34 **51**
Hounslow Central *Picc* BF45 **64**
Hounslow East *Picc* BG44 **64**

Hounslow West *Picc* BE44 **64**
Hyde Park Corner *Picc* BV41 **66**

Ickenham *Met & Picc* BA35 **44**
Island Gardens *Dock* CF42 **67**

Kennington *N'thn* BY42 **66**
Kensal Green *B'loo* BO38 **55**
Kensington (Olympia) *Dist* BR41 **65**
Kentish Town *N'thn* BW35 **47**
Kenton *B'loo* BJ32 **45**
Kew Gardens *Dist* BM44 **65**
Kilburn *J'lee* BR36 **55**
Kilburn Park *B'loo* BS37 **56**
Kingsbury *J'lee* BM32 **46**
King's Cross, St Pancras *N'thn, Picc, Met, Circle, Vic & Ham* BX38 **56**
Knightsbridge *Picc* BU41 **66**

Ladbroke Grove *Ham* BR39 **55**
Lambeth North *B'loo* BY41 **66**
Lancaster Gate *Cent* BT40 **56**
Latimer Road *Ham* BO40 **55**
Leicester Square *N'thn & Picc* BW40 **56**
Leyton *Cent* CF34 **48**
Leytonstone *Cent* CG33 **49**
Limehouse *Dock* CD39 **57**
Liverpool Street *Met, Ham Circle & Cent* CA39 **57**
London Bridge *N'thn* BZ40 **57**
Loughton *Cent* CK25 **31**

Maida Vale *B'loo* BS38 **56**
Manor House *Picc* BY33 **47**
Mansion House *Dist & Circle* BZ40 **57**
Marble Arch *Cent* BU39 **56**
Marylebone *B'loo* BU39 **56**
Mile End *Cent, Ham & Dist* CD38 **57**
Mill Hill East *N'thn* BR29 **37**
Monument *Dist & Circle* BZ40 **57**
Moorgate *N'thn, Met, Ham & Circle* BZ39 **57**
Moor Park *Met* BA27 **35**
Morden *N'thn* BS52 **86**
Mornington Crescent *N'thn* BW37 **56**
Mudchute *Dock* CE42 **67**

Neasden *J'lee* BO35 **46**
Newbury Park *Cent* CM26 **49**
New Cross *E. Lon* CD43 **67**
New Cross Gate *E. Lon* CD43 **67**
North Acton *Cent* BN39 **55**
North Ealing *Picc* BL39 **55**
Northfields *Picc* BK41 **64**
North Harrow *Met* BF32 **45**
Northolt *Cent* BF36 **54**
North Weald *Cent* CR17 **23**
North Wembley *B'loo* BK34 **45**
Northwick Park *Met* BJ33 **45**
Northwood *Met* BB29 **35**
Northwood Hills *Met* BC30 **35**
Notting Hill Gate *Cent, Dist & Circle* BS40 **56**

Oakwood *Picc* BW25 **29**
Old Street *N'thn* BZ38 **57**
Ongar *Cent* CX17 **24**
Osterley *Picc* BG43 **64**
Oval *N'thn* BY43 **66**
Oxford Circus *B'loo, Cent & Vic* BW39 **56**

Paddington *B'loo, Ham Dist & Circle* BT39 **56**
Park Royal *Picc* BM38 **55**
Parsons Green *Dist* BS44 **66**
Perrivale *Cent* BJ37 **54**
Piccadilly Circus *Picc & B'loo* BW40 **56**
Pimlico *N'thn* BW42 **66**
Pinner *Met* BE31 **45**
Plaistow *Ham & Dist* CG37 **58**
Poplar *Dock* CE40 **57**
Preston Road *Met* BL33 **46**
Putney Bridge *Dist* BR45 **65**

Queensbury *J'lee* BL31 **46**
Queen's Park *B'loo* BR37 **55**
Queensway *Cent* BS40 **56**

Ravenscourt Park *Dist* BP42 **65**
Rayners Lane *Met & Picc* BE33 **45**
Redbridge *Cent* CJ32 **49**
Regent's Park *B'loo* BV38 **56**
Richmond *Dist* BL45 **65**
Rickmansworth *Met* AX26 **35**
Roding Valley *Cent* CJ28 **40**
Rotherhithe *E. Lon* CC41 **67**
Royal Oak *Ham* BS39 **56**
Ruislip *Met & Picc* BB33 **44**
Ruislip Gardens *Cent* BC35 **44**
Ruislip Manor *Met & Picc* BC33 **44**
Russell Square *Picc* BX38 **56**

St. James's Park *Dist & Circle* BW41 **66**
St. John's Wood *J'lee* BT37 **56**
St. Pauls *Cent* BZ39 **57**
Seven Sisters *Vic* CA32 **48**
Shadwell *E. Lon & Dock* CB39 **57**
Shepherd's Bush *Cent & Ham* BO40 **55**
Shoreditch *E. Lon* CA38 **57**
Sloane Square *Dist & Circle* BV42 **66**
Snaresbrook *Cent* CH32 **49**
South Ealing *Picc* BK41 **64**
Southfields *Dist* BR47 **75**
Southgate *Picc* BW26 **38**
South Harrow *Picc* BG34 **45**
South Kensington *Picc, Dist & Circle* BT42 **66**
South Kenton *B'loo* BK33 **45**
South Quay *Dock* CE41 **67**
South Ruislip *Cent* BD35 **45**
South Wimbledon *N'thn* BS50 **76**
South Woodford *Cent* CH31 **49**
Stamford Brook *Dist* BO42 **65**
Stanmore *J'lee* BK28 **28**
Stepney Green *Dist & Ham* CC38 **57**
Stockwell *N'thn & Vic* BX44 **66**
Stonebridge Park *B'loo* BM36 **55**
Stratford *Cent* CF36 **57**

Sudbury Hill *Picc* BH35 **45**
Sudbury Town *Picc* BJ36 **54**
Surrey Quays *E. Lon* CC42 **67**
Swiss Cottage *J'lee* BT36 **56**

Temple *Circle & Dist* BX40 **56**
Theydon Bois *Cent* CN21 **31**
Tooting Bec *N'thn* BV48 **76**
Tooting Broadway *N'thn* BU49 **76**
Tottenham Court Road *Cent & N'thn* BW39 **56**
Tottenham Hale *Vic* CB31 **48**
Totteridge and Whetstone *N'thn* BT27 **38**
Tower Gateway *Dock* CA40 **57**
Tower Hill *Circle & Dist* CA40 **57**
Tufnell Park *N'thn* BW35 **47**
Turnham Green *Dist & Picc* BO42 **65**
Turnpike Lane *Picc* BY31 **47**

Upminster *Dist* CY34 **51**
Upminster Bridge *Dist* CX34 **51**
Upney *Dist* CN36 **58**
Upon Park *Dist & Ham* CJ37 **58**
Uxbridge *Met & Picc* AX36 **53**

Vauxhall *Vic* BX43 **66**
Victoria *Circle, Dist & Vic* BV41 **66**

Walthamstow Central *Vic* CE32 **48**
Wanstead *Cent* CH32 **49**
Wapping *E. Lon* CC40 **57**
Warren Street *N'thn & Vic* BW38 **56**
Warwick Avenue *B'loo* BT38 **56**
Waterloo *N'thn & B'loo* BY41 **66**
Watford *Met* BB24 **26**
Wembley Central *B'loo* BL36 **55**
Wembley Park *Met & J'lee* BM34 **46**
West Acton *Cent* BM39 **55**
Westbourne Park *Ham* BR39 **55**
West Brompton *Dist* BS42 **66**
Westferry *Dock* CE40 **57**
West Finchley *N'thn* BS29 **38**
West Ham *Ham & Dist* CG38 **58**
West Hampstead *J'lee* BS36 **56**
West Harrow *Met* BG32 **45**
West India Quay *Dock* CE40 **57**
West Kensington *Dist* BR42 **65**
Westminster *Circle & Dist* BX41 **66**
West Ruislip *Cent* BA34 **44**
Whitechapel *Ham, Dist & E. Lon* CB39 **57**
White City *Cent* BO40 **55**
Willesden Green *J'lee* BO36 **55**
Willesden Junction *B'loo* BO38 **55**
Wimbledon *Dist* BR50 **75**
Wimbledon Park *Dist* BS48 **76**
Woodford *Cent* CH29 **40**
Wood Green *Picc* BY30 **38**
Woodside Park *N'thn* BS28 **38**

PERSONAL INFORMATION

NAME AND ADDRESS	TELEPHONE	NOTES
Postcode		
Postcode		
Postcode		
Postcode		
Postcode		
Postcode		
Postcode		
Postcode		
Postcode		
Postcode		
Postcode		

PERSONAL INFORMATION

NAME AND ADDRESS	TELEPHONE	NOTES
Postcode		
Postcode		
Postcode		
Postcode		
Postcode		
Postcode		
Postcode		
Postcode		
Postcode		
Postcode		
Postcode		
Postcode		

PERSONAL INFORMATION

NAME AND ADDRESS	TELEPHONE	NOTES
Postcode		
Postcode		
Postcode		
Postcode		
Postcode		
Postcode		
Postcode		
Postcode		
Postcode		
Postcode		
Postcode		

PERSONAL INFORMATION

NAME AND ADDRESS	TELEPHONE	NOTES
Postcode		
Postcode		
Postcode		
Postcode		
Postcode		
Postcode		
Postcode		
Postcode		
Postcode		
Postcode		
Postcode		

PERSONAL INFORMATION

NAME AND ADDRESS	TELEPHONE	NOTES
Postcode		
Postcode		
Postcode		
Postcode		
Postcode		
Postcode		
Postcode		
Postcode		
Postcode		
Postcode		
Postcode		

PERSONAL INFORMATION

NAME AND ADDRESS	TELEPHONE	NOTES
Postcode		
Postcode		
Postcode		
Postcode		
Postcode		
Postcode		
Postcode		
Postcode		
Postcode		
Postcode		
Postcode		

PERSONAL INFORMATION

NAME AND ADDRESS	TELEPHONE	NOTES
Postcode		
Postcode		
Postcode		
Postcode		
Postcode		
Postcode		
Postcode		
Postcode		
Postcode		
Postcode		
Postcode		

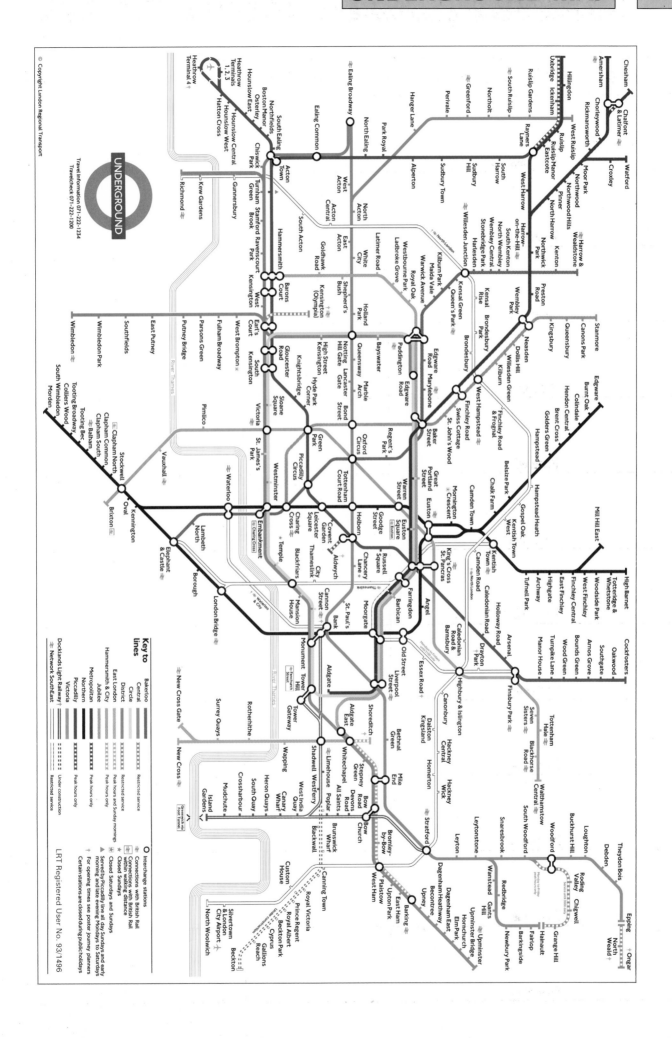
UNDERGROUND
Travel Information 071-222-1234
Travelcheck 071-222-1200
Key to lines
Bakerloo
Central
Restricted service
Circle
District
Restricted service
East London
Peak hours and Sunday mornings
Hammersmith & City
Peak hours only
Jubilee
Metropolitan
Peak hours only
Northern
Piccadilly
Peak hours only
Victoria
Docklands Light Railway
Under construction
Network SouthEast
Restricted service
Interchange stations
Connections with British Rail
Connections with British Rail within walking distance
Closed Sundays
Closed Saturdays and Sundays
Served by Piccadilly line all day Sundays and early morning and late evening Mondays to Saturdays
For opening times see poster journey planners
Certain stations are closed during public holidays
LRT Registered User No. 93/1496
© Copyright London Regional Transport

ADMINISTRATIVE AREAS

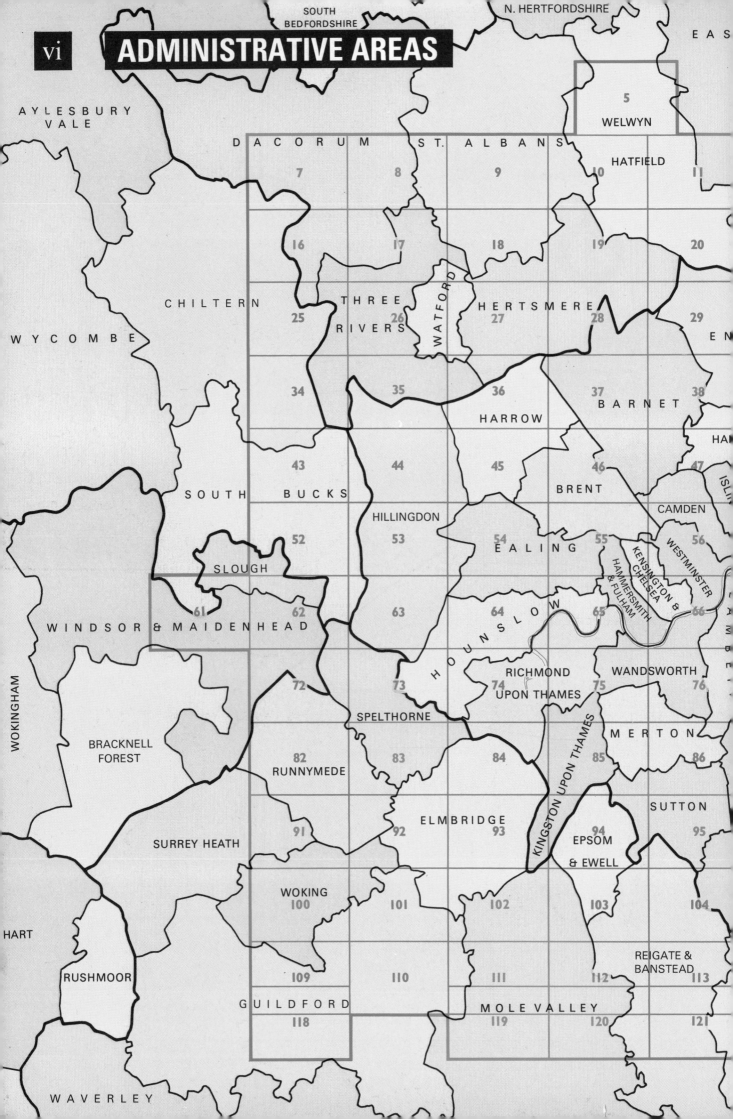

SOUTH BEDFORDSHIRE

N. HERTFORDSHIRE

EAS

AYLESBURY VALE

WELWYN 5

DACORUM 7

ST. ALBANS 9

8

10 HATFIELD

11

WYCOMBE

CHILTERN

THREE RIVERS 26

WATFORD

HERTSMERE 27

28

29

EN

16

17

18

19

20

25

34

35

36

37

BARNET

38

HARROW

43

SOUTH BUCKS

44

45

46

47

HA

BRENT

SLOUGH

HILLINGDON

52

53

EALING 54

55

CAMDEN

ISLI

56

WESTMINSTER

HAMMERSMITH & FULHAM

KENSINGTON & CHELSEA

61

WINDSOR & MAIDENHEAD

62

63

HOUNSLOW 64

65

66

WOKINGHAM

72

73

74 RICHMOND UPON THAMES

WANDSWORTH 75

76

SPELTHORNE

BRACKNELL FOREST

RUNNYMEDE 82

83

84

KINGSTON UPON THAMES

MERTON 85

86

SURREY HEATH

ELMBRIDGE

SUTTON

91

92

93

94 EPSOM & EWELL

95

WOKING 100

101

102

103

104

HART

RUSHMOOR

109

110

111

112

REIGATE & BANSTEAD 113

GUILDFORD 118

MOLE VALLEY 119

120

121

WAVERLEY

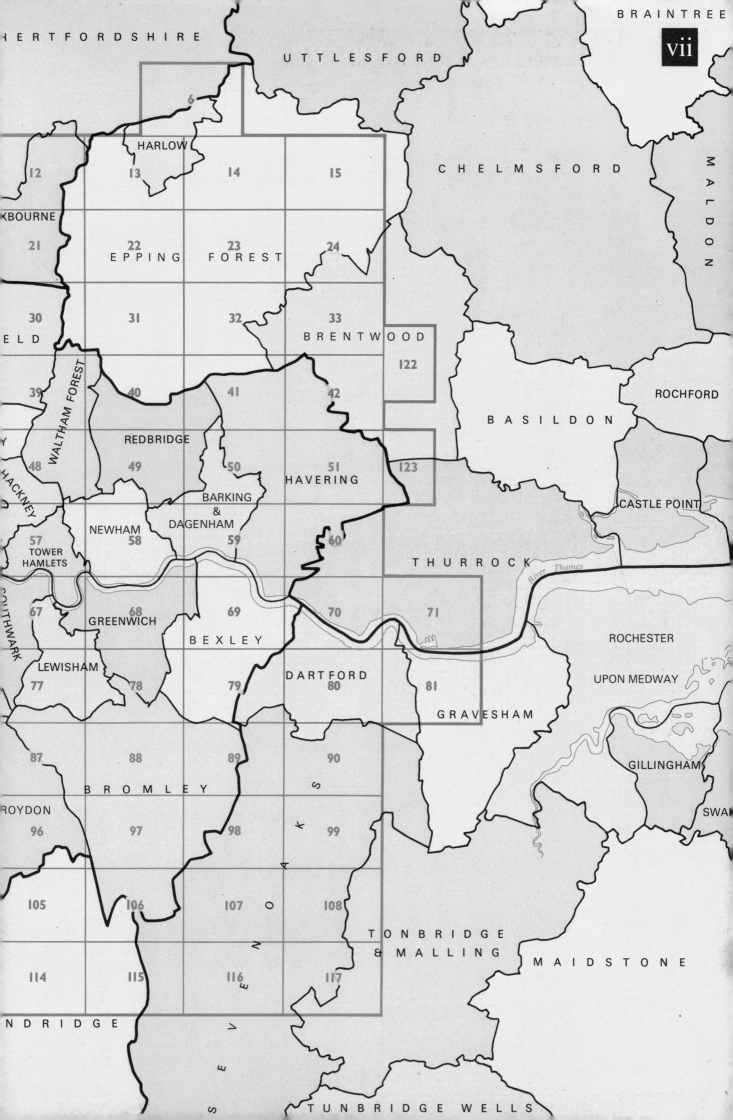
BRAINTREE
HERTFORDSHIRE
UTTLESFORD
6
HARLOW
12
13
14
15
CHELMSFORD
MALDON
KBOURNE
21
22
23
24
EPPING FOREST
30
31
32
33
ELD
BRENTWOOD
122
WALTHAM FOREST
39
40
41
42
ROCHFORD
BASILDON
REDBRIDGE
48
49
50
51
123
HAVERING
HACKNEY
BARKING & DAGENHAM
CASTLE POINT
NEWHAM
57
58
59
60
TOWER HAMLETS
THURROCK
River Thames
SOUTHWARK
67
68
69
70
71
GREENWICH
BEXLEY
ROCHESTER UPON MEDWAY
LEWISHAM
77
78
79
DARTFORD
80
81
GRAVESHAM
87
88
89
90
GILLINGHAM
BROMLEY
ROYDON
96
97
98
99
SWA
SEVENOAKS
105
106
107
108
TONBRIDGE & MALLING
MAIDSTONE
114
115
116
117
NDRIDGE
TUNBRIDGE WELLS